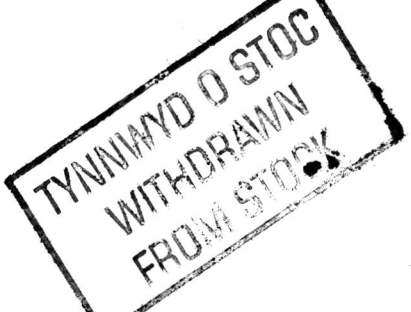

THE ROYAL
HORTICULTURAL SOCIETY

A–Z ENCYCLOPEDIA of GARDEN PLANTS

THE ROYAL HORTICULTURAL SOCIETY

A–Z ENCYCLOPEDIA of GARDEN PLANTS

CHRISTOPHER BRICKELL
Editor-in-Chief

VOLUME 2: K–Z

DK

LONDON, NEW YORK, MUNICH, MELBOURNE, DELHI

IMPORTANT NOTICE

This encyclopedia follows Royal Horticultural Society guidelines on potentially hazardous plants, although the properties of many garden plants have yet to be fully evaluated. Where a plant is known to have potentially harmful properties, a warning has been included in the appropriate alphabetical entry. However, any plant substance has the potential to cause an allergic reaction in some people, so due caution should be exercised when handling plants.

FIRST EDITION 1996

MANAGING EDITOR Jonathan Metcalf **SENIOR ART EDITORS** Peter Cross, Ina Stradins
EDITORS Polly Boyd, Monica Byles, Anna Cheifetz, Joanna Chisholm, Alison Copland, Clare Double, Peter Frances, Angeles Gavira, Richard Hammond, Maggie O'Hanlon, Lin Hawthorne, Sally Paxton, Lesley Riley, Harriet Stewart-Jones, Jo Weeks, Tony Whitehorn, Sarah Widdicombe, Fiona Wild
ART EDITORS Pauline Clarke, Elaine Hewson, Kate Poole, Helen Robson, Helen Taylor
PROOFREADING AND INDEXING Marion Dent, Ilse Gray, Jane Parker
DESIGN ASSISTANTS Robert Campbell, Murdo Culver
ADMINISTRATIVE SUPPORT Susila Baybars, Ian Hambleton, Paula Hardy, Simon Maughan, Paul Rundle
PRODUCTION CONTROLLER Michelle Thomas **PRODUCTION ASSISTANT** Hélène Lamassoure **DTP MANAGER** Mark Bracey
CULTIVATION EDITORS Cathy Buchanan, Lin Hawthorne, Andrew Mikolajski
HORTICULTURAL ADVISORS Peter Barnes, Roy Cheek, Sabina Knees, Nigel Rowland
PICTURE RESEARCHERS Denise Greig, Emily Hedges, Dr Alan Hemsley
ILLUSTRATORS Karen Cochrane, Martine Collings, Gill Tomblin
SENIOR MANAGING EDITOR Mary-Clare Jerram **MANAGING ART EDITOR** Amanda Lunn
EDITORIAL DIRECTOR Jackie Douglas **ART DIRECTOR** Peter Luff

REVISED EDITION 2003

SENIOR EDITOR Joanna Chisholm
SENIOR ART EDITOR Stephen Josland

EDITORS Polly Boyd, Lin Hawthorne, Lesley Riley
PROOFREADING Lynn Bresler, Monica Byles, Anna Cheifetz, Jo Weeks, Sarah Widdicombe
DTP DESIGNER Louise Waller
DESIGN ASSISTANT Maggie Aldred
PICTURE RESEARCH Samantha Nunn **PICTURE LIBRARY** Lucy Claxton, Richard Dabb
PRODUCTION Heather Hughes

SENIOR MANAGING EDITOR Anna Kruger
SENIOR MANAGING ART EDITOR Lee Griffiths

First edition published in Great Britain in 1996 by Dorling Kindersley Limited, London

This revised and expanded edition published in Great Britain in association with The Royal Horticultural Society by Dorling Kindersley Limited, 80 Strand, London WC2R 0RL
A Penguin Company
4 6 8 10 9 7 5 3

A CIP catalogue record for this book is available from the British Library

ISBN 0-7513-3738-2

Colour reproduction in Italy by GRB Editrice s.r.l. Printed and bound in China by Toppan Printing Co., (ShenZhen) Ltd.

Frontispiece: *Dahlia* 'Wootton Impact'

See our complete catalogue at
www.dk.com

CONTENTS

VOLUME 1

VOLUME 2

Editor-in-Chief

Christopher Brickell

CBE, BSc (Hort), FInstHort, VMH

Former Director General, The Royal Horticultural Society
Chairman, International Commission for the Nomenclature of Cultivated Plants

Contributors and Consultants

Susyn Andrews

George Argent

Roger S. Aylett
FIHort

David G. Barker
BSc

Larry Barlow

Peter Barnes

George Bartlett

Kenneth A. Beckett
VMM

Deni Bown

Jeffrey Brande

Cathy Buchanan
MA, DipHort (Kew), MIHort

David Burnie

Brian Burrow

Eric Catterall

Roy Cheek
MHort (RHS), FIHort

Ian Cooke
MHort (RHS)

Allen J. Coombes

Brian S. Duncan
MBE

Jack Elliott
VMH

Raymond J. Evison
VMH

Maurice Foster

John & Eileen Galbally

Richard W. Gilbert

Mike L. Grant

Pippa Greenwood
BSc, MSc

Diana Grenfell

Dr Christopher Grey-Wilson
BSc (Hort)

Dr Patricia Griggs

Peter Harkness
DHM

Lin Hawthorne

Tony Hender

Peter Hovenkamp

Clive Innes
VMH

Clive Jermy

Hazel Key

Ursula Key-Davis

Sabina G. Knees
BSc, MSc

W.A. Lord

Brian Mathew
VMH

Victoria Matthews

Peter R. Maynard

Margaret E. McKendrick

Tim Miles
MIHort

Diana Miller
BSc, MA

Jim Pearce

Martin Rickard
BSc (Botany)

Wilma Rittershausen

Peter Robinson
MHort (RHS), FIHort, DipHort (Edin)

Peter Q. Rose
MHort, FLS, MIHort

Keith Rushforth

Tony Schilling
MArb, FIHort, FLS, VMH

Christine Skelmersdale

David Small

Arthur Smith

Joyce Stewart
MSc, FIHort, FLS

Nigel Taylor

David Trehane
BSc (Hort)

W.B. Wade

Ray Waite

Dr Trevor G. Walker
DSc

Tim Whiteley

Photographers

Clive Boursnell

Deni Bown

Jonathan Buckley

Andrew Butler

Eric Crichton

Christine M. Douglas

John Fielding

Neil Fletcher

John Glover

Jerry Harpur

Sunniva Harte

C. Andrew Henley

Andrew Lawson

Andrew de Lory

Howard Rice

Bob Rundle

Juliette Wade

Matthew Ward

Dave Watts

Steven Wooster

THE A–Z PLANT DIRECTORY

K–Z

K

KADSURA

SCHISANDRACEAE

Genus of about 20 species of woody, twining, evergreen climbers from forest in E. and S.E. Asia. They are grown for their fleshy fruits and attractive, simple, glossy leaves, arranged alternately. Solitary, cup-shaped flowers are usually produced in the leaf axils; both male and female flowers, borne on separate plants, are required to produce the fruits. *K. japonica*, the only species commonly cultivated, is best grown in a sheltered position where it can be trained against a wall or pillar, or through a large shrub.

- **HARDINESS** Frost hardy.
- **CULTIVATION** Grow in fertile, moist but well-drained soil in full sun or partial shade. Pruning group 12, in winter.
- **PROPAGATION** Take semi-ripe cuttings in summer.
- **PESTS AND DISEASES** Trouble free.

K. japonica. Vigorous, evergreen climber with twining shoots and elliptic to ovate-lance-shaped, slightly toothed, glossy, dark green leaves, to 10cm (4in) long. Small, solitary, cup-shaped, yellowish white flowers, 2cm (¾in) across, are produced from summer to autumn, followed on female plants by red, blackberry-like fruit, 3cm (1¼in) across. ↕4m (12ft). China, Korea, Taiwan, Japan. ❄❄. **'Variegata'** has leaves that are broadly margined with creamy yellow and tinged pink, becoming creamy white in winter.

KAEMPFERIA

ZINGIBERACEAE

Genus of about 40 species of aromatic, rhizomatous perennials growing wild in the forests of tropical Asia. The leaves are simple and either 2-ranked on short stems or in basal clusters. White, pink, or lilac, 3-petalled flowers, each with a deeply 2-lobed lip, are borne in terminal spikes on short, leafy or scaly stems and are often fragrant. In frost-prone areas, grow in a warm greenhouse; in tropical and subtropical regions, use outdoors as ground cover.

- **HARDINESS** Frost tender.
- **CULTIVATION** Under glass, grow in loam-based potting compost (JI No.2) in bright filtered light. During the growing season, maintain moderate humidity and water freely, applying a balanced liquid fertilizer every 2–3 weeks. Keep completely dry in winter when dormant. Outdoors, grow in well-drained, humus-rich soil in partial shade.
- **PROPAGATION** Sow seed at 20°C (68°F) as soon as ripe, or divide rhizomes in spring.
- **PESTS AND DISEASES** Trouble free.

Kaempferia pulchra

K. pulchra ■ Low-growing, rhizomatous perennial with broadly elliptic, dark green leaves, about 15cm (6in) long, sometimes with silver markings. In summer, produces short spikes, to 5cm (2in) long, of 3-petalled, lilac or lilac-pink flowers, 4cm (1½in) across, amid the foliage. ↕15cm (6in), ↔30cm (12in). Thailand, Malaysia. ❄ (min. 10°C/50°F)

K. roscoeana (Dwarf ginger lily, Peacock lily). Low-growing, rhizomatous perennial with usually 2 rounded leaves, 10cm (4in) across, deep green with lighter green markings above, mid-green tinged red beneath. From summer to autumn, bears short spikes, 5cm (2in) long, of 3-petalled white flowers, 2.5–5cm (1–2in) across, amid the foliage. ↕15cm (6in), ↔20cm (8in). Burma. ❄ (min. 10°C/50°F)

K. rotunda (Resurrection lily). Erect, rhizomatous perennial with lance-shaped leaves, to 40cm (16in) long, with long, sharp points, silver-green and unmarked above, purple beneath. In summer, produces spikes, 8cm (3in) long, of up to 6 lilac-lipped, 3-petalled white flowers, 5cm (2in) across, above the foliage. ↕15cm (6in), ↔45cm (18in). S.E. Asia. ❄ (min. 10°C/50°F)

▷ **Kaffirboom,**
Cape see *Erythrina caffra*
Transvaal see *Erythrina lysistemon*
▷ **Kaffir bread** see *Encephalartos caffer*
▷ **Kaki** see *Diospyros kaki*

KALANCHOE

syn. BRYOPHYLLUM

CRASSULACEAE

Genus of about 130 species of annual, biennial, and perennial succulents, shrubs, climbers, and small trees, occurring in semi-desert or shady areas of Saudi Arabia, Yemen (including Socotra), C. Africa, South Africa, Madagascar, Asia, Australia, and tropical America. Some are tree-like or shrubby, others are more spreading in habit. All have fleshy stems bearing simple to 2-pinnatisect, rarely pinnate, toothed or scalloped, fleshy leaves, arranged in opposite pairs, rarely alternate or whorled. Diurnal, showy, bell-shaped, urn-shaped, or tubular, 4-lobed flowers, often swollen in the middle or at the bases, are borne in terminal, occasionally lateral, cyme-like or corymb-like panicles. Where temperatures drop below 12°C (54°F), grow as houseplants or in a temperate or warm greenhouse; some spreading species are particularly effective in a hanging basket. In warmer climates, grow outdoors in a shrub border or in beds.

Kalanchoe beharensis

- **HARDINESS** Frost tender.
- **CULTIVATION** Under glass, grow in loam-based potting compost (JI No.2) with additional grit, in bright filtered light. During the growing season, water moderately and apply a balanced liquid fertilizer 3 or 4 times; keep just moist in winter. Outdoors, grow in well-drained, humus-rich, moderately fertile soil in partial shade. See also pp.48–49.
- **PROPAGATION** Sow seed at 21°C (70°F) in early spring. Remove offsets and plantlets from leaves or inflorescences, or take stem cuttings, in spring or summer.
- **PESTS AND DISEASES** Susceptible to mealybugs, aphids, downy mildew, and leaf spot.

K. beharensis ■ Bushy, often tree-like, perennial succulent with broadly triangular to lance-shaped, slightly toothed, long-stalked leaves, to 35cm (14in) long, usually concave and brown above, convex and silvery beneath, and covered with minute, fine, silver or golden hairs. In late winter, mature plants bear many lateral, cyme-like panicles of urn-shaped, green-yellow flowers, 7mm (¼in) long, which are violet-veined inside. ↕↔1m (3ft) or more. Madagascar. ❄ (min. 10°C/50°F)

Kalanchoe daigremontiana

K. blossfeldiana ■ Bushy, perennial succulent with oval to oblong-ovate, softly toothed, glossy, dark green leaves, 8cm (3in) long, on long stalks. Tubular scarlet flowers, 1.5cm (½in) long, are produced in early spring, mostly in crowded, corymb-like panicles. ↕↔ to 40cm (16in). Madagascar. ❄ (min. 12°C/54°F). Many hybrids have been developed, with flowers in white, yellow, pink, and other shades.

K. daigremontiana ■ syn. *Bryophyllum daigremontianum* (Mexican hat plant). Erect, perennial succulent with lance-shaped leaves, 15–20cm (6–8in) long, usually spotted reddish brown, that produce adventitious plantlets on the toothed margins. Pendent, broadly tubular, greyish violet flowers, to 2cm (¾in) long, are produced in cyme-like panicles in winter. ↕1m (3ft), ↔30cm (12in). S.W. Madagascar. ❄ (min. 10°C/50°F)

K

Kalanchoe blossfeldiana

Kalanchoe fedtschenkoi 'Variegata'

K. delagoensis, syn. *Bryophyllum tubiflorum, K. tubiflora.* Erect, sparsely branched, perennial succulent with almost cylindrical leaves, to 15cm (6in) long, grey-green, spotted reddish brown; leaves have notched tips that produce adventitious plantlets. In late winter and early spring, produces cyme-like panicles of pendent, tubular-bell-shaped, purple-grey to pale orange-yellow flowers, to 2cm (¾in) or more long. ↕ 1m (3ft) or more, ↔ 30cm (12in) or more. Madagascar. ❀ (min. 10°C/50°F)
K. eriophylla. Bushy, perennial succulent with slender stems covered with white hairs, except at the bases. Bears ovate-oblong, very thick, white-woolly, mid-green leaves, 3cm (1¼in) long. Young leaves may have red tips. In spring, bears narrowly bell-shaped, blue-violet flowers, 6cm (2½in) long, in more or less erect, corymb-like panicles. ↕↔ 20cm (8in). Madagascar. ❀ (min. 15°C/59°F)
K. fedtschenkoi. Upright to decumbent, perennial succulent bearing hairless, obovate to oblong, blue-green leaves, 1–6cm (½–2½in) long, each with 2–8 prominent teeth. Pendent, bell-shaped, dull red or purple flowers, to 2cm (¾in) long, are produced in small, loose, corymb-like panicles in summer. ↕ 50cm (20in), ↔ 25cm (10in). Madagascar. ❀ (min. 12°C/54°F). **'Variegata'** ■ is bushy or semi-erect, with scalloped leaves margined creamy white and often flushed pink and mottled yellow; ↕↔ 50cm (20in).
K. grandiflora. Erect, perennial succulent with ovate to obovate, weakly scalloped, glaucous, mid-green leaves, 4–10cm (1½–4in) long. Tubular, bright yellow flowers, 1cm (½in) long, are borne in compact, cyme-like panicles in summer. ↕ 80cm (32in), ↔ 40cm (16in). S. India. ❀ (min. 10°C/50°F)
K. jongmansii. Bushy, woody-stemmed, spreading, perennial succulent with oblong to linear-elliptic, mid-green leaves, to 4.5cm (1¾in) long, rounded above, with entire or partly scalloped margins. In early spring, produces cyme-like panicles of bell-shaped, more or less erect yellow flowers, 3cm (1¼in) long. ↕↔ 30cm (12in). Madagascar. ❀ (min. 12°C/54°F)
K. laciniata, syn. *K. schweinfurthii.* Erect, perennial succulent with pinnatisect, occasionally pinnate, hairless, mid-green leaves, to 20cm (8in) long, each with 3–5 entire or lobed, ovate to elliptic segments. In summer, bears corymb-like panicles of tubular, greenish white to pale orange flowers, 0.8–1.5cm (⅜–½in) long. ↕ 1.2m (4ft), ↔ 60cm (24in). Namibia to Ethiopia, S. India, Thailand. ❀ (min. 10°C/50°F)
K. manginii. Semi-erect then pendent, free-branching, perennial succulent with obovate to ovate-spoon-shaped, entire or notched, mid-green leaves, 3cm (1¼in) long, minutely hairy when young. In spring, bears few-flowered, cyme-like panicles of tubular, urn-shaped, bright red flowers, 2–3cm (¾–1¼in) or more long. ↕↔ 30cm (12in). Madagascar. ❀ (min. 12°C/54°F)
K. marmorata, syn. *K. somaliensis.* Erect or decumbent, perennial succulent, branching from the base, bearing obovate, toothed, grey-frosted leaves, 6–20cm (2½–8in) long, with large, purple-brown marks. In spring, bears cyme-like panicles of narrowly tubular, erect, white, sometimes pink- or yellow-tinged flowers, 6–8cm (2½–3in) long. ↕↔ to 40cm (16in). Sudan to Zaire, Ethiopia, Somalia. ❀ (min. 12°C/54°F)
K. pinnata. Bushy, erect, perennial succulent with ovate, toothed, red-tinged, greyish green leaves, to 20cm (8in) long, which later produce adventitious, marginal plantlets. The lower leaves are simple, the upper ones pinnate, each with 3–5 scalloped, hairless leaflets. Pendent, tubular to bell-shaped, red-tinted, greenish white flowers, to 3.5cm (1½in) long, are produced in cyme-like panicles in late summer. ↕ to 1m (3ft) or more, ↔ to 45cm (18in). Widespread in the tropics. ❀ (min. 12°C/54°F)
K. pubescens. Bushy, erect, perennial succulent with hairy stems that are sometimes glandular. Mid-green leaves, to 4cm (1½in) or more long, are ovate-lance-shaped, toothed, and minutely hairy. Cyme-like panicles of pendent, bell-shaped, triangular-lobed, yellow to red flowers, 5mm (¼in) long, are borne in spring. Small, adventitious plantlets form abundantly in the flower clusters as the flowers fade. ↕ 1m (3ft.), ↔ 45cm (18in). N., C., and E. Madagascar. ❀ (min. 12°C/54°F)

Kalanchoe 'Tessa'

K. pumila. Semi-pendent, spreading, succulent subshrub with ovate to obovate, chalky, white-frosted, mid-green leaves, to 3.5cm (1½in) long, narrowing towards the bases, and with toothed margins at the tips. Urn-shaped flowers, 1cm (½in) long, pink with purple lines, are borne in few-flowered, corymb-like panicles in spring. ↕ 20cm (8in), ↔ to 45cm (18in). Madagascar. ❀ (min. 12°C/54°F)
K. schweinfurthii see *K. laciniata.*
K. somaliensis see *K. marmorata.*
***K.* 'Tessa'** ■ Pendent, perennial succulent bearing narrowly oval, mid-green leaves, 3cm (1¼in) long, with red margins. In late winter and early spring, produces cyme-like panicles of pendent, tubular, orange-red flowers, 2cm (¾in) long. ↕ 30cm (12in), ↔ 60cm (24in). ❀ (min. 12°C/54°F)
K. thyrsiflora. Bushy, white-frosted, perennial succulent, increasing by offsets. It is densely covered with oval to inversely lance-shaped, red-margined, pale green leaves, 10–15cm (4–6in) long, with blunt, rounded tips and leaf pairs united at the bases. In spring, bears cyme-like panicles of erect to spreading, tubular to urn-shaped, fragrant yellow flowers, 1–2cm (½–¾in) long. ↕ 60cm (24in), ↔ 30cm (12in). South Africa (Northern Cape, Western Cape, Eastern Cape). ❀ (min. 12°C/54°F)
K. tomentosa. Erect, bushy, densely white-felted, perennial succulent with thick, oblong, entire grey leaves, 2–9cm (¾–3½in) long, coarsely toothed at the tips, grooved above, and often finely margined reddish brown with furry silver hairs. Bell-shaped, green-yellow flowers, 1.5cm (½in) long, with red glandular hairs and lobes tinged purple, are borne in cyme-like panicles in early spring. ↕ to 1m (3ft), ↔ 20cm (8in). Madagascar. ❀ (min. 12°C/54°F)
K. tubiflora see *K. delagoensis.*
K. uniflora, syn. *Bryophyllum uniflorum.* Prostrate, perennial succulent with rounded, mid-green leaves, 4–15mm (⅛–½in) long, convex on both sides, and with a few uneven, rounded teeth. Pendent, urn-shaped, red to purple flowers, 1–2cm (½–¾in) long, are borne in few-flowered, corymb-like panicles in summer. ↕ 15cm (6in), ↔ 60cm (24in). Madagascar. ❀ (min. 10°C/50°F)
***K.* 'Wendy'** ■ Pendent to semi-erect, perennial succulent with ovate to oblong-ovate, slightly scalloped, glossy, mid-green leaves, to 7cm (3in) long. Corymb-like panicles of bell-shaped, orange- to yellow-tipped, purple-red flowers, 3cm (1¼in) long, are borne in late winter and early spring. ↕↔ 30cm (12in). ❀ (min. 10°C/50°F)

Kalanchoe 'Wendy'

KALIMERIS

ASTERACEAE/COMPOSITAE

Genus of about 10 species of erect, rhizomatous perennials, often with an overwintering rosette of leaves, from grassland and open woodland in E. Asia. The mid-green leaves, arranged alternately, are oblong to elliptic or heart-shaped, range from entire to pinnate, and may be hairy or hairless; leaves on the upper stems are usually shorter, linear-lance-shaped, and entire. Closely related to *Aster*, they bear loose corymbs of daisy-like flowerheads, with white, rose-pink, purple, or blue ray-florets and yellow to almost orange disc-florets, from summer to autumn. Depending on size, grow at the front, middle, or back of an herbaceous border.

- **HARDINESS** Fully hardy.
- **CULTIVATION** Grow in moderately fertile, humus-rich, well-drained soil in full sun or partial shade.
- **PROPAGATION** Sow seed in containers in a cold frame in spring or autumn. Divide or separate runners in spring.
- **PESTS AND DISEASES** Susceptible to mildew.

K. incisa ■ syn. *Boltonia incisa.* Slightly hairy, clump-forming perennial with oblong-lance-shaped or inversely lance-shaped, usually shallowly toothed, short-stalked or stalkless leaves, mostly 3–8cm (1¼–3in) long. From summer to autumn, produces flowerheads, 3–4cm (1¼–1½in) across, with light violet-blue or white ray-florets and yellow or, in white-rayed plants, greenish yellow disc-florets. ↕ 1.5m (5ft), ↔ 30–70cm (12–28in). E. Asia. ✻✻✻
K. integrifolia. Clump-forming perennial with lance-shaped or inversely lance-shaped to linear-lance-shaped, entire leaves, 5–7cm (2–3in) long, tapering at the base, and finely hairy above, downy beneath. Long-stalked blue flowerheads, 2cm (¾in) across, with yellow disc-florets, are borne from late summer to autumn. ↕ to 70cm (28in), ↔ 15–30cm (6–12in). E. Siberia. ✻✻✻
K. mongolica, syn. *Aster mongolicus.* Clump-forming perennial with oblong, deeply pinnatifid, stalked leaves, 10–15cm (4–6in) long, with hairy margins. Bears purple-tinged white flowerheads, 2–3cm (¾–1¼in) across, with yellow disc-florets, from summer to early autumn. ↕ 1.5–1.8m (5–6ft), ↔ 30–40cm (12–16in). China (Mongolia). ✻✻✻
K. pinnatifida, syn. *Aster pinnatifidus.* Clump-forming perennial with oblong to ovate-oblong or diamond-shaped, pinnatifid, hairy, stalkless leaves, 8cm (3in) long. Flowerheads, to 3cm (1¼in) wide, with pale violet or pale pink ray-florets and yellow disc-florets, are borne from summer to autumn. ↕ to 1.5m (5ft), ↔ 20–60cm (8–24in). Japan (Honshu). ✻✻✻
K. yomena, syn. *Aster yomena.* Clump-forming perennial, scattered with fine

Kalimeris incisa

Kalimeris yomena 'Shogun'

hairs, bearing oblong-lance-shaped or inversely lance-shaped, mostly shallowly toothed, short-stalked leaves, 3–6cm (1¼–2½in) long. Light violet-blue or white flowerheads, 3–4cm (1¼–1½in) across, with yellow or, in white-rayed plants, greenish yellow disc-florets, are produced from summer to autumn. Similar to *K. incisa* but has shorter, broader leaves, more of which are stalked. ↕ to 1m (36in), ↔ 15–30cm (6–12in). Japan, Korea. ❄❄❄. **'Shogun'** ■ has cream-variegated leaves in spring, eventually turning cream overall during summer, and becoming yellow in autumn; ↕ 45–70cm (18–28in), ↔ 25–35cm (10–14in).

KALMIA

ERICACEAE

Genus of 7 species of evergreen shrubs found in woodland, swamps, and meadows in North America and Cuba. They have leathery leaves, which may be alternate, in opposite pairs, or in whorls, and showy, bowl-, cup-, or saucer-shaped flowers borne in corymbs or racemes. They are useful for a shrub border or woodland garden; the dwarf species and cultivars are suitable for a peat or heather garden. All parts may cause severe discomfort if ingested.

- **HARDINESS** Fully hardy.
- **CULTIVATION** Grow in moist, humus-rich, acid soil in partial shade, or in sun where soils remain reliably moist. Mulch annually in spring with leaf mould or pine needles. Pruning group 8. *K. angustifolia* tolerates hard pruning; renovate all other species over several seasons.
- **PROPAGATION** Sow seed at 6–12°C (43–54°F) in spring. Take greenwood cuttings in late spring and semi-ripe cuttings in midsummer. Layer in late summer.
- **PESTS AND DISEASES** Trouble free.

K. angustifolia ■ (Sheep laurel). Mound-forming shrub with oblong to elliptic, dark green leaves, to 6cm (2½in) long, in opposite pairs or whorls of 3. Small, bowl- or cup-shaped, pale to deep red, occasionally white flowers, to 1cm (½in) across, are produced in corymbs, 5cm (2in) across, in early summer. ↕ 60cm (24in), ↔ 1.5m (5ft). E. North America. ❄❄❄. **f. *rubra*** has deep red flowers.

Kalmia angustifolia

Kalmia latifolia (inset: flower detail)

K. latifolia ■ (Calico bush, Mountain laurel). Dense, bushy shrub with alternate, oval to elliptic-lance-shaped, glossy, dark green leaves, to 12cm (5in) long. From late spring to midsummer, large corymbs, 8–10cm (3–4in) or more across, of bowl- or cup-shaped, pale to deep pink, or occasionally white flowers, 2–2.5cm (¾–1in) across, are produced from distinctively crimped, often dark pink or red buds. May take several years to recover from hard pruning. ↕↔ 3m (10ft). E. USA. ❄❄❄. **'Bullseye'** has white flowers heavily banded red-purple within. **'Carousel'** has white flowers conspicuously banded red and intricately patterned red or white within. **'Clementine Churchill'** ■ has rich pink flowers opening from dark pink buds. **'Elf'** is compact, with small leaves, 3cm (1¼in) long, and white flowers opening from pale pink buds; ↕↔ 1m (3ft). **'Freckles'** has pale pink flowers ringed with small, red-purple spots just inside the rim. **f. *fuscata*** ■ has a conspicuous deep maroon, purple, or cinnamon ring inside each of the white flowers. **f. *myrtifolia*** is dense, with small leaves, to 5cm (2in) long, and pale pink flowers; ↕↔ 1.2m (4ft) or more. **'Nipmuck'** has pale green leaves and nearly white flowers opening from dark red buds. **'Olympic Fire'** has wavy-margined leaves and large pink flowers, 2.5cm (1in) across, opening from red buds. **'Ostbo Red'** ■ has pale pink flowers opening from bright red buds. **'Shooting Star'** has unusual white flowers, each deeply cut into 5 lobes that reflex after the blooms open. **'Silver**

Kalmia latifolia 'Clementine Churchill'

Kalmia latifolia f. *fuscata*

K

Kalmia latifolia 'Ostbo Red'

Kalmia polifolia

Dollar' has very large white flowers, to 4cm (1½in) long.

K. microphylla, syn. *K. polifolia* var. *microphylla* (Western laurel). Sparsely branched, dwarf shrub with opposite, leathery, flat, ovate to oval leaves, 0.6–3.5cm (¼–1½in) long. Bears terminal racemes of saucer-shaped, pink to rose-purple flowers, to 3cm (1¼in) across, in late spring and early summer. ↕ to 15cm (6in), occasionally to 60cm (24in) in very wet, boggy conditions, ↔ 15–30cm (6–12in). USA (Alaska to California). ❄❄❄

K. polifolia ■ (Eastern bog laurel). Small, sparsely branched shrub with linear to oblong, glossy, dark green leaves, to 4cm (1½in) long, in opposite pairs or whorls of 3, with rolled-back margins and glandular hairs beneath. Bears racemes, 2.5–4cm (1–1½in) across, of up to 12 saucer-shaped, purple-pink flowers, 1–2cm (½–¾in) across, in mid- and late spring. Requires moist soil. ↕ 60cm (24in), ↔ 90cm (36in). Canada, N.E. USA. ❄❄❄. **var. *microphylla*** see *K. microphylla.*

KALMIOPSIS

ERICACEAE

Genus of one species of evergreen shrub from Oregon, USA, where it grows on rocky ledges on mountain cliffs. It has simple leaves, arranged alternately, and is cultivated for its terminal racemes of small, cup-shaped flowers. Suitable for a cool position in a peat garden.

• **HARDINESS** Fully hardy.

• **CULTIVATION** Grow in moist but well-drained, humus-rich, lime-free

Kalmiopsis leachiana 'La Piniec'

soil in full sun (provided that the soil remains cool and moist) or in partial shade. Pruning group 8.

• **PROPAGATION** Sow seed at 6–12°C (43–54°F) in spring, or take semi-ripe cuttings in summer.

• **PESTS AND DISEASES** Trouble free.

K. leachiana. Dwarf, evergreen shrub with alternate, oval to obovate, bright deep green leaves, to 3cm (1¼in) long, glandular beneath. Small, cup-shaped, rose-red to purple-pink flowers, to 2cm (¾in) across, are produced in terminal racemes, 2.5–5cm (1–2in) long, from early to late spring. ↕↔ 30cm (12in). USA (Oregon). ❄❄❄. **'La Piniec'** ■ has glossy, dark green leaves, to 2cm (¾in) long. **'Umpqua Valley'** is compact, vigorous, and free-flowering.

x KALMIOTHAMNUS

ERICACEAE

Hybrid genus of dwarf evergreen shrubs, resulting from crosses between *Kalmiopsis leachiana* and *Rhodothamnus chamaecistus.* They have small, narrow, dark green leaves and produce short racemes of 5-lobed, saucer-shaped flowers in late spring and summer. Grow in a heather or woodland garden.

• **HARDINESS** Fully hardy.

• **CULTIVATION** Grow in moist but well-drained, moderately fertile, humus-rich, lime-free soil in full sun or partial shade. Pruning group 8.

• **PROPAGATION** Take semi-ripe cuttings in summer.

• **PESTS AND DISEASES** Trouble free.

x *Kalmiothamnus ornithomma*

x ***K. ornithomma*** ■ Dwarf, rounded shrub with narrowly elliptic, hairless, deep green leaves, to 1.5cm (½in) long, pale green beneath. Saucer-shaped, pink to red-purple flowers, 2.5cm (1in) across, with crimson eyes, are borne in short, terminal racemes from late spring to early summer. ↕↔ 15cm (6in). Garden origin. ❄❄❄

KALOPANAX

ARALIACEAE

Genus of one species of deciduous tree from forests in E. Asia. It has a spreading habit and large, variably shaped, palmately lobed leaves, which are arranged alternately and vary from hairless to very hairy beneath. Large, terminal, umbel-like panicles of usually white, 4- or 5-petalled flowers, are borne in late summer, and are followed by spherical, blue-black fruit. It is a fine specimen tree.

• **HARDINESS** Fully hardy, but young growth may be damaged by late frosts.

• **CULTIVATION** Grow in fertile, moist but well-drained soil in full sun or partial shade, preferably sheltered by other trees and shrubs. Pruning group 1.

• **PROPAGATION** Sow seed in containers in a cold frame in autumn, or take greenwood cuttings in early summer.

• **PESTS AND DISEASES** Trouble free.

K. pictus see *K. septemlobus.*
K. ricinifolius see *K. septemlobus.*
K. septemlobus ■ Q syn. *Acanthopanax ricinifolius, Eleutherococcus pictus, Kalopanax pictus, K. ricinifolius.* Spreading, deciduous tree with spines on the trunk and shoots, and variably shaped, shallowly to deeply 5- to 7-lobed, dark green leaves, to 35cm (14in) or more across, which vary from hairless to very hairy beneath. Large, umbel-like panicles, 20–30cm (8–12in) long, of small, 4- or 5-petalled white flowers, 2mm (1/16in) across, are produced in late summer, followed by spherical, blue-black fruit, 4mm (⅛in) across. ↕↔ 10m (30ft). China, Korea, Russia (S. Kurile Islands, Sakhalin), Japan (Ryukyu Islands). ❄❄❄. **var. *magnificus*** has ovate leaves that are shallowly lobed and densely hairy on the lower leaf sides; W. China. **var. *maximowiczii*** is similar to var. *magnificus*, but has deeply lobed, lance-shaped leaves.

▷ **Kangaroo paw** see *Anigozanthos*
Black see *Macropidia fuliginosa*
Green see *Anigozanthos viridis*
Little see *Anigozanthos bicolor*
Mangles' see *Anigozanthos manglesii*
Yellow see *Anigozanthos pulcherrimus*
▷ **Kangaroo thorn** see *Acacia paradoxa*
▷ **Kangaroo vine** see *Cissus antarctica*
▷ **Kansas feather** see *Liatris pycnostachya*
▷ **Kapok** see *Ceiba pentandra*
▷ **Karaka** see *Corynocarpus laevigatus*
▷ **Karo** see *Pittosporum crassifolium*
▷ **Kassod tree** see *Senna siamea*
▷ **Katsura tree** see *Cercidiphyllum japonicum*
▷ **Kawaka** see *Libocedrus plumosa*
▷ **Kawa kawa** see *Macropiper excelsum*

Kalopanax septemlobus

KECKIELLA

SCROPHULARIACEAE

Genus of about 7 species of branching, deciduous, semi-evergreen, and evergreen shrubs and subshrubs from W. USA and Mexico, where they grow on dry hillsides. Closely related to *Penstemon*, they are usually grown for their habit and dense, terminal panicles or spike-like racemes of tubular or trumpet-shaped, yellow to red flowers borne in summer. They have opposite, lance-shaped to ovate, mid- to dark green leaves. *K. cordifolia* is best trained on a warm wall; other species are suitable for a mixed border.

• **HARDINESS** Frost hardy.

• **CULTIVATION** Grow in a sheltered site in moderately fertile, well-drained soil in full sun. Pruning group 1, or 13 if wall-trained.

• **PROPAGATION** Sow seed in containers in a cold frame in late winter or early spring. Take softwood cuttings in early summer or semi-ripe cuttings in midsummer.

• **PESTS AND DISEASES** Trouble free.

K. cordifolia, syn. *Penstemon cordifolius.* Loosely branched, scrambling, semi-evergreen shrub with lance-shaped to ovate, sharply toothed, dark green leaves, to 5cm (2in) long, heart-shaped at the bases. In midsummer, bears racemes of pendent, tubular, hooded red flowers, to 4cm (1½in) long, with dense yellow-brown beards on the lower staminodes. ↕ 1–3m (3–10ft), ↔ 60cm (2ft). USA (California). ❄❄

KELSEYA

ROSACEAE

Genus of one species of evergreen, cushion-forming subshrub found in rock crevices and scree in the Rocky Mountains, USA. Cultivated for its neat rosettes of silvery green foliage, it also has solitary, star-shaped flowers, produced in early summer. It resents winter wet, and is best grown in an alpine house, although it may be grown outdoors in a scree bed, trough, or vertical rock crevice.

• **HARDINESS** Fully hardy.

• **CULTIVATION** In an alpine house, grow in a mix of 3 parts grit and 1 part each of loam and leaf mould. Outdoors, grow in very gritty, humus-rich, moist but sharply drained, preferably alkaline soil, in full sun; provide overhead protection from rain in winter.

• **PROPAGATION** Sow seed in containers in an open frame in autumn, or take soft-tip cuttings in spring.

• **PESTS AND DISEASES** Susceptible to aphids and red spider mites under glass, and to grey mould (*Botrytis*) in damp conditions.

K. uniflora. Slow-growing, cushion-forming subshrub with tight rosettes of overlapping, ovate, leathery, dark green leaves, to 3mm (1/8in) long, clothed in silky silver hairs. Solitary, stemless, star-shaped, white or pink-flushed flowers, 8mm (3/8in) across, are produced from pink buds just above the leaf rosettes in early summer. Does not always flower freely. ↕ to 8cm (3in), ↔ to 15cm (6in). USA (Rocky Mountains). ✻✻✻

▷**Kenaf** see *Hibiscus cannabinus*

KENNEDIA *syn.* KENNEDYA

Coral pea

LEGUMINOSAE/PAPILIONACEAE

Genus of 16 species of herbaceous and woody-stemmed climbing and trailing perennials from a variety of habitats, including rainforest, open forest, shrubland, heathland, and semi-desert, in Australia and New Guinea. They are grown for their long-keeled, pea-like flowers, produced singly, in pairs, umbels, or racemes in the leaf axils. The leaves, arranged alternately, each have 3 leaflets and a pair of distinctive stipules at the base of the stalk. In frost-prone areas, grow in a cool or temperate greenhouse. In milder regions, train over a pergola or arch. The trailers are also good as ground cover on a bank.

• **HARDINESS** Half hardy to frost tender.

• **CULTIVATION** Under glass, grow in loam-based potting compost (JI No.2) with added sharp sand, in bright filtered light. In growth, water moderately and apply a balanced liquid fertilizer monthly; water sparingly in winter. Provide support for the climbing stems. Outdoors, grow in fertile, moist, but well-drained soil in partial shade. Pruning group 12, after flowering or in late winter.

• **PROPAGATION** Sow seed at 18–21°C (64–70°F) in spring, ideally after soaking in freshly boiled water for 12 hours.

• **PESTS AND DISEASES** Prone to red spider mites and whiteflies under glass.

Kennedia rubicunda

K. coccinea (Common coral vine). Woody-stemmed, twining climber or trailer, with leaves 3–10cm (1¼–4in) long, each divided into 3 broadly oblong to linear-wedge-shaped, occasionally lobed, slightly leathery, deep green leaflets. From spring to early summer, produces axillary and terminal, umbel-like racemes, 10cm (4in) long, of 4–20 coral-red flowers, 1.5cm (½in) wide, the standard petals marked with yellow and purple-margined at the bases, opening from buds covered with soft red hairs. Tolerates coastal sites and alkaline soil. ↕ 2m (6ft). Australia (Western Australia). ❀ (min. 5–7°C/41–45°F)

K. nigricans (Black coral pea). Vigorous, woody, twining climber with leaves 5–15cm (2–6in) long, each divided into 3 ovate, leathery, rich green leaflets, heart-shaped at the bases. From late winter to late spring or early summer, produces one-sided, axillary racemes, 15cm (6in) long, of elongated, velvety, purple-black flowers, to 3cm (1¼in) long, the standard petals reflexed and boldly splashed yellow. Thrives in poor sandy soil; tolerates coastal sites. ↕ 4–6m (12–20ft). Australia (Western Australia). ❀ (min. 5–7°C/41–45°F)

K. prostrata (Running postman, Scarlet runner). Prostrate to mat-forming trailer, with numerous, often sparsely branched, densely softly hairy stems radiating from a woody rootstock. The leaves, to 10cm (4in) long, are each composed of 3 ovate-rounded to rounded, wavy-margined, bright green leaflets. From spring to summer, sometimes also in autumn, scarlet flowers, to 2.5cm (1in) long, the standard petals each with a small, greenish yellow mark at the base, are borne in loose racemes, to 8cm (3in) long. ↔ to 1.5m (5ft). Australia (Western Australia). ❀ (min. 5°C/41°F)

K. rubicunda ■ (Dusky coral pea). Twining climber or mat-forming perennial with slender, hairy stems, becoming dense and tangled with age. The leaves, to 16cm (6in) long, are each composed of 3 ovate, hairy, mid-green leaflets. From spring to summer, dark red flowers, 3–4cm (1¼–1½in) long, with pointed keel petals and swept-back standards marked pale tan at the bases, are produced in loose, axillary racemes, to 8cm (3in) long. ↕ to 3m (10ft) or more. Australia (New South Wales, Victoria). ❀ (min. 5–7°C/41–45°F)

▷***Kennedya*** see *Kennedia*
▷***Kentia acuminata*** see *Carpentaria acuminata*
▷***Kentia canterburyana*** see *Hedyscepe canterburyana*
▷***Kentia forsteriana*** see *Howea forsteriana*
▷***Kentia joannis*** see *Veitchia joannis*
▷**Kerosene bush** see *Ozothamnus ledifolius*

KERRIA

Jew's mantle

ROSACEAE

Genus of one species of deciduous shrub, found in thickets and woodland in China and Japan. It has simple leaves, which are arranged alternately, and solitary, cup- or saucer-shaped yellow flowers. Kerrias are grown for their foliage and flowers, and are suitable

Kerria japonica 'Golden Guinea' (inset: flower detail)

for a shrub border or an open position in a woodland garden.

• **HARDINESS** Fully hardy.

• **CULTIVATION** Grow in fertile, well-drained soil in full sun or partial shade. Pruning group 3.

• **PROPAGATION** Take greenwood cuttings in summer. Divide in autumn.

• **PESTS AND DISEASES** Trouble free.

K. japonica. Suckering shrub with arching green shoots and ovate, pointed, sharply toothed, bright green leaves, to 10cm (4in) long. In mid- and late spring, produces solitary, single or double, golden yellow flowers, 3–5cm (1¼–2in) across. ↕ 2m (6ft), ↔ 2.5m (8ft). China, Japan. ✻✻✻. **'Golden Guinea'** ■ has very large, single flowers, 5–6cm (2–2½in) across. **'Picta'**, syn. 'Variegata', has grey-green leaves margined creamy white; ↕ 1.5m (5ft), ↔ 2m (6ft). **'Pleniflora'** is very vigorous and upright, with large, pompon-like, double flowers, 3cm (1¼in) across; ↕↔ 3m (10ft). **'Variegata'** see 'Picta'.

KETELEERIA

PINACEAE

Genus of 3–7 species of conical, monoecious, evergreen, coniferous trees, resembling *Abies*, found in warm temperate regions of China, Laos, Vietnam, and Taiwan. Most grow in wet or rocky habitats on poor, acid soil. They bear spirally arranged, flattened, oblong-linear, linear, or lance-shaped, shiny, mid- to dark green leaves, which are mostly spread into 2 comb-like rows, leaving circular leaf-scars on the branches. The female cones, borne in terminal or axillary clusters, are erect, cylindrical, and reddish brown when young, maturing pale brown or glaucous, blue-green, and they remain whole, eventually falling intact. The much smaller male cones are yellowish brown and often clustered at the tips of side branches. Keteleerias are fine specimen trees, and are best grown in regions where summers are long and hot.

• **HARDINESS** Fully hardy, but young shoots are prone to damage by late spring frosts.

• **CULTIVATION** Grow in fertile, moist but well-drained, neutral to slightly acid soil in full sun, preferably with shelter from cold, drying winds. Pruning group 1.

• **PROPAGATION** Sow seed in containers in a cold frame as soon as ripe or in late winter. Graft in mid- to late winter or from late summer to early autumn.

• **PESTS AND DISEASES** Prone to adelgids and honey fungus.

K. davidiana ■ ◊ Conical tree, becoming flat-topped and often producing buttress-like roots with age, with grey or grey-brown bark, becoming fissured as the tree develops. Oblong-linear, mid- to dark green leaves are spine-tipped and 4–6cm (1½–2½in) long on young plants, blunter and 2–4cm (¾–1½in) long on older trees. Cylindrical female cones, 12–20cm (5–8in) long, are reddish brown when young, maturing pale brown. ↕ 15–25m (50–80ft), ↔ 10m (30ft). China. ✻✻✻

Keteleeria davidiana

KIGELIA

Sausage tree

BIGNONIACEAE

Genus of one species of variable, evergreen tree from tropical woodland and more open areas in Africa. It has large, pinnate leaves, borne in opposite pairs, and loose, pendent panicles, 1–2m (3–6ft) long, of open, trumpet-shaped flowers, followed by long, woody pods. Where temperatures drop below 16°C (61°F), grow in a warm greenhouse, mainly for its foliage, although flowers may form on specimens reaching 3m (10ft) or more high. In tropical areas, it is an attractive specimen or shade tree.

- **HARDINESS** Frost tender.
- **CULTIVATION** Under glass, grow in loam-based potting compost (JI No.3) in full light but screened from the hottest summer sun, at least during the early years. During the growing season, water moderately and apply a balanced liquid fertilizer monthly; water sparingly in winter. Outdoors, grow in fertile, well-drained soil in full sun. Pruning group 1; plants under glass need restrictive pruning in late winter or after flowering.
- **PROPAGATION** Sow seed at 21–23°C (70–73°F) in spring.
- **PESTS AND DISEASES** Red spider mites, whiteflies, and mealybugs may be troublesome under glass.

K. pinnata ▣ ♡ Rounded to broadly columnar, usually freely branching tree with robust stems. Bears pinnate leaves, to 50cm (20in) long, each composed of 7–11 oblong to obovate, leathery, mid- to deep green leaflets, sometimes notched at the tips. Loose, pendent panicles of bat-pollinated flowers, each 10cm (4in) across, are produced in summer. Yellowish green in bud, they open to rich brownish red at night, when they have an unpleasant smell that is attractive to bats. The cylindrical, woody fruit, to 35–60cm (14–24in) or more long, may weigh 5–7kg (11–15lb), and are pale brown when ripe. They remain on the thickened flowering stems for many months. ↕ 15m (50ft) or more, ↔ 5–10m (15–30ft). Tropical Africa. ❀ (min. 16°C/61°F)

Kigelia pinnata

▷ **Kilmarnock willow** see *Salix caprea* 'Kilmarnock'
▷ **Kindling bark, Broad-leaved** see *Eucalyptus dalrympleana*
▷ **Kingcup** see *Caltha, C. palustris*
▷ **King protea** see *Protea cynaroides*
▷ **King's crown** see *Justicia carnea*
▷ **King's mantle** see *Thunbergia erecta*
▷ **King's spear** see *Asphodeline lutea*
▷ **Kinnikinnick** see *Arctostaphylos uva-ursi*

KIRENGESHOMA

HYDRANGEACEAE

Genus of 2 species of clump-forming perennials, with short rhizomes, from woodland in Korea and Japan. They have broadly tubular, waxy, pale or bright yellow flowers, borne on slender stalks in nodding, terminal cymes above pairs of elegant, sycamore-like leaves. They are suitable for a shady border, peat bed, or woodland garden.

- **HARDINESS** Fully hardy.
- **CULTIVATION** Grow in moist, lime-free soil, enriched with leaf mould, in partial shade sheltered from wind.
- **PROPAGATION** Sow seed in containers in a cold frame as soon as ripe or in spring (germination may be slow and erratic). Divide as growth begins in spring, taking care not to damage tender young shoots.
- **PESTS AND DISEASES** Slugs and snails may attack young growth and leaves.

K. palmata ▣ Clump-forming perennial with short rhizomes and arching, smooth, reddish purple stems. These bear broadly ovate, palmately lobed, slightly hairy, pale green leaves, 10–20cm (4–8in) long, becoming smaller, simple, and almost stalkless towards the stem tips. Nodding, terminal cymes of 3 broadly tubular, pale yellow flowers, to 3.5cm (1½in) long, with slightly recurved lobes and fleshy petals that overlap at the bases, are borne in late summer and early autumn. ↕ 60–120cm (24–48in), ↔ 75cm (30in). Japan. ❄❄❄

▷ **Kiss-me-over-the-garden-gate** see *Persicaria orientale*

Kirengeshoma palmata

Kitaibela vitifolia

KITAIBELA syn. KITAIBELIA

MALVACEAE

Genus of two species of imposing, often short-lived herbaceous perennials found in damp meadows and scrub from Slovenia to Macedonia. They have palmately lobed, vine-like leaves and showy, mallow-like flowers, produced singly or in axillary cymes. They are suitable for a wild or meadow garden.

- **HARDINESS** Fully hardy.
- **CULTIVATION** Grow in deep, moderately fertile, moist but well-drained soil in full sun or partial shade.
- **PROPAGATION** Sow seed in containers in a cold frame in spring or autumn. Root basal or softwood cuttings in spring.
- **PESTS AND DISEASES** Trouble free.

K. vitifolia ▣ Clump-forming, woody-based, softly white-hairy perennial with erect stems bearing 5- to 7-lobed, coarsely toothed leaves, to 17cm (7in) long. Mallow-like, open cup-shaped, 5-petalled, white to rose-red flowers, 4.5cm (1¾in) across, are produced singly or in few-flowered, axillary cymes from midsummer to early autumn. ↕ to 2.5m (8ft), ↔ 5m (15ft). Slovenia to Macedonia. ❄❄❄

▷ ***Kitaibelia*** see *Kitaibela*
▷ **Kiwi fruit** see *Actinidia deliciosa*
▷ **Klapperbos** see *Nymania capensis*

KLEINIA

ASTERACEAE/COMPOSITAE

Genus of 40 species of succulent perennials, closely related to *Senecio*, from lowlands and mountains in tropical Africa, N.W. Africa, the Canary Islands, southern Africa, Madagascar, and the Arabian Peninsula. Many species have tuberous roots and prostrate to upright, cylindrical to angular stems, with flat or cylindrical, succulent, usually entire leaves. Colourful, thistle-like flowerheads appear singly or in branched, terminal or axillary corymbs in summer. Where temperatures drop below 10°C (50°F), grow as houseplants or in a warm greenhouse. In warmer climates, grow in a desert garden.

- **HARDINESS** Frost tender.
- **CULTIVATION** Under glass, grow in a mix of 2 parts leaf mould and 1 part each loam and gritty sand, in full light. In growth, water moderately and apply a balanced liquid fertilizer 2 or 3 times. Keep dry when dormant. Outdoors, grow in sharply drained, gritty, humus-rich soil in full sun. See also pp.48–49.
- **PROPAGATION** Sow seed at 20°C (68°F), or take cuttings, in spring or summer.
- **PESTS AND DISEASES** Susceptible to scale insects.

Kleinia stapeliiformis

K. repens see *Senecio serpens.*
K. rowleyana see *Senecio rowleyanus.*
K. stapeliiformis ▣ syn. *Senecio stapeliiformis.* Erect succulent branching from the base, with new shoots growing underground at first. Thick, fleshy, 5- to 7-angled branches, glaucous green with purple staining, bear very slender, oblong, thread-like, fleshy, grey-green leaves, often flushed purple with dark green lines along their lengths. The leaves, 5mm (¼in) long, become thorny as they age. Solitary, thistle-like, red or orange-red flowerheads, to 4cm (1½in) long, are produced in summer. ↕↔ 20–30cm (8–12in). E. South Africa (KwaZulu/Natal). ❀ (min. 10°C/50°F)

▷ **Knapweed** see *Centaurea*
Greater see *C. scabiosa*

KNAUTIA

DIPSACACEAE

Genus of 40 or more species of scabious-like annuals and perennials from limestone grassland, scrub, and woodland in Europe, Caucasus, Russia (Siberia), and N. Africa. They have overwintering rosettes of simple to pinnatifid basal leaves, and opposite pairs of stem leaves, which are usually deeply pinnatifid, although the uppermost leaves may be simple. Tall stems bear cup-shaped involucres of bracts, with bristly hairs or teeth, surrounding dense, bluish lilac or reddish purple flowerheads. The flowers have unequally lobed corollas and stamens protruding in "pincushion" style. They are attractive to bees. Grow in a border, or a wild or cottage garden.

Knautia macedonica

• **HARDINESS** Fully hardy.
• **CULTIVATION** Grow in moderately fertile, well-drained, preferably alkaline soil in full sun.
• **PROPAGATION** Sow seed in containers in a cold frame in spring, or take basal cuttings in spring.
• **PESTS AND DISEASES** Prone to aphids.

K. arvensis, syn. *Scabiosa arvensis* (Field scabious). Clump-forming, deeply tap-rooted perennial with erect but often lax, hairless stems, the lower parts bristly. Produces simple to pinnatifid, hairy, dull green leaves, 5–25cm (2–10in) long, simple or pinnatifid higher up the stem. Flat-topped, bluish lilac flowerheads, 3–4cm (1¼–1½in) across, with softly bristly, involucral bracts, are borne from midsummer to early autumn. ↕ to 1.5m (5ft), ↔ 30cm (12in). Europe, Caucasus, Iran to C. Asia, Russia (Siberia). ✻✻✻
K. macedonica ■ syn. *Scabiosa rumelica*. Clump-forming perennial with slender, branched stems, pinnatifid basal leaves, 8cm (3in) long, each with a large, terminal lobe, and simple or pinnatifid stem leaves, 2–15cm (¾–6in) long. Numerous long-lasting, purple-red flowerheads, 1.5–3cm (½–1¼in) across, with softly bristly, involucral bracts, are produced in mid- and late summer. ↕ 60–80cm (24–32in), ↔ 45cm (18in). C. Balkans into Romania. ✻✻✻

KNIGHTIA

PROTEACEAE

Genus of 3 species of evergreen trees or shrubs from lowland to low mountain forest, one from New Zealand, 2 from New Caledonia. The leathery, entire or toothed leaves are arranged alternately and vary in shape with age: young plants have long, thin leaves; adults have shorter, thicker ones. Tubular flowers, with 4 petal-like tepals that roll up like springs, are borne in dense racemes. In frost-prone areas, grow in a cool or temperate greenhouse. In milder climates, use as a specimen tree.
• **HARDINESS** Frost tender; may survive short periods around 0°C (32°F).
• **CULTIVATION** Under glass, grow in loam-based potting compost (JI No.2) in full light, with shade from hot sun and with good ventilation. During the growing season, water moderately and apply a balanced liquid fertilizer every month; water sparingly in winter. Outdoors, grow in fertile, well-drained, neutral to acid soil, in full sun or partial shade, with shelter from cold winds. Pruning group 1.
• **PROPAGATION** Sow seed at 13–16°C (55–61°F) in spring. Root semi-ripe cuttings with bottom heat in summer (rooting may be slow).
• **PESTS AND DISEASES** Red spider mites may be a problem under glass.

K. excelsa ♀ (New Zealand honeysuckle, Rewarewa). Tall, usually columnar tree, with many short, lateral branches. Adult leaves are narrowly oblong to obovate-oblong, 10–15cm (4–6in) long, blunt-toothed and stiff. From spring to summer, produces few to many tubular red flowers, 2.5–4cm (1–1½in) long, in racemes 10cm (4in) long, covered with short, velvety, red-brown hairs, followed by narrow seed pods, which split open down one side only. ↕ to 30m (100ft), ↔ 7–10m (22–30ft). New Zealand. ❀ (min. 3–7°C/37–45°F)

KNIPHOFIA

Red hot poker, Torch lily

ASPHODELACEAE/LILIACEAE

Genus of about 70 species of evergreen or deciduous, rhizomatous perennials from mountainous or upland areas, often in moist places in rough grass or along streamsides, in southern and tropical Africa. Most are clump-forming, with arching, tufted, linear to strap-shaped, light to mid-green or blue-green leaves. In deciduous species and hybrids these leaves are usually thin, grass-like, and 10–100cm (4–39in) long; in evergreens, they are broader, keeled or strap-shaped, and to 1.5m (5ft) long. Erect, usually dense, spike-like racemes, 5–40cm (2–16in) long, of numerous pendent, occasionally erect, tubular or cylindrical flowers, 0.3–5cm (⅛–2in) long, are borne well above the foliage. They are attractive to bees. The flowers are red, orange, yellow, white, or greenish white; some open red, then turn to yellow, bearing striking, 2-coloured racemes. Numerous cultivars have been raised, ranging in size from dwarf plants, 50cm (20in) high, to tall plants, to 1.8m (6ft) high. Grow in a herbaceous border; in frost-prone areas, grow tender species in a cool or temperate greenhouse.
• **HARDINESS** Fully hardy to frost tender.
• **CULTIVATION** Grow in deep, fertile, humus-rich, moist but well-drained, preferably sandy soil, in full sun or partial shade. Mulch young plants with straw or leaves for the first winter.
• **PROPAGATION** Sow seed in containers in a cold frame in spring (although cultivars seldom come true from seed). Divide established clumps in late spring. Stimulate offshoots from slow-growing, woody-based, evergreen red hot pokers by cutting off crowns; leave offshoots in place to develop for 2 years before separating from parent plants, or use new shoots as basal cuttings.
• **PESTS AND DISEASES** Thrips may cause mottling of the foliage. Violet root rot may be a problem.

Kniphofia 'Atlanta'

Kniphofia 'Bees' Sunset'

***K.* 'Ada'.** Deciduous perennial with tawny orange-yellow flowers borne in late summer and early autumn. ↕ 90cm (36in), ↔ 60cm (24in). ✻✻✻
***K.* 'Atlanta'** ■ Evergreen perennial with grey-green leaves, and orange-red flowers, fading to pale yellow, borne in late spring and early summer. ↕ 1.2m (4ft), ↔ 75cm (30in). ✻✻✻
***K.* 'Bees' Lemon'.** Deciduous perennial with toothed leaves, and lemon-yellow flowers, green in bud, borne in late summer and early autumn. ↕ 90cm (36in), ↔ 60cm (24in). ✻✻✻
***K.* 'Bees' Sunset'** ■ Deciduous perennial with toothed leaves, and soft yellowish orange flowers borne from early to late summer. ↕ 90cm (36in), ↔ 60cm (24in). ✻✻✻
***K.* 'Border Ballet'.** Deciduous perennial with cream to pink flowers borne in late summer and early autumn. ↕↔ 60cm (24in). ✻✻✻
***K.* 'Bressingham Comet'.** Deciduous perennial with red-tipped orange flowers, yellow at the bases, borne in early and mid-autumn. ↕ 45cm (18in), ↔ 22cm (9in). ✻✻✻
***K.* 'Buttercup'.** Deciduous perennial with green buds, opening to clear yellow flowers in early summer. ↕↔ 75cm (30in). ✻✻✻
K. caulescens ■ Evergreen perennial with short, thick, woody-based stems and arching, linear, keeled, finely toothed, glaucous leaves, to 1m (3ft) long, purple at the bases. Coral-red flowers, 2.5cm (1in) long, fading to pale yellow, with protruding stamens, are borne in short, oblong-cylindrical racemes from late summer to mid-autumn. ↕ to 1.2m (4ft), ↔ 60cm (24in). South Africa (N. Eastern Cape, Free State, KwaZulu/Natal), Lesotho. ✻✻✻
***K.* 'C.M. Prichard' of gardens** see *K. rooperi.*
***K.* 'Corallina'.** Deciduous perennial with deep green leaves, and coral-red flowers borne in early summer. ↕ 90cm (36in), ↔ 60cm (24in). ✻✻✻
***K.* 'Early Buttercup'.** Deciduous perennial with yellow flowers borne in late spring and early summer. ↕ 90cm (36in), ↔ 60cm (24in). ✻✻✻
***K. ensifolia*.** Robust, evergreen perennial forming clumps of arching, narrowly elliptic, finely toothed, glaucous leaves, to 1.5m (5ft) long. Bears greenish white flowers, 1.5–2cm (½–¾in) long, often red in bud, in dense, cylindrical racemes from late summer to mid-autumn. ↕ 1.2m (4ft) or more, ↔ 60cm (24in). South Africa (Western Cape, Eastern Cape,

Kniphofia caulescens

KNIPHOFIA

Kniphofia 'Erecta'

K

KwaZulu/Natal, Mpumalanga, Limpopo). ❄❄❄
***K.* 'Erecta'** ■ Deciduous perennial with bright coral-red flowers, turning upwards after opening, borne in late summer and early autumn. ↕90cm (36in), ↔ 60cm (24in). ❄❄❄
***K.* 'Fiery Fred'.** Deciduous perennial with orange-red flowers borne from early to late summer. ↕to 1.2m (4ft), ↔ 60cm (24in). ❄❄❄
***K. galpinii* of gardens** see *K. triangularis.*
***K.* 'Goldelse'.** Deciduous perennial with grass-like leaves, and yellow flowers borne in racemes in early summer. ↕75cm (30in), ↔ 30cm (12in). ❄❄❄
***K.* 'Green Jade'** ■ Robust, evergreen perennial with keeled leaves, and green

Kniphofia 'Ice Queen'

flowers, becoming cream and then white, borne in racemes in late summer and early autumn. ↕to 1.5m (5ft), ↔ 60–75cm (24–30in). ❄❄❄
K. hirsuta. Evergreen perennial with linear, spreading, hairy, dark green leaves, 40–60cm (16–24in) long, red at the bases. Pinkish red flowers, 2–3cm (¾–1¼in) long, becoming yellow, are produced in conical racemes in mid-spring. ↕40cm (16in), ↔ 45cm (18in). Lesotho. ❄❄
***K.* 'Ice Queen'** ■ Robust, deciduous perennial bearing green-budded flowers opening to pale primrose yellow, fading to ivory, in early and mid-autumn. ↕to 1.5m (5ft), ↔ 75cm (30in). ❄❄❄
***K.* 'Jenny Bloom'.** Deciduous perennial with pink flowers, shading to cream and coral-pink, borne from late summer to mid-autumn. ↕1m (3ft), ↔ 30cm (12in). ❄❄❄
***K.* 'Limelight'.** Deciduous perennial with grass-like foliage, and canary-yellow flowers, greenish yellow in bud, borne in early autumn. ↕90cm (36in), ↔ 45cm (18in). ❄❄❄
***K.* 'Little Maid'** ■ Deciduous perennial with grass-like leaves, and racemes of flowers, pale green in bud, opening to

Kniphofia 'Percy's Pride'

buff-tinted pale yellow and ageing to ivory, borne in late summer and early autumn. ↕60cm (24in), ↔ 45cm (18in). ❄❄❄
K. macowanii see *K. triangularis.*
***K.* 'Maid of Orleans'.** Deciduous perennial bearing long-lasting flowers, pale primrose in bud, opening to deeper yellow, and maturing to ivory, borne in mid- and late summer. ↕to 1.2m (4ft), ↔ 45cm (18in). ❄❄❄
***K.* 'Mount Etna'.** Deciduous perennial with broad racemes of pale greenish yellow flowers, scarlet in bud, borne in late summer and early autumn. ↕to 1.2m (4ft), ↔ 90cm (36in). ❄❄❄
K. nelsonii see *K. triangularis.*
K. northiae. Evergreen perennial forming thick-stemmed, solitary plants, not clumps, with arching, linear, broad, unkeeled, glaucous leaves, to 1.5m (5ft) long. Pale yellow flowers, 2.5–3cm (1–1¼in) long, opening from red buds, are produced in oblong, very dense racemes from early to late summer. ↕1.5m (5ft), ↔ 90cm (36in). South Africa (Eastern Cape, KwaZulu/Natal), Lesotho. ❄❄❄
***K.* 'Percy's Pride'** ■ Deciduous perennial with keeled leaves, and canary-yellow flowers, green-tinted yellow in bud, opening to cream, borne in late summer and early autumn. ↕1.2m (4ft), ↔ 60cm (24in). ❄❄❄
***K.* 'Prince Igor'** ■ Deciduous perennial with glowing, deep orange-red flowers borne in racemes in early and mid-autumn. ↕1.8m (6ft), ↔ 90cm (36in). ❄❄❄
K. rooperi ■ syn. *K.* 'C.M. Prichard' of gardens. Robust, evergreen perennial with arching, broad, linear, acutely pointed, deeply keeled, dark green leaves. Orange-red flowers, 3.5–4.5cm (1½–1¾in) long, becoming orange-yellow, are borne in broadly ellipsoid, shiny racemes from early to late autumn. ↕1.2m (4ft), ↔ 60cm (24in). South Africa (Eastern Cape). ❄❄❄

Kniphofia 'Green Jade'

Kniphofia 'Little Maid'

Kniphofia 'Prince Igor'

Kniphofia rooperi

Kniphofia 'Royal Standard'

***K.* 'Royal Standard'** ▣ Deciduous perennial with bright yellow flowers, scarlet in bud, borne on stout stems in mid- and late summer. ↕ 90–100cm (36–39in), ↔ 60cm (24in). ❄❄❄

***K.* 'Samuel's Sensation'.** Deciduous perennial with bright scarlet flowers, tinged with yellow as they fade, borne in racemes in late summer and early autumn. ↕ 1.5m (5ft), ↔ 60–75cm (24–30in). ❄❄❄

***K.* 'Shining Sceptre'.** Deciduous perennial with clear yellow flowers, becoming ivory, borne in midsummer. ↕ 1.2m (4ft), ↔ 60cm (24in). ❄❄❄

***K. snowdenii* of gardens** see *K. thompsonii* var. *snowdenii.*

***K.* 'Strawberries and Cream'** ▣ Deciduous perennial with cream flowers, coral-pink in bud, borne in late summer and early autumn. ↕ 60cm (24in), ↔ 30cm (12in). ❄❄❄

***K.* 'Sunningdale Yellow'.** Deciduous perennial with long-lasting racemes of yellow flowers produced in mid- and late summer. ↕ 90cm (36in), ↔ 45cm (18in). ❄❄❄

***K. thompsonii* var. *snowdenii*,** syn. *K. snowdenii* of gardens. Gently spreading, deciduous, rhizomatous

Kniphofia 'Strawberries and Cream'

Kniphofia triangularis

perennial forming tufts of upright, linear leaves, to 60cm (24in) long. From midsummer to late autumn, produces a succession of few-flowered, open racemes of curved, yellowish orange or coral-pink flowers, to 3.5cm (1½in) long. ↕ to 90cm (36in), ↔ 45cm (18in). Uganda, Kenya. ❄❄

K. triangularis ▣ syn. *K. galpinii* of gardens, *K. macowanii, K. nelsonii.* Variable, deciduous perennial with arching, linear, grass-like leaves. Wiry stems, freely borne in moist conditions, produce dense racemes of reddish orange flowers, 2.5–3.5cm (1–1½in) long, becoming slightly yellower around the mouths, in early and mid-autumn. ↕ 60–90cm (24–36in), ↔ 45cm (18in). South Africa (Eastern Cape, Free State, KwaZulu/Natal), Lesotho. ❄❄❄

K. uvaria. Evergreen perennial with lax, linear, keeled, finely toothed, coarse leaves, to 60cm (24in) long. Flowers, 3–4cm (1¼–1½in) long, red in bud, opening to orange, and fading to yellow, are borne in slender, oblong-ovoid racemes in early autumn. ↕ 1.2m (4ft), ↔ 60cm (24in). South Africa (S. Western Cape). ❄❄❄. **'Nobilis'** has longer racemes of rich orange-red flowers, borne from midsummer to early autumn. ↕ 1.5–2m (5–6ft), ↔ 1m (3ft).

***K.* 'Wrexham Buttercup'** ▣ Deciduous perennial with clear, bright yellow flowers, borne in dense racemes in midsummer. ↕ 1.2m (4ft), ↔ 60cm (24in). ❄❄❄

▷ ***Kochia trichophylla*** see *Bassia scoparia* f. *trichophylla*

Kniphofia 'Wrexham Buttercup'

KOELERIA

GRAMINEAE / POACEAE

Genus of about 30 species of annual and perennial grasses from chalky and sandy grassland in N. and S. temperate zones and in tropical Africa. Several species are cultivated for their ornamental leaves and narrow panicles of silvery green or blue-green spikelets. They are suitable for a rock garden or the front of a border, either individually or in groups.

• **HARDINESS** Fully hardy.

• **CULTIVATION** Grow in medium to light, not too fertile, well-drained soil in full sun or light dappled shade. Koelerias thrive in alkaline and shallow, chalky soil. Cut back flowering stems either before seeding or in autumn.

• **PROPAGATION** Sow seed *in situ* in spring or autumn, or divide from mid-spring to early summer.

• **PESTS AND DISEASES** *Verticillium* wilt may be a problem.

K. glauca (Glaucous hair grass). Densely tufted, semi-evergreen, perennial grass, forming a compact mound of narrowly linear, glaucous grey-green leaves, to 20cm (8in) long, with inrolled margins. In early and midsummer, produces numerous erect stems bearing cylindrical panicles, to 10cm (4in) long, of shining, silver-green spikelets, which age to buff. ↕ to 40cm (16in) or more, ↔ 30cm (12in). W. and C. Europe to Russia (Siberia). ❄❄❄

KOELREUTERIA

SAPINDACEAE

Genus of 3 species of deciduous trees or shrubs from dry valley woodlands in China, Korea, and Taiwan. They have alternate, pinnate to 2-pinnate leaves, and large, pyramidal panicles, 10–35cm (4–14in) long, of shallowly bowl-shaped flowers, followed by unusual, inflated fruit capsules. They are fine specimen trees, flowering best in areas with hot summers.

• **HARDINESS** Fully hardy to frost hardy, provided the wood has been well ripened in summer.

• **CULTIVATION** Grow in fertile, well-drained soil in full sun. Pruning group 1; prune only to remove damaged or dead wood when dormant in winter.

• **PROPAGATION** Sow seed in containers in a cold frame in autumn. Take root cuttings in late winter.

• **PESTS AND DISEASES** Trouble free.

K. bipinnata ♀ Spreading tree with large, 2-pinnate, mid-green leaves, to 50cm (20in) long, comprising numerous oval-oblong, finely toothed leaflets. Red-spotted yellow flowers, 1cm (½in) across, are produced in large panicles, to 30cm (12in) long, from summer to autumn, followed by bladder-like fruit capsules, to 5cm (2in) long, red-brown when ripe. ↕ 10m (30ft), ↔ 8m (25ft). S.W. China. ❄❄

K. paniculata ▣ ♀ (Golden-rain tree, Pride of India). Spreading tree with pinnate leaves, to 45cm (18in) long, each consisting of 7–15 or more, ovate-oblong, scalloped leaflets. Emerging leaves are pink-red, becoming mid-green, and turning butter-yellow in autumn. Small yellow flowers, 1cm

Koelreuteria paniculata

(½in) across, are produced in large, pyramidal panicles, to 30cm (12in) long, in mid- and late summer; they are followed by bladder-like, pink- or red-flushed fruit capsules, to 5cm (2in) long. ↕↔ 10m (30ft) or more. China, Korea. ❄❄❄. **var. *apiculata*** has 2-pinnate leaves and light yellow flowers.

KOHLERIA

GESNERIACEAE

Genus of about 50 species of usually erect, rhizomatous perennials and subshrubs from rainforest of tropical regions of North America, Central America, and South America. They are grown for their foxglove-like flowers, which are bell-shaped or tubular, flaring out into 5 rounded lobes, usually produced from the leaf axils singly, in pairs, or in pendent, umbel-like racemes. Elliptic-lance-shaped to ovate leaves, opposite or in whorls of 3, are usually dark green, sometimes with silver markings, and have toothed or scalloped margins. All parts are hairy, including the flowers. In frost-prone climates, grow taller species in a warm greenhouse or conservatory; use compact species and cultivars as houseplants. In humid, tropical areas, grow in shaded sites in beds or borders.

• **HARDINESS** Frost tender.

• **CULTIVATION** Under glass, start into growth at 21°C (70°F) in early spring. Grow in loamless potting compost in bright filtered light, with high humidity. Using soft water, water moderately at first, then freely when in full growth. When flower buds appear, apply a high potash fertilizer every 2 weeks. In autumn, remove dying top growth and keep almost completely dry. Outdoors, grow in moist, well-drained, humus-rich soil in partial shade.

• **PROPAGATION** Divide in early spring.

• **PESTS AND DISEASES** The growing tips may be infested by aphids. Rhizome rot may occur in winter if conditions are too moist, or in spring if replanted rhizomes are slow to start into growth.

K. amabilis. Erect to prostrate, rhizomatous perennial with ovate, scalloped leaves, 10cm (4in) long, veined silver and purple-brown. In summer, bell-shaped, deep pink flowers, 2.5cm (1in) long, with purple and brick-red bars and stripes on the lobes and throats, are borne singly or in few-flowered, umbel-like racemes. May need

Kohleria digitaliflora

support. ↕↔ 60cm (24in). Colombia. ❄ (min. 15°C/59°F)

K. bogotensis. Erect, rhizomatous perennial with ovate, toothed, velvety, dark green leaves, 8cm (3in) long, marked paler green or white above. Bell-shaped, red-and-yellow flowers, 2.5cm (1in) long, with mouths spotted red, are borne singly or in pairs, from autumn to early winter. ↕ 60cm (24in), ↔ 45cm (18in). Colombia. ❄ (min. 15°C/59°F)

***K.* 'Connecticut Belle'.** Erect, compact, rhizomatous perennial with lance-shaped, toothed leaves, 7cm (3in) long, red beneath. Bell-shaped flowers, 2.5cm (1in) long, with bright red tubes, purple upper lobes, and purple-spotted, bright pink lower lobes, are produced singly or in pairs in summer. ↕ 40cm (16in), ↔ 20cm (8in). ❄ (min. 15°C/59°F)

K. digitaliflora ▣ Erect to spreading, rhizomatous perennial with lance-shaped, elliptic-lance-shaped to ovate, scalloped leaves, 20cm (8in) long, marked paler green. From summer to autumn, produces umbel-like racemes of up to 6, occasionally solitary, tubular, purple-pink flowers, 2.5–3cm (1–1¼in) long, white on the inside of the tubes, and with lobes spotted with dark, purplish green. ↕ 60cm (24in), ↔ 40cm (16in). Colombia. ❄ (min. 15°C/59°F)

K. eriantha ▣ Robust, bushy, rhizomatous perennial with ovate to ovate-lance-shaped, scalloped leaves, 7–13cm (3–5in) long. The leaves have prominent red hairs on the margins, and undersides that are paler and red-veined. In summer, produces tubular, orange-red flowers, 2.5cm (1in) long, with yellow-spotted lower lobes, either singly or in umbel-like racemes. ↕ to 1.2m (4ft), ↔ 30cm (12in) or more. Colombia. ❄ (min. 15°C/59°F)

Kohleria eriantha

▷ **Kohuhu** see *Pittosporum tenuifolium*

KOLKWITZIA

Beauty bush

CAPRIFOLIACEAE

Genus of one species of deciduous shrub from rocky, mountainous areas of Hubei, China. It has simple leaves, borne in opposite pairs, and is cultivated for its profusion of bell-shaped flowers borne in dense corymbs. Good for a shrub border or as a specimen plant.

- **HARDINESS** Fully hardy, but foliage may be damaged by late frosts.
- **CULTIVATION** Grow in fertile, well-drained soil, preferably in full sun, although some shade is tolerated. Pruning group 2.
- **PROPAGATION** Take greenwood cuttings in late spring or early summer, or remove suckers in spring.
- **PESTS AND DISEASES** Trouble free.

K. amabilis. Deciduous, suckering shrub with long, arching shoots and broadly ovate, tapered, dark green leaves, to 7cm (3in) long. Masses of bell-shaped, pale to deep pink flowers, to 1.5cm (½in) across, with yellow-flushed throats, are produced in terminal corymbs, 5–8cm (2–3in) across, in late spring and early summer. ↕ 3m (10ft), ↔ 4m (12ft). China (Hubei). ❄❄❄. **'Pink Cloud'** ▣ has bright, deep pink flowers.

▷ **Korokio** see *Corokia buddlejoides*
▷ ***Korolkowia sewerzowii*** see *Fritillaria sewerzowii*
▷ **Kowhai** see *Sophora tetraptera*
▷ **Krauss's spikemoss** see *Selaginella kraussiana*
▷ **Kris plant** see *Alocasia sanderiana*
▷ **Kudzu vine** see *Pueraria lobata*
▷ **Kumquat** see *Fortunella*
Round see *F. japonica*

Kolkwitzia amabilis 'Pink Cloud' (inset: flower detail)

Kunzea baxteri (inset: flower detail)

KUNZEA

MYRTACEAE

Genus of 25 species of evergreen shrubs and small trees from sands or sandy loam areas of mostly coastal habitats in Australia. They have small, often crowded, simple, entire, leathery leaves, and bear terminal "bottlebrush" spikes or heads of flowers. Each flower is composed of 5 small petals and a crown of conspicuous stamens, which in some species give the flowerheads their main colour. Where temperatures drop below 5°C (41°F), grow in a cool greenhouse, moving plants in containers outdoors during the warmer summer months. In milder climates, grow at the base of a house wall or in a shrub border.

- **HARDINESS** Frost tender; *K. baxteri* and *K. capitata* may survive short spells around 0°C (32°F).
- **CULTIVATION** Under glass, grow in lime-free (ericaceous) potting compost in full light, with good ventilation. In growth, water moderately and apply a balanced liquid fertilizer every month; water sparingly in winter. Outdoors, grow in moderately fertile, neutral to acid, well-drained, sandy soil in full sun; shelter from strong and dry winds. Pruning group 1; under glass, may need restrictive pruning after flowering.
- **PROPAGATION** Surface-sow seed at 16°C (61°F) in spring, or root semi-ripe cuttings with bottom heat in summer.
- **PESTS AND DISEASES** Trouble free.

K. baxteri ▣ Freely branching shrub, erect at first then spreading to a domed or rounded outline. Bears narrowly oblong, spreading, mid- to deep green leaves, 2cm (¾in) long, with white margins. Scarlet flowers, 2.5cm (1in) across, with long red stamens and yellow anthers, are produced in many short, dense spikes, to 10cm (4in) long, from spring to early summer. Thrives in seaside gardens. ↕↔ 1–2m (3–6ft) or more. Australia (Western Australia). ❄ (min. 5°C/41°F)

K. capitata. Bushy, rounded, freely branching shrub, erect at first but soon spreading, with upright, narrowly obovate to elliptic, mid-green leaves, 5–10mm (¼–½in) long, with arching tips. From spring to early summer, bears many small, rounded heads, 2cm (¾in) across, of deep mauve-pink flowers, 1cm (½in) long, with long stamens of the same colour tipped with cream anthers. ↕↔ 1–1.5m (3–5ft). Australia (New South Wales, Queensland). ❄ (min. 5°C/41°F)

▷ **Kurrajong** see *Brachychiton, B. discolor, B. populneus*
Flame see *B. acerifolius*
▷ **Kusamaki** see *Podocarpus macrophyllus*
▷ **Kyo-Chiku** see *Dendrocalamus giganteus*

L

LABLAB *syn.* DOLICHOS

LEGUMINOSAE/PAPILIONACEAE

Genus of one species of short-lived, herbaceous, perennial climber found in scrub in tropical Africa. Twining stems bear alternate, 3-palmate leaves and short, axillary racemes of fragrant, pea-like flowers. *L. purpureus* is extensively cultivated in Asia and North Africa for its edible fruit pods. In frost-prone areas, grow as a tender annual, or in a cool or temperate greenhouse. In warmer areas, train over a pergola or wall.

- **HARDINESS** Frost tender.
- **CULTIVATION** Under glass, grow in loam-based potting compost (JI No.2) in full light. When in growth, water freely and apply a balanced liquid fertilizer every 10–14 days until flowering; water sparingly in winter. Outdoors, grow in any well-drained soil in full sun (for the best crop of beans, water and fertilize as for plants under glass). Provide support of netting or trellis. Pruning group 11, in spring.
- **PROPAGATION** In cool climates, sow seed at 19–24°C (66–75°F) in spring. In warm climates, sow *in situ* when warm enough (19–24°C/66–75°F).
- **PESTS AND DISEASES** Trouble free.

L. purpureus ■ syn. *Dolichos lablab, D. niger, D. purpureus* (Egyptian bean, Indian bean). Fast-growing, twining, perennial climber producing 3-palmate, mid- to dark green leaves, composed of ovate to triangular leaflets, 10–15cm (4–6in) long. Bears fragrant, purple or white flowers, 1–2.5cm (½–1in) long, in racemes 20–40cm (8–16in) long, mainly in summer and autumn. Edible green pods, 10–15cm (4–6in) long, are often flushed purple, and contain 3–6 white to buff, reddish brown, brown, or black beans. ↕ 2–6m (6–20ft). Tropical Africa. ❀ (min. 7°C/45°F)

+ LABURNOCYTISUS

LEGUMINOSAE/PAPILIONACEAE

Deciduous tree, a graft hybrid, grown for its colourful, pea-like flowers borne in late spring and early summer. The leaves are alternate and 3-palmate. An ideal specimen tree, + *L.* 'Adamii' is also effective planted in small groups. All parts are highly toxic if ingested.

- **HARDINESS** Fully hardy.
- **CULTIVATION** Grow in moderately fertile, moist but well-drained soil in full sun. Pruning group 1; remove suckers.
- **PROPAGATION** Graft on to *Laburnum* seedlings in winter.
- **PESTS AND DISEASES** Trouble free.

+ *L.* 'Adamii' ■ (*Chamaecytisus purpureus* + *Laburnum anagyroides*). Spreading, deciduous tree with 3-palmate, dark green leaves, consisting of oval leaflets, to 6cm (2½in) long. Pea-like flowers occur in 3 colours, each borne in separate racemes in late spring and early summer: 2 are single colours, yellow and purple, true to each parent; the third is purple-pink with a yellow flush. ↕ 8m (25ft), ↔ 6m (20ft). Garden origin. ❄❄❄

+ *Laburnocytisus* 'Adamii'

Lablab purpureus

LABURNUM

Golden rain

LEGUMINOSAE/PAPILIONACEAE

Genus of 2 species of deciduous trees from woodland and thickets in the mountains of S. central Europe, S.E. Europe, and W. Asia. They are grown for their profuse, pendent, usually axillary racemes of pea-like yellow flowers, produced in late spring and early summer. The leaves are alternate and 3-palmate. Useful in a small garden as specimen trees or to form a pergola. All parts are highly toxic if ingested.

- **HARDINESS** Fully hardy.
- **CULTIVATION** Grow in moderately fertile, well-drained soil in full sun. Pruning group 1.
- **PROPAGATION** Sow seed (species only) in containers in a cold frame in autumn. Graft in late winter, or bud in summer.
- **PESTS AND DISEASES** Black fly, leaf miners, honey fungus, powdery mildew, and silver leaf may be troublesome.

L. alpinum (Scotch laburnum). Spreading tree with almost hairless, glossy, dark green leaves, consisting of 3 elliptic-ovate leaflets, to 8cm (3in) long. In late spring and early summer, bright yellow flowers are produced in slender racemes, 15–40cm (6–16in) long. ↕↔ 8m (25ft). S. central Europe, Italy, W. Balkans. ❄❄❄. **'Pendulum'** has weeping branches; ↕↔ 2m (6ft).

L. anagyroides syn. *L. vulgare* (Common laburnum). Spreading tree with hairy, grey-green young shoots, and dark green leaves composed of 3 elliptic-obovate leaflets, to 8cm (3in) long, hairy beneath. In late spring and early summer, produces bright yellow flowers in dense racemes, 10–30cm (4–12in) long. ↕↔ 8m (25ft). E. France to Italy, S. central Europe, Slovenia, Croatia. ❄❄❄

L. vulgare see *L. anagyroides*.

L. x watereri (*L. alpinum* x *L. anagyroides*). Spreading tree with virtually hairless young shoots, and dark green leaves composed of 3 elliptic-obovate leaflets, to 8cm (3in) long. Produces yellow flowers in dense racemes, to 50cm (20in) long, in late spring and early summer. ↕↔ 8m (25ft). Garden origin (also occurs in the wild where parents grow together). ❄❄❄. **'Vossii'** ■ has hairy young shoots, and bears racemes, to 60cm (24in) long, of golden yellow flowers.

Laburnum x *watereri* 'Vossii'

▷**Laburnum,**
Common see *Laburnum anagyroides*
Dalmatian see *Petteria ramentacea*
East African see *Calpurnia aurea*
Evergreen see *Piptanthus nepalensis*
Indian see *Cassia fistula*
Natal see *Calpurnia aurea*
Scotch see *Laburnum alpinum*

LACCOSPADIX

ARECACEAE/PALMAE

Genus of one species of single- or cluster-stemmed palm from rainforest in N.E. Australia. Arching, pinnate leaves are borne in a terminal cluster and die *in situ*, forming a skirt-like mass below the living crown. Spikes of bowl-shaped, 3-petalled flowers are borne between the leaves. In frost-prone areas, grow in a temperate or warm greenhouse; in warmer areas, grow as a specimen tree.

- **HARDINESS** Frost tender.
- **CULTIVATION** Under glass, grow in loam-based potting compost (JI No.3) in full light. In growth, water freely and apply a balanced liquid fertilizer monthly; water sparingly in winter. Pot on or top-dress in spring. Outdoors, grow in moderately fertile, moist but well-drained soil in full sun.
- **PROPAGATION** Sow seed at 27°C (81°F) in spring.
- **PESTS AND DISEASES** Red spider mites may be troublesome under glass.

L. australasica Slow-growing palm, usually with a single stem but sometimes with small clusters of stems, ringed with conspicuous leaf scars. Long-stalked, pinnate leaves, 2–3m (6–10ft) long,

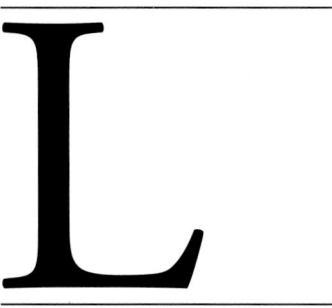

L

consist of many narrowly linear-lance-shaped, sparsely scaly, mid- to deep green leaflets. Yellow flowers are borne in spikes, 1m (3ft) or more long, usually in summer. ↕ 6m (20ft) occasionally more, ↔ 3–5m (10–15ft). Australia (Queensland). ❀ (min. 13°C/55°F)

▷ **Lace-bark** see *Hoheria populnea*
▷ **Lacebark, Queensland** see *Brachychiton discolor*
▷ **Lace plant** see *Aponogeton madagascariensis*

LACHENALIA

Cape Cowslip

HYACINTHACEAE/LILIACEAE

Genus of 90 species of bulbous perennials from grassland or rocky sites, on often seasonally moist ground, in South Africa. They are grown for their spikes or racemes of showy, tubular, bell-shaped, or cylindrical flowers, borne on often mottled stems from autumn to spring. Leaves are basal, very variably shaped, and frequently attractively spotted. In frost-prone areas, grow in a cool greenhouse or a conservatory. In frost-free areas, grow in a rock garden or in an open site among low shrubs.

• **HARDINESS** Half hardy.

• **CULTIVATION** Plant bulbs 10cm (4in) deep. Under glass, grow in loam-based potting compost (JI No.2) in full light. Water moderately until in full growth, then water freely, adding a balanced liquid fertilizer every 10–14 days. Reduce watering as the leaves fade, then keep dry until fresh growth starts in autumn. Outdoors, grow in light, well-drained soil in full sun.

L

• **PROPAGATION** Sow seed at 13–18°C (55–64°F) as soon as ripe, or remove bulblets in summer or autumn just before replanting or repotting.

• **PESTS AND DISEASES** Trouble free.

L. aloides ▣ syn. *L. tricolor*. Bulbous perennial with semi-erect, broadly lance- to strap-shaped, purple-spotted, slightly

Lachenalia aloides

Lachenalia aloides 'Nelsonii'

glaucous, mid-green leaves, 20cm (8in) long. In winter or early spring, produces racemes of up to 20 pendent, tubular yellow flowers, 2–3.5cm (1–1½in) long, that shade to scarlet at the tips. ↕ 15–28cm (6–11in), ↔ 5cm (2in). South Africa (Western Cape). ✲. **'Nelsonii'** ▣ has golden yellow flowers and unspotted leaves. **'Pearsonii'** is robust, with semi-erect, strap-shaped, mid-green leaves, to 25cm (10in) long, mottled with brown, and produces apricot flowers, to 3cm (1¼in) long, with the inner tepals tipped red to maroon; ↕ 30–40cm (12–16in). **var. *quadricolor*** has reddish orange buds opening to reddish orange-based, yellow-and-green flowers, with purple-maroon tips to the inner segments.

L. angustifolia see *L. contaminata*.

L. bulbifera, syn. *L. pendula*. Robust, bulbous perennial with semi-erect, ovate, lance-shaped, or strap-shaped, mid-green leaves, to 30cm (12in) long, usually heavily spotted brown-purple. In winter or spring, produces loose racemes of few to many pendent, cylindrical, red or orange flowers, 3–4cm (1¼–1½in) long, with green and purple tips. ↕ 30cm (12in), ↔ 5cm (2in). South Africa (Western Cape). ✲

L. contaminata, syn. *L. angustifolia*. Bulbous perennial with erect or semi-erect, narrow, grass-like, unmarked, mid- to deep green leaves, to 20cm (8in) long. In spring, bears racemes or spikes of few to many, open bell-shaped, slightly scented white flowers, 5–8mm (¼–⅜in) long, with maroon tips and stripes, held at right-angles to the stems. ↕ 6–25cm (2½–10in), ↔ 5cm (2in). South Africa (Western Cape). ✲

L. glaucina see *L. orchioides* var. *glaucina*.

L. glaucina* var. *pallida see *L. orchioides*.

L. mutabilis. Bulbous perennial with usually one semi-erect, lance-shaped, sometimes glaucous, mid-green leaf, to 20cm (8in) long, occasionally faintly spotted maroon. In winter or spring, produces dense spikes of up to 25 horizontal, stalkless, urn- to bell-shaped flowers, 1cm (½in) long, pale blue and white, with dark yellow inner tepals and dark tips, or rarely entirely greenish white. ↕ 10–45cm (4–18in), ↔ 5cm (2in). South Africa (Northern Cape, Western Cape). ✲

L. orchioides, syn. *L. glaucina* var. *pallida*. Bulbous perennial with 1 or 2 semi-erect, lance- or strap-shaped, mid-green leaves, to 28cm (11in) long, sometimes spotted brown. In late winter or spring, produces dense spikes of many semi-erect, oblong-cylindrical, fragrant, white, greenish yellow, or creamy yellow flowers, 1cm (½in) long, with flared tepals, fading to dull red as they mature. ↕ 15–40cm (6–16in), ↔ 5cm (2in). South Africa (Western Cape). ✲. **var. *glaucina***, syn. *L. glaucina*, has blue- or purple-shaded flowers with a fainter scent.

L. pendula see *L. bulbifera*.

L. rubida. Bulbous perennial with semi-erect, lance- to strap-shaped, mid- to deep green leaves, to 14cm (5½in) long, mottled deep purple. In autumn or early winter, produces racemes of few to many pendent, cylindrical, bright pink or ruby-red flowers, 2–3cm (¾–1¼in) long, shading to purple at the tips. ↕ 6–25cm (2½–10in), ↔ 5cm (2in). South Africa (Western Cape, Eastern Cape). ✲

L. tricolor see *L. aloides*.

L. unicolor. Very variable, bulbous perennial with lance- to strap-shaped, pale to dark green leaves, to 15cm (6in) long, usually with maroon warts above. In spring, bears racemes of many oblong-bell-shaped flowers, 5–8mm (¼–⅜in) long, that vary from cream with green tips, to pink, lilac-pink, magenta, blue, or purple, with darker tips. ↕ 8–30cm (3–12in), ↔ 5cm (2in). South Africa (Western Cape). ✲

▷ ***Lactuca alpina*** see *Cicerbita alpina*
▷ ***Lactuca plumieri*** see *Cicerbita plumieri*
▷ **Ladies' tresses, Nodding** see *Spiranthes cernua*
▷ **Lad's love** see *Artemisia abrotanum*
▷ **Lady of the night** see *Brunfelsia americana*
▷ **Lady palm** see *Rhapis*
▷ **Lady's mantle** see *Alchemilla*
Alpine see *A. alpina*
▷ **Lady's slipper orchid** see *Cypripedium, C. calceolus*
▷ **Lady's smock** see *Cardamine pratensis*

LAELIA

ORCHIDACEAE

Genus of about 50 species of evergreen, epiphytic or terrestrial orchids occurring in coastal regions up to altitudes of 2,600m (8,300ft), often in oak woodland, from Mexico and Central America to Brazil and Argentina. They have robust or slender, elongated pseudobulbs, each bearing 1 or 2 (sometimes 3) semi-rigid, narrowly oval, club-shaped, oblong, strap-shaped, or linear leaves. Brightly coloured flowers are usually produced in racemes from the apex of the pseudobulb. Many intergeneric hybrids derived from crosses with *Cattleya* and other related genera are also available.

• **HARDINESS** Frost tender.

• **CULTIVATION** Cool-growing orchids. Grow large species in epiphytic orchid compost in a slatted basket, and small ones epiphytically on a slab of bark. In summer, provide moist, shady conditions; water freely, adding fertilizer at every third watering, and mist once or twice daily. In winter, provide full light and water sparingly. See also p.46.

• **PROPAGATION** Divide when the plants overflow their containers. Remove

Laelia anceps

backbulbs of the Mexican species and pot up each one separately.

• **PESTS AND DISEASES** Scale insects, red spider mites, aphids, and mealybugs may be troublesome.

L. anceps ▣ Epiphytic orchid with ovate-oblong pseudobulbs, each with 1, or occasionally 2, lance-shaped, leathery leaves, 15cm (6in) long. In winter, produces racemes, to 60cm (24in) long, of 2–5 light rose-pink flowers, 6cm (2½in) across, with reddish purple lips and yellow throats with purple veining. ↕ 45–60cm (18–24in), ↔ 30cm (12in). C. Mexico. ❀ (min. 10°C/50°F; max. 30°C/86°F)

L. autumnalis. Epiphytic orchid with ovate-oblong pseudobulbs, each with 2 or 3 oblong to lance-shaped, leathery leaves, 12–20cm (5–8in) long. In winter, bears long-stemmed racemes, 30–100cm (12–39in) long, of 4–10 rose-pink flowers, 6cm (2½in) across, with rose-purple lips. ↕ 30–100cm (12–39in), ↔ 30cm (12in). Mexico. ❀ (min. 10°C/50°F; max. 30°C/86°F)

L. cinnabarina ▣ Epiphytic orchid with cylindrical, stem-like pseudobulbs, each with 1 or 2 linear to oblong, dark green leaves, 10–25cm (4–10in) long. Racemes, to 40cm (16in) long, of 5–15 brilliant cinnabar-red flowers, 4.5cm (1¾in) across, are produced in winter. ↕ 40cm (16in), ↔ 15cm (6in). S.E. Brazil. ❀ (min. 13°C/55°F; max. 30°C/86°F)

L. crispa. Epiphytic orchid with slender pseudobulbs, each with one oblong to strap-shaped, leathery leaf, 18cm (7in) long. In summer, bears racemes,

Laelia cinnabarina

10–25cm (4–10in) long, of 2 or 3 white flowers, 10cm (4in) across, with deep magenta veining on frilly lips. ↕ 40cm (16in), ↔ 30cm (12in). S. Brazil. ❀ (min. 13°C/55°F; max. 30°C/86°F)
L. flava. Epiphytic orchid with cylindrical, stem-like pseudobulbs, each with one lance-shaped to oblong, dark green leaf, 8–15cm (3–6in) long. In spring, bears upright racemes, 30–45cm (12–18in) long, of 5–10 yellow flowers, 3–4.5cm (1¼–1¾in) across. ↕ 30–45cm (12–18in), ↔ 15cm (6in). S.E. Brazil. ❀ (min. 13°C/55°F; max. 30°C/86°F)
L. majalis see *L. speciosa.*
L. pumila. Epiphytic orchid with ovoid pseudobulbs, each with one linear to oblong leaf, 8–12cm (3–5in) long. In autumn, lilac-rose flowers, 6cm (2½in) across, with rose-purple on the lips, are borne singly, or rarely in twos, on stems 4–10cm (1½–4in) tall, at the apex of each pseudobulb. ↕ 20cm (8in), ↔ 23cm (9in). S.E. Brazil. ❀ (min. 13°C/55°F; max. 30°C/86°F)
L. purpurata. Epiphytic orchid with slender pseudobulbs, each with one oblong, leathery leaf, 20–30cm (8–12in) long. In early summer, bears racemes, to 30cm (12in) long, of 2–7 white flowers, 15cm (6in) across, with purple in the lip centres. ↕ 45cm (18in), ↔ 30cm (12in). Brazil. ❀ (min. 13°C/55°F; max. 30°C/86°F)
L. speciosa, syn. *L. majalis.* Epiphytic orchid with stout, ovoid pseudobulbs, each with one oblong to lance-shaped, stiff leaf, 10–15cm (4–6in) long. In early summer, pale rose-lilac to rich magenta flowers, 9cm (3½in) across, are borne singly or in twos, on slender stems, 10–20cm (4–8in) tall, from the apex of each pseudobulb. ↕↔ 15–20cm (6–8in). C. Mexico. ❀ (min. 10°C/50°F; max. 30°C/86°F)

x LAELIOCATTLEYA

ORCHIDACEAE

Bigeneric hybrid genus of evergreen orchids, derived from crosses between *Laelia* and *Cattleya*. Racemes of large, showy flowers, in a range of bright colours, are borne at the tips of the pseudobulbs, above the foliage. They mostly produce a single, lance-shaped, leathery leaf, but may also bear 2 on each elongated pseudobulb, depending on the parentage of the hybrid. Often referred to colloquially as cattleyas.
• **HARDINESS** Frost tender.
• **CULTIVATION** Cool-growing orchids. Grow in epiphytic orchid compost in a slatted basket. In summer, provide high humidity and bright filtered light; water freely, adding fertilizer at every third watering, and mist once or twice daily. In winter, provide full light and water more sparingly. See also p.46.
• **PROPAGATION** Divide when the plants overflow their containers, or remove backbulbs and pot up separately.
• **PESTS AND DISEASES** Scale insects, red spider mites, aphids, and mealybugs may be troublesome.

x *Laeliocattleya* Trick or Treat 'Orange Princess'

x *L.* Rojo 'Mont Millais' (*Cattleya aurantiaca* x *Laelia milleri*). Evergreen orchid with cylindrical pseudobulbs and 1 or 2 ovate leaves, 10cm (4in) long. Bears slender, deep cinnabar-red flowers, 6cm (2½in) across, in short racemes in winter. ↕↔ 30cm (12in). ❀ (min. 13°C/55°F; max. 30°C/86°F)
x *L.* Trick or Treat 'Orange Princess' ■ (x *L.* Icarus x x *L.* Chit Chat). Evergreen orchid with cylindrical pseudobulbs and 2 narrowly oval leaves, 10cm (4in) long. Produces star-shaped, bright orange flowers, 4cm (1½in) across, in short racemes in spring. ↕↔ 30cm (12in). ❀ (min. 13°C/55°F; max. 30°C/86°F)

LAGAROSIPHON

Curly water thyme

HYDROCHARITACEAE

Genus of 9 species of semi-evergreen, submerged aquatic perennials occurring in still or slow-moving water in Africa. Used extensively as oxygenators in aquaria and in outdoor pools, they form dense, submerged masses of branched stems that support numerous linear-lance-shaped, recurved, often spirally arranged leaves and very small, white or pink flowers. In frost-prone climates, grow half-hardy species in a cold-water aquarium.
• **HARDINESS** Fully hardy to half hardy.
• **CULTIVATION** In an aquarium, admit full light, but do not provide additional heat; plants tend to become leggy in temperatures above 20°C (68°F). In an outdoor pond, grow in a submerged basket of loamy soil in full sun. Cut back regularly to restrict spread, and remove dead stems to prevent them from decomposing in the water.
• **PROPAGATION** Take stem-tip cuttings in spring or summer.
• **PESTS AND DISEASES** Trouble free.

L. major ■ syn. *Elodea crispa* of gardens. Submerged aquatic perennial with branched, fragile stems, to 1m (3ft) long, covered in linear to lance-shaped, recurved, dark green leaves, 0.6–2.5cm (¼–1in) long. Tubular, pink-tinged green flowers, 3mm (⅛in) long, develop inside translucent spathes in summer. ↔ indefinite. Southern Africa. ✲✲✲

Lagarosiphon major

LAGENOPHORA

ASTERACEAE/COMPOSITAE

Genus of about 15 species of low-growing, herbaceous perennials found mostly in open sites in scrub, grassland, and at forest margins, from lowland to subalpine altitudes, in Asia, Australasia, and Central and South America. They are cultivated for their solitary, daisy-like, white to purple flowerheads, borne over long periods in summer. The mostly basal leaves are oblong to broadly ovate, and may be entire or toothed to pinnatifid. Grow in a rock garden, on a sunny bank, or at the front of a border.
• **HARDINESS** Hardy to about -10°C (14°F).
• **CULTIVATION** Grow in well-drained soil in full sun. Propagate regularly, as they are often short-lived.
• **PROPAGATION** Sow seed in containers in a cold frame as soon as ripe.
• **PESTS AND DISEASES** Slugs and snails may be a probem.

L. pinnatifida. Mat-forming herbaceous perennial with rosettes of obovate to oblong, pinnatifid, sometimes toothed or further lobed, hairy, bronze-tinted, mid-green leaves, to 6cm (2½in) long. In summer, bears solitary, off-white flowerheads, to 1.5cm (½in) across, on stems 5–10cm (2–4in) long, sometimes to 25cm (10in) long. ↕ to 10cm (4in), ↔ to 15cm (6in). Mountain grassland in New Zealand. ✲✲

LAGERSTROEMIA

LYTHRACEAE

Genus of approximately 50 species of deciduous or evergreen shrubs and trees occurring in deciduous woodland, often near rivers, in warm-temperate and tropical regions from Asia to Australia. They are cultivated for their conical, brightly coloured panicles of flowers, with characteristic crinkled petals, and their often peeling bark. The leaves vary greatly in shape within the genus, but are usually opposite. In frost-prone areas, grow against a warm, sunny wall, or overwinter in a cool or temperate greenhouse. In warmer climates, grow as specimens, in group plantings, or as a hedge or screen.
• **HARDINESS** Half hardy, or frost hardy in areas with very hot summers where the wood can ripen fully.
• **CULTIVATION** Under glass, grow in loam-based potting compost (JI No.3) in full light. During the growing season, water freely and apply a balanced liquid fertilizer every 6–8 weeks; water sparingly at other times. Outdoors, grow in moderately fertile, well-drained soil in full sun. Pruning group 1; will withstand hard pruning if renovation is required.
• **PROPAGATION** Sow seed at 10–13°C (50–55°F) in spring. Root softwood cuttings in late spring, or semi-ripe cuttings with bottom heat in summer.
• **PESTS AND DISEASES** Mealybugs, red spider mites, and whiteflies may be a problem under glass.

Lagerstroemia fauriei

L. fauriei ■ ♀ Upright, many-stemmed, deciduous tree with peeling, red-brown bark and oblong, dark green leaves, to 10cm (4in) long. In summer, white flowers, 1cm (½in) across, are produced in panicles 5–10cm (2–4in) long. ↕↔ 8m (25ft). Japan. ✲✲
L. indica ♀ (Crepe flower, Crepe myrtle). Upright, deciduous tree or large shrub with peeling, grey-and-brown bark and obovate to oblong, dark green leaves, to 8cm (3in) long, bronze when young. From summer to autumn, white, pink, red, or purple flowers, 2–2.5cm (¾–1in) across, are produced in panicles to 20cm (8in) long. ↕↔ 8m (25ft). China. ✲✲. Some of the following are thought to be hybrids of *L. indica* and *L. fauriei.* **'Catawba'** produces purple flowers and orange-red autumn leaves; ↕↔ to 2m (6ft); ✲. **'Dallas Red'** is particularly hardy and fast-growing, and produces dark red flowers. **'Lavender Dwarf'** is a spreading shrub, bearing a profusion of light lavender-purple flowers; ↕↔ to 2m (6ft); ✲. **'Miami'** ■ is of hybrid origin, and bears dark pink flowers from midsummer to early autumn; ↕ 5m (15ft), ↔ 2.5m (8ft). **'Natchez'** ■ is a vigorous hybrid with

Lagerstroemia indica 'Miami'

L

Lagerstroemia indica 'Natchez'

white flowers; ↕↔ to 2m (6ft); ✲. **'Near East'** produces pale pink flowers; ↕↔ 5m (15ft). **'Seminole'** ■ is compact, and produces mid-pink flowers from mid-summer to early autumn; ↕ 2.2–2.5m (7–8ft), ↔ 6–7m (20–22ft). **'Sioux'** is of hybrid origin, with very large pink flowers, 5cm (2in) across; ↕↔ to 2.5m (8ft); ✲. **'Tuskegee'** is a hybrid with spreading branches; it bears large panicles, to 35cm (14in) long, of dark pink flowers; ↕↔ 5m (15ft). **'White Dwarf'** is a low mound-forming shrub, and freely bears white blooms; ↕↔ 1m (3ft); ✲. **'Wichita'** is vase-shaped, sometimes forming a small tree; it bears lavender-blue flowers from summer to late autumn; ↕↔ 3.5m (11ft); ✲

L. speciosa ♀ (Giant crepe myrtle, Pride of India, Queen's crepe myrtle). Spreading, freely branching, evergreen tree with peeling, light brown bark. Ovate to elliptic-oblong leaves, 8–20cm (3–8in) long, are grey-green above, sepia-flushed beneath. From spring to autumn, produces erect, open panicles, to 40cm (16in) long, of many pink, mauve, purple, or white flowers, to 5cm (3in) wide. ↕ 10–24m (30–78ft), ↔ 5–10m (15–30ft). Tropical Asia. ✲

LAGUNARIA

Norfolk Island hibiscus

MALVACEAE

Genus, allied to *Hibiscus,* of one species of evergreen tree from coastal woodland in E. Australia. It is grown for its habit, its alternate, simple, entire, leathery leaves, and its solitary, 5-petalled, hibiscus-like flowers, produced from the upper leaf axils. In frost-prone areas, grow in a cool greenhouse. In warmer areas, grow as a specimen tree, or as a windbreak in a coastal garden. Contact with the seeds may irritate skin.

- **HARDINESS** Frost tender; may survive short periods just below 0°C (32°F) if the wood is well ripened in summer.
- **CULTIVATION** Under glass, grow in loam-based potting compost (JI No.3) in full light. When in full growth, water freely and apply a balanced liquid fertilizer monthly; water sparingly at other times. Outdoors, grow in moderately fertile, well-drained soil in full sun. Pruning group 1; may need restrictive pruning under glass.
- **PROPAGATION** Sow seed at 16°C (61°F) in spring, or root greenwood cuttings with bottom heat in summer.
- **PESTS AND DISEASES** Scale insects may be a problem under glass.

L. patersonii ♤ (Cow itch tree, Queensland pyramid tree). Pyramidal to columnar tree, loosely branched when young, denser when mature, with ovate to broadly lance-shaped, blunt-tipped leaves, 5–10cm (2–4in) long, matt, almost olive-green above, densely whitish grey-scaled beneath. Bears a succession of cup- to trumpet-shaped, pink to rose-pink flowers, 4–6cm (1½–2½in) across, mainly in summer, followed by ovoid seed capsules, 2.5cm (1in) long. More than one plant is needed to produce seed. ↕ to 15m (50ft), ↔ 8–12m (25–40ft). E. Australia (including Lord Howe Island, Norfolk Island). ❀ (min. 3–5°C/37–41°F)

Lagerstroemia indica 'Seminole' (inset: flower detail)

Lagurus ovatus

LAGURUS

Hare's tail

GRAMINEAE/POACEAE

Genus of one species of annual grass occurring on maritime sands on the Mediterranean coast of S. Europe and, more rarely, on dry wasteland inland. Valued for its ornamental flowerheads in summer, it is effective in groups in a herbaceous or mixed border. The flowerheads are also useful in fresh or dried arrangements; pick them before fully mature for drying.

- **HARDINESS** Fully hardy.
- **CULTIVATION** Grow in light, ideally sandy, moderately fertile, well-drained soil in full sun.
- **PROPAGATION** Sow seed *in situ* in spring, or in containers in a cold frame in autumn.
- **PESTS AND DISEASES** Trouble free.

L. ovatus ■ (Hare's tail). Tufted grass with arching, linear to narrowly lance-shaped, flat, pale green leaves, to 20cm (8in) long. Throughout summer, bears dense, ovoid to oblong-cylindrical, spike-like panicles, to 6cm (2½in) long, of softly hairy, often purple-tinged, pale green spikelets, which mature to pale creamy buff. ↕ to 50cm (20in), ↔ 30cm (12in). Mediterranean. ✲✲✲. **'Nanus'** is much more compact; ↕ to 12cm (5in).

LAMARCKIA

GRAMINEAE/POACEAE

Genus of one species of annual grass occurring in open habitats in the Mediterranean region. It has twisted, linear leaves and one-sided panicles of attractively coloured spikelets. Grow in a herbaceous, mixed, or annual border for its distinctive inflorescences, which are useful in both fresh and dried flower arrangements.

- **HARDINESS** Fully hardy.
- **CULTIVATION** Grow in light, sandy, well-drained soil in full sun.

Lamarckia aurea

- **PROPAGATION** Make successional sowings *in situ* from early to late spring. Alternatively, sow in containers in a cold frame in late spring and transfer to the flowering site, to replace earlier sown plants after they have flowered. Plants from early sowings are usually past their best by midsummer.
- **PESTS AND DISEASES** Trouble free.

L. aurea ■ (Golden top, Toothbrush grass). Loosely tufted grass with wiry stems and flat, twisted, broadly linear, pale green leaves, to 12cm (5in) long. From mid-spring to summer, produces one-sided, oblong panicles, to 7cm (3in) long, of densely packed, downswept, bristled spikelets, shimmering golden yellow or whitish green, becoming silvery, and often purple flushed when mature. ↕ 30cm (12in), ↔ 25cm (10in). Mediterranean. ✲✲✲

LAMBERTIA

PROTEACEAE

Genus of 9 or 10 species of evergreen shrubs found on sandy or gravelly soils in heathland and woodland in Australia. They are cultivated for their slender, tubular flowers, which are solitary or borne in terminal clusters of 2–7, and surrounded by often colourful bracts; each flower has 4 narrow tepals that roll back like watch springs on opening. Leaves are usually narrow, simple, and entire, and are borne in pairs or whorls of 3. In frost-prone areas, grow in a cool or temperate greenhouse. In warmer climates, grow outdoors in a border.

- **HARDINESS** Generally frost tender; *L. formosa* may survive short periods near 0°C (32°F), provided the wood has been well ripened in summer.
- **CULTIVATION** Under glass, grow in a mix of 1 part loam and 3 parts each grit (or perlite) and peat, in full light. From spring to summer, water freely and apply a phosphate-free liquid fertilizer monthly; water sparingly in winter. Outdoors, grow in poor to moderately fertile, sharply drained, neutral to acid soil in full sun. Pruning group 1; may need restrictive pruning under glass.
- **PROPAGATION** Sow seed at 18°C (64°F) in spring, ideally singly in small containers. Root softwood cuttings in spring, or semi-ripe cuttings with bottom heat in summer; rooting may be slow and unreliable.
- **PESTS AND DISEASES** *Phytophthora* root rot may be a problem in moist soil.

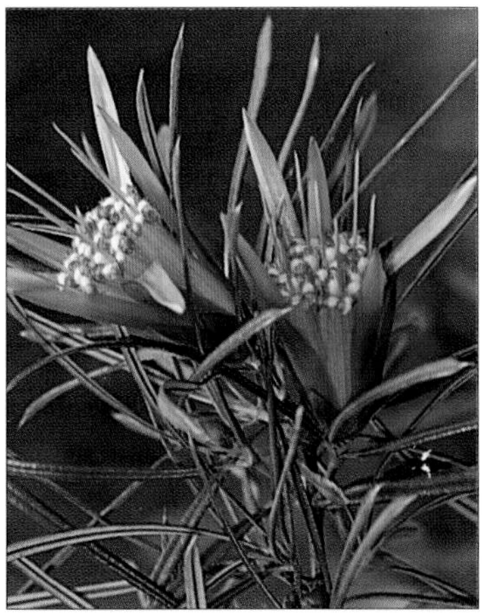
Lambertia formosa

L. formosa ■ (Mountain devil). Erect, open shrub, spreading with age, growing from a thickened, underground rootstock. Linear, sharp-tipped leaves, to 5cm (2in) long, usually in whorls of 3, are glossy, mid- to deep green above, white downy beneath. Bears clusters of up to 7 red flowers, 3–5cm (1¼–2in) long, surrounded by narrow, spreading, pink-flushed green bracts, some shorter than the flowers, some much longer, mainly from spring to summer, but often at other times of year. ↕ to 2m (6ft), ↔ to 1.5m (5ft). Australia (New South Wales). ❄ (borderline)

▷ **Lambs' ears** see *Stachys byzantina*
▷ **Lambs' lugs** see *Stachys byzantina*
▷ **Lambs' tails** see *Stachys byzantina*
▷ **Lambs' tongues** see *Stachys byzantina*
▷ ***Lamiastrum*** see *Lamium*
L. galeobdolon see *L. galeobdolon*

LAMIUM

syn. GALEOBDOLON, LAMIASTRUM
Dead nettle
LABIATAE/LAMIACEAE

Genus of about 50 species of annuals and usually rhizomatous perennials, occurring in habitats ranging from dry, open scrub to moist woodland, from Europe to Asia, and widespread in the Mediterranean and N. Africa. They have square stems and opposite, mainly ovate or kidney-shaped, coarsely toothed, wrinkled leaves, sometimes with coloured markings. The 2-lipped flowers are solitary, or borne in whorls in dense, leafy, spike-like inflorescences ("spikes"), mainly from late spring to summer.

Lamium galeobdolon 'Hermann's Pride'

Lamium maculatum

Grown mainly for their foliage, they provide good ground cover among shrubs or robust perennials. The larger species can be very invasive in moist, moderately fertile soils, but are less vigorous in poor soils; they may also be used in a border or in light woodland. Grow smaller, non-invasive species in a scree bed, rock garden, or alpine house.

- **HARDINESS** Fully hardy.
- **CULTIVATION** Grow the vigorous, ground-covering species in moist but well-drained soil in deep or partial shade. Site away from other small plants, and dig out rhizomes when necessary to confine spread. Grow *L. armenum* and *L. garganicum* subsp. *striatum* in sharply drained soil in full sun or partial shade. Protect *L. armenum* from excessive winter wet.
- **PROPAGATION** Sow seed in containers in a cold frame in autumn or spring. Divide in autumn or early spring. For small species, take stem-tip cuttings of non-flowering shoots in early summer.
- **PESTS AND DISEASES** Foliage may be damaged by slugs and snails.

L. armenum. Slow-growing, non-invasive, mat-forming or tufted perennial with obovate to diamond-shaped, scalloped, sometimes palmately lobed, mid-green leaves, 1cm (½in) long. In summer, produces solitary, long-tubed and hooded, pale pink to white flowers, to 5cm (2in) long, from the upper leaf axils. ↕ 5cm (2in), ↔ to 10cm (4in). Turkey (Anatolia). ❄❄❄
L. galeobdolon, syn. *Galeobdolon luteum*, *Lamiastrum galeobdolon* (Yellow archangel). Very invasive, rhizomatous

Lamium maculatum f. *albiflora*

Lamium maculatum 'Beacon Silver'

and often stoloniferous perennial with erect or creeping stems bearing very broadly ovate or diamond-shaped, sometimes heart-shaped, toothed, mid-green leaves, to 6cm (2½in) long, often marked silver. Spikes of whorled, brown-spotted yellow flowers, to 2cm (¾in) long, are produced in summer. ↕ 60cm (24in), ↔ indefinite. Europe to W. Asia. ❄❄❄. The following cultivars are less invasive, but still require careful siting. **'Hermann's Pride'** ■ forms a dense mat of small, ovate, heavily silver-streaked leaves, 3cm (1¼in) long. **'Silver Angel'** is more prostrate, with silver leaves; ↕ to 50cm (20in).
L. garganicum. Mat- to clump-forming perennial with upright stems that bear heart-shaped, broadly ovate, toothed, mid-green leaves, to 7cm (3in) long. Produces upright spikes of whorled, pale pink flowers, to 3cm (1¼in) long, from the upper leaf axils in early summer. ↕ 45cm (18in), ↔ 50cm (20in). Italy, Greece to Turkey and Iraq. ❄❄❄. **'Golden Carpet'** has mid-green leaves variegated with gold, and produces pink-and-white striped flowers. **subsp. *striatum*** is compact, with abundant spikes of pink flowers, heavily spotted and streaked dark purple; ↕ to 15cm (6in), ↔ to 20cm (8in).
L. maculatum ■ Low-growing, rhizomatous and stoloniferous perennial with prostrate and ascending stems bearing triangular-ovate, toothed, matt, mid-green leaves, 2–8cm (¾–3in) long, heart-shaped at the bases, and often mottled or zoned silvery white or pink. In summer, bears spikes of whorled, red-purple, sometimes white or pink flowers,

Lamium orvala

to 2cm (¾in) long. Excellent ground cover. ↕ 20cm (8in), ↔ 1m (3ft). Europe and North Africa to W. Asia. ❄❄❄. **f. *albiflora*** ■ syn. 'Album', is mat-forming, with matt, mid-green leaves, zoned silvery white, and white flowers from mid-spring to midsummer; ↕ 15cm (6in), ↔ 60cm (24in); Europe. **'Album'** see f. *albiflora*. **'Aureum'**, syn. 'Gold Leaf', has yellow leaves with paler white centres, and bears pink flowers. **'Beacon Silver'** ■ has silver leaves, narrowly margined green, and bears clear pale pink flowers. **'Cannon's Gold'** has gold leaves and purple flowers. **'Gold Leaf'** see 'Aureum'. **'Red Nancy'** has silver leaves with narrow, mid-green margins, and bears purplish red flowers. **'Sterling Silver'** has silver leaves and purple flowers. **'White Nancy'** produces pure white flowers above silver leaves that are narrowly margined green; ↕ to 15cm (6in), ↔ to 1m (3ft) or more.
L. orvala ■ Non-invasive, clump-forming perennial with broadly ovate to triangular, toothed, softly hairy, dark green leaves, 10–15cm (4–6in) long. Produces spikes of whorled, pinkish purple flowers, 3–4cm (1¼–1½in) long, from late spring to summer. ↕ to 60cm (24in), usually less, ↔ 30cm (12in). Central S. Europe. ❄❄❄. **f. *albiflorum***, syn. 'Album', bears white flowers. **'Album'** see f. *albiflorum*.

LAMPRANTHUS

AIZOACEAE

Genus of 180 or more species of erect or prostrate, perennial succulents from semi-desert areas of South Africa, especially the coastal belt. The opposite, cylindrical or 3-angled leaves often redden in full sun. Daisy-like flowers are profusely borne from summer to early autumn. In frost-prone areas, grow in a temperate greenhouse; they may also be used for summer bedding, especially in arid conditions. In warmer areas, grow in a desert garden or in a border with other succulents.

- **HARDINESS** Frost tender.
- **CULTIVATION** Under glass, grow in standard cactus compost in full light. From late spring to late summer, water moderately and apply low-nitrogen fertilizer every 4–6 weeks; water very sparingly at other times. Outdoors, grow in poor, sharply drained soil in full sun. In frost-prone climates, lift in autumn and overwinter under glass. See also pp.48–49.

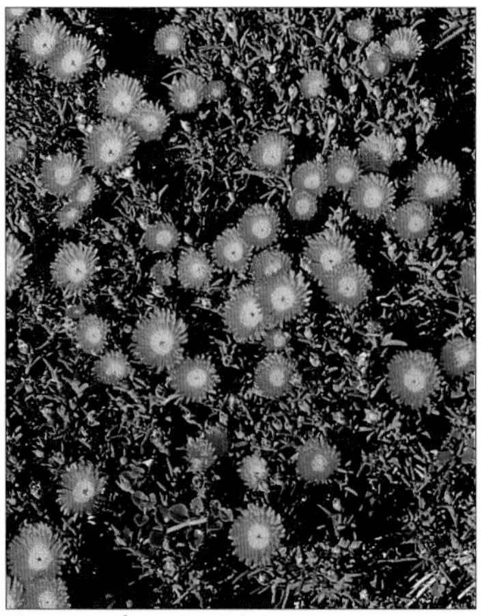
Lampranthus aurantiacus

Lampranthus deltoides

Lampranthus purpureus

Lantana camara 'Radiation'

L

• **PROPAGATION** Sow seed at 19–24°C (66–75°F) in spring. Root sections of stem in spring and summer.
• **PESTS AND DISEASES** Susceptible to mealybugs and, in flower, greenfly.

L. aurantiacus ■ Spreading, shrubby, sparsely branched succulent with semi-cylindrical, tapering, minutely spotted, grey-frosted, mid-green leaves, 2–3cm (¾–1¼in) long. Orange flowers, 4–5cm (1¼–2in) across, open in full sun from summer to early autumn. ↕ to 45cm (18in), ↔ indefinite. South Africa (Western Cape, Eastern Cape). ❄ (min. 7°C/45°F)
L. deltoides ■ syn. *Oscularia deltoides.* Spreading succulent with a mass of short stems bearing 3-angled, toothed, bluish grey leaves, 1cm (½in) long. From summer to early autumn, produces sometimes fragrant, pink to red flowers, 1.5–2cm (½–¾in) across. ↕ to 30cm (12in), ↔ indefinite. South Africa (Western Cape). ❄ (min. 7°C/45°F)
L. falcatus. Spreading, prostrate succulent with a mass of slender, tangled stems and 3-angled, curved, spotted, greyish green leaves, 6mm (¼in) long. Fragrant, purplish pink flowers, to 1.5cm (½in) across, are borne from summer to early autumn. ↕ to 30cm (12in), ↔ indefinite. South Africa (Western Cape). ❄ (min. 7°C/45°F)
L. haworthii ■ Trailing or semi-erect, freely branching succulent with semi-cylindrical, tapering, densely grey-frosted, pale green leaves, 2.5–4cm (1–1½in) long. Bright purplish pink flowers, to 7cm (3in) across, are borne from summer to early autumn. ↕ to 50cm (20in), ↔ indefinite. South Africa (Western Cape, Eastern Cape). ❄ (min. 7°C/45°F)
L. purpureus ■ Trailing or semi-erect succulent with slender stems and branches bearing rounded, rough, bluish green leaves, to 3.5cm (1½in) long, shortly tapered at the tips. From summer to early autumn, produces pinkish purple flowers, to 3cm (1¼in) across. ↕ to 40cm (16in), ↔ indefinite. South Africa (Western Cape). ❄ (min. 7°C/45°F)
L. roseus, syn. *Mesembryanthemum multiradiatum.* Creeping or semi-erect succulent with 3-angled, mid-green to glaucous, grey-green leaves, 3cm (1¼in) long, covered with prominent, translucent dots. Bears pale rose-pink flowers, 4cm (1½in) across, from summer to early autumn. ↕ to 50cm (20in), ↔ indefinite. South Africa (Western Cape, Eastern Cape). ❄ (min. 7°C/45°F)
L. spectabilis ■ Variable, spreading, prostrate succulent with narrowly 3-angled to cylindrical, keeled, mid-green leaves, 5–8cm (2–3in) long, partly tinged red. Produces reddish purple or, occasionally, white flowers, 5–7cm (2–3in) across, from summer to early autumn. ↕ to 30cm (12in), ↔ indefinite. South Africa (Western Cape). ❄ (min. 7°C/45°F)

▷**Lancewood** see *Pseudopanax crassifolius*
Toothed see *P. ferox*

LANTANA

VERBENACEAE

Genus of 150 species of evergreen shrubs and perennials from tropical North, Central, and South America, and South Africa, usually occurring in pine woodland and on disturbed ground. They are grown for their small, 5-lobed, salverform flowers, grouped tightly into rounded, flattened, or domed, terminal heads. Leaves are simple and toothed, often wrinkled, and borne in opposite pairs or whorls of 3. In frost-prone areas, grow in a temperate greenhouse, or use as summer bedding. In warmer areas, grow in a border; low, spreading species are good ground cover on a bank or between shrubs. All parts may cause severe discomfort if ingested, and contact with foliage may irritate skin.

• **HARDINESS** Frost tender.
• **CULTIVATION** Under glass, grow in loam-based potting compost (JI No.3) in full light. During the growing season, water freely and apply a balanced liquid fertilizer monthly; keep just moist in winter. Outdoors, grow in fertile, moist but well-drained soil in full sun. Pruning group 9; may need restrictive pruning in late winter under glass.
• **PROPAGATION** Sow seed at 16–18°C (61–64°F) in spring, or root semi-ripe cuttings with bottom heat in summer.
• **PESTS AND DISEASES** Whiteflies, red spider mites, and powdery mildew may be troublesome under glass.

L. aculeata* f. *varia see *L. camara* f. *varia.*
***L. camara* cultivars.** Variable, often prickly-stemmed shrubs with ovate, finely wrinkled, slightly toothed, deep green leaves, 5–10cm (2–4in) long. Flowerheads 2.5–5cm (1–2in) across, in colours ranging from white to yellow and salmon-pink to red or purple, are borne from late spring to late autumn. ↕↔ 1–2m (3–6ft). ❄ (min. 10°C/50°F). **'Cream Carpet'** is low and spreading, with creamy white flowers; ↕ 30cm (12in), ↔ 75cm (30in). **'Fabiola'** bears bicoloured, salmon-pink and yellow flowers. **'Feston Rose'** ■ has bicoloured, pink and yellow flowers. **'Goldmine'** see 'Mine d'Or'. **'Mine d'Or'**, syn. 'Goldmine', produces golden yellow flowers. **'Radiation'** ■ bears bicoloured, orange and red flowers. **'Schloss Ortenburg'** bears bicoloured, brick-red and orange-yellow flowers. **'Snow White'** ■ bears white flowers.

Lampranthus haworthii

Lampranthus spectabilis

Lantana camara 'Feston Rose'

Lantana camara 'Snow White'

Lantana montevidensis

'Spreading Sunset' produces orange-yellow flowers that take on reddish pink tints with age. **f. *varia***, syn. *L. aculeata* f. *varia*, bears yellow flowers turning purple on the outside, orange inside.
L. delicatissima see *L. montevidensis*.
L. montevidensis ■ syn. *L. delicatissima, L. sellowiana*. Spreading shrub, often forming a dense mat, with slender, flexible stems, usually covered with coarse, short hairs. Ovate to oblong or lance-shaped, coarsely toothed, mid- to deep green leaves are 2.5–3.5cm (1–1½in) long. Bears long-stalked, domed flowerheads, 2–3cm (¾–1¼in) wide, of yellow-eyed, lilac-pink to violet flowers, to 1cm (½in) across, mainly in summer. ↕ 20–100cm (8–39in), ↔ 60–120cm (2–4ft). Tropical South America. ❀ (min. 10°C/50°F)
L. sellowiana see *L. montevidensis*.
***L.* 'Tangerine'** ■ Low, spreading, often prickly stemmed shrub, probably a cultivar of *L. camara*, with ovate to ovate-oblong, finely wrinkled, slightly toothed, deep green leaves, 5–10cm (2–4in) long. Bears orange flowerheads, 2.5–5cm (1–2in) across, from late spring to late autumn. ↕↔ 1–2m (3–6ft). ❀ (min. 10°C/50°F)

Lantana 'Tangerine'

L. tiliifolia. Coarsely hairy shrub with broadly ovate to elliptic or rounded, wrinkled, scalloped or toothed, mid-green leaves, 10cm (4in) long. Yellow or orange flowers, to 1cm (½in) across, ageing to brick red, are produced in short-stalked, domed flowerheads, to 6cm (2½in) wide, mainly in summer. ↕↔ 1.5m (5ft). Brazil. ❀ (min. 10°C/50°F)

▷**Lantern,**
Chinese see *Physalis alkekengi*
Japanese see *Hibiscus schizopetalus, Physalis alkekengi*
▷**Lanterns, Chinese** see *Nymania capensis*
▷**Lantern tree** see *Crinodendron hookerianum*

LAPAGERIA

LILIACEAE/PHILESIACEAE

Genus of one species of woody, twining, evergreen climber occurring in moist forest habitats in Chile. It is grown for its very showy, pendent, oblong-bell-shaped flowers. The leaves are alternate and ovate. In frost-prone climates, grow in a cool greenhouse; elsewhere, it is best grown against a shady wall.
• **HARDINESS** Frost hardy to half hardy.
• **CULTIVATION** Under glass, grow in lime-free (ericaceous) potting compost with added sharp sand, in bright filtered light. During the growing season, water moderately and apply a balanced liquid fertilizer monthly; water sparingly in winter. Outdoors, grow in humus-rich, moist but well-drained, neutral to acid soil in partial shade. In frost-prone areas, shelter from cold, drying winds and protect with a dry mulch in winter. Provide support. Pruning group 11, after flowering, but best left unpruned.
• **PROPAGATION** Sow seed that has been soaked in water for 48 hours, at 13–18°C (55–64°F) in spring. Take semi-ripe cuttings in late summer, or layer in autumn.
• **PESTS AND DISEASES** Aphids, mealybugs, scale insects, and thrips may be a problem, particularly under glass.

L. rosea ■ (Chilean bellflower). Twining climber, spreading slowly by suckers, with ovate, dark green leaves, to 12cm (5in) long. From summer to late autumn, oblong-bell-shaped, fleshy, pink to red flowers, to 9cm (3½in) long, are borne singly or in twos or threes in the upper leaf axils. ↕ 5m (15ft). Chile.

Lapageria rosea

Lapageria rosea var. *albiflora*

❄❄ (borderline). **var. *albiflora*** ■ bears white flowers. **'Nash Court'** has soft pink flowers with deeper mottling.

▷***Lapeirousia cruenta*** see *Anomatheca laxa*
▷***Lapeirousia laxa*** see *Anomatheca laxa*
▷**Larch** see *Larix*
Dunkeld see *Larix* x *marschlinsii*
European see *Larix decidua*
Golden see *Pseudolarix amabilis*
Hybrid see *Larix* x *marschlinsii*
Japanese see *Larix kaempferi*
Siberian see *Larix sibirica*
Western see *Larix occidentalis*

LARDIZABALA

LARDIZABALACEAE

Genus of 2 species of monoecious, woody, twining, evergreen climbers from woodland in Chile. They are grown mainly for their ternate to 3-ternate, dark green leaves and striking flowers with 6 fleshy tepals. Train on a pergola or trellis, or against a wall.
• **HARDINESS** Frost hardy.
• **CULTIVATION** Grow in moderately fertile, well-drained soil in full sun or partial shade. In frost-prone areas, shelter from cold, drying winds. Pruning group 11, after flowering.
• **PROPAGATION** Sow seed in containers in a cold frame in spring, or take semi-ripe cuttings in late summer or autumn.
• **PESTS AND DISEASES** Trouble free.

L. biternata see *L. funaria*.
L. funaria, syn. *L. biternata*. Monoecious, sometimes dioecious climber. Ternate to 3-ternate, dark green leaves are composed of up to 9 ovate, rigid leaflets, 5–10cm (2–4in) long. From late autumn to winter, bears reflexed, 6-tepalled, purple-brown and white flowers, 2–2.5cm (¾–1in) across. Male flowers are borne in pendent racemes, 8–10cm (3–4in) long; female flowers are borne singly from the leaf axils. Edible, sausage-shaped purple berries are 5–8cm (2–3in) long. ↕ 3–4m (10–12ft). Chile. ❄❄

LARIX

Larch

PINACEAE

Genus of 10–14 species of upright, deciduous, monoecious, coniferous trees from coniferous forests of the N. hemisphere. They have attractive young foliage and normally brilliant, yellow to red autumn colour. The needle-shaped

Larix decidua

leaves are borne in loose spirals on long shoots, and near-whorls on short shoots. Terminal, erect, cylindrical or ovoid to conical, usually purple female cones are produced in spring, and turn woody and brown in the first season, usually persisting on the tree. Male cones are spherical to ovoid, and pink or yellow. Larches are useful as specimen trees, and tolerate a wide range of conditions.
• **HARDINESS** Fully hardy.
• **CULTIVATION** Grow in any deep, well-drained soil in full sun.
• **PROPAGATION** Sow seed in a seedbed in early spring, graft in winter, or root semi-ripe cuttings in summer under mist; cuttings are difficult to root.
• **PESTS AND DISEASES** Honey fungus and adelgids may be a problem. Canker may cause dieback.

L. decidua ■ ♤ syn. *L. europaea* (European larch). Conical, coniferous tree, often with a large, spreading crown when old, and with smooth, scaly grey bark, ridged on old trees. Linear, soft, pale green leaves, to 3.5cm (1½in) long, are borne on hairless shoots, which are straw-yellow during the first winter. Cylindrical to conical female cones, to

Larix occidentalis

L

3.5cm (1½in) long, have 40–50 scales, and protruding bracts. ↕ 30m (100ft) or more, ↔ 4–6m (12–20ft). Mountains of continental Europe. ❄❄❄. **'Corley'** is a dwarf, spreading or rounded shrub. Suitable for a rock garden; ↕↔ 1m (3ft).
L. x eurolepis see *L.* x *marschlinsii.*
L. europaea see *L. decidua.*
L. kaempferi ♤ syn. *L. leptolepis* (Japanese larch). Conical, coniferous tree with fissured and scaly, rust-brown to grey bark. Very similar to *L. decidua*, but with purplish red winter shoots covered in a waxy bloom. Hairless shoots bear linear, grey-green or bluish green leaves, to 4cm (1½in) long. Conical female cones, to 3cm (1¼in) long, have reflexed scales and concealed bracts. ↕ 30m (100ft) or more, ↔ 4–6m (12–20ft). Japan. ❄❄❄. **'Blue Haze'** has brighter foliage.
L. leptolepis see *L. kaempferi.*
L. x marschlinsii ♤ (*L. decidua* x *L. kaempferi*) syn. *L.* x *eurolepis* (Dunkeld larch, Hybrid larch). Fast-growing, conical, coniferous tree with bloomed, slightly hairy yellow shoots, and linear, grey-green leaves, to 4cm (1½in) long. Conical female cones, to 3cm (1¼in) long, have slightly reflexed scales and only a few visible bract scales. ↕ to 30m (100ft), ↔ to 6m (20ft). Garden origin. ❄❄❄
L. occidentalis ▣ ♤ (Western larch). Coniferous tree with a narrowly conical crown and scaly, red-brown to brown bark, becoming furrowed and fissured with age. Pointed, linear, blue-green to grey-green leaves, 2.5–4cm (1–1½in) long, each with 2 white bands beneath, are held on stout, orange-brown shoots, which are hairy when young. Female cones, 2.5–4.5cm (1–1¾in) long, are cylindrical to ovoid, with protruding bracts. ↕ to 25m (80ft) or more, ↔ to 5m (15ft). W. North America. ❄❄❄
L. russica see *L. sibirica.*
L. sibirica ♤ syn. *L. russica* (Siberian larch). Conical, coniferous tree with scaly, rust-brown bark and bright yellow or yellowish grey shoots, which are hairy when young. Narrowly linear leaves, 2–4cm (¾–1½in) long, are bright green, each with 2 white bands beneath. Ovoid female cones, 3–4cm (1¼–1½in) long, have hairy scales. ↕ 10–30m (30–100ft), ↔ to 5m (15ft). N.E. Europe to Russia (Siberia) and China. ❄❄❄

▷**Larkspur** see *Consolida, C. ajacis*

LATANIA
Latan palm

ARECACEAE/PALMAE

Genus of 3 species of single-stemmed palms from seasonally dry areas, often near the coast, in the Mascarene Islands. Fan-shaped, grey- to light green leaves are borne in terminal clusters, with bowl-shaped, 3-petalled flowers borne on separate male and female panicles between them. Where temperatures fall below 16°C (61°F), grow in a warm greenhouse; in warmer climates, grow as specimen plants.
• **HARDINESS** Frost tender.
• **CULTIVATION** Under glass, grow in loam-based potting compost (JI No.3) with added leaf mould and sharp sand, in full light with shade from the hottest sun. In growth, water freely and apply a balanced liquid fertilizer monthly; water

Latania lontaroides

sparingly in winter. Pot on or top-dress in spring. Outdoors, grow in moderately fertile, well-drained soil in full sun.
• **PROPAGATION** Sow seed at 27°C (81°F) in spring.
• **PESTS AND DISEASES** Red spider mites may be troublesome under glass.

L. loddigesii Ψ Small to medium-sized palm with blue-green leaf-blades, to 1.5m (5ft) across, deeply divided into many narrow lobes. Bears pale green or greenish white flowers in panicles to 1.5m (5ft) long, usually in summer. ↕ 10–16m (30–52ft), ↔ 3–3.5m (10–11ft). Mascarene Islands (Mauritius). ❁ (min. 16°C/61°F)
L. lontaroides ▣ Ψ Small to medium-sized palm with deeply lobed, grey-green leaf-blades, to 1.5m (5ft) across, with red-purple-flushed bases and leaf-stalks. Greenish white to cream flowers are borne in panicles to 1.5m (5ft) long, usually in summer. ↕ 10–16m (30–52ft), ↔ 3–3.5m (10–11ft). Mascarene Islands (Réunion). ❁ (min. 16°C/61°F)
L. verschaffeltii Ψ Small to medium-sized palm with yellow-margined, light green leaf-blades, to 1.2m (4ft) across, deeply divided into many slender lobes. Bears greenish white to cream flowers, usually in summer; male panicles are up to 3m (10ft) long, females to 1.7m (5½ft) long. ↕ 12–16m (40–52ft), ↔ 4m (12ft). Mascarene Islands (Rodrigues). ❁ (min. 16°C/61°F)

▷**Latan palm** see *Latania*

LATHRAEA

SCROPHULARIACEAE

Genus of 7 species of leafless, mainly subterranean, parasitic perennials from damp woodland in temperate Europe and Asia. Branching rhizomes bear usually rounded, scale-like, fleshy, ivory to mauve leaves. They are cultivated for their tubular, 2-lipped flowers, borne in raceme-like inflorescences at ground level in spring. Grow at the base of a

Lathraea clandestina

tree or shrub. *L. clandestina* is parasitic on willow (*Salix*), poplar (*Populus*), and alder (*Alnus*). Other species parasitize other trees and are usually host-specific.
• **HARDINESS** Fully hardy.
• **CULTIVATION** Grow in moist but well-drained soil in partial shade. Mulch with leaf mould in autumn.
• **PROPAGATION** Scatter seed at the base of a suitable host plant as soon as ripe.
• **PESTS AND DISEASES** Trouble free.

L. clandestina ▣ (Purple toothwort). Parasitic, rhizomatous perennial with opposite, kidney-shaped, stem-clasping, scale-like white leaves, 5mm (¼in) long. Racemes of 4–8 tubular, 2-lipped mauve flowers, to 3cm (1¼in) long, are borne just above the ground in early and mid-spring. ↕ 2cm (¾in), ↔ indefinite. W. Europe. ❄❄❄

LATHYRUS
Everlasting pea

LEGUMINOSAE/PAPILIONACEAE

Genus of 150 species of annuals and herbaceous or evergreen perennials from sunny, sandy or shingle banks, grassy slopes, wasteland, or open woodland in N. temperate regions, N. and E. Africa, and temperate South America. They are grown for their showy, pea-like, often scented flowers, in many colours, which are produced from the leaf axils, either singly or in racemes. Stems are usually winged, and bear alternate, pinnate leaves. Many are climbers (with tendrils); others are clump-forming. The climbers are useful for growing through shrubs or over a bank. Sweet peas (*L. odoratus*) are suitable for a trellis or arch, or an annual border for cut flowers and exhibition. Clump-forming species and cultivars are suitable for a rock garden, woodland garden, or herbaceous border. Seeds may cause mild stomach upset if ingested.
• **HARDINESS** Fully hardy to frost hardy.
• **CULTIVATION** Grow in fertile, humus-rich, well-drained soil in full sun or light dappled shade. Climbers need support. For the best flowers from *L. odoratus*, incorporate well-rotted organic matter in the season before planting, and apply a balanced liquid fertilizer every 2 weeks while in growth. Dead-head regularly. Sweet peas are usually grown on cane pyramids or trellis. Long-stemmed, exhibition-quality blooms are grown as cordons in beds prepared in autumn. Bush sweet peas are dwarf, largely self-supporting, non-climbing cultivars.
• **PROPAGATION** Soak seed and sow in containers in a cold frame in early spring; seed of annuals may also be sown *in situ* in mid-spring. Sweet peas may also be sown in autumn: pre-soak or chip seed and sow *in situ* in mild areas, or in containers in a cold frame where frosts are severe. Divide perennials in early spring, although they sometimes resent disturbance.
• **PESTS AND DISEASES** Aphids, slugs, snails, and thrips may be troublesome. *L. odoratus* may suffer from powdery mildew, *Fusarium* wilt, foot rot, root rot, and viruses.

L. aureus, syn. *L. luteus* of gardens, *L. vernus* var. *aurantiacus, Orobus aureus*. Clump-forming herbaceous perennial with upright, unwinged stems, and dark green leaves divided into 3–5 pairs of elliptic leaflets, 3.5–5cm (1½–2in) long. Produces one-sided racemes of 8–25 yellow-orange flowers, 1.5–2cm (½–¾in) long, from late spring to early summer. ↕ to 60cm (24in), ↔ 30cm (12in). Ukraine (Crimea), Caucasus, N. Turkey. ❄❄❄
L. chloranthus. Erect or scrambling, sparsely branched, annual climber with slender, winged stems, and mid-green leaves composed of one pair of elliptic leaflets, 2–6cm (¾–2½in) long. Sulphur- to bright yellow flowers, 1.5–2.5cm (½–1in) long, are produced singly or in pairs in summer. ↕ to 70cm (28in), sometimes more. C. and E. Turkey, N. Iraq, Iran, Armenia. ❄
L. gmelinii, syn. *L. luteus.* Clump-forming herbaceous perennial, similar to *L. aureus*, with upright, unwinged stems, and mid-green leaves divided into 3–6 pairs of oval leaflets, to 10cm (4in) long. Produces one-sided racemes of 4–15 brown-striped, orange-yellow flowers, 2.5–3cm (1–1¼in) long, from late spring to midsummer. ↕ to 90cm (36in), ↔ 30cm (12in). C. and S. Urals, Mountains of C. Asia. ❄❄❄
L. grandiflorus ▣ (Everlasting pea). Herbaceous, perennial climber,

Lathyrus grandiflorus

Lathyrus latifolius

spreading by suckers, with unwinged stems. Mid-green leaves usually consist of one pair of ovate to elliptic leaflets, to 5cm (2in) long. Racemes of 1 or 2 (sometimes up to 4) pink-purple and red flowers, to 3cm (1¼in) long, are produced in summer. ↕ 1.5m (5ft). Italy (including Sicily), Slovenia to Albania, Bulgaria. ❄❄❄

L. latifolius ■ (Everlasting pea, Perennial pea). Herbaceous, perennial climber with winged stems. Blue-green leaves consist of one pair of oblong-elliptic leaflets, 8–11cm (3–4½in) long, with 2 broad stipules. Racemes of 6–11 pink to purple flowers, 1.5–3cm (½–1¼in) long, are produced from summer to early autumn. ↕ 2m (6ft) or more. S. Europe. ❄❄❄. **'Blushing Bride'** produces pink-flushed white flowers. **'White Pearl'** bears pure white flowers.

L. linifolius* var. *montanus, syn. *L. montanus* (Bitter vetch). Tufted herbaceous perennial with upright, winged stems, and blue-green leaves divided into 1–4 pairs of oval to linear leaflets, to 5cm (2in) long. From spring to early summer, produces long-stalked racemes of 2–6 reddish purple flowers, 1.5cm (½in) long. Suitable for a wild-flower garden. ↕ 30–40cm (12–16in), ↔ 20–40cm (8–16in). W. and C. Europe, Asia. ❄❄❄

L. luteus see *L. gmelinii*.

***L. luteus* of gardens** see *L. aureus*.

***L. magellanicus* of gardens** see *L. nervosus*.

L. montanus see *L. linifolius* var. *montanus*.

L. nervosus ■ syn. *L. magellanicus* of gardens (Lord Anson's blue pea). Herbaceous, perennial climber with unwinged stems. Prominently veined, leathery, grey-green leaves consist of one pair of ovate leaflets, to 4cm (1½in) long, with prominent stipules. Long-stalked racemes of 3 fragrant, purplish blue flowers, to 2cm (¾in) long, are produced in summer. ↕ 5m (15ft). South America. ❄❄

L. odoratus (Sweet pea). Annual climber with winged stems, and mid- to dark green leaves consisting of one pair of ovate-elliptic leaflets, 5–6cm (2–2½in) long. From summer to early autumn, produces racemes of 2–4 fragrant flowers, to 3.5cm (1½in) long, with wine-red standard petals and purple wings and keels. ↕ to 2m (6ft). Italy (including Sicily). ❄❄❄. Many cultivars have been developed. "Old-

Lathyrus nervosus

fashioned", sweet peas were the earliest, selected mainly for their scent and intense colours; they have prominent stipules, and produce racemes of up to 4 small, highly scented flowers in single or mixed shades of white, red, pink, and blue. They are suitable for growing as a bush and for cutting. ↕ 2–2.5m (6–8ft). Newer developments, of which by far the most widely grown are the Spencer cultivars, have led to greater variety in the colour of the blooms, which occur in most colours except yellow. Spencer cultivars are vigorous, with prominent stipules, and bear racemes of 4 or 5 variably scented flowers, which may be single colours, bicoloured, picotee, or variably marked in contrasting colours, with upright standards and spreading wing petals, both waved. They are excellent for cut flowers. ↕ 2–2.5m (6–8ft), much more as cordons.

Cultivars of **Bijou Group** ■ are bushy, with prominent stipules; they bear racemes of up to 4 slightly scented flowers, to 3.5cm (1½in) long, with small, wavy petals, in shades of pink, blue, red, or white. Require only limited support. ↕↔ to 45cm (18in). Cultivars of **Continental Group** are semi-climbing and vigorous, with prominent stipules, and bear racemes of up to 5 flowers in shades of red, blue, pink, or white, with flat standards and slightly waved, spreading wing petals. Suitable as a bush and for cutting. Require support. ↕ 1–1.1m (3–3½ft). **Early Multiflora** cultivars are vigorous, with prominent stipules, and bear racemes of 5–8 waved, lightly scented flowers in deep rose-pink, salmon-pink, lavender-blue, mid-blue, scarlet, or white. Suitable as a bush and ideal for cutting. Best in a cool greenhouse. ↕ 2–2.5m (6–8ft). **Explorer Group** cultivars have prominent stipules, and produce racemes of up to 4 waved flowers in mid-blue, navy blue, crimson, scarlet, rose-pink, light pink, purple, or white. Dead-head to prolong flowering. Grow as a bush, for cut flowers, or as ground cover if sown in autumn and pinched out twice. ↕ 60cm (24in), ↔ to 1m (3ft). Cultivars of **Galaxy Group** are vigorous, with prominent stipules, and bear racemes of up to 8 waved flowers in rose-pink, salmon-pink, scarlet, white, or lavender-blue. Grow as a bush (with support); ideal for cutting. ↕ 2–2.5m (6–8ft). **'Jayne Amanda'** ■ (Spencer cultivar) bears racemes of usually 4,

Lathyrus odoratus 'Jayne Amanda'

rarely 5, rose-pink flowers. Suitable as a cordon or bush. Cultivars of **Jet Set Group** are bushy, with prominent stipules, and bear racemes of up to 5 flowers in shades of red, blue, pink, and white; the upright standards and spreading wing petals are both slightly waved. Grow as a bush, or in rows for cutting (with support). ↕ 1–1.2 (3–4ft). Cultivars of **Knee-hi Group** are bushy, with prominent stipules, and bear racemes of up to 4 flowers in shades of red, blue, pink, and white, with the upright standards and spreading wing petals both slightly waved. Suitable as a bush with support. ↕ to 1m (3ft). **'Lady Fairbairn'** (Spencer cultivar) produces racemes of usually 4 lilac-pink flowers. Suitable as a cordon or bush. ↕ 2–2.5m (6–8ft). **'Mrs. Bernard Jones'** (Spencer cultivar) bears racemes of usually 4, occasionally 5, white-flushed, almond-pink flowers. Suitable as a cordon or bush. **Multiflora** cultivars are vigorous, with prominent stipules, and bear racemes of 5–8 waved, lightly scented flowers in mid-blue, lavender-blue, deep rose-pink, salmon-pink, scarlet, or white. Suitable as a bush and for cutting. Best in a cool greenhouse. ↕ 2–2.5m (6–8ft). **'Noel Sutton'** ■ (Spencer cultivar) produces racemes of 4, sometimes 5, heavily scented, mid-blue flowers, tinged mauve. Grow as a cordon or bush. **'Pink Cupid'** has prominent stipules, and bears racemes of 3–6 small, plain, strongly scented flowers, with pink standards and whitish pink wing petals. Ideal for growing in a tub, trough, or hanging basket. ↕ 15cm (6in), ↔ 45cm (18in). **'Quito'** (Old-

Lathyrus odoratus Bijou Group

Lathyrus odoratus 'Noel Sutton'

L

Lathyrus odoratus 'White Supreme'

fashioned) has prominent stipules, and bears racemes of up to 4 small, plain, strongly scented flowers, with maroon standards and variously coloured wing petals. **Snoopea Group** cultivars lack tendrils, have prominent stipules, and bear racemes of up to 4 waved flowers in shades of red, blue, pink, and white. Dead-head to prolong flowering. Grow as a bush, or as ground cover if sown in autumn and pinched out twice. ↕ 60cm (24in), ↔ to 1m (3ft). Cultivars of **Supersnoop Group** are similar to Snoopea Group, but slightly stronger-growing. **'White Supreme'** ■ (Spencer cultivar) is vigorous, and bears racemes of usually 4, rarely 5, lightly scented white flowers. Grow as a cordon or bush; ideal for cutting.

L. pratensis (Common vetchling, Meadow vetchling). Variable, herbaceous, perennial climber with unwinged stems. Bluish green leaves are composed of one pair of linear-lance-shaped to elliptic leaflets, to 4cm (1½in) long. From late spring to summer, bears long-stalked racemes of 2–12 yellow flowers, to 1.5cm (½in) long. Suitable for a wildflower garden. ↕ 70–120cm (28–48in), ↔ to 2m (6ft). Europe, N. Africa to W. Asia. ❄❄❄

L. pubescens ■ Herbaceous, perennial climber with unwinged stems. Mid- to dark green leaves are composed of 1 pair (sometimes 2) of elliptic to lance-shaped leaflets, to 8cm (3in) long, with prominent stipules. In summer, bears long-stalked racemes of 6–16 pale to deep lilac-blue flowers, 0.8–1.5cm (⅜–½in) long. ↕ 3m (10ft). Chile, Argentina. ❄❄

Lathyrus pubescens

Lathyrus vernus

L. rotundifolius (Persian everlasting pea). Herbaceous, perennial climber with winged stems. Mid-green leaves consist of one pair of ovate to elliptic leaflets, 3–4.5cm (1¼–1¾in) long. Small racemes of 4–11 dark purplish pink to brownish red flowers, 1.5–2cm (½–¾in) long, are produced in summer. ↕ 1m (3ft). Ukraine (Crimea), Caucasus, E. Turkey, Iraq, Iran. ❄❄❄

L. sativus (Chickling pea). Scrambling, annual climber with angular, winged stems, and mid-green leaves divided into 2 or 3 pairs of narrowly elliptic, pointed leaflets, 4–6cm (1½–2½in) long. In summer, produces solitary, dainty blue flowers, to 1.5cm (½in) long, that fade to white and sometimes have pink veins. Largely grown for animal fodder, but suitable for a mixed or herbaceous border. ↕ to 1m (3ft), ↔ to 45cm (18in). C. and S. Europe, N. Africa, S.W. Asia. ❄❄❄

L. sylvestris (Perennial pea). Herbaceous, perennial climber with winged stems. Mid-green leaves consist of one pair of slender, linear-elliptic leaflets, 5–15cm (2–6in) long, with one pair of narrow stipules. Long-stalked racemes of 3–8 pink flowers, to 2cm (¾in) long, with purplish pink wing petals, are produced from summer to early autumn. ↕ 2m (6ft). Europe, N.W. Africa, Caucasus. ❄❄❄.

L. tingitanus. Herbaceous, perennial climber with slender, winged stems, and mid- to deep green leaves divided into one pair of narrowly elliptic to oblong-elliptic or linear-elliptic leaflets, 4–8cm (1½–3in) long. Pale pink or crimson-magenta flowers, 2–3cm (¾–1¼in) long, are produced singly or in twos or threes, in summer. ↕ to 1.5m (5ft). Spain, Portugal, Azores, Canary Islands, Morocco, Algeria, Sardinia. ❄❄

L. vernus ■ syn. *Orobus vernus* (Spring vetchling). Dense, clump-forming herbaceous perennial with unwinged, upright stems, and mid- to dark green leaves divided into 2–4 pairs of ovate to elliptic, sharp-pointed leaflets, 3–8cm (1¼–3in) long. In spring, bears one-sided racemes of 3–6 purplish blue flowers, to 2cm (¾in) long, that become almost greenish blue. ↕ 20–45cm (8–18in), ↔ 45cm (18in). Continental Europe, Turkey, Caucasus, Russia (Siberia). ❄❄❄. **'Alboroseus'** ■ bears pink-and-white flowers. **f. *albus*** bears white flowers. **var. *aurantiacus*** see *L. aureus.*

Lathyrus vernus 'Alboroseus'

▷**Lattice leaf plant** see *Aponogeton madagascariensis*
▷**Laudanum** see *Cistus ladanifer*
▷**Laurel** see *Prunus laurocerasus, P. lusitanica*
Alexandrian see *Danae racemosa*
Bay see *Laurus nobilis*
California see *Umbellularia californica*
Cherry see *Prunus laurocerasus*
Diamond-leaved see *Pittosporum rhombifolium*
Eastern bog see *Kalmia polifolia*
Indian see *Ficus microcarpa*
Mountain see *Kalmia latifolia*
Portugal see *Prunus lusitanica*
Sheep see *Kalmia angustifolia*
Sierra see *Leucothoe davisiae*
Spotted see *Aucuba japonica*
Spurge see *Daphne laureola*
Tasmanian see *Anopterus glandulosus*
Western see *Kalmia microphylla*

LAURELIA

ATHEROSPERMATACEAE/ MONIMIACEAE

Genus of 3 species of evergreen shrubs and trees occurring in forest and on streambanks in New Zealand, Chile, and Argentina. They are cultivated for their opposite, elliptic, entire or toothed, leathery, aromatic leaves. In summer, inconspicuous, often dioecious flowers are borne in axillary panicles or racemes. Grow in a shrub border, in a woodland garden, or against a warm, sunny wall.

- **HARDINESS** Fully hardy to frost hardy.
- **CULTIVATION** Grow in moist but well-drained, moderately fertile soil in full sun or partial shade, in a site that is sheltered from cold, drying winds. Pruning group 1.
- **PROPAGATION** Take semi-ripe cuttings in summer.
- **PESTS AND DISEASES** Trouble free.

L. sempervirens ◊ syn. *L. serrata* of gardens. Dense, conical shrub or tree with narrowly elliptic to elliptic, very aromatic, bright green leaves, to 10cm (4in) long, with toothed margins, except near the bases. Axillary panicles of tiny, cup-shaped green flowers are produced in early summer. ↕ 15m (50ft), ↔ 10m (30ft), usually less. Chile, Argentina. ❄❄❄ (borderline)

***L. serrata* of gardens** see *L. sempervirens.*

▷***Laurentia axillaris*** see *Isotoma axillaris*

LAURUS

LAURACEAE

Genus of 2 species of evergreen shrubs and trees from woodland, scrub, and rocky places in the Azores, the Canary Islands, and the Mediterranean. They are valued for their aromatic, alternate, ovate leaves. Small, greenish yellow male and female flowers are borne on separate plants. In areas with prolonged frosts, grow in a container and move into a cool greenhouse during winter and early spring. In warmer areas, grow as specimen trees, in a woodland garden, against a warm, sunny wall, or as a windbreak. They are effective in a container in a patio, as they tolerate clipping well.

- **HARDINESS** Frost hardy. Foliage may be damaged by strong, cold winds.
- **CULTIVATION** Grow in fertile, moist but well-drained soil in full sun or partial shade, sheltered from cold, drying winds. Pruning group 1; clip topiary specimens twice during summer.
- **PROPAGATION** Sow seed in containers in a cold frame in autumn, or take semi-ripe cuttings in summer.
- **PESTS AND DISEASES** Bay sucker, scale insects, tortrix moth caterpillars, powdery mildew, and leaf spot may be troublesome.

L. nobilis △ (Bay laurel, Sweet bay). Conical tree or large shrub with aromatic, narrowly ovate, glossy, dark green leaves, to 10cm (4in) long. In spring, bears clusters of greenish yellow flowers, 5mm (¼in) across, followed on female plants by broadly ovoid black berries, to 1.5cm (½in) long. Leaves are often used as a flavouring in cooking. Contact with foliage may aggravate skin allergies. ↕ 12m (40ft), ↔ 10m (30ft). Mediterranean. ❄❄. **'Aurea'** ■ has golden yellow foliage.

▷**Laurustinus** see *Viburnum tinus*
▷**Lavandin** see *Lavandula* x *intermedia*

Laurus nobilis 'Aurea'

LAVANDULA

Lavender

LABIATAE/LAMIACEAE

Genus of about 25 species of aromatic, evergreen shrubs and subshrubs occurring in dry, sunny, exposed, rocky habitats from the Canary Islands, the Mediterranean, and N.E. Africa to S.W. Asia and India. The leaves are opposite, and may be simple and entire, or toothed to pinnatifid, pinnate, or 2-pinnate, with the margins usually rolled under. They are cultivated for their mainly long-stalked spikes of fragrant, tubular, 2-lipped flowers, which, in many species, have a very high nectar content, making them particularly attractive to bees. In warm areas, lavenders are suitable for a variety of situations, from a shrub border to a rock garden, and are useful for edging and as a low hedge. In frost-prone climates, the half-hardy species should be grown at the base of a warm, sunny wall, or in a container which can be overwintered in a cool greenhouse or conservatory. The leaves and flowerheads are often dried for use in sachets or pot-pourri. If grown for drying, cut the flowerheads before they are fully open.

- **Hardiness** Fully hardy to half hardy.
- **Cultivation** Grow in moderately fertile, well-drained soil in full sun. Pruning group 10, in early or mid-spring.
- **Propagation** Sow seed in containers in a cold frame in spring, or take semi-ripe cuttings in summer.
- **Pests and diseases** Froghoppers, honey fungus, and grey mould (*Botrytis*) may be troublesome.

L. angustifolia (Lavender). Compact, bushy shrub with linear, grey-green leaves, to 5cm (2in) long. In mid- and late summer, long, unbranched stalks produce fragrant, pale to deep purple flowers in dense spikes, to 8cm (3in) long. ↕1m (3ft), ↔ 1.2m (4ft). W. Mediterranean. ❄❄❄. **'Hidcote'** ■ is more compact, and produces silvery grey leaves and dark purple flowers; ↕60cm (24in), ↔ 75cm (30in). **'Jean Davis'** produces pale pink flowers. **'Loddon Pink'** ■ is more compact, and produces soft pink flowers; ↕45cm (18in), ↔ 60cm (24in). **'Munstead'** produces blue-purple flowers; ↕45cm (18in), ↔ 60cm (24in). **'Nana Alba'** is very compact, and produces spikes of white

Lavandula angustifolia 'Hidcote'

Lavandula angustifolia 'Loddon Pink'

flowers; ↕↔ 30cm (12in). **'Twickel Purple'** ■ has narrowly oblong leaves, to 5cm (2in) long, and bears purple flowers in midsummer; ↕60cm (24in), ↔ 1m (3ft).

L. dentata ■ Spreading, bushy shrub with linear-oblong, scalloped, dark green leaves, to 4cm (1½in) long. In mid- and late summer, long, unbranched stalks produce dense spikes, to 5cm (2in) long, of slightly fragrant, purple-blue flowers, tipped with purple bracts. ↕1m (3ft), ↔ 1.5m (5ft). Atlantic islands, W. Mediterranean, Arabian Peninsula. ❄❄

L. x intermedia (*L. angustifolia* x *L. latifolia*) (English lavender, Lavandin). Rounded shrub with branching stems bearing oblong to lance-shaped to almost spoon-shaped, aromatic, grey-green leaves, 4–6cm (1½–2½in) long, covered in fine, silvery grey hairs. In summer, light blue to violet flowers are produced in spikes 10–20cm (4–8in) long. ↕↔ 30–50cm (12–20in). Garden origin. ❄❄❄. **'Grappenhall'** has narrowly oblong leaves, to 6cm (2½in) long, and bears spikes, to 7cm (3in) long, of slightly fragrant, blue-purple flowers; ↕1m (3ft), ↔ 1.5m (5ft); ❄❄. **'Seal'** bears pale purple flowers.

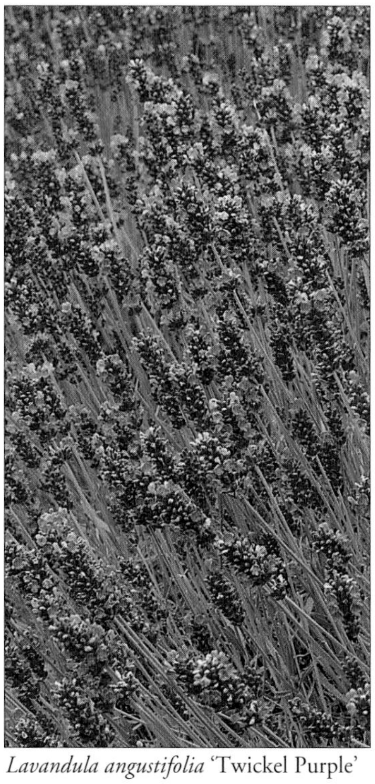

Lavandula angustifolia 'Twickel Purple'

Lavandula dentata

L. lanata. Rounded, bushy shrub with linear to inversely lance-shaped, densely white-woolly leaves, to 5cm (2in) long. Dense spikes, to 10cm (4in) long, of fragrant, dark purple flowers are produced on long, unbranched stalks in late summer. ↕75cm (30in), ↔ 90cm (36in). S. Spain. ❄❄

L. latifolia (Spike lavender). Upright, bushy shrub or subshrub with slender, elliptic or spoon-shaped to oblong-lance-shaped, grey-green leaves, to 6cm (2½in) long. In mid- and late summer, long, branched stalks produce fragrant, mauve-blue flowers in narrow, branching spikes, to 20cm (8in) long. ↕1m (3ft), ↔ 1.2m (4ft). W. Mediterranean. ❄❄

L. pinnata. Spreading, bushy shrub with pinnate, white-hairy, grey-green leaves, to 8cm (3in) long, consisting of numerous, oblong leaflets. In late summer, long, unbranched stalks bear fragrant, blue-purple flowers in spikes to 9cm (3½in) long. ↕↔ 1m (3ft). Canary Islands. ❄❄

L. stoechas ■ (French lavender). Compact, bushy shrub with linear, grey-green leaves, to 4cm (1½in) long. Dense, ovoid-oblong spikes, to 3cm (1¼in) long, of fragrant, dark purple flowers, topped by conspicuous, purple bracts, are borne on very short, unbranched stalks from late spring to summer. ↕↔ 60cm (24in). Mediterranean. ❄❄❄ (borderline). **subsp. *pedunculata*** has flower spikes borne on long stalks well above the foliage; Portugal, Spain.

L. viridis. Upright, bushy shrub with oblong, pale green leaves, to 5cm (2in) long. In mid- and late summer, small white flowers emerge from short-stemmed, unbranched, dense spikes, 2–3cm (¾–1¼in) long, each with a cluster of green bracts at the tip. ↕60cm (24in), ↔ 75cm (30in). Portugal, Spain, Madeira. ❄❄

Lavandula stoechas

LAVATERA

Mallow

MALVACEAE

Genus of approximately 25 species of annuals, biennials, herbaceous, semi-evergreen, or evergreen perennials, and deciduous, semi-evergreen, or evergreen subshrubs and shrubs. They have a wide distribution, occurring from the Azores, Canary Islands, W. Europe, and the Mediterranean to C. Asia, Russia (E. Siberia), Australia, and California, USA, and usually grow in dry, rocky places, often near coasts. They are cultivated for their showy, 5-petalled, saucer- or funnel-shaped flowers (similar to those of *Malva*), borne singly or in racemes, mainly in summer. Leaves are alternate, variably shaped, long-stalked, and usually palmately lobed. The annual, biennial, and short-lived perennial species are suitable for a herbaceous border or for summer bedding; shrubby lavateras are best grown in a shrub border or, in areas prone to severe frost, against a warm, sunny wall.

- **Hardiness** Fully hardy to frost hardy.
- **Cultivation** Grow in ideally light, moderately fertile, well-drained soil in full sun. Shelter from cold, drying winds in frost-prone areas. Pruning group 6.
- **Propagation** Sow seed of annuals *in situ* in mid- to late spring, or under glass in mid-spring. Sow seed of biennials in a cold frame in midsummer. Take softwood and greenwood cuttings of perennials in spring, and of subshrubs and shrubs in early summer. Propagate regularly as shrubs and perennials are often short-lived.
- **Pests and diseases** Prone to stem rot, rust, and soil-borne fungal diseases.

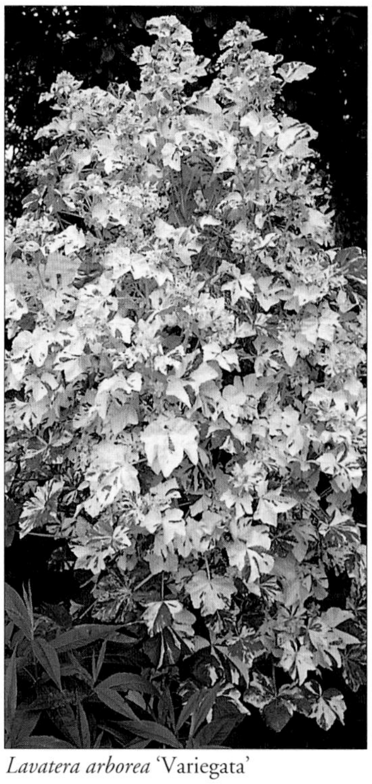

Lavatera arborea 'Variegata'

LAVATERA

Lavatera 'Barnsley'

L. arborea (Tree mallow). Tree-like, woody-stemmed annual, biennial, or short-lived, evergreen perennial with stout stems and rounded, palmately 5- to 7-lobed, mid-green leaves, to 20cm (8in) long. Racemes of 2–7 funnel-shaped, purple-pink flowers, to 6cm (2½in) across, with darker veins, are profusely borne throughout summer. May be grown as a windbreak in a coastal garden. ↕ 3m (10ft), ↔ 1.5m (5ft). W. Europe, Mediterranean. ✽✽. **'Variegata'** ▣ has conspicuous white markings on the leaves.

L. assurgentiflora. Deciduous or semi-evergreen shrub with twisted shoots and palmately 5- to 7-lobed, mid-green leaves, to 15cm (6in) long, with heart-shaped bases and white-hairy lower surfaces. In midsummer, produces funnel-shaped, dark cerise-pink flowers, to 8cm (3in) across, with darker veins, singly or in racemes of 2–4. A good windbreak in coastal gardens. ↕ 2m (6ft), ↔ 1.5m (5ft). USA (California, Santa Catalina Islands). ✽✽

***L.* 'Barnsley'** ▣ Vigorous, semi-evergreen subshrub with palmately 3- to 5-lobed, grey-green leaves, to 12cm (5in) long. Throughout summer, bears profuse racemes of open funnel-shaped, red-eyed white flowers, to 7cm (3in) across, ageing to soft pink, with deeply notched petals. ↕↔ 2m (6ft). ✽✽✽

L. bicolor see *L. maritima.*

***L.* 'Bredon Springs'** ▣ Vigorous, semi-evergreen subshrub with palmately 3- to 5-lobed, grey-green leaves, to 12cm (5in) long. Funnel-shaped, mauve-flushed, dusky pink flowers, to 7cm (3in) across, are borne in profuse

Lavatera 'Bredon Springs'

Lavatera cachemiriana

racemes throughout summer. ↕↔ 2m (6ft). ✽✽✽

***L.* 'Bressingham Pink'.** Upright, shrubby, semi-evergreen perennial with rounded-heart-shaped, shallowly lobed, hairy, pale grey-green leaves, 9cm (3½in) long. From midsummer to early autumn, produces racemes of many saucer-shaped, pale pink flowers, 5–10cm (2–4in) across. ↕ 1.8m (6ft), ↔ 1.2m (4ft). ✽✽✽

***L.* 'Burgundy Wine'.** Vigorous, semi-evergreen subshrub with palmately 3- to 5-lobed, grey-green leaves, to 12cm (5in) long. Profuse racemes of funnel-shaped, rich dark pink flowers, to 7cm (3in) across, with darker veins, are produced throughout summer. ↕↔ 2m (6ft). ✽✽✽

L. cachemiriana ▣ syn. *L. cachemirica.* Annual, or short-lived, woody-based, semi-evergreen perennial, with rounded to heart-shaped, palmately 3- to 5-lobed, blunt-toothed leaves, 7–16cm (3–6in) long, mid-green above, downy beneath. Racemes of many open funnel-shaped, silky-textured, clear rose-pink flowers, to 8cm (3in) across, are borne in summer. ↕ to 2.5m (8ft), ↔ to 1.2m (4ft). India (Kashmir). ✽✽✽

Lavatera 'Kew Rose'

Lavatera trimestris 'Mont Blanc'

L. cachemirica see *L. cachemiriana.*

***L.* 'Candy Floss'.** Vigorous, semi-evergreen subshrub with palmately 3- to 5-lobed, grey-green leaves, to 12cm (5in) long. Profuse racemes of funnel-shaped, pale pink flowers, to 7cm (3in) across, are borne throughout summer. ↕↔ 2m (6ft). ✽✽

***L.* 'Kew Rose'** ▣ Vigorous, semi-evergreen subshrub with purplish green shoots and palmately 3- to 5-lobed, grey-green leaves, to 12cm (5in) long. Profuse racemes of funnel-shaped, bright pink flowers, to 7cm (3in) across, with darker veins, are borne throughout summer. ↕↔ 2m (6ft). ✽✽

L. maritima, syn. *L. bicolor, L. maritima* var. *bicolor.* Upright, shrubby, evergreen perennial that bears almost rounded, shallowly lobed, toothed, hairy, grey-green leaves, to 6cm (2½in) long. From late summer to mid-autumn, produces solitary, axillary, saucer-shaped, pink, lilac-pink, or white flowers, 4–8cm (1½–3in) across, with magenta veins, each petal notched and with a magenta basal mark. ↕ 1.5m (5ft), ↔ 1m (3ft). W. Mediterranean. ✽✽.

var. *bicolor* see *L. maritima.*

L. mauritanica. Downy annual with rounded to heart-shaped, shallowly 5- to 7-lobed, toothed, mid-green leaves, 3–5cm (1¼–2in) long. Racemes of many funnel-shaped purple flowers, to 3cm (1¼in) across, are produced in summer. ↕ 80cm (32in), ↔ to 30cm (12in). Algeria, Morocco. ✽✽

***L. olbia* 'Rosea'** see *L.* 'Rosea'.

***L.* 'Peppermint Ice'** see *L. thuringiaca* 'Ice Cool'.

***L.* 'Rosea'**, syn. *L. olbia* 'Rosea'. Vigorous, semi-evergreen subshrub with palmately 3- to 5-lobed, grey-green leaves, to 12cm (5in) long. Produces racemes of many funnel-shaped, dark pink flowers, to 7cm (3in) across, throughout summer. ↕↔ 2m (6ft). ✽✽✽

***L.* 'Shorty'.** Semi-erect, semi-evergreen perennial with heart-shaped, lobed, hairy, pale green leaves, 5–8cm (2–3in) long. Racemes of many saucer-shaped, white or rose-pink flowers, to 5cm (2in) across, are produced from midsummer to early autumn. ↕↔ to 1m (3ft). ✽✽✽

L. thuringiaca (Tree lavatera). Upright herbaceous perennial with finely grey-hairy stems. Mid-green leaves, 9cm (3½in) long, are rounded with heart-shaped bases; basal leaves are unlobed, stem leaves are palmately 3- to 5-lobed. In summer, bears open funnel-shaped,

Lavatera trimestris 'Pink Beauty'

Lavatera trimestris 'Silver Cup'

long-stalked, purple-pink flowers, to 8cm (3in) across, either singly in the leaf axils or in loose racemes. ↕ to 2m (6ft), ↔ 1.8m (6ft). C. and S.E. Europe. ✽✽✽. **'Ice Cool'**, syn. *L.* 'Peppermint Ice', produces pure white flowers; ↕↔ 1.5m (5ft).

***L. trimestris* cultivars.** Softly hairy annuals bearing rounded, shallowly 3-, 5-, or 7-lobed, mid- to dark green leaves, 3–6cm (1¼–2½in) long, with heart-shaped bases. Open funnel-shaped, pink, reddish pink, or white flowers, 7–10cm (3–4in) across, are produced singly from the upper leaf axils in summer. They provide good cut flowers. ↕ to 1.2m (4ft), ↔ to 45cm (18in). Mediterranean. ✽✽✽. **'Loveliness'** produces deep rose-pink flowers; ↕ 0.9–1.2m (3–4ft). **'Mont Blanc'** ▣ is compact, with very dark green foliage and white flowers; ↕ 50cm (20in). **'Pink Beauty'** ▣ bears purple-centred, very pale pink flowers, with purple veining; ↕ to 60cm (24in). **'Ruby Regis'** bears deep reddish pink flowers; ↕ to 60cm (24in). **'Silver Cup'** ▣ produces bright rose-pink flowers, to 12cm (5in) across, with darker veining; ↕ to 75cm (30in).

▷ **Lavatera, Tree** see *Lavatera thuringiaca*

▷ **Lavender** see *Lavandula, L. angustifolia*

Cotton see *Santolina chamaecyparissus*

English see *Lavandula* x *intermedia*

French see *Lavandula stoechas*

Sea see *Limonium, L. latifolium*

Spike see *Lavandula latifolia*

LAWSONIA

Henna tree, Mignonette tree

LYTHRACEAE

Genus of one species of evergreen shrub or small tree occurring in tropical forest from N. Africa to S.W. Asia and N. Australia. It has opposite, simple, entire leaves and large, terminal panicles of small, 4-petalled, fragrant flowers. Where temperatures drop below 13°C (55°F), grow *L. inermis* in a temperate or warm greenhouse. In warmer areas, grow in a shrub border or as a hedge. Widely cultivated in tropical regions, it is a source of the orange-red dye henna.

- **HARDINESS** Frost tender.
- **CULTIVATION** Under glass, grow in loam-based potting compost (JI No.3) with added sharp sand, in full light. In full growth, water moderately and apply a balanced liquid fertilizer monthly; water sparingly in winter. Outdoors, grow in moderately fertile, well-drained soil in full sun. Pruning group 1; may need restrictive pruning under glass. Clip hedges in early summer.
- **PROPAGATION** Sow seed at 18–21°C (64–70°F) in spring. Take softwood cuttings in spring or hardwood cuttings in autumn.
- **PESTS AND DISEASES** Whiteflies and red spider mites may be troublesome under glass.

L. alba see *L. inermis.*

L. inermis ♀ syn. *L. alba.* Often spiny, open, large shrub or small tree. Elliptic to narrowly obovate or broadly lance-shaped, slender-pointed, mid- to dark green leaves are 2–5cm (¾–2in) long. Many tiny, fragrant flowers, with 4 crumpled, clawed, broadly ovate or spoon-shaped, white, pink, or cinnabar-red petals, are borne in pyramidal panicles, 20–40cm (8–16in) long, mainly in summer. ↕ 3–6m (10–20ft), ↔ 2–4m (6–12ft). N. Africa to S.W. Asia, N. Australia. ❀ (min. 13°C/55°F)

LAYIA

ASTERACEAE/COMPOSITAE

Genus of 15 species of erect to spreading, well-branched annuals, usually found in moist, grassy meadows, but also on sandy and gravelly soils in woodland or in stream washes, in W. USA. They are cultivated for their daisy-like, single, terminal flowerheads, which are composed of white, yellow, or white-tipped yellow ray-florets (each 3-toothed at the tip), and yellow disc-florets, and are profusely borne, mainly in summer. The alternate leaves are narrowly linear to oblong, and entire to finely divided or pinnatifid. Grow in a hot, dry border, or on a bank. They provide long-lasting cut flowers.

- **HARDINESS** Fully hardy to half hardy.
- **CULTIVATION** Grow in moist but well-drained, ideally light, sandy, moderately fertile to poor soil in full sun. Very fertile soil encourages lax growth.
- **PROPAGATION** Sow seed *in situ* in early spring or autumn. In frost-prone areas, protect autumn sowings with cloches.
- **PESTS AND DISEASES** Trouble free.

L. elegans see *L. platyglossa.*

L. platyglossa, syn. *L. elegans* (Tidy tips). Almost succulent-stemmed annual with usually linear to narrowly lance-shaped, toothed to pinnatifid, softly hairy, grey-green leaves, to 3cm (1¼in) long. From summer to autumn, bears flowerheads, to 5cm (2in) across, with white-tipped yellow ray-florets and deep golden yellow disc-florets. ↕ 30–45cm (12–18in), ↔ 24–30cm (10–12in). USA (California). ❄❄❄

▷ **Leadwort** see *Plumbago*
Cape see *P. auriculata*
Scarlet see *P. indica*
▷ **Leatherleaf** see *Chamaedaphne calyculata*
▷ **Leatherwood** see *Cyrilla racemiflora, Dirca palustris*
▷ ***Lechenaultia*** see *Leschenaultia*

LEDEBOURIA

HYACINTHACEAE/LILIACEAE

Genus of 16 species of semi-evergreen or evergreen, bulbous perennials occurring in seasonally dry, open areas or river valleys in South Africa. They are cultivated for their attractively marked leaves and their racemes of small, bell- or urn-shaped flowers, reminiscent of lily-of-the-valley (*Convallaria*); the flowers are produced in spring or summer. In areas where temperatures drop below 7°C (45°F), they are best grown in a conservatory or cool greenhouse. In warmer areas, grow in open sites in a rock or desert garden.

- **HARDINESS** Half hardy to frost tender.
- **CULTIVATION** Plant bulbs with the necks above soil level. Under glass, grow in loam-based potting compost (JI No.2), with added sharp sand, in full light. When in full growth, water freely and apply a high-potash fertilizer every 4 weeks; keep just moist in winter. Outdoors, grow in moderately fertile, well-drained soil in full sun.
- **PROPAGATION** Sow seed under glass in spring or autumn. Remove offsets in spring.
- **PESTS AND DISEASES** Trouble free.

L. cooperi, syn. *Scilla adlamii, S. cooperi.* Very variable, semi-evergreen, bulbous perennial producing semi-erect, ovate to ovate-oblong or linear, mid- to dark green, basal leaves, 5–25cm (2–10in) long, with bold purple stripes. In summer, bears racemes of up to 50 bell-shaped, purple-pink flowers, 6mm (¼in) long, tipped or striped green. ↕ 5–10cm (2–4in), ↔ 5cm (2in). South Africa. ❄

Ledebouria socialis

L. socialis ▣ syn. *Scilla socialis, S. violacea.* Evergreen, bulbous perennial bearing erect, broadly lance-shaped, fleshy, pale silvery green, basal leaves, to 10cm (4in) long, with large, dark green marks above, purple beneath. Racemes of up to 25 bell-shaped, purplish green flowers, 5mm (¼in) long, are produced in late spring or summer. ↕ 5–10cm (2–4in), ↔ 5cm (2in). South Africa (Northern Cape, Western Cape). ❄

x LEDODENDRON

ERICACEAE

Bigeneric hybrid genus of one evergreen shrub, a cross between *Rhododendron trichostomum* and *Ledum glandulosum* var. *columbianum*, with characteristics intermediate between those of its parents. It is grown for its lance-shaped, dark green leaves and large, terminal corymbs of tubular flowers. Grow in a woodland garden, or at the front of a shrub border or peat bank; associates well with dwarf rhododendrons.

- **HARDINESS** Fully hardy.
- **CULTIVATION** Grow in humus-rich, moist but well-drained, acid soil in partial shade. Dead-head after flowering. Pinch out the stem tips on young plants to encourage a bushy habit. Pruning group 8.
- **PROPAGATION** Take semi-ripe cuttings in early summer.
- **PESTS AND DISEASES** Trouble free.

x *L.* 'Arctic Tern', syn. *Rhododendron* 'Arctic Tern'. Upright to spreading shrub with lance-shaped, hairy, dark green leaves, to 5cm (2in) long. Bears rounded corymbs of tubular, 5-lobed, pure white flowers, to 2cm (¾in) long, in late spring and early summer. ↕↔ to 60cm (24in). ❄❄❄

LEDUM

ERICACEAE

Genus of approximately 4 species of evergreen shrubs widely distributed in bogs, marshes, and moist, often coniferous woodland in cool-temperate regions of the N. hemisphere. They are cultivated for their compact habit, aromatic leaves (which are alternate, and may be linear, ovate, oval, or oblong), and their dense, terminal, umbel-like corymbs of small, 5-petalled white flowers, produced in spring or early summer. Suitable for a cool position in a heather garden or peat bed.

Ledum groenlandicum

- **HARDINESS** Fully hardy.
- **CULTIVATION** Grow in humus-rich, moist but well-drained, acid to neutral soil in full sun or partial shade. Pruning group 8.
- **PROPAGATION** Surface-sow seed in containers under glass in spring or autumn. Take semi-ripe cuttings in late summer. Layer in autumn.
- **PESTS AND DISEASES** Trouble free.

L. glandulosum, syn. *Rhododendron neoglandulosum.* Bushy, rounded shrub with smooth shoots and ovate to oval leaves, to 5cm (2in) long, deeply veined and dark green above, white scaly beneath. In late spring, produces white flowers, to 1.5cm (½in) across, in rounded, terminal corymbs, 5cm (2in) across. ↕ 90cm (36in), ↔ 1.2m (4ft). W. North America. ❄❄❄

L. groenlandicum ▣ syn. *Rhododendron groenlandicum* (Labrador tea). Bushy, rounded shrub with rusty-woolly shoots and narrowly oval to elliptic-oblong leaves, to 5cm (2in) long, dark green above, densely rusty-felted beneath, with recurved margins. White flowers, 1–2cm (½–¾in) across, are borne in rounded, terminal corymbs, 5cm (2in) across, in late spring. ↕ 90cm (36in), ↔ 1.2m (4ft). Greenland, North America (Alaska, Canada south to N. USA). ❄❄❄

L. palustre, syn. *Rhododendron tomentosum* (Marsh ledum). Bushy, erect to spreading, usually rounded shrub with rusty-hairy shoots and narrowly oblong to linear leaves, 1–5cm (½–2in) long, dark green above, rusty-hairy beneath, with recurved margins. In late spring, bears white flowers, to 1.5cm (½in) across, in rounded, terminal corymbs, 5cm (2in) across. ↕ 0.3–1.2m (1–4ft), ↔ to 75cm (30in). N. Europe, N. Asia, North America. ❄❄❄.

subsp. *decumbens* is mat-forming, with linear leaves, to 2cm (¾in) long; ↕ 20cm (8in), ↔ 1m (3ft).

▷ **Ledum, Marsh** see *Ledum palustre*

L

LEEA

LEEACEAE

Genus of about 40 species of evergreen shrubs and small trees found in humid forest in tropical Africa, Madagascar, and from India to Malaysia. The alternate or opposite, often velvety leaves are simple to 3-pinnate, and are often flushed red to bronze when young. Small flowers, with tubular bases and 5, sometimes only 4, petal lobes, are borne in flattened, axillary or terminal cymes. Where temperatures drop below 16°C (61°F), grow mainly for their foliage, as houseplants or in a warm greenhouse. In warmer areas, they are distinctive specimens for a small lawn, and are also useful for hedging.

- **HARDINESS** Frost tender.
- **CULTIVATION** Under glass, grow in loam-based potting compost (JI No.3) in bright filtered light and moderate humidity. When in full growth, water freely and apply a balanced liquid fertilizer monthly; water sparingly in winter. Outdoors, grow in moderately fertile, moist but well-drained soil in partial or dappled shade. Pruning group 9; need restrictive pruning under glass. Prune hedges in spring.
- **PROPAGATION** Sow seed at 18°C (64°F) in spring, take semi-ripe cuttings in summer, or air layer in spring or early autumn.
- **PESTS AND DISEASES** Red spider mites may be a problem under glass.

L

L. coccinea (West Indian holly). Open shrub, becoming denser with age, bearing 2- or 3-pinnate leaves, to 60cm (24in) long, with numerous, oblong-lance-shaped to elliptic or obovate, slender-pointed, toothed leaflets, bronzed when young, maturing to glossy, deep green. Even when young, bears terminal cymes, 8–12cm (3–5in) across, of rounded scarlet buds opening to small pink flowers with yellow anthers, mainly in summer. ↕ 1.5–2.5m (5–8ft), ↔ 1–1.5m (3–5ft). Burma. ❁ (min. 16°C/61°F)

▷ **Leek, Roundheaded** see *Allium sphaerocephalon*

LEGOUSIA

CAMPANULACEAE

Genus of about 15 species of small, erect or spreading, unbranched or bushy annuals occurring on arable or stony ground in N. Africa, from Spain to Greece, and in the Caucasus, Turkey, Cyprus, Syria, Iraq, and Iran. They have ovate, oblong, or lance-shaped, wavy-margined, light to mid-green leaves, and produce small, 5-lobed, saucer- to bell-shaped flowers, singly or in delicate panicles or corymbs. Suitable for an annual border or wildflower garden. They provide unusual cut flowers.

- **HARDINESS** Fully hardy.
- **CULTIVATION** Grow in light, well-drained soil in full sun or partial shade.
- **PROPAGATION** Sow seed *in situ* in autumn or mid-spring.
- **PESTS AND DISEASES** Trouble free.

L. speculum-veneris, syn. *Specularia speculum-veneris* (Venus's looking glass). Erect, bushy annual with oblong to inversely lance-shaped, toothed leaves, 1.5–5cm (½–2in) long. From early summer to autumn, saucer-shaped, white-centred, violet-blue, occasionally white or pale purple flowers, to 2cm (¾in) across, with prominent, reflexed sepals, are profusely borne, either singly or in corymbs of 2 or 3, at the tips of branching stems. ↕ to 30cm (12in), ↔ 10cm (4in). C. and S. Europe, N. Africa, Cyprus, W. Syria, N. Iraq, Caucasus. ❄❄❄

LEIOPHYLLUM

ERICACEAE

Genus of one species of upright to mat-forming, evergreen shrub from acid woodland in E. USA. It is grown for its glossy foliage and abundance of star-shaped white flowers borne in terminal, umbel-like corymbs. Grow in a peat bed, shrub border, or woodland garden. It may spread widely by suckers.

- **HARDINESS** Fully hardy.
- **CULTIVATION** Grow in humus-rich, moist but well-drained, acid soil in partial or deep shade. In frost-prone areas, protect from cold, drying winds. Pruning group 8.
- **PROPAGATION** Surface-sow seed in containers outdoors in spring, take softwood cuttings in early summer, or pot up rooted suckers in spring.
- **PESTS AND DISEASES** Trouble free.

L. buxifolium ▣ (Sand myrtle). Bushy, usually suckering shrub with upright and spreading stems. Oblong or ovate, glossy, dark green leaves, to 1cm (½in) long, are tinted bronze in winter. In late spring and early summer, bears pink-budded white flowers, 6mm (¼in) across, in dense corymbs, to 2.5cm (1in) across. ↕ 30–60cm (12–24in), ↔ 60cm (24in) or more. USA (New Jersey to Florida). ❄❄❄. **'Nanum'** is compact, with pink flowers; ↕ 5–10cm (2–4in), ↔ 30cm (12in) or more.

LEIPOLDTIA

AIZOACEAE

Genus of about 20 species of erect or prostrate, shrubby, perennial succulents from periodically very dry areas of Namibia and South Africa. Leaves are opposite, often laterally compressed, thicker than wide, and often marked with raised spots. Daisy-like, pink or reddish purple flowers are borne singly or in cymes of 2–5 in summer, followed by ovoid green capsules with rough, papillose seeds. In frost-prone areas, they are best grown in a bowl garden or a warm greenhouse. In frost-free climates, they are effective in a desert garden.

- **HARDINESS** Frost tender.
- **CULTIVATION** Under glass, grow in standard cactus compost in full light. When in full growth, water sparingly and apply low-nitrogen fertilizer every 4–6 weeks; keep dry when dormant. Outdoors, grow in poor, sharply drained soil in full sun. Protect from winter wet. See also pp.48–49.
- **PROPAGATION** Sow seed at 19–24°C (66–75°F) in spring, or take cuttings of stem sections in late spring.
- **PESTS AND DISEASES** Vulnerable to greenfly and other aphids while flowering.

Leiophyllum buxifolium (inset: flower detail)

L. weigangiana. Erect, perennial succulent with woody stems, 3mm (⅛in) thick, and yellowish white bark. The boat-shaped, 3-angled, spotted, bluish green leaves are 1.5cm (½in) long and 5mm (¼in) thick. Solitary, violet to pink flowers, 2cm (¾in) across, are produced in summer. ↕ to 50cm (20in), ↔ 25cm (10in). Namibia. ❁ (min. 10°C/50°F)

▷ ***Lemaireocereus euphorbioides*** see *Neobuxbaumia euphorbioides*

LEMBOGLOSSUM

ORCHIDACEAE

Genus of about 14 species of evergreen, mostly epiphytic, rhizomatous orchids (often included within the genus *Odontoglossum*) occurring in humid forests at altitudes of 1,300–3,000m (4,300–10,000ft) in Mexico and Central and South America. They have broadly ovoid to oblong-ovoid, clustered pseudobulbs, each producing up to 3 linear, lance-shaped, ovate, or elliptic leaves. Flowers are produced in racemes from the bases of the pseudobulbs.

- **HARDINESS** Frost tender.
- **CULTIVATION** Cool- to intermediate-growing orchids. Grow in fine-grade epiphytic orchid compost in a container that constricts the roots. In summer, provide high humidity and bright filtered light, water freely, apply fertilizer at every third watering, and mist once or twice daily. In winter, provide full light and water sparingly. See also p.46.
- **PROPAGATION** Divide when the plants fill and overflow their containers.
- **PESTS AND DISEASES** Susceptible to red spider mites, aphids, and mealybugs.

L. bictoniense ▣ syn. *Odontoglossum bictoniense*. Epiphytic orchid with ovoid, compressed pseudobulbs, each with 2 or 3 elliptic-oblong to linear leaves, 10–45cm (4–18in) long. Light green flowers, 2.5cm (1in) across, heavily barred with brown, with heart-shaped, white or pink lips, are borne in tall, upright racemes from winter to spring. ↕ 60cm (24in), ↔ 30cm (12in). Mexico, Guatemala, El Salvador. ❁ (min. 10°C/50°F; max. 24°C/75°F)

L. cervantesii, syn. *Odontoglossum cervantesii*. Epiphytic orchid with ovoid pseudobulbs, each with one ovate-lance-shaped to elliptic-oblong leaf, 4–30cm (1½–12in) long. From winter to spring,

Lemboglossum bictoniense

Lemboglossum rossii

bears short, arching racemes of white to pink flowers, 4–6cm (1½–2½in) across, with narrow, central red spots and bands. ↕↔ 15cm (6in). S. Mexico, Guatemala. ❄ (min. 10°C/50°F; max. 24°C/75°F)
L. cordatum, syn. *Odontoglossum cordatum*. Epiphytic orchid with oblong, compressed, furrowed pseudobulbs, each with one narrowly elliptic, leathery leaf, 9–30cm (3½–12in) long. Brown-marked, green, white, or yellow flowers, to 6cm (2½in) across, are borne in erect racemes in late summer. ↕ 20cm (8in), ↔ 15cm (6in). Central America, Venezuela. ❄ (min. 10°C/50°F; max. 24°C/75°F)
L. rossii ■ syn. *Odontoglossum rossii*. Epiphytic orchid with ovoid pseudobulbs, each with one elliptic or elliptic-lance-shaped leaf, 5–20cm (2–8in) long. White, pink, or sometimes yellow flowers, 5–7cm (2–3in) across, with brown to pink-brown bars or spots on the sepals and petal bases, are borne in short, arching racemes from late winter to spring. ↕↔ 15cm (6in). Mexico, Guatemala, Honduras, Nicaragua. ❄ (min. 10°C/50°F; max. 24°C/75°F)
L. stellatum, syn. *Odontoglossum stellatum*. Epiphytic orchid with narrowly oblong pseudobulbs, each with one ovate to elliptic or inversely lance-shaped leaf, 6–15cm (2½–6in) long. From winter to spring, produces short, arching racemes of yellowish white flowers, 4cm (1½in) across, barred with brown (or sometimes entirely brown), with large, pink or white lips spotted deep pink. ↕↔ 15cm (6in). Mexico, Guatemala, El Salvador. ❄ (min. 10°C/50°F; max. 24°C/75°F)

▷ ***Lembotropis nigricans*** see *Cytisus nigricans*
▷ **Lemon** see *Citrus limon*
Meyer's see *C. limon* 'Meyer'
▷ **Lemon balm** see *Melissa officinalis*
▷ **Lemon verbena** see *Aloysia triphylla*
▷ **Lemonwood** see *Pittosporum eugenioides*

LENOPHYLLUM

CRASSULACEAE

Genus of about 6 species of clustering, perennial succulents from low-lying, often scrub or woodland areas of California, Texas, and New Mexico, USA, and Mexico. Very variably shaped, fleshy leaves are borne mainly in opposite pairs, forming loose, basal rosettes. Sparsely leafy flowering stems produce small, 5-petalled flowers, borne singly or in terminal racemes or panicles, from summer to winter. In areas where temperatures drop below 5°C (41°F), they may be grown outdoors in summer, but need to be protected in a temperate greenhouse at other times. In warmer climates, grow permanently outdoors in a shrub border or a desert garden.
• **HARDINESS** Frost tender.
• **CULTIVATION** Under glass, grow in standard cactus compost in full light. From spring to late summer, water freely and apply a balanced liquid fertilizer every 6–8 weeks. Water moderately in autumn and keep just moist in winter. Outdoors, grow in moderately fertile, sharply drained soil in full sun. See also pp.48–49.
• **PROPAGATION** Sow seed at 19–24°C (66–75°F), or divide offsets, in spring or early summer. Root leaf cuttings in summer.
• **PESTS AND DISEASES** Prone to greenfly while flowering.

L. guttatum. Rosetted, perennial succulent with ovate-elliptic to diamond-shaped, blunt-tipped, grey-green leaves, 2–3.5cm (¾–1½in) long, with purple-black spots, the upper surfaces broadly grooved. Cup-shaped, thick-sepalled, pale yellow flowers, to 1cm (½in) across, later tinged red, are produced in open, sparsely branched panicles from summer to autumn. ↕↔ 10–12cm (4–5in). N.E. Mexico. ❄ (min. 5°C/41°F)
L. texanum. Perennial succulent with loose rosettes of very thick, lance-shaped to ovate, mid-green leaves, 1.5–3cm (½–1¼in) long. Cup-shaped, fleshy, primrose-yellow flowers, 6–8mm (¼–⅜in) across, with red-tipped petals, are borne in few-branched panicles from late summer to early winter. ↕ to 10cm (4in), ↔ to 20cm (8in). USA (Texas), N.E. Mexico. ❄ (min. 5°C/41°F)

▷ **Lenten rose** see *Helleborus orientalis*
▷ **Lentisc** see *Pistacia lentiscus*

LEONOTIS

LABIATAE/LAMIACEAE

Genus of about 30 species of aromatic annuals, perennials, and evergreen to semi-evergreen subshrubs and shrubs (deciduous in cold climates) from upland grassland and rocky areas, mainly in South Africa, with one species widely distributed in tropical regions. They have square stems and opposite, lance-shaped to ovate leaves, and are cultivated for their showy whorls of 2-lipped flowers produced in terminal, leafy, raceme-like inflorescences. In frost-prone climates, they may be treated as tender perennials and grown in a cool greenhouse, or planted outdoors once there is little risk of frost. In warmer areas, grow outdoors in a border or against a warm wall.
• **HARDINESS** Half hardy.
• **CULTIVATION** Under glass, grow in loam-based potting compost (JI No.2) in full light. When in full growth, water freely and apply a balanced liquid fertilizer every 6–8 weeks; water sparingly in winter. Outdoors, grow in moderately fertile, well-drained soil in full sun. Pruning group 10, in spring, if grown permanently outdoors; if grown under glass or as tender perennials, cut to ground level in early spring.
• **PROPAGATION** Sow seed at 13–18°C (55–64°F) in spring, or take greenwood cuttings in late spring or summer.
• **PESTS AND DISEASES** Susceptible to grey mould (*Botrytis*), red spider mites, and whiteflies under glass.

L. leonurus ■ (Lion's ear). Upright, semi-evergreen or deciduous shrub or subshrub with lance-shaped to inversely lance-shaped, entire or scalloped, mid- to deep green leaves, 6–12cm (2½–5in) long. From autumn to early winter, produces whorls of tubular, 2-lipped, orange-red to scarlet flowers, 6cm (2½in) long. ↕ 2m (6ft) or more, ↔ 1m (3ft) or more. South Africa (except Gauteng and North-West Province). ✼.
'Harrismith White' bears white flowers.
L. ocymifolia. Woody-based, herbaceous perennial with ovate, toothed or scalloped, mid-green leaves, to 8cm (3in) long, with very hairy undersides. From late summer to autumn, produces dense whorls of tubular, 2-lipped, velvety-haired orange flowers, to 4cm (1½in) long, with the upper lip twice as long as the lower. ↕ to 3m (10ft), ↔ 1m (3ft). South Africa (except Free State, Gauteng, and North-West Province). ✼

Leonotis leonurus

LEONTICE

BERBERIDACEAE

Genus of 3 species of tuberous perennials occurring on dry hillsides in N. Africa, the E. Mediterranean, the Middle East, and S.W. and C. Asia. They are cultivated for their large, axillary or terminal racemes or panicles of small, cup-shaped flowers held above 3-palmate or pinnate leaves. Grow in an alpine house or bulb frame.
• **HARDINESS** Frost hardy.
• **CULTIVATION** Plant tubers 20cm (8in) deep in autumn. Under glass, grow in loam-based potting compost (JI No.2) with added grit, in full light. When in growth, water moderately and apply a low-nitrogen fertilizer every 6–8 weeks; keep dry when dormant. Outdoors, grow in any well-drained soil in full sun.
• **PROPAGATION** Sow seed in containers in a cold frame as soon as ripe.
• **PESTS AND DISEASES** Trouble free.

L. leontopetalum. Tuberous perennial with grey-green, basal leaves, to 25cm (10in) wide, each usually divided into 3 broadly obovate leaflets. From spring to early summer, produces panicles of cup-shaped yellow flowers, to 1.5cm (½in) across, which open flat. ↕ 20–80cm (8–32in), ↔ 15cm (6in). N. Africa, E. Mediterranean to Iran. ✼✼

LEONTOPODIUM

Edelweiss

ASTERACEAE/COMPOSITAE

Genus of approximately 35 species of perennials found in grassland and stony habitats in the mountains of Europe and Asia. They have simple, entire, hairy, mainly basal leaves. Upright stems bear compact, terminal cymes of small flowerheads consisting only of yellowish white disc-florets, surrounded by leaf-like, usually white-felted bracts. Easily grown, most species are suitable for a rock garden, raised bed, or alpine house.
• **HARDINESS** Fully hardy.
• **CULTIVATION** Grow in sharply drained, neutral to alkaline soil in full sun. Protect from excessive winter wet. In an alpine house, grow in loam-based potting compost (JI No.1) with added grit or sharp sand.
• **PROPAGATION** Sow seed in containers in an open frame as soon as ripe. Divide in early spring, although divisions are slow to establish.
• **PESTS AND DISEASES** Susceptible to slugs and snails outdoors, and to aphids and red spider mites under glass.

L. aloysiodorum see *L. haplophylloides*.
L. alpinum ■ (Edelweiss). Clump-forming perennial with linear to oblong-lance-shaped, grey-green, basal leaves, to 4cm (1½in) long. In spring or early summer, bears conspicuous heads of yellowish white flowers surrounded by stars of flannel-textured, grey-white bracts, 3–10cm (1¼–4in) across. ↕ 20cm (8in) ↔ 10cm (4in). Mountains of Europe. ✼✼✼. **subsp. *nivale***, syn. *L. nivale*, has densely white-hairy leaves,

Leontopodium alpinum

and bears woolly, pure white flowerheads and bracts, on short stems; ↕↔ to 15cm (6in); C. Apennines, mountains of Bulgaria and former Yugoslavia.

L. haplophylloides, syn. *L. aloysiodorum*. Erect, clump-forming or tufted perennial with linear-lance-shaped, lemon-scented, hairy, grey-green leaves, 5–7cm (2–3in) long, spotted black beneath. In early summer, bears yellowish white flowers surrounded by stars of many white-hairy, grey-green bracts, 5cm (2in) across. More tolerant of winter wet than *L. alpinum*. ↕ 30cm (12in), ↔ to 20cm (8in). Mountains of C. and S.W. China. ❄❄❄

L. nivale see *L. alpinum* subsp. *nivale*.

L. stracheyi. Mound-forming perennial with ovate-lance-shaped to linear leaves, to 4.5cm (1¾in) long, sparsely grey-hairy above, grey-downy beneath. In spring, bears short-stemmed heads of glistening, yellowish white flowers and many white-felted bracts, to 6cm (2½in) across. ↕ to 50cm (20in), ↔ to 30cm (12in). Himalayas, Mountains of India (Uttar Pradesh) to S.W. China. ❄❄❄

- ▷ **Leopard lily** see *Belamcanda chinensis*, *Lilium pardalinum*
- ▷ **Leopard's bane** see *Doronicum*
- ▷ ***Leopoldia comosa*** see *Muscari comosum*
- ▷ ***Lepachys columnifera*** see *Ratibida columnifera*
- ▷ ***Lepachys pinnata*** see *Ratibida pinnata*

LEPIDOZAMIA

ZAMIACEAE

Genus of 2 species of palm-like, dioecious cycads from slopes, gullies, and rainforest in E. Australia. The erect trunks are clad in old leaf bases, with the pinnate, light or deep green leaves borne in terminal whorls. Narrow, cone-like, green to brown, male or female flowerheads ("cones") are borne in the centres of the leaf rosettes. In frost-prone climates, grow in a temperate or warm greenhouse, or as houseplants. In frost-free climates, grow as specimen plants.

- **HARDINESS** Frost tender.
- **CULTIVATION** Under glass, grow in a mix of equal parts garden compost, loam, and coarse bark, with added slow-release fertilizer, grit, and charcoal, in bright filtered light. Water moderately when in growth, sparingly in winter. Outdoors, grow in moderately fertile, moist but well-drained soil in full sun or partial shade.
- **PROPAGATION** Sow seed at 24°C (75°F) in spring.
- **PESTS AND DISEASES** Red spider mites, mealybugs, and scale insects may be troublesome under glass.

Lepidozamia hopei

L. hopei ▣ ♈ Medium-sized to tall cycad with ascending to arching, pinnate, light green leaves, to 3m (10ft) long, each consisting of many lance-shaped, curved, lustrous leaflets. Green to brown flowering cones are borne usually in summer: the ovoid females to 60cm (24in) long, the cylindrical males to 80cm (32in) long. ↕ to 20m (70ft), ↔ to 6m (20ft). Australia (N.E. Queensland). ❀ (min. 13–15°C/ 55–59°F)

L. peroffskyana ♈ Medium-sized to tall cycad with pinnate, deep green leaves, to 3m (10ft) long, composed of linear to lance-shaped, lustrous leaflets, each with a yellow basal gland. Green to brown flowering cones are borne in summer: the ovoid females to 60cm (24in) long, the cylindrical males to 80cm (32in) long. ↕ to 20m (70ft), ↔ to 6m (20ft). Australia (Queensland, New South Wales). ❀ (min. 13–15°C/55–59°F)

LEPTINELLA

ASTERACEAE/COMPOSITAE

Genus of approximately 30 species of annuals and creeping, tufted, or mat-forming perennials from subalpine grassland and rocky areas in Australasia and South America. They form low carpets of pinnatifid, pinnatisect, or pinnate, often aromatic leaves, and bear solitary, button-like flowerheads on short stalks from late spring to summer.

Leptinella atrata

Effective as low ground cover and tolerant of some treading, they are suitable for paving crevices or gravel gardens, but are mostly too invasive for a rock garden. *L. atrata* is suitable for a scree bed or alpine house.

- **HARDINESS** Fully hardy.
- **CULTIVATION** Grow in moderately fertile, sharply drained soil in full sun.
- **PROPAGATION** Sow seed in containers in an open frame as soon as ripe. Divide in spring.
- **PESTS AND DISEASES** Trouble free.

L. atrata ▣ syn. *Cotula atrata*. Creeping, tufted perennial with fern-like, broadly elliptic, 2-pinnatifid, purple-tinged, grey-green leaves, to 8cm (3in) long. In late spring and early summer, bears hemispherical, purplish black flowerheads, to 1.5cm (½in) across, with yellow anthers that become prominent as the flowers mature. ↕ to 15cm (6in), ↔ to 20cm (8in). New Zealand. ❄❄❄. **subsp. *luteola*** has less deeply divided leaves, and bears conical flowerheads with dark red-brown centres and very prominent, creamy white stigmas.

L. pectinata. Tufted or mat-forming perennial with narrowly oblong, hairy or hairless, sometimes toothed, pinnatifid to pinnate leaves, 4cm (1½in) long, with linear to lance-shaped leaflets or lobes. White or pale yellow-red flowerheads, to 8mm (⅜in) across, are produced in late spring and early summer. ↕ to 15cm (6in), ↔ to 45cm (18in). New Zealand. ❄❄❄

LEPTOSPERMUM

Tea tree

MYRTACEAE

Genus of about 80 species of evergreen shrubs and trees occurring in rainforest and semi-arid areas mainly in Australia, but also from S.E. Asia to New Zealand. They are cultivated for their usually aromatic, neat foliage and their small, sometimes profusely borne flowers. The variably shaped leaves are alternate, entire, and hairless to densely silky-hairy. The flowers are produced from the leaf axils, either singly or in clusters of 2 or 3, and are shallowly cup-shaped to star-shaped, each with 5 white, red, or pink, clawed, usually broadly ovate petals. In frost-prone areas, grow hardy species against a warm, sunny wall, and half-hardy and frost-tender species in a cool greenhouse or conservatory. A few are also suitable for an alpine house. In warmer areas, grow in a shrub border.

- **HARDINESS** Fully hardy (borderline) to frost tender.
- **CULTIVATION** Under glass, grow in loam-based potting compost (JI No.3) in full light or bright filtered light. When in active growth, water freely and apply a balanced liquid fertilizer every 4 weeks; water sparingly in winter. Outdoors, grow in moderately fertile, well-drained soil in full sun or partial shade. Pruning group 8; may need restrictive pruning under glass.
- **PROPAGATION** Sow seed at 13–16°C (55–61°F) in autumn or spring, or root semi-ripe cuttings with bottom heat in summer.
- **PESTS AND DISEASES** Trouble free.

L. flavescens see *L. polygalifolium*.

L. grandiflorum, syn. *L. rodwayanum*. Upright shrub with white-hairy stems and ovate to elliptic, aromatic, silky-hairy, grey-green leaves, to 1.5cm (½in) long. Solitary, saucer-shaped, white or, rarely, pale pink flowers, to 2cm (¾in) across, are produced in mid- and late summer. ↕ 4m (12ft), ↔ 2m (6ft). Australia (Tasmania). ❄❄

L. humifusum see *L. rupestre*.

L. lanigerum ▣♀ syn. *L. pubescens* (Woolly tea tree). Freely branching, erect shrub or tree with softly hairy and often red-flushed green stems. Crowded, more or less spreading, obovate-oblong to oval, aromatic leaves, 0.5–1.5cm (¼–½in) long, often have recurved points, and are usually grey silky-hairy, at least beneath. From late spring to summer, bears solitary, shallowly cup-

Leptospermum lanigerum

Leptospermum rupestre

shaped white flowers, to 1.5cm (½in) across, with prominent red-brown calyces. ↕3–5m (10–15ft), ↔1.5–3m (5–10ft). Australia (New South Wales, Victoria, Tasmania). ✲✲

L. polygalifolium ♀ syn. *L. flavescens.* Erect to spreading, freely branching shrub or tree. Crowded, spreading or occasionally reflexed, mid- to deep green leaves, 0.5–2cm (¼–¾in) long, are linear to inversely lance-shaped-elliptic, with conspicuous oil glands, and sometimes lightly aromatic. From late spring to summer, bears a profusion of solitary, cup-shaped, white or cream, sometimes green- or pink-tinted flowers, 1cm (½in) across. ↕2–7m (6–22ft), ↔1–3m (3–10ft). Australia (Queensland, New South Wales, Lord Howe Island). ✲

L. prostratum see *L. rupestre.*

Leptospermum scoparium 'Gaiety Girl'

L. pubescens see *L. lanigerum.*

L. rodwayanum see *L. grandiflorum.*

L. rupestre ▣ syn. *L. humifusum, L. prostratum, L. scoparium* var. *prostratum* of gardens. Prostrate shrub, sometimes mounded and bushy, with dense foliage. Broadly to narrowly elliptic or obovate, glossy, deep green leaves, 0.7–2cm (¼–¾in) long, are spreading and aromatic. Star-shaped white flowers, to 1cm (½in) across, are borne singly or in pairs from late spring to summer. ↕0.3–1.5m (1–5ft), ↔0.9–1.5m (3–5ft). Australia (Tasmania). ✲✲✲ (borderline)

L. scoparium ▣ (Manuka, New Zealand tea tree). Compact shrub, rarely tree-like, with arching shoots and ascending to widely spreading, elliptic, broadly lance-shaped, or inversely lance-shaped, aromatic, mid- to dark green leaves, 0.7–2cm (¼–¾in) long, often silver-hairy when young. Solitary, shallowly cup- to saucer-shaped, white or pink-tinged white flowers, 1.5cm (½in) across, are profusely borne in late spring and early summer. ↕↔3m (10ft). S.E. Australia, New Zealand. ✲. **'Apple Blossom'** has white flowers overlaid with pink; ✲✲. **'Gaiety Girl'** ▣ bears semi-double flowers, deep pink outside, paler within; ✲✲. **'Huia'** is compact, with dark pink flowers. Suitable for a rock garden or alpine house; ↕30cm (12in), ↔45cm (18in). **'Keatleyi'** has pale pink flowers, 2.5cm (1in) across. **'Kiwi'** ▣ has purple-tinged young foliage and dark crimson flowers. Suitable for a rock garden or alpine house; ↕↔1m (3ft). **'Nicholsii'** has purple-tinged foliage and crimson flowers. **'Pink Cascade'** has a weeping habit, and produces pink flowers; ✲✲. **var. *prostratum*** of gardens see *L. rupestre.* **'Red Damask'** has dark green leaves and double, dark red flowers. **'Snow Flurry'** has double white flowers.

Leptospermum scoparium

Leptospermum scoparium 'Kiwi'

LESCHENAULTIA

syn. LECHENAULTIA

GOODENIACEAE

Genus of about 20 species of evergreen shrubs, subshrubs, and perennials from semi-arid or arid areas of Australia. The usually linear leaves are entire, stalkless, and alternate or spiralling on the wiry stems. The showy, terminal flowers are solitary or borne in corymbs; they each have 5 free, often centrally "winged", white, yellow to red, or blue petals, 2 small and 3 large, which form a basal tube. In frost-prone areas, grow in a cool or temperate greenhouse. In frost-free climates, grow in a shrub border or as ground cover.

- **HARDINESS** Frost tender, although *L. biloba* and *L. formosa* may survive temperatures near to 0°C (32°F) if kept almost dry.
- **CULTIVATION** Under glass, grow in a mix of 1 part loam-based potting compost (JI No.1) and 3 parts each grit (or perlite) and peat, in full light with shade from hot sun and with good ventilation. In active growth, water moderately and apply a phosphate-free liquid fertilizer monthly; water sparingly in winter. Outdoors, grow in sharply drained soil that is low in nitrates and phosphates, in full sun with some mid-day shade. Pruning group 8 for shrubs.
- **PROPAGATION** Sow seed at 13–18°C (55–64°F) in spring, or root softwood cuttings in spring with bottom heat.
- **PESTS AND DISEASES** Under glass, red spider mites may be troublesome, and poor ventilation in winter will encourage grey mould (*Botrytis*).

Leschenaultia formosa

L. biloba. Open shrub with linear, soft, mid-green to grey-green leaves, 1cm (½in) long. Bright blue, sometimes white flowers, 3cm (1¼in) across, are borne in leafy corymbs, to 8cm (3in) across, in late spring and early summer. Each petal lobe is roughly the shape of a fish-tail, the "tail fins" having sharp to blunt points. ↕↔30–60cm (12–24in). Australia (open eucalyptus forest in Western Australia). ❀ (min. 5–7°C/41–45°F)

L. floribunda. Erect, shrubby, woody-based perennial or short-lived shrub with alternate, narrowly oblong to linear, mid-green leaves, 3–8mm (⅛–⅜in) long. Blue or white flowers, 1.5cm (½in) across, are borne in loose corymbs, to 10cm (4in) across, from late spring to midsummer. ↕45cm (18in), ↔35cm (14in). Australia (coastal plains of Western Australia). ❀ (min. 5–7°C/41–45°F)

L. formosa ▣ Suckering, many-branched, spreading shrub with linear, blunt-tipped or pointed, light to grey-green leaves, to 1cm (½in) long. In late spring and early summer, produces solitary flowers, 2cm (¾in) across, in shades of bright red, orange, or orange-yellow. Usually short-lived, especially under glass. ↕↔30–60cm (12–24in). Australia (dry heathland in acid, quartzite sand in Western Australia). ❀ (min. 5–7°C/41–45°F)

LESPEDEZA

Bush clover

LEGUMINOSAE/PAPILIONACEAE

Genus of about 40 species of annuals, perennials, and deciduous subshrubs and shrubs found in meadows, grassland, and rocky places in E. Asia, Australia, and North America. They are cultivated for their small, pea-like flowers, profusely borne in axillary or terminal racemes. Leaves are alternate and 3-palmate. Excellent late-flowering plants for a mixed or shrub border.

- **HARDINESS** Fully hardy.
- **CULTIVATION** Grow in light, moderately fertile, well-drained soil in full sun. Pruning group 6 for shrubs;

Lespedeza thunbergii

treat as perennials in very cold areas, where shrubby species may be cut to the ground by frost in winter.
• **PROPAGATION** Sow seed in containers outdoors in spring, or take greenwood cuttings in early summer. *L. thunbergii* may also be divided in spring.
• **PESTS AND DISEASES** Trouble free.

L. bicolor. Upright shrub with arching shoots and 3-palmate, mid- to dark green leaves consisting of broadly oval to obovate leaflets, to 5cm (2in) long. In mid- and late summer, purple-pink flowers, to 1cm (½in) long, are borne in slender racemes, 5–12cm (2–5in) or more long, from the upper leaf axils. ↕↔ 2m (6ft). E. Asia. ❄❄❄
L. thunbergii ▣ Woody-based perennial or subshrub with long, arching shoots and 3-palmate, blue-green leaves consisting of oval or oval-lance-shaped leaflets, to 5cm (2in) long. In early autumn, purple-pink flowers, to 1.5cm (½in) long, are profusely borne in pendent, terminal racemes, to 15cm (6in) long. ↕ 2m (6ft), ↔ 3m (10ft). N. China, Japan. ❄❄❄

▷**Lettuce, Water** see *Pistia, P. stratiotes*

LEUCADENDRON

PROTEACEAE

Genus of 80 species of small, dioecious, evergreen shrubs and trees from varied habitats, ranging from sea plains to mountain slopes in dry or moist sites, in South Africa. They are grown mainly for their dense, cone-like, terminal clusters of small, tubular flowers, surrounded by large, leaf-like, often coloured or tinted bracts. Leaves are alternate or spiralling, stalkless, entire, leathery, and variably shaped. Both male and female plants are needed for fruiting cones to develop. Where temperatures fall below 5°C (41°F), grow in a cool or temperate greenhouse, although they seldom bear flowers or fruits in the former. In warm, dry areas, grow in a courtyard garden or against a sunny wall; the larger species are spectacular specimen plants.
• **HARDINESS** Frost tender.
• **CULTIVATION** Under glass, grow in a mix of 1 part lime-free (ericaceous) potting compost and 3 parts each grit (or perlite) and peat, in full light and low humidity. During the growing season, water moderately and apply magnesium sulphate and urea at half the recommended strength in spring and autumn; water sparingly in winter. Outdoors, grow in poor, well-drained, neutral to acid soil in full sun. May become chlorotic in magnesium-deficient soil. Pruning group 1.
• **PROPAGATION** Stratify seed below 5°C (41°F), then sow at 13–16°C (55–61°F) in a mix of equal parts peat and grit in spring. Root semi-ripe cuttings with bottom heat in summer.
• **PESTS AND DISEASES** Red spider mites may be a problem under glass.

L. argenteum ♤ (Silver tree). Erect, pyramidal to columnar tree with robust stems densely covered with lance-shaped, sharp-pointed, brilliant, silvery-hairy leaves, 10–15cm (4–6in) long. From spring to summer, bears spherical flowerheads, to 4cm (1½in) across, yellowish green on male trees, greenish silver on females, surrounded by leaf-like but broader and more lustrous bracts, to 2cm (¾in) long. The silvery cones often persist on the tree for several years. ↕ 6–10m (20–30ft), ↔ 2–4m (6–12ft). South Africa (Northern Cape, Western Cape, Eastern Cape). ❀ (min. 5–7°C/41–45°F)
L. discolor. Erect, open shrub with grooved, often purple-red stems and inversely lance-shaped, rigid, leathery, densely short-hairy, greyish green leaves, 2.5–4cm (1–1½in) long, often tipped and margined purple. From spring to early summer, bears ovoid to spherical flowerheads, 3cm (1¼in) across, purple-red to red on male shrubs, whitish green on females, surrounded by ivory to creamy white bracts, 4–5cm (1½–2in) long, with purple-red tips or margins (usually more boldly coloured in males). Cones are brown. ↕ 1.5–2.5m (5–8ft), ↔ 1–2m (3–6ft). South Africa (Northern Cape, Western Cape, Eastern Cape). ❀ (min. 5–7°C/41–45°F)
L. 'Safari Sunset' ▣ Vigorous, erect, freely branching shrub with narrowly oblong leaves, to 9cm (3½in) long, deep green flushed purple-red, more colourful when young. From summer to autumn, produces ovoid, sterile, yellowish green female flowerheads, 4cm (1½in) across, surrounded by light red bracts, 10–20cm (4–8in) long, maturing to purple-red and fading to golden yellow. ↕ to 2.5m (8ft), ↔ to 1.8m (6ft) or more. ❀ (min. 5–7°C/41–45°F)
L. tinctum. Spreading, freely branching shrub with robust stems, bent towards their bases, and oblong, dark green leaves, 8cm (3in) long, increasing in size towards the stem tips. From spring to summer, bears ovoid, greenish yellow flowerheads, to 3cm (1¼in) across, surrounded by glossy yellow bracts, 8cm (3in) long, which reflex after the flowers have faded. Cones have a sweet, spicy aroma. ↕↔ to 1.2m (4ft). South Africa (Northern Cape, Western Cape, Eastern Cape). ❀ (min. 5–7°C/41–45°F)

LEUCANTHEMELLA

ASTERACEAE/COMPOSITAE

Genus of 2 species of hairy perennials found in wet meadows or marshy places, one species in S.E. Europe, the other in E. Asia. They have tall stems, which bear numerous alternate, lance-shaped to broadly elliptic or oblong, entire to sharply toothed leaves. They are grown mainly for their chrysanthemum-like flowerheads, borne singly or in 2- to 8-flowered corymbs in autumn. Grow in a mixed or herbaceous border. Also good for cutting.
• **HARDINESS** Fully hardy.
• **CULTIVATION** Grow in any reliably moist soil in full sun or partial shade.
• **PROPAGATION** Divide, or take basal cuttings, in spring.
• **PESTS AND DISEASES** Susceptible to slugs; thrips may damage leaves.

Leucadendron 'Safari Sunset' (inset: flowerhead detail)

Leucanthemella serotina

L. serotina ▣ syn. *Chrysanthemum serotinum, C. uliginosum.* Strong-growing, erect perennial with simple, lance-shaped to broadly elliptic or oblong, toothed leaves, 6–12cm (2½–5in) long. From early to late autumn, white flowerheads, to 7cm (3in) across, with greenish yellow centres, are borne singly or in lax corymbs of 2–8. ↕ to 1.5m (5ft), ↔ 90cm (36in). S.E. Europe. ❄❄❄

LEUCANTHEMOPSIS

ASTERACEAE/COMPOSITAE

Genus of 6 species of dwarf, tufted, clump- or mat-forming, often short-lived perennials from mountain habitats in Europe and North Africa. They have pinnatisect, pinnatifid, or palmately lobed leaves, and bear solitary, daisy-like, white or yellow flowerheads in summer. Suitable for a rock garden, scree bed, or alpine house.
• **HARDINESS** Fully hardy (borderline).
• **CULTIVATION** Grow in any sharply drained soil in full sun. In an alpine house, grow in equal parts loam, leaf mould, and grit.
• **PROPAGATION** Sow seed in containers in an open frame as soon as ripe. Divide, or take basal cuttings, in spring.
• **PESTS AND DISEASES** Susceptible to aphids and red spider mites under glass.

L. alpina, syn. *Chrysanthemum alpinum* (Alpine chrysanthemum). Mat-forming, rhizomatous perennial with variable, ovate to spoon-shaped, pinnatisect, deeply pinnatifid, or palmately lobed, silvery grey leaves, to 4cm (1½in) long. In mid- and late summer, produces short-stemmed flowerheads, to 4cm (1½in) across, with white ray-florets, sometimes turning pink with age, and orange-yellow disc-florets. Best grown in a scree bed. ↕ 10cm (4in), ↔ to 20cm (8in). Pyrenees, Alps, Apennines, Carpathians. ❄❄❄

L

Leucanthemopsis pectinata

L. pectinata ■ syn. *Chrysanthemum pectinata, L. radicans, Pyrethrum radicans.* Densely tufted perennial, spreading by runners, with pinnatifid, grey-green to silvery green leaves, 7–14cm (3–6in) long, with 5–9 lobes. In summer, bears flowerheads to 2cm (¾in) across, with yellow-orange disc-florets, and golden yellow ray-florets that turn orange-red. ↕ 15cm (6in), ↔ to 30cm (12in). Spain (Sierra Nevada). ✻✻✻ (borderline)
L. radicans see *L. pectinata.*

LEUCANTHEMUM

ASTERACEAE/COMPOSITAE

Genus of 26 species of annuals and perennials from rocky alpine slopes and moist meadows, grassland, and wasteland in Europe and temperate Asia. They have alternate, entire, deeply pinnatifid, toothed, scalloped, or lobed leaves, and solitary, daisy-like, terminal flowerheads, which are usually white with yellow disc-florets. Grow alpine species in a scree bed or rock garden, taller perennials in a wild garden. Some hybrids and cultivars are useful in a herbaceous border and for cut flowers.

Leucanthemum paludosum 'Show Star'

• **HARDINESS** Fully hardy to frost hardy.
• **CULTIVATION** Grow in moderately fertile, moist but well-drained soil in full sun or partial shade. Alpine species need sharply drained soil in full sun. Many of the taller plants need support.
• **PROPAGATION** Sow seed of annuals *in situ* in spring. Sow seed of perennials in containers in a cold frame in autumn or spring. Divide perennials in early spring or late summer.
• **PESTS AND DISEASES** Aphids, slugs, earwigs, chrysanthemum eelworm, and leaf spots may be troublesome.

L. atratum, syn. *Chrysanthemum atratum.* Variable, clump- or mat-forming perennial with spoon-shaped, scalloped or lobed, dark green basal leaves, to 5cm (2in) long, and shorter, oblong to linear, deeply toothed to pinnatifid stem leaves, with toothed tips. In summer, upright stems bear solitary flowerheads, to 5cm (2in) across, with yellow disc-florets and white ray-florets. ↕↔ to 30cm (12in). Alps, Apennines, mountains of Slovenia, Bosnia & Herzegovina, and Yugoslavia (Serbia and Montenegro). ✻✻✻
L. hosmariense see *Rhodanthemum hosmariense.*
L. paludosum, syn. *Chrysanthemum paludosum.* Hairless, bushy annual with obovate, spoon-shaped, grey-green basal leaves, to 12cm (5in) long, and shorter, oblong-wedge-shaped stem leaves; all leaves are toothed to pinnatifid. In summer, produces solitary flowerheads, 2–3cm (¾–1¼in) across, with yellow or yellowish white ray-florets and deeper yellow disc-florets. ↕ 5–15cm (2–6in),

Leucanthemum x *superbum* 'Cobham Gold'

Leucanthemum x *superbum* 'Horace Read'

↔ 20cm (8in). S. Portugal, S. and S.E. Spain, Balearic Islands. ✻✻✻. **'Show Star'** ■ has wavy-margined, toothed, mid-green leaves and bright yellow flowerheads.
L.* x *superbum (*L. lacustre* x *L. maximum*) syn. *Chrysanthemum maximum* of gardens, *C.* x *superbum* (Shasta daisy). Robust, clump-forming perennial with inversely lance-shaped, toothed, glossy, almost fleshy, dark green basal leaves, to 30cm (12in) long, and shorter, lance-shaped, stalkless stem leaves. From early summer to early autumn, bears solitary, single or double white flowerheads, 10–12cm (4–5in) across, with yellow disc-florets, paler in the double-flowered forms. Good for cutting. ↕ 90cm (36in), ↔ 60cm (24in). Garden origin. ✻✻✻. **'Aglaia'** produces fringed, semi-double flowerheads; ↕ 60cm (24in). **'Bishopstone'** has feathery, single flowerheads with narrow, cut ray-florets. **'Cobham Gold'** ■ has double flowerheads; ↕ 60cm (24in). **'Esther Read'** has double, pure white flowerheads; ↕↔ 50–60cm (20–24in). **'Everest'** see 'Mount Everest'. **'Fiona Coghill'** has double flowerheads. **'Horace Read'** ■ has double white flowerheads with incurved disc-florets; ↕ 60cm (24in). **'Little Silver Princess'** see 'Silberprinzesschen'. **'Mount Everest'**, syn. 'Everest', bears single flowerheads, to 10cm (4in) across. **'Phyllis Smith'** ■ has single flower-heads with twisted, recurved ray-florets. **'Silberprinzesschen'**, syn. 'Little Silver Princess', has single flowerheads; ↕↔ 30cm (12in). **'Snowcap'** very freely bears single flowerheads, to 10cm (4in)

Leucanthemum x *superbum* 'Phyllis Smith'

Leucanthemum x *superbum* 'Wirral Pride'

across; ↕↔ 45cm (18in). **'Snow Lady'** is a fast-growing, erect, bushy perennial usually grown as an annual, with oval to lance-shaped, deeply toothed leaves; produces single white flowerheads in summer; ↕ 25–45cm (10–18in), ↔ 30cm (12in). **'T.E. Killin'** has double flowerheads, to 10cm (4in) across, with yellow anemone centres. **'Wirral Pride'** ■ has double flower-heads with anemone centres; ↔ 75cm (30in). **'Wirral Supreme'** has dense, double flowerheads with slightly shorter centre ray-florets; ↔ 75cm (30in).
L. vulgare, syn. *Chrysanthemum leucanthemum* (Marguerite, Ox-eye daisy). Extremely variable, rhizomatous perennial with obovate-spoon-shaped, toothed, smooth, dark green basal leaves, 2–10cm (¾–4in) long, and shorter, sometimes pinnatifid stem leaves. Solitary flowerheads, 2.5–5cm (1–2in) across, with bright yellow disc-florets and white ray-florets, are borne in late spring and early summer. ↕ 30–90cm (12–36in), ↔ 60cm (24in). Most of Europe, temperate Asia. ✻✻✻

LEUCHTENBERGIA

CACTACEAE

Genus of one species of perennial cactus with a thick, forked, tuberous rootstock, sometimes branching from the base, from hilly regions in central N. Mexico. The plant is covered with narrowly triangular, spirally arranged tubercles, each tipped by an areole bearing papery, twisted spines. The areoles on young tubercles produce fragrant flowers by day from summer to autumn. Where temperatures drop below 10°C (50°F), grow in a warm greenhouse; in warmer climates, grow in a desert garden.
• **HARDINESS** Frost tender.
• **CULTIVATION** Under glass, grow in standard cactus compost in full light. From mid-spring to early autumn, water moderately and apply a balanced liquid fertilizer every 6–8 weeks; keep

L

Leuchtenbergia principis

completely dry from mid-autumn to early spring. Outdoors, grow in moderately fertile, sharply drained, ideally alkaline soil, in full sun. Protect from winter wet. See also pp.48–49.
• **PROPAGATION** Sow seed at 19–24°C (66–75°F) in spring.
• **PESTS AND DISEASES** Susceptible to scale insects when in growth.

L. principis ■ Simple or branching cactus with a thick, cylindrical, fleshy root, appearing woody when mature, and spherical to short cylindrical stems. Narrowly triangular, glaucous, bluish green tubercles, 10–12cm (4–5in) long, cover the stems. Large grey areoles bear 8–14 radial spines, to 5cm (2in) long, and 1 or 2 centrals, to 15cm (6in) long. From summer to autumn, bears funnel-shaped, bright yellow flowers, to 8cm (3in) long. ↕30–60cm (12–24in), ↔ 30cm (12in). Central N. Mexico. ❄ (min. 10°C/50°F)

L

LEUCOCORYNE

ALLIACEAE/LILIACEAE

Genus of 12 species of garlic-scented, bulbous perennials from dry scrub and rocky hillsides in Chile. They are grown for their umbels of large, open funnel-shaped, scented, blue, white, or purple flowers, borne in spring. Each bulb produces 2–5 linear, often channelled, basal leaves, smelling of garlic. In frost-prone areas, grow in a cool greenhouse; in warmer areas, grow in a rock garden.
• **HARDINESS** Frost tender.
• **CULTIVATION** Plant bulbs 10cm (4in) deep. Under glass, grow in loam-based potting compost (JI No.2) with added sharp sand, in full light with good ventilation. When in growth, water moderately and apply a balanced liquid fertilizer monthly when in leaf. Reduce water after flowering and keep almost dry when dormant in summer. Pot on every 2 years in autumn. Outdoors, grow in moderately fertile, sharply drained soil in full sun.
• **PROPAGATION** Sow seed at 19–24°C (66–75°F) as soon as ripe, or remove offsets in autumn before repotting.
• **PESTS AND DISEASES** Trouble free.

Leucocoryne ixioides

L. ixioides ■ (Glory of the sun). Bulbous perennial with narrow, grass-like, basal leaves, to 45cm (18in) long, which wither as the flowers open. In spring, produces umbels of up to 12 outward-facing, open funnel-shaped, scented flowers, 2cm (¾in) across, white with purple veins, or lilac-blue with white throats. ↕45cm (18in), ↔ 8cm (3in). Chile. ❄ (min. 5–7°C/41–45°F)
L. purpurea. Bulbous perennial with narrow, grass-like, basal leaves, to 30cm (12in) long, which wither as the flowers open. In spring, produces umbels of 2–7 open funnel-shaped, scented, pale lilac flowers, 2.5cm (1in) across, with broad, red-purple centres. ↕45cm (18in), ↔ 8cm (3in). Chile. ❄ (min. 5–7°C/ 41–45°F)

LEUCOGENES

New Zealand edelweiss

ASTERACEAE/COMPOSITAE

Genus of 3 or 4 species of dwarf, hummock-, mat-, or clump-forming perennials from screes or rocky, fell-fields in the mountains of New Zealand. They have obovate-wedge-shaped or linear to lance-shaped, closely over-lapping, intensely silver-hairy leaves and, in summer, bear small, flat yellow flowerheads surrounded by collars of white-woolly bracts. Effective in a peat bed, rock garden, or alpine house, but difficult to grow in dry climates.
• **HARDINESS** Hardy to -10°C (14°F), possibly more.
• **CULTIVATION** Grow in gritty, humus-rich, moist but sharply drained soil in full sun. They grow best in cool, moist climates and resent a dry atmosphere in summer. Protect from winter wet. In an alpine house, grow in a mix of equal parts loam, leaf mould, and coarse sand.
• **PROPAGATION** Sow seed in containers in an open frame as soon as ripe. Take stem-tip cuttings in late summer.
• **PESTS AND DISEASES** Susceptible to red spider mites under glass; may be damaged by slugs and snails outdoors.

L. grandiceps ■ Mat-forming perennial with closely overlapping, obovate-wedge-shaped, silver-downy leaves, to 1cm (½in) long, that obscure the stems. In early summer, bears yellow flowerheads, 0.9–1.5cm (⅜–½in) across, near the shoot tips, each surrounded by a collar, 1cm (½in) across, of densely white-woolly bracts. ↕↔ 10–15cm (4–6in). New Zealand (South Island). ❄❄❄ (borderline)
L. leontopodium, syn. *Raoulia leontopodium*. Hummock-forming perennial with linear to lance-shaped-oblong leaves, to 2cm (¾in) long, clothed in yellowish or greyish silver or

Leucogenes grandiceps

silvery white down. In early summer, produces yellow flowerheads, to 2.5cm (1in) across, near the shoot tips, each surrounded by a collar, to 1.5cm (½in) across, of white-woolly bracts. ↕↔ 10–15cm (4–6in). New Zealand. ❄❄❄ (borderline)

LEUCOJUM

Snowflake

AMARYLLIDACEAE

Genus of about 10 species of mainly spring- or autumn-flowering, bulbous perennials from a variety of habitats, including woodland, shaded hillsides, wet sites, dunes, rocky grassland, and scrub, from W. Europe to the Middle East and N. Africa. They are related and similar to snowdrops (*Galanthus*), with usually 1 or 2, occasionally up to 8 flowers per stem, but the nodding or pendent, bell-shaped, usually white, sometimes pink flowers have 6 equal segments. Leaves are basal and strap-shaped to linear, or occasionally narrowly cylindrical. Small species are suitable for a rock garden, alpine house, or bulb frame, while larger species such as *L. aestivum* and *L. vernum* are excellent in a border, near water, or naturalized in grass.
• **HARDINESS** Fully hardy to frost hardy.
• **CULTIVATION** Plant dry bulbs 8–10cm (3–4in) deep in autumn. Grow in any moist but well-drained soil in full sun, apart from *L. aestivum* and *L. vernum*, which need reliably moist, humus-rich soil. In an alpine house, grow in equal parts loam, leaf mould, and sharp sand.
• **PROPAGATION** Sow seed in containers in a cold frame in autumn, or remove offsets once the leaves have died down.
• **PESTS AND DISEASES** Prone to slugs and narcissus bulb fly.

L. aestivum (Summer snowflake). Robust, bulbous perennial with erect, strap-shaped, glossy, dark green leaves, to 40cm (16in) long. In spring, leafless stems bear up to 8 bell-shaped, faintly chocolate-scented white flowers, 2cm (¾in) long, with green tips. ↕45–60cm (18–24in), ↔ 8cm (3in). Ireland, UK, Belgium, France, C. and E. Europe, N. Turkey, Ukraine (Crimea), Caucasus, N. and N.W. Iran. ❄❄❄.
'Gravetye Giant' ■ is more robust; ↕90cm (36in), especially when grown near water.
L. autumnale ■ Slender, bulbous perennial with erect, narrow, grass-like

Leucojum aestivum 'Gravetye Giant'

leaves, to 16cm (6in) long, produced with or just after the flowers. In late summer and early autumn, each bulb produces up to 4 leafless stems, each bearing 2–4 bell-shaped white flowers, 1cm (½in) long, with red-tinged bases. ↕10–15cm (4–6in), ↔ 5cm (2in). S.W. Europe, N. Africa. ❄❄❄
L. hiemale see *L. nicaeense.*
L. nicaeense, syn. *L. hiemale.* Bulbous perennial with 2–4 almost prostrate, curled, narrowly linear leaves, to 30cm (12in) long. In early spring, leafless stems produce 1 or 2 bell-shaped, waxy white flowers, 1cm (½in) long. Survives outside in a sunny, sheltered site, but is best grown in an alpine house. ↕10cm (4in), ↔ 5cm (2in). S.E. France. ❄❄
L. roseum. Bulbous perennial with leafless stems bearing 1 or 2 bell-shaped, pale pink flowers, 1cm (½in) long, in late summer or autumn. Erect, thread-like, narrowly linear leaves, to 10cm (4in) long, appear just after the flowers. Best in an alpine house, especially in areas that experience prolonged frost. ↕10cm (4in), ↔ 5cm (2in). Corsica, Sardinia. ❄❄
L. trichophyllum. Bulbous perennial with 3 linear leaves, 5–20cm (2–8in)

Leucojum autumnale

Leucojum vernum var. *vagneri*

long, that appear before or with the flowers. From winter to spring, slender, leafless stems bear 2–4 bell-shaped white flowers, to 2cm (¾in) long, sometimes flushed pink or purple. Best in an alpine house. ↕ 10–30cm (4–12in), ↔ 5cm (2in). S. Portugal, S.W. Spain, Morocco. ❄❄

L. valentinum. Bulbous perennial with narrowly linear, grey-green leaves, to 25cm (10in) long, produced after the flowers. In autumn, leafless stems bear 1–3 bell-shaped white flowers, 1cm (½in) long. ↕ 15cm (6in), ↔ 3–5cm (1¼–2in). C. Spain, N.W. Greece, Ionian Islands. ❄❄❄ (borderline)

L. vernum (Spring snowflake). Bulbous perennial with erect, strap-shaped, glossy, dark green leaves, to 25cm (10in) long. In early spring, produces stout, leafless stems with usually 1, occasionally 2, bell-shaped, green-tipped white flowers, 2.5cm (1in) long. ↕ 20–30cm (8–12in), ↔ 8cm (3in). S. and E. Europe. ❄❄❄. **var. *carpathicum*** produces 1 or 2 flowers per stem, each with yellow-tipped tepals. **var. *vagneri*** ■ is robust, and flowers in late winter and early spring, bearing 2 flowers per stem; ↕ 20cm (8in).

LEUCOPHYTA

syn. CALOCEPHALUS

Cushion bush

ASTERACEAE/COMPOSITAE

Genus of 18 species of annuals and evergreen perennials and small shrubs from rocky coastal habitats, often exposed to salt spray, in Australia. They are cultivated for their alternate, very narrow, entire, often white-woolly leaves and spherical, rayless flowerheads, which are clustered into terminal corymbs. In frost-prone climates, grow in a cool greenhouse, or as summer bedding or edging foliage plants. In warmer climates, they are useful for adding a silver edging to a shrub border.

- **HARDINESS** Frost tender; may withstand short periods down to 0°C (32°F).
- **CULTIVATION** Under glass, grow in loam-based potting compost (JI No.1) with added grit, in full light. Pot on or top-dress in spring, or plant outside in early summer. When in growth, water moderately and apply a balanced liquid fertilizer monthly; water sparingly in winter. Outdoors, grow in sharply drained, moderately fertile soil in full sun. Pinch out stem tips of young plants to promote bushiness. Pruning group 10, in spring.
- **PROPAGATION** Root semi-ripe cuttings in summer.
- **PESTS AND DISEASES** Prone to grey mould (*Botrytis*) in damp conditions.

L. brownii ■ syn. *Calocephalus brownii.* Bushy shrub with intricately branched, slender, silvery white-downy stems. Scale-like, silvery grey leaves, 5mm (¼in) long, are pressed closely against the stems, so that the bush appears leafless. In summer, produces small, rounded, terminal corymbs of creamy white, rarely purple flowerheads, 1cm (½in) across. ↕ 40–75cm (16–30in), ↔ 40–90cm (16–36in). Australia (Western Australia to New South Wales, Tasmania). ❁ (min. 5–7°C/41–45°F)

Leucophyta brownii

LEUCOPOGON

EPACRIDACEAE

Genus of about 150 species of erect or spreading, evergreen shrubs and small trees from heathland and forest in S. Asia and Australasia. They have variably shaped, entire leaves, and bear tubular flowers, with reflexed lobes, either singly or in spikes, followed by small, fleshy, berry-like fruits. Grow in a rock garden. In frost-prone areas, grow tender species in a cool greenhouse.

- **HARDINESS** Fully hardy to frost tender.
- **CULTIVATION** Grow in humus-rich, moist but well-drained, acid soil in full sun or partial shade. Pruning group 8 or 9.
- **PROPAGATION** Sow seed in containers outdoors as soon as ripe, or take greenwood cuttings in early summer.
- **PESTS AND DISEASES** Trouble free.

L. colensoi see *Cyathodes colensoi.*

L. fraseri, syn. *Cyathodes fraseri.* Creeping subshrub with densely overlapping, heath-like, obovate, short-stalked, glossy, dark green leaves, 5–10mm (¼–½in) long, often tinted red in autumn, with bristles on the tips and margins. Bears axillary, solitary, 5-lobed, fragrant white flowers, 5–10mm (¼–½in) across, towards the tips of upright shoots in summer. In autumn, produces edible, sweet-tasting, spherical, fleshy, pale orange fruit, 6–9mm (¼–⅜in) across. ↕ 10–15cm (4–6in), ↔ to 30cm (12in). New Zealand. ❄❄

x LEUCORAOULIA

ASTERACEAE/COMPOSITAE

Bigeneric hybrid genus between *Leucogenes leontopodium* and *Raoulia rubra*, from the Tararua mountains of New Zealand. Grown for its cushions of silvery, rosetted foliage, it is suitable for a scree bed or alpine house.

- **HARDINESS** Fully hardy.
- **CULTIVATION** Grow in gritty, sharply drained soil in full sun. Protect from winter wet. Under glass, grow in a mix of equal parts loam, leaf mould, and grit; top-dress with grit. Water freely from spring to summer; resents a hot, dry atmosphere in summer, so mist in hot weather. Keep just moist in winter.
- **PROPAGATION** Detach individual rosettes and root as cuttings in spring.
- **PESTS AND DISEASES** Susceptible to mildew, especially in dry conditions.

x *Leucoraoulia loganii*

x *L. loganii* ■ syn. *Raoulia* x *loganii.* Dense, cushion-forming perennial with neat, symmetrical, almost columnar rosettes of tiny, overlapping, densely hairy, silvery white leaves, to 2mm (1⁄16in) long. Produces insignificant pink flowerheads in summer in the wild, but very seldom in cultivation. ↕ 8cm (3in), ↔ 10cm (4in). New Zealand. ❄❄❄

LEUCOSPERMUM

Pincushion

PROTEACEAE

Genus of 47 species of evergreen shrubs and small trees from varied habitats, including scrub, subtropical coastal dune forest, evergreen temperate forest, and mountain slopes, in Zimbabwe and South Africa. The alternate, leathery, simple, entire or toothed leaves may be linear to elliptic, inversely lance-shaped, oval, ovate, obovate, oblong, or spoon-shaped. Dense, cone-like, clustered or solitary, terminal flowerheads are borne on short axillary shoots and have very prominent, red, orange, pink, yellow, or white styles. Where temperatures fall below 5°C (41°F), grow in a cool or temperate greenhouse. In warmer, dry areas, plant in a shrub border. The larger species are good specimen plants.

- **HARDINESS** Frost tender.
- **CULTIVATION** Under glass, grow in a mix of 1 part loam-based potting compost (JI No.1) and 3 parts each grit (or perlite) and peat, in full light. In active growth, water moderately and apply magnesium sulphate and urea at half the recommended strength in spring and autumn; water sparingly in winter, never allowing the compost to dry out. Outdoors, grow in well-drained, neutral to acid soil, with low levels of phosphates and nitrates, in full sun. Magnesium deficiency may lead to chlorosis. Pruning group 1; may need restrictive pruning under glass.
- **PROPAGATION** Stratify ripe seed below 5°C (41°F), then sow at 13–16°C (55–61°F) in spring. Root semi-ripe cuttings in summer with bottom heat.
- **PESTS AND DISEASES** Red spider mites may be a problem under glass.

L. catherinae (Catherine's pincushion). Densely bushy, erect shrub with a short, stout trunk. Crowded, inversely lance-shaped to elliptic, stalked, hairless leaves, 9–14cm (3½–5½in) long, each with 3 or 4 teeth at the tip, are usually mid- to deep green, tinted yellow or grey, with often red-flushed tips and margins. From spring to early summer, bears solitary, conical flowerheads, 10–15cm (4–6in) across, with erect, then arching styles that are light orange, tipped mauve-pink, ageing to deep reddish gold. ↕↔ 2.5m (8ft). South Africa (Western Cape). ❁ (min. 5°C/41°F)

L. cordifolium ■ syn. *L. nutans.* Rounded, spreading shrub with ovate to oblong, entire, stalkless, mid-green leaves, to 8cm (3in) long, heart-shaped at the bases, sometimes with 3–6 teeth at the tips, and initially downy, later almost smooth. From early spring to midsummer, horizontal to downward-arching stems, which bend sharply upwards at their tips, produce solitary, spherical flowerheads, 10–12cm (4–5in) wide, with numerous forward-arching, usually orange, but also crimson or

Leucospermum cordifolium

yellow styles. ↕ to 2m (6ft), ↔ 1.5–3.5m (5–11ft). South Africa (Northern Cape, Western Cape, Eastern Cape, on acid soils). ❀ (min. 5°C/41°F)

L. nutans see *L. cordifolium.*

L. reflexum. Rounded, moderately open shrub, thickening with age. Oblong-elliptic to inversely lance-shaped, hairy, grey-green leaves, 2–6cm (¾–2½in) long, sometimes have 2 or 3 teeth at the tips. From early spring to early summer, erect shoots produce solitary or paired, ovoid to spherical flowerheads, 4.5–6cm (1¾–2½in) across, composed of initially outward- and upward-curving orange styles, which are later strongly reflexed and deep crimson. ↕ to 3m (10ft), ↔ 2–4m (6–12ft). South Africa (Cedar Berg mountains in Western Cape). ❀ (min. 5°C/41°F)

LEUCOTHOE

ERICACEAE

Genus of about 50 species of deciduous, semi-evergreen, or evergreen shrubs from woodland, thickets, swamps, and streambanks in Madagascar, the Himalayas, E. Asia, and North and South America. They are grown for their alternate, very variably shaped, simple, often glossy, dark green leaves, and for their cylindrical to urn-shaped, usually white flowers, borne in terminal or axillary racemes or panicles. Effective in a peat bed or acid woodland garden.

• **HARDINESS** Fully hardy to frost hardy.

• **CULTIVATION** Grow in humus-rich, reliably moist, acid soil in deep or partial shade. Pruning group 1.

Leucothoe fontanesiana 'Rainbow'

Leucothoe fontanesiana SCARLETTA ('Zeblid')

• **PROPAGATION** Sow seed in containers in a cold frame in spring. Root semi-ripe cuttings with bottom heat in summer. Divide suckering species in spring.

• **PESTS AND DISEASES** Trouble free.

***L. catesbeyi* of gardens** see *L. fontanesiana.*

L. davisiae (Sierra laurel). Upright, suckering, evergreen shrub with ovate-oblong, glossy, dark green leaves, to 8cm (3in) long. Urn-shaped white flowers, 5mm (¼in) long, are produced in erect, axillary racemes, 5–15cm (2–6in) long, in early summer. ↕ 1m (3ft), ↔ 1.5m (5ft). USA (California, Oregon). ❄❄❄

L. fontanesiana, syn. *L. catesbeyi* of gardens, *L. walteri* (Switch ivy). Upright, evergreen shrub with arching branches and oblong-lance-shaped to ovate-lance-shaped, toothed, leathery leaves, 6–16cm (2½–6in) long, glossy, dark green above, paler below. In spring, bears almost cylindrical white flowers, 5mm (¼in) long, in axillary racemes, 4–6cm (1½–2½in) long. ↕ 1–2m (3–6ft), ↔ 3m (10ft). S.E. USA. ❄❄❄.

'Rainbow' ■ is thicket-forming, with lance-shaped, dark green leaves mottled cream and pink. Flowers are produced in late spring; ↕ 1.5m (5ft), ↔ 2m (6ft).

'Rollissonii' has narrowly elliptic-lance-shaped leaves, to 10cm (4in) long.

SCARLETTA ('Zeblid') ■ syn. *L.* SCARLETTA ('Zeblid'), has dark red-purple young foliage, which turns dark green, then bronze in winter.

L. keiskei. Clump-forming, evergreen shrub with upright to prostrate shoots and narrowly ovate to ovate-lance-shaped, slenderly tapered, glossy, dark green leaves, to 9cm (3½in) long, red when young. Urn-shaped white flowers, to 1cm (½in) long, are borne in nodding racemes, to 5cm (2in) long, at or near the ends of young shoots in midsummer. Suitable for a peat bed. ↕↔ 60cm (24in). Japan. ❄❄❄

L. racemosa (Fetter bush, Sweetbells). Bushy, suckering, deciduous or semi-evergreen shrub with upright shoots and oblong to ovate or elliptic, pointed, glossy, dark green leaves, to 6cm (2½in) long. In early summer, urn-shaped white flowers, 6mm (¼in) long, are profusely borne in upright to spreading, usually terminal racemes, to 10cm (4in) long. ↕↔ 1.5m (5ft). E. USA. ❄❄❄

***L.* SCARLETTA ('Zeblid')** see *L. fontanesiana* SCARLETTA ('Zeblid').

L. walteri see *L. fontanesiana.*

▷ ***Leuzea centauroides*** see *Stemmacantha centauroides*

LEVISTICUM

Lovage

APIACEAE/UMBELLIFERAE

Genus of one species of hairless perennial occurring in mountain regions in the E. Mediterranean. It has 2- or 3-pinnate, dark green leaves, and umbels of star-shaped flowers produced in midsummer. The strongly celery-scented roots and shoots are used as a vegetable or in salads, and the seeds are used for flavouring. Suitable for a herb garden. Contact with the foliage may cause photodermatitis.

• **HARDINESS** Fully hardy.

• **CULTIVATION** Tolerant of most soils, but best in deep, moderately fertile, moist but well-drained soil in full sun.

• **PROPAGATION** Sow seed in a seedbed as soon as ripe, or divide in early spring.

• **PESTS AND DISEASES** Leaf miners may be troublesome.

L. officinale. Robust perennial with stout, hollow, finely ribbed stems and 2- or 3-pinnate, triangular to diamond-shaped, dark green leaves, to 70cm (28in) long, with ovate, toothed leaflets. Star-shaped, greenish yellow flowers are borne in umbels, to 15cm (6in) across, in midsummer, followed by ovoid, slightly winged green fruit. ↕ 2m (6ft), ↔ 1m (3ft). E. Mediterranean. ❄❄❄

LEWISIA

PORTULACACEAE

Genus of about 20 species of deciduous or evergreen perennials from W. North America, with fleshy rootstocks, and rosettes or tufts of fleshy leaves that vary in shape. Deciduous species occur in open, stony meadows or grassland, and die down after flowering; evergreens are more commonly found in partial shade among rocks or in crevices. The funnel-shaped to open funnel-shaped flowers, with 5–9, sometimes up to 19 petals, are pink, magenta, purple, orange, yellow, or white. They are usually borne in cymes or panicles in spring and summer, often over long periods. Grow in an alpine house or rock garden, or in the crevices of a retaining wall.

• **HARDINESS** Fully hardy.

• **CULTIVATION** Grow in moderately fertile, humus-rich, sharply drained, neutral to acid soil: deciduous species and hybrids in full sun, evergreens in light shade. Protect all from winter wet; protect deciduous lewisias from rain in summer, when dormant. In an alpine house, grow in equal parts loam, leaf mould, and sharp sand.

• **PROPAGATION** Sow seed in containers in a cold frame in autumn, or remove offsets (evergreen species only) in early summer. Seed of *L.* Cotyledon Hybrids does not come true to colour, and many species hybridize freely in cultivation.

• **PESTS AND DISEASES** Susceptible to aphids under glass, and to slugs and snails outdoors. Prone to neck rot in wet conditions.

L. brachycalyx ■ Dwarf, tufted, deciduous perennial with a basal rosette of inversely lance-shaped, dark green leaves, 3–8cm (1¼–3in) long. In late spring and early summer, numerous solitary, funnel-shaped, white, sometimes pale pink flowers, 2.5–5cm (1–2in) across, are borne on scapes to 6cm (2½in) long. ↕↔ to 8cm (3in). USA (S. California, Arizona). ❄❄❄

L. columbiana. Evergreen perennial with compact rosettes of inversely lance-shaped or linear, dark green leaves, 2–10cm (¾–4in) long. From spring to summer, bears panicles of many open funnel-shaped, usually deep magenta-pink flowers, to 2.5cm (1in) across, sometimes pale pink with darker veins. ↕↔ to 15cm (6in). Canada (British Columbia), USA (Oregon). ❄❄❄

L. cotyledon. Evergreen perennial with flat rosettes of spoon-shaped or inversely

Lewisia brachycalyx

Lewisia Cotyledon Hybrids

lance-shaped or obovate, slightly glaucous, dark green leaves, 3–14cm (1¼–5½in) long. From spring to summer, produces compact panicles of many open funnel-shaped, paler and darker striped, usually pinkish purple, sometimes white, cream, yellow, or apricot flowers, to 2.5cm (1in) across. ↕30cm (12in), ↔ to 25cm (10in). USA (N.W. California). ❄❄❄. **f. *alba*** has pure white flowers. **var. *howellii*** has leaves with wavy, toothed margins, and pale pink flowers with darker veining.

***L.* Cotyledon Hybrids** ■ Clump-forming, evergreen perennials that produce rosettes of thick, variably shaped, mid- to dark green leaves, 3–14cm (1¼–5½in) long, with toothed or wavy margins. From late spring to summer, funnel-shaped flowers, 2–4cm (¾–1½in) across, in a range of bright colours, including shades of pink, deep magenta, yellow, and orange, are borne in compact panicles. ↕15–30cm (6–12in), ↔ 20–40cm (8–16in). ❄❄❄

***L.* 'George Henley'** ■ Clump-forming, evergreen perennial with rosettes of narrowly spoon-shaped, fleshy, dark green leaves, to 8cm (3in) long. From late spring to late summer, produces many-flowered cymes of funnel-shaped, purplish pink flowers, to 2.5cm (1in) across, with magenta veining. ↕10cm (4in) or more, ↔ 10cm (4in). ❄❄❄

L. longipetala, syn. *L. pygmaea* subsp. *longipetala*. Deciduous perennial with basal tufts of narrowly linear or linear-inversely lance-shaped, dark green leaves, 2–5cm (¾–2in) long. In late spring or early summer, produces several scapes, 3–6cm (1¼–2½in) long, bearing

Lewisia 'George Henley'

Lewisia tweedyi

cymes of 1–3 open funnel-shaped, star-like, pure white or pink-flushed white flowers, 2.5–4cm (1–1½in) across, with red-tinted sepals. Similar to, but easier to grow than *L. brachycalyx*. ↕↔ to 10cm (4in). USA (California). ❄❄❄

L. nevadensis. Deciduous perennial with loose, basal rosettes of narrowly linear, suberect, dark green leaves, 4–15cm (1½–6in) long. From late spring to summer, bears solitary, broadly funnel-shaped, star-like, white, rarely pink flowers, to 3.5cm (1½in) across, on scapes 10–15cm (4–6in) long. ↕↔ to 10cm (4in). W. USA. ❄❄❄

L. pygmaea. Deciduous perennial with tufts of linear or linear-inversely lance-shaped, erect, dark green leaves, 3–9cm (1¼–3½in) long. In summer, prostrate or semi-erect scapes, 1–6cm (½–2½in) long, bear cymes of 1–7 funnel-shaped, deep purplish pink, occasionally white or pale pink flowers, 1.5–2cm (½–¾in) across. ↕↔ to 8cm (3in). Canada, USA (Alaska to New Mexico). ❄❄❄. **subsp. *longipetala*** see *L. longipetala*.

L. rediviva (Bitterroot). Deciduous perennial with tufts of linear or club-shaped, dark green leaves, 1.5–5cm (½–2in) long, dying back rapidly at or after flowering. From early spring to summer, bears several solitary, broadly funnel-shaped, pink or white flowers, 5cm (2in) across, with 12–19 narrow petals, on scapes 1–3cm (½–1¼in) long. ↕5cm (2in), ↔ 10cm (4in). Canada (British Columbia), USA (California, Nevada, Utah). ❄❄❄

L. tweedyi ■ Rosette-forming, evergreen perennial with broad, inversely lance-shaped or obovate, purple-tinted, mid-green leaves, to 10cm (4in) long. From spring to early summer, scapes, 10–20cm (4–8in) long, bear open funnel-shaped, white to peach-pink flowers, to 6cm (2½in) across, singly or in cymes of up to 4. ↕20cm (8in), ↔ 30cm (12in). N.W. USA. ❄❄❄. **f. *alba*** has pure white to ivory flowers.

LEYCESTERIA

CAPRIFOLIACEAE

Genus of about 6 species of suckering, deciduous shrubs, with hollow, cane-like stems, from cliffs and mountain woodland in India, the Himalayas, China, and Burma. They are cultivated for their terminal or axillary racemes or spikes of whorled, tubular, 5-lobed flowers; *L. formosa* also has long-persistent, claret-red bracts below the blooms. The leaves are opposite, narrowly ovate to ovate, and long-pointed, with entire or toothed margins. Grow in a woodland garden or shrub border. In frost-prone areas, grow half-hardy species in a cool greenhouse.

- **HARDINESS** Fully hardy (borderline) to half hardy.
- **CULTIVATION** Grow in moderately fertile, well-drained soil in full sun or partial shade. Protect from cold, drying winds and mulch deeply in autumn where frosts are severe. Pruning group 3 or 6.
- **PROPAGATION** Sow seed in containers in a cold frame in autumn, or take softwood cuttings in summer.
- **PESTS AND DISEASES** Trouble free.

Leycesteria formosa (inset: flower detail)

L. crocothyrsos. Upright shrub with arching shoots and ovate, tapered leaves, to 15cm (6in) long. Golden yellow flowers, to 2cm (¾in) long, with wide-spreading lobes, are produced in arching, terminal racemes, 12–17cm (5–7in) long, from late spring to late summer, followed by small, spherical green berries. ↕↔ 2m (6ft). India (Assam), N. Burma. ❄❄

L. formosa ■ (Himalayan honeysuckle). Upright, thicket-forming shrub with attractive, bamboo-like, blue-green first-year shoots, and ovate, tapered, dark green leaves, to 17cm (7in) long. Pendent spikes, to 10cm (4in) long, of white flowers among dark purple-red bracts, are borne terminally or from the upper leaf axils, from summer to early autumn. Flowers are followed by spherical, red-purple berries. ↕↔ 2m (6ft). Himalayas, W. China. ❄❄❄ (borderline)

LEYMUS

GRAMINEAE/POACEAE

Genus of approximately 40 species of rhizomatous, perennial grasses, formerly included in *Elymus*. They occur mainly in grassland in N. temperate regions, with one species from Argentina. They have linear, flat or rolled, stiff, glaucous leaves, and bear narrowly linear racemes of usually paired, sometimes solitary spikelets in summer. The ornamental species are grown for the architectural value of their blue-green leaves; although invasive, they are also suitable for a mixed or herbaceous border.

- **HARDINESS** Fully hardy.
- **CULTIVATION** Grow in moderately fertile but not heavy, well-drained soil in full sun. Cut down dead growth in autumn.
- **PROPAGATION** Divide from mid-spring to early autumn.
- **PESTS AND DISEASES** Trouble free.

L. arenarius ■ syn. *Elymus arenarius*. Densely tufted grass with long rhizomes, forming loose, spreading clumps of arching, broadly linear, flat, pale blue-grey leaves, to 60cm (24in) long. Throughout summer, stiff, erect stems bear spike-like racemes, to 35cm (14in) long, of paired, blue-grey, then buff spikelets. ↕ to 1.5cm (5ft), ↔ indefinite. N. and W. Europe, Eurasia. ❄❄❄

L. giganteus see *L. racemosus*.

L. racemosus, syn. *Elymus racemosus*, *L. giganteus*. Rhizomatous grass with arching, broadly linear, flat, blue-green leaves, to 30cm (12in) long, rough

L

Leymus arenarius

textured above, smooth beneath. Throughout summer, stiff, upright stems produce spike-like racemes, to 35cm (14in) long, of flattened, softly hairy, initially bluish green, later buff spikelets, in clusters of 6. ↕ to 1.2m (4ft), ↔ 75cm (30in) or more. N. Europe, Eurasia. ❄❄❄. **'Glaucus'** is less invasive, and has erect or arching, clear, pale blue-green leaves; ↕ 75cm (30in).

▷ **Liana** see *Semele androgyna*

LIATRIS

Blazing star, Gayfeather

ASTERACEAE/COMPOSITAE

Genus of approximately 40 species of perennials with tuber- or corm-like, swollen, flattened stems. They occur mainly in prairie or open woodland, on dry, stony ground (although *L. spicata* grows in damper sites), in E. and C. North America. Linear to ovate-lance-shaped leaves are borne in basal tufts, and arranged alternately on the stiff stems. The numerous button-like flowerheads, produced in corymb-like spikes or racemes, are composed of dense clusters of tubular, pinkish purple or white disc-florets, and are unusual in that they open from the top of the inflorescence downwards. Suitable for a mixed or herbaceous border, and also good for cutting. The flowerheads are attractive to bees.

• **HARDINESS** Fully hardy.
• **CULTIVATION** Grow in light, moderately fertile, moist but well-drained soil in full sun; *L. spicata* needs reliably moist soil. Liable to rot in wet winters in heavy soils.
• **PROPAGATION** Sow seed in containers in a cold frame in autumn. Divide in spring.
• **PESTS AND DISEASES** Susceptible to slugs, snails, and mice (which eat the rootstocks).

Liatris spicata 'Kobold'

***L. callilepis* of gardens** see *L. spicata.*
L. pycnostachya (Kansas feather). Perennial with densely clustered, linear basal leaves, 10–30cm (4–12in) long, which reduce in size up the robust, hairy stems. Bears dense spikes, 45cm (18in) long, of bright purple flowerheads, 1cm (½in) across, from midsummer to early autumn. ↕ to 1.5m (5ft), ↔ 45cm (18in). C. and S.E. USA. ❄❄❄
L. scariosa. Perennial with densely clustered, lance-shaped to narrowly ovate or obovate, rough basal leaves, to 25cm (10in) long, reducing in size and inversely lance-shaped on the robust, hairy stems. Similar to *L. pycnostachya*, but with less dense spikes, 45cm (18in) long, of reddish purple flowerheads, 2.5cm (1in) across, in early autumn. ↕ 0.6–1.2m (2–4ft), ↔ 45cm (18in). N.E. and S.E. USA. ❄❄❄. **'September Glory'** has deep purple flowerheads; ↕ 1.3m (4½ft).
L. spicata ◼ syn. *L. callilepis* of gardens (Gayfeather). Perennial with hairless stems and linear or linear-lance-shaped basal leaves, 30–40cm (12–16in) long; stem leaves are smaller and linear. Long-lasting, pink-purple or white flower-heads, to 1cm (½in) across, are borne in dense spikes, 45–70cm (18–28in) long, in late summer and early autumn. ↕ to 1.5m (5ft), ↔ 45cm (18in). E. and S. USA. ❄❄❄. **'Blue Bird'** has blue-purple flowerheads. **'Floristan Weiss'** has white flowerheads; ↕ to 90cm (36in). **'Goblin'** see 'Kobold'. **'Kobold'** ◼ syn. 'Goblin', produces deep purple flower-heads; ↕ 40–50cm (16–20in). **'Snow Queen'** produces white flowerheads; ↕ 75cm (30in).

Liatris spicata

LIBERTIA

IRIDACEAE

Genus of 20 species of fibrous-rooted, clump-forming, rhizomatous, evergreen perennials occurring in moist, grassy areas and scrub in New Caledonia, New Zealand, and temperate North and South America. They have linear, leathery, 2-ranked, overlapping, mainly basal leaves; leaves on the stiff flowering stems are sparse and smaller. They are cultivated for their saucer-shaped, white or blue flowers, each usually with 3 small outer tepals, 3 broad inner tepals, and sheathing bracts, produced in panicles and followed by glossy, light brown seed heads. Grow the larger libertias in a herbaceous or mixed border, or in a gravel garden; the smaller species are suitable for a rock garden.

• **HARDINESS** Fully hardy (borderline) to frost hardy. *L. ixioides* may survive to -10°C (14°F).
• **CULTIVATION** Grow in moderately fertile, humus-rich, moist but well-drained soil in full sun. In frost-prone areas, protect in winter with a dry mulch.
• **PROPAGATION** Sow seed in containers outdoors as soon as ripe, or divide in spring.
• **PESTS AND DISEASES** Trouble free.

L. caerulescens. Clump-forming, rhizomatous perennial with linear, rigid, leathery leaves, 30–45cm (12–18in) long. In late spring, flowering stems bear 1 or 2 short leaves, and terminal, short-branched panicles consisting of umbel-like clusters of many pale blue flowers, 1cm (½in) across. ↕ to 60cm (24in), ↔ 30cm (12in). Chile. ❄❄
L. chilensis see *L. formosa.*
L. formosa, syn. *L. chilensis.* Rhizomatous perennial forming large clumps of linear, stiff, leathery, deep green leaves, 15–45cm (6–18in) long. Dense panicles composed of umbel-like clusters of 3–8 white or pale yellow-white flowers, 3.5cm (1½in) across, are borne in long succession from late spring to midsummer. ↕ 90cm (36in), ↔ 60cm (24in). Chile. ❄❄❄ (borderline)
L. grandiflora ◼ Rhizomatous perennial forming dense clumps of linear, leathery leaves, 30–75cm (12–30in) long. In late spring and early summer, bears long panicles composed of dense, umbel-like clusters of 3–6 white flowers, 3cm (1¼in) across, the outer tepals with olive or bronze keels. ↕ to 90cm (36in), ↔ 60cm (24in). New Zealand. ❄❄❄ (borderline)
L. ixioides. Rhizomatous perennial, similar to *L. grandiflora*, forming dense clumps of linear, leathery leaves, 20–30cm (8–12in) long. Leaves of some variants turn orange-brown in winter. In late spring and early summer, produces dense panicles composed of umbel-like clusters of usually 2–10 white flowers, 7–8mm (¼–⅜in) across, the outer tepals tinted brown or green. ↕↔ 60cm (24in). New Zealand (including Chatham Island). ❄❄

Libertia grandiflora

LIBOCEDRUS

CUPRESSACEAE

Genus of 6 species of conical, monoecious, evergreen, coniferous trees and shrubs from forest in New Zealand, New Caledonia, and South America. In the past, species of *Austrocedrus* and *Calocedrus* were included in the genus *Libocedrus.* The linear juvenile leaves and usually scale-like adult leaves are arranged in sets of 2 pairs, one on either side of the shoot (spreading pair), and one above and below (facial pair), forming 4 rows. Female cones are solitary, ovoid, and usually 4-scaled, with 2 pairs of enlarged, bract-like leaves at the bases; male cones are small, oblong, and borne at the tips of short shoots. Grow as specimen trees. In frost-prone areas, grow half-hardy species in a sheltered site or in a cool greenhouse.

• **HARDINESS** Fully hardy to half hardy.
• **CULTIVATION** Grow in any deep, moist but well-drained soil in full sun.

L. uvifera tolerates and often prefers a wet site or copious water supply. In frost-prone climates, shelter from cold, drying winds.

• **PROPAGATION** Sow seed in containers in a cold frame in spring, or take semi-ripe cuttings in summer.

• **PESTS AND DISEASES** Trouble free.

L. bidwillii ◊ Conical, coniferous tree at lower elevations, reduced to a shrub at altitudes above 1,000m (3,200ft). It has fibrous bark and scale-like, glossy, yellow-green adult leaves, to 2mm (1/16in) long, lying flat along the shoots. Ovoid female cones, 1cm (½in) long, have a green terminal spine on each scale. ↕ to 15m (50ft), ↔ to 3m (10ft). New Zealand. ❄❄

L. chilensis see *Austrocedrus chilensis.*

L. decurrens see *Calocedrus decurrens.*

L. plumosa ◊ (Kawaka). Conical, coniferous tree with fibrous bark and unequal pairs of scale-like, glossy, bright green adult leaves; the spreading pair, 3–5mm (⅛–¼in) long, is larger than the facial pair. Ovoid female cones are 1–2cm (½–¾in) long. ↕ to 15m (50ft), ↔ to 3m (10ft). New Zealand. ❄❄

L. uvifera ◊ syn. *Pilgerodendron uviferum.* Slow-growing, conical, coniferous shrub or small tree with thin bark, peeling in strips. Green shoots bear narrowly wedge-shaped leaves, to 5mm (¼in) long, with fine, tapered points, whitish green on the inner side, dark green on the outer. Ovoid female cones are 1cm (½in) long. ↕ to 6m (20ft), ↔ to 2m (6ft). S. Chile, S. Argentina (Andes and Tierra del Fuego). ❄❄❄ (borderline)

▷***Libonia*** see *Justicia*
L. floribunda see *J. rizzinii*

LICUALA

ARECACEAE/PALMAE

Genus of approximately 100 species of single- or cluster-stemmed palms found in rainforest and swamps, in low-lying areas from S.E. Asia to Malaysia, the New Hebrides, and Australia. Rounded, fan-like or palmately lobed leaves are arranged spirally along the upper parts of the stems; fibrous leaf bases remain on the stems after the leaves have withered. Spikes of cup-shaped, 3-petalled flowers are produced from the leaf axils. Where temperatures fall below 15–16°C (59–61°F), grow in a warm greenhouse. In warmer areas, grow the shrubby, suckering species in a border or in plantings against a wall, and the larger, single-stemmed species as lawn specimens or in a courtyard garden.

• **HARDINESS** Frost tender.

• **CULTIVATION** Under glass, grow in loam-based potting compost (JI No.3), with added peat or leaf mould and sharp sand, in bright filtered light and high humidity. When in growth, water freely and apply a balanced liquid fertilizer monthly. Mist twice a day in summer. Water moderately in winter. Pot on or top-dress in spring. Outdoors, grow in moderately fertile, moist but well-drained soil in partial shade.

• **PROPAGATION** In spring, sow seed at 24°C (75°F), or remove suckers.

• **PESTS AND DISEASES** Red spider mites and mealybugs may be troublesome under glass.

Licuala grandis

L. grandis ▣ 🌴 Small palm with a single, slender, erect trunk clad in fibrous leaf bases. Long-stalked, rounded leaf-blades, 1m (3ft) across, are glossy, mid- to pale green with notched margins, and are occasionally divided into 3 broadly wedge-shaped to rounded, wavy-margined segments. Green to greenish white flowers, 1cm (½in) across, are borne in pendent spikes, longer than the leaves, usually in summer. Flowers are followed by spherical, glossy red fruit. ↕ to 3m (10ft), ↔ 1.5–2.5m (5–8ft). New Hebrides. ❀ (min. 15–16°C/59–61°F)

L. muelleri see *L. ramsayi.*

L. ramsayi 🌴 syn. *L. muelleri.* Medium-sized palm with a single, erect stem, the upper part clad with fibrous leaf bases, the lower part smooth. Long, spiny leaf-stalks bear rounded leaf-blades, to 1m (3ft) across, divided into many wedge-shaped, radiating, rich green segments, some of which may be joined at the tips. Cream flowers, 1cm (½in) across, are borne in spikes, as long as, or longer than the leaves, usually in summer, and are followed by spherical, orange-red fruit. ↕ to 12m (40ft), ↔ 3–5m (10–15ft). Australia (N.E. Queensland). ❀ (min. 15–16°C/59–61°F)

L. spinosa ✲ Small, cluster-stemmed palm forming clumps of cane-like stems. These bear spirals of leaves, and are clad with fibrous leaf bases in the upper parts. Long, spiny-stalked, rounded leaf-blades, to 1.5m (5ft) across, are divided into 12–20 narrow, deep green, wedge-shaped segments with squared-off tips. Greenish white flowers, 1cm (½in) across, are borne in branched spikes, to 2m (6ft) long, mainly in summer, followed by ovoid red fruit. ↕↔ to 5m (15ft). Thailand, Malaysian peninsula, Indonesia, Philippines. ❀ (min. 15–16°C/59–61°F)

▷**Lignum, Climbing** see *Muehlenbeckia adpressa*

LIGULARIA

ASTERACEAE/COMPOSITAE

Genus of about 150 species of large, robust, often coarse perennials, mostly from C. and E. Asia, with a few from Europe, found in moist or wet grassland, open, wet scrub and woodland, by mountain streams, and in ditches. They have, ovate-oblong or elliptic to kidney-shaped or rounded, sometimes

Ligularia 'Gregynog Gold'

Ligularia przewalskii

palmately lobed, often toothed basal leaves, borne on long leaf-stalks, and smaller, alternate stem leaves. Erect stems bear terminal corymbs or racemes of few to many, showy, daisy-like, yellow or orange flowerheads, with yellow or brown disc-florets. Grow in a mixed or herbaceous border, or naturalize in moist soil; they are also imposing waterside plants.

• **HARDINESS** Fully hardy.

• **CULTIVATION** Grow in moderately fertile, deep, reliably moist soil, in full sun with some midday shade. Shelter from strong winds.

• **PROPAGATION** Sow seed of species in containers outdoors in autumn or spring, or divide species and cultivars in spring or after flowering. When seed-raised, *L. dentata* 'Desdemona' and *L. dentata* 'Othello' will often produce similar seedlings.

• **PESTS AND DISEASES** Slugs and snails may damage emerging leaves in spring.

L. clivorum see *L. dentata.*

L. dentata, syn. *L. clivorum, Senecio clivorum* (Golden groundsel). Clump-forming perennial with kidney-shaped to rounded, toothed, mid-green leaves, to 30cm (12in) long, deeply heart-shaped at the bases; the basal leaves have red leaf-stalks. Flat corymbs of many red-stalked, brown-centred, orange-yellow flowerheads, 10cm (4in) across, are borne from midsummer to early autumn. ↕ 1–1.5m (3–5ft), ↔ 1m (3ft). China, Japan. ❄❄❄. **'Desdemona'** has deep orange flowerheads and rounded, brownish green leaves that are deep maroon-purple beneath; ↕ 1m (3ft).

L

'Othello' is similar to 'Desdemona', but with deep purplish green leaves, purple-red beneath; ↕ 1m (3ft).
***L.* 'Gregynog Gold'** ▣ Clump-forming perennial with rounded, toothed leaves, to 35cm (14in) long, heart-shaped at the bases. In late summer and early autumn, bears tall, pyramidal racemes of many brown-centred, golden orange flowerheads, to 10cm (4in) across. ↕ to 1.8m (6ft), ↔ 1m (3ft). ❄❄❄
L. hodgsonii. Clump-forming perennial with kidney-shaped, toothed leaves, to 12cm (5in) across, heart-shaped at the bases. In mid- and late summer, bears corymbs of many yellow-orange flowerheads, 5cm (2in) across, with reddish brown centres, on stems often marked purple towards the bases. ↕ 90cm (36in), ↔ 60cm (24in). Japan. ❄❄❄
L. przewalskii ▣ syn. *Senecio przewalskii.* Clump-forming perennial with palmately lobed leaves, to 30cm (12in) long, deeply cut and irregularly lobed and toothed. In mid- and late summer, dark purple-green stems bear slender, dense racemes of yellow flowerheads, 2cm (¾in) across. ↕ to 2m (6ft), ↔ 1m (3ft). N. China. ❄❄❄
L. stenocephala. Clump-forming perennial with triangular, pointed, toothed leaves, to 35cm (14in) long, with heart-shaped bases. In early and late summer, tall, slender racemes of numerous yellow flowerheads, to 4cm (1½in) across, with orange-yellow centres, are borne on black-green stems. ↕ 1.5m (5ft), ↔ 1m (3ft). N. China, Taiwan, Japan. ❄❄❄. **'The Rocket'**, of hybrid origin, has tall black flower stems and boldly toothed leaves; ↕ 1.8m (6ft). **'Weihenstephan'**, of hybrid origin, has golden yellow flowerheads, 6–7cm (2½–3in) across; ↕ 1.8m (6ft).
L. tangutica see *Sinacalia tangutica.*
L. tussilaginea see *Farfugium japonicum.*
L. veitchiana. Clump-forming perennial bearing triangular to heart-shaped leaves, 30–35cm (12–14in) long, with wavy, toothed margins. Pyramidal racemes of numerous brown-centred yellow flowerheads, to 7cm (3in) across, are borne in mid- and late summer, followed by conspicuous, fluffy, purple-brown fruit. ↕ 1.8m (6ft), ↔ 1.2m (4ft). W. China. ❄❄❄

L

LIGUSTRUM

Privet

OLEACEAE

Genus of about 50 species of deciduous, semi-evergreen, or evergreen shrubs and trees found in woodland and thickets in Europe, N. Africa, the Himalayas, S.W. and E. Asia, and Australia. They bear opposite, variably shaped, often glossy leaves, and terminal panicles of small, tubular, 4-lobed, unpleasantly scented white flowers, followed by spherical or ovoid fruit. Grown for their foliage and flowers, they are good for a shrub border or as specimen plants; most species may be used for hedging. All parts may cause severe discomfort if ingested.

• **HARDINESS** Fully hardy to frost hardy.
• **CULTIVATION** Grow in any well-drained soil in full sun or partial shade; variegated privets colour better in sun. Pruning group 1; clip hedges twice in summer.

Ligustrum japonicum 'Rotundifolium'

• **PROPAGATION** Sow seed in containers in a cold frame in autumn or spring. Take semi-ripe cuttings in summer or hardwood cuttings in winter.
• **PESTS AND DISEASES** Susceptible to aphids, scale insects, leaf miners, and thrips, and prone to leaf spots, honey fungus, and wilt.

L. amurense (Amur privet). Dense, upright, deciduous or semi-evergreen shrub with elliptic, mid-green leaves, to 5cm (2in) long. White flowers are produced in panicles, 4–5cm (1½–2in) long, in late spring and early summer, followed by small, ovoid black fruit. Useful for hedging. ↕↔ 5m (15ft). N. China. ❄❄❄
L. chenaultii see *L. compactum.*

Ligustrum lucidum

Ligustrum lucidum 'Excelsum Superbum'

L. compactum ♤ syn. *L. chenaultii.* Vigorous, broadly conical, semi-evergreen tree with lance-shaped, occasionally notched, dark green leaves, 15cm (6in) or more long. White flowers are borne in panicles, 15–18cm (6–7in) long, in midsummer, followed by small, spherical black fruit. ↕ 10m (30ft), ↔ 8m (25ft). S.W. China. ❄❄
L. delavayanum. Compact, spreading, evergreen shrub with ovate, oval, or oblong, dark green leaves, to 3cm (1¼in) long. White flowers are produced in panicles, to 5cm (2in) long, in early summer, followed by spherical to ovoid, blue-black fruit. Useful for hedging. ↕ 2m (6ft), ↔ 3m (10ft). W. China (Sichuan, Yunnan). ❄❄❄
L. x ibolium (*L. obtusifolium* x *L. ovalifolium*). Upright, deciduous to semi-evergreen shrub with oval, glossy, mid-green leaves, to 6cm (2½in) long. White flowers are produced in panicles, 5–8cm (2–3in) long, in midsummer. Useful for hedging. ↕↔ 3m (10ft). Garden origin. ❄❄❄
L. japonicum (Japanese privet). Upright, dense, evergreen shrub with ovate, glossy, very dark green leaves, to 10cm (4in) long. Bears white flowers in panicles, to 15cm (6in) long, from mid-summer to early autumn, followed by ovoid-oblong black fruit. ↕ 3m (10ft), ↔ 2.5m (8ft). N. China, Korea, Japan. ❄❄❄. **'Rotundifolium'** ▣ is slow-growing and stiffly branched, with rounded, very leathery leaves, to 6cm (2½in) long; ↕ 1.5m (5ft), ↔ 1m (3ft).
L. lucidum ▣ ♤ (Chinese privet). Conical, evergreen tree or shrub with ovate or oval, tapered, glossy, dark green leaves, to 15cm (6in) long. White flowers are produced in panicles, to 20cm (8in) long, in late summer and early autumn, followed by ovoid-oblong, blue-black fruit. ↕↔ 10m (30ft). China. Korea, Japan. ❄❄❄. **'Excelsum Superbum'** ▣ has yellow-margined, bright green leaves. **'Tricolor'** has narrow, green and grey-green leaves with white margins (pink when young).
L. obtusifolium. Spreading, deciduous shrub with oval, dark green leaves, to 5cm (2in) long, often tinged purple in autumn. White flowers are produced in nodding panicles, to 5cm (2in) long, in midsummer, followed by spherical, blue-black fruit. Useful for hedging. ↕ 3m (10ft), ↔ 4m (12ft). Japan. ❄❄❄
L. ovalifolium. Vigorous, upright, evergreen or semi-evergreen shrub with

Ligustrum sinense

oval, rich green leaves, to 6cm (2½in) long. White flowers are borne in dense panicles, to 10cm (4in) long, in mid-summer, followed by spherical, shiny black fruit. Useful for hedging. ↕↔ 4m (12ft). Japan. ❄❄❄. **'Argenteum'** has leaves margined creamy white. **'Aureum'**, syn. 'Aureomarginatum' (Golden privet), has leaves with broad, bright yellow margins.
L. quihoui. Upright then rounded, deciduous shrub with slender, arching branches and narrowly oval to obovate, glossy, mid-green leaves, to 5cm (2in) long. Fragrant white flowers are produced in open panicles, 20cm (8in) or more long, in late summer and early autumn, followed by ovoid, glossy, black-purple fruit. Useful for hedging. ↕↔ 5m (15ft). China. ❄❄❄
L. sinense ▣ Vigorous, bushy, tree-like, deciduous or semi-evergreen shrub with arching branches and elliptic-oblong or lance-shaped, pale green leaves, to 7cm (3in) long. White flowers are profusely borne in panicles, to 10cm (4in) long, in midsummer, and are followed by spherical, purple-black fruit. Useful for hedging. ↕↔ 4m (12ft). China. ❄❄❄. **'Variegatum'** has white-margined, pale green leaves. **'Wimbei'** is compact and slow-growing, with upright leaves, to 1cm (½in) long. Rarely flowers; ↕ 1.5m (5ft), ↔ 1.2m (4ft).
***L.* 'Vicaryi'.** Dense, bushy, semi-evergreen shrub with broadly oval, golden yellow leaves, to 9cm (3½in) long. White flowers are produced in panicles, to 7cm (3in) long, in mid-summer, followed by spherical, blue-black fruit. ↕↔ 3m (10ft). ❄❄❄
L. vulgare (Common privet). Bushy, deciduous or semi-evergreen shrub with narrowly oval to lance-shaped, dark green leaves, to 6cm (2½in) long. Bears white flowers in panicles, to 5cm (2in) long, in early and midsummer, followed by spherical to ovoid black fruit. Useful for hedging. ↕↔ 3m (10ft). Europe, N. Africa, S.W. Asia. ❄❄❄. **'Aureum'** has golden yellow foliage; ↕↔ 2m (6ft).

▷ **Lilac** see *Syringa*
California see *Ceanothus*
Common see *Syringa vulgaris*
Himalayan see *Syringa emodi*
Persian see *Melia azedarach*, *Syringa* x *persica*
Rouen see *Syringa* x *chinensis*
St. Vincent see *Solanum seaforthianum*

LILIUM

Lily

LILIACEAE

Genus of approximately 100 species of bulbous perennials, mainly from woodland and scrub in Europe, Asia south to the Philippines, and North America; there are also innumerable garden hybrids. They are grown for their showy, sometimes very fragrant flowers, borne from late spring (or earlier with protection) to early autumn; these are followed by 3-parted capsules containing flat, papery seeds. The bulbs are composed of overlapping, fleshy scales and are sometimes rhizomatous or stoloniform with slender, horizontal stems that travel underground before becoming erect. The flower stems are unbranched and erect; in some lilies, roots develop on the stems just above the bulb. The elliptic to lance-shaped or linear, glossy, usually mid- to dark green leaves are arranged in whorls or spirals, or are scattered alternately up the stems. Most lilies vary between 1m (3ft) and 2m (6ft) in height, although a few may reach 3m (10ft). They do not spread widely (therefore only height measurements are given below).

The flowers are solitary or borne in racemes, panicles, or umbels, and may be upward-facing, horizontal or outward-facing, nodding, or pendent. They may be cup- to bowl- or bell-shaped, trumpet-shaped, funnel-shaped, turkscap (with strongly reflexed tepals), or occasionally star-shaped; each has 6 stamens and 6 tepals (see panel above). The tepals, occurring in most colours except blue, may be plain or marked with lines, spots, or papillae. Three categories of flower size – small, medium, and large – are used in the descriptions below. For turkscap, bowl-, cup-, and star-shaped flowers: small is up to 5cm (2in) across; medium is 5–7cm (2–3in) across; large is over 7cm (3in) across. For trumpet- and funnel-shaped flowers: small is up to 7cm (3in) long; medium is 7–10cm (3–4in) long; large is over 10cm (4in) long.

Lilies may be grown in many sites, including woodland or wild gardens and among shrubs or herbaceous plants. A few are suitable for a rock garden. Many also grow well in a large container. Lilies are often grown for exhibition and are excellent as cut flowers, particularly the triploid and tetraploid lilies, specially bred to be larger, sturdier, and more cold-tolerant than standard, diploid lilies. In frost-prone climates, grow half-hardy lilies in a cool greenhouse.

Lilies are classified into 9 divisions:

Division 1 (Asiatic hybrids)
These lilies are derived from various Asiatic species, including *L. bulbiferum*, *L. cernuum*, *L. concolor*, *L. davidii*, *L. lancifolium*, and *L. maculatum*. The flowers are borne in racemes or umbels, and are usually unscented. The leaves are narrowly ovate and arranged alternately. There are 3 subdivisions: **1a**) upward-facing flowers; **1b**) outward-facing flowers; **1c**) pendent flowers.

Division 2 (Martagon hybrids)
Derived primarily from *L. hansonii* and *L. martagon*, these lilies produce racemes of turkscap, sometimes scented flowers, and have whorls of elliptic leaves.

LILY FLOWERS

Lilies are valued for their very showy, often fragrant flowers. The 6 plain or strikingly marked tepals are variably curved, giving rise to the different shapes shown here, and to forms intermediate between them.

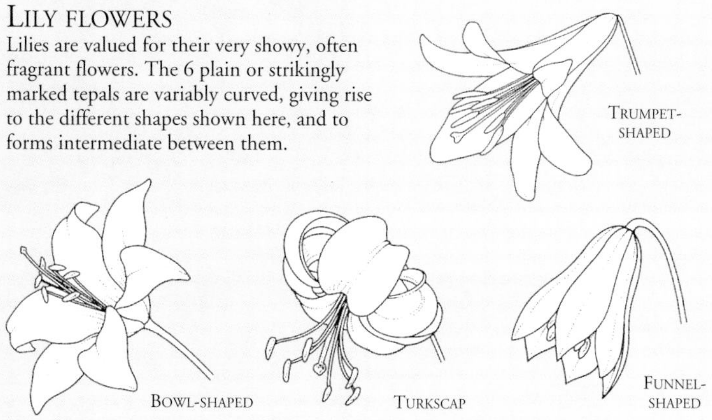

Division 3 (Candidum hybrids)
Derived from *L. candidum* and other European species, except *L. martagon*, these lilies produce sometimes scented, mostly turkscap flowers, singly or in umbels or racemes. Leaves are elliptic, and spirally arranged or scattered.

Division 4 (American hybrids)
Derived from American species, these lilies bear racemes of sometimes scented, mostly turkscap, but occasionally funnel-shaped flowers, and have whorls of lance-shaped to elliptic leaves.

Division 5 (Longiflorum hybrids)
Derived from *L. formosanum* and *L. longiflorum*, these lilies bear racemes or umbels of large, often sweetly scented, trumpet- or funnel-shaped flowers, sometimes only 2 or 3 per stem. Leaves are linear to narrowly lance-shaped, and scattered.

Division 6 (Trumpet and Aurelian hybrids)
Derived from Asiatic species, including *L. regale*, *L. henryi*, and *L. sargentiae*, these lilies bear racemes or umbels of usually scented flowers. Leaves are elliptic to linear, and alternate or spirally arranged. There are 4 subdivisions: **6a**) trumpet-shaped flowers; **6b**) bowl-shaped flowers; **6c**) very shallowly bowl-shaped flowers, some almost flat; **6d**) distinctly recurved flowers.

Division 7 (Oriental hybrids)
These lilies are derived from E. Asian species, such as *L. auratum*, *L. japonicum*, and *L. speciosum*, as well as their hybrids with *L. henryi*. Flowers are borne in racemes or panicles, and are often scented. Leaves are lance-shaped and alternate. There are 4 subdivisions: **7a**) trumpet-shaped flowers; **7b**) bowl-shaped flowers; **7c**) flat or very shallowly bowl-shaped flowers; **7d**) turkscap or variously recurved flowers.

Division 8. Other hybrids.

Division 9. All true species.

• **HARDINESS** Fully hardy to half hardy, but young growth may be damaged by frost.

• **CULTIVATION** Grow in well-drained soil enriched with leaf mould or well-rotted organic matter. Most prefer acid to neutral soil, but some are lime-tolerant or prefer alkaline soils. Most like a position in full sun, with the base of the plant in shade; a few prefer partial shade in light, open woodland. Under glass, grow in loam-based potting compost (JI No.2), with added grit and leaf mould, in full light with shade from hot sun. In active growth, water freely and apply a high-potash liquid fertilizer every 2 weeks. Keep moist in winter. Plant most bulbs in autumn, at a depth of 2–3 times their height, and with a distance between them equivalent to 3 times the diameter of the bulb; plant bulbs of stem-rooting lilies at a depth of at least 3 times the bulb height. Plant *L. candidum* and *L.* x *testaceum* very close to the soil surface; they also tolerate drier soil than other lilies.

• **PROPAGATION** Sow seed as soon as ripe; sow seed of hardy lilies in containers in a cold frame, and of half-hardy lilies at 13–18°C (55–64°F). Germination may be epigeal, in which the first growth appears above the compost, or hypogeal, in which the first growth is downwards and nothing appears above the compost until the first true leaf; in either case it may take 18 months to 2 years for growth to emerge. Detach bulblets from parent bulbs as plants become dormant and pot on. Remove bulbils from the leaf axils before plants die down, and pot on. Remove scales from healthy bulbs, lightly dust with sulphur, and place in trays of damp vermiculite at 20°C (68°F); pot on when small bulbs have formed, in 10–12 weeks.

• **PESTS AND DISEASES** Lily beetle, aphids, slugs, thrips, leatherjackets, and wireworms, as well as small mammals such as rabbits and voles, may be a problem. Various fungi can infect lilies either below or above ground. Grey mould (*Botrytis*) is sometimes a problem, especially in a wet, cool spring. Viruses may be troublesome, although some cultivars are virus-tolerant and grow well despite infection.

***L.* 'African Queen'** ▣ Vigorous Division 6a lily with erect stems. In mid- and late summer, large, fragrant, outward-facing to nodding, trumpet-shaped flowers, brownish purple outside, yellow or orange-apricot inside, are borne in pyramid-shaped racemes. ↕1.5–2m (5–6ft). ❄❄

***L.* 'Amber Gold'.** Division 1c lily bearing racemes, in early and mid-summer, of medium-sized, unscented, turkscap, bright orange-yellow flowers, spotted maroon in the centres and with reddish brown anthers. ↕1.2–1.5m (4–5ft). ❄❄❄

***L.* 'Angela North'** ▣ Clump-forming, moderately vigorous, triploid Division 1c lily. In midsummer, bears racemes of medium-sized, faintly scented, turkscap, deep wine-red flowers, with some darker spotting. ↕70–120cm (28–48in). ❄❄❄

***L.* 'Ariadne'** ▣ Triploid Division 1c lily with slender stems. In midsummer, produces racemes of small, scented, turkscap, pale orange flowers, flushed purple towards the tips of the tepals. ↕0.8–1.4m (2¾–4½ft). ❄❄❄

L. auratum (Golden-rayed lily). Vigorous Division 9 lily with stiff stems bearing scattered, lance-shaped, deep green leaves, 22cm (9in) long. In late summer and early autumn, produces racemes of usually up to 12, sometimes up to 30, sweetly fragrant, open bowl-shaped flowers, to 30cm (12in) across; the white tepals are recurved towards the tips, have a prominent central gold band, and are often crimson-speckled. Susceptible to virus. ↕0.6–1.5m (2–5ft).

Lilium bulbiferum var. *croceum*

L

Lilium 'African Queen'

Lilium 'Angela North'

Lilium 'Ariadne'

Lilium auratum var. *platyphyllum*

Lilium Bellingham Hybrids

Lilium 'Black Beauty'

Lilium 'Bright Star'

Lilium 'Bronwen North'

Lilium canadense

Lilium candidum

Lilium chalcedonicum

Lilium 'Connecticut King'

L

Japan. ❄❄❄. **'Crimson Beauty'** produces flowers with a crimson band along the centre of each tepal; ↕ to 1m (3ft). **'Golden Ray'** produces large flowers, to 35cm (14in) across, with a deep yellow band along each tepal; ↕ to 2m (6ft). **var. *platyphyllum*** ▣ has broadly lance-shaped leaves, and bears flowers with a yellow band along each tepal but few spots; ↕ to 1.5m (5ft).

***L.* 'Barbara North'.** Sturdy, clump-forming Division 1c lily. In mid-summer, produces racemes of medium-sized, slightly scented, broad, turkscap, mid-pink flowers, with paler throats and a scattering of small, dark red spots. ↕ 70–120cm (28–48in). ❄❄❄

***L.* Bellingham Hybrids** ▣ (*L. humboldtii* x *L. pardalinum* x *L. parryi*). Vigorous Division 4 lilies with rhizomatous bulbs. In early and mid-summer, produce racemes of medium-sized, unscented, turkscap flowers, ranging from yellow to orange and red, spotted with brown or deep red. They increase rapidly but require acid soil and partial shade. ↕ 1.8–2.2m (6–7ft). ❄❄❄

***L.* 'Black Beauty'** ▣ Vigorous Division 7d lily. In midsummer, bears racemes of medium-sized, scented, turkscap, dark blackish red flowers, with green centres and white tepal margins. ↕ 1.4–2m (4½–6ft). ❄❄❄

***L.* 'Black Dragon'.** Division 6a lily bearing stout racemes of large, scented, outward-facing, trumpet-shaped flowers, dark purplish red outside, white within, in early summer. ↕ 1.5m (5ft). ❄❄❄

***L.* 'Bright Star'** ▣ Division 6d lily bearing racemes of large, scented, outward-facing, ivory-white flowers in mid- and late summer; spreading tepals are recurved at the tips and each has an orange central band, producing a star-like effect. Lime-tolerant. ↕ 1–1.5m (3–5ft). ❄❄❄

***L.* 'Bronwen North'** ▣ Triploid Division 1c lily bearing racemes of medium-sized, slightly scented, turkscap, pale mauve-pink flowers, the throats pale pink with purple spots and lines, in early summer. ↕ 80–100cm (32–39in). ❄❄❄

***L.* 'Brushmarks'.** Division 1a lily producing racemes of large, upward-facing, cup-shaped orange flowers, with deep red marks and green throats, in early summer. ↕ to 1m (3ft). ❄❄❄

L. bulbiferum (Orange lily). Vigorous, clump-forming Division 9 lily with scattered, narrowly to broadly lance-shaped, bright green leaves, 5–15cm (2–6in) long, with marginal hairs; bulbils are borne in the upper leaf axils. In early and midsummer, produces usually 1- to 5-flowered umbels (sometimes many-flowered, dense racemes) of unscented, erect, bowl-shaped, bright orange-red flowers, 10–15cm (4–6in) across; the tepals are broad, with black or maroon spots and darker bases and tips. Grows well in acid or alkaline soil. ↕ 40–150cm (16–60in). S. Europe. ❄❄❄. **var. *croceum*** ▣ has orange flowers and does not produce bulbils.

L. canadense ▣ (Meadow lily). Division 9 lily with rhizomatous bulbs and whorls of lance-shaped to inversely lance-shaped, mid-green leaves, 15cm (6in) long, each with 5–7 parallel veins. In mid- and late summer, produces umbels, or occasionally racemes, of up to 30 faintly scented, narrowly to broadly trumpet-shaped yellow flowers, 5–8cm (2–3in) long, with recurved tips and maroon spots in the centres. ↕ 1–1.6m (3–5½ft). E. North America. ❄❄❄. **var. *coccineum***, syn. var. *rubrum*, bears bright red flowers with yellow throats. **var. *editorum*** has broader leaves and red flowers. **var. *rubrum*** see var. *coccineum*.

L. candidum ▣ (Madonna lily). Division 9 lily with broad, inversely lance-shaped, shiny, bright green basal leaves, 22cm (9in) long, appearing in autumn. Stiffly erect stems bear smaller, scattered or spirally arranged, often somewhat twisted, lance-shaped leaves, to 8cm (3in) long. In midsummer, produces a raceme of 5–20 sweetly fragrant, broadly trumpet-shaped, pure white flowers, 5–8cm (2–3in) long, with yellowish bases and bright yellow anthers. Produces overwintering basal leaves (the only lily with this character). Requires neutral to alkaline soil. ↕ 1–1.8m (3–6ft). S.E. Europe to E. Mediterranean. ❄❄❄

L. carniolicum see *L. pyrenaicum* subsp. *carniolicum*.

***L.* 'Casa Blanca'.** Division 7b lily, derived from *L. auratum,* with stout, stiff stems. In mid- and late summer, large, sweetly fragrant, bowl-shaped, pure white flowers, with widely spreading tepals that are recurved near the tips, are produced in umbels; they have white papillae near the bases inside, and orange-red anthers. ↕ 1–1.2m (3–4ft). ❄❄❄

L. cernuum (Nodding lily). Small, stem-rooting Division 9 lily. Scattered, linear, mid-green leaves, 8–18cm (3–7in) long, are mostly concentrated in the middle third of the slender stem. In early and midsummer, bears racemes of usually up to 6 (occasionally up to 15) fragrant, turkscap, pale lilac, pink, or purple flowers, 3–5cm (1¼–2in) across. Lime-tolerant, but prefers moist, peaty soil. ↕ 40–60cm (16–24in). Russia (N.E. Siberia) to Korea. ❄❄❄

L. chalcedonicum ▣ syn. *L. heldreichii* (Scarlet turkscap lily). Relatively small, stem-rooting Division 9 lily with spirally arranged, lance-shaped, deep green leaves, 12cm (5in) long, with silver-hairy margins; the lower leaves are spreading, the upper ones erect. In midsummer, produces racemes of up to 12 small, pungently scented, turkscap, sealing-wax-red flowers, 8cm (3in) across, unspotted, but with self-coloured papillae at the bases. Grow in any soil, in full sun or partial shade. ↕ 0.6–1.5m (2–5ft). N. Greece, Albania. ❄❄❄

***L.* 'Chinook'.** Moderately vigorous Division 1a lily. In early and mid-summer, bears umbels of medium-sized, unscented, bowl-shaped, pale apricot-buff flowers. ↕ 1–1.2m (3–4ft). ❄❄❄

***L.* 'Citronella'** ▣ Vigorous, clump-forming Division 1c lily. In mid-summer, bears racemes or panicles of medium-sized, turkscap, bright yellow to lemon-yellow flowers, speckled with faint black or reddish spots inside. ↕ 1.2–1.5m (4–5ft). ❄❄❄

L. concolor (Morning star lily). Stem-rooting Division 9 lily with reddish green stems bearing scattered, linear to linear-lance-shaped, dark green leaves, to 9cm (3½in) long, slightly hairy on the margins and beneath. In early and mid-summer, produces racemes or umbels of up to 10 fragrant, upward-facing, star-shaped, glossy scarlet flowers, 3–4cm (1¼–1½in) across. ↕ 30–90cm (12–36in). W. China. ❄❄❄

***L.* 'Connecticut Beauty'.** Moderately vigorous Division 1a lily. In early and midsummer, bears umbels of medium-sized, slightly scented, bowl-shaped yellow flowers, darker along the centre of each tepal and with some darker spotting. ↕ 60–100cm (24–39in). ❄❄❄

***L.* 'Connecticut King'** ▣ Vigorous, clump-forming Division 1a lily. In early and midsummer, produces racemes of medium-sized, unscented, long-lasting, star-shaped, rich deep yellow flowers, paling slightly towards the tips of the spreading, somewhat recurved tepals. ↕ 1m (3ft). ❄❄❄

***L.* 'Connecticut Yankee'.** Elegant Division 1c lily bearing racemes of medium-sized, unscented, turkscap, rich orange-red flowers, with a few darker spots within, in midsummer. ↕ 1.2–2m (4–6ft). ❄❄❄

L. cordatum see *Cardiocrinum cordatum.*

L.* x *dalhansonii ▣ (*L. hansonii* x *L. martagon* var. *cattaniae*). Division 8 lily bearing whorls of inversely lance-shaped, dark green leaves, 15–18cm (6–7in) long. In early summer, bears racemes of numerous small, pungently scented, turkscap, maroon flowers, 3–5cm (1¼–2in) across, spotted and suffused orange in the centres. ↕ 1–1.5m (3–5ft). Garden origin. ❄❄❄

L. dauricum. Stem-rooting Division 9 lily with rhizomatous bulbs and brown-spotted green stems. Lance-shaped to linear, hairy-margined, dark green leaves, 5cm (2in) long, are scattered, but with the uppermost in a whorl below the flowers. In early and midsummer,

Lilium 'Citronella'

Lilium x *dalhansonii*

Lilium davidii var. *willmottiae*

Lilium duchartrei

Lilium 'Enchantment'

Lilium 'Fire King'

Lilium formosanum var. *pricei*

Lilium grayi

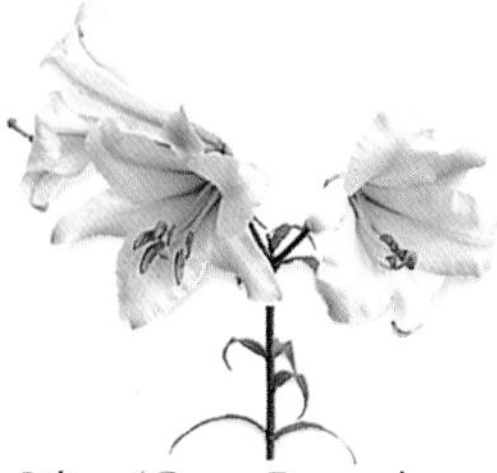

Lilium 'Green Dragon'

Lilium hansonii

Lilium henryi

Lilium lancifolium

Lilium lankongense

Lilium longiflorum

Lilium mackliniae

Lilium 'Marie North'

Lilium martagon

Lilium martagon var. *album*

Lilium medeoloides

produces umbels of up to 6 medium-sized, unscented, upward-facing, bowl-shaped, deep orange-scarlet flowers, to 10cm (4in) across, with yellowish orange centres, brownish red or purple spots, and hairy stalks. Best in acid soil, in full sun or partial shade. ↕ 50–70cm (20–28in). N.E. Asia. ❄❄❄

L. davidii. Sometimes rhizomatous Division 9 lily, with brown-spotted green stems bearing scattered, linear, finely toothed, dark green leaves, 6–10cm (2½–4in) long, hairy beneath. In summer, produces racemes of 10–20 unscented, long-stalked, turkscap, vermilion-red flowers, to 8cm (3in) across, with purple-black spots. ↕ 1–1.2m (3–4ft). W. China. ❄❄❄. **var. *unicolor*** is shorter, with unspotted or only faintly spotted flowers; ↕ 90cm (3ft). **var. *willmottiae*** ■ has rhizomatous bulbs, tall, arching stems with broader leaves, and up to 40 flowers per raceme; ↕ to 2m (6ft); China.

***L.* 'Destiny'.** Vigorous, clump-forming Division 1a lily. In early summer, bears umbels of medium-sized, unscented, bowl-shaped yellow flowers, with brown spots and tepals recurved towards the tips. ↕ 1–1.2m (3–4ft). ❄❄❄

L. duchartrei ■ Stoloniform, stem-rooting Division 9 lily with rhizomatous bulbs and ribbed, brown-flushed green stems bearing scattered, lance-shaped, stalkless, dark green leaves, to 10cm (4in) long, with rough margins. In summer, bears umbels of up to 12 scented, long-stalked, nodding, turkscap white flowers, 6–8cm (2½–3in) across, deep purple-spotted inside, and purple-flushed, ageing to red outside. ↕ 60–100cm (24–39in). China (Gansu, Sichuan, Yunnan). ❄❄❄

***L.* 'Enchantment'** ■ Very vigorous, clump-forming Division 1a lily. In early summer, produces umbels of medium-sized, unscented, cup-shaped, rich bright orange flowers with black spots inside. Easy to grow and good for cutting. ↕ 60–100cm (24–39in). ❄❄❄

***L.* 'Eros'.** Division 1c lily bearing racemes of small, unscented, turkscap buff flowers in midsummer. ↕ 0.9–1.1m (3–3½ft). ❄❄❄

***L.* 'Fire King'** ■ Vigorous Division 1b lily. In midsummer, produces racemes of large, unscented, shallowly funnel-shaped, bright reddish orange flowers, spotted purple inside and with recurved tepal tips. Excellent in a container. ↕ 1–1.2m (3–4ft). ❄❄❄

L. formosanum. Elegant, stem-rooting Division 9 lily with rhizomatous bulbs, and green stems that are purplish brown towards the bases. Numerous linear to narrowly oblong-lance-shaped, shiny, dark green leaves, 8–20cm (3–8in) long, are scattered, and sparse towards the stem tops. Slender, very fragrant, trumpet-shaped white flowers, 12–20cm (5–8in) long, flushed reddish purple outside, and with flared and somewhat recurved tepal tips, are borne singly, in pairs, or in umbels of up to 10, in late summer and early autumn. Requires moist, acid soil. Suitable for a conservatory. ↕ 0.6–1.5m (2–5ft). Taiwan. ❄❄. **var. *pricei*** ■ produces solitary flowers or clusters of up to 3 flowers, which are more strongly flushed purple on the outside, and borne earlier in the summer; ↕ 10–30cm (4–12in).

L. giganteum see *Cardiocrinum giganteum.*

***L.* Golden Splendor Group** ■ Vigorous, variable Division 6a lilies. In midsummer, strong, sturdy stems produce umbels of large, scented, outward-facing, shallowly trumpet-shaped, almost bowl-shaped flowers, in shades of yellow with dark burgundy-red bands outside. ↕ 1.2–2m (4–6ft). ❄❄❄

***L.* 'Gran Paradiso'.** Division 1a lily. Racemes of medium-sized, unscented, bowl-shaped red flowers with slightly recurved tepals are borne in mid-summer. ↕ 1m (3ft). ❄❄❄

L. grayi ■ Division 9 lily with rhizomatous bulbs and whorls of lance-shaped to oblong-lance-shaped, bright green leaves, 5–10cm (2–4in) long. In midsummer, bears tiered umbels of up to 12 scented, tubular-funnel-shaped, nodding red flowers, 6cm (2½in) long, paler inside, with yellowish centres and purple spots. Requires moist, acid soil. ↕ 1–1.7m (3–5½ft). E. USA. ❄❄❄

***L.* 'Green Dragon'** ■ Stout Division 6a lily, derived from the Olympic Hybrids. In midsummer, bears short racemes of large, fragrant, trumpet-shaped white flowers flushed greenish brown outside and stained yellow in the centres. ↕ 1.5–2.2m (5–7ft). ❄❄❄

L. hansonii ■ Vigorous, early-flowering, stem-rooting Division 9 lily. Inversely lance-shaped to elliptic, mid- to dark green leaves, to 18cm (7in) long, are borne in dense whorls of 12–20. In early summer, produces racemes of up to 12 small, fragrant, nodding, turkscap, brilliant orange-yellow flowers, 3–4cm

Lilium Golden Splendor Group

(1¼–1½in) across, with thick, recurved tepals spotted purplish brown near the bases. Grow in well-drained soil in partial shade. ↕1–1.5m (3–5ft). Russia (E. Siberia), Korea, Japan. ❄❄❄
L. heldreichii see *L. chalcedonicum*.
L. henryi ■ Vigorous, stem-rooting, clump-forming Division 9 lily with purple-marked green stems. Ovate-lance-shaped to lance-shaped, shiny, dark green leaves, 8–15cm (3–6in) long, are scattered; the lower leaves have short stalks, the upper ones are crowded below the flowers. In late summer, produces racemes of up to 10 (occasionally up to 20) faintly scented, turkscap, deep orange flowers, 6–8cm (2½–3in) across, spotted black, with deep red anthers. Easy to grow in neutral to alkaline soil in partial shade. ↕1–3m (3–10ft). C. China. ❄❄❄
***L.* 'Imperial Gold'.** Division 7c lily bearing racemes, in late summer, of large, fragrant, star-shaped, glistening white flowers, each tepal with recurved tips and a yellow stripe down the centre. ↕2m (6ft). ❄❄❄
***L.* 'Imperial Silver'.** Division 7c lily with the stems often spotted red. In late summer, produces racemes of large, fragrant, broad, shallowly bowl-shaped white flowers, with wide-spreading, burgundy-spotted tepals with recurved tips, and orange-red anthers. ↕1.5–2m (5–6ft). ❄❄❄
***L.* 'Iowa Rose'.** Vigorous Division 1b lily. In midsummer, bears racemes of medium-sized, unscented, bowl-shaped pink flowers, with recurved tepals, orange-yellow throats, and brown anthers. ↕1–1.2m (3–4ft). ❄❄❄
***L.* 'Jetfire'.** Early-flowering Division 1a lily bearing umbels of medium-sized, unscented, cup-shaped, rich orange flowers, with yellow centres, in early and midsummer. ↕80–120cm (32–48in). ❄❄❄
***L.* 'Journey's End'** ■ Stout Division 7d lily producing racemes of large, unscented, broad, turkscap flowers in late summer; the spreading tepals are deep pink, with maroon spots and white margins and tips. ↕1–2m (3–6ft). ❄❄❄
***L.* 'Karen North'.** Elegant, triploid Division 1c lily producing lax racemes of medium-sized, unscented, turkscap, orange-pink flowers with deep pink spots, in midsummer. ↕1–1.4m (3–4½ft). ❄❄❄
***L.* 'King Pete'.** Vigorous, clump-forming Division 1b lily. In mid-summer, produces umbels of medium-sized, unscented, broad, bowl-shaped cream flowers, marked and spotted orange and with orange-red anthers. Long-lasting in flower and good for cutting. ↕90cm (3ft). ❄❄❄
L. lancifolium ■ syn. *L. tigrinum* (Tiger lily). Robust, stem-rooting, clump-forming Division 9 lily with dark purple, often white-hairy stems. Scattered, narrowly lance-shaped, shiny, dark green leaves, 12–20cm (5–8in) long, have rough margins; the upper ones produce dark purplish black bulbils in the axils. Up to 40 unscented, nodding, turkscap, orange-red flowers, 12cm (5in) across, with dark purple spots and papillae, are produced in racemes in late summer and early autumn. The clone most often grown is triploid. Prefers moist, acid soil, but tolerates some lime. ↕0.6–1.5m (2–5ft).

Lilium 'Journey's End'

E. China, Korea, Japan. ❄❄❄. **var. *flaviflorum*** produces yellow flowers; Japan. **'Flore Pleno'** bears double flowers with 24–36 tepals and no stamens. **var. *splendens*** is exceptionally vigorous, with up to 25 large, black-spotted, deep orange-red flowers on downy stems. **'Yellow Tiger'** is a selection from var. *flaviflorum*, with purple-spotted, bright yellow flowers.
L. lankongense ■ Stoloniform Division 9 lily with scattered, lance-shaped, dark green leaves, 10cm (4in) long. Racemes of up to 15 small, unscented, turkscap pink flowers with darker spots are borne in midsummer. Tolerates lime if soil is humus-rich. ↕90–150cm (3–5ft). China (Yunnan). ❄❄❄
***L.* 'Lavender Mist'.** Tetraploid Division 7b lily. In late summer produces racemes of large, fragrant, bowl-shaped, heavily red-spotted white flowers, with reflexed tepals; nectaries are yellow blending to red. ↕1.2m (4ft). ❄❄❄
***L.* 'Limelight'.** Moderately robust Division 6a lily. In midsummer, bears short racemes of large, fragrant, slightly pendent, trumpet-shaped, lime-yellow flowers that are flushed with green, especially outside. ↕1–2m (3–6ft). ❄❄❄
L. longiflorum ■ (Easter lily). Vigorous, stem-rooting Division 9 lily with scattered, lance-shaped to oblong-lance-shaped, shiny, deep green leaves, to 18cm (7in) long. In midsummer, bears short racemes of 1–6 very fragrant, trumpet-shaped, horizontally placed, pure white flowers, to 18cm (7in) long, with yellow anthers. Widely grown for cut flowers; excellent in a container. Lime-tolerant. Grow in partial shade. ↕40–100cm (16–39in). S. Japan, Taiwan. ❄. **'Casa Rosa'** bears white flowers, flushed rose-pink. **'White American'** produces white flowers with green tips and deep yellow anthers.
L. mackliniae ■ Small, stem-rooting Division 9 lily with slender green stems, sometimes tinged purple, and linear-lance-shaped to narrowly elliptic, mid-green leaves, 3–6cm (1¼–2½in) long, scattered or whorled near the tops of the stems. In early and midsummer, bears racemes of up to 6 unscented, semi-pendent, bowl-shaped, purple-flushed, rose-pink flowers, 5cm (2in) across, with purple anthers. ↕30–60cm (12–24in). N.E. India (Assam). ❄❄❄
L. maculatum, syn. *L. thunbergianum*. Short, stem-rooting Division 9 lily with ribbed stems and scattered, elliptic to lance-shaped, dark green leaves, 5–10cm (2–4in) long. In early and midsummer, produces umbels of faintly scented, bowl-shaped, orange, red, or yellow flowers, 8–10cm (3–4in) across, with varying amounts of darker spotting. Prefers neutral to alkaline soil. ↕50–60cm (20–24in). Japan. ❄❄❄. **var. *flavum*** produces yellow flowers.
***L.* 'Magic Pink'** ■ Clump-forming Division 7b lily. In midsummer, produces short racemes of large, slightly scented, half-nodding, bowl-shaped, soft pink flowers, with a darker centre to each tepal. ↕1.2m (4ft). ❄❄❄
***L.* 'Marhan'.** Stout Division 2 lily producing racemes, in early summer, of medium-sized, pungently scented, turkscap, orange flowers, with reddish brown spotting. ↕1.5–2m (5–6ft). ❄❄❄
***L.* 'Marie North'** ■ Clump-forming, triploid Division 1c lily producing racemes of medium-sized, slightly scented, turkscap flowers in midsummer; dark pink in bud, the flowers open white, suffused pinkish mauve with some deeper speckling in the centres. Bulbils are sometimes produced. ↕80–120cm (32–48in). ❄❄❄
L. martagon ■ (Common turkscap lily). Vigorous, clump-forming, stem-rooting Division 9 lily producing stiff, purple- or red-flushed green stems. Elliptic to inversely lance-shaped, dark green leaves, to 16cm (6in) long, often hairy on the undersides, are mostly borne in dense whorls. In early and midsummer, produces narrow racemes of up to 50 small, pungently scented, pendent or nodding, turkscap, glossy, pink to purplish red flowers, to 5cm (2in) across, with some darker coloured spotting or flecking. Grow in almost any well-drained soil in full sun or partial shade. ↕0.9–2m (3–6ft). Europe to Mongolia. ❄❄❄. **var. *album*** ■ has bright green stems bearing pure white flowers, to 4cm (1½in) across. **var. *cattaniae***, syn. var. *dalmaticum*, has hairy stems and buds, and produces deep maroon flowers. **var. *dalmaticum*** see var. *cattaniae*. **var. *daugava*** bears purple flowers on short-hairy stems; ↕to 90cm (3ft); Latvia. **'Inshriach Ivory'** bears ivory-white flowers. **'Inshriach Rose'** has stout stems bearing deep rose-purple flowers with darker spots.
***L.* 'Maxwill'.** Striking Division 1c lily. In midsummer, stout stems produce racemes of small, unscented, turkscap, black-spotted, brilliant orange-red flowers, with strongly recurved tepals. ↕1.5–2.2m (5–7ft). ❄❄❄
L. medeoloides ■ Stem-rooting Division 9 lily with hollow green stems and stalkless, lance-shaped, dark green leaves, 12cm (5in) long, mostly in 1 or 2 whorls on the lower parts of the stems, with a few scattered on the upper parts. In midsummer, produces short racemes or umbels of up to 10 unscented, turkscap, orange-red to apricot flowers, 4.5cm (1¾in) across, with darker spots and purple anthers. Requires acid soil and partial shade. ↕40–75cm (16–30in). Russia (E. Siberia), N. China, Korea, Japan. ❄❄❄
L. monadelphum ■ syn. *L. szovitsianum*. Stout, clump-forming, sparsely stem-rooting Division 9 lily with stiff stems and scattered, lance-shaped to inversely lance-shaped or ovate, bright green leaves, to 14cm (5½in) long. In early summer, bears racemes of up to 30 large, nodding, fragrant, broadly trumpet-shaped yellow flowers, to 10cm (4in) across, flecked and spotted maroon or purple inside, flushed purplish brown outside. Tepals are moderately to prominently recurved. Lime-tolerant. Thrives in fairly heavy soil, and survives in drier, sunnier conditions than most lilies. ↕1–1.5m (3–5ft). N.E. Turkey, Caucasus. ❄❄❄
***L.* 'Mont Blanc'** ■ Short Division 1a lily producing umbels of large, unscented, wide, bowl-shaped white flowers, slightly brown-spotted in the centres, in early and midsummer. ↕60–70cm (24–28in). ❄❄❄

Lilium 'Magic Pink'

Lilium monadelphum

Lilium 'Mont Blanc'

Lilium nepalense

Lilium 'Olivia'

Lilium oxypetalum

Lilium pardalinum

Lilium 'Peggy North'

Lilium Pink Perfection Group

Lilium 'Pink Tiger'

Lilium pomponium

Lilium pyrenaicum

Lilium pyrenaicum subsp. *carniolicum* var. *albanicum*

Lilium regale

Lilium 'Rosemary North'

Lilium speciosum var. *rubrum*

Lilium 'Star Gazer'

Lilium 'Sun Ray'

Lilium tsingtauense

***L.* 'Montreux'.** Short Division 1a lily bearing umbels, in midsummer, of medium-sized, unscented, cup-shaped pink flowers, with brown dots in the centres and buff-yellow anthers. ↕80–100cm (32–39in). ❄❄❄

L. nanum ▣ syn. *Nomocharis nana*. Small Division 9 lily with slender stems and scattered, linear, mid-green leaves, to 12cm (5in) long. Bears solitary, scented, bell-shaped, pale pink to rose-purple flowers, 1–4cm (½–1½in) long, often with darker markings or spots, in early summer. Requires cool, moist, acid soil and partial shade. ↕6–30cm (2½–12in). Himalayas, W. China. ❄❄❄. **var. *flavidum*** bears pale yellow flowers.

L. nepalense ▣ Stoloniform, stem-rooting Division 9 lily with rhizomatous bulbs, erect or arching, smooth stems, and scattered, lance-shaped to oblong-lance-shaped, deep green leaves, to 15cm (6in) long. In early and mid-summer, bears unscented or pungently scented, funnel-shaped, yellow, greenish yellow, or greenish white flowers, singly or occasionally in groups of 2 or 3 in the upper leaf axils. The tepals later reflex, and are either flecked and spotted reddish purple, or are entirely reddish purple or maroon in the centres. Needs cool, acid soil and partial shade. ↕60–100cm (24–39in). N. India to Nepal and Bhutan (Himalayas). ❄

Lilium nanum

***L.* 'Olivia'** ▣ Division 7b lily with racemes of medium-sized, scented, slightly reflexed, bowl-shaped, pure white flowers in late summer. Shorter than many other Oriental hybrids. ↕75–100cm (30–39in). ❄❄❄

***L.* Olympic Hybrids.** Vigorous Division 6a lilies. A group of hybrids derived from various Asiatic species, including *L. brownii*, *L. leucanthum*, and *L. sargentiae*. In mid- and late summer, they bear racemes of up to 15 large, sweetly fragrant, trumpet-shaped flowers, ranging from white, greenish white, cream, and yellow, to pink and purple, often yellow in the throats. Tepals are flushed pink or purplish red on the outside. ↕1.2–2m (4–6ft). ❄❄❄

***L.* 'Omega'.** Division 7d lily with short stems producing short racemes, in late summer, of large, rose-pink flowers, with yellowish centres and sparse red spotting; the tepals are spreading and slightly recurved. ↕60–80cm (24–32in). ❄❄❄

L. oxypetalum ▣ syn. *Nomocharis oxypetala*. Small Division 9 lily with slender stems and scattered, linear to linear-lance-shaped, deep green leaves, to 7cm (3in) long, sometimes whorled below the flowers. In early summer, each slender stem produces 1 or 2 small, unscented, semi-pendent, shallowly bowl-shaped yellow flowers, to 5cm (2in) across, usually with some purple dots in the centres. Needs cool, moist, acid soil and partial shade. ↕20–30cm (8–12in). N.W. Himalayas. ❄❄❄. **var. *insigne*** produces purple flowers.

***L.* 'Pan'.** Delicate Division 1c lily bearing racemes of small, pleasantly scented, turkscap white flowers in midsummer. ↕1–1.2m (3–4ft). ❄❄❄

L. pardalinum ▣ (Leopard lily, Panther lily). Vigorous, clump-forming, rhizomatous Division 9 lily. Strong stems bear dense whorls of elliptic to inversely lance-shaped, deep green leaves, to 18cm (7in) long. In midsummer, produces racemes of up to 10 unscented, nodding, turkscap, orange-red to crimson flowers, 9cm (3½in) across, paler towards the bases and with large maroon spots (some encircled with yellow). Prefers moist soil in full sun or partial shade; lime-tolerant, but not in dry soil. ↕1.5–2.5m (5–8ft). W. USA. ❄❄❄. **var. *giganteum*** is particularly vigorous, with as many as 30 flowers per stem; they are crimson, and yellow towards the bases with crimson spots; ↕to 3m (10ft).

***L.* 'Peggy North'** ▣ Moderately vigorous, clump-forming, triploid Division 1c lily. In midsummer, bears racemes of medium-sized, faintly scented, turkscap, orange flowers, finely speckled dark brown. ↕1.2–1.5m (4–5ft). ❄❄❄

***L.* Pink Perfection Group** ▣ Division 6a lilies with stout stems. In mid-summer, produce short racemes or umbels of large, scented, slightly nodding, trumpet-shaped flowers, which are deep purplish red or purple-pink, with bright orange anthers. ↕1.5–2m (5–6ft). ❄❄❄

***L.* 'Pink Tiger'** ▣ Vigorous Division 1b lily with racemes of medium-sized, unscented, turkscap pink flowers in late summer. ↕1.2m (4ft). ❄❄❄

***L.* 'Pirate'.** Division 1a lily with slender stems bearing umbels of medium-sized, unscented, star-shaped, orange-red flowers in early summer. ↕1–1.2m (3–4ft). ❄❄❄

L. pomponium ▣ Slender, stem-rooting Division 9 lily with green stems that are spotted purple on the lower halves. Scattered, linear, mid-green leaves, to 15cm (6in) long, have silver-hairy margins. In early and midsummer, produces racemes of up to 6 (rarely up to 10) pungently scented, pendent, turkscap, sealing-wax-red flowers, 5cm (2in) across, generally with black spots and streaks in the throats. Prefers alkaline soil in full sun or partial shade. ↕1m (3ft). French and Italian Alps. ❄❄❄

L. ponticum see *L. pyrenaicum* subsp. *ponticum*.

L. pumilum, syn. *L. tenuifolium*. Stem-rooting Division 9 lily with slender stems bearing numerous scattered, linear, mid-green leaves, to 10cm (4in) long. In early summer, bears racemes of up to 30 fragrant, nodding to pendent, turkscap, scarlet flowers, 5cm (2in) across, unspotted or with a few black spots in the centres. Requires acid soil and full sun or partial shade. ↕15–45cm

Lilium 'Sterling Star'

L

(6–18in). Russia (Siberia) to Mongolia, N. China, and N. Korea. ✻✻✻
L. pyrenaicum ■ Stem-rooting, clump-forming Division 9 lily with green stems, sometimes spotted purple, and numerous scattered, linear to linear-lance-shaped, bright green leaves, 15cm (6in) long, often with silver-hairy margins. In early and midsummer, bears racemes of up to 12 pungent, pendent, turkscap, yellow or greenish yellow flowers, 5cm (2in) across, flecked and spotted dark maroon in the throats. Needs neutral to alkaline soil and full sun or partial shade. ↕30–100cm (12–39in). Pyrenees. ✻✻✻. **subsp. *carniolicum***, syn. *L. carniolicum*, has leaves with densely downy veins on the undersides, and produces orange or red flowers, spotted purple-brown; ↕to 1.2m (4ft); Alps, former Yugoslavia. **subsp. *carniolicum* var. *albanicum*** ■ has leaves that are hairless beneath, and bears plain yellow flowers; ↕rarely more than 40cm (16in); N. Greece, Albania. **subsp. *ponticum***, syn. *L. ponticum*, bears leaves 3–8cm (1¼–3in) long, with hairs beneath, and deep yellow flowers, flecked and spotted reddish brown or purple; ↕to 90cm (36in); N.E. Turkey. **var. *rubrum*** bears orange-red flowers.
L. regale ■ (Regal lily). Vigorous, stem-rooting Division 9 lily with erect or arching, purple-flushed, grey-green stems and numerous scattered, linear, shiny, deep green leaves, 5–13cm (2–5in) long. In midsummer, produces umbels of up to 25, very fragrant, broadly trumpet-shaped white flowers, 12–15cm (5–6in) long, flushed purple or purple-brown outside, with yellow centres and gold anthers. Grow in most well-drained soils, except very alkaline; prefers full sun. ↕0.6–2m (2–6ft). W. China. ✻✻✻. **var. *album*** bears almost pure white flowers with orange anthers.
***L.* 'Rosemary North'** ■ Triploid Division 1c lily producing racemes, in early and midsummer, of medium-sized, slightly scented, turkscap ochre flowers with a few dark ochre spots on the outside. ↕90–100cm (36–39in). ✻✻✻
***L.* 'Scheherazade'.** Vigorous, tetraploid Division 8 lily. In late summer, bears racemes of large, slightly scented, flat-faced, red and gold flowers with white margins and recurved tips. ↕2.5m (8ft). ✻✻✻
***L.* 'Shuksan'.** Stem-rooting Division 4 lily with stout stems bearing racemes, in midsummer, of medium-sized, slightly scented, turkscap, orange-yellow flowers, with large black or reddish brown spots. Good in partial shade, especially in acid soil. ↕1.4–2m (4½–6ft). ✻✻✻
***L.* 'Silk Road'.** Vigorous, tetraploid Division 7b lily. In midsummer, bears racemes of large, scented, open bowl-shaped red flowers with white tips. ↕1–1.5m (3–5ft). ✻✻✻
L. speciosum. Vigorous, stem-rooting Division 9 lily with erect to ascending, purple-flushed green stems. Short-stalked, dark green leaves, to 18cm (7in) long, are scattered and broadly lance-shaped to almost ovate. In late summer and early autumn, produces racemes of usually up to 12, sometimes more, large, fragrant, pendent or outward-facing, turkscap, pale pink or white flowers, to 18cm (7in) across, flushed deeper pink in the centres, and with papillae and pink or crimson spots. Needs moist,

L

Lilium superbum

acid soil and partial shade. ↕1–1.7m (3–5½ft). E. China, Japan, Taiwan. ✻✻✻. **var. *album*** produces white flowers and purple stems. **var. *gloriosoides*** has flowers with strongly reflexed, twisted tepals, bright scarlet at the base; China. **'Grand Commander'** has red-spotted, lilac-purple flowers with white-margined tepals. **var. *roseum*** has rose-pink flowers and green stems. **var. *rubrum*** ■ produces purple-brown stems and deep carmine-red flowers. **'Uchida'** bears crimson-red flowers with delicate, darker red spotting.
***L.* 'Star Gazer'** ■ Vigorous Division 7d lily bearing racemes, in midsummer, of large, highly scented, star-shaped red flowers with spreading tepals, recurved at the tips and marked with darker spots. Good in a container and for forcing. ↕1–1.5m (3–5ft). ✻✻✻
***L.* 'Sterling Star'** ■ Vigorous Division 1a lily. In early and midsummer, bears short racemes of large, faintly scented, cup-shaped, off-white flowers, flushed cream and speckled brown. ↕1–1.2m (3–4ft). ✻✻✻
***L.* 'Sun Ray'** ■ Division 1a lily bearing umbels of medium-sized, unscented, bowl-shaped yellow flowers, with a sparse scattering of brown dots, in early and midsummer. ↕1m (3ft). ✻✻✻
L. superbum ■ (American turkscap lily). Vigorous, stem-rooting Division 9 lily with rhizomatous bulbs, purple-mottled green stems, and linear-lance-shaped to elliptic, bright green leaves, 3.5–11cm (1½–4½in) long, mostly produced in dense whorls. In late summer and early autumn, bears long racemes of up to 40 unscented, pendent, turkscap flowers, to 7cm (3in) across; tepals are red-flushed orange, with maroon spots, and green towards the bases. Prefers moist, acid soil, and full sun or partial shade. ↕1.5–3m (5–10ft). E. USA. ✻✻✻
L. szovitsianum see *L. monadelphum.*
L. tenuifolium see *L. pumilum.*
L. x testaceum ■ (*L. candidum* x *L. chalcedonicum*) (Nankeen lily). Division 3 lily with alternate, somewhat twisted, lance-shaped, mid-green leaves. In early and midsummer, bears racemes of up to 12 scented, nodding, turkscap, pale apricot-orange flowers, to 8cm (3in) across, with faint red markings in the centres and red anthers. Lime-tolerant; grow in full sun or partial shade. ↕1–1.5m (3–5ft). Garden origin. ✻✻✻
***L.* 'Theodore Haber'.** Division 2 lily with racemes of small, slightly scented, turkscap, shiny, rich red flowers in early summer. ↕1m (3ft). ✻✻✻
L. thunbergianum see *L. maculatum.*
L. tigrinum see *L. lancifolium.*
***L.* 'Trance'.** Relatively short Division 7b lily. In early and midsummer, bears racemes of medium-sized, unscented, outward-facing, bowl-shaped pink flowers, with pale spots in the centres; tepals are dark pink along the centres, fading to almost white at the margins. ↕60–100cm (24–39in). ✻✻✻
L. tsingtauense ■ Stem-rooting Division 9 lily with hollow stems and inversely lance-shaped, hairless, dark green leaves, to 13cm (5in) long, mostly in 2 whorls. In midsummer, bears loose umbels of up to 15 unscented, upright, shallowly trumpet-shaped, maroon-

Lilium x *testaceum*

spotted, orange or orange-red flowers, 5–8cm (2–3in) across, with narrow tepals. Lime-tolerant, but best in moist, acid soil in full sun or partial shade. ↕70–100cm (28–39in). E. China, Korea. ✻✻✻
L. wallichianum. Stem-rooting Division 9 lily with stiff green stems that are tinged purple and bear scattered, linear to lance-shaped, deep green leaves, to 25cm (10in) long. In autumn, bears umbels of up to 4 large, horizontal, very fragrant, trumpet-shaped, white or cream flowers, tinged yellow or green, to 20cm (8in) across. Prefers moist, acid soil. ↕1–2m (3–6ft). Himalayas. ✻
***L.* 'White Henryi'.** Vigorous Division 6d lily producing racemes of large, slightly scented, bowl-shaped white flowers, with recurved tepals and orange nectaries and throats, in midsummer. ↕1.5m (5ft). ✻✻✻
L. wigginsii. Stem-rooting Division 9 lily with hairless stems and linear-lance-shaped, deep green leaves, to 22cm (9in) long, that are scattered and in 2–4 whorls roughly halfway up the stems. In midsummer, produces few-flowered racemes of unscented, pendent, turkscap, deep yellow flowers, 7cm (3in) across, with purple spots. Needs moist, acid soil and partial shade. ↕0.9–1.2m (3–4ft). W. USA. ✻✻✻
***L.* 'Yellow Blaze'.** Moderately vigorous Division 1a lily producing umbels of medium-sized, unscented, bowl-shaped, bright yellow flowers with red-brown spots, in mid- and late summer. ↕1.2–1.5m (4–5ft). ✻✻✻

▷**Lillypilly** see *Acmena smithii*
▷**Lily** see *Lilium*
African blue see *Agapanthus*
Amazon see *Eucharis* x *grandiflora*
American trout see *Erythronium revolutum*
American turkscap see *Lilium superbum*
Arum see *Zantedeschia, Z. aethiopica*
Atamasco see *Zephyranthes atamasca*
Aztec see *Sprekelia formosissima*
Belladonna see *Amaryllis belladonna*
Blackberry see *Belamcanda chinensis*
Blood see *Haemanthus, Scadoxus*
Common turkscap see *Lilium martagon*
Corn see *Clintonia borealis, Ixia*
Desert see *Hesperocallis undulata*
Dwarf ginger see *Kaempferia roscoeana*
Easter see *Lilium longiflorum*
Fire see *Cyrtanthus*
Florida swamp see *Crinum americanum*
Foxtail see *Eremurus*
Garland see *Hedychium*
Giant see *Cardiocrinum*
Ginger see *Alpinia, Hedychium*
Glory see *Gloriosa*
Golden-rayed see *Lilium auratum*
Golden spider see *Lycoris aurea*
Guernsey see *Nerine sarniensis*
Impala see *Adenium*
Jaburan see *Ophiopogon jaburan*
Jacobean see *Sprekelia formosissima*
Japanese pond see *Nuphar japonica*
Kaffir see *Schizostylis*
Lent see *Narcissus pseudonarcissus*
Leopard see *Belamcanda chinensis, Lilium pardalinum*
Madonna see *Lilium candidum*
May see *Maianthemum*
Meadow see *Lilium canadense*

▷**Lily cont.**
Mexican see *Hippeastrum reginae*
Morning star see *Lilium concolor*
Mount Cook see *Ranunculus lyallii*
Nankeen see *Lilium* x *testaceum*
Nodding see *Lilium cernuum*
Orange see *Lilium bulbiferum*
Painted wood see *Trillium undulatum*
Panther see *Lilium pardalinum*
Paradise see *Paradisea*
Peace see *Spathiphyllum, S. wallisii*
Peacock see *Kaempferia roscoeana*
Peruvian see *Alstroemeria*
Pineapple see *Eucomis*
Pink porcelain see *Alpinia zerumbet*
Plantain see *Hosta*
Pyjama see *Crinum macowanii*
Queen see *Curcuma petiolata, Phaedranassa*
Red spider see *Lycoris radiata*
Regal see *Lilium regale*
Resurrection see *Kaempferia rotunda, Lycoris squamigera*
St. Bernard's see *Anthericum liliago*
St. Bruno's see *Paradisea*
St. Joseph's see *Hippeastrum vittatum*
Scarborough see *Cyrtanthus elatus*
Scarlet turkscap see *Lilium chalcedonicum*
Sea see *Pancratium*
Slime see *Albuca*
Snowdon see *Lloydia serotina*
Spear see *Doryanthes*
Spider see *Hymenocallis*
Tiger see *Lilium lancifolium*
Toad see *Tricyrtis*
Torch see *Kniphofia*
Trout see *Erythronium*
Voodoo see *Sauromatum venosum*
Water see *Nymphaea*
Wood see *Trillium*
Yellow pond see *Nuphar, N. lutea*
▷**Lily-of-the-valley** see *Convallaria*
False see *Maianthemum bifolium*
Wild see *Pyrola rotundifolia*
▷**Lily-of-the-valley tree** see *Clethra arborea*
▷**Lily tree** see *Magnolia denudata*
▷**Lilyturf** see *Liriope, Ophiopogon*
White *Ophiopogon jaburan*
▷**Lime** see *Tilia*
American see *T. americana*
Common see *T.* x *europaea*
European white see *T. tomentosa*
Japanese see *T. japonica*
Large-leaved see *T. platyphyllos*
Mongolian see *T. mongolica*
Pendulous silver see *T.* 'Petiolaris'
Red-twigged see *T. platyphyllos* 'Rubra'
Silver see *T. tomentosa*
Small-leaved see *T. cordata*
▷***Limnanthemum nymphoides*** see *Nymphoides peltata*
▷***Limnanthemum peltatum*** see *Nymphoides peltata*

LIMNANTHES

Poached egg plant

LIMNANTHACEAE

Genus of about 17 species of low-growing annuals from moist habitats in W. USA. They have 2-pinnatifid, bright green leaves, and produce cup-shaped, 5-petalled flowers from summer to autumn. *L. douglasii*, the only species usually cultivated, is suitable for a rock garden and as path edging. It self-seeds freely. The nectar-rich flowers are attractive to bees and hoverflies.

Limnanthes douglasii

• **HARDINESS** Fully hardy.
• **CULTIVATION** Grow in fertile, moist but well-drained soil in full sun.
• **PROPAGATION** Sow seed *in situ* in spring or autumn. Protect autumn sowings in frost-prone areas.
• **PESTS AND DISEASES** Trouble free.

L. douglasii ■ (Poached egg plant). Slender-stemmed, erect to spreading annual with 2-pinnatifid, finely toothed, fleshy, glossy, bright yellow-green leaves, 5–12cm (2–5in) long. Bears numerous shallowly cup-shaped, fragrant, yellow-centred white flowers, to 2.5cm (1in) across, from summer to autumn. ↕↔ to 15cm (6in) or more. USA (California, Oregon). ❄❄❄

LIMNOCHARIS

LIMNOCHARITACEAE

Genus of 2 species of evergreen and deciduous aquatic annuals and perennials, found in the shallow margins of tropical pools in S.E. Asia, South America, and the West Indies. They produce rosettes of lance-shaped to ovate leaves, and umbels of saucer-shaped yellow flowers. In areas where temperatures fall below 10°C (50°F), grow in an indoor pool. In mild, temperate areas, use for temporary summer planting around an outdoor pool; in warmer climates grow permanently outdoors. They self-seed freely, the stems that bear the seed capsules bending over to water level, where each throws up another shoot.

• **HARDINESS** Frost tender.
• **CULTIVATION** Under glass, grow in baskets of heavy loam at the margins of a pool, in slightly acid water, at 20–25°C (68–77°F), in bright filtered light. Outdoors, grow in deep, acid, permanently wet soil in full sun. See also pp.52–53.
• **PROPAGATION** Scatter seed on the water surface as soon as ripe. Divide in summer.
• **PESTS AND DISEASES** Trouble free.

L. flava. Evergreen, marginal aquatic perennial with upright, long-stalked, lance-shaped to ovate leaves, to 20cm (8in) long, with heart-shaped bases. Umbels of 2–12 saucer-shaped yellow flowers, 2.5cm (1in) across, with off-white margins, are produced several times during summer. ↕↔ 60cm (24in). Tropical South America, West Indies. ❀ (min. 10°C/50°F)

LIMONIUM

Sea lavender, Statice

PLUMBAGINACEAE

Genus of 150 species of annuals, biennials, and deciduous and evergreen perennials and subshrubs from coasts, salt marshes, and deserts worldwide. Simple, entire or pinnatifid, tapering leaves, often appearing almost stalkless, are mostly borne in basal rosettes. Spikelets composed of small, stalkless, papery flowers and bracts are borne in usually one-sided, corymb-like panicles in summer and autumn; the calyces are tubular, the corollas have 5 lobed petals joined only at the bases. The calyces are usually a different colour from the corollas, and persist after the petals have fallen. Long-flowering plants, they are suitable for a sunny herbaceous or annual border, and for naturalizing in a gravel garden. They are also good for cutting and drying. The larger perennials grow well in coastal sites; the dwarf species are effective in a trough or rock garden, the less hardy ones being suitable for an alpine house.

• **HARDINESS** Fully hardy to frost tender.
• **CULTIVATION** Outdoors, grow in preferably sandy, well-drained soil in full sun. Large perennials tolerate dry, stony soil. Protect dwarf species from winter wet. In an alpine house, grow in a mix of equal parts loam-based potting compost (JI No.1) and grit.
• **PROPAGATION** Sow seed in early spring: sow perennials in containers outdoors and annuals at 13–18°C (55–64°F). Divide perennials in spring.
• **PESTS AND DISEASES** Susceptible to powdery mildew.

L. aureum **'Supernova'.** Erect perennial, often grown as an annual, with narrowly spoon- to lance-shaped, mostly basal, grey-green leaves, 1–5cm (½–2in) long, tapering gradually to leaf-stalks. In summer, stiff, branched stems bear panicles of small, terminal spikelets, each with tiny, funnel-shaped, orange-yellow flowers, to 5mm (¼in) long, enclosed in hairy white, papery calyces. Good for cut flowers. ↕ to 30cm (12in), ↔ to 23cm (9in). ❄❄❄

Limonium sinuatum California Series 'Iceberg'

L. bellidifolium, syn. *L. reticulata, Statice bellidifolia*. Compact, dome-forming, evergreen, woody-based perennial with spoon-shaped, dark green leaves, to 5cm (2in) long. Open panicles of dense spikelets that consist of tiny, trumpet-shaped, pale violet or blue-violet flowers, 5mm (¼in) long, with white, papery calyces, are borne on wiry, branched stems in early summer. Suitable for a rock garden, trough, or alpine house. ↕↔ to 15cm (6in). Coasts from E. England to the Mediterranean and the Black Sea. ❄❄❄

L. latifolium ■ syn. *L. platyphyllum* (Sea lavender). Rosette-forming perennial with elliptic to spoon-shaped, mid- to dark green leaves, usually to 30cm (12in) long, occasionally to 60cm (24in). In late summer, branched, wiry stems bear panicles of spikelets that consist of shortly tubular, deep lavender-blue flowers, 6mm (¼in) long, with white calyces. ↕ 60cm (24in) or more,

Limonium latifolium

L

Limonium sinuatum Forever Series 'Forever Gold'

↔ 45cm (18in). E. Bulgaria to S.E. Russia. ❄❄❄. **'Blue Cloud'** produces mauve flowers, 7mm (¼in) across. **'Violetta'** produces deep violet flowers.
L. minutum, syn. *Statice minuta.* Woody-based, evergreen perennial with cushion-like rosettes of spoon-shaped, dark green leaves, to 1cm (½in) long, with incurved margins. In early summer, short, slightly woody, branched stems bear panicles of spikelets with 1–4 tiny purple flowers, 5mm (¼in) long. ↕ 10cm (4in), ↔ 15cm (6in). S.E. France. ❄❄❄
L. platyphyllum see. *L. latifolium.*
L. reticulata see. *L. bellidifolium.*
L. sinuatum (Statice). Erect, densely hairy perennial, usually grown as an annual, with basal rosettes of oblong to lance-shaped, deeply lobed, wavy-margined, dark green leaves, 15cm (6in) long. In summer and early autumn, stiff, branched, winged, slightly leafy, bright green stems bear panicles of clustered spikelets that consist of tiny, funnel-shaped, pink, white, or blue flowers, 0.9–1.5cm (⅜–½in) long, enclosed in hairy, white or pale violet calyces. Good for cut flowers. ↕ to 40cm (16in), ↔ 30cm (12in). Mediterranean. ❄❄. **'Art Shades'** bears flowers in orange, salmon-pink, yellow, rose-pink, red, carmine-red, blue, creamy white, or lavender-blue. **California Series** cultivars have 9 strongly toned colour forms, each coming true from seed, ranging from rich, deep purple to the clear white flowers of **'Iceberg'** ▣. Cultivars of **Forever Series** bear large, tightly packed flower spikes in a mixture of 6 or 7 colours, including blue, pink, and yellow; **'Forever Gold'** ▣ has yellow flowers; ↕ to 60cm (24in). **Fortress Series** ▣ cultivars are freely branched, and bear flowers in about 6 vivid shades, including bright blues, pastels, and unusual apricot-yellows; ↕ to 60cm (24in). Cultivars of **Pacific Series** have flowers in deep rose-pink, apricot, yellow, sky blue, white, deep blue, or lavender blue. Cultivars of **Petite Bouquet Series** are very dwarf, with tightly bunched spikelets in blue, purple, deep salmon-pink, pure white, creamy white, lemon-yellow, or golden yellow; ↕ to 30cm (12in). **Sunburst Series** cultivars have flowers in warm colours, including orange-peach, apricot-yellow, and rose-red; good for cutting; ↕ to 75cm (30in).
L. spicatum see *Psylliostachys spicata.*

Limonium sinuatum Fortress Series

L. suworowii see *Psylliostachys suworowii.*
L. tataricum see *Goniolimon tataricum.*
L. tetragonum. Erect biennial with basal rosettes of narrowly spoon-shaped to oblong, leathery leaves, 8–15cm (3–6in) long. In autumn, stiff, branched stems bear panicles of small, terminal spikelets that consist of tiny, funnel-shaped pink flowers, 4–6mm (⅛–¼in) long, with white-hairy calyces. Good for cut flowers. ↕ 45cm (18in), ↔ 30cm (12in). China, Korea, Japan. ❄❄. **'Confetti'** has lemon-yellow flowers. **'Stardust'** is very tolerant of adverse weather, and bears up to 30 flowering stems per plant; ↕ to 60cm (24in).

LINANTHUS

POLEMONIACEAE

Genus of about 35 species of annuals and perennials, usually found in sandy and gravelly sites in grassland or scrub in W. USA, Mexico, and Chile. They have branched stems with alternate or opposite leaves, which are sometimes simple, but usually pinnately or palmately lobed, or fully divided, with linear segments. Bell- or funnel-shaped, white, blue, lilac, pink, or yellow flowers are borne singly or in loose cymes or dense heads, from spring to summer. Grow the perennial species in a rock garden; the annuals are suitable for an annual border or a wild garden.

- **HARDINESS** Fully hardy to frost hardy. The perennials are hardy to -8°C (18°F).
- **CULTIVATION** Grow in any light, well-drained soil in full sun.
- **PROPAGATION** Sow seed *in situ*: perennial species in autumn, annuals in spring. Take stem-tip cuttings of *L. nuttallii* in early summer.
- **PESTS AND DISEASES** Trouble free.

L. dianthiflorus (Ground pink). Erect, slender, branching, downy annual with mostly opposite, narrowly linear leaves, 1–2cm (½–¾in) long. Funnel-shaped then spreading, yellow-throated, white, pink, or lilac-blue flowers, to 2.5cm (1in) across, the petals lobed, toothed, and spotted at the bases, are borne singly or in short, few-flowered, leafy cymes from spring to summer. ↕ 5–12cm (2–5in), ↔ to 5cm (2in). USA (S. California) to Mexico (Baja California). ❄❄❄
L. grandiflorus (Mountain phlox). Erect, slender, branching, downy to almost smooth annual with alternate or opposite, palmately lobed leaves, to 10cm (4in) long, with 5–11 linear lobes, 1–3cm (½–1¼in) long. From spring to summer, bears dense heads of funnel-shaped then spreading, lavender-pink, lilac, or white flowers, to 3cm (1¼in) across, the petals lobed, toothed, and flecked with white. Good for cut flowers. ↕ 30–50cm (12–20in), ↔ to 23cm (9in). USA (S. California). ❄❄❄
L. nuttallii. Compact, bushy perennial with opposite, palmately lobed, pale green leaves, to 8cm (3in) long, with 5–9 pointed, linear lobes, to 1.5cm (½in) long, on densely branched stems. In early summer, bears abundant cymes of funnel-shaped to salverform white flowers, to 1.5cm (½in) across, with spreading lobes. ↕ to 15cm (6in), ↔ to 20cm (8in). USA (Washington State to California). ❄❄

LINARIA

Toadflax

SCROPHULARIACEAE

Genus of approximately 100 species of annuals, biennials, and herbaceous perennials from dry, sunny habitats, including scree, in temperate regions of the N. hemisphere, especially the Mediterranean. They have erect, sometimes trailing, branched stems, with simple, ovate or linear to lance-shaped, stalkless, often grey-green leaves, the lower ones usually whorled or opposite, the upper more or less alternate. They are grown for their irregular, 2-lipped, spurred, white, pink, red, purple, orange, or yellow flowers, resembling snapdragons (*Antirrhinum*), which are borne in terminal racemes from spring to autumn. The taller toadflaxes are useful for a herbaceous border, or for naturalizing in stony soil or a gravel garden. The smaller, alpine species are suitable for a rock garden, scree bed, or wall crevice. In frost-prone areas, grow half-hardy species in a cool greenhouse.

- **HARDINESS** Fully hardy to half hardy.
- **CULTIVATION** Grow in moderately fertile, light, well-drained, preferably sandy soil, in full sun.
- **PROPAGATION** Sow seed of annuals *in situ* in early spring; they self-seed freely. Sow seed of perennials in containers in a cold frame in early spring and plant out with care. Divide perennials, or take basal softwood cuttings, in spring.
- **PESTS AND DISEASES** Aphids and powdery mildew may be a problem.

L. alpina ▣ (Alpine toadflax). Trailing, short-lived perennial with linear-lance-shaped, blue-green leaves, 0.5–1.5cm (¼–½in) long, the lower leaves whorled, the upper ones alternate. In summer, produces 3- to 15-flowered racemes of 2-lipped, bicoloured, violet and deep yellow flowers, 1.5–2.5cm (½–1in) long, sometimes entirely violet, pink, or yellowish white, with spurs 8–10mm (⅜–½in) long. ↕ 8cm (3in), ↔ to 15cm (6in). C. and S. Europe. ❄❄❄
L. dalmatica see *L. genistifolia* subsp. *dalmatica.*
L. x dominii (*L. purpurea* x *L. repens*). Erect to spreading, branching perennial with opposite, simple, linear or linear-lance-shaped, mid-green leaves, 1–5cm (½–2in) long, the upper leaves sometimes whorled. From early summer to mid-autumn, produces branching

Linaria alpina

L

flowerheads of tubular, 2-lipped, pale lilac to purplish violet flowers, 0.8–1.5cm (3/8–1/2in) long, with spurs to 5mm (1/4in) long. ↕ to 1m (3ft), ↔ 60cm (2ft). Europe. ❄❄❄
L. genistifolia. Upright, branching perennial with alternate, semi-erect, linear to ovate, pointed, mid-green leaves, 9–18cm (3½–7in) long. From early to late summer, bears racemes of 2-lipped, lemon-yellow to orange flowers, 1.5–2cm (½–¾in) long, with spurs to 2.5cm (1in) long. ↕ 1m (3ft), ↔ 60cm (24in). Italy to Russia, Turkey. ❄❄❄. **subsp. *dalmatica*** ■ syn. *L. dalmatica*, has shorter, ovate to lance-shaped, glaucous leaves and yellow flowers, 2–5cm (¾–2in) long, in loose racemes; S. Italy, Balkan Peninsula, Romania.
L. glareosum see *Chaenorhinum glareosum.*
L. maroccana. Erect, sticky-hairy annual with alternate, narrowly linear, light green leaves, to 4cm (1½in) long. In summer, bears slender, slightly lax racemes of tiny, 2-lipped, violet-purple, occasionally pink or white flowers, to 1.5cm (½in) long, the lower lips marked orange to yellow, paler at the centres. ↕ 23–45cm (9–18in), ↔ to 15cm (6in). Morocco. ❄❄❄. **'Fairy Bouquet'** freely produces flowers, to 2cm (¾in) long, in yellow, rose-pink, salmon-pink, orange, carmine, lavender, and white; ↕ to 23cm (9in). **'Northern Lights'** ■ occurs in the same colours as 'Fairy Bouquet' but is long-flowering; ↕ to 60cm (24in). **'White Pearl'** has pure white flowers, to 2cm (¾in) long; ↕ to 23cm (9in).
L. purpurea. Erect, slender perennial with linear, mid-green leaves, 2–6cm (¾–2½in) long, the lower whorled, the upper alternate. From early summer to early autumn, 2-lipped, violet-purple flowers, 1.5cm (½in) long, with curved spurs to 5mm (¼in) long, are borne in long, slender, dense racemes. Self-seeds freely. ↕ to 90cm (36in), ↔ 30cm (12in). S. Europe. ❄❄❄. **'Canon J. Went'** ■ syn. 'Canon Went', bears pale pink flowers. Self-seeds true if isolated from the species. **'Springside White'**, syn. 'Radcliffe Innocence', has white flowers.
L. reticulata (Purple-net toadflax). Erect annual with whorls of linear, blue-green leaves, to 1cm (½in) long, deeply channelled at the centres. In late spring and summer, bears short, dense, tapering racemes of 2-lipped, downy, deep purple flowers, to 1.5cm (½in) long, finely veined yellow, each with a large, purple-veined, copper-orange or yellow mark

Linaria maroccana 'Northern Lights'

on the lower lip, and a spur 5–8mm (¼–3/8in) long. Often confused with *L. aeruginea* in gardens. ↕ 0.6–1.2m (2–4ft), ↔ to 23cm (9in). N. Africa. ❄❄❄. **'Aureo-purpurea'** has dark, rich purple flowers, each with a purple-veined, orange or yellow mark on the lower lip. **'Crown Jewels'** has maroon-red, orange, red, or golden yellow flowers; ↕ to 23cm (9in). **'Flamenco'** has purple, maroon-red, red, golden yellow, or orange, often bicoloured flowers, covered in a fine network of dark purple veins; good for cut flowers.
L. triornithophora. Erect perennial bearing whorls of lance-shaped to ovate-lance-shaped, mid-green leaves, 2.5–8cm (1–3in) long. From early or midsummer to early autumn, produces loose racemes of 2-lipped, purple-and-yellow flowers, 5–8cm (2–3in) long, usually in whorls of 3, with brownish purple spurs, 1.5–2.5cm (½–1in) long. ↕ 90cm (36in) or more, ↔ 60cm (24in). N. and C. Portugal, W. Spain. ❄❄
***L. tristis* 'Toubkal'.** Mound-forming perennial with decumbent stems bearing linear to oblong-lance-shaped, blue-green leaves, 1–4cm (½–1½in) long, the lower leaves in whorls, the upper alternate. In summer, produces racemes of 2-lipped, yellow-green flowers, 2.5cm (1in) long, each with a brown-purple mark on the lower lip and a spur 1cm (½in) long. Self-sterile. ↕ 8cm (3in), ↔ to 15cm (6in). ❄❄❄
L. vulgaris (Toadflax). Erect perennial, spreading by runners, with stiff, branched or unbranched stems bearing linear to narrowly elliptic, pale green leaves, 2–6cm (¾–2½in) long. From late spring to mid-autumn, bears pale yellow flowers, to 4.5cm (1¾in) long, with spurs 1cm (½in) long, in dense racemes. Self-seeds freely. ↕ 30–90cm (12–36in), ↔ 30cm (12in). Europe (except extreme north and much of Mediterranean). ❄❄❄

Linaria genistifolia subsp. *dalmatica*

Linaria purpurea 'Canon J. Went'

LINDELOFIA
BORAGINACEAE

Genus of about 12 species of clump-forming, hairy perennials, sometimes with short rhizomes, found on dry, stony slopes or in scrub from C. Asia to the Himalayas. They have lance-shaped, long-stalked basal leaves and alternate, ovate to oblong-lance-shaped, stalkless stem leaves. From spring to autumn, tubular, 2-lipped, brilliant blue to purple flowers, with 5 spreading lobes, are borne in terminal or axillary, one-sided cymes. Grow in a sunny border or gravel garden, or naturalize on a dry bank.
• **HARDINESS** Fully hardy.
• **CULTIVATION** Grow in moderately fertile, well-drained soil in full sun.
• **PROPAGATION** Sow seed in containers outdoors in early spring, or divide in spring.
• **PESTS AND DISEASES** Powdery mildew may be a problem.

***L. anchusiflora* of gardens** see *L. longiflora.*
***L. anchusoides* of gardens** see *L. longiflora.*
L. longiflora, syn. *Cynoglossum longiflorum*, *L. anchusiflora* of gardens, *L. anchusoides* of gardens, *L. spectabilis.* Clump-forming, branched perennial with short rhizomes and long-stalked, lance-shaped, mid-green basal leaves, 7–25cm (3–10in) long; stem leaves are shorter, and clasp the stems. In late spring and early summer, bears deep blue, sometimes purple flowers, to 1.5cm (½in) long, with protruding stamens, in one-sided, terminal cymes. ↕↔ 60cm (24in). W. Himalayas. ❄❄❄. **'Hartington White'** has grey-green leaves and white flowers; ↕↔ to 30cm (12in).
L. spectabilis see *L. longiflora.*

▷**Linden** see *Tilia*

L

LINDERA
LAURACEAE

Genus of about 80 species of deciduous and evergreen, dioecious trees and shrubs occurring in woodland and on river-banks in E. Asia and North America. They are cultivated for their aromatic, alternate, entire or 3-lobed leaves, often colouring well in autumn on deciduous species, and for their star-shaped flowers, which are borne in axillary umbels, rarely singly, early in the year. Grow in a woodland garden. In frost-prone areas,

Lindera benzoin

grow half-hardy species in a cool greenhouse or against a warm wall. Male and female plants need to be planted together in order to bear fruits.
• **HARDINESS** Fully hardy to frost tender.
• **CULTIVATION** Grow in fertile, moist but well-drained, acid soil in partial shade. Pruning group 1.
• **PROPAGATION** Sow seed in containers in a cold frame in autumn. Take greenwood cuttings in early summer.
• **PESTS AND DISEASES** Trouble free.

L. benzoin ■ (Spice bush). Rounded, deciduous shrub with upright branches and obovate, aromatic, bright green leaves, to 12cm (5in) long, turning yellow in autumn. Umbels of tiny, star-shaped, greenish yellow flowers, 4mm (⅛in) across, are borne in mid-spring, followed by ovoid red berries on female plants. ↕↔ 3m (10ft). S.E. Canada, E. USA. ✲✲✲
L. obtusiloba ♀ Spreading, deciduous shrub or small tree with ovate to rounded, entire or 3-lobed, aromatic, glossy, dark green leaves, to 12cm (5in) long. Bears umbels of tiny, star-shaped, dark yellow flowers, 3mm (⅛in) across, in early and mid-spring, before the leaves, followed by spherical, glossy, red-brown berries on female plants. ↕↔ 6m (20ft). China, Korea, Japan. ✲✲✲

LINDHEIMERA
Star daisy
ASTERACEAE/COMPOSITAE

Genus of 1, possibly 2 species of erect, branched, roughly hairy annuals from dry, limestone prairies in Texas, USA. They are grown for their small, daisy-like yellow flowerheads, profusely borne in lax, long-stalked corymbs. They have alternate, ovate-lance-shaped, entire to coarsely pinnatifid leaves, which are smaller and finer on the flowering stems. Persistent bright green, bract-like leaves surround the seed heads. Grow in an informal mixed or annual border.
• **HARDINESS** Fully hardy.

Lindheimera texana

• **CULTIVATION** Grow in moderately fertile, light, well-drained soil in full sun.
• **PROPAGATION** Sow seed in containers in a cold frame in early spring, or *in situ* in mid-spring.
• **PESTS AND DISEASES** Trouble free.

L. texana ■ (Star daisy). Tall, erect annual with branching red stems. Bears ovate-lance-shaped, pinnatifid, often toothed basal leaves, 4cm (1½in) long, and smaller, entire leaves on the upper stems and flower-stalks. Lax corymbs of broad-petalled, yellow-centred, golden yellow to creamy yellow flowerheads, to 2.5cm (1in) across, are borne in late spring and summer. ↕ to 60cm (24in), ↔ to 30cm (12in). USA (Texas). ✲✲✲

▷**Ling** see *Calluna, C. vulgaris*

LINNAEA
Twin-flower
CAPRIFOLIACEAE

Genus of one species of slender, prostrate, mat-forming, evergreen shrub, with stems that root where they touch the soil. It is native to woodland, heaths, and tundra in N. Eurasia and North America. Cultivated for its neat foliage and bell-shaped flowers, it is suitable for ground cover in a peat bed, woodland garden, or large rock garden.
• **HARDINESS** Fully hardy.
• **CULTIVATION** Grow in moderately fertile, humus-rich, reliably moist, acid soil in partial shade.
• **PROPAGATION** Sow seed in containers outdoors in autumn. Take softwood cuttings in early summer. Remove rooted runners between autumn and spring and pot up until established.
• **PESTS AND DISEASES** Trouble free.

L. borealis. Prostrate, mat-forming shrub with opposite, oval to rounded, scalloped leaves, to 1.5cm (½in) long, glossy, dark green above, buff to pale green beneath. In summer, pairs of nodding, narrowly bell- or funnel-shaped, pale pink flowers, to 1cm (½in) long, are produced on stalks, 5cm (2in) long, from the tips of leafy side shoots. ↕ to 8cm (3in), ↔ to 1m (3ft) or more. N. Eurasia, North America. ✲✲✲.
subsp. *americana* ■ has rounded, lobed, mid-green leaves, 2.5cm (1in) long, and bears funnel-shaped, white or pale pink flowers, to 1cm (½in) long, in late spring; ↕ 10cm (4in), ↔ to 30cm (12in); North America.

Linnaea borealis subsp. *americana*

LINOSPADIX
ARECACEAE/PALMAE

Genus of about 11 species of slender, single- or cluster-stemmed palms from rainforest and upland or coastal sands in New Guinea and Australia. Pinnate leaves are loosely clustered at the tops of the stems, and axillary, 3-petalled flowers are borne in slim, erect spikes. Where temperatures drop below 13°C (55°F), grow in a warm greenhouse. In tropical areas, grow as specimen plants;
• **HARDINESS** Frost tender.
• **CULTIVATION** Under glass, grow in loam-based potting compost (JI No.3) in bright filtered light. Pot on or top-dress in spring. In growth, water freely and apply a balanced liquid fertilizer every month. Water moderately in winter. Outdoors, grow in moderately fertile, humus-rich, moist but well-drained, acid soil in partial shade.
• **PROPAGATION** Sow seed at 24°C (75°F) in spring.
• **PESTS AND DISEASES** Red spider mites may be troublesome under glass.

L. monostachya ♈ (Walking stick palm). Small palm with a slender, erect stem and spreading to arching, pinnate, lustrous, mid- to deep green leaves, to 1m (3ft) long, with irregularly shaped leaflets. Greenish yellow flowers are borne in initially erect, then pendent, catkin-like spikes, to 1m (3ft) long, from spring to summer. ↕ 2–3m (6–10ft), ↔ 1–2m (3–6ft). Australia (Queensland, New South Wales). ❀ (min. 13–15°C/55–59°F)

LINUM
Flax
LINACEAE

Genus of about 200 species of annuals, biennials, and semi-evergreen, evergreen, and deciduous perennials, shrubs, and subshrubs, mainly from grassland, scrub, and dry slopes in temperate areas of the N. hemisphere. They are cultivated for their terminal or axillary racemes, panicles, cymes, or corymbs of colourful, 5-petalled, funnel- to saucer-shaped flowers, which are usually blue, yellow, or white, sometimes pink or red, and are borne over long periods. The simple, mainly alternate, sometimes opposite leaves are usually hairless, and deciduous unless otherwise stated. The smaller species are suitable for a rock garden, the larger ones for a border. Grow annuals in an annual border or as fillers in a herbaceous border.
• **HARDINESS** Fully hardy to frost hardy.
• **CULTIVATION** Grow in light, moderately fertile, humus-rich, well-drained soil (sharply drained for alpines) in full sun. Protect from winter wet.
• **PROPAGATION** Sow seed in spring or autumn: sow annuals *in situ*, perennials and shrubs in containers in a cold frame. Take stem-tip cuttings of perennials in early summer, and semi-ripe cuttings of subshrubs and shrubs in summer.
• **PESTS AND DISEASES** Susceptible to slugs, snails, and occasionally aphids.

L. arboreum ■ Dwarf, evergreen shrub with elliptic or spoon-shaped, thick, glaucous, bluish green leaves, 2–4cm (¾–1½in) long, often in

Linum arboreum

crowded rosettes. Compact, few-flowered, terminal cymes of funnel-shaped, deep yellow flowers, 2–3cm (¾–1¼in) across, are produced in succession in late spring and summer. ↕↔ to 30cm (12in). Greece (S. Aegean to Crete), W. Turkey. ✲✲
L. capitatum. Sturdy, rhizomatous perennial, sometimes confused with *L. flavum*, with rosettes of oblong-spoon-shaped basal leaves, and lance-shaped stem leaves, all dark green and 2–3.5cm (¾–1½in) long. During summer, produces compact, terminal cymes of upward-facing, funnel-shaped yellow flowers, to 2.5cm (1in) across. ↕ 40cm (16in), ↔ 25cm (10in). Balkan Peninsula, S. Italy. ✲✲✲
L. flavum (Golden flax, Yellow flax). Upright, woody-based perennial with spoon- to lance-shaped, dark green leaves, 2–3.5cm (¾–1½in) long. Bears dense, many-branched, terminal cymes of upward-facing, funnel-shaped, golden yellow flowers, to 2.5cm (1in) across, which open in sunshine in summer. ↕ 30cm (12in), ↔ to 20cm (8in). C. and S. Europe. ✲✲✲. **'Compactum'** ■ is more compact, and produces bright yellow flowers; ↕↔ 15cm (6in).

Linum flavum 'Compactum'

L

Linum grandiflorum 'Rubrum'

***L.* 'Gemmell's Hybrid'.** Semi-evergreen, dome-forming perennial that has a woody rootstock and bears ovate, glaucous, bluish green leaves, to 5cm (2in) long. Short-stalked, broadly funnel-shaped, chrome-yellow flowers, 3cm (1¼in) across, are profusely borne in terminal cymes over long periods in summer. ↕15cm (6in), ↔ to 20cm (8in). ❄❄

L. grandiflorum (Flowering flax). Erect, slender, basally branching, slightly downy annual with narrowly lance-shaped to ovate-lance-shaped, grey-green leaves, to 3cm (1¼in) long. Bears saucer-shaped, clear rose-pink flowers, to 4cm (1½in) across, with darker eyes, in loose, terminal panicles in summer. ↕40–75cm (16–30in), ↔ 15cm (6in). N. Africa. ❄❄❄. **'Bright Eyes'** produces ivory-white flowers, to 5cm (2in) across, with brownish red eyes; ↕ to 45cm (18in). **'Caeruleum'** produces blue-purple flowers. **'Rubrum'** ▣ produces brilliant crimson-red flowers; ↕ to 45cm (18in).

L. narbonense ▣ Clump-forming, short-lived perennial with wiry stems that bear erect, narrowly lance-shaped, pointed, glaucous, mid-green leaves, to 2cm (¾in) long. Few-flowered, terminal cymes of saucer-shaped, white-eyed, rich blue flowers, 3–4cm (1¼–1½in) across, individually fading by afternoon, are produced continuously in early and mid-summer. ↕30–60cm (12–24in), ↔ 45cm (18in). W. and C. Mediterranean. ❄❄❄ (borderline)

L. perenne (Perennial flax). Variable, clump-forming perennial, similar to *L. narbonense*, with slender stems bearing narrow, linear to lance-shaped, glaucous, bluish green leaves, to 2.5cm (1in) long. Terminal panicles of wide, funnel-shaped, clear blue flowers, 2–3cm (¾–1¼in) across, individually fading by afternoon, are produced continuously in early and midsummer. ↕10–60cm (4–24in), ↔ 30cm (12in). Europe to C. Asia. ❄❄❄. **'Blau Saphir'**, syn. 'Blue Sapphire', produces sky-blue flowers; ↕ to 30cm (12in).

L. salsoloides see *L. suffruticosum* subsp. *salsoloides*.

L. suffruticosum* subsp. *salsoloides, syn. *L. salsoloides*. Low-cushion-forming, woody-based perennial with branching stems bearing narrowly linear, greyish green leaves, to 4.5cm (1¾in) long. Loose, terminal cymes of saucer-shaped, pearl-white flowers, 3cm (1¼in) across, sometimes faintly veined purple, are produced in succession during summer. ↕10cm (4in), ↔ to 15cm (6in). Spain to N. Italy. ❄❄

▷**Lion's ear** see *Leonotis leonurus*
▷***Lippia citriodora*** see *Aloysia triphylla*
▷**Lipstick plant** see *Aeschynanthus pulcher*
▷**Lipstick tree** see *Bixa orellana*
▷**Lipstick vine** see *Aeschynanthus radicans* var. *lobbianus*

LIQUIDAMBAR

HAMAMELIDACEAE

Genus of 4 species of deciduous, monoecious trees occurring in moist woodland in E. and S.W. Asia, North America, and Mexico. They are cultivated particularly for their attractive foliage, which colours well in autumn, and for their upright but open habit. The maple-like leaves are alternate and palmately 3- to 7-lobed. Inconspicuous, yellow-green flowers are produced in rounded heads in late spring; the female flowers are followed by spiky, spherical fruit clusters. Liquidambars are excellent as part of a woodland planting, or as specimen trees isolated in grass.

- **HARDINESS** Fully hardy to frost hardy.
- **CULTIVATION** Grow in moderately fertile, preferably acid or neutral, moist but well-drained soil, in full sun for best autumn colour, or partial shade. Lime-tolerant, given a good depth of soil. Pruning group 1.
- **PROPAGATION** Sow seed in containers in a cold frame in autumn. Take greenwood cuttings in summer.
- **PESTS AND DISEASES** Trouble free.

Liquidambar styraciflua 'Golden Treasure'

L. formosana ♤ syn. *L. formosana* var. *monticola*. Broadly conical tree with palmately 3-lobed leaves, to 12cm (5in) across, purple when young, turning dark green, then orange, red, and purple in autumn. Plants from China grown as var. *monticola* are considered to be hardier than those from Taiwan. ↕12m (40ft), ↔ 10m (30ft). China, Taiwan. ❄❄. **var. *monticola*** see *L. formosana*.

L. orientalis ▣♤ (Oriental sweet gum). Small, slow-growing, bushy tree with palmately 5-lobed, mid-green leaves, to 7–10cm (3–4in) across, turning yellow and orange in autumn. ↕6m (20ft), ↔ 4m (12ft). S.W. Asia. ❄❄❄ (borderline)

L. styraciflua ♤ (Sweet gum). Broadly conical tree with young shoots often with corky wings. Palmately 5- or 7-lobed, glossy, mid-green leaves, to 15cm (6in) across, turn orange, red, and purple in autumn. ↕25m (80ft), ↔ 12m (40ft). E. USA, Mexico. ❄❄❄. **'Burgundy'** has dark red-purple autumn colour. **'Golden Treasure'** ▣ is slow-growing, with mid-green leaves margined dark yellow, becoming yellow-margined red-purple in autumn; ↕10m (30ft), ↔ 6m (20ft). **'Lane Roberts'** has dark blackish red leaves over a long period in autumn. **'Moonbeam'** is slow-growing, with creamy yellow leaves turning red, yellow, and purple in autumn; ↕10m (30ft), ↔ 6m (20ft). **'Palo Alto'** has orange-red autumn colour. **'Variegata'** has leaves striped and mottled yellow; ↕15m (50ft), ↔ 8m (25ft). **'Worplesdon'** ▣ has deeply lobed leaves turning purple then orange-yellow in autumn.

▷**Liquorice** see *Glycyrrhiza glabra*
Wild see *Astragalus glycyphyllos*

LIRIODENDRON

Tulip tree

MAGNOLIACEAE

Genus of 2 species of deciduous trees from woodland in China, Vietnam, and North America. They are cultivated for their stately habit and curiously shaped, alternate leaves, which colour well in autumn. The solitary, cup-shaped flowers, inconspicuous from a distance, add interest in summer, but are not produced on young plants; they are followed by cone-like fruits. Excellent grown as specimen trees.

L

Linum narbonense

Liquidambar orientalis

Liquidambar styraciflua 'Worplesdon' (inset: leaf detail)

Liriodendron tulipifera

- **HARDINESS** Fully hardy.
- **CULTIVATION** Grow in moderately fertile, preferably slightly acid, moist but well-drained soil in full sun or partial shade. Pruning group 1.
- **PROPAGATION** Sow seed (of species only) in containers in a cold frame in autumn. Graft in early spring, or bud in late summer.
- **PESTS AND DISEASES** Leaf spot and *Verticillium* wilt may be a problem.

L. chinense ♀ (Chinese tulip tree). Vigorous, broadly columnar, deciduous tree with saddle-shaped, dark green leaves, to 15cm (6in) long, turning yellow in autumn; the leaves are more or less square, and indistinctly lobed at the tips, hollowed at the bases, with a pointed lobe at each side. Cup-shaped green flowers, 4cm (1½in) long, with yellow veins, are produced in midsummer. ↕ 25m (80ft), ↔ 12m (40ft). China, Vietnam. ❄❄❄

L. tulipifera ■ ♀ (Tulip tree). Vigorous, broadly columnar to conical, deciduous tree with saddle-shaped, dark green leaves, to 15cm (6in) long, that turn yellow in autumn; the leaves are more or less square, and lobed at the tips, hollowed at the bases, with a pointed lobe at each side. Cup-shaped, pale green flowers, 6cm (2½in) long, orange-banded at the bases, are borne in midsummer. ↕ 30m (100ft), ↔ 15m (50ft). E. North America. ❄❄❄. **'Aureomarginatum'** ■ has leaves with broad, golden yellow margins; ↕ 20m (70ft), ↔ 10m (30ft). **'Fastigiatum'** ◊ is narrowly conical, with upright branches; ↕ 20m (70ft), ↔ 8m (25ft).

Liriodendron tulipifera 'Aureomarginatum'

L

LIRIOPE

Lilyturf

CONVALLARIACEAE/LILIACEAE

Genus of 5 or 6 species of tufted, rhizomatous and tuberous, evergreen and semi-evergreen perennials, found in usually acid woodland habitats in China, Vietnam, Taiwan, and Japan. They have arching, linear, grass-like, radical leaves, forming dense clumps or mats. Small, ovoid to spherical flowers, opening only slightly, are clustered in short, dense spikes or racemes, and are followed by black berries. Grow in a border or as ground cover.

- **HARDINESS** Fully hardy.
- **CULTIVATION** Grow in light, moderately fertile, preferably acid, moist but well-drained soil in partial or full shade, sheltered from cold, drying winds. Tolerant of drought.
- **PROPAGATION** Sow seed in containers outdoors, or divide, both in spring.
- **PESTS AND DISEASES** Young growth is susceptible to slug damage.

***L. exiliflora* 'Ariaka-janshige'**, syn. *L. exiliflora* 'Silvery Sunproof'. Clump-forming, evergreen, rhizomatous perennial with linear, mid-green leaves, to 40cm (16in) long, striped white and gold. Lax racemes of pale violet-purple flowers, to 6mm (¼in) across, are borne on violet-brown stems in late summer. ↕ 22–30cm (9–12in), ↔ 30cm (12in). ❄❄❄

***L. exiliflora* 'Silvery Sunproof'** see *L. exiliflora* 'Ariaka-janshige'.

L. graminifolia* var. *densiflora see *L. muscari.*

L. muscari ■ syn. *L. graminifolia* var. *densiflora*, *L. platyphylla*. Stout, tufted, evergreen, tuberous perennial with dense clumps of linear to strap-shaped, dark green leaves, 25–45cm (10–18in) long. From early to late autumn, purple-green stems bear dense spikes of bright violet-mauve flowers, 5–8mm (¼–⅜in) across. ↕ 30cm (12in), ↔ 45cm (18in). China, Taiwan, Japan. ❄❄❄. **'John Burch'** has gold-variegated foliage, and bears tall spikes of large flowers. **'Majestic'** has narrower leaves, and produces tall, sometimes fused and flattened spikes of rich lavender-blue flowers. **'Monroe White'** produces numerous green-stalked racemes of white flowers, to 9mm (⅜in) across. Requires full shade.

L. platyphylla see *L. muscari.*

L. spicata, syn. *Ophiopogon spicatus*. Rhizomatous, semi-evergreen perennial forming a dense mat of grassy, dark green leaves, 20–40cm (8–16in) long, with tiny marginal teeth. Violet-brown stems bear racemes of pale violet to white flowers, 7–8mm (¼–⅜in) across, in late summer. ↕ 25cm (10in), ↔ 45cm (18in). China, Vietnam, Japan. ❄❄❄

Liriope muscari

▷ ***Lisianthius*** see *Eustoma*
L. russellianus see *E. grandiflorum*

LITHOCARPUS

FAGACEAE

Genus of about 300 species of oak-like, evergreen trees and shrubs from forest and mountain slopes, mainly in E. and S.E. Asia, with one species in the W. USA. Leaves are alternate, leathery, and mostly entire, but occasionally toothed. Cylindrical male and female flowers (either unisexual or bisexual) are borne in erect spikes at or near the ends of the branches, and are followed by clusters of acorns, usually closely packed on the spikes. Cultivated for their handsome foliage, they are effective both as specimen trees and in an open site in a woodland garden.

- **HARDINESS** Fully hardy to frost hardy.
- **CULTIVATION** Grow in moderately fertile, acid to neutral, moist but well-drained soil in full sun or partial shade. In frost-prone areas, shelter from cold, drying winds. Pruning group 1.
- **PROPAGATION** Sow seed in containers in a cold frame in autumn.
- **PESTS AND DISEASES** Trouble free.

L. densiflorus ♀ (Tanbark oak). Spreading, evergreen tree with oblong, toothed, prominently veined, leathery, dark green leaves, to 12cm (5in) long, downy at first, becoming hairless and glossy with age. In summer, produces tiny, cylindrical white flowers in upright spikes, to 10cm (4in) long, sometimes followed by solitary or paired acorns, to 2.5cm (1in) long, in autumn. ↕↔ 10m (30ft). USA (Oregon, California). ❄❄❄

L. henryi ■ ♤ Slow-growing, broadly conical, evergreen tree with narrowly oblong to elliptic-oblong, tapered, entire, leathery leaves, to 25cm (10in) long, pale green at first, later dark green. Tiny white flowers are borne in upright spikes, to 15cm (6in) long, in autumn or winter. Bears clustered acorns, to 2.5cm (1in) long, in upright spikes in winter. ↕↔ 10m (30ft). China. ❄❄

Lithocarpus henryi (inset: leaf detail)

LITHODORA

BORAGINACEAE

Genus of about 7 species of low-growing, spreading or upright, evergreen shrubs and subshrubs, found in scrub, thickets, and woodland margins, and on mountains, from S.W. Europe to S. Greece, Turkey, and Algeria. They are cultivated for their 5-lobed, funnel-shaped, blue or white flowers, produced in leafy, terminal cymes, mainly in summer. Leaves are linear, lance-shaped, elliptic, or obovate, and hairy. The hardiest species are ideal for an open position in a rock garden or raised bed. Where temperatures fall below -5°C (23°F), grow frost-hardy species in an alpine house.

- **HARDINESS** Fully hardy to frost hardy; *L. zahnii* is hardy to at least -7°C (20°F).
- **CULTIVATION** Grow most species in well-drained, ideally alkaline to neutral soil, in full sun; *L. diffusa* 'Heavenly Blue' needs acid, humus-rich soil. In an alpine house, grow in a mix of equal parts loam, leaf mould, and sharp sand. Pruning group 8; or 10, after flowering.
- **PROPAGATION** Take semi-ripe cuttings in summer. Remove rooted suckers of *L. oleifolia* in spring.
- **PESTS AND DISEASES** Prone to aphids and red spider mites under glass.

***L. diffusa* 'Heavenly Blue'** ■ syn. *Lithospermum diffusum* 'Heavenly Blue'. Prostrate, spreading, many-branched, evergreen shrub with elliptic to narrowly oblong, deep green leaves, 1–3.5cm (½–1½in) long, hairy above and beneath. Bears a profusion of deep azure-blue flowers, 1cm (½in) across, in terminal cymes over long periods in late spring and summer. ↕ 15cm (6in), ↔ to 60cm (24in) or more. ***
L. graminifolia see *Moltkia suffruticosa.*
L. x intermedia see *Moltkia* x *intermedia.*
L. oleifolia ■ syn. *Lithospermum oleifolium.* Semi-upright, loosely

Lithodora diffusa 'Heavenly Blue'

Lithodora oleifolia

branched, suckering, evergreen shrub with obovate to oblong, dull, dark green leaves, 1cm (½in) long, silky-hairy beneath. Bears loose, terminal cymes of 3–7 sky-blue flowers, 9mm (⅜in) across, opening from pink-tinted buds in early summer. ↕ 20cm (8in), ↔ 30cm (12in) or more. E. Pyrenees. ***
L. rosmarinifolia, syn. *Lithospermum rosmarinifolium.* Domed, tufted, evergreen subshrub with upright, branching stems and lance-shaped to linear, dark green leaves, 2.5–6cm (1–2½in) long, grey-bristly beneath. Produces loose, open, terminal cymes of gentian-blue flowers, 2cm (¾in) across, in summer. ↕ 30cm (12in), ↔ 40cm (16in). S. Italy, Algeria. **
L. zahnii, syn. *Lithospermum zahnii.* Upright, many-branched, evergreen shrub with linear or narrowly oblong, leathery, dark grey-green leaves, to 4cm (1½in) long, grey-bristly beneath. Produces few-flowered, terminal cymes of blue or white flowers, 1.5cm (½in) across, in succession during summer, then intermittently until mid-autumn. ↕ 30cm (12in), ↔ 40cm (16in). S. Greece. **

LITHOPHRAGMA

Woodland star

SAXIFRAGACEAE

Genus of about 9 species of rosette-forming perennials from woodland in W. North America. They have fibrous rootstocks with basal bulbils, and kidney-shaped to rounded, palmately 3- to 5-lobed leaves, the lobes often toothed or further lobed. Simple or branched, upright stems bear racemes of small, campion-like, 5-petalled flowers in late spring. Grow in a peat bed, woodland garden, or rock garden.

Lithophragma parviflorum

- **HARDINESS** Fully hardy.
- **CULTIVATION** Grow in moderately fertile, humus-rich, sharply drained soil in partial or deep shade.
- **PROPAGATION** Sow seed in containers outdoors in autumn. Divide, or separate bulbils, in spring or autumn.
- **PESTS AND DISEASES** New growth may be eaten by slugs in spring.

L. parviflorum ■ (Prairie star). Clump-forming perennial producing basal bulbils and rounded, palmately 3- to 5-lobed, hairy, dark green, basal leaves, 1–3cm (½–1¼in) long. In late spring, unbranched stems produce open racemes of 4–14 nodding, white or pale pink flowers, 3cm (1¼in) across, with 3-lobed petals. ↕ 15cm (6in), ↔ to 30cm (12in). USA (California). ***

LITHOPS

Living stones, Stone plant

AIZOACEAE

Genus of about 40 species of dwarf, almost stemless, succulent perennials occurring among rocks and pebbles in semi-desert regions of Namibia and South Africa. They have thick, soft rootstocks that produce usually inversely cone-shaped "bodies", each composed of a pair of very fleshy leaves, 2–3cm (¾–1¼in) across, with a fissure usually running along much of their lengths. On the upper surface of each leaf is a window-like, translucent panel of dots, lines, or patches. Solitary, occasionally 2 or 3, daisy-like flowers, usually 2–3cm (¾–1¼in) across, sometimes larger, emerge from each fissure, mainly from midsummer to mid-autumn. They are followed by small, ovoid, fleshy capsules, containing tiny seeds. In areas where temperatures drop below 12°C (54°F), grow in a warm greenhouse or as houseplants; in warmer climates, grow in a desert garden.

- **HARDINESS** Frost tender.
- **CULTIVATION** Under glass, grow in standard cactus compost with added leaf mould, in full light. From early summer to late autumn, water freely and apply a half-strength balanced liquid fertilizer monthly. Keep dry at other times. Outdoors, grow in moderately fertile, sharply drained soil in full sun. See also pp.48–49.
- **PROPAGATION** Sow seed at 19–24°C (66–75°F) in spring or early summer, or remove offsets in early summer.
- **PESTS AND DISEASES** Susceptible to aphids and mealybugs when flowering.

L. aucampiae. Clump-forming succulent with pairs of reddish to sandy brown or ochre leaves forming inversely cone-shaped bodies, with darker marks on the flat upper surfaces. Yellow flowers are produced from late summer to mid-autumn. ↕ 3cm (1¼in), ↔ to 10cm (4in). South Africa (Northern Cape, Limpopo, Mpumalanga). ❀ (min. 12°C/54°F)
L. bella see *L. karasmontana* subsp. *bella.*
L. dinteri ■ Clustering succulent with pairs of reddish or greyish yellow leaves forming inversely cone-shaped bodies with convex upper surfaces. Each leaf has a conspicuous panel with 5–15 red spots. Bears yellow flowers from late summer to mid-autumn. ↕ 3cm (1¼in), ↔ 10cm (4in). Namibia, South Africa (Northern Cape, Western Cape). ❀ (min. 12°C/54°F)
L. dorotheae ■ Clustering succulent with pairs of unequally sized, beige or buff leaves forming inversely cone-shaped bodies with almost flat or convex upper surfaces. Each leaf has a translucent grey-green or olive panel marked with red lines and dots. Yellow flowers are produced in late summer. ↕ 2–3cm (¾–1¼in), ↔ 10cm (4in). South Africa (Northern Cape). ❀ (min. 12°C/54°F)
L. hookeri, syn. *L. turbiniformis.* Variable, clump-forming succulent with pairs of brown, buff, or grey leaves forming ovoid bodies with warty, flat or convex upper surfaces, each with a deeply grooved, rich brown panel. Red-tipped, straw-coloured flowers, 3–4.5cm (1¼–1½in) across, are borne from late summer to mid-autumn. ↕ to 2.5cm (1in), ↔ 15cm (6in) or more. South Africa (Northern Cape, Eastern Cape). ❀ (min. 12°C/54°F)
L. insularis. Solitary or clump-forming succulent with pairs of greenish brown leaves united into ovoid bodies with flat to concave upper surfaces. Each leaf has a translucent, dark green panel pitted with large red dots or lines. Bears yellow flowers, to 4cm (1½in) across, from late summer to mid-autumn. ↕ 1.5cm (½in), ↔ 3–8cm (1¼–3in) or more. South Africa (Western Cape, Eastern Cape). ❀ (min. 12°C/54°F)
L. julii. Clump-forming succulent with pairs of faintly red-tinged, whitish grey to dark grey leaves forming spherical bodies with flat to slightly concave, furrowed upper surfaces and brown-marked fissures. Each leaf has dark brown to pale green panels with broad markings and red dots. White flowers are borne from late summer to mid-autumn. ↕ 3cm (1¼in), ↔ indefinite. Namibia, South Africa (Northern Cape, Western Cape). ❀ (min. 12°C/54°F)
L. karasmontana ■ Clump-forming succulent with pairs of pale red-brown leaves forming inversely cone-shaped bodies, with dark brown markings and wrinkles on the flat to convex upper surfaces. Bears white flowers, 2.5–4cm (1–1½in) across, from late summer to mid-autumn. ↕ to 4cm (1½in), ↔ indefinite. Namibia, South Africa (Northern Cape, Western Cape).

Lithops dinteri

Lithops dorotheae

Lithops karasmontana

Lithops lesliei var. *hornii*

Lithops pseudotruncatella var. *dendritica*

Lithops schwantesii

❄ (min. 12°C/54°F). **subsp. *bella***, syn. *L. bella*, has yellowish brown leaves, with dull olive-green marks on the convex, uneven upper surfaces; ↕ to 3cm (1¼in).
L. kuibisensis see *L. schwantesii*.
L. lesliei. Clump-forming succulent with pairs of grey-green to buff to pale terracotta leaves, that form inversely cone-shaped bodies with convex upper surfaces. Each leaf has a pale to dark olive-green panel, with transparent dots. Yellow, rarely white flowers are borne from late summer to mid-autumn. ↕ to 1.5cm (½in), ↔ to 4cm (1½in). South Africa (Northern Cape, Free State, Limpopo, Mpumalanga). ❄ (min. 12°C/54°F). **var. *hornii*** ■ has light to dark brown or greenish brown leaves, the upper surfaces with tiny panels and irregular channels of opaque, dark greyish brown to reddish brown. Flowers are yellow and up to 4cm (1½in) across. ↕ to 3.5cm (1½in), ↔ 4cm (1½in). South Africa (Northern Cape). **var. *rubrobrunnea*** has reddish brown bodies, with greenish brown panels on flat to slightly convex upper surfaces. ↕ 3cm (1¼in), ↔ 6–8cm (2½–3in). South Africa (Limpopo, Mpumalanga).
L. marmorata ■ Mainly solitary succulent with a pair of pale grey or beige, sometimes grey-green or lilac leaves forming an inversely cone-shaped body, with greyish green lines on the slightly convex, deeply fissured upper surface. Scented white flowers are produced from late summer to mid-autumn. ↕ 3cm (1¼in), ↔ 5cm (2in) or more. South Africa (Northern Cape). ❄ (min. 12°C/54°F)
L. optica. Mat-forming succulent with pairs of sometimes uneven, greyish purple to grey-green leaves forming ovoid bodies, with convex, deeply fissured upper surfaces and greenish white panels. From late summer to mid-autumn, bears white, often pink-tipped flowers. ↕ 3cm (1¼in), ↔ indefinite. Namibia, South Africa (Northern Cape, Western Cape). ❄ (min. 12°C/54°F)
L. otzeniana. Clump-forming succulent. Pairs of greyish violet leaves form inversely cone-shaped bodies, with pale green to violet panels on the convex, deep-fissured upper surfaces. From late summer to mid-autumn, bears bright yellow flowers, 2cm (¾in) across. ↕ 3cm (1¼in), ↔ indefinite. South Africa (Northern Cape). ❄ (min. 12°C/54°F)
L. pseudotruncatella* var. *dendritica ■ syn. *L. pseudotruncatella* var. *pulmonuncula*. Usually solitary succulent producing a pair of unequal, brownish grey leaves that form an inversely cone-shaped body, with an indistinct panel lined and dotted with brownish green. From late summer to mid-autumn, produces golden yellow flowers, to 3.5cm (1½in) across. ↕↔ to 3cm (1¼in). Namibia, South Africa (Northern Cape, Western Cape). ❄ (min. 12°C/54°F). **var. *pulmonuncula*** see *L. pseudotruncatella* var. *dendritica*.
L. schwantesii ■ syn. *L. kuibisensis*, *L. schwantesii* var. *kuibisensis*. Very variable, mat-forming succulent with pairs of leaves forming inversely cone-shaped bodies, varying from light to dark grey, to yellowish green, orange, or reddish brown, with pink margins and dark green or pinkish red dots on the flat to slightly convex, often blue-tinged upper surfaces. Bright yellow flowers are borne from late summer to mid-autumn. The "type" of the species (pictured) has silvery blue-grey bodies, with red or blue-grey marks on the flat upper surfaces. ↕ 4cm (1½in), ↔ 15cm (6in). Namibia, South Africa (Northern Cape, Western Cape). ❄ (min. 12°C/54°F). **var. *kuibisensis*** see *L. schwantesii*.
L. turbiniformis see *L. hookeri*.
L. vallis-mariae. Clump-forming succulent with pairs of yellowish green to bluish white leaves forming inversely cone-shaped bodies, with slightly convex or flat upper surfaces marked with a network of grey lines or dots. Produces yellow flowers, 2.5–3.5cm (1–1½in) across, in summer. ↕ to 2–4cm (¾–1½in), ↔ 5–10cm (2–4in). Namibia. ❄ (min. 12°C/54°F)

Lithops marmorata

▷ ***Lithospermum diffusum* 'Heavenly Blue'** see *Lithodora diffusa* 'Heavenly Blue'
▷ ***Lithospermum doerfleri*** see *Moltkia doerfleri*
▷ ***Lithospermum graminifolium*** see *Moltkia suffruticosa*
▷ ***Lithospermum oleifolium*** see *Lithodora oleifolia*
▷ ***Lithospermum purpureocaeruleum*** see *Buglossoides purpurocaerulea*
▷ ***Lithospermum rosmarinifolium*** see *Lithodora rosmarinifolia*
▷ ***Lithospermum zahnii*** see *Lithodora zahnii*
▷ ***Litocarpus cordifolia*** see *Aptenia cordifolia*
▷ ***Litsea glauca*** see *Neolitsea sericea*
▷ **Little pickles** see *Othonna capensis*

LITTONIA

LILIACEAE/COLCHICACEAE

Genus of 8 species of tuberous, perennial, tendril climbers occurring in scrub and sandy, often coastal areas in Senegal, South Africa, and the Arabian Peninsula. They are cultivated for their pendent, bell-shaped flowers, which are borne in summer. Ovate-lance-shaped to linear leaves are alternate or opposite on the upper parts of the stems, and often almost whorled on the lower parts; they taper to tendrils at the tips. In frost-prone areas, grow in a temperate greenhouse or conservatory. In warmer areas, grow among low shrubs.

- **HARDINESS** Frost tender.
- **CULTIVATION** Plant tubers 10–15cm (4–6in) deep in autumn or early spring. Under glass, grow in loam-based potting compost (JI No.2) with added grit, in full light. As growth begins, water freely, then apply a half-strength balanced liquid fertilizer every 3–4 weeks. Reduce watering as the leaves fade, then keep just moist in winter. The brittle tubers resent disturbance, so pot on only when necessary. Outdoors, grow in moderately fertile, humus-rich, well-drained soil in full sun. Stems require support.
- **PROPAGATION** Sow seed at 19–24°C (66–75°F) in spring, or divide tubers with care when dormant.
- **PESTS AND DISEASES** Trouble free.

L. modesta ■ Tuberous tendril climber with slender stems bearing whorled or alternate, linear to ovate-lance-shaped, mid-green leaves, to 15cm (6in) long, with tendrils at their tips. Pendent, bell-shaped orange flowers, to 5cm (2in) long, are produced singly from the leaf axils in summer. ↕ 1–2m (3–6ft). South Africa (Limpopo, Mpumalanga, KwaZulu/Natal, Free State). ❄ (min. 8°C/46°F)

▷ **Living baseball** see *Euphorbia obesa*
▷ **Living granite** see *Pleiospilos*
▷ **Living rock** see *Ariocarpus fissuratus*
▷ **Living stones** see *Lithops*

Littonia modesta

L

LIVISTONA

ARECACEAE/PALMAE

Genus of about 28 species of single-stemmed palms, found in habitats ranging from streambanks and swamps to woodland, rainforest, and inland gorges, in the warmer parts of Asia and Australasia. Fan-shaped leaves are borne in often dense, terminal heads, and bowl-shaped, 3-petalled flowers are produced in panicles between them. In frost-prone climates, grow in a cool or warm greenhouse, or as houseplants. In warmer regions, they are suitable for growing as specimen plants.

- **HARDINESS** Frost tender.
- **CULTIVATION** Under glass, grow in loam-based potting compost (JI No.3) in full or bright indirect light. In the growing season, water freely and apply a balanced liquid fertilizer every month. Water sparingly in winter. Outdoors, grow in fertile, moist but well-drained soil in full sun or partial shade.
- **PROPAGATION** Sow seed at 23°C (73°F) in spring.
- **PESTS AND DISEASES** Red spider mites and scale insects may be troublesome under glass.

L. australis ▣ 🌴 (Australian fan palm, Cabbage palm). Large palm with an erect, robust trunk that is initially covered with a skirt of dead leaves and rough or almost prickly fibres. Long, spiny leaf-stalks support longer, lustrous, deep green blades, to 1.7m (5½ft) long, divided for two-thirds of their length into many linear lobes, often arching at the tips. From spring to summer, cream flowers are produced in panicles as long as, or shorter than the leaves; they are followed by spherical, brownish red to black fruit, 2cm (¾in) across. ↕ to 25m (80ft), ↔ to 5m (15ft). Coastal forest in E. Australia. ❀ (min. 3–5°C/37–41°F)

L. chinensis ▣ 🌴 (Chinese fan palm). Medium-sized palm with an erect, robust trunk swollen at the base, the upper part covered with fibrous leaf bases, at least at first. Glossy, rich green leaves, to 2m (6ft) long, with shorter, spiny leaf-stalks, are divided for up to two-thirds of their length into many linear, pendent segments. Cream flowers are borne in panicles to 1m (3ft) or more long, usually in summer, followed by ovoid to spherical, glossy, blue-green to grey-pink fruit, 2–2.5cm (¾–1in) across. ↕ to 12m (40ft), ↔ to 5m (15ft). S. Japan (including Ryukyu and Bonin Islands) to S. Taiwan. ❀ (min. 3–5°C/37–41°F)

L. mariae 🌴 (Red fan palm). Tall palm with a slim trunk, swollen at the base, and bearing old leaf bases, at least in the upper part. Spiny leaf-stalks, 2m (6ft) long, support prominently ribbed blades, 2m (6ft) long, divided to about half their length into linear, pendent lobes, initially flushed red to bronze-red, maturing to bluish green. In spring and summer, bears cream to pale yellow flowers in erect panicles, shorter than the leaves, followed by spherical, glossy black fruit, 2cm (¾in) across. ↕ to 30m (100ft), ↔ to 8m (25ft). C. Australia. ❀ (min. 13–15°C/55–59°F)

L. rotundifolia 🌴 Medium-sized to large palm with a slim trunk bearing prominent leaf scars. Spiny leaf-stalks, 2m (6ft) long, support shorter, rounded, lustrous, deep green blades, divided for about two-thirds of their length into many linear, rigid, shallowly notched lobes. Cream flowers are produced in panicles shorter than the leaves, usually in summer, and are followed by spherical, scarlet fruit, 2cm (¾in) across, which ripen to black. ↕ to 25m (80ft), ↔ to 8m (25ft). Philippines, Malaysia (Sabah), Indonesia (Sulawesi, Moluccas). ❀ (min. 13–15°C/55–59°F)

Livistona chinensis

Livistona australis

▷**Lizard plant** see *Tetrastigma voinierianum*
▷**Lizard tail** see *Crassula muscosa*

LLOYDIA

LILIACEAE

Genus of approximately 12 species of bulbous perennials from damp upland meadows and screes in temperate and arctic areas of the N. hemisphere. They have narrowly linear leaves and solitary or paired, bell-shaped flowers borne in spring or summer. Grow in an alpine house, bulb frame, or open rock garden.

- **HARDINESS** Fully hardy.
- **CULTIVATION** Plant bulbs 7cm (3in) deep in autumn. Grow in poor, peaty, humus-rich, moist but sharply drained soil in partial shade. In an alpine house use a mix of 1 part loam, 1 part leaf mould or peat, and 2 parts grit.
- **PROPAGATION** Sow seed in containers in an open frame in spring.
- **PESTS AND DISEASES** Trouble free.

L. graeca see *Gagea graeca*.

L. serotina (Snowdon lily). Bulbous perennial with erect, thread-like leaves, to 20cm (8in) long. In late spring and early summer, upright stems bear solitary or paired, upward-facing, bell-shaped white flowers, to 1.5cm (½in) long, with purple-red veins and pale yellow bases. ↕ 5–15cm (2–6in), ↔ 5cm (2in). Arctic and European mountains, Himalayas, S.W. China. ❄❄❄

LOASA

LOASACEAE

Genus of about 100 species of usually bushy, occasionally spreading or twining annuals, biennials, perennials, and subshrubs from open habitats, often by roads or on gravelly slopes, in Mexico and temperate South America. They have opposite or alternate, entire to palmately lobed, sometimes 3-palmate leaves, and bear nodding, yellow, white, or red flowers singly or in racemes. Each flower has 5 boat-shaped petals, which are inflated in appearance, and nectar scales banded in contrasting colours. Some species are covered in stinging hairs. Best in containers on a patio; grow alpine species in an alpine house.

- **HARDINESS** Frost hardy to half hardy.
- **CULTIVATION** Grow in fertile, reliably moist but well-drained soil in full sun.
- **PROPAGATION** Sow seed at 13–18°C (55–64°F) in mid-spring or *in situ* in late spring.
- **PESTS AND DISEASES** Trouble free.

***L. triphylla* var. *volcanica*.** Erect, bushy to loosely twining, densely glandular-hairy annual, with shallowly to deeply 3- to 5-lobed, coarsely toothed leaves, 7–15cm (3–6in) across, becoming less lobed on the upper parts of the stems. In summer, bears open, leafy racemes of nodding, hooded white flowers, to 5cm (2in) across, each with golden yellow nectar scales, crossbanded red and white, that form a central disc with concentric rings. Covered in stinging hairs. ↕ 60–90cm (24–36in), ↔ to 30cm (12in). Ecuador. ❄❄

▷***Lobeira macdougallii*** see *Nopalxochia macdougallii*

LOBELIA

CAMPANULACEAE/LOBELIACEAE

Genus of about 370 species of annuals, perennials (including some aquatics), and shrubs, found in tropical and temperate areas worldwide, especially in North, Central, and South America. Their habitats range from marshes, wet meadows, and riverbanks, to woodland, well-drained hilly and mountainous slopes, and deserts. Valued for their often brightly coloured flowers, lobelias vary enormously, but all have simple, alternate, often stalkless leaves and 2-lipped, tubular flowers, each with 5 lobes, the upper 2 lobes often erect, the lower 3 often spreading and fan-like; the calyx tubes are sometimes swollen. The flowers are usually borne in terminal racemes or panicles, but may also be solitary. The popular Bowden Hybrids, sometimes grouped under *L.* x *speciosa*, are perennials with ovate-lance-shaped, pointed leaves, 10–15cm (4–6in) long, which are sometimes red-purple with matching stems. Their flowers,

Lobelia 'Bees' Flame'

L

Lobelia 'Cherry Ripe'

2.5–3.5cm (1–1½in) across, are borne in terminal racemes, 15–20cm (6–8in) long, from midsummer to early autumn.

Perennials are effective beside water, or in a mixed border. Annuals are suitable for edging, or for a hanging basket or window-box. Aquatic species are useful in a wildlife pool. The shrubby and tree-like species are seldom grown. All parts may cause severe discomfort if ingested (although *L. erinus* is thought to be non-toxic); contact with the milky sap may irritate skin.

• **HARDINESS** Fully hardy to frost tender. *L. tupa* is hardy to -10°C (14°F).

• **CULTIVATION** Grow in deep, fertile, reliably moist soil in full sun or partial shade. To improve the flowering performance of annuals, apply a balanced liquid fertilizer every 2 weeks in spring and early summer, then a nitrogen-free fertilizer every 2 weeks from midsummer onwards. In frost-prone areas, protect half-hardy perennials with a dry winter mulch. Grow aquatics in baskets of acid soil at the margins of a pool or stream.

• **PROPAGATION** Sow seed at 13–18°C (55–64°F): sow seed of annuals in late winter, of perennials as soon as ripe.

Lobelia erinus 'Crystal Palace'

Divide border perennials in spring, aquatics in summer. Take bud cuttings of *L. cardinalis* in midsummer.

• **PESTS AND DISEASES** Susceptible to slugs and leaf blotch, the latter especially on *L. siphilitica*. Crowns may rot in damp, mild conditions. *L. cardinalis* may be affected by viruses.

L. angulata see *Pratia angulata*.

***L.* 'Bees' Flame'** ▣ Clump-forming, slightly hairy perennial with reddish purple stems and linear-lance-shaped, reddish purple leaves, to 15cm (6in) long. In mid- and late summer, produces racemes, to 45cm (18in) long, of tubular, 2-lipped, bright crimson flowers, 3.5–4.5cm (1½–1¾in) across. ↕75cm (30in), ↔ 30cm (12in). ✻✻✻

L. cardinalis, syn. *L. fulgens, L. splendens* (Cardinal flower). Short-lived, clump-forming perennial, with short rhizomes, often reddish purple stems, and narrowly ovate to oblong-lance-shaped, toothed, often glossy, bronze-tinged, bright green leaves, to 10cm (4in) long. In summer and early autumn, bears racemes, 35cm (14in) long, of tubular, 2-lipped, brilliant scarlet-red flowers, 5cm (2in) long, with

Lobelia erinus Cascade Series

Lobelia erinus 'Lilac Fountain'

reddish purple bracts. ↕90cm (36in), ↔ 30cm (12in). E. Canada (New Brunswick) to USA (Michigan to Florida to Texas, California), Mexico. ✻✻✻. **f. *alba*** has white flowers. **f. *rosea*** has pink flowers.

***L.* 'Cherry Ripe'** ▣ Bowden Hybrid with mid-green leaves, often suffused maroon. Bears tubular, 2-lipped, cherry-red flowers in mid- and late summer. ↕90cm (36in), ↔ 30cm (12in). ✻✻✻

***L.* 'Dark Crusader'.** Bowden Hybrid with maroon stems and leaves. Bears tubular, 2-lipped, velvety, deep red flowers in mid- and late summer. ↕60–90cm (24–36in), ↔ 30cm (12in). ✻✻✻

L. dortmanna (Water lobelia). Partly submerged aquatic perennial producing hollow, almost leafless stems and a mat of rosette-forming, oblong, dark green leaves, 3–7cm (1¼–3in) long. Pendent, tubular, 2-lipped, pale blue to pale violet flowers, to 2cm (¾in) long, are borne in loose racemes, 5cm (2in) long, above the water in summer. ↕60cm (24in), ↔ 30cm (12in). W. Europe, North America. ✻✻✻

***L. erinus* cultivars.** Low-growing, bushy, or trailing perennials, grown as annuals, with tiny, ovate to narrowly linear, or linear-obovate, toothed, mid- to dark green or bronze-flushed leaves, 1.5cm (½in) long. From summer to autumn, they bear small, loose racemes, 5cm (2in) long, of tubular, 2-lipped, blue, violet, white, pink, red, or purple flowers, to 1cm (½in) across, with white or yellow eyes and broad, fan-shaped lower lips. ↕10–23cm (4–9in), ↔ 10–15cm (4–6in). ✻. Cultivars of **Cascade Series** ▣ are trailing, with carmine-red, violet-blue, blue, pink, or white flowers; ↕15cm (6in). **'Cobalt Blue'** is compact, with very early, intensely mid-blue flowers; ↕to 12cm (5in). **'Crystal Palace'** ▣ is compact, and has dark blue flowers and dark green foliage; ↕to 10cm (4in). **'Lilac Fountain'** ▣ is trailing, and profusely bears lilac-pink flowers; ↕15cm (6in). **Moon Series** cultivars are early-flowering, with white, blue-and-white, or deep blue flowers. **'Mrs. Clibran'** is compact, with brilliant blue, white-eyed flowers; ↕10–15cm (4–6in). Cultivars of **Palace Series** have neat, blue to dark blue or white flowers, some with white eyes; ↕to 12cm (5in). Cultivars of **Regatta Series** are trailing, and bear blue, pink, crimson, or white flowers over a very long season. They bloom

Lobelia erinus 'Sapphire'

early; ↕to 20cm (8in). **Riviera Series** cultivars bear very early flowers in lilac-blue, sky-blue, or a mottled blue with picotee margins; ↕10–15cm (4–6in). **'Rosamund'** is compact, and produces white-eyed, cherry-red flowers; ↕10–15cm (4–6in). **'Sapphire'** ▣ is trailing, with bright blue, white-eyed flowers; ↕to 15cm (6in).

L. fulgens see *L. cardinalis*.

L.* x *gerardii see *L.* x *speciosa*.

***L.* 'Illumination'.** Clump-forming perennial with short rhizomes, downy, dark red stems, and linear-lance-shaped, dark green leaves, to 15cm (6in) long. In summer, bears tubular, 2-lipped scarlet flowers, 2.5–3cm (1–1¼in) across, in one-sided racemes, to 35cm (14in) long. ↕90cm (36in), ↔ 30cm (12in). ✻✻

L. laxiflora*.** Spreading, hairy, sub-shrubby, rhizomatous perennial with arching, red-tinted stems bearing linear-lance-shaped to elliptic, finely toothed, light green leaves, to 8cm (3in) long, with long, sharp points. In late spring and summer, bears semi-pendent, tubular, 2-lipped, red and yellow flowers, 4cm (1½in) long, usually singly, from the upper leaf axils. ↕to 90cm (36in), ↔ 2m (6ft) or more. Mexico, Central America. ✻✻ (borderline). **var. *angustifolia ▣ bears linear leaves, to 7cm (3in) long; ↕to 60cm (24in), ↔ 45cm (18in); USA (Arizona).

L. lutea see *Monopsis lutea*.

L. paludosa (Swamp lobelia). Marginal aquatic perennial bearing inversely lance-shaped, bright mid-green leaves, 15–22cm (6–9in) long. In summer, produces tubular, 2-lipped, pale blue flowers, to 1.5cm (½in) long, in racemes

Lobelia laxiflora var. *angustifolia*

L

Lobelia x *speciosa* 'Vedrariensis'

to 30cm (12in) long. ↕ 30–120cm (12–48in), ↔ 90cm (36in). USA (Georgia, Florida). ✻✻✻
L. pedunculata see *Pratia pedunculata.*
L. perpusilla see *Pratia perpusilla.*
***L.* 'Queen Victoria'.** Clump-forming, short-lived perennial with deep purple-red stems and lance-shaped, deep purple-red leaves, 10–15cm (4–6in) long. From late summer to mid-autumn, bears tubular, 2-lipped scarlet flowers, 2.5–3.5cm (1–1½in) long, in slightly one-sided racemes, to 45cm (18in) long. ↕ 90cm (36in), ↔ 30cm (12in). ✻✻✻
L. richardsonii. Bushy then trailing, evergreen perennial with pendent shoots clothed with narrowly elliptic, sparsely toothed, mid- to dark green leaves, to 5cm (2in) long. In summer and autumn, bears numerous long-stalked, tubular, 2-lipped, white-throated, bright lilac-blue flowers, to 2cm (¾in) long, singly in the leaf axils. ↕ 10cm (4in), ↔ 30cm (12in). Origin unknown. ✻
L. siphilitica (Blue cardinal flower). Clump-forming perennial with erect, leafy stems and ovate, oblong, or broadly lance-shaped, irregularly toothed, softly hairy, light green leaves, 10–15cm (4–6in) long. From late summer to mid-autumn, long-lasting, tubular, 2-lipped, bright blue flowers, 2.5–3.5cm (1–1½in) across, with leafy green bracts, are borne in dense racemes, 10–50cm (4–20in) long. ↕ 60–120cm (24–48in), ↔ 30cm (12in). E. USA. ✻✻✻.
f. *albiflora* bears white flowers.
L.* x *speciosa, syn. *L.* x *gerardii.* Clump-forming, slightly hairy perennial, often grown as an annual or biennial, with basal rosettes of oval to oblong-obovate,

Lobelia tupa

Lobelia 'Will Scarlet'

pointed, mid-green to red-flushed or ruby-red leaves, to 12cm (5in) long. From summer to autumn, bears tubular, 2-lipped, red, pink, or mauve-blue flowers, 3–4cm (1¼–1½in) across, in erect, dense, leafy racemes, to 35cm (14in) long. ↕ 1.2m (4ft), ↔ 30cm (12in). ✻✻✻. **Compliment Series** cultivars have dark green foliage and long-stemmed, loose racemes of scarlet, deep red, or blue-purple flowers; ↕ 75cm (30in) or more, ↔ to 23cm (9in). Cultivars of **Fan Series** have bronze-green or dark green leaves and compact, dense racemes, branching at the bases, of narrow-petalled flowers, to 2.5cm (1in) long, in pink, deep carmine-pink, scarlet, or deep red; ↕ 50–60cm (20–24in), ↔ to 23cm (9in). **'Vedrariensis'** ■ has dark green leaves often suffused red, and bears many-flowered racemes, to 45cm (18in) long, of violet-purple flowers.
L. splendens see *L. cardinalis.*
L. tupa ■ Robust, upright, clump-forming perennial with red-purple stems and ovate-lance-shaped to lance-shaped, downy, light grey-green leaves, to 30cm (12in) long. Narrowly tubular, 2-lipped, brick-red to orange-red flowers, 6cm (2½in) long, with red-purple calyces, are borne in racemes, to 45cm (18in) long, from mid- or late summer to mid-autumn. ↕ to 2m (6ft), ↔ 90cm (36in). Chile. ✻✻
***L.* 'Will Scarlet'** ■ Bowden Hybrid with mid-green leaves, suffused maroon and tubular, 2-lipped, bright blood-red flowers, borne from midsummer to early autumn. ↕ 90cm (36in), ↔ 30cm (12in). ✻✻✻

▷ **Lobelia,**
 False see *Monopsis*
 Gold see *Monopsis lutea*
 Swamp see *Lobelia paludosa*
 Water see *Lobelia dortmanna*
 Yellow see *Monopsis lutea*
▷ ***Lobivia backebergii*** see *Echinopsis backebergii*
▷ ***Lobivia caespitosa*** see *Echinopsis maximiliana*
▷ ***Lobivia cinnabarina*** see *Echinopsis cinnabarina*
▷ ***Lobivia ferox*** see *Echinopsis ferox*
▷ ***Lobivia pentlandii*** see *Echinopsis pentlandii*
▷ ***Lobivia silvestrii*** see *Echinopsis chamaecereus*
▷ **Loblolly bay** see *Gordonia lasianthus*
▷ **Lobster claw** see *Clianthus puniceus, Vriesea carinata*

LOBULARIA

Sweet Alison, Sweet alyssum

BRASSICACEAE/CRUCIFERAE

Genus of 5 species of low, mound-forming or spreading, hairy annuals and perennials from seashores, disturbed ground, and stony slopes in the Canary Islands and Mediterranean. They have narrow, linear-lance-shaped to oblong, light to mid-green leaves. In summer and early autumn, they produce cross-shaped, 4-petalled, often scented white flowers in compact, sometimes corymb-like, terminal racemes that elongate in fruit. Useful for the edges of a gravel drive or to fill paving cracks, and very tolerant of maritime conditions. *L. maritima* cultivars are particularly good summer bedding plants.
• **HARDINESS** Fully hardy.
• **CULTIVATION** Grow in light, moderately fertile, well-drained soil in full sun. Clip over after the first flush of bloom to encourage further flowering.
• **PROPAGATION** Sow seed *in situ* in late spring.
• **PESTS AND DISEASES** Downy mildew, slugs, flea beetles, clubroot, and white blister may be troublesome.

L. maritima, syn. *Alyssum maritimum.* Freely branching, usually compact, low-growing annual or short-lived perennial with linear-lance-shaped, slightly hairy, grey-green leaves, 3cm (1¼in) long. In summer, produces tiny, cross-shaped, slightly cupped, scented, white, occasionally pale purple-pink flowers in rounded, corymb-like racemes, 2.5–8cm (1–3in) across. ↕ 5–30cm (2–12in), ↔ 20–30cm (8–12in). Mediterranean, Canary Islands. ✻✻✻. **Alice Series** cultivars are compact, and bear white, purple, or rose-pink flowers; ↕ 8cm (3in). **'Carpet of Snow'** is loosely branched and ground-hugging, with white flowers; ↕ to 10cm (4in). Cultivars of **Easter Bonnet Series** ■ are very compact, bearing early, white, reddish

Lobularia maritima Easter Bonnet Series

Lobularia maritima 'Little Dorrit'

purple, or pink flowers; ↕ 8–10cm (3–4in). **'Little Dorrit'** ■ is loosely branched and spreading, with white flowers; ↕ to 10cm (4in). **'Navy Blue'** is very compact, with deep purple flowers; ↕ to 10cm (4in). **'New Purple'** is very compact and long-flowering, with purple flowers, shading to a lighter tone at the petal margins; ↕ to 10cm (4in). **'Rosario'** is vigorous and compact, with rose-pink flowers; ↕ 10cm (4in). **'Snowcloth'** is spreading, with white flowers. **'Snow Crystals'** is mound-forming and compact, and bears white flowers; ↕ to 25cm (10in). **'Wonderland Rose'** is less densely branched and more compact than 'Snowcloth', and bears rose-pink flowers; ↕ to 15cm (6in).

▷ **Locust** see *Robinia pseudoacacia*
 Black see *Robinia pseudoacacia*
 Bristly see *Robinia hispida*
 Caspian see *Gleditsia caspica*
 Honey see *Gleditsia triacanthos*
 New Mexico see *Robinia neomexicana*

LODOICEA

Coco-de-mer, Double coconut

ARECACEAE/PALMAE

Genus of one species of single-stemmed, dioecious palm found in wooded valleys in the Seychelles. It produces terminal clusters of fan-shaped leaves, and spikes of 3-petalled flowers between the lower leaves, followed by very large, coconut-like fruit. In frost-prone climates, grow in a warm greenhouse. In tropical climates, grow as a specimen plant.
• **HARDINESS** Frost tender.
• **CULTIVATION** Under glass, grow in loam-based potting compost (JI No.3) with added leaf mould, in full light. In the growing season, water freely and apply a balanced liquid fertilizer every month; water sparingly in winter. Outdoors, grow in fertile, moist but well-drained soil in full sun.
• **PROPAGATION** Sow seed at 24°C (75°F) in spring, half-buried in damp sand, in containers at least 1m (3ft) deep to allow room for the roots to develop.
• **PESTS AND DISEASES** Trouble free.

L. maldivica ♈ syn. *L. seychellarum.* Large palm with a columnar trunk that is slightly swollen at the base and ringed with old leaf scars. Robust leaf-stalks, 3–4m (10–12ft) long, support fan-shaped blades, to 7m (22ft) long, glossy, rich green above, matt and densely

woolly beneath, and divided for up to one-third of their length into many narrow, often pendent lobes. Green flowers are borne in spikes, to 2m (6ft) long, at intervals throughout the year, followed on female trees by heavy, woody, broadly heart-shaped, green then brown fruit, to 50cm (20in) across, which take 6 years to mature. ↕ to 30m (100ft), ↔ 15–20m (50–70ft). Seychelles. ❀ (min. 20°C/68°F)
L. seychellarum see *L. maldivica.*

LOESELIA

POLEMONIACEAE

Genus of 9 species of upright, branched annuals and bushy herbaceous, sometimes woody-based, perennials, from open, dry, rocky places in S. USA and N. and C. South America. The lance-shaped to elliptic or ovate, grey-green leaves are simple and toothed, the lower leaves opposite, the upper ones usually alternate. The trumpet-shaped, slightly 2-lipped flowers, with long, protruding stamens, are solitary or borne in clusters from the leaf axils in summer. Grow in a sunny, sheltered border; in frost-prone areas, grow half-hardy species in a cold or cool greenhouse.

- **HARDINESS** Frost hardy to half hardy.
- **CULTIVATION** Grow in very well-drained, fertile soil in full sun.
- **PROPAGATION** Sow seed in containers in a cold frame in late winter. Take softwood cuttings in spring or stem-tip cuttings in summer.
- **PESTS AND DISEASES** Trouble free.

L

L. mexicana. Upright, woody-based perennial with sharply toothed, spine-tipped, lance-shaped or elliptic, grey-green leaves, 2.5–4cm (1–1½in) long. In early summer, solitary, bright red flowers, 2.5cm (1in) long, with protruding stamens, are produced from the leaf axils. ↕ 1.5m (5ft), ↔ 50cm (20in). S. USA, Mexico. ❄❄

LOISELEURIA

Alpine azalea, Trailing azalea

ERICACEAE

Genus of one species of mat-forming, evergreen shrub from high alpine and subarctic regions in Europe, Japan, and North America. Cultivated for its foliage and flowers, it is suitable for a rock garden, peat bed, or alpine house, but is difficult to grow in dry climates.

- **HARDINESS** Fully hardy.
- **CULTIVATION** Grow in moderately fertile, humus-rich, moist but well-drained, acid soil in full sun. In an alpine house, use a mix of 4 parts peat or leaf mould and 1 part sharp sand.
- **PROPAGATION** Root softwood cuttings in early summer, or semi-ripe cuttings in midsummer. Layer in spring.
- **PESTS AND DISEASES** Trouble free.

L. procumbens. Prostrate shrub forming tight mats of crowded, oval to oblong, glossy, dark green leaves, to 1cm (½in) long. Terminal, upturned, broadly cup-shaped, rose-pink to white flowers, 6mm (¼in) across, are borne singly or in small umbels in early summer. ↕ 8cm (3in), ↔ to 30cm (12in). Europe, Japan, North America. ❄❄❄

▷**Lollipop plant** see *Pachystachys lutea*

LOMANDRA

Mat rush

LOMANDRACEAE

Genus of over 50 species of tuft- or tussock-forming, rhizomatous perennials found in a wide range of habitats in Australia, Papua New Guinea, and New Caledonia. They have linear, flat or cylindrical, hairy or hairless leaves. The male and female flowers, borne in spikes, racemes, or panicles, are often inconspicuous and not long-lasting. Some species are aromatic, others have an overpowering smell. Grow for mass planting or as individual accent plants. In damp, frost-prone areas, grow in a cool greenhouse or conservatory.

- **HARDINESS** Frost hardy to frost tender.
- **CULTIVATION** Outdoors, grow in any well-drained soil in full sun, or in partial shade in very hot regions. Rejuvenate old clumps by burning off the foliage. Under glass, grow in well-drained loam-based potting compost (JI No.2) in full light. Water moderately during the growing season, sparingly in winter.
- **PROPAGATION** Sow seed at 13–18°C (55–64°F) as soon as ripe. Divide in spring.
- **PESTS AND DISEASES** Trouble free.

L. glauca (Pale mat rush). Tussock-forming perennial with linear, mainly flat, mid-green leaves, 8–20cm (3–8in) long. In summer, bears cylindrical or tubular, purple-flushed yellow flowers, 5mm (¼in) long: the male flowers clustered in spikes 10–15cm (4–6in) long, the female flowers borne in spherical heads 1.5cm (½in) across. ↕ 20cm (8in), ↔ 35cm (14in). Australia (New South Wales). ❄❄
L. longifolia ▣ (Spiny-headed mat rush). Dense, tussock-forming perennial with linear, flat or nearly flat, yellow-green to dark green leaves, 1m (3ft) long. In summer, cylindrical, often fragrant, yellow or cream, male and female flowers, 4mm (⅛in) long, are borne in racemes or panicles 30–90cm (12–36in) long. ↕ 1m (3ft), ↔ 2m (6ft). Australia (E. South Australia, New South Wales, E. Tasmania). ❄❄

Lomandra longifolia

▷***Lomaria gibba*** see *Blechnum gibbum*

LOMATIA

PROTEACEAE

Genus of about 12 species of evergreen trees and shrubs from moist woodland in Australasia and South America. They have opposite or alternate, entire to pinnatifid, or pinnate to 3-pinnate leaves, and racemes of initially tubular, later star-shaped flowers, with 4 narrow, twisted lobes and prominent, curved styles. Grow in a woodland garden or shrub border.

- **HARDINESS** Frost hardy.
- **CULTIVATION** Grow in poor to moderately fertile, moist but well-drained, acid to neutral soil in full sun or partial shade. Shelter from cold winds in frost-prone areas. Pruning group 1.
- **PROPAGATION** Take softwood cuttings in early summer, or semi-ripe cuttings in midsummer.
- **PESTS AND DISEASES** Trouble free.

L. ferruginea ▣♀ Upright, bushy shrub or small tree with felted brown shoots and oblong to oval, 2-pinnate, dark green leaves, to 50cm (20in) long, the ovate-lance-shaped leaflets sometimes deeply lobed and fawn-felted beneath. In midsummer, bears yellow-and-red flowers, 1.5cm (½in) long, in axillary racemes to 5cm (2in) long. ↕ 10m (30ft), ↔ 5m (15ft). Chile, Argentina. ❄❄

Lomatia silaifolia

L. silaifolia ▣ Bushy shrub with upright branches bearing 2- or 3-pinnate, dark green leaves, to 30cm (12in) long, composed of lance-shaped leaflets with margins rolled under. In mid- and late summer, bears fragrant, creamy white flowers, 1.5cm (½in) long, in erect racemes or panicles, to 30cm (12in) long. ↕↔ 2m (6ft). S.E. Australia. ❄❄
L. tinctoria. Small, bushy, often suckering shrub with ovate to triangular, pinnate or 2-pinnate (rarely simple), dark green leaves, to 8cm (3in) long, deeply and finely cut into linear-lance-shaped leaflets. Fragrant, creamy white flowers, 1cm (½in) long, are borne in racemes to 10cm (4in) or more long, in midsummer. ↕ 1m (3ft), ↔ 1.5m (5ft). Australia (Tasmania). ❄❄

Lomatia ferruginea (inset: flower detail)

LOMATIUM

APIACEAE/UMBELLIFERAE

Genus of approximately 60 species of tap-rooted herbaceous perennials from open areas and rock crevices in W. North America. Cultivated for their foliage and flowers, they have finely divided, pinnate to 4-pinnate, fern-like leaves, and produce compound umbels of tiny, yellow, green, purple, or white flowers in spring and summer. Suitable for a rock garden or raised bed.

- **HARDINESS** Fully hardy to frost hardy.
- **CULTIVATION** Grow in moderately fertile, sharply drained soil in full sun.
- **PROPAGATION** Sow seed in containers in a cold frame as soon as ripe.
- **PESTS AND DISEASES** Trouble free.

L. dissectum. Low-growing perennial with triangular, 2- to 4-pinnate, fresh mid-green leaves, to 15–35cm (6–14in) long, composed of oblong leaflets. Bright yellow or purple flowers are borne in rounded, compound umbels, 3–13cm (1¼–5in) across, very early in spring, as the leaves develop. ↕ 15cm (6in) in flower, to 40cm (16in) or more later, ↔ to 20cm (8in). USA (Rocky Mountains). ❄❄❄

LOMATOPHYLLUM

ALOACEAE

Genus of about 11 species of mainly stemless, succulent perennials occurring on low, hilly terrain in Madagascar and Mauritius. They have fleshy leaves forming loose rosettes, similar to those of many *Aloe* species, and bear racemes or panicles of diurnal, bell-shaped or tubular flowers in summer. Where temperatures drop below 12°C (54°F), grow as houseplants or in a warm greenhouse; in warmer climates, grow in a shrub border or desert garden.

- **HARDINESS** Frost tender.
- **CULTIVATION** Under glass, grow in loam-based potting compost (JI No.2) with added leaf mould and grit, in full light. From early spring to early autumn, water freely and apply a half-strength balanced liquid fertilizer every 6–8 weeks. Keep barely moist at other times. Outdoors, grow in moderately fertile, sharply drained soil in full sun. See also pp.48–49.
- **PROPAGATION** Sow seed at 19–24°C (66–75°F), or detach offsets, in spring.
- **PESTS AND DISEASES** Susceptible to scale insects.

L. citreum see *L. occidentale* var. *citreum.*

L. occidentale. Stemless or short-stemmed, succulent perennial forming rosettes of 15–20 stiff, spreading, lance-shaped, mid-green leaves, 80–100cm (32–39in) long, with recurved, toothed or sparsely spiny margins. In summer, produces dense panicles of 50 or more tubular, deep pink flowers, 2–3cm (¾–1¼in) long. ↕ to 1m (3ft), ↔ to 1.5m (5ft). W. Madagascar. ❀ (min. 12°C/54°F). **var. *citreum***, syn. *L. citreum,* has a short stem, dark green leaves, 30cm (12in) long, and yellowish green flowers; ↕ 45–50cm (18–20in), ↔ 60cm (24in).

▷**London pride** see *Saxifraga* x *urbium*

LONICERA

Honeysuckle

CAPRIFOLIACEAE

Genus of about 180 species of deciduous and evergreen shrubs and twining climbers, widely distributed in the N. hemisphere, where they grow in varied habitats ranging from woodland and thickets to rocky places. They are cultivated mainly for their tubular or funnel- to bell-shaped, often fragrant flowers, which are usually 2-lipped or have 5 small, spreading lobes. The leaves are borne in opposite pairs and are usually simple. Honeysuckles may be grown in a variety of situations: train climbers on a wall or fence, or into a large shrub or small tree; grow shrubs in a shrub border, or use for hedging or ground cover. In frost-prone climates, grow half-hardy species in a cool greenhouse. The berries may cause mild stomach upset if ingested.

- **HARDINESS** Fully hardy to half hardy.
- **CULTIVATION** Grow shrubs in any well-drained soil in full sun or partial shade; grow climbers in fertile, humus-rich, moist but well-drained soil. All will tolerate full sun, but are less prone to aphids in partial shade. Under glass, grow in loam-based potting compost (JI No.3) in bright filtered light. When in growth, water freely and apply a balanced liquid fertilizer monthly; water sparingly in winter. Pruning group 2 for shrubs; group 11 for climbers (those flowering on the previous year's shoots, such as *L. periclymenum*, are best pruned back to strong young growth immediately after flowering each year). Trim hedges twice during summer.
- **PROPAGATION** Sow seed of hardy species in containers in a cold frame as soon as ripe; sow *L. hildebrandiana* at 13–18°C (55–64°F) in spring. Take semi-ripe cuttings of evergreens in summer, and greenwood or hardwood cuttings of deciduous honeysuckles in summer or autumn respectively.
- **PESTS AND DISEASES** Aphids may be a problem, particularly on some climbers.

L.* x *americana ▣ Vigorous, woody, deciduous, twining climber with paired, oval, dark green leaves, to 8cm (3in) long, the upper pairs united. Large whorls of tubular, 2-lipped, very fragrant yellow flowers, to 5cm (2in) long, strongly flushed red-purple, are borne in the leaf axils in summer and early autumn, followed by red berries. ↕ 7m (22ft). Garden origin. ❄❄❄

L.* x *bella. Upright, deciduous shrub with paired, ovate, pointed, mid-green leaves, to 5cm (2in) long. Axillary pairs of tubular, 5-lobed, pink or red flowers, 1.5–3cm (½–1¼in) long, becoming yellow, are produced in summer, and are followed by red berries. ↕ 2.5m (8ft), ↔ 3m (10ft). Garden origin. ❄❄❄. **'Atrorosea'** bears dark pink flowers with paler margins, in late spring. **'Candida'** bears white flowers.

L.* x *brownii (*L. hirsuta* x *L. sempervirens*) (Scarlet trumpet honeysuckle). Deciduous or semi-evergreen, twining climber with paired, ovate, blue-green leaves, to 8cm (3in) long. Bears terminal whorls of tubular, 2-lipped, slightly fragrant, orange to red flowers, 3.5cm (1½in) long, in summer, sometimes followed by red berries. ↕ 4m (12ft). Garden origin. ❄❄❄. **'Dropmore Scarlet'** ▣ bears long, trumpet-shaped, bright scarlet flowers over a long period. **'Fuchsioides'** has orange-scarlet flowers.

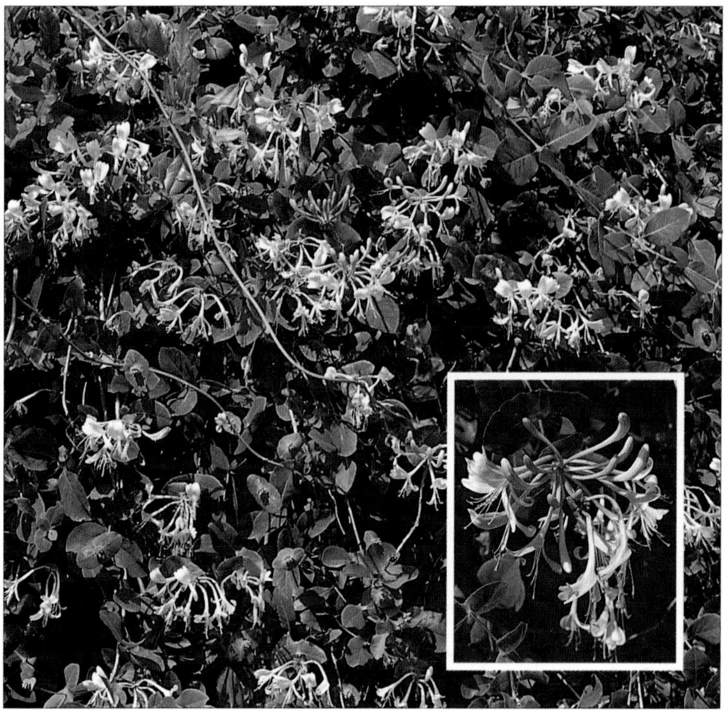

Lonicera x *americana* (inset: flower detail)

L. caprifolium (Italian honeysuckle). Woody, deciduous, twining climber with paired, oval to obovate, grey-green leaves, to 10cm (4in) long, the upper pairs united. Whorls of tubular, 2-lipped, very fragrant, pink-flushed, creamy white to yellow flowers, to 5cm (2in) long, are borne from the leaf axils in summer, and are followed by orange-red berries. ↕ 6m (20ft). Europe, W. Asia. ❄❄❄. **'Praecox'** bears creamy white flowers in late spring; they are often tinted light red, and turn yellow.

L. chaetocarpa. Upright, deciduous shrub with bristly shoots and paired, ovate to oblong, bristly, mid-green leaves, to 8cm (3in) long. In early summer, paired, sometimes solitary, funnel-shaped, 5-lobed, primrose-yellow flowers, to 3cm (1¼in) long, with large, leafy, pale green bracts, are borne in the leaf axils; the berries are red and cupped by the persistent, now red-tinted bracts. ↕↔ 2m (6ft). W. China. ❄❄❄

Lonicera x *brownii* 'Dropmore Scarlet'

L. etrusca (Etruscan honeysuckle). Vigorous, woody, twining, deciduous or semi-evergreen climber with paired, oval or obovate, mid-green leaves, to 10cm (4in) long, blue-green beneath, the upper pairs united. Tubular, 2-lipped, fragrant yellow flowers, 5cm (2in) long, flushed red and darkening with age, are produced in terminal and axillary whorls from midsummer to autumn, and are followed by red berries. Grows best in full sun. ↕ 4m (12ft). Mediterranean. ❄❄❄ (borderline). **'Donald Waterer'** produces flowers that are red outside, becoming orange-yellow, and white inside. **'Superba'** ▣ is vigorous, and produces large clusters of cream flowers that turn orange.

L. fragrantissima. Bushy, spreading, deciduous or semi-evergreen shrub with paired, oval leaves, to 7cm (3in) long, dull, dark green above, blue-green beneath, with bristly margins when young. Tubular, 2-lipped, very fragrant, creamy white flowers, 1cm (½in) long, are produced in pairs from the leaf axils in winter and early spring, but are often sparsely produced unless grown against a wall. Berries are dull red. ↕ 2m (6ft), ↔ 3m (10ft). China. ❄❄❄

Lonicera etrusca 'Superba'

L

Lonicera x *heckrottii*

L. giraldii. Evergreen, twining climber with densely hairy shoots and paired, narrowly oblong, velvet-textured, dark green leaves, to 8cm (3in) long, with long, sharp points and heart-shaped bases. Dense, terminal whorls of tubular, 2-lipped, purple-red flowers, to 2cm (¾in) long, with yellow stamens, are produced in early and midsummer, followed by white-frosted, purple-black berries. ↕5m (15ft). China. ❄❄❄
***L.* 'Gold Flame'** see *L.* x *heckrottii* 'Gold Flame'.
L.* x *heckrottii ■ (*L.* x *americana* x *L. sempervirens*). Deciduous or semi-evergreen, twining climber with paired, oblong to oval or elliptic, dark green leaves, to 6cm (2½in) long, blue-green beneath, with the upper pairs united. Tubular, 2-lipped, fragrant flowers, 4cm (1½in) long, pink outside, orange-yellow inside, are borne in terminal whorls during summer, and are sometimes followed by red berries. ↕5m (15ft). Garden origin. ❄❄❄. **'Gold Flame'**, syn. *L.* 'Gold Flame', is more vigorous, with brighter coloured flowers.
L. henryi. Vigorous, woody, evergreen, twining climber with paired, oblong-lance-shaped to oblong-ovate, tapered, glossy, dark green leaves, to 10cm (4in) long. Terminal or axillary whorls of tubular, 2-lipped, yellow-throated, purplish red flowers, to 2cm (¾in) long, are produced in early and midsummer, followed by purple-black berries. ↕10m (30ft). W. China. ❄❄❄ (borderline)
L. hildebrandiana ■ (Giant Burmese honeysuckle). Very vigorous, evergreen or semi-evergreen, twining climber with paired, broadly ovate or oval, dark green leaves, to 15cm (6in) long. Tubular, 2-lipped, very fragrant, creamy white flowers, to 8–15cm (3–6in) long, ageing to orange, are borne in pairs in terminal and axillary racemes in summer, and are followed by red berries. ↕10m (30ft) or more. China, S.E. Asia. ❄
L. involucrata (Twinberry). Dense, bushy, deciduous shrub with stout shoots and paired, ovate to oblong or lance-shaped, bright mid-green leaves, to 12cm (5in) long. Tubular, dark yellow, often red-suffused flowers, 1cm (½in) long, each with 5 short lobes, are borne in pairs from the leaf axils in late spring; they are surrounded by large green bracts that soon turn red, and are followed by glossy black berries. ↕2m (6ft), ↔3m (10ft). W. North America, Mexico. ❄❄❄
L. japonica (Japanese honeysuckle). Vigorous, woody, evergreen or semi-evergreen, twining climber with paired, broadly elliptic to ovate, sometimes deeply lobed, dark green leaves, to 8cm (3in) long. Tubular, 2-lipped, very fragrant, often purple-flushed, white flowers, to 4cm (1½in) long, ageing to yellow, are borne in pairs from the leaf axils over a long period from spring to late summer, followed by blue-black berries. ↕10m (30ft). E. Asia. ❄❄❄. **'Aureoreticulata'** has leaves attractively veined yellow; ↕6m (20ft); ❄❄. **'Dart's World'** is a particularly hardy evergreen cultivar of bushy, spreading habit, with dark green leaves and very fragrant, strongly red-flushed white flowers that turn yellow. **'Halliana'** ■ is very vigorous, with pure white flowers that age to dark yellow. **var. *repens*** has purple-tinged foliage, and produces white flowers heavily flushed red-purple. **var. *repens* 'Red Coral'** see 'Superba'. **'Superba'**, syn. var. *repens* 'Red Coral', has mid-green leaves, 5cm (2in) long, and bears scarlet flowers, 4–5cm (1½–2in) long.
L. korolkowii ■ Open, spreading, deciduous shrub with arching shoots and paired, ovate or oval leaves, to 3cm (1¼in) long, with long, sharp points, glaucous pale green above, glaucous blue-green beneath. In early summer, bears tubular, 2-lipped, pale rose-pink flowers, 1.5cm (½in) long, in pairs along the shoots, followed by bright red berries. ↕3m (10ft), ↔5m (15ft). Mountains of C. Asia, Afghanistan, Pakistan. ❄❄❄. **var. *zabelii* of gardens**, syn. *L. tatarica* 'Zabelii', bears bright pink flowers.

Lonicera korolkowii

L. ledebourii ■ Dense, bushy, deciduous shrub with stout shoots and paired, ovate-oblong, dark green leaves, to 12cm (5in) long. Funnel-shaped, 5-lobed, red-flushed, deep orange-yellow flowers, to 2cm (¾in) long, each with 2 large, persistent red bracts, are borne from the leaf axils in late spring and early summer, followed by glossy black berries. ↕3m (10ft), ↔4m (12ft). USA (California). ❄❄❄
L. maackii. Vigorous, upright, often tree-like, deciduous shrub with paired, oval-lance-shaped, tapered, dark green leaves, to 8cm (3in) long. Tubular, 2-lipped, fragrant white flowers, to 2cm (¾in) long, ageing to yellow, are borne in axillary pairs along the shoots in early summer, followed by dark red berries. ↕↔5m (15ft). China, Korea, Japan. ❄❄❄
L. morrowii. Spreading, deciduous shrub with arching branches and paired, oblong or ovate to elliptic, dull mid-green leaves, to 6cm (2½in) long, purple-tinged when young. Pairs of tubular, creamy white flowers, 1.5cm (½in) long, ageing to yellow, each with 5 short lobes, are borne along the shoots in late spring and early summer,

Lonicera periclymenum 'Graham Thomas'

followed by red berries. ↕2m (6ft), ↔3m (10ft). Japan. ❄❄❄
L. nitida. Bushy, evergreen shrub with paired, ovate to broadly ovate leaves, to 1cm (½in) long, glossy, dark green above, lighter beneath. Produces pairs of tubular, creamy white flowers, to 1cm (½in) long, from the leaf axils in spring, followed by glossy, blue-purple berries. Good for hedging. ↕to 3.5m (11ft), ↔3m (10ft). S.W. China. ❄❄❄. **'Baggesen's Gold'** has long, arching shoots and ovate, bright yellow leaves; ↕↔1.5m (5ft). **'Ernest Wilson'** is vigorous and spreading, with tiny, ovate, dark green leaves, 3–6mm (⅛–¼in) long; ↕2m (6ft). **'Yunnan'** is broad and upright, with larger leaves, 2cm (¾in) long, and with abundant flowers and berries; ↕↔2m (6ft).
L. periclymenum (Common honeysuckle, Woodbine). Vigorous, woody, deciduous, twining climber with paired, ovate, oval, or obovate, mid-green leaves, to 6cm (2½in) long, glaucous beneath. Terminal whorls of tubular, 2-lipped, very fragrant, white to yellow, often red-flushed flowers, to 5cm (2in) long, are borne in mid- and late summer, followed by bright red berries. ↕7m (22ft). Europe, North Africa, Turkey, Caucasus. ❄❄❄. **'Belgica'** (Early Dutch honeysuckle) produces white flowers that turn yellow, and are richly streaked red outside. **'Graham Thomas'** ■ has white flowers turning yellow, borne over a long period. **'Serotina'** ■ (Late Dutch honeysuckle) produces creamy white flowers streaked dark red-purple.

Lonicera hildebrandiana

Lonicera japonica 'Halliana'

Lonicera ledebourii

Lonicera periclymenum 'Serotina'

L. pileata. Dense, spreading, evergreen shrub with paired, ovate-oblong to oblong-lance-shaped, glossy, dark green leaves, to 3cm (1¼in) long. Funnel-shaped, 5-lobed, creamy white flowers, to 8mm (⅜in) long, are produced in pairs from the leaf axils in late spring, followed by violet-purple berries. Good ground cover. ↕ 60cm (24in), ↔ 2.5m (8ft). China. ❄❄❄

***L.* x *purpusii* 'Winter Beauty'.** Rounded, deciduous or semi-evergreen shrub with red-purple shoots and paired, ovate, dark green leaves, to 8cm (3in) long. Tubular, 2-lipped, very fragrant white flowers, 2cm (¾in) long, with conspicuous yellow anthers, are borne in small, axillary clusters in winter and early spring. Berries are rarely produced. ↕ 2m (6ft), ↔ 2.5m (8ft). ❄❄❄

L. rupicola* var. *syringantha see *L. syringantha.*

L. sempervirens ■ (Coral honeysuckle, Trumpet honeysuckle). Woody, deciduous or evergreen, twining climber with paired, oval or obovate leaves, to 7cm (3in) long, dark green above, blue-green beneath, the upper pairs united. Tubular flowers, to 5cm (2in) long, with 2 short lips, rich scarlet-orange outside, yellowish orange inside, are produced in terminal whorls in summer and autumn, and are followed by bright red berries. ↕ 4m (12ft). E. and S. USA. ❄❄❄ (borderline). **f. *sulphurea*** produces yellow flowers.

L. standishii. Upright, deciduous or semi-evergreen shrub with paired, oblong-lance-shaped, bristly, dark green leaves, to 10cm (4in) long, with long, slender points. Tubular, 2-lipped, fragrant, creamy white flowers, 3cm (1¼in) long, sometimes tinged very pale pink, are produced in axillary pairs along the shoots from late autumn to early spring, followed by red berries. ↕↔ 2m (6ft). China. ❄❄❄

Lonicera sempervirens

Lonicera tatarica

Lonicera x *tellmanniana*

L. syringantha, syn. *L. rupicola* var. *syringantha.* Graceful, rounded, deciduous shrub with oblong-ovate, grey-green leaves, to 2.5cm (1in) long, usually paired, sometimes in threes. Small, tubular-bell-shaped, 5-lobed, very fragrant, lilac-pink flowers, to 1cm (½in) across, are produced in pairs from the leaf axils in late spring and early summer, followed by red berries. ↕ 2–3m (6–10ft), ↔ 2m (6ft). W. China, Tibet. ❄❄❄

L. tatarica ■ Upright, bushy, deciduous shrub with paired, oblong-ovate to lance-shaped, dark green leaves, to 6cm (2½in) long, glaucous beneath. Axillary pairs of tubular, 5-lobed, white to pink or red flowers, to 2.5cm (1in) long, are profusely borne along the shoots in late spring and early summer, followed by scarlet to yellow-orange berries. ↕ 4m (12ft), ↔ 2.5m (8ft). S. Russia to C. Asia. ❄❄❄. **'Arnold Pink'** produces dark rose-pink flowers. **'Hack's Red'** bears very dark purplish red flowers. **'Zabelii'** see *L. korolkowii* var. *zabelii* of gardens.

L.* x *tellmanniana ■ (*L. sempervirens* 'Superba' x *L. tragophylla*). Woody, deciduous, twining climber with paired, elliptic-ovate to oblong, deep green leaves, to 10cm (4in) long, blue-white beneath, the upper pairs united. Terminal whorls of tubular, 2-lipped, bright copper-orange flowers, to 5cm (2in) long, are produced from late spring to midsummer. ↕ 5m (15ft). Garden origin. ❄❄❄

L. tragophylla. Woody, deciduous, twining climber with paired, oval to oblong, mid-green leaves, to 12cm (5in) long, blue-white beneath, the upper pairs united. Long-tubed, 2-lipped, bright yellow or orange-yellow flowers, to 8cm (3in) long, red-tinted above, are produced in large, terminal whorls in mid- and late summer, followed by red berries. ↕ 6m (20ft). C. China. ❄❄❄

***L.* x *xylosteoides* 'Clavey's Dwarf'.** Slow-growing, dense, upright, rounded, deciduous shrub with paired, oval to obovate, grey-green leaves, to 6cm (2½in) long. Pairs of small, tubular, 2-lipped white flowers, 1cm (½in) long, are produced from the leaf axils in late spring and early summer, followed by red berries. Suitable for hedging. ↕ 1.5m (5ft), ↔ 1m (3ft). ❄❄❄

L. xylosteum ■ (Fly honeysuckle). Dense, bushy, deciduous shrub with paired, ovate to obovate or oblong, grey-green leaves, to 6cm (2½in) long. Tubular, 2-lipped, creamy white flowers, to 1cm (½in) long, are produced in pairs along the shoots in late spring and early summer, followed by showy red, rarely yellow berries. ↕↔ 3m (10ft). Europe, Caucasus, Russia (Siberia). ❄❄❄

Lonicera xylosteum

▷ **Looking glass plant** see *Coprosma repens*

▷ **Loosestrife** see *Lysimachia, Lythrum*
Purple see *Lythrum salicaria*
Yellow see *Lysimachia vulgaris*

▷ ***Lophocereus*** see *Pachycereus*
L. schottii see *P. schottii*

LOPHOMYRTUS

MYRTACEAE

Genus of 2 species of evergreen shrubs or small trees, closely related to the genus *Myrtus*, occurring in coastal and lowland forest in New Zealand. They are cultivated for their flowers, foliage, and fruits. The leaves are opposite, simple, and leathery. In summer, 4-petalled flowers, each with a boss of prominent stamens, are borne singly from all the upper leaf axils, followed by many-seeded, purple-black to red berries. In frost-prone areas, grow in a cool greenhouse or against a warm wall. In milder areas, plant in a shrub border.

• **HARDINESS** Frost hardy to frost tender.

• **CULTIVATION** Under glass, grow in loam-based potting compost (JI No.2) in bright filtered light. During the growing season, water freely and apply a balanced liquid fertilizer monthly. Water sparingly in winter. Outdoors, grow in fertile, humus-rich, moist but well-drained soil in partial shade. Pruning group 1; may need restrictive pruning under glass.

• **PROPAGATION** Sow seed at 13–18°C (55–64°F) as soon as ripe. Root semi-ripe cuttings, with heels, in summer with bottom heat.

• **PESTS AND DISEASES** Red spider mites may be a problem under glass.

L. bullata ♀ syn. *Myrtus bullata.* Rounded, moderately bushy or open, large shrub or small tree with downy stems. Broadly ovate to rounded leaves, 1.5–3cm (½–1¼in) long, sometimes more, are strongly puckered or blistered between the veins, and bronze- to red-tinted when young, maturing to glossy, dark green. In summer, produces open cup-shaped white flowers, 1cm (½in) wide, usually followed by broadly ovoid, deep black-red berries, 7–10mm (¼–½in) long. ↕ 3–8m (10–25ft), ↔ 1–3m (3–10ft). New Zealand. ❄

L.* x *ralphii ♀ (*L. bullata* x *L. obcordata*). Large, rounded, vigorous shrub or small tree, of open habit. Broadly oblong-ovate, dark green leaves, usually 1.5–2.5cm (½–1in) long, are flat or slightly blistered between the veins. Mature plants produce open cup-shaped white flowers, 1cm (½in) wide, in summer, followed by dark black-red berries, 4–8mm (⅛–⅜in) long. ↕ 2–5m (6–15ft), ↔ 1.5–2.5m (5–8ft). Garden origin. ❄❄ (borderline). **'Gloriosa'** see 'Variegata'. **'Indian Chief'** has rounded, lustrous, reddish green leaves, to 1cm

Lophomyrtus x *ralphii* 'Variegata' (inset: leaf detail)

L

(½in) long. **'Kathryn'** has blistered leaves, flushed rich purple. **'Purpurea'** has slightly blistered, bronze-purple to deep purple-red leaves. **'Sundae'**, syn. 'Tricolor', has almost flat, rich green- and yellow-variegated leaves, with pink or bronze-red overtones, especially in sunny sites. **'Tricolor'** see 'Sundae'. **'Variegata'** ▣ syn. 'Gloriosa', *Myrtus bullata* 'Gloriosa', *Myrtus* x *ralphii* 'Variegata', has rounded, lustrous, deep green leaves, barely 1cm (½in) long, with creamy yellow variegation.

LOPHOPHORA

CACTACEAE

Genus of 2 species of variable, perennial cacti occurring in semi-arid areas of S. Texas (USA), and N. and E. Mexico. They have thick, tuberous rootstocks, and flattened-spherical stems that may become more cylindrical with age. Areoles bear a few weak spines when young, later just a few white hairs. Diurnal, solitary, bell-shaped flowers are produced at the tips of the stems and last 2–3 days. Where temperatures drop below 10°C (50°F), grow in a warm greenhouse or as houseplants; in warmer climates, plant outdoors in a desert garden, preferably on sloping ground.

- **HARDINESS** Frost tender.
- **CULTIVATION** Under glass, grow in standard cactus compost with added limestone chippings, in full light. From mid-spring to late summer, water freely and apply a balanced liquid fertilizer every 6–8 weeks. Keep dry at other times. Outdoors, grow in moderately fertile, sharply drained, alkaline soil in full sun. See also pp.48–49.
- **PROPAGATION** Sow seed at 19–24°C (66–75°F) in spring.
- **PESTS AND DISEASES** Trouble free.

L. echinata see *L. williamsii.*
L. lutea see *L. williamsii.*
L. williamsii ▣ syn. *L. echinata*, *L. lutea* (Dumpling cactus). Variable cactus, sometimes solitary, but usually forming large groups. Dark blue-green stems, 5–8cm (2–3in) thick, each have 4–14 low ribs, divided by narrow furrows, with prominent tubercles and white-woolly areoles. Bell-shaped, pink to carmine-red flowers, to 2.5cm (1in) across, sometimes with paler margins, are borne at the crowns from spring to autumn. ↕ to 5cm (2in), ↔ to 30cm (12in), in groups. USA (S. Texas), N. and N.E. Mexico. ❁ (min. 10°C/50°F)

Lophophora williamsii

Lophospermum erubescens

LOPHOSPERMUM

SCROPHULARIACEAE

Genus of 8 species of deciduous and evergreen, perennial climbers and shrubs from rocky slopes in North and Central America. They have entire or toothed, triangular to rounded leaves, and bear solitary, axillary, tubular to funnel- or trumpet-shaped, white to purple flowers. In temperate areas, grow in a cool greenhouse. In warmer areas, grow through a shrub or small tree.

- **HARDINESS** Half hardy to frost tender.
- **CULTIVATION** Under glass, grow in loam-based potting compost (JI No.2) with added sharp sand, in full light. In growth, water moderately and apply a balanced liquid fertilizer monthly. Water sparingly in winter. Outdoors, grow in moderately fertile, ideally sandy, moist but well-drained soil in full sun.
- **PROPAGATION** Sow seed at 19–24°C (66–75°F) in spring. Root semi-ripe cuttings in late summer.
- **PESTS AND DISEASES** Trouble free.

L. erubescens ▣ syn. *Asarina erubescens*, *Maurandya erubescens* (Creeping gloxinia). Scandent, evergreen, perennial climber (deciduous in cool areas), often grown as an annual, with soft, woody-based stems and triangular, toothed, downy, grey-green leaves, to 7cm (3in) long, with twining leaf-stalks. Bears trumpet-shaped, rose-pink flowers, 7cm (3in) long, in summer and autumn. ↕ 3m (10ft) or more. Mexico. ❁ (min. 3–5°C/37–41°F)

LOPHOSTEMON

MYRTACEAE

Genus of 4–6 species of evergreen trees or tall shrubs, closely related to *Tristania* and *Eucalyptus*. They occur in heavy, moist soil, frequently in rainforest or along the borders of streams, in N. and E. Australia and S. New Guinea. Leaves are simple, usually entire, and borne alternately or in whorls, often more densely towards the stem tips. The flowers have 5 spreading petals and many stamens fused into 5 separate bundles, and are produced in axillary cymes; they are followed by small, woody, cup- or top-shaped, 3-celled seed capsules. In frost-prone areas, grow as foliage plants in a cool or warm greenhouse; flowers are likely to form only on plants 2–3m (6–10ft) tall. In milder areas, lophostemons are good specimen and shade trees, and are effective as a windbreak or hedge.

- **HARDINESS** Half hardy to frost tender.
- **CULTIVATION** Under glass, grow in lime-free (ericaceous) potting compost with added sharp sand, in full or bright filtered light. During the growing season, water freely and apply a half-strength, balanced liquid fertilizer every month; water sparingly in winter. Outdoors, grow in poor to moderately fertile, neutral to acid, moist but well-drained soil in full sun or partial shade. Pruning group 1; trim hedges in late summer.
- **PROPAGATION** Sow seed at 13–18°C (55–64°F) in spring. Root semi-ripe cuttings in summer with bottom heat.
- **PESTS AND DISEASES** Red spider mites may be a problem under glass.

Lophostemon confertus (inset: flower detail)

L. confertus ▣ ▢ syn. *Tristania conferta* (Brush box). Bushy, round-headed tree with lance-shaped to ovate, smooth, bright green leaves, 7–15cm (3–6in) long, usually in whorls of 3–5. Bears cymes of 3–7 star-shaped white flowers, 2.5–4cm (1–1½in) across, in spring and summer, followed by top-shaped seed capsules, 1.5cm (½in) across. ↕ 10–15m (30–50ft), or to 40m (130ft) in moist, warm climates, ↔ 3–10m (10–30ft) or more. Australia (Queensland, New South Wales). ✲. **'Perth Gold'** has bright green leaves, strongly variegated yellow.

▷**Loquat** see *Eriobotrya japonica*
▷**Lords and ladies** see *Arum*

LOROPETALUM

HAMAMELIDACEAE

Genus of 1, possibly up to 3 species of rounded, evergreen shrubs or small trees found in woodland in the Himalayas, China, and Japan. The alternate leaves are ovate or oval, mid-green and rough above, paler beneath. Clusters of fragrant, spider-like white flowers, with 4 narrow, strap-shaped petals, are borne in terminal cymes in late winter and early spring. Grow in a woodland garden or shrub border.

- **HARDINESS** Frost hardy to half hardy.
- **CULTIVATION** Grow in fertile, humus-rich, moist but well-drained soil in partial shade. Pruning group 8.
- **PROPAGATION** Sow seed in containers in an open frame as soon as ripe. Root semi-ripe cuttings in summer with bottom heat.
- **PESTS AND DISEASES** Trouble free.

L. chinense. Bushy shrub with ovate or oval leaves, 2.5–6cm (1–2½in) long. In late winter or early spring, bears sweetly scented, spider-like white flowers, 2cm (¾in) across, in small, crowded cymes of 3–6. ↕↔ 2m (6ft). China, Burma, Japan. ✲✲ (borderline)

LOTUS syn. DORYCNIUM

LEGUMINOSAE/PAPILIONACEAE

Diverse genus of about 150 species of annuals, short-lived perennials, and deciduous, semi-evergreen, or evergreen subshrubs, found throughout most of the world, some in pasture, others in dryish, rocky areas. The alternate leaves are simple, palmate, or pinnate. Pea-like flowers, in a range of colours, occur either singly from the leaf axils or in terminal or axillary clusters. Suitable for a variety of sites, including a wild garden, rock garden, or shrub border; trailing species are useful for a hanging basket. In frost-prone areas, grow tender species in a cool greenhouse.

• **HARDINESS** Fully hardy to frost tender.
• **CULTIVATION** Under glass, grow in loam-based potting compost (JI No.2) with added grit, in full light. In growth, water freely and apply a balanced liquid fertilizer monthly; water sparingly in winter. Outdoors, grow in moderately fertile, well-drained soil in full sun. Pruning group 9 for shrubs (although most do not need pruning); may need restrictive pruning under glass.
• **PROPAGATION** Sow seed of hardy species in containers outdoors in spring or autumn. Sow seed of half-hardy and frost-tender species at 19–24°C (66–75°F) in spring. Take semi-ripe cuttings of shrubs in summer.
• **PESTS AND DISEASES** Mealybugs, aphids, and red spider mites may be a problem under glass.

L. berthelotii ▣ (Coral gem, Parrot's beak, Pelican's beak). Prostrate or trailing, evergreen subshrub with long stems densely clothed with palmate, silver-grey leaves, each with 3–5 linear leaflets, 1–2cm (½–¾in) long. In spring and early summer, freely bears solitary or paired, orange-red to scarlet, black-centred flowers, 3–4cm (1¼–1½in) long, resembling lobster claws. ↕ 20cm (8in), ↔ indefinite. Canary Islands, Cape Verde Islands. ❄ (borderline)
***L. corniculatus* 'Plenus'** (Double bird's foot trefoil). Spreading perennial with upright or prostrate stems bearing pinnate, mid- to bluish green leaves, each with 5 obovate to rounded leaflets, 0.5–1.5cm (¼–½in) long, the upper 3 separated from the lower 2 by a short stalk. In spring and early summer, produces axillary, umbel-like racemes of 3–8 pea-like, double yellow flowers, 1.5cm (½in) long, orange in bud, and often reddening with age. Less vigorous than the species. Suitable for a rock garden. ↕ 20–30cm (8–12in), ↔ to 30cm (12in) or more. ❄❄❄
L. hirsutus ▣ syn. *Dorycnium hirsutum* (Hairy canary clover). Rounded to spreading, evergreen or semi-evergreen,

Lotus berthelotii

Lotus hirsutus

silver-hairy subshrub with pinnate, densely hairy, grey-green leaves, each consisting of 5 elliptic to narrowly obovate leaflets, to 2cm (¾in) long. In summer and early autumn, produces axillary and terminal umbels of 4–10 pea-like, pink-flushed, creamy white flowers, 2cm (¾in) long, followed by reddish brown seed pods. Dislikes wet soil in winter. ↕ to 60cm (24in), ↔ to 1m (3ft). S. Portugal, Mediterranean. ❄❄❄ (borderline)
L. jacobaeus. Erect perennial with grey-hairy, sometimes pendent stems. Bears pinnate, mid-green leaves, each composed of 5 linear to narrowly obovate leaflets, 4cm (1½in) long, the upper 3 separated from the lower 2 by a short stalk. Pea-like, chocolate- to purple-brown flowers, to 1.5cm (½in) long, with brown-streaked yellow standard petals, are borne in axillary clusters of up to 6, on stalks longer than the leaves, from spring to autumn, but mainly in summer. ↕ 90cm (36in), ↔ 50cm (20in). Cape Verde Islands. ❄
L. maculatus. Trailing perennial, similar to *L. berthelotii,* with palmate, mid-green leaves, each consisting of 3–5 linear leaflets, 1–2cm (½–¾in) long. In spring and early summer, red- or orange-tipped yellow flowers, 2.5cm (1in) long and shaped like lobster claws, are borne singly or in clusters of 2–5 from the leaf axils. ↕ 20cm (8in), ↔ indefinite. Canary Islands (Tenerife). ❀ (min. 5°C/41°F)
***L. mascaensis* of gardens** see *L. sessilifolius.*
L. sessilifolius, syn. *L. mascaensis* of gardens. Low-growing, spreading, shrubby perennial with stalkless, 5-palmate, silver-grey leaves, each with oblong-lance-shaped leaflets, 5–10mm (¼–½in) long. Pea-like, vivid yellow flowers, 7mm (¼in) long, are borne in terminal and axillary clusters of 3–5 for several weeks in spring. ↕ to 60cm (24in), ↔ to 1.5m (5ft). Canary Islands. ❀ (min. 5°C/41°F)

▷ **Lotus** see *Nelumbo*
  American see *Nelumbo lutea*
  Blue see *Nymphaea caerulea*
  Sacred see *Nelumbo nucifera*
▷ **Lovage** see *Levisticum*
▷ **Love-in-a-mist** see *Nigella, N. damascena*
▷ **Love-in-a-puff** see *Cardiospermum halicacabum*
▷ **Love-in-idleness** see *Viola tricolor*
▷ **Love-lies-bleeding** see *Amaranthus caudatus*
▷ **Lucerne** see *Medicago sativa*

LUCULIA

RUBIACEAE

Genus of 5 species of deciduous and evergreen shrubs and small trees from E. Asia, found mostly in upland scrub and woodland and forest margins. They have large, prominently veined leaves, borne in opposite pairs, and terminal panicles or corymbs of salverform, waxy, fragrant flowers with 5 spreading lobes. In frost-prone climates, grow in a cool or temperate greenhouse. In milder climates, grow in a shrub border.
• **HARDINESS** Half hardy to frost tender.
• **CULTIVATION** Under glass, grow in loam-based potting compost (JI No.3) in full light. In spring, pot on or top-dress, and water moderately as growth begins. From summer to autumn, mist daily and water freely, applying a balanced liquid fertilizer monthly; keep just moist in winter. Outdoors, grow in moderately fertile, moist but well-drained soil in full sun. Pruning group 8 or group 9; may need restrictive pruning under glass.
• **PROPAGATION** Sow seed at 13–18°C (55–64°F) in spring. Root greenwood cuttings in summer with bottom heat.
• **PESTS AND DISEASES** Red spider mites, whiteflies, and mealybugs may be troublesome under glass.

L. grandifolia ♀ Erect to spreading, bushy, deciduous, large shrub or small tree. Ovate to elliptic, mid-green leaves, 20–35cm (8–14in) long, have red to brownish red stalks, veins, and margins, colouring richly in autumn. In summer, fragrant, salverform, greenish white to pure white flowers, 6–7cm (2½–3in) long, are borne in corymbs 10–20cm (4–8in) wide. ↕ 4–6m (12–20ft), ↔ 2–4m (6–12ft). Bhutan. ❀ (min. 5–7°C/41–45°F)
L. gratissima ♀ Erect then spreading, semi-evergreen or evergreen, large shrub or sometimes small tree, with downy, red-flushed green stems. Lance-shaped to ovate-oblong, long-pointed, prominently veined, mid- to deep green leaves are 10–20cm (4–8in) long, and downy beneath. Fragrant, salverform pink flowers, 2.5–4cm (1–1½in) long, with very slender tubes, are produced in corymbs, 10–20cm (4–8in) wide, from autumn to winter. ↕ 3–6m (10–20ft), ↔ 1.5–3m (5–10ft). Himalayas. ❀ (min. 7–10°C/45–50°F)

LUDWIGIA

ONAGRACEAE

Genus of 75 species of marginal and submerged aquatic perennials, occurring throughout the world, but mainly in warmer regions of North America. They have usually alternate, rarely opposite, simple, mainly stalkless leaves, borne on horizontal or upright, often floating stems. Small, sometimes showy, yellow or white flowers are produced singly from the leaf axils or in terminal clusters. In warm-temperate areas, grow at the margins of a wildlife pool. In cooler climates, grow tender species in an indoor pool or aquarium; *L. peploides* is particularly effective in an aquarium, where it may develop vertical, spongy, white, respiratory roots.
• **HARDINESS** Frost hardy to frost tender.

Ludwigia peploides

• **CULTIVATION** Grow in mud at the margins of a pool, in baskets of heavy loam in water 15–30cm (6–12in) deep, or in fertile soil in a bog garden, in full sun or dappled shade. In an aquarium, grow in bunches in an inert medium, at about 20°C (68°F), in full light. See also pp.52–53.
• **PROPAGATION** Divide in early spring. Take softwood cuttings in spring.
• **PESTS AND DISEASES** Trouble free.

L. longifolia, syn. *Jussiaea longifolia.* Upright, marginal aquatic perennial with narrowly winged stems sparsely covered with lance-shaped, mid-green leaves, 10–20cm (4–8in) long. Bears solitary, bell-shaped, pale yellow flowers, 3–5cm (1¼–2in) across, from the upper leaf axils in summer. ↕ 2m (6ft), ↔ 1m (3ft). Brazil to Argentina. ❀ (min. 13°C/55°F)
L. palustris (Water purslane). Marginal aquatic perennial with weak stems: either floating, to 50cm (20in) long, in water; or branched, creeping, and mat-forming on mud. Lance-shaped to elliptic-ovate leaves, 2–5cm (¾–2in) long, shiny, bright green above, dark olive-green to red-purple beneath, have long, sharp points. Axillary, paired, bell-shaped, yellowish green flowers, 2mm ($\frac{1}{16}$in) across, are borne in summer. ↕ 50cm (20in), ↔ indefinite. Europe, Asia, North and South America. ❄❄
L. peploides ▣ syn. *Jussiaea repens.* Scrambling, marginal aquatic perennial with horizontal shoots, to 60cm (24in) long, that root at the nodes or float. Elliptic, mid-green leaves, to 6cm (2½in) long, occasionally have vertical, spongy respiratory roots. In summer, bears axillary, solitary, cup-shaped, bright golden yellow flowers, 5cm (2in) across, with darker yellow spots at the bases. ↕ 60cm (24in), ↔ indefinite. North and South America. ❄

LUMA

MYRTACEAE

Genus of 4 species of evergreen shrubs and small trees from woodland in Chile and Argentina. They are mainly grown for their aromatic, leathery leaves, borne in opposite pairs, and their axillary, 4- or 5-petalled, cup-shaped white flowers; *L. apiculata* is also grown for its peeling bark. Grow as lawn specimens or in a small group; in frost-prone areas, grow in a sheltered border or against a wall. They may also be used for hedging.

Luma apiculata

- **HARDINESS** Frost hardy.
- **CULTIVATION** Grow in fertile, ideally humus-rich, well-drained soil in full sun or partial shade. Pruning group 1.
- **PROPAGATION** Sow seed in containers in a cold frame in spring. *L. apiculata* may self-seed. Take semi-ripe cuttings in late summer.
- **PESTS AND DISEASES** Trouble free.

L. apiculata ■ ♀ syn. *Myrtus apiculata, M. luma.* Vigorous, upright, bushy shrub or tree with peeling, cinnamon-brown and creamy white bark, and broadly elliptic, aromatic, glossy, dark green leaves, to 2.5cm (1in) long. Cup-shaped, 5-petalled white flowers, 2cm (¾in) long, are produced singly or in few-flowered cymes from midsummer to mid-autumn, followed by spherical purple berries. ↕↔ 10–15m (30–50ft) or more. Chile, Argentina. ❄❄.
'Glanleam Gold' is less vigorous, and has leaves with creamy yellow margins, pink-tinged when young; ↕↔ 3m (10ft).
L. chequen ♀ syn. *Myrtus chequen.* Upright shrub or small tree with broadly elliptic or broadly ovate, wavy-margined, aromatic, dark green leaves, to 2.5cm (1in) long. Cup-shaped, 4- or 5-petalled white flowers, 1.5cm (½in) across, are produced singly or in 3-flowered cymes in late summer and early autumn, followed by spherical black berries. ↕ 6m (20ft), ↔ 5m (15ft). Chile. ❄❄

LUNARIA

Honesty, Satin flower

BRASSICACEAE/CRUCIFERAE

Genus of 3 species of erect, branching annuals, biennials, and perennials occurring on disturbed ground and in uncultivated fields in Europe and W. Asia. They have alternate, ovate to triangular-heart-shaped, toothed leaves, and bear tall, open, terminal racemes of many 4-petalled, cross-shaped, violet-blue to white flowers in late spring and summer. Valued for their flowers, they may be naturalized in a shrub border, in woodland, or in a wild garden, where they self-seed. *L. annua* and *L. rediviva* have translucent seed pods that are excellent for dried flower arrangements.

- **HARDINESS** Fully hardy.
- **CULTIVATION** Grow in fertile, moist but well-drained soil in full sun or partial shade.
- **PROPAGATION** Sow seed in a seedbed: *L. rediviva* in spring, *L. annua* in early summer. Divide *L. rediviva* in spring.

Lunaria annua 'Munstead Purple'

- **PESTS AND DISEASES** Clubroot, white blister, and viruses may cause problems.

L. annua, syn. *L. biennis* (Honesty, Satin flower). Annual or biennial with ovate to heart-shaped, coarsely toothed, light to mid-green leaves, to 15cm (6in) long. In late spring and summer, cross-shaped, white to light purple flowers, to 1cm (½in) across, are borne in broad, leafy racemes, to 18cm (7in) long. Flat seed pods, 2.5–8cm (1–3in) long, are rounded and silvery. ↕ to 90cm (36in), ↔ to 30cm (12in). Europe. ❄❄❄.
var. *albiflora* bears white flowers.
var. *albiflora* 'Alba Variegata' has leaves variegated and margined creamy white, and white flowers. **'Munstead Purple'** ■ has deep reddish purple flowers. **'Variegata'** ■ bears leaves variegated and margined creamy white, and purple or red-purple flowers.
L. biennis see *L. annua.*
L. rediviva ■ (Perennial honesty). Clump-forming perennial with triangular-heart-shaped, finely toothed, dark green leaves, to 20cm (8in) long. Leafy stems bear loose racemes, to 18cm (7in) long, of fragrant, lilac-white flowers, 2.5cm (1in) across, in late spring and early summer, followed by flat, elliptic seed pods, to 5–8cm (2–3in) long, ripening to beige. ↕ 60–90cm (24–36in), ↔ 30cm (12in). Europe, Russia (W. Siberia). ❄❄❄

Lunaria rediviva

▷**Lungwort** see *Pulmonaria*
▷**Lupin** see *Lupinus*
Carolina see *Thermopsis villosa*
Tree see *Lupinus arboreus*

Lunaria annua 'Variegata'

LUPINUS

Lupin

LEGUMINOSAE/PAPILIONACEAE

Genus of about 200 species of annuals, perennials, and semi-evergreen and evergreen subshrubs or shrubs, mostly from the Mediterranean, North Africa, and North, Central, and South America; they are found in dry, hilly grassland and open woodland, on coastal sands or cliffs, and on riverbanks. Most have short-stemmed, palmate, often softly hairy, mid-green, mainly basal leaves, with lance-shaped leaflets; some alpines have silvery green leaves. Long, terminal racemes or spikes of pea-like flowers in many colours, including bicolours, are borne mainly in summer. There are numerous hybrid perennials (including the popular Russell lupins), which form dense clumps of palmate leaves and bear colourful flowers, 2.5cm (1in) long, in racemes or spikes 20–60cm (8–24in) long. Grow larger lupins in a border or wild garden, smaller species in a rock garden or scree bed; where winters are wet, grow the densely silver-hairy species in an alpine house. The seeds may cause severe discomfort if ingested.

- **HARDINESS** Fully hardy to half hardy.
- **CULTIVATION** Grow in moderately fertile, light and slightly acid, well-drained, sandy soil in full sun or partial shade. In an alpine house, grow in equal parts loam, leaf mould, and grit.
- **PROPAGATION** Sow seed in spring or autumn: for annuals and larger species, nick or soak for 24 hours and sow in a seedbed; for alpines and smaller species, sow in containers in a cold frame. Take basal cuttings of cultivars in mid-spring.
- **PESTS AND DISEASES** Fungal and bacterial rot, gall, mildew, leaf spot, virus, and slugs may be a problem.

L. albifrons ■ Erect to semi-erect, evergreen subshrub with 7- to 10-palmate, silver silky-hairy leaves, composed of inversely lance-shaped to

Lupinus albifrons

L

spoon-shaped leaflets, to 3cm (1¼in) long. In summer, pea-like, pale blue to red-purple flowers, 0.9–1.5cm (⅜–½in) across, with white-marked wing petals, are borne in racemes 10–30cm (4–12in) long. ↕↔ to 75cm (30in) or more. USA (California). ❄❄ (hardy to -7°C/20°F, but needs excellent drainage and full sun). **var. *collinus*** is lower-growing and much more compact; ↕↔ 10cm (4in).
L. arboreus ▣ (Tree lupin). Bushy, vigorous, evergreen or semi-evergreen shrub or subshrub, with silky shoots and 5- to 12-palmate, grey-green leaves, composed of obovate-oblong leaflets, to 6cm (2½in) long, silky-hairy beneath. Bears pea-like, fragrant, yellow, or rarely blue flowers, to 1.5cm (½in) long, in dense to lax, upright racemes, to 30cm (12in) long, in late spring and summer. ↕↔ 2m (6ft). USA (California). ❄❄. **'Mauve Queen'** has lilac flowers. **'Snow Queen'** has white flowers.
***L.* 'Band of Nobles'.** Clump-forming perennial bearing racemes of flowers in white, yellow, pink, red, blue, or bicolours (usually white or yellow in combination with another colour), in early and midsummer. ↕ to 1.5m (5ft), ↔ 75cm (30in). ❄❄❄
***L.* 'Beryl, Viscountess Cowdray'** ▣ Clump-forming perennial bearing dense racemes of bicoloured, rich pink and red flowers in early and midsummer. ↕ 90cm (36in), ↔ 75cm (30in). ❄❄❄
***L.* 'Blushing Bride'.** Clump-forming perennial bearing dense racemes of pink-tinged, ivory-white flowers in early and midsummer. ↕ 90cm (36in), ↔ 75cm (30in). ❄❄❄
***L. breweri*.** Tufted, mat-forming, short-lived, woody-based perennial with 7- to 10-palmate, densely silky-hairy, silver-green leaves, with inversely lance-shaped leaflets, to 2cm (¾in) long. In summer, bears dense racemes, to 5cm (2in) long, of pea-like, white-throated, violet-blue flowers, 6–9mm (¼–⅜in) long. ↕ 10cm (4in), ↔ to 20cm (8in). W. USA. ❄❄❄
***L.* 'Catherine of York'.** Clump-forming perennial bearing racemes of bicoloured,

Lupinus 'Beryl, Viscountess Cowdray'

pure salmon-orange and yellow flowers in early and midsummer. ↕ 90cm (36in), ↔ 75cm (30in). ❄❄❄
***L.* 'Chandelier'** ▣ Clump-forming perennial producing racemes of bright yellow flowers in early and midsummer. ↕ 90cm (36in), ↔ 75cm (30in). ❄❄❄
L. cruckshankii see *L. mutabilis.*
***L.* 'Lady Fayre'.** Clump-forming perennial bearing racemes of deep rose-pink flowers in early and midsummer. ↕ 90cm (36in), ↔ 75cm (30in). ❄❄❄
L. lepidus* var. *lobbii, syn. *L. lyallii.* Semi-prostrate to mat-forming, short-lived perennial bearing 5- to 7-palmate, silky-hairy, silver-green leaves, with inversely lance-shaped leaflets, to 1cm (½in) long. In late summer, bears dense racemes, to 5cm (2in) long, of pea-like, bright blue flowers, 1cm (½in) long, each standard petal with a white spot. ↕ 10cm (4in), ↔ to 20cm (8in). USA (Washington State to California). ❄❄❄
***L. luteus* 'Yellow Javelin'.** Erect, bushy annual with densely hairy stems and 7- to 11-palmate leaves, each with obovate-oblong, round-tipped, softly hairy, mid-green leaflets, 3–6cm (1¼–2½in) long. In summer, bears pea-like, bright golden yellow flowers, to 2cm (¾in) long, in

Lupinus arboreus

Lupinus 'Chandelier'

tall racemes, to 25cm (10in) long. ↕ to 60cm (24in), ↔ 30cm (12in). ❄❄❄
L. lyallii see *L. lepidus* var. *lobbii.*
***L.* 'Moonraker'.** Clump-forming perennial bearing racemes of lemon-yellow flowers in early and midsummer. ↕ 90cm (36in), ↔ 75cm (30in). ❄❄❄
L. mutabilis, syn. *L. cruckshankii.* Erect, bushy annual, with 7- to 9-palmate leaves, with inversely lance-shaped to spoon-shaped, round-tipped, blue-green leaflets, to 5–6cm (2–2½in) long, softly hairy beneath. In summer, bears racemes, 10–20cm (4–8in) long, of pea-like flowers, 2–3cm (¾–1¼in) long, with pale purple-blue keel petals, yellow standard petals, and deep blue wing petals. ↕ 1–1.1m (3–3½ft), ↔ 45–60cm (18–24in). ❄❄
***L.* 'My Castle'.** Clump-forming perennial bearing racemes of deep rose-pink flowers in early and midsummer. ↕ 90cm (36in), ↔ 75cm (30in). ❄❄❄
***L. nanus* 'Pixie Delight'** ▣ Erect, single-stemmed to bushy annual with 5- to 7-palmate leaves, composed of linear-lance-shaped, pointed, softly hairy, mid-green leaflets, to 3cm (1¼in) long. In summer, bears racemes, to 20cm (8in) long, of pea-like, pink, blue, lavender-

Lupinus 'The Chatelaine'

blue, white, or bicoloured flowers, 1.5cm (½in) across, the standard petals often with purple-dotted white marks or yellow spots. ↕ 50cm (20in), ↔ to 23cm (9in). ❄❄❄
***L.* 'Noble Maiden'.** Clump-forming perennial bearing racemes of creamy white flowers in early and midsummer. ↕ 90cm (36in), ↔ 75cm (30in). ❄❄❄
L. texensis (Texas bluebonnet). Erect to spreading, bushy annual with softly hairy stems and 5-palmate, mid-green leaves, each with lance-shaped, pointed leaflets, to 3cm (1¼in) long, hairy beneath and on the margins. Compact, crowded racemes, to 8cm (3in) long, of pea-like, deep blue to blue-purple flowers, 1cm (½in) across, are produced in summer. ↕ 25–30cm (10–12in), ↔ to 23cm (9in). USA (Texas). ❄❄❄
***L.* 'The Chatelaine'** ▣ Clump-forming perennial producing racemes of bicoloured, pink and white flowers in early and midsummer. ↕ 90cm (36in), ↔ 75cm (30in). ❄❄❄
***L.* 'The Governor'.** Clump-forming perennial producing racemes of bicoloured, deep blue and white flowers in early and midsummer. ↕ 90cm (36in), ↔ 75cm (30in). ❄❄❄

Lupinus nanus 'Pixie Delight'

Lupinus 'The Page'

L. 'The Page' ■ Clump-forming perennial producing racemes of rich carmine-red flowers in early and midsummer. ↕ 90cm (36in), ↔ 75cm (30in). ❄❄❄

L. 'Thundercloud'. Clump-forming perennial producing racemes of deep violet-blue flowers in early and midsummer. ↕ 90cm (36in), ↔ 75cm (30in). ❄❄❄

L

LUZULA

Woodrush

JUNCACEAE

Genus of about 80 species of mostly evergreen, tufted, grass-like perennials (rarely annuals), sometimes with short rhizomes or stolons. Woodrushes are widely distributed on heaths and moors, in fens and bogs, and in scrub, woodland, and mountain grassland throughout temperate regions. Broadly linear basal and stem leaves are flat or grooved along their lengths, and have fringes of zigzagged white hairs at the margins, which distinguish them from rushes (*Juncus*). Tiny flowers are borne in terminal, panicle-, corymb-, or cyme-like clusters, in spring or summer. Valued for their shade tolerance, woodrushes provide useful ground cover in damp shade, either in a mixed border or in a woodland garden. *L. ulophylla* is also suitable for a trough or rock garden.

• **HARDINESS** Most are fully hardy; *L. ulophylla* is hardy to -8°C (18°F) for short periods.

• **CULTIVATION** Grow in poor to moderately fertile, humus-rich, moist but well-drained soil in partial or deep shade (or in full sun where the soil is reliably moist). *L. nivea* prefers full sun.

• **PROPAGATION** Sow seed in containers outdoors in spring or autumn. Divide between mid-spring and early summer.

• **PESTS AND DISEASES** Trouble free.

L. maxima see *L. sylvatica*.

L. nivea ■ (Snowy woodrush). Slowly spreading, loosely tufted, evergreen

Luzula nivea

perennial forming loose clumps of flat, linear, deep green basal leaves, to 30cm (12in) long; stem leaves are to 20cm (8in) long. In early and midsummer, bears lax panicles, to 5cm (2in) long, of shiny, pure white flowers in tight clusters of up to 20. May be dried. ↕ to 60cm (24in), ↔ 45cm (18in). Spain, France, Italy, Slovenia, C. Europe. ❄❄❄

L. sylvatica, syn. *L. maxima* (Greater woodrush). Densely tufted, tussock-forming, evergreen perennial with linear, channelled, glossy, dark green leaves, to 30cm (12in) long. Groups of 2–5 small, chestnut-brown flowers are produced in open panicles, to 8cm (3in) long, from mid-spring to early summer. ↕ to 70–80cm (28–32in), ↔ 45cm (18in). S., W., and C. Europe, S.W. Asia. ❄❄❄. The following cultivars provide useful, dense ground cover.

'Aurea' ■ syn. *L. maxima* 'Aurea', has broad leaves that are bright, shiny yellow in winter, yellow-green in summer.

'Aureomarginata' see 'Marginata'.

'Marginata', syn. 'Aureomarginata', has a dense habit, rich green leaves with neat cream margins, and pendent, brown and gold spikelets.

Luzula sylvatica 'Aurea'

L. ulophylla. Dwarf, densely tufted, evergreen perennial forming a low mound of linear, deep green leaves, to 3–7cm (1¼–3in) long, V-shaped in cross-section, with conspicuous silvery hairs beneath and on the margins. In early summer, very dark brown flowers, the tepals with white membranous margins, are produced in short, stubby clusters, to 2cm (¾in) long. ↕ to 15cm (6in), ↔ 30cm (12in). New Zealand. ❄❄

LYCASTE

ORCHIDACEAE

Genus of about 45 species of deciduous, epiphytic or terrestrial orchids found in cloud forest at altitudes of 600–2,200m (2,000–7,700ft) in Mexico, Central and South America, and the West Indies. They produce robust, ovoid or ellipsoid, compressed pseudobulbs, and a number of broad, lance-shaped to oblong-elliptic, often soft, folded leaves. Large, waxy, fragrant flowers, produced singly on leafless stems from the bases, are typically triangular in shape, with the sepals framing the smaller, cupped petals and 3-lobed lips.

• **HARDINESS** Frost tender.

• **CULTIVATION** Cool-growing orchids. Grow in containers of crushed bark or loamless potting compost, or grow epiphytically on bark slabs. Throughout summer, provide high humidity and water freely (keeping the foliage dry); apply a balanced liquid fertilizer at every third watering. During winter, provide bright filtered light and keep dry. See also p.46.

• **PROPAGATION** Divide when plants overflow their containers, or remove and pot up backbulbs.

• **PESTS AND DISEASES** Red spider mites, aphids, whiteflies, and mealybugs may be troublesome.

L. aromatica. Epiphytic orchid with lance-shaped leaves, to 30–40cm (12–16in) long. Cinnamon-scented flowers, 4–6cm (1½–2½in) across, with deep golden to orange-yellow petals, yellowish green sepals, and lips with orange dots, are produced in abundance from spring to summer. ↕↔ 30cm (12in). Mexico, Guatemala, Belize, Honduras. ✽ (min. 11–12°C/52–54°F; max. 30°C/86°F)

L. brevispatha, syn. *L. candida* of gardens. Epiphytic orchid with lance-shaped leaves, to 50cm (20in) long. From winter to spring, produces an abundance of flowers, to 10cm (4in) across, with light green sepals with reddish brown spots, brown-spotted white petals, and white lips suffused and spotted pink. ↕↔ 30cm (12in). Guatemala, Nicaragua, Costa Rica, Panama. ✽ (min. 11–12°C/52–54°F; max. 30°C/86°F)

L. candida of gardens see *L. brevispatha*.

L. cruenta ■ Epiphytic orchid with lance-shaped leaves, to 35cm (18in) long. From spring to summer, produces an abundance of faintly cinnamon-scented flowers, to 7cm (3in) across, with greenish yellow sepals, yellowish orange petals with red spots near the bases, and orange lips with red spots and red triangular patches at the bases. ↕↔ 45cm (18in). Mexico, Guatemala,

Lycaste cruenta

El Salvador, Costa Rica. ✽ (min. 11–12°C/52–54°F; max. 30°C/86°F)

L. deppei ■ Epiphytic orchid with lance-shaped leaves, 30–50cm (12–20in) long. From spring to summer, produces abundant flowers, 9cm (3½in) across, with green sepals spotted red-brown, white petals flecked red-brown at the bases, and red-spotted, deep yellow lips, striped and dotted red at the bases. ↕↔ 30cm (12in). Mexico, Guatemala. ✽ (min. 11–12°C/52–54°F; max. 30°C/86°F)

L. gigantea see *L. longipetala*.

L. longipetala, syn. *L. gigantea*. Epiphytic orchid with lance-shaped leaves, to 60cm (24in) long. In summer, bears large, fleshy flowers, to 16cm (6in) across, with pale green sepals suffused brown, darker green petals, and red-brown lips with light orange margins; the flowers do not open fully. ↕↔ 45cm (18in). Venezuela, Colombia, Ecuador, Peru. ✽ (min. 11–12°C/52–54°F; max. 30°C/86°F)

L. skinneri, syn. *L. virginalis*. Epiphytic orchid with lance-shaped leaves, 50–60cm (20–24in) long. From winter to spring, produces flowers 12–15cm (5–6in) across, with cream sepals shaded lavender-pink to pink, reddish purple petals, and pink lips sometimes mottled purple. ↕↔ 30cm (12in). Mexico, Guatemala, Honduras, El Salvador. ✽ (min. 11–12°C/52–54°F; max. 30°C/86°F)

L. virginalis see *L. skinneri*.

L. Wyldfire (*L.* Balliae x *L.* Wyld Court). Robust, epiphytic orchid with lance-shaped leaves, 40cm (16in) long. In spring, produces an abundance of deep wine-red flowers, 12cm (5in) across, with darker lips. ↕↔ 45cm (18in). ✽ (min. 11–12°C/52–54°F; max. 30°C/86°F)

Lycaste deppei

LYCHNIS syn. VISCARIA

Campion, Catchfly

CARYOPHYLLACEAE

Genus of 15–20 species of biennials and perennials found in sites ranging from damp meadows and woodland to alpine habitats, in N. temperate and arctic regions. They have erect, usually branched stems, and opposite, simple, often hairy leaves. The 5-petalled, salverform to tubular or star-shaped flowers occur in scarlet, purple, pink, or white, and are either solitary or borne in terminal cymes or occasionally panicles. Grow larger perennials in a sunny border or wild garden, smaller, alpine species in a rock garden, and biennials in an annual or herbaceous border.

- **HARDINESS** Fully hardy.
- **CULTIVATION** Grow in any moderately fertile, well-drained soil in full sun or partial shade. *L. chalcedonica*, *L.* x *haageana*, and *L. viscaria* prefer moist, fertile soil; grey-leaved species produce their best leaf colour in dry soil in full sun. Dead-head to prolong flowering.
- **PROPAGATION** Sow seed in containers in a cold frame as soon as ripe or in spring; *L.* x *haageana* will flower the same year and may be treated as an annual. Divide or take basal cuttings in early spring.
- **PESTS AND DISEASES** Slugs may be a problem.

L. alpina ▣ (Alpine campion, Alpine catchfly). Dwarf, tufted perennial with rosettes of oblong-lance-shaped to elliptic-lance-shaped, dark green leaves, to 4cm (1½in) long. In summer, bears dense, rounded, terminal cymes of 6–20 salverform, purplish pink flowers, to 2cm (¾in) across, with frilled, 2-lobed petals. ↕↔ to 15cm (6in). Mountains of N. hemisphere, subarctic regions. ❄❄❄

Lychnis alpina

Lychnis x *arkwrightii* 'Vesuvius'

Lychnis chalcedonica

***L.* x *arkwrightii* 'Vesuvius'** ▣ Short-lived, clump-forming perennial with ovate-lance-shaped, hairy, dark brownish green leaves, 8cm (3in) long. In early and midsummer, bears terminal cymes of 5–10 star-shaped, orange-scarlet flowers, 3–4cm (1¼–1½in) across, with notched petals. ↕45cm (18in), ↔ 30cm (12in). ❄❄❄

L. chalcedonica ▣ (Jerusalem cross, Maltese cross). Erect, stiff perennial with ovate, mid-green basal leaves, and hairy, unbranched stems bearing clasping, ovate leaves, 5–8cm (2–3in) long, with heart-shaped bases. In early and midsummer, produces terminal, rounded, umbel-like cymes of 10–30 star-shaped scarlet flowers, 1.5cm (½in) across, each petal with 2 deep notches. Requires support. Self-seeds. ↕0.9–1.2m (3–4ft), ↔ 30cm (12in). European Russia. ❄❄❄. **'Rosea'** has rose-pink flowers.

L. coeli-rosa see *Silene coeli-rosa.*

L. coronaria ▣ (Dusty miller, Rose campion). Erect, woolly, silver-grey biennial or short-lived perennial with ovate-lance-shaped, silver-grey leaves: the basal leaves to 18cm (7in) long, the stem leaves to 10cm (4in). In late summer, bears few-flowered, terminal cymes of salverform, rounded, purple-red or pale purple flowers, 3cm (1¼in) across, with slightly reflexed, shallowly 2-lobed petals; they open singly, but in long succession. Self-seeds freely. ↕80cm (32in), ↔ 45cm (18in). S.E. Europe. ❄❄❄. **'Alba'** has white flowers.

Lychnis coronaria

Lychnis flos-jovis

L. coronata* var. *sieboldii see *L. sieboldii.*

L. flos-cuculi (Ragged robin). Slender, upright or spreading, sparsely hairy perennial with inversely lance-shaped, mid- to bluish green basal leaves, to 12cm (5in) long, and smaller, oblong-lance-shaped stem-clasping leaves. In late spring and early summer, produces loose, few-flowered, branched, terminal cymes of star-shaped, pale to bright purplish pink, sometimes white flowers, to 4cm (1½in) across, with petals deeply cut into 4 linear segments. Suitable for a wild garden. ↕ to 75cm (30in), ↔ to 80cm (32in). Damp places in Europe, Caucasus, and Russia (Siberia). ❄❄❄

L. flos-jovis ▣ (Flower of Jove, Flower of Jupiter). Mat-forming perennial with usually unbranched, erect, white-hairy stems, and lance- to spoon-shaped basal and stem-clasping leaves, to 10cm (4in) long. From early to late summer, bears loosely rounded cymes of 4–10 rounded, pink, white, or scarlet flowers, 2.5cm (1in) across, with slightly reflexed, notched petals. ↕20–60cm (8–24in) or more, ↔ 45cm (18in). C. Alps. ❄❄❄. **'Hort's Variety'** has rose-pink flowers; ↕30cm (12in).

L.* x *haageana (*L. fulgens* x *L. sieboldii*). Short-lived, clump-forming, hairy perennial with lance-shaped, mid-green leaves, 4–8cm (1½–3in) long. In mid- and late summer, salverform, brilliant red or orange flowers, 5cm (2in) across, with notched petals, are borne in few-flowered, loose, terminal cymes. ↕45–60cm (18–24in), ↔ 30cm (12in). Garden origin. ❄❄❄ (borderline)

L. sieboldii, syn. *L. coronata* var. *sieboldii*. Clump-forming, hairy perennial bearing inversely lance-shaped to elliptic, mid-green leaves, 5–8cm (2–3in) long. Clustered, terminal cymes of many flat, rounded, deep red flowers, 5cm (2in) across, the petals with shallowly toothed lobes, are produced in summer and early autumn. ↕60cm (24in), ↔ 30cm (12in). Japan. ❄❄❄

L. viscaria ▣ syn. *Viscaria vulgaris* (German catchfly). Mat-forming to tufted perennial with elliptic-lance-shaped to oblong-lance-shaped, hairless, dark green basal leaves, to 8cm (3in) long. The usually unbranched stems are sticky, with a few lance-shaped leaves. In early and midsummer, bears narrow, spike-like panicles of numerous salverform, purplish pink flowers, 2cm (¾in) across, with notched petals. ↕↔ 45cm (18in). Europe to W. Asia. ❄❄❄. **'Flore Pleno'** see 'Splendens Plena'. **'Fontaine'** produces large, double, pale red flowers, 2.5cm (1in) across. **'Snowbird'** produces white flowers. **'Splendens Plena'**, syn. 'Flore Pleno', bears double, bright pinkish magenta flowers, 2.5cm (1in) across.

***L.* x *walkeri* 'Abbotswood Rose'.** Clump-forming, woolly, silver-grey perennial, similar to *L. coronaria* but more spreading and shorter, with ovate, silver-grey basal leaves, to 8cm (3in) long, and smaller stem leaves. From early to late summer, produces terminal cymes of numerous salverform, rose-pink flowers, 3cm (1¼in) across, with slightly reflexed, shallowly notched petals. ↕40cm (16in) or more, ↔ 45cm (18in). ❄❄❄

Lychnis viscaria

▷ ***Lycianthes*** see *Solanum*
L. rantonnetii see *S. rantonnei*

LYCIUM

SOLANACEAE

Genus of about 100 species of sometimes spiny, deciduous and evergreen, often scandent shrubs, occurring throughout temperate and subtropical regions, usually in dry soil. Leaves are entire and alternate, and funnel-shaped or tubular flowers are borne singly or in clusters of up to 4 from the leaf axils. Cultivated for their habit, flowers, and fruits, they are useful for a shrub border or for covering a dry bank; they are particularly effective as a windbreak or hedge in a coastal garden. In frost-prone areas, grow tender species in a cool or temperate greenhouse.

- **HARDINESS** Fully hardy to frost tender.
- **CULTIVATION** Grow in moderately fertile, well-drained soil in full sun. Pruning group 1, or, for scandent species, group 11, in winter or early spring. Cut back hedges hard in spring; trim in early summer.
- **PROPAGATION** Sow seed in containers outdoors in autumn. Take hardwood cuttings in winter, or softwood cuttings in early summer.
- **PESTS AND DISEASES** Trouble free.

L. barbarum, syn. *L. halimifolium* (Chinese box thorn, Duke of Argyll's tea-tree). Variable, vigorous, erect or wide-spreading, sometimes scandent, often spiny, deciduous shrub. Long, arching branches bear narrowly oblong-lance-shaped, elliptic, or ovate, mid-green to grey-green leaves, to 6cm (2½in) long. Small clusters of 1–4 funnel-shaped, purple, lilac, or pink flowers, 9mm (⅜in) long, are produced in late spring and summer, followed by ovoid, orange-red or yellow berries, to 2cm (¾in) long. ↕ 3.5m (11ft) or more, ↔ 5m (15ft). China. ❄❄❄
L. halimifolium see *L. barbarum*.

LYCOPODIUM

Club moss

LYCOPODIACEAE

Genus of 100 or more species of rhizomatous, evergreen, terrestrial or epiphytic, moss-like perennials, found in most parts of the world in a very wide range of habitats, but mainly in tropical or temperate rainforest or cloud forest. They have erect, pendent, or creeping stems, which are usually repeatedly forked, and bear small, simple, linear-lance-shaped to ovate-triangular leaves, overlapping or in whorls. Spores are produced in the leaf axils, or sometimes in terminal cones on the smaller leaves. Only the epiphytic species are cultivated. In frost-prone areas, grow in a temperate or warm greenhouse. In frost-free climates, grow as epiphytes in shaded, damp sites.

- **HARDINESS** Frost tender.
- **CULTIVATION** Under glass, grow in slatted wooden baskets in equal parts peat, roughly chopped sphagnum moss, charcoal, and broken crocks, in bright indirect light. In the growing season, water moderately (avoiding the foliage), mist daily in summer, and apply a half-strength, seaweed-based liquid fertilizer

Lycopodium phlegmaria

as a foliar spray every month. Reduce watering in winter but do not allow the compost to dry out. Outdoors, grow epiphytically in a permanently damp niche on a tree, in partial shade.
- **PROPAGATION** Layer tips of fertile leaves at any time of year. See also p.51.
- **PESTS AND DISEASES** Slugs, snails, or mites may eat the soft, tender tips of growing stems. Fern scale may be a serious problem.

L. phlegmaria ▣ Epiphytic perennial with initially upright, later pendent stems, to 1m (3ft) long, forked several times. Produces often upright, broadly ovate-triangular, yellow- to olive-green leaves, to 2cm (¾in) long. Spores are formed in branched, terminal cones, to 1.5cm (½in) across, on small leaves. Probably an aggregate of several species. ↕ 90cm (36in), ↔ 1m (3ft). Asia, Australia, Pacific islands. ❀ (min. 10°C/50°F)

LYCORIS

AMARYLLIDACEAE

Genus of 10–12 species of bulbous perennials from wooded hills or rocky sites in low mountains, and the margins of cultivated fields, in China and Japan. They are grown for their showy umbels of tubular-funnel-shaped flowers, with narrow, spreading, sometimes reflexed tepal lobes, borne on leafless stems from spring to early autumn. The leaves are linear or strap-shaped. In areas with dry summers, grow in a sunny border or rock garden. Where summers are wet, they are best grown as container plants in a conservatory or cool greenhouse, but do not always flower regularly.

- **HARDINESS** Frost hardy to half hardy. *L. aurea*, *L. radiata*, and *L. squamigera* tolerate occasional temperatures to -15°C (5°F).
- **CULTIVATION** Plant in autumn with the necks of the bulbs at the surface. Under glass, grow in loam-based potting compost (JI No.2) in full light. Top-dress when growth begins, then water freely and apply a balanced liquid fertilizer monthly until the leaves die down. Keep dry in summer when dormant. Outdoors, grow in fertile, well-drained soil that dries out in summer, in full sun. In frost-prone areas, protect with a dry winter mulch.
- **PROPAGATION** Sow seed at 6–12°C (45–54°F) as soon as ripe. Remove offsets after flowering.
- **PESTS AND DISEASES** Trouble free.

L. albiflora. Bulbous perennial bearing umbels of 4–6 small, tubular-funnel-shaped white flowers, 4–5cm (1½–2in) long, with strongly reflexed, wavy-margined tepals and protruding stamens, in late summer and early autumn. Semi-erect, strap-shaped, glaucous, mid-green leaves, 30–60cm (12–24in) long, are produced after the flowers. Similar to *L. radiata*, and probably a variety of it. ↕ 45cm (18in), ↔ 20cm (8in). Japan. ❄
L. aurea ▣ (Golden spider lily). Bulbous perennial producing umbels, from spring to summer, of 5 or 6 tubular-funnel-shaped, wavy-margined yellow flowers, 10cm (4in) across, with the tepals reflexed at the tips, and

Lycoris aurea

Lycoris radiata

protruding stamens. Semi-erect, strap-shaped, fleshy, glaucous, mid-green leaves, to 60cm (24in) long, appear after the flowers. ↕ to 60cm (24in), ↔ 20cm (8in). China, Japan. ❄❄
L. radiata ▣ (Red spider lily). Bulbous perennial with wavy-margined, rose-red or deep red flowers, 4–5cm (1½–2in) long, with strongly reflexed tepals and conspicuous, protruding stamens, borne in umbels of 4–6 in late summer and early autumn. Semi-erect, strap-shaped, dark green leaves, 30–60cm (12–24in) long, appear after the flowers. ↕ 30–50cm (12–20in), ↔ 20cm (8in). Japan. ❄❄
L. sanguinea. Bulbous perennial producing umbels of up to 6 funnel-shaped, wavy-margined, bright red flowers, 5–6cm (2–2½in) across, the tepals with slightly reflexed tips, in summer and early autumn. Semi-erect, linear, dark green leaves, to 60cm (24in) long, appear after the flowers. ↕ to 50cm (20in), ↔ 20cm (8in). China, Japan. ❄
L. squamigera (Resurrection lily). Bulbous perennial with almost erect, tubular-funnel-shaped, slightly wavy, fragrant, pale rose-red flowers, 9–10cm (3½–4in) across, flushed or veined blue or purple, the tepals with reflexed tips, borne in umbels of up to 8 in summer. Semi-erect, strap-shaped, mid-green leaves, 30cm (12in) long, are produced the following spring. ↕ 45–70cm (18–28in), ↔ 30cm (12in). Japan. ❄❄

LYGODIUM

Climbing fern

SCHIZAEACEAE

Genus of 40 species of semi-evergreen and deciduous, scrambling or climbing ferns from tropical and subtropical forests worldwide. A single, palmately lobed or pinnate frond arises from the creeping, branching rhizomes. The midrib of the frond continues to grow, producing new pinnae in distant pairs; each pinna has a long, often forked stalk and a varying number of leaf-like segments. Spores are produced in small spikes at the segment margins. In frost-prone areas, grow in a warm greenhouse. In warmer areas, grow in moist woodland.

- **HARDINESS** Half hardy to frost tender. *L. palmatum* will withstand short periods at -5°C (23°F).
- **CULTIVATION** Under glass, grow in a mix of equal parts coarse leaf mould or peat, loam-based potting compost (JI No.2), chopped sphagnum moss,

Lygodium japonicum

and charcoal, in bright filtered light. Support on wires and provide plenty of space to climb. During the growing season, water freely, apply a balanced liquid fertilizer monthly, and mist daily. Reduce watering in winter but do not allow the compost to dry out. Outdoors, grow in moderately fertile, moist, peaty soil in deep or partial shade. *L. palmatum* needs lime-free soil.
- **PROPAGATION** Sow spores at 21°C (70°F) as soon as ripe. Divide plants before the leaves develop. See also p.51.
- **PESTS AND DISEASES** Trouble free.

L. japonicum ■ (Japanese climbing fern). Deciduous, climbing fern producing 2- or 3-pinnate, very finely divided fronds. Sterile pinnae, 5–12cm (2–5in) long, are irregularly and deeply lobed to pinnate; fertile pinnae are similar, or more finely divided. ↕ 2–3m (6–10ft) or more. India, China, Korea, Japan. ❀ (min. 5°C/41°F)
L. palmatum. Deciduous, climbing fern with palmately 3- to 7-lobed fronds, to 4cm (1½in) long. Fertile pinnae are much more finely divided than sterile ones. ↕ to 2m (6ft) or more. E. USA (N. Carolina to Florida). ✻

▷ ***Lygos*** see *Retama*

LYONIA

ERICACEAE

Genus of approximately 35 species of deciduous and evergreen shrubs, sometimes small trees, from the Himalayas, E. Asia, USA, Mexico, and the Antilles, generally occurring in woodland. They have simple, glossy, leathery leaves, borne alternately, and are cultivated for their dense, axillary racemes or clusters of often urn-shaped, sometimes bell-shaped, ovoid, or cylindrical flowers, borne on the previous year's shoots. Suitable for a woodland garden or peat garden.
- **HARDINESS** Fully hardy to frost hardy.
- **CULTIVATION** Grow in acid to neutral, moderately fertile, humus-rich, moist but well-drained soil in partial or deep shade. Pruning group 1 or 8.
- **PROPAGATION** Sow seed in containers outdoors in autumn. Take semi-ripe cuttings in summer. Layer in spring.
- **PESTS AND DISEASES** Trouble free.

L. ferruginea ⚲ (Rusty lyonia). Spreading, bushy, evergreen shrub or small tree with elliptic to ovate or obovate, leathery, dark green leaves, to 9cm (3½in) long, usually with the margins rolled under. The shoots and undersides of the leaves are covered with red-brown scales. Pendent clusters of up to 10 urn-shaped white flowers, 4mm (⅛in) long, are produced in late winter or spring. ↕ 5m (15ft), usually less, ↔ 2m (6ft). S.E. USA. ✻✻

Lyonia mariana

L. mariana ■ (Stagger-bush). Rounded, deciduous shrub with oblong, elliptic, or narrowly obovate, leathery, dark green leaves, to 8cm (3in) long, red in autumn, dotted with brown glands beneath. Pendent, ovoid-cylindrical, white to pale pink flowers, 0.8–1.5cm (⅜–½in) long, are borne in many-flowered, umbel-like racemes in late spring and early summer. ↕ to 2m (6ft), ↔ 1.2m (4ft). E. USA. ✻✻✻
L. ovalifolia ⚲ Bushy, rounded, deciduous or semi-evergreen shrub or small tree with red shoots. Paired, ovate-elliptic, ovate, or ovate-oblong, leathery, dark green leaves, to 15cm (6in) long, are often finely downy beneath. In late spring or summer, bears ovoid white flowers, to 1cm (½in) long, in racemes 5–10cm (2–4in) long. ↕ 3m (10ft), ↔ 2m (6ft) as a shrub; ↕ 12m (40ft), ↔ 8m (25ft) as a tree. Himalayas, China, Japan, Taiwan. ✻✻✻

▷ **Lyonia, Rusty** see *Lyonia ferruginea*

LYONOTHAMNUS

ROSACEAE

Genus of one species of evergreen tree, growing wild in canyons and on dry slopes in California, USA. Cultivated mainly for its habit, attractive bark, and simple to pinnate, thick, glossy leaves, borne in opposite pairs, it is effective as a specimen tree or in woodland.
- **HARDINESS** Frost hardy.
- **CULTIVATION** Grow in fertile, moist but well-drained soil in full sun or partial shade. Shelter from cold, drying winds in frost-prone areas. Pruning group 1.
- **PROPAGATION** Sow seed in containers outdoors in autumn, or take greenwood cuttings in summer.
- **PESTS AND DISEASES** Trouble free.

L. floribundus ♢ (Catalina ironwood). Conical, evergreen tree with peeling, red-brown bark and oblong to lance-shaped, glossy, deep green leaves, to 20cm (8in) long, softly hairy beneath; leaves are simple, or sometimes partially or fully pinnate on the same tree. From spring to summer, bears large, terminal, corymb-like panicles, to 20cm (8in) across, of small, 5-petalled, star-shaped white flowers. ↕ 12m (40ft), ↔ 6m (20ft). USA (California, Santa Catalina Island). ✻✻. **subsp. *aspleniifolius*** has pinnate or 2-pinnate leaves, often with pinnatifid leaflets; USA (islands off the coast of California).

▷ **Lyre flower** see *Dicentra spectabilis*

LYSICHITON

Skunk cabbage

ARACEAE

Genus of 2 species of robust, marginal aquatic perennials, with short rhizomes, from N.E. Asia and W. North America. They are grown for their basal clusters of large, ovate-oblong, glossy, mid- to dark green leaves, and yellow or white spathes that surround spadices bearing small, bisexual green flowers. They have a musky smell. Grow beside a stream or pool. All parts may cause severe discomfort if ingested; contact with the sap may irritate the skin and eyes.
- **HARDINESS** Fully hardy.
- **CULTIVATION** Grow in fertile, humus-rich soil at the margins of a stream or pool, in full sun or partial shade. Allow ample room for the leaves to develop. See also pp.52–53.
- **PROPAGATION** Sow seed on a tray of wet soil in a cold frame as soon as ripe. Remove offsets at the bases of the main stems in spring or summer.
- **PESTS AND DISEASES** Trouble free.

Lysichiton americanus

Lysichiton camtschatcensis

L. americanus ■ (Yellow skunk cabbage). Marginal aquatic perennial with rosettes of ovate-oblong, strongly veined, leathery, glossy, mid- to dark green leaves, 50–120cm (20–48in) long. Ovate to narrowly ovate, bright yellow spathes, to 40cm (16in) long, are borne in early spring. ↕ 1m (3ft), ↔ 1.2m (4ft). W. North America. ✻✻✻
L. camtschatcensis ■ (White skunk cabbage). Marginal aquatic perennial with rosettes of ovate-oblong, strongly veined, leathery, glossy, mid- to dark green leaves, 50–100cm (20–39in) long. In early spring, produces ovate to broadly lance-shaped, usually pointed white spathes, to 40cm (16in) long. ↕↔ 75cm (30in). N.E. Asia. ✻✻✻

LYSIMACHIA

Loosestrife

PRIMULACEAE

Genus of about 150 species of herbaceous and evergreen perennials and shrubs, mainly growing in damp grassland and woodland or by water, in subtropical regions, including South Africa, and N. temperate regions. They have opposite, alternate, or whorled, simple, entire or sometimes toothed or scalloped, often hairy leaves. The 5-petalled flowers vary from star-shaped to saucer- or cup-shaped, and are usually white or yellow, sometimes pink or purple, and either solitary and axillary or borne in terminal racemes or panicles. Larger species are suitable for a moist herbaceous border, bog garden, or pond margin, or for naturalizing in a wild or woodland garden. Low-growing species provide good ground cover. In frost-prone climates, grow tender species in a cool greenhouse.
- **HARDINESS** Fully hardy to frost tender.
- **CULTIVATION** Grow in humus-rich, preferably moist but well-drained soil that does not dry out in summer, in full sun or partial shade. Tall species may need support.
- **PROPAGATION** Sow seed in containers outdoors in spring. Divide in spring or autumn.
- **PESTS AND DISEASES** May be damaged by slugs and snails.

L. barystachys. Erect herbaceous perennial with softly hairy stems and alternate, rarely opposite, linear-oblong to lance-shaped, hairy, mid-green leaves, to 8cm (3in) long, glaucous beneath. Dense, pendent then erect, terminal

Lysimachia clethroides

racemes, to 30cm (12in) long, of star-shaped white flowers, 7–10mm (¼–½in) across, are borne in mid- and late summer. ↕ 60cm (24in), ↔ 45cm (18in). E. Russia, China, Korea, Japan. ❄❄❄

L. ciliata, syn. *Steironema ciliata.* Erect, rhizomatous herbaceous perennial with opposite or whorled, ovate-lance-shaped to ovate, hairy, mid-green leaves, to 15cm (6in) long, with hairy leaf-stalks. Solitary or paired, slightly pendent, star-shaped yellow flowers, 2.5cm (1in) across, with small, reddish brown centres, are produced on slender stalks from the upper leaf axils in midsummer. ↕ 1.2m (4ft), ↔ 60cm (24in). North America. ❄❄❄. **'Purpurea'** has purple-brown leaves that emerge almost black; ↕ 60–80cm (24–32in).

L. clethroides ■ Spreading, softly hairy, rhizomatous herbaceous perennial with erect stems bearing alternate, narrowly ovate-lance-shaped, pointed leaves, to 13cm (5in) long, mid-green above, pale green beneath. In mid- and late summer, saucer-shaped white flowers, 1cm (½in) across, are produced in dense, tapering, terminal racemes, 10–20cm (4–8in) long, which are

L

Lysimachia ephemerum

Lysimachia nummularia 'Aurea'

pendent before the flowers open but become upright with arching tips as they mature. ↕ 90cm (36in), ↔ 60cm (24in). China, Korea, Japan. ❄❄❄

L. ephemerum ■ Clump-forming herbaceous perennial with erect stems and opposite, linear-lance-shaped to linear-spoon-shaped, hairless, glaucous, grey-green, stem-clasping leaves, 15cm (6in) long. Saucer-shaped white flowers, 1cm (½in) across, are borne in slender, upright, dense, terminal racemes, to 40cm (16in) long, in early and mid-summer. Provide protection in severe winters. ↕ 1m (3ft), ↔ 30cm (12in). W. Portugal, S., C., and E. Spain, Pyrenees. ❄❄❄ (borderline)

***L. nummularia* 'Aurea'** ■ (Golden creeping Jenny). Rampant, prostrate, stem-rooting, evergreen perennial with opposite, broadly ovate to rounded, golden yellow leaves, to 2cm (¾in) long, heart-shaped at the bases. During summer, produces usually solitary, upturned, cup-shaped, bright yellow flowers, to 2cm (¾in) across. ↕ to 5cm (2in), ↔ indefinite. ❄❄❄

L. punctata ■ Erect, rhizomatous, softly hairy herbaceous perennial with opposite or whorled, elliptic to lance-

Lysimachia punctata

shaped, dark green leaves, 8cm (3in) long. Whorls of cup-shaped yellow flowers, 2.5cm (1in) across, are borne on short stalks from the leaf axils in mid- and late summer. May be invasive. ↕ to 1m (3ft), ↔ 60cm (24in). C. and S. Europe to Turkey. ❄❄❄

L. vulgaris (Yellow loosestrife). Stoloniferous, softly hairy herbaceous perennial with erect stems bearing opposite or whorled, ovate to lance-shaped, mid- to bright green leaves, to 9cm (3½in) long. In summer, cupped yellow flowers, to 1.5cm (½in) across, are produced in leafy, terminal panicles, 10–30cm (4–12in) long. ↕ to 1.2m (4ft), ↔ to 1m (3ft). Europe, W. Asia. ❄❄❄

LYTHRUM

Loosestrife

LYTHRACEAE

Genus of 38 species of annuals and perennials found in moist meadows and scrub, and in ditches and riversides, in N. temperate regions. They have 4-angled stems and usually opposite, ovate to lance-shaped or linear, stalkless leaves, which are occasionally softly hairy. Small, star-shaped or shallowly funnel-shaped, purple, pink, or rarely white flowers are produced singly or in groups from the leaf axils, sometimes forming spike-like racemes. Loosestrifes are long-flowering, and effective in a moist border, or bog garden, or naturalized near water. Some provide attractive autumn colour. A few species have become noxious weeds in the USA.

- **HARDINESS** Fully hardy.
- **CULTIVATION** Grow in any (preferably fertile), moist soil in full sun. Remove flowered stems to prevent self-seeding.
- **PROPAGATION** Sow seed at 13–18°C (55–64°F) in spring. Divide in spring. Take basal cuttings in spring or early summer.
- **PESTS AND DISEASES** Slugs and snails may damage young shoots.

***L.* 'Morden Pink'.** Clump-forming perennial with erect, branched stems and linear-lance-shaped, hairless leaves, 10cm (4in) long. In summer, bears star-shaped, clear pink flowers, 1cm (½in) across, in loose, spike-like racemes, to 45cm (18in) long. ↕ to 80cm (32in), ↔ 45cm (18in). ❄❄❄

L. salicaria (Purple loosestrife). Clump-forming perennial with erect, stiff, branched stems bearing lance-shaped, downy leaves, 10cm (4in) long. From midsummer to early autumn, produces star-shaped, bright purple-red to purple-pink flowers, 2cm (¾in) across, in spike-like racemes, to 45cm (18in) long. ↕ 1.2m (4ft), ↔ 45cm (18in). Europe, temperate Asia. ❄❄❄. **'Feuerkerze'**, syn. 'Firecandle', bears intense rose-red flowers in slender racemes; ↕ to 90cm (36in). **'Firecandle'** see 'Feuerkerze'. **'Happy'** has dark pink flowers; ↕ 45cm (18in). **'Robert'** produces bright pink flowers; ↕ 90cm (36in).

L. virgatum. Clump-forming perennial with erect, branched stems and linear-lance-shaped, hairless leaves, 10cm (4in) long. From early to late summer, star-shaped, purple-red flowers, 1cm (½in) across, are borne in slender, spike-like racemes, to 30cm (12in) long. ↕ 90cm (36in), ↔ 45cm (18in). E. Europe, W. and C. Asia, N.W. China. ❄❄❄. **'Rose

Lythrum virgatum 'The Rocket'

Queen'** produces bright rose-pink flowers, purple in bud; ↕ 60cm (24in). **'The Rocket'** ■ produces deep pink flowers; ↕ 80cm (32in).

LYTOCARYUM

ARECACEAE/PALMACEAE

Genus of 3 species of single- or multi-stemmed palms occurring in open woodland in seasonally dry areas, or among shrubs on rocky ridges, in southern Brazil. The upright stems each bear a terminal rosette of lance-shaped, pinnate, bright mid-green leaves, with about 60 pairs of linear leaflets. Small, cup-shaped flowers are borne in panicles, to 1.5m (5ft) long, arising from the leaf bases. They are followed by spherical green fruits, which split when ripe to reveal nut-like seeds. In frost-prone areas, grow in a temperate or warm greenhouse. In frost-free areas, grow as specimen trees.

- **HARDINESS** Frost tender.
- **CULTIVATION** Under glass, grow in loam-based potting compost (JI No.2) in full light, with moderate humidity. Water moderately when in growth, sparingly when dormant. Apply a balanced liquid fertilizer monthly when in growth. Outdoors, grow in fertile, well-drained soil in full sun or partial shade; shelter from cold, drying winds.
- **PROPAGATION** Sow seed at 18–24°C (64–75°F) in spring.
- **PESTS AND DISEASES** Trouble free.

L. weddellianum ♈ syn. *Microcoelum weddellianum, Syagrus weddelliana* (Weddell palm). Small palm with a slender, erect stem. Pinnate leaves, to 1.2m (4ft) long, have red-black scales along the stalks and midribs, and are composed of many narrowly linear leaflets, bright green above, greyish green beneath. Cup-shaped, 3-petalled green flowers are borne in panicles to 1m (3ft) long, usually in summer. ↕ 2–3m (6–10ft), ↔ 1–2m (3–6ft). Brazil. ❀ (min. 13°C/55°F)

M

MAACKIA

LEGUMINOSAE/PAPILIONACEAE

Genus of about 8 species of deciduous trees or shrubs occurring in woodland in E. Asia. Maackias are cultivated both for their foliage and flowers. The leaves are alternate and pinnate, each with up to 17 pairs of leaflets and a single terminal one. The small, pea-like flowers are produced in dense, terminal racemes or panicles in summer, and are followed by compressed, linear-oblong seed pods. Maackias are unusual specimen trees.

- **HARDINESS** Fully hardy.
- **CULTIVATION** Grow in moderately fertile, well-drained, neutral to acid soil in full sun. Pruning group 1.
- **PROPAGATION** Sow seed outdoors in containers or in a seedbed, in autumn. Insert greenwood cuttings in early or midsummer.
- **PESTS AND DISEASES** Trouble free.

M. amurensis ■ ♀ Open, spreading tree with pinnate, dark green leaves, 20–30cm (8–12in) long, with 7–11 ovate leaflets. In mid- and late summer, white flowers, to 1cm (½in) long, are produced in upright racemes, 10–15cm (4–6in) long, followed by flattened seed pods, to 5cm (2in) long, with ridged seams. ↕ to 15m (50ft), ↔ to 10m (30ft). N.E. China. ❄❄❄

M. chinensis ♀ Rounded, sometimes flat-topped tree bearing pinnate, dark green leaves, to 20cm (8in) long, with 9–13 oblong to elliptic leaflets, silvery grey-blue when they unfold. In mid- and late summer, white flowers, to 1cm (½in) long, are produced in upright panicles, 15–20cm (6–8in) long, followed by oblong to elliptic seed pods, to 7cm (3in) long. ↕↔ 10m (30ft). China (Hubei, Sichuan). ❄❄❄

MACFADYENA

syn. DOXANTHA

Cat's claw vine

BIGNONIACEAE

Genus of 3 or 4 species of evergreen climbers found in tropical forest and dry woodland from Mexico and the West Indies to Uruguay and Argentina. The leaves are borne in opposite pairs, each with 2 spreading leaflets and a short, 3-clawed tendril. Tubular-bell-shaped flowers, with 5 spreading lobes, are solitary or produced in axillary cymes from spring to summer. In frost-prone climates, grow these attractive climbers in a temperate greenhouse. In warm areas, grow over a fence, pergola, arch, or trellis, or use for ground cover.

- **HARDINESS** Frost tender.
- **CULTIVATION** Under glass, grow in loam-based potting compost (JI No.2) in bright filtered light, or full light with shade from hot sun. In the growing season, water freely and apply a balanced liquid fertilizer monthly; water sparingly in winter. Outdoors, grow in moderately fertile, moist but well-drained, slightly acid to slightly alkaline soil in full sun. Provide shelter from cold, drying winds. Pruning group 11, after flowering.
- **PROPAGATION** Sow seed at 16–21°C (61–70°F) as soon as ripe or in spring. Root semi-ripe cuttings with bottom heat in summer. Layer in spring.
- **PESTS AND DISEASES** Red spider mites, whiteflies, and mealybugs may prove troublesome under glass.

M. unguis-cati ■ syn. *Bignonia unguis-cati, Doxantha unguis-cati* (Common cat's claw vine). Slender-stemmed, vigorous climber with lance-shaped to ovate leaflets, 5–10cm (2–4in) or more long. From spring to summer, produces tubular, bright yellow flowers, 10cm (4in) across, usually with orange lines in the throats, followed by slender, bean-like seed pods, 25–90cm (10–36in) long. ↕ 6–10m (20–30ft). Mexico and West Indies to Argentina. ❀ (min. 7°C/45°F)

Maackia amurensis

Macfadyena unguis-cati

MACHAERANTHERA

Spine aster

ASTERACEAE/COMPOSITAE

Genus of about 25 species of annuals, biennials, herbaceous perennials, and deciduous shrubs, found in dry, open places in low mountains in W. North America. They are grown for their showy, daisy-like flowerheads, borne on branched stems in summer and early autumn. The oblong, lance-shaped, narrowly obovate, or spoon-shaped leaves, borne alternately, are simple and entire or toothed, or pinnatisect, and are usually hairy. Suitable for a sunny position in a border, although the smaller species are best grown in a rock garden or alpine house.

- **HARDINESS** Fully hardy.
- **CULTIVATION** Grow in very well-drained, moderately fertile soil in full sun. Species with hairy leaves may require protection from excessive winter wet. In an alpine house grow in a well-drained mix of equal parts loam-based potting compost (JI No.2) and grit.
- **PROPAGATION** Sow seed in containers in a cold frame in spring.
- **PESTS AND DISEASES** Trouble free.

M. bigelovii. Annual or biennial with slightly sticky stems bearing oblong or lance-shaped, toothed, hairless, bright green leaves, to 10cm (4in) long. Loose corymbs of daisy-like flowerheads, to 6cm (2½in) across, with rich purple to violet ray-florets and yellow disc-florets, are produced from late summer to early autumn. ↕ 90cm (36in), ↔ 45cm (18in). USA (Colorado, Arizona, New Mexico, Texas). ❄❄❄

M. shastensis. Biennial or short-lived perennial with ascending to decumbent, branching stems bearing inversely lance-shaped to spoon-shaped, entire or toothed, hairy, grey-green leaves, to 6cm (2½in) long. From late summer to early autumn, bears loose corymbs of yellow-centred, daisy-like flowerheads, to 2.5cm (1in) across, with violet ray-florets. ↕ 25cm (10in), ↔ 30cm (12in). W. USA. ❄❄❄

▷ ***Machaerocereus eruca*** see *Stenocereus eruca*

MACKAYA

ACANTHACEAE

Genus of one species of evergreen shrub occurring in dry, open, mixed forest in southern Africa. *M. bella* is cultivated for its opposite, slender-pointed, elliptic leaves and for its arching, terminal racemes of tubular-funnel-shaped flowers, each with 5 large, flared lobes, usually produced from spring to autumn. In frost-prone areas, grow in a temperate or warm greenhouse. In warmer climates, grow in a shrub border or as specimen plants.

- **HARDINESS** Frost tender.
- **CULTIVATION** Under glass, grow in loam-based potting compost (JI No.2) in bright filtered light, or full light with shade from hot sun. In growth, water freely and apply a balanced liquid fertilizer monthly; water sparingly in winter. Outdoors, grow in moderately fertile, moist but well-drained, neutral to slightly acid or alkaline soil in full sun or light dappled shade. Pruning group 9; plants under glass need restrictive pruning in late winter.
- **PROPAGATION** Sow seed at 16°C (61°F) in spring. Root semi-ripe cuttings with bottom heat in summer.
- **PESTS AND DISEASES** Red spider mites and whiteflies may be troublesome under glass.

M. bella ■ syn. *Asystasia bella.* Erect then spreading shrub, with elliptic, slender-pointed, wavy-margined, lustrous, deep green leaves, 8–12cm (3–5in) long, with prominent veins. Terminal racemes of narrowly funnel-shaped flowers, to 5cm (2in) across, with large, pale lilac petal lobes finely veined dark purple, are mainly produced

Mackaya bella

from spring to autumn. ↕ 1–2m (3–6ft), ↔ 1–1.5m (3–5ft). South Africa (Limpopo, Mpumalanga, E. Northern Cape, KwaZulu/Natal), Swaziland. ❀ (min. 10°C/50°F)

MACLEANIA

ERICACEAE

Genus of 40 species of evergreen shrubs and climbers, some scrambling or semi-scandent, and sometimes epiphytic, occurring in tropical forest in Central and South America. They are cultivated for their waxy, tubular flowers, each with 5 short petal lobes, which are produced in pendent racemes from the upper leaf axils. The simple, leathery leaves are arranged alternately. In areas where temperatures fall below 10°C (50°F), grow in a temperate or warm greenhouse. In frost-free climates, train over an arch or pergola, or grow against a wall.

• **HARDINESS** Frost tender.
• **CULTIVATION** Under glass, grow in lime-free (ericaceous) potting compost in bright filtered light. In the growing season, water moderately and apply a balanced liquid fertilizer monthly; water sparingly in winter. Outdoors, grow in moderately fertile, humus-rich, moist but well-drained, acid soil in partial shade. Pruning group 11 for climbers, immediately after flowering; group 8 for shrubs.
• **PROPAGATION** Surface-sow seed at 13–16°C (55–61°F) in spring. Root semi-ripe cuttings with bottom heat in early summer. Air layer in spring.
• **PESTS AND DISEASES** Scale insects may be a problem under glass.

M. insignis. Semi-scandent, sparsely branched shrub with a woody, tuberous base, often epiphytic in the wild. Ovate to elliptic leaves, 5–10cm (2–4in) long, are red-tinted when young, maturing to deep green. Orange to deep scarlet flowers, 2.5–4cm (1–1½in) long, with small, triangular petal lobes and softly hairy mouths, are produced in short, leafy racemes, mainly in summer. ↕ 2–4m (6–12ft), ↔ 1–1.5m (3–5ft). S. Mexico, Honduras, Guatemala. ❀ (min. 10°C/50°F)

MACLEAYA syn. BOCCONIA

Plume poppy

PAPAVERACEAE

Genus of 2 or 3 species of rhizomatous perennials found in grassy meadows, scrub, and woodland in China and Japan. They are cultivated for their foliage and graceful inflorescences. Erect, glaucous stems bear alternate, heart-shaped, palmately lobed, glaucous, grey-green to olive-green leaves, to 25cm (10in) long, with rounded, toothed lobes and prominent veins. Numerous petalless, tubular flowers, to 1cm (½in) long, with 2 or 4 sepals and a cluster of stamens, are borne in airy, plume-like panicles. The stems and leaf-stalks produce a yellowish orange latex. Grow plume poppies in a mixed or herbaceous border or as free-standing specimens; they may also be grown among shrubs or used to form a tall screen. They can be invasive.

• **HARDINESS** Fully hardy, but new growth may be damaged by late frosts.

Macleaya microcarpa 'Kelway's Coral Plume'

• **CULTIVATION** Grow in moderately fertile, moist but well-drained soil in full sun, although they will tolerate most soils and partial shade. Provide shelter from cold, drying winds.
• **PROPAGATION** Sow seed in containers in a cold frame in spring. Divide in late autumn or spring. Separate and transplant rooted rhizomes when dormant. Insert root cuttings in winter.
• **PESTS AND DISEASES** Slugs may attack young growth.

M. cordata, syn. *Bocconia cordata* (Plume poppy). Rhizomatous perennial with 5- to 7-lobed, grey- to olive-green leaves, white-downy beneath. In mid- and late summer, produces large, plume-like panicles of pendent, buff-white flowers, each with 25–40 stamens, on grey-green stems. ↕ to 2.5m (8ft), ↔ 1m (3ft). China, Japan. ❄❄❄. **'Flamingo'** has pink buds and buff-pink flowers.

M. x kewensis (*M. cordata* x *M. microcarpa*). Rhizomatous perennial with 5- to 9-lobed, grey-green leaves. Creamy buff flowers, each with 12–18 stamens, are produced in loose, terminal panicles in early and late summer. ↕ 2.5m (8ft), ↔ 1m (3ft) or more. Garden origin. ❄❄❄

***M. microcarpa* 'Kelway's Coral Plume'** ■ Rhizomatous perennial with 5- to 7-lobed, grey- to olive-green leaves, white-downy beneath. Large, loose panicles of pendent, deep buff- to coral-pink flowers, each with 8–15 stamens, open from pink buds in early and midsummer. ↕ 2.2m (7ft), ↔ 1m (3ft) or more. ❄❄❄

MACLURA syn. CUDRANIA

MORACEAE

Genus of 15 species of usually thorny, evergreen or deciduous, dioecious trees, shrubs, or climbers, the branches often reduced to spines, found in woodland and clearings, and by roadsides, from E. Asia to Australia, and from S. central USA to South America. The alternate or spiralling leaves are obovate or narrowly to broadly ovate. Racemes or clusters of small, spherical or cup-shaped, usually green flowers are followed by fleshy, spherical fruits, which are surrounded by enlarged bracts. Grow in a shrub border or as specimens; *M. pomifera* is also used for hedging. They need long, hot summers to grow well and produce fruit.

• **HARDINESS** Fully hardy. Unripened wood, particularly of young plants, may be susceptible to frost damage.
• **CULTIVATION** Grow in moderately fertile, well-drained soil in full sun. Pruning group 1.
• **PROPAGATION** Sow seed in containers in an open frame as soon as ripe. Root semi-ripe cuttings with bottom heat in summer, or take root cuttings in winter.
• **PESTS AND DISEASES** Trouble free.

M. aurantiaca see *M. pomifera*.

M. pomifera ♀ syn. *M. aurantiaca* (Osage orange). Rounded, deciduous tree, thorny when young, becoming less so with age, with ovate, pointed, dark green leaves, to 10cm (4in) long, turning yellow in autumn. Tiny, cup-shaped, yellow-green flowers – the females in short racemes, the males in dense, spherical clusters – are borne in early summer, followed on female trees by large, wrinkled, yellow-green fruit, to 12cm (5in) across. ↕ 15m (50ft), ↔ 12m (40ft). S. central USA. ❄❄❄

M. tricuspidata ♀ syn. *Cudrania tricuspidata*. Compact, rounded, deciduous shrub or small tree with ovate or obovate, dark green leaves, to 10cm (4in) long, sometimes 3-lobed at the apexes. In summer, spherical clusters of tiny green flowers are produced singly or in pairs from the leaf axils of the current year's growth, followed on female trees by glossy, edible, orange-red fruit, 2–5cm (¾–2in) across. ↕ 7m (22ft), ↔ 6m (20ft). C. China, Korea. ❄❄❄

▷**Macqui** see *Aristotelia chilensis*

MACROPIDIA

HAEMODORACEAE

Genus of one species of evergreen, rhizomatous perennial from Australia, found in open ground at the edges of scrub. It has fans of sword-shaped, basal leaves, and produces panicles of woolly, swollen, tubular flowers, with sharply reflexed segments often likened to a kangaroo's foot. In frost-prone areas, grow in a cool or temperate greenhouse. In warmer climates, it is an unusual and effective border plant.

• **HARDINESS** Frost tender.
• **CULTIVATION** Under glass, grow in loam-based potting compost (JI No.2), with added grit, in bright filtered light, or full light with shade from hot sun, with low humidity. In the growing season, water moderately and apply a balanced liquid fertilizer monthly; water sparingly in winter. Outdoors, grow in moderately fertile, well-drained, neutral to slightly acid soil in full sun, with shade from midday sun. Protect from excessive winter wet.
• **PROPAGATION** Sow seed at 10°C (50°F) as soon as ripe or in spring. Divide as growth starts in spring.
• **PESTS AND DISEASES** Trouble free.

M. fuliginosa (Black kangaroo paw). Perennial with short rhizomes and fan-shaped tufts of linear to narrowly strap-shaped, bluish green leaves, to 30cm (12in) long. Panicles of yellow flowers, 4.5cm (1¾in) long, covered in plume-like black hairs, are borne on stout, branched stems, to 1.2m (4ft) long, in summer. ↕ 1.2m (4ft), ↔ 60cm (24in). S.W. Australia. ❀ (min. 7°C/45°F)

MACROPIPER

PIPERACEAE

Genus of 9 species of spreading or rounded, evergreen, aromatic shrubs and small trees, occurring in lowland forest in the Pacific region from New Guinea to Polynesia and New Zealand. They are grown for their handsome, usually alternate (sometimes opposite), ovate to rounded, prominently veined, entire leaves, and for their showy, axillary spikes of small yellow or orange berries, which follow the insignificant unisexual flowers borne intermittently throughout the year. In frost-prone areas grow in a cool to intermediate greenhouse. In warmer climates, they are suitable for specimen shrubs.

• **HARDINESS** Half hardy to frost tender.
• **CULTIVATION** Under glass, grow in loam-based potting compost (JI No.3) in bright filtered light. In the growing season, water freely and apply a balanced liquid fertilizer every month; water sparingly in winter. Outdoors, grow in fertile, well-drained soil in light, dappled shade. Pruning group 8.
• **PROPAGATION** Sow seed at 13–18°C (55–64°F) as soon as ripe. Root semi-ripe cuttings with bottom heat in summer.
• **PESTS AND DISEASES** Mealybugs, scale insects, and red spider mites may be troublesome under glass.

M. excelsum (Kawa kawa, Pepper tree). Bushy, evergreen shrub with dark green young shoots, swollen at the nodes, and opposite, rounded to broadly ovate, aromatic, glossy, dark green leaves, 5–12cm (2–5in) long, with 5–7 prominent veins radiating from the base. Intermittently throughout the year, the upper leaf axils bear dense spikes, 5–8cm (2–3in) long, of tiny cream, male or female flowers, the females developing into spherical, orange or yellow berries, 2–3mm (1/16–1/8in) across. ↕↔ 2–3m (6–10ft). New Zealand. ❄ (borderline)

▷ ***Macrotomia echioides*** see *Arnebia pulchra*

MACROZAMIA

ZAMIACEAE

Genus of 12 species of dioecious cycads from well-drained sites in open forest in Australia. Some species have a palm-like stem; in others, the stem is short and completely or partly buried. Evergreen, pinnate leaves, with linear to lance-shaped, leathery, light to mid-green leaflets, are borne in terminal whorls or rosettes. Male or female inflorescences ("cones") are borne among the leaves. In frost-prone areas, grow in a temperate or warm greenhouse. In warmer climates, grow as specimen trees.

• **HARDINESS** Frost tender.
• **CULTIVATION** Under glass, grow in loam-based potting compost (JI No.2), with added grit, in full light with shade from hot sun, and with low to moderate humidity. Pot on or top-dress in spring. In growth, water moderately and apply a balanced liquid fertilizer monthly; water sparingly in winter. Outdoors, grow in poor to moderately fertile, well-drained, neutral to slightly acid soil in full sun, with shade from midday sun.
• **PROPAGATION** Sow seed at 21–30°C (70–86°F) as soon as ripe or in spring.
• **PESTS AND DISEASES** Trouble free.

M. communis ▣ (Burrawong). Cycad with a robust stem, buried at first then slowly elongating. Whorled leaves, to 2m (6ft) long, have linear, sharply pointed, lustrous, rich green leaflets. Cylindrical, green to brown flowering cones usually appear in summer: male cones are 20–45cm (8–18in) long, females to 45cm (18in) long. They are followed by ovoid fruit containing large, fleshy red seeds. ↕ 2–3m (6–10ft), ↔ to 4m (12ft). Australia (New South Wales). ❀ (min. 10°C/50°F)
M. corallipes see *M. spiralis*.
M. moorei ✾ Palm-like cycad with a thick, columnar trunk and whorled leaves, to 3m (10ft) long, with narrowly lance-shaped, deep green, often bluish green leaflets. Bears cylindrical, usually green flowering cones in summer: the males to 30cm (12in) long, the females to 90cm (36in) long. Flowers are followed by ovoid fruit with bright red seeds. ↕ to 9m (28ft), ↔ to 6m (20ft). Australia (New South Wales, Queensland). ❀ (min. 10°C/50°F)
M. spiralis, syn. *M. corallipes*. Small cycad with a largely underground stem, with only the growing point above the surface. Leaves, to 90cm (36in) or more long, have stalks with pink, red, or orange bases, and consist of many linear, matt, deep green leaflets that spiral longitudinally, at least when young. Cylindrical to ellipsoid green flowering

Macrozamia communis

cones, 15–20cm (6–8in) long, appear in summer, followed by ovoid fruit with orange to scarlet seeds. ↕ 1m (3ft) or more, ↔ to 2m (6ft). Australia (New South Wales). ❀ (min. 10°C/50°F)

MADIA

ASTERACEAE/COMPOSITAE

Genus of 18 species of erect, tar-scented annuals, biennials, and herbaceous perennials, found in dry, open habitats in W. North America and Chile. The linear to elliptic-oblong leaves are entire or toothed, the lower leaves opposite, the upper ones usually alternate. In summer, solitary, daisy-like yellow flowerheads are borne on leafy, branched stems, forming loose corymbs. In many species the flowers close at midday. Grow in a mixed or herbaceous border.

• **HARDINESS** Frost hardy.
• **CULTIVATION** Grow in moderately fertile, well-drained soil in full sun.
• **PROPAGATION** Sow seed *in situ* in late spring.
• **PESTS AND DISEASES** Trouble free.

M. elegans ▣ Erect annual with glandular hairs on the upper stems, and linear or narrowly lance-shaped leaves, to 15cm (6in) long. In summer, bears long-stalked, daisy-like flowerheads, 3–4cm (1¼–1½in) across, with yellow ray-florets, often with a red spot near the base, and yellow or maroon disc-florets. Flowers close at midday. ↕ 1.2m (4ft), ↔ 30cm (1ft). W. North America. ❄❄

Madia elegans

▷ **Madroño** see *Arbutus menziesii*.

MAGNOLIA

MAGNOLIACEAE

Genus of about 125 species of deciduous and evergreen trees and shrubs, occurring in woodland, in scrub, and on riverbanks from the Himalayas to E. and S.E. Asia, and from E. North America to tropical North and South America. They are grown for their showy, solitary, fragrant, usually erect, sometimes pendent or horizontal, cup-, saucer-, goblet-, or star-shaped flowers (see panel below), often borne before the leaves. The flowers have usually 6–9 tepals; colours include pure white, white flushed or stained pink or purple, pink, rich purple, creamy yellow, greenish yellow, glaucous green, and light to mid-yellow. The alternate leaves are usually obovate to ovate, oblong, or elliptic. Cone-like fruits, often with red-coated seeds, are attractive in autumn.

Grow magnolias as specimens or among other trees and shrubs. In frost-prone climates, grow tender species in a cool or temperate greenhouse. Many magnolias take 8–10 years to flower from seed; the early-flowering tree magnolias such as *M. sargentiana* var. *robusta* normally take 12–15 years, and *M. campbellii* can take much longer. Most budded or grafted plants will normally flower at 8 or 9 years.

• **HARDINESS** Fully hardy to frost tender. Flowers, and sometimes young foliage, of early-flowering magnolias may be damaged by late frosts.
• **CULTIVATION** Grow in moist, well-drained, humus-rich, preferably acid to neutral soil in sun or partial shade, with shelter from strong winds. *M. delavayi* and *M. grandiflora* will tolerate dry, alkaline soil; *M. kobus*, *M.* x *loebneri*, *M. sieboldii*, *M. stellata*, and *M. wilsonii* will grow in moist, alkaline soils. Mulch with manure and leaf mould in early spring, particularly on dry soils. Pruning group 1 for trees and deciduous shrubs; group 9 for evergreen shrubs.
• **PROPAGATION** Sow seed in a seedbed in autumn. Stratified seeds germinate freely. For deciduous magnolias, root greenwood cuttings in early summer, or semi-ripe cuttings in late summer. For evergreens, root semi-ripe cuttings from late summer to early autumn. Graft in winter. Bud in summer. Layer in early spring.
• **PESTS AND DISEASES** Prone to coral spot and scale insects.

M. acuminata ▣ ♢ (Cucumber tree). Vigorous, conical, deciduous tree with ovate to elliptic or oblong-ovate leaves, dark green above, lighter and softly hairy beneath, to 25cm (10in) long. In late spring and early summer, produces small, cup-shaped, yellow-green or glaucous green flowers, to 9cm (3½in) across, among the leaves, followed by red or brown fruit. ↕ 20m (70ft), ↔ 10m (30ft). E. North America. ❄❄❄.
'Golden Glow' has yellow flowers. **var. *subcordata***, syn. *M. cordata*, is shrubby, with smaller leaves, to 15cm (6in) long, and pale yellow to yellow-green flowers; ↕ 8m (25ft), ↔ 6m (20ft); S.E. USA.
***M.* 'Apollo'** ▣ ♢ Vigorous, upright, deciduous tree with ovate to elliptic, mid-green leaves, to 25cm (10in) long. In mid-spring, before the leaves, bears large, star-shaped flowers, to 20cm (8in) across, each with 9–12 broad, spreading tepals, deep violet-rose outside, paler inside. ↕ 6m (20ft), ↔ 5m (15ft). ❄❄❄
M. ashei see *M. macrophylla* subsp. *ashei*.
***M.* 'Betty'.** Vigorous, rounded, deciduous shrub with broadly ovate, mid-green leaves, to 15cm (6in) long. In mid-spring, bears large, cup-shaped flowers, to 20cm (8in) across, with up to 19 tepals, purple-red outside and white inside. ↕↔ 4m (12ft). ❄❄❄
***M.* x *brooklynensis* 'Woodsman'** ♢ Conical, later spreading, deciduous tree with ovate, mid-green leaves, to 25cm (10in) long. In late spring and early summer, bears narrowly cup-shaped flowers, to 12cm (5in) across, the outer 3 tepals green, the middle 3 green-flushed purple, and the central 3 pale pink. ↕ 10m (30ft), ↔ 6m (20ft). ❄❄❄
M. campbellii ▣ ♢ Vigorous, conical then spreading deciduous tree with

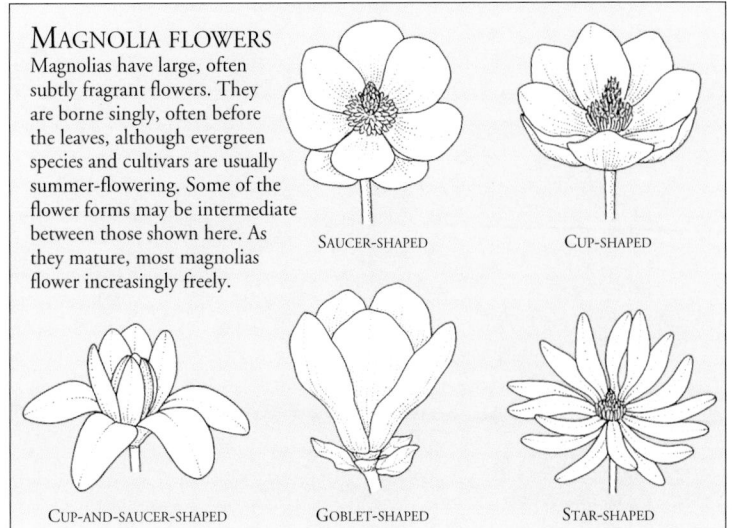

MAGNOLIA FLOWERS

Magnolias have large, often subtly fragrant flowers. They are borne singly, often before the leaves, although evergreen species and cultivars are usually summer-flowering. Some of the flower forms may be intermediate between those shown here. As they mature, most magnolias flower increasingly freely.

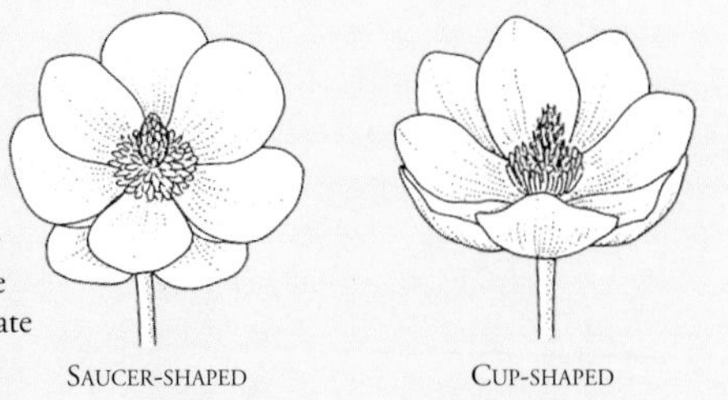

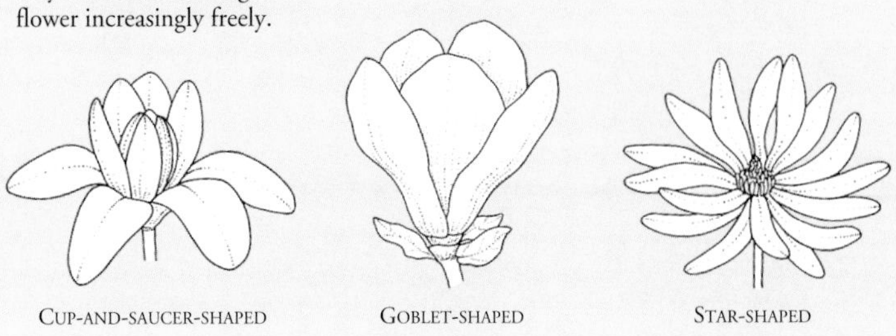

M

elliptic-ovate to oblong-elliptic, mid-green leaves, to 25cm (10in) long. Cup-and-saucer-shaped, white or crimson to rose-pink flowers, to 30cm (12in) across, with up to 16 tepals, are borne from late winter to spring, before the leaves. ↕15m (50ft), ↔10m (30ft). Nepal, India (Sikkim), Bhutan. ✽✽✽. **var. *alba*** has white flowers. **'Charles Raffill'** ▣ has purple-pink flowers. **'Darjeeling'** ▣ produces very dark pink flowers. **'Kew's Surprise'** has dark purple-pink flowers. **'Lanarth'** has rich purple flowers. **'Maharajah'** has large white flowers with purple bases. **subsp. *mollicomata*** ▣ bears purple-pink flowers at an earlier age and slightly later in the year; S.W. Tibet, N. Burma, China (Yunnan). **'Strybing White'** has large white flowers.

***M.* 'Charles Coates'** ▣ Vigorous, open, spreading, deciduous shrub with ovate leaves, clustered at the shoot tips, dark green above and slightly glaucous green beneath, to 25cm (10in) long. In late spring and early summer, produces erect or horizontal, fragrant, saucer-shaped, creamy white flowers, to 10cm (4in) across, with red anthers and 9–12 tepals. ↕10m (30ft), ↔6m (20ft). ✽✽✽

M. cordata see *M. acuminata* var. *subcordata*.

M. cylindrica Deciduous shrub or small, spreading tree with elliptic to oblong-elliptic, or obovate to inversely lance-shaped, shiny, dark green leaves, 8–14cm (3–5½in) long, paler and often glaucous beneath. Goblet- to cup-shaped white flowers, to 10cm (4in) long, flushed light pink to dark purple at the bases, are borne in spring, before the young leaves. ↕10m (30ft), ↔7m (22ft). E. China. ✽✽✽

***M. cylindrica* of gardens** see *M.* 'Pegasus'.

***M.* 'David Clulow'** Upright, later spreading, deciduous shrub or small tree with broadly ovate, mid-green leaves, to 25cm (10in) long. From mid- to late spring, before and with the unfurling leaves, bears large, cup-and-saucer-shaped flowers, to 20cm (8in) across, each with 9–12 white tepals faintly pink-flushed at the bases. Some weather-resistance. ↕↔6m (20ft). ✽✽✽

M. dawsoniana Broadly oval-headed, deciduous tree, occasionally a large shrub, with obovate, dark green leaves, to 15cm (6in) long, slightly glaucous beneath. Large, horizontal to pendent, saucer-shaped, pale lilac-pink flowers, to 12cm (5in) across, are borne in early spring, before the leaves. ↕15m (50ft), ↔10m (30ft). China. ✽✽. **'Chyverton'** ▣ has deep purplish pink tepals, white or very pale pink at the tips and within, and crimson anthers; ✽✽✽

M. delavayi ▣ Dense, rounded, evergreen shrub or tree with ovate to oblong, dark green leaves, to 30cm (12in) long. Short-lived, cup-shaped, creamy or yellowish white flowers, to 20cm (8in) across, are borne in late summer. Grows well against a wall. ↕↔10m (30ft). China. ✽✽

M. denudata ▣ syn. *M. heptapeta* (Lily tree, Yulan). Spreading, deciduous shrub or tree with obovate, mid-green leaves, to 15cm (6in) long. Cup-shaped, pure white flowers, to 15cm (6in) across, are borne in spring, before the leaves. ↕↔10m (30ft). China. ✽✽✽

Magnolia acuminata (inset: flower detail)

Magnolia 'Apollo'

***M.* 'Elizabeth'** ▣ Conical, deciduous tree with obovate leaves, to 20cm (8in) long, bronze when young, maturing to dark green. Cup-shaped, clear primrose-yellow flowers, to 15cm (6in) across, are produced in mid- and late spring, before and with the young leaves. ↕10m (30ft), ↔6m (20ft). ✽✽✽

M. fraseri ▣ Open, spreading, deciduous tree with obovate leaves, usually to 25cm (10in) long, but occasionally much larger, with distinct auricles, bronze when young, maturing to mid-green. Narrowly cup- or goblet-shaped, green-flushed, creamy white flowers, 15–20cm (6–8in) across, are borne in late spring and early summer. ↕↔10m (30ft). S.E. USA. ✽✽✽

***M.* 'Galaxy'** Fast-growing, broadly conical, deciduous tree with obovate, mid-green leaves, to 20cm (8in) long. Large, goblet-shaped, rich purple-pink flowers, to 12cm (5in) across, are borne in mid-spring, before the leaves. ↕12m (40ft), ↔8m (25ft). ✽✽✽

M. glauca see *M. virginiana*.

M. globosa Rounded, deciduous shrub or tree with rust-red young branches and elliptic to obovate, glossy, dark green leaves, to 20cm (8in) long. Pendent, rounded, cup-shaped white flowers, to 12cm (5in) across, with red anthers and 9–12 tepals, are produced in early summer. ↕↔5m (15ft). Himalayas, W. China. ✽✽

***M.* 'Gold Star'** Fast-growing, upright, deciduous shrub or small tree with elliptic to ovate, mid-green leaves, to 18cm (7in) long, reddish bronze when young. Star-shaped, creamy yellow flowers, to 10cm (4in) across, each with up to 14 strap-shaped tepals, are borne before the leaves in mid-spring. ↕6m (20ft), ↔5m (15ft). ✽✽✽

M. grandiflora (Bull bay). Dense, broadly conical, evergreen tree with narrowly elliptic to broadly ovate, leathery, glossy, dark green leaves, to 20cm (8in) long, with paler green and often rusty-hairy undersides. Large, cup-shaped, creamy white flowers, to 25cm (10in) across, with 9–12 tepals, are produced from late summer to autumn. ↕6–18m (20–60ft), ↔ to 15m (50ft). S.E. USA. ✽✽. **'Exmouth'** is particularly hardy, with narrowly ovate, light green leaves, thinly hairy beneath. **'Ferruginea'** ▣ has dark green leaves, rusty-hairy beneath. **'Goliath'** ▣ has broad, slightly twisted leaves and very large flowers, 20–30cm (8–12in) across. **'Little Gem'** is compact and upright, with elliptic to oval, dark green leaves, to 12cm (5in) long, rusty-hairy beneath, and small flowers; ↕6m (20ft), ↔3m (10ft). **'Russet'** has upright, dark green leaves, orange-brown beneath. **'Samuel Sommer'** has glossy, dark green leaves, rusty-hairy beneath, and very large flowers, to 35cm (14in) across.

***M.* 'Heaven Scent'** Spreading, deciduous tree or large shrub with broadly elliptic, glossy, mid-green leaves, to 20cm (8in) long. Goblet-shaped flowers, to 12cm (5in) long, with 9–12 tepals, pink outside and white inside, are produced from mid-spring to early summer. ↕↔10m (30ft). ✽✽✽

M. heptapeta see *M. denudata*.

M. hypoleuca see *M. obovata*

M. insignis see *Manglietia insignis*.

***M.* 'Iolanthe'** Vigorous, upright, deciduous tree with obovate, mid-green leaves, to 25cm (10in) long. From an early age, very large, cup-shaped flowers, to 25cm (10in) across, rose-pink outside and creamy white inside, are borne in mid-spring. ↕12m (40ft), ↔8m (25ft). ✽✽✽

***M.* 'Jane'.** Upright, deciduous shrub with ovate, glossy, mid-green leaves, to 15cm (6in) long. Cup-shaped, very fragrant flowers, to 10cm (4in) across, with 10 tepals, red-purple outside and white inside, are produced from slender, erect, red-purple buds in late spring. ↕4m (12ft), ↔3m (10ft). ✽✽✽

M. kobus ▣ Broadly conical, deciduous tree with narrowly obovate, often puckered, aromatic, mid-green leaves, to 20cm (8in) long. Goblet- to saucer-shaped white flowers, to 10cm (4in) across, occasionally flushed pink at the bases, are borne profusely in mid-spring. ↕12m (40ft), ↔10m (30ft). Japan. ✽✽✽

M. liliiflora, syn. *M. quinquepeta*. Bushy, deciduous shrub with elliptic to obovate, dark green leaves, to 20cm (8in) long. Goblet-shaped, purplish pink flowers, to 7cm (3in) across, are borne from mid-spring to midsummer. ↕3m (10ft), ↔4m (12ft). China. ✽✽✽. **'Nigra'** ▣ is compact, and flowers when young, bearing very dark purple-red flowers in early summer and intermittently into autumn; ↔2.5m (8ft).

M. x loebneri (*M. kobus* x *M. stellata*). Small, slender-branched, upright, deciduous tree or large shrub, with narrowly obovate, mid-green leaves, 10–15cm (4–6in) long. Star-shaped flowers, 8–13cm (3–5in) across, with 10–14 slender white tepals, sometimes suffused lilac-purple outside and pale pink inside, are produced before the leaves in mid-spring. ↕10m (30ft), ↔7m (22ft). Garden origin. ✽✽✽. **'Ballerina'** is more compact, with fragrant white flowers with up to 30 tepals; ↕3m (10ft), ↔6m (20ft). **'Leonard Messel'** ▣ is more rounded in habit, and produces abundant 12-tepalled, pale lilac-pink flowers in mid-spring; ↕8m (25ft), ↔6m (20ft). **'Merrill'** ▣ is vigorous, with broader leaves; flowers are initially goblet-shaped, then star-shaped, with 15 broad white tepals; ↔8m (25ft).

M. macrophylla (Great-leaved magnolia, Umbrella tree). Broadly upright, later rounded, deciduous tree with stout, blue-grey shoots and very large, obovate leaves, to 1m (3ft) long, light green above, silvery grey beneath.

M

MAGNOLIA

In early summer, produces open-cup-shaped, fragrant, creamy white flowers, to 30cm (12in) or more across, with 6 tepals, the inner 3 marked maroon at the bases. ↕↔ 10m (30ft). S.E. USA. ❄❄. **subsp. *ashei*** ▣ ◇ syn. *M. ashei*, is a more spreading shrub or small tree with glossy, light green leaves, glaucous beneath, to 60cm (24in) long. Produces saucer-shaped white flowers, 20–25cm (8–10in) across, the tepals stained maroon at the bases, followed by cylindrical to ovoid (not spherical) fruit; ↕ 10–20m (30–70ft), ↔ 8–15m (25–50ft); USA (N.W. Florida); ❄❄❄

***M.* 'Manchu Fan'** ▣ ◇ Spreading, deciduous tree or shrub with obovate, mid-green leaves, to 20cm (8in) long. In late spring, bears large, goblet-shaped, creamy white flowers, to 12cm (5in) across, each with 9 tepals, the inner ones flushed purple-pink at the bases. ↕ 6m (20ft), ↔ 5m (15ft). ❄❄❄

***M.* 'Maryland'** ◇ Broadly conical, evergreen shrub or tree with oblong, slightly wavy-margined, glossy, mid-green leaves, to 23cm (9in) long. Bears cup-shaped, strongly fragrant white flowers, to 15cm (6in) across, in late summer. Flowers when young. ↕ 6m (20ft) or more, ↔ 5m (15ft). ❄❄❄

***M.* 'Norman Gould'** ▣ ◇ Small, open, spreading, deciduous tree with obovate, mid-green leaves, to 12cm (5in) long. Goblet-shaped white flowers, to 12cm (5in) across, with 9–12 broad tepals, faintly streaked pink on the outside, are borne horizontally in early and mid-spring. ↕↔ 5m (15ft). ❄❄❄

M. obovata ▣ ◇ syn. *M. hypoleuca* (Japanese big-leaf magnolia). Vigorous, deciduous tree, conical when young, wide-spreading when mature, with large, obovate, mid-green leaves, to 50cm (20in) long, clustered at the ends of the shoots. Large, cup-shaped, very fragrant,

Magnolia kobus

creamy white flowers, to 20cm (8in) across, each with 9–12 tepals and crimson stamens, are produced in late spring and early summer, after the leaves. ↕ 15–30m (50–100ft), ↔ 10–15m (30–50ft). Japan. ❄❄❄

M. parviflora see *M. sieboldii*.

***M.* 'Pegasus'** ▣ ◇ syn. *M. cylindrica* of gardens. Deciduous shrub or multi-stemmed tree, initially vase-shaped, later spreading, with elliptic leaves, to 15cm (6in) long, dark green above and pale green beneath. In spring, before and with the young leaves, bears cup-shaped, creamy white or yellowish white flowers, to 10cm (4in) long, suffused purplish pink at the bases, with 6 large inner tepals and 3 smaller, membranous outer tepals. ↕↔ 6m (20ft). ❄❄❄

***M.* 'Peppermint Stick'** ◇ Conical, deciduous tree or large shrub, with obovate, mid-green leaves, to 20cm (8in) long. From mid-spring to early summer, large, cup-and-saucer-shaped flowers, to 11cm (4½in) across, with creamy white tepals, flushed dark purple-pink at the bases, are produced from long, slender buds. ↕ 10m (30ft), ↔ 6m (20ft). ❄❄❄

***M.* 'Princess Margaret'** ◇ Deciduous tree, conical when young, spreading when mature, with oblong-elliptic, mid-green leaves, to 25cm (10in) long. In early spring, before the leaves, bears large, cup-and-saucer-shaped flowers, to 28cm (11in) across, with 11 tepals, rich rose-pink outside and white inside. ↕ 15m (50ft), ↔ 10m (30ft). ❄❄❄

M.* x *proctoriana ◇ (*M. salicifolia* x *M. stellata*). Conical, deciduous tree with oval, aromatic leaves, to 12cm (5in) long, mid-green above and pale green beneath. Erect or horizontal, star-shaped white flowers, to 10cm (4in) across, with up to 12 tepals, are produced in mid-spring. ↕ 8m (25ft), ↔ 6m (20ft). Garden origin. ❄❄❄

M. quinquepeta see *M. liliiflora*.

***M.* 'Ricki'** ▣ Upright, deciduous shrub with broadly ovate, mid-green leaves, to 15cm (6in) long. Goblet-shaped flowers, to 15cm (6in) across, with 15 twisted tepals, pink to dark purple-pink at the bases, are produced from dark purple-pink buds in mid-spring. ↕↔ 4m (12ft). ❄❄❄

M. salicifolia ▣ ◇ (Willow-leaved magnolia). Conical, deciduous tree with narrowly elliptic to lance-shaped, lemon-scented leaves, dull green above and grey-white beneath, to 15cm (6in) long. Abundant star-shaped, fragrant, pure white flowers, to 10cm (4in) across, are borne in mid-spring, before the leaves. ↕ 10m (30ft), ↔ 6m (20ft). Japan. ❄❄❄. **'Jermyns'** is shrubby and spreading, with flowers to 13cm (5in) across, and broad leaves; ↕ 5m (15ft).

M. sargentiana ◇ Broadly conical, deciduous tree with obovate, light to mid-green leaves, to 18cm (7in) long.

Magnolia x *loebneri* 'Merrill'

Large, horizontal to nodding, goblet- to cup-shaped, 12- to 14-tepalled flowers, to 20cm (8in) across, white inside and purple-pink outside, are borne in mid- and late spring, before the leaves. ↕ 15m (50ft), ↔ 10m (30ft). W. China. ❄❄❄. **var. *robusta*** ◇ is usually more spreading, with oblong-obovate, mid-green leaves, to 20cm (8in) long, and large flowers, 22–30cm (9–12in) across, each with 12–16 white to rose-purple tepals, borne in early spring; ↕↔ 12m (40ft). **var. *robusta* 'Blood Moon'** ◇ is upright, with deep rose-purple flowers, 20–25cm (8–10in) across; ↕ 12m (40ft).

***M.* 'Sayonara'** ◇ Spreading, deciduous tree or shrub with obovate, mid-green leaves, to 20cm (8in) long. Large, broadly goblet-shaped, creamy white flowers, to 12cm (5in) across, the inner tepals faintly flushed purple-pink at the bases, are borne in mid- and late spring. ↕ 6m (20ft), ↔ 5m (15ft). ❄❄❄

M. sieboldii, syn. *M. parviflora*. Spreading, deciduous shrub with oblong

Magnolia campbellii

Magnolia campbellii 'Charles Raffill'

Magnolia campbellii 'Darjeeling'

Magnolia campbellii subsp. *mollicomata*

Magnolia 'Charles Coates'

Magnolia dawsoniana 'Chyverton'

Magnolia delavayi

Magnolia denudata

Magnolia 'Elizabeth'

Magnolia fraseri

Magnolia grandiflora 'Ferruginea'

Magnolia grandiflora 'Goliath'

Magnolia liliiflora 'Nigra'

Magnolia x *loebneri* 'Leonard Messel'

Magnolia macrophylla subsp. *ashei*

Magnolia 'Manchu Fan'

Magnolia 'Norman Gould'

Magnolia obovata

Magnolia 'Ricki' (inset: flower detail)

to ovate-elliptic leaves, to 15cm (6in) long, dark green above, grey-green and downy beneath. From late spring to late summer, bears cup-shaped, erect then horizontal or slightly nodding, fragrant white flowers, to 10cm (4in) across, with 12 tepals and crimson anthers. ↕8m (25ft), ↔ 12m (40ft). China, Korea, Japan. ❄❄❄. **subsp. *sinensis***, syn. *M. sinensis*, produces slightly larger, fully pendent flowers and more rounded, oval leaves; W. China.

M. sinensis see *M. sieboldii* subsp. *sinensis*.

M.* x *soulangeana ▣♧ (*M. denudata* x *M. liliiflora*). Variable, deciduous shrub or spreading tree with obovate, dark green leaves, to 20cm (8in) long. Large, goblet-shaped flowers, 8–30cm (3–6in) across, varying from deep rose-pink to violet-purple or pure white, are borne in mid- and late spring, before and with the young leaves. ↕↔ 6m (20ft). Garden origin. ❄❄❄. **'Alba Superba'** ♤ syn. 'Alba', is upright, with large, fragrant white flowers, slightly purple-flushed at the bases; ↕7m (22ft), ↔ 5m (15ft). **'Alexandrina'** ♤ is upright, with deeply saucer-shaped white flowers, to 10cm (4in) across, purple-flushed outside. **'Brozzoni'** ♤ is tree-like, with white flowers, to 13cm (5in) across, faintly purple-flushed outside; ↕8m (25ft). **'Burgundy'** bears profuse deep purple-pink flowers, 10cm (4in) across. **'Lennei'** has dark purple-pink flowers, to 10cm (4in) across, white within. **'Lennei Alba'** ▣ bears ivory-white flowers, 10cm (4in) across. **'Picture'** ♤ is compact and upright, with flowers, 10–13cm (4–5in) across, richly streaked dark reddish purple, white within, and flowering when only 1m (3ft) high; ↕8m (25ft). **'Rubra'** see 'Rustica Rubra'. **'Rustica Rubra'** ▣ syn. 'Rubra', has deeply goblet-shaped, dark purplish red flowers, 10–13cm (4–5in) across, milky white within. **'San José'** bears creamy white flowers, 10–13cm (4–5in) across, heavily flushed dark pink outside.

M. sprengeri ▣♧ Spreading, deciduous tree with obovate, dark green leaves, to 15cm (6in) long. Bears large, cup-shaped, white to pink flowers, to 15cm (6in) across, with 12–15 tepals, in mid-spring, before the leaves. ↕15m (50ft), ↔ 10m (30ft). China. ❄❄❄. **'Burncoose'** has rose-pink to red-purple flowers, to 17cm (7in) across. **'Copeland Court'** has clear deep pink flowers, to 20cm (8in) across. **'Diva'** has rich deep pink flowers, paler inside. **'Eric Savill'** is a small tree with rich reddish pink flowers, to 20cm (8in) across, each with 12 semi-pendent tepals; ↕12m (40ft).

***M.* 'Star Wars'** ▣♤ Broadly conical, deciduous tree with obovate to elliptic or ovate, mid-green leaves, to 20cm (8in) long. In spring, before and with the young leaves, produces large, broadly star-shaped flowers, 20cm (8in) across, each with 12 rich dark pink tepals. Flowers freely even when young. ↕↔ 6m (20ft). ❄❄❄

M. stellata ▣ (Star magnolia). Compact, bushy then spreading, deciduous shrub with obovate-oblong to inversely lance-shaped, mid-green leaves, to 10cm (4in) long. Silky buds open to star-shaped, mostly erect but sometimes horizontal, pure white, sometimes faintly pink-flushed flowers, 12cm (5in) across, with up to 15 tepals; flowers are borne profusely in early and mid-spring, before the leaves. ↕3m (10ft), ↔ 4m (12ft). Japan. ❄❄❄. **'Centennial'** bears white flowers, to 14cm (5½in) across, with 28–32 tepals. **'Jane Platt'** is vigorous and bushy, and has rich pink flowers, to 10cm (4in) across, with up to 32 tepals. **'Royal Star'** ▣ has faintly pink buds and white flowers, 12cm (5in) across, with 25–30 tepals. **'Rubra'** has dark pink flowers, to 12cm (5in) across. **'Waterlily'** has white flowers, to 12cm (5in) across, with up to 32 tepals.

***M.* 'Susan'** ▣ Upright, deciduous shrub bearing ovate, mid-green leaves, to 15cm (6in) long. In mid-spring, narrowly goblet-shaped, fragrant flowers, to 15cm (6in) across, with usually slightly twisted tepals, purple-red outside and paler inside, are produced from slender, dark red-purple buds. ↕4m (12ft), ↔ 3m (10ft). ❄❄❄

M. tripetala ♤ (Elkwood, Umbrella tree). Broadly conical, deciduous tree with obovate to inversely lance-shaped, dark green leaves, to 60cm (24in) long,

Magnolia x *soulangeana*

clustered at the ends of the shoots. Cup-shaped, unpleasantly scented, creamy white flowers, to 15cm (6in) across, with 9–16 tepals, are produced in late spring and early summer. ↕↔ 10m (30ft). E. USA. ❄❄❄

M.* x *veitchii ♤ (*M. campbellii* x *M. denudata*). Large, upright, deciduous tree with purple-green juvenile foliage and branches. Leaves are obovate or oblong, 15–30cm (6–12in) long, mostly rounded at the bases and pointed at the tips, and dark green when mature. Bears goblet-shaped, pink to white flowers, 15cm (6in) long, on bare branches in mid-spring. ↕30m (100ft), ↔ 3–10m (10–30ft). Garden origin. ❄❄. **'Isca'** has obovate leaves and satin-textured white flowers, faintly pink-tinged at the petal bases; ↕25m (80ft), ↔ 15m (50ft). **'Peter Veitch'** ▣ has pale pink flowers, shading to white at the petal tips.

M. virginiana ▣♤ syn. *M. glauca* (Sweet bay). Conical, deciduous or semi-evergreen shrub or small tree with elliptic to ovate, glossy, bright green leaves, to 15cm (6in) long, glaucous beneath. From early summer to early autumn, bears almost spherical, deeply cup-shaped, very fragrant flowers, to 6cm (2½in) across, with 8 or 9 creamy white tepals and an outer row of up to 6 smaller, greenish white tepals. ↕9m (28ft), ↔ 6m (20ft). E. USA. ❄❄❄

***M.* 'Wada's Memory'** ▣♤ Compact, broadly conical, deciduous tree with narrowly ovate, dark green leaves, to

M

Magnolia 'Pegasus'

Magnolia salicifolia

Magnolia x *soulangeana* 'Lennei Alba'

Magnolia x *soulangeana* 'Rustica Rubra'

Magnolia sprengeri

Magnolia stellata 'Royal Star'

Magnolia 'Susan'

Magnolia x *veitchii* 'Peter Veitch'

Magnolia virginiana

Magnolia 'Wada's Memory'

Magnolia x *wieseneri*

Magnolia wilsonii

Magnolia 'Star Wars'

18cm (7in) long, bronze when young. Open cup-shaped white flowers, to 15cm (6in) across, are freely produced in mid- and late spring, before the leaves. ↕9m (28ft), ↔7m (22ft). ❄❄❄
M.* x *watsonii see *M.* x *wieseneri.*
M.* x *wieseneri ▣ ⌓ (*M. hypoleuca* x *M. sieboldii*), syn. *M.* x *watsonii.* Spreading, deciduous shrub or tree with obovate, leathery, bright green leaves, to 20cm (8in) long, glaucous beneath. In early and midsummer, spherical white buds open to deeply cup-shaped, strongly fragrant flowers, 15cm (6in) across, with 6–9 ivory-white inner tepals, 3 smaller, pink-flushed outer tepals, and rose-crimson anthers. ↕6m (20ft), ↔5m (15ft). Garden origin. ❄❄❄
M. wilsonii ▣ ⌓ Spreading, deciduous shrub or small tree with red-purple shoots and elliptic or ovate to lance-shaped, dark green leaves, to 15cm (6in) long, felted red-brown beneath. In late spring and early summer, bears pendent, cup-shaped white flowers, to 10cm (4in) across, with crimson stamens. ↕↔6m (20ft). W. China. ❄❄❄
***M.* 'Yellow Bird'** ⌂ Conical, later spreading, deciduous tree with ovate, mid-green leaves, to 25cm (10in) long. Deeply cup-shaped, pure yellow flowers, to 12cm (5in) across, are borne in late spring and early summer. ↕10m (30ft), ↔6m (20ft). ❄❄❄

Magnolia stellata

▷**Magnolia,**
Great-leaved see *Magnolia macrophylla*
Japanese big-leaf see *Magnolia obovata*
Star see *Magnolia stellata*
Willow-leaved see *Magnolia salicifolia*

x MAHOBERBERIS

BERBERIDACEAE

Hybrid genus of 4 upright or rounded, evergreen shrubs, derived from crosses between species of *Berberis* and *Mahonia*, grown mainly for their foliage, which is usually very variable, individual plants having both simple and 3-palmate or pinnate leaves, which may be finely or coarsely toothed. Small clusters of cup-shaped yellow flowers produced in spring or summer are sometimes followed by usually infertile, spherical black berries. They are easily grown, and suitable for a shrub border or a woodland garden.
• **HARDINESS** Fully hardy.
• **CULTIVATION** Grow in moderately fertile, well-drained soil in partial shade. Pruning group 8.
• **PROPAGATION** Root semi-ripe cuttings in late summer or autumn.
• **PESTS AND DISEASES** Prone to powdery mildew.

x ***M. aquisargentii.*** Upright shrub of dense habit, with glossy, dark green leaves, paler beneath, of two types: rigid, 3-palmate, spine-toothed leaves, 6–8cm (2½–3in) long, and thinner, oblong, simple, finely toothed leaves, to 20cm (8in) long. Small yellow flowers, about 1cm (½in) across, are borne in terminal clusters in early summer, followed by black berries. Seldom affected by powdery mildew. ↕2.5m (8ft), ↔2m (6ft). Garden origin. ❄❄❄
x ***M. neubertii.*** Open, rounded shrub with bluish green foliage, sometimes bronzed in cold weather. Leaves, 5–8cm (2–4in) long, are of two types: some are rigid, ovate, simple or pinnate with ovate leaflets, and coarsely toothed; others are thinner, obovate, simple, and finely toothed. Not known to flower. ↕2m (6ft), ↔1.5m (5ft). Garden origin. ❄❄

MAHONIA

BERBERIDACEAE

Genus of about 70 species of evergreen shrubs occurring in rocky places and woodland in the Himalayas, E. Asia, and North and Central America. They are grown for their handsome foliage, fragrant flowers, decorative fruits, and, in tall species and cultivars, for their deeply fissured bark. The alternate, pinnate or occasionally 3-palmate, usually spiny-margined leaves are light grey-green to dark green, and sometimes purplish red or orange-red when young. Racemes or panicles (see panel below) of cup-shaped, usually yellow flowers, 0.8–1.5cm (⅜–½in) across, are followed by spherical or ovoid, mainly purple to black berries. Mahonias are useful for a variety of situations: use low-growing species and cultivars as ground cover, and taller ones as specimens in a shrub border or woodland garden.
• **HARDINESS** Fully hardy to frost hardy.
• **CULTIVATION** Grow in moderately fertile, humus-rich, moist but well-drained soil. Most mahonias prefer full or partial shade, but will tolerate sun if the soil is not too dry. *M. fremontii* and *M. nevinii* require very well-drained soil and full sun. Shelter *M. fortunei*, *M.* x *lindsayae*, and *M. lomariifolia* from cold, drying winds. Pruning group 8.
• **PROPAGATION** Sow seed outdoors in a seedbed or containers, in autumn or as soon as ripe. Stratified seeds germinate freely. Root semi-ripe or leaf-bud cuttings from late summer to autumn.
• **PESTS AND DISEASES** Rust and mildew may attack *M. aquifolium.*

M. acanthifolia see *M. napaulensis.*
M. aquifolium (Oregon grape). Open, suckering shrub with pinnate, bright green leaves, to 30cm (12in) long, with up to 9 obliquely ovate, spiny-toothed leaflets, often turning red-purple in winter. Bears yellow flowers in densely clustered racemes, to 8cm (3in) long, in spring, followed by spherical blue-black berries. ↕1m (3ft), ↔1.5m (5ft). W. North America. ❄❄❄. **'Atropurpurea'** has leaves that turn red-purple in winter. **'Fascicularis'** see *M.* x *wagneri* 'Pinnacle'. **'Orange Flame'** has rust-orange young foliage, turning red in winter; ↕60cm (24in), ↔1m (3ft). **'Smaragd'** ▣ is compact, bearing bright yellow flowers in large clusters, to 10cm (4in) long; ↕to 60cm (24in), ↔to 1m (3ft).
M. bealei see *M. japonica* 'Bealei'.
M. fortunei. Upright shrub with pinnate, dark green leaves, to 20cm (8in) long, with up to 13 slender, sharply toothed, elliptic-lance-shaped leaflets. Bright yellow flowers are produced in dense, upright racemes, to 7cm (3in) long, in early and mid-autumn, followed by ovoid to spherical,

Mahonia aquifolium 'Smaragd'

M

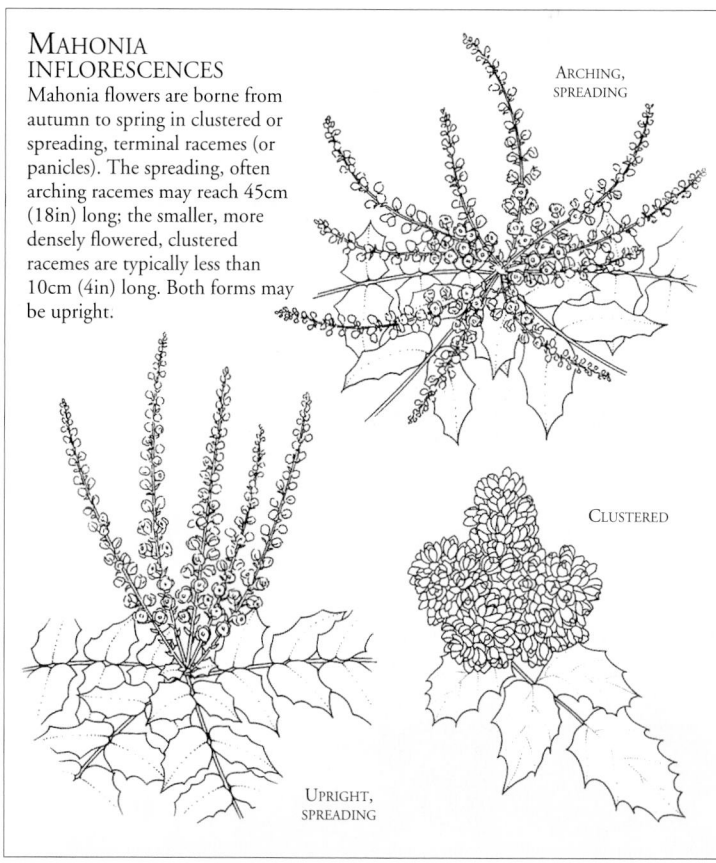

MAHONIA INFLORESCENCES

Mahonia flowers are borne from autumn to spring in clustered or spreading, terminal racemes (or panicles). The spreading, often arching racemes may reach 45cm (18in) long; the smaller, more densely flowered, clustered racemes are typically less than 10cm (4in) long. Both forms may be upright.

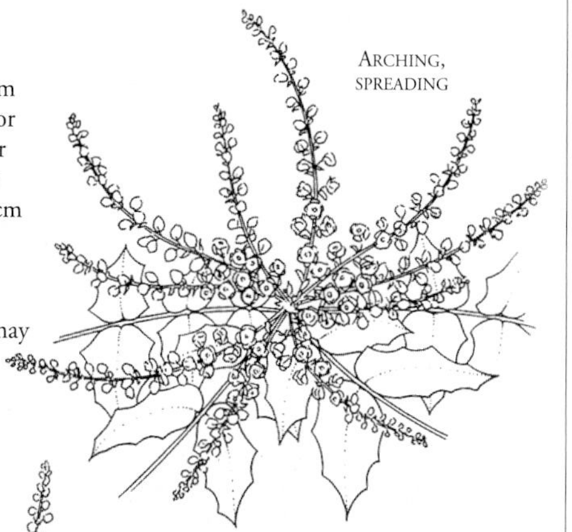

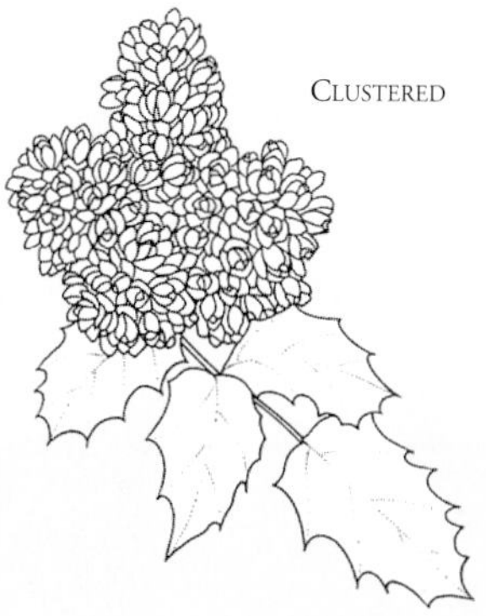

white-frosted, dark blue berries. ↕ 1.2m (4ft), ↔ 1m (3ft). China. ✽✽

M. fremontii. Upright, stiffly branched shrub bearing pinnate leaves, to 10cm (4in) long, with 3–7 wavy-margined, sharply toothed, oblong-lance-shaped, glaucous, grey-green leaflets. In summer, bears densely clustered racemes, to 5cm (2in) long, of yellow flowers, followed by ovoid, white-frosted, dark blue berries. ↕↔ 2m (6ft). S.W. USA, Mexico. ✽✽

***M.* 'Heterophylla'.** Upright shrub with red-purple shoots and pinnate, glossy, bright green leaves, to 30cm (12in) long, with up to 7 slender, ovate, lance-shaped to narrowly oblong-ovate, twisted leaflets, turning red-purple in winter. Yellow flowers are borne in clustered racemes, to 8cm (3in) long, in spring. Seldom produces fruit. ↕ 1m (3ft), ↔ 1.5m (5ft). ✽✽

M. japonica. Erect shrub with stout, upright branches and pinnate, dark green leaves, to 45cm (18in) long, with up to 19 sharply toothed, ovate-oblong to lance-shaped leaflets. Fragrant, pale yellow flowers are produced in arching, then spreading racemes, to 25cm (10in) long, from late autumn to early spring, followed by ovoid, blue-purple berries. ↕ 2m (6ft), ↔ 3m (10ft). China. ✽✽✽. **'Bealei'**, syn. *M. bealei*, has blue-green leaves divided into broad leaflets, and produces flowers in shorter, upright racemes, to 10cm (4in) long.

***M. x lindsayae* 'Cantab'.** Stoutly branched shrub bearing large, arching, pinnate, glossy, rich, deep green leaves, to 60cm (24in) long, with up to 15 ovate-oblong, sharply toothed leaflets, some turning red in winter. Fragrant, lemon-yellow flowers are produced in spreading racemes, to 30cm (12in) long, in late autumn and early winter. ↕↔ 2.5m (8ft). ✽✽

M. lomariifolia. Erect shrub with stout, upright shoots bearing pinnate, dark green leaves, to 60cm (24in) long, with up to 41 oblong-ovate to oblong-lance-shaped, sharply toothed leaflets. Fragrant yellow flowers are produced in densely clustered, upright racemes, 20cm (8in) long, from late autumn to winter, followed by ovoid, blue-black berries. ↕ 3m (10ft), ↔ 2m (6ft). W. China (S. Sichuan, Yunnan). ✽✽

M. x media (*M. japonica* x *M. lomariifolia*). Erect shrub with pinnate leaves, to 45cm (18in) long, with 17–21 ovate to lance-shaped, sharply toothed, dark green leaflets. Bright yellow to lemon-yellow flowers are borne in erect

Mahonia x *media* 'Buckland'

Mahonia x *media* 'Charity'

then spreading racemes, 25–35cm (10–14in) long, from late autumn to late winter. ↕ to 5m (15ft), ↔ to 4m (12ft). Garden origin. ✽✽✽. **'Arthur Menzies'** produces lemon-yellow flowers in upright, later spreading racemes, to 25cm (10in) long, in late autumn and early winter; ↕ 4m (12ft). **'Buckland'** ■ bears bright yellow flowers in arching racemes, to 45cm (18in) long. **'Charity'** ■ has densely clustered, upright then spreading racemes. **'Lionel Fortescue'** bears bright yellow flowers in upright racemes, to 40cm (16in) long. **'Winter Sun'** bears bright yellow flowers in densely clustered, arching racemes.

M. napaulensis, syn. *M. acanthifolia.* Open, upright shrub with pinnate, glossy, dark green leaves, to 50cm (20in) long, with up to 15 lance-shaped to narrowly ovate, sharply toothed leaflets. In early and mid-spring, bears yellow flowers in spreading racemes, to 20cm (8in) long, followed by ovoid, white-frosted, blue-black berries. ↕ 2.5m (8ft), ↔ 3m (10ft). Himalayas. ✽✽

M. nervosa. Dwarf, suckering shrub with pinnate, glossy, dark green leaves, to 60cm (24in) long, with up to 23

Mahonia x *wagneri* 'Pinnacle'

ovate-oblong to lance-shaped leaflets, often red-purple in winter. Bears yellow flowers in dense racemes, to 20cm (8in) long, in late spring and early summer, followed by spherical, blue-black berries. ↕ 45cm (18in), ↔ 1m (3ft). W. North America. ✽✽✽

M. nevinii. Upright shrub with purplish green shoots and pinnate leaves, grey-green to blue-green above, greyish white beneath, to 10cm (4in) long, with 5 lance-shaped, sharply toothed leaflets. Bright yellow flowers are produced in small, dense racemes, to 5cm (2in) long, in early and mid-spring, followed by spherical, dark red berries. ↕↔ 2m (6ft). USA (S. California). ✽✽

***M. pinnata* of gardens** see *M.* x *wagneri* 'Pinnacle'.

M. pumila. Low, dense, suckering shrub bearing pinnate, grey-green leaves, to 15cm (6in) long, with up to 9 ovate-oblong, sharply toothed leaflets, wedge-shaped at the bases, with long, pointed tips. Dark yellow flowers are produced in densely clustered racemes, to 5cm (2in) long, in spring, followed by ellipsoid, blue-black berries. ↕ 30cm (12in), ↔ 1m (3ft). USA (California, Oregon). ✽✽✽

Mahonia repens 'Rotundifolia' (inset: flower detail)

M. repens. Upright, suckering shrub bearing pinnate, matt green leaves, to 25cm (10in) long, with up to 7 pointed, ovate, wavy-margined, sharply toothed leaflets. Dark yellow flowers are borne in dense, upright racemes, to 8cm (3in) long, in mid- and late spring, followed by spherical, blue-black berries. ↕ 30cm (12in), ↔ 1m (3ft). W. North America. ✽✽✽. **'Rotundifolia'** ■ is taller, with broadly ovate, almost entire, rounded leaflets; ↕ 1.5m (5ft), ↔ 2m (6ft).

***M.* 'Undulata'** see *M.* x *wagneri* 'Undulata'.

M. x wagneri (*M. aquifolium* x *M. pinnata*). Upright shrub bearing pinnate leaves, to 20cm (8in) long, with 7–11 ovate, sharply toothed, dull to dark green leaflets. Yellow flowers are borne in dense racemes, to 8cm (3in) long, in spring, followed by spherical, white-frosted, blue-black berries. ↕ 80cm (32in), ↔ 1m (3ft). Garden origin. ✽✽✽. **'Moseri'** has pale green leaves, flushed pink or red. **'Pinnacle'** ■ syn. *M. aquifolium* 'Fascicularis', *M. pinnata* of gardens, is taller, with bronze juvenile leaves, maturing to bright green; ↕↔ 1.5m (5ft). **'Undulata'** syn. *M.* 'Undulata', has leaves with glossy, dark green, wavy-margined leaflets, turning red-purple in winter, and produces rich yellow flowers; ↕↔ 2m (6ft).

MAIANTHEMUM

May lily

CONVALLARIACEAE/LILIACEAE

Genus of 3 species of creeping, rhizomatous perennials from woodland in the N. hemisphere. They bear alternate, heart-shaped leaves on upright stems, and dense, terminal racemes of tiny, fluffy, star-shaped, 4-tepalled white flowers, followed by red berries. Use for ground cover in a woodland garden.

- **HARDINESS** Fully hardy.
- **CULTIVATION** Grow in humus-rich, leafy, moist but well-drained, neutral to acid soil in light dappled or deep shade.
- **PROPAGATION** Sow seed in containers in a cold frame as soon as ripe. Separate rooted runners in spring.
- **PESTS AND DISEASES** Slugs and snails may attack young leaves.

M. bifolium ■ (False lily-of-the-valley). Spreading perennial with 2 broadly heart-shaped to ovate, thin, glossy, dark green leaves, to 8cm (3in) across. Bears racemes of 8–20 white flowers in early summer, followed by small, spherical

Maianthemum bifolium

berries. ↕15cm (6in), ↔ indefinite. W. Europe to Japan. ❄❄❄
M. racemosum see *Smilacina racemosa.*

▷**Maidenhair fern** see *Adiantum*
Aleutian see *A. aleuticum*
Australian see *A. formosum*
Barbados see *A. tenerum* 'Farleyense'
Brittle see *A. tenerum*
Delta see *A. raddianum*
Diamond see *A. trapeziforme*
Dwarf see *A. aleuticum* var. *subpumilum*
Giant see *A. formosum*, *A. trapeziforme*
Himalayan see *A. venustum*
Northern see *A. aleuticum*
Silver dollar see *A. peruvianum*
Tassel see *A. raddianum* 'Grandiceps'
Trailing see *A. caudatum*
True see *A. capillus-veneris*
Walking see *A. caudatum*
▷**Maidenhair tree** see *Ginkgo*, *G. biloba*

MAIHUENIA

CACTACEAE

Genus of 3–5 species of dwarf, clustering, perennial cacti found in the Andes of S. Chile and S. Argentina. Cylindrical or spherical, fleshy, jointed stems bear small, ovate, slender, ever-green leaves. Diurnal, cup-shaped flowers are produced from near-terminal areoles in summer, followed by soft berries, to 5cm (2in) across, containing numerous black-coated seeds. Where temperatures fall below 0°C (32°F), grow in a cool or temperate greenhouse; elsewhere, grow in a rock or desert garden. Needs long, hot summers to produce flowers.
- **HARDINESS** Half hardy.
- **CULTIVATION** Under glass, grow in standard cactus compost in bright filtered light, or full light with shade from hot sun, with low humidity. From spring to summer, water moderately and apply a dilute fertilizer monthly; at other times, keep almost dry. Outdoors, grow in moderately fertile, sharply drained soil in dappled shade, or full sun with shade from midday sun. Protect from excessive winter wet. See also pp.48–49.
- **PROPAGATION** Sow seed at 19–24°C (66–75°F) in spring. Root stem cuttings in spring and summer.
- **PESTS AND DISEASES** Mealybugs may cause problems.

M. poeppigii ■ Clustering cactus with many short, cylindrical stems and fleshy, evergreen leaves, 5mm (¼in) long.

Maihuenia poeppigii

Areoles bear 3 or 4 slender, generally short, stiff spines, one of which grows to 2cm (¾in) long. Produces bright yellow flowers, 3–4.5cm (1¼–1¾in) long, in summer. ↕6cm (2½in), ↔ 30cm (12in). S. Chile, S. Argentina. ❄

▷**Maiten** see *Maytenus boaria*
▷**Maize** see *Zea mays*
▷***Majorana onites*** see *Origanum onites*
▷**Malanga** see *Xanthosoma*
▷**Malanga blanca** see *Xanthosoma sagittifolium*

MALCOLMIA

BRASSICACEAE/CRUCIFERAE

Genus of 35 species of bushy, sometimes prostrate annuals and perennials found on rocky slopes and as wild species in cultivated and disturbed ground, from the Mediterranean region to Afghanistan. They are grown for their short racemes of narrow, cross-shaped, 4-petalled, white, purple, or red flowers, borne from spring to autumn; they self-seed freely. Leaves are linear-oblong to ovate, spoon-shaped, or pinnatisect with lance-shaped lobes. Suitable for the front of an annual or mixed border, and for paving crevices, edging, or a gravel path; they thrive in coastal gardens.
- **HARDINESS** Fully hardy.
- **CULTIVATION** Grow in moderately fertile, well-drained soil in full sun, with shade from midday sun. Flowering is poor in regions with hot, humid summers, unless seed is sown early.
- **PROPAGATION** Sow seed thinly *in situ* from late spring. For a succession of flowers, repeat sowings at intervals of 4–6 weeks.
- **PESTS AND DISEASES** Downy mildew may be troublesome.

M. maritima (Virginia stock). Low-growing, erect to spreading, basally branching annual, with oval to elliptic, hairy-toothed or entire, blunt-tipped, grey-green leaves, to 5cm (2in) long. From spring to autumn, produces open, many-flowered, slender-stemmed spikes of sweetly fragrant, red or purple flowers, to 1cm (½in) across, each petal notched at the apex. ↕20–40cm (8–16in), ↔ 10–15cm (4–6in). Mediterranean. ❄❄❄. **Compacta Series** ■ cultivars have white, pink, red, or purple flowers; ↕40cm (16in).

Malcolmia maritima Compacta Series

MALEPHORA

AIZOACEAE

Genus of about 15 species of bushy, prostrate to erect, woody-based, perennial succulents from dry, hilly areas of southern Africa. The stems have prominent internodes. The opposite, semi-cylindrical or bluntly 3-angled, soft, fleshy, pale to mid-green leaves are united at the bases and coated with blue or white wax. Short-stalked, star-shaped, terminal or axillary flowers open in day-time from late summer to autumn. In frost-prone climates, grow in a cool or temperate greenhouse. In warmer areas, grow in a rock garden or desert garden.
- **HARDINESS** Frost tender.
- **CULTIVATION** Under glass, grow in standard cactus compost in full light with shade from hot sun, and with low humidity. From late spring to early autumn, water freely and apply a balanced liquid fertilizer monthly. Keep just moist at other times. Outdoors, grow in poor or moderately fertile soil in full sun. Provide protection from excessive winter wet. See also pp.48–49.
- **PROPAGATION** Sow seed at 19–24°C (66–75°F) in spring. Root leaf cuttings or stem segments in spring or summer.
- **PESTS AND DISEASES** Susceptible to mealybugs.

Malephora crocea

M. crocea ■ Semi-prostrate or erect, woody-based succulent with a thick, gnarled stem and greyish brown branches. Bears clusters of blunt-tipped, white-frosted, mealy, pale green leaves, to 4.5cm (1¾in) long, on short shoots. Solitary, golden yellow flowers, 3cm (1¼in) across, with red-backed petals, are produced in late summer. ↕20cm (8in), ↔ indefinite. South Africa (Western Cape). ❀ (min. 7°C/45°F)

▷**Mallow** see *Lavatera*, *Malva*
Annual see *Malope*, *M. trifida*
Common rose see *Hibiscus moscheutos*
Confederate rose see *Hibiscus mutabilis*
False see *Sidalcea*, *Sphaeralcea*
Globe see *Sphaeralcea*
Hollyhock see *Malva alcea*
Indian see *Abutilon*
Marsh see *Althaea officinalis*
Musk see *Abelmoschus moschatus*, *Malva moschata*
Poppy see *Callirhoe*
Prairie see *Sidalcea*, *Sphaeralcea coccinea*
Prairie poppy see *Callirhoe involucrata*
Sleepy see *Malvaviscus*
Swamp rose see *Hibiscus moscheutos*
Tree see *Lavatera arborea*
Wax see *Malvaviscus arboreus*

MALOPE

Annual mallow

MALVACEAE

Genus of 4 species of tall, bushy to almost unbranched annuals and perennials found on rocky limestone slopes, in thickets of prickly shrubs, and growing wild in arable fields, from the Mediterranean region to W. Asia. The ovate leaves are entire or lobed, and the showy, axillary flowers are long-stalked, broadly trumpet-shaped, and paper thin,

Malope trifida 'Vulcan'

ranging from pink or violet-blue to white, often veined in a deeper shade. Annual mallows thrive in coastal gardens, although they do poorly in hot, humid summer conditions. Grow at the front of an annual or mixed border; they self-seed freely and provide long-lasting cut flowers.

- **HARDINESS** Fully hardy.
- **CULTIVATION** Grow in moderately fertile, moist but well-drained soil in full sun, although partial shade is tolerated. Dead-head to prolong flowering. Give brushwood support in exposed sites.
- **PROPAGATION** Sow seed at 13–18°C (55–64°F) in early spring, or *in situ* in mid-spring.
- **PESTS AND DISEASES** Aphids and rust may be troublesome.

M. trifida (Annual mallow). Erect, branching to almost unbranched, stout-stemmed annual with hairy stems and leaves. Ovate, mid-green leaves, to 10cm (4in) long, are entire near the stem bases but 3- to 5-lobed higher up. From summer to autumn, produces broadly trumpet-shaped, pale to dark purple-red flowers, 5–8cm (2–3in) across, heavily veined dark purple, the petals narrowing at the bases to reveal bright green sepals below. ↕ to 90cm (36in), ↔ 23cm (9in). W. Mediterranean. ❄❄❄. **'Rosea'** has rose-red flowers. **'Vulcan'** ■ bears abundant bright magenta-pink flowers, to 8cm (3in) across. **'White Queen'** has pure white flowers, 5cm (2in) across.

MALPIGHIA

MALPIGHIACEAE

Genus of about 45 species of evergreen shrubs and small trees found in dry woodland in tropical North, Central, and South America, especially the Caribbean. They are grown for their opposite, simple, often toothed and leathery leaves, and their star-shaped to shallowly trumpet-shaped flowers, each with 5 unequally sized, clawed petals, often with crimped, waved, or fringed tips or margins. Flowers are borne singly or in axillary or terminal corymbs, followed by colourful, edible fruits. Where temperatures fall below 16°C (61°F), grow in a temperate or warm greenhouse. Elsewhere, use as specimen trees, in a shrub border, or for hedging.

- **HARDINESS** Frost tender.
- **CULTIVATION** Under glass, grow in loam-based potting compost (JI No.2) in full light, with shade from hot sun. In spring and summer, water moderately and apply a balanced liquid fertilizer monthly; water sparingly in winter. Outdoors, grow in moderately fertile, moist but well-drained soil in full sun with midday shade. Pruning group 9.
- **PROPAGATION** Sow seed at 18–24°C (64–75°F) in spring. Root semi-ripe cuttings with bottom heat in summer.
- **PESTS AND DISEASES** Red spider mites may be troublesome under glass.

M. coccigera (Miniature holly, Singapore holly). Small, bushy shrub, often prostrate unless regularly trimmed. Elliptic to obovate or rounded leaves, 1–2cm (½–¾in) long, are wavy-margined, spiny-toothed, and lustrous, deep green. Shallowly trumpet-shaped, pink or lilac-pink flowers, 1.5cm (½in) across, are produced singly or in pairs from all the upper leaf axils in summer, and usually followed by broadly ovoid red berries, 0.5–1.5cm (¼–½in) across. ↕ 30–150cm (1–5ft), ↔ 1–2m (3–6ft) or more. West Indies. ❁ (min. 16°C/61°F)
M. glabra (Barbados cherry). Upright, bushy shrub with ovate to elliptic-lance-shaped, entire, lustrous, dark green leaves, 2.5–7cm (1–3in) long. In summer, produces star-shaped pink flowers, 1.5cm (½in) across, with fringed margins, in axillary or terminal corymbs of 3–8 flowers, followed by spherical red berries, 1.5cm (½in) across. ↕ 3m (10ft), ↔ 1.5m (5ft). USA (Texas) to West Indies and N. South America. ❁ (min. 16°C/61°F)

▷**Maltese cross** see *Lychnis chalcedonica*

MALUS

Apple, Crab apple

ROSACEAE

Genus of about 35 species of deciduous trees and shrubs from woodland and thickets in Europe, Asia, and North America. They are grown for their often fragrant flowers, mostly 2–5cm (¾–2in) across, borne singly or in umbel-like corymbs, for their attractive, more or less spherical, edible fruits (although some are unpalatable if uncooked), and sometimes for their purple foliage and autumn colour. The flowers are usually shallowly cup-shaped and 5-petalled; in some cultivars, they may be semi-double or double. The leaves are alternate, oval to ovate or elliptic, mostly toothed, rarely entire, and occasionally lobed. Crab apples are ideal specimen trees, many of them suitable for small gardens. Apples of commerce, *Malus* x *domestica* and its cultivars, are not described here.

- **HARDINESS** Fully hardy.
- **CULTIVATION** Grow in moderately fertile, moist but well-drained soil in full sun, although partial shade is tolerated. Purple-leaved forms colour best in full sun. Pruning group 1.
- **PROPAGATION** Sow seed in a seedbed in autumn. Bud in late summer. Graft in midwinter.
- **PESTS AND DISEASES** Aphids, red spider mites, caterpillars, apple scab, honey fungus, canker, fireblight, and mildew may cause problems.

***M.* 'Aldenhamensis'** ♀ Spreading tree with ovate to shallowly lobed leaves, to 10cm (4in) long, red-purple when young, later bronze-green. Single or semi-double, dark red flowers are produced in late spring, followed by broadly ovoid, red-purple fruit, to 3cm (1¼in) long. ↕↔ 8m (25ft). ❄❄❄
***M.* 'Almey'** ■ ♀ Rounded tree with ovate leaves, to 8cm (3in) long, red-purple when young, later dark green. Deep rose-pink flowers, paler at the

Malus x *arnoldiana*

bases, are produced in late spring, followed by orange-red fruit, to 2.5cm (1in) across. ↕↔ 8m (25ft). ❄❄❄
M.* x *arnoldiana ■ ♀ (*M. baccata* x *M. floribunda*). Low, spreading tree with long, arching branches and oval, mid-green leaves, to 8cm (3in) long. In mid- and late spring, red buds open to fragrant pink flowers, fading to white, followed by ovoid, red-flushed yellow fruit, to 2cm (¾in) long. ↕ 5m (15ft), ↔ 8m (25ft). Garden origin. ❄❄❄
M.* x *atrosanguinea ♀ (*M. halliana* x *M. sieboldii*). Spreading tree with oval or slightly lobed, glossy, dark green leaves, to 8cm (3in) long. Rich pink flowers are produced from red buds in mid-spring, followed by long-stalked, yellow-flushed red fruit, to 1cm (½in) across. ↕↔ 6m (20ft). Garden origin. ❄❄❄
M. baccata ♀ (Siberian crab apple). Vigorous, rounded tree with oval, dark green leaves, paler beneath, to 9cm (3½in) long. Abundant white flowers are produced in mid- and late spring, followed by long-stalked, red or yellow fruit, 1cm (½in) across. ↕↔ 15m (50ft). E. Asia. ❄❄❄. **var. *mandshurica*** ■ (Manchurian crab apple) has more sparsely toothed leaves, downy beneath.

Malus 'Almey' (inset: flower detail)

Malus baccata var. *mandshurica*

M. 'Baskatong' Small, rounded tree with oval, dark green leaves, to 8cm (3in) long. Purple-red flowers, with paler centres, are produced from darker buds in late spring, followed by dark purple-red fruit, to 2.5cm (1in) across. ↕↔ 8m (25ft). ❄❄❄
M. bhutanica see *M. toringoides*.
M. 'Brandywine' Rounded tree with ovate, red-flushed, dark green leaves, to 9cm (3½in) long. Fragrant, double pink flowers are freely borne in late spring, followed by yellow-green fruit, to 2.5cm (1in) across. ↕↔ 6m (20ft). ❄❄❄
M. 'Butterball' ▣ Spreading tree with broadly ovate to heart-shaped, bright green leaves, to 8cm (3in) long, grey-green when young. Pink-flushed white flowers are borne in late spring, followed by striking, orange-yellow fruit, red-flushed at first, 3cm (1¼in) across. ↕↔ 8m (25ft). ❄❄❄
M. 'Candied Apple' syn. *M.* 'Weeping Candied Apple'. Small, spreading tree with weeping branches and ovate, red-flushed, dark green leaves, to 8cm (3in) long. Pink flowers are produced from red buds in late spring, followed by long-lasting, bright red fruit, 1cm (½in) across. ↕↔ 5m (15ft). ❄❄❄
M. 'Centurion' Narrowly upright tree, developing an oval head with age. Ovate, bronze-green leaves, to 10cm (4in) long, are red when young. Bears rose-red flowers in late spring, followed by long-lasting cerise fruit, to 1cm (½in) across. ↕ 8m (25ft), ↔ 6m (20ft). ❄❄❄
M. 'Chilko' Spreading tree with oval, dark green leaves, 8–9cm (3–3½in) long, red-purple when young. Dark rose-pink flowers are produced in mid-spring, followed by bright crimson fruit, 5cm (2in) across. ↕↔ 8m (25ft). ❄❄❄
M. coronaria (Wild sweet crab apple). Spreading tree producing ovate, toothed, sometimes shallowly lobed, dark green leaves, to 10cm (4in) long, red-tinged when young, turning scarlet-red and orange in autumn. Violet-scented pink flowers are borne in late spring, followed by acid-tasting, yellow-green fruit, 4cm (1½in) across. ↕↔ 9m (28ft). E. North America. ❄❄❄.
'Charlottae' has semi-double flowers.
M. 'Cowichan' ▣ Spreading tree with oval, glossy, dark green leaves, to 11cm (4½in) long, red-purple when young. Rose-pink, later almost white flowers are produced in mid-spring, followed by bright red-purple fruit, 4cm (1½in) across. ↕↔ 8m (25ft). ❄❄❄

Malus 'Butterball' (inset: fruit detail)

M. 'Crittenden' Compact, spreading tree with oval, dark green leaves, to 9cm (3½in) long. Pink-flushed white flowers are produced in late spring, followed by profuse, glossy, scarlet fruit, 2.5cm (1in) across, which last well into winter. ↕ 7m (22ft), ↔ 8m (25ft). ❄❄❄
M. 'Dartmouth' Vigorous, broadly upright to rounded tree with elliptic to broadly ovate, dark green leaves, to 11cm (4½in) long. White flowers are produced from pink buds in late spring, followed by large, smooth, red-purple fruit, to 5cm (2in) across. ↕ 8m (25ft), ↔ 7m (22ft). ❄❄❄
M. 'Dolgo' Vigorous, spreading tree with ovate, dark green leaves, to 8cm (3in) long. Fragrant white flowers are produced from pink buds in late spring, followed by ovoid-spherical, bright red-purple fruit, 5cm (2in) long. ↕ 11m (35ft), ↔ 10m (30ft). ❄❄❄
M. 'Dorothea' Spreading tree with oval, dark green leaves, to 8cm (3in) long. Semi-double to double, silvery pink flowers are produced from darker buds in late spring, followed by yellow fruit, 1cm (½in) across. Slow-growing and susceptible to scab. ↕↔ 8m (25ft). ❄❄❄

Malus 'Cowichan'

M. 'Echtermeyer' ▣ syn. *M.* 'Okonomierat Echtermeyer'. Weeping tree with oval, sometimes slightly lobed, bronze-green leaves, 8–10cm (3–4in) long, bronze-purple when young. Dark red-purple flowers are produced in late spring, followed by ovoid-spherical, purple-red fruit, 2.5cm (1in) long. ↕↔ 5m (15ft). ❄❄❄
M. 'Eleyi' Spreading tree with oval, purple-green leaves, to 10cm (4in) long, bronze-purple when young. Dark red-purple flowers are produced in late spring, followed by obovoid purple fruit, 2.5cm (1in) long. ↕↔ 8m (25ft). ❄❄❄
M. 'Evereste' Conical tree with oval, sometimes lobed, dark green leaves, 8–11cm (3–4½in) long. White flowers are freely produced from red buds in late spring, followed by red-flushed, orange-yellow fruit, 2.5cm (1in) across. ↕ 7m (22ft), ↔ 6m (20ft). ❄❄❄
M. floribunda ▣ (Japanese crab apple). Dense, spreading tree with ovate, sometimes lobed, dark green leaves, to 8cm (3in) long. Pale pink flowers are produced in mid- and late spring, from red buds, followed by very small, pea-like yellow fruit, 2cm (¾in) across. ↕↔ 10m (30ft). Japan. ❄❄❄

Malus 'Echtermeyer'

Malus floribunda

M. 'Frettingham's Victoria' Upright tree with oval, dark green leaves, to 8cm (3in) long. White flowers are produced in late spring, followed by red-flushed yellow fruit, 4cm (1½in) across. ↕ 8m (25ft), ↔ 4m (12ft). ❄❄❄
M. 'Golden Hornet' Rounded tree with oval, sharply toothed, bright green leaves, to 9cm (3½in) long. White flowers are produced from pink buds in late spring, followed by long-lasting, ovoid-spherical, golden yellow fruit, 2.5cm (1in) long. ↕ 10m (30ft), ↔ 8m (25ft). ❄❄❄
M. 'Hopa' Spreading tree with oval, dark green leaves, to 10cm (4in) long, red-purple when young. Dark pink flowers, with white centres, open from red-purple buds in mid-spring, followed by bright red fruit, to 2.5cm (1in) across. ↕↔ 10m (30ft). ❄❄❄
M. hupehensis ▣ Vigorous, spreading tree with elliptic to ovate, dark green leaves, to 10cm (4in) long. Fragrant white flowers are produced from pink buds in mid- and late spring, followed by cherry-like red fruit, 1cm (½in) across. ↕↔ 12m (40ft). China. ❄❄❄
M. 'Indian Magic' Rounded tree with ovate, dark green leaves, 8–10cm (3–4in) long. Rose-pink flowers open from red buds in late spring, followed by long-lasting, ellipsoid, glossy red, later orange fruit, 1cm (½in) across. ↕↔ 6m (20ft). ❄❄❄
M. 'Jewelberry' Dense, rounded tree or shrub with ovate, dark green leaves,

Malus hupehensis

Malus 'John Downie'

Malus 'Lemoinei'

Malus 'Liset'

Malus 'Marshall Oyama'

7–9cm (3–3½in) long. White flowers open from pink buds in late spring, followed by glossy red fruit, 1cm (½in) across, profusely borne, even on young trees. ↕↔ 5m (15ft). ❄❄❄
M. 'John Downie' ■ Narrow, upright tree, broadly conical when mature, with ovate, bright green leaves, to 10cm (4in) long. White flowers open from pale pink buds in late spring, followed by ovoid, orange and red fruit, to 3cm (1¼in) long. ↕ 10m (30ft), ↔ 6m (20ft). ❄❄❄
M. 'Katherine' ■ Open, rounded tree with oval, dark green leaves, to 8cm (3in) long. Large, double, pale pink flowers, maturing to white, are borne in mid- and late spring, followed by very small, pea-like, red-flushed yellow fruit, 1cm (½in) across. ↕↔ 6m (20ft). ❄❄❄
M. 'Lemoinei' ■ Spreading tree with ovate or slightly lobed, dark red-purple leaves, to 8cm (3in) long, turning purple-green. Dark wine-red flowers are produced in late spring, followed by cherry-like, dark red-purple fruit, 1.5cm (½in) across. ↕↔ 8m (25ft). ❄❄❄
M. 'Liset' ■ Rounded tree with ovate, often lobed, bronze-green leaves, to 8cm (3in) long, reddish purple when young. Dark purple-pink flowers open from dark red buds in late spring, followed by cherry-like, dark purple-red fruit, 1cm (½in) across. ↕↔ 6m (20ft). ❄❄❄
M. 'Magdeburgensis' ■ Spreading tree with ovate, dark green leaves, to 8cm (3in) long. Dense clusters of semi-double, deep pink flowers are produced in late spring, sometimes followed by yellow fruit, 1cm (½in) across. ↕ 6m (20ft), ↔ 6m (20ft). ❄❄❄
M. 'Marshall Oyama' ■ Broadly conical tree with elliptic, dark green leaves, to 8cm (3in) long. Pink-flushed white flowers are borne in late spring, followed by ovoid-spherical, yellow-flushed red fruit, to 4cm (1½in) long. ↕ 8m (25ft), ↔ 6m (20ft). ❄❄❄
M. 'Molten Lava' Weeping tree with yellowish green winter bark and ovate, dark green leaves, 6–10cm (2½–4in) long. White flowers open from dark red buds in late spring, followed by orange-red fruit, 1cm (½in) across. ↕ 5m (15ft), ↔ 4m (12ft). ❄❄❄
M. 'Neville Copeman' Spreading tree with oval, dark green leaves, to 10cm (4in) long, purplish red when young. Dark purple-pink flowers are borne in mid- and late spring, followed by orange-red to crimson fruit, 3.5cm (1½in) across. ↕↔ 9m (28ft). ❄❄❄
M. niedzwetskyana ■ syn. *M. pumila* var. *niedzwetskyana*. Spreading tree with oval, purple-green leaves, red when young, to 12cm (5in) long. Dark red-purple flowers are produced in late spring, followed by conical, red-purple fruit, to 5cm (2in) long. ↕ 6m (20ft), ↔ 8m (25ft). C. Asia. ❄❄❄
M. 'Okonomierat Echtermeyer' see *M.* 'Echtermeyer'.
M. 'Pink Spires' Narrowly upright tree with ovate, red-purple young leaves, 6–12cm (2½–5in) long, maturing to bronze-green in summer. Lavender-pink flowers are produced from darker buds in mid- and late spring, followed by long-lasting, purple-red fruit, 1cm (½in) across. ↕ 6m (20ft), ↔ 4m (12ft). ❄❄❄
M. prattii Broadly conical, upright tree, spreading with age, with ovate, tapered, mid-green leaves, to 12cm (5in) long, turning orange and red in autumn. Bears white flowers in late spring, followed by spherical to ovoid, white-speckled red fruit, 1cm (½in) across. ↕↔ 10m (30ft). W. China. ❄❄❄
M. 'Professor Sprenger' ■ Dense, rounded tree with broadly ovate, glossy, bright green leaves, to 8cm (3in) long, turning yellow in late autumn. In mid- and late spring, pink buds open to very fragrant white flowers, followed by long-lasting, orange-red fruit, to 1.5cm (½in) across. ↕↔ 7m (22ft). ❄❄❄
M. 'Profusion' Spreading tree with elliptic, bronze-green leaves, to 8cm (3in) long, purple-red when young. Dark purple-pink flowers are freely

M

Malus 'Katherine' (inset: flower detail)

Malus niedzwetskyana

Malus 'Magdeburgensis'

Malus 'Professor Sprenger'

Malus prunifolia

produced in late spring, followed by cherry-like, reddish purple fruit, 1cm (½in) across. ↕↔ 10m (30ft). ❄❄❄

M. prunifolia ▣ Spreading tree with elliptic to ovate, dark green leaves, to 10cm (4in) long. Fragrant white flowers open from pink buds in mid-spring, followed by long-lasting, spherical to ovoid, red or sometimes yellow fruit, 2.5cm (1in) across. ↕↔ 9m (28ft). Probably China. ❄❄❄

M. pumila* var. *niedzwetskyana see *M. niedzwetskyana*.

M.* x *purpurea (*M. atrosanguinea* x *M. niedzwetskyana*). Erect, open tree with broadly ovate, sometimes lobed, dark green leaves, to 10cm (4in) long. The young wood and spring foliage are both purplish red. Purplish pink flowers open from ruby-red buds in mid-spring, followed by dark red fruit, 2–2.5cm (¾–1in) across. Several cultivars listed here under their own names, *M.* 'Aldenhamensis', *M.* 'Eleyi', and *M.* 'Lemoinei', are sometimes referred to this hybrid. ↕ 4–7m (12–22ft), ↔ 2–4m (6–12ft). Garden origin. ❄❄❄

***M.* 'Red Barron'** Broadly upright tree with ovate, bronze-green leaves, 6–10cm (2½–4in) long, purple when young. Dark pink flowers open from dark red buds in late spring, followed by glossy, dark red fruit, 1cm (½in) across. ↕↔ 6m (20ft). ❄❄❄

***M.* 'Red Jade'** Weeping tree with ovate, tapered, glossy, mid-green leaves, to 9cm (3½in) long. White or pink-flushed flowers are produced from red buds in late spring, followed by ovoid, glossy, bright red fruit, to 1.5cm (½in) long. ↕ 4m (12ft), ↔ 6m (20ft). ❄❄❄

Malus 'Royalty' (inset: flower detail)

***M.* 'Red Sentinel'** ▣ Broadly upright tree with ovate, dark green leaves, to 8cm (3in) long. White flowers are produced in late spring, followed by long-lasting, yellow-flushed red, later glossy, dark red fruit, 2.5cm (1in) across. ↕↔ 7m (22ft). ❄❄❄

***M.* 'Red Siberian'** see *M.* x *robusta* 'Red Siberian'.

***M.* 'Red Silver'** Spreading tree with ovate leaves, grey-hairy at first, turning purple-red and hairless, then dark green, to 8cm (3in) long. Dark red-purple flowers are produced in late spring, followed by purple fruit, 2cm (¾in) across. ↕ 6m (20ft), ↔ 7m (22ft). ❄❄❄

***M.* x *robusta* 'Red Siberian'** syn. *M.* 'Red Siberian'. Vigorous, spreading tree with oval, dark green leaves, to 10cm (4in) long. In mid- and late spring, produces abundant pink-tinged white flowers followed by long-lasting red fruit, 2cm (¾in) across. ↕ 12m (40ft), ↔ 10m (30ft). ❄❄❄. **'Yellow Siberian'**, syn. *M.* 'Yellow Siberian', has yellow fruit.

***M.* 'Royal Beauty'** Small, weeping tree with elliptic, reddish purple leaves, to 6cm (2½in) long, turning dark green, purple beneath. Dark red-purple flowers are produced in late spring, followed by dark red fruit, 1cm (½in) across. ↕ 2m (6ft), ↔ 2.5m (8ft). ❄❄❄

***M.* 'Royalty'** ▣ Spreading tree with ovate, dark red-purple leaves, to 10cm (4in) long, retaining colour well and turning red in autumn, the larger leaves often slightly lobed. Crimson-purple flowers are produced in mid- and late spring, followed by dark red fruit, 1.5cm (½in) across. ↕↔ 8m (25ft). ❄❄❄

***M.* 'Rudolph'** Upright tree with ovate, glossy, dark green leaves, to 7cm (3in) long, reddish purple when young. Rose-red flowers open from darker red buds in late spring, followed by long-lasting, orange-yellow fruit, 1.5cm (½in) long. ↕ 7m (22ft), ↔ 4m (12ft). ❄❄❄

M. sargentii syn. *M. toringo* subsp. *sargentii*. Spreading shrub or tree with ovate or 3-lobed, dark green leaves, to 8cm (3in) long. White flowers are freely borne in late spring, followed by dark red fruit, 8mm (⅜in) across. ↕ 4m (12ft), ↔ 5m (15ft). Japan. ❄❄❄

M. sieboldii ▣ syn. *M. toringo*. Spreading shrub with arching branches and ovate to deeply 3- to 5-lobed leaves, to 6cm (2½in) long. Fragrant white flowers open from pink buds in mid-spring, followed by slender-stalked, red or yellow fruit, 1cm (½in) across. ↕ 2.5m (8ft), ↔ 3m (10ft). Japan. ❄❄❄.

'Calocarpa' see *M.* x *zumi* 'Calocarpa'.

***M.* 'Snowdrift'** Dense, rounded tree with elliptic to ovate, glossy, dark green leaves, to 10cm (4in) long. Abundant white flowers open from pink buds in late spring, followed by long-lasting, glossy, orange-red fruit, 1.5cm (½in) across. ↕↔ 6m (20ft). ❄❄❄

M. spectabilis Rounded tree with oval, glossy, dark green leaves, to 9cm (3½in) long. Blush-pink flowers are produced from rose-red buds in mid- and late spring, followed by yellow fruit, to 2.5cm (1in) across. ↕↔ 10m (30ft). Probably China. ❄❄❄

***M.* 'Spring Snow'** Dense, upright tree with oval, bright green leaves, 3–8cm (1¼–3in) long. Abundant fragrant white flowers are borne in late spring. Fruit are seldom produced. ↕ 8m (25ft), ↔ 6m (20ft). ❄❄❄

***M.* 'Striped Beauty'** ▣ Spreading tree with broadly elliptic, dark green leaves, to 12cm (5in) long. Bears white flowers in late spring, followed by red-striped yellow fruit, 2.5cm (1in) across. ↕↔ 7m (22ft). ❄❄❄

M. sylvestris (Common crab apple, Wild crab apple). Rounded, sometimes thorny tree with ovate, mid-green leaves, 4–8cm (1½–3in) long. Pink-flushed white flowers are produced in late spring, followed by greenish yellow, red-flushed fruit, to 2.5cm (1in) across. ↕ 9m (28ft), ↔ 7m (22ft). Europe. ❄❄❄

M. toringo see *M. sieboldii*.

M. toringo* subsp. *sargentii see *M. sargentii*.

M. toringoides syn. *M. bhutanica*. Spreading tree with ovate to lance-shaped, usually deeply 3- to 7-lobed, mid-green leaves, to 9cm (3½in) long. Slightly fragrant, creamy white flowers are produced in late spring, followed by spherical to ovoid yellow fruit, to 1.5cm (½in) long. ↕ 8m (25ft), ↔ 10m (30ft). W. China. ❄❄❄

M. transitoria ▣ Elegant, spreading tree with oblong to deeply 3-lobed, bright green leaves, 2–3cm (¾–1¼in) long, turning yellow in autumn. In late spring, white flowers open from pink buds, followed by very small, pea-like yellow fruit, 8mm (⅜in) long, on slender red stalks. ↕ 8m (25ft), ↔ 10m (30ft). N.W. China. ❄❄❄

M. trilobata Conical tree with maple-like, 3-lobed, glossy, bright green leaves, to 9cm (3½in) long, the lobes

Malus 'Red Sentinel'

Malus sieboldii

Malus 'Striped Beauty'

Malus transitoria

M

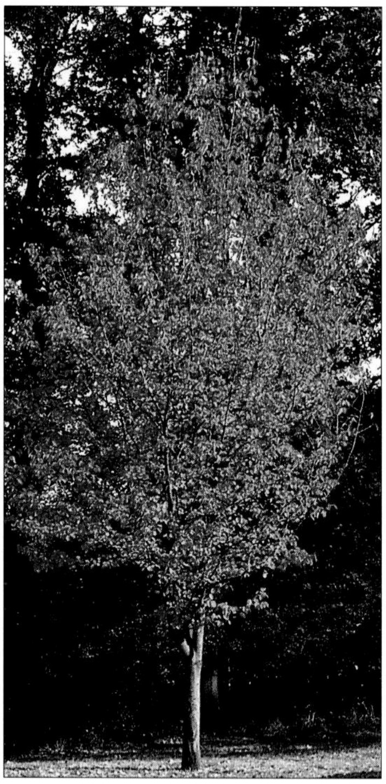
Malus tschonoskii

sometimes further lobed, turning yellow, red, and purple in autumn. White flowers are produced in early summer, followed by ellipsoid, red-flushed green fruit, 2cm (¾in) long. ↕15m (50ft), ↔7m (22ft). Greece, Syria, Lebanon, Israel. ❄❄❄

M. tschonoskii ▣ Erect tree with broadly ovate, glossy, mid-green leaves, to 12cm (5in) long, turning brilliant orange, red, and purple in autumn. In late spring, bears pink-flushed white flowers, followed by red-flushed, yellow-green fruit, 3cm (1¼in) across. ↕12m (40ft), ↔7m (22ft). Japan. ❄❄❄

***M.* 'Van Eseltine'** Upright tree with ovate, glossy, mid-green leaves, to 9cm (3½in) long. Double pink flowers are produced in late spring, followed by red-flushed yellow fruit, 1.5cm (½in) across, which fall early. ↕8m (25ft), ↔6m (20ft). ❄❄❄

***M.* 'Veitch's Scarlet'** ▣ Upright, spreading tree with ovate to elliptic, dark green leaves, to 8cm (3in) long. White flowers are produced in late spring, followed by ellipsoid, crimson-flushed scarlet fruit, 4.5cm (1¾in) long. ↕↔9m (28ft). ❄❄❄

***M.* 'Weeping Candied Apple'** see *M.* 'Candied Apple'.

***M.* 'White Cascade'** Weeping tree with ovate, dark green leaves, 6–10cm (2½–4in) long. Abundant white flowers open from pink buds in late spring, followed by small, greenish yellow fruit, 1cm (½in) across. ↕↔5m (15ft). ❄❄❄

***M.* 'Winter Gold'** Rounded tree with elliptic, often slightly lobed leaves, to 7cm (3in) long, bronze-tinged when young. White flowers open from pink buds in mid- and late spring, followed by long-lasting, lemon-yellow fruit, 1cm (½in) across. ↕↔6m (20ft). ❄❄❄

***M.* 'Wisley'** Rounded tree with elliptic to obovate leaves, to 10cm (4in) long, bronze-red at first, turning dark green. Lightly fragrant, dark purple-red flowers are produced in late spring, followed by large, conical, dark red fruit, 7cm (3in) long. ↕↔6m (20ft). ❄❄❄

Malus 'Veitch's Scarlet'

***M.* 'Yellow Siberian'** see *M.* x *robusta* 'Yellow Siberian'.

M. yunnanensis Broadly upright tree with ovate, sometimes shallowly lobed, pale green leaves, to 12cm (5in) long, with pale brown, felted hairs beneath, turning orange, red, and purple in autumn. White, sometimes pink-tinged flowers are borne in late spring, followed by speckled red fruit, 1.5cm (½in) across. ↕6–12m (20–40ft), ↔6m (20ft). S.W. China. ❄❄❄

***M.* x *zumi* 'Calocarpa'** syn. *M. sieboldii* 'Calocarpa'. Upright, pyramidal to rounded tree with ovate, frequently deeply lobed, dark green leaves, to 9cm (3½in) long. White flowers open from pink buds in late spring, followed by long-lasting, cherry-like, bright red fruit, 1cm (½in) across. ↕9m (28ft), ↔8m (25ft). ❄❄❄

MALVA
Mallow

MALVACEAE

Genus of about 30 species of annuals, biennials, and perennials, sometimes woody-based, occurring in dry, open habitats, waste ground, roadsides, and hedge banks in Europe, N. Africa, and temperate Asia, and widely naturalized elsewhere. The alternate, rounded or heart- or kidney-shaped leaves are entire, toothed, or shallowly 3- to 9-lobed, sometimes pinnatisect. The 5-petalled, shallowly funnel-shaped, or saucer- to cup-shaped, purple, blue, pink, or white flowers are produced singly, in clusters from the leaf axils, or sometimes in leafy, terminal racemes. An involucre of 1–3 distinct bracts is usually produced below the flowers (distinguishing *Malva* species and cultivars from those of the genus *Lavatera*, which have 3–9 joined bracts). Mallows are easily grown and produce long-lasting, often showy flowers; they are suitable for an annual, herbaceous, mixed, or shrub border, or for a wildflower garden.

- **HARDINESS** Fully hardy.
- **CULTIVATION** Grow in moderately fertile, moist but well-drained soil in full sun. Provide support, especially in rich soils. Perennials are often short-lived, but will self-seed.
- **PROPAGATION** Sow seed *in situ* or in containers in early spring or early summer. Root basal cuttings of perennials in spring.
- **PESTS AND DISEASES** Susceptible to rust and leaf spot.

Malva moschata

M. alcea (Hollyhock mallow). Erect, bushy, hairy, woody-based perennial with heart-shaped, scalloped, light green lower leaves, to 30cm (12in) long, and deeply pinnatisect upper leaves, to 15cm (6in) long. From early summer to early autumn, open funnel-shaped, purplish pink flowers, 5–7cm (2–3in) across, the petals slightly notched, are produced in terminal racemes and axillary clusters. ↕1.2m (4ft), ↔60cm (24in). S. Europe. ❄❄❄. **var. *fastigiata*** is narrow and upright, bearing deep pink flowers well into autumn; ↕to 80cm (32in).

M. moschata ▣ (Musk mallow). Erect, bushy, woody-based perennial with slightly musk-scented leaves, to 10cm (4in) long, the lower ones heart-shaped and the upper ones pinnatisect. From early summer to early autumn, bears saucer-shaped, pale pink or white flowers, 4–6cm (1½–2½in) across, in axillary clusters. ↕90cm (36in), ↔60cm (24in). Europe, N.W. Africa. ❄❄❄

M. nicaeensis. Erect, slightly hairy annual or biennial with semi-circular, shallowly 3- to 7-lobed, blunt-toothed leaves, to 10cm (4in) long, the leaf-stalks often considerably longer than the leaf-blades. In summer, saucer-shaped

Malva sylvestris 'Primley Blue'

pink or lilac-pink flowers, to 3.5cm (1½in) across, with hairy petal bases, are borne singly or in clusters from the upper leaf axils. ↕to 50cm (20in), ↔23cm (9in). Mediterranean, Arabian Peninsula to Iran, S. Russia. ❄❄❄

M. sylvestris. Erect to spreading, bushy, hairy, woody-based perennial, occasionally biennial. Broadly heart-shaped to rounded, shallowly 3- to 7-lobed leaves are dark green, to 10cm (4in) long. From late spring to mid-autumn, produces axillary clusters of open funnel-shaped, pinkish purple flowers, to 6cm (2½in) across, with notched petals and darker purple veins. ↕to 1.2m (4ft), ↔60cm (24in). N. Europe, N. Africa, S.W. Asia. ❄❄❄. **f. *alba*** has white flowers; ↕to 80cm (32in). **'Brave Heart'** is upright, with large purple flowers, to 8cm (3in) across, with strong veins and dark purple centres; ↕to 90cm (36in). **'Cottenham Blue'** is early-flowering, and has pale blue flowers, veined darker blue; ↕to 75cm (30in). **'Primley Blue'** ▣ is prostrate, and produces pale blue-violet flowers, veined darker blue; ↕to 20cm (8in), ↔30–60cm (12–24in).

MALVASTRUM

MALVACEAE

Genus of about 30 species of spreading to erect, evergreen, sometimes semi-evergreen perennials and shrubs, found on rock outcrops, rocky areas of prairies, and alluvial soils in arid and semi-arid areas of North and South America. The alternate, entire or lobed leaves are lance-shaped to rounded, 2.5–11cm (1–4½in) long, often with toothed margins. They are usually cultivated for their attractive, funnel- or cup-shaped, yellow, orange, pink, or red flowers, either solitary and axillary, or borne in terminal or axillary racemes or spikes. Grow in a sunny border or on a bank. In frost-prone areas, grow tender species in a cool greenhouse.

- **HARDINESS** Fully hardy to frost tender.
- **CULTIVATION** Grow in well-drained soil in full sun. Trim back any excess growth or dead shoots in spring.
- **PROPAGATION** Sow seed in containers in spring. Insert softwood cuttings in late spring or summer.
- **PESTS AND DISEASES** Trouble free.

M. capensis see *Anisodontea capensis*.

M. coccineum see *Sphaeralcea coccinea*.

M. lateritium. Prostrate perennial with alternate, rounded leaves, 8cm (3in) long, with 3–5 wedge-shaped to oblong lobes. Solitary, cup-shaped, peach-coloured flowers, 5cm (2in) across, with yellow anthers and deep yellow centres surrounded by deep rose-pink bands, are produced from late spring to summer. ↕20cm (8in), ↔1.5m (5ft). Argentina, Uruguay. ❄❄❄ (borderline)

MALVAVISCUS
Sleepy mallow

MALVACEAE

Genus of 3 species of evergreen shrubs found in coppices and thickets, often in coastal areas, in tropical North and South America. They have alternate, simple to palmately lobed, toothed, pale to mid-green leaves, and produce solitary, axillary or terminal racemes

Malvaviscus arboreus

of long-stemmed, pendent, red, pink, or white flowers. The flowers are similar to those of *Hibiscus*, although the long petals only partially unfurl, producing a narrowly funnel-shaped outline. In frost-prone climates, grow in a temperate or warm greenhouse. In warmer areas, grow in a shrub border or as an informal hedge.
• **HARDINESS** Frost tender.
• **CULTIVATION** Under glass, grow in loam-based potting compost (JI No.2) in bright filtered light, or full light with shade from hot sun. In growth, water freely, and apply a balanced liquid fertilizer monthly; water sparingly in winter. Outdoors, grow in moderately fertile, moist but well-drained soil in full sun; tolerates partial shade. Pruning group 8.
• **PROPAGATION** Sow seed at 15–21°C (59–70°F) in spring. Root softwood cuttings with bottom heat in spring, or semi-ripe cuttings in summer.
• **PESTS AND DISEASES** Susceptible to red spider mites, whiteflies, and mealybugs under glass.

M. arboreus ▣ syn. *M. mollis* (Wax mallow). Large, erect to spreading, usually freely branching shrub with densely velvety, downy stems and leaves. Bright green leaves are broadly ovate to heart-shaped, 6–12cm (2½–5in) long, and sometimes 3-lobed. Axillary, bright red flowers, to 5cm (2in) long, are borne mainly in late summer and early autumn. ↕ to 4m (12ft) or more, ↔ 1.5–3m (5–10ft). S.E. USA, Mexico to Colombia, Peru, Brazil. ❄ (min. 10°C/50°F). **var. *drummondii***, syn. *M. conzattii*, *M. grandiflorus*, has rounded, symmetrically lobed leaves, and flowers to 3cm (1¼in) long; S.W. USA, Mexico to Colombia. **var. *mexicanus*** is almost hairless, with lance-shaped to ovate leaves; Mexico to Colombia.
M. candidus. Erect, freely branching shrub with hairy stems. Hairy, mid-green leaves, to 18cm (7in) long, are broadly ovate to rounded, with 5-lobed, heart-shaped bases. Red flowers, 3cm (1¼in) long, are produced in terminal racemes in summer. ↕ to 4m (12ft), ↔ to 2m (6ft). Mexico. ❄ (min. 8°C/46°F).
M. conzattii see *M. arboreus* var. *drummondii*.
M. grandiflorus see *M. arboreus* var. *drummondii*.
M. mollis see *M. arboreus*.

MAMMILLARIA

CACTACEAE

Genus of about 150 species of spherical to cylindrical or columnar, perennial cacti from semi-desert regions, mainly in Mexico, but also in S. USA, the West Indies, Central America, Colombia, and Venezuela. Most offset freely to form clusters. Conical, cylindrical, or somewhat flattened tubercles encircle spined stems. The funnel-shaped, diurnal, white to yellow, orange, red, pink, or purple flowers are mostly borne in a ring around the crown. The berry-like fruits are oblong-ovoid to club-shaped. In frost-prone areas, grow in a temperate greenhouse or as houseplants. Elsewhere, grow in a desert garden.
• **HARDINESS** Frost tender.
• **CULTIVATION** Under glass, grow in standard cactus compost in full light with shade from hot sun. Provide low humidity. From mid-spring to autumn, water freely, applying a balanced liquid fertilizer monthly in late spring and summer; water sparingly in winter. Outdoors, grow in poor or moderately fertile, sharply drained soil in full sun. Protect from excessive winter wet. See also pp.48–49.
• **PROPAGATION** Sow seed at 19–24°C (66–75°F) in late winter or early spring. Remove offsets in early spring.
• **PESTS AND DISEASES** Vulnerable to mealybugs and root mealybugs.

M. albiflora see *M. herrerae* var. *albiflora*.
M. armillata. Clustering or solitary cactus with narrowly columnar, dull green stems, 4.5cm (1¾in) thick, and brown or brown-yellow spines (9–15 radials, one or more of which is hooked, and 1–4 centrals). Pale pink, creamy white, or pale yellow flowers, 2cm (¾in) long, are borne in summer. ↕ to 30cm (12in), ↔ indefinite. N.W. Mexico. ❄ (min. 7–10°C/45–50°F)
M. baumii, syn. *Dolichothele baumii*. Clustering cactus with spherical to ovoid, mid-green stems, 3–6cm (1¼–2½in) thick. Areoles bear 30–35 fine white radial spines and 5 or 6 longer, pale yellow centrals. In summer, bears bright yellow flowers, 3cm (1¼in) long. ↕ 8cm (3in), ↔ 12cm (5in). N.E. Mexico. ❄ (min. 7–10°C/45–50°F)
M. blossfeldiana, syn. *M. shurliana*. Solitary or clustering cactus with spherical to short, cylindrical, dark green stems, 4cm (1½in) thick, bearing close-set areoles with 15–20 black-tipped yellow radial spines and 3 or 4 black centrals, one of which is hooked. In summer, bears pale pink flowers, 3.5cm (1½in) long, with deep carmine-red median lines. ↕↔ 4cm (1½in). N.W. Mexico. ❄ (min. 7–10°C/45–50°F)
M. bocasana ▣ (Snowball cactus). Clump-forming cactus with spherical, white-hairy, dark bluish green stems, to 5cm (2in) thick. Close-set areoles bear 25–50 spreading white radial spines and 1 or 2 (sometimes up to 5) red or brown-yellow centrals. From spring to summer, bears yellowish white flowers, 1.5cm (½in) long, with red or pink median lines and often red-tipped petals. ↕ 5cm (2in), ↔ indefinite. C. Mexico. ❄ (min. 7–10°C/45–50°F)
M. bombycina ▣ Densely clustering cactus with spherical to cylindrical, mid-green stems, 5–8cm (2–3in) thick, densely white-woolly in the axils. Areoles bear 30–40 white radial spines and 2–4 longer, white to yellow or red-brown centrals, one of which is hooked and twice as long as the other centrals. Produces reddish purple flowers, 1.5cm (½in) long, from spring to summer. ↕ 20cm (8in), ↔ indefinite. W. central Mexico. ❄ (min. 7–10°C/45–50°F)
M. camptotricha ▣ syn. *Dolichothele camptotricha*, *M. decipiens* subsp. *camptotricha*. Freely clustering cactus with spherical, deep green stems, 7cm (3in) thick, the areoles with 2–8 pale yellow radial spines, but no centrals. Produces scented white flowers, to 2cm (¾in) long, each with a green median

Mammillaria bombycina

Mammillaria bocasana

Mammillaria camptotricha

M

line, from summer to autumn. ↕ to 8cm (3in), ↔ 20cm (8in). E. central Mexico. ❀ (min. 7–10°C/45–50°F)

M. candida, syn. *Mammilloydia candida* (Snowball cushion cactus). Slow-growing, solitary or clustering cactus with spherical to cylindrical, mid-green stems, 6–12cm (2½–5in) thick, with 4–7 white bristles in each axil. White-felted areoles bear white, often brown- or pink-tipped spines (50 radials and 8–12 centrals). Bears rose-pink flowers, 2cm (¾in) long, with white margins, from spring to summer. ↕↔ 15cm (6in). N.E. Mexico. ❀ (min. 7–10°C/45–50°F)

M. carmenae ▣ Clustering cactus with spherical to ovoid, mid-green stems, 3–4cm (1¼–1½in) thick, with white wool and long white bristles in the axils. The areoles bear 100 or more white or cream radial spines but no centrals. Has pink- or cream-flushed white flowers, 1cm (½in) long, in spring and summer. ↕ to 8cm (3in), ↔ 15cm (6in). E. central Mexico. ❀ (min. 7–10°C/45–50°F)

M. centricirrha see *M. magnimamma.*

M. conoidea see *Neolloydia conoidea.*

M. crinita see *M. zeilmanniana.*

M. crucigera. Clustering, branching cactus with depressed spherical or cylindrical to obovoid, dark brownish green stems, 3–5cm (1¼–2in) thick, with white-woolly axils and areoles. The areoles bear 24 or more needle-like white radial spines and usually 4 longer, thicker, waxy-yellow, brown- or black-tipped centrals. Pinkish purple flowers, 1.5cm (½in) long, are produced in summer. ↕ to 15cm (6in), ↔ indefinite. S. Mexico. ❀ (min. 7–10°C/45–50°F)

M. dealbata see *M. haageana.*

M. decipiens* subsp. *camptotricha see *M. camptotricha.*

M. densispina. Solitary cactus with spherical or cylindrical, dark green stems, to 10cm (4in) thick, and white-woolly areoles bearing about 25 yellow or pale brown radial spines and 5 or 6 longer, reddish brown, black-tipped centrals. Sulphur-yellow flowers, 2cm (¾in) long, often with red-flushed outer petals, are produced from spring to summer. ↕↔ 10cm (4in). C. Mexico. ❀ (min. 7–10°C/45–50°F)

M. elongata (Gold lace cactus). Variable, densely clustering cactus with cylindrical, mid-green stems, 1–3cm (½–1¼in) thick, and white, yellow, or dark reddish brown spines (15–20 radials and up to 3 centrals, although the centrals may be absent). Bears white

Mammillaria carmenae

Mammillaria geminispina

or yellow, sometimes faintly pink-striped flowers, to 1.5cm (½in) long, in summer. ↕ 15cm (6in), ↔ 30cm (12in). C. Mexico. ❀ (min. 7–10°C/45–50°F)

M. geminispina ▣ Solitary cactus, later offsetting and forming mounds, producing spherical, mid-green stems, 8cm (3in) thick, becoming cylindrical. The white-woolly areoles bear white spines (16–20 radials and 2–4 longer, often brown-tipped centrals). White to creamy white flowers, 1.5cm (½in) or more long, with carmine-red stripes, are produced from summer to autumn. ↕ 25cm (10in), ↔ 50cm (20in). C. Mexico. ❀ (min. 7–10°C/45–50°F)

M. gracilis, syn. *M. vetula* subsp. *gracilis.* Freely clustering cactus producing cylindrical, fresh green stems, 3–4.5cm (1¼–1¾in) thick, and slightly

Mammillaria magnimamma

woolly areoles with 3–5 brown central spines and 12–17 shorter, yellowish white radials. From spring to summer, bears yellowish white flowers, 1.5cm (½in) long, with pink or white median lines. Offsets fall away at the least touch. ↕ 5cm (2in), ↔ 20cm (8in). E. central Mexico. ❀ (min. 7–10°C/45–50°F). **var. *fragilis*** has 2 brown-tipped white central spines per areole; ↕ to 4cm (1½in), ↔ to 12cm (5in).

M. haageana, syn. *M. dealbata.* Cactus offsetting from the base and sides, with spherical or cylindrical, mid-green stems, 10cm (4in) thick, with slightly woolly axils. Areoles bear 18–20 thin white radial spines and 1 or 2 longer, black-tipped, red-brown centrals. Bears carmine-red flowers, 1.5cm (½in) long, from spring to summer. ↕ 15cm (6in),

Mammillaria hahniana

Mammillaria microhelia

↔ 24cm (10in). C. and S.E. Mexico. ❀ (min. 7–10°C/45–50°F)

M. hahniana ▣ (Old lady cactus). Solitary cactus, forming groups when mature, with spherical, mid-green stems, 12cm (5in) thick, coated with long white hairs, bristles, and spines (20–30 fine, hair-like radials and 1–3 or more shorter, dark-tipped centrals). Purplish red flowers, to 1cm (½in) long, are produced from spring to summer. ↕ to 20cm (8in), ↔ to 40cm (16in). C. Mexico. ❀ (min. 7–10°C/45–50°F)

M. herrerae. Solitary or clustering cactus with spherical, mid-green stems, 2–3cm (¾–1¼in) thick, occasionally elongating slightly with age, and densely coated with about 100 near-white radial spines but no centrals. Bears pale pink to reddish violet flowers, 2.5cm (1in) long, from spring to summer. ↕↔ 3–4cm (1¼–1½in). C. Mexico. ❀ (min. 7–10°C/45–50°F). **var. *albiflora***, syn. *M. albiflora*, has pure white flowers.

M. magnimamma ▣ syn. *M. centricirrha.* Extremely variable, freely clustering cactus with spherical, greyish green stems, 10–15cm (4–6in) thick, and white-woolly axils and areoles, the latter with 3–6 brown-tipped, yellowish white radial spines of unequal length, but no centrals. From spring to summer, bears purple-red to pink or brownish yellow flowers, 2.5cm (1in) long. ↕ to 30cm (12in), ↔ to 60cm (24in). C. Mexico. ❀ (min. 7–10°C/45–50°F)

M. mazatlanensis. Clustering cactus with cylindrical, greyish green stems, 4cm (1½in) thick. Rounded, woolly areoles bear 12–15 white radial spines and 3 or 4 longer, hooked, glossy, reddish brown centrals with cream bases. Bright carmine-red flowers, 4cm (1½in) long, develop in summer. ↕ 12cm (5in), ↔ 30cm (12in). W. Mexico. ❀ (min. 7–10°C/45–50°F)

M. microhelia ▣ Solitary or clustering cactus with cylindrical, greyish green stems, 3.5–5cm (1½–2in) thick, densely covered with spines (up to 50 golden yellow to pale brown-white radials and up to 8, shorter, dark red-brown centrals, although these may be absent). Bears creamy white, occasionally pink-suffused flowers, to 1.5cm (½in) long, from spring to summer. ↕↔ 15cm (6in). C. Mexico. ❀ (min. 7–10°C/45–50°F)

M. mystax. Clustering or solitary cactus with spherical to cylindrical, grey-green stems, 10cm (4in) thick, with white wool and bristles in the axils. The areoles bear 5–10 brown-tipped white

Mammillaria plumosa

radial spines and 3 or 4 longer, purplish grey centrals. From spring to summer, bears purplish pink flowers, 2.5cm (1in) long. ↕ to 15cm (6in), ↔ 24cm (10in). S. Mexico. ❄ (min. 7–10°C/45–50°F)
M. plumosa ■ Clustering cactus with spherical, mid-green stems, 7cm (3in) thick, and white-woolly axils. The areoles bear about 40 feathery white radial spines but no centrals. Greenish white or pale yellow flowers, 1.5cm (½in) long, with reddish brown median lines, are borne in late summer. ↕ 12cm (5in), ↔ 40cm (16in). N.E. Mexico. ❄ (min. 7–10°C/45–50°F)
M. rhodantha. Solitary cactus with mostly spherical to cylindrical, mid-green stems, 10–12cm (4–5in) thick, and white-woolly axils. The areoles bear 16–24 straight, glossy, white to yellow radial spines and 4–7 longer, often curved, red-brown, occasionally straw-coloured or golden yellow centrals. Purplish pink flowers, 2cm (¾in) long, are borne in summer. ↕↔ 40cm (16in). C. Mexico. ❄ (min. 7–10°C/45–50°F)
M. schiedeana. Solitary or clustering cactus with slightly depressed spherical, mid-green stems, 4–6cm (1½–2½in) thick, with long, woolly hairs in the axils. The areoles bear 70–80 yellow to white radial spines but no centrals. Cream flowers, 2cm (¾in) long, are produced from summer to autumn. ↕ 10cm (4in), ↔ 30cm (12in). C. Mexico. ❄ (min. 7–10°C/45–50°F)
M. sempervivi. Solitary to clump-forming cactus with depressed spherical to short, cylindrical, dark green stems, to 10cm (4in) thick, often elongating, and densely woolly in the axils. The areoles bear 3–7 white radial spines and 2–4 slightly longer, yellow-brown or red centrals. White or yellowish pink flowers, 1cm (½in) long, with red median lines, are borne from spring to summer. ↕↔ 8cm (3in). C. Mexico. ❄ (min. 7–10°C/45–50°F)
M. senilis. Slow-growing, solitary cactus, eventually clustering, with spherical to cylindrical, pale green stems, 6–10cm (2½–4in) thick, white-woolly, bristly axils, and white spines (30–40 radials and 4–6 longer centrals, 1 or 2 of which are hooked). Violet- or orange-red flowers, 6cm (2½in) long, with slender tubes, are borne from spring to summer. ↕ 15cm (6in), ↔ to 40cm (16in). N.W. Mexico. ❄ (min. 7–10°C/45–50°F)
M. shurliana see *M. blossfeldiana.*
M. vetula* subsp. *gracilis see *M. gracilis.*
M. zeilmanniana ■ syn. *M. crinita.* Clustering cactus with spherical, dark green stems, 4.5cm (1¾in) thick, with bare axils. Areoles bear 15–18 hair-like white radial spines and 4 shorter, reddish brown centrals, 1 of which is hooked. Reddish violet, pink, or white flowers, to 2cm (¾in) long, are borne in summer. ↕ 15cm (6in), ↔ 30cm (12in). C. Mexico. ❄ (min. 7–10°C/45–50°F)

Mammillaria zeilmanniana

▷***Mammilloydia candida*** see *Mammillaria candida*
▷**Mandarin** see *Citrus reticulata*

MANDEVILLA
syn. DIPLADENIA
APOCYNACEAE

Genus of about 120 species of mainly tuberous-rooted, woody-stemmed, twining climbers, with some perennials, from tropical woodland in Central and South America. Opposite, simple leaves are borne on stems containing a milky latex. They have often showy, funnel-shaped to tubular-salverform flowers, each with 5 broad, spreading petal lobes, borne mainly in axillary racemes. Grow on a pergola or trellis, or as a screen. In frost-prone climates, grow in a temperate or warm greenhouse. Contact with the sap may irritate skin; all parts may cause mild stomach upset if ingested.

- **HARDINESS** Frost tender; *M. laxa* may survive temperatures near to 0°C (32°F).
- **CULTIVATION** Under glass, grow in loam-based potting compost (JI No.3), in full light with shade from hot sun. In the growing season, water moderately, and apply a balanced liquid fertilizer monthly; water sparingly in winter. Outdoors, grow in moderately fertile, moist but well-drained soil in full sun with some midday shade. Pruning group 12, in late winter or early spring.
- **PROPAGATION** Sow seed at 18–23°C (64–73°F) in spring. Root softwood cuttings in late spring or semi-ripe cuttings in summer, with bottom heat.
- **PESTS AND DISEASES** Red spider mites, whiteflies, and mealybugs may be troublesome under glass.

***M.* x *amabilis* 'Alice du Pont'** see *M.* x *amoena* 'Alice du Pont'.
***M.* x *amoena* 'Alice du Pont'** ■ syn. *M.* x *amabilis* 'Alice du Pont'. Woody-stemmed, twining climber bearing elliptic-oblong to ovate-oblong, slightly wrinkled, mid- to deep green leaves, 9–18cm (3½–7in) long, with short points. Racemes of up to 20 narrowly funnel-shaped, glowing pink flowers, 8–10cm (3–4in) across, are freely produced in summer. ↕ to 7m (22ft). ❄ (min. 10–15°C/50–59°F)

Mandevilla x *amoena* 'Alice du Pont'

M. boliviensis, syn. *Dipladenia boliviensis.* Slender-stemmed, usually freely branching, woody, twining climber with elliptic to oblong or elliptic-obovate, slender-pointed, shiny, mid-green leaves, 5–10cm (2–4in) long. In mid- and late summer, bears racemes of 3–7 white flowers, 5–7cm (2–3in) across, with yellow eyes and angular petal lobes. ↕ 3–4m (10–12ft). Ecuador, Bolivia. ❄ (min. 10–15°C/50–59°F)
M. laxa, syn. *M. suaveolens, M. tweediana* (Chilean jasmine). Vigorous, freely branching, woody-stemmed, twining climber. Ovate to oblong leaves, 5–10cm (2–4in) long, have heart-shaped bases and slender-pointed tips, lustrous, rich green above and purple or grey-green beneath. From summer to early autumn, bears racemes of 5–15 tubular, strongly fragrant, pure white or creamy white flowers, 5–9cm (2–3½in) across, with broad, rounded, often crimped petal lobes. ↕ 3–5m (10–15ft). Peru, Bolivia, Argentina. ❄ (min. 5°C/41°F)
M. splendens ■ syn. *Dipladenia splendens.* Vigorous, moderately to freely branching, woody-stemmed, twining climber with downy young stems and broadly elliptic, lustrous, mid-green leaves, 10–20cm (4–8in) long, with heart-shaped bases and slender-pointed tips. In summer, produces racemes of 3–5 narrowly funnel-shaped flowers, to 10cm (4in) across, with rounded, rose-pink petal lobes and white and yellow throats. ↕ 3–6m (10–20ft). S.E. Brazil. ❄ (min. 10–15°C/50–59°F). **'Rosacea'** has rose-pink flowers, margined and flushed deep purplish pink, with the tops of the throats ringed brighter pink.
M. suaveolens see *M. laxa.*
M. tweediana see *M. laxa.*

Mandevilla splendens

MANDRAGORA
Mandrake
SOLANACEAE

Genus of 6 species of perennials, with fleshy tap roots, found in dry, stony areas from the Mediterranean region to the Himalayas. They have large, basal rosettes of ovate to lance-shaped leaves, and stemless or short-stemmed, tubular-bell-shaped flowers, with triangular lobes, borne singly or in basal clusters from autumn to early spring. The fleshy fruits are spherical or ellipsoid. Grow in a rock garden or at the base of a warm, sunny wall. Alkaloids in the plant may be harmful if ingested.

- **HARDINESS** Hardy to -10°C (14°F).
- **CULTIVATION** Grow in deep, moderately fertile, well-drained soil in full sun. Shelter from cold, drying winds and protect from excessive winter wet. Avoid disturbance once established.
- **PROPAGATION** Sow seed in containers in an open frame as soon as ripe or in autumn. Insert root cuttings in winter.
- **PESTS AND DISEASES** Slugs and snails may damage leaves and fruits.

M. autumnalis (Autumn mandrake). Perennial with rosettes of oblong to lance-shaped, dark green leaves, to 25cm (10in) long. From autumn to winter, produces basal clusters of tubular-bell-shaped, violet or white flowers, to 3cm (1¼in) across, often with green or white streaks, followed by ellipsoid, orange or yellow fruit, to 3cm (1¼in) long. ↕ 15cm (6in), ↔ to 30cm (12in). Portugal, Spain, E. Mediterranean. ❄❄
M. officinarum ■ (Common mandrake, Devil's apples, Love apple). Perennial with rosettes of ovate to lance-shaped, wavy-margined, dark green leaves, to 30cm (12in) long, upright at first, then lying flat on the ground. In spring, bears basal clusters of upward-facing, tubular-bell-shaped, greenish white flowers, to 2.5cm (1in) across, sometimes stained purple, followed by spherical yellow fruit, to 3cm (1¼in) across. ↕ 15cm (6in), ↔ to 30cm (12in). N. Italy, W. Balkans, Greece, W. Turkey. ❄❄

Mandragora officinarum

▷ **Mandrake** see *Mandragora*
American see *Podophyllum peltatum*
Autumn see *Mandragora autumnalis*
Common see *Mandragora officinarum*

MANETTIA

RUBIACEAE

Genus of about 80 species of evergreen perennials and woody-stemmed, twining climbers from moist woodland or rainforest in tropical North and South America, and the West Indies. They have opposite, usually simple, sometimes toothed leaves, and tubular to funnel-shaped flowers, with 4 short lobes, borne singly or in axillary panicles or cymes. In frost-prone areas, grow in a cool or temperate greenhouse. Elsewhere, grow on an arch or wall or through small trees.
• **HARDINESS** Frost tender.
• **CULTIVATION** Under glass, grow in loam-based potting compost (JI No.2) in full light or bright filtered light. In growth, water moderately and apply a balanced liquid fertilizer every 3–4 weeks; water sparingly in winter. Outdoors, grow in moderately fertile, moist but well-drained soil, ideally in full sun, but will tolerate partial shade. Pruning group 12, in late winter or early spring.
• **PROPAGATION** Sow seed at 13–18°C (55–64°F) in spring. Root stem-tips of softwood cuttings in late spring or summer.
• **PESTS AND DISEASES** Whiteflies may be a problem under glass.

M. bicolor see *M. luteorubra.*
M. cordifolia (Firecracker vine). Vigorous climber with thin, oblong to lance-shaped, ovate, or heart-shaped leaves, to 8cm (3in) long, lustrous, bright green above, paler and downy or hairless beneath. From late winter to summer, tubular, brilliant red to deep orange flowers, 3–5cm (1¼–2in) long, the lobes sometimes yellow-flushed, are borne singly or in crowded, leafy panicles. ↕2–4m (6–12ft). Peru, Bolivia, Argentina. ❄ (min. 7°C/45°F)
M. inflata see *M. luteorubra.*
M. luteorubra ■ syn. *M. bicolor*, *M. inflata* (Brazilian firecracker). Fast-growing climber with angular, slightly sticky, hairy stems bearing ovate to lance-shaped, light to dark green leaves, 3.5–15cm (1½–6in) long. In summer, bears usually solitary, tubular, bright red, yellow-lobed flowers, 2.5–5cm (1–2in) long, inflated at the bases and with dense velvety hairs. ↕2–4m (6–12ft). Paraguay, Uruguay. ❄ (min. 7°C/45°F)

Manettia luteorubra

MANGLIETIA

MAGNOLIACEAE

Genus of 25 species of upright to spreading, evergreen trees and shrubs found in mountain woodland from the Himalayas to S. and W. China and Malaysia. They have alternate, mostly oblong-ovate to elliptic or inversely lance-shaped, glossy, light or dark green leaves. They are usually cultivated for their magnolia-like flowers, borne singly at the tips of the branches, and followed by cone-like heads containing oblong to ovoid, fleshy-coated seeds. Grow as specimen plants. In frost-prone areas, grow in a cool or temperate greenhouse.
• **HARDINESS** Frost tender, although *M. insignis* may survive short periods near to 0°C (32°F).
• **CULTIVATION** Under glass, grow in loam-based potting compost (JI No.2) in bright filtered or indirect light. In growth, water moderately and apply a balanced liquid fertilizer monthly; water sparingly in winter. Outdoors, grow in humus-rich, moist but well-drained soil in partial shade, or in full sun in humid conditions. Pruning group 1; need restrictive pruning under glass, after flowering.
• **PROPAGATION** Sow seed at 5–9°C (41–48°F) as soon as ripe. Root softwood cuttings with bottom heat in spring. Layer or air layer one-year-old stems in spring.
• **PESTS AND DISEASES** Scale insects may be a problem under glass.

M. insignis ♀ syn. *Magnolia insignis.* Erect then spreading, many-branched tree with grey-downy young shoots. The narrowly oval to inversely lance-shaped, leathery leaves, 10–20cm (4–8in) long, are glossy, rich green above and slightly glaucous beneath. Bears erect, cup-shaped, cream-tinted, pink to rose-pink or carmine-red flowers, 8cm (3in) across, with 9–12 tepals, from spring to early summer, sometimes followed by purple fruit, 5–10cm (2–4in) long. ↕8–12m (25–40ft), ↔3–5m (10–15ft). C. Himalayas to N. Vietnam and W. China. ❄ (min. 5°C/41°F)

▷ **Manuka** see *Leptospermum scoparium*
▷ **Manzanita** see *Arbutus*, *Arctostaphylos*, *A. manzanita*
Bigberry see *Arctostaphylos glauca*
Dune see *Arctostaphylos pumila*
Eastwood see *Arctostaphylos glandulosa*
Greenleaf see *Arctostaphylos patula*
Parry see *Arctostaphylos manzanita*
Pine-mat see *Arctostaphylos nevadensis*
Stanford see *Arctostaphylos stanfordiana*

▷ **Maple** see *Acer*
Amur see *Acer tataricum* subsp. *ginnala*
Ash-leaved see *Acer negundo*
Big-leaf see *Acer macrophyllum*
Canyon see *Acer saccharum* subsp. *grandidentatum*
Cappadocian see *Acer cappadocicum*
Caucasian see *Acer cappadocicum*
Eagle's claw see *Acer platanoides* 'Laciniatum'
Flowering see *Abutilon*
Full-moon see *Acer japonicum*
Greek see *Acer heldreichii* subsp. *trautvetteri*
Hawthorn see *Acer crataegifolium*
Hornbeam see *Acer carpinifolium*
Italian see *Acer opalus*
Japanese see *Acer japonicum*, *A. palmatum*
Korean see *Acer pseudosieboldianum*
Lobel's see *Acer cappadocicum* subsp. *lobelii*
Montpellier see *Acer monspessulanum*
Mountain see *Acer spicatum*
Nikko see *Acer maximowiczianum*
Norway see *Acer platanoides*
Oregon see *Acer macrophyllum*
Paper-bark see *Acer griseum*
Parlour see *Abutilon*
Père David's see *Acer davidii*
Red see *Acer rubrum*
Red bud see *Acer heldreichii* subsp. *trautvetteri*
Rock see *Acer saccharum*
Scarlet see *Acer rubrum*
Shantung see *Acer truncatum*
Silver see *Acer saccharinum*
Snake-bark see *Acer capillipes*, *A. davidii*, *A. rufinerve*
Striped see *Acer pensylvanicum*
Sugar see *Acer saccharum*
Swamp see *Acer rubrum*
Tatarian see *Acer tataricum*
Three-toothed see *Acer buergerianum*
Trident see *Acer buergerianum*
Vine see *Acer circinatum*
▷ **Maracuja de refresco** see *Passiflora alata*

MARANTA

MARANTACEAE

Genus of about 20 species of evergreen, rhizomatous perennials from rainforest in tropical Central and South America. They are cultivated for their crowded clumps of blunt-ended, elliptic leaves, spreading by day and raised to an erect position in the evening. Small, tubular, 2-lipped white flowers are produced in pairs in loose racemes. In frost-prone areas, grow as houseplants or in a warm greenhouse, either in hanging baskets or trained up moss poles. In warmer climates, use as ground cover among shrubs in shade.
• **HARDINESS** Frost tender.
• **CULTIVATION** Under glass, grow in loamless or loam-based potting compost (JI No.2) in bright filtered or bright indirect light, in half-pots or pans to accommodate the shallow root system. Provide high humidity at all times. In the growing season, water moderately and apply a balanced liquid fertilizer monthly; water sparingly in winter. Outdoors, grow in humus-rich, moist but well-drained soil in deep or partial shade.
• **PROPAGATION** Sow seed at 13–18°C (55–64°F) as soon as ripe. Divide in spring. Take basal cuttings, 7–10cm (3–4in) long, and root with bottom heat in spring.
• **PESTS AND DISEASES** Red spider mites may be troublesome under glass.

Maranta leuconeura 'Erythroneura'

Maranta leuconeura 'Kerchoveana'

M. kerchoveana see *M. leuconeura* 'Kerchoveana'.
M. leuconeura (Prayer plant). Very variable, clump-forming perennial with elliptic to obovate, dark green leaves, 12cm (5in) long, with silver lines that fan from the midribs to the margins; the undersides are deep purple or grey-green. ↕↔30cm (12in). Brazil. ❄ (min. 15°C/59°F). **'Erythroneura'** ■ syn. 'Erythrophylla' (Herringbone plant), bears oblong-obovate to obovate, velvety, olive- and black-green leaves with bright red midribs and veins, and jagged, light yellow-green markings around the midribs; the undersides are deep red. **'Kerchoveana'** ■ syn. *M. kerchoveana* (Rabbit's foot, Rabbit's tracks), bears broadly oblong-elliptic, light grey-green leaves with roughly square brown marks, turning green with age, either side of the pale green midribs; the undersides are pale blue-grey. **'Massangeana'**, syn. var. *massangeana*, produces broadly elliptic, blackish green leaves with silver-grey feathering along the midribs and veins; the undersides are purple.
M. makoyana see *Calathea makoyana.*

▷ ***Marginatocereus marginatus*** see *Stenocereus marginatus*
▷ **Marguerite** see *Leucanthemum vulgare*
Golden see *Anthemis tinctoria*

MARGYRICARPUS

ROSACEAE

Genus of one species of dwarf, evergreen shrub from dry, open sites in northern mountains and southern lowlands of the Andes. It produces pinnate leaves and insignificant flowers, and is valued for its long-lasting fruit. Suitable for growing in a scree bed, a rock garden, or an alpine house.

• **HARDINESS** Hardy to -7°C (19°F) in well-drained soil.

• **CULTIVATION** Grow in moderately fertile, acid, moist but well-drained soil in full sun with some midday shade. In an alpine house, grow in lime-free (ericaceous) compost. Shelter from cold, drying winds and protect from excessive winter wet. Pruning group 1.

• **PROPAGATION** Sow seed in containers in a cold frame in autumn or as soon as ripe. Layer or root softwood cuttings in late spring or early summer.

• **PESTS AND DISEASES** Susceptible to aphids and whiteflies under glass.

M. pinnatus, syn. *M. setosus* (Pearl berry). Spreading, densely branched shrub bearing sharply pointed, pinnate leaves, to 2cm (¾in) long, with linear, dark green leaflets with inrolled, silky-hairy margins. In early summer, bears axillary clusters of 1–3 tiny green flowers, followed by spherical, leathery, purple-tinted white fruit, to 7mm (¼in) across. ↕ to 30cm (12in), ↔ to 45cm (18in). Andes. ❄❄

M. setosus see *M. pinnatus.*

▷**Marigold** see *Calendula*
  African see *Tagetes* African Group
  Afro-French see *Tagetes* Afro-French Group
  Corn see *Xanthophthalmum segetum*
  English see *Calendula*
  French see *Tagetes* French Group
  Marsh see *Caltha, C. palustris*
  Pot see *Calendula*
  Signet see *Tagetes* Signet Group
▷**Mariposa, Yellow** see *Calochortus luteus*
▷**Mariposa tulip** see *Calochortus*
▷**Marjoram** see *Origanum*
  Compact see *O. vulgare* 'Compactum'
  French see *O. onites*
  Golden wild see *O. vulgare* 'Aureum'
  Hop see *O. dictamnus*
  Pot see *O. onites*
  Sweet see *O. majorana*
  Wild see *O. vulgare*
▷**Marlberry** see *Ardisia japonica*
▷**Marmalade bush** see *Streptosolen jamesonii*
▷***Marniera chrysocardium*** see *Epiphyllum chrysocardium*

MARRUBIUM

Horehound

LABIATAE/LAMIACEAE

Genus of about 40 species of woolly perennials from Mediterranean Europe and temperate Asia, mainly found in dry, sunny, stony wasteland. They have square stems, opposite, usually ovate or ovate-oblong, often malodorous leaves, and tubular, 2-lipped flowers in axillary whorls. Grow in a large rock garden or a mixed border; they are particularly effective in a Mediterranean garden.

• **HARDINESS** Hardy to -10°C (14°F).

• **CULTIVATION** Grow in poor, well-drained soil in full sun. Provide shelter from cold, drying winds and protection from excessive winter wet.

• **PROPAGATION** Sow seed in containers in a cold frame in late spring, although germination is erratic. Root softwood cuttings in spring.

• **PESTS AND DISEASES** Trouble free.

***M. candidissimum* of gardens** see *M. incanum.*

M. incanum, syn. *M. candidissimum* of gardens. Spreading, silky-hairy perennial with many erect, densely white-hairy shoots bearing oblong-ovate, scalloped or toothed, grey-green leaves, white-felted beneath. In early summer, produces congested whorls of very pale lilac, almost white flowers, to 1.5cm (½in) long, within grey-woolly calyces. ↕ 20–50cm (8–20in), ↔ 60cm (24in). Italy, Sicily, Balkan Peninsula. ❄❄

▷***Marsdenia*** see *Cionura*
  M. erecta see *C. erecta*
▷**Marsh mallow** see *Althaea officinalis*
▷**Marsh marigold** see *Caltha, C. palustris*
  Giant see *C. palustris* var. *palustris*
▷**Marsh orchid** see *Dactylorhiza*
  Robust see *D. elata*

MARSILEA

Pepperwort, Water clover

MARSILEACEAE

Genus of 65 species of rhizomatous, terrestrial, amphibious, and aquatic perennial ferns from warm-temperate Europe, tropical W. Africa, N. Asia, Australia, and E. USA. They grow in large numbers, mainly beside rivers but also in lakes, where the elongated rhizomes grow upwards, producing a canopy of surface leaves that develop a terrestrial form if the water recedes. Triangular to ovate, 4-lobed leaves each bear a spore case at the base, and close up at night when submerged. Grow at

Marsilea quadrifolia

the margins of a pool. In frost-prone areas, grow tender species in an indoor pool in a warm greenhouse or conservatory, or in a tropical aquarium; *M. quadrifolia* is suitable for a cold-water aquarium.

• **HARDINESS** Fully hardy to frost tender.

• **CULTIVATION** Outdoors, grow in the muddy margins of a pool, or in lattice baskets filled with loamy soil, in full sun, at a depth of 15cm (6in). Under glass, grow in baskets of fertile soil at the pool margins, in slightly acid water at 20–26°C (68–79°F), in full light. In an aquarium, root in containers of fine sand or peat; feed with a proprietary aquatic fertilizer. See also pp.52–53.

• **PROPAGATION** Cut the rhizomes into sections and anchor to the substrate in shallow water.

• **PESTS AND DISEASES** Trouble free.

M. drummondii ■ (Common nardoo). Creeping, terrestrial or aquatic, perennial fern with fan-shaped leaves, 1–4cm (½–1½in) across, with 4 leaflets, and upright stems, to 30cm (12in) long, produced singly from the rhizomes. ↕ to 15cm (6in), ↔ indefinite. Australia. ❀ (min. 18°C/64°F)

Marsilea drummondii

M. quadrifolia ■ (Water clover). Creeping, aquatic, perennial fern with long rhizomes, and leaves to 3cm (1¼in) across, with 4 soft, triangular, sometimes overlapping leaflets, downy when young; when submerged, they float on the surface, on stalks to 15cm (6in) long. ↕ to 15cm (6in), ↔ indefinite. Europe, N. Asia, E. USA. ❄❄❄

▷**Marvel of Peru** see *Mirabilis jalapa*
▷***Mascarena lagenicaulis*** see *Hyophorbe lagenicaulis*

MASDEVALLIA

ORCHIDACEAE

Genus of approximately 340 species of evergreen, epiphytic, terrestrial, or lithophytic orchids, mainly found in cloud forest at 800–4,200m (2,600–13,700ft), from Mexico to Central and South America. They lack pseudobulbs but have short, erect stems, each supporting a single, oblong to ovate or linear to lance-shaped, curved or upright, rigid, fleshy leaf. Flowers are borne singly or in racemes, among or usually above the foliage, mostly from spring to summer. Enlarged, often long-tailed sepals surround the minute petals and lips, giving the flowers a triangular shape.

• **HARDINESS** Frost tender.

• **CULTIVATION** Cool-growing orchids. Grow in small pots of epiphytic orchid compost made with fine-grade bark. Provide full light and ample ventilation. In summer, provide moist shade, water freely, feed at every third watering, and mist once or twice daily. In winter, water more sparingly, but do not allow to dry out. See also p.46.

• **PROPAGATION** Not suitable for division, although cuttings or offshoots may be rooted successfully.

• **PESTS AND DISEASES** Red spider mites, aphids, mealybugs, and yellow bean virus may be troublesome.

M. Angel Frost ■ (*M. strobelii* x *M. veitchiana*). Epiphytic orchid with upright, oblong to narrowly ovate leaves, 15cm (6in) long. Bears racemes of orange flowers, 8cm (3in) long, in spring. ↕ 23cm (9in), ↔ 15cm (6in). ❀ (min. 11°C/52°F; max. 24°C/75°F)

M. Angel Heart (*M. ignea* x *M. infracta*). Epiphytic orchid with upright, linear to lance-shaped leaves, 15cm (6in) long. Red flowers, 8cm (3in) long, are borne singly or in racemes, in spring.

Masdevallia Angel Frost

Masdevallia coccinea

↕23cm (9in), ↔15cm (6in). ❄ (min. 11°C/52°F; max. 24°C/75°F)
M. coccinea ▣ Terrestrial orchid with upright, oblong to lance-shaped leaves, 15–20cm (6–8in) long. In summer, bears solitary flowers, 6–10cm (2½–4in) long, with purple-pink, crimson, red-orange, yellow, or white sepals, and white petals. ↕40cm (16in), ↔30cm (12in). Colombia, Peru. ❄ (min. 11°C/52°F; max. 24°C/75°F)
M. elephanticeps* var. *pachysepala see *M. mooreana.*
***M.* Hugh Rogers** ▣ (*M. amabilis* x *M. yungasensis*). Epiphytic orchid with upright, oblong to lance-shaped leaves, 15cm (6in) long. In spring, bears racemes of orange or red flowers, 8cm (3in) long, with darker veins in the same colour. ↕23cm (9in), ↔15cm (6in). ❄ (min. 11°C/52°F; max. 24°C/75°F)
M. ignea see *M. militaris.*
M. infracta ▣ Epiphytic orchid with upright, oblong to lance-shaped leaves, 8–14cm (3–5½in) long. Bears racemes of cupped, yellow-flushed, dull red to purplish pink flowers, 10–15cm (4–6in) long, with long, pale yellow tails, in summer. ↕↔15cm (6in). Peru, Brazil. ❄ (min. 11°C/52°F; max. 24°C/75°F)
***M.* Measuresiana** (*M. amabilis* x *M. tovarensis*). Epiphytic orchid with upright, oblong to lance-shaped leaves, 10–15cm (4–6in) long. Bears racemes of long-tailed white flowers, 8cm (3in) long, flushed pale pink, in succession in winter. ↕23cm (9in), ↔15cm (6in). ❄ (min. 11°C/52°F; max. 24°C/75°F)

Masdevallia Hugh Rogers

Masdevallia infracta

M. militaris, syn. *M. ignea.* Lithophytic orchid with upright, oblong to lance-shaped leaves, to 15cm (6in) long. Orange-scarlet to red-brown flowers, 4.5cm (1¾in) long, are borne singly in summer. ↕30cm (12in), ↔23cm (9in). Venezuela, Colombia. ❄ (min. 11°C/52°F; max. 24°C/75°F)
M. mooreana, syn. *M. elephanticeps* var. *pachysepala.* Epiphytic orchid with upright, linear-oblong leaves, to 20cm (8in) long. Greenish yellow flowers, to 9cm (3½in) across, spotted dull purple, with bright yellow tails, are borne singly in summer. ↕↔15cm (6in). Venezuela, Colombia. ❄ (min. 11°C/52°F; max. 24°C/75°F)
M. rolfeana. Epiphytic orchid with upright, obovate to elliptic leaves, 11–14cm (4½–5½in) long. Dark reddish purple flowers, 6cm (2½in) long, with short yellow tails, are borne singly from spring to summer. ↕↔15cm (6in). Costa Rica. ❄ (min. 11°C/52°F; max. 24°C/75°F)
M. tovarensis ▣ Epiphytic orchid with upright, obovate to lance-shaped leaves, to 15cm (6in) long. Milk-white flowers, 8cm (3in) long, with short tails, are produced in short racemes in winter. ↕↔15cm (6in). Venezuela. ❄ (min. 11°C/52°F; max. 24°C/75°F)
M. veitchiana. Lithophytic orchid with upright, oblong to narrowly obovate leaves, 15–25cm (6–10in) long. Bright orange-red, purple-hairy flowers, 10–15cm (4–6in) long, shot with crimson, with short tails, are borne singly from spring to summer. ↕30cm (12in), ↔23cm (9in). Peru. ❄ (min. 11°C/52°F; max. 24°C/75°F)

Masdevallia tovarensis

▷**Mask flower** see *Alonsoa*
▷**Masterwort** see *Astrantia*
▷**Mastic, Chinese** see *Pistacia chinensis*
▷**Mastic tree** see *Pistacia lentiscus*
Peruvian see *Schinus molle*
▷**Mat rush** see *Lomandra*
Pale see *L. glauca*
Spiny-headed see *L. longifolia*

MATTEUCCIA

DRYOPTERIDACEAE/WOODSIACEAE

Genus of 3 or 4 species of deciduous, terrestrial ferns, commonly occurring in deciduous woodland in Europe, E. Asia, and North America. In spring, the erect or creeping rhizomes produce lance-shaped, pinnate to 2-pinnatifid sterile fronds in regular "shuttlecocks". These are followed in mid- and late summer by distinctive, smaller, more erect, darker, and longer-stalked fertile fronds, which persist over winter. Grow in moist shade in a woodland garden, a damp border, or at the edge of a pond.
• **HARDINESS** Fully hardy.
• **CULTIVATION** Grow in humus-rich, moist but well-drained, neutral to slightly acid soil in partial or light dappled shade.
• **PROPAGATION** Sow spores at 15°C (59°F) as soon as ripe. Divide established clumps in early spring.
• **PESTS AND DISEASES** Trouble free.

M. struthiopteris ▣ (Ostrich fern, Shuttlecock fern). Rhizomatous fern with erect "shuttlecocks" of broadly lance-shaped, pinnate, pale green sterile fronds, 1.2m (4ft) or more long, with narrowly lance-shaped, pinnatifid pinnae. Shorter, dark brown fertile fronds, 30cm (12in) or more long, have linear pinnae with strongly inrolled margins, and appear in late summer. Spreads by horizontal rhizomes, producing separate "shuttlecocks" 10–20cm (4–8in) from the parent plant. ↕1.7m (5½ft), ↔to 1m (3ft). Europe, E. Asia, E. North America. ❄❄❄

Matteuccia struthiopteris

MATTHIOLA

Gillyflower, Stock

BRASSICACEAE/CRUCIFERAE

Genus of 55 species of bushy, erect annuals and perennials, occasionally subshrubs, from scrub and hilly areas in W. Europe, South Africa, and C. and S.W. Asia. The leaves are simple, usually lance-shaped, sometimes pinnatifid or shallowly lobed, and grey-green to mid-green. *Matthiola* species and cultivars are grown for their usually sweetly scented, pastel pink, purple, or white flowers. The flowers are cross-shaped (double in some cultivar selections), and borne in terminal, spike-like racemes or panicles. Grow in a mixed or annual border.

Cultivars of *M. incana* are useful spring and summer bedding plants, and provide attractive cut flowers. They are often divided by horticulturists into the following 4 groups. Brompton stocks, grown as biennials, bear tall panicles of single or double flowers. East Lothian stocks may be grown as biennials or spring-sown annuals; more compact and smaller-flowered than Brompton Group stocks, they produce spike-like racemes of single or double flowers. Ten Week stocks are grown as annuals, and may be dwarf or tall: dwarf cultivars, suitable for bedding or containers, bear single or double flowers, usually in panicles; tall cultivars bear mostly double flowers in dense, usually unbranched, spike-like racemes. Column stocks are generally grown under glass for cut flowers, and produce long, dense, upright, spike-like racemes of mainly double flowers.
• **HARDINESS** Fully hardy to frost hardy.
• **CULTIVATION** Grow in moderately fertile, moist but well-drained, preferably neutral to slightly alkaline soil in a sheltered position in full sun. Give support to tall cultivars.
• **PROPAGATION** Sow seed of *M. longipetala* subsp. *bicornis in situ* in spring, and repeat for a succession of flowers. For bedding, sow seed of *M. incana* Cinderella Series, Midget Series, and Ten Week Mixed at 10–18°C (50–64°F) in early spring. Sow seed of *M. incana* Legacy Series, Sentinel Series, and Excelsior Mammoth Column Series in a seedbed or in containers in a cold frame in midsummer; overwinter under cloches in cold climates and plant out in spring. Seedlings are prone to "damping off". Sow seed of perennials in containers in a cold frame in spring or summer; overwinter in a cold frame and plant out in the following spring.
• **PESTS AND DISEASES** Susceptible to aphids, flea beetles, cabbage root flies, clubroot, downy mildew, grey mould (*Botrytis*), seed-borne infections of bacterial leaf spot, root and stem rots, and cucumber mosaic virus.

M. bicornis see *M. longipetala* subsp. *bicornis.*
M. fruticulosa. Dwarf, lax or tufted, woody-based, hairy to densely white-woolly perennial with simple or pinnatifid, linear to oblong, grey-green leaves, to 12cm (5in) long. In summer, bears long, upright, spike-like racemes of flowers, 1.5–3cm (½–1¼in) across, varying from yellow to purplish violet. ↕to 60cm (24in), ↔to 20cm (8in). C. and S. Europe, Turkey (in Europe

M

Matthiola incana Cinderella Series

only), Cyprus, Lebanon, N.W. Africa. ❄❄❄. **subsp. *valesiaca*** is tufted, spreads by underground runners, and bears dense racemes of mauve-purple to red-purple flowers; prefers acid soil; ↕25cm (10in), ↔ 30cm (12in); N. and E. Spain, Pyrenees, S. Alps, Balkans.
M. incana (Gillyflower, Stock). Woody-based perennial or subshrub, sometimes short-lived, with entire, occasionally pinnatifid or lobed, inversely lance-shaped to linear-lance-shaped, grey-green to white-hairy leaves, 5–10cm (2–4in) long. Upright racemes of sweet-scented, mauve, purple, violet, pink, or white flowers, to 2.5cm (1in) across, are borne from late spring to summer. ↕ to 80cm (32in), ↔ to 40cm (16in). Coastal S. and W. Europe, from Spain to W. Turkey, Cyprus, Arabian Peninsula, Egypt. ❄❄❄ (borderline). The many cultivars of *M. incana*, sometimes resulting from crosses with *M. sinuata*, are grown as annuals or biennials, and produce single or fully double, almost rosette-like, scented flowers in dense, spike-like racemes or panicles, 15–45cm (6–18in) tall, in summer. *M. incana* cultivars are sometimes divided into informal groups (see introduction). **Cinderella Series** ■ cultivars bear double, dark blue-purple, lavender-blue, red, rose-pink, silvery blue, or white flowers in racemes 15cm (6in) long; ↕20–25cm (8–10in), ↔ to 25cm (10in). **Excelsior Mammoth Column Series** cultivars bear mostly double, pink, red, pale blue, or white flowers in spike-like racemes, 30cm (12in) long; ↕ to 75cm (30in), ↔ to 30cm (12in). **Legacy Series** cultivars bear mainly double flowers in scarlet-red, crimson-red, rose-pink, lavender-blue, white, and creamy yellow, in panicles 30cm (12in) long; ↕30–45cm (12–18in) or more, ↔ to 30cm (12in). **Midget Series** cultivars produce double flowers in a range of pastel and deeper tones, including rose-red, red, violet, and white, in spikes 15cm (6in) long; ↕↔ to 25cm (10in). **Sentinel Series** cultivars produce racemes 30cm (12in) long, of double flowers in colours including white, pink, carmine-red, and light to dark blue; ↕ to 75cm (30in), ↔ to 30cm (12in). **Ten Week Mixed** ■ bears mainly double flowers in shades of crimson, pink, lavender-pink, purple, and white, in racemes 15cm (6in) long; ↕30cm (12in), ↔ to 25cm (10in).

Matthiola incana Ten Week Mixed

M. longipetala* subsp. *bicornis, syn. *M. bicornis* (Night-scented stock). Erect to spreading, single-stemmed to branching annual with narrowly linear, sometimes pinnatifid, grey-green leaves, to 8cm (3in) long. In summer, produces open racemes of pink, mauve, or purple flowers, to 2cm (¾in) across, which are strongly fragrant at night. ↕30–35cm (12–14in), ↔ 23cm (9in). Greece to S.W. Asia. ❄❄❄

▷***Matucana aurantiaca*** see *Oreocereus aurantiacus*
▷***Matucana haynei*** see *Oreocereus haynei*
▷***Matucana intertexta*** see *Oreocereus intertexta*

MAURANDELLA

SCROPHULARIACEAE

Genus of one species of twining, herbaceous, perennial climber from dry desert riverbeds, subject to flooding, in limestone areas of S.W. USA and Mexico. It has hairless, slender, many-branched stems, to 2.2m (7ft) long, and ovate-triangular, lobed leaves. Tubular flowers are borne singly from the leaf axils throughout summer and autumn. In frost-prone climates, grow as a half-hardy annual or in a cool greenhouse. In warmer areas, use to clothe a pergola, arch, or trellis, or grow against a wall.
• **HARDINESS** Half hardy.
• **CULTIVATION** Under glass and when grown as an annual, grow in loam-based potting compost (JI No.2) in full light with shade from hot sun. In growth, water moderately and apply a balanced liquid fertilizer monthly; water sparingly in winter. Outdoors, grow in moderately fertile, moist but well-drained soil in full sun with some midday shade, or in light dappled shade. Shelter from cold, drying winds. Remove dead top growth.
• **PROPAGATION** Sow seed at 13–18°C (55–64°F) in spring. Root softwood cuttings with bottom heat in late spring.
• **PESTS AND DISEASES** Trouble free.

M. antirrhiniflora ■ syn. *Asarina antirrhiniflora* (Violet twining snapdragon). Wiry-stemmed climber with shallowly lobed, bright to mid-green leaves, 2.5–10cm (1–4in) or more long. Produces snapdragon-like flowers, to 4.5cm (1¾in) long, with white tubes and usually violet or purple, occasionally pink lobes, in summer and autumn. ↕1–2m (3–6ft). S.W. USA, Mexico. ❄

Maurandella antirrhiniflora

MAURANDYA

SCROPHULARIACEAE

Genus of 2 species of twining, woody-based, herbaceous, perennial climbers found in rocky areas and woodland in Mexico and Central America. The leaves are triangular to broadly ovate, sometimes heart-shaped at the bases, and sometimes 5-lobed. Solitary, trumpet-shaped blooms are borne in the leaf axils throughout summer and autumn. Use to clothe a trellis, or grow against a wall. In frost-prone areas, grow in a cool greenhouse or outdoors as annuals.
• **HARDINESS** Half hardy.
• **CULTIVATION** Under glass, grow in loam-based potting compost (JI No.2) in full light with shade from hot sun, or in bright filtered light. In growth, water freely; apply a balanced liquid fertilizer monthly. Keep just moist in winter. Outdoors, grow in moderately fertile, moist but well-drained soil in full sun. Remove dead top growth in autumn.
• **PROPAGATION** Sow seed at 13–18°C (55–64°F) in spring. Root softwood cuttings with bottom heat in late spring.
• **PESTS AND DISEASES** Trouble free.

M. barclayana ■ syn. *Asarina barclayana*. Medium-sized, erect, free-flowering climber with angular to shallowly lobed, ovate, mid- to light green leaves, 2.5–4.5cm (1–1¾in) long, with heart-shaped bases. From summer to autumn, produces flowers, 4–7cm (1½–3in) long, with white or green-tinted white tubes and white, pink, or deep purple lobes. ↕2–5m (6–15ft). Mexico. ❄
M. erubescens see *Lophospermum erubescens*.
M. purpusii, syn. *Asarina purpusii*. Tuberous climber with triangular-ovate, softly hairy, mid-green leaves, 4–8cm (1½–3in) long, sometimes coarsely toothed. Produces purplish pink flowers, 4cm (1½in) long, throughout summer and autumn. ↕60cm (24in). Mexico. ❄

Maurandya barclayana

MAXILLARIA

ORCHIDACEAE

Genus of about 250 species of evergreen, rhizomatous, epiphytic or terrestrial orchids from tropical and subtropical Central and South America, found from sea level to over 3,000m (10,000ft), sometimes in cloud forest. Solitary or clustered, usually laterally compressed, ovoid to spherical, sometimes oblong pseudobulbs produce 1 or 2 thin to leathery, grass-like or broadly oblong, usually mid-green leaves. Flowers are borne singly or in clusters on scapes produced from long or short rhizomes. They range from white to dark red or yellow, and usually appear intermittently throughout summer.

• **HARDINESS** Frost tender.
• **CULTIVATION** Cool- or intermediate-growing orchids. Grow in epiphytic orchid compost in pots or slatted baskets, or epiphytically on slabs of bark. In summer, grow in moist partial shade, water freely, feed at every third watering, and mist once or twice daily. Admit full light in winter; keep moist throughout the year. See also p.46.
• **PROPAGATION** Divide when plants fill the containers and "flow" over the sides.
• **PESTS AND DISEASES** Susceptible to red spider mites, aphids, and mealybugs.

M. cucullata, syn. *M. meleagris*. Very variable, epiphytic orchid with small, ovoid pseudobulbs producing 1, occasionally 2, strap-shaped leaves, to 30cm (12in) long. From summer to autumn, bears deep red, occasionally yellow, pink, or black-maroon flowers with yellow to white lips, heavily spotted and striped dark red, on scapes 12–16cm (5–6in) long. ↕↔ 15cm (6in). Mexico, Guatemala, Panama. ❀ (min. 10°C/50°F; max. 30°C/86°F)
M. grandiflora. Epiphytic orchid with compressed, ovoid pseudobulbs and one strap-shaped, apical leaf, 25–50cm (10–20in) long. White flowers, 6cm (2½in) across, with white or yellow, pink- or purple-margined lips, are borne on scapes 10–30cm (4–12in) long, from spring to early summer. ↕↔ 30cm (12in). N.W. South America. ❀ (min. 10°C/50°F; max. 30°C/86°F)
M. meleagris see *M. cucullata*.
M. picta. Epiphytic orchid with conical pseudobulbs and one narrowly oblong leaf, to 30cm (12in) long. Fragrant, deep yellow to white flowers, spotted purple, dark red, or brown, to 4cm (1½in) across, are borne on scapes 15cm (6in) long, from spring to summer. ↕↔ 23cm (9in). Colombia, Brazil. ❀ (min. 10°C/50°F; max. 30°C/86°F)
M. porphyrostele ■ Epiphytic orchid with ovoid pseudobulbs and 2 lance-shaped, apical leaves, 20cm (8in) long. From winter to spring, slightly fragrant, light yellow flowers, 2.5cm (1in) across, with purple-striped throats, are borne on scapes 8cm (3in) long. ↕↔ 15cm (6in). Brazil. ❀ (min. 10°C/50°F; max. 30°C/86°F)
M. sanderiana. Epiphytic or terrestrial orchid with compressed, ovoid pseudobulbs, with one narrowly oblong leaf, to 40cm (16in) long. Bears fragrant white flowers, 12cm (5in) across, with heavy red basal spotting, on short, horizontal or erect scapes, to 25cm (10in) long, from summer to early autumn. ↕↔ 45cm (18in). Ecuador, Peru. ❀ (min. 10°C/50°F; max. 30°C/86°F)

Maxillaria porphyrostele

▷**May** see *Crataegus laevigata*, *C. monogyna*
▷**May apple** see *Podophyllum peltatum*
Chinese see *P. pleianthum*
▷**Mayflower** see *Epigaea repens*
▷**Maypops** see *Passiflora incarnata*

MAYTENUS

CELASTRACEAE

Genus of about 225 species of evergreen, mainly dioecious trees and shrubs from forest in North and South America and tropical Africa. The variably shaped, alternate leaves are entire or toothed. Tiny, star-shaped to tubular flowers are produced in axillary cymes, racemes, or panicles, or sometimes singly. Grow as specimen trees or in woodland. In frost-prone areas, grow tender species in a cool or temperate greenhouse. Long, hot summers are needed for production of flowers and fruits.

• **HARDINESS** Fully hardy to frost tender.
• **CULTIVATION** Grow in moderately fertile, moist but well-drained soil in full sun with midday shade. Shelter from cold, drying winds. Pruning group 1.
• **PROPAGATION** Sow seed under glass in autumn. Remove suckers, which may appear at some distance from the parent plant, in spring. Root semi-ripe cuttings with bottom heat in summer.
• **PESTS AND DISEASES** Trouble free.

M. boaria ♀–♀ syn. *M. chilensis* (Maiten). Tree or shrub, of variable habit, with pendent or upright branches and narrowly elliptic to lance-shaped, glossy, dark green, finely toothed leaves, to 5cm (2in) long. Bears small clusters of tiny, tubular, pale green flowers, the males with yellow anthers, in mid- and late spring; on the same plant, female flowers produce orange-red capsules, which open to release red seeds. ↕ 20m (70ft), ↔ to 10m (30ft). Chile. ❄❄❄
M. chilensis see *M. boaria*.

MAZUS

SCROPHULARIACEAE

Genus of about 30 species of annuals and creeping, usually mat-forming, prostrate perennials, which root at the nodes. They are found in wet habitats from lowland to mountainous regions of the Himalayas, India, Pakistan,

Mazus reptans

China, Taiwan, Japan, S.E. Asia, and Australasia. The leaves, 1–5cm (½–2in) long, borne in opposite pairs, are mostly linear to spoon-shaped or obovate, toothed, and usually mid-green. Narrowly tubular flowers, with erect upper lips and large, spreading, 3-lobed lower lips, are produced singly or in few-flowered racemes from the leaf axils. *Mazus* species are suitable for ground cover in a sheltered rock garden or in paving crevices, or as pan plants in an alpine house.

• **HARDINESS** Hardy to -10°C (14°F).
• **CULTIVATION** Grow in moderately fertile, moist but well-drained soil in a sheltered site in full sun. In an alpine house, grow in shallow containers of loam-based potting compost (JI No.2).
• **PROPAGATION** Sow seed in containers in a cold frame in spring or autumn. Divide in spring.
• **PESTS AND DISEASES** Slugs and snails may be a problem.

M. reptans ■ Mat-forming perennial with lance-shaped to elliptic or obovate, coarsely toothed leaves, 1–3cm (½–1¼in) long. From late spring to summer, produces 2- to 5-flowered racemes of purple-blue flowers, 1.5–2cm (½–¾in) long, with yellow- and red-spotted white lower lips. ↕ to 5cm (2in), ↔ to 30cm (12in) or more. Himalayas. ❄❄

▷**Meadow beauty** see *Rhexia*, *R. virginica*
▷**Meadow rue** see *Thalictrum*
Yellow see *T. flavum*
▷**Meadowsweet** see *Filipendula ulmaria*

MECONOPSIS

PAPAVERACEAE

Genus of about 45 species of annuals, biennials, and deciduous or evergreen, often short-lived or monocarpic perennials. They occur in moist, shady mountainous areas, alpine meadows, woodland, scrub, scree, and rocky slopes in the Himalayas, Burma, and China, with one species from W. Europe. Usually hairy or bristly, they produce basal rosettes of pinnate or simple leaves, which may be entire, toothed, lobed, or pinnatisect. The lower leaves are long-stalked, the upper ones short-stalked or stalkless. The flowering stems, usually one per leaf rosette, are either leafless and unbranched, each bearing a solitary flower, or leafy and branched near the top, bearing flowers singly or in short racemes or panicles, the uppermost opening first. The flowers are generally pendent, saucer- to cup-shaped, poppy-like, and silky, with numerous stamens and usually 4, but sometimes up to 9 petals. The flower-stalks lengthen after flowering as the fruits develop.

Meconopsis species grow best in areas with cool, damp summers. Most are suitable for growing in large groups in a moist, cool woodland garden, but also perform well in a moist peat bed or terrace. *M. cambrica* is suitable for a wildflower garden but will thrive almost anywhere, except in very dry soils.

• **HARDINESS** Fully hardy; young growth may be damaged by late frosts.
• **CULTIVATION** Grow in humus-rich, leafy, moist but well-drained, neutral to slightly acid soil, open enough to prevent stagnation and rot in winter; site in partial shade with shelter from cold, drying winds. Mulch generously, and water in dry spells in summer. Short-lived perennials, e.g. *M. betonicifolia*, are less likely to be monocarpic in moist conditions, and if flowering is prevented until several crowns have been formed.
• **PROPAGATION** Sow seed in containers in a cold frame, preferably as soon as ripe or in spring. Use loamless seed compost, sow thinly, and keep moist; light is needed for germination. Over winter, keep young plants produced from autumn sowings in a cold greenhouse or frame. Seedlings are prone to damping off.

Divide after flowering. Root vegetative buds of *M. chelidoniifolia* when they appear in the upper leaf axils.

Meconopsis betonicifolia

M

MECONOPSIS

Meconopsis cambrica

• **PESTS AND DISEASES** Susceptible to downy mildew and to damage caused by slugs and snails.

M. betonicifolia ▣ (Himalayan blue poppy, Tibetan blue poppy). Deciduous perennial, sometimes short-lived, with loose rosettes of oblong to ovate, toothed, light bluish green leaves, 15–30cm (6–12in) long, heart-shaped or truncate at the bases and covered with rust-coloured hairs. In early summer, pendent to horizontal, saucer-shaped, bright blue, sometimes purple-blue or white flowers, 8–10cm (3–4in) across, with yellow stamens, are borne singly on bristly stalks, to 20cm (8in) long, sometimes clustered towards the tops of the stems. ↕ 1.2m (4ft), occasionally more, ↔ 45cm (18in). Tibet, S.W. China, Burma. ❄❄❄
M. cambrica ▣ (Welsh poppy). Tap-rooted, deciduous perennial. Elliptic, pinnatisect to pinnatifid or irregularly lobed, pale to bluish green, hairless to hairy leaves, to 20cm (8in) long, are borne on branched stems and in basal tufts. From mid-spring to mid-autumn, produces solitary, shallowly cup-shaped, lemon-yellow to orange flowers, 5–6cm (2–2½in) across, on slender stalks, to 25cm (10in) long, from the upper leaf axils. ↕ 45cm (18in) occasionally more, ↔ 25cm (10in). W. Europe. ❄❄❄. **var. *aurantiaca*** has orange flowers. **'Flore Pleno'** has double yellow flowers.
M. chelidoniifolia ▣ Deciduous perennial, spreading by offset buds to form clumps of slender, semi-scandent, leafy, branched stems. The hairy, pale green leaves, to 40cm (16in) long at the base and 3–12cm (1¼–5in) on the stems, are pinnatisect with pinnatifid lobes. In mid- and late summer, nodding, saucer-shaped, pale yellow flowers, 2.5–3.5cm (1–1½in) across, are produced from the upper leaf axils, on stalks 4–5cm (1½–2in) long. ↕ 1m (3ft), ↔ 60cm (24in). China (W. Sichuan). ❄❄❄
M. dhwojii. Monocarpic, evergreen perennial forming basal rosettes of pinnatisect leaves, to 30cm (12in) long, with elliptic-oblong or inversely lance-shaped, lobed segments, covered with bristly, black-based yellow hairs. Branched, leafy stems, to 60cm (24in) long, bear numerous nodding, shallowly cup-shaped, pale yellow flowers, 4–5cm (1½–2in) across, with stalks to 15cm (6in) long, in early summer. The upper flowers are solitary; those on the lower branches are in short racemes of up to 5 flowers. ↕ to 90cm (36in), ↔ 30cm (12in). E. Nepal. ❄❄❄
M. grandis ▣ (Himalayan blue poppy). Clump-forming, deciduous perennial with erect, elliptic, irregularly toothed leaves, 15–25cm (6–10in) long, tapered at the bases. The leaves are borne in basal rosettes and on branched stems, the uppermost forming a whorl below the flowers; they are mid-to dark green, with red-brown or rust-coloured hairs. In early summer, nodding, shallowly cup-shaped, rich blue to purplish red flowers, 12–15cm (5–6in) across, each with up to 9 petals and clusters of yellow anthers, are produced singly from the upper leaf axils on stalks to 40cm (16in) long. Monocarpic in dry conditions. ↕ 1–1.2m (3–4ft), ↔ 60cm (24in). E. Tibet, E. Nepal to India (Sikkim) and Bhutan. ❄❄❄
M. horridula ▣ Monocarpic, deciduous perennial with loose rosettes of simple, entire, elliptic to narrowly inversely lance-shaped, wavy-margined, mid- to grey-green leaves, to 25cm (10in) long, covered with yellow to purple spines. In early and midsummer, branched, leafless, spiny stems bear numerous semi-pendent, cup-shaped, pale to deep blue or reddish blue (rarely white) flowers, 5–8cm (2–3in) across, usually in racemes, on stalks to 15cm (6in) long. ↕ 20–90cm (8–36in), ↔ 45cm (18in). W. Nepal to S.E. Tibet and China (Gansu, Sichuan, Yunnan). ❄❄❄
M. integrifolia ▣ Monocarpic, deciduous perennial covered in downy, red-brown or yellow hairs, and forming rosettes of entire, inversely lance-shaped to obovate or linear, pale green, strongly 3-veined leaves, 35cm (14in) long, yellow-hairy when young, almost hairless when mature. From late spring to midsummer, stout, sometimes branched stems bear leaves in a loose whorl below 2–10 erect flowers. The shallowly cup-shaped, 6- to 8-petalled flowers, to 23cm (9in) across, are pale to rich lemon-yellow with dark yellow or orange stamens, and borne on stalks to 45cm (18in) long. ↕ to 90cm (36in), ↔ 45–60cm (18–24in). N.E. Tibet, China (Gansu, Sichuan, Yunnan). ❄❄❄
M. napaulensis ▣ Monocarpic, evergreen perennial forming rosettes of pinnatisect, yellow-green, red-bristly basal leaves, to 50cm (20in) long, with oblong, lobed segments; the upper stem leaves are pinnatifid or simple. From late spring to midsummer, branching stems bear semi-pendent, bowl-shaped, pink, red, or purple (rarely white) flowers, 6–8cm (2½–3in) across; flowers are borne on stalks to 8cm (3in) long, often in racemes of up to 17 on the lower branches but singly near the stem tops. ↕ 2.5m (8ft), ↔ 60–90cm (24–36in). C. Nepal to China (W. Sichuan). ❄❄❄
M. paniculata. Monocarpic, evergreen perennial, similar to *M. napaulensis*, with rosettes of pinnatisect or pinnatifid, greyish green leaves, to 60cm (24in) long, covered with rough yellow hairs. From late spring to midsummer, tall, branched stems bear shallowly lobed leaves and many-flowered racemes or panicle-like cymes of pendent, shallowly cup-shaped, pale yellow flowers, 5–9cm (2–3½in) across. ↕ to 2m (6ft), ↔ 60cm

Meconopsis chelidoniifolia

Meconopsis grandis

Meconopsis horridula

Meconopsis integrifolia

Meconopsis napaulensis

Meconopsis regia

(24in). E. Nepal to India (Assam). ❄❄❄

M. punicea. Tap-rooted, deciduous perennial with crowded rosettes of entire, inversely lance-shaped, densely grey-hairy, mid-green, basal leaves, 15–35cm (6–14in) long. From midsummer to early autumn, unbranched scapes, to 45cm (18in) long, up to 6 per rosette, bear solitary, pendent, narrowly funnel-shaped, vivid crimson flowers, to 10cm (4in) long, with 4–6 long, somewhat flared petals. Monocarpic in dry conditions. ↕ to 75cm (30in), ↔ 30cm (12in). N.E. Tibet, W. China. ❄❄❄

M. quintuplinervia (Harebell poppy). Slowly clump-forming, deciduous perennial forming rosettes of entire, obovate to narrowly inversely lance-shaped or lance-shaped, mid- to dark green, basal leaves, to 25cm (10in) long, with dense golden to rust-coloured bristles. From early to late summer, pendent, cup-shaped, pale lavender-blue or purplish blue (rarely white) flowers, 3.5cm (1½in) across, are produced singly, or rarely in twos or threes, on unbranched, slender scapes, to 35cm (14in) long. ↕ 45cm (18in), ↔ 30cm (12in). N.E. Tibet, W. China (Gansu, N.W. Sichuan to C. Shaanxi). ❄❄❄

M. regia ▣ Monocarpic, evergreen perennial with branched, leafy, hairy stems, and rosettes of simple, narrowly elliptic, finely but deeply toothed, densely silver- or gold-hairy leaves, to 60cm (24in) long. From late spring to midsummer, bears numerous outward-facing, cup-shaped, soft yellow or red flowers, 9–13cm (3½–5in) across, with 4, occasionally 6, overlapping, rounded petals. Upper flowers are solitary; the lower ones are grouped on lateral branches in the upper leaf axils. ↕ to 2m (6ft), ↔ 1m (3ft). C. Nepal. ❄❄❄

M. x sarsonsii (*M. betonicifolia* x *M. integrifolia*). Deciduous, sometimes monocarpic, fertile perennial with ovate, toothed, mid-green leaves, to 15cm (6in) long, covered with rust-coloured hairs and arranged in loose rosettes. In early summer, branched stems produce solitary, pendent to erect, saucer-shaped, pale creamy yellow flowers, 7–10cm (3–4in) across, on stalks to 40cm (16in) long, produced from the axils of loose whorls of stem leaves. ↕ 1.2m (4ft), ↔ 90cm (3ft). Garden origin. ❄❄❄

M. x sheldonii (*M. betonicifolia* x *M. grandis*). Rosette-forming, hairy perennial with elliptic-oblong to lance-shaped, toothed, dark green basal and stem leaves, 15–30cm (6–12in) long. In late spring and early summer, shallowly cup-shaped, deep rich to pale blue flowers, 6–10cm (2½–4in) across, are borne singly in the upper leaf axils of the branched stems, on stalks 20–50cm (8–20in) long. ↕ 1.2–1.5m (4–5ft), ↔ 60cm (24in). Garden origin. ❄❄❄. The following cultivars, often listed under *M.* x *sheldonii*, have a different parentage but are placed here for convenience. **'Branklyn'** has coarsely toothed leaves, and produces vivid blue flowers, to 12cm (5in) across; ↕ to 1.8m (6ft). **'Slieve Donard'** is vigorous and free-flowering, with entire leaves and brilliant, rich blue flowers with long, pointed petals; ↕ to 1m (3ft).

M. villosa, syn. *Cathcartia villosa.* Rosette-forming, evergreen perennial with ovate to rounded, hairy, light green basal and stem leaves, to 12cm (5in) long, palmately 3- to 5-lobed and sparsely toothed. In late spring and early summer, semi-pendent, saucer-shaped yellow flowers, 4–5cm (1½–2in) across, on stalks to 13cm (5in) long, are borne singly from the upper leaf axils of hairy, branched stems. ↕ 60cm (24in), ↔ 30cm (12in). E. Nepal to Bhutan. ❄❄❄

MEDICAGO
Medick

LEGUMINOSAE/PAPILIONACEAE

Genus of 50–60 species of annuals, perennials, and small shrubs from dry, sunny grassland in Europe and W. and S.W. Asia. They have 3-palmate, light or yellow-green to mid-green or bluish green leaves, sometimes with red spots, and bear short, axillary racemes of pea-like flowers. Annuals and perennials are suitable for a wild garden; shrubby species tolerate coastal conditions, and are best grown in a sunny, open border or against a warm wall. *M. sativa* is grown as a crop plant, as sprouted seeds for salads, and as a "green manure". The flowers attract bees and butterflies.

• **HARDINESS** Fully hardy to frost hardy.

• **CULTIVATION** Grow in poor to moderately fertile, well-drained soil in full sun. Pruning group 1; remove dead wood in spring.

• **PROPAGATION** Sow seed of perennials *in situ* in spring or autumn. Sow seed of shrubs in containers in a cold frame in spring or autumn. Root greenwood cuttings with bottom heat in early summer.

• **PESTS AND DISEASES** Trouble free.

M. arborea (Moon trefoil). Dense, bushy, evergreen shrub with dark green leaves with obovate leaflets, 0.6–2cm (¼–¾in) long, silky-hairy when young. From late spring to early autumn, bears dense racemes of 4–8 yellow flowers, 1.5–2cm (½–¾in) long, followed by flattened, spiralled, green, later brown seed pods. ↕↔ 2m (6ft). Canary Islands, S. Europe and Mediterranean to S.W. Asia. ❄❄ (borderline)

M. sativa (Alfalfa, Lucerne). Erect or spreading, hairy, slender-stemmed perennial bearing bluish green leaves with obovate to linear leaflets, to 3cm (1¼in) long. In summer and early autumn, produces long-stalked racemes of pale mauve to violet flowers, to 1cm (½in) long, followed by small, spiralled or sickle-shaped, deep brown seed pods. ↕ to 80cm (32in), ↔ 30–80cm (12–32in). Europe, W. Asia. ❄❄❄

▷**Medick** see *Medicago*

MEDINILLA

MELASTOMATACEAE

Genus of about 150 species of evergreen shrubs and scandent climbers, some epiphytic, from rainforest in tropical Africa, S.E. Asia, and the Pacific. They have simple, entire, boldly veined leaves, borne in whorls or opposite pairs. Small, star- to bowl-shaped, 4- to 6-petalled flowers, often with large, coloured bracts, are borne in pendent or upright panicles or cymes. Where temperatures fall below 15°C (59°F), grow in a warm greenhouse. In moist, tropical areas, grow climbing species over an arch or pergola; the shrubs are suitable for specimen planting or a shrub border. Long, hot summers are required for production of flowers and fruits.

• **HARDINESS** Frost tender.

• **CULTIVATION** Under glass, grow in loam-based potting compost (JI No.2) in bright filtered light, or full light with shade from hot sun; provide high humidity. In growth, water moderately and apply a balanced liquid fertilizer monthly; water sparingly in winter. Outdoors, grow in moderately fertile, moist but well-drained soil in dappled shade, or full sun with some midday shade. Pruning group 11 for climbers, after flowering; group 8 for shrubs.

• **PROPAGATION** Sow seed at 19–24°C (66–75°F) in spring. Root softwood cuttings in spring or semi-ripe cuttings with bottom heat in summer. Air layer in spring.

• **PESTS AND DISEASES** Scale insects may be troublesome under glass.

Medinilla magnifica

M. magnifica ▣ Erect, sparsely branched, epiphytic shrub with robust, ribbed to strongly winged stems bearing broadly ovate to obovate, leathery, lustrous, deep green leaves, 20–30cm (8–12in) long, with prominent, pale green veins. From spring to summer, yellow-stamened, pink to coral-red flowers, to 2.5cm (1in) across, are borne in dense, pendent panicles, 25–40cm (10–16in) long, with several pairs of large, cupped pink basal bracts. ↕ 1–2m (3–6ft), ↔ 0.6–1.5m (2–5ft). Philippines. ❀ (min. 15°C/59°F)

▷**Mediterranean heath** see *Erica erigena*
▷**Medlar** see *Mespilus germanica*
▷**Medusa's head** see *Euphorbia caput-medusae*

MEEHANIA

LABIATAE/LAMIACEAE

Genus of 6 species of stoloniferous, clump-forming perennials found in moist, deciduous woodland in Asia and North America. Square stems bear opposite pairs of ovate to heart-shaped, finely hairy leaves. Tubular, 2-lipped, violet or blue flowers are produced from the leaf axils from late spring to summer. Grow in a shady border or as ground cover in a woodland garden.

• **HARDINESS** Fully hardy.

• **CULTIVATION** Grow in humus-rich, moist but well-drained soil in full to light dappled shade.

• **PROPAGATION** Sow seed in containers in a cold frame in spring. Separate stolons in early spring or autumn. Root stem-tip cuttings in spring.

• **PESTS AND DISEASES** Susceptible to damage by slugs.

M. urticifolia ▣ Stoloniferous, clump-forming perennial, spreading widely, with broadly ovate, heart-shaped, wrinkled, softly hairy leaves, 3–6cm (1¼–2½in) long, with scalloped margins. One-sided spikes of 3–12 deep violet flowers, 4–5cm (1½–2in) long, sometimes with white lines and the lower lips spotted dark purple, are produced in late spring and early summer. ↕ 30–45cm (12–18in), ↔ to 2.5m (8ft). Japan. ❄❄❄

Meehania urticifolia

MEGACODON

GENTIANACEAE

Genus of one species of clump-forming perennial found in damp pastures and streamsides from C. Nepal to S.W. China. It has basal rosettes of elliptic to broadly elliptic leaves, and bears smaller leaves on stout, erect stems. Broadly bell-shaped flowers are produced in summer. Grow in a woodland or bog garden, or plant near pools and streams.

- **HARDINESS** Fully hardy.
- **CULTIVATION** Grow in humus-rich, moist but well-drained soil in partial or light dappled shade. Provide a dry winter mulch and shelter from cold, drying winds.
- **PROPAGATION** Sow seed in containers in a cold frame as soon as ripe. Basal shoots can be rooted in spring, although seldom successfully. Like the large herbaceous gentians (*Gentiana*), *M. stylophorus* does not transplant readily.
- **PESTS AND DISEASES** Susceptible to damage by slugs.

M. stylophorus, syn. *Gentiana stylophora*. Upright, clump-forming perennial with basal rosettes of elliptic to broadly elliptic, glossy, dark green leaves, 30cm (12in) long, and pairs of smaller leaves, 10–15cm (4–6in) long, joined at their bases around the stems. In mid- and late summer, pale to mid-yellow flowers, 6–8cm (2½–3in) long, with green lines inside, are borne in pairs from the upper leaf axils. ↕ to 2m (6ft), ↔ 60cm (24in). C. Nepal to China (Yunnan). ❄❄❄

▷***Megalonium*** see *Aeonium*
M. nobile see *A. nobile*
▷***Megasea*** see *Bergenia*

MEGASKEPASMA

ACANTHACEAE

Genus of one species of evergreen shrub from tropical woodland in Venezuela. It has opposite, simple, entire leaves, and is grown for its colourful, terminal, spike-like cymes of 2-lipped, tubular flowers surrounded by crimson bracts. Where temperatures fall below 15°C (59°F), grow in a temperate or warm greenhouse; in warmer areas, grow in a courtyard garden or a shrub border.

- **HARDINESS** Frost tender.
- **CULTIVATION** Under glass, grow in loam-based potting compost (JI No.2 or No.3) in full light, with high humidity. In the growing season, water freely and apply a balanced liquid fertilizer monthly; water sparingly in winter. Outdoors, grow in moderately fertile, moist, well-drained soil in full sun. Pruning group 8; withstands restrictive pruning and renovation well.
- **PROPAGATION** Sow seed at 18–21°C (64–70°F) in spring. Root greenwood cuttings in early summer, or semi-ripe cuttings with bottom heat in late summer.
- **PESTS AND DISEASES** Red spider mites, whiteflies, and mealybugs may be troublesome under glass.

M. erythrochlamys ▣ (Brazilian red cloak, Red justicia). Erect, robust-stemmed shrub, sparsely branched unless regularly pruned, with ovate to

Megaskepasma erythrochlamys

broadly elliptic or lance-shaped, boldly veined, mid-green leaves, 12–30cm (5–12in) long. From early autumn to winter, terminal, columnar to narrowly pyramidal, spike-like cymes, 20–30cm (8–12in) long, of tubular, 2-lipped, white or pink flowers, to 8cm (3in) long, are produced from the axils of broadly ovate crimson bracts, to 4cm (1½in) long. ↕ 2–3m (3–10ft), ↔ 1–2m (3–6ft). Venezuela. ❄ (min. 15°C/59°F)

MELALEUCA

Paperbark

MYRTACEAE

Genus of at least 150 species of evergreen shrubs and trees, allied to *Callistemon*, found in habitats ranging from rainforest to semi-arid areas in tropical to cool-temperate zones, mainly in Australia but also in New Caledonia, New Guinea, and Malaysia. Many species have several layers of paper-thin, corky bark, which is shed continuously. The small, flat or cylindrical, often leathery leaves are mainly alternate, or sometimes opposite or whorled. Small flowers, each with 5 short petals and numerous conspicuous, coloured stamens, arranged in 5 fused bundles, are borne in dense, axillary spikes, resembling those of bottlebrushes. In frost-prone areas, grow in a cool or temperate greenhouse. Elsewhere, grow in a shrub border or as specimen trees. Long, hot summers are required for production of flowers and fruits.

- **HARDINESS** Half hardy to frost tender.
- **CULTIVATION** Under glass, grow in loam-based potting compost (JI No.2), with added leaf mould, in full light with shade from hot sun. In the growing season, water moderately and apply a balanced liquid fertilizer monthly; water sparingly in winter. Outdoors, grow in moderately fertile, well-drained soil in full sun with some midday shade. Shelter from cold, drying winds. Pruning group 1; plants under glass need restrictive pruning after flowering.
- **PROPAGATION** Sow seed at 13–24°C (55–75°F) in spring. Root semi-ripe cuttings with bottom heat in summer.
- **PESTS AND DISEASES** Prone to scale insects and red spider mites under glass.

M. elliptica ▣ (Granite bottlebrush). Many-branched shrub, erect at first, then spreading or rounded, with furrowed, peeling bark. The opposite,

Melaleuca elliptica

Melaleuca nesophila

broadly elliptic to elliptic-oblong leaves, 0.5–1.5cm (¼–¾in) long, are mid- to deep green above and paler beneath. From spring to early summer, small, bright pink to crimson flowers, with stamens of the same colour, are borne in abundant short, dense spikes, to 4cm (1½in) or more long. ↕↔ 1–3m (3–10ft). Australia (Western Australia). ❄ (min. 5–7°C/41–45°F)

M. hypericifolia ○ Many-branched, large shrub or small tree, erect at first, then spreading, with very firm, papery bark and opposite, sometimes arching, narrowly oblong-elliptic or obovate leaves, 1–4cm (½–1½in) long. From spring to summer, small red flowers, with crimson stamens, are produced in loose, feathery, lateral spikes, 5–8cm (2–3in) long. ↕ 2–5m (6–15ft), ↔ 1.5–2.5m (5–8ft). Australia (New South Wales). ❄ (min. 5–7°C/41–45°F)

M. nesophila ▣ ○ syn. *M. nesophylla* (Western tea myrtle). Erect to spreading, large shrub or small tree with freely branching stems and spongy, peeling bark. Alternate, mid- to deep green leaves are narrowly obovate, 2–3cm (¾–1¼in) long, with 1–3 faint veins. From spring to summer, bears lavender-pink to rose-pink flowers in dense, spherical spikes, to 2.5cm (1in) or more across. ↕ 3–7m (10–22ft), ↔ 2–4m (6–12ft). Australia (Western Australia). ❄ (min. 5–7°C/41–45°F)

M. nesophylla see *M. nesophila.*

▷***Melandrium elisabethae*** see *Silene elisabethae*

MELASPHAERULA

IRIDACEAE

Genus of one species of spring-flowering, cormous perennial from shaded woodland in South Africa. It has narrow, grass-like leaves, and produces spikes of star-shaped flowers. In frost-prone areas, grow in a cool greenhouse or in a bulb frame. In warmer climates, grow at the base of a warm, sunny wall.

• **HARDINESS** Half hardy.
• **CULTIVATION** Plant 10–15cm (4–6in) deep. Under glass, grow in loam-based potting compost (JI No.2), with additional sharp sand, in full light. Water sparingly until the flower spikes appear, then water moderately; apply a balanced liquid fertilizer every 6–8 weeks in the growing season; keep just moist in winter. Outdoors, grow in moderately fertile, well-drained soil in full sun. In mild areas, plant in autumn, providing a dry winter mulch; in areas with prolonged frosts, plant in early spring and lift in autumn, after the leaves die down. Protect from excessive winter wet.
• **PROPAGATION** Sow seed at 6–12°C (43–54°F) in autumn. Remove offsets when dormant in autumn.
• **PESTS AND DISEASES** Trouble free.

M. graminea see *M. ramosa*.
M. ramosa, syn. *M. graminea*. Cormous perennial with spreading, branched stems bearing erect, grass-like leaves, 5–25cm (2–10in) long. Spikes of up to 7 star-shaped, creamy white or yellowish flowers, 2–3cm (¾–1¼in) across, often veined purple, are produced in spring. ↕20–50cm (8–20in), ↔ 8cm (3in). South Africa (S. Western Cape). ✲

MELASTOMA

MELASTOMATACEAE

Genus of up to 70 species of evergreen shrubs, small trees, and a few herbaceous perennials from moist woodland, often in hilly areas, in India, S.E. Asia, and adjacent Pacific islands. The opposite leaves are lance-shaped to oblong or elliptic, mostly dark green, and often leathery. Usually 5-petalled, open bowl- to saucer-shaped, purple, red, pink, or white flowers are produced in terminal cymes of 3–7 or, rarely, are borne singly; the flowers are followed by fleshy berries. Where temperatures fall below 13–15°C (55–59°F), grow in a warm greenhouse. In warmer regions, grow as free-standing specimen plants or among other shrubs. Long, hot summers are required for the production of flowers and fruits.
• **HARDINESS** Frost tender.
• **CULTIVATION** Under glass, grow in loam-based potting compost (JI No.2) in full light with shade from hot sun. Provide moderate humidity. In the growing season, water moderately and apply a balanced liquid fertilizer monthly; water sparingly in winter. Outdoors, grow in moderately fertile, moist but well-drained soil in full sun with some midday shade. Shelter from cold, drying winds. Pruning group 1 or 8; need restrictive pruning under glass.
• **PROPAGATION** Sow seed at 6–12°C (43–54°F) in spring. Root semi-ripe cuttings with bottom heat in summer.
• **PESTS AND DISEASES** Scale insects and red spider mites may be troublesome under glass.

M. malabathricum (Indian rhododendron). Many-branched, spreading shrub with densely scaly-hairy stems and ovate to broadly lance-shaped, coarsely hairy, dark green leaves, 7–10cm (3–4in) long, with prominent veins. Produces shallowly bowl-shaped purple flowers, 3cm (1¼in) across, singly or in cymes of 2–5, from spring to summer, sometimes followed by spherical, red-pulped berries, 8mm (⅜in) across. ↕2–3m (6–10ft), ↔ 1.5–2.5m (5–8ft). India, S.E. Asia. ❀ (min. 13°C/55°F)

MELIA

MELIACEAE

Genus of 3–5 species of deciduous or semi-evergreen trees and shrubs from India to China, S.E. Asia, and N. Australia. They have alternate, pinnate or 2-pinnate leaves, and bear small, star-shaped flowers in large, axillary panicles. Each flower has 5 or 6 spreading petals and 10–12 stamens, the filaments of which are fused into a tube with the anthers arranged around the rim. The attractive, bead-like, spherical, single-seeded berries are poisonous. In frost-prone areas, grow in a temperate greenhouse mainly for their foliage, although plants in large containers may flower when 2–3m (6–10ft) tall. In warmer areas, grow as specimen or shade trees.
• **HARDINESS** Frost tender.
• **CULTIVATION** Under glass, grow in loam-based potting compost (JI No.2) in full light. In the growing season, water freely and apply a balanced liquid fertilizer monthly; water sparingly in winter. Outdoors, grow in moderately fertile, well-drained soil in full sun. Provide shelter from cold, drying winds. Pruning group 1; plants under glass may need restrictive pruning.
• **PROPAGATION** Sow seed at 13–18°C (55–64°F) in spring. Root softwood cuttings with bottom heat in summer.
• **PESTS AND DISEASES** Red spider mites may be a problem under glass.

M. azedarach ▣ ♡ (Bead-tree, Persian lilac, Pride of India). Fast-growing, many-branched, spreading, round-headed, deciduous tree with fissured grey bark. Pinnate or 2-pinnate leaves, 30–60cm (12–24in) long, have many ovate to elliptic, sharply toothed, sometimes lobed, mid- to bright green leaflets. Produces a profusion of star-shaped, fragrant lilac flowers, 2cm (¾in) across, in arching to pendent panicles, 10–20cm (4–8in) long, from spring to early summer; they are followed by spherical to broadly ovoid yellow fruit, 1cm (½in) long. Seeds are used as beads in Asia. ↕10–15m (30–50ft), ↔ 5–8m (15–25ft). N. India, China. ❀ (min. 7°C/45°F)

Melia azedarach

MELIANTHUS

MELIANTHACEAE

Genus of 6 species of evergreen shrubs from grassland in hilly areas of southern Africa. The alternate, pinnate, light green, grey-green, or blue-green leaves have prominent stipules. Small flowers, producing profuse quantities of nectar, are borne in erect, terminal and axillary racemes; each has 5 irregular sepals and petals, the upper ones often forming a hood or tube, and the lower ones making a short spur. Grow in a border or as specimen plants; they are particularly suited to a coastal garden. In frost-prone areas, grow tender species as foliage plants in a cold greenhouse, and stand or plant outside in summer. Alternatively, treat them as herbaceous perennials; where temperatures do not fall much below -5°C (23°F), they will usually re-sprout annually from the base.
• **HARDINESS** Frost hardy to frost tender; *M. major* may survive temperatures just below 0°C (32°F), if the wood has been well ripened in summer.
• **CULTIVATION** Under glass, grow in loam-based potting compost (JI No.2) in full light. Provide low humidity. In growth, water freely and apply a balanced liquid fertilizer monthly; water sparingly in winter. Outdoors, grow in moderately fertile, moist but well-drained soil in full sun. Provide a dry winter mulch and protect from excessive winter wet. Shelter from cold, drying winds. Pruning group 7 or 8.
• **PROPAGATION** Sow seed at 13–18°C (55–64°F) in spring. Root basal or softwood cuttings in late spring or early summer. Remove any rooted suckers in spring.
• **PESTS AND DISEASES** Susceptible to red spider mites and whiteflies under glass.

M. major ▣ (Honey bush). Tall, erect to spreading shrub with robust, hollow stems, most of them near ground level and branching sparingly. Spreading, pinnate leaves, 30–50cm (12–20in) long, have 9–17 closely set, ovate, sharply and boldly toothed, grey-green to bright blue-grey leaflets. From late spring to midsummer, produces spike-like racemes, 30–80cm (12–32in) long, of brownish crimson to deep brick-red flowers, 2.5cm (1in) long. ↕2–3m (6–10ft), ↔ 1–3m (3–10ft). South Africa (Northern Cape, Western Cape, Eastern Cape). ✲

Melianthus major

Melica altissima 'Atropurpurea'

MELICA

Melick

GRAMINEAE/POACEAE

Genus of about 75 species of deciduous, rhizomatous, clump-forming, perennial grasses occurring in grasslands of most temperate regions, except Australia. In summer, panicles of laterally compressed spikelets are borne on erect stems among clumps of linear, flat or inrolled, arching leaves. Grow in a mixed or herbaceous border, or in a woodland garden.
• **HARDINESS** Fully hardy.
• **CULTIVATION** Grow in moderately fertile, moist but well-drained soil. *M. altissima* thrives in full sun or light dappled shade; *M. nutans* prefers light shade; *M. uniflora* will tolerate full shade and drier conditions. Protect from excessive winter wet.
• **PROPAGATION** Sow seed *in situ* in spring or as soon as ripe. Divide as growth starts in early or mid-spring.
• **PESTS AND DISEASES** Trouble free.

M. altissima (Siberian melick). Tufted, perennial grass with creeping rhizomes and pointed, linear, pale to mid-green leaves, 10–23cm (4–9in) long, with rough surfaces. In summer, green spikelets are produced in erect, one-sided panicles, 10–25cm (4–10in) long, with densely flowered tips. ↕0.6–1.5m (2–5ft), ↔ 40–80cm (16–32in). Europe. ✲✲✲. **'Alba'** has pale green leaves, and produces conspicuous, pale greenish white spikelets from late spring to late summer. **'Atropurpurea'** ▣ has lustrous, deep purple spikelets that become paler with age. Good for drying.
M. nutans (Mountain melick, Wood melick). Slowly creeping, perennial grass forming loose clumps of shiny, fresh green leaves, to 20cm (8in) long. Gracefully arching stems bear one-sided panicles, to 15cm (6in) long, of bead-like, brown and cream spikelets from late spring to midsummer. ↕45cm (18in), ↔ 30cm (12in) or more. Europe, N. and S.W. Asia. ✲✲✲
M. uniflora. Perennial grass with slender, creeping rhizomes forming loose tufts of linear, pointed, bright green leaves, 5–20cm (2–8in) long, with hairy upper surfaces. Purple or brown spikelets are borne in sparsely branched, erect or nodding panicles, 2.5–20cm (1–8in) long, in summer. ↕20–60cm (8–24in), ↔ to 60cm (24in). Europe, S.W. Asia. ✲✲✲. **'Variegata'** has fresh

M

green leaves with creamy white central stripes and purple-flushed bases, and bears dark purplish brown spikelets from late spring to midsummer.

▷**Melick** see *Melica*
Mountain see *M. nutans*
Siberian see *M. altissima*
Wood see *M. nutans*

MELICYTUS
syn. HYMENANTHERA

VIOLACEAE

Genus of about 7 species of evergreen or semi-evergreen shrubs from Australasia, found in rocky sites from mountains to woodland, dry riverbeds, and coasts. They have alternate, lance-shaped to broadly ovate, elliptic, or oblong, sweetly fragrant leaves. Small male and female flowers, with 5 spreading petals, are usually borne on separate plants. *M. crassifolius* and *M. dentatus* are grown for their attractive habits and their decorative fruits. Grow in an open, sunny site in a shrub border. In frost-prone areas, grow tender species in a cool greenhouse. Need long, hot summers to flower and fruit well.
• **HARDINESS** Fully hardy to frost tender.
• **CULTIVATION** Grow in moderately fertile, moist but well-drained soil in full sun. Protect from cold, drying winds. Pruning group 8 or 9.
• **PROPAGATION** Sow seed in containers in a cold frame in spring. Root semi-ripe cuttings in summer.
• **PESTS AND DISEASES** Trouble free.

M. crassifolius, syn. *Hymenanthera crassifolia.* Densely branched, twiggy, and often slightly spiny shrub with obovate to oblong-elliptic, leathery, dark green leaves, to 2cm (¾in) long. In late spring and early summer, bears tiny yellow flowers, followed by ovoid purple berries, 5mm (¼in) across. ↕↔ 1.2m (4ft). New Zealand. ❄❄❄ (borderline)
M. dentatus, syn. *Hymenanthera dentata.* Dense shrub with oblong, leathery, dark green leaves, to 4cm (1½in) long. Tiny, yellow to greenish white flowers are borne in late spring, followed by spherical purple berries, 5mm (¼in) across. ↕ 1.5m (5ft), ↔ 2m (6ft) or more. S.E. Australia. ❄❄

MELINIS syn. RHYNCHELYTRUM

GRAMINEAE/POACEAE

Genus of about 15 species of clump-forming, annual or perennial grasses from savannah grasslands of tropical Africa and S.E. Asia. They have flat, linear to thread-like leaves, and produce compact or open panicles of spikelets from summer to autumn. *M. repens*, the only species in general cultivation, is grown for its brightly coloured flower-heads, which may be cut for fresh flowers. Grow at the front of a border; in frost-prone areas, treat as an annual, or lift and keep frost-free in winter.
• **HARDINESS** Half hardy to frost tender; *M. repens* may tolerate short periods below 0°C (32°F).
• **CULTIVATION** Grow in moderately fertile, light, well-drained soil in full sun. In areas with light frosts, provide a deep, dry winter mulch. In colder areas, lift in late autumn and pot up in a loam-based potting compost (JI No.1); keep barely moist and frost-free in winter, and plant out again in spring when danger of frost has passed.
• **PROPAGATION** Sow seed at 13–18°C (55–64°F) in late winter, harden off, and plant out after all danger of frost has passed. Divide in spring.
• **PESTS AND DISEASES** Trouble free.

M. repens, syn. *Rhynchelytrum repens, R. roseum* (Natal grass). Loosely tufted, annual or short-lived, perennial grass. Upright, ascending stems bear flat, linear, long-pointed leaves, to 30cm (12in) long. From midsummer to early autumn, bears cylindrical to ovoid panicles, to 20cm (8in) long, of keeled, flattened spikelets, densely clothed in silky white hairs and strongly tinted bright purple to rose-red. ↕ 45–120cm (18–48in), ↔ 60–100cm (24–39in). Tropical Africa. ❄

MELIOSMA

MELIOSMACEAE

Genus of 20–25 species of evergreen and deciduous trees and shrubs occurring in forests from India and Sri Lanka to Japan, and in Mexico, Central America, and tropical South America. The alternate leaves are simple, sometimes pinnate, and mid- to dark green. Large panicles of tiny, cup- and saucer-shaped, 5-petalled, fragrant flowers are borne in spring or summer. Grow as specimen plants in a shrub border or woodland garden, or against a warm, sunny wall.
• **HARDINESS** Fully hardy to frost hardy; young foliage may be damaged by late frosts.
• **CULTIVATION** Grow in moderately fertile, moist but well-drained, neutral to slightly acid soil, in full sun with some midday shade. Shelter from cold, drying winds. Pruning group 1, or 13 if grown as a wall specimen.
• **PROPAGATION** Sow seed in containers in a cold frame in autumn. Root greenwood cuttings in early summer.
• **PESTS AND DISEASES** Trouble free.

M. myriantha ♀ Spreading, deciduous, small tree or shrub with arching branches and simple, narrowly elliptic to ovate-lance-shaped, sharply toothed, mid-green leaves, to 20cm (8in) long; these have soft, red-brown hairs on the midribs and leaf-stalks. Very fragrant, minute, creamy white flowers are borne in panicles, 30cm (12in) long, in midsummer, followed by small, peppercorn-like, dark red fruit, to 2mm ($\frac{1}{16}$in) across. ↕ 2.5m (8ft) or more, ↔ 4m (12ft). China, Korea, Japan. ❄❄❄
M. oldhamii see *M. pinnata* var. *oldhamii.*
M. pinnata* var. *oldhamii ♀ syn. *M. oldhamii.* Stoutly branched, deciduous tree, upright when young, later spreading, with pinnate, dark green leaves, to 35cm (14in) long, with up to 13 broadly ovate to obovate leaflets. White flowers are borne in panicles, to 30cm (12in) long, in early summer, followed by small, black or dark red fruit, 5mm (¼in) across. ↕ 10m (30ft), ↔ 6m (20ft). China, Korea. ❄❄❄
M. veitchiorum ▣♀ Slow-growing, deciduous tree, upright when young, later spreading, with pinnate, dark green leaves, to 75cm (30in) long, with up to 11 ovate or oblong leaflets and red

Meliosma veitchiorum

stalks. Creamy white flowers are borne in dense panicles, to 45cm (18in) long, in late spring, followed by spherical violet fruit, to 8mm (⅜in) across. ↕ 10m (30ft), ↔ 8m (25ft). W. China. ❄❄❄

MELISSA
Balm

LABIATAE/LAMIACEAE

Genus of 3 species of herbaceous perennials occurring from Europe to C. Asia on damp wasteland, from sea level to mountains. Toothed, ovate, pale or mid-green leaves, which smell strongly of lemons when bruised, are borne in opposite pairs on square, branching stems. Leafy, whorled spikes of tubular, 2-lipped, pale yellow or white flowers are borne in summer. *M. officinalis* is a decorative, drought-tolerant plant, useful for a herbaceous or mixed border, or a herb garden. The flowers attract bees and other insects, and the leaves may be used in pot-pourri or for herb tea.
• **HARDINESS** Fully hardy.
• **CULTIVATION** Grow in poor, well-drained soil in full sun, with protection from excessive winter wet. In early summer, cut back variegated forms to encourage strongly coloured growth.
• **PROPAGATION** Sow seed in containers in a cold frame in spring. Divide as growth starts in spring, or in autumn.
• **PESTS AND DISEASES** Trouble free.

M. officinalis (Bee balm, Lemon balm). Bushy, upright perennial with hairy, glandular stems and wrinkled, ovate, light green leaves, to 7cm (3in) long. Throughout summer, produces irregular spikes of pale yellow flowers, becoming white or lilac-tinted white, to 1.5cm (½in) long. ↕ 60–120cm (2–4ft), ↔ 30–45cm (12–18in). S. Europe. ❄❄❄. **'All Gold'** has golden yellow leaves and white flowers, tinted pale lilac. **'Aurea'** ▣ syn. 'Variegata' of gardens, has dark green leaves, heavily splashed gold at the margins.

MELITTIS
Bastard balm

LABIATAE/LAMIACEAE

Genus of one species of clump-forming perennial occurring in light woodland throughout Europe, except the extreme north, as far as the Ukraine. It has leafy, square stems, bearing opposite pairs of leaves, and produces 2-lipped flowers in

Melissa officinalis 'Aurea'

Melittis melissophyllum

white, pink, or purple, or white with pink or purple lips, in whorls from the upper leaf axils. Grow *M. melissophyllum* in a shady, mixed or herbaceous border, or in a woodland garden. The flowers are attractive to bees.
- **Hardiness** Fully hardy.
- **Cultivation** Grow in moderately fertile, moist but well-drained soil in partial shade; avoid excessively dry soil.
- **Propagation** Sow seed in containers in a cold frame as soon as ripe or in spring. Divide as new growth starts in spring.
- **Pests and diseases** Trouble free.

M. melissophyllum ■ Herbaceous perennial with erect, hairy or glandular stems. The oval, scalloped, aromatic, honey-scented leaves, to 8cm (3in) long, are hairy and wrinkled, with prominent veins. In late spring and early summer, produces whorls of 2–6 tubular, 2-lipped flowers, 4cm (1½in) long, in pink, purple, or white, or creamy white with pink or purple lips and spots. ↕20–70cm (8–28in), ↔50cm (20in). Europe to Ukraine. ❄❄❄

MELOCACTUS
Turk's cap cactus

CACTACEAE

Genus of 20 or more species of spherical, rarely elongated, simple, occasionally branching, perennial cacti from coastal areas of Central and South America, Cuba, and the West Indies. They have prominently spined ribs. As plants mature, a cephalium, consisting of a mass of wool and bristles, which in some species gradually elongates to over 1m (3ft) tall, forms on the crown of each stem. The plant body apparently does not develop further once the cephalium appears. Spreading, funnel-shaped, diurnal flowers are borne on the cephalium in summer, followed by berry-like fruits with glossy, black-coated seeds. Where temperatures fall below 16°C (61°F), grow in a warm greenhouse. Elsewhere, grow in a desert garden.
- **Hardiness** Frost tender.
- **Cultivation** Under glass, grow in standard cactus compost in full light and away from draughts. In growth, water sparingly, mist very occasionally, and apply fertilizer monthly. Plants are prone to root rot if overwatered, or will rot if too cold. Water very sparingly in winter. Outdoors, grow in moderately fertile, gritty, sharply drained soil in full sun. See also pp.48–49.
- **Propagation** Sow seed at 19–24°C (66–75°F) in spring.
- **Pests and diseases** Trouble free.

M. actinacanthus see *M. matanzanus.*
M. azureus. Cactus with a spherical to cylindrical, mid- to grey-green, often glaucous stem with 9–12 ribs bearing white spines (1–3 centrals and 7–11 radials). The white-woolly cephalium bears conspicuous red bristles. Pink flowers, 1.5–2cm (½–¾in) across, are borne in summer, followed by white to pale pink fruit. ↕14–30cm (5½–12in), ↔14–20cm (5½–8in). E. Brazil. ❄ (min. 16°C/61°F)
M. communis see *M. intortus.*
M. curvispinus, syn. *M. oaxacensis.* Cactus with a spherical or ovoid, dull green stem bearing 10–15 furrowed ribs and reddish brown spines (8–12 radials and 1 or 2 longer centrals). The low-set cephalium has dense brown bristles and a white-woolly top. Dark rose-pink flowers, 2–4cm (¾–1½in) across, are produced in summer. ↕↔15cm (6in). S. and E. Mexico, Guatemala. ❄ (min. 16°C/61°F)
M. intortus ■ syn. *M. communis.* Cactus with a flattened-spherical, dark green stem, elongating with age, bearing 12–24 ribs and yellow-brown spines (10–14 radials and 1–3 centrals). Rose-pink flowers, 1.5–2cm (½–¾in) across, are borne from the cylindrical, brown-bristly cephalium in summer. ↕1m (3ft) or more, ↔25cm (10in). West Indies. ❄ (min. 16°C/61°F)
M. macrodiscus see *M. zehntneri.*
M. matanzanus, syn. *M. actinacanthus.* Cactus with a spherical, dark green stem bearing 8–13 straight ribs and brownish white or grey spines (5–9 radials and 1 longer central). The low-set cephalium has dense, orange-red bristles. Pink flowers, 1.5–2cm (½–¾in) across, are borne in summer. ↕8cm (3in), ↔9cm (3½in). N. Cuba. ❄ (min. 16°C/61°F)
M. oaxacensis see *M. curvispinus.*
M. zehntneri, syn. *M. macrodiscus.* Cactus with a spherical, bluish green stem with 10 ribs and pale brown spines (6–10 radials and 1 central, although the central one may be absent). The low-set, white-woolly cephalium is often slow to develop. Rose-red flowers, 1.5–2.5cm (½–1in) across, are borne in summer, followed by reddish violet fruit. ↕14cm (5½in), ↔18cm (7in). E. Brazil. ❄ (min. 16°C/61°F)

Melocactus intortus

MENISPERMUM
Moonseed

MENISPERMACEAE

Genus of 2 species of twining, suckering, semi-woody, sometimes herbaceous, deciduous, dioecious climbers from woodland in E. Asia and E. North America. They are grown for their long racemes or panicles of grape-like, glossy black fruits. The alternate, peltate leaves are ovate-heart-shaped to almost rounded. Tiny, bowl-shaped, male and female flowers are borne in racemes or panicles. Grow on a trellis, against a wall, or through small trees. The fruits may cause severe discomfort if ingested.
- **Hardiness** Fully hardy; unripened growth may be damaged by frost.
- **Cultivation** Grow in moderately fertile, moist but well-drained soil in full sun or dappled shade. Provide support. Pruning group 11, in early spring.
- **Propagation** Sow seed in containers outdoors in autumn. Transplant suckers in autumn or spring.
- **Pests and diseases** Trouble free.

M. canadense (Canadian moonseed, Yellow parilla). Usually semi-woody, suckering climber with slender shoots and long-stalked, ovate-heart-shaped to rounded, 3- to 7-angled leaves, 8–15cm (3–6in) long. In summer, produces tiny, yellow-green flowers in axillary racemes or panicles, followed on female plants by grape-like, glossy black fruit, to 1cm (½in) long. ↕5m (15ft). E. North America. ❄❄❄

MENTHA
Mint

LABIATAE/LAMIACEAE

Genus of 25 species of aromatic, rhizomatous perennials, rarely annuals, found in Europe, Africa, and Asia, often in shallow water or wet or moist soil. Erect, branching stems bear lance-shaped to rounded, light to dark green, purple-, blue-, or grey-green leaves. The tubular to bell-shaped flowers are weakly 2-lipped, with 4 spreading lobes and leafy bracts. They are borne in summer, in spikes of whorl-like clusters, or occasionally in a single, terminal cluster. Mints are widely used as culinary herbs.

Grow in a herb or vegetable garden; less invasive species are also suitable for a border. Use *M. aquatica* for stabilizing the muddy edges of a pool, *M. pulegium* as ground cover, and *M. requienii* in a rock garden. All attract bees; most dry well for use in pot-pourri.
- **Hardiness** Fully hardy.
- **Cultivation** Grow in poor, moist soil in full sun. Restrict spread of invasive species by planting in deep containers and plunging in the soil, or by growing in small beds to restrict root run. *M. aquatica* can be grown in containers submerged in water up to 15cm (6in) deep. See also pp.52–53.
- **Propagation** Sow seed in containers in a cold frame in spring. Divide in spring or autumn. Portions of rhizome will root at any time during the growing season; pot up until established. Root tip cuttings in spring or summer.
- **Pests and diseases** Powdery mildew, especially during drought, and rust are troublesome.

Mentha aquatica

M. aquatica ■ (Watermint). Marginal aquatic or semi-aquatic perennial with long, thin, segmented rhizomes, often reddish purple stems, and ovate to ovate-lance-shaped, toothed, aromatic, sometimes hairy, dark green leaves, to 6cm (2½in) long, occasionally to 9cm (3½in). In summer, produces whorls of shallowly tubular lilac flowers, to 5mm (¼in) long, in dense, spherical, terminal clusters. ↕15–90cm (6–36in), ↔1m (3ft) or more. Eurasia. ❄❄❄
M. citrata see *M.* x *piperita* f. *citrata.*
M. corsica see *M. requienii.*
***M.* x *gentilis* 'Aurea'** see *M.* x *gracilis* 'Variegata'.
***M.* x *gentilis* 'Variegata'** see *M.* x *gracilis* 'Variegata'.
***M.* x *gracilis* 'Aurea'** see *M.* x *gracilis* 'Variegata'.
***M.* x *gracilis* 'Variegata'** (*M. arvensis* x *M. spicata*), syn. *M.* x *gentilis* 'Aurea', *M.* x *gentilis* 'Variegata', *M.* x *gracilis* 'Aurea' (Ginger mint, Red mint). Spreading perennial with erect, often red-tinted stems and short-stalked, ovate-lance-shaped to elliptic-oblong leaves, 3–7cm (1¼–3in) long, striped and flecked gold, and strongly aromatic and ginger-flavoured. In summer, bears dense, whorled clusters of tubular lilac flowers, to 4mm (⅛in) long, widely spaced on upright stems. ↕30cm (12in) or more, ↔ to 1m (3ft) or more. ❄❄❄
M. longifolia, syn. *M. sylvestris* (Horsemint). Vigorous, creeping perennial with grey-hairy stems and oblong-elliptic, toothed, strongly aromatic, musty-scented, green to silver-grey leaves, 6–9cm (2½–3½in) long, with unbranched hairs. In summer,

Mentha x*smithiana*

M

Mentha suaveolens 'Variegata'

tubular, lilac or white flowers, to 5mm (¼in) long, are borne in dense whorls in terminal, tapering spikes. ↕ to 1.2m (4ft), ↔ 1m (3ft) or more. Europe, Turkey, Caucasus, N.W. Iran. ***
M. odorata see *M.* x *piperita* f. *citrata*.
M. x piperita f. citrata (*M. aquatica* x *M. spicata*), syn. *M. citrata, M. odorata, M. piperita* var. *citriodora* (Eau de Cologne mint, Lemon mint). Vigorous, spreading, eau de Cologne-scented perennial with hairless stems and thin-textured, ovate, dark green leaves, 4–9cm (1½–3½in) long, tinged reddish purple in sun or copper-red in shade. Bears dense, terminal, oblong spikes of congested whorls of tubular, pinkish purple flowers, 4mm (⅛in) long, in late summer. ↕ 50cm (20in), ↔ 1m (3ft) or more. Garden origin. ***
M. piperita var. citriodora see *M.* x *piperita* f. *citrata*.
M. pulegium (Pennyroyal). Spreading perennial with upright and procumbent stems bearing short-stalked, narrowly elliptic to rounded, sharply aromatic, bright green leaves, to 3cm (1¼in) long, hairy beneath. Widely spaced, leafy whorls of tubular lilac flowers, 4–6mm (⅛–¼in) long, are borne in spikes in summer. ↕ 10–40cm (4–16in), ↔ to 50cm (20in). S.W. and C. Europe, Mediterranean to Iran. ***
M. requienii, syn. *M. corsica* (Corsican mint). Procumbent, mat-forming, hairy or hairless perennial with slender, creeping, rooting stems bearing broadly ovate to rounded, peppermint-scented, bright green leaves, to 7mm (¼in) across. In summer, bears whorls of tiny, tubular lilac flowers, 2mm (1/16in) long, in short spikes. Prefers shade. ↕ to 1cm (½in), ↔ indefinite. France (Corsica), Italy (including Sardinia). ***
M. rotundifolia of gardens see *M. suaveolens*.
M. rubra var. raripila see *M.* x *smithiana*.
M. x smithiana ■ (*M. aquatica* x *M. arvensis* x *M. spicata*), syn. *M. rubra* var. *raripila* (Red raripila). Vigorous, spreading perennial with ovate, toothed, sweet-smelling, sparsely hairy, dark green, red-tinted leaves, 3–9cm (1¼–3½in) long. In summer, produces spikes of dense whorls of tubular lilac flowers, to 5mm (¼in) long, usually well spaced, sometimes clustered at the stem tips. ↕ to 1m (3ft), ↔ 1.2m (4ft) or more. N. and C. Europe. ***
M. spicata, syn. *M. viridis* (Spearmint). Spreading perennial with stalkless, lance-shaped to oblong-ovate, toothed, aromatic (usually sweet-smelling but sometimes pungent), bright green leaves, 5–9cm (2–3½in) long, hairless or with branched and unbranched hairs beneath. Bears dense, cylindrical spikes of usually separated whorls of tubular to bell-shaped, pink, lilac, or white flowers, to 3mm (⅛in) long, in summer. ↕ to 1m (3ft), ↔ indefinite. W. and C. Europe, Mediterranean. ***
M. suaveolens, syn. *M. rotundifolia* of gardens (Apple mint). Vigorous, spreading, apple-scented perennial with often white-hairy stems and toothed, oblong-ovate to rounded, irregularly wrinkled and softly hairy, greyish green leaves, to 3cm (1¼in) long, the margins sometimes rolled under and wavy. In summer, bears tubular, pink or white flowers, to 2mm (1/16 in) long, in dense whorls in terminal, often branched spikes. ↕ to 1m (3ft), ↔ indefinite. W. and S. Europe, Mediterranean. ***.
'Variegata' ■ (Pineapple mint) has leaves with broad cream streaks and margins, and a rich, fruity fragrance.
M. sylvestris see *M. longifolia*.
M. x villosa var. alopecuroides (*M. spicata* x *M. suaveolens*) (Bowles' mint). Variable, spreading perennial with softly hairy, broadly ovate or rounded, aromatic, toothed, bright green leaves, 4–8cm (1½–3in) long. In summer, whorls of tubular pink flowers, 2–3mm (1/16–⅛in) long, are produced in large, leafy spikes. ↕ 30–90cm (12–36in), ↔ indefinite. Garden origin. ***
M. viridis see *M. spicata*.

MENTZELIA

Starflower

LOASACEAE

Genus of 60 species of spreading to erect, freely branching, densely stiff-haired annuals, biennials, perennials, and subshrubs, mostly from dry, sandy, or rocky scrub in S.W. USA, Mexico, and the West Indies. Alternate, mainly lance-shaped, coarsely toothed, light to mid-green leaves may be simple, lobed, or pinnatifid. The poppy-like, 5- to 10-petalled, bright orange, yellow, or white flowers, often night-scented or opening only in strong sunlight, are borne singly or in loose cymes in summer. Grow in an annual or mixed border, or a wild garden; they need long, hot summers to flower well. In frost-prone areas, grow tender species in a cool greenhouse.
• **HARDINESS** Fully hardy to frost tender.
• **CULTIVATION** Grow in moderately fertile, well-drained soil in a warm, sheltered site in full sun. Water freely in the growing season for repeat flowering. After first flush of bloom, cut annuals back to 5cm (2in).
• **PROPAGATION** Sow seed of annuals *in situ* in spring.
• **PESTS AND DISEASES** Trouble free.

M. lindleyi ■ syn. *Bartonia aurea* (Blazing star). Erect, freely branching annual with lance-shaped to oval, pinnatifid, mid-green to grey leaves, to 15cm (6in) long, the lobes sometimes toothed. In summer, 5-petalled, very fragrant, night-scented, golden yellow blooms, 5–9cm (2–3½in) across, are borne singly from the leaf axils or in 2- or 3-flowered cymes at the stem tips; petals are flushed orange-red at the bases. ↕ 15–70cm (6–28in), ↔ to 23cm (9in). USA (California). ***

MENYANTHES

MENYANTHACEAE

Genus of one species of rhizomatous, aquatic or semi-aquatic perennial from the N. hemisphere, especially in Europe. It forms large, spreading, floating mats that extend over the shallow, still or slow-moving water of lakes or ponds, and sometimes across the muddy margins. *M. trifoliata* has 3-palmate leaves and bears racemes of star-shaped flowers. It is a decorative plant for ponds and for the margins of a wildlife pool, and is useful for disguising hard edges.
• **HARDINESS** Fully hardy.
• **CULTIVATION** In a large pool, grow in an aquatic planting basket, at a depth of 15–23cm (6–9in), or in muddy pond margins. Provide a site in full sun to encourage production of the short-lived flowers. See also pp.52–53.
• **PROPAGATION** Sow seed in winter in containers standing in water. In summer, divide young rhizomes into pieces, 23–30cm (9–12in) long, and place them horizontally on soft mud in an aquatic planting basket or in shallow water; push in and peg down.
• **PESTS AND DISEASES** Trouble free.

M. trifoliata ■ (Bogbean). Aquatic perennial with extensive, creeping rhizomes, to 1.2m (4ft) long, and 3-palmate leaves with elliptic to ovate or obovate leaflets, to 6cm (2½in) long. In summer, bears erect racemes of 10–20 white flowers, 2.5cm (1in) across, pink outside and in bud, with very finely fringed and bearded petals. ↕ 20–30cm (8–12in), ↔ indefinite. Europe, N. Asia, N.W. India, North America. ***

MENZIESIA

ERICACEAE

Genus of about 7 species of freely branching, spreading to upright, deciduous shrubs, found in woodland in E. Asia and North America. The ovate to elliptic or oblong leaves are arranged alternately and often clustered at the shoot tips. Small, nodding, urn- to bell-shaped, 4- or 5-lobed flowers are borne in umbels in late spring and early summer. Grow *Menziesia* species in a peat bed or woodland garden; they grow best in areas with cool, damp summers.
• **HARDINESS** Fully hardy, although young growth may be damaged by late frosts.
• **CULTIVATION** Grow in moist but well-drained, humus-rich, acid soil in partial shade. Shelter from cold, drying winds. Pruning group 8.
• **PROPAGATION** Sow seed in containers in spring at 13°C (55°F), or in a cold

Mentzelia lindleyi

Menyanthes trifoliata

Menziesia ciliicalyx var. *purpurea*

frame outdoors in autumn. Root greenwood cuttings with bottom heat in early summer.
• **PESTS AND DISEASES** Trouble free.

M. ciliicalyx var. lasiophylla see *M. ciliicalyx* var. *purpurea*.
M. ciliicalyx var. purpurea ■ syn. *M. ciliicalyx* var. *lasiophylla*. Slow-growing, bushy shrub with clustered, obovate to oval, bright green leaves, to 7cm (3in) long. In late spring and early summer, bears umbels of 3–8 urn-shaped, dark purple-pink flowers, 1.5cm (½in) long. ‡↔ 1m (3ft). Japan. ❄❄❄
M. ferruginea (Fool's huckleberry, Rusty leaf). Upright, twiggy shrub with clustered, obovate to elliptic, mid-green leaves, to 6cm (2½in) long, covered in soft, rust-brown hairs and turning red in autumn. From late spring to summer, bears umbels of 2–5 urn-shaped, red-flushed yellow flowers, 7mm (¼in) long. ‡ 2m (6ft), ↔ 1.5m (5ft). N.W. North America (Alaska to N. California). ❄❄❄

MERENDERA

COLCHICACEAE/LILIACEAE

Genus of about 10 species of bulbous perennials from subalpine meadows and dry sites in open woodland in the Mediterranean region, N. Africa, the Middle East, and W. Asia. The semi-erect, basal leaves are linear to linear-lance-shaped, strap-shaped, or inversely lance-shaped, and elongate after flowering. Small, funnel-shaped flowers, with separate, often narrow, star-shaped tepals, are borne at ground level, with or before the leaves in spring or autumn. Grow in a raised bed, alpine house, or bulb frame; *M. montana* is suitable for a sunny rock garden.
• **HARDINESS** Fully hardy to half hardy.
• **CULTIVATION** Plant 5–7cm (2–3in) deep in late summer. Outdoors, grow in moist but well-drained soil in full sun. In a bulb frame, grow in loam-based potting compost (JI No.2) with added sharp sand. Water moderately in the growing season. *Merendera* species require a hot, dry period of summer dormancy. Repot annually in summer.
• **PROPAGATION** Sow seed in containers in a cold frame: in spring for autumn-flowering species, in autumn for spring-flowering species. Remove offsets during summer dormancy.
• **PESTS AND DISEASES** Trouble free.

M. bulbocodium see *M. montana*.
M. caucasica see *M. trigyna*.
M. eichleri see *M. trigyna*.
M. montana ■ syn. *M. bulbocodium*, *M. pyrenaica*. Cormous perennial with 3 or 4 linear, channelled leaves, to 22cm (9in) long, borne with or after the flowers. In autumn, produces 1 or 2 upright, funnel-shaped, purple to red-purple flowers, to 7cm (3in) long, sometimes with white bases. ‡↔ 5cm (2in). C. Pyrenees, Iberian peninsula. ❄❄❄
M. pyrenaica see *M. montana*.
M. raddeana see *M. trigyna*.
M. robusta. Cormous perennial bearing 3–6 linear to lance-shaped leaves, to 25cm (10in) long, with the flowers. Produces 1–4 upright, funnel-shaped, deep pink to lilac or white flowers,

Merendera montana

2–4cm (¾–1½in) long, in spring. ‡ 8cm (3in), ↔ 5cm (2in). Iran, Afghanistan, Turkmenistan, N. India. ❄❄
M. trigyna, syn. *M. caucasica*, *M. eichleri*, *M. raddeana*. Bulbous perennial with linear to linear-lance-shaped leaves, to 17cm (7in) long, borne with the flowers. In spring, bears 1–3 funnel-shaped, purple-pink to white flowers, 2–3cm (¾–1¼in) long, with narrow, inversely lance-shaped tepals. ‡↔ 5cm (2in). Turkey, Caucasus, Iran. ❄❄

MERREMIA

CONVOLVULACEAE

Genus of at least 70 species of woody, evergreen and herbaceous, mainly twining climbers found in tropical regions in diverse habitats, including mudflats, grassland, and woodland. The alternate or spiralling leaves are entire or palmately lobed or divided. Funnel- to bell-shaped flowers are borne singly or in small clusters from the upper leaf axils. In frost-prone areas, grow in a temperate greenhouse, or treat as tender annuals and grow outdoors. Elsewhere, grow over a pergola, arch, or trellis.
• **HARDINESS** Frost tender.
• **CULTIVATION** Under glass, grow in loam-based potting compost (JI No.2), in full light with shade from hot sun. In growth, water moderately and apply a balanced liquid fertilizer monthly; water sparingly in winter. Outdoors, grow in moderately fertile, moist but well-drained soil in full sun with some midday shade. Shelter from cold, drying winds. Pruning group 11, in late winter or early spring.
• **PROPAGATION** Sow seed at 18–24°C (64–75°F) in spring.
• **PESTS AND DISEASES** Susceptible to red spider mites and whiteflies under glass.

M. tuberosa, syn. *Ipomoea tuberosa*, *Operculina tuberosa* (Spanish morning glory, Wood rose, Yellow morning glory). Vigorous, woody-stemmed, evergreen twining climber. Palmately 5- to 7-lobed, bright to mid-green leaves have oblong-lance-shaped lobes, to 15cm (6in) long. Bears funnel-shaped yellow flowers, 5–6cm (2–2½in) across, usually in stalked clusters of 3–9, but sometimes also singly, mainly in summer. Spherical fruit, to 4cm (1½in) across, develop from the woody sepals. ‡ 10–20m (30–70ft). Mexico to tropical South America. ❀ (min. 7–10°C/45–50°F)

▷**Merrybells** see *Uvularia*
Large see *U. grandiflora*

MERTENSIA

BORAGINACEAE

Genus of about 50 species of clump-forming, mound-forming, or prostrate perennials from wet meadows, woodland, and coasts in Europe, Asia, North America, and Greenland. The alternate, lance-shaped to rounded leaves, sometimes with heart-shaped bases, are light to dark green or greyish or bluish green. Pendent, tubular or bell-shaped, 5-lobed blue flowers, with flared, funnel-shaped mouths, are borne in terminal or axillary cymes. Grow the smaller species in a gravel bed, rock garden, or alpine house, the larger ones in a peat bed, herbaceous border, or woodland garden.
• **HARDINESS** Fully hardy.

Mertensia ciliata

• **CULTIVATION** Grow in moist but well-drained, humus-rich soil in light dappled shade. Alpine species, such as *M. echioides,* require humus-rich, gritty soil; *M. maritima* and *M. simplicissima* prefer low-fertility, sharply drained, very gritty or sandy soil. All prefer full sun with some midday shade.
• **PROPAGATION** Sow seed in containers in a cold frame in autumn; keep young plants shaded and do not allow the soil to dry out. Divide clumps carefully as new growth commences in spring. Take root cuttings of *M. pulmonarioides* when dormant, in autumn or early winter.
• **PESTS AND DISEASES** Slugs and snails may cause damage.

M. asiatica see *M. simplicissima*.
M. ciliata ■ Upright perennial with stemless, ovate, lance-shaped, or oblong, bluish green basal leaves, to 15cm (6in) long, and ovate to lance-shaped stem leaves. Axillary cymes of bell-shaped, clear blue flowers, to 8mm (⅜in) long, are borne in summer. ‡ to 60cm (24in), ↔ to 30cm (12in). W. USA. ❄❄❄
M. echioides. Clump-forming perennial with spoon-shaped or ovate to lance-shaped or oblong, dark green leaves, to 9cm (3½in) long. Many-flowered, curving cymes, to 12cm (5in) long, of funnel-shaped, deep blue flowers, to 7mm (¼in) long, are borne on upright stems in summer. ‡ 15cm (6in), ↔ to 10cm (4in). Himalayas. ❄❄❄
M. maritima (Oyster plant). Spreading, prostrate perennial with fleshy, spoon-shaped to oblong-ovate, very glaucous, blue-green leaves, to 10cm (4in) long. Bell-shaped, bright blue flowers, to

Mertensia simplicissima

8mm (3/8in) across, open from pink buds in branching, terminal cymes in early summer. ↕ 10cm (4in), ↔ to 30cm (12in). Coasts of E. North America, Greenland, and N. Europe. ✻✻✻.
subsp. *asiatica* see *M. simplicissima.*
M. pterocarpa see *M. sibirica.*
M. pulmonarioides see *M. virginica.*
M. sibirica, syn. *M. pterocarpa.* Clump-forming perennial with broadly elliptic, broadly ovate, or heart-shaped, light green basal leaves, 5–10cm (2–4in) long. The erect, unbranched, hairless, light green stems bear more oval, pointed leaves. From late spring to midsummer, terminal cymes of flared, tubular, deep blue or purple-blue flowers, to 1cm (1/2in) long, are borne on long, axillary flower-stalks. ↕ 60cm (24in), ↔ 30cm (12in). E. Siberia, E. Asia. ✻✻✻
M. simplicissima ▣ syn. *M. asiatica, M. maritima* subsp. *asiatica.* Prostrate perennial with procumbent, leafy shoots and rosettes of obovate to broadly ovate, glaucous, blue-green leaves, 3–8cm (1¼–3in) long. From late spring to early autumn, bears terminal cymes of flared, tubular, turquoise-blue flowers, 1cm (1/2in) long, on spreading stems. ↕ to 90cm (36in), ↔ 30cm (12in). Russia (Sakhalin), Korea, Japan. ✻✻✻
M. virginica, syn. *M. pulmonarioides* (Blue bells, Virginia cowslip). Clump-forming perennial with erect, branching stems bearing elliptic to ovate, soft, hairless, bluish green leaves, to 15cm (6in) long. Terminal cymes of flared, long-tubed, violet-blue or white flowers, 2–2.5cm (3/4–1in) long, are borne in mid- and late spring. ↕ 45cm (18in), ↔ 25cm (10in). North America. ✻✻✻

▷ ***Mesembryanthemum cordifolium*** see *Aptenia cordifolia*
▷ ***Mesembryanthemum criniflorum*** see *Dorotheanthus bellidiformis*
▷ ***Mesembryanthemum derenbergianum*** see *Ebracteola derenbergiana*
▷ ***Mesembryanthemum multiradiatum*** see *Lampranthus roseus*
▷ ***Mesembryanthemum tricolor*** see *Dorotheanthus gramineus*

MESPILUS

ROSACEAE

Genus of one species of deciduous tree or large shrub found in woodland and thickets in mountainous regions of S.E. Europe and S.W. Asia. It is grown for its attractive, spreading habit, colourful autumn foliage, bowl-shaped flowers, borne singly at the ends of short shoots, and flattened, apple-like fruit, which have prominent, persistent calyces. Grow as a specimen tree. The fruit are edible following the first frosts in late autumn, when well-ripened and partly rotten.
• **HARDINESS** Fully hardy.
• **CULTIVATION** Grow in moderately fertile, moist but well-drained soil in full sun or light shade. Pruning group 1.
• **PROPAGATION** Sow seed in a seedbed in autumn. Bud in late summer.
• **PESTS AND DISEASES** Aphids, brown rot, caterpillars, and powdery mildew may cause problems.

M. germanica ▣ ♀ (Medlar). Spreading tree or large shrub with alternate, lance-shaped to oblong-oval, dark green leaves, to 15cm (6in) long,

Mespilus germanica

turning yellow-brown in autumn. Bears white, sometimes pink-tinged flowers, to 5cm (2in) across, in late spring and early summer. Almost spherical, fleshy brown fruit grow up to 5cm (2in) or more across. ↕ 6m (20ft), ↔ 8m (25ft). S.E. Europe, S.W. Asia. ✻✻✻. **'Dutch'** has russet-brown fruit. **'Nottingham'** has brown fruit, 4cm (1½in) across.

▷ **Mespilus, Snowy** see *Amelanchier*

METASEQUOIA

CUPRESSACEAE/TAXODIACEAE

Genus of one species of deciduous, monoecious, coniferous tree from valley forests of C. China. It has 2-ranked, linear leaves that turn gold to red-brown in autumn. The shoots, leaves, and cone scales grow in opposite pairs. It is an excellent specimen tree, growing quickly to a considerable height.
• **HARDINESS** Fully hardy.
• **CULTIVATION** Grow in humus-rich, moist but well-drained soil in full sun. Initial growth is fast, but on dry sites is slower after plants reach 10m (30ft) tall.
• **PROPAGATION** Sow seed in a seedbed in autumn. Root hardwood cuttings in

Metasequoia glyptostroboides

winter, or semi-ripe cuttings with bottom heat in midsummer.
• **PESTS AND DISEASES** Trouble free.

M. glyptostroboides ▣ ♀ (Dawn redwood). Conical tree with ascending branches and fibrous, orange-brown bark, often fluted in cultivation. Soft, spreading leaves are bright fresh green, to 1.5cm (1/2in) long on mature trees, 2cm (3/4in) or more on seedlings, with 2 light green bands beneath. Deciduous shoots are green, without growth buds; permanent shoots, bearing growth buds, are pink-brown, later brown. Produces ovoid, light brown female cones, 2cm (3/4in) long, on stalks 2–4cm (3/4–1½in) long, and pendent, spherical brown male cones, 0.5–1.5cm (1/4–1/2in) long, with 15–20 scales, in the upper crown. ↕ 20–40m (70–130ft), ↔ 5m (15ft) or more. China (N.W. Hubei). ✻✻✻

METROSIDEROS

Pohutakawa, Rata

MYRTACEAE

Genus of 50 species of dwarf to tall, upright, evergreen shrubs, trees, and climbers found in rainforest, dry river valleys, and subalpine areas from South Africa to Malaysia, Australasia, and the Pacific islands (including Hawaii). The simple, mostly entire, leathery leaves are borne in opposite pairs. Small, trumpet-shaped flowers, with insignificant petals and conspicuous, brush-like tufts of stamens with coloured filaments, are borne in terminal or axillary cymes or racemes. In frost-prone areas, grow in a cool greenhouse. Elsewhere, grow as specimens, or as a hedge or screen.
• **HARDINESS** Frost hardy to frost tender; *M. excelsus* and *M. robustus* survive short spells several degrees below 0°C (32°F).
• **CULTIVATION** Under glass, grow in loam-based potting compost (JI No.2) in full light, with shade from hot sun. In growth, water freely and apply a balanced liquid fertilizer monthly; water sparingly in winter. Outdoors, grow in humus-rich, moderately fertile, moist but well-drained, neutral to acid soil, in full sun. Shelter from cold, drying winds. Pruning group 1; plants under glass need restrictive pruning.
• **PROPAGATION** Surface-sow seed at 13–15°C (55–59°F) in spring. Root semi-ripe cuttings with bottom heat in summer. Air layer in spring.
• **PESTS AND DISEASES** Scale insects may be a problem under glass.

M. excelsus ▣ ♀ syn. *M. tomentosus* (Christmas tree, Common pohutakawa). Erect, freely branching tree, spreading with age, with elliptic to oblong leaves, 5–10cm (2–4in) long, semi-glossy, dark green above, densely white-felted beneath. It has broad, compact, many-flowered, terminal cymes of flowers, 3–4cm (1¼–1½in) long, with crimson filaments and golden anthers, borne throughout summer. ↕ to 20m (70ft), ↔ 10–20m (30–70ft). New Zealand (North Island). ✻. **'Aureus'** has rich yellow filaments.
M. kermadecensis ♀ Bushy, rounded to spreading tree with broadly ovate to oblong-elliptic leaves, 2.5–5cm (1–2in) long, with recurved margins, dark green above and densely white-felted beneath. In summer, produces abundant dense,

Metrosideros excelsus

terminal cymes of flowers 2cm (3/4in) long, with crimson filaments and yellow anthers. ↕ to 20m (70ft), ↔ 8–12m (25–40ft). New Zealand, including Raoul Island. ✻. **'Sunninghill'** has variegated leaves, irregularly splashed creamy yellow. **'Variegatus'** has leaves marbled dark green and grey-green, with broad, irregular, creamy white margins.
M. robustus ♀ (Northern rata, Rata). Erect, freely branching tree, often epiphytic when young, spreading with age. Elliptic to ovate-oblong leaves, 2.5–5cm (1–2in) long, are semi-glossy, dark green above and hairless and paler beneath. In summer, flowers 3cm (1¼in) long, with matt crimson filaments and yellow anthers, are borne in dense, terminal cymes on 4-angled stems. ↕ to 30m (100ft), ↔ to 12m (40ft). New Zealand. ✻
M. tomentosus see *M. excelsus.*

MEUM

APIACEAE/UMBELLIFERAE

Genus of one species of clump-forming perennial from mountain slopes, poor grassland, and roadsides in W. and C. Europe. The hairless, aromatic, mainly basal leaves are pinnate, with whorled, hair-like segments. Small, star-shaped flowers are borne in compound umbels in summer. Grow as a foliage plant in a mixed or herbaceous border.
• **HARDINESS** Fully hardy.
• **CULTIVATION** Grow in moderately fertile, well-drained, preferably alkaline soil in full sun.
• **PROPAGATION** Sow seed in containers in a cold frame as soon as ripe. Divide in spring; pot up until established.
• **PESTS AND DISEASES** Slugs and snails may damage young growth. Aphids may also be a problem.

M. athamanticum (Baldmoney, Spignel). Perennial with oblong, 3- or 4-pinnate, light to mid-green leaves, with finely cut leaflets, 5mm (1/4in) long. In early and midsummer, bears tiny, white or purple-tinged white flowers in small umbels, 3–6cm (1¼–2½in) across, grouped into larger, compound umbels. ↕ 20–60cm (8–24in), ↔ 30cm (12in). W. and C. Europe. ***

▷**Mexican bush** see *Salvia leucantha*
▷**Mexican creeper** see *Antigonon leptopus*
▷**Mexican hat** see *Ratibida*
▷**Mexican hat plant** see *Kalanchoe daigremontiana*
▷**Mexican orange blossom** see *Choisya, C. ternata*
▷**Mezereon** see *Daphne mezereum*
▷**Michaelmas daisy** see *Aster novi-belgii*

Michauxia

CAMPANULACEAE

Genus of 7 species of imposing biennials or short-lived, monocarpic perennials from sunny, well-drained, stony sites in the E. Mediterranean region and S.W. Asia. The toothed, hairy, rosette-forming leaves are pinnatisect or pinnatifid, each leaf with a single large, terminal lobe. Racemes or panicles of white or blue flowers, with spreading or reflexed corollas consisting of many narrow petals, are produced on stout, leafy stems. Grow in a mixed border.

• **Hardiness** Fully hardy.
• **Cultivation** Grow in moderately fertile, well-drained, alkaline soil in full sun. Provide a dry winter mulch.
• **Propagation** Sow seed *in situ* in spring. May also self-seed.
• **Pests and diseases** Trouble free.

M. campanuloides. Perennial with robust, branched stems and lance-shaped, pinnatifid leaves, to 20cm (8in) long. Pendent, purple-tinged white flowers, 2–4cm (¾–1½in) across, with narrow, reflexed corolla lobes and protruding, tubular, hairy styles, are borne in panicles in early summer. ↕ to 1.5m (5ft), ↔ 45cm (18in). E. Mediterranean (Turkey, Syria). ***

M. tchihatchewii ■ Perennial with long-stalked, oblong to broadly lance-shaped, coarsely toothed leaves, 15–20cm (6–8in) long. In midsummer, robust, stiff, branching stems, one per rosette, bear dense, spike-like racemes of nodding, initially broadly bell-shaped, white or blue flowers, to 3cm (1¼in) across, with mildly reflexed corollas, the lobes divided only to one-third of their length. ↕ 1.5m (5ft) or more, ↔ 45cm (18in). Turkey. ***

Michelia

MAGNOLIACEAE

Genus of 45 species of deciduous and evergreen, rounded, spreading shrubs and upright trees from broad-leaved woodland in India and Sri Lanka, and from the Himalayas to China and S.E. Asia. They are grown for their usually fragrant, magnolia-like flowers, borne singly from the leaf axils in spring or summer. The oblong, oval-oblong, or elliptic, leathery leaves are alternate or spiralling. In frost-prone areas, grow in a cool greenhouse or conservatory. Elsewhere, grow the shrubs in a border or small courtyard garden, and the trees in a woodland garden or as specimen plants.

• **Hardiness** Half hardy to frost tender; *M. doltsopa* and *M. figo* may survive short spells near to 0°C (32°F).
• **Cultivation** Under glass, grow in loam-based potting compost (JI No.2), with added peat or composted bark, in full light with shade from hot sun, and low or moderate humidity. In growth, water moderately and apply a balanced liquid fertilizer monthly; water sparingly in winter. Outdoors, grow in humus-rich, moist but well-drained, neutral to acid soil, in full sun with some midday shade, or in partial shade. Shelter from cold, drying winds. Pruning group 1.
• **Propagation** Sow seed in containers in a cold frame or under glass either in autumn or as soon as ripe. Root greenwood cuttings in early summer or semi-ripe cuttings in mid- or late summer. Layer in spring.
• **Pests and diseases** Prone to scale insects and red spider mites under glass.

M. doltsopa ■ Small, evergreen tree, sometimes shrubby. It is erect, bushy, and pyramidal when young, with slightly warty stems, spreading with age. Leaves are oval-oblong to lance-shaped, 8–18cm (3–7in) long, lustrous, dark green above, silky, grey-hairy beneath. Bowl-shaped, fragrant, white to very pale yellow flowers, 7–10cm (3–4in) across, are borne from spring to early summer. ↕ 8–15m (25–50ft), ↔ 5–10m (15–30ft). E. Himalayas, Tibet, W. and S.W. China. ❀ (min. 5°C/41°F)

M. figo ■ Rounded, bushy, freely branching, evergreen shrub with downy, yellowish brown stems and elliptic-oblong to slightly obovate or oval leaves, 5–10cm (2–4in) long, lustrous, dark green above, paler beneath. From spring to summer, bears cup-shaped, banana-scented, yellowish green to ivory-white flowers, 3cm (1¼in) across, with dark red or maroon petal margins. Flowers are initially enclosed in woolly brown bracts. ↕ 3–6m (10–20ft), ↔ 1.5–3.5m (5–11ft). China. ❀ (min. 5°C/41°F)

Michelia figo

▷**Mickey Mouse plant** see *Ochna serrulata*

Microbiota

CUPRESSACEAE

Genus of one species of prostrate to low mound-forming, evergreen, dioecious or monoecious, coniferous shrub from open slopes in S.E. Siberia. It has scale-like, broadly triangular, pointed leaves that turn bronze over winter; this can be a striking feature, although it sometimes appears that the plant is dying. The minute, ovoid cones have leathery scales, each one opening to release a single seed. Grow in a shrub border or as a specimen shrub; *M. decussata* is also a useful ground-cover plant, similar to the spreading junipers (*Juniperus*).

• **Hardiness** Fully hardy.
• **Cultivation** Grow in moderately fertile, moist but well-drained soil in full sun. Pruning is not required.
• **Propagation** Sow seed in a seedbed in autumn. Root semi-ripe cuttings in summer.
• **Pests and diseases** Trouble free.

M. decussata ■ Spreading coniferous shrub with green shoots, later turning red-brown, and flat sprays of bright mid-green leaves, to 3mm (⅛in) long, paler below, in symmetrical pairs. Female cones, 3mm (⅛in) long, each have 2–4 scales, one of which is fertile; male cones, 2–4mm (1/16–⅛in) long, are pale yellow. ↕ to 1m (3ft), ↔ indefinite. Russia (S.E. Siberia). ***

Microcachrys

PODOCARPACEAE

Genus of one species of monoecious, evergreen, spreading, coniferous shrub, found on 2 mountain summits in W. Tasmania. It is cultivated for its small, scale-like, triangular leaves, borne on procumbent, snake-like branches, and, to a lesser extent, for its small, mulberry-like cones. *M. tetragona* is suitable for a shrub border or rock garden, or for ground cover.

Michauxia tchihatchewii

Michelia doltsopa

Microbiota decussata

Microcachrys tetragona

- **HARDINESS** Frost hardy.
- **CULTIVATION** Grow in humus-rich, moist but well-drained, neutral to slightly acid soil in full sun, with some midday shade.
- **PROPAGATION** Sow seed as soon as ripe in a seedbed, or in containers in a cold frame. Root semi-ripe cuttings in summer.
- **PESTS AND DISEASES** Trouble free.

M. tetragona ■ Spreading, coniferous shrub with overlapping, dark green leaves, 2–3mm (1/16–⅛in) long, arranged spirally in 4 rows on the shoots. Ovoid female cones, 1cm (½in) long, have whorls of 4 rounded scales, becoming fleshy and translucent red, each with a single seed; oblong male cones, 3mm (⅛in) long, are borne at the ends of the shoots. ↕ to 50cm (20in), ↔ 1m (3ft). Australia (W. Tasmania). ❄❄

▷ ***Microcoelum weddellianum*** see *Lytocaryum weddellianum*
▷ ***Microglossa*** see *Aster*
M. albescens see *A. albescens*

MICROLEPIA

DENNSTAEDTIACEAE

Genus of about 45 species of terrestrial, evergreen ferns from tropical regions worldwide, mainly found at forest margins. Long-creeping rhizomes produce soft, usually dark green fronds. These are pinnate to 3-pinnate, the pinnae sometimes shallowly to deeply lobed. The round sori are formed within the margins of the leaf-blade. In frost-prone areas, grow in a temperate greenhouse. In warmer climates, *Microlepia* species and cultivars are suitable for a peat bed or woodland garden.

- **HARDINESS** Frost tender.
- **CULTIVATION** Under glass, grow in 1 part coarse leaf mould (or peat) and charcoal, and 2 parts loam-based potting compost (JI No.2), in bright indirect light with high humidity. In the growing season, water freely and apply a balanced liquid fertilizer monthly; water sparingly in winter. Outdoors, grow in humus-rich, moist but well-drained soil in light dappled or partial shade. See also p.51.
- **PROPAGATION** Sow spores in containers at 20°C (68°F) as soon as ripe. Divide rhizomes of well-established plants in spring, before new growth commences.
- **PESTS AND DISEASES** Trouble free.

Microlepia speluncae

M. speluncae ■ Large, terrestrial, clump-forming fern producing long-stalked, triangular, 2- or 3-pinnate, dark green fronds, 0.8–1.5m (32–60in) long, which consist of triangular or lance-shaped to oblong pinnae without raised veins. ↕ to 1.5m (5ft), ↔ to 3m (10ft). S.E. Asia to Australia. ❁ (min. 5–10°C/41–50°F)

M. strigosa. Terrestrial fern producing ovate to lance-shaped, 2- or 3-pinnate, dark green fronds, 70–90cm (28–36in) long, consisting of linear to lance-shaped pinnae. Fronds are small and often arching, and have raised veins on their lower surfaces. ↕ to 1m (3ft), ↔ to 2m (6ft). N. India to Japan and Polynesia. ❁ (min. 5–10°C/41–50°F). **'Cristata'** produces fronds with lobed pinnae, which are crested at the tips.

MICROMERIA

LABIATAE/LAMIACEAE

Genus of about 70 species of annuals, perennials, and dwarf, evergreen shrubs (which at one time included species now placed in the genus *Acinos*). They occur in dry, rocky sites in the Mediterranean region, the Caucasus, and S.W. China. The ovate, linear, or lance-shaped, often aromatic, light to dark green leaves are arranged in opposite pairs. Spike-like racemes of small, tubular, 2-lipped, white to purple flowers are produced in short-stalked whorls in summer. *Micromeria* species are suitable for a rock garden, or at the front of a mixed border.

- **HARDINESS** Hardy to -10°C (14°F).
- **CULTIVATION** Grow in moderately fertile, well-drained soil in full sun, with protection from excessive winter wet. Pruning group 10, in early spring or after flowering.
- **PROPAGATION** Sow seed of perennials in containers in a cold frame in spring; sow seed of annuals *in situ* in late spring. Divide perennials in spring. Root softwood cuttings in early summer.
- **PESTS AND DISEASES** Trouble free.

M. corsica see *Acinos corsicus.*
M. juliana. Rounded, evergreen, downy shrub with stalkless, ovate to linear or lance-shaped, aromatic, dark green leaves, 5–10mm (¼–½in) long. In summer, upright, spike-like racemes, comprising whorls of up to 20 purplish pink flowers, to 4mm (⅛in) long, are borne at the stem tips. ↕↔ 10–40cm (4–16in). Mediterranean. ❄❄

▷ **Mignonette** see *Reseda*
Common see *R. odorata*
▷ **Mignonette tree** see *Lawsonia*

MIKANIA

ASTERACEAE/COMPOSITAE

Genus of about 300 species of woody-stemmed and herbaceous, deciduous or evergreen, twining or scandent climbers, allied to *Eupatorium*. They occur in tropical to warm-temperate regions worldwide in a broad range of habitats, from prairies and grassland to deciduous and tropical woodland. The usually opposite leaves are simple, and may be entire, toothed, or shallowly to palmately lobed. Hemispherical flowerheads, similar to those of groundsel (*Senecio*), lack ray-florets, and are borne in spikes, racemes, corymbs, or panicles. In frost-prone areas, grow in a temperate greenhouse. In warmer climates, grow in a woodland garden, use to clothe an arch or pergola, or allow to scramble through shrubs.

- **HARDINESS** Frost tender; *M. scandens* may survive short periods at 0°C (32°F).
- **CULTIVATION** Under glass, grow in loam-based potting compost (JI No.2) in bright filtered light. In the growing season, water freely and apply a balanced liquid fertilizer monthly; water sparingly in winter. Outdoors, grow in moderately fertile, moist but well-drained soil in light dappled shade. Pruning group 11, in early spring.
- **PROPAGATION** Sow seed at 13–15°C (55–59°F) in spring. Insert softwood cuttings in late spring.
- **PESTS AND DISEASES** Red spider mites and whiteflies may prove troublesome under glass.

M. scandens (Climbing hempweed, Hemp vine). Twining climber, often semi- or fully evergreen in tropical areas, with triangular to heart-shaped, glossy, mid- to bright green leaves, 5–10cm (2–4in) long, with entire or irregularly toothed margins. From late summer to late autumn, small but dense corymbs, 2–5cm (¾–2in) long, of vanilla-scented, usually white to pale flesh-pink, sometimes lilac to purple or yellow-tinted white flowerheads are produced from the upper leaf axils. ↕ 2–5m (6–15ft). Tropical North and South America. ❁ (min. 5°C/41°F)

▷ **Mile-a-minute plant** see *Fallopia aubertii, F. baldschuanica*
▷ **Milfoil** see *Myriophyllum*
Diamond see *M. aquaticum*
Western see *M. hippuroides*

MILIUM

GRAMINEAE/POACEAE

Genus of 6 species of annual and tussock-forming, perennial grasses found mainly in woodland in temperate regions of Europe, Asia, and E. North America. They have flat, linear to lance-shaped, light to yellow-green leaves, and produce open, spreading panicles of well-spaced, single-flowered spikelets from late spring to midsummer. Grow in a herbaceous or mixed border, or in woodland.

- **HARDINESS** Fully hardy.
- **CULTIVATION** Grow in humus-rich, moist but well-drained soil in partial shade; will tolerate sun where soils remain reliably moist. May self-seed, but not in profusion.
- **PROPAGATION** Sow seed *in situ* in spring; *M. effusum* 'Aureum' comes true from seed. Divide in early spring and early summer.
- **PESTS AND DISEASES** Trouble free.

***M. effusum* 'Aureum'** (Bowles' golden grass, Golden wood millet). Slowly spreading, loosely tufted, semi-evergreen, perennial grass. Smooth, flat strap-shaped to linear leaves, to 30cm (12in) long, are rich golden yellow, particularly in spring. From late spring to midsummer, tiny golden spikelets are produced in delicate, slender, golden-stemmed, nodding panicles, 30cm (12in) long. ↕ to 60cm (24in), ↔ 30cm (12in). ❄❄❄

▷ **Milk bush** see *Gomphocarpus fruticosus*
▷ **Milkmaids** see *Burchardia*
▷ **Milkweed** see *Asclepias, Euphorbia*
Swamp see *Asclepias incarnata*
▷ **Milkwort** see *Polygala, P. calcarea*

MILLA

ALLIACEAE/LILIACEAE

Genus of about 6 species of bulbous perennials, related to *Brodiaea*, often found on dry slopes in S. USA, Mexico, and Central America. They have cylindrical or flat, linear leaves. Umbels of erect, tubular, scented flowers, each with 6 spreading tepals, are produced from summer to autumn. In frost-prone areas, lift and overwinter in frost-free conditions, or grow in a cool greenhouse or alpine house. In warmer climates, grow in a sheltered bed under a wall, or in a herbaceous border.

- **HARDINESS** Half hardy.
- **CULTIVATION** In frost-prone areas, plant 8cm (3in) deep in well-drained soil in spring. Provide a sheltered site in full sun. Lift after flowering, and keep frost free during winter. Under glass, grow in a mix of equal parts loam, leaf mould, and sharp sand, in full light. Water sparingly until shoots appear, then apply a balanced liquid fertilizer every 4–6 weeks and water moderately. Reduce water as leaves wither and keep dry in winter. In frost-free areas, plant 10cm (4in) deep in autumn, in a well-drained, sheltered site in full sun.
- **PROPAGATION** Sow seed at 13–18°C (55–64°F) in spring. Remove offsets when dormant.
- **PESTS AND DISEASES** Trouble free.

M. biflora. Bulbous perennial with semi-erect, narrowly linear, glaucous, mid-green, basal leaves, 10–50cm (4–20in) long. In summer, bears umbels of 1–6, occasionally 8, white or white-flushed lilac or pink flowers, 1.5–3.5cm (½–1½in) long, with green central veins on the flat, spreading, reflexed tepals. ↕ 30cm (12in), ↔ 5cm (2in). S.W. USA, Mexico, Central America. ✻

▷**Millet** see *Panicum miliaceum*
Golden wood see *Milium effusum* 'Aureum'

MILLETTIA

LEGUMINOSAE/PAPILIONACEAE

Genus of about 120 species of deciduous and evergreen trees, shrubs, and woody-stemmed climbers from deciduous and evergreen woodland in Africa, Madagascar, India, and E. Asia. They have pinnate leaves, with lance-shaped to broadly ovate leaflets, borne alternately or in opposite pairs. Pea-like flowers are produced in terminal and lateral racemes or panicles, similar to those of wisterias. In frost-prone areas, grow in a cool or temperate greenhouse. In milder areas, grow as specimen trees or shrubs, and use climbers to clothe a fence, arch, pergola, or trellis.

- **HARDINESS** Half hardy to frost tender; *M. reticulata* will survive short periods at 0°C (32°F).
- **CULTIVATION** Under glass, grow in loam-based potting compost (JI No.2) in full light, with shade from hot sun. In the growing season, water freely and apply a balanced liquid fertilizer monthly; water sparingly in winter. Outdoors, grow in moderately fertile, well-drained soil in full sun. Pruning group 1 for trees and shrubs; group 11 for climbers, after flowering; group 13 for wall-trained plants.
- **PROPAGATION** Sow seed at 6–12°C (43–54°F) as soon as ripe. Root semi-ripe cuttings with bottom heat in summer.
- **PESTS AND DISEASES** Whiteflies, aphids, and red spider mites may be troublesome under glass.

M. reticulata. Twining, woody climber or scandent shrub bearing pinnate leaves with 5–9 lance-shaped to elliptic, semi-leathery leaflets, 3–9cm (1¼–3½in) long. In summer, produces pea-like, rose-pink, red, or blue flowers, to 1cm (½in) long, in dense racemes or panicles, 15–20cm (6–8in) long. ↕ 5m (15ft) or more, ↔ 1–2m (3–6ft). S. China, Taiwan. ❀ (min. 5°C/41°F)

MILTONIA

ORCHIDACEAE

Genus of about 15 species of evergreen, epiphytic orchids (which at one time included species now in *Miltoniopsis*), occurring mainly in warm, moist forests in Brazil. They produce ovoid to cylindrical, compressed pseudobulbs, each with 2 linear, oblong, oblong-linear, or oblong-lance-shaped, apical, usually mid-green leaves. Often star-shaped, sometimes fragrant flowers are produced in usually erect racemes from the bases of the pseudobulbs, at various times of the year.

- **HARDINESS** Frost tender.
- **CULTIVATION** Intermediate-growing orchids. Grow in containers of epiphytic compost, epiphytically on bark, or in slatted baskets. In summer, provide humid conditions with partial shade, water freely, feed at every third watering, and mist once or twice daily. In winter, admit full light and water moderately. See also p.46.
- **PROPAGATION** Divide when the plant fills the pot and "flows" over the sides.
- **PESTS AND DISEASES** Prone to aphids, red spider mites, and mealybugs.

***M.* Bluntii** (*M. clowesii* x *M. spectabilis*). Naturally occurring, epiphytic hybrid orchid with elongated pseudobulbs and linear leaves, 15cm (6in) long. In autumn, produces racemes of 3–7 star-shaped, fragrant, light yellow flowers, 8cm (3in) long, with red-brown markings, white lips, and purplish crimson bases. ↕↔ 23cm (9in). Brazil. ❀ (min. 13°C/55°F; max. 30°C/86°F)
M. candida, syn. *Anneliesia candida*. Epiphytic orchid with oblong-ovoid pseudobulbs and linear-lance-shaped leaves, 30cm (12in) long. In autumn, produces racemes of 2–8 star-shaped, greenish yellow flowers, 8cm (3in) across, spotted chestnut-brown and yellow, with lips sometimes flushed white or pink. ↕↔ 23cm (9in). Brazil. ❀ (min. 13°C/55°F; max. 30°C/86°F)
M. clowesii ■ Epiphytic orchid with narrowly ovoid pseudobulbs and linear leaves, 30cm (12in) long. In autumn, bears long racemes of 3–7 star-shaped, greenish yellow flowers, 5cm (2in) across, each barred chestnut-brown, with white lips tinted violet-purple at the bases. ↕↔ 23cm (9in). Brazil. ❀ (min. 13°C/55°F; max. 30°C/86°F)
M. phalaenopsis see *Miltoniopsis phalaenopsis*.
M. roezlii see *Miltoniopsis roezlii*.
M. spectabilis. Epiphytic orchid producing elongated pseudobulbs and linear-oblong leaves, 15cm (6in) long. Throughout summer, white, red, or purple flowers, 8cm (3in) across, with red or purple lips, each with 3 yellow ridges at the base, are borne singly or occasionally in pairs. ↕↔ 23cm (9in). Brazil. ❀ (min. 13°C/55°F; max. 30°C/86°F)

Miltonia clowesii

MILTONIOPSIS

Pansy orchid

ORCHIDACEAE

Genus of 5 species of evergreen, epiphytic or lithophytic orchids (often included in *Miltonia*) from Central and South America, found in mountainous regions from 300m (1,000ft) to over 2,000m (7,000ft). The fleshy, ovoid pseudobulbs are partially covered by soft-textured, linear, grey-green, basal leaves. Decorative, fragrant flowers, with large, flat lips, are produced in racemes from the bases of the pseudobulbs. There are many colourful hybrids, often blooming twice a year, with up to 6 flowers in a raceme.

- **HARDINESS** Frost tender.
- **CULTIVATION** Cool-growing orchids. Grow in containers of epiphytic orchid compost. In summer, provide humid, shady conditions with plenty of fresh air, water freely, and feed at every third watering; water sparingly in winter. Do not spray the foliage, as it may become spotted. See also p.46.
- **PROPAGATION** Divide when the plant fills the pot and "flows" over the sides.
- **PESTS AND DISEASES** Red spider mites, aphids, and mealybugs may prove troublesome.

Miltoniopsis Robert Strauss 'Ardingly'

***M.* Anjou 'St. Patrick'** ■ (*M.* Hoggar x *M.* Piccadilly). Epiphytic orchid with ovoid pseudobulbs and linear leaves, 20cm (8in) long. Deep red flowers, 8cm (3in) across, with white and orange-red marks at the bases of the lips, are borne in racemes, mostly in summer. ↕↔ 23cm (9in). ❀ (min. 11°C/52°F; max. 24°C/75°F)
***M.* Emotion 'Redbreast'** (*M.* Emoi x *M.* Nyasa). Epiphytic orchid with ovoid pseudobulbs and linear leaves, 20cm (8in) long. Bears racemes of bright cream flowers, 8cm (3in) across, with attractive brownish red flushing on the lips, mostly in summer. ↕↔ 23cm (9in). ❀ (min. 11°C/52°F; max. 24°C/75°F)
***M.* Jersey** (*M.* Hamburg x *M.* Hannover). Epiphytic orchid with ovoid pseudobulbs and linear leaves, 20cm (8in) long. Produces racemes of dark red flowers, 8cm (3in) across, with red lips, mostly in summer. ↕↔ 23cm (9in). ❀ (min. 11°C/52°F; max. 24°C/75°F)
M. phalaenopsis, syn. *Miltonia phalaenopsis*. Epiphytic orchid with compressed, ovoid pseudobulbs and narrowly linear leaves, 15–22cm (6–9in) long. Racemes of 2–4 white flowers, 5cm (2in) across, with bold, red-purple splashes on the lips, are produced in autumn. ↕↔ 15cm (6in). Colombia. ❀ (min. 11°C/52°F; max. 24°C/75°F)
***M.* Robert Strauss 'Ardingly'** ■ (*M.* Augusta x *M.* Gattonensis). Epiphytic orchid with ovoid pseudobulbs and linear leaves, 20cm (8in) long. White flowers, 8cm (3in) across, highlighted with yellow, with red or pink petal bases, and flushed orange at the bases of the lips, are produced in racemes,

Miltoniopsis Anjou 'St. Patrick'

mostly in summer. ↕↔ 23cm (9in). ❄ (min. 11°C/52°F; max. 24°C/75°F)

M. roezlii, syn. *Miltonia roezlii*. Epiphytic orchid with ovoid pseudobulbs. Linear leaves, 15–25cm (6–10in) long, have dark green longitudinal lines beneath. In autumn and winter, bears 4- to 6-flowered racemes of white flowers, 6cm (2½in) across, with purple or red-mauve patches at the bases of the petals. ↕↔ 15cm (6in). Colombia. ❄ (min. 11°C/52°F; max. 24°C/75°F)

MIMETES

PROTEACEAE

Genus of 11 species of upright, evergreen shrubs or subshrubs from heath and scrub, often exposed, in South Africa. Alternate or spiralling, narrowly to broadly ovate, oblong, or lance-shaped, mid- to blue-green or silvery leaves are usually crowded and overlap to varying degrees. Tubular flowers enclosed in overlapping, leaf-like bracts, often with protruding perianth segments and styles, are borne terminally or in the upper leaf axils. In frost-prone climates, grow in a cool or temperate greenhouse. Elsewhere, grow in a shrub border.

- **HARDINESS** Frost tender; may survive brief spells near 0°C (32°F).
- **CULTIVATION** Under glass, grow in a mix of equal parts loam, leaf mould, and grit or perlite, with added charcoal, in full light and with good ventilation. Water moderately in growth, sparingly in winter. In spring and early autumn, apply a liquid fertilizer of magnesium sulphate and urea. Outdoors, grow in moist but well-drained, neutral to slightly acid, poor or moderately fertile soil with low levels of phosphates and nitrates, in full sun. Pruning group 1.
- **PROPAGATION** Sow seed at 6–12°C (43–54°F) as soon as ripe, in equal parts of grit and peat. Prick out seedlings into individual containers as soon as possible.
- **PESTS AND DISEASES** Red spider mites may be a problem under glass.

M. cucullatus ▣ syn. *M. lyrigera* (Rooistompie). Usually erect, sometimes decumbent shrub with densely downy stems that branch from near the base. Spiralling, narrowly oblong, slightly glaucous, mid-green leaves, 3–8cm (1–3in) long, have rounded, irregularly notched, orange-brown tips. In summer, bears axillary, or sometimes terminal flowerheads, 5–7cm (2–3in) long, which consist of overlapping, red and yellow leaf-like bracts and flowers with perianth segments in the same colours but with protruding, feathery, silver-white tips and red styles. Grows on stony slopes. ↕↔ to 1.5m (5ft). South Africa (Western Cape). ❄ (min. 5°C/41°F)

M. hirtus. Erect shrub with stems that branch near the base and spiralling, ovate, very hairy, mid-green leaves, 1–6cm (½–2½in) long, often pinkish brown when young. In summer, bears terminal or axillary flowerheads, 5cm (2in) long, consisting of overlapping green leaf-like bracts, and flowers with prominent, silvery white and red-tipped, bright yellow perianth segments and red styles. Grows in marshy ground. ↕↔ to 1.5m (5ft). South Africa (Western Cape). ❄ (min. 10°C/50°F)

M. lyrigera see *M. cucullatus.*

Mimetes cucullatus

MIMOSA

LEGUMINOSAE/MIMOSACEAE

Genus of about 400 species of annuals, evergreen perennials, shrubs (sometimes scandent or trailing), and small trees, found in habitats ranging from forest to dry savannah in tropical regions. The often spiny stems bear alternate, 2-pinnate leaves, which in some species are sensitive to touch. Tiny, pea-like flowers, each with 4 or 5 petals and up to 10 long stamens, are lightly clustered in spherical heads, which are borne singly, or in spikes or panicles. The seed pods are sometimes twisted, curled, or spiny. Where temperatures fall below 13–16°C (55–61°F), grow in a warm greenhouse or as houseplants. In warmer areas, grow the annuals and perennials as ground cover, the shrubs in a border, and the trees as specimen plants. Need long, hot summers if they are to flower and fruit. (For the yellow-flowered florists' mimosa, see *Acacia dealbata*.)

- **HARDINESS** Frost tender.
- **CULTIVATION** Under glass, grow in loam-based potting compost (JI No.2) in full light, with shade from hot sun. In the growing season, water moderately and apply a balanced liquid fertilizer monthly; water sparingly in winter. Outdoors, grow in moderately fertile, well-drained soil in full sun, although they will tolerate light dappled shade. Pruning group 1.
- **PROPAGATION** Sow seed at 18–24°C (64–75°F) in spring. Alternatively, root softwood cuttings with bottom heat in early summer.
- **PESTS AND DISEASES** Red spider mites may be troublesome under glass.

M. distachya see *Paraserianthes lophantha.*

M. pudica ▣ (Humble plant, Sensitive plant). Bushy, mat-forming annual or short-lived, evergreen perennial with slender, prickly, branching stems. Bright green to greyish green leaves, 5–10cm (2–4in) long, each have 4 radiating linear leaflets divided into 10–25 pairs of narrow, oblong segments that fold up when touched. Spherical, light pink to lilac flowerheads, 1–2cm (½–¾in) across, are produced mainly in summer. ↕ 30–75cm (12–30in), ↔ 40–90cm (16–36in). Tropical North and South America. ❄ (min. 13°C/55°F)

▷**Mimosa** see *Acacia dealbata*

Mimosa pudica

MIMULUS syn. DIPLACUS

Monkey flower, Musk

SCROPHULARIACEAE

Genus of about 150 species of annuals, perennials, and evergreen shrubs found in southern Africa, Asia, Australia, and North, Central, and South America, usually occurring in damp areas but sometimes found in chaparral or deserts. The opposite, entire or toothed leaves are linear to nearly rounded, and mostly pale to dark green. Snapdragon-like, 5-lobed, 2-lipped, tubular or trumpet- or funnel-shaped flowers, often heavily spotted in contrasting colours, are borne from spring to autumn on upright stems, either in the axils or in spike-like racemes. The smaller species and cultivars are suitable for a damp pocket in a rock garden; grow most of the larger ones in a damp border or bog garden. Use the shrubs in a warm border. In frost-prone areas, grow the tender perennials in a cold greenhouse or as bedding annuals, and the tender shrubs in a cool greenhouse or conservatory.

- **HARDINESS** Fully hardy to frost tender.
- **CULTIVATION** Outdoors, grow most species in fertile, humus-rich, very moist soil in full sun or light dappled shade. *M. aurantiacus*, *M. longiflorus*, and *M. puniceus* need well-drained soil and full sun; *M. cardinalis* and *M. lewisii* tolerate drier soils. *M. luteus* can be grown in water to 7cm (3in) deep, *M. ringens* to 15cm (6in). Under glass, grow in loam-based potting compost (JI No.2) in full light, with shade from hot sun and good ventilation. In the growing season, water freely and apply a balanced liquid fertilizer monthly; keep moist in winter. Monkey flowers are often short-lived, so propagate regularly. Pruning group 9 for shrubs.
- **PROPAGATION** Sow seed of hardy species and variants in containers in a cold frame in autumn or early spring; sow seed of tender ones at 6–12°C (43–54°C) in spring; plant out after danger of frost has passed. Divide perennials in spring. Root softwood cuttings in early summer, and semi-ripe cuttings of shrubs in midsummer.
- **PESTS AND DISEASES** Slugs and snails may cause damage. Young plants are susceptible to powdery mildew.

M. 'Andean Nymph' ▣ syn. *M. naiandinus*. Spreading perennial with branching rhizomes and narrowly ovate

Mimulus 'Andean Nymph'

M

Mimulus aurantiacus

Mimulus x *hybridus* Magic Series

Mimulus luteus

to triangular-ovate, hairy, sparsely toothed, pale green leaves, to 3cm (1¼in) long. Leafy racemes of trumpet-shaped, white to cream flowers, to 2cm (¾in) across, the lobes heavily stained pink-purple, and with pink-spotted cream throats and lower lips, are borne over a long period in summer. ↕ to 20cm (8in), ↔ to 30cm (12in). Andes. ✻✻

M. aurantiacus ▣ syn. *Diplacus glutinosus, M. glutinosus*. Erect, often laxly branched shrub with lance-shaped to oblong, toothed, sticky, glossy, rich green leaves, to 7cm (3in) long. Bears open trumpet-shaped, orange, yellow, or dark red flowers, to 4.5cm (1¾in) long, with wavy margins, in leafy racemes from late summer to autumn. ↕↔ 1m (3ft). USA (Oregon, California). ✻✻

M.* x *bartonianus see *M.* x *harrisonii*.

M. cardinalis ▣ (Scarlet monkey flower). Creeping perennial with erect, branching, hairy stems bearing ovate to oblong-elliptic, sharply toothed, downy, light green leaves, to 10cm (4in) long. Throughout summer, produces solitary, axillary, tubular scarlet flowers, 4–5cm (1½–2in) long, sometimes with yellow throat markings; the lips are wide open but the tubular throats pinched. ↕ 90cm (36in), ↔ 60cm (24in). W. USA to Mexico. ✻✻✻ (borderline)

***M. cupreus* 'Whitecroft Scarlet'** see *M.* 'Whitecroft Scarlet'.

M. glutinosus see *M. aurantiacus*.

M. glutinosus* var. *puniceus see *M. puniceus*.

M. guttatus, syn. *M. langsdorffii*. Upright to spreading, vigorous perennial, with stolons that root at the nodes. Broadly ovate to oval, mid-green leaves, 1–8cm (½–3in) long, are coarsely or sometimes deeply toothed. Bears racemes of funnel-shaped yellow flowers, 1.5–2.5cm (½–1in) long, often tinged or marked red at the throats, in summer. ↕ to 30cm (12in), ↔ 50–120cm (20–48in). North America (Alaska to California). ✻✻✻

M.* x *harrisonii, syn. *M.* x *bartonianus* (*M. cardinalis* x *M. lewisii*). Upright perennial with elliptic, lobed, toothed, softly hairy, sticky, mid-green leaves, to 7cm (3in) long. From early summer to early autumn, produces solitary, axillary, tubular, bright clear pink to rose-red flowers, to 3cm (1¼in) long, with wide lips and with red-brown spots on the yellow throats. ↕ 60cm (24in), ↔ 45cm (18in). Garden origin. ✻✻

***M.* 'Highland Yellow'.** Upright perennial with branching rhizomes and narrowly ovate, sparsely toothed, hairy, pale green leaves, 3–8cm (1¼–3in) long. Trumpet-shaped, pale creamy yellow flowers, 2 per axil, each to 2.5cm (1in) across, usually with few spots, are produced over a long period in summer. ↕ to 20cm (8in), ↔ to 30cm (12in). ✻✻

***M.* x *hybridus* cultivars** (*M. guttatus* x *M. luteus*). Erect, basally branching, bushy, tender perennials, often grown as annuals, with oval to elliptic, toothed, mid- to dark green leaves, 3–7cm (1¼–3in) long. In summer, they bear axillary, solitary, tubular then flaring, open-mouthed, brightly coloured, usually spotted flowers, to 5cm (2in) across; the upper lips are 2-lobed, the lower ones 3-lobed. ↕ 12–30cm (5–12in), ↔ to 30cm (12in). ✻✻✻. **'Calypso'** is available as a mixture, and produces self-coloured, bicoloured, and spotted flowers in a wide colour range, including mixtures of orange, yellow, burgundy-red, and pink; ↕ 13–23cm (5–9in). **Magic Series** ▣ cultivars are early-flowering, producing small flowers in a broad range of colours, including bright oranges, yellows, and reds, as well as more unusual pastel shades and bicolours; ↕ 15–20cm (6–8in). **Mystic Series** cultivars are compact and early-flowering, producing wine-red or bright red, ivory-white, yellow, rose-pink, or orange flowers, almost entirely without marking or spotting; ↕ 13–23cm (5–9in). **'Viva'** is large and vigorous, with large, bright yellow flowers, with a broad red mark on each lobe; ↕ 20–30cm (8–12in).

M. langsdorffii see *M. guttatus*.

***M.* 'Leopard'.** Spreading perennial with branching rhizomes and narrowly ovate, sparsely toothed, hairy, pale green leaves, 3–8cm (1¼–3in) long. Solitary, axillary, trumpet-shaped yellow flowers, 2.5cm (1in) across, spotted reddish brown, are borne in summer. ↕ to 20cm (8in), ↔ to 30cm (12in). ✻✻

M. lewisii ▣ Upright perennial with oblong-elliptic, minutely toothed, stalkless, softly hairy, glandular, sticky, mid-green leaves, to 7cm (3in) long. Solitary, axillary, tubular, purple-pink to deep rose-pink, sometimes white flowers, 3–5cm (1¼–2in) long, with yellowish white throats, are produced throughout summer. ↕ 60cm (24in), ↔ 45cm (18in). North America (Alaska to California). ✻✻

M. longiflorus. Variable, erect-branched shrub with lance-shaped to oblong, toothed, sticky, pale green leaves, to 8cm (3in) long, with impressed veins. From spring to summer, bears trumpet-shaped, orange, lemon-yellow to cream, or dark red flowers, to 6cm (2½in) long, with dark orange bands at the mouths, in leafy racemes. ↕↔ 1m (3ft). USA (California), N.W. Mexico. ✻

M. luteus ▣ (Monkey musk, Yellow monkey flower). Vigorous, spreading perennial with decumbent or upright stems and toothed, broadly ovate to oblong, mid-green leaves, 2–3cm (¾–1¼in) long. Yellow flowers, 2–5cm (¾–2in) long, 2 per axil, with dark red or purple-red spots on the petal lobes and throats, are borne from late spring to summer. Self-seeds freely. ↕ 30cm (12in), ↔ to 60cm (24in). Chile, widely naturalized elsewhere. ✻✻✻

M. naiandinus see *M.* 'Andean Nymph'.

M. primuloides. Rhizomatous, mat-forming perennial with hairy, oblong to obovate, entire or toothed, light to mid-green leaves, 1–4cm (½–1½in) long. Trumpet-shaped yellow flowers, to 2cm (¾in) long, with red-spotted throats, are produced on short stems, usually 2 per axil, in summer. ↕ to 10cm (4in), ↔ to 20cm (8in). W. USA. ✻✻✻

M. puniceus, syn. *M. glutinosus* var. *puniceus*. Erect-branched shrub with narrowly lance-shaped, toothed, sticky, dark green leaves, to 7cm (3in) long. Funnel-shaped, brick-red to orange-red flowers, 5cm (2in) long, are produced in leafy racemes from spring to late summer. ↕ 1.5m (5ft). USA (California), N.W. Mexico. ✻✻

Mimulus cardinalis

Mimulus lewisii

Mimulus 'Whitecroft Scarlet'

M. ringens (Allegheny monkey flower). Erect, hairless perennial with square, branching stems and semi-clasping, lance-shaped to narrowly oblong or inversely lance-shaped, toothed, mid-green leaves, 5–10cm (2–4in) long. Bears solitary, axillary, tubular, violet, violet-blue, white, or rarely pink flowers, 3cm (1¼in) long, with narrow throats, from early to late summer. ↕ to 90cm (36in), ↔ 30cm (12in). E. North America. ❄❄❄
***M.* 'Whitecroft Scarlet'** ■ syn. *M. cupreus* 'Whitecroft Scarlet'. Short-lived, spreading perennial bearing ovate, mid-green leaves, 2–8cm (¾–3in) long, with toothed margins. Numerous trumpet-shaped, deep scarlet flowers, 2cm (¾in) across, are produced in many-flowered racemes from early to late summer. ↕ to 10cm (4in), ↔ to 15cm (6in). ❄❄
***M.* 'Wisley Red'.** Short-lived, spreading perennial with branching rhizomes and narrowly ovate to lance-shaped, hairy, pale green leaves, to 3cm (1¼in) long, with sparsely toothed margins. Solitary, axillary, trumpet-shaped, velvety, blood-red flowers, to 2cm (¾in) across, are produced in summer. ↕ 15cm (6in), ↔ to 20cm (8in). ❄❄

▷***Mina*** see *Ipomoea*
▷**Mind your own business** see *Soleirolia soleirolii*
▷**Mint** see *Mentha*
Apple see *M. suaveolens*
Bowles' see *M.* x *villosa* var. *alopecuroides*
Corsican see *M. requienii*
Eau de Cologne see *M.* x *piperita* f. *citrata*
Ginger see *M.* x *gracilis* 'Variegata'
Lemon see *M.* x *piperita* f. *citrata*
Pineapple see *M. suaveolens* 'Variegata'
Red see *M.* x *gracilis* 'Variegata'
▷**Mint bush** see *Prostanthera*
Alpine see *P. cuneata*
Oval-leaved see *P. ovalifolia*
Round-leaved see *P. rotundifolia*
Snowy see *P. nivea*
▷**Mintleaf** see *Plectranthus madagascariensis*

MIRABILIS

NYCTAGINACEAE

Genus of about 50 species of annuals and tuberous perennials from dry, open habitats in S.W. USA and Central and South America. Branched stems bear opposite, ovate leaves, and axillary corymbs or panicles of trumpet-shaped, often fragrant flowers, over a long period in summer. In frost-prone areas, grow most perennial species as annuals, lift after flowering, and overwinter in frost-free conditions; alternatively, grow in a cool greenhouse. In warmer climates, grow in a border. All parts may cause severe discomfort if ingested; contact with the sap may irritate skin.
• **HARDINESS** Frost hardy to frost tender.
• **CULTIVATION** Outdoors, grow in moderately fertile, well-drained soil in full sun, watering freely while in growth. Provide protection from excessive winter wet. In frost-prone areas, protect perennials with a mulch or lift tubers and store in frost-free conditions over winter, and then plant out in late spring. Under glass, grow in loam-based potting compost (JI No.2), with added grit, in

Mirabilis jalapa

full light. In the growing season, water freely and apply a balanced liquid fertilizer monthly; keep dry in winter.
• **PROPAGATION** Sow seed at 13–18°C (55–64°F) in early spring, or *in situ* after danger of frost has passed. Divide tubers in spring.
• **PESTS AND DISEASES** Slugs and aphids may be troublesome.

M. jalapa ■ (Four o'clock flower, Marvel of Peru). Bushy perennial with ovate leaves, 5–10cm (2–4in) long. Fragrant, red, pink, magenta, yellow, or white flowers, to 5cm (2in) long, some striped, and often with several colours present on the same plant, are borne from early to late summer. Individual flowers open in late afternoon and die by morning. ↕↔ 60cm (24in) or more. Peru, tropical North, Central, and South America. ❄❄ (borderline)

MISCANTHUS

GRAMINEAE/POACEAE

Genus of 17–20 species of deciduous or evergreen, tufted or rhizomatous, perennial grasses occurring in moist meadows and marshland from Africa to E. Asia. The reed-like stems bear linear or narrowly lance-shaped, folded, arching, light or mid-green, or blue- or purplish green leaves. Dense, terminal, arching panicles of silky-hairy spikelets are borne in late summer and autumn; flowerheads are more numerous following long, hot summers. In many cases, the dying growth provides russet autumn colours, and is sometimes attractive in winter. Grow as free-standing specimens, or in a mixed or herbaceous border. They may also be used for waterside planting or temporary summer screening. The flowerheads may be used for cutting.
• **HARDINESS** Fully hardy to frost hardy.
• **CULTIVATION** Tolerant of most conditions but best in moderately fertile, moist but well-drained soil in full sun. Protect from excessive winter wet. Where withered stems are left for winter effect, they should be cut to the ground by early spring; however, *M. floridulus* may lose dead foliage in strong winds.
• **PROPAGATION** Sow seed in containers in a cold frame in early spring. Divide as new growth commences in spring. May be slow to establish; pot on divisions or grow in a cold frame or cold or cool greenhouse until established.
• **PESTS AND DISEASES** Trouble free.

M. floridulus. Deciduous or ever-green, slowly spreading, clump-forming, perennial grass with sturdy, upright stems and downward-arching, linear, glaucous, pale green leaves, to 90cm (36in) long, with silver midribs. Erect, pyramidal panicles, to 50cm (20in) long, of silvery spikelets, are produced in autumn, although these are rarely borne in cooler regions. Often confused with *M. sacchariflorus*. ↕ 2.5m (9ft), ↔ 1.5m (5ft) or more. S.E. Asia. ❄❄❄
M. sacchariflorus (Silver banner grass). Deciduous, robust, clump-forming, perennial grass bearing stiff, flat, linear, blue-green leaves, to 90cm (36in) long, with pale, silver-green midribs. In late summer and early autumn, produces finely hairy, pyramidal or fan-shaped panicles, to 40cm (16in) long, of numerous silky-hairy, silvery white spikelets. ↕ 1.5–2.2m (5–7ft), ↔ 1.4m (4½ft). S.E. Asia. ❄❄
M. sinensis. Deciduous, clump-forming, perennial grass with erect stems and mostly basal, flat, erect or arching, linear, blue-green leaves, to 1.2m (4ft) long. Pyramidal panicles, to 40cm (16in) long, of silky-hairy, pale grey spikelets, tinted maroon or purple-brown, are produced in autumn. ↕ to 4m (12ft), ↔ 1.2m (4ft). S.E. Asia. ❄❄❄. **'Cabaret'** has broad, mid-green leaves with conspicuous white stripes; ↕ to 1.8m (6ft). **'Gracillimus'** (Maiden grass) has very narrow, curved leaves with white midribs, becoming bronzed in autumn; ↕ 1.3m (4½ft). **'Kleine Silberspinne'** is lower-growing, bearing open, spidery, white-tinged red panicles, fading to silver, from late summer to autumn; ↕ 1.2m (4ft). **'Morning Light'** resembles 'Gracillimus' but has narrow white leaf margins, giving a silvery effect; ↕ 1.2m (4ft). **'Pünktchen'** is stiffly upright, with creamy yellow horizontal bands on the leaves; ↕ 1.2m (4ft). **var. *purpurascens*** has leaves that turn purplish green, with pink midribs, in summer, and develop red and orange tones in autumn; ↕ 1.2m (4ft).

Miscanthus sinensis 'Zebrinus'

'Rotsilber' bears rich red-tinted silver panicles in late summer and early autumn, above narrow leaves with prominent silver midribs; ↕ 1.2m (4ft). **'Silberfeder'** ■ syn. 'Silver Feather', is free-flowering, bearing silvery to pale pinkish brown panicles in early and mid-autumn, remaining through winter; ↕ to 2.5m (8ft). **'Silver Feather'** see 'Silberfeder'. **'Variegatus'** has leaves with creamy white and pale green longitudinal bands; ↕ 1.8m (6ft). **'Zebrinus'** ■ (Zebra grass) is broadly arching, with creamy white or pale yellow horizontal bands on the leaves; ↕ to 1.2m (4ft).
M. yakushimensis. Dense, clump-forming, deciduous, perennial grass with narrowly linear leaves, to 60cm (24in) long; leaves are light green, with silvery pink midribs, and turn yellow in autumn. Slender, open, conical or fan-shaped silvery panicles, to 50cm (20in) long, are produced in late summer and early autumn. ↕ 60–75cm (24–30in), ↔ 75cm (30in). Japan. ❄❄❄

▷**Mission bells** see *Fritillaria biflora*
▷**Miss Willmott's ghost** see *Eryngium giganteum*

Miscanthus sinensis 'Silberfeder'

MITCHELLA

Partridge berry

RUBIACEAE

Genus of 2 species of trailing, evergreen perennials found in woodland in North America and Japan. The trailing stems root at the nodes and bear opposite, broadly ovate to lance-shaped leaves. Small, funnel-shaped, fragrant white flowers, borne in pairs in summer, are followed by ornamental red berries. Grow in a rock garden or woodland garden, or on a peat terrace.

• **HARDINESS** Fully hardy.
• **CULTIVATION** Grow in moist but well-drained, humus-rich, acid soil in light dappled or partial shade.
• **PROPAGATION** Sow seed in containers in a cold frame in autumn; keep moist after sowing. Separate rooted runners in spring.
• **PESTS AND DISEASES** Trouble free.

M. repens (Creeping box, Partridge berry). Prostrate, mat-forming perennial with broadly ovate, glossy, dark green, white-veined leaves, to 2cm (¾in) long. White, often pink-flushed flowers, 1cm (½in) long, are borne in early summer, followed by spherical, bright red berries, to 1cm (½in) across. ↕ 5cm (2in), ↔ to 30cm (12in). North America. ❄❄❄

MITELLA

Bishop's cap, Mitrewort

SAXIFRAGACEAE

Genus of 20 species of clump-forming, rhizomatous perennials occurring in woodland in E. Asia and North America. The long-stalked, lobed, ovate, glossy, mid- or dark green, basal leaves are heart-shaped at the bases. Slender, often one-sided, occasionally leafy racemes of tiny, pendent or horizontal, bell-shaped flowers, each with 5 fringed petals, are borne in summer. Use for ground cover in a woodland garden.

• **HARDINESS** Fully hardy.
• **CULTIVATION** Grow in moist but well-drained, leafy, acid soil in partial or dappled shade. They self-seed freely.
• **PROPAGATION** Sow seed in containers in a cold frame in autumn. Divide in spring.
• **PESTS AND DISEASES** Slugs and snails may be a problem.

M. breweri ■ Perennial with hairy, indistinctly lobed, broadly ovate, mid-green leaves, 5–10cm (2–4in) long. In late spring and summer, bears racemes of 20–40 yellowish green flowers, 2mm (1/16in) long, with fringed, comb-like petals, on stems to 15cm (6in) tall. ↕ 15cm (6in), ↔ to 20cm (8in). W. to C. North America. ❄❄❄

M. stauropetala. Vigorous perennial with broadly ovate, slightly lobed, often purple-tinged, mid-green leaves, 4–10cm (1½–4in) long. In summer, bears racemes of 10–35 white or purple flowers, to 4mm (⅛in) long, with deeply cut and fringed petals, on stems to 50cm (20in) tall. ↕ to 50cm (20in), ↔ to 30cm (12in). North America (Rocky Mountains). ❄❄❄

Mitella breweri

MITRARIA

GESNERIACEAE

Genus of one species of woody, evergreen, scandent or spreading shrub from moist woodland in Chile and Argentina. The leaves are opposite and ovate, and the showy flowers are tubular. *M. coccinea* prefers cool, humid climates. Grow in a woodland garden or sheltered shrub border. Where frosts are severe, grow in a cool greenhouse.

• **HARDINESS** Frost hardy (borderline).
• **CULTIVATION** Under glass, grow in lime-free (ericaceous) potting compost in bright filtered light, with moderate to high humidity. In growth, water freely and apply a balanced liquid fertilizer monthly; water sparingly in winter but do not allow to dry out. Outdoors, grow in moist but well-drained, humus-rich, acid soil in light dappled shade. Shelter from cold, drying winds. Keep roots cool and shaded, but allow the top to grow into sunlight. Pruning group 9.
• **PROPAGATION** Sow seed in containers in a cold frame in spring. Root semi-ripe cuttings with bottom heat in summer.
• **PESTS AND DISEASES** Trouble free.

M. coccinea ■ Weakly scandent shrub with opposite, ovate, toothed, leathery, glossy, dark green leaves, to 2.5cm (1in) long. Scarlet flowers, 3cm (1¼in) long, each with 5 small lobes, are borne singly from the leaf axils over a long period from late spring to autumn. ↕↔ to 2m (6ft). Chile, Argentina. ❄❄ (borderline)

Mitraria coccinea

▷ **Mitrewort** see *Mitella*
▷ **Mock orange** see *Philadelphus*, *P. coronarius*
Australian see *Pittosporum undulatum*
Japanese see *Pittosporum tobira*
▷ ***Modecca digitata*** see *Adenia digitata*
▷ **Mole plant** see *Euphorbia lathyris*

MOLINIA

GRAMINEAE/POACEAE

Genus of 2 species of loosely or densely tufted, perennial grasses found in damp moorland in Europe and N. and S.W. Asia. They are grown for their attractive habit, autumn foliage, and graceful, dense to open panicles of compressed spikelets, each with 4 florets, held well above the foliage. Grow in a mixed or herbaceous border, or woodland garden.

• **HARDINESS** Fully hardy.
• **CULTIVATION** Grow in any moist but well-drained, preferably acid to neutral soil, in full sun or partial shade.
• **PROPAGATION** Sow seed of species in containers in a cold frame in spring. Divide species and cultivars in spring, and pot up until established.
• **PESTS AND DISEASES** Trouble free.

M. caerulea (Purple moor grass). Tufted perennial with dense clumps of flat, linear-oblong, mid-green leaves, to 45cm (18in) long, with purple bases. From spring to autumn, bears dense, narrow panicles, 40cm (16in) long, of purple spikelets on yellow-tinted stems. ↕ to 1.5m (5ft), ↔ 40cm (16in). Europe, N. and S.W. Asia. ❄❄❄. **subsp. *arundinacea* 'Karl Foerster'** ■ has leaves to 80cm (32in) long, and open panicles of purple spikelets on arching stems. **subsp. *arundinacea* 'Skyracer'** has leaves, to 1m (3ft) long, that turn clear gold in autumn; ↕ to 2.2m (7ft). **'Moorhexe'** is very upright, with dark purple spikelets held tightly against erect stems; ↕ 45cm (18in). **'Variegata'** is tufted and compact, with dark green, cream-striped leaves, ochre stems, and purple spikelets; ↕ 45–60cm (18–24in).

MOLTKIA

BORAGINACEAE

Genus of about 6 species of perennials or shrubs, some evergreen, found in alkaline soils in rock crevices or on open hillsides from N. Italy and Greece to S.W. Asia. They have alternate, oblong or linear to lance-shaped or inversely lance-shaped, hairy, mid- or dark green leaves. Tubular or funnel-shaped, blue, purple, or yellow flowers are borne in short, one-sided, terminal cymes from late spring to summer. Grow in a Mediterranean or rock garden, or at the front of a mixed or shrub border.

• **HARDINESS** Fully hardy to frost hardy.
• **CULTIVATION** Grow in poor, well-drained, preferably alkaline soil in full sun. Protect from excessive winter wet and shelter from cold, drying winds. Pruning group 10, after flowering, if required.

Molinia caerulea subsp. *arundinacea* 'Karl Foerster'

M

Moltkia doerfleri

• **PROPAGATION** Sow seed under glass or in containers in a cold frame in autumn. Root softwood cuttings in early summer. Layer woody species in spring.
• **PESTS AND DISEASES** Susceptible to aphids and whiteflies under glass.

M. doerfleri ■ syn. *Lithospermum doerfleri*. Rhizomatous, woody-based perennial with wiry, upright stems and lance-shaped, mid-green leaves, to 5cm (2in) long. Bears cymes of pendent, narrowly tubular, deep purple flowers, to 2.5cm (1in) long, from late spring to midsummer. ↕↔ 30–50cm (12–20in). N.E. Albania. ✻✻✻
M.* x *intermedia (*M. petraea* x *M. suffruticosa*), syn. *Lithodora* x *intermedia*. Evergreen, dome-shaped subshrub with linear or narrowly oblong, dark green leaves, to 10cm (4in) long. In early summer, bears compact cymes of open funnel-shaped, bright blue flowers, 1.5cm (½in) long, often pink-tinged in bud. ↕ 15–30cm (6–12in), ↔ to 30cm (12in). Garden origin. ✻✻✻
M. petraea. Semi-evergreen, dwarf shrub with oblong-lance-shaped to linear, inrolled leaves, to 5cm (2in) long, dark green above and white beneath. In summer, pink-purple buds open to funnel-shaped, deep blue or violet-blue flowers, to 8mm (⅜in) long, with prominent stamens, borne in compact cymes. ↕↔ 20–40cm (8–16in). Former Yugoslavia, Albania, Greece. ✻✻✻
M. suffruticosa ■ syn. *Lithodora graminifolia*, *Lithospermum graminifolium*. Deciduous, upright, loosely branched shrub with narrowly linear, bristly, dark green leaves, to 15cm (6in) long. In summer, tubular, bright blue to purple-blue flowers, to 1.5cm (½in) long, are borne in dense, clustered cymes. ↕↔ to 30cm (12in). N. Italy. ✻✻✻

MOLUCCELLA

LABIATAE/LAMIACEAE

Genus of 4 species of erect, branching annuals and short-lived perennials found in fallow fields and on stony slopes from the Mediterranean to N.W. India. The 4-sided stems bear opposite, simple, rounded to ovate, incised or scalloped, mid- to pale green leaves. From summer to autumn, small, tubular, 2-lipped, hooded flowers, with expanded, bell-shaped calyces, are borne in whorls from the upper leaf axils. Grow in a mixed or annual border; the unusual flower spikes are useful for dried flower arrangements.
• **HARDINESS** Half hardy.
• **CULTIVATION** Grow in moderately fertile, moist but well-drained soil in full sun.
• **PROPAGATION** Sow seed at 13–18°C (55–64°F) in early or mid-spring, or *in situ* in late spring.
• **PESTS AND DISEASES** Trouble free.

Moluccella laevis

M. laevis ■ (Bells of Ireland, Shell flower). Annual with very broadly ovate, deeply scalloped, pale green leaves, to 6cm (2½in) long. In late summer, bears whorls of 6–8 fragrant, white to pale purplish pink flowers in spikes 23–30cm (9–12in) tall; each flower is cupped in a pale green calyx, which becomes white-veined and papery in fruit. ↕ 60–90cm (24–36in), ↔ 23cm (9in). Caucasus, Turkey, Syria, Iraq. ✻

MONADENIUM

EUPHORBIACEAE

Genus of about 50 species of bushy, tree-like, or trailing, monoecious, perennial succulents from low to high altitudes in tropical E. Africa, Angola, Namibia, South Africa, and Zimbabwe. Some species produce annual growth from a subterranean, thickened tuber or caudex; others retain fleshy stems all year. The fleshy or scaly leaves may fall quickly. In summer, unusual, small, petalless, diurnal flowers are borne in cup-like bracts within yellow, green, or brown-orange involucres. In areas where temperatures fall below 18°C (64°F), grow in a warm greenhouse. Elsewhere, grow in a rock or desert garden.
• **HARDINESS** Frost tender.
• **CULTIVATION** Under glass, grow in standard cactus compost in full light, with low humidity. From spring to summer, water moderately and apply a low-nitrogen liquid fertilizer monthly; keep dry in winter. Outdoors, grow in poor to moderately fertile, sharply drained soil in full sun. Protect from excessive winter wet. See also pp.48–49.
• **PROPAGATION** Sow seed at 19–24°C (66–75°F) in spring. Root cuttings of stem sections in spring and summer.
• **PESTS AND DISEASES** Trouble free.

M. ellenbeckii. Bushy succulent with thick, fleshy, cylindrical stems, and pitted branches, to 2.5cm (1in) thick, produced at or near the base. A few oval, stiff, fleshy, hairy, mid-green leaves, 1cm (½in) long, are borne at the branch tips and soon fall. Yellow-green involucres, with bract-cups 1cm (½in) across, form in summer. ↕ 1m (3ft), ↔ 45cm (18in). Ethiopia, Kenya. ❀ (min. 18°C/64°F)

Monadenium lugardae

M. lugardae ■ Erect succulent with a caudiciform base and a spineless stem, to 3cm (1¼in) thick, branching freely at or near the base. Thick, obovate, scalloped to toothed, fleshy leaves, to 9cm (3½in) long, form at the branch tips. Pale green involucres, yellow or orange-brown within, with bract-cups 7mm (¼in) across, are produced in summer. ↕ 60cm (24in), ↔ 45cm (18in). Namibia, South Africa (Limpopo, Mpumalanga, KwaZulu/Natal), Zimbabwe. ❀ (min. 18°C/64°F)

MONANTHES

CRASSULACEAE

Genus of about 12 species of mat-forming or shrubby, perennial or annual succulents from rocky, upland areas in N. Africa and the Canary Islands. Rosettes of fleshy, often warty leaves are crowded at the ends of thick, fleshy branches. Small, star-shaped, diurnal flowers, often in compact racemes or branched cymes, are borne from spring to summer. Where temperatures fall below 7°C (45°F), grow in a temperate greenhouse throughout the year, or use for outdoor bedding from spring to summer. In warmer climates, grow in a rock or desert garden.
• **HARDINESS** Frost tender.
• **CULTIVATION** Under glass, grow in standard cactus compost in full light. From spring to autumn, water moderately and apply a low-nitrogen liquid fertilizer monthly; keep dry in winter. Outdoors, grow in poor, sharply drained soil in full sun. Protect from excessive winter wet. See also pp.48–49.
• **PROPAGATION** Sow seed at 19–24°C (66–75°F) in spring. Root stem-tip or leaf cuttings in spring or summer.
• **PESTS AND DISEASES** Trouble free.

M. dasyphylla. Semi-prostrate succulent with thick, inversely lance-shaped, softly hairy, reddish green to dark green leaves, to 2cm (¾in) long, with purple stripes and spots, the inner leaves shorter and incurved. Suberect racemes of 2–5 yellow, red-striped flowers, to 5mm (¼in) across, are produced in summer. ↕ to 5cm (2in), ↔ 15cm (6in). Canary Islands (Tenerife). ❀ (min. 7°C/45°F)

Moltkia suffruticosa

Monanthes muralis

M. laxiflora. Shrubby, slightly pendent succulent with opposite, ovate, wrinkled, dark green leaves, to 1.5cm (½in) long. Suberect racemes of 6–10 yellow, sometimes purple flowers, to 1cm (½in) across, with minute red spots, are produced from spring to summer. ↕↔ 10cm (4in) or more. Canary Islands. ❁ (min. 7°C/45°F)

M. muralis ▣ Shrubby succulent with dense rosettes of obovate, warty leaves, to 1cm (½in) long, marked deep greyish purple or red. From spring to summer, produces racemes of 3–7 yellowish white flowers, 1cm (½in) across, with red tufted stamens. ↕ 10cm (4in), ↔ 15cm (6in) or more. Canary Islands (Hierro, Gomera). ❁ (min. 7°C/45°F)

M. polyphylla. Mat- or cushion-forming succulent with cylindrical to club-shaped, pale green leaves, to 1cm (½in) long. From spring to summer, produces erect racemes, usually with 1–4 red flowers, 1cm (½in) across, with white-hairy stalks and calyces. ↕ to 12cm (5in), ↔ indefinite. Canary Islands. ❁ (min. 7°C/45°F)

▷**Monarch of the East** see *Sauromatum venosum*

▷**Monarch of the veldt** see *Arctotis fastuosa*

MONARDA

Bergamot

LABIATAE/LAMIACEAE

Genus of about 15 species of annuals and clump-forming, rhizomatous herbaceous perennials occurring in dry scrub, prairies, and woodland in North America. Simple or sparsely branching, square stems bear opposite, lance-shaped to oval, usually toothed but sometimes entire, aromatic, mid- to dark green or purple-green leaves with conspicuous veins. From midsummer to early autumn, tubular, sage-like, white, pink, red, or violet flowers, often with coloured bracts, are borne in terminal whorls. Each flower has 2 lips, the upper one hooded and erect, the lower one 3-lobed and more spreading. Most monardas in general cultivation (including those described below) are derived from *M. didyma*, or are hybrids with *M. fistulosa*. They have ovate, toothed, usually dark green leaves, to 14cm (5½in) long, sometimes softly hairy beneath. Flowers, to 5cm (2in) long, are borne in whorls, with usually red-tinged bracts. Long-flowering and colourful, monardas are suitable for a mixed or herbaceous border; the flowers attract bees.

Monarda 'Beauty of Cobham'

• **HARDINESS** Fully hardy.
• **CULTIVATION** Grow in moderately fertile, humus-rich, moist but well-drained soil in full sun or light dappled shade. Protect from excessive winter wet; do not allow to dry out in summer.
• **PROPAGATION** Sow seed in containers in a cold frame in spring or autumn. Divide clumps in spring, before new growth begins. Root basal cuttings in spring.
• **PESTS AND DISEASES** Susceptible to slugs, especially in spring, and to powdery mildew in hot, dry summers. Some cultivars are mildew-resistant.

***M.* 'Adam'.** Clump-forming perennial bearing cherry-red flowers from midsummer to early autumn. ↕ 90cm (36in), ↔ 45cm (18in). ❄❄❄

***M.* 'Beauty of Cobham'** ▣ Clump-forming perennial with purplish green leaves. Pale pink flowers, with purple-pink bracts, are produced from midsummer to early autumn. ↕ 90cm (36in), ↔ 45cm (18in). ❄❄❄

***M.* 'Blaustrumpf'**, syn. *M.* 'Blue Stocking'. Clump-forming perennial bearing deep violet-purple flowers, with purple bracts, from midsummer to early autumn. ↕ 90cm (36in), ↔ 45cm (18in). ❄❄❄

***M.* 'Blue Stocking'** see *M.* 'Blaustrumpf'.

***M.* 'Cambridge Scarlet'** ▣ Clump-forming perennial bearing rich scarlet-red flowers, with brownish red calyces, from midsummer to early autumn. ↕ 90cm (36in), ↔ 45cm (18in). ❄❄❄

***M.* 'Croftway Pink'** ▣ Clump-forming perennial producing clear rose-pink flowers, with pink-tinged bracts, from midsummer to early autumn. ↕ 90cm (36in), ↔ 45cm (18in). ❄❄❄

M. didyma (Bee balm, Bergamot, Oswego tea). Bushy, clump-forming perennial with branching, square stems and ovate to ovate-lance-shaped, dull, mid-green leaves, to 14cm (5½in) long, softly hairy beneath. From mid- to late summer, each flowering stem bears 2 whorls of bright scarlet or pink flowers, 3–4.5cm (1¼–1¾in) long, with red-tinged bracts. ↕ 90cm (36in) or more, ↔ 45cm (18in). E. North America. ❄❄❄

M. fistulosa (Wild bergamot). Bushy, clump-forming perennial with branching stems, more rounded than *M. didyma*. Bears ovate to ovate-lance-shaped, softly hairy, dull, mid-green leaves, 4–10cm (1½–4in) long. From mid- to late summer or early autumn, bears lilac-purple or pale pink flowers, 2–3cm (¾–1¼in) long, with purple-tinged bracts. ↕ 1.2m (4ft), ↔ 45cm (18in). E. North America. ❄❄❄

***M.* 'Loddon Crown'.** Clump-forming perennial bearing rich, dark red-purple flowers, with purplish brown bracts and calyces, from midsummer to early autumn. ↕ 90cm (36in), ↔ 45cm (18in). ❄❄❄

***M.* 'Mahogany'** ▣ Clump-forming perennial bearing wine-red flowers, with brownish red bracts, from midsummer to early autumn. ↕ 90cm (36in), ↔ 45cm (18in). ❄❄❄

***M.* 'Prairie Night'** see *M.* 'Prärienacht'.

***M.* 'Prärienacht'** ▣ syn. *M.* 'Prairie Night'. Clump-forming perennial bearing purple-lilac flowers, with green, slightly red-tinged bracts, from midsummer to early autumn. ↕ 90cm (36in), ↔ 45cm (18in). ❄❄❄

***M.* 'Schneewittchen'**, syn. *M.* 'Snow Maiden'. Clump-forming perennial bearing white flowers, with green bracts,

Monarda 'Cambridge Scarlet'

Monarda 'Croftway Pink'

Monarda 'Mahogany'

Monarda 'Prärienacht'

from midsummer to early autumn. ↕90cm (36in), ↔45cm (18in). ***

***M.* 'Snow Maiden'** see *M.* 'Schneewittchen'.

***M.* 'Vintage Wine'.** Clump-forming perennial bearing red-purple flowers, with brownish green bracts and calyces, from midsummer to early autumn. ↕90cm (36in), ↔45cm (18in). ***

MONARDELLA

LABIATAE/LAMIACEAE

Genus of about 20 species of annuals and herbaceous perennials, often with creeping stems, occurring mainly on dry, stony slopes in W. North America. The small, opposite, aromatic, entire or toothed leaves are linear to diamond-lance-shaped, oblong, ovate, or elliptic. Terminal, spherical whorls of 2-lipped, tubular flowers (the upper lip 2-lobed and the lower one 3-lobed), often with purplish red, leaf-like bracts, are produced in summer. Suitable for a Mediterranean or rock garden, the front of a mixed border, or an alpine house.

- **HARDINESS** Fully hardy to frost hardy.
- **CULTIVATION** Grow in poor, sharply drained soil in full sun. In an alpine house, grow in shallow containers in a mix of equal parts loam-based potting compost (JI No.2) and grit. Protect from excessive winter wet and shelter from cold, drying winds.
- **PROPAGATION** Sow seed under glass in autumn. Divide, or root basal or soft-wood cuttings in spring, both with bottom heat.
- **PESTS AND DISEASES** Susceptible to aphids and whiteflies under glass.

M. macrantha. Deciduous, decumbent, woody-based perennial with spreading branches and ovate to elliptic, toothed, hairy, slightly leathery, mid-green leaves, to 3cm (1¼in) long. In mid- and late summer, bears scarlet flowers, 1cm (½in) long, in whorled flowerheads, 3–4cm (1¼–1½in) across, surrounded by purplish red bracts. ↕15cm (6in), ↔ to 20cm (8in). USA (California). **

▷**Monkey cup** see *Nepenthes*
▷**Monkey flower** see *Mimulus*
Allegheny see *M. ringens*
Scarlet see *M. cardinalis*
Yellow see *M. luteus*
▷**Monkey plant** see *Ruellia makoyana*
▷**Monkey puzzle** see *Araucaria araucana*
▷**Monkshood** see *Aconitum, A. napellus*

MONOPSIS

False lobelia

CAMPANULACEAE

Genus of 18 species of low-growing or weakly erect, slender annuals and perennials from tropical and southern Africa, occurring in open, damp areas and at streamsides or on rocky slopes. Sometimes included in *Lobelia*, they have opposite or alternate, usually stalkless, lance-shaped or narrowly ovate leaves. Tubular flowers, either 2-lipped and lobelia-like, with erect upper lobes and spreading lower lobes, or nearly symmetrical, with 5 rounded lobes, are produced from summer into autumn, either singly in the leaf axils or in loose racemes at the stem tips. Grow in a rock garden, or at the front of a border, or in containers or hanging baskets.

- **HARDINESS** Half hardy to frost tender.
- **CULTIVATION** Grow in moderately fertile, moist but well-drained soil in full sun. In containers, grow in loam-based potting compost (JI No.1) in full sun. Water freely in the growing season and apply a balanced liquid fertilizer monthly; keep just moist in winter.
- **PROPAGATION** Sow seed at 18–21°C (64–70°F) in spring. Take stem-tip cuttings in summer. Propagate regularly.
- **PESTS AND DISEASES** Slugs and snails may damage young plants.

M. lutea, syn. *Lobelia lutea* (Gold lobelia, Yellow lobelia). Low-growing, weakly erect or trailing perennial, grown as an annual, with alternate, stalkless, lance-shaped, toothed, mid-green leaves, 0.5–2cm (¼–¾in) long. From early summer to autumn, bears loose racemes, to 9cm (3½in) long, of tubular, 2-lipped yellow flowers, 0.5–1cm (¼–½in) across. ↕ to 30cm (12in), ↔ to 60cm (24in). Southern Africa. *

MONSTERA

ARACEAE

Genus of about 40 species of evergreen, often epiphytic root climbers found in rainforest in tropical Central and South America, and the West Indies. The alternate, mid- to deep green leaves usually differ in size and shape on young and mature plants, but are mainly ovate and entire, lobed, or deeply pinnatifid. On mature plants, arum-like spathes, each enclosing a spadix of tiny, star-shaped, petalless flowers, are produced from the leaf axils, followed by aromatic, sometimes edible, cylindrical fruit packed with berries. Where temperatures fall below 15°C (59°F), grow in a warm greenhouse or as houseplants (plants in containers rarely flower or fruit). In warmer climates, grow up a palm tree or on an arch or pergola. The fruit of *M. deliciosa* tastes of pineapple when fully ripe. Other parts of the plant may cause mild stomach upset if ingested, and contact with the sap may irritate skin or eyes.

Monstera deliciosa

- **HARDINESS** Frost tender.
- **CULTIVATION** Under glass, grow in loam-based potting compost (JI No.2), in bright indirect light with moderate to high humidity. In the growing season, water freely and apply a balanced liquid fertilizer monthly; water sparingly in winter. Outdoors, grow in moderately fertile, humus-rich, moist but well-drained soil in partial shade. Pruning group 11, in spring; plants grown under glass may require restrictive pruning.
- **PROPAGATION** Sow seed at 18–24°C (64–75°F) as soon as ripe. Root tip or leaf cuttings with bottom heat in summer. Layer in autumn.
- **PESTS AND DISEASES** Scale insects and red spider mites may be troublesome under glass.

M. deliciosa ▣ (Ceriman, Mexican breadfruit, Swiss cheese plant). Robust, epiphytic climber with thick, sparingly branched stems. Mature plants have long-stalked, broadly ovate to heart-shaped, pinnatifid, leathery, glossy, mid- to deep green leaves, 30–90cm (12–36in) long, often perforated with elliptic to oblong holes. Juvenile leaves are shorter-stalked, much smaller, and entire. Bears creamy white spathes, 20–30cm (8–12in) long, usually from spring to summer, sometimes followed by aromatic, edible, cream fruit, to 25cm (10in) long. ↕10–20m (30–70ft). S. Mexico to Panama. ❀ (min. 15°C/59°F). **'Variegata'** produces leaves splashed and marbled ivory or yellow, but is very liable to revert to green.

***M. latevaginata* of gardens** see *Rhaphidophora korthalsii.*

M. obliqua. Slender, sparsely branched, epiphytic climber, cultivated only in its mature form when it has lance-shaped to ovate, deep green leaves, 14–35cm (5½–14in) long, uneven at the bases. Leaf blades are entire but often perforated with irregular holes. Bears bright yellow spathes, 4–7cm (1½–3in) long, in summer, sometimes followed by deep orange fruit, 4–8cm (1½–3in) long. Rarely flowers or fruits in cultivation. ↕10–20m (30–70ft). Tropical South America, West Indies. ❀ (min. 15°C/59°F)

▷**Montbretia** see *Crocosmia, C. x crocosmiiflora*
▷***Montia australasica*** see *Neopaxia australasica*
▷**Moon carrot** see *Seseli*
▷**Moonflower** see *Ipomoea alba*
▷**Moonseed** see *Menispermum*
Canadian see *M. canadense*
▷**Moor grass,**
Balkan see *Sesleria heufleriana*
Blue see *Sesleria albicans*
Nest see *Sesleria nitida*
Purple see *Molinia caerulea*
▷**Moosewood** see *Acer pensylvanicum*

Moraea huttonii

MORAEA

IRIDACEAE

Genus of about 120 species of deciduous or semi-deciduous, cormous perennials, occurring in seasonally moist grassland throughout Africa. The linear or lance-shaped, flat or rolled, often channelled, light to mid-green leaves may be basal or borne on the stems. From spring to summer, a succession of short-lived, colourful, iris-like flowers are produced in clusters within pairs of large bracts. In frost-free climates, some species, such as *M. angusta*, *M. moggii*, and *M. spathulata*, are evergreen. In frost-prone areas, grow the half-hardy species in a cool greenhouse. In warmer climates, the frost-hardy species are best in a mixed border or at the base of warm, sunny wall; grow half-hardy species in a mixed border or a rock garden.

- **HARDINESS** Frost hardy to half hardy.
- **CULTIVATION** Plant 7cm (3in) deep in spring or autumn. Outdoors, grow frost-hardy species in well-drained, humus-rich, moderately fertile soil in full sun with some midday shade. Protect from excessive winter wet. In areas prone to severe frosts, grow under glass, as for half-hardy species. Under glass, grow half-hardy species in loam-based potting compost (JI No.2), with added sharp sand, in full light. Water sparingly as growth begins, freely when in full growth. Dry off as leaves wither, to ensure a dry dormancy from midsummer to autumn. In warmer areas, grow outdoors, as for frost-hardy species.

Moraea polystachya

Moraea ramosissima

• **PROPAGATION** Sow seed of frost-hardy species in containers in a cold frame in spring; sow seed of half-hardy species under glass in autumn. Separate offsets when dormant.
• **PESTS AND DISEASES** Trouble free.

M. angusta. Cormous perennial producing a solitary, erect, linear, rolled, stem leaf, to 60cm (24in) long. Brown- or grey-tinged yellow flowers, 6–8cm (2½–3in) across, are produced in spring. ↕ 20–40cm (8–16in), ↔ 8cm (3in). South Africa (S. Western Cape). *
M. aristata, syn. *M. glaucopis.* Cormous perennial producing a solitary, erect, narrowly linear, flat, basal leaf, to 45cm (18in) long. Produces white flowers, 5–7cm (2–3in) across, with conspicuous, green, blue, or violet central eyes on the outer tepals, on occasionally branched stems in late spring. ↕ 25–35cm (10–14in), ↔ 8cm (3in). South Africa. *
M. glaucopis see *M. aristata.*
M. huttonii ▣ Cormous perennial with a solitary, semi-erect, narrowly linear, flat or channelled, basal leaf, to 1m (3ft) long. Scented, golden yellow flowers, to 8cm (3in) across, with brown marks and deeper yellow eyes towards the centres, are borne on occasionally branched stems from spring to early summer. Similar to *M. spathulata*, but with purple-brown marks on the styles. ↕ 70–90cm (28–36in), ↔ 8cm (3in). South Africa (KwaZulu/Natal), Lesotho. **
M. moggii. Robust, cormous perennial with a solitary, erect, narrowly linear, basal leaf, to 60cm (24in) long, channelled at the base and rolled at the tip. Yellow, sometimes cream or white flowers, to 5cm (2in) across, with bright yellow and purple veins on the outer tepals, are borne in late summer. One of the easiest species to grow. ↕ 70cm (28in), ↔ 8cm (3in). South Africa (KwaZulu/Natal), Swaziland. **
M. natalensis. Cormous perennial with a solitary, narrowly linear, channelled leaf, to 20cm (8in) long, borne near the top of the stem. In summer, produces lilac or violet-blue flowers, 2.5–3cm (1–1¼in) across, with a conspicuous yellow central mark, ringed dark mauve, on each outer tepal. ↕ to 45cm (18in), ↔ 8cm (3in). Zaire, Zambia, Malawi, Zimbabwe, Mozambique, South Africa (KwaZulu/Natal, Mpumalanga). *
M. polystachya ▣ Cormous perennial bearing 3–5 erect but later spreading, linear, channelled to almost flat leaves, to 80cm (32in) long, on branching stems. In summer, bears violet to pale blue flowers, 6–8cm (2½–3in) across, with a white-margined yellow mark at the centre of each outer tepal. ↕ to 80cm (32in), ↔ 8cm (3in). Namibia, Botswana, South Africa (Northern Cape, Eastern Cape, W. Limpopo). *
M. ramosissima ▣ Cormous perennial with numerous semi-erect, narrowly linear, channelled, basal leaves, 30–50cm (12–20in) long. Produces yellow flowers, 4–6cm (1½–2½in) across, with deeper yellow centres, on many-branched stems from spring to early summer. Produces offset corms. ↕ 50–120cm (20–48in), ↔ 10cm (4in). South Africa. *
M. spathacea see *M. spathulata.*
M. spathulata, syn. *M. spathacea.* Robust, cormous perennial with a solitary, semi-erect, narrowly linear, flat or channelled, basal leaf, to 80cm (32in) long. Bears golden yellow flowers, to 9cm (3½in) across, in early and mid-summer. Outer tepals each have a deep yellow to orange-yellow central mark and purple-brown margins. Similar to *M. huttonii* but more robust and with larger flowers. ↕ 50–90cm (20–36in), ↔ 8cm (3in). Zimbabwe, Mozambique, Swaziland, Lesotho, South Africa (KwaZulu/Natal, Limpopo, Mpumalanga, Eastern Cape). **
M. villosa. Variable, cormous perennial with a solitary, trailing, narrowly linear, channelled, basal leaf, 20–50cm (8–20in) long. In early spring, branched stems bear white, cream, pink, orange, vivid blue, lilac, or purple flowers, 5–7cm (2–3in) across. Outer tepals each have a yellow central mark, surrounded by 1 or 2 darker yellow, purple, or black bands. ↕ 15–40cm (6–16in), ↔ 5cm (2in). South Africa (Northern Cape, Western Cape, Eastern Cape). *

MORICANDIA

BRASSICACEAE/CRUCIFERAE

Genus of about 7 species of usually low-growing, branching annuals or short-lived perennials found in fields and by pathways in the Mediterranean region and the Middle East. They have opposite, obovate to ovate, fleshy, hairless, grey-green leaves that are usually stalkless, the upper leaves clasping the stems, and they produce loose, terminal racemes of cross-shaped, violet to purple (occasionally purplish white) flowers in summer. Grow in a rock garden or mixed border.
• **HARDINESS** Frost hardy.
• **CULTIVATION** Grow in moderately fertile, moist but well-drained, lime-rich soil in full sun.
• **PROPAGATION** Sow seed in containers in a cold frame in spring or autumn.
• **PESTS AND DISEASES** Trouble free.

M. arvensis ▣ syn. *Brassica arvensis.* Branching annual or short-lived perennial bearing obovate, grey-green leaves, to 50cm (20in) long, with rounded tips and wavy margins. Loose racemes of 10–20 purple flowers, to 2.5cm (1in) across, are borne from early to midsummer. ↕ 25–50cm (10–20in), ↔ 20cm (8in). W. Mediterranean. **
M. moricandioides, syn. *Brassica moricandioides, M. ramburii* (Violet cabbage). Branching, short-lived perennial with obovate, wavy-margined, grey-green leaves, to 50cm (20in) long, rounded at the tips. From early to midsummer, produces loose racemes of 20–40 purple flowers, to 2.5cm (1in) across. ↕ to 60cm (24in), ↔ 30cm (12in). Spain. **
M. ramburii see *M. moricandioides.*

Moricandia arvensis

MORINA *syn.* ACANTHOCALYX

MORINACEAE

Genus of 4 or 5 species of evergreen perennials found on open, rocky and grassy slopes and in open woodland in E. Europe, Turkey to C. Asia, the Himalayas, and S.W. China. They have rosettes of lance-shaped, glossy, mid- to dark green leaves with spiny-toothed, wavy margins; the leaves become smaller near the tops of the stems. Whorled, spiny bracts are held immediately below spikes of tubular, red, pink, white, or yellow flowers, borne in whorled clusters. Each flower has a long perianth tube and a wide, 2-lipped mouth. Grow in a mixed or herbaceous border; *M. persica* is useful for a rock or Mediterranean garden. The seed heads are useful for dried flower arrangements.

Morina longifolia

• **HARDINESS** Fully hardy.
• **CULTIVATION** Grow in poor or moderately fertile, sharply drained soil in full sun. Protect from winter wet.
• **PROPAGATION** Sow seed in a cold frame as soon as ripe, with one seed per container of gritty seed compost. *M. persica* is difficult to germinate. Over-winter young plants in a well-ventilated cold frame. Insert root cuttings in winter.
• **PESTS AND DISEASES** Susceptible to slug damage and rot, especially in shade.

M. longifolia ▣ (Whorlflower). Rosette-forming perennial with linear to oblong, pinnatifid, aromatic, glossy, dark green, basal leaves, to 25cm (10in) long, with sharp marginal spines. In midsummer, tiered, whorled clusters of waxy white flowers, 3cm (1¼in) long, are produced in spikes; flowers become rose-pink then red after fertilization. ↕ to 90cm (36in) or more, ↔ 30cm (12in). Himalayas. ***
M. persica. Rosette-forming perennial with linear to elliptic, deeply lobed to pinnatifid, very spiny, dark green, basal leaves, to 20cm (8in) long. In mid- and late summer, numerous flowering stems bear dense whorls of bracts below spikes of whorled clusters of scented flowers, 3–3.5cm (1¼–1½in) long; flowers are white, sometimes with yellow-flushed throats, and become pink or reddish pink after fertilization. ↕ to 1.5m (5ft), ↔ 60cm (24in). S. and E. Balkans, Turkey, Iran. ***

MORISIA

BRASSICACEAE/CRUCIFERAE

Genus of one species of compact, rosette-forming, tap-rooted perennial occurring in sandy areas of Corsica and Sardinia. It produces pinnatifid leaves and almost stemless, cross-shaped flowers. Grow in a rock garden, scree bed, trough, or alpine house.
• **HARDINESS** Fully hardy.
• **CULTIVATION** Grow in moderately fertile, sharply drained soil in full sun. Protect from excessive winter wet. In an alpine house, use a mix of equal parts loam-based potting compost (JI No.1) and grit.
• **PROPAGATION** Sow seed in containers in a cold frame in spring. Insert root cuttings in a cold frame in winter.
• **PESTS AND DISEASES** Neck rot may be a problem in very damp conditions.

M. hypogaea see *M. monanthos.*
M. monanthos, syn. *M. hypogaea.* Perennial forming neat rosettes of lance-shaped, pinnatifid, slightly fleshy, glossy, dark green leaves, 5–8cm (2–3in) long, with oblong segments. In late spring and early summer, bears almost stemless, golden yellow flowers, to 1.5cm (½in) across. ↕ 5cm (2in), ↔ to 10cm (4in). France (Corsica), Italy (Sardinia). ***.
'Fred Hemingway' ▣ has flowers to 2cm (¾in) across.

▷**Morning glory** see *Ipomoea, I. tricolor*
Common see *Ipomoea purpurea*
Red see *Ipomoea coccinea*
Spanish see *Merremia tuberosa*
Star see *Ipomoea coccinea*
Woolly see *Argyreia nervosa*
Yellow see *Merremia tuberosa*
▷**Mortiña** see *Vaccinium floribundum*

Morisia monanthos 'Fred Hemingway'

MORUS

Mulberry

MORACEAE

Genus of about 10 species of upright to rounded, deciduous shrubs and trees found mainly in woodland in Africa, Asia, and North and South America. The alternate, ovate to rounded, toothed leaves, often lobed and heart-shaped at the bases, are light to dark green. In late spring and early summer, tiny, cup-shaped, pale green male and female flowers are borne in separate catkins on the same plant; each female flower cluster develops into a single, spherical to oblong, edible, raspberry-like fruit. Grow as specimen trees; *M. alba* 'Pendula' is particularly suitable for a small garden; *M. nigra* is the best species for edible fruit. In frost-prone areas, grow tender species in a temperate greenhouse. The leaves of several species are used to feed silkworms.

• **HARDINESS** Fully hardy to frost tender; unripened wood may be damaged by frost.

• **CULTIVATION** Grow in moderately fertile, moist but well-drained soil in full sun. Shelter from cold, drying winds. Pruning group 1, in late autumn or early winter, as trees "bleed" at other times.

• **PROPAGATION** Sow seed in containers outdoors during autumn. Root semi-ripe cuttings in summer. Root hardwood cuttings in a prepared bed in a cold frame in autumn; thick pieces of 2- to 4-year-old wood, known as "truncheons", will also root if treated as hardwood cuttings. Bud cultivars in summer.

• **PESTS AND DISEASES** Susceptible to bacterial blight, canker, coral spot, and powdery mildew.

M. alba Q syn. *M. bombycis* (White mulberry). Spreading tree with ovate to heart-shaped, sometimes lobed, glossy, bright green leaves, to 20cm (8in) long, turning yellow in autumn. Ovoid, insipid-tasting white fruit, to 2.5cm (1in) long, ripening to pink and red, are borne in late summer. ‡↔ 10m (30ft). China. ❄❄❄. **'Laciniata'** has deeply lobed leaves. **'Pendula'** ♀ is weeping, and produces pendent shoots; ‡ 3m (10ft), ↔ 5m (15ft).
M. bombycis see *M. alba*.
M. nigra ■ Q (Black mulberry). Rounded tree with ovate to heart-shaped, often doubly toothed, mid-green leaves, to 15cm (6in) long, rough-textured above. Ovoid green fruit, to 2.5cm (1in) long, turn red then dark purple in late summer, and have a pleasant, slightly acidic flavour. ‡ 12m (40ft), ↔ 15m (50ft). Origin uncertain (probably S.W. Asia). ❄❄❄
M. rubra Q (Red mulberry). Rounded tree with broadly ovate, sometimes lobed leaves, usually to 12cm (5in) long but sometimes more, with heart-shaped bases and abruptly pointed tips; they are dark green, turning yellow in autumn. Cylindrical, sweet-tasting fruit, to 3cm (1¼in) long, ripen to dark purple in late summer. ‡ 12m (40ft), ↔ 15m (50ft). S.E. Canada, E. USA. ❄❄❄

Morus nigra

▷ **Moses-in-the-cradle** see *Tradescantia spathacea*
▷ **Mosquito bills** see *Dodecatheon hendersonii*
▷ **Mosquito grass** see *Bouteloua gracilis*
▷ **Mosquito plant** see *Azolla filiculoides*
▷ **Moss,**
Club see *Lycopodium*
Fairy see *Azolla filiculoides*
Rose see *Portulaca, P. grandiflora*
Spanish see *Tillandsia usneoides*
▷ **Moss rose, Common** see *Rosa* x *centifolia* 'Muscosa'
▷ **Mother-in-law's cushion** see *Echinocactus grusonii*
▷ **Mother-in-law's tongue** see *Dieffenbachia, Sansevieria trifasciata*
▷ **Mother of pearl plant** see *Graptopetalum paraguayense*
▷ **Mother of thousands** see *Saxifraga stolonifera* 'Tricolor', *Soleirolia soleirolii*
▷ **Mother of thyme** see *Acinos arvensis*
▷ **Mottlecah** see *Eucalyptus macrocarpa*
▷ **Mountain ash** see *Sorbus aucuparia*
American see *S. americana*
Korean see *S. alnifolia*
▷ **Mountain devil** see *Lambertia formosa*
▷ **Mountain fringe** see *Adlumia fungosa*
▷ **Mountain pine** see *Pinus uncinata*
Dwarf see *P. mugo*
▷ **Mountain spinach, Red** see *Atriplex hortensis*
▷ **Mourning widow** see *Geranium phaeum*
▷ **Mouse plant** see *Arisarum proboscideum*
▷ **Moutan** see *Paeonia suffruticosa*
▷ **Mrs. Robb's bonnet** see *Euphorbia amygdaloides* var. *robbiae*

MUCUNA

LEGUMINOSAE/PAPILIONACEAE

Genus of about 100 species of herbaceous and woody-stemmed, evergreen, twining climbers and shrubs from woodland in tropical regions worldwide. The 3-palmate leaves are alternate or arranged in spirals. *Mucuna* species are grown for their large, pea-like flowers, with prominent, curved and pointed, keeled petals, which are borne in showy, pendent, axillary racemes. Where temperatures fall below the minimum levels given below, grow in a temperate or warm greenhouse. In warmer areas, use to clothe an arch, pergola, or trellis.

• **HARDINESS** Frost tender.

• **CULTIVATION** Under glass, grow in loam-based potting compost (JI No.2) in bright filtered light. In growth, water freely and apply a balanced liquid fertilizer monthly; water sparingly in winter. Outdoors, grow in moderately fertile, moist but well-drained soil in full sun, with some midday shade. Pruning group 11 or 12 outdoors; group 12 under glass. Prune after flowering.

Mucuna bennettii

• **PROPAGATION** Sow seed at 18–24°C (64–75°F) in spring.

• **PESTS AND DISEASES** Susceptible to red spider mites and whiteflies under glass.

M. bennettii ■ (New Guinea creeper). Fast-growing, woody-stemmed climber with sparingly to moderately branched, wrinkled stems, and dark green leaves with elliptic to oblong leaflets, 11–14cm (4½–5½in) long. Short, dense racemes of scarlet to flame-red flowers, 8–13cm (3–5in) long, with downy orange calyces, are borne mainly in summer. ‡ to 20m (70ft) or more. New Guinea. ❀ (min. 15°C/59°F)
M. pruriens. Semi-woody, annual or short-lived perennial climber bearing branched stems with a rough covering of long, bristly hairs when young, eventually becoming hairless. Leaves are mid-green with elliptic to oblong leaflets, 5–16cm (2–6in) long. From late spring to summer, produces racemes of deep blackish purple to lilac or white flowers, 2–4cm (¾–1½in) long, with downy, pale brown calyces. ‡ 4m (12ft). Tropical Asia, widely naturalized elsewhere. ❀ (min. 8°C/46°F)

MUEHLENBECKIA

POLYGONACEAE

Genus of 20 species of dioecious, deciduous and evergreen shrubs (sometimes mat-forming with runners) and twining, woody climbers, from rocky areas and woodland in New Guinea, Australia, New Zealand, and South America. They are grown for their intricate habit, their minute, alternate, linear to rounded leaves (absent in some species), and their tiny, cup-shaped, sweet-scented flowers, which are produced singly or in pairs, in axillary clusters or spikes, or in terminal or

axillary racemes or panicles. The shrubs are suitable for a border, the climbing species for clothing an arch, pergola, or trellis. *M. complexa* is also useful as ground cover. In frost-prone climates, grow tender species in containers in a temperate greenhouse.
• **HARDINESS** Frost hardy to frost tender.
• **CULTIVATION** Grow in moderately fertile, moist but well-drained soil in full sun, with some midday shade. Provide shelter from cold, drying winds and suitable support where required. Pruning group 11, after flowering; may need restrictive pruning under glass.
• **PROPAGATION** Sow seed at 19–24°C (66–75°F) as soon as ripe. Root semi-ripe cuttings with bottom heat in summer.
• **PESTS AND DISEASES** Trouble free.

M. adpressa (Climbing lignum, Macquarie vine). Small, deciduous, wiry-stemmed climber with lance-shaped to broadly ovate, glossy, dark green leaves, 1–6cm (½–2½in) long, with crinkly margins and often heart-shaped bases. From spring to summer, whitish green flowers are produced in short, axillary spikes, 2.5–8cm (1–3in) long. ↕ 2m (6ft) or more. Coastal, temperate Australia. ❄
M. axillaris. Small, deciduous, prostrate or spreading, many-branched shrub, often rooting at the nodes, with broadly ovate-oblong to rounded, mid-green leaves, 5–10cm (2–4in) long. Cup-shaped, yellowish green flowers are produced singly or in pairs from the leaf axils, from summer to early autumn. ↕ 20cm (8in), ↔ 80cm (32in). S.E. Australia, New Zealand. ❄❄
***M. axillaris* of gardens** see *M. complexa.*
M. complexa, syn. *M. axillaris* of gardens. Vigorous, deciduous, creeping shrub or twining climber with slender shoots and rounded to violin-shaped, dark green leaves, 0.5–1.5cm (¼–½in) long. Bears greenish white flowers in terminal and axillary racemes, 2.5–3cm (1–1¼in) long, in summer, followed by fleshy white fruit, 5mm (¼in) across. ↕ 3m (10ft). New Zealand. ❄❄
M. platyclados see *Homalocladium platycladum.*

▷ **Mugga** see *Eucalyptus sideroxylon*
▷ **Mugwort** see *Artemisia*
  Western see *A. ludoviciana*
  White see *A. lactiflora*

M

MUHLENBERGIA
Muhly

GRAMINEAE/POACEAE

Genus of 160 species of annual and evergreen perennial, clump-forming, or occasionally creeping, grasses from rocky slopes, prairies, and scrub in North, Central, and South America and central and E. Asia. Most of the clump-forming species form dense mounds of stiff, linear leaves from which arise slender or open panicles of often pinkish green or purplish green spikelets. Others have erect, bamboo-like stems bearing pendent masses of small leaves, or produce weakly upright stems that eventually trail. The clump-forming and erect species are good specimen plants in a hot, dry garden; the trailing species look attractive as ground cover or cascading from tall containers.

Muhlenbergia capillaris

• **HARDINESS** Fully hardy to frost hardy.
• **CULTIVATION** Grow in moderately fertile, well-drained soil in full sun. In containers, grow in loam-based potting compost (JI No.2) in full light.
• **PROPAGATION** Sow seed at 13–16°C (55–61°F) in late winter or early spring. Divide in spring.
• **PESTS AND DISEASES** Trouble free.

M. capillaris ■ (Hairawn muhly, Pink muhly). Densely tufted, perennial grass forming a mound of linear, dark green leaves, to 30cm (12in) long. From mid- to late autumn, produces airy, open panicles, 20–50cm (8–20in) long, of pink spikelets on slender branches. ↕ 60–100cm (24–36in), ↔ 1m (3ft). S.E. North America. ❄❄. **REGAL MIST ('Lenca')** ■ has deeper pink spikelets.
M. dumosa ■ (Bamboo muhly). Slowly spreading, rhizomatous, perennial grass with upright or arching, woody-based stems. Clusters of branchlets at the upper nodes bear numerous linear, bright green leaves, to 10cm (4in) long, giving a bamboo-like effect. In late spring and early summer, small, narrow panicles, 1–4cm (½–1½in) long, of pinkish green, then straw-coloured

Muhlenbergia capillaris REGAL MIST ('Lenca')

Muhlenbergia dumosa

spikelets are borne among the leaves. ↕ 1–2m (3–6ft), ↔ indefinite. S.W. North America. ❄❄
M. japonica (Japanese muhly). Loosely tufted, perennial grass with lax stems, initially erect but eventually trailing, bearing linear, greyish green leaves, 5–15cm (2–6in) long. From mid-summer to mid-autumn, bears narrow panicles, 7–15cm (3–6in) long, of glaucous, purplish green spikelets. ↕ to 20cm (8in), ↔ to 1.2m (4ft). China, Korea, Japan. ❄❄. **'Cream Delight'**, syn. 'Variegata' (Striped Japanese muhly), has leaves with cream margins, narrow cream stripes, and yellow stems.
M. mexicana (Mexican muhly, Wirestem muhly). Creeping, rhizomatous, perennial grass with upright stems, branching at the upper nodes and bearing linear, greyish green leaves, to 20cm (8in) long. From midsummer to early autumn, produces narrow panicles, 10–15cm (4–6in) long, of purplish green spikelets. ↕ 40–100cm (16–39in), ↔ indefinite. Mid North America. ❄❄❄

▷ **Muhly** see *Muhlenbergia*
  Bamboo see *M. dumosa*
  Hairawn see *M. capillaris*
  Japanese see *M. japonica*
  Mexican see *M. mexicana*
  Pink see *M. capillaris*
  Striped Japanese see *M. japonica* 'Cream Delight'
  Wirestem *M. mexicana*

MUKDENIA
syn. ACERIPHYLLUM

SAXIFRAGACEAE

Genus of 2 species of slowly spreading herbaceous perennials from woodland in N.E. Asia. They have short, thick rhizomes and large, long-stalked, palmately 5- to 9-lobed, toothed leaves. Leafless panicles or racemes of small, bell-shaped, 5- to 6-petalled white flowers are borne in spring. *Mukdenia* species are suitable for a woodland garden or peat terrace, and grow best in areas with cool, damp summers.
• **HARDINESS** Fully hardy.
• **CULTIVATION** Grow in leafy, moist but well-drained soil in light dappled or partial shade.
• **PROPAGATION** Sow seed in containers in a cold frame in autumn. Divide in spring, just before buds expand.
• **PESTS AND DISEASES** Slugs and snails may damage young leaves.

M. rossii, syn. *Aceriphyllum rossii.* Perennial with short, thick rhizomes and palmately 5- to 9-lobed, bronze-tinted, mid-green leaves, 15cm (6in) across. Dense, short-branched panicles of creamy white flowers, to 5mm (¼in) across, are borne above the leaves in spring. ↕ to 35cm (14in), ↔ to 40cm (16in) or more. N. China, Korea. ❄❄❄

▷ **Mulberry** see *Morus*
  Black see *Morus nigra*
  Paper see *Broussonetia papyrifera*
  Red see *Morus rubra*
  White see *Morus alba*
▷ ***Mulgedium alpinum*** see *Cicerbita alpina*
▷ ***Mulgedium plumieri*** see *Cicerbita plumieri*
▷ **Mulla mulla, Pink** see *Ptilotus exaltatus*
▷ **Mullein** see *Verbascum*
  Dark see *V. nigrum*
  Great see *V. thapsus*
  Nettle-leaved see *V. chaixii*
  Purple see *V. phoeniceum*

MURRAYA

RUTACEAE

Genus of 4 or 5 species of small, rounded trees and bushy to open shrubs with evergreen, aromatic foliage, found in dry, broadleaved forest in S.E. Asia, from India to China and Malaysia, and the Pacific Islands. They have alternate, pinnate leaves with leathery, glossy, dark green leaflets. They are grown for their showy, often fragrant flowers, borne intermittently through the year, and for their small, ovoid to nearly spherical berries. The trumpet-shaped flowers, with 4 or 5 recurved petals, are either solitary or in clusters, and are produced from the leaf axils or at the stem tips. In frost-prone areas, grow in a temperate greenhouse or as houseplants; in warmer climates, grow as specimen plants.
• **HARDINESS** Frost tender.
• **CULTIVATION** Under glass, grow in loam-based potting compost (JI No.2) in full light with shade from hot sun. In spring and summer, apply a balanced liquid fertilizer monthly. Keep just moist in winter. Outdoors, grow in fertile, well-drained soil in full sun. Pruning group 1.
• **PROPAGATION** Root semi-ripe cuttings in summer.
• **PESTS AND DISEASES** Prone to red spider mites, whiteflies, and mealybugs under glass.

Murraya paniculata

M. exotica see *M. paniculata*.
M. paniculata ■ syn. *M. exotica* (Chinese box, Orange jasmine). Large, bushy shrub bearing oblong-elliptic or oblong-obovate, glossy, dark green leaves, 10–15cm (4–6in) long, with 3–9 elliptic or obovate leaflets. Fragrant white flowers, 1.5–2cm (½–¾in) long, with recurved petals, are produced in terminal clusters intermittently throughout the year, sometimes followed by bright orange or red berries, 1.5cm (½in) long. S.E. Asia. ↕ 5m (15ft), ↔ 3m (10ft). ❀ (min. 3°C/37°F)

MUSA
Banana, Plantain
MUSACEAE

Genus of 40 species of evergreen, palm-like, suckering perennials found in light woodland and at forest margins, in N.E. India and Bangladesh, and from S.E. Asia to Japan and N. Australia. The leaf-blades are huge and often paddle-shaped (although the shape may vary) and light to mid-green, or grey-green; the leaf-sheaths form false stems. In summer, clusters of tubular flowers are produced from the axils of broad, coloured bracts in erect or pendent spikes. The cylindrical fruits are edible; several species and cultivars produce the bananas of commerce. In frost-prone areas, grow in a temperate greenhouse, or use in a summer bedding scheme. In warmer climates, grow as specimen plants.
• **HARDINESS** Frost hardy to frost tender.
• **CULTIVATION** Under glass, grow in loam-based potting compost (JI No.3) in full light, with shade from hot sun. From spring to summer, water freely and apply a balanced liquid fertilizer monthly; keep just moist in winter. Repot ornamental species annually or every other year, in spring. For bedding, plant out when danger of frost has passed; lift and pot-up in autumn. Outdoors, grow in a sheltered site in humus-rich soil in full sun.
• **PROPAGATION** Sow seed as soon as ripe at 21–24°C (70–75°F). Pre-soak spring-sown seed for 24 hours. Separate suckers in early spring, removing older leaves. Divide established clumps every 5 years.
• **PESTS AND DISEASES** Red spider mites, mealybugs, and aphids may be trouble-some, particularly under glass.

M. acuminata ✲ syn. *M. cavendishii*, *M. nana* of gardens. Upright, very variable, suckering perennial with false

Musa basjoo

Musa ornata

stems and paddle-shaped, glaucous, mid-green leaf-blades, 2–3m (6–10ft) long, with brown, papery margins. In summer, pendent, pear-shaped, white, cream, or yellow flowers, 2–3cm (¾–1¼in) long, with dull purple bracts, are borne in 2 rows per bract, followed by edible fruit, 15–20cm (6–8in) long, which are yellow when ripe. ↕ 4–6m (12–20ft), ↔ 2–3m (6–10ft). S.E. Asia to N. Australia. ❀ (min. 7°C/45°F). **'Dwarf Cavendish'**, syn. 'Basrai', *M. nana* of gardens, *M.* x *paradisiaca* 'Dwarf Cavendish' (Edible banana, French plantain), has oblong, mid-green leaf-blades, to 1.5m (5ft) long. Pendent clusters of yellow flowers, with reddish purple bracts, are produced irregularly throughout the year. Seedless yellow fruit, to 20cm (8in) long, borne in long bunches, have sweet-tasting white pulp. The most suitable cultivar for general garden cultivation; should produce fruit annually if a minimum temperature of 15–18°C (59–64°F) is maintained. ↕↔ to 3m (10ft).
M. arnoldiana see *Ensete ventricosum*.
M. basjoo ■✲ syn. *M. japonica* (Japanese banana). Suckering perennial with slender false stems, green at first, becoming papery with age, and arching, oblong-lance-shaped, bright green leaf-blades, to 3m (10ft) long. In summer, produces pale yellow or cream flowers, 2–3cm (¾–1¼in) long, with large brown bracts, in pendent, terminal spikes, followed by unpalatable, yellowish green fruit, 6cm (2½in) long, with black seeds in white pulp. ↕ to 5m (15ft), ↔ to 4m (12ft). Japan (including Ryukyu Islands). ✲✲
M. cavendishii see *M. acuminata*.
M. coccinea see *M. uranoscopus*.
M. ensete see *Ensete ventricosum*.
M. japonica see *M. basjoo*.
***M. nana* of gardens** see *M. acuminata*, *M. acuminata* 'Dwarf Cavendish'.
M. ornata ■✲ (Flowering banana). Suckering perennial with oblong to elliptic, waxy, slightly glaucous, blue-green leaf-blades, 2m (6ft) long. Produces yellowish orange flowers, 3cm (1¼in) long, with purplish pink bracts, on short, erect false stems at various times of year, followed by greenish yellow fruit, 6cm (2½in) long, with black seeds. ↕ to 3m (10ft), ↔ to 4m (12ft). Bangladesh. ❀ (min. 7°C/45°F)
***M.* x *paradisiaca* 'Dwarf Cavendish'** see *M. acuminata* 'Dwarf Cavendish'.
M. uranoscopus, syn. *M. coccinea* (Scarlet banana). Suckering perennial with reddish green false stems, becoming papery with age. Produces oval to elliptic leaf-blades, 1m (3ft) long, glossy, bright green above, paler and waxy beneath. In summer, bears erect spirals of tubular yellow flowers, 2–3cm (¾–1¼in) long, enclosed in bright red bracts, followed by orange-yellow fruit, 5cm (2in) long, with black seeds. Good for containers and cut flowers. ↕↔ 1.5m (5ft). S.E. Asia (S. China, Vietnam, Laos, Cambodia). ❀ (min. 7°C/45°F)

MUSCARI *syn.* MUSCARIMIA
Grape hyacinth
HYACINTHACEAE/LILIACEAE

Genus of 30 species of bulbous perennials occurring from sea level to subalpine areas, in woodland and on steppes, stony slopes, and screes, in the Mediterranean region and S.W. Asia. The fleshy leaves, arranged in basal clusters, are linear to inversely lance-shaped, or sickle- or spoon-shaped, mostly channelled, and mid-green, or blue- or grey-green. Flowers are borne in terminal racemes on leafless stems in spring or, occasionally, autumn; the lower fertile flowers are sometimes crowned by smaller, paler sterile ones. They may be tubular, bell-shaped, or spherical, often with constricted mouths, and are 4–8mm (⅛–⅜in) long, occasionally to 1cm (½in) long. Grow in massed displays in a mixed border; they are also suitable for a deciduous woodland garden, a wild garden, or for naturalizing in grassland. Use the smaller species in a rock garden.
• **HARDINESS** Fully hardy to frost hardy.
• **CULTIVATION** Plant 10cm (4in) deep in groups in autumn, in moderately fertile, moist but well-drained soil in full sun. Lift and divide congested clumps to maintain vigour, when dormant in summer.
• **PROPAGATION** Sow seed in containers in a cold frame in autumn. Remove offsets in summer.
• **PESTS AND DISEASES** Prone to viruses.

Muscari armeniacum 'Blue Spike'

M. armeniacum ■ Vigorous, bulbous perennial with semi-erect, narrowly linear to linear-inversely lance-shaped, mid-green leaves, 30cm (12in) long, in autumn. Tubular, bright blue flowers with constricted white mouths are borne in dense racemes, 2–8cm (¾–3in) long, in spring. May be invasive. ↕ 20cm (8in), ↔ 5cm (2in). S.E. Europe to Caucasus. ✲✲✲. **'Argaei'** has bright blue flowers. **'Blue Spike'** ■ has large, densely bunched, double, blue flowers.
M. aucheri ■ syn. *M. lingulatum*. Bulbous perennial with erect or semi-erect, narrowly sickle- to narrowly spoon-shaped, mid-green leaves, 5–20cm (2–8in) long. In spring, bears tight racemes, 1–4cm (½–1½in) long, of tubular, bright blue flowers with constricted white mouths, usually crowned with paler blue, sterile flowers. ↕ 10–15cm (4–6in), ↔ 5cm (2in). Turkey. ✲✲✲. **'Tubergenianum'**, syn. *M. tubergenianum*, is more robust, with a conspicuous crown of sterile flowers; ↕ 20cm (8in).
M. azureum, syn. *Hyacinthus azureus*, *Pseudomuscari azureum*. Bulbous perennial with erect, narrowly inversely lance-shaped, greyish green leaves,

M

Muscari armeniacum

Muscari aucheri

6–20cm (2½–8in) long. In spring, bears shortly bell-shaped, bright sky-blue flowers with a darker stripe on each lobe and scarcely constricted mouths, in dense, conical to ovoid racemes, 1–3cm (½–1¼in) long. May self-seed freely. ↕ 10cm (4in), ↔ 5cm (2in). Turkey. ❄❄❄. **f. *album*** has pure white flowers.
M. botryoides. Slender perennial with semi-erect, narrowly spoon-shaped, mid-green leaves, 5–25cm (2–10in) long. In spring, bears spherical, bright blue flowers with constricted white mouths, in dense racemes 2–5cm (¾–2in) long. ↕ 15–20cm (6–8in), ↔ 5cm (2in). C. and S.E. Europe. ❄❄❄. **f. *album*** ▣ has slender racemes of fragrant white flowers.
M. comosum, syn. *Leopoldia comosa* (Tassel grape hyacinth). Bulbous perennial with spreading, linear, mid-green leaves, to 15cm (6in) long. In spring, bears oblong-urn-shaped, creamy brown flowers with constricted mouths, in racemes 6–30cm (2½–12in) long. Spherical, bright violet, upper, sterile flowers are borne in tassels on long, upright stalks. ↕ 20–60cm (8–24in), ↔ 5cm (2in). S. Europe, Turkey, Iran. ❄❄. **'Plumosum'**, syn. 'Monstrosum', has feathery heads composed entirely of purple, sterile threads.
M. latifolium. Bulbous perennial with solitary, semi-erect, inversely lance-shaped, mid-green leaves, 7–30cm (3–12in) long. In spring, bears dense racemes, 2–6cm (¾–2½in) long, of oblong-urn-shaped, violet-black flowers, constricted at the mouths, and crowns of paler, sterile flowers. ↕ 20cm (8in), ↔ 5cm (2in). S.W. Asia. ❄❄
M. lingulatum see *M. aucheri*.

Muscari botryoides f. *album*

Muscari macrocarpum

M. macrocarpum ▣ syn. *M. moschatum* var. *flavum*, *M. muscarimi* var. *flavum*. Bulbous perennial with thick, fleshy, persistent roots and semi-erect, linear, greyish green leaves, to 30cm (12in) long. In spring, produces tubular, strongly fragrant yellow flowers, with constricted mouths, opening from purplish brown buds, in racemes 4–6cm (1¾–2½in) long. Requires a hot, dry summer dormancy to flower well. ↕ 10–15cm (4–6in), ↔ 8cm (3in). Greece (Aegean islands), W. Turkey. ❄❄
M. moschatum* var. *flavum see *M. macrocarpum*.
M. muscarimi* var. *flavum see *M. macrocarpum*.
M. neglectum, syn. *M. racemosum*. Bulbous perennial with many semi-erect, linear, channelled to almost cylindrical, bright, mid-green leaves, 6–40cm (2½–16in) long, often produced in autumn. In spring, bears blue-black flowers with constricted white mouths, in dense racemes 1–5cm (½–2in) long. Increases rapidly. ↕ 10–20cm (4–8in), ↔ 5cm (2in). Europe, N. Africa, S.W. Asia. ❄❄❄
***M. paradoxum* of gardens** see *Bellevalia pycnantha.*
M. pycnantha see *Bellevalia pycnantha*.
M. racemosum see *M. neglectum*.
M. tubergenianum see *M. aucheri* 'Tubergenianum'.

▷ ***Muscarimia*** see *Muscari*
▷ **Musk** see *Mimulus*
Monkey see *M. luteus*

MUSSAENDA

RUBIACEAE

Genus of about 100 species of evergreen perennials, shrubs, subshrubs, and twining climbers found in woodland from tropical Africa and Asia to Malaysia. The opposite or whorled, membranous, lance-shaped to elliptic, or ovate or oblong, usually mid-green leaves are often hairy on the lower surfaces. Tubular or funnel-shaped, yellow, red, pink, or white flowers, each with 5 spreading lobes, are borne in often large, terminal or axillary panicles or cymes. One sepal of each flower is often greatly enlarged and colourful. Where temperatures fall below 15°C (59°F), grow in a warm greenhouse. In warmer areas, grow as free-standing specimens or in a shrub border, or use climbers to clothe an arch or pergola.
• **HARDINESS** Frost tender.

Mussaenda 'Don Leonila'

• **CULTIVATION** Under glass, grow in loam-based potting compost (JI No.2) in full light, with shade from hot sun. In growth, water freely and apply a balanced liquid fertilizer monthly; water sparingly in winter. Outdoors, grow in moderately fertile, moist but well-drained soil in full sun, with some midday shade. Pruning group 1 for shrubs; group 12, after flowering, for climbers under glass.
• **PROPAGATION** Sow seed at 19–24°C (66–75°F) in spring. Root semi-ripe cuttings with bottom heat in summer.
• **PESTS AND DISEASES** Susceptible to red spider mites and whiteflies under glass.

***M.* 'Aurorae'**, syn. *M. phillippica* 'Aurorae'. Rounded, evergreen shrub with opposite, ovate, prominently veined, downy leaves, 8–15cm (3–6in) long. Narrowly funnel-shaped, deep golden yellow flowers, with pendent, obovate white sepals, to 8cm (3in) long, are borne in terminal cymes, 8cm (3in) long, in summer, or throughout the year in warm regions. ↕↔ 1.5m (5ft). ❀ (min. 12°C/54°F)
***M.* 'Don Leonila'** ▣ Rounded, evergreen shrub with opposite, ovate, downy leaves, 8–15cm (3–6in) long, with prominent veins. In summer, bears narrowly funnel-shaped, deep yellow flowers, with obovate, creamy white sepals, to 8cm (3in) long, in terminal cymes, 8cm (3in) long. ↕ 3m (10ft), ↔ 1.5m (5ft). ❀ (min. 12°C/54°F)
M. erythrophylla ▣ Twining climber, usually grown as a shrub, with ovate or broadly elliptic to broadly ovate, softly hairy, red-veined, dark green leaves, 10–18cm (4–7in) long. In summer, bears small, creamy white, red-centred flowers, each with one broadly ovate sepal, 5–10cm (2–4in) long, in large, dense panicles, 4cm (1½in) long. ↕ 2–3m (6–10ft) (as a shrub), 8–10m (25–30ft) (as a climber); ↔ 1.5–2.5m (5–8ft). Tropical Africa. ❀ (min. 15°C/59°F). **'Queen Sirikit'** bears pendent flowers, with numerous large, wavy, deep pink to ivory sepals, on arching branches.
***M. phillippica* 'Aurorae'** see *M.* 'Aurorae'.

Mussaenda erythrophylla

MUTISIA

ASTERACEAE/COMPOSITAE

Genus of about 60 species of evergreen shrubs and tendril climbers occurring in woodland and scrub in South America. The leaves are alternate, linear to oblong-ovate, sometimes pinnate, and mid- or dark green. Showy, daisy-like flowerheads are borne singly from the leaf axils from summer to autumn. Grow in a small courtyard garden or through shrubs in a border, or use to clothe a fence or trellis. In frost-prone areas, grow frost-hardy species in a cool or temperate greenhouse.
• **HARDINESS** Frost hardy to half hardy.
• **CULTIVATION** Under glass, grow in loam-based potting compost (JI No.2) in bright filtered light, or full light with shade from hot sun. In growth, water moderately and apply a balanced liquid fertilizer monthly; keep just moist in winter. Outdoors, grow in moderately fertile, moist but well-drained soil in full sun. Protect from excessive winter wet and shelter from cold, dry winds. Keep roots cool and moist. Pruning group 11, in spring, if necessary to restrict size.
• **PROPAGATION** Sow seed in autumn: frost-hardy species in containers in a cold frame; half-hardy species at 13–18°C (55–64°F). Can be difficult to germinate. Root stem-tip cuttings in late spring or summer. Layer in autumn. Separate suckers in spring.
• **PESTS AND DISEASES** Trouble free.

M. decurrens ▣ Suckering climber with winged stems and narrowly oblong, entire or toothed, dark green leaves, to 12cm (5in) long, each ending in a 2-lobed tendril. Bright orange flower-heads, to 12cm (5in) across, are borne in summer. Best propagated from suckers. ↕ 3m (10ft). Chile, Argentina. ❄❄
M. ilicifolia. Climber with winged shoots and holly-like, ovate to ovate-

Mutisia decurrens

M

Mutisia oligodon

elliptic, bright green leaves, to 6cm (2½in) long, each ending in a long, unbranched tendril. Short-stalked, pale pink flowerheads, to 7cm (3in) across, with yellow centres, are borne from summer to autumn and often irregularly during the year. ↕ 3m (10ft). Chile. ❄❄
M. oligodon ▣ Climber with oblong, sharply toothed, glossy, dark green leaves, white woolly beneath, to 3.5cm (1½in) long, each ending in a long tendril. Long-stalked pink flowerheads, to 7cm (3in) across, with yellow centres, are produced from summer to autumn. ↕ 1.5m (5ft). Chile, Argentina. ❄❄

▷**Myall, Weeping** see *Acacia pendula*

MYOPORUM

MYOPORACEAE

Genus of about 30 species of spreading, prostrate to upright, evergreen shrubs and trees from open, dry areas, usually at low altitudes, from E. Asia to Australia, New Zealand, and Hawaii. The alternate, variably shaped, entire or toothed, light to mid-green leaves are dotted with glands. Small, bell-shaped or tubular-bell-shaped flowers, each with 5 spreading lobes, are borne singly or in short cymes from the leaf axils, followed by small, succulent berries. In frost-prone areas, grow in a temperate or warm greenhouse, mainly for foliage. Elsewhere, they are suitable for a shrub border, and are ideal as informal hedges and windbreaks, especially near the sea.
• **HARDINESS** Frost tender; may survive brief spells near 0°C (32°F).
• **CULTIVATION** Under glass, grow in loam-based potting compost (JI No.2) in full light, with shade from hot sun, or in bright filtered light. In growth, water freely; apply a balanced liquid fertilizer monthly. Water sparingly in winter. Outdoors, grow in moderately fertile, moist but well-drained soil in full sun, with midday shade. Pruning group 9.
• **PROPAGATION** Sow seed at 6–12°C (45–54°F) as soon as ripe. Root semi-ripe cuttings with bottom heat in summer.
• **PESTS AND DISEASES** Scale insects may be a problem under glass.

M. laetum ♀ (Ngaio). Large shrub or small tree of dense habit, with sticky stem tips and thick, furrowed brown bark when mature. Fleshy, bright green leaves are lance-shaped to oblong or obovate, 4–10cm (1½–4in) long. Bears

Myoporum parvifolium

cymes of 2–6 bell-shaped, purple-spotted white flowers, 1cm (½in) across, in summer. Narrowly ovoid berries are pale to deep reddish purple, 6–9mm (¼–⅜in) long. ↕ 5–10m (15–30ft), ↔ 2–5m (6–15ft). New Zealand. ❄ (min. 2°C/36°C). **var. *decumbens*** is spreading or prostrate, and useful for ground cover; ↕ to 1m (3ft).
M. parvifolium ▣ Small, spreading, bushy shrub with reddish green, sticky stems, and narrowly spoon-shaped to linear, fleshy, bright green leaves, to 3cm (1¼in) long, with prominent glands. In summer, produces bell-shaped, honey-scented, white, occasionally lilac flowers, 1cm (½in) across, usually purple-dotted, singly or in twos or threes, followed by broadly ovoid purple berries, 7mm (¼in) long. ↕ to 60cm (24in), ↔ 60–90cm (24–36in). Australia (South Australia, Victoria, Tasmania). ❄ (min. 2°C/36°C)

MYOSOTIDIUM

BORAGINACEAE

Genus of one species of evergreen perennial from rocky or sandy coasts on Chatham Island, New Zealand. It has thick, fleshy stems and leaves, the latter large, simple, and glossy, and forget-me-not-like flowers. Grow in a peat bed or rock garden; it can be difficult to grow as it needs cool, damp conditions, preferably in a coastal location. In frost-prone areas, grow in a cool greenhouse.
• **HARDINESS** Half hardy, although will survive temperatures just below 0°C (32°F) with some protection.
• **CULTIVATION** Under glass, grow in loam-based potting compost (JI No.2) in bright filtered light. In growth, water freely and apply a seaweed-based fertilizer monthly; keep just moist in winter. Outdoors, grow in humus-rich, gritty, moist but well-drained soil with a seaweed mulch, in light dappled shade. Provide shelter from cold, drying winds.
• **PROPAGATION** Sow seed under glass in autumn or as soon as ripe. Divide in spring.
• **PESTS AND DISEASES** Prone to slugs.

M. hortensia ▣ syn. *M. nobile* (Chatham Island forget-me-not). Clump-forming, evergreen perennial with very glossy, ovate to heart-shaped, ribbed, basal leaves, to 30cm (12in) long, with conspicuous veins and wavy margins. In early summer, bears dense, corymb-like cymes of open bell-shaped, pale to dark blue flowers, 1cm (½in) across, sometimes with white-margined lobes. ↕↔ to 60cm (24in). New Zealand (Chatham Island). ❄
M. nobile see *M. hortensia*.

MYOSOTIS

Forget-me-not

BORAGINACEAE

Genus of 50 or more species of annuals, biennials, and clump- or mat-forming perennials found in woods, meadows, swampy soils, and at pond margins in Europe, Asia, Australasia, and North and South America. They produce alternate, variably shaped, hairy leaves, and usually paired cymes of 5-lobed, salverform, occasionally funnel-shaped flowers in blue, yellow, or white, mostly with yellow or white eyes. The dwarf perennials are mainly short-lived but self-seed freely; they are useful for a rock garden, bank, scree bed, or alpine house. Grow *M. scorpioides* at the margins of a pond. *M. sylvatica* is suitable for a mixed or wildflower border; its cultivars are useful for spring bedding.
• **HARDINESS** Fully hardy; *M. alpestris* and *M. explanata* need gritty, sharply drained soil to survive wet winters.
• **CULTIVATION** Grow in moderately fertile or poor, moist but well-drained soil in full sun, with some midday shade, or in partial shade. Dwarf perennials may become coarse in rich soils; in an alpine house, grow in a mix of equal parts loam, leaf mould, and grit. Grow *M. scorpioides* in wet soil, or in an aquatic planting basket as a shallow-water marginal, at a maximum depth of 10cm (4in); see also pp.52–53.

Myosotis alpestris

• **PROPAGATION** Sow seed of annuals and biennials *in situ* in spring or, for spring bedding, in containers in a cold frame or seedbed in early summer. Sow seed of perennials in containers in a cold frame in spring; divide when dormant. Sow seed of *M. scorpioides in situ* in mud at pond margins, or in moist compost in containers in a cold frame, in spring; divide and replant in mud or in baskets in shallow water.
• **PESTS AND DISEASES** Susceptible to powdery and downy mildew. Slugs and snails may cause damage outdoors.

M. alpestris ▣ syn. *M. rupicola* (Alpine forget-me-not). Short-lived, clump-forming perennial with oblong-lance-shaped or spoon-shaped, bright green leaves, to 8cm (3in) long. Dense cymes of salverform, bright blue, yellow-eyed flowers, to 9mm (⅜in) across, are borne from spring to early summer. ↕ 20cm (8in), ↔ to 15cm (6in). Europe. ❄❄❄
M. explanata. Clump- to hummock-forming perennial with rosettes of obovate to spoon-shaped, white-hairy, grey-green leaves, to 7cm (3in) long. In early summer, spreading stems bear large cymes of salverform to funnel-shaped white flowers, to 1cm (½in) across. ↕ to 20cm (8in), ↔ to 15cm (6in). New Zealand (South Island). ❄❄❄
M. palustris see *M. scorpioides*.
M. rupicola see *M. alpestris*.
M. scorpioides, syn. *M. palustris* (Water forget-me-not). Marginal aquatic perennial with creeping rhizomes and upright or semi-upright, angular stems. Leaves are narrowly ovate and mid-green, to 10cm (4in) long at the bases,

Myosotidium hortensia

Myosotis sylvatica 'Music'

Myosotis sylvatica Victoria Series 'Victoria Rose'

becoming slightly longer up the stem. In early summer, bears open cymes of salverform, bright blue flowers, to 8mm (3/8in) across, each with a white, pink, or yellow eye. ↕ 15–30cm (6–12in) or more, ↔ 30cm (12in). Europe, Asia, North America. ✽✽✽. **'Mermaid'** is strong-stemmed and more compact, with dark green leaves, 4–6cm (1½–2½in) long, and bright blue, yellow-eyed flowers; ↕ 15–23cm (6–9in).

M. sylvatica. Tufted, hairy biennial or short-lived perennial, usually grown as a biennial, with ovate to elliptic or lance-shaped, grey-green leaves, to 11cm (4½in) long. From spring to early summer, bears saucer-shaped, yellow-eyed, blue or occasionally white flowers, to 9mm (3/8in) across, in dense cymes. ↕ 12–30cm (5–12in), ↔ to 15cm (6in). Europe. ✽✽✽. Cultivars of **Ball Series** are ball-shaped and compact; ↕ 15cm (6in); **'Blue Ball'** has azure flowers, and **'Snowball'** has white flowers. **'Blue Basket'** is tall and erect, with deep azure flowers; ↕ 25–30cm (10–12in). **'Music'** ■ is vigorous and erect, with large, very bright blue flowers; ↕ to 25cm (10in). **'Pompadour'** is compact and ball-shaped, with large, deep rose-pink flowers; ↕ 15–20cm (6–8in). **'Ultramarine'** is dwarf and compact, with deep indigo-blue flowers; ↕ to 15cm (6in). **Victoria Series** cultivars are dwarf and compact, with white, blue, or pink flowers; **'Victoria Rose'** ■ has bright rose-pink flowers; ↕ 10cm (4in).

▷**Myriad leaf** see *Myriophyllum verticillatum*

MYRICA

MYRICACEAE

Genus of about 50 species of dioecious or monoecious, deciduous and evergreen, usually suckering shrubs and erect trees, found in moist ground worldwide. They have alternate, lance-shaped to ovate, usually aromatic, dark green leaves. *M. cerifera* and *M. gale* are both effective when grown in groups. *M. cerifera* may also be used as a screening plant; *M. gale* is a useful bog garden plant.

- **HARDINESS** Fully hardy to frost hardy.
- **CULTIVATION** Grow in humus-rich, moist soil. *M. gale* will also grow in permanently waterlogged, acid soil. Pruning group 1.
- **PROPAGATION** Sow seed in containers outdoors as soon as ripe. Root greenwood cuttings in early to midsummer. Layer in spring.
- **PESTS AND DISEASES** Trouble free.

M. cerifera (Wax myrtle). Rounded, deciduous or evergreen shrub with upright branches and obovate or narrowly inversely lance-shaped, aromatic leaves, to 10cm (4in) long. In spring, produces inconspicuous, yellow-green male catkins, to 2cm (¾in) long, followed by spherical, waxy, grey-white fruit, 3mm (1/8in) across, borne in dense clusters along the shoots and persisting over winter. ↕↔ 5m (15ft). S.E. USA. ✽✽

M. gale (Bog myrtle, Sweet gale). Thicket-forming, suckering, deciduous shrub with upright branches and inversely lance-shaped, toothed, aromatic leaves, to 6cm (2½in) long. Yellow-brown male catkins, to 1.5cm (½in) long, are borne in mid- and late spring, followed by spherical, yellow-brown fruit, to 3mm (1/8in) across, dotted with resin. ↕↔ 1.5m (5ft). Europe, Asia, North America. ✽✽✽

MYRIOPHYLLUM

Milfoil

HALORAGACEAE

Genus of 45 species of submerged or marginal aquatic annuals and perennials occurring in wet ground, ponds, and streams, widely distributed but mainly found in the S. hemisphere. The foliage is highly decorative, with long, submerged, delicate stems bearing alternate, opposite, or whorled leaves. The submerged leaves are linear to oblong or rounded, and pinnatifid with fine, hair-like segments; the emergent leaves are entire or toothed, and lance-shaped to ovate or linear. Milfoils provide refuge for fish fry, as well as oxygenating the water. Grow in an outdoor pool, or use *M. aquaticum* in a tropical aquarium and *M. hippuroides* and *M. verticillatum* in a cold-water aquarium.

- **HARDINESS** Fully hardy to frost hardy.
- **CULTIVATION** In an aquarium, grow in an inert medium in full light, preferably in hard water, at 10–15°C (50–59°F) for *M. hippuroides* and *M. verticillatum*, 18–24°C (64–75°F) for *M. aquaticum*. Outdoors, grow in baskets of loamy soil in full sun, at a depth of 1m (3ft) for *M. aquaticum* and *M. verticillatum*, and 45cm (18in) for *M. hippuroides*. Top growth may be damaged by frost but should re-emerge below the surface in spring. See also pp.52–53.
- **PROPAGATION** Root cuttings (young tips, or segments) by inserting in the bottom sand.
- **PESTS AND DISEASES** Young growth may be eaten by fishes. Algae or detritus in the water chokes the leaves.

M. aquaticum ■ syn. *M. brasiliense*, *M. proserpinacoides* (Diamond milfoil, Parrot feather). Aquatic perennial with rarely branched stems, to 2m (6ft) long, becoming woody at the bases and often creeping out of shallow water. Rounded, pinnatifid, bright yellowish green submerged leaves, to 4cm (1½in) long, each have 4–8 segments and are arranged in whorls of 4 or 5; rounded, bluish green emergent leaves are shorter. In summer, minute, monoecious, bright yellow-green flowers are produced in spikes from the axils of the submerged leaves. ↔ indefinite. Indonesia (Java), Australia, New Zealand, South America. ✽✽

M. brasiliense see *M. aquaticum.*

M. hippuroides ■ (Western milfoil). Aquatic perennial with thin stems, to 60cm (24in) long. Bears lance-shaped to ovate, pinnatifid, yellow-green submerged leaves, to 2cm (¾in) long, each with up to 25 segments. Linear to lance-shaped, finely divided, olive-green to red emergent leaves, 5cm (2in) long, borne in whorls of 4–6, are usually upward-pointing. Bears minute white flowers from the axils of the emergent leaves in summer. ↔ indefinite. S.W. USA. ✽✽

Myriophyllum aquaticum

Myriophyllum hippuroides

M. proserpinacoides see *M. aquaticum.*

M. verticillatum (Myriad leaf). Aquatic perennial with stems to 1m (3ft) long. Linear, pinnatifid, tightly packed, bright green submerged leaves, to 4cm (1½in) long, are arranged in whorls of 4–6, with 8–16 pairs of opposite segments. Emergent leaves are pinnatifid and comb-like, to 2.5cm (1in) long. In summer, bears yellowish flowers in a spike, to 15cm (6in) tall, just above the water surface. ↔ indefinite. Europe, Asia, North America. ✽✽✽

▷***Myrmecophila tibicinis*** see *Schomburgkia tibicinis*
▷**Myrobalan** see *Prunus cerasifera*
▷**Myrrh, Garden** see *Myrrhis odorata*

MYRRHIS

Sweet Cicely

APIACEAE/UMBELLIFERAE

Genus of one species of aromatic herbaceous perennial originally found in mountains of S. Europe, now widespread in damp sites in Europe and Asia. It has compound umbels of small white flowers and delicate, fern-like foliage. Grow in a mixed border, or in a herb or wildflower garden. Self-seeds freely.

- **HARDINESS** Fully hardy.
- **CULTIVATION** Grow in moderately fertile, moist but well-drained soil in dappled shade. Harvest leaves from early spring to late summer. To improve the flavour and quality of the leaves, remove the flowering stems as they develop.

Myrrhis odorata

• **PROPAGATION** Sow seed in containers in a cold frame in spring or as soon as ripe. Divide in spring or autumn.
• **PESTS AND DISEASES** Trouble free.

M. odorata ■ (Garden myrrh, Sweet Cicely). Perennial with stout, hairy, hollow stems and soft, 2- or 3-pinnate, bright green leaves, to 45cm (18in) long, comprising deeply toothed, oblong to lance-shaped pinnae. Compound umbels of small, star-shaped white flowers, are produced in early summer, followed by ridged, beaked, shiny brown fruit, to 2cm (¾in) long. Aniseed-flavoured leaves and young shoots provide sweetness when cooked with fruit. ↕ 2m (6ft), ↔ 1.5m (5ft). S. Europe. ❄❄❄

MYRSINE

MYRSINACEAE

Genus of about 5 species of dioecious, evergreen, many-branched, upright or rounded shrubs and small trees, found in forest and scrub in Africa, the Azores, the Himalayas, China, and New Zealand. They are mainly cultivated for their alternate, linear or lance-shaped to rounded, usually entire, leathery, sometimes glossy, mid- or dark green leaves. Inconspicuous male and female flowers are borne in umbels on separate plants; both are needed to produce fruit. Grow in a shrub border, against a wall, or in a rock, peat, or woodland garden. In frost-prone areas, grow half-hardy and frost-tender species in a temperate greenhouse.
• **HARDINESS** Frost hardy to frost tender.
• **CULTIVATION** Grow in humus-rich, moist but well-drained soil in full sun or light dappled shade. *M. africana* is lime-tolerant, but will not thrive on shallow, dry, chalk soil. Pruning group 1 or 8.
• **PROPAGATION** Sow seed in containers in a cold frame in autumn. Root semi-ripe cuttings with bottom heat in summer.
• **PESTS AND DISEASES** Trouble free.

M. africana (African boxwood, Cape myrtle). Slow-growing, densely leafy, upright shrub with narrowly obovate to elliptic, aromatic, glossy, dark green leaves, to 2cm (¾in) long. In late spring, produces umbels of 3–6 tiny, yellow-brown flowers. Female plants bear spherical, pale blue fruit, 5mm (¼in) across. ↕ 1.2m (4ft), ↔ 75cm (30in). Azores, E. and S. Africa, Himalayas, China. ❄❄

MYRTEOLA

MYRTACEAE

Genus of 12 species of dwarf, evergreen, mat-forming to rounded, bushy shrubs or subshrubs from upland slopes and raised bogs in South America. They are grown for their attractive fruits and glossy foliage. Leaves are opposite, ovate to rounded, and mid- to dark green. Cup-shaped, 4- or 5-petalled, pale yellow to white flowers are borne singly from the leaf axils from late spring to summer, followed by spherical, pink to dark red berries in autumn. Grow in a peat bed, or a rock or woodland garden.
• **HARDINESS** Fully hardy.
• **CULTIVATION** Grow in humus-rich, moist but well-drained, acid soil in full sun, with some midday shade, or in

Myrteola nummularia

dappled shade. Pruning is not required; trim wayward shoots if necessary.
• **PROPAGATION** Sow seed in containers in an open frame in autumn. Root semi-ripe cuttings, taken with a heel, with bottom heat in summer.
• **PESTS AND DISEASES** Trouble free.

M. nummularia ■ syn. *Myrtus nummularia*. Mat-forming subshrub with branching stems and ovate, dark green leaves, to 8mm (⅜in) long. In early summer, bears white flowers, 8mm (⅜in) across, followed by spherical to ellipsoid pink berries, 7–10mm (¼–½in) long. ↕ 5cm (2in), ↔ 30cm (12in). S. Chile, S. Argentina, Falkland Islands. ❄❄❄

MYRTILLOCACTUS

CACTACEAE

Genus of 4 species of shrubby or tree-like perennial cacti from semi-arid areas of Mexico and Guatemala. They have deep bluish green stems and thick, erect branches with 5–8 ribs and spiny, felted areoles. Open funnel-shaped, short-tubed flowers are borne from the upper lateral areoles in summer, followed by ovoid, purplish blue fruits. Where temperatures drop below 10°C (50°F), grow in a warm greenhouse. In warmer areas, grow in a rock or desert garden.
• **HARDINESS** Frost tender.
• **CULTIVATION** Under glass, grow in standard cactus compost in full light with low humidity. From mid-spring to early autumn, water moderately and apply a low-nitrogen fertilizer monthly; keep just moist at other times. Outdoors, grow in poor to moderately

Myrtillocactus geometrizans

fertile, sharply drained soil in full sun. Provide protection from excessive winter wet. See also pp.48–49.
• **PROPAGATION** Sow seed at 19–24°C (66–75°F), or take stem cuttings, both in spring.
• **PESTS AND DISEASES** Susceptible to damage by mealybugs.

M. cochal. Tree-like cactus with mid-green stems, 15cm (6in) or more thick, with 6–8 shallow-grooved ribs and grey or black spines (3–5 radials and sometimes 1 longer central). White or pale yellow flowers, 2.5cm (1in) across, tinged green or purple, are borne both diurnally and nocturnally in early and midsummer. ↕ 1m (3ft), ↔ 45cm (18in). N.W. Mexico. ❁ (min. 10°C/50°F)
M. geometrizans ■ Tree-like cactus with bluish green stems, to 10cm (4in) thick, branching from about 30cm (12in) above ground level. Each has 5–6 smooth, acute ribs with 5–9 red-brown then grey radial spines and 1 longer, almost black central spine. White or cream flowers, 2.5–3.5cm (1–1½in) across, are produced diurnally in early and midsummer. ↕ 4m (12ft), ↔ 2m (6ft). Mexico. ❁ (min. 10°C/50°F)

▷**Myrtle** see *Myrtus*
Bog see *Myrica gale*
Cape see *Myrsine africana*, *Phylica*
Common see *Myrtus communis*
Crepe see *Lagerstroemia indica*
Giant crepe see *Lagerstroemia speciosa*
Heath see *Thryptomene*
Lemon-scented see *Backhousia citriodora*, *Darwinia citriodora*
Queen's crepe see *Lagerstroemia speciosa*
Sand see *Leiophyllum buxifolium*
Sea see *Baccharis halimifolia*
Snow see *Calytrix alpestris*
Tarentum see *Myrtus communis* subsp. *tarentina*
Wax see *Myrica cerifera*
Western tea see *Melaleuca nesophila*

MYRTUS

Myrtle

MYRTACEAE

Genus of one species of rounded, evergreen shrub occurring in scrub, woodland, and woodland margins in the Mediterranean region. Myrtles are cultivated for their aromatic leaves and their solitary, bowl-shaped, fragrant white flowers, which are borne from summer to autumn. They are suitable for a mixed or shrub border, or for growing against a wall. They may also be grown as free-standing specimen shrubs or as an informal hedge. They need long, hot summers to produce flowers and fruits.
• **HARDINESS** Frost hardy.
• **CULTIVATION** Grow in moderately fertile, moist but well-drained soil in full sun, sheltered from cold, drying winds. Pruning group 9, or group 13 if wall-trained.
• **PROPAGATION** Sow seed in containers in a cold frame in autumn. Root semi-ripe cuttings with bottom heat in late summer.
• **PESTS AND DISEASES** Trouble free.

M. apiculata see *Luma apiculata*.
M. bullata see *Lophomyrtus bullata*.
***M. bullata* 'Gloriosa'** see *Lophomyrtus* x *ralphii* 'Variegata'.
M. chequen see *Luma chequen*.
M. communis ■ (Common myrtle). Upright, bushy shrub, arching with age, bearing opposite, ovate, glossy, dark green leaves, to 5cm (2in) long. From mid- to late summer or early autumn, produces solitary, 5-petalled flowers, 2cm (¾in) across, with conspicuous central tufts of white stamens; the flowers are followed by oblong-ellipsoid, purple-black berries, 1cm (½in) long. ↕↔ 3m (10ft). Mediterranean. ❄❄. **var. *acutifolia*** is more erect in habit, with long-pointed, lance-shaped leaves. **'Flore Pleno'** has double white flowers. **'Jenny Reitenbach'** see subsp. *tarentina*. **'Leucocarpa'** has white berries. **'Microphylla'** see subsp. *tarentina*. **'Nana'** see subsp. *tarentina*. **subsp. *tarentina***, syn. 'Jenny Reitenbach', 'Microphylla', 'Nana' (Tarentum myrtle), is more compact and rounded, with narrowly elliptic leaves, to 2cm (¾in) long, and pink-tinted cream flowers, followed by white berries; ↕↔ 1.5m (5ft). **subsp. *tarentina* 'Microphylla Variegata'** is similar to subsp. *tarentina*, but has white-margined leaves. **'Variegata'** has leaves margined creamy white.
M. lechleriana see *Amomyrtus luma*.
M. luma see *Luma apiculata*.
***M. luma* of gardens** see *Amomyrtus luma*.
M. nummularia see *Myrteola nummularia*.
***M.* x *ralphii* 'Variegata'** see *Lophomyrtus* x *ralphii* 'Variegata'.
M. ugni see *Ugni molinae*.

Myrtus communis

N

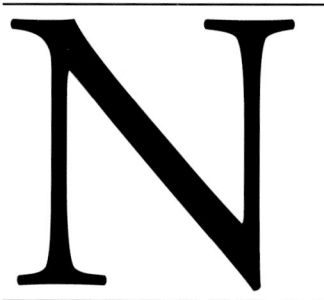

▷ ***Naegelia cinnabarina*** see *Smithiantha cinnabarina*
▷ ***Naegelia zebrina*** see *Smithiantha zebrina*
▷ **Naked ladies** see *Colchicum*
▷ ***Nananthus rubrolineata*** see *Aloinopsis rubrolineata*
▷ ***Nananthus schooneesii*** see *Aloinopsis schooneesii*

NANDINA

BERBERIDACEAE

Genus of one species of evergreen or semi-evergreen shrub, with alternate, pinnate leaves, from mountain valleys in India, China, and Japan. *N. domestica* is grown for its flowers, fruit, and elegant foliage. Grow in a shrub border; low-growing cultivars are fine ground cover.

• **HARDINESS** Frost hardy.
• **CULTIVATION** Grow in a sheltered site in moist but well-drained soil, preferably in full sun. Pruning group 9.
• **PROPAGATION** Sow seed in containers in a cold frame as soon as ripe. Root semi-ripe cuttings in summer.
• **PESTS AND DISEASES** Viruses can cause narrow, distorted leaflets to develop.

N. domestica ▣ (Heavenly bamboo). Evergreen or semi-evergreen shrub with upright shoots and pinnate to 3-pinnate leaves, to 90cm (36in) long, with lance-shaped leaflets, red to reddish purple when young and in winter. In mid-summer, bears conical panicles, to 40cm (16in) long, of small, star-shaped white flowers, to 1cm (½in) across, with large yellow anthers, followed by long-lasting, spherical, bright red fruit, 8mm (⅜in) across. ↕ 2m (6ft), ↔ 1.5m (5ft). India, China, Japan. ✲✲. **'Fire Power'** is dwarf and compact, with bright red leaves; ↕ 45cm (18in), ↔ 60cm (24in). **'Harbor Dwarf'** is compact; ↕ 1m (3ft), ↔ 1.2m (4ft). **'Umpqua Chief'** is compact; ↕ 1.5m (5ft), ↔ 1.2m (4ft).

Nandina domestica

NARCISSUS

Daffodil

AMARYLLIDACEAE

Genus of about 150 species of bulbous perennials from Europe and N. Africa, usually found in meadows from sea level to subalpine altitudes, and in woodland, river silts, and rock crevices. Thousands of cultivars have been developed. All are grown for their attractive flowers, borne in spring, sometimes autumn or winter. Leafless stems bear between 1 and 20 flowers, each with 6 spreading perianth segments (petals) surrounding an almost flat or long and narrow corona (the cup or trumpet). The flowers are mostly yellow or white, occasionally green; some have red, orange, or pink coronas. The leaves are basal, often strap-shaped or cylindrical, and 15–75cm (6–30in) long, depending on the species.

Most daffodils are suitable for planting between shrubs or in a border, or for growing in containers; many are easily naturalized in grass or in a woodland garden. They are excellent for cutting. Smaller species, hybrids, and cultivars are good rock garden plants; some can be naturalized in fine, short grass. *N. cantabricus, N. romieuxii,* and *N. rupicola* either need a warm, dry summer dormancy or produce delicate flowers early in the year, and are therefore best grown in an alpine house or bulb frame. In frost-prone areas, grow the less hardy members of Division 8 in a cool greenhouse. Contact with the sap of daffodils may irritate skin; all parts may cause severe discomfort if ingested.

For horticultural purposes, daffodils are split into 13 divisions, each with distinct characteristics. All are of garden origin, except for Division 13 species. The spreads given for each division provide a guide to planting distance.

Division 1. Trumpet
Flowers are solitary, each with a trumpet (corona) as long as, or longer than, the perianth segments. Usually early and mid-spring-flowering. ↔ 8–16cm (3–6in).
Division 2. Large-cupped
Flowers are solitary, each with a cup (corona) more than one-third the length of, but not as long as, the perianth segments. Some are scented. Spring-flowering. ↔ 16cm (6in).
Division 3. Small-cupped
Flowers are solitary, each with a cup (corona) up to one-third the length of the perianth segments. Some are scented. Spring-flowering. ↔ 16cm (6in).
Division 4. Double
Each stem has one or more flowers, with doubling of the perianth segments or the corona or both. Some are sweetly scented. Usually early and mid-spring-flowering. ↔ 16cm (6in).
Division 5. Triandrus
Each stem produces 2 or more nodding flowers, with reflexed perianth segments and relatively short cups (coronas). Mid- and late spring-flowering. ↔ 5–8cm (2–3in).
Division 6. Cyclamineus
Flowers are solitary, each acutely angled to the stem, with significantly reflexed perianth segments and usually a long cup or trumpet (corona). Usually early spring-flowering. ↔ 8cm (3in).
Division 7. Jonquilla and Apodanthus
Each stem produces 1–5 (rarely 8) usually scented flowers, with spreading or reflexed perianth segments, and with cup-shaped, funnel-shaped, or flared coronas usually wider than they are long. Usually mid- and late spring-flowering. ↔ 8cm (3in).
Division 8. Tazetta
Small-flowered cultivars produce 3–20 flowers per stem; larger-flowered cultivars bear 3 or 4 flowers per stem. They have stout stems, wide leaves, broad perianth segments, and small cups (coronas). They are usually scented, and are good as cut flowers. Some cultivars are half-hardy and should be grown in a cool greenhouse. Late autumn- to late spring-flowering. ↔ 8cm (3in).
Division 9. Poeticus
Flowers are usually fragrant, and usually solitary, with pure white perianth segments. The small, open cups (coronas) usually have green and/or yellow centres and red rims, but may be of a single colour. Late spring- and early summer-flowering. ↔ 16cm (6in).
Division 10. Bulbocodium
Flowers are usually solitary, with dominant cups (coronas) and relatively small perianth segments. Winter- and early spring-flowering. ↔ 5–8cm (2–3in), or 16cm (6in) for larger bulbs.
Division 11. Split-corona
Flowers are usually solitary, with the corona usually split for more than half its length. Spring-flowering. ↔ 16cm (6in). There are 2 subdivisions:
Division 11a. Collar – The corona segments are opposite the perianth segments.
Division 11b. Papillon – The corona segments are alternate to the perianth segments.
Division 12. Other daffodil cultivars
Includes daffodil cultivars that do not fit the definition of any other division. ↔ 5–8cm (2–3in) or 16cm (6in), depending on the size of the bulbs.
Division 13. Daffodils distinguished solely by botanical name
Includes all wild daffodils and their wild hybrids, such as the single-flowered *N. pseudonarcissus* and the multi-headed *N. tazetta.* Some are difficult to grow in an open garden. Autumn- to spring-flowering. ↔ 5–8cm (2–3in), or 16cm (6in) for larger bulbs.

• **HARDINESS** Fully hardy to half hardy.
• **CULTIVATION** Plant bulbs at one-and-a-half times their own depth in autumn, slightly deeper in light soils and in grass.

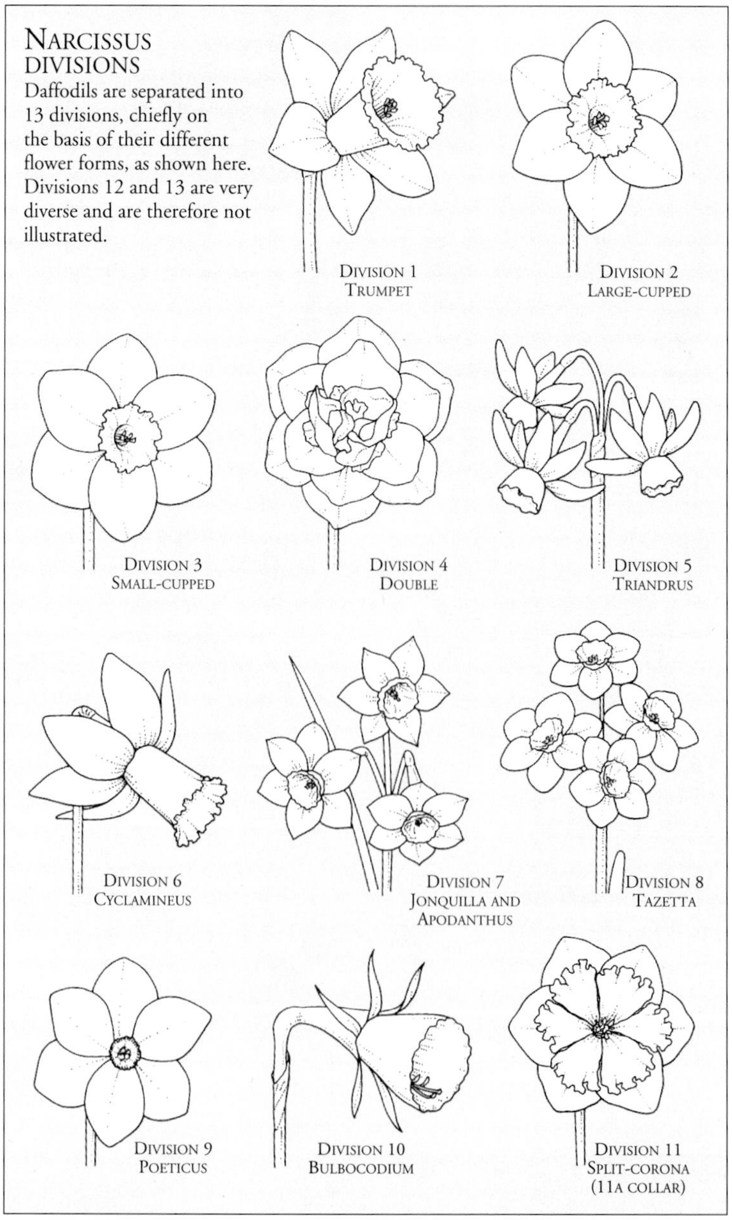

N

NARCISSUS

Narcissus 'Acropolis'

Narcissus 'Actaea'

Narcissus 'Altruist

Narcissus 'Altun Ha'

Narcissus 'Arkle'

Narcissus 'Avalanche'

Narcissus 'Beryl'

Narcissus 'Border Beauty'

Narcissus 'Bravoure'

Most grow best in moderately fertile soil, well-drained but moist in the growing season. *N. asturiensis*, *N. bulbocodium*, *N. cyclamineus*, *N. triandrus*, and their cultivars need neutral to acid soils. *N. jonquilla* and *N. tazetta* prefer slightly alkaline soils. Most daffodils thrive in full sun or dappled part-day shade. *N. assoanus* and *N. asturiensis* require full sun. Division 6 daffodils like cooler conditions and do well in grass. Division 7 and 8 daffodils flower best in full sun and drier soils. Water late-flowering daffodils in dry spring weather (flowers may abort in dry conditions). Dead-head plants as flowers fade, and allow leaves to die down naturally for at least 6 weeks. Apply a low-nitrogen, high-potash fertilizer after flowering if bulbs are not performing well. Lift and divide clumps when flowering becomes sparse or the clumps congested. If daffodils are naturalized in grass, delay the first cut until 4–6 weeks after flowers have faded; for species such as *N. bulbocodium*, *N. cyclamineus*, and *N. pseudonarcissus*, delay cutting until seeds have dispersed.

Under glass, grow in a mix of 2 parts loam-based potting compost (JI No.2) and 1 part grit. Plunge containers outdoors in a cool, shady spot and keep dry when dormant.

For indoor display, plant bulbs 5cm (2in) deep in early autumn in loamless or loam-based potting compost (JI No.2). Plunge in a cold frame outdoors until the roots are well-established and shoots appear. Keep cool and moist, and protect from frost. Move into a cool greenhouse in full light, and gradually increase the temperature to 10°C (50°F), then to no more than 18°C (64°F) when flowering. Water freely and apply a half-strength, high-potash fertilizer weekly. Bring indoors as the buds begin to open. Discard or plant out into the garden after flowering.

• **PROPAGATION** Sow seed of species as soon as ripe in deep containers in a cold frame. Cultivars do not come true from seed, but new cultivars are often selected from seed of crosses between cultivars, or from open-pollinated seed. After germination, keep frost-free, cool, and moist. After 2 years, transfer seedlings to a nursery bed and grow on until they reach flowering size, which may take up to 7 years. Alternatively, separate and replant offsets as leaves fade in early summer, or in early autumn before new roots are produced.

• **PESTS AND DISEASES** The most serious problems include large narcissus bulb fly, narcissus eelworm, slugs, narcissus basal rot and other fungal infections, viruses (including narcissus yellow stripe virus), and bulb scale mite on bulbs forced for early flowering.

***N.* 'Acropolis'** ▣ Division 4 daffodil bearing well-formed, double flowers, 11cm (4½in) across, in mid-spring. Numerous snow-white segments are interspersed with bright orange-red ones. ↕45cm (18in). ***

***N.* 'Actaea'** ▣ Division 9 daffodil producing strongly scented flowers, 8.5cm (3¼in) across, in late spring. Open, wavy, pure white perianth segments surround the red ribbon-like margin of each flattened, bowl-shaped yellow corona. ↕45cm (18in). ***

***N.* 'Albus Plenus Odoratus'** see *N. poeticus* 'Plenus'.

***N.* 'Altruist'** ▣ Division 3 daffodil flowering in mid-spring. Flowers, 8–8.5cm (3–3¼in) across, have pointed, pale apricot perianth segments and fluted, bright orange-red cups. Colour fades rapidly in sunlight. ↕45cm (18in). ***

***N.* 'Altun Ha'** ▣ Division 2 daffodil producing soft greenish lemon-yellow flowers, 12cm (5in) across, with rounded, overlapping perianth segments and wide, fluted cups, in mid-spring. Cups gradually fade to white. ↕40cm (16in). ***

***N.* 'Arctic Gold'.** Division 1 daffodil. In mid-spring, bears smooth, waxy, rich golden yellow flowers, 9.5cm (3¾in) across, with widely flanged, deeply notched trumpets. ↕40cm (16in). ***

***N.* 'Arkle'** ▣ Strong, vigorous Division 1 daffodil. Flowers, 12.5cm (5in) across, among the largest of the yellow trumpet daffodils, are borne in mid-spring. Perianth segments are smooth and each corona is slightly flared, with a roll at the mouth. ↕40cm (16in). ***

N. assoanus, syn. *N. juncifolius*, *N. requienii* (Rush-leaved jonquil). Tiny Division 13 daffodil with thin, cylindrical leaves, to 20cm (8in) long. In mid-spring, bears circular, scented, golden yellow flowers, 2cm (¾in) across, singly or in pairs. ↕15cm (6in). S. France, S. and E. Spain. ***

N. asturiensis, syn. *N. minimus* of gardens. Division 13 daffodil with spreading, channelled, glaucous, mid-green leaves, to 15cm (6in) long. In late winter and early spring, bears solitary, pale yellow flowers, 3.5cm (1½in) across, with narrow perianth segments and waisted trumpets. ↕8cm (3in). N. Portugal, N. and C. Spain. ***

***N.* 'Avalanche'** ▣ Division 8 daffodil producing 10 or more sweetly scented flowers, 3.5cm (1½in) across, with pure white perianth segments and lemon-yellow cups, in mid-spring. Long-lasting as cut flowers. ↕35cm (14in). **

***N.* 'Avalon'** ▣ Division 2 daffodil flowering in mid-spring. Circular, bright lemon-yellow flowers, 11cm (4½in) across, have wide, fluted coronas that become white with age. ↕35cm (14in). ***

***N.* 'Badbury Rings'.** Division 3 daffodil with slightly scented flowers, 10cm (4in) across, in mid-spring. Has broadly ovate, smooth, deep yellow perianth segments, and shallowly bowl-shaped, vivid yellow cups with clearly defined, bright orange-red rims. ↕45cm (18in). ***

***N.* 'Bantam'.** Division 2 daffodil with well-shaped flowers, 5.5cm (2¼in) across, on stiff stems, produced in mid-spring. Short, bright golden yellow perianth segments surround short, flared, intense orange cups with orange-red rims. ↕20–24cm (8–10in). ***

***N.* 'Barnum'.** Very vigorous Division 1 daffodil. In early spring, produces deep golden yellow flowers, 12cm (5in) across, with very broad, spreading perianth segments and wide, cylindrical trumpets, generously flanged and indented at the mouths. ↕50cm (20in). ***

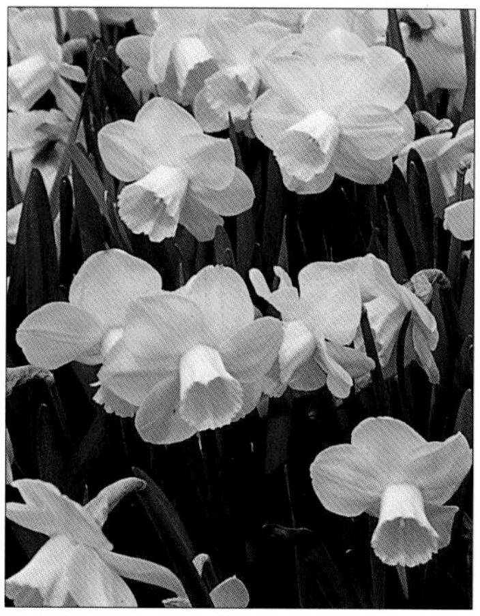

Narcissus 'Avalon'

***N.* 'Bell Song'.** Division 7 daffodil. In mid- and late spring, produces 2 or 3 flower stems, each with 1 or 2 nodding white flowers, 4cm (1½in) across, with pale pink cups. ↕30cm (12in). ***

***N.* 'Berlin'.** Division 2 daffodil flowering in mid-spring. Flowers, 8.25cm (3¼in) across, have rounded, greenish yellow perianth segments and vivid yellow coronas, each with a broad band of orange at the frilled mouth. ↕40cm (16in). ***

***N.* 'Beryl'** ▣ Vigorous Division 6 daffodil flowering in early spring Flowers, 7.5cm (3in) across, have reflexed perianth segments, opening yellow but quickly fading to creamy white, and small yellow and orange cups. ↕20cm (8in). ***

***N.* 'Bobbysoxer'.** Division 7 daffodil producing 1 or 2 flowers per stem, in late spring. Flowers, 3cm (1¼in) across, have primrose-yellow perianth segments and yellow and orange cups. ↕18cm (7in). ***

***N.* 'Border Beauty'** ▣ Division 2 daffodil flowering in mid-spring. Flowers, 11cm (4½in) across, have triangular, overlapping, deep yellow perianth segments and shallowly bowl-shaped, deep orange-red coronas, wavy at the mouths and reflexed at the rims. ↕45cm (18in). ***

***N.* 'Bravoure'** ▣ Division 1 daffodil flowering in mid-spring. Flowers, 12cm (5in) across, have unusually long and slender yellow trumpets and slightly pointed, overlapping white perianth segments. ↕45cm (18in). ***

***N.* 'Broomhill'.** Long-lasting Division 2 daffodil producing robust, well-proportioned, smooth, waxy, pure white flowers, 10cm (4in) across, in mid-spring. ↕40cm (16in). ***

***N.* 'Bryanston'.** Vigorous Division 2 daffodil bearing yellow flowers, 9.5–10cm (3¾–4in) across, in mid-spring. Pointed, smooth, wide perianth segments lie very flat; cups are indented. ↕40cm (16in). ***

N. bulbocodium ▣ (Hoop-petticoat daffodil). Small Division 13 daffodil with narrow, semi-cylindrical, dark green leaves, 10–40cm (4–16in) long. In mid-spring, bears funnel-shaped, pale yellow to deep yellow flowers, 3.5cm (1½in) across, with expanded trumpets and tiny, pointed perianth segments. Can be naturalized in damp grass that dries out in summer. ↕10–15cm (4–6in). S.W. and W. France, Portugal, Spain, N. Africa. ***. **var. *citrinus*** has pale lemon-yellow flowers. **'Golden Bells'** ▣ syn *N.* 'Golden Bells', is an exceptionally vigorous Division 10 daffodil producing long-lasting, weather-resistant, deep yellow flowers, 10cm (4in) across, on strong stems in early spring; ↕17cm (7in).

***N.* 'Burning Bush'** ▣ Robust Division 3 daffodil. In late spring, produces flowers, 11cm (4½in) across, with rounded, spreading, deep golden yellow perianth segments and very shallowly bowl-shaped, deep red cups. ↕50cm (20in). ***

Narcissus bulbocodium

Narcissus bulbocodium 'Golden Bells'

Narcissus 'Burning Bush'

Narcissus 'Camelot'

Narcissus 'Camoro'

Narcissus 'Cantabile'

Narcissus 'Cassata'

Narcissus 'Charity May'

Narcissus 'Cheerfulness'

Narcissus 'Chit Chat'

Narcissus 'Cool Crystal'

Narcissus cyclamineus

***N.* 'Camelot'** ■ Division 2 daffodil producing clear, deep yellow flowers, 11cm (4½in) across, in mid-spring. Perianth segments are very broadly ovate, with blunt tips; coronas are funnel-shaped, flared, and loosely frilled at the mouths. ↕35cm (14in). ***

***N.* 'Camoro'** ■ Division 10 daffodil producing flowers, 3cm (1¼in) across, in very early spring. Almost insignificant perianth segments are creamy white with green at the bases and at the midribs; wide, funnel-shaped coronas are pale creamy white. ↕15cm (6in). ***

N. campernelli see *N.* x *odorus*.

***N.* 'Cantabile'** ■ Division 9 daffodil. In late spring, stiff stems bear neat, well-rounded white flowers, 4cm (1½in) across, with tiny, red-rimmed, green and yellow cups. ↕25cm (10in). ***

N. cantabricus ■ (White hoop-petticoat daffodil). Division 13 daffodil with narrow, semi-cylindrical, slightly channelled leaves, to 15cm (6in) long. In winter, bears funnel-shaped white flowers, 3.5cm (1½in) across, with tiny, pointed perianth segments and expanded trumpets. ↕15–20cm (6–8in). S. Spain, N. Africa. ***

***N.* 'Cantatrice'.** Division 1 daffodil with pure white flowers, 11cm (4½in) across, in mid-spring. Perianth segments are pointed; trumpets are smooth and slender. ↕40cm (16in). ***

***N.* 'Capax Plenus'** see *N.* 'Eystettensis'.

***N.* 'Cassata'** ■ Division 11a daffodil. In mid-spring, produces flowers 10cm (4in) across, with pure white perianth segments nearly obscured by flattened corona segments, which open lemon-yellow and become white. ↕40cm (16in). ***

***N.* 'Castanets'.** Robust Division 8 daffodil. In early spring, each stem bears 4–8 scented flowers, 5cm (2in) across, with broadly ovate, slightly reflexed, deep golden yellow perianth segments and shallowly bowl-shaped orange coronas, wavy at the mouths. ↕35cm (14in). ***

***N.* 'Cedric Morris'.** Division 1 daffodil. In early winter, bears lemon-yellow flowers, 8cm (3in) across, with narrow perianth segments and waisted trumpets. ↕15cm (6in). ***

***N.* 'Charity May'** ■ Division 6 daffodil bearing lemon-yellow flowers, 9cm (3½in) across, with broad, reflexed perianth segments and long cups, in early spring. ↕30cm (12in). ***

***N.* 'Cheerfulness'** ■ Division 4 daffodil flowering in mid-spring. Each stem bears several sweetly scented, double white flowers, 5.5cm (2¼in) across, with clusters of cream segments in the centres. ↕40cm (16in). ***

***N.* 'Cherrygardens'.** Division 2 daffodil flowering in mid-spring. Flowers, 10.5cm (4¼in) across, have overlapping, sparkling white perianth segments and intense pink coronas, with darker rims and green eyes. ↕40cm (16in). ***

***N.* 'Chit Chat'** ■ Free-flowering Division 7 daffodil producing sweetly scented, golden yellow flowers, 3cm (1¼in) across, in late spring. Each slender stem bears 2–3 flowers with rounded, overlapping perianth segments and expanded, shallowly bowl-shaped coronas. ↕17cm (7in) ***

***N.* 'Conestoga'.** Division 2 daffodil flowering in mid-spring. Circular flowers, 9cm (3½in), across, have very broad, rounded white perianth segments and shallow, ribbed coronas that open orange and soon become apricot-yellow, with green at the bases and orange at the rims. ↕40cm (16in). ***

***N.* 'Cool Crystal'** ■ Division 3 daffodil with white flowers, 10.5cm (4¼in) across, produced in mid-spring. Bowl-shaped coronas have green eyes. ↕50cm (20in). ***

***N.* 'Crackington'.** Very vigorous and free-flowering Division 4 daffodil with double flowers, 10.5cm (4¼in) across, in early spring. Each flower consists of neat whorls of yellow perianth segments interspersed with corona segments, which open orange and become paler with age. ↕40cm (16in). ***

***N.* 'Crowndale'.** Division 4 daffodil flowering in early spring. Bears double flowers, 9.5cm (3¾in) across, with whorls of yellow perianth segments intermingled with short, bright orange-red corona segments. ↕40cm (16in). ***

***N.* 'Cryptic'.** Division 1 daffodil. In mid-spring, produces well-shaped flowers, 11cm (4½in) across, with broad white perianth segments and long, apple-blossom-pink trumpets. ↕40cm (16in). ***

N. cyclamineus ■ Robust, vigorous Division 13 daffodil with spreading, narrow, keeled, bright green leaves, 12–30cm (5–12in) long. Bears solitary, nodding, golden yellow flowers, 4.5cm (1¾in) long, in early spring. Narrow perianth segments are completely reflexed from the long, narrow-waisted trumpets. ↕15–20cm (6–8in). N.W. Portugal, N.W. Spain. ***

***N.* 'Daydream'.** Division 2 daffodil flowering in mid-spring. Flowers, 8cm (3in) across, have greenish yellow perianth segments; each cup has a white halo surrounding the base. At maturity, cups become almost white. ↕35cm (14in). ***

***N.* 'Decoy'.** Division 2 daffodil freely producing flowers, 9.5cm (3¾in) across, in mid-spring. Broadly ovate white perianth segments surround short, funnel-shaped, finely frilled, deep rose-red cups. ↕40cm (16in). ***

***N.* 'Diversity'.** Free-flowering Division 11a daffodil. In mid-spring, produces flowers, 9.5cm (3¾in) across, with broad, flat, pure white perianth segments and large, shallowly bowl-shaped, apple-blossom-pink coronas, each with 6 reflexed lobes, shading to white at the centres and at the rims. ↕40cm (16in). ***

***N.* 'Dove Wings'** ■ Division 6 daffodil flowering in early spring. Flowers, 8.5cm (3¼in) across, have broad, creamy white perianth segments swept back from long, clear lemon-yellow cups. ↕30cm (12in). ***

***N.* 'Dr. Hugh'.** Division 3 daffodil flowering in mid-spring. Flowers, 11cm (4½in) across, have smooth white perianth segments surrounding small orange cups with clear green eyes. ↕50cm (20in). ***

***N.* 'Dutch Delight'** ■ Strong, vigorous Division 2 daffodil flowering in early or mid-spring. Flowers, 10cm (4in) across, have broadly ovate, slightly pointed, deep golden yellow perianth segments and long, flared, trumpet-shaped, deep orange-red coronas, slightly frilled at the mouths. ↕45cm (18in). ***

***N.* 'Dutch Master'.** Prolific Division 1 daffodil. In mid-spring, bears golden yellow flowers, 11cm (4½in) across, with broadly ovate perianth segments and coronas expanded at the deeply indented mouths. ↕45cm (18in). ***

***N.* 'Electrus'.** Division 11a daffodil. In mid-spring bears flowers, 10cm (4in) across, with broadly ovate, slightly reflexed white perianth segments and large, flat coronas, each with 6 reflexed, bright pinkish orange segments, enhanced by a green eye. ↕40cm (16in). ***

***N.* 'Elizabeth Ann'** ■ Division 6 daffodil. In mid-spring, bears flowers, 8cm (3in) across, with reflexed white perianth segments and bowl-shaped, lightly ribbed white coronas, with green eyes and sharply defined, apple-blossom-pink rims. ↕25cm (10in). ***

***N.* 'Empress of Ireland'** ■ Division 1 daffodil flowering in mid-spring. Produces white flowers, 10–11cm (4–4½in) across, with very broad, triangular, overlapping perianth segments and narrow, widely flanged

Narcissus cantabricus

N

trumpets. Among the largest white trumpet daffodils. ↕40cm (16in). ❄❄❄
N. 'Ethos' ■ Vigorous, upright Division 1 daffodil bearing golden yellow flowers, 11cm (4½in) across, in mid-spring. Has long, cylindrical, slightly expanding trumpets backed by gently reflexed, triangular, spreading perianth segments. ↕50cm (20in). ❄❄❄
N. 'Eystettensis', syn. *N.* 'Capax Plenus' (Queen Anne's double daffodil). Division 4 daffodil with fully double, lemon-yellow flowers, 6cm (2½in) across, with many rows of evenly overlapping perianth segments, borne in mid-spring. ↕23cm (9in). ❄❄❄
N. 'Falconet'. Division 8 daffodil. In early spring, each stem bears 3–5 fragrant flowers, 4cm (1½in) across, with overlapping, deep yellow perianth segments and small, bowl-shaped, bright orange coronas. ↕40cm (16in). ❄❄❄
N. 'February Gold' ■ Vigorous Division 6 daffodil flowering in early spring. Flowers, 7.5cm (3in) across, have reflexed, golden yellow perianth segments and long, slightly darker trumpets. ↕30cm (12in). ❄❄❄
N. 'Foundling'. Division 6 daffodil flowering in mid-spring. Flowers, 7cm (3in) across, have broad white perianth segments, well-reflexed from short, clear rose-pink cups. ↕30cm (12in). ❄❄❄
N. 'Fragrant Rose' ■ Fragrant Division 2 daffodil flowering in late spring. Each flower is 9.5cm (3¾in) across, with rounded white perianth segments, pink-tinted with age, and a green-eyed conical cup of deep reddish pink. ↕45cm (18in). ❄❄❄
N. 'Gay Kybo'. Division 4 daffodil producing well-formed, double flowers, 10.5cm (4¼in) across, in mid-spring. Regularly arranged, creamy white perianth segments surround shorter, rich orange corona segments. ↕45cm (18in). ❄❄❄
N. 'Geranium'. Division 8 daffodil bearing up to 6 scented, glistening white flowers, 5.5cm (2¼in) across, with

Narcissus 'High Society'

bright orange-red cups, in mid- and late spring. Excellent for cutting. ↕35cm (14in). ❄❄❄
N. 'Glenfarclas'. Division 1 daffodil flowering in mid-spring. Flowers, 11cm (4½in) across, have broad, deep yellow perianth segments and cylindrical, deep orange trumpets, slightly expanded at the rims. ↕38cm (15in). ❄❄❄
N. 'Gold Bond' ■ Robust Division 2 daffodil. In mid-spring, bears deep golden yellow flowers, 11cm (4½in) across, with smooth, spreading perianth segments and slightly frilled and expanded, cylindrical coronas. ↕50cm (20in). ❄❄❄
N. 'Gold Convention' ■ Division 2 daffodil flowering in mid-spring. Each golden yellow flower, 11cm (4½in) across, has broadly ovate, blunt-tipped perianth segments and a long, cylindrical corona, expanded and lightly frilled at the mouth, and turning almost orange with age. ↕50cm (20in). ❄❄❄
N. 'Golden Aura'. Division 2 daffodil producing rich golden yellow flowers, 9.5cm (3¾in) across, in mid-spring. Flowers have smooth, flat perianth segments and large, well-proportioned, bell-shaped cups. ↕40cm (16in). ❄❄❄
N. 'Golden Bells' see *N. bulbocodium* 'Golden Bells'.
N. 'Golden Ducat' ■ Division 4 daffodil bearing double, golden yellow flowers, 11cm (4½in) across, with many layers of pointed segments, in mid-spring. ↕35cm (14in). ❄❄❄
N. 'Golden Vale'. Division 1 daffodil. In mid-spring, bears rich golden yellow flowers, 12cm (5in) across, with the trumpets expanding towards the indented mouths. ↕45cm (18in). ❄❄❄
N. 'Goldfinger' ■ Vigorous Division 1 daffodil. In mid-spring, bears long-lasting, deep yellow flowers, 11cm (4½in) across, with broad, rounded perianth segments and neatly expanded, cylindrical trumpets. ↕43cm (17in). ❄❄❄
N. 'Grand Soleil d'Or' ■ Division 8 daffodil with each stem bearing many scented, double, gold and tangerine-orange flowers, 4.5cm (1¾in) across, in early spring. ↕45cm (18in). ❄❄
N. 'Gull'. Division 2 daffodil producing flowers, 11cm (4½in) across, in mid-spring. Has triangular, smooth, pure white perianth segments and funnel-shaped, loosely frilled white coronas, shaded green at the bases. ↕45cm (18in). ❄❄❄
N. 'Halley's Comet'. Division 3 daffodil. In mid-spring produces flowers, 10cm (4in) across, with rounded, milk-white perianth segments and very shallowly bowl-shaped, deep yellow cups, green at the bases. ↕45cm (18in). ❄❄❄
N. 'Hartlebury'. Division 3 daffodil flowering in mid-spring. Each flower, 10cm (4in) across, has broadly ovate, overlapping, pure white perianth segments and a disc-shaped, ribbed, deep red corona, orange at the base. ↕40cm (16in). ❄❄❄
N. 'Hawera' ■ Slender Division 5 daffodil with multiple stems per bulb, each bearing up to 5 canary-yellow flowers, 3–5cm (1¼–2in) across, with slightly reflexed perianth segments, in late spring. ↕18cm (7in). ❄❄
N. 'Highfield Beauty'. Division 8 daffodil producing stems with up to 3

Narcissus 'Dove Wings'

Narcissus 'Dutch Delight'

Narcissus 'Elizabeth Ann'

Narcissus 'Empress of Ireland'

Narcissus 'Ethos'

Narcissus 'February Gold'

Narcissus 'Fragrant Rose'

Narcissus 'Gold Bond'

Narcissus 'Gold Convention'

Narcissus 'Golden Ducat'

Narcissus 'Goldfinger'

Narcissus 'Grand Soleil d'Or'

slightly scented, butter-yellow flowers, 6.5cm (2½in) across, in mid-spring. The small cups are several shades darker than the smooth, overlapping perianth segments. ↕50cm (20in). ❄❄❄
N. 'High Society' ■ Vigorous Division 2 daffodil producing flowers, 11cm (4½in) across, in mid-spring. Perianth segments are broadly ovate, overlapping, and white. Cup-shaped coronas are yellow fading to white, with green bases, and slightly flanged and indented, deep rose-pink rims. ↕55cm (22in). ❄❄❄
N. 'Hillstar'. Prolific Division 7 daffodil. In mid-spring, each stem bears 2–3 flowers, 6.5cm (2¾in) across. Broad, overlapping perianth segments are bright lemon-yellow with a deep band of white at the bases; funnel-shaped coronas are ivory-white shading to buff-yellow at the bases. ↕35cm (14in). ❄❄❄
N. 'Ice Follies' ■ Division 2 daffodil flowering in mid-spring. Flowers, 9.5cm (3¾in) across, have large, creamy white perianth segments and wide cups, frilled at the mouths, that open lemon-yellow and fade almost to white. Very prolific. ↕40cm (16in). ❄❄❄
N. 'Ice Wings' ■ Division 5 daffodil. In mid-spring, bears 2 or 3 pure white flowers, 4cm (1½in) across, with strongly reflexed perianth segments and relatively long, straight-sided trumpets. ↕35cm (14in). ❄❄❄
N. 'Intrigue'. Division 7 daffodil flowering in mid-spring, with each stem bearing 2–3 scented flowers, 5–6.5cm (2–2¾in) across. Broadly ovate, overlapping, smooth perianth segments are brilliant greenish yellow, with a white halo at the bases. Shallowly funnel-shaped, yellow coronas rapidly become white. ↕40cm (16in). ❄❄❄
N. 'Jack Snipe' ■ Vigorous Division 6 daffodil. In early and mid-spring, produces long-lasting flowers, 4cm (1½in) across, with reflexed white perianth segments and short, lemon-yellow trumpets. Increases rapidly. ↕20cm (8in). ❄❄❄
N. 'Jack Wood'. Division 11a daffodil flowering in early spring. Flowers, 11cm (4½in) across, have very broad, overlapping, flat, mid-yellow perianth segments and large, flat, reflexed, golden yellow coronas, each with 6 uniform segments. ↕50cm (20in). ❄❄❄
N. 'Jake'. Vigorous Division 3 daffodil. In late spring, freely produces flowers, 10.5cm (4¼in) across, with smooth, mid-yellow perianth segments, broadly ovate and overlapping, and shallowly bowl-shaped, rich reddish orange coronas, olive-green at the bases. ↕45cm (18in). ❄❄❄
N. 'Jenny'. Division 6 daffodil. In early and mid-spring, bears flowers 5cm (2in) across, with strongly reflexed, pointed, creamy white perianth segments and

N

Narcissus 'Hawera'

Narcissus 'Ice Follies'

Narcissus 'Ice Wings'

Narcissus 'Jack Snipe'

Narcissus 'Jetfire'

Narcissus 'Jumblie'

Narcissus 'Liberty Bells'

Narcissus 'Little Beauty'

Narcissus 'Little Witch'

Narcissus 'Merlin'

Narcissus 'Minnow'

Narcissus 'Mount Hood'

long, clear lemon-yellow trumpets that fade to cream. Similar to *N.* 'Dove Wings' but perianth segments are more pointed. ↕30cm (12in). ❄❄❄

***N.* 'Jetfire'** ▣ Division 6 daffodil. In early spring, bears flowers 7.5cm (3in) across, with strongly reflexed, golden yellow perianth segments and long, bright orange trumpets, which fade in bright sun. ↕20cm (8in). ❄❄❄

***N.* 'Jingle Bells'.** Division 5 daffodil. In mid-spring, each stem bears 2–3 nodding flowers, 5cm (2in) across, with broadly ovate, pointed, and slightly reflexed white perianth segments and goblet-shaped, deep lemon-yellow coronas. ↕30cm (12in). ❄❄❄

N. jonquilla (Wild jonquil). Division 13 daffodil with erect to spreading, narrow, semi-cylindrical leaves, 40–45cm (16–18in) long. In late spring, bears heads of up to 5 strongly scented, golden yellow flowers, 3cm (1¼in) across, with small, pointed perianth segments and tiny, flat cups. ↕30cm (12in). Spain. ❄❄❄

***N.* 'Jumblie'** ▣ Small Division 12 daffodil. In early spring, bears multiple stems per bulb, each with up to 3 nodding flowers, 3cm (1¼in) across, with strongly reflexed, bright golden yellow perianth segments and deeper yellow-orange cups. ↕17cm (7in). ❄❄

N. juncifolius see *N. assoanus.*

***N.* 'Kaydee'.** Division 6 daffodil producing slightly pendent, reflexed flowers, 8cm (3in) across, in mid-spring. Has broadly ovate, glistening, pure white perianth segments, with sharp points at the rounded tips, and cylindrical, fiery pink coronas, widely expanded and even at the mouths. ↕35cm (14in). ❄❄❄

***N.* 'Killearnan'.** Large Division 9 daffodil producing fragrant flowers, 7.5cm (3in) across, in late spring. Pure white perianth segments are broadly ovate and overlapping. Very shallow, ribbed, green-eyed yellow coronas have narrow red rims and are tightly frilled at the mouths. ↕45cm (18in). ❄❄❄

***N.* 'Ladies' Choice'.** Division 7 daffodil, each stem bearing 2–3 scented, pure white flowers, 7.5cm (3in) across, in late spring. Perianth segments are ovate, spreading, and smooth; coronas are short, cylindrical, and even at the mouths and have dark grey-green bases. ↕40cm (16in). ❄❄❄

***N.* 'Liberty Bells'** ▣ Sturdy Division 5 daffodil bearing 2 nodding, clear lemon-yellow flowers, 9cm (3½in) across, with spreading perianth segments, in mid-spring. ↕30cm (12in). ❄❄❄

***N.* 'Lighthouse Reef'.** Division 1 daffodil. In mid-spring, produces greenish sulphur-yellow flowers, 11cm (4½in) across, with widely cylindrical trumpets, each surrounded by a greenish white halo at the junction with the perianth segments. Trumpets become white with age. ↕38cm (15in). ❄❄❄

***N.* 'Limbo'.** Free-flowering Division 2 daffodil. In mid-spring produces flowers, 10cm (4in) across, with broadly ovate, overlapping, apricot-orange perianth segments and shallowly bowl-shaped, finely ribbed, deep orange-red cups. ↕40cm (16in). ❄❄❄

***N.* 'Lintie'.** Division 7 daffodil. In mid-spring, produces 1 or 2 unscented, primrose-yellow flowers, 5.5cm (2¼in) across, with orange cups. Similar to *N.* 'Bobbysoxer' but the flowers are slightly larger and each cup has a distinct green eye. ↕25cm (10in). ❄❄❄

***N.* 'Little Beauty'** ▣ Sturdy, dwarf Division 1 daffodil bearing well-formed, flowers, 3cm (1¼in) across, with creamy white perianth segments and clear yellow trumpets, in early spring. ↕14cm (5½in). ❄❄❄

***N.* 'Little Gem'.** Dwarf Division 1 daffodil bearing golden yellow flowers, 4.5cm (1¾in) across, in early spring. Similar to *N. minor* and probably a selection from it. ↕13cm (5in). ❄❄❄

Narcissus 'Manly'

***N.* 'Little Witch'** ▣ Vigorous, sturdy Division 6 daffodil. In early and mid-spring, produces long-lasting, golden yellow flowers, 4cm (1½in) across, with strongly reflexed perianth segments and long trumpets. ↕22cm (9in). ❄❄❄

***N.* 'Lorikeet'.** Division 1 daffodil flowering in mid-spring. Each flower, 10cm (4in) across, has deep lemon-yellow perianth segments and a neatly expanded, deep salmon-pink trumpet. ↕35cm (14in). ❄❄❄

***N.* 'Manly'** ▣ Large, strong-stemmed Division 4 daffodil bearing double flowers, 11.5cm (4¾in) across, in early to mid-spring. Broadly ovate, overlapping, greenish yellow perianth segments, arranged in whorls, decreasing in size towards the centres, are interspersed with short, bright orange corona segments. ↕45cm (18in). ❄❄❄

***N.* 'Merlin'** ▣ Division 3 daffodil flowering in mid-spring. Flowers, 7.5cm (3in) across, have rounded, pure white perianth segments and flattened, pale yellow cups, each trimmed with a band of intense red. ↕45cm (18in). ❄❄❄

***N. minimus* of gardens** see *N. asturiensis.*

***N.* 'Minnow'** ▣ Dwarf Division 8 daffodil. In mid-spring, bears up to 5 flowers, 2.5cm (1in) across, with cream perianth segments and pale yellow cups fading to cream. Increases rapidly; may be shy to flower. ↕18cm (7in). ❄❄❄

N. minor ▣ syn. *N. nanus* of gardens. Dwarf Division 13 daffodil with erect, narrow, flat or channelled, grey-green leaves, 8–15cm (3–6in) long, and yellow flowers, 3cm (1¼in) across, borne in early spring. Increases well. ↕10–15cm (4–6in). France, N. Spain. ❄❄❄

***N.* 'Mission Bells'.** Ivory-white Division 5 daffodil flowering in mid-spring. Each stem bears 1–3 flowers, 7.5cm (3in) across, with broadly ovate, slightly reflexed perianth segments and long, cup-shaped coronas, with a hint of yellow-green inside. ↕25cm (10in). ❄❄❄

***N.* 'Misty Glen'.** Division 2 daffodil producing flowers, 10cm (4in) across, in mid-spring. Perianth segments are broadly ovate, rounded at the tips, much

Narcissus minor

N

overlapping, and smooth. Bluish white coronas are long, cup-shaped, straight at the mouths, and distinctly green at the bases inside. ↕40cm (16in). ❄❄❄

***N.* 'Monza'.** Tall, weather-resistant Division 4 daffodil bearing double flowers, 10cm (4in) across, in early spring. Deep golden yellow perianth segments are rounded and arranged in whorls, giving each flower a domed profile; in the centres, these are interspersed with deep orange-red corona segments. ↕50cm (20in). ❄❄❄

***N.* 'Mount Hood'** ■ Division 1 daffodil flowering in mid-spring. Flowers, 10cm (4in) across, have well-formed, broadly overlapping, off-white perianth segments and creamy white trumpets, soon fading to off-white; each trumpet broadens towards the mouth. ↕45cm (18in). ❄❄❄

***N. nanus* of gardens** see *N. minor.*

***N.* 'Nonchalant'.** Division 3 daffodil with flowers, 9.5cm (3¾in) across, in mid- to late spring. Brilliant greenish yellow perianth segments are broadly ovate, blunt-tipped, and overlapping; short, flared, and frilled coronas are a slightly deeper shade of yellow. ↕45cm (18in). ❄❄❄

***N.* 'Notre Dame'.** Very floriferous Division 2 daffodil producing flowers, 10cm (4in) across, in late spring. Very smooth, overlapping white perianth segments are slightly concave and reflexed. Each long, cup-shaped corona, slightly constricted at the mouth, is pinkish yellow with green at the base and a band of orange-pink at the rim. ↕45cm (18in). ❄❄❄

***N. obvallaris*,** syn. *N. pseudonarcissus* subsp. *obvallaris* (Tenby daffodil). Sturdy Division 13 daffodil with erect, glaucous, mid-green leaves, 30cm (12in) long, and stiff stems that bear neat, golden yellow flowers, 4cm (1½in) across, in early spring. Excellent for naturalizing. ↕30cm (12in). UK (S. Wales), W. Europe. ❄❄❄

N. x odorus (*N. jonquilla* x *N. pseudonarcissus*), syn. *N. campernelli* (Campernelle jonquil). Division 13 daffodil with narrow, strap-shaped, strongly keeled leaves, to 50cm (20in) long. In early spring, bears 1 or 2 strongly scented, golden yellow flowers, 4cm (1½in) across, with large cups and narrow perianth segments. ↕25cm (10in). Garden origin. ❄❄❄. **'Rugulosus'** see *N.* 'Rugulosus'.

***N.* 'Osmington'.** Division 2 daffodil flowering in mid-spring. Flowers, 9.5cm (3¾in) across, have broad, smooth white perianth segments and bright red coronas. ↕40cm (16in). ❄❄❄

***N.* 'Pacific Coast'.** Dwarf Division 8 daffodil bearing flowers, 3.5cm (1½in) across, in late spring. Has rounded, light greenish yellow perianth segments and shallowly bowl-shaped, vivid yellow coronas. Flowers best in warmer areas. ↕15cm (6in). ❄❄❄

***N.* 'Pacific Rim'.** Division 2 daffodil with flowers, 9cm (3½in) across, in mid-spring. Broadly ovate, clear yellow perianth segments are smooth and spreading; shallowly bowl-shaped coronas are deeper yellow with clearly defined, rich orange-red rims. ↕40cm (16in). ❄❄❄

***N.* 'Panache'** ■ Division 1 daffodil producing among the largest white daffodil flowers, 11.5cm (4½in) across, in mid-spring. Flowers are pure white, with well-balanced trumpets tinged green at the bases, and broad, overlapping perianth segments. ↕40cm (16in). ❄❄❄

***N.* 'Paper White'** see *N. papyraceus.*

***N. papyraceus*,** syn. *N.* 'Paper White' (Paper-white narcissus). Division 13 daffodil with erect, keeled, glaucous, mid-green leaves, 30cm (12in) long. Bears clusters of up to 10 strongly fragrant, glistening white flowers, 1.5cm (½in) across, from winter to early spring. ↕35cm (14in). S. France, S. Spain, N. Africa. ❄❄. **'Ziva'**, syn. *N.* 'Ziva', is a clone of *N. papyraceus* used for forcing and bowl culture.

***N.* 'Patabundy'.** Vigorous Division 2 daffodil. In mid-spring, bears flowers, 10cm (4in) across, with broadly ovate, pointed, deep golden yellow perianth segments and conical, deep orange-red coronas that retain their colour well. ↕50cm (20in). ❄❄❄

***N.* 'Patois'** ■ Division 9 daffodil bearing flowers, 8cm (3in) across, in late spring to early summer. Has very broad, rounded, pure white perianth segments and disc-shaped, ribbed, greenish lemon-yellow coronas, darker green at the bases, with narrow, deep red rims that retain their colour well. ↕45cm (18in). ❄❄❄

***N.* 'Pencrebar'** ■ Small Division 4 daffodil with circular, fragrant, double, golden yellow flowers, 3cm (1¼in) across, often 2 per stem, borne in mid-spring. ↕18cm (7in). ❄❄❄

***N.* 'Petrel'.** Division 5 daffodil producing clusters of up to 7 nodding, pure white flowers, 3cm (1¼in) across, with slightly reflexed perianth segments, in late spring. ↕25cm (10in). ❄❄❄

***N.* 'Pink Paradise'** ■ Vigorous, strong-stemmed Division 4 daffodil with double flowers, 9.5cm (3¾in) across, in mid-spring. White perianth segments are arranged in whorls, reducing in size towards the centres, and are interspersed with short, bright rose-pink corona segments. ↕50cm (20in). ❄❄❄

***N.* 'Pinza'.** Division 2 daffodil. In early spring, bears flowers, 9.5cm (3¾in) across, with broadly ovate, smooth, slightly pointed perianth segments and cup-shaped, orange-yellow coronas, lightly ribbed, frilled, and expanded, each with a broad band of bright orange at the rim. Retains its colour well. ↕40cm (16in). ❄❄❄

***N.* 'Pipit'** ■ Division 7 daffodil bearing 2 or 3 sweetly scented, lemon-yellow flowers, 7cm (3in) across, in mid- and late spring. Cups quickly fade to cream. ↕25cm (10in). ❄❄❄

N. poeticus (Poet's narcissus). Robust, variable Division 13 daffodil with erect, narrow, strap-shaped, channelled leaves, to 45cm (18in) long. In late spring, bears solitary, fragrant flowers, 4.5–7cm (1¾–3in) across, with flat, pure white perianth segments and tiny, red-rimmed yellow cups. ↕20–50cm (8–20in). France, Switzerland, Italy (widely naturalized in S. Europe). ❄❄❄. **'Plenus'**, syn. *N.* 'Albus Plenus Odoratus', has strongly fragrant, untidy, double, pure white flowers, 4cm (1½in) across. Occasionally, the remains of the red cups are visible between the perianth segments. Excellent for cutting; ↕40cm (16in). **var. *recurvus*** ■ (Old pheasant's eye) has flowers 4cm (1½in) across, with

Narcissus 'Panache'

Narcissus 'Patois'

Narcissus 'Pencrebar'

Narcissus 'Pink Paradise'

Narcissus 'Pipit'

Narcissus poeticus var. *recurvus*

recurved, glistening white perianth segments; ↕35cm (14in); Switzerland.

***N.* 'Pops Legacy'.** Sturdy Division 1 daffodil flowering in early spring. Each flower, 11cm (4½in) across, has broad, overlapping white perianth segments and a well-proportioned, indented, deep yellow trumpet, expanded at the mouth. ↕35cm (14in). ❄❄❄

***N.* 'Precocious'** ■ Vigorous Division 2 daffodil bearing flowers, 10cm (4in) across, in mid-spring. Broadly ovate white perianth segments are spreading and slightly concave; deep reddish rose-pink coronas are bowl-shaped, expanded at the mouths, and heavily frilled. ↕40cm (16in). ❄❄❄

N. pseudonarcissus (Lent lily, Wild daffodil). Very variable Division 13 daffodil with erect, strap-shaped, usually glaucous, mid-green leaves, 8–50cm (3–20in) long. Nodding flowers, 4–7cm (1½–3in) across, with yellow trumpets and narrow, twisted cream perianth segments, are produced in early spring. Good for naturalizing. ↕15–35cm (6–14in). Europe. ❄❄❄. **subsp. *obvallaris*** see *N. obvallaris.*

***N. pumilus* 'Plenus'** see *N.* 'Rip van Winkle'.

***N.* 'Purbeck'.** Division 3 daffodil flowering in mid-spring. Flowers, 9.5cm (3¾in) across, have broad, bright white perianth segments and small, goblet-shaped yellow cups, each with a green-tinged throat, fringed with a bright orange band. ↕45cm (18in). ❄❄❄

Narcissus 'Precocious'

***N.* 'Quail'.** Robust Division 7 daffodil. In mid-spring, bears 2 or 3 scented, golden yellow flowers, 4cm (1½in) across, with long cups and neat perianth segments. ↕40cm (16in). ❄❄❄

***N.* 'Queen's Guard'.** Large Division 1 daffodil with exceptionally durable flowers, 11.5cm (4¾in) across, in early spring. Has expanded, deep yellow trumpets, even at the mouths, set at right-angles to broadly overlapping, pure white perianth segments. ↕40cm (16in). ❄❄❄

***N.* 'Quiet Waters'.** Vigorous Division 1 daffodil. In mid-spring, produces snow-white flowers, 10.5cm (4¼in) across, with broadly ovate perianth segments and straight-sided, slightly expanded, fluted trumpets. ↕35cm (14in). ❄❄❄

***N.* 'Quince'** ■ Division 12 daffodil producing 1–3 soft yellow flowers, 3cm (1¼in) across, with short, frilled, golden yellow cups, in early and mid-spring. Each bulb bears a succession of flower stems. ↕16cm (6in). ❄❄

***N.* 'Rainbow'** ■ Vigorous Division 2 daffodil flowering in mid-spring. Bears consistently good-quality flowers, 10cm (4in) across, with fine-textured white perianth segments and white cups, each with a broad band of copper-pink at the slightly indented mouth. ↕45cm (18in). ❄❄❄

***N.* 'Rapture'.** Division 6 daffodil with deep golden yellow flowers, 8cm (3in) across, in early spring. Ovate, pointed, and overlapping perianth segments are strongly reflexed from long, cylindrical coronas, which are slightly constricted towards the mouths and flared at the rims. ↕35cm (14in). ❄❄❄

***N.* 'Reggae'.** Prolific Division 6 daffodil with flowers, 6cm (2½in) across, borne in mid-spring, held well above the foliage. Overlapping white perianth segments are strongly reflexed; small, funnel-shaped, deep pink coronas are fluted and slightly frilled. ↕25cm (10in). ❄❄❄

***N.* 'Replete'.** Division 4 daffodil with double flowers, 10.5cm (4¼in) across, borne on tall stems in early spring. White perianth segments, arranged in whorls, decreasing in size towards the centres, are intermingled with short, ruffled, bright reddish pink corona segments. ↕45cm (18in). ❄❄❄

N. requienii see *N. assoanus.*

Narcissus 'Quince'

Narcissus 'Rainbow'

Narcissus 'Rip van Winkle'

Narcissus 'Rockall'

Narcissus romieuxii

Narcissus 'Rugulosus'

Narcissus rupicola

Narcissus rupicola subsp. *watieri*

Narcissus 'Salome'

Narcissus 'Stratosphere'

Narcissus 'Suzy'

Narcissus 'Sweetness'

***N.* 'Rijnveld's Early Sensation'.** Division 1 daffodil producing yellow flowers, 9cm (3½in) across, in late winter. Very early-flowering and long-lasting. ↕25–35cm (10–14in). ❄❄❄
***N.* 'Rip van Winkle'** ■ syn. *N. pumilus* 'Plenus'. Division 4 daffodil bearing double, greenish yellow flowers, 5cm (2in) across, with irregular, pointed perianth segments, in early spring. ↕14cm (5½in). ❄❄❄
***N.* 'Rockall'** ■ Division 3 daffodil flowering in mid-spring. Flowers, 11cm (4½in) across, have large, overlapping, slightly pointed white perianth segments and saucer-shaped, finely fluted, rich orange-red coronas. ↕50cm (20in). ❄❄❄
N. romieuxii ■ Small Division 13 daffodil with erect or spreading, narrow, semi-cylindrical, dark green leaves, to 20cm (8in) long. In early spring, bears funnel-shaped flowers, 3.5cm (1¼in) across, which vary from pale straw-yellow to pale primrose-yellow. Similar to *N. bulbocodium*, which has deeper yellow flowers. ↕8–10cm (3–4in). N. Africa. ❄❄
***N.* 'Royal Marine'.** Division 2 daffodil. In mid-spring, bears flowers, 11cm (4½in) across, with broadly ovate, smooth, overlapping, pure white perianth segments and shallowly cup-shaped, finely ribbed, deep orange coronas, yellow at the bases. ↕45cm (18in). ❄❄❄
***N.* 'Rugulosus'** ■ syn. *N.* x *odorus* 'Rugulosus'. Robust Division 7 daffodil. In early spring, each stem bears up to 4 strongly scented, large-cupped, golden yellow flowers, 5.5cm (2¼in) across, with narrow perianth segments. ↕30cm (12in). ❄❄❄
N. rupicola ■ Division 13 daffodil with erect, thin, cylindrical, keeled, grey-green leaves, 18cm (7in) long. Circular, golden yellow flowers, 3cm (1¼in) across, with shallow, 6-lobed cups, are produced in mid-spring. ↕15cm (6in). Portugal, Spain. ❄❄❄. **subsp. *watieri*** ■ syn. *N. watieri*, has pure white flowers, 1.5cm (½in) across, with flat perianth segments and widely funnel-shaped coronas; ↕10cm (4in); N. Africa; ❄❄
***N.* 'Salome'** ■ Division 2 daffodil flowering in mid-spring. Produces consistently good-quality flowers, 9cm (3½in) across, with smooth, waxy, pale cream perianth segments and large, almost trumpet-shaped, peach-pink cups. ↕45cm (18in). ❄❄❄
***N.* 'Savoir Faire'.** Vigorous Division 2 daffodil producing flowers, 11cm (4½in) across, in mid-spring. White perianth segments are spreading, rounded, and overlapping; bowl-shaped coronas, each with 6 sometimes overlapping lobes, open yellow and gradually become white, with green at the bases and a broad band of pink at the rolled rims. ↕50cm (20in). ❄❄❄
***N.* 'Serena Lodge'.** Division 4 daffodil flowering in mid- to late spring. Double flowers, 10.5cm (4¼in) across, have broadly ovate, milk-white perianth segments in whorls, interspersed with short, deep buff-yellow corona segments. ↕50cm (20in). ❄❄❄
***N.* 'Sheelagh Rowan'.** Large Division 2 daffodil with flowers, 13cm (5in) across, in mid- to late spring. Off-white perianth segments are broad and spreading; purer white coronas are cylindrical with shallow, overlapping lobes at the lightly frilled mouths. ↕55cm (22in). ❄❄❄
***N.* 'Sherpa'.** Robust Division 1 daffodil with white flowers, 12cm (5in) across, borne on strong stems in mid-spring. Has very broad, pointed perianth segments and cylindrical trumpets slightly expanded and frilled at the mouths. ↕40cm (16in). ❄❄❄
***N.* 'Silent Valley'.** Division 1 daffodil bearing snow-white flowers, 11.5cm (4½in) across, in mid-spring. Broad, pointed, strongly overlapping, smooth perianth segments surround trumpets highlighted by striking green eyes. ↕40cm (16in). ❄❄❄
***N.* 'Silver Crystal'.** Division 3 daffodil producing white flowers, 11.5cm (4¾in) across, in mid- to late spring. Each flower has broadly ovate, pointed perianth segments and a shallowly bowl-shaped, ribbed, slightly frilled corona, with a moss-green eye. ↕55cm (22in). ❄❄❄
***N.* 'Small Talk'.** Free-flowering Division 1 daffodil of miniature proportions, with golden yellow flowers, 4.5cm (1¾in) across, borne on sturdy stems in early spring. Perianth segments are narrow and trumpets are slightly flared and notched. ↕15cm (6in). ❄❄❄
***N.* 'Sorbet'.** Division 11b daffodil with flowers, 10cm (4in) across, borne in late spring. Broad, overlapping, slightly creased white perianth segments alternate with corona segments; these are buttercup-yellow with orange flecks and white patches. ↕45cm (18in). ❄❄❄
***N.* 'Spellbinder'.** Vigorous Division 1 daffodil bearing sulphur-yellow flowers, 10–11.5cm (4–4½in) across, in mid-spring. Coronas gradually fade to white, with whitish green at the mouths. ↕50cm (20in). ❄❄❄
***N.* 'Sportsman'.** Division 2 daffodil producing flowers, 10cm (4in) across, in early spring. Deep yellow perianth segments are broadly ovate and rounded at the tips. Deep orange-red coronas are narrowly bowl-shaped, flared, and lightly frilled at the mouths. ↕45cm (18in). ❄❄❄
***N.* 'Stratosphere'** ■ Division 7 daffodil. In mid-spring, each tall, strong stem bears up to 3 scented blooms, to 6.5cm (2½in) across, with smooth yellow perianth segments and small, rich deep gold cups. ↕65cm (26in). ❄❄❄

Narcissus 'Tahiti'

***N.* 'Sun Disc'.** Neat, dwarf Division 7 daffodil with stiff stems, each bearing a single, perfectly circular, mid-yellow flower, 5cm (2in) across, in mid-spring. Perianth segments fade to cream with age. ↕18cm (7in). ❄❄❄
***N.* 'Suzy'** ■ Division 7 daffodil producing 1 or 2 scented flowers, 6cm (2½in) across, with primrose-yellow perianth segments and rich orange cups, in mid-spring. ↕40cm (16in). ❄❄❄
***N.* 'Sweetness'** ■ Vigorous Division 7 daffodil with stiff stems bearing solitary, strongly fragrant, golden yellow flowers, 4cm (1½in) across, in mid-spring. Long-lasting as a cut flower. ↕40cm (16in). ❄❄❄
***N.* 'Tahiti'** ■ Division 4 daffodil with double flowers, 11cm (4½in) across, borne in mid-spring. Regular, rounded, rich golden yellow perianth segments surround a cluster of bright red-orange corona segments. ↕45cm (18in). ❄❄❄
N. tazetta. Very variable Division 13 daffodil with erect, broad, twisted, keeled, glaucous, mid-green leaves, 20–50cm (8–20in) long. In winter or spring, bears up to 20 sweetly scented flowers, 4cm (1½in) across, with white perianth segments and yellow cups. ↕15–50cm (6–20in). Mediterranean region. Widely naturalized. ❄❄
***N.* 'Telamonius Plenus'**, syn. *N.* 'Van Sion'. Vigorous Division 4 daffodil producing double, greenish yellow flowers, 10cm (4in) across, in early spring. This very old cultivar is variable in flower shape: it is occasionally fully double; sometimes the trumpet is filled with segments, but the perianth segments remain distinct. Excellent for naturalizing. ↕35cm (14in). ❄❄❄
***N.* 'Tête-à-Tête'** ■ Vigorous, dwarf Division 12 daffodil bearing 1–3 flowers, 6.5cm (2½in) across, in early spring. They have deep golden yellow perianth segments, slightly reflexed from deeper yellow cups. ↕15cm (6in). ❄❄❄
***N.* 'Thalia'** ■ Division 5 daffodil flowering in mid-spring. Bears 2 milk-white flowers, 5cm (2in) across, with narrow, twisted, slightly reflexed perianth segments and open cups. ↕35cm (14in). ❄❄❄
***N.* 'Trena'** ■ Prolific Division 6 daffodil with flowers, 8cm (3in) across,

Narcissus 'Tête-à-Tête'

Narcissus 'Thalia'

Narcissus 'Trena'

Narcissus triandrus

Narcissus 'Yellow Cheerfulness'

Narcissus 'Young Blood'

in early spring. Has ovate, overlapping, pure white perianth segments, which are curving and reflexed, and narrowly cylindrical, vivid yellow coronas, flared at the mouths. ↕35cm (14in). ❄❄❄
***N.* 'Trevithian'.** Vigorous Division 7 daffodil bearing 1–3 scented, soft lemon-yellow flowers, 7cm (3in) across, in mid-spring. Perianth segments are well-rounded; cups are short and flared. ↕45cm (18in). ❄❄❄
N. triandrus ▣ (Angel's tears). Small Division 13 daffodil with decumbent or erect, narrow, flat or channelled leaves, 20–30cm (8–12in) long. In mid-spring, bears 1–6 nodding cream flowers, 6cm (2½in) across, with reflexed perianth segments and rounded cups. ↕10–25cm (4–10in). Portugal, Spain. ❄❄❄
***N.* 'Tripartite'.** Division 11a daffodil bearing stems of up to 3 golden yellow flowers, 6.5cm (2½in) across, in late spring. Each expanded corona is split into 6 segments that lie flat against the perianth segments. ↕45cm (18in). ❄❄❄
***N.* 'Triple Crown'.** Free-flowering Division 3 daffodil with deep golden yellow flowers, 9.5cm (3¾in) across, in mid-spring. Perianth segments are very broad, spreading, and rounded at the tips. Shallowly bowl-shaped coronas each have a deep green base and a narrow band of red at the rim. ↕50cm (20in). ❄❄❄
***N.* 'Trumpet Warrior'.** Division 1 daffodil blooming in early spring. Each flower, 10cm (4in) across, has deep lemon-yellow perianth segments and widely flanged, indented, pure white trumpets. ↕40cm (16in). ❄❄❄
***N.* 'Tuesday's Child'.** Division 5 daffodil bearing 1–3 slightly pendent flowers, 6cm (2½in) across, in mid-spring. Pointed white perianth segments are swept back from short, lemon-yellow coronas. ↕35cm (14in). ❄❄❄
***N.* 'Tyrone Gold'.** Robust Division 1 daffodil bearing deep golden yellow flowers, 12cm (5in) across, with spreading perianth segments and flared, cylindrical, and indented trumpets, in early spring. ↕45cm (18in). ❄❄❄
***N.* 'Uncle Duncan'.** Division 1 daffodil with flowers, 9.5cm (3¾in) across, in early spring. Has smooth, mid-yellow perianth segments and funnel-shaped orange coronas with neatly ribbed, expanded mouths, tinted apple-green inside. ↕40cm (16in). ❄❄❄
***N.* 'Unique'.** Division 4 daffodil producing well-formed, double flowers, 10.5cm (4¼in) across, in mid-spring. They are circular, with broad, rounded white perianth segments, interleaved with rich yellow corona segments in the centres. ↕50cm (20in). ❄❄❄
***N.* 'Van Sion'** see *N.* 'Telamonius Plenus'.
***N.* 'Verona'.** Division 3 daffodil flowering in mid-spring. Bears circular flowers, 9.5–10cm (3¾–4in) across, with broadly overlapping white perianth segments. Flattish, fluted cups open cream and soon fade to white. ↕45cm (18in). ❄❄❄
***N.* 'Viking'.** Division 1 daffodil. In mid-spring, produces deep golden yellow flowers, 11.5cm (4½in) across, each with broad, pointed perianth segments and a long, slightly expanded trumpet, frilled at the mouth. ↕45cm (18in). ❄❄❄
***N.* 'Vulcan'.** Division 2 daffodil flowering in mid-spring. Flowers, 9.5cm (3¾in) across, have rounded, smooth, rich golden yellow perianth segments and fiery orange-red cups with slightly widened, jagged mouths. ↕50cm (20in). ❄❄❄
N. watieri see *N. rupicola* subsp. *watieri*.
***N.* 'White Ideal'.** Division 1 daffodil bearing very large, all-white flowers, 12.5cm (5in) across, in mid-spring. Broad perianth segments are overlapping and slightly pointed; long, cylindrical trumpets are generously expanded and frilled at the mouths. ↕40cm (16in). ❄❄❄
***N.* 'W.P. Milner'.** Sturdy Division 1 daffodil bearing nodding flowers, 6cm (2½in) across, in early and mid-spring. Forward-pointing, cream perianth segments surround pale, creamy white trumpets. ↕23cm (9in). ❄❄❄
***N.* 'Yellow Cheerfulness'** ▣ Division 4 daffodil producing strong stems of 3 or 4 sweetly scented, circular, double, golden yellow flowers, 2cm (¾in) across, in mid-spring. ↕45cm (18in). ❄❄❄
***N.* 'Young Blood'** ▣ Division 2 daffodil with flowers, 10cm (4in) across, in late spring. White perianth segments are very broad and overlapping, blunt-tipped, and slightly concave. Bowl-shaped, deep orange-red coronas have indented rims. ↕40cm (16in). ❄❄❄
***N.* 'Ziva'** see *N. papyraceus* 'Ziva'.

▷**Narcissus,**
Paper-white see *Narcissus papyraceus*
Poet's see *Narcissus poeticus*
▷**Nardoo, Common** see *Marsilea drummondii*
▷**Nasturtium** see *Tropaeolum majus*
Flame see *T. speciosum*

NAUTILOCALYX

GESNERIACEAE

Genus of 38 species of evergreen perennials, often woody at the bases, from open woodland in the West Indies, Central America, and tropical South America. They are grown for their opposite, prominently veined, glossy leaves and tubular, 5-lobed flowers, borne singly or in clustered cymes in the upper leaf axils. In frost-prone areas, grow in a warm greenhouse. In warmer areas, plant among shrubs or trees.
• **HARDINESS** Frost tender.
• **CULTIVATION** Under glass, grow in loamless potting compost in bright filtered light and high humidity. During growth, water freely with soft water and apply a balanced liquid fertilizer monthly. Water moderately in winter. Outdoors, grow in moist but well-drained, humus-rich soil in light shade.
• **PROPAGATION** Root softwood or stem-tip cuttings in spring or summer.
• **PESTS AND DISEASES** Mealybugs and tarsonemid mites may be troublesome.

N. bullatus, syn. *N. tessellatus*. Erect perennial with elliptic, finely toothed, puckered, dark green leaves, to 23cm (9in) long, purple beneath. From spring to summer, bears cymes of up to 10 hairy, pale yellow flowers, 3cm (1¼in) across. ↕60cm (24in), ↔35cm (14in). Peru. ❅ (min. 16°C/61°F)
N. lynchii ▣ Erect, branched perennial with elliptic-lance-shaped, toothed, very dark green, sometimes red-purple leaves, 12cm (5in) long, red-purple beneath. In summer, bears cymes of 2 or 3 yellow flowers, to 3cm (1¼in) across, with red hairs outside, purple streaks inside, and maroon sepals. ↕60cm (24in), ↔30cm (12in). Colombia. ❅ (min. 16°C/61°F)
N. tessellatus see *N. bullatus*.

▷**Navelwort** see *Omphalodes*
Venus's see *O. linifolia*
▷***Neanthe bella*** see *Chamaedorea elegans*

Nautilocalyx lynchii

Nectaroscordum siculum subsp. *bulgaricum*

NECTAROSCORDUM

ALLIACEAE/LILIACEAE

Genus of 3 species of bulbous perennials from damp or shady woodland, rocky places, and dry mountain slopes of S. Europe and W. Asia. They have linear, deeply channelled or keeled leaves, which smell of garlic. Loose umbels of bell-shaped flowers, 2–2.5cm (¾–1in) long, are borne in summer. Grow in a wild garden or herbaceous border.
• **HARDINESS** Fully hardy.
• **CULTIVATION** Grow in any moderately fertile, well-drained soil in full sun or partial shade. May self-seed freely.
• **PROPAGATION** Sow seed in containers in a cold frame in autumn or spring. Remove offsets in summer.
• **PESTS AND DISEASES** Trouble free.

N. dioscoridis see *N. siculum* subsp. *bulgaricum*.
N. siculum, syn. *Allium siculum*. Robust, bulbous perennial with linear, sharply keeled, basal leaves, 30–40cm (12–16in) long. In summer, stout stems bear umbels of 10–30 pendulous, open bell-shaped, white or cream flowers, 1.5–2.5cm (½–1in) long, flushed pink or purplish red, and tinted green at the bases. Seed pods become erect as flowers fade. ↕to 1.2m (4ft), ↔10cm (4in). France, Italy. ❄❄❄. **subsp. *bulgaricum*** ▣ syn. *Allium bulgaricum*, *N. dioscoridis*, has off-white flowers, flushed green and purple. S.E. Europe, N.W. Turkey, Ukraine (Crimea).

NEILLIA

ROSACEAE

Genus of 10 species of deciduous shrubs and subshrubs, with branching, zigzag stems, found in scrub and at rocky stream margins in the Himalayas and E. Asia. The alternate, dark, glossy leaves are irregularly toothed and have up to 5, but usually 3 lobes. They are

Neillia thibetica

cultivated for their graceful, arching habit and their racemes or panicles of small, bell-shaped or tubular flowers, profusely borne in late spring and early summer. Grow in a shrub border or woodland garden.

- **HARDINESS** Fully hardy.
- **CULTIVATION** Grow in fertile, well-drained soil in full sun or partial shade. Pruning group 2 or 3, after flowering.
- **PROPAGATION** Take greenwood cuttings in early summer. Remove suckers in autumn.
- **PESTS AND DISEASES** Trouble free.

N. longiracemosa see *N. thibetica.*
N. sinensis. Thicket-forming, suckering shrub with arching shoots and peeling brown bark. Leaves are usually 3-lobed, ovate to oblong, sharply toothed, and long-pointed, to 10cm (4in) long. In late spring and early summer, small, tubular, pinkish white flowers, to 12mm (½in) long, are produced in slender, 12- to 20-flowered racemes, to 6cm (2½in) long. ↕↔ 2m (6ft). C. China. ✲✲✲
N. thibetica ■ syn. *N. longiracemosa.* Thicket-forming, suckering shrub with arching shoots and ovate or ovate-oblong, 3-lobed, long-pointed, toothed, bright green leaves, to 10cm (4in) long. In early summer, small, tubular-bell-shaped, rose-pink flowers, to 8mm (⅜in) long, are produced in arching racemes, to 15cm (6in) long. ↕↔ 2m (6ft). W. China. ✲✲✲

NELUMBO
Lotus
NELUMBONACEAE

Genus of 2 species of rhizomatous, marginal aquatic perennials from Asia, N. Australia, and E. North America, found at the shallow margins or on the muddy banks of pools. They are widely cultivated and naturalized in subtropical and tropical areas. The handsome, horizontally held, peltate, waxy-bloomed, almost circular leaves are held well above the water. The showy, solitary, fragrant, water lily-like flowers are borne on long stalks, and develop distinctive, flat-topped seed pods that may be dried for use in flower arrangements. They are excellent as specimen plants in an outdoor pool. In frost-prone areas, grow *N. nucifera* with giant water lilies (*Victoria*) in an indoor tropical pool, or in large, water-filled half-barrels on a patio outdoors; overwinter in frost-free conditions.

Nelumbo lutea

- **HARDINESS** Half hardy to frost tender; in cold climates, *N. lutea* and some *N. nucifera* cultivars can be overwintered outdoors given sufficient summer warmth to ripen the rhizomatous roots; these will survive if well below any frozen soil or water.
- **CULTIVATION** In an outdoor pool, grow in large containers in heavy loam enriched with well-rotted farmyard manure or compost, in full sun. As growth proceeds, gradually lower the containers to increase the water depth to 40–60cm (16–24in), or 15–22cm (6–9in) for smaller cultivars. Remove fading foliage. In very cold areas, reduce the water level gradually in autumn, remove the containers, and overwinter in frost-free conditions, keeping the rhizomes just moist. Under glass, grow in large containers in an indoor pool in full light. See also pp.52–53.
- **PROPAGATION** Sow seed in spring, preferably scarified before sowing, at a minimum temperature of 25°C (77°F), in small containers of loam covered by 5cm (2in) of water. Increase water depth and container size until plants are large enough to plant in the flowering site.
  Carefully divide the fragile rhizomes, which resent disturbance. In spring, plant rootstock horizontally just below the soil surface, and barely submerge until growth starts.
- **PESTS AND DISEASES** Outdoors, leaves may be attacked by corn-borers and woolly-bear caterpillars, and by various leaf-spotting diseases, particularly brown spot and dry brown spot. Red spider mites and whiteflies may be a problem under glass.

Nelumbo 'Mrs. Perry D. Slocum'

N. lutea ■ (American lotus, Water chinquapin, Yanquapin). Aquatic perennial with radical, concave-circular, bluish green leaves, 50cm (20in) across, prominently veined beneath, held on stalks to 2m (6ft) long. In summer, produces rose-like yellow flowers, to 25cm (10in) across. ↕ 2m (6ft), ↔ indefinite. North America. ❁ (min. 7°C/45°F)
N. 'Mrs. Perry D. Slocum' ■ Aquatic perennial with rounded, flat or wavy-margined, glaucous, grey-green leaves, 80cm (32in) across, on stalks to 1.4m (4½ft) long. In summer, freely produces deep pink flowers, to 30cm (12in) across, turning yellow over a period of several days. ↕ 1.2–1.5m (4–5ft). ↔ indefinite. ❁ (min. 5°C/41°F)
N. nucifera (Sacred lotus). Aquatic perennial with flat or concave-circular, wavy-margined, glaucous, mid-green leaves, 80cm (32in) across, on stalks to 2m (6ft) long. Peony-like, sometimes double, pink or white flowers, to 30cm (12in) across, are produced in summer on long stalks with short, fleshy prickles. ↕ 0.7–1.5m (28–60in), above water level, ↔ indefinite. Asia (Iran to Japan), N. Australia. ❁ (min. 5°C/41°F). **'Alba Grandiflora'** has wavy-margined, dark green leaves and white flowers, 22–25cm (9–10in) across, sometimes hidden in the foliage; ↕ 1.2–1.8m (4–6ft). **'Alba Striata'** has white flowers, with jagged red margins. **'Charles Thomas'** has lavender-pink flowers, 15–20cm (6–8in) across. Grow in a tub or small pool; ↕ 60–90cm (26–36in). **'Kermesina'** has fully double, rose-pink to bright red flowers, 15–20cm (6–8in) across, produced on stiff stems well above the leaves; ↕ 60–90cm (26–36in). **'Momo Botan'** has long-lasting flowers, to 15cm (6in) across, with dark rose-pink petals, yellow towards the bases. Suitable for a small pool or half-barrel. ↕ 60–120cm (2–4ft). **'Rosea Plena'** produces double, dark rose-pink flowers, 25–35cm (10–14in) across, yellowish towards the bases; ↕ 1.2–1.5m (4–5ft).

NEMATANTHUS
GESNERIACEAE

Genus of about 30 species of scandent or trailing, evergreen, usually epiphytic subshrubs, often becoming woody at the bases, from tropical rainforest in South America. They have opposite, sometimes whorled, elliptic to obovate, entire to toothed, fleshy leaves. The colourful flowers, borne singly or in clustered cymes in the leaf axils, are tubular and pouched. In frost-prone areas, grow in a warm greenhouse or as houseplants. Elsewhere, grow epiphytically on trees or shrubs, or underplant among them.

- **HARDINESS** Frost tender.
- **CULTIVATION** Under glass, grow in loamless potting compost in bright filtered light, or full light with shade from hot sun, with moderate humidity. Water moderately with soft water (less in winter), and feed actively growing plants every month with a balanced liquid fertilizer. For sporadic flowering through winter, maintain a minimum temperature of 15–16°C (59–61°F). Tip-prune young plants when young to encourage branching. Outdoors, grow in moist but well-drained, humus-rich soil in partial shade.

Nematanthus gregarius

- **PROPAGATION** Take stem-tip cuttings in spring.
- **PESTS AND DISEASES** Aphids may infest new growth, including calyces and flowers.

N. gregarius ■ syn. *Hypocyrta radicans, N. radicans.* Trailing to pendent or scandent subshrub with elliptic to obovate, fleshy, glossy, rich green leaves, 2–4cm (¾–1½in) long, borne in opposite pairs or whorls of 3. Clusters of 1–3 tubular, pouched, bright orange flowers, 2.5cm (1in) long, with purple-brown stripes and green, orange-tipped calyces, are borne in summer. ↕ to 80cm (32in), ↔ 90cm (36in) or more. Brazil. ❁ (min. 10–15°C/50–59°F)
N. radicans see *N. gregarius.*
N. strigillosus, syn. *Hypocyrta strigillosa.* Scandent to trailing subshrub, woody at the base, with opposite, elliptic, mid- to deep green leaves, to 3.5cm (1½in) long, sparsely hairy above, pale green and densely downy beneath. Solitary, tubular, orange and yellow flowers, to 2cm (¾in) long, with prominent pouches and green calyces flushed brownish red, are produced mainly in summer. Becomes pendent if grown in a hanging basket. ↕ to 1.5m (5ft), ↔ to 90cm (36in), or more if trailing. Brazil. ❁ (min. 10–15°C/50–59°F)
N. 'Tropicana' ■ Erect, freely-branching subshrub with purple stems and opposite, obovate, thick, fleshy, glossy, dark green leaves, 3cm (1¼in) long. Tubular, pouched, glossy, dark yellow flowers, 2.5cm (1in) long, with maroon stripes, enclosed in long-lasting, leafy, bright red calyces, are produced throughout the year. ↕ 30cm (12in), ↔ 45cm (18in). ❁ (min. 13°C/55°F)

Nematanthus 'Tropicana'

NEMESIA

SCROPHULARIACEAE

Genus of 50 or more species of bushy, erect annuals, perennials, and subshrubs from South Africa, where they grow in sandy soils near the coast or in scrubby, often disturbed soil inland. The leaves are opposite, simple, usually linear to lance-shaped, frequently toothed. The showy, almost trumpet-shaped, 2-lipped flowers (the upper lip 4-lobed, the lower lip unlobed or 2-lobed) are borne singly in the upper leaf axils or in short terminal racemes. Annual cultivars are colourful summer bedding plants outdoors, or may be grown as short-lived, early spring-flowering container plants in a cool greenhouse. They are good for cutting. *N. caerulea* is suitable for a raised bed or herbaceous border, and is often used as a container plant.

- **HARDINESS** Frost hardy to half hardy.
- **CULTIVATION** Grow in moist but well-drained, moderately fertile, slightly acidic soil in full sun. Water annuals freely in dry weather to maintain flower production. Under glass, grow in loam-based potting compost (JI No.2) in full light. Water moderately during growth. Pinch out growing tips to promote bushiness.
- **PROPAGATION** Sow seed at 15°C (59°F) from early to late spring, or in autumn for spring-flowering container plants. Take tip cuttings of unflowered shoots from perennial species in late summer; overwinter young plants in frost-free conditions.
- **PESTS AND DISEASES** Foot rot and root rot may cause problems.

N. caerulea ■ syn. *N. foetens* of gardens, *N. fruticans* of gardens. Woody-based perennial with erect or spreading stems and entire or toothed, linear to lance-shaped leaves, 4cm (1½in) long. Produces terminal racemes of short-tubed, 2-lipped, pink, pale blue, lavender-blue, or white

Nemesia strumosa Carnival Series

flowers, to 1.5cm (½in) long, with yellow throats, from early summer to autumn. ↕ to 60cm (24in), ↔ 30cm (12in). South Africa (Limpopo, Mpumalanga, Free State, KwaZulu/Natal), Lesotho. ✻✻. **'Innocence'** has white flowers. **'Joan Wilder'** has deep lavender-blue flowers.

***N. foetens* of gardens** see *N. caerulea*.

***N. fruticans* of gardens** see *N. caerulea*.

N. strumosa. Basally branching annual with lance-shaped, entire to coarsely toothed, slightly hairy leaves, to 7cm (3in) long. In mid- and late summer, produces terminal racemes of 2-lipped red, yellow, pink, blue, purple, or white flowers, to 2.5cm (1in) across. The flowers may be in single colours, or bicolours with the upper and lower lips in contrasting colours; they often have external purple veins and yellow, "bearded" throats with darker marks. ↕ 18–30cm (7–12in), ↔ 10–16cm (4–6in). South Africa . ✻. **'Blue Gem'** bears bright blue flowers. **Carnival Series** ■ cultivars are compact and dwarf, with purple-veined yellow, red, bronze-yellow, orange, pink, or white flowers; ↕ 17–23cm (7–9in). **'Danish Flag'** has bicoloured flowers in red and white. **'KLM'** ■ has bicoloured flowers in blue and white, with yellow throats. **'National Ensign'** is a bicoloured cultivar with deep pink-red and white flowers. **'Prince of Orange'** produces orange flowers with purple veins; ↕ to 20cm (8in).

Nemesia caerulea

Nemesia strumosa 'KLM'

NEMOPHILA

HYDROPHYLLACEAE

Genus of 11 species of spreading to erect, slender, fleshy-stemmed, sometimes sticky-hairy annuals found in variable habitats in W. North America, from coastal sands to chaparral and redwood forest. The mid-green or grey-green leaves are opposite, lobed or pinnate, ovate to rounded, spoon-shaped, or oblong, and toothed. Small, saucer- or bell-shaped, blue or white flowers are borne singly in the upper leaf axils in summer. Grow as edging in a border, or in a window-box or other container.

- **HARDINESS** Fully hardy.
- **CULTIVATION** Grow in fertile, moist but well-drained soil in full sun or partial shade. May cease flowering in hot, dry weather if not watered.
- **PROPAGATION** Sow seed *in situ* in early spring or autumn; they self-seed freely.
- **PESTS AND DISEASES** Aphids may be troublesome.

N. insignis see *N. menziesii*.

N. maculata ■ (Five-spot). Fleshy-stemmed, sometimes slightly downy annual with 5- to 9-pinnate leaves, oblong to oval in outline and 1–3cm (½–1¼in) long. In summer, produces solitary, saucer-shaped white flowers, to 4.5cm (1¾in) across, borne on long stalks; each petal is tipped with a small, violet-blue mark, and is sometimes faintly veined or tinted mauve-blue. ↕↔ 15–30cm (6–12in). USA (California). ✻✻✻

N. menziesii, syn. *N. insignis* (Baby blue-eyes). Fleshy-stemmed, downy annual with 9- to 11-pinnate, toothed,

Nemophila maculata

grey-green leaves, oval to oblong in outline, 2–5cm (¾–2in) long. In summer, bears solitary, long-stalked, saucer-shaped, bright blue flowers, to 4cm (1½in) across, with lighter blue centres often stained white or yellow, and with darker blue or deep purple spots or marks on the petals. ↕ 20cm (8in), ↔ 30cm (12in). USA (California). ✻✻✻. **subsp. *atromaria*** has white flowers, to 3cm (1¼in) across, with black or dark purple spots. **'Coelestis'** has white flowers margined sky-blue. **'Oculata'** has pale blue flowers with deep purple centres.

▷ ***Neobesseya asperispina*** see *Escobaria asperispina*

▷ ***Neobesseya macdougallii*** see *Ortegocactus macdougallii*

NEOBUXBAUMIA

CACTACEAE

Genus of about 8 species of columnar or tree-like, perennial cacti from dry to humid areas of Mexico. The stems are cylindrical and the ribs usually low-set; the areoles bear numerous bristles and bristly spines. The nocturnal, white, pink, or red flowers, produced in summer, are followed by angular fruits, which open like stars when ripe. In areas where temperatures drop below 15°C (59°F), grow in a warm greenhouse. In warmer climates, grow in a courtyard or border.

- **HARDINESS** Frost tender.
- **CULTIVATION** Under glass, grow in standard cactus compost with added grit, in full light with shade from hot sun, and with low humidity. From mid-spring to late summer, water freely and apply a dilute liquid fertilizer monthly. Keep completely dry at other times. Outdoors, grow in sharply drained, gritty, poor to moderately fertile, humus-rich soil in full sun. See also pp.48–49.
- **PROPAGATION** Sow seed at 19–24°C (66–75°F) in spring.
- **PESTS AND DISEASES** Susceptible to scale insects.

N. euphorbioides ■ syn. *Cephalocereus euphorbioides*, *Lemaireocereus euphorbioides*, *Rooksbya euphorbioides*. Simple, tree-like cactus with a columnar, greyish green, dark green, or blue-green, sometimes red-tinged stem, 10–15cm (4–6in) thick, with 8–10 acute, straight ribs. White-woolly areoles produce

N

Neobuxbaumia euphorbioides

bristly, black to dark grey spines (1–5 radials and sometimes 1 central), becoming white. Funnel-shaped flowers, 8–10cm (3–4in) long, with reddish pink tubes, wine-red outer tepals, and cream throats, are borne in summer. ↕ 1–2m (3–6ft), ↔ 15cm (6in). E. Mexico. ❀ (min. 15°C/59°F)
N. polylopha. Usually simple, columnar cactus producing a pale green stem, 35cm (14in) or more thick, bearing 20–50 slightly rounded ribs with white-woolly areoles, yellow bristles, and yellow spines (7–9 radials and 1 shorter central). Funnel-shaped, red or pink flowers, to 5–8cm (2–3in) long, with purple-brown tubes, develop in summer. ↕ 2–3m (6–10ft), ↔ 35cm (14in). C. Mexico. ❀ (min. 15°C/59°F)

▷ ***Neochilenia chilensis*** see *Neoporteria chilensis*
▷ ***Neochilenia mitis* of gardens** see *Neoporteria napina*

NEOLITSEA

LAURACEAE

Genus of 60 species of evergreen, dioecious shrubs and trees from tropical woodland in E. and S.E. Asia, Malaysia, and Indonesia. Only *N. sericea* is usually cultivated, for its handsome, simple, alternate, leathery leaves. Flowers are insignificant, each having 4 sepals that fall on opening; on female plants these are followed by red or black berries. In very cold areas, grow in a cool greenhouse as foliage plants. In milder climates, grow at the base of a warm, sunny wall, in a woodland garden, or as specimen plants; they also make useful screens or hedges.
• **HARDINESS** Frost hardy to frost tender.
• **CULTIVATION** Under glass, grow in loam-based potting compost (JI No.3) in full light or bright filtered light. During growth, water moderately and apply a balanced liquid fertilizer monthly. Water sparingly in winter. Outdoors, grow in fertile, moist but well-drained soil in full sun or partial shade, with shelter from cold, dry winds. Pruning group 1; may need restrictive pruning under glass.
• **PROPAGATION** Sow seed in containers in a cool greenhouse as soon as ripe. Root semi-ripe cuttings with bottom heat in summer.
• **PESTS AND DISEASES** Scale insects may be a problem under glass.

N. glauca see *N. sericea*.
N. sericea ◌ syn. *Litsea glauca, N. glauca.* Large shrub or small tree, ovoid to columnar, later spreading, with yellow-brown, silky-hairy shoots. Leaves are ovate to oblong-elliptic, 10–18cm (4–7in) long, with 3 prominent veins; they are softly golden-hairy above when young, becoming deep green above and glaucous beneath. In late summer, produces small, star-shaped yellow flowers in stalkless umbels, followed in autumn by red berries, 1.5cm (½in) long, on female plants. ↕ to 6m (20ft), ↔ to 3m (10ft) or more. China, Taiwan, Korea, Japan. ✻

NEOLLOYDIA

CACTACEAE

Genus of 10–14 species of spherical or cylindrical, perennial cacti found on low hillsides in S.W. Texas, USA, and in E. and N.E. Mexico. They frequently form clumps by offsetting. The ribs bear spined tubercles, often spirally arranged, sometimes with dense hairs or wool in the axils. The wide-spreading, funnel-shaped, diurnal flowers are produced from spring to summer. In areas where temperatures drop below 15°C (59°F), cultivate in a warm greenhouse. In warmer climates, grow in a border or desert garden.
• **HARDINESS** Frost tender.
• **CULTIVATION** Under glass, grow in standard cactus compost in full light. From mid-spring to early autumn, water moderately and apply a dilute, balanced liquid fertilizer monthly. Keep dry at other times. Outdoors, grow in sharply drained, humus-rich, moderately fertile soil in full sun. See also pp.48–49.
• **PROPAGATION** Sow seed at 19–24°C (66–75°F) in spring.
• **PESTS AND DISEASES** Susceptible to root mealybugs when container-grown.

N. conoidea ■ syn. *Coryphantha conoidea, Mammillaria conoidea.* Often offsetting, variable cactus with spherical to cylindrical, bluish grey or yellow-green stems, to 7cm (3in) thick. Ovoid tubercles have woolly axils and white-woolly areoles (8–28 white to grey radial spines, 0–6 longer black centrals). In summer, produces reddish violet, magenta, or deep purple flowers, to 6cm (2½in) across. ↕ to 10cm (4in), ↔ 15cm (6in) in clusters. S.W. Texas, E. and N.E. Mexico. ❀ (min. 15°C/59°F)
N. schmiedickeana, syn. *Turbinicarpus schmiedickeanus.* Variable, simple or clump-forming cactus with spherical or short-cylindrical, dark blue to grey-green stems, to 5cm (2in) thick; they have 10–12 ribs divided into pyramidal, 4-angled tubercles with bare axils. White-woolly areoles, later bare, produce 1–8 incurved grey spines. In spring, bears white, yellow, or pink to magenta flowers, 1–3cm (½–1¼in) across, with violet mid-lines on the inner petals. ↕ to 5cm (2in), ↔ to 15cm (6in). Mexico. ❀ (min. 15°C/59°F)

Neolloydia conoidea

NEOMARICA

IRIDACEAE

Genus of about 15 species of rhizomatous, herbaceous perennials from often mountainous habitats in tropical Central and South America. They are cultivated for their short-lived, iris-like flowers, borne in summer on erect stems. The erect, sword-shaped leaves are ribbed or heavily veined, and arranged in basal fans. In frost-prone areas, grow in a temperate or warm greenhouse. In warmer climates, grow in a border or among shrubs.
• **HARDINESS** Frost tender.
• **CULTIVATION** Under glass, grow in loam-based potting compost (JI No.2), with added sharp sand and leaf mould, in bright filtered light, or in full light with shade from the hottest sun. Water moderately in summer, sparingly in winter. Apply a balanced liquid fertilizer monthly when in full growth. Outdoors, grow in well-drained, moderately fertile, humus-rich soil in partial shade.
• **PROPAGATION** Sow seed at 15–18°C (59–64°F) in spring, or divide in spring.
• **PESTS AND DISEASES** Trouble free.

N. caerulea ■ Rhizomatous perennial with a basal fan of sword-shaped, dark green leaves, to 1.6m (5½ft) long. In summer, bears a succession of flat, scented, mid-blue flowers, 8–10cm (3–4in) across, striped white, yellow, and brown in the centres. ↕↔ 60cm (24in). Brazil. ❀ (min. 10°C/50°F)

▷ ***Neopanax arboreum*** see *Pseudopanax arboreus*

NEOPAXIA

PORTULACACEAE

Genus of one variable species of prostrate, stoloniferous, mat-forming, herbaceous perennial found in moist habitats, including bogs, swamps, and streams, at high altitudes in Australia and New Zealand. It is grown for its erect, alternate, fleshy leaves and its saucer-shaped, white or pale pink flowers, borne from spring to summer. Grow at the margins of streams and ponds, or in any other moist, boggy soil.
• **HARDINESS** Fully hardy.
• **CULTIVATION** Grow in moderately fertile, moist soil, preferably in full sun.
• **PROPAGATION** Sow seed as soon as ripe in containers in a cold frame. Divide mats in spring.
• **PESTS AND DISEASES** Trouble free.

N. australasica, syn. *Montia australasica.* Prostrate, stoloniferous, mat-forming perennial with alternate, linear to spoon-shaped, fleshy, deep green to bright light green, or grey-green leaves, 3–10cm (1¼–4in) long. From spring to early summer, bears saucer-shaped, white or pink flowers, 1–2cm (½–¾in) across, borne singly or in few-flowered cymes. ↕ 10cm (4in), ↔ 40cm (16in). Australia (Western Australia, South Australia, Victoria, Tasmania), New Zealand. ✻✻✻

Neomarica caerulea

N

NEOPORTERIA

CACTACEAE

Genus of 20–30 species of simple, sometimes clustering, perennial cacti, most from rocky, coastal sites in Chile, a few from S. Peru and W. Argentina. They have spherical to short-cylindrical, ribbed, spiny stems and usually solitary, funnel- or bell-shaped flowers produced from or close to the crowns. Where temperatures drop below 10°C (50°F), grow in a warm greenhouse or as houseplants; elsewhere, use in a desert garden.
- **HARDINESS** Frost tender.
- **CULTIVATION** Under glass, grow in standard cactus compost in full light, with low humidity. From mid-spring to early autumn, water moderately and apply a dilute liquid fertilizer monthly. Keep dry at other times. Outdoors, grow in sharply drained, poor to moderately fertile, humus-rich soil in full sun. See also pp.48–49.
- **PROPAGATION** Sow seed at 19–24°C (66–75°F) in spring or summer.
- **PESTS AND DISEASES** Vulnerable to root mealybugs and mealybugs, especially when container-grown.

N. chilensis, syn. *Echinocactus chilensis, Eriosyce chilensis, Neochilenia chilensis.* Simple or clustering cactus with spherical to short-cylindrical, pale green stems, each with about 20 ribs. Areoles each bear about 20 glassy white radial spines and 6–8 longer, yellowish brown centrals. From late spring to early autumn, bears broadly funnel-shaped, white or pink flowers, 5cm (2in) across, with carmine-red outer petals. ↕ 30cm (12in), ↔ 10cm (4in). Chile. ❄ (min. 10°C/50°F)
N. crispa, syn. *Eriosyce crispa, Pyrrhocactus crispus.* Simple cactus with a tuberous rootstock. The spherical, dark green stem has 13–16 ribs, and black or grey spines (6–10 radials, 2–4 longer centrals). Funnel-shaped red flowers, 3.5cm (1½in) across, with a deeper red mid-stripe to each inner petal, are borne from late summer to autumn. ↕↔ 7cm (3in). Chile. ❄ (min. 10°C/50°F)
N. litoralis see *N. subgibbosa.*
N. mitis see *N. napina.*
N. napina ■ syn. *Eriosyce napina, Neochilenia mitis* of gardens, *Neoporteria mitis.* Variable, simple cactus with a spherical, brownish green stem, sometimes tinged red, divided into chin-like tubercles, and with dark brownish

Neoporteria napina

Neoporteria villosa

black spines (3–9 radials, no centrals). From late spring to early autumn, bell- to funnel-shaped, pale yellow, sometimes pink-flushed flowers, 3–4cm (1¼–1½in) across, open from green-woolly buds. ↕ 2.5cm (1in), ↔ 3.5cm (1½in). Chile. ❄ (min. 10°C/50°F)
N. nidus, syn. *Eriosyce kunzei.* Simple cactus with a spherical to short-cylindrical, dark green stem, rarely elongating, bearing 16–18 deeply scalloped ribs hidden by about 30 upward-curved, pale grey, cream, or yellow spines per areole. Tubular-funnel-shaped, red or pink flowers, 4cm (1½in) across, with prominently pointed petals, are produced from late spring to early autumn. ↕ to 30cm (12in), ↔ to 10cm (4in). Chile. ❄ (min. 10°C/50°F)
N. subgibbosa, syn. *Eriosyce subgibbosa, N. litoralis.* Variable, simple cactus producing a spherical, mid-green to grey-green stem, later elongating and often decumbent; the stem bears 16–20 warty ribs and deep orange-yellow, brown, or black spines (16–30 thin radials, 4–8 much thicker centrals). Funnel-shaped, carmine-pink flowers, 4cm (1½in) across, with paler, almost white throats, develop from late spring to early autumn. ↕ to 30cm (12in), ↔ 10cm (4in). Chile. ❄ (min. 10°C/50°F)
N. taltalensis, syn. *Eriosyce taltalensis.* Simple cactus with a spherical, dull dark green stem, 10–16 warty ribs, and pale yellowish brown areoles bearing 6–20 curving to twisted, brown, later white radial spines and up to 6 dark greyish brown to black centrals. Bears funnel-shaped, purplish pink, yellow, or white flowers, 3cm (1¼in) across, in summer. ↕↔ 8cm (3in). Chile. ❄ (min. 10°C/50°F)
N. villosa ■ syn. *Eriosyce villosa.* Simple or clustering cactus with spherical then short-cylindrical, grey-green stems turning black-purple; the stems bear 13–15 ribs covered with upward-curved, hair-like, yellowish grey or pale brown spines (12–16 or more radials, 4 thicker centrals). Funnel-shaped, white-throated pink flowers, to 3cm (1¼in) across, are borne from late spring to summer. ↕ 15cm (6in), ↔ to 10cm (4in). Chile. ❄ (min. 10°C/50°F)

NEOREGELIA syn. AREGELIA

BROMELIACEAE

Genus of about 70 species of evergreen, sometimes rhizomatous or stoloniferous, epiphytic or terrestrial perennials (bromeliads) from coastal scrub, woodland, and rainforest, to 1,600m (5,000ft) high, in South America. They are grown for the striking colour of their central leaves and bracts when flowering. Variable, usually spiny-margined leaves are borne in rosettes; large sheaths totally enclose the scape and its bracts. An umbel-like, sometimes raceme- or corymb-like, inflorescence nestles within each leaf rosette and, in summer, bears long-lasting, tubular flowers. Offsets form around the flowering rosettes. Where temperatures drop below 10°C (50°F), grow in a temperate greenhouse, or as houseplants. In warm climates, grow in a shady, moist site.
- **HARDINESS** Frost tender.
- **CULTIVATION** Under glass, grow in epiphytic or terrestrial bromeliad compost in bright filtered light. During growth, water freely with soft water. Apply a low-nitrogen liquid fertilizer monthly from spring to late autumn. Keep rosette cups filled with soft water from spring to early autumn. Water sparingly in winter. Sever spent leaf rosettes at the bases. Outdoors, grow in gritty, leafy soil in an open site with partial shade, or grow epiphytically in a tree. See also p.47.
- **PROPAGATION** Sow seed at 27°C (81°F) as soon as ripe. Separate offsets in spring or summer.
- **PESTS AND DISEASES** Susceptible to scale insects.

N. ampullacea. Stoloniferous, terrestrial bromeliad with dense, funnel-shaped rosettes of 6–15 tongue-shaped, sometimes red-banded, mid-green leaves, 15–20cm (6–8in) long. Tubular flowers, to 2.5cm (1in) long, with blue, white-based petals and white-margined green sepals, are borne in summer. Stolons appear from beneath the rosettes; at the tips, further rosettes develop. ↕↔ 40cm (16in). Brazil. ❄ (min. 10°C/50°F)
N. carolinae, syn. *Aregelia carolinae, Nidularium carolinae* (Blushing

Neoregelia carolinae 'Tricolor'

Neoregelia concentrica

bromeliad). Epiphytic bromeliad with open rosettes of 12–20 strap-shaped, toothed, copper-suffused, mid-green leaves, 40–60cm (16–24in) long; at flowering time, the central leaves turn crimson. Red bracts surround violet-purple to lavender-blue flowers, to 4cm (1½in) long, in summer. ↕ 20–30cm (8–12in), ↔ 40–60cm (16–24in). Brazil. ❄ (min. 10°C/50°F). **'Tricolor'** ■ syn. f. *tricolor*, var. *tricolor*, has leaves striped ivory-white, green, and rose-red.
N. concentrica ■ Rhizomatous, epiphytic bromeliad with dense rosettes of 7–30 broadly strap-shaped, spreading, glossy, mid- to dark green leaves, 20–40cm (8–16in) long, often marked dark purple at the tips, and with black marginal spines. Yellow-white bracts, suffused violet or purple, turn purple-pink in summer, when the pale blue or white flowers, 4–5cm (1½–2in) long, are produced. ↕ to 30cm (12in), ↔ to 70cm (28in). Brazil. ❄ (min. 10°C/50°F). **var. *plutonis*** ■ syn. 'Plutonis', has spreading rosettes of broad, mid-green, sometimes pale green leaves, which are flushed magenta-red during flowering; the flowers are pale lavender; ↔ 40cm (16in) or more.
N. eleutheropetala ■ Stoloniferous, terrestrial or epiphytic bromeliad with rosettes of about 30 tongue-shaped, mid-green leaves, 50–70cm (20–28in) long, turning reddish green towards the bases, and with sharp marginal spines and brown sheaths. The innermost, purple-brown leaves surround dense, umbel-like inflorescences of white flowers, to 3.5cm (1½in) long, borne in summer and interspersed with long,

Neoregelia concentrica var. *plutonis*

Neoregelia eleutheropetala

purple-tipped bracts. ↕↔ to 70cm (28in). Venezuela, Colombia, Peru, Amazonian Brazil. ❀ (min. 10°C/50°F)
N. pineliana. Epiphytic bromeliad with a short stem producing ascending stolons, which bear leaves along their lengths. The rosettes have up to 12 narrowly lance-shaped to linear, grey-scaly, mid-green leaves, to 50cm (20in) long, with minute marginal spines and purple sheaths. In summer, the central leaves turn red, and dense umbels of blue, white-based flowers, to 6cm (2½in) long, darkening towards the tips, are produced. ↕↔ 40cm (16in) or more. Possibly Brazil. ❀ (min. 10°C/50°F)
N. princeps. Epiphytic or terrestrial bromeliad with spreading rosettes of 15–20 strap-shaped, pointed, minutely scaly, laxly toothed, mid-green leaves, 50cm (20in) long, with densely grey-scaly sheaths; the inner leaves are smaller and bright red. Bears white flowers, 3–4cm (1¼–1½in) long, with deep blue tips and red sepals, in summer. ↕↔ 75cm (30in). S. Brazil. ❀ (min. 10°C/50°F)
N. spectabilis (Fingernail plant). Terrestrial bromeliad producing funnel-shaped rosettes of 20–30 arching, strap-shaped, grey-scaly, red-tipped, glossy, olive-green leaves, 40–45cm (16–18in) long, with smooth or minutely spiny margins and grey-white cross-banding beneath. Inner leaves are red, often margined purple, with white bases. In summer, bears blue flowers, 4–4.5cm (1½–1¾in) long, with red or purple bracts. ↕ to 40cm (16in), ↔ to 80cm (32in). S. Brazil. ❀ (min. 10°C/50°F)

NEPENTHES

Monkey cup, Tropical pitcher plant

NEPENTHACEAE

Genus of over 70 species and numerous hybrids of dioecious, evergreen, carnivorous, climbing, terrestrial or epiphytic perennials from Madagascar, the Seychelles, S.E. Asia, Borneo, and Queensland, Australia. They are found in moist, acid, organic soils in open grassland or forest, and sometimes grow epiphytically on trees. The usually lance-shaped or strap-shaped leaves, 5–65cm (2–26in) long, each have a prolonged midrib, which acts as a tendril and may be terminated by a hanging, hollow "pitcher", 5–35cm (2–14in) long, with 2 vertical ridges, or "wings", at the front. Pitchers vary greatly in shape and colour, from pale yellow to green or purplish red, and are frequently mottled; upper and lower pitchers often differ in colour on the same plant. The colourful, thickened rim of a pitcher secretes nectar to attract insects, small mammals, and even birds, which become trapped inside. Its apex forms a lid to deflect excess rain. The tiny, petalless male and female flowers, with green or brown sepals, are borne in spike-like racemes. In frost-prone areas, grow in a warm greenhouse or conservatory; in tropical climates, grow climbers through trees, or attach epiphytes to branches. Heights vary greatly according to conditions and support; in cultivation, most are cut back to encourage young foliage and the development of large pitchers.
• **HARDINESS** Frost tender.
• **CULTIVATION** Lowland species and hybrids from sea level to 1,000m (3,300ft) need daytime temperatures of 24°C (75°F), and night-time temperatures of 15°C (59°F) in winter, 21°C (70°F) in summer. Provide ventilation when over 38°C (100°F). Highland species and hybrids from 1,000–3,000m (3,300–9,900ft) need daytime temperatures of 18°C (64°F), and 10°C (50°F) at night. Ventilate when over 21°C (70°F). Under glass, grow in slatted baskets in a mix of 2 parts bark, 2 parts perlite, and 1 part coarse peat or coconut fibre, or in clean, live sphagnum moss. Provide bright filtered light, or full light with shade from hot sun, and high humidity. In summer, apply a high-nitrogen liquid fertilizer weekly. Prune mature plants in spring, reducing stems by two-thirds of their length, to induce vigorous, pitcher-producing shoots. Outdoors, grow in moist, open, leafy soil in partial shade, or as epiphytes.
• **PROPAGATION** Sow seed as soon as ripe on the surface of moist peat or fine coir compost, and place in a tray of water in a shaded propagator; maintain a temperature of 27°C (81°F). In spring, insert cuttings with 3 or 4 leaves into nepenthes compost (described above) and maintain at 21–27°C (70–81°F). Air layer in spring or summer.
• **PESTS AND DISEASES** Mealybugs may be troublesome. Grey mould (*Botrytis*) may affect leaves.

N. ampullaria. Lowland climber with rounded, squat, deep red or green, sometimes mottled pitchers, to 5cm (2in) long, with round, horizontal mouths and small, narrow, reflexed lids. Wings are broad, spreading, and toothed. Pitchers are produced only from the basal leaves or in clusters from the rhizomes, not from climbing shoots. ↕ to 20m (70ft). Malaysia to New Guinea. ❀ (min. day: 24°C/75°F; night: 15°C/59°F in winter, 21°C/70°F in summer)
N. x coccinea (*N.* x *dominii* x *N. mirabilis*). Lowland climber with yellow-green pitchers, to 15cm (6in) long, mottled purple-red, with inflated bases and oblique mouths. The green lids have red markings. ↕ to 6m (20ft). Garden origin. ❀ (min. day: 24°C/75°F; night: 15°C/59°F in winter, 21°C/70°F in summer)
***N.* 'Director G.T. Moore'** ▣ Lowland climber with pear-shaped, light green pitchers, to 13cm (5in) long, with dense purple-red mottling, oblique mouths, and fringed, mottled wings. ↕ 3m (10ft). ❀ (min. day: 24°C/75°F; night: 15°C/59°F in winter, 21°C/70°F in summer)
N. gracilis. Slender, lowland climber with linear to elliptic leaves and numerous pitchers. Lower pitchers are small, cylindrical, light green, sometimes suffused pink or maroon, to 7cm (3in) long, with narrow lips, round lids, and narrow wings. Upper pitchers, to 15cm (6in) long, are dark mahogany-red and narrow in the middle. Even young plants bear inflorescences, 15cm (6in) long, of red-brown flowers. ↕ to 2m (6ft). Philippines to Indonesia. ❀ (min. day: 24°C/75°F; night: 15°C/59°F in winter, 21°C/70°F in summer)
N. x hookeriana (*N. ampullaria* x *N. rafflesiana*). Lowland climber producing ovoid lower pitchers with broad wings and rim, and funnel-shaped upper pitchers. Both are pale green with dark red spots, and have oblique mouths. Upper pitchers grow to 13cm (5in) long, lower to 11cm (4¼in). ↕ 3m (10ft). Malaysia to Borneo. ❀ (min. day: 24°C/75°F; night: 15°C/59°F in winter, 21°C/70°F in summer)
N. mirabilis. Lowland climber or terrestrial perennial with cylindrical pitchers, to 18cm (7in) long, red, or pale green with red blotches; each has an oblique, round mouth and an oval lid. ↕ to 10m (30ft). S. China, S.E. Asia to Australia (N. Queensland). ❀ (min. day: 24°C/75°F; night: 15°C/59°F in winter, 21°C/70°F in summer)
N. rafflesiana ▣ Lowland climber with creamy green pitchers, marked chocolate-red, each with a striped rim.

Nepenthes 'Director G.T. Moore'

Lower pitchers, to 13cm (5in) long, each have a rounded base, an oblique, oval mouth with the rim rising vertically at the back to form a stalk for the lid, and large, toothed wings. Upper pitchers, to 30cm (12in) long, with small wings, are tapered at the bases. ↕ to 9m (28ft). Sumatra to Borneo. ❀ (min. day: 24°C/75°F; night: 15°C/59°F in winter, 21°C/70°F in summer)
N. rajah. Rare, highland climber with large green pitchers, to 35cm (14in) long, mottled red to red-purple, each with an elliptic and oblique mouth, a broad, wavy rim, and a large, oval lid. Lower pitchers are ellipsoid, while upper ones are tapered only at the bases. The pitchers have been known to catch rats. Commercial trading in this species is strictly regulated. ↕ 2m (6ft). Borneo (Mt. Kinabalu). ❀ (min. day: 18°C/64°F; night: 10°C/50°F)
N. ventricosa. Highland, terrestrial or epiphytic perennial producing numerous cylindrical pitchers, to 18cm (7in) long, each narrower in the middle, with a round to oval mouth and small green lid, suffused red. ↕ 4m (12ft). Philippines. ❀ (min. day: 18°C/64°F; night: 10°C/50°F)

Nepenthes rafflesiana

N

NEPETA

Catmint

LABIATAE/LAMIACEAE

Genus of approximately 250 species of perennials, rarely annuals, native to a variety of habitats, from cool and moist to hot and dry sites in scrub, on grassy banks and stony slopes, or in high mountains, in non-tropical parts of the N. hemisphere. Ovate to lance-shaped, entire, scalloped, or toothed, often aromatic leaves are borne in opposite pairs; some are hairy, producing a silvery or greyish green effect. The spike-like cymes (sometimes racemes or panicles) of tubular, irregularly 2-lipped flowers, in white and shades of blue and purple, occasionally yellow, are borne in interrupted axillary whorls along the flower stems, often over long periods. Grow taller catmints in a mixed or herbaceous border, the shorter ones in a rock garden. Some species attract cats; most are attractive to bees.

- **HARDINESS** Fully hardy to half hardy.
- **CULTIVATION** Grow in any well-drained soil in full sun or partial shade. *N. govaniana* and *N. subsessilis* prefer moist, cool soils. *N. sibirica* likes fairly dry conditions. Grow *N. phyllochlamys* in a hot, dry rock crevice or in a trough. Provide support for taller catmints; trim *N. nervosa* and *N.* x *faassenii* after flowering to keep plants compact and to induce a second flowering.
- **PROPAGATION** Sow seed in a seedbed, or in containers in a cold frame, in autumn; some catmints self-seed freely. Divide in spring or autumn. Take softwood cuttings in early summer.
- **PESTS AND DISEASES** Slugs may damage young growth. Powdery mildew may be a problem in dry summers.

***N.* 'Blue Beauty'** see *N.* 'Souvenir d'André Chaudron'.
N.* x *faassenii ■ (*N. nepetella* x *N. racemosa*), syn. *N. mussinii* of gardens. Clump-forming perennial with erect to spreading, branched stems and narrowly ovate to lance-shaped, scalloped, wrinkled, hairy, aromatic, silvery grey-green leaves, to 3cm (1¼in) long. From early summer to early autumn, freely bears spike-like, whorled cymes of pale lavender-blue flowers, to 12mm (½in) long, with darker purple spots. ↕↔ to 45cm (18in) Garden origin. ❄❄❄
***N. glechoma* 'Variegata'** see *Glechoma hederacea* 'Variegata'.

Nepeta x *faassenii*

Nepeta govaniana

N. govaniana ■ syn. *Dracocephalum govanianum*. Clump-forming perennial bearing erect, branching, hairy stems and ovate to oblong-elliptic, pointed, scalloped, softly hairy, aromatic leaves, to 10cm (4in) long. From midsummer to early autumn, bears long, lax racemes or panicles of light yellow flowers, to 3cm (1¼in) long. ↕ 90cm (36in), ↔ 60cm (24in). W. Himalayas. ❄❄❄
N. grandiflora. Clump-forming perennial with erect, sparsely branched stems and ovate, scalloped, softly hairy, aromatic leaves, 10cm (4in) long. In early summer, produces spike-like, whorled cymes of violet-blue flowers, to 2cm (¾in) long. ↕ 75cm (30in), ↔ 30cm (12in). Caucasus. ❄❄❄
***N. hederacea* 'Variegata'** see *Glechoma hederacea* 'Variegata'.
N. macrantha see *N. sibirica.*
N. mussinii see *N. racemosa.*
***N. mussinii* of gardens** see *N.* x *faassenii.*
N. nervosa ■ Bushy perennial bearing erect, unbranched stems with narrowly lance-shaped, entire to slightly toothed, conspicuously veined, hairy, faintly aromatic, mid- to grey-green leaves, to 10cm (4in) long. Dense, cylindrical,

Nepeta nervosa

Nepeta sibirica

spike-like, whorled cymes of purplish blue, rarely yellow flowers, to 12mm (½in) long, are borne from midsummer to early autumn. ↕ 45–60cm (18–24in), ↔ 30cm (12in). India (Kashmir). ❄❄❄
N. phyllochlamys. Spreading perennial with decumbent stems and triangular-ovate, scalloped, intensely white-downy, aromatic leaves, to 1.5cm (½in) long. In summer, bears short, spike-like, whorled cymes of lilac-pink flowers, 1cm (½in) long, with white-felted bracts. Requires very sharply drained soil. ↕ to 10cm (4in), ↔ to 20cm (8in). Turkey. ❄❄❄
N. racemosa, syn. *N. mussinii.* Spreading to upright perennial with ovate, scalloped, finely hairy, aromatic, mid-green leaves, 1–3cm (½–1¼in) long, with heart-shaped bases. In summer, produces raceme-like, whorled cymes of deep violet- to lilac-blue flowers, 1–2cm (½–¾in) long. ↕ to 30cm (12in), ↔ to 45cm (18in). Caucasus, Turkey, N. and N.W. Iran. ❄❄❄. **'Little Titch'** has pale lavender-blue flowers; ↕↔ 15cm (6in).
N. sibirica ■ syn. *Dracocephalum sibiricum, N. macrantha.* Erect, leafy perennial with branching stems bearing oblong-lance-shaped, toothed, aromatic, dark green leaves, to 9cm (3½in) long, minutely hairy at the margins. In mid- and late summer, bears long, raceme-like, whorled cymes of blue to lavender-blue flowers, to 4cm (1½in) long. ↕ 90cm (36in), ↔ 45cm (18in). Russia (Siberia), E. Asia. ❄❄❄
***N.* 'Six Hills Giant'.** Vigorous, clump-forming perennial with narrowly ovate, toothed, hairy, aromatic, light grey-green leaves, to 4cm (1½in) long. In summer, bears abundant spike-like, whorled cymes of lavender-blue flowers, 2cm (¾in) long. ↕ to 90cm (36in), ↔ 60cm (24in). ❄❄❄
***N.* 'Souvenir d'André Chaudron'**, syn. *N.* 'Blue Beauty'. Spreading, clump-forming perennial with oval to lance-shaped, toothed, smooth, aromatic, grey-green leaves, to 8cm (3in) long. Throughout summer, bears spike-like, whorled cymes of large, dark lavender-blue flowers, 4cm (1½in) long. ↕↔ 45cm (18in). ❄❄❄
N. subsessilis. Clump-forming perennial with erect, unbranched stems bearing ovate, toothed, hairless, aromatic, dark green leaves, 8–10cm (3–4in) long. Spike-like, whorled cymes of bright blue flowers, 3cm (1¼in) long, appear from midsummer to early autumn. ↕ to 90cm (36in), ↔ 30cm (12in). Japan. ❄❄❄

NEPHROLEPIS

Sword fern

NEPHROLEPIDACEAE/OLEANDRACEAE

Genus of about 30 species of evergreen or semi-evergreen, epiphytic and terrestrial ferns from rainforest or more open habitats in tropical and subtropical regions worldwide. They have short, erect rhizomes, usually with numerous runners. The dense clusters of pinnate fronds may be erect, spreading, or pendent. Pinnae are usually linear and simple, but may be divided, forked, or crisped in cultivars, of which there are many. In frost-prone areas, grow in a temperate greenhouse or as houseplants; in warmer climates, grow in moist, shady sites among shrubs.

- **HARDINESS** Mostly frost tender. *N. cordifolia* is half hardy.
- **CULTIVATION** Under glass, grow in a mix of 1 part loam, 2 parts sharp sand, and 3 parts leaf mould in bright filtered light, with moderate to high humidity and good ventilation. During the growing season, water moderately with soft water and apply a half-strength, balanced liquid fertilizer monthly. Water sparingly in winter. Outdoors, grow in moderately fertile, moist but well-drained, humus-rich soil in partial shade.
- **PROPAGATION** Sow spores at 21°C (70°F) as soon as ripe. Many cultivars are sterile, or do not come true from spores. Separate rooted runners in late winter or early spring. See also p.51.
- **PESTS AND DISEASES** Some cultivars are susceptible to fern scale, as well as rot, when fronds become too wet.

N. cordifolia ■ Tufted fern bearing erect to arching or pendent, lance-shaped to linear fronds, to 80cm (32in) long, with up to 70 pairs of oblong to linear pinnae, sometimes toothed at the tips. ↕ 80cm (32in), ↔ to 1.5m (5ft). Tropical regions. ❄. **'Duffii'** has short, rounded pinnae, and its fronds are often

Nephrolepis cordifolia

Nephrolepis exaltata 'Bostoniensis'

N

forked at the tips. **'Plumosa'** is slow-growing, with lobed pinnae.
N. exaltata. Tufted fern with widely arching to erect, linear fronds, to 2m (7ft) long, with shallowly toothed, sickle-shaped pinnae. It is the source of nearly all *Nephrolepis* cultivars. ↕↔ to 2m (7ft). USA (Florida), Mexico, West Indies, Central America, tropical South America, Polynesia, and Africa. ❀ (min. 7–10°C/45–50°F). **'Aurea'** see 'Golden Boston'. **'Bostoniensis'** ■ (Boston fern) has broader, lance-shaped fronds, erect at first, then arching to pendent. A very tolerant houseplant. **'Childsii'** has very broad, 3- or 4-pinnate, closely overlapping fronds. **'Elegantissima'** has 2-pinnate fronds. **'Golden Boston'** ■ syn. 'Aurea', is similar to 'Bostoniensis' but with golden yellow fronds. **'Gracillima'** has lacy, 3-pinnate fronds. **'Hillii'** is very vigorous, with 2-pinnate or 2-pinnatifid fronds, the pinnae variously lobed or crisped; ↕ to 1m (3ft), ↔ to 2m (6ft). **'Mini Ruffle'** is a very compact cultivar with 2- or 3-pinnate fronds; ↕ to 5cm (2in), ↔ 8cm (3in). **'Silver Balls'** has fronds covered with dense, silvery scales as they unfurl. **'Verona'** has dense, pendent, 3- or 4-pinnate fronds.
N. falcata. Tufted fern with arching to pendent, lance-shaped, glossy, dark green fronds, 2.5m (8ft) long, divided into close-set, sickle-shaped pinnae. ↕ to 2.5m (8ft), ↔ to 1m (36in). S.E. Asia. ❀ (min. 7–10°C/45–50°F). **f. *furcans*** ■ has pinnae with 1 or 2 forks at the tips.

▷ ***Nephthytis triphylla* of gardens** see *Syngonium podophyllum*

Nephrolepis exaltata 'Golden Boston'

Nephrolepis falcata f. *furcans*

NERINE

AMARYLLIDACEAE

Genus of about 30 species of bulbous perennials, some evergreen, found on screes, on rock ledges, and in other well-drained or arid sites in southern Africa. They have spherical umbels of lily-like flowers, with reflexed, often wavy-margined tepals; in herbaceous species, these appear before or with the strap-shaped leaves. Many cultivars with large, colourful flowers have been developed; flowers are borne in umbels, 10–20cm (4–8in) across, of up to 25 flowers, followed by semi-erect, basal leaves. Grow *N. bowdenii* at the base of a sunny wall. *N. sarniensis* and *N. undulata* thrive where frosts are rare. Grow *N. filifolia* and *N. masoniorum* in a rock garden. All are ideal greenhouse plants, and are good as cut flowers. If ingested, all parts may cause mild stomach upset.
• **HARDINESS** Fully hardy to half hardy.
• **CULTIVATION** Under glass, plant in autumn or spring with the tips of the bulbs above the surface of the loam-based potting compost (JI No. 2); they flower best when bulbs are congested. Provide full light. Water freely during active growth. Keep warm and dry when dormant in summer. After flowering, apply a low-nitrogen liquid fertilizer. Outdoors, plant in well-drained soil in full sun in early spring. Provide a deep, dry winter mulch in cold areas.
• **PROPAGATION** Sow seed at 10–13°C (50–55°F) as soon as ripe. Divide clumps after flowering.
• **PESTS AND DISEASES** Prone to attack by slugs.

***N.* 'Baghdad'.** Bulbous perennial bearing loose umbels of crimson flowers with paler centres in autumn. ↕ 60cm (24in), ↔ 8cm (3in). ✲
***N.* 'Blanchefleur'.** Bulbous perennial bearing glistening white flowers in compact umbels in autumn. ↕ 50cm (20in), ↔ 8cm (3in). ✲
N. bowdenii ■ Robust, bulbous perennial with broad, strap-shaped leaves, to 30cm (12in) long. In autumn, bears open umbels of up to 7 or more funnel-shaped, faintly scented pink flowers, to 8cm (3in) across, with recurved, wavy-margined tepals. ↕ 45cm (18in), ↔ 8cm (3in). South Africa (Eastern Cape, KwaZulu/Natal, Free State). ✲✲✲. **f. *alba*** ■ has white flowers, sometimes flushed pale pink.

Nerine bowdenii

Nerine bowdenii f. *alba*

'Mark Fenwick', syn. 'Fenwick's Variety', has pink flowers on dark stalks.
***N.* 'Corusca Major'**, syn. *N. sarniensis* var. *corusca* 'Major'. Bulbous perennial bearing compact umbels of scarlet flowers with bold stamens in early autumn. Grown commercially for cutting. ↕ 60cm (24in), ↔ 8cm (3in). ✲
N. crispa see *N. undulata.*
***N.* 'Early Snow'.** Bulbous perennial with compact umbels of pure white flowers, borne in early autumn. ↕ 60cm (24in), ↔ 8cm (3in). ✲
N. filifolia ■ Bulbous perennial with narrow, grass-like leaves, 20cm (8in) long. In autumn, bears compact umbels of 5–10 small, bright pink to white flowers, to 2.5cm (1in) across, with wavy-margined tepals. Bears new leaves as old ones fade, so the plant is virtually evergreen. ↕ 30cm (12in), ↔ 5cm (2in). South Africa (Free State). ✲
N. flexuosa. Bulbous perennial with arching, narrow, strap-shaped leaves, to 30cm (12in) long. In late autumn, bears compact umbels of 10–20 dark-veined pink flowers, to 3cm (1¼in) across, with wavy-margined tepals, the upper ones recurved. ↕ 45cm (18in), ↔ 8cm (3in). South Africa (Eastern Cape, KwaZulu/Natal, Free State). ✲. **'Alba'** has white flowers.
***N.* 'Fothergillii Major'.** Bulbous perennial bearing large, compact umbels of 10–20 bright orange-red flowers, with wavy-margined tepals, in late summer and early autumn. ↕ 50cm (20in), ↔ 8cm (3in). ✲
N. masoniorum. Slender, bulbous perennial with narrow, grass-like, almost evergreen leaves, to 20cm (8in) long. In

Nerine filifolia

Nerine sarniensis

autumn, downy stems bear compact umbels of 4–15 bright pink flowers, to 2cm (¾in) across, with a deep rose-red vein down the centre of each wavy-margined petal. ↕ 30cm (12in), ↔ 5cm (2in). South Africa (Eastern Cape). ✲
N. 'Radiant Queen'. Bulbous perennial with loose umbels of rose-pink flowers in autumn. ↕ 60cm (24in), ↔ 8cm (3in). ✲
N. 'Salmon Supreme'. Bulbous perennial bearing compact umbels of salmon-pink flowers in autumn. ↕ 60cm (24in), ↔ 8cm (3in). ✲
N. sarniensis ▣ (Guernsey lily). Bulbous perennial with erect, strap-shaped, bright green leaves, to 30cm (12in) long. In early autumn, bears compact umbels of 10–20 crimson to orange-red flowers, 3–4cm (1¼–1½in) across, with wavy-margined tepals and conspicuous stamens. ↕ 45cm (18in), ↔ 8cm (3in). South Africa (Northern Cape, Western Cape). ✲. **var. *corusca* 'Major'** see *N.* 'Corusca Major'.
N. undulata, syn. *N. crispa*. Bulbous perennial with strap-shaped leaves, to 45cm (18in) long. In autumn, bears umbels of 8–12 slender, mid-pink flowers, 4–5cm (1½–2in) across, with narrow, crinkled tepals. ↕ 45cm (18in), ↔ 8cm (3in). South Africa (Eastern Cape). ✲

NERIUM

Oleander

APOCYNACEAE

Genus of 1 or 2 species of evergreen shrubs or small trees found in seasonally dry stream beds and margins from the Mediterranean to China. They are grown for their often large, terminal cymes of colourful, narrowly funnel-shaped or salverform flowers, which each have 5 broad, spreading, angular petal lobes, and are followed by forked, elongated, bean-like seed pods. Lance-shaped leaves are narrow, leathery, and borne in opposite pairs or whorls of 3. *N. oleander* has been widely naturalized. Numerous cultivars have been raised, both single- and double-flowered, with white, yellow, apricot, pink, red, purple-red, and lilac flowers. In frost-prone areas, grow *N. oleander* in a cool greenhouse and move outdoors in summer; in warmer areas, use as a specimen plant, or grow in a shrub border or as a hedge. All parts are highly toxic if ingested; contact with foliage may irritate skin.
• **HARDINESS** Most are frost tender, but may survive short periods at 0°C (32°F).

Nerium oleander

N. oleander 'Little Red' is hardy to -12°C (10°F).
• **CULTIVATION** Under glass, grow in loam-based potting compost (JI No.3) in full light; ventilate well. During growth, water moderately and apply a balanced liquid fertilizer monthly. Water sparingly in winter. Outdoors, grow in fertile, moist but well-drained soil in full sun. Pruning group 9; plants under glass may need restrictive pruning in late winter; will tolerate hard pruning.
• **PROPAGATION** Sow seed at 16°C (61°F) in spring. Root semi-ripe cuttings in summer, with bottom heat. Air layer in spring.
• **PESTS AND DISEASES** Scale insects, mealybugs, and red spider mites may be a problem under glass.

N. obesum see *Adenium obesum.*
N. oleander ▣♀ (Rose bay). Tall, erect to spreading shrub or small tree with lance-shaped, deep green to greyish green leaves, 6–20cm (2½–8in) long. In summer, bears cymes of up to 80 pink, red, or white flowers, 3–5cm (1½–2in) across. ↕ 2–6m (6–20ft), ↔ 1–3m (3–10ft). E. Mediterranean (possibly to W. China); widely naturalized. ❀ (min. 2–5°C/36–41°F). **'Carneum Plenum'**, syn. 'Mrs. Roeding', is dwarf, with double, salmon-pink flowers; ↕ 1–2m (3–6ft), ↔ 60–100cm (24–39in). **'Casablanca'** ▣ syn. 'Monca', has single white flowers, sometimes suffused pink. **'Little Red'** has single red flowers; ✲✲✲ (borderline). **'Monca'** see 'Casablanca'. **'Monta'** see 'Tangier'. **'Monvis'** see 'Ruby Lace'. **'Mrs. Roeding'** see 'Carneum Plenum'.

Nerium oleander 'Casablanca'

Nerium oleander 'Petite Salmon' (inset: flower detail)

'Petite Pink' is dwarf, with single, pale pink flowers; ↕ 1–2m (3–6ft), ↔ 60–100cm (24–39in). **'Petite Salmon'** ▣ is dwarf, with large, single, salmon-pink flowers; ↕ 1–2m (3–6ft), ↔ 60–100cm (24–39in). **'Ruby Lace'**, syn. 'Monvis', has showy clusters of large, single, deep red flowers, 8cm (3in) across, with fringed lips and wavy edges. **'Tangier'**, syn. 'Monta', bears single, light pink flowers. **'Variegatum'** has leaves with white to pale yellow margins, and double pink flowers.

NERTERA

RUBIACEAE

Genus of approximately 6 species of mat-forming perennials from moist lowland to mountainous forest, and moist grassland and scrub, in S. China, S.E. Asia to Australasia, the Antarctic, and Mexico to South America. They have very small, broadly ovate to lance-shaped leaves, tiny funnel- or bell-shaped flowers, and fleshy, spherical to pear-shaped fruits. In frost-prone areas, grow as houseplants, or in an alpine house or cool greenhouse. Elsewhere, grow as ground cover in a rock garden.
• **HARDINESS** Fully hardy to frost tender; *N. granadensis* tolerates temperatures to -3°C (27°F) for short periods.
• **CULTIVATION** Under glass, grow in loamless potting compost in bright filtered light or indirect light. During growth, water freely and apply a balanced liquid fertilizer monthly. Water sparingly in winter. Outdoors, grow in humus-rich, gritty, moist but well-drained soil in partial shade. Protect from excessive winter wet.
• **PROPAGATION** Sow seed at 13–16°C (55–61°F), or divide, in spring.
• **PESTS AND DISEASES** May be infested by aphids or red spider mites.

N. granadensis ▣ (Bead plant). Stem-rooting, moss-like perennial with broadly ovate, bright green leaves, to 8mm (⅜in) long. In summer, bears small, stemless, bell-shaped, yellowish green flowers, 3mm (⅛in) across, followed by masses of spherical, shiny, orange or red berries, 5mm (¼in) across. (Populations from South America, New Zealand, and Australia are sometimes considered a distinct species, *N. depressa*.) ↕ 2cm (¾in), ↔ to 20cm (8in). Mexico, Central America. ✲

Nertera granadensis

N

▷ **Nerve plant** see *Fittonia*
▷ **Net bush** see *Calothamnus*
Common see *C. quadrifidus*
▷ **Net leaf,**
Painted see *Fittonia*
Silver see *Fittonia albivensis* Argyroneura group
▷ **Nettle,**
Dead see *Lamium*
Flame see *Solenostemon, S. scutellarioides*
Hedge see *Stachys*
Painted see *Solenostemon, S. scutellarioides*
Pyrenean dead see *Horminum pyrenaicum*
▷ **Nettle tree** see *Celtis*
Southern see *C. australis*
▷ **Never-never plant** see *Ctenanthe oppenheimiana* 'Tricolor'
▷ **New Guinea creeper** see *Mucuna bennettii*
▷ **New Zealand daisy** see *Celmisia*
▷ **New Zealand flax** see *Phormium tenax*
▷ **Ngaio** see *Myoporum laetum*

NICANDRA

Apple of Peru, Shoo-fly

SOLANACEAE

Genus of one species of upright, branching annual from open sites and wasteland in Peru. It has alternate, solitary, oval to elliptic-lance-shaped or ovate, toothed leaves. The short-lived, bell-shaped flowers are followed by brown berries borne in green, lantern-like calyces. Grow in a wild garden or a mixed border. Fruiting branches can be dried for use in winter arrangements.

- **HARDINESS** Fully hardy.
- **CULTIVATION** Grow in fertile, moist but well-drained soil in full sun.
- **PROPAGATION** Sow seed at 15°C (59°F) in early spring, or *in situ* in mid-spring; self-seeds freely.
- **PESTS AND DISEASES** Trouble free.

N. physalodes (Apple of Peru, Shoo-fly). Erect, vigorous annual with wavy-margined leaves, to 10cm (4in) or more long. White-throated, light violet-blue flowers, to 3.5cm (1½in) across, are borne profusely in the upper leaf axils, from summer to autumn, followed by round berries that are enclosed in green calyces, 3–4cm (1¼–1½in) across. Peru. ↕ to 90cm (36in), ↔ 30cm (12in). ✻✻✻. **'Violacea'** has indigo-blue and white flowers.

▷ ***Nicodemia madagascariensis*** see *Buddleja madagascariensis*
▷ ***Nicolaia elatior*** see *Etlingera elatior*

NICOTIANA

Tobacco plant

SOLANACEAE

Genus of about 67 species of erect, frequently rosette-forming annuals, biennials, perennials, and shrubs from Australia, North America, and tropical South America, where they grow on mountain slopes and valley floors, often in moist soils. They have alternate, linear or oblong-lance-shaped to broadly ovate, glandular-hairy leaves. Flowers are tubular to trumpet-shaped or salverform, occasionally scented, and borne in racemes or panicles, usually in summer, sometimes in autumn. They usually

Nicotiana langsdorffii

open only in the early evening and at night; flowers of some cultivars remain open during the day if in partial shade. Cultivars derived from *N. alata* and *N.* x *sanderae* are ideal summer bedding annuals, their upward- or horizontally-facing blooms remaining open in full sun. Grow *N. sylvestris* in a border or semi-wild garden. All parts may cause severe discomfort if ingested; contact with the foliage may irritate skin.

- **HARDINESS** Frost hardy to half hardy.
- **CULTIVATION** Grow in fertile, moist but well-drained soil in full sun or partial shade. Stake tall plants in open positions. Although half hardy, *N. alata* and *N. sylvestris* can be overwintered outdoors where temperatures only occasionally fall to -5°C (23°F); they will resprout from rootstocks the following spring. Provide a dry winter mulch. Pruning group 6 for shrubs.
- **PROPAGATION** Surface-sow seed at 18°C (64°F) in mid-spring.
- **PESTS AND DISEASES** Prone to aphids, whiteflies, leafhoppers, and grey mould (*Botrytis*), particularly under glass. Also prone to viruses, especially mosaic virus.

N. affinis see *N. alata*.
N. alata, syn. *N. affinis*. Short-lived, rosette-forming perennial, grown as an annual, with spoon-shaped to ovate leaves, to 25cm (10in) long, becoming smaller up the stems. Tubular, greenish yellow flowers, to 10cm (4in) long, with funnel-shaped mouths, white within, are produced in open racemes, and are strongly fragrant at night. ↕ to 1.5m (5ft), ↔ 30cm (12in). S. Brazil, N. Argentina. ✻

Nicotiana 'Lime Green'

Nicotiana x *sanderae* Domino Series 'Salmon Pink'

N. glauca. Fast-growing, gaunt, semi-evergreen shrub with long, arching, smooth, glaucous shoots and ovate, fleshy, blue-grey leaves, 10cm (4in) or more long. Bears tubular, bright yellow flowers, to 4cm (1½in) long. ↕↔ 2.5–3m (8–10ft). S. Bolivia to N. Argentina. ✻
N. langsdorffii ■ Well-branched, sticky annual with a basal rosette of ovate leaves, to 25cm (10in) long. Bears nodding, slender panicles of tubular, apple-green flowers, to 5cm (2in) long, with spreading, 5-lobed mouths. ↕ to 1.5m (5ft), ↔ to 35cm (14in). Brazil. ✻
***N.* 'Lime Green'** ■ Upright annual with spoon-shaped leaves, 5–20cm (2–8in) long, the upper leaves oblong-lance-shaped. Produces salverform, lime-green flowers, to 12cm (5in) long, each with an abruptly flattened limb. ↕ 60cm (24in), ↔ 25cm (10in). ✻
N.* x *sanderae (*N. alata* x *N. forgetiana*). Upright, woody-based, sticky annual or short-lived perennial with spoon-shaped to oblong-ovate, wavy-edged basal leaves, 5–25cm (2–10in) long, the upper leaves oblong-lance-shaped. Bears open racemes or panicles of red, occasionally white, rose-pink, or purple, salverform

Nicotiana x *sanderae* Starship Series

Nicotiana sylvestris

flowers, to 5cm (2in) across. ↕ to 60cm (24in), ↔ 30–40cm (12–16in). Garden origin. ✻. **Domino Series** cultivars have upward-facing flowers in red, white, crimson-pink, lime-green, pink with white eyes, purple, purple with white eyes, salmon-pink, or white with rose-pink margins; ↕ 30–45cm (12–18in). **Domino Series 'Salmon Pink'** ■ has salmon-pink flowers. **Havana Series** cultivars are compact; colours include pale pink with deep rose-pink reverse, and lime-green with rose-pink reverse; ↕ 30–35cm (12–14in). **Merlin Series** cultivars are dwarf, bred for containers; colours include purple, purple with white eyes, crimson-pink, lime-green, and white; ↕ 23–30cm (9–12in). **Metro Series** cultivars have rose-pink, red, lime-green, white, or lilac-pink flowers; ↕ to 35cm (14in). **Starship Series** ■ cultivars have pink, red, rose-pink, white, or lime-green flowers, and good all-weather tolerance; ↕ 30cm (12in).
N. sylvestris ■ Many-branched, stout-stemmed biennial or short-lived perennial with a basal rosette of dark green, oblong-elliptic to elliptic-ovate leaves, to 35cm (14in) long. Produces short, densely packed panicles of nodding, sweet-scented, long-tubed, trumpet-shaped white flowers, to 9cm (3½in) long, with 5 spreading lobes. Flowers close in full sun. ↕ to 1.5m (5ft), ↔ to 60cm (24in). Argentina. ✻

NIDULARIUM

Bird's-nest bromeliad

BROMELIACEAE

Genus of about 25 species of rosette-forming, evergreen, usually epiphytic perennials (bromeliads), sometimes rhizomatous, related to *Neoregelia*, from woodland and rainforest, to 2,000m (6,500ft) high, mainly in Brazil. The toothed leaves are narrow to broadly strap-shaped. The conspicuous leaf sheaths surround tubular flowers, usually borne in summer; they nestle in a cluster of large bracts, resembling a bird's nest. Where temperatures drop below 12°C (54°F), grow in a warm greenhouse or as houseplants; in warmer areas, grow in a moist, shady border.

- **HARDINESS** Frost tender.
- **CULTIVATION** Under glass, grow in epiphytic bromeliad compost in bright filtered light with moderate to high humidity. In growth, water freely with soft water. Apply a low-nitrogen liquid fertilizer monthly from spring to late

Nidularium procerum var. *kermesianum*

autumn. Keep rosette cups filled with water from spring to early autumn; keep just moist in winter. Outdoors, grow in an open site, in moderately fertile, gritty, leafy soil in partial shade, or grow epiphytically on a tree. See also p.47.
• **PROPAGATION** Sow seed at 27°C (81°F) as soon as ripe. Separate offsets in spring or summer.
• **PESTS AND DISEASES** Susceptible to scale insects.

N. carolinae see *Neoregelia carolinae.*
N. fulgens (Blushing bromeliad). Epiphytic, rhizomatous bromeliad with spreading rosettes of 15–20 strap-shaped, sparsely and sharply toothed, pointed, bright pale green leaves, to 40cm (16in) long, slightly scaly beneath. Bears clusters of tubular white flowers, 5cm (2in) long, with purple-blue tips and bright red sepals, among the lance-shaped, brilliant red bracts. ↕ 40cm (16in), ↔ to 60cm (24in). S. Brazil. ❄ (min. 12°C/54°F)
N. innocentii. Very variable, epiphytic bromeliad with funnel-shaped rosettes of 30 or more sword- or strap-shaped, minutely toothed, dark green or reddish green leaves, 20–60cm (8–24in) long,

Nidularium regelioides

widening towards the tips, with dark red undersides. Produces clusters of tubular, white- or pink-sepalled, green-based white flowers, to 6cm (2½in) long, in rosettes of bright red or green-tipped red bracts. ↕ 20–30cm (8–12in), ↔ 60cm (24in). Brazil. ❄ (min. 12°C/54°F)
N. procerum. Epiphytic bromeliad with erect rosettes of 12–40 sharp-pointed, finely toothed, waxy, copper-suffused, pale green leaves, 40–100cm (16–39in) long. Bears 25–30 or more tubular, blue-tipped vermilion flowers, to 3cm (1¼in) long, among clusters of red floral bracts. ↕ 20–30cm (8–12in), ↔ to 75cm (30in). Brazil. ❄ (min. 12°C/54°F). **var. *kermesianum*** ■ has red-suffused, often narrower, shorter leaves, to 40cm (16in) long; ↔ to 45cm (18in).
N. regelioides ■ Terrestrial or epiphytic bromeliad with tubular rosettes of 12–20 strap-shaped, pointed, toothed, bright green leaves, 35–40cm (14–16in) long, suffused deeper green. Bright red bracts surround clusters of 5–8 tubular red flowers, 4–5cm (1½–2in) long, with purple-tipped white sepals. ↕ 30cm (12in), ↔ 45cm (18in). S. Brazil. ❄ (min. 12°C/54°F)

NIEREMBERGIA

Cup flower

SOLANACEAE

Genus of over 20 species of annuals, perennials, and shrubs from moist, sunny habitats in temperate South America. Slender, spreading or upright stems bear alternate, entire leaves and colourful, open cup- or bell-shaped, sometimes tubular flowers in summer. Most perennial species are frost tender, but are easily propagated and are often grown as annuals; use as bedding, as border edging, or in containers under glass for early spring flowers. In warm areas, grow in open sites among shrubs. Grow *N. repens* in a rock garden or in paving crevices; may become invasive.
• **HARDINESS** Fully hardy to frost tender.
• **CULTIVATION** Outdoors, grow in a sheltered site in moist but well-drained soil in full sun. *N. repens* prefers dry, sandy soils. Under glass, grow in loam-based potting compost (JI No.1) in full light. During growth, water moderately and apply a balanced liquid fertilizer monthly. Water sparingly in winter. Trim lightly after flowering.
• **PROPAGATION** Sow seed in autumn for spring flowering, or in spring at 15°C (59°F). Take stem-tip cuttings of tender perennials at any time during summer. Divide *N. repens* in spring.
• **PESTS AND DISEASES** Susceptible to aphids and whiteflies under glass, and may be damaged by slugs and snails outdoors. May be affected by viruses, especially tobacco mosaic virus.

N. caerulea see *N. linariifolia.*
N. frutescens see *N. scoparia.*
N. hippomanica see *N. linariifolia.*
N. linariifolia, syn. *N. caerulea, N. hippomanica.* Erect, branching, downy-stemmed perennial with narrowly spoon-shaped, pointed leaves, to 8mm (⅜in) long. In summer, bears cup-shaped, lavender-blue flowers, to 2cm (¾in) across, with yellow throats. ↕↔ to 20cm (8in). Argentina. ✻
N. repens, syn. *N. rivularis* (White cup). Creeping, mat-forming, stem-rooting

Nierembergia scoparia 'Mont Blanc'

perennial with rounded, spoon-shaped, light green leaves, to 3cm (1¼in) long. Bears open bell-shaped, yellow-centred white flowers, 2.5–5cm (1–2in) across, in summer. ↕ 5cm (2in), ↔ 60cm (24in) or more. Andes, warm-temperate South America. ✻✻. **'Violet Queen'** produces rich purple flowers.
N. rivularis see *N. repens.*
N. scoparia, syn. *N. frutescens.* Shrubby perennial with well-branched stems and stalkless, linear to narrowly spoon-shaped leaves, to 5cm (2in) long. From midsummer to early autumn, bears wide-mouthed, tubular, pale blue flowers, 2.5cm (1in) across, fading to white at the margins. ↕ to 45cm (18in) or more, ↔ 30cm (12in). Chile. ✻✻. **'Mont Blanc'** ■ has white flowers. **'Purple Robe'** has rich violet-blue flowers; ✻✻✻. **'Violacea'** has longer leaves and deep violet-blue flowers.

NIGELLA

Devil-in-a-bush, Love-in-a-mist

RANUNCULACEAE

Genus of 20 species of stiffly erect, bushy annuals found on rocky slopes, wasteland, and in fallow fields in the Mediterranean, Eurasia, and N. Africa. Leaves are alternate, feathery, pinnatisect to 3-pinnatisect. The solitary, sometimes paired, terminal or axillary flowers, borne mainly in summer, are pink, blue, yellow, or white, with 5 petal-like sepals and 5–10 smaller, 2-lipped true petals; they sometimes nestle within a showy, ruff-like surround of strongly veined leaves with hair-like, wispy divisions at each tip. The decorative, sometimes inflated capsules with persistent styles can be dried for flower arrangements. Grow in an informal, mixed or annual border; self-seeding may occur. They also provide long-lasting cut flowers.
• **HARDINESS** Fully hardy.
• **CULTIVATION** Grow in any well-drained soil in full sun.
• **PROPAGATION** Sow seed *in situ* in mid-spring or autumn. Provide cloche

Nigella damascena 'Miss Jekyll'

protection in winter for plants sown in autumn.
• **PESTS AND DISEASES** Trouble free.

N. damascena (Devil-in-a-bush, Love-in-a-mist). Single-stemmed or branching annual with ovate, finely divided, 2- or 3-pinnatisect, bright green leaves, 12cm (5in) long. In summer, bears terminal, saucer-shaped, pale blue flowers, to 4.5cm (1¾in) across, becoming sky-blue with age, each with a "ruff" of foliage, finely divided at the tips. ↕ to 50cm (20in), ↔ to 23cm (9in). S. Europe, N. Africa. ✻✻✻. **'Blue Midget'** is dwarf; ↕ 25cm (10in). **'Dwarf Moody Blue'** is dwarf, with violet flowers fading to sky-blue; ↕ 20cm (8in). **'Miss Jekyll'** ■ is tall, with sky-blue flowers; ↕ to 45cm (18in). **'Mulberry Rose'** has large, creamy pink flowers deepening to rose-pink; ↕ to 45cm (18in). **Persian Jewel Series** ■ cultivars have sky-blue, deep violet-blue, rose-pink, deep pink, or white flowers; ↕ to 40cm (16in).
***N. hispanica* 'Curiosity'.** Bushy annual bearing broadly ovate, finely divided, 2- or 3-pinnatisect, dark green leaves, to 14cm (5½in) long. Terminal, scented, saucer-shaped, bright blue flowers, to 6cm (2½in) across, with dark eyes and deep maroon-red stamens, are borne singly or in pairs, in summer. ↕ 60–75cm (24–30in), ↔ to 45cm (18in). ✻✻✻
***N. orientalis* 'Transformer'.** Bushy annual with finely divided, 2- or 3-pinnatisect, broadly ovate, bluish green leaves, to 14cm (5½in) long. In late spring and early summer, bears terminal, solitary yellow flowers, to 4.5cm (1¾in) across. The strongly ribbed seed pods

Nigella damascena Persian Jewel Series

resemble umbrellas when turned inside out, making an unusual addition to dried flower arrangements. ↕ to 45cm (18in), ↔ 22–30cm (9–12in). ❄❄❄

▷**Nightshade, Stinking** see *Hyoscyamus niger*
▷**Ninebark** see *Physocarpus opulifolius*

NIPPONANTHEMUM

ASTERACEAE/COMPOSITAE

Genus of one species of herbaceous or subshrubby perennial from sandy, coastal regions of Japan. It has erect or spreading stems bearing alternate, aromatic leaves crowded together at the ends of the branches. Solitary, daisy-like white flowerheads are borne in summer. Grow in a mixed or herbaceous border, or at the base of a warm, sunny wall.
• **HARDINESS** Frost hardy; may survive temperatures down to -10°C (14°F).
• **CULTIVATION** Grow in very well-drained, moderately fertile soil in full sun. In frost-prone areas, provide a winter mulch over the roots, and protect the leaves with evergreen branches.
• **PROPAGATION** Sow seed at 13°C (55°F) in spring. Divide in early summer.
• **PESTS AND DISEASES** Slugs and aphids may be troublesome.

N. nipponicum. Almost subshrubby perennial with erect or spreading, sparsely branched stems and stalkless, narrowly spoon-shaped, irregularly toothed, aromatic, mid- to dark green leaves, to 9cm (3½in) long. From late summer to late autumn, bears daisy-like white flowerheads, to 6cm (2½in) across, with green disc-florets maturing yellow. ↕↔ 60cm (24in). Japan. ❄❄

N

▷**Nirre** see *Nothofagus antarctica*
▷**Nodding catchfly** see *Silene pendula*
▷**Nodding ladies' tresses** see *Spiranthes cernua*

NOLANA

SOLANACEAE

Genus of 18 species of often glandular-hairy, erect to spreading annuals, perennials, and subshrubs, usually grown as annuals, found in semi-desert and coastal areas in Peru and Chile. They have simple, alternate or whorled, sometimes succulent leaves. The broadly trumpet-shaped, 5-petalled, blue, pink, or white flowers are borne singly or in clusters in the leaf axils. Grow in a border, or as short-lived container plants in a cool greenhouse. In warm climates, grow perennials in a rock garden.
• **HARDINESS** Half hardy.
• **CULTIVATION** Outdoors, grow in any moderately fertile soil in full sun. Under glass, grow in loam-based potting compost (JI No.2) in full light. Water moderately during the growing season.
• **PROPAGATION** Sow seed at 13–15°C (55–59°F) in early spring, *in situ* in late spring, or in autumn for spring-flowering container plants.
• **PESTS AND DISEASES** Prone to aphids.

N. humifusa. Spreading, sticky, glandular-hairy annual, perennial, or subshrub with a basal rosette of stalkless, elliptic to spoon-shaped leaves, to 2.5cm (1in) long, and elliptic stem leaves. In summer, bears lilac-blue flowers, to

Nolana paradoxa

1.7cm (⅔in) across, with broad white throats, streaked lilac-blue. ↕ to 15cm (6in), ↔ to 45cm (18in). Peru, Chile. ❄. **'Little Bells'** has inversely lance-shaped basal leaves and larger flowers, to 2.5cm (1in) across.
N. paradoxa ▣ Spreading, fleshy, glandular-hairy annual or perennial with a basal rosette of stalkless, inversely lance-shaped leaves, 5cm (2in) long, and ovate to elliptic stem leaves. In summer, bears dark blue, sometimes purple or purple-blue flowers, to 5cm (2in) across, with yellow throats and white eyes, only opening in full sun. ↕ 20–25cm (8–10in), ↔ to 60cm (24in). Chile. ❄

▷***Nolina bigelowii*** see *Beaucarnea bigelowii*
▷***Nolina longifolia*** see *Beaucarnea longifolia*
▷***Nolina recurvata*** see *Beaucarnea recurvata*
▷***Nolina stricta*** see *Beaucarnea stricta*
▷***Nolina texana*** see *Beaucarnea texana*
▷***Nolina tuberculata*** see *Beaucarnea recurvata*

NOMOCHARIS

LILIACEAE

Genus of about 7 species of bulbous perennials from seasonally moist meadows, rocks, and woodland in mountainous areas of W. China, S.E. Tibet, Burma, and N. India. They have linear to lance-shaped or oblong-ovate leaves borne in whorls on the upper parts of the stems, or scattered along them in pairs or threes. In summer, they bear loose racemes of often spotted, saucer-

Nomocharis pardanthina

shaped to flat, 6-tepalled flowers, 5–7cm (2–3in) across. They are ideal for a cool woodland garden and are effective grown with rhododendrons.
• **HARDINESS** Fully hardy.
• **CULTIVATION** Plant 15cm (6in) deep in winter or spring, in humus-rich, acid soil in partial shade; in cool areas, they may be grown in full sun. Ensure soil is moist in summer but never waterlogged.
• **PROPAGATION** Sow seed at 7–10°C (45–50°F) in autumn or spring. Flowers appear about 4 years after germination.
• **PESTS AND DISEASES** Susceptible to slug damage.

N. aperta. Bulbous perennial with lance-shaped leaves, 6–10cm (2½–4in) long, in pairs along the stem. In early summer, produces racemes of 5 or 6 nodding, flattish, pale pink flowers, 5–10cm (2–4in) across, spotted deep purple. ↕ 30–80cm (12–32in), ↔ 10cm (4in). W. China. ❄❄❄
N. farreri. Bulbous perennial with linear to lance-shaped leaves, 3.5cm (1½in) long, in whorls up the stem. In early summer, bears racemes of up to 20 nodding, saucer-shaped, white or pale pink flowers, 5–11cm (2–4½in) across, with heavy reddish purple spotting and dark centres. Similar to *N. pardanthina*, but the petals have smooth margins and the leaves are narrower. ↕ 90cm (36in), ↔ 10cm (4in). N.E. Burma. ❄❄❄
N. mairei see *N. pardanthina.*
N. nana see *Lilium nanum.*
N. oxypetala see *Lilium oxypetalum.*
N. pardanthina ▣ syn. *N. mairei.* Bulbous perennial with whorls of elliptic to lance-shaped leaves, 2.5–11cm (1–4½in) long. In early summer, bears racemes of 2–20 nodding, saucer-shaped then flat, white or pale pink flowers, 5–9cm (2–3½in) across; they are heavily spotted reddish purple, and have dark centres and fringed petals. ↕ 90cm (36in), ↔ 10cm (4in). W. China. ❄❄❄
N. saluenensis. Bulbous perennial with elliptic leaves, 2–4cm (¾–1½in) long, scattered up the stem. In early summer, bears racemes of 1–6 nodding, saucer-shaped flowers, 6–9cm (2½–3½in) across, that vary from pale to mid-pink or white, with light maroon spotting towards the dark purple centres. ↕ 90cm (36in), ↔ 10cm (4in). W. China, N.E. Burma. ❄❄❄

▷***Nopalea cochenillifera*** see *Opuntia cochenillifera*

NOPALXOCHIA

CACTACEAE

Genus of 4 species of freely branching, epiphytic, perennial cacti, often included in *Disocactus*, from forest in S. Mexico and Central America. They have strap-shaped, jointed, spineless stems, often cylindrical at the bases, with notched margins. In late spring and early summer, funnel- to bell- or cup-shaped, diurnal flowers are borne on slender tubes from the marginal areoles. The flowers last for 3–4 days and are followed in the species by ovoid red fruits, containing seeds encased in jelly-like pulp. Below 10°C (50°F), grow in a temperate or warm greenhouse, or as houseplants. In warmer climates, grow in a courtyard or in a shady border.
• **HARDINESS** Frost tender.
• **CULTIVATION** Under glass, grow in slightly acid, epiphytic cactus compost in bright filtered light, with moderate humidity, away from draughts. During growth, water freely and apply a dilute balanced liquid fertilizer monthly. Keep barely moist when dormant. Outdoors, grow in moist but sharply drained, leafy, gritty soil in a sheltered site in partial shade. See also pp.48–49.
• **PROPAGATION** Sow seed at 19–24°C (66–75°F) in spring. Take cuttings of stem sections after flowering.
• **PESTS AND DISEASES** Vulnerable to mealybugs, especially in early spring.

N. 'Achievement'. Semi-erect, perennial cactus producing strap-shaped stems with rounded margins. Bears yellow flowers, 14cm (5½in) across, with frilled petals. ↕ 45cm (18in) or more, ↔ 40cm (16in). ❀ (min. 10°C/50°F)
N. ackermannii ▣ syn. *Disocactus ackermannii, Epiphyllum ackermannii.* Erect, perennial cactus with flat, thin, slightly scalloped, fleshy stems, rarely 3-ribbed. The crimson or orange-red flowers have pale yellow-green tubes, 12cm (5in) long, with short pink styles and white stigma lobes. ↕ 45cm (18in) or more, ↔ 40cm (16in). S. Mexico. ❀ (min. 10°C/50°F)
N. 'Alba Superba'. Erect, perennial cactus producing strap-shaped stems with rounded margins. Bears flowers 15–20cm (6–8in) across, with pure white inner petals and pinkish white outer segments. ↕↔ to 50cm (20in). ❀ (min. 10°C/50°F)
N. 'Calypso'. Semi-erect, perennial cactus producing strap-shaped stems with rounded margins and lilac-pink flowers, 12cm (5in) or more across. ↕↔ to 30cm (12in). ❀ (min. 10°C/50°F)
N. 'Celestine'. Erect, perennial cactus producing strap-shaped stems with rounded margins. Bears ruffled, pale reddish pink flowers, 12cm (5in) across. ↕↔ 35cm (14in). ❀ (min. 10°C/50°F)
N. 'Chauncey'. Erect, perennial cactus producing strap-shaped stems with rounded margins. Bears flowers, 15cm (6in) across, with purple inner petals, each with a red mid-line, and dark red outer segments. ↕ to 60cm (24in), ↔ 45cm (18in). ❀ (min. 10°C/50°F)
N. 'Dreamland'. Erect, perennial cactus with strap-shaped, round-margined stems. Flowers, 12cm (5in) across, have pinkish orange petals, each with a deeper, almost red mid-line, and rose-red throats. ↕↔ 50cm (20in). ❀ (min. 10°C/50°F)

Nopalxochia ackermannii

Nopalxochia 'Gloria'

***N.* 'Gloria'** ■ Erect then pendent, perennial cactus bearing slender, strap-shaped stems with minutely notched margins. Produces deep, rich reddish pink flowers, paler in the throats, 10cm (4in) across. ↕30cm (12in), ↔45cm (18in). ❀ (min. 10°C/50°F)
***N.* 'Helena'.** Erect, perennial cactus with 3-angled, notched stems and minutely spiny areoles. Bears red to violet flowers, 12cm (5in) across, with frilled petals. ↕↔45cm (18in). ❀ (min. 10°C/50°F)
***N.* 'Jennifer Ann'** ■ Erect then pendent, perennial cactus with strap-shaped, strongly notched stems. Bears yellow flowers, paler in the throats, to 15cm (6in) across. ↕30cm (12in), ↔50cm (20in). ❀ (min. 10°C/50°F)

Nopalxochia 'Jennifer Ann'

Nopalxochia 'Kismet'

Nopalxochia phyllanthoides 'Deutsche Kaiserin'

***N.* 'King Midas'.** Erect, perennial cactus with strap-shaped or angular stems. Bears bright yellow flowers, to 20cm (8in) across, each with a deep golden mid-stripe and yellowish orange sepals. ↕to 1m (3ft), ↔50cm (20in). ❀ (min. 10°C/50°F)
***N.* 'Kismet'** ■ Perennial cactus producing wide, strap-shaped stems with rounded margins. Bears widely cup-shaped flowers, 16cm (6in) across, in shades of pale purple in the throats and deepening to dark, rich scarlet in the outer segments. ↕↔ to 40cm (16in). ❀ (min. 10°C/50°F)
***N. macdougallii*,** syn. *Disocactus macdougallii, Epiphyllum macdougallii, Lobeira macdougallii.* Semi-erect, perennial cactus producing flat, 2-winged, scalloped, fleshy stems with inset, marginal areoles. Bears narrowly trumpet-shaped, lilac-rose flowers, to 8cm (3in) across, with brown-green tubes. ↕30cm (12in), ↔45cm (18in). S.E. Mexico. ❀ (min. 10°C/50°F)
***N.* 'M.A. Jeans'.** Erect then slightly pendent, perennial cactus producing strap-shaped stems with minutely notched margins. Bears deep pink flowers, 8cm (3in) across. ↕30cm (12in), ↔50cm (20in). ❀ (min. 10°C/50°F)
***N.* 'Moonlight Sonata'.** Erect, perennial cactus producing strap-shaped stems with rounded margins. Bears flowers, 18cm (7in) across, with white bases, purple-pink petals, and dark violet sepals. ↕45cm (18in), ↔30cm (12in). ❀ (min. 10°C/50°F)

Nopalxochia 'Zoe'

***N. phyllanthoides* 'Deutsche Kaiserin'** ■ syn. *Disocactus phyllanthoides* 'Deutsche Kaiserin'. Semi-erect, perennial cactus with strap-shaped, scalloped, fleshy, deep green stems, tapering towards the ends. Bears pink flowers, 7–9cm (3–3½in) across, with white centres. ↕to 45cm (18in), ↔24cm (10in). ❀ (min. 10°C/50°F)
***N.* 'Queen Anne'.** Semi-pendent, perennial cactus producing strap-shaped stems with rounded margins. Bears yellow flowers, 10cm (4in) across. ↕24cm (10in), ↔40cm (16in). ❀ (min. 10°C/50°F)
***N.* 'Soraya'.** Erect, perennial cactus producing strap-shaped stems with rounded margins. Bears brilliant deep scarlet flowers, 11cm (4½in) across, with broad, almost oval petals. ↕24cm (10in), ↔20cm (8in). ❀ (min. 10°C/50°F)
***N.* 'Tyke'.** Erect, untidy, perennial cactus producing strap-shaped stems with rounded margins. Reddish orange flowers, 12cm (5in) across, have wide-spreading, twisted petals. ↕to 50cm (20in), ↔45cm (18in). ❀ (min. 10°C/50°F)
***N.* 'Zoe'** ■ Semi-prostrate, perennial cactus producing strap-shaped stems with rounded margins. Bears peach-orange flowers, to 12cm (5in) across, each with 3 rows of petals. ↕↔40–50cm (16–20in). ❀ (min. 10°C/50°F)

▷**Nordmann fir** see *Abies nordmanniana*
▷**Norway spruce** see *Picea abies*

NOTHOFAGUS

Southern beech

FAGACEAE

Genus of 20 or more species of evergreen or deciduous trees and shrubs from the S. hemisphere (New Guinea and New Caledonia to Australia, New Zealand, and South America), where they occur as forest trees from sea level to the mountains. Leaves are alternate, simple, entire or toothed, sometimes with wavy margins. Flowers and fruits are inconspicuous. They are grown for their habit and foliage, and, in the case of deciduous species, for their attractive autumn colour. Grow as specimen trees in a large garden or woodland garden. In the wild, they often attain much greater heights than in cultivation.

- **HARDINESS** Fully hardy to frost hardy.
- **CULTIVATION** Grow in fertile, moist but well-drained, lime-free soil in full sun. Shelter evergreen species from strong cold winds. Pruning group 1.
- **PROPAGATION** Sow seed in a seedbed in autumn. Seed from garden sources may give rise to hybrids.
- **PESTS AND DISEASES** Root rot may be a problem.

***N. alpina* of gardens** see *N. procera.*
N. antarctica ■♤ (Antarctic beech, Nirre). Broadly conical, often many-stemmed, deciduous tree or shrub bearing ovate to broadly ovate, glossy, dark green leaves, to 3cm (1¼in) long. Leaves are finely toothed and crinkle-margined, and turn yellow in autumn. ↕15m (50ft), ↔10m (30ft). S. Chile, S. Argentina. ❄❄❄
N. betuloides ■♤ Dense, broadly columnar, evergreen tree with ovate to broadly ovate, blunt-toothed, dark blackish green leaves, to 2.5cm (1in) long, often unequal at the bases, borne on sticky red shoots. ↕15m (50ft), ↔6m (20ft). Chile, Argentina. ❄❄
N. cunninghamii ♤ (Myrtle beech). Conical, evergreen tree with slender, downy shoots and ovate to triangular-ovate, blunt-toothed, glossy leaves, to 2cm (¾in) long, bronze-red in summer when young. ↕12m (40ft), ↔8m (25ft). Australia (Victoria, Tasmania). ❄❄
N. dombeyi ■♤–♤ Broadly columnar to conical, evergreen tree. Shoots, which are pendulous at the tips, bear narrowly ovate-lance-shaped, finely toothed, dark green leaves, 2–4cm (¾–1½in) long, often unequal at the bases. ↕20m (70ft), ↔10m (30ft). Chile, Argentina. ❄❄
N. menziesii ♤ (Silver beech). Dense, conical, evergreen tree with silvery white bark when young. Bears broadly ovate to rounded, leathery, dark green leaves, to 2cm (¾in) long, toothed at the

Nothofagus antarctica

Nothofagus betuloides

Nothofagus dombeyi

N

Nothofagus procera

margins, pale green when young. ↕ 15m (50ft), ↔ 8m (25ft). New Zealand. ❄❄
N. obliqua ♤ (Roblé). Fast-growing, narrowly to broadly conical, deciduous tree with arching shoots. Oblong or oblong-lance-shaped, dark green leaves, to 7cm (3in) long, blue-green beneath, with usually 8–10 pairs of veins and doubly toothed margins, turn yellow to orange or red in autumn. ↕ 20m (70ft), ↔ 15m (50ft). Chile, Argentina. ❄❄❄
N. procera ▣ ♤ syn. *N. alpina* of gardens (Rauli). Fast-growing, broadly conical, deciduous tree. Bears oblong-lance-shaped to elliptic-lance-shaped, matt, slightly scalloped, deep green leaves, to 10cm (4in) or more long, conspicuously marked with 15–18 pairs of veins. Leaves are bronze when young, turning yellow to orange or red in autumn. ↕ 25m (80ft), ↔ 15m (50ft). Chile, Argentina (Andes). ❄❄❄
N. pumilio ▣ ♤–♀ Columnar, sometimes shrubby, often several-stemmed, deciduous tree bearing oblong to obovate, dark green leaves, to 4cm (1½in) long; each has 5–7 pairs of veins with 2 rounded teeth between each vein. ↕ 15m (50ft), ↔ 10m (30ft). Chile, Argentina (Andes). ❄❄❄
N. solanderi ♤ (Black beech). Broadly conical, evergreen tree with ovate-elliptic to elliptic-oblong, entire, dark blackish green leaves, to 1.5cm (½in) long, grey-hairy beneath, ending in a short point. ↕ 15m (50ft), ↔ 10m (30ft). New Zealand. ❄❄. **var. *cliffortioides*** (Mountain beech) has ovate, twisted, more sharply pointed leaves.

Nothofagus pumilio (inset: leaf detail)

NOTHOLIRION

LILIACEAE

Genus of 6 species of bulbous perennials, related to *Fritillaria* and *Lilium*, found in open woodland, scrub, and rocky mountains from Afghanistan to W. China. They have basal tufts of narrowly lance-shaped leaves in winter, and racemes of nodding, trumpet- or funnel-shaped flowers in summer. In frost-prone areas, grow in a cool, protected site, or in a cool greenhouse. They grow best in areas with cool summers.
• **HARDINESS** Frost hardy, but leaves are susceptible to frost damage.
• **CULTIVATION** Plant 10–15cm (4–6in) deep in autumn. Outdoors, plant in deep, humus-rich, well-drained soil in partial shade. Provide protection during periods of prolonged frost. Under glass, plant in large containers in loamless potting compost with added leaf mould and sharp sand, in bright filtered light. Water freely during growth. Keep barely moist when dormant. Bulbs are monocarpic and die after flowering, leaving offsets or a cluster of bulblets that take some time to reach flowering size.
• **PROPAGATION** Sow seed or grow on bulblets in late summer in containers in a cold frame. Remove offsets in autumn.
• **PESTS AND DISEASES** Trouble free.

N. bulbuliferum. Bulbous perennial with narrow, lance-shaped, basal leaves, to 45cm (18in) long. In summer, bears racemes of 10–30 trumpet-shaped, pale lilac flowers, to 4cm (1½in) long, with green tips. ↕ to 1.5m (5ft). ↔ 15cm (6in). Nepal to W. China. ❄❄
N. campanulatum. Bulbous perennial with narrow, lance-shaped, basal leaves, to 30cm (12in) long. In summer, bears racemes of up to 20 pendent, deep crimson-purple, green-tipped flowers, to 5cm (2in) long. ↕ 80cm (32in), ↔ 15cm (6in). N. Burma, W. China. ❄❄

NOTHOSCORDUM

False garlic

ALLIACEAE/LILIACEAE

Genus of about 20 species of bulbous perennials from rocky hillsides and disturbed ground in North and South America. They have linear, basal leaves and, from spring to summer, loose umbels of 6-tepalled, funnel-, bell-, or almost star-shaped flowers, borne on erect, leafless stems. They resemble *Allium* but without its characteristic smell. Grow in a rock garden or raised bed. *N. gracile* is best in a wild garden as it increases freely; may become invasive.
• **HARDINESS** Hardy to -10°C (14°F).
• **CULTIVATION** Plant 7cm (3in) deep in any soil in full sun or partial shade in autumn.
• **PROPAGATION** Sow seed as soon as ripe in containers in a cold frame. Remove offsets in autumn.
• **PESTS AND DISEASES** Trouble free.

N. fragrans see *N. gracile.*
N. gracile, syn. *N. fragrans*, *N. inodorum* of gardens. Very vigorous, bulbous perennial with narrow, linear, basal leaves, 20–40cm (8–16in) long. Fragrant umbels of 8–15 small, funnel-shaped, brown- or pink-striped, white or occasionally lilac flowers, 0.9–1.5cm (⅜–½in) long, are borne from spring to summer. ↕ 25–70cm (10–28in), ↔ 5cm (2in). Mexico, South America. ❄❄
***N. inodorum* of gardens** see *N. gracile.*
N. neriniflorum see *Calloscordum neriniflorum.*

▷ ***Notocactus*** see *Parodia*
N. apricus see *P. concinna*
N. brevihamatus see *P. brevihamata*
N. concinnus see *P. concinna*
N. graessneri see *P. graessneri*
N. haselbergii see *P. haselbergii*
N. magnifica see *P. magnifica*
N. mammulosus see *P. mammulosa*
N. mutabilis see *P. mutabilis*
N. ottonis see *P. ottonis*
N. penicillata see *P. penicillata*
N. rutilans see *P. rutilans*
N. scopa see *P. scopa*
N. submammulosus see *P. mammulosa*

Notospartium glabrescens

NOTOSPARTIUM

LEGUMINOSAE/PAPILIONACEAE

Genus of 3 species of leafless shrubs or trees found on valley sides and river terraces in South Island, New Zealand. They are grown for their elegant habit, green, leafless branches, and pendulous racemes of colourful, pea-like flowers, borne in summer. Grow in a shrub border or at the base of a sunny wall.
• **HARDINESS** Frost hardy.
• **CULTIVATION** Grow in moist but well-drained soil in full sun; shelter from strong winds. Pruning group 9.
• **PROPAGATION** Sow seed in containers in a cold frame in autumn or spring. Take semi-ripe cuttings in summer, with bottom heat.
• **PESTS AND DISEASES** Trouble free.

N. carmichaeliae (Pink broom). Weeping shrub with slender, pendulous, leafless green shoots. Pea-like, purple-veined pink flowers, 8mm (⅜in) long, with broad, standard petals, are borne in dense, slender racemes, to 5cm (2in) long. ↕ 2–4m (6–12ft), ↔ 1.5m (5ft). New Zealand (South Island). ❄❄
N. glabrescens ▣ ♀ Upright shrub or small tree with pendulous lower branches and slightly flattened, slender, dark blue-green shoots. Pea-like pink flowers, to 1cm (½in) long, flushed and veined purple, are produced in open racemes, to 5cm (2in) long. ↕ 3m (10ft), ↔ 2m (6ft) or more. New Zealand (South Island). ❄❄

NUPHAR

Spatterdock, Yellow pond lily

NYMPHAEACEAE

Genus of 25 species of deciduous, submerged, aquatic perennials, mainly from temperate regions of the N. hemisphere. They have stout, creeping rhizomes, and both leathery floating leaves and membranous submerged leaves. In summer, they bear solitary,

N

almost spherical flowers, held above the water surface. The flowers are followed by berry-like, ovoid to flask-shaped fruits. Generally more vigorous than water lilies (*Nymphaea*), they thrive in deeper, cooler water, forming robust groups of foliage on large natural lakes, where they may cover the water surface completely.

- **HARDINESS** Fully hardy to frost hardy.
- **CULTIVATION** Outdoors, grow vigorous species in water 2m (6ft) deep, anchoring the thick rhizomes in the mud at the bottom. Grow less vigorous species in acid water about 30cm (12in) deep, providing a free root-run. Grow in full sun, and divide frequently for optimum flower production.
- **PROPAGATION** Separate pieces of rhizome that have a growing point attached, and transplant.
- **PESTS AND DISEASES** Trouble free.

N. advena (American spatterdock). Aquatic perennial with floating or upright, thick, tough, leathery, broadly ovate to oblong leaves, to 30cm (12in) long. In summer, bears red-tinged yellow flowers, 4cm (1½in) across, with coppery-red stamens. ↔ indefinite. C. and E. USA. ✽✽✽

N. japonica ■ (Japanese pond lily). Aquatic perennial with narrowly ovate to oblong floating leaves, to 40cm (16in) long, arrow-shaped at the bases, and distinctive, narrow, arrow-shaped, wavy submerged leaves, to 30cm (12in) long. Produces yellow, red-tinted flowers, 5cm (2in) across, in summer. ↔ 1m (3ft). Japan. ✽✽

N. kalmiana. Aquatic perennial with broadly rounded floating leaves, 10cm (4in) long, softly hairy beneath, and distinctive, thin, rounded submerged leaves. In summer, bears orange flowers, 2cm (¾in) across, with yellow margins. ↔ 60–90cm (24–36in). E. USA. ✽✽

N. lutea ■ syn. *N. luteum* (Yellow pond lily). Aquatic perennial with ovate-oblong to rounded, thick, mid- to deep green floating leaves, 40cm (16in) long, and broadly ovate to rounded, wavy-margined, translucent, pale green submerged leaves, each with a deep sinus. In summer, bears yellow flowers, 6cm (2½in) across, with a distinctive, unpleasant smell. ↔ 2m (6ft). Eurasia, N. Africa, E. USA, West Indies. ✽✽✽

N. luteum see *N. lutea.*

N. pumila. Aquatic perennial with broadly ovate floating leaves, 14cm (5½in) long, and broadly ovate to

Nuphar japonica

Nuphar lutea

rounded, wavy-margined, translucent, pale green submerged leaves. In summer, bears yellow flowers, to 3cm (1¼in) across. Suitable for a small pool. ↔ 1.4m (4½ft). Europe, Russia (W. Siberia), Japan. ✽✽✽

▷**Nutmeg tree, California** see *Torreya californica*
▷**Nutmeg yew** see *Torreya*
▷***Nuttallia*** see *Oemleria*
N. cerasiformis see *O. cerasiformis*
▷***Nyctocereus serpentinus*** see *Peniocereus serpentinus*

NYMANIA

MELIACEAE

Genus of one species of evergreen shrub from hot, dry areas of South Africa. It is grown for its small, 4-petalled flowers, with 8 long stamens, produced singly from the leaf axils, and its colourful, bladder-like seed pods. The leaves are very narrow and arranged alternately. In frost-prone areas, grow *N. capensis* in a cool greenhouse or conservatory. In warm, dry climates, grow in a border or as a specimen plant.

- **HARDINESS** Frost tender, but may survive short periods at 0°C (32°F).
- **CULTIVATION** Under glass, grow in loam-based potting compost (JI No.2) in full light. In spring and summer, water moderately and apply a balanced liquid fertilizer every month. Water sparingly in winter. Outdoors, grow in fertile, well-drained soil in full sun. Pruning group 8; may need restrictive pruning under glass after fruiting.
- **PROPAGATION** Sow seed at 16°C (61°F) in spring. Root semi-ripe cuttings in summer, with bottom heat.
- **PESTS AND DISEASES** Usually trouble free, although scale insects may be a problem under glass.

N. capensis 🏆 (Chinese lanterns, Klapperbos). Erect to ascending, large shrub or sometimes small tree, usually very open, with rigid branches. The stems are crowded with linear to narrowly oblong leaves, to 5cm (2in) long. Bears 4-petalled flowers, 1.5cm (½in) long, with erect, carmine-red to rose-pink petals, from late winter to early summer. Inflated seed capsules, 2.5–3cm (1–1¼in) long, are off-white, and heavily mottled and suffused carmine-red. ↕ 2–3m (6–10ft) or more, ↔ 1–2m (3–6ft). South Africa (Eastern Cape). ❀ (min. 5–7°C/41–45°F)

NYMPHAEA

Water lily

NYMPHAEACEAE

Genus of 50 species of herbaceous, submerged aquatic perennials occurring worldwide, cultivated for their showy, sometimes fragrant flowers and floating leaves. Water lilies have horizontal or upright rhizomes or stoloniferous tubers, and broadly ovate to rounded, floating leaves, each cleft into 2 lobes, with a basal sinus and a long leaf-stalk. The mostly white, yellow, pink, red, or, in the non-hardy species, blue flowers, borne in summer, each have 4 sepals and numerous narrow petals and stamens. Berry-like fruits, with many seeds, mature under water.

Hardy water lilies, usually day-blooming and with floating flowers, include 2 subgroups: the robust Marliacea Group hybrids, probably derived from *N. alba*, *N. odorata*, *N. tuberosa*, and *N. mexicana*, have rounded leaves, and flowers held just above the water; hybrids in the less vigorous Laydekeri Group, derived from *N. alba* and *N. tetragona*, have flowers held on or just above the water, and rounded, often mottled leaves. Tender, tropical water lilies are either day-blooming or night-blooming, with larger, often toothed leaves, and generally bear their flowers well above the water.

Water lilies are a decorative addition to any pool; the shade of their leaves is useful in reducing algae growth. In frost-prone areas, grow tender water lilies in a conservatory in full sun.

- **HARDINESS** Fully hardy to frost tender.
- **CULTIVATION** Grow in undisturbed water in full sun. In summer, plant hardy water lilies in firm, loamy soil; insert the rhizomes just under the surface and cover with washed pea gravel or chippings. Submerge freshly planted containers so that 15–25cm (6–10in) of water covers the young crowns, either by temporarily lowering the water level or by raising the containers on brick plinths. For small rhizomes, reduce the depth to 8cm (3in); increase to 50cm (20in) for the largest rhizomes. Once plants are established, gradually increase the water depth above the crowns to twice the initial planting depth. Contain vigorous water lilies in an aquatic planting basket, or in a specially constructed, permanent planting station, about 1m (3ft) across and 45cm (18in)

Nymphaea 'Blue Beauty'

deep. During active growth, feed container-grown water lilies with proprietary aquatic fertilizer according to the manufacturer's instructions. Remove yellow leaves and dead-head regularly. Divide established plants, whose leaves thrust vertically above the water surface, to maintain flowering.

In frost-prone areas, grow tropical water lilies year-round in baskets in an indoor pool with a minimum temperature of 10°C (50°F) in winter, and 21°C (70°F) in summer. In frost-free areas, plant in an outdoor pool in summer, remove the tubers in autumn, and overwinter in damp sand at a minimum of 10°C (50°F). Restart young plants in spring when dividing overwintered tubers. See also pp.52–53.

- **PROPAGATION** Surface-sow seed as soon as ripe, and cover with 2.5cm (1in) of water; germinate hardy species at 10–13°C (50–55°F), tropical species at 23–27°C (73–81°F). The seed heads sink as seeds ripen; enclose in a muslin bag to avoid losses. Divide rhizomes of older plants, or separate offsets. Remove young plantlets from viviparous water lilies in summer, and pot individually in shallow water until established.
- **PESTS AND DISEASES** Susceptible to brown china-mark moth, false leaf-mining midge, water lily beetle, water lily aphid (which overwinters on *Prunus* species), and brown spot, crown rot, and water lily leaf spot.

N. alba ■ (White water lily). Aquatic perennial with rounded, dark green leaves, often red-green beneath, 30cm (12in) across, with open sinuses. The faintly fragrant white flowers, 20cm (8in) across, with yellow stamens, are cup-shaped, later star-shaped, and day-blooming. ↔ 1.7m (5½ft). Eurasia, N. Africa. ✽✽✽

N. 'Albida' ■ syn. *N.* 'Marliacea Albida'. Aquatic perennial (Marliacea Group) with rounded, dark green leaves, 22cm (9in) across, slightly bronzed when young, with open sinuses. The fragrant, cup-shaped white flowers, 12–15cm (5–6in) across, have yellow stamens. ↔ 0.9–1.2m (3–4ft). ✽✽✽

N. 'Amabilis'. Aquatic perennial with rounded leaves, 24cm (10in) across, with open sinuses, reddish purple when young, maturing to dark green with red-margined, light green undersides. Star-shaped flowers, 15–19cm (6–7in) across, are pink with light pink tips and dark yellow stamens. ↔ 1.5–2.2m (5–7ft). ✽✽✽

N. 'American Star' ■ Aquatic perennial bearing rounded leaves, 25–27cm (10–11in) across, with open sinuses, purple-green when young, with red undersides, maturing to light green. Star-shaped flowers, 15–17cm (6–7in) across, with long, salmon-pink petals tipped paler pink, yellow inner stamens, and pinkish orange outer stamens, are borne well above the water surface. ↔ 1.2–1.5m (4–5ft). ✽✽✽

N. 'Attraction' ■ Aquatic perennial bearing oval, light bronze leaves, to 25–30cm (10–12in) long, with overlapping lobes, one of which is distinctly raised. Cup-shaped, later star-shaped flowers, to 23cm (9in) across, have dark garnet-red inner petals, lighter towards the margins, and orange-red stamens. ↔ 1.2–1.5m (4–5ft). ✽✽✽

N

NYMPHAEA

***N.* 'Aurora'** ■ Aquatic perennial with oval, mid-green leaves with maroon mottling, to 16cm (6in) long, with open sinuses. Cup-shaped, later flattened flowers, 10cm (4in) across, with orange stamens, change from yellowish apricot-red through orange-red to a slightly flecked burgundy-red. ↔ 0.9–1.5m (3–5ft). ❄❄❄

***N.* 'Blue Beauty'** ■ Aquatic perennial with oval, toothed, wavy-margined, dark green leaves lightly speckled brown above, to 35cm (14in) across, with partly overlapping lobes. Day-blooming, star-shaped, fragrant, mid-blue flowers, 20–28cm (8–11in) across, have dark yellow stamens. ↔ 1.2–2.2m (4–7ft). ❀ (min. 10°C/50°F)

N. caerulea (Blue lotus). Aquatic perennial with ovate, mid-green leaves, 30–40cm (12–16in) long, purple-spotted beneath, with overlapping lobes. Day-blooming, star-shaped, pale blue flowers, 15cm (6in) across, have paler inner petals and yellow stamens. ↔ 2.5–3m (8–10ft). N. and tropical Africa. ❄

N. capensis ■ (Cape blue water lily). Aquatic perennial with rounded, toothed, wavy-margined, mid-green leaves, 25–40cm (10–16in) across, with slightly overlapping lobes. The young leaves are purple-spotted beneath. Produces day-blooming, star-shaped, fragrant, light blue flowers, 21–25cm (8–10in) across, with dark yellow stamens. ↔ 1.5–2.5m (5–8ft). E. Africa, southern Africa, Madagascar. ❀ (min. 5°C/41°F). **'Rosea'** has leaves tinted red beneath and red-flushed, pale pink flowers.

***N.* 'Carnea'**, syn. *N.* 'Marliacea Carnea'. Aquatic perennial (Marliacea Group) with dark green leaves, 19–20cm (7–8in) across, purplish when young, and light pink flowers, 11–12cm (4½–5in) across, with yellow stamens. ↔ 1.2–1.5m (4–5ft). ❄❄❄

***N. caroliniana* 'Nivea'** ■ syn. *N.* 'Caroliniana Nivea'. Aquatic perennial bearing rounded, pale green leaves, 20–25cm (8–10in) across, with slightly open sinuses. Star-shaped, fragrant ivory-white flowers, 12–15cm (5–6in) across, have yellow stamens. ↔ 1.2–1.5m (4–5ft). ❄❄❄

***N.* 'Caroliniana Nivea'** see *N. caroliniana* 'Nivea'.

***N.* 'Charlene Strawn'.** Aquatic perennial with rounded leaves, 20–22cm (8–9in) across, red with purple mottling when young, maturing to mid-green, sometimes marked with purple, and with overlapping lobes. Star-shaped, highly fragrant, yellow flowers, 15–20cm (6–8in) across, have yellow stamens. ↔ 0.9–1.5m (3–5ft). ❄❄❄

***N.* 'Charles de Meurville'.** Aquatic perennial with oval, dark green leaves, 25cm (10in) long, with long, deep sinuses. Star-shaped flowers, 15–17cm (6–7in) across, are dark pinkish red in the centre, fading to pink towards the margins, with orange stamens. ↔ 1.2–1.5m (4–5ft). ❄❄❄

***N.* 'Chromatella'** ■ syn. *N.* 'Marliacea Chromatella'. Aquatic perennial (Marliacea Group) bearing olive-green leaves with bronze markings, 15–20cm (6–8in) across, coppery with purple streaks when young. Canary-yellow flowers, 15cm (6in) across, have broad, incurved petals and golden stamens. ↔ 1.2–1.5m (4–5ft). ❄❄❄

N.* x *daubenyana (*N. caerulea* x *N. micrantha*). Aquatic, viviparous, hybrid perennial producing ovate, olive- to bronze-green leaves, to 30cm (12in) long, with wavy margins and overlapping lobes, many bearing a plantlet. Day-blooming, cup-shaped, fragrant flowers, 10–18cm (4–7in) across, are light blue with dark margins and yellow stamens. ↔ 0.9–1.2m (3–4ft). Garden origin. ❀ (min. 10°C/50°F)

***N.* 'Ellisiana'.** Aquatic perennial with oval, mid-green leaves, 17–20cm (7–8in) long, with open sinuses; young leaves are dark green, marked purple. Star-shaped, fragrant, bright red flowers, 10–12cm (4–5in) across, have orange-red stamens. ↔ 90cm (36in). ❄❄❄

***N.* 'Emily Grant Hutchings'.** Aquatic perennial bearing rounded, wavy-margined leaves, 25–30cm (10–12in) across, bronze-green above, olive-green beneath, with overlapping nodes. Night-blooming, cup-shaped, dark pink flowers, 15–20cm (6–8in) across, have red stamens. ↔ 1.8–2.2m (6–7ft). ❀ (min. 10°C/50°F)

***N.* 'Escarboucle'** ■ Aquatic perennial with rounded, mid-green leaves, 25–27cm (10–11in) across, brown-tinged when young, with overlapping lobes. Cup-shaped, later star-shaped, vermilion-red flowers, about 15–17cm (6–7in) across, have white-tipped outer petals and dark orange stamens. ↔ 1.2–1.5m (4–5ft). ❄❄❄

Nymphaea 'Froebelii'

***N.* 'Fire Crest'** ■ Aquatic perennial with rounded, mid-green leaves, 22cm (9in) across, dark purple when young, with open sinuses. Star-shaped, deep pink flowers, 15cm (6in) across, with lavender-pink inner petals, have orange inner stamens and pink outer stamens. ↔ 1.2m (4ft). ❄❄❄

N. flava see *N. mexicana.*

***N.* 'Froebelii'** ■ Aquatic perennial with rounded, pale green leaves, 15cm (6in) across, bronzed when young, with open sinuses. Cup-shaped, later star-shaped, burgundy-red flowers, 10–12cm (4–5in) across, have orange-red stamens. ↔ 90cm (36in). ❄❄❄

***N.* 'Fulgens'** ■ syn. *N.* 'Laydekeri Fulgens'. Aquatic perennial (Laydekeri Group) with broadly ovate, dark green leaves, 21cm (8in) long, with overlapping lobes; young leaves are purplish green, marked dark purple. Cup-shaped, burgundy-red flowers, 12–15cm (5–6in) across, have orange-red stamens. ↔ 1.2–1.5m (4–5ft). ❄❄❄

***N.* 'General Pershing'** ■ Aquatic perennial bearing rounded, wavy-margined, olive-green, purple-marked leaves, 23–25cm (9–10in) across, with almost closed sinuses. Day-blooming, cup-shaped, later flat, highly fragrant, lavender-pink flowers, 20–27cm (8–11in) across, have yellow stamens. ↔ 1.5–1.8m (5–6ft). ❀ (min. 10°C/50°F)

N. gigantea (Australian water lily). Aquatic perennial with rounded, toothed, wavy-margined, veined, mid-green leaves, to 60cm (24in) across, tinged pink to purple beneath, with often overlapping lobes. Day-blooming, star-shaped, sky-blue to purplish blue flowers, to 30cm (12in) across, have bright yellow stamens. ↔ 2–3m (6–10ft). N. Papua New Guinea, tropical Australia. ❀ (min. 10°C/50°F)

***N.* 'Gladstoneana'.** Aquatic perennial with rounded, wavy-margined, dark

N

Nymphaea alba

Nymphaea 'Albida'

Nymphaea 'American Star'

Nymphaea 'Attraction'

Nymphaea 'Aurora'

Nymphaea capensis

Nymphaea caroliniana 'Nivea'

Nymphaea 'Chromatella'

Nymphaea 'Escarboucle'

Nymphaea 'Fire Crest'

Nymphaea 'Fulgens'

Nymphaea 'General Pershing'

green leaves, 27–30cm (11–12in) across, with toothed margins along the overlapping lobes, and bronzed when young. Star-shaped white flowers, 12–17cm (5–7in) across, have yellow stamens. ↔ 1.5–2.5m (5–8ft). ❄❄❄

***N.* 'Gloriosa'.** Aquatic perennial with broadly ovate, bronze-green leaves, 20–22cm (8–9in) long, with open sinuses; young leaves are light-purple with darker markings and have overlapping lobes. Cup-shaped to star-shaped, bright red flowers, 12cm (5in) across, have orange-red stamens. ↔ 1.5m (5ft). ❄❄❄

***N.* 'Gonnère'** ▣ Aquatic perennial with rounded, light green leaves, 15–22cm (6–9in) across, with open sinuses; young leaves are bronzed. Globe-shaped, fragrant white flowers, 10–15cm (4–6in) across, have yellow stamens. ↔ 0.9–1.2m (3–4ft). ❄❄❄

***N.* 'Indiana'.** Aquatic perennial with rounded, olive-green leaves, 12cm (5in) long, with open sinuses; young leaves are heavily marked with purplish green. Cup-shaped flowers, gradually flattening to 9–10cm (3½–4in) across, turn from apricot, through apricot-orange, to dark orange-red, and have orange stamens. ↔ 75cm (30in). ❄❄❄

***N.* 'James Brydon'** ▣ Aquatic perennial with rounded, bronze-green leaves, 17cm (7in) across, with overlapping lobes; young leaves are purplish brown with dark purple markings. Cup-shaped, vivid rose-red flowers, 10–12cm (4–5in) across, have orange-red stamens. ↔ 0.9–1.2m (3–4ft). ❄❄❄

***N.* 'Laydekeri Fulgens'** see *N.* 'Fulgens'.

N. lotus (Egyptian water lily). Aquatic perennial with rounded, toothed, dark green leaves, to 50cm (20in) across, softly hairy beneath, with wavy margins and overlapping nodes. Bears day- or night-blooming, star-shaped, pink-tinged white flowers, to 25cm (10in) across. ↔ 2–3m (6–10ft). Egypt to tropical and S.E. Africa. ❀ (min. 10°C/50°F)

***N.* 'Louise'.** Aquatic perennial with rounded, mid-green leaves, 22–25cm (9–10in) across, with open sinuses; young leaves are slightly bronzed. Cup-shaped, sweetly fragrant red flowers, 15cm (6in) across, have dark yellow stamens. ↔ 1.2–1.5m (4–5ft). ❄❄❄

Nymphaea 'Lucida'

***N.* 'Lucida'** ▣ Aquatic perennial with broadly ovate, mid-green leaves, to 25cm (10in) long, with large purple markings and open sinuses. Star-shaped flowers, 12–15cm (5–6in) across, have red inner petals, pink-veined, whitish pink outer petals, and yellow stamens. ↔ 1.2–1.5m (4–5ft). ❄❄❄

***N.* 'Marliacea Albida'** see *N.* 'Albida'.

***N.* 'Marliacea Carnea'** see *N.* 'Carnea'.

***N.* 'Marliacea Chromatella'** see *N.* 'Chromatella'.

N. mexicana, syn. *N. flava* (Yellow water lily). Aquatic perennial with ovate to rounded, wavy, toothed, leathery, mid-green leaves, to 18cm (7in) across, with brown marks above, purple beneath, and with open sinuses and overlapping lobes. Bears both floating and aerial, day-blooming, cup-shaped, later star-shaped, slightly fragrant, pale to bright yellow flowers, to 13cm (5in) across. ↔ 2–3m (6–10ft). S. USA, Mexico. ❀ (min. 10°C/50°F)

***N.* 'Mme Wilfon Gonnère'.** Aquatic perennial with rounded leaves, 23–25cm (9–10in) across, with overlapping lobes, slightly bronzed when young, maturing to mid-green; each has a broad yellow stripe in spring that disappears in summer. Peony-like pink flowers, 12cm (5in) across, have light pink outer petals and gold stamens. ↔ 1.2m (4ft). ❄❄❄

N. odorata. Aquatic perennial with ovate to rounded, leathery, glossy, mid-green leaves, 15–30cm (6–12in) across, with open sinuses. Day-blooming, cup-shaped or later star-shaped, fragrant white flowers, 10–22cm (4–9in) across, have yellow stamens. ↔ 1.2–1.8m (4–6ft). N.E. USA. ❄❄❄. **'Sulphurea'** has purple-marked, bronze-green leaves, and fragrant yellow flowers, held slightly above the water. ↔ 0.9–1.2m (3–4ft). **'Sulphurea Grandiflora'** ▣ is similar to 'Sulphurea', with marbled, dark green leaves and very large, star-shaped, bright rich yellow flowers. **'Turicensis'** has rounded leaves, 12–15cm (5–6in) across, with rounded lobes and open sinuses, and bears star-shaped, fragrant, soft pink flowers; ↔ 70cm (28in).

***N.* 'Paul Hariot'.** Aquatic perennial with oval leaves, 15–17cm (6–7in) long, with rounded tips and open sinuses; leaves are purple-speckled olive-green, maturing to purple-marked dark green. Cup-shaped flowers, 10–12cm (4–5in) across, are creamy apricot, turning light pink, and have orange stamens. ↔ 0.9–1.2m (3–4ft). ❄❄❄

***N.* 'Pearl of the Pool'** ▣ Aquatic perennial with rounded, deep green leaves, 25cm (10in) across, with lobes sometimes overlapping and raised, bronzed when young. Star-shaped, fragrant pink flowers, 12–15cm (5–6in) across, have pinkish orange stamens. ↔ 1.2–1.5m (4–5ft). ❄❄❄

***N.* 'Pink Sensation'** ▣ Aquatic perennial with rounded, mid-green leaves, to 25cm (10in) across, with narrow sinuses; young leaves are purple-green. Cup-shaped, later star-shaped pink flowers, 12–15cm (5–6in) across, have yellow inner stamens and pink outer stamens. ↔ 1.2m (4ft). ❄❄❄

N. pygmaea see *N. tetragona.*

***N.* 'Pygmaea Alba'** see *N. tetragona.*

***N.* 'Radiant Red'.** Aquatic perennial with rounded, mid-green leaves, to 25cm (10in) across, with partly open sinuses. Star-shaped red flowers, 12–15cm (5–6in) across, have long, flecked petals and orange stamens. ↔ 0.9–1.2m (3–4ft). ❄❄❄

***N.* 'Red Flare'.** Aquatic perennial with rounded, heavily toothed, reddish bronze leaves, 25–30cm (10–12in) across, with wavy margins and open sinuses. Night-blooming, flat, dark red flowers, 17–25cm (7–10in) across, have light pink or yellowish stamens, and are held well above the water. ↔ 1.5–1.8m (5–6ft). ❀ (min. 10°C/50°F)

***N.* 'Rembrandt'.** Aquatic perennial with rounded, mid-green leaves, 22–25cm (9–10in) across, with open sinuses; young leaves are purplish green. Bears peony-like red flowers, 15–20cm (6–8in) across, with yellow stamens. ↔ 70–120cm (28in–48in). ❄❄❄

***N.* 'René Gérard'** ▣ Aquatic perennial with rounded, mid-green leaves, to 25–27cm (10–11in) across, bronzed when young, with partly open sinuses. Star-shaped, rosy-red flowers, 15–22cm (6–9in) across, have strongly flecked, paler outer petals and yellow stamens. ↔ 1.5m (5ft). ❄❄❄

N

Nymphaea 'Gonnère'

Nymphaea 'James Brydon'

Nymphaea odorata 'Sulphurea Grandiflora'

Nymphaea 'Pearl of the Pool'

Nymphaea 'Pink Sensation'

Nymphaea 'René Gérard'

Nymphaea 'Rose Arey'

Nymphaea 'Sunrise'

Nymphaea tetragona

Nymphaea tetragona 'Helvola'

Nymphaea 'Vésuve'

Nymphaea 'Virginalis'

***N.* 'Rose Arey'** ■ Aquatic perennial with rounded, bronze-green leaves, 22cm (9in) across, purple when young, with narrow sinuses. Bears star-shaped, fragrant, deep rose-pink flowers, 17–20cm (7–8in) across, orange-pink toward the margins, with golden stamens. ↔ 1.2–1.5m (4–5ft). ❄❄❄
***N.* 'St. Louis'.** Aquatic perennial with broadly ovate, light green leaves, to 50cm (20in) long, sometimes with wavy margins, purple-marked when young, with open sinuses. Day-blooming, star-shaped, fragrant, lemon-yellow flowers, 20–27cm (8–11in) across, have golden yellow stamens. ↔ 2.5–3m (8–10ft). ❀ (min. 10°C/50°F)
***N.* 'Sunrise'** ■ Aquatic perennial with broadly ovate, dark green leaves, 27cm (11in) long, with open sinuses; young leaves have purple mottling. Bears star-shaped, bright yellow flowers, 17–23cm (7–9in) across, with long, narrow petals and yellow stamens. ↔ 1.2–1.5m (4–5ft). ❄❄
N. tetragona ■ syn. *N. pygmaea*, *N.* 'Pygmaea Alba'. Aquatic perennial with ovate, dark green, purple-blotched leaves, to 8cm (3in) across, with open sinuses. Day-blooming, cup-shaped, slightly fragrant flowers, 2.5–5cm (1–2in) across, are white with yellow stamens. ↔ 25–40cm (10–16in). N.E. Europe, N. Asia to Japan, N. America. ❄❄. **'Helvola'** ■ has heavily mottled, purple-marked leaves, 12cm (5in) long. Slightly fragrant, vivid yellow flowers, 5–7cm (2–3in) across, have orange-yellow stamens and become star-shaped.
***N. tuberosa*.** Aquatic perennial with rounded, bright green leaves, 10–40cm (4–16in) across, with open sinuses. Day-blooming, cup-shaped, slightly scented white flowers, 10–22cm (4–9in) across, with yellow stamens, are sometimes held 5–8cm (2–3in) above the water. N.E. USA. ↔ to 2.2m (7ft). ❄❄. **'Richardsonii'** has mid-green leaves, 40cm (16in) across, with overlapping lobes. Peony-like white flowers have yellow stamens. ❄❄❄
***N.* 'Vésuve'** ■ Aquatic perennial with rounded, mid-green leaves, 22–25cm (9–10in) across, with open sinuses. Star-shaped, fragrant red flowers, 17cm (7in) across, darkening with age, have inward-curving petals and orange-red stamens. ↔ 1.2m (4ft). ❄❄❄
***N.* 'Virginalis'** ■ Aquatic perennial with rounded, pale green leaves, 22cm (9in) across, purple or bronze when young, with overlapping lobes. Star-shaped, fragrant white flowers, 11–14cm (4½–5½in) across, have yellow stamens. ↔ 0.9–1.2m (3–4ft). ❄❄❄
***N.* 'Virginia'.** Aquatic perennial with ovate, mid-green leaves, 25cm (10in) long, heavily marked with purple, mainly at the margins of older leaves, with open sinuses. Star-shaped, fragrant flowers, 17–20cm (7–8in) across, pale yellow in the centres and off-white towards the outsides, have yellow stamens. ↔ 1.5–1.8m (5–6ft). ❄❄❄
***N.* 'Wood's White Knight'.** Aquatic perennial bearing rounded, mid-green leaves, 30–40cm (12–16in) across, with scalloped, wavy margins and open sinuses. Produces night-blooming, peony-like, fragrant white flowers, 25–30cm (10–12in) across, with yellow stamens. ↔ 2.5–3m (8–10ft). ❀ (min. 10°C/50°F)

NYMPHOIDES

Floating heart

MENYANTHACEAE

Genus of 20 species of rhizomatous, herbaceous, submerged aquatic perennials occurring worldwide. They are often found in shallow, still water in lakes and ponds, where they spread rapidly, the leaves forming a floating carpet. Leaves are rounded with heart-shaped bases, or kidney-shaped, and grow from thin, creeping, branched rhizomes. The yellow or white, fringed flowers, resembling miniature water lilies (*Nymphaea*), are held above the surface of the water. Grow in a wildlife pool with water lilies or *Nuphar* species. In frost-prone areas, grow tender species in a greenhouse pool or aquarium.

- **HARDINESS** Fully hardy to frost tender.
- **CULTIVATION** Outdoors, grow hardy species, and tender species in frost-free areas, in water no deeper than 60cm (2ft). In a small pool, contain within an aquatic planting basket; in a larger pool or lake, growth is limited to the shallow margins. In frost-prone areas, grow tender species in an inert medium in a large aquarium or indoor pool in full light; most are tolerant of a range of water qualities. See also pp.52–53.
- **PROPAGATION** Separate runners during summer.
- **PESTS AND DISEASES** Trouble free.

***N. humboldtiana*.** Rhizomatous, aquatic perennial with spreading runners and kidney-shaped, shiny, pale green leaves, 15cm (6in) across, reddish green beneath, borne on stalks to 1m (3ft) long. In summer, bears funnel-shaped white flowers, to 4cm (1½in) across, with fringed petals. ↔ indefinite. Mexico, West Indies, Central America and tropical South America. ❀ (min. 5°C/41°F)
N. indica (Water snowflake). Rhizomatous, aquatic perennial bearing rounded, glossy, pale green leaves, 5–20cm (2–8in) across, with heart-shaped bases. In summer, bears funnel-shaped white flowers, to 2cm (¾in) across, with yellow centres, and fringed petals covered with hairy white glands. ↔ indefinite. Tropical regions worldwide. ❀ (min. 5°C/41°F)
N. peltata ■ syn. *Limnanthemum nymphoides*, *L. peltatum*, *Villarsia nymphoides* (Water fringe, Yellow floating heart). Rhizomatous, aquatic perennial with runners, to 2m (6ft) long, bearing ovate to rounded, mottled, bright mid-green leaves, 5–10cm (2–4in) across. Funnel-shaped, bright golden yellow flowers, 2cm (¾in) across, are produced on long stalks in summer. It is the only species regularly grown outdoors in frost-prone areas. ↔ indefinite. Europe, Asia. ❄❄❄

Nymphoides peltata

NYSSA

Tupelo

CORNACEAE/NYSSACEAE

Genus of about 5 species of deciduous trees from woodland and swampland in E. Asia and E. North America. Leaves are simple and alternate. Small, inconspicuous green flowers, borne in clusters in early summer, are followed by small, ovoid blue fruits, about 1cm (½in) long. Grown for their attractive foliage and brilliant autumn colour, they are ideal as specimen trees or in group plantings, and are effective near water.

- **HARDINESS** Fully hardy, but do best in areas with hot summers.
- **CULTIVATION** Grow in fertile, moist but well-drained, neutral to acid soil in sun or partial shade, with shelter from cold, dry winds. Plant as small plants, to 30cm (12in) tall, from containers; it is difficult to transplant them successfully. Pruning group 1; in cool-maritime climates, if it is difficult to maintain a leader, grow as multi-stemmed trees.
- **PROPAGATION** Sow seed in a seedbed in autumn. Take greenwood cuttings in early summer, or semi-ripe cuttings in midsummer.
- **PESTS AND DISEASES** Trouble free.

Nyssa sylvatica

N. sinensis ■ (Chinese tupelo). Broadly conical, deciduous tree, sometimes with several stems. Oblong to elliptic, entire, slenderly tapered, dark green leaves, to 20cm (8in) long, are sparsely hairy and bronze-red when young, turning brilliant shades of orange, red, and yellow in autumn, and becoming nearly hairless when mature. ↕↔ 10m (30ft). C. China. ❄❄❄
N. sylvatica ■ (Black gum, Sour gum, Tupelo). Broadly conical to columnar, deciduous tree with often drooping lower branches. Bears ovate to obovate, matt or glossy, dark green leaves, to 15cm (6in) long, downy beneath when young, with short, blunt points. Leaves turn vivid orange, yellow, or red in autumn. ↕ 20m (70ft), ↔ 10m (30ft). E. North America. ❄❄❄

Nyssa sinensis (inset: leaf detail)

O

OBREGONIA

CACTACEAE

Genus of one species of low-growing, simple, sometimes clustering perennial cactus, closely related to *Ariocarpus*, found on periodically dry, rocky hillsides in N.E. Mexico. Its stems are covered by leaf-like, spirally arranged tubercles. Funnel-shaped flowers are produced from the woolly, depressed centre of each crown during daytime in summer; they are followed by white berries containing pear-shaped, slightly curved seeds. Below 10°C (50°F), grow in a temperate greenhouse; in warm, dry climates, use in a desert garden.
• **HARDINESS** Frost tender.

Obregonia denegrii

• **CULTIVATION** Under glass, grow in standard cactus compost in full light with shade from hot sun. From mid-spring to late summer, water moderately and apply a low-nitrogen liquid fertilizer every 4–5 weeks. In autumn, reduce water gradually, then keep completely dry until early spring. Outdoors, grow in sharply drained, neutral to slightly alkaline, gritty, poor, humus-rich soil in full sun. See also pp.48–49.
• **PROPAGATION** Sow seed at 21°C (70°F) in spring or summer.
• **PESTS AND DISEASES** Susceptible to aphids, especially while flowering.

O. denegrii ■ Perennial cactus with a thick, tuberous rootstock and flattened-spherical, greyish green or brownish green stems. Triangular tubercles have woolly hairs in the axils, and areoles at their tips, from which a few bristly spines emerge, but quickly fall. In summer, bears solitary, broadly funnel-shaped, very narrow-petalled, white or pale pink flowers, 2–3.5cm (¾–1½in) across, with yellow centres. ↕ 7–10cm (3–4in), ↔ 12cm (5in). N.E. Mexico. ❀ (min. 7–10°C/45–50°F)

OCHAGAVIA

BROMELIACEAE

Genus of 3 species of evergreen, terrestrial perennials (bromeliads) found on exposed, coastal rock faces in Chile. They have almost stemless, spreading rosettes of stiff, spiny-toothed leaves. The spherical inflorescences, produced in summer, sit low in the centres of the rosettes and have conspicuous, narrow bracts and tubular, red or yellow flowers; these are followed by ovoid green berries containing large, spherical brown seeds. Where temperatures regularly drop below 5°C (41°F), grow in a cool greenhouse or as houseplants; in warmer climates, use outdoors in a desert garden.
• **HARDINESS** Frost tender; will sometimes withstand short periods at 0°C (32°F) in a sheltered site.
• **CULTIVATION** Under glass, grow in terrestrial bromeliad compost in full light with low humidity. In growth, water moderately with soft water (avoiding the crown), and apply a half-strength, low-nitrogen liquid fertilizer every 3–4 weeks; keep dry when dormant. Outdoors, grow in moderately

Ochagavia carnea

fertile, humus-rich, gritty, sharply drained soil in full sun. See also p.47.
• **PROPAGATION** Sow seed at 27°C (81°F) as soon as ripe.
• **PESTS AND DISEASES** Susceptible to scale insects.

O. carnea ■ syn. *O. lindleyana.* Terrestrial bromeliad with wide-spreading, dense rosettes of 30–50 stiff, very narrow, linear-lance-shaped, spiny-toothed leaves, 50cm (20in) long, tapering to pointed tips; they are bright dark green above, sometimes with grey-white scales, and densely covered with grey-white scales beneath. In summer, produces many tubular, rose-pink flowers, to 5cm (2in) long, in congested, short-stalked, spherical inflorescences, each with a collar of white and pink bracts. ↕↔ 60cm (24in). C. Chile. ❀ (min. 5°C/41°F)
O. lindleyana see *O. carnea.*

OCHNA

Bird's eye bush

OCHNACEAE

Genus of over 80 species of deciduous or semi-evergreen trees and shrubs from tropical woodland in Africa and Asia, grown for their flowers and fruits. The leathery, often shiny leaves are alternate, simple, and usually minutely toothed. The 5- to 10-petalled, saucer-shaped flowers are solitary, or borne in racemes, panicles, cymes, or umbels. After the petals fall, the calyces and receptacles enlarge and become thick and colourful, contrasting with the shiny, purplish black or black, usually spherical, one-

Ochna serrulata

seeded fruits, borne 3–12 on each receptacle. In frost-prone areas, grow in a conservatory or temperate greenhouse; elsewhere, use in a shrub border.
• **HARDINESS** Frost tender.
• **CULTIVATION** Under glass, grow in loam-based potting compost (JI No.3) in full light with shade from hot sun. In growth, water moderately and apply a balanced liquid fertilizer monthly; water sparingly in winter. Outdoors, grow in fertile, moist but well-drained soil in full sun. Pruning group 8; plants under glass need restrictive pruning after flowering.
• **PROPAGATION** Sow seed at 16°C (61°F) in spring. Root semi-ripe cuttings with bottom heat in summer, or air layer in spring.
• **PESTS AND DISEASES** Red spider mites may infest plants under glass.

O. multiflora see *O. serrulata.*
***O. serratifolia* of gardens** see *O. serrulata.*
O. serrulata ■ ♀ syn. *O. multiflora, O. serratifolia* of gardens (Mickey Mouse plant). Bushy, semi-evergreen shrub or small tree, with bronze shoots covered with close-set, raised, corky dots. Shiny, bright green leaves, 6cm (2½in) long, are narrowly elliptic and finely toothed. Saucer-shaped flowers, to 2cm (¾in) across, each with 5 or 6 spreading, bright yellow petals, are borne singly or in small cymes, mainly in late spring and summer; after the petals fall, the receptacle and sepals turn glossy red. Produces pendent clusters of 5 or 6 spherical, lustrous black fruit. ↕ 1.5–2.5m (5–8ft), ↔ 1–2m (3–6ft). South Africa. ❀ (min. 7°C/45°F)

OCIMUM

LABIATAE/LAMIACEAE

Genus of 35 species of aromatic annuals and evergreen perennials and shrubs occurring in hot, dry scrub in tropical Africa and Asia. They have erect, usually branching stems, with linear to almost rounded leaves, borne in opposite pairs. The tubular flowers, usually in whorls of 6, are arranged in loose or dense spikes, and have small to large, occasionally brightly coloured bracts. Most species and cultivars have medicinal or culinary uses; *O. basilicum* (basil) and its cultivars are grown as culinary herbs. Grow as annuals in a herb or vegetable garden.
• **HARDINESS** Half hardy to frost tender.
• **CULTIVATION** Grow in light, fertile, well-drained soil in a warm, sheltered site in full sun. Water freely during dry periods in summer. Pinch out flower-heads as soon as they appear, to ensure continued leaf growth.
• **PROPAGATION** Sow seed at 13°C (55°F) in early spring, or sow *in situ* in early summer.
• **PESTS AND DISEASES** May be infested with aphids, and sometimes affected by mildew in hot, dry summers.

O. basilicum (Basil, Sweet basil). Erect, bushy, aromatic annual or short-lived perennial. Narrowly oval to elliptic leaves, to 5cm (2in) long, are entire or toothed, sometimes slightly hairy, and bright green, occasionally flushed deep purple. Produces whorls of 6 tubular, 2-lipped, sometimes pink-purple-tinged, white flowers, to 1cm (½in) long, in lax, slightly hairy spikes in late summer.

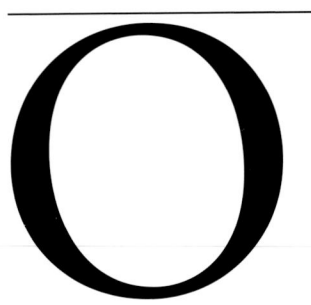

Ocimum basilicum 'Dark Opal'

↕ 30–60cm (12–24in), ↔ 30cm (12in) if grown as an annual. Tropical and subtropical Asia; widely grown in tropical, subtropical, and Mediterranean climates. ✻. **'Dark Opal'** ■ has red-purple leaves and pink flowers. **var. *minimum*** (Greek bush basil) is compact and rounded, bearing ovate leaves, less than 1cm (½in) long, and flowers 2–3mm (1/16–⅛in) long; ↕↔ 15–30cm (6–12in). **'Purple Ruffles'** has purple leaves, curled and fringed at the margins.

O

▷ **Oconee bells** see *Shortia galacifolia*
▷ **Ocotillo** see *Fouquieria splendens*
▷ **Octopus tree** see *Schefflera actinophylla*

x ODONTIODA

ORCHIDACEAE

Hybrid genus of epiphytic, evergreen orchids derived from crosses between *Odontoglossum* and *Cochlioda*; they are vegetatively indistinguishable from *Odontoglossum*. They have ovoid, compressed pseudobulbs, each with 2 linear, mid-green leaves, 20cm (8in) long, at the tip. Erect to arching racemes, 30–45cm (12–18in) tall, of 12 or more rounded to star-shaped flowers, 8cm (3in) across, often with ruffled or crisped margins, arise from the bases of the pseudobulbs at almost any time of the year, most commonly in spring. The flowers range in colour from pastel shades to deep reds, and are often spotted or marked red or yellow.

- **HARDINESS** Frost tender.
- **CULTIVATION** As *Odontoglossum.*
- **PROPAGATION** Divide when the plant fills the pot and "flows" over the sides.
- **PESTS AND DISEASES** Susceptible to red spider mites, aphids, and mealybugs.

x *Odontioda* Mount Bingham

x *O.* City of Birmingham (x *O.* Gold Wood x *Odontoglossum harryanum*). Epiphytic orchid with yellow flowers marked purple and bronze. ↕ 45cm (18in), ↔ 30cm (12in). ❄ (min. 10°C/50°F; max. 24°C/75°F)
x *O.* Durham Castle 'Lyoth Supreme' (x *O.* Ingmar x x *O.* Trixon). Epiphytic orchid producing brilliantly coloured flowers in rich red and mauve shades. ↕ 45cm (18in), ↔ 30cm (12in). ❄ (min. 10°C/50°F; max. 24°C/75°F)
x *O.* Eric Young (x *O.* Golden Rialto x *Odontoglossum* Niamalto). Epiphytic orchid producing light yellow flowers, spotted with deeper yellow. ↕ 45cm (18in), ↔ 30cm (12in). ❄ (min. 10°C/50°F; max. 24°C/75°F)
x *O.* Le Nez Point (x *O.* Brocade x x *O.* Trixon). Epiphytic orchid with solid, dark red flowers. ↕ 45cm (18in), ↔ 30cm (12in). ❄ (min. 10°C/50°F; max. 24°C/75°F)
x *O.* Mount Bingham ■ (x *O.* Ingera x x *O.* Marzorka). Epiphytic orchid with flowers patterned in red and lilac. ↕ 45cm (18in), ↔ 30cm (12in). ❄ (min. 10°C/50°F; max. 24°C/75°F)
x *O.* Petit Port ■ (x *O.* Colwell x x *O.* Margia). Epiphytic orchid bearing rich red flowers with pink-, yellow-, or brown-patterned lips. ↕ 45cm (18in), ↔ 30cm (12in). ❄ (min. 10°C/50°F; max. 24°C/75°F)
x *O.* Red Rum (x *O.* Brocade x x *O.* Ingera). Epiphytic orchid with flowers richly patterned in red-mauve and purple. ↕ 45cm (18in), ↔ 30cm (12in). ❄ (min. 10°C/50°F; max. 24°C/75°F)

x *Odontioda* Petit Port

x ODONTOCIDIUM

ORCHIDACEAE

Hybrid genus of epiphytic, evergreen orchids derived from crosses between *Odontoglossum* and *Oncidium*; they are vegetatively indistinguishable from *Odontoglossum*. They have rounded or ovoid to conical pseudobulbs (all those described are rounded and compressed), each with 2 linear, mid-green leaves, 23cm (9in) long, at the tip. Tall, arching racemes or panicles of 12 or more flowers, 8cm (3in) across, arise from the base. The predominantly yellow, yellow-brown, or russet-red flowers have large, flared lips.

- **HARDINESS** Frost tender.
- **CULTIVATION** As *Odontoglossum.*
- **PROPAGATION** Divide when the plants overflow their containers.
- **PESTS AND DISEASES** Prone to red spider mites, aphids, and mealybugs.

x *O.* Artur Elle 'Columbien' ■ (*Odontoglossum* Hambühren Gold x *Oncidium tigrinum*). Epiphytic orchid bearing yellow flowers, delicately patterned with chestnut-brown, all year round. ↕ 45cm (18in), ↔ 30cm (12in). ❄ (min. 10°C/50°F; max. 24°C/75°F)
x *O.* 'Crowborough' (*Odontoglossum* Golden Guinea x *Oncidium leucochilum*). Epiphytic orchid bearing deep brown and yellow flowers with white lips, mainly in spring. ↕ 45cm (18in), ↔ 30cm (12in). ❄ (min. 10°C/50°F; max. 24°C/75°F)
x *O.* 'Purbeck Gold' (*Odontoglossum* Gold Cup x *Oncidium tigrinum*). Epiphytic orchid bearing deep yellow, brown-spotted flowers, with flared yellow lips, mainly in autumn. ↕ 45cm (18in), ↔ 30cm (12in). ❄ (min. 10°C/50°F; max. 24°C/75°F)
x *O.* Tiger Hambühren ■ (*Odontoglossum* Goldrausch x *Oncidium tigrinum*). Epiphytic orchid bearing rich yellow flowers, heavily spotted and barred with chestnut-brown, mainly in autumn. ↕ 45cm (18in), ↔ 30cm (12in). ❄ (min. 10°C/50°F; max. 24°C/75°F)
x *O.* Tigersun 'Orbec' ■ (*Odontoglossum* Sunmar x *Oncidium tigrinum*). Epiphytic orchid bearing yellow flowers, lightly marked with chestnut-brown, mainly in autumn. ↕ 45cm (18in), ↔ 30cm (12in). ❄ (min. 10°C/50°F; max. 24°C/75°F)

x *Odontocidium* Artur Elle 'Columbien'

x *Odontocidium* Tiger Hambühren

x *Odontocidium* Tigersun 'Orbec'

ODONTOGLOSSUM

ORCHIDACEAE

Genus of about 200 species of evergreen, epiphytic or lithophytic, rhizomatous orchids from mountainous regions, at altitudes of 2,000–3,000m (7,000–10,000ft), in Central and South America. They produce ovoid or oblong-ellipsoid to conical pseudobulbs, each with 1–3 variably shaped, thinly leathery, mid-green leaves at the tip. Flowers are borne in tall or short, erect or arching racemes or panicles arising from the bases of the pseudobulbs, and are highly variable in colour and shape. Many hybrids have been produced that will flower at almost any time of year, with 12 or more flowers in a raceme.

- **HARDINESS** Frost tender.
- **CULTIVATION** Cool-growing orchids. Grow in small pots of epiphytic orchid compost, preferably made with fine-grade bark to suit the fine root system. In summer, provide bright filtered light and high humidity; water and mist freely, and apply fertilizer at every third watering. In winter, provide full light and water sparingly. See also p.46.
- **PROPAGATION** Divide when the plant fills the pot and "flows" over the sides. Hybrids are better retained as one plant; pot on, in late summer or early spring.
- **PESTS AND DISEASES** Prone to red spider mites, aphids, and mealybugs.

Odontoglossum crispum

O. bictoniense see *Lemboglossum bictoniense.*
***O.* Buttercrisp** (*O.* Brimstone Butterfly x *O.* Crispania). Epiphytic orchid with ovoid, compressed pseudobulbs and narrowly oval leaves, 15cm (6in) long. Clear yellow flowers, 6cm (2½in) across, with a few brown spots and brown-spotted, white-margined lips, appear at any time of year. ↕ 30cm (12in), ↔ 25cm (10in). ❄ (min. 10°C/50°F; max. 24°C/75°F)
O. cariniferum. Epiphytic orchid with oblong-ellipsoid, compressed, furrowed pseudobulbs and oblong-elliptic leaves, to 30cm (12in) long. In spring, bears yellow-margined brown flowers, 5cm (2in) across, in erect or arching panicles, 0.6–1.2m (2–4ft) long. ↕ to 1.2m (4ft), ↔ 30cm (12in). Costa Rica, Panama, Colombia, Venezuela. ❄ (min. 10°C/50°F; max. 24°C/75°F)
O. cervantesii see *Lemboglossum cervantesii.*
O. cordatum see *Lemboglossum cordatum.*
O. crispum ■ Epiphytic orchid with ovoid pseudobulbs and linear-elliptic leaves, to 40cm (16in) long. In winter, white flowers, 8cm (3in) across, the lips sometimes yellow and spotted red in the centres, are produced in racemes to 50cm (20in) long. ↕ 50cm (20in), ↔ 25cm (10in). Colombia. ❄ (min. 10°C/50°F; max. 24°C/75°F)
O. grande see *Rossioglossum grande.*
O. harryanum. Epiphytic orchid with slender, ovoid pseudobulbs and elliptic-oblong leaves, to 45cm (18in) long. Flowers, 8cm (3in) across, varying from olive-green to buff or chestnut-brown, with lips lined purplish mauve, appear in racemes to 1–1.2m (3–4ft) long, in winter. ↕ 1–1.2m (3–4ft), ↔ 23cm (9in). Colombia, Peru. ❄ (min. 10°C/50°F; max. 24°C/75°F)

Odontoglossum Royal Occasion

O. odoratum. Epiphytic orchid with ovoid pseudobulbs and narrowly lance-shaped leaves, to 30cm (12in) long. Star-shaped, fragrant flowers, 6cm (2½in) across, pale to deep yellow, dotted and marked dark maroon or red-brown, are produced in panicles to 75cm (30in) long, in spring. ↕ 75cm (30in), ↔ 20cm (8in). Colombia, Venezuela. ❄ (min. 10°C/50°F; max. 24°C/75°F)
O. rossii see *Lemboglossum rossii.*
***O.* Royal Occasion** ■ (*O.* Ardentissimum x *O.* Pumistor). Epiphytic orchid with ovoid pseudobulbs and narrowly oval leaves, 30cm (12in) long. White flowers, 6cm (2½in) across, with deep yellow markings in the centres of the lips, are produced in early summer. ↕ 30cm (12in), ↔ 25cm (10in). ❄ (min. 10°C/50°F; max. 24°C/75°F)
***O.* Saint Brelade 'Jersey'** (*Lemboglossum rossii* x *O.* Ophyras). Epiphytic orchid with ovoid pseudobulbs and narrowly oval leaves, 15cm (6in) long. Highly decorative, pale mauve flowers, 6cm (2½in) across, with deeper mauve or maroon markings and pale mauve lips marked with white and maroon, are produced in late spring. ↕ 30cm (12in), ↔ 25cm (10in). ❄ (min. 10°C/50°F; max. 24°C/75°F)
O. spectatissimum, syn. *O. triumphans.* Epiphytic orchid producing ovoid pseudobulbs and narrowly elliptic leaves, 40cm (16in) long. In spring, bears erect or arching racemes, to 90cm (36in) long, of golden yellow flowers, heavily barred and spotted chestnut-brown, 10cm (4in) across. ↕ 90cm (36in), ↔ 20cm (8in). Colombia, Venezuela. ❄ (min. 10°C/50°F; max. 24°C/75°F)
O. stellatum see *Lemboglossum stellatum.*
O. triumphans see *O. spectatissimum.*

ODONTONEMA

ACANTHACEAE

Genus of 26 species of evergreen perennials and shrubs from woodland in tropical America. They are grown for their terminal racemes or panicles of tubular, brightly coloured flowers, which are 2-lipped or symmetrical. The simple, entire leaves are borne in opposite pairs. Where temperatures fall below 13°C (55°F), grow in a warm greenhouse. In warmer climates, grow in a shrub border.

- **HARDINESS** Frost tender.
- **CULTIVATION** Under glass, grow in loam-based potting compost (JI No.3) in full light with shade from hot sun, and with moderate humidity. During the growing season, water moderately and apply a balanced liquid fertilizer every month; water sparingly in winter. Outdoors, grow in fertile, moist but well-drained soil in full sun. Pruning group 8; plants under glass need restrictive pruning after flowering.
- **PROPAGATION** Sow seed at 16–18°C (61–64°F) in spring. Root greenwood cuttings in early summer, or semi-ripe cuttings with bottom heat in summer.
- **PESTS AND DISEASES** Prone to whiteflies and red spider mites under glass.

O. strictum. Erect shrub, with robust, sparsely branched, rigid stems and oblong, wavy-margined, glossy, deep green leaves, 10–15cm (4–6in) long, with long, sharp points. In winter and spring, bears tubular, 2-lipped, waxy crimson flowers, 2.5cm (1in) long, in slender, erect, compact panicles, to 30cm (12in) long. ↕ 2m (6ft) or more (if unpruned), ↔ 60–100cm (24–39in). Central America. ❄ (min. 13°C/55°F)

x ODONTONIA

ORCHIDACEAE

Hybrid genus of epiphytic, evergreen orchids derived from crosses between *Odontoglossum* and *Miltonia*; they are vegetatively indistinguishable from *Odontoglossum*. They produce ovoid to conical pseudobulbs, each with 2 leaves at the tip. The flowers have large, flat lips and are produced in tall, arching racemes arising from the bases of the pseudobulbs at almost any time of year.

- **HARDINESS** Frost tender.
- **CULTIVATION** As *Odontoglossum.*
- **PROPAGATION** Divide when the plants overflow their containers.
- **PESTS AND DISEASES** Prone to red spider mites, aphids, and mealybugs.

x *O.* Olga (*Odontoglossum crispum* x x *Odontonia* Thisbe). Epiphytic orchid producing ovoid pseudobulbs and narrowly oval leaves, 30cm (12in) long. White flowers, 8cm (3in) across, with lips marked nut-brown, are borne in tall, arching racemes in winter. ↕ 30cm (12in), ↔ 25cm (10in). ❄ (min. 10°C/50°F; max. 24°C/75°F)

OEMLERIA syn. NUTTALLIA, OSMARONIA

ROSACEAE

Genus of one species of deciduous shrub found in forest and canyons in W. North America. It is grown for its simple, alternate, glossy leaves, and its pendent racemes of bell-shaped flowers, both of which appear very early in the year (it is one of the first plants to come into leaf, often in late winter). Male and female flowers are borne on separate plants and both must be grown to bear the small, black, plum-like fruit. Grow in a shrub border or woodland garden.

- **HARDINESS** Fully hardy.
- **CULTIVATION** Grow in fertile, moist but well-drained soil in sun or partial shade. In moist soil, vigorously growing plants may sucker extensively; remove excess suckers to restrict growth. Pruning group 1 or 2.
- **PROPAGATION** Sow seed in a seedbed as soon as ripe. Take greenwood cuttings in early summer. Transplant suckers in autumn.
- **PESTS AND DISEASES** May become chlorotic in shallow, chalky soil.

O. cerasiformis ■ syn. *Nuttallia cerasiformis, Osmaronia cerasiformis* (Indian plum, Oregon plum, Oso berry). Suckering shrub, forming a thicket of upright, eventually arching shoots. These bear narrowly oblong, or lance-shaped to inversely lance-shaped, glossy, dark green leaves, to 9cm (3½in) long, grey-green and softly hairy beneath. Small, bell-shaped, almond-scented

Oemleria cerasiformis (inset: flower detail)

white flowers are produced in pendent racemes, to 10cm (4in) long, in early spring. They are followed on female plants by ovoid, plum-like, purple-black fruit, 2cm (¾in) long. ↕ 2.5m (8ft) or more, ↔ 4m (12ft). W. North America (British Columbia to California). ❄❄❄

OENANTHE

APIACEAE/UMBELLIFERAE

Genus of about 30 species of moisture-loving, hairless perennials from wet meadows, marshland, and shallow water in the N. hemisphere, South Africa, and Australia. Most have alternate, pinnate leaves and bear compound umbels of small, star-shaped white flowers, each with 5 notched petals. They are suitable for damp soil in a bog garden, or for planting as ground cover near a stream or pool. In frost-prone areas, grow tender species in a cool greenhouse. In some species, all parts may cause severe discomfort if ingested; some species are deadly. *O. javanica* is the exception; it is grown as a vegetable in areas where it grows naturally.

- **HARDINESS** Fully hardy to frost tender; *O. javanica* often survives temperatures to -10°C (14°F).
- **CULTIVATION** Grow in any moderately fertile, preferably moist or wet soil, in full sun or partial shade, although quite dry soil is tolerated, especially in partial shade. Shelter from cold, drying winds. In frost-prone areas, provide a dry winter mulch; take cuttings and overwinter in a cold greenhouse to insure against losses.
- **PROPAGATION** Divide in late spring, as growth begins. Take stem-tip cuttings in spring.
- **PESTS AND DISEASES** Susceptible to aphids, and may be damaged by slugs and snails.

O. japonica see *O. javanica.*
O. javanica, syn. *O. japonica.* Spreading perennial with horizontal, rooting stems and celery-like, triangular, pinnate or 2-pinnate leaves, 7–15cm (3–6in) long, with narrowly ovate, toothed, mid-green segments. Compound umbels of star-shaped white flowers, 3mm (⅛in) long, are produced in late summer. ↕ 20–40cm (8–16in), ↔ 90cm (36in). India to Japan, Malaysia, Australia (Queensland). ❄❄. **'Flamingo'** ▣ is grown for its attractive foliage, which is variegated pink, cream, and white.

Oenanthe javanica 'Flamingo'

OENOTHERA

Evening primrose, Sundrops

ONAGRACEAE

Genus of about 125 species of annuals, biennials, and perennials, some with tap roots or fibrous roots and a few with rhizomes or runners. Mostly from North America, with a few from South America, they grow in well-drained, sunny sites, such as mountain slopes, although some are from deserts. They have upright or decumbent stems bearing alternate, more or less lance-shaped, simple or pinnatifid, entire or toothed stem leaves, and occasionally basal rosettes of slightly larger leaves. Evening primroses are cultivated for their flowers, which are mainly produced over long periods in summer; they are often fragrant, white, yellow, or pink, and are large, saucer- to cup-shaped, sometimes trumpet-shaped. Each flower has a long tube and 4 petals, and is either solitary and axillary, or borne in terminal racemes. Individual flowers open at dawn or dusk and fade quickly. Taller species are suitable for a sunny, mixed or herbaceous border; low-growing ones are better for border edging. *O. acaulis*, *O. caespitosa*, and *O. macrocarpa* are excellent for a scree bed or rock garden.

- **HARDINESS** Fully hardy to frost hardy.
- **CULTIVATION** Grow in poor to moderately fertile, well-drained, even stony soil in full sun. *O. fruticosa* prefers slightly more fertile soil. Protect rock garden plants and *O. speciosa* from excessive winter wet.
- **PROPAGATION** Sow seed in containers in a cold frame: annuals and perennials in early spring, biennials in early summer; or sow annuals and biennials *in situ* in autumn. *O. glazioviana* self-seeds prolifically. Divide in early spring, or take softwood cuttings of unflowered shoots of perennials from late spring to midsummer. To avoid damage to tap-rooted species, grow on seedlings and cuttings individually in pots before planting out.
- **PESTS AND DISEASES** Prone to slugs, and sometimes affected by leaf spot and mildew. Root rot may be a problem in wet, heavy soil.

O. acaulis, syn. *O. taraxacifolia.* Clump-forming, short-lived perennial with rosettes of inversely lance-shaped, irregularly pinnatifid, mid-green leaves, 12–20cm (5–8in) long, and a few decumbent stems, to 30cm (12in) or more long. In summer, bears 2–5 trumpet-shaped white flowers, to 8cm (3in) across, from the leaf axils; they open at sunset, and turn pink next day. ↕ 15cm (6in), ↔ to 20cm (8in). Chile. ❄❄❄ (borderline)
O. albicaulis. Spreading annual, biennial, or short-lived perennial, usually grown as a biennial, with basal rosettes of spoon-shaped to ovate, grey-green leaves, to 5cm (2in) long, and white-hairy stems bearing lance-shaped, pinnatifid leaves. In summer, produces solitary, bowl-shaped, scented flowers, to 8cm (3in) across, which open in the evening and are initially white, then cream, and finally pale pink. ↕ 15–30cm (6–12in), ↔ to 30cm (12in). N. America (Rocky Mountains). ❄❄❄

Oenothera fruticosa 'Fyrverkeri'

O. biennis (Evening primrose). Erect, hairy annual or biennial, usually grown as a biennial. Produces large rosettes of oblong to lance-shaped, shallowly toothed, slightly sticky, red-veined, mid-green leaves, 10–30cm (4–12in) long, and lance-shaped stem leaves, to 15cm (6in) long. Bowl-shaped, fragrant flowers, to 5cm (2in) across, initially pale yellow, ageing to dark golden yellow, and opening in the evening, are borne in leafy, spike-like racemes from summer to autumn. Seeds are used to produce evening primrose oil. ↕ 1–1.5m (3–5ft), ↔ to 60cm (24in). E. North America; naturalized in many parts of the world. ❄❄❄
O. caespitosa. Clump-forming biennial or perennial with numerous rosettes of inversely lance-shaped to diamond- or spoon-shaped, entire or irregularly toothed, grey-green leaves, 2–25cm (¾–10in) long. In summer, produces cup-shaped, fragrant white flowers, to 10cm (4in) across, from the rosette leaf axils, several opening at once at sunset; they turn pink with age. ↕↔ to 20cm (8in). W. USA. ❄❄❄
O. cinaeus see *O. fruticosa* subsp. *glauca.*
O. deltoides (Desert evening primrose). Erect annual or perennial, branching from the base, with triangularly ovate to lance-shaped, entire to pinnatifid, mid-green leaves, 5–10cm (2–4in) long. Often produces decumbent basal branches in addition to erect stems. In summer, bears solitary, bowl-shaped flowers, 4–8cm (1½–3in) across, initially white then pink, opening in the morning. Needs sharply drained soil. ↕ to 30cm (12in), ↔ to 20cm (8in). USA (Arizona), Mexico (Baja California). ❄❄
O. elata* subsp. *hookeri, syn. *O. hookeri.* Erect perennial or biennial bearing basal rosettes of lance-shaped, slightly toothed, mid-green leaves, 5–12cm (2–5in) long, and hairy, branching stems with smaller leaves. Throughout summer, bears numerous, cup-shaped flowers, 5–7cm (2–3in) across, initially pale yellow becoming orange-red, which open at dusk in terminal spikes. ↕ 90cm (36in), ↔ 30cm (12in). W. North America. ❄❄❄
O. fraseri see *O. fruticosa* subsp. *glauca.*
O. fruticosa, syn. *O. linearis* (Sundrops). Erect perennial or biennial with branched, softly hairy, red-tinged stems bearing lance-shaped to ovate, toothed, mid-green leaves, 2.5–11cm (1–4½in) long, the basal leaves inversely lance-shaped to obovate. From late spring to late summer, produces racemes of 3–10 saucer- to cup-shaped, deep yellow flowers, 2.5–5cm (1–2in) across, opening during the day. ↕ 30–90cm (12–36in), ↔ 30cm (12in). E. North America. ❄❄❄. **'Fireworks'** see 'Fyrverkeri'. **'Fyrverkeri'** ▣ syn. 'Fireworks', has purple-brown-flushed leaves, and yellow flowers opening from red buds. **subsp. *glauca***, syn. *O. cinaeus, O. fraseri, O. glauca, O. tetragona*, has broader, only sparsely hairy, sometimes glaucous leaves, red-tinted when young, and light yellow flowers; E. USA. **'Highlight'** see 'Hoheslicht'. **'Hoheslicht'**, syn. 'Highlight', produces an abundance of bright yellow flowers; ↕ 60cm (24in). **'Yellow River'** has red stems and large, canary-yellow flowers, 4–6cm (1½–2½in) across.
O. glauca see *O. fruticosa* subsp. *glauca.*
O. glazioviana, syn. *O. glazouana.* Erect biennial or short-lived perennial bearing basal rosettes of ovate-lance-shaped, hairy, mid-green leaves, to 20cm (8in) long, with conspicuous white midribs above, red beneath; slightly smaller leaves are borne on the hairy, unbranched, red-spotted stems. In mid- and late summer, produces racemes of bowl-shaped yellow flowers, 5–8cm (2–3in) across, with red-tinged calyces, opening at dusk. ↕ to 1.5m (5ft), ↔ 60cm (24in). N. America. ❄❄❄
O. glazouana see *O. glazioviana.*
O. hookeri see *O. elata* subsp. *hookeri.*
O. linearis see *O. fruticosa.*
O. macrocarpa ▣ syn. *O. missouriensis* (Ozark sundrops). Vigorous perennial with trailing, hairy, often red-tinted stems, branching from a central rootstock. Leaves are lance-shaped to ovate, toothed, pale to mid-green, 2–8cm (¾–3in) long, with white midribs. From late spring to early autumn, produces a long succession of solitary, cup-shaped, bright golden yellow flowers, to 12cm (5in) across, with red-flecked calyces, remaining

Oenothera macrocarpa

Oenothera perennis

open in daytime. ↕ 15cm (6in), ↔ to 50cm (20in). S. Central USA. ❄❄❄
O. missouriensis see *O. macrocarpa.*
O. perennis ▣ syn. *O. pumila* (Sundrops). Clump-forming perennial with rosettes of spoon-shaped to inversely lance-shaped, mid-green leaves, 2.5–5cm (1–2in) long. Loose, leafy, upright, few-flowered racemes of funnel-shaped yellow flowers, to 2cm (¾in) across, open during the day in summer. ↕↔ to 20cm (8in) or more. E. North America. ❄❄❄
O. pumila see *O. perennis.*
O. speciosa. Sometimes invasive perennial, spreading by runners, with basal rosettes of oblong-lance-shaped to lance-shaped, toothed or pinnatifid, mid-green leaves, 2.5–5cm (1–2in) long, and arching stems bearing slightly smaller leaves. Solitary, saucer-shaped to shallowly cup-shaped, very fragrant white flowers, 2.5–6cm (1–2½in) across, sometimes ageing to pink, are produced from early summer to early autumn, opening during the day. ↕↔ 30cm (12in). S.W. USA to Mexico. ❄❄❄. **var. *childsii*** ▣ syn. 'Rosea', has smaller white flowers, 4–5cm (1½–2in) across, strongly suffused pink, with deep pink veins and yellow petal bases.
'Rosea' see var. *childsii.*
O. taraxacifolia see *O. acaulis.*
O. tetragona see *O. fruticosa* subsp. *glauca.*

▷ **Oil palm** see *Elaeis*
  African see *E. guineensis*
▷ **Oil tree,**
  Karum see *Pongamia pinnata*
  Macassar see *Cananga odorata*
  Poona see *Pongamia pinnata*
▷ **Old maid** see *Catharanthus roseus*
▷ **Old man** see *Artemisia abrotanum*
▷ **Old-man-live-forever** see *Pelargonium cotyledonis*
▷ **Old man's beard** see *Clematis*
▷ **Old pheasant's eye** see *Narcissus poeticus* var. *recurvus*

Olea

Olive

OLEACEAE

Genus of about 20 species of evergreen trees and shrubs often found in dry, rocky places in the Mediterranean and Africa to C. Asia and Australasia. They have opposite, leathery leaves, which may be entire or toothed, and produce terminal or axillary panicles of small, 4-lobed, white or off-white flowers; these are followed by edible, ovoid or spherical fruits. Thriving only in areas with a Mediterranean or similar climate, *O. europaea,* the only species cultivated, is of great economic importance for its fruit (olives) and the oil extracted from them. Grow as a specimen tree or in a border; in frost-prone areas, grow in a cool greenhouse or conservatory, or at the base of a sunny, sheltered wall.
• **Hardiness** Frost hardy.
• **Cultivation** Under glass, grow in loam-based potting compost (JI No.3) with additional sharp sand, in full light. During the growing season, water moderately and apply a balanced liquid fertilizer every month; water sparingly in winter. Outdoors, grow in deep, fertile, sharply drained soil in full sun. Pruning group 1; plants under glass need restrictive pruning in spring.
• **Propagation** Sow seed at 13–15°C (55–59°F) in spring. Take semi-ripe cuttings in summer.
• **Pests and diseases** May be infested with scale insects.

Oenothera speciosa var. *childsii*

O. europaea ♀ (Olive). Slow-growing, evergreen tree, developing a rounded head, with opposite, leathery, elliptic to lance-shaped, irregularly toothed leaves, to 8cm (3in) long, grey-green above, silvery grey-green beneath. Tiny, fragrant, creamy white flowers are borne in axillary panicles, to 5cm (2in) long, in summer, followed by edible, spherical to ovoid green fruit (olives), to 4cm (1½in) long, ripening to black. ↕↔ 10m (30ft). Mediterranean. ❄❄

▷ **Oleander** see *Nerium*

Olearia

Daisy bush

ASTERACEAE/COMPOSITAE

Genus of about 130 species of evergreen shrubs and small trees, and some herbaceous perennials, from a variety of habitats, including coastal areas, bogs, forest, riverbanks, and mountain scrub, in Australia. They have generally alternate, occasionally clustered, simple, usually leathery leaves, and are cultivated for their daisy-like flowerheads, borne singly, or in corymbs or panicles, in spring or summer. Olearias are suitable for planting in a shrub border, or in a sheltered site if not fully hardy. Some, such as *O.* x *haastii, O. macrodonta,* and *O. traversii,* may be grown as hedges and windbreaks, particularly in coastal areas. In frost-prone climates, grow tender species in a cool or temperate greenhouse.
• **Hardiness** Fully hardy to frost tender.
• **Cultivation** Outdoors, grow in fertile, well-drained soil in full sun, with shelter from cold, drying winds. Under glass, grow in loam-based potting compost (JI No.3) in full light. When in growth, water moderately and apply a balanced liquid fertilizer monthly; water sparingly in winter. Pruning group 8 for early-flowering species, group 9 for late-flowering species; trim lightly to maintain a compact habit. Most species break freely from old wood and tolerate hard pruning.
• **Propagation** Root semi-ripe cuttings in summer, using bottom heat for tender species.
• **Pests and diseases** Trouble free.

O. albida ♀ (Tanguru). Vigorous, upright shrub or small tree with alternate, oblong to ovate-oblong, wavy-margined leaves, to 10cm (4in) long, dark green above, white-felted beneath. Small, daisy-like white flowerheads, to 7mm (¼in) across, each with 1–5 ray-florets, are borne in panicles, to 5cm (2in) across, in summer. ↕ 5m (15ft), ↔ 3m (10ft). New Zealand (North Island). ❄
***O. albida* of gardens** see *O.* 'Talbot de Malahide'.
O. avicenniifolia ♀ Rounded, bushy shrub or small tree with alternate, elliptic to lance-shaped, dark grey-green leaves, to 10cm (4in) long, pale yellow- or white-felted beneath. Small, daisy-like, fragrant white flowerheads, to 5mm (¼in) across, each with usually 1 or 2 ray-florets, are borne in broad corymbs, to 8cm (3in) across, in late summer and early autumn. ↕ 3m (10ft), ↔ 5m (15ft). New Zealand (South Island, Stewart Island). ❄❄❄ (borderline)

Olearia cheesemanii

O. cheesemanii ▣ ♀ syn. *O. rani* of gardens. Upright-branched shrub or small tree with alternate, oblong or elliptic to lance-shaped, slightly toothed, leathery, glossy, dark green leaves, to 9cm (3½in) long, white-felted beneath. Daisy-like white flowerheads, to 9mm (⅜in) across, with yellow centres, are borne in large corymbs, to 20cm (8in) across, in mid- and late spring. ↕ 4m (12ft), ↔ 3m (10ft). New Zealand. ❄❄
O. ciliata. Upright shrub with rough shoots and clustered, rigid, linear, deep green leaves, to 1.5cm (½in) long, the margins strongly rolled back. Solitary, long-stalked, daisy-like flowerheads, 2.5cm (1in) across, blue or white with yellow centres, are produced in spring. ↕ 30cm (12in), ↔ 20cm (8in). Temperate regions of Australia. ❄❄
O. erubescens. Upright shrub with alternate, oblong to lance-shaped, toothed, sometimes lobed, glossy, dark green leaves, to 4cm (1½in) long, sometimes red-tinged when young. In late spring and early summer, daisy-like, yellow-centred white flowerheads, 2.5cm (1in) across, appear singly or in clusters of 2–5, forming leafy panicles, to 45cm (18in) long. ↕ 1.5m (5ft), ↔ 60cm (24in). S.E. Australia. ❄❄
O. frostii. Spreading shrub with alternate, obovate, entire or wavy-toothed, grey-green leaves, to 2.5cm

Olearia x *haastii*

O

Olearia macrodonta

(1in) long, covered with star-like hairs. In midsummer, very showy, yellow-centred mauve flowerheads, resembling Michaelmas daisies, to 4cm (1½in) across, are borne singly or in groups of 2 or 3. ↕60cm (24in), ↔1m (3ft). S.E. Australia (Victoria). ❄

O. gunniana see *O. phlogopappa.*

O.* x *haastii ▣ (*O. avicenniifolia* x *O. moschata*). Dense, bushy shrub with alternate, oval or ovate, glossy, dark green leaves, to 2.5cm (1in) long, white-felted beneath. Dense corymbs, to 8cm (3in) across, of daisy-like, yellow-centred white flowerheads, to 8mm (⅜in) across, appear in mid- and late summer. ↕2m (6ft), ↔3m (10ft) or more. Natural hybrid from New Zealand (South Island). ❄❄❄

***O.* 'Henry Travers'**, syn. *O. semidentata* of gardens. Rounded shrub with slender, white-felted shoots and alternate, lance-shaped, leathery, grey-green leaves, to 8cm (3in) long, white-felted beneath. Solitary, daisy-like flowerheads, 5cm (2in) across, with purple centres and numerous lilac ray-florets, are produced in early and midsummer. ↕2.5m (8ft), ↔2m (6ft). Natural hybrid from New Zealand (Chatham Islands). ❄❄

O. ilicifolia 🌳 (Mountain holly). Dense, spreading, bushy shrub or small tree with alternate, stiff and leathery, narrowly oblong, wavy-margined, sharply toothed, grey-green leaves, to 10cm (4in) long. Daisy-like, fragrant white flowerheads, to 1.5cm (½in) across, with yellow centres, are produced in large corymbs, to 10cm (4in) across, in summer. ↕↔5m (15ft). New Zealand. ❄❄❄ (borderline)

O. insignis see *Pachystegia insignis.*

O. lacunosa. Rounded, strongly branched shrub with densely grey-woolly branchlets. Bears alternate, slender, linear to linear-oblong, sharp-pointed, leathery leaves, 8–17cm (3–7in) long, dark green with yellow midribs above, silver-hairy to pale brown-hairy beneath. Small, daisy-like white flowerheads, 5mm (¼in) across, with yellow centres, are produced in spherical, corymb-like panicles, to 20cm (8in) across, in summer; they are borne more freely in warm, but not dry climates. ↕2–3m (6–10ft), sometimes 4–5m (12–15ft), ↔3m (10ft). New Zealand. ❄❄

O. macrodonta ▣🌳 (Arorangi). Vigorous, upright shrub or small tree with alternate, holly-like, ovate-oblong, sharply toothed and pointed, glossy, dark green leaves, to 10cm (4in) long, silver-white-felted beneath. In summer, bears large corymbs, to 15cm (6in) across, of daisy-like, fragrant white flowerheads, to 1cm (½in) across, with reddish brown centres. ↕6m (20ft), ↔5m (15ft). New Zealand. ❄❄❄ (borderline)

***O.* x *mollis* 'Zennorensis'**, syn. *O.* 'Zennorensis'. Dense, rounded shrub with alternate, lance-shaped, sharply toothed leaves, to 10cm (4in) long, glossy, dark olive-green above, densely white-woolly beneath. Daisy-like white flowerheads, 1.5–2cm (½–¾in) across, with yellow centres, are produced in spherical corymbs, 15–20cm (6–8in) across, in late spring. ↕↔2m (6ft). ❄❄❄ (borderline)

Olearia phlogopappa 'Comber's Pink'

O. moschata (Incense plant). Dense, upright, bushy shrub with alternate, obovate to oblong, leathery, musk-scented, grey-tinged green leaves, to 1.5cm (½in) long, densely white-hairy on both surfaces. Produces dense corymbs of 12–30 daisy-like, yellow-centred white flowerheads, each to 1cm (½in) across, in midsummer. ↕1–2m (3–6ft), ↔1m (3ft). New Zealand (South Island). ❄❄

O. nummulariifolia ▣ Dense, rounded, slow-growing shrub with stout, upright shoots. Bears alternate, small, obovate to rounded, very leathery leaves, to 1cm (½in) long, the margins rolled back, and bright green when young, becoming dark green, and densely white-woolly to buff- or yellow-woolly beneath. Daisy-like, fragrant white flowerheads, 2cm (¾in) across, with cream or pale yellow centres, are produced singly or in clusters of 2 or 3 at the shoot tips in midsummer. ↕↔2m (6ft). New Zealand. ❄❄❄ (borderline)

O. phlogopappa, syn. *O. gunniana, O. stellulata* of gardens. Compact, upright shrub with alternate, oblong to narrowly obovate, wavy-margined, shallowly toothed leaves, to 5cm (2in) long, grey-

Olearia x *scilloniensis*

green above, densely white-woolly or grey-white-woolly beneath. Daisy-like, usually white, sometimes blue, mauve, or pink flowerheads, 3cm (1¼in) across, with yellow centres, are freely borne in loose, erect corymbs, to 7cm (3in) across, in spring and early summer. ↕↔2m (6ft). S.E. Australia. ❄❄. **'Comber's Blue'** has mid-blue ray-florets. **'Comber's Pink'** ▣ has pink ray-florets.

O. ramulosa ▣ Arching, slender-branched shrub bearing alternate, linear to linear-obovate, dark green leaves, to 1cm (½in) long, the margins rolled back, and densely hairy beneath. Solitary, daisy-like, white, or sometimes blue, mauve, or pink flowerheads, 1.5cm (½in) across, with white centres, are produced in spring, or in late winter under glass. ↕↔1.5m (5ft). Australia. ❅ (min. 5°C/41°F)

***O. rani* of gardens** see *O. cheesemanii.*

O.* x *scilloniensis ▣ (*O. lirata* x *O. phlogopappa*). Dense, initially upright then rounded shrub, with alternate, elliptic-oblong, wavy-margined, dark green leaves, to 10cm (4in) long, pale green and densely felted beneath. In late spring, daisy-like white flowerheads, to 6cm (2½in) across, with yellow centres, are very profusely borne in corymbs to 7cm (3in) across. ↕↔2m (6ft). Garden origin. ❄❄. **'Master Michael'** has grey-green foliage and blue flowerheads.

***O. semidentata* of gardens** see *O.* 'Henry Travers'.

O. solandri ▣🌳 Dense, upright, bushy shrub or small tree with slender, sticky, yellow-hairy shoots and heather-like, opposite, narrowly spoon-shaped to

Olearia nummulariifolia

Olearia ramulosa

Olearia solandri

Olearia 'Talbot de Malahide' (inset: flower detail)

narrowly obovate or linear, dark green leaves, to 8mm (⅜in) long, densely white- to yellow-felted beneath. Solitary, daisy-like, very strongly fragrant, pale yellow flowerheads, 8mm (⅜in) across, with about 20 tiny florets, are produced from summer to autumn. ↕↔ 2m (6ft). New Zealand. ❄❄
O. stellulata of gardens see *O. phlogopappa.*
O. 'Talbot de Malahide' ■ syn. *O. albida* of gardens. Dense, upright, bushy shrub with alternate, narrowly ovate, glossy, dark green leaves, to 10cm (4in) long, white- or yellowish-white-felted beneath. Small, daisy-like, fragrant white flowerheads, to 1cm (½in) across, each with up to 6 ray-florets and an inconspicuous, brownish yellow centre, are borne in broad corymbs, to 10cm (4in) across, in late summer and early autumn. ↕ 3m (10ft), ↔ 5m (15ft). ❄❄
O. traversii ♡ Dense, upright shrub, sometimes a small tree, with stout, angled shoots and opposite, oval to ovate-oblong leaves, to 6cm (2½in) long, glossy, dark green above, white-felted beneath. In early summer, bears relatively inconspicuous, daisy-like, grey-white flowerheads, to 6mm (¼in) across, without ray-florets, in panicles to 5cm (2in) long. Useful for coastal hedging. ↕ 5–10m (15–30ft), ↔ 3–5m (10–15ft), or more. New Zealand (Chatham Islands). ❄❄❄ (borderline)
O. virgata ■ Arching shrub with smooth, slender, wiry shoots and opposite, narrowly obovate to linear, dark green leaves, to 2cm (¾in) long, densely white-felted beneath. In summer, small, daisy-like, fragrant, yellowish white flowerheads, 1cm (½in) across, each with 3–6 ray-florets and an inconspicuous centre, are profusely borne in opposite clusters, to 4cm (1½in) across, along the branches. ↕↔ 5m (15ft). New Zealand. ❄❄❄ (borderline). **var. *lineata*** has pendulous, softly hairy branchlets with linear leaves, to 4cm (1½in) long, the margins strongly rolled back, and flowerheads with 8–14 ray-florets; ↕ to 2m (6ft); New Zealand (South Island).
O. 'Zennorensis' see *O.* x *mollis* 'Zennorensis'.

Olearia virgata

▷**Oleaster** see *Elaeagnus angustifolia*
▷**Olive** see *Olea, O. europaea*
Fragrant see *Osmanthus fragrans*
▷***Oliveranthus elegans*** see *Echeveria harmsii*

OLSYNIUM

IRIDACEAE

Genus of about 12 species of fibrous-rooted, clump-forming perennials, often included in *Sisyrinchium*, found in moist grassland from sea level to subalpine regions in North and South America. They have mostly basal, stem-clasping, linear or lance-shaped leaves, and are grown for their nodding, trumpet-shaped to bell-shaped flowers which are borne in spring. Grow in a shady rock garden, peat bed, or alpine house.
• **HARDINESS** Fully hardy.
• **CULTIVATION** Grow in moist, humus-rich, moderately fertile soil in partial shade. In an alpine house, use a mix of equal parts loam, leaf mould, and grit.
• **PROPAGATION** Sow seed in containers in a cold frame in autumn. Young plants take 2 or 3 years to flower.
• **PESTS AND DISEASES** Trouble free.

O. biflorum, syn. *Phaiophleps biflora, Sisyrinchium odoratissimum.* Slender, clump-forming perennial, with short rhizomes producing upright stems with narrow, rush-like leaves, 4–22cm (1½–9in) long. In late spring or summer, bears cymes of usually 2, occasionally more, trumpet-shaped, fragrant, red-veined, creamy yellow flowers, 2.5cm (1in) long. ↕ 20–35cm (8–14in), ↔ 5cm (2in). Argentina (Patagonia). ❄❄❄
O. douglasii, syn. *Sisyrinchium douglasii, S. grandiflorum* (Grass widow). Clump-forming perennial with upright, slender, rush-like stems sheathed with linear, greyish green leaves, to 10cm (4in) long. In early spring, nodding, bell-shaped, satin-textured, rich purple flowers, to 2cm (¾in) long, are borne in several terminal spathes, each with 1–4 flowers. ↕ 15–30cm (6–12in), ↔ to 10cm (4in). W. North America. ❄❄❄. **var. *album*** has white flowers.

OMPHALODES

Navelwort

BORAGINACEAE

Genus of about 28 species of annuals, biennials, and perennials, some of which are evergreen or semi-evergreen, from a wide range of habitats in Europe, N. Africa, and Asia. They have clusters of simple leaves either in basal tufts or arranged alternately on stems. In spring and summer, they produce blue or white flowers, similar to forget-me-nots (*Myosotis*), each with a short tube and 5 spreading lobes, usually in terminal racemes or cymes, sometimes singly from the leaf axils. Most are shade-loving, used as ground cover in a border, or rock or woodland garden. Grow *O. luciliae* in a rock garden, scree bed, tufa, or alpine house; use *O. linifolia* in an annual border or for cutting.
• **HARDINESS** Fully hardy.
• **CULTIVATION** Most of the perennials thrive in moist, moderately fertile, humus-rich soil in partial shade. Grow *O. linifolia* in moderately fertile, well-drained soil in sun. Grow *O. luciliae* in tufa, or in very gritty, alkaline soil, in full sun; in an alpine house, use a mix of equal parts loam, leaf mould, and grit, with added limestone chippings.

Omphalodes cappadocica

Omphalodes cappadocica 'Cherry Ingram'

• **PROPAGATION** Sow seed in spring: sow annuals *in situ*; sow perennials in containers in a cold frame. Divide perennials in early spring.
• **PESTS AND DISEASES** Very susceptible to damage by slugs and snails.

O. cappadocica ■ Clump-forming, rhizomatous, evergreen perennial with ovate to heart-shaped, pointed, finely hairy, mid-green, basal leaves, to 10cm (4in) long. Produces loose, terminal racemes, to 25cm (10in) long, of 3–12 white-eyed, azure-blue flowers, each to 5mm (¼in) across, in early spring. ↕ to 25cm (10in), ↔ to 40cm (16in). Woodland in Turkey. ❄❄❄. **'Cherry Ingram'** ■ is more compact, with larger, deep blue flowers, 7mm (¼in) across. **'Starry Eyes'** also has larger flowers, to 7mm (¼in) across, with a central white stripe on each petal.
O. linifolia ■ (Venus's navelwort). Erect annual, branching from the base, with narrowly lance-shaped to spoon-shaped, sparsely white-hairy, glaucous basal leaves, to 10cm (4in) long, and smaller, very narrow, stalkless stem leaves. From spring to summer, produces loose, terminal racemes of

Omphalodes linifolia

5–15 tiny, slightly scented, white, or very occasionally pale blue flowers, to 1.5cm (½in) across. Self-seeds readily. ↕30–40cm (12–16in), ↔ to 15cm (6in). Dry, open sites, often in alkaline soil, in S.W. Europe. ❄❄❄

O. luciliae. Clump-forming, semi-evergreen perennial with upright to prostrate stems and ovate to elliptic or oblong, pale grey-blue, basal leaves, to 10cm (4in) long. Produces loose, terminal cymes of 3–15 clear light blue flowers, to 8mm (⅜in) across, often opening pink, over long periods in summer. May be difficult to establish. ↕10cm (4in) or more, ↔ to 15cm (6in). Vertical limestone cliffs, generally in shade, in Greece and Turkey. ❄❄❄

O. verna (Blue-eyed Mary, Creeping forget-me-not). Clump-forming, stoloniferous, semi-evergreen perennial with heart-shaped, ovate to ovate-lance-shaped, pointed, hairy, mid-green, basal leaves, to 20cm (8in) long. Terminal racemes of 5–20 white-eyed, deep bright blue flowers, to 1cm (½in) across, appear in spring. ↕ to 20cm (8in), ↔ 30cm (12in) or more. Moist woodland in S.E. Alps to N. Apennines and to mountains of Romania. ❄❄❄

OMPHALOGRAMMA

PRIMULACEAE

Genus of about 15 species of usually rhizomatous perennials, related to *Primula*, from the Himalayas and the mountains of China. They are grown for their solitary, horizontally borne, salverform flowers, with long tubes and 6–8 spreading lobes, borne in spring or early summer. The lance-shaped to ovate or elliptic, often white-hairy, primula-like, mid- to dark green leaves are borne in rosettes, and arise from a large, dormant winter bud surrounded by scales. They grow best in cool, moist climates; grow in a peat bed, shady rock garden, or in an alpine house.

- **HARDINESS** Fully hardy.
- **CULTIVATION** Grow in cool, moist conditions, in open, moderately fertile, humus-rich, well-drained soil in partial shade. In an alpine house, use a mix of equal parts loam, leaf mould, and grit; move plants to a cool, shady site outdoors during summer.
- **PROPAGATION** Sow seed in containers in an open frame as soon as ripe.
- **PESTS AND DISEASES** Prone to aphids and whiteflies under glass. Young leaves are susceptible to slug and snail damage.

Omphalogramma vinciflorum

O. vinciflorum ■ Rosette-forming perennial, lacking a rhizome but with a large, dormant winter bud. Bears obovate-oblong to oblong, entire to scalloped, hairy, mid-green leaves, to 20cm (8in) long. In spring, produces solitary, salverform flowers, spreading to 5cm (2in) across, with deep violet-purple lobes and darker throats. ↕20cm (8in), ↔ 10cm (4in). China (Yunnan, Sichuan). ❄❄❄

ONCIDIUM

ORCHIDACEAE

Genus of over 450 species of evergreen, terrestrial, epiphytic, or lithopythic orchids found in a variety of habitats, from sea level to altitudes of 3,000m (10,000ft), in Mexico, Central America, South America, and the West Indies. Some oncidiums are compact with fan-like foliage; others have pseudobulbs that bear either 1 large, rigid leaf or 2 smaller, flexible leaves. The flowers are typically yellow, with prominent lips, and are produced in short or tall racemes or panicles from the bases of the plants.

- **HARDINESS** Frost tender.
- **CULTIVATION** Cool- to intermediate-growing orchids. Grow compact species in pots of epiphytic orchid compost; grow those with large, leathery leaves and elongated habit (e.g. *O. flexuosum*) epiphytically on bark or in baskets. In summer, provide high humidity and bright filtered light; those with leathery leaves prefer full light. During the growing season, mist daily and water freely, applying a half-strength fertilizer at every third watering. Provide full light in winter. Keep oncidiums with large pseudobulbs dry in winter; those with small pseudobulbs, or none, require watering all year round. See also p.46.
- **PROPAGATION** Divide when the plants overflow their containers, or remove backbulbs (produced by *O. flexuosum* and *O. tigrinum*) and pot up separately.
- **PESTS AND DISEASES** Prone to aphids, mealybugs, and red spider mites.

O. cavendishianum. Epiphytic orchid with very small pseudobulbs (sometimes none), each with one elliptic to broadly lance-shaped, rigid, leathery leaf, 15–45cm (6–18in) long. In spring, fragrant, waxy, red-spotted yellow flowers, 4cm (1½in) across, with deep yellow lips, are produced in panicles 1.5m (5ft) or more tall. ↕60cm (24in), ↔ 30cm (12in). S. Mexico, Guatemala, Honduras. ❀ (min. 13°C/55°F; max. 30°C/86°F)

O. crispum. Epiphytic orchid with ovoid pseudobulbs, each with 2 narrowly lance-shaped, leathery leaves, 20cm (8in) long. Chestnut-brown and yellow-spotted flowers, to 8cm (3in) across, are produced in erect to pendent panicles, to 1.1m (3½ft) long, from autumn to spring. ↕60cm (24in), ↔ 30cm (12in). Brazil. ❀ (min. 13°C/55°F; max. 30°C/86°F)

***O.* Fire Opal** (*O.* Persian Red x *O.* Susan Perreira). Epiphytic orchid with a fan of overlapping, rigid, flattened, linear-oblong leaves, 10cm (4in) long. Highly decorative flowers, 2.5cm (1in) or more across, in shades of rich pink over creamy white, are produced in long racemes several times during the

Oncidium flexuosum

year. ↕30cm (12in), ↔ 15cm (6in). ❀ (min. 13°C/55°F; max. 30°C/86°F)

O. flexuosum ■ (Dancing doll orchid). Epiphytic orchid with ovoid-oblong pseudobulbs, each with 1 or 2 linear, leathery leaves, to 10–20cm (4–8in) long. From autumn to winter, rich canary-yellow flowers, 2cm (¾in) across, with red-brown markings on the sepals and petals, are clustered towards the tips of panicles to 80cm (32in) long. ↕60cm (24in), ↔ 30cm (12in). S.E. Brazil, Paraguay, Argentina, Uruguay. ❀ (min. 13°C/55°F; max. 30°C/86°F)

***O.* Gypsy Beauty** (*O.* Phyllis Hetfield x *O.* Thelma Beaumont). Epiphytic orchid with a fan of overlapping, rigid, flattened, linear-oblong leaves, 10cm (4in) long. Highly decorative white and burgundy-red flowers, 2.5cm (1in) or more across, with raspberry lips, are produced in clusters towards the ends of racemes several times during the year. ↕30cm (12in), ↔ 15cm (6in). ❀ (min. 13°C/55°F; max. 30°C/86°F)

O. longipes. Epiphytic orchid with slender, oblong-ovoid pseudobulbs, each with 2 oblong, soft leaves, to 15cm (6in) long. In spring, produces short racemes of 2–6 yellow flowers, 3.5cm (1½in) across, heavily spotted and streaked red-brown, with yellow lips. ↕12cm (5in), ↔ 15cm (6in). S.E. Brazil. ❀ (min. 13°C/55°F; max. 30°C/86°F)

O. macranthum, syn. *Cyrtochilum macranthum.* Epiphytic orchid with oblong-conical, fleshy pseudobulbs, each with 2 narrowly inversely lance-shaped to oblong leaves, 25–50cm (10–20in) long. Yellow to brown-gold flowers, 8cm (3in) across, with yellowish white

Oncidium ornithorrhynchum

Oncidium tigrinum

lips bordered violet-purple, are borne in lax, spreading panicles, to 3m (10ft) tall, in summer. ↕1m (3ft), ↔ 60cm (24in). Colombia, Ecuador, Peru. ❀ (min. 13°C/55°F; max. 30°C/86°F)

O. ornithorrhynchum ■ Epiphytic orchid producing ovoid or ellipsoid pseudobulbs, each with 2 linear-lance-shaped to linear-elliptic, soft leaves, 10–40cm (4–16in) long. In autumn, fragrant, white, pink, or purple-pink flowers, 2–2.5cm (¾–1in) across, with darker pink or lilac-pink lips, are produced in strongly arching panicles, to 50cm (20in) long. ↕15cm (6in), ↔ 23cm (9in). S. Mexico, Guatemala, El Salvador, Costa Rica. ❀ (min. 13°C/55°F; max. 30°C/86°F)

O. papilio see *Psychopsis papilio.*

O. pusillum, syn. *Psygmorchis pusilla.* Epiphytic orchid with a flattened fan of linear-oblong to oblong-elliptic, fleshy leaves, 6cm (2½in) long. Bears axillary racemes, to 6cm (2½in) long, of 1–4 bright yellow flowers, marked rust-red, to 3cm (1¼in) across, intermittently all year round. ↕↔ 8cm (3in). Central America, South America, West Indies. ❀ (min. 13°C/55°F; max. 30°C/86°F)

O. sphacelatum. Epiphytic orchid with ribbed, ovoid-ellipsoid pseudobulbs, each with 2 linear-oblong to linear-lance-shaped, semi-leathery leaves, to 1m (3ft) long. In spring, deep yellow flowers, to 3cm (1¼in) across, marked and spotted red-brown, with golden yellow lips, are produced in dense, upright panicles, to 1.5m (5ft) tall. ↕↔ 60cm (24in). Central America, Venezuela. ❀ (min. 13°C/55°F; max. 30°C/86°F)

O. tigrinum ■ Epiphytic orchid with spherical pseudobulbs, each with 1 or 2 linear-oblong, leathery leaves, 30–50cm (12–20in) long. Fragrant yellow flowers, 5cm (2in) across, with sepals and petals heavily suffused dark red-brown, and with large yellow lips, are produced in long, stout, usually erect panicles, to 1.5m (5ft) tall, in winter. ↕45cm (18in), ↔ 30cm (12in). Mexico. ❀ (min. 13°C/55°F; max. 30°C/86°F)

▷**Onion** see *Allium*
False sea see *Ornithogalum longibracteatum*
Nodding see *Allium cernuum*
Sea see *Urginea maritima*
Wild see *Allium cernuum*
▷**Onion couch** see *Arrhenatherum elatius* subsp. *bulbosum* 'Variegatum'

O

Onoclea sensibilis

Onoclea

WOODSIACEAE

Genus of one species of deciduous, terrestrial fern found in damp sites in E. Asia and E. North America. In spring, long-stalked, pinnate or deeply pinnatisect sterile fronds arise singly at short intervals from creeping rhizomes, dying down at the first frost. The fertile fronds are 2-pinnate, with contracted, bead-like black segments curled in to cover the sori, and are borne in late summer, persisting throughout winter. *O. sensibilis* will thrive at the edge of water, or in a damp, shady border.

- **Hardiness** Fully hardy.
- **Cultivation** Grow in a sheltered site in moist, fertile, humus-rich, preferably acid soil, in light dappled shade (the fronds will burn if exposed to too much sun).
- **Propagation** Sow spores at 15–16°C (59–60°F) as soon as ripe, or divide in spring. See also p.51.
- **Pests and diseases** Trouble free.

O. sensibilis ▣ (Sensitive fern). Deciduous fern, producing upright then arching, broadly lance-shaped or triangular, pinnate to deeply pinnatisect, pale green sterile fronds, to 1m (3ft) long, in spring; these each have 8–12 pairs of pinnae, which are lobed to wavy-margined or entire. Fertile fronds are borne in late summer, and are stiffly erect, lance-shaped, and 2-pinnate, to 60cm (24in) long; the pinnae are reduced to bead-like black lobes enclosing the sori. The emerging fronds may sometimes be pinkish bronze in spring. ↕ 60cm (24in), ↔ indefinite. E. Asia, E. North America. ✻✻✻

Ononis

Restharrow

LEGUMINOSAE/PAPILIONACEAE

Genus of about 75 species of annuals, perennials, and dwarf shrubs occurring in dry, rocky sites or in grassland, often in alkaline soil, in Europe, the Mediterranean, the Canary Islands, and from N. Africa to Iran. They have alternate, simple or 3-palmate, usually toothed and hairy, clover-like, mostly mid-green leaves, and are grown for their pea-like flowers, borne in panicles, spikes, or racemes in summer. Grow in a rock garden, wall, or sunny bank, or at the front of a mixed or shrub border.

Ononis fruticosa

- **Hardiness** Fully hardy.
- **Cultivation** Grow in a warm, sunny position in moderately fertile, well-drained soil. They may be short-lived, so propagate regularly.
- **Propagation** Sow seed in containers in an open frame in autumn or spring. Take greenwood cuttings of shrubby species in early summer.
- **Pests and diseases** May be infested with red spider mites under glass.

O. fruticosa ▣ (Shrubby restharrow). Short-lived, deciduous shrub with 3-palmate, leathery leaves, 4cm (1½in) long, composed of leaflets that are oblong-lance-shaped and unevenly toothed. Nodding clusters, 5–8cm (2–3in) long, of pea-like pink flowers, each to 2cm (¾in) long, with dark central markings and paler wings, are borne over long periods in summer. ↕↔ to 60cm (24in), occasionally to 1m (3ft). S.E. France, C. Pyrenees, C. and E. Spain. ✻✻✻

O. repens (Common restharrow). Upright or spreading, often stem-rooting, deciduous subshrub, sometimes with soft spines, bearing ovate, simple or 3-palmate leaves, to 2cm (¾in) long, composed of leaflets that are ovate, hairy, and toothed. Open, leafy racemes of pea-like, pink or pink-purple flowers, each to 2cm (¾in) long, are produced throughout summer. ↕ 30–60cm (12–24in), ↔ 50–80cm (20–32in) or more. Europe. ✻✻✻

O. rotundifolia. Upright, deciduous or semi-evergreen, dwarf shrub with 3-palmate leaves, 3cm (1¼in) long, composed of broadly elliptic to rounded, coarsely toothed, hairy leaflets, the terminal leaflet long-stalked. In summer, produces axillary racemes or panicles of pea-like, pale to deep pink or white flowers, to 2cm (¾in) long, striped darker pink. ↕ to 50cm (20in), ↔ to 30cm (12in). S. Europe (S.E. Spain to E. Austria, C. Italy). ✻✻✻

▷ ***Onopordon*** see *Onopordum*

Onopordum

syn. Onopordon

Cotton thistle, Scotch thistle

ASTERACEAE/COMPOSITAE

Genus of about 40 erect, rosette-forming biennials from steppes, stony slopes, fallow fields, and disturbed ground in Europe, the Mediterranean, and W. Asia. They have simple to pinnatifid or pinnatisect, spiny-toothed leaves covered in cobweb-like, soft grey hair; the leaves are borne alternately on coarse, usually freely branching, mostly white-woolly stems, the leaf bases often continuing down the stems as very conspicuous wings. Large, round flowerheads, typically thistle-like and without ray-florets, are produced singly or in tight clusters at the stem tips in summer. They may be bright purple, blue-violet, rose-pink, or occasionally white, and are attractive to bees. Cotton thistles readily self-seed and may be grown in a large border, or in a semi-wild or gravel garden.

- **Hardiness** Fully hardy.
- **Cultivation** Grow in fertile, well-drained, neutral to slightly alkaline soil in full sun.
- **Propagation** Sow seed in containers in a cold frame or *in situ* in autumn or spring.
- **Pests and diseases** Slugs and snails may damage the foliage.

O. acanthium ▣ Tap-rooted, rosette-forming biennial with oblong-ovate to lance-shaped or ovate, pinnatifid, spiny-toothed, grey-green leaves, to 35cm (14in) long, sparsely hairy above. In the second year, produces massive, branching, 2- to 4-winged, spiny, hairy, yellow-green stems; in summer, these produce solitary or clustered, round, thistle-like, pale purple or white flower-heads, 4–5cm (1½–2in) across, encased in spine-tipped bracts. ↕ to 3m (10ft), ↔ 1m (3ft). W. Europe to W. and C. Asia. ✻✻✻

O. arabicum see *O. nervosum.*

O. nervosum, syn. *O. arabicum.* Tap-rooted, rosette-forming biennial with oblong-lance-shaped, pinnatisect, spiny toothed, silver-grey leaves, to 50cm (20in) long; they have prominent pale veins and are sparsely hairy beneath. In the second year, produces massive, branching, broad-winged, deeply veined, densely hairy, yellow-tinged stems; in summer, these bear clusters of round, thistle-like, bright purple-red to purple-pink flowerheads, to 3.5cm (1½in) across, encased in spine-tipped bracts. ↕ to 2.5m (9ft), ↔ 1m (3ft). Portugal, Spain. ✻✻✻

Onopordum acanthium

Onosma

BORAGINACEAE

Genus of about 150 species of biennials and often woody-based perennials found in sunny, rocky sites, often rock crevices, from the Mediterranean to Turkey. They are grown for their nodding cymes of narrowly tubular to cylindrical-bell-shaped flowers, mainly yellow, pink, red, or white. The simple, alternate leaves are covered in fine hairs, contact with which may irritate skin. Grow in a scree bed, or in a rock or wall crevice; in wet climates, they grow best in an alpine house or cold greenhouse.

- **Hardiness** Frost hardy; most will withstand tempertures to -10°C (14°F).
- **Cultivation** Outdoors, grow in full sun in a very gritty scree bed, or grow plants on their sides in vertical wall or rock crevices. Protect from excessive rainfall. Under glass, grow in a mix of equal parts loam, leaf mould, and grit; avoid wetting the foliage when watering.
- **Propagation** Sow seed in containers in an open frame in autumn. Take softwood or greenwood cuttings of shrubs in late spring or early summer.
- **Pests and diseases** May be infested with aphids or whiteflies under glass.

O. alborosea ▣ Evergreen, clump-forming perennial with white-hairy, branching stems bearing densely white-bristly-hairy, grey-green leaves, which are spoon- to lance-shaped or obovate to oblong, and to 6cm (2½in) long. In summer, produces congested, terminal cymes of nodding, narrowly tubular-bell-shaped white flowers, to 3cm (1¼in) long; the petal tips quickly darken to pink and sometimes mature to deep purple or violet-blue. ↕↔ 25cm (10in). S.W. Asia. ✻✻

O. frutescens. Upright perennial with unbranched stems covered with tiny, soft hairs. The bristly-hairy, greyish green leaves, to 7cm (3in) long, are lance-shaped to oblong-lance-shaped or linear, with margins rolled back. In summer, bears cymes of cylindrical-bell-shaped, bright yellow flowers, to 2cm (¾in) long, maturing to orange-brown or reddish brown. ↕ 25cm (10in), ↔ to 60cm (24in). Greece, Turkey, Syria. ✻✻

Onosma alborosea

Oophytum

AIZOACEAE

Genus of 2 species of succulent perennials, similar to *Conophytum*, found in dry, hilly areas in Western Cape, South Africa. They have pairs of erect, thick, soft, fleshy leaves, which join to form ovoid, egg-like "bodies" that wither during the dormant period (the name *Oophytum* means "egg plant"). Solitary, daisy-like flowers are produced from a cleft at the top of each body in late summer. In areas where temperatures drop below 7°C (45°F), grow in a temperate greenhouse; in warm, dry climates, grow in a scree bed, raised bed, or desert garden.

• **Hardiness** Frost tender.

• **Cultivation** Under glass, grow in a mix of 2 parts loam to 1 part each sharp sand and leaf mould, in full light with shade from hot sun. Water moderately from late summer to early autumn, and sparingly on warm days from mid-autumn to spring. Keep barely moist when semi-dormant from late spring to midsummer. Outdoors, grow in gritty, poor, humus-rich soil, in full sun with some midday shade. See also pp.48–49.

• **Propagation** Sow seed at 20–25°C (68–77°F), or separate and root complete bodies, in spring or summer.

• **Pests and diseases** Susceptible to greenflies, especially while flowering.

O. oviforme. Clump-forming, succulent perennial with papillose, glossy, olive-green to bright reddish green leaves, united in pairs to form ovoid bodies, 1cm (½in) across. In late summer, bears daisy-like white flowers, 2cm (¾in) across, with purplish pink tips. ↕ 2cm (¾in), ↔ 10cm (4in). South Africa (Western Cape). ❀ (min. 7°C/45°F)

▷ ***Operculina tuberosa*** see *Merremia tuberosa*

Ophiopogon

Lilyturf

CONVALLARIACEAE/LILIACEAE

Genus of about 50 species of evergreen, rhizomatous or tufted perennials, often with swollen, fleshy roots, sometimes also stoloniferous, from shady scrub or woodland in E. Asia, especially China and Japan. They are grown mainly for their dense tufts of somewhat grass-like leaves. Racemes of numerous small, 6-tepalled, semi-spherical to bell-shaped, pinkish white, lilac, or white flowers are produced on leafless stems in summer, followed by spherical to oblong-ellipsoid, glossy, blue or black fruits. Grow as grassy ground cover, for border edging, or in a rock garden or peat bed. In frost-prone areas, grow the less hardy species for seasonal bedding, or in a cool or temperate greenhouse.

• **Hardiness** Fully hardy to half hardy.

• **Cultivation** Outdoors, grow in moist but well-drained, slightly acid, fertile, humus-rich soil in full sun or partial shade. Top-dress annually with leaf mould in autumn. Under glass, grow in loam-based potting compost (JI No.2) in full light or bright indirect light. In growth, water freely and apply a balanced liquid fertilizer monthly; water sparingly in winter.

Ophiopogon jaburan 'Vittatus' (inset: flower detail)

• **Propagation** Sow seed in containers in a cold frame as soon as ripe. Divide in spring as growth resumes.

• **Pests and diseases** Slugs may damage young leaves.

O. jaburan (Jaburan lily, White lilyturf). Tufted, stoloniferous perennial with strap-shaped, leathery, dark green leaves, to 60cm (24in) long. Short bell-shaped, white, sometimes lilac-tinted flowers, 1cm (½in) long, are produced in racemes, to 15cm (6in) long and occasionally curled, in late summer, followed by oblong-ellipsoid, violet-blue fruit, 1cm (½in) long. ↕ to 60cm (24in), ↔ to 30cm (12in). Japan. ❄❄. **'Argenteovittatus'** see 'Vittatus'. **'Javanensis'** see 'Vittatus'. **'Variegatus'** see 'Vittatus'. **'Vittatus'** ■ syn. 'Argenteovittatus', 'Javanensis', 'Variegatus', has pale green leaves that are striped and margined cream, yellow, or white. **'White Dragon'** has leaves boldly striped with white, almost obliterating the green.

O. japonicus. Tuberous-rooted, rhizomatous perennial forming clumps of narrowly linear, curved, rigid, dark green leaves, 20–30cm (8–12in) long.

Ophiopogon planiscapus 'Nigrescens'

In summer, bears short racemes, 5–8cm (2–3in) long, of small, bell-shaped, white, occasionally lilac-tinged flowers, 5mm (¼in) across, followed by spherical, blue-black berries, 5mm (¼in) across. ↕ 20–30cm (8–12in), ↔ 30cm (12in). Japan. ❄❄❄. **'Kyoto Dwarf'** is compact; ↕↔ 10cm (4in). **'Silver Dragon'** has white-variegated leaves; ↕ to 30cm (12in), ↔ to 15cm (6in).

O. planiscapus. Clump-forming, spreading, rhizomatous perennial with strap-shaped, curving, dark green leaves, 10–35cm (4–14in) long. Short bell-shaped, pale purplish white flowers, to 7mm (¼in) long, are borne in racemes, 4–8cm (1½–3in) long, in summer, followed by spherical, fleshy, dark blue-black fruit, 3–5mm (⅛–¼in) across. ↕ 20cm (8in), ↔ 30cm (12in). ❄❄❄. **'Nigrescens'** ■ syn. 'Arabicus', 'Black Dragon', 'Ebony Knight', has almost black leaves.

O. spicatus see *Liriope spicata.*

Ophrys

ORCHIDACEAE

Genus of about 30 species of deciduous, tuberous, terrestrial orchids from Europe, Mediterranean islands, N. Africa, and W. Asia, occurring in habitats ranging from marshes and grassland to woodland and mountain-sides. They produce rosettes of oblong-ovate, ovate, or lance-shaped, mid-green leaves. From the rosettes arise erect inflorescences with small, bract-like leaves and racemes of 2–12 flowers; each has 3 spreading sepals, 2 petals, and a large lip, often strikingly coloured and resembling the abdomen of a bee or other insect. *Ophrys* species are suitable for a rock garden or for naturalizing in fine turf; in wet, frost-prone climates, they are best grown in an alpine house.

• **Hardiness** Fully hardy to frost hardy.

• **Cultivation** Outdoors, grow in sharply drained, gritty, leafy, humus-rich soil in partial shade. Plant dormant tubers in autumn, at least 5cm (2in)

Ophrys apifera

deep. In frost-prone areas, provide a dry winter mulch. In an alpine house, grow in terrestrial orchid compost in bright filtered light. During the growing season, water moderately; keep dry and frost-free when dormant. See also p.46.

• **Propagation** Separate offsets in autumn.

• **Pests and diseases** Slugs and snails may cause problems.

O. apifera ■ (Bee orchid). Terrestrial orchid with oblong-ovate leaves, 6cm (2½in) long. Erect racemes, to 30cm (12in) tall, of 2–11 flowers, 2.5cm (1in) across, each with green or purplish pink sepals and petals, and a lip marked red-purple and yellow, are borne in mid-spring and early summer. ↕ 30cm (12in), ↔ 15cm (6in). W., S., and C. Europe, N. Africa, W. Asia. ❄❄❄

O. aranifera see *O. sphegodes.*

O. fuciflora see *O. holoserica.*

O. fusca (Sombre bee orchid). Terrestrial orchid with oblong-ovate or lance-shaped leaves, 6cm (2½in) long. In mid- and late spring, produces erect racemes, to 30cm (12in) tall, of up to 8 variable green or yellow-green flowers, 5cm (2in) across, each with a yellow- or white-margined, bluish, brown, purple, or purplish red lip. ↕ 30cm (12in), ↔ 15cm (6in). Mediterranean, S.W. Romania. ❄❄. **subsp. *iricolor*** ■ has racemes of up to 4 flowers, each with

Ophrys fusca subsp. *iricolor*

a longer lip that has 2 elongated, iridescent blue patches.
O. holoserica, syn. *O. fuciflora* (Late spider orchid). Terrestrial orchid with ovate-oblong leaves, 6cm (2½in) long. From mid-spring to midsummer, produces short, erect racemes, to 30cm (12in) tall, of 2–6 flowers, 3cm (1¼in) across; each has green, bright pink, or white sepals, pink to purple-pink petals, and a dark brown to dark maroon or ochre lip, sometimes with yellow margins. ↕30cm (12in), ↔ 15cm (6in). W., S.W., and C. Europe. ❄❄
O. lutea. Terrestrial orchid with ovate leaves, 6cm (2½in) long. Erect racemes, to 30cm (12in) tall, of 2–7 yellow-green flowers, 2.5cm (1in) across, each with a bright yellow lip, dark brown or purplish black in the centre, are borne from mid-spring to early summer. ↕30cm (12in), ↔ 15cm (6in). Portugal, Mediterranean. ❄❄
O. speculum see *O. vernixia.*
O. sphegodes, syn. *O. aranifera* (Early spider orchid). Variable, terrestrial orchid with ovate-lance-shaped leaves, 8cm (3in) long. From late spring to midsummer, produces erect racemes, to 45cm (18in) long, of up to 10 flowers, to 2.5cm (1in) across; each has green, occasionally brownish green sepals and petals, and a pale to blackish brown, velvety lip. ↕↔ 15cm (6in). Europe. ❄❄
O. vernixia, syn. *O. speculum* (Mirror orchid). Terrestrial orchid with oblong to lance-shaped leaves, 6cm (2½in) long. In late spring and early summer, produces erect racemes, to 30cm (12in) tall, of up to 15 green flowers, 2.5cm (1in) across, with dark brown stripes; the lip is velvety, black- or brown-margined, with glossy, deep blue, yellow-bordered centres. ↕30cm (12in), ↔ 15cm (6in). Portugal, N. Africa, Mediterranean. ❄❄

OPHTHALMOPHYLLUM

AIZOACEAE

Genus of 19 species of perennial succulents, closely related to *Conophytum* and growing wild in dry, hilly areas of Namibia and South Africa. They bear "bodies" of paired, erect, compressed-cylindrical, very fleshy leaves, united for most of their length, with transparent "windows" on the usually flat tops. Solitary, daisy-like flowers are borne from clefts between the paired lobes, during the day in late summer and autumn. In areas where temperatures drop below 10°C (50°F), grow in a temperate greenhouse; in warm, dry climates, grow in a desert garden or in a scree bed or raised bed.
• **HARDINESS** Frost tender.
• **CULTIVATION** Under glass, grow in a mix of 2 parts loam to 1 part each sharp sand and leaf mould, in full light. From late spring to early autumn, water sparingly and apply a dilute, low-nitrogen liquid fertilizer every 4–6 weeks. Reduce water from mid- to late autumn; keep completely dry from winter to mid-spring. Outdoors, grow in gritty, poor, humus-rich soil in full sun. See also pp.48–49.
• **PROPAGATION** Sow seed at 20–25°C (68–77°F), or separate and root complete bodies, in spring or summer.
• **PESTS AND DISEASES** Trouble free.

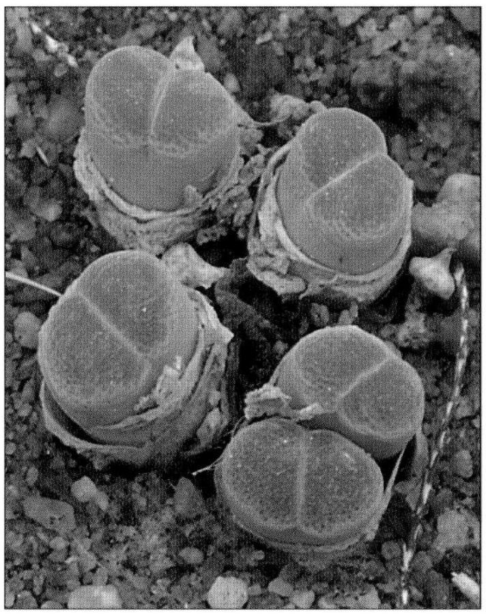
Ophthalmophyllum longum

O. longum ▣ syn. *Conophytum longum.* Clump-forming, perennial succulent with grey-green to brown bodies, 2cm (¾in) across, consisting of rounded lobes with translucent dots above and keeled undersides. Daisy-like, white to pale pink flowers, 2cm (¾in) across, are borne in late summer and autumn. ↕3cm (1¼in), ↔ indefinite. Namibia, South Africa. ❁ (min. 5–7°C/41–45°F)
O. maughanii. Clump-forming, perennial succulent producing yellowish green bodies, 2cm (¾in) across, with short, conical lobes. In late summer and autumn, produces daisy-like white flowers, 1.5cm (½in) across. ↕4cm (1½in), ↔ indefinite. Namibia, South Africa. ❁ (min. 5–7°C/41–45°F)

▷**Opium poppy** see *Papaver somniferum*

OPLISMENUS

GRAMINEAE/POACEAE

Genus of 6 species of trailing, annual or perennial grasses from subtropical and tropical forests of Africa, Asia, Polynesia, and Central and South America. They have slender, rooting, leafy stems with flat, lance-shaped to ovate leaves, and bear one-sided racemes of insignificant flowers. Only *O. africanus* 'Variegatus' is of decorative value: in warm areas, it provides excellent ground cover, and is also a useful edging plant; in frost-prone areas, grow as an ornamental plant in a hanging basket in a temperate greenhouse or conservatory.
• **HARDINESS** Frost tender.
• **CULTIVATION** Under glass, grow in loamless or loam-based potting compost (JI No.2) in bright filtered or full light. In growth, water freely and apply a balanced liquid fertilizer every 4 weeks. Water sparingly in winter. Outdoors, grow in any moist but well-drained soil in full sun or partial shade.
• **PROPAGATION** Separate rooted stems in spring; pot up and keep in a propagating case until established.
• **PESTS AND DISEASES** Trouble free.

O. africanus, syn. *O. hirtellus.* Evergreen perennial with wiry stems, spreading and rooting at the nodes, bearing narrowly lance-shaped to ovate, softly hairy, mid-green leaves, to 5cm (2in) long, with long points. Small flowers are produced in one-sided racemes, to 15cm (6in) long, from summer to winter. ↕15cm (6in), but may form mounds to 90cm

Oplismenus africanus 'Variegatus'

(36in), ↔ indefinite. Africa, Polynesia, tropical Central and South America. ❁ (min. 5°C/41°F). **'Variegatus'** ▣ syn. 'Vittatus', has white-striped leaves, flushed purple-pink.
O. hirtellus see *O. africanus.*

OPUNTIA

CACTACEAE

Genus of about 200 species of perennial cacti, ranging from alpine and ground-cover plants to bushy and tree-like species, from often very arid regions in North, Central, and South America, and the West Indies. They have usually pad-like and flattened, or sometimes cylindrical, club-shaped, or spherical, segmented branches, with areoles producing spines and glochids (barbed spines); a few species have leaf-like scales, which soon fall. On mature plants, funnel- or bowl-shaped flowers are produced singly from the areoles at the tips or sides of the segments; they appear during the day in spring or summer, and are followed by usually spiny, obovoid or spherical fruits (prickly pears). In a few species, these are edible, and contain large, smooth white seeds in pulp.
In areas where temperatures drop below 10°C (50°F), grow tender species in a cool or temperate greenhouse. In warmer areas, grow opuntias in a desert garden or in a border with other cacti. They are not suitable as houseplants; contact with the bristles causes intense irritation to skin, and they are difficult to remove.
• **HARDINESS** Fully hardy (if kept dry in winter) to frost tender.
• **CULTIVATION** Under glass, grow in standard cactus compost in full light or bright filtered light. Large species are best planted directly into a greenhouse border; all dislike root restriction. From early spring to mid-autumn, water freely and apply a balanced liquid fertilizer 3 or 4 times. Keep dry at other times. Outdoors, grow in moderately fertile, sharply drained, gritty, humus-rich soil in full sun. See also pp.48–49.
• **PROPAGATION** Sow pre-soaked seed at 21°C (70°F) in spring. Separate and root stem segments. Handle plants using folded newspaper; dispose of it after use.
• **PESTS AND DISEASES** Vulnerable to scale insects and mealybugs.

O. argentina ▣ syn. *Brasiliopuntia brasiliensis.* Tree-like, perennial cactus with thick, bright green stems, cylindrical branches, and flat, oblong segments, 5–12cm (2–5in) long, each with pale brown glochids and usually one spine which is red at first, becoming brown. Wide-spreading, funnel-shaped yellow flowers, 3–4cm (1¼–1½in) across, are produced in summer, followed by edible, ovoid, spineless, purplish red fruit, 5cm (2in) long. ↕ to 15m (50ft), ↔ 3m (10ft). N. Argentina. ❁ (min. 7–10°C/45–50°F)
O. basilaris. Clump-forming, perennial cactus with velvety, bluish green or pale reddish green stems divided into flat, obovate to nearly rounded segments, 10–20cm (4–8in) long. Brown areoles each have reddish brown glochids and none or 1, rarely up to 5, spines. Bowl-shaped, usually deep purple-red flowers, 6–8cm (2½–3in) across, are borne in summer, followed by spherical to ovoid, dry, velvety, grey-green fruit, 3–4cm (1¼–1½in) long. ↕1m (3ft), ↔ to 75cm (30in) or more. S. USA, N. Mexico. ❁ (min. 7–10°C/45–50°F)
O. chlorotica. Bushy or tree-like, perennial cactus with pale bluish green stems composed of flattened, rounded to obovate segments, to 20cm (8in) long. Grey areoles each bear yellow glochids and 1–6 or more pale yellow or brown spines, which blacken with age. Broadly funnel-shaped yellow flowers, 7cm (3in) across, flushed red outside, are produced from spring to summer; they are followed by ovoid purple fruit, 4cm (1½in) long, with short spines that are lost as the fruit mature. ↕ to 2m (6ft), ↔ 75cm (30in). USA (California, Nevada, New Mexico), N. Mexico. ❁ (min. 7–10°C/45–50°F)
O. clavarioides. Semi-prostrate, tuberous-rooted, many-branched, perennial cactus with stems divided into cylindrical, inversely conical, flat, or fan-shaped, greyish brown segments, 2cm (¾in) or more long. Whitish grey areoles bear leaf-like, deciduous red scales, to 2mm (1/16in) long, and each areole has 4–10 minute, fine white spines, but no glochids. In late spring and summer, produces funnel-shaped, brownish green flowers, 6cm (2½in) across, followed by ellipsoid, spineless, greyish brown fruit, 1.5cm (½in) long. ↕↔ to 10cm (4in). Argentina. ❁ (min. 7–10°C/45–50°F)
O. cochenillifera, syn. *Nopalea cochenillifera.* Shrubby or tree-like, perennial cactus with stems composed of flattened, elliptic to obovate, glossy,

Opuntia argentina

Opuntia erinacea

dark green segments, 8–25cm (3–10in) long. Mid-green areoles produce yellow glochids, and sometimes 1–3 yellow spines, usually none. Narrowly funnel-shaped, bright red flowers, to 4cm (1½in) across, are produced in late spring and summer, followed by ellipsoid, fleshy, spineless red fruit, 2.5–4cm (1–1½in) long. ↕ to 4m (12ft), ↔ 1m (3ft). Mexico. ❀ (min. 7–10°C/45–50°F)

O. compressa see *O. ficus-indica.*

***O. engelmannii* of gardens** see *O. phaeacantha.*

O. erinacea ▣ syn. *O. hystricina, O. polyacantha* var. *erinacea.* Clump-forming, perennial cactus with bluish green stems composed of flattened, rounded to broadly obovate segments, 5–10cm (2–4in) long. Brown or white areoles each have yellow glochids and 9 or more thread-like white spines, to 10cm (4in) long. Shallowly bowl-shaped, red, pink, purplish pink, or yellow flowers, 6cm (2½in) across, are borne in summer; they are followed by ovoid, light green, very spiny fruit, to 2cm (¾in) long. ↕ 50cm (20in), ↔ 1.5m (5ft). S.W. USA. ❀ (min. 7–10°C/45–50°F).
var. *ursina* ▣ (Grizzly bear cactus) bears oblong-elliptic stem segments with numerous very long, thread-like, deflexed spines, to 10cm (4in) long, and produces orange or pink flowers; ↕↔ to 45cm (18in). USA (California, Nevada, Arizona).

O. falcata, syn. *Consolea falcata.* Tree-like, perennial cactus with glossy, dark green stems composed of flattened, oblong to lance-shaped segments, to 35cm (14in) long, marked with small tubercles. White areoles each bear a few brownish white glochids and 2–8 needle-like, rough, pale yellow or yellowish brown spines. Bowl-shaped red flowers, 3–5cm (1¼–2in) across, are borne in late spring and summer, and are followed by ovoid, spineless, dark green fruit, to 4cm (1½in) long. ↕ to 1.5m (5ft), ↔ 75cm (30in). Haiti. ❀ (min. 7–10°C/45–50°F)

O. ficus-indica, syn. *O. compressa* (Indian fig, Prickly pear). Bushy or tree-like, perennial cactus with stems composed of flattened, obovate to oblong, greyish green or mid-green segments, 10–40cm (4–16in) long, with white areoles producing yellow glochids and usually 1 or 2 spines. Bowl-shaped yellow flowers, 10cm (4in) across, are produced in late spring and summer, and are followed by edible, ovoid, spineless purple fruit, to 10cm (4in) long. Some cultivars have yellow, orange, or red fruit. ↕↔ 5m (15ft). Mexico. ❀ (min. 7–10°C/45–50°F)

Opuntia erinacea var. *ursina*

Opuntia microdasys var. *albispina*

O. humifusa. Clump-forming, semi-prostrate, perennial cactus with stems divided into flattened, elliptic to obovate or rounded, greyish green segments, 5–13cm (2–5in) long, often tinged purple, and bearing narrowly wedge-shaped leaves, to 7mm (¼in) long. Brown areoles produce brown glochids, and sometimes 1 or 2 black-tipped white spines. Produces broadly funnel-shaped, bright yellow flowers, 4–6cm (1½–2½in) across, in late spring and summer; they are followed by obovoid, spineless, edible purple or red fruit, 2.5–4cm (1–1½in) long. ↕ 10–30cm (4–12in), ↔ to 1m (3ft) or more. C. and E. USA. ❀ (min. 3–5°C/37–51°F)

O. hystricina see *O. erinacea.*

O. imbricata, syn. *Cylindropuntia imbricata.* Variable, many-branched, perennial cactus with cylindrical, mid-green to bluish green stem segments, 10–40cm (4–16in) long, with very prominent tubercles, and cylindrical leaves, 1.5cm (½in) long. Large yellow areoles each bear yellow glochids and 8–30 brown-sheathed, reddish yellow or white spines. Broadly funnel-shaped, purple or red flowers, usually 4–8cm (1½–3in) across, are produced in late spring and summer, followed by nearly spherical, spineless yellow fruit, 3cm (1¼in) long. ↕ to 3m (10ft), ↔ 1m (3ft). S.W. USA, Mexico. ❀ (min. 7–10°C/45–50°F)

O. microdasys. Bushy, perennial cactus with stems comprising flattened, oblong, obovate, or almost rounded, velvety, pale to mid-green segments, 6–15cm (2½–6in) long; these are thickly dotted with white areoles bearing minute, yellow, white, or reddish brown glochids and usually no spines. Bowl-shaped, bright yellow flowers, 4–5cm (1½–2in) across, often tinged red on the outside, are produced from spring to summer; they are followed by oblong-ellipsoid, spineless, light purplish red fruit, to 4.5cm (1¾in) long. ↕↔ 40–60cm (16–24in). N. and C. Mexico. ❀ (min. 7–10°C/45–50°F).
var. *albispina* ▣ has dark green stem pads, white glochids, whitish yellow flowers, and darker purple-red fruit.
var. *pallida* (Bunny ears) has thin, greyish green stem segments, 8–15cm (3–6in) long, with yellow areoles and glochids; ↕↔ 60cm (24in). **var. *rufida***, syn. *O. rufida*, has reddish brown areoles and glochids, and no spines, and produces bowl-shaped, yellow or orange-yellow flowers; ↕↔ 50cm (20in); S. USA, N.W. Mexico.

O. paraguayensis. Semi-erect, perennial cactus with glossy, dark green stems composed of flattened, inversely lance-shaped or narrowly elliptic segments, 18–30cm (7–12in) long, with prominent, yellowish white areoles, tufts of yellow glochids, and usually no spines or one pale yellow spine. Broadly bowl-shaped orange flowers, 8cm (3in) across, are produced in late spring and summer, and are followed by conical, spineless, dark purple fruit, to 7cm (3in) long. ↕ to 2m (6ft), ↔ 1.5m (5ft). Paraguay, Argentina. ❀ (min. 7–10°C/45–50°F)

O. phaeacantha, syn. *O. engelmannii* of gardens. Variable, perennial cactus with stems divided into flattened, obovate or rounded, pale to bluish green, sometimes purple-tinged segments, 10–40cm (4–16in) long. Brown areoles each have a tuft of brown glochids and 1–8 sheathed, brown or red-brown spines. Produces broadly funnel-shaped, sulphur-yellow flowers, 5cm (2in) across, sometimes red-tinged inside, in late spring and summer, followed by ovoid, spineless red fruit, to 4cm (1½in) long. ↕ to 1.5m (5ft), ↔ to 2m (6ft). S.W. USA, N. Mexico. ❀ (min. 7–10°C/45–50°F)

O. polyacantha* var. *erinacea see *O. erinacea.*

O. pycnantha. Bushy, semi-prostrate, perennial cactus with stems composed of flattened, rounded, slightly softly hairy, dark green segments, 10–18cm (4–7in) long; they are covered with pale brown areoles, each bearing brownish yellow glochids and 3–12 reflexed, yellow or red-brown spines. From spring to summer, produces broadly funnel-shaped, greenish yellow, often red-tinged flowers, 4.5cm (1¾in) across; they are followed by ovoid, very prickly, spiny, dull green fruit, 4cm (1½in) long. ↕↔ 45cm (18in). Mexico (Baja California). ❀ (min. 7–10°C/45–50°F)

O. robusta ▣ Variable, shrubby or tree-like, perennial cactus with stems composed of flat, thick, oval to almost rounded, greyish or bluish green segments, to 40cm (16in) across. Brown areoles bear reddish brown glochids and, in each upper areole, 2–12 sheathed

O

Opuntia robusta

white, pale brown, or yellow spines. Shallowly bowl-shaped yellow flowers, 7cm (3in) across, are produced in late spring and summer, followed by spherical to ellipsoid, spineless, deep red fruit, 8cm (3in) long. ↕↔ 2m (6ft) or more. C. Mexico. ❀ (min. 7–10°C/45–50°F)

O. rufida see *O. microdasys* var. *rufida*.

O. subulata, syn. *Austrocylindropuntia subulata*. Freely branching, tree-like, perennial cactus, with cylindrical, unsegmented, dark green stems, 5–7cm (2–3in) in diameter; they are covered with oblong tubercles and, on the upper stems, semi-cylindrical, sharp-pointed, more or less evergreen leaves, 5cm (2in) or more long. Yellow areoles each have yellow glochids and 1 or 2 pale yellow spines. Cup-shaped red flowers, 7cm (3in) across, are produced from spring to summer, followed by persistent, oblong-ellipsoid, spineless, dark green fruit, 6–10cm (2½–4in) long. ↕ to 4m (12ft), ↔ to 1.5m (5ft). S. Peru. ❀ (min. 7–10°C/45–50°F)

O. tunicata ▣ syn. *Cylindropuntia tunicata*. Densely bushy, freely branching, perennial cactus with whorls of glaucous green stems divided into cylindrical segments, 6–15cm (2½–6in) long. Prominent white areoles have yellow glochids and 6–10 sheathed, off-white or yellow spines. From spring to summer, bears cup-shaped yellow flowers, 3–5cm (1¼–2in) across, followed by spherical to broadly club-shaped, spineless, glaucous green fruit, to 3cm (1¼in) long. ↕ 60cm (24in), ↔ 1m (3ft). C. Mexico. ❀ (min. 7–10°C/45–50°F)

Opuntia tunicata

Opuntia verschaffeltii

O. verschaffeltii ▣ syn. *Austrocylindropuntia verschaffeltii*. Clump-forming, perennial cactus with dull green stems composed of cylindrical segments, 10–20cm (4–8in) or more long, with low tubercles and bearing persistent, cylindrical leaves, to 3cm (1¼in) long. White areoles have yellow glochids and 1–3 or more, hair-like white spines. Cup-shaped, red or orange-red flowers, 4cm (1½in) across, are produced from spring to summer, followed by spherical, spineless red fruit, to 3cm (1¼in) long. ↕ 15cm (6in), ↔ 1m (3ft). Bolivia, N. Argentina. ❀ (min. 7–10°C/45–50°F)

O. vestita, syn. *Austrocylindropuntia vestita* (Cotton-pole cactus). Low-growing, perennial cactus with fragile, warty, pale green stems, and cylindrical segments to 20cm (8in) long. Yellow areoles, the upper ones with cylindrical, more or less evergreen leaves, 1cm (½in) long, each produce white glochids and 4–8 white spines intermingled with many fine white hairs, which envelop the stems. Cup-shaped, dark violet-red flowers, 4cm (1½in) across, are produced from late spring to summer, followed by spherical, spineless red fruit, to 2cm (¾in) long. ↕↔ 1m (3ft). Bolivia. ❀ (min. 7–10°C/45–50°F)

▷**Orache, Red** see *Atriplex hortensis*
▷**Orange,**
Australian mock see *Pittosporum undulatum*
Japanese bitter see *Poncirus trifoliata*
Japanese mock see *Pittosporum tobira*
Mock see *Philadelphus, P. coronarius*
Osage see *Maclura pomifera*
Panama see x *Citrofortunella microcarpa*
Seville see *Citrus aurantium*
Sweet see *Citrus sinensis* 'Washington'
▷**Orange ball tree** see *Buddleja globosa*
▷**Orange blossom, Mexican** see *Choisya, C. ternata*

ORBEA

ASCLEPIADACEAE

Genus of about 20 species of dwarf, erect to decumbent, mainly clump-forming, leafless, perennial succulents, closely related to *Stapelia*, from semi-arid, hilly, often rocky terrain in E. Africa and South Africa. They have large, warty teeth along the angled stem margins, and produce funnel-shaped, usually 5-lobed, often unpleasantly scented flowers, which attract blue-bottles. The diurnal flowers, borne singly or in few-flowered cymes from summer to autumn, each have a slightly wrinkled, usually flattened corolla, surrounded by a very pronounced, smooth annulus. Below 11°C (52°F), grow in a warm greenhouse; in warm, dry climates, use in a desert garden.

- **HARDINESS** Frost tender.
- **CULTIVATION** Under glass, grow in standard cactus compost, top-dressed with grit. Provide low humidity, with bright filtered light in summer, full light in winter. From spring to early autumn, water moderately, applying a low-nitrogen fertilizer every 3–4 weeks. Keep dry at other times, but water sparingly on warm winter days to prevent shrivelling. Outdoors, grow in gritty, loamy, moderately fertile, humus-rich soil in partial shade. See also pp.48–49.
- **PROPAGATION** Sow seed at 18–21°C (64–70°F) in spring. Take stem-segment cuttings in spring and summer.
- **PESTS AND DISEASES** Susceptible to mealybugs and root mealybugs, and to black rot if overwatered.

O. ciliata, syn. *Diplocyathus ciliata*. Mat-forming succulent with erect, 4-angled, toothed, mid-green stems, the tips tinged red. In summer, bears solitary, bowl-shaped, pale yellow flowers, to 8cm (3in) across, with dark purple-spotted annuli. ↕ 5cm (2in), ↔ to 15cm (6in). South Africa (Northern Cape, Eastern Cape). ❀ (min. 11°C/52°F)

O. variegata ▣ syn. *Stapelia variegata* (Starfish cactus, Toad cactus). Variable, clump-forming succulent with erect, obtusely angled, prominently toothed, greyish green stems, often mottled purple. In summer, produces cymes of up to 5 funnel-shaped, flat, densely wrinkled, dark brownish red flowers, 5–9cm (2–3½in) across, patterned white or yellowish white. ↕ 10cm (4in), ↔ to 30cm (12in). South Africa (Eastern Cape). ❀ (min. 11°C/52°F)

ORBEOPSIS

ASCLEPIADACEAE

Genus of about 10 species of leafless, perennial succulents from dry hillsides in Angola, Mozambique, and South Africa. They have angled, freely branching, usually greyish green stems, and bear umbel-like clusters of star-shaped, malodorous flowers during the day in early summer. In areas where temperatures drop below 10°C (50°F), grow in a warm greenhouse; in warm, dry climates, grow in a desert border.

- **HARDINESS** Frost tender.
- **CULTIVATION** Under glass, grow in standard cactus compost and top-dress with grit. Provide low humidity and full light with shade from hot sun. From spring to early autumn, water moderately and apply a low-nitrogen fertilizer every 4 or 5 weeks. Keep dry at other times, but water sparingly on warm winter days to prevent shrivelling. Outdoors, grow in moderately fertile, gritty, loamy, and humus-rich soil, in full sun. See also pp.48–49.
- **PROPAGATION** Sow seed at 18–21°C (64–70°F) in spring. Take stem-segment cuttings in spring and summer.
- **PESTS AND DISEASES** Trouble free.

O. albocastanea, syn. *Caralluma albocastanea*. Semi-erect, succulent perennial that offsets from the base, producing 4-angled, upward-curving, reddish brown stems with pale spots and large, projecting teeth. In early summer,

Orbea variegata

star-shaped flowers, 2.5–3cm (1–1¼in) across, are borne in umbel-like clusters of 3–6; they are green outside with red spots, and cream inside with brownish purple spots, the margins having thick, dark red hairs. They have dark brown coronas. ↕ 8cm (3in), ↔ 18cm (7in). Namibia. ❀ (min. 10°C/50°F)
O. lutea, syn. *Caralluma lutea*. Variable, mat-forming, succulent perennial with 4-angled, coarsely toothed, greyish green stems. In early summer, bears dense, umbel-like clusters of 3–26 star-shaped flowers, 4–8cm (1½–3in) across, ranging in colour from reddish brown to maroon or pale lemon-yellow, with yellow-hairy margins and yellow coronas. ↕ 10cm (4in), ↔ 24cm (10in). Southern Africa. ❀ (min. 10°C/50°F)

▷ **Orchid,**
Bee see *Ophrys apifera*
Butterfly see *Orchis papilionacea*
Clown see *Rossioglossum grande*
Cradle see *Anguloa*
Dancing doll see *Oncidium flexuosum*
Early purple see *Orchis mascula*
Early spider see *Ophrys sphegodes*
Golden chain see *Dendrochilum*
Green-veined see *Orchis morio*
Heart-lipped tongue see *Serapias cordigera*
Heath spotted see *Dactylorhiza maculata*
Jewel see *Goodyera*
Lady's slipper see *Cypripedium, C. calceolus*
Late spider see *Ophrys holoserica*
Marsh see *Dactylorhiza*
Mirror see *Ophrys vernixia*
Moth see *Phalaenopsis*
Pansy see *Miltoniopsis*
Poor man's see *Schizanthus, S. pinnatus*
Robust marsh see *Dactylorhiza elata*
Scorpion see *Arachnis*
Shower see *Congea tomentosa*
Showy lady's slipper see *Cypripedium reginae*
Slipper see *Paphiopedilum*
Sombre bee see *Ophrys fusca*
Spider see *Brassia lawrenceana*
Spotted see *Dactylorhiza*
Swan see *Cycnoches*
Tiger see *Rossioglossum grande*
Tongue see *Serapias*
Tulip see *Anguloa*
▷ **Orchids** see p.46
▷ **Orchid tree** see *Amherstia nobilis, Bauhinia variegata*

ORCHIS

ORCHIDACEAE

Genus of about 35 species of deciduous, terrestrial orchids from Europe and Asia, mostly occurring in open, grassy places, frequently in poor, dry soil. They have 2 or 3 spherical or ovoid tubers, and rosettes of linear-lance-shaped to oblong-ovate, sometimes purple-spotted, light to dark green leaves. Dense, erect racemes of delicate purple, red, pink, yellow, green, or white flowers, each with a short spur, and sometimes with a pungent odour, are produced from spring to summer. They are suitable for a rock garden or woodland garden, but are usually grown in an alpine house.
• **HARDINESS** Fully hardy to frost hardy.
• **CULTIVATION** In an alpine house, grow in terrestrial orchid compost in bright

Orchis morio

filtered light. Water moderately in growth; keep dry and frost-free when dormant. Outdoors, grow in fertile, well-drained, gritty, humus-rich soil in partial shade. *O. morio* and *O. papilionacea* prefer slightly acid to slightly alkaline soil; *O. mascula* prefers moist, neutral to slightly acid soil. Plant dormant tubers in autumn, at least 8cm (3in) deep. In frost-prone areas, provide a dry winter mulch. See also p.46.
• **PROPAGATION** Separate offsets in spring.
• **PESTS AND DISEASES** Slugs and snails may be troublesome.

O. elata see *Dactylorhiza elata*.
O. maderensis see *Dactylorhiza foliosa*.
O. mascula (Early purple orchid). Terrestrial orchid with mid-green, often purple-spotted leaves, 15cm (6in) long. From spring to midsummer, bears light to dark purple flowers, 2cm (¾in) long, in erect racemes, to 30cm (12in) tall. ↕ 30cm (12in), ↔ 15cm (6in). Europe. ❄❄❄
O. morio ▣ (Green-veined orchid). Terrestrial orchid with pale to mid-green leaves, 6cm (2½in) long. Pale to deep purple flowers, 2cm (¾in) long, with green veins on the cupped sepals, are borne in erect racemes, to 15cm (6in) tall, from spring to midsummer. ↕ 15–30cm (6–12in), ↔ 8cm (3in). Europe to W. Iran. ❄❄
O. papilionacea (Butterfly orchid). Terrestrial orchid with mid-green leaves, 6cm (2½in) long. In spring and early summer, bears erect racemes, to 15cm (6in) tall, of pale purple to lilac, sometimes reddish brown, darker veined flowers, 2cm (¾in) long, with large, pink-veined lips. ↕ 15–30cm (6–12in), ↔ 8cm (3in). S. Europe to S.W. Asia. ❄❄❄

▷ **Oregano** see *Origanum, O. vulgare*

OREOCEREUS

syn. BORZICACTUS

CACTACEAE

Genus of about 6 species of mainly columnar, perennial cacti from mountainous regions in South America. The thick, cylindrical, many-ribbed stems, usually branching from the bases, have tubercles and spiny areoles and, in some species, are covered in long hairs. Solitary, tubular-funnel-shaped flowers are produced during the day in summer, usually near the stem tips. Below 10°C

Oreocereus aurantiacus

(50°F), grow as houseplants or in a warm greenhouse; in warm, dry climates, grow in a desert garden.
• **HARDINESS** Frost tender.
• **CULTIVATION** Under glass, grow in a mix of 4 parts standard cactus compost and 1 part limestone chippings, in full light. From spring to summer, water freely; apply a balanced liquid fertilizer monthly. Keep dry at other times. Outdoors, grow in moderately fertile, slightly alkaline, sharply drained, humus-rich soil in full sun. See also pp.48–49.
• **PROPAGATION** Sow seed at 21°C (70°F) in spring or summer.
• **PESTS AND DISEASES** Vulnerable to scale insects.

O. aurantiacus ▣ syn. *Borzicactus aurantiacus, Matucana aurantiaca*. Solitary or clustering, perennial cactus with spherical to flattened-spherical or short-cylindrical, warty, dark green stems, each with 11–28 ribs. Elliptic areoles bear 16–22 yellow to reddish brown radial spines, but no centrals. In summer, produces solitary, red-throated, bright orange-red or orange-yellow flowers, to 9cm (3½in) long. ↕↔ 15cm (6in). N. Peru. ❀ (min. 10°C/50°F).
O. celsianus ▣ syn. *Borzicactus celsianus*. Slow-growing, clump-forming, perennial cactus with cylindrical, erect stems branching from the bases, each with 10–17 warty ribs. Grey-woolly areoles bear white hairs and yellow to reddish brown spines (7–9 radials and 1–4 much longer centrals). In summer, produces solitary, pale purplish pink flowers, 7–9cm (3–3½in) long, brownish red outside. ↕ 1–3m (3–10ft), ↔ 45cm (18in) or more. Bolivia, N.W. Argentina. ❀ (min. 10°C/50°F)
O. haynei ▣ syn. *Borzicactus haynei, Matucana haynei*. Solitary, occasionally clustering, perennial cactus with spherical to cylindrical, grass-green stems, each with 25–30 ribs and low-set tubercles. Ovoid, thickly set areoles bear yellow wool and spreading, stiff, white to yellowish brown spines (30 or more radials and 3 centrals). Solitary, red and orange to purplish crimson flowers, to 6–7cm (2½–3in) long, are produced in summer. ↕ to 30cm (12in), ↔ 10cm (4in). N. Peru. ❀ (min. 10°C/50°F)
O. hempelianus, syn. *Arequipa hempeliana*. Solitary, perennial cactus with branching, spherical then short-cylindrical, erect or semi-prostrate, greyish green or glaucous green stems, each with 10–20 warty ribs and yellow wool at the tips. White areoles each bear 11–40 spines (8–30 radials and 3–10 longer centrals). Solitary, bright scarlet to purplish red flowers, to 8cm (3in) long, appear in summer. ↕ to 40cm (16in), ↔ 10cm (4in). Mountains of S. Peru, N. Chile. ❀ (min. 10°C/50°F)
O. intertexta, syn. *Matucana intertexta*. Clump-forming, perennial cactus with erect, spherical to short-cylindrical, shiny, dark green stems, each with 14–18 warty ribs, often somewhat spiralled. Elliptic areoles each bear yellow spines, reddish brown beneath (16–18 radials and 3–7 longer centrals). Solitary, orange-red flowers, 5–7cm (2–3in) across, are produced in summer. ↕↔ to 15cm (6in). Peru. ❀ (min. 10°C/50°F)
O. peruviana see *Oroya peruviana*.

Oreocereus celsianus

Oreocereus haynei

ORIGANUM

Marjoram, Oregano

LABIATAE/LAMIACEAE

Genus of about 20 species of often rhizomatous, summer-flowering, herbaceous perennials and deciduous and evergreen subshrubs from open habitats, often in mountainous areas of the Mediterranean and S.W. Asia. They have spreading to upright stems bearing simple, aromatic leaves in opposite pairs, and inflorescences in spiked whorls, which are sometimes panicle- or corymb-like. The elongated, tubular or funnel-shaped, 2-lipped flowers are borne amid conspicuous, often brightly coloured bracts, which remain attractive for many weeks. Some origanums, *O. dictamnus*, *O. majorana*, *O. onites*, and *O. vulgare* and their cultivars, are used as culinary herbs. Grow smaller species in a rock garden, scree bed, alpine house, or at the front of a border; grow larger ones in a herbaceous border or herb garden. All attract bees and other insects.

• **HARDINESS** Fully hardy to frost hardy.

• **CULTIVATION** Outdoors, grow in full sun in poor to moderately fertile, well-drained, preferably alkaline soil. Grow dwarf perennials and subshrubs in free-draining soil. Some fully hardy species and cultivars resent winter wet, and are best grown in an alpine house; grow in a mix of equal parts loam, leaf mould, and sharp sand. Cut back old, flowered stems in early spring.

• **PROPAGATION** Sow seed in containers in a cold frame in autumn, or at 10–13°C (50–55°F) in spring. Divide in spring, or take basal cuttings in late spring.

• **PESTS AND DISEASES** Susceptible to aphids and red spider mites under glass.

O. amanum ■ Low-spreading, evergreen subshrub with ovate, bright green leaves, to 1.5cm (½in) long, and heart-shaped at the bases. In summer and autumn, curved, funnel-shaped pink flowers, 4cm (1½in) long, with small spreading lobes, are produced in congested, terminal whorls among green bracts, to 2cm (¾in) long, which become flushed purple-pink with age. ↕ 10–20cm (4–8in), ↔ to 30cm (12in). E. Mediterranean, Turkey. ❄❄❄

Origanum 'Kent Beauty'

***O.* 'Barbara Tingey'.** Dense, mound-forming, semi-evergreen subshrub, similar to *O. rotundifolium*. Produces rounded, bluish green leaves, purple beneath, 2cm (¾in) long. From summer to autumn, nodding whorls of tubular pink flowers, 1.5cm (½in) long and flared at the mouths, are borne among green bracts, 2cm (¾in) long, which age to deep purple-pink. ↕ 10cm (4in), ↔ to 20cm (8in). ❄❄❄

***O.* 'Buckland'.** Upright perennial, with rounded, hairy, grey-green leaves, 1.5cm (½in) long. In summer, whorls of tubular pink flowers, 1.5cm (½in) long, are borne among bracts, 2cm (¾in) long, which are pink from an early age. ↕ 20cm (8in), ↔ to 15cm (6in). ❄❄❄

O. dictamnus (Cretan dittany, Hop marjoram). Dome-forming, evergreen subshrub with arching, branching stems bearing rounded-ovate to rounded, densely white-felted, mid-green, sometimes purple-mottled leaves, to 2.5cm (1in) long. In mid- and late summer, bears dense, pendent, panicle-like whorls of small, open funnel-shaped pink flowers, 1cm (½in) long, among hop-like purple bracts, 9–10mm (⅜–½in) long. In wet climates, grow in an alpine house. ↕ 15cm (6in), ↔ to 20cm (8in). Crete. ❄❄

Origanum laevigatum

O. heracleoticum see *O. vulgare* subsp. *hirtum*.

***O.* 'Kent Beauty'** ■ Prostrate, semi-evergreen subshrub with trailing stems clothed in rounded-ovate, bright green leaves, to 2cm (¾in) long. In summer, produces whorls of small, tubular, pale pink to mauve flowers, 1.5cm (½in) long, among deep rose-pink bracts, 2cm (¾in) long. ↕ 10cm (4in), ↔ to 20cm (8in). ❄❄❄

O. laevigatum ■ Woody-based perennial with erect, wiry, red-purple stems and ovate to elliptic, dark green leaves, 1.5–2cm (½–¾in) long, hairy only along the midribs beneath. Loose, panicle-like whorls of numerous tubular, scarcely 2-lipped, purplish pink flowers, 1.5cm (½in) long, are produced from late spring to autumn. The flowers have darker purple calyces, surrounded by red-purple bracts, 1cm (½in) long. ↕ to 50–60cm (20–24in), ↔ 45cm (18in). Turkey, Cyprus. ❄❄❄. **'Herrenhausen'** ■ has purple-flushed young leaves and winter foliage, and denser whorls of pink flowers; ↕ 45cm (18in). **'Hopleys'** has large, deep pink flowers, 2cm (¾in) long, and large bracts, 1.5cm (½in) long, borne in narrow whorls; ↕ 60cm (24in).

O. majorana (Sweet marjoram). Upright, evergreen subshrub, often grown as an annual or biennial, with branching stems bearing ovate or elliptic, softly hairy, grey-green leaves, 0.3–3cm (⅛–1¼in) long. Panicles of tubular, white or pink flowers, 8mm (⅜in) long, with grey-green bracts, to 4mm (⅛in) long, appear from early to late summer. ↕ to 80cm (32in), ↔ 45cm (18in). S.W. Europe, Turkey. ❄❄

O. microphyllum. Domed, spreading, evergreen subshrub with ovate, downy grey leaves, to 5mm (¼in) long, on slender branches. In summer, bears loose, panicle-like whorls of tubular, pink to purple flowers, 5mm (¼in) long, among purple bracts, to 4mm (⅛in) long. ↕ 25cm (10in), ↔ to 30cm (12in). Crete. ❄❄

O. onites, syn. *Majorana onites* (French marjoram, Pot marjoram). Small, mound-forming, semi-evergreen subshrub with red-hairy stems and ovate to elliptic, bright green leaves, to 2cm (¾in) long, rounded to heart-shaped at the bases. In late summer, produces tubular white flowers, to 6mm (¼in) long, in dense, corymb-like whorls, with green bracts, to 4mm (⅛in) long. Popular herb for Mediterranean dishes. ↕ 60cm (24in), ↔ 30cm (12in). E. Mediterranean. ❄❄

O. rotundifolium. Rhizomatous, woody-based perennial or deciduous, rounded subshrub, with rounded to heart-shaped, blue-grey leaves, to 2.5cm (1in) long. Throughout summer, produces nodding, hop-like whorls of small, tubular, pale pink flowers, to 1.5cm (½in) long, among pale lemon-green bracts, to 2.5cm (1in) long. ↕ 10–30cm (4–12in), ↔ to 30cm (12in). Turkey, Armenia, Georgia. ❄❄❄

O. vulgare ■ (Oregano, Wild marjoram). Bushy, rhizomatous, woody-based perennial with upright to spreading stems bearing very aromatic, rounded to ovate, dark green leaves, to 4cm (1½in) long. From midsummer to early autumn, bears loose panicle- or corymb-like whorls of tubular flowers,

Origanum amanum

Origanum laevigatum 'Herrenhausen'

Origanum vulgare

Origanum vulgare 'Aureum'

to 4mm (⅛in) long, varying from deep to pale pink or white, with whorls of leafy, purple-tinted green bracts, to 1cm (½in) long. ↕↔ 30–90cm (12–36in). Europe. ✻✻✻. **'Aureum'** ■ (Golden wild marjoram) has golden leaves and pink flowers, and spreads less vigorously than the species; ↔ to 30cm (12in). **'Aureum Crispum'** is more spreading than the species, with curly golden leaves; ↔ 45cm (18in). **'Compactum'** (Compact marjoram) is dense, compact, and dome-forming, with smaller leaves, to 2cm (¾in) long; ↕ to 15cm (6in), ↔ to 30cm (12in). **'Gold Tip'**, syn. 'Variegatum', is like 'Aureum Crispum', but the leaves are yellow only at their tips; ↕ 40cm (16in), ↔ 45cm (18in). **'Heiderose'** is upright and bushy in habit, with pink flowers; ↕ to 40cm (16in). **subsp. *hirtum***, syn. *O. heracleoticum*, has a compact habit, with hairy leaves, hairy green bracts, and small heads of white flowers; ↕ 30–70cm (12–28in), ↔ 20–45cm (8–18in); Greece, Turkey. **'Variegatum'** see 'Gold Tip'.

ORIXA

RUTACEAE

Genus of one species of deciduous, spreading, dioecious shrub from woodland and thickets in mountainous regions of China, Korea, and Japan. Cultivated for its elegant, aromatic foliage, it is suitable for a shrub border or woodland garden.

- **HARDINESS** Fully hardy.
- **CULTIVATION** Grow in fertile, well-drained soil in sun or shade. Tolerant of dry soils and exposed positions. Pruning group 1.
- **PROPAGATION** Sow seed in containers in a cold frame in spring. Take semi-ripe cuttings in midsummer.
- **PESTS AND DISEASES** Trouble free.

O. japonica. Spreading, slender-branched, deciduous shrub with simple, alternate, obovate to inversely lance-shaped, aromatic, dark green leaves, to 12cm (5in) long, pale yellow in autumn. Cup-shaped, 4-petalled green flowers, to 5mm (¼in) across, are borne in the leaf axils as the leaves emerge in spring; the males are borne in small panicles, to 3cm (1¼in) long, the females singly. Female plants bear 4-lobed brown fruit, 2cm (¾in) across. ↕ 2.5m (8ft), ↔ 4m (12ft). China, Korea, Japan. ✻✻✻

ORNITHOGALUM

Star-of-Bethlehem

HYACINTHACEAE/LILIACEAE

Genus of 80 species of bulbous perennials found in a variety of habitats, ranging from dry, rocky hillsides to meadows and woodland, in C. and S. Europe, the Mediterranean, former USSR, W. and S.W. Asia, tropical Africa, and South Africa. They are grown for their sometimes corymb-like racemes of often star-, cup-, or funnel-shaped, occasionally scented flowers; usually white, sometimes yellow or orange, they are borne on leafless stems in spring or summer. The leaves are basal, and vary from linear to obovate, sometimes with a silver stripe down the centre. Smaller species are suitable for a rock garden; taller ones for a herbaceous border. In ideal growing conditions, *O. nutans* and *O. umbellatum* may become invasive, but, as with *O. montanum*, are suitable for naturalizing in short turf or beneath shrubs. In frost-prone areas, grow tender species in a cool greenhouse, or grow outdoors and lift in autumn. All parts may cause severe discomfort if ingested, and the sap may irritate skin.

- **HARDINESS** Fully hardy to frost tender.
- **CULTIVATION** Plant bulbs 10cm (4in) deep. Outdoors, plant fully hardy and frost-hardy species in autumn, in moderately fertile, well-drained soil, in a sunny situation. *O. nutans* and *O. umbellatum* tolerate partial shade. Plant half-hardy species in spring for summer flowering; in growth, water freely and lift after flowering; keep frost-free over winter. Under glass, grow tender species in large containers of loam-based potting compost (JI No.2), in full light with shade from hot sun. When in growth, water freely; keep dry when dormant, and repot annually in spring. *O. thyrsoides* may be planted under glass in autumn for spring flowering.
- **PROPAGATION** Sow seed in containers in a cold frame in autumn or spring. Remove offsets when dormant.
- **PESTS AND DISEASES** Trouble free.

O. arabicum. Bulbous perennial with basal rosettes of semi-erect, broadly linear, dark green leaves, to 60cm (24in) long. In early summer, bears corymb-like racemes of 6–25 cup-shaped, scented, white or cream flowers, 3cm (1¼in) across, each with a conspicuous

Ornithogalum balansae

Ornithogalum lanceolatum

black ovary. ↕ 30–80cm (12–32in), ↔ 8cm (3in). Mediterranean. ✻

O. balansae ■ syn. *O. oligophyllum* of gardens. Slender, bulbous perennial with almost prostrate, inversely lance-shaped, glossy, mid-green, basal leaves, to 15cm (6in) long. In early spring, bears corymb-like racemes of 2–5 cup-shaped flowers, 3cm (1¼in) across, glistening white inside, bright green outside. ↕ to 8cm (3in), ↔ 10cm (4in). Balkans, Turkey, Georgia. ✻✻✻

O. caudatum see *O. longibracteatum.*

O. lanceolatum ■ Dwarf, bulbous perennial producing basal rosettes of prostrate, lance-shaped, shiny, mid-green leaves, 10–12cm (4–5in) long. In spring, bears compact, almost stemless racemes of 5–13 star-shaped white flowers, 2–3cm (¾–1¼in) across, striped green on the outsides. ↕ 5–10cm (2–4in), ↔ 10cm (4in). Turkey, Syria, Lebanon. ✻✻✻

O. longibracteatum, syn. *O. caudatum* (False sea onion). Bulbous perennial with lax, strap-shaped, semi-succulent, pale green, basal leaves, to 60cm (24in) long. In summer, bears tall racemes of up to 300 bell-shaped white flowers, to 1.5cm (½in) across, striped green outside, with bracts extending far beyond the flowers. ↕ 1–1.5m (3–5ft), ↔ 15cm (6in). Tropical Africa, South Africa (Northern Cape, Eastern Cape). ✻✻

O. montanum ■ Bulbous perennial producing basal rosettes of prostrate, linear, shiny, pale to greyish green leaves, 10–15cm (4–6in) long. In spring, bears corymb-like racemes of 10–20 star-shaped white flowers, 2cm

Ornithogalum montanum

Ornithogalum narbonense

(¾in) across, striped green on the outsides. ↕ 10–25cm (4–10in), ↔ 10cm (4in). S. Europe, Turkey, Lebanon, Israel. ✻✻

O. narbonense ■ Bulbous perennial with semi-erect, linear, grey-green, basal leaves, to 60cm (24in) long. Produces upright, narrowly pyramidal racemes of 25–75 star-shaped white flowers, 2cm (¾in) across, in late spring and early summer. ↕ 30–90cm (12–36in), ↔ 5cm (2in). Mediterranean, Turkey, Caucasus, Iran. ✻✻✻

O. nutans. Bulbous perennial with semi-erect, strap-shaped, bright mid-green, basal leaves, 30–40cm (12–16in) long, each with a central silver stripe above. In spring, bears one-sided racemes of up to 20 semi-pendent, funnel-shaped, silvery white flowers, 3cm (1¼in) across, broadly striped green outside. ↕ 20–60cm (8–24in), ↔ 5cm (2in). Europe, S.W. Asia. ✻✻✻

***O. oligophyllum* of gardens** see *O. balansae.*

O. pyramidale. Bulbous perennial with basal clusters of semi-erect, linear, glossy, mid-green leaves, to 60cm (24in) long, which wither as the flowers open. In late spring and early summer, produces stiff racemes of numerous star-shaped white flowers, 1–2cm (½–¾in) across, striped green on the outsides. ↕ 30–120cm (12–48in), ↔ 7cm (3in). C. Europe, Balkans. ✻✻✻

O. pyrenaicum (Bath asparagus). Bulbous perennial with basal tufts of semi-erect, narrowly linear, grey-green leaves, 20–35cm (8–14in) long, often withering as the flowers open. Long racemes of 25–40 star-shaped, pale yellow flowers, to 1cm (½in) across, broadly or narrowly striped green outside, are produced in early summer. ↕ to 1m (3ft), ↔ 10cm (4in). Europe, Turkey, Caucasus. ✻✻✻

O. saundersiae. Robust, bulbous perennial with erect, strap-shaped, dark green, sometimes greyish green, basal leaves, 60cm (24in) long. In winter or spring, produces dense, corymb-like

Ornithogalum umbellatum

racemes of cup-shaped, white or creamy white flowers, 2–3cm (¾–1¼in) across, with black or greenish black ovaries. ↕ to 1m (3ft), ↔ 10cm (4in). South Africa (Limpopo, Mpumalanga, KwaZulu/Natal), Swaziland. ✻

O. sintenisii. Small, bulbous perennial with basal rosettes of nearly prostrate, linear, recurved and often twisted, mid-green leaves, 20–30cm (8–12in) long. In spring, produces almost stemless racemes of 4–12 open star-shaped white flowers, 2cm (¾in) across, striped green on the outsides. ↕↔ 10cm (4in). Russia, Georgia, Azerbaijan, Iran. ✻✻✻

O. thyrsoides (Chincherinchee). Robust, bulbous perennial with semi-erect, linear to narrowly lance-shaped, mid-green, basal leaves, to 30cm (12in) long, with hairy margins, withering before the flowers open. In spring and early summer, bears dense racemes of many cup-shaped white flowers, 2cm (¾in) across, tinted cream or green at the bases. Excellent for cut flowers. ↕ to 70cm (28in), ↔ 10cm (4in). South Africa (Western Cape). ✻

O. umbellatum ▣ (Star-of-Bethlehem). Bulbous perennial with semi-erect, linear, white-veined, mid-green, basal leaves, to 30cm (12in) long, each with a central silver stripe above; the leaves wither as the flowers open in early summer. Produces corymb-like racemes of 6–20 long-stalked, star-shaped white flowers, 2cm (¾in) across, striped green outside. Increases rapidly. ↕ 10–30cm (4–12in), ↔ 10cm (4in). Europe, Turkey, Syria, Lebanon, Israel, N. Africa. ✻✻✻

ORNITHOPHORA

ORCHIDACEAE

Genus of 1 or possibly 2 species of evergreen, epiphytic orchids from Brazil, occurring in warm, moist, forested areas. They have slender, compressed, ovoid pseudobulbs, each with 2 linear leaves at the tip, and a fine mat of aerial roots. Tiny flowers are borne in slender racemes arising from the bases of the pseudobulbs, and resemble a swarm of insects hovering above the plant.

• **HARDINESS** Frost tender.
• **CULTIVATION** Cool- to intermediate-growing orchids. Grow in epiphytic orchid compost in shallow pots or slatted baskets, or epiphytically on slabs of bark. Provide high humidity and bright filtered light all year. In summer, mist daily, water freely, and apply a quarter-strength fertilizer at every third watering. In winter, water more sparingly, and do not allow to dry out completely. See also p.46.
• **PROPAGATION** Divide when the plant fills the pot and "flows" over the sides.
• **PESTS AND DISEASES** Susceptible to red spider mites, aphids, and mealybugs.

O. radicans, syn. *Sigmatostalix radicans.* Epiphytic orchid with grass-like leaves, 10–18cm (4–7in) long. Intricately patterned, slightly fragrant, white-green or green-yellow flowers, to 8mm (⅜in) across, with cream lips, are borne in racemes 7–15cm (3–6in) long, in autumn. ↕ 10cm (4in), ↔ 30cm (12in). Brazil. ⌂ (min. 13°C/55°F; max. 30°C/86°F)

▷ ***Orobus aureus*** see *Lathyrus aureus*
▷ ***Orobus vernus*** see *Lathyrus vernus*

ORONTIUM

Golden club

ARACEAE

Genus of one species of marginal aquatic perennial from E. USA. It has large, thick rhizomes producing oblong to narrowly elliptic, submerged, floating, or aerial leaves, and curious, pencil-like spadices that stand well above the water. Ideal for the margins of an informal pool, it associates well with waterside irises and primulas in early summer.

• **HARDINESS** Fully hardy.
• **CULTIVATION** Grow in deep mud at a pool margin with ample room to spread, or in baskets of loamy soil, in water no

Orontium aquaticum

deeper than 45cm (18in), and in full sun to develop the beauty of the glaucous leaves. Remove the short-lived flower spikes when they fade. See also pp.52–53.
• **PROPAGATION** Sow seed as soon as ripe in a cold frame in trays of loam-based seed compost, and cover with no more than 1–3cm (½–1¼in) of water. Divide the rhizomes in spring.
• **PESTS AND DISEASES** Trouble free.

O. aquaticum ▣ Rhizomatous, marginal aquatic perennial with oblong to narrowly elliptic, submerged, aerial, or floating leaves, to 25cm (10in) long, mid-green and glaucous, often purple-tinted beneath. From late spring to midsummer, bears small, bright yellow flowers near the tops of numerous cylindrical white spadices, 18cm (7in) tall. ↕ 30–45cm (12–18in), ↔ 60–75cm (24–30in). E. USA. ✻✻✻

OROSTACHYS

CRASSULACEAE

Genus of about 10 species of freely offsetting, monocarpic perennials, closely related to *Sedum*, from low to mountainous, rocky areas of Russia, China, North Korea, South Korea, and Japan. They have dense, hemispherical to spherical rosettes of fleshy leaves, and produce erect stems bearing terminal, spike-like racemes or panicles of short-stalked, star-shaped flowers during summer or autumn. The rosettes die after flowering and fruiting. Below 8°C (46°F), grow in a cool greenhouse; in warmer climates, grow in a bed or border with other succulents.

• **HARDINESS** Half hardy to frost tender.
• **CULTIVATION** Under glass, grow in standard cactus compost in full light. From spring to autumn, water freely and apply a half-strength, balanced liquid fertilizer every 4 weeks. Keep almost dry in winter. Outdoors, grow in poor, well-drained soil in full sun. See also pp.48–49.
• **PROPAGATION** Sow seed at 13–18°C (55–64°F), or divide offsets, in spring.
• **PESTS AND DISEASES** Susceptible to mealybugs.

O. chanetii. Clump-forming, perennial succulent with a stoloniferous rootstock and compact, basal rosettes of linear, greyish green leaves, 4cm (1½in) long. Dense, pyramidal, spike-like racemes or panicles, to 20cm (8in) long, of star-shaped white flowers, 1–2cm (½–¾in) across, reddish pink outside, are borne in summer and autumn. ↕ to 20cm (8in) sometimes more, ↔ 10cm (4in). China. ⌂ (min. 8°C/46°F)

OROYA

CACTACEAE

Genus of 2 or 3 species of perennial cacti from dry, stony slopes, screes, and cliffs, at altitudes to 4,000m (13,000ft), in Peru. They have flattened-spherical to very short-cylindrical, rarely offsetting stems with numerous warty ribs and spined areoles. Bell- or funnel-shaped flowers are usually borne in a ring around the crown of each stem in summer, followed by obovoid to ovoid red or yellow berries containing black-coated seeds. Where temperatures drop below 13°C (55°F), grow in a warm greenhouse; in warm, dry climates, use in a desert garden.

• **HARDINESS** Frost tender.
• **CULTIVATION** Under glass, grow in standard cactus compost in full light. From spring to autumn, water freely and apply half-strength, balanced liquid fertilizer 3 or 4 times. Keep barely moist in winter. Outdoors, grow in sharply drained, neutral to slightly alkaline, poor, humus-rich soil in full sun. See also pp.48–49.
• **PROPAGATION** Sow seed at 18–21°C (64–70°F) in spring.
• **PESTS AND DISEASES** Susceptible to aphids while flowering.

O. neoperuviana see *O. peruviana.*

O. peruviana ▣ syn. *Oreocereus peruviana, Oroya neoperuviana.* Perennial cactus producing solitary, dull green or bluish green stems, each with up to 35 rounded ribs notched into long tubercles. Linear areoles bear brownish yellow spines (10–30 radials, in comb-like formation, and up to 6 longer centrals). Bell-shaped, pale carmine-red to vermilion, usually yellow-based flowers, 1.5–3cm (½–1¼in) long, are borne in summer. ↕ 15–20cm (6–8in), occasionally more, ↔ to 15cm (6in). Peru. ⌂ (min. 13°C/55°F)

▷ ***Orphanidesia*** see *Epigaea*
O. gaultherioides see *E. gaultherioides*
▷ **Orpine** see *Sedum telephium*
Stone see *S. rupestre*
▷ **Orris root** see *Iris germanica* 'Florentina'

Oroya peruviana

ORTEGOCACTUS

CACTACEAE

Genus of one species of perennial cactus, closely related to *Mammillaria*, from dry areas of S.W. Mexico. It has spherical to short-cylindrical stems, which often offset to form small clusters, with spirally arranged, warty ribs and prominently spined areoles. Solitary, funnel-shaped yellow flowers are produced in summer, followed by orange-yellow or dull red fruit. In areas where temperatures drop below 15°C (59°F), grow in a warm greenhouse; in warm, dry climates, grow in a border with other cacti, or in a raised bed or desert garden.

- **HARDINESS** Frost tender.
- **CULTIVATION** Under glass, grow in standard cactus compost in full light. From spring to early autumn, water freely and apply half-strength, balanced liquid fertilizer every 4–5 weeks. Keep dry at other times. Outdoors, grow in moderately fertile, sharply drained, humus-rich, slightly acid soil in full sun. See also pp.48–49.
- **PROPAGATION** Sow seed at 21°C (70°F) in spring.
- **PESTS AND DISEASES** Vulnerable to mealybugs.

O. macdougallii ■ syn. *Neobesseya macdougallii*. Clustering, perennial cactus producing spherical to short-cylindrical, pale greyish green stems, 3–4cm (1¼–1½in) thick, covered with large, diamond-shaped tubercles. White-woolly areoles bear black-tipped, white or totally black spines (7 or 8 radials and 1 shorter central spine). Solitary, funnel-shaped yellow flowers, to 3cm (1¼in) long, the outer tepals tinted purple outside, are produced in summer; they are followed by spherical-ellipsoid, orange-yellow or dull red fruit with black-coated seeds. ↕ to 6cm (2½in), ↔ 12cm (5in). S.W. Mexico. ❀ (min. 15°C/59°F)

ORTHOPHYTUM

BROMELIACEAE

Genus of about 18 species of mat-forming, evergreen, semi-succulent, terrestrial perennials (bromeliads) from dry, rocky slopes, to 1,200m (4,000ft) high, in E. Brazil. They spread by stolons to form wide rosettes of usually stemless, softly spiny leaves. In summer, they produce varyingly branched inflorescences with leafy bracts and small, dense clusters of slender, tubular, mainly white flowers. In areas where temperatures drop below 15°C (59°F), grow in a warm greenhouse; in warm, dry climates use in a desert garden.

- **HARDINESS** Frost tender.
- **CULTIVATION** Under glass, grow in terrestrial bromeliad compost in full light. In the growing season, water moderately with soft water, applying half-strength, balanced liquid fertilizer every 3–4 weeks. Keep plants dry in winter. Outdoors, grow in sharply drained, moderately fertile, humus-rich soil in full sun. See also p.47.
- **PROPAGATION** Sow seed at 27°C (81°F) in early spring. Separate offsets in spring.
- **PESTS AND DISEASES** Susceptible to aphids while flowering.

O. navioides, syn. *Cryptanthopsis navioides*. Stemless bromeliad that spreads by stolons to form clustered rosettes of narrowly lance-shaped, finely toothed, sparsely scaly, mid-green leaves, to 30cm (12in) long. In summer, tubular white flowers, to 3cm (1¼in) long, with pale yellowish green sepals and bracts, are produced in few-flowered clusters, sunk in the centre of each rosette. The whole plant often turns bright red or red-purple as the flowers mature. ↕ to 20cm (8in), ↔ to 60cm (24in). E. Brazil. ❀ (min. 15°C/59°F)

O. saxicola. Stemless bromeliad, spreading by stolons to form large clusters of rosettes. Narrowly triangular,

Ortegocactus macdougallii

Orthophytum vagans

toothed, pale bright green leaves, 3–6cm (1¼–2½in) long, are usually thick and fleshy. In summer, produces head-like clusters of thick, fleshy bracts and short-stalked, tubular white flowers, to 2cm (¾in) long, with white-margined green sepals, and petals with 2 basal projections. Both the bracts and the flowers are almost hidden in the rosettes. ↕ 8cm (3in), ↔ indefinite. E. Brazil. ❀ (min. 15°C/59°F)

O. vagans ■ Trailing bromeliad with an elongated, branching caudex, the branches rooting down and forming large, spreading groups. Produces loosely rosetted rows of narrowly triangular, deeply channelled, slightly toothed, bright green leaves, to 10cm (4in) long, scaly beneath, turning red-purple with age. In summer, produces stemless inflorescences of red or orange bracts and 15–30 tubular, apple-green flowers, 2cm (¾in) long, with white-woolly sepals, and stalks 5cm (2in) long. ↕ to 20cm (8in), ↔ indefinite. E. Brazil. ❀ (min. 15°C/59°F)

ORTHROSANTHUS

IRIDACEAE

Genus of 7 species of evergreen perennials occurring in sandy soils in Australia and tropical America. They have narrowly strap-shaped or linear, rigid or arching leaves, arising from short, woody rhizomes. They are grown for their bowl-shaped to open saucer-shaped, 6-tepalled blue flowers, borne in loose, terminal panicles on slender, erect stalks. The flowers are short-lived, but open in succession for 2 weeks or more from late spring to summer. In frost-prone areas, grow in a cool greenhouse or conservatory; in warmer areas, grow in a warm, sunny border.

- **HARDINESS** Half hardy to frost tender.
- **CULTIVATION** Under glass, grow in loam-based potting compost (JI No.2), with additional sharp sand and leaf mould, in full light. Water moderately when in growth; keep almost dry when dormant. Repot or top-dress in spring. Outdoors, grow in light, fertile, well-drained, humus-rich soil in full sun.
- **PROPAGATION** Sow seed at 13–18°C (55–64°F), or divide, in spring.
- **PESTS AND DISEASES** Trouble free.

O. chimboracensis. Rhizomatous perennial with stiff, leathery, linear, basal leaves, to 40cm (16in) long, rough to the touch. Loose panicles of shallowly

Orthrosanthus multiflorus

bowl-shaped, lavender-blue flowers, 4cm (1½in) across, are produced in summer. ↕ 30–60cm (12–24in), ↔ 30cm (12in). Mexico to Peru. ✲

O. multiflorus ■ Rhizomatous perennial with rigid, linear, basal leaves, to 45cm (18in) long, with smooth margins. From late spring to summer, bears narrow panicles of open saucer-shaped, pale blue to violet-blue flowers, to 4cm (1½in) across. ↕ 60cm (24in), ↔ 30cm (12in). S.W. Australia. ✲

ORYCHOPHRAGMUS

BRASSICACEAE/CRUCIFERAE

Genus of 2 species of annuals or biennials occurring in fallow fields and on wasteland in C. Asia and China. They have thin, pinnatifid, lower leaves and entire stem-clasping leaves. Cross-shaped flowers, with 4-clawed violet petals, are produced in terminal racemes from late spring to summer. Grow outdoors as a bedding annual or biennial, or, for flowers in late winter and early spring, grow as a short-lived container plant in a cool or temperate greenhouse.

- **HARDINESS** Half hardy.
- **CULTIVATION** Outdoors, grow in fertile, well-drained soil in a warm, sunny site. Under glass, grow in loam-based potting compost (JI No.2) in full light. In growth, water moderately.
- **PROPAGATION** Sow seed *in situ* in spring or early summer or, in frost-free climates, in autumn.
- **PESTS AND DISEASES** Trouble free.

O. violaceus. Annual or biennial with an upright habit, and moderately fast-growing, branching stems bearing thin, pinnatifid, pale green basal leaves, 12–15cm (5–6in) or more long, and smaller, entire, pale green stem-clasping leaves. Produces terminal racemes of 5–25 cross-shaped violet flowers, to 2.5cm (1in) across, in late spring and early summer. ↕ 30–60cm (12–24in), ↔ 30cm (12in). China. ✲

ORYZA

Rice

GRAMINEAE/POACEAE

Genus of about 20 species of annual or perennial, rhizomatous grasses with flat, linear leaves, and panicles of laterally compressed spikelets producing rice-grain seeds when ripe. They are native to tropical and subtropical Africa and Asia, and are widely cultivated in subtropical and tropical regions. *O. sativa* 'Nigrescens' has unusually coloured leaves, and is the only *Oryza* grown for ornamental reasons. Where temperatures fall below 10°C (50°F), grow in a warm greenhouse or conservatory; in warmer areas, grow as a pond marginal or in a bog garden.

- **HARDINESS** Frost tender.
- **CULTIVATION** Under glass, provide full light and use loam-based potting compost (JI No.3) in shallow clay pots, or in fibreglass trays with drainage holes. Keep the soil surface submerged to a depth of about 2.5cm (1in), and refresh water regularly; maintain water temperature at 20–30°C (68–86°F). Drain off as flowerheads form, and keep evenly moist. Algal growth on the soil surface is unsightly but not harmful. Outdoors, grow in very moist, fertile, clay-loam soil, or in pots in shallow water at a pond margin, in full sun.
- **PROPAGATION** Surface-sow seed at 19–24°C (66–75°F) in late winter, in pots standing in containers of water.
- **PESTS AND DISEASES** Trouble free.

***O. sativa* 'Nigrescens'.** Loosely tufted annual, rhizomatous grass with strong, erect stems bearing arching, broadly linear, dark brownish purple leaves, to 1m (3ft) long. Produces spikelets in open, arching panicles, 35cm (14in) long, from midsummer to mid-autumn. ↕75cm (30in), ↔ 30cm (12in). S.E. Asia. ❀ (min. 10°C/50°F)

OSBECKIA

MELASTOMATACEAE

Genus of 40–60 species of evergreen perennials, subshrubs, and shrubs from Africa to China, and southwards from Japan to Australia, where they thrive in habitats from grassland to woodland. They are grown for their often showy, 4- or 5-petalled flowers, borne in terminal, leafy panicles or cymes, or sometimes singly, and for their simple, opposite, usually entire, somewhat leathery and bristly-hairy, strongly 3- to 7-veined leaves. Below 13–15°C (55–59°F), grow in a warm greenhouse; in warmer areas, use in a border.

- **HARDINESS** Frost tender.
- **CULTIVATION** Under glass, grow in loam-based potting compost (JI No.3) in bright filtered light, or full light with shade from hot sun. In growth, water freely and apply a balanced liquid fertilizer monthly; water moderately in winter. Outdoors, grow in fertile, moist but well-drained, humus-rich, neutral to acid soil in partial shade or with some midday shade. Pruning group 9; plants under glass need restrictive pruning in early spring.
- **PROPAGATION** Sow seed at 18°C (64°F) in spring. Root semi-ripe cuttings with bottom heat in summer.
- **PESTS AND DISEASES** Prone to scale insects and red spider mites under glass.

O. stellata. Erect shrub, spreading with age, with moderately branched, finely hairy stems and narrowly ovate, hairy-margined, deep green leaves, 6–15cm (2½–6in) long, with long, sharp points; each leaf has 5–7 prominent veins. Bears loose cymes of 4-petalled, saucer-shaped, blue-purple to reddish lilac, pink, or white flowers, 5cm (2in) across, mainly in summer. ↕1.2–1.8m (4–6ft), ↔ 1–1.5m (3–5ft). India to China. ❀ (min. 13°C/55°F)

▷***Oscularia deltoides*** see *Lampranthus deltoides*
▷**Osier,**
Common see *Salix viminalis*
Green see *Cornus alternifolia*
Purple see *Salix purpurea*

OSMANTHUS

syn. x OSMAREA

OLEACEAE

Genus of about 15–20 species of evergreen shrubs and small trees from woodland in Asia, the Pacific islands, and S. USA. They are grown for their foliage and flowers: the leaves are lance-shaped to ovate, borne in opposite pairs; the small, tubular, 4-lobed, usually fragrant, white, occasionally yellow or orange flowers are produced in mainly axillary clusters or terminal panicles. The flowers are usually followed by ovoid, blue-black fruits. *Osmanthus* species and cultivars are ideal for a shrub border or woodland garden. *O. delavayi* may be wall-trained; *O.* x *burkwoodii*, *O. delavayi*, and *O. heterophyllus* are very good for hedging and topiary. In frost-prone areas, grow the tender species in a cool or temperate greenhouse.

- **HARDINESS** Fully hardy to frost tender.
- **CULTIVATION** Outdoors, grow in fertile, well-drained soil in sun or partial shade, with shelter from cold, drying winds. Under glass, grow in loam-based potting compost (JI No.3) in full light with shade from hot sun. When in growth, water freely and apply a balanced liquid fertilizer monthly; water sparingly in winter. Pruning group 8 for early-flowering species; group 9 for late-flowering species; all tolerate hard pruning. Trim hedges after flowering, or in spring for *O. heterophyllus*.
- **PROPAGATION** Sow seed in containers in a cold frame as soon as ripe. Root semi-ripe cuttings in summer with bottom heat. Layer in autumn or spring.
- **PESTS AND DISEASES** Trouble free.

Osmanthus x *burkwoodii*

Osmanthus decorus

O. armatus. Dense, rounded shrub with oblong-lance-shaped, sharply spine-toothed, leathery, glossy, dark green leaves, to 15cm (6in) long. Broadly tubular, fragrant, creamy white flowers, with spreading lobes, to 5mm (¼in) across, are borne in axillary clusters in autumn, followed by ovoid, dark violet fruit, to 2cm (¾in) long. ↕2.5–5m (8–15ft), ↔ 4m (12ft). W. China. ❄❄

O.* x *burkwoodii ■ (*O. decorus* x *O. delavayi*), syn. x *Osmarea burkwoodii*. Dense, rounded shrub with oval to ovate, slightly toothed, leathery, glossy, dark green leaves, to 5cm (2in) long. Tubular, very fragrant white flowers, the lobes to 5mm (¼in) across, are profusely borne in small, axillary clusters in mid- and late spring. Seldom produces fruit. ↕↔ 3m (10ft). Garden origin. ❄❄❄

O. decorus ■ syn. *Phillyrea decora*. Dense, rounded, spreading shrub with narrowly oval to oblong, pointed, leathery, glossy, dark green leaves, to 12cm (5in) long, very occasionally with a few teeth. Tubular white flowers, the lobes to 8mm (⅜in) across, are borne in dense, axillary clusters in mid-spring, followed by ellipsoid, blue-black fruit, to 1.5cm (½in) long. ↕3m (10ft), ↔ 5m (15ft). Georgia, N.E. Turkey. ❄❄❄

O. delavayi ■ syn. *Siphonosmanthus delavayi*. Rounded, bushy shrub with arching branches and ovate, finely toothed, leathery, glossy, dark green leaves, to 2.5cm (1in) long. Tubular, very fragrant white flowers, the lobes to 1cm (½in) across, are produced in axillary and terminal clusters in mid- and late spring, followed by ovoid, blue-black fruit, to 1cm (½in) long. ↕2–6m (6–20ft), ↔ 4m (12ft) or more. W. China (Sichuan, Yunnan). ❄❄❄

Osmanthus delavayi

Osmanthus heterophyllus 'Aureomarginatus'

O. forrestii see *O. yunnanensis*.

O.* x *fortunei (*O. fragrans* x *O. heterophyllus*). Upright shrub with holly-like, oval to ovate, leathery, glossy, dark green leaves, to 10cm (4in) long, with spiny margins, but spineless towards the tops of mature plants. Tubular, fragrant white flowers, the lobes to 1cm (½in) across, are produced in axillary clusters from late summer to autumn. Seldom produces fruit. ↕ to 2m (6ft), sometimes to 6m (20ft), ↔ 5m (15ft). Garden origin. ❄❄. **'San José'** has narrower, more spiny leaves.

O. fragrans ♀ (Fragrant olive, Sweet tea). Vigorous, upright shrub or small tree with oblong to oblong-lance-shaped, leathery, entire or finely toothed, glossy, dark green leaves, 10–12cm (4–5in) long. Tubular, very fragrant white flowers, the lobes to 1cm (½in) across, appear singly or in few-flowered, axillary clusters in autumn, and sometimes in spring and summer; they are followed by ovoid, blue-black fruit, to 1cm (½in) long. ↕↔ 6m (20ft). Himalayas, China, Japan. ❄. **f. *aurantiacus*** has orange flowers.

O. heterophyllus. Dense, rounded shrub with holly-like, oval to elliptic-oblong, sharply toothed, leathery, glossy, dark green leaves, to 6cm (2½in) long, often spineless on mature plants. Tubular, fragrant white flowers, the lobes to 5mm (¼in) across, are produced in small, axillary clusters from late summer to autumn, followed by ovoid, blue-black fruit, to 1cm (½in) long. ↕↔ 5m (15ft). Japan, Taiwan. ❄❄. **'Aureomarginatus'** ■ syn. 'Aureus', has yellow-margined leaves. **'Gulftide'** is compact, with very spiny leaves; ↕2.5m (8ft), ↔ 3m (10ft). **'Myrtifolius'** has

O

Osmanthus heterophyllus 'Purpureus'

entire, spine-tipped leaves, to 5cm (2in) long; ↕↔ 3m (10ft). **'Purpureus'** ▣ has dark blackish purple young leaves. **'Rotundifolius'** has small, spineless leaves, to 4cm (1½in) long, rounded at the tips; ↕↔ 3m (10ft).
O. yunnanensis syn. *O. forrestii.* Large shrub or small tree, broadly upright at first, later spreading. The oblong to ovate-lance-shaped, spiny-toothed to entire leaves, to 20cm (8in) long, have long, sharp points and are leathery, glossy, dark green, spotted black beneath. Broadly tubular, very fragrant, creamy white flowers, with lobes to 8mm (⅜in) across, are borne in small, axillary clusters in late winter and early spring; they are followed by ovoid, dark purple fruit, to 1.5cm (½in) long, with a white bloom. ↕↔ 10m (30ft) or more. W. China. ❄❄❄ (borderline)

▷**x *Osmarea*** see *Osmanthus*
x *O. burkwoodii* see *O.* x *burkwoodii*
▷***Osmaronia*** see *Oemleria*
O. cerasiformis see *O. cerasiformis*

OSMUNDA

OSMUNDACEAE

Genus of about 12 species of deciduous, terrestrial ferns found in damp places and watersides in all continents except Australasia. Broadly lance-shaped to triangular-ovate or ovate, pinnate, 2-pinnate, or 2-pinnatifid sterile fronds arise from large, erect rhizomes and turn yellow or golden brown in autumn. Distinctive, partially or wholly fertile fronds produce branched clusters of spherical greenish sporangia, which turn rust-brown or blackish on reduced pinnae. Grow in a damp border, or at the margins of a pond or stream.
• **HARDINESS** Fully hardy.
• **CULTIVATION** Grow in moist, fertile, humus-rich, preferably acid soil, in light dappled shade. *O. regalis* prefers a wetter site, but does well in full sun as long as water is plentiful.
• **PROPAGATION** Sow spores at 15–16°C (59–61°F) within 3 days of ripening in summer; they lose viability quickly. Divide clumps from established colonies in autumn or early spring. See also p.51.
• **PESTS AND DISEASES** Trouble free.

O. cinnamomea (Cinnamon fern). Deciduous fern bearing "shuttlecocks" of ovate-lance-shaped, pinnate, pale blue-green sterile fronds, 0.6–1.5m (2–5ft) long, with pinnatifid segments,

Osmunda regalis

surrounding much narrower, erect fertile fronds, to 1m (3ft) long. The top of each fertile frond is a mass of cinnamon-brown sporangia in summer. ↕ 90cm (36in), ↔ 60cm (24in). E. North America. ❄❄❄
O. claytoniana (Interrupted fern). Deciduous fern bearing "shuttlecocks" of ovate-lance-shaped, pinnate, pale blue-green sterile fronds, to 90cm (36in) long, with pinnatifid segments; they surround taller fertile fronds, similar but with some of the middle pinnae reduced and, in summer, covered in sporangia, which are initially blackish, later yellow-green, then rust-brown. ↕ 90cm (36in), ↔ 60cm (24in). E. North America. ❄❄❄
O. regalis ▣ (Flowering fern, Royal fern). Deciduous fern producing dense clumps of broadly triangular-ovate, 2-pinnate, bright green sterile fronds, 1m (3ft) or more long. In summer, partially fertile fronds, to 2m (6ft) long, have tassel-like tips, with brown or rust-coloured sporangia covering the much smaller pinnae. The fibrous rootstock is the source of osmunda fibre, used as a potting compost for orchids. ↕ 2m (6ft), ↔ 4m (12ft). Temperate and subtropical regions. ❄❄❄. **'Cristata'** has pinnae and segments with crested tips; ↕↔ 1.2m (4ft). **'Purpurascens'** bears attractive red-purple-flushed fronds in spring; ↕↔ 1.2m (4ft). **'Undulata'** bears fronds with wavy segments; ↕↔ 1.2m (4ft).

▷**Oso berry** see *Oemleria cerasiformis*

OSTEOMELES

ROSACEAE

Genus of 3 species of deciduous, semi-evergreen, or evergreen shrubs or small trees from river valleys in China, Japan, Hawaii, and New Zealand. They have alternate, finely pinnate leaves and terminal corymbs of small, cup-shaped, 5-petalled white flowers, followed by spherical to ovoid, red-brown, black, or blue-black fruits, to 8mm (⅜in) across.

Osteomeles schweriniae

They are best grown in a sheltered shrub border or against a wall. In very cold areas, grow in a cool greenhouse.
• **HARDINESS** Frost hardy to half hardy.
• **CULTIVATION** Outdoors, grow in fertile, well-drained soil in full sun or partial shade, sheltered from strong, cold winds. Under glass, grow in loam-based potting compost (JI No.2) in full light. In growth, water freely and apply a balanced liquid fertilizer monthly; water sparingly in winter. Pruning group 8; may need restrictive pruning under glass.
• **PROPAGATION** Sow seed in containers in a cold frame in autumn. Take semi-ripe cuttings in summer.
• **PESTS AND DISEASES** Trouble free.

O. schweriniae ▣ Deciduous or semi-evergreen, arching shrub with long, slender shoots and ovate to oblong-ovate, pinnate leaves, to 7cm (3in) long, consisting of 15–31 ovate-oblong leaflets. In early summer, small, cup-shaped white flowers, to 1.5cm (½in) across, are produced in corymbs, to 8cm (3in) across, at the shoot tips; they are followed by spherical, red-brown, later blue-black fruit. ↕↔ 3m (10ft). S.W. China (Yunnan). ❄❄

OSTEOSPERMUM

ASTERACEAE/COMPOSITAE

Genus of about 70 species of evergreen subshrubs, perennials, and annuals, mostly from southern Africa, but also from the Arabian Peninsula, mainly found in grassland, on rocky mountains, or at forest margins. The alternate leaves are linear to broadly obovate, with entire, toothed, or lobed margins. Osteospermums are grown for their daisy-like, usually white, pink, or yellow flowerheads, sometimes with disc-florets in a contrasting colour, borne singly or in open panicles from late spring to autumn. Numerous cultivars have been selected and named; they have ray-florets varying from deep magenta through deep or pale pink to white or yellow. Grow osteospermums in a border; in frost-prone areas, the half-hardy perennials and subshrubs are best grown as annuals.
• **HARDINESS** Fully hardy to frost tender. Many cultivars will withstand short spells down to -10°C (14°F).
• **CULTIVATION** Grow in light, moderately fertile, well-drained soil in a warm, sheltered site in full sun. Dead-head regularly to prolong flowering. In frost-prone climates, propagate annually and overwinter in frost-free conditions.
• **PROPAGATION** Sow seed at 18°C (64°F) in spring. Root softwood cuttings in late spring or semi-ripe cuttings in late summer.
• **PESTS AND DISEASES** Prone to aphids, downy mildew, and *Verticillium* wilt.

***O. barberae* of gardens** see *O. jucundum.*
***O.* 'Bodegas Pink'.** Semi-upright subshrub with mostly inversely lance-shaped, toothed, mid-green leaves with pale yellow margins. From late spring to autumn, bears solitary, daisy-like flowerheads, 5cm (2in) across, with mauve-pink ray-florets, mauve-purple on the reverse, and dark bluish mauve disc-florets. ↕↔ 45cm (18in). ❄
***O.* 'Buttermilk'** ▣ Upright subshrub with mostly inversely lance-shaped, sparsely toothed, mid-green leaves. Solitary, daisy-like flowerheads, 5cm (2in) across, with white-based, primrose-yellow ray-florets, bronze-yellow on the reverse, and dark bluish mauve disc-florets, are borne from late spring to autumn. ↕↔ 60cm (24in). ❄❄
***O.* 'Cannington Roy'.** Densely spreading subshrub with obovate, sparsely toothed, mid-green leaves. From late spring to autumn, bears solitary, daisy-like flowerheads, 5cm (2in) across, with purple-tipped white ray-florets that age to mauve-pink, mauve-purple on the reverse, and with purple disc-florets. Good ground cover. ↕ 15cm (6in), ↔ 60cm (24in). ❄❄
O. caulescens, syn. *O. ecklonis* var. *prostratum* of gardens. Prostrate subshrub with inversely lance-shaped, toothed, mid-green leaves, to 10cm (4in) long. From late spring to autumn, bears solitary, daisy-like flowerheads, 5–6cm (2–2½in) across, with white ray-florets, flushed purple on the reverse, and blue-grey disc-florets. ↕ 10cm (4in), ↔ 60cm (24in). South Africa. ❄❄
O. ecklonis, syn. *Dimorphotheca ecklonis.* Variable, erect to almost prostrate subshrub with inversely lance-shaped, toothed, grey-green leaves, to 10cm (4in) long. From late spring to autumn, bears solitary, daisy-like flower-heads, 5–8cm (2–3in) across, with white ray-florets, indigo-blue on the reverse, and dark blue disc-florets. ↕ 0.6–1.5m (2–5ft), ↔ 0.6–1.2m (2–4ft). South Africa (Eastern Cape). ❄❄. **'Blue Streak'** has slate-blue disc-florets and

Osteospermum 'Buttermilk'

Osteospermum jucundum

white ray-florets, slate-blue on the reverse; ↕↔ 60cm (2ft). **var. *prostratum* of gardens** see *O. caulescens.*

O. fruticosum. Woody-based perennial with erect or decumbent stems and obovate to spoon-shaped, slightly fleshy, entire or minutely toothed, mid-green leaves, to 10cm (4in) long, mainly in basal rosettes. Solitary, daisy-like flowerheads, 6–7cm (2½–3in) across, the ray-florets white with purple bases, the disc-florets purplish violet, are borne from late spring to mid-autumn. ↕ to 60cm (24in), ↔ 75cm (30in). South Africa (Western Cape, Eastern Cape, KwaZulu/Natal). ✲✲

O. jucundum ▣ syn. *Dimorphotheca barberae* of gardens, *O. barberae* of gardens. Neat, clump-forming perennial, spreading by surface rhizomes, with linear to inversely lance-shaped, entire or sparsely toothed, greyish green leaves, 8–10cm (3–4in) long. From late spring to autumn, bears solitary, long-stalked, daisy-like flowerheads, 5cm (2in) across, with mauve-pink to magenta-purple ray-florets, bronze-purple to purple-pink on the reverse, and purple disc-florets that age to gold. ↕ 10–50cm (4–20in), ↔ 50–90cm (20–36in). South Africa

Osteospermum 'Whirlygig'

(Limpopo, Free State, KwaZulu/Natal), Swaziland, Lesotho. ✲✲✲. **var. *compactum*** forms neat, compact mats; ↕ 10–20cm (4–8in). **var. *compactum* 'Blackthorn'**, syn. var. *compactum* 'Blackthorn Seedling', has dark purple florets.

***O.* 'Nairobi Purple'** ▣ syn. *O.* 'Tresco Purple'. Spreading subshrub with broadly obovate to spoon-shaped, sparsely toothed, bright green leaves, and purplish green stems. From late spring to autumn, bears daisy-like, dark purple flowerheads, 5cm (2in) across, with purple ray-florets, flushed white on the reverse, and black disc-florets. ↕ 15cm (6in), ↔ 90cm (36in). ✲

***O.* 'Tauranga'** see *O.* 'Whirlygig'.

***O.* 'Tresco Purple'** see *O.* 'Nairobi Purple'.

***O.* 'Whirlygig'** ▣ syn. *O.* 'Tauranga'. Spreading subshrub with inversely lance-shaped, toothed, grey-green leaves. From late spring to autumn, bears solitary, daisy-like flowerheads, 5–8cm (2–3in) across, with crimped and spoon-shaped white ray-florets, slate-blue or powder-blue on the reverse, and slate-blue disc-florets. ↕↔ 60cm (24in). ✲

OSTROWSKIA

Giant bellflower

CAMPANULACEAE

Genus of one species of tap-rooted perennial from well-drained, stony hillsides in Uzbekistan and Tajikistan. It has thick, unbranched stems which produce whorls of ovate, toothed leaves, and is grown mainly for its racemes of outward-facing, bell-shaped, deep to pale milky-blue flowers. Grow in a sunny, herbaceous or mixed border.

- **HARDINESS** Fully hardy; young growth may be damaged by late frosts.
- **CULTIVATION** Grow in deep, moderately fertile, moist but well-drained soil in full sun. Dies back soon after flowering; when dormant, protect from wet, and provide a dry winter mulch.
- **PROPAGATION** Sow seed singly in containers in a cold frame as soon as ripe; only seed-leaves are produced in the first year. Take care to avoid root damage when potting on and planting out. May produce flowers in the third or fourth year. Take root cuttings in late autumn; they may be slow to become established.
- **PESTS AND DISEASES** Susceptible to slug damage.

O. magnifica ▣ Erect, clump-forming perennial with thick, unbranched stems bearing whorls of 4 or 5 ovate, toothed, hairless, somewhat glaucous leaves, 10–15cm (4–6in) long. In early and midsummer, produces few-flowered racemes of outward-facing, open bell-shaped, silver-sheened, pale to deep milky-blue or pale purple flowers, 12–15cm (5–6in) across, veined and suffused lilac. ↕ to 1.5m (5ft), ↔ 45cm (18in). Uzbekistan, Tajikistan. ✲✲✲

OSTRYA

BETULACEAE/CORYLACEAE

Genus of approximately 10 species of monoecious, deciduous trees occurring in woodland in Europe, Asia, North America, and Central America. They have simple, ovate to ovate-oblong or ovate-lance-shaped leaves, arranged alternately. The flowers are produced in catkins, males and females on the same tree, but only the males are conspicuous. Female catkins develop into hop-like fruits in late summer. They are excellent specimen trees for a woodland garden.

- **HARDINESS** Fully hardy.
- **CULTIVATION** Grow in fertile, well-drained soil in sun or partial shade. Pruning group 1.
- **PROPAGATION** Sow seed as soon as ripe in containers in a cold frame, or in a seedbed.
- **PESTS AND DISEASES** Trouble free.

O. carpinifolia ♤–♡ (Hop hornbeam). Broadly conical to rounded tree with hairy shoots and ovate, doubly toothed, lustrous, dark green leaves, to 10cm (4in) long, each with 15–20 pairs of veins; the leaves turn yellow in autumn. Pendulous, yellow male catkins, to 7cm (3in) long, are formed in autumn and open in mid-spring. Hop-like white fruit clusters, 5cm (2in) long, develop in summer and turn brown in autumn. ↕↔ 20m (70ft). S. Europe, Turkey, Syria, Caucasus. ✲✲✲

O. virginiana ▣ ♤ (American hop hornbeam, Ironwood). Conical tree with glandular-hairy shoots and ovate-lance-shaped, sharply, sometimes doubly toothed, dark green leaves, to 12cm (5in) long, each with 11–15 pairs of veins. Pendulous, yellow male catkins, to 5cm (2in) long, are formed in autumn and open in mid-spring; hop-like white fruit clusters, to 5cm (2in) long, develop in summer and turn brown in autumn. ↕ 15m (50ft), ↔ 12m (40ft). E. North America. ✲✲✲

OTHONNA

ASTERACEAE/COMPOSITAE

Genus of about 150 species of evergreen or deciduous, shrubby, succulent perennials and small shrubs, often arising from caudices or thick, tuberous rootstocks. They are found in dry, hilly areas of Tunisia, Algeria, Namibia, and South Africa. They have entire or dissected, fleshy leaves, which are lobed or toothed, and terminal, daisy-like, usually yellow, rarely white or purple flowerheads, produced singly or in corymbs from summer to winter. In areas where temperatures drop below 10°C (50°F), grow tender species as houseplants or in a temperate greenhouse; in warm, dry climates, use in a desert border. Grow *O. cheirifolia* in a raised bed or rock garden, or in a sunny border.

- **HARDINESS** Fully hardy to frost tender.
- **CULTIVATION** Under glass, grow in standard cactus compost in full light. Water moderately during the growing season, more sparingly in winter. Apply a balanced liquid fertilizer 3 or 4 times during summer and autumn. Outdoors, grow in sharply drained, moderately fertile, gritty soil in full sun. See also pp.48–49.
- **PROPAGATION** Sow seed at 18–21°C (64–70°F) in spring. Insert basal or semi-ripe cuttings with bottom heat in late summer. Take basal cuttings of *O. cheirifolia* in early summer.

O

Osteospermum 'Nairobi Purple'

Ostrowskia magnifica

Ostrya virginiana

Othonna cheirifolia

Othonna herrei

• **PESTS AND DISEASES** Prone to red spider mites and aphids.

O. capensis (Little pickles). Evergreen, perennial succulent with cylindrical to cylindrical-obovoid, entire, fleshy, pale green leaves, to 2.5cm (1in) long, often clustered on slender, trailing stems. In summer, bears few-flowered corymbs of daisy-like yellow flowerheads, 1cm (½in) across, which open only in sun. Excellent for a hanging basket. ↕ 20cm (8in), ↔ 1m (3ft). South Africa (Eastern Cape). ❅ (min. 5°C/41°F)
O. cheirifolia ▣ syn. *Othonnopsis cheirifolia*. Spreading, evergreen shrub with branching stems bearing lance- to spoon-shaped, entire, fleshy, pale grey-green leaves, to 8cm (3in) long. In summer, bears solitary, daisy-like yellow flowerheads, about 4cm (1½in) across. ↕ 30cm (12in), ↔ 60cm (24in). N. Africa. ❄❄
O. herrei ▣ Deciduous, perennial succulent with thickened stems and prominent, woody nodules formed from persistent leaf bases. Bears irregularly obovate, wavy-margined, toothed, fleshy, bluish green leaves, 5cm (2in) long, at the tips of short branches. Produces corymbs of daisy-like yellow flowerheads, 2cm (¾in) across, in late autumn and early winter. ↕↔ 10cm (4in). Namibia, South Africa (Northern Cape). ❅ (min. 7–10°C/45–50°F)

▷ ***Othonnopsis cheirifolia*** see *Othonna cheirifolia*

OURISIA

SCROPHULARIACEAE

Genus of approximately 25 species of low-growing, mainly rhizomatous, evergreen or semi-evergreen perennials occurring in alpine regions of Tasmania, New Zealand, South America, and Antarctica. They have mostly radical leaves, which are usually conspicuously veined, but are cultivated for their usually short-tubed flowers, each with 5 spreading lobes, the 3 lower lobes larger than the upper 2. The flowers are produced singly from the leaf axils, or in whorls or racemes on leafless stems. Ourisias grow best in cool, moist climates, and are suitable for a shady rock garden, peat bed, shaded wall, or alpine house.
• **HARDINESS** Fully hardy.
• **CULTIVATION** Grow in reliably moist, fertile, humus-rich soil in partial shade.

Ourisia macrophylla

Rhizomatous species quickly exhaust soil nutrients, so divide and replant them when they begin to deteriorate. In an alpine house, grow in a mix of 1 part each loam and grit with 2 parts leaf mould, and keep slightly moist in winter; they resent a dry atmosphere.
• **PROPAGATION** Sow seed in containers in a cold frame, as soon as ripe or in early spring. Divide rhizomatous species, or separate rooted sections, in spring. Take stem-tip cuttings of *O. microphylla* in early summer.
• **PESTS AND DISEASES** Often damaged by slugs and snails.

O. caespitosa. Dwarf, mat-forming, evergreen perennial with broadly ovate-spoon-shaped, entire or notched, grey-green leaves, 4–8mm (⅛–⅜in) long. Leafless stems bear up to 5-flowered whorls of tubular, yellow-throated white flowers, to 1.5cm (½in) across, in early summer. ↕ 5cm (2in), ↔ to 20cm (8in). New Zealand. ❄❄❄. **var. *gracilis*** is more compact, with leaves to 6mm (¼in) long, and solitary flowers; ↕ 3cm (1¼in), ↔ 15cm (6in).
O. coccinea. Mat-forming, evergreen perennial with rosettes of broadly elliptic or oblong, toothed, strongly veined, light green leaves, 3–6mm (⅛–¼in) long. Throughout summer, produces loose, terminal racemes of pendent, long-tubed, noticeably 2-lipped scarlet flowers, to 4cm (1½in) long. May spread widely in cool, moist conditions. ↕ 20cm (8in), ↔ 40cm (16in) or more. Chilean Andes. ❄❄❄
***O.* 'Loch Ewe'.** Vigorous, spreading, evergreen perennial, similar to *O. coccinea*, with tight rosettes of broadly oval, leathery, mid-green leaves, 3–6cm (1¼–2½in) long, heart-shaped at the bases. Dense, spike-like racemes of tubular, clear pale pink flowers, 2.5cm (1in) across, are borne in late spring and early summer. ↕ to 20cm (8in), ↔ 30cm (12in). ❄❄❄
O. macrophylla ▣ Mat-forming, evergreen, rhizomatous perennial with ovate to rounded-oblong, coarsely veined, bright green leaves, to 22cm (9in) long. Upright stems produce whorled racemes of many yellow-throated white flowers, to 2cm (¾in) across, in summer. ↕ 30cm (12in) or more, ↔ 40cm (16in) or more. New Zealand. ❄❄❄
O. microphylla ▣ Cushion-forming, semi-evergreen perennial with slender, branching stems clothed in heath-like, pale green leaves, 2mm (1/16in) long, pressed closely to the stems. In late spring and early summer, produces a profusion of solitary, small, tubular, pale pink flowers, 1cm (½in) across, with white centres. ↕ 5cm (2in), ↔ to 15cm (6in). Chile, Argentina. ❄❄❄
***O.* 'Snowflake'.** Robust, mat-forming, evergreen perennial, similar to *O. caespitosa*, with obovate, spoon-shaped, glossy, dark green leaves, to 1cm (½in) long. Clusters of tubular white flowers, 1–2cm (½–¾in) across, are produced in summer. ↕ 10cm (4in), ↔ to 25cm (10in). ❄❄❄

▷ **Our Lord's candle** see *Yucca whipplei*
▷ **Owl's eyes** see *Huernia zebrina*

Ourisia microphylla

OXALIS

Shamrock, Sorrel

OXALIDACEAE

Genus of about 500 species of fibrous-rooted, bulbous, rhizomatous, or tuberous annuals and perennials, some of which are very invasive weeds. They occur in open habitats or in woodland, and are widely distributed, with many species from southern Africa and South America. Those grown as ornamentals are valued for their palmate, clover-like foliage (some have leaves that fold at night), and for their funnel- to cup- or bowl-shaped, 5-petalled flowers; these are furled umbrella-like in bud, are borne singly or in cymes, sometimes umbel-like, and usually open only in sunlight, closing in dull weather or at night. Woodland species, such as *O. acetosella* and *O. oregana*, are suitable for naturalizing in a shady site. Many of the hardy species from southern Africa and South America, as well as various cultivars, are suitable for a rock garden, raised bed, trough, or alpine house. In frost-prone areas, grow the less hardy species in a temperate or warm greenhouse.
• **HARDINESS** Fully hardy to frost tender.
• **CULTIVATION** Grow hardy woodland species in moist, fertile, humus-rich soil in full or partial shade. Other hardy species need full sun and well-drained, moderately fertile, humus-rich soil. Under glass, grow in loam-based potting compost (JI No.2) with added grit, in bright filtered light and low humidity. When in growth, water moderately and apply a balanced liquid fertilizer every month. Keep all container-grown plants barely moist when dormant. In an alpine house, grow in a mix of equal parts loam, leaf mould, and grit.
• **PROPAGATION** Sow seed at 13–18°C (55–64°F) in late winter or early spring. Divide in spring; small sections of rhizomatous species root readily with bottom heat.
• **PESTS AND DISEASES** Prone to rust. May be damaged by slugs and snails.

O. acetosella* var. *purpurascens see *O. acetosella* var. *subpurpurascens*.
O. acetosella* var. *rosea see *O. acetosella* var. *subpurpurascens*.
O. acetosella* var. *subpurpurascens ▣ syn. *O. acetosella* var. *purpurascens*, *O. acetosella* var. *rosea*. Creeping, mat-forming, rhizomatous perennial

Oxalis acetosella var. *subpurpurascens*

Oxalis adenophylla

with clover-like, pale green leaves, each with 3 inversely heart-shaped, sparsely hairy leaflets, to 2cm (¾in) long. In spring, bears solitary, cup-shaped, dark-veined, rose-pink flowers, 2cm (¾in) across. ↕ 5cm (2in), ↔ indefinite. Woodland in N. hemisphere. ✲✲✲

O. adenophylla ■ Clump-forming perennial with fibre-covered bulbs that produce grey-green leaves, each consisting of 9–22 narrowly and inversely heart-shaped leaflets, to 2cm (¾in) long. In late spring, bears solitary, widely funnel-shaped, purplish pink flowers, about 2.5cm (1in) across, with darker veins and purple throats. ↕ 10cm (4in), ↔ to 15cm (6in). Andes, Chile, Argentina. ✲✲✲

O. bowiei, syn. *O. purpurata* var. *bowiei*. Clump-forming, bulbous perennial with long-stalked, clover-like, leathery leaves, each with 3 rounded to inversely heart-shaped, notched leaflets, 1–2.5cm (½–1in) long, mid-green above, hairy and often purple beneath. Bears loose, umbel-like cymes of 3–12 funnel-shaped, deep purplish pink flowers, to 4cm (1½in) across, with yellow-green tubes, in summer. Very similar to *O. purpurata*, which produces runners and may be invasive. ↕ to 25cm (10in), ↔ to 15cm (6in). South Africa (Western Cape, Eastern Cape, KwaZulu/Natal). ✲✲

O. carnosa see *O. megalorrhiza*.

O. chrysantha. Fibrous-rooted, mat-forming perennial with creeping and rooting, slender stems and white-hairy, light green leaves, each divided into 3 triangular to inversely heart-shaped leaflets, 8mm (⅜in) long. Produces

Oxalis depressa

Oxalis enneaphylla 'Rosea'

solitary, funnel-shaped, bright yellow flowers, 1.5–2cm (½–¾in) across, with red markings at the mouths, throughout summer and into autumn. ↕ 5cm (2in), ↔ 30cm (12in) or more. Brazil. ✲✲

O. deppei see *O. tetraphylla*.

O. depressa ■ syn. *O. inops*. Clump-forming, bulbous perennial with short runners and short-stalked, sometimes sparsely hairy and dark-spotted, grey-green leaves, each divided into 3 triangular-obovate leaflets, to 1cm (½in) long. In summer, bears solitary, widely funnel-shaped, deep rose-pink to purple-pink flowers, to 2cm (¾in) across, with yellow tubes. ↕ 5cm (2in), ↔ to 20cm (8in) or more. Southern Africa. ✲✲✲ (borderline)

O. enneaphylla. Clump-forming perennial with scaly, branching rhizomes, producing tufts of umbrella-like, somewhat fleshy, hairy, blue-grey leaves, each consisting of 9–20 narrowly oblong, pleated leaflets, to 2cm (¾in) long. Solitary, widely funnel-shaped, fragrant, white to deep red-pink flowers, 2–2.5cm (¾–1in) across, are produced in late spring and early summer. ↕ 8cm (3in), ↔ to 15cm (6in). Patagonia, Falkland Islands. ✲✲✲. **'Minutifolia'** has a more compact habit, with much smaller leaflets, to 1cm (½in) long, and white flowers; ↕ 5cm (2in), ↔ 10cm (4in). **'Rosea'** ■ has light purple-pink flowers.

O. hedysaroides. Semi-evergreen subshrub with upright, branching, leafy stems, bearing light green leaves, glaucous beneath, each with 3 broadly ovate leaflets, to 2.5cm (1in) long. Produces axillary cymes of 3–6 widely funnel-shaped yellow flowers, to 1.5cm (½in) across, in summer. Suitable for a cool greenhouse. ↕ to 1m (3ft), ↔ to 45cm (18in). Central America. ✲

O. herrerae, syn. *O. succulenta*. Erect, succulent perennial with short-branched, scaly stems. Bears clusters of broad, hairless, mid-green leaves, each with 3 inversely heart-shaped, fleshy leaflets, to 1cm (½in) long, often slightly hairy beneath, on stalks 2–5cm (¾–2in) long. Short-branched cymes of 5–7 bowl-shaped, red-veined yellow flowers, to 1.5cm (½in) across, appear in summer. ↕ to 30cm (12in), ↔ 21cm (8in). Peru, Chile. ❀ (min. 10°C/50°F)

O. hirta. Variable, bulbous perennial with upright or decumbent, leafy stems bearing almost stalkless, hairy, pale green leaves, each with 3 linear to oblong or obovate leaflets, to 1.5cm (½in) long. In autumn and winter, bears solitary, open funnel-shaped, white, red-pink, or purple flowers, 2cm (¾in) across, with yellow throats. Best in a cool greenhouse in frost-prone climates. ↕ 30cm (12in), ↔ 10cm (4in). South Africa (Western Cape). ✲✲

O. inops see *O. depressa*.

***O.* 'Ione Hecker'.** Clump-forming, rhizomatous perennial, similar to *O. enneaphylla*, with grey-green leaves, each consisting of 9–15 narrowly oblong leaflets, to 1.5cm (½in) long. In summer, produces solitary, widely funnel-shaped, blue-violet flowers, to 3cm (1¼in) across, conspicuously veined dark purple, and with dark purple throats. ↕ 8cm (3in), ↔ 10cm (4in). ✲✲✲

O. laciniata, syn. *O. squamosoradicosa*. Tuft-forming, rhizomatous perennial, with tiny bulbils, producing tufts of blue-grey, often purple-margined leaves, each with 8–12 inversely heart-shaped, folded, crinkly-margined leaflets, to 1.5cm (½in) long. Solitary, widely funnel-shaped, scented, violet-blue, lilac-blue, red, pink, or white flowers, with light green throats, and to 2.5cm (1in) across, are produced in late spring and summer. Prefers cool conditions. ↕ 5–10cm (2–4in), ↔ 10cm (4in). Patagonia. ✲✲✲

O. lobata ■ syn. *O. perdicaria*. Clump-forming, bulbous perennial with tuberous roots, producing compact clusters of bright green leaves, each with 3 inversely heart-shaped leaflets, 7mm (¼in) long. The leaves, which appear in spring, die down quickly and reappear

Oxalis lobata

in late summer and autumn at the same time as the solitary, funnel-shaped, bright yellow flowers, often dotted and veined red, 1–2cm (½–¾in) across. ↕↔ to 10cm (4in). Chile. ✲✲

O. megalorrhiza, syn. *O. carnosa*. Slow-growing, succulent perennial with fleshy rhizomes and few-branched, fleshy stems, later becoming woody. These produce terminal clusters of fleshy, glossy, mid-green leaves, each with 3 inversely heart-shaped leaflets, 1–2cm (½–¾in) long. Umbel-like cymes of 2–5 bowl-shaped yellow flowers, to 2cm (¾in) across, are borne in summer and autumn. ↕ 15cm (6in), to 40cm (16in) with age, ↔ to 20cm (8in). Coastal regions of Galapagos Islands, and Peru, Chile, Bolivia. ❀ (min. 10°C/50°F)

O. obtusa ■ Slowly spreading, mat-forming, bulbous perennial with runners producing bulbils. It is similar to *O. depressa*, but with shorter-stemmed, hairy, grey-green leaves, each with 3 rounded to triangular-obovate leaflets, 0.5–2.5cm (¼–1in) long. Solitary, widely funnel-shaped, rose-pink, brick-red, or yellow flowers, to 2cm (¾in) across, appear in summer. ↕ 5cm (2in), ↔ 20cm (8in). Namibia, South Africa (Eastern Cape, Southern Cape). ✲✲

O. oregana. Creeping, rhizomatous perennial with hairy, mid-green leaves, each divided into 3 inversely heart-shaped leaflets, 1–3cm (½–1¼in) long. Solitary, cup-shaped, rose-pink, lilac, occasionally white flowers, 2.5cm (1in) across, are produced on slender stems from spring to autumn. ↕ to 20cm (8in), ↔ indefinite. Woodland in W. North America. ✲✲✲

Oxalis obtusa

Oxalis tetraphylla

O. perdicaria see *O. lobata.*
O. purpurata* var. *bowiei see *O. bowiei.*
O. purpurea. Variable, bulbous perennial with clusters of silky, white-hairy, dark green leaves, each with 3 diamond-shaped to rounded or broadly obovate leaflets; these are often deep purple beneath, 2cm (¾in) long, and hairy at the margins and on the surfaces. Solitary, widely funnel-shaped, cream, white, pink, or purple flowers, 3–5cm (1¼–2in) across, are produced in autumn and winter. ↕ 10cm (4in), ↔ 15cm (6in). South Africa (Limpopo, Mpumalanga, Eastern Cape), Swaziland. ❄❄. **'Ken Aslet'** has bright, deep yellow flowers.
O. squamosoradicosa see *O. laciniata.*
O. succulenta see *O. herrerae.*
O. tetraphylla ■ syn. *O. deppei* (Good luck plant, Lucky clover). Clump-forming, bulbous perennial with mid-green leaves, each consisting of 4 strap-shaped to inversely triangular, entire or notched leaflets, 2–7cm (¾–3in) long, usually banded purple at the bases. In summer, produces loose, umbel-like cymes of 4–12 widely funnel-shaped, reddish purple flowers, with greenish yellow throats, 2–3cm (¾–1¼in) across. ↕↔ to 15cm (6in). Mexico. ❄❄. **'Iron Cross'** ■ has leaflets that each have a V-shaped, dark purple band at the base, combining to form a distinctive cross over the 4 leaflets.
O. versicolor. Clump-forming, bulbous perennial with mid-green leaves, each divided into 3 wedge-shaped-linear to linear, almost hairless leaflets, 1–2cm (½–¾in) long. A profusion of solitary, funnel-shaped white flowers, 2–3cm (¾–1¼in) across, crimson-margined on the reverse and crimson-striped in bud, are produced from late summer to winter. Suitable for an alpine house. ↕ 8cm (3in), ↔ 20cm (8in) or more. Southern Africa. ❄

Oxalis tetraphylla 'Iron Cross'

▷ **Ox eye** see *Heliopsis*
▷ **Oxlip** see *Primula elatior*

OXYDENDRUM

ERICACEAE

Genus of one species of deciduous, large shrub or small tree from woodland and streamsides in E. North America. It has rusty-red to grey bark, simple, alternate leaves, which turn vivid red in autumn, and large, terminal panicles of cylindrical to urn-shaped white flowers. Cultivated for the autumn colour of its foliage and for its flowers, it is best grown in an open glade in a woodland garden.
• **HARDINESS** Fully hardy.
• **CULTIVATION** Grow in fertile, moist but well-drained, acid soil, preferably avoiding exposed sites. Pruning group 1.
• **PROPAGATION** Sow seed in containers in a cold frame in autumn. Take semi-ripe cuttings in summer.
• **PESTS AND DISEASES** Trouble free.

O. arboreum ■◊ (Sorrel tree, Sourwood). Conical to columnar shrub or tree with elliptic to oblong-lance-shaped, toothed, glossy, dark green leaves, to 20cm (8in) long, turning brilliant shades of red, yellow, and purple in autumn. Cylindrical to urn-shaped white flowers, to 6mm (¼in) long, are borne in large panicles, to 25cm (10in) long, in late summer and early autumn. ↕ 10–15m (30–50ft), ↔ 8m (25ft). E. North America. ❄❄❄

▷ ***Oxypetalum*** see *Tweedia*
  O. caeruleum see *T. caerulea*
▷ **Oyster plant** see *Mertensia maritima*
▷ **Ozark sundrops** see *Oenothera macrocarpa*

Oxydendrum arboreum

OZOTHAMNUS

ASTERACEAE/COMPOSITAE

Genus of about 50 species of evergreen shrubs and woody-based perennials, closely related to *Helichrysum*, from Australia and New Zealand, where they grow in rocky places and on heathland, from the coast to the mountains. They are cultivated for their often aromatic, usually small, heath-like, alternate leaves, and for their solitary or corymb-like flowerheads, displaying white disc-florets. Grow larger species in a shrub border; smaller species are good in a trough, rock garden, or alpine house.
• **HARDINESS** Fully hardy to half hardy.
• **CULTIVATION** Grow in moderately fertile, well-drained soil in a sheltered site in full sun. *O. coralloides* and *O. selago* need gritty, sharply drained soil; protect from excessive winter wet. In an alpine house, use a mix of equal parts loam, leaf mould, and grit. Pruning group 8.
• **PROPAGATION** Sow seed in containers in an open frame as soon as ripe. Take semi-ripe cuttings in summer.
• **PESTS AND DISEASES** Trouble free.

O. coralloides ■ syn. *Helichrysum coralloides.* Compact, rounded shrub with diamond-shaped, scale-like, leathery leaves, 5mm (¼in) long, white-woolly beneath, and pressed flat to the cylindrical branches. Solitary, terminal, yellowish white, cylindrical flowerheads, 6mm (¼in) across, appear in summer. ↕↔ 60cm (24in). New Zealand. ❄❄
O. ledifolius ■ syn. *Helichrysum ledifolium* (Kerosene bush). Compact, rounded shrub with yellowish green shoots densely covered with oblong-linear, aromatic, dark green leaves, to 1cm (½in) long, yellow-downy beneath, the margins strongly curved under. In early summer, bears white flowerheads, 5mm (¼in) across, in dense, terminal corymbs, 3–5cm (1¼–2in) across. ↕↔ 1m (3ft). Australia (Tasmania). ❄❄
O. rosmarinifolius ■ syn. *Helichrysum rosmarinifolium.* Compact, upright shrub with rosemary-like, linear, dark green leaves, to 4cm (1½in) long, woolly beneath, the margins curved under. Fragrant white flowerheads, 4mm (⅛in) across, red in bud, are borne in dense, terminal corymbs, 4cm (1½in) across, in early summer. ↕ 2–3m (6–10ft), ↔ 1.5m (5ft). S.E. Australia. ❄❄. **'Silver Jubilee'** has silvery grey leaves.

Ozothamnus coralloides

Ozothamnus ledifolius

O. selago ■ syn. *Helichrysum selago.* Dense, upright shrub with rigid shoots densely covered in tiny, ovate to triangular, aromatic leaves, 3mm (⅛in) long, pressed flat to the shoots. Terminal, solitary cream flowerheads, 7mm (¼in) across, are produced in summer. ↕ to 40cm (16in), ↔ 25cm (10in). New Zealand (South Island). ❄❄❄
O. thyrsoideus, syn. *Helichrysum thyrsoideum* (Snow in summer). Upright shrub with linear, aromatic, dark green leaves, to 5cm (2in) long, pressed flat to the shoots. Over a long period in summer, pure white flowerheads, about 4mm (⅛in) across, are produced in dense, rounded corymbs, 2cm (¾in) across, at the shoot tips. ↕ to 3m (10ft), ↔ 2m (6ft). S.E. Australia. ❄❄

Ozothamnus rosmarinifolius

Ozothamnus selago

P

Pachycereus

syn. Lophocereus

CACTACEAE

Genus of possibly 9 species of columnar, often tree-like, ribbed, perennial cacti from semi-desert areas of the USA and Mexico. These often massive cacti branch from the bases of the main stems, and have large, spiny, usually scaly areoles, sometimes woolly or bristly in the axils. The nocturnal or diurnal, funnel- or bell-shaped, or short, tubular flowers are produced only on mature plants. The bristly, spherical, fleshy fruits contain large, black-coated seeds. Where temperatures drop below 10°C (50°F), grow in a temperate or warm greenhouse. In warmer climates, use in a desert garden.
• **Hardiness** Frost tender.
• **Cultivation** Under glass, grow in standard cactus compost in full light. From spring to summer, water moderately and apply a low-nitrogen liquid fertilizer every 4–5 weeks. Keep dry at other times. Outdoors, grow in moderately fertile, sharply drained soil in full sun. See also pp.48–49.
• **Propagation** Sow seed at 19–24°C (66–75°F) in spring. Take stem-tip cuttings in summer.
• **Pests and diseases** Vulnerable to scale insects and occasionally mealybugs.

P. marginatus, syn. *Stenocereus marginatus.* Erect cactus with sometimes sparsely branched, 4- to 7-ribbed, dark

Pachycereus pringlei

Pachycereus schottii

green stems, 8–15cm (3–6in) across, with grey-white areoles and brown to grey spines (5–8 radials, 1 or 2 longer centrals). Bears nocturnal and diurnal, tubular, greenish white or pink flowers, 3–5cm (1¼–2in) across, in summer. ↕ to 3–7m (10–22ft), ↔ 1m (3ft). C. and S. Mexico. ❀ (min. 10°C/50°F)
P. pecten-aboriginum. Erect, tree-like cactus with branched, dark bluish green stems, 30cm (12in) thick, each with 10 or 11 acute ribs and grey-white areoles bearing stiff brown spines, fading to grey (8 or 9 radials, 1 or 2 longer centrals). In summer, bears nocturnal and diurnal, funnel-shaped white flowers, 6–8cm (2½–3in) across, with greenish red outer petals. ↕ to 8m (25ft), ↔ 3m (10ft). W. Mexico. ❀ (min. 10°C/50°F)
P. pringlei ■ Tree-like cactus with dark blue-green stems, 1m (3ft) or more thick, and erect branches, each with 10–17 rounded ribs. Grey areoles have reddish to dark brown spines, fading to grey (about 20 radials, 1–3 slightly longer centrals). In summer, bears nocturnal, bell- to funnel-shaped white flowers, 8cm (3in) across, with greenish red outer petals. ↕ to 12–15m (40–50ft), ↔ 3m (10ft). N.W. Mexico. ❀ (min. 10°C/50°F)
P. schottii ■ syn. *Lophocereus schottii.* Erect, columnar cactus with dull dark green stems, to 10–15cm (4–6in) thick, each with 4–9 ribs. Grey-woolly areoles produce almost black spines, fading to grey (4–7 radials, often 1 central). As the plant matures, a spiny, hairy pseudocephalium forms; in summer, it produces nocturnal, slender, funnel-shaped, red, pink, or white flowers, 3–4cm (1¼–1½in) across, green outside, with an unpleasant smell. ↕ 7m (22ft), ↔ 3m (10ft). USA (S. Arizona), N.W. Mexico. ❀ (min. 10°C/50°F).
'Monstrosus' has misshapen stems, irregular ribs, and spineless areoles; ↕ to 3m (10ft), ↔ 1m (3ft).
P. weberi. Tree-like cactus producing glaucous, blue-green stems, 20cm (8in) or more thick, and erect, 8- to 10-ribbed branches. White-woolly areoles each produce up to 13 spines (6–12 yellowish white, later reddish brown or black radials, 1 longer grey central). In mid-summer, bears nocturnal, funnel-shaped white flowers, yellowish white outside, to 10cm (4in) long. ↕ 10m (30ft), ↔ 3m (10ft) or more. S. Mexico. ❀ (min. 10°C/50°F)

Pachycormus

ANACARDIACEAE

Genus of one species of very variable, slow-growing, deciduous, perennial succulent from desert or semi-desert areas of Mexico. Grey- or silver-barked branches bear pinnate, feathery leaves. Dense, terminal racemes of tiny, cup-shaped flowers are produced by day in summer. Where temperatures drop below 15°C (59°F), grow in a warm greenhouse. In warmer climates, use in a desert garden.
• **Hardiness** Frost tender.
• **Cultivation** Under glass, grow in loam-based potting compost (JI No.2), with added grit, in full light. From mid-spring until the leaves fall, water freely and apply a balanced liquid fertilizer every 6–8 weeks. Keep just moist at other times. Outdoors, grow in sharply drained, moderately fertile soil in full sun. See also pp.48–49.
• **Propagation** Sow seed at 19–24°C (66–75°F) in spring.
• **Pests and diseases** Young growth is vulnerable to red spider mites.

P. discolor ■ (Elephant tree). Free-branching succulent. The trunk and branches are very swollen, and both contain sponge-like wood and white latex. Pinnate, mid-green leaves, to 8cm (3in) long, consist of 6–8 oval, slightly toothed or lobed leaflets, hairy towards the tips. In summer, bears lax, dense racemes of cup-shaped, white to yellow or red flowers, to 6mm (¼in) long. ↕ 4m (12ft), ↔ 45cm (18in) or more. N.W. Mexico. ❀ (min. 15°C/59°F)

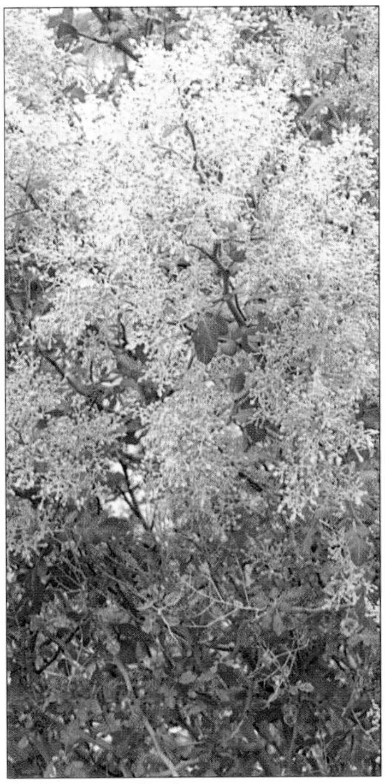

Pachycormus discolor

Pachycymbium

ASCLEPIADACEAE

Genus of about 30 species of leafless, perennial succulents, formerly classified under *Caralluma*, from mostly hilly terrain in the Arabian Peninsula, E. Africa, Zimbabwe, and South Africa. They have erect or prostrate, 4-angled or rounded, prominently toothed stems, and produce compact cymes of diurnal, bell- or cup-shaped flowers, usually near the stem tips, in summer. Where temperatures drop below 10°C (50°F), grow in a warm greenhouse. In warmer climates, use in a desert garden.
• **Hardiness** Frost tender.
• **Cultivation** Under glass, grow in loam-based potting compost (JI No.2), with added grit or sharp sand, in full light. From mid-spring to early autumn, water moderately and apply a low-nitrogen liquid fertilizer every 6–8 weeks. Keep just moist at other times. Outdoors, grow in moderately fertile, sharply drained soil in full sun. See also pp.48–49.
• **Propagation** Sow seed at 19–24°C (66–75°F) in spring. Take stem-tip cuttings in spring or early summer.
• **Pests and diseases** Prone to ant damage while flowering.

P. dummeri, syn. *Caralluma dummeri.* Erect, spreading succulent with 4-angled or slightly rounded, greyish green stems, 1.5cm (½in) thick, with dark red stripes. In summer, produces cymes of 1–4, sometimes up to 6, bell-shaped, olive-green to dark green flowers, 4cm (1½in) across, with tapering, spreading lobes, hairy inside, smooth outside. ↕ 10cm (4in), ↔ to 15cm (6in). Uganda, Kenya, Tanzania. ❀ (min. 10°C/50°F)

Pachyphragma

BRASSICACEAE/CRUCIFERAE

Genus of one species of semi-evergreen, rhizomatous perennial found in moist beech woods in N.E. Turkey and the Caucasus. It produces long-stalked, basal leaves, glossy, dark green at first, becoming duller. Broad, terminal corymbs of 4-petalled white flowers appear just as the leaves develop; the stems later elongate so that the flattened fruit are held above the foliage. A slow-growing, ground-cover plant, *P. macrophyllum* is suitable for planting beneath trees and deciduous shrubs.

Pachyphragma macrophyllum

- **HARDINESS** Fully hardy.
- **CULTIVATION** Grow in moderately fertile, moist, leafy soil, preferably in partial shade.
- **PROPAGATION** Sow seed in containers in a cold frame in autumn. Divide in spring. Take basal stem cuttings in late spring.
- **PESTS AND DISEASES** Slugs may be a problem.

P. macrophyllum ■ syn. *Thlaspi macrophyllum*. Semi-evergreen perennial with ovate to rounded, scalloped leaves, 2.5–10cm (1–4in) long, produced in basal clusters that partially persist over winter. Flat corymbs of cross-shaped, 4-petalled, unpleasantly scented white flowers, 2cm (¾in) across, with pale green veins, are borne in early spring, followed by distinctive, flat, inversely heart-shaped fruit. ↕20–40cm (8–16in), ↔ 60–90cm (24–36in). Caucasus, N.E. Turkey. ✲✲✲

PACHYPHYTUM

CRASSULACEAE

Genus of 12 or more species of rosette-forming, perennial succulents from arid areas of Mexico, closely resembling *Echeveria*, with which it hybridizes. The semi-erect, usually branching, spreading stems become decumbent with age, and bear variably shaped, swollen, fleshy, mid- to dark or grey-green, frequently white-frosted leaves. Racemes of diurnal, bell-shaped flowers are borne on fleshy, sometimes sparsely branched stems, mainly in spring. Where temperatures drop below 7°C (45°F), grow in a temperate greenhouse. In warmer climates, use in a desert garden.

- **HARDINESS** Frost tender.
- **CULTIVATION** Under glass, grow in standard cactus compost in full light, with shade from hot sun. In the growing season, water moderately and apply a low-nitrogen liquid fertilizer every 6–8 weeks. Keep almost dry at other times. Outdoors, grow in moderately fertile, sharply drained soil in full sun, with some midday shade. See also pp.48–49.
- **PROPAGATION** Sow seed at 19–24°C (66–75°F) in spring. Take leaf or stem-tip cuttings in spring or summer.
- **PESTS AND DISEASES** Trouble free.

P. compactum ■ Compact succulent with short-stemmed rosettes of oblong to lance-shaped, white-frosted, dark green leaves, 2–3cm (¾–1¼in) long,

Pachyphytum longifolium

sometimes tinged red-purple, with rounded, angular margins. Racemes of 3–10 pendent, blue-tipped, orange-red flowers, 1cm (½in) long, with pink or green calyces, develop in spring. ↕10–15cm (4–6in), ↔ 30cm (12in) or more. Mexico. ❄ (min. 7°C/45°F)

P. hookeri. Clump-forming, long-stemmed succulent with scattered, almost cylindrical, pointed, mid-green leaves, to 5cm (2in) long, with a blue-grey to white bloom; they are slightly flattened on the upper surfaces, with blunt to rounded margins. Racemes of 5–18 yellowish pink flowers, to 1.5cm (½in) long, flushed pale purple-red, with green-tipped pink sepals, are borne in spring. ↕60cm (24in), ↔ indefinite. Mexico. ❄ (min. 7°C/45°F)

P. longifolium ■ Rosette-forming succulent with inversely lance-shaped, grey-green leaves, 6–11cm (2½–4½in) long, with a blue-glaucous bloom, blunt or pointed at the tips, and grooved beneath. Racemes of 10–50 white flowers, 1cm (½in) long, strongly suffused red, develop mainly in spring, but also irregularly throughout the year. ↕15cm (6in) or more, ↔ 20cm (8in) or more. Mexico. ❄ (min. 7°C/45°F)

P. oviferum ■ (Sugar-almond plant). Clump-forming succulent producing short-stemmed rosettes of obovoid, white-frosted, light green leaves, 2–5cm (¾–2in) long, flushed lavender-blue. Racemes of 10–15 vivid orange-red or greenish red flowers, 1.5cm (½in) long, with pale blue-white calyces, are borne from winter to spring. ↕10–12cm (4–5in), ↔ 30cm (12in) or more. Mexico. ❄ (min. 7°C/45°F)

PACHYPODIUM

APOCYNACEAE

Genus of 13 species of shrubby or tree-like, perennial succulents from mostly arid regions of Namibia, South Africa, and Madagascar. Many have swollen, irregularly shaped caudices and very thick, thorny stems. Leaves are simple, entire, and variably shaped; they are usually deciduous but may persist in cultivation. Diurnal, salverform to funnel- or bell-shaped flowers are borne usually in terminal clusters, in summer. Where temperatures drop below 15°C (59°F), grow in a warm greenhouse. In warmer climates, use in a desert garden or as focal points on a lawn.

- **HARDINESS** Frost tender.
- **CULTIVATION** Under glass, grow in standard cactus compost in full light. From late spring to early autumn, water moderately and apply a low-nitrogen liquid fertilizer every 4–5 weeks. Keep dry at other times. Outdoors, grow in moderately fertile, sharply drained soil in full sun. See also pp.48–49.
- **PROPAGATION** Sow seed at 19–24°C (66–75°F), or take stem-tip cuttings, in late spring.
- **PESTS AND DISEASES** Susceptible to aphids while flowering.

P. baronii. Tree-like succulent with a massive, stout, thorny caudex and thick, thorny stems bearing obovate to elliptic, tapering, greyish green leaves, to 15cm (6in) long. Salverform, bright red flowers, to 6cm (2½in) across, develop in summer. ↕3m (10ft), ↔ to 1m (3ft). N. Madagascar. ❄ (min. 15°C/59°F)

P. bispinosum. Shrubby succulent with a rugged, partly underground caudex and thin, thorny, fleshy branches bearing lance-shaped to narrowly lance-shaped, roughly hairy, mid-green leaves, 4–8cm (1½–3in) long. Broadly bell-shaped, pink to purple flowers, 3cm (1¼in) across, with recurving white lobes, are produced in summer. ↕45cm (18in), ↔ 18cm (7in). South Africa (Eastern Cape). ❄ (min. 15°C/59°F)

P. densiflorum. Shrubby, slow-growing succulent with a thorny caudex, short stem, and short, thick, thorny branches. The obovate to oblong-ovate leaves, to 10cm (4in) long, are mid- to dark green, grey-felted beneath. In summer, bears salverform, bright yellow flowers, to 3cm (1¼in) across, each with prominent yellow anthers forming a cone. ↕ to 45cm (18in), ↔ 12cm (5in) or more. Madagascar. ❄ (min. 15°C/59°F)

P. geayi. Tree-like succulent with a thorny caudex, branching near the top with age. Thorny branches bear linear, greyish green leaves, to 40cm (16in) long, silver-grey-hairy beneath. Salverform, pure white flowers, 8cm (3in) across, are produced in summer. ↕ to 8m (25ft), ↔ to 2m (6ft). S.W. Madagascar. ❄ (min. 15°C/59°F)

P. lamerei ■ Tree-like succulent with a thick caudex branching near the top, with thorns generally in groups of 3. Bears terminal clusters of linear to lance-shaped, shining, dark green leaves, 25–40cm (10–16in) long. Salverform, yellow-throated, creamy white flowers, to 11cm (4½in) across, are borne in summer. ↕ to 6m (20ft), ↔ 2m (6ft). S. and S.W. Madagascar. ❄ (min. 15°C/59°F)

P. namaquanum. Tree-like succulent with a thick, fleshy, thorny, caudex-like trunk, rarely branching, with spirally arranged tubercles, and thorns in groups of 3. Produces terminal rosettes of lance-shaped, slightly hairy, pale green leaves, 12cm (5in) long, with wavy, crisped

P

Pachyphytum compactum

Pachyphytum oviferum

Pachypodium lamerei

Pachypodium succulentum

margins. In summer, bears tubular, yellow-green and purple-red flowers, striped yellow inside, to 2cm (¾in) long. ↕ to 2.5m (8ft), ↔ 1.5m (5ft). S. Namibia, South Africa (Northern Cape). ❀ (min. 15°C/59°F)
P. rosulatum. Variable, shrubby succulent with a spherical or irregularly shaped, thorny caudex, branching stems, and elliptic, mid- to dark green leaves, to 8cm (3in) long, slightly hairy above. Salverform yellow flowers, to 1.5cm (½in) across, with rounded, flat lobes, are produced in summer. ↕ to 1.5m (5ft), ↔ 1m (3ft) or more. Madagascar. ❀ (min. 15°C/59°F). **var. *horombense*** has inflated, bell-shaped flowers.
P. succulentum ▣ Shrubby succulent with a mainly underground caudex. Strong, sturdy branches bear paired thorns and narrowly lance-shaped, minutely hairy, mid- to dark green leaves, to 6cm (2½in) long. Salverform, pink, white, sometimes red-striped, or red flowers, 4cm (1½in) across, with narrow, spreading lobes, develop in summer. ↕↔ 60–90cm (24–36in). South Africa (Free State to Western Cape and Eastern Cape). ❀ (min. 15°C/59°F)

PACHYSANDRA

BUXACEAE

Genus of 4 species of evergreen or semi-evergreen perennials and subshrubs occurring in woodland in China and Japan. They have often rhizome-like, fleshy green stems and upright branches with alternate, broadly ovate to obovate, entire or coarsely toothed, grey- to dark green leaves clustered at their tips. Terminal or axillary spikes of small, unisexual, petalless flowers (the females greenish white, the males with white stamens) are produced in spring or early summer. Cultivated for their foliage, they are useful as ground cover in a shrub border or woodland garden. They spread freely, especially in moist, humus-rich soil.
- **HARDINESS** Fully hardy.
- **CULTIVATION** Grow in any but very dry soil in full or partial shade.
- **PROPAGATION** Divide in spring. Root softwood cuttings in early summer.
- **PESTS AND DISEASES** May be damaged by slugs and snails.

P. terminalis ▣ Spreading, evergreen perennial with obovate, coarsely toothed, glossy, dark green leaves, to 10cm (4in)

Pachysandra terminalis

long, clustered at the ends of short, smooth stems. Produces tiny white male flowers in spikes, 2–3cm (¾–1¼in) long, in early summer. ↕ 20cm (8in), ↔ indefinite. N. China, Japan. ✽✽✽. **'Green Carpet'** is more compact, with smaller, finely toothed leaves, to 7cm (3in) long; ↕ 15cm (6in), ↔ to 60cm (24in). **'Variegata'** is slower-growing, and produces attractive white-margined leaves; ↕ 25cm (10in), ↔ to 60cm (24in).

PACHYSTACHYS

ACANTHACEAE

Genus of 12 species of evergreen perennials and shrubs, closely allied to *Justicia*, from woodland or rainforest in the West Indies and tropical Central and South America. They are cultivated for their tubular, 2-lipped flowers, borne in erect, terminal spikes with large, overlapping, usually brightly coloured bracts. Leaves are opposite and simple, ovate to lance-shaped, and mid- to dark green. Where temperatures drop below 10–15°C (50–59°F), grow in a warm or temperate greenhouse, or as houseplants. In warmer areas, use in a border.
- **HARDINESS** Frost tender.
- **CULTIVATION** Under glass, grow in loam-based potting compost (JI No.2) in full light, with high humidity. During the growing season, water freely and apply a balanced liquid fertilizer monthly. Water moderately in winter. Outdoors, grow in fertile, moist but well-drained soil in full sun. Pruning group 8; may need restrictive pruning under glass.

Pachystachys coccinea

Pachystachys lutea

- **PROPAGATION** Root softwood cuttings with bottom heat in summer.
- **PESTS AND DISEASES** Whiteflies and red spider mites may be troublesome under glass.

P. cardinalis see *P. coccinea.*
P. coccinea ▣ syn. *Jacobinia coccinea, Justicia coccinea, P. cardinalis* (Cardinal's guard). Erect shrub producing robust, simple or sparsely branched stems and ovate-elliptic, strongly veined, lightly wrinkled, dark green leaves, 15–20cm (6–8in) long. In winter, tubular, strongly 2-lipped scarlet flowers, 5cm (2in) long, are produced in terminal spikes, 15cm (6in) long, with 4-ranked, pale green bracts. ↕ to 2m (6ft) or more, ↔ 60–90cm (24–36in). West Indies, N. South America. ❀ (min. 13°C/55°F)
P. lutea ▣ (Lollipop plant). Erect shrub with moderately to sparsely branched stems and narrowly ovate, elliptic, or lance-shaped, slender-pointed, strongly veined, mid- to deep green leaves, 8–15cm (3–6in) long. In spring and summer, produces tubular, strongly 2-lipped white flowers, 4–5cm (1½–2in) long, borne in terminal spikes, 10cm (4in) long, with 4-ranked, bright golden yellow bracts. ↕ to 1m (3ft), ↔ 45–75cm (18–30in). Peru. ❀ (min. 13°C/55°F)

PACHYSTEGIA

ASTERACEAE/COMPOSITAE

Genus of one species of evergreen shrub, related to *Olearia*, occurring on cliffs and riverbanks and in rocky places from sea level to mountains in New Zealand. It has alternate, simple leaves, and bears terminal or axillary, solitary flowerheads, to 6cm (2½in) across, with white ray-florets and yellow disc-florets. Grown for its foliage and showy flowers, it is suitable for a rock garden.
- **HARDINESS** Frost hardy.
- **CULTIVATION** Grow in fertile, well-drained soil in full sun; shelter from cold, drying winds. Pruning group 1.
- **PROPAGATION** Sow seed in containers in a cold frame in autumn. Take semi-ripe cuttings in summer.
- **PESTS AND DISEASES** Trouble free.

P. insignis, syn. *Olearia insignis* (Marlborough rock daisy). Spreading shrub with stout, white- or brown-felted shoots and oval to obovate, glossy, dark green leaves, to 15cm (6in) long, grey-green when young, and clustered at the tips of the shoots. In summer, bears long-stalked, daisy-like, solitary white flowerheads, to 6cm (2½in) across, with yellow centres. ↕ 90cm (36in), ↔ 1.2m (4ft). New Zealand (South Island). ✽✽

▷ ***Pachystima*** see *Paxistima*

x PACHYVERIA

CRASSULACEAE

Hybrid genus of mainly rosetted, sometimes clump-forming, perennial succulents, the result of crosses between *Pachyphytum* and *Echeveria*. They have alternate, fleshy, light to mid- or grey-green leaves in very variable shapes, sometimes forming rosettes. Diurnal, bell- or star-shaped flowers are borne in one-sided cymes, in spring or summer. Where temperatures drop below 7°C (45°F), grow in a temperate greenhouse. In warmer areas, use in a desert garden.
- **HARDINESS** Frost tender.
- **CULTIVATION** Under glass, grow in standard cactus compost in full light, with shade from hot sun. From mid-spring to late summer, water moderately and apply a low-nitrogen liquid fertilizer every 6–8 weeks. Keep almost dry at other times. Outdoors, grow in moderately fertile, sharply drained soil in full sun, with some midday shade. See also pp.48–49.
- **PROPAGATION** Take leaf or stem-tip cuttings in spring or summer.
- **PESTS AND DISEASES** Susceptible to mealybugs, especially while flowering.

x ***P. glauca*** ▣ syn. *Echeveria* x *fruticosa*. Rosetted, offsetting succulent with semi-cylindrical, red-tipped, blue-green, white-frosted leaves, to 6cm (2½in) long, with darker markings. Pendent, star-shaped yellow flowers, 1.5cm (½in) long, with recurving red tips, open in terminal, one-sided cymes in spring. ↕ 30cm (12in), ↔ indefinite. ❀ (min. 7°C/45°F)

▷ **Pacific grindelia** see *Grindelia stricta*

x *Pachyveria glauca*

PAEONIA

Peony

PAEONIACEAE

Genus of 30 or more species of clump-forming herbaceous perennials and deciduous, sometimes suckering shrubs or subshrubs ("tree peonies") found in meadows, scrub, and rocky places from Europe to E. Asia, and in W. North America. They are grown for their large, brightly coloured, sometimes fragrant, showy flowers and bold, dissected leaves. Some bear pod-like fruits, each with 2–5 lobes and large, red or black seeds. Herbaceous peonies, with tuberous root-stocks, comprise the majority of species and cultivars; most cultivars are derived from *P. lactiflora*. Tree peonies have woody stems, often with lax branches.

Peonies have mid- to dark green, sometimes silver-, bluish, or grey-green leaves; these are 2-ternate or occasionally pinnate, with few to many, usually oval to obovate, sometimes linear, entire or lobed leaflets, occasionally softly hairy, especially on the veins beneath.

Peony flowers are usually erect and solitary, or sometimes borne several to a stem. They are saucer-, cup-, or bowl-shaped, sometimes spherical when first open, and each single flower has 5 green sepals and 5–10 brightly coloured petals. Most have a crowded central boss of usually cream or yellow stamens; those with double flowers have either no stamens or a few hidden among the petals. The flowers can be divided into 4 major groups: single, semi-double, double, and anemone-form (see panel). In the descriptions below, flower sizes of herbaceous cultivars are defined as: "small", 5–10cm (2–4in) across; "medium-sized", 10–15cm (4–6in) across; "large", 15–20cm (6–8in) across; or "very large", over 20cm (8in) across. Tree peonies have single to double flowers, 5–30cm (2–12in) across.

Peonies are long-lived plants but often resent disturbance. Most flower in early summer (exceptions to this are indicated below). They are ideal for a mixed, herbaceous, or shrub border. If ingested, all parts can cause mild stomach upset.

Paeonia 'Argosy'

• **HARDINESS** Fully hardy to frost hardy; young foliage and flower buds may be damaged by late spring frosts.
• **CULTIVATION** Grow in deep, fertile, humus-rich, moist but well-drained soil in full sun or partial shade. Shelter tree peonies from cold, drying winds. Large-flowered cultivars may need support. Pruning group 1 for tree peonies.
• **PROPAGATION** Sow seed in containers outdoors in autumn or early winter (may take 2 or 3 years to germinate). Divide herbaceous peonies in autumn or early spring, or take root cuttings in winter. Take semi-ripe cuttings of tree peonies in summer, or graft in winter.
• **PESTS AND DISEASES** Susceptible to viruses, eelworms, and swift moth larvae. Honey fungus may cause rapid death. Peony grey mould blight (peony wilt) may destroy shoots and buds.

***P.* 'Albert Crousse'.** Herbaceous perennial with deep green leaves and large, double, frilly, rose-pink flowers, flecked with carmine-red in the centres; the outer petals are spreading, the inner ones crowded and ruffled. ‡↔ 85–90cm (34–36in). ✲✲✲
P. albiflora see *P. lactiflora*.
***P.* 'Alice Harding'.** Herbaceous perennial with mid-green leaves and large, double, fragrant, creamy white, amber-tinted flowers with slightly frilled petals, the inner ones incurved. ‡↔ 80–100cm (32–39in). ✲✲✲
***P.* 'America'.** Herbaceous perennial with mid-green leaves and large, single, bowl-shaped, deep crimson flowers, with broad, slightly frilled petals. ‡↔ 0.9–1.1m (3–3½ft). ✲✲✲
P. anomala. Herbaceous perennial with dark green leaves, grey-green beneath, each with 9 narrow-oblong, pinnatifid leaflets, with bristly veins above. Bears single, cup-shaped, bright reddish purple flowers, 7–10cm (3–4in) across, with rounded, wavy petals and golden yellow stamens. ‡↔ 50–60cm (20–24in). Kyrgyzstan, China (E. Tien Shan Mountains). ✲✲✲
***P.* 'Argosy'** ■ syn. *P.* x *lemoinei* 'Argosy'. Compact, deciduous shrub (tree peony) with mid-green leaves, deeply divided into pointed lobes. Bears single, cup-shaped, lemon-yellow flowers, marked crimson-purple at the bases, 18cm (7in) across. Difficult to propagate. ‡↔ 2m (6ft). ✲✲✲
P. arietina see *P. mascula* subsp. *arietina*.
***P.* 'Artemis'.** Upright, sparsely branched, deciduous shrub (tree peony) with red-tinged shoots and dark green, red-stalked leaves, blue-green beneath, deeply cut into pointed lobes. Single, cup-shaped, silky yellow flowers, 15cm (6in) across, are borne in late spring. ‡ 2m (6ft), ↔ 1.5m (5ft). ✲✲✲
***P.* 'Auguste Dessert'** ■ Herbaceous perennial with deep green leaves, turning crimson in autumn, and large, semi-double to double, carmine-red flowers, flushed salmon-pink, the silver margins slightly ruffled and uneven. ‡↔ 70–80cm (28–32in). ✲✲✲
***P.* 'Avant Garde'** ■ Herbaceous perennial with abundant mid-green leaves and large, single, bowl-shaped, rose-pink, darker-veined flowers, with

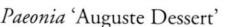

Paeonia 'Auguste Dessert'

Paeonia 'Avant Garde'

Paeonia 'Ballerina'

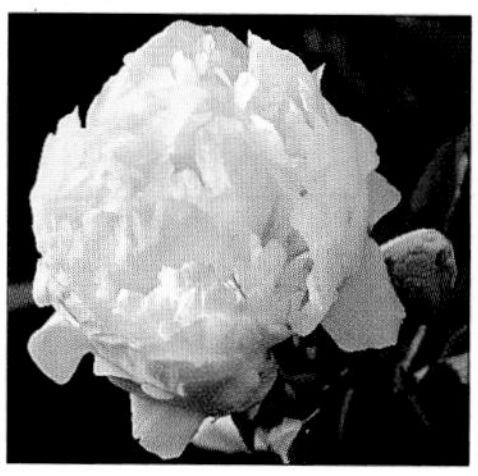

Paeonia 'Baroness Schröder'

Paeonia 'Bowl of Beauty'

Paeonia cambessedesii

yellow stamens. Good for cutting. ‡↔ 90–100cm (36–39in). ✲✲✲
***P.* 'Ballerina'** ■ Herbaceous perennial with deep green leaves, turning red in autumn, and large, double, pink, lilac-flushed flowers, fading almost to white; the outer petals are broad and incurved, the inner ones narrower, curved, and ruffled at the tips. ‡↔ 90–100cm (36–39in). ✲✲✲
***P.* 'Baroness Schröder'** ■ Free-flowering herbaceous perennial with deep green leaves, and large, double, pale pink flowers that fade to white; the outer petals are broad and spreading, the inner ones crowded and incurved, with ruffled margins. ‡↔ 90–100cm (36–39in). ✲✲✲
***P.* 'Barrymore'.** Herbaceous perennial with mid-green leaves and large, anemone-form flowers with pale pink outer petals, fading to pure white as the buds open, and golden yellow petaloids. ‡↔ 80–90cm (32–36cm). ✲✲✲
***P.* 'Bowl of Beauty'** ■ Herbaceous perennial with mid-green leaves. Produces very large, anemone-form, carmine-red, pink-tinted flowers with dense, creamy white centres consisting of many crowded, narrow petaloids. ‡↔ 80–100cm (32–39in). ✲✲✲
P. broteroi. Herbaceous perennial with semi-glossy, mid-green leaves, glaucous beneath, each with 9 leaflets, the lower leaves cut into 2 or 3 narrow, pointed lobes, the upper leaves unlobed. In late spring and early summer, bears single, cup-shaped, pink flowers, 10–13cm (4–5in) across, with oval petals and yellow stamens. ‡↔ 40–50cm (16–20in). Portugal, W. and S. Spain. ✲✲
***P.* 'Bunker Hill'.** Herbaceous perennial with deep green leaves and large, double, bright red flowers with ruffled petals. ‡↔ 70–75cm (28–30in). ✲✲✲
P. cambessedesii ■ (Majorcan peony). Herbaceous perennial, usually flushed red or purple. Purple-veined leaves, dark green above, reddish purple beneath, are each divided into 9 pointed, lance-shaped, elliptic, or ovate leaflets. Produces single, bowl-shaped, deep pink flowers, 6–10cm (2½–4in) across, with wavy-margined petals and yellow stamens with red filaments, in mid- and late spring. ‡↔ 45–55cm (18–22in). Balearic Islands (Majorca). ✲✲
***P.* 'Captivation'.** Herbaceous perennial with deep green leaves. Produces very large, single, bowl-shaped, cherry-red flowers with a silver sheen. ‡↔ 0.9–1.1m (3–3½ft). ✲✲✲

PEONY FLOWER FORMS

Peony flowers may be saucer-, cup-, or bowl-shaped, in one of the following forms: **single** – with a whorl of 5–10 broad, overlapping, often slightly incurved petals, and a large, central boss of stamens; **semi-double** – like single peonies, but with 2 or 3 whorls of similar petals; **double** – large, spherical flowers, with narrower, overlapping, often crowded, ruffled petals filling the centres, and stamens inconspicuous or absent; or **anemone-form** (also known as imperial or Japanese) – single or semi-double flowers, with the stamens replaced by narrow, crowded, petal-like structures, known as petaloids (or staminodes).

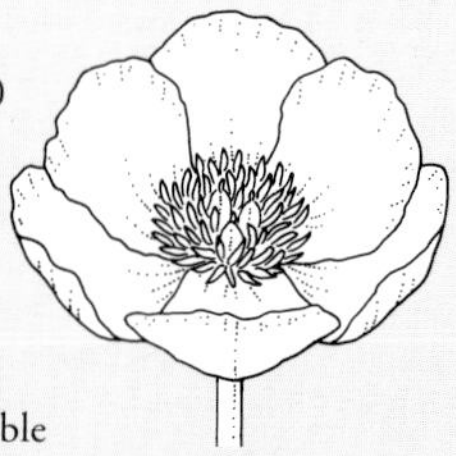

SINGLE

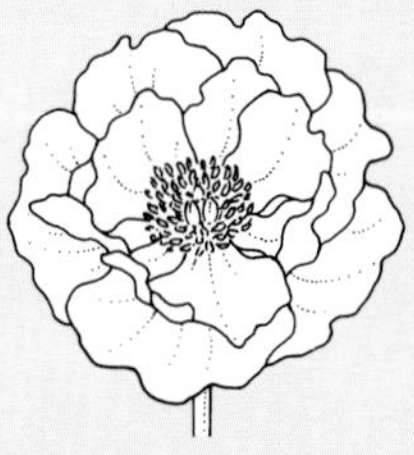

SEMI-DOUBLE

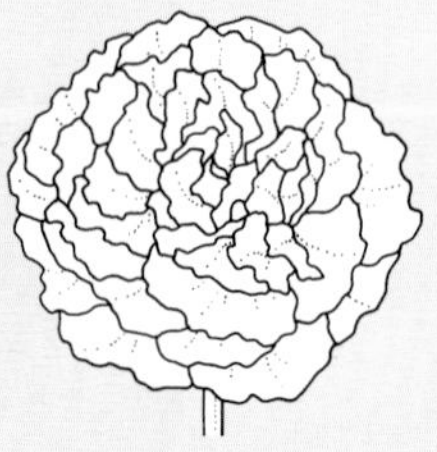

DOUBLE

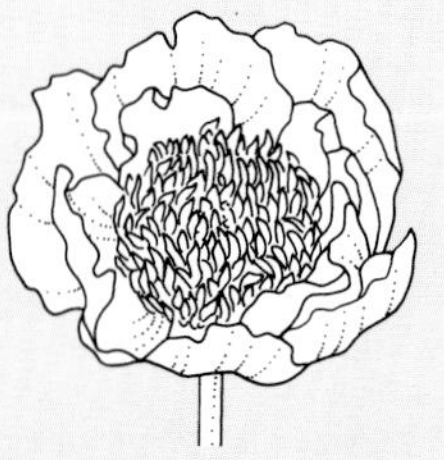

ANEMONE-FORM

P

Paeonia 'Cornelia Shaylor'

Paeonia delavayi

Paeonia 'Duchesse de Nemours'

Paeonia 'Evening World'

Paeonia 'Globe of Light'

Paeonia 'Instituteur Doriat'

Paeonia 'Kelway's Supreme'

Paeonia 'Krinkled White'

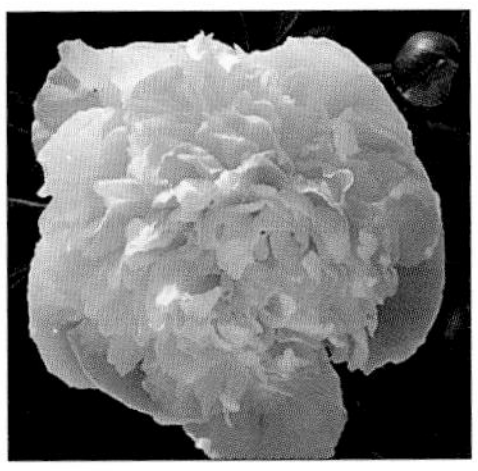
Paeonia 'Laura Dessert'

Paeonia lutea var. *ludlowii*

Paeonia 'Magic Orb'

Paeonia mlokosewitschii

Paeonia 'Mme Louis Henri'

Paeonia obovata var. *alba*

Paeonia officinalis 'Crimson Globe'

Paeonia officinalis 'Rubra Plena'

Paeonia peregrina

Paeonia potaninii var. *trollioides*

Paeonia 'Sarah Bernhardt'

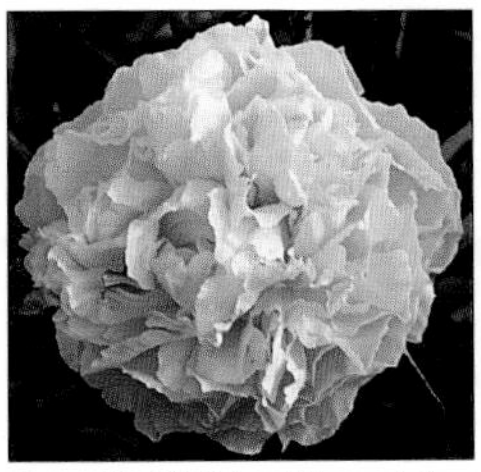
Paeonia 'Shirley Temple'

Paeonia 'Sir Edward Elgar'

P. 'Carnival'. Herbaceous perennial with deep green leaves. Produces large, double, carmine-red flowers, each with a central mass of dissected, ruffled, cream and rose-pink petals. ↕↔ 80–90cm (32–36in). ❄❄❄

P. 'Cheddar Cheese'. Herbaceous perennial with mid-green leaves. Bears large, double flowers with incurving, ivory-white inner petals and shorter, slightly ruffled yellow outer petals. ↕↔ 90–100cm (36–39in). ❄❄❄

P. 'Chocolate Soldier'. Herbaceous perennial with deep green leaves, flushed bronze when young. Bears large, satiny, deeply cupped, semi-double, deep purple-red flowers with golden stamens. ↕↔ 90–100cm (36–39in). ❄❄❄

P. corallina see *P. mascula.*

P. 'Cornelia Shaylor' ▣ Herbaceous perennial with deep green foliage. Bears large, fragrant, double flowers, opening rose-pink but soon fading to bluish white, with dense, ruffled central petals. ↕↔ 80–90cm (32–36in). ❄❄❄

P. 'Dayspring'. Herbaceous perennial with mid-green leaves and medium-sized, single, cup-shaped, fragrant, pale pink flowers, borne several to a stem. ↕↔ 60–70cm (24–28in). ❄❄❄

P. decora see *P. peregrina.*

P. 'Defender'. Herbaceous perennial with glossy, deep green leaves and medium-sized, single, cup-shaped, deep crimson flowers, with golden yellow stamens. ↕↔ 90–100cm (36–39in). ❄❄❄

P. delavayi ▣ Upright, sparsely branched, deciduous shrub (tree peony) with 2-pinnate, dark green leaves, blue-green beneath, the leaflets deeply cut into pointed lobes. Bears horizontal to nodding, single, cup-shaped, rich dark red flowers, 10cm (4in) across. ↕ 2m (6ft), ↔ 1.2m (4ft). China. ❄❄❄. **var. *ludlowii*** see *P. lutea* var. *ludlowii.*

P. 'Double Cherry' see *P. suffruticosa* 'Yae-zakura'.

P. 'Dresden'. Vigorous herbaceous perennial with stout stems and deep green leaves that turn red in autumn. Produces large, single, bowl-shaped, ivory-white flowers, flushed rose-pink. ↕↔ 80–85cm (32–34in). ❄❄❄

P. 'Duchesse de Nemours' ▣ syn. *P.* 'Mrs. Gwyn Lewis'. Robust herbaceous perennial with deep green leaves. Bears large, fragrant, double, pure white flowers, flushed green in bud, with spreading outer petals and dense, unevenly ruffled, yellow-based inner petals. ↕↔ 70–80cm (28–32in). ❄❄❄

P. emodi ▣ (Himalayan peony). Herbaceous perennial with erect to arching stems and dark green leaves, each divided into 9 narrow, sometimes 2- or 3-lobed, elliptic leaflets. Semi-pendent, single, cup-shaped, pure white flowers, 10–17cm (4–7in) across, with golden yellow stamens, are borne several to a stem in late spring. ↕↔ 60–80cm (24–32in). W. Himalayas. ❄❄❄

P. 'Emperor of India'. Herbaceous perennial with deep green foliage and large, anemone-form, rich dark red flowers with golden yellow petaloids. ↕↔ 85–90cm (34–36in). ❄❄❄

P. 'Evening World' ▣ Herbaceous perennial with mid-green leaves. Bears large, anemone-form flowers with spreading, soft pink outer petals and narrow, paler flesh-pink petaloids. ↕↔ 90–100cm (36–39in). ❄❄❄

P. 'Félix Crousse', syn. *P.* 'Victor Hugo'. Herbaceous perennial with deep green leaves and large, fragrant, double, deep crimson-pink flowers, with darker centres and ruffled, silver-margined petals. ↕↔ 70–75cm (28–30in). ❄❄❄

P. 'Festiva Maxima'. Herbaceous perennial with strong, erect stems and abundant mid-green foliage. Bears very large, fragrant, double white flowers, with loosely arranged, irregularly margined petals, the inner petals with crimson marks at their bases. ↕↔ 90–100cm (36–39in). ❄❄❄

P. 'Flamingo'. Herbaceous perennial with deep green leaves, turning red in autumn. Bears large, double, clear salmon-pink flowers. ↕↔ 75–85cm (30–34in). ❄❄❄

P. 'Flight of Cranes' see *P. suffruticosa* 'Renkaku'.

P. 'Floral Rivalry' see *P. suffruticosa* 'Hana-kisoi'.

P. 'Gay Ladye'. Herbaceous perennial with deep green leaves. Bears medium-sized, single, cup-shaped, vivid deep rose-red flowers with wide-spreading petals. ↕↔ 80–90cm (32–36in). ❄❄❄

P. 'Globe of Light' ▣ Herbaceous perennial with mid-green leaves. Bears large, fragrant, anemone-form, rose-pink flowers with golden yellow petaloids. ↕↔ 90–100cm (36–39in). ❄❄❄

P. humilis, syn. *P. officinalis* subsp. *humilis*, *P. officinalis* subsp. *microcarpa*. Herbaceous perennial with hairy stems and leaf-stalks, and mid-green leaves, pale green and densely hairy beneath, each with 9 leaflets deeply cut into narrowly elliptic to oblong lobes. Bears single, bowl- or cup-shaped, purple-red flowers, 10–13cm (4–5in) across, with yellow stamens. ↕↔ 70–80cm (28–32in). S.W. Europe. ❄❄❄

P. 'Instituteur Doriat' ▣ Herbaceous perennial with deep green foliage, turning red in autumn. Produces large, anemone-form, velvety, crimson-red flowers with broad, ruffled, silver-margined pink petaloids. ↕↔ 90–100cm (36–39in). ❄❄❄

***P. japonica* of gardens** see *P. lactiflora.*

P. 'Kamada Brocade' see *P. suffruticosa* 'Kamada-nishiki'.

P. 'Karl Rosenfield'. Herbaceous perennial with hairy stems and leaf-stalks, and mid-green leaves with leaflets deeply cut into narrowly elliptic to oblong lobes. Bears large, double, bright deep red flowers, 10–13cm (4–5in) across. ↕↔ 70–80cm (28–32in). ❄❄❄

P. 'Kelway's Majestic'. Herbaceous perennial with deep green leaves. Bears large, anemone-form, fragrant, bright crimson-pink flowers with slightly ruffled, silver- or gold-flecked, lilac-pink petaloids. ↕↔ 90–100cm (36–39cm). ❄❄❄

P. 'Kelway's Supreme' ▣ Robust herbaceous perennial with mid-green foliage. Bears large, fragrant, double or semi-double, pale pink flowers, fading to white, with broad, overlapping petals, often borne in clusters over a long period. ↕↔ 90–100cm (36–39in). ❄❄❄

P. 'Knighthood'. Herbaceous perennial with deep green leaves. Produces large, double, intense wine-red flowers with narrow, crowded, slightly ruffled petals. ↕↔ 70–80cm (28–32in). ❄❄❄

P. 'Krinkled White' ▣ Herbaceous perennial with mid-green leaves and strong stems bearing large, single, cup-

P

Paeonia emodi

shaped white, occasionally pink-flushed flowers, with slightly ruffled petals and golden yellow stamens. ↕↔ 75–80cm (30–32in). ❄❄❄

***P.* 'Kronos'.** Upright, sparsely branched, deciduous shrub (tree peony) with red-tinged shoots and red-stalked, dark green leaves, blue-green beneath, deeply cut into pointed lobes. Semi-double, dark red, blue-tinged flowers, 15cm (6in) across, are borne in late spring. ↕ 2m (6ft), ↔ 1.5m (5ft). ❄❄❄

P. lactiflora, syn. *P. albiflora*, *P. japonica* of gardens. Herbaceous perennial with erect, red-mottled stems and dark green leaves, each with 9 elliptic or lance-shaped, rough-margined leaflets, paler and slightly hairy beneath. In early and midsummer, bears usually solitary, single, cup- or bowl-shaped, fragrant, white to pale pink flowers, 7–10cm (3–4in) across, with pale yellow stamens. ↕↔ 50–70cm (20–28in). Russia (E. Siberia), Mongolia, N. and W. China, Tibet. ❄❄❄

***P.* 'Laura Dessert'** ▣ Herbaceous perennial with pale to mid-green leaves. Bears large, fragrant, double flowers with spreading, pink-flushed, creamy white outer petals and pale canary-yellow, incurving inner petals. ↕↔ 70–75cm (28–30in). ❄❄❄

P.* x *lemoinei (*P. lutea* x *P. suffruticosa*). Upright to spreading, sparsely branched, deciduous shrub (tree peony) with dark green leaves, deeply divided into pointed lobes. Single to double, cup-shaped flowers, 15–20cm (6–8in) across, are white to yellow, often with orange, red, or pink marks. ↕↔ 1.5m (5ft). Garden origin. ❄❄❄. **'Argosy'** see *P.* 'Argosy'. **'L'Espérance'** see *P.* 'L'Espérance'. **'Mme Louis Henri'** see *P.* 'Mme Louis Henri'. **'Souvenir de Maxime Cornu'** see *P.* 'Souvenir de Maxime Cornu'.

***P.* 'L'Espérance'**, syn. *P.* x *lemoinei* 'L'Espérance'. Upright, deciduous shrub (tree peony) with mid-green leaves, each with several deep, pointed lobes. Bears single, cup-shaped, primrose-yellow flowers, 20cm (8in) across, carmine-red at the bases, with red filaments and golden yellow anthers. ↕ 2m (6ft), ↔ 1.5m (5ft). ❄❄❄

P. lobata see *P. peregrina*.

P. lutea*.** Upright, sparsely branched, deciduous shrub (tree peony) with dark green leaves, blue-green beneath, each with 9 leaflets, deeply cut into pointed lobes. Bears horizontal to nodding, single, cup-shaped, vivid yellow flowers, 6cm (2½in) across. ↕↔ 1.5m (5ft). S.W. China. ❄❄❄. **var. *ludlowii ▣ syn. *P. delavayi* var. *ludlowii*, is more widely grown and more vigorous than the species, with bright green foliage and larger flowers, to 12cm (5in) across, borne in late spring; ↕↔ 2.5m (8ft); S.E. Tibet. **'Superba'** has bronze young foliage, and pink-flushed yellow flowers with red filaments and orange anthers.

***P.* 'Magic Orb'** ▣ Herbaceous perennial producing deep green leaves, turning red in autumn. Bears large, fragrant, double flowers with broad, vivid rose-pink outer petals and narrower, more ruffled, incurved, pink-suffused, creamy white inner petals. ↕↔ 90–100cm (36–39in). ❄❄❄

***P.* 'Magnificent Flower'** see *P. suffruticosa* 'Hana-daijin'.

P. mascula ▣ syn. *P. corallina*. Erect herbaceous perennial with leaves divided into 9 broadly ovate, obovate, or elliptic leaflets, bluish green above, paler green beneath. Cup- to bowl-shaped flowers are single, deep purplish red, sometimes rose-pink, 7–13cm (3–5in) across, with deep yellow stamens. ↕↔ 60–100cm (24–39in). S. Europe. ❄❄❄. **subsp. *arietina***, syn. *P. arietina*, has narrower, often lobed leaflets, hairy beneath, and reddish pink flowers; ↕↔ 50–75cm (20–30in); E. Europe, Turkey. **subsp. *arietina* 'Northern Glory'** has grey-green leaves and deep pink-purple flowers; ↕↔ 60–70cm (24–28in).

P. mlokosewitschii ▣ (Caucasian peony). Erect herbaceous perennial with bluish green leaves, each divided into 9 broadly elliptic, ovate, or obovate, blunt, sometimes red-margined leaflets, paler and slightly hairy beneath. In late spring and early summer, bears single, bowl-shaped, lemon-yellow flowers, 10–12cm (4–5in) across, with broad, oval petals and pale yellow stamens. ↕↔ 65–90cm (26–36in). Caucasus. ❄❄❄

***P.* 'Mme Louis Henri'** ▣ syn. *P.* x *lemoinei* 'Mme Louis Henri'. Upright, deciduous shrub (tree peony) with mid-green leaves divided into pointed lobes. Bears semi-double, warm orange-yellow flowers, to 17cm (7in) across, heavily flushed orange-red. ↕ 2m (6ft), ↔ 1.5m (5ft). ❄❄❄

***P.* 'Monsieur Jules Elie'.** Herbaceous perennial with deep green leaves and very large, rounded, double, deep rose-red flowers with a silver sheen. ↕↔ 90–100cm (36–39in). ❄❄❄

***P.* 'Mother of Pearl'.** Herbaceous perennial with attractive, pale bluish green, often red-margined leaves and large, single, cup-shaped, pink-flushed, pale yellow flowers. ↕↔ 70–75cm (28–30in). ❄❄❄

***P.* 'Mrs. Gwyn Lewis'** see *P.* 'Duchesse de Nemours'.

P. obovata*.** Herbaceous perennial with erect stems and large, deep green leaves, each with 9 uneven, broadly elliptic leaflets, pale grey-green and slightly hairy beneath. Bears single, cup-shaped, white to purplish red flowers, 7–10cm (3–4in) across, with yellow anthers and green-white or purple filaments. ↕↔ 60–70cm (24–28in). China. ❄❄❄. **var. *alba ▣ has white flowers with purple filaments; ↕↔ 70–90cm (28–36in).

P. officinalis (Common peony). Herbaceous perennial with erect stems, slightly hairy at first, and deep green leaves, each divided into 9 leaflets with elliptic to oblong lobes, paler and sometimes hairy beneath. Single, cup-shaped, shiny, deep red or rose-pink flowers, 10–13cm (4–5in) across, with yellow stamens, are borne in early and midsummer. ↕↔ 60–70cm (24–28in). Europe. ❄❄❄. **'Alba Plena'** has large, double white flowers, sometimes flushed pink, the slightly ruffled petals spreading to reveal the carpels at the centre of each flower; ↕↔ 70–75cm (28–30in). **'China Rose'** has dark green leaves and single, deeply cup-shaped, deep salmon-pink flowers with golden yellow stamens; ↕↔ 45–50cm (18–20in). **'Crimson Globe'** ▣ produces single, garnet-red flowers with golden yellow stamens; ↕↔ 70–85cm (28–34in). **subsp. *humilis*** see *P. humilis*. **'James Crawford Weguelin'** has bowl-shaped, garnet-red flowers with yellow stamens. **subsp. *microcarpa*** see *P. humilis*. **'Rosea Superba Plena'** has large, double, deep rose-pink flowers with slightly ruffled petals. **'Rubra Plena'** ▣ has leaves with deep green leaflets, divided into broad, oval segments, and large, double, vivid crimson flowers with satiny, ruffled petals; ↕↔ 70–75cm (28–30in).

Paeonia mascula

P. peregrina ▣ syn. *P. decora*, *P. lobata*. Herbaceous perennial with erect stems and stiff, lustrous, deep green leaves, each with 9 notched or deeply lobed leaflets, bristly on the veins above, usually hairless beneath. Single, bowl-shaped, glistening, deep red flowers, 10–13cm (4–5in) across, with yellow stamens, are borne in late spring and early summer. ↕↔ 50–60cm (20–24in). S. Europe. ❄❄❄. **'Otto Froebel'**, syn. 'Sunshine', produces deep vermilion flowers with deep yellow stamens. **'Sunshine'** see 'Otto Froebel'.

P. potaninii*.** Low-growing, deciduous subshrub (tree peony), spreading by suckers, bearing 2-pinnate, dark green leaves with slender lobes. Produces nodding, single, cup- or bowl-shaped, deep maroon-red flowers, 5cm (2in) across, with red filaments. ↕ 60cm (24in), ↔ 1.5m (5ft) or more. W. China. ❄❄❄. **f. *alba has white flowers with green filaments. **var. *trollioides*** ▣ produces deeply cup-shaped yellow flowers in late spring.

***P.* 'Président Poincaré'.** Herbaceous perennial with deep green leaves, turning red in autumn. Bears large, fragrant, double, deep crimson flowers with ruffled petals in the centres. ↕↔ 90–100cm (36–39in). ❄❄❄

P. rockii see *P. suffruticosa* subsp. *rockii*.

***P.* 'Sarah Bernhardt'** ▣ Robust herbaceous perennial with erect stems, mid-green leaves, and very large, double, fragrant, rose-pink flowers, the inner petals with ruffled and silvered margins. ↕↔ 90–100cm (36–39in). ❄❄❄

***P.* 'Savage Splendour'.** Upright, sparsely branched, deciduous shrub (tree peony) with mid-green leaves, bluish green beneath, deeply cut into pointed lobes. In late spring or early summer, bears large, solitary, single, cup-shaped white flowers, flushed rose- or lavender-pink. ↕ 2m (6ft), ↔ 1.5m (5ft). ❄❄❄

***P.* 'Shirley Temple'** ▣ Herbaceous perennial with deep green leaves. Bears large, double, rose-pink flowers, fading to buff-white, with whorled petals, the innermost paler, narrower, and loosely arranged. ↕↔ 80–85cm (32–34in). ❄❄❄

***P.* 'Silver Flare'.** Herbaceous perennial with deep green leaves and large, single, deeply cup-shaped, fragrant, carmine-red flowers, with silver-margined petals and golden yellow stamens. ↕↔ 90–100cm (36–39in). ❄❄❄

***P.* 'Sir Edward Elgar'** ▣ Herbaceous perennial with glossy, dark green leaves, turning red in autumn. Bears abundant large, single, cup-shaped, dark brownish crimson flowers with lemon-yellow stamens. ↕↔ 70–80cm (28–32in). ❄❄❄

P.* x *smouthii (*P. lactiflora* x *P. tenuifolia*). Erect herbaceous perennial with bright green leaves, each divided into 9 leaflets with many, very narrow segments. In late spring, bears single, cup-shaped, fragrant, bright red flowers, 7–10cm (3–4in) across, with yellow stamens. A sterile hybrid. ↕↔ 60–80cm (24–32in). Garden origin. ❄❄❄

Paeonia 'Souvenir de Maxime Cornu'

Paeonia suffruticosa 'Cardinal Vaughan'

Paeonia suffruticosa 'Godaishu'

Paeonia suffruticosa 'Reine Elisabeth'

Paeonia suffruticosa subsp. *rockii*

Paeonia tenuifolia

Paeonia veitchii

Paeonia 'White Wings'

Paeonia wittmanniana

***P.* 'Souvenir de Maxime Cornu'** ■ syn. *P.* x *lemoinei* 'Souvenir de Maxime Cornu'. Upright, deciduous shrub (tree peony) with mid-green leaves divided into pointed lobes. Bears double, very fragrant, golden yellow flowers, 20cm (8in) across, the ruffled petal margins strongly suffused dull reddish orange. ↕ 2m (6ft), ↔ 1.5m (5ft). ❄❄❄

P. suffruticosa (Moutan). Upright, sparsely branched, deciduous shrub (tree peony) with dark green leaves, blue-green beneath, each with 9 elliptic or ovate leaflets, deeply cut into pointed lobes. In late spring and early summer, bears single, cup- to bowl-shaped, sometimes scented, white, pink, red, or purple flowers, 15–30cm (6–12in) across, some with maroon marks at the bases. ↕↔ to 2.2m (7ft). China. ❄❄❄. **'Banksii'** has double, purple-red flowers with white tips. **'Cardinal Vaughan'** ■ has semi-double, ruby-purple flowers. **'Five Continents'** see 'Godaishu'. **'Godaishu'** ■ syn. 'Five Continents', has semi-double white flowers. **'Hana-daijin'**, syn. *P.* 'Magnificent Flower', has double, violet-purple flowers. **'Hana-kisoi'**, syn. *P.* 'Floral Rivalry', has semi-double, shell-pink flowers. **'Joseph Rock'** see subsp. *rockii*. **'Kamada-nishiki'**, syn. *P.* 'Kamada Brocade', has double, reddish mauve flowers. **'Mrs. William Kelway'** produces double white flowers. **'Reine Elisabeth'** ■ has semi-double to double, salmon-pink flowers tinged red, with ruffled margins. **'Renkaku'**, syn. *P.* 'Flight of Cranes', has dense, double white flowers with deep yellow stamens. **subsp. *rockii*** ■ syn. 'Joseph Rock', 'Rock's Variety', *P. rockii*, has semi-double white flowers, marked deep maroon at the bases. **'Rock's Variety'** see subsp. *rockii*. **'Yae-zakura'**, syn. *P.* 'Double Cherry', has double, soft pink flowers.

P. tenuifolia ■ Herbaceous perennial with deep green leaves, pale and grey-green beneath, with many pointed, linear segments. In late spring and early summer, bears single, cup-shaped, deep red flowers, 7–9cm (3–3½in) across, with yellow stamens. ↕↔ 50–70cm (20–28in). S.E. Europe to S. Russia. ❄❄❄. **'Plena'** has long-lasting, double, rich red flowers.

P. veitchii ■ Herbaceous perennial with hairless stems and deep green leaves, each divided into 9 lance-shaped, pointed leaflets, hairy along the veins above, pale grey-green and hairless beneath. Usually solitary, semi-pendent, single, cup-shaped, white or pink to pale magenta-pink flowers, 7–9cm (3–3½in) across, with pale lemon stamens, open widely in late spring and early summer. ↕↔ 50–60cm (20–24in). W. China. ❄❄❄. **f. *alba*** has white flowers with yellow stamens; ↕↔ 70–75cm (28–30in). **var. *woodwardii*** is shorter, with hairy stems and leaves hairy beneath, and bears rose-pink flowers; ↕↔ 30–40cm (12–16in).

***P.* 'Victor Hugo'** see *P.* 'Félix Crousse'.

***P.* 'White Wings'** ■ Herbaceous perennial with glossy, deep green leaves, red in autumn. Large, single, deeply cup-shaped, fragrant, yellowish white flowers have broad, slightly ruffled petals. ↕↔ 75–85cm (30–34in). ❄❄❄

***P.* 'Whitleyi Major'.** Herbaceous perennial with deep green leaves flushed reddish brown. Bears large, single, cup-shaped, ivory-white flowers with broad, wide-spreading petals and yellow stamens. ↕↔ 80–85cm (32–34in). ❄❄❄

P. wittmanniana ■ Herbaceous perennial with stiff, hairless stems and shiny, dark green leaves with broadly ovate to broadly elliptic leaflets, paler and downy beneath. In late spring and early summer, bears deeply cup-shaped to almost hemispherical, single, primrose-yellow flowers, 10–13cm (4–5in) across, with yellow anthers and red filaments. ↕↔ 80–110cm (32–42in). N.W. Caucasus. ❄❄❄

▷ **Pagoda flower** see *Clerodendrum paniculatum*
▷ **Pagoda tree** see *Plumeria*
  Japanese see *Sophora japonica*
▷ **Paint brush, White** see *Haemanthus albiflos*
▷ **Painted drop-tongue** see *Aglaonema crispum*
▷ **Painted leaf** see *Euphorbia cyathophora*
▷ **Painted net leaf** see *Fittonia*
▷ **Palas** see *Butea monosperma*

PALIURUS

RHAMNACEAE

Genus of about 8 species of spiny, deciduous or evergreen shrubs and trees occurring in dry and rocky places in woodland and at stream margins from S. Europe to E. Asia. The glossy, mid- to dark green leaves are alternate, ovate to broadly ovate, entire or toothed, often with heart-shaped bases. Star-shaped, 5-petalled, yellowish green flowers are produced in small, axillary cymes. The fruits are large, flat, winged discs. Reputed to have been used for Christ's "crown of thorns", *P. spina-christi* is cultivated for its foliage, small flowers, and unusual fruit. Grow in a shrub border or against a wall; can be used for hedging in regions with hot summers.

• **HARDINESS** Frost hardy, but may be hardier in areas with very hot summers.
• **CULTIVATION** Grow in full sun in any well-drained soil. Pruning group 1.
• **PROPAGATION** Sow seed in containers in a cold frame in autumn. Take softwood cuttings in summer.
• **PESTS AND DISEASES** Trouble free.

P. spina-christi ■ (Christ's thorn, Jerusalem thorn). Bushy, deciduous shrub with slender, thorny shoots and ovate, 3-veined, glossy, bright dark green leaves, to 4cm (1½in) long. Small cymes of tiny, star-shaped yellow flowers are produced in summer, followed by woody fruit, to 2.5cm (1in) across, each with a rounded green wing, turning brown. ↕ 4m (12ft), ↔ 3m (10ft). S. Europe to N. China. ❄❄

▷ **Palm,**
  African oil see *Elaeis guineensis*
  Alexander see *Archontophoenix alexandrae, Ptychosperma elegans*

Paliurus spina-christi

Areca see *Chrysalidocarpus lutescens*
Australian fan see *Livistona australis*
Australian ivy see *Schefflera actinophylla*
Bangalow see *Archontophoenix cunninghamiana*
Barbel see *Acanthophoenix*
Betel nut see *Areca catechu*
Blue fan see *Brahea armata*
Blue hesper see *Brahea armata*
Bottle see *Beaucarnea recurvata, Hyophorbe, H. lagenicaulis*
Broom see *Thrinax parviflora*
Burmese fish-tail see *Caryota mitis*
Butterfly see *Chrysalidocarpus lutescens*
Cabbage see *Cordyline, Livistona australis*
Canary Island date see *Phoenix canariensis*
Cardboard see *Zamia furfuracea*
Chilean wine see *Jubaea*
Chinese fan see *Livistona chinensis*
Christmas see *Veitchia merrillii*
Chusan see *Trachycarpus fortunei*
Clustered fish-tail see *Caryota mitis*
Coquito see *Jubaea chilensis*
Date see *Phoenix dactylifera*
Desert fan see *Washingtonia filifera*
Doum see *Hyphaene, H. coriacea*
Dwarf fan see *Chamaerops*
Everglades see *Acoelorraphe wrightii*
Feather duster see *Rhopalostylis sapida*
Fern see *Cycas, C. circinalis*
Fiji fan see *Pritchardia pacifica*
Fish-tail see *Caryota*
Florida silver see *Coccothrinax argentata*
Gingerbread see *Hyphaene thebaica*
Golden feather see *Chrysalidocarpus lutescens*
Grey goddess see *Brahea armata*
Hesper see *Brahea*
Honey see *Jubaea chilensis*
Illawarra see *Archontophoenix cunninghamiana*
Jaggery see *Caryota urens*
Japanese sago see *Cycas revoluta*
Jelly see *Butia capitata*
Kentia see *Howea forsteriana*
Key see *Thrinax morrisii*
King see *Archontophoenix*
Lady see *Rhapis*
Latan see *Latania*
Lipstick see *Cyrtostachys lakka*
Macaw fat see *Elaeis guineensis*
Manila see *Veitchia merrillii*
Mexican fern see *Dioon edule*
Miniature date see *Phoenix roebelenii*
Miniature fan see *Rhapis excelsa*
Miniature fish-tail see *Chamaedorea metallica*
Needle see *Rhapidophyllum*
New Zealand cabbage see *Cordyline australis*
Nikau see *Rhopalostylis sapida*
Northern bangalow see *Archontophoenix alexandrae*
Oil see *Elaeis*
Palmyra see *Borassus flabellifer*
Panama hat see *Carludovica palmata*
Parlour see *Chamaedorea elegans*
Peach see *Bactris gasipaes*
Petticoat see *Copernicia macroglossa*
Piccabeen see *Archontophoenix cunninghamiana*
Porcupine see *Rhapidophyllum hystrix*
Princess see *Dictyosperma*

▷ **Palm cont.**
Pygmy date see *Phoenix roebelenii*
Queen see *Syagrus romanzoffiana*
Red fan see *Livistona mariae*
Reed see *Chamaedorea seifrizii*
Royal see *Roystonea*
Ruffle see *Aiphanes*
Sago see *Caryota urens, Cycas, C. circinalis*
San Jose hesper see *Brahea brandegeei*
Saw see *Acoelorraphe*
Saw cabbage see *Acoelorraphe wrightii*
Sealing wax see *Cyrtostachys lakka*
Sentry see *Howea*
Silver saw see *Acoelorraphe wrightii*
Snake see *Amorphophallus, A. konjac*
Solitaire see *Ptychosperma elegans*
Spine see *Aiphanes caryotifolia*
Spiny club see *Bactris*
Sugar see *Arenga pinnata*
Talipot see *Corypha umbraculifera*
Thatch see *Coccothrinax, Thrinax, T. parviflora*
Thatch leaf see *Howea forsteriana*
Thread see *Washingtonia robusta*
Toddy see *Borassus flabellifer, Caryota urens*
Umbrella see *Hedyscepe*
Walking stick see *Linospadix monostachya*
Wax see *Copernicia*
Weddell see *Lytocaryum weddellianum*
Window see *Reinhardtia, R. gracilis*
Wine see *Borassus flabellifer, Caryota urens*
Yellow see *Chrysalidocarpus*
Zamia see *Cycas media*
▷ **Palmetto** see *Sabal*
Blue see *Rhapidophyllum hystrix*
Cabbage see *Sabal palmetto*
Common blue see *Sabal palmetto*
Dwarf see *Sabal minor*
Scrub see *Sabal minor*
Texas see *Sabal mexicana*
▷ **Palmito do campo** see *Syagrus flexuosa*
▷ **Palms** see p.50

P

PAMIANTHE

AMARYLLIDACEAE

Genus of 2 or 3 species of evergreen or deciduous, bulbous perennials from moist, sandy but rocky areas at altitudes of 1,000–2,000m (3,250–7,000ft) in South America. They have false stems formed from the bases of the strap-shaped, keeled leaves, and are grown for their umbels of large, fragrant white spring flowers, resembling daffodils (*Narcissus*), each with 6 spreading outer tepals and an inner "cup". In frost-prone areas, grow in a temperate or warm greenhouse. In warmer regions, grow among small shrubs or in a border.

• **HARDINESS** Frost tender.

• **CULTIVATION** Plant in late summer or early autumn, with the neck of each bulb just above soil level. Under glass, grow in loam-based potting compost (JI No.2), with added grit and well-rotted organic matter, in full light. When in growth, water moderately and apply a balanced liquid fertilizer every month. Water sparingly at other times. Outdoors, grow in moderately fertile, moist but sharply drained soil in full sun.

• **PROPAGATION** Sow seed at 16–21°C (61–70°F) when ripe. Remove offsets in autumn.

• **PESTS AND DISEASES** Trouble free.

P. peruviana ▣ Deciduous, bulbous perennial with a false stem formed by the bases of the semi-erect, strap-shaped, mid-green leaves, 50cm (20in) long, with rounded keels. In spring, produces terminal umbels of 2–4 large, strongly fragrant flowers, 12cm (5in) across, with spreading, creamy white outer petals and bell-shaped, split white "cups" with green central stripes. ↕ to 1.2m (4ft), ↔ 30cm (12in). Peruvian Andes. ❀ (min. 15°C/59°F)

▷ **Pampas grass** see *Cortaderia, C. selloana*
▷ **Panamiga** see *Pilea involucrata*

Pamianthe peruviana

Pancratium illyricum

PANCRATIUM

Sea lily

AMARYLLIDACEAE

Genus of about 16 species of bulbous perennials found in sandy or rocky sites from the Canary Islands, W. Africa to Namibia, and the Mediterranean to tropical Asia. They have 2-ranked, linear to strap-shaped, basal leaves, and produce terminal umbels of showy, fragrant flowers, each with 6 spreading outer petals and a central "cup". Grow against a warm, sunny wall or, in frost-prone areas, in a cool greenhouse.

• **HARDINESS** Half hardy to frost tender. Half-hardy species may withstand occasional temperatures to -5°C (23°F).

• **CULTIVATION** Plant bulbs 15–20cm (6–8in) deep when dormant. Under glass, grow in loam-based potting compost (JI No.2) with added grit, in deep containers or in a greenhouse border, in full light. When in growth, water freely and apply a balanced liquid fertilizer monthly. Keep dry in summer when dormant. Water sparingly in autumn and winter. Outdoors, grow in any sharply drained soil in full sun.

• **PROPAGATION** Sow seed at 13–18°C (55–64°F) when ripe, or remove offsets when dormant.

• **PESTS AND DISEASES** Trouble free.

P. illyricum ▣ Bulbous perennial with semi-erect, broad, strap-shaped, mid-green, glaucous, basal leaves, to 50cm (20in) long. Bears umbels of 10–15 white flowers, 8cm (3in) across, in late spring and early summer. ↕ 40cm (16in), ↔ 15cm (6in). Corsica, Sardinia. ❄

P. maritimum (Sea daffodil). Bulbous perennial with long-necked bulbs and semi-erect, narrow, strap-shaped, grey-green, basal leaves, to 50cm (20in) long. Bears umbels of up to 6 fragrant white flowers, to 10cm (4in) across, in late summer. ↕↔ 30cm (12in). Coastal S.W. Europe, Mediterranean. ❄

PANDANUS

Screw pine

PANDANACEAE

Genus of 250 or more species of dioecious, evergreen shrubs and trees occurring in dry and moist sites throughout tropical regions of Africa, India, Asia, Australasia, and the Pacific islands. The sparsely branched stems of mature plants are often supported by stilt roots. Screw pines are grown for their attractive foliage: the linear, light to dark green leaves are tough and usually spiny-toothed, and borne in 3 spiralling ranks forming terminal rosettes. The small and petalless male and female flowers are produced on separate plants, males in slender, often branched spikes, and females in short, dense, cone-like heads, which develop into small fruits, resembling pineapples when fertilized. Where temperatures fall below 13°C (55°F), grow young plants in a warm greenhouse or as houseplants. In warmer regions, use as specimen plants.

• **HARDINESS** Frost tender.

• **CULTIVATION** Under glass, grow in loam-based potting compost (JI No.2), with added leaf mould and charcoal, in full light, with moderate to high humidity. From spring to summer, water moderately and apply a balanced liquid fertilizer every month. Water sparingly in winter. Outdoors, grow in fertile, moist but well-drained soil in full sun. Pruning group 1.

• **PROPAGATION** Sow seed at 18°C (64°F) as soon as ripe or in spring, first soaking them for 24 hours. Remove suckers or offsets in spring.

• **PESTS AND DISEASES** Scale insects and red spider mites may cause problems under glass.

P. odoratissimus see *P. tectorius*.

P. sanderi. Slow-growing, suckering shrub that seldom branches and rarely flowers. Bears rosettes of arching, linear, minutely spiny yellow leaves, 45–75cm (18–30in) long, becoming green with pale yellow stripes when mature. ↕ 1m (3ft), ↔ 0.75–1.5m (30–60in). Malaysia, possibly Indonesia (Timor). ❀ (min. 13°C/55°F). **'Roehrsianus'** is more robust, and produces leaves to 1m (3ft) long.

P. tectorius ▣❀ syn. *P. odoratissimus*. Many-branched, upright tree with thick stilt roots. Whorls of robust branches bear rosettes of linear, long-pointed,

Pandanus tectorius

stiffly leathery, bluish green leaves, 1–1.5m (3–5ft) long, with spines along the margins and midribs beneath. Each male flower spike, 20–30cm (8–12in) long, is branched and sheathed in a fragrant white spathe; female flower-heads are small and solitary, about 5cm (2in) across. Flowers are borne mainly in summer, followed by spherical to broadly ovoid fruit, 15–25cm (6–10in) long; they may be yellow or light green, flushed red. ↕ 3–6m (10–20ft), ↔ 2–4m (6–12ft). S.E. Asia, Pacific islands. ❀ (min. 13°C/55°F). **var. *bulbosus*** is larger, with fleshier fruit; widely grown in the Pacific; ↕ 4–6m (12–20ft). **var. *laevis*** has spineless leaves.

▷ **Panda plant** see *Philodendron bipennifolium*

PANDOREA

BIGNONIACEAE

Genus of 6 species of woody-stemmed, evergreen, twining climbers, rarely shrubs, related to *Tecomaria* and *Tecoma*. They occur in rainforest from sea level to 3,000m (10,000ft) in Malaysia, Papua New Guinea, Australia, and New Caledonia, and are grown for their attractive flowers and foliage. Leaves are opposite or whorled, pinnate, and mid- or dark green, each with up to 7 pairs of leaflets. The fragrant, tubular flowers, each with 5 broad, spreading, petal lobes, the upper 2 smaller than the lower 3, are borne usually in terminal, cyme-like panicles or racemes. In mild climates, they are suitable for a pergola or arch, or look especially effective cascading from a tree. In frost-prone areas, grow in a cool greenhouse.

• **HARDINESS** Frost tender; but *P. jasminoides* and *P. pandorana* may survive temperatures around 0°C (32°F) for short periods, if the wood has been well-ripened in summer.

• **CULTIVATION** Under glass, grow in loam-based potting compost (JI No.3) in full light. When in growth, water moderately and apply a balanced liquid fertilizer monthly. Water sparingly in winter. Outdoors, grow in fertile, moist but well-drained soil in full sun. Provide support for climbing stems. Pruning group 11, after flowering.

• **PROPAGATION** Sow seed at 13–18°C (55–64°F) in spring. Root greenwood cuttings with bottom heat in summer. Layer in spring.

• **PESTS AND DISEASES** Susceptible to red spider mites and aphids under glass.

Pandorea jasminoides

P. jasminoides ▣ syn. *Bignonia jasminoides* (Bower plant). Vigorous, twining climber with wiry, branching stems, and pinnate leaves composed of 5–9 ovate to lance-shaped, glossy, bright green leaflets, 2.5–5cm (1–2in) long. Tubular flowers with spreading lobes, 4–5cm (1½–2in) across, are white, flushed crimson-pink in the throats, and freely produced in small, cyme-like panicles from spring to summer. ↕ 5m (15ft) or more. Australia (Queensland, New South Wales). ❀ (min. 5°C/41°F). **'Alba'** has pure white flowers. **'Lady Di'** has white flowers with creamy yellow, sometimes orange-yellow throats. **'Rosea'** has pink flowers with deeper pink throats. **'Rosea Superba'** produces large pink flowers, to 6cm (2½in) long, with purple-spotted, deep pink throats.

P. lindleyana see *Clytostoma calystegioides*.

P. pandorana, syn. *Bignonia pandorana*, *Tecoma australis* (Wonga wonga vine). Strong-growing, twining climber with slender, branching stems. Pinnate leaves have usually 6 pairs of ovate to broadly lance-shaped, mid-green leaflets, 3–10cm (1¼–4in) long, deeply and narrowly lobed when young, entire or sometimes scalloped when mature. Tubular, creamy yellow flowers spotted and streaked reddish purple, 1.5–3cm (½–1¼in) across, with spreading lobes, are borne in terminal and axillary cyme-like racemes in winter and spring. ↕ 6m (20ft) or more. E. Australia (including Tasmania), Papua New Guinea, Pacific islands. ❀ (min. 5°C/41°F)

P. ricasoliana see *Podranea ricasoliana*.

PANICUM

Crab grass

GRAMINEAE/POACEAE

Genus of about 470 annual or perennial, deciduous or evergreen grasses occurring in open grassland or woodland, often in rocky, moist limestone soil, in tropical areas worldwide, in Europe, and in temperate North America. The leaves are thread-like in bud, usually becoming flat and linear-ovate, and may be light to mid-green, grey-green, or purple. In late summer and autumn, they bear finely branching panicles or racemes of 2-flowered spikelets. Ornamental species are valued mainly for their light, airy flowerheads, suitable for cutting and drying; some species, such as millet (*P. miliaceum*), are also valuable fodder crops. Grow in a sunny, mixed or herbaceous border.

• **HARDINESS** Fully hardy to half hardy.

• **CULTIVATION** Grow in moderately fertile, well-drained soil in full sun.

• **PROPAGATION** Sow seed at 13–18°C (55–64°F) in spring. Divide perennials

Panicum capillare

between mid-spring and early summer.

• **PESTS AND DISEASES** Trouble free.

P. capillare ▣ (Witch grass). Lax, loosely tufted annual with clumps of flat, linear to narrowly lance-shaped, mid-green leaves, to 30cm (12in) long. In late summer and autumn, produces dense panicles, to 45cm (18in) long, of tiny, greenish brown spikelets on hair-fine branchlets. ↕ 60–100cm (24–39in), ↔ 60cm (24in). North America. ✻

P. miliaceum (Millet). Erect, clump-forming annual with flat, narrow, lance-shaped, mid-green, sometimes purple-flushed leaves, to 40cm (16in) long. Produces rigid, intricately branched panicles, to 30cm (12in) long, of slightly pendent, purple-tinged green flowers, borne in small spikelets, to 6mm (¼in) long, in late summer. ↕ to 90cm (36in), ↔ to 23cm (9in). C., S., and E. Europe. ✻✻✻. **'Violaceum'**, syn. *P. violaceum*, has purple-violet leaves and spikelets.

P. violaceum see *P. miliaceum* 'Violaceum'.

P. virgatum (Switch grass). Narrowly upright, rhizomatous, deciduous, perennial grass forming clumps of purple to glaucous, mid-green stems that bear upright, flat, linear, mid-green leaves, to 60cm (24in) long. Leaves turn yellow in autumn and light brown in winter. Produces broad, diffuse, weeping panicles, to 50cm (20in) long, of tiny, purple-green spikelets in early autumn. ↕ 1m (3ft), ↔ 75cm (30in). S. Canada, USA to Central America. ✻✻✻. **'Hänse Herms'**, syn. 'Haense Herms', has a fountain-like habit, and rich reddish purple autumn foliage. **'Heavy Metal'** has stiffer, more erect, metallic blue-grey leaves, turning yellow in autumn. **'Strictum'** is narrowly upright, with leaves that turn bright yellow in autumn; ↕ 1.2m (4ft), ↔ 60cm (24in).

▷ **Pansy** see *Viola*, *V.* x *wittrockiana*
Mountain see *V. lutea*
Wild see *V. tricolor*
▷ **Panther lily** see *Lilium pardalinum*

PAPAVER

Poppy

PAPAVERACEAE

Genus of 70 species of annuals, biennials, and perennials occurring in a wide range of habitats from lowlands to high mountains; most are from C. and S. Europe and temperate Asia, a few from South Africa, Australia, W. North America, and subarctic regions. Some annuals are common weeds of arable fields. The usually unbranched, wiry, sometimes hairy stems, which exude latex if damaged, produce a few alternate, mostly radical leaves, which may be simple and toothed, or pinnate to 3-pinnate, pinnatifid, or pinnatisect, bristly or smooth, and grey-green or light to dark green. The short-lived flowers are wide-spreading, bowl-, cup-, or saucer-shaped, usually 4-petalled, and brightly coloured, sometimes with basal marks or spots. They are borne singly or in panicles or racemes, the buds often pendent, and are followed by distinctive "pepper-pot" seed pods. Most larger species are spectacular plants for a mixed or herbaceous border; several of the smaller poppies are suitable for a rock garden or an annual border.

• **HARDINESS** Fully hardy to frost hardy.

• **CULTIVATION** Grow in deep, fertile, well-drained soil in full sun, except *P. alpinum* and its cultivars, which require very sharply drained soil.

• **PROPAGATION** Sow seed in spring: for annuals and biennials, sow seed *in situ*; for perennials, sow seed in containers in a cold frame. Divide perennials in spring, or take root cuttings from them in late autumn or early winter.

• **PESTS AND DISEASES** Prone to aphids, pedicel necrosis and fungal wilts, and, in damp conditions, downy mildew.

P. alpinum ▣ (Alpine poppy). Tuft-forming, short-lived perennial with variable, 2- or 3-pinnate, sometimes pinnatisect, hairy, grey-green leaves, to

Papaver alpinum

Papaver atlanticum

20cm (8in) long, with linear segments. Solitary, cup- to saucer-shaped, white, yellow, orange, or red flowers, to 4cm (1½in) across, are produced in summer. The name *P. alpinum* is often used to include a range of plants that are now considered distinct species. ↕ 15–20cm (6–8in), ↔ 10cm (4in). Europe (Pyrenees, Alps, Carpathian Mountains). ❄❄❄. **subsp. *burseri*** see *P. burseri*. **subsp. *rhaeticum*** see *P. rhaeticum*.

P. atlanticum ■ Erect, clump-forming, short-lived perennial with oblong to lance-shaped, coarsely toothed, mid-green leaves, to 15cm (6in) long, very hairy, particularly beneath. In summer, bears solitary, saucer-shaped, soft orange flowers, to 5cm (2in) across, with very hairy sepals. ↕ 30cm (12in), ↔ 15cm (6in). Morocco. ❄❄❄

P. bracteatum. Upright, clump-forming, bristly perennial producing pinnatisect, mid-green leaves, 25–45cm (10–18in) long, with lance-shaped, toothed segments. In early summer, bears solitary, bowl-shaped, blood-red flowers, 10–18cm (4–7in) across, with 4–6 petals, each with a large, elongated black spot at the base. Similar to *P. orientale* but with taller, stiffer stems,

Papaver fauriei

sepal-like bracts below the flowers, and longer spots on the petals. ↕ to 1.2m (4ft), ↔ 90cm (36in). N. Iran. ❄❄❄

P. burseri, syn. *P. alpinum* subsp. *burseri*. Tuft-forming, almost hairless, semi-evergreen, short-lived perennial with 2- or 3-pinnate, grey-green leaves, to 20cm (8in) long, consisting of linear to lance-shaped segments. In summer, produces solitary, saucer-shaped white flowers, to 4cm (1½in) across, with yellow stamens. ↕ 15cm (6in), ↔ 10cm (4in). Europe (Alps, Carpathian Mountains). ❄❄❄

P. commutatum. Erect, branching annual with oval to oblong, pinnatisect, downy, mid-green leaves, to 15cm (6in) long, with lance-shaped segments. Solitary, bowl-shaped, brilliant red flowers, to 8cm (3in) across, spotted black at the petal bases, are borne on softly grey-hairy stems in summer. ↕ to 45cm (18in), ↔ 15cm (6in). Greece (Crete), Turkey, Caucasus, N. Iran. ❄❄❄

P. croceum, syn. *P. nudicaule* of gardens (Arctic poppy, Icelandic poppy). Erect, tuft-forming, hairy perennial, usually grown as a biennial, producing oval, pinnatifid to pinnatisect, densely hairy,

Papaver croceum 'Summer Breeze'

Papaver 'Fireball'

blue-green leaves, 3–15cm (1¼–6in) long, with oblong segments. Solitary, bowl-shaped, occasionally double, fragrant, yellow or white, sometimes orange or pale red flowers, to 8cm (3in) across, are borne on short, hairy stalks in summer. ↕ to 30cm (12in), ↔ to 15cm (6in). Subarctic regions. ❄❄❄. **Champagne Bubbles Group** has large flowers, to 12cm (5in) across, in a range of mostly pastel shades, including red, bronze-yellow, apricot-yellow, pink, and yellow; ↕ to 45cm (18in). **Garden Gnome Group** is dwarf, with flowers mainly in bright shades, including orange-red, yellow, pink, salmon-pink, and white. **'Summer Breeze'** ■ bears orange, golden yellow, yellow, or white flowers over a very long flowering period; ↕ 30–35cm (12–14in). **Wonderland Series** is dwarf, with large, short-stalked, white, orange, yellow, or red flowers, and is ideal in containers; ↕ to 25cm (10in).

P. dubium (Long-headed poppy). Upright, slender-stemmed, hairy annual with pinnatisect, blue-green leaves, 10–15cm (4–6in) long, with ovate segments. Throughout summer, produces solitary, saucer-shaped, pale scarlet or pinkish red flowers, to 7cm (3in) across, sometimes marked black at the petal bases. ↕ to 60cm (24in), ↔ to 20cm (8in). Europe, W. Asia. ❄❄❄

P. fauriei ■ syn. *P. miyabeanum* of gardens. Compact, mound-forming, short-lived perennial, similar to *P. alpinum*, bearing pinnate, grey-green leaves, to 15cm (6in) long, with lance-shaped, deeply lobed leaflets. Solitary, bowl-shaped, pale yellow or greenish yellow flowers, 2–3cm (¾–1¼in) across, are produced in summer. ↕↔ to 10cm (4in). Russia (N. Kurile Islands), Japan. ❄❄❄

P. 'Fireball' ■ syn. *P.* 'Nanum Flore Pleno'. Upright, densely hairy perennial, spreading freely by runners, bearing lance-shaped, conspicuously toothed, bristly, mid-green leaves, to 20cm (8in) long. Solitary, hemispherical, semi-double to double, orange-scarlet flowers, 3–4cm (1¼–1½in) across, with narrow petals, are produced from late spring to midsummer. ↕↔ 30cm (12in). ❄❄❄

P. lateritium. Clump-forming, upright perennial with very hairy, oblong, deeply toothed, mid-green leaves, to 20cm (8in) long. Branching stems produce bowl-shaped, deep orange flowers, to 5cm (2in) across, usually solitary but occasionally in pairs, in mid- and late summer. ↕ 40cm (16in), ↔ 30cm (12in). Turkey. ❄❄❄

***P. miyabeanum* of gardens** see *P. fauriei*.

***P.* 'Nanum Flore Pleno'** see *P.* 'Fireball'.

***P. nudicaule* of gardens** see *P. croceum*.

P. orientale (Oriental poppy). Clump-forming perennial, spreading by runners, with erect, white-bristly stems and pinnatisect, mid-green leaves, to 30cm (12in) long, with lance-shaped, toothed segments. From late spring to midsummer, bears solitary, cup-shaped, orange-scarlet flowers, 10–16cm (4–6in) across, with no bracts; the 4–6 petals have large, bluish black or white basal spots, broader than they are long. ↕ 45–90cm (18–36in), ↔ 60–90cm (24–36in). Caucasus, N.E. Turkey, N. Iran. ❄❄❄. Most plants grown in gardens as cultivars of *P. orientale* are hybrids with *P. bracteatum* and the closely related *P. pseudoorientale;* they are listed here for easy reference. **'Allegro'** ■ has bright orange-scarlet flowers with bold, black basal marks. **'Beauty of Livermere'** ■ has large, crimson-scarlet flowers, to 20cm (8in) across, with a black mark at the base of

Papaver orientale 'Allegro'

Papaver orientale 'Beauty of Livermere'

Papaver orientale 'Black and White'

each petal; ↕0.9–1.2m (3–4ft), ↔ 90cm (36in). **'Black and White'** ■ produces white flowers with a crimson-black mark at the base of each petal. **'Cedric Morris'** ■ has grey-hairy leaves and very large, soft pink flowers, to 16cm (6in) across, the frilled petals each with a black basal mark. **'Indian Chief'** produces deep mahogany-red flowers without spots. **'May Queen'** bears double, orange-red flowers with slightly quilled, unmarked petals. **'Mrs. Perry'** has pale salmon-pink flowers with black basal marks. **'Perry's White'** has white flowers with maroon-purple centres. **'Picotée'** produces pure white flowers with creased petals that have broad, frilled, orange-pink margins.

P. rhaeticum, syn. *P. alpinum* subsp. *rhaeticum*. Tufted perennial, similar to *P. alpinum*, bearing pinnate, finely hairy, grey-green leaves, to 8cm (3in) long, composed of ovate to lance-shaped segments. Solitary, bowl-shaped, golden yellow or orange flowers, to 5cm (2in) across, are produced in summer. ↕15cm (6in), ↔ 10cm (4in). Pyrenees. ✽✽✽

P. rhoeas (Corn poppy, Field poppy, Flanders poppy). Erect, branching, sparsely hairy annual with oblong, pinnatifid to pinnatisect, downy, light green leaves, to 15cm (6in) long, with lance-shaped segments. Solitary, bowl-shaped, bright red flowers, to 8cm (3in) across, sometimes marked black at the petal bases, are borne on short, downy stalks in summer. ↕ to 90cm (36in), ↔ to 30cm (12in). Eurasia, N. Africa; also widely naturalized. ✽✽✽. **'Fairy Wings'** see 'Mother of Pearl'. **'Mother of Pearl'** ■ syn. 'Fairy Wings',

Papaver orientale 'Cedric Morris'

Papaver rhoeas 'Mother of Pearl'

produces dove-grey, soft pink, or lilac-blue flowers, with paler zoning. **Shirley Series** ■ cultivars have single, semi-double, or double flowers in yellow, pink, orange, or sometimes red, always unmarked at the bases; they need careful selection to maintain the true stock. **Shirley Series 'Reverend Wilks'** has single and semi-double flowers in red, pink, or white, with some picotees and bicolours.

P. rupifragum. Erect, clump-forming perennial with obovate, toothed or lobed, mid-green leaves, to 15cm (6in) long. In summer, bears solitary, bowl-shaped, pale brick-red flowers, to 8cm (3in) across. Similar to *P. atlanticum* except that leaves are hairy only on margins and veins beneath, and sepals are hairless. May self-seed freely. ↕45cm (18in), ↔ 20cm (8in). Spain. ✽✽✽

P. somniferum (Opium poppy). Erect annual with oblong, deeply lobed, glaucous, blue-green leaves, to 12cm (5in) or more long. In summer, leafy stems bear solitary, bowl-shaped, pink, mauve-purple, red, or white flowers, to 10cm (4in) across, sometimes with dark spots at the petal bases. They are followed by large, blue-green seed pods that are good for dried arrangements. All parts may cause mild stomach upset if ingested. ↕ to 1.2m (4ft), ↔ to 30cm (12in). Origin unknown; very widely cultivated and naturalized. ✽✽✽. **'Hen and Chickens'** is grown primarily for its seed heads, with very large pods surrounded by clusters of much smaller capsules. **'Paeony Flowered'** ■ has large, double, frilly flowers in red, purple, pink, salmon-pink, maroon-red,

Papaver rhoeas Shirley Series

Papaver somniferum 'Paeony Flowered'

or white. **'White Cloud'** produces double white flowers.

P. triniifolium. Erect, branching, hairless or sparsely hairy biennial. In the first year, forms a basal rosette of 3 or 4 ovate to oblong, pinnatisect, glaucous, blue-green leaves, to 7cm (3in) long, with linear segments covered in short yellow hairs. In the summer of the second year, many-branched, leafy stems produce solitary, cup-shaped, orange-pink flowers, to 5cm (2in) across. ↕ to 30cm (12in), ↔ 15cm (6in). E. and S. Turkey. ✽✽✽

▷ **Paperbark** see *Melaleuca*
▷ **Paper bush** see *Edgeworthia*
▷ **Paper mulberry** see *Broussonetia papyrifera*
▷ **Paper rush, Egyptian** see *Cyperus papyrus*

PAPHIOPEDILUM

Slipper orchid

ORCHIDACEAE

Genus of about 60 species of evergreen, mainly terrestrial orchids, some epiphytic or lithophytic, occurring at sea level to over 2,000m (7,000ft), from India to China, S.E. Asia, and Papua New Guinea. They are sympodial, lack pseudobulbs, and produce short stems bearing strap-shaped, lance-shaped, or elliptic to ovate, leathery, sometimes mottled, grey to pale, mid-, or dark green leaves. Each shoot ends in a distinctive solitary flower, or a raceme of 2–8 flowers, each with an upright upper sepal, 2 spreading petals, and 2 lateral sepals united under a variably shaped lip or "pouch". Many hybrids have been developed. Contact with foliage may aggravate skin allergies.

• **HARDINESS** Frost tender.

• **CULTIVATION** Cool- to intermediate-growing orchids. Grow in terrestrial orchid compost, with added crushed bark and dolomitic limestone chips, in pots that constrict the roots. In summer, provide high humidity and bright filtered light, water freely, and apply fertilizer at every third watering. Do not mist. In winter, provide full light and water sparingly; do not allow the compost to dry out completely between waterings. See also p.46.

• **PROPAGATION** Not suitable for division, although cuttings or offshoots may be rooted successfully.

• **PESTS AND DISEASES** Prone to red spider mites, aphids, and mealybugs.

P. appletonianum ■ Terrestrial orchid with elliptic, mottled, mid-green and purple leaves, to 20cm (8in) long. Solitary flowers, 12cm (5in) across, with slender green and rose-pink petals, pale green, darker veined upper sepals, and light brown pouches, appear in winter and spring. ↕30cm (12in), ↔ 15cm (6in). Laos, Thailand, Cambodia. ❀ (min. 13°C/55°F; max. 30°C/86°F)

P. argus. Terrestrial orchid with oblong-lance-shaped, pale green leaves with darker mottling, 12–20cm (5–8in) long. In spring, bears solitary flowers, 10cm (4in) across, with dark purple-spotted, off-white petals, pink at the tips; upper sepals have dark green or purple veining; dark green-veined pouches are red above the lips, yellow beneath. ↕30cm (12in), ↔ 15cm (6in). Philippines. ❀ (min. 13°C/55°F; max. 30°C/86°F)

P. bellatulum ■ Terrestrial orchid with rigid, leathery, elliptic to strap-shaped leaves, mottled green and grey, to 20cm (8in) long. Solitary, almost stemless, rounded, white or pale yellow flowers, 9cm (3½in) across, with large, dark red spots, are produced in spring. ↕12cm (5in), ↔ 15cm (6in). Burma, Thailand. ❀ (min. 13°C/55°F; max. 30°C/86°F)

***P.* Buckhurst 'Mont Millais'** ■ (*P.* Greenville x *P.* Spring Vigil). Terrestrial orchid with strap-shaped to ovate, mid-green leaves, 15cm (6in) long. Solitary yellow flowers, 12cm (5in) across, with white upper sepals, are usually produced in winter. ↕30cm (12in), ↔ 20cm (8in). ❀ (min. 13°C/55°F; max. 30°C/86°F)

P. callosum ■ Terrestrial orchid with strap-shaped to elliptic, greyish green leaves, to 25cm (10in) long, with dark green mottling. In spring, bears solitary, maroon and green flowers, 7–9cm (3–3½in) across, with white-striped maroon upper sepals and maroon lips. ↕30cm (12in), ↔ 15cm (6in). Thailand, Cambodia, S. Vietnam. ❀ (min. 13°C/55°F; max. 30°C/86°F)

P. delenatii. Terrestrial orchid with rigid, leathery, elliptic to strap-shaped leaves, 10–15cm (4–6in) long, mottled green and grey above, deep purple beneath. In spring, bears almost stalkless white flowers, 8cm (3in) across, with pink lips, singly or in pairs. ↕20cm (8in), ↔ 15cm (6in). C. Vietnam. ❀ (min. 13°C/55°F; max. 30°C/86°F)

***P.* Delrosi** (*P. delenatii* x *P. rothschildianum*). Terrestrial orchid with semi-rigid, strap-shaped, linear, purplish green leaves, 15cm (6in) long, lightly mottled greyish green and mid-green. In spring, bears richly coloured pink flowers, 10cm (4in) across, singly or in racemes. ↕↔ 30cm (12in). ❀ (min. 13°C/55°F; max. 30°C/86°F)

P. fairrieanum ■ Terrestrial orchid with strap-shaped, dark green leaves, 9–15cm (3½–6in) long. In autumn, bears solitary, purple-veined, pale green-white flowers, 6–8cm (2½–3in) across, with greenish yellow lips suffused purple brown. ↕↔ 15cm (6in). Himalayas, N.E. India (Sikkim), Bhutan. ❀ (min. 10°C/50°F; max. 30°C/86°F)

***P.* Freckles** ■ (*P.* Burleigh Mohur x *P.* F.C. Puddle). Terrestrial orchid with strap-shaped, mid-green leaves, 15cm (6in) long. In early winter, bears solitary cream flowers, 12cm (5in) across, spotted purple-brown, with pink-flushed lips. ↕30cm (12in), ↔ 20cm (8in). ❀ (min. 13°C/55°F; max. 30°C/86°F)

Paphiopedilum fairrieanum

***P.* Goultenianum 'Album'** ■ (*P. callosum* x *P. curtisii*). Terrestrial orchid with broadly ovate, mottled, grey-green and dark green leaves, 10cm (4in) long. Solitary, lime-green and white flowers, 10cm (4in) across, with striped upper sepals, are usually borne in spring. ↕ 30cm (12in), ↔ 20cm (8in). ❄ (min. 13°C/55°F; max. 30°C/86°F)
P. haynaldianum ■ Terrestrial or lithophytic orchid with strap-shaped, light green leaves, to 40cm (16in) long. Racemes of up to 6 slender flowers, to 13cm (5in) across, with green petals tipped and spotted rose-pink, and with spotted upper sepals and greenish brown pouches, are borne in spring. ↕ 45cm (18in), ↔ 30cm (12in). Philippines. ❄ (min. 13°C/55°F; max. 30°C/86°F)
P. hirsutissimum. Terrestrial orchid with linear to strap-shaped, mid-green leaves, to 45cm (18in) long. Solitary flowers, to 14cm (5½in) across, with green and rose-mauve petals, green upper sepals, shaded brown, and greenish brown pouches, are borne in spring. ↕ 15cm (6in), ↔ 20cm (8in). N.E. India, S. China, Thailand. ❄ (min. 10°C/50°F; max. 30°C/86°F)
P. insigne. Terrestrial orchid with linear to lance-shaped, yellowish green leaves, 20–30cm (8–12in) long. Solitary flowers, 7–10cm (3–3½in) across, with yellow-bronze petals and pouches, and pale green-yellow, spotted upper sepals, appear from autumn to spring. ↕ 15cm (6in), ↔ 25cm (10in). E. Himalayas. ❄ (min. 10°C/50°F; max. 30°C/86°F)
***P.* Joanne's Wine** ■ (*P.* Maudiae x *P.* Vintner's Treasure). Terrestrial orchid with broadly ovate, greyish green leaves, 10cm (4in) long, with dark mottling. In spring, bears solitary flowers, 10cm (4in) across, mostly dark purple and light green. ↕ 23cm (9in), ↔ 20cm (8in). ❄ (min. 13°C/55°F; max. 30°C/86°F)
***P.* Lyric 'Glendora'** ■ (*P.* Lucid x *P.* Paeony). Terrestrial orchid with strap-shaped to ovate, mid-green leaves, 15cm (6in) long. Solitary, rounded flowers, 12cm (5in) across, with deep red and green petals, and white upper sepals with dark red centres, are usually produced in winter. ↕ 30cm (12in), ↔ 20cm (8in). ❄ (min. 13°C/55°F; max. 30°C/86°F)
***P.* Maudiae** (*P. callosum* x *P. lawrenceanum*). Terrestrial orchid with attractive, ovate leaves, mottled light and dark green, 12cm (5in) long. Solitary, green-and-white-striped flowers, 10cm (4in) across, are borne in spring or summer. ↕ 30cm (12in), ↔ 15cm (6in). ❄ (min. 13°C/55°F; max. 30°C/86°F). **'Coloratum'** ■ has wine-red flowers with striped upper sepals and greenish white centres.
***P.* Miller's Daughter** ■ (*P.* Chantal x *P.* Dusty Miller). Terrestrial orchid with strap-shaped to ovate, mid-green leaves, 15cm (6in) long. Solitary white flowers, 10cm (4in) across, with pink veins and spots, are usually produced in spring. ↕ 23cm (9in), ↔ 20cm (8in). ❄ (min. 13°C/55°F; max. 30°C/86°F)
P. niveum ■ Terrestrial orchid with rigid, leathery, elliptic to strap-shaped leaves, 10–15cm (4–6in) long, mottled green and grey. Solitary, powder-white flowers, 8cm (3in) across, with small red spots, are borne in summer. ↕↔ 15cm (6in). S. Thailand, N. Malaysia. ❄ (min. 13°C/55°F; max. 30°C/86°F)
P. rothschildianum. Terrestrial orchid with semi-rigid, elliptic to strap-shaped, shiny, mid-green leaves, to 50cm (20in) long. In spring and summer, produces racemes of 2–6 flowers, to 20cm (8in) across, with thin, purple-spotted cream petals, white upper sepals, spotted and striped dark purple, and purplish brown, yellow-rimmed pouches. ↕ 60cm (24in), ↔ 45cm (18in). N. Borneo. ❄ (min. 13°C/55°F; max. 30°C/86°F)
***P.* Silvara 'Jancis'** ■ (*P.* F.C. Puddle x *P.* Sungrove). Terrestrial orchid with narrowly ovate, mid-green leaves, 15cm (6in) long. Solitary white flowers, 10cm (4in) across, with upper sepals peppered orange-brown, are usually borne in spring. ↕ 23cm (9in), ↔ 20cm (8in). ❄ (min. 13°C/55°F; max. 30°C/86°F)
P. sukhakulii ■ Terrestrial orchid with narrowly elliptic, mottled, dark grey and mid- and dark green leaves, to 15cm (6in) long. In autumn, bears solitary flowers, 10–12cm (4–5in) across. They have green petals, heavily spotted purplish black, green-striped white upper sepals, and reddish brown pouches. ↕↔ 15cm (6in). Thailand. ❄ (min. 13°C/55°F; max. 30°C/86°F)
***P.* Vanda M. Pearman** ■ (*P. bellatum* x *P. delenatii*). Terrestrial orchid with elliptic to strap-shaped leaves, to 25cm (10in) long, mottled grey and dark green above, purple beneath. From spring to summer, white flowers, 9cm (3½in) across, with pink-flushed pouches, are borne singly or in pairs. ↕ 20cm (8in), ↔ 18cm (7in). ❄ (min. 13°C/55°F; max. 30°C/86°F)
P. venustum ■ Terrestrial orchid with ovate-lance-shaped leaves, to 25cm (10in) long, mottled grey-green and purple. From winter to spring, bears solitary flowers, 8cm (3in) across, with green and rose-red, maroon-spotted petals, green-striped white upper sepals, and yellowish green to reddish brown, prominently veined pouches. ↕↔ 15cm (6in). Himalayas. ❄ (min. 10°C/50°F; max. 30°C/86°F)
P. villosum ■ Terrestrial orchid with strap-shaped, dull mid-green leaves, 25–40cm (10–16in) long. Solitary, glossy, red-brown flowers, 8cm (3in) across, with green and brown upper sepals and light yellow-bronze to green pouches, appear from winter to spring. ↕↔ 15cm (6in). N.E. India, Burma, Thailand, Laos. ❄ (min. 13°C/55°F; max. 30°C/86°F)
***P.* Vintage Harvest 'Applemint'** ■ (*P.* Chianti x *P.* Golden Acres). Terrestrial orchid with strap-shaped, dark green leaves, 15cm (6in) long. In winter, bears solitary, green-yellow flowers, 12cm (5in) across, with cream margins on the upper sepals, turning gold. ↕ 30cm (12in), ↔ 20cm (8in). ❄ (min. 13°C/55°F; max. 30°C/86°F)

Paphiopedilum appletonianum

Paphiopedilum bellatulum

Paphiopedilum Buckhurst 'Mont Millais'

Paphiopedilum callosum

Paphiopedilum Freckles

Paphiopedilum Goultenianum 'Album'

Paphiopedilum haynaldianum

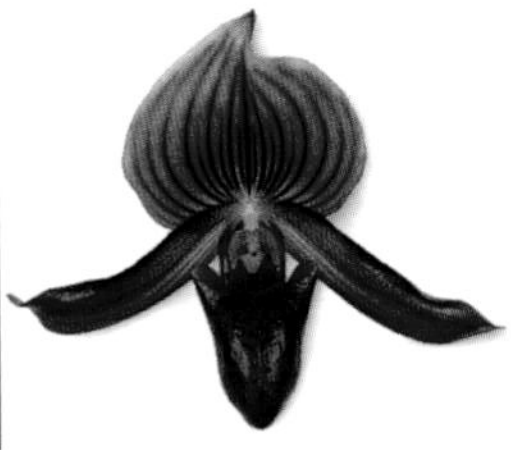

Paphiopedilum Joanne's Wine

Paphiopedilum Lyric 'Glendora'

Paphiopedilum Maudiae 'Coloratum'

Paphiopedilum Miller's Daughter

Paphiopedilum niveum

Paphiopedilum Silvara 'Jancis'

Paphiopedilum sukhakulii

Paphiopedilum Vanda M. Pearman

Paphiopedilum venustum

Paphiopedilum villosum

Paphiopedilum Vintage Harvest 'Applemint'

▷ **Paprika** see *Capsicum annuum*
▷ **Papyrus** see *Cyperus papyrus*
▷ **Parachute plant** see *Ceropegia sandersonii*

PARADISEA

Paradise lily, St. Bruno's lily

ASPHODELACEAE/LILIACEAE

Genus of 2 species of clump-forming perennials found in subalpine or damp meadows and woodland in S. Europe. They have short rhizomes with fleshy roots and linear, hairless, greyish green, basal leaves. They are grown for their loose racemes, borne on slender stems, of trumpet-shaped, 6-tepalled, fragrant flowers, which are good for cutting. Grow in a mixed or herbaceous border.

• **HARDINESS** Fully hardy.
• **CULTIVATION** Grow in humus-rich, fertile, moist but well-drained soil in full sun or dappled shade.
• **PROPAGATION** Sow seed in containers in a cold frame as soon as ripe or in spring. Divide after flowering, or in early spring.
• **PESTS AND DISEASES** Slugs may be a problem.

P. liliastrum. Clump-forming perennial producing short rhizomes and grass-like leaves, 12–25cm (5–10in) long. One-sided racemes of white flowers, 3–6cm (1¼–2½in) long, with conspicuous yellow anthers, are borne in late spring or early summer. ↕ 30–60cm (12–24in), ↔ 30cm (12in). Mountains of S. Europe. ❄❄❄. **'Major'** ▣ has larger flowers, 5–6cm (2–2½in) long.
P. lusitanicum. Upright, clump-forming perennial with basal rosettes of linear leaves, 30–40cm (12–16in) long. Racemes of 20–25 white flowers, 2cm (¾in) long, are borne in summer. ↕ 80–120cm (32–48in), ↔ 30–40cm (12–16in). Portugal, Spain. ❄❄❄

▷ **Paradise flower** see *Solanum wendlandii*

Paradisea liliastrum 'Major'

PARAHEBE syn. DERWENTIA

SCROPHULARIACEAE

Genus of about 30 species of evergreen or semi-evergreen subshrubs and perennials, often classified under *Hebe* or *Veronica.* Most are from Australia and New Zealand, with a few from Papua New Guinea, occurring mainly in sunny and dry, stony habitats or scree. They have woody-based stems, and produce opposite, usually more or less ovate, toothed, mid- to dark green or blue-green leaves, stalkless or with very short stalks. They are cultivated for their erect, axillary racemes of small, saucer-shaped, usually white, pink, lilac, or blue flowers, frequently with contrasting markings; each flower has 4, rarely 5, often pointed, unequal petals. Often mat-forming or decumbent, they are effective tumbling over walls or large rocks, or growing through shrubs, and are also suitable for a gravel bed.

• **HARDINESS** Fully hardy to frost hardy.
• **CULTIVATION** Grow in well-drained, poor to moderately fertile soil in full sun. In frost-prone climates, shelter from cold, drying winds.
• **PROPAGATION** Sow seed in containers in a cold frame as soon as ripe or in spring. Take semi-ripe cuttings in early or midsummer.
• **PESTS AND DISEASES** Slugs may eat young growth.

***P. x bidwillii* 'Kea'.** Prostrate, mat-forming, evergreen subshrub with oblong to obovate, leathery, dark green leaves, to 6mm (¼in) long. Produces short, slender racemes of saucer-shaped, crimson-veined white flowers, to 8mm (⅜in) across, in summer. ↕ 10cm (4in), ↔ 15cm (6in). ❄❄❄
P. catarractae ▣ Decumbent or upright, evergreen subshrub with ovate to elliptic or lance-shaped, shallowly to sharply toothed, dark green leaves, to 4cm (1½in) long, tinged purple when young. In summer, produces racemes

Parahebe perfoliata

of saucer-shaped, purple-veined white flowers, 1cm (½in) across, with red eyes. ↕↔ to 30cm (12in). New Zealand. ❄❄❄
P. densifolia see *Chionohebe densifolia.*
P. hookeriana. Mat-forming, evergreen subshrub with crowded, overlapping, broadly ovate to oblong or oval, deeply toothed, leathery, sparsely hairy, mid-green leaves, to 1.5cm (½in) long. Saucer-shaped, white to lavender-blue flowers, to 1cm (½in) across, each usually with a crimson eye, are borne in racemes in summer. ↕ 15cm (6in), ↔ 50cm (20in). New Zealand (North Island). ❄❄❄
P. lyallii. Variable, prostrate, stem-rooting, semi-evergreen shrub with rounded to ovate, leathery, toothed to scalloped, dark green leaves, to 1cm (½in) long. In early summer, bears dense racemes of saucer-shaped, usually purple-veined, white to pink flowers, 1cm (½in) across, with red eyes. ↕ 25cm (10in), ↔ 50cm (20in). New Zealand. ❄❄❄
P. perfoliata ▣ syn. *Veronica perfoliata* (Digger's speedwell). Woody-based, evergreen perennial with arching, spreading stems. Bears pairs of broadly ovate, toothed, slightly leathery, glaucous, blue- or grey-green leaves, 5cm (2in) long, overlapping at the bases, each pair arranged at right-angles to the next pair. In late summer, produces racemes of saucer-shaped blue flowers, 6–10mm (¼–½in) across. ↕ 60–75cm (24–30in), ↔ 45cm (18in). S.E. Australia. ❄❄

Parahebe catarractae

▷ **Parapara** see *Pisonia umbellifera*

PARAQUILEGIA

RANUNCULACEAE

Genus of 4–6 species of tufted perennials occurring in rock crevices and scree in the Himalayas and mountains of C. Asia and China. They are grown for their solitary, short-stalked, cup-shaped flowers, produced in spring, and for their fern-like, ternate to 3-ternate, often grey or blue-green leaves, arranged alternately. These attractive alpines are suitable for a scree bed, trough, or alpine house, but may be difficult to establish; they grow best in climates with cool summers and cold, dry winters.

• **HARDINESS** Fully hardy.
• **CULTIVATION** Outdoors, grow in poor, sharply drained, alkaline soil in full sun. Protect from winter wet. In an alpine house, grow in a mix of equal parts loam, leaf mould, and grit.
• **PROPAGATION** Sow seed in containers in an open frame as soon as ripe.
• **PESTS AND DISEASES** Susceptible to aphids and red spider mites under glass, and prone to damage by slugs and snails.

P. anemonoides ▣ syn. *P. grandiflora.* Tufted perennial producing long-stalked, 2- or 3-ternate, blue-green leaves, 3cm (1¼in) long, with many, deeply lobed segments. In late spring, produces violet-blue, purple-blue, or pale lilac, occasionally white flowers, 2.5cm (1in) across, with golden nectaries and yellow anthers. ↕↔ to 10cm (4in). C. Asia, Himalayas, W. China. ❄❄❄
P. grandiflora see *P. anemonoides.*

Paraquilegia anemonoides

P

PARASERIANTHES

LEGUMINOSAE/MIMOSACEAE

Genus of one species of deciduous large shrub or small tree from coastal scrub in Western Australia. It is cultivated for its fine, fern-like foliage and delicate cylindrical flowerheads, which consist of many small florets with long protruding stamens and are produced in spring. The alternate, 2-pinnate leaves have numerous oblong to sickle-shaped leaflets. In frost-prone areas, grow paraserianthes in a cool greenhouse; in warmer climates, grow as a specimen plant.

• **HARDINESS** Frost tender.
• **CULTIVATION** Under glass, grow in loam-based potting compost (JI No.2) in full light. When in growth, water moderately and apply a balanced liquid fertilizer monthly; maintain low humidity. Water sparingly in winter. Outdoors, grow in moderately fertile, well-drained soil in full sun. Pruning group 1, or 13 if wall-trained; plants under glass may need restrictive pruning in early spring.
• **PROPAGATION** Sow seed at 16–18°C (61–64°F) in spring, after soaking for 24 hours in warm water. Root softwood cuttings in summer.
• **PESTS AND DISEASES** Red spider mites and whiteflies may be troublesome under glass.

Paraserianthes lophantha ♀ syn. *Albizia distachya, A. lophantha, Mimosa distachya* (Cape wattle, Swamp wattle). Erect to spreading, large shrub or small tree with fern-like, bright green leaves, 30cm (12in) long, with numerous small, oblong-ovate, lop-sidedly pointed leaflets. In spring, bears tiny, yellow-green or gold flowerheads in cylindrical, axillary spikes, 3–6cm (1¼–2½in) long. ↕ 2–10m (6–30ft), ↔ 1–3m (3–10ft). Australia (Western Australia). ❀ (min. 4–5°C/39–41°F)

P

▷ **Parasol tree, Chinese** see *Firmiana simplex*
▷ **Parilla, Yellow** see *Menispermum canadense*

PARIS syn. DAISWA

TRILLIACEAE

Genus of about 20 species of rhizomatous perennials occurring in woodland from Europe to the Caucasus, and from the Himalayas to E. Asia. Erect stems each bear a whorl of 4 or more very variable, lance-shaped to ovate, mid- or dark green leaves, just below a solitary, terminal, wheel-shaped, spider-like, or star-shaped flower, with protruding stamens. The flowers are followed by fleshy, capsular fruits with shiny, black or red seeds; these may cause mild stomach upset if ingested. Suitable for a woodland or peat garden.

• **HARDINESS** Fully hardy.
• **CULTIVATION** Grow in moist, fertile, leafy soil in full or partial shade. Leave plants undisturbed to increase year by year.
• **PROPAGATION** Sow seed in containers outdoors in autumn. Divide after the foliage has died down.
• **PESTS AND DISEASES** Slugs may attack rhizomes and young growth.

P. polyphylla, syn. *Daiswa polyphylla*. Slowly spreading perennial with short rhizomes and erect, smooth stems, each producing a whorl of 6–12 oblong to inversely lance-shaped, mid-green leaves, 8–18cm (3–7in) long, rounded at the bases. Solitary, spider-like flowers, each consisting of 4–8 narrow green outer tepals, 2.5–10cm (1–4in) long, and thread-like, yellowish green inner tepals, to 10cm (4in) long, with numerous stamens, are borne in summer. Angled, almost spherical green capsules, to 2cm (¾in) across, split to reveal shiny red seeds when ripe. ↕ 60–90cm (24–36in), ↔ 30cm (12in). Himalayas to Burma, Thailand, W. China. ❄❄❄

P. quadrifolia. Upright perennial with creeping rhizomes and erect stems, each with a whorl of usually 4, sometimes 5 or 6, ovate, mid-green leaves, 5–15cm (2–6in) long. In late spring, bears solitary, star-shaped flowers, 4–7cm (1½–3in) across, with mid-green outer tepals, white inner tepals, and twice as many stamens as inner tepals. Bears blue-black, spherical, berry-like capsules, 1cm (½in) across. ↕ 15–40cm (6–16in), ↔ 30cm (12in). Eurasia. ❄❄❄

PARKINSONIA

CAESALPINIACEAE/LEGUMINOSAE

Genus of more than 12 species of deciduous or evergreen shrubs and trees from dry savannah or scrubland in the drier regions of Africa, S. North America, and Central America. They are grown for their flowers and delicate foliage. The branches have pairs of spines at each node, and bear alternate, 2- or 3-pinnate leaves with very small, light to mid- or yellow-green leaflets. The mostly yellow, red-spotted flowers, with spreading, clawed petals, are borne in short, usually axillary racemes from the upper leaf nodes, followed by leathery or woody, pea-like pods. Grow as specimen trees. In frost-prone areas, grow in a cool or temperate greenhouse.

• **HARDINESS** Frost tender.
• **CULTIVATION** Under glass, grow in loam-based potting compost (JI No.3) in full light, with low humidity. From spring to summer, water moderately and apply a balanced liquid fertilizer every month. Water sparingly in winter. Outdoors, grow in fertile, well-drained soil in full sun. Pruning group 1; may need restrictive pruning under glass, after flowering.
• **PROPAGATION** Sow seed at 18–21°C (64–70°F) in spring.
• **PESTS AND DISEASES** Red spider mites may be a problem under glass.

P. aculeata ▣ ♀ (Jerusalem thorn). Small, spreading, often weeping, deciduous tree, or occasionally large shrub, bearing spiny green stems and branchlets. Slender, 2-pinnate, stalkless, mid-green leaves, to 30cm (12in) long, have distinctive flat midribs and many tiny, ovate to oblong leaflets, 2–5mm (¹⁄₁₆–¼in) long, often quickly deciduous; they fold up at night. In spring, bears racemes of 2–15 cup-shaped, bright yellow flowers, to 2cm (¾in) across, with orange-spotted standard petals and orange-red stamens. ↕ to 10m (30ft), ↔ 5–8m (15–25ft). S. USA, Mexico; widely naturalized in tropical and subtropical regions. ❀ (min. 5°C/41°F)

Parkinsonia aculeata

PARNASSIA

Bog star, Grass of Parnassus

PARNASSIACEAE/SAXIFRAGACEAE

Genus of 15 species of herbaceous perennials found in bogs in temperate regions in the N. hemisphere. They produce basal rosettes of broadly ovate, heart-, or kidney-shaped, mid- to dark green leaves. They are grown for their large, solitary, bowl- or saucer-shaped, white to pale yellow flowers, with yellow, nectar-bearing staminodes, borne on upright stems in spring, summer, or early autumn. Grow in wet soil in a rock garden or bog garden.

• **HARDINESS** Fully hardy.
• **CULTIVATION** Grow in humus-rich, poor to moderately fertile, wet but not stagnant soil in full sun.
• **PROPAGATION** Sow seed in containers in a cold frame in autumn; keep moist. Divide in autumn or spring.
• **PESTS AND DISEASES** Susceptible to slug and snail damage.

P. fimbriata. Rosette-forming perennial with kidney-shaped, mid-green basal leaves, 2–5cm (¾–2in) long, and long-stalked, broadly ovate stem leaves, 2cm (¾in) long. Solitary, bowl-shaped white flowers, 3–4cm (1¼–1½in) across, are borne in late summer and early autumn. ↕↔ 20–60cm (8–24in). North America (Alaska to California). ❄❄❄

P. palustris ▣ (Grass of Parnassus). Rosette-forming perennial with ovate, heart-shaped, pale green leaves, to 3cm (1¼in) long. Slender stems bear solitary, green-veined white flowers, 2.5cm (1in) across, with yellow nectar glands, in late spring and early summer. ↕ 20cm (8in), ↔ 10cm (4in). N. temperate regions. ❄❄❄

Parnassia palustris

PAROCHETUS

LEGUMINOSAE/PAPILIONACEAE

Genus of 2 species (often confused in cultivation) of trailing, deciduous or evergreen perennials found in montane habitats in E. Africa, the Himalayas to Sri Lanka, S.W. China, and S.E. Asia. They are grown for their clover-like leaves and bright blue, occasionally white, pea-like flowers. Grow in a rock garden or alpine house. *P. africana* is ideal in a hanging basket.

• **HARDINESS** Fully hardy to half hardy.
• **CULTIVATION** Grow in any moist but well-drained soil in partial shade, but protect from winter wet. Plants may be short-lived, so propagate regularly and overwinter young plants under glass. In an alpine house, grow in a mix of equal parts loam-based potting compost (JI No.2), leaf mould, and grit.
• **PROPAGATION** Divide in spring, or separate rooted runners when in growth.
• **PESTS AND DISEASES** May be damaged by slugs and snails.

P. africanus ▣ (Shamrock pea). Prostrate, mat-forming, non-tuberous, evergreen perennial with freely rooting stems. Each leaf has 3 inversely heart-shaped, rich dark green leaflets, to 3cm (1¼in) long, with bold, dark brown horseshoe markings. Solitary or paired, bright blue flowers, 2.5cm (1in) across, are borne mainly from late autumn to late spring. ↕ 10cm (4in), ↔ 60–100cm (24–39in). Mountains of E. Africa. ❄

P. communis. Prostrate, tuberous-rooted, deciduous perennial with trailing stems. Leaves are divided into 3 inversely heart-shaped, mid-green leaflets, to 2cm (¾in) long, with irregular bronze-brown horseshoe markings. Produces a succession of solitary or paired, bright blue flowers, 2.5cm (1in)

Parochetus africanus

across, in late summer and autumn. ↕10cm (4in), ↔ 30cm (12in) or more. Himalayas to Sri Lanka, S.W. China, S.E. Asia. ✲✲✲

PARODIA *syn.* ERIOCACTUS, NOTOCACTUS, WIGGINSIA

CACTACEAE

Genus of 35–50 species of simple or clustering, mainly spherical, many-ribbed, spiny, perennial cacti, sometimes becoming columnar and sometimes offsetting from the bases. The genus includes many species transferred from *Eriocactus*, *Notocactus*, and *Wigginsia*. They occur mainly in the highlands of Colombia, Brazil, Bolivia, Paraguay, Argentina, and Uruguay. Solitary, diurnal, bell- to funnel-shaped flowers develop near or at the crowns. Where temperatures drop below 10°C (50°F), grow in a warm greenhouse. In warmer climates, use in a desert garden.

- **HARDINESS** Frost tender.
- **CULTIVATION** Under glass, grow in standard cactus compost in full or bright filtered light. From mid-spring to late summer, water moderately and apply a low-nitrogen liquid fertilizer every 6–8 weeks. Keep barely moist at other times. Outdoors, grow in sharply drained, moderately fertile soil in full sun, with some midday shade. See also pp.48–49.
- **PROPAGATION** Sow seed at 19–24°C (66–75°F) in spring or summer.
- **PESTS AND DISEASES** Vulnerable to mealybugs and, while flowering, aphids.

P. brevihamata ■ syn. *Notocactus brevihamatus*. Simple or clustering

Parodia brevihamata

Parodia chrysacanthion

Parodia erinacea

cactus producing spherical, olive-green stems, each with 20–26 closely set ribs, rounded tubercles, white to yellow areoles, and yellow, later brownish yellow spines (about 16 radials, 1–4 slightly longer centrals). Funnel-shaped, lemon-yellow, sometimes red-tinted flowers, 4cm (1½in) across, are borne in spring. ↕↔ to 6cm (2½in). S. Brazil. ❄ (min. 10°C/50°F)

P. chrysacanthion ■ Simple cactus producing a spherical to depressed-spherical, pale green stem with about 24 spirally arranged, warty ribs, and the crown covered with thick yellow wool. Yellowish white areoles bear yellow spines (30–40 fine radials, 1 or more centrals). Funnel-shaped yellow flowers, 2cm (¾in) across, develop in spring. ↕8–12cm (3–5in), ↔ 10cm (4in). N. Argentina. ❄ (min. 10°C/50°F)

P. concinna, syn. *Eriocactus apricus*, *Notocactus apricus*, *N. concinnus*. Simple cactus producing a flattened-spherical, 15- to 32-ribbed, dark green stem with a woolly crown, white areoles, and white, pale yellow, brown, or red-brown spines (10–12 radials, 4–6 or more, longer, slightly darker centrals). Funnel-shaped, red-tipped, deep lemon-yellow flowers, 5–8cm (2–3in) across, are produced in spring. ↕ to 6cm (2½in), ↔ 10cm (4in). S. Brazil, Uruguay. ❄ (min. 10°C/50°F)

P. erinacea ■ syn. *Wigginsia erinacea*, *W. vorwerkiana*. Freely offsetting cactus with spherical to short-cylindrical, light to dark green stems, 6–30cm (2½–12in) thick, each with 15–30 spiralling ribs, grey areoles, and off-white, grey, or brown spines (2–12 radials, 1 longer central). In summer, bears funnel-

Parodia haselbergii

Parodia leninghausii

shaped, glossy yellow flowers, 4cm (1½in) across. ↕15cm (6in) or more, ↔ 25cm (10in). S. Brazil, Uruguay, N.E. Argentina. ❄ (min. 10°C/50°F)

P. graessneri, syn. *Notocactus graessneri*. Simple cactus producing a spherical, dark green stem with an angled, spiny crown and 50–60 heavily warty ribs. White areoles bear both pale to golden yellow and pale brown to white spines (about 55 radials, 5 or 6 centrals). In spring, bears funnel-shaped, pale yellow-green flowers, 2cm (¾in) across. ↕10–15cm (4–6in), ↔ 10cm (4in). S. Brazil. ❄ (min. 10°C/50°F)

P. haselbergii ■ syn. *Notocactus haselbergii* (Scarlet ball cactus). Simple cactus, rarely offsetting from the base, with a spherical, greyish green stem, to 15cm (6in) thick, with a woolly crown set at an angle, and with 30–60 or more ribs. White-woolly areoles produce yellowish white to yellow spines (25–60 radials, 3–5 slightly longer centrals). Funnel-shaped, bright orange-red or orange-yellow flowers, 1.5cm (½in) across, appear from winter to spring. ↕4–15cm (1½–6in), ↔ 18cm (7in) in clusters. S. Brazil. ❄ (min. 10°C/50°F)

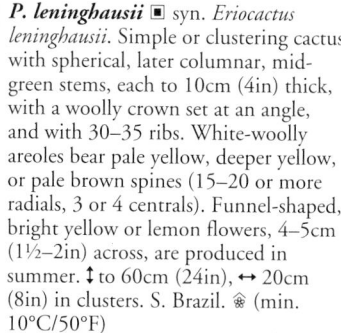

P. leninghausii ■ syn. *Eriocactus leninghausii*. Simple or clustering cactus with spherical, later columnar, mid-green stems, each to 10cm (4in) thick, with a woolly crown set at an angle, and with 30–35 ribs. White-woolly areoles bear pale yellow, deeper yellow, or pale brown spines (15–20 or more radials, 3 or 4 centrals). Funnel-shaped, bright yellow or lemon flowers, 4–5cm (1½–2in) across, are produced in summer. ↕ to 60cm (24in), ↔ 20cm (8in) in clusters. S. Brazil. ❄ (min. 10°C/50°F)

P. liliputana see *Blossfeldia liliputana*.

P. magnifica, syn. *Notocactus magnifica*. Simple, sometimes clustering cactus with spherical, later columnar, 11- to 15-ribbed, bluish green stems, to 15cm (6in) thick. Grey-felted areoles bear yellow or brown spines (12–15 or more radials, up to 12 longer centrals). Funnel-shaped, sulphur-yellow flowers, 5cm (2in) across, develop in summer. ↕7–15cm (3–6in), ↔ to 45cm (18in). S. Brazil. ❄ (min. 10°C/50°F)

P. mammulosa ■ syn. *Notocactus mammulosus*, *N. submammulosus*. Simple cactus producing a spherical, dark green stem with a woolly crown and 13–21 heavily warty ribs. White areoles bear white, off-white, grey, or pale brown spines (6–25 radials, 2–4 longer centrals). Funnel-shaped, pale to golden yellow flowers, 3.5–5cm (1½–2in) across, with bold red stigmas, develop in summer. ↕10–13cm (4–5in), ↔ 6cm (2½in). S. Brazil, Uruguay, N.E. Argentina. ❄ (min. 10°C/50°F)

P. microsperma, syn. *P. mutabilis* var. *sanguiniflora*, *P. sanguiniflora*. Simple cactus producing a depressed-spherical to spherical, sometimes cylindrical, mid-green stem with 15–21 warty ribs. White areoles bear white and red to brown spines (10–25 radials, 3 or 4 longer centrals). Funnel-shaped, yellow or red flowers, 3.5cm (1½in) across, are borne from spring to summer. ↕20cm (8in), ↔ 10cm (4in). N. Argentina. ❄ (min. 10°C/50°F)

P

Parodia mammulosa

P. mutabilis, syn. *Notocactus mutabilis*. Simple cactus producing a spherical, glaucous, mid-green stem with a white-woolly, brown-spiny crown and 25 or more, spirally arranged, warty ribs. White-woolly areoles bear white and yellow, reddish brown, or orange-brown spines (20–50 fine, almost hair-like, radials, 4–10 strong, sometimes hooked centrals). Funnel-shaped, golden yellow flowers, 3–5cm (1¼–2in) across, are produced from spring to summer. ↕↔ 8cm (3in). N. Argentina. ❄ (min. 10°C/50°F). **var. *sanguiniflora*** see *P. microsperma*.
P. nivosa ▣ Simple cactus producing a spherical to short-cylindrical, dull green stem with a white-woolly crown and 16–20 spirally arranged, warty ribs. White-felted areoles have white spines (15–20 radials, 3–5 longer centrals). Funnel-shaped, brilliant red flowers, 3cm (1¼in) across, develop in spring. ↕ 15cm (6in), ↔ 6cm (2½in). N. Argentina. ❄ (min. 10°C/50°F)
P. ocampoi. Clustering cactus with spherical to short-cylindrical, 13- to 20-ribbed, dark green stems, 6cm (2½in) thick, with grey areoles and pale reddish brown spines (8 or 9 radials, 1 smaller central). Funnel-shaped, golden yellow flowers, 3cm (1¼in) across, are borne from spring to summer. ↕ 7–20cm (3–8in), ↔ 15cm (6in). C. Bolivia. ❄ (min. 10°C/50°F)
P. ottonis, syn. *Notocactus ottonis*. Variable, simple, later clustering cactus with spherical or cylindrical, 6- to 15-ribbed, light or dark green or bluish or purplish green stems, 5–15cm (2–6in) thick, each with a white-woolly crown. Pale brown-woolly areoles produce off-white to yellow and brown spines (10–18 radials, 3–6 centrals). Funnel-shaped, deep yellow, rarely orange-red flowers, 4–6cm (1½–2½in) across, are borne in summer. ↕ 3–15cm (1¼–6in), ↔ 18cm (7in). S. Brazil, S. Paraguay, N.E. Argentina, Uruguay. ❄ (min. 10°C/50°F)
P. penicillata, syn. *Notocactus penicillata*. Simple, spherical, later cylindrical cactus producing a mid-green stem with about 17–20 spiralling ribs and close-set tubercles. Brown-woolly areoles bear white, off-white, pale yellow, or pale brown spines (about 40 radials, 10–20 centrals). In summer, bears funnel-shaped, orange-yellow or vermilion-red flowers, 5cm (2in) across. ↕ 30cm (12in), ↔ 12cm (5in). N. Argentina. ❄ (min. 10°C/50°F)

Parodia nivosa

Parodia rutilans

P. rutilans ▣ syn. *Notocactus rutilans*. Simple cactus producing a spherical to cylindrical, bluish dark green stem with a slightly sunken, white-woolly crown and 18–24 spirally arranged ribs. White-woolly areoles produce reddish brown and brown-tipped white spines (14–16 radials, 2 slightly longer centrals). In summer, bears funnel-shaped flowers, 3–4cm (1¼–1½in) across, with pink-tipped petals and yellowish white throats. ↕↔ 5cm (2in). N. Uruguay. ❄ (min. 10°C/50°F)
P. sanguiniflora see *P. microsperma*.
P. schumanniana. Usually simple cactus producing a spherical to cylindrical, mid-green stem with 21–48 straight, acute ribs. White-woolly areoles bear golden yellow, brown, or reddish brown, later grey spines (about 4 radials, 3 or 4 shorter centrals). Produces funnel-shaped, lemon to golden yellow flowers, 4.5–7cm (1¾–3in) across, in summer. ↕ to 1.8m (6ft), ↔ 30cm (12in). S. Paraguay, N.E. Argentina. ❄ (min. 10°C/50°F)
P. scopa, syn. *Notocactus scopa* (Silver ball cactus). Simple or clustering cactus with spherical to cylindrical, 25- to 40-ribbed, dark green stems with spiny, woolly crowns. Grey areoles produce white, pale yellow, red, or brown spines (35–40 or more radials, 3 or 4 longer centrals). Funnel-shaped, bright yellow flowers, 4cm (1½in) across, appear in summer. ↕ 5–50cm (2–20in), ↔ 10cm (4in). S. Brazil, Uruguay. ❄ (min. 10°C/50°F)

PARONYCHIA

Whitlow-wort

CARYOPHYLLACEAE/ILLECEBRACEAE

Genus of about 50 species of annuals and evergreen, mat-forming perennials found mainly in hot, dry habitats around the Mediterranean and in N. Africa, with some in North America. They have linear to lance-shaped, silvery green leaves and dense, axillary cymes of very small, cup-shaped flowers surrounded by conspicuous, translucent silver bracts. Cultivated for their flowers and foliage, they are good carpeting plants for a rock garden.

- **HARDINESS** Fully hardy to half hardy.
- **CULTIVATION** Grow in sharply drained, poor to moderately fertile soil in full sun.
- **PROPAGATION** Divide in spring. Take stem-tip cuttings in early summer.
- **PESTS AND DISEASES** Trouble free.

P. capitata, syn. *P. nivea*. Vigorous, mat-forming perennial with linear-lance-shaped to oblong, silvery grey-green leaves, to 6mm (¼in) long. In summer, bears tiny green flowers in cymes to 1cm (½in) across, enclosed by ornamental, ovate, silvery, papery bracts. ↕ 5cm (2in), ↔ to 30cm (12in). Mediterranean. ✻✻✻
***P. kapela* subsp. *serpyllifolia*.** Very compact, mat-forming perennial with ovate to lance-shaped or elliptic, silvery bluish green leaves, to 4mm (⅛in) long. In summer, bears tiny, greenish white flowers in cymes to 2cm (¾in) across, enclosed by silvery white, papery bracts. ↕ to 5cm (2in), ↔ to 20cm (8in). Mediterranean. ✻✻✻
P. nivea see *P. capitata*.

▷ **Parrot feather** see *Myriophyllum aquaticum*

PARROTIA

HAMAMELIDACEAE

Genus of one species of deciduous tree occurring in forests in the Caucasus and N. Iran. *P. persica* is cultivated for its simple, alternate, rich green foliage, attractively coloured in autumn, for its peeling bark, and for its petalless flowers with bright red stamens, borne in dense clusters along the branches in late winter or early spring. Grow as a specimen tree, or in an open site in woodland.

- **HARDINESS** Fully hardy, but flower buds may be damaged by harsh frosts.
- **CULTIVATION** Grow in deep, fertile, moist but well-drained soil in full sun or partial shade. Grow in acid soil for best autumn colour. Pruning group 1.
- **PROPAGATION** Sow seed in containers in a cold frame in autumn. Take green-wood cuttings in early summer, or semi-ripe cuttings in mid- and late summer.
- **PESTS AND DISEASES** Trouble free.

P. persica ▣ ♀ (Persian ironwood). Dense, spreading, short-trunked tree with peeling, grey and fawn bark when mature. Obovate, glossy, rich green leaves, to 12cm (5in) long, turn yellow, orange, and red-purple in autumn. Tiny, spider-like red flowers are produced in spherical clusters, 1cm (½in) across, in late winter or early spring, before the leaves appear. ↕ 8m (25ft), ↔ 10m (30ft). Caucasus, N. Iran. ✻✻✻. **'Pendula'** ♀ is very compact and weeping. ↕ 1.5m (5ft), ↔ 3m (10ft).

PARROTIOPSIS

HAMAMELIDACEAE

Genus of one species of deciduous shrub occurring in forests in the W. Himalayas. It is cultivated for its showy flowerheads of petalless flowers, each with 20 or more yellow stamens surrounded by large bracts. Leaves are simple and arranged alternately. Grow as a specimen shrub.

- **HARDINESS** Fully hardy; but late frosts may damage flowerheads.
- **CULTIVATION** Grow in deep, fertile, preferably lime-free, moist but well-drained soil in full sun or partial shade. Pruning group 1.
- **PROPAGATION** Sow seed in containers in a cold frame in autumn. Take green-wood cuttings in early summer, or semi-ripe cuttings in late summer.
- **PESTS AND DISEASES** Trouble free.

P. jacquemontiana ♀ Upright shrub, or occasionally small tree, with very broadly ovate to ovate, mid-green leaves, to 10cm (4in) long. From mid-spring to early summer, produces spider-like flowerheads, to 5cm (2in) across, consisting of yellow-anthered stamens surrounded by conspicuous white bracts. ↕ 6m (20ft), ↔ 4m (12ft). W. Himalayas. ✻✻✻

▷ **Parrot leaf** see *Alternanthera ficoidea*
▷ **Parrot's beak** see *Lotus berthelotii*
▷ **Parrot's bill** see *Clianthus puniceus*
▷ **Parrot's flower** see *Heliconia psittacorum*

Parrotia persica (inset: leaf detail)

P

▷ **Parsley** see *Petroselinum, P. crispum*
Cow see *Anthriscus sylvestris*
French see *Petroselinum crispum* var. *neapolitanum*
Hamburg see *Petroselinum crispum* var. *tuberosum*
Italian see *Petroselinum crispum* var. *neapolitanum*

PARTHENOCISSUS

Virginia creeper

VITACEAE

Genus of about 10 species of deciduous tendril climbers found in forests in the Himalayas, E. Asia, and North America. Some species are twining, but more commonly they cling by disc-like suckers on the tips of tendrils. They are grown for their lobed or fully divided, palmate leaves, usually brightly coloured in autumn. Clusters of inconspicuous flowers, with 5, sometimes 4, short, thick green petals, are produced in summer, and may be followed by dark blue or black berries, to 8mm (3/8in) across. Grow through a large tree or use to cover a wall or fence. The foliage of wall-grown plants often harbours a variety of wildlife. The berries may cause mild stomach upset if ingested.

• **HARDINESS** Fully hardy; *P. henryana* is frost hardy if not grown against a wall.
• **CULTIVATION** Grow in any fertile, well-drained soil in shade or sun; *P. henryana* usually colours best in partial shade. Young plants may need support initially. Pruning group 11, in early winter and, if necessary, also in summer.
• **PROPAGATION** Sow seed in containers in a cold frame in autumn. Take softwood cuttings in early summer, greenwood cuttings in midsummer, or hardwood cuttings in winter.
• **PESTS AND DISEASES** Trouble free.

Parthenocissus henryana

Parthenocissus thomsonii

Parthenocissus tricuspidata

P. henryana ■ syn. *Vitis henryana* (Chinese Virginia creeper). Woody climber with palmate, dark green leaves composed of 3–5 oval, toothed leaflets, to 12cm (5in) long, conspicuously veined white, and sometimes pink in the centres, turning bright red in autumn. ↕10m (30ft). China. ✱✱✱ (borderline)

P. quinquefolia, syn. *Vitis quinquefolia* (Virginia creeper). Vigorous, woody climber with palmate, dull, mid-green leaves composed of usually 5 oval, sharply toothed leaflets, to 10cm (4in) long, turning brilliant red in autumn. ↕15m (50ft) or more. E. North America. ✱✱✱

Parthenocissus tricuspidata 'Lowii'

P. striata see *Cissus striata*.

P. thomsonii ■ syn. *Cayratia thomsonii, Vitis thomsonii.* Woody climber with palmate, dark green leaves consisting of usually 5 oval, sharply toothed leaflets, to 10cm (4in) long, reddish purple when young, turning purple-green in summer and bright red in autumn. ↕10m (30ft). China, Himalayas. ✱✱✱

P. tricuspidata ■ (Boston ivy). Vigorous, woody climber with variable, broadly ovate, deeply toothed, bright green leaves, to 20cm (8in) long, either 3-lobed or with 3 ovate leaflets, turning brilliant red to purple in autumn. ↕20m (70ft). China, Korea, Japan. ✱✱✱. **'Beverley Brook'** has purple-tinged summer foliage, turning brilliant red in autumn. **'Lowii'** ■ has small, deeply 3- to 7-lobed leaves, 10cm (4in) long. **'Veitchii'** ■ syn. *Ampelopsis veitchii*, has dark red-purple foliage in autumn.

▷ **Partridge berry** see *Mitchella, M. repens*
▷ **Pasque flower** see *Pulsatilla vulgaris*
Alpine see *P. alpina*
Eastern see *P. patens*

Parthenocissus tricuspidata 'Veitchii'

PASSIFLORA

Granadilla, Passion flower

PASSIFLORACEAE

Genus of more than 400 species of mostly evergreen tendril climbers, and a few annuals, perennials, shrubs, and trees. They occur usually in tropical woodland, on rocks, and in grassland, mainly in tropical North, Central, and South America, and also in tropical Asia, Australia, New Zealand, and the Pacific islands. The leaves are usually alternate, simple or 2- to 9-lobed (mainly 3- or 5-lobed), elliptic to rounded or broadly ovate, and often with prominent nectar glands on the margins or stalks. The exotic flowers are mostly produced singly, sometimes in racemes, from the upper leaf axils. Each has a wide, tubular base and 10, sometimes 5 tepals, that spread out flat, reflex, or form a saucer or bowl shape. A stalk in the centre of each flower bears the ovary and stamens, and is surrounded by one or several rings of fleshy filaments (the corona). The ovoid to spherical, edible, usually yellow fruits are very variable in size. Hardy species are ideal for clothing a wall or trellis. In frost-prone areas, grow tender species in a cool to warm greenhouse. In warmer climates, train over a pergola or arch, or through a tree.

• **HARDINESS** Fully hardy to frost tender. *P.* 'Amethyst', *P. manicata*, and *P.* 'Star of Bristol' may survive temperatures down to 0°C (32°F) if the wood has been well-ripened in summer.
• **CULTIVATION** Under glass, plant in a greenhouse border or in large tubs of loam-based potting compost (JI No.3) in full light, with shade from hot sun. Water freely when in growth, sparingly in winter. Top-dress annually in spring. Outdoors, grow in moderately fertile, moist but well-drained soil in full sun or partial shade, with shelter from cold, drying winds. Pruning group 11 or 12, if necessary, in early spring.
• **PROPAGATION** Sow seed at 13–18°C (55–64°F) in spring. Take semi-ripe cuttings in summer. Layer in spring or autumn.
• **PESTS AND DISEASES** Prone to viruses, especially cucumber mosaic virus, and to red spider mites, whiteflies, mealybugs, and scale insects under glass.

P. alata (Maracuja de refresco, Winged-stem passion flower). Robust climber with sparsely branched, 4-winged stems

Passiflora 'Amethyst'

P

and broadly ovate or oblong-ovate, sometimes finely toothed, rich to light green leaves, 8–15cm (3–6in) long. From spring to late summer, bears nodding, fragrant, bowl-shaped, bright carmine-red flowers, 10–12cm (4–5in) across, with curved outer tepals, opening from light crimson buds; coronas have purple, red, and white zones. Bears ovoid to pear-shaped, yellow fruit, 10–15cm (4–6in) long. ↕ to 6m (20ft) or more. Peru to E. Brazil. ❀ (min. 5–7°C/41–45°F)

P.* x *alatocaerulea see *P.* x *belotii.*

P.* x *allardii (*P. caerulea* 'Constance Elliott' x *P. quadrangularis*). Vigorous, woody tendril climber with 3-lobed, dark green leaves, to 15cm (6in) long. Bowl-shaped, pink-flushed white flowers, to 10cm (4in) or more across, with coronas banded purple, red, and white, are produced from summer to autumn. Bears ovoid, bright orange fruit, to 6cm (2½in) long, without seeds. ↕ 10m (30ft). Garden origin. ✲

***P.* 'Amethyst'** ▣ syn. *P. amethystina* of gardens, *P.* 'Lavender Lady', *P. violacea* of gardens. Vigorous climber with smooth, slender stems and deeply 3-lobed, membranous, rich green leaves, 6–8cm (2½–3in) long. In late summer and autumn, produces bowl-shaped, purple to purple-blue flowers, to 11cm (4½in) across, with green anthers, tepals that reflex as the flower fades, and darker corona filaments. Bears ellipsoid orange fruit, to 6cm (2½in) long. ↕ 4m (12ft) or more. Garden origin. ❀ (min. 5°C/41°F)

***P. amethystina* of gardens** see *P.* 'Amethyst'.

P. antioquiensis ▣ syn. *Tacsonia van-volxemii* (Red banana passion flower). Vigorous climber with slender, branched stems and finely toothed, deeply 3-lobed, mid- to deep green leaves, 10–15cm (4–6in) long, downy beneath, each lobe with a slender point; occasionally produces simple, ovate to lance-shaped leaves. Bears long-tubed, bright rose-red, rarely pink flowers, to 14cm (5½in) across, with small violet coronas, mainly in summer. Ellipsoid yellow fruit, to 10cm (4in) long, have a delicate flavour. ↕ 5m (15ft) or more. Colombia. ❀ (min. 5–7°C/41–45°F)

P.* x *belotii (*P. alata* x *P. caerulea*) syn. *P.* x *alatocaerulea*, *P.* 'Empress Eugenie'. Vigorous climber with slender, 4- or 5-winged, often red-tinted stems. Mid-green leaves, 14cm (5½in) long, each have 3 deep, ovate lobes, the central one

Passiflora antioquiensis

Passiflora caerulea

largest. From summer to autumn, bears fragrant, bowl-shaped white flowers, 11–13cm (4½–5in) across, the longer inner tepals tinted or dotted purple or red; coronas have blue, purple, and white zones. ↕ 5m (15ft) or more. Garden origin. ❀ (min. 5°C/41°F)

P. caerulea ▣ (Blue passion flower). Fast-growing climber with moderately branching, slender, 4-angled, grooved stems bearing rich green leaves, to 10cm (4in) long, divided almost to the base into 3–9, usually 5, oblong lobes. From summer to autumn, bears bowl-shaped, white, sometimes pink-tinged flowers, 7–10cm (3–4in) across, with purple-, blue-, and white-zoned coronas. Ovoid, orange-yellow fruit, to 6cm (2½in) long, are edible but not flavoursome. ↕ 10m (30ft) or more. C. and W. South America. ✲✲. **'Constance Elliott'** ▣ has fragrant white flowers with pale blue or white filaments. **'Grandiflora'** has flowers to 15cm (6in) across.

P.* x *caeruleoracemosa ▣ (*P. caerulea* x *P. racemosa*). Variable, vigorous climber with branching, slender, smooth stems and deeply 3- to 5-lobed, rich green leaves, 12–15cm (5–6in) long. From summer to autumn, bears bowl-shaped,

Passiflora caerulea 'Constance Elliott'

Passiflora x *caeruleoracemosa*

red-purple flowers, 10–13cm (4–5in) wide, with spreading corona filaments, deep purple to black at the bases and white above. Produces ovoid green fruit, to 6cm (2½in) long. ↕ 6m (20ft) or more. Garden origin. ❀ (min. 5°C/41°F).

P. coccinea ▣ syn. *P. fulgens*, *P. velutina* (Red granadilla). Vigorous climber with very slender, smooth, red to purple stems, and oblong-ovate, mid-green leaves, 6–14cm (2½–5½in) long, with soft, red-brown hairs and large, lobe-like teeth. From midsummer to autumn, produces saucer-shaped scarlet flowers, 8–10cm (3–4in) across; coronas have purple, pale pink, and white zones. Spherical to ovoid, finely white-woolly fruit, 5cm (2in) long, ripen orange or yellow with darker stripes. ↕ 4m (12ft) or more. N.W. South America. ❀ (min. 10–13°C/50–55°F)

P. edulis (Passion fruit, Purple granadilla). Vigorous, woody climber with 3-lobed, toothed, glossy, mid-green leaves, to 20cm (8in) long. In summer, produces bowl-shaped white flowers, 7cm (3in) across, green beneath, with wavy, purple-zoned white coronas and ovoid, yellow to purple fruit, 5cm (2in)

Passiflora coccinea

long. ↕ 5m (15ft). Brazil. ❀ (min. 16°C/61°F)

***P.* 'Empress Eugenie'** see *P.* x *belotii.*

P.* x *exoniensis (*P. antioquiensis* x *P. mollissima*) syn. *Tacsonia* x *exoniensis.* Robust climber with branching, slender stems. Downy, rich green leaves, 10cm (4in) long, each have 3 wide-spreading, narrowly lance-shaped, toothed lobes. In summer, produces semi-pendent, long-tubed flowers, 10–13cm (4–5in) wide, dark pink in bud, opening to rose-pink, with short white coronas. Bears banana-shaped fruit, to 9cm (3½in) long, yellow when ripe. ↕ 6m (20ft) or more. Garden origin. ❀ (min. 5°C/41°F)

P. fulgens see *P. coccinea.*

P. incarnata (Maypops). Tendril climber with deeply 3- to 5-lobed, finely toothed, dark green leaves, to 15cm (6in) long. Bowl-shaped, scented, pale purple to nearly white flowers, 8cm (3in) across, with purple and white coronas, are produced in summer, followed by ovoid yellow fruit, to 6cm (2½in) long. ↕ 2m (6ft). E. USA. ✲✲✲

***P.* 'Lavender Lady'** see *P.* 'Amethyst'.

P. manicata ▣ Robust climber with branching, angular stems bearing glossy, rich green leaves, to 10cm (4in) long,

Passiflora manicata

Passiflora quadrangularis

with 3 broad, ovate, sharply toothed lobes, densely woolly beneath. From spring to autumn, produces saucer-shaped, bright red flowers, 10cm (4in) across, white at the bases, with short, purple-blue and white coronas. Bears ovoid, glossy, deep green fruit, to 5cm (2in) long. ↕ 3m (10ft). N. South America. ❄ (min. 5–7°C/41–45°F)

P. mollissima, syn. *Tacsonia mollissima* (Banana passion flower). Fast-growing climber with moderately branching, slender, downy stems. Softly white-downy, ovate-oblong, mid-green leaves, 10cm (4in) long, have heart-shaped bases and 3 broad, toothed lobes. From midsummer to late autumn, bears pendent, long-tubed, bowl-shaped, pink to coral-pink flowers, 6–9cm (2½–3½in) across; the inner 5 tepals are shorter and darker-tinted than the outer 5, and the corona is reduced to a purple, warty ring. Produces oblong-ovoid, flavoursome yellow fruit, to 8cm (3in) long. ↕ 5m (15ft) or more. N. South America. ❄ (min. 7°C/45°F)

P. organensis. Woody climber with variable, 2-lobed, rarely 3-lobed, usually broadly wedge-shaped, mid-green leaves, 2–4cm (¾–1½in) long, flecked cream and pink above, purple beneath. In summer, bears bowl-shaped, cream to dark purple flowers, 5cm (2in) across, with similarly coloured coronas. Produces spherical, yellow-green fruit, to 1.5cm (½in) across. ↕ 2.5m (8ft). Brazil. ❄ (min. 16°C/61°F)

Passiflora racemosa

P. quadrangularis ▣ (Giant granadilla). Strong-growing, tuberous-rooted climber with sparsely branched, 4-angled, winged stems and broadly ovate, rich green leaves, 10–25cm (4–10in) long, with abrupt, slender points. From midsummer to autumn, bears nodding, fragrant, bowl-shaped, pale to deep red flowers, to 12cm (5in) across; they have massive coronas of wavy filaments, 6cm (2½in) long, banded red-purple and white with pink, red, or violet mottling. Greenish yellow to orange, oblong-ovoid fruit, 20–30cm (8–12in) long, have sweetly acid pulp. ↕ 15m (50ft) or more. Central and South America, West Indies. ❄ (min. 13°C/55°F)

P. racemosa ▣ (Red passion flower). Vigorous, woody climber with slender, angled stems. The leathery, glossy, mid-green leaves, to 10cm (4in) long, are ovate and simple, or with 3 oblong lobes. Bowl-shaped, bright red flowers, 12cm (5in) across, with purple and white coronas, are borne in pendent racemes, to 30cm (12in) long, in summer and autumn. Produces oblong, deep green fruit, to 8cm (3in) long, becoming paler as they ripen. ↕ 5m (15ft). Brazil. ❄ (min. 16°C/61°F)

P. sanguinea see *P. vitifolia*.

***P.* 'Star of Bristol'.** Vigorous climber with sparsely branched, slender stems, and rounded, 3- to 5-lobed, dark green leaves, 8–10cm (3–4in) long, the central lobe longest. From summer to autumn, produces saucer- or star-shaped, rich mauve flowers, 10–11cm (4–4½in) across, with darker, spreading coronas. Bears ovoid, bright orange fruit, 5cm (2in) long. ↕ to 4m (12ft). ❄ (min. 5–7°C/41–45°F)

P. velutina see *P. coccinea*.

***P. violacea* of gardens** see *P.* 'Amethyst'.

P. vitifolia, syn. *P. sanguinea*. Vigorous climber with moderately branching, slender, downy, reddish brown stems. Glossy, dark green leaves, 7–14cm (3–5½in) long, have 3 ovate, toothed or scalloped lobes, minutely hairy on the veins. From early summer to autumn, bears bowl-shaped, glowing, bright red flowers, 12–19cm (5–7in) across, with coronas of short, pale red or white filaments and longer, dark red or yellow ones. Produces ovoid, downy, yellow-green fruit, 6cm (2½in) long, with white mottling. ↕ 5m (15ft) or more. Nicaragua to Peru. ❄ (min. 13°C/55°F)

▷ **Passion flower** see *Passiflora*
Banana see *P. mollissima*
Blue see *P. caerulea*
Red see *P. racemosa*
Red banana see *P. antioquiensis*
Winged-stem see *P. alata*
▷ **Passion fruit** see *Passiflora edulis*

PATERSONIA

IRIDACEAE

Genus of 13–18 species of tufted, evergreen, rhizomatous perennials occurring in dry grassland or scrub in Borneo, New Guinea, and Australia. They are cultivated for their short-lived, iris-like, blue or purple, occasionally yellow or white flowers, with 3 broad, spreading outer tepals and 3 smaller, erect inner tepals, the inner ones sometimes absent. They are produced few to many in each inflorescence, on erect to spreading stems in spring or summer. Fans of linear, mid- to grey-green leaves arise from the bases of the stems. In frost-prone areas, grow in a cool greenhouse or conservatory. In warmer areas, grow in a border.

- **HARDINESS** Frost tender.
- **CULTIVATION** Under glass, grow in loam-based potting compost (JI No.2), with added grit, in full light. During the growing season, water freely and apply a balanced liquid fertilizer monthly. Water sparingly in winter. Outdoors, grow in light, fertile, well-drained soil in full sun.
- **PROPAGATION** Sow seed at 13–18°C (55–64°F), or divide, in autumn.
- **PESTS AND DISEASES** Trouble free.

P. glabrata. Rhizomatous perennial with very narrow, mid-green leaves, to 30cm (12in) long. Purple flowers, to 3.5cm (1½in) long, are produced in summer on stems 15cm (6in) long. ↕ to 30cm (12in), ↔ 23cm (9in). Australia (Victoria, New South Wales, Queensland). ❄ (min. 5°C/41°F)

Patersonia sericea

P. occidentalis. Tuft-forming, rhizomatous perennial with few or many mid-green leaves, to 40cm (16in) long. In spring and summer, purple or deep blue flowers, 3.5cm (1½in) long, are borne on stems to 50cm (20in) long. ↕ to 50cm (20in), ↔ 30cm (12in). Australia (Western Australia). ❄ (min. 5°C/41°F)

P. sericea ▣ Rhizomatous perennial with very rigid, erect, mid-green leaves, 55cm (22in) long. Deep purple-blue flowers, 3.5cm (1½in) long, are produced on woolly stems, to 50cm (20in) long, in summer. ↕ 30cm (12in), ↔ 23cm (9in). Australia (Victoria, New South Wales, Queensland). ❄ (min. 5°C/41°F)

P. umbrosa. Rhizomatous perennial with rigid, mid-green leaves, 60–100cm (24–39in) long. In summer, produces blue flowers, 3–4cm (1¼–1½in) long, on stems 80cm (32in) long. ↕ to 1m (3ft), ↔ 30cm (12in). Australia (Western Australia). ❄ (min. 5°C/41°F). **f. *xanthina*** has yellow flowers.

PATRINIA

VALERIANACEAE

Genus of about 15 species of clump-forming herbaceous perennials occurring in grassy mountain habitats in Siberia and Japan. They are cultivated for their long-stemmed, sometimes corymb-like panicles of small, 5-lobed, cup-shaped, yellow or white flowers, produced in summer. The leaves are mainly basal, ovate to rounded, lobed, palmate, or pinnate, rarely entire, and mid- to dark green. Grow in a woodland garden or rock garden, in a mixed or herbaceous border, or as ground cover.

- **HARDINESS** Fully hardy.
- **CULTIVATION** Grow in fertile, humus-rich, moist soil in partial or deep shade.

Patrinia triloba var. *palmata*

• **PROPAGATION** Sow seed as soon as ripe in containers in a cold frame. Divide in spring.
• **PESTS AND DISEASES** Young leaves may be damaged by slugs and snails.

P. triloba. Clump-forming, stoloniferous perennial with palmately 3- to 5-lobed, mid-green leaves, 6–10cm (2½–4in) across, turning yellow in autumn. In mid- and late summer, branching, red-tinted stems produce panicles, to 10cm (4in) across, of small, fragrant, cup-shaped yellow flowers, each with a short tube and 5 spreading lobes. ↕ 20–50cm (8–20in), ↔ 15–30cm (6–12in). Japan. ❄❄❄. **var. *palmata*** ▣ has flowers with short spurs.

PAULOWNIA

SCROPHULARIACEAE

Genus of 6 species of deciduous trees occurring in woodland in E. Asia. They produce stout shoots and usually large, hairy, opposite, ovate or 3- to 5-lobed, mid- or yellow-green leaves, often with heart-shaped bases. The flower buds are formed in autumn, and open, before the leaves appear, to bell- to trumpet-shaped, foxglove-like flowers, borne in terminal panicles. Grown for their habit, attractive foliage, and showy flowers, they are fine specimen trees for a lawn. They grow and flower best in climates with long, hot summers. In frost-prone areas, grow paulownias as pollards, which will produce very large, ornamental leaves.
• **HARDINESS** Fully hardy; young plants may be damaged by frost.
• **CULTIVATION** Grow in fertile, well-drained soil in full sun. In frost-prone areas, shelter from cold, drying winds. Unripened growth and exposed flower buds may be damaged by late frosts. Pruning group 1, or group 7 if larger leaves are desired.
• **PROPAGATION** Sow seed in containers in a cold frame in autumn or spring. Take root cuttings in winter. Over-winter young plants under glass in their first year.
• **PESTS AND DISEASES** Canker, honey fungus, leaf spot, and powdery mildew may cause problems.

P. fortunei ♀ Broadly columnar tree with stout shoots and ovate, mid-green leaves, to 20cm (8in) long, glossy above and densely hairy beneath. Fragrant flowers, 10cm (4in) long, pale purple outside and creamy white with purple spots inside, are produced in upright panicles in late spring. ↕↔ 8m (25ft). China, Taiwan. ❄❄❄
P. imperialis see *P. tomentosa.*
P. tomentosa ▣♀ syn. *P. imperialis* (Empress tree, Foxglove tree, Princess tree). Fast-growing, broadly columnar tree with stout shoots and ovate, sometimes shallowly lobed, bright light green leaves, to 30cm (12in) long, hairy above, densely hairy beneath. Fragrant, pinkish lilac flowers, 5cm (2in) long, with purple and yellow marks inside, are borne in upright panicles in late spring. ↕ 12m (40ft), ↔ 10m (30ft). China. ❄❄❄

▷ ***Paurotis wrightii*** see *Acoelorraphe wrightii*

Paulownia tomentosa (inset: flower detail)

PAVETTA

RUBIACEAE

Genus of about 350 species of evergreen shrubs, subshrubs, and trees, related to *Ixora*, found in grassland, thickets, and woodland in tropical and subtropical Africa and Asia. They are grown for their variable, simple leaves, opposite or in whorls of 3, often membranous with tiny black glands, and for their small, tubular flowers with 4 spreading petal lobes (cylindrical to salverform or funnel-shaped), borne in terminal cymes or corymbs. Where temperatures fall below 7°C (45°F), grow in a temperate or warm greenhouse. In warmer regions, grow in a shrub border.
• **HARDINESS** Frost tender.
• **CULTIVATION** Under glass, grow in loam-based potting compost (JI No.3), with added sharp sand, in full light with shade from hot sun, and with high humidity. In spring and summer, water freely and apply a balanced liquid fertilizer monthly. Water sparingly in winter. Outdoors, grow in fertile, moist but well-drained soil in full sun. Pruning group 1; may need restrictive pruning under glass.
• **PROPAGATION** Sow seed at 18–21°C (64–70°F) in spring. Root semi-ripe cuttings in summer, with bottom heat.
• **PESTS AND DISEASES** Trouble free.

P. caffra see *P. capensis.*
P. capensis, syn. *P. caffra*. Bushy, erect then spreading shrub with white-downy stems and obovate, mid-green leaves, to 5cm (2in) long, with pointed tips. Dense, flattened corymbs, 2.5–4cm (1–1½in) across, of white flowers, 2cm (¾in) long, appear in summer, followed by spherical, glossy black fruit, to 1cm (½in) across. ↕↔ 1–2m (3–6ft). South Africa (Western Cape, Eastern Cape). ❀ (min. 7°C/45°F)

PAVONIA

MALVACEAE

Genus of about 150 species of evergreen perennials, subshrubs, and shrubs, often occurring on sandy soils in tropical and subtropical regions of Africa, Asia, the Pacific islands, and North and South America. They are grown for their brightly coloured flowers, solitary, axillary, or borne in terminal, spherical clusters or panicles, mainly in summer. Petals are spreading, or form a tube surrounded by a bell- or cup-shaped calyx, with a whorl of hairy bracts beneath; the stamens and anthers are often protruding. Most have alternate, linear to broadly ovate or oblong, light to dark green leaves, each with a bract-like stipule at the base of the leaf-stalk. In subtropical and tropical gardens, grow among shrubs or in a border. In cooler areas, grow in a warm greenhouse.
• **HARDINESS** Frost tender.
• **CULTIVATION** Under glass, grow in loam-based potting compost (JI No.3) in bright filtered light, with high humidity. When in growth, water freely and apply a balanced liquid fertilizer monthly. Water sparingly in winter. Outdoors, grow in fertile, humus-rich, well-drained soil in full sun or partial shade. Pruning group 1; may need restrictive pruning under glass.
• **PROPAGATION** Sow seed at 19–24°C (66–75°F) in spring. Root semi-ripe cuttings with bottom heat in summer.
• **PESTS AND DISEASES** Red spider mites and whiteflies may be troublesome.

P. x gledhillii (*P. mackoyana* x *P. multiflora*) syn. *P. intermedia* of gardens, *P. multiflora* of gardens. Sparsely branched shrub with pointed, elliptic to lance-shaped, glossy, light green leaves, 10–15cm (4–6in) long, with linear to lance-shaped stipules. In late summer, bears solitary, dark purple flowers, to 3cm (1¼in) long, enclosed in almost cylindrical, hairy calyces with grey-pink teeth, and each with a whorl of red bracts beneath; the stamens have red filaments and chalky, lilac-blue anthers. ↕ to 2m (6ft), ↔ 1m (3ft). Garden origin. ❀ (min. 16–18°C/61–64°F)
***P. intermedia* of gardens** see *P.* x *gledhillii.*
***P. multiflora* of gardens** see *P.* x *gledhillii.*

▷ **Pawpaw** see *Asimina triloba*

PAXISTIMA syn. PACHYSTIMA

CELASTRACEAE

Genus of 2 species of low-growing, evergreen shrubs found in rocky sites on mountains and in coniferous woodland in North America. They are grown for their small, opposite, linear to ovate or oblong, sometimes finely toothed, leathery leaves. Tiny, cross-shaped, 4-petalled, greenish white or white flowers, solitary or in axillary clusters, are produced in summer. Grow as ground cover in a rock garden or peat terrace.
• **HARDINESS** Fully hardy.
• **CULTIVATION** Grow in moderately fertile, humus-rich, moist but well-drained soil in full sun or light dappled shade.
• **PROPAGATION** Take semi-ripe cuttings in summer. Remove rooted suckers in spring or autumn.
• **PESTS AND DISEASES** Trouble free.

P. canbyi. Spreading, branching, stem-rooting shrub with stalkless, linear-oblong, sometimes finely toothed, glossy, dark green leaves, to 2cm (¾in) long, with incurved margins. Bears short, pendent clusters of greenish white flowers, 5mm (¼in) across, in summer. ↕ 40cm (16in), ↔ to 1m (3ft). C. North America. ❄❄❄

▷ **Pea,**
Balloon see *Sutherlandia frutescens*
Black coral see *Kennedia nigricans*
Blue see *Clitoria ternatea*
Bush see *Pultenaea procumbens*
Chickling see *Lathyrus sativus*
Coral see *Hardenbergia, Kennedia*
Dusky coral see *Kennedia rubicunda*
Everlasting see *Lathyrus, L. grandiflorus, L. latifolius*
Glory see *Clianthus formosus, C. puniceus*
Heart see *Cardiospermum halicacabum*
Lord Anson's blue see *Lathyrus nervosus*
Perennial see *Lathyrus latifolius, L. sylvestris*
Persian everlasting see *Lathyrus rotundifolius*

P

PEDILANTHUS

EUPHORBIACEAE

Genus of about 14 species of variable, bushy, succulent shrubs and small trees occurring mainly in low, rocky terrain in Mexico, Central and South America, the West Indies, and Florida, USA. Many species branch from the roots to form clumps. The fleshy, narrow to broadly ovate, light to mid-green, sometimes white-mottled leaves are usually quickly deciduous. Terminal or axillary cymes of flower-like, tubular bract-cups are borne during the day in summer. Where temperatures drop below 10°C (50°F), grow as houseplants or in a warm greenhouse. In warmer areas, use in a desert garden or shrub border. The stems and leaves contain a milky sap that may cause stomach upset if ingested.

• **HARDINESS** Frost tender.

Pedilanthus tithymaloides 'Variegatus'

• **CULTIVATION** Under glass, grow in loam-based potting compost (JI No.2), with added well-rotted organic matter and sharp sand, in bright filtered light. In spring and summer, water moderately and apply a balanced liquid fertilizer every month. Water sparingly in winter. Outdoors, grow in moderately fertile, sharply drained soil in full sun or partial shade. See also pp.48–49.

• **PROPAGATION** Sow seed at 19–24°C (66–75°F) in spring. Take stem-tip cuttings in summer.

• **PESTS AND DISEASES** Trouble free.

P. bracteatus. Bushy, succulent shrub, branching freely from the base, with straight stems. Deciduous, ovate to inversely lance-shaped, white-powdery, mid-green leaves, 10cm (4in) or more long, are keeled beneath, with blunt or pointed tips. In summer, produces green bract-cups, 1.5cm (½in) long, with crimson glands. ↕ 1–3m (3–10ft), ↔ 45cm (18in). N.W. Mexico. ❄ (min. 10°C/50°F)

P. tithymaloides. Upright, bushy, clump-forming, succulent shrub with thin, woody or fleshy, zigzagged stems. Evergreen or deciduous, ovate to elliptic, mid-green leaves, to 8cm (3in) long, are keeled and slightly hairy or powdery beneath. In summer, produces fleshy red bract-cups, to 1.5cm (½in) long, yellow-green at the bases. ↕ 2m (6ft), ↔ to 1m (3ft). USA (Florida) to Venezuela, West Indies. ❄ (min. 10°C/50°F).

'Variegatus' ■ has variably shaped leaves, to 15cm (6in) long, with white or pink variegation; ↔ to 45cm (18in).

PEDIOCACTUS

CACTACEAE

Genus of about 6 species of simple or clustering, spherical, perennial cacti occurring in rocky terrain in W. and S. USA. The spiny stems have spiralling, tuberculate ribs. Bell-shaped flowers are produced near or at the stem tips, followed by spherical, pink or greenish yellow fruits. Where temperatures drop below 2°C (36°F), grow as houseplants or in a cool greenhouse. In warmer areas, grow in a raised bed or desert garden.

• **HARDINESS** Frost tender.

• **CULTIVATION** Under glass, grow in standard cactus compost in full light. From spring to summer, water moderately and apply a low-nitrogen fertilizer every 6–8 weeks. Keep dry at other times. Outdoors, grow in moderately fertile, sharply drained soil in full sun. See also pp.48–49.

• **PROPAGATION** Sow seed at 19–24°C (66–75°F) in spring.

• **PESTS AND DISEASES** Susceptible to mealybugs early in the growing season.

P. simpsonii. Simple or clustering cactus with spherical to ovoid, mid-green stems, each with 12 ribs, and white-woolly areoles bearing fine spines (15–25 white radials and 5–10 slightly longer, reddish brown centrals). In spring, white, pink, magenta, yellow, or yellow-green flowers, 1–3cm (½–1¼in) long, are borne singly or in clusters by day. ↕ 12–15cm (5–6in), ↔ to 15cm (6in). W. USA. ❄ (min. 2°C/36°F)

PELARGONIUM

GERANIACEAE

Genus of about 230 species of mainly evergreen perennials, succulents, subshrubs, and shrubs, commonly but incorrectly known as geraniums. They occur in a variety of habitats, from mountains to deserts, mostly in South Africa. The many cultivars, derived from about 20 species, are popular garden plants; few species are grown. Leaves are variable, but are usually alternate, palmately lobed or pinnate, sometimes aromatic, often on long stalks. Erect stems bear 5-petalled flowers in terminal, umbel-like clusters (pseudoumbels) referred to in this account as "clusters". The flowers are saucer- or star-shaped, trumpet- or funnel-shaped, or "butterfly"-shaped (the upper 2 petals larger than the lower 3); they are usually borne from spring to summer, although many will flower throughout the year if kept above 7–10°C (45–50°F).

In frost-prone areas, use in containers outside in summer or as bedding plants, and overwinter in a cool greenhouse or conservatory. In frost-free areas, grow in a sunny border. Use scented-leaved cultivars as edging for a border or alongside a path. For winter flowers, grow in a temperate greenhouse or as houseplants. Contact with the foliage may occasionally aggravate skin allergies.

Most cultivars belong to one of the following 6 horticultural groups.

Angel
Very bushy, evergreen perennials and subshrubs, derived mainly from *P. crispum*. They have rounded, sometimes scented, usually mid-green leaves, 1–3cm (½–1¼in) long, and clusters of small, single flowers of the regal type (see panel), to 3cm (1¼in) across, in shades of pink, purple, mauve, or white.

Ivy-leaved
Trailing, evergreen perennials with lobed, sometimes pointed, stiff, fleshy, usually mid-green leaves, 2.5–12cm (1–5in) long, very similar to those of ivy (*Hedera helix*). Some cultivars have short-jointed stems. Clusters of single to double flowers, to 4cm (1½in) across, are produced in shades of red, pink, mauve, purple, or white.

Regal
Bushy, evergreen perennials and shrubs, some with short-jointed stems. The leaves are rounded, sometimes lobed or partially toothed, and mid-green, 5–9cm (2–3½in) long. Clusters of single, rarely double flowers, to 4cm (1½in) across, are produced in single or combined shades of red, pink, purple, orange, white, or reddish black.

Scented-leaved
Shrubby, evergreen perennials and shrubs grown mainly for their attractive leaves, which release scent when brushed; each cultivar has a distinct perfume. Leaves are mainly mid-green, sometimes variegated, or gold or silver, and are very variable in shape and size, usually 1.5–12cm (½–5in) long, sometimes toothed, lobed, or deeply incised. They bear clusters of small, single flowers, to 2.5cm (1in) across, in shades of mauve, pink, purple, or white.

Unique
Shrubby, evergreen perennials with rounded or lobed, sometimes incised, mid-green leaves, 5–14cm (2–5½in) across, often with a pungent scent when crushed. They produce clusters of trumpet-shaped, single, white, pink, red, purple, or orange flowers of the regal type (see panel), to 3cm (1¼in) across.

PELARGONIUM GROUPS

Leaves and flower clusters (pseudoumbels) of the 4 main pelargonium groups are shown here. Angel and unique pelargoniums have clusters similar to those of regal pelargoniums.

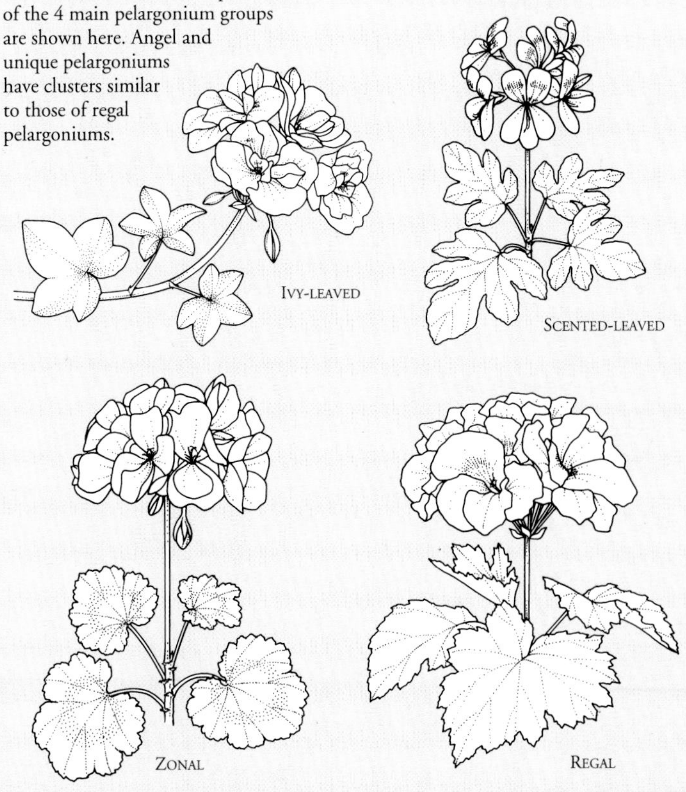

Pelargonium 'Apple Blossom Rosebud'

Zonal
Erect, bushy, succulent-stemmed, evergreen perennials, some with short-jointed stems, derived mainly from *P. inquinans* and *P. zonale*. The leaves are rounded, 4–14cm (1½–5½in) across, light to deep green, often bicoloured or multi-coloured, with zones of dark bronze-green or maroon. Flowers are single, semi-double, or double, to 2.5cm (1in) across, in shades of scarlet, purple, pink, white, orange, or rarely yellow. Rain may damage the blooms of some double-flowered cultivars; these should be grown under glass. As bedding plants, most grow to 60cm (24in) tall; dwarf cultivars are 12–20cm (5–8in) tall, miniature cultivars to 12cm (5in) tall.

There are 2 main groups of zonal pelargoniums: the seed-raised bedding types, mainly comprising the single-flowered F1 hybrids, which flower in the first year and come true to colour and type when raised from seed; and the large-flowered cultivars propagated only from cuttings, which are ideal container plants in a conservatory or as house-plants, or outdoors in frost-free periods.

Zonal pelargoniums can be separated into the following groups:
Cactus-flowered – Flowers, resembling those of cactus dahlias, are single or double, the petals twisted into quills.
Double- and semi-double-flowered – Flowers normally comprise 6 or more open petals.
Fancy-leaved – These are grown mainly for their foliage, which may be silver or gold tricoloured (silver or gold, usually with white and green), bronze and gold, almost black, or butterfly-leaved with a distinct hue in the leaf centre. Flowers are often small and single, rarely double.
Formosum hybrids – Flowers are flat, single or double, with narrow petals. Leaves are deeply incised.
Rosebud – Flowers are double, with rosebud-like centres (the central petals remaining unopened).
Single-flowered – Flowers usually have no more than 5 petals.
Stellar – Flowers are irregularly star-shaped, single or double: the bottom 3 petals are wedge-shaped and broad, the top 2 are much narrower and toothed. Leaves have pointed lobes and, in some cultivars, dark, often central zones.

• **HARDINESS** Mostly frost tender; there are 1 or 2 hardy species from Turkey.
• **CULTIVATION** Under glass, grow in loamless or loam-based potting compost (JI No.2) in full light, with shade from hot sun and good ventilation. Water moderately during growth; apply a balanced liquid fertilizer every 10–14 days in spring and early summer, and a high-potash fertilizer when in flower. Water sparingly in winter. If kept at 7–10°C (45–50°F), plants may flower over winter. Otherwise, cut back by up to two-thirds and keep almost dry. Outdoors, grow in fertile, neutral to alkaline, well-drained soil. Most prefer full sun; regal cultivars prefer partial shade, and zonals tolerate some shade. Lift bedding plants in autumn and over-winter in dry, frost-free conditions; cut back top-growth by one-third and repot in late winter as new growth resumes. Dead-head all pelargoniums regularly.
• **PROPAGATION** Sow seed of species and F1 zonal pelargoniums at 13–18°C (55–64°F) in late winter and early spring. Take softwood cuttings in spring, late summer, or early autumn.
• **PESTS AND DISEASES** Susceptible to vine weevils, leafhoppers, root mealy-bugs, aphids, caterpillars, western flower thrips, sciarid flies, grey mould (*Botrytis*), and black leg. Zonal pelargoniums are particularly prone to rust, and regal pelargoniums to whiteflies.

P. abrotanifolium. Bushy, erect, evergreen, woody-stemmed subshrub. Rounded, finely divided, grey-green leaves, to 1.5cm (½in) long, have linear lobes and smell like southernwood (*Artemisia abrotanum*). Bears star-shaped, white or pink flowers, 1.5cm (½in) across, in clusters of up to 5, to 5cm (2in) across, from spring to summer. ↕30–40cm (12–16in), ↔25–30cm (10–12in). South Africa (Free State, Northern Cape, Western Cape, Eastern Cape). ❄ (min. 2°C/36°F)

P. acetosum ■ Erect, evergreen perennial with succulent stems bearing obovate, toothed, fleshy, grey-green leaves, 2–6cm (¾–2½in) long, sometimes margined red. From spring to summer, star-shaped, salmon-pink flowers, 2–3.5cm (¾–1½in) across, with long, narrow petals, are borne in sparse clusters, 6–7cm (2½–3in) across. ↕50–60cm (20–24in), ↔20–25cm (8–10in). South Africa (Eastern Cape). ❄ (min. 2°C/36°F)

***P.* 'Amethyst'** ■ Vigorous, short-jointed ivy-leaved pelargonium. Semi-double purple flowers are produced in clusters, 9–10cm (3½–4in) across; the upper petals are marked with deep purple and white feathering. ↕25–30cm (10–12in), ↔20–25cm (8–10in). ❄ (min. 2°C/36°F)

***P.* 'Apple Blossom Rosebud'** ■ Rosebud zonal pelargonium bearing bicoloured white and pink flowers in clusters, to 8cm (3in) across. ↕30–40cm (12–16in), ↔20–25cm (8–10in). ❄ (min. 2°C/36°F)

***P.* 'Arctic Star'** ■ Upright, stellar zonal pelargonium with single white flowers in clusters, 5–8cm (2–3in) across. ↕25–30cm (10–12in), ↔15–20cm (6–8in). ❄ (min. 2°C/36°F)

***P.* 'Ardens'.** Prostrate, evergreen pelargonium with pinnate, bluntly lobed, grey-green leaves, 15cm (6in) long, with irregularly toothed margins. In early and midsummer, bears long-stemmed, saucer-shaped, crimson-red flowers, with black blotches, in clusters, 5–8cm (2–3in) across. ↕10–13cm (4–5in), ↔15–18cm (6–7in). Garden origin. ❄ (min. 2°C/36°F)

***P.* 'Aroma'.** Scented-leaved pelargonium with small, rounded, sweet-smelling, grey-green leaves. Bears white flowers in sparse clusters, 2–2.5cm (¾–1in) across. ↕20–25cm (8–10in), ↔15–20cm (6–8in). ❄ (min. 2°C/36°F)

***P.* 'Atomic Snowflake'.** Bushy scented-leaved pelargonium producing large, 3-lobed, mid-green leaves with yellow variegation and a lemon-rose fragrance. Produces mauve flowers in clusters, 2–2.5cm (¾–1in) across. ↕45–50cm (18–20in), ↔25–30cm (10–12in). ❄ (min. 2°C/36°F)

***P.* 'Attar of Roses'.** Scented-leaved pelargonium with 3-lobed, rose-scented leaves. Produces mauve flowers in clusters, 2.5–3cm (1–1¼in) across. ↕50–60cm (20–24in), ↔25–30cm (10–12in). ❄ (min. 2°C/36°F)

***P.* Avanti Series.** Early-flowering, seed-raised, single-flowered zonal pelargoniums with clusters, 10cm (4in) across, of flowers in white or shades of pink, salmon-pink, or red; also available as a mixture. ↕35cm (14in), ↔25cm (10in). ❄ (min. 2°C/36°F)

***P.* 'Avenida'.** Compact, single-flowered zonal pelargonium. Bears brown-zoned, mid-green leaves and bright red flowers in clusters, 5–8cm (2–3in) across. ↕↔20–25cm (8–10in). ❄ (min. 2°C/36°F)

***P.* 'Barbe Bleu'** ■ Ivy-leaved pelargonium with double, purple-black flowers, fading to wine-red in full sun, in clusters, 9–10cm (3½–4in) across. ↕50–60cm (20–24in), ↔20–25cm (8–10in). ❄ (min. 2°C/36°F)

***P.* 'Bird Dancer'** ■ Dwarf, stellar zonal pelargonium with dark-zoned leaves. Bears single flowers, with pale pink lower petals and salmon-pink upper petals, in clusters, to 8cm (3in) across. ↕15–20cm (6–8in), ↔12–15cm (5–6in). ❄ (min. 2°C/36°F)

***P.* 'Black Knight'** ■ Compact angel pelargonium with clusters, 2.5cm (1in) across, of white-edged, purple-black flowers. ↕↔13–18cm (5–7in). ❄ (min. 2°C/36°F)

***P.* 'Blazonry'** ■ Fancy-leaved zonal pelargonium producing rounded, deep cream leaves with rose-pink, mid-green, and purple zones. Single red flowers are borne in clusters, 8cm (3in) across. ↕25–30cm (10–12in), ↔15–20cm (6–8in). ❄ (min. 2°C/36°F)

***P.* BLUE-BLIZZARD ('Fisrain').** Compact, short-jointed ivy-leaved pelargonium. Single, white-eyed mauve flowers are produced in clusters, 5–8cm (2–3in) across. ↕↔20–25cm (8–10in). ❄ (min. 2°C/36°F)

***P.* BLUES ('Fisblu')** ■ Compact, semi-double-flowered zonal pelargonium bearing bright pink flowers in clusters, 5–8cm (2–3in) across. ↕↔15–20cm (6–8in). ❄ (min. 2°C/36°F)

Pelargonium acetosum

Pelargonium 'Amethyst'

Pelargonium 'Arctic Star'

Pelargonium 'Barbe Bleu'

Pelargonium 'Bird Dancer'

Pelargonium 'Black Knight'

***P.* 'Bold Romance'** ■ Spreading, semi-double-flowered zonal pelargonium with white-eyed, rose-pink flowers in clusters, 10–13cm (4–5in) across. ↕ 25–30cm (10–12in), ↔ 20–25cm (8–10in). ❄ (min. 2°C/36°F)
***P.* 'Brookside Primrose'** ■ Miniature, fancy-leaved zonal pelargonium with dark brown butterfly markings in the centre of each rounded leaf. Double, light pink flowers are borne in clusters, 7cm (3in) across. ↕ 10–12cm (4–5in), ↔ 7–10cm (3–4in). ❄ (min. 2°C/36°F)
***P.* 'Captain Starlight'** ■ Bushy angel pelargonium producing clusters, 2.5cm (1in) across, of pale mauve flowers with deep purple upper petals with red feathering. ↕↔ 18–23cm (7–9in). ❄ (min. 2°C/36°F)
***P.* 'Carisbrooke'** ■ Regal pelargonium with clusters, 9–10cm (3½–4in) across, of pale rose-pink flowers, feathered and blazed wine-red on the upper petals. ↕ 40–45cm (16–18in), ↔ 20–25cm (8–10in). ❄ (min. 2°C/36°F)
P. carnosum ■ Deciduous, perennial succulent with a smooth, swollen stem, 5cm (2in) thick, and fleshy branches, erect and swollen at the joints. Very variable, ovate-oblong, pinnate, stalked, slightly hairy, grey-green leaves, 7–14cm (3–5½in) long, have lobed segments with scalloped margins. Clusters, 4cm (1½in) across, of 2–8 star-shaped, white to pale yellow-green flowers, 1cm (½in) across, are borne in summer. ↕ 40cm (16in), ↔ 25cm (10in). Namibia, South Africa (Northern Cape, Western Cape, Eastern Cape). ❄ (min. 10°C/50°F)
***P.* 'Caroline Schmidt'** ■ Vigorous, upright, fancy-leaved zonal pelargonium with white-edged, mid-green leaves and double red flowers borne in clusters, 5–8cm (2–3in) across. ↕ 30–35cm (12–14in), ↔ 18–23cm (7–9in). ❄ (min. 2°C/36°F)
***P.* Century Series.** Compact, seed-raised, single-flowered zonal pelargoniums bearing flowers in shades of red, pink, or white, in clusters, to 15cm (6in) across, early in the season. ↕ to 45cm (18in), ↔ 30cm (12in). ❄ (min. 2°C/36°F). **'Century Hot Pink'** ■ has very bright pink flowers.
***P.* Challenge Series.** Compact, seed-raised, single-flowered zonal pelargoniums with clusters, to 12cm (5in) across, of flowers in white or

Pelargonium carnosum

shades of red or pink. ↕↔ to 30cm (12in). ❄ (min. 2°C/36°F).
***P.* 'Charity'.** Bushy scented-leaved pelargonium with deeply cut, mid-green leaves with broad gold margins and a sharp orange scent. Produces pale mauve flowers in clusters, 2–2.5cm (¾–1in) across. ↕ 20–25cm (8–10in), ↔ 15–20cm (6–8in). ❄ (min. 2°C/36°F)
***P.* Cheerio Series.** Seed-raised, single-flowered zonal pelargoniums bearing flowers in white or shades of pink, salmon-pink, red, or violet, in clusters, 10cm (4in) across. ↕↔ 30–40cm (12–16in). ❄ (min. 2°C/36°F)
***P.* 'Chelsworth'.** Miniature, double-flowered zonal pelargonium bearing clusters, 7cm (3in) across, of pinkish orange flowers. ↕ 10–12cm (4–5in), ↔ 7–10cm (3–4in). ❄ (min. 2°C/36°F)
***P.* 'Clorinda'** ■ Vigorous scented-leaved pelargonium with 3-lobed, cedar-scented leaves. Bears rose-pink flowers in clusters, 7cm (3in) across. ↕ 45–50cm (18–20in), ↔ 20–25cm (8–10in). ❄ (min. 2°C/36°F)
***P.* 'Coddenham'** ■ Miniature, double-flowered zonal pelargonium bearing orange-red flowers in clusters, 7cm (3in) across. ↕ 10–12cm (4–5in), ↔ 7–10cm (3–4in). ❄ (min. 2°C/36°F)
***P.* 'Contrast'** ■ Fancy-leaved zonal pelargonium with rounded, golden yellow, green, and red leaves. Single scarlet flowers are produced in clusters, to 8cm (3in) across. ↕ 25–30cm (10–12in), ↔ 15–20cm (6–8in). ❄ (min. 2°C/36°F)
***P.* 'Copthorne'.** Vigorous scented-leaved pelargonium with large-lobed leaves exuding an exotic, spicy scent. Bears clusters, 8–9cm (3–3½in) across, of mauve flowers with purple feathering on the upper petals. ↕ 45–50cm (18–20in), ↔ 20–25cm (8–10in). ❄ (min. 2°C/36°F)
P. cotyledonis (Old-man-live-forever). Bushy, deciduous, perennial succulent with short, rough, swollen stems, to 3cm (1¼in) thick. Rounded, rich deep green leaves, 1.5–2cm (½–¾in) long, are heart-shaped at the bases. Clusters, to 6cm (2½in) across, of 5–15 rounded, pure white flowers, to 1.5cm (½in) across, are borne in late spring and early summer. ↕ 30cm (12in), ↔ 15cm (6in). St. Helena. ❄ (min. 10°C/50°F)
***P.* 'Creamery'.** Short-lived, double-flowered zonal pelargonium with pointed leaves. Pale yellow flowers, in clusters, 6–7cm (2½–3in) across, colour best when grown in partial shade. ↕ 25–30cm (10–12in), ↔ 10–15cm (4–6in). ❄ (min. 2°C/36°F)
***P. crispum* 'Variegatum'** ■ (Variegated lemon-scented pelargonium). Upright scented-leaved pelargonium with cream-margined, mid-green leaves that release a lemon fragrance when brushed. Pale mauve flowers are produced in clusters, 2–2.5cm (¾–1in) across. ↕ 35–45cm (14–18in), ↔ 12–15cm (5–6in). ❄ (min. 2°C/36°F)
***P.* 'Crocodile'.** Compact, short-jointed ivy-leaved pelargonium with mid-green leaves overlaid with a creamy white mesh. Bears single, bright cerise-pink flowers in clusters, 5–8cm (2–3in) across. ↕↔ 15–20cm (6–8in). ❄ (min. 2°C/36°F)
***P.* 'Crystal Palace Gem'.** Prostrate, fancy-leaved zonal pelargonium bearing light yellow-green leaves, each with a deeper green splash. Produces clusters, 5cm (2in) across, of single, soft coral-red flowers. ↕ 13–15cm (5–6in), ↔ 18–20cm (7–8in). ❄ (min. 2°C/36°F)
P. cucullatum ■ Shrubby, evergreen perennial with cup-shaped, softly hairy, mid-green leaves, to 8cm (3in) long. Bears abundant trumpet-shaped, mauve-purple flowers, to 5cm (2in) across, in clusters, 8–9cm (3–3½in) across, from spring to summer. ↕ 60–90cm (24–36in), ↔ 20–25cm (8–10in). South Africa (Western Cape). ❄ (min. 2°C/36°F)
***P.* 'Dame Anna Neagle'.** Fancy-leaved zonal pelargonium (incorrectly registered as dwarf) producing rounded gold leaves with wide bronze zones. Double, light pink flowers are borne in clusters, 6–7cm (2½–3in) across. ↕ 20–25cm (8–10in), ↔ 15–20cm (6–8in). ❄ (min. 2°C/36°F)
***P.* 'Davina'.** Miniature, double-flowered zonal pelargonium. Bears clusters, 7cm (3in) across, of salmon-pink flowers, flushed and veined deeper salmon-pink. ↕ 10–12cm (4–5in), ↔ 7–10cm (3–4in). ❄ (min. 2°C/36°F)
***P.* 'Deacon Fireball'.** Compact, short-jointed, double-flowered zonal pelargonium bearing bright red flowers in clusters, 5–8cm (2–3in) across. ↕↔ 20–25cm (8–10in). ❄ (min. 2°C/36°F)
***P.* 'Deacon Lilac Mist'.** Compact, short-jointed, double-flowered zonal pelargonium with soft lilac-pink flowers in clusters, 5–8cm (2–3in) across. ↕↔ 13–18cm (5–7in). ❄ (min. 2°C/36°F)
***P.* 'Delhi'** see *P.* 'Delli'.
***P.* 'Delli'**, syn. *P.* 'Delhi'. Upright regal pelargonium bearing clusters, 10–13cm (4–5in) across, of frilly pink flowers with broad white margins. ↕ 30–40cm (12–16in), ↔ 30–35cm (12–14in). ❄ (min. 2°C/36°F)
P. denticulatum. Erect, branched, evergreen perennial with triangular, very deeply cut, irregularly toothed, sticky, dark green leaves, 6–8cm (2½–3in) long, sometimes darker along veins, smelling strongly of balsam. Bears clusters, 5cm (2in) across, of up to 6 spoon-shaped mauve flowers, 2.5cm (1in) across, from spring to summer. ↕ 1.5m (5ft), ↔ 75cm (2½ft). South Africa (S. Eastern Cape, S. Western Cape). ❄ (min. 2°C/36°F)
***P.* 'Dibbinsdale'** ■ Dwarf, double-flowered zonal pelargonium with rose-pink flowers in clusters, 2.5–5cm (1–2in) across. ↕↔ 13–15cm (5–6in). ❄ (min. 2°C/36°F)
***P.* 'Dolly Vardon'** ■ Fancy-leaved zonal pelargonium with rounded, white, red, and green leaves. Bears single scarlet flowers in clusters, 7cm (3in) across. ↕ 25–30cm (10–12in), ↔ 12–15cm (5–6in). ❄ (min. 2°C/36°F)

Pelargonium 'Blazonry'

Pelargonium BLUES ('Fisblu')

Pelargonium 'Bold Romance'

Pelargonium 'Brookside Primrose'

Pelargonium 'Captain Starlight'

Pelargonium 'Carisbrooke'

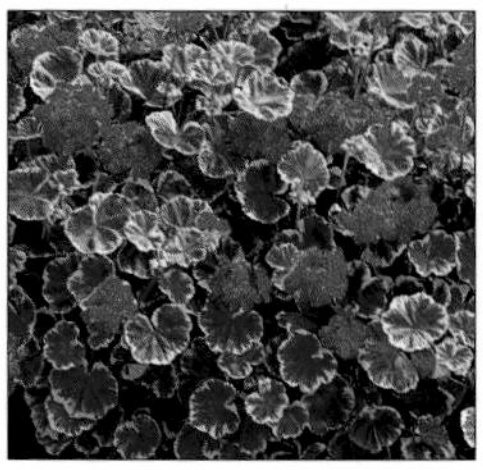

Pelargonium 'Caroline Schmidt'

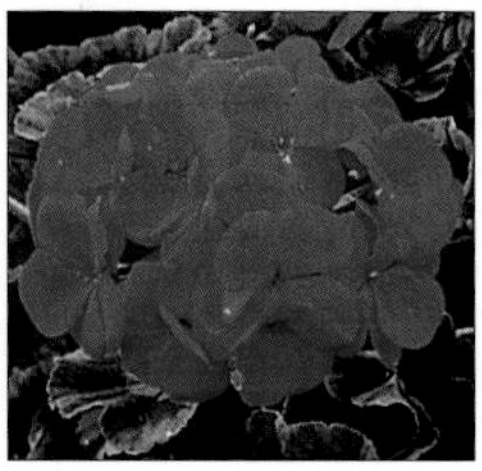

Pelargonium Century Series 'Century Hot Pink'

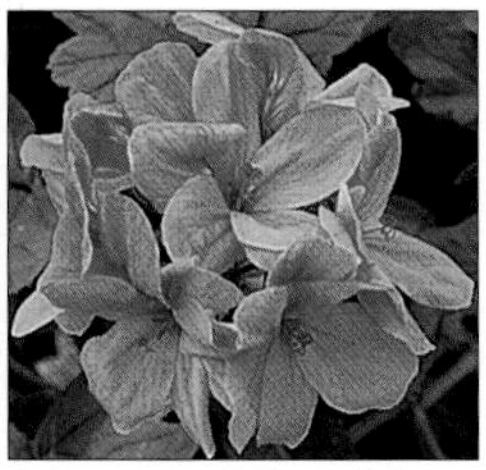

Pelargonium 'Clorinda'

Pelargonium 'Coddenham'

Pelargonium 'Contrast'

Pelargonium crispum 'Variegatum'

Pelargonium 'Fringed Aztec'

P. Dynamo Series. Seed-raised, single-flowered zonal pelargoniums bearing white, deep scarlet, deep rose-pink, or salmon-pink flowers in clusters, 12cm (5in) across. ↕ 40cm (16in), ↔ 30cm (12in). ❀ (min. 2°C/36°F)
P. echinatum. Shrubby, tuberous-rooted, deciduous, perennial succulent with an erect, swollen stem bearing a few grey branches, 1cm (½in) thick, covered with spiny stipules. Heart-shaped, scalloped, grey-green leaves, to 3cm (1¼in) long, with 3–5 shallow lobes, are hairy above, more so beneath. In spring and early summer, produces clusters, to 10cm (4in) across, of 3–8 small, star-shaped, white to pink flowers, 3cm (1¼in) across, with dark red marks on the upper petals. ↕ 30cm (12in) or more, ↔ to 30cm (12in). South Africa (Northern Cape). ❀ (min. 10°C/50°F)
P. Elite Series. Compact, sturdy, seed-raised, single-flowered zonal pelargoniums, most with attractive leaf zoning, producing clusters, 12cm (5in) across, of flowers in white, salmon-pink, or shades of red or pink. ↕↔ 25–35cm (10–14in). ❀ (min. 2°C/36°F)
P. 'Emma Jane Read' ■ Dwarf, double-flowered zonal pelargonium with light pink flowers in clusters, 2.5–5cm (1–2in) across. ↕↔ 10–13cm (4–5in). ❀ (min. 2°C/36°F)
P. 'Evka'. Bushy, short-jointed ivy-leaved pelargonium with small, light green leaves edged creamy white. Bears single, light red flowers in clusters, 5–8cm (2–3in) across. ↕ 20–25cm (8–10in), ↔ 15–20cm (6–8in). ❀ (min. 2°C/36°F)
P. 'Filicifolium'. Scented-leaved pelargonium producing very finely cut, fern-like, balsam-scented leaves. Bears pale mauve flowers in small clusters, 2–2.5cm (¾–1in) across. ↕ 25–30cm (10–12in) or more, ↔ 12–15cm (5–6in). ❀ (min. 2°C/36°F)
P. 'First Blush' ■ Bushy regal pelargonium bearing white flowers, each with a spreading blaze of red across the upper petals, in clusters, 8–10cm (3–4in) across. ↕↔ 20–25cm (8–10in). ❀ (min. 2°C/36°F)
P. 'Flower of Spring' ■ Fancy-leaved zonal pelargonium with rounded silver leaves. Bears single scarlet flowers in clusters, 7cm (3in) across. ↕ 45–60cm (18–24in), ↔ 20–25cm (8–10in). ❀ (min. 2°C/36°F)
P. x fragrans see *P.* 'Fragrans'.
P. 'Fragrans' ■ syn. *P. x fragrans*, *P.* Fragrans Group. Bushy scented-leaved pelargonium with pine-scented, grey-green foliage. Bears clusters, 2.5–3cm (1–1¼in) across, of white flowers. ↕ 20–25cm (8–10in), ↔ 15–20cm (6–8in). ❀ (min. 2°C/36°F)
P. Fragrans Group see *P.* 'Fragrans'.
P. 'Fragrans Variegatum'. Bushy scented-leaved pelargonium producing pine-scented, grey-green leaves with cream and white variegation. Bears clusters, 2.5–3cm (1–1¼in) across, of white flowers. ↕ 20–25cm (8–10in), ↔ 15–20cm (6–8in). ❀ (min. 2°C/36°F)
P. 'Francis Parrett' ■ Miniature, double-flowered zonal pelargonium bearing purple-pink flowers in clusters, 7cm (3in) across. ↕ 10–12cm (4–5in), ↔ 7–10cm (3–4in). ❀ (min. 2°C/36°F)
P. 'Friesdorf'. Dwarf, fancy-leaved zonal pelargonium with rounded, almost black leaves and narrow-petalled, single crimson flowers in clusters, 7cm (3in) across. ↕ 15–20cm (6–8in), ↔ 10–12cm (4–5in). ❀ (min. 2°C/36°F)
P. 'Frills'. Miniature, double-flowered zonal pelargonium with pale salmon-pink flowers borne in clusters, 4–4.5cm (1½–1¾in) across. ↕ 10–12cm (4–5in), ↔ 7–10cm (3–4in). ❀ (min. 2°C/36°F)
P. 'Fringed Aztec' ■ Compact regal pelargonium producing clusters, 5–8cm (2–3in) across, of white flowers with toothed petals, each splashed with red deepening to mahogany. ↕ 20–25cm (8–10in), ↔ 25–30cm (10–12in). ❀ (min. 2°C/36°F)
P. 'Gemini' ■ Bushy, stellar zonal pelargonium bearing star-shaped, double, white-eyed red flowers, with quilled petals, in clusters, 5–8cm (2–3in) across. ↕↔ 18–20cm (7–8in). ❀ (min. 2°C/36°F)
P. 'Golden Brilliantissimum'. Fancy-leaved zonal pelargonium producing rounded leaves with orange, mid-green, and dark wine-red zones. Bears double, cherry-red flowers in clusters, to 8cm

Pelargonium 'Hazel Cherry'

(3in) across. ↕ 25–30cm (10–12in), ↔ 12–15cm (5–6in). ❀ (min. 2°C/36°F)
P. 'Golden Lilac Mist'. Bushy, fancy-leaved zonal pelargonium with rounded, bronze-zoned gold leaves. Double, lavender-pink flowers are borne in clusters, 7cm (3in) across. ↕ 25–30cm (10–12in), ↔ 15–20cm (6–8in). ❀ (min. 2°C/36°F)
P. 'Graveolens' of gardens ■ (Rose geranium, Sweet-scented geranium). Vigorous, bushy, erect scented-leaved pelargonium with slightly rough, lobed and cut, mid-green leaves, which have a pungent lemon-rose scent. Sterile mauve flowers are borne in clusters, 2.5–3cm (1–1¼in) across. ↕ 45–60cm (18–24in), ↔ 20–40cm (8–16in). ❀ (min. 2°C/36°F)
P. 'Gustav Emich' ■ Double-flowered zonal pelargonium producing orange-scarlet flowers in clusters, 10–13cm (4–5in) across. ↕ 40–45cm (16–18in), ↔ 20–25cm (8–10in). ❀ (min. 2°C/36°F)
P. 'Happy Thought' ■ Fancy-leaved zonal pelargonium bearing rounded leaves, each with a greenish yellow butterfly marking in the centre. Single, light crimson flowers are produced in clusters, 8–9cm (3–3½in) across. ↕ 40–45cm (16–18in), ↔ 20–25cm (8–10in). ❀ (min. 2°C/36°F)
P. 'Hazel Cherry' ■ Spreading regal pelargonium bearing clusters, 8–10cm (3–4in) across, of bright red flowers with a large mahogany blaze on each

P

Pelargonium cucullatum

Pelargonium 'Dibbinsdale'

Pelargonium 'Dolly Vardon'

Pelargonium 'Emma Jane Read'

Pelargonium 'First Blush'

Pelargonium 'Flower of Spring'

Pelargonium 'Fragrans'

Pelargonium 'Francis Parrett'

Pelargonium 'Gemini'

Pelargonium 'Graveolens' of gardens

Pelargonium 'Gustav Emich'

Pelargonium 'Happy Thought'

Pelargonium Horizon Series

petal. ↕ 15–20cm (6–8in), ↔ 20–25cm (8–10in). ❀ (min. 2°C/36°F)
P. 'Highfield's Delight'. Upright, single-flowered zonal pelargonium bearing mid-green leaves with distinct brown zones, and light shell-pink flowers in clusters, 5–8cm (2–3in) across. ↕ 30–35cm (12–14in), ↔ 15–20cm (6–8in). ❀ (min. 2°C/36°F)
P. 'Highfield's Festival'. Compact, double-flowered zonal pelargonium with white-eyed pink flowers in clusters, 10–13cm (4–5in) across. ↕ 30–35cm (12–14in), ↔ 25–30cm (10–12in). ❀ (min. 2°C/36°F)
P. 'Highfield's Pride'. Upright, single-flowered zonal pelargonium with brown-zoned, mid-green leaves and light scarlet flowers in clusters, 5–8cm (2–3in) across. ↕ 30–35cm (12–14in), ↔ 15–20cm (6–8in). ❀ (min. 2°C/36°F)
P. Horizon Series ▣ Compact, bushy, seed-raised, single-flowered zonal pelargoniums with strongly zoned foliage. Bear flowers in white or shades of pink or red in clusters, to 12cm (5in) across, early in the season. Good wet-weather tolerance. ↕ to 30cm (12in), ↔ 25cm (10in). ❀ (min. 2°C/36°F). **'Horizon Scarlet'** produces dark, strongly zoned leaves and scarlet flowers.
P. 'Imperial Butterfly' ▣ Spreading angel pelargonium with lemon-scented leaves and clusters, 2.5cm (1in) across, of white flowers with purple feathering. ↕ 20–25cm (8–10in), ↔ 15–22cm (6–9in). ❀ (min. 2°C/36°F)
P. *inquinans*. Erect, evergreen perennial producing soft, woody stems and rounded, mid-green leaves, 5–6cm (2–2½in) across; they stain fingers red when handled. Saucer-shaped scarlet flowers, 4cm (1½in) across, are borne in clusters, 9cm (3½in) across, from spring to summer. One of the original parents of zonal pelargoniums. ↕ 60–90cm (24–36in), ↔ 20–25cm (8–10in). South Africa (Mpumalanga, KwaZulu/Natal, Eastern Cape). ❀ (min. 2°C/36°F)
P. 'Irene' ▣ Vigorous, semi-double-flowered zonal pelargonium producing light cerise-red flowers in clusters, 11cm (4½in) across. ↕ 40–45cm (16–18in), ↔ 25–30cm (10–12in). ❀ (min. 2°C/36°F)
P. 'Ivory Snow' ▣ Compact, fancy-leaved zonal pelargonium with bright green leaves margined creamy white. Bears double white flowers in clusters, 5–8cm (2–3in) across. ↕↔ 20–25cm (8–10in). ❀ (min. 2°C/36°F)
P. 'Jackie', syn. *P.* 'Jackie Gall'. Very bushy, slow-growing, short-jointed ivy-leaved pelargonium with small leaves. Bears clusters, 9cm (3½in) across, of rosebud-like, double, pale lavender-pink flowers. ↕↔ 15–20cm (6–8in). ❀ (min. 2°C/36°F)
P. 'Jackie Gall' see *P.* 'Jackie'.
P. 'Janet Hofman'. Compact, semi-double-flowered zonal pelargonium with salmon-pink flowers in clusters, 8–10cm (3–4in) across. ↕↔ 25–30cm (10–12in). ❀ (min. 2°C/36°F)
P. 'Joy' ▣ Upright regal pelargonium producing tight clusters, 5–8cm (2–3in) across, of very frilly, white-edged, deep pink flowers with white throats. ↕ 25–30cm (10–12in), ↔ 15–20cm (6–8in). ❀ (min. 2°C/36°F)
P. 'Just William'. Miniature, double-flowered zonal pelargonium with bright red flowers in clusters, 6–7cm (2½–3in) across. ↕ 10–12cm (4–5in), ↔ 7–10cm (3–4in). ❀ (min. 2°C/36°F)
P. 'Karl Hagele'. Spreading, double-flowered zonal pelargonium with white-eyed, light purple flowers in clusters, 5–8cm (2–3in) across. ↕↔ 20–25cm (8–10in). ❀ (min. 2°C/36°F)
P. 'King of Denmark'. Compact, double-flowered zonal pelargonium producing leaves with broad brown zones near the edges. Bears soft salmon-pink flowers in clusters, 5–8cm (2–3in) across. ↕↔ 20–25cm (8–10in). ❀ (min. 2°C/36°F)
P. 'Lachskönigin' ▣ Short-jointed ivy-leaved pelargonium with semi-double, rosy salmon-pink flowers borne in clusters, 11cm (4½in) across. ↕ 25–30cm (10–12in), ↔ 15–20cm (6–8in). ❀ (min. 2°C/36°F)
P. 'Lady Plymouth' ▣ Scented-leaved pelargonium with eucalyptus-scented, silver-margined leaves. Lavender-pink flowers are borne in clusters, 3–3.5cm (1¼–1½in) across. ↕ 30–40cm (12–16in), ↔ 15–20cm (6–8in). ❀ (min. 2°C/36°F)
P. 'La France'. Short-jointed ivy-leaved pelargonium with semi-double mauve flowers, in clusters, 8–10cm (3–4in) across. ↕ 25–30cm (10–12in), ↔ 20–25cm (8–10in). ❀ (min. 2°C/36°F)
P. 'Lara Starshine' ▣ Bushy, spreading scented-leaved pelargonium with deeply cut, sharply scented leaves. Bears clusters, 2.5–5cm (1–2in) across, of white-eyed pink flowers, the upper petals of each overlaid, veined, and feathered carmine-pink. ↕↔ 20–25cm (8–10in). ❀ (min. 2°C/36°F)
P. 'L'Elégante' ▣ Ivy-leaved pelargonium with silver-green leaves that turn cream-variegated, mid-green, and purple if kept very dry. Single white flowers are borne in clusters, to 8cm (3in) across. ↕ 20–25cm (8–10in), ↔ 15–20cm (6–8in). ❀ (min. 2°C/36°F)
P. 'Lemon Fancy'. Scented-leaved pelargonium with rough-textured, toothed leaves with a citrus fragrance. Produces mauve flowers in clusters, 3–3.5cm (1¼–1½in) across. ↕ 40–45cm (16–18in), ↔ 15–20cm (6–8in). ❀ (min. 2°C/36°F)
P. 'Lila Mini Cascade'. Thin-stemmed ivy-leaved pelargonium with single, lilac-pink flowers borne in clusters, 8–9cm (3–3½in) across. ↕ 45–50cm (18–20in), ↔ 15–20cm (6–8in). ❀ (min. 2°C/36°F)
P. 'Lilian Woodberry'. Upright, short-jointed, single-flowered zonal pelargonium producing clusters, 5–8cm (2–3in) across, of cerise flowers with large white eyes. ↕ 20–25cm (8–10in), ↔ 15–20cm (6–8in). ❀ (min. 2°C/36°F)
P. 'Lord Bute'. Regal pelargonium producing dark reddish black flowers, the petals with dark red margins, in clusters, to 10cm (4in) across. ↕ 45cm (18in), ↔ 30cm (12in). ❀ (min. 2°C/36°F)
P. 'Mabel Grey' ▣ Scented-leaved pelargonium with deeply cut, rough-textured leaves with a very strong lemon scent. Produces purple flowers in clusters, 5cm (2in) across. ↕ 30–35cm (12–14in), ↔ 12–15cm (5–6in). ❀ (min. 2°C/36°F)
P. 'Marmalade'. Miniature, double-flowered zonal pelargonium with dark green leaves zoned dark brown. Bears light orange flowers in clusters, 2.5–5cm

Pelargonium 'Joy'

Pelargonium 'Imperial Butterfly'

Pelargonium 'Irene'

Pelargonium 'Ivory Snow'

Pelargonium 'Lachskönigin'

Pelargonium 'Lady Plymouth'

Pelargonium 'L'Elégante'

PELARGONIUM

(1–2in) across. ↕↔ 10–13cm (4–5in). ❄ (min. 2°C/36°F)
P. 'Maxime Kovaleski' ▣ Upright, single-flowered zonal pelargonium with light green leaves and orange flowers in clusters, 5–8cm (2–3in) across. ↕ 30–35cm (12–14in), ↔ 15–20cm (6–8in). ❄ (min. 2°C/36°F)
P. 'Meadowside Midnight' ▣ Upright, stellar zonal pelargonium with very dark green, almost black leaves. Bears single, scarlet-orange flowers in clusters, 5cm (2in) across. ↕ 25–30cm (10–12in), ↔ 15–18cm (6–7in). ❄ (min. 2°C/36°F)
P. 'Mini Red'. Bushy, very short-jointed ivy-leaved pelargonium with small, pale green leaves. Produces small, single, light red flowers in clusters, 2.5–5cm (1–2in) across. ↕ 15–20cm (6–8in), ↔ 10–15cm (4–6in). ❄ (min. 2°C/36°F)
P. 'Minstrel Boy'. Compact regal pelargonium bearing deep mahogany-black flowers in clusters, 8–10cm (3–4in) across. ↕↔ 20–25cm (8–10in). ❄ (min. 2°C/36°F)
P. 'Miss Burdett Coutts'. Compact, fancy-leaved zonal pelargonium with cream, white, green, and red leaves and single, coral-red flowers in clusters, 2.5–5cm (1–2in) across. ↕↔ 15–20cm (6–8in). ❄ (min. 2°C/36°F)
P. 'Miss Wackles'. Miniature, double-flowered zonal pelargonium producing mid-green leaves with dark brown zones. Produces cerise-red flowers in clusters, 4.5–5cm (1¾–2in) across. ↕ 10–12cm (4–5in), ↔ 7–10cm (3–4in). ❄ (min. 2°C/36°F)
P. 'Mme Crousse'. Very long-jointed ivy-leaved pelargonium with semi-double, pale pink flowers in clusters, to 7cm (3in) across. ↕ 50–60cm (20–24in), ↔ 15–20cm (6–8in). ❄ (min. 2°C/36°F)
P. 'Mont Blanc'. Very compact, fancy-leaved zonal pelargonium with white-margined, dark green leaves and single white flowers in clusters, 2.5–5cm (1–2in) across. ↕↔ 15–20cm (6–8in). ❄ (min. 2°C/36°F)
P. 'Moon Maiden'. Upright angel pelargonium producing clusters, 2.5cm (1in) across, of lilac flowers with white throats and a light purple dot on each petal. ↕ 25–30cm (10–12in), ↔ 18–23cm (7–9in). ❄ (min. 2°C/36°F)
P. 'Morval' ▣ Dwarf, semi-double-flowered zonal pelargonium with light golden leaves and soft china-pink flowers in clusters, 2.5–5cm (1–2in) across. ↕↔ 13–15cm (5–6in). ❄ (min. 2°C/36°F)
P. 'Mr. Henry Cox' ▣ syn. *P.* 'Mrs. Henry Cox'. Fancy-leaved zonal pelargonium with rounded, golden yellow leaves marked with mid-green, dark purple, and red. Single pink flowers, with small white eyes, are borne in clusters, 7cm (3in) across. ↕ 25–30cm (10–12in), ↔ 10–12cm (4–5in). ❄ (min. 2°C/36°F)
P. 'Mrs. G.H. Smith'. Upright, compact angel pelargonium producing clusters, 2.5cm (1in) across, of white flowers with a crimson blotch on each upper petal. ↕ 20–25cm (8–10in), ↔ 15–20cm (6–8in). ❄ (min. 2°C/36°F)
P. 'Mrs. Henry Cox' see *P.* 'Mr. Henry Cox'.
P. 'Mrs. Quilter' ▣ Fancy-leaved zonal pelargonium bearing rounded gold leaves with wide bronze zones. Single, pale pink flowers are borne in clusters, 7cm (3in) across. Leaf colour deepens in full sun. ↕ 30–40cm (12–16in), ↔ 12–15cm (5–6in). ❄ (min. 2°C/36°F)
P. Multibloom Series ▣ Seed-raised, single-flowered zonal pelargoniums with abundant flowers in white or shades of pink or red, some with white eyes, borne in clusters, 8–12cm (3–5in) across. Early flowering over a long period; good wet-weather tolerance. ↕ 25–30cm (10–12in), ↔ 30cm (12in). ❄ (min. 2°C/36°F)
P. 'Occold Shield' ▣ Compact, fancy-leaved zonal pelargonium producing gold leaves, each with a dark brown medallion in the centre. Bears semi-double orange flowers in clusters, 5–8cm (2–3in) across. ↕ 25–30cm (10–12in), ↔ 20–25cm (8–10in). ❄ (min. 2°C/36°F)
P. odoratissimum. Bushy, spreading, evergreen perennial with rounded, light green leaves, 4–5cm (1½–2in) across, with a scent reminiscent of stored apples. Produces clusters, 2.5–3cm (1–1¼in) across, of 3–10 star-shaped white flowers, to 1.5cm (½in) across, from spring to summer. ↕ 20–25cm (8–10in), ↔ 45–60cm (18–24in). South Africa (KwaZulu/Natal, Limpopo, Eastern Cape, Western Cape). ❄ (min. 2°C/36°F)

Pelargonium 'Lara Starshine'

P. 'Old Spice' ▣ Bushy, erect scented-leaved pelargonium with rounded, spicy-scented leaves. Bears white flowers in clusters, 3–3.5cm (1¼–1½in) across. ↕ 25–30cm (10–12in), ↔ 12–15cm (5–6in). ❄ (min. 2°C/36°F)
P. 'Orange Appeal' ▣ Seed-raised, single flowered zonal pelargonium with clear, bright orange flowers borne in clusters, to 7cm (3in) across. ↕ 30–40cm (12–16in), ↔ 30cm (12in). ❄ (min. 2°C/36°F)
P. Orbit Series. Very early flowering, seed-raised, single-flowered zonal pelargoniums that branch from the base and have fine leaf zoning. Produce large clusters, 12–14cm (5–5½in) across, of flowers in white or shades of pink, orange, or red. ↕ to 35cm (14in), ↔ 25cm (10in). ❄ (min. 2°C/36°F). **'Cherry Orbit'** is upright, with purple-zoned leaves and cherry-red flowers.
P. 'Orion'. Miniature, double-flowered zonal pelargonium. Orange flowers are produced in clusters, 2.5–5cm (1–2in) across. ↕↔ 8–10cm (3–4in). ❄ (min. 2°C/36°F)
P. 'Paton's Unique' ▣ Vigorous unique pelargonium bearing coral-red and pale pink flowers, with small white eyes, in clusters, 4–4.5cm (1½–1¾in) across. The leaves release a pungent scent when bruised. ↕ 40–45cm (16–18in), ↔ 15–20cm (6–8in). ❄ (min. 2°C/36°F)
P. Pinto Series see *P.* Pulsar Series.
P. 'Prince of Orange'. Erect, thin-stemmed scented-leaved pelargonium with small, rounded, orange-scented leaves. Bears mauve flowers in clusters, 2.5–3cm (1–1¼in) across. ↕ 25–30cm (10–12in), ↔ 15–20cm (6–8in). ❄ (min. 2°C/36°F)
P. Pulsar Series, syn. *P.* Pinto Series. Seed-raised, single-flowered zonal pelargoniums with strongly zoned foliage. Flowers, in white or shades of pink or red, including bicolours, are borne in clusters, 12–14cm (5–5½in) across. ↕ 30–35cm (12–14in), ↔ 30cm (12in). ❄ (min. 2°C/36°F). **'Pulsar Scarlet'** ▣ has deep red flowers.
P. radens. Vigorous, upright, bushy, evergreen subshrub with triangular, deeply 2-pinnatifid, rough, strongly aromatic, grey-green leaves, 6cm (2½in) long, consisting of oblong segments with margins rolled under. Produces star-shaped, pale to purple-pink flowers, 1.5cm (½in) across, in 2- to 6-flowered clusters, to 6cm (2½in) across, in late spring and summer. ↕ 30–45cm (12–18in), ↔ 20–30cm (8–12in). South Africa (Western Cape, Eastern Cape). ❄ (min. 2°C/36°F)
P. 'Red Black Vesuvius'. Miniature, single-flowered zonal pelargonium with purple-black leaves and bright scarlet flowers in clusters, 2.5cm (1in) across. ↕ 8cm (3in), ↔ 8–10cm (3–4in). ❄ (min. 2°C/36°F)
P. 'Red Cascade'. Trailing ivy-leaved pelargonium with single red flowers in clusters, 5–8cm (2–3in) across. ↕ 25–30cm (10–12in), ↔ 20–25cm (8–10in). ❄ (min. 2°C/36°F)
P. 'Rembrandt'. Regal pelargonium producing clusters, 5–8cm (2–3in) across, of white-throated, light purple flowers, overlaid and feathered with purple-black. ↕ 35–40cm (14–16in), ↔ 23–25cm (9–10in). ❄ (min. 2°C/36°F)

Pelargonium 'Mabel Grey'

Pelargonium 'Maxime Kovaleski'

Pelargonium 'Meadowside Midnight'

Pelargonium 'Morval'

Pelargonium 'Mr. Henry Cox'

Pelargonium 'Mrs. Quilter'

Pelargonium Multibloom Series

Pelargonium 'Occold Shield'

Pelargonium 'Old Spice'

Pelargonium 'Orange Appeal'

Pelargonium 'Paton's Unique'

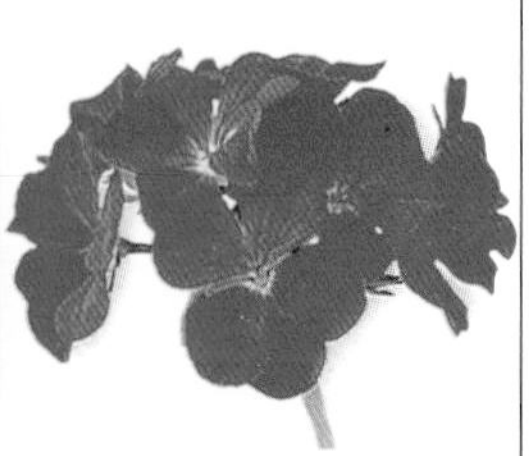

Pelargonium Pulsar Series 'Pulsar Scarlet'

P

P. 'Rimfire' ■ Spreading regal pelargonium with deep mahogany flowers, edged salmon-red, borne in clusters, 9–10cm (3¼–4in) across. ↕ 30–40cm (12–16in), ↔ 30–38cm (12–14in). ❀ (min. 2°C/36°F)

P. Ringo 2000 Series. Seed-raised, single-flowered zonal pelargoniums with very dark zoning on the leaves. Flowers, in white, shades of pink or red, or mixtures, are produced in clusters, 12–14cm (5–5½in) across. ↕ 30–40cm (12–16in), ↔ 25–35cm (10–14in). ❀ (min. 2°C/36°F)

P. ROKOKO ('Fisfid'). Bushy, semi-double-flowered zonal pelargonium with peach flowers in clusters, 10–12cm (4–5in) across. ↕ 30–35cm (12–14in), ↔ 20–25cm (8–10in). ❀ (min. 2°C/36°F)

P. 'Rollisson's Unique' ■ Unique pelargonium producing clusters, 7cm (3in) across, of red-purple flowers with deep purple and white feathering on the upper petals. ↕ 40–45cm (16–18in), ↔ 15–20cm (6–8in). ❀ (min. 2°C/36°F)

P. 'Rosmaroy' ■ Spreading regal pelargonium with frilly, mauve-pink flowers borne in clusters, 5–8cm (2–3in) across. ↕↔ 20–25cm (8–10in). ❀ (min. 2°C/36°F)

P. 'Rouletta' ■ Vigorous ivy-leaved pelargonium with semi-double, bicoloured light crimson and white flowers borne in clusters, 9cm (3½in) across. May temporarily revert to plain crimson in hot weather. ↕ 50–60cm (20–24in), ↔ 15–20cm (6–8in). ❀ (min. 2°C/36°F)

P. 'Royal Oak'. Scented-leaved pelargonium with dark green leaves, shaped like oak leaves, with dark central marks, and exuding an exotic, spicy scent. Bears mauve flowers in clusters, 2.5–3cm (1–1¼in) across. ↕ 30–40cm (12–16in), ↔ 25–30cm (10–12in). ❀ (min. 2°C/36°F)

P. 'Royal Sovereign'. Bushy, fancy-leaved zonal pelargonium with rounded bronze and gold leaves. Double red flowers are produced in clusters, 7cm (3in) across. ↕ 25–30cm (10–12in), ↔ 15–20cm (6–8in). ❀ (min. 2°C/36°F)

P. 'Sarah Don' ■ Upright angel pelargonium bearing gold-green leaves. Pink flowers, with each upper petal blotched and feathered with purple, are produced in clusters, 2.5cm (1in) across. ↕↔ 18–23cm (7–9in). ❀ (min. 2°C/36°F)

Pelargonium 'Sarah Don'

P. 'Saxifragoides'. Slow-growing, trailing, possibly ivy-leaved pelargonium with small, succulent leaves. Produces tiny, double, mauve and white flowers in clusters, 2.5–3cm (1–1¼in) across. ↕ 15–20cm (6–8in), ↔ 12–15cm (5–6in). ❀ (min. 2°C/36°F)

P. Sensation Series. Seed-raised, single-flowered zonal pelargoniums, flowering very early and over a long season, with good wet-weather tolerance. Produce clusters, 10–12cm (4–5in) across, of flowers in shades of pink, orange, or red, some with white eyes, including mixtures. ↕ to 30cm (12in), ↔ 25cm (10in). ❀ (min. 2°C/36°F). **'Sensation Rose'** has rose-pink flowers.

P. sibthorpiifolium. Stemless perennial arising from a caudex-like base. Stalked, heart-shaped, scalloped, dark green leaves, to 2cm (¾in) long, have minute, soft hairs. Clusters, to 4cm (1½in) across, of 2–6 rounded white flowers, 1.5cm (½in) across, marked and lined red, are borne in early summer. ↕↔ to 15cm (6in). Namibia, South Africa (Northern Cape). ❀ (min. 10°C/50°F)

P. 'Silver Wings'. Bushy, compact, fancy-leaved zonal pelargonium with mid-green leaves edged in creamy white. Bears single, lavender-pink blooms in clusters, 5cm (2in) across. ↕↔ 15–20cm (6–8in). ❀ (min. 2°C/36°F)

P. 'Something Special'. Bushy, semi-double-flowered zonal pelargonium with soft salmon-pink flowers in clusters, 10–13cm (4–5in) across. ↕↔ 25–30cm (10–12in). ❀ (min. 2°C/36°F)

P. 'Spanish Angel' ■ Upright angel pelargonium producing clusters, 2.5cm (1in) across, of dark purple flowers with narrow lilac margins. ↕ 18–23cm (7–9in), ↔ 13–18cm (5–7in). ❀ (min. 2°C/36°F)

P. 'Spellbound'. Vigorous regal pelargonium with clusters, 10–11cm (4–4½in) across, of pink flowers, overlaid wine-red on the upper petals. ↕ 30–40cm (12–16in), ↔ 15–20cm (6–8in). ❀ (min. 2°C/36°F)

P. 'Spitfire'. Cactus-flowered zonal pelargonium with silver leaves. Bears single scarlet flowers in clusters, 5–6cm (2–2½in) across. ↕ 25–30cm (10–12in), ↔ 12–15cm (5–6in). ❀ (min. 2°C/36°F)

P. 'Splendide' ■ Slow-growing, short-branching pelargonium. Butterfly-shaped flowers, 2–3cm (¾–1¼in) across, are borne singly or in clusters, 10–12cm (4–5in) across. Dark red upper petals each have a black spot at the base; lower petals are white, sometimes stained red. ↕ 25–30cm (10–12in), ↔ 15–20cm (6–8in). ❀ (min. 2°C/36°F)

P. 'Spot-on-bonanza'. Compact regal pelargonium bearing clusters, 5–8cm (2–3in) across, of very pale pink flowers spotted and splashed very dark pink. ↕ 30–35cm (12–14in), ↔ 15–20cm (6–8in). ❀ (min. 2°C/36°F)

P. 'Standout'. Vigorous, single-flowered zonal pelargonium producing white-centred, coral-pink flowers in clusters, 9–10cm (3½–4in) across. ↕ 45–50cm (18–20in), ↔ 20–25cm (8–10in). ❀ (min. 2°C/36°F)

P. 'Summer Showers'. Ivy-leaved pelargonium bearing single flowers in rose-pink, plum-pink, lavender-blue, or white, in clusters, to 12cm (5in) across. ↕ to 60cm (24in), ↔ trailing to 90cm (36in). ❀ (min. 2°C/36°F)

P. 'Super Nova'. Stellar zonal pelargonium with double, lilac-pink flowers in clusters, 7cm (3in) across. ↕ 30–40cm (12–16in), ↔ 20–25cm (8–10in). ❀ (min. 2°C/36°F)

P. 'Sweet Mimosa'. Scented-leaved pelargonium with deeply lobed, pungently-scented leaves and clusters, 5cm (2in) across, of mid-pink flowers with carmine splashes and feathering on the upper petals. ↕ 23–25cm (9–10in), ↔ 15–20cm (6–8in). ❀ (min. 2°C/36°F)

Pelargonium 'Splendide'

P. 'Sweet Miriam'. Spreading scented-leaved pelargonium with deeply lobed, pungently scented leaves and mid-pink flowers in clusters, 5cm (2in) across. ↕ 23–25cm (9–10in), ↔ 15–20cm (6–8in). ❀ (min. 2°C/36°F)

P. 'Tamie' ■ Dwarf, double-flowered zonal pelargonium producing pure white flowers in clusters, 2.5–5cm (1–2in) across. ↕↔ 13–15cm (5–6in). ❀ (min. 2°C/36°F)

P. tetragonum. Shrubby, deciduous, perennial succulent with 3- or 4-angled, erect, smooth, fleshy, pale green stems and broadly heart-shaped, 5-lobed, scalloped, mid-green leaves, 5cm (2in) long. In summer, butterfly-shaped, cream to pale pink flowers, 6cm (2½in) long, with purple-red veins, are borne usually in pairs. ↕ 70cm (28in), ↔ 50cm (20in). South Africa (Eastern Cape, Western Cape). ❀ (min. 10°C/50°F)

P. 'The Boar' ■ Lax, trailing, evergreen perennial producing rounded, mid-green leaves, 6cm (2½in) long, with dark purple-black centres. From spring

Pelargonium 'Rimfire'

Pelargonium 'Rollisson's Unique'

Pelargonium 'Rosmaroy'

Pelargonium 'Rouletta'

Pelargonium 'Spanish Angel'

Pelargonium 'Tamie'

Pelargonium 'The Boar'

Pelargonium 'Tip Top Duet'

Pelargonium tomentosum

Pelargonium Tornado Series

Pelargonium 'Vina'

Pelargonium 'Voodoo'

Pelargonium Video Series

to summer, bears masses of single, salmon-pink flowers in long-stalked, loose clusters, 7–9cm (3–3½in) across. ↕ 50–60cm (20–24in), ↔ 20–25cm (8–10in). ❀ (min. 2°C/36°F)

***P.* 'Tip Top Duet'** ■ Angel pelargonium bearing clusters, 4.5–5cm (1¾–2in) across, of very pale pink flowers, the lower petals veined and margined mauve, the upper petals feathered and blazed red-purple. ↕ 30–40cm (12–16in), ↔ 15–20cm (6–8in). ❀ (min. 2°C/36°F)

P. tomentosum ■ (Peppermint-scented geranium). Vigorous, evergreen perennial with heart-shaped, lobed, velvety, peppermint-scented, mid-green leaves, 4–6cm (1½–2½in) long, on scrambling stems. Clusters, 4.5–5cm (1¾–2in) across, of 4–15 butterfly-shaped white flowers, 1.5cm (½in) across, are produced from spring to summer. ↕ 75–90cm (30–36in), ↔ 60–75cm (24–30in). South Africa (Western Cape). ❀ (min. 2°C/36°F)

***P.* Tornado Series** ■ Neat, compact, early-flowering, seed-raised ivy-leaved pelargoniums. Single lilac or white flowers, in clusters 10–12cm (4–5in) across, are borne on trailing stems. ↕ to 25cm (10in), ↔ 20cm (8in). ❀ (min. 2°C/36°F)

P. triste. Tuberous-rooted herbaceous perennial producing finely pinnate, trailing, mid-green leaves, 18cm (7in) long. From spring to summer, bears clusters, 3–3.5cm (1¼–1½in) across, of 6–20 star-shaped, freesia-scented, nocturnal flowers, 2–3cm (¾–1¼in) across, in yellow, green, or pink, either in combination or with reddish black. ↕ 15–20cm (6–8in), ↔ 45–50cm (18–20in). South Africa (Western Cape, Northern Cape). ❀ (min. 2°C/36°F)

***P.* 'Vancouver Centennial'.** Stellar zonal pelargonium with bronze and brown leaves. Single orange-red flowers are borne in clusters 7cm (3in) across. ↕ 25–30cm (10–12in), ↔ 15–20cm (6–8in). ❀ (min. 2°C/36°F)

***P.* 'Variegated Petit Pierre'.** Upright and branching, miniature, single-flowered zonal pelargonium with white-edged mid-green leaves. Bright pink flowers are borne in clusters 2.5cm (1in) across. ↕ 13–15cm (5–6in), ↔ 8–10cm (3–4in). ❀ (min. 2°C/36°F)

***P.* Video Series** ■ Very dwarf and compact, seed-raised, single-flowered zonal pelargoniums with dark green, strongly zoned foliage. Bear clusters, 8–10cm (3–4in) across, of flowers in shades of pink, or red, salmon-pink, or mixtures. ↕ 20cm (8in), ↔ 18cm (7in). ❀ (min. 2°C/36°F)

***P.* 'Vina'** ■ Compact, upright fancy-leaved pelargonium with yellow leaves. Double, salmon-pink flowers, flushed coral-pink, are borne in clusters 5–8cm (2–3in) across. ↕ 25–30cm (10–12in), ↔ 20–25cm (8–10in). ❀ (min. 2°C/36°F)

***P.* 'Voodoo'** ■ Unique pelargonium bearing clusters, 7cm (3in) across, of light wine-red flowers, blazed purple-black on each petal. ↕ 50–60cm (20–24in), ↔ 20–25cm (8–10in). ❀ (min. 2°C/36°F)

***P.* 'Warrenorth Coral'.** Compact, fancy-leaved zonal pelargonium with creamy white and mid-green leaves, each with a broad, coral-pink zone in the centre. Double, coral-pink flowers are borne in clusters 2.5–5cm (1–2in) across. ↕↔ 15–20cm (6–8in). ❀ (min. 2°C/36°F)

***P.* 'Welling'.** Scented-leaved pelargonium producing broad, bluntly lobed, mid-green leaves, each with a small brown blotch in the centre, with a delicate, flowery scent. Light red flowers are borne in clusters 2.5–5cm (1–2in) across. ↕↔ 20–25cm (8–10in). ❀ (min. 2°C/36°F)

***P.* 'Yale'.** Long-jointed, trailing ivy-leaved pelargonium producing semi-double red flowers in clusters to 10cm (4in) across. ↕ 20–25cm (8–10in), ↔ 15–20cm (6–8in). ❀ (min. 2°C/36°F)

▷ **Pelargonium, Variegated lemon-scented** see *Pelargonium crispum* 'Variegatum'
▷ **Pelican's beak** see *Lotus berthelotii*

PELLAEA

ADIANTACEAE

Genus of about 80 species of deciduous or evergreen, terrestrial ferns occurring usually in sheltered sites in semi-desert regions, mainly in South Africa and South America, but also in Canada, the USA, and Australasia. Pinnate or 2-pinnate fronds arise from an erect rhizome in spring. Sori are produced around the segment margins. Grow in a terrace or rock garden. In cool climates, grow tender species in a cool to warm greenhouse.

- **HARDINESS** Frost hardy to frost tender.
- **CULTIVATION** Grow in moderately fertile, moist but well-drained soil in full sun, with some midday shade. In frost-prone areas, grow beneath an over-hanging rock and protect with a dry winter mulch.
- **PROPAGATION** Sow spores at 13–18°C (55–64°F) when ripe. See also p.51.
- **PESTS AND DISEASES** Trouble free.

P. rotundifolia (Button fern). Ever-green fern producing a tuft of narrowly oblong, pinnate, leathery, dull dark green fronds, 15–30cm (6–12in) long, with red-flushed midribs, and narrowly oblong to rounded pinnae with finely scalloped margins. Prefers moist, acid soil. ↕ to 30cm (12in), ↔ 40cm (16in). Australia, New Zealand. ❄❄

▷ ***Pellionia*** see *Elatostema*
P. daveauana see *E. repens*
P. pulchra see *E. pulchra*
P. repens see *E. repens*

PELTANDRA

Arrow arum

ARACEAE

Genus of 4 species of rhizomatous, monoecious, marginal aquatic perennials from marshland in E. North America. They have arrow-shaped or spear-shaped, glossy, mid- or dark green leaves. Tiny male and female flowers are borne on spadices, each surrounded by a longer, sometimes wavy-margined, green or white spathe; they are followed by clusters of green or red berries. Grow on the muddy banks of a wildlife pool or a bog garden; their horizontal surface rhizomes help to stabilize the soil. May become invasive.

- **HARDINESS** Fully hardy.
- **CULTIVATION** Grow in full sun, in the margins of a pond or in baskets of loamy soil in water to 20cm (8in) deep. See also pp.52–53.
- **PROPAGATION** Divide in spring.
- **PESTS AND DISEASES** Trouble free.

P. alba see *P. sagittifolia.*

P. sagittifolia, syn. *P. alba* (White arrow arum). Aquatic perennial producing arrow-shaped, bright green leaves, to 15cm (6in) long, on stalks to 50cm (20in) long. White spathes, 7–10cm (3–4in) long, which open widely, are borne in early summer, followed by red berries. ↕ 45cm (18in), ↔ 60cm (24in). S.E. USA. ❄❄❄

P. undulata see *P. virginica.*

P. virginica ■ syn. *P. undulata* (Green arrow arum). Aquatic perennial with narrowly arrow-shaped, strongly veined, mid-green leaves, 30cm (12in) long, borne on stalks to 45cm (18in) long. Green spathes, 20cm (8in) long, which open only slightly, have wavy, yellow or white margins; they are produced in early summer, and are followed by green berries. ↕ 90cm (36in), ↔ 60cm (24in). E. and S.E. USA. ❄❄❄

▷ ***Peltiphyllum*** see *Darmera*
P. peltatum see *D. peltata*

Peltandra virginica

PELTOBOYKINIA

SAXIFRAGACEAE

Genus of 2 species of rhizomatous perennials from mountain woodland in S. Japan. They have peltate, lobed or deeply cut, toothed, glossy, olive- to mid-green leaves: the basal leaves have long leaf-stalks; the stem leaves become progressively smaller and almost stalkless up the stem. Short-lived, small, open bell-shaped, pale greenish yellow flowers are borne in terminal cymes in summer. Grow as ground cover or as foliage plants in a moist, shady position.

- **HARDINESS** Fully hardy.
- **CULTIVATION** Grow in moist, moderately fertile, humus-rich soil in partial shade.
- **PROPAGATION** Sow seed in containers in a cold frame in spring. Divide in autumn or spring.
- **PESTS AND DISEASES** Trouble free.

P. tellimoides, syn. *Boykinia tellimoides.* Clump-forming perennial with rounded to heart-shaped, shallowly lobed, finely toothed, olive- to mid-green leaves, to 30cm (12in) long. Bears pale greenish yellow flowers, 6–10mm (¼–½in) across, in early summer. ↕ to 90cm (36in), ↔ 75cm (30in). Japan. ❄❄❄

PELTOPHORUM

CAESALPINIACEAE/LEGUMINOSAE

Genus of 9 species of evergreen trees, related to *Caesalpinia*, occurring in open savannah and dense woodland in tropical regions worldwide. Cultivated mainly as foliage plants, they have often large, alternate, 2-pinnate leaves. Yellow flowers, each with 5 frilled, spreading petals, are produced in racemes or panicles from the uppermost leaf axils. Where temperatures drop below 7°C (45°F), grow in a temperate greenhouse. In warmer climates, grow as specimen or shade trees.

- **HARDINESS** Frost tender.
- **CULTIVATION** Under glass, grow in loam-based potting compost (JI No.3), with added sharp sand, in full light. During growth, water moderately and apply a balanced liquid fertilizer monthly. Water sparingly in winter. Outdoors, grow in fertile, moist but well-drained soil in full sun. Pruning group 1; needs restrictive pruning under glass.
- **PROPAGATION** Sow pre-soaked or scarified seed at 18–21°C (64–70°F) in spring.
- **PESTS AND DISEASES** Prone to red spider mites and whiteflies under glass.

P. pterocarpum ⚲ (Flame tree, Yellow flamboyant tree). Fast-growing tree, wide-spreading and freely branching, with rust-red-downy stems. Large, 2-pinnate, deep green leaves are composed of 8–20 pairs of elliptic-oblong leaflets, 2cm (¾in) long. In summer, produces ascending racemes, to 45cm (18in) long, of fragrant, bright yellow flowers, 4cm (1½in) across, with obovate, crinkly petals, each with a central brownish red mark. Elliptic to oblong, winged, purple-brown seed pods are 8–10cm (3–4in) long. ↕ 15m (50ft), ↔ 8–10m (25–30ft). Sri Lanka to Malaysia and N. Australia (coast). ❀ (min. 7°C/45°F)

P

PENIOCEREUS

CACTACEAE

Genus (now incorporating the genus *Nyctocereus*) of 20 species of thin-stemmed, climbing or prostrate, perennial cacti, sometimes with thick, tuberous roots. They are found in semi-arid areas of S.W. USA, Mexico, and Central America. The branching, ribbed stems usually have only a few spines, and bear axillary, sometimes terminal, solitary, trumpet-shaped flowers, with wide-spreading petals, which open at night in summer. Where temperatures drop below 13°C (55°F), grow in a warm greenhouse. In warmer climates, grow in a desert garden or against a wall.
- **HARDINESS** Frost tender.
- **CULTIVATION** Under glass, grow in a mix of 4 parts standard cactus compost and 1 part well-rotted organic matter in full light, with shade from hot sun. From spring to summer, water freely and apply a low-nitrogen fertilizer every 6–8 weeks. Keep barely moist at other times. Outdoors, grow in sharply drained, moderately fertile soil in full sun, with some midday shade. Stake tall species. See also pp.48–49.
- **PROPAGATION** Sow seed at 19–24°C (66–75°F) in early spring.
- **PESTS AND DISEASES** Vulnerable to mealybugs and aphids, especially while flowering.

P. serpentinus, syn. *Nyctocereus serpentinus*. Climbing or slightly pendent cactus, sometimes branching from the base. Mid-green stems, 5cm (2in) thick, have 10–17 rounded ribs, with areoles bearing about 12 white or brown spines. White flowers, red outside, 15–20cm (6–8in) long, are borne in summer. ↕ 2–3m (6–10ft), ↔ 1m (3ft) or more. Mexico. ❁ (min. 13°C/55°F)

PENNISETUM

GRAMINEAE/POACEAE

Genus of approximately 120 species of rhizomatous or stoloniferous, clump-forming, annual and perennial grasses found in woodland and savannah in tropical, subtropical, and warm-temperate zones worldwide. They have linear leaves, and are grown for their feathery, spike-like panicles of clustered, oblong to lance-shaped spikelets, borne in summer and autumn, which are useful for both fresh and dried arrangements. Grow in a mixed border.
- **HARDINESS** Most are hardy to -10°C (14°F). *P. setaceum* is frost hardy. Some are frost tender.
- **CULTIVATION** Grow in preferably light, moderately fertile, well-drained soil in full sun. Cut back dead top-growth by early spring. In frost-prone areas, protect with a dry winter mulch.
- **PROPAGATION** Sow seed at 13–18°C (55–64°F) in early spring. Divide in late spring or early summer.
- **PESTS AND DISEASES** Trouble free.

P. alopecuroides, syn. *P. compressum* (Fountain grass). Clump-forming, densely tufted, evergreen perennial grass with flat, linear, pointed, mid- to dark green leaves, 30–60cm (12–24in) long. In summer and autumn, bears bristly,

Pennisetum alopecuroides 'Hameln'

yellow-green to dark purple spikelets in cylindrical to narrowly oblong panicles, to 20cm (8in) long. ↕ 0.6–1.5m (2–5ft), ↔ 0.6–1.2m (2–4ft). E. Asia to W. Australia. ❄❄. **'Hameln'** ▣ is compact and early flowering, with greenish white spikelets, grey-brown when mature, in panicles to 12cm (5in) long. Dark green leaves, to 15cm (6in) long, turn golden yellow in autumn.
P. compressum see *P. alopecuroides*.
P. longistylum see *P. villosum*.
P. macrourum. Densely tufted, clump-forming, evergreen perennial grass with flat or rolled, linear, mid-green leaves, to 60cm (24in) long. In late summer and early autumn, bears pale green, long-bristled spikelets, turning pale brown to purple when mature, in cylindrical, erect or inclined, dense panicles, to 30cm (12in) long. ↕ to 1.8m (6ft), ↔ 1.2m (4ft). Southern Africa. ❄❄
P. orientale. Mound-forming, densely tufted, deciduous perennial grass with upright or arching, narrowly linear, dark green leaves, to 10cm (4in) long. In mid- and late summer, bears softly long-bristled, pink spikelets in long, narrow panicles, to 14cm (5½in) long, resembling bottle brushes. ↕ 60cm (24in), ↔ 75cm (30in). C. and S.W. Asia to N. India. ❄❄
P. rueppellii see *P. setaceum*.
P. setaceum, syn. *P. rueppellii* (Fountain grass). Mound-forming, densely tufted, deciduous perennial grass, often grown as an annual, with upright, narrowly linear, flat or rolled, rough-textured, mid-green leaves, to 30cm (12in) long. From mid-summer to early autumn, bears pink to purplish pink spikelets in plumed, long-bristled, upright to nodding, narrow panicles, to 30cm (12in) long. ↕ 1m (3ft), ↔ 45cm (18in). Tropical Africa, S.W. Asia, Arabian Peninsula. ❄❄. **'Atropurpureum'** see 'Purpureum'. **'Burgundy Giant'** is larger, and is suffused deep burgundy-purple throughout; produces pendulous panicles more than 30cm (12in) long; ↕ 1.5m (5ft), ↔ 60cm (24in). **'Purpureum'**, syn. 'Atropurpureum', has dark purple leaves and deep crimson flowers.
P. villosum ▣ syn. *P. longistylum* (Feathertop). Loosely tufted, deciduous perennial grass, often grown as an annual, with upright or arching stems bearing flat or folded, narrowly linear, mid-green leaves, to 15cm (6in) long, and with long hairs just below the flowerheads. In late summer and early autumn, produces cylindrical to almost spherical, plume-like panicles, to 11cm (4½in) long, with soft, feathery pale green or white bristles, becoming purple when mature. ↕↔ 60cm (24in). Mountains of N.E. tropical Africa. ❄❄

▷ **Pennyroyal** see *Mentha pulegium*
▷ **Pennywort** see *Hydrocotyle*

Pennisetum villosum

PENSTEMON

SCROPHULARIACEAE

Genus of approximately 250 species of deciduous, semi-evergreen, or evergreen perennials and subshrubs occurring in a variety of habitats, from open plains to subalpine and alpine areas, in North and Central America. Leaves are stalked or stalkless, usually linear to lance-shaped, and borne in opposite pairs or whorls, or sometimes alternately on the upper parts of the shoots. They are grown for their racemes or panicles of tubular, tubular-bell-shaped, or tubular-funnel-shaped, 2-lipped flowers; the upper lip is usually 2-lobed, the lower lip 3-lobed.

Numerous, bushy, free-flowering cultivars have been developed; most are semi-evergreen with persistent basal growth, and produce racemes or panicles of foxglove-like flowers from early summer to mid-autumn. Other leaf and flower characteristics are very variable: in the descriptions below, leaves are defined simply as narrow or large, and flowers as small or large. Narrow leaves are linear-lance-shaped to lance-shaped, to 7cm (3in) long; large leaves are elliptic to narrowly ovate, usually 12cm (5in) or more long. Small flowers are 2.5–3cm (1–1¼in) long; large flowers are 5–7cm (2–3in) long.

Grow larger species and cultivars in a border or as bedding and smaller ones in a rock garden or at the front of a border.
- **HARDINESS** Fully hardy to half hardy.
- **CULTIVATION** Grow border perennials in fertile, well-drained soil in full sun or partial shade; grow shrubby and dwarf species in poor to moderately fertile, very gritty, sharply drained soil in full sun. In frost-prone areas, protect border perennials with a dry winter mulch. Unless seed is needed, dead-head after flowering to maintain vigour.
- **PROPAGATION** Sow seed in late winter or spring: sow seed of rock garden plants in containers in a cold frame; sow seed of border perennials at 13–18°C (55–64°F). Take softwood cuttings in early summer or semi-ripe cuttings in midsummer. Divide in spring.
- **PESTS AND DISEASES** May be damaged by slugs and snails, and infested with chrysanthemum eelworm. Powdery mildew may be a problem.

***P.* 'Alice Hindley'** ▣ Large-leaved perennial bearing large, tubular-bell-shaped, pale lilac-blue flowers, white

Penstemon 'Alice Hindley'

Penstemon 'Andenken an Friedrich Hahn'

inside, tinged mauve-pink outside, from midsummer to early or mid-autumn. ↕90cm (36in), ↔45cm (18in). ❄❄
P. 'Andenken an Friedrich Hahn' ■ syn. *P.* 'Garnet'. Vigorous, bushy, narrow-leaved perennial bearing small, tubular-bell-shaped, deep wine-red flowers from midsummer to early or mid-autumn. ↕75cm (30in), ↔60cm (24in). ❄❄❄ (borderline)
P. 'Apple Blossom' ■ Narrow-leaved perennial bearing small, tubular-bell-shaped, pale pink flowers, with white throats, from midsummer to early or mid-autumn. ↕↔45–60cm (18–24in). ❄❄❄ (borderline)
P. 'Barbara Barker' see *P.* 'Beech Park'.
P. barbatus ■ syn. *Chelone barbata* (Beardlip penstemon). Erect perennial with semi-evergreen basal rosettes and deciduous stems bearing lance-shaped to linear, entire, sometimes glaucous, mid-green leaves, to 20cm (8in) long. From early summer to early autumn, bears long panicles of pendent, tubular red flowers, tinged pink to carmine-red, 3–4cm (1¼–1½in) long, the reflexed lower lips with yellow beards, the upper ones projecting over them. ↕1.8m (6ft) or more, ↔30–50cm (12–20in). W. USA to Mexico. ❄❄❄
P. barrettiae. Bushy, clump-forming, semi-evergreen perennial with deciduous stems. Ovate to elliptic-ovate, toothed, glaucous, pale green leaves, 4–6cm (1½–2½in) long, are tinged red. In early summer, bears dense racemes of tubular-bell-shaped, lilac-purple flowers, 3.5cm (1½in) long. ↕20–40cm (8–16in), ↔25cm (10in). N.W. USA. ❄❄❄

Penstemon 'Apple Blossom'

Penstemon barbatus

P. 'Beech Park, syn. *P.* 'Barbara Barker'. Large-leaved perennial with large, tubular-bell-shaped, pink and white flowers borne from midsummer to early or mid-autumn. ↕75cm (30in), ↔45cm (18in). ❄❄
P. 'Burford Seedling' see *P.* 'Burgundy'.
P. 'Burgundy' ■ syn. *P.* 'Burford Seedling'. Large-leaved perennial bearing large, tubular-bell-shaped, wine-red flowers, with white styles and stigmas and white-marked, lighter red throats, from midsummer to early or mid-autumn. ↕90cm (36in), ↔45cm (18in). ❄❄
P. campanulatus, syn. *P. pulchellus.* Upright, semi-evergreen perennial with wiry stems bearing narrowly linear to lance-shaped, toothed, dark green leaves, to 10cm (4in) long. Loose racemes of tubular-bell-shaped, pinkish purple or violet flowers, to 3cm (1¼in) long, are borne in early summer. It is a parent of many hybrids. ↕30–60cm (12–24in), ↔45cm (18in). Mexico, Guatemala. ❄❄
P. cardwellii ■ Spreading, sometimes stem-rooting, evergreen subshrub with elliptic, finely toothed, mid-green leaves, to 4cm (1½in) long. In early summer, bears few-flowered, raceme-like panicles of slender, tubular-funnel-shaped, deep purple flowers, to 2.5cm (1in) long. ↕10–20cm (4–8in), ↔30cm (12in). USA (Washington, Oregon). ❄❄❄ (borderline)
P. 'Charles Rudd'. Narrow-leaved perennial with purple stems and small, tubular-bell-shaped, magenta-purple

Penstemon 'Burgundy'

Penstemon cardwellii

flowers, with white throats, borne from midsummer to early or mid-autumn. ↕60cm (24in), ↔45cm (18in). ❄❄❄
P. 'Chester Scarlet' ■ Large-leaved perennial bearing large, tubular-bell-shaped scarlet flowers from midsummer to mid-autumn. ↕60cm (24in), ↔45cm (18in). ❄
P. cordifolius see *Keckiella cordifolia.*
P. davidsonii. Prostrate, evergreen subshrub with rounded-elliptic, leathery, entire, mid-green leaves, to 1.5cm (½in) long. In late spring and early summer, bears raceme-like panicles of tubular-funnel-shaped, deep pink to purple flowers, to 4cm (1½in) long. ↕20cm (8in), ↔40cm (16in). Coastal W. USA. ❄❄❄ (borderline). **var. *menziesii*** is creeping, mat-forming, and semi-evergreen, with elliptic to rounded, minutely toothed leaves. In summer, bears few-flowered racemes of violet-purple flowers, to 3.5cm (1½in) long. ↕15cm (6in), ↔20cm (8in). W. Canada, N.W. USA.
P. diffusus see *P. serrulatus.*
P. digitalis. Vigorous perennial with semi-evergreen basal rosettes and semi-evergreen or deciduous stems often

Penstemon 'Evelyn'

marked reddish purple. Leaves are inversely lance-shaped, entire or sparsely toothed, mid-green, and 10–15cm (4–6in) long. Panicles of tubular-bell-shaped white flowers, 2.5cm (1in) long, sometimes flushed very pale violet, with purple lines inside, are borne from early to late summer. ↕to 1m (3ft), ↔45cm (18in). E. and S.E. USA. ❄❄❄.
'Husker Red' has maroon-red young leaves and pink-tinted white flowers; ↕50–75cm (20–30in), ↔30cm (12in).
'Woodville White' bears white flowers.
P. eatonii (Eaton's firecracker). Upright, woody-based, evergreen or semi-evergreen perennial with lance-shaped-oblong, leathery, mid-green or blue-green leaves, the basal leaves to 15cm (6in) long, the stem leaves shorter.

Penstemon 'Chester Scarlet'

Penstemon fruticosus subsp. *scouleri* f. *albus*

In late summer, bears erect, one-sided panicles of tubular, bright scarlet flowers, 2.5cm (1in) long. ↕ 30–100cm (12–39in), ↔ 30–35cm (12–14in). USA (California to Nevada and Utah). ❄❄
P. 'Evelyn' ■ Bushy, narrow-leaved perennial. Small, tubular, rose-pink flowers, paler inside and marked with darker pink lines, are borne from midsummer to early or mid-autumn. ↕ 45–60cm (18–24in), ↔ 30cm (12in). ❄❄❄
P. 'Firebird' see *P.* 'Schoenholzeri'.
P. fruticosus (Shrubby penstemon). Evergreen, spreading, semi-upright subshrub with lance-shaped to elliptic, toothed, glossy, mid-green leaves, to 5cm (2in) long. Dense racemes of tubular-funnel-shaped, purplish blue flowers, 2.5–3.5cm (1–1½in) long, are borne in late spring and early summer. ↕↔ to 40cm (16in). N. USA. ❄❄❄ (borderline). **subsp. *scouleri***, syn. *P. scouleri*, has pale to deep purple flowers, to 5cm (2in) long, in summer; W. Canada, N.W. USA. **subsp. *scouleri* f. *albus*** ■ bears white flowers; ↕↔ to 30cm (12in).
P. 'Garnet' see *P.* 'Andenken an Friedrich Hahn'.

Penstemon heterophyllus

P. 'George Home'. Narrow-leaved perennial with small, tubular-bell-shaped, wine-red flowers, with white throats, the white extending over the lips, borne from midsummer to early or mid-autumn. ↕ 75cm (30in), ↔ 45cm (18in). ❄❄❄ (borderline)
P. heterophyllus ■ (Foothill penstemon). Evergreen subshrub with linear to lance-shaped, entire, mid-green or bluish green leaves, 2–5cm (¾–2in) long, narrowing at the bases. In summer, produces racemes of tubular-funnel-shaped, pinkish blue flowers, 2.5–3.5cm (1–1½in) long, with blue or lilac lobes. ↕↔ 30–50cm (12–20in). USA (California). ❄❄❄ (borderline). **'Heavenly Blue'** has blue flowers. **subsp. *purdyi*** is compact, with loose racemes of sky-blue flowers; ↕↔ to 20cm (8in). **'True Blue'** is more lax, with racemes of pure bright blue flowers; ↕↔ to 40cm (16in).
P. 'Hidcote Pink'. Narrow-leaved perennial bearing small, tubular, pale pink flowers, with spreading lobes marked with crimson lines inside, from midsummer to early or mid-autumn. ↕ 60–75cm (24–30in), ↔ 45cm (18in). ❄❄❄ (borderline)

Penstemon hirsutus var. *pygmaeus*

Penstemon isophyllus

P. hirsutus. Spreading to upright, evergreen subshrub with lance-shaped, toothed, dark green leaves, to 10cm (4in) long. In summer, produces loose racemes of tubular-funnel-shaped, pale violet flowers, 2–5cm (¾–2in) long, with white throats. ↕ 40–80cm (16–32in), ↔ 30–60cm (12–24in). N.E. North America. ❄❄❄. **var. *pygmaeus*** ■ is compact and mat-forming, with purple-tinted leaves, 8cm (3in) long; ↕↔ 10cm (4in). **var. *pygmaeus* 'Purpureus'** produces bright clear purple flowers.
P. 'Hopleys Variegated'. Large-leaved perennial producing mid-green leaves with creamy yellow margins. Bears large, tubular-bell-shaped, lilac-blue flowers with white throats, from midsummer to early or mid-autumn. A variegated version of *P.* 'Alice Hindley'. ↕ 60cm (24in), ↔ 45cm (18in). ❄❄
P. isophyllus ■ Erect, sometimes spreading, evergreen subshrub with lance-shaped, purple-tinged, mid-green leaves, 3–5cm (1¼–2in) long. From early to late summer, produces tubular-bell-shaped, red to deep pink flowers, 4cm (1½in) long, slightly suffused white, in one-sided racemes, to 30cm (12in) long. ↕ to 70cm (28in), ↔ 45cm (18in). Mexico. ❄
P. 'King George V'. Narrow-leaved perennial bearing small, tubular-bell-shaped, bright red flowers, with red-marked white throats, from midsummer to early or mid-autumn. ↕ 60cm (24in), ↔ 45cm (18in). ❄❄
P. linarioides. Spreading, semi-evergreen subshrub with many slender, upright shoots bearing linear, mid-green

Penstemon 'Maurice Gibbs'

Penstemon newberryi

leaves, to 2.5cm (1in) long. In summer, produces narrow, spike-like racemes of narrowly tubular-funnel-shaped, pale to deep purple flowers, 1.5–2cm (½–¾in) long, with darker streaks in the throats. ↕ 50cm (20in), ↔ 25cm (10in). USA (New Mexico, Arizona). ❄❄❄ (borderline)
P. 'Maurice Gibbs' ■ Large-leaved perennial bearing large, tubular-bell-shaped, cerise-red flowers, with white throats, from midsummer to early or mid-autumn. ↕ 75cm (30in), ↔ 45cm (18in). ❄❄
P. 'Midnight'. Large-leaved perennial bearing large, tubular-bell-shaped, dark indigo-blue flowers from midsummer to early or mid-autumn. ↕ 90cm (36in), ↔ 45cm (18in). ❄❄
P. 'Mother of Pearl'. Narrow-leaved perennial. From midsummer to early or mid-autumn, produces small, tubular-bell-shaped, pearl-mauve flowers, tinted pink and white, with white throats and red lines. ↕ to 75cm (30in), ↔ 45cm (18in). ❄❄❄ (borderline)
P. 'Myddelton Gem'. Large-leaved perennial bearing pale green leaves. From midsummer to early or mid-autumn, produces large, tubular-bell-

Penstemon 'Pennington Gem'

Penstemon pinifolius 'Mersea Yellow'

shaped, pinkish purple flowers, with white throats. ↕75cm (30in), ↔ 45cm (18in). ✻✻

P. newberryi ■ Evergreen, mat-forming subshrub with elliptic to ovate, minutely toothed, leathery, dark green leaves, 1.5–4cm (½–1½in) long. In early summer, produces dense racemes of tubular-funnel-shaped, deep red-pink flowers, to 3cm (1¼in) long. ↕25cm (10in), ↔ 30cm (12in). USA (Nevada, California). ✻✻✻. **f. *humilior*** is more compact than the species; ↕15cm (6in), ↔ 20cm (8in).

***P.* 'Pennington Gem'** ■ Narrow-leaved perennial. Large, tubular-bell-shaped, mid-pink flowers, with white throats and purple anthers, are borne from midsummer to early or mid-autumn. ↕to 75cm (30in), ↔ 45cm (18in). ✻✻

P. pinifolius. Spreading, evergreen subshrub with crowded, needle-like, pale to mid-green leaves, 1–2.5cm (½–1in) long. In summer, produces loose, terminal, spike-like racemes of narrowly tubular, bright scarlet flowers, each 2.5cm (1in) long. ↕40cm (16in), ↔ 25cm (10in). S. USA, Mexico. ✻✻✻ (borderline). **'Mersea Yellow'** ■ has bright deep yellow flowers.

***P.* 'Pink Endurance'.** Upright, woody-based, large-leaved perennial with long, spike-like racemes of small, tubular-funnel-shaped, white-throated, rose-pink flowers, produced in summer. ↕40cm (16in), ↔ 30cm (12in). ✻✻✻ (borderline)

P. pulchellus see *P. campanulatus.*

P. rupicola (Rock penstemon). Prostrate, evergreen subshrub producing

Penstemon 'Schoenholzeri'

Penstemon serrulatus

elliptic to rounded, leathery, toothed, thick, blue-green leaves, to 2cm (¾in) long. Tubular-funnel-shaped, deep reddish pink flowers, 2.5–3.5cm (1–1½in) long, are borne in late spring or early summer. ↕to 10cm (4in), ↔ 45cm (18in). Coastal W. USA. ✻✻✻ (borderline). **'Diamond Lake'** is more robust, with pink flowers, 3.5cm (1½in) long. **'Pink Dragon'** is more compact, with pale salmon-pink flowers; ↕20cm (8in), ↔ 30cm (12in).

***P.* 'Schoenholzeri'** ■ syn. *P.* 'Firebird'. Narrow-leaved perennial bearing large, tubular-bell-shaped scarlet flowers, 7cm (3in) long, from midsummer to early or mid-autumn. ↕75cm (30in), ↔ 60cm (24in). ✻✻

P. scouleri see *P. fruticosus* subsp. *scouleri.*

P. serrulatus ■ syn. *P. diffusus* (Cascade penstemon). Spreading, semi-evergreen subshrub with ovate to lance-shaped or elliptic, toothed, glossy, dark green leaves, 2–9cm (¾–3½in) long. Broad, dense, one-sided panicles of narrowly tubular-bell-shaped, pinkish purple flowers, to 2.5cm (1in) long, are borne in late summer. ↕50cm (20in), ↔ 30cm (12in). USA (Alaska to Oregon). ✻✻✻

***P.* 'Six Hills'.** Prostrate, evergreen subshrub with rounded, fleshy, grey-green leaves, to 2.5cm (1in) long. In late spring and early summer, produces small, tubular-funnel-shaped, lavender-blue flowers. ↕15cm (6in), ↔ 20cm (8in). ✻✻✻

***P.* 'Snow Storm'** see *P.* 'White Bedder'.

***P.* 'Sour Grapes'** ■ Large-leaved perennial. Large, tubular-bell-shaped,

Penstemon 'Sour Grapes'

Penstemon 'Stapleford Gem'

greyish blue flowers, suffused rich purple and tinged green, are produced from midsummer to early or mid-autumn. ↕60cm (24in), ↔ 45cm (18in). ✻✻

***P.* 'Stapleford Gem'** ■ Large-leaved perennial. Large, tubular-bell-shaped, lilac-purple flowers are borne from midsummer to early or mid-autumn; upper lips are pale pink-lilac, and lower lips and throats are white with purple lines. ↕to 60cm (24in), ↔ 45cm (18in). ✻✻✻

P. venustus (Lovely penstemon). Evergreen subshrub with almost stalkless, lance-shaped to oblong, minutely toothed, bluish green leaves, to 8cm (3in) long. Spike-like panicles of tubular-funnel-shaped, pale to deep violet flowers, 2cm (¾in) long, are borne in early summer. ↕40–100cm (16–39in), ↔ 30cm (12in). N.W. USA. ✻✻✻ (borderline)

***P.* 'White Bedder'** ■ syn. *P.* 'Snow Storm'. Large-leaved perennial bearing large, tubular-funnel-shaped white flowers, becoming pink-tinged, with brown anthers, from midsummer to early or mid-autumn. ↕60cm (24in), ↔ 45cm (18in). ✻✻

Penstemon 'White Bedder'

▷**Penstemon,**
Beardlip see *Penstemon barbatus*
Cascade see *Penstemon serrulatus*
Foothill see *Penstemon heterophyllus*
Lovely see *Penstemon venustus*
Rock see *Penstemon rupicola*
Shrubby see *Penstemon fruticosus*

PENTACHONDRA

EPACRIDACEAE

Genus of 3 species of prostrate, evergreen shrubs from boggy meadows in Australia, Tasmania, and New Zealand. They are grown for their heath-like, linear to ovate or elliptic, mid- or dark green leaves, and for their solitary, axillary, small, tubular flowers; the colourful, berry-like fruits are seldom produced in cultivation. They are suitable for a rock garden or peat bank and grow best in cool climates with mild winters.

- **HARDINESS** Frost hardy.
- **CULTIVATION** Grow in moderately fertile, humus-rich, moist but well-drained soil in full sun.
- **PROPAGATION** Sow seed at 13–18°C (55–64°F) as soon as ripe. Take semi-ripe cuttings in summer.
- **PESTS AND DISEASES** Trouble free.

P. pumila. Procumbent shrub with crowded, obovate, hairy, purplish green leaves, to 5mm (¼in) long. In early summer, produces white flowers, to 6mm (¼in) long, with recurving lobes, occasionally followed by orange-red fruit. ↕8cm (3in), ↔ 30cm (12in). Australia, New Zealand. ✻✻

PENTAGLOTTIS

Green alkanet

BORAGINACEAE

Genus of one species of evergreen perennial, related to *Anchusa*, occurring in damp, shady habitats, and in hedgerows and woodland margins, in S.W. Europe; it is naturalized in the UK and Belgium. It is valued for its flowers, which resemble forget-me-nots, borne in spring and early summer. The simple leaves are long-stalked in basal rosettes, and stalkless along the branching, erect or ascending stems. Grow in a wild or woodland garden, or in a wildflower border; may self-seed freely.

- **HARDINESS** Fully hardy.
- **CULTIVATION** Grow in humus-rich, damp soil in partial or deep shade. Dead-head after flowering to prevent self-seeding.
- **PROPAGATION** Sow seed in containers in a cold frame when ripe or in early spring. Divide in early spring; the roots are brittle and any pieces left in the soil will sprout freely.
- **PESTS AND DISEASES** Trouble free.

P. sempervirens, syn. *Anchusa sempervirens* (Green alkanet). Bristly, tap-rooted perennial with erect to ascending stems arising from a basal rosette of pointed, ovate to ovate-oblong, mid-green leaves, 10–40cm (4–16in) long; stem leaves are smaller. From spring to early summer, bears leafy cymes of bright blue flowers, to 1cm (½in) across, each with a short tube and 5 spreading lobes. ↕↔ 70–100cm (28–39in). S.W. Europe. ✻✻✻

PENTAS

RUBIACEAE

Genus of up to 40 species of mainly evergreen perennials, biennials, and shrubs from forest margins and scrub in the Arabian Peninsula, tropical Africa, and Madagascar. They are grown for their flat or domed corymbs of salverform flowers, each with 5 spreading petals, which last well as cut flowers. Leaves are ovate to elliptic or lance-shaped, mostly mid-green, and opposite or whorled, on prostrate or erect stems, to 2m (6ft) long. In frost-prone climates, grow in a temperate greenhouse, or in containers outdoors in summer. In warmer areas, grow in a bed or border, or in containers on a patio.

- **HARDINESS** Frost tender.
- **CULTIVATION** Under glass, grow in loam-based potting compost (JI No.2), with added leaf mould and sharp sand, in bright filtered light. During growth, water freely and apply a balanced liquid fertilizer every month. Water sparingly in winter. Outdoors, grow in fertile, well-drained soil in full sun. Pruning group 9, in late winter; plants under glass need restrictive pruning.
- **PROPAGATION** Sow seed at 16–18°C (61–64°F) in spring. Take softwood cuttings at any time of year.
- **PESTS AND DISEASES** Aphids and red spider mites may be troublesome.

***P.* 'California Lavender'.** Dwarf, shrubby perennial with ovate to elliptic or lance-shaped leaves, to 15cm (6in) long. Large, flat corymbs of pale lavender flowers, to 2cm (¾in) across, are borne in summer. ↕35cm (14in), ↔45cm (18in). ❄ (min. 7°C/45°F)
***P.* 'California Pink'.** Compact herbaceous perennial with elliptic to lance-shaped leaves, 8–15cm (3–6in) long. In summer, bears flat corymbs of pink flowers, to 2cm (¾in) across. ↕↔40cm (16in). ❄ (min. 7°C/45°F)
P. carnea see *P. lanceolata*.
P. lanceolata ■ syn. *P. carnea* (Egyptian star cluster, Star cluster). Erect or prostrate, woody-based evergreen perennial or subshrub with ovate to elliptic or lance-shaped, hairy leaves, to 15cm (6in) long. From spring to autumn, bears flat or domed corymbs of long-tubed, pink, magenta, blue, lilac, or white flowers, to 1.5cm (½in) across. ↕2m (6ft), ↔1m (3ft). Yemen to tropical E. Africa. ❄ (min. 7°C/45°F).

Pentas lanceolata

Pentas lanceolata 'Kermesina'

'Avalanche' has white-variegated leaves, and white flowers. **'Kermesina'** ■ has red-throated, deep pink flowers. **'New Look'** ■ has dark green leaves and light pink flowers. **subsp. *quartiniana*** has short-tubed, pink to red flowers.
***P.* 'Orchid Star'.** Erect, shrubby perennial with elliptic or lance-shaped, light green leaves, 8–15cm (3–6in) long. Bears domed corymbs of lilac flowers, to 2cm (¾in) across, in summer. ↕45cm (18in), ↔50cm (20in). ❄ (min. 7°C/45°F)
***P.* 'Tu-tone'.** Compact, subshrubby perennial with elliptic or lance-shaped leaves, 8–15cm (3–6in) long. Large, domed corymbs of pink, red-centred flowers, 1–2cm (½–¾in) across, are borne in summer. ↕1m (3ft), ↔60cm (24in). ❄ (min. 7°C/45°F)

Pentas lanceolata 'New Look'

▷**Peony** see *Paeonia*
Caucasian see *P. mlokosewitschii*
Common see *P. officinalis*
Himalayan see *P. emodi*
Majorcan see *P. cambessedesii*

PEPEROMIA

PIPERACEAE

Genus of 1,000 or more species of evergreen, sometimes succulent, rosette-forming or erect perennials, some with trailing stems. They occur in tropical and subtropical regions worldwide, in habitats varying from high-altitude cloud forest to near-desert conditions. All have small, short-lived root systems, but absorb water from the atmosphere and store it in their leaf cells. They are grown mainly for their fleshy, often long-stalked, elliptic to ovate or heart-shaped, usually alternate leaves, sometimes in whorls or panicles. Small, white or greenish white flowers are produced in upright, sometimes branched and panicle-like spikes. Flowering is erratic but mainly in late summer. In frost-prone areas, grow in a warm greenhouse or as houseplants; grow trailing species in a hanging basket, and small species in a bottle garden. In tropical areas, grow as ground cover or in a border.

- **HARDINESS** Frost tender.
- **CULTIVATION** Under glass, grow in loamless or loam-based potting compost (JI No.1) in bright indirect light when in active growth, and in full light in winter. Water moderately in summer, sparingly in winter, preferably with tepid, soft water. From spring to summer, maintain moderate to high humidity, mist twice daily, and apply a balanced liquid fertilizer monthly. Outdoors, grow in humus-rich, moist but well-drained soil in partial shade. Most species tolerate poor light, and many of the thicker-leaved species will survive in dry conditions for some time.
- **PROPAGATION** Sow seed at 19–24°C (66–75°F) when ripe. During growth, take softwood, leaf, or leaf bud cuttings, or remove offsets of rosetted variants.
- **PESTS AND DISEASES** Trouble free.

Peperomia caperata

P. argyreia, syn. *P. sandersii* (Watermelon peperomia). Upright, rosette-forming perennial with heart-shaped, leathery, deep green, silver-striped leaves, 5–9cm (2–3½in) long, with long red stems. Bears small green flowers in spikes 5–8cm (2–3in) long. ↕20cm (8in), ↔15cm (6in). N. South America. ❄ (min. 15°C/59°F)
P. caperata ■ Mound-forming perennial with rosettes of long-stemmed, deeply corrugated, heart-shaped, dark green leaves, 2.5–4cm (1–1½in) long. Tiny white flowers are borne in spikes 5–8cm (2–3in) long. ↕↔20cm (8in). Brazil. ❄ (min. 15°C/59°F). **'Emerald**

Peperomia caperata 'Luna Red'

Peperomia clusiifolia

Ripple' has deep green leaves with darker stripes along the veins. **'Little Fantasy'** is dwarf, with dark green leaves; ↕↔ 8cm (3in). **'Luna Red'** ■ has dark crimson leaves and stems. **'Tricolor'** is slow-growing, and has pale green leaves with wide cream margins and central pink markings.
P. clusiifolia ■ Stiff, erect perennial with obovate, slightly concave, mid-green leaves, 4–11cm (1½–4½in) long, often purple-tinged when young. Pale green flowers are borne in spikes 12–19cm (5–7in) long. ↕ 25cm (10in), ↔ 15cm (6in). Brazil. ❄ (min. 15°C/59°F). **'Variegata'** has red-margined, cream-variegated, mid-green leaves.
P. dolabriformis (Prayer peperomia). Robust, erect perennial, becoming woody with age, with succulent, purse-shaped, bright green leaves, 4–5cm (1½–2in) long; the 2 halves of each leaf are folded upwards and fused along the dark green margins. Leafy stems produce panicle-like spikes, 3–7cm (1¼–3in) long, of white flowers. ↕ to 25cm (10in), ↔ 20cm (8in). Peru. ❄ (min. 15°C/59°F)
P. fraseri, syn. *P. resediflora* (Flowering peperomia). Upright, rosette-forming perennial with stiff, heart-shaped, shiny, dark green leaves, 2.5–4.5cm (1–1¾in) long, pale green beneath with red veins. Leafy stems bear panicle-like spikes, to 40cm (16in) long, of white flowers. The only species grown also for its flowers. ↕ 40cm (16in), ↔ 20cm (8in). Ecuador, Colombia. ❄ (min. 15°C/59°F)
P. glabella ■ (Wax privet peperomia). Spreading perennial with trailing stems and broadly elliptic to slightly obovate, mid-green leaves, 4–6cm (1½–2½in) long, dotted with black glands. Green flowers are borne in spikes 8–12cm (3–5in) long. ↕ 15cm (6in), ↔ 30cm (12in). West Indies, Central and South America. ❄ (min. 15°C/59°F). **'Variegata'** has leaves with creamy yellow margins.
P. griseoargentea, syn. *P. hederifolia* (Ivy-leaf peperomia). Rosette-forming perennial with heart-shaped, silvery grey leaves, 3–6cm (1¼–2½in) long, tinged copper along the veins. Green flowers are borne in spikes 5–9cm (2–3½in) long. ↕ 20cm (8in), ↔ 15cm (6in). Brazil. ❄ (min. 15°C/59°F)
P. hederifolia see *P. griseoargentea.*
P. incana (Felted peperomia). Stiff, semi-erect perennial, later spreading, with succulent, broadly ovate, grey-green leaves, 3–6cm (1¼–2½in) long, covered in white-woolly hairs. Produces green flowers with purple anthers, in spikes 15–20cm (6–8in) long. ↕↔ 30cm (12in). S.E. Brazil. ❄ (min. 15°C/59°F)
P. maculosa (Radiator plant). Robust, erect perennial, becoming untidy as it grows larger, with ovate, shiny, dark green leaves, 12–15cm (5–6in) long, on long stems. Bears spikes, 20cm (8in) or more long, of dark purple flowers. ↕↔ to 20cm (8in). West Indies, Panama, N. South America. ❄ (min. 15°C/59°F)
P. magnoliifolia see *P. obtusifolia.*
P. marmorata ■ syn. *P. verschaffeltii* (Sweetheart peperomia). Rosette-forming perennial with heart-shaped, dull, mid- or bluish green leaves, 7–12cm (3–5in) long, striped silver-grey, with indented veins. Bears green flowers in spikes to 9cm (3½in) long. ↕↔ to 25cm (10in). S. Brazil. ❄ (min. 15°C/59°F). **'Silver Heart'** has pale green leaves with broad silver stripes.
P. metallica (Red tree). Erect, bushy perennial with elliptic, dark red leaves, 2–3cm (¾–1¼in) long, each with a broad silver band down the centre. Bears red flowers in spikes 3–4cm (1¼–1½in) long. ↕ to 20cm (8in), ↔ 15cm (6in). Peru. ❄ (min. 15°C/59°F)
P. nivalis. Variable, creeping or erect, succulent perennial with fleshy stems containing aniseed-scented sap. Boat-shaped, keeled, fleshy, bright green leaves, 1.5cm (½in) long, white or white flushed pink beneath, are densely crowded at the tips of the stems. Tiny, dull yellow flowers develop in very compressed spikes, to 1.5cm (½in) long. ↕ 10–15cm (4–6in), ↔ indefinite. Peru. ❄ (min. 8°C/46°F)

P

Peperomia glabella

Peperomia marmorata

Peperomia obtusifolia 'Variegata'

P. nummulariifolia see *P. rotundifolia.*
P. obtusifolia syn. *P. magnoliifolia* (Pepper face). Stiff, upright perennial with elliptic, leathery, dull green leaves, 5–15cm (2–6in) long. White flowers are produced in spikes 9–12cm (3½–5in) long. ↕↔ 25cm (10in). ❄ (min. 15°C/59°F). **'Green and Gold'** has leaves with golden yellow margins. **'Variegata'** ■ has leaves with wide, white or yellow margins.
P. orba, syn. *P.* 'Princess Astrid'. Erect, bushy perennial with ovate, succulent, softly hairy, grey-green leaves, 4–5cm (1½–2in) long, each with a broad silver stripe down the centre. Bears green flowers in spikes 8–12cm (3–5in) long. ↕ to 15cm (6in), ↔ 20cm (8in). Origin unknown. ❄ (min. 15°C/59°F). **'Pixie'**, syn. 'Teardrop', is a dwarf cultivar, with leaves 2–3cm (¾–1¼in) long. Propagate from the smaller shoots. It may revert, producing larger leaves; shoots bearing these should be cut out as they appear. ↕ 8cm (3in), ↔ 10cm (4in). **'Teardrop'** see 'Pixie'.
***P.* 'Princess Astrid'** see *P. orba.*
P. resediflora see *P. fraseri.*
P. rotundifolia, syn. *P. nummulariifolia* (Creeping buttons). Creeping, usually epiphytic, succulent perennial with slender, fleshy stems, often covered with minute, fine hairs or bristles, and bearing rounded to broadly elliptic, fleshy, bright green leaves, 1cm (½in) long. Produces short spikes, 1cm (½in) long, of yellowish white flowers. ↕ 3cm (1¼in), ↔ to 25cm (10in). South Africa, West Indies, Central and South America. ❄ (min. 10°C/50°F)
P. rubella. Erect, branching perennial, becoming untidy with age, with whorls of 4 or 5 elliptic, pale-veined, pale to deep green leaves, to 1.5cm (½in) long, red beneath, giving a copper tinge to the foliage. Green flowers are borne in spikes 2–5cm (¾–2in) long. ↕ to 20cm (8in), ↔ 25cm (10in). West Indies. ❄ (min. 15°C/59°F)
P. sandersii see *P. argyreia.*
P. scandens (False philodendron). Trailing perennial with heart-shaped, pale green leaves, 5–7cm (2–3in) long. Produces green flowers in spikes 12–14cm (5–5½in) long. ↕ to 20cm (8in), ↔ 50cm (20in). Mexico to South America. ❄ (min. 15°C/59°F). **'Variegata'** produces leaves with broad yellow margins, but tends to revert to plain green.
P. velutina. Upright, bushy perennial with broadly elliptic, fleshy, velvety, dark green leaves, 2–4.5cm (¾–1¾in) long, with pale veins, and red beneath. Green flowers are produced in spikes 9–10cm (3½–4in) long. ↕ to 30cm (12in), ↔ 20cm (8in). Ecuador. ❄ (min. 15°C/59°F)
P. verschaffeltii see *P. marmorata.*
P. verticillata. Erect, fleshy perennial with rounded to obovate leaves, pale green above, red-pink beneath, 0.8–3cm (⅜–1¼in) long, and borne in whorls of 5 at the nodes. Leaves and the lower parts of stems are softly white-hairy. Green flowers are borne in spikes, 2–2.5cm (¾–1in) long. ↕ to 50cm (20in), ↔ to 45cm (18in). W. Indies. ❄ (min. 10°C/50°F)

▷ **Peperomia,**
Felted see *Peperomia incana*
Flowering see *Peperomia fraseri*
Ivy-leaf see *Peperomia griseoargentea*
Prayer see *Peperomia dolabriformis*
Sweetheart see *Peperomia marmorata*
Watermelon see *Peperomia argyreia*
Wax privet see *Peperomia glabella*
▷ **Pepper** see *Capsicum, Piper*
Bell see *Capsicum annuum* Grossum Group
Black see *Piper nigrum*
Cayenne see *Capsicum annuum* Longum Group
Cherry see *Capsicum annuum* Cerasiforme Group
Chilli see *Capsicum, C. annuum, C. annuum* Longum Group
Cone see *Capsicum annuum* Conioides Group
Japan see *Zanthoxylum piperitum*
Mountain see *Drimys lanceolata*
Red cone see *Capsicum annuum* Fasciculatum Group
White see *Piper nigrum*
▷ **Pepper bush, Sweet** see *Clethra, C. alnifolia*
▷ **Pepper face** see *Peperomia obtusifolia*
▷ **Peppermint,**
Mount Wellington see *Eucalyptus coccifera*
Narrow-leaved black see *Eucalyptus nicholii*
Sydney see *Eucalyptus piperita*
▷ **Pepper tree** see *Macropiper excelsum, Schinus molle*
Brazilian see *S. terebinthifolius*
▷ **Pepperwort** see *Marsilea*
▷ **Perennials** see pp.38–39

PERESKIA

CACTACEAE

Genus of 16 species of tree-like, scandent, or shrubby, perennial cacti occurring in wooded, often hilly regions of the USA (Florida), Mexico, Central America, tropical South America to N. Argentina, and the West Indies. They have spiny, slightly fleshy branches; some become woody with age. Some have tuberous roots. The fleshy, lance-shaped to rounded or oblong leaves are usually evergreen (deciduous in species with a dormant period). Bowl-shaped flowers, solitary or borne in axillary or terminal corymbs or panicles, open by day from spring to autumn. Where temperatures drop below 10–15°C (50–59°F), grow in a temperate or warm greenhouse. In warm, dry climates, use in a desert garden or courtyard garden.
• **HARDINESS** Frost tender.

Pereskia aculeata

• **CULTIVATION** Under glass, grow in standard cactus compost in full light, with shade from hot sun. From mid-spring to late summer, water moderately and apply a low-nitrogen fertilizer every 5–6 weeks. Water sparingly in winter. Provide support for stems of climbing species. Outdoors, grow in moderately fertile, sharply drained soil in light dappled shade. See also pp.48–49.
• **PROPAGATION** Sow seed at 19–24°C (66–75°F) in spring. From late spring to summer, take cuttings of stem sections.
• **PESTS AND DISEASES** Susceptible to mealybugs and, while flowering, aphids.

P. aculeata ■ (Barbados gooseberry). Vigorous, scandent, deciduous cactus producing spiny, fleshy stems and lance-shaped or elliptic to ovate, soft, dark green leaves, to 11cm (4½in) long. Brown areoles bear 1–3 yellowish brown spines. In autumn, produces panicles of long-lasting, scented, creamy white flowers, to 5cm (2in) across, with orange-red stamens. ↕ 8–10m (25–30ft), ↔ indefinite. USA (Florida), West Indies, Paraguay to S. Brazil. ❀ (min. 15°C/59°F). **'Godseffiana'**, syn. var. *godseffiana*, has glossy, peach-coloured leaves when young, often purplish red beneath; ↕ 2–3m (6–10ft), ↔ 1m (3ft).
P. amapola see *P. nemorosa*.
P. argentina see *P. nemorosa*.
P. grandiflorus see *P. grandifolia*.
P. grandifolia ■ syn. *P. grandiflorus*, *Rhodocactus grandifolius*. Shrubby, erect, evergreen cactus with thick, spiny stems and narrowly elliptic, ovate, or obovate to lance-shaped leaves, 9–23cm (3½–9in) long. Brown areoles bear up to 8 almost black spines. Corymbs of bright pink to purple-pink flowers, 3–5cm (1¼–2in) across, with white-based petals, are produced from spring to autumn. ↕ to 5m (15ft), ↔ 1m (3ft). Brazil. ❀ (min. 15°C/59°F)
P. nemorosa, syn. *P. amapola*, *P. argentina*, *P. sacharosa* of gardens. Shrubby, often tree-like, erect, evergreen cactus with smooth green branches and lance-shaped leaves, to 12cm (5in) long. Greyish white areoles bear 3 or more red spines. From spring to summer, bears corymbs of white or pink flowers, 8cm (3in) across. Often confused with *P. sacharosa*. ↕ 6–8m (20–25ft), ↔ 1m (3ft). S. Brazil, Paraguay, Argentina, Uruguay. ❀ (min. 15°C/59°F)
***P. sacharosa* of gardens** see *P. nemorosa*.

Pereskia grandifolia

PEREZIA

ASTERACEAE/COMPOSITAE

Genus of about 35 species of upright, tufted, sometimes rhizomatous perennials, and occasionally shrubs and annuals, found in open scree in the mountains of South America. The alternate leaves are entire, toothed, or pinnatifid or pinnatisect with toothed and often spiny margined lobes. Daisy- or thistle-like flowerheads are borne singly or in terminal cymes or panicles. Grow in a scree bed or an alpine house; they are intolerant of winter wet.
• **HARDINESS** Fully hardy.
• **CULTIVATION** Grow in fertile, humus-rich, gritty, sharply drained soil in full sun. Protect from winter wet. In an alpine house, grow in a mix of equal parts loam-based potting compost (JI No.1) and grit.
• **PROPAGATION** Sow seed in containers in a cold frame as soon as ripe. Take semi-ripe cuttings in early summer.
• **PESTS AND DISEASES** Aphids, whiteflies, and red spider mites may be a problem under glass.

P. linearis. Tufted, hairy-stemmed perennial with dark green leaves, to 3cm (1¼in) long, fringed with fine hairs; basal leaves are narrowly lance-shaped to spoon-shaped, stem leaves are lance-shaped. Bears solitary, short-stemmed, deep blue flowerheads, 2.5cm (1in) or more across, in winter or early spring. ↕ 10cm (4in), ↔ 15cm (6in). S. Andes. ❄❄❄

▷ **Perfoliate Alexanders** see *Smyrnium perfoliatum*

PERICALLIS

ASTERACEAE/COMPOSITAE

Genus of 15 species of perennials and subshrubs, sometimes grown as annuals, occurring in forests and on slopes and rocky outcrops in the Canary Islands, Madeira, and the Azores. They are grown for their daisy-like flowerheads, solitary or borne in corymbs, appearing from winter to early autumn. Stems are upright to spreading, simple or branching. Leaves are simple, rounded to broadly lance-shaped or arrow-shaped, arranged alternately or in basal rosettes. In frost-prone areas, grow in a cool greenhouse or as houseplants. In warmer climates, grow in a shrub border or use as summer bedding.
• **HARDINESS** Frost tender.
• **CULTIVATION** Under glass, grow in loam-based potting compost (JI No.2) in full light, with shade from hot sun. During growth, water moderately and apply a balanced liquid fertilizer every 2 weeks. Outdoors, grow in fertile, well-drained soil, in full sun with midday shade, or in partial shade. Remove spent blooms to prolong flowering; discard plants when flowering has ceased.
• **PROPAGATION** Sow seed at 13–18°C (55–64°F) from spring to midsummer. Root semi-ripe cuttings in summer.
• **PESTS AND DISEASES** Susceptible to aphids, red spider mites, thrips, whiteflies, and chrysanthemum leaf miner.

P. x hybrida, syn. *Cineraria cruentus* of gardens, *C. x hybrida*, *Senecio cruentus*, *S. x hybridus* (Florists' cineraria). Cushion-forming or loosely branched perennial, often grown as an annual, with alternate, ovate, triangular-heart-shaped, mid- to deep green leaves, 25–30cm (10–12in) long. From winter to spring, bears loose, terminal and axillary corymbs, 2.5–8cm (1–3in) across, of flowerheads in single colours and bicolours, in pink, red, blue, white, magenta, lavender-blue, and copper. ↕ 45–60cm (18–24in), ↔ 25–60cm (10–24in). Garden origin. ❀ (min. 7°C/45°F). **'Brilliant'** has large flowerheads, 5cm (2in) across, in a mixture of white, blue, deep red, copper, and rose-pink, and bicolours. **'Chloe'** is an early-flowering mixture, with flowerheads in shades of blue, carmine-red, and pink, and bicolours. **Cindy Series** cultivars are compact; flowerheads are in single colours, as well as in a mixture of blue, carmine-red, copper, and pink; ↕ 20cm (8in), ↔ 30cm (12in). **'Royalty'** is late-flowering, with flowerheads in sky-blue, cherry-red, lilac with a white eye, and bicolours. **'Spring Glory'** ■ is compact and early-flowering, with abundant flowerheads in blue, copper, carmine-red, and pink, as well as bicolours; ↕ 20cm (8in), ↔ 25cm (10in). **'Star Wars'** is compact, with flowerheads in a mixture of white, blue, rose-pink, carmine-red, and purple; ideal for small containers; ↕ 15cm (6in), ↔ 20cm (8in).

PERILLA

LABIATAE/LAMIACEAE

Genus of 6 species of erect, bushy, aromatic annuals, with 4-angled stems, found in variable habitats, usually in woodland, from India to Japan. They are cultivated for their opposite, simple, usually ovate, mid- or dark green leaves, often flushed or variegated red or bronze. Whorls of insignificant, 2-lipped, 5-lobed, bell-shaped flowers, each encased in a prominent, 2-lipped calyx, are borne in upright spikes in late summer and autumn. *P. frutescens* and its cultivars are the most commonly grown; their decorative, often purple and frilly foliage contrasts well with the flowers of summer bedding plants.
• **HARDINESS** Frost hardy.
• **CULTIVATION** Grow in fertile, moist but well-drained soil in full sun or partial shade.
• **PROPAGATION** Sow seed at 13–18°C (55–64°F) in spring.
• **PESTS AND DISEASES** Trouble free.

Pericallis x *hybrida* 'Spring Glory'

Perilla frutescens var. *crispa*

P. frutescens. Vigorous, hairy annual with broadly ovate, pointed, deeply toothed, long-stalked, mid-green, sometimes purple-flecked leaves, to 12cm (5in) long. Whorls of tiny white flowers are borne in spikes, to 10cm (4in) long, in summer. ↕ to 1m (3ft), ↔ to 30cm (12in). Himalayas to E. Asia. **. **var. *crispa*** ■ syn. var. *nankinensis*, has attractive, dark purple or dark bronze, sometimes dark green leaves with frilly margins. **var. *nankinensis*** see var. *crispa*.

PERIPLOCA

ASCLEPIADACEAE

Genus of 11 species of deciduous or evergreen shrubs and climbers found in woodland, in thickets, and on riverbanks in the Mediterranean, tropical Africa, and E. Asia. They are grown for their attractive, lance-shaped to broadly ovate leaves, borne in opposite pairs. Small, star-shaped flowers are produced in terminal or axillary corymbs or cymes. Train *P. graeca*, the most commonly grown species, on wires against a wall, or grow over a pergola, trellis, or similar support. The fruits and sap may cause stomach upset if ingested.

- **HARDINESS** Frost hardy.
- **CULTIVATION** Grow in any well-drained soil in a warm, sheltered site in full sun. Support climbing stems. Pruning group 11, in early spring.
- **PROPAGATION** Sow seed at 13–16°C (55–61°F) in spring. Take semi-ripe cuttings in summer.
- **PESTS AND DISEASES** Trouble free.

P. graeca (Silk vine). Twining, deciduous climber with ovate, glossy, dark green leaves, to 10cm (4in) long. Star-shaped, unpleasantly scented, 5-lobed flowers, 2.5cm (1in) across, greenish yellow outside and purple-brown inside, are borne in long-stalked corymbs of up to 12, in mid- and late summer. They are followed by slender seed pods, to 12cm (5in) long, which open to release silky-tufted seeds. ↕ 9m (28ft). S.E. Europe, S.W. Asia. **

▷**Periwinkle** see *Vinca*
Greater see *Vinca major*
Lesser see *Vinca minor*
Madagascar see *Catharanthus*, *C. roseus*
▷***Pernettya*** see *Gaultheria*
P. mucronata see *G. mucronata*
P. prostrata see *G. myrsinoides*
P. tasmanica see *G. tasmanica*

PEROVSKIA

LABIATAE/LAMIACEAE

Genus of 7 species of deciduous subshrubs occurring in rocky sites from C. Asia to the Himalayas. They are cultivated for their flowers and leaves, which are opposite, often finely cut and deeply divided, lance-shaped to ovate or oblong, aromatic, and grey-green. Terminal panicles of small, tubular, 2-lipped blue flowers are produced in late summer and early autumn. Grow in a mixed or herbaceous border.

- **HARDINESS** Fully hardy.
- **CULTIVATION** Grow in well-drained, poor to moderately fertile soil in full sun. They tolerate dry, chalky soil and coastal conditions. Pruning group 6.
- **PROPAGATION** Root softwood cuttings in late spring, or semi-ripe cuttings in summer.
- **PESTS AND DISEASES** Trouble free.

P. atriplicifolia. Upright subshrub with grey-white shoots and ovate, deeply cut and lobed, grey-green leaves, to 5cm (2in) long. Small, tubular, violet-blue flowers are borne in tall panicles, to 30cm (12in) long, in late summer and early autumn. ↕ 1.2m (4ft), ↔ 1m (3ft). Afghanistan. ***
***P.* 'Blue Spire'** ■ Upright subshrub with grey-white stems bearing ovate, very deeply divided, silver-grey leaves, to 5cm (2in) long. Tubular, violet-blue flowers, in panicles to 30cm (12in) long, are very profusely borne in late summer and early autumn. ↕ 1.2m (4ft), ↔ 1m (3ft). ***
***P.* 'Hybrida'.** Upright subshrub with grey-white shoots and ovate, deeply cut, grey-green leaves, to 5cm (2in) long. In late summer and early autumn, bears tubular, dark lavender-blue flowers in tall panicles, to 40cm (16in) long. ↕ 1m (3ft), ↔ 75cm (30in). ***

▷**Persian shield** see *Strobilanthes dyerianus*

Perovskia 'Blue Spire'

PERSICARIA

syn. ACONOGONON, BISTORTA, TOVARA

POLYGONACEAE

Genus of 50–80 species of annuals, often rhizomatous or stoloniferous perennials, and rarely subshrubs. They may be evergreen, semi-evergreen, or deciduous; some have attractive autumn leaf colour. They are found in a variety of habitats worldwide. Often spreading and sometimes invasive, they have usually fleshy stems and simple, entire, variably shaped, often conspicuously veined leaves comprising long-stalked basal leaves and fewer, smaller, alternate, stalkless leaves on the stems. Spikes or panicles of small, usually long-lasting, funnel-, bell-, or cup-shaped, white, pink, or red flowers are followed by distinctive, usually brownish red, 3-angled or ovoid fruits. Some of the larger perennials are undemanding plants for a border, or as ground cover, and are suitable for naturalizing in a meadow or woodland garden. Grow smaller species in a large rock garden, or at the front of a border. Contact with all parts may irritate skin; the sap may cause mild stomach upset if ingested.

- **HARDINESS** Fully hardy to frost hardy.
- **CULTIVATION** Grow in any moist soil in full sun or partial shade. *P. bistorta* tolerates dry soil.
- **PROPAGATION** Sow seed in containers in a cold frame in spring. Divide perennials in spring or autumn.
- **PESTS AND DISEASES** *P. campanulata* may attract blackfly; *P. virginiana* 'Painter's Palette' may suffer slug or snail damage.

P. affinis, syn. *Polygonum affine*. Mat-forming, evergreen perennial with elliptic-lance-shaped, dark green leaves, 5–15cm (2–6in) long, turning red-bronze in autumn. From midsummer to mid-autumn, bears spikes, 5–8cm (2–3in) long, of cup-shaped, bright rose-red flowers, to 5mm (¼in) long, fading to pale pink; flowers turn brown with age, providing colour during winter. ↕ to 25cm (10in), ↔ 60cm (24in) or more. Himalayas. ***. **'Darjeeling Red'** has large leaves, to 15cm (6in) long, and flowers that open pink and turn red when mature; ↔ 50cm (20in). **'Dimity'** has dense spikes of light pink flowers; leaves turn red in autumn; ↕ 10cm (4in), ↔ 45cm (18in). **'Donald Lowndes'** ■ has pointed leaves, and produces dense spikes of pale pink flowers, becoming darker when mature; ↕ to 20cm (8in), ↔ 30cm (12in). **'Superba'** ■ is vigorous, and has pale pink flowers, becoming deep pinkish red, with red calyces; leaves turn rich brown in autumn.

Persicaria affinis 'Superba'

Persicaria affinis 'Donald Lowndes'

P

Persicaria bistorta 'Superba'

P. amplexicaulis, syn. *Bistorta amplexicaulis, Polygonum amplexicaule* (Bistort). Robust, clump-forming, semi-evergreen perennial with ovate-lance-shaped, pointed, mid-green leaves, to 25cm (10in) long; they are slightly puckered and prominently veined above, downy beneath. Long-stalked, narrow spikes, to 10cm (4in) long, of narrowly bell-shaped, bright red to purple or white flowers, 5mm (¼in) long, are borne from midsummer to early autumn. ↕↔ to 1.2m (4ft). Himalayas. ❄❄❄. **'Arun Gem'** is low-growing, and produces pendent spikes of dark pink flowers with bronze tips; ↕ 30cm (12in), ↔ 90cm (36in). **'Firetail'** has bright red flowers. **'Inverleith'** forms mounds of dark green leaves, and produces short spikes of dark red flowers; ↕↔ to 45cm (18in).

P. bistorta, syn. *Polygonum bistorta* (Bistort). Vigorous, clump-forming, leafy, hairless, semi-evergreen perennial with broadly ovate, pointed, boldly veined, mid-green leaves, 10–30cm (4–12in) long. Narrowly bell-shaped, pale pink or white flowers, 5mm (¼in) long, are borne in short, dense, cylindrical spikes, 5–7cm (2–3in) long,

Persicaria campanulata

Persicaria macrophylla

from early summer to mid-autumn. ↕ 75cm (30in), ↔ 90cm (36in). Europe, N. and W. Asia. ❄❄❄. **subsp. *carnea***, syn. *Polygonum carneum*, has deeper pink flowers borne in more spherical spikes; ↕ 45–70cm (18–28in), ↔ 45cm (18in); Caucasus, N. and E. Turkey. **'Superba'** ■ has dense, spherical spikes of soft pink flowers, freely borne over a long period; ↕ to 90cm (36in).

P. campanulata ■ syn. *Polygonum campanulatum*. Clump-forming, stoloniferous, deciduous or semi-evergreen perennial with sparse, lance-shaped to elliptic-ovate basal leaves, to 15cm (6in) long, and numerous stem leaves; all are hairy, with conspicuous veins, and mid-green above, white or light brown beneath. From midsummer to early autumn, slender stems bear loose, short-stalked panicles, 15cm (6in) long, of bell-shaped, fragrant, pink or white flowers, 5mm (¼in) long. ↕↔ 90cm (36in). N. India, N. Burma, S.W. China. ❄❄❄. **'Southcombe White'** has white flowers.

P. capitata, syn. *Polygonum capitatum*. Branching, stem-rooting, evergreen to deciduous perennial with ovate to elliptic, dark green leaves, to 5cm (2in) long, each with a purple V-shaped band. Bears bell-shaped pink flowers, 2–3mm (1⁄16–⅛in) long, in dense, rounded, short-stemmed panicles, to 1.5cm (½in) across, in summer. Good ground cover; may be invasive. ↕ 8cm (3in), ↔ 50cm (20in) or more. Himalayas. ❄❄

P. macrophylla ■ syn. *Polygonum macrophyllum, P. sphaerostachyum*. Rosette-forming, semi-evergreen perennial with woody crowns and lance-

Persicaria milletii

Persicaria tenuicaulis

shaped, boldly veined, mid-green leaves, to 20cm (8in) long. Dense, cylindrical spikes, 1cm (½in) long, of bell-shaped, pink to red flowers, 5mm (¼in) long, are borne from early summer to early autumn. ↕↔ 30cm (12in). Himalayas to S.W. China. ❄❄❄

P. milletii ■ syn. *Polygonum milletii*. Clump-forming, erect, semi-evergreen perennial with linear-lance-shaped, pointed, dark green leaves, to 30cm (12in) long, with prominent midribs and long sheaths. From early summer to late autumn, bears dense, cylindrical spikes, to 4cm (1½in) long, of bell-shaped crimson flowers, 6mm (¼in) long. Similar to *P. macrophylla*, but longer-flowering. ↕↔ to 60cm (24in). Himalayas to S.W. China. ❄❄❄

P. orientale, syn. *Polygonum orientale* (Kiss-me-over-the-garden-gate, Prince's feather, Princess feather). Erect, stout-stemmed, branching, hairy annual with broadly ovate, pointed, mid-green leaves, 10–20cm (4–8in) long, heart-shaped at the bases. Bell-shaped, pink to rose-red or white flowers, to 4mm (⅛in) long, are borne in dense, branching, pendent spikes, 2–8cm (¾–3in) long, in late summer and autumn. ↕ to 1.2m (4ft), ↔ to 60cm (24in). E. and S.E. Asia, Australia. ❄❄❄

P. tenuicaulis ■ syn. *Polygonum tenuicaule*. Slow-growing, mat-forming, deciduous or semi-evergreen perennial with ovate-elliptic, dark green leaves, 3–8cm (1¼–3in) long. Bears short, dense spikes, about 3.5cm (1½in) long, of bell-shaped, fragrant white flowers, 3mm (⅛in) long, in late spring. ↕ 5cm (2in), ↔ 15cm (6in). Japan. ❄❄❄

Persicaria vacciniifolia

Persicaria virginiana 'Painter's Palette'

P. vacciniifolia ■ syn. *Polygonum vacciniifolium*. Creeping, semi-evergreen perennial with branching, red-tinted stems bearing ovate-elliptic, glossy, mid-green leaves, to 2.5cm (1in) long, turning red in autumn. Bell-shaped, deep pink flowers, 4–6mm (⅛–¼in) long, are produced in narrow, upright spikes, to 8cm (3in) long, in late summer and autumn. ↕ 20cm (8in), ↔ 50cm (20in) or more. Himalayas. ❄❄❄

P. virginiana, syn. *Polygonum virginianum, Tovara virginiana*. Upright herbaceous perennial with ovate to elliptic, mid-green leaves with dark green markings, 8–25cm (3–10in) long. In late summer and early autumn, produces slender, very loose, terminal and axillary spikes, 10–30cm (4–12in) long, of cup-shaped green flowers, 2–3mm (1⁄16–⅛in) across, turning red. ↕ 40–120cm (16–48in), ↔ 60–140cm (24–56in). Himalayas, Japan, E. North America. ❄❄❄. **'Painter's Palette'** ■ produces variegated leaves with central V-shaped brown marks, yellow patches, deep pinkish red tints, and red midribs and stalks.

▷ **Persimmon,**
Chinese see *Diospyros kaki*
Japanese see *Diospyros kaki*

PETASITES

Butterbur, Sweet coltsfoot

ASTERACEAE/COMPOSITAE

Genus of about 15 species of dioecious, rhizomatous perennials from Europe, Asia, and North America, some found in mountainous regions, others in swampy sites, by streams, and in moist woodland. They have long-stalked, heart- to kidney-shaped basal leaves and smaller, short-stalked or stalkless, scale-like stem leaves. Thick stems bear purple, white, or yellow flowerheads, which usually consist of a mixture of disc-florets, ray-florets, and thread-like florets (some fertile, some sterile); they

P

Petasites japonicus

are borne singly or in dense corymbs, racemes, or panicles. Individual plants are either male or female. Grown for their large leaves, they provide good ground cover beside a stream or pool, or in a wild garden, although they may become invasive. The flowers provide early nectar for bees.

• **HARDINESS** Fully hardy to frost hardy. Below -10°C (14°F), new growth of *P. fragrans* may die above ground, but the rhizomes will usually survive.

• **CULTIVATION** Grow in deep, humus-rich, fertile soil that is permanently moist but not stagnant, in partial or full shade. *P. fragrans* tolerates drier soil.

• **PROPAGATION** Divide in spring or autumn.

• **PESTS AND DISEASES** Trouble free.

P. fragrans (Winter heliotrope). Spreading perennial with fleshy rhizomes and kidney-shaped, toothed, basal leaves, to 12cm (5in) across, hairy beneath, borne on stalks to 30cm (12in) long. Short, lax panicles of about 10 strongly vanilla-scented, pale lilac to purple flowerheads, 1cm (½in) across, appear with the leaves from midwinter to early spring. ↕ to 30cm (12in), ↔ 1.5m (5ft). C. Mediterranean. ✲✲

P. japonicus ▣ Rhizomatous perennial with kidney-shaped, irregularly toothed, basal leaves, to 80cm (32in) across, hairy beneath, borne on stalks 1m (3ft) long. Densely clustered corymbs of yellowish white flowerheads, to 1.5cm (½in) across, with oblong bracts below, are borne before the leaves in late winter and early spring. May become invasive. ↕ 1.1m (3½ft) ↔ 1.5m (5ft). China, Korea, Japan. ✲✲✲

PETREA

VERBENACEAE

Genus of 30 species of deciduous or semi-evergreen climbers, shrubs, and small trees found in woodland from Mexico to tropical South America. They are grown for their salverform flowers, each with 5 petal lobes, produced in terminal racemes or from the uppermost leaf axils, sometimes forming panicles. Simple, elliptic leaves, with prominent veins, are borne in whorls or opposite pairs. Where temperatures fall below 10–13°C (50–55°F), grow in a warm or temperate greenhouse. In warmer areas, grow in open beds, in borders, or as specimen plants; climbing species look spectacular cascading from a tree.

Petrea volubilis

• **HARDINESS** Frost tender.

• **CULTIVATION** Under glass, grow in loam-based potting compost (JI No.3) in full light. When in growth, water moderately and apply a balanced liquid fertilizer every month. Water sparingly in winter. Outdoors, grow in fertile, moist but well-drained soil in full sun. Support climbing stems. Pruning group 11, in late winter or early spring.

• **PROPAGATION** Root semi-ripe cuttings with bottom heat in summer. Layer or air layer in late winter.

• **PESTS AND DISEASES** Scale insects, mealybugs, and red spider mites may be a problem under glass.

P. kohautiana. Woody-stemmed, semi-evergreen climber producing branching, twining stems and stalkless, oblong-elliptic, dark green leaves, 5–20cm (2–8in) long, with heart-shaped bases. Bears erect to nodding panicles, to 60cm (24in) long, of small, salverform, violet to white flowers, from late winter to summer. ↕ to 10m (30ft). West Indies. ❀ (min. 10°C/50°F).

P. volubilis ▣ (Purple wreath, Queen's wreath). Woody-stemmed, semi-evergreen climber with branching, twining stems and short-stalked, oblong-elliptic leaves, 10–20cm (4–8in) long, deep green above, paler beneath. Bears erect to arching panicles, 20–35cm (8–14in) long, of small, salverform, amethyst to deep violet flowers, with lilac calyx lobes, from late winter to summer. ↕ to 12m (40ft). Mexico, Central America, Lesser Antilles. ❀ (min. 10°C/50°F). **'Albiflora'** has white flowers.

PETROCALLIS

BRASSICACEAE/CRUCIFERAE

Genus of 2 species of cushion-forming perennials occurring at high altitudes in limestone screes and rocks in the Alps, Pyrenees, and Carpathian mountains. They have palmately 3- to 5-lobed leaves, produced in compact rosettes. Corymbs of 4-petalled flowers are borne on short leafless stems in spring. Grow in an alpine house, scree bed, or trough; they are intolerant of winter wet.

• **HARDINESS** Fully hardy.

• **CULTIVATION** In an alpine house, grow in a mix of 1 part each loam and leaf mould to 2 parts grit. Outdoors, grow in sharply drained, very gritty, poor soil in full sun. Provide protection from winter wet.

• **PROPAGATION** Sow seed in containers in an open frame in autumn. Root rosettes as cuttings in early summer.

• **PESTS AND DISEASES** Aphids, whiteflies, and red spider mites may be troublesome under glass.

P. pyrenaica. Cushion-forming evergreen perennial with dense rosettes of 3-lobed, grey-green leaves, to 6mm (¼in) long. Short-stemmed corymbs of cross-shaped, vanilla-scented, pink-purple, rarely white flowers, to 1cm (½in) across, are borne in spring. ↕ 5cm (2in), ↔ 10cm (4in). Europe (Alps, Pyrenees, Carpathian Mountains). ✲✲✲

PETROCOSMEA

GESNERIACEAE

Genus of about 30 species of evergreen perennials occurring on shady rocks in the mountains of Asia. They produce rosettes of variably shaped, usually lance-shaped to nearly rounded, felted leaves, and are grown for their 5-lobed, tubular to bell-shaped flowers produced in few-flowered, umbel-like clusters in spring. In frost-prone areas, grow in an alpine house or cold greenhouse. In frost-free climates, grow on a shady wall or in a rock crevice.

• **HARDINESS** Half hardy; may be hardy to -2°C (28°F) in a cold greenhouse.

• **CULTIVATION** Under glass, grow in loam-based potting compost (JI No.2), with added grit and leaf mould, in bright indirect light. When in growth, water moderately and apply a balanced liquid fertilizer monthly. Water sparingly in winter. Outdoors, grow in gritty, moderately fertile, humus-rich soil in partial shade.

• **PROPAGATION** Sow seed at 13–18°C (55–64°F) as soon as ripe. Take leaf cuttings in summer.

• **PESTS AND DISEASES** Susceptible to slugs and snails, aphids, and whiteflies.

P. kerrii ▣ Rosette-forming perennial with downy, ovate-lance-shaped to oblong, rich green leaves, to 10cm (4in)

Petrocosmea kerrii

long. In summer, produces short-stemmed, umbel-like clusters of 1–3 short-tubed white flowers, to 1cm (½in) across, with 2-lobed upper lips and 3-lobed lower lips, and yellow throats. ↕ 8cm (3in), ↔ 15cm (6in). Thailand. ✲

PETROPHILE

PROTEACEAE

Genus of about 40 species of evergreen shrubs, allied to *Isopogon*, occurring on heathland, in woodland, and on cliffs, in rocky or sandy soil in Australia. The alternate leaves are linear to broadly triangular, simple, lobed, or pinnate or 2-pinnate, and rigidly leathery. They are cultivated for their unusual flowers, borne in dense spikes or cone-like clusters, surrounded by small bracts, from winter to spring. Each flower is tubular in bud, then splits open to the base into 4 rolled sepals, each with a stamen attached. When the flowers fade, the bracts enlarge and become woody, enclosing the seed pods. In frost-prone areas, grow in a well-ventilated cool greenhouse. In warmer climates, use in a shrub border.

• **HARDINESS** Frost tender, although may survive short spells at 0°C (32°F).

• **CULTIVATION** Under glass, grow in a mix of equal parts loam-based potting compost (JI No.1), grit or perlite, and peat or coir, in full light. When in growth, water moderately and apply a phosphate-free liquid fertilizer every month. Water sparingly in winter. Outdoors, grow in poor, neutral to acid, well-drained, sandy or gritty soil that is low in phosphates and nitrates. Pruning group 1; may need restrictive pruning under glass.

• **PROPAGATION** Sow seed at 18°C (64°F) in spring. Take semi-ripe cuttings with bottom heat in summer.

• **PESTS AND DISEASES** Prone to *Phytophthora* root rot when grown in moist soil and high humidity.

P. linearis. Moderately bushy shrub with wiry stems bearing sickle-shaped, flat, thick, grey-green leaves, 3–8cm (1¼–3in) long, with rounded margins. In spring, produces terminal, ovoid heads, to 5cm (2in) long, of pink flowers, 2.5cm (1in) long; the flowers open to reveal swollen yellow stigmas that turn orange when mature. ↕ to 1m (3ft), ↔ to 80cm (32in). Australia (Western Australia). ❀ (min. 5–7°C/41–45°F)

▷ ***Petrophyton*** see *Petrophytum*

PETROPHYTUM

syn. PETROPHYTON

Rock spiraea

ROSACEAE

Genus of 3 species of evergreen sub-shrubs, related to *Spiraea*, occurring in screes or rock crevices in the mountains of W. North America. They are grown for their short, dense, spike-like racemes of tiny, fluffy, cup-shaped flowers, each with 5 overlapping petals, produced in summer, and for their neat, compact habit. They form dense mats or mounds of short, prostrate, branching shoots with densely packed, entire, inversely lance-shaped to spoon-shaped, leathery, hairy leaves. Grow in crevices in a rock

Petrophytum hendersonii

garden, or in tufa, in a trough, or in an alpine house.
• **HARDINESS** Fully hardy in very well-drained soil.
• **CULTIVATION** Grow in poor to moderately fertile, sharply drained, preferably slightly alkaline soil in full sun. In an alpine house, grow in a mix of 1 part each loam and leaf mould and 2 parts grit.
• **PROPAGATION** Sow seed in containers in an open frame in autumn. Take semi-ripe cuttings in early summer. Remove offsets in spring,
• **PESTS AND DISEASES** Aphids and red spider mites may be troublesome under glass.

P. caespitosum. Mat-forming subshrub with dense tufts of spoon-shaped, silky-hairy, bluish green leaves, to 1cm (½in) long. Tiny, cup-shaped, creamy white flowers, with prominent stamens, are produced in conical, spike-like racemes, to 10cm (4in) long, in summer. ↕ 5cm (2in), ↔ 30cm (12in). USA (Rocky Mountains). ❄❄❄
P. hendersonii ■ Dome-forming subshrub with branched stems bearing hairy, spoon-shaped, blue-green leaves, to 2cm (¾in) long. In summer, bears tiny, cup-shaped, white to creamy white flowers in dense, conical, spike-like racemes, to 8cm (3in) long. ↕ 10cm (4in), ↔ 20cm (8in). N.W. USA. ❄❄❄

PETRORHAGIA

CARYOPHYLLACEAE

Genus of about 30 species of annuals and perennials, allied to *Gypsophila* and *Dianthus*, occurring in rocky and sandy habitats in S. and C. Europe. They produce wiry stems, swollen at the nodes, and bear linear to lance-shaped or oblong, sometimes keeled leaves. They are cultivated for their terminal panicles or cymes of 5-petalled, salver-form, white, sometimes pink or yellow flowers, borne in summer. Grow in a sunny position on a bank, in a rock garden, or against a wall.
• **HARDINESS** Fully hardy in well-drained soil.
• **CULTIVATION** Grow in any poor to moderately fertile, well-drained soil in full sun.
• **PROPAGATION** Sow seed in containers in a cold frame in autumn. Take stem-tip cuttings in early summer.
• **PESTS AND DISEASES** May be damaged by slugs and snails.

Petrorhagia saxifraga

P. saxifraga ■ syn. *Tunica saxifraga* (Tunic flower). Mat-forming perennial with linear, pointed, grass-like, rich green leaves, about 1cm (½in) long. Delicate cymes of small, salverform, white or pink flowers, 1cm (½in) across, with darker veining, are borne over long periods in summer. C. and S. Europe. ↕ 10cm (4in), ↔ 20cm (8in). ❄❄❄. **'Rosette'** is more compact, with double pink flowers; ↕ 8cm (3in), ↔ 15cm (6in)

PETROSELINUM

Parsley

APIACEAE/UMBELLIFERAE

Genus of 3 species of biennials, with thick rootstocks, occurring in fallow fields and on rocky slopes and waste ground in Mediterranean Europe. The solid, ridged stems bear triangular, pinnate to 3-pinnate, mid-green leaves with toothed leaflets. Terminal, compound umbels of tiny, star-shaped, white or greenish yellow flowers, sometimes tinged red, are produced in the second year, followed by small, ovoid fruits. *P. crispum* (parsley) is grown as a culinary flavouring or garnish, and is widely naturalized in temperate regions; many cultivars are available. Parsley is usually grown as an annual, as the leaves become coarser in the second year. The tuberous-rooted Hamburg parsley (*P. crispum* var. *tuberosum*) is used as a root vegetable. Grow in a herb garden.
• **HARDINESS** Fully hardy.
• **CULTIVATION** Grow in fertile, moist but well-drained soil in full sun or partial shade. For best culinary yield, in winter in frost-prone areas, overwinter

Petroselinum crispum 'Afro'

in a cold greenhouse or provide cloche protection.
• **PROPAGATION** Sow seed *in situ* from spring to late summer, and keep well watered until germinated. In frost-prone areas, protect late sowings with cloches.
• **PESTS AND DISEASES** Carrot fly larvae may damage roots, and celery fly larvae may tunnel into leaves. The foliage may be affected by leaf spots and by viruses, some transmitted by aphids.

P. crispum (Parsley). Hairless, clump-forming biennial producing triangular, 3-pinnate, shiny, bright green leaves, divided into ovate, toothed segments, each to 3cm (1¼in) long. In summer of the second year, bears tiny, star-shaped, yellow-green flowers in flat-topped, terminal umbels, 1.5–4cm (½–1½in) across. ↕ 80cm (32in), ↔ 60cm (24in). S. Europe. ❄❄❄. **'Afro'** ■ is upright, with tightly curled, dark green leaves. **'Clivi'** is a compact, dwarf cultivar with dark green leaves; ↕ 20cm (8in), ↔ 30cm (12in). **var. *neapolitanum*** (French parsley, Italian parsley) has leaves with flat segments, and a stronger flavour. **var. *tuberosum*** (Hamburg parsley) produces enlarged, edible roots; ↕ to 35cm (14in), ↔ 30cm (12in).

PETTERIA

LEGUMINOSAE/PAPILIONACEAE

Genus of one species of deciduous shrub, related to *Laburnum*, occurring in mountain scrub in the Balkans, grown for its dense, erect, terminal racemes of fragrant, yellow, pea-like flowers, produced in late spring and summer. It has long-stalked, 3-palmate leaves arranged alternately. Grow in a mixed or shrub border. The seeds may cause stomach upset if ingested.
• **HARDINESS** Fully hardy.
• **CULTIVATION** Grow in well-drained, fertile soil in full sun. Pruning group 1.
• **PROPAGATION** Sow seed in containers outdoors in autumn. Take greenwood cuttings in early summer.
• **PESTS AND DISEASES** Trouble free.

P. ramentacea (Dalmatian laburnum). Upright shrub with 3-palmate, dark green leaves, to 9cm (3½in) long, lighter beneath, comprising elliptic to rounded leaflets. Fragrant yellow flowers, to 2cm (¾in) long, are produced in dense, upright racemes, to 8cm (3in) long, in late spring and early summer. ↕ 2m (6ft), ↔ 1m (3ft). Balkans. ❄❄❄

PETUNIA

SOLANACEAE

Genus of about 40 species of spreading to erect, branching, sticky-hairy annuals and perennials from stony slopes, steppes, and disturbed ground in South America. Simple, ovate to lance-shaped, mid- to dark green leaves are mostly alternate; upper leaves may be opposite. Showy, solitary, 5-lobed, fluted, single or double, saucer- or trumpet-shaped flowers are borne in the upper leaf axils.

Many cultivars have been produced, derived primarily from *P. axillaris*, *P. integrifolia*, and *P. violacea*. Although perennials, they are grown as annuals, and are particularly useful in coastal gardens or in poor soil. The flowers, 3–10cm (1¼–4in) across, are borne from late spring to late autumn, in a variety of colours, mainly pink, red, pale yellow, violet-blue, or white. Some have dark veining, central white "stars", "halos" (throats in contrasting colours), or picotee margins. Leaves are usually 5–12cm (2–5in) long.

The cultivars are divided into two groups. **Grandiflora** petunias have very large flowers, generally to 10cm (4in) across. Many are susceptible to rain damage, and are best grown in sheltered hanging baskets and containers. **Multiflora** petunias are bushier than Grandiflora petunias, with smaller flowers, to 5cm (2in) across, produced in greater quantity. They are usually more tolerant of wet weather, and are ideal for summer bedding or in a mixed border; individual plants may carpet an area up to 1m (3ft) across.
• **HARDINESS** Half hardy.
• **CULTIVATION** Under glass, grow in loam-based potting compost (JI No.1) in full light. When in growth, water freely and apply a high-potassium fertilizer every 2 weeks. Outdoors, grow in light, well-drained soil in full sun, with shelter from wind. Dead-head to prolong flowering.

Petunia Carpet Series

Petunia 'Purple Wave'

• **Propagation** Sow seed at 13–18°C (55–64°F) in autumn or mid-spring. Take softwood cuttings in summer; in frost-prone areas, overwinter young plants under glass.
• **Pests and diseases** Prone to aphids and slugs. May be affected by fungal foot rot, and many viruses, including alfalfa mosaic virus, tomato spotted wilt, tobacco mosaic virus, and potato viruses.

***P.* Aladdin Series** ▣ Grandiflora petunias producing flowers in a range of colours, including strong shades of red and salmon-pink. ↕ to 30cm (12in), ↔ 30–90cm (12–36in). ✻
***P.* Carillon Series** see *Calibrachoa* Carillon Series
***P.* Carpet Series** ▣ Multiflora petunias, very compact and spreading, producing flowers in a colour range that includes strong reds and oranges. Ideal for ground cover. ↕ 20–25cm (8–10in), ↔ 30–90cm (12–36in). ✻
***P.* Celebration Series** see *Calibrachoa* Celebration Series
***P.* Celebrity Series.** Compact, early-flowering Grandiflora petunias with blooms in a large range of colours, including shades of blue, pink, or red, or pale tones of pink, yellow, or white, some with attractive dark veining. ↕ 23–30cm (9–12in), ↔ 30–90cm (12–36in). ✻. **'Pink Morn'** has pink flowers with pale creamy yellow throats.
***P.* Daddy Series.** Early-flowering Grandiflora petunias bearing large, heavily veined flowers in pastel to deep pink, salmon-pink, purple, or lavender-blue. ↕ to 35cm (14in), ↔ 30–90cm (12–36in). ✻. **'Sugar Daddy'** ▣ has purple flowers with dark veins.
***P.* Dream Series.** Grandiflora petunias with white, pink, salmon-pink, red or magenta flowers. Good wet-weather tolerance for Grandiflora cultivars. ↕ 30–40cm (12–16in), ↔ 30–90cm (12–36in). ✻. **'Salmon Dream'** has salmon-pink flowers.
***P.* Duo Series.** Multiflora petunias with double flowers in a colour range that includes pink, lavender-pink, red, and burgundy, some with dark veining and some bicolours. Tolerate wet weather, but best in containers or under glass. ↕ to 30cm (12in), ↔ 30–90cm (12–36in). ✻. **'Peppermint'** ▣ has pink flowers with darker rose-pink veining.
***P.* Flash Series.** Compact, early-flowering Grandiflora petunias in a range of colours, including rose-pink, salmon-pink, coral-pink, scarlet, red, sky-blue, blue, and white, all with creamy yellow throats; bicolours are available. ↕ 23–40cm (9–16in), ↔ 30–90cm (12–36in). ✻
***P.* Horizon Series.** Multiflora petunias with flowers in a colour range, including white, blue, salmon-pink, and red, as well as "halo" cultivars, which have throats in white or shades of red or pink. ↕ 25–35cm (10–14in), ↔ 30–90cm (12–36in). ✻. **'Horizon Red Halo'** ▣ has red flowers with white throats.
***P.* Hula Hoop Series.** Early-flowering Grandiflora petunias with blooms in blue, purple, red, or rose-pink, all with broad, ruffled white margins; also available as a mixture. ↕ 30cm (12in), ↔ 35cm (14in). ✻
***P.* Merlin Series.** Multiflora petunias, very compact and remaining dwarf throughout the season, with flowers mainly in red, rose-pink, or blue, with some picotees. ↕ 20–25cm (8–10in), ↔ 30–90cm (12–36in). ✻
***P.* Million Bells Series** see *Calibrachoa* Million Bells Series
***P.* Mirage Series**. Multiflora petunias producing large flowers, to 7cm (3in) across, in white or shades of blue, pink, red, or purple, some with darker veining or with central stars. Good wet-weather tolerance. ↕ to 30cm (12in), ↔ 30–90cm (12–36in). ✻. **'Mirage Lavender'** ▣ has deep lavender-blue flowers.
***P.* Picotee Series.** Grandiflora petunias bearing flowers in rich blue, purple, red, or rose-pink, all with broad, ruffled white margins. ↕ 23–40cm (9–16in), ↔ 30–90cm (12–36in). ✻. **'Picotee Rose'** ▣ is compact, with deep rose-pink, white-margined flowers; ↕ to 20cm (8in), ↔ 45cm (18in).
***P.* Polo Series.** Compact Multiflora petunias with flowers in plain, strong colours, some veined; some bicolours. Excellent wet weather tolerance. ↕ to 25cm (10in), ↔ 30–90cm (12–36in). ✻
***P.* Primetime Series** ▣ Multiflora petunias with flowers in a range of 24 colours and 5 mixtures (one of the broadest ranges for a Multiflora series); colours include white or shades of blue, pink, salmon-pink, or red, some with dark veins or central stars, or picotee margins. ↕ to 35cm (14in), ↔ 30–90cm (12–36in). ✻. **'Red Veined'** has rose-pink flowers with red veining.
***P.* 'Purple Wave'** ▣ Multiflora petunia with a spreading habit and vibrant magenta flowers. Use as ground cover or in hanging baskets. ↕ 45cm (18in), ↔ 30–90cm (12–36in). ✻
***P.* Supercascade Series.** Grandiflora petunias, very free-flowering over a long period, with huge flowers, to 12cm (5in) across, in white and blue, lilac-pink, rose-pink, salmon-pink, or deep red. ↕ to 30cm (12in), ↔ 30–90cm (12–36in). ✻
***P.* Surfinia Series.** Grandiflora petunias, more vigorous and branching than other cultivars, with flowers in white and shades of pink, magenta, red, lavender-blue, and blue. They are free-flowering, with good wet-weather tolerance, and have a trailing habit ideal for hanging baskets. Available only as young plants, propagated from soft-wood cuttings. ↕ 23–40cm (9–16in), ↔ 30–90cm (12–36in). ✻. **'Surfinia Purple'** ▣ has magenta flowers with purple veining.
***P.* Ultra Series.** Early-flowering Grandiflora petunias, compact but spreading, with good wet-weather tolerance. They produce large flowers in a range of 17 colours, including white and shades of blue, pink, and red, or a mixture, some with central stars. ↕ 25–30cm (10–12in), ↔ 30–90cm (12–36in). ✻. **'Rose Star'** ▣ has rose-pink flowers, each with a broad, white central star, creating a striped effect.

Petunia Aladdin Series

Petunia Daddy Series 'Sugar Daddy'

Petunia Duo Series 'Peppermint'

Petunia Horizon Series 'Horizon Red Halo'

Petunia Mirage Series 'Mirage Lavender'

Petunia Picotee Series 'Picotee Rose'

Petunia Primetime Series

Petunia Surfinia Series 'Surfinia Purple'

Petunia Ultra Series 'Rose Star'

▷ ***Peucedanum graveolens*** see *Anethum graveolens*

Phacelia

Scorpion weed

HYDROPHYLLACEAE

Genus of about 150 species of usually erect annuals, biennials, and perennials from variable habitats, including stony slopes, scrub, and woodland, in North and South America. The usually pinnate, sometimes simple leaves are broadly ovate to elliptic or linear, and mostly alternate, the lower ones sometimes opposite. They produce terminal cymes, racemes, or panicles of tubular, bell-shaped, or bowl-shaped, blue, violet, white, or yellow flowers, each with 5 narrow, spreading lobes, and with prominent styles and stamens. The annual species are suitable for a border or a wildlife garden; their nectar-rich flowers attract bees and other insects. Grow *P. sericea* in an alpine house or scree bed; it resents winter wet. Contact with foliage may aggravate skin allergies.
• **Hardiness** Fully hardy.
• **Cultivation** Grow annuals in fertile, well-drained soil in full sun. Outdoors, grow *P. sericea* in gritty, sharply drained soil in full sun. Protect from winter wet; in an alpine house, grow in a mix of equal parts loam, leaf mould, and grit.
• **Propagation** Sow seed of annuals *in situ* in spring or early autumn. Sow seed of *P. sericea* in containers in a cold frame in autumn.
• **Pests and diseases** *P. sericea* is susceptible to aphids and red spider mites under glass.

P

Phacelia campanularia

P. campanularia ■ (Californian bluebell). Erect, compact, intricately branched, glandular-hairy, aromatic annual with simple, ovate to elliptic, coarsely toothed, dark green leaves, to 5cm (2in) long. Lax cymes of upturned, spreading, bell-shaped, dark blue, occasionally white flowers, to 2.5cm (1in) across, are borne in late spring and summer. ↕ 15–30cm (6–12in), ↔ 15cm (6in). USA (S. California). ❄❄❄
P. grandiflora. Vigorous, erect, glandular-hairy annual with simple, broadly ovate to elliptic, irregularly toothed, mid-green leaves, to 20cm (8in) long. Produces erect, densely flowered cymes of upturned, spreading, bell-shaped, lilac-blue or white flowers, to 2cm (¾in) across, in summer. ↕ to 90cm (36in), ↔ to 30cm (12in). USA (S. California). ❄❄❄
P. sericea. Rosette-forming biennial or short-lived perennial with silvery, silky-hairy, deeply pinnatifid leaves, to 10cm (4in) long, with oblong-lance-shaped lobes. Short, dense, panicle-like cymes of bell-shaped, indigo-blue flowers, 6–8mm (¼–⅜in) across, with pale blue anthers and protruding stamens, are produced in summer. ↕ to 55cm (22in), ↔ 10cm (4in). Canada, USA (Rocky Mountains). ❄❄❄
P. tanacetifolia. Erect, hairy annual, with pinnatifid to 2-pinnatifid or pinnate, mid-green leaves, to 25cm (10in) long, composed of lance-shaped lobes or pinnae. Dense, curved racemes of spreading, bell-shaped, blue or lavender-blue flowers, to 1.5cm (½in) across, are produced in summer. ↕ to 1.2m (4ft), ↔ to 45cm (18in). USA (California) to Mexico. ❄❄❄

PHAEDRANASSA
Queen lily
AMARYLLIDACEAE

Genus of about 6 species of bulbous perennials from meadows and rocky slopes at high altitudes in South America. They are grown for their colourful, tubular or narrowly funnel-shaped, pendent flowers, borne in terminal umbels of 3–11, from spring to summer. The leaves are basal, lance-shaped to elliptic, and up to 40cm (16in) long, developing with or after the flowers. In frost-prone areas, grow in a cool or temperate greenhouse. In warmer climates, grow in a warm, sunny position in a border.
• **HARDINESS** Frost tender, but will occasionally withstand temperatures to 0°C (32°F) for short periods.
• **CULTIVATION** Under glass, grow in loam-based potting compost (JI No.2) with added sharp sand and leaf mould, in full light. When in growth, water moderately and apply a balanced liquid fertilizer every month. Keep just moist when dormant in autumn and winter. Outdoors, grow in moderately fertile, well-drained soil that does not dry out in summer.
• **PROPAGATION** Sow seed at 13–18°C (55–64°F) when ripe. Remove offsets in autumn.
• **PESTS AND DISEASES** Trouble free.

Phaedranassa carmiolii

P. carmiolii ■ Bulbous perennial producing erect, lance-shaped, mid-green, basal leaves, to 40cm (16in) long, developing with the flowers. From spring to summer, bears umbels of 4–10 pendent, tubular, shiny crimson flowers, 3.5–4.5cm (1½–1¾in) long, with green and yellow tips, and with conspicuous, protruding white anthers. ↕ 50–70cm (20–28in), ↔ 8cm (3in). South America. ❀ (min. 7°C/45°F)
P. dubia. Bulbous perennial producing erect, elliptic, mid-green, basal leaves, to 50cm (20in) long, with the flowers. In summer, produces umbels of 7–9 pendent, tubular, green-tipped, purple-pink flowers, 4.5–5cm (1¾–2in) long, with protruding stamens. ↕ 50–70cm (20–28in), ↔ 8cm (3in). Peru. ❀ (min. 7°C/45°F)
P. tunguraguae. Bulbous perennial with ovoid bulbs and erect, lance-shaped or inversely lance-shaped, glossy, dark green, basal leaves, 30–40cm (12–16in) long, developing after the flowers. Bears umbels of 6–8 pendent, tubular, green-tipped, coral-red flowers, to 3cm (1¼in) long, in summer. ↕ 50–70cm (20–28in), ↔ 8cm (3in). Ecuador. ❀ (min. 7°C/45°F)
P. viridiflora. Bulbous perennial with erect, narrow, bright green, basal leaves, to 40cm (16in) long, appearing with the flowers. Umbels of 3–5 pendent, tubular, yellow and green flowers, 2.5cm (1in) long, are borne in summer. ↕ 60cm (24in), ↔ 8cm (3in). Ecuador, possibly Peru. ❀ (min. 7°C/45°F)

▷ ***Phaedranthus buccinatorius*** see *Distictis buccinatoria*
▷ ***Phaiophleps biflora*** see *Olsynium biflorum*
▷ ***Phaiophleps nigricans*** see *Sisyrinchium striatum*

PHAIUS
ORCHIDACEAE

Genus of about 30 species of deciduous to evergreen, terrestrial and epiphytic orchids from lowland and montane forests in Africa, Madagascar, Asia, Indonesia, N. Australia, and the Pacific islands. They have spherical to ovoid, sometimes stem-like pseudobulbs, each with 3–10 large, folded, lance-shaped to elliptic, mid-green leaves, arranged alternately. Colourful, often spectacular flowers, with entire or lobed lips and spreading petals, are produced in tall, upright, axillary, many-flowered racemes from near the bases of the plants.
• **HARDINESS** Frost tender.
• **CULTIVATION** Intermediate-growing orchids. Grow in terrestrial orchid compost in deep containers that allow room for the copious root system. In summer, provide high humidity and bright filtered light, and water freely, applying fertilizer at every third watering. Once the leaves are fully developed, mist twice daily. In winter, water sparingly and provide full light. See also p.46.
• **PROPAGATION** Divide when the plants "overflow" their containers (take care when dividing to avoid damaging the clustered pseudobulbs).
• **PESTS AND DISEASES** Scale insects, red spider mites, aphids, and mealybugs may be troublesome.

P. flavus, syn. *P. maculatus*. Semi-evergreen orchid with conical pseudo-bulbs and lance-shaped, mid-green leaves, to 60cm (24in) long, with yellow and white spots. Racemes of fragrant yellow flowers, 8cm (3in) across, with red-brown markings on the lips, are produced in spring. ↕ 1m (3ft), ↔ 60cm (24in). India, Thailand, Malaysia, Indonesia (Java). ❀ (min. 15°C/59°F; max. 30°C/86°F)
P. maculatus see *P. flavus*.
P. tankervilleae ■ Semi-evergreen orchid with ovoid pseudobulbs and several elliptic to lance-shaped, pointed, mid-green leaves, to 1m (3ft) long. In summer, produces racemes of nodding, fragrant, red-brown flowers, 8cm (3in) across, with pink to purplish red lips; throats are yellow and purplish red inside, silvery outside. ↕↔ 1m (3ft). C. China, N. India, Sri Lanka through S.E. Asia to Australia. ❀ (min. 15°C/59°F; max. 30°C/86°F)

Phaius tankervilleae

PHALAENOPSIS
Moth orchid
ORCHIDACEAE

Genus of approximately 50 species of mostly evergreen, mainly epiphytic, monopodial orchids occurring from sea level to lowland forests in the Himalayas, S.E. Asia, and N. Australia. They each have a short, upward-growing, stem-like rhizome, lacking pseudobulbs and producing 3–6 broadly obovate or oval, upright or semi-pendent, fleshy, mid- to dark green, sometimes mottled leaves. Flowers, in simple or branched racemes, are produced from the bases of the leaves, often throughout the year, remaining in bloom for many months. Many hybrids have been produced.
• **HARDINESS** Frost tender.
• **CULTIVATION** Warm-growing orchids. Grow epiphytically on slabs of bark, or in epiphytic orchid compost in a slatted basket to allow the aerial roots to hang outside. Provide high humidity and bright filtered light all year. From spring to autumn, water freely, mist daily, and apply a balanced fertilizer monthly. In winter, water sparingly, keeping the foliage dry. Support the racemes of flowers to prevent kinking, and cut back flowered stems to a lower node to encourage production of further flowers. See also p.46.
• **PROPAGATION** Not suitable for division, although cuttings or offshoots may be rooted successfully.
• **PESTS AND DISEASES** Red spider mites, aphids, and mealybugs may be a problem.

Phalaenopsis Allegria

Phalaenopsis cornu-cervi

P

Phalaenopsis Doris

P. Allegria ■ (*P.* Alice Gloria x *P.* Wilma Hughes). Epiphytic orchid with semi-pendent, broadly oval leaves, 30cm (12in) or more long. Numerous large, rounded, heavy, pure white flowers, to 12cm (5in) across, appear in pendent racemes, 1m (3ft) long, throughout the year. ↕ 1m (3ft), ↔ 45cm (18in). ❄ (min. 18°C/64°F; max. 30°C/86°F)
P. amabilis. Epiphytic orchid with semi-pendent, broadly oval leaves, 15–50cm (6–20in) long. Numerous white flowers, 6–10cm (2½–4in) across, with yellow-margined lips and red throat markings, appear in pendent, simple or branched racemes, 1m (3ft) long, from autumn to early spring. ↕↔ 30cm (12in). Philippines, Indonesia to Australia (N.E. Queensland). ❄ (min. 18°C/64°F; max. 30°C/86°F)
P. cornu-cervi ■ Epiphytic orchid with oblong-ovate leaves, to 25cm (10in) long. Star-shaped, fragrant, waxy, yellow-green flowers, 5cm (2in) across, overlaid with red-brown, are borne in succession throughout the year, in short, branched or simple racemes, 15cm (6in) long. ↕ 15cm (6in), ↔ 20cm (8in). Burma, S.E. Asia. ❄ (min. 18°C/64°F; max. 30°C/86°F)
P. Doris ■ (*P.* Elizabethae x *P.* Katherine Siegwart). Epiphytic orchid with semi-pendent, broadly oval, grey-green leaves, 30cm (12in) long. Pink flowers, 8cm (3in) across, with purple-red lips, are borne in arching racemes, 1m (3ft) long, throughout the year. ↕↔ 30cm (12in). ❄ (min. 18°C/64°F; max. 30°C/86°F)
P. equestris. Epiphytic orchid with oblong-ovate leaves, to 20cm (8in) long.

Phalaenopsis Lipperose

From spring to winter, bears simple or branched, erect to arching racemes, 35cm (14in) long, of small, rose-pink flowers, 2cm (¾in) across, with deep pink or purple lips, streaked dark red. ↕↔ 20cm (8in). Philippines, Taiwan. ❄ (min. 18°C/64°F; max. 30°C/86°F)
P. Esmé Hennessy (*P.* Anna Queen x *P.* Pekoe). Vigorous epiphytic orchid with semi-pendent, broadly oval leaves, 30cm (12in) or more long. White flowers, 8cm (3in) across, with faint yellow markings and crimson lips, appear in pendent racemes, 1m (3ft) long, mainly in winter. ↕↔ 30cm (12in). ❄ (min. 18°C/64°F; max. 30°C/86°F)
P. Golden Horizon 'Sunrise' ■ (*P.* Barbara Freed Saltzman x *P.* Golden Buddha). Epiphytic orchid with broadly oval leaves, to 25cm (10in) long. Fleshy, creamy yellow flowers, 6cm (2½in) across, with red-brown stripes and orange-red lips, are borne throughout the year in short racemes, 15cm (6in) long. ↕ 15cm (6in), ↔ 30cm (12in). ❄ (min. 18°C/64°F; max. 30°C/86°F)
P. Henriette Lecoufle 'Boule de Neige' (*P.* Lachésis x *P.* Ramona). Epiphytic orchid with semi-pendent, broadly oval leaves, 30cm (12in) long. Produces large, pure white flowers, 10–12cm (4–5in) across, in pendent racemes, 1m (3ft) long, mainly in winter. ↕ 1m (3ft), ↔ 30cm (12in). ❄ (min. 18°C/64°F; max. 30°C/86°F)
P. Lipperose ■ (*P.* Ruby Wells x *P.* Zada). Epiphytic orchid with semi-pendent, broadly oval leaves, 30cm (12in) long. Pink flowers, 10cm (4in) across, with red lips, appear throughout the year in many-flowered, pendent

Phalaenopsis stuartiana

racemes, 1m (3ft) long. ↕ 1m (3ft), ↔ 30cm (12in). ❄ (min. 18°C/64°F; max. 30°C/86°F)
P. lueddemanniana. Epiphytic orchid with oblong-ovate leaves, to 30cm (12in) long. In summer, full, rounded, fragrant, waxy white flowers, 5cm (2in) across, with brownish purple bands and pink to purple lips, are borne in succession in short, simple or branched racemes, 15cm (6in) long. ↕ 15cm (6in), ↔ 20cm (8in). Philippines. ❄ (min. 18°C/64°F; max. 30°C/86°F)
P. schilleriana ■ Epiphytic orchid with semi-pendent, broadly elliptic, fleshy leaves, to 45cm (18in) long, dark green spotted with silver-grey above, purple beneath. Numerous rose-pink flowers, 5cm (2in) or more across, with white or yellow lips spotted reddish purple, appear in branching racemes, 1m (3ft) long, in winter and spring. ↕ 60cm (24in), ↔ 30cm (12in). Philippines. ❄ (min. 18°C/64°F; max. 30°C/86°F)
P. stuartiana ■ Epiphytic orchid with semi-pendent, broadly oval, mid-green leaves, 35cm (14in) long, mottled grey-green above, purple beneath. In winter, bears branching racemes, 1m (3ft) long, of white flowers, 8cm (3in) across, with yellow marks and brownish red spots on the lower sepals and lips. ↕ 60cm (24in), ↔ 30cm (12in). Philippines. ❄ (min. 18°C/64°F; max. 30°C/86°F)
P. violacea. Epiphytic orchid with broadly oblong leaves, 20–25cm (8–10in) long. In spring and summer, star-shaped, fragrant, waxy, rich violet-purple, yellow, and white flowers, 6cm (2½in) across, with reddish purple lips, are borne in succession in short racemes, 15cm (6in) long. ↕ 15cm (6in), ↔ 30cm (12in). Malaysia, Indonesia (Sumatra), Borneo. ❄ (min. 18°C/64°F; max. 30°C/86°F)
P. Yukimai ■ (*P.* Grace Palm x *P.* Musashino). Epiphytic orchid with broadly oval leaves, 20cm (8in) long. White flowers, 8cm (3in) across, with yellow-tinted, sometimes purple-red lips, appear in racemes 30cm (12in) tall, throughout the year. ↕↔ 30cm (12in). ❄ (min. 18°C/64°F; max. 30°C/86°F)

PHALARIS

GRAMINEAE/POACEAE

Genus of about 15 species of tufted, annual grasses or spreading rhizomatous, perennial grasses found in extremely variable habitats in temperate regions, from dry slopes to moist lake margins. They produce compact panicles of ovate spikelets, each with 1–3 flowers. Leaves are pale to mid-green, usually broadly linear and flat, with short points. *P. arundinacea* and its cultivars need to be controlled if grown in a mixed or herbaceous border, but are good as ground cover, or planted at the side of a pond or stream.

- **HARDINESS** Fully hardy to frost hardy.
- **CULTIVATION** Grow in any soil in full sun or partial shade. Cut back dead foliage in early spring. On variegated cultivars, which may otherwise revert to plain green after midsummer, cut down all but the new young shoots in early summer to encourage fresh growth.
- **PROPAGATION** Divide from mid-spring to midsummer.
- **PESTS AND DISEASES** Trouble free.

P. arundinacea (Reed canary grass, Ribbon grass). Erect, evergreen, rhizomatous, perennial grass with flat, linear, short-pointed, mid-green leaves, to 35cm (14in) long, occasionally striped yellow. In early and midsummer, bears narrow panicles, to 17cm (7in) long, of pale green spikelets, fading to buff with age. ↕ to 1.5m (5ft) in flower, ↔ indefinite. Eurasia, Southern Africa, North America. ❄❄❄. **'Feesey'**, syn. 'Mervyn Feesey', is flushed pink at the stem bases, and has light green leaves with broad white stripes, and panicles with a faint purplish flush; less invasive than the species. **'Mervyn Feesey'** see 'Feesey'. **var. *picta*** ■ (Gardeners' garters) has a number of variants with white-striped leaves; ↕ to 1m (3ft).

Phalaenopsis Golden Horizon 'Sunrise'

Phalaenopsis schilleriana

Phalaenopsis Yukimai

Phalaris arundinacea var. *picta*

P

▷**Phanera** see *Bauhinia corymbosa*
▷***Phanerophlebia*** see *Cyrtomium*
P. falcata see *C. falcatum*
P. fortunei see *C. fortunei*
▷***Pharbitis*** see *Ipomoea*
P. hederacea see *I. hederacea*
P. purpurea see *I. purpurea*
▷***Phaseolus caracalla*** see *Vigna caracalla*
▷**Pheasant's eye** see *Adonis annua*
Old see *Narcissus poeticus* var. *recurvus*

PHEBALIUM

RUTACEAE

Genus of 45 species of evergreen trees and shrubs occurring in woodland or open, moist and dry habitats in Australia and New Zealand. They are grown for their foliage and flowers. The simple, alternate, often aromatic, light to dark green leaves are linear to rounded or oblong, sometimes cylindrical. Small, tubular, star- or bell-shaped, 4- or 5-petalled flowers are usually borne singly or in axillary and terminal, umbel-like clusters. Where temperatures regularly fall below 5°C (41°F), grow in a cool greenhouse. In milder climates, grow at the back of a border, or use as a barrier or hedge.

- **HARDINESS** Half hardy to frost tender.
- **CULTIVATION** Under glass, grow in lime-free (ericaceous) potting compost in full light. During growth, water moderately and apply a balanced liquid fertilizer monthly. Water sparingly in winter. Outdoors, grow in neutral to slightly acid, moderately fertile, humus-rich, moist but well-drained soil in full sun. Pruning group 1; may need restrictive pruning under glass after flowering.
- **PROPAGATION** Sow seed at 13–18°C (55–64°F) in spring. Root semi-ripe cuttings with bottom heat in summer.
- **PESTS AND DISEASES** Trouble free.

P. squameum ♀ (Bobie-bobie, Satinwood). Large shrub or small tree, erect and lightly to moderately branched if unpruned. Elliptic to oblong-lance-shaped, leathery leaves, 3–10cm (1¼–4in) long, are mid- to deep green above, silver-white scaly with translucent oil glands beneath. In spring or early summer, bears umbel-like clusters of star-shaped white flowers, 8–10mm (⅜–½in) across, with prominent stamens. ↕ 3–6m (10–20ft), ↔ 1.5–3m (5–10ft). Australia (Queensland to Tasmania). ❀ (min. 5°C/41°F)

PHEGOPTERIS

Beech fern

THELYPTERIDACEAE

Genus of 3 or 4 species of deciduous, terrestrial ferns found on shady banks and rocks in high rainfall areas throughout the N. hemisphere and in S.E. Asia. The pinnate to 2-pinnate or pinnatifid fronds, with pinnatifid or pinnatisect pinnae, arise at random from each erect to creeping rhizome, their fronds turning at right-angles to the light. Round sori, without protective indusia, are produced in 2 rows on the undersides of the frond segments. Beech ferns are ideal for growing in a moist, shady border, or among rocks where the soil does not dry out.

Phegopteris connectilis

- **HARDINESS** Fully hardy.
- **CULTIVATION** Grow in moderately fertile, humus-rich, reliably moist soil, preferably in deep shade.
- **PROPAGATION** Sow spores at 15°C (59°F) as soon as ripe. Divide in spring. See also p.51.
- **PESTS AND DISEASES** Trouble free.

P. connectilis ■ syn. *Thelypteris phegopteris* (Beech fern). Deciduous fern bearing long-stalked, arrow-shaped to triangular, pinnate, pale green fronds, 30cm (12in) long, with oblong or linear to lance-shaped, deeply pinnatifid pinnae, composed of oblong segments. The lowest pair of pinnae point forwards and downwards. ↕ 30cm (12in), ↔ indefinite. N. hemisphere. ❄❄❄
P. decursive-pinnata. Deciduous fern producing tufts of narrowly lance-shaped, pinnate or 2-pinnatifid, pale green fronds, to 80cm (32in) long, each tapering gradually to a stalk up to 20cm (8in) long. Pinnae are entire and linear, occasionally pinnatifid. ↕ 80cm (32in), ↔ 40cm (16in). E. Asia. ❄❄❄
P. hexagonoptera, syn. *Thelypteris hexagonoptera* (Broad beech fern). Deciduous fern with long-stalked, triangular, pinnate-pinnatifid fronds, 40cm (16in) long. Similar to *P. connectilis*, but fronds and pinnae are broader, and the lowest pair of pinnae do not point forwards or downwards. ↕ 40cm (16in), ↔ indefinite. E. North America. ❄❄❄

PHELLODENDRON

RUTACEAE

Genus of 10 species of deciduous, dioecious trees found in moist stream margins in the mountains of E. Asia. They have opposite, pinnate, dull yellowish green to dark green leaves. Small, cup-shaped green male and female flowers are borne in clusters on separate plants in summer, and both must be grown to produce the dark blue-black, spherical fruits, 1cm (½in) across. Grown for their habit and aromatic foliage, usually giving fine autumn colour, phellodendrons are best used as specimen trees in a garden large enough to accommodate their spreading habit. They thrive in areas with hot summers.

- **HARDINESS** Fully hardy, but young growth may be damaged by late frosts.
- **CULTIVATION** Grow in deep, fertile, well-drained soil in full sun. Pruning group 1.
- **PROPAGATION** Sow seed in containers outdoors in autumn. Root heeled semi-ripe cuttings in midsummer.
- **PESTS AND DISEASES** Trouble free.

P. amurense ♀ (Amur cork tree). Spreading tree with stout shoots, and with thick, corky, pale grey-brown bark when mature. Bears pinnate leaves, to 35cm (14in) long, with up to 13 ovate to lance-shaped, glossy, dark green leaflets, glaucous beneath, turning yellow in autumn. ↕ to 14m (46ft), ↔ 15m (50ft). N.E. Asia. ❄❄❄. **var *sachalinense*** see *P. sachalinense*.
P. chinense ■ ♀ Spreading tree with stout shoots and thin, dark grey-brown bark. Produces pinnate leaves, to 40cm (16in) long, with up to 13 oblong to lance-shaped leaflets, yellow-green above, light green and downy beneath, turning yellow in autumn. ↕ 10m (30ft), ↔ 12m (40ft). C. China. ❄❄❄
P. lavalleei ♀ Spreading tree with stout shoots and slightly corky, pale grey-brown bark when mature. Bears pinnate leaves, to 35cm (14in) long, with up to 11 oval to lance-shaped, tapered, matt, mid-green leaflets, downy on the veins beneath, turning yellow in autumn. ↕ 10m (30ft), ↔ 12m (40ft). Japan. ❄❄❄
P. sachalinense ♀ syn. *P. amurense* var. *sachalinense*. Spreading tree with stout shoots and thin, finely channelled, dark brown bark. Bears pinnate leaves, to 30cm (12in) long, with up to 13 ovate-oblong leaflets, dull green above, smooth and blue-green beneath, turning yellow in autumn. ↕ 10m (30ft), ↔ 12m (40ft). Russia (Sakhalin), Korea, Japan. ❄❄❄

Phellodendron chinense

PHILADELPHUS

Mock orange

HYDRANGEACEAE/PHILADELPHACEAE

Genus of about 40 species of mainly deciduous shrubs found in scrub and on rocky hillsides from E. Europe to the Himalayas, E. Asia, and North and Central America. They are cultivated for their usually fragrant, 4-petalled, cup- or bowl-shaped, sometimes cross-shaped, single, semi-double, or double flowers, produced singly or in racemes, panicles, or cymes. The leaves are simple, mostly ovate, and usually mid-green, arranged in opposite pairs. Grow in a shrub border, or as specimen plants in a woodland garden; larger species and cultivars may be used for screening. Grow *P. mexicanus* against a wall; in frost-prone climates, grow in a cool greenhouse.

- **HARDINESS** Fully hardy to half hardy.
- **CULTIVATION** Grow in any moderately fertile, well-drained soil in full sun or partial shade. *P. microphyllus* needs full sun. Under glass, grow in loam-based potting compost (JI No.3) in full light or bright filtered light. During the growing season, water freely and apply a balanced liquid fertilizer monthly. Keep just moist in winter. Pruning group 2.
- **PROPAGATION** Take softwood cuttings in summer, or hardwood cuttings in autumn or winter.
- **PESTS AND DISEASES** Powdery mildew and aphids may be a problem.

P. 'Avalanche'. Upright, spreading, deciduous shrub with arching branches and elliptic, entire leaves, to 2.5cm (1in) long. Racemes of up to 7 single, cup-shaped, fragrant white flowers, 2.5cm (1in) across, are borne profusely in mid- and late summer. ↕ to 1.5m (5ft), ↔ 3m (10ft). ❄❄❄
P. 'Beauclerk' ■ Slightly arching, deciduous shrub with broadly ovate, toothed leaves, to 6cm (2½in) long. Large, single, cup-shaped white flowers, 5cm (2in) across, with slightly pink-flushed centres, are borne singly or in racemes of 3–5, in early and mid-summer. ↕↔ 2.5m (8ft). ❄❄❄

Philadelphus 'Beauclerk'

P

Philadelphus 'Boule d'Argent'

Philadelphus 'Burfordensis'

***P.* 'Belle Etoile'.** Arching, deciduous shrub with narrowly ovate, tapered, entire leaves, to 9cm (3½in) long. Single, cup-shaped, very fragrant white flowers, 5cm (2in) across, marked pale purple in the centres, are freely borne singly or in 3- to 5-flowered racemes, in late spring and early summer. ↕1.2m (4ft), ↔2.5m (8ft). ✲✲✲

***P.* 'Boule d'Argent'** ■ Arching, compact, bushy, deciduous shrub with broadly ovate, entire, dark green leaves, to 6cm (2½in) long. In early and midsummer, slightly fragrant, semi-double to double, milk-white flowers, 4.5cm (1¾in) across, are profusely borne in racemes of 5–7. ↕↔1.5m (5ft). ✲✲✲

***P.* 'Bouquet Blanc'.** Upright, deciduous shrub with ovate, nearly entire leaves, to 5cm (2in) long. Semi-double to double, fragrant white flowers, 2.5cm (1in) across, are borne singly, in pairs, or in racemes of 3–5, in early or midsummer. ↕2m (6ft), ↔1.5m (5ft). ✲✲✲

***P.* 'Buckley's Quill'** ■ Upright, deciduous shrub with ovate, entire, dark green leaves, to 8cm (3in) long. Double, fragrant white flowers, 2.5cm (1in) across, each with about 30 quill-like petals, are produced singly or in racemes of 3–5, in early or midsummer. ↕2m (6ft), ↔1.2m (4ft). ✲✲✲

***P.* 'Burfordensis'** ■ Vigorous, upright, deciduous shrub with ovate, toothed, dark green leaves, to 11cm (4½in) long. Large, single, cup-shaped, slightly fragrant white flowers, to 7cm (3in) across, are profusely borne in racemes of 5–9, in early and midsummer. ↕3m (10ft), ↔2m (6ft). ✲✲✲

P. coronarius (Mock orange). Broadly upright, deciduous shrub with ovate, shallowly toothed leaves, to 10cm (4in) long. Short, terminal racemes of 5–9 cup-shaped, single, very fragrant, creamy white flowers, 2.5cm (1in) across, are produced in early summer. ↕3m (10ft), ↔2.5m (8ft). S. Europe, Caucasus. ✲✲✲. **'Aureus'** has golden yellow leaves, turning yellow-green in summer; foliage of flowering shoots may burn in full sun; ↕2.5m (8ft), ↔1.5m (5ft). **'Variegatus'** ■ has leaves with broad white margins, and white flowers; ↕2.5m (8ft), ↔2m (6ft)

***P.* 'Dame Blanche'** ■ Compact, arching, bushy, deciduous shrub with peeling, dark blackish brown bark and ovate, entire, dark green leaves, to 2cm (¾in) long. Semi-double to nearly double, fragrant, pure white flowers, to 2cm (¾in) across, are freely borne, usually in pairs or in 3- to 5-flowered racemes, in early or midsummer. ↕↔2m (6ft). ✲✲✲

Philadelphus coronarius 'Variegatus'

Philadelphus delavayi f. *melanocalyx*

P. delavayi. Upright, deciduous shrub with arching branches and ovate, tapered, sometimes toothed, dark green leaves, to 10cm (4in) or more long. In early or midsummer, bears racemes of 5–9 single, cup-shaped, very fragrant, pure white flowers, 4cm (1½in) across, often purple-flushed on the backs of the sepals. ↕3m (10ft), ↔2.5m (8ft). W. China, S.E. Tibet, N. Burma. ✲✲. **f. *melanocalyx*** ■ syn. *P. purpurascens*, produces white flowers with dark purple sepals.

***P.* 'Girandole'.** Upright, deciduous shrub with ovate leaves, to 5cm (2in) long, nearly entire or each with 1–6 teeth on both margins. Dense, double, fragrant, creamy white flowers, to 4cm (1½in) across, are borne in racemes of up to 7, in early and midsummer. ↕↔1.5m (5ft). ✲✲✲

***P.* 'Glacier'.** Upright, deciduous shrub with small, ovate, toothed leaves, to 4cm (1½in) long. Dense racemes of up to 9 double, fragrant white flowers, 2.5cm (1in) across, are borne in midsummer. ↕↔1.5m (5ft). ✲✲✲

***P.* 'Innocence'.** Upright, deciduous shrub with arching branches and ovate, entire leaves, to 5cm (2in) long, strongly mottled yellow. Single, or sometimes semi-double, cup-shaped, very fragrant white flowers, 3–3.5cm (1¼–1½in) across, usually in 3-flowered racemes, are produced in early or midsummer. ↕3m (10ft), ↔2m (6ft). ✲✲✲

***P.* 'Lemoinei'** ■ Upright, deciduous shrub with arching branches and ovate, tapered leaves, to 5cm (2in) long, each with 2 or 3 teeth on both margins. Small, single, cup-shaped, extremely fragrant, pure white flowers, 2.5cm (1in) across, are profusely borne in racemes of 3–5, in early or midsummer. ↕↔1.5m (5ft). ✲✲✲

P. lewisii. Spreading, deciduous shrub with arching branches and ovate, sometimes finely toothed, bright green leaves, to 10cm (4in) long. Racemes of 5–11 unscented or slightly fragrant, single, cup-shaped, pure white flowers, 4cm (1½in) across, are profusely borne in early or midsummer. ↕↔3m (10ft). W. North America (British Columbia to California). ✲✲✲

Philadelphus 'Buckley's Quill' (inset: flower detail)

Philadelphus 'Dame Blanche'

Philadelphus 'Lemoinei'

P

Philadelphus 'Manteau d'Hermine'

Philadelphus 'Virginal'

P. magdalenae. Spreading, bushy, deciduous shrub with ovate, short-pointed, entire leaves, to 6cm (2½in) long. Single, cup-shaped, slightly fragrant, pure white flowers, 2.5cm (1in) across, are borne in racemes of up to 11, in late spring and early summer. ↕↔ 4m (12ft). W. China. ❄❄❄

***P.* 'Manteau d'Hermine'** ▣ Bushy, compact, deciduous shrub with arching shoots and elliptic, pointed, entire, pale to mid-green leaves, to 2.5cm (1in) long. Produces double, very fragrant, creamy white flowers, 4cm (1½in) across, usually in racemes of 3, in early and midsummer. ↕ 75cm (30in), ↔ 1.5m (5ft). ❄❄❄

P. mexicanus. Spreading, evergreen shrub with pendent, bristly shoots and ovate, sometimes sparsely toothed leaves, to 11cm (4½in) long. Single, cup-shaped, strongly rose-scented, creamy white flowers, to 4cm (1½in) across, are borne singly or in racemes of 3, in summer. ↕↔ 2m (6ft) or more. Mexico, Guatemala. ❄. **'Rose Syringa'** has flowers with conspicuous purple-pink markings in the centres.

P. microphyllus ▣ Compact, upright, deciduous shrub with peeling, dark chestnut-brown bark and small, elliptic, entire, glossy, mid-green leaves, to 2cm (¾in) long. Solitary or paired, single, cross-shaped, very fragrant, pure white flowers, 2.5cm (1in) across, are borne in early and midsummer. ↕↔ 1m (3ft). S.W. USA. ❄❄❄

***P.* 'Mont Blanc'.** Upright, deciduous shrub with ovate, sparsely toothed leaves, to 3cm (1¼in) long. Single, cross-shaped, fragrant, pure white flowers, to 2.5cm (1in) across, are profusely borne singly or in racemes of up to 5, in early summer. ↕↔ 1m (3ft). ❄❄❄

Philadelphus microphyllus

P. purpurascens see *P. delavayi* f. *melanocalyx*.

***P.* 'Silberregen'**, syn. *P.* 'Silver Showers'. Rounded, deciduous shrub with upright, arching shoots and ovate, entire leaves, to 4cm (1½in) long. Solitary, single, cup-shaped, strawberry-scented, pure white flowers, 4cm (1½in) across, are profusely borne in early summer. ↕ 1.2m (4ft), ↔ 1.5m (5ft). ❄❄❄

***P.* 'Silver Showers'** see *P.* 'Silberregen'.

P. subcanus. Erect, deciduous shrub with smooth, grey-brown bark, later peeling, and ovate or ovate-lance-shaped, finely toothed leaves, 4–14cm (1½–5½in) long. In early summer, produces racemes of 5–20 or more shallowly cup-shaped, slightly fragrant white flowers, 2.5–3cm (1–1¼in) across. ↕ 6m (20ft), ↔ 2–3m (6–10ft). S.W. China. ❄

***P.* 'Sybille'.** Arching, deciduous shrub with broadly ovate, entire leaves, to 5cm (2in) long. In early or midsummer, single, cup-shaped, very fragrant white flowers, to 5cm (2in) across, with conspicuous purple marks in the centres, are profusely produced, either singly or in racemes of 3–5. ↕ 1.2m (4ft), ↔ 2m (6ft). ❄❄❄

***P.* 'Virginal'** ▣ Vigorous, upright, deciduous shrub with ovate, entire, dark green leaves, to 8cm (3in) or more long. Double, very fragrant, pure white flowers, 5cm (2in) across, are produced in loose racemes of 5–9, in early or midsummer. ↕ 3m (10ft) or more, ↔ 2.5m (8ft). ❄❄❄

x PHILAGERIA

LILIACEAE/PHILESIACEAE

Hybrid genus of one evergreen shrub, derived from crosses between *Philesia* and *Lapageria*. It is cultivated for its pendent, tubular flowers, which are produced in summer, and has entire, leathery leaves, which are arranged alternately. In frost-prone climates, grow in a cool greenhouse. In warmer areas, grow on a moist, shady bank or against a shaded wall.

- **HARDINESS** Frost tender.
- **CULTIVATION** Under glass, grow in lime-free (ericaceous) compost with added sharp sand, in bright indirect light. When in growth, water freely and apply a balanced liquid fertilizer every month. Water sparingly in winter. Outdoors, grow in moderately fertile, humus-rich, reliably moist, acid soil in partial shade. Support climbing stems. Pruning group 12, in spring.
- **PROPAGATION** Layer in autumn.
- **PESTS AND DISEASES** Trouble free.

x *P. veitchii* (*Lapageria rosea* x *Philesia magellanica*). Twining or scrambling, evergreen shrub producing oblong, 3-veined, glossy, dark green leaves, to 4cm (1½in) long. Pendent, tubular, bright rose-pink flowers, 5cm (2in) long, are borne singly from the leaf axils in summer. ↕ 3–4m (10–12ft). ⌂ (min. 2°C/36°F).

PHILESIA

PHILESIACEAE

Genus of one species of evergreen shrub occurring in moist forest in Chile. The alternate leaves are leathery and scale-like. Grown for its showy, trumpet-shaped flowers, produced from the leaf axils in summer and autumn, it is suitable for a moist, shady position.

- **HARDINESS** Frost hardy.
- **CULTIVATION** Grow in moderately fertile, humus-rich, moist but well-drained, acid soil in partial shade. Does not tolerate hot, dry conditions. Pruning group 9.
- **PROPAGATION** Take semi-ripe cuttings in summer, or remove suckers in spring.
- **PESTS AND DISEASES** Trouble free.

P. magellanica. Erect, suckering shrub or, in mild, moist areas, root climber, with oblong, rigid, dark green leaves, to 4cm (1½in) long, blue-white beneath. Trumpet-shaped, waxy, crimson-pink flowers, to 6cm (2½in) long, are borne singly in the leaf axils from midsummer to autumn. ↕ 1m (3ft), ↔ 2m (6ft). Chile. ❄❄

PHILLYREA

OLEACEAE

Genus of 4 species of evergreen shrubs and trees occurring in woodland and rocky places from the Mediterranean to S.W. Asia. Grown for their habit and foliage, they have opposite, linear to ovate-elliptic, yellow-green to dark green leaves. The 4-lobed, salverform white flowers are borne in axillary cymes, followed by spherical or ovoid, blue-black fruits. Grow in a shrub border or woodland garden, or as specimen plants. In frost-prone areas, grow against a sheltered wall.

- **HARDINESS** Fully hardy to frost hardy.
- **CULTIVATION** Grow in fertile, well-drained soil, ideally in full sun, with shelter from cold, dry winds. Tolerates partial shade. Pruning group 1 or 8.
- **PROPAGATION** Root semi-ripe cuttings with bottom heat in summer.
- **PESTS AND DISEASES** Whiteflies may be troublesome.

P. angustifolia. Dense, bushy shrub with narrowly linear, dark green leaves, to 6cm (2½in) long. Inconspicuous, fragrant, greenish white flowers are produced in cymes, 1cm (½in) across, in late spring and early summer, followed

Phillyrea latifolia

by spherical, blue-black fruit, 5mm (¼in) across. ↕↔ 3m (10ft). Mediterranean. ❄❄❄

P. decora see *Osmanthus decorus.*

P. latifolia ■ ○ Dense, rounded shrub or small tree with oval, glossy, dark green leaves, to 6cm (2½in) long. Inconspicuous, fragrant, greenish white flowers are borne in cymes, 1cm (½in) across, in late spring and early summer, followed by spherical, blue-black fruit, 5mm (¼in) across. ↕↔ to 9m (28ft). Mediterranean, S.W. Asia. ❄❄❄

PHILODENDRON

ARACEAE

Genus of over 500 species of often epiphytic, evergreen, sometimes tree-like perennials and root climbers from various habitats, usually rainforest, in the USA (Florida), Mexico, the West Indies, and Central and tropical South America. They are grown for their leathery, glossy leaves, which may be simple, entire, linear, ovate to oblong, heart-, arrow-, or broadly spear-shaped, and pinnatifid, bipinnatifid, or sometimes pedatisect; they are borne alternately, or in tufts or rosettes. Seed-raised species often have a distinct juvenile stage, with leaves quite unlike those of mature plants. Inflorescences, comprising tiny, petalless flowers borne on spadices and enclosed by spathes, are produced intermittently. Where temperatures fall below 15°C (59°F), grow in a warm greenhouse or as house-plants. In warmer areas, train climbing species through a tree or against a wall, and grow large species as specimen plants. Small epiphytes are suitable for a large hanging basket. All parts may cause severe discomfort if ingested; contact with sap may irritate skin.

- **HARDINESS** Frost tender.
- **CULTIVATION** Under glass, grow in well-drained, loamless potting compost in bright filtered or indirect light. During the growing season, water freely and apply a balanced liquid fertilizer every month. In summer, mist twice daily. Water sparingly in winter. Support climbing stems with a moss pole. Outdoors, grow in fertile, humus-rich, moist but well-drained soil in dappled or partial shade. Plants under glass may need restrictive pruning.
- **PROPAGATION** Surface-sow seed at 19–24°C (66–75°F) in spring. Take stem-tip or leaf bud cuttings in summer. Layer or air layer in spring.

Philodendron bipinnatifidum

Philodendron hederaceum

- **PESTS AND DISEASES** Prone to scale insects, mealy bugs, and red spider mites under glass.

P. andreanum see *P. melanochrysum.*

P. angustisectum, syn. *P. elegans.* Sparsely branched climber with ovate, pinnatisect, reflexed leaves, 30–60cm (12–24in) long, each with 16–32 slender, finger-like lobes, glossy, deep green above, paler beneath. Green spathes, 15cm (6in) long, are yellow inside, with pink-flushed margins. ↕ 5m (15ft). Colombia. ❀ (min.15°C/59°F)

***P. auritum* of gardens** see *Syngonium auritum.*

P. bipennifolium, syn. *P. panduriforme* (Fiddleleaf, Panda plant). Sparsely branched climber with ovate to arrow-shaped, reflexed, lustrous, deep green leaves, 30–45cm (12–18in) long, each with 5 broad lobes, the terminal one longest. Bears greenish cream spathes, to 11cm (4½in) long. ↕ to 5m (15ft) or more. S.E. Brazil. ❀ (min. 15°C/59°F)

P. bipinnatifidum ■ syn. *P. selloum* (Tree philodendron). Tree-like perennial, usually with a single, robust, erect stem, reclining with age. Very long-stalked, reflexed leaves, to 1m (3ft)

Philodendron melanochrysum

long, are broadly ovate, heart-shaped at the bases, and deeply pinnatisect, with many narrow, wavy-margined, semi-glossy, rich green lobes. Green to red-purple spathes, 30cm (12in) long, are cream with red margins inside. ↕↔ to 5m (15ft). S.E. Brazil, Paraguay, Argentina. ❄. **'German Selloum'** has narrower leaf lobes. **'Variegatum'** has leaves splashed yellow to light green.

P. cordatum see *P. hederaceum.*

P. domesticum, syn. *P. hastatum* of gardens (Elephant's ear). Usually sparsely branched climber with narrowly triangular to arrow-shaped, reflexed, glossy, bright green leaves, 45–60cm (18–24in) long. Spathes are 12–18cm (5–7in) long, green on the outside, cherry-red inside. ↕ 3–6m (10–20ft). Origin unknown. ❀ (min. 15°C/59°F)

P. elegans see *P. angustisectum.*

P. erubescens (Blushing philodendron, Red-leaf philodendron). Stout climber with red-purple stems and pinkish bracts when young. Ovate-triangular, glossy, dark green leaves, 25–40cm (10–16in) long, heart-shaped at the bases, are coppery red-purple beneath, with purple-tinged stalks. Bears red-purple spathes, 15cm (6in) long, crimson inside, with an unusual aroma. ↕ 3–6m (10–20ft). Colombia. ❀ (min. 15°C/59°F). **'Burgundy'** is slower-growing, with smaller, red-flushed leaves, to 30cm (12in) long. **'King of Spades'** has black-purple leaves.

***P. hastatum* of gardens** see *P. domesticum.*

P. hederaceum ■ syn. *P. cordatum, P. scandens* (Heart leaf, Sweetheart vine). Fast-growing, slender-stemmed climber with glossy, deep green leaves, 10–30cm (4–12in) long, heart-shaped, reflexed, and sometimes red-purple beneath. Produces purple spathes, to 5cm (2in) long. ↕ 3–6m (10–20ft). Central America, West Indies. ❀ (min. 15°C/59°F). **f. *micans***, syn. *P. micans*, has bronze leaves, red-tinted beneath, with larger, overlapping basal leaf lobes. **subsp. *oxycardium***, syn. *P. oxycardium*, has young leaves flushed bronze-brown; E. Mexico.

P. imbe, syn. *P. sellowianum.* Robust climber with long aerial roots and red-purple stems bearing ovate-oblong to arrow-shaped, reflexed leaves, to 35cm (14in) long; they are glossy, mid- to dark green above, often tinted red beneath. Spathes, 15–22cm (6–9in) long, are cream and green. ↕ 3–5m (10–15ft). S.E. Brazil. ❀ (min. 15°C/59°F)

P. laciniatum see *P. pedatum.*

P. melanochrysum ■ syn. *P. andreanum* (Black gold philodendron, Velour philodendron). Sparsely branched climber. Bears narrowly ovate to oblong-lance-shaped, pendent, velvety blackish green leaves, to 1m (3ft) long, with pale green veins; they have short, slender points and heart-shaped bases. Juvenile plants have much smaller, broader, coppery red leaves. Produces green and white spathes, to 20cm (8in) long. ↕ 3–6m (10–20ft). Colombia. ❀ (min. 15°C/59°F)

P. micans see *P. hederaceum* f. *micans.*

P. oxycardium see *P. hederaceum* subsp. *oxycardium.*

P. panduriforme see *P. bipennifolium.*

P. pedatum, syn. *P. laciniatum.* Robust, moderately branching climber. Reflexed, irregularly pinnatifid, glossy, deep green leaves, to 45cm (18in) long, are ovate, with 5–7 narrowly triangular lobes, the 2 basal lobes sometimes lobed and pointing backwards. Bears greenish white spathes, red-flushed at the bases and cream inside, 10–13cm (4–5in) long. ↕ 3–5m (10–15ft). Venezuela to Brazil. ❀ (min. 15°C/59°F)

P. scandens see *P. hederaceum.*

P. selloum see *P. bipinnatifidum.*

P. sellowianum see *P. imbe.*

P. trifoliatum see *Syngonium auritum.*

▷ **Philodendron,**
Black gold see *Philodendron melanochrysum*
Blushing see *Philodendron erubescens*
False see *Peperomia scandens*
Red-leaf see *Philodendron erubescens*
Tree see *Philodendron bipinnatifidum*
Velour see *Philodendron melanochrysum*

PHLEBODIUM

POLYPODIACEAE

Genus of 10 species of semi-evergreen ferns occurring on trees and rocks in the USA (Florida), Mexico, West Indies, and Central and tropical South America. They have thick, creeping rhizomes, densely covered with golden brown scales, and large, pinnate or pinnatifid, sometimes glaucous fronds. Spores are formed in groups, in one or more rows parallel to the midribs. In frost-prone climates, grow in a warm greenhouse or as houseplants; they are very effective in hanging baskets. In warmer regions, grow in a warm, sheltered border.

- **HARDINESS** Frost tender.
- **CULTIVATION** Under glass, grow in 1 part each loam, medium-grade bark, and charcoal, 2 parts sharp sand, and 3 parts coarse leaf mould. Provide full light or bright filtered light. During growth, water moderately and apply a balanced liquid fertilizer every month. Water sparingly in winter. Outdoors, grow in fertile, well-drained soil in full sun or light dappled shade.
- **PROPAGATION** Sow spores at 19–24°C (66–75°F) as soon as ripe. Divide rhizomes in spring. See also p.51.
- **PESTS AND DISEASES** Scale insects may be a problem.

P. aureum ■ syn. *Polypodium aureum* (Golden polypody, Hare's foot fern, Rabbit's foot fern). Large, creeping fern

Phlebodium aureum

P

Phlebodium aureum 'Mandaianum'

with arching, ovate to oblong or triangular, deeply pinnatifid, glaucous, grey-green fronds, to 1.5m (5ft) long, each with up to 35 narrowly linear to lance-shaped, oblong, or strap-shaped, wavy-margined segments. ↕ 75cm (30in), ↔ to 1.5m (5ft). USA (Florida), Mexico, West Indies, Central and tropical South America. ❀ (min. 10°C/50°F). **var. *areolatum***, syn. 'Glaucum', has leathery fronds, 60cm (24in) long, with a more pronounced glaucous bloom. **'Glaucum'** see var. *areolatum*. **'Mandaianum'** ■ (Blue fern) has slightly lobed fronds with wavy margins.

PHLOMIS

LABIATAE/LAMIACEAE

Genus of about 100 species of sage-like herbaceous perennials and evergreen shrubs or subshrubs found in rocky sites in Europe, North Africa, and Asia. Leaves are opposite, lance-shaped to ovate, light to grey-green, often with star-shaped hairs. They are grown for their foliage and showy, tubular, dead nettle-like, often hooded, white, yellow, or lilac flowers, borne in dense, axillary whorls on tall, erect stems; they are effective massed in a border. In frost-prone areas, grow against a wall. *P. lanata* is suitable for a rock garden. In winter, seed heads of herbaceous species may be left on for their ornamental effect.

• **HARDINESS** Fully hardy to frost hardy.

• **CULTIVATION** Grow in any fertile, well-drained soil in full sun; *P. russeliana* and *P. samia* tolerate some shade. Pruning group 8 or 9.

Phlomis cashmeriana

• **PROPAGATION** Sow seed at 13–18°C (55–64°F) in spring. Divide perennials in spring (preferably) or in autumn. Take softwood cuttings of shrubs in summer.

• **PESTS AND DISEASES** Leafhoppers may be troublesome.

P. bovei* subsp. *maroccana, syn. *P. samia* subsp. *maroccana*. Erect, sticky-hairy perennial with elliptic to oblong, scalloped, grey-green basal leaves, 6–8cm (2½–3in) long, heart-shaped at the bases, and smaller stem leaves. Purple-pink flowers, 4–4.5cm (1½–1¾in) long, with purple spots inside, white-woolly outside, are borne in summer. Similar to *P. samia* but more robust. ↕ to 1.5m (5ft), ↔ 1m (3ft). Morocco. ❄❄

P. cashmeriana ■ Erect, densely woolly perennial with ovate to lance-shaped basal leaves, 10–25cm (4–10in) long, yellow-grey above, paler beneath, and smaller stem leaves. In midsummer, hooded, lilac-purple flowers, 2.5cm (1in) long, are borne from the upper leaf axils. ↕ to 90cm (36in), ↔ 60cm (24in). India (Kashmir), W. Himalayas. ❄❄❄

P. chrysophylla. Rounded, evergreen shrub with stout, spreading branches and elliptic to broadly ovate, grey-green leaves, to 6cm (2½in) long, turning golden green in late summer. Golden yellow flowers, 3cm (1¼in) long, are produced in early summer. ↕ 1m (3ft), ↔ 1.2m (4ft). S.W. Asia. ❄❄

***P.* 'Edward Bowles'.** Upright, evergreen subshrub with large, heart-shaped, wrinkled, grey-green leaves, 15cm (6in) long, woolly beneath. Bears sulphur-yellow flowers, 3cm (1¼in) long, paler on the hoods, in early and midsummer. ↕ 1m (3ft), ↔ 1.5m (5ft). ❄❄

P. fruticosa ■ (Jerusalem sage). Mound-forming, evergreen shrub with upright shoots and sage-like, ovate-lance-shaped, wrinkled, grey-green leaves, to 10cm (4in) long, woolly beneath. In early and midsummer, bears dark golden yellow flowers, 3cm (1¼in) long. ↕ 1m (3ft), ↔ 1.5m (5ft). E. Mediterranean. ❄❄❄ (borderline)

Phlomis fruticosa (inset: flower detail)

Phlomis italica

P. italica ■ Upright, evergreen shrub bearing oblong-lance-shaped, grey-woolly leaves, to 5cm (2in) long. Lilac-pink flowers, 2cm (¾in) long, are borne in midsummer. ↕ 30cm (12in), ↔ 60cm (24in). Balearic Islands. ❄❄

P. lanata. Compact, mound-forming, evergreen shrub bearing oblong to rounded, deeply veined, scaly, sage-green leaves, to 2.5cm (1in) long. Golden yellow flowers, 2cm (¾in) long, covered with brown hairs, are produced in summer. ↕ 50cm (20in), ↔ 75cm (30in). Greece (Crete). ❄❄

P. longifolia. Spreading, evergreen shrub with white-woolly young shoots and lance-shaped, deeply veined, bright green leaves, to 7cm (3in) long, grey-woolly beneath. Dark yellow flowers, to 4cm (1½in) long, with calyx teeth to 3mm (⅛in) long, are produced in summer. ↕ 1.2m (4ft), ↔ 2m (6ft). S.W. Asia. ❄❄. **var. *bailanica*** has ovate leaves, and flowers with longer calyx teeth, 3–6mm (⅛–¼in) long.

P. purpurea ■ Upright, evergreen shrub with woolly shoots and lance-shaped, leathery, grey-green leaves, to 10cm (4in) long, with star-shaped hairs above, woolly beneath. Purple to pink,

Phlomis purpurea

occasionally white flowers, 2.5cm (1in) long, are produced in summer. ↕↔ to 60cm (24in). Spain, Portugal. ❄❄

P. russeliana ■ syn. *P. samia* of gardens, *P. viscosa* of gardens. Erect, hairy perennial, less woolly than *P. cashmeriana* (so appears greener), with mid-green leaves: basal leaves are ovate, 6–20cm (2½–8in) long, heart-shaped at the bases; stem leaves are smaller and scalloped. Hooded, pale yellow flowers, 2.5–3.5cm (1–1½in) long, are borne from late spring to early autumn, mainly in early summer. Often confused with *P. samia*. ↕ to 90cm (36in), ↔ 75cm (30in). Turkey, Syria. ❄❄❄

P. samia. Erect perennial producing ovate, scalloped, woolly basal leaves, 10–20cm (4–8in) long, heart-shaped at the bases, and mid-green above, grey beneath, and with smaller stem leaves. Hooded lilac flowers, 3–3.5cm (1¼–1½in) long, tinged rose-pink, especially on the lips, are borne from early to late summer. ↕ to 1m (3ft), ↔ 80cm (32in). S.E. Europe, Turkey. ❄❄❄. **subsp. *maroccana*** see *P. bovei* subsp. *maroccana*.

***P. samia* of gardens** see *P. russeliana*.

***P. viscosa* of gardens** see *P. russeliana*.

Phlomis russeliana

PHLOX

POLEMONIACEAE

Genus of 67 species of evergreen or herbaceous, low-growing or cushion-forming to erect perennials, as well as a few annuals and shrubs, found mostly in North America (one from Siberia, Russia). They are grown for their showy flowers, borne mainly in terminal corymbs or panicle-like cymes, sometimes singly. The flowers are salverform, occasionally funnel-shaped, each with a narrow, tubular base opening to 5 flat, ovate petal lobes, sometimes in a star-shaped arrangement. Leaves are simple, entire, linear to ovate, light to dark green, and often in opposite pairs, the upper leaves sometimes alternate. Mat- and cushion-forming species, from dry, rocky habitats, flower in spring or early summer; grow in a rock garden or alpine house, in a dry wall, or as edging. Woodland species are mainly trailing, and usually flower in early summer; grow in shady sites. The taller "border" phlox are mostly from moist riverside habitats, and produce large corymbs of flowers, usually in midsummer, which are good for cutting. Annuals, from dry rocky slopes and coastal sands, flower from late spring to autumn, and are useful for bedding.

• **HARDINESS** Fully hardy to half hardy.

• **CULTIVATION** Grow annuals in any fertile, well-drained soil in full sun. Perennials and shrubs have varying needs, which may be grouped as set out below. Cut back all tall herbaceous species to the ground in autumn. Deadhead *P. maculata* and *P. paniculata* to prolong flowering. Stake tall cultivars.

1. Grow in fertile, moist soil in full sun or partial shade.

2. Grow in humus-rich, fertile, moist but well-drained soil in partial shade.

3. Grow in well-drained, fertile soil in full sun, or in dappled shade in low rainfall areas.

4. Grow in gritty, sharply drained, poor to moderately fertile soil in full sun. In an alpine house, grow in a mix of equal parts loam, leaf mould, and sharp sand.

• **PROPAGATION** Sow seed of annuals at 13–18°C (55–64°F) in early spring; sow seed of perennials in containers in a cold frame when ripe or in spring. Divide *P. carolina*, *P. maculata*, and *P. paniculata*, and their cultivars, in autumn or spring. Insert basal cuttings in spring, or take root cuttings in early autumn or winter. Take softwood cuttings of non-flowering stems of cushion-forming perennials in spring. Detach rooted pieces of stem from trailing perennials in spring or early autumn.

• **PESTS AND DISEASES** Susceptible to leafy gall, stem eelworms, powdery mildew, and leaf spot.

P. adsurgens. Creeping, stem-rooting, semi-evergreen perennial with prostrate to ascending stems bearing stalkless, rounded to narrowly ovate, light to mid-green leaves, to 2.5cm (1in) long. In late spring and early summer, bears open cymes of salverform, broad-petalled, salmon-pink flowers, to 2.5cm (1in) across, with paler centres. Cultivation group 2. ↕↔ 30cm (12in). N.W. USA. ✽✽✽. **'Red Buttes'** has deep pink flowers with large, overlapping petal lobes. **'Wagon Wheel'** ▣ has salmon-pink flowers with very narrow petal lobes, resembling the spokes of a wheel.
***P. amoena* 'Variegata'** see *P.* x *procumbens* 'Variegata'.
P. bifida ▣ (Sand phlox). Mound-forming, evergreen perennial with hairy, needle-like, linear leaves, to 6cm (2½in) long. In spring and early summer, bears abundant cymes of salverform, fragrant, deep lavender-blue to white flowers, 2cm (¾in) across, with star-shaped, very deeply cleft petal lobes. Cultivation group 3 or 4. ↕ to 20cm (8in), ↔ 15cm (6in). C. USA. ✽✽✽. **'Colvin's White'** has pure white flowers.
P. bryoides. Cushion-forming, evergreen perennial with hairy, overlapping, lance-shaped leaves, to 5mm (¼in) long. In late spring and early summer, bears solitary, stalkless, salverform, pure white flowers, 1cm (½in) across, towards the shoot tips. May become lax and fail to flower freely in cultivation. Cultivation group 4. ↕ 2–5cm (¾–2in), ↔ 15cm (6in). High altitudes in USA (Oregon, W. Montana to Nevada, W. Nebraska). ✽✽✽
P. carolina (Thick-leaf phlox). Upright and spreading herbaceous perennial bearing thick, lance-shaped to ovate-oblong leaves, 13cm (5in) long. In summer, produces cymes of salverform,

Phlox bifida

purple to pink, rarely white flowers, to 2cm (¾in) across. Cultivation group 1. ↕ 1.2m (4ft), ↔ 45cm (18in). C. and E. USA. ✽✽✽. **'Bill Baker'** ▣ produces bright green leaves, to 15cm (6in) long, and bears pink flowers, to 2.5cm (1in) across, in early summer; ↕ 45cm (18in), ↔ 30cm (12in).
***P.* 'Chattahoochee'** ▣ Short-lived, prostrate, branching, semi-evergreen perennial with purple-tinted stems and lance-shaped leaves, 2–5cm (¾–2in) long, purple-flushed when young. Bears cymes of salverform, lavender-blue flowers, 2–2.5cm (¾–1in) across, with conspicuous red-purple eyes, over long periods in summer and early autumn. Cultivation group 2. ↕ 15cm (6in), ↔ 30cm (12in). ✽✽✽
P. divaricata (Blue phlox, Wild sweet William). Spreading, stem-rooting, semi-evergreen perennial with ovate, hairy leaves, to 5cm (2in) long, narrower on the flowering stems. In early summer, produces open cymes of salverform, lavender-blue to pale violet and white flowers, 2–3cm (¾–1¼in) across, with notched or unnotched petal lobes. Cultivation group 2. ↕ to 35cm (14in), ↔ 50cm (20in). Woodland in Canada, E. USA. ✽✽✽. **'Dirigo Ice'** ▣ has clear, pale blue flowers. **subsp. *laphamii*** ▣ has pale to deep lilac-blue flowers with narrow petal lobes.
P. douglasii. Mound-forming, evergreen perennial densely covered with stiff, narrowly lance-shaped, dark green leaves, to 1cm (½in) long. In late spring or early summer, produces salverform, white, lavender-blue, or pink flowers, 1.5cm (½in) across, singly or in twos or threes. Cultivation group 3. ↕ to 20cm (8in), ↔ 30cm (12in). USA (S. Washington to California). ✽✽✽. **'Boothman's Variety'** ▣ produces violet-pink flowers with dark eyes. **'Crackerjack'** ▣ is more compact, with reddish magenta flowers; ↕ to 12cm (5in), ↔ to 20cm (8in). **'Iceberg'** has white flowers, sometimes faintly tinged blue. **'Red Admiral'** ▣ bears deep crimson flowers. **'Violet Queen'** is compact, with deep violet-purple flowers; ↕ to 10cm (4in), ↔ to 15cm (6in). **'Waterloo'** has crimson flowers.
P. drummondii (Annual phlox). Erect to spreading, bushy, hairy annual with very variable, narrowly inversely lance-shaped to nearly ovate, almost stalkless, stem-clasping leaves, 2.5–8cm (1–3in) long. In late spring, produces cymes of salverform, hairy, purple, pink, red, lavender-blue, or white flowers, to 2.5cm (1in) across, often pale inside, with contrasting marks at the bases of the petal lobes. ↕ 10–45cm (4–18in), ↔ to 25cm (10in) or more. USA (E. Texas). ✽✽. **'African Sunset'** ▣ has dusky to deep red flowers. **'Chanal'** ▣ is spreading, but still compact, and bears double, almost rose-like pink flowers. **'Dwarf Beauty'** is early flowering, with abundant, very large blooms, to 3cm (1¼in) or more across, in colours including rose-pink, crimson-red, yellow, violet-blue, and white; ↔ 40cm (16in) or more. Cultivars in **Ethnie Pastel Shades Series** are ground-hugging, compact, and very uniform, with flowers in a range of pink and white shades. **Palona Series** cultivars are dwarf and bushy, forming spherical plants, with flowers in white, light blue, violet, salmon-pink, rose-pink, carmine-red, or crimson, some with contrasting eyes. **Palona Series 'Light Salmon'** ▣ has pale salmon-pink flowers. **'Petticoat'** is dwarf, with very small flowers, to 1.5cm (½in) across, available as a mixture of cream, rose-pink, salmon-pink, and carmine-pink, including bicolours; flowers late, but over a long season; ↕ to 10cm (4in). **'Promise Pink'** has semi-double, deep salmon-pink flowers. **'Sternenzauber'** ▣ syn.

Phlox adsurgens 'Wagon Wheel'

Phlox carolina 'Bill Baker'

Phlox 'Chattahoochee'

Phlox divaricata 'Dirigo Ice'

Phlox divaricata subsp. *laphamii*

Phlox douglasii 'Boothman's Variety'

Phlox douglasii 'Crackerjack'

Phlox douglasii 'Red Admiral'

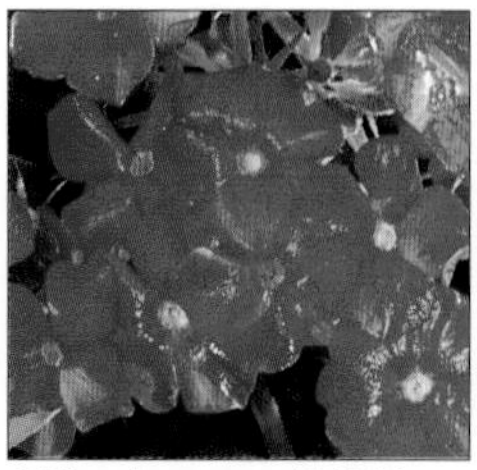

Phlox drummondii 'African Sunset'

Phlox drummondii 'Chanal'

Phlox drummondii Palona Series 'Light Salmon'

Phlox drummondii 'Sternenzauber'

P

Phlox nana 'Arroya'

'Twinkle', has tiny flowers, to 2cm (¾in) across, in shades including salmon-pink, rose-pink, and carmine-pink, as well as picotees; petal lobes are often fringed and pointed, appearing star-like. **'Twinkle'** see 'Sternenzauber'.
***P.* 'Emerald Cushion'.** Compact, mound-forming, evergreen perennial, similar to *P. subulata*, with linear to elliptic, light green leaves, to 2cm (¾in) long. In late spring and early summer, bears cymes of salverform, pale violet flowers, 2–2.5cm (¾–1in) across, with narrow, notched petal lobes. Cultivation group 3. ↕ 8cm (3in), ↔ 20cm (8in). ❄❄❄
***P.* 'Fuller's White'.** Clump-forming, semi-evergreen perennial, similar to, but more compact than *P. divaricata*, with ovate leaves, to 5cm (2in) long. In early summer, upright stems bear cymes of salverform, pure white flowers, 2–2.5cm (¾–1in) across, with notched petal lobes. Cultivation group 2. ↕↔ to 20cm (8in). ❄❄❄
***P. hoodii*.** Dwarf, tuft-forming, evergreen perennial with hairy, lance-shaped leaves, to 1cm (½in) long. Bears solitary, salverform, white to pale violet flowers, 1cm (½in) across, in late spring and early summer. Cultivation group 4. ↕ 5cm (2in), ↔ 10cm (4in). USA (Rocky Mountains). ❄❄❄
***P.* 'Kelly's Eye'** ■ Vigorous, mound-forming, evergreen perennial, similar to *P. douglasii*, with narrowly lance-shaped, dark green leaves, to 1.5cm (½in) long. In late spring and early summer, bears cymes of salverform, very pale pink flowers, 1.5cm (½in) across, with red-purple eyes. Cultivation group 3. ↕ 10cm (4in), ↔ 30cm (12in) or more. ❄❄❄
P. maculata (Meadow phlox). Erect herbaceous perennial with hairy stems, often red-spotted, and linear to ovate, smooth leaves, 6–13cm (2½–5in) long. In early and midsummer, bears narrowly conical, panicle-like cymes of salverform, fragrant, violet, pink, or white flowers, 2–2.5cm (¾–1in) across. Cultivation group 1. ↕ to 90cm (36in), ↔ 45cm (18in). E. USA. ❄❄❄. **'Alpha'** produces lilac-pink flowers. **'Omega'** ■ has white flowers with lilac-red eyes.
P. mesoleuca see *P. nana* subsp. *ensifolia*.
***P.* 'Millstream'** see *P.* x *procumbens* 'Millstream'.
P. nana (Santa Fe phlox). Deciduous or semi-evergreen perennial, spreading by runners, with trailing or upright shoots, to 20cm (8in) long, sparsely covered with linear to lance-shaped, downy, grey-green leaves, to 4cm (1½in) long. Produces abundant solitary, salverform, bright pink, purple, or white, rarely pale yellow flowers, to 2.5cm (1in) across, from summer to autumn. Cultivation group 4. ↕ to 20cm (8in), ↔ to 30cm (12in). S.W. USA, Mexico. ❄❄❄. **'Arroya'** ■ bears brilliant magenta flowers, with small white eyes, over long periods in summer. **subsp. *ensifolia***, syn. *P. mesoleuca*, produces white-eyed, soft pink, purple, soft yellow, or white flowers; slower-growing than the species, with shorter shoots, and more difficult to grow. **'Mary Maslin'** ■ has vivid scarlet flowers with yellow eyes. **'Paul Maslin'** has pale yellow flowers with deep purple eyes. **'Tangelo'** has brilliant orange-red flowers with yellow eyes.
P. nivalis ■ (Trailing phlox). Decumbent, evergreen perennial with trailing shoots, to 30cm (12in) long, and hairy, lance-shaped leaves, 2.5cm (1in) long. Bears cymes of salverform, purple, pink, or white flowers, to 1.5cm (½in) across, in summer. Cultivation group 3. ↕ 20cm (8in), ↔ 30cm (12in). C. USA. ❄❄❄. **'Camla'** has very pale pink, almost white flowers.
P. paniculata (Perennial phlox). Erect herbaceous perennial with ovate or lance-shaped to elliptic, toothed, thin leaves, 5–13cm (2–5in) long. Panicle-like cymes of salverform, fragrant, white or pale to dark lilac flowers, 1.5–2.5cm (½–1in) across, are borne from summer to early or mid-autumn. Cultivation group 1. ↕ 1.2m (4ft), ↔ 60–100cm (24–39in). E. USA. ❄❄❄. **'Aida'** has crimson flowers with purple eyes. **'Amethyst'** produces violet flowers. **'Balmoral'** ■ is vigorous, with large trusses of pink flowers; ↕ 90cm (36in). **'Blue Boy'** is strong-growing, and bears mauve-blue flowers with white eyes; ↕ 90cm (36in). **'Brigadier'** ■ has orange-tinged, pinkish red flowers, and deep green leaves. **'Bright Eyes'** has clear pale pink flowers with red eyes. **'Eva Cullum'** ■ is very free-blooming, producing bright deep pink flowers with darker pink centres. **'Eventide'** ■ has lavender-blue flowers; ↕ 90cm (36in). **'Fujiyama'** ■ syn. 'Mount Fuji', has white flowers; ↕ to 75cm (30in). **'Graf Zeppelin'** ■ has white flowers with red centres. **'Hampton Court'** ■ has dark green foliage and mauve-blue flowers. **'Harlequin'** ■ has leaves with broad, ivory-white margins, and produces reddish purple flowers. **'Le Mahdi'** has deep bluish purple flowers with darker eyes; ↕ 1.1m (3½ft). **'Mia Ruys'** ■ bears large white flowers, to 3cm (1¼in) across; ↕ 60cm (24in). **'Mother of Pearl'** ■ has pink-tinted white flowers; ↕ 75cm (30in). **'Mount Fuji'** see 'Fujiyama'. **'Norah Leigh'** ■ has extensively white-variegated leaves and small, pale lilac flowers, 1.5cm (½in) across, with deeper lilac-pink centres; ↕ 90cm (36in). **'Orange Perfection'** bears deep orange flowers. **'Prince of Orange'** has orange-red flowers; ↕ to 80cm (32in). **'Prospero'** has pale lilac flowers with almost white petal margins; ↕ to 90cm (36in). **'Sandringham'** has pale pink flowers with deeper pink centres and widely spaced petal lobes. **'Sir John Falstaff'** has deep salmon-pink flowers with wine-red eyes. **'Starfire'** has dark green leaves and deep crimson-red flowers; ↕ 90cm (36in). **'White Admiral'** bears white flowers; ↕ 90cm (36in). **'Windsor'** ■ has reddish pink flowers with purple-pink eyes.
P.* x *procumbens (*P. stolonifera* x *P. subulata*). Decumbent, mat-forming, semi-evergreen perennial with inversely lance-shaped to elliptic, glossy leaves, 2.5cm (1in) long. Bears open, flat cymes of salverform, bright purple flowers, 2cm (¾in) across, in early summer. Cultivation group 2 or 3. ↕ 10cm (4in), ↔ 30cm (12in). Garden origin. ❄❄❄. **'Millstream'**, syn. *P.* 'Millstream', bears a profusion of deep lavender-pink flowers. **'Variegata'**, syn. *P. amoena* 'Variegata', has leaves with cream margins, and bears deep pink flowers.
P. stolonifera (Creeping phlox). Stoloniferous, spreading herbaceous perennial with obovate, dark green leaves, to 5cm (2in) long. In early summer, upright stems produce open cymes of salverform, pale to deep purple flowers, to 3cm (1¼in) across. Cultivation group 2. ↕ 10–15cm (4–6in), ↔ 30cm (12in) or more. Woodland in C. USA. ❄❄❄. **'Ariane'** ■ has pale green leaves, and white flowers, 3cm (1¼in) or more across, with star-shaped petal lobes and small yellow eyes. **'Blue Ridge'** bears clear pale blue flowers. **'Mary Belle Frey'** has pink flowers.
P. subulata (Moss phlox). Dense, evergreen perennial forming cushions or mats of hairy, linear to elliptic, bright green leaves, 0.6–2cm (¼–¾in) long. Salverform, purple or red, sometimes violet-purple, lilac, pink, or white flowers, 1.5–2.5cm (½–1in) across, often with star-shaped petal lobes, are produced in few-flowered cymes, rarely singly, in late spring and early summer. Cultivation group 3. ↕ 5–15cm (2–6in),

P

Phlox 'Kelly's Eye'

Phlox maculata 'Omega'

Phlox nana 'Mary Maslin'

Phlox nivalis

Phlox paniculata 'Balmoral'

Phlox paniculata 'Brigadier'

Phlox paniculata 'Eva Cullum'

Phlox paniculata 'Eventide'

Phlox paniculata 'Fujiyama'

Phlox paniculata 'Graf Zeppelin'

Phlox paniculata 'Hampton Court'

Phlox paniculata 'Harlequin'

Phlox paniculata 'Windsor'

↔ 50cm (20in) or more. E. to C. USA. ✻✻✻. **'Amazing Grace'** has a lax habit, and bears pale pink flowers with deep pinkish purple eyes. **'G.F. Wilson'** ▣ is vigorous and cushion-forming, and produces deep lavender-blue flowers. **'Marjorie'** ▣ is mat-forming, and bears very large, narrow-petalled, deep pink flowers, 3cm (1¼in) across, each with a darker pink band around a yellow eye. **'McDaniel's Cushion'** is vigorous, cushion-forming, and extremely free-flowering, with very large, deep pink flowers, to 3.5cm (1½in) across. **'Scarlet Flame'** is vigorous and mat-forming, with deep scarlet flowers. **'Temiskaming'** is slow-growing and cushion-forming, with small, deep magenta flowers, 1.5cm (½in) across.

▷ **Phlox**
Annual see *Phlox drummondii*
Blue see *Phlox divaricata*
Creeping see *Phlox stolonifera*
Meadow see *Phlox maculata*
Moss see *Phlox subulata*
Mountain see *Linanthus grandiflorus*
Perennial see *Phlox paniculata*
Sand see *Phlox bifida*
Santa Fe see *Phlox nana*
Thick-leaf see *Phlox carolina*
Trailing see *Phlox nivalis*

Phlox paniculata 'Mia Ruys'

Phlox paniculata 'Mother of Pearl'

Phlox paniculata 'Norah Leigh'

Phlox stolonifera 'Ariane'

Phlox subulata 'G.F. Wilson'

Phlox subulata 'Marjorie'

PHOENIX

ARECACEAE/PALMAE

Genus of 17 species of single- and cluster-stemmed palms occurring in tropical and subtropical forest or low scrub thickets in the Canary Islands, Africa, Crete (Greece), and W. and S. Asia to the Philippines. They have linear to ovate or oblong, pinnate leaves, usually borne in dense, terminal clusters. The bowl-shaped, 3-petalled, cream to yellow flowers are produced in panicles from the lower axils, followed by yellow, orange, red, brown, or black fruits. In frost-prone climates, grow in a warm greenhouse or as houseplants. In warmer areas, use as specimen plants on a lawn.
- **HARDINESS** Frost tender.
- **CULTIVATION** Under glass, grow in loam-based potting compost (JI No.2) in full light, with shade from hot sun. Pot on or top-dress in spring. When in growth, water freely and apply a balanced liquid fertilizer monthly. Water sparingly in winter. Outdoors, grow in fertile, moist but well-drained soil in full sun, with some midday shade.
- **PROPAGATION** Sow seed at 19–24°C (66–75°F) in spring.
- **PESTS AND DISEASES** Prone to scale insects and red spider mites under glass.

P. canariensis Ψ (Canary Island date palm). Medium-sized palm with a stout, columnar trunk marked with oblong leaf scars wider than they are long. Spreading to broadly arching leaves, 4–6m (12–20ft) long, consist of many linear, bright mid- to deep green leaflets, set in a single plane. Bowl-shaped, cream to yellow flowers are borne in pendent panicles, 1–1.2m (3–4ft) long, in summer. Fruit are cylindrical to ellipsoid, and yellow flushed red, 2cm (¾in) long, with edible, sweet, but almost dry flesh. ↕ to 15m (50ft), ↔ 12m (40ft). Canary Islands. ❀ (min. 10–16°C/50–61°F)
P. dactylifera Ψ (Date palm). Tall, sometimes suckering palm producing a columnar trunk usually clad with old leaf bases, at least towards the top. Leaves, 4–6m (12–20ft) long, are composed of many linear, greyish green leaflets, the lowest ones reduced to spines, arranged in various planes giving a 3-dimensional effect. Bowl-shaped cream flowers appear in long-stalked panicles, 1.5–2m (5–6ft) long, in spring or summer. Ellipsoid to cylindrical, edible, sweet, fleshy, yellow to reddish brown fruit, 2.5–7cm (1–3in) long, are very variable both in texture and flavour. ↕ to 30m (100ft), ↔ 6–12m (20–40ft). Probably N. Africa and W. Asia. ❀ (min. 10–16°C/50–61°F)
P. humilis see *P. loureirii*.
P. loureirii ✲ syn. *P. humilis*. Small palm, often with clustered stems, bearing leaves to 2m (6ft) long or more, composed of linear, glaucous, bright mid-green leaflets, clustered along the midribs. Bowl-shaped cream flowers appear in panicles, to 1m (3ft) long, usually in summer, followed by ovoid, dry-fleshed, red to black fruit, 1.5–2cm (½–¾in) across. ↕ 2–5m (6–15ft), ↔ 2–4m (6–12ft). Sri Lanka, India to S. China. ❀ (min. 10–16°C/50–61°F)
P. reclinata ▣ ✲ Small, clustering palm with ascending or leaning, slender stems clad with fibrous, red-brown leaf remains. Leaves, to 2.5m (8ft) long, are composed of many linear, mid- to deep green leaflets, usually arranged in several planes. Bowl-shaped cream flowers are produced in panicles, to 1.5m (5ft) long, usually in summer, followed by cylindrical-ellipsoid, edible but dry, orange-red to black fruit, to 2cm (¾in) across. ↕↔ to 10m (30ft). Tropical Africa. ❀ (min. 10–16°C/50–61°F)

Phoenix reclinata

P. roebelenii Ψ (Miniature date palm, Pygmy date palm). Small, sometimes clustering palm, often with a narrow skirt of dead leaves. Living leaves, 1–1.2m (3–4ft) long, have many linear, bright deep green leaflets, sometimes with flattened, scale-like hairs beneath. Bowl-shaped cream flowers appear in panicles, to 45cm (18in) long, usually in summer, followed by ellipsoid, edible black fruit, to 1cm (½in) long. ↕ 2m (6ft) or more, ↔ to 2.5m (8ft). Laos. ❀ (min. 10–16°C/50–61°F)

PHORMIUM

AGAVACEAE/PHORMIACEAE

Genus of 2 species of evergreen perennials found in scrub and swamps, and on hillsides and riverbanks, in areas ranging from coasts to mountains in New Zealand. They form clumps of large, linear, keeled leaves, each folded into a V-shape at the base, and ranging in colour from yellow-green to dark green, with many fine stripes. Cultivars often have attractive coloured or variegated foliage. Abundant small, tubular, 6-tepalled flowers are produced in erect panicles on leafless stems in summer. They provide a focal point in a border, by a building, or at the edge of a lawn, and are ideal for a coastal garden.
- **HARDINESS** Frost hardy to half hardy; may tolerate temperatures to -12°C (10°F) if given a deep, dry winter mulch.
- **CULTIVATION** Grow in fertile, moist but well-drained soil in full sun. In frost-prone areas, provide a deep, dry mulch in winter.
- **PROPAGATION** Sow seed at 13–18°C (55–64°F) in spring. Divide in spring.
- **PESTS AND DISEASES** Mealybugs may be a problem.

P. colensoi see *P. cookianum*.
P. cookianum, syn. *P. colensoi* (Mountain flax). Clump-forming perennial with broad, arching, linear, light to yellowish green leaves, to 1.5m (5ft) long. Tubular, yellow-green

Phormium cookianum subsp. *hookeri* 'Tricolor'

Phormium tenax

flowers, to 4cm (1½in) long, are borne in upright panicles, 2m (6ft) long, in summer. ↕ to 2m (6ft), ↔ 3m (10ft). New Zealand. ✻✻. **subsp. *hookeri* 'Cream Delight'** has leaves with broad bands of creamy yellow in the centres and narrower bands towards the margins. **subsp. *hookeri* 'Tricolor'** ▣ has leaves conspicuously margined creamy yellow and red. **'Maori Chief'**, a hybrid of *P. cookianum*, has pink- and red-striped bronze leaves. **'Maori Sunrise**, a hybrid of *P. cookianum*, produces slender, apricot-and-pink-striped leaves with bronze margins. **'Variegatum'** has light green leaves with cream to lime-green stripes and margins.
***P.* 'Sundowner'** ▣ Clump-forming perennial with broad, upright, bronze-green leaves, to 1.5m (5ft) long, with dark rose-pink margins. Tubular, yellow-green flowers, to 4cm (1½in) long, are borne in upright panicles, 2m (6ft) long, in summer. ↕↔ to 2m (6ft). ✻✻
P. tenax ▣ (New Zealand flax). Clump-forming perennial with rigid, upright, linear leaves, to 3m (10ft) long, dark green above, blue-green beneath. Stout, red-purple panicles, to 4m (12ft) long, of tubular, dull red flowers, 5cm (2in) long, are borne in summer. ↕ 4m (12ft), ↔ 2m (6ft). New Zealand. ✻✻. **'Aurora'**, a hybrid of *P. tenax*, has arching bronze leaves striped red, salmon-pink, and yellow; ↕↔ 1.2m (4ft). **'Bronze Baby'**, a dwarf hybrid of *P. tenax*, produces bronze leaves, pendent at the tips; ↕↔ 60–80cm (24–32in). **'Dazzler'** ▣ a hybrid of *P. tenax*, has arching bronze leaves with red, orange, and pink stripes; ↕ 1m (3ft), ↔ 1.2m (4ft). **'Variegatum'** produces leaves with creamy yellow stripes at the margins. **'Veitchianum'** has leaves with broad, creamy white stripes.
***P.* 'Yellow Wave'.** Clump-forming perennial producing broad, arching, yellow-green leaves, to 1m (3ft) long, longitudinally striped mid-green. Tubular, dull red flowers, 5cm (2in) long, in stout, red-purple panicles, to 4m (12ft) long, are borne in summer. ↕ 4m (12ft), ↔ 2m (6ft). ✻✻

Phormium 'Sundowner'

Phormium tenax 'Dazzler'

PHOTINIA

syn. STRANVAESIA

ROSACEAE

Genus of about 60 species of deciduous or evergreen shrubs and trees found in woodland and thickets from the Himalayas to E. and S.E. Asia. Leaves are alternate, lance-shaped to broadly ovate, and mid- or dark green; evergreen leaves are attractive and glossy, often brightly coloured in shades of red when young; deciduous leaves often colour well in autumn. The small, 5-petalled flowers are saucer- to cup-shaped, and are borne in dense, terminal and axillary, corymb-like panicles, followed by spherical or ovoid, usually red fruits, 0.5–1cm (¼–½in) across. Grow deciduous species in a woodland garden, or as specimens on a lawn; grow evergreens in a shrub border or among other trees and shrubs. Use *P.* x *fraseri* cultivars for hedging. In frost-prone areas, grow evergreen shrubs against a wall or in the shelter of trees.

• **HARDINESS** Fully hardy to frost hardy. The early growth of *P. serratifolia* may be damaged by late frosts.
• **CULTIVATION** Grow in fertile, moist but well-drained soil in full sun or partial shade. *P. beauverdiana* and *P. villosa* need acid to neutral soil. Protect frost-hardy species from cold, drying winds. Pruning group 1.

Photinia davidiana

Photinia davidiana 'Palette'

• **PROPAGATION** Sow seed in containers in a cold frame in autumn. Root semi-ripe cuttings with bottom heat in summer.
• **PESTS AND DISEASES** May be affected by fireblight. Susceptible to leaf spot and powdery mildew.

P. arbutifolia see *Heteromeles salicifolia*.
P. beauverdiana ♀ Spreading, deciduous tree with elliptic to obovate, dark green leaves, to 12cm (5in) long, turning red in autumn. In late spring, bears small white flowers in corymb-like panicles, to 5cm (2in) across, followed by ovoid red fruit. ↕ to 10m (30ft), ↔ 6m (20ft). W. China. ✻✻✻
P. davidiana ▣♀ syn. *Stranvaesia davidiana*. Upright, evergreen tree or shrub with elliptic to inversely lance-shaped, tapered, dark green leaves, to 12cm (5in) long; older leaves turn red in autumn. In midsummer, small white flowers are produced in corymb-like panicles, 7cm (3in) across, followed by spherical, bright red fruit. ↕ 8m (25ft), ↔ 6m (20ft). China, Vietnam. ✻✻✻. **'Palette'** ▣ is slow-growing and shrubby, with leaves boldly marked creamy white; ↕ 5m (15ft), ↔ 3m (10ft). **var. *undulata* 'Fructu Luteo'** has yellow fruit.
P.* x *fraseri ♀ (*P. glabra* x *P. serratifolia*). Upright, evergreen shrub or small tree with inversely lance-shaped to elliptic, leathery, dark green leaves, 10–20cm (4–8in) long, bronze to bright red when young. In mid- and late spring, produces small white flowers in corymb-like panicles, to 15cm (6in) across. ↕↔ 5m (15ft). Garden origin. ✻✻.

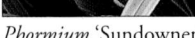

Photinia x *fraseri* 'Red Robin'

Photinia glabra 'Rubens'

'Birmingham' ♀ is bushy-headed, spreading, and often many-stemmed, with oblong to obovate leaves, bright purple-red when young; sometimes bears spherical red fruit. **'Red Robin'** ▣ is compact, with bright red young foliage.
P. glabra. Dense, rounded, evergreen shrub with elliptic to obovate, dark green leaves, to 9cm (3½in) long, red when young. In early summer, bears flattened, corymb-like panicles, 10cm (4in) across, of small white flowers, followed by spherical red fruit, turning black. ↕↔ 3m (10ft). Japan. ✻✻.
'Rubens' ▣ has bright red young leaves.
P. nussia ♀ syn. *Stranvaesia nussia.* Spreading, often rather spiny, evergreen tree with oblong to obovate, leathery, glossy, dark green leaves, to 10cm (4in) long, paler beneath. In midsummer, bears small white flowers in flattened, corymb-like panicles, to 10cm (4in) across, followed by spherical, downy, orange-red fruit. ↕↔ 6m (20ft). Himalayas to S.E. Asia. ✻✻
***P.* 'Redstart'** ♀ Upright, evergreen shrub or small tree bearing oblong to elliptic, dark green leaves, to 11cm (4½in) long, bronze-red when young, on red shoots. Small white flowers, in dense, corymb-like panicles, 10cm (4in) across, appear in early summer before spherical, yellow-flushed, orange-red fruit. ↕ 5m (15ft), ↔ 3m (10ft). ✻✻✻
P. serratifolia ♀ syn. *P. serrulata.* Spreading, evergreen tree with peeling, grey and red-brown bark when mature. Oblong to inversely lance-shaped, glossy, shallowly but sharply toothed, dark green leaves, to 20cm (8in) long, are red when young. Bears small white flowers, in flattened, corymb-like panicles, 10–18cm (4–7in) across, in late spring and early summer, followed by spherical red fruit. ↕ 10–12m (30–40ft), ↔ 8m (25ft). China. ✻✻
P. serrulata see *P. serratifolia.*
P. villosa ▣ ♀ Spreading, deciduous tree, sometimes shrubby, with elliptic to obovate, dark green leaves, to 7cm (3in) long, bronze when young, turning orange and red in autumn. Small white flowers in flattened, corymb-like panicles, 4cm (1½in) across, appear in late spring, before ovoid red fruit. ↕↔ 5m (15ft). China, Korea, Japan. ✻✻✻

PHRAGMIPEDIUM

ORCHIDACEAE

Genus of 15–20 species of large, evergreen, mainly terrestrial, occasionally lithophytic or epiphytic orchids from Mexico and Central and South America, often found in between rocks or near rivers at low altitudes. They have robust, fleshy, clustered shoots with fibrous roots, but lack pseudobulbs. Leaves are leathery, strap-shaped, often mid-green, and arranged in 2 ranks. Upright stems, arising from the centre of each shoot, bear one or several often brightly coloured flowers in terminal racemes or panicles; some have very long petals, and each has a significant, slipper-shaped lip.
• **HARDINESS** Frost tender.
• **CULTIVATION** Cool-growing orchids. Grow in epiphytic orchid compost in containers that restrict the roots. In summer, provide bright filtered light and high humidity, and apply fertilizer at every third watering. In winter, provide full light, with some midday shade, water sparingly, and apply fertilizer every 6–8 weeks. See also p.46.
• **PROPAGATION** Divide clustered shoots by separating offshoots before growth begins in late winter or early spring.
• **PESTS AND DISEASES** Prone to red spider mites, aphids, and mealybugs.

Phragmipedium Sedenii

P. besseae. Terrestrial or lithophytic orchid with 6–10 strap-shaped, leathery leaves, to 20cm (8in) long. Bright scarlet flowers, 6cm (2½in) across, are borne singly or in short, upright racemes in spring. ↕↔ 15cm (6in). Ecuador, Peru. ❁ (min. 14°C/57°F; max. 30°C/86°F)
P. caudatum. Epiphytic or lithophytic orchid with usually 6–9 strap-shaped, blunt-tipped, leathery, light green leaves, to 60cm (24in) long. In summer, bears upright racemes of very large flowers, 10–15cm (4–6in) across, with very narrow, ribbon-like, dark reddish to greenish brown, pendent petals, 60cm (24in) long, off-white to yellow-green sepals veined darker green or orange, and deep pinkish white lips with pink or brown veins and yellow rims. ↕↔ 60cm (24in). Mexico to Peru. ❁ (min. 14°C/57°F; max. 30°C/86°F)
P. longifolium. Terrestrial orchid with about 6 strap-shaped, leathery leaves, to 1m (3ft) long, with sharp-pointed tips. In autumn, bears racemes of pale yellow-green flowers, 15cm (6in) across, with wavy, purple-margined petals, dark green-veined sepals, and purple-flushed lips. ↕↔ 60cm (24in). Costa Rica, Panama, Colombia, Ecuador. ❁ (min. 14°C/57°F; max. 30°C/86°F)
***P.* Sedenii** ▣ (*P. longifolium* x *P. schlimii*). Terrestrial orchid with strap-shaped leaves, to 30cm (12in) long. Erect racemes of rounded, ivory-white flowers, 6cm (2½in) across, flushed and margined rose-pink, with twisted petals and rose-pink lips, appear sporadically throughout the year. ↕↔ 60cm (24in). ❁ (min. 14°C/57°F; max. 30°C/86°F)

PHRAGMITES

Reed

GRAMINEAE/POACEAE

Genus of approximately 4 species of rhizomatous, perennial reed grasses widely distributed in fen, marsh, and riverside habitats in temperate and tropical zones worldwide. They have robust stems bearing deciduous, flat, linear, mid- or slightly grey-green leaves.

Phragmites australis 'Variegatus'

From late summer to mid- or late autumn, they produce large, plumed, silky-hairy panicles of 3- to 11-flowered spikelets, which are useful for dried arrangements. *P. australis*, the only species commonly grown, is vigorous and invasive, especially at the water's edge. Grow in naturalistic lakeside plantings with ample space. Where space is limited, grow in large containers sunk in water to restrict growth.
• **HARDINESS** Fully hardy.
• **CULTIVATION** Grow in moderately fertile, reliably moist, deep soil in full sun. Cut back dead stems by late winter.
• **PROPAGATION** Divide from early spring to early summer.
• **PESTS AND DISEASES** Trouble free.

P. australis, syn. *P. communis* (Common reed, Norfolk reed). Vigorous, rhizomatous reed grass with robust stems bearing flat, linear, long-pointed, greyish green leaves, to 60cm (24in) long, turning golden russet in autumn. From late summer to mid-autumn, bears spikelets in plume-like, silky-hairy, glistening, dark brownish purple panicles, to 45cm (18in) long. ↕ to 3m (10ft) in flower, ↔ indefinite. Tropical and temperate regions worldwide. ✻✻✻. **'Variegatus'** ▣ is less invasive, and has leaves striped golden yellow, fading almost to white.
P. communis see *P. australis.*

PHUOPSIS *syn.* CRUCIANELLA

RUBIACEAE

Genus of one species of mat-forming, stem-rooting perennial found in open sites on hillsides in the Caucasus Mountains and N.E. Iran. It produces whorls of narrowly elliptic leaves, and is cultivated for its abundant clusters of small, tubular-funnel-shaped, scented flowers, each with 5 spreading petal lobes, borne at the tips of the stems in summer. Grow as ground cover on a bank, in a rock garden, or at the front of a border.
• **HARDINESS** Fully hardy.
• **CULTIVATION** Grow in moderately fertile, gritty, moist but well-drained soil in full sun or partial shade. Cut back after flowering to maintain a compact shape.
• **PROPAGATION** Sow seed in containers in an open frame in autumn. Divide or take stem-tip cuttings from spring to early summer.
• **PESTS AND DISEASES** Trouble free.

Photinia villosa (inset: leaf detail)

P

Phuopsis stylosa

P. stylosa ■ syn. *Crucianella stylosa.* Mat-forming perennial with slender, branching stems bearing whorls of 6–8 pointed, narrowly elliptic, musk-scented, pale green leaves, 1.5–2.5cm (½–1in) long. Produces rounded heads of many tiny, tubular-funnel-shaped pink flowers, 1.5–2cm (½–¾in) long, over long periods in summer. ↕ 15cm (6in), ↔ 50cm (20in) or more. Caucasus, N.E. Iran. ❄❄❄

PHYGELIUS

SCROPHULARIACEAE

Genus of 2 species of evergreen shrubs or subshrubs found on wet slopes and streambanks in South Africa. They are cultivated for their panicles of showy, tubular flowers, each with 5 recurved lobes, borne over a long period in summer and often into autumn. The ovate to lance-shaped, dark green leaves are mostly in opposite pairs, the upper leaves sometimes alternate. Grow in a shrub border or herbaceous border, or against a wall. Where temperatures regularly drop below 0°C (32°F), treat as herbaceous perennials. They may spread extensively by suckers, given ideal conditions.

• **HARDINESS** Frost hardy. *P. capensis* is hardy to -10°C (14°F).

• **CULTIVATION** Grow in fertile, moist but well-drained soil in full sun. Dead-head to encourage further flowering. In frost-prone areas, shelter from cold, drying winds, and provide a dry winter mulch. If grown as herbaceous perennials, cut back to the bases in spring; otherwise, pruning group 9.

Phygelius aequalis

Phygelius aequalis 'Yellow Trumpet'

• **PROPAGATION** Sow seed in containers in a cold frame in spring. Take softwood cuttings in late spring. Remove rooted suckers in spring. Overwinter young plants under glass in frost-prone areas.

• **PESTS AND DISEASES** Figwort weevils and capsid bugs may be a problem.

P. aequalis ■ Upright, suckering shrub with ovate, dark green leaves, to 11cm (4½in) long. In summer, produces upright panicles, to 25cm (10in) long, of nodding, dusky pink flowers, to 6cm (2½in) or more long, with crimson lobes and yellow throats. ↕↔ 1m (3ft). South Africa. ❄❄. **'Yellow Trumpet'** ■ has pale green leaves, and bears pale creamy yellow flowers.

P. capensis (Cape figwort). Upright, suckering shrub with ovate, dark green leaves, to 9cm (3½in) long. In summer, bears upright panicles, to 60cm (24in) long, of yellow-throated orange flowers, to 5cm (2½in) long, with orange-red lobes; the flowers turn back towards the stems. ↕ 1.2m (4ft), ↔ 1.5m (5ft). South Africa. ❄❄. **'Coccineus'** has scarlet flowers.

P. x rectus (*P. aequalis* x *P. capensis*). Upright, suckering shrub with ovate,

Phygelius x *rectus* 'Moonraker'

dark green leaves, to 10cm (4in) long. In summer, bears pale red flowers, to 6cm (2½in) long, in panicles 15–30cm (6–12in) long. ↕↔ to 1.5m (5ft). Garden origin. ❄❄. **'African Queen'** ■ bears pendent, pale red flowers, with orange-red lobes and yellow mouths, in upright panicles, 30cm (12in) or more long; ↕ 1m (3ft), ↔ 1.2m (4ft). **'Devil's Tears'** has pendent, deep red-pink flowers, turning back towards the stems, with orange-red lobes and yellow throats. **'Moonraker'** ■ has slightly downward-curved, pale creamy yellow flowers. **'Pink Elf'** produces slender, pale pink flowers, with spreading, dark crimson lobes, in panicles to 15cm (6in) long; ↕ 75cm (30in), ↔ 90cm (36in). **'Salmon Leap'** ■ has deeply lobed orange

Phygelius x *rectus* 'African Queen'

Phygelius x *rectus* 'Salmon Leap'

flowers, turning slightly back towards the stems, in panicles to 45cm (18in) long; ↕ 1.2m (4ft), ↔ 1.5m (5ft). **'Winchester Fanfare'** has pendent, dusky, red-pink flowers.

PHYLICA

Cape myrtle

RHAMNACEAE

Genus of about 150 species of heath-like, evergreen shrubs occurring in a range of habitats from seashores to rocky mountain slopes, mainly in South Africa but also in Madagascar and Tristan da Cunha. Leaves are small, alternate, often densely borne, usually narrow, simple, and entire, often with rolled margins. Each tiny flower either has 5 sometimes petal-like sepals and no petals, or has modified petals forming bristles or filaments. Where temperatures fall below 5°C (41°F), grow in a cool greenhouse. In warmer areas, use in a shrub border, or as a hedge or low windbreak.

• **HARDINESS** Frost tender, but may survive temperatures near 0°C (32°F) in a sheltered site, if the wood has been well ripened in summer.

• **CULTIVATION** Under glass, grow in lime-free (ericaceous) potting compost in full light; ventilate well. When in growth, water moderately and apply a balanced liquid fertilizer monthly. Keep just moist in winter. Outdoors, grow in moderately fertile, humus-rich, moist but well-drained, ideally neutral to acid soil in full sun. Pruning group 10, after flowering; clip hedges after flowering or in midsummer.

• **PROPAGATION** Sow seed at 13–18°C (55–64°F) in spring. Take greenwood cuttings in early summer.

• **PESTS AND DISEASES** Trouble free.

P. plumosa, syn. *P. pubescens.* Moderately bushy, downy shrub with wiry stems. Linear to lance-shaped, mid-green leaves, 1–3cm (½–1¼in) long, have rolled margins, and are dotted with glands above, long-hairy beneath. In spring, bears plume-like inflorescences of tiny, cup-shaped, dark brown flowers, surrounded by leaf-like bracts, 2–3cm (¾–1¼in) long, densely clothed in long, brownish white hairs. ↕ 1–2m (3–6ft), ↔ 0.75–1.5m (1½–5ft). South Africa. ❀ (min. 5°C/41°F)

P. pubescens see *P. plumosa.*

▷ ***Phyllanthus nivosus*** see *Breynia disticha*

x PHYLLIOPSIS

ERICACEAE

Hybrid genus of dwarf, evergreen shrubs, derived from crosses between *Phyllodoce* and *Kalmiopsis*. They are grown for their bell-shaped flowers, borne in spring. The stems are upright, bearing simple, alternate, glossy leaves. Grow in a peat bed, or in a shady site in a rock garden.
- **HARDINESS** Fully hardy.
- **CULTIVATION** Grow in moderately fertile, humus-rich, acid, reliably moist soil in deep or partial shade. Pruning group 10, after flowering.
- **PROPAGATION** Take semi-ripe cuttings in summer.
- **PESTS AND DISEASES** Trouble free.

x *P. hillieri* 'Pinocchio'. Upright shrub with branching, hairy shoots. Oblong-obovate, glossy, dark green leaves, 2cm (¾in) long, have margins slightly rolled under. Bears erect, terminal racemes of 5-lobed, widely bell-shaped, red-purple flowers, 1cm (½in) across, in late spring. ↕ 20cm (8in), ↔ to 30cm (12in). ❄❄❄

▷ ***Phyllitis*** see *Asplenium*
P. scolopendrium see *A. scolopendrium*
▷ ***Phyllocactus biformis*** see *Disocactus biformis*
▷ ***Phyllocactus eichlamii*** see *Disocactus eichlamii*

PHYLLOCLADUS

Celery pine

PHYLLOCLADACEAE/PODOCARPACEAE

Genus of 5 species of monoecious or dioecious, evergreen, coniferous trees and shrubs found in forests in Indonesia, Malaysia, the Philippines, Tasmania (Australia), and New Zealand. They have 2 kinds of shoots: normal shoots that produce radial, reduced, scale-like, non-functioning leaves, and flattened, modified shoots that form leaf-like, photosynthesizing elements called "phylloclades", which resemble the leaves of celery. Female cones each bear one to several seeds within fleshy, cup-like arils, usually on the edges of the phylloclades. Male cones are catkin-like, borne in terminal groups. Celery pines are unusual specimen plants, and are attractive in spring with their colourful male cones. In frost-prone areas, grow half-hardy species in a cool greenhouse.
- **HARDINESS** Frost hardy to half hardy.
- **CULTIVATION** Under glass, grow in loam-based potting compost (JI No.3), with added leaf mould, in full light. When in growth, water freely and apply a balanced liquid fertilizer every month. Water sparingly in winter. Outdoors, grow in any well-drained soil in full sun.
- **PROPAGATION** Sow seed at 6–12°C (43–54°F) in spring. Take semi-ripe cuttings in summer.
- **PESTS AND DISEASES** Trouble free.

P. trichomanoides ▣ ◊ (Tanekaha). Pyramidal tree with smooth, grey-black bark and whorled branches. Pinnate phylloclades, to 30cm (12in) long, each with 7–15 diamond-shaped segments, are reddish brown when young, then mid-green. In spring, produces spherical, dark blue or black female cones, 2cm (1in) long, and catkin-like,

Phyllocladus trichomanoides

cylindrical, purple male cones, 1cm (½in) long, ripening red then yellow, borne in clusters of 5–10. ↕ to 12m (40ft) or more, ↔ to 6m (20ft) or more. New Zealand. ❄

PHYLLODOCE

ERICACEAE

Genus of 8 species of spreading or erect, evergreen shrubs and subshrubs from alpine and arctic habitats in the N. hemisphere. Leaves are alternate, linear, leathery, downy beneath, with rolled, toothed margins. Bell-, urn-, or pitcher-shaped, nodding or horizontally held flowers are borne in terminal racemes or umbel-like clusters, sometimes solitary. Grow in a peat bed or rock garden.
- **HARDINESS** Fully hardy.
- **CULTIVATION** Grow in moderately fertile, humus-rich, moist but well-drained, acid soil in partial shade. Pruning group 10, after flowering.
- **PROPAGATION** Sow seed at 6–12°C (43–54°F) in early spring. Take semi-ripe cuttings in summer. Layer in spring.
- **PESTS AND DISEASES** Red spider mites may be a problem under glass.

P. aleutica. Decumbent or scrambling, mat-forming shrub with linear, minutely toothed, bright dark green leaves, 1.5cm (½in) long, softly yellow-downy and with a central white line beneath. In late spring and early summer, bears pendent, umbel-like clusters of urn-shaped, pale yellow-green flowers, to 8mm (⅜in) long. ↕ to 20cm (8in), ↔ 25cm (10in). Japan, Russia (Sakhalin, Kurile Islands, Kamchatka), USA (Alaska). ❄❄❄.

Phyllodoce x *intermedia* 'Drummondii'

P. caerulea, syn. *P. taxifolia*. Upright shrub with linear, fine-toothed, glossy, dark green leaves, to 1cm (½in) long, downy beneath. Pitcher-shaped, purplish pink flowers, 1cm (½in) long, are produced singly or in umbel-like clusters, in late spring and summer. ↕ 15–22cm (6–9in), ↔ 30cm (12in). Europe, Asia, USA. ❄❄❄
P. empetriformis ▣ Loose, mat-forming shrub with linear, glossy, bright green leaves, 1.5cm (½in) long, with glandular-toothed margins, downy beneath. Bears umbel-like clusters of long-stalked, bell-shaped, purple-pink to rose-red flowers, 9mm (½in) long, in late spring and early summer. ↕ 30cm (12in), ↔ to 40cm (16in). W. North America. ❄❄❄
P.* x *intermedia (*P. aleutica* var. *glanduliflora* x *P. empetriformis*). Bushy, low-spreading subshrub with linear, glossy, fine-toothed, dark green leaves, 1.5cm (½in) long, downy beneath. In mid-spring, bears umbel-like clusters of pendent, urn-shaped to narrowly bell-shaped, reddish purple to pink flowers, to 6mm (¼in) long, on slender red stalks. ↕ 15–23cm (6–9in), ↔ 35cm (14in). ❄❄❄. **'Drummondii'** ▣ has deep red-purple flowers.
P. nipponica. Erect subshrub with linear, dark green leaves, to 1cm (½in) long, with white-downy midribs beneath, and minutely glandular-toothed, rolled margins. Loose, umbel-like clusters of pendent, bell-shaped, white, sometimes pink-tinged flowers, 7mm (¼in) long, are borne on upright, red-tinted stalks in late spring and early summer. ↕↔ to 20cm (8in). Japan. ❄❄❄
P. taxifolia see *P. caerulea*.

Phyllodoce empetriformis

PHYLLOSTACHYS

GRAMINEAE/POACEAE

Genus of about 80 species of medium-sized to large, evergreen bamboos occurring in deciduous woodland and groves in E. Asia and the Himalayas. They have a branching habit and spreading rhizomes, although in cool-temperate climates they usually form compact clumps. The canes are hollow and grooved, and often zigzag from node to node on young plants. Leaves are yellow-green or light to dark green, narrowly lance-shaped, and tessellated. Valued for their elegant form and foliage, some also for their subtly coloured canes, they are suitable for growing in containers outdoors, as specimen plants, or in groups among shorter shrubs in a border. They thrive in a woodland garden, and may also be used to create a screen.
- **HARDINESS** Fully hardy.
- **CULTIVATION** Grow in fertile, humus-rich, moist but well-drained soil in full sun or dappled shade. In containers, use loam-based potting compost (JI No.3), and apply a balanced liquid fertilizer monthly. In frost-prone climates, shelter from cold, drying winds.
- **PROPAGATION** Divide in spring.
- **PESTS AND DISEASES** Emerging young shoots are sometimes damaged by slugs.

P. aurea (Fishpole bamboo, Golden bamboo). Clump-forming, stiffly upright bamboo with grooved canes, bright mid-green at first, becoming brown-yellow when mature; there are cup-shaped swellings beneath each node, and the lower nodes are asymmetrical, distorted, and often densely crowded. Produces narrowly lance-shaped, yellowish to golden green leaves, to 15cm (6in) long. ↕ 2–10m (6–30ft), ↔ indefinite. S.E. China. ❄❄❄
P. aureosulcata (Yellow-groove bamboo). Clump-forming bamboo producing rough, brownish green canes, often zigzagged at the bases, with yellow grooves and striped sheaths. Leaves are narrowly lance-shaped and mid-green, to 17cm (7in) long. ↕ 3–6m (10–20ft), ↔ indefinite. N.E. China. ❄❄❄.
var. *aureocaulis* ▣ has sulphur-yellow canes, occasionally with green stripes near the bases; C. China. **'Spectabilis'**

Phyllostachys aureosulcata var. *aureocaulis*

Phyllostachys bambusoides

produces thick yellow canes with green grooves.

P. bambusoides ▣ (Giant timber bamboo). Clump-forming bamboo with thick, shiny, deep green canes and large, thick leaf sheaths with kinked bristles. Bears broadly lance-shaped, glossy, dark green leaves, to 20cm (8in) long. ↕3–8m (10–25ft), ↔ indefinite. China, possibly also Japan. ✻✻✻. **'Allgold'** ▣ syn. 'Holochrysa', 'Sulphurea' of gardens, produces rich golden yellow canes, sometimes striped green; occasionally has yellow-striped leaves. **'Holochrysa'** see 'Allgold'. **'Sulphurea' of gardens** see 'Allgold'.

P. flexuosa ▣ (Zigzag bamboo). Clump-forming bamboo with slightly ribbed, slender, arching canes, often zigzagged between the nodes, bright green at first, turning yellow-brown to almost black with age, and with a waxy white bloom below the nodes. Bears narrowly lance-shaped, fresh green leaves, to 15cm (6in) long, which retain their colour throughout winter. ↕2–10m (6–30ft), ↔ indefinite. China. ✻✻✻

***P.* 'Henonis'** see *P. nigra* var. *henonis.*

P. nigra ▣ (Black bamboo). Clump-forming bamboo with arching, slender

Phyllostachys bambusoides 'Allgold'

Phyllostachys flexuosa

green canes that turn lustrous black in their second or third year. Produces abundant lance-shaped, dark green leaves, 4–13cm (1½–5in) long. ↕3–5m (10–15ft), ↔ 2–3m (6–10ft). E. and C. China. ✻✻✻. **'Boryana'** has green to yellowish green canes with purple-brown marks. **var. *henonis*** ▣ syn. *P.* 'Henonis', has bright green canes, turning yellow-green when mature, and glossy leaves, downy and rough when young.

P. violascens. Clump-forming then spreading bamboo with swollen green canes, finely striped purple, becoming violet with age. Bears narrowly lance-shaped, glossy, dark green leaves, to 12cm (5in) long, glaucous beneath. ↕to 5m (16ft) or more, ↔ 2m (6ft) or more. China. ✻✻✻

Phyllostachys nigra

Phyllostachys nigra var. *henonis*

x PHYLLOTHAMNUS

ERICACEAE

Hybrid genus of one upright, evergreen shrub, derived from crosses between *Phyllodoce* and *Rhodothamnus*, grown for its heath-like, alternate, linear leaves and its funnel-shaped flowers, borne in late spring and early summer. Grow in a peat garden or shady rock garden.

- **HARDINESS** Fully hardy.
- **CULTIVATION** Grow in acid, humus-rich, moderately fertile, moist but well-drained soil in partial shade. Shelter from cold, drying winds. Pruning group 10, after flowering.
- **PROPAGATION** Root semi-ripe cuttings in summer.
- **PESTS AND DISEASES** Red spider mites may be troublesome under glass.

x *P. erectus* (*Phyllodoce empetriformis* x *Rhodothamnus chamaecistus*). Evergreen shrub with linear, glossy, dark green leaves, to 1.5cm (½in) long. Produces terminal clusters of 2–10 widely funnel-shaped, deep rose-pink flowers, 1cm (½in) across, in late spring and early summer. ↕25cm (10in), ↔ to 30cm (12in). Garden origin. ✻✻✻

▷***Phyodina*** see *Callisia*

PHYSALIS

Ground cherry

SOLANACEAE

Genus of about 80 species of upright, bushy, sometimes rhizomatous annuals and perennials found in sunny or lightly shaded, well-drained habitats worldwide, although mostly in the Americas. They have alternate or whorled, entire or pinnatifid, mid-green leaves. Tiny, inconspicuous, bell-shaped flowers, with star-shaped mouths, are produced singly (rarely in small clusters) from the leaf axils; they are followed by spherical, bright red, yellow, or purple, sometimes edible berries, enclosed in decorative, papery, orange to scarlet calyces. In some species, the calyces skeletonize, and persist throughout winter with the berries inside, remaining attractive; they can be used in dried arrangements. They are suitable for a border, although they may become invasive. All parts of *P. alkekengi*, except the fully ripe fruit, may cause mild stomach upset if ingested; contact with foliage may irritate skin.

- **HARDINESS** Fully hardy to frost hardy.
- **CULTIVATION** Grow in any well-drained soil in full sun or partial shade. Cut stems for drying as the calyces begin to colour.
- **PROPAGATION** Sow seed of perennials in containers in a cold frame in spring; sow seed of annuals *in situ* in mid-spring. Divide in spring.
- **PESTS AND DISEASES** Caterpillars may be a problem.

P. alkekengi ▣ (Chinese lantern, Japanese lantern). Vigorous, spreading, rhizomatous perennial with triangular-ovate to diamond-shaped leaves, to 12cm (5in) long. Nodding, bell-shaped cream flowers, 2cm (¾in) long, with star-shaped mouths, are produced from the leaf axils in midsummer, followed by large, bright orange-scarlet berries enclosed in papery red calyces, to 5cm

Physalis alkekengi

(2in) across. ↕60–75cm (24–30in), ↔ 90cm (36in) or more. C. and S. Europe, W. Asia to Japan. ✻✻✻. **var. *franchetii*** has broadly ovate leaves, and tiny, solitary, creamy white flowers, to 6mm (¼in) long.

PHYSARIA

Bladderpod

BRASSICACEAE/CRUCIFERAE

Genus of 14 species of rosette-forming, often short-lived perennials occurring mainly in the mountains of W. North America, usually in rocky sites and open screes. They are cultivated for their unusual, bladder-like seed pods and their attractive symmetrical rosettes of obovate to lance-shaped, mid-green, often silver-hairy leaves. Raceme-like clusters of 4-petalled, cross-shaped yellow flowers are borne in summer, followed by the inflated seed pods. Grow in a scree bed or alpine house; they are intolerant of excessive winter wet.

- **HARDINESS** Fully hardy.
- **CULTIVATION** Grow in moderately fertile, gritty, sharply drained soil in full sun. Protect from winter wet. In an alpine house, grow in a mix of equal parts loam, leaf mould, and grit.
- **PROPAGATION** Sow seed in containers in an open frame as soon as ripe.
- **PESTS AND DISEASES** Prone to damage by slugs and snails. May be infested with aphids and red spider mites under glass.

P. didymocarpa. Rosette-forming perennial with obovate, silver-grey leaves, 1.5–4cm (½–1½in) long, with a suede-like texture. In summer, bears open clusters of cross-shaped, bright yellow flowers, 2cm (¾in) across, followed by large, inflated, grey-hairy seed pods, 1cm (½in) long. ↕8–10cm (3–4in), ↔ to 15cm (6in). W. North America. ✻✻✻

PHYSOCARPUS

ROSACEAE

Genus of about 10 species of deciduous shrubs occurring in thickets and on rocky slopes in E. Asia and North America. They have peeling bark and alternate, ovate to rounded or kidney-shaped, palmately lobed, mid- or dark green leaves. They are cultivated for their foliage and dense, terminal corymbs of small, cup-shaped white flowers, borne in early summer. Grow in a shrub border.

Physocarpus opulifolius 'Dart's Gold'

- **HARDINESS** Fully hardy.
- **CULTIVATION** Grow in preferably acid, fertile, moist but well-drained soil in full sun or partial shade. May become chlorotic if grown in shallow chalk soil. Pruning group 1 or 2.
- **PROPAGATION** Sow seed in containers outdoors in spring or autumn. Take greenwood cuttings in summer. Remove rooted suckers in autumn or spring.
- **PESTS AND DISEASES** Trouble free.

P. opulifolius, syn. *Spiraea opulifolius* (Ninebark). Compact, thicket-forming shrub, spreading by suckers, with arching branches and broadly ovate, 3-lobed, doubly toothed, mid-green leaves, to 8cm (3in) long. Small, cup-shaped, pink-tinged white flowers are produced in dense corymbs, 5cm (2in) across, in early summer, followed by clusters of bladder-like, green-flushed red fruit, 6mm (¼in) long. ↕ 3m (10ft), ↔ 5m (15ft). E. North America. ✲✲✲. **'Dart's Gold'** ■ has bright yellow young foliage; ↕ 2m (6ft), ↔ 2.5m (8ft).

PHYSOPLEXIS

CAMPANULACEAE

Genus of one species of tuft-forming, deciduous perennial found in rock crevices in the Alps. Clusters of unusual, bottle-shaped flowers arise from basal tufts of ovate to heart-shaped, toothed leaves. Grow in an alpine house, rock crevice, or scree bed; they are intolerant of winter wet.
- **HARDINESS** Fully hardy.
- **CULTIVATION** Grow in gritty, poor to moderately fertile, sharply drained, preferably alkaline soil in full sun, with some midday shade. Protect from winter wet. In an alpine house, grow in a mix of equal parts loam, leaf mould, and grit.
- **PROPAGATION** Sow seed in containers in an open frame in autumn.
- **PESTS AND DISEASES** Very susceptible to damage by slugs and snails.

Physoplexis comosa

P. comosa ■ syn. *Phyteuma comosum.* Tufted, deciduous perennial with ovate to heart-shaped, deeply toothed, mid- to dark green leaves, 2–5cm (¾–2in) long. In late summer, bears terminal clusters of 10–20 bottle-shaped, pale violet flowers, to 2cm (¾in) across, with inflated bases and narrow "necks", and with tapered, deep violet tips. ↕ 8cm (3in), ↔ to 10cm (4in). Europe (Alps). ✲✲✲

PHYSOSTEGIA

Obedient plant

LABIATAE/LAMIACEAE

Genus of about 12 species of erect, hairless, deciduous, rhizomatous perennials occurring in moist, sunny sites in E. North America. They have square stems and alternate pairs of variable, often toothed leaves. Almost stalkless, tubular, 2-lipped, purple, pink, or white flowers, with flattish upper lips, 3-lobed lower lips, and tubular calyces, are borne in sometimes branched racemes, mainly in summer. The flowers will remain in a new position if they are moved on the stalks, hence the common name. Grow in a border; good for cut flowers.
- **HARDINESS** Fully hardy to frost hardy.
- **CULTIVATION** Grow in fertile, reliably moist soil in full sun or partial shade.
- **PROPAGATION** Sow seed in containers in a cold frame in autumn. Divide in winter or early spring before new growth.
- **PESTS AND DISEASES** Slugs may cause damage. Fungal and bacterial rots may affect damaged rhizomes.

P. speciosa see *P. virginiana.*
P. virginiana, syn. *P. speciosa* (False dragonhead, Obedient plant). Spreading perennial with lance-shaped, elliptic, or spoon-shaped, sharply toothed, mid-green leaves, to 13cm (5in) long. Bears racemes of deep purple or bright lilac-pink, sometimes white flowers, 2–3cm (¾–1¼in) long, with inflated mouths, from midsummer to early autumn. ↕ to 1.2m (4ft), ↔ 60cm (24in) or more. E. North America. ✲✲✲. **'Bouquet Rose'** has pale, lilac-pink flowers. **'Galadriel'** is dwarf, with pale pink-purple flowers; ↕↔ to 45cm (18in). **subsp. *speciosa* 'Variegata'** see 'Variegata'. **'Summer Snow'** produces white flowers with green calyces; ↕↔ to 60cm (24in). **'Variegata'** ■ syn. subsp. *speciosa* 'Variegata', produces greyish green leaves with white margins, and magenta-pink flowers. **'Vivid'** ■ forms dense clumps, and bears bright purple-pink flowers; ↕ 30–60cm (12–24in), ↔ 30cm (12in).

Physostegia virginiana 'Variegata'

Physostegia virginiana 'Vivid'

PHYTEUMA

Horned rampion

CAMPANULACEAE

Genus of about 40 species of tuft- or clump-forming perennials from open mountain habitats, meadows, and light woodland in Europe and Asia. They have simple, often toothed basal leaves and erect stems with smaller leaves. They are cultivated for their terminal spikes or rounded clusters of stalkless, tubular, narrowly 5-lobed flowers, borne in summer, each flowerhead with a collar of leafy bracts. Grow in a sunny site in a rock garden or at the front of a border.
- **HARDINESS** Fully hardy.
- **CULTIVATION** Grow in moderately fertile, well-drained soil in full sun.
- **PROPAGATION** Sow seed in containers in a cold frame in autumn.
- **PESTS AND DISEASES** Prone to damage by slugs and snails.

Phyteuma scheuchzeri

P. comosum see *Physoplexis comosa.*
P. humile. Compact, tuft-forming perennial with linear-lance-shaped, sparsely toothed basal leaves, 5–10cm (2–4in) long, and a few shorter stem leaves. In summer, bears violet-blue flowers in rounded clusters, to 2.5cm (1in) across, with linear bracts. ↕ 15cm (6in), ↔ 20cm (8in). Europe (C. and S.W. Alps). ✲✲✲
P. scheuchzeri ■ Tuft-forming perennial with linear-lance-shaped, sparsely toothed basal leaves, 5–15cm (2–6in) long, and shorter stem leaves. In summer, bears rounded clusters, 2.5cm (1in) across, of violet-blue flowers with linear bracts. ↕ 40cm (16in), ↔ 30cm (12in). Europe (Alps, Apennines). ✲✲✲

PHYTOLACCA

Pokeweed

PHYTOLACCACEAE

Genus of about 25 species of perennials, shrubs, and trees found in open fields or woodland in tropical and subtropical areas of Africa, Asia, and North to South America. They are grown for their attractive autumn foliage colour and their decorative fruits. Leaves are alternate, ovate to elliptic, and entire, and most of the perennial species have coloured stems. Racemes or panicles of small, shallowly cup-shaped, petalless flowers are followed by spherical, dark red to blackish purple berries. Grow in a large border, light woodland, or a waterside planting. All parts may cause severe discomfort if ingested; the fruit of *P. americana* may be lethal if eaten. Contact with the sap may irritate skin.
- **HARDINESS** Fully hardy to half hardy.
- **CULTIVATION** Grow in any fertile, moist soil in full sun or partial shade.
- **PROPAGATION** Sow seed at 13–18°C (55–64°F) in early spring.
- **PESTS AND DISEASES** *P. americana* may be a carrier of several viruses, such as yellows, mosaic, and ringspot.

P. americana ■ syn. *P. decandra* (Pokeweed, Red ink plant). Erect, unpleasant-smelling perennial with branching, red-marked stems and fleshy roots. Ovate to lance-shaped, mid-green

Phytolacca americana

P

leaves, 15–30cm (6–12in) long, are purple-tinged in autumn. From mid-summer to early autumn, bears white to pink flowers, 8mm (3⁄8in) across, in racemes 20cm (8in) long; these elongate to 30cm (12in), and are sometimes pendent when bearing the blackish maroon berries (highly toxic if ingested). ↕ to 4m (12ft), ↔ 1m (3ft). E. North America to Mexico. ❄❄❄

P. clavigera see *P. polyandra.*

P. decandra see *P. americana.*

P. polyandra, syn. *P. clavigera*. Erect, shrubby perennial with stems becoming vivid crimson. Ovate to elliptic, mid-green leaves, to 30cm (12in) long, turn yellow in autumn. In late summer, purplish pink flowers, 8mm (3⁄8in) across, are produced in erect, compact racemes, to 18cm (7in) long, elongating to 30cm (12in) long when bearing the dense masses of black berries. ↕ 2m (6ft), ↔ 60cm (24in). China. ❄❄❄

PICEA

Spruce

PINACEAE

Genus of 30–40 species of monoecious, evergreen, coniferous trees occurring in forest in cool-temperate regions of the N. hemisphere. They have whorled branches and needle-like leaves set singly around the shoots. The woody, oval to oblong-cylindrical female cones, terminal on main shoots and sideshoots, are erect at flowering, later pendent; they ripen in a season from green or red when young, to purple or brown when mature. Ovoid, yellow to red-purple male cones, 2–3cm (3⁄4–11⁄4in) long, are borne in spring on the previous year's shoots. Spruces are useful for shelter planting or as specimen trees; several cultivars are dwarf or slow-growing.

- **HARDINESS** Fully hardy to frost hardy.
- **CULTIVATION** Grow in any deep, moist but well-drained, ideally neutral to acid soil in full sun. *P. omorika* tolerates alkaline soils; *P. morrisonicola* needs shelter from cold, drying winds.

Picea abies

- **PROPAGATION** Sow seed in containers in a cold frame in spring. Graft cultivars in winter. Take ripewood cuttings of dwarf cultivars in late summer.
- **PESTS AND DISEASES** Adelgids may cause galls, and aphids may cause needle loss. Red spider mites may be trouble-some. Susceptible to honey fungus.

P. abies ▣ ◊–◊ (Christmas tree, Norway spruce). Conical tree when young, columnar when mature, with red-brown bark and orange-brown shoots. Produces blunt, 4-sided, dark green leaves, to 2.5cm (1in) long, pointing forwards and upwards on the shoots, and cylindrical, deep green, later brown female cones, 10–20cm (4–8in) long. The most commonly cultivated spruce. ↕ 20–40m (70–130ft), ↔ 6m (20ft). S. Scandinavia to C. and S. Europe. ❄❄❄. **'Acrocona'** ◊ is small, with pendent branches, and produces abundant cones even on young plants; ↕ 1–3m (3–10ft), ↔ 3–4m (10–12ft). **'Gregoryana'** is a bushy, dwarf shrub, with a tight, rounded habit; ↕↔ 80cm (32in). **'Nidiformis'** is a spreading, slow-growing, bushy shrub with a hollow "nest" in the centre; ↕ to 1.5m (5ft), ↔ 3–4m (10–12ft). **'Ohlendorffii'** ▣ is a very slow-growing, rounded, bushy shrub, becoming more conical, with short leaves, to 8mm (3⁄8in) long; ↕ 3m (10ft), ↔ 2–5m (6–15ft). **'Reflexa'** ▣ is prostrate, unless trained on a stem, when it becomes pendent and weeping; ↕ to 15cm (6in), ↔ indefinite.

P. asperata ▣ △–◊ (Dragon spruce). Conical or columnar tree with scaly, purplish grey bark and thick, ridged, yellow-brown shoots, turning ash-grey. Stout, curved, 4-sided, glaucous, blue-green to dark green leaves, 1–2.5cm (1⁄2–1in) long, point upwards on the shoots. Cylindrical, green, later light brown female cones are 5–15cm (2–6in) long. ↕ 25m (80ft), ↔ 6m (20ft). W. China. ❄❄❄

P. brachytyla △ (Sargent spruce). Conical tree, becoming domed in old age, with cracked grey bark and slender, white or pale brown shoots. Pendent branchlets bear flattened, glossy, mid-green leaves, white beneath, 1–2.5cm (1⁄2–1in) long, spreading at the sides of the shoots. Bears cylindrical, green, later dark brown female cones, 6–15cm (21⁄2–6in) long. ↕ 25m (80ft), ↔ 6–8m (20–25ft). C. to W. China. ❄❄❄

P. breweriana ▣ ◊ (Brewer spruce). Slow-growing, columnar tree with level

Picea abies 'Ohlendorffii'

Picea abies 'Reflexa'

Picea breweriana

branches, grey bark, becoming scaly, and pendent side branchlets. Stout, blunt, flattened leaves, glossy, deep green above, whitish green beneath, 2.5–3.5cm (1–11⁄2in) long, are arranged radially on the shoots. Cylindrical, red-brown female cones are 7–14cm (3–51⁄2in) long. ↕ 10–15m (30–50ft), ↔ 3–4m (10–12ft). USA (N. California, S. Oregon). ❄❄❄

P. engelmannii △ (Engelmann spruce). Conical tree with short branches, scaly, red-brown bark, and pale brown shoots. Flexible, slender, 4-sided, bluish green to steel-blue leaves, 1.5–3cm (1⁄2–11⁄4in) long, are arranged radially, pointing slightly forwards along the shoots. Ovoid to cylindrical, stalkless, light brown female cones, 2.5–7cm (1–3in) long, have flexible scales. ↕ 20–40m (70–130ft), ↔ to 5m (15ft). North America (Rocky Mountains). ❄❄❄

P. glauca ◊–△ (White spruce). Narrowly or broadly conical tree with ash-grey bark, becoming scaly, and buff-white shoots. Four-sided, blue-green leaves, 1–2cm (1⁄2–3⁄4in) long, are spreading at the sides of the shoots, overlapping above. Ovoid, green, later light brown female cones are 4–6cm (11⁄2–21⁄2in) long. ↕ to 50m (160ft), ↔ 3–6m (10–20ft). Canada, N. USA. ❄❄❄. **var. *albertiana* 'Conica'** ▣ syn. 'Albertiana Conica', is a neat, cone-shaped, dwarf, bushy shrub; ↕ 2–6m (6–20ft), ↔ 1–2.5m (3–8ft).

P. jezoensis* subsp. *hondoensis △ (Hondo spruce). Conical tree, becoming gaunt in old age, with large, spreading branches, fissured grey bark, and dense,

Picea asperata (inset: leaf detail)

P

Picea glauca var. *albertiana* 'Conica'

pendent, white or pale brown shoots. Bears flattened, overlapping, glossy, dark green leaves, 1–2cm (½–¾in) long, bright silver beneath. Cylindrical, green, later pale reddish brown female cones, 4–6cm (1½–2½in) long, have thin, stiff scales. ↕ 30m (100ft), ↔ to 8m (25ft). Japan (Honshu). ❄❄❄

P. likiangensis ♢ (Lijiang spruce). Broadly conical tree with fissured or scaly grey bark and stout, pale brown shoots. Flattened, bluish green leaves, to 1.5cm (½in) long, overlap above the shoots, and spread below. Cylindrical, bright reddish purple, later brown female cones are 7–15cm (3–6in) long. Early-flowering if planted in poor, sandy soil. ↕ 30m (100ft), ↔ 6–9m (20–28ft). S. and W. China, S.E. Tibet. ❄❄❄

P. mariana ♢ (Black spruce). Conical tree with scaly, grey-brown bark and brown shoots with reddish brown hairs, the lower shoots often layering to form a skirt. Blunt, 4-sided, bluish green leaves are 0.5–2cm (¼–¾in) long. Ovoid, green, later grey-brown female cones, 2–3.5cm (¾–1½in) long, persist on the tree for 2–3 years. ↕ 10–20m (30–70ft), ↔ 2–3m (6–10ft). Canada, N.E. USA. ❄❄❄. **'Nana'** ▣ is a rounded, bushy, dwarf shrub with bluish grey foliage; ↕↔ to 50cm (20in).

P. morrisonicola ▣ ◊ (Taiwan spruce). Conical tree with pink-brown or grey-brown bark and very slender, ash-grey shoots. Slender, 4-sided, grass-green leaves, to 1.5cm (½in) long, lie flat on top of the shoots and are spreading below. Oblong-cylindrical purple female cones are 5–7cm (2–3in) long. ↕ to 20m (70ft), ↔ to 5m (15ft). Taiwan. ❄❄

Picea mariana 'Nana'

P

Picea morrisonicola

P. omorika ▣ ◊ (Serbian spruce). Narrow, spire-like tree with pendent branches ascending at the tips, brown bark cracking into square plates, and orange-brown shoots with black hairs. Flattened, dark to blue-green leaves, 1–2cm (½–¾in) long, white beneath, lie flat at the sides of the shoots and are spreading below. Bears ovate-oblong, red-brown, later brown female cones, 3–7cm (1¼–3in) long. ↕ 20m (70ft), ↔ 2–3m (6–10ft). Bosnia, Serbia (Drina River valley). ❄❄❄. **'Gnom'** is a dense, broadly conical, dwarf shrub; ↕ to 1.5m (5ft), ↔ 1m (3ft).

P. orientalis ◊–◊ (Caucasian spruce, Oriental spruce). Broadly columnar tree, conical when young, with smooth, pink-grey bark, becoming cracked with age, and hairy, grey-brown shoots. Very

Picea omorika

Picea orientalis 'Skylands'

short, blunt, 4-sided, dark green leaves, 6–8mm (¼–⅜in) long, are arranged radially on the shoots. Male cones are deep red. Ovoid-conical, dark purple, later brown female cones are 6–10cm (2½–4in) long. ↕ 30m (100ft), ↔ 6–8m (20–25ft). Caucasus, N.E. Turkey. ❄❄❄. **'Aurea'** has bright creamy gold young foliage for 6 weeks in spring. **'Skylands'** ▣ is similar to 'Aurea', but the creamy gold colour lasts all year.

P. pungens ◊–◊ (Colorado spruce). Conical to columnar tree with scaly, purplish grey bark and stout, orange-brown shoots. Stiff, stout, sharp-pointed, 4-sided, bluish grey-green leaves, 1.5–3cm (½–1¼in) long, arranged radially on the shoots, curve upwards, and are covered in glaucous wax. Cylindrical, green, later pale brown female cones are 7–12cm (3–5in) long, with flexible scales. ↕ 15m (50ft), ↔ to 5m (15ft). USA (S. Rocky Mountains from Wyoming to Colorado). ❄❄❄. **'Hoopsii'** has glaucous, blue-white foliage. **'Koster'** ▣ has glaucous, silvery blue foliage. **'Montgomery'** is a slow-growing, dwarf shrub, with grey-blue leaves and a broad, conical habit; ↕ to 1.5m (5ft), ↔ 1m (3ft). **'Mrs. Cesarini'** is dwarf, with blue-green leaves; ↕ to 2m (6ft), ↔ 1.5m (5ft).

P. purpurea ◊–♢ (Purple-cone spruce). Columnar or conical tree with flaky, orange-brown bark and slender, densely hairy, buff-white shoots. Slightly flattened, glossy, mid-green leaves, grey-white beneath, 7–12mm (¼–½in) long, lie flat on top of the shoots and are spreading below. Ovoid, purple, later purple-brown female cones are 2.5–4cm

Picea pungens 'Koster'

Picea smithiana

(1–1½in) long. ↕ to 20m (70ft), ↔ to 5m (15ft). N.W. China. ❄❄❄

P. sitchensis ◊ (Sitka spruce). Narrowly conical tree with wide-spreading branches when old, purple-brown bark becoming grey, and white shoots. Sharp-pointed, flattened, dark green leaves, white beneath, 2–2.5cm (¾–1in) long, overlap above the shoots, and spread below. Cylindrical, green, later pale brown female cones are 5–10cm (2–4in) long. ↕ 25–50m (80–160ft), ↔ 6–12m (20–40ft). Coastal W. North America (Alaska to California). ❄❄❄

P. smithiana ▣ ◊–◊ (Morinda spruce). Conical then columnar tree with spreading branches, pendent branchlets, scaly grey bark, and pale brown shoots. Sparse, incurved, 4-sided, dark green leaves, to 4cm (1½in) long, are arranged radially. Cylindrical, green, later bright brown female cones are 10–20cm (4–8in) long. ↕ 20–30m (70–100ft), ↔ 6–9m (20–28ft). E. Afghanistan to W. Nepal. ❄❄❄

▷ **Pick-a-back plant** see *Tolmiea*
▷ **Pickerel weed** see *Pontederia*, *P. cordata*
▷ **Pickles, Little** see *Othonna capensis*

PICRASMA

SIMAROUBACEAE

Genus of 8 species of deciduous trees occurring in forest in E. and S.E. Asia, the West Indies, Central America, and tropical South America. They have alternate, pinnate leaves, each with a terminal leaflet, and produce axillary, umbel-like panicles of bowl-shaped flowers. *P. quassioides*, the most commonly grown species, is valued for its autumn foliage colour; grow in an open position in a woodland garden, or at a woodland margin.

• **HARDINESS** Fully hardy.

• **CULTIVATION** Grow in fertile, well-drained soil in full sun or partial shade. In frost-prone climates, shelter from cold, drying winds. Pruning group 1.

Picrasma quassioides

Pieris formosa var. *forrestii* 'Wakehurst'

Pieris formosa 'Henry Price'

Pieris japonica 'Blush'

• **PROPAGATION** Sow seed in containers in a cold frame in autumn.
• **PESTS AND DISEASES** Trouble free.

P. ailanthoides see *P. quassioides*.
P. quassioides ■ ◊ syn. *P. ailanthoides* (Quassia). Upright tree with pinnate leaves, to 35cm (14in) long, composed of 9–15 ovate, sharply toothed, glossy, mid-green leaflets, turning yellow, orange, and red in autumn. Tiny, bowl-shaped green flowers are produced in umbel-like panicles, to 15cm (6in) long, in early summer. ↕↔ 8m (25ft). N. India, Nepal, Bhutan, China, Korea, Japan. ***

PIERIS

ERICACEAE

Genus of 7 species of evergreen shrubs occurring in forest and on hillsides in the Himalayas, E. Asia, North America, and the West Indies. They are grown for their alternate or whorled, oblong or lance-shaped to obovate, glossy, mid- to dark green leaves, often attractively coloured when young, and their terminal panicles of small, urn-shaped flowers, 5–9mm (¼–⅜in) long, usually borne in spring. Grow in a shrub border, or in a peat or woodland garden. Leaves may cause severe discomfort if ingested.
• **HARDINESS** Fully hardy to frost hardy; young growth may be damaged by late frosts.
• **CULTIVATION** Grow in moderately fertile, humus-rich, moist but well-drained, acid soil in full sun or light shade. In frost-prone areas, shelter from cold, drying winds. Pruning group 8.
• **PROPAGATION** Sow seed in containers in a cold frame in spring or autumn. Take greenwood cuttings in early summer, or semi-ripe cuttings in mid- to late summer, with bottom heat.
• **PESTS AND DISEASES** Leaf spot and *Phytophthora* root rot may be a problem.

***P.* 'Bert Chandler'.** Conical shrub with lance-shaped, finely toothed leaves, to 10cm (4in) long, bright pink when young, turning creamy yellow and white, then dark green. Small white flowers are produced only rarely, in pendent panicles to 10cm (4in) long, in spring. ↕ 2m (6ft), ↔ 1.5m (5ft). ***
***P.* 'Brouwer's Beauty'.** Dense, erect shrub with obovate to oblong-lance-shaped, lightly toothed, glossy, dark green leaves, 3–8cm (1¼–3in) long. In spring, bears white flowers in semi-erect or pendent, terminal panicles, 5–12cm (2–5in) long. ↕ to 3m (10ft), ↔ to 2m (6ft). ***
P. floribunda ■ Compact, rounded shrub with elliptic-ovate, toothed, glossy, dark green leaves, to 8cm (3in) long. White flowers, opening from greenish white buds, are borne in erect, terminal panicles, to 12cm (5in) long, at the shoot tips, in early and mid-spring. ↕ 2m (6ft), ↔ 3m (10ft). S.E. USA. ***
***P.* 'Forest Flame'.** Compact, upright shrub with slender, inversely lance-shaped, finely toothed, glossy, dark green leaves, to 12cm (5in) long, bright red when young, turning pink, then creamy white, and finally green. White flowers, in erect then pendent, terminal panicles, to 15cm (6in) long, are borne in mid- and late spring. ↕ 4m (12ft), ↔ 2m (6ft). **
P. formosa. Upright, often suckering, large shrub with oblong, finely toothed, glossy, dark green leaves, to 10cm (4in) long, bronze when young. White flowers are produced in large, semi-erect to pendent, terminal panicles, to 15cm (6in) long, in mid- and late spring. ↕ 5m (15ft), ↔ 4m (12ft). China, Himalayas. **. **var. *forrestii* 'Charles Michael'** has red young growth, and produces large flowers, 9–11mm (⅜–½in) long, in large panicles, to 18cm (7in) long. **var. *forrestii* 'Jermyns'** is spreading, with arching branches and dark red young foliage; produces pendent panicles of white flowers opening from dark red buds; ↕↔ 2.5m (8ft). **var. *forrestii* 'Wakehurst'** ■ has brilliant red young foliage. **'Henry Price'** ■ has deeply veined, very dark green leaves, dark bronze-red when young.
P. japonica ■ Compact, rounded shrub with narrowly obovate to elliptic, toothed, glossy, mid-green leaves, to 9cm (3½in) long. White flowers are produced in pendent or semi-erect, terminal panicles, to 15cm (6in) long, clustered at the tips of the shoots, in late winter and spring. ↕ 4m (12ft), ↔ 3m (10ft). E. China, Taiwan, Japan. ***. **'Blush'** ■ has very dark green leaves and pink-flushed white, later all-white flowers, opening from dark pink buds. **'Christmas Cheer'** has pink-stalked, crimped white flowers, with deep rose-red tips. **'Daisen'** has red flowers, opening from dark pink buds, and

Pieris japonica 'Flamingo'

Pieris floribunda (inset: flower detail)

Pieris japonica

Pieris japonica 'Scarlett O'Hara'

Pieris japonica 'White Cascade'

fading to pink. **'Debutante'** is compact and low-growing, with white flowers in dense, erect panicles, to 12cm (5in) long; ↕↔ 1m (3ft). **'Dorothy Wyckoff'** produces deeply veined, very dark green leaves, turning bronze in cold weather, and purple-red buds, opening pale pink, later turning white. **'Firecrest'** has deeply veined, dark green leaves, 10cm (4in) long, bright red when young; ↔ 2m (6ft); ✻✻. **'Flamingo'** ■ has dark red buds, opening dark pink. **'Grayswood'** has brownish red new growth, narrow, dark green leaves, and white flowers borne in long, dense panicles, to 18cm (7in) or more. **'Little Heath'** is dwarf and compact, with leaves to 3cm (1¼in) long, pink-flushed when young, and with silvery white margins; ↕↔ 60cm (24in). **'Mountain Fire'** has red young leaves, turning glossy chestnut-brown. **'Purity'** is compact, and produces white flowers in upright panicles, and pale green leaves when young; ↕↔ 1m (3ft). **'Scarlett O'Hara'** ■ has white flowers borne in dense panicles. **'Valley Valentine'** has large panicles of dark dusky red flowers. **'White Cascade'** ■ has white flowers in long panicles, 18cm (7in) or more long, borne over a long period.

P. nana, syn. *Arcterica nana*. Wiry-stemmed, slow-spreading, cushion-forming, dwarf shrub with ovate-elliptic, leathery, toothed, dark green leaves, to 1cm (½in) long, in pairs or whorls of 3, tinted red-bronze in winter. In late spring and early summer, produces fragrant white flowers in pendent, terminal panicles, to 6cm (2½in) long. ↕ 8cm (3in), ↔ to 30cm (12in). Russia (Kamchatka), Japan. ✻✻✻

P

▷ **Pigeon berry** see *Duranta erecta*

▷ **Pignut** see *Carya glabra*

▷ **Pikake** see *Jasminum sambac*

PILEA

URTICACEAE

Genus of about 600 erect or creeping, semi-succulent annuals and evergreen perennials, sometimes woody at the bases, found in rainforest throughout tropical regions worldwide, except Australia. Stems may be branched or unbranched. They are cultivated for their textured, occasionally fleshy, attractively marked, opposite leaves, which are very variable in shape and colour. They also produce wispy, usually insignificant, unisexual, 3- or 4-tepalled

Pilea cadierei

flowers in cymes or panicles, or sometimes singly, from the leaf axils. In frost-prone areas, grow in a warm greenhouse or as houseplants; use trailing species in a hanging basket. In warmer climates, grow as ground cover in a damp, shady border.

- **HARDINESS** Frost tender.
- **CULTIVATION** Under glass, grow in shallow pans of loamless potting compost in bright indirect light, with high humidity. During the growing season, water moderately, allowing the surface to dry out between waterings, and apply a balanced liquid fertilizer every month. Water sparingly in winter. Outdoors, grow in any reliably moist soil in partial or deep shade.
- **PROPAGATION** Sow seed at 19–24°C (66–75°F) in spring. Divide or detach rosettes in spring. Root stem-tip cuttings with bottom heat in spring.
- **PESTS AND DISEASES** May be affected by powdery mildew.

P. cadierei ■ (Aluminium plant). Erect perennial with branches becoming woody at the bases. The obovate to oblong-inversely-lance-shaped, toothed, dark green leaves, 8cm (3in) long, each

Pilea microphylla

have 4 rows of raised silver patches on the upper surface. ↕ 30cm (12in), ↔ 16–21cm (6–8in). Vietnam. ❀ (min. 15°C/59°F). **'Minima'** is compact; ↕ 15cm (6in).

P. grandifolia. Rounded to upright, shrubby perennial producing ovate, coarsely toothed, glossy, dark or bronze-green leaves, 10–20cm (4–8in) long, with pointed tips, sometimes puckered between the veins. ↕ to 1.5m (5ft), ↔ to 80cm (32in). Jamaica. ❀ (min. 10°C/50°F)

P. involucrata ■ syn. *P. mollis* (Friendship plant, Panamiga). Trailing or creeping perennial producing tight rosettes of virtually stalkless, ovate to obovate, toothed, dark green leaves, 6cm (2½in) long, with bronze-flushed,

Pilea involucrata

Pilea nummulariifolia

quilted surfaces, sometimes with paler margins. ↕ 3cm (1¼in), ↔ to 30cm (12in). Central and South America. ❀ (min. 15°C/59°F). **'Moon Valley'** is more upright and open in habit, and produces ovate, toothed, fresh green leaves, to 10cm (4in) long, with deep purple sunken veins; ↕↔ 30cm (12in).

P. microphylla ■ (Artillery plant). Densely branching, succulent annual or short-lived perennial with thick, almost erect, fleshy, hairless stems; these bear unequal pairs of obovate to rounded, semi-succulent, bright green leaves, to 1cm (½in) long, with blunt or pointed tips, or rounded leaves, to 3mm (⅛in) long. ↕↔ 30cm (12in). USA (Florida), Mexico, West Indies, South America. ❀ (min. 15°C/59°F)

P. mollis see *P. involucrata.*

P. nummulariifolia ■ (Creeping Charlie). Trailing or creeping perennial with frequently branching stems, rooting at the nodes. Rounded, deeply quilted, light green leaves, 2cm (¾in) long, fold inwards slightly at the midribs. ↕ 15cm (6in), ↔ 60cm (24in). West Indies, tropical South America. ❀ (min. 15°C/59°F)

P. peperomioides. Open-bushy, erect, perennial succulent with thick, fleshy stems covered with persistent stipules. Produces spirally arranged, long-stalked, elliptic to almost rounded, succulent, pale green leaves, 9cm (3½in) long. ↕↔ 30cm (12in) or more. China (Yunnan). ❀ (min. 10°C/50°F)

PILEOSTEGIA

HYDRANGEACEAE

Genus of 4 species of woody, evergreen root climbers, related to *Hydrangea* and *Schizophragma*, occurring on forest trees and cliffs in India and E. Asia. They have opposite, obovate to oblong, mid-green leaves, and produce dense, terminal, corymb-like panicles of small, cup- or star-shaped, 4- or 5-petalled, creamy white flowers, in late summer and autumn. *P. viburnoides*, the most commonly cultivated species, is valued for its foliage and flowers. Grow on a large tree trunk or a wall.

- **HARDINESS** Hardy to at least -10°C (14°F).
- **CULTIVATION** Grow in fertile, well-drained soil in sun or shade. Pruning group 11, in early spring.
- **PROPAGATION** Root semi-ripe cuttings in summer. Layer in spring.
- **PESTS AND DISEASES** Trouble free.

Pileostegia viburnoides

P. viburnoides ■ syn. *Schizophragma viburnoides*. Evergreen climber with oblong, leathery, dark green leaves, to 15cm (6in) long. Small, star-shaped, creamy white flowers, with prominent stamens, are borne in dense panicles, to 15cm (6in) across, in late summer and autumn. ↕6m (20ft). India, China, Taiwan. ❄❄

▷**Pilewort** see *Ranunculus ficaria*
▷***Pilgerodendron uviferum*** see *Libocedrus uvifera*
▷***Pilocereus senilis*** see *Cephalocereus senilis*

PILOSELLA

ASTERACEAE/COMPOSITAE

Genus of about 20 hairy, rhizomatous or stoloniferous herbaceous perennials from a variety of habitats in Eurasia and North Africa, including grassland, sand dunes, dry slopes, and open woodland. The ovate to narrowly lance-shaped or spoon-shaped, entire or toothed leaves are usually in basal rosettes, sometimes with smaller stem leaves. Greenish yellow or yellow to orange-red, rarely white or red, dandelion-like flowerheads are borne singly or in terminal clusters on usually leafless stems in summer. Grow in a wild garden or meadow, or on dry walls and banks.
• **HARDINESS** Fully hardy.
• **CULTIVATION** Grow in poor to moderately fertile, well-drained or dry soil in full sun or partial shade.
• **PROPAGATION** Sow seed in containers outdoors. Divide in autumn or spring.
• **PESTS AND DISEASES** Trouble free.

Pilosella aurantiaca

P. aurantiaca ■ syn. *Hieracium aurantiacum, H. brunneocroceum* (Fox and cubs, Orange hawkweed). Stoloniferous perennial with basal rosettes of elliptic to lance-shaped, bluish green leaves, to 20cm (8in) long. In summer, black-hairy stems bear dense clusters of 8–10 orange-red or orange-brown flowerheads, 1.5cm (½in) across. ↕to 20cm (8in), ↔90cm (36in). Grassy places in Europe. ❄❄❄

PILOSOCEREUS

CACTACEAE

Genus of 60 species of tree-like or bushy, perennial cacti, branching from the stems or the bases, found in warm, humid, moist areas of Mexico, Central and South America, and the West Indies. The many ribs have spiny, generally densely woolly, hairy areoles, sometimes as long as 5cm (2in), the wool forming skeins covering the ribs. In summer, nocturnal, tubular to bell-shaped flowers are borne from pseudocephaliums, from prominent areoles, or at the crowns, followed by fleshy, fig-like fruits. Below 15°C (59°F), grow in a warm greenhouse. In warmer areas, use as a focal point on a lawn or in a courtyard.
• **HARDINESS** Frost tender.
• **CULTIVATION** Under glass, grow in standard cactus compost in full light. From spring to summer, water freely and apply a balanced liquid fertilizer every 6–8 weeks. Keep just moist at other times. Outdoors, grow in gritty, moderately fertile, sharply drained soil in full sun. See also pp.48–49.
• **PROPAGATION** Sow seed at 19–24°C (66–75°F) in spring.
• **PESTS AND DISEASES** Vulnerable to mealybugs, and to ants if planted out.

P. leucocephalus see *P. palmeri*.
P. palmeri ■ syn. *P. leucocephalus*. Tree-like cactus with a blue-green stem, 5–10cm (2–4in) thick, with 7–9 rounded ribs. The areoles bear dark brown or greyish black spines (8–12 radials, 1 or 2 longer centrals), pale brown or yellow at first. Some areoles become covered with woolly grey hairs, borne more densely at the crown, forming a pseudocephalium. Pinkish purple flowers, 8cm (3in) long, purple-brown outside, are borne in summer. ↕to 6m (20ft), ↔1m (3ft). E. Mexico, Central America. ❀ (min. 15°C/59°F)

▷**Pilot plant** see *Silphium laciniatum*

Pilosocereus palmeri

PIMELEA

THYMELAEACEAE

Genus of about 80 species of evergreen shrubs and subshrubs found in scrub, rocky places, and grassland from coastal areas to mountains in Australasia. Those commonly cultivated usually have opposite pairs of ovate to oblong leaves. Tubular, sometimes fragrant flowers, each with 4 spreading lobes, are borne in flat to almost spherical, terminal heads, surrounded by often colourful bracts. They are followed in some species by white, red, green, or black fruits (one-seeded drupes or nuts). In frost-prone areas, grow in containers outdoors and bring under cover in winter, or grow in a cool greenhouse. In warmer climates, grow in a border or a rock garden.
• **HARDINESS** Frost hardy to frost tender.
• **CULTIVATION** Under glass, grow in lime-free (ericaceous) potting compost with added sharp sand, in full light. During growth, water moderately and apply a balanced liquid fertilizer every month. Water sparingly in winter. Outdoors, grow in fertile, well-drained, neutral to acid soil in full sun. Pruning group 8.
• **PROPAGATION** Sow seed in containers in a cold frame in spring. Root semi-ripe cuttings with bottom heat in summer.
• **PESTS AND DISEASES** Red spider mites may be a problem in dry conditions under glass.

P. ferruginea ■ Bushy, domed shrub, at least when young. Densely borne, glossy, mid-green leaves, to 1cm (½in) long, are ovate to oblong, with rolled margins. In late spring and early summer, bears almost spherical heads, to 4cm (1½in) across, of slender-tubed, white-hairy, rose-pink flowers, 8mm (⅜in) across, surrounded by pink to red bracts. ↕1–2m (3–6ft), ↔1–1.5m (3–5ft). Australia (Western Australia). ❄
P. prostrata ■ Compact, spreading shrub with dark shoots and densely clustered, ovate, grey-green, often red-margined, leathery leaves, to 6mm (¼in) long. In summer, bears flat heads, to 2cm (¾in) across, of tubular, fragrant white flowers, to 6mm (¼in) across, followed by tiny, fleshy, white or red fruit. ↕20cm (8in), ↔50cm (20in). New Zealand. ❄❄
P. traversii. Upright shrub with densely overlapping, oblong, leathery, grey-

Pimelea ferruginea

Pimelea prostrata

green, often red-margined leaves, to 1cm (½in) long. Flat heads, 2cm (¾in) across, of up to 20 silky-hairy, tubular, white or pink flowers, 6–8mm (¼–⅜in) across, are borne in summer. ↕↔50cm (20in). New Zealand. ❄❄

▷**Pimpernel** see *Anagallis*
Blue see *A. monellii*

PIMPINELLA

APIACEAE/UMBELLIFERAE

Genus of about 150 species of annuals, biennials, and perennials occurring in rough grassland, hedgerows, and woodland in Europe, N. Africa, Asia, and South America. Most have hairy stems, with simple or pinnate leaves, and bear compound umbels of tiny, star-shaped, usually white or yellow, sometimes pink or purple flowers, followed by ovoid-oblong to nearly spherical fruits. Most are suitable for naturalizing in a wild garden; *P. major* 'Rosea' is also effective in a border.
• **HARDINESS** Fully hardy.
• **CULTIVATION** Grow in any, but preferably fertile, moist soil in full sun or partial shade.

Pimpinella major 'Rosea'

• **PROPAGATION** Sow seed in containers in a cold frame as soon as ripe. Prick out into deep containers, to avoid damage to the tap roots when transplanting later.
• **PESTS AND DISEASES** Susceptible to aphids, slugs, and snails, and to powdery mildew in dry conditions.

P. major. Erect perennial producing triangular to rounded, pinnate, mid-green basal leaves, to 18cm (7in) long, each with 7–13 ovate to lance-shaped, lobed or toothed leaflets, 2–8cm (¾–3in) long, and smaller stem leaves. In mid- and late spring, ridged stems bear tiny, white, greenish white, or pink flowers in compound umbels, 6cm (2½cm) across. ↕ to 1.2m (4ft), ↔ 60cm (24in). Europe to Caucasus. ✲✲✲. **'Rosea'** ■ has both deep pink and pale pink flowers, in early and midsummer.

▷ **Pinang** see *Areca catechu*

PINANGA

ARECACEAE/PALMAE

Genus of about 120 species of single- or cluster-stemmed palms occurring in undergrowth in dense, tropical rain-forest at low to medium altitudes from the Himalayas to S. China, S.E. Asia, and Papua New Guinea. Simple or pinnate, variably shaped, light to dark green leaves are borne in terminal tufts above distinct crownshafts. Bowl-shaped, 3-petalled flowers are produced in spikes or panicles (erect at first, then becoming pendent) arising from the bases of the crownshafts. In frost-prone areas, grow in a warm greenhouse. In lowland, tropical areas, plant in a shady site near other trees or in a courtyard.
• **HARDINESS** Frost tender.
• **CULTIVATION** Under glass, grow in loam-based potting compost (JI No.3), with added peat and sharp sand, in bright filtered to low light. Pot on or top-dress in spring. During growth, water freely and apply a balanced liquid fertilizer monthly. Water moderately during winter. Outdoors, grow in fertile, moist but well-drained soil in dappled to deep shade.
• **PROPAGATION** Sow seed at 24°C (75°F) in spring.
• **PESTS AND DISEASES** Red spider mites may be troublesome under glass.

P. patula ■ ❀ Small, cluster-stemmed palm with erect, smooth, cane-like stems with swollen bases. Irregularly pinnate leaves, to 1.5m (5ft) long, each have 16–36 lance-shaped, bright green leaflets. Bowl-shaped green flowers, turning red with age, are borne in recurved panicles, to 1cm (½in) across, usually in summer. ↕↔ to 2.5m (8ft). Indonesia (Sumatra), Borneo. ❁ (min. 16–18°C/61–64°F)

Pinanga patula

▷ **Pincushion** see *Leucospermum*
Catherine's see *L. catherinae*
▷ **Pincushion flower** see *Isopogon dubius, Scabiosa, S. atropurpurea*
▷ **Pine** see *Pinus*
Aleppo see *Pinus halepensis*
Armand see *Pinus armandii*
Arolla see *Pinus cembra*
Australian see *Casuarina*
Austrian see *Pinus nigra*
Beach see *Pinus contorta*
Bhutan see *Pinus wallichiana*
Big-cone see *Pinus coulteri*
Bishop see *Pinus muricata*
Blue see *Pinus wallichiana*
Bosnian see *Pinus heldreichii*
Bristle cone see *Pinus aristata*
Canary Islands see *Pinus canariensis*
Celery see *Phyllocladus*
Chilean see *Araucaria araucana*
Chinese red see *Pinus tabuliformis*
Cook see *Araucaria columnaris*
Corsican see *Pinus nigra* subsp. *laricio*
Coulter see *Pinus coulteri*
Cowtail see *Cephalotaxus harringtonii*
Cypress see *Callitris*
Digger see *Pinus sabineana*
Dwarf mountain see *Pinus mugo*
Dwarf Siberian see *Pinus pumila*
Eastern white see *Pinus strobus*
European black see *Pinus nigra*
Foxtail see *Pinus balfouriana*
Holford see *Pinus* x *holfordiana*
Hoop see *Araucaria cunninghamii*
Jack see *Pinus banksiana*
Japanese black see *Pinus thunbergii*
Japanese red see *Pinus densiflora*
Japanese umbrella see *Sciadopitys verticillata*
Japanese white see *Pinus parviflora*
Jeffrey see *Pinus jeffreyi*
Kauri see *Agathis, A. australis*
King William see *Athrotaxis selaginoides*
Knobcone see *Pinus attenuata*
Korean see *Pinus koraiensis*
Lacebark see *Pinus bungeana*
Limber see *Pinus flexilis*
Lodgepole see *Pinus contorta, P. contorta* var. *latifolia*
Macedonian see *Pinus peuce*
Maritime see *Pinus pinaster*
Mexican weeping see *Pinus patula*
Mexican white see *Pinus ayacahuite*
Monterey see *Pinus radiata*
Montezuma see *Pinus montezumae*
Moreton Bay see *Araucaria cunninghamii*
Mountain see *Pinus uncinata*
New Caledonian see *Araucaria columnaris*
Norfolk Island see *Araucaria heterophylla*
Oyster bay cypress see *Callitris rhomboidea*
Pitch see *Pinus rigida*
Ponderosa see *Pinus ponderosa*
Prince's see *Chimaphila*
Radiata see *Pinus radiata*
Red see *Pinus resinosa*

▷ **Pine cont.**
Scots see *Pinus sylvestris*
Screw see *Pandanus*
Shore see *Pinus contorta*
Stone see *Pinus pinea*
Swiss stone see *Pinus cembra*
Tasmanian cypress see *Callitris oblonga*
Umbrella see *Pinus pinea*
Western white see *Pinus monticola*
Western yellow see *Pinus ponderosa*
Weymouth see *Pinus strobus*
Whitebark pine see *Pinus albicaulis*
▷ **Pineapple** see *Ananas*
Red see *A. bracteatus*
Wild see *A. bracteatus*
▷ **Pineapple flower** see *Eucomis*
Giant see *E. pallidiflora*
▷ **Pineapple guava** see *Acca sellowiana*

PINELLIA

ARACEAE

Genus of about 6 species of tuberous perennials found in deciduous forest, in cultivated fields, and at roadsides in China, Korea, and Japan. The simple, 3-palmate or pedate, basal leaves are rounded to ovate-lance-shaped or heart-shaped. Usually long, fine, black, green, or dark purple spadices, protruding from cylindrical spathes, are borne in summer. Grow in a peat bed or rock garden.
• **HARDINESS** Frost hardy.
• **CULTIVATION** Plant tubers 10–15cm (4–6in) deep in spring. Grow in fertile, humus-rich, well-drained soil in full sun or partial shade.
• **PROPAGATION** Sow seed in containers in a cold frame as soon as ripe. Remove offsets in autumn or early spring, or detach bulbils in late summer.
• **PESTS AND DISEASES** Trouble free.

P. pedatisecta. Tuberous perennial bearing pedate, mid-green leaves, each with 7–11 ovate to lance-shaped segments, 18cm (7in) long. Yellow-green spathes, 10–18cm (4–7in) long, each concealing a yellow-green spadix, rise above the leaves in summer. ↕ 18cm (7in), ↔ 8cm (3in). N. and W. China, Japan. ✲✲
P. ternata. Tuberous perennial with 3-palmate, mid-green leaves, composed of ovate-elliptic to oblong segments, 3–12cm (1¼–5in) long. Produces slightly hooded green spathes, to 7cm (3in) long, each with a protruding, slender green spadix, in summer. ↕ to 20cm (8in), ↔ 5cm (2in). China, Korea, Japan. ✲✲

PINGUICULA

Butterwort

LENTIBULARIACEAE

Genus of about 45 species of spring- or summer-flowering, insectivorous perennials from boggy habitats widely distributed in the N. hemisphere and in South America. They have rosettes of mucilage-secreting, lance-shaped to almost rounded leaves, and leafless stems bearing solitary, spurred, 2-lipped, trumpet-shaped flowers, the upper lip 2-lobed, the lower with 3 widely spreading lobes. Some species die back to resting buds in winter. The sticky leaves trap insects, which are then digested; under glass, butterworts may be used to assist in controlling aphids and whiteflies. In frost-prone areas, grow tender species as houseplants or in a temperate green-house. Hardy species are suitable for an alpine house or as bog plants.

Pinguicula moranensis

• **HARDINESS** Fully hardy to frost tender.
• **CULTIVATION** Under glass, grow in a mixture of equal parts chopped peat and sphagnum moss, with added broken clay pots, in bright filtered light. During growth, water freely and apply a balanced liquid fertilizer every month. Water sparingly during winter. Outdoors, grow in poor, peaty, permanently moist soil in full sun or partial shade.
• **PROPAGATION** Surface-sow seed on damp sphagnum moss at 13–18°C (55–64°F), as soon as ripe. Divide in late winter.
• **PESTS AND DISEASES** Slugs and snails may be troublesome.

P. grandiflora. Rosette-forming perennial with resting buds in winter. Obovate-oblong, sticky, pale green leaves are 3–4.5cm (1¼–1¾in) long. During summer, trumpet-shaped, spurred, dark blue flowers, 2.5cm (1in) across, with widely spreading lobes and white throats, are borne on slender stems. ↕ 15cm (6in), ↔ 10cm (4in). W. Europe. ✲✲✲
P. moranensis ■ Rosette-forming perennial with ovate, sticky, dull pale green leaves, 6–10cm (2½–4in) long, with inrolled, purple-green margins. Trumpet-shaped, deep carmine-red flowers, to 3cm (1¼in) across, are borne on slender stems in summer. ↕ 15cm (6in), ↔ 10cm (4in). Mexico. ❁ (min. 7°C/45°F)

▷ **Pink** see *Dianthus*
Alpine see *Dianthus alpinus*
Carthusian see *Dianthus carthusianorum*
Cheddar see *Dianthus gratianopolitanus*
Chinese see *Dianthus chinensis*
Deptford see *Dianthus armeria*
Fringed see *Dianthus monspessulanus*
Ground see *Linanthus dianthiflorus*
Indian see *Dianthus chinensis*
Maiden see *Dianthus deltoides*
Sea see *Armeria*
Swamp see *Helonias bullata*
▷ **Pink shower** see *Cassia javanica*
▷ **Piñon,**
Mexican see *Pinus cembroides*
Rocky Mountain see *Pinus edulis*
Single-leaf see *Pinus monophylla*

PINUS

Pine

PINACEAE

Genus of approximately 120 species of monoecious, evergreen, coniferous trees or shrubs, widely distributed in forests of the N. hemisphere from the Arctic Circle to Central America, Europe, N. Africa, and S.E. Asia. The bark is often fissured, and in some species is divided into irregular, plate-like sections. Pines have small bundles of 2–5, rarely 1 or 6–8, needle-like, light to dark green or yellow-green to bluish or grey-green leaves, which usually persist for 2–4 years, sometimes for longer. The winter buds are usually cylindrical or ovoid, and often resinous. Female cones take 2, or occasionally 3 years to ripen; the seeds are winged in most species. Male cones are yellow and catkin-like, clustered at the shoot bases. Pines are useful as specimen trees, and for shelter and windbreaks; some cultivars and slow-growing species are suitable for a rock garden.

- **HARDINESS** Fully hardy to frost hardy.
- **CULTIVATION** Grow in any well-drained soil in full sun. The 5-needled species may be short-lived in shallow, chalk soil.
- **PROPAGATION** Sow seed of species in containers in a cold frame in spring. Graft cultivars in late winter.
- **PESTS AND DISEASES** Prone to adelgids, aphids, sawfly larvae, honey fungus, pine shoot moth, and various needle cast diseases. Some 5-needled pines are susceptible to white pine blister rust.

P. albicaulis ♤ (Whitebark pine). Broadly conical tree with smooth, grey-white bark, developing a spreading crown and becoming scaly with age. Bears stout, flexible, hairy, reddish brown young shoots with ovoid, pointed, resinous buds and long, sharp, pointed, yellow-brown to red-brown scales. Dull, dark green leaves, 4–7mm (⅛–¼in) long, are clustered together in fives at the ends of the shoots and persist for several years. Near-spherical, purple-brown female cones, 4–8cm (1½–3in) long, have a stout, bristle-like protrusion on each scale; the cones fall intact without shedding the wingless, edible seeds. ↕ 15m (50ft), ↔ 6–9m (20–28ft). Rocky Mountains from S.W. Alberta and C. British Columbia to Sierra Nevada, California. ❄❄❄

Pinus aristata

P. aristata ▣ ♤ (Bristle cone pine). Dense, conical tree with upturned branch tips, smooth, dark grey bark, and red-brown shoots with pale hairs and ovoid buds. Bright green leaves, 2–4cm (¾–1½in) long, have flecks of white resin and are borne in fives; young needles have blue-white inner sides. Leaves are retained for up to 20 years. Long-ovoid brown female cones, 4–10cm (1½–4in) long, have a bristle-like prickle on each scale. ↕ to 10m (30ft), ↔ to 6m (20ft). USA (Arizona, New Mexico, Colorado). ❄❄❄

P. armandii ♤ (Armand pine). Broadly conical tree with an open, whorled habit, smooth bark, becoming cracked with age, and olive-green shoots with cylindrical-ovoid buds. Forward-pointing, pendent, shiny, deep green leaves, 10–20cm (4–8in) long, with white inner sides and curved at the bases, are borne in fives. Cylindrical-conical female cones, 12–20cm (5–8in) long, have wingless seeds. ↕ 15–20m (50–70ft), ↔ 6–8m (20–25ft). Tibet, N. Burma, China, Taiwan. ❄❄❄

P. attenuata ♤ (Knobcone pine). Conical tree with ascending branches, smooth grey bark, becoming fissured and scaly with age, and green-brown shoots with resinous, narrow, spindle-shaped buds. Stiff, slender, grey-green leaves, 8–18cm (3–7in) long, are borne in threes. Ovoid-conical, yellow-brown female cones, swollen on the outer sides, are 9–20cm (3½–8in) long, and may persist for over 20 years. ↕ to 25m (80ft), ↔ to 6–8m (20–25ft). North America (Oregon to Baja California). ❄❄❄

Pinus ayacahuite

Pinus bungeana

P. ayacahuite ▣ ♤ (Mexican white pine). Conical to broadly conical tree with smooth grey bark, becoming domed and scaly with age, and finely hairy, pale yellow-brown shoots with resinous, conical buds. Forward-pointing, pendent, shiny green leaves, 10–20cm (4–8in) long, with white bands on the inner sides, appear in fives. Very resinous, cylindrical female cones, 20–45cm (8–18in) long, have conical apexes and reflexed scales. ↕ to 30m (100ft), ↔ 6–8m (20–25ft). S. Mexico, Guatemala, Honduras. ❄❄❄

P. balfouriana ♤ (Foxtail pine). Broad, conical tree with ridged grey bark and hairy, orange-brown shoots with ovoid buds. Dark green leaves, 2–3cm (¾–1¼in) long, with faint white bands on the inner sides, are borne in fives,

Pinus canariensis

Pinus coulteri

and retained for 10–20 years. Oblong-cylindrical, purple-brown female cones, 8–14cm (3–5½in) long, have a short prickle on each scale. Similar to *P. aristata*, but does not have flecks of resin on its leaves. ↕ 15m (50ft), ↔ 6–8m (20–25ft). USA (California). ❄❄❄

P. banksiana ◊ (Jack pine). Narrow, conical tree when young, becoming irregular and scruffy with age. It has fissured, red-brown or grey bark, thin, flexible brown shoots, and very resinous, cylindrical buds. Stout, twisted, divergent, yellow-green leaves, 2–4cm (¾–1½in) long, are borne in pairs. Forward-pointing, ovoid-conical, strongly curved, yellow-buff to grey female cones, 4–6cm (1½–2½in) long, are persistent. ↕ 10–20m (30–70ft), ↔ 3–5m (10–15ft). North America (Yukon Territory to Atlantic), south into N.E. USA. ❄❄❄

P. bungeana ▣ ◊–♤ (Lacebark pine). Columnar or bushy-crowned, slow-growing tree with smooth bark, which flakes in small, round scales to reveal creamy patches that darken through purple to grey-green. Shoots are olive-green with ovoid to ellipsoid buds, and bear hard, shiny, yellow-green leaves, 5–10cm (2–4in) long, in threes. Ovoid female cones, 4–7cm (1½–3in) long, bear seeds with short, brittle wings. ↕ 10–15m (30–50ft), ↔ 5–6m (15–20ft). N. and C. China. ❄❄❄

P. canariensis ▣ ♤ (Canary Islands pine). Conical to broadly conical tree, becoming domed with age, with fissured, red-brown bark, yellow shoots, and large, ovate buds. Spreading, grass-green adult leaves, 15–30cm (6–12in) long, are borne in threes. Glaucous blue juvenile leaves are borne singly and are retained for several years. Ellipsoid-ovoid female cones, 9–20cm (3½–8in) long, are borne on long stalks, 2cm (¾in) long. ↕ to 25m (80ft), ↔ 6–9m (20–28ft). Canary Islands. ❄❄

P. cembra ◊–♤ (Arolla pine, Swiss stone pine). Narrow, columnar tree with smooth, dark grey bark, becoming fissured with age, and densely brown-hairy shoots with ovate, resinous buds. Dark green leaves, bluish white on the inner sides, 7–9cm (3–3½in) long, are borne in fives. Broad, oblong-conical, bluish green female cones, 6–8cm (2½–3in) long, are resinous, and bear edible, wingless seeds. ↕ 15–20m (50–70ft), ↔ 6–8m (20–25ft). C. Europe. ❄❄❄

P

Pinus densiflora 'Umbraculifera'

P. cembroides ○ (Mexican piñon). Domed, rounded tree with scaly, silver-grey bark, fissured red-brown, and orange-brown shoots with ellipsoid buds, which have tapered, reflexed scales. Radially arranged, dark green leaves, 3–6cm (1¼–2½in) long, with glaucous inner sides, are borne in threes, occasionally in pairs. Spherical green female cones, 2.5–4cm (1–1½in) across, ripen to brown, and have wingless seeds. ↕10–18m (30–60ft), ↔ 6–8m (20–25ft). S.W. USA, N. Mexico. **

P. chylla see *P. wallichiana.*

P. contorta ○ (Beach pine, Lodgepole pine, Shore pine). Broadly conical tree when young, becoming domed with age, with scaly, red-brown bark, shiny, greenish brown shoots, and very resinous, cylindrical buds. Dense, forward-pointing, deep green leaves, 4–5cm (1½–2in) long, are borne in pairs. Long-conical, yellow-brown to brown female cones, 2.5–7cm (1–3in) long, have reflexed scales, and are persistent. ↕ to 25m (80ft), ↔ to 8m (25ft). Coastal N.W. North America. ***. **var. *latifolia*** △ (Lodgepole pine) has a conical habit, flakier bark, and brighter green, spreading leaves, 6–9cm (2½–3½in) long, with ovoid cones, 4cm (1½in) long; Rocky Mountains. **'Spaan's Dwarf'** is dwarf, with a sloping trunk and an open habit, with erect branches; leaves are 1.5cm (½in) long; ↕↔ 75cm (30in).

P. coulteri ▣ ○ (Big-cone pine, Coulter pine). Domed tree with grey bark, becoming black-grey and fissured, and brown, glaucous shoots with long, cylindrical to ovoid buds. Radially arranged, stiff, grey-green or bluish green leaves, 20–30cm (8–12in) long, are borne in threes. Massive, ovoid, yellow-brown female cones, 20–35cm (8–14in) long, have stout, forward-pointing spines and large, wingless seeds. ↕ to 25m (80ft), ↔ 8–10m (25–30ft). USA (California), Mexico (Baja California). ***

P. densiflora △ (Japanese red pine). Broadly conical to rounded tree, becoming flat-topped, with reddish brown bark, flaky in the upper crown, grey and fissured at the base. The whitish pink shoots have slightly resinous, ovoid buds. Slender, bright green leaves, 8–12cm (3–5in) long, are borne in pairs. Bears long-ovoid, yellow-brown female cones, 3–6cm (1¼–2½in) long. ↕15–25m (50–80ft), ↔ 5–7m (15–22ft). N.E. Asia, Japan. ***. **'Alice Verkade'** is a globe-shaped, dwarf selection, with bright green leaves; it grows only about 7cm (3in) per year; ↕50cm (20in) or more, ↔ 1m (3ft) (when mature). **'Ja-nome'** see 'Oculus Draconis'. **'Oculus Draconis'**, syn. 'Ja-nome', is a large shrub or small tree, with 2 distinctive yellow bands ("dragon's eyes") on each leaf. Bears blue-green female cones. **'Tagyosho'** see 'Umbraculifera'. **'Umbraculifera'** ▣ ○ syn. 'Tagyosho', is a slow-growing, rounded to broadly spreading tree with a domed or umbrella-shaped crown; ↕4m (12ft), ↔ 6m (20ft).

P. edulis ○ (Rocky Mountain piñon). Compact, irregular, domed tree with silvery grey bark, orange, bloomed shoots, and ovoid buds. The dark green leaves, 3–6cm (1¼–2½in) long, glaucous on the inner sides, are borne mainly in pairs, and persist for 3–9 years. Spherical, pale brown or green-brown female cones are 3cm (1¼in) long, with wingless seeds. The piñon seeds, or pine kernels, of commerce come mainly from this species. ↕6–15m (20–50ft), ↔ 6–8m (20–25ft). S.W. USA. **

P. excelsa see *P. wallichiana.*

P. flexilis △ (Limber pine). Broadly conical tree, later domed at the top, with smooth grey bark, later fissured; very pliant, hairy green shoots have broadly cylindrical to ovoid buds. Dark green leaves, 4–9cm (1½–3½in) long, are produced in tight bundles of five, and persist for 5–6 years. Long-ovoid, yellow-ochre female cones are 7–15cm (3–6in) long, with wingless seeds. Male cones are red. ↕15–20m (50–70ft), ↔ 6–9m (20–28ft). Rocky Mountains from Alberta to Arizona. ***

P. griffithii see *P. wallichiana.*

P. halepensis △–○ (Aleppo pine). Conical tree, becoming rounded with age, with scaly, red-brown bark, glaucous grey shoots, and ovate buds with reflexed scales. Slender, sparse, bright green leaves, 6–11cm (2½–4½in) long, are borne in pairs. Long-ovoid, red-brown female cones are 5–12cm (2–5in) long. ↕ to 20m (70ft), ↔ to 6m (20ft). Mediterranean. **

P. heldreichii ◊ syn. *P. leucodermis* (Bosnian pine). Narrow, long-conical tree with scaly, ash-grey bark, glaucous shoots becoming white, and broad, non-resinous, ovoid buds. Dense, forward-pointing, very rigid, dark green leaves, 7–9cm (3–3½in) long, are borne in pairs. Long-conical female cones, 5–10cm (2–4in) long, are cobalt-blue in early summer, ripening to brown. ↕15–20m (50–70ft), ↔ 5–6m (15–20ft). Balkans. ***. **'Compact Gem'** is dense, with dark green-black leaves growing 2.5cm (1in) per year.

P.* x *holfordiana ▣ △ (*P. ayacahuite* x *P. wallichiana*) (Holford pine). Broadly conical tree with grey-brown bark, becoming fissured, and with hairy shoots and cylindrical-conical buds. Blue-green leaves, to 10–20cm (4–8in) long, are borne in fives. Ellipsoid green female cones, 25–30cm (10–12in) long, ripen to buff or yellow-brown. Differs from *P. ayacahuite* in having less reflexed cone scales and smaller seeds, and from *P. wallichiana* in having hairy shoots and wider cones. ↕ to 30m (100ft), ↔ 6–8m (20–25ft). Garden origin. ***

P. insignis see *P. radiata.*

P. jeffreyi ▣ △ (Jeffrey pine). Broadly conical tree with smooth, deeply fissured black bark and stout, glaucous, grey-green shoots with long, oblong-conical buds. Grey-green or bluish green leaves, 12–26cm (5–10in) long, are borne in threes. Long-ovoid, yellow-grey female cones, 13–30cm (5–12in) long, have rounded bases. ↕25–35m (80–120ft), ↔ 6–8m (20–25ft). North America (Oregon to Baja California). ***

P. koraiensis △ (Korean pine). Broadly conical tree with smooth, dark grey bark, becoming scaly with age, and green shoots with dense, orange-brown hairs and ovoid to cylindrical buds. Shiny, deep green leaves with silvery white bands on the inner sides, are borne in fives, and are 6–12cm (2½–5in) long. Long-conical, bright green female cones, 9–16cm (3½–6in) long, have large, free-tipped scales and large, wingless seeds. ↕ to 20m (70ft), ↔ to 8m (25ft). Pacific Russia, Korea, N.E. China. ***

P. leucodermis see *P. heldreichii.*

P. monophylla ○ (Single-leaf piñon). Slow-growing shrub or small tree with a domed crown, smooth, brown or grey bark, becoming fissured with age, and orange shoots with cylindrical-conical buds. Long-persistent, grey-green leaves, 2–5cm (¾–2in) long, are mainly produced singly, and are round in section (occasionally set in pairs and then half-moon-shaped in section). Ovoid, yellow-buff female cones, 8cm (3in) long, have large, wingless seeds. ↕5–10m (15–30ft), ↔ to 6m (20ft). S.W. USA. **

Pinus montezumae

Pinus x *holfordiana*

Pinus jeffreyi (inset: leaf detail)

P

Pinus mugo 'Mops'

P. montezumae ■ ♤ (Montezuma pine). Broadly conical tree, becoming domed when old; it has fissured, grey-brown bark, very stout, rough brown shoots, and ovoid, sharply pointed buds. Fresh green, pendent leaves, 15–30cm (6–12in) long, are produced in fives, rarely in sixes or sevens. Bears ovoid to ovoid-conical, yellow to rust-brown female cones, 13–20cm (5–8in) long. ↕ 15–30m (50–100ft), ↔ 6–9m (20–28ft). C. and S. Mexico to Guatemala. ❄❄ (borderline)

P. monticola ⇧ (Western white pine). Narrowly conical tree when young, becoming columnar with age. It has smooth, dark grey bark, becoming plate-like, and brownish green shoots with rust-brown hairs and cylindrical to spherical buds. Pale green leaves, 7–10cm (3–4in) long, with bluish green inner sides, are borne in fives. Narrowly conical female cones, 15–30cm (6–12in) long, are green to purple-green when young, yellow-brown when mature. ↕ 25–40m (80–130ft), ↔ 6–8m (20–25ft). North America (British Columbia to California). ❄❄❄

P. mugo ♧ (Dwarf mountain pine). Shrub or rounded to broadly spreading tree with thick, ascending or spreading branches, scaly grey bark, green shoots, becoming brown, and very resinous, ovoid-oblong buds. Well-spaced, dark to bright green leaves, 3–8cm (1¼–3in) long, are borne in pairs. Ovoid to long-conical, dark brown female cones are 2–6cm (¾–2½in) long and symmetrical at maturity. ↕ to 3.5m (11ft), ↔ to 5m (15ft). C. Europe. ❄❄❄. **'Gnom'** is a squat shrub when young, becoming

Pinus muricata

Pinus nigra

more rounded. **'Mops'** ■ is almost spherical, with green leaves; it grows approximately 6cm (2½in) per year. **subsp. *uncinata*** see *P. uncinata.*

P. muricata ■ ♤–♧ (Bishop pine). Conical tree, becoming broadly domed or columnar with age, with fissured, dark grey bark, orange-brown shoots, and conical to cylindrical buds. Stiff, grey-green or blue-green leaves, 10–15cm (4–6in) long, are borne in pairs, occasionally threes. Oblique, ovoid-conical, nut-brown female cones, 7–9cm (3–3½in) long, have stout spines on the outer scales and persist for 20–30 years. Northern populations in California have blue-green foliage and are faster-growing in cultivation. ↕ to 20m (70ft), ↔ 6–9m (20–28ft). USA (California). ❄❄❄

P. nigra ■ ♤–♧ (Austrian pine, European black pine). Domed tree with dense, spreading branches, fissured dark brown or black bark, brown shoots, and broadly ovoid, abruptly acute buds with papery scales. Dense, straight, rigid, dark green leaves, 8–16cm (3–6in) long, are borne in pairs. Long-ovoid, yellow-brown female cones are 6–8cm (2½–3in) long. ↕ to 30m (100ft), ↔ 6–8m (20–25ft). Austria, N. Italy to the Balkans. ❄❄❄. **subsp. *laricio***, syn. subsp. *maritima* (Corsican pine), is a narrowly conical tree, becoming columnar with age, with dark grey bark, yellow-brown shoots, and narrowly conical, tapered buds. Flexible, well-spaced, grey-green or green leaves are 11–18cm (4½–7in) long; ↕ to 40m (130ft), ↔ to 10m (30ft). France (Corsica), S. Italy (including Sicily). **subsp. *maritima*** see subsp. *laricio.*

P. parviflora ■ ♤ (Japanese white pine). Conical or columnar tree, often with a spreading crown, with scaly, purplish brown bark, greyish brown shoots, and ovoid buds. Deep green leaves, 2–6cm (¾–2½in) long, with whitish blue inner sides, are borne in fives. Ovoid-oblong, red-brown female cones, 5–7cm (2–3in) long, have short-winged seeds. ↕ 10–20m (30–70ft), ↔ 6–8m (20–25ft). Japan. ❄❄❄. **'Adcock's Dwarf'** is dense and slow-growing, with short, grey-green leaves, 1.5–2.5cm (½–1in) long. **f. *glauca***, syn. 'Glauca', is the most common variant in cultivation; it is small and spreading, with twisted, glaucous foliage.

P. patula ■ ♧ (Mexican weeping pine). Rounded to broadly spreading

Pinus parviflora (inset: cone detail)

Pinus patula

tree with scaly, reddish brown bark, pale green-brown, glaucous shoots, and cylindrical buds. Slender, pendent, shiny, light green leaves, 15–30cm (6–12in) long, are borne in threes, rarely fours or fives. Stalkless, long-conical, yellow to chestnut-brown female cones are 6–10cm (2½–4in) long. Frost tender when young. ↕ 15–20m (50–70ft), ↔ 6–10m (20–30ft). C. Mexico. ❄❄

P. peuce ■ ♤ (Macedonian pine). Conical or columnar tree with smooth, grey-green bark, becoming fissured with age, and green, slightly glaucous shoots with ovoid-conical buds. Stiff, grey-green leaves, 7–9cm (3–3½in) long, are borne in fives. Cylindrical-conical green female cones, ripening brown, are 7–16cm (3–6in) long. Tolerates a wide variety of conditions, including very poor soils and harsh climates. ↕ 25m (80ft), ↔ to 6–8m (20–25ft). S. Balkans to N. Greece. ❄❄❄

P. pinaster ♤ (Maritime pine). Conical tree, becoming domed, with deeply fissured, orange-brown to purple bark, brown shoots, and spindle-shaped buds that have reflexed scales. Paired, well-spaced, stout, stiff, grey-green leaves are 10–25cm (4–10in) long. Long-ovoid green female cones, 8–22cm (3–9in) long, ripen to chestnut-brown. ↕ to 20m (70ft), ↔ 6–8m (20–25ft). S.W. Europe, Mediterranean. ❄❄❄

P. pinea ■ ♧ (Stone pine, Umbrella pine). Conical tree when young, becoming domed, with stout, radiating branches, plate-like, orange-brown bark, orange-brown shoots, and ovate buds. Well-spaced, twisted, glossy green adult leaves, 12–15cm (5–6in) long, are borne in pairs. Solitary, glaucous blue juvenile leaves are retained for several years. Ovoid, shiny brown female cones, 12cm (5in) long, ripen in the third year and have wingless seeds. ↕ 15–20m (50–70ft), ↔ 6–12m (20–40ft). Mediterranean. ❄❄❄

P. ponderosa ♤–♧ (Ponderosa pine, Western yellow pine). Conical tree, becoming columnar, with deeply fissured bark with smooth, broad plates, and stout, green-brown shoots with oblong-cylindrical buds. Dense, rigid, grey-green leaves, 10–25cm (4–10in) long, are borne in threes, rarely pairs or fives. Ovoid or long-ovoid purple female cones, 6–16cm (2½–6in) long, age to brown. ↕ 25–35m (80–120ft), ↔ 6–8m (20–25ft). Rocky Mountains from British Columbia to California. ❄❄❄

Pinus peuce

Pinus pumila 'Compacta'

P. pumila (Dwarf Siberian pine). Spreading, low shrub with flexible branches that bend down in cold weather, and hairy, green-brown shoots with cylindrical-conical buds. Dark green leaves, 4–6cm (1½–2½in) long, with bright blue inner sides, are borne in fives. Ovoid female cones, violet-purple when young, becoming red- or yellow-brown, are 3–6cm (1¼–2½in) long, with wingless seeds. Male cones are bright red in spring. ↕↔ 2–6m (6–20ft). Russia (Siberia) to Japan, N.E. China. ❄❄❄. **'Compacta'** ▣ is a rounded bush, with very dense, grey-green leaves, 5–8cm (2–3in) long, grey-white beneath; ↕↔ 2–3m (6–10ft).

P. radiata △–▯ syn. *P. insignis* (Monterey pine, Radiata pine). Narrow, conical tree, becoming broadly domed, with heavily ridged black bark, grey-green shoots, and cylindrical buds. Slender, shiny, bright green leaves, 10–15cm (4–6in) long, are borne in threes. Very oblique, ovoid, glossy, yellow-brown female cones, 8–15cm (3–6in) long, with 20 swollen outer scales, persist for 20–30 years. Widely planted. ↕ 25–40m (80–130ft), ↔ 8–12m (25–40ft). USA (California). ❄❄❄

P

P. resinosa △ (Red pine). Conical tree with upswept branches, flaky red bark in the upper crown, scaly, pink-grey bark at the base, and stout, orange to red-brown shoots with ovoid to narrowly conical buds. Yellow-green leaves, 10–15cm (4–6in) long, are produced in pairs and persist for 4–5 years; they snap if bent. Long-ovoid female cones, 4–6cm (1½–2½in) long, are chestnut-brown. Male cones are purple. ↕ 15–25m (50–80ft), ↔ 6–8m (20–25ft). North America (Nova Scotia to West Virginia). ❄❄❄

P. rigida △ (Pitch pine). Conical or ovoid tree, becoming irregular, with fissured, dark grey bark, grey-brown shoots, and cylindrical to ovoid-oblong buds. Thick, stiff, grey-green leaves, 7–14cm (3–5½in) long, are borne in threes. Ovoid-conical, yellow-brown female cones, 3–9cm (1¼–3½in) long, often persist for several years. ↕ to 20m (70ft), ↔ 5–7m (15–22ft). North America (Maine and Ontario south to Georgia). ❄❄❄

P. sabineana △–▯ (Digger pine). Conical or domed tree with fissured grey bark, grey-bloomed shoots, and narrow, cylindrical buds. Flexible, sparse, blue-green or grey-green leaves, 15–30cm (6–12in) long, are borne in threes. Ovoid, dark brown female cones, 10–25cm (4–10in) long, each have a hooked spine and wingless seeds. ↕ to 20m (70ft), ↔ 5–6m (15–20ft). USA (California). ❄❄❄

Pinus pinea (inset: cone detail)

P. strobus △–▯ (Eastern white pine, Weymouth pine). Slender, conical tree with upswept branches when young, becoming more columnar. It has smooth grey bark, which turns black and cracked, and slender, olive-brown shoots with ovoid-oblong buds. Slender, grey-green leaves, 8–14cm (3–5½in) long, are borne in fives. Cylindrical, tapered green female cones, ripening to brown, are 8–15cm (3–6in) long. ↕ to 35m (120ft), ↔ 6–8m (20–25ft). North America (Newfoundland to Georgia). ❄❄❄. **'Fastigiata'** ▯ has a narrow, columnar crown of ascending branches.

P. sylvestris ▣ △–▯ (Scots pine). Conical to columnar-conical tree, becoming domed, with flaky, red-brown or orange bark in the upper crown, ridged, purple-grey bark at the base, and green-brown shoots with oblong-ovate buds. Twisted, blue-green or yellow-green leaves, 5–7cm (2–3in) long, are borne in pairs. Ovoid-conical green female cones, 3–7cm (1¼–3in) long, ripen to grey or red-brown. ↕ 15–30m (50–100ft), ↔ 6–9m (20–28ft). Europe (excluding the far north), temperate Asia. ❄❄❄. **'Argentea'** see 'Edwin Hillier'. **'Aurea'** has bright golden yellow foliage in winter, resuming normal colour in spring; ↕ 10–15m (30–50ft). **'Beuvronensis'** is a dwarf, rounded bush, to 1m (3ft) high. **'Edwin Hillier'**, syn. 'Argentea', bears bright, silvery blue leaves. **'Fastigiata'** ▯ is narrow and has an upright habit with ascending branches; ↕ to 8m (25ft), ↔ 1–3m (3–10ft). **'Gold Coin'** ▣ is a slow-growing shrub, with intense golden foliage; ↕↔ to 2m (6ft). **'Nana'** see 'Watereri'. **'Watereri'**, syn. 'Nana', is a slow-growing, small tree with an upright habit; ↕ 4m (12ft), ↔ 7m (22ft).

P. tabuliformis △–▯ (Chinese red pine). Conical tree when young, becoming flat-topped when old. It has scaly, red-brown bark in the upper crown, fissured grey bark at the base, and yellow-brown shoots with ovoid-conical buds. The leaves, 9–15cm (3½–6in) long, are produced in pairs. Broadly ovoid-conical, dark brown female cones are 4–9cm (1½–3½in) long. ↕ to 15–20m (50–70ft), ↔ 6–10m (20–30ft). N. China. ❄❄❄

P. thunbergiana see *P. thunbergii*.

P. thunbergii △ syn. *P. thunbergiana* (Japanese black pine). Conical tree, becoming rounded, with dark purplish grey bark, yellow-brown shoots, and cylindrical-ovoid buds covered with silky white scales. Thick, dark grey-green leaves, 7–15cm (3–6in) long, are borne in pairs. Long-ovoid, green-brown female cones are 4–7cm (1½–3in) long. Tolerates salt spray. ↕ 15–25m (50–80ft), ↔ 6–8m (20–25ft). N.E. China, Japan, Korea. ❄❄❄

P. uncinata △ syn. *P. mugo* subsp. *uncinata* (Mountain pine). Conical, upright tree, becoming domed with age; it produces scaly, grey-pink bark, orange-brown shoots, and very resinous, small, ovoid buds. Stiff, dark green leaves, 6cm (2½in) long, are produced

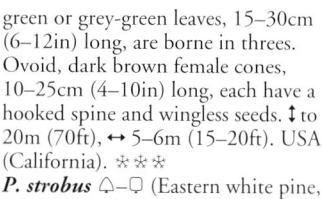

Pinus sylvestris

in pairs. Ovoid, strongly oblique, pale brown female cones are 4–6cm (1½–2½in) long. ↕ 15–20m (50–70ft), ↔ 6–8m (20–25ft). Alps to Spain. ❄❄❄

P. wallichiana △–▯ syn. *P. chylla*, *P. excelsa*, *P. griffithii* (Bhutan pine, Blue pine). Conical tree when young, developing a broad, domed crown. It has smooth grey bark, becoming scaly and dark brown, and stout, olive-green shoots with cylindrical-conical buds. Arching to pendent, grey-green to glaucous blue leaves are 11–20cm (4½–8in) long, and produced in fives. Ellipsoid green female cones, 10–30cm (4–12in) long, ripening to brown, have forward-pointing scales. ↕ 20–35m (70–120ft), ↔ 6–12m (20–40ft). Himalayas from Afghanistan to N.E. India. ❄❄❄

Pinus sylvestris 'Gold Coin'

PIPER

Pepper

PIPERACEAE

Genus of more than 1,000 species of shrubs, climbers, and small trees from highly variable habitats in tropical regions. Many have a pungent aroma, and some, including *P. nigrum*, are grown as spice crops in tropical areas. They bear alternate, asymmetric, very variable, but often narrowly to broadly ovate to rounded green leaves, heart-shaped at the bases, on stems that are swollen at the nodes. Cylindrical spikes of small (often unisexual) flowers without petals or sepals are followed by single-seeded fruit. In warm, humid, tropical areas with heavy, well-distributed rainfall, peppers are grown in fertile soils, with the shade and support of trees. Fruit is harvested at different stages of ripeness for different uses: dried, green mature fruit for black pepper; ripening green fruit for pickled pink peppercorns; ripened, red or yellow fruit (soaked to remove the outer layer of skin) for white pepper. In temperate zones, *P. nigrum* is grown in a conservatory or warm greenhouse; it may bear fruit under glass. Grow outdoors only in tropical areas.

• **HARDINESS** Frost tender.

• **CULTIVATION** Under glass, grow in loam-based potting compost (JI No.3) with added sharp sand, in bright filtered light and with high humidity. In the growing season, water moderately and apply a balanced liquid fertilizer every month; water sparingly in winter. Outdoors, grow in fertile, well-drained soil in dappled shade. Support climbing stems. Pruning group 11, in late winter.

• **PROPAGATION** Sow seed at 20–24°C (66–75°F) in early spring, or take semi-ripe cuttings in summer.

• **PESTS AND DISEASES** Susceptible to fungal root rot, pepper weevil, and pepper flea beetle.

P. nigrum ■ (Black pepper, White pepper). Evergreen, woody-stemmed, perennial climber with ovate, heart-shaped, leathery, deeply veined, dark green leaves, to 13cm (5in) long. In summer, bears small white flowers in spikes to 11cm (4½in) long, on the side of the swollen stem joint opposite the leaf, followed by spherical fruit that are red when ripe. ↕↔ 4m (12ft) or more. India, Sri Lanka. ❀ (min. 16°C/61°F)

Piper nigrum

PIPTANTHUS

LEGUMINOSAE/PAPILIONACEAE

Genus of 2 species of deciduous or semi-evergreen shrubs occurring in scrub and woodland in the mountains of China and the Himalayas. They have alternate, 3-palmate, mid- to dark green, sometimes grey- or blue-green leaves, occasionally with white hairs and a grey-green surface. Grown for their foliage and pea-like flowers, they are suitable for a shrub border, or for growing against, or training on, a wall.

• **HARDINESS** Frost hardy.

• **CULTIVATION** Grow in fertile, well-drained soil in sun or partial shade. In frost-prone areas, shelter from cold, drying winds. Pruning group 1, or group 13 if wall-trained.

• **PROPAGATION** Sow seed in containers in a cold frame in spring or autumn. Take heeled, semi-ripe basal cuttings in summer.

• **PESTS AND DISEASES** Trouble free.

P. laburnifolius see *P. nepalensis*.

P. nepalensis ■ syn. *P. laburnifolius* (Evergreen laburnum). Open, upright, deciduous or semi-evergreen shrub producing 3-palmate leaves composed of lance-shaped, dark blue-green leaflets, to 15cm (6in) long, blue-white beneath. Pea-like, bright yellow flowers, 4cm (1½in) long, are borne in upright, terminal racemes in late spring and early summer, followed by pendent green seed pods, to 22cm (9in) long. ↕ 2.5m (8ft), ↔ 2m (6ft). Himalayas, S.W. China. ❄❄

P. tomentosus. Open, upright, deciduous or semi-evergreen shrub with 3-palmate leaves composed of ovate, grey-green leaflets, to 15cm (6in) long, silky-hairy beneath. In late spring and early summer, bears pea-like, lemon-yellow flowers, 3cm (1¼in) long, in upright racemes, followed by pendent, woolly seed pods, to 8cm (3in) long. ↕ 2.5m (8ft), ↔ 2m (6ft). S.W. China. ❄❄

Piptanthus nepalensis (inset: flower detail)

PISONIA

syn. HEIMERLIODENDRON

NYCTAGINACEAE

Genus of 50 species of evergreen trees, shrubs, and climbers from chiefly maritime habitats in tropical regions worldwide, but mainly in North and South America. Cultivated for their attractive leaves, which are simple and entire, and borne alternately, in opposite pairs, or in whorls of 3, they also produce small, funnel-shaped, petalless flowers: the males with tufts of stamens, the females with solitary ovaries that develop into nutlets (achenes). In areas where temperatures fall below 10–13°C (50–55°F), grow in a temperate or warm greenhouse, or as houseplants. In warmer climates, grow as specimen trees, as windbreaks, or as a hedge.

• **HARDINESS** Frost tender.

• **CULTIVATION** Under glass, grow in loam-based potting compost (JI No.3) in full light or bright indirect light. When in growth, water freely and apply a balanced liquid fertilizer every month; water sparingly in winter. Outdoors, grow in fertile, humus-rich, well-drained soil in full sun or partial shade. Pruning

Pisonia umbellifera 'Variegata'

group 1; may need restrictive pruning under glass.

• **PROPAGATION** Sow seed at 15–18°C (59–64°F) in spring. Take greenwood cuttings in early summer, or semi-ripe cuttings in mid- to late summer. Air layer in spring.

• **PESTS AND DISEASES** Red spider mites and scale insects may infest greenhouse specimens.

P. brunoniana see *P. umbellifera*.

P. umbellifera ♡ syn. *Heimerliodendron brunonianum*, *P. brunoniana* (Bird-catcher tree, Parapara). Small tree or large shrub, erect at first, then spreading, and usually freely branching. Densely borne, opposite or whorled, elliptic to lance-shaped leaves, 10–40cm (4–16in) long, are thinly leathery, glossy, and rich green. Bears insignificant, funnel-shaped, pink or yellow flowers, about 4–7mm (⅛–¼in) long, in leafy panicles, intermittently throughout the year. Female sepals are sticky-glandular and elongate, enclosing the nutlets. ↕ 5–20m (15–70ft) sometimes more, ↔ 3–5m (10–15ft). Mauritius to Australia, New Zealand, and Japan (Ogasawara-Shoto). ❀ (min. 10°C/50°F). **'Variegata'** ■ has leaves irregularly splashed and margined creamy white, and pink-tinged stalks.

▷**Pistachio** see *Pistacia*

PISTACIA

Pistachio

ANACARDIACEAE

Genus of 11 species of rounded to upright, dioecious, deciduous and evergreen trees and shrubs from dry habitats in the Mediterranean, C. Asia to Japan, Malaysia, Mexico, and S. USA. They are grown for their foliage, flowers, and fruit (although *P. vera*, which produces the edible pistachio nut, is not grown ornamentally). The alternate leaves are usually pinnate, occasionally ternate or simple; the small, petalless, mostly mid-green flowers appear in usually axillary racemes or panicles, followed by the peppercorn-like fruit. Grow as specimen trees; they thrive in coastal conditions. In frost-prone areas, grow half-hardy species in a cool or warm greenhouse.

• **HARDINESS** Frost hardy to half hardy.

• **CULTIVATION** Under glass, grow in loam-based potting compost (JI No.3) with added sharp sand, in full light.

P

Pistacia lentiscus

During growth, water freely and apply a balanced liquid fertilizer monthly; water sparingly in winter. Outdoors, grow in moderately fertile, sharply drained soil in full sun. Pruning group 1; may need restrictive pruning under glass.
• **PROPAGATION** Sow seed at 25°C (77°F) in early spring. Take greenwood cuttings in late spring or early summer, or semi-ripe cuttings in summer.
• **PESTS AND DISEASES** Prone to fungal root rot; coral spot affects *P. chinensis.*

P. chinensis ♂ (Chinese mastic). Deciduous tree, erect at first, then spreading with age. Pinnate leaves, to 25cm (10in) long, each with 10–12 oblong-elliptic, toothed, leathery, glossy, dark green leaflets, with no terminal leaflet, colour well in autumn. Aromatic red flowers are produced with the young leaves in mid- and late spring; the males are borne in crowded panicles, to 10cm (4in) long, the females in looser panicles, 15–25cm (6–10in) long. The flowers are followed by spherical red fruit, about 3mm (⅛in) across, maturing blue. ↕ 15–25m (50–80ft), ↔ 7–10m (22–30ft). C. and W. China. ✻✻
P. lentiscus ▣ ♂ (Lentisc, Mastic tree). Evergreen, resinous, aromatic shrub or sometimes small, bushy tree. Pinnate leaves, 10cm (4in) long, with winged stalks and midribs, each have 2–7 pairs of narrowly oblong to ovate, ovate, oblong-lance-shaped, or elliptic, leathery, glossy, dark green leaflets, with no terminal leaflet. In spring or early summer, bears dense panicles, to 3cm (1¼in) long, of male flowers with red stamens, and looser panicles, 6cm (2½in) long, of brownish green female flowers. The flowers are followed by spherical red fruit, 5mm (¼in) across, ripening black. The sap yields mastic, the fragrant gum used in medicine, dentistry, and varnish. ↕↔ 1–3m (3–10ft). Morocco, Canary Islands, Portugal, S. Europe to Greece. ✻
P. terebinthus ♀ (Terebinth, Turpentine tree). Deciduous, freely branching tree, or sometimes large shrub, with pinnate leaves, 10–20cm (4–8in) long; these each consist of 3–6 pairs of oval, semi-glossy, mid- to rich green leaflets, with a terminal leaflet. In spring or ear y summer, bears greenish red flowers; the males in compact panicles, 6–10cm (2½–4in) long, the females in looser panicles, 5–15cm (2–6in) long. The flowers are surrounded by brown bracts, and are followed by obovoid, edible red to purple-brown fruit, to 7mm (¼in) long. The sap yields a fragrant gum, which is used in cancer treatments. ↕ 6m (20ft) or more, ↔ 2–6m (6–20ft). Portugal to Turkey, Canary Islands, Morocco to Egypt. ✻

PISTIA

Shell flower, Water lettuce

ARACEAE

Genus of one species of evergreen, floating aquatic perennial distributed worldwide in the tropics and subtropics. It is grown for its rosettes of attractive, wedge-shaped leaves, and for the exquisite colouring of its fine, feathery roots (which turn from white to purple, and finally black). Although regarded as a weed in some tropical areas, where its radiating stolons cover the surface of the water, it is an excellent ornamental plant for a sunny, temperate pool, for a greenhouse pool, or for a large aquarium.
• **HARDINESS** Frost tender.
• **CULTIVATION** Grow as a floating aquatic in full sun with some midday shade. In frost-prone areas, lift before the first frosts and overwinter at a minimum of 10°C (50°F); alternatively, grow under glass on the surface of an indoor pool (or in baskets at the pool margins), in full light, with shade from hot sun, maintaining a water temperature of 15–22°C (59–72°F). The higher the water temperature, the more rapid is the growth of the plant. See also pp.52–53.
• **PROPAGATION** Separate plantlets in summer.
• **PESTS AND DISEASES** Trouble free.

P. stratiotes ▣ (Shell flower, Water lettuce). Evergreen, floating aquatic perennial with spreading or semi-upright, wedge-shaped, glaucous leaves, to 20cm (8in) long, fluted above and ribbed beneath, borne in floating rosettes. Inconspicuous, tubular flowers are borne in leaf-like spathes in the leaf axils, irregularly throughout the year. ↕ 10cm (4in), ↔ indefinite. Tropics and subtropics. ❀ (min. 10°C/50°F)

PITCAIRNIA

BROMELIACEAE

Genus of over 260 species of very variable, rosette-forming, usually evergreen perennials (bromeliads), mostly terrestrial, a few epiphytic. All but one species occur in rocky, generally dry areas of Mexico, Central America, South America, and many West Indian islands. They are cultivated for their linear, lance-shaped, or strap-shaped leaves, which have smooth or spiny margins, and for their bell-shaped, white, yellow, orange, green, or red flowers, which are produced in spikes, racemes, or panicles on branched or unbranched stems. In areas where temperatures drop below 10°C (50°F), grow in a warm greenhouse; in warmer climates, pitcairnias are suitable for a desert garden or moist shrub border.
• **HARDINESS** Frost tender.
• **CULTIVATION** Under glass, grow in standard bromeliad compost in full or bright filtered light. From mid-spring to late autumn, water moderately and apply a nitrogen-based fertilizer every 6–8 weeks. Evergreen species require moderate to high humidity, deciduous species require low humidity. When dormant, protect from cold draughts, keeping deciduous species dry, and evergreen species just moist. Outdoors, grow in moderately fertile, sharply drained soil in sun or partial shade. See also p.47.
• **PROPAGATION** Sow seed at 19–24°C (66–75°F) in spring. Remove offsets in late spring or early summer.
• **PESTS AND DISEASES** Susceptible to scale insects and mealybugs, especially early in the growing season.

Pistia stratiotes

Pitcairnia heterophylla

P. atrorubens. Rosette-forming, epiphytic or terrestrial, evergreen bromeliad with variable leaves: the outer ones are much reduced, smooth-margined, ovate, and very pointed; the lance-shaped inner ones, 60–90cm (24–36in) long, have smooth margins and spiny black stalks. In summer, up to 20 bell-shaped, pale yellow flowers, surrounded by red-purple floral bracts, are produced in spikes, to 30cm (12in) long, on stems with pointed, brownish purple scape-bracts. ↕ to 90cm (36in), ↔ to 60cm (24in). Mexico, Central America, N.W. South America. ❀ (min. 10°C/50°F)
P. bifrons. Rosette-forming, terrestrial, evergreen bromeliad producing strap-shaped, smooth-margined leaves, to 70cm (28in) or more long. During summer, 20–30 bell-shaped, red, red-orange, or yellow flowers, with red or yellow floral bracts, are produced in racemes, 18–27cm (7–11in) long, on white-scaly scapes. ↕↔ 70cm (28in). West Indies (Leeward and Westward Islands, St. Kitts, Guadeloupe). ❀ (min. 10°C/50°F)
P. heterophylla ▣ Epiphytic or terrestrial bromeliad, evergreen for most of the year, but deciduous for a brief period, with a bulbous-based rosette of linear, viciously barbed, spiny outer leaves, to 20cm (8in) long, sometimes reduced to brown spines. Inner leaves, to 70cm (28in) long, are smooth-margined, linear, and white-woolly beneath. During summer, 3–12 bell-shaped, red-pink or white flowers are produced in spikes, to 15cm (6in) long, among red floral bracts, on very short scapes. ↕ 12cm (5in) or more, ↔ to 30cm (12in). Mexico to Venezuela and Peru. ❀ (min. 10°C/50°F)

▷ **Pitcher plant** see *Sarracenia*
Tropical see *Nepenthes*

PITTOSPORUM

PITTOSPORACEAE

Genus of approximately 200 species of usually evergreen shrubs and trees, a few epiphytic, found in habitats ranging from sandy savannah to rain-forest, mainly in Australasia, but also in southern Africa, S. and E. Asia, and the Pacific islands. They are grown for their attractive, glossy, often leathery leaves, which are simple, usually entire, and borne alternately or in whorls. The often fragrant, 5-petalled flowers are borne mostly singly in the leaf axils, or in axillary or terminal corymbs, umbels, panicles, or clusters; they are followed by nearly spherical, woody fruits (capsules) that contain usually black seeds embedded in a sticky, brownish yellow mucilage. Where temperatures fall below 0°C (32°F), grow in a cool greenhouse, moving the plants outdoors for the summer. In warmer climates, the trees are fine specimens for a lawn; the shrubs are suitable for a border, and make a good hedge or windbreak, especially in coastal regions.

• **HARDINESS** Frost hardy to frost tender. Half-hardy species may survive short spells at several degrees below 0°C (32°F), provided wood has been well ripened in summer.

• **CULTIVATION** Under glass, grow in loam-based potting compost (JI No.3) in full light. When in growth, water moderately and apply a balanced liquid fertilizer monthly; water sparingly in winter. Outdoors, grow in fertile, moist but well-drained soil in full sun or partial shade, although those with variegated or purple leaves produce the best leaf effect in full sun. In frost-prone climates, shelter from cold, drying winds. Pruning group 1; may need restrictive pruning under glass. Trim hedges in spring and midsummer.

• **PROPAGATION** Sow seed ideally as soon as ripe, or in spring in containers in a cold frame. Take semi-ripe cuttings in summer, or layer or air layer in spring.

• **PESTS AND DISEASES** Red spider mites and scale insects may infest greenhouse specimens. Leaf spot and powdery mildew may cause problems.

P. bicolor ♀ Large shrub or small tree, erect and bushy, with downy young stems. Alternate, oblong, leathery leaves, 2.5–6cm (1–2½in) long, have rolled margins, and are deep green above, white- to brown-felted beneath. Bears nodding, bell-shaped, fragrant, maroon-crimson flowers, about 1cm (½in) long, singly or in small, axillary clusters, mainly in spring; these are followed by dark red capsules, 1cm (½in) or more across. ↕ 4–5m (12–15ft), occasionally more, ↔ 2–5m (6–15ft). Australia (New South Wales, Victoria, Tasmania). ✲

P. colensoi see *P. tenuifolium* subsp. *colensoi*.

P. crassifolium ♀ (Karo). Large, monoecious shrub or small tree, usually bushy and erect. It has erect to ascending stems, white- to buff-felted when young, and alternate, leathery leaves, 5–7cm (2–3in) or more long, which are obovate to elliptic, and dark green above, white- or buff-felted beneath. Tubular-bell-shaped, dark red to purple flowers, to 1cm (½in) across, are borne in terminal clusters in early summer: the males in clusters of up to 10, the females in clusters of 5. The flowers are followed by almost spherical brown capsules, to 1.5cm (½in) across. ↕ 5–10m (15–30ft), ↔ 2–5m (6–15ft). New Zealand (North Island). ✲. **'Compactum'** is smaller, denser, and has grey-green leaves, 3–5cm (1¼–2in) long, in tight whorls; ↕ 1.5m (5ft), ↔ 1m (3ft). **'Variegatum'** ▣ has grey-green leaves with broad, irregular, creamy white margins; ↕ 2.5m (8ft).

P. dallii ♀ Small, broadly upright tree or sometimes large, rounded shrub, opening out with age, with reddish purple stems. Very deep green leaves, alternate, or whorled at the stem tips, are 6–11cm (2½–4½in) long, elliptic to elliptic-oblong, either coarsely and sharply toothed or virtually entire. In summer, produces small, shallowly cup-shaped, fragrant, yellow-green or white flowers, to 0.6–2cm (¼–¾in) across, in dense, terminal, compound umbels; they are followed by ovoid brown capsules, 1cm (½in) long. ↕ to 6m (20ft), ↔ 2–4m (6–12ft). New Zealand (South Island). ✲✲

P. eugenioides ⌂ (Lemonwood, Tarata). Small tree, erect and conical when young, becoming rounded with age. Alternate, elliptic to narrowly ovate, wavy-margined leaves, to 13cm (5in) long, are thinly leathery, glossy, light green, and lemon-scented when crushed. Produces star-shaped, fragrant, light greenish yellow flowers, 3mm (⅛in) across, in dense, terminal, compound umbels in summer, followed by ovoid

Pittosporum 'Garnettii'

brown capsules, 7mm (¼in) long. ↕ 5–12m (15–40ft), ↔ 2–5m (6–15ft). New Zealand. ✲. **'Variegatum'** ▣♀ produces leaves with bold, irregular, cream to creamy yellow margins. **'Zita Robinson'** ⌂ is similar to the species, but is dense and columnar, with wavy leaf margins.

P. 'Garnettii' ▣ Large, bushy shrub, erect at first, then spreading, with alternate, oblong to elliptic leaves, 4–6cm (1½–2½in) long, sparsely hairy below, almost hairless above, greyish green and pink-spotted, with slightly wavy, creamy white margins. In late spring and early summer, bell-shaped, dark purple flowers, about 1cm (½in) long, are borne singly from the leaf axils, followed by almost spherical brown capsules, 1cm (½in) long. ↕ 3–5m (10–15ft), ↔ 2–4m (6–12ft). ✲

P. phillyreoides ♀ (Desert willow, Weeping pittosporum). Large shrub or small tree of spreading, weeping habit, with softly hairy young stems and alternate, linear-oblong to narrowly lance-shaped, thick leaves, 5–10cm (2–4in) long, mid- to deep green above, paler beneath. In summer, bears bell-shaped, cream to yellow flowers, 1.5cm (½in) long, occasionally singly or more often in axillary, corymb-like clusters. They are followed by almost spherical yellow capsules, 1.5cm (½in) long, which split to disclose sticky, orange-red seeds. ↕ 6–10m (20–30ft), ↔ 3–5m (10–15ft). Dry areas of Australia. ✲

P. ralphii ▣♀ Fast-growing, large shrub or small tree, erect then spreading, with white- to buff-downy young stems, and alternate, elliptic, sometimes wavy-margined leaves, 7–13cm (3–5in) long, semi-lustrous, deep green above, white to buff-felted beneath. In late spring and early summer, bears tubular-bell-shaped, very dark red flowers, to 1cm (½in) long, in loose, terminal, umbel-like clusters, followed by ovoid, hairy, brown capsules, 1.5cm (½in) long. ↕ 3–4m (10–12ft), ↔ 1.5–2.5m (5–8ft). New Zealand (North Island). ✲✲. **'Variegatum'** has greyish green leaves with irregular, fairly wide, creamy white margins. **'Wheeler's Dwarf'** is smaller, very dense, and slow-growing; ↕ 1m (3ft), ↔ 60cm (24in).

P. revolutum. Large, bushy shrub with brown-downy young stems and alternate, ovate to lance-shaped, semi-lustrous, mid- to deep green leaves, 3–11cm (1¼–4½in) long, pale brown and densely woolly beneath, especially

Pittosporum ralphii

on the midribs. In late spring and early summer, produces bell-shaped yellow flowers, 8–10mm (⅜–½in) long, in small, compact, terminal, few-flowered umbels; they are sometimes followed by almost spherical orange capsules, 1cm (½in) or more long, which split to reveal sticky red seeds. ↕ 2–4m (6–12ft), much taller in a warm climate with high rainfall, ↔ 1.5–2.5m (5–8ft). Australia (Queensland, New South Wales). ✲

P. rhombifolium ♀ (Diamond-leaved laurel). Conical tree, moderately bushy when young, with long-stalked, broadly lance-shaped to diamond-shaped or narrowly oval, lustrous, mid- to deep green leaves, arranged alternately. In summer, produces bell-shaped white flowers, 8–10mm (⅜–½in) long, in axillary or terminal, many-flowered clusters; they are sometimes followed by spherical, bright orange capsules, 1cm (½in) long, which split to reveal the red capsule interior and sticky, glossy black seeds. ↕ 10–20m (30–70ft), ↔ 3–6m (10–20ft). Australia (moist coastal forest in Queensland). ✲

P. tenuifolium ▣♀–♀ (Kohuhu). Large, bushy shrub to small tree, erect and fast-growing when young, broader and slower-growing with age. Produces dark grey to black young stems and alternate, oblong-ovate to elliptic-obovate, usually wavy-margined, thinly leathery, glossy, mid-green leaves, 2.5–6cm (1–2½in) long. In late spring and early summer, bears bell-shaped, honey-scented, black-red flowers, 8–10mm (⅜–½in) across, singly or sometimes in small, few-flowered axillary clusters; they are followed by

Pittosporum crassifolium 'Variegatum'

Pittosporum eugenioides 'Variegatum'

Pittosporum tenuifolium

Pittosporum tenuifolium 'Irene Paterson'

grey-black capsules, 1.5cm (½in) long. ↕ 4–10m (12–30ft), ↔ 2–5m (6–15ft). New Zealand. ✻✻. **'Abbotsbury Gold'** has yellow leaves with irregular green margins; ↕ 3m (10ft), ↔ 1.5m (5ft). **subsp. *colensoi*,** syn. *P. colensoi*, produces softly hairy young stems and broader, thicker leaves, 5–10cm (2–4in) long; ↕ 8m (25ft), ↔ 1–4m (3–12ft). **'Deborah'** bears small leaves, 2.5cm (1in) long, with cream and green variegation; ↕ 2m (6ft), ↔ 1m (3ft). **'Golden King'** is erect, with light golden green leaves; ↕ to 3m (10ft), ↔ 1m (3ft). **'Irene Paterson'** ■ grows slowly, and bears white leaves speckled and mottled between the veins; ↕ to 1.2m (4ft), ↔ to 60cm (24in). **'Limelight'** bears elliptic, lime-green leaves with dark green, only slightly wavy margins. **'Margaret Turnbull'** is compact, bearing dark green leaves centrally splashed golden yellow; ↕ to 1.8m (6ft), ↔ 1m (3ft). **'Nigricans'** produces black twigs and deep bronze-purple mature leaves. **'Purpureum'** is similar to 'Nigricans' but more open in habit, with purple foliage; ↕ 3m (10ft), ↔ 1.5m (5ft). **'Silver Queen'** is compact in growth, and has grey-green leaves with irregular white margins; ↕ 1–4m (3–12ft), ↔ 2m (6ft). **'Tom Thumb'** ■ forms a low bush, and bears foliage flushed bronze-purple; ↕ to 1m (3ft), ↔ 60cm (24in). **'Warnham Gold'** has golden green leaves that mature golden yellow. **'Wendle Channon'** has light green leaves with cream-coloured margins.

P. tobira ■♀ (Japanese mock orange). Large shrub or small tree, usually rounded and dense, with erect, sturdy stems and alternate, obovate, leathery leaves, 3–10cm (1¼–4in) long, lustrous and deep green above, paler beneath, and with recurved margins. In late spring and early summer, bears large, handsome, terminal, umbel-like clusters of bell-shaped, very sweetly scented, creamy white flowers, to 2.5cm (1in) across, ageing yellow; they are followed by spherical, yellow-brown capsules with red seeds, 1.5cm (½in) long. ↕ 2–10m (6–30ft), ↔ 1.5–3m (5–10ft). China, Korea, Japan. ✻. **'Variegatum'** has congested stems and smaller leaves, 3cm (1¼in) long, with irregular white margins.

P. undulatum ♀ (Australian mock orange, Cheesewood). Dense, rounded tree with alternate, oblong-lance-shaped to narrowly oblong-ovate, wavy-margined leaves, 7–15cm (3–6in) long, glossy, deep green above, paler beneath. From late spring to midsummer, bears bell-shaped, fragrant, creamy white flowers, 1.5cm (½in) across, in terminal, umbel-like clusters; they are sometimes followed by spherical, orange to brown capsules, to 1cm (½in) across, which split to reveal sticky, ruby-red seeds. ↕ 8–15m (25–50ft), sometimes to 24m (80ft), ↔ 3–7m (10–22ft). Australia (Queensland to Tasmania). ✻. **'Variegatum'** has leaves with irregular white margins.

P. viridiflorum. Usually free-branching, large shrub or small tree, bearing hairy young stems and alternate, obovate, leathery leaves, 3–10cm (1¼–4in) long; the leaves are lustrous, deep green above, paler beneath, sometimes with margins rolled under. From late spring to mid-summer, produces terminal, corymb-like panicles of small, jasmine-scented, yellow-green flowers, to 6mm (¼in) across; they are short-tubed and open trumpet-shaped, with 5 spreading lobes, and are followed by almost spherical brown capsules, 1.5cm (½in) long. ↕ 3m (10ft), sometimes to 6m (20ft), ↔ 2–3m (6–10ft). South Africa. ❀ (min. 5°C/41°F)

Pittosporum tenuifolium 'Tom Thumb'

Pittosporum tobira

▷**Pittosporum, Weeping** see *Pittosporum phillyreoides*

PITYROGRAMMA

ADIANTACEAE/PTERIDACEAE

Genus of about 14 species of evergreen, terrestrial ferns, native to woodland and shady rocks in W. North America and tropical areas of Africa, Central America, and South America. They have creeping rhizomes that produce tufts of attractive, triangular, pinnate to 3-pinnate fronds, with a silvery white, yellow, or rarely pink, mealy powder on the undersides. Elongated sori are produced along the veins, without protective indusia. In frost-prone climates, grow in a warm greenhouse or as houseplants. In warmer regions, grow in a sheltered, shady border.

• **HARDINESS** Frost tender.

• **CULTIVATION** Under glass, grow in 1 part each of loam, medium-grade bark, and charcoal, 2 parts sharp sand, and 3 parts coarse leaf mould, in bright filtered light. In the growing season, water moderately, avoiding wetting the foliage, and apply a balanced liquid fertilizer every month. Water sparingly in winter. Outdoors, grow in humus-rich, moist but well-drained soil in partial shade.

• **PROPAGATION** Sow spores at 19–24°C (66–75°F) when ripe. Divide in spring. See also p.51.

• **PESTS AND DISEASES** Trouble free.

P. argentea ■ Tufted fern bearing long-stalked, arching, broadly triangular, 2- or 3-pinnate fronds, to 60cm (24in) long, with a silvery white or golden yellow bloom beneath. Pinnae are narrowly triangular-ovate, composed of wedge-shaped to broadly oblong-ovate and deeply pinnatifid secondary segments. ↕ to 60cm (24in), ↔ 1m (3ft). Africa, Madagascar, Mascarene Islands. ❀ (min. 10°C/50°F)

Pityrogramma argentea

P. calomelanos. Neat, tufted fern bearing triangular-ovate, very regularly 2-pinnate, mid-green fronds, to 80cm (32in) long, usually silvery white, rarely pink mealy, on the undersides, composed of narrowly diamond-shaped segments. ↕ to 30–90cm (12–36in), ↔ to 1m (3ft). Tropical Central America and South America. ❀ (min. 10°C/50°F). **var. *austroamericana*** has a yellow or orange bloom on the undersides of the fronds.

P. chrysophylla. Tufted fern producing very long-stalked, ovate or triangular-ovate, 2- or 3-pinnate, mid-green fronds, 20–60cm (8–24in) tall. Similar to *P. calomelanos*, but the frond undersides are covered with a bright yellow, waxy powder, and the segments are ovate to narrowly diamond-shaped. ↕↔ 10–40cm (4–16in). West Indies, South America. ❀ (min. 10°C/50°F)

P. triangularis, syn. *Gymnogramma triangularis* (Goldback fern). Tufted fern bearing triangular, 2-pinnate, mid- to yellow-green fronds, to 20cm (8in) long, rarely more, the undersides covered with a gold or silver, waxy powder. Pinnae are divided into narrow, triangular or oblong segments. ↕↔ 10–20cm (4–8in). S.W. USA, N.W. Mexico. ❀ (min. 10°C/50°F)

▷***Plagianthus lyallii*** see *Hoheria lyallii*
▷***Plagiorhegma*** see *Jeffersonia*
P. dubia see *J. dubia*
▷**Plane** see *Platanus*
London see *P.* x *hispanica*
Oriental see *P. orientalis*

PLANTAGO

Plantain

PLANTAGINACEAE

Genus of some 200 species of mostly rosette-forming annuals, biennials, evergreen perennials and shrubs, many of which are invasive, from very variable habitats worldwide. Grown mainly for their attractive basal rosettes of linear to almost rounded leaves, they also bear tiny, tubular flowers with 4 small petal lobes, in long-stemmed, spherical to oblong spikes, in summer. Grow larger species in a herbaceous border, smaller, alpine species in a rock garden or alpine house. In frost-prone areas, grow tender species in a cool greenhouse.

• **HARDINESS** Fully hardy to frost tender.

• **CULTIVATION** Under glass, grow in 4 parts peat or leaf mould to 1 part grit or sharp sand. Outdoors, grow in

Plantago nivalis

preferably neutral to acid, moderately fertile, sharply drained soil in full sun. Protect from winter wet.
• **PROPAGATION** Sow seed in containers in a cold frame in autumn, or divide in spring.
• **PESTS AND DISEASES** Prone to aphids and red spider mites under glass.

P. nivalis ■ Compact perennial with neat rosettes of lance-shaped, silky-hairy, silver-green leaves, to 1cm (½in) long. In summer, leafless stems, 10cm (4in) long, produce spikes, to 1cm (½in) across, of tubular, grey-brown flowers. ↕2.5cm (1in), ↔ 8cm (3in). S. Spain. ✻✻✻

▷ **Plantain** see *Musa, Plantago*
French see *Musa acuminata* 'Dwarf Cavendish'
Parrot's see *Heliconia psittacorum*
Water see *Alisma*

PLATANUS
Plane
PLATANACEAE

Genus of about 6 species of deciduous trees found predominantly in valley bottoms and watercourses in North America and Mexico, with one species occurring in S.E. Europe and one in S.E. Asia. Planes are cultivated for their imposing stature and open habit. They are also valued for their large, alternate, palmately lobed leaves, which turn golden brown in autumn, and their flaking bark. The flowers are inconspicuous, but spherical clusters of fruits hang from the shoots throughout winter. They are most suitable as street trees or for large gardens or parks. Planes thrive in urban conditions, but if planted too close to buildings their vigorous roots may cause damage to drains. Contact with the basal tufts of hair on the fruits may irritate the skin and respiratory system.
• **HARDINESS** Fully hardy to half hardy, but all grow better in climates with hot summers where the current year's shoots are well ripened.
• **CULTIVATION** Grow in fertile, well-drained soil in full sun. Pruning group 1.
• **PROPAGATION** Sow seed (of species only) in autumn. Take hardwood cuttings in winter.
• **PESTS AND DISEASES** All except *P. orientalis* are susceptible to plane anthracnose. The foliage is prone to lacebugs.

Platanus x *hispanica*

P.* x *acerifolia see *P.* x *hispanica.*
P.* x *hispanica ■ (*P. occidentalis* x *P. orientalis*), syn. *P.* x *acerifolia* (London plane). Vigorous, broadly columnar, deciduous tree with flaking brown, grey, and cream bark and very variable but usually sharply 3- to 5-lobed, bright green leaves, to 35cm (14in) long. Green, later brown fruit clusters, 2.5cm (1in) across, are borne in groups of up to 4, and persist during autumn and winter. ↕30m (100ft), ↔ 20m (70ft). Garden origin. ✻✻✻. **'Bloodgood'** is fast-growing, drought-tolerant, and relatively resistant to anthracnose. **'Suttneri'** has leaves marked creamy white; ↕20m (70ft), ↔ 15m (50ft).
P. occidentalis (American sycamore, Buttonwood). Vigorous, broadly columnar, deciduous tree with flaking brown, grey, and cream bark and usually 3-lobed, bright green leaves, to 20cm (8in) long. Green fruit clusters, 2.5cm (1in) across, later turning brown, are produced usually singly, but occasionally in pairs, and persist during autumn and winter. ↕25m (80ft), ↔ 20m (70ft) or more. E. and S. North America. ✻✻

P. orientalis ■ (Oriental plane). Vigorous, spreading, deciduous tree with flaking grey, brown, and cream bark and deeply 5-lobed, glossy green leaves, to 25cm (10in) long. Green fruit clusters, to 2.5cm (1in) across, later turning brown, are produced in groups of up to 6, and persist during autumn and winter. ↕↔ 30m (100ft) or more. S.E. Europe (widely planted in W. Asia). ✻✻✻
P. racemosa (California sycamore). Vigorous, broadly columnar tree with flaking grey bark and deeply 5-lobed, occasionally 3-lobed, dark green leaves, to 15–30cm (6–12in) long, velvety when young. Green fruit clusters, 2.5cm (1in) across, later turning brown, are produced in groups of 2–7, and persist throughout autumn and winter. ↕25m (80ft), ↔ 20m (70ft) or more. USA (S. California), Mexico. ✻

PLATYCARYA
JUGLANDACEAE

Genus of one species of deciduous, large shrub or small tree from forest in E. Asia. It is grown for its long, pinnate leaves, which turn yellow in autumn, its upright catkins, and its long-lasting, cone-like racemes of fruit. The bark is often used for making a black dye. Best grown as a specimen tree in woodland.
• **HARDINESS** Fully hardy, but young plants may be damaged by frost.
• **CULTIVATION** Grow in fertile, moist but well-drained soil in full sun. Pruning group 1.
• **PROPAGATION** Sow seed in containers in autumn.
• **PESTS AND DISEASES** Trouble free.

P. strobilacea Rounded tree with alternate, pinnate, mid-green leaves, to 30cm (12in) long, composed of 7 to 15 ovate to oblong-lance-shaped, toothed leaflets. In mid- and late summer, tiny flowers are borne in erect, yellow-green catkins: several males, to 10cm (4in) long, surround a single female. Small-winged, green, later brown fruit are borne in cone-like racemes to 4cm (1½in) long, in autumn, and survive until the following year. ↕↔ 15m (50ft). China, Taiwan, Korea, Japan. ✻✻✻

Platanus orientalis (inset: leaf detail)

PLATYCERIUM
Staghorn fern
POLYPODIACEAE

Genus of 15 or more species of evergreen, epiphytic ferns, with short-creeping rhizomes; most are found in temperate and tropical rainforest in Africa, Asia, and Australia, a few in South America. They are grown mainly for their attractive, often elegant foliage, each plant bearing both sterile and fertile fronds. The mid- to deep green sterile fronds are stalkless, rounded to oblong, and entire to irregularly lobed at the upper margins; they become brown and papery, and usually form a persistent "nest" or basket at the plant's base. The fertile fronds are spreading or pendent to erect, wedge-shaped at the bases, usually grey-green and leathery, and often repeatedly forked; they are shed naturally when old. All fronds are covered on both sides with small, star-shaped hairs. Spores are formed in large patches on the undersides of fertile fronds; in some species, new plants develop from runners on the sides of established nests. In frost-prone areas, grow in a conservatory or cool or temperate greenhouse, or as houseplants, preferably in hanging baskets. In warmer regions, grow epiphytically on a tree.
• **HARDINESS** Frost tender.
• **CULTIVATION** Under glass, grow epiphytically in equal parts coarse leaf mould (or peat), roughly chopped sphagnum moss, loam, and charcoal, in bright filtered light. When in growth, water freely, mist daily, and apply a balanced liquid fertilizer monthly; water sparingly in winter. Outdoors, grow epiphytically on a tree in partial shade.
• **PROPAGATION** Sow spores at 21°C (70°F) when ripe. Detach plantlets produced from root tips or runners as soon as nests have formed. See also p.51.
• **PESTS AND DISEASES** Scale insects can be a problem.

P. alcicorne (South American staghorn). Epiphytic fern with rounded to kidney-shaped, entire or partially lobed sterile fronds, 15–40cm (6–16in) long, which lie flat, and are mid- to deep green then brown. Leathery, grey-green fertile fronds, 60cm (24in) long, are erect, and divided 2 or 3 times. Spores are formed on frond forks. ↕↔ to 85cm (34in). E. Africa, Madagascar, Seychelles, Mauritius. ❀ (min. 5°C/41°F)
***P. alcicorne* of gardens** see *P. bifurcatum.*
P. bifurcatum ■ syn. *P. alcicorne* of gardens (Common staghorn fern). Very variable, epiphytic fern with erect or horizontal, rounded to heart- or kidney-shaped sterile fronds, 12–45cm (5–18in) long, which are mid- to deep green then brown, and are entire, wavy, or lobed at the upper margins. Grey-green fertile fronds, to 90cm (36in), are erect, spreading, or pendent, forked 2 or 3 times into strap-shaped, densely hairy segments. Very similar to *P. alcicorne.* ↕to 90cm (36in), ↔ 80cm (32in). Java to E. Australia. ❀ (min. 5°C/41°F)

Platycerium bifurcatum

Platycerium hillii

P. grande. Epiphytic fern with bronze to green sterile fronds, to 1m (3ft) tall, rounded to heart- or kidney-shaped, with deeply lobed upper margins; they are papery, may be spreading or lying flat to the branches, and form a crown. Grey-green fertile fronds, to 1.8m (6ft) tall, are pendent, wedge-shaped, leathery, and forked into strap-shaped segments. Spores form in 2 large semicircular patches on the second forks of fertile fronds. ↕ to 1.8m (6ft), ↔ 1.2m (4ft). Philippines, Malaysia, Australia. ❄ (min. 15°C/59°F)
P. hillii ■ Epiphytic fern with rounded, dark green sterile fronds, to 40cm (16in) long, shallowly lobed at the upper margins, and lying flat to the branches. Leathery, light grey-green fertile fronds are erect or arching, broadly wedge-shaped, irregularly forked or palmately lobed above, and 75cm (30in) or more tall. Sometimes considered a variety of *P. bifurcatum.* ↕ 70cm (28in) or more, ↔ 60cm (24in). N.W. Australia, New Guinea. ❄ (min. 10°C/50°F)

PLATYCLADUS
Oriental thuja
CUPRESSACEAE

Genus of one species of broadly conical to columnar, monoecious, evergreen coniferous tree, closely related to *Thuja*, found in forests of N.E. Asia. Scale-like, wedge- to diamond-shaped leaves, with blunt tips, produced in 2 ranks of opposite pairs, are slightly aromatic when bruised. Small, erect, ovoid to pear-shaped female cones have 3 or 4 pairs of scales, each scale having a recurved then reflexed hook just below its tip; male cones are small, about 1mm (1/16in) long, and ovoid. It is an excellent conifer for a difficult site and thrives in both alkaline and acid soils. Grow as specimen trees or for hedging. The dwarf cultivars may be grown in a rock garden or scree bed. Contact with the foliage may aggravate skin allergies.
• **HARDINESS** Fully hardy.
• **CULTIVATION** Grow in moist but well-drained soil in full sun, although tolerates dry, free-draining sites. Trim hedging in spring and late summer. Pruning group 1.
• **PROPAGATION** Sow seed in late winter or spring in containers in a cold frame. Insert semi-ripe cuttings with a heel from late summer to mid-autumn using bottom heat.
• **PESTS AND DISEASES** Prone to scale insects, aphids, and *Coryneum* canker. Leaves are susceptible to *Keithia* disease, which may occasionally be fatal in young seedlings.

P. orientalis ⇧–⇩ syn. *Biota orientalis, Thuja orientalis.* Conical or irregularly crowned tree with fibrous, red-brown bark and erect, irregularly arranged, flattened sprays of scale-like, wedge-diamond-shaped, blunt, slightly scented, mid- or yellow-green leaves, 2–3mm (1/16–1/8in) long, which frequently turn bronze in winter. Erect, ovoid to pear-shaped, grey-bloomed female cones, 2cm (3/4in) long, have 3 or 4 pairs of scales, each scale having a prominent hook just below its tip. ↕ to 15m (50ft), ↔ to 6m (20ft). Mongolia, China (N. China, Manchuria), N. Korea. ❄❄❄. **'Aurea Nana'** has a dwarf habit and produces yellow-green leaves, fading to bronze in winter; ↕↔ to 90cm (36in). **'Conspicua'** ■ has a dense, compact, conical habit and golden foliage when young, turning light green in maturity; retains its colour well throughout the year; ↕ 3m (10ft), ↔ 2m (6ft). **'Elegantissima'** is a conical bush, with golden yellow leaves that slowly mature to yellow-green and turn bronze during winter; ↕ to 5m (15ft), ↔ 1.5–2m (5–6ft). **'Golden Minaret'** ■ has a dense, conical habit, and produces golden yellow foliage that retains its colour well in winter; ↕ 3m (10ft), ↔ 90cm (36in). **'Semperaurea'** ■ is an ovoid bush, with golden yellow new growth; ↕ to 3m (10ft), ↔ 2m (6ft).

Platycladus orientalis 'Conspicua'

Platycladus orientalis 'Golden Minaret'

Platycladus orientalis 'Semperaurea'

PLATYCODON
Balloon flower
CAMPANULACEAE

Genus of one species of perennial, variable in habit and form, from grassy slopes and mountain meadows in E. Asia. Late emerging, it forms a neat clump of hairless stems with simple, ovate to ovate-lance-shaped, toothed, bluish green leaves. It is cultivated mainly for its clusters of bell-shaped, 5-petalled, mid-blue, dark blue, or lilac-purple flowers, which open from large, balloon-like buds. It is suitable for growing in a rock garden or the front of a herbaceous border. It is also good as a cut flower. Established plants resent disturbance.
• **HARDINESS** Fully hardy.
• **CULTIVATION** Grow in deep, light, fertile, loamy, reliably moist but well-drained soil in full sun or partial shade. Stems may require support.
• **PROPAGATION** Sow seed *in situ* or in containers, in spring. Divide in summer, or detach rooted basal shoots in early summer.
• **PESTS AND DISEASES** Slugs and snails attack young shoots.

Platycodon grandiflorus

P. grandiflorus ■ Compact, clump-forming perennial with ovate to ovate-lance-shaped, toothed, bluish green leaves, to 5cm (2in) long, produced in whorls on the lower stem, and arranged alternately higher up the plant. In late summer, clusters of large, balloon-like buds open to shallow, bell-shaped, 5-petalled, purple-blue flowers, to 5cm (2in) across, with darker blue veins and pointed tips to the petals. ↕ to 60cm (24in), ↔ 30cm (12in). Russia (E. Siberia), N. China (including Manchuria), Korea, Japan. ❄❄❄. **f. *albus*** produces white flowers with blue veins. **f. *apoyama*** bears deep violet flowers; ↕ 20cm (8in). **'Mother of Pearl'** see 'Perlmutterschale'. **'Park's Double Blue'** produces double, violet-blue flowers. **'Perlmutterschale'**, syn. 'Mother of Pearl', produces pale pink flowers.

PLATYSTEMON
Californian poppy, Creamcups
PAPAVERACEAE

Genus of one extremely variable species of erect to spreading, basally branching, hairy annual from grassland, desert margins, and chaparral in W. USA. It has almost stalkless, stem-clasping, entire leaves, which are sometimes produced in small whorls. The Californian poppy is cultivated for its short-lived, poppy-like flowers, each consisting of a central boss of flattened stamen filaments, which are borne in profusion where the climate is neither too hot nor too humid. Suitable for use in an annual border or a rock garden.
• **HARDINESS** Fully hardy.
• **CULTIVATION** Grow in very light, well-drained soil in full sun.
• **PROPAGATION** Sow seed *in situ* in spring.
• **PESTS AND DISEASES** Trouble free.

P. californicus (Californian poppy, Creamcups). Many-branched, spreading annual bearing linear-oblong to lance-shaped, densely hairy, strongly parallel-veined, grey-green leaves, to 8cm (3in) long. During spring, produces short-lived, single, slender-stemmed, 6-petalled, poppy-like, creamy yellow flowers, to 2.5cm (1in) across. ↕ 10–30cm (4–12in), ↔ to 23cm (9in). USA (California to Arizona, Utah). ❄❄❄

Plectranthus forsteri 'Marginatus'

PLECTRANTHUS

LABIATAE/LAMIACEAE

Genus of 350 species of annuals, evergreen perennials, semi-succulents, and shrubs occurring in Africa, Madagascar, Asia, Australasia, and Pacific islands. Cultivated mainly for their foliage and flowers, they are often upright in habit at first but become trailing or spreading as they mature. The heart-shaped to ovate or rounded leaves have usually scalloped, sometimes toothed or wavy margins; they are mostly soft, often slightly furry, and aromatic. The small, tubular, 2-lipped, whorled flowers are borne in terminal panicles, racemes, or spikes. In frost-prone climates, grow plectranthus in a cool or temperate greenhouse or conservatory, or as houseplants; grow trailing species in hanging baskets, which may be placed outside in summer and autumn. In warmer areas, grow in a sunny border.

- **HARDINESS** Frost tender.
- **CULTIVATION** Under glass, grow in loam-based potting compost (JI No.2) in full light, with shade from hot sun. During the growing season, water freely and apply a balanced liquid fertilizer every month; water moderately during winter. Outdoors, grow in moderately fertile, well-drained soil in dappled shade.
- **PROPAGATION** Sow seed at 19–24°C (66–75°F) when ripe. Divide in mid- or late spring. Take stem-tip cuttings at any time of year.
- **PESTS AND DISEASES** Trouble free.

Plectranthus oertendahlii

P. amboinicus. Spreading, often decumbent, evergreen, woody-based perennial with densely hairy, velvety, broadly ovate, pleasantly aromatic, fleshy mid-green leaves, to 4.5cm (1¾in) long, dotted with pale brown glands, and with finely scalloped margins. In summer, bears whorls of 4–10, tubular, 2-lipped, lilac-pink, mauve, or white flowers, 7–9cm (3–3½in) across, in terminal racemes, to 15cm (6in) long. Seldom flowers in cultivation. ↕ 30cm (12in), ↔ 1m (3ft). Tropical to Southern Africa (Kenya, Angola, Mozambique, Swaziland, N. KwaZulu/Natal). ❄ (min. 10°C/50°F)

P. argentatus. Erect to spreading, evergreen shrub with silver-hairy stems and densely pubescent, ovate, light grey-green leaves, 5–11cm (2–4½in) long, with scalloped margins. In summer, produces terminal racemes, to 30cm (12in) long, of whorled, tubular, pale bluish white flowers, 9–10mm (⅜–½in) across. ↕↔ 1m (3ft). Australia. ❄ (min. 10°C/50°F)

***P. australis* of gardens** see *P. verticillatus.*

***P. coleoides* of gardens** see *P. forsteri.*

***P. coleoides* 'Variegatus' of gardens** see *P. madagascariensis* 'Variegated Mintleaf'.

P. forsteri, syn. *P. coleoides* of gardens. Upright then trailing, evergreen perennial producing ovate to broadly ovate, hairy, light green leaves, 6–10cm (2½–4in) long, with scalloped margins. Intermittently bears terminal racemes, 15–20cm (6–8in) long, of whorled, tubular, pale mauve or white flowers, 3cm (1¼in) across. ↕ 25cm (10in), ↔ to 1m (3ft). E. Australia, Fiji, New Caledonia. ❄ (min. 10°C/50°F). **'Marginatus'** ▣ has leaves with broad, creamy white margins.

P. madagascariensis (Mintleaf). Creeping, shrubby, semi-succulent perennial with square brown stems and rounded, scalloped, firm, fleshy leaves, 3–4cm (1¼–1½in) long, sometimes wrinkled, and coated with white bristles; the leaves smell of mint when crushed. Terminal spikes, 10–15cm (4–6in) long, of whorled, tubular, 2-lipped, pale lavender-blue or white flowers, to 1½cm (½in) across, often dotted with red glands, are borne in early summer. ↕ to 30cm (12in), ↔ indefinite. S.E. Africa, Madagascar. ❄ (min.15°C/59°F). **'Variegated Mintleaf'**, syn. *P. coleoides* 'Variegatus' of gardens, has variegated white leaves.

P. oertendahlii ▣ (Candle plant, Swedish ivy). Trailing perennial with freely branching, reddish purple stems bearing ovate to almost rounded, scalloped, bronze-green leaves, 3–4cm (1¼–1½in) long, with pale veins above, and undersides with soft purple felting. Loose, terminal racemes, 20cm (8in) long, of whorled, white or light blue flowers, 5mm (¼in) long, are produced at intervals all year round. ↕ 20cm (8in), ↔ trailing to 1m (3ft) or more. South Africa (KwaZulu/Natal). ❄ (min. 10°C/50°F)

P. thyrsoideus, syn. *Coleus thyrsoideus, Solenostemon thyrsoideus.* Bushy, branching perennial or subshrub, often grown as an annual or a winter-flowering container plant, with hairy stems and heart-shaped, toothed, hairy, mid-green leaves, to 15cm (6in) long. Produces bright blue flowers, to 1cm (½in) long, in terminal spikes, to 9cm (3½in) long, at various times during the year. ↕ to 90cm (36in), ↔ to 60cm (24in). C. Africa. ❄ (min. 4°C/39°F)

P. verticillatus, syn. *P. australis* of gardens (Swedish ivy). Mat-forming, semi-succulent perennial with creeping stems rooting at the nodes. Ovate to rounded, coarsely toothed, soft, fleshy leaves, 1.5–4cm (½–1½in) long, have purplish green undersides. Terminal spikes, 16cm (6in) long, of whorled, tubular, 2-lipped, purple-speckled, white or pale mauve flowers, 1.5–2.5cm (½–1in) across, are produced in summer. ↕ 6–8cm (2½–3in), ↔ indefinite. South Africa (Limpopo, Mpumalanga, Eastern Cape), Swaziland, Mozambique. ❄ (min. 10°C/50°F)

PLEIOBLASTUS

GRAMINEAE/POACEAE

Genus of about 20 upright, evergreen, woody bamboos usually found in woodland and woodland margins in China and Japan. They are cultivated for their leaves, which are linear to lance-shaped, 5–35cm (2–14in) long, often tessellated, sometimes variegated, and usually white-bristled on the margins. They have generally vigorously spreading rhizomes, and produce thickets of erect, woody canes, round in section, and either hollow or almost solid; on the lower part of each cane there are 1–7 branches per node. Spikes or racemes of spikelets, each containing 5–13 florets, are sometimes produced, but flowering occurs only rarely. They are suitable for growing in open glades in a woodland garden.

- **HARDINESS** Fully hardy.
- **CULTIVATION** Grow in fertile, humus-rich, moist but well-drained soil in full sun, or in partial shade if not variegated. Provide shelter from cold, dry winds. Some are vigorous, requiring restraint.
- **PROPAGATION** Separate rhizomes in spring; keep divisions moist until they are well established.
- **PESTS AND DISEASES** Trouble free.

Pleioblastus auricomus

P. auricomus ▣ syn. *Arundinaria auricoma, A. viridistriata, P. viridistriatus.* Upright bamboo with short-running rhizomes and hollow, purple-green canes with hairy nodes. The leaves, to 18cm (7in) long, are linear, brilliant yellow with green stripes, and margined with fine bristles. ↕ to 1.5m (5ft), ↔ 1.5m (5ft). Japan. ✻✻✻

P. humilis, syn. *Arundinaria humilis, Sasa humilis.* Upright bamboo with hollow, dark green canes, 1–3 branches per node, and linear, mid-green leaves, to 20cm (8in) long, sometimes downy beneath. Can be very invasive. ↕ 1.5m (5ft), ↔ 2m (6ft) or more. Japan. ✻✻✻

P. pygmaeus, syn. *Arundinaria pygmaea* (Pygmy bamboo). Upright, woody bamboo with usually solid, mid-green canes, flattened above; they are purplish green at the tips, with 1 or 2 branches at each node. The leaves are linear, tessellated, downy, mid-green, and 8cm (3in) long. ↕ 40cm (16in), ↔ 1m (3ft). Japan. ✻✻✻. **var. *distichus*** ▣ syn. *Arundinaria disticha, A. pygmaea* var.

P

Pleioblastus pygmaeus var. *distichus*

Pleioblastus variegatus

disticha, has hollow canes and hairless leaves; ↕ 1m (3ft), ↔ 1.5m (5ft).
***P. simonii* 'Variegatus'**, syn. *Arundinaria simonii* 'Variegata', *P. simonii* f. *variegatus.* Upright, woody bamboo with hollow canes, which have a waxy bloom and 3 branches at each white node. Mid-green, linear to lance-shaped leaves, to 20cm (8in) long, are sometimes striped white, and are finely downy beneath. ↕ 3m (10ft), ↔ 2m (6ft) or more. Japan. ❄❄❄.
f. *variegatus* see *P. simonii* 'Variegatus'.
P. variegatus ■ syn. *Arundinaria fortunei, A. variegata.* Upright, woody bamboo with hollow, pale green canes; the nodes have a white, waxy bloom beneath and each bears 1 or 2 branches. Linear leaves, 14cm (5½in) long, are dark green with cream stripes, and have fine white hairs on both sides. ↕ 75cm (30in), ↔ 1.2m (4ft). Japan. ❄❄❄
P. viridistriatus see *P. auricomus.*

PLEIONE

ORCHIDACEAE

Genus of about 16–20 species of small, deciduous, epiphytic, terrestrial, or lithophytic orchids mainly from wet forest or woodland, at altitudes of 1,000–4,000m (3,250–13,000ft) or higher, from N. India to S. China and Taiwan. They produce short-lived, variably shaped pseudobulbs with 1 or 2 folded, lance-shaped to elliptic, mid-green leaves, 15cm (6in) long, which usually fall before flowering. The often solitary flowers, 8cm (3in) across, are borne on short stems, 5–10cm (2–4in) long, from new growth, at various times of the year. Grow most species in a cool or temperate greenhouse or alpine house, or as houseplants. In areas where temperatures seldom fall below -5°C (23°F), *P. formosana* may be grown in a sheltered rock garden.

• **HARDINESS** Half hardy; some are frost hardy in areas where frost is only sporadic.

• **CULTIVATION** Cool-growing orchids. Grow in shallow pans of terrestrial or epiphytic orchid compost. Repot annually before flowering. Water freely in spring and summer until the leaves begin to die down, then keep just moist and admit full light. In summer, provide bright filtered light and moderate humidity, mist twice daily, and feed at every third watering. In winter, allow a period of rest, reducing the temperature to 0–2°C (32–35°F). Outdoors, grow *P. formosana* in sharply drained,

Pleione bulbocodioides

moderately fertile, leafy, humus-rich soil in a sheltered site in partial shade. Plant in mid-spring. In cold areas, protect from severe weather and excessive wet with an open cloche, from early autumn to spring. See also p.46.

• **PROPAGATION** Divide annually when repotting, discarding old pseudobulbs.

• **PESTS AND DISEASES** Prone to aphids, red spider mites, slugs, and mealybugs.

***P.* Alishan** (*P. formosana* x *P.* Versailles). Epiphytic or lithophytic orchid producing spherical to ovoid pseudobulbs, each bearing one elliptic leaf, to 15cm (6in) long. In spring, bears solitary, pale to dark lilac-pink flowers, with brown or orange-brown spotted lips and usually white-tipped petals and sepals. ↕ 15cm (6in), ↔ 30cm (12in). ❄ (borderline)
P. bulbocodioides ■ Terrestrial or lithophytic orchid with almost spherical pseudobulbs, each bearing one folded, lance-shaped to elliptic leaf, to 14cm (5½in) long. In spring, bears solitary, rose-lilac flowers, with white to pink lips spotted with pale brown or purplish pink. ↕ 15cm (6in), ↔ 30cm (12in). Burma, China, Taiwan. ❄ (borderline)

Pleione Eiger

Pleione formosana

***P.* Eiger** ■ (*P. formosana* x *P. humilis*). Terrestrial or lithophytic orchid with large, pear-shaped pseudobulbs, each bearing one elliptic leaf, to 18cm (7in) long. In mid- and late winter, produces white flowers, shaded pink, 1 or 2 per stem, with white lips marked red, or red and yellow. ↕ 12cm (5in), ↔ 5cm (2in). ❄ (borderline)
P. formosana ■ Terrestrial or lithophytic orchid with almost spherical pseudobulbs, each bearing one folded, lance-shaped to elliptic leaf, to 14cm (5½in) long. In spring, produces solitary, pale rose-lilac flowers with white lips that have brownish markings, pink margins, and brown or purplish pink spots. ↕ 15cm (6in), ↔ 30cm (12in). E. China, Taiwan. ❄ (borderline)
P. forrestii ■ Terrestrial or lithophytic orchid with conical pseudobulbs, each bearing one folded, lance-shaped leaf, 10–15cm (4–6in) long. In winter and spring, produces solitary yellow flowers with red-dotted lips. ↕ 15cm (6in), ↔ 30cm (12in). China. ❄ (borderline)
P. hookeriana. Epiphytic or lithophytic orchid with conical to ovoid pseudobulbs, each bearing one folded, lance-shaped to elliptic leaf, 5–21cm (2–8in) long. In summer, produces very pale pink to pale purple flowers, 5cm (2in) across, with solitary, white to pale pink lips. ↕ 10cm (4in), ↔ 15cm (6in). Tibet, Nepal, N.E. India, Bhutan, Burma, Laos, N. Thailand, China. ❄ (borderline)
P. humilis. Epiphytic or lithophytic orchid with conical pseudobulbs, each bearing one folded, lance-shaped leaf, 20–30cm (8–12in) long. From winter to spring, produces solitary white flowers with red-streaked lips. ↕ 15cm (6in), ↔ 30cm (12in). Nepal, N.E. India, Burma. ❄ (borderline)
P.* x *lagenaria (*P. maculata* x *P. praecox*). Epiphytic or lithophytic orchid with inverted, cone-shaped pseudobulbs, each bearing 2 folded, lance-shaped leaves, to 30cm (12in) long. Fragrant, pink to rose-lilac to purple flowers, with a yellow central area and purple marks around the margins, are borne 1 or 2 per pseudobulb, in autumn. ↕ 15cm (6in), ↔ 30cm (12in). India (Assam), possibly S. China. ❄ (borderline)
P. limprichtii. Epiphytic or lithophytic orchid with conical, ovoid or pear-shaped pseudobulbs, each bearing one folded, conical to ovoid leaf, to 14cm (5½in) long. In spring, deep pink to pink-magenta flowers, with rose-red spotted lips, are borne 1 or rarely 2 per pseudobulb. ↕ 15cm (6in), ↔ 30cm (12in). S.W. China, possibly N. Burma. ❄ (borderline)
P. maculata. Epiphytic or lithophytic orchid with barrel-shaped pseudobulbs, each bearing 2 folded, lance-shaped to elliptic leaves, 15–30cm (6–12in) long. In autumn, produces solitary, white or pale cream flowers, sometimes streaked with pink, the lips white with purple markings and a central yellow patch. ↕ 15cm (6in), ↔ 30cm (12in). N. India, Bhutan, Burma, S.W. China, N. Thailand. ❄ (borderline)
P. praecox ■ Epiphytic or lithophytic orchid with bottle-shaped pseudobulbs, each bearing 2 folded, lance-shaped to narrowly elliptic leaves, to 20cm (8in)

Pleione forrestii

Pleione praecox

long. Solitary, bright rose-purple flowers are produced in autumn. ↕15cm (6in), ↔ 30cm (12in). Nepal, N. India (Sikkim), Bhutan, Burma, S.W. China, Thailand. ✲ (borderline)

P. Shantung (*P.* x *confusa* x *P. formosana*). Epiphytic or lithophytic orchid with conical pseudobulbs, each bearing one lance-shaped leaf, to 15cm (6in) long. The flowers, borne in spring, are usually yellow, with red spotting on the lips, but some selections of this grex are white or have yellow lips combined with pink petals and sepals. ↕15cm (6in), ↔ 30cm (12in). ✲ (borderline)

P. Stromboli 'Fireball' (*P. bulbocodioides* x *P. speciosa*). Epiphytic orchid with conical pseudobulbs, each bearing one folded, lance-shaped to narrowly elliptic leaf, to 25cm (10in) long. In spring, produces solitary, rose-lilac flowers with lips that have reddish pink markings. ↕15cm (6in), ↔ 30cm (12in). ✲ (borderline)

P. Versailles (*P. formosana* x *P. limprichtii*). Epiphytic or lithophytic orchid with flask-shaped pseudobulbs, each bearing one elliptic leaf, to 15cm (6in) long. In spring, bears solitary, mauve-pink flowers with orange-brown to purple-brown spotting on the lips, which are sometimes white. ↕15cm (6in), ↔ 30cm (12in). ✲ (borderline)

P. Vesuvius (*P. bulbocodioides* x *P.* x *confusa*). Epiphytic or lithophytic orchid with spherical to conical pseudobulbs, each bearing one lance-shaped leaf, to 15cm (6in) long. In spring, produces pale lavender-pink to dark mauve-pink flowers with red to brownish orange spotting on the lips. ↕15cm (6in), ↔ 30cm (12in). ✲ (borderline)

PLEIOSPILOS

Living granite

AIZOACEAE

Genus of about 35 species of solitary or clump-forming, stemless, perennial succulents from arid areas of South Africa. They are grown for their unusual form and attractive flowers. Most have 1 or 2, occasionally 3 pairs of often unequal, erect, very fleshy, greyish or yellowish green or brown to red leaves, often with variably coloured dots; they are usually flattened on the upper surfaces, keeled, rounded, or rounded and partly keeled beneath, and united at the bases. The daisy-like, diurnal, yellow or orange flowers, which sometimes have a coconut-like fragrance, open in late summer and early autumn. In areas where temperatures drop below 7°C (45°F), grow as houseplants or in a temperate greenhouse. In warm, dry climates, grow in a raised bed or succulent border.

- **HARDINESS** Frost tender.
- **CULTIVATION** Under glass, grow in standard cactus compost in full light. From early summer to late autumn, water sparingly but regularly and apply a low-nitrogen liquid fertilizer every 4–6 weeks. Keep dry at all other times. Outdoors, grow in low-fertility, sharply drained soil in full sun. See also pp.48–49.
- **PROPAGATION** Sow seed at 19–24°C (66–75°F), or detach offsets, from late spring to summer.
- **PESTS AND DISEASES** Vulnerable to aphids while flowering.

P. bolusii ▣ Usually solitary, perennial succulent with one pair of ovoid, grey-green leaves, 4–7cm (1½–3in) long, sometimes tinged red and with dark green dots; they are generally broader than long, with the undersides more rounded and partly keeled. Daisy-like, golden yellow flowers, 6–8cm (2½–3in) across, are solitary or produced in cymes of 2–4 in late summer and early autumn. ↕8cm (3in), ↔ 15cm (6in). South Africa (Eastern Cape). ❀ (min. 7°C/45°F)

P. nelii. Solitary, perennial succulent with up to 3 pairs of unequal, almost hemispherical, densely dotted, greyish green leaves, 4–8cm (1½–3in) long, with the tips of the very rounded undersides drawn over the flat upper surfaces. In late summer and early autumn, produces solitary, daisy-like, orange-pink flowers, 7cm (3in) across. ↕7cm (3in), ↔ 12cm (5in). South Africa (Western Cape, Eastern Cape). ❀ (min. 7°C/45°F)

Pleiospilos bolusii

Pleiospilos simulans

P. simulans ▣ Clump-forming, perennial succulent bearing one pair of slightly unequal, ovate to 3-angled, spreading, densely dotted, reddish, yellowish, or brownish green leaves, 5–8cm (2–3in) long, the keeled undersides thickening towards the tips. Daisy-like, scented, yellow or orange flowers, 6cm (2½in) across, are solitary or produced in cymes of 1–3 in late summer and early autumn. ↕10cm (4in), ↔ to 30cm (12in). South Africa (Eastern Cape). ❀ (min. 7°C/45°F)

▷ ***Pleroma macrantha*** see *Tibouchina urvilleana*

PLEUROSPERMUM

APIACEAE/UMBELLIFERAE

Genus of about 15 species of biennials and herbaceous perennials from E. Europe to E. Asia, where they grow in meadows and open woodland. They are grown for their large umbels of flowers, their finely cut leaves, and their statuesque appearance. They have solid, usually hairless stems and oblong to triangular, mid- to dark green leaves that are 2- to 4-pinnate or pinnatisect, with narrowly ovate to ovate lobes. Compound umbels of white or pink flowers, borne in summer, with obovate petals, are followed by ovoid-oblong to ellipsoid, laterally compressed, often narrowly winged fruit. Grow in a wild garden or herbaceous border.

- **HARDINESS** Fully hardy.
- **CULTIVATION** Grow in moderately fertile, moist but well-drained soil in full sun or light dappled shade.
- **PROPAGATION** Sow seed in containers in a cold frame as soon as ripe; prick out into deep pots as soon as possible to avoid tap-root damage.
- **PESTS AND DISEASES** Susceptible to slug and snail damage.

P. benthamii ▣ Very robust, upright, almost hairless herbaceous perennial with stems often tinged red, and 1- to 2-pinnate, mid- to dark green leaves, 40–60cm (16–24in) long, with narrowly ovate, irregularly and deeply cut lobes. Conspicuous, greenish or white winged bracts are borne around small pink, sometimes white, flowers in umbels, 3–15cm (1¼–6in) across, in summer. These are followed by ovoid-oblong to ellipsoid, scarcely winged, pale mid-brown fruit, 6–8mm (¼–⅜in) long. ↕1.3–1.6m (4½–5½ft), ↔ 50–80cm (20–32in). Bhutan, Sikkim, Nepal, S.W. China. ✲✲✲

Pleurospermum benthamii

P. brunonis. Upright herbaceous perennial with hairless or very sparsely hairy, mid-green stems and triangular, 2- or 3-pinnate, mid-green leaves, 10–35cm (4–14in) long, with ovate and irregularly cut or toothed lobes. Bracts and bracteoles have conspicuous, papery white wings. In summer, small white or pinkish white flowers are produced in umbels, about 20cm (8in) across, followed by ovoid-oblong to ellipsoid, narrowly winged, pale to mid-brown fruit, about 5mm (¼in) long. ↕1.5–1.8m (5–6ft), ↔ 60–100cm (24–39in). Pakistan to W. Nepal. ✲✲✲

PLEUROTHALLIS

ORCHIDACEAE

Genus of about 900 species of mainly small, evergreen, epiphytic or rarely lithophytic orchids found in tropical North, Central, and South America, from Mexico to Peru and Brazil; they occur in forest from low altitudes to over 2,500m (8,000ft). Although extremely variable in form and habit, they typically produce slender stems on creeping rhizomes, with a solitary, lance-shaped to almost rounded, leathery, mid-green leaf at the apex of each stem. One or many flowers, 1.5–3cm (½–1¼in) across, may be produced singly or in racemes from the base of each leaf.

- **HARDINESS** Frost tender.
- **CULTIVATION** Cool- to intermediate-growing orchids. Grow epiphytically on bark, or pot tightly into small containers of epiphytic orchid compost made with fine-grade bark. In summer, provide bright filtered light and high humidity; water freely, mist twice daily, and apply a balanced liquid fertilizer at every third watering. In winter, admit full light and water more sparingly. See also p.46.
- **PROPAGATION** Divide when the plant fills the pot and "flows" over the sides.
- **PESTS AND DISEASES** May be infested by red spider mites, aphids, and mealybugs.

P. grobyi. Small, epiphytic orchid bearing fleshy, lance-shaped to narrowly ovate leaves, 7cm (3in) long, with blunt or rounded tips. Loose racemes of translucent, pale yellow to green flowers, 1cm (½in) long, with scattered purple veins, streaked with brown, are produced above the foliage in summer. ↕ 8cm (3in), ↔ 10cm (4in). Mexico, West Indies, Central and South America. ❄ (min. 10°C/50°F; max. 24°C/75°F)

▷**Plum,**
Cherry see *Prunus cerasifera*
Date see *Diospyros lotus*
Indian see *Oemleria cerasiformis*
Natal see *Carissa macrocarpa*
Oregon see *Oemleria cerasiformis*

PLUMBAGO

Leadwort

PLUMBAGINACEAE

Genus of 10–15 species of annuals, perennials, and evergreen shrubs and scandent climbers from tropical woodland and scrub in warm-temperate to tropical regions worldwide. They have alternate, simple, entire leaves, and are grown for their terminal, sometimes corymb-like racemes of attractive, white, red, or blue, salverform flowers, each with 5 spreading petal lobes. Where temperatures fall below 7°C (45°F), grow in a cool or temperate greenhouse or conservatory; plants grown in containers can be moved outdoors in summer. In warmer climates, use shrub and perennial species in a mixed or shrub border; train climbers over a pergola or arch.

- **HARDINESS** Half hardy to frost tender.
- **CULTIVATION** Under glass, grow in loam-based potting compost (JI No.3) in full light. Top-dress or pot on in spring. During the growing season, water freely and apply a balanced liquid fertilizer every month; water sparingly in winter. Outdoors, grow in fertile, well-drained soil in full sun. Tie stems to supports. Pruning group 12 for climbers, in early spring; group 8 for shrubs. May need restrictive pruning under glass.
- **PROPAGATION** Sow seed at 13–18°C (55–64°F) in spring, or root semi-ripe cuttings in midsummer with bottom heat. Take softwood cuttings from *P. indica* in late spring or early summer, or insert root cuttings in late winter.
- **PESTS AND DISEASES** Red spider mites, whiteflies, and mealybugs may be a problem under glass.

P

P. auriculata ■ syn. *P. capensis* (Cape leadwort). Scandent, evergreen shrub, grown as a climber, with slender, whippy, moderately branching stems. Oblong to oblong-spoon-shaped leaves, 4–7cm (1½–3in) long, are mid- to bright matt green, sometimes with a blue-grey tone. Bears long-tubed, sky-blue flowers, 4cm (1½in) long, in dense, terminal, corymb-like racemes, 15cm (6in) across, from summer to late autumn. ↕ 3–6m (10–20ft), ↔ 1–3m (3–10ft). South Africa. ✲. **var. *alba*** bears pure white flowers.
P. capensis see *P. auriculata.*
P. indica, syn. *P. rosea* (Scarlet leadwort). Small, evergreen shrub becoming spreading or semi-scandent if not pruned annually. Ovate-elliptic leaves, 5–11cm (2–4½in) long, are mid- to deep green. Long-tubed, red to deep rose-pink flowers, 2.5cm (1in) long, are

Plumbago auriculata

borne in terminal racemes, 10–30cm (4–12in) long, in winter (earlier if unpruned). ↕ to 2m (6ft), ↔ to 1m (3ft). S.E. Asia. ❄ (min. 7°C/45°F)
P. larpentiae see *Ceratostigma plumbaginoides.*
P. rosea see *P. indica.*

▷**Plume,**
Brazilian see *Justicia carnea*
Scarlet see *Euphorbia fulgens*
▷**Plume plant** see *Calomeria amaranthoides*

PLUMERIA

Frangipani, Pagoda tree, West Indian jasmine

APOCYNACEAE

Genus of 7 or 8 species of deciduous or semi-evergreen shrubs and small trees, with succulent stems and very thick, fleshy branches, from tropical and subtropical America. The simple, entire leaves, clustered towards the stem tips, are alternately or spirally arranged. The fragrant, salverform flowers, each with 5 broad petal lobes, are borne in showy, terminal clusters or panicles, often on bare stems or with the young leaves. Below 10°C (50°F), grow in a temperate or warm greenhouse, or as houseplants. In warmer climates, use as specimen plants. The milky sap may cause mild stomach upset if ingested.

- **HARDINESS** Frost tender.
- **CULTIVATION** Under glass, grow in loam-based potting compost (JI No.2) with added sharp sand, in full light. In growth, water moderately and apply a balanced liquid fertilizer monthly; keep almost dry in winter. Outdoors, grow in moderately fertile, well-drained soil in full sun. Pruning group 1; need restrictive pruning under glass.
- **PROPAGATION** Sow seed at 18°C (64°F) in spring. Take ripe cuttings of leafless stem tips in early spring; allow these to dry at the bases before inserting.
- **PESTS AND DISEASES** Red spider mites may be troublesome under glass.

P. acuminata see *P. rubra* var. *acutifolia.*
P. acutifolia see *P. rubra* var. *acutifolia.*
P. alba ■ ♀ (West Indian jasmine). Large, deciduous shrub or small, spreading tree with robust, sparsely branched, very thick stems. Spirally arranged, lance-shaped, slightly wrinkled, rich green leaves, to 30cm (12in) long, are usually finely hairy beneath. Salverform, yellow-eyed white flowers, 6cm (2½in) across, are produced in terminal panicles from summer to autumn. ↕ to 6m (20ft), ↔ to 4m (12ft). Puerto Rico, Lesser Antilles. ❄ (min. 10–13°C/50–55°F)
P. rubra ■ ♀ (Common frangipani). Large, deciduous shrub or small, sparsely branched tree, upright in habit, with very thick stems bearing alternately arranged, broadly elliptic to oblong or inversely lance-shaped, mid-green leaves, 20–40cm (8–16in) long, with paler midribs. Salverform, yellow-eyed flowers, 7–10cm (3–4in) across, usually rose-pink but sometimes yellow or red to bronze, are produced in terminal panicles from summer to autumn. ↕ to 7m (22ft), ↔ to 5m (15ft). Mexico to Panama. ❄ (min. 10–13°C/50–55°F). **var. *acutifolia***, syn. *P. acuminata, P. acutifolia*, produces oblong-elliptic, pointed, dark green leaves, to 10cm (4in) long, on long stalks. Terminal panicles of salverform, very fragrant, yellow-centred white flowers, 8–9cm (3–3½in) across, with widely spreading petals, are produced from late summer to autumn. ↕ 4m (12ft), ↔ to 2m (6ft). Mexico to

Plumeria rubra

Panama, N. South America, West Indies. **f. *tricolor*** bears pink-margined white flowers with yellow eyes.

▷**Plum yew** see *Cephalotaxus, C. harringtonii, Prumnopitys andina*
Fortune see *Cephalotaxus fortunei*
▷**Plush plant** see *Echeveria pulvinata*

POA

Meadow grass, Spear grass

GRAMINEAE/POACEAE

Genus of about 500 species of mainly perennial grasses (some are annuals) found in cool-temperate regions in a wide range of habitats from seashores to alpine zones. They include a number of important fodder, lawn, and pasture

Plumeria alba

grasses. Of variable habit, they are grown for their narrowly linear, flat to folded leaves and open or compact, summer-flowering panicles. Most cultivated species are grown as turf grasses or for agricultural purposes. *P. alpina* var. *vivipara* is grown as a curiosity, either in a rock garden or at the front of a border. *P. chaixii* and other ornamental species are suitable for a border, and for naturalizing in woodland and other shady situations.
• **Hardiness** Fully hardy.
• **Cultivation** Grow in moderately fertile, medium to light, well-drained soil in full sun or partial shade. Remove flowering stems in autumn to prevent self-seeding; cut back dead foliage in early spring.
• **Propagation** Sow seed in containers in a cold frame in spring or autumn, or divide between mid-spring and early summer. Peg down mature flowerheads of *P. alpina* var. *vivipara* to allow plantlets to root.
• **Pests and diseases** Trouble free.

P. alpina (Alpine meadow grass). Densely tufted perennial with neat mounds of thick, flat, linear, short-pointed, mid-green leaves, 4–10cm (1½–4in) long. From early to late summer, produces dense, ovoid-pyramidal, short-branched, purplish green flowering panicles, to 7cm (3in) long. ↕ 30cm (12in), ↔ 20cm (8in). W. Europe to C. Asia. ❄❄❄. **var. *vivipara*** has panicles in which flower spikelets have been replaced by tiny plantlets.
P. chaixii. Densely tufted perennial bearing flat or folded, unusually broad, linear, glossy, bright green leaves, to 45cm (18in) long and 1cm (½in) wide, each abruptly contracted at the tip to form a "hood". In late spring and early summer, bears open, slightly nodding, straight-branched, ovate to ovate-oblong, pale green, often purple-tinted flowering panicles, to 25cm (10in) long, on strong, erect stems held well above the foliage. ↕ 1m (3ft), ↔ 45cm (18in). Europe, S.W. Asia, North America. ❄❄❄

▷ **Poached egg plant** see *Limnanthes, L. douglasii*

PODALYRIA

LEGUMINOSAE/PAPILIONACEAE

Genus of about 25 species of evergreen shrubs from woodland, forest margins, and streamsides in southern Africa. They have simple, usually densely hairy leaves with rolled margins, and are grown for their fragrant, pea-like flowers, borne singly or in pairs from the leaf axils. Where temperatures fall below 7°C (45°F), grow in a cool greenhouse. In warmer areas, grow in a shrub border or at the base of a house wall.
• **Hardiness** Frost tender.
• **Cultivation** Under glass, grow in loam-based potting compost (JI No.3) in full light. When in growth, water moderately and apply a balanced liquid fertilizer every month; water sparingly in winter. Outdoors, grow in moderately fertile, moist but well-drained soil in full sun. Pruning group 8; may need restrictive pruning under glass.
• **Propagation** Sow seed at 13–18°C (55–64°F) in spring. Root semi-ripe cuttings with bottom heat in summer.
• **Pests and diseases** Red spider mites may be troublesome under glass.

P. sericea. Spreading, densely leafy shrub with obovate leaves, 2cm (¾in) long, thickly covered with silver-silky hairs that age to gold. From autumn to spring, produces solitary, upright, pea-like, fragrant, lavender-blue to lavender-pink flowers, 1cm (½in) across, with a purple mark at each petal base. ↕ 45–90cm (18–36in), ↔ 45–100cm (18–39in). South Africa (Northern Cape, Western Cape, Eastern Cape). ❀ (min. 7°C/45°F)

▷ **Podocarp,**
Tasmanian see *Podocarpus lawrencii*
Willowleaf see *Podocarpus salignus*

PODOCARPUS

PODOCARPACEAE

Genus of about 100 species of dioecious, occasionally monoecious, evergreen, coniferous trees and shrubs from forests, mainly in warm-temperate to tropical zones. They are grown for their spirally arranged leaves, which are variable in shape and are mainly borne in 2 ranks. Male and female flowers are usually borne on separate trees: the males are yellow or red, solitary or in axillary clusters of up to 5, or, in some species, borne in narrow, catkin-like cones; the females are green and produced in cone-like structures. Male and female plants are both needed to produce the plum-shaped, rounded to oblong, usually single-seeded fruits, which have fleshy, often red arils at the bases.

Grow as specimens or in a woodland garden; *P. lawrencii* and *P. nivalis* are also suitable for a shrub border or large rock garden. *P. macrophyllus* needs long, hot, humid summers to achieve tree stature, remaining shrub-like in cooler areas; it is sometimes used for hedging. The frost-tender species are attractive specimens in warm climates, but need temperate or warm greenhouse protection in frost-prone areas.
• **Hardiness** Fully hardy to frost tender.
• **Cultivation** Tolerant of a range of soils but best in fertile, moist but well-drained, humus-rich soil in full sun, with shelter from cold, dry winds. Most species thrive best in humid or high-rainfall climates.
• **Propagation** Sow seed as soon as ripe, or in containers in an open frame in spring; germination may take as long as 12–18 months. Take semi-ripe cuttings from upright leading shoots in late summer.
• **Pests and diseases** Trouble free.

P. alpinus see *P. lawrencii.*
P. andinus see *Prumnopitys andina.*
P. lawrencii, syn. *P. alpinus* (Tasmanian podocarp). Spreading, dense, rounded shrub bearing slender green shoots. Linear, dull green leaves, 6–12mm (¼–½in) long, each with 2 grey bands beneath, are parted on either side of the shoots. Male flowers are produced in yellow, catkin-like cones, female flowers in green cone-like structures. Ovoid, bright red fruit, 6mm (¼in) long, are produced in autumn on female plants. ↕↔ to 2m (6ft). Australia (New South Wales, Tasmania). ❄❄❄

Podocarpus nivalis (inset: fruit detail)

P. macrophyllus ♢ (Kusamaki). Conical tree, becoming domed, with reddish brown bark and erect or spreading, yellowish green shoots. Lance-shaped, firm, leathery leaves, 6–10cm (2½–4in) long, are light green becoming dark green above, each with 2 glaucous bands beneath, and are erect or spreading on the shoots. Male flowers are borne in yellow, catkin-like cones, female flowers in green cone-like structures. Ovoid, reddish purple fruit, about 1cm (½in) long, are borne in autumn on female plants. ↕ to 15m (50ft), ↔ 6–8m (20–25ft). E. China, Japan. ❄❄
P. nivalis ▣ (Alpine totara). Spreading, dense, rounded shrub, very similar to *P. alpinus*, but with more rigid, linear, green-bronze leaves, 1–2cm (½–¾in) long, set radially around the slender, mid-green shoots, unparted on either side. Male flowers are borne in yellow, catkin-like cones, female flowers in green cone-like structures. Oblong, bright red fruit, 6mm (¼in) long, are produced in autumn on female plants. ↕↔ to 2m (6ft). New Zealand. ❄❄❄
P. salignus ▣ ♢ (Willowleaf podocarp). Columnar or broadly conical tree with spreading, later pendent branches, fibrous, peeling, red-brown bark, and green shoots that become grey-brown with age. Spreading, linear, often sickle-shaped leaves, 5–11cm (2–4½in) long, are dark bluish green (with a ridge above), and yellow-green beneath; they occur mainly near the shoot tips. The male flowers are borne in yellow, catkin-like cones, female flowers in green cone-like structures. Egg-shaped, green or dark violet fruit, 8mm (⅜in) long, are produced in autumn on female plants. Very graceful as a mature tree. ↕ to 20m (70ft), ↔ 6–9m (20–28ft). Chile. ❄❄❄

Podocarpus salignus

PODOPHYLLUM

BERBERIDACEAE

Genus of about 9 species of shade-loving, rhizomatous perennials, cultivated for their foliage and flowers, from scrub and forest in North America and from the Himalayas to China and Taiwan. Each plant has 1 or 2 peltate, palmately lobed, radical leaves, sometimes with purplish brown patches between the conspicuous veins; the leaves are pushed up by the lengthening leaf-stalks and emerge looking like tiny, folded umbrellas. Terminal, cup-shaped, pink, white, or red flowers are solitary or produced in small umbels, and are followed by red or yellow fruits, 2.5–5cm (1–2in) long. Podophyllums are suitable for a woodland garden or moist, shady border. All parts of the plants are highly toxic if ingested.
• **Hardiness** Fully hardy to frost hardy.
• **Cultivation** Grow in humus-rich, leafy, moist soil in full or partial shade (*P. peltatum* tolerates drier soil). In cold areas, protect frost-hardy species with a dry winter mulch.
• **Propagation** Sow seed in containers in an open frame as soon as ripe. Divide in spring or late summer.
• **Pests and diseases** Susceptible to slug damage in spring as the leaves emerge.

Podophyllum hexandrum

P. emodi see *P. hexandrum.*
P. hexandrum ■ syn. *P. emodi.* Rhizomatous perennial bearing long-stalked, 3- to 5-lobed, deeply toothed, mid-green leaves, to 25cm (10in) long, with purplish brown markings; they unfurl after flowering. Solitary, open cup-shaped, usually 6-petalled, white or pale pink flowers, 2.5–5cm (1–2in) across, with prominent yellow anthers, are borne from late spring to midsummer; they are followed by plum-like, ovoid, fleshy red fruit, to 5cm (2in) long. ↕45cm (18in), ↔ 30cm (12in). N. India (Himalayas) to China. ***
P. japonicum see *Ranzania japonica.*
P. peltatum (American mandrake, May apple). Creeping, rhizomatous perennial producing long-stalked, 5- to 9-lobed, toothed, sometimes 2-cleft, glossy leaves, to 30cm (12in) long, well-developed at flowering. Solitary, semi-pendent, shallowly cup-shaped, usually 9-petalled, fragrant, waxy white to pale pink flowers, 5cm (2in) across, are produced beneath the leaves from mid-spring to early summer; they are followed by edible, ovoid, yellowish green fruit, 2.5–5cm (1–2in) long. ↕45cm (18in), ↔ 1.2m (4ft) or more. North America (Ontario and Quebec to Texas and Florida). ***
P. pleianthum (Chinese may apple). Rhizomatous perennial with shallowly 6- to 10-lobed, finely toothed, glossy leaves, to 35cm (14in) long. Clusters of 5–8 cup-shaped, deep crimson to purple flowers are borne in the leaf axils in summer, followed by ovoid-spherical, dark red fruit, 2.5cm (1in) long. ↕75cm (30in), ↔ 45cm (18in). C. and S.E. China, Taiwan. **

PODRANEA

BIGNONIACEAE

Genus of 2 species of woody-stemmed, evergreen climbers from open woodland; one species from Zimbabwe, the other from South Africa. They have pinnate leaves, borne in opposite pairs, and are cultivated for their 5-lobed, trumpet-shaped, foxglove-like flowers. Where temperatures regularly fall below 0°C (32°F), grow in a cool or temperate greenhouse. In milder climates, they are suitable for a pergola or arch, or cascading from a tree.
• **HARDINESS** Frost tender; may survive short spells near to 0°C (32°F).
• **CULTIVATION** Under glass, grow in loam-based potting compost (JI No.3) in bright filtered light. In growth, water moderately and apply a balanced liquid fertilizer monthly; water sparingly in winter. Outdoors, grow in fertile, moist but well-drained soil in light dappled or partial shade. Pruning group 12, immediately after flowering.
• **PROPAGATION** Sow seed at 13–18°C (55–64°F) in spring, take semi-ripe cuttings in summer, or layer in spring.
• **PESTS AND DISEASES** Prone to red spider mites and mealybugs under glass.

P. ricasoliana, syn. *Pandorea ricasoliana, Tecoma ricasoliana* (Pink trumpet vine). Scandent, twining climber, becoming bushy with age, with pinnate leaves, to 25cm (10in) long, composed of 5–11 lance-shaped to ovate, unevenly toothed, rich green leaflets with slender points. Produces loose, terminal panicles of about 12 trumpet-shaped pink flowers, to 6cm (2½in) long, with red veins, paler tubes, and wavy-margined, round lobes, from winter to summer, depending on temperature. ↕3–5m (10–15ft). South Africa (Eastern Cape, KwaZulu/Natal). ❀ (min. 10°C/50°F)

▷**Pohutakawa** see *Metrosideros*
Common see *M. excelsus*
▷***Poinciana gilliesii*** see *Caesalpinia gilliesii*
▷***Poinciana pulcherrima*** see *Caesalpinia pulcherrima*
▷***Poinciana regia*** see *Delonix regia*
▷**Poinsettia** see *Euphorbia pulcherrima*
Annual see *E. cyathophora*
▷**Poison arrow plant** see *Acokanthera oblongifolia*
▷**Poison bulb** see *Crinum asiaticum*
▷**Poke, Indian** see *Veratrum viride*
▷**Pokeweed** see *Phytolacca, P. americana*
▷**Polar plant** see *Silphium laciniatum*

POLEMONIUM

Jacob's ladder

POLEMONIACEAE

Genus of about 25 species of deciduous, clump-forming or occasionally rhizomatous perennials and annuals, found in stony, arctic or alpine soils, often by streams, or in damp meadows, woodland, or scrub, in Europe, Asia, North America, and Central America. Most have basal clumps of unequally pinnate leaves, usually with numerous leaflets, and erect or decumbent stems bearing smaller leaves. They are grown for their spring and summer flowers,

Polemonium carneum

which are bell-shaped, saucer-shaped, narrowly tubular, or funnel-shaped and spreading at the mouths; they are usually white or blue, sometimes purple, pink, or yellow, and either solitary or in terminal or axillary cymes. Grow taller species in a border or wild garden, the smaller, alpine species in a rock garden, scree bed, or alpine house. *P. caeruleum* grows well in grass. *P. brandegeei* and *P. pauciflorum* are usually short-lived.
• **HARDINESS** Fully hardy.
• **CULTIVATION** Grow tall species in any fertile, well-drained but moist soil, preferably in full sun or partial shade. Grow small species in gritty, sharply drained soil in full sun with some midday shade. Dead-head regularly.
• **PROPAGATION** Sow seed in containers in a cold frame in autumn or spring, or divide in spring.
• **PESTS AND DISEASES** Powdery mildew may be a problem.

P. brandegeei. Clump-forming, perennial bearing mainly basal, sticky, pinnate leaves, to 10cm (4in) long, with many lance-shaped leaflets, each to 1.5cm (½in) long. In early summer, upright stems bear short, terminal cymes of long-tubed, funnel-shaped, pale to deep golden yellow, rarely white flowers, to 2.5cm (1in) long. ***. **subsp. *mellitum***, syn. *P. mellitum*, bears looser cymes of white or pale cream flowers in summer. ↕20cm (8in), ↔ 15cm (6in). USA (Rocky Mountains).
P. caeruleum ■ (Greek valerian, Jacob's ladder). Clump-forming perennial, mainly hairless but softly hairy near the inflorescences. Bears 2-pinnate leaves, to 40cm (16in) long, each composed of 19–27 oblong-lance-shaped leaflets, 1.5–4cm (½–1½in) long. Lax, terminal or axillary cymes of open bell-shaped, lavender-blue, rarely white flowers, 1–2.5cm (½–1in) across, are produced on erect, branched stems in early summer. ↕30–90cm (12–36in), ↔ 30cm (12in). N. and C. Europe, N. Asia, W. North America. ***. **var. *lacteum***, syn. var. *album*, has white flowers.
P. carneum ■ Hairless, clump-forming perennial bearing coarsely divided, pinnate leaves, to 20cm (8in) long, with 13–21 elliptic to ovate leaflets, each 0.7–2cm (¼–¾in) long. Lax, terminal cymes of shallowly bell-shaped, pale pink or yellow, sometimes dark purple or lavender flowers, 1–2.5cm (½–1in) across, with yellow centres, are borne on erect, branched stems in early summer. ↕10–40cm (4–16in), ↔ 20cm (8in). USA (Washington to California). ***
P. confertum see *P. viscosum.*
P. eximium, syn. *P. viscosum* var. *eximium.* Compact, clump-forming, perennial bearing crowded tufts of pinnate, glandular-sticky leaves, to 10cm (4in) long, with numerous leaflets, each 6–8mm (¼–⅜in) long, deeply cut into 3 or 5 segments. Erect, branched stems bear dense, terminal cymes of narrowly funnel-shaped to cylindrical, clear blue flowers, 1.5cm (½in) long, in summer. ↕10–30cm (4–12in), ↔ 15cm (6in). High altitudes in W. USA (California, Sierra Nevada). ***
P. foliosissimum. Leafy, clump-forming perennial producing a few erect, softly

Polemonium caeruleum

Polemonium 'Lambrook Mauve'

Polemonium pauciflorum

hairy stems. Pinnate leaves, to 15cm (6in) long, each have 11–25 elliptic-lance-shaped leaflets, 1–5cm (½–2in) long. Dense, axillary and terminal cymes of bell-shaped, blue-violet, cream, or white flowers, to 1.5cm (½in) across, are produced in midsummer. ↕75–80cm (30–32in), ↔ 60cm (24in). Central W. USA. ❄❄❄. **var. *flavum*** bears yellow flowers that are shaded orange-red outside; ↕40–70cm (16–28in). USA (S. Arizona, New Mexico).

***P.* 'Lambrook Mauve'** ▣ syn. *P. reptans* 'Lambrook Manor', *P. reptans* 'Lambrook Mauve'. Clump-forming perennial forming rounded mounds of neat, pinnate leaves, to 25cm (10in) long, each composed of 7–19 ovate or oblong leaflets, 3–5cm (1¼–2in) long. Erect, branched stems very freely bear lax, terminal cymes of bell-shaped, lilac-blue flowers, 1.5–2cm (½–¾in) across, in late spring and early summer. ↕↔ to 45cm (18in). ❄❄❄

P. mellitum see *P. brandegeei* subsp. *mellitum*.

P. pauciflorum ▣ Short-lived, clump-forming perennial with spreading to erect, branched, softly hairy stems and mainly pinnate leaves, to 15cm (6in)

Polemonium pulcherrimum

long, each composed of 11–25 elliptic-lance-shaped leaflets, to 2.5cm (1in) long. From early to late summer, bears horizontal to semi-pendent, narrowly tubular, red-tinted, pale yellow flowers, 4cm (1½in) across, with spreading mouths, either singly or in loose, few-flowered, terminal or axillary cymes. ↕↔ to 50cm (20in). USA (S.E. Arizona, New Mexico). ❄❄❄

P. pulcherrimum ▣ Clump-forming perennial with pinnate leaves, to 14cm (5½in) long, each composed of 11–25 ovate leaflets, to 3.5cm (1½in) long. Dense, terminal and axillary cymes of bell-shaped, light blue to purple-blue or white flowers, to 1cm (½in) across, with short tubes, yellow within, are borne on erect, branched stems in early summer. ↕↔ 30cm (12in). North America (Alaska to California). ❄❄❄

***P. reptans* 'Lambrook Manor'** see *P.* 'Lambrook Mauve'.

***P. reptans* 'Lambrook Mauve'** see *P.* 'Lambrook Mauve'.

P. viscosum, syn. *P. confertum*. Clump-forming perennial bearing mainly basal, pinnate leaves, to 20cm (8in) long, with whorls of many palmately 3- or 5-lobed leaflets, each to 1.5cm (½in) long. In summer, produces large, terminal cymes of funnel-shaped, deep blue flowers, to 2–3cm (¾–1¼in) across, on upright, branched stems. ↕5–50cm (2–20in), ↔ 5–20cm (2–8in). North America (mountains from Canada to New Mexico). ❄❄❄. **var. *eximium*** see *P. eximium*.

POLIANTHES

AGAVACEAE

Genus of 13 species of tuberous perennials found in open woodland and at roadsides in sandy areas in Mexico and Texas. They are grown for their showy, loose racemes or spikes of tubular flowers, borne in summer. The mostly basal leaves are lance-shaped or linear. In frost-prone climates, grow in a warm greenhouse or summer border; elsewhere, grow in a sheltered border.

- **HARDINESS** Frost tender.
- **CULTIVATION** Under glass, grow in loam-based potting compost (JI No.2) in full light. During the growing season, water moderately, and apply a balanced liquid fertilizer every 2 weeks. Reduce watering as the leaves die down, and keep dry when dormant. Outdoors, grow in moderately fertile, well-drained soil in full sun. Lift before first frosts and store tubers in sand in frost-free conditions.
- **PROPAGATION** Sow seed at 19–24°C (66–75°F) as soon as ripe. Remove offsets when the plants are dormant.
- **PESTS AND DISEASES** Prone to viruses.

P. geminiflora, syn. *Bravoa geminiflora*. Tuberous perennial with semi-erect, narrow, linear, basal leaves, 30–40cm (12–16in). In summer, produces lax racemes of paired, pendent, tubular, bright orange-red flowers, 2.5cm (1in) long. ↕ to 70cm (28in), ↔ 8cm (3in). Mexico. ❀ (min. 15°C/59°F)

P. tuberosa (Tuberose). Tuberous perennial with semi-erect, thin, linear-lance-shaped leaves, to 45cm (18in) long, in a basal rosette. Spikes of tubular, intensely fragrant, waxy white flowers, 3–6cm (1¼–2½in) long, are

Polianthes tuberosa 'The Pearl'

produced in summer. ↕ to 1.2m (4ft), ↔ 15cm (6in). Mexico. ❀ (min. 15°C/59°F). **'The Pearl'** ▣ produces semi-double to double flowers.

▷ **Policeman's helmet** see *Impatiens glandulifera*

POLIOTHYRSIS

FLACOURTIACEAE

Genus of one species of deciduous tree from mountain woodland in C. China. It is grown for its glossy, dark green leaves and fragrant, papery, greenish white then yellow summer flowers. Grow as a specimen or among trees.

- **HARDINESS** Fully hardy.
- **CULTIVATION** Grow in fertile, well-drained soil in full sun or partial shade, with shelter from cold, drying winds. Pruning group 1.
- **PROPAGATION** Sow seed in containers in an open frame in autumn, or take greenwood cuttings in summer.
- **PESTS AND DISEASES** Trouble free.

P. sinensis ▣ ♀ Spreading, deciduous tree with grey bark, which is deeply furrowed in mature trees. Ovate, slender-pointed, glossy, dark green leaves, to 15cm (6in) long, red-tinged when young, are arranged alternately, and are borne on red stalks. In mid- and late summer, white buds open to tiny, cup-shaped, fragrant, papery, greenish white then yellow flowers, produced in conical panicles, to 25cm (10in) long. ↕10m (30ft) or more, ↔ 6m (20ft). C. China. ❄❄❄

Poliothyrsis sinensis (inset: flower detail)

P

▷ **Polka dot plant** see *Hypoestes, H. phyllostachya*
▷ **Polvillo, Guayacan** see *Tabebuia serratifolia*
▷ **Polyanthus** see *Primula* Polyanthus Group

POLYGALA

Milkwort, Seneca, Snakeroot

POLYGALACEAE

Genus of about 500 species of annuals and evergreen perennials and shrubs found in a wide range of habitats worldwide, except in New Zealand, Polynesia, and arctic regions. They are grown for their terminal or axillary racemes of colourful, pea-like flowers, borne in late spring and summer, or in some species in autumn; each flower has 5 sepals, the inner two forming broad, petal-like "wings", and 5 petals, the lowest forming a keel with a fringed apex. The leaves are alternate, opposite, or whorled, linear to rounded, and usually leathery. Grow hardy species in a woodland or rock garden, or in an alpine house. In frost-prone areas, grow tender species in a cool greenhouse or conservatory; in warmer climates, use in a shrub border.

• **HARDINESS** Fully hardy to frost tender.
• **CULTIVATION** Under glass, grow in loamless potting compost in full light, with shade from hot sun. In growth, keep well-ventilated, water freely, and apply a balanced liquid fertilizer monthly; water sparingly in winter. Outdoors, grow in moderately fertile, humus-rich, sharply drained soil in full sun or partial shade. Pruning group 9 for *P.* x *dalmaisiana* and *P. myrtifolia.*
• **PROPAGATION** Sow seed of hardy species in containers in an open frame in autumn; sow seed of tender species at not less than 15°C (59°F) in spring. Take softwood cuttings in early summer, or semi-ripe cuttings in mid- to late summer.
• **PESTS AND DISEASES** Aphids and whiteflies may be a problem under glass.

P

Polygala calcarea

Polygala calcarea 'Bulley's Form'

P. calcarea ▣ (Milkwort). Prostrate, creeping, mat-forming, evergreen perennial with basal rosettes of obovate, leathery, mid-green leaves, 1–3.5cm (½–1½in) long. In late spring and early summer, trailing stems bear deep blue flowers, to 7mm (¼in) long, with white-fringed lips, in terminal racemes, to 3cm (1¼in) long. ↕ 5cm (2in), ↔ to 20cm (8in). W. Europe. ❄❄❄. The following cultivars are more robust and free-flowering than the species: **'Bulley's Form'** ▣ has larger flowers in a deeper blue. **'Lillet'** has a compact habit, and produces brighter blue flowers over a long period.

P. chamaebuxus. Small, spreading, evergreen shrub with lance-shaped, leathery, dark green leaves, 1.5–3cm (½–1¼in) long. The flowers, 1.5cm (½in) long, have bright yellow lips, white or pale yellow wings, and a bright yellow keel that ages to purple or brownish crimson; the flowers may be solitary or in pairs, and are produced in the upper leaf axils, mainly in late spring and early summer. ↕ 5–15cm (2–6in), ↔ to 30cm (12in). W. central Europe. ❄❄❄. **var. *grandiflora*** ▣ syn. var. *purpurea*, var. *rhodoptera*, produces flowers with deep purplish pink wings and yellow lips. Alps, Carpathians. **var. *purpurea*** see var. *grandiflora*. **var. *rhodoptera*** see var. *grandiflora*.

P. x dalmaisiana ▣ (*P. myrtifolia* x *P. oppositifolia*) syn. *P. myrtifolia* var. *grandiflora* of gardens. Erect, rounded, evergreen shrub, tending to spread with age. Elliptic, ovate, or lance-shaped, glaucous, mid- to deep green leaves, to 2.5cm (1in) long, can be alternate or opposite on the same plant. Leafy, terminal racemes of purple or rose-magenta flowers, 2.5cm (1in) long, with the bases of the keels white, are borne from midsummer to late autumn. ↕↔ 1–2.5m (3–8ft). Garden origin. ❁ (min. 5–7°C/41–45°F)

P. myrtifolia. Erect, bushy, evergreen shrub, spreading with age, with elliptic-oblong or obovate, leathery, mid- to deep green leaves, 2.5–5cm (1–2in) long. Short, leafy, terminal racemes of purple-veined, greenish white flowers, to 2cm (¾in) long, with crested keel petals, are borne from spring to autumn. ↕ 1–2.5m (3–8ft), ↔ 1–2m (3–6ft). South Africa. ❁ (min. 5–7°C/41–45°F). **var. *grandiflora* of gardens** see *P.* x *dalmaisiana.*

Polygala chamaebuxus var. *grandiflora*

Polygala x *dalmaisiana*

POLYGONATUM

Solomon's seal

CONVALLARIACEAE/LILIACEAE

Genus of about 50 species of rhizomatous perennials from woodland in temperate regions of Eurasia and N. America. Cultivated for their foliage and flowers, they have usually arching stems and alternate, opposite, or whorled, linear to broadly elliptic or ovate, parallel-veined leaves that turn yellow in autumn. Mostly pendent, sometimes erect, tubular to bell-shaped, mainly white or cream, occasionally purple-pink flowers, with green markings, are either solitary or produced in small clusters, often along the lower sides of the stems. The flowers are usually followed by berry-like, spherical, red or black fruits. Solomon's seals are suitable for a shady border, or for a woodland or rock garden. All parts may cause mild stomach upset if ingested.

• **HARDINESS** Fully hardy to frost hardy.
• **CULTIVATION** Grow in fertile, humus-rich, moist but well-drained soil in full or partial shade.
• **PROPAGATION** Sow seed in containers in a cold frame in autumn. Divide rhizomes when growth begins in spring, taking care to avoid damaging young, brittle shoots.
• **PESTS AND DISEASES** Susceptible to slugs and sawfly larvae.

P. biflorum, syn. *P. canaliculatum, P. commutatum, P. giganteum.* Rhizomatous perennial with arching, hairless stems with alternate, narrowly lance-shaped to broadly elliptic leaves, to 18cm (7in) long, with hairless or minutely hairy undersides that are glaucous along the veins. From late spring to midsummer, usually solitary or 2–4 pendent, tubular, greenish white flowers, 1–2.5cm (½–1in) long, are produced in the leaf axils; they are followed by spherical black fruit, 9mm (⅜in) across. ↕ 0.4–2m (16–72in), ↔ 60cm (24in). S. central Canada, E. North America. ❄❄❄

P. canaliculatum see *P. biflorum.*

P. commutatum see *P. biflorum.*

***P. cyrtonema* of gardens** see *Disporopsis pernyi.*

P. giganteum see *P. biflorum.*

P. hirtum ▣ syn. *P. latifolium.* Rhizomatous perennial producing erect stems with alternate, lance-shaped to ovate leaves, 8–15cm (3–6in) long,

Polygonatum hirtum

Polygonatum hookeri

slightly hairy beneath. From late spring to midsummer, produces 1–5 pendent, tubular, green-tipped white flowers, 2cm (¾in) long, in the leaf axils; they are followed by spherical black fruit, 6mm (¼in) across. ↕ to 1.2m (4ft), ↔ 60cm (24in). C. and S.E. Europe, Turkey, W. Russia, Caucasus. ***
P. hookeri ■ Creeping, slowly spreading perennial with upright stems bearing alternate, linear to narrowly elliptic leaves, to 4cm (1½in) long, hairless beneath. In late spring and early summer, produces solitary, erect, pale to deep pink, short-tubed flowers, 2cm (¾in) across, with wide-spreading tepals, in the upper leaf axils; they are followed by spherical black fruit, 3mm (⅛in) across. Suitable for a peat bed. ↕ to 10cm (4in), ↔ to 30cm (12in) or more. E. Himalayas, China. ***
P. humile. Rhizomatous perennial with upright stems bearing lance-shaped to ovate leaves, 4–7cm (1½–3in) long, arranged alternately, and finely hairy on the lower veins. In late spring, produces solitary or paired, pendent, tubular white flowers, to 2cm (¾in) long, in the upper leaf axils; they are followed by spherical, blue-black fruit, to 6mm

Polygonatum multiflorum 'Striatum'

Polygonatum stewartianum

(¼in) across. ↕ 20cm (8in), ↔ 50cm (20in) or more. E. Europe, W. Asia. ***
P. x hybridum (*P. multiflorum* x *P. odoratum*) syn. *P. multiflorum* of gardens (Common Solomon's seal). Rhizomatous perennial with scarcely arching, hairless stems bearing alternate, ovate-lance-shaped leaves, to 20cm (8in) long, held horizontally. Pendent, tubular, green-tipped, creamy white flowers, 2cm (¾in) long, slightly constricted around the middle, are produced in late spring, usually 4 per axil; they are followed by spherical, blue-black fruit, to 8mm (⅜in) across. ↕ to 1.5m (5ft), ↔ 30cm (12in). Garden origin. ***
P. latifolium see *P. hirtum.*
P. multiflorum. Rhizomatous perennial with arching, hairless stems bearing ovate-lance-shaped leaves, to 5–15cm (2–6in) long, arranged alternately. In late spring, each lower leaf axil produces 2–6 pendent, tubular, green-tipped white flowers, 1cm (½in) long; they are followed by spherical black fruit, 4–6mm (⅛–¼in) across. ↕ to 90cm (36in), ↔ 25cm (10in). Europe, temperate Asia. ***. **'Striatum'** ■ syn. 'Variegatum', has leaves striped creamy white.
***P. multiflorum* of gardens** see *P.* x *hybridum.*
P. odoratum, syn. *P. officinale.* Creeping, rhizomatous perennial with arching, angular stems bearing alternate, lance-shaped to ovate, hairless leaves, 5–15cm (2–6in) long, usually in 2 rows. In late spring and early summer, bears 1 or 2 pendent, tubular, fragrant, green-tipped white flowers, to 3cm (1¼in) long, in the upper leaf axils, followed by spherical black fruit, 6mm (¼in) across. ↕ to 85cm (34in), ↔ 30cm (12in). Europe, Caucasus, Russia (Siberia) to Japan. ***. **'Flore Pleno'** has double flowers with more extensive green markings. **'Gilt Edge'** has leaves with narrow yellow margins.
P. officinale see *P. odoratum.*
P. stewartianum ■ Rhizomatous perennial with short, erect, slightly angular, hairless stems bearing whorled, linear-lance-shaped leaves, to 10cm (4in) long. From late spring to midsummer, produces small clusters of 1–3 pendent, tubular, purple-pink flowers, to 1.5cm (½in) long, in the leaf axils. The spherical red fruit, to 6mm (¼in) across, are spotted purplish white. ↕ 20–90cm (8–36in), ↔ 25cm (10in). Europe, temperate Asia. ***
P. verticillatum (Whorled Solomon's seal). Rhizomatous perennial with erect, slightly angular, hairless stems bearing stalkless, mainly whorled, sometimes opposite, lance-shaped leaves, 6–15cm (2½–6in) long. From late spring to midsummer, produces 1–4 pendent, tubular, greenish white flowers, to 1.5cm (½in) long, in the upper leaf axils; they are followed by spherical red fruit, 5mm (¼in) across. ↕ 20–90cm (8–36in), ↔ 25cm (10in). Europe, Caucasus, Afghanistan. ***

▷ ***Polygonum affine*** see *Persicaria affinis*
▷ ***Polygonum amplexicaule*** see *Persicaria amplexicaulis*
▷ ***Polygonum aubertii*** see *Fallopia aubertii*
▷ ***Polygonum baldschuanicum*** see *Fallopia baldschuanica*
▷ ***Polygonum bistorta*** see *Persicaria bistorta*
▷ ***Polygonum campanulatum*** see *Persicaria campanulata*
▷ ***Polygonum capitatum*** see *Persicaria capitata*
▷ ***Polygonum carneum*** see *Persicaria bistorta* subsp. *carnea*
▷ ***Polygonum macrophyllum*** see *Persicaria macrophylla*
▷ ***Polygonum milletii*** see *Persicaria milletii*
▷ ***Polygonum orientale*** see *Persicaria orientale*
▷ ***Polygonum sphaerostachyum*** see *Persicaria macrophylla*
▷ ***Polygonum tenuicaule*** see *Persicaria tenuicaulis*
▷ ***Polygonum vacciniifolium*** see *Persicaria vacciniifolia*
▷ ***Polygonum virginianum*** see *Persicaria virginiana*

POLYPODIUM

POLYPODIACEAE

Genus of about 75 species of mostly evergreen, usually epiphytic, sometimes terrestrial ferns, mainly from tropical regions of the USA, Central America, and South America, but also from temperate and other tropical regions. They are often found growing on trees, rocks, walls, or well-drained banks and sand dunes. They are cultivated for their sculptural fronds, which are usually lance-shaped, simple to pinnatifid or pinnate, occasionally more divided, and borne at random in 2 rows along creeping, often surface rhizomes. Sori, without indusia, are arranged in rows on each side of the midrib of each frond or pinna. The hardy species are good for a rock garden, mixed border, or bank, especially where winter green and ground cover are required. In frost-prone climates, grow tender species in a warm greenhouse. Elewhere, the tropical species, which are mostly epiphytic, are suitable for growing in trees.

- **HARDINESS** Fully hardy to frost tender.
- **CULTIVATION** Under glass, grow in equal parts fine-grade bark, perlite, and charcoal. May be grown epiphytically in bright filtered light; wrap the rhizomes in moss and tie to a suitable rooting medium, such as osmunda fibre, and keep moist until established. Water moderately during the growing season; sparingly in winter. Outdoors, grow in moderately fertile, humus-rich, gritty or stony, well-drained soil (*P. cambricum* requires neutral to alkaline soil) in full sun or dappled shade, with shelter from cold, dry winds.
- **PROPAGATION** Sow spores at 15–16°C (59–61°F) when ripe. Divide in spring or early summer. See also p.51.
- **PESTS AND DISEASES** Trouble free.

P. aureum see *Phlebodium aureum.*
P. australe see *P. cambricum.*
P. cambricum, syn. *P. australe*, *P. vulgare* subsp. *serratum* (Southern polypody). Terrestrial, deciduous fern producing broadly lance-shaped to broadly triangular-ovate, pinnate, mid-green fronds, to 60cm (24in) long, with linear or oblong pinnae, the longest usually being the second pair from the base; the pinnae often have toothed margins. New fronds appear in late summer and die back in spring. Sori are conspicuously yellow in winter. ↕ 15–60cm (6–24in), ↔ indefinite. S. and W. Europe. ***. Sterile variants, producing yellow-green fronds with deeply cut margins, are often listed or grown as *P. cambricum.* **'Cristatum'** bears crested frond tips and pinnae. **'Grandiceps'** has much larger crests than 'Cristatum', with the crests at the tips usually wider than the rest of the fronds. **'Omnilacerum Oxford'** has tall, erect, oblong-lance-shaped fronds, to 60cm (24in) long, with lance-shaped pinnae cut irregularly almost to the midribs. **'Whilharris'** produces thick-textured, lance-shaped fronds, to 45cm (18in) long, with pinnae deeply divided into long segments.
P. formosanum. Epiphytic, evergreen fern with arching to pendent, ovate to oblong, pinnate, glaucous, pale green fronds, to 50cm (20in) long, composed of spreading, lance-shaped to linear pinnae. The rhizome is conspicuously glaucous, and is very sparsely covered with small scales. ↕↔ to 45cm (18in). China, Taiwan, Japan. *
P. glycyrrhiza ■ (Licorice fern). Terrestrial, evergreen fern producing

Polypodium glycyrrhiza

P

Polypodium polypodioides

lance-shaped, pinnate or very deeply pinnatifid, mid- to dark green fronds, to 35cm (14in) long, comprising sickle-shaped, linear pinnae. Similar to *P. vulgare*, except fronds are darker green, pinnae tips more pointed, and sori smaller. If chewed, the rhizome has a very sweet, licorice taste. ↕ 30cm (12in), ↔ indefinite. North America (Alaska to California). ✻✻✻. **'Longicaudatum'**, syn. *P. vulgare* 'Longicaudatum', has fronds with very long, pointed tips. **'Malahatense'** consists of fertile variants with deeply cut pinnae; they come true from spores.

P. polypodioides ▣ (Resurrection fern). Small, semi-evergreen, terrestrial or epiphytic fern with narrowly triangular or oblong, pinnate, fairly leathery, mid-green fronds, to 30cm (12in) tall, covered with scales, and composed of well-spaced, linear or oblong pinnae. Frond margins temporarily roll inwards during dry weather. ↕ to 30cm (12in), ↔ indefinite. Southern Africa, tropical regions of America. ✻

P. scouleri ▣ (Leathery polypody). Terrestrial, evergreen fern bearing broadly ovate to triangular, pinnate or very deeply pinnatifid, leathery, thick,

Polypodium scouleri

Polypodium vulgare

rigid, glossy, deep green fronds, 30cm (12in) long. Pinnae are spreading and narrowly oblong. Needs a sheltered site in frost-prone gardens. ↕ 30cm (12in), ↔ indefinite. N.W. North America (coastal belt). ✻✻

P. virginianum (Rockcap fern, Virginian polypody). Terrestrial or epiphytic, evergreen fern, very similar to *P. vulgare*, with arching or pendent, narrowly lance-shaped or triangular to oblong, pinnate or very deeply pinnatifid, leathery to thin, dark green fronds, 25cm (10in) long, composed of lance-shaped to linear or oblong pinnae. ↕ 25cm (10in), ↔ indefinite. E. Asia, North America. ✻✻✻

P. vulgare ▣ (Common polypody). Terrestrial or epiphytic, evergreen fern with lance-shaped to oblong, pinnate or very deeply pinnatifid, thin to leathery, dark green fronds, 40cm (16in) long, composed of close, spreading, oblong to linear pinnae. Replaced in warmer sites in Europe by the very similar species, *P. interjectum*, which has ovate-triangular, thin-textured fronds. ↕ 30cm (12in), ↔ indefinite. Mostly in northern regions or on higher ground in Europe, Africa, E. Asia. ✻✻✻. **'Bifidograndiceps'** has

Polypodium vulgare 'Cornubiense'

large, flat crests; ↕ 30–50cm (12–20in). **'Cornubiense'** ▣ is very vigorous, bears both pinnatifid and 3- or 4-pinnatifid fronds, and is excellent as ground cover; ↕ 30–40cm (12–16in). **'Cornubiense Grandiceps'** has 3-pinnate fronds, to 40cm (16in) long, with large, branched, terminal crests. **'Jean Taylor'** is crested, with pinnatifid and 4-pinnatifid fronds, moss-like in appearance; ↕ 20cm (8in). **'Longicaudatum'** see *P. glycyrrhiza* 'Longicaudatum'. **subsp. *serratum*** see *P. cambricum*. **'Trichomanoides Backhouse'** bears pinnatifid and 4-pinnatifid fronds; ↕ 20cm (8in).

▷ **Polypody,**
Common see *Polypodium vulgare*
Golden see *Phlebodium aureum*
Leathery see *Polypodium scouleri*
Limestone see *Gymnocarpium robertianum*
Southern see *Polypodium cambricum*
Virginian see *Polypodium virginianum*

POLYSCIAS

ARALIACEAE

Genus of about 100 species of rounded or upright, evergreen shrubs and small trees from tropical regions of Africa, Asia, and the Pacific. They are cultivated for their alternate or spiralling leaves, which may be simple, 3-palmate, or pinnate to 3-pinnate, and tend to be grouped towards the stem tips. The small, usually whitish green flowers have 4–15 tepals, and are most often produced in panicles composed of small umbels, or in terminal clusters; they are followed by small, usually purple to black berries. Below 16°C (61°F), grow in a warm greenhouse or as houseplants. In warmer climates, grow in a shrub border; strong-growing species are also effective for hedging. All parts may cause severe discomfort if ingested; contact with sap may irritate skin.

- **HARDINESS** Frost tender.
- **CULTIVATION** Under glass, grow in loam-based potting compost (JI No.3) in full light or bright filtered light. In growth, water freely, mist daily, and apply a balanced liquid fertilizer every month. Water sparingly in winter. Outdoors, grow in fertile, humus-rich, moist but well-drained soil in full sun or partial shade. Pruning group 1; trim hedges in late summer and, if necessary, in late winter or early spring; may need restrictive pruning under glass.
- **PROPAGATION** Sow seed at 19–24°C (66–75°F) in spring. Take greenwood cuttings in early summer, or root semi-ripe or ripe, leafless stem sections with bottom heat in summer.
- **PESTS AND DISEASES** Red spider mites, mealybugs, and root-knot eelworms may be troublesome under glass.

P. filicifolia ▣ (Chotito, Fern-leaf aralia). Erect, evergreen shrub, sparingly branched (at least when young) unless regularly tip-pruned. Young plants bear arching to semi-pendent, pinnate to 3-pinnate leaves, to 10cm (4in) long, with 9–17 narrowly elliptic, bright green leaflets with purple-tinted midribs. Mature plants produce leaves to 90cm (36in) long, composed of leaflets with entire or finely toothed margins. Star-shaped, whitish green flowers are borne

Polyscias filicifolia

(rarely) in terminal, umbel-like panicles, in summer, followed by black fruit. Probably a hybrid. ↕ to 2–2.5m (6–8ft) or more, ↔ to 1m (3ft) or more. S. Malaysia, Pacific. ⊛ (min. 16°C/61°F). **'Marginata'** has white-margined leaves.

P. guilfoylei ♀ (Coffee tree, Geranium aralia). Large, erect, evergreen shrub or small tree, generally sparsely branched, with foliage confined to the stem tips. Pinnate leaves, 30–45cm (12–18in) long, are each composed of 5–9 broadly ovate to oblong-elliptic, shallowly lobed, irregularly spiny-toothed, white- to cream-margined, mid-green leaflets. In summer, mature plants produce brown-budded, 5-petalled, star-shaped, yellow-green flowers in large, loose, terminal, umbel-like panicles, to 50cm (20in) long, followed by spherical, black-purple fruit, 5mm (¼in). ↕ 4–6m (12–20ft), ↔ 1–2.5m (3–8ft). E. Malaysia, W. Pacific. ⊛ (min. 16°C/61°F). **'Laciniata'** has pendent, 2-pinnate leaves composed of lance-shaped leaflets with white margins. **'Victoriae'** ▣ (Lace aralia) is compact, with much-dissected, fern-like leaves; each leaflet irregularly toothed and white-margined; ↕ 1.5m (5ft), ↔ 80cm (32in).

Polyscias guilfoylei 'Victoriae'

POLYSTICHUM

Holly fern, Shield fern

DRYOPTERIDACEAE

Genus of nearly 200 species of usually evergreen, terrestrial ferns found in a range of habitats from alpine cliffs to tropical forests worldwide. They are cultivated for their often lance-shaped, pinnate to 3-pinnate fronds, which arise from erect or short-creeping rhizomes, usually in shapely, "shuttlecock" crowns. The pinnae are holly-like, and sometimes lobed, each lobe ending in a sharp point or bristle. Sori are borne on the undersides of the fronds, each usually protected by a rounded indusium. Grow shield ferns in a rock garden, fernery, or well-drained border. In frost-prone areas, grow tender species in a cool, temperate, or warm greenhouse.

- **HARDINESS** Fully hardy to frost tender.
- **CULTIVATION** Grow in fertile, humus-rich, well-drained soil in deep or partial shade. Remove dead fronds before new ones unfurl. Protect the crowns from excessive winter wet.
- **PROPAGATION** Sow spores at 15–16°C (59–61°F) when ripe. Divide rhizomes in spring. Detach fronds bearing bulbils in autumn. See also p.51.
- **PESTS AND DISEASES** Susceptible to the fungal disease *Taphrina wettsteiniana.*

P. acrostichoides. Terrestrial, evergreen fern producing a shuttlecock of narrowly lance-shaped, pinnate, dark green fronds, 60cm (24in) long, with small, holly-like pinnae. Fertile fronds narrow abruptly towards tips where sori occur. ↕45cm (18in), ↔90cm (36in). N.E. North America. ❄❄❄

P. aculeatum (Hard shield fern, Prickly shield fern). Terrestrial, evergreen fern bearing narrowly lance-shaped, pinnate or 2-pinnate, often glossy, dark green fronds, 60cm (24in) long or more, forming shuttlecocks. Pinnae are oblong and pinnate or pinnatifid, with spiny-toothed lobes that are unstalked and acutely angled at the point of attachment to the midribs. Reliably evergreen. ↕60cm (24in), ↔90cm (36in). N.W. and C. Europe. ❄❄❄. **'Pulcherrimum'** see *P. setiferum* 'Pulcherrimum Bevis'.

P. munitum ▣ (Sword fern). Terrestrial, evergreen fern that bears narrowly lance-shaped, leathery, pinnate, dark green fronds, 90cm (36in) long or more, forming shuttlecocks. Pinnae are linear and spiny-toothed. Larger than *P. acrostichoides*, its fertile fronds do not narrow at the tips. ↕90cm (36in), rarely to 1.5m (5ft), ↔1.2m (4ft). N.W. North America. ❄❄❄

P. polyblepharum (Japanese tassel fern). Terrestrial, evergreen fern bearing shuttlecocks of spreading, lance-shaped, 2-pinnate, shiny, dark green fronds, 30–80cm (12–32in) long, covered with golden hairs when they unfurl. Pinnae lobes are oblong-ovate and have spiny-toothed margins. ↕60–80cm (24–32in), ↔90cm (36in). South Korea, Japan. ❄❄❄

P. rigens. Terrestrial, evergreen fern producing shuttlecocks of narrowly ovate-oblong, 2-pinnate, leathery, harsh-textured, dull green fronds, 30–45cm (12–18in) long. Broad, lance-shaped pinnae are divided into ovate, spiny-

Polystichum munitum

Polystichum setiferum Plumosodivisilobum Group

Polystichum setiferum 'Pulcherrimum Bevis'

toothed lobes. In spring, fronds are yellowish green. ↕40cm (16in), ↔60cm (24in). Japan. ❄❄❄

P. setiferum (Soft shield fern). Terrestrial, evergreen fern with soft, lance-shaped, 2-pinnate, dark green fronds, 30–120cm (12–48in) long, arranged in shuttlecocks. Pinnae lobes are ovate, bristle-toothed, stalked, and obtusely angled at the point of attachment to the midribs. ↕1.2m (4ft), ↔90cm (36in). Europe. ❄❄❄. Ferns of **Divisilobum Group** ▣ produce usually spreading, 3-pinnate fronds, comprising narrowed and leathery segments; bulbils often form along the frond midribs. ↕↔50–70cm (20–28in) or more. **'Dahlem'** bears almost erect fronds; ↕75cm (30in), ↔45cm (18in). **'Herrenhausen'** has broader, spreading fronds; ↕50cm (20in). **'Iveryanum'** has fronds crested at the tips; ↕50cm (20in), ↔60cm (24in). **Multilobum Group** ferns produce 3-pinnate fronds similar to those of the Divisilobum Group, but the frond segments are not narrowed or leathery; ↕↔60–80cm (24–32in). **Plumosodivisilobum Group** ▣ ferns bear fronds, 4-pinnate at the base, with segments narrowed towards the frond tips; lower pinnae often overlap. **'Plumosomultilobum'** has overlapping, very leafy pinnae, which give it a moss-like appearance; similar to the Plumosodivisilobum Group, but the segments are not narrowed. **'Plumosum Bevis'** see 'Pulcherrimum Bevis'. **'Pulcherrimum Bevis'** ▣ syn. 'Plumosum Bevis', *P. aculeatum* 'Pulcherrimum', has elongated pinnae and segments that sweep gracefully towards the tips. Only very rarely fertile; ↕↔60–80cm (24–32in).

P. tsussimense (Korean rock fern). Terrestrial, evergreen fern producing shuttlecocks of broadly lance-shaped, 2-pinnate, dark green fronds, 20–40cm (8–16in) long. The narrow, ovate to oblong-ovate, spiny-toothed pinnae are sharply and abruptly pointed. ↕↔40cm (16in). East Asia. ❄❄❄

Polystichum setiferum Divisilobum Group

▷**Pomegranate** see *Punica, P. granatum*
Wild see *Burchellia bubalina*

PONCIRUS syn. AEGLE

RUTACEAE

Genus of one species of spiny, deciduous shrub or small tree from woodland in China and Korea. It produces alternate, 3-palmate, dark green leaves, and is cultivated for its 5-petalled, fragrant white flowers and orange-like fruit. Grow in a shrub border or against a sunny wall, or as a very thick, thorny hedge. It is sometimes used as a rootstock for *Citrus* cultivars.

- **HARDINESS** Fully hardy.
- **CULTIVATION** Grow in fertile, well-drained soil in full sun, with shelter from cold, dry winds. Pruning group 1; trim hedges after flowering or fruiting.
- **PROPAGATION** Sow seed in containers in a cold frame in autumn. Take semi-ripe cuttings with bottom heat in summer.
- **PESTS AND DISEASES** Trouble free.

P. trifoliata 🗨 (Japanese bitter orange). Rounded, bushy, deciduous shrub or tree with rigid green shoots armed with very sharp spines. Alternate, 3-palmate leaves, 2.5–6cm (1–2½in) long, comprise 3 obovate, dark green leaflets, to 5cm (2in) long, turning yellow in autumn. Solitary, cup-shaped then saucer-shaped, fragrant white flowers, 5cm (2in) across, are borne in late spring and early summer, often again in autumn, followed by orange-like, inedible, green then orange fruit, 4cm (1½in) across. ↕↔5m (15ft). N. China, Korea. ❄❄❄

▷**Pondweed** see *Elodea*
Canadian see *Elodea canadensis*
Cape see *Aponogeton distachyos*
Curled see *Potamogeton crispus*

P

PONGAMIA

LEGUMINOSAE/PAPILIONACEAE

Genus of one species of wide-spreading, deciduous or semi-evergreen tree from seashores and riverbanks in Malaysia, Indonesia, N. Australia, and Pacific islands. It has pinnate leaves and axillary racemes of pea-like flowers. In frost-prone climates, grow in a warm greenhouse for its foliage. In tropical areas, it is a fine shade tree, suitable for coasts.

- **HARDINESS** Frost tender.
- **CULTIVATION** Under glass, grow in loam-based potting compost (JI No.3) with added sharp sand, in full light. In growth, water moderately and apply a balanced liquid fertilizer monthly; water sparingly in winter. Outdoors, grow in fertile, well-drained soil in full sun. Pruning group 1; may need restrictive pruning under glass.
- **PROPAGATION** Sow seed at 18–24°C (64–75°F) in spring. Root semi-ripe cuttings in summer with bottom heat.
- **PESTS AND DISEASES** Whiteflies may be a problem under glass.

P. pinnata ♀ (Karum oil tree, Poona oil tree). Many-branched, spreading, deciduous or semi-evergreen tree with a domed head and a usually short trunk. The pinnate, glossy, bright green leaves, 15–30cm (6–12in) long, comprise 5–9 ovate to elliptic leaflets, emerging pink-bronze. In summer and autumn, produces racemes, 13cm (5in) long, of pea-like, mauve-pink or cream flowers, strongly scented when crushed; they have rounded, standard petals, to 1.5cm (½in) across, often incurled. ↕ 20–25m (70–80ft), ↔ 15–25m (50–80ft). Malaysia, Indonesia, N. Australia, Pacific islands. ❀ (min. 16°C/61°F)

PONTEDERIA

Pickerel weed

PONTEDERIACEAE

P

Genus of 5 species of marginal aquatic perennials from freshwater marshes and swamp ditches in North, Central, and South America. They are grown for their neat habit, distinctive foliage, and highly coloured flowers. The thick rootstock produces clumps of often linear or lance-shaped leaves. Terminal spikes of tubular, 2-lipped, usually blue flowers are borne in summer and early autumn. Grow at the margins of a pond, or in a large, water-filled tub on a sunny, sheltered patio. Flower spikes may not open fully in cool, wet summers.

Pontederia cordata

- **HARDINESS** Fully hardy to frost hardy.
- **CULTIVATION** Grow in aquatic planting baskets of fertile, loamy soil at the margins of a pool; grow in no more than 10–12cm (4–5in) of water, in full sun. See also pp.52–53.
- **PROPAGATION** Sow seed in containers outdoors as soon as ripe. Divide in late spring when growth starts.
- **PESTS AND DISEASES** Trouble free.

P. cordata ■ (Pickerel weed). Marginal aquatic perennial with erect, lance-shaped, triangular to ovate, glossy, emergent, floating, or submerged leaves, 20cm (8in) wide, with heart-shaped bases, borne on stalks to 25cm (10in) long. In late summer, produces tubular blue flowers in closely packed spikes, 2–16cm (¾–6in) long, on flower-stalks to 35cm (14in) tall. ↕ 0.9–1.3m (3–4½ft), ↔ 60–75cm (24–30in). E. North America to Caribbean. ❄❄❄. **var. *lancifolia***, syn. *P. lanceolata*, has narrower leaves, to 12–20cm (5–8in) long, on stalks 60–70cm (24–28in) long. ↕ 1.2–1.5m (4–5ft), ↔ 1m (3ft). E. and S. USA, South America. ❄❄ (borderline)
P. lanceolata see *P. cordata* var. *lancifolia*.

▷**Ponytail** see *Beaucarnea recurvata*
▷**Poplar** see *Populus*
Balsam see *P. balsamifera*
Berlin see *P.* x *berolinensis*
Black see *P. nigra*
Canadian see *P.* x *canadensis*
Chinese necklace see *P. lasiocarpa*
Grey see *P.* x *canescens*
Lombardy see *P. nigra* var. *italica*
Necklace see *P. deltoides*
Western balsam see *P. trichocarpa*
White see *P. alba*
▷**Poppy** see *Papaver*
Alpine see *Papaver alpinum*
Arctic see *Papaver croceum*
California see *Eschscholzia, E. californica*
Californian see *Platystemon, P. californicus*
Celandine see *Stylophorum diphyllum*
Corn see *Papaver rhoeas*
Field see *Papaver rhoeas*
Flanders see *Papaver rhoeas*
Harebell see *Meconopsis quintuplinervia*
Himalayan blue see *Meconopsis betonicifolia, M. grandis*
Horned see *Glaucium*
Icelandic see *Papaver croceum*
Long-headed see *Papaver dubium*
Matilija see *Romneya*
Mexican tulip see *Hunnemannia fumariifolia*
Opium see *Papaver somniferum*
Oriental see *Papaver orientale*
Plume see *Macleaya, M. cordata*
Prickly see *Argemone, A. mexicana*
Red horned see *Glaucium corniculatum*
Snow see *Eomecon*
Tibetan blue see *Meconopsis betonicifolia*
Tree see *Dendromecon, Romneya*
Water see *Hydrocleys nymphoides*
Welsh see *Meconopsis cambrica*
Yellow horned see *Glaucium flavum*
▷**Poppy mallow** see *Callirhoe*
Prairie see *C. involucrata*

POPULUS

Aspen, Cottonwood, Poplar

SALICACEAE

Genus of about 35 species of usually dioecious, mainly deciduous trees found in woodland, valley bottoms, riverbanks, and swampland in N. temperate regions. They are cultivated for their very rapid growth as specimen trees, and for their alternate, ovate, triangular-ovate, or diamond-shaped leaves, often aromatic in bud and when unfolding. They have tiny flowers borne in catkins, generally 5–15cm (2–6in) long, mostly in late winter or spring, before the leaves. Male and female flowers are usually borne on separate trees, the females producing copious fluffy white seeds. Most poplars are useful as windbreaks; *P. alba* and *P.* x *canescens* will thrive in coastal sites. The vigorous root systems may damage drains and foundations, particularly on clay soil, so avoid growing poplars within 40m (130ft) of a building.

- **HARDINESS** Fully hardy.
- **CULTIVATION** Tolerant of any, except constantly waterlogged soil, although best in deep, fertile, moist but well-drained soil in full sun. *P. alba* and *P.* x *canescens* tolerate dry conditions. Pruning group 1.
- **PROPAGATION** Take hardwood cuttings in winter. Remove suckers in autumn or late winter.
- **PESTS AND DISEASES** Susceptible to bacterial canker, various fungal diseases (such as honey fungus, rust, and silver leaf), and a variety of insects (such as beetles) and caterpillars, which may eat the foliage or bore into the bark.

P. alba ■♀ (Abele, White poplar). Spreading, deciduous tree with white-hairy young shoots and broadly ovate to almost rounded, wavy-margined to maple-like, deeply 5-lobed leaves, to 10cm (4in) long, dark green above, thickly white-hairy beneath, and turning yellow in autumn. In early spring, bears pendent red male catkins, 7cm (3in) long, or green females, 5cm (2in) long. ↕ 20–40m (70–130ft), ↔ 15m (50ft). N. Africa, Turkey, C. and S. former USSR (including S.W. Siberia). ❄❄❄. **f. *pyramidalis*** ■▯ is pyramidal in shape; ↔ 5m (15ft). **'Raket'** ■▯ syn. 'Rocket', is narrowly conical; ↔ 8m (25ft). **'Richardii'** has leaves that are golden yellow above; ↕ 15m (50ft), ↔ 12m (40ft). **'Rocket'** see 'Raket'.

Populus alba

Populus alba f. *pyramidalis*

P. balsamifera ▯ (Balsam poplar, Tacamahac). Fast-growing, columnar, deciduous tree producing smooth, hairless shoots, balsam-scented buds, and ovate, glossy leaves, to 12cm (5in) long, dark green above, whitish green beneath. Pendent green catkins, the males to 5cm (2in) long, the females to 7cm (3in) long, are produced in early spring. ↕ 30m (100ft), ↔ 8m (25ft). North America. ❄❄❄. **var. *michauxii*** produces downy shoots; N. USA.
***P.* 'Balsam Spire'** ▯ syn. *P.* 'TT 32'. Very fast-growing, narrowly columnar, deciduous tree bearing ovate leaves, 5–12cm (2–5in) long, which are obtuse at the rounded bases and hairy beneath. Cylindrical green female catkins,

Populus alba 'Raket'

Populus x *canadensis* 'Robusta'

10–14cm (4–5½in) long, are produced from pleasantly aromatic buds in late winter or spring. ↕ 30m (100ft), ↔ 10m (30ft). ❄❄❄.

P.* x *berolinensis (*P. laurifolia* x *P. nigra* var. *italica*) (Berlin poplar). Columnar to broadly columnar, deciduous tree bearing upright branches and ovate, tapered leaves, to 12cm (5in) long, bright green above, whitish green beneath. Red male catkins, 7cm (3in) long, are borne in early spring. ↕ 30m (100ft), ↔ 8m (25ft). Garden origin. ❄❄❄

P.* x *canadensis (*P. deltoides* x *P. nigra*) (Canadian poplar). Fast-growing, conical to columnar, deciduous tree bearing triangular to ovate, scalloped, tapered, glossy, bright green leaves, to 10cm (4in) long, turning yellow in autumn. Red male or green female catkins, each to 10cm (4in) long, are produced in early spring. ↕ 30m (100ft), ↔ 12m (40ft). Garden origin. ❄❄❄. **'Aurea'** syn. 'Serotina Aurea', is columnar and male, producing bronze young leaves in late spring, later turning golden yellow; ↕ 25m (80ft), ↔ 10m (30ft). **'Robusta'** ▣ is narrowly conical and male, producing bronze-red young leaves in mid-spring. **'Serotina'** is similar to 'Aurea', but is broadly domed, with spreading branches, and produces grey-green foliage in summer. **'Serotina Aurea'** see 'Aurea'. **'Serotina de Selys'** syn. 'Serotina Erecta', has an upright habit, with pale green young leaves and red male catkins. **'Serotina Erecta'** see 'Serotina de Selys'.

***P.* x *candicans* of gardens** see *P.* x *jackii*.

P.* x *canescens ▣ (*P. alba* x *P. tremula*) (Grey poplar). Broadly columnar to spreading, deciduous tree bearing glossy, dark green leaves; these may be broadly ovate, grey-woolly beneath, and to 8cm (3in) long, or rounded, almost hairless, and to 6cm (2½in) long. Red male catkins, to 10cm (4in) long, are borne in early spring. Green catkins, 2–10cm (¾–4in) long, are borne on female trees, which are rarely seen. ↕ to 30m (100ft), rarely to 50m (160ft), ↔ 15m (50ft). Europe. ❄❄❄

P. deltoides ▣ (Eastern cottonwood, Necklace poplar). Fast-growing, spreading, deciduous tree bearing oval to triangular, glossy, bright green leaves, to 12cm (5in) long, strongly balsam-scented when young. Red male or green female catkins, each to 10cm (4in) long, are produced in early spring. ↕ 30m (100ft), ↔ 20m (70ft). E. North America. ❄❄❄. **'Siouxland'** is rust-resistant and male.

P. fremontii Fast-growing, round-headed, deciduous tree with spreading branches and glossy, yellow-green, broadly triangular leaves, to 8cm (3in) long, which turn yellow in autumn. Pendent red male or green female catkins, both to 10cm (4in) long, open in early spring. ↕ 25m (80ft), ↔ 15m (50ft). W. USA. ❄❄❄

P. glauca syn. *P. jacquemontii* var. *glauca*. Fast-growing, broadly conical, deciduous tree bearing broadly ovate, blue-green leaves, to 17cm (7in) long, on red leaf-stalks marked with darker red veins. The leaves emerge bronze in early spring, and turn yellow in autumn. Pendent catkins are produced in late spring, the red males to 12cm (5in), the green females to 15cm (6in) long. ↕ 20m (70ft), ↔ 10m (30ft). E. Himalayas. ❄❄❄

P. grandidentata (Bigtooth aspen). Spreading, deciduous tree with grey-hairy young shoots and ovate leaves, to 12cm (5in) long, grey-woolly at first, dark green above and pale green beneath. Red male catkins, to 6cm (2½in) long, or green females, to 10cm (4in) long, are produced in early spring. ↕ 20m (70ft), ↔ 12m (40ft). E. North America. ❄❄❄

P.* x *jackii (*P. balsamifera* x *P. deltoides*), syn. *P.* x *candicans* of gardens (Balm of Gilead). Broadly columnar, deciduous tree bearing broadly ovate leaves, to 15cm (6in) long, heart-shaped at the bases, dark green above, whitish green beneath. Green female catkins, to 16cm (6in) long, are produced in early spring. ↕ 25m (80ft), ↔ 15m (50ft). Garden origin. ❄❄❄. **'Aurora'** ▣ has leaves conspicuously marked white, cream, and pink; ↕ 15m (50ft), ↔ 6m (20ft).

P. jacquemontii* var. *glauca see *P. glauca*.

P. lasiocarpa (Chinese necklace poplar). Broadly conical, later round-headed, deciduous tree bearing stout shoots, hairy when young, and large, heart-shaped, tapered, dark green leaves, to 30cm (12in) long, produced on red stalks. Yellow-green catkins, to 10cm (4in) long, usually containing both male and female flowers, are produced in mid-spring. ↕ 20m (70ft), ↔ 12m (40ft). C. China. ❄❄❄

P. maximowiczii ▣ Fast-growing, conical, deciduous tree with hairy young shoots and ovate-elliptic leaves, to 12cm (5in) long, bright green above, whitish green beneath, with green veins. Red male catkins, to 10cm (4in) long, or green females, to 15cm (6in), are borne in early spring. ↕ to 30m (100ft) or more, ↔ 10m (30ft). N.E. Asia. ❄❄❄

Populus x *jackii* 'Aurora'

Populus x *canescens*

Populus deltoides (inset: leaf detail)

Populus maximowiczii

P

Populus nigra var. *italica*

P. nigra ♀ (Black poplar). Fast-growing, spreading, deciduous tree with dark bark and triangular to ovate, tapered, glossy, dark green leaves, to 10cm (4in) long, bronze when young, turning yellow in autumn. Red male or green female catkins, both 5cm (2in) long, are produced in early and mid-spring. ↕35m (120ft), ↔20m (70ft). Europe, N. Africa, C. Asia (including Kazakhstan), Russia (Siberia). ❄❄❄. **'Afghanica'** see 'Thevestina'. **var. *italica*** ▣ (Lombardy poplar) is male and narrowly columnar; ↕30m (100ft), ↔5m (15ft). **'Thevestina'** syn. 'Afghanica', is narrowly columnar and female, with striking white bark; ↕30m (100ft), ↔5m (15ft).
P. simonii Columnar, deciduous tree with diamond-shaped-ovate to elliptic,

Populus tremula 'Pendula'

Populus trichocarpa

tapered, dark green leaves, to 12cm (5in) long, emerging yellow-green and balsam-scented very early in spring. Red male or green female catkins, both to 3cm (1¼in) long, are produced in early spring. Susceptible to damage by late frosts. ↕12m (40ft), ↔6m (20ft). N. and W. China. ❄❄❄. **'Fastigiata'** is narrowly upright; ↔3m (10ft).
P. szechuanica Broadly columnar, deciduous tree with ovate-oblong to broadly lance-shaped, smooth, dark green leaves, to 30cm (12in) long, whitish green beneath, bronze when young. Red male catkins, to 10cm (4in) long, or green females, to 15cm (6in), are borne in mid-spring. ↕to 40m (130ft), ↔10m (30ft). W. China. ❄❄❄. **var. *tibetica*** has leaves that are downy beneath, with dark red veins and leaf-stalks.
P. tremula (Common aspen). Vigorous, spreading, deciduous tree or shrub with flat-stalked, rounded to ovate, coarsely toothed, dark green leaves, to 8cm (3in) long, bronze when young, turning yellow in autumn; they tremble and rattle in the breeze. Grey-red male or green female catkins, both to 7cm (3in) long, are produced in early spring. ↕20m (70ft), ↔10m (30ft). Temperate Europe and Asia to China and Japan. ❄❄❄. **'Pendula'** ▣ (Weeping aspen) has long, pendent branches; ↕6m (20ft), ↔8m (25ft).
P. tremuloides (American aspen, Quaking aspen). Vigorous, spreading, deciduous tree with flat-stalked, rounded to ovate, finely toothed, glossy, dark green leaves, to 6cm (2½in) long, bronze when young, turning yellow in autumn; light winds cause quivering and rattling of the leaves. Grey-red male or green female catkins, both to 6cm (2½in) long, are produced in early spring. ↕15m (50ft), ↔10m (30ft). W. North America. ❄❄❄
P. trichocarpa ▣ (Black cottonwood, Western balsam poplar). Fast-growing, conical, deciduous tree with ovate, glossy leaves, to 20cm (8in) long, dark green above, white beneath, turning yellow in autumn, and strongly balsam-scented when young. Red male catkins, 7cm (3in) long, or green females, to 15cm (6in) long, are borne in mid-spring. ↕30m (100ft) or more, ↔10m (30ft). W. North America. ❄❄❄
***P.* 'TT 32'** see *P.* 'Balsam Spire'.

PORANA

CONVOLVULACEAE

Genus of about 20 species of evergreen, twining climbers or shrubs, closely related to *Ipomoea*, from open or dense woodland in tropical Africa, Asia, and Australia. They have alternate, usually heart-shaped leaves, and are grown for their small, bell- to funnel-shaped, white, blue, or purple flowers, borne singly or in terminal panicles or cymes. Where temperatures drop below 7°C (45°F), grow in a cool or temperate greenhouse. In warmer regions, they are suitable for training over a pergola or arch, or through a shrub.

- **HARDINESS** Frost tender.
- **CULTIVATION** Under glass, grow in loam-based potting compost (JI No.2) in full light. During the growing season, water moderately and apply a balanced liquid fertilizer every 4 weeks; water sparingly in winter, after flowering. Outdoors, grow in fertile, moist but well-drained soil in full sun. Support the climbing stems. Pruning group 11, in early spring.
- **PROPAGATION** Soak seed and sow at 18°C (64°F) in spring. Root greenwood cuttings in early summer, or semi-ripe cuttings with bottom heat in late summer.
- **PESTS AND DISEASES** Prone to red spider mites and whiteflies under glass.

P. paniculata (Bridal bouquet, Snow in the jungle, White corallita). Strong-growing, twining climber bearing slender-pointed, heart-shaped, mid-green leaves, 8–15cm (3–6in) long, smooth above, white-powdery beneath when young. Produces large, terminal panicles, to 30cm (12in) long, of many funnel-shaped, elder-scented white flowers, 8mm (⅜in) across, from summer to early winter. ↕to 9m (28ft). N. India, N. Burma. ❀ (min. 7°C/45°F)

PORTEA

BROMELIACEAE

Genus of about 7 species of rosette-forming, evergreen, terrestrial perennials (bromeliads) from Brazil, where they usually grow in coastal shrubland and shaded forest, to 600m (2,000ft) high. They are cultivated for their foliage and flowers: the strap-shaped, spiny-margined, fairly stiff leaves are mostly scaly, especially beneath; the tubular, blue or violet flowers are borne in cylindrical heads on long, slender flower-stalks. Where temperatures fall below 15°C (59°F), grow in an indoor garden; in warmer climates, they are suitable for growing outdoors in a desert garden.

- **HARDINESS** Frost tender.
- **CULTIVATION** Under glass, grow in terrestrial bromeliad compost in full light, with shade from hot sun. Water moderately at all times; overwatering often causes root rot. During the growing season, apply a low-nitrogen fertilizer every 6–8 weeks. Outdoors, grow in humus-rich, leafy, loamy soil in full sun, with some midday shade. See also p.47.
- **PROPAGATION** Sow seed at 19–24°C (66–75°F) in spring or summer. Remove offsets in late spring.
- **PESTS AND DISEASES** Susceptible to beetles when grown outdoors. Scale insects sometimes attack new growth.

Portea petropolitana

P. petropolitana ▣ Terrestrial perennial bearing a rosette of strap-shaped, minutely scaly, mid- to dark green leaves, to 80cm (32in) long, with black marginal spines. Large-toothed leaf sheaths have dark brown scales. In summer, the stout, reddish brown scapes produce branched, pendent, compound, cylindrical inflorescences, to 40cm (16in) long, with rose-red bracts. The tubular flowers, to 3cm (1¼in) long, have blue-violet petals and red ovaries. ↕to 1m (3ft), ↔40cm (16in). E. Brazil. ❀ (min. 15°C/59°F). **var. *extensa*** has more open inflorescences with lilac-blue flowers and purple-tipped green ovaries, borne on arching, coral-red scapes.

▷ **Portia tree** see *Thespesia populnea*

PORTULACA

Purslane, Rose moss

PORTULACACEAE

Genus of 100 semi-succulent, mainly erect to trailing annuals, with a few perennials, found in dry, sandy soils in warm-temperate and tropical regions. They have small, fleshy, alternate to sometimes opposite, flat to cylindrical, almost moss-like leaves, which are very variable in colour, often white, green, or red. They are grown for their showy, cup-shaped, rose-like, 4- to 7-petalled, scarlet, carmine, purple, yellow, pink, apricot, or white flowers, which usually have a leafy rosette of foliage below each flowerhead; flowering is best in dry summers. Grow as annuals in a sunny,

Portulaca grandiflora Sundance Hybrids

dry border or bank, or in a window-box or other container.

• **HARDINESS** Half hardy to frost tender.
• **CULTIVATION** Outdoors, grow in poor, sandy, well-drained soil in full sun.
• **PROPAGATION** Sow seed at 13–18°C (55–64°F) in mid-spring.
• **PESTS AND DISEASES** Prone to aphids. Seedlings are susceptible to damping-off.

P. grandiflora (Rose moss, Sun plant). Spreading, red-stemmed annual with clusters of cylindrical, fleshy, bright green leaves, to 2.5cm (1in) long. In summer, produces single or double, mid- to dark green, satin-textured, rose-pink, red, yellow, or white flowers, to 2.5cm (1in) or more across, sometimes striped and flecked in a contrasting colour. ↕ 10–20cm (4–8in), ↔ 15cm (6in). Brazil, Argentina, Uruguay. ✲. **Minilaca Hybrids** have a neat and compact habit, with large, double flowers, to 5cm (2in) across, in scarlet-red, rose-pink, apricot-pink, creamy yellow, and golden yellow; they are good container plants; ↕ 10–15cm (4–6in). **Sundance Hybrids** ■ are semi-trailing, with large, semi-double or double flowers, to 5cm (2in) across, in a broad range of bright colours; ↕ to 15cm (6in). **Sundial Series** cultivars were bred for longer flowering in poor conditions and cooler climates; they have double flowers in a broad colour range, including an unusual bicolour: white, striped and flecked with lavender-blue.

PORTULACARIA

PORTULACACEAE

Genus of 1–3 species (often considered one variable species) of bushy, perennial, succulent shrubs from semi-arid, hilly lowland in Namibia, South Africa, Swaziland, and Mozambique. Grown mainly for their foliage, they have fleshy stems, leaves, and branches, and inconspicuous, cup- or saucer-shaped flowers in cymes or short racemes. In areas where temperatures fall below 10°C (50°F), grow in a warm greenhouse; in warm, dry climates, use in a shrub border or desert garden.

• **HARDINESS** Frost tender.
• **CULTIVATION** Under glass, grow in loam-based potting compost (JI No.2) with added grit, in full light or bright filtered light. From early spring to early autumn, water freely and apply a low-nitrogen liquid fertilizer every 6–8 weeks; keep almost completely dry at

Portulacaria afra 'Foliis Variegatis'

other times. Outdoors, grow in moderately fertile, sharply drained soil in full sun or partial shade. Pruning group 1. See also pp.48–49.

• **PROPAGATION** Root cuttings of stem sections in spring with bottom heat.
• **PESTS AND DISEASES** Susceptible to scale insects.

P. afra. Bushy, succulent shrub with thick, grey-barked stems and jointed, short, twig-like, projecting branches. The obovate, sometimes pointed, opposite, glossy green leaves, to 2cm (¾in) long, are flat above, convex below. Inconspicuous, saucer-shaped, pale pink flowers, 2mm (1/16in) across, are produced in summer. ↕ 2–3m (6–10ft), ↔ 1.5m (5ft). Namibia, South Africa (Northern Cape, Eastern Cape, Limpopo, Mpumalanga), Swaziland, Mozambique. ❀ (min. 10°C/50°F). **'Foliis Variegatis'** ■ syn. 'Variegatus', has yellow-mottled leaves.

POSOQUERIA

RUBIACEAE

Genus of 12–16 species of upright to rounded, evergreen shrubs and trees occurring in habitats from forest to moist ravines in tropical regions of America. They are cultivated for their simple, leathery leaves, produced in opposite pairs, and corymbs of tubular, pendent, salverform, fragrant, white, pink, or red flowers. The flowers each have 5 spreading petal lobes, and are borne in terminal corymbs; they are followed by yellow berries. In areas where temperatures fall below 5–7°C (41–45°F), grow in a cool or temperate greenhouse; elsewhere they are suitable for a shrub border, or as specimens.

• **HARDINESS** Frost tender.
• **CULTIVATION** Under glass, grow in a loam-based potting compost (JI No.2) with added grit, in full light or bright filtered light. From early spring to early autumn, water freely and apply a balanced liquid fertilizer every 6–8 weeks; keep just moist at other times. Outdoors, grow in moderately fertile, sharply drained soil in full sun or partial shade. Pruning group 8; plants under glass need restrictive pruning.
• **PROPAGATION** Take greenwood cuttings in early summer, or semi-ripe cuttings in mid- or late summer.
• **PESTS AND DISEASES** Susceptible to red spider mites, whiteflies, and mealybugs under glass.

P. latifolia ♢ Moderately bushy shrub, or sometimes small, broadly upright tree if unpruned, bearing ovate or oblong to elliptic, prominently veined, rich green leaves, 15–25cm (6–10in) long. In spring, produces dense corymbs of few to many slender-tubed, fragrant white flowers, with long, slender tubes to 15cm (6in) long, 6cm (2½in) across; they are followed by yellow berries, 4–8cm (1½–3in) across. ↕ 2–14m (6–45ft), ↔ 2–6m (6–20ft). Mexico to Brazil, West Indies. ❀ (min. 7°C/45°F)

▷ **Possum haw** see *Ilex decidua, Viburnum acerifolium*

POTAMOGETON

POTAMOGETONACEAE

Genus of 80–100 species of marginal to deep-water aquatic perennials, distributed almost throughout the world, flourishing in freshwater ditches, ponds, canals, and waterways. They are cultivated as oxygenators in water gardens and for their decorative effect in aquariums. The branched, creeping rhizomes spread rapidly in muddy pool bottoms, where they support an interwoven, mat-like network of translucent, linear to lance-shaped submerged leaves, and leathery, opaque, lance-shaped to rounded floating leaves. Inconspicuous flowers are borne in fleshy spikes just above the water.

Grow the hardy species as oxygenators in outdoor pools; *P. crispus* tolerates polluted water better than any other oxygenator, and can also be used in cold-water aquariums. In frost-prone climates, grow tender species in cool-water aquariums; in warmer climates, they are suitable for outdoor pools.

• **HARDINESS** Fully hardy to frost tender.
• **CULTIVATION** In an aquarium, grow in pots of an inert medium in full light. Feed with sachets of proprietary aquarium plant fertilizer. In an outdoor pool, grow in baskets of sandy loam, or root in a muddy pond bottom at a depth of 15–60cm (6–24in), ideally in full sun, or in partial shade. Cut back frequently and thin to keep in check. Submerged leaves may become encrusted with deposits of lime. See also pp.52–53.
• **PROPAGATION** Take cuttings of stem sections in late spring or early summer; the foliage becomes brittle from midsummer onwards.
• **PESTS AND DISEASES** Trouble free.

P. crispus (Curled pondweed). Marginal to deep-water aquatic perennial with cylindrical, branching stems, to 4m (12ft) long, bearing narrowly oblong, almost translucent submerged leaves, about 4cm (1½in) long, wavy-margined when mature, and stalked, pointed, leathery floating leaves. Spikes of inconspicuous, crimson and creamy white flowers, 0.5–1.5cm (¼–½in) across, are produced just above the water surface in summer. ↔ indefinite. Europe, Asia to Australasia. ✲✲✲

▷ **Potato bush, Blue** see *Solanum rantonnei*
▷ **Potato tree, Chilean** see *Solanum crispum*
▷ **Potato vine** see *Solanum laxum, S. wendlandii*

POTENTILLA *syn.* COMARUM

Cinquefoil

ROSACEAE

Genus of about 500 species of shrubs, herbaceous perennials, and a few annuals and biennials, found throughout the N. hemisphere, in habitats ranging from meadows to mountain screes. They are cultivated for their attractive, usually 5-petalled, saucer- to cup-shaped, occasionally star-shaped, white, yellow, orange, pink, or red flowers; they are produced over long periods from spring to autumn, either singly or, more often, in cymes or terminal panicles. The alternate leaves may be pinnate or 3- to 7-palmate, and are often strongly veined and wrinkled. The shrubby potentillas, mainly derived from *P. fruticosa*, are excellent, long-flowering plants for a mixed or shrub border and for low hedges. Many species are also suitable for rock gardens, raised beds, or mixed borders. Most clump-forming hybrids, derived mainly from *P. atrosanguinea* and *P. nepalensis*, are valued for their single, semi-double, or double, mainly red or yellow flowers providing summer and autumn colour in herbaceous borders: they have strawberry-like, 5-palmate, mid- to dark green leaves, 5–10cm (2–4in) long, conspicuously veined and toothed.

• **HARDINESS** Fully hardy.
• **CULTIVATION** Grow in poor to moderately fertile, well-drained soil in full sun. Rock-garden species prefer poor, gritty, sharply drained soil. Pruning group 10 for shrubs, in early or mid-spring.
• **PROPAGATION** Sow seed in containers in a cold frame in autumn or spring. Divide perennials in autumn or spring. Take greenwood cuttings of shrubs in early summer.
• **PESTS AND DISEASES** Trouble free.

P. alba ■ Clump-forming perennial with spreading stems, bearing 5-palmate

Potentilla alba

POTENTILLA

Potentilla atrosanguinea

Potentilla aurea

Potentilla eriocarpa

Potentilla fruticosa 'Abbotswood'

Potentilla fruticosa 'Daydawn'

Potentilla fruticosa 'Elizabeth'

Potentilla fruticosa 'Farrer's White'

Potentilla fruticosa 'Friedrichsenii'

Potentilla fruticosa 'Manchu'

Potentilla fruticosa 'Primrose Beauty'

Potentilla fruticosa 'Princess'

Potentilla fruticosa 'Red Ace'

Potentilla fruticosa 'Sunset'

Potentilla fruticosa 'Vilmoriniana'

Potentilla 'Gloire de Nancy'

Potentilla megalantha

Potentilla nepalensis 'Miss Willmott'

Potentilla neumanniana 'Goldrausch'

Potentilla recta 'Warrenii'

Potentilla 'William Rollison'

Potentilla 'Yellow Queen'

leaves, with oblong to obovate-lance-shaped leaflets, 2–4cm (¾–1½in) long, light green above, silver-silky-hairy beneath. In late spring and early summer, bears loose cymes of flat, saucer-shaped white flowers, 2.5cm (1in) across. ↕ 8cm (3in), ↔ to 30cm (12in). C. and S. Europe. ❄❄❄

P. arbuscula see *P. fruticosa* var. *arbuscula*.

***P. arbuscula* of gardens** see *P. fruticosa* 'Elizabeth'.

P. atrosanguinea ■ (Himalayan cinquefoil). Clump-forming, hairy perennial bearing 3-palmate, dark green leaves, 5–8cm (2–3in) long, with ovate to elliptic or obovate, toothed leaflets, grey-silky-hairy to densely white-hairy. From summer to autumn, panicle-like cymes of saucer-shaped, yellow, orange, or pale to deep red flowers, 3cm (1¼in) across, are borne on erect, branching, wiry stems. ↕ 45–90cm (18–36in), ↔ 60cm (24in). Himalayas. ❄❄❄. **var. *argyrophylla*** has leaves with 3–5 leaflets, and yellow or yellow-orange flowers.

P. aurea ■ Mat-forming perennial with 3- or 5-palmate, glossy, mid-green leaves, to 3cm (1¼in) long, composed of oblong leaflets with sharply toothed, silver-hairy margins. Produces cymes of flat, saucer-shaped, deep golden yellow flowers, 2cm (¾in) across, with overlapping petals, from late spring to summer. ↕ 10cm (4in), ↔ 20cm (8in). Pyrenees, Alps. ❄❄❄

***P. davurica* var. *mandschurica* of gardens** see *P. fruticosa* 'Manchu'.

***P. davurica* 'Veitchii'** see *P. fruticosa* var. *veitchii*.

P. erecta, syn. *P. tormentilla* (Tormentil). Low-growing perennial with trailing, non-rooting stems and usually 3-palmate, rarely 4- or 5-palmate leaves consisting of wedge- to lance-shaped, toothed leaflets, to 2cm (¾in) long, dark green above, silver-silky-hairy beneath. Loose, terminal cymes of slender-stemmed, 4-petalled, saucer-shaped yellow flowers, to 1cm (½in) across, are borne from late spring to summer. Suitable for a wildflower garden. ↕ 10–30cm (4–12in), ↔ to 60cm (24in). Europe, Asia. ❄❄❄

P. eriocarpa ■ Carpet-forming perennial with 3-palmate, bright green leaves, to 3cm (1¼in) long, composed of wedge-shaped, toothed leaflets. Solitary or clustered, short-stalked, cup-shaped, deep yellow flowers, to 4cm (1½in) across, are produced in early summer. ↕ 8cm (3in), ↔ 30cm (12in). Pakistan to China, Himalayas. ❄❄❄

***P.* 'Etna'.** Clump-forming perennial with silver-tinted, deep green leaves, and panicles of semi-double, deep velvety red flowers, 2.5–3cm (1–1¼in) across, with yellow margins, borne in midsummer. ↕ to 45cm (18in), ↔ 60cm (24in). ❄❄❄

***P.* 'Flamenco'.** Clump-forming perennial with deep green leaves, and panicles of single, bright scarlet flowers, 2.5–3cm (1–1¼in) across, borne from late spring to midsummer. ↕ to 45cm (18in), ↔ 60cm (24in). ❄❄❄

P. fragiformis see *P. megalantha*.

P. fruticosa*.** Compact, bushy, deciduous shrub with pinnate leaves, to 4cm (1½in) long, composed of usually 5 or 7 narrowly oblong, dark green leaflets. Saucer-shaped yellow flowers, to 4cm (1½in) across, are borne singly or in cymes of 3 over a long period from late spring to mid-autumn. ↕ 1m (3ft), ↔ 1.5m (5ft). Europe, N. Asia, North America. ❄❄❄. **'Abbotswood'** ■ has white flowers and dark blue-green leaves; ↕ 75cm (30in), ↔ 1.2m (4ft). **var. *arbuscula, syn. *P. arbuscula*, has grey-green to silvery grey foliage and golden yellow flowers, 4.5cm (1¾in) across; ↔ 1.2m (4ft); Himalayas, China. **'Beesii'**, syn. 'Nana Argentea', is slow-growing and compact, with silver-silky-hairy leaves and golden yellow flowers, 2cm (¾in) across; ↕ 60cm (24in), ↔ 1.2m (4ft). **'Blink'** see 'Princess'. **'Coronation Triumph'** bears profuse bright yellow flowers. **'Daydawn'** ■ has creamy yellow flowers that are flushed orange-pink; ↔ 1.2m (4ft). **'Elizabeth'** ■ syn. *P. arbuscula* of gardens, bears bright yellow flowers, to 4.5cm (1¾in) across. **'Farrer's White'** ■ bears profuse white flowers, 2.5cm (1in) across. **'Friedrichsenii'** ■ is vigorous and upright, with grey-green leaves and pale yellow flowers, 3cm (1¼in) across; ↕ 1.5m (5ft), ↔ 1.2m (4ft). **'Gold Drop'**, syn. 'Goldkugel', *P. parvifolia* 'Gold Drop', is upright, with profuse golden flowers, 2.5cm (1in) across; ↕↔ 1.2m (4ft). **'Goldfinger'** has large, rich yellow flowers, to 5cm (2in) across. **'Goldkugel'** see 'Gold Drop'. **'Jackman's Variety'** has bright yellow flowers, 3–4cm (1¼–1½in) across. **'Katherine Dykes'** has profusely borne, canary-yellow flowers. **'Klondike'** produces bright green leaves and bright yellow flowers. **'Longacre Variety'** is low-growing and spreading, with bright yellow flowers, to 4cm (1½in) or more across; ↕ 60cm (24in). **'Maanelys'**, syn. 'Moonlight', *P.* 'Manelys', has soft yellow flowers, 3cm (1¼in) across, and grey-green foliage; ↕ 1.2m (4ft), ↔ 2m (6ft). **'Manchu'** ■ syn. *P. davurica* var. *mandschurica* of gardens, is dwarf and mound-forming, with dark pink shoots, silvery grey, silky-hairy leaves, and white flowers, 2.5cm (1in) across; ↕ 30cm (12in), ↔ 75cm (30in). **'Moonlight'** see 'Maanelys'. **'Nana Argentea'** see 'Beesii'. **'Pretty Polly'** has pale pink flowers, 2cm (¾in) across; ↕ 50cm (20in), ↔ 75cm (30in). **'Primrose Beauty'** ■ has grey-green leaves and pale primrose-yellow flowers, 3.5cm (1½in) across. **'Princess'** ■ syn. 'Blink', is low-growing, with pale pink flowers, 2.5cm (1in) across, fading to white in full sun; ↕ 60cm (24in), ↔ 1m (3ft). **'Red Ace'** ■ has bright vermilion flowers, yellow on the backs of the petals, fading in full sun. **'Royal Flush'** has rich pink flowers with yellow centres, fading to white in full sun; ↕ 45cm (18in), ↔ 75cm (30in). **'Snowbird'** has double white flowers. **'Sunset'** ■ has dark orange flowers, 3cm (1¼in) across, fading in full sun; ↔ 1m (3ft). **'Tangerine'** has yellow flowers, 3cm (1¼in) across, flushed pale orange-red; ↔ 1m (3ft). **'Tilford Cream'** is dense and spreading, with creamy white flowers, 3.5cm (1½in) across; ↕ 60cm (24in), ↔ 1m (3ft). **var. *veitchii***, syn. *P. davurica* 'Veitchii', has white flowers, 2.5cm (1in) across. **'Vilmoriniana'** ■ is upright, with silvery grey leaves and creamy white flowers, 4cm (1½in) across; ↕ 1.2m (4ft), ↔ 1m (3ft). **'Yellow Gem'** has a low and spreading habit, producing grey foliage

Potentilla 'Gibson's Scarlet'

and ruffled, bright yellow flowers; ↕ 60cm (24in), ↔ 1.2m (4ft).
***P.* 'Gibson's Scarlet'** ■ Clump-forming perennial with soft green leaves and raceme-like cymes of single, very bright scarlet flowers, 3cm (1¼in) across, from early to late summer. ↕ to 45cm (18in), ↔ 60cm (24in). ❄❄❄
***P.* 'Gloire de Nancy'** ■ syn. *P.* 'Glory of Nancy'. Clump-forming perennial with dark green leaves, and racemes of double, reddish orange flowers, 2.5–3cm (1–1¼in) across, from early to late summer. ↕ to 45cm (18in), ↔ 60cm (24in). ❄❄❄
***P.* 'Glory of Nancy'** see *P.* 'Gloire de Nancy'.
***P.* 'Manelys'** see *P. fruticosa* 'Maanelys'.
P. megalantha ■ syn. *P. fragiformis.* Compact, clump-forming perennial producing 3-palmate leaves, to 8cm (3in) long, with broadly elliptic to obovate, coarsely scalloped leaflets, mid-green and slightly hairy above, grey-green and more hairy beneath. Erect cymes of 3–7 saucer-shaped yellow flowers, 3–4cm (1¼–1½in) across, are produced in mid- and late summer. ↕ 15–30cm (6–12in), ↔ 15cm (6in). E. Asia, Japan. ❄❄❄
***P.* 'Monsieur Rouillard'.** Clump-forming perennial with mid- to deep green leaves and raceme-like cymes of double, yellow-marked, deep blood-red flowers, 3cm (1¼in) across, borne from early to late summer. ↕ to 45cm (18in), ↔ 60cm (24in). ❄❄❄
P. nepalensis. Loose, clump-forming perennial with numerous branching, red-tinged, wiry stems bearing 5-palmate, mid-green leaves, 8–10cm (3–4in) long, composed of large, obovate or elliptic, coarsely toothed, hairy leaflets. Throughout summer, bears loose cymes of saucer-shaped, dark crimson flowers, 2.5cm (1in) across, on long leaf-stalks. ↕ 30–90cm (12–36in), ↔ 60cm (24in). W. Himalayas. ❄❄❄. **'Miss Willmott'** ■ has cherry-pink flowers suffused yellow, with darker pink centres; ↕ 30–45cm (12–18in). **'Roxana'** has copper-pink flowers with cherry-red centres; ↕ to 45cm (18in).
P. neumanniana, syn. *P. tabernaemontani*, *P. verna.* Procumbent, mat-forming perennial, similar to *P. eriocarpa*, with 5- or 7-palmate leaves, to 4cm (1½in) long, comprising inversely lance-shaped to obovate, toothed, mid-green leaflets. Bears loose cymes of up to 12 saucer-shaped yellow flowers, to 2.5cm (1in) across, over long periods from spring onwards. ↕ to 10cm (4in), ↔ 30cm (12in). Europe. ❄❄❄. **'Goldrausch'** ■ produces loose cymes of up to 10 bright golden yellow flowers from spring to early summer; ↕ 10cm (4in), ↔ 20cm (8in). **'Nana'** is more compact; ↕ 8cm (3in), ↔ 15cm (6in).
P. nitida. Densely tufted perennial with palmate, silver-hairy leaves, to 1.5cm (½in) long, comprising 3, rarely 4 or 5, inversely lance-shaped to obovate leaflets. In summer, bears solitary or paired, short-stemmed, saucer-shaped, deep pink, rarely white flowers, 2.5cm (1in) or more across. Attractive alpine for a scree bed; not always free-flowering. ↕ to 10cm (4in), ↔ 15cm (6in). S.W. and S.E. Alps, Apennines. ❄❄❄
P. palustris, syn. *Comarum palustre* (Marsh cinquefoil). Rhizomatous, woody-based perennial with upright, decumbent stems and pinnate leaves, 3–7cm (1¼–3in) long, composed of 5–7 toothed, oblong, grey-green leaflets, to 6cm (2½in) long. Produces lax cymes of bowl-shaped, purple to maroon flowers, to 3cm (1¼in) across, in early summer. Suitable for the margins of a wildlife pond. ↕ to 50cm (20in), ↔ to 80cm (32in) or more. Europe, W. Asia, North America. ❄❄❄
***P. parvifolia* 'Gold Drop'** see *P. fruticosa* 'Gold Drop'.
P. recta. Erect, clump-forming, hairy perennial producing 5- or 7-palmate leaves, 10cm (4in) long, with oblong to obovate, toothed, grey-green to mid-green leaflets. Flat cymes of saucer-shaped, pale yellow flowers, to 2.5cm (1in) across, are produced from early to late summer. ↕ 60cm (24in), ↔ 45cm (18in). Europe, Caucasus, Russia (Siberia). ❄❄❄. **'Citrina'** see var. *sulphurea.* **'Macrantha'** see 'Warrenii'. **var. *pallida*** see var. *sulphurea.* **var. *sulphurea***, syn. 'Citrina', var. *pallida*, produces pale yellow to cream flowers; ↕ 45cm (18in). **'Warrenii'** ■ syn. 'Macrantha', produces loose cymes of bright canary-yellow flowers.
P. tabernaemontani see *P. neumanniana.*
P.* x *tonguei (*P. anglica* x *P. nepalensis*). Clump-forming perennial with long, spreading stems bearing 3- or 5-palmate, dark green leaves, to 5cm (2in) long, composed of obovate leaflets. Over long periods in summer, produces solitary or loose, few-flowered cymes of rather flat, bowl-shaped, apricot-yellow flowers, 1.5cm (½in) across, with deep carmine-red eyes. ↕ 10cm (4in), ↔ to 30cm (12in). Garden origin. ❄❄❄
P. tormentilla see *P. erecta.*
P. verna see *P. neumanniana.*
***P.* 'William Rollison'** ■ Clump-forming perennial with mid-green leaves and raceme-like cymes of semi-double, yellow- or red-orange flowers, 2.5–3cm (1–1¼in) across, with yellow centres and petal backs, from early to late summer. ↕ to 45cm (18in), ↔ 60cm (24in). ❄❄❄
***P.* 'Yellow Queen'** ■ Clump-forming perennial with mid-green leaves and raceme-like cymes of double or semi-double, pure yellow flowers, 2.5–3cm (1–1¼in) across, from early to late summer. ↕ 30–45cm (12–18in), ↔ 60cm (24in). ❄❄❄

▷ ***Pothos celatocaulis*** see *Rhaphidophora korthalsii*
▷ **Pothos,**
Golden see *Epipremnum aureum*
Satin see *Scindapsus pictus*

x POTINARA

ORCHIDACEAE

Quadrigeneric hybrid genus of evergreen orchids derived from crosses between *Brassavola*, *Cattleya*, *Laelia*, and *Sophronitis*. They are vegetatively similar to the 4 parent genera, which are loosely referred to as "cattleyas", and have stout to slender pseudobulbs and 1 or 2 mostly broadly oblong, semi-rigid, leathery leaves. The short racemes of flowers, with usually strong, clear colours, often yellow or red, are borne at the bases of the leaves, with or without sheaths.
• **HARDINESS** Frost tender.

x *Potinara* Cherub 'Spring Daffodil'

• **CULTIVATION** Cool-growing orchids. Grow in pots of epiphytic orchid compost made with coarse bark. When in growth, provide high humidity and bright filtered light, water freely, and feed at every third watering. In winter, admit full light and water sparingly. See also p.46.
• **PROPAGATION** Divide or remove backbulbs in spring.
• **PESTS AND DISEASES** Scale insects, red spider mites, aphids, and mealybugs may be troublesome.

x *P.* Cherub 'Spring Daffodil' ■ (*Cattleya aurantiaca* x *Lowiara* Trinket). Epiphytic orchid with elongated pseudobulbs and semi-rigid, broadly oval leaves, 10cm (4in) long. Clear yellow flowers, 5cm (2in) across, are produced in short racemes in spring. ↕ 15cm (6in), ↔ 20cm (8in). ❀ (min. 13°C/55°F; max. 30°C/86°F)

▷ **Pouch flower** see *Calceolaria*
▷ **Poui,**
Pink see *Tabebuia rosea*
Yellow see *Tabebuia serratifolia*
▷ **Powder-puff tree** see *Calliandra*
▷ **Prairie coneflower** see *Ratibida*
▷ **Prairie star** see *Lithophragma parviflorum*

PRATIA

CAMPANULACEAE

Genus of about 20 species of prostrate, spreading, freely rooting, evergreen perennials, mostly from damp, shady habitats in Africa, Asia, Australia, New Zealand, and South America. They produce alternate, usually stalkless, often toothed, ovate to rounded leaves, and are grown for their mass of solitary, 2-lipped, star-shaped, usually white or blue-purple flowers. Good ground cover in damp soil, they are also suitable for a rock garden or paving crevice, but can be invasive. In areas prone to prolonged or severe frosts, grow frost-hardy species in an alpine house.
• **HARDINESS** Fully hardy to frost hardy.
• **CULTIVATION** Grow in fertile, loamy, reliably moist soil in partial or deep shade; *P. pedunculata* tolerates drier soils. In an alpine house, use a mix of equal parts loam, leaf mould, and grit.
• **PROPAGATION** Divide at any time of year. Keep divisions moist until well-established.
• **PESTS AND DISEASES** Prone to slugs and snails, and to aphids under glass.

Pratia pedunculata

P. angulata, syn. *Lobelia angulata.* Mat-forming, evergreen perennial with red-tinted stems that spread and root down freely. The broadly ovate to rounded, coarsely toothed leaves are very variable in size, but usually 5–10mm (¼–½in) long. In late spring and early summer, bears short-stalked, axillary, star-shaped, sometimes purple-streaked white flowers, to 1cm (½in) across; they are followed by spherical, red-purple, fleshy fruit, 4mm (⅛in) across. Moderately invasive in moist conditions. ↕ 5cm (2in), ↔ 30–60cm (12–24in). Malaysia, Indonesia, New Zealand. ✽✽✽. **'Treadwellii'**, syn. *P. treadwellii*, is larger in all its parts, and may be very invasive; ↕ 6cm (2½in), ↔ 1m (3ft).

P. pedunculata ▣ syn. *Lobelia pedunculata.* Ground-hugging perennial with ovate to rounded leaves, to 9mm (⅜in) long. Short-stalked, star-shaped, pale blue flowers, to 7mm (¼in) across, are borne over long periods in summer. Invasive, even in dry conditions, but not too rampant. ↕ 1.5cm (½in), ↔ indefinite. Australia. ✽✽✽

P. perpusilla, syn. *Lobelia perpusilla.* Mat-forming perennial bearing tiny, obovate leaves, 3–5mm (⅛–¼in) long, with deeply toothed margins. During summer, bears short-stalked, star-shaped white flowers, 6–10mm (¼–½in) across, with recurving lobes. ↕ to 2cm (¾in), ↔ indefinite. ✽✽. **'Fragrant Carpet'** produces fragrant flowers.

P. treadwellii see *P. angulata* 'Treadwellii'.

▷ **Prayer plant** see *Maranta leuconeura*
▷ **Prickle ear** see *Acanthostachys*
▷ **Prickly Moses** see *Acacia verticillata*
Western see *A. pulchella*
▷ **Prickly pear** see *Opuntia ficus-indica*
▷ **Pride of Bolivia** see *Tipuana tipu*
▷ **Pride of Burma** see *Amherstia nobilis*
▷ **Pride of India** see *Koelreuteria paniculata, Lagerstroemia speciosa, Melia azedarach*
▷ **Pride of Madeira** see *Echium candicans*
▷ **Primavera** see *Cybistax donnell-smithii*
▷ **Primrose** see *Primula, P. vulgaris*
Cape see *Streptocarpus*
Desert evening see *Oenothera deltoides*
Evening see *Oenothera, O. biennis*
Fairy see *Primula malacoides*
Japanese see *Primula japonica*

P

PRIMULA

Primrose

PRIMULACEAE

Genus of about 400 species of mainly herbaceous perennials, some woody-based and evergreen. Occurring in a wide range of habitats from bogs and marshland to alpine areas, they are widely distributed throughout the N. hemisphere, with almost half the species from the Himalayas; a few are also found in the S. hemisphere. They have linear to broadly ovate to obovate, pale to dark green leaves in basal rosettes, and attractive, often salverform, sometimes tubular, bell-shaped or funnel-shaped flowers, with usually spreading petals joined at the bases into tubes. The solitary flowers may be clustered together among the leaves, or borne on slender to stout flower-stalks in umbels, whorls, or racemes. In some primulas, the leaves, flower stems, and calyces may be covered with a white or yellow, waxy meal, or "farina". Primulas can be used for most garden sites, from bog and waterside plantings to borders, rock gardens, and bedding; they can also be grown in an alpine house. A few tender species are grown as cool or temperate greenhouse container plants, or as houseplants.

Primula is a complex genus, divided into many different botanical sections. In gardens, however, only the following 3 major groupings are recognised; they apply to many, but not all, primulas.

Auricula primulas
Evergreen primulas, developed from hybrids between *P. auricula* and *P. hirsuta*. They bear umbels of several, usually large, flat-faced, salverform flowers above smooth, leathery, often white-mealy foliage. There are 3 main subgroups: alpine, show, and border.

Alpine Auricula Group – These have the colour of the flower centres in sharp contrast to that of the petals. They may be classed as either light-centred (white or pale in the centres) or gold-centred (yellow or gold in the centres). There is no meal on either leaves or flowers. Grow in an alpine house or rock garden.

Show Auricula Group – These have a distinct circle of white meal, or "paste", in the centre of each flower. They may be described as self-coloured (one colour from the central paste to the petal margins), edged (the paste surrounded by black, feathering out to a green, grey, or white margin), or fancy (the paste surrounded by a colour other than black, with a green, grey, or white margin). Grow in an alpine house.

Border Auricula Group – These are generally robust, garden Auriculas, sometimes white-mealy, and often very fragrant. Grow in a mixed or herbaceous border; excellent for cottage gardens.

Candelabra primulas
Robust herbaceous perennials with several whorls of flowers arranged in tiers up tall, sturdy stems. They are deciduous, dying back to basal buds, or semi-evergreen, dying back to reduced rosettes. Grow in moist shade or woodland; they are seen at their best in groups by streams or in bog gardens.

Primrose-Polyanthus primulas
A very diverse grouping of evergreen, semi-evergreen, or deciduous, winter- to spring-flowering perennial hybrids derived from *P. elatior, P. juliae*, *P. veris*, and *P. vulgaris.* They have rosettes of broadly ovate to obovate leaves, and mainly large, salverform flowers borne in fascicles (bunched clusters) or umbels, sometimes with both types of inflorescence on the same plant. They occur in a wide range of colours, and are grown as biennials for bedding or containers, as greenhouse container plants, or as perennials for rock gardens, and herbaceous and mixed borders. They are divided into 2 main groups, although interbreeding blurs the distinction between the two.

Primrose Group – Mainly grown as herbaceous perennials, and similar in habit to the 2 main parents, *P. vulgaris* and *P. juliae.* Most produce solitary flowers clustered among the basal rosettes, although a few may have both solitary and umbel-like inflorescences. They are either spring-flowering, if grown without protection, or winter- to spring-flowering, if grown as biennial, greenhouse container plants.

Polyanthus Group – Perennials, usually grown as biennials from summer-sown seed and planted out in autumn to flower through winter and the following spring, or grown under glass as winter- and spring-flowering container plants. A few cultivars are grown as spring-flowering herbaceous perennials; they are propagated by division in autumn, or in spring immediately after flowering. Distinguished from Primrose Group primulas by their long-stalked umbels.

PRIMULA GROUPINGS

The genus *Primula* is classified into many botanical sections. In gardens, however, the 3 informal groupings shown here are the most commonly recognized.

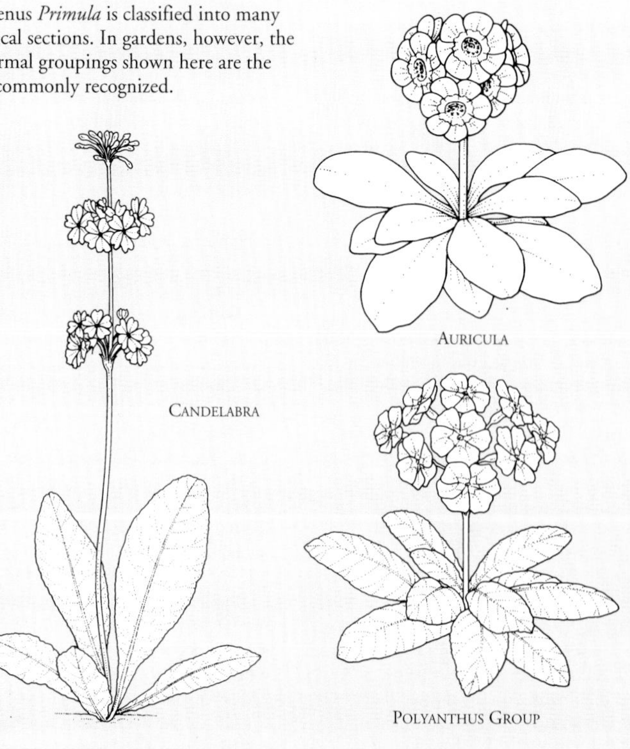

• **HARDINESS** Fully hardy to frost tender.
• **CULTIVATION** For ease of reference, cultivation requirements have been set out in groups, as follows:
1. Full sun or partial shade, in moderately fertile, moist but well-drained, humus-rich soil.
2. Partial shade, in deep, humus-rich, moist, neutral to acid loam soil, or peaty soil. Tolerates full sun if soil remains moist at all times.
3. Deep or partial shade in peaty, gritty, moist but sharply drained acid soil. Protect from excessive winter wet.
4. Under glass in an alpine house or frame. Use a mix of equal parts loam-based potting compost (JI No. 2), leaf mould or peat, and grit. Avoid wetting the foliage of mealy species and hybrids.
5. Full sun with some midday shade, or partial shade, in moist but sharply drained, gritty, humus-rich, slightly alkaline soil.
6. In a cool or temperate greenhouse, or as a houseplant. Use a mix of 4 parts loam-based potting compost (JI No.2) and 1 part each grit and leaf mould (or peat), in bright filtered light. In growth, water freely and apply a half-strength balanced liquid fertilizer every week.
• **PROPAGATION** Surface-sow seed of half-hardy and frost-tender species in early spring. Sow seed of hardy species in containers in an open frame, as soon as ripe or in late winter or early spring. Divide between autumn and early spring. Root basal cuttings or offsets in autumn or early spring. Take root cuttings when dormant in winter.
• **PESTS AND DISEASES** Prone to aphids, red spider mites, leafhoppers, vine weevil, slugs, viruses, primula brown core, and grey mould (*Botrytis*).

P. 'Adrian' ▣ Alpine Auricula primula with oval to rounded, mid-green leaves, to 10cm (4in) long. In spring, produces salverform, light-centred flowers, 3cm (1¼in) across, with purple-blue petals, paler at the margins. Cultivation group 1 or 4. ↕↔ 10cm (4in). ✽✽✽

P. 'Alice Haysom'. Self-coloured show Auricula primula with oval to rounded, mid-green leaves, to 10cm (4in) long. In spring, bears salverform flowers, 3cm

(1¼in) across, with cardinal-red petals and golden yellow tubes. Cultivation group 4. ↕↔ 10cm (4in). ❄❄❄

P. allionii ■ Rosette-forming, evergreen perennial with entire, sometimes scalloped or finely toothed, glandular-hairy, inversely lance-shaped, grey-green leaves, to 5cm (2in) long. In late winter and spring, produces 1- to 5-flowered umbels of salverform flowers, each to 3cm (1¼in) across, varying from white to pink to reddish purple. Each corolla has a flat face and a white eye. Cultivation group 4 (lime-loving). ↕ 7–10cm (3–4in), ↔ to 20cm (8in). Cliffs in S. France and N. Italy. ❄❄❄. There are many named cultivars. **'Snowflake'** is vigorous, with large white flowers, 2.5cm (1in) across, sometimes flushed pink at the margins.

P. alpicola ■ Rosette-forming, deciduous perennial with elliptic, toothed or scalloped, mid-green leaves, to 10cm (4in) long. In summer, white-mealy stems produce umbels of 6–12 pendent, tubular to funnel-shaped, fragrant, white, yellow, or violet flowers, 1–2.5cm (½–1in) across, with white-mealy eyes. Cultivation group 2. ↕ 50cm (20in), ↔ 30cm (12in). Moist alpine areas in S.E. Tibet. ❄❄❄

P. amoena see *P. elatior* subsp. *meyeri.*

P. anisodora see *P. wilsonii* var. *anisodora.*

***P.* 'Argus'** ■ Very vigorous alpine Auricula primula with oval to rounded, mid-green leaves, to 12cm (5in) long. In spring, produces salverform flowers, to 3cm (1¼in) across, with almost white centres, and petals shading from plum-red to beetroot-red. Cultivation group 1 or 4. ↕↔ 10cm (4in). ❄❄❄

P. aurantiaca. Small, rosette-forming, deciduous Candelabra primula with inversely lance-shaped to obovate, finely toothed, dark green leaves, to 20cm (8in) long, with red-purple midribs. In summer, red-tinged stems produce 2–6 whorls of 6–12 salverform, brilliant red-orange flowers, 1.5cm (½in) across. Cultivation group 2. ↕ 30cm (12in), ↔ 40cm (16in). Moist, shaded sites in S.W. China. ❄❄❄

P. aureata ■ Rosette-forming, evergreen perennial with spoon-shaped to oblong, toothed, white-mealy, mid-green leaves, to 8cm (3in) long. In spring, very short stems, hidden within the foliage, produce umbels of 2–10 salverform, cream to yellow flowers, 3–4cm (1¼–1½in) across, with large, darker yellow eyes. Cultivation group 3 or 4. ↕ 15cm (6in), ↔ 20cm (8in). Moist cliffs and rocky hillsides in Nepal. ❄❄

Primula 'Argus'

P. auricula. Rosette-forming, evergreen, sometimes white-mealy perennial, with usually obovate-spoon-shaped to rounded, entire to toothed, pale green to grey-green leaves, to 12cm (5in) long. Umbels of 2–30 salverform, fragrant, deep yellow flowers, 1.5–2.5cm (½–1in) across, are produced in spring. Cultivation group 1, 4, or 5. ↕ 20cm (8in), ↔ 25cm (10in). Alps, Apennines, Carpathians. ❄❄❄. **var. *albocincta*** ■ bears grey-green leaves with white margins; Dolomites.

***P.* 'Beatrice Wooster'.** Rosette-forming, evergreen perennial with obovate, scalloped or finely toothed, glandular-hairy, grey-green leaves, to 8cm (3in) long. Large, shallowly cup-shaped, clear pink flowers, to 3cm (1¼in) across, with white eyes, are borne in umbels of 2–10 on short stems in spring. Cultivation group 4 or 5. ↕ 10cm (4in), ↔ 20cm (8in). ❄❄❄

P. beesiana ■ syn. *P. bulleyana* subsp. *beesiana.* Rosette-forming, deciduous or semi-evergreen Candelabra primula that dies back to basal buds or reduced rosettes. The leaves are inversely lance-shaped to obovate, toothed, mid-green, and to 22cm (9in) long, with red midribs. In summer, stout, white-mealy stems each bear 2–8 whorls of 8–16 salverform, yellow-eyed, reddish pink flowers, 2cm (¾in) across. Cultivation group 2. ↕↔ 60cm (24in). Moist mountain meadows in China. ❄❄❄

P. x berninae (*P. hirsuta* x *P. latifolia*). Small, neat, rosette-forming, deciduous perennial with ovate, toothed, mid-green leaves, to 12cm (5in) long. In spring, very short stems produce tubular to cup-shaped purple flowers, 1.5cm (½in) across, singly or in umbels of up to 15. Cultivation group 1 or 4. ↕ 7cm (3in), ↔ 15cm (6in). Garden origin. ❄❄❄. **'Windrush'** produces white-eyed, red-purple flowers, 2cm (¾in) across.

***P.* 'Betty Green'.** Vigorous, rosette-forming, semi-evergreen Primrose Group primula bearing obovate, rich apple-green leaves, to 15cm (6in) long. Tubular to saucer-shaped, vivid crimson flowers, to 4cm (1½in) across, with clear yellow eyes, are produced freely in umbels of 3–25 in spring. Cultivation group 1 or 2. ↕ 10–15cm (4–6in), ↔ 30–40cm (12–16in). ❄❄❄

P. bhutanica. Rosette-forming, deciduous perennial, dying back to a large, white-mealy bud in winter. The spoon-shaped, finely toothed, slightly white-mealy, crinkled leaves are mid-green, and to 10cm (4in) long. In late winter and spring, very short stems, hidden within the foliage, each bear umbels of 2–10 salverform, yellow-eyed blue flowers, 2.5cm (1in) across. Cultivation group 3. ↕ 15cm (6in), ↔ 20cm (8in). Mixed forest in Tibet, Bhutan, and India (Assam). ❄❄❄

***P.* 'Blairside Yellow'** ■ Compact border Auricula primula, with rounded to oval, pale green leaves, to 12cm (5in) long. In early spring, produces open funnel-shaped yellow flowers, to 2.5cm (1in) across. Cultivation group 2 or 5. ↕ 10cm (4in), ↔ 20cm (8in). ❄❄❄

***P.* 'Blossom'** ■ Vigorous alpine Auricula primula with oval, dark green leaves, 12cm (5in) long. Produces salverform, gold-centred flowers, 2.5cm (1in) across, with shaded crimson petals, in spring. Cultivation group 1 or 4. ↕↔ 10cm (4in). ❄❄❄

Primula 'Adrian'

Primula allionii

Primula alpicola

Primula aureata

Primula auricula var. *albocincta*

Primula 'Blairside Yellow'

Primula 'Blossom'

Primula 'Buckland Wine'

Primula bulleyana

P. boothii. Rosette-forming, deciduous perennial with spoon-shaped to elliptic, toothed, dark green leaves, to 15cm (6in) long. Very short stems produce umbels of 2–25 saucer-shaped, yellow-eyed, purple-pink flowers, to 3cm (1¼in) across, in spring. Cultivation group 3 or 4. ↕ 10cm (4in), ↔ 20cm (8in). Moist, peaty areas in E. Himalayas. ❄❄

***P.* 'Broadwell Gold'.** Vigorous border Auricula primula bearing obovate, mid-green leaves, to 15cm (6in) long. In spring, bears salverform, golden yellow flowers, to 4cm (1½in) across, with white-mealy eyes. Cultivation group 1, 2, or 4. ↕↔ 25cm (10in). ❄❄❄

***P.* 'Buckland Wine'** ■ Compact, rosette-forming, semi-evergreen, Primrose Group primula with oval, bronze-green leaves, to 15cm (6in) long. In spring, produces salverform, wine-red flowers, to 4cm (1½in) across, in umbels of 3–15. Cultivation group 1, 2, or 4. ↕ 10cm (4in), ↔ 25cm (10in). ❄❄❄

P. bulleyana ■ Rosette-forming, semi-evergreen Candelabra primula with ovate to ovate-lance-shaped, toothed, mid-green leaves, to 30cm (12in) long. In summer, stout stems produce 5–7 whorls of 5 to many salverform flowers, 2cm (¾in) across, in crimson fading to orange. Cultivation group 2. ↕↔ 60cm (24in). Hillsides in China. ❄❄❄. **subsp. *beesiana*** see *P. beesiana.*

P. burmanica. Rosette-forming, deciduous Candelabra primula with inversely lance-shaped, toothed, dull, deep green leaves, to 30cm (12in) long. Stout stems produce up to 6 whorls of 10–18 salverform, yellow-eyed, red-purple flowers, 2cm (¾in) across, in late spring and early summer. Cultivation group 2. ↕↔ 60cm (24in). Meadows and forests in China and Burma. ❄❄❄

P. capitata ■ Rosette-forming, semi-evergreen, short-lived perennial, with inversely lance-shaped or oblong-lance-shaped, finely toothed, usually mealy, pale green leaves, to 15cm (6in) long, white-mealy beneath. Tubular, dark purple flowers, to 1cm (½in) long, with shallowly lobed petals, are borne in flattened, spherical racemes on white-mealy stems, from late spring to early autumn. Cultivation group 2. ↕↔ 40cm (16in). Moist alpine regions in Tibet,

Primula beesiana

P

Primula capitata

Primula chungensis

Primula clarkei

Primula clusiana

Primula 'Craddock White'

Primula denticulata var. *alba*

Primula elatior

Primula flaccida

Primula forrestii

Bhutan, and India (Sikkim). ✻✻✻. **subsp. *mooreana*** is vigorous, and larger in all parts; ↕↔ 60cm (24in).

P. chionantha. Rosette-forming, deciduous perennial with inversely lance-shaped, toothed or almost entire, mid-green leaves, to 25cm (10in) long, covered in yellow or white meal. From late spring to early summer, stout stems produce 1–4 many-flowered whorls of tubular to funnel-shaped, fragrant, milk-white flowers, with or without whitish eyes, to 2.5cm (1in) across. Cultivation group 1 or 2. ↕↔ 60cm (24in). Open, alpine meadows in China. ✻✻✻. **subsp. *melanops***, syn. *P. melanops*, has lance-shaped, toothed or scalloped, mid-green leaves, white-mealy beneath. In late spring, white-mealy stems each bear 1 or 2 umbels of 5–12 narrowly tubular to bell-shaped, fragrant, black-eyed purple flowers, 2cm (¾in) across; Cultivation group 2 or 4; ↕ 35cm (14in), ↔ 50cm (20in). **subsp. *sinopurpurea***, syn. *P. sinopurpurea*, bears oblong-lance-shaped, mid-green leaves, 5–35cm (2–14in) long, yellow-mealy beneath. In late spring and early summer, produces nodding, tubular to funnel-shaped, magenta, purple, and violet flowers, to 3cm (1¼in) across, with pale purple eyes, in umbels of 6–12; Cultivation group 2; ↕ 30–45cm (12–18in), ↔ 30–35cm (12–14in).

***P.* 'Chloe'.** Green-edged show Auricula primula with oval, dark green leaves, to 12cm (5in) long. Salverform, 5- to 7-petalled black flowers, 2.5cm (1in) across, are borne in spring. Cultivation group 4. ↕↔ 10cm (4in). ✻✻✻

P. chungensis ■ Vigorous, rosette-forming, deciduous Candelabra primula with oblong-obovate, toothed and shallowly lobed, mid-green leaves, to 30cm (12in) long. In early summer, stout stems bear 2–5 whorls of up to 12 salverform, fragrant, pale orange flowers, 1.5–2cm (½–¾in) across, with red tubes. Cultivation group 2. ↕ 80cm (32in), ↔ 60cm (24in). Wet, open forest in China and Bhutan. ✻✻✻

P. clarkei ■ Small, rosette-forming, deciduous perennial with rounded to ovate, toothed, pale green leaves, to 5cm (2in) long. In spring, flat, yellow-eyed, rose-pink flowers, to 2cm (¾in) across, are borne in sometimes short-stemmed umbels of 2–6. Cultivation group 2 or 4. ↕ 7cm (3in), ↔ 15cm (6in). Moist hillsides in India (Kashmir). ✻✻✻

P. clusiana ■ Small, rosette-forming, evergreen perennial with oblong to ovate, leathery, dark green leaves, to 8cm (3in) long. In spring, salverform, white-eyed, rose-pink to lilac flowers, to 4cm (1½in) across, are borne singly or in umbels of up to 4. Cultivation group 4 or 5. ↕ 8cm (3in), ↔ 15cm (6in). Austria (N. calcareous Alps). ✻✻✻

P. cockburniana. Rosette-forming, deciduous biennial or short-lived perennial Candelabra primula with oblong to oblong-obovate, mid-green leaves, to 15cm (6in) long, with small, toothed lobes. Slender stems bear 1–3 whorls of 3–8 salverform, red-tinged orange flowers, 1.5cm (½in) across, in summer. Cultivation group 1 or 2. ↕↔ 40cm (16in). Marshy, alpine meadows in China (S.W. Sichuan). ✻✻✻

P. cortusoides. Small, rosette-forming, deciduous perennial with ovate-oblong, softly hairy, toothed, mid-green leaves, to 9cm (3½in) long. Umbels of 2–15 salverform, rose-red, pink to red-violet flowers, to 2cm (¾in) across, are borne in late spring and early summer. Cultivation group 2. ↕↔ 30cm (12in). Woodland in Russia (W. Siberia). ✻✻✻

***P.* 'Craddock White'** ■ Rosette-forming, deciduous or semi-evergreen Primrose Group primula with oval, dark green, bronze-veined leaves, 15cm (6in) long. In spring, salverform, scented white flowers, to 4cm (1½in) across, with yellow eyes, are produced in umbels of 3–8. Cultivation group 2. ↕ 12cm (5in), ↔ 25cm (10in). ✻✻✻

P. cuneifolia. Rosette-forming, deciduous, short-lived perennial with inversely lance-shaped, obovate, or wedge-shaped, coarsely toothed, pale green leaves, to 8cm (3in) long. In summer, salverform, rose-red, yellow-eyed flowers, to 2cm (¾in) across, are borne singly or in umbels of up to 9, on stems ranging from tiny to 30cm (12in) tall. Cultivation group 2 or 4. ↕↔ to 30cm (12in). Russia (Siberia), Japan, North America (E. Alaska to British Columbia, Aleutian Islands). ✻✻✻

P. denticulata (Drumstick primula). Robust, rosette-forming, deciduous perennial with oblong-obovate or spoon-shaped, mid-green leaves, to 25cm (10in) long, finely toothed, and white-mealy beneath. Stout stems bear crowded, spherical umbels of tubular to trumpet- or bell-shaped, yellow-eyed, purple flowers, to 2cm (¾in) across, from mid-spring to summer. Cultivation group 1 or 2. ↕↔ 45cm (18in). Moist alpine regions from Afghanistan to S.E. Tibet, Burma, and China. ✻✻✻. **var. *alba*** ■ has white flowers. **'Rubra'** has red-purple flowers.

***P.* 'Dreamer'** ■ Rosette-forming, semi-evergreen or evergreen Primrose Group primula with inversely lance-shaped to obovate, mid-green leaves, 10cm (4in) long. In spring, produces salverform flowers, 4–5cm (1½–2in) across, in cream, apricot, pink, or rose-pink; all bicolours have darker eyes and yellow centres. Cultivation group 6. ↕ 8–10cm (3–4in), ↔ 15–20cm (6–8in). ✻

P. edgeworthii see *P. nana*.

P. elatior ■ (Oxlip). Variable, rosette-forming, evergreen or semi-evergreen perennial with ovate to oblong or elliptic, scalloped, mid-green leaves, to 20cm (8in) long, softly hairy beneath. In spring and summer, stiff, upright stems bear one-sided umbels of 2–12 tubular yellow flowers, to 2.5cm (1in) long. Cultivation group 1 or 2. ↕ 30cm (12in), ↔ 25cm (10in). Moist meadows and open woodland in Europe, Turkey to the Altai Mountains, and Russia (Siberia). ✻✻✻. **subsp. *meyeri***, syn. *P. amoena*. Rosette-forming, deciduous perennial with elliptic to spoon-shaped, scalloped or finely toothed leaves, to 17cm (7in) long, bright green above, usually densely hairy beneath. In early spring, hairy stems bear usually one-sided umbels of 6–10 flat to shallowly tubular to funnel-shaped, red-purple, violet-blue, or occasionally white flowers, 2.5cm (1in) across, with yellow eyes. Cultivation group 2 or 4; ↕↔ 15cm (6in); peaty banks and rocky hillsides in Caucasus and N.E. Turkey.

Primula 'Dreamer'

P. ellisiae. Rosette-forming, deciduous perennial with inversely lance-shaped to spoon-shaped, finely toothed, mid-green leaves, to 15cm (6in) long. In summer, sturdy stems produce umbels of 4–8 saucer-shaped, yellow-eyed, pinkish purple flowers, to 2.5cm (1in) across. Cultivation group 1 or 4. ↕↔ 30cm (12in). Moist crevices and ledges in USA (New Mexico). ✻✻✻

***P.* 'E.R. Janes'.** Vigorous, rosette-forming, semi-evergreen Primrose Group primula with broadly oval, toothed, mid-green leaves, to 15cm (6in) long. Masses of salverform, orange-flushed, salmon-pink flowers, 4cm (1½in) across, are borne in fascicles in spring, sometimes again in autumn. Has little foliage at spring flowering. Cultivation group 1 or 2. ↕ 10–15cm (4–6in), ↔ 30–40cm (12–16in). ✻✻✻

P. farinosa. Rosette-forming, deciduous perennial with inversely lance-shaped, sometimes toothed, mid-green leaves, to 10cm (4in) long, and white-mealy beneath. Bears compact umbels of 2–10 tubular, white-mealy, yellow-eyed, lilac-pink flowers, 1.5cm (½in) across, in late spring and early summer. Cultivation group 2 or 4. ↕↔ to 25cm (10in). Moist meadows in Europe, N. Asia, and N. Pacific. ✻✻✻

***P.* 'Finesse'.** Rosette-forming, evergreen or semi-evergreen perennial bearing inversely lance-shaped to obovate, mid-green leaves, 10cm (4in) long. In late winter and early spring, produces salverform flowers, 4.5cm (1¾in) across, in rose-pink, crimson-red, scarlet-red, mauve-blue, purple, light blue, or dark blue; each flower has a thin, "laced" margin in silver or gold. Cultivation group 6. ↕ 8–10cm (3–4in), ↔ 15–20cm (6–8in). ✻

P. flaccida ■ syn. *P. nutans* of gardens. Rosette-forming, deciduous, short-lived perennial with narrowly elliptic or obovate, downy, finely toothed, pale to mid-green leaves, to 20cm (8in) long. In summer, bears conical umbels of 5–15 pendent, broadly tubular to funnel-shaped, white-mealy, lavender-blue to violet flowers, 2.5cm (1in) across. Cultivation group 3 or 4. ↕ 50cm (20in), ↔ 30cm (12in). Open forest and alpine meadows in China. ✻✻✻

P. florindae ■ (Giant cowslip). Rosette-forming, deciduous perennial with ovate, toothed, mid-green leaves, to 45cm (18in) long. Umbels of up to 40 pendent, slender, tubular to funnel-shaped, white-mealy, fragrant, sulphur-yellow flowers, 1–2cm (½–¾in) across, are borne on stout stems in summer. Cultivation group 1 or 2. ↕ to 1.2m (4ft), ↔ 90cm (36in). Marshes and streams in S.E. Tibet. ✻✻✻

P. forrestii ■ Rosette-forming, evergreen, perennial subshrub with ovate-elliptic, scalloped to toothed, dark green leaves, to 20cm (8in) long, wrinkled above, white-mealy beneath. In late spring and summer, stout stems bear umbels of 10–25 salverform, orange-eyed, golden yellow flowers, 1.5–2.5cm

PRIMULA

(½–1in) across. Cultivation group 4 or 5. ↕ 60cm (24in), ↔ 45cm (18in). Dry, shady crevices in limestone cliffs in China. ❄❄❄

P.* x *forsteri* f. *bileckii (*P. hirsuta* x *P. minima*). Dwarf, rosette-forming, evergreen perennial with wedge-shaped, leathery, toothed, shiny, dark green leaves, 0.5–3cm (½–1¼in) long, with soft, glandular hairs. In late spring, bears umbels of 2 or 3 salverform, red-pink flowers, 1.5–3cm (½–1¼in) across, on very short stems. Cultivation group 2 or 4. ↕ 7cm (3in), ↔ 10cm (4in). Austria (Alps). ❄❄❄

P. frondosa ▣ Rosette-forming, deciduous perennial with spoon-shaped, finely toothed or lobed, mid-green leaves, to 10cm (4in) long, white-mealy beneath. In late spring and early summer, salverform, yellow-eyed, pale pinkish lilac to red-purple flowers, to 1.5cm (½in) across, are borne singly or in loose umbels of up to 30. Cultivation group 2 or 4. ↕ 15cm (6in), ↔ 25cm (10in). Bulgaria (Stara Planina plateau). ❄❄❄

***P.* 'Garryarde Guinevere'** ▣ Vigorous, rosette-forming, evergreen Polyanthus Group primula with oval, toothed, deep bronze leaves, 15cm (6in) long, and salverform, yellow-eyed, purplish pink flowers, 4cm (1½in) across, borne in umbels of 3–8 in spring. Cultivation group 2. ↕ 12cm (5in), ↔ 25cm (10in). ❄❄❄

P. geraniifolia. Rosette-forming, hairy, deciduous perennial with rounded, 7- to 9-lobed leaves, to 15cm (6in) long, with scalloped margins. Slender stems bear umbels of 2–12 semi-pendent, tubular to bell-shaped, pinkish purple flowers, to 2cm (¾in) across, in late spring and early summer. Cultivation group 2. ↕↔ 30cm (12in). Shady hillsides in India (Sikkim), Nepal, Bhutan, Tibet, and China. ❄❄❄

P. glutinosa. Rosette-forming, evergreen perennial with narrowly inversely lance-shaped to oblong, entire, leathery, sticky, glandular-hairy leaves, to 6cm (2½in) long. In late spring and early summer, cup-shaped, fragrant, blue-violet flowers, to 2cm (¾in) across, are borne singly or in umbels of up to 8. Cultivation group 1 or 4. ↕↔ 10cm (4in). Wet, acid alpine meadows in E. Alps and C. Balkans. ❄❄❄

***P.* Gold-laced Group** ▣ Erect, semi-evergreen or evergreen Polyanthus Group primula with oval, sometimes red-tinged, mid-green leaves, 18cm (7in) long. In spring, bears umbels of 3–12 salverform, golden-eyed, very dark mahogany-red or black flowers, to 3cm (1¼in) across, each petal with a narrow gold margin. Cultivation group 2 or 4. ↕ 25cm (10in), ↔ 30cm (12in). ❄❄❄

P. gracilipes ▣ Rosette-forming, evergreen or semi-evergreen perennial with oblong to spoon-shaped to elliptic, toothed, mid-green leaves, to 15cm (6in) long. From winter to early summer, umbels of salverform, purple-pink flowers, 1.5–2.5cm (½–1in) across, with white-bordered, orange-yellow eyes, are borne on very short stems hidden within the foliage. Cultivation group 3 or 4. ↕ 10cm (4in), ↔ 20cm (8in). Moist alpine regions in S.E. Tibet and C. Nepal. ❄❄❄

P. griffithii. Rosette-forming, deciduous perennial with ovate to arrow-shaped, toothed, dark bluish green leaves, to 25cm (10in) long, sparsely white-mealy beneath. Bears umbels of 5–12 salverform, yellow-eyed purple flowers, 2.5cm (1in) across, in spring. Cultivation group 3 or 4. ↕ 25cm (10in), ↔ 45cm (18in). Moist hillsides in Tibet and Bhutan. ❄❄❄

P. halleri. Rosette-forming, deciduous perennial with inversely lance-shaped, elliptic to obovate, sometimes finely toothed, white-mealy, mid-green leaves, to 8cm (3in) long. Stout stems bear umbels of up to 20 salverform, yellow-eyed, lilac-pink flowers, to 2cm (¾in) across, in late spring and early summer. Cultivation group 2 or 4. ↕ 30cm (12in), ↔ 25cm (10in). Stony alpine meadows in Alps, Carpathians, Balkans. ❄❄❄

Primula florindae

Primula frondosa

Primula 'Garryarde Guinevere'

Primula Gold-laced Group

Primula gracilipes

Primula hirsuta

Primula 'Inverewe'

Primula 'Iris Mainwaring'

Primula japonica 'Miller's Crimson'

Primula japonica 'Postford White'

P. heucherifolia. Rosette-forming, stoloniferous, hairy, deciduous perennial with long-stalked, rounded leaves, to 15cm (6in) long, with 7–11 triangular lobes. Slender stems bear 3–10 pendent, bell-shaped, mauve-pink to rich purple flowers, 1–2.5cm (½–1in) across, in early summer. Cultivation group 2. ↕↔ 30cm (12in). Shady, rocky hillsides in China (Sichuan). ❄❄❄

P. hirsuta ▣ syn. *P. rubra.* Rosette-forming, evergreen perennial with spoon-shaped to obovate, toothed, glandular-hairy, mid-green leaves, to 8cm (3in) long. In late spring and early summer, salverform, usually white-eyed, mauve-pink flowers, 1.5–2.5cm (½–1in) across, are borne singly or in umbels of up to 15, on short stems. Cultivation group 1, 2, or 4. ↕ 10cm (4in), ↔ 25cm (10in). Pyrenees, Alps. ❄❄❄

***P.* 'Hyacinthia'**, syn. *P. marginata* 'Hyacinthia'. Robust, rosette-forming, evergreen perennial with obovate, slightly white-mealy, light green leaves, to 12cm (5in) long. In spring, shallowly tubular to funnel-shaped, 6-lobed, hyacinth-blue flowers, to 3cm (1¼in) across, are borne in umbels of 2–20. Cultivation group 4 or 5. ↕ 15cm (6in), ↔ 20cm (8in). ❄❄❄

***P.* 'Inverewe'** ▣ Vigorous, rosette-forming, semi-evergreen Candelabra primula with oval to lance-shaped, toothed, coarse, mid-green leaves, to 20cm (8in) long. In summer, numerous stems each bear several whorls of 5–15 salverform, brilliant red flowers, to 3cm (1¼in) across. Cultivation group 2. ↕ 75cm (30in), ↔ 60cm (24in). ❄❄❄

P. involucrata. Rosette-forming, deciduous perennial with ovate to oblong, entire or finely toothed, mid-green leaves, to 15cm (6in) long. In late spring and early summer, long, slender stems produce umbels of 2–6 pendent, shallowly tubular to bell-shaped, yellow-eyed white flowers, 1.5–2cm (½–¾in) across. Cultivation group 2. ↕↔ 30cm (12in). Moist alpine meadows from Pakistan to S.W. China. ❄❄❄. **subsp. *yargongensis***, syn. *P. yargongensis,* produces umbels of 3–8 semi-pendent, mauve-pink flowers; S.E. Tibet, China.

P. ioessa. Rosette-forming, deciduous perennial with narrowly oblong or inversely lance-shaped to spoon-shaped, deeply toothed, mid-green leaves, to 20cm (8in) long. Bears umbels of 2–8 pendent, tubular to funnel-shaped, white-mealy, fragrant, mauve-pink to violet or white flowers, 2.5cm (1in) across, in summer. Cultivation group 2, 3, or 4. ↕↔ 30cm (12in). Wet alpine meadows in S.E. Tibet. ❄❄❄

***P.* 'Iris Mainwaring'** ▣ Compact, rosette-forming, evergreen or semi-evergreen Primrose Group primula with oval, deep green leaves, to 18cm (7in) long. In spring, delicate, salverform pink flowers, 4cm (1½in) across, with yellow centres, are borne in umbels of 3–8. Cultivation group 1, 2, or 4. ↕ 10–15cm (4–6in), ↔ 30–40cm (12–16in). ❄❄❄

P. japonica (Japanese primrose). Robust, rosette-forming, deciduous perennial with obovate, oblong, or broadly spoon-shaped, finely scalloped or toothed, pale green leaves, to 25cm (10in) long. Stout stems bearing 1–6 whorls of 5–25 salverform, red-purple to white flowers, 2cm (¾in) across, are borne in late spring and early summer. Cultivation group 2. ↕↔ 45cm (18in). Moist, shady places in Japan. ❄❄❄. **'Miller's Crimson'** ▣ has crimson flowers. **'Postford White'** ▣ is robust, and has red-eyed, clear white flowers.

P. jesoana. Rosette-forming, hairy, deciduous or semi-evergreen perennial with rounded, deeply 7- to 9-lobed, mid-green leaves, to 30cm (12in) long.

P

Primula Joker Series

Primula x *kewensis* 'Mountain Spring'

Primula 'Linda Pope'

Primula 'Linnet'

Primula marginata 'Kesselring's Variety'

Primula 'Mark'

Primula modesta var. *faurieae*

Primula obconica Cantata Series 'Cantata Lavender'

Primula obconica 'Queen of the Market'

Slender stems each bear 1–4 umbels of 2–6 shallowly tubular to bell-shaped, yellow-eyed, pinkish purple or white flowers, 2cm (¾in) across, in late spring and early summer. Cultivation group 2 or 4. ↕↔ 30cm (12in). Mountain areas in C. Japan. ✻✻

***P.* 'Johanna'.** Rosette-forming, deciduous perennial bearing inversely lance-shaped, mid-green leaves, to 2cm (¾in) long. In spring, produces few-flowered umbels of salverform, yellow-eyed, clear pink flowers, 1cm (½in) across. Cultivation group 2 or 4. ↕ 10cm (4in), ↔ 15cm (6in). ✻✻✻

***P.* Joker Series** ▣ Compact, rosette-forming, evergreen or semi-evergreen perennials with small, short-stemmed, inversely lance-shaped to obovate, mid-green leaves, 10cm (4in) long. Salverform flowers, 4.5cm (1¾in) across, in a range of colours, including numerous bicolours, with prominent yellow or creamy yellow eyes, are borne in spring. Cultivation group 6. ↕ 8–10cm (3–4in), ↔ 20cm (8in). ✻

P. juliae. Rosette-forming, semi-evergreen or deciduous perennial with rounded, scalloped, dark green leaves, to 10cm (4in) long, deeply heart-shaped at the bases. In spring and summer, bears solitary, long-stalked, saucer-shaped magenta flowers, to 3cm (1¼in) across, with yellow eyes. Cultivation group 1, 2, or 4. ↕ 7cm (3in), ↔ 25cm (10in). Rocky mountain forest in E. Caucasus. ✻✻✻

P.* x *kewensis (*P. floribunda* x *P. sinensis*). Rosette-forming, evergreen perennial with obovate to spoon-shaped, toothed, sparsely white-mealy, mid-green leaves, 15–20cm (6–8in) long. Each stem bears 2–5 whorls of 6–10 long-tubed, salverform, fragrant yellow flowers, to 2cm (¾in) across, in early spring. Cultivation group 6. ↕ to 45cm (18in), ↔ 20cm (8in). Garden origin. ✻. **'Mountain Spring'** ▣ is compact, with golden yellow flowers; ↕ to 25cm (10in). **'Thurgold'** produces lemon-yellow flowers.

***P.* 'Kinlough Beauty'.** Vigorous, evergreen or semi-evergreen Polyanthus Group primula with oval, dark green leaves, to 15cm (6in) long. In spring, salverform, salmon-pink flowers, 4cm (1½in) across, with cream stripes, are produced in umbels of 3–12. Cultivation group 1, 2, or 4. ↕ 10–15cm (4–6in), ↔ 30–40cm (12–16in). ✻✻✻

P. kisoana. Rosette-forming, hairy, deciduous perennial with rounded, shallowly lobed, mid-green leaves, to 15cm (6in) long. In spring and early summer, produces umbels of 2–6 tubular to funnel-shaped, pinkish purple flowers, to 3cm (1¼in) across. Cultivation group 2, 3, or 4. ↕ 20cm (8in), ↔ 40cm (16in). Woodland in S.W. Japan. ✻✻✻

***P.* 'Lady Greer'.** Dainty, evergreen or semi-evergreen Polyanthus Group primula with spoon-shaped, bottle-green leaves, to 12cm (5in) long. In spring, bears salverform, pale yellow flowers, 2cm (¾in) across. Cultivation group 2 or 3. ↕ 10–15cm (4–6in), ↔ 30–40cm (12–16in). ✻✻✻

P. latifolia. Rosette-forming, deciduous perennial with broadly lance-shaped, glandular-hairy, dull green leaves, to 15cm (6in) long, sometimes toothed at the tips. One-sided umbels of 2–25 salverform, sometimes white-mealy, fragrant, red-purple flowers, 1.5–2cm (½–¾in) across, are produced in late spring and early summer. Cultivation group 1, 2, or 4. ↕ 20cm (8in), ↔ 30cm (12in). Moist, shady, acid cliffs in Pyrenees and Alps. ✻✻✻

***P.* 'Linda Pope'** ▣ syn. *P. marginata* 'Linda Pope'. Vigorous, rosette-forming, evergreen or semi-evergreen perennial with oval, toothed, white-mealy, mid-green leaves, 10cm (4in) long. Umbels of 4–16 salverform, mauve-blue flowers, to 3cm (1¼in) across, with white-mealy eyes, are borne in spring. Cultivation group 4 or 5. ↕ 15cm (6in), ↔ 30cm (12in). ✻✻✻

***P.* 'Lingwood Beauty'.** Rosette-forming, evergreen or semi-evergreen, Primrose Group primula with oval, bright green leaves, to 12cm (5in) long. Umbels of 3–12 salverform crimson flowers, 2.5cm (1in) across, with deep orange eyes, are borne in late spring. Cultivation group 2 or 4. ↕ 10–15cm (4–6in), ↔ 30–40cm (12–16in). ✻✻✻

***P.* 'Linnet'** ▣ Rosette-forming, evergreen perennial bearing obovate, mid-green leaves, to 8cm (3in) long. In spring, bears umbels of salverform, yellow-eyed, orange to rose-pink flowers, 3cm (1¼in) across. Cultivation group 3 or 4. ↕ 10cm (4in), ↔ 20cm (8in). ✻✻✻

***P.* 'Lismore Yellow'.** Rosette-forming, evergreen perennial with ovate, dark green leaves, to 3cm (1¼in) long. In spring, short stems bear umbels of 2–5 open funnel-shaped, pale yellow flowers, 2.5cm (1in) across. Cultivation group 4 or 5. ↕ 10cm (4in), ↔ 15cm (6in). ✻✻✻

P. luteola. Rosette-forming, evergreen or semi-evergreen perennial with lance-shaped, sharply double-toothed, mid-green leaves, to 30cm (12in) long. In spring, robust, white-mealy stems bear symmetrical to spherical umbels of 10–25 salverform yellow flowers, 1.5cm (½in) across. Cultivation group 1 or 2. ↕ 35cm (14in), ↔ 45cm (18in). Moist meadows in E. Caucasus. ✻✻✻

P. macrophylla. Short-lived, rosette-forming, deciduous perennial with lance-shaped to inversely lance-shaped, entire or finely scalloped, mid-green leaves, to 25cm (10in) long, usually white-mealy beneath. In spring, white-mealy stems bear umbels of 5–25 salverform purple flowers, 2cm (¾in) across; the eyes are usually darker or tinged yellow. Cultivation group 2 or 4. ↕ 25cm (10in), ↔ 30cm (12in). Rocky alpine meadows in Himalayas. ✻✻✻

P. malacoides (Fairy primrose). Erect, rosette-forming, evergreen perennial, usually grown as an annual, with dainty, oval, slightly frilly-margined, softly downy, pale green leaves, to 10cm (4in) long. In winter and spring, flat, single or double, pale lilac-purple, reddish pink, and white flowers, to 1cm (½in) across, are borne in whorls of decreasing size up slender, softly hairy stems. Cultivation group 6. ↕ 30–45cm (12–18in), ↔ 20cm (8in). China. ✻. **'Benary's Special'** is compact, with blue, yellow, golden orange, scarlet, red-pink, rose-pink, or white flowers; ↕ to 30cm (12in).

P. marginata. Rosette-forming, evergreen or semi-evergreen perennial with obovate to oblong, toothed, leathery, mid-green leaves, to 10cm (4in) long, white-mealy on the margins. In spring, white-mealy stems each bear a symmetrical umbel of 2–20 shallowly tubular to funnel-shaped, faintly fragrant, lavender-blue flowers, to 3cm (1¼in) across, with white-mealy eyes. Cultivation group 4 or 5. ↕ 15cm (6in), ↔ 30cm (12in). Europe (Alps). ✻✻✻. **'Holden's Variety'**, syn. 'Holden Clough', is compact, with small, tubular to funnel-shaped, dark blue flowers,

Primula Polyanthus Group Cowichan Series

2cm (¾in) across. **'Hyacinthia'** see *P.* 'Hyacinthia'. **'Ivy Agee'** is vigorous, with heavily white-mealy leaves and lilac-blue flowers with cream eyes. **'Kesselring's Variety'** ▣ is moderately vigorous, with deep lavender-blue flowers. **'Linda Pope'** see *P.* 'Linda Pope'.

***P.* 'Mark'** ▣ Vigorous alpine Auricula primula with oval, vibrant green leaves, to 12cm (5in) long. In spring, bears salverform, light-centred, wine-purple to pink flowers, 2.5cm (1in) across. Cultivation group 4. ↕↔ 10cm (4in). ✻✻✻

***P.* 'Marven'.** Rosette-forming, evergreen or semi-evergreen perennial with white-mealy, ovate or obovate-oblong, light green leaves, to 10cm (4in) long. In spring, produces umbels of up to 15 tubular to funnel-shaped, deep violet-blue flowers, 3cm (1¼in) across, each with a very dark eye, bordered by a white-mealy zone. Cultivation group 4 or 5. ↕ 10cm (4in), ↔ 25cm (10in). ✻✻✻

***P.* 'McWatt's Cream'.** Rosette-forming, evergreen or semi-evergreen Polyanthus Group primula with short scapes and spoon-shaped, deep green leaves, 12cm (5in) long. In spring, bears 3- to 12-flowered umbels of salverform cream flowers, 2cm (¾in) across. Cultivation group 1, 2, or 4. ↕ 10–15cm (4–6in), ↔ 30–40cm (12–16in). ✻✻✻

P. melanops see *P. chionantha* subsp. *melanops*.

P. minima. Dwarf, rosette-forming, evergreen perennial with wedge-shaped, leathery, sharply toothed, shiny, dark green leaves, to 3cm (1¼in) long. In late spring, very short stems each produce sometimes 2 salverform, white-eyed, rose-pink, lilac, or white flowers, to 3cm (1¼in) across. Cultivation group 2 or 4. ↕ 7cm (3in), ↔ 20cm (8in). Alpine meadows in E. Alps and Balkans. ✻✻✻

P. modesta. Rosette-forming, deciduous perennial with elliptic to spoon-shaped, wavy-margined or toothed, mid-green leaves, to 8cm (3in) long, white-mealy beneath. In spring and early summer, produces umbels of 2–15 salverform, purple-pink flowers, 1.5cm (½in) across. Cultivation group 1 or 4. ↕↔ 20cm (8in). Moist alpine meadows in Japan. ✻✻✻. **var. *faurieae*** ▣ is smaller, with yellow-eyed, pinkish purple flowers, and broadly ovate, white-mealy leaves with rolled back margins.

P. nana, syn. *P. edgeworthii*. Rosette-forming, deciduous perennial with spoon-shaped to triangular-ovate, pale green leaves, to 12cm (5in) long, forming a tight rosette or crown in winter. From late winter to spring, very short stems bear umbels of flat, blue, lilac, pink, or white flowers, 3.5cm (1½in) across, with yellow and white eyes. Cultivation group 3 or 4. ↕ 10cm (4in), ↔ 15cm (6in). W. Himalayas. ❄❄❄

***P. nutans* of gardens** see *P. flaccida*.

P. obconica. Erect, rosette-forming, evergreen perennial, usually grown as an annual, with fairly coarse, oval to heart-shaped, toothed, mid-green leaves, to 15cm (6in) long. In winter and spring, produces salverform, pink, lilac-blue, red, or white flowers, 2.5–5cm (1–2in) across, sometimes with slightly frilled petal margins, in whorls of decreasing size up stout, hairy stems. Contact with the foliage may irritate skin, and the foliage may cause mild stomach upset if ingested. Cultivation group 6. ↕ 23–40cm (9–16in), ↔ to 25cm (10in). China. ❄❄. **'Appleblossom'**, syn. 'Apricot Brandy', produces large flowers in pale pink, flushing to salmon-pink, then deeper red-pink; ↕ to 20cm (8in). **'Apricot Brandy'** see 'Appleblossom'. **Cantata Series** cultivars are long-blooming, with flowers in carmine-red, pink, rose-pink, apricot-pink, lavender-blue, or white; ↕ 25–30cm (10–12in); **'Cantata Lavender'** ■ bears lavender-blue flowers. **'Pin Up'** has rose-pink flowers, and is free-flowering. **'Queen of the Market'** ■ has red-pink flowers; ↕ to 20cm (8in).

***P.* 'Old Yellow Dusty Miller'**. Vigorous border Auricula primula with spoon-shaped, white-mealy, mid-green leaves, to 12cm (5in) long. In spring, produces salverform yellow flowers, 3cm (1¼in) across, with white-mealy eyes. Cultivation group 1. ↕ 15cm (6in), ↔ 25cm (10in). ❄❄❄

***P.* 'Orb'**. Neat show Auricula primula with spoon-shaped or oval, dark green leaves, 12cm (5in) long. In spring, bears salverform, green-margined black flowers, 3cm (1¼in) across. Vigorous and easy to grow. Cultivation group 4. ↕↔ 10cm (4in). ❄❄❄

Primula pulverulenta 'Bartley'

***P.* 'Our Pat'**. Rosette-forming, evergreen or semi-evergreen Polyanthus Group primula with oval, purple-tinted, bronze-green leaves, to 15cm (6in) long. Umbels of 3–8 rounded, double, dark claret-red flowers, 4cm (1½in) across, are produced very freely in spring. Cultivation group 1, 2, or 4. ↕ 10–15cm (4–6in), ↔ 30–40cm (12–16in). ❄❄❄

P. palinuri ■ Rosette-forming, evergreen perennial with spoon-shaped to oblong-ovate, sometimes glandular-hairy, more or less toothed, fleshy, mid-green leaves, to 20cm (8in) long. In late winter and early spring, stout stems bear umbels of 3–40 nodding, narrowly funnel-shaped, scented yellow flowers, 1.5cm (½in) across, with white-mealy eyes. Cultivation group 1 or 4; requires full sun. ↕↔ 30cm (12in). Coastal cliffs in S. Italy. ❄❄❄

P. parryi. Rosette-forming, deciduous perennial with obovate to inversely lance-shaped, leathery, entire or finely toothed, mid-green leaves, to 35cm (14in) long, covered in short glands. In spring and summer, stout, erect stems bear one-sided umbels of 3–20 pendent, funnel-shaped, strongly scented, red-purple to magenta flowers, to 3cm (1¼in) across; these are yellow-eyed with dark haloes. Cultivation group 2 or 4. ↕↔ 45cm (18in). Shady mountain areas in W. USA. ❄❄❄

***P.* 'Peter Klein'**. Rosette-forming, semi-evergreen or deciduous perennial with rounded to ovate, bright mid-green leaves, to 6cm (2½in) long. In spring, stout stems produce umbels of 2–5 salverform, bright, deep pink flowers, 2.5cm (1in) across. Cultivation group 2 or 4. ↕↔ 15cm (6in). ❄❄❄

P. petiolaris ■ Rosette-forming, evergreen perennial with spoon-shaped, finely toothed, mid-green leaves, to 10cm (4in) long. In spring, salverform, magenta-purple flowers, 2cm (¾in) across, yellow-eyed and with thin white borders, are borne singly on short stalks, 2–5cm (¾–2in) long. Cultivation group 3 or 4. ↕ 10cm (4in), ↔ 20cm (8in). Himalayas. ❄❄❄

***P.* Polyanthus Group** (Polyanthus). Rosette-forming, evergreen to semi-evergreen perennials of garden origin, with a complicated parentage believed to include *P. veris*, *P. elatior*, *P. vulgaris*, and the red-flowered European primula, *P. juliae*. They form sturdy rosettes of oval, heavily veined, dark green leaves, to 18cm (7in) long, almost corrugated in appearance. Large, salverform, mostly yellow-centred, red, blue, orange, yellow, white, or pink flowers, to 5cm (2in) across, are borne in umbels of 3–15 on thick, hairy stems, to 15cm (6in) long, from late winter to mid-spring. Some seed mixtures are available that produce hardy spring bedding plants. Cultivation group 1, 2, 4, or 6. **Cowichan Series** ■ cultivars bear bronze-flushed foliage, and flowers in strong, velvety, yellow, blue, red, maroon, or purple, without central yellow eyes. **Crescendo Series** ■ cultivars are winter-hardy, with large, yellow-centred flowers, 5cm (2in) across, available in a number of separate ranges, classified by colour. **Rainbow Series** cultivars are short-stemmed, with yellow-centred flowers in blue, creamy yellow, pink, carmine-red, scarlet-red, white, or yellow, as well as some unusual rusty orange shades.

Primula palinuri

Primula petiolaris

Primula Polyanthus Group Crescendo Series

Primula polyneura

Primula prolifera

Primula Prominent Series

Primula x *pubescens* 'Mrs. J.H. Wilson'

Primula pulverulenta

Primula reidii var. *williamsii*

P. polyneura ■ Rosette-forming, deciduous perennial with ovate to rounded, 7- to 11-lobed, mid-green leaves, to 30cm (12in) long. Each stem produces 1–3 umbels, each with 2–12 salverform, yellow-eyed, purplish pink flowers, 2.5cm (1in) across, in late spring and summer. Cultivation group 2. ↕↔ 45cm (18in). Woodland in W. China. ❄❄❄

P. prolifera ■ Rosette-forming, evergreen Candelabra primula with spoon- to diamond-shaped, finely toothed, deep green leaves, to 35cm (14in) long. In early summer, stout stems each produce 1–7 whorls of 3–12 salverform, fragrant, white-mealy, pale to golden yellow or occasionally dull violet flowers, 2.5cm (1in) across. Cultivation group 2. ↕↔ 60cm (24in). Moist, shady alpine areas from India (Assam) to S.W. China, N. Burma, and Indonesia (Sumatra, Java). ❄❄❄

***P.* Prominent Series** ■ Dwarf, compact, semi-evergreen or evergreen perennials with inversely lance-shaped to obovate, mid-green leaves, 10cm (4in) long. In mid- and late winter, salverform flowers, 4–5cm (1½–2in) across, are borne in a very wide range of colours, including bicolours. Cultivation group 6. ↕ 8–10cm (3–4in), ↔ 15–20cm (6–8in). ❄

P.* x *pubescens (*P. auricula* x *P. hirsuta*). Vigorous, rosette-forming, evergreen perennial with obovate to broadly spoon-shaped, sometimes entire, white-mealy, usually mid-green leaves, to 10cm (4in) long. Umbels of few to many salverform flowers, 1.5–2.5cm (½–1in) across, in white, yellow, pink, red, purple, or brown, are borne very freely in spring. Cultivation group 1 or 4. ↕ to 15cm (6in), ↔ 30cm (12in). Garden origin. ❄❄❄. **'Faldonside'** produces dusky red-pink flowers with white eyes; ↕ 7–10cm (3–4in). **'Harlow Car'** has shallowly toothed leaves and large, creamy white flowers, 3cm (1¼in) across; ↕ 7–10cm (3–4in). **'Mrs. J.H. Wilson'** ■ bears compact rosettes of lance-shaped to obovate, rather thick, grey-green leaves, and fragrant, white-eyed purple flowers; ↕ 7cm (3in). **'Rufus'** produces shallowly toothed, pale green leaves, and umbels of up to 16 large, almost brick-red flowers, to 3cm (1¼in) across, with golden yellow eyes; ↕ 8–10cm (3–4in).

P. pulverulenta ■ Rosette-forming, deciduous Candelabra primula with obovate or inversely lance-shaped, finely toothed, mid-green leaves, to 30cm (12in) long. In late spring and early summer, stout, white-mealy stems each bear several whorls of tubular, deep red or red-purple flowers, 2.5cm (1in) across, with darker red or purple eyes. Cultivation group 2. ↕ to 1m (3ft), ↔ 60cm (24in). Wet hillsides in China (Sichuan). ❄❄❄. **'Bartley'** ■ has shell-pink flowers with red eyes.

P. reidii. Robust, rosette-forming, deciduous perennial with oblong to oblong-lance-shaped, scalloped or lobed leaves, to 20cm (8in) long. In summer, produces compact umbels of 3–10 pendent, bell-shaped, fragrant white flowers, 2.5cm (1in) across, often white-mealy on the outsides. Cultivation group 3 or 4. ↕ 5–15cm (2–6in), ↔ 10–15cm (5–6in). N.E. India to C. Nepal (Himalayas). ❄❄❄. **var. *williamsii*** ■ is more robust, producing flowers that are pale blue to white; ↕↔ 15cm (6in); W. and C. Nepal.

Primula rosea

Primula rusbyi

Primula secundiflora

Primula sieboldii 'Wine Lady'

Primula sonchifolia

Primula veris

Primula vulgaris 'Double Sulphur'

Primula 'Wanda'

Primula warshenewskiana

P. rosea ▣ Rosette-forming, deciduous perennial with obovate to inversely lance-shaped, scalloped or finely toothed, mid-green, often bronze-flushed leaves, to 20cm (8in) long, tinted red-bronze at first, emerging after the flowers. Umbels of 4–12 salverform, yellow-eyed, red-pink flowers, to 2.5cm (1in) across, are borne in spring. Cultivation group 2. ↕↔ 20cm (8in). Wet meadows from Afghanistan to Nepal. ❄❄❄. **'Grandiflora'** is vigorous, producing larger flowers, to 3cm (1¼in) across; ↕ to 20cm (8in).

P

Primula vialii

P. rubra see *P. hirsuta.*
P. rusbyi ▣ Rosette-forming, deciduous perennial with elliptic to spoon-shaped, entire or toothed, glandular-hairy, mid-green leaves, 3–10cm (1¼–4in) long. One-sided umbels of 4–12 salverform, rose-red to deep purple flowers, 3cm (1¼in) across, with incurved petals, are produced in spring and summer. Cultivation group 2 or 4. ↕ 20cm (8in), ↔ 35cm (14in). S.E. Arizona, S.W. New Mexico. ❄❄❄
P.* x *scapeosa (*P. bracteosa* x *P. scapigera*)**.** Vigorous, rosette-forming perennial bearing oblong to spoon-shaped, toothed, mid-green leaves, to 15cm (6in) long. In spring, salverform, pink-purple flowers, 2.5cm (1in) across, are produced singly on short stalks. Cultivation group 3 or 4. ↕ 10cm (4in), ↔ 25cm (10in). Garden origin. ❄❄❄
***P.* 'Schneekissen'**, syn. *P.* 'Snow Cushion'. Very compact, rosette-forming, evergreen Primrose Group primula with rounded, pale green leaves, 10cm (4in) long. Short stems bear umbels of 3–8 salverform, pure white flowers, 2.5cm (1in) across, in spring. Cultivation group 1, 2, or 4. ↕ 8–10cm (3–4in), ↔ 20cm (8in). ❄❄❄
P. secundiflora ▣ Rosette-forming, evergreen or semi-evergreen perennial with oblong to obovate or inversely lance-shaped, mid-green leaves, to 30cm (12in) long, with scalloped to toothed margins, and yellow-mealy beneath when young. In summer, stout stems produce one-sided umbels of 5–20 nodding, tubular to bell-shaped, red-purple or deep rose-red flowers, 2.5cm (1in) across. Cultivation group 2. ↕ 60–90cm (24–36in), ↔ 60cm (24in). Wet alpine meadows in S.E. Tibet and W. China. ❄❄❄
P. sieboldii. Rosette-forming, deciduous perennial with oblong-ovate, lobed, toothed, downy, pale green leaves, to 20cm (8in) long. In late spring and early summer, bears umbels of 2–15 salverform flowers, 2.5cm (1in) across; the flowers are rose-violet to lilac-purple or deep crimson, with white eyes, sometimes pure white. Cultivation group 2. ↕ 30cm (12in), ↔ 45cm (18in). Moist meadows and woodland in Japan. ❄❄❄. **'Musashino'** is vigorous, and bears large, pale rose-pink flowers, 3.5cm (1½in) across, darker beneath. **'Shi-un'** produces fringed flowers that are dark lavender-pink, fading to lavender-blue. **'Snowflake'** is vigorous, producing large white flowers, 3.5cm (1½in) across, with deeply cut petals. **'Sumina'** bears large, wisteria-blue flowers, 3cm (1¼in) across. **'Wine Lady'** ▣ produces white flowers, flushed with purple-red.
P. sikkimensis (Himalayan cowslip). Rosette-forming, deciduous perennial with oblong to lance-shaped, elliptic or oblong to inversely lance-shaped, toothed, shining, pale green leaves, to 30cm (12in) long. Produces umbels of numerous pendent, funnel-shaped, white-mealy, yellow or cream flowers, 2.5cm (1in) across, in late spring and early summer. Cultivation group 2. ↕ 60–90cm (24–36in), ↔ 60cm (24in). Wet meadows in Himalayas (W. Nepal to S.W. China). ❄❄❄
P. sinensis. Erect, rosette-forming, evergreen perennial, usually grown as an annual, bearing broadly ovate to rounded, toothed, hairy, bright mid-green leaves, 8–10cm (3–4in) long, often red beneath. In winter and early spring, bears salverform, wavy-margined, purple to pink flowers, to 4cm (1½in) across, in 6- to 10-flowered whorls of decreasing size on thick, hairy stems. ↕↔ 15–20cm (6–8in). Cultivation group 6. Possibly N. China. ❄. **Single Superb Mixed** has flowers in white, pink, red, and lilac-blue; ↕ to 25cm (10in), ↔ to 15cm (6in).
P. sinopurpurea see *P. chionantha* subsp. *sinopurpurea.*
***P.* 'Snow Cushion'** see *P.* 'Schneekissen'.
P. sonchifolia ▣ Rosette-forming, deciduous perennial with oblong to obovate, mid-green leaves, to 20cm (8in) long, with small, toothed lobes. In spring, very short stems (elongating in fruit) bear umbels of 3–20 salverform, yellow-eyed, white-margined, lavender-blue flowers, 2.5cm (1in) across. Overwinters as large, white-mealy buds. Cultivation group 3 or 4. ↕ 5cm (2in), ↔ 30cm (12in). Open meadows near the snow line in China, S.E. Tibet, and Burma. ❄❄❄
P. suffrutescens. Mat-forming, evergreen perennial with long rhizomes, and rosettes of wedge-shaped to spoon-shaped, scalloped to toothed, fleshy, dusky green leaves, to 5cm (2in) long. In summer, produces umbels of 2–10 salverform, yellow-eyed, rose-pink to red or purple flowers, 2cm (¾in) across. Cultivation group 1 or 4. ↕ 15cm (6in), ↔ 30cm (12in). USA (California, Sierra Nevada mountains). ❄❄❄
***P.* 'Tawny Port'.** Very dwarf, rosette-forming, evergreen or semi-evergreen Polyanthus Group primula bearing rounded to oval, toothed, maroon-green leaves, 15cm (6in) long. Short stems produce salverform, dark port-wine-coloured flowers, 3.5cm (1½in) across, singly or in umbels of up to 5, over a long period from early to late spring. Cultivation group 1, 2, or 4. ↕ 10–15cm (4–6in), ↔ 15–20cm (6–8in). ❄❄❄
P. veris ▣ (Cowslip). Very variable, rosette-forming, evergreen or semi-evergreen perennial with oblong-ovate to ovate, sometimes scalloped, mid-green leaves, to 20cm (8in) long. In mid- and late spring, produces umbels of 2–16 salverform, nodding, fragrant, deep yellow flowers, 1.5–2.5cm (½–1in) across. Cultivation group 1 or 2. ↕↔ 25cm (10in). Europe to W. Asia. ❄❄❄
P. vialii ▣ Rosette-forming, deciduous, often short-lived perennial with broadly lance-shaped to oblong, toothed, softly hairy, mid-green leaves, to 30cm (12in) long. Stiff, stout, white-mealy stems produce dense spikes, to 15cm (6in) long, of many pendent, tubular, blue-violet flowers, 1cm (½in) across, in summer. In bud, the calyces are bright crimson. Cultivation group 2. ↕ 30–60cm (12–24in), ↔ 30cm (12in). Moist mountain areas in China (Sichuan, Yunnan). ❄❄❄
P. villosa. Rosette-forming, evergreen perennial bearing obovate or spoon-shaped to oblong, toothed, fleshy, glandular-hairy leaves, 2–15cm (¾–6in) long. In early summer, red-hairy stems produce umbels of 4–12 salverform, white-eyed, pink to lilac flowers, to 2.5cm (1in) across. Cultivation group 2 or 4. ↕↔ 15cm (6in). Austria (Tyrol). ❄❄❄
P. vulgaris (Primrose). Rosette-forming, evergreen or semi-evergreen perennial with inversely lance-shaped to obovate, toothed to scalloped, deeply veined, bright green leaves, to 25cm (10in) long, softly hairy beneath. From early to late spring, produces clusters of 3–25 salverform, often fragrant, usually pale yellow flowers, 2.5–4cm (1–1½in) across. Cultivation group 2. ↕ 20cm (8in), ↔ 35cm (14in). Open woodland and shady banks in Europe and W. Turkey. ❄❄❄. Many cultivars have been produced, of which some are hybrids, but with a similar habit to the species, and with double flowers. **'Alba Plena'**, syn. 'Double White', is vigorous and free-flowering, with fully double white flowers on long stalks. **'Double Sulphur'** ▣ is vigorous, bearing sage-

Primula vulgaris 'Miss Indigo'

green leaves and double yellow flowers. **'Double White'** see 'Alba Plena'. **'Jack in the Green'** has single yellow blooms, each backed by a ring of bract-like leaves. **'Ken Dearman'** has double orange flowers, flushed with yellow and copper. **'Marie Crousse'** is vigorous, with large, scented, double violet flowers, 3cm (1¼in) across, splashed white. **'Miss Indigo'** ■ is vigorous, and bears double, deep rich purple flowers with creamy white tips. **subsp. *sibthorpii*** ■ has wedge-shaped leaves, with usually rose-pink, red, lilac, purple, or white flowers; Balkans, Ukraine (Crimea), Caucasus, Turkey, Armenia.

***P.* 'Wanda'** ■ Very vigorous, long-flowering, rosette-forming, evergreen or semi-evergreen perennial with oval, toothed, purplish green leaves, to 12cm (5in) long. Produces clusters of solitary, salverform, dark claret-red flowers, to 3.5cm (1½in) across, in spring. Thrives well in both sun and shade. Cultivation group 1 or 2. ↕10–15cm (4–6in), ↔ 30–40cm (12–16in). ❄❄❄

***P.* Wanda Supreme Series** ■ Evergreen or semi-evergreen perennials with small, inversely lance-shaped to obovate, bronze to dark green leaves, 8–10cm (3–4in) long. From winter to mid-spring, bears flowers, 4–5cm (1½–2in) across, in a mixture of different shades of blue, yellow, purple, burgundy, red, rose, and pink bicolours. Cultivation group 1 or 2. ↕8–10cm (3–4in), ↔ 15cm (6in). ❄❄

P. warshenewskiana ■ Rosette-forming, deciduous perennial with oblong to inversely lance-shaped, finely toothed, dark green leaves, to 7cm (3in)

Primula Wanda Supreme Series

long. Salverform, rose-pink flowers, 1.5cm (½in) across, with white-ringed yellow eyes, are borne singly or in umbels of up to 8, on short stems in late spring to summer. Cultivation group 2 or 4. ↕7cm (3in), ↔ 15cm (6in). Streamsides and wet ground from Tajikistan to Pakistan. ❄❄❄

***P. wilsonii* var. *anisodora*,** syn. *P. anisodora.* Rosette-forming, semi-evergreen Candelabra primula with obovate, finely toothed, aniseed-scented, mid-green leaves, to 25cm (10in) long. Stout stems produce 3–5 whorls of 8–10 pendent, tubular to bell-shaped, brown-purple flowers with green eyes, 1.5cm (½in) across, in summer. Cultivation group 2. ↕↔ 60cm (24in). Wet meadows in S.W. China. ❄❄❄

Primula vulgaris subsp. *sibthorpii*

P. wulfeniana. Rosette-forming, evergreen perennial with lance-shaped or elliptic to inversely lance-shaped or obovate, leathery, glandular-hairy, dark green leaves, 1.5–4cm (½–1½in) long. In spring, produces solitary or paired, salverform, rose-red to lilac flowers, to 2.5cm (1in) across, with deeply notched petal lobes. Cultivation group 4 or 5. ↕7cm (3in), ↔ 8cm (3in). Austrian Alps to S. Carpathians. ❄❄❄

P. yargongensis see *P. involucrata* subsp. *yargongensis.*

▷ **Primula, Drumstick** see *Primula denticulata*

▷ **Prince's feather** see *Amaranthus cruentus, Persicaria orientale*

▷ **Princess feather** see *Persicaria orientale*

▷ **Princess tree** see *Paulownia tomentosa*

PRINSEPIA

ROSACEAE

Genus of 4 species of arching, spiny, deciduous shrubs found in woodland and thickets in the Himalayas and China. They are cultivated for their linear to elliptic or oblong-lance-shaped leaves, which are rich green on opening, later glossy or dull dark green. They are also valued for their fragrant, cup-shaped, white to yellow flowers, and for their cherry-like, spherical or ovoid, purple or red fruits. Grow in a shrub border, against a wall, or as a hedge; the leaves appear early, and are an excellent foil for other early flowering shrubs.

- **HARDINESS** Fully hardy.
- **CULTIVATION** Grow in fertile, well-drained but not dry soil in full sun, in an open position with room to spread. Pruning group 1; cut out dead wood in summer.
- **PROPAGATION** Sow seed in containers in an open frame in autumn. Take greenwood cuttings in early summer.
- **PESTS AND DISEASES** Trouble free.

P. uniflora ■ Spreading, deciduous shrub with arching shoots bearing sharp spines and alternate, narrowly oblong to linear-oblong, glossy, rich dark green leaves, to 6cm (2½in) long. From early spring to summer, cup-shaped, fragrant white flowers, 1.5cm (½in) across, are produced singly or in clusters of up to 8, along the shoots; they are followed by cherry-like, red or purple fruit, 1cm (½in) across. ↕1.5m (5ft), ↔ 2.5m (8ft). China (N.W. China, Inner Mongolia). ❄❄❄

Prinsepia uniflora

PRITCHARDIA

ARECACEAE/PALMAE

Genus of about 37 species of single-stemmed palms from upland areas with high rainfall, on moist hillsides, and in rainforest valleys on volcanic soils in Fiji, Hawaii, and adjacent Pacific islands. They are cultivated for their fan-shaped, rich, mid-green or silvery or greyish green leaves, which are borne in terminal tufts. They produce small, bell-shaped, white, cream, yellow, or orange flowers in spikes or panicles between the leaves. In frost-prone climates, grow in a warm greenhouse. In tropical areas, they are suitable for growing as lawn specimens or in other strategic sites.

- **HARDINESS** Frost tender.
- **CULTIVATION** Under glass, grow in loam-based potting compost (JI No.3) with added sharp sand, in bright filtered light. During the growing season, water freely and apply a liquid feed every month; water sparingly in winter. Outdoors, grow in fertile, moist but well-drained soil in partial shade.
- **PROPAGATION** Sow seed at 24°C (75°F) in spring.
- **PESTS AND DISEASES** Prone to scale insects and red spider mites under glass.

P. gaudichaudii ■ 🌴 Small palm with an erect, columnar trunk and long-stalked, fan-shaped leaves, 1–1.2m (3–4ft) long, deeply cut into many slender lobes, brown-hairy beneath, rich to silvery green above. Bell-shaped yellow flowers are borne in spikes up to 1m (3ft) long, usually in summer. ↕2–5m (6–15ft), ↔ 2.5–3.5m (8–11ft). Hawaii. ❁ (min. 16–18°C/61–64°F)

P. pacifica 🌴 (Fiji fan palm). Small to medium-sized palm with a smooth, slim, columnar trunk. Long-stalked, fan-shaped leaves, 1m (3ft) or more long, are white-downy when young, then smooth, rich green; they are divided for about one-third of their length into slender, pointed lobes. Bell-shaped, white to yellow flowers are borne in stiff panicles, 1m (3ft) long, in summer. ↕to 10m (30ft), ↔ 4–5m (12–15ft). Fiji. ❁ (min. 16–18°C/61–64°F)

▷ **Privet** see *Ligustrum*
Amur see *L. amurense*
Chinese see *L. lucidum*
Common see *L. vulgare*
Golden see *L. ovalifolium* 'Aureum'
Japanese see *L. japonicum*

Pritchardia gaudichaudii

P

PROBOSCIDEA

Elephant's tusk, Proboscis flower, Unicorn plant

PEDALIACEAE

Genus of about 9 species of erect to spreading, robust, frequently sticky-hairy annuals and perennials found in open plains in tropical North, Central, and South America. They are grown for the tropical effect of their foliage and fruits; the fruits can be dried and used for winter arrangements. The opposite, occasionally alternate, long-stemmed, fairly coarse leaves are rounded to ovate-lance-shaped, entire to palmately or pinnately lobed, and strongly veined. The flowers are borne in racemes, and are funnel- to bell-shaped, 5-lobed, reddish purple, lavender-pink, creamy white, or orange-yellow, with enclosing calyces split to the bases on one side; they are followed by unusually shaped fruits, which each have a pair of strongly upcurved, slender, horn-like beaks or projections at one end, and a fringed crest along the centre of the capsule body. The cultivated species are annuals, and are suitable for a mixed border; they may also be grown as decorative container plants in a cool or temperate greenhouse or conservatory.

- **HARDINESS** Half hardy.
- **CULTIVATION** Under glass, grow in loam-based potting compost (JI No.2) in full light. During the growing season, water freely and apply a balanced liquid fertilizer every 4 weeks. Discard after flowering. Outdoors, grow in fertile, moist but well-drained soil in full sun.
- **PROPAGATION** Sow seed at 21–24°C (70–75°F) in spring.
- **PESTS AND DISEASES** Trouble free.

P. fragrans. Spreading, thick-stemmed, softly hairy annual bearing rounded, broadly ovate to broadly triangular, 5-lobed leaves, to 25cm (10in) long. In summer, produces loose racemes of 8–20 funnel-shaped, fragrant, reddish purple to purple flowers, to 5cm (2in) across; the upper lobes are marked dark purple, each with a strong yellow band extending into the throat. The flowers are followed by narrow, canoe-shaped, crested fruit, to 6cm (2½in) long, with beak-like projections, to 18cm (7in) long, at one end. ↕ to 45cm (18in), ↔ to 90cm (36in). USA (Texas) to Mexico. ✲

P. jussieui see *P. louisianica.*

P. louisianica, syn. *P. jussieui*, *P. proboscidea* (Common devil's claw, Common unicorn plant, Ram's horn). Erect to spreading, thick-stemmed, softly hairy annual with rounded to broadly ovate, unlobed, wavy-margined leaves, 6–20cm (2½–8in) long. In summer, bears open racemes of 8–20 funnel-shaped, creamy white to purple flowers, 3.5–5cm (1½–2in) across, flecked reddish purple and marked yellow within the throats; they are followed by crested, boat-shaped fruit, 10–20cm (4–8in) long, each with a pair of horn-like projections at one end that are longer than the fruit body. ↕ to 45cm (18in), ↔ to 90cm (36in). C. and S.E. USA. ✲

P. proboscidea see *P. louisianica.*

▷**Proboscis flower** see *Proboscidea*

Promenaea xanthina

PROMENAEA

ORCHIDACEAE

Genus of about 15 species of small, evergreen, epiphytic orchids from Brazil, occurring in forest areas at an altitude of around 1,500m (5,000ft). They produce oval pseudobulbs with 1–3 soft-textured, ovate-lance-shaped, light green, apical leaves. Usually yellow or white flowers are borne in ones or twos, rarely more, in short racemes from the bases of the pseudobulbs, mostly in summer and autumn.

- **HARDINESS** Frost tender.
- **CULTIVATION** Cool-growing orchids. Grow in small pots of epiphytic orchid compost made with fine bark, or epiphytically on slabs of bark. During summer, provide high humidity and bright filtered light, water freely (taking care not to overwater), and feed at every third watering. In winter, admit full light and water sparingly. See also p.46.
- **PROPAGATION** Divide when the plant fills the pot and "flows" over the sides, or remove backbulbs.
- **PESTS AND DISEASES** Prone to red spider mites, aphids, and mealybugs.

P. xanthina ■ Epiphytic orchid with clustered, oval pseudobulbs each with 2 broadly oval, soft-textured, light green leaves, 5cm (2in) long. Fragrant, lemon-yellow flowers, 4cm (1½in) across, with red-dotted lips, are borne in summer. ↕ 8cm (3in), ↔ 15cm (6in). Brazil. ❀ (min. 13°C/55°F; max. 30°C/86°F)

▷**Propeller plant** see *Crassula perfoliata* var. *minor*

▷**Prophet flower** see *Arnebia pulchra*

▷***Prosartes*** see *Disporum*

PROSTANTHERA

Mint bush

LABIATAE/LAMIACEAE

Genus of 50 species of bushy, evergreen shrubs and small trees from heathland and dry forest to rainforest and seashore (some species at subalpine and alpine level) in Australia. They are grown for their simple, entire or toothed, aromatic leaves, borne in opposite pairs, and leafy, terminal racemes or panicles of broadly tubular, cup- or bell-shaped, 2-lipped, 5-lobed, white, blue, or purple, occasionally red, yellow, or green flowers. In frost-prone climates, grow all but *P. cuneata* in a cool greenhouse. In warmer areas, grow in a mixed or shrub border, or at the base of a house wall.

Prostanthera cuneata (inset: flower detail)

- **HARDINESS** Frost hardy to half hardy.
- **CULTIVATION** Under glass, grow in loam-based potting compost (JI No.2) in full light. When in growth, water moderately and apply a balanced liquid fertilizer monthly; water sparingly in winter. Outdoors, grow in moderately fertile, moist but well-drained soil in full sun. Pruning group 8, after flowering; hard pruning may be detrimental.
- **PROPAGATION** Sow seed at 13–18°C (55–64°F) in spring, or take semi-ripe cuttings in summer.
- **PESTS AND DISEASES** Prone to red spider mites and whiteflies under glass.

P. cuneata ■ (Alpine mint bush). Bushy, erect to spreading shrub producing woody shoots. Tiny, obovate to rounded, entire leaves, 6mm (¼in) long, with wedge-shaped bases and rolled margins, are glossy, mid- to dark green, and strongly aromatic when crushed. In summer, bears racemes, 20cm (8in) long, of numerous broadly tubular white flowers, 1.5cm (½in) across, with purple and yellow markings within the wide tubes. ↕↔ 30–90cm (12–36in). Australia (subalpine and alpine levels from New South Wales to Tasmania). ✲✲

P. nivea (Snowy mint bush). Moderately bushy shrub, erect at first, then spreading, with slender, square-sectioned stems and entire, narrowly lance-shaped to linear, inrolled, bright green leaves, 2.5–4cm (1–1½in) long. In spring and early summer, bears bell-shaped, pure white, sometimes lavender-blue-tinted flowers, to 2cm (¾in) across, in racemes to 15cm (6in) long. ↕ 2–3m (6–10ft), ↔ 1.5–2m (5–6ft). S.E. Australia. ✲. **var. *induta*** produces lilac flowers and silvery green foliage.

P. ovalifolia ■ (Oval-leaved mint bush). Bushy shrub with erect stems and lance-shaped to inversely lance-shaped, entire, matt, grey-green leaves, to 1.5cm (½in) long. In late spring and early summer, an abundance of cup-shaped purple flowers, 1cm (½in) across, sometimes mauve, or white tinged with lilac, are borne in leafy, terminal racemes, 6–7cm (2½–3in) long. ↕ 2.5–4m (8–12ft), ↔ 1.5–2.5m (5–8ft). E. Australia. ✲

P. rotundifolia ■ (Round-leaved mint bush). Bushy, spreading shrub with

Prostanthera ovalifolia

P

Prostanthera rotundifolia

slender, hoary stems and rounded to ovate, scarcely toothed leaves, to 1.5cm (½in) long, deep green above, paler beneath. In late spring and early summer, bears bell-shaped, purple to lilac-purple flowers, 1cm (½in) across, in numerous short racemes, to 7cm (3in) long. ↕2–4m (6–12ft), ↔1–3m (3–10ft). S.E. Australia (including Tasmania). ✼. **var. *rosea***, syn. 'Chelsea Girl', produces grey-green leaves and light rose-pink flowers with mauve anthers.

PROTEA

PROTEACEAE

Genus of 115 species of evergreen shrubs and, rarely, small, usually upright trees found on rocky hillsides and dry scrub from tropical Africa to South Africa. The leaves are alternate to spiralling, simple, entire, and leathery. Proteas are cultivated for their usually solitary and terminal, mainly cone-like clusters or flat heads of small flowers surrounded by petal-like, green, white, pink to purple, or yellow bracts, each cluster resembling a single, large flower. Each floret is tubular, splitting into 4 sepals to reveal the long, straight or curved, usually coloured style. In frost-prone areas, grow in a cool, well-ventilated greenhouse. In warmer areas, use in a mixed or shrub border. Larger species are also fine specimen plants.

• **HARDINESS** Half hardy to frost tender.

• **CULTIVATION** Under glass, grow in a mixture of 1 part loam with added charcoal and 3 parts equal measures of grit (or perlite) and peat, in full light.

Protea cynaroides

Protea eximia

Water moderately during spring and summer; apply a liquid fertilizer of magnesium sulphate and urea, both at half recommended strength, once in spring and again in early autumn. Water sparingly in winter. Outdoors, grow in poor, neutral to acid, well-drained soil in full sun. Pruning group 1; may need restrictive pruning under glass.

• **PROPAGATION** Sow seed at 13–18°C (55–64°F) as soon as ripe or in spring, or take semi-ripe cuttings in summer.

• **PESTS AND DISEASES** Magnesium deficiency may result in chlorosis of the leaves. Die-back and general failure to thrive usually indicate that the rooting medium is too rich.

P. barbata see *P. speciosa*.
P. barbigera see *P. magnifica*.
P. compacta. Erect, moderately bushy shrub with oblong to elliptic, stalkless, horny-margined leaves, 5–13cm (2–5in) long. In spring and summer, oblong buds open to obovoid flowerheads, 7–10cm (3–4in) across, with bright pink, rarely white bracts, fringed with white hairs. ↕2.5–3.5m (8–11ft), ↔1.5–2.5m (5–8ft). South Africa (Western Cape). ✼
P. cynaroides ▣ (King protea). Robust-stemmed, sparsely to moderately branched shrub, often spreading with age. Rounded to elliptic leaves are 8–14cm (3–5½in) long, and are borne on stalks 4–18cm (1½–7in) long. From late spring to summer, produces goblet- or bowl-shaped flowerheads, 12–30cm (5–12in) across, with deep crimson-red to pink or cream bracts. ↕↔1–2m (3–6ft). South Africa (Western Cape, Eastern Cape). ✼
P. eximia ▣♀ Large shrub or small tree, rounded to broadly columnar, with fairly robust, sparsely branched stems. Ovate leaves are purple-flushed, silvery green, and glaucous, 6–10cm (2½–4in) long, sometimes with red margins, and heart-shaped at the bases. In spring and summer, bears oblong to inversely cone-shaped flowerheads, to 14cm (5½in) across, with red or red-tinted pink bracts, fringed with white hairs. ↕3–5m (10–15ft), ↔2–3m (6–10ft). South Africa (Western Cape). ✼
P. longifolia, syn. *P. minor*. Erect to spreading shrub with linear, ascending, stalkless, mid- to deep green leaves, 9–20cm (3½–8in) long. During summer, produces oblong to inversely conical flowerheads, 10cm (4in) long, with greenish white to pink bracts, the inner ones fringed with hairs. ↕2–3m (6–10ft), ↔1.5–2.5m (5–8ft). South Africa (Western Cape). ✼
P. magnifica, syn. *P. barbigera* (Woolly-bearded protea). Erect shrub, often spreading when young, with robust stems and oblong or lance-shaped, wavy-margined, greyish green leaves, 10cm (4in) or more long. From spring to summer, produces densely packed flowerheads, 15cm (6in) across, initially narrowly bell-shaped, opening to cup-shaped, with black-tipped white inner bracts and clear pink outer bracts, fringed with white hairs. ↕↔1.5–2.5m (5–8ft). South Africa (Western Cape). ✼
P. mellifera see *P. repens*.
P. minor see *P. longifolia*.
P. repens ▣♀ syn. *P. mellifera* (Sugarbush). Erect, moderately bushy shrub or sometimes small tree bearing erect, linear to lance-shaped leaves, to 15cm (6in) long. From spring to summer, produces flowerheads, obovoid in bud, goblet-shaped when open, to 9cm (3½in) across, with hairless bracts, uniformly cream-white or tipped with dark red to pink, and coated with a sticky resin. ↕2–4m (6–12ft), ↔1.5–3m (5–10ft). South Africa (Western Cape, Eastern Cape). ✼
P. scolymocephala. Rounded shrub with linear to spoon-shaped, tapered, wavy-margined, olive-green leaves, 4–9cm (1½–3½in) long. From late spring to summer, bears bowl-shaped flowerheads, to 5cm (2in) across, with creamy green bracts flushed pink at the tips. ↕0.9–1.5m (3–5ft), ↔75–120cm (30–48in). South Africa (Western Cape). ✼
P. speciosa, syn. *P. barbata*. Erect, moderately branched shrub with elliptic, leathery, orange-margined, mid-green leaves, 11cm (4½in) long. From summer to autumn, bears oblong-goblet-shaped flowerheads, 8cm (3in) across, with bearded, bright pink to creamy yellow bracts, fringed with tawny brown hairs. ↕1m (3ft), ↔80cm (32in). South Africa (Western Cape). ✼

▷**Protea,**
King see *Protea cynaroides*
Woolly-bearded see *Protea magnifica*

PRUMNOPITYS

PODOCARPACEAE

Genus of 10 species of dioecious, occasionally monoecious, evergreen, coniferous trees from forest in Puerto Rico through the Andes to southern Argentina, and from Malaysia to New Zealand. They are upright trees with whorled shoots, grown mainly for their linear or oblong, yew-like foliage. Male and female cones are borne at various times of the year: ovoid or cylindrical male cones are solitary or in groups of 2–20; spherical or ovoid female cones are solitary or borne in groups of up to 8. The fruits are like small, upright plums, but with only a thin, fleshy layer around the seed, and are borne in the leaf axils of short sideshoots. Grow as specimen trees or for hedging. In frost-prone areas, grow tender species in a cool or temperate greenhouse.

• **HARDINESS** Fully hardy to frost tender.

• **CULTIVATION** Grow in moderately fertile, moist but well-drained soil in full sun, with shelter from cold, drying winds. Clip hedges in early summer or midsummer.

• **PROPAGATION** Sow seed in containers outdoors in spring. Take semi-ripe cuttings in late summer.

• **PESTS AND DISEASES** Trouble free.

P. andina ♤ syn. *Podocarpus andinus* (Plum yew). Dioecious, ovoid tree, conical when young, frequently with several stems, with smooth, grey-brown bark and shoots that are green for 3 years. Linear, soft, dull bluish green leaves, 2–3cm (¾–1¼in) long, parted below the shoot, are more upright above, especially in the sun; each has 2 white bands beneath. Ovoid, white-tinged yellow male cones, 1–2.5cm

Protea repens (inset: flower detail)

(½–1in) long, are produced in racemes of 5–20 at various times of the year. Plum-shaped, yellowish white fruit, 2cm (¾in) long, have thin, fleshy, edible layers. ↕ 10–20m (30–70ft), ↔ 6–8m (20–25ft). Chile, Argentina. ❄❄❄

PRUNELLA
Self-heal

LABIATAE/LAMIACEAE

Genus of 7 species of spreading, semi-evergreen perennials, rooting freely at the nodes, found on dry grassland, on sunny banks, and in open woodland in Europe, Asia, North Africa, and North America. They are grown for their dense, upright spikes or heads of tubular, 2-lipped, white, pink, or violet flowers. The leaves are linear-lance-shaped to broadly ovate, simple or deeply lobed, often rounded at the bases, and either basal or in tufts on the stems. Self-heals make useful ground cover for banks, the front of a border, or a wild garden, where they attract bees and other beneficial insects. They are very vigorous, and must be sited where they will not swamp smaller plants.

- **HARDINESS** Fully hardy.
- **CULTIVATION** Grow in any soil in full sun or partial shade. Dead-head to prevent self-seeding.
- **PROPAGATION** Sow seed at 6–12°C (43–54°F) in spring. Divide in spring or autumn.
- **PESTS AND DISEASES** Susceptible to slugs and snails.

P. grandiflora ▣ (Large self-heal). Vigorous, spreading perennial bearing simple, ovate to ovate-lance-shaped, sparsely toothed, deep green leaves, 10cm (4in) long. In summer, leafy stems produce whorls of purple flowers, to 3cm (1¼in) long, with darker lips, in dense, upright spikes. ↕ 15cm (6in), ↔ 1m (3ft) or more. Europe. ❄❄❄. **'Pink Loveliness'** produces clear pink flowers. **'White Loveliness'** produces pure white flowers.

Prunella grandiflora

PRUNUS *syn.* AMYGDALUS
Ornamental cherry

ROSACEAE

Genus of more than 200 species of deciduous or evergreen, upright, rounded, or occasionally spreading trees or shrubs, widely distributed in N. temperate regions and to the Andes of South America and mountains of S.E. Asia. They occur mainly in woodland, woodland margins, and thickets, but also in a range of other habitats, including coastal sands, rocky places, and cliffs. They have alternate, broadly ovate to lance-shaped, elliptic, oblong, or obovate to almost rounded, usually toothed leaves. Ornamental cherries are cultivated mainly for their white, sometimes pink or red flowers, which are saucer-, bowl-, or cup-shaped, with 5 petals (more in semi-double or double forms); they are usually followed by fleshy, spherical or ovoid fruits. Some, such as *P. maackii* and *P. serrula*, are also grown for their shiny, coloured bark; many, including *P. sargentii*, have good autumn leaf colour. Certain *Prunus* species and cultivars, notably the plum (*P.* x *domestica*), cultivars of the almond (*P. dulcis*), and the peach (*P. persica*), are grown for their edible fruits. Leaves and fruits of most other species may cause severe discomfort if ingested.

They are excellent specimen trees, many being suitable for a small garden. Dense, bushy species, such as *P. laurocerasus* and *P. lusitanica,* are useful for screening and ground cover. *P. cerasifera*, *P.* x *cistena*, *P. incisa*, and *P. spinosa* are suitable for hedging. Grow shrubby species and their cultivars, such as *P. glandulosa* and *P. triloba,* against a wall or in a shrub border.

- **HARDINESS** Fully hardy to frost hardy.
- **CULTIVATION** Grow in any moist but well-drained, moderately fertile soil: deciduous species and cultivars in full sun, evergreens in full sun or partial shade. *P. glandulosa* needs hot sun to ripen its wood. *P. laurocerasus* may become chlorotic on shallow chalk soil. Pruning group 1 for trees and most deciduous shrubs (prune in midsummer in areas where silver leaf is a problem); group 5 for *P. glandulosa* and *P. triloba* (group 13 if wall-trained); group 8 for evergreen shrubs. Trim deciduous hedges after flowering, evergreens in early to mid-spring.
- **PROPAGATION** Sow seed of species in containers outdoors in autumn. Root greenwood cuttings of deciduous species in early summer, and semi-ripe cuttings of evergreens in midsummer, both with bottom heat. Bud cultivars in summer, or graft in early spring.
- **PESTS AND DISEASES** Susceptible to damage from aphids, caterpillars, and bullfinches. Diseases include peach leaf curl (on *P. dulcis* and *P. persica*), silver leaf, honey fungus, blossom wilt, bacterial canker, and *Taphrina wiesneri*, which causes witches' brooms.

***P.* 'Accolade'** ▣ ⌓ Spreading, deciduous tree with oblong, tapered, dark green leaves, to 10cm (4in) long. Clusters of 3 semi-double, pale pink flowers, 4cm (1½in) across, open from dark pink buds in early spring. ↕↔ 8m (25ft). ❄❄❄

***P.* 'Amanogawa'** ▯ Upright, deciduous tree bearing obovate leaves, to 12cm (5in) long, yellowish bronze in spring while still folded, often red, yellow, and green on the same tree, at the same time, in autumn. In late spring, bears dense clusters of saucer-shaped or semi-double, fragrant, pale pink flowers, 4cm (1½in) across, held vertically on stout stalks. ↕ 8m (25ft), ↔ 4m (12ft). ❄❄❄

P.* x *amygdalopersica ⌓ (*P. dulcis* x *P. persica*) syn. *P.* x *persicoides*. Spreading, deciduous tree bearing lance-shaped, tapered, mid-green leaves, to 12cm (5in) long, with sharply toothed margins. Solitary, saucer-shaped, light pink flowers, 5cm (2in) across, are borne in early and mid-spring, followed by spherical, peach-like, dry-fleshed green fruit, 4cm (1½in) across. ↕↔ 7m (22ft). Garden origin. ❄❄❄. **'Pollardii'** bears large, rich pink flowers in early spring.

P. avium ▣ ⌓ (Gean, Wild cherry). Spreading, deciduous tree with red-banded bark and ovate-oblong, dark green leaves, to 15cm (6in) long, bronze when young, turning red and yellow in autumn. Bowl-shaped white flowers, 3cm (1¼in) across, are borne in umbels in mid-spring, followed by heart-shaped to ovoid red fruit, 1cm (½in) across. ↕ 20m (70ft), ↔ 10m (30ft). Europe, N. Africa, S.W. Asia, Russia (W. Siberia). ❄❄❄. **'Plena'** ▣ has double flowers and red autumn colour; ↕↔ 12m (40ft).

P.* x *blireana ⌓ Spreading, deciduous shrub or small tree bearing ovate, red-purple leaves, to 6cm (2½in) long, turning dark green in summer. Solitary, double pink flowers, 3cm (1¼in) across, are produced before the leaves in early and mid-spring. ↕↔ 4m (12ft). Garden origin. ❄❄❄

P. campanulata ⌓ (Bell-flowered cherry, Taiwan cherry). Spreading, deciduous tree bearing ovate, tapered mid-green leaves, to 10cm (4in) long. Shallowly bowl-shaped, pink or red flowers, 2cm (¾in) across, in umbels of 2–5, are borne before or with the leaves in early and mid-spring, followed by ovoid, cherry-like red fruit, to 1.5cm (½in) across. ↕↔ 8m (25ft). S. China, Taiwan, S. Japan. ❄❄

P. cerasifera ⌓ (Cherry plum, Myrobalan). Rounded, deciduous tree with ovate to obovate, dark green leaves, to 6cm (2½in) long. Solitary, bowl-shaped white flowers, 2.5cm (1in) across, are borne along bare shoots in early spring, with the leaves, and are sometimes followed by spherical, plum-like, edible, red or yellow fruit, 3cm (1¼in) across. ↕↔ 10m (30ft). S.E. Europe, S.W. Asia. ❄❄❄. **'Nigra'** ▣ syn. 'Pissardii Nigra', has dark purple leaves, red when young, and pink flowers. **'Pissardii'**, syn. *P. pissardii*, has dark red-purple leaves, and pale pink flowers that fade to white. **'Pissardii Nigra'** see 'Nigra'. **'Thundercloud'** ▣ has pink flowers and dark purple foliage.

***P.* 'Cheal's Weeping'** ▣ ♀ syn. *P.* 'Kiku-shidare-zakura'. Weeping, deciduous tree bearing lance-shaped, tapered, mid-green leaves, to 10cm (4in) long, bronze when young. Fully double, bright pink flowers, 4cm (1½in) across, are borne in dense clusters, before or with the leaves, in mid- and late spring. ↕↔ 3m (10ft). ❄❄❄

Prunus cerasifera 'Nigra'

P

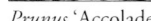

Prunus 'Accolade'

Prunus avium

Prunus avium 'Plena'

Prunus cerasifera 'Thundercloud'

Prunus 'Cheal's Weeping'

Prunus x *cistena*

Prunus dulcis 'Roseoplena'

Prunus glandulosa 'Alba Plena'

Prunus 'Hokusai'

Prunus incisa

Prunus jamasakura

Prunus 'Kanzan'

***P.* 'Chôshû-hizakura'** ♀ Broadly upright, deciduous tree with elliptic, tapered, dark green leaves, to 15cm (6in) long, bronze-red when young. Bowl-shaped or semi-double, mid-pink flowers, 3cm (1¼in) across, are borne in clusters of 2–4 in mid-spring. ↕7m (22ft), ↔6m (20ft). ❄❄❄
P.* x *cistena ▣ (*P. cerasifera* 'Atropurpurea' x *P. pumila*). Slow-growing, upright, deciduous shrub with oval, red-purple leaves, to 6cm (2½in) long, red when young. Solitary, bowl-shaped white flowers, 1cm (½in) across, are produced in late spring, sometimes followed by spherical, cherry-like, dark purple fruit, 2cm (¾in) across. ↕↔1.5m (5ft). Garden origin. ❄❄❄
P. davidiana ♀ Spreading, deciduous tree with slender, lance-shaped, long-pointed, somewhat glossy, dark green leaves, to 12cm (5in) long. Solitary, saucer-shaped, white or pale pink flowers, 2.5cm (1in) across, stalkless or almost so, are borne before the leaves in early spring, followed by spherical, woolly yellow fruit, to 3cm (1¼in) across. Flowers may be damaged by late frosts. ↕↔8m (25ft). China. ❄❄❄
P. dulcis ♀ (Common almond). Upright, spreading, deciduous tree with lance-shaped, finely toothed, tapered, dark green leaves, to 12cm (5in) long. Solitary or paired, bowl-shaped, pink or white flowers, 5cm (2in) across, are produced on bare shoots in early spring, followed by ovoid, velvety green fruit, to 6cm (2½in) long, each containing an edible nut. ↕↔8m (25ft). N. Africa, C. and S.W. Asia. ❄❄❄. **'Roseoplena'** ▣ bears double pink flowers.
***P.* 'Fudan-zakura'** ♀ syn. *P. serrulata* f. *semperflorens*. Small, spreading, deciduous tree with ovate, mid-green leaves, 6–12cm (2½–5in) long, rough on the upper surfaces. Intermittently from late autumn to mid-spring, soft pink buds open to shallowly cup-shaped, single white flowers, 4cm (1½in) across, in short-stalked clusters. ↕↔5m (15ft). ❄❄❄
P. glandulosa. Rounded, deciduous shrub bearing narrowly ovate or elliptic, finely toothed, pale to mid-green leaves, to 10cm (4in) long. In late spring, bowl-shaped, white to pale pink flowers, to 1cm (½in) across, are borne singly or in pairs, densely clustered along the branches; they are followed by spherical, dark red fruit, to 1cm (½in) across. ↕↔1.5m (5ft). N. and C. China, Japan. ❄❄❄. **'Alba Plena'** ▣ has double, pure white flowers. **'Rosea Plena'** see 'Sinensis'. **'Sinensis'**, syn. 'Rosea Plena', has double pink flowers.
***P.* 'Hally Jolivette'** ▣♀ Rounded, bushy, deciduous tree or shrub with ovate, dark green leaves, to 5cm (2in) long. Double white flowers, 3cm (1¼in) across, in clusters of up to 5, open from pink buds in mid- and late spring. ↕↔5m (15ft). ❄❄❄
***P.* 'Hillieri'** ♀ Spreading, deciduous tree with elliptic, dark green leaves, to 10cm (4in) long, bronze when young, orange-red in autumn. Many bowl-shaped, soft pink flowers, 4cm (1½in) across, are produced in clusters of up to 4, in mid-spring. ↕↔10m (30ft). ❄❄❄
***P.* x *hillieri* 'Spire'** see *P.* 'Spire'.
***P.* 'Hokusai'** ▣♀ syn. *P.* 'Uzuzakura'. Spreading, deciduous tree with oval, dark green leaves, to 12cm (5in) long, bronze when young, orange and red in autumn. In mid- and late spring, bears double, pale pink flowers, 5cm (2in) across, singly or in dense clusters of up to 6. ↕6m (20ft), ↔8m (25ft). ❄❄❄
***P.* 'Hosokawa'** see *P.* 'Mount Fuji'.
***P.* 'Ichiyo'** ♀ Spreading, deciduous tree with elliptic, dark green leaves, to 10cm (4in) long, bronze when young. Wide-open, double, soft pink flowers, 5cm (2in) across, are borne in long, pendent clusters of 3 or 4 in mid- and late spring. ↕↔8m (25ft). ❄❄❄
P. ilicifolia ♀ (Holly-leaved cherry). Compact, spreading, rounded, evergreen shrub or small tree with broadly lance-shaped to ovate, holly-like, sharply toothed, leathery, glossy, dark green leaves, to 5–7cm (2–3in) long. In summer, bowl-shaped white flowers, to 8mm (⅜in) across, are borne in racemes to 7cm (3in) long. Spherical, cherry-like red fruit, to 1.5cm (½in) across, ripen to blue-black. ↕to 9m (28ft), ↔6m (20ft). USA (California). ❄❄
P. incisa ▣♀ (Fuji cherry). Spreading, deciduous, rounded shrub, rarely tree-like, with ovate to obovate, sharply toothed, dark green leaves, to 6cm (2½in) long, bronze-red when young, turning orange-red in autumn. Saucer-shaped, white or pale pink flowers, 2cm (¾in) across, solitary or in clusters of 2 or 3, are borne before the leaves in early and mid-spring; they are followed by ovoid, cherry-like, purple-black fruit, to 8mm (⅜in) long. ↕↔8m (25ft). S.W. Japan. ❄❄❄. **'February Pink'** bears pale pink flowers over a long period in winter and early spring. **'Kojo-no-mai'** has oblong to lance-shaped leaves, 0.6–3cm (¼–1¼in) long, yellow-green when young, turning mid-green in summer. Light red buds open to pale red flowers, 1.5cm (½in) across, borne singly or in pairs. ↕↔2.5m (8ft). **'Praecox'** has pink buds that open to white flowers in late winter.

Prunus 'Hally Jolivette' (inset: flower detail)

P. jamasakura ▣♀ syn. *P. serrulata* var. *spontanea* (Hill cherry). Spreading, deciduous tree with oblong, dark green leaves, to 12cm (5in) long, bronze-red when young, turning red and yellow in autumn. In mid- and late spring, bears a profusion of cup-shaped white flowers, 3cm (1¼in) across, in clusters of 3–5, followed by ovoid, cherry-like, magenta-red fruit, to 1cm (½in) long. ↕↔12m (40ft). China, Korea, Japan. ❄❄❄
***P.* 'Jo-nioi'** ♀ Spreading, deciduous tree with elliptic, mid-green leaves, to 10cm (4in) long, pale bronze when young. Bowl-shaped, fragrant white flowers, 4cm (1½in) across, in clusters of 3–5, open from pink buds in mid-spring. ↕↔10m (30ft). ❄❄❄
***P.* 'Kanzan'** ▣♀ Upright, deciduous tree, vase-shaped when young, spreading wider with age, with ovate, dark green leaves, to 12cm (5in) long, bronze when young. Double, deep pink flowers, 5cm (2in) across, are profusely borne in clusters of 2–5 in mid- and late spring, before and as the leaves emerge. ↕↔10m (30ft). ❄❄❄
***P.* 'Kiku-shidare-zakura'** see *P.* 'Cheal's Weeping'.
***P.* 'Kursar'** ♀ Spreading, deciduous tree with elliptic, dark green leaves, to 12cm (5in) long, bronze when young. Saucer-shaped, dark pink flowers, 2cm (¾in) across, are profusely borne in clusters of 3 or 4 in early spring, before the leaves. ↕↔8m (25ft). ❄❄❄

P

Prunus laurocerasus

Prunus laurocerasus 'Otto Luyken'

Prunus laurocerasus 'Zabeliana'

Prunus lusitanica subsp. *azorica*

Prunus lusitanica 'Variegata'

Prunus mahaleb

Prunus 'Mount Fuji'

Prunus mume 'Beni-chidori'

Prunus mume 'Omoi-no-mama'

Prunus 'Okame'

Prunus padus

Prunus padus 'Colorata'

P. laurocerasus ■ (Cherry laurel, Laurel). Dense, bushy, evergreen shrub, becoming spreading and tree-like with age, with oblong, glossy leaves, to 15cm (6in) long, dark green above, pale green beneath. In mid- and late spring, cup-shaped, fragrant white flowers, 8mm (3/8in) across, are produced in upright racemes, 5–12cm (2–5in) long, followed by conical, cherry-like red fruit, 1cm (1/2in) across, ripening to black. ↕ 8m (25ft), ↔ 10m (30ft). E. Europe, S.W. Asia. ❄❄❄. **'Camelliifolia'** is upright, with conspicuously twisted leaves; ↔ 4m (12ft). **'Castlewellan'**, syn. 'Marbled White', has leaves conspicuously marked white; ↕↔ 5m (15ft). **'Green Carpet'** see 'Grünerteppich'. **'Grünerteppich'**, syn. 'Green Carpet', is low and spreading, with leaves to 12cm (5in) long; ↕ 1m (3ft), ↔ 3m (10ft). **'Herbergii'** has a compact habit, with narrow leaves; ↕↔ 3m (10ft). **'Marbled White'** see 'Castlewellan'. **'Otto Luyken'** ■ is very compact, with narrow, pointed, dark green leaves, to 11cm (4½in) long; frequently flowers again in autumn; ↕ 1m (3ft), ↔ 1.5m (5ft). **'Rotundifolia'** is vigorous and upright, excellent for hedging; ↕ 5m (15ft), ↔ 4m (12ft). **'Schipkaensis'** is spreading, and flowers profusely; ↕ 2m (6ft), ↔ 3m (10ft). **'Zabeliana'** ■ has a low and wide-spreading habit, very narrow leaves, and often flowers again in autumn; ↕ 1m (3ft), ↔ 2.5m (8ft).

P. lusitanica ♀ (Laurel, Portugal laurel). Dense, bushy, evergreen shrub or tree with red-stalked, ovate to elliptic, glossy, dark green leaves, to 12cm (5in) long. Cup-shaped, fragrant white flowers, 1.5cm (1/2in) across, are borne in slender, ascending, spreading, or pendent racemes, to 25cm (10in) long, in early summer, followed by ovoid, cherry-like red fruit, 1cm (1/2in) across, ripening to black. ↕↔ to 20m (70ft). S.W. Europe. ❄❄. **subsp. *azorica*** ■ has broader leaves, and racemes to 10cm (4in) long; Azores. **'Variegata'** ■ has leaves narrowly margined with white.

P. maackii ■ ♀ (Manchurian cherry). Conical, deciduous tree or shrub with peeling, yellow-brown bark and ovate, dark green leaves, to 8cm (3in) long, turning yellow in autumn. In mid-spring, produces dense racemes, 5–8cm (2–3in) long, each with 6–10 bowl-shaped, fragrant white flowers, 1cm (1/2in) across; they are followed by spherical, cherry-like, glossy black fruit, 5mm (1/4in) across. ↕ 10m (30ft), ↔ 8m (25ft). N.E. Asia. ❄❄❄

P. mahaleb ■ ♀ (St. Lucie cherry). Spreading, deciduous tree with rounded, glossy, dark green leaves, to 6cm (2½in) long, turning yellow in autumn. In mid- and late spring, bowl-shaped, very fragrant white flowers, 1.5cm (1/2in) across, are produced in racemes to 5cm (2in) long; they are followed by ovoid, glossy red cherries, 6mm (1/4in) long, ripening to black. ↕ 10m (30ft), ↔ 8m (25ft). Europe. ❄❄❄

Prunus maackii (inset: bark detail)

***P.* 'Mount Fuji'** ■ ♀ syn. *P.* 'Hosokawa', *P.* 'Shirotae'. Spreading, deciduous tree with slightly arching branches and elliptic, dark green leaves, to 12cm (5in) long, pale green when young, orange and red in autumn. In mid-spring, bears cup-shaped or semi-double, fragrant white flowers, 5cm (2in) across, in pendent clusters of 2 or 3. ↕ 6m (20ft), ↔ 8m (25ft). ❄❄❄

P. mume ♀ (Japanese apricot). Spreading, deciduous tree producing green shoots and rounded, tapered, dark green leaves, to 10cm (4in) long. Bowl-shaped, fragrant, white to dark pink flowers, 2.5cm (1in) across, are produced singly or in pairs, on bare shoots, in late winter and early spring; they are followed by spherical, softly hairy, apricot-like, sour to bitter, edible yellow fruit, to 3cm (1¼in) across. ↕↔ 9m (28ft). China, Korea. ❄❄❄. **'Beni-chidori'** ■ syn. 'Benishidore', is upright and shrubby, with dark pink flowers; ↕↔ 2.5m (8ft). **'Dawn'** bears double, ruffled pink flowers. **'Omoi-no-mama'** ■ syn. 'Omoi-no-wac', is upright and shrubby, with semi-double, pink-flushed white flowers; ↕↔ 2.5m (8ft). **'Pendula'** ♀ has weeping branches and pink flowers; ↕↔ 6m (20ft). **'W.B. Clarke'** ♀ is weeping, with double pink flowers; ↕↔ 6m (20ft).

***P.* 'Okame'** ■ ♀ Bushy, deciduous tree or shrub with narrowly oval, sharply toothed, dark green leaves, to 8cm (3in) long, turning orange and red in autumn. In early spring, profuse, cup-shaped, carmine-pink flowers, 2–2.5cm (3/4–1in) across, are borne in clusters of 2–5. ↕ 10m (30ft), ↔ 8m (25ft). ❄❄❄

P. padus ■ ♀ (Bird cherry). Spreading, deciduous tree or shrub, conical when young. Elliptic, dark green leaves, to 10cm (4in) long, turn red or yellow in autumn. Pendent racemes, to 15cm (6in) long, of cup-shaped, fragrant white flowers, to 1.5cm (1/2in) across, are produced in late spring, followed by spherical, pea-like, glossy black fruit, 8mm (3/8in) across. ↕ 15m (50ft), ↔ 10m (30ft). Europe, N. Asia to C. Japan. ❄❄❄. **'Albertii'** bears abundant flowers in dense racemes. **'Colorata'** ■ has reddish purple young foliage and pink flowers. **'Plena'** has double flowers. **'Watereri'** ■ has flowers in slender racemes, to 20cm (8in) long.

***P.* 'Pandora'** ■ ♀ Spreading, deciduous tree, upright when young, with oval, dark green leaves, to 7cm (3in) long, bronze when young, turning orange and red in autumn. In early spring, masses of solitary, cup-shaped, pale pink flowers, 3cm (1¼in) across, open before the leaves, from dark pink buds. ↕ 10m (30ft), ↔ 8m (25ft). ❄❄❄

***P. pendula* 'Pendula Rosea'** see *P.* x *subhirtella* 'Pendula Rosea'.

***P. pendula* 'Pendula Rubra'** see *P.* x *subhirtella* 'Pendula Rubra'.

P. pensylvanica ♀ (Pin cherry). Spreading, deciduous tree or shrub with peeling, red-banded bark and ovate to

P

Prunus padus 'Watereri'

Prunus 'Pandora'

Prunus persica 'Klara Mayer'

Prunus persica 'Prince Charming'

Prunus 'Pink Perfection'

Prunus sargentii

Prunus 'Shirofugen'

Prunus 'Shôgetsu'

Prunus spinosa 'Purpurea'

Prunus 'Spire'

Prunus x *subhirtella* 'Autumnalis Rosea'

Prunus x *subhirtella* 'Pendula Rosea'

oblong-lance-shaped, bright green leaves, to 11cm (4½in) long, turning yellow and red in autumn. In mid- and late spring, cup-shaped white flowers, 1.5cm (½in) across, are borne before or with the leaves, in stalkless umbels of 3–6, followed by spherical red fruit, 5mm (¼in) across. ↕↔ to 10m (30ft). North America. ***. **'Stockton'** has double flowers and red autumn colour.

P. persica (Peach). Spreading, deciduous tree with narrowly elliptic, slender-pointed, glossy, mid- to dark green leaves, to 15cm (6in) long. Bears solitary, bowl-shaped, pink or red flowers, 4cm (1½in) across, in late spring, before the leaves, followed by spherical, downy, edible, red-blushed yellow fruit, 8cm (3in) across. ↕↔ 8m (25ft). China. ***. **'Helen Borchers'** has semi-double, rose-pink flowers, 6cm (2½in) across. **'Klara Mayer'** ■ has double, bright pink flowers. **'Peppermint Stick'** bears double white flowers with red stripes. **'Prince Charming'** ■ is upright, with double, dark pink flowers; ↕ 4m (12ft), ↔ 1.5m (5ft).

P.* x *persicoides see *P.* x *amygdalopersica*.

***P.* 'Pink Perfection'** ■ Spreading, deciduous tree with oblong, dark green leaves, to 12cm (5in) long, bronze when young. Double pink flowers, 5cm (2in) across, open in long, pendent clusters of 3–5 in late spring. ↕↔ 8m (25ft). ***

***P.* 'Pink Star'** see *P.* x *subhirtella* 'Stellata'.

P. pissardii see *P. cerasifera* 'Pissardii'.

Prunus serrula

P. sargentii ■ (Sargent cherry). Spreading, deciduous tree with elliptic, tapered, dark green leaves, to 12cm (5in) long, red when young, turning brilliant orange-red in early autumn. Bowl-shaped, pale pink flowers, 4cm (1½in) across, are produced in umbels of 2–4 in mid-spring; they are followed by ovoid, cherry-like, glossy crimson fruit, to 1cm (½in) long. ↕ to 20m (70ft), ↔ 15m (50ft). Russia (Sakhalin), Korea, Japan. ***. **'Columnaris'** is narrow and upright; ↔ 3m (10ft).

P. serotina (Black cherry, Wild rum cherry). Broadly columnar, deciduous tree with elliptic, glossy, dark green leaves, to 12cm (5in) long, turning yellow or red in autumn. In late spring and early summer, bowl-shaped, fragrant white flowers, 1.5cm (½in) across, are borne in racemes to 15cm (6in) long; they are followed by spherical, edible red fruit, 1cm (½in) across, ripening to black. ↕ to 35m (120ft), ↔ 12–18m (40–60ft). North America. ***

P. serrula ■ Rounded, deciduous tree with peeling, glossy, copper-brown bark and lance-shaped, tapered, dark green leaves, to 10cm (4in) long, turning yellow in autumn. Bowl-shaped white flowers, 2cm (¾in) across, solitary or in umbels of 2–4, are borne as the leaves emerge in late spring, followed by ovoid, cherry-like fruit, 1cm (½in) long. ↕↔ 10m (30ft). W. China. ***

P. serrulata* f. *semperflorens see *P.* 'Fudan-zakura'.

P. serrulata* var. *spontanea see *P. jamasakura*.

***P.* 'Shirofugen'** ■ Spreading, deciduous tree bearing oblong, dark green leaves, to 12cm (5in) long, bronze-red when young, turning orange-red in autumn. Clusters of 3–5 double, fragrant white flowers, 5cm (2in) across, open from pink buds in late spring; they turn pink before they fall. ↕ 8m (25ft), ↔ 10m (30ft). ***

***P.* 'Shirotae'** see *P.* 'Mount Fuji'.

***P.* 'Shôgetsu'** ■ Rounded, deciduous tree bearing oblong, mid-green leaves, to 12cm (5in) long, bronze when young, then orange and red. Frilly-margined, double, pink and white flowers, 5cm (2in) across, in pendent clusters of 3–6, open from pink buds in late spring. ↕ 5m (15ft), ↔ 8m (25ft). ***

P. spinosa (Blackthorn, Sloe). Dense, bushy, spiny, deciduous shrub or tree with elliptic to obovate, mid- to deep green leaves, to 5cm (2in) long. Solitary, rarely paired, bowl-shaped white flowers, to 1.5cm (½in) across, are borne before the leaves in early and mid-spring; they are followed by spherical, edible, glaucous black fruit, 1.5cm (½in) across. ↕ 5m (15ft), ↔ 4m (12ft). Europe to Russia (W. Siberia), Mediterranean. ***. **'Purpurea'** ■ has red leaves, later turning dark red-purple, and pale pink flowers.

***P.* 'Spire'** ■ syn. *P.* x *hillieri* 'Spire'. Vase-shaped, deciduous tree, conical when young, with obovate, dark green leaves, to 10cm (4in) long, bronze when young, turning orange and red in autumn. Bowl-shaped, pale pink flowers, 4cm (1½in) across, in clusters of 3–5, are produced as the leaves emerge in mid-spring. ↕ 10m (30ft), ↔ 6m (20ft). ***

P.* x *subhirtella (*P. incisa* x *P. pendula*) (Higan cherry, Rosebud cherry). Spreading, deciduous tree with broadly elliptic or ovate, sometimes 3-lobed, sharply toothed, dark green leaves, to 8cm (3in) long, pale bronze when young, turning yellow in autumn. Bowl-shaped, white or pink flowers, 2cm (¾in) across, are borne in clusters of 2–5, intermittently from autumn to spring, before or with the leaves; they are sometimes followed by ovoid, cherry-like, red, later nearly black fruit, 8mm (⅜in) long. ↕↔ 8m (25ft). Japan. ***. **'Autumnalis'** bears semi-double, pink-tinged white flowers in mild periods between autumn and spring. **'Autumnalis Rosea'** ■ is similar to 'Autumnalis' but produces pink flowers. **'Fukubana'** produces semi-double, dark rose-pink flowers. **'Pendula Rosea'** ■ syn. *P. pendula* 'Pendula Rosea', has weeping branches and rose-pink flowers. **'Pendula Rosea Plena'** ■ has weeping branches and semi-double, rose-pink flowers. **'Pendula Rubra'** syn. *P. pendula* 'Pendula Rubra', has weeping branches and dark pink flowers.

P

Prunus x *subhirtella* 'Pendula Rosea Plena' (inset: flower detail)

Prunus x *subhirtella* 'Stellata'

Prunus 'Taihaku'

Prunus tenella

Prunus 'Ukon'

Prunus 'Yae-murasaki'

Prunus x *yedoensis*

'Stellata' ▣ syn. *P.* 'Pink Star', has pale pink flowers, red in bud, with narrow, pointed petals.
***P.* 'Taihaku'** ▣ (Great white cherry). Vigorous, spreading, deciduous tree bearing elliptic, dark green leaves, to 20cm (8in) long, bronze when young. Bowl-shaped white flowers, to 6cm (2½in) across, are produced in clusters of up to 4 in mid-spring. ↕ 8m (25ft), ↔ 10m (30ft). ❄❄❄
P. tenella ▣ (Dwarf Russian almond). Bushy, deciduous shrub with upright shoots and obovate to inversely lance-shaped, glossy, dark green leaves, to 8cm (3in) long. Bowl-shaped, bright pink flowers, to 3cm (1¼in) across, solitary or in profuse clusters of 2 or 3, are produced with the young leaves in mid- and late spring; they are followed by ovoid, almond-like, velvety, grey-yellow fruit, to 2.5cm (1in) long. ↕ to 1.5m (5ft), ↔ 1.5m (5ft). C. Europe to Russia (Siberia). ❄❄❄. **'Fire Hill'** has very dark pink flowers.
***P.* 'Trailblazer'** Broadly upright, deciduous tree with oval, red-purple leaves, to 8cm (3in) long. Solitary, bowl-shaped, white or pale pink flowers, 2cm (¾in) across, are borne before the leaves in mid-spring, and are sometimes followed by plum-like, edible red fruit, 6cm (2½in) across. ↕ 10m (30ft), ↔ 6m (20ft). ❄❄❄

Prunus 'Umineko' (inset: flower detail)

P. triloba (Flowering almond). Densely branched, deciduous shrub or small tree bearing broadly elliptic, often 3-lobed leaves, 4–8cm (1½–3in) long, dark green above, mid-green and softly hairy beneath. Solitary or paired, bowl-shaped pink flowers, 2–3.5cm (¾–1½in) across, are produced in early and mid-spring; they are followed by spherical red fruit, 1cm (½in) across. ↕↔ 3m (10ft). China. ❄❄❄.
'Multiplex' is spreading, bearing oval leaves, to 6cm (2½in) long. Double pink flowers, 4cm (1½in) across, are produced in mid-spring. ↕↔ 4m (12ft).
***P.* 'Ukon'** ▣ Vigorous, spreading, deciduous tree with elliptic, tapered, dark green leaves, to 12cm (5in) long, bronze when young. Clusters of 3–6 double flowers, 4cm (1½in) across, yellowish white on the outsides and slightly pink at the tips, open from pink buds in mid-spring. ↕ 8m (25ft), ↔ 10m (30ft). ❄❄❄
***P.* 'Umineko'** ▣ Upright, deciduous tree with ovate, sharply toothed, dark green leaves, to 7cm (3in) long, pale green when young. Cup-shaped white flowers, 4cm (1½in) across, are borne in clusters of 2 or 3 in mid-spring, with the young leaves. ↕ 8m (25ft), ↔ 3m (10ft). ❄❄❄
***P.* 'Uzuzakura'** see *P.* 'Hokusai'.
P. virginiana (Choke cherry, Virginian bird cherry). Conical, often suckering, deciduous tree or shrub with broadly obovate to broadly elliptic, glossy, mid- to dark green leaves, to 10cm (4in) long. In late spring, bears cup-shaped white flowers, 1cm (½in) across, in dense racemes, to 10cm (4in) long; they are followed by spherical, red to purple fruit, 8mm (⅜in) across. ↕ 10m (30ft), ↔ 8m (25ft). North America. ❄❄❄. **'Schubert'** produces leaves that turn dark red-purple in summer.
***P.* 'Yae-murasaki'** ▣ Spreading, very slow-growing, deciduous tree with elliptic, tapered, mid-green leaves, to 12cm (5in) long, bronze when young, turning orange-red in autumn. In mid-spring, bears semi-double, dark pink flowers, 4cm (1½in) across, in clusters of 2–4. ↕ 5m (15ft), ↔ 8m (25ft). ❄❄❄
P.* x *yedoensis ▣ (*P. speciosa* x *P.* x *subhirtella*) (Yoshino cherry). Spreading, deciduous tree with arching branches and elliptic, dark green leaves, to 11cm (4½in) long. In early spring, before the leaves, produces a profusion of racemes of 5 or 6 bowl-shaped, pale pink flowers, 4cm (1½in) across, fading to nearly white. ↕ to 15m (50ft), ↔ 10m (30ft). Japan. ❄❄❄. **'Pendula'** see 'Shidare-yoshino'. **'Perpendens'** see 'Shidare-yoshino'. **'Shidare-yoshino'** syn. 'Pendula', 'Perpendens', has weeping branches arching to the ground.

PSEUDERANTHEMUM

ACANTHACEAE

Genus of about 60 species of evergreen perennials, subshrubs, and shrubs from woodland habitats in tropical regions worldwide. They are grown primarily for their variegated or coloured leaves, which are opposite, simple, and entire or toothed. The long, tubular, 2-lipped, white, blue, purple, or red flowers, sometimes marked with yellow, are produced in spikes, racemes, or cymes.

Pseuderanthemum atropurpureum 'Variegatum'

In areas where temperatures fall below 13°C (55°F), grow as foliage plants in a warm greenhouse. In tropical climates, they are suitable for a shrub border.
• **HARDINESS** Frost tender.
• **CULTIVATION** Under glass, grow in loam-based potting compost (JI No.2) in bright filtered light, providing high humidity. During the growing season, water moderately and apply a balanced liquid fertilizer every month; water sparingly in winter. Outdoors, grow in fertile, moist, but well-drained soil in full sun with some midday shade, or in partial shade. Pruning group 9; needs restrictive pruning under glass.
• **PROPAGATION** Root semi-ripe cuttings in midsummer with bottom heat.
• **PESTS AND DISEASES** Prone to red spider mites and whiteflies under glass.

P. atropurpureum, syn. *Eranthemum atropurpureum*. Erect, open shrub, the stems sparsely branched unless pinched out at intervals when young. Ovate to broadly elliptic leaves, 10–15cm (4–6in) long, are deep purple, sometimes metallic green, spotted yellow, pinkish purple, pink, green, and white. During summer, tubular white flowers, spotted rose-red or purple at the bases, 2.5cm (1in) long, are borne in dense, terminal spikes, to 18cm (7in) long. ↕ 0.9–1.5m (3–5ft), ↔ 30–75cm (12–30in). Polynesia. ❀ (min. 13°C/55°F).
'Tricolor' see 'Variegatum'.
'Variegatum' ▣ syn. 'Tricolor', bears bronze-purple leaves, splashed and suffused creamy yellow and pink, and has pink flowers.

PSEUDOCYDONIA

ROSACEAE

Genus of one species of deciduous or semi-evergreen shrub or tree from temperate woodland in China. It has simple, dark green leaves, but is grown mainly for its peeling bark, cup-shaped pink flowers, and large, edible yellow fruit. It is best cultivated as a specimen tree, but will achieve tree stature only in regions with long, hot summers; in areas with cool summers, it remains shrubby and is best trained against a warm, sunny wall.
• **HARDINESS** Fully hardy in areas with hot summers, but otherwise frost hardy.
• **CULTIVATION** Grow in fertile, well-drained soil in full sun. Provide a warm site, sheltered from severe frost, and, in

areas with cool summers, sheltered from cold, drying winds. Pruning group 1, or group 13 if wall-grown.
• **PROPAGATION** Sow seed in containers outdoors in autumn.
• **PESTS AND DISEASES** Trouble free.

P. sinensis ♀ syn. *Cydonia sinensis*. Spreading shrub or small tree bearing peeling grey and white bark, and oval, finely toothed, dark green leaves, to 10cm (4in) long. Solitary, cup-shaped pink flowers, 4cm (1½in) across, are produced in mid- and late spring, followed, after hot summers, by ovoid yellow fruit, 15cm (6in) long. ↕↔ 6m (20ft). China. ❄❄

▷ ***Pseudodrynaria coronans*** see *Aglaomorpha coronans*
▷ ***Pseudofumaria*** see *Corydalis*
P. lutea see *C. lutea*
▷ ***Pseudogynoxys chenopodioides*** see *Senecio confusus*

PSEUDOLARIX

PINACEAE

Genus of one species of monoecious, deciduous, coniferous tree occurring in forest in China, with linear leaves borne in rosettes on short shoots (as in *Larix*). It is grown mainly for the outstanding golden orange colour of its autumn foliage. The female cones have large, triangular green scales and release the seeds by disintegrating; the male cones are catkin-like and clustered on short shoots. It is an excellent specimen tree, but is initially slow-growing, and is best grown in regions with long, hot summers.
• **HARDINESS** Fully hardy.
• **CULTIVATION** Grow in deep, fertile, acid to neutral, well-drained soil in a warm, sheltered site in full sun. Protect from cold, drying winds.
• **PROPAGATION** Sow seed in containers outoors in spring. Take greenwood cuttings in early summer.
• **PESTS AND DISEASES** Trouble free.

Pseudolarix amabilis

P. amabilis ■ ♀ syn. *P. kaempferi* (Golden larch). Broadly conical or flattened, open-crowned tree with spreading branches, grey bark furrowed with raised, plate-like pieces, and purple, later greyish purple shoots with ovoid buds. Linear, soft, fresh green leaves, 2–5cm (¾–2in) long, turning golden orange in autumn, are borne on both long and short shoots. Erect, ovoid, yellow-green female cones, 6–8cm (2½–3in) long, ripening to brown, are spiky due to the free tips of the scales. ↕ to 15–20m (50–70ft), ↔ 6–12m (20–40ft). S. and E. China. ❄❄❄
P. kaempferi see *P. amabilis*.

▷ ***Pseudomuscari azureum*** see *Muscari azureum*

PSEUDOPANAX

ARALIACEAE

Genus of 12–20 species of evergreen trees and shrubs from forest and scrub in Tasmania (Australia), New Zealand, and Chile. Cultivated for their upright habit, foliage, and fruits, they are valuable architectural or specimen plants. The alternate, simple or palmate, entire or variously toothed leaves may vary greatly in shape, depending on the age of the plant. Inconspicuous, 4- or 5-petalled green flowers are borne mainly in winter, in terminal or, less commonly, lateral umbels, clusters, racemes, or mixtures of these. Male and female flowers usually grow on separate plants; both are required to produce the fruits, which are drupe-like, each with 2–5 stones. Grow in a warm, sheltered shrub border. In frost-prone areas, grow tender species in a cool greenhouse or conservatory.
• **HARDINESS** Frost hardy to frost tender.
• **CULTIVATION** Under glass, grow in loam-based potting compost (JI No.3), with added sharp sand, in full light with shade from hot sun, or in bright filtered light. In growth, water moderately and apply a balanced liquid fertilizer every month; water sparingly in winter. Outdoors, grow in fertile, well-drained soil in full sun or partial shade. In frost-prone areas, shelter from cold, drying winds. Pruning group 1; may need restrictive pruning under glass.
• **PROPAGATION** Sow seed in autumn or spring: seed of tender species at 19–24°C (66–75°F); seed of hardy species in containers in a cold frame. Take semi-ripe cuttings, or air layer, in summer.
• **PESTS AND DISEASES** Trouble free.

P. arboreus ♀ syn. *Neopanax arboreum* (Five finger, Whauwhaupaku). Bushy, round-headed, evergreen tree or sometimes large shrub, with long-stalked, 5- or 7-palmate, glossy, deep green leaves, composed of stalked, narrowly oblong to oblong-obovate, toothed leaflets, 10–20cm (4–8in) long. In winter, bears star-shaped, purple-budded cream flowers in compound umbels, to 20cm (8in) across, followed by black-purple fruit, 6mm (¼in) across. ↕ 4–8m (12–25ft), ↔ 2.5–5m (8–15ft). New Zealand. ⚘ (min. 2°C/36°F)
P. crassifolius ♀ (Lancewood). Evergreen tree, unbranched for many years, with long, slender seedling leaves, to 60cm (24in) long, and downward-

Pseudopanax ferox

pointing, dark green mature leaves, to 1m (3ft) long or more. Seedling leaves are simple, ovate to lance-shaped, membranous, coarsely toothed or lobed; mature leaves are linear, rigid, somewhat variegated, with red midribs and spine-tipped teeth. Mature plants develop a rounded head and narrow, spreading, linear to linear-obovate, 3- or 5-palmate, leathery leaves, with linear or sword-shaped leaflets, 20cm (8in) long. Star-shaped, greenish white flowers are produced in umbels, 7–10cm (3–4in) across, in summer and early autumn; they are followed on female or hermaphrodite flowers by spherical black fruit, 5mm (¼in) across. ↕ to 15m (50ft) ↔ 2m (6ft). New Zealand. ❄❄
P. ferox ■ ♀ (Toothed lancewood). Upright, dioecious, evergreen tree, later developing a small, rounded head. Young plants produce simple, pendent, narrow, linear, sharply pointed, coarsely and jaggedly toothed, dark bronze-green mature leaves, to 45cm (18in) long, marked white or grey. Mature plants bear spreading, linear, dark green leaves, to 15cm (6in) long. Green flowers are borne in umbel-like panicles, to 10cm (4in) across, in summer and early

Pseudopanax lessonii 'Gold Splash'

autumn; they are followed on female plants by ovoid black fruit, 8mm (⅜in) across. ↕ 5m (15ft), ↔ 2m (6ft). New Zealand. ❄❄
P. laetus ♀ Rounded, dioecious, evergreen tree or shrub with stout shoots, and 5- or 7-palmate leaves composed of long-stalked, obovate, leathery, dark green leaflets, to 30cm (12in) long. In winter, bears greenish purple flowers in compound umbels, to 20cm (8in) across, followed on female plants by spherical, purple-black fruit, 5mm (¼in) across. ↕ 6m (20ft), ↔ 3m (10ft). New Zealand (North Island). ❄❄
P. lessonii ♀ (Houpara). Erect to spreading, evergreen, large shrub or small tree, with stout branches. The deep green leaves are 3- or 5-palmate: on juvenile plants they have 5 lance-shaped, coarsely and irregularly toothed leaflets, to 12cm (5in) long; on mature plants, they comprise 3 smaller, stalkless, obovate, entire to sparsely toothed leaflets, to 10cm (4in) long. Yellowish green flowers are borne in compound umbels, 10cm (4in) across, in summer; they are followed by oblong, purple-black fruit, 5mm (¼in) long. ↕ 3–6m (10–20ft), ↔ 2–4m (6–12ft). New Zealand (North Island, Three Kings Island). ⚘ (min. 2°C/36°F). **'Gold Splash'** ■ has yellow-marked leaves. **'Purpureus'** has bronze-purple foliage.

▷ ***Pseudorhipsalis alata*** see *Disocactus alatus*
▷ ***Pseudorhipsalis macrantha*** see *Disocactus macranthus*

PSEUDOSASA

GRAMINEAE/POACEAE

Genus of 3–6 species of woody, upright, spreading to clump-forming, evergreen, rhizomatous, perennial bamboos, often thicket-forming, found in woodland and along roads or tracks in China, Japan, and Taiwan. They are cultivated for their woody canes, which are erect, cylindrical, simple-branched or sometimes 3-branched at each upper node, and to 6m (20ft) high. The mid- or dark green leaves are lance-shaped or oblong, hairless, and somewhat tessellated. Rarely, spikelets of 2 to 8 flowers are borne in terminal, lax panicles. Grow in a woodland or wild garden, or as screening plants; they can be vigorous and invasive, and need room to spread.
• **HARDINESS** Fully hardy.
• **CULTIVATION** Grow in fertile, moist but well-drained soil in full sun or partial shade. If plants do flower, cut back to the bases, and apply a general-purpose fertilizer and deep organic mulch; this usually restores vigour.
• **PROPAGATION** Divide clumps in spring; keep moist until established.
• **PESTS AND DISEASES** Trouble free.

P. japonica. Upright, eventually thicket-forming, spreading, rhizomatous bamboo. Canes are olive green when young, maturing to pale beige. Lance-shaped or oblong, tessellated, dark green leaves, to 35cm (14in) long, are silver-grey beneath and have yellow midribs. Bears spikelets of 2–8 green flowers in lax panicles, but flowering is rare. ↕ 6m (20ft), ↔ indeterminate. Japan. ❄❄❄
P. orthotropa see *Sinobambusa orthotropa*.

Pseudotsuga menziesii 'Fretsii'

PSEUDOTSUGA

PINACEAE

Genus of 6–8 species of tall, evergreen, coniferous trees from forest in China, Taiwan, Japan, W. North America, and Mexico. The linear leaves, arranged radially on the shoots, develop from pointed, many-scaled buds that are unique to the genus. The female cones have protruding, trident-shaped bract scales; the male cones are cylindrical. They are imposing specimen trees.

- **HARDINESS** Fully hardy.
- **CULTIVATION** Grow in any well-drained, non-chalky soil, in full sun.
- **PROPAGATION** Sow seed in containers outdoors in spring. Graft cultivars in late winter.
- **PESTS AND DISEASES** The foliage is attacked by Douglas fir adelgids.

P. douglasii see *P. menziesii.*
P. menziesii syn. *P. douglasii, P. taxifolia* (Douglas fir). Broadly conical tree when young, becoming columnar with spreading branches. The bark is smooth and grey at first, then thick, corky, deeply ridged, and red-brown. Ovoid, sharp-pointed, red-brown buds open to linear, soft, dark green leaves, 1.5–3cm (½–1¼in) long, loosely parted on the shoots, each with 2 white bands beneath. Ovoid-conical female cones, 7–10cm (3–4in) long, have long, erect bracts. ↕ 25–50m (80–160ft), ↔ 6–10m (20–30ft). W. North America (British Columbia to California). ✻✻✻.
'Fretsii' ▣ is slow-growing, forming a small, spreading, conical tree, with dull green leaves, 0.8–1cm (⅜–½in) long; ↕ to 6m (20ft). **var. *glauca*** ▣ (Blue Douglas fir) has smaller cones, 4.5–6cm (1¾–2½in) long, with reflexed bracts; the leaves are blue-glaucous, and the grey or black bark is thinner and more scaly. **'Oudemansii'** is slow-growing, with short leaves, 1.5–2cm (½–¾in) long; ↕ 5–10m (15–30ft).
P. taxifolia see *P. menziesii.*

PSEUDOWINTERA

WINTERACEAE

Genus of 3 species of aromatic, evergreen trees and shrubs from mountain forest in New Zealand. They are cultivated mainly for their alternate, broadly elliptic, leathery leaves, which have obvious glands. Cup-shaped, greenish yellow to white flowers are produced in axillary clusters, and are followed by spherical, dark red or black fruits. Pseudowinteras grow best in a sheltered border or woodland situation. In frost-prone areas, grow less hardy species in a cool greenhouse.

Pseudotsuga menziesii var. *glauca* (inset: cone detail)

Pseudowintera colorata

- **HARDINESS** Frost hardy to half hardy.
- **CULTIVATION** Under glass, grow in loam-based potting compost (JI No.3) in full light or bright filtered light. During growth, water freely, applying a balanced liquid fertilizer monthly; water sparingly at all other times. Outdoors, grow in humus-rich, preferably neutral to acid, moist but well-drained soil in full sun or partial shade. Pruning group 8; may need restrictive pruning under glass.
- **PROPAGATION** Sow seed at 13–18°C (55–64°F) in autumn or spring. Root semi-ripe cuttings in midsummer with bottom heat.
- **PESTS AND DISEASES** Trouble free.

P. colorata ▣ syn. *Drimys colorata.* Spreading, bushy shrub bearing broadly elliptic, leathery, yellow-green leaves, to 8cm (3in) long, marked pink and margined dark red-purple above, glaucous beneath. In mid-spring, bears clusters of 2–5 or more, cup-shaped, greenish yellow flowers, 1cm (½in) across, followed by spherical red, later black berries, 5mm (¼in) across. ↕ 1m (3ft), ↔ 1.5m (5ft). New Zealand. ✻✻

▷ ***Pseudozygocactus epiphylloides*** see *Hatiora epiphylloides*

PSILOTUM

Fork fern

PSILOTACEAE

Genus of 2 species of terrestrial or epiphytic, evergreen, rhizomatous, fern-like perennials from moist tropical and warm-temperate forest or woodland worldwide. They are grown for their upright, spreading, or pendent habit, and for their distinctive, repeatedly forked, triangular or flattened, yellow-green stems, 1–3mm (1/16–⅛in) thick, which may die back in winter. The leaves are very small and inconspicuous, and the stems sometimes bear small, spherical, 3-lobed sporangia in the axils of minute bracts. In frost-prone areas, grow in a cool or temperate greenhouse, and leave undisturbed for long periods; in warmer areas, grow beneath shrubs or tree ferns.

Psilotum nudum

- **HARDINESS** Frost tender.
- **CULTIVATION** Under glass, grow in 1 part each of loam, medium-grade bark, and charcoal, 2 parts sharp sand, and 3 parts coarse leaf mould; or grow epiphytically on tree-fern bark. Provide bright filtered light and high humidity. In growth, water and mist freely, and apply a balanced liquid fertilizer every month; water sparingly in winter. Outdoors, grow in moderately fertile, moist but well-drained soil in light dappled shade.
- **PROPAGATION** Sow spores at 21°C (70°F) when ripe. Divide established plants in spring. See also p.51.
- **PESTS AND DISEASES** Trouble free.

P. nudum ▣ Bushy, evergreen, fern-like perennial with upright, spreading, or pendent, branching, yellow-green, triangular stems, to 60cm (24in) long. Dull yellow sporangia, 3mm (⅛in) wide, are produced on the upper parts of the stems. Leaves are sparse and scale-like, 2mm (1/16in) long. ↕↔ 60cm (24in). Tropical to warm-temperate areas worldwide. ❁ (min. 5°C/41°F)

PSYCHOPSIS

ORCHIDACEAE

Genus of about 5 species of small, evergreen, epiphytic orchids from lowland to mountainous forest, at altitudes of up to 1,000m (3,250ft), in Central America, South America, and Trinidad. They have compressed, clustered, oval pseudobulbs, and solitary, semi-rigid, oblong-elliptic leaves, which are mottled dark green and dull purple. Butterfly-

Psychopsis papilio

P

like flowers are borne over a long period in long, slender, few-flowered, jointed racemes, occasionally singly, from the base of each pseudobulb.
- **HARDINESS** Frost tender.
- **CULTIVATION** Intermediate-growing orchids. Grow in epiphytic orchid compost or epiphytically on slabs of bark. Throughout the year, provide full light and high humidity, and water sparingly. During summer, mist rather than water, and feed every week. See also p.46.
- **PROPAGATION** Divide when the plant fills the pot and "flows" over the sides.
- **PESTS AND DISEASES** May be infested by red spider mites, aphids, and mealybugs.

P. papilio ■ syn. *Oncidium papilio.* Epiphytic orchid with spherical pseudobulbs, each producing a single, ovate to elliptic leaf, 12–25cm (5–10in) long. Orange-brown flowers, 15cm (6in) across, slightly mottled greenish yellow, with yellow and brown mottled lips, are borne in few-flowered racemes, to 1.2m (4ft) long, throughout the year. ↕60cm (24in), ↔30cm (12in). Trinidad, Venezuela, Colombia, Ecuador, Peru. ❁ (min. 10°C/50°F; max. 30°C/86°F)

▷ ***Psygmorchis pusilla*** see *Oncidium pusillum*

PSYLLIOSTACHYS
Statice

PLUMBAGINACEAE

Genus of about 6–8 species of erect, usually rosette-forming annuals found in sandy soils on plains and in foothills from Syria to Iran and C. Asia. They have mostly basal, deeply lobed or occasionally simple and entire, oblong or lance-shaped to obovate, light to mid-green leaves. From spring to autumn, they produce branching or simple spikes of tiny, tubular, pink or white flowers, each with 5 spreading lobes. Statices are suitable for the front of an annual border, and are tolerant of coastal conditions. They are also excellent for cutting and drying.
- **HARDINESS** Fully hardy to half hardy.
- **CULTIVATION** Grow in fertile, moist but well-drained soil in a warm, sheltered site in full sun.
- **PROPAGATION** Sow seed at 21°C (70°F) in spring.
- **PESTS AND DISEASES** Prone to grey mould (*Botrytis*) and powdery mildew.

P. spicata, syn. *Limonium spicatum, Statice spicata.* Rosette-forming annual with deeply lobed, inversely lance-shaped leaves, 5–15cm (2–6in) long; the leaf-stalks and midribs are densely clothed in long hairs. Rose-pink flowers are borne in terminal spikes, to 9cm (3½in) long, and shorter, lateral spikes, from summer to early autumn. ↕30–45cm (12–18in), ↔ to 30cm (12in). Ukraine (Crimea), Caucasus, Iran. ❄

P. suworowii ■ syn. *Limonium suworowii, Statice suworowii.* Rosette-forming annual bearing simple, basal, inversely lance-shaped to oblong-obovate, wavy-margined to slightly lobed, light green leaves, to 15cm (6in) long. Rose-pink flowers, are borne in narrow, cylindrical, branching spikes, to 20cm (8in) long, from summer to early autumn. ↕30–45cm (12–18in), ↔ to 30cm (12in). Iran, W. Turkmenistan, N. Afghanistan, C. Asia. ❄

Psylliostachys suworowii

PTELEA

RUTACEAE

Genus of 3 or more species of aromatic, deciduous trees and shrubs found in thickets and on rocky slopes in North America. Cultivated for their 3-palmate, strongly scented leaves, they also bear corymbs of inconspicuous, cup-shaped or star-shaped, sometimes unisexual, greenish white flowers, followed by winged, more or less rounded and flattened fruits. Suitable for growing in a shrub border or as lawn specimens.
- **HARDINESS** Fully hardy to frost hardy.
- **CULTIVATION** Grow in fertile, well-drained soil in full sun or dappled shade. Pruning group 1.
- **PROPAGATION** Sow seed in containers outdoors in autumn or spring. Take greenwood cuttings in early summer.
- **PESTS AND DISEASES** Trouble free.

P. trifoliata (Hop tree). Upright, deciduous shrub with aromatic bark and alternate, 3-palmate, scented, dark green leaves, to 12cm (5in) long, with ovate to elliptic leaflets. Corymbs of star-shaped, greenish white flowers are borne in summer, followed by winged, rounded and flattened, pale green fruit, to 2.5cm (1in) across. ↕8m (25ft), ↔4m (12ft). North America (Ontario to Connecticut, Michigan, Iowa, Florida, Texas, and N. Mexico). ❄❄❄. **'Aurea'** ■ bears bright yellow to yellow-green leaves, turning dark green, then yellow in autumn; ↕5m (15ft).

Ptelea trifoliata 'Aurea'

PTERIS
Brake

ADIANTACEAE/PTERIDACEAE

Genus of approximately 280 species of deciduous, semi-evergreen, and evergreen, terrestrial ferns, found mainly in tropical and subtropical forests throughout the world. The rhizomes are stout and erect to slender and short-creeping. Brakes are cultivated for their closely spaced fronds, which are pinnatisect or pinnate to 4-pinnate, and range from less than 30cm (12in) long to 3m (10ft). Spores form at the frond margins, which curl under to protect them. In frost-prone climates, grow the tender species and cultivars in a cool or temperate greenhouse, or as houseplants. In warmer areas, use singly as feature plants, or in mixed foliage plantings.
- **HARDINESS** Frost hardy to frost tender.
- **CULTIVATION** Under glass, grow in 1 part each of sharp sand, coarse leaf mould, and charcoal, and 2 parts loam-based potting compost (JI No.2), in bright filtered light and high humidity; *P. cretica* and *P. vittata* prefer slightly alkaline soil, so add limestone chips. In growth, water freely, applying a high-nitrogen liquid fertilizer monthly; water sparingly in winter. Outdoors, grow in any moist but well-drained soil (except chalky soil), with added leaf mould, in partial or deep shade.
- **PROPAGATION** Sow spores at 21°C (70°F) when ripe. Divide plants with creeping, branched rhizomes in spring. See also p.51.
- **PESTS AND DISEASES** Prone to scale insects and leaf eelworms under glass. In still, humid conditions, sooty mould may occur if water settles on the fronds.

P. argyraea ■ (Silver brake). Evergreen fern with erect rhizomes bearing erect, pinnate or 2-pinnate fronds, 60–100cm (24–39in) long, each with up to 6 pairs

Pteris argyraea

of oblong, dark green pinnae with broad, silvery white stripes down their centres. The pinnatisect pinnae are composed of numerous linear-oblong lobes; the lowest pair are usually forked. Requires shade. ↕↔ to 1m (3ft). Tropics. ❁ (min. 10°C/50°F)

P. biaurita. Evergreen fern with erect rhizomes producing erect, oblong or triangular-oblong, pinnate, light apple-green fronds, to 1.3m (4½ft) long, each with 5–15 pairs of pinnatisect pinnae, the lowest pair usually forked. Similar to *P. argyraea*, but pinnae lack the central white streaks. Thrives in damp shade. ↕0.6–1.5m (24–60in), ↔40–150cm (16–60in). Tropics. ❁ (min. 10°C/50°F)

P. cretica. Evergreen fern with a short-creeping, many-branched rhizome. Produces arching, crowded, ovate or rounded, pinnate, pale green fronds, 30–70cm (12–28in) long, each with 1–5 pairs of narrowly lance-shaped, simple or forked pinnae. Fertile fronds are taller and have narrower pinnae than sterile fronds. Some clones are half hardy. ↕ to 75cm (30in), ↔60cm (24in). Europe, Africa, Asia. ❁ (min. 2°C/36°F). **'Albolineata'** ■ has a broad white band along the centre of each

Pteris cretica 'Albolineata'

Pteris multifida

pinna, and is easier to grow than the species; ❄❄ (borderline). **'Childsii'** has broader pinnae than the species, with incised margins and small crested tips. Possibly of hybrid origin; ↕ to 50cm (20in), ↔ 30cm (12in). **'Distinction'** is smaller than the species, and has deeply lobed pinnae with branched tips; ↕↔ 40cm (16in). **'Mayi'** is similar to 'Albolineata', but has crested pinnae tips. **'Parkeri'** is a vigorous cultivar, with broader, mid- to dark green pinnae; ↕ to 90cm (36in), ↔ 60cm (24in). **'Rivertoniana'** is strong-growing, with pinnae margins that are deeply but irregularly cut into narrow lobes. **'Wimsettii'** has a compact habit; the margins of the pinnae are deeply and irregularly lobed, with the tips often crested; ↕↔ 45cm (18in).

P. dentata. Evergreen fern that forms clumps of triangular to ovate, very variably divided, 2- or 3-pinnate, bright green fronds, to 1.5m (5ft) long, arising from short-creeping to erect rhizomes. Sterile fronds have pinnae segments with finely toothed margins, but on fertile fronds the margins are entire. ↕ 0.5–1.8m (20–72in), ↔ 0.6–1.5m (24–60in). Tropical Africa, South Africa, Arabian Peninsula. ❀ (min. 10°C/50°F)

P. ensiformis (Sword brake). Evergreen fern with short-creeping, branched rhizomes producing narrow-triangular, 2-pinnate, dark green fronds, often greyish white around the midribs. Fertile fronds, up to 40cm (16in) long, have 4 or 5 pairs of linear pinnae, each with a few toothed segments at the base. Sterile fronds are shorter, and have narrower pinnae with entire margins. ↕↔ 30cm (12in). Himalayas to Japan, Philippines, Polynesia, tropical Australia. ❀ (min. 10°C/50°F). **'Arguta'** has dark green fronds with strongly contrasting silver-white central midribs. **'Evergemiensis'** has silver markings similar to 'Arguta'. **'Victoriae'** has white bands running either side of the midribs.

P. fauriei. Small, neat, evergreen fern with erect rhizomes producing arching, broadly triangular to ovate, mid-green fronds, 20–60cm (8–24in) long, each with 3–5 pairs of oblong, deeply pinnatisect pinnae. ↕ to 45cm (18in), ↔ 60cm (24in). China, Japan. ❀ (min. 10°C/50°F)

P. multifida ■ (Spider brake). Evergreen fern with short-creeping to erect, many-branched rhizomes producing numerous erect, ovate, light green fronds, 20–50cm (8–20in) long. Each frond is 2-pinnate at the base, pinnatisect above, with 3–5 pairs of pinnae. Pinnae are linear, with long, tapering tips, the upper ones decurrent to the stem. ↕ to 45cm (18in), ↔ 23cm (9in). China, Korea, Japan to Taiwan, Indonesia. ❀ (min. 10°C/50°F). **'Corymbifera'** has crested pinnae tips.

P. tremula (Shaking brake, Tender brake). Evergreen fern with an erect rhizome producing ovate, arching, light green fronds, to 2m (6ft) tall, 3- or 4-pinnate at the base, with overlapping pinnae giving a feathery appearance. Pinnae are narrowly oblong to linear, with finely toothed margins. Fast-growing, and may become invasive. ↕ to 1.5m (5ft), ↔ 1m (3ft). New Zealand, Australia, Fiji. ❀ (min. 10°C/ 50°F)

Pteris tricolor

Pteris vittata

P. tricolor ■ (Painted brake). Evergreen fern with erect, ovate, pinnate fronds, 40–60cm (16–24in) long, arising from creeping, branched rhizomes. Fertile fronds have 2–5 pairs of pinnatisect, oblong pinnae; they are red-purple when young, ageing to mid-green, but stalks and midribs remain purple. ↕ to 60cm (24in), ↔ 60cm (24in). Malacca. ❀ (min. 10°C/50°F)

P. umbrosa (Jungle brake). Evergreen fern with short-creeping, many-branched rhizomes. Triangular-ovate, shining, dark green, erect fronds, to 1m (3ft) tall, are 2-pinnatisect with 3–7 pairs of narrowly lance-shaped lobes, the lower ones divided into 3 or 5 segments. The fronds are similar in appearance to those of *P. cretica*, but are much more robust and luxuriant. ↕ to 1.2m (4ft), ↔ 1m (3ft). Australia. ❀ (min. 10°C/50°F)

P. vittata ■ Evergreen fern with short-creeping rhizomes covered with golden scales. Fronds are erect, oblong, pinnate, to 1m (3ft) tall, with up to 40 pairs of simple, linear, dark green pinnae. Tolerates chalk and some exposure to sun. ↕ to 1m (3ft), ↔ 60cm (24in). Tropical and warm-temperate regions of Europe, Africa, Asia, Australasia. ❀ (min. 2°C/36°F)

PTEROCACTUS

CACTACEAE

Genus of 9 species of dwarf, shrub-like cacti occurring in hilly regions of Argentina. They arise from tuberous rootstocks, and branch from the bases to produce somewhat club-shaped stems. The areoles bear very fine, almost hair-like spines and minute glochids. Small, white or yellow to reddish brown and coppery, diurnal flowers, without tubes, are produced terminally in early summer. In frost-prone climates, grow in a cool greenhouse or in a bowl garden; in warmer regions, they are suitable for growing outdoors in a desert garden.

- **HARDINESS** Frost tender.
- **CULTIVATION** Under glass, grow in standard cactus compost in full light. From spring to summer, water moderately and apply a low-nitrogen liquid fertilizer every 4 or 5 weeks. Keep completely dry at other times. Outdoors, grow in poor, sharply drained soil in full sun. See also pp.48–49.
- **PROPAGATION** Sow seed at 19–24°C (66–75°F) in spring. Take basal cuttings in spring or early summer.
- **PESTS AND DISEASES** Susceptible to mealybugs.

P. fischeri. Short-stemmed, shrub-like cactus producing spherical or ovoid, cylindrical, jointed, brown-green stems, 2cm (¾in) thick. White areoles bear about 16 spines (12 yellow radial spines and 4 longer, brownish yellow centrals). White flowers, 4cm (1½in) or more across, are produced in early summer. ↕ 15cm (6in), ↔ to 20cm (8in). S. Argentina. (Neuquen, Rio Negro). ❀ (min. 2–7°C/36–45°F)

P. kuntzei see *P. tuberosus.*

P. tuberosus ■ syn. *P. kuntzei.* Shrub-like cactus producing cylindrical, brown or green-brown stems, to 0.8–1.5cm (⅜–½in) thick, with a vertical violet line below each areole. The grey areoles bear minute, off-white spines that lie flat on the stems. Pale yellow flowers, 3–5cm (1¼–2in) across, sometimes tinged orange-brown or coppery brown, are produced in early summer. ↕↔ to 40cm (16in). Argentina (Mendoza). ❀ (min. 2–7°C/36–45°F)

Pterocactus tuberosus

PTEROCARYA

Wing nut

JUGLANDACEAE

Genus of about 10 species of fast-growing, deciduous trees found in woodland and on riverbanks, mainly in the mountains of Asia, from the Caucasus to Japan. They are cultivated for their attractive, spreading habit, for their large, alternate, more or less oblong, pinnate leaves, composed of 5–27 leaflets, which colour yellow in autumn, and for their long, pendent spikes of winged fruit, which are produced over a long period in summer. Inconspicuous green male and female flowers are produced in separate catkins in spring as the leaves emerge. Wing nuts grow to a considerable size, so site in a large garden or park.

- **HARDINESS** Fully hardy, but foliage may be damaged by late frosts.
- **CULTIVATION** Grow in deep, fertile, moist but well-drained soil in full sun. Pruning group 1; remove unwanted suckers as they appear.
- **PROPAGATION** Sow seed in containers outdoors in autumn. Remove rooted suckers in autumn.
- **PESTS AND DISEASES** Trouble free.

P. fraxinifolia 🌳 (Caucasian wing nut). Vigorous, spreading tree bearing pinnate leaves, to 40cm (16in) long, with cylindrical midribs; the leaves are composed of 23 or more, oblong to ovate, glossy, dark green leaflets. Small, winged green fruit are produced in pendent spikes, to 50cm (20in) long, in summer. ↕ 25m (80ft), ↔ 20m (70ft). Caucasus, N. Iran. ❄❄❄

P. x rehderiana 🌳 (*P. fraxinifolia* x *P. stenoptera*). Very vigorous, spreading, strongly suckering tree bearing pinnate leaves, to 20cm (8in) long, with slightly winged midribs; the leaves are composed of up to 21 oblong to ovate, glossy, dark green leaflets. Small, winged green fruit are produced in pendent spikes, to 45cm (18in) long, in summer. ↕ 25m (80ft), ↔ 20m (70ft). Garden origin. ❄❄❄

P. rhoifolia 🌳 (Japanese wing nut). Spreading tree with pinnate leaves, to 40cm (16in) long; the leaves are composed of up to 21 ovate-oblong, tapered, glossy, mid-green leaflets. Small, winged green fruit are produced in pendent spikes, to 30cm (12in) long, in summer. ↕ 30m (100ft), ↔ 25m (80ft). Japan. ❄❄❄

P. stenoptera ▣ 🌳 (Chinese wing nut). Spreading tree with pinnate leaves, to 40cm (16in) long, with winged midribs; the leaves comprise up to 21 oblong, bright green leaflets, the terminal leaflet often absent. Small, winged green fruit are produced in pendent spikes, to 30cm (12in) long, in summer. ↕ 25m (80ft), ↔ 15m (50ft). China. ❄❄❄

Pterocarya stenoptera (inset: fruit detail)

PTEROCELTIS

ULMACEAE

Genus of one species of deciduous tree found near streams, in rocky places, and in valleys in the mountains of China. It is cultivated for its attractive habit, peeling bark, bright green foliage, and winged green fruit. Inconspicuous, very small green flowers are produced in spring. Pteroceltis is best grown as a specimen tree.

- **HARDINESS** Fully hardy.
- **CULTIVATION** Grow in fertile, moist but well-drained soil in full sun. Pruning group 1.
- **PROPAGATION** Sow seed in containers outdoors in autumn.
- **PESTS AND DISEASES** Trouble free.

P. tatarinowii 🌳 Spreading tree with arching branches, flaking grey bark, and ovate, tapered, 3-veined, bright green leaves, to 10cm (4in) long, with toothed margins. The tiny, green male flowers are produced in stalkless clusters; the very small, green female flowers are solitary. Both male and female flowers are produced in spring, from the leaf axils; they are followed by round, winged green fruit, 2cm (¾in) across, in autumn. ↕↔ 10m (30ft). N. and C. China. ❄❄❄

PTEROCEPHALUS

DIPSACACEAE

Genus of approximately 25 species of annuals, perennials, and evergreen shrubs, occurring on rocky slopes, roadsides, and waste ground from the Mediterranean and tropical Africa to C. Asia, the Himalayas, and W. China. They have opposite, simple, entire or pinnatifid leaves, sometimes with scalloped margins. They are cultivated for their scabious-like, pink or mauve flowerheads, produced on long stems in summer, and the attractive, papery seed heads that follow. *P. perennis*, the only species widely grown, is suitable for a rock garden or the front of a border.

- **HARDINESS** Fully hardy.
- **CULTIVATION** Grow in any well-drained soil in full sun.
- **PROPAGATION** Sow seed in containers in a cold frame in autumn. Take stem-tip cuttings in summer.
- **PESTS AND DISEASES** Trouble free.

P. perennis ▣ syn. *P. parnassi*. Evergreen, mat-forming perennial bearing opposite, ovate to fiddle-shaped, hairy, grey-green leaves, to 4cm (1½in) long, scalloped at the margins. During summer, long stems, to 8cm (3in) long, bear solitary, dense, flattened heads of tubular, pale pinkish purple flowers, to 4cm (1½in) across; they are followed by papery seed heads. ↕ 8cm (3in), ↔ 20cm (8in). Greece. ❄❄❄

P. parnassi see *P. perennis*.

Pterocephalus perennis

PTERODISCUS

PEDALIACEAE

Genus of 18 species of succulent perennials and subshrubs found in semi-desert, rocky regions from tropical E. to S.W. Africa. They have a swollen caudex, tuberous roots, and solitary or branching stems. They are grown for their foliage and flowers: the leaves are very variable, light to dark green, and have entire, toothed, or deeply cut margins; the 5-lobed, funnel- to bell-shaped flowers are slightly 2-lipped, diurnal, usually yellow, orange, red, purple, or white, and are produced singly from the leaf axils in summer. In areas where temperatures fall below 15°C (59°F), grow as houseplants or in a warm greenhouse; in warm, dry climates, grow in a succulent border.

- **HARDINESS** Frost tender.
- **CULTIVATION** Under glass, grow in standard cactus compost in full light. From spring to summer, water sparingly and apply a low-nitrogen liquid fertilizer every 4–6 weeks. Keep dry at other times. Outdoors, grow in moderately fertile, sharply drained soil in full sun. Protect from excessive wet. See also pp.48–49.
- **PROPAGATION** Sow seed in spring at 19–24°C (66–75°F).
- **PESTS AND DISEASES** Trouble free.

P. luridus. Succulent with a conical, fleshy caudex, 8cm (3in) thick towards the base, covered with a smooth grey bark. Spreading, slightly white-frosted stems bear oblong, dark green leaves, 8cm (3in) long, with white or blue undersides and entire margins. Funnel-shaped yellow flowers, 2.5–5cm (1–2in) long, spotted red outside, are produced in summer. ↕ 50cm (20in), ↔ 15cm (6in). S.W. Africa. ❀ (min. 15°C/59°F)

P. speciosus. Succulent with a conical to spherical, fleshy caudex, 6cm (2½in) thick towards the base, and stems bearing linear-oblong, dark green leaves, to 6cm (2½in) long, with irregularly toothed margins. Funnel-shaped, pale reddish purple flowers, 3cm (1¼in) long, are produced in summer. ↕ 15cm (6in), ↔ 10cm (4in). South Africa (Limpopo, Eastern Cape). ❀ (min. 15°C/59°F)

PTEROPOGON

ASTERACEAE/COMPOSITAE

Genus of 10 erect to slightly spreading, slender-stemmed, white-woolly annuals, previously part of the genus *Helipterum*, from semi-arid regions of South Africa and Australia. They bear alternate, narrowly lance-shaped, light to mid-green, white-woolly leaves, but are cultivated for their long-stemmed, leafy clusters of small, rounded, papery, daisy-like, usually yellow flowerheads, borne from summer to early autumn. Suitable for an annual or mixed border. The flowerheads are good for drying, the clustered blooms of *P. humboldtianus* turning an attractive metallic green.

- **HARDINESS** Half hardy.
- **CULTIVATION** Grow in poor, sharply drained soil in full sun.
- **PROPAGATION** Sow seed *in situ* in late spring.
- **PESTS AND DISEASES** Prone to aphids.

P. humboldtianus, syn. *Helipterum humboldtianum*. Erect, single-stemmed or slightly branching annual with narrowly lance-shaped, white-woolly leaves, to 3cm (1¼in) long. Slightly fragrant, straw-textured yellow flowers are produced in flowerheads to 8cm (3in) across, from summer to early autumn. ↕ to 45cm (18in), ↔ to 15cm (6in). S. Australia. ❄

PTEROSTYRAX

STYRACACEAE

Genus of 4 species of spreading, deciduous trees or shrubs, with peeling, aromatic bark, occurring in mountain woodland in China and Japan. They are cultivated for their alternate, oblong to ovate, pale green leaves, pendent panicles of fragrant, 5-lobed white flowers, and unusual, ribbed or winged fruits. Grow as shrubs or as single- or multiple-stemmed specimen trees in a lawn or woodland setting.
• **HARDINESS** Fully hardy.
• **CULTIVATION** Grow in deep, fertile, well-drained, neutral to acid soil in full sun or partial shade. Pruning group 1.
• **PROPAGATION** Sow seed in containers outdoors in autumn. Take semi-ripe cuttings in summer.
• **PESTS AND DISEASES** Trouble free.

P. hispida ♀ (Epaulette tree). Spreading tree or shrub with peeling, aromatic grey bark and oblong to ovate, pale green leaves, to 20cm (8in) long. Bell-shaped, fragrant white flowers, 1cm (½in) across, each with 5 lobes divided almost to the base, are borne in pendent panicles, to 20cm (8in) long, in early and midsummer, followed by oblong, 5-ribbed fruit, to 1cm (½in) long, covered in yellow-brown bristles. ↕ 15m (50ft), ↔ 12m (40ft). China, Japan. ❄❄❄

▷ ***Ptilotrichum spinosum*** see *Alyssum spinosum*

P

PTILOTUS

AMARANTHACEAE

Genus of about 100 species of annuals, herbaceous perennials, and subshrubs from open scrub in Australia. They are grown for their dense, rounded, ovoid or conical to cylindrical spikes of tiny, 5-tepalled, white, yellow, pink, mauve, purple, or green flowers, often enhanced by long white hairs. The leaves are alternate and usually narrow. In frost-prone areas, grow in a cool greenhouse or in an alpine house, or as annual summer bedding plants; in warmer areas, grow in a border or rock garden.
• **HARDINESS** Frost hardy.
• **CULTIVATION** Under glass, grow in loam-based potting compost (JI No.2) in full light. During the growing season, water moderately and apply a balanced liquid fertilizer monthly; keep almost dry in winter. Outdoors, grow in fertile, sharply drained soil in full sun; avoid wet conditions.
• **PROPAGATION** Sow seed at 13–16°C (55–61°F) in spring. Take root cuttings in early spring.
• **PESTS AND DISEASES** Trouble free.

P. exaltatus (Pink mulla mulla). Robust, bushy perennial with rosettes of oblong-lance-shaped, thick, wavy-margined, bluish green leaves, to 8cm (3in) long, often tinged red. Very small, white to pink or red flowers, with hairy brown bracts, are borne in conical, later cylindrical spikes, to 15cm (6in) long, from winter to summer. ↕ to 30cm (12in) or more, ↔ 60cm (24in). Australia. ❄❄
P. manglesii, syn. *Trichinium manglesii*. Erect or spreading perennial bearing rosettes of narrow to broadly ovate, thick, smooth-margined, white-hairy, mid-green leaves, 2.5–8cm (1–3in) long. The lower leaves are borne on long stalks; the upper leaves are smaller and stalkless. In summer, very small, pink to violet flowers, with dark brown bracts, are produced in round to ovoid, white-hairy spikes, 8–10cm (3–4in) long. ↕↔ 10–40cm (4–16in). Australia. ❄❄

PTYCHOSPERMA

ARECACEAE/PALMAE

Genus of about 30 species of single- or cluster-stemmed palms found in moist forest habitats from coastal lowlands to mountain valleys, from Micronesia to Australia, New Guinea, and the Solomon Islands. Pinnate, oblong-elliptic, glossy leaves are composed of linear leaflets. Greenish white or greenish yellow, 3-petalled flowers are produced in panicles below the leaves, followed by spherical to ovoid, red, orange, or purplish black fruits. In frost-prone climates, grow in a warm greenhouse, or as houseplants. In tropical regions, grow as specimens in a small lawn, or to add height and interest to a shrub border.
• **HARDINESS** Frost tender.
• **CULTIVATION** Under glass, grow in loam-based potting compost (JI No.3) with added well-rotted organic matter and sharp sand, in bright indirect light. Pot on or top-dress in spring; during the growing season, water freely and apply a balanced liquid fertilizer every month. Water sparingly in winter. Outdoors, grow in fertile, moist but well-drained soil in partial shade.
• **PROPAGATION** Sow seed at 24°C (75°F) in spring.
• **PESTS AND DISEASES** Prone to scale insects and red spider mites under glass.

P. alexandrae see *Archontophoenix alexandrae*.
P. elegans ♀ syn. *Seaforthia elegans* (Alexander palm, Solitaire palm). Small to medium-sized palm with a slender, columnar trunk, ringed with old leaf scars. The woolly crownshaft produces pinnate, short-stalked leaves, 1–2.5m (3–8ft) long, composed of many broadly linear, mid-green leaflets with notched or toothed tips. In summer, fragrant, greenish white flowers, each to 8mm (⅜in) across, are produced in nodding panicles, 30–60cm (12–24in) long; they are followed by ovoid, bright red fruit, 2cm (¾in) across. ↕ 8–12m (25–40ft), ↔ 2–4m (6–12ft). N.E. Australia. ❁ (min. 16°C/61°F)
P. macarthurii ▣ ❁ Small, cluster-stemmed palm with slender, ring-scarred trunks. Pinnate, short-stalked leaves, 1.5m (5ft) long, are composed of many linear, bright green leaflets with ragged-toothed tips. Greenish yellow flowers, each to 8mm (⅜in) across, are produced in panicles 30–45cm (12–18in) long,

Ptychosperma macarthurii

usually in summer; they are followed by ovoid red fruit, 1.5cm (½in) long. ↕ 3–7m (10–22ft), ↔ 2–4m (6–12ft). New Guinea, N.E. Australia (Cape York Peninsula). ❁ (min. 16°C/61°F)

▷ **Puccoon, Red** see *Sanguinaria*
▷ **Pudding pipe-tree** see *Cassia fistula*

PUERARIA

LEGUMINOSAE/PAPILIONACEAE

Genus of 17 species of mainly woody-stemmed, deciduous or evergreen, twining climbers from thickets and woodland in S.E. Asia and Japan. They are grown for their alternate, 3-palmate or pinnate leaves and for their axillary or terminal racemes of pea-like flowers. *P. lobata*, the only species commonly cultivated, is extremely vigorous and must be sited with care. It is suitable for growing as ground cover, for screening an unsightly building, or for covering a tall tree stump. In frost-prone areas, it may also be grown as an annual.
• **HARDINESS** Frost hardy to frost tender.
• **CULTIVATION** Grow in fertile, moist but well-drained soil in full sun or partial shade. Support twining stems. Pruning group 11, in spring.
• **PROPAGATION** Sow seed at 13–18°C (55–64°F) in spring.
• **PESTS AND DISEASES** Trouble free.

P. hirsuta see *P. lobata*.
P. lobata, syn. *P. hirsuta*, *P. thunbergiana* (Japanese arrowroot, Kudzu vine). Very vigorous, deciduous, twining climber, with a large tuber, sometimes grown as an annual. Bears 3-palmate leaves composed of ovate to diamond-shaped, lobed leaflets, the central one largest, to 18cm (7in) long. In autumn, fragrant, pea-like purple flowers, 2cm (¾in) long, are produced in erect racemes, to 25cm (10in) long. ↕ to 20m (70ft) or more (sometimes reaches half this in one year). China, Japan, Pacific islands. ❄❄
P. thunbergiana see *P. lobata*.

PULMONARIA

Lungwort

BORAGINACEAE

Genus of about 14 species of deciduous or evergreen, low-growing perennials, with slowly spreading rhizomes. They are found in Europe and Asia, on acid to alkaline soils in a wide range of habitats, including mountainous areas, moist, subalpine woodland, and streamsides. They are grown for their early flowers, often among the first perennial blooms, in late winter or spring, and for their simple, ovate to elliptic or oblong, hairy basal leaves, which are often attractively spotted white or silver. The stem leaves are few, smaller, and more or less stalkless. Regular, funnel-shaped flowers, 5–10mm (¼–½in) across, with 5 spreading lobes, are borne in terminal cymes; the flowers may be pink, red, violet, purple, blue, or white, with either long (pin) or short (thrum) styles; blue, purple, or violet flowers may often be pink in bud. After flowering, new "summer" leaves develop, showing the markings at their best. Lungworts are good ground-cover plants for a shady position: grow in woodland, among shrubs, in a wild garden, or at the front of a border. They are attractive to bees.
• **HARDINESS** Fully hardy.
• **CULTIVATION** Grow in humus-rich, fertile, moist but not waterlogged soil, in full or partial shade; *P. officinalis* will tolerate full sun. Remove old leaves after flowering. Divide every 3–5 years.
• **PROPAGATION** Sow seed in containers outdoors as soon as ripe. Lungworts hybridize freely in cultivation, and plants raised from seed of species in gardens often do not come true. Divide after flowering, or in autumn. Take root cuttings in midwinter.
• **PESTS AND DISEASES** Prone to powdery mildew in dry conditions. Slugs and snails may damage new growth.

P. angustifolia (Blue cowslip). Open clump-forming, rhizomatous, usually deciduous perennial with lance-shaped, unspotted, mid- to dark green leaves, 40cm (16in) long. Funnel-shaped, rich blue flowers are borne profusely on erect then spreading stems, from early to late spring. ↕ 25–30cm (10–12in), ↔ 45cm (18in). C., N.E., and E. Europe. ❄❄❄. **subsp. *azurea*** ▣ syn. *P. azurea*, has brighter blue flowers, tinted red in bud; ↕ to 25cm (10in). **'Beth's Pink'** see

Pulmonaria angustifolia subsp. *azurea*

Pulmonaria 'Lewis Palmer'

P. 'Beth's Pink'. **'Blaues Meer'** produces bright blue flowers very freely.
P. azurea see *P. angustifolia* subsp. *azurea*.
***P.* 'Beth's Pink'**, syn. *P. angustifolia* 'Beth's Pink'. Clump-forming, rhizomatous, deciduous perennial with ovate, white-spotted, dark green leaves, to 25cm (10in) long, narrowing abruptly to the leaf-stalks. In mid- and late spring, bears funnel-shaped, deep coral-pink flowers. ↕ to 30cm (12in), ↔ 45cm (18in). ✼✼✼
***P.* 'Blue Ensign'.** Clump-forming, rhizomatous, deciduous perennial with ovate, unspotted, dark green leaves, to 25cm (10in) long, and large, blue-violet flowers, borne in spring. ↕ to 35cm (14in), ↔ to 45cm (18in). ✼✼✼
***P.* 'Lewis Palmer'** ▣ syn. *P. longifolia* 'Lewis Palmer'. Clump-forming, rhizomatous, deciduous perennial with lance-shaped, softly hairy, dark green basal leaves, to 30cm (12in) long, irregularly splashed and spotted greenish white, and ovate-lance-shaped stem leaves. In early spring, bears funnel-shaped flowers that open pink and become bright blue. ↕ 35cm (14in), ↔ 45cm (18in). ✼✼✼

Pulmonaria officinalis 'Sissinghurst White'

P. longifolia. Densely clump-forming, rhizomatous, deciduous perennial with narrowly lance-shaped, dark green leaves, to 45cm (18in) long, spotted silvery white. Dense cymes of long-lasting, funnel-shaped, blue-purple to almost blue flowers are borne from late winter to late spring. ↕ to 30cm (12in), ↔ 45cm (18in). S. England, France, Portugal, Spain. ✼✼✼. **'Bertram Anderson'** has longer, narrower, more strongly marked leaves, and brighter blue flowers. **'Lewis Palmer'** see *P.* 'Lewis Palmer'.
***P.* 'Mawson's Blue'** ▣ syn. *P.* 'Mawson's Variety'. Erect to spreading, rhizomatous, deciduous perennial bearing ovate to elliptic, softly hairy, unspotted, dark green leaves, to 30cm (12in) long. Produces dark blue flowers in spring. ↕ to 35cm (14in), ↔ to 45cm (18in). ✼✼✼
***P.* 'Mawson's Variety'** see *P.* 'Mawson's Blue'.
P. mollis, syn. *P. montana*. Vigorous, clump-forming, rhizomatous, deciduous perennial bearing elliptic to narrowly ovate, softly hairy, unspotted, mid-green leaves, to 45cm (18in) long. From late winter to mid-spring, produces funnel-shaped, rich blue flowers, sometimes pink-tinged fading to purplish blue. ↕ to 45cm (18in), ↔ 60cm (24in). Belgium, N.W. France, W. Germany, W. Switzerland. ✼✼✼
P. montana see *P. mollis.*
P. officinalis (Jerusalem cowslip, Soldiers and sailors, Spotted dog). Open clump-forming, rhizomatous, evergreen perennial with ovate, bristly, white-

Pulmonaria saccharata

spotted, bright mid-green leaves, 10–13cm (4–5in) long, heart-shaped at the bases. From early to late spring, bears funnel-shaped flowers, opening pink and becoming reddish violet then blue. ↕ 25cm (10in), ↔ 45cm (18in). Europe. ✼✼✼. **'Cambridge Blue'**, syn. 'Cambridge', bears heart-shaped leaves and abundant pale blue flowers, pink-tinted on opening; ↕ to 30cm (12in). **'Sissinghurst White'** ▣ syn. *P. saccharata* 'Sissinghurst White', bears leaves 20–25cm (8–10in) long, with numerous white spots, and pure white flowers opening from pale pink buds; ↕ to 30cm (12in). **'White Wings'** bears pink-eyed white flowers in late spring.
P. rubra. Loosely clump-forming, rhizomatous, leafy, evergreen perennial with elliptic, almost diamond-shaped, velvety, unspotted, matt, bright green leaves, to 60cm (24in) long. Funnel-shaped, bright brick-red to salmon-red flowers are borne over a long period from late winter to mid-spring. ↕ to 40cm (16in), ↔ 90cm (36in). S.E. Europe. ✼✼✼. **var. *alba*** see var. *albocorollata*. **var. *albocorollata***, syn. var. *alba*, has white flowers; ↕ to 30cm (12in). **'Barfield Pink'** has pink-and-white-striped flowers; ↕ to 30cm (1.2in). **'Bowles' Red'** has leaves with pale green spots, and coral-red flowers. **'David Ward'** has strongly white-variegated, sage-green leaves, with cream margins, and coral-red flowers; ↕ to 30cm (12in). **'Redstart'** ▣ has coral-red flowers, and is often the first pulmonaria to flower, in midwinter.
P. saccharata ▣ (Jerusalem sage). Clump-forming, rhizomatous, evergreen perennial with elliptic, white-spotted, mid-green leaves, to 27cm (11in) long, the stem leaves nearly as large as the basal leaves. From late winter to late spring, bears funnel-shaped, red-violet, violet, or white flowers, with dark green calyces. ↕ 30cm (12in), ↔ 60cm (24in). S.E. France, N. and C. Italy. ✼✼✼. Cultivars in **Argentea Group** have almost completely silver leaves, and flowers opening red, ageing to dark violet. **'Frühlingshimmel'** ▣ has many-spotted leaves, and light blue flowers with darker blue-purple eyes and calyces; ↕ 25cm (10in). **'Leopard'** has many-spotted, dark green leaves and red, pink-tinted flowers. **'Mrs. Moon'** has pink buds opening to bluish lilac flowers. **'Pink Dawn'** bears deep pink flowers ageing to violet. **'Sissinghurst White'** see *P. officinalis* 'Sissinghurst White'.
P. vallarsae. Clump-forming, rhizomatous, deciduous perennial with elliptic-oblong, wavy-margined, densely softly hairy, dark green leaves, 20cm (8in) long, narrowing abruptly to the leaf-stalks; they have bright green or whitish green spots, in rare cases none. Funnel-shaped violet flowers, becoming more purple with age, are borne on glandular-hairy stems from early to late spring. ↕ 15–30cm (6–12in), ↔ 60cm (24in). Italy. ✼✼✼. **'Margery Fish'** has bright green leaves, 15cm (6in) long, densely silvered on the upper surfaces, with the midribs and margins spotted. The flowers are coral-pink to red-violet, becoming violet; ↕ 18–28cm (7–11in).

Pulmonaria 'Mawson's Blue'

Pulmonaria rubra 'Redstart'

Pulmonaria saccharata 'Frühlingshimmel'

PULSATILLA

RANUNCULACEAE

Genus of about 30 species of clump-forming, deciduous perennials (sometimes with a few overwintering leaves) with a coarsely fibrous rootstock, found mainly in short turf and alpine meadows in Eurasia and N. America. They are cultivated for their finely dissected, fern-like leaves and their solitary, usually silky-hairy, bell- or cup-shaped flowers, produced in spring and early summer. The flowers are followed by spherical seed heads with silver-silky, plume-like styles, borne on stems that often elongate considerably after flowering; heights given below are for plants in flower. Grow in a rock garden, scree bed, or alpine house. All parts of the plant may cause mild stomach upset if ingested, and, in rare instances, contact with the sap may irritate skin.

- **HARDINESS** Fully hardy.
- **CULTIVATION** Grow in fertile, very well-drained soil in full sun; *P. vernalis* needs very gritty, moist but sharply drained soil in a scree bed, and requires protection from excessive winter wet. Pulsatillas resent root disturbance and may be difficult to establish, so plant when small and leave undisturbed. In an alpine house, use a mix of equal parts loam-based potting compost (JI No.1) and grit.
- **PROPAGATION** Sow seed as soon as ripe in containers in an open frame. Take root cuttings in winter.
- **PESTS AND DISEASES** Young growth may be attacked by slugs and snails.

Pulsatilla alpina

Pulsatilla halleri

Pulsatilla vernalis

P. alpina ■ (Alpine pasque flower). Clump-forming perennial with finely divided, 2-pinnate, hairy, mid-green leaves, 6–12cm (2½–5in) long, composed of 30–80 toothed leaflets. In spring, bears cup-shaped white flowers, to 6cm (2½in) across, with silky-hairy petals, blue-tinted on the reverse, and yellow stamens, followed by ornamental seed heads (pictured). ↕15–30cm (6–12in), ↔20cm (8in). Mountains in C. Europe. ❄❄❄. **subsp. *apiifolia***, syn. subsp. *sulphurea*, has pale yellow flowers, and usually occurs in acid soils. **subsp. *sulphurea*** see subsp. *apiifolia*.

P. halleri ■ Tufted perennial, densely clothed in long silver hairs, with pinnate, light green leaves, 5–18cm (2–7in) long, comprising 3–5 pinnatifid leaflets with oblong-lance-shaped lobes; the terminal leaflet is long-stalked. Erect, silky-hairy, bell-shaped, violet-purple to lavender-blue flowers, to 9cm (3½in) across, are produced with the leaves in late spring. ↕20cm (8in), ↔15cm (6in). C. and S.E. Europe, Crimea. ❄❄❄. **subsp. *grandis***, syn. *P. vulgaris* subsp. *grandis*, has silvery golden brown hairs. It bears very finely divided leaves after the shallowly bell-shaped, lavender-blue flowers, which have rounded segments; C. Europe, Ukraine.

P. patens (Eastern pasque flower). Clump-forming perennial with rounded-heart-shaped, roughly hairy, 3- to 7-palmate, mid-green leaves, to 12cm (5in) long; each of the leaflets is divided into 15–80 linear to linear-lance-shaped segments. In late spring, bears erect, broadly cup-shaped, blue-violet, lilac, or occasionally yellowish or yellowish white flowers, 5–8cm (2–3in) across. ↕15cm (6in), ↔10cm (4in). E. Europe, Russia (Siberia), North America. ❄❄❄

Pulsatilla vulgaris

Pulsatilla vulgaris f. *alba*

P. vernalis ■ Clump-forming perennial (with basal leaves overwintering) producing clusters of finely cut, very sparsely hairy, pinnate, light green leaves, 6–12cm (2½–5in) long, comprising 3–5 deeply toothed leaflets. In spring, pendent buds open to erect, bell-shaped white flowers, to 6cm (2½in) across, deeply flushed with bluish violet and silky on the outside. ↕↔ to 10cm (4in). Mountains from Spain to Scandinavia, Bulgaria, and Russia (Siberia). ❄❄❄

P. vulgaris ■ (Pasque flower). Clump-forming perennial with finely divided, pinnate, light green leaves, 8–20cm (3–8in) long, comprising 7–9 leaflets, each 2- or 3-pinnatisect; the lobes are linear to linear-lance-shaped, very hairy when young. In spring, bears upright or semi-pendent, bell-shaped or narrowly bell-shaped, silky-hairy flowers, 4–9cm (1½–3½in) across, in shades of deep to pale purple, occasionally white. ↕10–20cm (4–8in), ↔20cm (8in). UK, W. France to Ukraine. ❄❄❄. **f. *alba*** ■ produces pure white flowers of variable size. **subsp. *grandis*** see *P. halleri* subsp. *grandis*. **'Rode Klokke'**, syn. 'Rote Glocke', bears deep red flowers. **'Rote Glocke'** see 'Rode Klokke'.

PULTENAEA

LEGUMINOSAE/PAPILIONACEAE

Genus of about 120 species of evergreen shrubs from dry forest in Australia. They are cultivated for their usually alternate, occasionally opposite, linear to almost rounded leaves, and for their pea-like flowers. The axillary, usually yellow or pink flowers have notched standard petals, and are produced singly or in clusters, which are often crowded into apparently terminal heads. In frost-prone areas, grow in a cool greenhouse; in warmer areas, grow in a shrub border, or at the base of a wall.

- **HARDINESS** Half hardy to frost tender.
- **CULTIVATION** Under glass, grow in loamless potting compost with added sharp sand, in full light. In growth, water moderately and apply a balanced liquid fertilizer every month; water sparingly in winter. Outdoors, grow in moderately fertile, well-drained soil in full sun. Pruning group 8; may need restrictive pruning under glass.
- **PROPAGATION** Sow seed at 13–18°C (55–64°F) in autumn or spring. Root semi-ripe cuttings with bottom heat in summer.
- **PESTS AND DISEASES** Grey mould may be a problem in damp conditions.

P. procumbens (Bush pea, Eggs and bacon). Low, spreading to mat-forming shrub with alternate, narrowly elliptic, mid- to deep greyish green leaves, 0.8–1cm (⅜–½in) long, with upfolded sides and reflexed points. In spring and early summer, pea-like, orange-red flowers, 1cm (½in) across, shaded orange-yellow, are produced in small, apparently terminal heads. ↕15–30cm (6–12in), ↔40cm (16in) or more. Australia (New South Wales, Victoria). ❄ (min. 5°C/41°F)

PUNICA

Pomegranate

LYTHRACEAE/PUNICACEAE

Genus of 2 species of rounded, deciduous shrubs or trees found in scrub, one species occurring from S.E. Europe and S.W. Asia to the Himalayas, the other from Socotra (Yemen). They have mostly opposite, narrowly oblong, entire leaves, and are grown for their showy, funnel-shaped, bright red flowers and large, spherical, edible fruits. In frost-prone areas, grow in a cool greenhouse or against a sunny wall, either as free-standing shrubs or fan-trained; in warmer areas, use as specimen trees, in a shrub border, or as hedging.

- **HARDINESS** Frost hardy; they require long, hot summers to produce fruit.

Punica granatum var. *nana*

P

• **CULTIVATION** Under glass, plant directly in a greenhouse border or in large containers of loam-based potting compost (JI No.2) in full light. When in growth, water freely and apply a balanced liquid fertilizer every month; water sparingly in winter. A temperature of 13–16°C (55–61°F) in autumn is required for fruit to ripen. Outdoors, grow in fertile, well-drained soil in full sun. Pruning group 1, from spring to summer; group 13 if wall-trained. Remove wayward shoots in spring.
• **PROPAGATION** Sow seed at 13–18°C (55–64°F) in spring. Root semi-ripe cuttings with bottom heat in summer.
• **PESTS AND DISEASES** Trouble free.

P. granatum ♀ (Pomegranate). Upright, sometimes spiny shrub or small, rounded tree with opposite, narrowly oblong, glossy, bright green leaves, to 8cm (3in) long, coppery or red-veined when young. Over a long period in summer, bears funnel-shaped, 5-petalled, bright orange-red flowers, to 4cm (1½in) across, singly or in clusters of up to 5, followed by spherical, yellow-brown, edible fruit, to 12cm (5in) across. ↕6m (20ft), ↔5m (15ft). S.E. Europe to Himalayas. ❄❄. **var. *nana*** ▣ is a compact, rounded shrub that fruits very freely; ↕↔30–100cm (12–39in). **f. *plena*** produces double flowers.

▷**Purslane** see *Claytonia*, *Portulaca*
Rock see *Calandrinia umbellata*
Tree see *Atriplex halimus*
Water see *Ludwigia palustris*

PUSCHKINIA

HYACINTHACEAE/LILIACEAE

Genus of one species of bulbous perennial, related to *Chionodoxa* and *Scilla*, occurring in the Middle East, in damp flushes in grassland where snow has recently melted. It is grown for its small, densely packed racemes of bell-shaped, pale blue flowers with darker blue stripes, borne in spring. The bulbs

Puschkinia scilloides var. *libanotica*

each have 2 semi-erect, basal leaves. Grow in a rock garden or among shrubs.
• **HARDINESS** Fully hardy.
• **CULTIVATION** Grow in any well-drained soil in full sun or light dappled shade.
• **PROPAGATION** Sow seed in containers in a cold frame in summer or autumn. Remove offsets in summer as the leaves die down.
• **PESTS AND DISEASES** Prone to viruses.

P. libanotica see *P. scilloides* var. *libanotica*.
P. scilloides ▣ Small, bulbous perennial with 2 semi-erect, linear, basal leaves, 15cm (6in) long. In spring, produces compact racemes of 4–10 open bell-shaped, very pale, bluish white flowers, 1cm (½in) across, with a dark blue stripe on each petal. ↕to 20cm (8in), ↔5cm (2in). Caucasus, Turkey, Lebanon, N. Iraq, N. Iran. ❄❄❄. **var. *libanotica*** ▣ syn. *P. libanotica*, has smaller white flowers, 7–8mm (¼–⅜in) across, rarely striped blue, with long, sharply pointed lobes; Turkey, Lebanon.

▷**Pussy ears** see *Cyanotis somaliensis*
▷**Pussy-toes** see *Antennaria*

Puschkinia scilloides

PUTORIA

RUBIACEAE

Genus of 3 species of dwarf, evergreen shrubs occurring in sunny, rocky areas around the Mediterranean. They bear opposite, lance-shaped to obovate or oblong, malodorous, leathery, lustrous, rich, mid-green leaves, but they are cultivated for their long-tubed, funnel-shaped, pink to purple flowers, produced singly or in clusters from early to late summer. *P. calabrica*, the only cultivated species, is suitable for growing in a rock garden or at the base of a warm, sunny wall.
• **HARDINESS** Fully hardy.
• **CULTIVATION** Grow in any well-drained soil in full sun.
• **PROPAGATION** Sow seed in containers in a cold frame in spring. Take softwood cuttings in early summer.
• **PESTS AND DISEASES** Trouble free.

P. calabrica (Stinking madder). Slow-growing, spreading shrub with elliptic-lance-shaped, leathery, mid-green leaves, 2cm (¾in) long, foetid if crushed. Produces dense, terminal clusters of funnel-shaped pink flowers, to 1.5cm (½in) long, from early to late summer. ↕8cm (3in), ↔ to 30cm (12in). Mediterranean. ❄❄❄

PUYA

BROMELIACEAE

Genus of about 170 species of terrestrial, evergreen perennials (bromeliads) from rocky slopes, to 2,000m (6,500ft) high, in Andean South America, Costa Rica, Colombia, Guyana, N. Brazil, and N. central Argentina. They have erect or widely spreading rosettes of linear leaves with coarse marginal spines; young leaf-blades are upright, mature ones are outspread. The leaf sheaths are prominent, often forming bulbous bases. The flowers are trumpet- or bell-shaped, in colours from white, greenish yellow, and sea-green to ice-blue or violet; they are usually produced in erect panicles, the branches having sterile tips (which act as perches for humming-bird pollinators). Flowers are followed by green fruit capsules containing winged seeds. Puyas tolerate cold better than most bromeliads. In frost-prone areas, grow in a conservatory or cool green-house; in warmer climates, use in a raised bed.
• **HARDINESS** Frost hardy (borderline) to frost tender.
• **CULTIVATION** Under glass, grow in terrestrial bromeliad compost in full light. From mid-spring to late summer, water moderately and apply a low-nitrogen liquid fertilizer every 6–8 weeks; water sparingly at other times. Outdoors, grow in any well-drained soil in full sun. Protect from winter wet. See also p.47.
• **PROPAGATION** Sow seed at 19–24°C (66–75°F) as soon as ripe.
• **PESTS AND DISEASES** New growth is susceptible to scale insects.

P. berteroniana ▣ Bromeliad with a caudex-like stem bearing spreading, terminal rosettes of lance-shaped, arching, dark green leaves, 60–100cm (24–39in) long, white-scaly beneath. In

Puya berteroniana

early summer, produces loose, pyramidal panicles, over 1m (3ft) long, of funnel-shaped, rich bluish green or deep blue-green flowers, 5cm (2in) long, with bright orange-yellow stamens. Will tolerate brief periods below 0°C (32°F). ↕to 2m (6ft), ↔3m (10ft). C. Chile. ❄❄ (borderline)
P. caerulea see *P. coerulea*.
P. chilensis ▣ Bromeliad with a very woody, caudex-like stem, sometimes branched, bearing spreading, dense, terminal rosettes of lance-shaped, stiff, leathery, mid-green leaves, 1m (3ft) long, with marginal spines. In summer, produces bell- to trumpet-shaped, yellow or green flowers, to 5cm (2in) long, with green sepals, in loosely branched panicles, 1.5m (5ft) long; the

P

Puya chilensis

Puya mirabilis

upper parts of the panicle branches are covered with reduced bracts. ↕ 5m (15ft), ↔ 2m (6ft) or more. C. Chile. ❄
P. coerulea, syn. *P. caerulea*. Extremely variable bromeliad producing well-developed, erect, stout stems, each with terminal, spreading rosettes of lance-shaped leaves, to 60cm (24in) long, the leaf-blades ash-white, the margins with hooked, reddish brown spines, to 5mm (¼in) long. In summer, produces tubular, erect, stalked, dark blue flowers, 5cm (2in) or more long, in racemes or panicles, 40cm (16in) or more long. ↕↔ to 2m (6ft). C. Chile. ❄
P. mirabilis ▣ Stemless bromeliad bearing terminal, spreading rosettes of loose, linear-lance-shaped, finely toothed, white to brownish green leaves, to 60cm (24in) long. In summer, bears loose, simple racemes, to 50cm (20in) long, of funnel-shaped, yellowish green flowers, 10cm (4in) long. ↕↔ to 60cm (24in). Bolivia, N. Argentina. ❈ (min. 5°C/41°F)
P. raimondii ▣ Bromeliad with a thick, caudex-like stem, to 50cm (20in) across. Produces broadly lance-shaped, often red-suffused, bright green leaves, to 2m (6ft) long, densely scaly beneath,

Puya raimondii

in a dense, globular, terminal rosette. In summer, tubular, greenish white, rarely purple flowers, 5cm (2in) long, are borne in a cylindrical, compound raceme, to 5m (15ft) long. ↕ to 2m (6ft), ↔ 1m (3ft). Peru, Bolivia. ❈ (min. 5°C/41°F)

PYCNOSORUS

Billy buttons, Drumsticks

ASTERACEAE/COMPOSITAE

Genus of 6 species of annuals, rosette-forming perennials, and subshrubs from Australia, where they occur in low-lying, open habitats. Their strap-shaped leaves are alternate, decreasing in size up the stems, the basal leaves soon withering. They are grown for their white-haired, mid-green leaves and compound, spherical yellow flowerheads, produced in summer. *P. globosus* is ideal for growing in an annual border, while other species are better grown in a rock garden or scree bed.
• **HARDINESS** Frost hardy.
• **CULTIVATION** Grow annuals in well-drained soil in full sun and perennials and subshrubs in moderately fertile, well-drained soil in full sun. Protect from excessive winter wet.
• **PROPAGATION** Sow seed at 13–18°C (55–64°F) in spring. Divide perennials in spring.
• **PESTS AND DISEASES** Slugs and snails may attack young growth.

P. globosus, syn. *Craspedia globosa* (Bachelor's buttons, Drumsticks). Rosette-forming, white-woolly perennial, usually grown as an annual, with narrowly strap-shaped, light green leaves, to 30cm (12in) long, covered in white hairs. Mustard-yellow flowerheads, to 3cm (1¼in) across, are produced in summer at the tips of long, rigid, hairy stems. ↕ 60–90cm (24–36in), ↔ to 12cm (5in). Australia (W. Victoria, New South Wales, Queensland, South Australia). ❄❄❄

PYCNOSTACHYS

LABIATAE/LAMIACEAE

Genus of 40 species of erect, evergreen perennials or soft-stemmed shrubs occurring in forest margins in tropical and southern Africa and Madagascar. They are cultivated for their dense, terminal spikes of 2-lipped, tubular, deep blue flowers. The leaves are opposite or in whorls, linear, lance-

Pycnostachys dawei

shaped, or ovate, and are rather pungent when crushed. In frost-prone areas, grow in a warm greenhouse or conservatory. In warmer areas, they are suitable for growing in a shrub border.
• **HARDINESS** Frost tender.
• **CULTIVATION** Under glass, grow in loam-based potting compost (JI No.2) with added sharp sand, in full light. During the growing season, water freely and apply a balanced liquid fertilizer every month; water sparingly in winter. Outdoors, grow in fertile, well-drained soil in full sun.
• **PROPAGATION** Sow seed at 15–18°C (59–64°F) in spring. Take softwood cuttings at any time.
• **PESTS AND DISEASES** Whiteflies may be troublesome.

P. dawei ▣ Pyramidal, evergreen perennial bearing opposite, linear, mid-green leaves, to 30cm (12in) long, red beneath, with long, sharp points and toothed margins. In summer, produces tubular, cobalt-blue flowers, to 2.5cm (1in) long, in dense, terminal spikes, 15cm (6in) long. ↕ 1.8m (6ft), ↔ 90cm (36in). Tropical Africa. ❈ (min. 12°C/54°F)
P. urticifolia. Erect, soft-stemmed, evergreen shrub, becoming somewhat woody at the base and branching freely, with opposite, narrowly ovate, hairless or softly hairy, mid-green leaves, to 12cm (5in) long, often with toothed margins. In winter, tubular, deep blue flowers, 1–2cm (½–¾in) long, sometimes white with a blue tinge, are produced in dense, terminal spikes, to 10cm (4in) long. ↕ 2.5m (8ft), ↔ 1.2m (4ft). Tropical Africa and Mozambique. ❈ (min. 12°C/54°F)

▷ ***Pygmea armstrongii*** see *Chionohebe armstrongii*
▷ ***Pygmea pulvinaris*** see *Chionohebe pulvinaris*
▷ ***Pygmea tetragona*** see *Chionohebe densifolia*

PYRACANTHA

Firethorn

ROSACEAE

Genus of 7 species of spiny, evergreen, spreading to erect shrubs, occasionally trees, found in scrub and woodland margins from S. Europe to S.W. Asia, the Himalayas, China, and Taiwan. They are cultivated for their foliage, flowers, and, in particular, fruit: the variably shaped leaves are alternate and often have toothed margins; the 5-petalled white flowers are hawthorn-like and borne in compound corymbs; the showy, spherical berries that follow them in autumn are yellow, orange, or red. Grow firethorns as free-standing shrubs in a shrub border, or against a wall, or for hedging. The seeds may cause mild stomach upset if ingested.
• **HARDINESS** Fully hardy to frost hardy.
• **CULTIVATION** Grow in fertile, well-drained soil in full sun or partial shade. In frost-prone areas, shelter from cold, drying winds. Pruning group 1 for free-standing shrubs. Trim hedging in early to midsummer. On wall-trained plants, tie in any shoots needed to extend the framework, and cut back unwanted shoots to the main stem. After flowering in midsummer, shorten lateral shoots to

Pyracantha 'Golden Charmer'

2 or 3 leaves from the base to expose the developing berries. In spring, remove old fruit trusses to make way for new growth.
• **PROPAGATION** Sow seed in containers in a cold frame in autumn. Root semi-ripe cuttings with bottom heat in summer.
• **PESTS AND DISEASES** Susceptible to aphids, caterpillars, scale insects, leaf miners, coral spot, fireblight, and scab.

P. angustifolia. Dense, bushy shrub with narrowly oblong or obovate, dark green leaves, to 5cm (2in) long, grey-felted beneath. Small white flowers are produced in corymbs in midsummer; they are followed by orange-yellow berries, 8mm (⅜in) across. ↕↔ 3m (10ft). W. China. ❄❄

Pyracantha atalantioides 'Aurea'

Pyracantha 'Golden Dome'

P. atalantioides. Vigorous shrub with upright, arching shoots and oblong-elliptic to lance-shaped, glossy, dark green leaves, to 8cm (3in) long. In spring, small white flowers are borne in corymbs; they are followed by persistent, bright orange-red berries, to 7mm (¼in) across. ↕ to 6m (20ft), ↔ 4m (12ft). C. China. ❄❄. **'Aurea'** ■ bears yellow berries.
P. coccinea. Dense, bushy shrub with ovate-lance-shaped, dark green leaves, 2–4cm (¾–1½in) long. Small, creamy white flowers are borne in corymbs in early summer, followed by bright scarlet berries, 5mm (¼in) across. ↕↔ 4m (12ft). S.E. Europe to Caucasus. ❄❄❄. **'Lalandei'** has an upright habit and a profusion of bright orange-red berries, 7–8mm (¼–⅜in) across; ↕ to 6m (20ft).
***P.* 'Golden Charmer'** ■ Vigorous, bushy shrub with arching branches and inversely lance-shaped, glossy, bright green leaves, to 5cm (2in) long. Small white flowers are produced in corymbs in early summer, followed by bright orange-red berries, 9mm (⅜in) across. ↕↔ 3m (10ft). ❄❄❄
***P.* 'Golden Dome'** ■ Spreading shrub, forming a dense mound of arching branches bearing oblong, glossy, dark green leaves, to 6cm (2½in) long. In early summer, small white flowers are produced in corymbs; they are followed by an abundance of golden yellow berries, 5mm (¼in) across. ↕ 2m (6ft), ↔ 3m (10ft). ❄❄❄
***P.* 'Harlequin'.** Spreading shrub with oblong, dark green leaves, 5cm (2in) long, strikingly marked creamy white, flushed pink when young. Small white

Pyracantha 'Mohave'

Pyracantha 'Orange Glow'

flowers are produced in corymbs in early summer, followed by red berries, 5mm (¼in) across. Best grown against a wall. ↕ 1.5m (5ft), ↔ 2m (6ft). ❄❄
P. koidzumii. Erect shrub with inversely lance-shaped, glossy, dark green leaves, to 5cm (2in) long. Small white flowers are produced in corymbs in early summer, followed by orange-red berries, 7mm (¼in) across. ↕ 3m (10ft), ↔ 4m (12ft). Taiwan. ❄❄. **'Rosedale'** has arching branches and bright red berries, 9mm (⅜in) across.
***P.* 'Mohave'** ■ Vigorous, bushy shrub with oval, dark green leaves, to 6cm (2½in) long. In early summer, small white flowers are produced in corymbs, followed by long-lasting red berries, 9mm (⅜in) across. ↕ 4m (12ft), ↔ 5m (15ft). ❄❄
***P.* 'Orange Charmer'.** Vigorous, bushy shrub with arching branches and elliptic to obovate, glossy, bright green leaves, to 5cm (2in) long. Small white flowers are borne in corymbs in early summer, followed by dark orange berries, 9mm (⅜in) across. ↕↔ 3m (10ft). ❄❄❄
***P.* 'Orange Glow'** ■ Upright, later spreading, loosely branched shrub with broadly elliptic to obovate, glossy, dark

Pyracantha 'Soleil d'Or'

Pyracantha x *watereri*

green leaves, 2–4cm (¾–1½in) long. Small white flowers are produced in corymbs in late spring, followed by a profusion of persistent, orange-red to dark orange berries, 7–8mm (¼–⅜in) across. ↕↔ 3m (10ft). Probably a cultivar of *P. fortuneana*. ❄❄❄
P. rogersiana. Spreading shrub with arching branches and inversely lance-shaped to narrowly obovate, glossy, bright green leaves, to 4cm (1½in) long. Small white flowers are produced in corymbs in spring, followed by orange-red berries, 8mm (⅜in) across. ↕↔ 4m (12ft). W. China. ❄❄. **f. *flava*** has yellow berries.
***P.* 'Santa Cruz'.** Low, compact, spreading shrub with oblong, dark green leaves, to 8cm (3in) long. Small white flowers are produced in corymbs in early summer, followed by small red berries, 6–8mm (¼–⅜in) across. ↕ 1m (3ft), ↔ 2m (6ft). ❄❄
***P.* 'Shawnee'.** Spreading shrub with narrowly elliptic, glossy, dark green leaves, to 5cm (2in) long. Small white flowers are borne in corymbs in early summer, followed by slightly flattened, orange-yellow berries, 9mm (⅜in) across. ↕ 3m (10ft), ↔ 4m (12ft). ❄❄
***P.* 'Soleil d'Or'** ■ Upright shrub with red-tinged shoots and broadly elliptic, glossy, dark green leaves, 6cm (2½in) long. Small white flowers are borne in corymbs in early summer, followed by golden yellow berries, 1cm (½in) across. ↕ 3m (10ft), ↔ 2.5m (8ft). ❄❄❄
***P.* 'Teton'.** Vigorous, upright shrub with oblong, wavy-margined, glossy, bright green leaves, to 5cm (2in) long. Small white flowers are produced in corymbs in early summer, followed by an abundance of yellow-orange berries, 6mm (¼in) across. ↕ 5m (15ft), ↔ 3m (10ft). ❄❄❄
P.* x *watereri ■ (*P. atalantioides* x *P. rogersiana*). Dense, upright shrub with elliptic, dark green leaves, to 6cm (2½in) long. In early summer, small white flowers are produced in corymbs, followed by bright red berries, 8mm (⅜in) across. ↕↔ 2.5m (8ft). Garden origin. ❄❄❄

▷ **Pyramid tree, Queensland** see *Lagunaria patersonia*
▷ ***Pyrethropsis*** see *Rhodanthemum*
P. atlantica see *R. atlanticum*
P. catananche see *R. catananche*
P. gayana see *R. gayanum*
P. hosmariensis see *R. hosmariense*
P. maresii see *R. maresii*
▷ ***Pyrethrum*** see *Tanacetum*
P. coccineum see *Tanacetum coccineum*
P. parthenium see *Tanacetum parthenium*
P. ptarmiciflorum see *Tanacetum ptarmiciflorum*
P. radicans see *Leucanthemopsis pectinata*
P. roseum see *Tanacetum coccineum*
▷ **Pyrethrum** see *Tanacetum coccineum*

PYROLA

Shinleaf, Wintergreen

ERICACEAE/PYROLACEAE

Genus of 35 species of creeping, rhizomatous, evergreen perennials from woodland and moorland in the N. hemisphere. They are grown for their basal clusters of alternate, simple, usually rounded to ovate, long-stalked, mid- to dark green leaves, and upright racemes of cup- to bowl-shaped, white, pink, or red flowers, borne in summer. They can be hard to establish, possibly needing a mycorrhizal association with specific, soil-dwelling fungi. Grow in a woodland garden, peat bed, or rock garden.
• **HARDINESS** Fully hardy.
• **CULTIVATION** Grow in fertile, acid, leafy, moist but well-drained soil in partial or dappled shade.
• **PROPAGATION** Surface-sow seed in containers of damp sphagnum moss as soon as ripe. Divide with care in spring; roots resent disturbance.
• **PESTS AND DISEASES** Very susceptible to attack by slugs and snails.

P. rotundifolia (Round-leaved wintergreen, Wild lily-of-the-valley). Creeping perennial with basal clusters of rounded or broadly oval, mid- to dark green leaves, 2–6cm (¾–2½in) long. In summer, produces upright stems bearing loose racemes of up to 20 cup-shaped, pure white, rarely pink-tinged flowers, 0.8–1.5cm (⅜–½in) across, with incurving petals. ↕ 20cm (8in), ↔ 15cm (6in). Europe, North America. ❄❄❄

PYROSTEGIA

BIGNONIACEAE

Genus of 3 or 4 species of woody-stemmed, evergreen tendril climbers found in tropical woodland in South America. Leaves, produced in opposite pairs, each have 2 or 3 leaflets and sometimes a terminal, 3-branched tendril. The tubular or bell-shaped, usually orange or red flowers each have a tapered base and club-like tip, with 5 short petal lobes. Where temperatures fall below 10–13°C (50–55°F), grow in a temperate or warm greenhouse. In warmer areas, grow over a pergola or arch, or allow to cascade from a tree.
• **HARDINESS** Frost tender.
• **CULTIVATION** Under glass, grow in loam-based potting compost (JI No.2) with added leaf mould and sharp sand, in full light. During the growing season, water moderately and apply a balanced liquid fertilizer monthly; water sparingly in winter. Outdoors, grow in fertile, moist but well-drained soil in full sun. Support climbing stems. Pruning group 11 or 12, after flowering.
• **PROPAGATION** Sow seed at 16°C (61°F) in spring. Root semi-ripe cuttings with bottom heat in summer.

P

Pyrostegia venusta

• **PESTS AND DISEASES** May be infested with scale insects and red spider mites under glass.

P. ignea see *P. venusta*.
P. venusta ■ syn. *P. ignea* (Golden shower). Very vigorous climber with numerous slender stems, and opposite leaves composed of ovate to oblong-lance-shaped, rich green leaflets, to 8cm (3in) long. Bears a profusion of curved, tubular, waxy, golden to reddish orange flowers, 6cm (2½in) long, in terminal clusters, mainly in winter. ↕ 10m (30ft) or more. Bolivia to Brazil, Paraguay, N. Argentina. ❀ (min. 10–13°C/50–55°F)

▷ ***Pyrrhocactus crispus*** see *Neoporteria crispa*

PYRROSIA
Felt fern
POLYPODIACEAE

Genus of about 100 species of epiphytic and terrestrial, evergreen ferns with long-creeping rhizomes, mainly from tropical forest in North and South America, but also found in temperate areas in E. Asia. They are cultivated for their very small to large, mostly simple, linear to almost rounded, sometimes palmately lobed, thick, leathery fronds, the undersides of which are usually densely covered with matted and felt-like, star-shaped, branched hairs. In frost-prone climates, grow in a container or hanging basket in a temperate greenhouse; elsewhere, grow epiphytically on a tree or on other mossy supports, or in a sheltered, shady border.

• **HARDINESS** Frost hardy to frost tender.
• **CULTIVATION** Under glass, grow in a mix of 1 part each loam, medium-grade bark, and charcoal, 2 parts sharp sand, and 3 parts coarse leaf mould. Provide bright filtered or indirect light, with high humidity. In growth, water freely and apply a balanced liquid fertilizer monthly; water sparingly in winter. Outdoors, grow in moderately fertile, leafy, well-drained soil in partial shade.
• **PROPAGATION** Sow spores at 21°C (70°F) when ripe. Divide in spring. See also p.51.
• **PESTS AND DISEASES** Scale insects may be troublesome.

P. lingua ■ (Japanese felt fern, Tongue fern). Evergreen fern bearing simple, lance-shaped to ovate, leathery, glossy, dark green fronds, to 30cm (12in) long, sparsely hairy above, densely covered with star-shaped hairs beneath. Spores form in patches over a large part of the undersides of the fronds. ↕ 10–20cm (4–8in), ↔ 30cm (12in). E. Asia, China, Taiwan, Japan (Ryukyu Islands). ❀ (min. 10°C/50°F). **'Cristata'** has fronds repeatedly forked at the tips.

Pyrrosia lingua

PYRUS
Pear
ROSACEAE

Genus of about 30 species of upright, mainly deciduous trees and shrubs, found in woodland, in rocky places, and on hillsides in Europe, W. to E. Asia, and N. Africa. They are grown for their habit, flowers, and fruits. The leaves are alternate, entire or very rarely lobed, ovate to oblong, elliptic, or oval, the margins often with forward-pointing teeth; some have good autumn colour. The 5-petalled, saucer- to bowl-shaped flowers, borne in umbel-like racemes, are white, occasionally pink, and usually have red anthers. The fruits are spherical to typically pear-shaped; many cultivars have been bred specifically for the production of culinary and dessert pears. Ornamental pears are best grown as specimen trees on a lawn; the smaller or narrower ones, such as *P. salicifolia* 'Pendula' and *P. calleryana* 'Chanticleer', are particularly good for a small garden.
• **HARDINESS** Fully hardy.
• **CULTIVATION** Grow in fertile, well-drained soil in full sun. Pruning group 1.
• **PROPAGATION** Sow seed in an open frame or in a seedbed in autumn. Bud in summer, or graft in winter.

Pyrus calleryana 'Chanticleer'

Pyrus communis

• **PESTS AND DISEASES** Susceptible to aphids, caterpillars, leaf midges, mites, fireblight, honey fungus, powdery mildew, canker, brown rot, and scab.

P. calleryana △ Broadly conical, often very thorny, deciduous tree with ovate to broadly ovate, finely scalloped or toothed, glossy, dark green leaves, to 8cm (3in) long, turning red in late autumn. White flowers, 2cm (¾in) across, are borne in umbel-like racemes of up to 12, in early and mid-spring, followed in autumn by spherical brown fruit, 1cm (½in) across. ↕↔ 15m (50ft). China. ❄❄❄. **'Autumn Blaze'** has red-purple autumn colour. **'Bradford'** ◊ is narrowly conical, becoming broader with age, and thornless; ↔ 12m (40ft). **'Capital'** ◊ is narrowly conical, with copper autumn colour; ↕ 12m (40ft), ↔ 5m (15ft). **'Chanticleer'** ■◊ is narrowly conical; ↔ 6m (20ft).
P. communis ■△ (Common pear). Columnar, occasionally thorny, deciduous tree with ovate to elliptic, glossy, dark green leaves, to 10cm (4in) long, with fine, forward-pointing teeth. White flowers, 4cm (1½in) across, often tinged pink in bud, are borne in umbel-like racemes of 5–9 in mid-spring; they are followed by edible, pear-shaped to spherical, green to yellow fruit, to 10cm (4in) long. ↕ 15m (50ft), ↔ 10m (30ft). S. Europe, S.W. Asia. ❄❄❄. **'Beech Hill'** ◊ is narrowly conical, with leaves that turn orange and red in autumn; ↕ 10m (30ft), ↔ 7m (22ft).
P. japonica see *Chaenomeles speciosa*.
P. nivalis △ (Snow pear). Broadly conical, thornless, deciduous tree with elliptic to obovate, entire or shallowly scalloped, silvery grey leaves, to 8cm (3in) long, white-hairy beneath. In mid-spring, bears white flowers, 3cm (1¼in) across, in umbel-like racemes of 6–9, followed by spherical, yellow-green fruit, 4cm (1½in) across. ↕ 12m (40ft), ↔ 8m (25ft). C. and S.E. Europe. ❄❄❄
P. salicifolia ○ Spreading, deciduous tree with pendent shoots and lance-shaped to narrowly elliptic, willow-like, grey-felted leaves, to 9cm (3½in) long, becoming hairless with age. Creamy white flowers, 2cm (¾in) across, are borne in dense, umbel-like racemes of 6–8 in spring, followed by pear-shaped green fruit, 3cm (1¼in) long. ↕ 8m (25ft), ↔ 6m (20ft). S.E. Europe, Caucasus, Turkey, N.W. Iran. ❄❄❄. **'Pendula'** ■☂ has stiffly weeping branches; ↕ 5m (15ft), ↔ 4m (12ft).
P. ussuriensis △ Broadly conical, deciduous tree with broadly oval, glossy, dark green leaves, to 10cm (4in) long. White flowers, 3cm (1¼in) across, are borne in umbel-like racemes of 6–9 in mid-spring, followed by almost spherical green fruit, 4cm (1½in) across. ↕ 12m (40ft), ↔ 8m (25ft). N.E. Asia. ❄❄❄

Pyrus salicifolia 'Pendula'

Q

▷ **Quaking grass** see *Briza*
Common see *B. media*
Greater see *B. maxima*
Lesser see *B. minor*
▷ **Quamash** see *Camassia*, *C. quamash*
▷ ***Quamoclit coccinea*** see *Ipomoea coccinea*
▷ ***Quamoclit lobata*** see *Ipomoea lobata*
▷ ***Quamoclit pennata*** see *Ipomoea quamoclit*

QUAQUA

ASCLEPIADACEAE

Genus of 14 species of perennial succulents, closely related to *Caralluma*, from hilly, often rocky terrain in S. Namibia and South Africa, grown for their lobed, bowl-shaped flowers, borne singly or in clusters during daytime in early summer. Where temperatures fall below 10°C (50°F), grow in a warm greenhouse; in warm, dry climates, use in a raised bed with other succulents.
• **HARDINESS** Frost tender.
• **CULTIVATION** Under glass, grow in a mix of equal parts loam-based potting compost (JI No.2) and sharp grit, in full light with shade from hot sun. During growth, water freely and apply a dilute balanced fertilizer 2 or 3 times. Keep barely moist in winter. Outdoors, grow in gritty, sharply drained, moderately fertile soil in full sun with some midday shade. See also pp.48–49.
• **PROPAGATION** Sow seed at 18–21°C (64–70°F) in spring. Take stem cuttings in late summer.
• **PESTS AND DISEASES** Prone to aphids.

Q. pillansii, syn. *Caralluma pillansii*. Erect, freely branching succulent with 4-angled, sturdy, dark grey-green stems, to 2.5cm (1in) thick, spotted red, and with compressed brown teeth with spine-like tips. Dense clusters of 4–20 bowl-shaped, purple-brown flowers, to 2.5cm (1in) across, with purple- or red-spotted, greyish green lobes, develop from the stem grooves in early summer. ‡↔ to 30cm (12in). S. Namibia, South Africa (Western Cape). ⌂ (min. 10°C/50°F)

▷ **Quassia** see *Picrasma quassioides*
▷ **Queen Anne's lace** see *Anthriscus sylvestris*
▷ **Queen Anne's thimbles** see *Gilia capitata*
▷ **Queen anthurium** see *Anthurium veitchii*
▷ **Queencup** see *Clintonia uniflora*
▷ **Queen of the meadows** see *Filipendula ulmaria*
▷ **Queen of the night** see *Selenicereus grandiflorus*
▷ **Queen of the prairies** see *Filipendula rubra*
▷ **Queen's tears** see *Billbergia nutans*

QUERCUS

Oak

FAGACEAE

Genus of about 600 species of monoecious, deciduous, semi-evergreen or evergreen trees and shrubs, widely distributed in woodland and scrub in the N. hemisphere, and grown for their habit and foliage. They have usually fissured bark, downy to hairless shoots, and alternate, entire, lobed, or toothed leaves, which in some deciduous species give excellent autumn colour. The tiny male and female flowers are produced separately on the same plant in late spring and early summer; the males are borne in pendent catkins, the females singly, in pairs, or in racemes, followed by usually ovoid brown nuts (acorns) in scaly cups. The acorns are mostly 1–3cm (½–1¼in) long, sometimes more, and solitary or paired, but in some species are borne in racemes. Oak trees are best as specimens in a large garden or a park.
• **HARDINESS** Fully hardy to frost hardy.
• **CULTIVATION** Grow in deep, fertile, well-drained soil in sun or partial shade; evergreen species prefer full sun. Shelter oaks of borderline hardiness from frost and cold winds. They are lime-tolerant unless stated otherwise. Pruning group 1.
• **PROPAGATION** Sow seed in containers in a cold frame or seedbed as soon as ripe. Graft in mid-autumn or late winter.
• **PESTS AND DISEASES** Susceptible to oak wilt, honey fungus, powdery mildew, aphids, gall wasps, and various bracket fungi. Knopper gall can disfigure acorns.

Q. acutissima ⚲ Rounded, deciduous tree with fissured, corky, ashen-grey to black bark and long-lasting, sweet-chestnut-like, oblong-lance-shaped to obovate, glossy, mid-green leaves, to 20cm (8in) long, margined with bristle-tipped teeth. Solitary, ovoid acorns are borne in cups covered with slender, long, hairy scales. ‡↔ 15–20m (50–70ft). Himalayas, China, Korea, Japan. ✻✻✻
Q. aegilops see *Q. macrolepis*.
Q. agrifolia ▣ ⚲ (Californian live oak). Spreading, evergreen tree or shrub with ridged, grey to reddish brown bark and convex, ovate-elliptic to broadly elliptic, spiny-toothed, glossy, dark green leaves, to 7cm (3in) long. Bears solitary, slender, ovoid, pointed acorns, to 3.5cm (1½in) long. ‡↔ 10m (30ft). USA (California). ✻✻✻
Q. alba ⚲ (American white oak). Spreading, deciduous tree with peeling, pale grey to brown bark. The obovate, oblong, or elliptic, deeply lobed, bright green leaves, to 22cm (9in) long, often pink-tinged when young, turn purple-red in autumn. Solitary acorns are ovoid-oblong. Needs lime-free soil. ‡↔ 30m (100ft). E. North America. ✻✻✻
Q. aliena ⚲ Spreading, deciduous tree with fissured, grey-brown bark, obovate, prominently toothed and veined, glossy, bright green leaves, to 20cm (8in) long, blue-green beneath, and stalked, ovoid acorns. ‡ 25m (80ft), ↔ 12m (40ft). China, Korea, Japan. ✻✻✻
Q. bicolor ⚲ (Swamp white oak). Spreading, deciduous tree with peeling, fissured, grey-brown bark and oblong-obovate or obovate, shallowly lobed, glossy, dark green leaves, to 16cm (6in) long, white-hairy beneath when young, orange to bright red in autumn. Long-stalked acorns are oblong-ovoid. ‡ 20m (70ft), ↔ 15m (50ft). S.E. USA. ✻✻✻
Q. borealis see *Q. rubra*.
Q. canariensis ▣ ⬮ (Mirbeck's oak). Deciduous or semi-evergreen tree, narrow when young, broadening with age, with rugged, thick black bark. Obovate-oblong to obovate, shallowly lobed, rich green leaves, to 18cm (7in) long, turn yellow-brown in autumn. Ovoid acorns are borne in clusters. ‡ 30m (100ft), ↔ 15m (50ft). S.W. Europe, N. Africa. ✻✻✻
Q. castaneifolia ▣ ⚲ (Chestnut-leaved oak). Fast-growing, spreading, deciduous tree with rough, corky brown bark and sweet-chestnut-like, elliptic-oblong to oblong-lance-shaped, triangular-toothed, glossy, dark green leaves, to 16cm (6in) long, grey beneath. Ovoid acorns, in long-scaled cups, are solitary or in groups of up to 5. ‡ 25m (80ft), ↔ 20m (70ft). Caucasus, N. Iran. ✻✻✻. **'Green Spire'** ⬮ has upright branches; ↔ 10m (30ft).
Q. cerris ⚲ (Turkey oak). Fast-growing, spreading, deciduous, very variable tree with grey-white bark, splitting into thick plates, and oblong-elliptic to oblong-lance-shaped, deeply lobed or toothed, dark green leaves, to 12cm (5in) long, pale green beneath and yellow-brown in autumn. Ellipsoid acqrns, 2.5–4cm (1–1½in) long, in cups densely covered with long, slender scales, are solitary or in groups of 2–4. ‡ 30m (100ft), ↔ 25m (80ft). C. and S. Europe. ✻✻✻. **'Argenteovariegata'** ▣ syn. 'Variegata', has leaves margined with creamy yellow, later creamy white; ‡ 15m (50ft), ↔ 12m (40ft).
Q. chrysolepis ⚲ (Canyon oak). Spreading, evergreen tree or shrub with scaly, whitish grey or red-tinted bark and oblong-ovate to elliptic, spiny-toothed, leathery, glossy, dark green leaves, to 6cm (2½in) long, grey- or yellow-hairy beneath. Ovoid to oblong-ovoid acorns, 2.5–5cm (1–2in) long, are borne in felted cups. ‡ 20m (70ft), ↔ 10m (30ft). USA (California). ✻✻
Q. coccifera ⚲ (Kermes oak). Bushy, compact, evergreen shrub or tree with smooth grey bark, cracking with age, and holly-like, ovate to oblong-lance-shaped, spiny-margined, glossy, dark green leaves, 3–5cm (1¼–2in) long.

Quercus canariensis

Bears solitary, spherical or ovoid acorns in very spiny cups. ‡ to 10m (30ft), ↔ 4–6m (12–20ft). Mediterranean. ✻✻
Q. coccinea ▣ ⚲ (Scarlet oak). Rounded, deciduous tree with pale grey-brown bark in scaly plates. Glossy, dark green leaves, to 15cm (6in) long, are elliptic, with deep lobes ending in bristle-tipped teeth, and tufts of hairs in the vein axils beneath; the leaves turn bright red in autumn. Acorns are ovoid to nearly spherical. Requires lime-free soil. ‡ 20m (70ft), ↔ 15m (50ft). E. North America. ✻✻✻. **'Splendens'** is very dark red in autumn.
Q. conferta see *Q. frainetto*.
Q. dentata ▣ ⚲ (Daimio oak). Rugged, spreading, stoutly branched, deciduous tree with fissured brown bark, splitting into grey, scaly plates. Produces obovate, shallowly lobed to wavy-margined, dark green leaves, to 30cm (12in) or more long. Bears ovoid to nearly spherical, solitary acorns. Requires acid soil. ‡ 15m (50ft), ↔ 10m (30ft). E. Asia. ✻✻✻
Q. ellipsoidalis ▣ ⚲ (Northern pin oak). Spreading, deciduous tree with

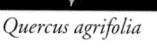

Quercus agrifolia

Quercus castaneifolia

Quercus cerris 'Argenteovariegata'

Quercus coccinea

Quercus dentata

Quercus ellipsoidalis

Q

QUERCUS

Quercus ilex

smooth grey bark. Glossy, dark green leaves, to 13cm (5in) long, are elliptic with wedge-shaped bases, and deeply cut into bristle-tipped lobes; they turn red-purple in autumn. Acorns are ellipsoid. Needs lime-free soil. ↕20m (70ft), ↔15m (50ft). Central N. USA. ❄❄❄
Q. falcata 🌳 Spreading, deciduous tree with fissured, grey-brown bark. Elliptic, dark green leaves, 9–22cm (3½–9in) long, white- or grey-hairy beneath, are deeply cut into bristle-tipped, usually curved lobes, the terminal lobe often long. Bears broadly ellipsoid to spherical acorns. Requires lime-free soil. ↕15m (50ft), ↔12m (40ft). S.E. USA. ❄❄❄
Q. frainetto 🌳 syn. *Q. conferta* (Hungarian oak). Fast-growing, spreading, deciduous tree with rugged, dark grey bark and obovate, dark green leaves, to 20cm (8in) long, cut into many rounded lobes and turning yellow-brown in autumn. Bears ellipsoid to ovoid-oblong acorns in clusters. ↕30m (100ft), ↔20m (70ft). S.E. Europe. ❄❄❄. **'Hungarian Crown'** 🌳 is compact and upright; ↕20m (70ft), ↔10m (30ft).
Q. garryana ▣🌳 (Oregon oak). Rounded, deciduous tree with shallowly cracked, pale grey bark and orange-red, hairy young shoots. Glossy, oblong-obovate, dark green leaves, to 15cm (6in) long, have up to 5 deep, entire lobes each side. The solitary, ovoid acorns are sweet and edible. ↕↔10m (30ft). W. North America. ❄❄❄
Q. x heterophylla ▣🌳 (*Q. phellos* x *Q. rubra*). Spreading, deciduous tree with smooth, pale grey bark. Oblong-lance-shaped to obovate, entire to shallowly bristle-toothed, glossy, mid-green leaves, are to 15cm (6in) long, turning orange to red in autumn. Bears ovoid acorns in very shallow cups. Requires lime-free soil. ↕20m (70ft), ↔15m (50ft). E. USA. ❄❄❄
Q. x hispanica 🌳 (*Q. cerris* x *Q. suber*), syn. *Q.* x *pseudosuber*. Upright, semi-evergreen tree with corky, grey-brown bark and very variable (often fiddle-shaped, lobed, or oblong-elliptic), glossy, dark green leaves, to 5cm (2in) long, white-hairy beneath. Oblong-ovoid acorns are to 4cm (1½in) long. ↕12m (40ft), ↔8m (25ft). Garden origin. ❄❄❄. **'Diversifolia'**, syn. *Q.* x *lucombeana* 'Diversifolia', has unusual leaves: in some, the central portions are reduced to narrow strips; others are fiddle- or spoon-shaped; ↔4–5m (12–15ft). **'Lucombeana'** ▣🌳 syn. *Q.* x *lucombeana*, *Q.* x *lucombeana* 'William Lucombe' (Lucombe oak) has ovate to oblong leaves, to 12cm (5in) long; ↕25m (80ft), ↔20m (70ft).
Q. ilex ▣🌳 (Holm oak). Rounded, evergreen tree with smooth, dark grey bark and very variable, usually oblong-ovate to lance-shaped, entire or toothed, glossy, dark green leaves, to 8cm (3in) long, grey-hairy beneath, and silvery grey when young. Bears oblong-ovoid to nearly rounded acorns, solitary or in groups of 2 or 3. ↕25m (80ft), ↔20m (70ft). S.W. Europe. ❄❄. **'Fordii'** has narrowly oblong, wavy-margined leaves.
Q. ilicifolia 🌳 Spreading, deciduous small tree or shrub with smooth grey bark and obovate to elliptic leaves, to 10cm (4in) long, each with usually 5 bristle-tipped, triangular lobes, dark green above and grey-hairy beneath; they turn red or yellow in autumn. Bears paired, ovoid to nearly spherical acorns. ↕6m (20ft), ↔5m (15ft). E. USA. ❄❄❄
Q. imbricaria 🌳 (Shingle oak). Spreading, deciduous tree with smooth, grey-brown bark and oblong to lance-shaped or obovate, entire, glossy, dark green leaves, to 18cm (7in) long, grey-hairy beneath, and turning yellow-brown in autumn. Bears solitary, nearly spherical acorns. ↕20m (70ft), ↔15m (50ft). C. and E. USA. ❄❄❄
Q. ithaburensis* subsp. *macrolepis see *Q. macrolepis*.
Q. kelloggii 🌳 (Californian black oak). Rounded, deciduous tree with cracked, dark brown bark and elliptic, deeply lobed, glossy, dark green leaves, 8–22cm (3–9in) long; they each have usually 7 bristle-tipped lobes, and turn yellow-brown in autumn. Produces ovoid-oblong acorns, to 3.5cm (1½in) long. ↕20m (70ft), ↔15m (50ft). USA (Oregon, California). ❄❄❄
Q. laurifolia ▣🌳 Rounded, deciduous tree with fissured, grey-black bark and narrowly oblong to obovate, entire to 3-lobed, smooth, glossy, dark green leaves, to 10cm (4in) long, bronze when young, lasting well into winter. Bears spherical-ovoid acorns. Requires lime-free soil. ↕↔20m (70ft). S.E. USA. ❄❄❄
***Q. x libanerris* 'Rotterdam'** 🌳 Fast-growing, spreading, deciduous tree with fissured grey bark and oblong, sharply toothed and lobed, glossy, dark green leaves, to 12cm (5in) long, grey-hairy beneath. Acorns are similar to those of *Q. cerris*. ↕probably 20m (70ft), ↔15m (50ft). Recent garden origin. ❄❄❄
Q. libani 🌳 (Lebanon oak). Rounded, deciduous or semi-evergreen tree with smooth, later fissured, grey bark and slender shoots. Chestnut-like, oblong-lance-shaped to oblong, glossy, dark green leaves, to 10cm (4in) long, with numerous bristly marginal teeth, last well into winter. Acorns are ovoid to cylindrical. ↕↔15m (50ft). Turkey, Syria, N. Iraq, N. Iran. ❄❄❄
Q. lobata 🌳 Slow-growing, spreading, deciduous tree with deeply furrowed, grey to brown bark. Obovate, dark green leaves, to 8cm (3in) long, are each deeply divided into 11 rounded lobes, and are finely hairy beneath. Bears ovoid, sweet, edible acorns, to 4cm (1½in) long. ↕16m (52ft), ↔15m (50ft). USA (California). ❄❄❄
Q. x lucombeana see *Q.* x *hispanica* 'Lucombeana'.
***Q. x lucombeana* 'Diversifolia'** see *Q.* x *hispanica* 'Diversifolia'.
***Q. x lucombeana* 'William Lucombe'** see *Q.* x *hispanica* 'Lucombeana'.
Q. macranthera ▣🌳 Fast-growing, spreading, deciduous tree with fissured, grey-brown bark and stout, hairy shoots. Obovate, mid- to dark green leaves, to 19cm (7in) long, have many rounded lobes, cut more deeply towards the bases. Bears solitary, ovoid-ellipsoid acorns. ↕20m (70ft), ↔15m (50ft). Caucasus, N. Iran. ❄❄❄
Q. macrocarpa ▣🌳 Slow-growing, spreading, deciduous tree with ridged, dark brown bark and corky, hairy shoots. Glossy, dark green leaves, to 25cm (10in) long, white-hairy beneath, are obovate to oblong-obovate, with deep and irregular lobes. Solitary, ovoid

Quercus myrsinifolia

Quercus phellos (inset: autumn leaf colour)

Q

acorns, to 5cm (2in) long, are borne in large, fringed cups. ↕ 15m (50ft), ↔ 10m (30ft). E. North America. ❄❄❄

Q. macrolepis ▣ ⚲ syn. *Q. aegilops*, *Q. ithaburensis* subsp. *macrolepis*. Spreading, deciduous or semi-evergreen, often broad-crowned tree with fissured, dark grey bark. Ovate to oblong, grey-green leaves, to 10cm (4in) long, with angular, bristle-tipped lobes, are densely white-hairy or yellowish white-hairy on both surfaces. Bears acorns, to 4.5cm (1¾in) long, singly or in clusters, in unusually large, scaly cups, to 6cm (2½in) across. ↕ 15m (50ft), ↔ 12m (40ft). S.E. Europe, Turkey. ❄❄

Q. marilandica ▣ ⚲ (Black Jack oak). Spreading, deciduous small tree with very rough, black-brown bark. Broadly obovate, glossy, dark green leaves, 6–17cm (2½–7in) long, each end in 3 bristle-tipped lobes, and turn yellow, red, or brown in autumn. Produces ovoid acorns. Requires lime-free soil. ↕ 12m (40ft), ↔ 15m (50ft). S.E. USA. ❄❄❄

Q. mongolica ⚲ Spreading, deciduous tree with rough grey bark and obovate, dark green leaves, to 20cm (8in) or more long, with rounded lobes. Produces ovoid to ellipsoid acorns. ↕ 20m (70ft), ↔ 15m (50ft). E. Asia. ❄❄❄. **subsp. *crispula* var. *grosseserrata*** has leaves with acutely triangular, tooth-like lobes.

Q. muehlenbergii ▣ ⚲ (Chinkapin oak). Rounded, deciduous tree with grey, scaly bark and elliptic to obovate, pointed, glossy, dark green or yellow-green leaves, to 15cm (6in) long, whitish green beneath, triangularly lobed and with curved teeth, turning yellow-brown in autumn. Bears ovoid acorns. ↕ 15m (50ft), ↔ 12m (40ft). E. USA. ❄❄❄

Quercus robur f. *fastigiata*

Q. myrsinifolia ▣ ⚲ Rounded, evergreen tree or shrub with smooth, dark grey bark and lance-shaped, tapered, weakly toothed, glossy, dark green leaves, to 12cm (5in) long, bronze-red when young. Solitary, ovoid-oblong acorns are borne in distinctively ringed cups. ↕ 12m (40ft), ↔ 10m (30ft). S. China, Laos, Japan. ❄❄

Q. nigra ▣ △ (Water oak). Broadly conical, deciduous tree with smooth, brown then dark grey bark. Variable, dark green leaves, 4–15cm (1½–6in) long, are narrowly obovate or spoon-shaped, rarely elliptic, usually 3-lobed, and retained late on the tree. Acorns are spherical. Needs lime-free soil. ↕ 15m (50ft), ↔ 12m (40ft). S.E. USA. ❄❄❄

Q. palustris ▣ △ (Pin oak). Fast-growing, broadly conical, deciduous tree with pendent lower branches and smooth grey bark. Elliptic, deeply lobed, glossy, mid-green leaves, to 15cm (6in) long, are broadly tapered at the bases; they have large tufts of hairs in the leaf vein axils beneath, and turn scarlet to red-brown in autumn. Acorns are nearly spherical. ↕ 20m (70ft), ↔ 12m (40ft). E. USA. ❄❄❄. **'Sovereign'** has spreading lower branches.

Q. pedunculata see *Q. robur*.

Q. petraea ⚲ syn. *Q. sessiliflora* (Sessile oak). Spreading, deciduous tree with ridged grey bark and yellow-stalked, ovate, obovate, or oblong, dark green leaves, 6–17cm (2½–7in) long, with rounded lobes. Bears stalkless, ovoid to oblong-ovoid acorns singly or in clusters. ↕ 30m (100ft), ↔ 25m (80ft). Europe. ❄❄❄. **'Columna'** ◊ syn. *Q.* x *rosacea* 'Columna', is upright and columnar, with oblong, lobed or entire, bluish green leaves; ↕ 20m (70ft), ↔ 6m (20ft).

Q. phellos ▣ ⚲ syn. *Q. pumila* (Willow oak). Spreading, deciduous tree with smooth grey bark and willow-like, entire or slightly wavy-margined, slender, linear to narrowly oblong, bright dark green leaves, to 12cm (5in) long; in autumn, they turn yellow, then brown. Acorns are spherical. ↕ 20m (70ft), ↔ 15m (50ft). E. USA. ❄❄❄

Q. phillyreoides ▣ ⚲ Spreading, evergreen tree with smooth, brownish grey to dark grey bark and oblong to ovate-oblong, toothed, dark green leaves, to 6cm (2½in) long, often bronze when young. Ovoid acorns are borne in cone-shaped cups. ↕↔ 10m (30ft). China, S. Japan. ❄❄❄

Q. pontica ▯ (Armenian oak). Shrubby or oval-headed, deciduous, small tree with shallowly fissured, pale grey-brown bark and stout reddish shoots. Obovate or elliptic to broadly elliptic, bright mid-green leaves, to 25cm (10in) long, with numerous parallel veins ending in small, pointed teeth, turn yellow-brown in autumn. Ovoid acorns are borne singly or in stout-stalked clusters, at the shoot tips. ↕ 6m (20ft), ↔ 5m (15ft). N.E. Turkey, Caucasus. ❄❄❄

Q.* x *pseudosuber see *Q.* x *hispanica*.

Q. pubescens ⚲ Spreading, deciduous tree with deeply furrowed, grey to black bark and densely hairy shoots. Oblong-ovate, grey-green leaves, to 10cm (4in) long, hairy beneath, have rounded lobes ending in small, pointed teeth. Ovoid acorns are borne singly or in groups of up to 4. ↕ 10–20m (30–70ft), ↔ 15m (50ft). C. and S. Europe, Turkey, Ukraine (Crimea). ❄❄❄

Quercus garryana

Quercus x *heterophylla*

Quercus x *hispanica* 'Lucombeana'

Quercus laurifolia

Quercus macranthera

Quercus macrocarpa

Quercus macrolepis

Quercus marilandica

Quercus muehlenbergii

Quercus nigra

Quercus palustris

Quercus phillyreoides

Quercus robur 'Concordia'

Quercus rubra

Quercus rubra 'Aurea'

Q. pumila see *Q. phellos*.

Q. pyrenaica ▯ Broadly columnar, deciduous tree with furrowed, brown to black bark and often pendent, downy shoots. Obovate, elliptic, or broadly oblong, deeply lobed and toothed, glossy, dark green leaves, to 16cm (6in) long, downy when young, emerge in late spring. The oblong-ovoid acorns are produced in clusters. ↕ 20m (70ft), ↔ 12m (40ft). France, Spain, Portugal, Morocco. ❄❄❄

Q. robur ⚲ syn. *Q. pedunculata* (Common oak, English oak, Pedunculate oak). Rugged, spreading, deciduous tree with fissured, grey-brown bark. Dark green, short-stalked leaves, to 14cm (5½in) long, are ovate-oblong, with rounded lobes, each base with two small, ear-like lobes. Ovoid acorns are borne singly or in clusters. ↕ 35m (120ft), ↔ 25m (80ft). Europe. ❄❄❄. **'Concordia'** ▣ has bright yellow young foliage, turning green; ↕↔ 10m (30ft). **f. *fastigiata*** ▣ ◊ has upright branches; ↕↔ 15m (50ft). **f. *pendula*** ⚲ has weeping shoots.

***Q.* x *rosacea* 'Columna'** see *Q. petraea* 'Columna'.

Q. rubra ▣ ⚲ syn. *Q. borealis* (Red oak). Fast-growing, spreading, deciduous tree with smooth, greyish brown or dark grey bark. Elliptic, matt, dark green leaves, to 20cm (8in) long, cut into bristle-tipped lobes, turn yellow- to red-brown in autumn. Acorns are hemispherical. Requires lime-free soil. ↕ 25m (80ft), ↔ 20m (70ft). E. North America. ❄❄❄. **'Aurea'** ▣ has golden yellow leaves in spring, turning green; ↕ 15m (50ft), ↔ 10m (30ft).

Q. sessiliflora see *Q. petraea*.

Q. shumardii ▯ Broadly columnar, deciduous tree with smooth grey bark.

Q

Quercus suber

Leaves are glossy, dark green, to 18cm (7in) long, elliptic to elliptic-obovate, truncate, each with up to 9 lobes ending in bristle-tipped teeth, and turn red to red-brown in autumn. Acorns are ovoid. Requires lime-free soil. ↕ 20m (70ft), ↔ 12m (40ft). S.E. USA. ❄❄❄

Q. suber ■ ⚲ (Cork oak). Rounded, evergreen tree with thick, corky bark (the cork of commerce). Ovate-oblong, toothed, rigid, dark green leaves, to 7cm (3in) long, are grey-hairy beneath. Bears ovoid-oblong acorns. ↕↔ 20m (70ft). W. Mediterranean, N. Africa. ❄❄

Q. x turneri ⚲ (*Q. ilex* x *Q. robur*). Dense, rounded, semi-evergreen tree with fissured, brownish grey to dark grey bark and obovate, shallowly lobed, dark green leaves, to 12cm (5in) long. Bears ovoid acorns in clusters. ↕↔ 20m (70ft). Garden origin. ❄❄❄

Q. velutina ⚲ (Black oak). Fast-growing, spreading, deciduous tree with ridged, dark brown, almost black bark. Elliptic, glossy, dark green leaves, to 25cm (10in) long, each with up to 7 pointed, deep lobes, turn red-brown in autumn. Acorns are almost spherical. Requires lime-free soil. ↕ 30m (100ft), ↔ 25m (80ft). E. North America. ❄❄❄

Q. wislizeni ■ ⚲ Spreading, evergreen tree or shrub with blackish or reddish brown bark and broadly lance-shaped to broadly elliptic, usually spiny-toothed, glossy, dark green leaves, 2.5–4cm (1–1½in) long. Bears solitary, oblong-ellipsoid acorns, to 4cm (1½in) long. ↕ to 20m (70ft), ↔ 12m (40ft). USA (California). ❄❄

QUESNELIA

BROMELIACEAE

Genus of approximately 15 species of almost stemless, evergreen, terrestrial or epiphytic perennials (bromeliads), some rhizomatous, found in scrub, woodland, or rainforest in E. Brazil, to 2,000m (6,500ft). They are cultivated for their rosetted, lance-shaped, spiny-margined, thick, stiff leaves and their upright or pendent, ellipsoid or cylindrical, dense or lax inflorescences of ovoid or tubular flowers, borne among showy bracts from late spring to summer. Below 13°C (55°F), grow as houseplants or in a warm greenhouse; elsewhere, grow in a humid, moist part of the garden.

- **HARDINESS** Frost tender.
- **CULTIVATION** Under glass, grow in epiphytic or terrestrial bromeliad compost in bright filtered light. Water moderately at all times and regularly mist lightly. Apply a nitrogen-based fertilizer monthly during the growing season. Outdoors, grow in open, coarse, humus-rich, moist but well-drained soil in partial shade. See also p.47.
- **PROPAGATION** Sow seed at 27°C (81°F) as soon as ripe. Remove offsets in late spring or summer.
- **PESTS AND DISEASES** Young growth is vulnerable to scale insects.

Q. liboniana ■ Epiphytic perennial with funnel-shaped rosettes of lance-shaped, stiff, minutely brown-scaly, dark green leaves, 75–80cm (30–32in) long, margined with straight or curved spines. From late spring to summer, bears simple or few-branched inflorescences,

Quercus wislizeni (inset: acorn detail)

Quesnelia liboniana

10cm (4in) long, comprising orange-red bracts and tubular, deep purple-blue flowers, 5cm (2in) long, with yellow sepals, flushed orange-red. ↕↔ 75cm (30in). E. Brazil. ❀ (min. 13°C/55°F)

Q. marmorata, syn. *Aechmea marmorata*. Epiphytic, rhizomatous perennial with tubular rosettes of thick, 2-ranked, lance-shaped, greyish green leaves, 40–60cm (16–24in) long, marbled and banded lilac and green, with pinkish grey marginal spines. From late spring to summer, bears pyramid-shaped, terminal inflorescences, 20cm (8in) long, consisting of tiny pink floral bracts and ovoid, blue or purple flowers, 3cm (1¼in) long, with blue-purple sepals. ↕ 60cm (24in), ↔ 30cm (12in) or more. E. Brazil. ❀ (min. 13°C/55°F)

Q. quesneliana. Rhizomatous, terrestrial perennial with broad rosettes of 6–10 lance-shaped, brown-spiny, bright green leaves, 70–90cm (28–36in) long, cross-banded with greyish lilac scales beneath. From late spring to summer, bears cylindrical or narrowly ellipsoid inflorescences, 15cm (6in) long; these consist of overlapping pink, later white scales and spirally arranged, wavy-margined, red to rose-pink bracts, which almost hide the oval, blue-margined white flowers, 3.5cm (1½in) long, with red sepals. ↕↔ to 75cm (30in) or more. E. Brazil. ❀ (min. 13°C/55°F)

▷**Quick** see *Crataegus monogyna*
▷**Quickthorn** see *Crataegus monogyna*
▷**Quince** see *Cydonia*
Common see *Cydonia oblonga*
Flowering see *Chaenomeles*
Japanese see *Chaenomeles, C. japonica*
Maule's see *Chaenomeles japonica*

QUISQUALIS

COMBRETACEAE

Genus of about 16 species of woody-stemmed, evergreen climbers or scandent shrubs from tropical forest in Africa, South Africa, Indonesia, and Malaysia. They are cultivated for their small, tubular, 5-lobed flowers, borne in terminal or axillary racemes or panicles. Leaves are simple and usually produced in opposite pairs. Where temperatures fall below 13°C (55°F), grow in a warm greenhouse. In tropical climates, use to clothe an arch or wall.

- **HARDINESS** Frost tender.
- **CULTIVATION** Under glass, grow in loam-based potting compost (JI No.3) in full light with shade from hot sun. In growth, water freely and apply a balanced liquid fertilizer every month. Water sparingly in winter. Outdoors, grow in moderately fertile, moist but well-drained soil in full sun with some midday shade. Pruning group 11, in late winter or early spring.
- **PROPAGATION** Sow seed at 18°C (64°F) in spring. Root softwood cuttings with bottom heat in late spring. Layer in spring.
- **PESTS AND DISEASES** Prone to red spider mites and mealybugs under glass.

Q. indica ■ (Rangoon creeper). Freely branching, perennial climber, erect and shrub-like when young. Mid- to deep green leaves, 8–18cm (3–7in) long, are elliptic to elliptic-oblong with rounded to heart-shaped bases, long, sharp tips, and prominent veins. In summer and autumn, bears slender-tubed, fragrant flowers, 4–7cm (1½–3in) long, with 5 spreading lobes, in pendent, terminal racemes, 10cm (4in) long; initially white, they change to pink and purplish red then bright red over a 3-day period. ↕ to 20m (70ft) or more. Tropical Africa and S.E. Asia. ❀ (min. 13°C/55°F)

Quisqualis indica

Q

R

- ▷ **Rabbit's foot** see *Maranta leuconeura* 'Kerchoveana'
- ▷ **Rabbit's tracks** see *Maranta leuconeura* 'Kerchoveana'
- ▷ **Radiator plant** see *Peperomia maculosa*
- ▷ **Raffia** see *Raphia*
- ▷ **Ragged robin** see *Lychnis flos-cuculi*
- ▷ **Ragwort,**
  - **Chinese** see *Sinacalia tangutica*
  - **Leopard's bane** see *Senecio doronicum*
- ▷ **Rainbow plant, Marbled** see *Billbergia* Fantasia Group
- ▷ **Rainbow star** see *Cryptanthus bromelioides*
- ▷ **Rain flower** see *Zephyranthes*
- ▷ **Raisin-tree** see *Hovenia dulcis*

RAMONDA

GESNERIACEAE

Genus of 3 species of rosette-forming, evergreen perennials from shady rock crevices and cliff faces in N.E. Spain, the Pyrenees, and Balkan mountains. They are grown for their hairy, crinkled leaves, of variable shape and colour, and their flat or shallowly cup-shaped, colourful flowers. The flowers are often slightly 2-lipped, with 4 or 5, rarely 6 petals, and are borne singly or in cyme-like panicles on slender, leafless stems, in late spring and early summer. Grow in a rock garden, a peat bed, in crevices in a stone wall, or in an alpine house.

• **HARDINESS** Fully hardy, but intolerant of excessive winter wet.

• **CULTIVATION** In an alpine house, grow in equal parts loam, leaf mould, and grit, in bright filtered light with shade from hot sun. Outdoors, grow in moist but well-drained, humus-rich, moderately fertile soil in partial shade. Plants are best grown on their sides to avoid accumulations of moisture in the rosettes, which may cause rotting in winter. Leaves wither in dry conditions, but recover if watered thoroughly.

Ramonda myconi

• **PROPAGATION** Sow seed very thinly in containers in a cold frame as soon as ripe. Seedlings develop slowly, so do not prick out until they have several leaves. Root rosettes in early summer, or root leaf cuttings in early autumn.

• **PESTS AND DISEASES** Very susceptible to slug and snail damage.

R. myconi ▣ syn. *R. pyrenaica*. Rosette-forming, evergreen perennial with elliptic to very broadly ovate, hairy, slightly crinkled, dark green leaves, to 8cm (3in) long. Cyme-like panicles of outward-facing, flat, 5-petalled flowers, 2.5cm (1in) across, usually deep violet-blue with yellow anthers, are borne in late spring and early summer; pink and white variants also occur. ↕ 10cm (4in), ↔ to 20cm (8in). Pyrenees, N.E. Spain. ❄❄❄

R. nathaliae. Rosette-forming, evergreen perennial with elliptic to broadly ovate, hairy, slightly crinkled, glossy, pale green leaves, to 5cm (2in) long, entire or with slightly scalloped margins. In late spring and early summer, bears cyme-like panicles of outward-facing, flattish, 4-petalled, deep mauve-blue flowers, to 3.5cm (1½in) across, with orange-yellow eyes and yellow anthers. ↕↔ 10cm (4in). Bosnia & Herzegovina, Macedonia, N. Greece. ❄❄❄

R. pyrenaica see *R. myconi*.

R. serbica. Rosette-forming, evergreen perennial with narrowly obovate, hairy, crinkled, irregularly scalloped, pale green leaves, to 5cm (2in) long. In late spring and early summer, outward-facing, saucer- to cup-shaped, lilac-blue flowers, 3.5cm (1½in) across, each with 5, sometimes 6 petals and violet-blue anthers, open singly or in pairs in cyme-like panicles. ↕ 10cm (4in), ↔ 15cm (6in). Croatia, Yugoslavia, Albania, W. Greece, N.W. Bulgaria. ❄❄❄

- ▷ **Rampion, Horned** see *Phyteuma*
- ▷ **Ram's horn** see *Proboscidea louisianica*
- ▷ **Rangoon creeper** see *Quisqualis indica*

RANUNCULUS

Buttercup, Crowfoot

RANUNCULACEAE

Genus of about 400 species of annuals, biennials, and mainly deciduous, sometimes evergreen perennials, widely distributed in temperate regions of the world. They are found in a range of habitats, varying from damp woodland to grassland, and from mountain screes and summer-dry sites to bogs or shallow water. They may be rhizomatous, tuberous, fibrous-rooted, or spread by runners. The leaves form basal rosettes or are sometimes stem-clasping; they are very variable in shape, and may be simple and entire, toothed to palmately lobed, or pinnatisect. Buttercups are grown for their bowl-shaped, or cup- to saucer-shaped, usually 5-petalled, mainly yellow, but also white, pink, orange, or red flowers, which are borne singly or in cyme-like panicles in spring, summer, or occasionally autumn. They are suitable for a wide range of sites. Contact with the sap may irritate skin.

• **HARDINESS** Most are fully hardy. *R. asiaticus* is half hardy.

• **CULTIVATION** Buttercups have a range of cultivation requirements; for ease of reference, they have been divided into groups as follows:

Ranunculus aconitifolius

1. Woodland buttercups, best in partial or full shade in moist, humus-rich soil.
2. Buttercups easily grown in sun or partial shade, in fertile, moist but well-drained soil; grow in a border or rock garden.
3. High alpine buttercups, best grown in gritty, humus-rich, sharply drained soil in a scree bed in full sun, or in an alpine house in a mix of equal parts loam, leaf mould, and grit in full light.
4. Aquatic or bog plants, best grown in mud at a pond margin or streamside. Grow *R. aquatilis* in 15–60cm (6–24in) of still or fast-moving water; grow *R. lingua* and *R. flammula* in 15–22cm (6–9in) of still or slow-moving water.
5. Tuberous buttercups (except *R. ficaria*) that require a dry, dormant period in summer; best in a bulb frame or alpine house in a mix of equal parts loam, leaf mould, and grit in full light.

• **PROPAGATION** Sow seed of most alpine species in pans in an open frame when seed is still slightly green; germination is erratic, and pans should be retained for several years if seeds fail to germinate in the first year. Sow seed of perennials, aquatic perennials, and mat-forming alpines in containers in a cold frame as soon as ripe, or divide in spring or autumn. Divide tuberous species, or detach basal bulbils (where these form), in spring or autumn.

• **PESTS AND DISEASES** Vulnerable to slug and snail damage, aphids, and powdery mildew.

R. aconitifolius ▣ (Bachelor's buttons). Clump-forming, hairy, fibrous-rooted perennial producing palmately 3- to 5-lobed, toothed, glossy, dark green, basal leaves, to 20cm (8in) long. In late spring and early summer, freely branched stems bear numerous red-tinged buds that open to panicles of saucer-shaped white flowers, 1–2cm (½–¾in) across, with red- or purple-backed sepals. Cultivation group 1 or 2. ↕ 60cm (24in), ↔ 45cm (18in). C. Europe. ❄❄❄. **'Flore Pleno'** ▣ (Fair maids of France, Fair maids of Kent, White bachelor's buttons) has long-lasting, double white flowers with numerous small petals.

R. acris (Meadow buttercup). Erect, hairy, fibrous-rooted perennial, sometimes with short rhizomes. The long-stalked, broadly ovate, palmately 3- to 7-lobed, mid-green, basal leaves, 8cm (3in) long, have toothed lobes, which are sometimes further subdivided. Many-branched stems bear panicles of numerous saucer-shaped, glossy, golden yellow flowers, to 2.5cm (1in) across, in early and midsummer. Cultivation group 1 or 2. ↕ 20–90cm (8–36in), ↔ 22cm (9in). Europe and W. Asia. ❄❄❄. **'Farrer's Yellow'** has pale yellow flowers. **'Flore Pleno'** ▣ bears double, rosetted, many-petalled yellow flowers.

Ranunculus acris 'Flore Pleno'

Ranunculus aconitifolius 'Flore Pleno'

Ranunculus alpestris

Ranunculus asiaticus

Ranunculus constantinopolitanus 'Plenus'

R. alpestris ■ Short-lived, tufted, occasionally evergreen perennial with fibrous roots. The kidney-shaped, palmately 3- to 5-lobed, basal leaves, are 3–5cm (1¼–2in) long, round-toothed, glossy, and dark green. From late spring to midsummer, bears cup-shaped white flowers, to 2cm (¾in) across, singly or occasionally in clusters of 2 or 3. Cultivation group 3. ↕↔ to 10cm (4in). Mountains of C. and S. Europe. ❄❄❄
R. amplexicaulis. Clump-forming perennial with fibrous roots and ovate-lance-shaped, entire, sometimes sparsely hairy, grey-green basal leaves, to 7cm (3in) long, and smaller leaves clasping the upright, branching stems. In early summer, bears cyme-like panicles of up to 5 cup-shaped white flowers, each 2–2.5cm (¾–1in) across. Cultivation group 2. ↕ to 30cm (12in), ↔ 20cm (8in). Pyrenees, N. and C. Spain. ❄❄❄
R. aquatilis ■ (Water crowfoot). Aquatic annual or usually evergreen perennial with submerged, branched, slender stems and dark green leaves, 3–8cm (1¼–3in) long. The kidney-shaped to rounded, floating leaves are deeply divided into 3–7 lobes; the submerged leaves have many thread-like segments. Solitary, bowl- or saucer-shaped, white-based yellow flowers, 2cm (¾in) across, are borne on the water's surface in midsummer. Cultivation group 4. ↔ indefinite. Europe. ❄❄❄
R. asiaticus ■ (Persian buttercup). Tuberous, fibrous-rooted perennial with long-stalked, broadly ovate to rounded, deeply 3-lobed, hairy, pale to dark green, basal leaves, to 14cm (5½in) long, the lobes further subdivided and toothed. Branching flowering stems bear 1–4 cup-shaped, red, pink, yellow, or white flowers, 3–5cm (1¼–2in) across, with purple-black centres, in late spring and early summer. Cultivation group 5. ↕ 20–45cm (8–18in), ↔ 20cm (8in). E. Mediterranean, N.E. Africa, S.W. Asia. ❄. **Turban Group** cultivars have double flowers.
R. bulbosus (Bulbous buttercup). Erect, hairy, sometimes semi-evergreen perennial with fibrous roots and a swollen, corm-like stem base. Ovate, 3-lobed, dark green basal and lower stem leaves, to 12cm (5in) long, each have a long-stalked middle segment. In late spring and early summer, bears branched, cyme-like panicles of several saucer-shaped, rich golden yellow flowers, 2–3cm (¾–1¼in) across, with reflexed, paler yellow sepals. Cultivation group 2. ↕ 15–40cm (6–16in), sometimes to 80cm (32in), ↔ 30cm (12in). Europe, N. Africa, Caucasus. ❄❄❄. **var. *farreri*** see 'F.M. Burton'. **'F.M. Burton'**, syn. var. *farreri*, bears glossy, pale creamy yellow flowers. **'Speciosus Plenus' of gardens** see *R. constantinopolitanus* 'Plenus'.
R. bullatus. Tuberous perennial with broadly obovate, puckered, glossy, dark green, basal leaves, to 10cm (4in) long, hairy beneath, and often with 3 shallow lobes or teeth at the tips. In autumn, short, unbranched stems each bear 1 or 2 bowl-shaped, violet-scented, shining yellow flowers, 2.5cm (1in) across. Unusual in being autumn-flowering and scented. Cultivation group 5. ↕↔ to 10cm (4in). W. to E. Mediterranean, (including Spain and Portugal). ❄❄

R. calandrinioides ■ Clump-forming perennial with thick, fleshy roots and broadly lance-shaped to ovate-lance-shaped, hairless, blue-green leaves, to 7cm (3in) long, dying down in summer. In late winter and early spring, unbranched stems bear short, cyme-like panicles of up to 3 cup-shaped, usually pink-flushed white flowers, to 5cm (2in) across. Cultivation group 3 or 5. ↕ 20cm (8in), ↔ 15cm (6in). Atlas Mountains. ❄❄❄
R. constantinopolitanus. Clump-forming perennial with short rhizomes and deeply 3-lobed, mid-green basal and lower stem leaves, 3–10cm (1¼–4in) long. From mid-spring to midsummer, branched stems bear cyme-like panicles of 3–8 bowl-shaped, glossy, bright yellow flowers, to 3cm (1¼in) across, with reflexed, pale yellow sepals. Cultivation group 1 or 2. ↕ 30–70cm (12–28in), ↔ 30cm (12in). E. Europe, Balkans, Cyprus, Syria, Iraq, Iran, Caucasus, Ukraine (Crimea). ❄❄❄. **'Plenus'** ■ syn. *R. bulbosus* 'Speciosus Plenus' of gardens, *R. gouanii* 'Plenus', *R. speciosus* 'Flore Pleno', produces double yellow flowers; ↕ 30cm (12in), ↔ 15cm (6in).

R. crenatus. Rosette-forming, semi-evergreen perennial with fibrous roots and rounded, glossy, mid-green leaves, 5–15mm (¼–½in) long, toothed or shallowly 3-lobed at the tips. In summer, flowering stems bear solitary, or occasionally pairs of shallowly cup-shaped white flowers, 2.5cm (1in) across. Cultivation group 3. ↕↔ to 8cm (3in). E. Alps, C. Apennines, mountains of Balkan peninsula, S. and E. Carpathians. ❄❄❄
R. ficaria (Lesser celandine, Pilewort). Very variable, tuberous perennial with long-stalked, broadly heart-shaped, glossy, usually dark green, basal leaves, 2–5cm (¾–2in) long, often with silver or bronze markings and scalloped or toothed margins. In early spring, bears usually solitary, shallowly cup-shaped, brilliant, shining, golden yellow flowers, 2–3cm (¾–1¼in) across, fading to white with age. The leaves die down after flowering. Some variants produce axillary bulbils and are extremely invasive. Cultivation group 1. ↕ 5cm (2in), ↔ to 30cm (12in) or more. Europe, N.W. Africa, S.W. Asia. ❄❄❄. **f. *albus*** ■ has very pale yellow flowers, fading to white, and leaves marked dark bronze. **f. *aurantiacus*** ■ syn. 'Cupreus', has silvery leaves, each with a bronze central mark, and deep coppery orange flowers, darker on the reverse. **'Brazen Hussy'** produces glossy, deep chocolate-brown leaves, and shining, golden yellow flowers with a bronze reverse. Seedlings often have bronze leaves. **'Collarette'** produces leaves with bronze central bands, and double yellow flowers with anemone-form centres. **'Cupreus'** see f. *aurantiacus*. **'Double Bronze'** bears double yellow flowers with a bronze reverse to the petals. **'Double Cream'** see 'Double Mud'. **'Double Mud'**, syn. 'Double Cream', has double cream flowers, with a grey-tinted reverse to the petals. **'Salmon's White'** bears pale green leaves with bronze marks, and cream flowers, tinted blue-purple on the reverse of the petals.

Ranunculus aquatilis

Ranunculus calandrinioides

Ranunculus ficaria f. *albus*

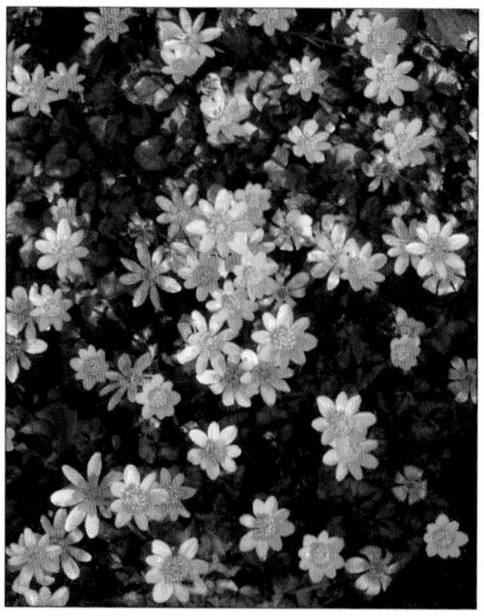

Ranunculus ficaria f. *aurantiacus*

R. flammula (Lesser spearwort). Marginal aquatic perennial with semi-erect, red-tinted green stems bearing broadly ovate to linear-lance-shaped, dark green leaves, 1–2.5cm (½–1in) long. Shallowly cup-shaped, bright yellow flowers, 2cm (¾in) across, are borne in few-flowered, cyme-like panicles, or sometimes singly, in early summer. Cultivation group 4. ↕70cm (28in), ↔ 75cm (30in). Europe, Asia. ❄❄❄

R. glacialis. Hummock-forming perennial with fibrous roots and very broadly ovate, deeply 3-lobed, slightly fleshy, hairless, dark green leaves, 3–8cm (1¼–3in) long. In late spring and early summer, flowering stems bear solitary, occasionally 2 or 3, shallowly cup-shaped, white or pink flowers, 2–3cm (¾–1¼in) across, flushed deep pink after fertilization. Protect from excessive winter wet. Cultivation group 3. ↕5–25cm (2–10in), ↔ 5cm (2in). Spain (Sierra Nevada), Pyrenees, Alps, Greenland. ❄❄❄

***R. gouanii* 'Plenus'** see *R. constantinopolitanus* 'Plenus'.

R. gramineus ◼ Clump-forming perennial, very variable in size and habit, with basal clusters of grass-like, linear to lance-shaped, very finely hairy, glaucous leaves, to 20cm (8in) long. In late spring and early summer, branched flowering stems bear 1–3 cup-shaped, lemon-yellow flowers, to 2cm (¾in) across. Cultivation group 2. ↕to 30cm (12in), ↔ to 15cm (6in). S.W. Europe. ❄❄❄

R. insignis. Semi-evergreen, clump-forming perennial, similar to *R. lyallii*, with ovate-lance-shaped, leathery, dark green, basal leaves, to 15cm (6in) long, brown-hairy beneath. In summer, bears panicles of 5–20 shallowly cup-shaped, deep yellow flowers, 2–5cm (¾–2in) across. Cultivation group 1 or 2. ↕to 60cm (24in), ↔ to 30cm (12in). New Zealand. ❄❄❄

R. lingua ◼ (Greater spearwort). Marginal aquatic perennial with erect, hollow stems. Non-flowering stems bear long-stalked, ovate to ovate-oblong, blue-green leaves, to 20cm (8in) long, with heart-shaped bases. In early summer, branched flowering stems, with short-stalked, linear to lance-shaped leaves, bear cup-shaped, golden yellow flowers, 5cm (2in) across, singly or in few-flowered, cyme-like panicles. Cultivation group 4. ↕1.5m (5ft), ↔ 2m (6ft). Europe to Siberia. ❄❄❄

R. lyallii (Giant buttercup, Mount Cook lily). Semi-evergreen, clump-forming, rhizomatous perennial with peltate, rounded, scalloped, leathery, dark green, basal leaves, to 30cm (12in) long, becoming progressively smaller up the branching stems. Cyme-like panicles of 5–15 cup-shaped white flowers, 5cm (2in) across, are borne in summer. Requires cool conditions. Cultivation group 1 or 2. ↕to 1m (3ft), ↔ to 35cm (14in). Rocky areas in New Zealand. ❄❄❄ (borderline)

Ranunculus lingua

Ranunculus gramineus

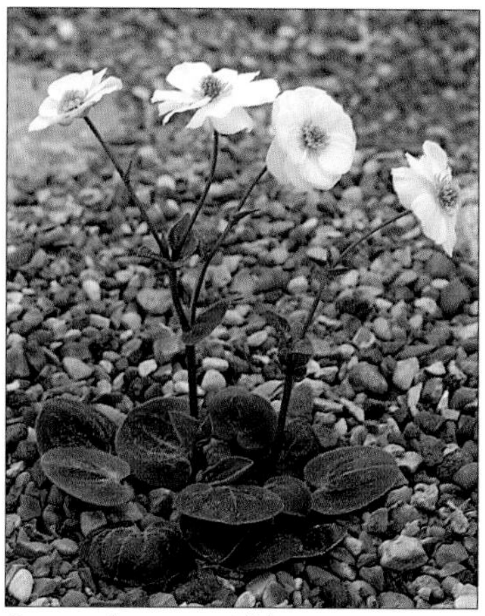

Ranunculus parnassiifolius

***R. montanus* 'Molten Gold'.** Vigorous, mat-forming, rhizomatous perennial producing rounded-obovate, 3- to 5-lobed, glossy, deep green basal leaves, to 4cm (1½in) long, and narrower stem leaves. In early summer, short flowering stems each bear 1–3 shallowly cup-shaped, shining, bright gold-yellow flowers, 2–3cm (¾–1¼in) across. Cultivation group 2. ↕10cm (4in), ↔ 30cm (12in). ❄❄❄

R. parnassiifolius ◼ Rosette-forming perennial with fibrous roots and broadly lance-shaped to ovate-heart-shaped, hairy, dark green, basal leaves, to 5cm (2in) long. In early summer, stems bear solitary, occasionally 2 or 3, cup-shaped flowers, 2.5cm (1in) across, opening white but often turning pink with age, usually finely pink- or red-veined. Cultivation group 3. ↕15cm (6in), ↔ 10cm (4in). High screes in the Alps, Pyrenees, N. Spain. ❄❄❄

***R. repens* 'Pleniflorus'** see *R. repens* var. *pleniflorus.*

***R. repens* var. *pleniflorus*,** syn. *R. repens* 'Pleniflorus' (Double creeping buttercup). Erect, fast-spreading, hairy, stoloniferous perennial. Long-stalked, triangular-ovate, mid-green basal and lower stem leaves, 9cm (3½in) long, each have 3 lobes, further cut into 3 toothed segments, the middle lobe long-stalked. Branched stems bear cyme-like panicles of double, glossy, bright yellow flowers, 1.5–2cm (½–¾in) across, with tightly packed petals and pale yellow sepals, from late spring to midsummer. Cultivation group 1 or 2. ↕30–60cm (12–24in), ↔ 2m (6ft). ❄❄❄

***R. speciosus* 'Flore Pleno'** see *R. constantinopolitanus* 'Plenus'.

RANZANIA

BERBERIDACEAE

Genus of one species of herbaceous perennial found in deciduous mountain woodland in S. Japan. It has short rhizomes, and is grown for its attractive foliage and flowers. Smooth stems, with opposite, 3-palmate leaves at their tips, bear pendent, bell-shaped flowers, either singly or in few-flowered cymes, before the leaves have fully developed; the long flower-stalks become upright as berries form. Grow in a woodland garden or shady border.

- **HARDINESS** Hardy to -10°C (14°F), but late frosts may damage new growth.
- **CULTIVATION** Grow in moist, leafy, humus-rich soil in partial or deep shade.
- **PROPAGATION** Sow seed in containers in a cold frame in autumn; seedlings will flower in about 4 years. Divide in early spring.
- **PESTS AND DISEASES** Susceptible to slug damage in spring.

***R. japonica*,** syn. *Podophyllum japonicum.* Rhizomatous perennial with smooth stems, each bearing 2 or 3 opposite, broadly triangular leaves, to 8cm (3in) long, composed of 3 broadly ovate to heart-shaped leaflets, mid-green above, bluish green beneath. In mid- and late spring, long flower-stalks bear pendent, bowl-shaped, pale mauve-blue flowers, 2.5–3cm (1–1¼in) across, each with 6 large, pointed tepals and 6 small petals that recurve with age. The flowers are followed by elliptic white berries, to 1.5cm (½in) long. ↕to 30cm (12in), ↔ 20cm (8in). S. Japan (N. Hondo). ❄❄

RAOULIA

ASTERACEAE/COMPOSITAE

Genus of about 20 species of evergreen perennials or subshrubs from screes and open rocky places at high and low altitudes in New Zealand. They form mats or cushions of dense, overlapping, linear to diamond- or spoon-shaped, silvery leaves. The usually small, disc-shaped flowerheads are borne singly or in few-flowered, terminal clusters. They thrive in regions with cool summers and mild winters, and are excellent foliage plants for a rock garden, raised bed or scree bed, or for an alpine house.

- **HARDINESS** Hardy to about -10°C (14°F) in well-drained soil.
- **CULTIVATION** Under glass, grow in a mix of equal parts loam, leaf mould, and sharp sand, with a top dressing of grit, in bright filtered light. When in growth, water freely (avoiding the foliage); keep just moist in winter. Outdoors, grow in gritty, humus-rich, moist but sharply drained soil in full sun, or in partial shade in warm, dry areas. Protect from excessive winter wet.
- **PROPAGATION** Divide or separate rooted stems of mat-forming species in spring. Root new rosettes of cushion-forming species as cuttings in early summer in partial shade; water carefully and moderately until rooted.
- **PESTS AND DISEASES** Prone to red spider mites and aphids under glass.

R. australis ◼ syn. *R. lutescens.* Prostrate, mat-forming, grey-silver perennial with branching, rooting stems, densely clothed in overlapping, spoon-shaped, silver-hairy leaves, 2mm (1/16in) long. In summer, bears sulphur-yellow flowerheads, 5mm (¼in) across. Plants sold under this name are often variants of *R. hookeri.* ↕1cm (½in), ↔ 30cm (12in) or more. New Zealand. ❄❄

R. eximia (Vegetable sheep). Extremely dense, cushion-forming perennial with tightly packed rosettes of overlapping, oblong to ovate, grey-hairy leaves, to 2mm (1/16in) long. Yellowish white flowerheads, to 3mm (⅛in) across, are borne in late spring or summer. Resents winter wet; best grown in an alpine

Raoulia australis

R

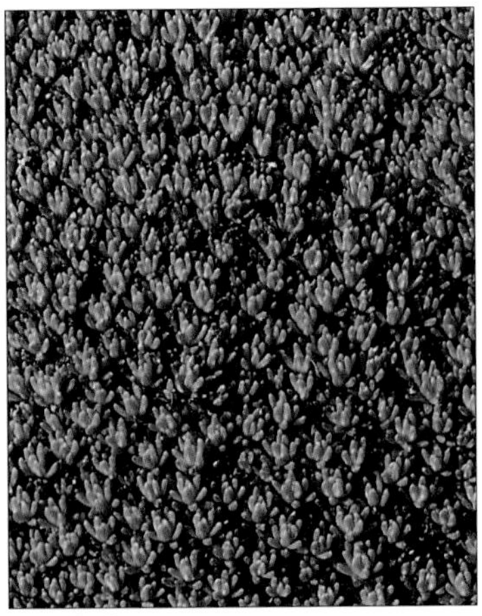
Raoulia haastii

Raoulia hookeri var. *albosericea*

house. ↕ 5cm (2in), ↔ to 10cm (4in). New Zealand. ❄❄
R. haastii ▣ Dense, cushion-forming perennial with loosely overlapping, ovate to linear-oblong, silky-hairy leaves, to 5mm (¼in) long; pale green at first, they darken in summer, becoming brown-tinted in winter. In spring, bears yellow flowerheads, to 5mm (¼in) across. ↕ 1cm (½in), ↔ 30cm (12in) or more. New Zealand. ❄❄
R. hookeri* var. *albosericea ▣ Mat-forming perennial producing branching, rooting stems clothed in closely overlapping, narrowly obovate-spoon-shaped leaves, 2mm (1⁄16in) long, covered with white-silky hairs. Silky-hairy, pale green or straw-coloured flowerheads, to 7mm (¼in) across, are borne briefly in summer. Similar to, but less tolerant of winter wet than *R. australis.* ↕ 1cm (½in), ↔ to 20cm (8in). New Zealand (North Island). ❄❄
R. leontopodium see *Leucogenes leontopodium.*
R. x loganii see x *Leucoraoulia loganii.*
R. lutescens see *R. australis.*

RAPHIA
Raffia
ARECACEAE/PALMAE

Genus of about 30 species of massive, single- or cluster-stemmed, spreading, monocarpic palms, mainly found in moist, wet, or swampy sites and by streams in Central and South America, Africa, and Madagascar. Some species have short, underground stems (caudices) and appear to be stemless. The pinnate, light to mid-green leaves, with folded linear leaflets, are produced in terminal heads or tufts. Panicles of bowl-shaped, 3-petalled flowers are borne either between the leaves or just beneath the lowest leaf. In frost-prone areas, grow young specimens as house-plants, or in a warm greenhouse or conservatory. In tropical areas, use the stemless species in a border, and those with stems as specimens on a lawn.
• **HARDINESS** Frost tender.
• **CULTIVATION** Under glass, grow in loamless potting compost in bright filtered light. In the growing season, water freely and apply a balanced liquid fertilizer monthly; water moderately in winter. Pot on or top-dress in spring. Outdoors, grow in moist, moderately fertile, humus-rich soil in partial shade.
• **PROPAGATION** Sow seed at 27°C (81°F) in spring.
• **PESTS AND DISEASES** Red spider mites may be a problem under glass.

R. farinifera Large, spreading palm with a sturdy trunk covered in old leaf bases. Erect to arching leaves, to 20m (70ft) long, each have numerous linear leaflets to 2m (6ft) long; they are waxy, light to mid-green above, and waxy, powdery white beneath. Green flowers, 8–15mm (⅜–½in) across, are borne in panicles to 3m (10ft) long, in summer, followed by ovoid to ellipsoid, scaly orange fruit, 7–10cm (3–4in) long. ↕ to 25m (80ft), ↔ to 20m (70ft) or more. Tropical Africa, Madagascar. ❀ (min. 16°C/61°F)

▷ ***Raphidophora*** see *Rhaphidophora*
▷ **Raripila, Red** see *Mentha* x *smithiana*
▷ **Raspberry, Flowering** see *Rubus odoratus*
▷ **Rasp fern, Common** see *Doodia media*
▷ **Rata** see *Metrosideros, M. robustus*
Northern see *M. robustus*

RATIBIDA
Mexican hat, Prairie coneflower
ASTERACEAE/COMPOSITAE

Genus of 5 or 6 species of biennials and perennials, mainly found on prairies in North America and Mexico. Woody-based crowns produce erect stems, branching above the middle, that bear alternate, pinnate to pinnatifid leaves and solitary, terminal flowerheads. They are cultivated for their daisy-like flowerheads, which have a few long, yellow or yellow-brown ray-florets and prominent, spherical or cone-shaped centres of brown disc-florets. Grow in a sunny border, gravel garden, or wild-flower meadow. The flowerheads are good for cutting.
• **HARDINESS** Fully hardy.
• **CULTIVATION** Grow in dry, well-drained, neutral to slightly alkaline, moderately fertile soil in full sun. Ratibidas are drought-resistant.
• **PROPAGATION** Sow seed in containers in a cold frame in early spring. Divide perennials in spring when young (the roots become woody with age).
• **PESTS AND DISEASES** Trouble free.

R. columnifera ▣ syn. *Lepachys columnifera, Rudbeckia columnifera.* Erect perennial, sometimes grown as a biennial or annual, with pinnate, hairy, greyish green leaves, 3–15cm (1¼–6in) long; the leaflets are usually linear, entire, and often pinnatifid. From early summer to early autumn, long, thin, branching stems bear daisy-like flower-heads, to 8cm (3in) across, with reflexed yellow ray-florets and large, columnar centres of green, then brown disc-florets. ↕ to 80cm (32in), ↔ 30cm (12in). S.W. Canada, W. and C. USA to New Mexico. ❄❄❄ **f. *pulcherrima*** bears flowerheads with purple-brown or reddish brown ray-florets; ↕ 30cm (12in), ↔ 20cm (8in).

Ratibida columnifera

R. pinnata, syn. *Lepachys pinnata* (Drooping coneflower, Grey-head coneflower). Upright, stout-stemmed, branching perennial, sometimes grown as a biennial or annual. Pinnate, toothed, bluish green leaves, 2–12cm (¾–5in) long, with lance-shaped, sparsely hairy leaflets, are borne mainly on the lower, unbranched portion of the stems. From summer to autumn, bears long-stemmed, daisy-like flowerheads, to 12cm (5in) across, with bright yellow ray-florets and red-brown disc-florets forming prominent, oval, cone-shaped centres. ↕ to 1.2m (4ft), ↔ to 45cm (18in). C. North America. ❄❄❄

▷ **Rattan cane** see *Calamus rotang*
▷ **Rattan vine** see *Berchemia scandens*
▷ **Rattlebox** see *Crotalaria*
▷ **Rattlesnake plant** see *Calathea lancifolia*
▷ **Rauli** see *Nothofagus procera*

RAVENALA
Traveller's tree
STRELITZIACEAE

Genus of one species of small, evergreen tree, occurring in open rainforest or deforested areas in Madagascar, grown for its foliage, spathes, and palm-like habit. The large, alternate, long-stalked, banana-like leaves have expanded leaf bases that accumulate water. Boat-shaped spathes, enclosing cymes of tiny, 3-petalled flowers, are borne from the leaf axils. Where temperatures fall below 16–18°C (61–64°F), grow in a warm greenhouse. In tropical regions, use as a specimen tree.
• **HARDINESS** Frost tender.
• **CULTIVATION** Under glass, grow in loam-based potting compost (JI No.3) in full light, with high humidity. Water freely in spring and summer, applying a balanced liquid fertilizer monthly; water more sparingly in winter. Outdoors, grow in fertile, moist, but well-drained soil in full sun. Provide shelter from strong winds.
• **PROPAGATION** Sow seed at 20–21°C (68–70°F), or remove rooted suckers, in spring.
• **PESTS AND DISEASES** Red spider mites may be a problem under glass.

R. madagascariensis Large, erect tree with an unbranched, palm-like trunk topped by a fan-shaped crown of 2-ranked, paddle-shaped, leathery, lustrous, rich green leaves. The oblong leaf-blades, 2–4m (6–12ft) long, are borne on thick, grooved stalks, of about the same length, closely overlapping at the bases. On mature plants, tiny, narrow white flowers, each with 6 tepals, emerge from pointed, boat-shaped, greenish white spathes, a few at a time, in summer; they are followed by fruit capsules that contain seeds with bright blue arils. ↕ 10–16m (30–52ft), ↔ 3–6m (10–20ft). Madagascar. ❀ (min. 16–18°C/61–64°F)

REBUTIA
syn. SULCOREBUTIA, WEINGARTIA
CACTACEAE

Genus of about 40 species of mostly dwarf, clump-forming, simple or clustering, perennial cacti found in mountainous terrain, to 4,000m (13,000ft) high, in Bolivia and N. and N.W. Argentina. They are cultivated for their habit and colourful flowers. The spherical to short-cylindrical, ribbed stems are divided into low tubercles in some species. The areoles have mainly short, bristly spines and, in summer, those near the stem bases bear many trumpet-shaped, diurnal flowers. In frost-prone regions, grow in a temperate greenhouse or as houseplants. In warm, dry areas, use in a desert garden or a raised bed.
• **HARDINESS** Frost tender.
• **CULTIVATION** Under glass, grow in standard cactus compost in full light, with low humidity. From spring to summer, water moderately and apply a balanced liquid fertilizer 3 or 4 times; keep completely dry at other times. Outdoors, grow in moderately fertile, gritty, sharply drained soil in full sun. See also pp.48–49.
• **PROPAGATION** Sow seed at 21°C (70°F) in early spring, or remove offsets in spring or summer.
• **PESTS AND DISEASES** Prone to mealy-bugs early in the growing season.

Rebutia aureiflora

Rebutia fiebrigii

Rebutia violaciflora

Rebutia tiraquensis

R. aureiflora ▣ Freely clustering cactus with depressed-spherical to spherical, mid-green to greenish violet, often red-tinged stems, to 3.5cm (1½in) thick. Stems are covered with spirally arranged tubercles set with white areoles and greyish white spines (10–16 radials and 1–4 longer centrals). Bears white-throated, yellow or yellowish orange, sometimes orange, red, or purple flowers, 4cm (1½in) across, in summer. ↕ 10cm (4in), ↔ to 20cm (8in). N.W. Argentina. ❀ (min. 5°C/41°F)
R. fiebrigii ▣ syn. *R. muscula.* Variable, clustering cactus with spherical to ovoid or depressed-spherical, dark green stems, 6cm (2½in) thick, with up to 18 ribs. White areoles bear 30–40 white radial spines and 2–5 longer, brownish white centrals. Bright yellowish brown or bright orange to red flowers, 2–3.5cm (¾–1½in) across, are borne in summer. ↕ 10cm (4in), ↔ to 15cm (6in). Bolivia, N.W. Argentina. ❀ (min. 5°C/41°F)
R. heliosa. Simple, later clustering cactus with depressed-spherical to cone-shaped, greyish green stems, to 2.5cm (1in) thick, with 15–40 low-tubercled, spirally arranged ribs. Brown-felted areoles have 24–26 tiny, comb-like, undifferentiated white spines. In summer, bears orange or deep rose-red flowers, 4cm (1½in) across; inner petals often have a central lilac stripe. ↕ 10cm (4in), ↔ 15cm (6in). Bolivia. ❀ (min. 5°C/41°F)
R. krainziana see *R. marsoneri.*
R. marsoneri ▣ syn. *R. krainziana.* Clustering cactus with warty, depressed-spherical, bright to dull green stems, 4cm (1½in) thick, with 20 or more spirally arranged ribs and close-set white areoles with 8–12 tiny, undifferentiated white spines. Bears bright red flowers, to 5cm (2in) across, sometimes with a violet sheen and violet throats, in summer. ↕ 5cm (2in), ↔ 20cm (8in). Probably of garden origin. ❀ (min. 5°C/41°F)
R. minuscula* subsp. *violaciflora see *R. violaciflora.*
R. muscula see *R. fiebrigii.*
R. neocumingii ▣ syn. *Weingartia neocumingii.* Simple, variable cactus, with hemispherical to spherical, bright dark green stems, 10cm (4in) thick. The stems have 16–18 warty ribs, white areoles, and brown-tipped yellow spines (16–20 radials and 3–10 thicker centrals). Orange or yellow flowers, 2cm (¾in) or more across, are borne in summer. ↕ 20cm (8in), ↔ 10cm (4in). Bolivia. ❀ (min. 5°C/41°F)
R. pygmaea. Simple or clustering cactus producing ovoid to short-cylindrical, mid- to dark green stems, 1–2cm (½–¾in) thick, with tubercles arranged in 8–12 spiral rows and white spines, 2–3mm (1⁄16–⅛in) long (9–11 radials, no centrals). Solitary, pink-purple flowers, 2–2.5cm (¾–1in) across, are borne on the lower parts of the stems in summer. ↕ 4cm (1½in), ↔ 8cm (3in). N.W. Argentina. ❀ (min. 10°C/50°F)
R. rauschii see *R. steinmannii.*
R. senilis. Freely offsetting cactus (sometimes included in *R. miniscula*) with depressed-spherical, dark green stems, to 7cm (3in) thick, with about 18 warty, spirally arranged ribs, and white areoles bearing 25–30 long, fine, yellowish white or chalky white, undifferentiated spines. Lemon-yellow, or white-throated, carmine-red flowers, 3.5cm (1½in) across, are borne in summer. ↕ 8cm (3in), ↔ 15cm (6in). N. Argentina. ❀ (min. 5–7°C/41–45°F)
R. spegazziniana ▣ Clustering cactus with spherical, pale to deep green stems, 5cm (2in) thick, with about 18 warty ribs, white-felted areoles, and white spines (14 radials and 3–6 shorter centrals). Bears pale vermilion to dark red flowers, 2.5–3cm (1–1¼in) across, in summer. ↕ to 10cm (4in), ↔ to 20cm (8in). N.W. Argentina. ❀ (min. 5–7°C/41–45°F)
R. spinosissima. Freely offsetting cactus with spherical, bright green stems, 5–6cm (2–2½in) thick, with 15 or more warty, spirally arranged ribs, white-hairy areoles, and white spines (numerous radials and 5 or 6 thicker, brown-tipped centrals). Bears pale orange to mid-red flowers, 3–4cm (1¼–1½in) across, in summer. ↕ to 10cm (4in), ↔ 15cm (6in). N. Argentina. ❀ (min. 5–7°C/41–45°F)
R. steinbachii* subsp. *tiraquensis see *R. tiraquensis.*
R. steinmannii, syn. *R. rauschii.* Offsetting cactus with a tuberous rootstock and ovoid, blackish green to violet stems, 3cm (1¼in) thick, with up to 16, spirally arranged, low-tubercled ribs. White-felted areoles bear yellow or black spines (up to 11 radials, no centrals). Carmine-red flowers, 3cm (1¼in) across, often with paler red or white throats, are borne in summer. ↕ 5cm (2in), ↔ 10cm (4in). Bolivia. ❀ (min. 5°C/41°F)
R. tiraquensis ▣ syn. *R. steinbachii* subsp. *tiraquensis.* Upright cactus with mid-green stems, simple at first, but eventually clump-forming, covered in spirally arranged tubercles. Elongated areoles, to 7mm (¼in) long, bear 2–4 reddish brown central spines, 6–7cm (2½–3in) long, and 14–18 glassy white radials. Solitary, funnel-shaped, purple or magenta flowers, 3.5cm (1½in) across, are borne in summer. ↕ 9–10cm (3½–4in), ↔ 10cm (4in). Bolivia. ❀ (min. 7–10°C/45–50°F)
R. violaciflora ▣ syn. *R. minuscula* subsp. *violaciflora.* Freely clustering cactus with slightly flattened, spherical, dull mid- to dark green stems, 5cm (2in) thick, with 16–20 warty, spirally arranged ribs, and brown areoles bearing 25–30 undifferentiated white spines. Red or bright pinkish purple flowers, 3–4cm (1¼–1½in) across, are produced in summer. ↕ 5cm (2in), ↔ 12cm (5in). N. Argentina. ❀ (min. 5°C/41°F)

Rebutia marsoneri

Rebutia neocumingii

Rebutia spegazziniana

R

▷ ***Rechsteineria leucotricha*** see *Sinningia canescens*
▷ **Redbud,**
California see *Cercis occidentalis*
Chinese see *Cercis chinensis*
Eastern see *Cercis canadensis*
Western see *Cercis occidentalis*
▷ **Red cloak, Brazilian** see *Megaskepasma erythrochlamys*
▷ **Red hot poker** see *Kniphofia*
▷ **Red ink plant** see *Phytolacca americana*
▷ **Red pine** see *Pinus resinosa*
Chinese see *P. tabuliformis*
Japanese see *P. densiflora*
▷ **Red tree** see *Peperomia metallica*
▷ **Redwood,**
Coastal see *Sequoia sempervirens*
Dawn see *Metasequoia glyptostroboides*
Giant see *Sequoiadendron giganteum*
Sierra see *Sequoiadendron giganteum*
▷ **Reed** see *Phragmites*
Burr see *Sparganium*
Common see *Phragmites australis*
Giant see *Arundo donax*
Norfolk see *Phragmites australis*
Roof *see Chondropetalum tectorum, Thamnochortus insignis*
▷ **Reedmace** see *Typha*
Narrow-leaved see *T. angustifolia*

REHDERODENDRON

STYRACACEAE

Genus of 9 species of deciduous shrubs and trees from mountain woodland in China and Vietnam. They are valued for their cup-shaped, 5-petalled white flowers, borne in leafless, axillary, cyme-like panicles or racemes, and their oblong or elliptic, ribbed, woody fruits. The leaves are alternate and finely toothed. *R. macrocarpum*, the only species usually grown, is ideal for a woodland garden.
• **HARDINESS** Hardy to -10°C (14°F).
• **CULTIVATION** Grow in fertile, moist but well-drained, neutral to acid soil in sun or partial shade, sheltered from cold, dry winds. Pruning group 1.
• **PROPAGATION** Sow seed in containers in a cold frame as soon as ripe. Root semi-ripe cuttings in summer.
• **PESTS AND DISEASES** Trouble free.

R

R. macrocarpum ♀ Small, broadly upright, deciduous tree with red young shoots and elliptic to oblong, glossy, dark green leaves, to 15cm (6in) long. As the leaves emerge in late spring, bears cyme-like racemes of 6–10 cup-shaped, fragrant, creamy white flowers, 6cm (2½in) across. Flowers are followed by pendent, ellipsoid, green, then red fruit, to 7cm (3in) long. ↕ 10m (30ft), ↔ 7m (22ft). W. China. ❄❄

REHMANNIA

GESNERIACEAE/SCROPHULARIACEAE

Genus of 8 or 9 species of perennials, sometimes grown as biennials, from woodland and stony sites in China. They are cultivated for their large, foxglove-like flowers, which are 2-lipped and borne singly or in clusters in the leaf axils, sometimes forming leafy, raceme-like inflorescences. The leaves, arranged in basal rosettes, are large, obovate to oblong, shallowly lobed or toothed, conspicuously veined, and hairy. Grow at the front of a sunny

Rehmannia elata

border; in regions with mild, damp winters grow permanently, or over-winter, in a cool greenhouse.
• **HARDINESS** Fully hardy to frost hardy.
• **CULTIVATION** Under glass, grow in loam-based potting compost (JI No.2) in bright filtered light. When in growth, water freely and apply a balanced liquid fertilizer monthly; keep just moist in winter. Outdoors, grow in well-drained, moderately fertile, humus-rich soil in a sheltered site in full sun. In regions where winters are mild and damp, lift in autumn, pot up, and overwinter in a cool, dry, frost-free place.
• **PROPAGATION** Sow seed at 13–16°C (55–61°F) in late winter; seedlings will flower in 12–14 months. Take root cuttings in late autumn, or softwood cuttings from basal shoots before flowering. Separate and pot up runners in spring.
• **PESTS AND DISEASES** Susceptible to slug and snail damage.

***R. angulata* of gardens** see *R. elata.*
R. elata ▣ syn. *R. angulata* of gardens (Chinese foxglove). Rosette-forming perennial with obovate, lobed or toothed, conspicuously veined, hairy, mid-green, basal leaves, 20–25cm (8–10in) long. Bears racemes of semi-pendent, tubular flowers, 7–10cm (3–4in) long, from summer to autumn. The flowers have bright pinkish purple lips and paler tubes; they are red-spotted, especially in the throats. ↕ to 1.5m (5ft), ↔ 50cm (20in). China. ❄❄❄
R. glutinosa. Sticky, purple-hairy perennial with slender runners and rosettes of obovate, scalloped, veined, basal leaves, to 10cm (4in) long, mid-green above and often red-tinted beneath. From mid-spring to summer, pendent, tubular flowers, to 5cm (2in) long, are borne singly or in few-flowered clusters in the leaf axils. The flowers have reddish brown tubes, marked with darker reddish purple veins, and pale yellow-brown lips. ↕ 15–30cm (6–12in), ↔ to 30cm (12in). N. China. ❄❄❄

REINECKEA

CONVALLARIACEAE/LILIACEAE

Genus of one species of rhizomatous, evergreen perennial from deciduous woodland or sandy, open areas among shrubs in China and Japan. It is grown for its arching, pale green leaves and spikes of tiny, fragrant pink flowers. *R. carnea* provides attractive, leafy ground cover, but rarely flowers freely or bears its spherical red berries in areas with cool summers.
• **HARDINESS** Fully hardy.
• **CULTIVATION** Grow in moist but well-drained, humus-rich, neutral or acid soil in partial shade.
• **PROPAGATION** Sow seed in containers in a cold frame as soon as ripe. Separate rhizomes from the margins of established clumps in spring.
• **PESTS AND DISEASES** Susceptible to damage from slugs and snails.

R. carnea. Evergreen, rhizomatous perennial with tufts of arching, linear-lance-shaped, glossy, mid- to dark green leaves, 15–35cm (6–14in) long, borne in 2 ranks at the ends of the rhizomes. In late spring, bears dense, terminal spikes of shallowly cup-shaped, pale to deep pink flowers, to 1cm (½in) across, each with 6 segments, the tips reflexing with age. In areas with warm summers, spherical red berries, 8–10mm (⅜–½in) across, are produced in autumn. ↕ 20cm (8in), ↔ 40cm (16in) or more. China, Japan. ❄❄❄

REINHARDTIA

Window palm

ARECACEAE/PALMAE

Genus of 6 species of single- and cluster-stemmed, monoecious palms from tropical rainforest from S. Mexico to Colombia, seldom exceeding 8m (25ft) in height. The mid- or dark green leaves are entire, pinnately ribbed or pinnate and divided into oblong to wedge-shaped, lobe-like leaflets. Bowl-shaped, 3-petalled flowers are borne in panicles or on solitary spikes between the leaves, usually with 2 male flowers and one female flower in a group. In frost-prone areas, grow in a warm greenhouse or as houseplants; elsewhere, use them in a shady site under trees or in a courtyard garden.
• **HARDINESS** Frost tender.
• **CULTIVATION** Under glass, grow in loamless potting compost in bright filtered or indirect light with high humidity. Water freely and apply a balanced liquid fertilizer monthly when in growth; water moderately in winter. Pot on or top-dress in spring. Outdoors, grow in humus-rich, moist but well-drained soil in partial to full shade.
• **PROPAGATION** Sow seed at 27°C (81°F) in spring.
• **PESTS AND DISEASES** Red spider mites may be a problem under glass.

R. gracilis 🌴 (Window palm). Small palm with single or clustered, cane-like stems bearing persistent leaf sheaths near the apex of the stems, smooth below. Bright green leaves, to 60cm (24in) long, are divided into 2 or 4 boldly toothed lobes or leaflets each side of the leaf-stalk, with small holes ("windows") where they join the midrib; the 2 larger, apical lobes are fused at their bases into a fishtail shape, the 2 smaller basal lobes (sometimes very narrow or missing) extend at right angles. Bears creamy white flowers, 5cm (2in) across, in panicles, to 60cm (24in) long, usually in summer, followed by obovoid, purple-black fruit, to 1.5cm (½in) long. ↕ 1.5–2.5m (5–8ft), ↔ 1.2–2m (4–6ft). S. Mexico to Honduras. ❀ (min. 13°C/55°F)

REINWARDTIA

LINACEAE

Genus of 1 or 2 species of evergreen shrubs or subshrubs, related to flaxes (*Linum*), found in mountain woodland from Pakistan to S.W. China and S.E. Asia. The alternate, elliptic- to oblong-obovate leaves may be entire or toothed. They are grown for their funnel-shaped flowers, each with 5 spreading petal lobes, borne in terminal or axillary, cyme-like clusters, occasionally singly. Where temperatures fall below 7°C (45°F), grow in a temperate greenhouse. In milder regions, grow at the base of a sunny wall, or in a courtyard garden.

Reinwardtia indica

• **HARDINESS** Frost tender.
• **CULTIVATION** Under glass, grow in loamless or loam-based potting compost (JI No.3) in full light, with shade from hot sun and moderate humidity. In growth, mist regularly, water freely, and apply a balanced liquid fertilizer monthly; water moderately at other times. Winter flowers are borne most freely with a minimum temperature of 13°C (55°F). Outdoors, grow in fertile, moist but well-drained, humus-rich soil in full sun. Pruning group 8; tip-prune young plants to encourage branching.
• **PROPAGATION** Sow seed at 16–18°C (61–64°F) in spring. Root softwood cuttings in early summer.
• **PESTS AND DISEASES** Red spider mites may be a problem under glass.

R. indica ■ syn. *R. tetragyna*, *R. trigyna* (Yellow flax). Open, erect to spreading shrub with elliptic- to oblong-obovate, finely toothed, deep green to greyish green leaves, 3–8cm (1¼–3in) long. From autumn to late spring, produces funnel-shaped, bright golden yellow flowers, 3–5cm (1¼–2in) across, singly or in short, cyme-like clusters from the leaf axils. ↕↔ 60–90cm (24–36in). Pakistan, N. India, Burma, S.W. China, S.E. Asia. ⊛ (min. 7°C/45°F)
R. tetragyna see *R. indica*.
R. trigyna see *R. indica*.

RENANTHERA

ORCHIDACEAE

Genus of about 15 species of evergreen, epiphytic orchids from mostly moist forest areas, sometimes on rocks, in S.E. Asia. They produce upright, extending rhizomes, with branched, monopodial stems up to 1m (3ft) long. The leaves are spirally arranged or in 2 ranks and are narrowly ovate to linear-oblong, semi-rigid, leathery, mid-green, and unequally 2-lobed at the tips. Long panicles of typically red flowers with narrow sepals and tiny lips arise opposite the leaf bases.
• **HARDINESS** Frost tender.
• **CULTIVATION** Intermediate-growing orchids. Grow in epiphytic orchid compost in slatted baskets in full light with shade from hot sun. In summer, water freely, apply fertilizer at every third watering, and mist plants twice daily. Water moderately in winter. See also p.46.
• **PROPAGATION** Divide when the plant fills the pot and "flows" over the sides; laboratory conditions required if grown from seed.
• **PESTS AND DISEASES** Red spider mites, aphids, whiteflies, and mealybugs may be a problem.

Renanthera Brookie Chandler

***R.* Brookie Chandler** ■ (*R. monachica* x *R. storiei*) Epiphytic orchid with rigid stems and 2-ranked, oblong leaves, 10–12cm (4–5in) long. Dark red, red-spotted flowers, 8cm (3in) long, are produced in panicles, 45cm (18in) long, mainly during summer. ↕ 1.2m (4ft), ↔ 30cm (12in). ⊛ (min. 13°C/55°F; max. 30°C/86°F)
R. coccinea. Epiphytic orchid with rigid stems and 2-ranked, linear-oblong leaves, 9–12cm (3½–5in) long. In spring and autumn, produces panicles, to 70cm (28in) long, of flowers, 7cm (3in) long; some sepals are pale pink speckled orange-yellow and bright red, while other sepals are vivid red. ↕ 4m (12ft), ↔ 30cm (12in). S.E. Asia (Thailand, Laos, Vietnam, S. China). ⊛ (min. 13°C/55°F; max. 30°C/86°F)
R. imschootiana ■ Epiphytic orchid with rigid stems and 2-ranked, oblong leaves, 10cm (4in) long. Red and yellow, often spotted flowers, 5cm (2in) long, are produced in panicles, to 45cm (18in) long, in summer. ↕ 45cm (18in), ↔ 30cm (12in). N.E. India, Burma, Laos. ⊛ (min. 13°C/55°F; max. 30°C/86°F)

RESEDA

Mignonette

RESEDACEAE

Genus of 55–60 species of erect to spreading, branching, and occasionally rosette-forming annuals and perennials from stony hillsides, scrub, or field margins, mainly in the Mediterranean and S.W. Asia, but also in E. Africa and N.W. India. They have alternate, small, variably shaped, entire, toothed, or pinnatifid, veined, mostly mid-green leaves. Star-shaped, greenish white, greenish yellow, or yellow, sometimes red-tinged flowers, with 4–10 narrow petals, are borne in long, unbranched or branching, spike-like racemes from spring to autumn. *R. odorata* has been grown for centuries, mainly for its fragrant flowers, which hold their scent for months even when cut and dried; modern cultivars have larger, more strongly coloured flowers, which tend to be less fragrant. All are attractive to bees, and are ideal for a mixed or herbaceous border, or for a wildflower garden.
• **HARDINESS** Fully hardy.
• **CULTIVATION** Grow in well-drained, moderately fertile, preferably alkaline soil in full sun or partial shade. Deadhead to prolong flowering.
• **PROPAGATION** Sow seed at 13°C (55°F) in late winter, or *in situ* in early spring or autumn. Where temperatures fall below -5°C (23°F), provide cloche protection for autumn-sown seedlings.
• **PESTS AND DISEASES** Trouble free.

R. odorata ■ (Common mignonette). Erect to slightly spreading, hairless annual with branching, strongly ribbed stems and entire, elliptic to spoon-shaped, sometimes 3-lobed leaves, to 10cm (4in) long. From summer to early autumn, bears loose, conical, raceme-like heads of tiny, star-shaped, highly fragrant, yellowish green or white to reddish green flowers, to 7mm (¼in) across; each flower has 4–7 petals and a central tuft of orange stamens. ↕ 30–60cm (12–24in), ↔ to 23cm (9in). N. Africa. Widely naturalized. ***

▷ **Restharrow** see *Ononis*
Common see *O. repens*
Shrubby see *O. fruticosa*

RESTIO

RESTIONACEAE

Genus of about 90 species of rush-like, tufted, dioecious, rhizomatous perennials from cool or damp, grassy places in the foothills of coastal mountains in southern Africa. They are grown for their graceful, slender green stems, sometimes branched and feathery in appearance, and for their delicate, grass-like inflorescences in summer. The leaves are reduced to persistent, sheath-like structures that are split to the base and surround the flowering stems. The flowers are borne in brown spikelets in summer, the males and females on separate plants. In frost-prone climates, grow as a specimen plant in a container; in warmer climates, grow as a specimen plant or in a border.
• **HARDINESS** Half hardy.
• **CULTIVATION** Under glass, grow in loam-based potting compost (JI No.2) in full light. When in growth, water moderately and apply a balanced liquid fertilizer every 4 weeks; maintain low humidity. Water sparingly in winter.

Renanthera imschootiana

Reseda odorata

Outdoors, grow in moderately fertile, well-drained, preferably acid soil in full sun. In frost-prone areas, plant out after last frosts; lift and pot up in autumn and overwinter in a cool, dry place.
• **PROPAGATION** Sow seed at 16–18°C (61–64°F) in spring, after soaking for 24 hours in warm water. Divide rhizomes in early spring.
• **PESTS AND DISEASES** Prone to red spider mites and whiteflies under glass.

R. dispar. Tufted, rhizomatous perennial with sparsely warty, mid-green stems, rounded in cross-section, with brown sheaths. Male inflorescences bear numerous reddish brown spikelets in summer, slightly overtopped by mid-brown spathes. Female inflorescences have fewer spikelets per stem, overtopped by long, reddish maroon spathes. ↕ 1.5–2m (5–6ft), ↔ to 2m (6ft). South Africa (Western Cape). ❄
R. quadratus. Tufted rhizomatous perennial with smooth, light green stems, distinctly 4-angled in cross-section, with light brown sheaths. Male and female inflorescences are superficially similar but differ in the females having hairless lateral sepals. Dark brown spikelets, 4–6mm (1/8–1/4in) long, are borne at the tips of stem branches in summer. ↕ 1.5–2m (5–6ft), ↔ to 2m (6ft). South Africa (Western Cape). ❄

▷ **Resurrection plant** see *Selaginella lepidophylla*

RETAMA syn. LYGOS

LEGUMINOSAE/PAPILIONACEAE

Genus, related to *Genista*, of 4 species of deciduous shrubs found on sandy and rocky soils in the Canary Islands, the Mediterranean, and W. Asia. They have willowy, dark green stems with alternate, mid-green leaves that soon fall, and pea-like, yellow or white flowers borne in dense, axillary racemes. *R. monosperma*, the only species usually cultivated, has an elegant, arching habit and fragrant flowers. In frost-prone areas, grow in a cool greenhouse. In warmer areas, grow in a sheltered border or at the base of a warm, sunny wall.
• **HARDINESS** Half hardy.
• **CULTIVATION** Under glass, grow in loam-based potting compost (JI No.2) in full light. When in growth, water moderately; keep just moist in winter. Outdoors, grow in moderately fertile, sharply drained soil in full sun, in a sheltered site. Pruning group 3, but rarely needed; do not cut back old wood.
• **PROPAGATION** Sow seed in containers in a cold frame in spring. Root semi-ripe cuttings in summer.
• **PESTS AND DISEASES** Trouble free.

R. monosperma, syn. *Genista monosperma*. Graceful, deciduous shrub with slender, arching, silky grey stems and a few linear leaves, to 2cm (3/4in) long, which soon fall. Small, very fragrant, pea-like white flowers are produced in dense, axillary racemes, to 4cm (1½in) long, in early spring. ↕ to 4m (12ft), ↔ 1.5m (5ft). Portugal, Spain, N. Africa, Canary Islands. ❄

▷ **Rewarewa** see *Knightia excelsa*
▷ ***Reynoutria*** see *Fallopia*

RHAMNUS

RHAMNACEAE

Genus of 125 or more species of usually thorny, deciduous or evergreen shrubs and trees, widely distributed in N. temperate regions, with a few in the S. hemisphere. They occur in woodland, heathland, scrub, fens, bogs, or rocky places, often on alkaline soils. They are cultivated mainly for their foliage, which has good autumn colour in some deciduous species, and for their decorative fruits. The leaves are opposite or alternate. Tiny, hermaphrodite or unisexual, cup-shaped flowers, 2–4mm (1/16–1/8in) across, with 4 or 5 petals, are borne in axillary racemes or umbel-like clusters; they are often fragrant and usually yellowish white, greenish white, or white. Some flowers, particularly those of *R. frangula*, are very attractive to bees. Grow in a shrub border; *R. cathartica* and *R. frangula* may be used as hedging, or in a wild or woodland garden. All parts may cause severe discomfort if ingested.
• **HARDINESS** Fully hardy to frost hardy.
• **CULTIVATION** Grow in moderately fertile soil in full sun or partial shade. *R. cathartica*, *R. frangula*, and *R. imeretina* prefer moist soils. *R. alaternus* needs well-drained soil in full sun. Pruning group 1; trim hedges in early spring. Cut out reverting shoots on *R. alaternus* 'Argenteovariegata' when seen.
• **PROPAGATION** Sow seed in containers in a cold frame as soon as ripe. Root semi-ripe cuttings of evergreen species in summer. Root greenwood cuttings of deciduous species in early summer, or layer in autumn or spring.
• **PESTS AND DISEASES** Trouble free.

R. alaternus (Italian buckthorn). Erect to spreading, evergreen shrub with ovate to oblong, leathery, glossy, dark green leaves, to 7cm (3in) long. Unisexual and hermaphrodite, yellow-green flowers are borne in axillary clusters in late spring and early summer; they are followed by spherical red fruit, 6mm (1/4in) across, ripening to black in late summer. ↕ 5m (15ft), ↔ 4m (12ft). Portugal, Morocco, Mediterranean, Ukraine (Crimea). ❄❄. **'Argenteovariegata'** ▣ syn. 'Variegata', has grey-green leaves with white margins.
R. californica (Coffeeberry). Upright, evergreen or semi-evergreen shrub with red shoots and oblong to oval, glossy, mid-green leaves, to 8cm (3in) long. In late spring and early summer, bears axillary clusters of hermaphrodite, yellowish white flowers. Spherical red fruit, 6mm (1/4in) across, ripen to purple-black in late summer and autumn. ↕ 4m (12ft), ↔ 3m (10ft). W. USA. ❄❄
R. cathartica (Common buckthorn). Dense, thicket-forming, spiny, deciduous shrub, sometimes a small tree, with oval to ovate or elliptic, glossy, dark green leaves, to 6cm (2½in) long, turning yellow in autumn. Axillary clusters of unisexual, yellowish green flowers are borne in late spring and early summer. In autumn, bears spherical red fruit, to 6mm (1/4in) across, ripening to black. ↕ 6m (20ft), ↔ 5m (15ft). Europe, N.W. Africa, Asia. ❄❄❄
R. frangula (Alder buckthorn). Bushy, spreading, deciduous shrub with oval to obovate, glossy, dark green leaves, to 7cm (3in) long, turning red in autumn. In late spring and early summer, bears axillary clusters of hermaphrodite green flowers, followed by fleshy, spherical red fruit, to 1cm (½in) across, ripening to black. ↕↔ 5m (15ft). Europe, N. Africa, Russia to Altai Mountains. ❄❄❄ **'Aspleniifolia'** ▣ is slow-growing and has fern-like, linear, irregularly scalloped leaves; ↕ 3–4m (10–12ft), ↔ 2–3m (6–10ft). **'Columnaris'** (Tallhedge buckthorn) is narrow and upright and is primarily used as hedging.
R. imeretina. Open, spreading, deciduous shrub with stout shoots and oblong to oval, conspicuously veined, dark green leaves, to 30cm (12in) long, turning bronze-purple in autumn. In early summer, bears unisexual green flowers in axillary clusters, followed in late summer and autumn by spherical red fruit, 5mm (1/4in) across, ripening to black. ↕ 3m (10ft), ↔ 5m (15ft). Georgia, E. Turkey, Armenia. ❄❄❄
R. saxatilis. Variable, low-growing, deciduous shrub with densely hairy, spine-tipped shoots and opposite to almost opposite or clustered, ovate to obovate, hairless or sparsely hairy, finely toothed, mid- to dark green leaves, 2–3cm (3/4–1¼in) long. Small, 4-parted, unisexual, greenish or pale green flowers, usually borne in cyme-like axillary clusters but occasionally solitary, are produced from spring to early summer, followed by spherical black fruit, to 6mm (1/4in) across. ↕↔ 50–100cm (20–39in). S. Europe (submontane and mountainous areas in France and Spain to Greece and Bulgaria). ❄❄❄

Rhamnus frangula 'Aspleniifolia'

Rhamnus alaternus 'Argenteovariegata'

RHAPHIDOPHORA

syn. RAPHIDOPHORA

ARACEAE

Genus of about 120 species of evergreen root climbers and trailers from subtropical and tropical forest in Africa, S.E. Asia, Australasia, and the Pacific islands. They are cultivated for their attractive leaves, which are short-stalked and entire on young plants, and long-stalked, larger, and pinnatifid or perforated on mature specimens. In summer, mature plants grown outdoors produce yellow spadices of tiny, petalless flowers, surrounded by boat-shaped, yellow to green spathes. In frost-prone regions, grow as house-plants, or in a warm greenhouse or

R

conservatory. In tropical areas, grow up a tree or on a damp shady wall. All parts may cause severe discomfort if ingested; contact with sap may irritate skin.

- **HARDINESS** Frost tender.
- **CULTIVATION** Under glass, grow in equal parts loam, leaf mould, bark, and sharp sand in bright filtered light. Provide moderate humidity, draught-free conditions, and the support of a moss pole or similar structure. When in full growth, water moderately, mist regularly, and apply a balanced liquid fertilizer every 2–3 weeks; water sparingly in winter. Outdoors, grow in moist, humus-rich soil in partial shade. Pruning group 11, after flowering.
- **PROPAGATION** Sow seed at 18–21°C (64–70°F) in spring. Root stem-tip or leaf-bud cuttings, or air layer, in spring or early summer.
- **PESTS AND DISEASES** Prone to scale insects and red spider mites under glass.

R. celatocaulis see *R. korthalsii.*
R. decursiva ▣ Erect, robust climber usually grown in its adult phase, when it has thick, stiff, sparsely branched stems and oblong, pinnatifid, leathery, glossy dark green leaves, 50–90cm (20–36in) long. Juvenile leaves are arranged in 2 ranks and are broadly ovate, entire, and mid-green, to 30cm (12in) long. Fleshy yellow spathes, 14–18cm (5½–7in) long, are borne singly from the leaf axils in summer. ↕ to 10m (30ft). N. Burma, India, Sri Lanka. ❀ (min. 15°C/59°F)
R. korthalsii, syn. *Monstera latevaginata* of gardens, *Pothos celatocaulis, R. celatocaulis, R. pinnata* (Shingle plant). Erect, sparsely branched climber mostly grown in its juvenile phase, when it has short-stalked, elliptic-ovate, entire, blue-green leaves, to 10cm (4in) long, closely overlapping and lying flat along the stems. Mature leaves are entire or pinnatifid, and 20–40cm (8–16in) long, with stalks of the same length. In summer, produces fleshy yellow spathes, to 15cm (6in) long, singly from the leaf axils on long stalks. ↕ 10m (30ft). Borneo. ❀ (min. 15°C/59°F)
R. pinnata see *R. korthalsii.*

Rhaphidophora decursiva

RHAPHIOLEPIS

ROSACEAE

Genus of about 3–5, possibly up to 15 species of evergreen shrubs and trees from scrub in S.E. and E. Asia. They are grown for their alternate, often toothed leaves, which are glossy, dark green, and leathery, and for their fragrant, apple-blossom-like, star-shaped flowers borne in erect, terminal racemes or panicles in spring or summer. Grow in a sheltered border, or at the base of a warm, sunny wall. In frost-prone areas, grow half-hardy species in a cool greenhouse.

- **HARDINESS** Frost hardy to half hardy.
- **CULTIVATION** Under glass, grow in loam-based potting compost (JI No.3) in full light. In the growing season, water moderately and apply a balanced liquid fertilizer monthly; water sparingly in winter. Outdoors, grow in moist but well-drained, moderately fertile soil in full sun, with shelter from cold, drying winds. Pruning group 8.
- **PROPAGATION** Root semi-ripe cuttings in late summer. Layer in autumn.
- **PESTS AND DISEASES** Trouble free.

R. x delacourii (*R. indica* x *R. umbellata*). Dome-shaped, evergreen shrub with broadly obovate to inversely lance-shaped, shallowly toothed, leathery, dark green leaves, to 7cm (3in) long. Star-shaped pink flowers, to 2cm (¾in) across, are produced in erect, broadly conical panicles, to 10cm (4in) long, in spring or summer. ↕ 2m (6ft), ↔ 2.5m (8ft). Garden origin. ❄❄. **'Coates' Crimson'** bears dark pink flowers. **'Enchantress'** is compact, with rose-pink flowers. **'Indian Princess'** produces bright pink flowers fading to white. **'Spring Song'** bears pale pink flowers over an extended period. **'White Enchantress'** is dwarf and compact, bearing pure white flowers.
R. indica (Indian hawthorn). Bushy, spreading, evergreen shrub producing narrowly elliptic to lance-shaped, deeply toothed, leathery, glossy, dark green leaves, to 7–11cm (3–4½in) long. In spring or early summer, bears white flowers, to 1.5cm (½in) across, with pink-flushed centres, in loose racemes or panicles, to 8cm (3in) long. ↕ 1.5m (5ft), ↔ 2m (6ft). China. ❄
R. japonica see *R. umbellata.*
R. ovata see *R. umbellata.*
R. umbellata ▣ syn. *R. japonica, R. ovata.* Bushy, evergreen shrub with oval to obovate or inversely lance-shaped, leathery, dark green, shallowly toothed leaves, to 9cm (3½in) long. White flowers, to 2cm (¾in) across, sometimes tinted rose-pink, are borne in conical racemes, to 10cm (4in) long, in early summer. ↕↔ 1.5m (5ft). Korea, Japan. ❄❄

Rhaphiolepis umbellata

RHAPIDOPHYLLUM

Needle palm

ARECACEAE/PALMAE

Genus of one species of almost stemless palm from wooded, swampy areas in coastal S.E. USA. It is grown for its fan-shaped, palmately lobed leaves, cut almost to the midribs. The tiny, bowl-shaped, 3-petalled flowers are borne in small panicles among the leaf sheaths. In frost-prone areas, grow in a cool or temperate greenhouse. In warmer areas, use as a lawn or courtyard specimen.

- **HARDINESS** Frost tender, but will survive short spells around 0°C (32°F), if ripened by warm summers.
- **CULTIVATION** Under glass, grow in loam-based potting compost (JI No.2) in bright filtered light. When in growth, water freely and apply a balanced liquid fertilizer monthly; water more sparingly in winter. Pot on or top-dress in spring. Outdoors, grow in any moderately fertile, moist but well-drained soil in partial shade.
- **PROPAGATION** Sow seed at 16–18°C (61–64°F) in spring. Remove smaller suckers in spring.
- **PESTS AND DISEASES** Red spider mites, mealybugs, and scale insects may be a problem under glass.

Rhapidophyllum hystrix

R. hystrix ▣❋ (Blue palmetto, Porcupine palm). Small, slow-growing, clump-forming palm with a short-branching stem system below or at the soil surface. Sheaths at the bases of the leaf-stalks bear long, erect spines; each smooth, erect leaf-stalk bears a deeply lobed leaf-blade, to 1m (3ft) long, with 5–12 lobes, bright green above, tinted blue-grey beneath. Tiny, bowl-shaped, purplish red flowers, borne in summer, are hidden by the foliage. ↕ 1.5–2m (5–6ft), ↔ 2–4m (6–12ft). USA (S. Carolina to Florida and Mississippi). ❀ (min. 7–10°C/45–50°F)

RHAPIS

Lady palm

ARECACEAE/PALMAE

Genus of 12 species of small, cluster-stemmed palms found in shady tropical and subtropical forest from S. China to S.E. Asia. The light or mid-green leaves, arranged in spirals or loose tufts at the stem tips, are divided almost to the bases into 2–10 or more lobes. Bowl-shaped, 3-petalled flowers are borne in short panicles between the leaves. In frost-prone areas, grow in a temperate or warm greenhouse, or as houseplants. In frost-free regions, use in a shady border or to add foliage interest to other plantings.

- **HARDINESS** Frost tender.
- **CULTIVATION** Under glass, grow in loamless potting compost in bright filtered light. In the growing season, water freely and apply a balanced liquid fertilizer monthly; water moderately in winter. Pot on or top-dress in spring. Outdoors, grow in any moderately fertile, moist but well-drained soil in dappled shade.
- **PROPAGATION** Sow seed at 27°C (81°F), or divide, in spring.
- **PESTS AND DISEASES** Red spider mites may be a problem under glass.

Rhapis excelsa

R. excelsa ▣❋ syn. *R. flabelliformis* (Miniature fan palm). Small, clump-forming palm with slender, erect, bamboo- or reed-like stems. The long-stalked, deeply lobed, lustrous, dark green leaves, 20–30cm (8–12in) long, each have 3–10 broadly to narrowly lance-shaped, puckered lobes. Tiny, bowl-shaped cream flowers are borne in panicles, to 12cm (5in) long, among the leaves, in summer. ↕↔ 1.5–5m (5–15ft). S. China. ❀ (min. 10–13°C/50–55°F). **'Variegata'** has leaves with white-striped lobes. **'Zuikonishiki'** has leaves with yellow-variegated lobes; ↕ to 60cm (24in), rarely more.
R. flabelliformis see *R. excelsa.*

▷ ***Rhazya*** see *Amsonia*
R. orientalis see *A. orientalis*

RHEUM
Rhubarb
POLYGONACEAE

Genus of about 50 species of rhizomatous, often tough or woody perennials found in a range of habitats, from marshy meadows and streamsides to scrub and rocky slopes, in E. Europe and C. Asia to the Himalayas and China. Unlike *R.* x *hybridum*, which is grown for its edible leaf-stalks, the rhubarbs described below are cultivated for their imposing, large, basal leaves and tall flower panicles. A few species from mountainous regions in Asia are dwarf with small flower spikes. The rounded, entire to palmately lobed leaves often emerge from bright red buds; the leaves are sometimes crimson-purple when young, usually with coarse teeth and conspicuous veins and midribs. Large panicles of tiny, petalless, star-shaped flowers are borne on hollow, leafless, flowering stems in summer; they have large, colourful, showy bracts in some species. The flowers are followed by small, triangular, winged, usually brown fruits. Grow rhubarbs near water, or in a moist border or woodland garden. The leaves may cause severe discomfort if ingested.
• **HARDINESS** Fully hardy.
• **CULTIVATION** Grow in deep, moist, humus-rich soil in full sun or partial shade. *R. alexandrae* prefers wet, marshy soil. Mulch annually in early spring with well-rotted organic matter. *R. nobile* may prove difficult to establish.
• **PROPAGATION** Sow seed in containers in a cold frame in autumn. Divide in early spring.
• **PESTS AND DISEASES** Susceptible to damage by slugs, and prone to crown rot and viruses.

***R.* 'Ace of Hearts'** ▣ syn. *R.* 'Ace of Spades'. Rhizomatous perennial with elongated, heart-shaped, entire, dark green leaves, to 35cm (14in) long, red-veined above and purple-red beneath. In mid- and late summer, numerous tiny, star-shaped, very pale pink to white flowers open in panicles to 1.2m (4ft) long. ↕ to 1.2m (4ft), ↔ 90cm (36in). ❄❄❄
***R.* 'Ace of Spades'** see *R.* 'Ace of Hearts'.
R. alexandrae. Rhizomatous perennial with rosetted, oblong-ovate, entire, glossy, dark green leaves, to 20cm (8in) long, with heart-shaped bases and prominent veins. In early summer, bears narrow, arching, then pendent panicles, 60cm (24in) long, of tiny, star-shaped, yellow-green flowers, which are almost hidden by creamy white or greenish cream bracts, to 10cm (4in) or more long. ↕ to 1.5m (5ft), ↔ 60cm (24in). W. China, Tibet. ❄❄❄
R. nobile. Rhizomatous perennial, similar to *R. alexandrae*, with broadly ovate, entire, glossy, dark green leaves, to 30cm (12in) or more long, veined and margined red. In midsummer, bears panicles, 60cm (24in) long, of showy, arching to pendent, overlapping cream bracts, to 15cm (6in) long, which conceal short, erect clusters of tiny, star-shaped green flowers. ↕ to 2m (6ft), ↔ 60cm (24in). Himalayas, Nepal to S.E. Tibet. ❄❄❄
R. palmatum (Chinese rhubarb). Rhizomatous perennial with a massive rootstock and thick leaf-stalks that bear broadly ovate to rounded, palmately 3–9 lobed, coarsely toothed, dark green leaves, to 90cm (36in) long, purple-red or red and softly hairy beneath. In early summer, numerous tiny, star-shaped, creamy green to deep red flowers are borne in panicles to 2m (6ft) long. ↕ to 2.5m (8ft), ↔ to 1.8m (6ft). N.W. China, N.E. Tibet. ❄❄❄.
'Atropurpureum' see 'Atrosanguineum'.
'Atrosanguineum' ▣ syn. 'Atropurpureum', has leaves that emerge from almost scarlet buds; the leaves are vivid crimson-purple when young, fading gradually to dark green above. Bears clustered panicles of rich cerise-pink flowers. **'Bowles' Crimson'** has darker red flowers, and leaves that are crimson beneath. **var. *tanguticum*** has leaves with jagged leaflets, emerging reddish green and becoming dark green, often purple-tinted, with age. Massive flowering stems bear erect panicles of numerous white, pink, or crimson flowers; ↕ 2m (6ft).

▷ **Rheumatism root** see *Jeffersonia diphylla*

RHEXIA
Meadow beauty
MELASTOMATACEAE

Genus of about 10 species of bristly perennials, some tuberous, others woody-based, from swamps or moist meadows in E. North America. They have square stems and opposite, oblong to ovate-lance-shaped, almost stalkless leaves with entire, usually hairy to bristly margins. They are cultivated for their shallowly saucer-shaped flowers, each with a short tube, 4 widely parted petals, and 8 prominent stamens, borne singly or in terminal cymes in summer. Grow in a sheltered border, bog garden, or wild garden.
• **HARDINESS** Fully hardy to frost hardy.
• **CULTIVATION** Grow in constantly moist, acid soil in full sun. In frost-prone areas that do not experience snow cover, protect the crown with a deep winter mulch. They dislike disturbance.
• **PROPAGATION** Sow seed at 13–18°C (55–64°F) in spring; before planting out, grow seedlings on, in containers in a cold frame, for up to 2 years to obtain strong plants. Divide in spring.
• **PESTS AND DISEASES** Susceptible to slug damage.

R. virginica (Meadow beauty). Bristly, tuberous perennial with square, slightly winged stems. Almost stalkless, oval to oblong-lance-shaped, mid-green leaves, to 5cm (2in) long, are hairy above, with

Rheum 'Ace of Hearts'

Rheum palmatum 'Atrosanguineum'

R

3–5 prominent veins and hair-fringed margins. In mid- and late summer, few-flowered cymes of shallowly saucer-shaped, short-tubed purple flowers, 4cm (1½in) across, open from red-bristly buds. ↕ 22–45cm (9–18in), ↔ 15cm (6in). E. North America (Nova Scotia to Texas). ❄❄❄

▷ ***Rhipsalidopsis*** see *Hatiora*
R. gaertneri see *H. gaertneri*
R. rosea see *H. rosea*

RHIPSALIS

CACTACEAE

Genus of about 50 species of mostly epiphytic or rock-dwelling perennial cacti from wooded and forested areas of Central and South America and the West Indies, with one species found in tropical Africa, Madagascar, and Sri Lanka. They often have aerial roots and freely branching stems, which vary in shape from cylindrical to winged, or flat and leaf-like, and may be ribbed or angled, some having spines or bristles. Small, funnel-shaped, diurnal flowers are borne singly or in small clusters from the areoles, mainly from spring to summer. These are followed by fleshy, berry-like, usually spherical fruits. In frost-prone areas, grow as houseplants in containers or hanging baskets, or in a temperate or warm greenhouse. In frost-free regions, grow epiphytically on a tree, or in a sheltered, humid border.

- **HARDINESS** Frost tender.
- **CULTIVATION** Under glass, grow in epiphytic cactus compost in bright filtered or indirect light with moderate to high humidity. Mist daily in warm weather. In growth, water freely and apply a balanced liquid fertilizer 3 or 4 times; water sparingly at other times. Outdoors, grow in an open site in fertile, humus-rich, moist but sharply drained soil in partial shade. See also pp.48–49.
- **PROPAGATION** Sow seed at 19–24°C (66–75°F), or root cuttings of stem sections, in spring or summer.
- **PESTS AND DISEASES** Susceptible to mealybugs.

R. baccifera, syn. *R. cassutha* (Mistletoe cactus). Pendent, epiphytic cactus with aerial roots and cylindrical, sparsely branched, mid-green stems, 4–6mm (⅛–¼in) thick. Minute areoles bear clusters of funnel-shaped white flowers, 5–10mm (¼–½in) long, from winter to

Rhipsalis cereuscula

Rhipsalis floccosa

spring, then spherical, translucent white or pale pink fruit, 5–8mm (¼–⅜in) across. ↕ to 4m (12ft), ↔ 60cm (24in). Africa, Madagascar, Sri Lanka, Tropical America. ❄ (min. 7–12°C/ 45–54°F)
R. capilliformis see *R. teres*.
R. cassutha see *R. baccifera*.
R. cereuscula ▣ Erect then pendent, epiphytic cactus producing cylindrical, many-branched, mid-green stems, 4mm (⅛in) thick, with whorls of short, jointed branches. In spring, woolly, few-bristled areoles at the tips of the short branches bear usually solitary, narrowly funnel-shaped white flowers, 1.5cm (½in) long, with pinkish green sepals. These are followed by obovoid white fruit, 5mm (¼in) across. ↕ to 60cm (24in), ↔ 40cm (16in). Brazil, Paraguay, Argentina. ❄ (min. 7–12°C/45–54°F)
R. crispata. Semi-pendent, epiphytic cactus producing branching, flat, leaf-like, light green stems, 2–4cm (¾–1½in) thick, with elliptic, inversely lance-shaped or obovate segments, with sometimes 3-winged, scalloped margins. In early summer, minute, spineless areoles bear solitary, funnel-shaped, creamy white flowers, 1.5cm (½in) across, followed by spherical white, sometimes red-flushed fruit, 8–10mm (⅜–½in) across. ↕ 60cm (24in), ↔ indefinite. S.E. Brazil. ❄ (min. 7–12°C/45–54°F)
R. fasciculata. Erect or semi-pendent, epiphytic cactus (sometimes included in *R. baccifera*) producing cylindrical, branching, pale bluish green stems, 6mm (¼in) thick, with woolly, few-bristled areoles along the margins. In early summer, the areoles bear funnel-shaped, white or pale greenish white flowers, to 8mm (⅜in) long, singly or in small clusters. The spherical white fruit are 4–5mm (⅛–¼in) across. ↕ to 60cm (24in), ↔ to 30cm (12in). Brazil. ❄ (min. 7–12°C/ 45–54°F)
R. floccosa ▣ syn. *R. tucumanensis.* Pendent, epiphytic cactus with aerial roots and cylindrical, branching, mid-green stems, to 1cm (½in) thick. Stem segments are arranged in whorls of 2–6, and have slightly woolly, sunken areoles bearing solitary, funnel-shaped, pink-tipped, white or creamy white flowers, 1.5cm (½in) long, from winter to spring. These are followed by spherical white, sometimes pink-tinged fruit, 5–10mm (¼–½in) across. ↕ 45cm (18in), ↔ 24cm (10in). Brazil, Bolivia, N. Paraguay, Argentina. ❄ (min. 7–12°C/45–54°F)
R. paradoxa. Pendent, epiphytic cactus with aerial roots and branching, mid-green stems, 3–5cm (1¼–2in) thick. Stems have long, 3-angled segments, twisted into shorter segments every 2–6cm (¾–2½in), with white wool at the top of each angle. Funnel-shaped white flowers, 2cm (¾in) across, are borne singly from sunken areoles in late spring. They are followed by spherical red fruit, 8mm (⅜in) across. ↕ 1m (3ft) or more, ↔ indefinite. S.E. Brazil. ❄ (min. 7–12°C/45–54°F)
R. teres ▣ syn. *R. capilliformis.* Pendent, epiphytic cactus producing cylindrical, jointed, pale green stems with bunches of side branches, 2–3mm (¹⁄₁₆–⅛in) thick. The stems have slightly woolly, bristly areoles and, near the tips of the joints, minute, bristleless areoles bearing clusters of funnel-shaped, glossy, greenish white flowers, to 8mm (⅜in) long, in late spring. These are followed by spherical white fruit, 4–5mm (⅛–¼in) across. ↕ 40cm (16in) or more, ↔ 30cm (12in). E. Brazil. ❄ (min. 7–12°C/45–54°F)
R. tucumanensis see *R. floccosa.*

Rhipsalis teres

RHODANTHE

syn. ACROCLINIUM
Strawflower

ASTERACEAE/COMPOSITAE

Genus of over 40 species of erect, drought-tolerant annuals, perennials, and subshrubs, frequently included in the genera *Acroclinium* and *Helipterum*, occurring in arid areas of Australia. They are cultivated for their solitary or corymb-like clusters of daisy-like, straw-

Rhodanthe chlorocephala subsp. *rosea*

Rhodanthe manglesii

textured, "everlasting", single to double, yellow, white, or pink flowerheads, borne mainly in summer. The alternate leaves are entire, linear to oblong or obovate, and mid- to grey-green. Grow strawflowers in an annual or mixed border; the perennials and subshrubs are usually grown as annuals, even in frost-free areas. The flowerheads are excellent for using in dried flower arrangements.

- **HARDINESS** Half hardy.
- **CULTIVATION** Grow in light, well-drained, preferably poor soil in full sun. Cut for drying before flowerheads are fully open, and hang upside down in a cool, dry, dark place.
- **PROPAGATION** Sow seed at 16°C (61°F) in early spring and plant out when all danger of frost has passed, or sow *in situ* in mid-spring.
- **PESTS AND DISEASES** Seedlings and young plants are prone to aphids and slug damage.

R. chlorocephala* subsp. *rosea ▣ syn. *Acroclinium roseum, Helipterum roseum.* Fast-growing, erect annual producing linear, pointed, stem-clasping, grey-green leaves, to 3.5cm (1½in) long. In summer, bears solitary, daisy-like flowerheads, 2.5–8cm (1–3in) across, with yellow disc-florets surrounded by spreading, papery, white or rose-pink bracts, often with white bases. The flowerheads close in dull weather. ↕ 30–60cm (12–24in), ↔ 15cm (6in). S.W. Australia. ❄
R. manglesii ▣ syn. *Helipterum manglesii.* Erect, bushy annual with oblong to ovate, pointed, grey-green leaves, to 10cm (4in) long. From summer to early autumn, bears stiff-stemmed clusters of small, daisy-like flowerheads, to 3cm (1¼in) across, with light yellow disc-florets surrounded by decorative, spreading, papery, red, pink, or white bracts. ↕ 60cm (24in), ↔ 15cm (6in). W. Australia. ❄

RHODANTHEMUM

syn. CHRYSANTHEMOPSIS, PYRETHROPSIS

ASTERACEAE/COMPOSITAE

Genus of about 10 species of mat-forming, often rhizomatous perennials and subshrubs, previously included in the genera *Chrysanthemum* or *Leucanthemum*, from exposed rocky areas in N. Africa, with one species from Spain. They are cultivated for their solitary, large, daisy-like flowerheads,

R

Rhodanthemum hosmariense

Rhodiola rosea

surrounded by prominent, usually green bracts, borne on erect, branched or unbranched stems, mainly in spring and summer. The deeply or shallowly 3-lobed leaves are hairy and sometimes silvery. Grow in a sunny rock garden, a raised bed, at the base of a warm, sunny wall, or in an alpine house.

- **HARDINESS** Most are hardy to -10°C (14°F) in very well-drained soil, but resent excessive winter wet.
- **CULTIVATION** Under glass, grow in loam-based potting compost (JI No.2) in full light. In the growing season, water freely and apply a balanced liquid fertilizer monthly; water moderately in winter. Outdoors, grow in moderately fertile, very well-drained soil in full sun.
- **PROPAGATION** Sow seed in containers in a cold frame in spring. Root softwood cuttings in early summer.
- **PESTS AND DISEASES** Susceptible to aphids and red spider mites under glass.

R. atlanticum, syn. *Chrysanthemum atlanticum, Pyrethropsis atlantica.* Prostrate, rhizomatous perennial with unbranched stems and 3-lobed, hairy, mid-green leaves, to 4cm (1½in) long, the middle lobe divided into 3, the outer lobes finely divided. In summer, bears solitary, daisy-like flowerheads, 3cm (1¼in) across, with white ray-florets, flushed pink beneath, and yellow disc-florets. ↕ 8cm (3in), ↔ 30cm (12in). Morocco. ❄❄

R. catananche, syn. *Chrysanthemum catananche, Pyrethropsis catananche.* Rhizomatous perennial producing unbranched stems and hairy, silver-grey leaves, to 6cm (2½in) long, irregularly cut into 3 toothed lobes. In summer, bears solitary, daisy-like flowerheads, to 5cm (2in) across, with cream ray-florets, each with a maroon stripe, surrounding deep yellow disc-florets. ↕ 15cm (6in), ↔ 30cm (12in). Morocco. ❄❄

R. gayanum, syn. *Chrysanthemum gayanum, Pyrethropsis gayana.* Semi-erect subshrub with branching stems and deeply 3-lobed, softly hairy, grey-green leaves, 2.5cm (1in) long. In summer, freely bears solitary, daisy-like flowerheads, 2.5–4cm (1–1½in) across, with rose-pink or white, pink-backed ray-florets and brown disc-florets. ↕↔ to 30cm (12in). Morocco, Algeria. ❄❄

R. hosmariense ■ syn. *Chrysanthemum hosmariense, Leucanthemum hosmariense, Pyrethropsis hosmariensis.* Spreading, bushy subshrub with stalkless, softly hairy, intensely silver, deeply 3-lobed leaves, to 4cm (1½in) long. From early spring to autumn, bears solitary, short-stemmed, daisy-like flowerheads, to 5cm (2in) across, with white ray-florets and wide centres of yellow disc-florets. The flowerheads are surrounded by silvery bracts, the outer ones with black margins. It is the easiest species to grow in the open garden; in an alpine house it flowers for most of the year, if deadheaded. ↕ 10–30cm (4–12in), ↔ 30cm (12in). Morocco (Atlas Mountains). ❄❄

R. maresii, syn. *Chrysanthemum maresii, Pyrethropsis maresii.* Spreading subshrub, similar to *R. hosmariense*, with deeply 3-lobed, softly hairy, silver-green leaves, to 6cm (2½in) long. In summer, bears solitary, daisy-like flowerheads, 2–4cm (¾–1½in) across, with yellow ray-florets and yellow disc-florets that become increasingly purple-tinged with age. ↕ 10–30cm (4–12in), ↔ 30cm (12in). Algeria. ❄❄

RHODIOLA

CRASSULACEAE

Genus of about 50 species of perennials, some dioecious, widely distributed in the N. hemisphere in sunny, rocky habitats. They have thick, fleshy rhizomes producing scaly brown basal leaves, and stiffly erect, unbranched or occasionally branched stems that bear alternate, triangular-ovate to lance-shaped, often toothed, fleshy, grey-green stem leaves. The small, star-shaped, green, yellow, orange, or red flowers, with 8–10 prominent stamens, are borne in dense, rounded, terminal, corymb- or raceme-like heads, and may be unisexual or bisexual. Rhodiolas are cultivated for their foliage and flowers, and are suitable for a rock garden, or the front of a mixed or herbaceous border.

- **HARDINESS** Fully hardy.
- **CULTIVATION** Grow in moderately fertile soil in full sun.
- **PROPAGATION** Sow seed in containers in a cold frame in spring or autumn. Divide rhizomes in spring or early summer. Root leaf cuttings in summer.
- **PESTS AND DISEASES** Prone to aphids.

Rhodiola heterodonta

R. heterodonta ■ syn. *Sedum heterodontum, S. rosea* var. *heterodontum.* Erect, hairless, dioecious, rhizomatous perennial with branching stems of ovate, fleshy, greyish green leaves, 2.5–3cm (1–1¼in) long, either entire or with a few coarse teeth. In late spring and early summer, bears dense, terminal cymes of numerous star-shaped yellow flowers, 3mm (⅛in) across, opening from rounded red buds in late spring and early summer. Male flowers have red or purple-red anthers that colour the whole of the flowerheads; females have purple-tipped carpels. ↕↔ to 40cm (16in). Afghanistan, Pamir Mountains, W. Himalayas, Tibet. ❄❄❄

R. rosea ■ syn. *Sedum rosea, S. rhodiola* (Roseroot). Variable, clump-forming, dioecious, rhizomatous perennial with purple stems bearing broadly ovate to narrowly inversely lance-shaped, entire or irregularly toothed, glaucous, fleshy, grey-green leaves, to 4cm (1½in) long, with red-tinted tips. In summer, bears dense, terminal, corymb- or umbel-like heads of numerous male or female, yellow-green flowers, 6mm (¼in) across, opening from slightly pink buds. ↕ 5–30cm (2–12in), ↔ 20cm (8in). Throughout N. hemisphere. ❄❄❄. **subsp. *integrifolia*** has smaller leaves, and red-purple, sometimes green flowers often borne on reddish green stems.

R. wallichiana, syn. *Sedum crassipes, S. wallichianum.* Erect, rhizomatous, hairless perennial with linear-lance-shaped, slightly toothed, mid-green leaves, 1–3cm (½–1¼in) long. In early summer, bears dense but few-flowered, terminal, corymb-like flowerheads with bisexual, star-shaped, pale yellow to greenish white flowers, 5–10mm (¼–½in) across, sometimes tinged pink. ↕ to 35cm (14in), ↔ 30cm (12in). W. Himalayas, W. China, Tibet. ❄❄❄

▷ ***Rhodocactus grandifolius*** see *Pereskia grandifolia*

RHODOCHITON

SCROPHULARIACEAE

Genus of 3 species of deciduous, perennial climbers found in woodland in Mexico. They are cultivated for their flowers, which have pendent, long-tubed corollas, with 5 rounded segments, and inflated calyces. Twining leaf-stalks bear alternate, simple, sparsely toothed leaves. In frost-prone areas, grow as annuals outdoors, or in a cool greenhouse. In frost-free areas, use to cover a pergola or arch.

- **HARDINESS** Frost tender.
- **CULTIVATION** Under glass, grow in loam-based potting compost (JI No.2) in full light with shade from hot sun. When in growth, water freely and apply a balanced liquid fertilizer monthly; keep just moist in winter. Pot on in spring. Outdoors, grow in fertile, humus-rich, moist but well-drained soil in full sun.
- **PROPAGATION** Sow seed at 15–18°C (59–64°F) as soon as ripe or in spring.
- **PESTS AND DISEASES** Prone to red spider mites and whiteflies under glass.

R. atrosanguineus ■ syn. *R. volubile.* Slender-stemmed climber producing heart-shaped, rich green leaves, 4–8cm (1½–3in) long. Long, pendent stalks bear solitary, tubular, black to reddish purple flowers, 4.5cm (1¾in) long, with cup-shaped, rose-pink or mauve calyces, from summer to autumn. ↕ to 3m (10ft), sometimes more. Mexico. ❀ (min. 3–5°C/37–41°F)

R. volubile see *R. atrosanguineus.*

Rhodochiton atrosanguineus

R

RHODODENDRON

syn. AZALEA

ERICACEAE

Genus of 500–900 species of evergreen and deciduous trees and shrubs, sometimes epiphytic, from Europe, Asia, Australasia, and North America, particularly S.W. China, Tibet, Burma, N. India, and New Guinea. They occur in diverse habitats, from dense forest to alpine tundra, and from sea level to high altitudes. They vary greatly in habit (see panel below), and may reach a height of 25m (80ft) or creep at ground level to form prostrate shrubs.

The leaves are mostly lance-shaped and mid- to dark green, ranging in size from 4mm (⅛in) to 75cm (30in) long. All hybrids described below conform to one of the following leaf length ranges: very large, 45–75cm (18–30in) long; large, 15–45cm (6–18in) long; medium-sized, 5–15cm (2–6in) long; small, 1–5cm (½–2in) long; very small, 4–10mm (⅛–½in) long. Some have leaves and young stems covered with an indumentum (a dense woolly covering of hairs or scales); a few have leaves that are aromatic when crushed.

Rhododendrons are grown mainly for their spectacular, sometimes strongly scented flowers, which are borne singly or in lateral or terminal racemes (known as trusses), from late autumn to late summer. The individual flowers vary greatly in size and shape (see panel below), but are usually 5-lobed, and often marked with flares or spots inside, on the upper or lower lobes or in the throats; some also have conspicuous or brightly coloured, basal nectar pouches inside. There are thousands of hybrids, encompassing nearly every flower colour. Some rhododendrons also have attractive young growth, which ranges in colour from red to bronze-brown or metallic blue-green; a few have decorative, exfoliating bark, which may be any colour from brown-pink or deep maroon to silvery grey. A number of the deciduous rhododendrons are valued for their autumn colour.

Rhododendrons have a wide range of garden uses: dwarf alpine varieties are effective in a rock garden; larger woodland rhododendrons are excellent for brightening shady areas; the "iron-clad" (or "hardy hybrid") rhododendrons are tolerant of more exposed sites and also suitable for hedges or informal screens; and many of the modern compact hybrids are ideal for growing on shaded patios, or in containers or tubs. In frost-prone areas, tender rhododendrons, including Vireyas, are best grown in a conservatory or cool greenhouse. The nectar of some rhododendron flowers may cause severe discomfort if ingested.

In horticulture, rhododendrons are often divided into 4 main groups: evergreen rhododendrons, Vireya rhododendrons, azaleas, and azaleodendrons.

RHODODENDRON FLOWER FORMS

Rhododendron flowers are tubular-, funnel-, trumpet-, or bell-shaped, or may take a form between these shapes. A few have saucer-shaped or hose-in-hose flowers (with 2 flower tubes, one inside the other).

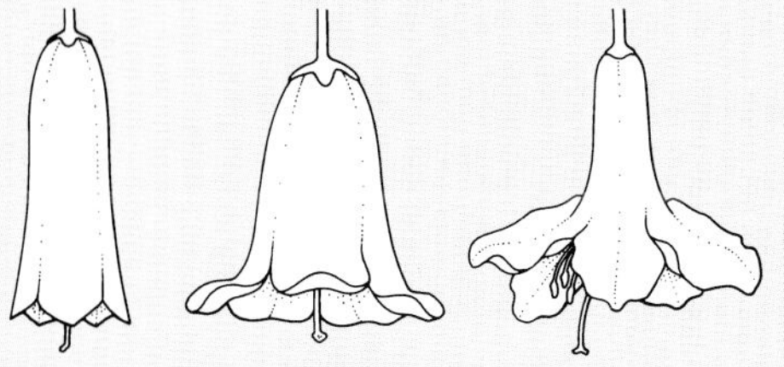

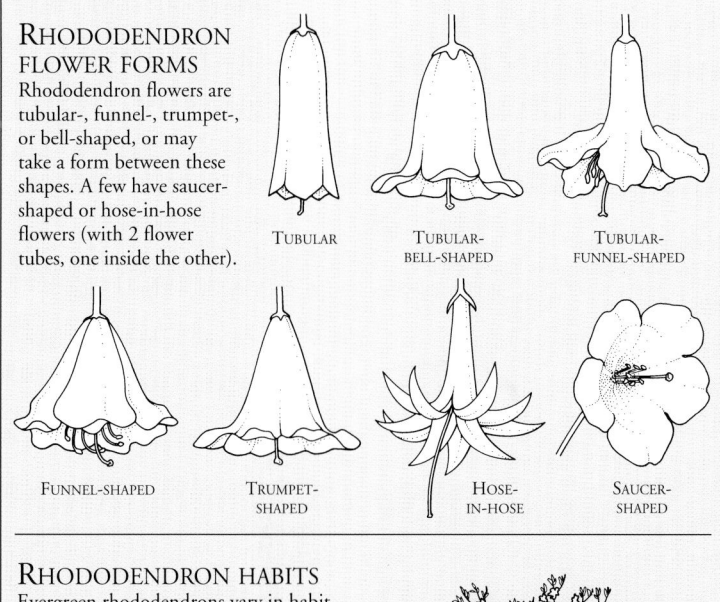

TUBULAR — TUBULAR-BELL-SHAPED — TUBULAR-FUNNEL-SHAPED

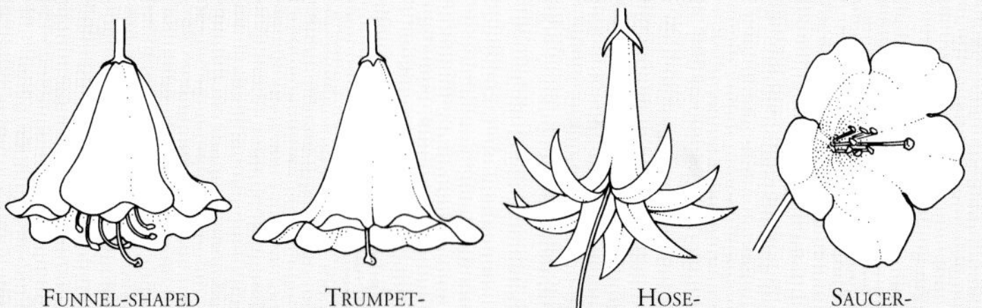

FUNNEL-SHAPED — TRUMPET-SHAPED — HOSE-IN-HOSE — SAUCER-SHAPED

RHODODENDRON HABITS

Evergreen rhododendrons vary in habit from small shrubs to large trees. Azaleas and Vireyas are both shrubby.

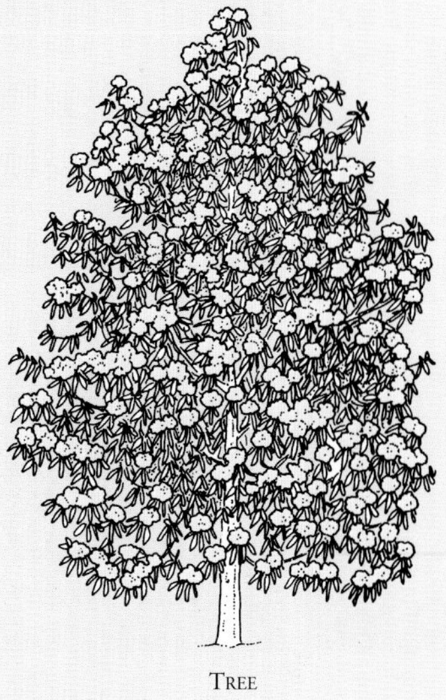

TREE

DECIDUOUS AZALEA

SMALL ROUNDED SHRUB

Evergreen rhododendrons
Unless otherwise stated, all evergreen shrubs and trees described on the following pages fall into this group, which includes the "iron-clad" rhododendrons (often known as "hardy hybrids"), derived from *R. catawbiense*, *R. caucasicum*, and *R. ponticum* crosses. Evergreen rhododendrons vary in habit from small, cushion-forming shrubs to tree rhododendrons. They have small to large leaves and flowers in a variety of shapes, sizes, and colours.

Vireya rhododendrons
Sometimes known as Malesian rhododendrons, these are evergreen, usually epiphytic shrubs from tropical areas of S.E. Asia, and are frost tender. They have scaly leaves and stems. The flowers are extremely varied in shape, colour, and season; a range of plants will give flowers throughout the year. Grow in a cool greenhouse or conservatory. Containers will restrict the spread of larger plants.

Evergreen and deciduous azaleas
These are small to medium-leaved shrubs belonging to the botanical Section *Azalea* within the genus *Rhododendron*, and commonly known to gardeners as azaleas. They bear a profusion of small to large trusses of usually small flowers in a variety of shapes. Azalea hybrids may be further divided into the following subgroups:
***Deciduous hybrid azaleas* – Ghent (Gandavense) hybrids** are Belgian-raised, fully hardy azaleas, resulting from crosses between American azalea species and *R. luteum.* The funnel-shaped, white, yellow, orange, pink, or red flowers, borne in early summer, are long-tubed, sometimes double, and usually scented. **Knap Hill-Exbury hybrids** are English hybrid azaleas with complex origins (American azalea species x *R. molle*), characterized by large trusses of trumpet-shaped, scented or scentless flowers, in a wide range of bright colours, borne in mid- to late spring. **Mollis hybrids** have Dutch and Belgian origins, and are a result of crossing selections of *R. molle* subsp. *japonicum* and *R. molle.* Funnel-shaped, unscented flowers, in a wide range of colours, including cream, yellow, pink, orange, or red, are borne before the leaves in late spring. **New Zealand Ilam hybrids** are a further selection developed from Knap Hill-Exbury hybrids. **Occidentale hybrids** are English azaleas, raised by crossing Mollis hybrids with *R. occidentale.* Funnel-shaped, usually scented, pink or white flowers are borne in summer, later than those of Ghent hybrids. **Rustica (Rustica Flore Pleno) hybrids** are sweet-scented, double-flowered azaleas, resulting from crosses between double-flowered Ghent hybrids and *R. molle* subsp. *japonicum.* Funnel-shaped, hose-in-hose, yellow, cream, white, pink, or red flowers are borne in late spring and early summer on compact bushes.
***Evergreen hybrid azaleas* – Gable hybrids** are azaleas raised by Joseph B. Gable in Pennsylvania, USA, using mainly *R. kaempferi* and *R. yedoense* var. *poukhanense* with other species and hybrids. The unscented flowers are funnel-shaped, mostly pink, red, or white, and borne in late spring and early summer. **Glenn Dale hybrids** are varied, complex azaleas raised in Glenn Dale, Maryland, USA. The relatively large, scented, funnel-shaped flowers, usually white or pink to red, are borne from spring to early summer. Some are frilled, semi-double, or multicoloured. **Indian (Indica) hybrids** are complex azaleas, mostly of Belgian origin, bred from *R. indicum*, *R. mucronatum*, *R. simsii*, and other species. In winter, they produce large, funnel-shaped, unscented flowers in a wide range of colours, and are popular for growing indoors in containers for winter decoration. **Kaempferi hybrids** are Dutch azaleas raised from *R. kaempferi*, *R.* 'Malvaticum', and *R.* 'Maxwellii'. They are taller, more hardy, and later-flowering than Kurume hybrids (below), which are also derived from *R. kaempferi.* They bear funnel-shaped, unscented, white, pink, or red flowers in spring, on bushes about 1.2m (4ft) tall. **Kurume hybrids** are Japanese-raised dwarf azaleas, originating from crosses between *R. kaempferi*, *R. kiusianum*, and *R.* 'Obtusum'. Numerous, very small, funnel-shaped, unscented flowers are borne in a wide range of colours in spring. They are particularly effective in massed plantings. **Kyushu hybrids** are very hardy Japanese azaleas. They are the result of a complex breeding programme, using *R. kiusianum* with other dwarf species to produce low-growing, compact plants with small, shiny leaves. They are exceptionally hardy, to -30°C (-22°F), and ideal for cold climates. Small, funnel-shaped, unscented flowers, in a wide range of colours, are borne in spring. **Oldhamii hybrids** are dwarf azaleas raised at Exbury, England. The large, funnel-shaped flowers are unscented and borne in a wide range of colours in spring. **Satsuki hybrids** are Japanese-raised azaleas, originally used for bonsai work. They have been bred using mainly *R. indicum* and *R. simsii.* Half hardy with a low, twiggy habit, they bear large, funnel-shaped, unscented flowers in white, pink, red, or purple, in summer. They have a tendency to sport. **Shammarello hybrids** were raised by Shammarello in N. Ohio, USA. They are ideal for growing in very cold climates, and are hardy from -20 to -26°C (-10 to -20°F). Many have been raised by crossing *R.* 'Hino-crimson' with *R. yedoense* var. *poukhanense.* They have small, trumpet-shaped, unscented flowers in a range of colours, borne in late spring. **Vuyk (Vuykiana) hybrids** were bred by Vuyk van Nes Nurseries in Holland, using a complex cross of *R. kaempferi* and *R. mucronulatum*, and probably other species. They bear very showy, medium-sized, funnel-shaped, unscented flowers in a range of colours, in late spring.

Azaleodendrons
This is a group of hybrids between deciduous azaleas and evergreen hybrid rhododendrons. They are generally fully hardy, semi-evergreen shrubs, 1–2.5m (3–8ft) tall, flowering in late spring and early summer. They produce cream, yellow, pink, or mauve flowers, some of which are fragrant.
• **HARDINESS** Fully hardy to frost tender.
• **CULTIVATION** Under glass, grow tender rhododendrons in lime-free (ericaceous) potting compost in bright filtered light with moderate to high humidity. When in growth, water freely with soft water and apply a balanced liquid fertilizer monthly; keep just moist in winter.

For Vireyas, use well-crocked containers and incorporate granulated bark, rotted bracken litter, or conifer needles to keep the compost open. Vireyas will tolerate a maximum day temperature of 32°C (90°F).

Indian hybrids grown as winter-flowering houseplants should be misted daily until the flower buds show colour; provide a maximum temperature of 13–16°C (55–61°F) when in bloom. Remove spent flowers and repot after flowering, then transfer to a cool greenhouse or window-sill in bright, indirect light. For the summer months, plunge pots in a shaded, well-ventilated cold frame and keep cool, moist, and humid; protect from any autumn frosts; bring plants indoors in early winter.

Outdoors, grow rhododendrons in moist but well-drained, leafy, humus-rich, acid soil (ideally pH4.5–5.5). Shallow planting is essential: all rhododendrons are surface-rooting and will not tolerate deep planting. Most large-leaved species and hybrids require dappled shade in sheltered woodland conditions; avoid the deep shade beneath a tree canopy. Most of the other groups, including the "iron clads" or "hardy hybrids", thrive in light dappled shade or part-day shade, but not in early morning sun; they will tolerate a more open site if given shelter from cold, dry winds. Most dwarf alpine species will tolerate full sun in cooler climates, provided the soil remains moist. Avoid frost pockets to reduce the risks of waterlogging and bark split. Mulch annually with leaf mould. After flowering, dead-head where practical, to promote vegetative growth rather than seed production. Pruning group 1 (deciduous), pruning group 8 (evergreen).
• **PROPAGATION** Surface-sow seed at 13–18°C (55–64°F) in ericaceous (lime-free) propagating compost or fine moss peat, as soon as ripe or in early spring. Sow seed of hardy dwarf species and hybrids in containers in a cold frame as soon as ripe. Rhododendrons hybridize freely and garden-collected seed may not come true; however, seed collected from species in the wild or from hand-pollinated garden plants will generally produce plants that are true to type. Root semi-ripe cuttings in late summer. Layer in autumn. Graft in late winter or late summer.
• **PESTS AND DISEASES** Susceptible to vine weevil, rhododendron and azalea whiteflies, leafhoppers, lacebugs, scale insects, caterpillars, aphids, powdery mildew, bud blast, honey fungus, rust, leafy gall, petal blight, silver leaf, *Phytophthora* root rot, and lime-induced chlorosis (if soil is not sufficiently acid).

***R.* 'A. Bedford'** see *R.* 'Arthur Bedford'.
R. aberconwayi. Upright, evergreen shrub with elliptic, leathery, dark green leaves, 3–7cm (1¼–3in) long. In mid-spring, bears trusses of 6–12, openly bell-shaped to saucer-shaped, white or pale pink flowers, to 10cm (4in) across, often purple-flecked inside. ↕↔ 1.5–2m (5–6ft). W. China. ❄❄❄
***R.* 'Addy Wery'.** Evergreen Kurume azalea with small leaves. In mid- and late spring, bears an abundance of funnel-shaped, vermilion-red flowers, 4.5cm (1¾in) long, in small trusses. ↕↔ 1.2m (4ft). ❄❄❄
R. adenogynum ♀ syn. *R. adenophorum.* Evergreen shrub or small tree with elliptic or narrowly elliptic, dark green leaves, 6–11cm (2½–4½in) long; the undersides have a thick, tawny indumentum, yellowish brown at first, becoming olive-brown when mature. Trusses of 4–12 funnel-shaped, pink-tinged white flowers, 3–4.5cm (1¼–1¾in) long, spotted crimson inside, or each with a reddish pink mark, are borne in mid-spring. ↕↔ 2.5m (8ft). S.W. China. ❄❄❄
R. adenophorum see *R. adenogynum.*
R. albrechtii ■ Twiggy, deciduous azalea with obovate, finely toothed, dark green leaves, 4–12cm (1½–5in) long, grey-downy beneath. Trusses of 3–5 widely bell-shaped, deep to purplish rose-pink flowers, 4–5cm (1½–2in) across, spotted olive-green inside, are borne in mid-spring. Tolerates full sun. ↕↔ 2.5m (8ft). Japan. ❄❄❄
***R.* 'Alison Johnstone'** ■ Evergreen shrub producing small, elliptic leaves with a metallic lustre. In spring, bears loose trusses of pendent, tubular-bell-shaped, pale yellow flowers, 4cm (1½in) long, flushed peach-pink inside. Prefers a sunny, sheltered site. ↕↔ 2m (6ft). ❄❄❄
***R.* 'Angelo'.** Tall, evergreen shrub with an open habit and medium-sized to large leaves. Trusses of 9–10 funnel-shaped, fragrant, very pale pink or white flowers, 13cm (5in) long, open in late spring and early summer. ↕↔ 4m (12ft). ❄❄❄
***R.* 'Anna Baldsiefen'.** Dwarf, compact, evergreen shrub of upright habit, with small, oblong-ovate leaves, turning bronze-red in winter. In early spring, bears dense trusses of numerous funnel-shaped, bright pink flowers, 3cm (1¼in) long, with deeper pink margins. ↕↔ 1m (3ft). ❄❄❄
***R.* 'Anna Rose Whitney'.** Evergreen shrub with large leaves. In late spring, bears loose, rounded trusses of widely funnel-shaped, deep rose-pink flowers, 6–10cm (2½–4in) across, spotted brown inside. ↕↔ 4m (12ft). ❄❄❄
R. anthopogon. Small, compact, evergreen shrub with ovate, elliptic, or rarely rounded, aromatic leaves, 1–3.5cm (½–1½in) long, dark green above, reddish brown and scaly beneath. In mid- and late spring bears dense clusters of 5–15 tubular white, pink, or rarely pale yellow flowers, 1–2cm (½–¾in) long, with spreading petal-lobes. ↕↔ to 1.5m (5ft). N. India, Nepal, Bhutan, W. China. ❄❄❄
R. anwheiense, syn. *R. maculiferum* subsp. *anwheiense.* Evergreen, rounded shrub with elliptic to oblong-elliptic, pale green leaves, 3–10cm (1¼–4in) long. In mid- and late spring, produces trusses of 6–12 openly bell-shaped, white flushed pink flowers, 2.5–4cm (1–1½in) long, spotted reddish purple inside. ↕↔ 1–2.5m (3–8ft). E. China. ❄❄❄
R. arborescens (Smooth azalea, Sweet azalea). Upright, deciduous shrub or small tree with obovate to elliptic, glossy, mid-green leaves, 4.5–10cm (1¾–4in) long, turning reddish green in autumn. In early summer, bears trusses of 3–7 funnel-shaped, cinnamon-scented, white to light pink flowers, 4–5cm (1½–2in) long, often with red stamens and a yellow blotch on the upper corolla lobe. ↕↔ 2.5–6m (8–20ft). S.E. and E. North America. ❄❄❄
R. arboreum ■♀ Evergreen tree producing inversely lance-shaped, dark green leaves, 7–19cm (3–7in) long, with a silvery, fawn, or cinnamon-brown indumentum beneath. Dense trusses of tubular-bell-shaped, red, pink, or white flowers, 3–5cm (1¼–2in) long, with black nectar pouches and black spots inside, are borne in early spring. ↕ 12m (40ft), ↔ 4m (12ft). China to Thailand, N. India, Bhutan, Sri Lanka. ❄❄
***R.* 'Arctic Tern'** see x *Ledodendron* 'Arctic Tern'.
***R.* 'Argosy'.** Late-flowering, vigorous, evergreen shrub or small tree with large inversely lanceolate, dark green leaves, to 18cm (7in) long. Bears trusses of 6–12 funnel-shaped, fragrant white flowers, 8–10cm (3–4in) long, with cream throats, in midsummer. ↕↔ 4m (12ft). ❄❄❄
R. argyrophyllum ■ Evergreen shrub with oblong to lance-shaped, dark green leaves, 3–6cm (1¼–2½in) long, with grey-white hairs beneath. In mid- and late spring, bears lax trusses of funnel- to bell-shaped, mid- to pale pink flowers, 3–6cm (1¼–2½in) long, spotted deep pink inside. ↕ 6m (20ft), ↔ 2.5m (8ft). S.W. China. ❄❄❄
R. arizelum see *R. rex* subsp. *arizelum.*
***R.* 'Arthur Bedford'**, syn. *R.* 'A. Bedford'. Vigorous, evergreen shrub with large leaves. In early summer, bears pyramid-shaped trusses of funnel-shaped, light mauve flowers, 5–9cm (2–3½in) long, each with a deep brown-red flare in the throat. Tolerant of sun. ↕↔ 3m (10ft). ❄❄❄
R. atlanticum (Coast azalea, Dwarf azalea). Suckering, deciduous shrub with ovate or obovate to elliptic, bluish green leaves, 3–5cm (1¼–2in) long. Trusses of 4–13 funnel-shaped, strongly musk-scented, white or pinkish white flowers, 3–4cm (1¼–1½in) long, are borne with or just before the leaves in late spring to early summer. ↕↔ 1–2m (3–6ft). S.E. North America. ❄❄❄
***R.* Augfast Group.** Compact, rounded evergreen shrubs with small, elliptic to ovate, dark green leaves, to 3cm (1¼in) long. In mid-spring bears trusses of about 15 broadly funnel-shaped, lavender-blue flowers, 1.5cm (½in) long. ↕↔ 80cm (32in). ❄❄❄
R. augustinii ■♀ Bushy, evergreen shrub or small tree producing oblong to lance-shaped, mid- to dark green leaves, 4–11cm (1½–4½in) long. Trusses of 2–5 broadly funnel-shaped, pale to deep blue or lavender-blue flowers, to 7cm (3in) across, spotted greenish brown inside, open in mid-spring. Will grow in full sun. ↕↔ 2.2m (7ft). China. ❄❄❄
R. auriculatum ♀ Multi-stemmed, spreading, evergreen shrub or small tree producing oblong to lance-shaped, dark green leaves, 15–30cm (6–12in) long, with ear-like lobes at their bases. In late summer, bears loose trusses of funnel-shaped, 7-lobed, very fragrant white flowers, 8–11cm (3–4½in) long, tinted green inside. ↕ to 10m (30ft), ↔ 5m (15ft). W. China. ❄❄❄
R. austrinum. Deciduous azalea with ovate to elliptic-obovate, dark green leaves, 5–10cm (2–4in) long, densely hairy and grey-green beneath. Trusses of 5–9 tubular-funnel-shaped, yellow to orange flowers, 3.5cm (1½in) long, with dark pink tubes, are borne in mid- to late spring. Will tolerate full sun. ↕↔ 3–5m (10–15ft). S. USA (Florida to Mississippi). ❄❄❄
***R.* 'Azor'.** Vigorous, evergreen shrub of open habit, with medium-sized leaves. In midsummer, bears loose trusses of funnel-shaped, fragrant, salmon-pink flowers, 6–9cm (2½–3½in) long, spotted red-brown inside. ↕↔ 4m (12ft). ❄❄❄
***R.* 'Azuma-kagami'** ■ Compact, evergreen Kurume azalea with small leaves. In mid-spring, bears numerous small trusses of hose-in-hose, bright pink flowers, 3cm (1¼in) long. ↕↔ 1.2m (4ft). ❄❄❄
***R.* 'Baden-Baden'.** Compact, spreading, evergreen shrub with medium-sized, often slightly twisted, elliptic, dark green leaves, to 9cm (3½in) long. In late

Rhododendron albrechtii

Rhododendron 'Alison Johnstone'

Rhododendron arboreum

Rhododendron argyrophyllum

Rhododendron augustinii

Rhododendron 'Azuma-kagami'

R

RHODODENDRON

spring bears loose trusses of broadly funnel-shaped, waxy, cherry red flowers, 3–4cm (1¼–1½in) long. ↕ 1m (3ft), ↔ 1.5m (5ft). ❄❄❄

R. barbatum ◯ Multi-stemmed, tall, evergreen shrub or small tree with bristly leaf-stalks and young stems, and peeling, reddish purple bark. Produces elliptic to obovate, dark green leaves, 9–19cm (3½–7in) long. Tight trusses of tubular to bell-shaped, bright scarlet flowers, 3.5–5cm (1½–2in) long, with crimson-black nectar pouches inside, are borne in early spring. ↕↔ 6m (20ft). Himalayas. ❄❄❄

***R.* 'Beauty of Littleworth'** ■ Vigorous, showy, evergreen shrub with large leaves. In late spring, bears cone-shaped trusses of funnel-shaped, fragrant white flowers, 10–15cm (4–6in) long, spotted crimson inside. Only suitable for dappled shade. ↕↔ 4m (12ft). ❄❄❄

***R.* 'Beethoven'** ■ Dwarf, evergreen Vuyk azalea with small leaves. In late spring, bears lax trusses of funnel-shaped, fringe-petalled, magenta-pink flowers, 5cm (2in) long, each with a deeper mauve mark inside. ↕↔ 1.3m (4½ft). ❄❄❄

***R.* 'Berryrose'.** Mound-forming, evergreen shrub with sparse, medium-sized leaves. Compact trusses of tubular-funnel-shaped, bright apricot-orange flowers, 10cm (4in) long, are borne in late spring. ↕↔ 1.5m (5ft). ❄❄❄

***R.* 'Blue Diamond'** ■ Dwarf, small-leaved, evergreen shrub with a compact, upright habit. In mid- and late spring, bears trusses of up to 5 funnel-shaped, violet-blue flowers, 5cm (2in) long. Prefers full sun. ↕↔ 1.5m (5ft). ❄❄❄

***R.* 'Blue Peter'** ■ Large-leaved, evergreen shrub of open habit. In early summer, bears tight, rounded trusses of funnel-shaped, lavender-blue flowers, 7cm (3in) long, with frilled petals and purple marks inside. Tolerates full sun. ↕↔ 3m (10ft). ❄❄❄

***R.* 'Blue Tit'.** Dwarf, compact, evergreen shrub with small leaves that are a distinctive yellowish green when young, mid-green when mature. Trusses of 2 or 3 funnel-shaped, grey-blue flowers, 0.7–2.5cm (¼–1in) long, are borne at the tips of the shoots in early and mid-spring. Suitable for a rock garden in full sun. ↕↔ 1m (3ft). ❄❄❄

***R.* 'Bow Bells'.** Free-flowering, compact, evergreen shrub with small to medium-sized, broadly ovate to rounded leaves, reddish bronze when young, mid-green when mature. In late spring, bears lax trusses of long-stalked, bell-shaped, light pink flowers, 5–6cm (2–2½in) long. ↕↔ 2m (6ft). ❄❄❄

R. brachysiphon see *R. maddenii.*

***R.* 'Britannia'.** Low but relatively broad, evergreen shrub with medium-sized, pale green leaves. Dense trusses of bell-shaped, bright scarlet flowers, 5–7cm (2–3in) long, are borne in early summer. ↕ 1.5m (5ft), ↔ 2.2m (7ft). ❄❄❄

R. bullatum see *R. edgeworthii.*

R. bureaui see *R. bureavii.*

R. bureavii ■ syn. *R. bureaui.* Multi-stemmed, evergreen shrub producing ovate to lance-shaped, dark green leaves, 4.5–12cm (1¾–5in) long, initially covered with a light brown indumentum above and a woolly, bright orange-brown indumentum beneath. In mid-spring, produces neat trusses of tubular-

Rhododendron 'Blue Diamond'

bell-shaped, white or soft pink flowers, 2.5–4cm (1–1½in) long, spotted crimson. ↕↔ 3m (10ft). S.W. China. ❄❄❄

R. calendulaceum. Robust, deciduous azalea with elliptic-oblong, mid-green leaves, 3.5–9cm (1½–3½in) long, softly hairy on both sides. In late spring and early summer, bears lax trusses of funnel-shaped, bright orange to scarlet flowers, to 5cm (2in) long, usually opening with the leaves, or just after they emerge. Prefers full sun. ↕↔ 2.5m (8ft). E. USA. ❄❄❄

R. calophytum ■◯ Many-stemmed, evergreen shrub or small tree with oblong to inversely lance-shaped, dark green leaves, 14–30cm (5½–12in) long. In early spring, bears large trusses of broadly bell-shaped, 5- to 7-lobed, fragrant, pale pink flowers, to 7cm (3in) across, with basal, carmine-red marks in the throats. ↕ 10m (30ft), ↔ 6m (20ft). S.W. China, Tibet. ❄❄❄

R. calostrotum ■ Compact, dwarf, evergreen shrub with oblong-ovate to rounded leaves, 1–3cm (½–1¼in) long, scaly and glaucous above, with dense brown scales beneath. In late spring and early summer, freely bears solitary or pairs of saucer-shaped, bright rose-purple flowers, 2–4cm (¾–1½in) across, often with purple spots on the upper lobes. Tolerates full sun if kept moist. ↕ 75cm (30in), ↔ 90cm (36in). N.E. India, Tibet, W. China. ❄❄❄. **subsp. *keleticum*,** syn. *R. keleticum*, is almost prostrate, with glossy, dark green leaves, 2–9mm (1/16–3/8in) long, densely brown-scaly beneath. Bears trusses of up to 3 widely funnel-shaped, purplish crimson flowers, crimson-spotted inside; ↕ 30cm (12in), ↔ 90cm (36in). S.E. Tibet, S.W. China, N.E. Burma.

R. campanulatum ■◯ Vigorous, evergreen shrub or small tree producing oblong-elliptic, dark green leaves, 7–14cm (3–5½in) long, with a dense, suede-like brown indumentum beneath. In mid-spring, bears trusses of 8–15 broadly bell-shaped, lilac-blue, some-times white flowers, 5cm (2in) across, with darker spots inside. ↕↔ 4m (12ft). Himalayas. ❄❄❄

R. campylocarpum ■◯ Robust, evergreen shrub or small tree with neat, elliptic-ovate, dark green leaves, 3–10cm (1¼–4in) long, pale grey-green beneath. Trusses of 3–15 delicate, bell-shaped, pale to mid-yellow flowers, 2.5–4cm (1–1½in) long, are borne in mid-spring. Some variants have deep red basal marks inside. ↕ to 5m (15ft), ↔ 4m (12ft). S.E. Tibet, S.W. China, N.E. Burma. ❄❄❄

R. campylogynum. Dwarf, compact, evergreen shrub with inversely lance-shaped leaves, 1–3.5cm (½–1½in) long, glossy, dark green above, often off-white or silver beneath. In late spring, bears small trusses of long-stemmed, nodding, broadly bell-shaped flowers, 1–2.5cm (½–1in) long, varying in colour from white or pink to purple or purplish black. Suitable for growing in a rock garden in full sun. ↕↔ 75cm (30in). E. India (Arunachal Pradesh), Tibet, W. China, N.E. Burma. ❄❄❄

R. camtschaticum. Deciduous shrub with an unusual, dwarf, procumbent habit and obovate, hairy-margined, mid-green leaves, 2–5cm (¾–2in) long, on hairy shoots. Saucer-shaped, reddish purple or pink flowers, 2.5cm (1in) across, each with a leafy calyx, are borne singly or in pairs in late spring and early summer. ↕ to 30cm (12in), ↔ 90cm (36in). E. Asia, Alaska. ❄❄❄

***R.* 'Carita'** ■ Neat, evergreen shrub, becoming more open with age, with medium-sized leaves. In mid-spring, bears flat-topped trusses of funnel-shaped flowers, 5cm (2in) long, pale pink to pale lemon yellow, each with a small, cerise-red, basal flash in the throat. ↕↔ 2.5m (8ft). ❄❄❄

***R.* 'Carmen'.** Dwarf, evergreen shrub with small, dark green leaves. Loose trusses of 2–5 tubular-bell-shaped, waxy, dark red flowers, 3–6cm (1¼–2½in) long, are produced in mid-spring. ↕ 1m (3ft), ↔ 1.2m (4ft). ❄❄❄

R. carolinianum see *R. minus.*

R. catawbiense. Evergreen shrub with oblong-ovate, glossy, dark green leaves, 7–15cm (3–6in) long, paler beneath. Large trusses of funnel-bell-shaped, reddish purple flowers, 3–4.5cm (1¼–1¾in) long, are produced in late spring and early summer. Thrives in full sun; very hardy. ↕↔ 3m (10ft). E. North America. ❄❄❄

***R.* 'Catawbiense Album'.** Vigorous, shrubby, evergreen "iron-clad" rhododendron with medium-sized leaves. In early summer, pale lilac buds open to conical trusses of bell-shaped white flowers, 6–8cm (2½–3in) long, with green flashes in the throats. Tolerates sun and wind. ↕↔ 3m (10ft). ❄❄❄

***R.* 'Cécile'** ■ Vigorous, deciduous Knap Hill-Exbury azalea with medium-sized leaves. In late spring, dark salmon-pink buds open to dense, rounded trusses of tubular-funnel-shaped, clear salmon-pink flowers, 5cm (2in) long, with yellow flares in the throats. ↕↔ 2.2m (7ft). ❄❄❄

***R.* 'Chikor'.** Dwarf, evergreen shrub with a neat habit and small, dark green leaves, bronze-tinted in winter. Trusses of 3–6 saucer-shaped, clear yellow flowers, 3cm (1¼in) across, are borne in mid-spring. ↕↔ 60cm (24in). ❄❄❄

***R.* 'Chionoides'.** Dense, evergreen shrub with medium-sized leaves. In mid- and late spring, bears dense trusses of funnel-shaped, pure white flowers, 5cm (2in) long, each with a conspicuous yellow flare on the inside of the upper lobe. Tolerant of wind, sun, and heat. ↕↔ 2m (6ft). ❄❄❄

***R.* 'Christmas Cheer'.** Dense, compact, evergreen shrub with medium-sized leaves. Numerous trusses of funnel-shaped, whitish pink flowers, 4.5cm (1¾in) long, open in late winter and early spring. ↕↔ 2m (6ft). ❄❄❄

R. ciliatum. Semi-dwarf, compact, evergreen shrub with oblong-elliptic leaves, 4.5–9cm (1¾–3½in) long, dark green above, paler green beneath, and with hairy margins. Small trusses of 2–4 tubular-bell-shaped, pinkish white flowers, 2–3cm (¾–1¼in) long, open in early and mid-spring. Tolerates full sun. ↕↔ 2m (6ft). E. Himalayas. ❄❄

***R.* 'Cilpinense'** ■ Showy, compact, small-leaved, evergreen shrub. In early spring, bears profuse trusses of up to 3 funnel-shaped, pale to mid-pink flowers, 4.5–5cm (1¾–2in) long. Flowers are vulnerable to early frosts. ↕↔ 1.1m (3½ft). ❄❄❄

R. cinnabarinum ■ Vigorous, erect, evergreen shrub producing neat, aromatic, elliptic-obovate, hairless, dark green leaves, 3–9cm (1¼–3½in) long, with a metallic grey-green sheen above, scaly beneath. Loose trusses of pendent, narrowly tubular-bell-shaped, waxy, red, some-times yellow, orange, apricot-pink, or reddish purple flowers, 2.5–3.5cm (1–1½in) long, are borne from mid-spring to early summer. ↕ 6m (20ft), ↔ 2m (6ft). Himalayas to N. Burma. ❄❄❄. **subsp. *xanthocodon*** ■ syn. *R. xanthocodon*, bears trusses of 5–10 rich yellow flowers. E. India, Bhutan, Tibet, China.

***R.* 'Cinnkeys'.** Erect, evergreen shrub with medium-sized, narrowly oblong, glossy leaves. In mid- and late spring, bears multiple trusses of narrowly tubular flowers, 4cm (1½in) long, with clear red tubes and yellow lobes with a light, waxy bloom. ↕↔ 2.2m (7ft). ❄❄❄

***R.* 'Coccineum Speciosum'.** Bushy, deciduous Ghent azalea with small, dark green leaves, turning yellow or orange in autumn. In early summer, bears lax trusses of funnel-shaped, fragrant, rich orange-red flowers, to 5cm (2in) long. ↕↔ 2m (6ft). ❄❄❄

***R.* 'Corneille'** ■ Deciduous, tall-growing Ghent azalea of open habit, with small leaves. Domed trusses of open trumpet-shaped, honeysuckle-like, fragrant cream flowers, 4cm (1½in) long, strongly suffused pink on the outside, are borne in early summer. ↕↔ 1.5–2.5m (5–8ft). ❄❄❄

***R.* 'Cottage Garden's Pride'** see *R.* 'Mrs. G.W. Leak'.

***R.* 'Crest'** ■ syn. *R.* (Hawk Group) 'Crest'. Evergreen shrub of open habit, with medium-sized leaves. In mid-spring, orange-yellow buds open to trusses of up to 12 long-lasting, broadly funnel-shaped, primrose-yellow flowers, 10cm (4in) long. ↕↔ 3.5m (11ft). ❄❄❄

R. cubittii ■ Evergreen shrub (now included in *R. veitchianum*) with purple-brown young shoots and oblong-elliptic, leathery, sparsely scaly, mid- to dark green leaves, to 10cm (4in) long. In mid- and late spring, bears funnel-shaped, white to pale pink flowers, to 10cm (4in) long, with brownish or orange-yellow markings. ↕ 1.5m (5ft), ↔ to 1m (3ft). N. Burma. ❄

***R.* 'Cunningham's White'.** Compact, evergreen shrub with medium-sized leaves. In late spring, mauve buds open to lax trusses of funnel-shaped white flowers, 5–6cm (2–2½in) long, with yellow to green-brown markings inside. ↕↔ 2.2m (7ft). ❄❄❄

***R.* 'Curlew'.** Dwarf, spreading, small-leaved, evergreen shrub. In mid-spring, bears numerous trusses of 2 or 3 broadly funnel-shaped, bright yellow flowers, 5cm (2in) across, spotted greenish brown inside. ↕↔ 60cm (24in). ❄❄❄

***R.* 'Cynthia'** ■ syn. *R.* 'Lord Palmerston'. Large, evergreen shrub with large leaves. In late spring, bears pyramidal trusses of funnel-shaped, deep rose-pink to magenta flowers, 8cm (3in) long, with deep crimson markings on the insides of the upper lobes. Grows well in sun. ↕↔ 6m (20ft). ❄❄❄

R. dauricum. Deciduous or semi-evergreen shrub with small, elliptic, leathery, glossy, dark green leaves, 1–3.5cm (½–1½in) long, scaly beneath, turning purple-brown in winter. In mid- and late winter, bears small trusses of funnel-shaped, vivid rose-purple flowers, 1.5–2cm (½–¾in) long. Very hardy; suitable for an open site. ↕↔ 1.5m (5ft). E. Asia. ❄❄❄

R. davidsonianum ■ Vigorous, evergreen shrub producing lance-shaped to oblong-lance-shaped, glossy, dark green leaves, 3–7cm (1¼–3in) long, densely brown-scaly beneath. In mid-spring, bears trusses of 2–6 broadly funnel-shaped, pale pink to purplish pink flowers, to 4.5cm (1¾in) across, sometimes spotted red inside. Grow in full sun or partial shade. ↕ to 4m (12ft), ↔ 3m (10ft). W. China. ❄❄❄

***R.* 'Daviesii'.** Compact, deciduous Ghent azalea with small leaves. In late spring and early summer, bears lax trusses of tubular to funnel-shaped, fragrant white flowers, to 7cm (3in) long, with yellow flares inside. ↕↔ 1.5m (5ft). ❄❄❄

R. decorum ■♀ Large shrub or small tree with rough, fissured bark and oblong-ovate, dark green leaves, 6–20cm (2½–8in) long, glaucous beneath. In late spring and early summer, bears trusses of 7–10 funnel- to bell-shaped, 6- or 7-lobed, strongly scented white flowers, 4.5–11cm (1¾–4½in) long, sometimes faintly tinged pink, often with greenish yellow bases. ↕ 6m (20ft), ↔ 2.5m (8ft). China. ❄❄❄

R. degronianum* subsp. *heptamerum see *R. metternichii.*

R. degronianum* subsp. *yakushimanum see *R. yakushimanum.*

R. dichroanthum. Compact, evergreen shrub producing obovate to inversely lance-shaped, dark green leaves, 4–4.5cm (1½–1¾in) long, with a thin, pale fawn indumentum beneath. In late spring and early summer, bears trusses of 4–8 fleshy, tubular to bell-shaped, yellow to orange or orange-red flowers, 3.5–5cm (1½–2in) long. Grows well in full sun. ↕ to 2m (6ft), ↔ 2.2m (7ft). N.E. Burma, W. China. ❄❄❄

R. discolor see *R. fortunei* subsp. *discolor.*

***R.* 'Doc'** ■ Small, compact, evergreen shrub with medium-sized leaves. In late spring, bears rounded trusses of funnel-shaped, wavy-margined, rose-pink flowers, 4cm (1½in) long, with deeper pink margins and spots, fading to white. ↕↔ 1.2m (4ft). ❄❄❄

***R.* 'Doncaster'.** Evergreen shrub with distinctive, concave, wavy-margined, medium-sized leaves. Full, dense trusses of funnel-shaped, dark red flowers, to 8cm (3in) long, each with a black-spotted flare inside, are borne in mid- and late spring. ↕↔ 2.2m (7ft). ❄❄❄

***R.* 'Dopey'.** Upright, compact, evergreen shrub with medium-sized leaves. In late spring, bears neat, full trusses of long-lasting, bell-shaped, glossy red flowers, 5–7cm (2–3in) long, with dark brown spots inside, paler towards the margins. ↕↔ 2m (6ft). ❄❄❄

***R.* 'Dora Amateis'** ■ Reliable, semi-dwarf, compact, evergreen shrub with small leaves. In spring, bears lax trusses of 6–8 broadly funnel-shaped white flowers, 2–3cm (¾–1¼in) long, the insides flushed pink with small green flecks. ↕↔ 60cm (24in). ❄❄❄

***R.* 'Dr. Herman Sleumer'.** Evergreen Vireya rhododendron with medium-sized leaves. Intermittently bears trusses of 5 or 6 bell-shaped pink flowers, 4–6cm (1½–2½in) long, with cream throats, from winter to summer. ↕ 1.2m (4ft), ↔ 1m (3ft). ❅ (min. 5°C/41°F)

R. edgeworthii, syn. *R. bullatum.* Evergreen, epiphytic shrub with elliptic to ovate, wrinkled, dark green leaves, 5–10cm (2–4in) long; the shoots and undersides of the leaves have a thick, tawny indumentum. In mid-spring, bears trusses of 2 or 3 broadly funnel-shaped, strongly scented flowers, 6–15cm (2½–6in) across, white to pale pink or pink, flushed deep red outside. ↕↔ 2.5m (8ft). E. Himalayas. ❄❄

***R.* 'Edmund de Rothschild'.** Vigorous, upright, leggy, evergreen shrub with medium-sized leaves. In early summer, bears dense trusses of 20 or more funnel-shaped, deep red flowers, 9cm (3½in) long, heavily spotted darker red inside. ↕↔ 3m (10ft). ❄❄❄

Rhododendron 'Beauty of Littleworth'

Rhododendron 'Beethoven'

Rhododendron 'Blue Peter'

Rhododendron bureavii

Rhododendron calophytum

Rhododendron calostrotum

Rhododendron campanulatum

Rhododendron campylocarpum

Rhododendron 'Carita'

Rhododendron 'Cécile'

Rhododendron 'Cilpinense'

Rhododendron cinnabarinum

Rhododendron cinnabarinum subsp. *xanthocodon*

Rhododendron 'Corneille'

Rhododendron 'Crest'

Rhododendron cubittii

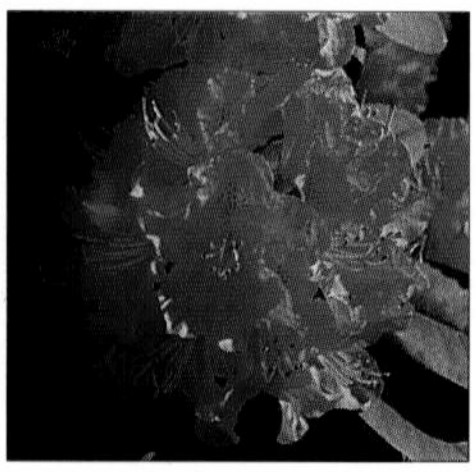

Rhododendron 'Cynthia'

Rhododendron davidsonianum

Rhododendron decorum

Rhododendron 'Doc'

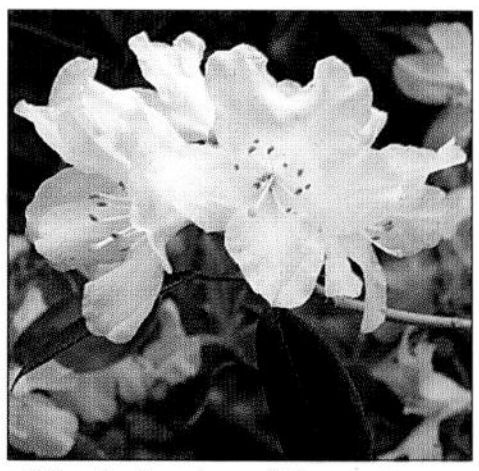

Rhododendron 'Dora Amateis'

R

***R.* 'Elisabeth Hobbie'.** Dense, compact, semi-dwarf, evergreen shrub with medium-sized, rounded leaves. In early and mid-spring, produces lax trusses of 6–10 narrowly funnel-shaped, scarlet-red flowers, 6cm (2½in) long, faintly spotted darker red inside. ↕↔ 75cm (30in). ❄❄❄
***R.* 'Elizabeth'** ▣ Compact, dwarf, evergreen shrub with small leaves. In spring, bears trusses of up to 5 funnel-shaped, bright red flowers, 6–8cm (2½–3in) long, in such abundance that they may almost hide the foliage. Suitable for sun. ↕↔ 1m (3ft). ❄❄❄
***R.* 'Elizabeth Lockhart'.** Compact, semi-dwarf, evergreen shrub with small, rounded, shiny, deep maroon-purple leaves. In mid-spring, bears loose trusses of bell-shaped, cherry-red flowers, 5cm (2in) long. Remove any growth that reverts to green. ↕↔ 1m (3ft). ❄❄❄
***R.* 'Elsie Lee'.** Dwarf, evergreen Shammarello azalea with small leaves. In late spring, bears numerous small trusses of broadly funnel-shaped, semi-double, light reddish-purple flowers, 5–7cm (2–3in) across. Suitable for full sun and exposed sites. Very hardy. ↕↔ 1m (3ft). ❄❄❄
R. eriogynum see *R. facetum.*
***R.* 'Fabia'** ▣ Evergreen shrub with medium-sized leaves. Loose trusses of long-lasting, funnel-shaped, orange-red flowers, to 7cm (3in) long, marked pale brown inside, are borne in late spring. ↕↔ 2m (6ft). ❄❄
R. facetum ♀ syn. *R. eriogynum.* Evergreen shrub or small tree with a woolly white indumentum on young shoots. Oblong-elliptic to inversely lance-shaped leaves, 10–19cm (4–7in) long, are matt, mid-green above, glossy beneath. In early summer, produces trusses of 8–16 tubular-bell-shaped, bright scarlet flowers, 4–5cm (1½–2in) long, with deep purple nectar pouches. ↕ 10m (30ft), ↔ 2.5m (8ft). Burma, China. ❄❄
R. falconeri ▣♀ Multi-stemmed, evergreen tree with flaking, red-brown bark. Broadly elliptic to obovate, dark green leaves, 18–35cm (7–14in) long, have a dense, woolly brown indumentum beneath and on the leaf-stalks. In mid-spring, bears large trusses of 20–25 widely bell-shaped, fleshy, creamy white or yellow flowers, 4–5cm (1½–2in) long, sometimes pink-tinged, often with purple marks inside. ↕ to 12m (40ft), ↔ 5m (15ft). E. Himalayas. ❄❄❄
R. fastigiatum. Compact, dwarf, alpine rhododendron with broadly elliptic to ovate-oblong, glaucous, mid-green leaves, 0.5–1.5cm (¼–½in) long, with tan scales beneath. Abundant trusses of up to 5 funnel-shaped, purplish blue flowers, 1–2cm (½–¾in) long, are borne in mid-spring. Suitable for full sun. ↕↔ 1m (3ft). W. China. ❄❄❄
***R.* 'Fastuosum Flore Pleno'** ▣ Dome-shaped, shrubby, "iron-clad" rhododendron with medium-sized leaves. Long-lasting trusses of funnel-shaped, wavy-margined, double mauve flowers, 5–7cm (2–3in) long, with brown-crimson flashes inside, are borne in late spring and early summer. ↕↔ 4m (12ft). ❄❄❄
R. ferrugineum (Alpenrose). Compact, evergreen shrub with elliptic, glossy, dark green leaves, 2–4cm (1–1½in) long, the leaf-stalks and undersides covered in red-brown scales. In early summer, bears trusses of 6–8 tubular, rose-pink to crimson, sometimes white flowers, 1.5cm (½in) long, with spreading lobes. Prefers full sun. ↕ to 1.5m (5ft), ↔ 1.2m (4ft). C. Europe. ❄❄❄
R. fictolacteum see *R. rex* subsp. *fictolacteum.*
***R.* 'Firefly'** see *R.* 'Hexe'.
R. forrestii. Prostrate, creeping, evergreen shrub with neat, broadly obovate to rounded, glossy, dark green leaves, 1–3cm (½–1¼in) long, purple beneath. Tubular to bell-shaped, fleshy scarlet flowers, 3–3.5cm (1¼–1½in) long, with dark carmine-red nectar pouches, are borne singly or in pairs in mid-spring. ↕ 20cm (8in), ↔ 1.5m (5ft). Tibet, China (Yunnan), N.E. Burma. ❄❄❄
R. fortunei ♀ Evergreen shrub or small tree with oblong-elliptic to oblong leaves, 8–18cm (3–7in) long, matt, dark green above, paler green beneath. Trusses of 6–12 broadly funnel-shaped, 7-lobed, fragrant, pink or lilac-pink flowers, 6–8cm (2½–3in) across, are borne in mid- and late spring. ↕ 10m (30ft), ↔ 2.5m (8ft). China. ❄❄❄.
subsp. *discolor* ▣ syn. *R. discolor,* has a more open habit, and bears trusses of 8–10 funnel- to bell-shaped, white, pink, or rose-pink flowers, in early and midsummer; ↕ 6m (20ft), ↔ 3m (10ft).
***R.* 'Fragrantissimum'** ▣ Lax, evergreen shrub with hairy, medium-sized leaves. In mid-spring, bears trusses of up to 4 broadly funnel-shaped, nutmeg-scented, white, sometimes pink-flushed flowers, 6cm (2½in) long, with yellow throats. ↕↔ 2m (6ft). ❄

Rhododendron falconeri

Rhododendron 'Golden Torch'

***R.* 'Freya'** ▣ Deciduous, compact, bushy Rustica azalea with small leaves. Flat-domed trusses of funnel-shaped, hose-in-hose, fragrant, pink-flushed, salmon-orange flowers, 4cm (1½in) long, are borne in late spring and early summer. Suitable for sun. ↕↔ 1.5m (5ft). ❄❄❄
***R.* 'Frome'** ▣ Deciduous Knap Hill-Exbury azalea of open habit, with medium-sized leaves. In late spring, bears frilled, wavy-margined, broadly funnel-shaped, saffron-yellow flowers, 7cm (3in) long, overlaid with red in their throats. Suitable for an open site. ↕↔ 1.5m (5ft). ❄❄❄
R. fulgens. Rounded, evergreen shrub with smooth, peeling, pink-grey to red-brown bark. The broadly ovate to obovate, glossy, dark green leaves, 7–11cm (3–4½in) long, have a dense, reddish brown indumentum beneath. Compact trusses of 10–15 tubular to bell-shaped, crimson-scarlet flowers, 2–3.5cm (¾–1½in) long, with black-red nectar pouches, are borne in early spring. ↕ 4m (12ft), ↔ 3m (10ft). E. Himalayas, Tibet. ❄❄❄
R. fulvum ▣♀ Large, evergreen shrub or small tree with inversely lance-shaped to elliptic leaves, 8–22cm (3–9in) long, glossy, dark green above, with a red-brown to fawn indumentum beneath. Compact trusses of up to 20 tubular-bell-shaped white flowers, 2.5–4.5cm (1–1¾in) long, flushed rose-pink to deep rose-pink, sometimes each with a basal crimson mark, open in early and mid-spring. ↕ 5m (15ft), ↔ 3m (10ft). E. Himalayas, China. ❄❄❄
***R.* 'Furnivall's Daughter'** ▣ Upright, rounded, showy, evergreen shrub with medium-sized leaves. In late spring and early summer, bears compact trusses of funnel-shaped, bright pink flowers, 9cm (3½in) long, each with a bold, strawberry-red flare in the throat. ↕↔ 3m (10ft). ❄❄❄
***R.* 'George Budgen'.** Vigorous, evergreen, compact Vireya rhododendron with medium-sized leaves. Trusses of up to 5 tubular-funnel-shaped flowers, 8cm (3in) long, bright orange at the petal tips, shading to rich yellow at the centres, are borne intermittently from winter to summer. ↕ 1.3m (4½ft), ↔ 1–1.2m (3–4ft). ❀ (min. 5°C/41°F)
***R.* 'George Reynolds'** ▣ Deciduous, bushy Knap Hill-Exbury azalea with medium-sized leaves. Large trusses of broadly funnel-shaped yellow flowers, 6–8cm (2½–3in) long, flushed pink in bud, are borne with or before the leaves, in mid-spring. Suitable for full sun. ↕↔ 2m (6ft). ❄❄❄
***R.* 'Gibraltar'.** Vigorous, deciduous Knap Hill-Exbury azalea with medium-sized leaves. In spring, crimson-orange buds open to dense trusses of funnel-shaped, brilliant orange flowers, 6–8cm (2½–3in) long, each with a distinct yellow flash and crinkled petals. Suitable for full sun. ↕↔ 1.5m (5ft). ❄❄❄
***R.* 'Ginny Gee'.** Dwarf, evergreen shrub forming dense, cushion-like mats of small, dark green leaves. Multiple trusses of tubular-funnel-shaped, pale purplish pink flowers, 2.5cm (1in) long, fading to white-pink, cover the leaves in mid-spring. Suitable for sun. ↕↔ 60–90cm (24–36in). ❄❄❄
R. glaucophyllum. Compact, semi-dwarf, evergreen shrub with oblong to elliptic-lance-shaped, aromatic leaves, 3.5–6cm (1½–2½in) long, matt, dark green above, white-glaucous and scaly beneath. In mid-spring, bears lax trusses of 4–10 bell-shaped, white, rose-pink, or pinkish purple flowers, 1–3cm (½–1¼in) long. Suitable for full sun. ↕↔ 1.5m (5ft). E. Himalayas. ❄❄❄
***R.* 'Gloria Mundi'** ▣ Deciduous, twiggy Ghent azalea with small leaves. In early summer, bears lax trusses of honeysuckle-like, tubular-funnel-shaped, fragrant orange flowers, 4–7cm (1½–3in) long, with yellow flares inside and frilled margins. Suitable for full sun. ↕↔ 2m (6ft). ❄❄❄
***R.* 'Glory of Littleworth'** ▣ Semi-evergreen azaleodendron of untidy habit,

R

with medium-sized leaves. Compact trusses of broadly funnel-shaped, creamy white flowers, 5–6cm (2–2½in) long, with bright orange-red flashes on the upper petals, open from mid-spring to early summer. ↕↔ 1.5m (5ft). ❄❄❄

***R.* 'Glowing Embers'** ■ Striking, deciduous Knap Hill-Exbury azalea with medium-sized leaves. Conical trusses of broadly funnel-shaped, vivid reddish orange flowers, 7cm (3in) long, each marked orange in the throat, are produced in mid-spring. Suitable for sun. ↕↔ 2m (6ft). ❄❄❄

***R.* 'Goldbukett'**, syn. *R.* 'Golden Bouquet'. Evergreen shrub producing medium-sized leaves. In late spring and early summer, bears loose trusses of 10–14 funnel-shaped, creamy yellow flowers, 5–6cm (2–2½in) long, spotted red-purple inside. Very hardy. ↕↔ 2m (6ft). ❄❄❄

***R.* 'Gold Crown'** see *R.* 'Goldkrone'.

***R.* 'Golden Bouquet'** see *R.* 'Goldbukett'.

***R.* 'Golden Fleece' of gardens** see *R.* 'Princess Anne'.

***R.* 'Golden Torch'** ■ Compact, upright, evergreen shrub with medium-sized leaves. In late spring and early summer, salmon-pink buds open to rounded trusses of funnel-shaped, soft yellow flowers, 4–5cm (1½–2in) long, fading to pale yellow or cream. ↕↔ 1.5m (5ft). ❄❄❄

***R.* 'Goldkrone'** ■ syn *R.* 'Gold Crown'. Low-growing, compact, evergreen shrub with medium-sized leaves. Trusses of 16–18 funnel- to bell-shaped, bright golden yellow flowers, 5–7cm (2–3in) long, delicately spotted ruby-red inside, are borne in succession in mid-spring. Very hardy. ↕↔ 1.5m (5ft). ❄❄❄

***R.* 'Goldsworth Orange'.** Upright, evergreen shrub, of dense, compact habit, with medium-sized leaves. In early summer, bears full trusses of tubular-funnel-shaped, salmon-pink flowers, 6cm (2½in) long, with subtle orange shading. ↕↔ 2m (6ft). ❄❄❄

***R.* 'Gomer Waterer'.** Compact, evergreen shrub with medium-sized leaves. In late spring and early summer, lilac-pink buds open to hemispherical trusses of funnel-shaped white flowers, to 8cm (3in) long, flushed mauve-pink at the margins, each with a bold yellow-brown flare in the throat. Very tolerant of sun, heat, and wind. ↕↔ 2m (6ft). ❄❄❄

***R.* 'Grace Seabrook'.** Vigorous, evergreen shrub with medium-sized leaves. In early and mid-spring, bears tight trusses of funnel-shaped, deep blood-red flowers, 8cm (3in) long, paling at the margins. Very hardy. ↕↔ 2m (6ft). ❄❄❄

***R.* 'Greeting'.** Dwarf, evergreen Glenn Dale azalea with small leaves. In early and mid-spring, bears lax trusses of funnel-shaped, wavy-margined, bright orange-red flowers, 5cm (2in) long. Grow in full sun or partial shade. ↕↔ 1m (3ft). ❄❄❄

R. griersonianum ■ Striking, evergreen shrub with bristly, woolly shoots. Elliptic to oblong-lance-shaped, matt, olive-green leaves, 10–20cm (4–8in) long, have a loose brown indumentum beneath. In late spring and early summer, trusses of 5–12 tubular-bell-shaped scarlet flowers, 6–8cm (2½–3in) long, open from buds with long, tapering scales. ↕↔ 3m (10ft). W. China, N.E Burma. ❄❄❄

R. griffithianum 🌳 Evergreen, large shrub or tree with peeling, smooth, red-brown bark. Oblong-elliptic, pale green leaves, 10–30cm (4–12in) long, are slightly glaucous beneath. Trusses of 3–6 open bell-shaped, fragrant, white or pale pink flowers, 4.5–8cm (1¾–3in) long, spotted green inside, open in mid-spring. ↕ 6m (20ft), ↔ 2.5m (8ft). C. and E. Himalayas, Bhutan. ❄❄

R. groenlandicum see *Ledum groenlandicum*.

***R.* 'Gumpo'**, syn. *R. indicum* var. *eriocarpum* 'Gumpo'. Late-flowering, dwarf, evergreen Satsuki azalea with small leaves. In early summer, bears few-flowered trusses of funnel-shaped, wavy-petalled, white, sometimes pink or pink-flushed white flowers, 6–8cm (2½–3in) long. Heat-tolerant. ↕↔ 1m (3ft). ❄❄❄

R. haematodes. Slow-growing, compact, evergreen shrub producing oblong-obovate, dark green leaves, 4.5–10cm (1¾–4in) long, with a dense, reddish-brown indumentum beneath. In late spring, bears lax trusses of 6–10 tubular-bell-shaped, fleshy crimson flowers, 3.5–4.5cm (1½–1¾in) long. ↕↔ 2m (6ft). China (Yunnan). ❄❄❄

***R.* 'Halfdan Lem'** ■ Very vigorous, lax, evergreen shrub with large leaves. In mid- and late spring, bears tight trusses of broadly funnel-shaped red flowers, 9cm (3½in) long, spotted dark red, fading to pink. ↕↔ 2.5m (8ft). ❄❄❄

***R.* 'Hatsugiri'** ■ Compact, dwarf, evergreen Kurume azalea with tiny leaves. In spring, bears trusses of up to 3 broadly funnel-shaped, bright crimson-purple flowers, 0.7–2.5cm (¼–1in) long. Tolerates sun. ↕↔ 60cm (24in). ❄❄❄

***R.* (Hawk Group) 'Crest'** see *R.* 'Crest'.

***R.* 'Hexe'**, syn. *R.* 'Firefly'. Dwarf, evergreen Indian azalea of neat habit, with small leaves. In spring, bears lax trusses of numerous hose-in-hose, glowing crimson flowers, 3–4cm (1¼–1½in) long. ↕↔ 60cm (24in). ❄❄

***R.* 'Hino-crimson'.** Dwarf, evergreen Kurume azalea of dense habit, with small leaves. In spring, bears abundant funnel-shaped, brilliant red flowers, 0.7–2.5cm (¼–1in) long, in rounded trusses. ↕↔ 60cm (24in). ❄❄❄

***R.* 'Hinode-giri'** ■ Compact, dwarf, evergreen Kurume azalea with small leaves. In spring, bears domed trusses of numerous broadly funnel-shaped, bright crimson flowers, 1–2.5cm (½–1in) long. Prefers full sun. ↕↔ 60cm (24in). ❄❄❄

***R.* 'Hinomayo'** ■ Dwarf, small-leaved, evergreen Kurume azalea of dense, compact habit. From mid-spring to early summer, produces lax trusses of broadly funnel-shaped, clear pink flowers, 1–2.5cm (½–1in) long. Will tolerate full sun. ↕↔ 60cm (24in). ❄❄❄

R. hippophaeoides ■ Upright, semi-dwarf, evergreen shrub with narrowly lance-shaped, aromatic, scaly, grey-green leaves, 2–3cm (¾–1¼in) long. In early and mid-spring, bears trusses of 6–8 funnel-shaped, lavender-blue or pale lilac flowers, 0.5–2.5cm (¼–1in) long. Prefers full sun. ↕ 1.5m (5ft), ↔ 75cm (30in). S.W. China. ❄❄❄

R. hodgsonii 🌳 Evergreen tree or large shrub with attractive, peeling, red-brown to grey bark and oblong-elliptic leaves, 17–24cm (7–10in) long, glossy, dark green above, with a pale brown indumentum beneath. Compact trusses

Rhododendron 'Elizabeth'

Rhododendron 'Fabia'

Rhododendron 'Fastuosum Flore Pleno'

Rhododendron fortunei subsp. *discolor*

Rhododendron 'Fragrantissimum'

Rhododendron 'Freya'

Rhododendron 'Frome'

Rhododendron fulvum

Rhododendron 'Furnivall's Daughter'

Rhododendron 'George Reynolds'

Rhododendron 'Gloria Mundi'

Rhododendron 'Glory of Littleworth'

Rhododendron 'Glowing Embers'

Rhododendron 'Goldkrone'

Rhododendron griersonianum

Rhododendron 'Halfdan Lem'

Rhododendron 'Hatsugiri'

Rhododendron 'Hinode-giri'

Rhododendron 'Hinomayo'

Rhododendron hippophaeoides

Rhododendron 'Homebush'

R

of 15–20 tubular-bell-shaped, fleshy, crimson, purple, or rose-purple flowers, 3–5cm (1¼–2in) long, each usually with 7 or 8, occasionally up to 10 lobes, open in mid- and late spring. ↕ to 11m (35ft), ↔ 6m (20ft). E. Himalayas. ❄❄❄

***R.* 'Homebush'** ■ Compact, bushy, deciduous Knap Hill-Exbury azalea with medium-sized leaves. In late spring, bears tight, rounded trusses of trumpet-shaped, semi-double, bright pink flowers, 3cm (1¼in) long, with paler pink shading. ↕↔ 1.5m (5ft). ❄❄❄

***R.* 'Hotei'.** Dense, evergreen shrub with medium-sized leaves. In mid- and late spring, bears slightly open trusses of funnel-shaped, deep yellow flowers, 5cm (2in) long, each with a prominent calyx. ↕↔ 1.5–2.5m (5–8ft). ❄❄❄

***R.* 'Humming Bird'.** Neat, compact, dome-shaped, evergreen shrub with small, rounded, glossy leaves. In early and mid-spring, bears loose trusses of 4 or more, nodding, widely bell-shaped, cherry-red flowers, 5–6cm (2–2½in) across. ↕↔ 1.5m (5ft). ❄❄❄

***R.* 'Hydon Dawn'** ■ Very compact, low-growing, evergreen shrub with medium-sized leaves. From mid-spring to early summer, bears tight trusses of funnel-shaped, frilled, pale pink flowers, 5cm (2in) long, fading to white. Tolerates full sun. ↕↔ 1.5m (5ft). ❄❄❄

***R.* 'Hydon Hunter'.** Vigorous, open shrub with medium-sized leaves. In early summer, bears compact trusses of narrowly bell-shaped flowers, 5cm (2in) long, with red rims fading to pink in the centres and spotted orange inside. Grow in sun. ↕↔ 1.5m (5ft). ❄❄❄

***R.* 'Ilam Cream'** ■ Evergreen shrub producing large leaves. Lax trusses of lilac-pink buds open to funnel-shaped, fragrant, creamy yellow flowers, 6–9cm (2½–3½in) long, in late spring and early summer. ↕↔ 4m (12ft). ❄❄❄

R. impeditum. Compact, dwarf, evergreen shrub with tiny, elliptic-ovate, aromatic, scaly, grey-green leaves, 4–15mm (⅛–½in) long. In mid- and late spring, bears abundant broadly funnel-shaped, purplish blue flowers, 2–2.5cm (¾–½in) long, singly or in pairs. ↕↔ 60cm (24in). W. China. ❄❄❄

***R.* 'I.M.S.'** see *R.* 'Irene Stead'.

***R. indicum* var. *eriocarpum* 'Gumpo'** see *R.* 'Gumpo'.

R. insigne. Compact, dome-shaped, evergreen shrub with elliptic to lance-shaped, stiff leaves, 7–13cm (3–5in) long, glossy, dark green above, copper beneath. In late spring and early summer, bears trusses of 8–15 bell-shaped, pinkish white flowers, to 4cm (1½in) long, the insides striped rose-pink with crimson spots. Tolerates full sun. ↕↔ 4m (12ft). W. China. ❄❄❄

***R.* 'Irene Koster'** ■ Deciduous Occidentale azalea with medium-sized leaves. Bold trusses of delicate, funnel-shaped, fragrant, pink-suffused yellow flowers, 6cm (2½in) long, with orange-yellow flashes inside, open in late spring and early summer. ↕↔ 2m (6ft). ❄❄❄

***R.* 'Irene Stead'** ■ syn. *R.* 'I.M.S.'. Vigorous, evergreen shrub with large leaves and deep purple leaf-stalks. In late spring, flower buds open to very large trusses of funnel-shaped, fragrant, soft pink flowers, 6–9cm (2½–3½in) long. ↕↔ 4m (12ft). ❄❄❄

***R.* 'Irohayama'** ■ Compact, dwarf, small-leaved, evergreen Kurume azalea. Small trusses of abundant funnel-shaped white flowers, 4–5cm (1½–2in) long, margined pale lavender, open in spring. Grow in sun. ↕↔ 60cm (24in). ❄❄❄

R. irroratum ○ Evergreen, large shrub or small tree with inversely lance-shaped to elliptic leaves, 7–14cm (3–5½in) long, mid-green above, paler beneath. Trusses of up to 15 tubular-bell-shaped white flowers, 3.5–5cm (1½–2in) long, sometimes suffused pale pink, and variably crimson-spotted within, open in early spring. Grow in sun. ↕ 8m (25ft), ↔ 4m (12ft). China (Yunnan, Sichuan), Vietnam, Indonesia, Laos. ❄❄❄

***R.* Jalisco Group.** Evergreen shrub of open habit, with medium-sized leaves. In late spring and early summer, bears semi-pendent trusses of funnel-shaped, yellow or apricot-yellow flowers, 6cm (2½in) long, marked and streaked red-brown in the throats. ↕↔ 2.2m (7ft). ❄❄

R. japonicum see *R. molle* subsp. *japonicum.*

R. jasminiflorum. Evergreen Vireya rhododendron with a lax, untidy habit. Elliptic to lance-shaped or oblong, dark green leaves, 2.5–5cm (1–2in) long, arranged in whorls of 3–5, have small but distinct brown scales beneath. Trusses of 5–12 trumpet-shaped, sweet-scented flowers, 3.5–5cm (1½–2in) long, often opening pale pink and fading to white, with red flower-stalks, are borne intermittently from summer to winter. ↕ 1m (3ft), ↔ 1–2m (3–6ft). W. Malaysia, Philippines, Sumatra. ❀ (min. 5°C/41°F)

***R.* 'Jean Marie Montague'** see *R.* 'The Hon. Jean Marie de Montague'.

***R.* 'John Cairns'** ■ Striking, robust, small-leaved, evergreen Kaempferi azalea, of compact, upright habit. Flat-headed trusses of abundant funnel-shaped, orange-red flowers, 4–4.5cm (1½–1¾in) long, are borne in spring. Grow in sun. ↕↔ 1.5m (5ft). ❄❄❄

R. kaempferi ■ Loosely branched, erect, semi-evergreen azalea with glossy, mid-green leaves, 1–5cm (1½–2in) long, ovate to lance-shaped in spring, smaller and elliptic-obovate in summer. In late spring and early summer, bears trusses of 2–4 broadly funnel-shaped flowers, 2–3cm (¾–1¼in) long, in shades of red. Prefers full sun. ↕ 3m (10ft), ↔ 1.5m (5ft). Korea, Japan. ❄❄❄

R. keiskei ■ Compact, dwarf or semi-dwarf, evergreen shrub with small, oblong-lance-shaped, dark green leaves, 2.5–8cm (1–3in) long, slightly scaly above, densely scaly beneath. Trusses of 2–5 broadly funnel-shaped, pale to lemon-yellow flowers, to 5cm (2in) across, are borne freely in mid- and late spring. ↕ 25–90cm (10–36in), ↔ 1.2m (4ft). S. Japan. ❄❄❄. **'Yaku Fairy'** is prostrate; ↕ 15cm (6in).

R. keleticum see *R. calostrotum* subsp. *keleticum.*

***R.* 'Ken Janeck'** see *R. yakushimanum* 'Ken Janeck'.

R. kesangiae ○ Vigorous, evergreen shrub or small tree with very large, broadly elliptic to obovate, glossy, dark green leaves, 20–30cm (8–12in) long, with a silver-fawn indumentum beneath. In mid- and late spring, bears compact trusses of 15–25 bell-shaped, rose-pink flowers, 3–5cm (1¼–2in) long, with red nectar pouches. ↕ 12m (40ft), ↔ 8m (25ft). Bhutan. ❄❄❄

***R.* 'Kilimanjaro'** ■ Vigorous, evergreen shrub with medium-sized leaves. From mid-spring to early summer, bears very large trusses of funnel-shaped, bright deep red flowers, 15cm (6in) long, spotted crimson on the lobes. ↕↔ 2.2m (7ft). ❄❄❄

***R.* 'Kirin'** ■ Free-flowering, evergreen, compact, dwarf Kurume azalea with small leaves. In mid-spring, bears small trusses of hose-in-hose, deep pink flowers, 3cm (1¼in) long, shaded a delicate silvery rose-pink. Suitable for sun. ↕↔ 1.5m (5ft). ❄❄❄

R. kiusianum ■ Dwarf, semi-evergreen shrub with variable, broadly elliptic to obovate, short-bristled, mid-green leaves, 0.5–2cm (¼–¾in) long, larger in spring than in summer. Trusses of 2 or 3 funnel-shaped, pink or purple, sometimes white flowers, 1.5–2cm (½–¾in) long, are borne in late spring and early summer. Prefers full sun. ↕↔ 1.2m (4ft). Japan. ❄❄❄

***R.* 'Klondyke'.** Striking, deciduous Knap Hill-Exbury azalea with medium-sized leaves. In late spring, red-flushed buds open to large trusses of funnel-shaped, glowing orange-gold flowers, 6cm (2½in) long, tinted red on the reverse of the petals. Grow in full sun. ↕↔ 2m (6ft). ❄❄❄

***R.* 'Kluis Sensation'.** Relatively slow-growing, evergreen shrub with medium-sized leaves. In late spring and early summer, bears tight trusses of funnel-shaped, slightly frilled, dark red-scarlet flowers, 4.5–5cm (1¾–2in) long, spotted crimson inside. Particularly tolerant of heat and sun. ↕↔ 2.2m (7ft). ❄❄❄

R. konori. Erect, evergreen Vireya rhododendron producing obovate to broadly elliptic, dull, mid-green leaves, 11–14cm (4½–5½in) long, with small brown scales beneath. From summer to winter, intermittently bears trusses of 4–7 elongated, funnel-shaped, usually 7-lobed, fragrant flowers, 7–9cm (3–3½in) long, pale to deep pink, or pink fading to white, with prominent cream stamens. ↕ 2m (6ft), ↔ 1.5m (5ft). New Guinea. ❀ (min. 5°C/41°F)

***R.* 'Kure-no-yuki'** ■ syn. *R.* 'Snowflake'. Compact, dwarf, evergreen Kurume azalea with small leaves. Freely bears trusses of 2 or 3 hose-in-hose white flowers, 0.5–2.5cm (¼–1in) long, in mid-spring. ↕↔ 1m (3ft). ❄❄❄

R. lacteum. Large, densely branched, evergreen shrub producing oblong-elliptic, dark green leaves, 8–17cm (3–7in) long, with a brown indumentum beneath. Trusses of 20–30 broadly bell-shaped, pale yellow flowers, 5cm (2in) across, sometimes with crimson marks inside, are borne in mid- and late spring. ↕↔ 5m (15ft). China (Sichuan, Yunnan), Burma. ❄❄❄

***R.* 'Lady Alice Fitzwilliam'.** Open, evergreen shrub with medium-sized leaves. In mid-spring, bears trusses of 2 or 3 funnel-shaped, nutmeg-scented pink flowers, 10cm (4in) long, maturing to white with yellow-marked throats. ↕↔ 2m (6ft). ❄❄

***R.* 'Lady Clementine Mitford'.** Shrubby, spreading, evergreen "iron-clad" rhododendron, with medium-sized leaves. In late spring and early summer, bears compact trusses of funnel-shaped flowers, to 8cm (3in) long, peach-pink at the margins of the petals, shading to white at the centres, with V-shaped markings of red-brown to green spots in the throats. ↕↔ 2.5m (8ft). ❄❄❄

***R.* 'Lady Eleanor Cathcart'** ○ Shrubby, evergreen "iron-clad" rhododendron with arching, medium-sized leaves. In late spring, bears rounded trusses of funnel-shaped, pale pink flowers, 5–6cm (2–2½in) long, with dark maroon flares inside. Suitable for sun. ↕↔ 4m (12ft). ❄❄❄

R. laetum ■ Erect, evergreen Vireya rhododendron with elliptic to broadly elliptic, glossy, dark green leaves, 5–9cm (2–3½in) long, with tiny scales beneath. In spring, bears trusses of 5–12 funnel-shaped, golden yellow flowers, 4.5cm (1¾in) long, later suffused orange-red, on red flower-stalks. ↕↔ 1.5m (5ft). N.W. New Guinea. ❀ (min. 5°C/41°F)

Rhododendron luteum

***R.* 'Lavender Girl'** ■ Evergreen, large-leaved shrub with domed trusses of funnel-shaped, fragrant, pink-mauve flowers, to 10cm (4in) long, fading to near white in the centres. Blooms open in late spring and early summer, earlier than most similar-coloured hybrids. Grow in an open site. ↕↔ 2.5m (8ft). ❄❄❄

***R.* 'Ledifolium'** see *R.* x *mucronatum.*

***R.* 'Lem's Cameo'** ■ Evergreen shrub producing medium-sized leaves, brown-bronze when young. In mid-spring, bears large, domed trusses of funnel-shaped, frilled, pale peach flowers, 9cm (3½in) long, fading to apricot-cream or pink, and marked and spotted red in the throats. ↕↔ 2.2m (7ft). ❄❄❄

R. lepidostylum. Dome-shaped, dwarf, evergreen shrub with densely bristly shoots. Small, oblong-oval, obovate, or ovate leaves, 3–3.5cm (1¼–1½in) long, intensely glaucous above, golden scaly beneath, have margins fringed with hairs. Broadly funnel-shaped yellow flowers, 4cm (1½in) across, sparsely bristly outside, are borne singly or in pairs, in late spring and early summer. ↕↔ 1m (3ft). W. China. ❄❄❄

R. leucaspis ■ Densely branched, dwarf, evergreen shrub with bristly calyces and shoots, and broadly elliptic, dark green leaves, 3–4.5cm (1¼–1¾in) long, bristly above, scaly and yellowish green beneath. In early spring, bears trusses of up to 3 saucer-shaped white flowers, 5cm (2in) across, with chocolate-brown anthers. ↕ 1m (3ft), ↔ 1.5m (5ft). S.E. Tibet. ❄❄

R. lindleyi. Evergreen, epiphytic shrub, of untidy habit, with peeling, reddish brown bark. Lance-shaped to oblong-lance-shaped, olive-green leaves, 9–13cm (3½–5in) long, are glaucous and scaly beneath. In late spring and early summer, bears trusses of up to 6 tubular to funnel-shaped, scented white flowers, 7–10cm (3–4in) long, each with a yellow or orange flare within. ↕ 3m (10ft), ↔ 2m (6ft). E. Himalayas. ❄❄

***R.* 'Lionel's Triumph'.** Tall, large-leaved evergreen shrub with an open habit. Large trusses of funnel-shaped, creamy yellow flowers, 10cm (4in) long, with crimson-spotted throats and pink-flushed margins, open from pink buds in mid-spring. Grow in partial shade. ↕↔ 4m (12ft). ❄❄❄

R

***R.* 'Loderi King George'** ■ Large, evergreen shrub of open habit, with large leaves. In late spring and early summer, pale pink buds open to huge trusses of funnel-shaped, fragrant, pure white flowers, 9–11cm (3½–4½in) long, with subtle green markings in the throats. ↕↔ 4m (12ft). ❄❄❄

***R.* 'Loderi Venus'.** Evergreen, large-leaved shrub of open habit. In late spring and early summer, bears large trusses of funnel-shaped, fragrant, mid-pink flowers, 9–11cm (3½–4½in) long, fading to pale pink, the throats slightly green-marked. ↕↔ 4m (12ft). ❄❄❄

***R.* 'Loder's White'.** Vigorous, evergreen shrub with large leaves. In midsummer, bears large, conical trusses of long-lasting, funnel-shaped, slightly fragrant white flowers, 9–10cm (3½–4in) long, with red flecks inside. Thrives in sun. ↕↔ 3m (10ft). ❄❄❄

***R.* 'Lord Palmerston'** see *R.* 'Cynthia'.

***R.* 'Louise Dowdle'** ■ Compact, evergreen Glenn Dale azalea with medium-sized leaves. In spring, bears compact trusses of funnel-shaped, vivid red-purple flowers, 4cm (1½in) long, the throats with bright rose-red marks. Suitable for full sun. ↕↔ 1m (3ft). ❄❄❄

R. lutescens ■ Graceful, bushy, erect, semi-evergreen shrub with ovate-oblong to lance-shaped, sparsely scaly leaves, 5–9cm (2–3½in) long, bronze when young, maturing to dull green, and paler green with yellow scales beneath. In early spring, bears trusses of 3–6 broadly funnel-shaped, primrose-yellow flowers, 2.5cm (1in) across, spotted green inside. ↕↔ 5m (15ft). S.W. China. ❄❄❄

R. luteum ■ Deciduous azalea of open habit, with oblong to lance-shaped, mid-green leaves, 5–10cm (2–4in) long, sparsely hairy above and beneath. Trusses of 7–12 funnel-shaped, strongly scented, sticky yellow flowers, 3.5cm (1½in) long, open in late spring and early summer. Prefers full sun. ↕↔ 4m (12ft). E. Europe to Caucasus. ❄❄❄

R. macabeanum ♀ Evergreen shrub or tree with large, oblong-ovate, dark green leaves, 20–30cm (8–12in) long, with a woolly, pale fawn indumentum beneath. In mid-spring, bears huge trusses of up to 20 broadly bell-shaped, creamy to deep yellow flowers, 5–6cm (2–2½in) across, with purple marks inside, and purple nectar pouches. ↕ 15m (50ft), ↔ 6m (20ft). India (Manipur). ❄❄❄

R. macgregoriae ■ Bushy, evergreen Vireya rhododendron with ovate-lance-shaped to ovate-elliptic, glossy, dark green leaves, 4–9cm (1½–3½in) long, minutely scaly beneath. Trusses of up to 25 short, widely funnel- to bell-shaped, usually yellow or orange, occasionally pink flowers, to 1–3cm (½–1¼in) long, with protruding brown stamens, open in winter. ↕ to 5m (15ft), ↔ 1–2m (3–6ft). New Guinea. ❀ (min. 5°C/41°F)

R. macrophyllum. Large, free-flowering, evergreen shrub with oblong-obovate to elliptic leaves, 7–17cm (3–7in) long, dark green above, paler green beneath. In late spring and early summer, bears compact trusses of 15–20 funnel-shaped, rose-purple to pink, sometimes white flowers, 3–4cm (1¼–1½in) long, with red-brown spots inside. Suitable for sun. ↕↔ to 5m (15ft). W. North America. ❄❄❄

R. maculiferum* subsp. *anwheiense see *R. anwheiense.*

R. maddenii, syn. *R. brachysiphon.* Multi-stemmed, evergreen shrub with peeling, grey-brown bark. Leaves, varying from lance-shaped or obovate to elliptic, are 6–18cm (2½–7in) long, dark green above, and densely brown-scaly beneath. In late spring and early summer, bears trusses of 2–4 funnel-shaped, strongly scented white flowers, 6–10cm (2½–4in) long, sometimes flushed rose-pink. ↕↔ 2.5m (8ft). Himalayas, S.W. China, Burma. ❄❄

R. mallotum ♀ Evergreen, upright shrub or small tree producing obovate, stiff leaves, 10–13cm (4–5in) long, dark green and hairless above, with a woolly, reddish brown indumentum beneath. Trusses of up to 15 tubular-bell-shaped, fleshy scarlet flowers, 4–4.5cm (1½–1¾in) long, are borne in early spring. ↕ 6–7m (20–22ft), ↔ 3m (10ft). W. China, N.E. Burma. ❄❄❄

***R.* 'Martha Isaacson'.** Sturdy, semi-evergreen azaleodendron with medium-sized, maroon-tinted leaves. In late spring and early summer, bears rounded

Rhododendron 'Hydon Dawn'

Rhododendron 'Ilam Cream'

Rhododendron 'Irene Koster'

Rhododendron 'Irene Stead'

Rhododendron 'Irohayama'

Rhododendron 'John Cairns'

Rhododendron kaempferi

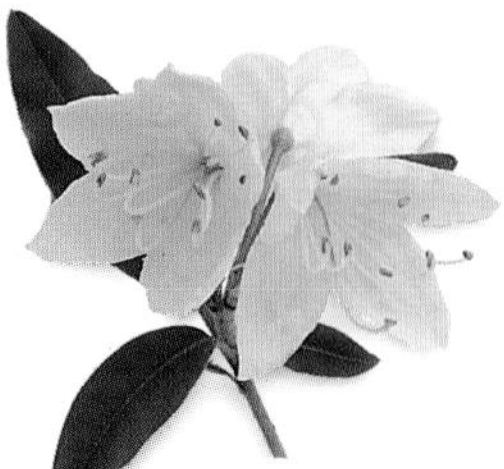
Rhododendron keiskei

Rhododendron 'Kilimanjaro'

Rhododendron 'Kirin'

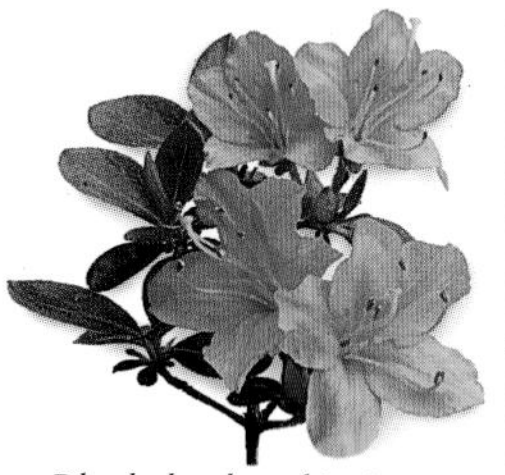
Rhododendron kiusianum

Rhododendron 'Kure-no-yuki'

Rhododendron laetum

Rhododendron 'Lavender Girl'

Rhododendron 'Lem's Cameo'

Rhododendron leucaspis

Rhododendron 'Loderi King George'

Rhododendron 'Louise Dowdle'

Rhododendron lutescens

Rhododendron macgregoriae

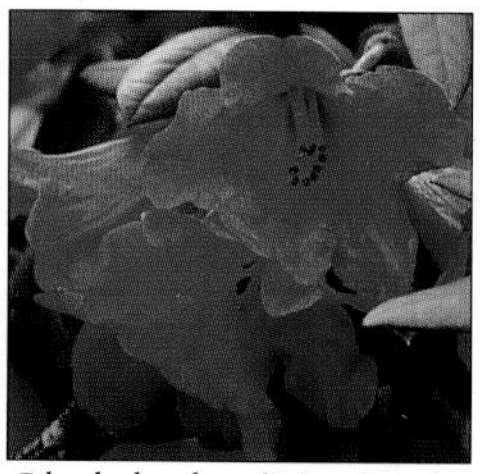
Rhododendron 'May Day'

trusses of funnel-shaped, slightly scented white flowers, 4cm (1½in) long, with vivid pink stripes. Prefers full sun. ↕↔ 2.5m (8ft). ✻✻✻

***R.* 'May Day'** ▣ Low-growing, spreading, large-leaved evergreen shrub. In mid-spring, freely bears loose trusses of funnel-shaped scarlet flowers, 7cm (3in) long, with petal-like calyces. Tolerates full sun. ↕↔ 1.5m (5ft). ✻✻✻

***R.* 'Medway'** ▣ Deciduous, bushy Knap Hill-Exbury azalea of open habit, with medium-sized leaves. In late spring, bears trusses of trumpet-shaped, pale pink flowers, 6cm (2½in) long, with darker margins, orange-flashed throats, and frilled petals. ↕↔ 1.5–2.5m (5–8ft). ✻✻✻

***R. mekongense* Viridescens Group**, syn. *R. viridescens.* Distinctive, semi-dwarf, evergreen shrubs with oblong-oval, pale blue-green leaves, 5cm (2in) long, glaucous above, paler and scaly beneath. Trusses of 4 or 5 broadly funnel-shaped, pale yellow flowers, 2cm (¾in) long, with green spots inside, are borne in late spring and early summer. Suitable for full sun. ↕↔ 1.2m (4ft). S.E. Tibet, S.W. China. ✻✻✻

R. metternichii ▣ syn. *R. degronianum* subsp. *heptamerum.* Evergreen shrub with oblong to inversely lance-shaped leaves, 8–14cm (3–5½in) long, often red when young, maturing to glossy, deep green above, with a thick brown indumentum beneath. In mid-spring, bears trusses of up to 12 funnel- to bell-shaped, 5- to 7-lobed, pale to deep pink flowers, 3–4.5cm (1¼–1¾in) long, sometimes deeper pink inside. Tolerates full sun. ↕↔ 2m (6ft). N. Japan. ✻✻✻

R. minus, syn. *R. carolinianum.* Evergreen shrub with ovate-elliptic to elliptic, dark green leaves, 5–11cm (2–4½in) long, brown-scaly beneath. In late spring and early summer, bears trusses of 6–12 funnel- to bell-shaped, pink-purple, pink, or white flowers, 2–3.5cm (¾–1½in) long, with green-brown spots. Very hardy; suitable for an open site. ↕↔ 4m (12ft). E. North America. ✻✻✻

***R.* 'Moerheim'.** Free-flowering, dwarf, evergreen shrub with small, dark green leaves that turn maroon in winter. Bears small trusses of funnel-shaped, violet-blue flowers, 3cm (1¼in) long, in abundance in mid-spring. Very hardy; prefers full sun. ↕↔ 60cm (24in). ✻✻✻

R. molle* subsp. *japonicum, syn. *R. japonicum.* Vigorous, deciduous azalea of upright habit, with obovate, obovate-oblong, or inversely lance-shaped leaves, 5–10cm (2–4in) long, mid-green above, paler bluish green beneath. Trusses of 2–12 widely funnel-shaped, often scented, orange-red, occasionally yellow flowers, 6–9cm (2½–3½in) long, softly hairy outside, are borne before the leaves, in late spring. Tolerates full sun. ↕↔ 2.2m (7ft). C. and E. Japan. ✻✻✻

***R.* 'Moonshine Crescent'.** Evergreen shrub of open, upright habit, with medium-sized leaves. In mid-spring, dome-shaped trusses of bell-shaped, primrose-yellow flowers, 5–7cm (2–3in) long, open from red winter buds. ↕↔ 2–2.5m (6–8ft). ✻✻✻

R. moupinense. Compact, dwarf, evergreen shrub with narrowly ovate, elliptic, or obovate, glossy, dark green leaves, 3–5cm (1¼–2in) long, paler green and minutely scaly beneath. Trusses of up to 3 funnel-shaped, white,

Rhododendron 'Polar Bear' (inset: flower detail)

pink, or deep rose-pink flowers, 3–4cm (1¼–1½in) long, sometimes spotted purple inside, are borne in late winter and early spring. ↕↔ 1.2m (4ft). W. China. ✻✻✻

***R.* 'Mrs. A.T. de la Mare'.** Upright, compact, evergreen shrub with medium-sized leaves. Domed trusses of funnel-shaped, frilled, slightly fragrant, pale pink flowers, 9cm (3½in) long, fading to white, with green-spotted throats, are borne in late spring. ↕↔ 3m (10ft). ✻✻✻

***R.* 'Mrs. Furnivall'** ▣ Compact, evergreen shrub with medium-sized leaves. From an early age, bears neat trusses of funnel-shaped, light rose-pink flowers, to 8cm (3in) long, each with a bold, brownish red flare inside, in late spring. Suitable for partial shade or full sun. ↕↔ 2.2m (7ft). ✻✻✻

***R.* 'Mrs. G.W. Leak'** ▣ syn. *R.* 'Cottage Garden's Pride'. Compact, evergreen shrub with medium-sized leaves. In mid-spring, bears upright trusses of funnel-shaped, light rose-pink flowers, 10–15cm (4–6in) long, each with a deep brown and crimson central flare. ↕↔ 4m (12ft). ✻✻✻

***R.* 'Mrs. T.H. Lowinsky'** ▣ Free-flowering, vigorous, evergreen shrub with medium-sized leaves. Dense trusses of funnel-shaped, pink-flushed white flowers, to 8cm (3in) long, each with a bright orange-brown flare inside and reflexed lobes, open from lavender-pink buds in early summer. Grow in sun. ↕↔ 2.2–3m (7–10ft). ✻✻✻

R.* x *mucronatum ▣ syn. *R.* 'Ledifolium'. Spreading, semi-evergreen shrub with lance-shaped to ovate- or oblong-lance-shaped, hairy, mid-green leaves, 3–6cm (1¼–2½in) long. In mid-spring, freely bears trusses of 2 or 3 widely funnel-shaped, fragrant white, occasionally pink flowers, 6–7cm (2½–3in) across. Grows well in full sun. ↕↔ 1.2–1.5m (4–5ft). Origin uncertain. ✻✻✻

R. mucronulatum. Dwarf to medium-sized, deciduous shrub of erect habit, with lance-shaped, dark green leaves, 4–6cm (1½–2½in) long, scaly beneath. Solitary, funnel-shaped, pinkish purple, pink, or occasionally white flowers, 2–2.5cm (¾–1in) long, are borne from midwinter to early spring. Grow in full sun. ↕ 0.3–2.5m (1–8ft), ↔ 1m (3ft). E. Russia, N. and C. China, Mongolia. ✻✻✻

R. nakaharae. Prostrate, compact, evergreen shrub with small, bristly leaves, 2.5cm (1in) long, shiny, dark green above, paler green beneath. Trusses of up to 3 funnel- to bell-shaped, dark orange-red to rose-red flowers, 1–2cm (½–¾in) long, are borne in early and midsummer. ↕ 30cm (12in), ↔ 2m (6ft). Taiwan. ✻✻✻

***R.* 'Naomi'** ▣ ◯ Tall, evergreen shrub or small tree with medium-sized leaves. In mid-spring, produces large trusses of widely funnel-shaped, fragrant, pale lavender-pink flowers, 9cm (3½in) across, shading to greenish yellow in the throats and each with a subtle brown stripe. ↕↔ 5m (15ft). ✻✻✻

***R.* 'Narcissiflorum'** ▣ Compact, vigorous, deciduous Ghent azalea with medium-sized leaves. In late spring and early summer, bears compact trusses of hose-in-hose, sweetly scented, pale yellow flowers, 3cm (1¼in) long, darker yellow towards the centres and on the outsides of the petals. ↕↔ 1.5–2.5m (5–8ft). ✻✻✻

R. neoglandulosum see *Ledum glandulosum.*

***R.* 'Ne Plus Ultra'.** Vigorous, upright, evergreen Vireya rhododendron with medium-sized leaves. Trusses of up to 14 tubular-funnel-shaped, bright red flowers, 5–6cm (2–2½in) long, with purplish pink throats, are produced intermittently from summer to winter. ↕ 1.5m (5ft), ↔ 1m (3ft). ❀ (min. 5°C/41°F)

R. neriiflorum ▣ Evergreen shrub producing elliptic to oblong or inversely lance-shaped, dark green leaves, 4–11cm (1½–4½in) long, glaucous beneath. In mid- and late spring, bears trusses of 5–12 tubular-bell-shaped, fleshy, bright scarlet to crimson flowers, 3.5–4.5cm (1½–1¾in) long. Suitable for full sun. ↕ to 6m (20ft), ↔ 4m (12ft). Tibet, China, Burma. ✻✻✻

R. niveum ◯ Distinctive, evergreen shrub or tree with white-felted shoots and inversely lance-shaped to elliptic leaves, 11–17cm (4½–7in) long, dark green above, with a white-fawn indumentum beneath. In mid-spring, bears compact trusses of 15–30 tubular-bell-shaped, smoky blue to purple-lilac flowers, 3–3.5cm (1¼–1½in) long, with dark purple nectar pouches inside. ↕ to 6m (20ft), ↔ 4m (12ft). India (Sikkim), Bhutan. ✻✻✻

***R.* Nobleanum Group** ▣ ◯ syn. *R.* x *pulcherrimum.* Robust, evergreen shrubs or small trees producing medium-sized to large leaves. Compact trusses of broadly funnel-shaped flowers, 5cm (2in) across, which may be rose-red, pink, or white (depending on the clone), are borne intermittently in mild weather, from late autumn to early spring. ↕↔ 5m (15ft). ✻✻✻

***R.* 'Nova Zembla'** ▣ Evergreen shrub with medium-sized leaves. Full, rounded trusses of broadly funnel-shaped, deep red flowers, 4–5cm (1½–2in) long, spotted darker red inside, are produced in mid- and late spring. ↕↔ 1.5–3m (5–10ft). ✻✻✻

R. nuttallii ◯ Evergreen shrub or small tree of open habit, with oblong to oblong-ovate, puckered leaves, 17–26cm (7–10in) long, dark green above, densely scaly beneath. Trusses of 3–6 very large, tubular to bell-shaped, strongly scented, yellow or creamy white flowers, 8–13cm (3–5in) long, suffused yellow in the throats, are borne in mid-spring. ↕↔ to 10m (30ft). N.E. India to W. China. ✻

R. occidentale ▣ Deciduous shrub with elliptic to oblong-lance-shaped leaves, 3–9cm (1¼–3½in) long, glossy, mid-green above, glaucous beneath. In early summer, bears trusses of 6–12 broadly funnel-shaped, sweetly scented, usually creamy white or pale pink flowers, 6–8cm (2½–3in) across, each with a yellow or yellow-orange mark inside. Grow in sun. ↕↔ 3m (10ft). W. North America. ✻✻✻

***R.* 'Odee Wright'** ▣ Compact, sometimes low-growing, dense, evergreen shrub with medium-sized leaves. In mid-spring, peach-coloured buds open to trusses of up to 15 broadly funnel-shaped, greenish yellow flowers, to 15cm (6in) long, tinted pink, and spotted carmine-red in the throats. Grow in full sun. ↕↔ 1.5m (5ft). ✻✻✻

***R.* 'Olive'** ▣ Free-flowering, upright, small to medium-sized, evergreen shrub producing small, ovate-elliptic leaves, mid-green above, paler green beneath. Trusses of 2 or 3 funnel-shaped flowers, 4cm (1½in) long, mauve-pink with deeper spots inside, are borne in early spring. ↕ 1.2m (4ft), ↔ 1m (3ft). ❄❄❄

R. orbiculare ⚲ Evergreen shrub or tree producing distinctive, rounded, matt, mid-green leaves, 7–13cm (3–5in) long, glaucous beneath, with heart- or ear-shaped bases. Loose trusses of 7–12 broadly bell-shaped, rose- to deep pink flowers, 5–7cm (2–3in) long, are borne in mid- and late spring. Grow in sun. ↕↔ 3m (10ft). W. China. ❄❄❄

R. oreodoxa ▣⚲ Evergreen shrub or small tree with obovate-elliptic, dark green leaves, 6–9cm (2½–3½in) long, pale bluish green and glaucous beneath. In mid-spring, bears abundant trusses of 10–12 tubular- to broadly bell-shaped, usually 7-lobed pink flowers, 5cm (2in) long, sometimes purple-spotted inside. Tolerates full sun. ↕ 3–5m (10–15ft), ↔ 3m (10ft). W. China. ❄❄❄

R. oreotrephes ▣ Evergreen shrub producing oblong-elliptic, mid- or grey-green leaves, 2–8cm (¾–3in) long, usually with purple, red-brown, or grey scales, and glaucous beneath. In mid- and late spring, bears trusses of 3–11 funnel- to bell-shaped, mauve, purple, or rose-pink flowers, 2.5–3.5cm (1–1½in) long, sometimes purple-spotted inside. Thrives in sun. ↕↔ 5m (15ft). Tibet, China, Burma. ❄❄❄

R. pachysanthum ▣ Evergreen, mound-forming shrub. Lance-shaped to oval leaves, 4–10cm (1½–4in) long, have a conspicuous silver-brown indumentum above, and a dense silver indumentum beneath, later becoming rich brown. In mid-spring, bears trusses of 11 or more funnel- to bell-shaped, pale rose-pink flowers, to 4cm (1½in) long, with variable markings inside. Grow in sun. ↕ 1.5–2.5m (5–8ft), ↔ 2.5m (8ft). Taiwan. ❄❄❄

***R.* 'Palestrina'** ▣ Compact, evergreen Vuyk azalea with small leaves. Trusses of 2 or 3 open funnel-shaped, pure white flowers, 6–10cm (2½–4in) long, with faint green markings in the throats, are borne freely in late spring. ↕↔ 1.2m (4ft). ❄❄❄

***R.* 'Patty Bee'.** Free-flowering, dwarf, evergreen shrub, of compact, rounded habit, with small leaves turning purple-bronze in winter. Compact trusses of broadly funnel-shaped, clear pale yellow flowers, 5cm (2in) across, appear in early and mid-spring. Prefers full sun; very hardy. ↕↔ 75cm (30in). ❄❄❄

R. pemakoense. Dwarf, dense, compact, evergreen shrub with small, elliptic to obovate leaves, 2–3cm (¾–1¼in) long, glossy, dark green above, glaucous beneath. Abundant trusses of up to 3 bell-shaped, pink to rose-purple flowers, 3.5–4.5cm (1½–1¾in) long, open in early and mid-spring. ↕↔ 60cm (24in). N.E. India, S.E. Tibet. ❄❄❄

***R.* 'Penheale Blue'.** Free-flowering, low-growing, compact, evergreen shrub with small leaves. Clustered trusses of funnel-shaped, red-flushed, bright violet-blue flowers, 2.5cm (1in) long, are borne in early and mid-spring. Good in full sun. ↕↔ 1–1.2m (3–4ft). ❄❄❄

***R.* 'Percy Wiseman'.** Low-growing, compact, evergreen shrub with medium-sized leaves. In mid- and late spring, bears rounded trusses of funnel-shaped, peach-pink and cream flowers, 5cm (2in) long, fading to creamy white, with green markings in the throats. Suitable for full sun. ↕↔ 2m (6ft). ❄❄❄

***R.* 'Persil'** ▣ Deciduous, bushy Knap Hill-Exbury azalea producing medium-sized leaves. Funnel-shaped, pure white flowers, to 6cm (2½in) long, each with a bold orange-yellow flare inside, open in mid-spring. ↕↔ 2m (6ft). ❄❄❄

***R.* 'Peter John Mezitt'**, syn. *R.* 'P.J. Mezitt'. Dwarf, compact, evergreen shrub with small, ovate, dark green leaves, which turn brownish purple in winter if grown in full sun. Trusses of 4–9 small, frost-resistant, broadly funnel-shaped, bright lavender-pink flowers, 4.5cm (1¾in) long, are borne in very early spring. Very hardy. ↕↔ 1.2m (4ft). ❄❄❄

***R.* 'Pink Pearl'** ▣ Vigorous, evergreen shrub of open, erect habit, with large leaves. In mid- and late spring, bears abundant tall trusses of funnel-shaped, soft pink flowers, 10–12cm (4–5in) long, fading to white. Thrives in sun. ↕↔ 4m (12ft). ❄❄❄

***R.* 'P.J. Mezitt'** see *R.* 'Peter John Mezitt'.

***R.* 'Polar Bear'** ▣⚲ Late-flowering, vigorous, multi-stemmed, evergreen shrub or small tree with large leaves. In late summer, bears large trusses of tubular-funnel-shaped, strongly scented white flowers, 4.5–10cm (1¾–4in) long, with light brown-flecked, pale green throats. ↕ 5m (15ft), ↔ 4m (12ft). ❄❄❄

R. ponticum. Vigorous, evergreen shrub with inversely lance-shaped to broadly elliptic leaves, 6–18cm (2½–7in) long, glossy, dark green above, paler beneath. In early summer, bears trusses of 10–15 broadly funnel-shaped, reddish purple, occasionally white flowers, to 5cm (2in) long, often spotted yellowish green inside. ↕ 6–8m (20–25ft), ↔ 6m (20ft). Portugal, Spain, Lebanon, Turkey, Armenia, Caucasus. ❄❄❄

R.* x *praecox see *R.* 'Praecox'.

***R.* 'Praecox'**, syn. *R.* x *praecox.* Early-flowering, sometimes low-growing, evergreen shrub producing small leaves. In late winter and early spring, trusses of 2 or 3 widely funnel-shaped, rose-purple flowers, 4–4.5cm (1½–1¾in) across, are borne at the shoot tips. Thrives in full sun; suitable as a hedge. ↕↔ 1.3m (4½ft). ❄❄❄

***R.* 'President Roosevelt'** ▣ Slow-growing, weakly branched, evergreen shrub with splashes of bright yellow on its medium-sized, glossy, dark green leaves. In early and mid-spring, bears conical trusses of funnel-shaped, bright red flowers, 4–5cm (1½–2in) long, fading to white in the centres. ↕↔ 2m (6ft). ❄❄❄

***R.* 'Princess Anne'**, syn. *R.* 'Golden Fleece' of gardens. Compact, rounded, semi-dwarf, evergreen shrub with small, ovate, mid-green leaves, bronze when young and during cold winters. Domed trusses of funnel-shaped, pale yellow, green-tinged flowers, 5cm (2in) long, are borne in abundance in mid-spring. Prefers full sun. ↕↔ 75–120cm (30–48in). ❄❄❄

R. pseudochrysanthum. Dome-shaped, evergreen shrub producing ovate to elliptic, rigid, thick, dark green leaves, 3–8cm (1¼–3in) long, with a thin grey

Rhododendron 'Medway'

Rhododendron metternichii

Rhododendron 'Mrs. Furnivall'

Rhododendron 'Mrs. G.W. Leak'

Rhododendron 'Mrs. T.H. Lowinsky'

Rhododendron mucronatum

Rhododendron 'Naomi'

Rhododendron 'Narcissiflorum'

Rhododendron neriiflorum

Rhododendron Nobleanum Group

Rhododendron 'Nova Zembla'

Rhododendron occidentale

Rhododendron 'Odee Wright'

Rhododendron 'Olive'

Rhododendron oreodoxa

Rhododendron oreotrephes

Rhododendron pachysanthum

Rhododendron 'Palestrina'

Rhododendron 'Persil'

Rhododendron 'Pink Pearl'

Rhododendron 'President Roosevelt'

R

indumentum above; the undersides are glossy, with midrib indumentum only. In mid-spring, bears trusses of 5–10 bell-shaped, pale pink or white flowers, 3–4cm (1¼–1½in) long, deeply lined with dark pink outside and spotted with dark pink inside. Suitable for full sun. ↕↔ to 3m (10ft). Taiwan. ❄❄❄

***R.* 'Ptarmigan'** ▣ Free-flowering, drought-resistant, dwarf, evergreen shrub with a spreading habit and small, dark green leaves. Clustered trusses of funnel-shaped, pure white flowers, 2.5cm (1in) long, virtually smother the foliage in early and mid-spring. ↕↔ 45–90cm (18–36in). ❄❄❄

R.* x *pulcherrimum see *R.* Nobleanum Group.

***R.* 'Purple Splendour'** ▣ Evergreen shrub with medium-sized leaves. In late spring and early summer, bears trusses of about 15 striking, frilled, funnel-shaped, deep purple-blue flowers, to 8cm (3in) long, each with a purple-black basal mark inside. Suitable for full sun. ↕↔ 3m (10ft). ❄❄❄

***R.* 'Queen Elizabeth II'** ▣ Strong-growing, evergreen shrub of open habit, with medium-sized leaves. Full trusses of 10–12 funnel-shaped, very pale, clear greenish yellow flowers, 11–12cm (4½–5in) long, are borne in mid- and late spring. ↕↔ 1.5–3m (5–10ft). ❄❄❄

R. racemosum ▣ Stiffly branched, evergreen shrub producing broadly obovate to oblong-elliptic, mid- to dark green leaves, 1.5–5cm (½–2in) long, glaucous beneath. Bears abundant trusses of up to 4 widely funnel-shaped, deep rose-red, pink, or white flowers, to 3cm (1¼in) across, along the stems in early and mid-spring. ↕↔ 2m (6ft). W. China. ❄❄❄

***R.* 'Razorbill'.** Free-flowering, compact, semi-dwarf, evergreen shrub with small, crinkled, dark green leaves. In early and mid-spring, bears conical trusses of distinctive, upward-facing, tubular, light rose-pink flowers, 2cm (¾in) long, flushed deep pink inside. ↕↔ 1.1–1.3m (3½–4½ft). ❄❄❄

R. rex ♀ Evergreen, large shrub or small tree producing inversely lance-shaped leaves, 25–45cm (10–18in) long, with a cinnamon-brown indumentum above when young, becoming wrinkled, dark green, with a thick, cinnamon-brown or darker brown indumentum beneath. In mid- and late spring, bears trusses of 12–25 bell-shaped, 7- or 8-lobed, white-tinged pink flowers, 4–5cm (1½–2in) long, each with a crimson basal mark and sometimes heavily spotted crimson. Requires a sheltered site in light woodland. ↕↔ 12m (40ft). China (Sichuan, Yunnan). ❄❄❄. **subsp. *arizelum*** ▣ syn. *R. arizelum*, has obovate leaves, 13–22cm (5–9in) long, and usually yellow, sometimes pink, rarely white flowers, with crimson marks in the throats; ↕↔ 8m (25ft), China (W. Yunnan), N.E. Burma. **subsp. *fictolacteum*** ▣ syn. *R. fictolacteum*, has oblong-ovate to lance-shaped leaves, 11–30cm (4½–12in) long, and bears trusses of 12–25 white, sometimes pink-tinged flowers with crimson throats and sometimes crimson spotting; S.E. Tibet, China (W. Yunnan), N.E. Burma.

***R.* 'Rose Bud'** ▣ Compact, low-growing, evergreen Kurume azalea with small leaves. In mid-spring, bears an abundance of small trusses of rosebud-like, funnel-shaped, rose-pink flowers, 3cm (1¼in) long. Thrives in sun. ↕↔ 60–90cm (24–36in). ❄❄❄

***R.* 'Roza Harrison'** see *R.* 'Roza Stevenson'.

***R.* 'Roza Stevenson'** ▣ syn. *R.* 'Roza Harrison'. Vigorous, open, erect, evergreen shrub with medium-sized leaves. In mid- and late spring, bears abundant loose trusses of 10–12 saucer-shaped, clear lemon-yellow flowers, 15cm (6in) across. ↕↔ 1.5–4m (5–12ft). ❄❄❄

R. rubiginosum ♀ Evergreen shrub or small tree with lance-shaped or oblong to elliptic-lance-shaped, dark green leaves, 5–12cm (2–5in) long, red-brown and scaly beneath. In mid- and late spring, bears trusses of 4–8 funnel- to bell-shaped, rose-pink to lilac-purple flowers, 1.5–3.5cm (½–1½in) long, brown-spotted inside. Thrives in sun. ↕ 10m (30ft) or more, ↔ 6m (20ft). S.E. Tibet, S.W. China, N. Burma. ❄❄❄

R. russatum ▣ Dwarf, compact, evergreen shrub with narrowly to broadly elliptic or oblong, dark green leaves, to 4cm (1½in) long, brown to red-brown and scaly beneath. In mid- and late spring, bears trusses of 4–6 broadly funnel-shaped, reddish purple to indigo-blue, occasionally white flowers, 1–2cm (½–¾in) across. Prefers sun. ↕ to 1.5m (5ft), ↔ 1.2m (4ft). S.W. China. ❄❄❄

***R.* 'St. Valentine'** ▣ Evergreen azalea of spreading habit, with small, elliptic leaves. Trusses of 3–5 pendent, tubular-bell-shaped, bright red flowers, 4cm (1½in) long, are borne in spring. ↕ 1.5m (5ft), ↔ 2m (6ft). ❀ (min. 5°C/41°F)

***R.* 'Sappho'** ▣ Free-flowering, tall, evergreen shrub with medium-sized leaves. Funnel-shaped white flowers, 7–9cm (3–3½in) long, attractively flared purple-black in the throats, are borne in high-domed trusses in early summer. Grow in full sun. ↕↔ 3m (10ft). ❄❄❄

R. sargentianum. Compact, dwarf, evergreen shrub with bristly, scaly shoots and broadly elliptic, aromatic leaves, to 1.5cm (½in) long, glossy mid-green above, densely golden scaly beneath. From mid-spring to early summer, bears

Rhododendron 'Temple Belle'

flattened trusses of 5–7 tubular, lemon-yellow or cream flowers, to 1cm (½in) long, with spreading lobes. ↕↔ 60cm (24in). W. China. ❄❄❄

***R.* 'Satan'.** Bushy, free-flowering, deciduous Knap Hill-Exbury azalea with medium-sized leaves. In mid-spring, produces bold trusses of funnel-shaped, bright red flowers, 5cm (2in) long. Grow in full sun. ↕↔ 2m (6ft). ❄❄❄

***R.* 'Scarlet Wonder'.** Free-flowering, compact, semi-dwarf, evergreen shrub with small leaves. In mid-spring, bears loose trusses of 4–7 funnel-shaped, slightly frilled, bright cardinal-red flowers, 5cm (2in) long. ↕↔ 1.2–2m (4–6ft). ❄❄❄

R. schlippenbachii. Deciduous, densely branched azalea with obovate or broadly ovate leaves, 2.5–11cm (1–4½in) long, dark green above, paler green beneath, borne in whorls of 5 at the branch tips. In mid- and late spring, produces trusses of 3–6 flat or saucer-shaped, pale pink or rose-pink, sometimes white flowers, 3–5cm (1¼–2in) across, spotted reddish pink on the upper lobes. ↕↔ to 5m (15ft). China (N. Manchuria), Korea. ❄❄❄

***R.* 'Scintillation'.** Evergreen shrub with medium-sized leaves. In early summer, bears dense, rounded trusses of funnel-shaped, pale pink flowers, 6–7cm (2½–3in) long, each with a bronze to pinkish brown flare in the throat. ↕↔ 2.2m (7ft). ❄❄❄

***R.* 'Seta'** ▣ Free-flowering, evergreen shrub of open habit, with small leaves. In early spring, bears upright, clustered trusses of tubular-bell-shaped, light pink flowers, 3.5cm (1½in) long, striped deep pink on the outsides. ↕↔ 1–1.5m (3–5ft). ❄❄❄

***R.* 'Seven Stars'** ▣ Vigorous, upright, evergreen shrub with medium-sized leaves. In mid-spring, bears rounded trusses of funnel-shaped, pale pinkish white flowers, 5cm (2in) across, flushed deep red-purple on the outsides on opening. ↕↔ 4m (12ft). ❄❄

***R.* 'Shamrock'.** Free-flowering, compact, dwarf, spreading, evergreen shrub with small leaves. In early and mid-spring, pale green buds open to trusses of 5–9 funnel-shaped, pale yellow flowers, 0.7–2.5cm (¼–1in) across, tinged green and spotted yellow inside. Very hardy; tolerates sun and drought. ↕↔ 75cm (30in). ❄❄❄

***R.* 'Silver Moon'.** Dwarf, broadly spreading, evergreen Glenn Dale azalea with small leaves. Abundant, funnel-shaped white flowers, 6–8cm (2½–3in) long, marked pale green inside, are borne in rounded trusses in mid-spring. Grow in sun. ↕↔ 1–1.5m (3–5ft). ❄❄❄

***R.* 'Silver Slipper'.** Bushy, deciduous Knap Hill-Exbury azalea producing medium-sized leaves. Domed trusses of funnel-shaped white flowers, 6cm

Rhododendron 'Rose Bud'

RHODODENDRON

(2½in) across, flushed pink with central orange flares inside, are borne freely in mid-spring. Suitable for sun. ‡↔ 2m (6ft). ❄❄❄

R. sinogrande ■ ☊ Evergreen shrub or small tree with very large, oblong to lance-shaped, glossy, dark green leaves, to 75cm (30in) long, with a smooth, silver to buff indumentum beneath. In mid- and late spring, bears trusses of 20–30 widely bell-shaped, pale yellow to creamy white flowers, 5cm (2in) long, marked crimson inside. ‡↔ 10m (30ft). Tibet, China, Burma. ❄❄❄

R. 'Sir Charles Lemon'. Tall, erect, evergreen shrub producing medium-sized, dark green leaves with a cinnamon-brown indumentum beneath. In mid- and late spring, bears abundant dense trusses of funnel-shaped, pure white flowers, 4cm (1½in) across, speckled red inside. Grow in full sun. ‡ 6m (20ft), ↔ 4m (12ft). ❄❄❄

R. smirnowii. Evergreen shrub producing oblong to lance-shaped, dark green leaves, 7–14cm (3–5½in) long, with a thick, woolly, fawn indumentum beneath. Trusses of 10–12 funnel- to bell-shaped, pale to deep rose-purple flowers, to 4cm (1½in) long, are borne in late spring and early summer. Very hardy. ‡ to 4m (12ft), ↔ 5m (15ft). N.E. Turkey, Georgia, Caucasus. ❄❄❄

R. 'Snowdrift'. Deciduous, bushy Mollis azalea with medium-sized leaves. Dense trusses of narrowly funnel-shaped white flowers, with yellow-orange marks in the throats, are borne in spring before the leaves. Suitable for full sun. ‡↔ 2.5m (8ft). ❄❄❄

R. 'Snowflake' see *R.* 'Kure-no-yuki'.

R. 'Snow Lady'. Compact, evergreen, semi-dwarf shrub with medium-sized leaves. In early spring, freely bears lax trusses of 2–5 funnel-shaped, pure white flowers, 2.5–4cm (1–1½in) long. Flowers best in a sunny, but sheltered site. ‡↔ 1m (3ft). ❄❄❄

R. 'Songbird'. Evergreen, compact, semi-dwarf shrub with small leaves. Neat trusses of small, funnel-shaped, vivid violet-blue flowers are borne in early spring. Very hardy; suitable for full sun. ‡↔ 1.2m (4ft). ❄❄❄

R. souliei ■ Evergreen shrub with ovate-rounded leaves, 6–8cm (2½–3in) long, metallic blue-green above when young, becoming mid-green with age, light green and glaucous beneath. In late spring and early summer, bears trusses of 5–8 saucer-shaped, pink or rose-red, occasionally white flowers, 5–8cm (2–3in) long. ‡ to 5m (15ft), ↔ 4m (12ft). W. China. ❄❄❄

R. 'Spek's Brilliant' ■ Deciduous Mollis azalea with medium-sized leaves. In late spring and early summer, produces full trusses of funnel-shaped, bright orange-scarlet flowers, 2.5–6cm (1–2½in) across, with deeper orange-scarlet flares inside. Suitable for full sun. ‡↔ 2.5m (8ft). ❄❄❄

R. 'Spek's Orange' ■ Deciduous, bushy Mollis azalea with medium-sized leaves. In late spring and early summer, bears dense trusses of broadly funnel-shaped, bright reddish orange flowers, 6cm (2½in) long. Suitable for full sun. ‡↔ 2.5m (8ft). ❄❄❄

R. 'Strawberry Ice' ■ Bushy, deciduous Knap Hill-Exbury azalea with medium-sized leaves. Rounded trusses of broadly funnel-shaped, pale flesh pink flowers, 6–7cm (2½–3in) long, heavily veined and mottled deeper pink at the petal margins, with deep yellow-marked throats, are borne in late spring. Thrives in full sun. ‡↔ 2m (6ft). ❄❄❄

R. strigillosum. Large, dome-shaped, evergreen shrub with densely bristly shoots and recurved, oblong to lance-shaped leaves, 7–14cm (3–5½in) long, bright green above, scaly and brown-hairy beneath. From late winter to mid-spring, bears trusses of 8–12 tubular-bell-shaped, glossy crimson-scarlet flowers, 4–6cm (1½–2½in) long. ‡↔ 6m (20ft). W. China. ❄❄❄

R. 'Susan' ■ Vigorous but compact, evergreen shrub with medium-sized leaves. In mid-spring, bears trusses of 12–16 funnel-shaped, cool mauve-blue flowers, 6cm (2½in) long, with darker margins, fading to near white. ‡↔ 3m (10ft). ❄❄❄

R. sutchuenense ■ ☊ Spreading, evergreen shrub or small tree with oblong to lance-shaped leaves, 11–25cm (4½–10in) long, matt, mid-green above, paler green beneath. From late winter to mid-spring, bears trusses of 8–12 broadly bell-shaped, rose-pink or pale lilac flowers, to 8cm (3in) across, often with purple spots inside. ‡↔ 8m (25ft). W. China. ❄❄❄

R. 'Taylorii'. Erect, evergreen Vireya rhododendron with medium-sized, narrowly elliptic leaves. From winter to spring, intermittently bears rounded trusses of up to 15 funnel-shaped pink flowers, 5–8cm (2–3in) long. ‡ 1.5m (5ft), ↔ 1m (3ft). ❅ (min. 5°C/41°F)

R. 'Temple Belle' ■ Low-growing, compact, evergreen shrub producing medium-sized, rounded, pale green leaves. Loose trusses of 3–5 bell-shaped, clear pink flowers, 5–6cm (2–2½in) long, are borne freely in early and mid-spring. ‡↔ 2m (6ft). ❄❄❄

R. 'Tessa Roza'. Early-flowering, low-growing, upright, evergreen shrub with small leaves. In late winter and early spring, produces trusses of 3 funnel-shaped, deep rose-pink flowers, 3–4cm (1¼–1½in) long, spotted deep carmine-red inside. ‡↔ 1.5m (5ft). ❄❄❄

R. 'The Hon. Jean Marie de Montague', syn. *R.* 'Jean Marie Montague'. Free-flowering, compact, evergreen shrub with medium-sized leaves. Dense trusses of funnel-shaped, scarlet-crimson flowers, 5–7cm (2–3in) long, are borne in mid-spring. Tolerates heat, sun, and an exposed site. ‡↔ 2.5m (8ft). ❄❄❄

R. thomsonii ■ ☊ Evergreen shrub or small tree with smooth, peeling, purple-brown bark and broadly ovate leaves, 3–11cm (1¼–4½in) long, dark green above, glaucous beneath. Pendent trusses of 6–12 bell-shaped, waxy, fleshy, deep blood-red flowers, 3.5–5cm (1½–2in) long, with large calyces, open in mid- and late spring. ‡↔ 6m (20ft). Himalayas, W. China. ❄❄❄

R. 'Titian Beauty' ■ Low-growing, compact, evergreen shrub producing medium-sized, deep green leaves, with a thin brown indumentum beneath. Lax trusses of tubular-bell-shaped, waxy, rich red flowers, 3.5–5cm (1½–2in) long, are borne on long flower-stalks above the foliage, in late spring and early summer. Suitable for full sun. ‡↔ 2m (6ft). ❄❄❄

R. tomentosum see *Ledum palustre*.

Rhododendron 'Ptarmigan'

Rhododendron 'Purple Splendour'

Rhododendron 'Queen Elizabeth II'

Rhododendron racemosum

Rhododendron rex subsp. *arizelum*

Rhododendron rex subsp. *fictolacteum*

Rhododendron 'Roza Stevenson'

Rhododendron russatum

Rhododendron 'St. Valentine'

Rhododendron 'Sappho'

Rhododendron 'Seta'

Rhododendron 'Seven Stars'

Rhododendron sinogrande

Rhododendron souliei

Rhododendron 'Spek's Brilliant'

Rhododendron 'Spek's Orange'

Rhododendron 'Strawberry Ice'

Rhododendron 'Susan'

Rhododendron sutchuenense

Rhododendron thomsonii

Rhododendron 'Titian Beauty'

R

Rhododendron 'Vanessa Pastel'

Rhododendron vernicosum

Rhododendron 'Vuyk's Rosyred'

Rhododendron 'Vuyk's Scarlet'

Rhododendron wardii

Rhododendron yakushimanum

Rhododendron yakushimanum 'Ken Janeck'

Rhododendron 'Yellow Hammer'

Rhododendron yunnanense

R. tsariense. Evergreen shrub producing elliptic-obovate, dark green leaves, 3.5–6cm (1½–2½in) long, with a rich cinnamon-brown indumentum beneath. Trusses of 3 or 4 bell-shaped white flowers, 2.5–3.5cm (1–1½in) long, tinged pink and frequently spotted red inside, are borne from early to late spring. ↕↔ 4m (12ft). E. Himalayas, Tibet, Bhutan. ✻✻✻

***R.* 'Vanessa Pastel'** ■ Free-flowering, compact, evergreen shrub producing medium-sized leaves. In early summer, bears lax trusses of funnel-shaped, creamy pink flowers, 6cm (2½in) long, stained red on the outsides and with red-marked throats. ↕↔ 2m (6ft). ✻✻

R. vaseyi. Deciduous azalea with elliptic to elliptic-oblong, hairless, shiny, dark green leaves, 5–12cm (2–5in) long, paler green beneath. In mid- and late spring, trusses of 4–8 broadly funnel-shaped, rose-pink, pale pink, or white flowers, 4cm (1½in) long, spotted red, are produced before the leaves. Suitable for full sun. ↕↔ 5m (15ft). E. North America. ✻✻✻

R. vernicosum ■♀ Evergreen shrub or small tree of variable habit, with elliptic to ovate-elliptic or obovate-elliptic, dull, mid-green leaves, 5–10cm (2–4in) long, slightly glaucous beneath. In late spring, produces trusses of 6–12 funnel- to bell-shaped, 6- or 7-lobed flowers, 3.5–5cm (1½–2in) long, bright rose-pink, lavender-pink, or white, sometimes marked crimson inside. ↕↔ 6m (20ft). W. China. ✻✻✻

***R.* 'Vida Brown'.** Slow-growing, evergreen Kurume azalea of low, compact habit, with small leaves. Hose-in-hose, rose-pink flowers, 4cm (1½in) long, are borne in small trusses in mid-spring. ↕ 75cm (30in), ↔ 1.2m (4ft). ✻✻✻

R. viridescens see *R. mekongense* Viridescens Group.

R. viscosum. Deciduous azalea with hairy shoots and elliptic-obovate to oblong-obovate, dark green leaves, 1.5–3cm (½–1¼in) long, often glaucous beneath. In early and midsummer, bears trusses of 4–12 narrowly tubular to funnel-shaped, fragrant, pink-suffused white flowers, 2–3cm (¾–1¼in) long. Thrives in damp soil in sun. ↕↔ 2.5m (8ft). E. North America. ✻✻✻

***R.* 'Vuyk's Rosyred'** ■ Low-growing, dwarf, evergreen Vuyk azalea with small leaves. Bears a profusion of funnel-shaped, satiny, deep rose-pink flowers, 5cm (2in) long, each with a darker pink flare inside, in pairs in mid-spring. Suitable for full sun. ↕ 75cm (30in), ↔ 1.2m (4ft). ✻✻✻

***R.* 'Vuyk's Scarlet'** ■ Dwarf, evergreen Vuyk azalea with small leaves. In mid-spring, bears abundant solitary or paired, funnel-shaped, crimson-scarlet flowers, 6–7cm (2½–3in) long, with wavy-margined lobes. Tolerates full sun, especially in frost-prone areas. ↕ 75cm (30in), ↔ 1.2m (4ft). ✻✻✻

R. wardii ■♀ Evergreen shrub or small tree with oblong-elliptic to broadly obovate, hairless, dark green leaves, 6–11cm (2½–4½in) long, paler green beneath. Trusses of 7–14 broadly funnel-shaped flowers, 4–5cm (1½–2in) long, in various shades of yellow, sometimes with basal crimson marks inside, are borne in late spring and early summer. ↕ 6m (20ft), ↔ 5m (15ft). S.E. Tibet, S.W. China. ✻✻✻

***R.* 'Wigeon'.** Free-flowering, semi-dwarf, evergreen shrub with small leaves. In mid-spring, bears neat trusses of numerous saucer-shaped, rich lavender-pink flowers, 2.5cm (1in) long, with deeper spotting on the upper lobes inside. Very hardy; suitable for full sun. ↕↔ 1.2m (4ft). ✻✻✻

R. williamsianum. Dome-shaped, evergreen shrub with ovate-rounded leaves, 2–4.5cm (¾–1¾in) long, brown when young, bright green above and glaucous beneath when mature. Loose trusses of 2 or 3 bell-shaped pink or occasionally white flowers, 3–4cm (1¼–1½in) long, are borne in mid- and late spring. Thrives in full sun. ↕ to 1.5m (5ft), ↔ 1.2m (4ft). W. China. ✻✻✻

***R.* 'Winsome'** ■ Compact, dense, sometimes low-growing, evergreen shrub with medium-sized, mid-green leaves, bronze when young. Loose trusses of funnel-shaped, cherry-pink flowers, 5–6cm (2–2½in) long, open in early and mid-spring. Suitable for sun or partial shade. ↕↔ 1.5m (5ft). ✻✻✻

***R.* 'Wombat'** ■ Prostrate, vigorous, evergreen azalea with small leaves. Lax trusses of funnel-shaped pink flowers, 1–2cm (½–¾in) long, are produced in abundance in early summer. Provides excellent ground cover in full sun. ↕ 25cm (10in), ↔ 1.2m (4ft). ✻✻✻

Rhododendron 'Winsome'

Rhododendron 'Wombat'

R. xanthocodon see *R. cinnabarinum* subsp. *xanthocodon.*

***R.* 'Yaku Princess'.** Dense, compact, low-growing, evergreen shrub producing medium-sized, olive-green leaves, with a buff indumentum beneath. Spherical trusses of funnel-shaped, pinkish white flowers, 5–6cm (2–2½in) long, each with a deeper pink mark and greenish spots inside, are borne in mid- and late spring. Suitable for full sun. ↕↔ 1.5m (5ft). ✻✻✻

R. yakushimanum ■ syn. *R. degronianum* subsp. *yakushimanum.* Tightly dome-shaped, evergreen shrub with recurved, linear to lance-shaped, glossy, dark green leaves, 8–14cm (3–5½in) long, with a thick, reddish brown indumentum beneath. Young foliage has a pale cinnamon-brown indumentum on the upper surfaces, which is lost as the leaves mature. In mid-spring, trusses of 5–10 deep rose-pink buds open to tubular-funnel-shaped flowers, 3–4.5cm (1¼–1¾in) long, fading to pale pink or white. Very hardy; suitable for full sun. ↕↔ to 2m (6ft). Japan (Yakushima Island). ✻✻✻. **'Ken Janeck'** ■ syn. *R.* 'Ken Janeck', is low-growing, bearing full trusses of funnel-shaped white flowers, 4–5cm (1½–2in) long, lined with pinkish purple and spotted with green; ↕ 1.2m (4ft), ↔ 1.3m (4½ft).

***R.* 'Yellow Hammer'** ■ Erect, free-flowering, evergreen shrub with tiny leaves. Bears small, tightly packed trusses of 2 or 3 tubular, canary-yellow flowers, 2.5–3cm (1–1¼in) long, in early and mid-spring, and often again in autumn. Grow in sun. ↕↔ 2m (6ft). ✻✻✻

R. yunnanense ■ Vigorous, evergreen or semi-evergreen shrub with lance-shaped, narrowly elliptic, or elliptic, scaly leaves, 3–10cm (1¼–4in) long, bright green above, paler green beneath. In late spring, bears trusses of 3–5 broadly funnel-shaped, pink, pale rose-pink, lavender-pink, or white flowers, 2–3cm (¾–1¼in) long, sometimes with crimson marks, or crimson-spotted inside. Thrives in sun. ↕ to 6m (20ft), ↔ 4m (12ft). S.E. Tibet, W. China, Burma. ✻✻✻

▷ **Rhododendron, Indian** see *Melastoma malabathricum*

R

RHODOHYPOXIS

HYPOXIDACEAE

Genus of 6 species of small, clump-forming herbaceous perennials, with corm-like rootstocks, from open meadows in areas with heavy summer rainfall in the eastern provinces of South Africa, and Swaziland. The basal leaves are lance-shaped and hairy. Short-stalked, almost flat, white, pink, red, or deep purple flowers are produced over long periods in summer. Each flower has 6 overlapping tepals, arranged in 2 ranks of 3, which are fused at the bases to form a tube; the outer tepals are broader than the inner ones. Grow in a trough, rock garden, or alpine house.

• **HARDINESS** Fully hardy to frost hardy; to survive lower temperatures, plants must be kept almost dry in winter.

• **CULTIVATION** Under glass, grow in a mix of equal parts lime-free (ericaceous) potting compost, leaf mould, and sharp sand, in full light. When in growth, water freely and apply a balanced liquid fertilizer monthly; keep just moist in winter. Outdoors, grow in well-drained, moderately fertile, humus-rich soil in full sun, with protection from excessive winter wet. *R. milloides* thrives in damp conditions, and will tolerate more winter wet.

• **PROPAGATION** Sow seed at 6–12°C (45–54°F) as soon as ripe or in spring. Divide established clumps, or separate offsets, in late autumn.

• **PESTS AND DISEASES** Susceptible to red spider mites and thrips under glass.

R. baurii. Clump-forming perennial with basal clusters of narrowly lance-shaped, keeled, folded leaves, to 10cm (4in) long. The leaves are dull greyish green, and very hairy on both surfaces and at the margins. Solitary, pale to deep reddish pink flowers, to 2cm (¾in) across, are produced on stalks 5–10cm (2–4in) tall, throughout summer. ↕↔ 10cm (4in). South Africa. ❄❄. The

Rhodohypoxis baurii 'Albrighton'

Rhodohypoxis baurii 'Margaret Rose'

following cultivars, derived mainly from *R. baurii* and *R. baurii* var. *platypetala*, are generally large-flowered and vigorous. **'Albrighton'** ▣ has deep red-pink flowers. **'Harlequin'** has pink-flushed white flowers, to 1.5cm (½in) across, with distinct pink margins. **'Helen'**, syn. *R.* 'Tetra White', has very large white flowers, 3cm (1¼in) or more across. **'Margaret Rose'** ▣ has clear pink flowers. **var. *platypetala*** is more robust than *R. baurii*, with wider, grey-green leaves and white, rarely pink flowers, to 3cm (1¼in) across; ↕ 12cm (5in), ↔ 15cm (6in). **'Tetra Pink'** and **'Tetra Red'** have large flowers, 3cm (1¼in) or more across, in pink and reddish purple, respectively; flowers become smaller after 2–3 years.

R. milloides. Vigorous, clump-forming perennial with runners, and with erect, hairless or sparsely hairy, linear-lance-shaped, keeled, folded, light green, basal leaves, to 17cm (7in) long. Cerise or dark crimson, occasionally deep pink or white flowers, to 3.5cm (1½in) across, are produced on hairy flower-stalks, to 12cm (5in) or more tall, over long periods in summer. ↕ 15cm (6in), ↔ 20cm (8in). South Africa. ❄❄❄

***R.* 'Tetra White'** see *R. baurii* 'Helen'.

RHODOPHIALA

AMARYLLIDACEAE

Genus, closely related to *Hippeastrum*, of about 35 species of bulbous perennials from coastal sands to rocky, dry sites in the mountains of Uruguay, Argentina, and Chile. They are grown for their funnel-shaped flowers, borne in umbels on leafless stems in summer or autumn. The basal leaves are linear and mid-green. Grow in an alpine house; in frost-free areas, however, *R. advena* and *R. pratensis* may be grown outdoors against a warm, sunny wall.

• **HARDINESS** Half hardy to frost tender; *R. advena*, *R. bifida*, and *R. pratensis* may withstand occasional falls to around -5°C (23°F).

Rhodophiala advena

• **CULTIVATION** Under glass, plant bulbs with the necks and shoulders above soil level, in autumn. Grow in loam-based potting compost (JI No.2) in full light or bright filtered light. Water sparingly until plants are in active growth, then water moderately and apply a half-strength balanced liquid fertilizer every 2–3 weeks. Keep dry when dormant. Avoid root disturbance; pot on only every 3 years. Outdoors, plant bulbs 15–20cm (6–8in) deep in moderately fertile, well-drained soil in full sun. Provide a deep, dry winter mulch in cold areas.

• **PROPAGATION** Sow seed at 16°C (61°F) as soon as ripe. Remove offsets in autumn or winter.

• **PESTS AND DISEASES** Trouble free.

R. advena ▣ syn. *Hippeastrum advenum.* Bulbous perennial producing umbels of 2–6 horizontal, open funnel-shaped, red, yellow, or pink flowers, 5cm (2in) across, in late summer and early autumn, just before the semi-erect, linear, basal leaves, 15–30cm (6–12in) long, emerge. ↕ 30–50cm (12–20in), ↔ 10cm (4in). Chile. ❄

R. bifida, syn. *Hippeastrum bifidum.* Bulbous perennial producing umbels of up to 5 erect, narrowly funnel-shaped, bright deep red flowers, 5cm (2in) long, in summer; flowers are borne as, or just before, the semi-erect, linear, basal leaves, to 45cm (18in) long, emerge. ↕ to 30cm (12in), ↔ 10cm (4in). Argentina, Uruguay. ❄

R. pratensis, syn. *Hippeastrum pratense.* Bulbous perennial bearing umbels of 2–8 horizontal, broadly funnel-shaped red flowers, 5–7cm (2–3in) across, in early summer, at the same time as the semi-erect, linear, basal leaves, 30–50cm (12–20in) long. ↕ to 60cm (24in), ↔ 10cm (4in). Chile. ❄

RHODOTHAMNUS

ERICACEAE

Genus of 2 species of dwarf, evergreen shrubs found in pockets of humus-rich soil, often among limestone rocks, in the eastern Alps and Turkey. They have glossy, dark green foliage, and are grown for their solitary, occasionally clustered, cup-shaped pink flowers, produced in profusion from the leaf axils in early summer. Grow in a rock garden, peat bed, or alpine house. They are not easy to establish.

• **HARDINESS** Fully hardy.

• **CULTIVATION** Under glass, grow in loam-based potting compost (JI No.2) with additional leaf mould, in full light. In the growing season, water freely and apply a balanced liquid fertilizer monthly; water more sparingly in winter. Outdoors, grow in moderately fertile, humus-rich, acid or alkaline, moist soil with a cool root run. They prefer full sun, but partial shade is tolerated, especially in drier areas. Avoid root disturbance.

• **PROPAGATION** Sow seed in containers in an open frame in autumn. Root semi-ripe cuttings in summer.

• **PESTS AND DISEASES** Susceptible to aphids and red spider mites under glass.

R. chamaecistus. Semi-prostrate, evergreen shrub with elliptic to inversely lance-shaped, glossy, bright dark green leaves, 6–10mm (¼–½in) long, paler beneath, fringed with bristly white hairs. In late spring and early summer, abundant cup-shaped, 5-petalled, pale clear pink flowers, to 3cm (1¼in) across, with red eyes, are produced singly from the leaf axils or in few-flowered terminal clusters. ↕ 20cm (8in), ↔ 25cm (10in). E. Alps. ❄❄❄

RHODOTYPOS

ROSACEAE

Genus of one species of deciduous shrub occurring in scrub and woodland in China and Japan. It has opposite, ovate, toothed leaves, but is cultivated mainly for its large, papery, 4-petalled white flowers, borne over a long period from spring to summer, and its shiny black berries. Grow in a shrub border or woodland garden.

• **HARDINESS** Fully hardy.

• **CULTIVATION** Grow in moderately fertile, moist but well-drained soil, preferably in sun, although partial shade is tolerated. Pruning group 1 or 2.

• **PROPAGATION** Sow seed in a seedbed, or in containers in a cold frame, in autumn. Root greenwood cuttings in early summer, or semi-ripe cuttings in late summer.

• **PESTS AND DISEASES** Trouble free.

R. kerrioides see *R. scandens.*

R. scandens ▣ syn. *R. kerrioides.* Deciduous shrub with arching shoots and ovate, tapered, sharply toothed, deeply veined, mid-green leaves, to 6cm (2½in) long. In late spring and early summer, 4-petalled white flowers, 4cm

Rhodotypos scandens

R

(1½in) across, are produced singly from the shoot tips; they are followed by spherical, glossy black berries, to 8mm (⅜in) across. ‡↔ 1.5m (5ft). China, Japan. ❄❄❄

x RHODOXIS

HYPOXIDACEAE

Hybrid genus of herbaceous perennials resulting from crosses between *Hypoxis* and *Rhodohypoxis*, with corm-like rootstocks. The mid-green leaves are basal and linear, with generally hairy margins. In summer, 1 or 2 white, pale pink, or red flowers, with 6 spreading tepals and prominent yellow anthers, are produced on scapes 5–10cm (2–4in) long. Grow in a trough, rock garden, or alpine house.

- **HARDINESS** Frost hardy.
- **CULTIVATION** In an alpine house, grow in a mix of equal parts lime-free (ericaceous) potting compost, leaf mould, and sharp sand in full light. Water freely in growth, applying a balanced liquid fertilizer monthly; keep just moist in winter. Outdoors, grow in fertile, well-drained, humus-rich soil in full sun. Provide protection from excessive winter wet.
- **PROPAGATION** Separate offsets in late autumn.
- **PESTS AND DISEASES** Susceptible to red spider mites and thrips under glass.

x ***R.* 'Hebron Farm Cerise'** ▣ (*Hypoxis milloides* x *Rhodohypoxis parvula*). Clump-forming perennial with 3–5 basal, erect or slightly curved, narrowly linear, hairless, mid-green leaves, 5–10cm (2–4in) long. In summer, star-shaped, flat flowers, to 1.5cm (½in) across, deep red with yellow anthers, are produced usually singly on scapes 5–8cm (2–3in) long. ‡↔ 10cm (4in). South Africa (KwaZulu/Natal). ❄❄

x ***R. hybrida*** (*Hypoxis parvula* x *Rhodohypoxis baurii*). Clump-forming perennial with a basal cluster of up to 5

x *Rhodoxis* 'Hebron Farm Cerise'

x *Rhodoxis hybrida* 'Hebron Farm Pink'

x *Rhodoxis hybrida* 'Hebron Farm Red Eye'

linear leaves, 5–10cm (2–4in) long, with long marginal hairs. In summer, star-shaped, white or pale pink flowers, 2cm (¾in) across, greenish beneath and with a central boss of yellow anthers, are produced on scapes, 5cm (2in) long. ‡↔ 10cm (4in). South Africa (KwaZulu/Natal). ❄❄. **'Hebron Farm Pink'** ▣ has pale pink flowers with yellow anthers, the tepals deeper pink on the underside. **'Hebron Farm Red Eye'** ▣ produces white flowers, with a small red zone around yellow anthers.

▷ ***Rhoeo discolor*** see *Tradescantia spathacea*
▷ ***Rhoeo spathacea*** see *Tradescantia spathacea*

RHOICISSUS

VITACEAE

Genus of 10–12 species of evergreen trees and woody-stemmed tendril climbers or scramblers from woodland in tropical Africa and South Africa. The leaves are alternate, and simple or 3-, occasionally 5-palmate, with entire or toothed leaflets. Tendrils are produced opposite the leaves. Tiny, yellowish green flowers are borne in small cymes that are almost hidden by the leaves; they are followed by red to purple berries. Where temperatures fall below 7°C (45°F), grow in a cool or temperate greenhouse, or as houseplants; elsewhere, use to clothe a wall, pergola, or arch.

- **HARDINESS** Frost tender.
- **CULTIVATION** Under glass, grow in loam-based potting compost (JI No.2) in full light. In the growing season, water moderately and apply a balanced liquid fertilizer monthly; water sparingly in winter. Outdoors, grow in fertile, moist but well-drained soil in full sun. Pruning group 11, in early spring.
- **PROPAGATION** Sow seed at 13°C (55°F) in spring. Root semi-ripe cuttings with bottom heat in summer. Layer in spring.
- **PESTS AND DISEASES** Red spider mites and powdery mildew may be a problem.

R. capensis ▣ syn. *Cissus capensis*, *Vitis capensis* (Cape grape). Robust climber with tuberous roots and very long, forked tendrils. Leathery, lustrous, dark green leaves, 10–20cm (4–8in) long, are rounded to kidney-shaped, and bluntly 5-angled, with broad, wavy teeth.

Rhoicissus capensis

Insignificant, yellowish green flowers are borne in spring, and are followed by grape-like, spherical, blackish red berries. ‡ 5m (15ft) or more. South Africa. ❁ (min. 7°C/45°F)

R. rhombifolia see *Cissus rhombifolia*.

RHOMBOPHYLLUM

AIZOACEAE

Genus of 3 species of very fleshy, usually compact, mat-forming, perennial succulents occurring on hillsides and often in the lowlands of South Africa. The crowded, fleshy leaves are linear or semi-cylindrical, expanded towards the middle, and opposite or united at the bases; they are mid- to dark greyish green, with white or translucent spots, and margins that are entire or have 1 or 2 short teeth. Attractive, daisy-like, bright golden yellow flowers, which open during the day, are produced singly or in cymes of 3–7 in summer. In frost-prone regions, grow in a temperate greenhouse. In warm, dry climates, grow outdoors in a raised bed or desert garden.

- **HARDINESS** Frost tender.
- **CULTIVATION** Under glass, grow in standard cactus compost in full light with low humidity. In spring and summer, water moderately and apply a dilute, low-nitrogen fertilizer monthly; keep completely dry at other times. Outdoors, grow in poor to moderately fertile, sharply drained soil in full sun. See also pp.48–49.
- **PROPAGATION** Sow seed at 19–24°C (66–75°F), or divide offsets, in spring or summer.
- **PESTS AND DISEASES** Prone to aphids while flowering.

R. rhomboideum ▣ Clump-forming succulent with 4 or 5 uneven pairs of semi-cylindrical, white-spotted, dark greyish green leaves, 2.5–5cm (1–2in) long; the upper surfaces of the leaves are more or less flat, the undersurfaces are rounded, thickened, and keeled towards

Rhombophyllum rhomboideum

the tips, with paler green, occasionally toothed margins. Golden yellow flowers, 3cm (1¼in) across, tinged red on the reverse of the petals, are produced in summer. ↕ 5cm (2in), ↔ 15cm (6in). South Africa (Eastern Cape). ❀ (min. 7°C/45°F)

RHOPALOSTYLIS

ARECACEAE/PALMAE

Genus of 3 species of erect, single-stemmed, monoecious palms, occurring in lowland and coastal forests in New Zealand and Norfolk Island. They are grown for their attractive, smooth, grey-green trunks and large tufts of oblong, pinnate, erect to arching, dark green leaves, which arise from a bulbous crownshaft. Tiny, bowl-shaped to spherical, purplish pink, lilac, cream, or white flowers are borne in panicles beneath the foliage in summer and autumn. In frost-prone areas, grow young plants in a warm greenhouse or conservatory; in warmer areas, grow as specimen trees.

• **HARDINESS** Half hardy to frost tender.
• **CULTIVATION** Under glass, grow in loamless potting compost in bright, filtered light with moderate humidity. In the growing season, water freely and apply a balanced liquid fertilizer monthly; water sparingly in winter. Pot on in spring. Outdoors, grow in deep, fertile, humus-rich, moist but well-drained soil in a sheltered position in partial shade.
• **PROPAGATION** Sow seed at 19–24°C (66–75°F) in spring.
• **PESTS AND DISEASES** Red spider mites, scale insects, and thrips may be troublesome under glass.

R. sapida 🌴 (Feather duster palm, Nikau palm). Slow-growing palm with a solitary, stout, unbranched trunk bearing a tuft of oblong, erect, dark green leaves, to 3m (10ft) long, pinnately divided into linear segments, to 90cm (3ft) long. In summer and autumn, produces dense panicles, to 60cm (24in) long, of bowl-shaped to spherical, purplish pink, lilac, or cream flowers, 6mm (¼in) across, followed by ellipsoid, brick-red fruit, 1cm (½in) long. ↕ 8m (25ft), ↔ 4m (12ft). New Zealand, Chatham Island. ❄ (borderline)

▷ **Rhubarb** see *Rheum*
Chinese see *R. palmatum*

RHUS syn. TOXICODENDRON

Sumach

ANACARDIACEAE

Genus of about 200 species of deciduous or evergreen shrubs, trees, and woody climbers, widely distributed in temperate and subtropical North America, South Africa, E. Asia, and N.E. Australia. They are found in woodland, thickets, dry sites, bogs, and on rocky slopes. Sumachs are cultivated primarily for their attractive, alternate leaves, which may be simple, pinnate, or palmate. In many species and cultivars the foliage turns brilliant shades of yellow, red, or orange in autumn; some also produce showy fruit clusters. The inconspicuous flowers, usually 2mm (1⁄16in) across, are borne in spring or summer in terminal, normally erect, ovoid, or conical to pyramidal panicles. In autumn, they are followed by spherical, usually red fruits, 4–6mm (⅛–¼in) across. *R. glabra*, *R.* x *pulvinata*, and *R. typhina* usually produce male and female flowers on separate plants; plants of both sexes must be grown together to obtain fruit. Grow in a shrub border or woodland garden, or as specimen plants. In frost-prone areas, grow tender species in a cool greenhouse. All parts of *R. radicans* and *R. verniciflua* are highly toxic if ingested; contact with their foliage, and that of a number of related species, including *R. succedanea*, may aggravate skin allergies.

• **HARDINESS** Fully hardy to frost tender.
• **CULTIVATION** Grow in moist but well-drained, moderately fertile soil, in full sun to obtain best autumn colour. Suckering species, such as *R. typhina*, may be invasive. Pruning group 1, or group 7 for *R. typhina*, *R.* x *pulvinata*, and *R. glabra*.
• **PROPAGATION** Sow seed in a seedbed in autumn. Root semi-ripe cuttings in summer, or insert root cuttings in winter. Separate suckers when dormant.

Rhus trichocarpa

• **PESTS AND DISEASES** Prone to coral spot and *Verticillium* wilt.

R. aromatica (Fragrant sumach). Mound-forming, suckering, deciduous shrub with spreading shoots. The 3-palmate, aromatic leaves, to 10cm (4in) long, are softly hairy or almost hairless, with ovate or obovate, sharply toothed, dark green leaflets, turning orange to red-purple in autumn. Tiny yellow flowers are borne in small, erect, ovoid panicles, 2cm (¾in) long, in mid-spring, followed by spherical red fruit. ↕ 1–1.5m (3–5ft), ↔ 1.5m (5ft). E. North America. ❄❄❄

R. chinensis ♀ Upright, deciduous tree with stout, downy shoots bearing pinnate leaves, to 40cm (16in) long, with winged stalks and 7–13 ovate-oblong, mid-green leaflets, turning red in autumn. In late summer, bears yellowish white flowers in erect, conical panicles, to 25cm (10in) long, followed by spherical, orange-red fruit. ↕↔ 6m (20ft). E. Asia. ❄❄❄ (borderline)

R. copallina ♀ (Dwarf sumach, Shining sumach). Upright, deciduous shrub or tree with long, branching, softly hairy, reddish green shoots. Pinnate leaves, to 35cm (14in) long, have winged stalks, and 9–15 oblong-lance-shaped, glossy, dark green leaflets, turning bright red in autumn. In summer, bears yellow-green flowers in erect, conical panicles, to 15cm (6in) long, followed by spherical red fruit. ↕↔ 1.5m (5ft) or more. E. North America. ❄❄❄

R. cotinoides see *Cotinus obovatus.*

R. cotinus see *Cotinus coggygria.*

R. glabra ■ (Scarlet sumach, Smooth sumach). Bushy, suckering, deciduous shrub producing smooth, hairless shoots and pinnate leaves, to 45cm (18in) long, with 15–31 oblong-lance-shaped, toothed, glossy, bluish green leaflets, turning rich red in autumn. In summer, bears yellow-green flowers in upright, conical panicles, to 25cm (10in) long; they are followed on female plants by

Rhus glabra

Rhus typhina

R

spherical red fruit. ↕↔ 2.5m (8ft) or more. North America, Mexico. ❄❄❄.
'Laciniata' of gardens see *R.* x *pulvinata* 'Red Autumn Lace'.
R. potaninii ♀ Rounded, deciduous tree with hairless or finely hairy shoots and pinnate leaves, to 35cm (14in) long, composed of 7–11 oblong to oblong-lance-shaped, dark green leaflets, turning red in autumn. Creamy white flowers are borne in pendent, pyramidal panicles, 20cm (8in) long, in summer, followed by spherical, hairy red fruit. ↕ 12m (40ft), ↔ 8m (25ft). China. ❄❄❄
***R.* x *pulvinata* 'Red Autumn Lace'**, syn. *R. glabra* 'Laciniata' of gardens. Spreading, suckering, deciduous shrub with smooth shoots and pinnate leaves, to 50cm (20in) or more long, composed of 11–13 oblong-lance-shaped, rich green leaflets, turning orange to red-purple in autumn. Yellow-green flowers are borne in erect, conical panicles, to 20cm (8in) long, in summer, followed by spherical, bristly red fruit. ↕ 3m (10ft), ↔ 5m (15ft). ❄❄❄
R. succedanea ♀ syn. *Toxicodendron succedaneum* (Wax tree). Spreading, deciduous tree with softly hairy young shoots. Pinnate leaves, to 30cm (12in) long, have 9–15 ovate-oblong, glossy, dark green leaflets, turning red in autumn. Yellow-green flowers are borne in dense, erect, conical panicles, to 12cm (5in) long, in summer, followed by spherical, waxy, yellow-brown fruit. ↕↔ 10m (30ft). E. Asia. ❄❄
R. trichocarpa ▣ ♀ Spreading, deciduous tree or shrub with softly hairy young shoots, later becoming hairless. Pinnate leaves, to 50cm (20in) long, have 13–17 broadly ovate, usually entire, dark green leaflets, pink-tinged when young, turning red-purple to orange in autumn. In summer, bears yellow flowers in erect, conical panicles, to 10cm (4in) long, followed by spherical, bristly, brownish yellow fruit. ↕↔ 6m (20ft). C. China, Korea, Japan. ❄❄❄
R. typhina ▣ ♀ (Stag's horn sumach, Velvet sumach). Upright, suckering, deciduous shrub or tree with densely velvety red shoots, resembling a stag's horns. Pinnate leaves, to 60cm (24in) long, have 11–31 oblong-lance-shaped, dark green leaflets, turning brilliant orange-red in autumn. Yellow-green flowers are produced in erect, conical panicles, to 20cm (8in) long, in summer; they are followed on female plants by dense clusters of spherical, hairy, deep crimson-red fruit. ↕ 5m (15ft) or more, ↔ 6m (20ft). E. North America. ❄❄❄. **'Dissecta'**, syn. 'Laciniata' of gardens, is female and shrubby, with finely cut leaflets; ↕ 2m (6ft), ↔ 3m (10ft).
R. verniciflua ▣ ♀ syn. *Toxicodendron vernicifluum* (Varnish tree). Spreading, deciduous tree with softly hairy young shoots, later becoming hairless. Pinnate leaves, to 60cm (24in) long, have 7–13 broadly ovate, glossy, bright green leaflets, turning red in autumn. Yellow-green flowers are produced in lax, semi-pendent panicles, to 20cm (8in) long, in summer, followed by spherical, pale yellow fruit. ↕ 15m (50ft), ↔ 10m (30ft). E. Asia. ❄❄❄

Rhus verniciflua

▷ ***Rhynchelytrum*** see *Melinis*
R. repens see *M. repens*
R. roseum see *M. repens*

RHYNCHOLAELIA

ORCHIDACEAE

Genus of 2 evergreen, epiphytic or lithophytic orchids (sometimes included in *Brassavola*) from South America, Mexico, and Central America, where they are found in mountainous forest up to 1,500m (5,000ft). They have elongated, cylindrical pseudobulbs, which each produce a single stout, rigid, elliptic-oblong, grey-green or dull green leaf, 7–15cm (3–6in) long, and a solitary terminal flower. Both the flower and leaf are borne from a sheath at the apex of the pseudobulb. Species of this genus have been crossed many times with the closely related *Cattleya* and *Laelia*.

• **HARDINESS** Frost tender.
• **CULTIVATION** Cool- to intermediate-growing orchids. Grow in epiphytic orchid compost in a slatted basket, or epiphytically on a bark slab. Provide moist, unshaded conditions all year. In summer, water freely, applying fertilizer at every third watering, and mist twice daily. Keep dry in winter. See also p.46.
• **PROPAGATION** Divide when plants fill their pots and "flow" over the sides.
• **PESTS AND DISEASES** Red spider mites, aphids, whiteflies, and mealybugs may be a problem.

R. digbyana ▣ syn. *Brassavola digbyana*. Epiphytic orchid with ridged pseudobulbs, to 15cm (6in) long, each producing a single, elliptic-oblong, powdery grey-green leaf, to 20cm (8in) long. Strongly scented, solitary, pale yellow-green flowers, 17cm (7in) across, each with a fringed white lip, are borne in spring. ↕↔ 30cm (12in). Mexico, Belize. ❀ (min. 13°C/55°F; max. 30°C/86°F)
R. glauca, syn. *Brassavola glauca*. Epiphytic orchid with compressed pseudobulbs, to 9cm (3½in) long, each producing one elliptic-oblong, dull-green glaucous leaf, to 12cm (5in) long, and, in spring, a solitary flower, 10cm (4in) across. Flower has white, pale lavender, or olive-green sepals and petals, and a white or creamy yellow lip with a purplish mark at its base. ↕↔ 15cm (6in). Mexico, Guatemala, Honduras. ❀ (min. 13°C/55°F; max. 30°C/86°F)

Rhyncholaelia digbyana

RHYNCHOSTYLIS

ORCHIDACEAE

Genus of about 6 species of evergreen, monopodial, epiphytic orchids from warm, moist forest in India, Malaysia, Indonesia, the Philippines, Thailand, Laos, Burma, and Sri Lanka. They have thick, rigid, aerial roots, and produce 8–10 pairs of semi-rigid, linear to strap-shaped leaves at the apexes of short, stout stems. Many small flowers are borne in dense, upright or pendent racemes that arise laterally from the bases of the leaves from spring to winter.

• **HARDINESS** Frost tender.
• **CULTIVATION** Intermediate-growing orchids. Grow in epiphytic orchid compost in a half-pot or (preferably) in a slatted basket. Provide high humidity, full light, and shade from hot sun. In summer, water freely, mist daily, and apply a balanced liquid fertilizer at every third watering; water moderately in winter. Disturb as little as possible. See also p.46.
• **PROPAGATION** Divide when the plant fills the container and "flows" over the sides. Cuttings or offshoots may be rooted successfully.
• **PESTS AND DISEASES** Red spider mites, aphids, and mealybugs may be a problem.

R. gigantea. Epiphytic orchid with linear, mid-green leaves, 25cm (10in) long. Fragrant, waxy, pale purple-spotted, white or deep violet flowers, to 4cm (1½in) across, are borne in pendent racemes, 20–25cm (8–10in) long, from autumn to winter. ↕↔ 30cm (12in). Burma, Thailand, Laos. ❀ (min. 13–15°C/55–59°F; max. 30°C/86°F)
R. retusa. Epiphytic orchid with linear to oblong, bluish green leaves, 25cm (10in) long. Fragrant, waxy white flowers, to 3cm (1¼in) across, spotted purple or pink, with purple lips, are produced in pendent racemes, to 30cm (12in) long, in summer. ↕ 15cm (6in), ↔ 25cm (10in). India, Burma, Sri Lanka to Malaysia, Philippines. ❀ (min. 13–15°C/55–59°F; max. 30°C/86°F)

▷ **Ribbon bush** see *Homalocladium*, *Hypoestes aristata*
▷ **Ribbon grass** see *Phalaris arundinacea*
▷ **Ribbon plant** see *Chlorophytum comosum*, *Dracaena sanderiana*
▷ **Ribbonwood** see *Hoheria sexstylosa*

RIBES

Flowering currant

GROSSULARIACEAE/SAXIFRAGACEAE

Genus of about 150 species of mainly deciduous, occasionally evergreen, sometimes spiny shrubs, widely distributed in woodland, scrub, and rocky places. Most are found in N. temperate regions; some occur in South America. Some species, such as blackcurrant (*R. nigrum*), redcurrant (*R. rubrum*), and gooseberry (*R. uva-crispa*), are grown for their edible fruits; those described below are cultivated primarily for their flowers. The leaves are alternate and often 3- to 5-lobed. Small, tubular, cup- or bell-shaped flowers, each with small petals and 4, rarely 5, larger, spreading sepals, are borne singly or in pendent racemes, mostly in spring or summer. The berry-like fruits are spherical or ovoid, and vary in colour from red or black to green or white. Grow in a shrub border; *R. speciosum* is best grown against a wall. *R. sanguineum* may be used as informal hedging.

• **HARDINESS** Fully hardy to frost hardy.
• **CULTIVATION** Grow in moderately fertile, well-drained soil in full sun. *R. laurifolium* will grow well in partial shade; *R. sanguineum* 'Brocklebankii' should be shaded from the hottest sun. Pruning group 2; group 13 if wall-grown, in late summer. Trim hedges after flowering.
• **PROPAGATION** Root hardwood cuttings of deciduous flowering currants in winter. Root semi-ripe cuttings of evergreens in summer.
• **PESTS AND DISEASES** Aphids, leaf spot, powdery mildew, honey fungus, and coral spot may be a problem.

R. alpinum. Compact, mound-forming, much-branched, deciduous shrub with spineless shoots and broadly ovate, 3- to 5-lobed, mid-green leaves, to 5cm (2in) long, often smaller. In spring, bears bell-shaped, greenish yellow flowers (males and females on separate plants) in erect racemes, to 4cm (1½in) long; they are followed on female plants by spherical, dark red fruit, 7mm (¼in) long. ↕ 60cm (24in), ↔ 90cm (36in). N. Europe to Russia (Siberia). ❄❄❄. **'Aureum'** ▣ is female, and has bright yellow leaves, becoming paler in summer.
***R. aureum* of gardens** see *R. odoratum*.
R.* x *gordonianum (*R. petraeum* x *R. sanguineum*). Spreading, spineless,

Ribes alpinum 'Aureum'

R

Ribes laurifolium

deciduous shrub with rounded, 3- to 5-lobed, toothed, aromatic, dark green leaves, to 5cm (2in) long. Tubular, 5-lobed flowers, red outside and yellow within, open in dense, pendent racemes, to 7cm (3in) long, in early summer. It is not known to produce fruit and is probably sterile. ↕ 2m (6ft), ↔ 2.5m (8ft). Garden origin. ✽✽✽

R. laurifolium ■ Spreading, spineless, dioecious, evergreen shrub with ovate-oblong, scalloped, leathery, dark green leaves, 5–10cm (2–4in) long. In late winter and early spring, bears cup-shaped, greenish yellow flowers in pendent racemes, the males to 5cm (2in) long, the females to 2.5cm (1in) long. Female flowers are followed by ovoid fruit, to 1cm (½in) long, red at first, ripening to black. ↕ 1m (3ft), ↔ 1.5m (5ft). W. China. ✽✽✽

R. odoratum ■ syn. *R. aureum* of gardens (Buffalo currant). Spineless, erect, deciduous shrub with hairy young shoots (hairless in the true *R. aureum*). Broadly ovate, 3- to 5-lobed, toothed, bright green leaves, to 8cm (3in) long, turn red and purple in autumn. In mid- and late spring, bears tubular, fragrant yellow flowers in pendent racemes, to 5cm (2in) long, followed by spherical black fruit, to 1cm (½in) across. ↕↔ 2m (6ft). C. USA. ✽✽✽

R. sanguineum (Flowering currant). Upright, spineless, deciduous shrub with rounded, 3- to 5-lobed, toothed, aromatic, dark green leaves, 5–10cm (2–4in) long, heart-shaped at the bases, and slightly hairy above, white-hairy beneath. Tubular, deep pinkish red flowers are borne in pendent racemes,

Ribes odoratum

Ribes sanguineum 'Brocklebankii' (inset: leaf and flower detail)

5–10cm (2–4in) long, in spring, followed by spherical, glaucous, blue-black fruit, 5mm (¼in) across. ↕↔ 2m (6ft). W. North America. ✽✽✽. **'Brocklebankii'** ■ is slow-growing, with bright yellow leaves, paler in summer, and pale pink flowers; ↕↔ 1.2m (4ft). **'King Edward VII'** is compact and upright, with dark red flowers. **'Pulborough Scarlet'** ■ is vigorous, and bears dark red, white-centred flowers; ↕ 3m (10ft), ↔ 2.5m (8ft). **'Tydeman's White'** has pure white flowers; ↕↔ 2.5m (8ft).

R. speciosum (Fuchsia-flowered currant). Upright, spiny, deciduous shrub with bristly shoots, red when young, and broadly ovate, 3- to 5-lobed, glossy, mid-green leaves, 1–4cm (½–1½in) long. In mid- and late spring, bears slender, bell-shaped, dark red flowers, with protruding red stamens, in small, pendent racemes, 2.5cm (1in) long. Flowers are followed by spherical, bristly red fruit, to 1cm (½in) across. ↕ 2m (6ft), sometimes more, ↔ 2m (6ft). USA (California). ✽✽✽ (borderline)

Ribes sanguineum 'Pulborough Scarlet'

▷ **Rice** see *Oryza*
Annual wild see *Zizania aquatica*
Canadian wild see *Zizania aquatica*
Water see *Zizania aquatica*
Wild see *Zizania*
▷ **Rice-paper plant** see *Tetrapanax papyrifer*

RICHEA

EPACRIDACEAE

Genus of 11 species of evergreen shrubs and small trees found in moist forest in Australia, often at high altitudes. They have crowded branches with spiralling, alternate, narrow leaves, overlapping at the bases. The small, ovoid to conical or bottle-shaped flowers are borne in terminal spikes, racemes, or panicles; they are open at the bases and almost closed at the tips, quickly losing their petals and leaving the stamens and stigmas exposed. In frost-prone areas, grow half-hardy and tender species in a cool greenhouse or conservatory. In frost-free areas, grow the shrubby species at the base of a sunny wall or in a shrub border; use the trees as specimen plants.

- **HARDINESS** Frost hardy to half hardy.
- **CULTIVATION** Under glass, grow in lime-free (ericaceous) potting compost in full light. When in growth, water freely and apply a half-strength balanced liquid fertilizer monthly; water sparingly in winter. Outdoors, grow in moist but well-drained, poor to moderately fertile, humus-rich, neutral to acid soil in full sun; shelter from cold, dry winds. Pruning group 9.
- **PROPAGATION** Surface-sow seed in containers outdoors, ideally as soon as ripe or in spring (germination is

Richea dracophylla

unreliable). Root semi-ripe cuttings with bottom heat in late summer.
- **PESTS AND DISEASES** Trouble free.

R. dracophylla ■ ♀ Medium to large shrub or small tree with sparse, erect branches. Spreading, spiralling, flexuous, lance-shaped, dark green leaves, 15–30cm (6–12in) long, with tapering, red-tinged tips, are crowded at the ends of the stems. Small, obovoid white flowers are produced in dense, upright panicles, 15–25cm (6–10in) long, in summer. ↕ 2–5m (6–15ft), ↔ 0.6–1.5m (2–5ft). Australia (Tasmania). ✽

R. scoparia. Rounded, erect, many-branched, dense shrub, with narrowly lance-shaped, semi-rigid, spine-tipped, mid- to deep green leaves, 3–6cm (1¼–2½in) long. Small, ovoid flowers, ranging in colour from white to pink, red, or orange, often with darker petal tips, are borne in erect, dense, cylindrical racemes, to 12cm (5in) long, in summer. ↕↔ to 1.5m (5ft). Australia (Tasmania). ✽✽✽ (borderline)

RICINUS

EUPHORBIACEAE

Genus of one species of erect, very fast-growing, mound-forming, suckering, monoecious, evergreen shrub, widely naturalized in wasteland, at roadsides, and on stony slopes, from N.E. Africa to W. Asia. It is grown mainly for its large, glossy, palmately lobed leaves. Spikes of small, cup-shaped flowers are followed by prickly, ovoid capsules. In frost-prone areas, grow as an annual in a cool greenhouse or conservatory, or as a specimen

Ricinus communis

R

Ricinus communis 'Impala'

plant for summer bedding. In warmer climates, grow in a border. All parts of *R. communis*, particularly the seeds, are highly toxic if ingested; contact with the foliage may aggravate skin allergies.

- **HARDINESS** Half hardy.
- **CULTIVATION** Under glass, grow in loam-based potting compost (JI No.2) in full light. In growth, water freely and apply a balanced liquid fertilizer monthly; water sparingly in winter. Outdoors, grow in fertile, humus-rich, well-drained soil in full sun. Stake in exposed sites. Plants grown on poor soils tend to produce flowers at the expense of vegetative growth and bear smaller leaves. Pruning group 9; plants grown under glass may need restrictive pruning.
- **PROPAGATION** Soak seed for 24 hours before sowing in late spring; sow singly into 9cm (3½in) pots, at 21°C (70°F). Grow young plants on at 13°C (55°F); pot on into 13cm (5in) pots before they become pot-bound, to prevent premature flower production. Plant out when all danger of frost has passed.
- **PESTS AND DISEASES** Red spider mites may be a problem under glass.

R. communis ■ (Castor oil plant). Erect, branching shrub, usually grown as an annual, with alternate, very broadly ovate, deeply 5- to 12-lobed, toothed, glossy, mid-green, reddish purple, or bronze-red leaves, 15–45cm (6–18in) long. Greenish yellow flowers, to 2.5cm (1in) long, are borne in ovoid spikes, to 15cm (6in) long, in summer; the female flowers are borne above the males at the tips of the spikes, and each female has a prominent red stigma. The flowers are followed by spherical, reddish brown capsules, covered with soft brown spines. ↕ to 1.8m (6ft) or more, ↔ to 1m (3ft) as an annual; ↕ to 10m (30ft), ↔ to 4m (12ft) as a shrub. N.E. Africa to W. Asia. ✲. Heights given for cultivars are for annual growth. **'Carmencita'** is tall and well-branched, with dark bronze-red foliage and bright red female flowers; ↕ 2–3m (6–10ft). **'Impala'** ■ is compact, with reddish purple foliage and yellowish green male flowers; young shoots and leaves are carmine-red; ↕ 1.2m (4ft). **'Red Spire'** is tall, with red stems and bronze-flushed leaves; ↕ 2–3m (6–10ft). **'Zanzibariensis'** ■ is tall, producing large, white-veined, mid-green leaves, 50cm (20in) long; ↕ 2–3m (6–10ft).

Ricinus communis 'Zanzibariensis'

RIGIDELLA

IRIDACEAE

Genus, closely related to *Tigridia*, of 4 species of bulbous perennials from dry pine to cloud forest in Central America. They are cultivated for their iris-like, brightly coloured flowers, borne in succession in spring or summer. The long, broadly lance-shaped, many-folded leaves are reduced to short, sharp-pointed, leaf-like bracts on the flowering stems. In frost-prone areas, grow in a cool greenhouse. In warmer areas, grow at the base of a sunny wall, or in a warm site where the soil dries out in summer.

- **HARDINESS** Half hardy, but may withstand short spells at -5°C (23°F).
- **CULTIVATION** Plant bulbs 10cm (4in) deep in spring. Under glass, grow in deep containers of loam-based potting compost (JI No.2) with added sharp sand, in full light. Water moderately in growth; keep completely dry in winter. Pot on in spring. Outdoors, grow in humus-rich, well-drained soil in full sun; in frost-prone regions, lift for frost-free winter storage.
- **PROPAGATION** Sow seed at 13–18°C (55–64°F) in spring.
- **PESTS AND DISEASES** Trouble free.

R. flammea. Bulbous perennial with lance-shaped basal leaves, to 30cm (12in) long, and shorter, sheathing stem leaves. Short-lived, iris-like, semi-pendent, brilliant scarlet flowers, 10cm (4in) across, with striking purple markings at the bases of the petals, are borne in succession before the leaves in spring or early summer. ↕ 1–1.5m (3–5ft), ↔ 30cm (12in). Mexico. ✲

▷ **Rimu** see *Dacrydium cupressinum*

ROBINIA

LEGUMINOSAE/PAPILIONACEAE

Genus of about 20 species (or only 4, according to some authorities) of deciduous, sometimes bristly or thorny trees and shrubs found in woodland and thickets in the USA. They are cultivated for their alternate, pinnate leaves, and pendent racemes of pea-like flowers, borne in late spring and early summer. Grow the trees as specimen plants; shrubby robinias are suitable for a large shrub border. *R. hispida* is effective grown against a sunny wall. All parts may cause severe discomfort if ingested.

- **HARDINESS** Fully hardy.
- **CULTIVATION** Grow in full sun in moderately fertile, moist but well-drained soil; they will tolerate poor, dry soils. Shelter from strong winds, as the branches are brittle. Suckers from *R. pseudoacacia* may be a problem. Pruning group 1; *R. pseudoacacia* 'Frisia' also group 7. Prune in late summer or early autumn to prevent bleeding.
- **PROPAGATION** Sow seed in containers in a cold frame in autumn. Insert root cuttings, or graft, in winter. Remove suckers in autumn.
- **PESTS AND DISEASES** Trouble free.

Robinia hispida

***R. x ambigua* 'Decaisneana'** ⚲ Spreading, nearly thornless tree with pinnate, dark green leaves, to 25cm (10in) long, composed of up to 23 ovate leaflets. Pale pink flowers, 2.5cm (1in) long, are borne in pendent racemes, to 15cm (6in) long, in early summer, followed by smooth, dark brown seed pods, 10cm (4in) long. ↕ 15m (50ft), ↔ 10m (30ft). ✲✲✲
R. fertilis see *R. hispida* var. *fertilis.*
R. hispida ■ (Bristly locust, Rose acacia). Upright, suckering shrub with bristly shoots and pinnate, dark green leaves, to 30cm (12in) long, composed of 9–13 ovate to broadly elliptic leaflets. In late spring and early summer, bears light rose-pink flowers, 3cm (1¼in) long, in pendent racemes, to 12cm (5in) long, followed by bristly brown seed pods, 4–6cm (1½–2½in) long. ↕ 2.5m (8ft), ↔ 3m (10ft). S.E. USA. ✲✲✲. **var. *fertilis***, syn. *R. fertilis*, has dense, spreading bristles on shoots and leaves, and narrow, oblong-ovate to elliptic leaflets; ↕↔ 2m (6ft). **var. *fertilis* 'Monument'** is compact and conical, with sparsely bristly shoots and lilac-pink flowers; ↕ 4m (12ft). **var. *kelseyi***, syn. *R. kelseyi*, is similar to *R. hispida* but has bristles only on the flower-stalks and raceme axes; leaves have oblong to ovate leaflets. It bears bright rose-pink flowers very freely.
***R.* 'Idaho'** ■⚲ Open, spreading tree with arching branches and pinnate, mid- to dark green leaves, to 25cm (10in) long, with 15 oval leaflets. In late spring and early summer, produces fragrant, dark pink flowers, 2.5cm (1in) long, in pendent racemes, to 20cm (8in) long. It is sterile and does not bear seed pods. ↕ 12m (40ft), ↔ 10m (30ft). ✲✲✲
R. kelseyi see *R. hispida* var. *kelseyi.*
R. luxurians see *R. neomexicana.*
R. x margaretta see *R. x slavinii.*
***R. x margaretta* 'Casque Rouge'** see *R. x slavinii* 'Casque Rouge'.

Robinia 'Idaho'

***R. x margaretta* 'Pink Cascade'** see *R. x slavinii* 'Casque Rouge'.
R. neomexicana ⚲ syn. *R. luxurians* (New Mexico locust). Upright, thicket-forming, spiny shrub or small tree with pinnate, hairy, blue-green leaves, to 20cm (8in) long, composed of 13 to 25 lance-shaped, narrowly ovate or oblong leaflets. In early summer, bears pink flowers, 2.5cm (1in) long, in pendent racemes, to 10cm (4in) long, followed by sparsely glandular brown seed pods, to 10cm (4in) long. ↕ 6m (20ft), ↔ 5m (15ft). USA (New Mexico, Arizona). ✲✲✲
R. pseudoacacia ⚲ (Black locust, False acacia, Locust). Fast-growing, suckering, broadly columnar tree with usually spiny shoots. Pinnate, dark green leaves, to 30cm (12in) long, have up to 23 lance-shaped or elliptic to ovate, blunt leaflets. In early and midsummer, bears fragrant white flowers, 2cm (¾in) long, in pendent racemes, to 20cm (8in) long, followed by smooth, dark brown seed pods, 10cm (4in) long. ↕ 25m (80ft), ↔ 15m (50ft). E. USA. ✲✲✲. **'Bessoniana'** ⚲ is erect then rounded; ↕ 15m (50ft), ↔ 10m (30ft). **'Fastigiata'** see 'Pyramidalis'. **'Frisia'** ■⚲ has golden

Robinia pseudoacacia 'Frisia'

yellow foliage, turning yellow-green in summer, then orange-yellow in autumn; ↕ 15m (50ft), ↔ 8m (25ft). **'Inermis' of gardens** see 'Umbraculifera'. **'Pyramidalis'** syn. 'Fastigiata', is narrowly columnar, with upright, spineless shoots; ↕ 15m (50ft), ↔ 3m (10ft). **'Tortuosa'** is slow-growing, with twisted shoots; ↕ 15m (50ft), ↔ 10m (30ft). **'Umbraculifera'** syn. 'Inermis' of gardens (Mop-head acacia), has a rounded crown; ↕↔ 6m (20ft).
R. x slavinii (*R. hispida* var. *kelseyi* x *R. pseudoacacia*), syn. *R.* x *margaretta.* Open, rounded, spiny tree or shrub with bristly young branches and pinnate, dark green leaves, to 20cm (8in) long, composed of up to 19 ovate leaflets. Fragrant, lilac-pink to dark pink flowers, 2cm (¾in) long, are borne in pendent racemes, to 15cm (6in) long, in late spring; they are followed by brown, warty seed pods, to 10cm (4in) long. ↕↔ 10m (30ft). Garden origin. ❄❄❄. **'Casque Rouge'** syn. *R.* x *margaretta* 'Casque Rouge', *R.* x *margaretta* 'Pink Cascade', has dark purple-pink flowers.

▷ **Roblé** see *Nothofagus obliqua*
▷ ***Rochea coccinea*** see *Crassula coccinea*
▷ ***Rochea falcata*** see *Crassula perfoliata* var. *minor*
▷ **Rock cress** see *Arabis*
▷ **Rocket, Sweet** see *Hesperis matronalis*
▷ **Rock rose** see *Cistus, Helianthemum*
Montpellier see *Cistus monspeliensis*
Sydney see *Boronia serrulata*

RODGERSIA

SAXIFRAGACEAE

Genus of 6 species of vigorous, clump-forming, rhizomatous perennials occurring in moist woodland and scrub, and at streamsides, in the mountains of Burma, China, Korea, and Japan. They have large, long-stalked, palmate or pinnate, sometimes bronze-tinted, basal leaves, in some species turning shades of red and brown in autumn. In summer, tall stems bear star-shaped, petalless, white or pink flowers, each 7–8mm (¼–⅜in) across, in large, fluffy, pyramidal panicles. These are followed by dark red or brown, capsular fruits. Grow near water, in a bog garden or moist border, or use for naturalizing at woodland margins.
• **HARDINESS** Fully hardy, but young leaves may be damaged by late frosts.
• **CULTIVATION** Grow in humus-rich, moist soil in full sun or partial shade, sheltered from cold, drying winds. They resent drought, but will tolerate drier conditions with more shade.
• **PROPAGATION** Sow seed in containers in a cold frame in spring. Divide in early spring.
• **PESTS AND DISEASES** Slugs may damage young leaves.

Rodgersia pinnata 'Superba'

R. aesculifolia ▣ Clump-forming, rhizomatous perennial producing horse-chestnut-like, palmate, crinkled, mid-green leaves, to 25cm (10in) long. The leaves have densely woolly, red-brown stalks and veins, and usually 7, sometimes 5–9, obovate, toothed leaflets. In midsummer, bears numerous star-shaped, white or pink flowers in large panicles, to 60cm (24in) long. ↕ to 2m (6ft), ↔ 1m (3ft). N. China. ❄❄❄
R. japonica see *R. podophylla.*
R. pinnata. Rhizomatous, clump-forming perennial producing pinnate, or partially pinnate or palmate, crinkled, heavily veined, glossy, dark green leaves, to 90cm (36in) long; leaves have reddish green stalks and 5–9 obovate-inversely-lance-shaped leaflets. In mid- and late summer, reddish green stems bear star-shaped, yellowish white, pink, or red flowers in panicles 30–70cm (12–28in) long. ↕ to 1.2m (4ft), ↔ 75cm (30in). China (Sichuan, Yunnan). ❄❄❄. **'Superba'** ▣ has purplish bronze young leaves, sometimes with fewer leaflets than in the species, and bright pink flowers.
R. podophylla ▣ syn. *R. japonica.* Clump-forming, rhizomatous perennial with palmate leaves, to 40cm (16in) long, composed of usually 5 large, jagged, obovate, 3- to 5-lobed leaflets, crinkled and bronze when young, becoming smoother, glossy, and mid-green, with brown hairs. The leaves turn bronze-red in autumn. In mid- and late summer, bears star-shaped, creamy green flowers in panicles 30cm (12in) long. ↕ to 1.5m (5ft), ↔ to 1.8m (6ft). Korea, Japan. ❄❄❄
R. sambucifolia ▣ Clump-forming, rhizomatous perennial with elder-like, pinnate, hairy, dark green leaves, to 75cm (30in) long, with usually 7, sometimes 3–11, oblong-lance-shaped, toothed leaflets. In early and mid-summer, bears star-shaped, white or pink flowers in dense panicles, to 45cm (18in) long, arching at the tips. ↕↔ 90cm (36in). W. China. ❄❄❄
R. tabularis see *Astilboides tabularis.*

Rodgersia aesculifolia

Rodgersia podophylla

Rodgersia sambucifolia

RODRIGUEZIA

ORCHIDACEAE

Genus of about 30 species of evergreen, rhizomatous, epiphytic orchids from warm, moist, forest areas of Central and South America. They have fine, aerial, sometimes mat-forming roots, ovoid pseudobulbs partially enveloped by overlapping leaf-sheaths, and narrowly strap-shaped to oblong, leathery, mid-green leaves. They are grown mainly for their fragrant flowers, borne in pendent racemes arising from the bases of the pseudobulbs.
• **HARDINESS** Frost tender.
• **CULTIVATION** Intermediate-growing orchids. Grow in small containers of epiphytic orchid compost made with fine-grade bark, or grow epiphytically on bark. Provide full light with shade from hot sun, and high humidity. In summer, water freely, mist daily, and apply a balanced liquid fertilizer at every third watering; water more sparingly in winter. See also p.46.
• **PROPAGATION** Divide when the plant fills the pot and "flows" over the sides.
• **PESTS AND DISEASES** Prone to red spider mites, aphids, and mealybugs.

R. venusta. Epiphytic orchid with compressed, ovoid pseudobulbs, each producing several narrowly oblong, leathery leaves, 15cm (6in) long. Arching racemes of many very fragrant, pure white flowers, 3cm (1¼in) across, with yellow-marked lips, are borne in autumn. ↕↔ 15cm (6in). E. Brazil. ❀ (13°C/55°F; max. 30°C/86°F)

ROHDEA

CONVALLARIACEAE/LILIACEAE

Genus of one species of rhizomatous perennial from woodland in S.W. China and Japan, grown for its basal rosettes of fleshy, dark green leaves, and erect spikes of narrowly bell-shaped flowers, borne in early spring. Grow in a woodland garden or damp, shady border.
• **HARDINESS** Frost hardy; will tolerate occasional falls in temperature to around -10°C (14°F).
• **CULTIVATION** Grow in humus-rich, moist, moderately fertile soil in deep or partial shade.
• **PROPAGATION** Sow seed in containers in a cold frame in autumn. Divide in spring.
• **PESTS AND DISEASES** Prone to damage by slugs, snails, and vine weevil larvae.

R. japonica. Rosetted, rhizomatous perennial with thick, semi-erect, usually inversely lance-shaped, leathery, dark green leaves, 28–45cm (11–18in) long. In early spring, erect stems bear dense spikes, 2.5–5cm (1–2in) long, of narrowly bell-shaped, greenish white flowers, to 5mm (¼in) across, followed by fleshy red berries. ↕25cm (10in), ↔ 20cm (8in). S.W. China, Japan. ❄❄

ROMANZOFFIA

HYDROPHYLLACEAE

Genus of 4 species of low-growing, clump-forming perennials, with tuber-like roots, from shaded, rocky, alpine, or woodland habitats in W. North America and the Aleutian Islands. They produce tufts of rounded or kidney-shaped, lobed or deeply scalloped leaves, which die back after flowering and re-emerge in autumn. The bell- or funnel-shaped flowers, each with 5 rounded petal lobes and conspicuous anthers, are borne in raceme-like cymes in early summer. Suitable for a woodland garden, rock garden, peat bed, or for growing in an alpine house.

- **HARDINESS** Fully hardy.
- **CULTIVATION** Grow in moist but well-drained, humus-rich, neutral to acid soil in deep or partial shade.
- **PROPAGATION** Sow seed in containers in an open frame as soon as ripe. Divide in early spring.
- **PESTS AND DISEASES** Susceptible to damage by slugs and snails.

R. sitchensis, syn. *R. suksdorfii.* Tufted perennial with swollen roots and kidney-shaped, deeply lobed, glossy, dark green leaves, 2.5cm (1in) long. In early summer, bears small, funnel-shaped white flowers, 8mm (⅜in) long, with yellow petal bases and deep yellow anthers, in branching, terminal, raceme-like cymes, to 15cm (6in) long. ↕30cm (12in), ↔ to 15cm (6in). W. North America (Alaska to Montana). ❄❄❄
R. suksdorfii see *R. sitchensis.*

ROMNEYA

Matilija poppy, Tree poppy

PAPAVERACEAE

Genus of 2 species of suckering, woody-based, subshrubby perennials found in chaparral and sage scrub in S. California, USA, and N. Mexico. They are grown for their glaucous foliage and fragrant, showy white flowers. The leaves are alternate, and pinnatifid to pinnatisect; the poppy-like, solitary, terminal, 6-petalled flowers, with bright yellow stamens, are borne in summer. Grow in a border or, in frost-prone areas, against a warm, sunny wall.

- **HARDINESS** Frost hardy.
- **CULTIVATION** Grow in fertile, well-drained soil in full sun, sheltered from strong, cold winds. Provide a deep, dry winter mulch. Tree poppies are sometimes difficult to establish and resent transplanting, but may eventually spread vigorously by suckers. Usually cut back to the base by frost; in warmer areas, pruning group 6.
- **PROPAGATION** Sow seed at 13–16°C (55–61°F) in spring. Root basal cuttings in spring; insert root cuttings in winter.
- **PESTS AND DISEASES** *Verticillium* wilt and caterpillars may be a problem.

Romneya coulteri 'White Cloud'

R. coulteri. Upright, deciduous subshrub producing ovate to rounded, pinnatifid, intensely glaucous, grey-green leaves, to 12cm (5in) long, with 3–5 lance-shaped to ovate lobes. Solitary, shallowly cup-shaped white flowers, to 12cm (5in) across, with prominent yellow stamens, are borne over a long period in summer. ↕1–2.5m (3–8ft), ↔ indefinite. ❄❄. **'White Cloud'** ■ is vigorous and fast-spreading, with very glaucous foliage.

ROMULEA

IRIDACEAE

Genus of about 80 species of small, cormous perennials from a range of habitats including mountainous areas and coastal cliff tops in Europe, the Mediterranean, N. Africa, and South Africa. They are grown for their colourful, crocus-like flowers, produced in spring on very short, slender stems. The flowers often open only at midday, closing in the evening. Each plant produces up to 6 erect, or recurved and arching, thread-like, basal leaves, 5–40cm (2–16in) long. Grow in a sunny rock garden, or in containers in an alpine house. Half-hardy species are best grown in a cool greenhouse.

- **HARDINESS** Frost hardy to half hardy.
- **CULTIVATION** Plant corms 8cm (3in) deep in autumn. Under glass, grow in loam-based potting compost (JI No.2) with additional grit, in full light. In the growing season, water moderately and apply a balanced liquid fertilizer monthly. After flowering, reduce water gradually; keep completely dry when dormant in summer. Outdoors, grow in moderately fertile, well-drained soil in full sun.
- **PROPAGATION** Sow seed at 6–12°C (45–54°F) in autumn, or remove offsets when dormant.
- **PESTS AND DISEASES** Trouble free.

Romulea bulbocodium

Romulea sabulosa

***R. bulbocodioides* of gardens** see *R. flava.*
R. bulbocodium ■ syn. *R. grandiflora.* Small, cormous perennial with recurved, linear, channelled, mid-green, basal leaves. In spring, stems bear up to 5 upright, funnel-shaped, pale to deep lilac-purple flowers, 2.5cm (1in) long, with white or yellow centres. ↕5–10cm (2–4in), ↔ 5cm (2in). Mediterranean, Portugal, N.W. Spain, Bulgaria. ❄❄. **var. *crocea*** has yellow flowers.
R. flava, syn. *R. bulbocodioides* of gardens. Cormous perennial with upright, sheathing, linear, mid-green, basal leaves. In spring, produces up to 4 solitary, funnel-shaped, yellowish green, sometimes white or blue flowers, 3–4cm (1¼–1½in) long, with yellow centres. ↕10cm (4in), ↔ 5cm (2in). South Africa (Western Cape, Northern Cape, Eastern Cape). ❄
R. grandiflora see *R. bulbocodium.*
R. longituba see *R. macowanii* var. *alticola.*
R. macowanii* var. *alticola, syn. *R. longituba.* Cormous perennial with erect or recurved, linear, mid-green, basal leaves. In summer, stems bear up to 3 tubular, bright yellow flowers, 3–6cm (1¼–2½in) long, with orange-yellow centres. ↕8cm (3in), ↔ 5cm (2in). Lesotho (Drakensberg mountains), South Africa. ❄❄
R. requienii. Cormous perennial with arching to almost prostrate, linear, mid-green, basal leaves. Stems with up to 3 funnel-shaped violet flowers, 5cm (2in) long, sometimes veined darker violet, and with paler violet or white centres, are produced in spring. ↕↔ 12cm (5in), ↔ 5cm (2in). Mediterranean, France (Corsica), Italy (Sardinia). ❄❄
R. sabulosa ■ Showy, cormous perennial with upright or recurved, linear, mid-green, basal leaves. In early spring and summer, stems bear up to 4 funnel-shaped flowers, 5cm (2in) long; the flowers are bright shining scarlet to ruby red, with black centres, sometimes with paler margins, and open wide in the sun. ↕10–20cm (4–8in), ↔ 5cm (2in). South Africa (Western Cape, Eastern Cape). ❄

RONDELETIA

RUBIACEAE

Genus of 125–150 species of evergreen shrubs and trees from tropical woodland in Central and South America. The simple, leathery to paper-thin leaves are borne in opposite pairs or whorls of 3. They are grown for their small, tubular to salverform, sometimes fragrant flowers, each with 4–6 spreading petal lobes, which are borne in large, axillary or terminal panicles, cymes, or corymbs. Where temperatures fall below 12°C (54°F), grow in a temperate or warm greenhouse. In warmer areas, grow in a shrub border.

- **HARDINESS** Frost tender.
- **CULTIVATION** Under glass, grow in loam-based potting compost (JI No.3) with added leaf mould, in full light with shade from hot sun. Water freely in growth, and apply a balanced liquid fertilizer monthly; water moderately in winter. Outdoors, grow in fertile, moist but well-drained soil in sun or partial shade. Pruning group 9; plants under glass may need restrictive pruning.
- **PROPAGATION** Root semi-ripe cuttings with bottom heat in summer.
- **PESTS AND DISEASES** Prone to red spider mites, mealybugs, and whiteflies.

R. amoena ■ ♀ Bushy, rounded shrub or small tree with smooth to downy stems and elliptic or ovate-oblong leaves, 8–15cm (3–6in) long, glossy, mid-green above, brown-hairy or hairless beneath. In summer, bears axillary or terminal cymes or panicles, 5–15cm (2–6in) long, of small, salverform, fragrant, pink or white flowers with bearded yellow throats. ↕1.5–5m (5–15ft) or more, ↔ 1.5–4m (5–12ft). Mexico, Guatemala, Panama. ❀ (min. 12°C/54°F)
R. odorata, syn. *R. speciosa.* Bushy shrub, often with downy to felted stems, producing ovate to oblong, puckered, wavy-margined leaves, to 10cm (4in) long, deep green above, paler green beneath. Tubular, fragrant, orange to red, yellow-throated flowers are borne in dense, terminal cymes, corymbs, or panicles, 10cm (4in) long, in autumn. ↕to 3m (10ft), ↔ to 2.5m (8ft). Cuba, Panama. ❀ (min. 12°C/54°F)
R. speciosa see *R. odorata.*

▷***Rooksbya euphorbioides*** see *Neobuxbaumia euphorbioides*
▷**Rooistompie** see *Mimetes cucullatus*

Rondeletia amoena

R

ROSA

Rose

ROSACEAE

Genus of about 150 species of semi-evergreen or deciduous, perennial shrubs and climbers. They are found in a wide variety of habitats in Asia, Europe, N. Africa, and North America. Roses have erect, arching, scrambling, or sometimes trailing, often thorny or prickly stems. The alternate leaves range from 2.5–18cm (1–7in) or more long; each leaf usually has 5 or 7 often toothed, variably shaped leaflets.

Roses are grown for their attractive, often very fragrant flowers, borne mainly in summer and autumn, and sometimes also for their fruits, or hips. The flowers are solitary or borne in corymbs (referred to here as clusters), are sometimes remontant, and vary greatly in colour, size, and form (see panel below). Roses are suitable for a range of garden uses: as specimen plants or standards, for a shrub or mixed border, as hedges, or as climbers to clothe walls, trees, pillars, pergolas, and arbours. Groups of roses are often grown together in a single bed; a well-chosen mix of cultivars will ensure a long summer display. Miniature roses are suitable for a rock garden, raised bed, or containers. The flowers of all roses are good for cutting.

Rose species and cultivars are often regarded as 2 separate groups. Cultivars are further divided into Old Garden and Modern roses. Cultivars, derived initially from crossing Species roses, number many thousands, and are very varied in habit. In the subgroup descriptions below, leaflet lengths are defined as: small, up to 4cm (1½in); medium-sized, 4–7cm (1½–3in); large, over 7cm (3in). The flowers, in a range of shapes, are borne mainly in summer, over a longer period than Species roses; they are often remontant. Flowers are single (having 8 petals or fewer), semi-double (8–20 petals), double (20 petals or more), or fully double (over 30 petals). "Single to fully double", as used below, means that the flowers may be single, semi-double, double, or fully double.

Many modern rose cultivars are sold under names other than the registered Plant Breeder's Rights (PBR) names; where this is the case, the plant is listed under its trade name, with the PBR name in brackets afterwards.

Species roses
Also known as wild roses, Species roses (including those interspecific hybrids that share most of the characteristics of their parent species) are either shrubs or climbers, mostly bearing single, 5-petalled, often fragrant flowers in early summer, usually in one flush on short shoots from second-year wood; the flowers are followed by red or black hips.

Old Garden roses
This category is so large that it is divided into two groups. Roses in Group A are mostly of European origin, while those in Group B are hybrids between Oriental and European roses.

ROSE FLOWER FORMS

Flat – Open, usually single or semi-double flowers with petals that are almost flat.
Cupped – Open, single to fully double flowers with petals that curve outwards and upwards from the centre.
Rounded – Usually double or fully double flowers with even-sized, overlapping petals forming a bowl shape or more rounded form.
High-centred – Semi-double to fully double flowers with high, tight centres.
Urn-shaped – Semi-double to fully double flowers with inner petals that curve inwards to form an urn-shape, and outer petals that are flatter and more spreading.
Rosette-shaped – Almost flat, double or fully double flowers with slightly overlapping, often uneven petals.
Quartered-rosette – Almost flat, double or fully double flowers with the petals, often of uneven size, arranged so that the flower appears divided into 4 sections.
Pompon – Small, rounded, double or fully double flowers, usually in clusters, with masses of small petals.

FLAT

CUPPED

ROUNDED

HIGH-CENTRED

URN-SHAPED

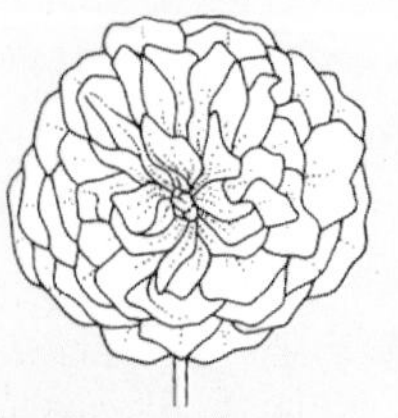

ROSETTE-SHAPED

QUARTERED-ROSETTE

POMPON

GROUP A
Alba – Large, free-branching shrub roses, varying greatly in size, with only a few prickles on the stems. They have greyish green leaves with medium to large, ovate leaflets, and bear clusters of 5–7 semi- to fully double, scented flowers in midsummer, on shoots from second-year wood. Very hardy. Most are suitable for a border, as hedges, or as specimen plants.
Centifolia (Provence) – Lax, thorny shrub roses producing matt, dark green leaves with small to medium-sized, ovate leaflets. Double or fully double, often scented flowers, are borne singly or in clusters of 3 in summer, on shoots from second-year wood. Grow in a border.
Damask – Open shrub roses with prickly stems and downy leaves with medium to large, ovate leaflets. They bear semi- to fully double, often very fragrant flowers, singly or in loose clusters of 5–7, mainly in summer, on shoots from second-year wood; a few also flower on new wood in autumn. Ideal for a border or for training against a support.
Gallica – Shrub roses of dense, free-branching habit, with usually thorny stems, and mostly dull, dark green leaves with medium-sized, ovate leaflets. In summer, they bear single to fully double, mostly scented flowers, often in clusters of 3, on shoots from second-year wood. Use in a bed or as hedges.
Moss – Often lax shrub roses with moss-like, furry growth on the stems and calyces, and mostly dark green leaves with medium to large, ovate leaflets. Semi- to fully double, usually fragrant flowers, often in clusters of 3 or more, are borne on very thorny shoots from second-year wood in summer. Suitable for a bed or border.
Scots (or ***Scotch***) – Suckering shrub roses, selections or hybrids of *R. pimpinellifolia*, of low, spreading, rarely upright habit, with prickly stems and dark green leaves comprising small to medium-sized, ovate leaflets. The single to double, occasionally scented flowers are solitary or borne in clusters of 3 or more, on short stems from second-year wood, usually in early summer. Suitable for a bed or border.
Sweet Briar – Vigorous, free-branching shrub roses with usually thorny stems and sweetly scented, dark green leaves comprising small to medium-sized, ovate leaflets. In summer, they bear single to double, usually scented flowers, singly or in clusters of up to 7, on short shoots from second-year wood. Use as hedges, as specimen plants, or in a large border.

GROUP B
Bourbon – Large, open, remontant shrub and climbing roses, often with long, smooth or prickly stems, which may be trained to climb. They have often glossy leaves with medium-sized, ovate leaflets, and most bear numerous scented, double or fully double flowers, usually in clusters of 3, in flushes in summer and usually autumn. Flowers are borne on short shoots from second-year wood and on new wood. Ideal for a border, or for training on a fence, wall, or pillar.
Boursault – Climbing roses with long, arching, usually smooth stems, and dark green leaves with medium to large, ovate leaflets. They bear semi-double or double, slightly scented flowers, singly or in clusters of 3, in early summer, on short shoots from second-year wood. Grow against a sheltered wall or fence.
China – Spindly, remontant shrub roses with mostly smooth stems, bearing only a few reddish brown prickles, and glossy leaves composed of small to medium-sized, lance-shaped leaflets. They bear single to fully double, sometimes scented flowers, singly or in clusters of 3–13, in flushes from summer to autumn. Flowers are borne on short shoots from second-year wood and on new wood. Use in a border, or grow against a low wall in a sheltered site.
Hybrid Musk – Vigorous, remontant shrub roses with prickly stems and abundant foliage comprising medium to large, ovate leaflets. They produce mainly double blooms, often very fragrant, either singly or in clusters of 2–7 or more, in flushes from midsummer to autumn. Good for a shrub border, or can be trained on a wall.
Hybrid Perpetual – Free-branching, remontant shrub roses with upright, prickly growth and dark green leaves with medium to large, ovate leaflets. They bear often scented, fully double flowers, singly or in clusters of 3, in flushes from summer to autumn, on shoots from second-year wood and on new wood. Ideal for a bed or border.
Noisette – Remontant climbing roses with smooth stems and usually glossy leaves comprising medium to large, ovate or lance-shaped leaflets. They bear large clusters of 3–15 slightly spice-scented, normally double to fully double flowers, in flushes from summer to autumn. Flowers are borne on shoots from second-year wood, occasionally on new wood. Grow on a sheltered wall.
Portland – Upright, compact, remontant shrub roses with thorny stems and usually dark green leaves composed of medium to large, ovate leaflets. Semi- to fully double, usually scented flowers are borne, singly or in clusters of 3, in flushes from summer to autumn, mainly on shoots from second-year wood. Grow in a bed or border.
Sempervirens – Vigorous, semi-evergreen climbing or rambler roses with shiny, light green leaves composed of small to medium-sized, lance-shaped leaflets. Arching, thorny stems bear clusters of 3–15 unscented, semi- to fully double flowers in summer, on short stems from second-year wood. Use to clothe a fence or pergola, or in informal, unconfined plantings.
Tea – Remontant shrub and climbing roses with smooth to thorny stems, sometimes bearing a few large red prickles, and glossy, light or sometimes dark green leaves with medium-sized, lance-shaped leaflets. Semi- to fully double, spice-scented flowers are borne singly or in clusters of 3, in flushes from summer to autumn, on shoots from second-year wood and on new wood. Grow in a sheltered site in a bed or border, or against a wall.

Modern roses
Climber – Often vigorous climbing roses with thorny, arching, stiff stems

and often dense, glossy, mid- to dark green foliage. They bear often scented flowers in a variety of forms, singly or in clusters of 3–7 or more. Some bloom in summer only, on short shoots from second-year wood; many are remontant and also flower on new wood. Train against a wall or fence, or use to cover garden structures.

Climbing Miniature – Remontant climbing roses with restrained, sparsely thorny growth, and leaves composed of very small, lance-shaped leaflets. Clusters of 3–9 tiny, single to fully double, rarely scented flowers are borne in flushes from summer to autumn, on shoots from second-year wood and on new wood. Grow against a low wall, fence, or pillar.

Floribunda (Cluster-flowered bush) – Remontant, free-branching bush roses of upright or bushy habit, usually with prickly stems and glossy, dark green leaves composed of medium-sized, ovate or lance-shaped leaflets. The single to fully double, sometimes scented flowers are usually in clusters of 3–25, rarely solitary, and borne continuously from summer to autumn on shoots from second-year wood and on new wood. Use in a border or as hedges.

Ground-cover – Spreading and trailing roses, mostly with prickly stems, producing often glossy leaves with small to medium-sized, lance-shaped leaflets. They bear clusters of numerous single to fully double, sometimes scented flowers; some flower in summer only, on short shoots from second-year wood; some are remontant, and also flower on new wood. Many bear flowers all along the stems. Ideal for a bed, bank, or container, or for trailing over walls.

Hybrid Tea (Large-flowered bush) – Remontant, free-branching bush roses of upright or bushy habit, with usually thorny stems and glossy or matt, mid- to dark green leaves with medium-sized to large, ovate or lance-shaped leaflets. Large, usually double, often scented flowers are solitary or borne in clusters of 3 in flushes from summer to autumn, on shoots from second-year wood and on new wood. Use as hedges or in a formal bed, and for cut flowers.

Miniature – Remontant bush roses with very compact, rarely spreading, sparsely thorny, short growth, and leaves with tiny, usually lance-shaped leaflets. Sprays of 3–11 tiny, single to fully double, rarely scented flowers are borne in flushes from summer to autumn, on very short shoots from second-year wood and on new wood. Ideal for edging paths or driveways, or for a raised bed, rock garden, or container.

Patio (Dwarf cluster-flowered bush) – Remontant bush roses with compact growth, sometimes prickly stems, and usually glossy leaves composed of small to medium, ovate or lance-shaped leaflets. They bear clusters of 3–11 single to double, usually unscented flowers in flushes from summer to autumn, on shoots from second-year wood and on new wood. Suitable for a bed, border, or container, or as a hedge.

Polyantha – Remontant, compact-growing bush or shrub roses with sparsely thorny stems, and glossy leaves with small, lance-shaped leaflets. Sprays of many small, single to double, rarely scented flowers are borne in flushes from summer to autumn, on short shoots from second-year wood and on new wood. Suitable for a bed or border, as hedges, and for containers.

Rambler – A diverse group of vigorous roses with long, arching, thorny, sometimes lax stems and dense foliage. They have usually glossy leaves with small, lance-shaped leaflets, and bear clusters of 3–21 single to fully double, sometimes scented flowers, mainly in summer, on short shoots from second-year wood. Train over a fence or pergola, on walls, or into a tree.

Rugosa – Hardy shrub roses with tough, wrinkled, usually bright green leaves with medium to large, ovate or lance-shaped leaflets and prickly stems. Most bear single or semi-double, scented flowers, in clusters of 3–11, throughout summer and autumn, on shoots from second-year wood and on new wood. They are often followed by tomato-like, usually red hips. Use as hedges, for a bed or border, or as specimen plants.

Rosa Abraham Darby ('Auscot')

Shrub – Roses in this diverse group are usually larger than bush roses (a general term used to describe Floribundas, Hybrid Teas, Miniatures, Patio roses, and occasionally Ground-cover roses). They often have thorny stems, and bear leaves with medium-sized to large, ovate or lance-shaped leaflets. The usually scented, semi-double to double flowers are borne in few- to many-flowered clusters, sometimes singly, from summer to autumn; some bloom in summer only from second-year wood; most are remontant and also flower on new wood. Ideal for hedges, for a border or bed, or as specimen plants.

• **Hardiness** Fully hardy to frost hardy.
• **Cultivation** Roses tolerate a wide range of conditions, but usually prefer an open site in full sun. They thrive in moderately fertile, humus-rich, moist but well-drained soil. Soil in which roses have recently been grown is unsuitable for new plantings because of the build-up of harmful soil organisms. In such cases, either use fresh soil or sterilize the soil with a proprietary remedy, or choose a fresh planting site. The best time for planting is winter or early spring, during a frost-free spell. For best flowering, apply a balanced fertilizer and mulch in late winter or early spring. In spring and summer, apply a balanced liquid fertilizer every 3 weeks. The heights and spreads given in the rose descriptions are for pruned plants; unpruned, roses grow much larger.

Most roses sold have been budded on the rootstock of a wild rose to ensure vigorous growth. The rootstock may produce shoots, known as "suckers", which should be removed at their point of origin as soon as seen. To identify a sucker, check that it originates from the rootstock itself, and not from above the point where the plant was budded.

Rain may damage the flowers, causing the petals to form "balls". Since they can develop mildew and other fungi, they need to be removed as soon as possible, cutting back to a strong-growing bud.
• **Propagation** Root hardwood cuttings in autumn. Bud in summer.
• **Pests and diseases** Susceptible to aphids, leafhoppers, red spider mites, scale insects, caterpillars, sawfly larvae, and leaf-cutting bees; rabbits and deer may cause damage. Prone to black spot, rust, powdery mildew, die-back, canker, crown gall, honey fungus, soil sickness, viruses, and downy mildew.

Pruning requirements

On planting, shorten thick roots to 25cm (10in) and remove damaged ones. Reduce top-growth to 3–5 strong shoots, and cut these back to outward-facing buds: to 8–15cm (3–6in) above ground for Hybrid Tea and Floribunda roses and dwarf variants; to 40cm (16in) for ramblers; to 20–30cm (8–12in) for other groups. For climbers and standards, remove only dead, diseased, damaged, weak, or crossing shoots.

When in growth, remove dead, damaged, and diseased wood, suckers, and blind shoots, and prune as below. Dead-head all roses unless hips are wanted. In autumn, trim long shoots back by 15–30cm (6–12in) to reduce wind rock. Avoid pruning in frosty weather when roses are dormant; delay until early spring in areas with severe winters. Prune in the cooler months in warm climates, to simulate dormancy.

The pruning chart below gives specific advice for individual rose groups. For standard roses, prune according to the type of rose that forms the head; leave weeping standards unpruned on planting and for 2 subsequent years, to develop their form.

Group	Season	For maintenance	For renewal
Hybrid Tea, Tea, Hybrid Perpetual	Late winter to early spring	Cut back main stems to 20–25cm (8–10in) above ground in temperate climates; to 45–60cm (18–24in) in warm climates. Reduce sideshoots to 2 or 3 buds or 10–15cm (4–6in). Remove weak, spindly shoots.	Cut back ⅓ of oldest stems almost to the base; repeat for rest of old stems over next 2 or 3 years.
Floribunda, Miniature, Patio, Polyantha	Late winter to early spring	Cut back main stems to 25–45cm (10–18in) above ground; reduce sideshoots to 2 or 3 buds. Cut back stems and sideshoots of Patio roses and Miniatures by ⅓–½.	As above.
Climbers (inc. Climbing Miniatures), Boursault, Noisette, and Climbing Bourbon	Late autumn to early spring	In the first 2 years, cut out only dead, diseased, or damaged wood; train stems on to wires or other, preferably horizontal supports. From year 3, prune main shoots to within designated area for growth; reduce sideshoots by ⅔, or to 3 or 4 buds.	Cut back 1 or 2 of oldest stems to 30–45cm (12–18in) above ground. Repeat every 1–3 years.
Rambler, Sempervirens	Summer, after flowering	In the first 2 years, train stems on to support; reduce sideshoots only, by ⅔ or to 2–4 buds. In year 3, reduce sideshoots as before, and begin renewal pruning.	Cut out ¼–⅓ of flowered stems at the base. New shoots arise from base.
Ground-cover	Late winter to early spring	Cut back to outward-facing buds to confine to designated area for growth. Shorten sideshoots if overcrowded.	Cut out ⅕–¼ of oldest flowered stems.
Species, Shrub, Miniature, Rugosa	Late summer, after flowering	For non-remontant roses, prune main stems lightly, or cut back by up to ⅓, as necessary; reduce sideshoots by ½–⅔. For remontant roses, see below.	As above.
Bourbon, China, Portland; & remontant roses of group above	Late winter to early spring	As for category above, but during the dormant season.	As above.
Alba, Centifolia, Damask, Moss, Scots, Sweet Briar	Late summer	Immediately after flowering, prune main stems lightly or cut back by ¼–⅓, as necessary; reduce sideshoots by ⅔.	Cut out up to ¼ of oldest stems; cut back rest by ⅓.
Gallica, Hybrid Musk	Late summer	Cut back overlong shoots by up to ⅓; reduce sideshoots by ⅔.	Cut out 1 or 2 of oldest stems every 1–3 years.

R

Rosa 'Agnes'

Rosa 'Alba Maxima'

Rosa 'Albéric Barbier'

Rosa 'Albertine'

Rosa Alec's Red ('Cored')

Rosa 'Alister Stella Gray'

Rosa 'Aloha'

Rosa 'Alpine Sunset'

Rosa Amber Queen ('Harroony')

Rosa 'American Pillar'

Rosa Angela Rippon ('Ocaru')

Rosa Anisley Dickson ('Dickimono')

***R.* Abbeyfield Rose ('Cocbrose').** Compact Hybrid Tea rose with glossy, dark green leaves. High-centred, double, deep rose-pink flowers, 10cm (4in) across, are borne freely from summer to autumn. ↕↔ 60cm (24in). ✲✲✲

***R.* Abraham Darby ('Auscot')** ■ Shrub rose with a strong, bushy habit and large, glossy, dark green leaves. Cupped, fully double, fruit-scented, apricot-pink flowers, 11cm (4½in) across, are borne from summer to autumn. ↕↔ 1.5m (5ft). ✲✲✲

***R.* 'Adélaïde d'Orléans'.** Sempervirens rambler rose with long, slender stems and matt, light green leaves. Clusters of pendent, cupped, semi-double, lightly scented, light pink flowers, 4cm (1½in) across, are borne in midsummer. ↕ 5m (15ft), ↔ 3m (10ft). ✲✲

***R.* 'Agnes'** ■ Rugosa rose with upright stems, dark green leaves, and cupped, double, scented, light yellow flowers, 10cm (4in) across, produced in summer (a few borne later). ↕ 2m (6ft), ↔ 1.2m (4ft). ✲✲✲

***R.* 'Aimée Vibert'**, syn. *R.* 'Bouquet de la Mariée'. Noisette climbing rose with long stems and glossy, dark green leaves. Cupped, fully double, lightly scented white flowers, 8cm (3in) across, are borne in large clusters from summer to autumn. Prune to maintain as a shrub. ↕ 3–5m (10–15ft), ↔ 3m (10ft). ✲✲

***R.* 'Alba Maxima'** ■ syn. *R.* x *alba* 'Maxima' (Great white rose, Jacobite rose, White rose of York). Alba rose of vigorous, upright habit, with greyish green leaves. Flat, double, sweet-scented, creamy white flowers, 8cm (3in) across, are borne in midsummer. ↕ 2.2m (7ft), ↔ 1.5m (5ft). ✲✲✲

***R.* x *alba* 'Maxima'** see *R.* 'Alba Maxima'.

***R.* x *alba* 'Semiplena'** see *R.* 'Alba Semiplena'.

***R.* 'Alba Semiplena'**, syn. *R.* x *alba* 'Semiplena'. Alba rose of vigorous, bushy habit, with greyish green leaves. In midsummer, produces flat, semi-double, scented white flowers, 8cm (3in) across. ↕ 2.2m (7ft), ↔ 1.5m (5ft). ✲✲✲

***R.* 'Albéric Barbier'** ■ Vigorous, pendent, semi-evergreen Rambler with glossy, dark green leaves. Bears clusters of rosette-shaped, fully double, slightly fragrant, creamy white flowers, 8cm (3in) across, ageing to white, in summer. ↕ to 5m (15ft), ↔ 3m (10ft). ✲✲✲

***R.* 'Albertine'** ■ Vigorous, rampant Rambler with arching, prickly, reddish green stems and mid-green leaves. Rounded to cupped, fully double, sweetly scented, light salmon-pink flowers, 8cm (3in) across, are borne freely in midsummer. ↕ to 5m (15ft), ↔ 4m (12ft). ✲✲✲

***R.* 'Alchymist'.** Vigorous, free-branching Climber with glossy, deep green leaves, coppery when young. Flat, fully double, fragrant yellow flowers, 10cm (4in) across, deepening to orange-pink, are borne freely in summer. ↕ 2.5m (8ft), ↔ 1.2m (4ft). ✲✲✲

***R.* Alec's Red ('Cored')** ■ Hybrid Tea rose with mid-green leaves and high-centred, fully double, strongly fragrant red flowers, 15cm (6in) across, borne from summer to autumn. ↕ 1m (3ft), ↔ 60cm (24in). ✲✲✲

***R.* Alexander ('Harlex')** ■ Vigorous Hybrid Tea rose with glossy, dark green foliage. Urn-shaped, double, bright red flowers, 12cm (5in) across, often with scalloped petals, are borne on long stems from summer to autumn. ↕ to 2m (6ft), ↔ 80cm (32in). ✲✲

***R.* 'Alister Stella Gray'** ■ syn. *R.* 'Golden Rambler'. Noisette climbing rose with long, vigorous, arching stems and mid-green foliage. Quartered-rosette, fully double, musk-scented flowers, 6cm (2½in) across, yolk-yellow fading to white, are borne freely from summer to autumn. ↕ to 5m (15ft), ↔ 3m (10ft). ✲✲

***R.* 'Allgold'.** Upright, narrow Floribunda rose with glossy, bright green leaves. Flat, double, lightly scented, bright yellow flowers, 8cm (3in) across, are produced from summer to autumn. ↕ 60cm (24in), ↔ 50cm (20in). ✲✲✲

***R.* 'Aloha'** ■ Strong-stemmed Climber with leathery, dark green leaves. Bears rounded, fully double, sweetly scented, rose-pink and salmon-pink flowers, 9cm (3½in) across, from summer to autumn. Prune to maintain as a shrub. ↕ to 3m (10ft), ↔ 2.5m (8ft). ✲✲✲

***R.* 'Alpine Sunset'** ■ Compact Hybrid Tea rose with glossy, light green leaves. From summer to autumn, bears rounded, fully double, fragrant, light peach-yellow flowers, 18cm (7in) across, edged pink. ↕↔ 60cm (24in). ✲✲✲

***R.* Altissimo ('Delmur').** Climber with dark green leaves and cupped, single, bright red flowers, 12cm (5in) across, showing yellow stamens, borne from summer to autumn. ↕ 3m (10ft), ↔ 2.5m (8ft). ✲✲✲

***R.* 'Amberlight'** see *R.* Fyvie Castle ('Cocbamber').

***R.* Amber Queen ('Harroony')** ■ syn. *R.* 'Prinz Eugen van Savoyen'. Floribunda rose of neat, spreading habit, with leathery, dark green foliage, reddish green when young. Cupped, fully double, fragrant, amber-yellow flowers, 8cm (3in) across, are borne from summer to autumn. ↕ 50cm (20in), ↔ 60cm (24in). ✲✲✲

Rosa Alexander ('Harlex')

***R.* 'American Pillar'** ■ Rampant Rambler with long stems and leathery, glossy, mid-green foliage. Large clusters of cupped, single, carmine-red flowers, 5cm (2in) across, with white eyes, are borne freely in midsummer. ↕ to 5m (15ft), ↔ 4m (12ft). ✲✲✲

***R.* x *anemonoides* 'Ramona'** see *R.* 'Ramona'.

***R.* Angela Rippon ('Ocaru')** ■ syn. *R.* 'Ocarina'. Miniature rose of upright habit, with many dark green leaves. Bears urn-shaped, fully double, rose- to salmon-pink flowers, 4cm (1½in) across, from summer to autumn. ↕ 45cm (18in), ↔ 30cm (12in). ✲✲✲

***R.* Anisley Dickson ('Dickimono')** ■ syn. *R.* 'Dicky'. Vigorous Floribunda rose with glossy, dark green leaves and clusters of high-centred, double, deep reddish salmon-pink flowers, 8cm (3in) across, borne from summer to autumn. ↕ 1m (3ft), ↔ 75cm (30in). ✲✲✲

***R.* Anna Ford ('Harpiccolo')** ■ Dwarf Floribunda rose of compact habit, with dark green leaves. Bears many urn-shaped, semi-double, orange-red flowers, 4cm (1½in) across, opening flat, from summer to autumn. ↕ 45cm (18in), ↔ 40cm (16in). ✲✲✲

***R.* Anna Livia ('Kormetter')**, syn. *R.* 'Trier 2000'. Vigorous Floribunda rose with leathery, mid-green foliage. Large sprays of rounded, double pink flowers, 8cm (3in) across, are borne freely from summer to autumn. ↕ 75cm (30in), ↔ 60cm (24in). ✲✲✲

***R.* Anne Harkness ('Harkaramel')** ■ Floribunda rose of vigorous, tall habit, with mid-green foliage. Urn-shaped, double, apricot-yellow flowers, 8cm (3in) across, are borne in many-flowered sprays from late summer to autumn. ↕ 1.2m (4ft), ↔ 60cm (24in). ✲✲✲

***R.* 'Apricot Nectar'.** Floribunda rose with mid-green leaves and rounded, fully double, scented, apricot to apricot-pink flowers, 10cm (4in) across, borne in tight clusters from summer to autumn. ↕ to 80cm (32in), ↔ 65cm (26in). ✲✲✲

***R.* Armada ('Haruseful')** ■ Vigorous, free-branching Shrub rose with glossy, dark green leaves. Cupped, semi-double, scented, deep rose-pink flowers, 8cm (3in) across, are borne from summer to autumn. ↕ 1.5m (5ft), ↔ 1.2m (4ft). ✲✲✲

Rosa ANNA FORD ('Harpiccolo')

Rosa ANNE HARKNESS ('Harkaramel')

Rosa ARMADA ('Haruseful')

Rosa 'Arthur Bell'

Rosa AWAKENING ('Probuzini')

Rosa BABY MASQUERADE ('Tanba')

Rosa banksiae 'Lutea'

Rosa 'Bantry Bay'

Rosa 'Baron Girod de l'Ain'

Rosa BARONNE EDMOND DE ROTHSCHILD ('Meigriso')

Rosa 'Belle de Crécy'

Rosa 'Blairii Number Two'

***R.* 'Arthur Bell'** ■ Floribunda rose with glossy, bright green leaves. Cupped, double, fragrant, yellow to cream flowers, 8cm (3in) across, are produced from summer to autumn. ↕ 1m (3ft), ↔ 60cm (24in). ❄❄❄
***R.* AVON ('Poulmulti')**, syn. *R.* 'Fairy Lights', *R.* 'Sunnyside'. Ground-cover rose of compact habit, with dark green leaves. Clusters of flat, semi-double, pale pink to pearl-white flowers, 4.5cm (1¾in) across, are borne along the stems from summer to autumn. ↕ 35cm (14in), ↔ 1m (3ft). ❄❄❄
***R.* AWAKENING ('Probuzini')** ■ Climber with glossy, mid-green leaves. Clusters of cupped, fully double, fragrant, pale pearl-pink flowers, 8cm (3in) across, are borne from summer to autumn. Tolerates a partially shaded site. ↕ 3m (10ft), ↔ 2.5m (8ft). ❄❄❄
***R.* 'Ayrshire Splendens'** see *R.* 'Splendens'.
***R.* 'Baby Blanket'** see *R.* OXFORDSHIRE ('Korfullwind').
***R.* 'Baby Carnival'** see *R.* BABY MASQUERADE ('Tanba').
***R.* BABY LOVE ('Scrivluv').** Patio rose of shrubby growth and dense, upright habit. Shallowly cupped, single, bright yellow flowers, 5cm (2in) across, are borne freely close to the mid-green foliage, from summer to autumn. ↕ 1.1m (3½ft), ↔ 75cm (30in). ❄❄❄
***R.* BABY MASQUERADE ('Tanba')** ■ syn. *R.* 'Baby Carnival'. Miniature rose of dense, twiggy habit, with dark green leaves and clusters of many rosette-shaped, double, yellow-pink flowers, 2.5cm (1in) across, borne from summer to autumn. ↕↔ 40cm (16in). ❄❄❄
***R.* 'Bad Nauheim'** see *R.* 'National Trust'.
***R.* 'Ballerina'** ■ Polyantha rose of dense, spreading habit, with mid-green leaves. Spectacular in flower, it bears many shallowly cupped, single, white-centred, light pink flowers, 3cm (1¼in) across, in mop-headed clusters, from summer to autumn. ↕ to 1.5m (5ft), ↔ 1.2m (4ft). ❄❄❄
R. banksiae, syn. *R. banksiae* var. *alba*, *R. banksiae* 'Alba Plena' (Double white banksian rose). Climbing Species rose with long, slender, smooth stems and small, pale green leaves composed of 3–7 oblong-lance-shaped to elliptic-ovate leaflets, 3–6cm (1¼–2½in) long. Clusters of many rosette-shaped, double, violet-scented white flowers, 2.5cm (1in) across, with notched petals, are borne in late spring. Protect from frost. Prune spent wood only. ↕ to 12m (40ft), ↔ to 6m (20ft). W. and C. China. ❄❄. **var. *alba*** see *R. banksiae*. **'Alba Plena'** see *R. banksiae*. **'Lutea'** ■ syn. var. *lutea* (Yellow banksian rose) bears fully double yellow flowers, 2cm (¾in) across. Needs a sheltered wall; ↕↔ to 6m (20ft). **'Lutescens'**, syn. f. *lutescens*, bears single, strongly scented yellow flowers. **var. *normalis*** (Single white banksian rose) bears single, fragrant white flowers on prickly stems; ↕↔ to 12m (40ft).
***R.* 'Bantry Bay'** ■ Upright, free-branching Climber with dark green leaves. Clusters of cupped, semi-double, lightly scented, deep pink flowers, 9cm (3½in) across, are borne from summer to autumn. ↕ 4m (12ft), ↔ 2.5m (8ft). ❄❄❄
***R.* 'Baron Girod de l'Ain'** ■ Hybrid Perpetual rose of vigorous habit, with moderately prickly stems and leathery, dark green leaves. From summer to autumn, bears cupped, fully double, scented crimson, white-edged flowers, 10cm (4in) across, with wavy-margined petals. ↕ 1.2m (4ft), ↔ 1m (3ft). ❄❄❄
***R.* BARONNE EDMOND DE ROTHSCHILD ('Meigriso')** ■ Vigorous Hybrid Tea rose with leathery, glossy, mid-green foliage. Rounded, fully double, fragrant, ruby-red flowers, 12cm (5in) across, with a pale pink reverse to the petals, are borne from summer to autumn. ↕ 90cm (36in), ↔ 75cm (30in). ❄❄❄
***R.* 'Baronne Prévost'.** Erect Hybrid Perpetual rose with prickly stems and dark green leaves. Quartered-rosette, fully double, scented pink flowers, 10cm (4in) across, are borne from summer to autumn. ↕ to 1.5m (5ft), ↔ 1m (3ft). ❄❄❄
***R.* BEAUTIFUL BRITAIN ('Dicfire').** Upright Floribunda rose with sparse, mid-green leaves. Bears cupped, double, lightly scented, tomato-red flowers, 7cm (3in) across, from summer to autumn. ↕ 75cm (30in), ↔ 60cm (24in). ❄❄❄
***R.* 'Beauty of Glazenwood'** see *R.* x *odorata* 'Pseudindica'.
***R.* BEAUTY STAR ('Frystar')**, syn. *R.* 'Liverpool Remembers'. Compact, upright Hybrid Tea rose with glossy, dark green leaves. High-centred, double, strongly scented vermilion flowers, 10cm (4in) across, are produced from summer to autumn. ↕ 90cm (36in), ↔ 60cm (24in). ❄❄❄
***R.* 'Belle Amour'.** Upright Alba rose with grey-green foliage. Camellia-like, rounded, semi-double, myrrh-scented, light salmon-pink flowers, 9cm (3½in) across, cupped on opening, are borne in midsummer, followed by spherical red hips. ↕ 2m (6ft), ↔ 1.2m (4ft). ❄❄❄
***R.* 'Belle Courtisane'** see *R.* 'Königin von Dänemark'.
***R.* 'Belle de Crécy'** ■ Gallica rose of lax habit, with bristly stems and greyish green leaves. In summer, bears quartered-rosette, full-petalled, fully double, fragrant, deep pink to purple flowers, 8cm (3in) across, showing green centres as they open. ↕ 1.2m (4ft), ↔ 1m (3ft). ❄❄❄
***R.* 'Belle de Londres'** see *R.* 'Compassion' .
***R.* BELLE EPOQUE ('Fryyaboo')** ■p.935. Vigorous, upright Hybrid Tea rose with dark green foliage. High-centred, double, fragrant flowers, 10cm (4in) across, of bronze-orange, deeper on petal reverses, are borne from summer to autumn. ↕ 1.1m (3½ft), ↔ 60cm (24in). ❄❄❄
***R.* 'Belle of Portugal'** see *R.* 'Belle Portugaise'.
***R.* 'Belle Portugaise'**, syn. *R.* 'Belle of Portugal'. Very vigorous, climbing Tea rose with glossy, olive green leaves and high-centred, semi-double, fragrant, light salmon-pink flowers, 12cm (5in) across, borne in summer. ↕ to 5m (15ft), ↔ 3m (10ft). ❄❄
***R.* 'Berkeley'** see *R.* TOURNAMENT OF ROSES ('Jacient').
***R.* BERKSHIRE ('Korpinka')**, syn. *R.* 'Pink Sunsation', *R.* 'Sommermärchen'. Prostrate Ground-cover rose with glossy, dark green leaves. Flat, semi-double, scented, cherry-pink flowers, 5cm (2in) across, with gold stamens, are borne from summer to autumn. ↕ 60cm (24in), ↔ 1.2m (4ft). ❄❄❄
***R.* BETTY HARKNESS ('Harette').** Vigorous, upright Floribunda rose with glossy, dark green leaves. Bears many cupped, double, sweet-scented, coral-orange flowers, 9cm (3½in) across, from summer to autumn. ↕ 1.5m (5ft), ↔ 75cm (30in). ❄❄❄
***R.* BIG PURPLE ('Stebigpu')**, syn. *R.* 'Nuit d'Orient'. Vigorous Hybrid Tea rose with dark green leaves. Bears high-centred, fully double, strongly scented, deep beetroot-purple flowers, 12cm (5in) across, from summer to autumn. ↕ 1.1m (3½ft), ↔ 70cm (28in). ❄❄❄
***R.* BIRTHDAY GIRL ('Meilasso')**, syn. *R.* 'Cocorico'. Bushy Floribunda rose with mid-green foliage. Cupped, semi-double, lightly scented, carmine-pink and yellow flowers, 8cm (3in) across, are produced from summer to autumn. ↕ 75cm (30in), ↔ 60cm (24in). ❄❄❄
***R.* 'Bizarre Triomphant'** see *R.* 'Charles de Mills'.
***R.* 'Blairii Number Two'** ■ Vigorous, climbing Bourbon rose with mid-green

Rosa 'Ballerina'

R

Rosa 'Blessings'

Rosa 'Bobbie James'

Rosa Bonica ('Meidomonac')

Rosa 'Boule de Neige'

Rosa 'Bourbon Queen'

Rosa Breath of Life ('Harquanne')

Rosa Bright Smile ('Dicdance')

Rosa Brown Velvet ('Maccultra')

Rosa 'Buff Beauty'

Rosa 'Camaïeux'

Rosa 'Cardinal de Richelieu'

Rosa Cardinal Hume ('Harregale')

leaves, reddish green when young. In summer, bears clusters of usually 3–5 double, fragrant, light pink flowers, 8cm (3in) across, rounded at first, opening flat. Prone to mildew. ↕ to 4m (12ft), ↔ 2m (6ft). ❄❄❄

***R.* 'Blanc Double de Coubert'.** Rugosa rose of dense, spreading habit, with leathery, mid-green foliage. From summer to autumn, bears loose-petalled, cupped to flat, semi-double, fragrant white flowers, 8cm (3in) across, with yellow stamens, followed in some years by spherical red hips. ↕ 1.5m (5ft), ↔ 1.2m (4ft). ❄❄❄

***R.* 'Blanche Moreau'.** Moss rose of lax growth, with dark green leaves. In summer, bears cupped, fully double, fragrant white flowers, 10cm (4in) across, with brownish green mossing on the stems and calyces. ↕ 1.5m (5ft), ↔ 1.2m (4ft). ❄❄❄

***R.* 'Blessings'** ■ Vigorous Hybrid Tea rose with dark green leaves. Bears urn-shaped, fully double, scented, salmon-pink flowers, 10cm (4in) across, from summer to autumn. ↕ 1.1m (3½ft), ↔ 75cm (30in). ❄❄❄

***R.* 'Bleu Magenta'.** Lax, arching Rambler with glossy, dark green foliage. Cupped, double, lightly scented, purple to violet flowers, 5cm (2in) across, with yellow stamens, are borne freely in summer. ↕ 3.5m (11ft), ↔ 3m (10ft). ❄❄❄

***R.* Blue Moon ('Tannacht'),** syn. *R.* 'Mainzer Fastnacht', *R.* 'Sissi'. Branching Hybrid Tea rose with dark green leaves. Bears high-centred, fully double, fragrant, lilac-mauve flowers, 10cm (4in) across, from summer to autumn. ↕ 1m (3ft), ↔ 70cm (28in). ❄❄❄

***R.* 'Blue Rambler'** see *R.* 'Veilchenblau'.

***R.* 'Blush Noisette'** see *R.* 'Noisette Carnée'.

***R.* 'Blush Rambler'.** Vigorous Rambler with long, arching stems and masses of glossy, mid-green leaves. Large, dense clusters of cupped, semi-double, light pink flowers, 4cm (1½in) across, are borne in late summer. ↕ 4m (12ft), ↔ 5m (15ft). ❄❄❄

***R.* 'Bobbie James'** ■ Rampant Rambler producing glossy leaves, reddish green when young, maturing mid-green. Large clusters of cupped, semi-double, scented, creamy white flowers, 5cm (2in) across, are produced in summer. ↕ to 10m (30ft), ↔ 6m (20ft). ❄❄❄

***R.* Bonica ('Meidomonac')** ■ syn. *R.* 'Bonica '82'. Vigorous Shrub rose of low, spreading habit, with dense, glossy, rich green foliage. Large sprays of cupped, fully double, rose-pink flowers, 7cm (3in) across, are borne from summer to autumn. ↕ 85cm (34in), ↔ 1.1m (3½ft). ❄❄❄

***R.* 'Bonica '82'** see *R.* Bonica ('Meidomonac').

***R.* 'Boule de Neige'** ■ Bourbon rose of vigorous, uneven growth, with glossy, dark green leaves. From summer to autumn, bears cupped to rosette-shaped, fully double, fragrant white flowers, 8cm (3in) across, tinged pink. ↕ 1.5m (5ft), ↔ 1.2m (4ft). ❄❄❄

***R.* 'Bouquet de la Mariée'** see *R.* 'Aimée Vibert'.

***R.* 'Bourbon Queen'** ■ syn. *R.* 'Souvenir de la Princesse de Lamballe'. Vigorous Bourbon rose with long, leafy stems and mid-green foliage. Clusters of numerous cupped, double, scented, magenta to rose-pink flowers, 8cm (3in) across, are borne mainly in summer. ↕ to 2.5m (8ft), ↔ 1.5m (5ft). ❄❄❄

R. bracteata (Chickasaw rose, Macartney rose). Fast-growing, semi-evergreen Species rose with prickly, brownish green stems and glossy, dark green leaves, each with 5–11 obovate to elliptic leaflets, 2–5cm (¾–2in) long. From summer to autumn, bears cupped to flat, single, lightly scented white flowers, 9cm (3½in) across, with gold stamens and curling petals, followed by spherical orange hips. ↕↔ to 6m (20ft). S.E. China, Taiwan. ❄❄

***R.* 'Brass Ring'** see *R.* Peek A Boo ('Dicgrow').

***R.* Braveheart ('Cocjabby'),** syn. *R.* 'Gordon's College'. Vigorous, upright Floribunda rose with glossy, purplish green leaves. Bears high-centred, double, scented, reddish salmon flowers, 9cm (3½in) across, from summer to autumn. ↕ 75cm (30in), ↔ 60cm (24in). ❄❄❄

***R.* Breath of Life ('Harquanne')** ■ Upright Climber with mid-green leaves and rounded, fully double, scented, apricot to apricot-pink flowers, 10cm (4in) across, borne from summer to autumn. ↕ 2.5m (8ft), ↔ 2.2m (7ft). ❄❄❄

***R.* Bride ('Fryyearn').** Bushy, upright Hybrid Tea rose with dark green leaves. High-centred, double, strongly scented, blush-pink flowers, 9cm (3½in) across, are borne from summer to autumn. ↕ 80cm (32in), ↔ 60cm (24in). ❄❄❄

***R.* Bridge of Sighs ('Harglowing').** Upright, arching Climber with small, glossy, dark green leaves. Clusters of flat, semi-double, scented, apricot flowers, 5cm (2in) across, are produced from summer to autumn. ↕ 2.5m (8ft), ↔ 1.8m (6ft). ❄❄❄

***R.* Bright Smile ('Dicdance')** ■ Low-growing Floribunda rose with glossy, bright green leaves. Well-spaced clusters of flat, semi-double, scented yellow flowers, 8cm (3in) across, are borne freely from summer to autumn. ↕↔ 45cm (18in). ❄❄❄

***R.* 'Brite Lites'** see *R.* Princess Alice ('Hartanna').

***R.* Broadlands ('Tanmirsch'),** syn. *R.* 'Sonnenschirm'. Vigorous, spreading Ground-cover rose with glossy, light green foliage. Cupped, double, scented, light yellow flowers, 8cm (3in) across, are borne from summer to autumn. ↕ 1m (3ft), ↔ 1.5m (5ft). ❄❄❄

***R.* Brother Cadfael ('Ausglobe').** Upright Shrub rose with large, dark green leaves. Bears deeply cupped, double, fragrant, rose-pink flowers, 12cm (5in) across, from summer to autumn. ↕ 1.1m (3½ft), ↔ 90cm (36in). ❄❄❄

***R.* Brown Velvet ('Maccultra')** ■ syn. *R.* 'Colorbreak'. Floribunda rose with glossy, dark green leaves. Bears quartered-rosette, fully double, brownish orange flowers, 8cm (3in) across, from summer to autumn. ↕ 1m (3ft), ↔ 60cm (24in). ❄❄❄

***R.* 'Buffalo Bill'** see *R.* Regensberg ('Macyoumis').

***R.* 'Buff Beauty'** ■ Hybrid Musk rose of rounded habit, with dense, dark green leaves. Freely bears large clusters of cupped, fully double, lightly fragrant flowers, 9cm (3½in) across, apricot fading to buff, in summer (with a few borne later). ↕↔ 1.2m (4ft). ❄❄❄

***R.* 'Burgund '81'** see *R.* Loving Memory ('Korgund').

***R.* 'Burning Sky'** see *R.* Paradise ('Weizeip').

R. californica. Shrubby Species rose with bristly shoots and dull, mid-green leaves, each composed of 5–7 ovate to broadly elliptic leaflets, 1–3cm (½–1¼in) long. Clusters of flat, single, scented, lilac-pink flowers, 4cm (1½in) across, are borne freely in summer, a few later in autumn, before the spherical, orange-red hips. ↕ 1.5–2.5m (5–8ft), ↔ 1.2–2m (4–6ft). USA (S. Oregon to S. California), N.W. Mexico. ❄❄❄. **'Plena'**, often confused with *R. nutkana* of gardens, has grey-green foliage and cupped to flat, semi-double, fragrant, lilac-purple flowers, 5cm (2in) across, with white at the petal bases, in summer; ↕ 1.8m (6ft), ↔ 1.5m (5ft).

***R.* 'Camaïeux'** ■ Gallica rose of dense habit, with mid-green foliage. Cupped, fully double, scented, light pink flowers, 9cm (3½in) across, striped with crimson-purple to lilac-grey, are borne in summer. ↕↔ 80cm (32in). ❄❄❄

***R.* Cambridgeshire ('Korhaugen'),** syn. *R.* 'Carpet of Colour'. Spreading Ground-cover rose with glossy, dark green leaves. Cupped, semi-double, lightly scented, gold and cerise-pink flowers, 6cm (2½in) across, are borne freely from summer to autumn. ↕ 50cm (20in), ↔ 90cm (36in). ❄❄❄

***R.* 'Canary Bird'** see *R. xanthina* 'Canary Bird'.

***R.* 'Cantabrigiensis'.** Vigorous, upright Species hybrid with ferny, mid-green foliage. Cupped, single, scented, primrose-yellow flowers, 5cm (2in) across, are borne in late spring. ↕ 3m (10ft), ↔ 2m (6ft). ❄❄❄

***R.* 'Capitaine John Ingram'.** Vigorous, bushy Moss rose with dark green leaves and clusters of peony-like, pompon-shaped, fully double, fragrant, dark crimson to purple flowers, 8cm (3in) across, with a lilac-pink reverse to the petals, borne in summer. ↕ 1.2m (4ft), ↔ 1m (3ft). ❄❄❄

***R.* 'Cardinal de Richelieu'** ■ Gallica rose of vigorous, compact, lax habit, with smooth stems and dense, dark green foliage. Rounded, fully double, fragrant, deep burgundy-purple flowers, 8cm (3in) across, are borne in summer. ↕ 1m (3ft), ↔ 1.2m (4ft). ❄❄❄

***R.* Cardinal Hume ('Harregale')** ■ Vigorous Shrub rose of spreading habit, with dense, dark green leaves. Bears dense clusters of cupped, double, lightly scented, reddish purple flowers, 8cm (3in) across, from summer to autumn. ↕ 80cm (32in), ↔ 1.1m (3½ft). ❄❄❄

Rosa CASINO ('Macca')

Rosa 'Cécile Brunner'

Rosa 'Céleste'

Rosa x *centifolia* 'Muscosa'

Rosa 'Cerise Bouquet'

Rosa CHAMPAGNE COCKTAIL ('Horflash')

Rosa CHERRY BRANDY '85 ('Tanryrandy')

Rosa CHILTERNS ('Kortemma')

Rosa 'Chinatown'

Rosa CIDER CUP ('Dicladida')

Rosa CITY GIRL ('Harzorba')

Rosa CITY OF LONDON ('Harukfore')

***R.* 'Caribia'** see *R.* 'Harry Wheatcroft'.
***R.* 'Carl Philip'** see *R.* THE TIMES ROSE ('Korpeahn').
***R.* 'Caroline Testout'** see *R.* 'Mme Caroline Testout'.
***R.* 'Carpet of Colour'** see *R.* CAMBRIDGESHIRE ('Korhaugen').
***R.* CASINO ('Macca')** ■ syn. *R.* 'Gerbe d'Or'. Climber with sparse, dark green leaves and rounded, fully double, fragrant yellow flowers, 9cm (3½in) across, sometimes opening quartered-rosette, borne from summer to autumn. ↕3m (10ft), ↔ 2.2m (7ft). ❄❄❄
***R.* 'Catherine Mermet'.** Vigorous, shrubby Tea rose with glossy, mid-green leaves and high-centred, fully double, scented, beige-pink flowers, 10cm (4in) across, with a mauve tinge, borne from summer to autumn. ↕1.2m (4ft), ↔ 1.1m (3½ft). ❄❄
***R.* 'Cécile Brunner'** ■ syn. *R.* 'Mignon', *R.* 'Sweetheart Rose'. China rose of upright growth, with sparse, dark green leaves. Perfectly formed, urn-shaped, fully double, light pink flowers, 4cm (1½in) across, are borne from summer to autumn. ↕75cm (30in), ↔ 60cm (24in). ❄❄❄
***R.* 'Céleste'** ■ syn. *R.* 'Celestial'. Vigorous, spreading Alba rose with greyish green foliage. Clusters of cupped, double, fragrant, light pink flowers, 8cm (3in) across, are produced in midsummer. ↕1.5m (5ft), ↔ 1.2m (4ft). ❄❄❄
***R.* 'Celestial'** see *R.* 'Céleste'.
R.* x *centifolia*.** Vigorous Centifolia rose of branching habit, with arching, dull, mid-green leaves comprising 5–7 broadly ovate leaflets, to 5cm (2in) long. In summer, bears cupped, fully double, very fragrant, deep rose-pink, sometimes red or white flowers, 9cm (3½in) across. ↕1.5m (5ft), ↔ 1.2m (4ft). Garden origin. ❄❄❄. **'Cristata'**, syn. *R.* 'Chapeau de Napoleon', *R.* 'Cristata' (Crested moss rose) has a lax, branching habit, and double, rose-pink flowers on bowing stems. It has no true moss, but mossy tufts on the calyces. Best grown on a support. **'Muscosa'** ■ (Common moss rose) is a vigorous, branching Moss rose, with dull, dark green leaves and dense moss on the stems and calyces. Rounded to cupped pink flowers are 8cm (3in) across. **var. *pomponia see *R.* 'De Meaux'.
***R.* 'Cerise Bouquet'** ■ Very vigorous Shrub rose of arching habit, producing small, greyish green leaves. In summer, bears a spectacular display of flat, semi-double, cherry-red flowers, 6cm (2½in) across. ↕↔ to 3.5m (11ft). ❄❄❄
***R.* 'C.F. Meyer'** see *R.* 'Conrad Ferdinand Meyer'.

Rosa 'Charles de Mills'

***R.* CHAMPAGNE COCKTAIL ('Horflash')** ■ Floribunda rose with dark green leaves. From summer to autumn, bears open clusters of cupped, double, scented, light yellow flowers, 9cm (3½in) across, with pink markings. ↕1m (3ft), ↔ 70cm (28in). ❄❄❄
***R.* 'Champneys' Pink Cluster'.** Vigorous Noisette climbing rose with arching, smooth stems and glossy, light green leaves. From summer to autumn, bears large clusters of cupped, double, fragrant pink flowers, 5cm (2in) across. ↕2.5–4m (8–12ft), ↔ 2.5m (8ft). ❄❄
***R.* 'Chapeau de Napoleon'** see *R.* x *centifolia* 'Cristata'.
***R.* 'Charles de Mills'** ■ syn. *R.* 'Bizarre Triomphant'. Upright, arching Gallica rose with smooth stems and mid-green foliage. In summer, pink buds open to quartered-rosette, fully double, fragrant, mulberry-coloured flowers, 10cm (4in) across. ↕↔ 1.2m (4ft) or more. ❄❄❄
***R.* CHATSWORTH ('Tanotari', 'Tanotax')**, syn. *R.* 'Footloose', *R.* 'Mirato'. Spreading Ground-cover rose with glossy, dark green leaves. Bears flat, semi-double, scented pink flowers, 7cm (3in) across, from summer to autumn. ↕75cm (30in), ↔ 1m (3ft). ❄❄❄
***R.* CHERRY BRANDY '85 ('Tanryrandy')** ■ Fast-growing Hybrid Tea rose of uneven habit, with dense, glossy, bright green leaves. High-centred to cupped, double orange flowers, 9cm (3½in) across, suffused salmon-pink, are borne singly and in open clusters from summer to autumn. ↕75cm (30in), ↔ 60cm (24in). ❄❄❄
***R.* CHILTERNS ('Kortemma')** ■ syn. *R.* 'Fiery Sunsation', *R.* 'Mainaufeuer', *R.* 'Red Ribbons'. Vigorous, spreading Ground-cover rose with glossy, bright green foliage. Cupped to flat, semi-double, lightly scented, deep crimson flowers, 6cm (2½in) across, are borne from summer to autumn. ↕75cm (30in), ↔ 2.2m (7ft). ❄❄❄
***R.* 'Chinatown'** ■ syn. *R.* 'Ville de Chine'. Vigorous Floribunda rose with strong, uneven growth and abundant glossy, dark green leaves. From summer to autumn, produces rounded, double, scented yellow flowers, 10cm (4in) across, flushed pink. ↕1.2m (4ft), ↔ 1m (3ft). ❄❄❄
R. chinensis* var. *minima see *R.* 'Rouletii'.
***R. chinensis* 'Mutabilis'** see *R.* x *odorata* 'Mutabilis'.
***R. chinensis* 'Semperflorens'** see *R.* x *odorata* 'Semperflorens'.
***R. chinensis* 'Viridiflora'** see *R.* x *odorata* 'Viridiflora'.
***R.* 'Christian IV'** see *R.* THE TIMES ROSE ('Korpeahn').
***R.* 'Chrysler Imperial'.** Upright Hybrid Tea rose producing dark green leaves. From summer to autumn, bears high-centred, fully double, very fragrant, deep red flowers, 12cm (5in) across. Prefers a sheltered site. ↕1m (3ft), ↔ 60cm (24in). ❄❄❄
***R.* CIDER CUP ('Dicladida')** ■ Dwarf Floribunda rose of compact habit, with dense, glossy, mid-green foliage. From summer to autumn, bears well-spaced clusters of high-centred, double, deep apricot-pink flowers, 4cm (1½in) across. ↕45cm (18in), ↔ 30cm (12in). ❄❄❄
***R.* CITY GIRL ('Harzorba')** ■ Free-branching Climber with glossy, dark green leaves. From summer to autumn, bears clusters of cupped, semi-double, scented, salmon-pink flowers, 11cm (4½in) across. ↕↔ 2.2m (7ft). ❄❄❄
***R.* CITY OF BELFAST ('Macci').** Floribunda rose of compact habit, with glossy, dark green foliage and cupped, double scarlet flowers, 6cm (2½in) across, borne from summer to autumn. ↕↔ 60cm (24in). ❄❄❄
***R.* 'City of Leeds'.** Vigorous Floribunda rose producing dark green foliage. Freely bears cupped to flat, semi-double, salmon-pink flowers, 9cm (3½in) across, from summer to autumn. ↕75cm (30in), ↔ 60cm (24in). ❄❄❄
***R.* CITY OF LONDON ('Harukfore')** ■ Floribunda rose or climbing rose of spreading, uneven habit, with glossy mid-green leaves. Bears loosely formed, rounded to flat, semi-double to double, fragrant, light pink flowers, 8cm (3in) across, from summer to autumn. ↕80cm (32in), ↔ 75cm (30in). ❄❄❄
***R.* 'City of Portland'** see *R.* 'Mme Caroline Testout'.
***R.* CLAIRE ROSE ('Auslight').** Upright Shrub rose with large, light green leaves. Cupped to flat, double, lightly scented, blush-pink flowers, 11cm (4½in) across, appear from summer to autumn. ↕1.2m (4ft), ↔ 90cm (36in). ❄❄❄
***R.* CLAIR MATIN ('Meimont').** Upright Shrub rose or Climber with glossy, dark

R

Rosa 'Climbing Mrs. Sam McGredy'

Rosa 'Compassion'

Rosa 'Complicata'

Rosa CONGRATULATIONS ('Korlift')

Rosa 'Conrad Ferdinand Meyer'

Rosa CONSTANCE SPRY ('Austance')

Rosa CORDON BLEU ('Harubasil')

Rosa 'Cornelia'

Rosa 'Crimson Glory'

Rosa 'Crimson Shower'

Rosa x *damascena* var. *semperflorens*

Rosa 'Danse du Feu'

green foliage. Bears cupped to flat, semi-double, fragrant, light pink flowers, 7cm (3in) across, from summer to autumn. ↕2.2m (7ft), ↔ 1.2m (4ft). ***

***R.* CLARISSA ('Harprocrustes').** Floribunda rose producing many small, glossy, dark green leaves. Abundant urn-shaped, fully double apricot flowers, 5cm (2in) across, are borne on long stems from summer to autumn. ↕80cm (32in), ↔ 45cm (18in). ***

***R.* 'Climbing Cécile Brunner'.** Vigorous Climber with strong growth and sparse, dark green leaves composed of lance-shaped leaflets. From summer to autumn, bears exquisitely formed, urn-shaped, double, light pink flowers, 4cm (1½in) across. ↕↔ 4m (12ft). ***

***R.* 'Climbing Crimson Glory'.** Climber of branching habit, with fairly sparse, mildew-prone, dark green leaves and prickly stems. Cupped, fully double, intensely fragrant, dark crimson flowers, 11cm (4½in) across, are borne on bowing stems from summer to autumn. ↕ to 5m (15ft), ↔ 2.5m (8ft). ***

***R.* 'Climbing Ena Harkness'.** Climber of branching habit, with mid-green foliage and high-centred, fully double, fragrant, bright crimson flowers, 12cm (5in) across, from summer to autumn. ↕5m (15ft), ↔ 2.5m (8ft). ***

***R.* 'Climbing Etoile de Hollande'.** Climber with rampant, open growth, dark green foliage, and cupped, double, very fragrant, dark crimson flowers, 11cm (4½in) across, borne mainly in summer. ↕ to 6m (20ft), ↔ 5m (15ft). ***

***R.* 'Climbing Iceberg'** ■ Climber with strong, well-branched growth and dense, light green foliage. Showy clusters of cupped, double white flowers, 8cm (3in) across, are borne freely from summer to autumn. ↕↔ 3m (10ft). ***

***R.* 'Climbing Lady Hillingdon'.** Climbing Tea rose with stiff, vigorous growth, purplish green wood, and glossy, dark green foliage. From summer to autumn, high-centred to cupped, semi-double to double, fragrant, light apricot-yellow flowers, 9cm (3½in) across, are borne on nodding stems. ↕ to 5m (15ft), ↔ 2.5m (8ft). ***

***R.* 'Climbing Little White Pet'** see *R.* 'Félicité Perpétue'.

***R.* 'Climbing Mrs. Sam McGredy'** ■ Vigorous Climber with a stiff, branching habit and sparse, dark green foliage. Urn-shaped, fully double, copper-red to salmon-pink flowers, 11cm (4½in) across, are borne mainly in summer. ↕↔ 3m (10ft). ***

***R.* 'Climbing Orange Meillandina'** see *R.* CLIMBING ORANGE SUNBLAZE ('Meijikatarsar').

***R.* CLIMBING ORANGE SUNBLAZE ('Meijikatarsar')**, syn. *R.* 'Climbing Orange Meillandina'. Climbing Miniature rose with upright, branching growth and many dark green leaves. Cupped, fully double, bright orange-red flowers, 4cm (1½in) across, are borne from summer to autumn. ↕1.5m (5ft), ↔ 1.2m (4ft). ***

***R.* 'Climbing Paul Lédé'.** Vigorous, free-branching Climber with dark green leaves. In summer and autumn, bears pointed, high-centred to cupped, double, scented, buff-yellow flowers, 9cm (3½in) across, tinged carmine-red. ↕5m (15ft), ↔ 2.5m (8ft). ***

***R.* 'Climbing Pompon de Paris'.** Vigorous, miniature China climbing rose with spreading, arching growth and abundant matt, mid-green foliage. Many-flowered clusters of cupped, fully double, rose-red flowers, 2.5cm (1in) across, are borne in early summer. ↕ to 4m (12ft), ↔ 2.5m (8ft). ***

***R.* 'Climbing Shot Silk'.** Branching Climber with glossy, deep green foliage. Urn-shaped to cupped, double, sweet-scented flowers, 10cm (4in) across, salmon-pink suffused yellow, are borne mainly in summer. ↕3m (10ft), ↔ 2.5m (8ft). ***

Rosa 'Climbing Iceberg'

***R.* 'Cocorico'** see *R.* BIRTHDAY GIRL ('Meilasso').

***R.* 'Colorbreak'** see *R.* BROWN VELVET ('Maccultra').

***R.* 'Commandant Beaurepaire'**, syn. *R.* 'Panachée d'Angers'. Vigorous, bushy, spreading Bourbon rose with wavy, pale green leaves. From summer to autumn, bears cupped, double, fragrant pink flowers, 10cm (4in) across, with purple and white stripes. ↕↔ 1.2m (4ft). ***

***R.* 'Compassion'** ■ syn. *R.* 'Belle de Londres'. Climber with upright, free-branching growth and dark green leaves. Bears rounded, fully double, fragrant flowers, 10cm (4in) across, salmon-pink suffused apricot, from summer to autumn. ↕3m (10ft), ↔ 2.5m (8ft). ***

***R.* 'Complicata'** ■ Very vigorous Gallica rose with strong, arching, open growth and greyish green leaves. In summer, bears clusters of cupped to flat, single pink flowers, 11cm (4½in) across, with paler centres and folded petals. ↕2.2m (7ft), ↔ 2.5m (8ft). ***

***R.* 'Comte de Chambord'** see *R.* 'Mme Knorr'.

***R.* 'Comtesse de Labarthe'** see *R.* 'Duchesse de Brabant'.

***R.* 'Comtesse Ouwaroff'** see *R.* 'Duchesse de Brabant'.

***R.* CONGRATULATIONS ('Korlift')** ■ syn. *R.* 'Sylvia'. Tall, vigorous Hybrid Tea rose with dark green leaves. Neatly formed, urn-shaped, fully double, rose-pink flowers, 11cm (4½in) across, are borne on long stems from summer to autumn. ↕1.5m (5ft), ↔ 1m (3ft). ***

***R.* 'Conrad Ferdinand Meyer'** ■ syn. *R.* 'C.F. Meyer'. Strong, vigorous Shrub rose with prickly, arching stems and coarse, greyish green leaves. Bears cupped, fully double, fragrant, silvery pink flowers, 10cm (4in) across, mainly in summer, a few in autumn. Prone to rust. ↕2.5m (8ft), ↔ 2m (6ft). ***

***R.* CONSERVATION ('Cocdimple')** ■ Vigorous, dwarf Floribunda rose with glossy, mid-green leaves. From summer to autumn, freely bears dense clusters of cupped, semi-double, apricot-pink flowers, 6cm (2½in) across. ↕↔ 45cm (18in). ***

***R.* CONSTANCE SPRY ('Austance')** ■ Shrub rose of arching habit, which will climb if supported, with dense, greyish green leaves. Rounded, fully double, myrrh-scented pink flowers, 12cm (5in) across, are borne on nodding stems in summer. ↕2m (6ft), ↔ 1.5m (5ft) as a shrub; ↕↔ 3m (10ft) as a climber. ***

R.* x *cooperi see *R.* 'Cooperi'.

***R.* 'Cooperi'**, syn. *R.* x *cooperi*, *R.* 'Cooper's Burmese Rose', *R. gigantea* 'Cooperi'. Arching Climber with large, dark green leaves. Bears cupped, single, scented, creamy white flowers, 10cm (4in) across, in summer; a few are borne later in autumn. ↕6m (20ft), ↔ 5m (15ft). **

***R.* 'Cooper's Burmese Rose'** see *R.* 'Cooperi'.

***R.* CORDON BLEU ('Harubasil')** ■ Hybrid Tea rose with dark green foliage and cupped, double, scented, reddish apricot flowers, 10cm (4in) across, borne from summer to autumn. ↕1m (3ft), ↔ 60cm (24in). ***

***R.* 'Cornelia'** ■ Vigorous Hybrid Musk rose of arching, spreading habit, producing dense, dark green leaves with lance-shaped leaflets. From summer to autumn, bears large clusters of many rosette-shaped, double, pink-tinged flowers, 5cm (2in) across, copper at the centres. ↕↔ 1.5m (5ft). ***

***R.* 'Country Lass'** see *R.* OXFORDSHIRE ('Korfullwind').

***R.* CRIMSON CASCADE ('Fryclimbdown').** Stiffly branching Climber with glossy, deep green foliage. Cupped, double, lightly scented, bright crimson flowers, 9cm (3½in) across, are borne from summer to autumn. ↕2.5m (8ft), ↔ 1.8m (6ft). ***

***R.* 'Crimson Glory'** ■ Hybrid Tea rose of branching habit, with sparse, mildew-prone, dark green leaves and prickly stems. Cupped, fully double, intensely fragrant, dark crimson flowers, 11cm (4½in) across, are borne on bowing stems from summer to autumn. ↕↔ 60cm (24in). ***

***R.* 'Crimson Shower'** ■ Rambler with lax stems and many glossy, bright green leaves. Dense clusters of rosette-shaped, double crimson flowers, 3cm (1¼in) across, are produced from late summer to autumn. ↕ to 2.5m (8ft), ↔ 2.2m (7ft). ***

***R.* 'Cristata'** see *R.* x *centifolia* 'Cristata'.

***R.* 'Cuisse de Nymphe'** see *R.* 'Great Maiden's Blush'.

Rosa 'De la Maître Ecole'

Rosa DELLA BALFOUR ('Harblend')

Rosa 'Desprez à Fleur Jaune'

Rosa 'Doris Tysterman'

Rosa 'Dortmund'

Rosa DOUBLE DELIGHT ('Andeli')

Rosa DUBLIN BAY ('Macdub')

Rosa 'Duc de Guiche'

Rosa 'Duchesse de Brabant'

Rosa 'Dupontii'

Rosa 'Dutch Gold'

Rosa ecae

***R.* 'Dainty Bess'.** Branching Hybrid Tea rose with leathery, dark green leaves. Bears flat, single, scented, pale pink flowers, 9cm (3½in) across, with maroon stamens, from summer to autumn. ↕1m (3ft), ↔ 60cm (24in). ✻✻✻
R.* x *damascena*,** syn. *R.* 'Kazanlik', *R.* 'Trigintipetala' (Damask rose, Summer damask rose). Vigorous Damask rose with arching, prickly stems and dull, greyish green leaves, each composed of 5, rarely 7, ovate to elliptic leaflets, to 6cm (2½in) long. In summer, bears clusters of 3–11 cupped to flat, semi-double, fragrant, pale pink to white flowers, 8cm (3in) across. ↕2m (6ft), ↔ 1.5m (5ft). Middle East. ✻✻✻. **var. *bifera see var. *semperflorens*. **var. *semperflorens*** ▣ syn. var. *bifera*, *R.* 'Quatre Saisons' (Autumn damask rose, Four seasons rose, Rose of Castille) has an open, arching habit and light green leaves. Bears loosely formed, rose-pink flowers, 9cm (3½in) across, in lax clusters, in summer and sporadically in autumn. Best in a sunny position; ↕1.5m (5ft), ↔ 1.2m (4ft). **'Versicolor'** (York and Lancaster rose) has a twiggy, untidy habit, and bears loosely cupped, double, pink-tinged white flowers, 6cm (2½in) across; ↕1.5m (5ft), ↔ 1.2m (4ft).
***R.* 'Danse du Feu'** ▣ syn. *R.* 'Spectacular'. Stiffly branched Climber with abundant glossy, mid-green leaves. Bears rounded, double scarlet flowers, 8cm (3in) across, from summer to autumn. ↕↔ 2.5m (8ft). ✻✻✻

Rosa CONSERVATION ('Cocdimple')

***R.* DARLING FLAME ('Meilucca'),** syn. *R.* 'Minuetto'. Bushy, well-branched Miniature rose producing glossy, dark green leaves. Bears urn-shaped, double, orange-red flowers, 4cm (1½in) across, freely from summer to autumn. ↕40cm (16in), ↔ 30cm (12in). ✻✻✻
***R.* DAWN CHORUS ('Dicquasar').** Bushy, upright Hybrid Tea rose with dark green foliage. Bears high-centred, double, scented, reddish orange flowers, 9cm (3½in) across, from summer to autumn. ↕75cm (30in), ↔ 60cm (24in). ✻✻✻
***R.* 'Dearest'.** Floribunda rose of compact, spreading habit, with dark green leaves. Large clusters of camellia-like, rounded, double, fragrant, light rose-pink flowers, 8cm (3in) across, are borne from summer to autumn. ↕↔ 60cm (24in). ✻✻✻
***R.* 'Deep Secret',** syn. *R.* 'Mildred Scheel'. Vigorous Hybrid Tea rose with glossy, dark green foliage. Rounded, fully double, scented, deep crimson flowers, 10cm (4in) across, are borne from summer to autumn. ↕1m (3ft), ↔ 75cm (30in). ✻✻✻
***R.* 'De la Maître Ecole'** ▣ Gallica rose of bushy, spreading habit, with mid-green foliage. Quartered-rosette, fully double, fragrant, carmine-red to light pink flowers, 10cm (4in) across, are borne on bowed stems in summer. ↕1m (3ft), ↔ 1.1m (3½ft). ✻✻✻
***R.* DELLA BALFOUR ('Harblend')** ▣ Stiffly branching Climber with leathery, dark green leaves. Bears high-centred, double, scented, orange-pink flowers, 10cm (4in) across, from summer to autumn. ↕2.2m (7ft), ↔ 2m (6ft). ✻✻✻
***R.* 'De Meaux',** syn. *R.* x *centifolia* var. *pomponia*, *R.* 'Rose de Meaux' (Pompon rose). Dwarf Centifolia rose of upright habit, with bright green leaves. Clusters of pompon, fully double, scented, rose-pink flowers, 4cm (1½in) across, are borne in summer. ↕1m (3ft), ↔ 75cm (30in). ✻✻✻
***R.* 'Desprez à Fleur Jaune'** ▣ syn. *R.* 'Jaune Desprez'. Vigorous Noisette climbing rose with arching growth and light green leaves. Flat, fully double, scented, pale creamy apricot flowers, 8cm (3in) across, are borne mainly in summer. ↕↔ 5m (15ft). ✻✻
***R.* 'Dianthiflora'** see *R.* 'Fimbriata'.
***R.* 'Dicky'** see *R.* ANISLEY DICKSON ('Dickimono').

***R.* 'Doris Tysterman'** ▣ Tall Hybrid Tea rose producing glossy, dark green foliage. High-centred, double, orange-red flowers, 10cm (4in) across, are borne from summer to autumn. ↕1.2m (4ft), ↔ 75cm (30in). ✻✻✻
***R.* 'Dorothy Perkins'.** Lax Rambler with glossy, dark green leaves. Bears dense clusters of rosette-shaped, double, rose-pink flowers, 2cm (¾in) across, in late summer. ↕↔ to 3m (10ft). ✻✻✻
***R.* 'Dortmund'** ▣ Upright Climber with dense, glossy, dark green leaves. Showy clusters of flat, single red flowers, 10cm (4in) across, each with a white eye, are borne freely from summer to autumn. ↕3m (10ft), ↔ 2m (6ft). ✻✻✻
***R.* DOUBLE DELIGHT ('Andeli')** ▣ Hybrid Tea rose of uneven, branching habit, with dull, mid-green foliage. From summer to autumn, bears rounded, fully double, sweet-scented flowers, 12cm (5in) across, pale pink, margined and flushed carmine-red. ↕1m (3ft), ↔ 60cm (24in). ✻✻✻
***R.* 'Dreaming Spires'.** Free-branching Climber with dark green leaves. Bears cupped, double, fragrant, bronze-yellow flowers, 8cm (3in) across, from summer to autumn. ↕3m (10ft), ↔ 2.2m (7ft). ✻✻✻
***R.* 'Dresden China'** see *R.* 'Sophie's Perpetual'.
***R.* DRUMMER BOY ('Harvacity').** Spreading, dwarf Floribunda rose producing mid-green foliage. Dense sprays of cupped, double, bright crimson flowers, 5cm (2in) across, are borne freely from summer to autumn. ↕↔ 50cm (20in). ✻✻✻
***R.* DUBLIN BAY ('Macdub')** ▣ Free-branching Climber, which may be pruned to form a shrub. Bears glossy, dark green leaves and clusters of cupped, double, bright crimson flowers, 10cm (4in) across, from summer to autumn. ↕↔ 2.2m (7ft). ✻✻✻
***R.* 'Duc de Guiche'** ▣ Gallica rose of spreading habit, with dark green leaves. Flat quartered-rosette, fully double, crimson-purple flowers, 10cm (4in) across, are produced in summer. ↕↔ 1.2m (4ft). ✻✻✻
***R.* 'Duchesse de Brabant'** ▣ syn. *R.* 'Comtesse de Labarthe', *R.* 'Comtesse Ouwaroff'. Tea rose of spreading, shrubby habit, with mid- to dark green leaves. Bears cupped, silky-petalled, double, scented, rose-pink flowers, 11cm (4½in) across, from summer to autumn. ↕1.2m (4ft) or more, ↔ 1m (3ft). ✻✻
***R.* 'Duchesse de Montebello'.** Lax, shrubby Gallica rose with greyish green leaves. Cupped, double, fragrant, rose-pink flowers, 6cm (2½in) across, are borne in summer. ↕1.5m (5ft), ↔ 1m (3ft). ✻✻✻
***R.* 'Duchesse d'Istrie'** see *R.* 'William Lobb'.
***R.* 'Duchess of Portland'** see *R.* 'Portlandica'.
***R.* 'Duchess of York'** see *R.* SUNSEEKER ('Dicracer').
***R.* 'Duftzauber '84'** see *R.* ROYAL WILLIAM ('Korzaun').
***R.* 'Dunwich Rose'** see *R.* *pimpinellifolia* 'Dunwich Rose'.
***R.* 'Dupontii'** ▣ syn. *R. moschata* var. *nivea* (Snowbush rose). Shrub rose of upright, shrubby habit, with grey-green foliage. Cupped to flat, single, fragrant, creamy white flowers, 6cm (2½in) across, showing yellow anthers, are borne freely in midsummer. ↕↔ 2.2m (7ft). ✻✻✻
***R.* 'Dutch Gold'** ▣ Vigorous Hybrid Tea rose producing large, dark green leaves. Rounded, fully double, scented yellow flowers, 15cm (6in) across, are borne from summer to autumn. ↕1.1m (3½ft), ↔ 75cm (30in). ✻✻✻
***R.* 'Easlea's Golden Rambler'.** Rambler with leathery, dark green leaves and loose, rounded, fully double, scented flowers, 10cm (4in) across, bright yellow flecked with red, borne in summer. ↕to 6m (20ft), ↔ 5m (15ft). ✻✻✻
***R.* 'Easter Morn'** see *R.* 'Easter Morning'.
***R.* 'Easter Morning',** syn. *R.* 'Easter Morn'. Compact, upright Miniature rose with glossy, dark green foliage. Urn-shaped, double, lightly scented, ivory flowers, 2.5cm (1in) across, are borne from summer to autumn. ↕40cm (16in), ↔ 25cm (10in). ✻✻✻
***R.* EASY GOING ('Harflow').** Bushy, upright Floribunda rose with glossy, dark green foliage. Cupped, double, scented, bronze-yellow flowers, 9cm (3½in) across, are produced from summer to autumn. ↕75cm (30in), ↔ 60cm (24in). ✻✻✻
R. ecae ▣ Erect, wiry, suckering Species rose with red stems and small, fern-like,

R

Rosa 'Eden Rose'

Rosa Eglantyne ('Ausmak')

Rosa Elina ('Dicjana')

Rosa 'Elizabeth Harkness'

Rosa 'Emily Gray'

Rosa 'Empereur du Maroc'

Rosa 'Ena Harkness'

Rosa English Garden ('Ausbuff')

Rosa 'English Miss'

Rosa 'Ernest H. Morse'

Rosa Escapade ('Harpade')

Rosa Eye Paint ('Maceye')

mid-green leaves, each composed of 5–9 broadly elliptic to obovate leaflets, 4–8mm (⅛–⅜in) long. Cupped, single, musk-scented, bright yellow flowers, 2cm (¾in) across, are produced along the stems in late spring. Prone to die-back. ↕1.5m (5ft), ↔1.2m (4ft). Turkmenistan, Uzbekistan, Tajikistan, N.E. Afghanistan, N.W. Pakistan. ✻✻

***R.* 'Eden Rose'** ■ Upright Hybrid Tea rose of vigorous growth with large, olive-green leaves. Bears high-centred, fully double, scented, deep pink flowers, 10cm (4in) across, lighter pink on petal reverse, from summer to autumn. ↕1.1m (3½ft), ↔ 75cm (30in). ✻✻✻

***R.* Eden Rose '88 ('Meiviolin')**, syn. *R.* 'Pierre de Ronsard'. Stiffly branching Climber with large, dark green leaves. Bears rounded, fully double, lightly scented, creamy white to lavender-pink flowers, 11cm (4½in) across, from summer to autumn. ↕2.5m (8ft), ↔ 1.8m (6ft). ✻✻✻

R. eglanteria see *R. rubiginosa.*

***R.* Eglantyne ('Ausmak')** ■ syn. *R.* 'Eglantyne Jebb'. Bushy, upright Shrub rose with mid-green leaves. Quartered-rosette, double, scented, light pink flowers, 10cm (4in) across, are produced from summer to autumn. ↕1.1m (3½ft), ↔ 90cm (36in). ✻✻✻

***R.* 'Eglantyne Jebb'** see *R.* Eglantyne ('Ausmak').

***R.* 'E.H. Morse'** see *R.* 'Ernest H. Morse'.

***R. elegantula* 'Persetosa'**, syn. *R. elegantula* f. *persetosa*, *R. farreri* f. *persetosa.* Upright Species rose with wiry stems, red-bristled when young, and pale grey-green leaves, each composed of 7–11 narrowly ovate to elliptic, fern-like leaflets, 1.5cm (½in) long, reddening in autumn. Shallowly cupped, single, light pink flowers, 2cm (¾in) across, are produced in summer; they are followed by ovoid, orange-red hips. ↕↔ 2m (6ft). N.W. China. ✻✻✻

R. elegantula* f. *persetosa see *R. elegantula* 'Persetosa'.

***R.* Elina ('Dicjana')** ■ syn. *R.* 'Peaudouce'. Vigorous Hybrid Tea rose with abundant dark green foliage. Rounded, fully double, scented, ivory-white flowers, 15cm (6in) across, with lemon-yellow centres, are borne freely from summer to autumn. ↕1.1m (3½ft), ↔ 75cm (30in). ✻✻✻

***R.* 'Elizabeth Harkness'** ■ Hybrid Tea rose of compact habit, with dark green leaves. High-centred to rounded, fully double, fragrant, creamy pink flowers, 12cm (5in) across, are produced from summer to autumn. ↕80cm (32in), ↔ 60cm (24in). ✻✻✻

***R.* Elizabeth of Glamis ('Macel')**, syn. *R.* 'Irish Beauty'. Floribunda rose producing mid-green foliage. From summer to autumn, bears well-spaced sprays of cupped, double, scented, light orange-pink flowers, 9cm (3½in) across. ↕75cm (30in), ↔ 60cm (24in). ✻✻✻

***R.* 'Emera Blanc'** see *R.* White Flower Carpet ('Noaschnee').

***R.* 'Emily Gray'** ■ Semi-evergreen Rambler with lax stems covered in lustrous, dark green leaves. In summer, bears small clusters of loosely formed, rounded, double, scented, butter-yellow flowers, 5cm (2in) across. ↕to 5m (15ft), ↔ 3m (10ft). ✻✻✻

***R.* 'Empereur du Maroc'** ■ Hybrid Perpetual rose of compact, shrubby habit, with mid-green leaves. Quartered-rosette, fully double, fragrant, maroon-crimson flowers, 8cm (3in) across, are borne freely on bowed stems in summer, sparsely in autumn. ↕1.2m (4ft), ↔ 1m (3ft). ✻✻✻

***R.* 'Empress Josephine'** see *R.* x *francofurtana.*

***R.* 'Ena Harkness'** ■ Hybrid Tea rose of branching habit, with mid-green leaves. High-centred, double, fragrant, bright crimson flowers, 10cm (4in) across, are borne from summer to autumn. ↕75cm (30in), ↔ 60cm (24in). ✻✻✻

***R.* English Garden ('Ausbuff')** ■ Upright Shrub rose with light green leaves and rosette-shaped, double, lightly scented flowers, 10cm (4in) across, buff-yellow, paling towards the edges, are produced from summer to autumn. ↕1m (3ft), ↔ 75cm (30in). ✻✻✻

***R.* 'English Miss'** ■ Floribunda rose of compact, spreading habit, with leathery, dark green leaves. Bears wide clusters of camellia-like, cupped, fully double, fragrant, pale pink flowers, 8cm (3in) across, from summer to autumn. ↕75cm (30in), ↔ 60cm (24in). ✻✻✻

***R.* 'Ernest H. Morse'** ■ syn. *R.* 'E.H. Morse'. Hybrid Tea rose with semi-glossy, dark green foliage. High-centred, double, very fragrant crimson flowers, 12cm (5in) across, are freely produced from summer to autumn. ↕75cm (30in), ↔ 60cm (24in). ✻✻✻

***R.* Escapade ('Harpade')** ■ Vigorous Floribunda rose of dense habit, with abundant light green foliage. Showy, cupped, semi-double, scented, pink-violet flowers, 8cm (3in) across, each with a white eye, are borne freely from summer to autumn. ↕75cm (30in), ↔ 60cm (24in). ✻✻✻

***R.* 'Esmeralda'** see *R.* Keepsake ('Kormalda').

***R.* Especially for You ('Fryworthy')**. Upright Hybrid Tea rose with dark green foliage. High-centred to cupped, double, scented, bright yellow flowers, 9cm (3½in) across, appear from summer to autumn. ↕1.2m (4ft), ↔ 75cm (30in). ✻✻✻

***R.* Essex ('Poulnoz')**, syn. *R.* 'Pink Cover'. Ground-cover rose of dense habit, with dark green leaves. From summer to autumn, clusters of many small, cupped, single, light reddish pink flowers, 2.5cm (1in) across, with whitish pink centres, are borne freely along the stems. ↕60cm (24in), ↔ 1.2m (4ft). ✻✻✻

***R.* Euphrates ('Harunique')**. Prickly, hummock-forming Shrub rose with light green leaves composed of narrow leaflets. In summer, produces clusters of numerous cupped, single, salmon- to rose-pink flowers, 2cm (¾in) across, with scarlet at the petal bases. ↕60cm (24in), ↔ 75cm (30in). ✻✻✻

***R.* Evelyn ('Aussaucer')**. Upright Shrub rose with mid-green leaves. Bears quartered-rosette, double, fragrant, light apricot flowers, 9cm (3½in) across, from summer to autumn. ↕1.1m (3½ft), ↔ 90cm (36in). ✻✻✻

***R.* Evelyn Fison ('Macev')**, syn. *R.* 'Irish Wonder'. Floribunda rose with sparse, glossy, dark green foliage. Many neatly formed, rounded, double, bright deep red flowers, 6cm (2½in) across, are borne from summer to autumn. ↕70cm (28in), ↔ 60cm (24in). ✻✻✻

***R.* 'Excelsa'**, syn. *R.* 'Red Dorothy Perkins'. Lax Rambler with abundant glossy, mid-green leaves. In summer, bears dense clusters of rosette-shaped, fully double crimson flowers, 2cm (¾in) across. Prone to mildew. ↕4m (12ft), ↔ 3m (10ft). ✻✻✻

***R.* Eye Paint ('Maceye')** ■ syn. *R.* 'Tapis Persan'. Vigorous Floribunda or Shrub rose with dense, dark green foliage. Large clusters of cupped to flat, single scarlet flowers, 5cm (2in) across, with white eyes, are borne from summer to autumn. ↕1.1m (3½ft), ↔ 75cm (30in). ✻✻✻

***R.* Fairyland ('Harlayalong')**. Polyantha rose of vigorous, arching, spreading habit, with small, dark green leaves. Large sprays of many rosette-shaped, double, scented, pale pink flowers, 4cm (1½in) across, are borne from summer to autumn. ↕75cm (30in), ↔ 1.2m (4ft). ✻✻✻

***R.* 'Fairy Lights'** see *R.* Avon ('Poulmulti').

***R.* 'Fanny Bias'** see *R.* 'Gloire de France'.

***R.* 'Fantin-Latour'** ■ Vigorous Centifolia rose of open habit, producing broad, dark green leaves. Cupped to flat, fully double, fragrant, light pink flowers, 10cm (4in) across, each with a green button eye, are borne in summer. ↕1.5m (5ft), ↔ 1.2m (4ft). ✻✻✻

R. farreri* f. *persetosa see *R. elegantula* 'Persetosa'.

***R.* Fascination ('Poulmax')**, syn. *R.* 'Fredensborg'. Bushy Floribunda rose with glossy, dark green leaves. Bears cupped, double, lightly scented, shrimp-pink flowers, 6cm (2½in) across, from summer to autumn. ↕75cm (30in), ↔ 60cm (24in). ✻✻✻

R. fedtschenkoana. Very vigorous, suckering Species rose with arching, bristly stems and pale grey-green leaves, with 5–9 elliptic to obovate leaflets, 2.5cm (1in) long. Flat, single white flowers, 4.5cm (1¾in) across, with yellow stamens, are borne in clusters of up to 4 blooms, mainly in summer; they are followed by pear-shaped, orange-red hips. ↕↔ 2.2m (7ft). C. Asia. ✻✻✻

***R.* 'Fée des Neiges'** see *R.* Iceberg ('Korbin').

***R.* 'Felicia'** ■ Vigorous Hybrid Musk rose with abundant dark green leaves. Large clusters of cupped, double, scented, light pink flowers, 8cm (3in) across, flushed yellow-apricot, are borne from summer to autumn. ↕1.5m (5ft), ↔ 2.2m (7ft). ✻✻✻

***R.* 'Félicité et Perpétue'** see *R.* 'Félicité Perpétue'.

R

Rosa 'Fantin-Latour'

Rosa 'Felicia'

Rosa 'Félicité Parmentier'

Rosa 'Félicité Perpétue'

Rosa FELLOWSHIP ('Harwelcome')

Rosa 'Ferdinand Pichard'

Rosa 'Fire Princess'

Rosa foetida

Rosa foetida 'Persiana'

Rosa FRAGRANT CLOUD ('Tanellis')

Rosa 'Francis E. Lester'

Rosa 'François Juranville'

***R.* 'Félicité Parmentier'** ■ Vigorous Alba rose of upright, compact habit, producing abundant grey-green leaves. In midsummer, bears quartered-rosette, fully double, fragrant, cream to pale pink flowers, 6cm (2½in) across. ↕ 1.3m (4½ft), ↔ 1.2m (4ft). ❄❄❄
***R.* 'Félicité Perpétue'** ■ syn. *R.* 'Climbing Little White Pet', *R.* 'Félicité et Perpétue'. Sempervirens rambler rose with long, slender stems clothed in dense, dark green leaves. Rosette-shaped, fully double, pale pink to white flowers, 4cm (1½in) across, are borne freely in summer. ↕ to 5m (15ft), ↔ to 4m (12ft). ❄❄❄
***R.* FELLOWSHIP ('Harwelcome')** ■ Vigorous Floribunda rose producing even growth and abundant glossy, mid-green foliage. Well-spaced clusters of cupped, double, scented, deep orange flowers, 9cm (3½in) across, are borne freely from summer to autumn. ↕ 75cm (30in), ↔ 60cm (24in). ❄❄❄
***R.* 'Ferdi'** see *R.* FERDY ('Keitoli').
***R.* 'Ferdinand Pichard'** ■ Upright, compact Hybrid Perpetual rose with smooth stems and long, light green leaves. Cupped, double, fragrant, pale pink flowers, 8cm (3in) across, with pink and red stripes, are produced from summer to autumn. ↕ 1.5m (5ft), ↔ 1.2m (4ft). ❄❄❄
***R.* FERDY ('Keitoli')** ■ syn. *R.* 'Ferdi'. Shrub rose with an uneven, spiky habit and fine-cut, mid-green leaves. Dense clusters of cupped to flat, double, bright pink flowers, 2.5cm (1in) across, wreathe the stems from summer to autumn. ↕ 80cm (32in), ↔ 1.2m (4ft). ❄❄❄
***R.* FESTIVAL ('Kordialo').** Compact Floribunda rose with abundant dark green leaves. From summer to autumn, bears dense clusters of rounded, semi-double, crimson-scarlet flowers, 4.5cm (1¾in) across, with a silvery white reverse to the petals. ↕ 60cm (24in), ↔ 50cm (20in). ❄❄❄
***R.* 'Fiery Sunsation'** see *R.* CHILTERNS ('Kortemma').
***R. filipes* 'Kiftsgate'** ■ syn. *R.* 'Kiftsgate'. Rampant Climber producing abundant glossy, light green leaves, each composed of 5–7 narrowly elliptic to narrowly ovate leaflets, 5–8cm (2–3in) long. Large clusters of cupped, single, fragrant, creamy white flowers, 2.5cm (1in) across, are borne in late summer. ↕ to 10m (30ft), ↔ 6m (20ft). ❄❄❄
***R.* 'Fimbriata'**, syn. *R.* 'Dianthiflora', *R.* 'Phoebe's Frilled Pink'. Vigorous Rugosa rose of arching habit with light green leaves. Flat, dianthus-like, double, scented white to blush-pink flowers, 4.5cm (1¾in) across, with small, frilled petals, are borne in summer and autumn. ↕ 1.5m (5ft), ↔ 1.2m (4ft). ❄❄❄
***R.* FIONA ('Meibeluxen').** Shrub rose with a wide, spreading habit and glossy, dark green leaves. Large clusters of cupped to flat, double red flowers, 6cm (2½in) across, are borne from summer to autumn. ↕ 80cm (32in), ↔ 1.2m (4ft). ❄❄❄
***R.* 'Fire Princess'** ■ Upright Miniature rose with glossy, mid-green leaves. Rosette-shaped, fully double scarlet flowers, 4cm (1½in) across, are borne from summer to autumn. ↕ 45cm (18in), ↔ 30cm (12in). ❄❄❄
***R.* 'F.J. Grootendorst'**, syn. *R.* 'Nelkenrose'. Rugosa rose of upright, dense habit, with prickly stems and coarse, leathery, dark green leaves. Crowded clusters of rosette-shaped, double crimson flowers, 4cm (1½in) across, with frilled petals, are borne from summer to autumn. ↕ 1.5m (5ft), ↔ 1.2m (4ft). ❄❄❄
***R.* 'Flower Carpet'** see *R.* PINK FLOWER CARPET ('Noatraum').
***R.* FLOWER POWER ('Frycassia').** Compact Patio rose with mid-green foliage. Cupped, double, lightly scented, peach-salmon flowers, 6cm (2½in) across, appear from summer to autumn. ↕↔ 35cm (14in). ❄❄❄
R. foetida ■ (Austrian briar, Austrian yellow rose). Species rose of upright, open habit, with arching, brownish green stems and pale green leaves, each composed of 5–7 elliptic to obovate leaflets, 2–4cm (¾–1½in) long. Cupped, single, pungent, bright yellow flowers, 5cm (2in) across, are borne in early summer; the flowers are followed by spherical red hips. Susceptible to die-back in hard winters. ↕↔ 1.5m (5ft). W. to C. Asia. ❄❄. **'Bicolor'**, syn. *R.* 'Rose Capucine' (Austrian copper rose), a sport of *R. foetida*, has vivid nasturtium-orange flowers with a yellow reverse to the petals. **'Persiana'** ■ syn. var. *persiana* (Persian yellow rose) has gaunt, arching growth, small, fern-like leaves, and fully double yellow flowers, 6cm (2½in) across; ↔ 1.2m (4ft).
***R.* 'Fontaine'** see *R.* 'Fountain'.
***R.* 'Footloose'** see *R.* CHATSWORTH ('Tanotari', 'Tanotax').
***R.* 'Fountain'**, syn. *R.* 'Fontaine', *R.* 'Red Prince'. Vigorous Shrub rose with strong, upright growth and glossy, dark green leaves. From summer to autumn, bears large clusters of cupped, double, scented, bright crimson flowers, 12cm (5in) across. ↕ 2m (6ft), ↔ 1.2m (4ft). ❄❄❄
***R.* FRAGRANT CLOUD ('Tanellis')** ■ Hybrid Tea rose with branching growth and abundant dark green leaves. Rounded, double, intensely fragrant, dusky scarlet flowers, 11cm (4½in) across, are borne freely from summer to autumn. ↕ 75cm (30in), ↔ 60cm (24in). ❄❄❄

Rosa FERDY ('Keitoli')

***R.* 'Fragrant Delight'.** Floribunda rose of willowy, uneven habit, with abundant reddish green foliage. Freely bears large sprays of urn-shaped, double, scented, salmon-pink flowers, 8cm (3in) across, from summer to autumn. ↕ 1m (3ft), ↔ 75cm (30in). ❄❄❄
***R.* FRAGRANT DREAM ('Dicodour').** Upright, branching Hybrid Tea rose producing dark green foliage. High-centred to rounded, double, fragrant, light apricot flowers, 12cm (5in) across, are borne from summer to autumn. ↕ 80cm (32in), ↔ 75cm (30in). ❄❄❄
***R.* 'Fragrant Surprise'** see *R.* SAMARITAN ('Harverag').
***R.* FRANCINE AUSTIN ('Ausram').** Shrub rose with an arching, open habit and long, light green leaves. Small sprays of many pompon, double, scented white flowers, 4cm (1½in) across, are borne on bowed stems from summer to autumn. ↕ 1m (3ft), ↔ 1.2m (4ft). ❄❄❄
***R.* 'Francis E. Lester'** ■ Vigorous, arching Rambler producing glossy, dark green foliage. Large clusters of cupped, single, fragrant, blush-pink flowers, 5cm (2in) across, are borne freely in summer. ↕ 6m (20ft), ↔ 4m (12ft). ❄❄❄
R.* x *francofurtana, syn. *R.* 'Empress Josephine'. Bushy, wide-spreading Gallica rose with smooth stems and greyish green leaves composed of 5–7 broadly ovate leaflets, to 5cm (2in) long. Loosely formed, rounded, semi-double flowers, 9cm (3½in) across, with wavy-margined, bright pink petals and deeper pink veining, open in summer, followed by inversely cone-shaped red hips. ↕↔ 1.2m (4ft). Garden origin. ❄❄❄
***R.* 'François Juranville'** ■ Rambler with abundant glossy, dark green leaves and clusters of rosette-shaped, fully double, apple-scented, light salmon-pink flowers, 8cm (3in) across, borne in summer. ↕ 6m (20ft), ↔ 5m (15ft). ❄❄❄
***R.* 'Frau Dagmar Hartopp'** see *R.* 'Fru Dagmar Hastrup'.

Rosa 'Frau Karl Druschki'

Rosa FREEDOM ('Dicjem')

Rosa 'Fru Dagmar Hastrup'

Rosa 'Frühlingsmorgen'

Rosa FULTON MACKAY ('Cocdana')

Rosa gallica var. *officinalis*

Rosa gallica var. *officinalis* 'Versicolor'

Rosa GENTLE TOUCH ('Diclulu')

Rosa glauca

Rosa 'Glenfiddich'

Rosa 'Gloire de Dijon'

Rosa 'Golden Chersonese'

***R.* 'Frau Karl Druschki'** ▣ syn. *R.* 'Reine des Neiges', *R.* 'Snow Queen', *R.* 'White American Beauty'. Vigorous Hybrid Perpetual rose with strong, arching stems, mid-green leaves, and high-centred, fully double, milk-white flowers, 11cm (4½in) across, borne from summer to autumn. ↕ to 1.5m (5ft), ↔ 1.2m (4ft). ❄❄❄

***R.* 'Fredensborg'** see *R.* FASCINATION ('Poulmax').

***R.* 'Fred Loads'.** Vigorous Floribunda rose with dark green leaves. Bears many showy, cupped to flat, semi-double, vermilion-orange flowers, 9cm (3½in) across, from summer to autumn. ↕ 2m (6ft), ↔ 1m (3ft). ❄❄❄

***R.* FREEDOM ('Dicjem')** ▣ Hybrid Tea rose of uneven growth, with many shoots and abundant glossy, mid-green foliage. Rounded, double, stiff-petalled, bright yellow flowers, 9cm (3½in) across, are borne freely from summer to autumn. ↕ 75cm (30in), ↔ 60cm (24in). ❄❄❄

***R.* FRIEND FOR LIFE ('Cocnanne').** Compact, bushy Floribunda rose with glossy, dark green leaves. Cupped, semi-double, lightly scented, rose-pink flowers, 8cm (3in) across, appear from summer to autumn. ↕ 75cm (30in), ↔ 60cm (24in). ❄❄❄

***R.* 'Friesia'** see *R.* 'Korresia'.

***R.* 'Fritz Nobis'.** Vigorous, upright Shrub rose with greyish green leaves. In summer, bears cupped, double, scented, light rose-pink flowers, 6cm (2½in) across, tinged with salmon-pink. ↕ 2.2m (7ft), ↔ 1.8m (6ft). ❄❄❄

***R.* 'Fru Dagmar Hastrup'** ▣ syn. *R.* 'Frau Dagmar Hartopp'. Sturdy Rugosa rose of spreading habit, producing leathery, mid-green leaves. Shallowly cupped, single, clove-scented, light pink flowers, 9cm (3½in) across, are borne mainly in summer, followed by tomato-shaped, dark red hips in autumn. ↕ 1m (3ft), ↔ 1.2m (4ft). ❄❄❄

***R.* 'Frühlingsgold'**, syn. *R.* 'Spring Gold'. Vigorous Shrub rose with strong, arching branches, covered in downy red bristles when young, and with toothed, matt, light green leaves. Cupped, semi-double, scented, pale yellow flowers, 10cm (4in) across, with golden stamens, are borne mainly in early summer. ↕ 2.5m (8ft), ↔ 2.2m (7ft). ❄❄❄

***R.* 'Frühlingsmorgen'** ▣ syn. *R.* 'Spring Morning'. Open, free-branching Shrub rose with greyish green leaves. Shallowly cupped, single, hay-scented pink flowers, 12cm (5in) across, with primrose-yellow centres and maroon stamens, are produced in early summer. ↕ 2m (6ft), ↔ 1.5m (5ft). ❄❄❄

***R.* FULTON MACKAY ('Cocdana')** ▣ Hybrid Tea rose with handsome, glossy, mid-green foliage. High-centred, double, scented, golden apricot, pink-flushed flowers, 12cm (5in) across, are borne from summer to autumn. ↕ 75cm (30in), ↔ 60cm (24in). ❄❄❄

***R.* FYVIE CASTLE ('Cocbamber')**, syn. *R.* 'Amberlight'. Hybrid Tea rose of compact, branching habit, with mid-green foliage. Rounded, fully double, scented flowers, 13cm (5in) across, apricot-pink flushed amber, are borne from summer to autumn. ↕↔ 60cm (24in). ❄❄❄

R. gallica* var. *officinalis ▣ syn. *R. officinalis* (Apothecary's rose, Crimson damask rose, Provins rose, Red rose of Lancaster). Species rose of compact, rounded habit, producing rough, dark green leaves with 3–5, rarely 7, broadly elliptic to almost rounded leaflets, 2.5–8cm (1–3in) long. Cupped to flat, semi-double, scented, pinkish red flowers, 8cm (3in) across, are borne singly or in clusters of 2–4 in summer, followed by spherical to ellipsoid, orange-red hips. ↕ 80cm (32in), ↔ 1m (3ft). ❄❄❄. **'Versicolor'** ▣ (Rosa mundi rose) is compact, with pale pink flowers, striped reddish pink.

***R.* GALWAY BAY ('Macba').** Free-branching Climber with dark green foliage. Cupped, double, lightly scented, salmon-pink flowers, 8cm (3in) across, are borne from summer to autumn. ↕ 3m (10ft), ↔ 2.2m (7ft). ❄❄❄

***R.* GARDEN PARTY.** Vigorous Hybrid Tea rose with mid-green leaves. From summer to autumn, bears high-centred, double, fragrant white flowers, 12cm (5in) across, margined pale pink. ↕ 1.2m (4ft), ↔ 80cm (32in). ❄❄❄

***R.* GENTLE TOUCH ('Diclulu')** ▣ Dwarf Floribunda rose of compact habit, producing dark green leaves. Sprays of urn-shaped, semi-double, pale salmon-pink flowers, 5cm (2in) across, are borne close to the foliage from summer to autumn. ↕ 50cm (20in), ↔ 40cm (16in). ❄❄❄

***R.* 'Gerbe d'Or'** see *R.* CASINO ('Macca').

***R.* GERTRUDE JEKYLL ('Ausbord').** Lanky Shrub rose with greyish green leaves. Cupped, double, fragrant, deep pink flowers, 10cm (4in) across, with infolded petals, are borne from summer to autumn. ↕ 1.5m (5ft), ↔ 1m (3ft). ❄❄❄

***R.* 'Ghislaine de Féligonde'.** Free-branching Shrub rose or Rambler with large, glossy, mid-green leaves. Bears large clusters of cupped, double, scented, buff-yellow flowers, 6cm (2½in) across, in early summer, a few flowers borne later. ↕↔ 2.5m (8ft). ❄❄❄

***R. gigantea* 'Cooperi'** see *R.* 'Cooperi'.

***R.* GINGERNUT ('Coccrazy').** Dwarf Floribunda rose of vigorous, short, spreading habit, with glossy, mid-green leaves. From summer to autumn, freely bears cupped, double flowers, 6cm (2½in) across, bronze-orange, with reddish tints on the reverse of the petals. ↕ 40cm (16in), ↔ 45cm (18in). ❄❄❄

***R.* GINGER SYLLABUB ('Harjolina').** Vigorous, arching Climber with mid-green leaves. Quartered-rosette, double, scented, pearl-pink flowers, 10cm (4in) across, with apricot centres, appear from summer to autumn. ↕ 3m (10ft), ↔ 2.2m (7ft). ❄❄❄

***R.* 'Gioia'** see *R.* PEACE ('Mme A. Meilland').

***R.* 'Gipsy Boy'** see *R.* 'Zigeunerknabe'.

R. glauca ▣ syn. *R. rubrifolia.* Vigorous, arching Species rose with reddish green stems and greyish purple leaves, each composed of 5–9 ovate to narrowly elliptic leaflets, 2.5–4cm (1–1½in) long. Flat, single, cerise-pink flowers, 4cm (1½in) across, with paler pink centres and gold stamens, are borne in small clusters in summer; they are followed by many spherical red hips in autumn. ↕ 2m (6ft), ↔ 1.5m (5ft). Mountains of C. and S. Europe. ❄❄❄

***R.* 'Glenfiddich'** ▣ Floribunda rose with glossy, dark green leaves. Produces clusters of urn-shaped, double, scented, amber to yellow flowers, 10cm (4in) across, from summer to autumn. ↕ 80cm (32in), ↔ 60cm (24in). ❄❄❄

***R.* 'Gloire de Dijon'** ▣ (Old glory rose). Vigorous, stiffly branching Noisette or climbing Tea rose with glossy, dark green leaves. Quartered-rosette, fully double, scented, creamy buff flowers, 10cm (4in) across, are borne from summer to autumn. ↕ to 5m (15ft), ↔ 4m (12ft). ❄❄❄

***R.* 'Gloire de France'**, syn. *R.* 'Fanny Bias'. Lax Gallica rose with crisp, dark green foliage. Quartered-rosette, fully double, fragrant, lilac-pink flowers, 8cm (3in) across, are borne freely in summer. ↕ 1m (3ft), ↔ 1.2m (4ft). ❄❄❄

***R.* 'Gloire des Mousseuses'**, syn. *R.* 'Gloire des Mousseux'. Vigorous, upright Moss rose with light green leaves. Bears cupped to flat, double, fragrant pink flowers, 10cm (4in) across, in summer. ↕ 1.2m (4ft), ↔ 90cm (36in). ❄❄❄

***R.* 'Gloire des Mousseux'** see *R.* 'Gloire des Mousseuses'.

***R.* 'Gloria Dei'** see *R.* PEACE ('Mme A. Meilland').

***R.* GLORIANA '97 ('Chewpope').** Vigorous Climbing Miniature rose with dark green leaves. Bears cupped, double, fragrant, mauve and lilac flowers, 6cm (2½in) across, from summer to autumn. ↕ 2.5m (8ft), ↔ 1.8m (6ft). ❄❄❄

***R.* GOLDEN CELEBRATION ('Ausgold').** Rounded Shrub rose with glossy, dark

Rosa filipes 'Kiftsgate'

Rosa 'Golden Showers'

Rosa 'Goldfinch'

Rosa GRAHAM THOMAS ('Ausmas')

Rosa 'Grandpa Dickson'

Rosa GREAT EXPECTATIONS ('Mackalves')

Rosa 'Great Maiden's Blush'

Rosa GROUSE ('Korimro')

Rosa 'Gruss an Aachen'

Rosa 'Hakuun'

Rosa HANDEL ('Macha')

Rosa HANNAH GORDON ('Korweiso')

Rosa 'Harry Wheatcroft'

green leaves. Deeply cupped, double, fragrant, golden yellow flowers, 9cm (3½in) across, are produced from summer to autumn. ↕↔ 1.2m (4ft). ❄❄❄

***R.* 'Golden Cherry'** see *R. laevigata.*

***R.* 'Golden Chersonese'** ■ syn. *R.* 'Hilgold'. Vigorous, upright Shrub rose with arching, reddish green stems and fern-like, mid-green leaves. Cupped to flat, single, bright yellow flowers, 4cm (1½in) across, are borne along the branches in early summer. ↕ 2.2m (7ft), ↔ 1.5m (5ft). ❄❄❄

***R.* 'Golden Rambler'** see *R.* 'Alister Stella Gray'.

***R.* 'Golden Showers'** ■ Stiff, upright Climber with glossy, dark green leaves. Numerous cupped, double, fragrant, clear yellow flowers, 10cm (4in) across, are borne from summer to autumn. ↕ to 3m (10ft), ↔ 2m (6ft). ❄❄❄

***R.* 'Golden Sunblaze'** see *R.* 'Rise 'n' Shine'.

***R.* GOLDEN WEDDING ('Arokris').** Vigorous, upright Floribunda rose with mid-green foliage. Bears cupped, double, lightly scented, deep yellow flowers, 9cm (3½in) across, from summer to autumn. ↕ 80cm (32in), ↔ 60cm (24in). ❄❄❄

***R.* 'Golden Wings'** ■ Dense, spreading Shrub rose with many prickly stems and light green leaves. Shallowly cupped, single, scented, pale yellow flowers, 12cm (5in) across, are borne from summer to autumn. ↕ 1.1m (3½ft), ↔ 1.3m (4½ft). ❄❄❄

***R.* 'Goldfinch'** ■ Vigorous, arching Rambler producing abundant light green leaves. Masses of rosette-shaped, double, scented flowers, 4cm (1½in) across, deep yellow fading to creamy white, are borne in summer. ↕ 2.5m (8ft), ↔ 2m (6ft). ❄❄❄

***R.* 'Gold of Ophir'** see *R.* x *odorata* 'Pseudindica'.

***R.* 'Goldsmith'** see *R.* SIMBA ('Korbelma').

***R.* GOOD AS GOLD ('Chewsunbeam').** Stiffly branching Climbing Miniature rose with narrow, dark green leaves. Cupped, double, scented, golden yellow flowers, 5cm (2in) across, appear from summer to autumn. ↕ 1.8m (6ft), ↔ 1.5m (5ft). ❄❄❄

***R.* 'Gordon's College'** see *R.* BRAVEHEART ('Cocjabby').

***R.* GRAHAM THOMAS ('Ausmas')** ■ Vigorous Shrub rose of lax, arching habit, with bright green leaves. Bears quartered-rosette to cupped, fully double, scented yellow flowers, 11cm (4½in) across, from summer to autumn. ↕ 1.2m (4ft), ↔ 1.5m (5ft). ❄❄❄

***R.* 'Grandiflora'** see *R. pimpinellifolia* 'Grandiflora'.

***R.* 'Grandpa Dickson'** ■ syn. *R.* 'Irish Gold'. Hybrid Tea rose of compact habit, with glossy, light green leaves. High-centred, fully double, primrose-yellow flowers, 18cm (7in) across, are borne from summer to autumn. ↕ 75cm (30in), ↔ 60cm (24in). ❄❄❄

***R.* GREAT EXPECTATIONS ('Mackalves')** ■ Compact, free-branching Floribunda rose with glossy, dark green leaves, reddish when young. Bears cupped, double, scented, apricot-pink flowers, 8cm (3in) across, from summer to autumn. ↕ 90cm (36in), ↔ 75cm (30in). ❄❄❄

***R.* 'Great Maiden's Blush'** ■ syn. *R.* 'Cuisse de Nymphe', *R.* 'La Séduisante'. Vigorous Alba rose with strong, arching stems and grey-green leaves. Cupped, fully double, very fragrant, pinkish white flowers, 8cm (3in) across, with infolded petals, are borne freely in midsummer. ↕ 2m (6ft), ↔ 1.3m (4½ft). ❄❄❄

***R.* GROUSE ('Korimro')** ■ syn. *R.* 'Immensee', *R.* 'Lac Rose'. Very vigorous, trailing Ground-cover rose with glossy, dark green leaves. Flat, single, scented, light pink to near white flowers, 4cm (1½in) across, are borne close to the stems in summer. ↕ 60cm (24in), ↔ 3m (10ft). ❄❄❄

***R.* 'Gruss an Aachen'** ■ Erect Floribunda rose with leathery, dark green foliage. Rounded, fully double, scented, pale pink to creamy white flowers, 8cm (3in) across, are borne from summer to autumn. ↕↔ 45cm (18in). ❄❄

***R.* 'Guinée'.** Vigorous, stiffly branched Climber producing leathery, dark green leaves. In summer, bears cupped, fully double, fragrant, blackish red flowers, 11cm (4½in) across. ↕ 5m (15ft), ↔ 2.2m (7ft). ❄❄❄

Rosa 'Golden Wings'

***R.* 'Gypsy Boy'** see *R.* 'Zigeunerknabe'.

***R.* 'Hakuun'** ■ Dwarf Floribunda rose of low, compact habit, with light green foliage. Masses of high-centred to rounded, semi-double, buff to creamy white flowers, 6cm (2½in) across, open from summer to autumn. ↕ 40cm (16in), ↔ 45cm (18in). ❄❄❄

***R.* HAMPSHIRE ('Korhamp')** ■ Prostrate Ground-cover rose producing glossy, mid-green leaves. From summer to autumn, bears clusters of many flat, single scarlet flowers, 5cm (2in) across, with yellow centres fading to white. ↕ 30cm (12in), ↔ 75cm (30in). ❄❄❄

***R.* HANDEL ('Macha')** ■ Climber of stiff, erect habit, with glossy, dark green leaves. Bears open clusters of urn-shaped, double, lightly scented cream flowers, 8cm (3in) across, with pinkish red margins, from summer to autumn. ↕ 3m (10ft), ↔ 2.2m (7ft). ❄❄❄

***R.* HAND IN HAND ('Haraztec').** Upright Patio rose with small, mid-green leaves. Bears clusters of cupped, double, lightly scented red flowers, 5cm (2in) across, from summer to autumn. ↕ 60cm (24in), ↔ 40cm (16in). ❄❄❄

***R.* HANNAH GORDON ('Korweiso')** ■ syn. *R.* 'Raspberry Ice'. Floribunda rose of spreading, open habit, with dark green leaves. From summer to autumn, bears sprays of cupped, double, pale pink flowers, 8cm (3in) across, margined reddish pink. ↕ 80cm (32in), ↔ 65cm (26in). ❄❄❄

***R.* 'Harisonii'** see *R.* x *harisonii* 'Harison's Yellow'.

***R.* x *harisonii* 'Harison's Yellow'**, syn. *R.* 'Harisonii'. Suckering Scots rose of gaunt habit, with prickly, dark brown stems and small, fern-like, mid-green leaves with 5–7 oval leaflets, 2cm (¾in) long. In summer, bears cupped, semi-double, bright deep yellow flowers, 5cm (2in) across, on short stems, followed by spherical-oblong, blackish red hips. ↕ 2m (6ft), ↔ 1.2m (4ft). ❄❄❄. **'Williams' Double Yellow'**, syn. *R.* 'Williams' Double Yellow', has a suckering, branching habit, and bears loosely double, fragrant flowers.

***R.* 'Harry Wheatcroft'** ■ syn. *R.* 'Caribia'. Vigorous Hybrid Tea rose with glossy, reddish green leaves. Bears high-centred, double, scarlet-red

R

Rosa helenae

Rosa 'Henri Martin'

Rosa Heritage ('Ausblush')

Rosa 'Hermosa'

Rosa Hertfordshire ('Kortenay')

Rosa High Hopes ('Haryup')

Rosa 'Hula Girl'

Rosa Iceberg ('Korbin')

Rosa 'Iced Ginger'

Rosa Ingrid Bergman ('Poulman')

Rosa Intrigue ('Korlech')

Rosa Invincible ('Runatru')

flowers, 12cm (5in) across, with yellow-striped petals, from summer to autumn. ↕1m (3ft), ↔60cm (24in). ✻✻✻

***R.* Harvest Fayre ('Dicnorth').** Floribunda rose with uneven growth and yellowish green leaves. Showy, rounded, double, apricot-orange flowers, 6cm (2½in) across, are borne freely from summer to autumn. ↕75cm (30in), ↔60cm (24in). ✻✻✻

***R.* 'Heart Throb'** see *R.* Paul Shirville ('Harqueterwife').

***R.* 'Heckenzauber'** see *R.* Sexy Rexy ('Macrexy').

***R.* 'Heidekönigin'** see *R.* Pheasant ('Kordapt').

***R.* 'Heideröslein'** see *R.* 'Nozomi'.

***R.* 'Heidetraum'** see *R.* Pink Flower Carpet ('Noatraum').

R. helenae ■ Trailing or climbing Species rose with dark greyish green leaves. Bears corymbs of cupped to flat, single, fragrant white flowers, 4cm (1½in) across, with yellow stamens, early in summer. ↕6m (20ft), ↔3m (10ft). ✻✻

***R.* 'Helmut Schmidt'** see *R.* Simba ('Korbelma').

***R.* 'Henri Martin'** ■ (Red moss rose). Vigorous Moss rose of arching growth, with rough, dark green leaves. Rounded, double, scented crimson flowers, 8cm (3in) across, with light green moss on the stems and sepals, open in summer. ↕to 2m (6ft), ↔1.2m (4ft). ✻✻✻

***R.* Heritage ('Ausblush')** ■ Vigorous Shrub rose with dark green leaves. Open clusters of cupped, fully double, lemon-scented, light pink flowers, 11cm (4½in) across, with infolded petals, are borne from summer to autumn. ↕↔1.2m (4ft). ✻✻✻

***R.* 'Hermosa'** ■ syn. *R.* 'Mélanie Lemaire', *R.* 'Mme Neumann'. Upright, bushy China rose with greyish green leaves and rounded, double, scented, rose-pink flowers, 7cm (3in) across, borne freely from summer to autumn. ↕1m (3ft), ↔60cm (24in). ✻✻✻

***R.* Hertfordshire ('Kortenay')** ■ Ground-cover rose of compact, uneven, spiky habit, with dense, bright green leaves. Flat, single, carmine-pink flowers, 4.5cm (1¾in) across, with paler pink centres, are borne freely in large clusters on short stems, from summer to autumn. ↕45cm (18in), ↔1m (3ft). ✻✻✻

***R.* 'Highdownensis'**, syn. *R. moyesii* 'Highdownensis'. Vigorous Shrub rose with dense growth and mid-green leaves, reddish green when young. Flat, single, deep pink flowers, 5cm (2in) across, with yellow stamens, borne close to the branches in summer, are followed by large, flask-shaped scarlet hips. ↕3m (10ft), ↔2m (6ft). ✻✻✻

***R.* High Hopes ('Haryup')** ■ Stiff, vigorous, arching Climber with glossy, dark green leaves. Urn-shaped to rounded, double, scented, light rose-pink flowers, 8cm (3in) across, are borne freely from summer to autumn. ↕4m (12ft), ↔2.5m (8ft). ✻✻✻

***R.* 'Hilgold'** see *R.* 'Golden Chersonese'.

***R.* 'Hugh Dickson'.** Vigorous Hybrid Perpetual rose with lanky, arching, prickly stems and rough, dark green leaves. Rounded, fully double, fragrant crimson flowers, 10cm (4in) across, are borne from summer to autumn. ↕2.5m (8ft), ↔1.5m (5ft), trained against a support; ↕1.5m (5ft), ↔2.5m (8ft), if pegged down. ✻✻✻

R. hugonis see *R. xanthina* f. *hugonis.*

***R.* 'Hula Girl'** ■ Miniature rose of compact, upright habit, with semi-glossy, mid-green foliage. Urn-shaped, fully double, lightly scented, pale orange-pink flowers, 3cm (1¼in) across, are borne from summer to autumn. ↕50cm (20in), ↔30cm (12in). ✻✻✻

***R.* Iceberg ('Korbin')** ■ syn. *R.* 'Fée des Neiges', *R.* 'Schneewittchen'. Vigorous Floribunda rose of rounded habit, with abundant light green foliage. Bears large clusters of cupped, double, creamy to pure white flowers, 7cm (3in) across, from summer to autumn. ↕80cm (32in), ↔65cm (26in). ✻✻✻

***R.* Ice Cream ('Korzuri')**, syn. *R.* 'Memoire'. Vigorous, bushy, upright Hybrid Tea rose with dark green leaves. Cupped, double, scented, creamy white flowers, 12cm (5in) across, are borne from summer to autumn. ↕80cm (32in), ↔65cm (26in). ✻✻✻

***R.* 'Iced Ginger'** ■ Floribunda rose of lanky habit, with sparse, light green foliage. Bears high-centred, fully double, buff to copper-pink flowers, 11cm (4½in) across, from summer to autumn. ↕1m (3ft), ↔70cm (28in). ✻✻✻

***R.* 'Immensee'** see *R.* Grouse ('Korimro').

***R.* 'Impressionist'** see *R.* Purple Tiger ('Jacpurr').

***R.* 'Incarnata'** see *R.* 'Maiden's Blush'.

***R.* Indian Summer ('Peaperfume').** Hybrid Tea rose of compact habit and uneven growth, with dark green foliage. Rounded, fully double, fragrant, creamy orange flowers, 11cm (4½in) across, are borne from summer to autumn. ↕55cm (22in), ↔60cm (24in). ✻✻✻

***R.* Ingrid Bergman ('Poulman')** ■ Hybrid Tea rose of branching habit, with leathery, dark green leaves. High-centred, fully double, dark red flowers, 11cm (4½in) across, are produced from summer to autumn. ↕80cm (32in), ↔65cm (26in). ✻✻✻

***R.* 'Integrity'** see *R.* Savoy Hotel ('Harvintage').

***R.* Intrigue ('Korlech')** ■ syn. *R.* 'Lavaglut'. Vigorous Floribunda rose of compact habit, with glossy, purplish green leaves. Rounded, double, dark red flowers, 7cm (3in) across, are borne in large clusters from summer to autumn. ↕70cm (28in), ↔60cm (24in). ✻✻

***R.* Invincible ('Runatru')** ■ Floribunda rose of compact habit, with glossy, dark green foliage. Cupped, double, bright crimson flowers, 9cm (3½in) across, are borne in open clusters from summer to autumn. ↕70cm (28in), ↔50cm (20in). ✻✻✻

***R.* 'Irish Beauty'** see *R.* Elizabeth of Glamis ('Macel').

***R.* Irish Eyes ('Dicwitness').** Bushy, compact Floribunda rose with semi-glossy, mid-green foliage. Cupped, double, lightly scented, yellow and scarlet flowers, 6cm (2½in) across, are borne from summer to autumn. ↕75cm (30in), ↔85cm (34in). ✻✻✻

***R.* 'Irish Gold'** see *R.* 'Grandpa Dickson'.

***R.* 'Irish Wonder'** see *R.* Evelyn Fison ('Macev').

***R.* 'Ispahan'** ■ syn. *R.* 'Pompon des Princes', *R.* 'Rose d'Isfahan'. Vigorous Damask rose with grey-green foliage and cupped, double, fragrant, clear pink flowers, 8cm (3in) across, in summer. ↕1.5m (5ft), ↔1.2m (4ft). ✻✻✻

***R.* Jacqueline du Pré ('Harwanna')** ■ Vigorous, arching Shrub rose with glossy, dark green leaves. Cupped, semi-double, musk-scented ivory flowers, 10cm (4in) across, with scalloped petals and red stamens, are borne from early summer to autumn. ↕1.5m (5ft), ↔1.2m (4ft). ✻✻✻

***R.* 'Jacques Cartier'** see *R.* 'Marchesa Boccella'.

Rosa Hampshire ('Korhamp')

R

Rosa 'Ispahan'

Rosa JACQUELINE DU PRÉ ('Harwanna')

Rosa 'John Cabot'

Rosa 'Julia's Rose'

Rosa 'Just Joey'

Rosa KEEPSAKE ('Kormalda')

Rosa KENT ('Poulcov')

Rosa 'Königin von Dänemark'

Rosa 'Korresia'

Rosa 'Lamarque'

Rosa LAURA FORD ('Chewarvel')

Rosa 'Lavender Jewel'

***R.* 'Jaune Desprez'** see *R.* 'Desprez à Fleur Jaune'.
***R.* 'Jenny Duval'** see *R.* 'Président de Sèze'.
***R.* 'John Cabot'** ▣ Vigorous Shrub rose producing abundant light green leaves. Clusters of cupped, double, scented magenta flowers, 6cm (2½in) across, are borne from summer to autumn. ↕ 1.5m (5ft), ↔ 1.2m (4ft). ✻✻✻
***R.* 'Josephine Bruce'.** Hybrid Tea rose with short, splayed growth and dark green foliage. From summer to autumn, bears high-centred, double, fragrant, rich blackish crimson flowers, 12cm (5in) across. Prone to mildew. ↕ 75cm (30in), ↔ 60cm (24in). ✻✻✻
***R.* 'Joseph's Coat'.** Vigorous, branching Climber or Shrub rose with dark green leaves. Showy clusters of urn-shaped to cupped, double yellow flowers, 8cm (3in) across, suffused orange-pink and red, are borne from summer to autumn. ↕↔ 3m (10ft) as a climber; ↕ to 1.2m (4ft), ↔ 1m (3ft) as a shrub. ✻✻✻
***R.* 'Julia's Rose'** ▣ Hybrid Tea rose with spindly, branching growth and sparse, reddish green foliage. High-centred, double, brownish pink to buff flowers, 10cm (4in) across, are borne from summer to autumn. ↕ 75cm (30in), ↔ 45cm (18in). ✻✻✻
***R.* 'Just Joey'** ▣ Hybrid Tea rose of open, branching habit, with sparse, dark green foliage. Rounded, fully double, fragrant, copper-pink flowers, 12cm (5in) across, with wavy-margined petals, are borne from summer to autumn. ↕ 75cm (30in), ↔ 70cm (28in). ✻✻✻
***R.* 'Karen Blixen'** see *R.* SILVER ANNIVERSARY ('Poulari').
***R.* 'Katharina Zeimet'**, syn. *R.* 'White Baby Rambler'. Vigorous Polyantha bush rose producing abundant dark green leaves. From summer to autumn, bears dense clusters of cupped, double white flowers, 4.5cm (1¾in) across. ↕↔ 50cm (20in) or more. ✻✻✻
***R.* 'Kathleen Harrop'.** Bourbon rose of arching, lax habit, with dark green leaves. Cupped, double, fragrant, pale pink flowers, 8cm (3in) across, are borne from summer to autumn. Susceptible to mildew. ↕ 2.5m (8ft), ↔ 2m (6ft). ✻✻✻
***R.* 'Kazanlik'** see *R.* x *damascena*.
***R.* KEEPSAKE ('Kormalda')** ▣ syn. *R.* 'Esmeralda'. Hybrid Tea rose of uneven habit, with dark green leaves. From summer to autumn, bears high-centred, fully double, lightly scented, deep pink flowers, 12cm (5in) across. ↕ 75cm (30in), ↔ 60cm (24in). ✻✻✻
***R.* KENT ('Poulcov')** ▣ syn. *R.* 'Pyrenees', *R.* 'White Cover'. Compact, spreading, Ground-cover rose with glossy, dark green leaves. Cupped to flat, semi-double white flowers, 4.5cm (1¾in) across, are borne on short stems from summer to autumn. ↕ 45cm (18in), ↔ 1m (3ft). ✻✻✻
***R.* 'Kew Rambler'.** Vigorous Rambler with stiff but pliable growth and dense, grey-green leaves. Clusters of cupped, single, scented pink flowers, 4cm (1½in) across, each with a white eye and yellow stamens, are borne in summer. ↕ 5m (15ft), ↔ 4m (12ft). ✻✻✻
***R.* 'Kiftsgate'** see *R. filipes* 'Kiftsgate'.
***R.* 'King's Ransom'.** Hybrid Tea rose producing leathery, glossy, dark green leaves. Bears urn-shaped to cupped, fully double, lightly scented yellow flowers, 12cm (5in) across, on long stems from summer to autumn. ↕ 75cm (30in), ↔ 60cm (24in). ✻✻✻
***R.* 'Königin von Dänemark'** ▣ syn. *R.* 'Belle Courtisane', *R.* 'Queen of Denmark'. Vigorous, lax Alba rose with dull, bluish green leaves. In midsummer, bears quartered-rosette, fully double, very fragrant, deep to light pink flowers, 9cm (3½in) across, with green button eyes. ↕ 1.5m (5ft), ↔ 1.2m (4ft). ✻✻✻
***R.* 'Königliche Hoheit'** see *R.* 'Royal Highness'.
***R.* 'Kordes Robusta'** see *R.* ROBUSTA ('Korgosa').
***R.* 'Korresia'** ▣ syn. *R.* 'Friesia', *R.* 'Sunsprite'. Compact Floribunda rose with light green leaves. Sprays of urn-shaped to cupped, double, fragrant, bright yellow flowers, 8cm (3in) across, with wavy-margined petals, are borne from summer to autumn. ↕ 75cm (30in), ↔ 60cm (24in). ✻✻✻
***R.* 'La Belle Sultane'** see *R.* 'Violacea'.
***R.* 'Lac Rose'** see *R.* GROUSE ('Korimro').
***R.* 'Lady Penzance'.** Vigorous, twiggy, free-branching Sweet Briar rose with apple-scented, glossy, dark green leaves. Cupped, single, copper-pink and yellow flowers, 4cm (1½in) across, are borne briefly in midsummer, followed by ovoid red hips. ↕↔ 2m (6ft). ✻✻✻
***R. laevigata*,** syn. *R.* 'Golden Cherry' (Camellia rose, Cherokee rose). Vigorous Species rose with large prickles, arching stems, and attractive, glossy, dark green leaves, each with 3, rarely 5, lance-shaped to elliptic or ovate leaflets, 3–6cm (1¼–2½in) long. Solitary, flat, single, scented white flowers, to 10cm (4in) across, with scalloped petals and gold stamens, are borne in summer; they are followed by pear-shaped, bristly, brownish orange-red hips. Evergreen in mild climates. ↕↔ 2–6m (6–20ft). E. and S. China, Taiwan, S.E. Asia. ✻✻

Rosa LAURA ASHLEY ('Chewharla')

***R.* L'AIMANT ('Harzola')** ▣p.929. Vigorous Floribunda rose with dark green foliage. Cupped, double, fragrant, reddish salmon-pink flowers, 9cm (3½in) across, are borne from summer to autumn. ↕ 1m (3ft), ↔ 75cm (30in). ✻✻✻
***R.* 'Lamarque'** ▣ Vigorous Noisette climbing rose with smooth stems and limp, glossy, bright green foliage. Flat, quartered-rosette, fully double, fragrant, yellowish white flowers, 9cm (3½in) across, are borne on nodding stems from summer to autumn. ↕ to 5m (15ft), ↔ 2.5m (8ft). ✻✻
***R.* 'La Reine Victoria'** see *R.* 'Reine Victoria'.
***R.* 'La Royale'** see *R.* 'Maiden's Blush'.
***R.* 'La Séduisante'** see *R.* 'Great Maiden's Blush'.
***R.* LAURA ASHLEY ('Chewharla')** ▣ Dense, compact Ground-cover rose producing abundant mid-green leaves. Large clusters of cupped to flat, single, magenta-pink to lilac flowers, 3cm (1¼in) across, with pale yellow centres, are borne from summer to autumn. ↕ 60cm (24in), ↔ 1.2m (4ft). ✻✻✻
***R.* LAURA FORD ('Chewarvel')** ▣ Stiff, upright, Climbing Miniature rose with abundant glossy, light green leaves. From summer to autumn, bears clusters of urn-shaped to flat, semi-double, lightly scented yellow flowers, 4.5cm (1¾in) across, becoming pink tinged with age. ↕ 2.2m (7ft), ↔ 1.2m (4ft). ✻✻✻
***R.* 'Lavaglut'** see *R.* INTRIGUE ('Korlech').
***R.* 'Lavender Jewel'** ▣ Miniature rose of compact, spreading habit, with dark green foliage. Cupped, double, lavender-pink flowers, 4cm (1½in) across, are produced in clusters from summer to autumn. ↕↔ 30cm (12in). ✻✻✻

Rosa 'Lavender Lassie'

Rosa Lawinia ('Tanklewi')

Rosa Leaping Salmon ('Peamight')

Rosa Little Bo-Peep ('Poullen')

Rosa Lovely Lady ('Dicjubell')

Rosa 'Lovers' Meeting'

Rosa Loving Memory ('Korgund')

Rosa 'Maiden's Blush'

Rosa 'Maigold'

Rosa Many Happy Returns ('Harwanted')

Rosa 'Marchesa Boccella'

Rosa 'Maréchal Niel'

***R.* 'Lavender Lassie'** ■ Vigorous, free-branching Shrub rose producing dark green leaves. Cupped to flat, double, fragrant, lavender-pink flowers, 7cm (3in) across, are borne from summer to autumn. ↕1.5m (5ft), ↔ 1.2m (4ft). ✽✽✽

***R.* Lawinia ('Tanklewi')** ■ Stiffly branching Climber with mid-green leaves. Cupped, double, fragrant pink flowers, 9cm (3½in) across, are borne from summer to autumn. ↕4m (12ft), ↔ 2.5m (8ft). ✽✽✽

***R.* L.D. Braithwaite ('Auscrim').** Open Shrub rose producing greyish green leaves. Loosely formed, rosette-shaped, fully double, scented, bright crimson flowers, 9cm (3½in) across, with infolded petals, are borne from summer to autumn. ↕1m (3ft), ↔ 1.2m (4ft). ✽✽✽

***R.* Leaping Salmon ('Peamight')** ■ Stiffly branching Climber with glossy, dark green foliage. High-centred, double, fragrant, salmon-pink flowers, 10cm (4in) across, are borne from summer to autumn. ↕3m (10ft), ↔ 1.8m (6ft). ✽✽✽

***R.* 'Leda'** (Painted damask rose). Lax Damask rose with prickly stems and grey-green leaves. In summer, bears rosette-shaped, fully double, fragrant, carmine-tipped white flowers, 7cm (3in) across, with button centres, reflexing into a ball. ↕↔ 1m (3ft). ✽✽✽

***R.* 'Lemon Pillar'** see *R.* 'Paul's Lemon Pillar'.

***R.* 'Leverkusen'.** Vigorous, arching Climber producing toothed, glossy, deep green leaves. Clusters of wide-opening, rosette-shaped, double, lightly scented, pale yellow flowers, 8cm (3in) across, are borne from summer to autumn. Prune to maintain as a shrub. ↕3m (10ft), ↔ 2.2m (7ft). ✽✽✽

***R.* Little Bo-Peep ('Poullen')** ■ Patio rose of low, spreading habit, with dark green foliage. dense clusters of many rounded to flat, semi-double, light pink flowers, 4cm (1½in) across, are borne close to the plant from summer to autumn. ↕30cm (12in), ↔ 50cm (20in). ✽✽✽

***R.* Little Rambler ('Chewramb').** Lax, arching Climbing Miniature rose with small, dark green leaves. Clusters of rosette-shaped, double, fragrant, blush-pink flowers, 4cm (1½in) across, are produced from summer to autumn. ↕2.5m (8ft), ↔ 2.2m (7ft). ✽✽✽

***R.* 'Little White Pet'** see *R.* 'White Pet'.

***R.* 'Liverpool Remembers'** see *R.* Beauty Star ('Frystar').

***R. longicuspis* of gardens** see *R. mulliganii.*

***R.* 'Louise Odier'**, syn. *R.* 'Mme de Stella'. Bourbon rose of slender, arching growth, with light grey-green foliage. Camellia-like, rosette-shaped, fully double, fragrant pink flowers, 9cm (3½in) across, with lilac tints, are borne from summer to autumn. ↕2m (6ft), ↔ 1.2m (4ft). ✽✽✽

***R.* Lovely Lady ('Dicjubell')** ■ Hybrid Tea rose with a vigorous, free-branching habit and abundant glossy, mid-green leaves. Urn-shaped, fully double, scented, salmon-pink flowers, 10cm (4in) across, are borne from summer to autumn. ↕75cm (30in), ↔ 60cm (24in). ✽✽✽

***R.* 'Lovers' Meeting'** ■ Free-branching Hybrid Tea rose of vigorous, spreading habit, with bronze-green foliage. High-centred, double, reddish orange flowers, 9cm (3½in) across, are borne singly and in wide sprays from summer to autumn. ↕↔ 75cm (30in). ✽✽✽

***R.* Loving Memory ('Korgund')** ■ syn. *R.* 'Burgund '81'. Robust Hybrid Tea rose with dull, dark green leaves. High-centred, fully double, lightly scented, dark red flowers, 12cm (5in) across, are borne on strong, stiff stems from summer to autumn. ↕1.1m (3½ft), ↔ 75cm (30in). ✽✽✽

R. lucida see *R. virginiana.*

***R.* 'Lü E'** see *R.* x *odorata* 'Viridiflora'.

***R.* 'Macrantha Raubritter'** see *R.* 'Raubritter'.

R. macrophylla. Vigorous Species rose producing red stems and mid-green leaves, each composed of 7–11 oval leaflets, to 6cm (2½in) long. Flat, single, scented red flowers, 5–7cm (2–3in) across, are borne singly or in clusters of up to 5 in summer, followed by flask-shaped red hips. ↕4m (12ft), ↔ 3m (10ft). Himalayas, from Pakistan to W. China. ✽✽✽

***R.* 'Magenta'.** Shrubby, spreading Floribunda rose with leathery, dark green leaves. Quartered-rosette, fully double, fragrant, pink-magenta flowers, 9cm (3½in) across, are borne in heavy clusters on bowed stems from summer to autumn. ↕1.5m (5ft), ↔ 1.2m (4ft). ✽✽✽

***R.* Magic Carpet ('Jaclover').** Spreading Ground-cover rose with glossy, dark green foliage. Cupped, semi-double, spicy-scented, lavender-pink flowers, 5cm (2in) across, are borne from summer to autumn. ↕50cm (20in), ↔ 1.5m (5ft). ✽✽✽

***R.* Magic Carrousel ('Moorcar').** Miniature rose of compact, bushy habit, producing glossy, mid-green leaves. Rosette-shaped, double, pale yellow flowers, 4cm (1½in) across, with crimson edging, are borne from summer to autumn. ↕40cm (16in), ↔ 30cm (12in). ✽✽✽

***R.* 'Maiden's Blush'** ■ syn. *R.* 'Incarnata', *R.* 'La Royale'. Vigorous, upright, arching Alba rose with dull, bluish green foliage. Cupped, fully double, fragrant, very pale pink flowers, 7cm (3in) across, with irregular centres, are borne in midsummer. ↕1.2m (4ft), ↔ 90cm (36in). ✽✽✽

***R.* 'Maigold'** ■ Strong, stiff-growing Climber with very prickly, arching stems and leathery, dark green leaves. Cupped, semi-double, scented, bronze-yellow flowers, 10cm (4in) across, are borne freely in early summer and sparsely again in autumn. ↕↔ 2.5m (8ft). ✽✽✽

***R.* 'Mainaufeuer'** see *R.* Chilterns ('Kortemma').

***R.* 'Mainzer Fastnacht'** see *R.* Blue Moon ('Tannacht').

***R.* Many Happy Returns ('Harwanted')** ■ syn. *R.* 'Prima'. Floribunda rose of shrubby habit, with attractive, glossy, mid-green foliage. Cupped, semi-double, scented, pale pink flowers, 10cm (4in) across, are borne in dense clusters from summer to autumn. ↕↔ 75cm (30in). ✽✽✽

***R.* 'Marchesa Boccella'** ■ syn. *R.* 'Jacques Cartier'. Portland rose of dense habit, with abundant light green foliage. Quartered-rosette, fully double, scented, rose-pink flowers, 11cm (4½in) across, are borne on short stems from summer to autumn. ↕1.2m (4ft), ↔ 1m (3ft). ✽✽✽

***R.* 'Maréchal Niel'** ■ Vigorous Noisette or climbing Tea rose with long, glossy, rich green leaves. High-centred, fully double, scented, clear yellow flowers, 10cm (4in) across, are produced on nodding stems from summer to autumn. ↕to 5m (15ft), ↔ 2.5m (8ft). ✽✽✽ (borderline)

***R.* Margaret Merril ('Harkuly')** ■ Floribunda rose with crisp, dark green leaves. Bears high-centred to cupped, double, fragrant, pale pink to white flowers, 10cm (4in) across, with maroon stamens, singly or in clusters from summer to autumn. ↕80cm (32in), ↔ 60cm (24in). ✽✽✽

***R.* 'Marguerite Hilling'** ■ syn. *R.* 'Pink Nevada'. Vigorous, arching Shrub rose with red stems and dense, light green foliage. Flat, semi-double, scented, rose-pink flowers, 10cm (4in) across, with deeper shading, are borne freely in early summer and sparsely in autumn. ↕↔ 2.2m (7ft). ✽✽✽

***R.* 'Mariandel'** see *R.* The Times Rose ('Korpeahn').

***R.* Marjorie Fair ('Harhero')**, syn. *R.* 'Red Ballerina', *R.* 'Red Yesterday'. Dense Polyantha rose with glossy, mid-green leaves. Mop-headed clusters of many cupped, single, wine-red flowers, 4.5cm (1¾in) across, each with a white eye, are borne from summer to autumn. ↕↔ 1.2m (4ft). ✽✽✽

***R.* 'Marlena'.** Floribunda rose of compact habit, with dark green leaves. Sprays of cupped, double, bright crimson flowers, 6cm (2½in) across, are borne freely from summer to autumn. ↕↔ 45cm (18in). ✽✽✽

***R.* Mary Rose ('Ausmary')** ■ Shrub rose of upright, uneven growth, with matt, mid-green leaves. Cupped, double, scented, deep rose-pink flowers, 9cm (3½in) across, are borne from summer to autumn. ↕1.2m (4ft), ↔ 1m (3ft). ✽✽✽

***R.* 'Masquerade'.** Vigorous Floribunda rose of compact habit, with leathery, dark green leaves. From summer to autumn, bears sprays of cupped to flat, semi-double flowers, to 6cm (2½in) across, changing in colour from yellow to pink and dark red. ↕80cm (32in), ↔ 60cm (24in). ✽✽✽

***R.* Matangi ('Macman').** Compact Floribunda rose producing abundant glossy, dark green leaves. Showy, open-cupped, double, rich orange-red flowers, 9cm (3½in) across, with white in the centres and on the reverse of the petals, are borne from summer to autumn. ↕80cm (32in), ↔ 60cm (24in). ✽✽✽

Rosa

Rosa MARGARET MERRIL ('Harkuly')

Rosa 'Marguerite Hilling'

Rosa MARY ROSE ('Ausmary')

Rosa 'Max Graf'

Rosa 'May Queen'

Rosa MELODY MAKER ('Dicqueen')

Rosa 'Mme Alfred Carrière'

Rosa 'Mme de Sancy de Parabère'

Rosa 'Mme Hardy'

Rosa 'Mme Isaac Pereire'

Rosa 'Mme Knorr'

Rosa MOLINEUX ('Ausmol')

***R.* 'Max Graf'** ■ Trailing Groundcover rose with glossy, dark green foliage. Cupped, single, scented pink flowers, 8cm (3in) across, with pale centres, are borne in summer. ↕60cm (24in), ↔ 2.5m (8ft). ✻✻✻
***R.* 'May Queen'** ■ Vigorous, arching Rambler with abundant glossy, mid-green foliage. In summer, bears clusters of quartered-rosette, double, apple-scented, clear rose-pink flowers, 8cm (3in) across. ↕4m (12ft), ↔ 3m (10ft). ✻✻✻
***R.* 'Meg'.** Stiff, vigorous Climber with dark green leaves. Bears open clusters of cupped to flat, semi-double, fragrant, pink-apricot to pink flowers, 12cm (5in) across, with red stamens, from summer to autumn. ↕↔ 4m (12ft). ✻✻✻
***R.* 'Mélanie Lemaire'** see *R.* 'Hermosa'.
***R.* MELODY MAKER ('Dicqueen')** ■ Floribunda rose of dense habit, with abundant dark green foliage. Freely bears rounded, fully double, light scarlet flowers, 9cm (3½in) across, from summer to autumn. ↕70cm (28in), ↔ 60cm (24in). ✻✻✻
***R.* 'Memoire'** see *R.* ICE CREAM ('Korzuri').
***R.* 'Mermaid'.** Vigorous, slow-growing Climber with stiff, red-brown stems, hooked thorns, and glossy, dark green leaves. From summer to autumn, bears cupped to flat, single, primrose-yellow flowers, 11cm (4½in) across, with sulphur-yellow stamens. ↕↔ to 6m (20ft). ✻✻✻
***R.* 'Mevrouw Nathalie Nypels'.** Bushy Polyantha rose with a compact habit and glossy, mid-green leaves. Freely bears cupped, semi-double, rose-pink flowers, 6cm (2½in) across, from summer to autumn. ↕75cm (30in), ↔ 60cm (24in). ✻✻✻
***R.* 'Mignon'** see *R.* 'Cécile Brunner'.
***R.* 'Mildred Scheel'** see *R.* 'Deep Secret'.
***R.* 'Minuetto'** see *R.* DARLING FLAME ('Meilucca').
***R.* 'Mirato'** see *R.* CHATSWORTH ('Tanotari', 'Tanotax').
***R.* MISCHIEF ('Macmi').** Hybrid Tea rose producing abundant but rust-prone, mid-green leaves. Urn-shaped, double, scented, pink-orange to pink flowers, 10cm (4in) across, are borne from summer to autumn. ↕1m (3ft), ↔ 60cm (24in). ✻✻✻
***R.* 'Mme Alfred Carrière'** ■ Noisette climbing rose with slender, smooth stems and pale green foliage. Rounded, fully double, fragrant, pale pink to white flowers, 6cm (2½in) across, are borne from summer to autumn. ↕5m (15ft), ↔ 3m (10ft). ✻✻✻
***R.* 'Mme Butterfly'.** Hybrid Tea rose with stiff growth and sparse, mid-green foliage. Neatly formed, urn-shaped to cupped, double, fragrant, light pink flowers, 8cm (3in) across, are borne from summer to autumn. ↕1m (3ft), ↔ 60cm (24in). ✻✻✻
***R.* 'Mme Caroline Testout'** ■ syn. *R.* 'Caroline Testout', *R.* 'City of Portland'. Vigorous, branching Hybrid Tea rose with large, mid-green leaves. Rounded, double, scented, bright rose-pink flowers, 11cm (4½in) across, tinged carmine-red, are borne from summer to autumn. ↕1m (3ft), ↔ 75cm (30in). ✻✻✻
***R.* 'Mme de la Roche-Lambert'** see *R.* 'Mme Delaroche-Lambert'.
***R.* 'Mme Delaroche-Lambert'**, syn. *R.* 'Mme de la Roche-Lambert'. Upright, arching Moss rose with rough, dull, light to mid-green leaves and brownish green moss. Rounded, fully double, scented, purplish pink flowers, 8cm (3in) across, some with button centres, are borne mainly in summer, sometimes also in autumn. ↕1.2m (4ft), ↔ 1m (3ft). ✻✻✻

Rosa 'Mme Caroline Testout'

***R.* 'Mme de Sancy de Parabère'** ■ Vigorous, arching Boursault climbing rose with smooth green wood and dark green leaves. Rosette-shaped, double, clear rose-pink flowers, 12cm (5in) across, are borne in early summer. ↕5m (15ft), ↔ 3m (10ft). ✻✻
***R.* 'Mme de Stella'** see *R.* 'Louise Odier'.
***R.* 'Mme Grégoire Staechelin'** ■ syn. *R.* 'Spanish Beauty'. Very vigorous, arching Climber with masses of large, dark green leaves. Rounded, fully double flowers, 12cm (5in) across, with ruffled, red-flushed, clear pink petals, are borne in early summer. Flowers are followed by large, spherical red hips. ↕ to 6m (20ft), ↔ 4m (12ft). ✻✻✻
***R.* 'Mme Hardy'** ■ Vigorous, upright Damask rose with abundant leathery, dark green leaves. Quartered-rosette, fully double, fragrant white flowers, 10cm (4in) across, each with a green button eye, are produced in summer. ↕1.5m (5ft), ↔ 1.2m (4ft). ✻✻✻
***R.* 'Mme Hébert'** see *R.* 'Président de Sèze'.
***R.* 'Mme Isaac Pereire'** ■ Vigorous, arching Bourbon shrub or climbing rose with large, dark green leaves. From summer to autumn, bears quartered-rosette, fully double, fragrant, deep purplish pink flowers, 15cm (6in) across. ↕2.2m (7ft), ↔ 2m (6ft). ✻✻✻
***R.* 'Mme Knorr'** ■ syn. *R.* 'Comte de Chambord'. Bushy, leafy, vigorous Portland rose with mid-green foliage. From summer to autumn, produces quartered-rosette, fully double, fragrant, pink, darker-centred flowers, 10cm (4in) across. ↕1.2m (4ft), ↔ 1m (3ft). ✻✻✻
***R.* 'Mme Legras de St. Germain'.** Upright Alba rose with smooth stems and greyish green leaves. Rosette-shaped, fully double, fragrant, lemon-white flowers, 9cm (3½in) across, are borne in midsummer. May be trained on a support. ↕↔ 2m (6ft) as a shrub; ↕ to 5m (15ft) as a climber. ✻✻✻
***R.* 'Mme Neumann'** see *R.* 'Hermosa'.
***R.* 'Mme Pierre Oger'.** Lax Bourbon rose with slender stems and light green leaves. From summer to autumn, produces cupped, double, scented, creamy pink flowers, 8cm (3in) across, marked with lilac. ↕2m (6ft), ↔ 1.2m (4ft). ✻✻✻
***R.* 'Mme Plantier'** ■ Vigorous, arching Alba shrub or Noisette climbing rose producing long, smooth, mid-green leaves. In midsummer, bears clusters of cupped, fully double, scented white flowers, 7cm (3in) across, reflexing into a ball. ↕↔ to 6m (20ft) on a support, ↕2m (6ft), ↔ 2.5m (8ft) grown as a shrub. ✻✻✻
***R.* MOLINEUX ('Ausmol')** ■ Upright, bushy Shrub rose with bright green leaves. Bears cupped to flat, double, scented yellow flowers, 10cm (4in) across, from summer to autumn. ↕↔ 1m (3ft). ✻✻✻
***R.* 'Moonlight'** ■ Hybrid Musk rose of dense habit, with stems and leaves both reddish green. Clusters of flat, semi-

Rosa 'Mme Grégoire Staechelin'

Rosa 'Moonlight'

Rosa 'Morning Jewel'

Rosa moschata

Rosa MOUNTBATTEN ('Harmantelle')

Rosa moyesii 'Geranium'

Rosa 'Mrs. John Laing'

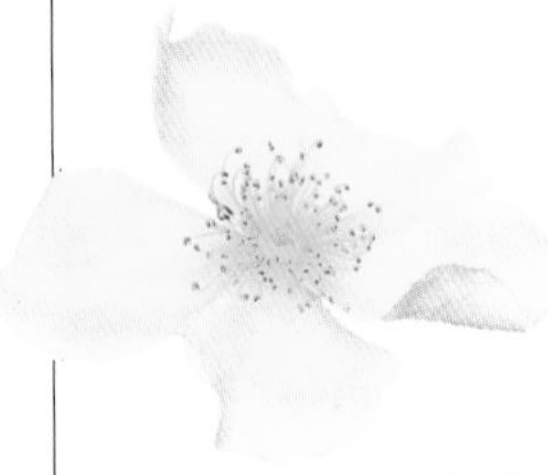
Rosa 'Mrs. Oakley Fisher'

Rosa mulliganii

Rosa 'National Trust'

Rosa 'Nevada'

Rosa 'New Dawn'

Rosa NEWS ('Legnews')

double, scented, lemon-white flowers, 4.5cm (1¾in) across, are borne freely from summer to autumn. ↕↔ 1.2m (4ft). ❄❄❄

***R.* 'Morning Jewel'** ■ Vigorous, free-branching Climber producing glossy, mid-green leaves. Clusters of cupped, double, scented, bright pink flowers, 9cm (3½in) across, are borne from summer to autumn. Tolerates partial shade. ↕ 3m (10ft), ↔ 2.5m (8ft). ❄❄❄

R. moschata ■ (Musk rose). Species rose of tall, lax habit, with dark green stems and purplish green leaves, each comprising 5–7 broadly ovate to broadly elliptic leaflets, 1.5–4cm (½–1½in) long. Few-flowered, loose clusters of flat, single to semi-double, musk-scented, milk-white flowers, 5cm (2in) across, are borne from late summer to autumn; they are followed by spherical to ovoid, orange-red hips. ↕↔ to 3m (10ft). W. Asia. ❄❄. **var. *nivea*** see *R.* 'Dupontii'.

***R.* MOUNTBATTEN ('Harmantelle')** ■ Vigorous Floribunda rose of shrubby habit, with crisp, leathery, bright green leaves. Rounded, fully double, scented yellow flowers, 10cm (4in) across, are produced from summer to autumn. ↕ 1.2m (4ft), ↔ 75cm (30in). ❄❄❄

R. moyesii. Vigorous, arching Species rose producing mid- to dark green leaves, each comprising 7–13 small, broadly elliptic to ovate leaflets, 1–4cm (½–1½in) long. Flat or cupped, single, deep scarlet or pink flowers, 5cm (2in) across, with yellow stamens, are borne singly or in small clusters in summer; they are followed by large, flask-shaped red hips. ↕ 4m (12ft), ↔ 3m (10ft). W. China. ❄❄❄. **var. *fargesii*** is less vigorous, and has pink flowers; ↕ 2.5m (8ft), ↔ 1.5m (5ft). **'Geranium'** ■ has a compact habit, and bears brighter, cherry-red flowers with cream stamens, followed by orange-red hips; ↕ 2.5m (8ft), ↔ 1.5m (5ft). **'Highdownensis'** see *R.* 'Highdownensis'.

***R.* 'Mr. Lincoln'.** Stiff-stemmed Hybrid Tea rose of upright habit, producing leathery, dull, dark green foliage. High-centred to cupped, fully double, fragrant, dark velvety red flowers, 12cm (5in) across, are borne from summer to autumn. ↕ 1.1m (3½ft), ↔ 60cm (24in). ❄❄❄

***R.* 'Mrs. John Laing'** ■ Hybrid Perpetual rose with abundant light green foliage. From summer to autumn, bears rounded, fully double, fragrant, silvery pink flowers, 12cm (5in) across. ↕ 1m (3ft), ↔ 75cm (30in). ❄❄❄

***R.* 'Mrs. Oakley Fisher'** ■ Hybrid Tea rose with spindly stems and sparse, bronze-green foliage. From summer to autumn, bears cupped to flat, single, scented apricot flowers, 7cm (3in) across, fading to pale buff with age. ↕↔ to 1m (3ft). ❄❄❄

R. mulliganii ■ syn. *R. longicuspis* of gardens. Rampant Species rose with large, glossy, greyish green leaves, each comprising 5–7 elliptic-ovate to oblong-ovate leaflets, to 6cm (2½in) long. Large clusters of many pendent, cupped to flat, single white flowers, to 6cm (2½in) across, are borne on slender flower-stalks in summer. ↕ to 6m (20ft), ↔ 3m (10ft). W. China. ❄❄❄

R. multiflora. Upright, arching, very vigorous Species rose producing masses of dull, light to mid-green leaves, each with 7–9, rarely 5–11, obovate or elliptic leaflets, 1.5–5cm (½–2in) long. Large clusters of cupped to flat, single, fruit-scented white flowers, to 3cm (1¼in) across, fading to red, are borne freely but fleetingly in summer, followed by ovoid to spherical red hips, to 7mm (¼in) long. ↕ to 5m (15ft), ↔ 3m (10ft). Japan, Korea. ❄❄❄

***R.* 'Mutabilis'** see *R.* x *odorata* 'Mutabilis'.

***R.* 'National Trust'** ■ syn. *R.* 'Bad Nauheim'. Compact Hybrid Tea rose with abundant dark green foliage. Bears neatly formed, urn-shaped, fully double, scarlet-crimson flowers, 10cm (4in) across, freely from summer to autumn. ↕↔ 60cm (24in). ❄❄❄

***R.* 'Nelkenrose'** see *R.* 'F.J. Grootendorst'.

***R.* 'Nevada'** ■ Vigorous, arching Shrub rose with red stems and dense, light green leaves. Flat, semi-double, scented, creamy white flowers, 10cm (4in) across, are borne freely in early summer and sparsely in autumn. ↕↔ 2.2m (7ft). ❄❄❄

***R.* 'New Dawn'** ■ syn. *R.* 'The New Dawn'. Climber of vigorous, arching habit, with glossy, mid-green leaves. From summer to autumn, bears clusters of cupped, double, fragrant, pale pearl-pink flowers, 8cm (3in) across. Tolerates a partially shaded site. ↕ 3m (10ft), ↔ 2.5m (8ft). ❄❄❄

***R.* NEWS ('Legnews')** ■ Floribunda rose with dark green foliage. Cupped, wide-opening, double, scented, bright beetroot-purple flowers, 8cm (3in) across, are borne from summer to autumn. ↕ 60cm (24in), ↔ 50cm (20in). ❄❄❄

***R.* NICE DAY ('Chewsea'),** syn. *R.* 'Patio Queen'. Stiffly branching Climbing Miniature rose with small, glossy, dark green leaves. Cupped, double, scented, salmon-pink flowers, 5cm (2in) across, are produced from summer to autumn. ↕ 2.2m (7ft), ↔ 1.2m (4ft). ❄❄❄

***R.* 'Niphetos'.** Branching, climbing Tea rose with lance-shaped, pale green leaves. Pointed buds open to rounded, double, scented, creamy white flowers, 12cm (5in) across, produced on nodding stems, mainly in summer, a few later. ↕ 3m (10ft), ↔ 2.5m (8ft). ❄❄❄

***R.* 'Noisette Carnée'** ■ syn. *R.* 'Blush Noisette'. Branching Noisette rose with lax stems and matt, mid-green foliage. Cupped, double, spice-scented, pale pink flowers, 4cm (1½in) across, are produced from summer to autumn. Prune to maintain as a shrub. ↕ 2–4m (6–12ft), ↔ 2–2.5m (6–8ft). ❄❄❄

***R.* 'Normandica'** see *R.* 'Petite de Hollande'.

***R.* NORTHAMPTONSHIRE ('Mattdor').** Spreading Ground-cover rose with glossy, dark green foliage. Large sprays of cupped, semi-double, pearl-white

Rosa 'Mme Plantier'

R

Rosa 'Noisette Carnée'

Rosa 'Nozomi'

Rosa nutkana 'Plena'

Rosa OCTAVIA HILL ('Harzeal')

Rosa x *odorata* 'Mutabilis'

Rosa x *odorata* 'Pallida'

Rosa x *odorata* 'Viridiflora'

Rosa 'Ophelia'

Rosa ORANGES AND LEMONS ('Macoranlem')

Rosa ORANGE SUNBLAZE ('Meijikitar')

Rosa OXFORDSHIRE ('Korfullwind')

Rosa PAINTED MOON ('Dicpaint')

flowers, 4.5cm (1¾in) across, are borne freely from summer to autumn. ↕45cm (18in), ↔ 1m (3ft). ***

***R.* 'Nozomi'** ▣ syn. *R.* 'Heideröslein'. Trailing Ground-cover rose producing glossy, dark green leaves. Clusters of flat, single, pale pink-white flowers, 2.5cm (1in) across, cover the plant in summer. ↕45cm (18in), or to 1.5m (5ft) when trained on a pillar, ↔ 1.2m (4ft). ***

***R.* 'Nuit d'Orient'** see *R.* BIG PURPLE ('Stebigpu').

***R.* 'Nuits de Young'** (Old black rose). Erect Moss rose with wiry stems, brownish green mossing, and dark green leaves. In summer, bears flat, double, scented, dark maroon-purple flowers, 5cm (2in) across, showing yellow stamens. ↕1.2m (4ft), ↔ 1m (3ft). ***

R. nutkana (Nootka rose). Robust Species rose with brownish green stems and toothed, mid-green leaves, each with 5–9 ovate to elliptic leaflets, 2–5cm (¾–2in) long. In summer, bears usually solitary, cupped, single, reddish pink flowers, 5–7cm (2–3in) across, followed by spherical, purplish red hips. ↕ to 3m (10ft), ↔ 2m (6ft). North America (Alaska to N. California). ***.
'Plena' ▣ has semi-double pink flowers; ↕1.5–2.5m (5–8ft), ↔ 1.2–2m (4–6ft).

***R.* 'Ocarina'** see *R.* ANGELA RIPPON ('Ocaru').

***R.* OCTAVIA HILL ('Harzeal')** ▣ Vigorous Shrub rose with abundant glossy, dark green leaves. Sprays of several quartered-rosette, double, scented, clear rose-pink flowers, 8cm (3in) across, are borne from summer to autumn. ↕↔ 1.1m (3½ft). ***

R.* x *odorata (*R. chinensis* x *R. gigantea*). Shrubby or climbing China rose with lax, prickly stems and light green leaves comprising 3–5 narrowly ovate leaflets, 4–6cm (1½–2½in) long. From summer to autumn, bears rounded, double, white, pale pink, or pale yellow flowers, 5–8cm (2–3in) across. ↕↔ 2m (6ft) as a shrub; ↕5m (15ft), ↔ 3–4m (10–12ft) as a climber. Garden origin. **.
'Mutabilis' ▣ syn. *R. chinensis* 'Mutabilis', *R.* 'Mutabilis', *R.* 'Tipo Ideale', is shrubby, with reddish purple, sparsely prickly stems that will climb if supported, and glossy, dark green leaves, flushed purple. It produces cupped, single flowers, 6cm (2½in) across, which change from light yellow to copper-pink, and then to deep pink; ↕1.2m (4ft), ↔ 1m (3ft) as a shrub; ↕ to 3m (10ft), ↔ 2m (6ft) as a climber; *** (borderline). **'Pallida'** ▣ (Old blush China rose, Parsons' pink China rose) is bushy, with glossy, mid-green leaves. It freely bears cupped, double pink flowers, 6cm (2½in) across; ↕1m (3ft), sometimes to 3m (10ft) in mild climates, ↔ 80cm (32in); ***. **'Pseudindica'**, syn. *R.* 'Beauty of Glazenwood', *R.* 'Gold of Ophir', *R.* 'San Rafael' (Fortune's double yellow rose) is a lax Climber with glossy, light green leaves. It bears high-centred to cupped, semi-double, scented, copper-red to yellow flowers, 5cm (2in) across; ↕2.5–5m (8–15ft), ↔ 1.5–3m (5–10ft).
'Semperflorens', syn. *R. chinensis* 'Semperflorens' (Slater's crimson China rose) is open-branched, with dark green leaves and semi-double, crimson-red flowers, 6cm (2½in) across; ↕↔ 1m (3ft).
'Viridiflora' ▣ syn. *R. chinensis* 'Viridiflora', *R.* 'Lü E', *R.* 'Viridiflora' (Green rose) is upright, with glossy, dark green leaves and sprays of rosette-shaped, double flowers, 5cm (2in) across, green turning purplish green, with narrow petals that resemble sepals; ↕75cm (30in), ↔ 60cm (24in); ***

R. officinalis see *R. gallica* var. *officinalis*.

Rosa OPEN ARMS ('Chewpixcel')

R. omeiensis* f. *pteracantha see *R. sericea* subsp. *omeiensis* f. *pteracantha*.

***R.* 'Opalia'** see *R.* WHITE FLOWER CARPET ('Noaschnee').

***R.* 'Opa Pötschke'** see *R.* 'Precious Platinum'.

***R.* OPEN ARMS ('Chewpixcel')** ▣ Vigorous, arching Climbing Miniature rose with narrow, pointed, deep green leaves. Cupped, single, scented, light pink flowers, 4.5cm (1¾in) across, are borne from summer to autumn. ↕↔ 1.5m (5ft). ***

***R.* 'Ophelia'** ▣ Hybrid Tea rose with stiff growth and sparse, dark green foliage. Neatly formed, urn-shaped to cupped, double, fragrant, creamy pale pink flowers, 8cm (3in) across, are produced from summer to autumn. ↕1m (3ft), ↔ 60cm (24in). ***

***R.* ORANGES AND LEMONS ('Macoranlem')** ▣ Vigorous Floribunda rose with glossy, dark green foliage, reddish green when young. From summer to autumn, bears rounded, fully double flowers, 10cm (4in) across, with stiff, infolded, orange-yellow petals, striped scarlet, fading to pinkish red. ↕80cm (32in), ↔ 60cm (24in). ***

***R.* 'Orange Sensation'.** Vigorous, spreading Floribunda rose producing glossy, light green foliage. Rounded, double, scented, bright orange-red flowers, 8cm (3in) across, are borne from summer to autumn. ↕70cm (28in), ↔ 60cm (24in). ***

***R.* ORANGE SUNBLAZE ('Meijikitar')** ▣ syn. *R.* 'Sunblaze'. Miniature rose of compact habit, with dense, dark green leaves. Cupped, fully double, bright orange-red flowers, 4cm (1½in) across, are borne from summer to autumn. ↕↔ 30cm (12in). ***

***R.* OXFORDSHIRE ('Korfullwind')** ▣ syn. *R.* 'Baby Blanket', *R.* 'Country Lass', *R.* 'Sommermorgen'. Dense, spreading Ground-cover rose with dark green foliage. Bears cupped, double, lightly scented, pale pink flowers, 6cm (2½in) across, with gold stamens, from summer to autumn. ↕65cm (26in), ↔ 1.2m (4ft). ***

***R.* 'Paestana'** see *R.* 'Portlandica'.

***R.* PAINTED MOON ('Dicpaint')** ▣ Leafy, spreading Hybrid Tea rose producing mid-green foliage. Wide sprays of cupped, double flowers, 9cm

R

Rosa 'Paul Neyron'

Rosa PAUL SHIRVILLE ('Harqueterwife')

Rosa 'Paul's Lemon Pillar'

Rosa PEACE ('Mme A. Meilland')

Rosa PEARL DRIFT ('Leggab')

Rosa 'Penelope'

Rosa 'Perle d'Or'

Rosa PHEASANT ('Kordapt')

Rosa PICCADILLY ('Macar')

Rosa pimpinellifolia 'Dunwich Rose'

Rosa pimpinellifolia 'Grandiflora'

Rosa pimpinellifolia 'Plena'

(3½in) across, light yellow, strongly suffused pink and crimson, are borne from summer to autumn. ↕75cm (30in), ↔ 60cm (24in). ***

R. 'Panachée d'Angers' see *R.* 'Commandant Beaurepaire'.

R. PAPA MEILLAND ('Meisar'). Hybrid Tea rose with a lanky habit and olive-green leaves. High-centred, fully double, very fragrant, dark velvet-crimson flowers, 12cm (5in) across, are borne on long stems from summer to autumn. Susceptible to mildew. ↕1m (3ft), ↔ 60cm (24in). **

R. PARADISE ('Weizeip'), syn. *R.* 'Burning Sky'. Vigorous Hybrid Tea rose producing glossy, dark green leaves. From summer to autumn, bears high-centred, double, scented, lavender-pink flowers, 10cm (4in) across, edged ruby-red. ↕1.2m (4ft), ↔ 70cm (28in). ***

R. 'Para Ti' see *R.* 'Pour Toi'.

R. 'Parkdirektor Riggers'. Stiff, vigorous Climber with glossy, dark green leaves. Large clusters of cupped, semi-double scarlet flowers, 6cm (2½in) across, with wavy-margined petals, are borne from summer to autumn. ↕4m (12ft), ↔ 2.5m (8ft). ***

R. PASCALI ('Lenip'). Hybrid Tea rose with sparse, dark green foliage. Neatly formed, urn-shaped, double white flowers, 9cm (3½in) across, are borne from summer to autumn. ↕75cm (30in), ↔ 50cm (20in). ***

R. 'Patio Queen' see *R.* NICE DAY ('Chewsea').

R. 'Paul Neyron' ▣ Vigorous, upright Hybrid Perpetual rose with olive-green leaves. Rounded, fully double, scented flowers, to 15cm (6in) across, with ruffled, lilac-tinged, deep pink petals, are borne from summer to autumn. ↕1.5m (5ft), ↔ 1.2m (4ft). ***

R. 'Paul's Himalayan Musk', syn. *R.* 'Paul's Himalayan Rambler'. Rampant Rambler with trailing shoots and arching, dark green leaves. Large clusters of rosette-shaped, double, pale pink flowers, 4cm (1½in) across, are borne freely in summer. Effective trained on a tree. ↕↔ 10m (30ft). ***

R. 'Paul's Himalayan Rambler' see *R.* 'Paul's Himalayan Musk'.

R. PAUL SHIRVILLE ('Harqueterwife') ▣ syn. *R.* 'Heart Throb'. Hybrid Tea rose of spreading, shrubby habit, with dark reddish green foliage. High-centred, double, fragrant, rose-pink to salmon-pink flowers, 10cm (4in) across, are borne from summer to autumn. ↕1m (3ft), ↔ 75cm (30in). ***

R. 'Paul's Lemon Pillar' ▣ syn. *R.* 'Lemon Pillar'. Stiff, upright Climber with dark green leaves and high-centred to rounded, fully double, lemon-scented white flowers, 12cm (5in) across, borne in summer. ↕4m (12ft), ↔ 3m (10ft). ***

R. 'Paul's Scarlet Climber'. Very vigorous, arching Climber with dense, semi-glossy, mid-green foliage. Clusters of many cupped, double, bright red flowers, 8cm (3in) across, are borne freely in summer. ↕↔ 3m (10ft). ***

R. 'Paul Transon'. Vigorous, lax Rambler producing glossy, dark green foliage. Flat, fully double, scented, copper- to salmon-pink flowers, 8cm (3in) across, with pleated petals, are borne in summer, also later in warm sites. ↕3m (10ft), ↔ 2.5m (8ft). ***

R. PEACE ('Mme A. Meilland') ▣ syn. *R.* 'Gioia', *R.* 'Gloria Dei'. Vigorous, shrubby Hybrid Tea rose with glossy, dark green foliage. High-centred to rounded, fully double, scented, pink-tinged yellow flowers, 15cm (6in) across, are produced from summer to autumn. ↕1.2m (4ft), ↔ 1m (3ft). ***

R. PEARL ANNIVERSARY ('Whitston'). Compact, bushy Patio rose with mid-green leaves. Bears cupped, double, slightly scented, pearl-pink flowers, 5cm (2in) across, from summer to autumn. ↕↔ 45cm (18in). ***

Rosa PENNY LANE ('Hardwell')

R. PEARL DRIFT ('Leggab') ▣ Vigorous Shrub rose of spreading habit, with abundant glossy, dark green leaves. From summer to autumn, bears clusters of cupped, semi-double, scented, pale pink flowers, 10cm (4in) across. ↕1m (3ft), ↔ 1.2m (4ft). ***

R. 'Peaudouce' see *R.* ELINA ('Dicjana').

R. PEEK A BOO ('Dicgrow'), syn. *R.* 'Brass Ring'. Dense, cushion-forming Patio rose with narrow, dark green leaves. Sprays of many urn-shaped, double, apricot-pink flowers, 4cm (1½in) across, are borne freely from summer to autumn. ↕↔ 45cm (18in). ***

R. PEER GYNT ('Korol'). Vigorous Hybrid Tea rose with abundant rich green foliage. Rounded, fully double, lightly scented yellow flowers, 11cm (4½in) across, edged reddish pink, are borne from summer to autumn. ↕80cm (32in), ↔ 60cm (24in). ***

R. 'Penelope' ▣ Bushy, dense Hybrid Musk rose with dark green leaves. Large clusters of well-spaced, cupped to flat, semi-double, scented, pale creamy pink flowers, 7cm (3in) across, are borne from summer to autumn. ↕↔ 1.1m (3½ft). ***

R. PENNY LANE ('Hardwell') ▣ Vigorous, free-branching Climber with glossy, dark green leaves. Quartered-rosette, double, scented, pearl-pink flowers, 10cm (4in) across, tinged light apricot, are borne from summer to autumn. ↕3m (10ft), ↔ 1.8m (6ft). ***

R. 'Perle d'Or' ▣ syn. *R.* 'Yellow Cécile Brunner'. China rose forming a leafy, twiggy shrub with glossy, dark green foliage. From summer to autumn, neatly formed, urn-shaped, fully double, pale apricot flowers, 4cm (1½in) across, are borne in clusters on slender stems. ↕to 1.2m (4ft), ↔ 1m (3ft). ***

R. 'Perpetual White Moss' see *R.* 'Quatre Saisons Blanche Mousseuse'.

R. 'Petite de Hollande', syn. *R.* 'Normandica', *R.* 'Petite Junon de Hollande', *R.* 'Pompon des Dames'. Vigorous, compact, bushy Centifolia rose with mid-green leaves. Clusters of rounded, fully double, many-petalled, fragrant, rose-pink flowers, 5cm (2in) across, are borne in summer. ↕↔ 1m (3ft). ***

R. 'Petite Junon de Hollande' see *R.* 'Petite de Hollande'.

R. 'Petite Lisette'. Damask rose with toothed, greyish green leaves. Well-spaced clusters of pompon, fully double, scented, rose-pink flowers, 2.5cm (1in) across, with infolded centre petals, are borne in summer. ↕↔ 1m (3ft). ***

R. PHEASANT ('Kordapt') ▣ syn. *R.* 'Heidekönigin'. Ground-cover rose of creeping habit, producing abundant glossy, mid-green leaves. Cupped, double pink flowers, 5cm (2in) across, showing yellow stamens, are borne in clusters along the stems in summer. ↕50cm (20in), ↔ 3m (10ft). ***

R. 'Phoebe's Frilled Pink' see *R.* 'Fimbriata'.

R. 'Phyllis Bide'. Vigorous Climber with many lax shoots and glossy, mid-green leaves with narrow leaflets. From summer to autumn, bears wide clusters of rosette-shaped, double flowers, yellow flushed pink, 5cm (2in) across. ↕2.5m (8ft), ↔ 1.5m (5ft). ***

R. PICCADILLY ('Macar') ▣ Vigorous Hybrid Tea rose producing abundant glossy, reddish green foliage. From summer to autumn, bears high-centred, double, bicoloured, red and yellow flowers, 12cm (5in) across. ↕80cm (32in), ↔ 60cm (24in). ***

R. PICCOLO ('Tanolokip'). Floribunda rose with glossy, dark green leaves. Cupped to flat, double, orange-red flowers, 6cm (2½in) across, are borne from summer to autumn. ↕↔ 50cm (20in). ***

R. 'Pierre de Ronsard' see *R.* EDEN ROSE '88 ('Meiviolin').

R. pimpinellifolia, syn. *R. spinosissima* (Burnet rose, Scotch rose, Scots rose). Dense, spreading, prickly Species rose of suckering habit, with small, fern-like, dark green leaves composed of 7–9, rarely 11, broadly elliptic or broadly obovate to almost rounded leaflets, 0.5–2cm (¼–¾in) long. Solitary, cupped, single, creamy white flowers, 5cm (2in) across, are borne freely in early summer, followed by spherical, purplish black hips. ↕to 1m (3ft), ↔ 1.2m (4ft). W. and S. Europe, S.W. and C. Asia to China and Korea. ***. **var. *altaica*** see 'Grandiflora'. **'Dunwichensis'** see 'Dunwich Rose'.

Rosa Pink Bells ('Poulbells')

Rosa 'Pink Favorite'

Rosa Pink Flower Carpet ('Noatraum')

Rosa 'Pink Grootendorst'

Rosa 'Pink Perpetue'

Rosa L'Aimant ('Harzola')

Rosa Polar Star ('Tanlarpost')

Rosa 'Portlandica'

Rosa Pot o' Gold ('Dicdivine')

Rosa 'Precious Platinum'

Rosa 'Président de Sèze'

Rosa Pretty Polly ('Meitonje')

'Dunwich Rose' ■ syn. *R.* 'Dunwich Rose', *R. pimpinellifolia* 'Dunwichensis', is vigorous and twiggy, with a low, hummock-forming habit and masses of short-stemmed, cupped to flat, scented, creamy white flowers, 5cm (2in) across, with prominent gold stamens; ↕ 65cm (26in). **'Grandiflora'** ■ syn. *R.* 'Grandiflora', *R. pimpinellifolia* var. *altaica*, is vigorous and of upright habit, with twiggy stems and cupped to flat, creamy white flowers, 6cm (2½in) across, with yellow stamens; ↕ to 2m (6ft). **'Plena'** ■ has double white flowers.
***R.* Pink Bells ('Poulbells')** ■ Vigorous, spreading Ground-cover rose of dense habit, with abundant mid-green foliage. Pompon, fully double, bright pink flowers, 2.5cm (1in) across, are borne along the stems in summer. ↕ 75cm (30in), ↔ 1.5m (5ft). ❄❄❄
***R.* 'Pink Cover'** see *R.* Essex ('Poulnoz').
***R.* 'Pink Favorite'** ■ Branching Hybrid Tea rose with long, glossy, dark green leaves. High-centred to cupped, double, bright rose-pink flowers, deeper in bud, 9cm (3½in) across, are borne freely from summer to autumn. ↕ 75cm (30in), ↔ 60cm (24in). ❄❄❄
***R.* Pink Flower Carpet ('Noatraum')** ■ syn. *R.* 'Flower Carpet', *R.* 'Heidetraum'. Vigorous Ground-cover rose with abundant glossy, bright green leaves. Showy clusters of cupped, double, deep rose-pink flowers, 5cm (2in) across, are borne freely along the stems from summer to autumn. ↕ 75cm (30in), ↔ 1.2m (4ft). ❄❄❄
***R.* 'Pink Grootendorst'** ■ Rugosa rose of upright, dense habit, with prickly stems and coarse, leathery, dark green leaves. Crowded clusters of rosette-shaped, double, rose-pink flowers, 4cm (1½in) across, with frilled petals, are borne from summer to autumn. ↕ 1.3m (4½ft), ↔ 1.1m (3½ft). ❄❄❄
***R.* 'Pink Nevada'** see *R.* 'Marguerite Hilling'.
***R.* 'Pink Parfait'.** Floribunda rose of compact habit producing mid-green foliage. High-centred to cupped, double flowers, 9cm (3½in) across, in shades of light pink, are borne freely from summer to autumn. ↕ 70cm (28in), ↔ 60cm (24in). ❄❄❄

Rosa 'Pour Toi'

***R.* 'Pink Perpetue'** ■ Stiffly branched Climber with leathery, dark green leaves. Rounded to cupped, double, scented pink flowers, 8cm (3in) across, with a deeper pink reverse to the petals, are borne from summer to autumn. ↕ to 3m (10ft), ↔ 2.5m (8ft). ❄❄❄
***R.* 'Pink Sunsation'** see *R.* Berkshire ('Korpinka').
***R.* 'Pink Symphony'** see *R.* Pretty Polly ('Meitonje').
***R.* 'Poesie'** see *R.* Tournament of Roses ('Jacient').
***R.* Poetry in Motion ('Harelan')** ■ Vigorous, upright Hybrid Tea rose with large, leathery, deep green leaves. Bears high-centred, double, scented yellow flowers, 11cm (4½in) across, edged pale rose-red, from summer to autumn. ↕ 1m (3ft), ↔ 60cm (24in). ❄❄❄
***R.* Polar Star ('Tanlarpost')** ■ syn. *R.* 'Polarstern'. Vigorous, free-branching Hybrid Tea rose with dark green leaves. High-centred, fully double, creamy white flowers, 11cm (4½in) across, are borne on long, stiff stems, from summer to autumn. ↕ 1m (3ft), ↔ 70cm (28in). ❄❄❄
***R.* 'Polarstern'** see *R.* Polar Star ('Tanlarpost').
***R.* 'Pompon de Paris'** see *R.* 'Rouletii'.
***R.* 'Pompon des Dames'** see *R.* 'Petite de Hollande'.
***R.* 'Pompon des Princes'** see *R.* 'Ispahan'.
***R.* 'Portlandica'** ■ syn. *R.* 'Duchess of Portland', *R.* 'Paestana' (Portland rose). Vigorous Portland rose of shrubby habit, with dark green leaves. Cupped, single to semi-double, cerise-red flowers, 8cm (3in) across, with golden stamens, are borne in summer, and again in autumn if dead-headed. ↕↔ 1m (3ft). ❄❄❄
***R.* Pot o' Gold ('Dicdivine')** ■ Hybrid Tea rose of compact, spreading habit, with abundant mid-green foliage. Rounded, fully double, fragrant, golden yellow flowers, 9cm (3½in) across, are borne from summer to autumn. ↕ 75cm (30in), ↔ 60cm (24in). ❄❄❄
***R.* 'Pour Toi'** ■ syn. *R.* 'Para Ti'. Upright Miniature rose with dark green leaves. Urn-shaped, double, lightly scented, creamy white flowers, 3cm (1¼in) across, are produced from summer to autumn. ↕ 30cm (12in), ↔ 25cm (10in). ❄❄❄
***R.* 'Precious Platinum'** ■ syn. *R.* 'Opa Pötschke'. Vigorous Hybrid Tea rose of uneven growth, producing glossy, dark green leaves. Rounded, fully double, bright crimson-scarlet flowers, 10cm (4in) across, are borne from summer to autumn. ↕ 1m (3ft), ↔ 65cm (26in). ❄❄❄
***R.* 'Président de Sèze'** ■ syn. *R.* 'Jenny Duval', *R.* 'Mme Hébert'. Vigorous Gallica rose of open habit, with greyish green foliage. Quartered-rosette, fully double, fragrant, pale lilac-pink flowers, 10cm (4in) across, with deep magenta margins, are borne in summer. ↕↔ 1.2m (4ft). ❄❄❄
***R.* Pretty Lady ('Scrivo').** Bushy, rounded Floribunda rose with dark green foliage. Cupped, semi-double, slightly fragrant, pearl-pink flowers, 9cm (3½in) across, are borne from summer to autumn. ↕ 90cm (36in), ↔ 75cm (30in). ❄❄❄
***R.* Pretty Polly ('Meitonje')** ■ syn. *R.* 'Pink Symphony', *R.* 'Sweet Sunblaze'. Compact, rounded Patio rose with abundant dark green leaves. Many cupped, fully double, rose-pink flowers, 4.5cm (1¾in) across, are borne from summer to autumn. ↕ 40cm (16in), ↔ 45cm (18in). ❄❄❄
***R.* Pride of England ('Harencore')** ■ Vigorous, upright Hybrid Tea rose with mid-green foliage. High-centred to

Rosa Pride of England ('Harencore')

Rosa primula

Rosa PRINCESS MICHAEL OF KENT ('Harlightly')

Rosa PRINCESS OF WALES ('Hardinkum')

Rosa PRISTINE ('Jacpico')

Rosa PURPLE TIGER ('Jacpurr')

Rosa 'Queen Elizabeth'

Rosa QUEEN MOTHER ('Korquemu')

Rosa 'Ramona'

Rosa 'Raubritter'

Rosa RED BLANKET ('Intercell')

Rosa REGENSBERG ('Macyoumis')

Rosa 'Reine des Violettes'

cupped, double, lightly scented, deep red flowers, 12cm (5in) across, are borne from summer to autumn. ↕ 1.1m (3½ft), ↔ 65cm (26in). ❄❄❄

***R.* 'Prima'** see *R.* MANY HAPPY RETURNS ('Harwanted').

***R.* 'Prima Ballerina'.** Vigorous Hybrid Tea rose, often with scaly marks on the stems, producing leathery, mid-green leaves. Urn-shaped, double, fragrant, warm rose-pink flowers, 10cm (4in) across, are borne from summer to autumn. ↕ 1m (3ft), ↔ 60cm (24in). ❄❄❄

R. primula ▣ (Incense rose). Erect to arching Species rose with aromatic, dense, fern-like, mid-green leaves comprising 9, rarely 7–13, elliptic to obovate or inversely lance-shaped leaflets, to 2cm (¾in) long, on slender, reddish green stems. Solitary, cupped, single, scented, pale primrose-yellow flowers, to 5cm (2in) across, are borne in late spring; they are followed by spherical to inversely cone-shaped, brownish maroon hips. ↕ to 3m (10ft), ↔ 2m (6ft). Asia (Turkmenistan to N. China). ❄❄❄ (borderline)

***R.* 'Prince Charles'.** Arching, lax Bourbon rose with smooth stems and leathery, dark green leaves. Loosely formed, rounded to cupped, double, fragrant, crimson-purple flowers, 10cm (4in) across, fading to lilac-red, are borne in summer. ↕ to 1.5m (5ft), ↔ 1.3m (4ft). ❄❄❄

***R.* PRINCESS ALICE ('Hartanna')** ▣ syn. *R.* 'Brite Lites', *R.* 'Zonta Rose'. Floribunda rose of narrow habit, with mid-green leaves comprising lance-shaped leaflets. Long-stemmed sprays of rounded, double, bright yellow flowers, 6cm (2½in) across, are borne from summer to autumn. ↕ 1.1m (3½ft), ↔ 60cm (24in). ❄❄❄

***R.* PRINCESS MICHAEL OF KENT ('Harlightly')** ▣ Compact Floribunda rose with glossy, bright green foliage. Rounded, fully double, scented yellow flowers, 9cm (3½in) across, are borne from summer to autumn. ↕ 60cm (24in), ↔ 50cm (20in). ❄❄❄

Rosa PRINCESS ALICE ('Hartanna')

***R.* PRINCESS OF WALES ('Hardinkum')** ▣ Dense, compact Floribunda rose with glossy, dark green leaves. Bears cupped, double, scented white flowers, 10cm (4in) across, from summer to autumn. ↕ 75cm (30in), ↔ 60cm (24in). ❄❄❄

***R.* 'Prinz Eugen van Savoyen'** see *R.* AMBER QUEEN ('Harroony').

***R.* PRISTINE ('Jacpico')** ▣ Vigorous Hybrid Tea rose producing dark green leaves with very large leaflets. From summer to autumn, bears high-centred, double, scented flowers, 12cm (5in) across, ivory flushed pale pink with long, overlapping petals. ↕ 1.2m (4ft), ↔ 75cm (30in). ❄❄❄

***R.* 'Prosperity'.** Dense, arching Hybrid Musk rose with many dark green leaves. From summer to autumn, bears large clusters of rosette-shaped, double, scented, creamy white flowers, 5cm (2in) across, flushed pale pink. ↕ to 2.5m (8ft), ↔ 1.2m (4ft). ❄❄❄

***R.* PURPLE TIGER ('Jacpurr')** ▣ syn. *R.* 'Impressionist'. Bushy Floribunda rose with glossy, mid-green leaves. Cupped, double, lightly scented, purple flowers, 6cm (2½in) across, with blush-pink stripes, are produced from summer to autumn. ↕ 75cm (30in), ↔ 55cm (22in). ❄❄❄

***R.* 'Pyrenees'** see *R.* KENT ('Poulcov').

***R.* 'Quatre Saisons'** see *R.* x *damascena* var. *semperflorens.*

***R.* 'Quatre Saisons Blanche Mousseuse'**, syn. *R.* 'Perpetual White Moss', *R.* 'Rosier de Thionville'. Open, arching Moss rose, a sport of *R.* x *damascena* var. *semperflorens*, with light green leaves, and stems and buds covered with stiff, brownish green moss. Loosely formed, cupped to flat, double, fragrant white flowers, 9cm (3½in) across, are borne in summer, and sporadically in autumn. ↕ 1.5m (5ft), ↔ 1.2m (4ft). ❄❄❄

***R.* 'Queen Elizabeth'** ▣ syn. *R.* 'The Queen Elizabeth'. Vigorous Floribunda rose with leathery, dark green leaves. Rounded, fully double pink flowers, 10cm (4in) across, are borne on long, stiff stems from summer to autumn. ↕ to 2.2m (7ft), ↔ 1m (3ft). ❄❄❄

***R.* QUEEN MOTHER ('Korquemu')** ▣ Patio rose of spreading habit, with abundant glossy, mid-green foliage. Many cupped to flat, semi-double, clear pink flowers, 6cm (2½in) across, are borne from summer to autumn. ↕ 40cm (16in), ↔ 60cm (24in). ❄❄❄

***R.* 'Queen of Beauty & Fragrance'** see *R.* 'Souvenir de la Malmaison'.

***R.* 'Queen of Denmark'** see *R.* 'Königin von Dänemark'.

***R.* 'Queen of the Violets'** see *R.* 'Reine des Violettes'.

***R.* 'Rambling Rector'** ▣ Rampant Rambler with strong, arching stems and abundant grey-green foliage. Clusters of many cupped to flat, semi-double, scented, creamy white flowers, 4cm (1½in) across, showing golden stamens, are borne in summer, followed by spherical red hips in autumn. ↕↔ 6m (20ft). ❄❄❄

***R.* 'Ramona'** ▣ syn. *R.* x *anemonoides* 'Ramona', *R.* 'Red Cherokee'. Stiff, open Climber with sparse, dark green leaves. Flat, single, carmine-red flowers, 10cm (4in) across, with a greyish red reverse to the petals and gold stamens, are borne in early summer. ↕ 2.5m (8ft), ↔ 3m (10ft). ❄❄

***R.* 'Raspberry Ice'** see *R.* HANNAH GORDON ('Korweiso').

***R.* 'Raubritter'** ▣ syn. *R.* 'Macrantha Raubritter'. Shrub rose of lax, spreading habit, with dark greyish green leaves. Clusters of many rounded, semi-double pink flowers, 5cm (2in) across, are borne in summer. ↕ to 1m (3ft), ↔ 2m (6ft). ❄❄❄

***R.* 'Red Ballerina'** see *R.* MARJORIE FAIR ('Harhero').

***R.* RED BLANKET ('Intercell')** ▣ Ground-cover rose of spreading habit, with abundant dark green leaves. Cupped, then flat, semi-double flowers, to 7cm (3in) across, are rose-red paling to white at the petal bases, are produced in wide, showy clusters from summer to autumn. ↕ 75cm (30in), ↔ 1.2m (4ft). ❄❄❄

***R.* 'Red Cherokee'** see *R.* 'Ramona'.

***R.* 'Red Dorothy Perkins'** see *R.* 'Excelsa'.

***R.* 'Red Prince'** see *R.* 'Fountain'.

***R.* 'Red Ribbons'** see *R.* CHILTERNS ('Kortemma').

***R.* 'Red Yesterday'** see *R.* MARJORIE FAIR ('Harhero').

***R.* REGENSBERG ('Macyoumis')** ▣ syn. *R.* 'Buffalo Bill', *R.* 'Young Mistress'. Floribunda rose of short, dense habit, with glossy, mid-green leaves. Cupped,

Rosa 'Reine Victoria'

Rosa REMEMBER ME ('Cocdestin')

Rosa RENAISSANCE ('Harzart')

Rosa 'Rise 'n' Shine'

Rosa ROBIN REDBREAST ('Interrob')

Rosa ROB ROY ('Cocrob')

Rosa ROBUSTA ('Korgosa')

Rosa 'Roger Lambelin'

Rosa ROSEMARY HARKNESS ('Harrowbond')

Rosa 'Roseraie de l'Haÿ'

Rosa ROSY CUSHION ('Interall')

Rosa 'Rosy Mantle'

double flowers, opening to 11cm (4½in) across, deep pink marked with white, are borne in dense clusters from summer to autumn. ↕ 40cm (16in), ↔ 50cm (20in). ❄❄❄

***R.* 'Reine des Neiges'** see *R.* 'Frau Karl Druschki'.

***R.* 'Reine des Violettes'** ■ syn. *R.* 'Queen of the Violets'. Arching Hybrid Perpetual rose with smooth stems and greyish green leaves. From summer to autumn, bears quartered-rosette, fully double, fragrant, violet-purple flowers, 8cm (3in) across. ↕ 1.5m (5ft), ↔ 1.2m (4ft). ❄❄❄

***R.* 'Reine Victoria'** ■ syn. *R.* 'La Reine Victoria'. Lax Bourbon rose with slender stems and light green leaves. Cupped, double, scented, light rose-pink flowers, 8cm (3in) across, are borne from summer to autumn. ↕ 2m (6ft), ↔ 1.2m (4ft). ❄❄❄

***R.* REMEMBER ME ('Cocdestin')** ■ Vigorous Hybrid Tea rose of stiff habit, with abundant glossy, dark green leaves. High-centred, fully double, copper-orange flowers, 9cm (3½in) across, are borne singly and in wide sprays from summer to autumn. ↕ 1m (3ft), ↔ 60cm (24in). ❄❄❄

***R.* REMEMBRANCE ('Harxampton').** Compact Floribunda rose with glossy, dark green leaves. Cupped, double, lightly scented, bright deep scarlet flowers, 9cm (3½in) across, are borne from summer to autumn. ↕ 60cm (24in), ↔ 55cm (22in). ❄❄❄

***R.* RENAISSANCE ('Harzart')** ■ Vigorous, bushy Hybrid Tea rose with large, dark green leaves. Cupped, double, very fragrant, blush-pink to white flowers, 10cm (4in) across, are produced from summer to autumn. ↕↔ 75cm (30in). ❄❄❄

***R.* RHAPSODY IN BLUE ('Frantasia').** Upright Shrub rose of uneven habit, with leathery, light green foliage. Cupped, semi-double, very fragrant, bright purple flowers, 8cm (3in) across, are borne from summer to autumn. ↕ 1.6m (5½ft), ↔ 90cm (36in). ❄❄❄

***R.* 'Rise 'n' Shine'** ■ syn. *R.* 'Golden Sunblaze'. Miniature rose of upright habit, with dark green leaves. Urn-shaped, fully double yellow flowers, 4cm (1½in) across, are borne from summer to autumn. ↕ 40cm (16in), ↔ 25cm (10in). ❄❄❄

***R.* 'Robert le Diable'.** Centifolia rose of bushy, lax habit, with narrow, dark green leaves. In summer, bears cupped to flat, semi-double, scented purple flowers, 8cm (3in) across, shaded slate-grey and splashed with cerise-red. ↕↔ 1m (3ft). ❄❄❄

***R.* ROBIN REDBREAST ('Interrob')** ■ Dwarf Ground-cover rose of dense habit, with many glossy, mid-green leaves. Dense clusters of cupped to flat, single, dark red flowers, 4.5cm (1¾in) across, with pale white centres, are produced from summer to autumn. ↕ 45cm (18in), ↔ 60cm (24in). ❄❄❄

***R.* ROB ROY ('Cocrob')** ■ Upright Floribunda rose with glossy, dark green leaves. High-centred to cupped, double, lightly scented, crimson-scarlet flowers, 9cm (3½in) across, are borne from summer to autumn. ↕ 90cm (36in), ↔ 60cm (24in). ❄❄❄

***R.* ROBUSTA ('Korgosa')** ■ syn. *R.* 'Kordes Robusta'. Vigorous, stiff-growing Rugosa rose with prickly stems and leathery, dark green leaves. Clusters of cupped, single, wine-red flowers, 6cm (2½in) across, with wavy-margined petals, are produced from summer to autumn. ↕ 1.5m (5ft), ↔ 1m (3ft). ❄❄❄

***R.* 'Roger Lambelin'** ■ Hybrid Perpetual rose with a shrubby habit, producing dark green leaves. Loosely formed, rounded, double, fragrant flowers, 7cm (3in) across, with maroon, white-margined petals, are borne predominantly in summer. Prone to rust. ↕↔ 1m (3ft). ❄❄❄

***R.* 'Rose Capucine'** see *R. foetida* 'Bicolor'.

***R.* 'Rose de Meaux'** see *R.* 'De Meaux'.

***R.* 'Rose des Maures'** see *R.* 'Sissinghurst Castle'.

***R.* 'Rose d'Isfahan'** see *R.* 'Ispahan'.

***R.* ROSE GAUJARD ('Gaumo').** Strong-growing Hybrid Tea rose with abundant glossy, dark green foliage. Urn-shaped, double, cherry-red flowers, 10cm (4in) across, with a pale pink reverse to the petals, are borne from summer to autumn. ↕ 1m (3ft), ↔ 75cm (30in). ❄❄❄

Rosa 'Rambling Rector'

***R.* 'Rose-Marie Viaud'.** Vigorous Rambler with conspicuously veined, light green leaves. Sprays of rosette-shaped, double, lavender-pink to purple flowers, 4cm (1½in) across, fading to greyish mauve, are produced in summer. ↕ to 5m (15ft), ↔ 2.5m (8ft). ❄❄❄

***R.* ROSEMARY HARKNESS ('Harrowbond')** ■ Vigorous Hybrid Tea rose of shrubby habit, with glossy, dark green foliage. Urn-shaped buds open to rounded, double, fragrant, orange to salmon-pink flowers, 10cm (4in) across, from summer to autumn. ↕↔ 80cm (32in). ❄❄❄

***R.* 'Roseraie de l'Haÿ'** ■ Vigorous, dense Rugosa rose with leathery, wrinkled, light green leaves. Cupped to flat, double, strongly scented, rich purple-red flowers, 11cm (4½in) across, are borne from summer to autumn. ↕ 2.2m (7ft), ↔ 2m (6ft). ❄❄❄

***R.* 'Rosier de Thionville'** see *R.* 'Quatre Saisons Blanche Mousseuse'.

***R.* ROSY CUSHION ('Interall')** ■ Dense, spreading Shrub rose with abundant glossy, dark green leaves. From summer to autumn, bears clusters of cupped, semi-double, scented pink flowers, 6cm (2½in) across, with off-white centres. ↕ 1m (3ft), ↔ 1.2m (4ft). ❄❄❄

***R.* ROSY FUTURE ('Harwaderox').** Upright Patio rose of uneven habit, with small, glossy, dark green leaves. Bears urn-shaped, semi-double, scented, pinkish red flowers, 6cm (2½in) across, from summer to autumn. ↕ 55cm (22in), ↔ 40cm (16in). ❄❄❄

***R.* 'Rosy Mantle'** ■ Stiff Climber of open habit, with sparse, dark green leaves. High-centred, fully double, fragrant, rose- to salmon-pink flowers, 10cm (4in) across, are borne from summer to autumn. ↕ 2.5m (8ft), ↔ 2m (6ft). ❄❄❄

***R.* 'Rouletii'**, syn. *R. chinensis* var. *minima*, *R.* 'Pompon de Paris'. Compact, Miniature rose with thin stems and mid-green leaves comprising many lance-shaped leaflets. Cupped, double, deep pink flowers, 2cm (¾in) across, are borne freely from summer to autumn. ↕↔ 20cm (8in). ❄❄❄

R. roxburghii ■ syn. *R. roxburghii* 'Plena' (Burr rose, Chestnut rose, Chinquapin rose). Vigorous, stiff-

Rosa roxburghii

Rosa ROYAL WILLIAM ('Korzaun')

Rosa rubiginosa

Rosa rugosa

Rosa 'Salet'

Rosa 'Sally Holmes'

Rosa 'Sanders' White Rambler'

Rosa 'Sarah van Fleet'

Rosa SAVOY HOTEL ('Harvintage')

Rosa 'Seagull'

Rosa SEXY REXY ('Macrexy')

Rosa SHEILA'S PERFUME ('Harsherry')

growing Species rose with flaky bark and light to mid-green leaves, each composed of 7, rarely 17–19, narrowly ovate to obovate leaflets, 1.5–2.5cm (½–1in) long. Solitary, neatly formed, rounded, double, lilac-pink flowers, 8cm (3in) across, open from prickly buds in summer. ↕↔ 2m (6ft). E. Asia. ❄❄❄. **'Plena'** see *R. roxburghii.*
***R.* 'Royal Dane'** see *R.* TROIKA ('Poumidor').
***R.* 'Royal Highness'**, syn. *R.* 'Königliche Hoheit'. Hybrid Tea rose producing strong stems and leathery, dark green leaves. High-centred, fully double, fragrant, pearl-pink flowers, 12cm (5in) across, are borne from summer to autumn. ↕ 1.1m (3½ft), ↔ 60cm (24in). ❄❄❄
***R.* ROYAL WILLIAM ('Korzaun')** ▣ syn. *R.* 'Duftzauber '84'. Vigorous Hybrid Tea rose with dark green leaves. High-centred, fully double, fragrant, deep crimson flowers, 12cm (5in) across, are borne from summer to autumn. ↕ 1m (3ft), ↔ 75cm (30in). ❄❄❄
R. rubiginosa ▣ syn. *R. eglanteria* (Eglantine rose, Sweet briar). Vigorous, arching, prickly Species rose with apple-scented, dark green leaves composed of 5–9 ovate leaflets, 2.5–4cm (1–1½in) long. Cupped, single, rose-pink flowers, 2.5cm (1in) across, are produced in midsummer, followed by ovoid to spherical red hips in autumn. ↕↔ to 2.5m (8ft). Europe, N. Africa to W. Asia. ❄❄❄

Rosa rugosa var. *rosea*

R. rubrifolia see *R. glauca.*
R. rugosa ▣ (Hedgehog rose, Japanese rose, Ramanas rose). Vigorous, dense Species rose with very prickly stems and wrinkled, leathery, dark green leaves, each composed of 7–9, rarely up to 11, narrowly oblong leaflets, 2.5–5cm (1–2in) long. Cupped, single, fragrant, violet-carmine-red flowers, 8cm (3in) across, showing yellow stamens, are borne singly or in small clusters from summer to autumn, followed by tomato-shaped, red to orange-red hips. Good as a hedge. ↕↔ 1–2.5m (3–8ft). E. Russia, N. China, Korea, Japan. ❄❄❄. **var. *alba*** has white flowers, to 9cm (3½in) across, opening from pale pink buds. **var. *rosea*** ▣ has rose-pink flowers. **var. *rubra***, syn. f. *rubra*, has purplish red flowers. **'Scabrosa'** see *R.* 'Scabrosa'.
***R.* ST. CECILIA ('Ausmit').** Upright Shrub rose with mid-green leaves and neatly spaced, cupped, fully double, myrrh-scented, pale apricot-pink to white flowers, 10cm (4in) across, borne on bowed stems from summer to autumn. ↕ 1m (3ft), ↔ 75cm (30in). ❄❄❄
***R.* 'St. Nicholas'.** Vigorous, erect, prickly Damask rose with abundant downy, dark green foliage. Cupped, semi-double, scented, rose-pink flowers, 12cm (5in) across, with golden stamens, are borne in summer, followed by ellipsoid, orange-red hips. ↕ to 2m (6ft), ↔ 1.2m (4ft). ❄❄❄
***R.* 'Salet'** ▣ Upright, arching Moss rose with lightly mossed stems and matt, pale green foliage. Bears rounded, double, fragrant, clear rose-pink flowers, 7cm (3in) across, mainly in summer. ↕ 1.2m (4ft), ↔ 1m (3ft). ❄❄❄
***R.* 'Sally Holmes'** ▣ Upright, narrow Shrub rose with glossy, dark green leaves. Large clusters of many wide, cupped, single, scented, creamy white flowers, 9cm (3½in) across, are borne on long stems from summer to autumn. ↕ 2m (6ft), ↔ 1m (3ft). ❄❄❄
***R.* SAMARITAN ('Harverag')**, syn. *R.* 'Fragrant Surprise'. Hybrid Tea rose with abundant glossy, mid-green foliage. From summer to autumn, wide sprays of pointed buds open to quartered-rosette, fully double, scented flowers, 9cm (3½in) across, which age from apricot-pink to orange-red. ↕ 70cm (28in), ↔ 60cm (24in). ❄❄❄

***R.* 'Sanders' White Rambler'** ▣ Vigorous, arching Rambler of lax growth, with abundant glossy, light green leaves. Bears sprays of many rosette-shaped, fully double, scented white flowers, 5cm (2in) across, in late summer. ↕↔ to 4m (12ft). ❄❄❄
***R.* 'San Rafael'** see *R.* x *odorata* 'Pseudindica'.
***R.* 'Sarah van Fleet'** ▣ Vigorous, erect to arching Rugosa rose producing large, wrinkled, bronze-green leaves. Cupped, semi-double, fragrant, clear light pink flowers, 8cm (3in) across, showing yellow stamens, are borne from summer to autumn. ↕ 2.5m (8ft), ↔ 1.5m (5ft). ❄❄❄
***R.* SAVOY HOTEL ('Harvintage')** ▣ syn. *R.* 'Integrity'. Vigorous Hybrid Tea rose producing strong stems and dark green leaves. From summer to autumn, bears high-centred to rounded, fully double, light pink flowers, 11cm (4½in) across, with a deeper pink reverse to the petals. ↕ 80cm (32in), ↔ 60cm (24in). ❄❄❄
***R.* 'Scabrosa'**, syn. *R. rugosa* 'Scabrosa'. Vigorous, dense-growing Rugosa rose of rounded habit, with wrinkled, leathery, light green leaves. Cupped, single, fragrant, reddish mauve flowers, 10cm (4in) across, with prominent yellow stamens, are borne from summer to autumn, followed by tomato-shaped red hips. ↕↔ 1.7m (5½ft). ❄❄❄
***R.* 'Scarlet Fire'** see *R.* 'Scharlachglut'.
***R.* 'Scarlet Glow'** see *R.* 'Scharlachglut'.
***R.* 'Scharlachglut'**, syn. *R.* 'Scarlet Fire', *R.* 'Scarlet Glow'. Very vigorous, arching Shrub rose or Climber of open habit, with dark green leaves. Showy, cupped, single, bright crimson-scarlet flowers, 12cm (5in) across, with golden stamens, are borne freely in summer, followed by pear-shaped, bright red hips. Prune to maintain as a shrub. ↕ to 3m (10ft), ↔ 2m (6ft). ❄❄❄
***R.* 'Schneeflocke'** see *R.* WHITE FLOWER CARPET ('Noaschnee').
***R.* 'Schneewittchen'** see *R.* ICEBERG ('Korbin').
***R.* 'Schneezwerg'**, syn. *R.* 'Snow Dwarf'. Rugosa rose of dense, bushy, even habit, with wrinkled, mid-green leaves. From summer to autumn, bears flat, semi-double, scented white flowers, 8cm (3in) across, showing yellow stamens; they are followed by tomato-shaped, orange-red hips. ↕ 1.2m (4ft), ↔ 1.5m (5ft). ❄❄❄
***R.* 'Schoolgirl'.** Stiff, lanky Climber producing sparse, deep green leaves. High-centred to rounded, fully double, scented, deep apricot flowers, 10cm (4in) across, are borne from summer to autumn. ↕ 3m (10ft), ↔ 2.5m (8ft). ❄❄❄
***R.* 'Schwanensee'** see *R.* SWAN LAKE ('Macmed').
***R.* 'Seagull'** ▣ Rampant Rambler of arching habit, with greyish green leaves. Large clusters of numerous cupped to flat, single to semi-double white flowers, 2.5cm (1in) across, with golden stamens, cover the plant in summer. ↕ to 6m (20ft), ↔ 4m (12ft). ❄❄❄
R. sericea* subsp. *omeiensis* f. *pteracantha, syn. *R. omeiensis* f. *pteracantha* (Winged thorn rose). Stiff, upright, vigorous Species rose with large, translucent red prickles, to 3cm (1¼in) or more wide and 2cm (¾in) tall, on young stems. Small, fern-like, light green leaves each have 11–17 elliptic, oblong, or obovate leaflets, 1–3cm (½–1¼in) long. Solitary, flat, usually 4-petalled white flowers, 2.5–6cm (1–2½in) across, are borne briefly along the stems in summer. ↕ 2.5m (8ft), ↔ 2.2m (7ft). W. China. ❄❄❄
***R.* SEXY REXY ('Macrexy')** ▣ syn. *R.* 'Heckenzauber'. Floribunda rose producing abundant glossy, dark green foliage. Showy, heavy heads of camellia-like, rounded, fully double, rose-pink flowers, 8cm (3in) across, are borne from summer to autumn. ↕ 70cm (28in), ↔ 60cm (24in). ❄❄❄
***R.* SHEILA'S PERFUME ('Harsherry')** ▣ Floribunda rose with glossy, dark green leaves. Urn-shaped, double, fragrant yellow flowers, 9cm (3½in) across, strongly marked and veined with red, are borne singly or in open clusters from summer to autumn. ↕ 75cm (30in), ↔ 60cm (24in). ❄❄❄
***R.* SHINE ON ('Dictalent').** Compact Patio rose with small, semi-glossy, bright green leaves. Cupped, double, lightly scented, orange-yellow flowers, 6cm (2½in) across, flushed rose-pink, are borne from summer to autumn. ↕↔ 40cm (16in). ❄❄❄
***R.* SHOCKING BLUE ('Korblue').** Floribunda rose with dark green leaves.

Rosa 'Silver Jubilee'

Rosa SIMBA ('Korbelma')

Rosa SIMPLY THE BEST ('Macamster')

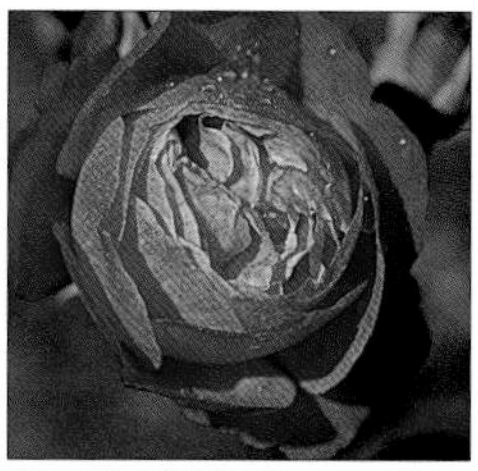

Rosa 'Sophie's Perpetual'

Rosa 'Southampton'

Rosa 'Souvenir de la Malmaison'

Rosa 'Souvenir de St. Anne's'

Rosa 'Souvenir du Docteur Jamain'

Rosa 'Stanwell Perpetual'

Rosa SUMMER WINE ('Korizont')

Rosa SUNBLEST ('Landora')

Rosa SUNSEEKER ('Dicracer')

Urn-shaped buds open to rounded, fully double, fragrant, lilac-purple flowers, 10cm (4in) across, borne singly or in clusters from summer to autumn. ↕75cm (30in), ↔ 60cm (24in). ❄❄❄

***R.* SILVER ANNIVERSARY ('Poulari')**, syn. *R.* 'Karen Blixen'. Free-branching Hybrid Tea rose with glossy, light green leaves. Urn-shaped, double, lightly scented white flowers, 10cm (4in) across, are produced from summer to autumn. ↕70cm (28in), ↔ 60cm (24in). ❄❄❄

***R.* 'Silver Jubilee'** ▣ Hybrid Tea rose of dense, leafy habit, with dark green leaves. High-centred, fully double, rose-pink flowers, to 12cm (5in) across, flushed peach- or salmon-pink, are borne singly or in open clusters on strong stems from summer to autumn. ↕1.1m (3½ft), ↔ 60cm (24in). ❄❄❄

***R.* SIMBA ('Korbelma')** ▣ syn. *R.* 'Goldsmith', *R.* 'Helmut Schmidt'. Hybrid Tea rose of compact habit, with mid-green leaves. Urn-shaped buds open to well-formed, rounded, fully double yellow flowers, 9cm (3½in) across, borne from summer to autumn. ↕60cm (24in), ↔ 50cm (20in). ❄❄❄

***R.* SIMPLY THE BEST ('Macamster')** ▣ Vigorous, bushy, upright Hybrid Tea rose with large, glossy, mid-green leaves. Cupped, double, scented, copper-orange flowers, 9cm (3½in) across, are borne from summer to autumn. ↕90cm (36in), ↔ 75cm (30in). ❄❄❄

***R.* 'Sissi'** see *R.* BLUE MOON ('Tannacht').

***R.* 'Sissinghurst Castle'**, syn. *R.* 'Rose des Maures'. Gallica rose of upright, free-suckering habit, with slender, firm stems and dark green leaves. Cupped to flat, semi-double, scented, deep maroon-crimson flowers, 6cm (2½in) across, showing yellow stamens, are borne in summer. ↕↔ 1m (3ft). ❄❄❄

***R.* SNOW CARPET ('Maccarpe')**. Prostrate, creeping Miniature rose with bright green leaves. In summer, bears pompon, fully double, creamy white flowers, 3cm (1¼in) across. ↕15cm (6in), ↔ 45cm (18in). ❄❄❄

***R.* 'Snow Dwarf'** see *R.* 'Schneezwerg'.

***R.* 'Snow Queen'** see *R.* 'Frau Karl Druschki'.

***R.* 'Sombreuil'**. Vigorous, free-branching, climbing Tea or Shrub rose with leathery, dark green leaves. Flat, quartered-rosette, double, fragrant, blush-pink to white flowers, 9cm (3½in) across, are borne from summer to autumn. Prune to maintain as a shrub. ↕ to 3m (10ft), ↔ 1.8m (6ft). ❄❄

***R.* 'Sommermärchen'** see *R.* BERKSHIRE ('Korpinka').

***R.* 'Sommermorgen'** see *R.* OXFORDSHIRE ('Korfullwind').

***R.* 'Sommerwind'** see *R.* SURREY ('Korlanum').

***R.* 'Sonnenschirm'** see *R.* BROADLANDS ('Tanmirsch').

***R.* 'Sophie's Perpetual'** ▣ syn. *R.* 'Dresden China'. Vigorous, shrubby China rose with dark green leaves. Cupped, double, fragrant, blush-pink flowers, 7cm (3in) across, overlaid cerise, are borne in summer and autumn. Climbs with support. ↕ to 2.2m (7ft), ↔ 1.2m (4ft). ❄❄❄

***R.* 'Southampton'** ▣ syn. *R.* 'Susan Ann'. Floribunda rose with glossy, dark green leaves. High-centred, double, scented apricot flowers, 8cm (3in) across, flushed with red, are borne singly or in clusters on firm stems from summer to autumn. ↕1.1m (3½ft), ↔ 70cm (28in). ❄❄❄

***R.* 'Souvenir de la Malmaison'** ▣ syn. *R.* 'Queen of Beauty & Fragrance'. Dense, spreading Bourbon rose with dark green foliage and quartered-rosette, fully double, spice-scented, pale pink to white flowers, 12cm (5in) across, produced from summer to autumn. Rain may spoil flowers. ↕↔ to 1.5m (5ft). ❄❄❄

***R.* 'Souvenir de la Princesse de Lamballe'** see *R.* 'Bourbon Queen'.

***R.* 'Souvenir de St. Anne's'** ▣ Vigorous Bourbon rose producing abundant dark green foliage. Wide-opening, cupped, semi-double, scented, pearl-pink flowers, 9cm (3½in) across, are borne freely from summer to autumn. ↕1.5m (5ft), ↔ 1.2m (4ft). ❄❄❄

***R.* 'Souvenir du Docteur Jamain'** ▣ Arching, shrubby Hybrid Perpetual rose with dark green leaves. Bears cupped, double, fragrant, velvet-textured red flowers, 9cm (3½in) across, in summer and autumn. Climbs with support. ↕ to 3m (10ft), ↔ to 2.5m (8ft). ❄❄❄

***R.* 'Spanish Beauty'** see *R.* 'Mme Grégoire Staechelin'.

***R.* 'Spectacular'** see *R.* 'Danse du Feu'.

R. spinosissima see *R. pimpinellifolia*.

***R.* 'Splendens'**, syn. *R.* 'Ayrshire Splendens' (Myrrh-scented rose). Vigorous Climber with dark green leaves. In summer, purple-red buds open to loosely formed, cupped, double, myrrh-scented, pale creamy pink flowers, 4.5cm (1¾in) across, with orange-yellow stamens. ↕ to 8m (25ft), ↔ 3m (10ft). ❄❄❄

***R.* 'Spring Gold'** see *R.* 'Frühlingsgold'.

***R.* 'Spring Morning'** see *R.* 'Frühlingsmorgen'.

***R.* 'Stanwell Perpetual'** ▣ Scots rose of spreading, twiggy habit, with prickly stems and fern-like, dark greyish green leaves. Loosely formed, cupped, fully double, scented, pale pink flowers, 8cm (3in) across, are borne singly on thin stems from summer to autumn. ↕1m (3ft), ↔ 1.2m (4ft). ❄❄❄

R. stellata* var. *mirifica (Sacramento rose). Species rose of suckering habit, with springy, wiry, prickly stems and mid-green leaves, each with 3–5 deeply cut, gooseberry-like, wedge-shaped leaflets, 0.7–1cm (¼–½in) long. In summer bears solitary, wide-opening, cupped to flat, single, scented, pink to deep rose-purple flowers, 3.5–6cm (1½–2¼in) across. ↕ to 1.1m (3½ft), ↔ 1.2m (4ft). USA (New Mexico). ❄❄❄

***R.* SUMA ('Harsuma')** ▣ Prostrate Ground-cover rose with glossy, dark green foliage, turning burnished crimson in autumn. Clusters of rosette-shaped, double, ruby-red to deep pink flowers, 3cm (1¼in) across, are borne along the stems from summer to autumn. ↕50cm (20in), ↔ 1.5m (5ft). ❄❄❄

Rosa SUMA ('Harsuma')

***R.* SUMMER WINE ('Korizont')** ▣ Climber with stiff, branching growth and mid-green leaves. Cupped, single, scented, coral-pink flowers, 10cm (4in) across, shaded yellow at the bases and with folded petals, are produced from summer to autumn. ↕3m (10ft), ↔ 2.2m (7ft). ❄❄❄

***R.* 'Sunblaze'** see *R.* ORANGE SUNBLAZE ('Meijikitar').

***R.* SUNBLEST ('Landora')** ▣ Hybrid Tea rose producing glossy, mid-green leaves. Pointed buds open to cupped, double yellow flowers, 9cm (3½in) across, borne freely from summer to autumn. ↕1m (3ft), ↔ 60cm (24in). ❄❄❄

***R.* 'Sunnyside'** see *R.* AVON ('Poulmulti').

***R.* SUNRISE ('Kormarter')**. Arching Climber with bronze foliage. Cupped, double, scented apricot flowers, shaded pink, 9cm (3½in) across, are produced from summer to autumn. ↕2.5m (8ft), ↔ 1.8m (6ft). ❄❄❄

***R.* SUNSEEKER ('Dicracer')** ▣ syn. *R.* 'Duchess of York'. Vigorous, dense Patio rose with dark green leaves. Cupped, semi-double, lightly scented, orange-red flowers, 6cm (2½in) across, with yellow stamens, are borne from summer to autumn. ↕75cm (30in), ↔ 50cm (20in). ❄❄❄

***R.* SUNSET BOULEVARD ('Harbabble')**. Bushy Floribunda rose with glossy, mid-green leaves. Produces cupped, double, lightly scented, pale orange-salmon flowers, 9cm (3½in) across, from summer to autumn. ↕90cm (36in), ↔ 60cm (24in). ❄❄❄

***R.* 'Sunsprite'** see *R.* 'Korresia'.

***R.* SUPER EXCELSA ('Helexa')**. Vigorous, arching Rambler producing mid-green foliage. Cupped, double, slightly scented crimson flowers, 3.5cm (1¼in) across, are borne from summer to autumn. ↕4m (12ft), ↔ 2.5m (8ft). ❄❄❄

***R.* SUPER FAIRY ('Helsufair')** ▣ Vigorous, arching Rambler with glossy, mid-green leaves. Bears cupped, double, lightly scented, pale rose-pink flowers, 3.5cm (1½in) across, from summer to autumn. ↕4m (12ft), ↔ 2.5m (8ft). ❄❄❄

Rosa Surrey ('Korlanum')

Rosa Swan Lake ('Macmed')

Rosa Swany ('Meiburenac')

Rosa Sweet Dream ('Fryminicot')

Rosa Sweetheart ('Cocapeer')

Rosa Sweet Magic ('Dicmagic')

Rosa Sweet Memories ('Whamemo')

Rosa Tear Drop ('Dicomo')

Rosa Tequila Sunrise ('Dicobey')

Rosa 'The Fairy'

Rosa The Times Rose ('Korpeahn')

Rosa Tigris ('Harprier')

***R.* Super Star ('Tanorstar')**, syn. *R.* 'Tropicana'. Hybrid Tea rose of open, uneven habit, with small, dark green leaves. Rounded, fully double, lightly scented, vermilion to pale scarlet flowers, 11cm (4½in) across, are borne from summer to autumn. ↕ 1.1m (3½ft), ↔ 1m (3ft). ✻✻✻

***R.* Surrey ('Korlanum')** ■ syn. *R.* 'Sommerwind', *R.* 'Vent d'Eté'. Vigorous, mound-forming Ground-cover rose with abundant dark green foliage. Clusters of cupped, double, rose-pink flowers, 6cm (2½in) across, are borne along the stems from summer to autumn. ↕ 80cm (32in), ↔ 1.2m (4ft). ✻✻✻

***R.* 'Susan Ann'** see *R.* 'Southampton'.

***R.* 'Sutter's Gold'.** Spindly Hybrid Tea rose with sparse, leathery, dark green foliage. High-centred buds open to loosely formed, high-centred, double, fragrant, golden orange flowers, 11cm (4½in) across, overlaid with red, from summer to autumn. ↕ 1m (3ft), ↔ 60cm (24in). ✻✻✻

Rosa Super Fairy ('Helsufair')

***R.* Swan Lake ('Macmed')** ■ syn. *R.* 'Schwanensee'. Stiffly branching Climber with deep green leaves. Cupped, double, lightly scented, blush-pink to white flowers, 10cm (4in) across, are borne from summer to autumn. ↕ 3m (10ft), ↔ 1.8m (6ft). ✻✻✻

***R.* Swany ('Meiburenac')** ■ Vigorous, dense Ground-cover rose with glossy, dark green leaves. Profuse clusters of numerous flat, fully double white flowers, 5cm (2in) across, are borne from summer to autumn. ↕ to 75cm (30in), ↔ to 1.7m (5½ft). ✻✻✻

***R.* Sweet Dream ('Fryminicot')** ■ Patio rose of compact, leafy habit, with mid-green foliage. Dense clusters of cupped, fully double, peach-apricot flowers, 6cm (2½in) across, are borne on stiff stems from summer to autumn. ↕ 40cm (16in), ↔ 35cm (14in). ✻✻✻

***R.* Sweetheart ('Cocapeer')** ■ Hybrid Tea rose of upright habit, with dense, light green foliage. Rounded, double, fragrant, rose-pink flowers, 11cm (4½in) across, are borne from summer to autumn. ↕ 90cm (36in), ↔ 60cm (24in). ✻✻✻

***R.* 'Sweetheart Rose'** see *R.* 'Cécile Brunner'.

***R.* Sweet Juliet ('Ausleap').** Extremely vigorous Shrub rose with mid-green leaves. Cupped, fully double, tea-scented, apricot-yellow flowers, 10cm (4in) across, are borne from summer to autumn. ↕ 1.1m (3½ft), ↔ 1m (3ft). ✻✻✻

***R.* Sweet Magic ('Dicmagic')** ■ Compact Patio rose with bright green leaves. From summer to autumn, well-spaced clusters of urn-shaped buds open to cupped, double, apricot-orange and yellow flowers, 4cm (1½in) across. ↕↔ 35cm (14in). ✻✻✻

***R.* Sweet Memories ('Whamemo')** ■ Compact, leafy Patio rose with mid-green foliage. Bears cupped, double, lightly scented, lemon-yellow flowers, 6cm (2½in) across, from summer to autumn. ↕ 40cm (16in), ↔ 35cm (14in). ✻✻✻

***R.* 'Sweet Sunblaze'** see *R.* Pretty Polly ('Meitonje').

***R.* 'Sylvia'** see *R.* Congratulations ('Korlift').

***R.* 'Sympathie'** ■ Free-branching, vigorous Climber with dense, glossy, dark green foliage. Cupped, fully double, bright deep red flowers, 8cm (3in) across, are borne from summer to autumn, usually in clusters. ↕ 3m (10ft), ↔ 2.5m (8ft). ✻✻✻

***R.* Tall Story ('Dickooky').** Ground-cover rose with abundant glossy, light green leaves. Graceful sprays of cupped, semi-double, scented, light primrose-yellow flowers, 6cm (2½in) across, are borne on bowed stems from summer to autumn. ↕ 75cm (30in), ↔ 1.2m (4ft). ✻✻✻

***R.* 'Tapis d'Orient'** see *R.* 'Yesterday'.

***R.* 'Tapis Persan'** see *R.* Eye Paint ('Maceye').

***R.* Tear Drop ('Dicomo')** ■ Compact Patio rose with small, glossy, dark green leaves. Flat, semi-double, lightly scented, blush-pink to white flowers, 4cm (1½in) across, are produced from summer to autumn. ↕ 30cm (12in), ↔ 40cm (16in). ✻✻✻

***R.* Tequila Sunrise ('Dicobey')** ■ Hybrid Tea rose of open habit, with glossy, dark green leaves. Wide sprays of rounded, fully double yellow flowers, 10cm (4in) across, with scarlet-margined petals, are borne freely from summer to autumn. ↕ 75cm (30in), ↔ 60cm (24in). ✻✻✻

Rosa 'Sympathie'

***R.* 'The Fairy'** ■ Polyantha rose of dense, cushion-forming habit, with abundant glossy, mid-green leaves. Rosette-shaped, double, light pink flowers, 2.5cm (1in) across, are borne freely from late summer to autumn. ↕↔ 60–90cm (24–36in). ✻✻✻

***R.* 'The New Dawn'** see *R.* 'New Dawn'.

***R.* 'The Queen Elizabeth'** see *R.* 'Queen Elizabeth'.

***R.* The Times Rose ('Korpeahn')** ■ syn. *R.* 'Carl Philip', *R.* 'Christian IV', *R.* 'Mariandel'. Floribunda rose of spreading habit, with abundant purplish green leaves. Cupped to flat, double, dark crimson flowers, 8cm (3in) across, are borne in wide clusters from summer to autumn. ↕ 60cm (24in), ↔ 75cm (30in). ✻✻✻

***R.* 'Thisbe'.** Leafy, bushy, Hybrid Musk rose producing mid-green leaves with lance-shaped leaflets. Rosette-shaped, fully double, scented, buff-yellow flowers, 4.5cm (1¾in) across, fading to cream and showing amber stamens, are produced in clusters from summer to autumn. ↕↔ 1.2m (4ft). ✻✻✻

***R.* Tigris ('Harprier')** ■ Cushion-forming, spreading Shrub rose producing wiry, prickly, gooseberry-like stems and pale green leaves. In summer, bears pompon, double, canary-yellow flowers, 3cm (1¼in) across, with dark red eyes. ↕ 45cm (18in), ↔ 60cm (24in). ✻✻✻

***R.* 'Tipo Ideale'** see *R.* x *odorata* 'Mutabilis'.

***R.* Top Marks ('Fryministar')** ■ Compact Patio rose with uneven habit and small, glossy, mid-green leaves. Bears rosette-shaped, double, lightly scented vermilion flowers, 4cm (1½in) across, from summer to autumn. ↕ 40cm (16in), ↔ 45cm (18in). ✻✻✻

***R.* 'Tour de Malakoff'** ■ Centifolia rose of lax, spreading habit, with dark green leaves. Cupped, double, fragrant flowers, 12cm (5in) across, purplish magenta fading to greyish violet, are borne in summer. ↕ 2m (6ft), ↔ 1.5m (5ft). ✻✻✻

Rosa Top Marks ('Fryministar')

Rosa 'Tour de Malakoff'

Rosa 'Tricolore de Flandre'

Rosa Troika ('Poumidor')

Rosa Trumpeter ('Mactru')

Rosa 'Tuscany Superb'

Rosa Valencia ('Koreklia')

Rosa Valentine Heart ('Dicogle')

Rosa 'Veilchenblau'

Rosa Belle Epoque ('Fryyaboo')

Rosa Westerland ('Korwest')

Rosa 'White Cockade'

***R.* Tournament of Roses ('Jacient')**, syn. *R.* 'Berkeley', *R.* 'Poesie'. Strong-growing Hybrid Tea rose with glossy, dark green leaves. Rounded, double, light rose- to salmon-pink flowers, 10cm (4in) across, are borne from summer to autumn. ↕ 1.1m (3½ft), ↔ 60cm (24in). ❄❄❄

***R.* 'Tricolore de Flandre'** ▣ Vigorous Gallica rose of bushy, upright habit, with dull, dark green leaves. Cupped to flat, fully double, fragrant, pale pink flowers, 6cm (2½in) across, striped with pink and purple, are borne in summer. ↕↔ 1m (3ft). ❄❄❄

***R.* 'Trier 2000'** see *R.* Anna Livia ('Kormetter').

***R.* 'Trigintipetala'** see *R.* x *damascena.*

***R.* Troika ('Poumidor')** ▣ syn. *R.* 'Royal Dane'. Vigorous, branching Hybrid Tea rose with abundant semi-glossy, mid-green leaves. High-centred, double, fragrant, reddish orange flowers, 15cm (6in) across, with pink flushes, are produced from summer to autumn. ↕ 1m (3ft), ↔ 75cm (30in). ❄❄❄

***R.* 'Tropicana'** see *R.* Super Star ('Tanorstar').

***R.* Trumpeter ('Mactru')** ▣ Floribunda rose of compact habit, with deep green foliage. Showy, cupped, fully double, vivid orange-red flowers, 6cm (2½in) across, are borne from summer to autumn. ↕ 60cm (24in), ↔ 50cm (20in). ❄❄❄

***R.* 'Tuscany Superb'** ▣ (Double velvet rose). Vigorous, rounded Gallica rose with dark green leaves. In summer, erect stems bear cupped to flat, double, scented, deep crimson-maroon to purple flowers, 5cm (2in) across, showing gold stamens. ↕↔ 1m (3ft). ❄❄❄

***R.* Valencia ('Koreklia')** ▣ Hybrid Tea rose of open habit, with leathery, glossy, dark green foliage. From summer to autumn, bears high-centred, fully double, fragrant, amber-yellow flowers, 10cm (4in) across. ↕ 75cm (30in), ↔ 65cm (26in). ❄❄❄

***R.* Valentine Heart ('Dicogle')** ▣ Floribunda rose of open habit, producing dark green foliage. From summer to autumn, pale scarlet buds open to cupped, semi-double, scented, pale pink and deeper pink flowers, 7cm (3in) across, with infolded, frilled petals at the centres. ↕ 60cm (24in), ↔ 50cm (20in). ❄❄❄

***R.* 'Variegata di Bologna'.** Willowy, arching, smooth-wooded Bourbon rose with pale green leaves. Quartered-rosette, fully double, fragrant flowers, 8cm (3in) across, pale pink stippled with purple-crimson, are borne from summer to autumn. Prone to black spot. ↕ 2.2m (7ft), ↔ 1.5m (5ft). ❄❄❄

***R.* Variety Club ('Haredge')** ▣ Compact, upright Patio rose with glossy, mid-green leaves. Rosette-shaped, double, lightly scented, pale vermilion flowers, 5cm (2in) across, are borne from summer to autumn. ↕ 70cm (28in), ↔ 50cm (20in). ❄❄❄

***R.* 'Veilchenblau'** ▣ syn. *R.* 'Blue Rambler', *R.* 'Violet Blue'. Vigorous Rambler with light green leaves. In summer, bears large clusters of many cupped, double, fruit-scented violet flowers, 3cm (1¼in) across, streaked with white. ↕↔ 4m (12ft). ❄❄❄

***R.* Velvet Fragrance ('Fryperdee').** Vigorous, free-branching Hybrid Tea rose with large, dark green leaves. High-centred, double, very fragrant, deep red flowers, 10cm (4in) across, are borne from summer to autumn. ↕ 1m (3ft), ↔ 70cm (28in). ❄❄❄

***R.* 'Vent d'Eté'** see *R.* Surrey ('Korlanum').

***R.* 'Vick's Caprice'.** Upright, bushy Hybrid Perpetual rose with light green leaves. Pink buds open to cupped, fully double, fragrant, pale pink flowers, 10cm (4in) across, striped with pink and with irregular centres, from summer to autumn. Flowers may ball in rain. ↕ 1.2m (4ft), ↔ 1m (3ft). ❄❄❄

***R.* 'Ville de Chine'** see *R.* 'Chinatown'.

***R.* 'Violacea'**, syn. *R.* 'La Belle Sultane'. Tall, smooth-stemmed Gallica rose with sparse, grey-green foliage. In summer, bears cupped to flat, single, fragrant, violet-purple flowers, 10cm (4in) across, with golden stamens. ↕ 2.2m (7ft), ↔ 1.5m (5ft). ❄❄❄

***R.* 'Violet Blue'** see *R.* 'Veilchenblau'.

R. virginiana, syn. *R. lucida.* Species rose of erect, suckering habit, with glossy, light to mid-green leaves composed of 5–9 obovate to oblong-elliptic leaflets, 2.5–6cm (1–2½in) long, reddening in autumn. Cupped to flat, single, pale to bright pink flowers, 5–7cm (2–3in) across, are produced singly or in clusters of up to 8 blooms in summer; they are followed by spherical, ruby-red hips in autumn. ↕ 1.2m (4ft), ↔ 1.5m (5ft). E. North America. ❄❄❄

***R.* 'Viridiflora'** see *R.* x *odorata* 'Viridiflora'.

***R.* Warm Welcome ('Chewizz').** Stiff, arching Climbing Miniature rose with many dark green leaves. Small clusters of urn-shaped, semi-double, orange-red flowers, 4cm (1½in) across, are borne freely from summer to autumn. ↕↔ 2.2m (7ft). ❄❄❄

***R.* Warm Wishes ('Fryxotic').** Vigorous, bushy, upright Hybrid Tea rose with deep green foliage. Cupped, double, fragrant, peach-salmon flowers, 10cm (4in) across, are borne from summer to autumn. ↕ 1.1m (3½ft), ↔ 70cm (28in). ❄❄❄

***R.* 'Wedding Day'.** Rampant Rambler producing glossy, mid-green leaves with lance-shaped leaflets. Large clusters of flat, single, fruit-scented, creamy white flowers, 2.5cm (1in) across, ageing to pale pink, are borne in summer. ↕ to 8m (25ft), ↔ 4m (12ft). ❄❄❄

Rosa Variety Club ('Haredge')

***R.* Wee Jock ('Cocabest').** Dense, compact Patio rose with abundant dark green leaves. From summer to autumn, high-centred buds open to rosette-shaped, fully double, deep crimson flowers, 4cm (1½in) across. ↕↔ 35cm (14in). ❄❄❄

***R.* 'Wendy Cussons'.** Strong-branching Hybrid Tea rose with dark green leaves. Cherry-red buds open to high-centred, double, fragrant, cerise-pink flowers, 12cm (5in) across, from summer to autumn. ↕ 1m (3ft), ↔ 70cm (28in). ❄❄❄

***R.* Westerland ('Korwest')** ▣ Vigorous, stiff-stemmed Shrub or climbing rose with bright green leaves. From summer to autumn, bears bold clusters of loosely formed, cupped, double, scented, apricot-orange flowers, 8cm (3in) across, suffused yellow. ↕ 2m (6ft), ↔ 1.2m (4ft) as a shrub; ↕ to 2.5m (8ft) as a climber. ❄❄❄

***R.* 'Whisky'** see *R.* Whisky Mac ('Tanky').

***R.* Whisky Mac ('Tanky')**, syn. *R.* 'Whisky'. Hybrid Tea rose with reddish green stems and glossy, dark green foliage. From summer to autumn, produces rounded, double, fragrant, light amber-yellow flowers, 10cm (4in) across. Prone to mildew. ↕ 75cm (30in), ↔ 60cm (24in). ❄❄

***R.* 'White American Beauty'** see *R.* 'Frau Karl Druschki'.

***R.* 'White Baby Rambler'** see *R.* 'Katharina Zeimet'.

***R.* 'White Cockade'** ▣ Upright, shrubby Climber with dark green leaves. From summer to autumn, produces rounded, fully double, milk-white flowers, 9cm (3½in) across. ↕ 2.2m (7ft), ↔ 1.5m (5ft). ❄❄❄

***R.* 'White Cover'** see *R.* Kent ('Poulcov').

***R.* White Flower Carpet ('Noaschnee')**, syn. *R.* 'Emera Blanc', *R.* 'Opalia', *R.* Schneeflocke'. Lax, spreading Ground-cover rose, with glossy, deep green foliage. Cupped, semi-double, fragrant white flowers, 10cm (4in) across, are borne from summer to autumn. ↕ 60cm (24in), ↔ 1.2m (4ft). ❄❄❄

***R.* 'White Pet'** ▣ syn. *R.* 'Little White Pet'. Vigorous, free-branching Polyantha rose with deep green foliage. From summer to autumn, red buds

Rosa 'White Pet'

open to dense sprays of rosette-shaped, fully double white flowers, 4cm (1½in) across. ↕45cm (18in), ↔ 55cm (22in) with hard pruning. ❄❄❄

***R.* 'White Wings'.** Hybrid Tea rose with dark green leaves. Cupped to flat, single, scented white flowers, 8cm (3in) across, with chocolate-brown stamens, open from summer to autumn. ↕1m (3ft), ↔ 60cm (24in). ❄❄❄

R. wichuraiana see *R. wichurana.*

R. wichurana, syn. *R. wichuraiana* (Memorial rose). Vigorous, climbing, semi-evergreen Species rose, mound-forming as ground cover, producing numerous small, glossy, dark green leaves composed of 5–9 elliptic to broadly ovate leaflets, to 2.5cm (1in) long. Cupped to flat, single, clover-scented white flowers, 4.5cm (1¾in) across, with prominent, golden yellow stamens, are borne in loose clusters of 6–10 in late summer. Ovoid to spherical hips are orange-red to dark red, and to 1.5cm (½in) long. ↕2m (6ft), ↔ 6m (20ft). E. China, Korea, Japan, Taiwan. ❄❄❄

***R.* 'William Allen Richardson'.** Noisette climbing rose with arching, branching growth and glossy, dark green leaves. From summer to autumn, urn-shaped buds open to quartered-rosette, double, scented, apricot-yellow flowers, 4.5cm (1¾in) across, paler towards the petal margins. ↕3m (10ft), ↔ 2.5m (8ft). ❄❄❄

R

***R.* 'William Lobb'**, syn. *R.* 'Duchesse d'Istrie'. Vigorous Moss rose with arching, prickly stems, abundant mossy growth, and mid-green leaves. Cupped,

Rosa WINCHESTER CATHEDRAL ('Auscat')

fully double, scented, purple to lavender-grey flowers, 8cm (3in) across, are borne in summer. Best grown on a support. ↕↔ 2m (6ft). ❄❄❄

***R.* 'Williams' Double Yellow'** see *R.* x *harisonii* 'Williams' Double Yellow'.

***R.* 'William III'.** Suckering, spreading Scots rose with wiry stems and grey-green leaves. In early summer, bears cupped, semi-double, scented flowers, 4.5cm (1¾in) across, magenta-crimson shaded purplish red or lilac, followed by spherical, brownish red hips in autumn. ↕50cm (20in), ↔ 80cm (32in). ❄❄❄

***R.* WILTSHIRE ('Kormuse')** ▣ Spreading Ground-cover rose with glossy, mid-green foliage. Bears cupped, double, scented, reddish pink flowers, 7cm (3in) across, from summer to autumn. ↕60cm (24in), ↔ 1.2m (4ft). ❄❄❄

***R.* WINCHESTER CATHEDRAL ('Auscat')** ▣ Upright Shrub rose with uneven habit and matt, mid-green leaves. Cupped, double, scented white flowers, 9cm (3½in) across, tinged buff, are produced from summer to autumn. ↕1.2m (4ft), ↔ 1m (3ft). ❄❄❄

***R.* WORCESTERSHIRE ('Korlalon').** Spreading Ground-cover rose with glossy, mid-green leaves. Cupped to flat, semi-double, scented yellow flowers, 6cm (2½in) across, paling at the petal edges, are borne from summer to autumn. ↕60cm (24in), ↔ 90cm (36in). ❄❄❄

R. xanthina. Species rose of shrubby, dense growth, with reddish green stems and fern-like, greyish green leaves, each with 7–13 broadly elliptic to obovate leaflets, 1–2cm (½–¾in) long. Loosely formed, cupped to flat, semi-double, scented yellow flowers, 5cm (2in) across, are borne (usually singly) along the stems in late spring. ↕↔ 2.5m (8ft). N. China, Korea. ❄❄❄. **'Canary Bird'**, syn. *R.* 'Canary Bird', is arching in habit, with cupped, single, musk-scented yellow flowers borne in spring, sometimes sparsely later; ↕3m (10ft), ↔ to 4m (12ft). **f. *hugonis***, syn. *R. hugonis* (Father Hugo's rose, Golden rose of China) produces cupped, single, lightly scented, pale yellow flowers, 4.5cm (1¾in) across, in late spring; ↔ 2m (6ft); W. and C. China. **f. *normalis*** bears single flowers.

***R.* 'Yellow Cécile Brunner'** see *R.* 'Perle d'Or'.

***R.* 'Yesterday'**, syn. *R.* 'Tapis d'Orient'. Polyantha bush rose of uneven growth, with glossy, mid-green leaves. Sprays of rosette-shaped, semi-double, scented, lilac-pink to rose-violet flowers, 2.5cm (1in) across, are borne very freely from summer to autumn. ↕↔ 1–1.5m (3–5ft). ❄❄❄

***R.* 'Young Mistress'** see *R.* REGENSBERG ('Macyoumis').

***R.* 'Yvonne Rabier'.** Compact Polyantha rose with abundant bright green leaves. From summer to autumn, bears rounded, fully double, lightly scented, creamy white flowers, 4.5cm (1¾in) across. ↕↔ 40cm (16in). ❄❄❄

***R.* 'Zéphirine Drouhin'** ▣ (Thornless rose). Bourbon rose with lax, open, thorn-free growth and mid-green leaves. From summer to autumn, freely bears loosely cupped, double, fragrant, deep pink flowers, 8cm (3in) across. Good as a climber or hedge. ↕ to 3m (10ft), ↔ 2m (6ft). ❄❄❄

***R.* 'Zigeunerknabe'**, syn. *R.* 'Gipsy Boy', *R.* 'Gypsy Boy'. Vigorous, lanky Bourbon rose with coarse, dark green leaves. Cupped to flat, double, scented, purplish crimson flowers, 8cm (3in) across, with prominent, golden yellow stamens, are borne from summer to autumn. ↕2m (6ft), ↔ 1.2m (4ft). ❄❄❄

***R.* 'Zonta Rose'** see *R.* PRINCESS ALICE ('Hartanna').

Rosa WILTSHIRE ('Kormuse')

Rosa 'Zéphirine Drouhin'

ROSCOEA

ZINGIBERACEAE

Genus of about 18 species of tuberous perennials from meadows, slopes, and partially forested areas in the Himalayas and China. They are cultivated for their unusual, hooded, orchid-like flowers, which have prominent, entire or 2-lobed lips. The flowers are surrounded by overlapping bracts, and are produced on leafy stems from the leaf axils in summer or autumn. The arching leaves are stem-sheathing and linear, or lance-shaped to oblong-ovate. Roscoeas thrive in cool climates; grow in a peat bed, a woodland garden, or a damp, shady border.

- **HARDINESS** Fully hardy to frost hardy; will survive temperatures to -20°C (-4°F) if planted very deep.
- **CULTIVATION** Plant tubers 15cm (6in) deep in winter or early spring. Grow in moderately fertile, humus-rich, leafy, moist but well-drained soil, in a cool, sheltered site in partial shade. In frost-prone areas, apply a deep winter mulch.
- **PROPAGATION** Sow seed in containers in a cold frame as soon as ripe. Divide in spring.

Roscoea cautleyoides

Roscoea humeana

Roscoea purpurea

• **PESTS AND DISEASES** Slugs and vine weevils may be a problem.

R. auriculata. Tuberous perennial with 3–10 linear to broadly lance-shaped, dark green leaves, to 25cm (10in) long. Bears rich purple flowers, 3.5cm (1½in) across, from the upper leaf axils in late summer or autumn. ↕25–55cm (10–22in), ↔ 15cm (6in). Nepal, India (Sikkim). ✻✻✻ (borderline)
***R. capitata* of gardens** see *R. scillifolia.*
R. cautleoides see *R. cautleyoides.*
R. cautleyoides ▣ syn. *R. cautleoides.* Tuberous perennial with 1–4 linear to lance-shaped, deep to mid-green leaves, 40cm (16in) long, usually to 15cm (6in) long at flowering. In midsummer, bears yellow, white, or purple flowers, 4cm (1½in) across, from the upper leaf axils. ↕to 55cm (22in), ↔ 15cm (6in). China (Sichuan, Yunnan). ✻✻✻ (borderline)
R. humeana ▣ Sturdy, tuberous perennial bearing a succession of up to 10 rich purple flowers, 4cm (1½in) across, from the upper leaf axils in early summer. The 1 or 2, rarely 3, oblong to ovate, deep green leaves, to 22cm (9in) long, are usually only partially developed at flowering time. ↕15–25cm (6–10in), ↔ 15cm (6in). China (Sichuan, Yunnan). ✻✻✻ (borderline)
R. procera see *R. purpurea.*
R. purpurea ▣ syn. *R. procera, R. purpurea* var. *procera.* Tuberous perennial with 4–8 lance-shaped to oblong-ovate, deep green leaves, to 25cm (10in) long. Purple, or sometimes white or bicoloured flowers, 6cm (2½in) across, are produced in succession from the upper leaf axils in early and mid-summer. ↕25–40cm (10–16in), ↔ 15cm (6in). Himalayas. ✻✻✻ (borderline).
var. *procera* see *R. purpurea.*
R. scillifolia, syn. *R. capitata* of gardens. Slender, tuberous perennial with 1–5 linear to linear-lance-shaped, mid-green leaves, 6–12cm (2½–5in) long. In summer, produces 2–4 blackish pink or purplish pink flowers, 2cm (¾in) across, on leafless stalks above the leaves. May seed freely. ↕35cm (14in), ↔ 8cm (3in). China (Yunnan). ✻✻✻ (borderline)

▷**Rose** see *Rosa*
Apothecary's see *Rosa gallica* var. *officinalis*
Austrian copper see *Rosa foetida* 'Bicolor'
Austrian yellow see *Rosa foetida*
Autumn damask see *Rosa* x *damascena* var. *semperflorens*

▷**Rose cont.**
Burnet see *Rosa pimpinellifolia*
Burr see *Rosa roxburghii*
Camellia see *Rosa laevigata*
Cherokee see *Rosa laevigata*
Chestnut see *Rosa roxburghii*
Chickasaw see *Rosa bracteata*
Chinquapin see *Rosa roxburghii*
Christmas see *Helleborus niger*
Common moss see *Rosa* x *centifolia* 'Muscosa'
Cotton see *Hibiscus mutabilis*
Crested moss see *Rosa* x *centifolia* 'Cristata'
Crimson damask see *Rosa gallica* var. *officinalis*
Damask see *Rosa* x *damascena*
Desert see *Adenium*
Double velvet see *Rosa* 'Tuscany Superb'
Double white banksian see *Rosa banksiae*
Eglantine see *Rosa rubiginosa*
Father Hugo's see *Rosa xanthina* f. *hugonis*
Fortune's double yellow see *Rosa* x *odorata* 'Pseudindica'
Four seasons see *Rosa* x *damascena* var. *semperflorens*
Great white see *Rosa* 'Alba Maxima'
Green see *Rosa* x *odorata* 'Viridiflora'
Guelder see *Viburnum opulus*
Hedgehog see *Rosa rugosa*
Incense see *Rosa primula*
Jacobite see *Rosa* 'Alba Maxima'
Japanese see *Rosa rugosa*
Lenten see *Helleborus orientalis*
Macartney see *Rosa bracteata*
Memorial see *Rosa wichurana*
Montpellier rock see *Cistus monspeliensis*
Musk see *Rosa moschata*
Myrrh-scented see *Rosa* 'Splendens'
Nootka see *Rosa nutkana*
Old black see *Rosa* 'Nuits de Young'
Old blush China see *Rosa* x *odorata* 'Pallida'
Old glory see *Rosa* 'Gloire de Dijon'
Painted damask see *Rosa* 'Leda'
Parsons' pink China see *Rosa* x *odorata* 'Pallida'
Persian yellow see *Rosa foetida* 'Persiana'
Pompon see *Rosa* 'De Meaux'
Portland see *Rosa* 'Portlandica'
Provins see *Rosa gallica* var. *officinalis*
Ramanas see *Rosa rugosa*
Red moss see *Rosa* 'Henri Martin'
Rock see *Cistus, Helianthemum*
Rosa mundi see *Rosa gallica* var. *officinalis* 'Versicolor'
Sacramento see *Rosa stellata* var. *mirifica*
Scotch see *Rosa pimpinellifolia*
Scots see *Rosa pimpinellifolia*
Single white banksian see *Rosa banksiae* var. *normalis*
Slater's crimson China see *Rosa* x *odorata* 'Semperflorens'
Snowbush see *Rosa* 'Dupontii'
Summer damask see *Rosa* x *damascena*
Sun see *Cistus, Helianthemum*
Sydney rock see *Boronia serrulata*
Thornless see *Rosa* 'Zéphirine Drouhin'
Winged thorn see *Rosa sericea* subsp. *omeiensis* f. *pteracantha*
Wood see *Merremia tuberosa*
Yellow banksian see *Rosa banksiae* 'Lutea'
York and Lancaster see *Rosa* x *damascena* 'Versicolor'

▷**Rose bay** see *Nerium oleander*
▷**Rosebay, East Indian** see *Tabernaemontana divaricata*
▷**Rose campion** see *Lychnis coronaria*
▷**Rosemary** see *Rosmarinus, R. officinalis*
Australian see *Westringia fruticosa*
Bog see *Andromeda*
Common bog see *Andromeda polifolia*
Wild see *Dampiera rosmarinifolia*
▷***Roseocactus fissuratus*** see *Ariocarpus fissuratus*
▷**Rose of Castille** see *Rosa* x *damascena* var. *semperflorens*
▷**Rose of China** see *Hibiscus rosa-sinensis*
Golden see *Rosa xanthina* f. *hugonis*
▷**Rose of heaven** see *Silene coeli-rosa*
▷**Rose of Jericho** see *Selaginella lepidophylla*
▷**Rose of Lancaster, Red** see *Rosa gallica* var. *officinalis*
▷**Rose of Sharon** see *Hypericum calycinum*
▷**Rose of York, White** see *Rosa* 'Alba Maxima'
▷**Roseroot** see *Rhodiola rosea*
▷**Rosewood, Brazilian** see *Tipuana tipu*
▷**Rosinweed** see *Grindelia, Silphium*

ROSMARINUS

Rosemary

LABIATAE/LAMIACEAE

Genus of 2 species of evergreen shrubs found in rocky sites, woodland, and scrub in the Mediterranean region, and cultivated for their attractive, aromatic foliage and flowers. The leaves are opposite and narrowly linear; the 2-lipped, tubular flowers are produced in short, few-flowered, axillary whorls. Grow in a shrub or mixed border, in a herb garden, against a warm, sunny wall, or use as hedging. Low-growing cultivars, such as *R. officinalis* 'Prostratus', are suitable for growing in a rock garden or along the top of a dry wall. The leaves of rosemary are commonly dried and used as a culinary herb.
• **HARDINESS** Frost hardy; *R. officinalis* and most cultivars will withstand falls to -10°C (14°F) in well-drained soil.
• **CULTIVATION** Grow in well-drained, poor to moderately fertile soil in full sun. Pruning group 9. Trim hedges after flowering.
• **PROPAGATION** Sow seed in containers in a cold frame in spring. Root semi-ripe cuttings in summer.
• **PESTS AND DISEASES** Honey fungus may be a problem.

Rosmarinus officinalis

***R. eriocalyx* of gardens** see *R. officinalis* 'Prostratus'.
***R. lavandulaceus* of gardens** see *R. officinalis* 'Prostratus'.
R. officinalis ▣ (Rosemary). Upright to rounded, dense, bushy, aromatic, evergreen shrub with linear, leathery, dark green leaves, to 5cm (2in) long, white-felted beneath. Whorls of tubular, 2-lipped, purple-blue to white flowers, 1cm (½in) long, are produced from the upper leaf axils from mid-spring to early summer, and often again in autumn. ↕↔ 1.5m (5ft). Mediterranean. ✻✻. **'Aureovariegatus'** see 'Aureus'. **'Aureus'**, syn. 'Aureovariegatus', 'Gilded', produces yellow-marked leaves. **'Benenden Blue'**, syn. 'Collingwood Ingram', has narrow, dark green leaves and vivid blue flowers. **'Collingwood Ingram'** see 'Benenden Blue'. **'Fastigiatus'** see 'Miss Jessopp's Upright'. **'Gilded'** see 'Aureus'. **'Miss Jessopp's Upright'**, syn. 'Fastigiatus', f. *pyramidalis*, is vigorous and has an upright habit; ↕↔ 2m (6ft). **'Prostratus'** ▣ syn. *R. eriocalyx* of gardens, *R. lavandulaceus* of gardens, is prostrate and the least hardy variant; ↕15cm (6in). **f. *pyramidalis*** see 'Miss Jessopp's

R

Rosmarinus officinalis 'Prostratus'

Upright'. **'Roseus'** produces pink flowers. **'Severn Sea'** has a spreading habit, with arching branches and bright blue flowers; ↕ 1m (3ft). **'Tuscan Blue'** is upright, bearing dark blue flowers.

ROSSIOGLOSSUM

ORCHIDACEAE

Genus of 6 species of epiphytic, evergreen orchids from rainforest, up to altitudes of 2,700m (9,000ft), in Central America. At its apex, each conical to ovoid, dark grey-green pseudobulb produces 1–3 broadly oval, dark green to grey- or bluish green leaves, marked brown at the bases. Erect or arching, few-flowered racemes of showy, yellow and brown flowers are produced from the base of new growth from autumn to winter. Use as houseplants.

• **HARDINESS** Frost tender.

• **CULTIVATION** Cool-growing orchids. Grow in epiphytic orchid compost, with added leaf mould and sphagnum, in bright filtered light. In summer, provide good ventilation and, as new growth begins, water freely, applying a balanced liquid fertilizer monthly; keep just moist in winter. See also p.46.

• **PROPAGATION** Divide when the plant fills the pot and "flows" over the sides.

• **PESTS AND DISEASES** Prone to red spider mites, aphids, and mealybugs.

R. grande, syn. *Odontoglossum grande* (Clown orchid, Tiger orchid). Epiphytic orchid with elliptic to lance-shaped, leathery, dark or bluish green leaves, 10–20cm (4–8in) long. From autumn to winter, bears erect racemes of 4–8 rich, glossy, chestnut-brown and yellow flowers, 12cm (5in) across, spotted red, brown, or yellow, with white lips. ↕ 35cm (14in), ↔ 20cm (8in). Mexico, Guatemala. ⊛ (min. 10°C/50°F; max. 30°C/86°F)

ROSULARIA

CRASSULACEAE

Genus of about 25 species of evergreen succulent perennials from the mountains of S.W. Europe, N. Africa, and Central Asia to the Himalayas. They produce mat-forming, clump-forming, or solitary rosettes of oblong to spoon-shaped, fleshy leaves, which are frequently pale green and may be entire or minutely toothed. In summer, panicles of funnel-, saucer-, or bell-shaped, white, yellow, or pink flowers are borne on erect leafy stems, which may be lateral or terminal on the rosette. The rosettes of some species die after flowering. Grow rosularias in a rock garden, scree bed, or trough, or in an alpine house.

R

• **HARDINESS** Frost hardy to frost tender.

• **CULTIVATION** Outdoors, grow in moderately fertile, sharply drained soil, with added grit, in full sun. Protect from excessive winter wet (a rock crevice, sheltered from rain, is ideal). In an alpine house, grow in a shallow container in loam-based potting compost (JI No.2), with added grit, in full light. Water moderately in growth, applying a balanced liquid fertilizer at half strength monthly; keep just moist in winter.

• **PROPAGATION** Sow seed under glass in spring. Detach and root offsets in summer or early autumn.

• **PESTS AND DISEASES** May be damaged by vine weevil and aphids.

R. chrysantha. Mat-forming, succulent perennial with rosettes, 1.5–3cm (½–1¼in) across, of oblong-spoon-shaped, entire, glandular-hairy to glabrous, pale green leaves, 1–2cm (½–¾in) long. In early summer, bears narrowly funnel-shaped, white or pale creamy yellow flowers, 1.5cm (½in) long, in terminal panicles on erect stems, the rosettes dying after flowering. ↕ 15cm (6in), ↔ 20cm (8in). Turkey. ❄❄

R. sedoides, syn. *Sempervivella sedoides.* Mat-forming, succulent perennial with rosettes, 2–4cm (¾–1½in) across, of spoon-shaped to ovoid, entire, glandular-hairy leaves, 1–2cm (½–¾in) long, bright green becoming red-tinged in summer, each rosette producing small offsets on thread-like stolons. In summer, saucer-shaped white flowers, to 1.5cm (½in) across, are borne in lateral panicles just above the foliage. ↕ 10cm (4in), ↔ 20cm (8in). S. Himalayas (Kashmir). ❄❄

R. sempervivum. Variable, clump-forming, succulent perennial with flat, loose rosettes, 4–8cm (1½–3in) across, composed of spoon-shaped, entire, fleshy, glandular-hairy, dark green leaves, 1.5–4.5cm (½–1¾in) long, with few offsets. In summer, funnel-shaped, deep pink flowers, 8–10mm (⅜–½in) long, are borne in lateral panicles. ↕ 10cm (4in), ↔ 10–15cm (4–6in). E. Mediterranean (Turkey, Iran). ⊛ (min. 5°C/41°F)

ROTHMANNIA

RUBIACEAE

Genus of 25–30 species of evergreen shrubs and small trees from woodland and open savannah in tropical Africa, the Seychelles, Madagascar, and Asia. The leaves are simple and usually in opposite pairs, but sometimes in threes. They are cultivated for their bell- or funnel-shaped flowers, each with 5 spreading petal lobes, borne singly or in terminal and axillary clusters or cymes. Where temperatures fall below 7–10°C (45–50°F), grow in a cool or temperate greenhouse. In milder climates, grow at the base of a warm, sunny wall or in a shrub border.

• **HARDINESS** Frost tender.

• **CULTIVATION** Under glass, grow in loamless or loam-based potting compost (JI No.2) in full light, with shade from hot sun. When in growth, water freely with soft water and apply a balanced liquid fertilizer monthly; water sparingly in winter. Outdoors, grow in moist but well-drained, fertile, neutral to acid soil in full sun with some midday shade. Pruning group 1; plants under glass may need restrictive pruning.

• **PROPAGATION** Sow seed at 16°C (61°F) in spring. Root semi-ripe cuttings with bottom heat in summer.

• **PESTS AND DISEASES** Whiteflies, stem mealybugs, and root mealybugs may be a problem under glass.

R. capensis 🌳 syn. *Gardenia capensis, G. rothmannia* (Candlewood). Spreading tree with grey to brown bark. The broadly lance-shaped or elliptic to ovate leaves, 5–10cm (2–4in) long, are lustrous, deep green with conspicuous, sunken veins above, paler green beneath. Solitary, funnel-shaped, fragrant, white, cream, or yellow flowers, to 8cm (3in) long, are borne in summer. ↕ to 14m (46ft), ↔ to 7m (22ft). South Africa. ⊛ (min. 7–10°C/45–50°F)

R. globosa 🌳 syn. *Gardenia globosa* (September bells). Spreading, large shrub or small tree with dark grey to brown bark. Inversely lance-shaped to lance-shaped or elliptic leaves, 6–12cm (2½–5in) long, are bright green with yellow, pink, or maroon veins, more obvious beneath than above. Narrowly bell-shaped, fragrant, ivory to white, occasionally pink-tinged flowers, to 4cm (1½in) long, with arching to reflexed petal lobes, are borne singly or in small clusters in the leaf axils in summer. ↕ 3–7m (10–22ft), ↔ 2–3.5m (6–11ft). South Africa. ⊛ (min. 7–10°C/45–50°F)

▷ **Rowan** see *Sorbus aucuparia*
Hubei see *S. hupehensis*

ROYSTONEA

Royal palm

ARECACEAE/PALMAE

Genus of about 10 species of single-stemmed palms occurring in moist, rich soil on the Caribbean islands and adjacent coasts. The trunks may be columnar, or swollen in the middle or at the base. Each trunk is topped by a crownshaft and a tuft of pinnate, feather-shaped, bright mid-green leaves. The tiny, cup-shaped, 3-petalled flowers are borne in panicles just below the crownshaft. In frost-prone climates, grow young plants in a warm greenhouse. In tropical regions, use royal palms as lawn specimens or grow them in an avenue.

• **HARDINESS** Frost tender.

• **CULTIVATION** Under glass, grow in loamless potting compost in full light, shaded from hot sun. When in growth, water freely and apply a balanced liquid fertilizer monthly; water moderately in winter. Pot on or top-dress in spring.

Roystonea regia

Outdoors, grow in moderately fertile, moist but well-drained soil in full sun.

• **PROPAGATION** Sow seed at 27°C (81°F) in spring.

• **PESTS AND DISEASES** Red spider mites, mealybugs, and scale insects may be a problem under glass.

R. borinquena 🌴 syn. *R. caribaea.* Medium-sized palm with a spindle-shaped trunk ringed with old leaf scars. The arching leaves, up to 3m (10ft) long, have many narrow, linear, rich green leaflets in 2 double ranks. Cup-shaped cream flowers, with green-purple anthers, are borne in panicles, 1m (3ft) long, usually in summer. ↕ to 18m (60ft), ↔ to 6m (20ft). Puerto Rico (including Vieques), US Virgin Islands (St. Croix). ⊛ (min. 15°C/59°F)

R. caribaea see *R. borinquena.*

R. regia ▣ 🌴 Tall palm with a sturdy trunk, usually thickened at the base and again in the middle, becoming thinner towards the crownshaft. Leaves 3–5m (10–15ft) long, have many linear, rich green leaflets arranged in several ranks. Cup-shaped white flowers are borne in panicles, to 1m (3ft) long, usually in summer. ↕ to 25m (80ft), ↔ to 10m (30ft). Cuba. ⊛ (min. 15°C/59°F)

▷ **Rubber plant** see *Ficus elastica*

RUBUS

ROSACEAE

Genus of 250 or more species of often prickly or bristly, deciduous or evergreen shrubs and climbers, occasionally herbaceous perennials, found worldwide in a range of habitats from coastal sand dunes to thickets, woodland, forest, and mountain slopes. The leaves are alternate and entire, lobed, palmate, or pinnate, each with 3 to many, usually toothed leaflets. The saucer- to cup-shaped, 4- or 5-petalled flowers are borne in racemes or panicles, sometimes singly or in few-flowered clusters, and are pink, white, red, or purple.

Blackberries or brambles (*R. fruticosus*), raspberries (*R. idaeus*), and hybrids between these and other species are grown for their edible fruits. Ornamental species are cultivated for their flowers, their foliage, and sometimes their attractive winter shoots, and are suitable for growing in a shrub border. Prostrate species provide good ground cover in sun or shade. Vigorous species are best grown in a wild or woodland garden.

• **HARDINESS** Fully hardy to frost hardy.

• **CULTIVATION** Grow in well-drained, moderately fertile soil. Grow deciduous species that are cultivated for their winter shoots in full sun; grow evergreen or semi-evergreen species in sun or partial shade. Pruning group 7 for *R. biflorus, R. cockburnianus, R. thibetanus*; group 2 for other deciduous species and cultivars; group 11 for *R. henryi*, after flowering, although pruning is seldom required.

• **PROPAGATION** Divide *R. odoratus* in autumn. Root greenwood cuttings of deciduous species and cultivars in summer, or hardwood cuttings in early winter. Root semi-ripe cuttings of evergreens in summer. Detach rooted pieces of prostrate evergreens between autumn and spring.

Rubus 'Benenden'

• **PESTS AND DISEASES** Grey mould (*Botrytis*) may be a problem.

***R.* 'Benenden'** ▣ Spreading, deciduous shrub with arching, thornless branches, peeling bark, and broadly ovate, shallowly 3- to 5-lobed, dark green leaves, 6–8m (2½–3in) long. Solitary, rose-like, saucer-shaped, pure white flowers, to 7cm (3in) across, are borne profusely in late spring and early summer. ↕↔ 3m (10ft). ❄❄❄
***R.* 'Betty Ashburner'.** Prostrate, evergreen shrub with erect then arching shoots, densely covered in red bristles. Heart-shaped, shallowly 5-lobed, wavy-margined, glossy, mid-green leaves, 6cm (2½in) long, are deeply veined above, glaucous beneath. In summer, produces racemes of saucer-shaped white flowers, 2cm (¾in) across, from the leaf axils. ↕ 30cm (12in), ↔ indefinite. ❄❄❄
R. biflorus ▣ Erect, prickly, deciduous shrub with chalky-white-bloomed young shoots, particularly conspicuous in winter. Ovate, pinnate leaves, to 25cm (10in) long, each have 3, sometimes 5, ovate to elliptic, dark green leaflets, white-felted beneath. In summer, produces saucer-shaped white flowers,

Rubus biflorus

Rubus henryi var. *bambusarum*

2cm (¾in) across, singly or in clusters of 2 or 3 from the leaf axils, followed by edible, spherical yellow fruit, to 2cm (¾in) across. ↕↔ 3m (10ft). Himalayas, China. ❄❄❄. **var. *quinqueflorus*** has intensely white stems, and bears clusters of 5 or more flowers.
R. calycinoides see *R. pentalobus.*
R. cockburnianus. Thicket-forming, deciduous shrub producing arching, prickly shoots with a brilliant white bloom in winter. Ovate, pinnate leaves, to 20cm (8in) long, with 5–7, sometimes 9, diamond-shaped or ovate-lance-shaped leaflets, are dark green above and white-hairy beneath, appearing greenish white overall. In summer, bears terminal racemes of saucer-shaped purple flowers, 1cm (½in) across, followed by spherical black, unpalatable fruit, to 1.5cm (½in) across. ↕↔ 2.5m (8ft). China. ❄❄❄
***R. fockeanus* of gardens** see *R. pentalobus.*
R. henryi* var. *bambusarum ▣ Scrambling, evergreen climber with slender, spiny, white-hairy shoots and lance-shaped, deeply 3-lobed, glossy, dark green leaves, to 12cm (5in) long, white-felted beneath. Long racemes of cup-shaped pink flowers, 2cm (¾in) across, are borne in summer, followed by spherical, glossy black fruit, 1.5cm (½in) across. ↕ 6m (20ft). W. and C. China. ❄❄❄
R. odoratus (Flowering raspberry). Fast-growing, thicket-forming, deciduous shrub with spineless shoots and large, broadly ovate, 5-lobed, velvety, dark green leaves, to 24cm (10in) long. From early summer to early autumn, bears panicles of shallowly cup-shaped,

Rubus spectabilis 'Olympic Double'

fragrant, purple-pink flowers, to 5cm (2in) across; they are followed by tasteless, flattened hemispherical red fruit, to 2cm (¾in) across. ↕↔ 2.5m (8ft) or more. E. North America. ❄❄❄
R. pentalobus, syn. *R. calycinoides*, *R. fockeanus* of gardens. Prostrate, evergreen shrub with sparsely prickly shoots that root as they creep along the ground. The rounded, shallowly 3- to 5-lobed, glossy, dark green leaves, to 5cm (2in) long, are heart-shaped at the bases, with deeply impressed veins and wrinkled margins. In summer, bears solitary, saucer-shaped white flowers, 2cm (¾in) across, sometimes followed by spherical red fruit, to 10mm (½in) across. ↕ 10cm (4in), ↔ indefinite. Taiwan. ❄❄❄
***R. spectabilis* 'Flore Pleno'** see *R. spectabilis* 'Olympic Double'.
***R. spectabilis* 'Olympic Double'** ▣ syn. *R. spectabilis* 'Flore Pleno'. Thicket-forming, deciduous shrub with upright, slightly prickly shoots and 3-palmate leaves, to 15cm (6in) long, composed of ovate, glossy, mid-green leaflets. Usually solitary, very showy, double, bright purple-pink flowers, 5cm (2in) across, open in mid-spring. ↕↔ 2m (6ft). ❄❄❄
R. thibetanus. Erect, thicket-forming, deciduous shrub with arching, prickly shoots, conspicuously white-bloomed in winter. Triangular, pinnate, dark green leaves, to 22cm (9in) long, have 7–13 lance-shaped to ovate leaflets, densely grey-hairy above, densely white-hairy beneath. In summer, saucer-shaped, red-purple flowers, 1cm (½in) across, are borne singly from the upper leaf axils or in few-flowered terminal racemes, followed by spherical black fruit, to 1.5cm (½in) across, with a whitish bloom. ↕↔ 2.5m (8ft). W. China. ❄❄❄
R. tricolor. Prostrate, evergreen shrub with both creeping and arching shoots, covered in conspicuous red bristles. Ovate, entire or very shallowly 3- to 5-lobed, glossy, dark green leaves, to 10cm (4in) long, are heart-shaped at the bases and white-hairy beneath. Saucer-shaped white flowers, 2.5cm (1in) across, open singly or in few-flowered terminal racemes in summer, followed by edible, raspberry-like red fruit, to 2.5cm (1in) across. ↕ 60cm (24in), ↔ indefinite. China (Sichuan, Yunnan). ❄❄❄
***R. ulmifolius* 'Bellidiflorus'.** Fast-growing, deciduous or semi-evergreen shrub of open habit, with long, arching, thorny shoots and 3- to 5-palmate leaves, to 12cm (5in) long, composed of ovate, dark green leaflets. Large panicles of hemispherical, double pink flowers, to 1.5cm (½in) across, are produced in mid- and late summer. ↕ 2.5m (8ft), ↔ 4m (12ft). ❄❄❄

RUDBECKIA

Coneflower

ASTERACEAE/COMPOSITAE

Genus of about 20 species of annuals, biennials, and perennials (some of which may be grown as annuals), with short rhizomes, from moist meadows and light woodland in North America. They have branched or unbranched stems, and most have alternate, simple to pinnatifid, occasionally pinnate, prominently veined leaves, toothed towards the tips. Usually solitary, daisy-like flowerheads, often with reflexed yellow ray-florets and conical centres

Rudbeckia fulgida var. *sullivantii* 'Goldsturm'

consisting of black, brown, or green disc-florets, are borne on long stems over a long period from summer to autumn. Most are good for cut flowers. Grow in a border, or naturalize in a meadow or woodland garden. Most cultivars of *R. hirta* are grown as annuals, and are good for bedding or for infilling in borders.
• **HARDINESS** Fully hardy to half hardy.
• **CULTIVATION** Grow in moderately fertile, preferably heavy but well-drained soil that does not dry out, in full sun or partial shade. *R. fulgida* var. *deamii* is more drought-tolerant than other species. On fertile soils, *R. laciniata* 'Golden Glow' may become invasive.
• **PROPAGATION** Sow seed of perennials in containers in a cold frame in early spring, or divide in autumn or spring. Sow seed of annuals and biennials at 16–18°C (61–64°F) in spring.
• **PESTS AND DISEASES** Slugs may damage young growth. *R. laciniata* 'Golden Glow' is susceptible to aphids.

***R.* 'Autumn Sun'** see *R.* 'Herbstsonne'.
R. columnifera see *Ratibida columnifera.*
R. deamii see *R. fulgida* var. *deamii.*
R. fulgida (Black-eyed Susan). Rhizomatous perennial with branched stems, long-stalked, oblong to lance-shaped, entire basal leaves, to 12cm (5in) long, and lance-shaped, toothed stem leaves; both are mid-green and slightly hairy with prominent veins. Daisy-like flowerheads, to 7cm (3in) across, with orange-yellow ray-florets and conical, blackish brown disc-florets, are borne from late summer to mid-autumn. ↕ to 90cm (36in), ↔ 45cm (18in). E. USA. ❄❄❄. **var. *deamii***, syn. *R. deamii*, is free-flowering, and has very hairy stems with long-pointed, ovate or oval-ovate, toothed, rough basal and stem leaves; ↕ to 60cm (24in). USA (Indiana). **var. *speciosa***, syn. *R. newmanii*, *R. speciosa*, has elliptic to lance-shaped, almost sickle-shaped basal leaves and coarsely toothed stem leaves; USA (New Jersey to Alabama and Georgia). **var. *sullivantii***, syn. *R. sullivantii*, has broadly ovate to narrowly ovate-lance-shaped, less hairy, coarsely toothed, dark green basal leaves and stem leaves, which become progressively smaller up the stems. The flowerheads are 8–9cm (3–3½in) across. USA (Michigan to Missouri, Connecticut to W. Virginia). **var. *sullivantii***

Rudbeckia 'Herbstsonne'

'Goldsturm' ■ has large, golden yellow flowerheads, 9–12cm (3½–5in) across, on shorter stems than the species; ↕ to 60cm (24in).
R. gloriosa see *R. hirta.*
***R.* 'Herbstsonne'** ■ syn. *R.* 'Autumn Sun'. Upright, rhizomatous, clump-forming perennial with oval, toothed or slightly lobed, prominently veined, glossy, mid-green leaves, to 15cm (6in) long. From midsummer to early autumn, branching stems produce daisy-like flowerheads, 10–12cm (4–5in) across, with bright yellow ray-florets and high, conical centres of green disc-florets, becoming yellowish brown with age. ↕ to 2m (6ft), ↔ 90cm (36in). ❄❄❄
R. hirta, syn. *R. gloriosa* (Black-eyed Susan). Upright, stout-stemmed, branching, bristly biennial or short-lived perennial, often grown as an annual, with mid-green leaves. The basal leaves are ovate to diamond-shaped, sometimes slightly toothed, strongly 3-veined, and to 10cm (4in) long; the stem leaves are usually narrower and ovate to lance-shaped. Daisy-like flowerheads, to 7cm (3in) across, with pale to golden yellow ray-florets and prominent, conical centres of deep brown-purple disc-florets, are produced between summer and early autumn. ↕ 30–90cm (12–36in), ↔ 30–45cm (12–18in). C. USA. ❄❄❄. **'Bambi'** produces flowerheads with bronze-brown, chestnut-brown, and golden yellow ray-florets; ↕ to 30cm (12in). **Becky Mixed** ■ is very dwarf, and produces flowerheads with ray-florets in shades of lemon-yellow, golden yellow, and dark red or reddish brown; ↕ to 25cm (10in). **'Goldilocks'** produces double and semi-double flowerheads with golden-orange ray-florets; ↕ to 60cm (24in). **'Green Eyes'** see 'Irish Eyes'. **'Irish Eyes'**, syn. 'Green Eyes', bears flowerheads with bright yellow ray-florets and green disc-florets; ↕ 60–75cm (24–30in). **'Kelvedon Star'** produces flowerheads with deep golden yellow ray-florets, zoned in brownish red. **'Marmalade'** is bushy and compact, with flowerheads of generous size, sometimes to 13cm (5in) across, with deep golden orange ray-florets; ↕ to 45cm (18in). **'Rustic Dwarfs'** ■ produces flowerheads with golden yellow, brownish red, or bronze-orange ray-florets, with some bicolours; ↕ to 60cm (24in). **'Sonora'** is compact, producing flowerheads with bright yellow ray-florets; ↕ to 40cm (16in).
R. laciniata. Rhizomatous, hairless, glaucous perennial, forming loose clumps of tall, wiry stems, branched towards their tips. Basal leaves, to 10cm (4in) long, are pinnate or pinnatisect, each with deeply 3- to 5-lobed, toothed leaflets and prominent veins; stem leaves become less deeply lobed higher up the stems. Daisy-like flowerheads, 7–15cm (3–6in) across, with reflexed, pale yellow ray-florets and hemispherical to conical centres of greenish yellow disc-florets, are produced between midsummer and mid-autumn. ↕ 1.5m–3m (5–10ft), ↔ 1m (3ft). C. and E. North America. ❄❄❄. **'Golden Fountain'** see 'Goldquelle'. **'Golden Glow'** is extremely vigorous, producing fully double flowerheads with yellow ray-florets; ↕ to 1.8m (6ft), ↔ 2–2.5m (6–8ft). **'Goldquelle'** ■ syn. 'Golden Fountain', is compact, bearing double flowerheads with lemon-yellow ray-florets, and green disc-florets that turn yellow as the flowerheads open; ↕ to 90cm (36in), ↔ 45cm (18in). **var. *hortensia***, syn. 'Hortensia', is the name applied to all variants of *R. laciniata* that bear double flowerheads.
R. newmanii see *R. fulgida* var. *speciosa.*
R. purpurea see *Echinacea purpurea.*
R. speciosa see *R. fulgida* var. *speciosa.*
R. sullivantii see *R. fulgida* var. *sullivantii.*

Rudbeckia laciniata 'Goldquelle'

Rudbeckia hirta Becky Mixed

Rudbeckia hirta 'Rustic Dwarfs'

▷ **Rue** see *Ruta*
Common see *Ruta graveolens*
Fringed see *Ruta chalepensis*
Goat's see *Galega*

RUELLIA

syn. DIPTERACANTHUS

ACANTHACEAE

Diverse genus of about 150 species of evergreen perennials and soft-stemmed or woody shrubs and subshrubs, widely distributed in tropical America, warm parts of North America, and Africa and Asia, where they are found in meadows and at woodland margins. The leaves are opposite and entire, and may be stalked or stalkless. Funnel-shaped flowers are produced singly, in clusters from the leaf axils, or in terminal panicles. The tropical species, in particular, are cultivated for their attractive foliage and flowers, and are suitable for informal borders or plantings. In frost-prone climates, grow tender species in a warm greenhouse.

- **HARDINESS** Fully hardy to frost tender.
- **CULTIVATION** Under glass, grow in loamless potting compost in bright filtered light with high humidity. In the growing season, water freely and apply a balanced liquid fertilizer monthly; water moderately in winter. Pinch out the young shoots to encourage branching. Pruning group 10, after flowering. Outdoors, grow in any fertile, humus-rich, moist soil in a site in full sun or partial shade.
- **PROPAGATION** Sow seed at 19–24°C (66–75°F) in spring. Root softwood cuttings in spring or early summer.
- **PESTS AND DISEASES** Trouble free.

R. amoena see *R. graecizans.*
R. devosiana ■ Hairy shrub with soft, purple-flushed stems and broadly lance-shaped, pale-veined, dark green leaves, to 8cm (3in) long, purple beneath. Funnel-shaped, lavender-blue-flushed white flowers, 4–5cm (1½–2in) long, with slender tubes and notched, spreading, purple-veined lobes, are produced singly from the leaf axils from spring to summer. ↕ 45cm (18in), ↔ 30cm (12in). Brazil. ❀ (min. 12°C/54°F)
R. graecizans, syn. *R. amoena.* Bushy shrub with soft, spreading stems and ovate to oblong, hairless, mid-green leaves, to 18cm (7in) long. Funnel-shaped scarlet flowers, 2.5cm (1in) long, each with one enlarged sepal, are borne in axillary clusters on long stalks from spring to summer. ↕ 60cm (24in), ↔ 45cm (18in). South America. ❀ (min. 12°C/54°F)

Ruellia devosiana

Ruellia macrantha

R. macrantha ■ (Christmas pride). Erect, soft-stemmed subshrub with lance-shaped, hairy, dull, dark green leaves, to 15cm (6in) long. From autumn to winter, funnel-shaped but slightly curved, rich purplish pink flowers, to 8cm (3in) long, with darker veins, are produced singly from the leaf axils. ↕ to 2m (6ft), ↔ 45cm (18in). Brazil. ❄ (min. 12°C/54°F)
R. makoyana (Monkey plant, Trailing velvet plant). Slender- and soft-stemmed, spreading, hairy perennial with ovate, silver-veined purple leaves, to 8cm (3in) long, dark purple beneath. In summer, produces funnel-shaped, carmine-pink flowers, 5cm (2in) long, singly from the leaf axils. ↕ to 60cm (24in), ↔ 45cm (18in). Brazil. ❄ (min. 12°C/54°F)

RUMEX

Dock

POLYGONACEAE

Genus of about 200 species of annuals, biennials, and usually tap-rooted, sometimes rhizomatous perennials from a range of habitats including mountains, wasteland, cultivated ground, and streamsides in N. temperate regions. Docks have simple, variably shaped, mainly basal leaves, which occasionally have wavy margins. In summer, the tiny, star-shaped, bisexual or unisexual flowers are borne in whorls in usually erect, dense, terminal panicles or racemes. They are followed by small, triangular, brown to red-brown fruit. Some species are invasive weeds; a few are grown for their decorative foliage or as herbs. Grow in a herbaceous or mixed border. All parts of docks may cause mild stomach upset if ingested; contact with the foliage may irritate skin.
• **HARDINESS** Fully hardy to half hardy.
• **CULTIVATION** Grow in moderately fertile, well-drained soil in full sun.
• **PROPAGATION** Sow seed *in situ* in spring. Docks also self-seed freely.
• **PESTS AND DISEASES** Susceptible to slug damage and aphids.

R. sanguineus ■ (Bloody dock, Red-veined dock). Tap-rooted, rosette-forming perennial with oblong-lance-shaped, mid- to dark green leaves, 5–15cm (2–6in) long, conspicuously veined blood-red or purple. In early and midsummer, erect, red-tinted flower stems bear panicles of tiny, star-shaped, green then red-brown flowers, 4mm (⅛in) across, followed by dark brown fruit. ↕ to 90cm (36in), ↔ 30cm (12in). Europe, N. Africa, S.W. Asia. ❄❄❄

RUMOHRA

DRYOPTERIDACEAE

Genus of 50 species of epiphytic or terrestrial, rock-dwelling, evergreen ferns occurring in cool woodland or scrub in tropical regions of the S. hemisphere. They have scaly, creeping rhizomes covered in golden brown scales, and triangular, pinnate or 2- or 3-pinnate, leathery fronds. Spores are formed in conspicuous, large, circular spots, each covered with a centrally attached indusium. In frost-prone climates, grow in a warm greenhouse; in warmer areas, grow epiphytically or in a damp, shady border. The fronds are popular for flower arrangements.
• **HARDINESS** Frost tender.
• **CULTIVATION** Under glass, grow epiphytically on bark, or in shallow pots or hanging baskets in a mix of 1 part each of loam, medium-grade bark, and charcoal, 2 parts sharp sand, and 3 parts coarse leaf mould. Provide bright filtered light and moderate humidity. In growth, mist regularly, water freely, and apply a half-strength balanced liquid fertilizer monthly; water sparingly in winter. Outdoors, grow epiphytically or in moist, leafy, open, humus-rich soil in partial or light dappled shade.
• **PROPAGATION** Sow spores at 21°C (70°F) as soon as ripe, or separate rooted sections of rhizomes in early summer. See also p.51.
• **PESTS AND DISEASES** Trouble free.

R. adiantiformis ■ (Leather fern). Evergreen, terrestrial or epiphytic fern, very variable in size, producing ovate or triangular, 2- or 3-pinnate, leathery, dark green fronds, to 90cm (36in) or more long; the fronds have narrowly diamond-shaped to oblong pinnae. ↕ 0.5–1.5m (20–60in), ↔ to 1m (3ft). Tropical and subtropical areas of S. hemisphere. ❄ (min. 10–13°C/ 50–55°F)

▷**Running postman** see *Kennedia prostrata*

RUPICAPNOS

PAPAVERACEAE

Genus of about 30 species of almost stemless, evergreen perennials found on sunny mountain slopes or cliff faces in Spain and N. Africa. They have pinnate, finely dissected leaves with pinnatisect leaflets, and bear corymb-like racemes of tubular, 4-petalled, spurred flowers in summer. The short-lived *R. africana* is the most commonly cultivated species, and can be successfully grown in a scree bed or alpine house.
• **HARDINESS** Frost hardy. Will survive temperatures to -10°C (14°F), but will not tolerate winter wet.
• **CULTIVATION** Under glass, grow in a mix of 1 part each of loam and leaf mould and 2 parts grit, with additional tufa chippings, in full light. Water moderately in the growing season; keep just moist in winter. Self-seed freely under glass. Outdoors, grow in gritty, sharply drained soil in a scree bed, in full sun with protection from excessive winter wet.
• **PROPAGATION** Collect seed when almost ripe but still green, and sow immediately in containers in a cold frame.
• **PESTS AND DISEASES** Trouble free.

R. africana ■ Short-lived perennial producing basal clumps of fern-like, pinnate, bright grey-blue leaves, 8–10cm (3–4in) long, finely divided into pinnatisect leaflets, which may be linear, ovate, or oblong. Delicate, corymb-like racemes of 4-petalled, spurred, pinkish-purple flowers, to 1.5cm (½in) long, with dark purple tips, are borne over a long period in summer. ↕ 15cm (6in), ↔ 20cm (8in). Morocco (Rif Mountains). ❄❄. **subsp. *decipiens*** bears yellow-marked white flowers; S.W. Spain.

RUSCHIA

AIZOACEAE

Genus of about 350 species of shrubby or stemless, mat-forming, perennial succulents from semi-desert regions of Namibia and South Africa. Many species branch freely to form tufts or mats; others become shrubby, to 1m (3ft) tall. The leaves are arranged in pairs and are often boat-shaped. Daisy-like flowers open during the day in summer. In warm, dry climates, grow in a raised bed or desert garden. In frost-prone areas, grow prostrate species in a temperate greenhouse, or treat as frost-tender annuals and use for bedding, window-boxes, or hanging baskets.
• **HARDINESS** Frost tender.
• **CULTIVATION** Under glass, grow in standard cactus compost in full light with low humidity. Water moderately from spring to autumn, applying a dilute balanced liquid fertilizer once in late spring and once in late summer; keep dry in winter. Outdoors, grow in poor, gritty, sharply drained soil in full sun. See also pp.48–49.
• **PROPAGATION** Sow seed at 21°C (70°F) in early spring. Plant out seedlings to be grown as annuals when all danger of frost has passed. Root cuttings of stem sections from spring to summer.
• **PESTS AND DISEASES** Susceptible to mealybugs.

R. acuminata. Shrubby succulent with erect or almost prostrate, woody stems. Produces pairs of ovoid, bluntly keeled, sometimes toothed leaves, to 2.5cm (1in) long, with convex sides, narrowing towards the tips. They are roughly papillose, fleshy, and blue-green marked with dull green spots. In summer, bears solitary, terminal or axillary, daisy-like, white or pale pink flowers, 3cm (1¼in) across. ↕ 20cm (8in), ↔ 50cm (20in). South Africa (Eastern Cape). ❄ (min. 7°C/45°F)
R. derenbergiana see *Ebracteola derenbergiana.*
R. macowanii ■ Shrubby succulent with short, prostrate, woody stems and erect, fleshy branches. The fleshy, grey-green leaves, to 3.5cm (1½in) long, are boat-shaped to cylindrical, flat above and keeled beneath. In summer, bears solitary, terminal, daisy-like pink flowers, 2cm (¾in) across, with a darker pink stripe on each petal. ↕ 20cm (8in), ↔ 45cm (18in). South Africa (Western Cape, Northern Cape, Eastern Cape). ❄ (min. 7°C/45°F)
R. pusilla. Tufted, prostrate, almost stemless succulent with nearly spherical, fleshy, bright green leaves, 4mm (⅛in) long, keeled beneath. Solitary, terminal or axillary, daisy-like, pale pinkish white flowers, 1cm (½in) across, are produced in summer. ↕↔ 7cm (3in). South Africa (Western Cape, Northern Cape, Eastern Cape). ❄ (min. 7°C/45°F)
R. pygmaea. Mat-forming, prostrate succulent with very short, fleshy stems bearing 1 or 2 dissimilar pairs of ovoid or ellipsoid, fleshy, bright green leaves, to 5mm (¼in) long, keeled beneath, and more or less united almost to the tips. The leaf skins gradually shrivel to disclose a second pair of leaves, which are not united, and these become the

Rumex sanguineus

Rumohra adiantiformis

Rupicapnos africana

Ruschia macowanii

first pair of leaves of the following year's growth. Solitary, terminal or axillary, daisy-like, whitish pink flowers, to 2cm (¾in) across, are borne in summer. ↕↔ 8cm (3in). Namibia, South Africa (Western Cape, Northern Cape, Eastern Cape). ❀ (min. 7°C/45°F)

RUSCUS
Broom

LILIACEAE/RUSCACEAE

Genus of 6 species of rhizomatous, evergreen subshrubs from woodland in Madeira and the Azores, through Europe and N. Africa to Iran. The tiny, true leaves are replaced by flattened, leaf-like shoots (cladophylls) on which the flowers and showy red fruits are borne. The inconspicuous, star-shaped, green or greenish white flowers, to 2mm (1/16in) across, each have 6 tepals. *Ruscus* species are usually dioecious, and plants of both sexes are normally needed to obtain fruit; however, *R. aculeatus* sometimes bears hermaphrodite, self-fertile flowers. Grow in a dry, shady site. The stems may be dried in glycerine and used in floral arrangements. The berries of *R. aculeatus* may cause mild stomach upset if ingested.

- **HARDINESS** Fully hardy to frost hardy.
- **CULTIVATION** Grow in any but water-logged soil in sun or partial or full shade. Individual shoots are short-lived, but new ones are produced annually; cut out dead stems at the base in spring.
- **PROPAGATION** Sow seed in a seedbed, or in containers in a cold frame, as soon as ripe. Divide in spring.
- **PESTS AND DISEASES** Trouble free.

R

Ruscus hypoglossum

R. aculeatus (Butcher's broom). Clump-forming, rhizomatous subshrub with upright, branched shoots bearing ovate, spine-tipped, glossy, dark green cladophylls, to 2.5cm (1in) long. From late summer to winter, female plants produce spherical, bright red berries, 8mm (⅜in) across, on the upper sides of the cladophylls. ↕ 75cm (30in), ↔ 1m (3ft). Europe, N. Turkey, N. Africa, Azores. ❄❄❄

R. hypoglossum ■ Clump-forming, rhizomatous subshrub producing arching, unbranched shoots and obovate to broadly ovate, glossy, mid-green cladophylls, to 10cm (4in) long. Female plants bear spherical red berries, 1cm (½in) across, on the upper sides of the cladophylls, from autumn to winter. ↕ 45cm (18in), ↔ 1m (3ft). Italy, Czech Republic to Turkey. ❄❄

R. hypophyllum. Rhizomatous, clump-forming subshrub with upright shoots and ovate, pointed, dark green cladophylls, to 10cm (4in) long. Female plants bear spherical red berries, 1cm (½in) across, on the upper or lower side of the cladophylls, from late summer to winter. Male and female flowers may be borne on the same plant. ↕ 60cm (24in), ↔ 1m (3ft). S.E. France, S. Spain, N. Africa, Sicily. ❄❄

▷ **Rush** see *Juncus*
Corkscrew see *Juncus effusus* f. *spiralis*
Dwarf Japanese see *Acorus gramineus* var. *pusillus*
Egyptian paper see *Cyperus papyrus*
Flowering see *Butomus*
Japanese see *Acorus gramineus*
Jointed see *Juncus articulatus*
Mat see *Lomandra*
Pale mat see *Lomandra glauca*
Spiny-headed mat see *Lomandra longifolia*
Variegated Japanese see *Acorus gramineus* 'Variegatus'
▷ **Rushes** see p.54

RUSSELIA

SCROPHULARIACEAE

Genus of about 50 species of evergreen or deciduous shrubs and subshrubs found at forest margins from Mexico and Cuba to Colombia. The pendent, rush-like stems bear opposite or whorled, often scale-like leaves. Showy, tubular, red, pink, or white flowers are borne in axillary cymes, or sometimes singly. *R. equisetiformis* is the only species commonly cultivated. In frost-prone areas, grow as houseplants, in a cool or temperate greenhouse, or in hanging baskets. In warmer climates, grow at the front of a shrub border, or allow to trail over the edges of a raised bed or wall.

- **HARDINESS** Frost tender.
- **CULTIVATION** Under glass, grow in loam-based potting compost (JI No.2) in full or bright filtered light. When in growth, water moderately and apply a balanced liquid fertilizer monthly; water sparingly in winter. Outdoors, grow in a sheltered site in well-drained, humus-rich, moderately fertile soil in full sun. Pruning group 9.
- **PROPAGATION** Divide rooted layers in spring; root softwood cuttings at any time of year.
- **PESTS AND DISEASES** Trouble free.

Russelia equisetiformis

R. equisetiformis ■ syn. *R. juncea* (Coral plant, Firecracker plant). Deciduous, branching subshrub with rush-like, erect and pendent, mid-green stems. The elliptic, scale-like, mid-green leaves, to 1.5cm (½in) long, fall early. Tubular scarlet flowers, to 3cm (1¼in) long, are borne in pendent cymes from spring to autumn. ↕ 1.5m (5ft), ↔ 2.5m (8ft). Mexico. ❀ (min. 10°C/50°F)

R. juncea see *R. equisetiformis.*

▷ **Russian vine** see *Fallopia baldschuanica*
▷ **Rusty leaf** see *Menziesia ferruginea*

RUTA
Rue

RUTACEAE

Genus of 8 species of deciduous or evergreen shrubs, subshrubs, and woody-based herbaceous perennials, occurring in dry, rocky habitats in the Canary Islands, the Mediterranean region, N.E. Africa, and S.W. Asia. They are cultivated for their aromatic foliage and flowers. The leaves are alternate, occasionally opposite, broadly ovate to rounded, and pinnatisect to pinnate. The unusual, 4- or 5-petalled, fringed or toothed yellow flowers are produced in terminal cymes. Rue is suitable for growing in a mixed or herbaceous border, or in a rock garden or herb garden. The foliage is sometimes used medicinally or very sparingly as a culinary flavouring. All parts of rue may cause severe discomfort if ingested; the foliage may cause photodermatitis on contact.

- **HARDINESS** Fully hardy to frost hardy.
- **CULTIVATION** Grow in moderately fertile, very well-drained soil in full sun or partial shade. Rue will thrive in a hot, dry site. Pruning group 10, in spring or after flowering.
- **PROPAGATION** Sow seed in containers in a cold frame in spring. Root semi-ripe cuttings in summer.
- **PESTS AND DISEASES** *Phytophthora* root rot may be a problem.

R. chalepensis (Fringed rue). Upright subshrub producing broadly ovate, 2- or 3-pinnatisect, aromatic, blue-green leaves, to 12cm (5in) long, with numerous oblong-lance-shaped or obovate lobes. Cup-shaped, dark yellow flowers, 2cm (¾in) across, each with 4 petals fringed with long hairs, are borne in open cymes in summer. ↕↔ 60cm (24in). S. Europe, N.E. Africa, S.W. Asia. ❄❄.

'Dimension Two' is more spreading than the species, and almost prostrate.

R. graveolens (Common rue). Rounded to erect, evergreen shrub with alternate, broadly ovate to rounded, 2-pinnatisect, aromatic, glaucous, blue-green leaves, to 15cm (6in) long, with numerous obovate lobes. Cymes of cup-shaped, 4-petalled, dull yellow flowers, 2cm (¾in) across, are borne in summer. ↕ 1m (3ft), ↔ 75cm (30in). S.E. Europe. ❄❄❄.

'Jackman's Blue' ■ more compact than the species, with more intensely glaucous, blue-green foliage; ↕ 60cm (24in).

▷ ***Ruyschiana spicata*** see *Dracocephalum ruyschiana*
▷ **Rye,**
Canadian wild see *Elymus canadensis*
Wild see *Elymus*

Ruta graveolens 'Jackman's Blue'

S

SABAL

Palmetto

ARECACEAE/PALMAE

Genus of 14 species of single-stemmed or stemless palms, chiefly from low-lying or swampy areas in tropical forest, from S. USA to N. South America, and from the West Indies. They have deeply divided, fan-shaped leaves, which often remain *in situ* when they die, forming a skirt-like bundle just below each crown. Panicles of 3-petalled flowers are borne between the leaves, usually in summer. In frost-prone areas, grow in a cool to warm greenhouse, a conservatory, or as houseplants. In warmer areas, plant the trees as lawn specimens and the stemless species in a shrub border.

- **HARDINESS** Frost tender.
- **CULTIVATION** Under glass, grow in well-drained, loam-based potting compost (JI No.2) in bright indirect light. During the growing season, water moderately and apply a balanced liquid fertilizer monthly. Pot on or top-dress in spring. Mist over lightly every day in summer. Keep just moist in winter. Outdoors, grow in moderately fertile, moist but well-drained soil in full sun with some midday shade.
- **PROPAGATION** Sow seed at 19–24°C (66–75°F) in spring.
- **PESTS AND DISEASES** Prone to scale insects and red spider mites under glass.

S. glabra see *S. minor.*
S. guatemalensis see *S. mexicana.*
S. mexicana 🌴 syn. *S. guatemalensis, S. texana* (Texas palmetto). Medium-sized palm with a columnar trunk that bears old leaf bases for several years. Fan-shaped, bright green, often yellowish green leaves, 1m (3ft) long, are divided up to halfway into many slender, pointed lobes. Bears cream flowers in panicles as long as or longer than the leaves, usually in summer. ↕ to 18m (60ft), ↔ to 4m (12ft). USA (Texas), Mexico, Guatemala. ❀ (min. 10–13°C/50–55°F)
S. minima see *S. minor.*
S. minor ■ ✻ syn. *S. glabra, S. minima, S. pumila* (Dwarf palmetto, Scrub palmetto). Small palm with a short, buried stem (only the tip visible above the ground) and long-stalked, fan-shaped, blue-green leaves, 1–1.5m (3–5ft) long, divided at least to two-thirds into many slender lobes. Cream flowers are borne, usually in summer, in erect to arching panicles, to 2m (6ft) long. ↕ 1–2m (3–6ft), ↔ to 3m (10ft). S.E. USA. ❀ (min. 3–5°C/37–41°F)
S. palmetto ■ 🌴 (Cabbage palmetto, Common blue palmetto). Large palm with a rough trunk, to 60cm (24in) in diameter. Bears compact, spherical heads of many fan-shaped, rich green leaves, to 2m (6ft) long, divided into

Sabal palmetto

numerous long, 2-lobed segments with thread-like filaments hanging between them. Cream flowers are borne in panicles just longer than the leaves, usually in summer. ↕ to 30m (100ft), ↔ 5–7m (15–22ft). USA (N. Carolina to Florida). ❀ (min. 5–7°C/41–45°F)
S. pumila see *S. minor.*
S. texana see *S. mexicana.*

Sabal minor

▷ ***Sabina*** see *Juniperus*

SACCHARUM

syn. ERIANTHUS

Plume grass

GRAMINEAE/POACEAE

Genus of about 20 species of reed-like, tufted, clump-forming, or rhizomatous, perennial grasses found by riversides and in valley bottoms, widely distributed in warm-temperate and tropical regions. They are grown for their inflorescences and foliage. Leaves are narrowly lance-shaped to linear. Large, plume-like panicles of crowded flower spikes with silky-hairy spikelets are borne in pairs in summer and autumn. Effective at the back of a herbaceous or mixed border, against a warm, sunny wall, or as free-standing specimens. The cut panicles are useful in fresh and dried arrangements.

- **HARDINESS** Fully hardy to frost tender.
- **CULTIVATION** Grow in moderately fertile, well-drained soil in full sun, with shelter from cold, drying winds. Protect crowns from extreme cold with dry mulch or horticultural fleece. Remove any flowerheads left for winter effect by early spring. *S. ravennae* flowers most reliably after a long, hot summer.
- **PROPAGATION** Sow seed in containers under glass or in a cold frame in spring. Divide in mid-spring or early summer.
- **PESTS AND DISEASES** Trouble free.

S. ravennae. Robust, densely tufted, perennial grass with arching, linear leaves, 60–90cm (24–36in) long, that are grey-green with central white stripes, purple-tinted in autumn. In late summer and autumn, erect stems bear dense, upright panicles, to 60cm (24in) long, of softly hairy, silver-grey to purple flower spikes. ↕ 2–3m (6–10ft), ↔ 1.2m (4ft). Mediterranean to N. Africa. ✻✻ (hardy to about -8°C/18°F)

▷ **Sacred flower of the Incas** see *Cantua buxifolia*
▷ **Sacred fig** see *Ficus religiosa*
▷ **Sacred lotus** see *Nelumbo nucifera*

SADLERIA

BLECHNACEAE

Genus of 7 species of evergreen, tree-like ferns from rainforest and exposed sites on lava flows in Hawaii. They each have a stout rhizome, crowned with large, divided fronds. The spores, unlike those of other tree ferns, such as *Cyathea* and *Dicksonia,* are borne in lines along the midribs of the frond segments. *S. cyatheoides* is the only species generally grown. In frost-prone areas, grow in a temperate greenhouse, a conservatory, or as houseplants. In warmer areas, grow in a shrub border, a woodland garden, or as a free-standing specimen.

- **HARDINESS** Frost tender.
- **CULTIVATION** Under glass, grow in equal parts medium-grade bark, perlite, and charcoal, in bright indirect to moderate light, and with moderate to high humidity. In growth, water moderately and apply a balanced liquid fertilizer monthly; keep just moist in winter. Outdoors, grow in moderately fertile, humus-rich, moist but well-drained, acid to neutral soil in partial to deep shade; shelter from cold, dry winds.
- **PROPAGATION** Sow spores at 21°C (70°F) as soon as ripe. See also p.51.
- **PESTS AND DISEASES** Trouble free.

S. cyatheoides. Tree-like fern with ovate, 2-pinnate, leathery fronds, 90cm (36in) long, dark green above, glaucous beneath; they have narrowly oblong pinnae, and numerous linear segments with the margins rolled under. ↕ 1.5m (5ft), ↔ 1.8m (6ft). USA (Hawaii). ❀ (min. 10°C/50°F)

▷ **Safflower** see *Carthamus, C. tinctorius*
▷ **Saffron,**
  False see *Carthamus tinctorius*
  Meadow see *Colchicum autumnale*
▷ **Saffron-spike** see *Aphelandra squarrosa*
▷ **Sage** see *Salvia*
  Autumn see *Salvia greggii*
  Blue see *Eranthemum pulchellum*
  Bog see *Salvia uliginosa*
  Common see *Salvia officinalis*
  Jerusalem see *Phlomis fruticosa, Pulmonaria saccharata*
  Jim see *Salvia clevelandii*
  Mealy see *Salvia farinacea*
  Pineapple see *Salvia elegans* 'Scarlet Pineapple'
  Purple see *Salvia officinalis* 'Purpurascens'
  Scarlet see *Salvia splendens*
▷ **Sagebrush** see *Artemisia, Seriphidium tridentatum*
▷ **Sage wood, South African** see *Buddleja salviifolia*

SAGINA

Pearlwort

CARYOPHYLLACEAE

Genus of about 20 species of compact, low-growing annuals and perennials found in a wide range of habitats, extensively distributed throughout the temperate regions of the N. hemisphere. They have linear to narrowly wedge-shaped leaves, arranged in pairs and joined at the bases around the stems. Minute, 4- or 5-petalled, rarely petalless white flowers are produced either singly or in few-flowered cymes. The majority of pearlworts are weeds; those described

Sagina boydii

here are cultivated mainly for their dense mats or cushions of leaves, which provide effective ground cover. They are suitable for growing in a rock garden or paving crevice. Alternatively, grow in an alpine house.

• **HARDINESS** Fully hardy.

• **CULTIVATION** Grow in poor to moderately fertile, acid to neutral, moist but well-drained soil in full sun with some midday shade. *S. boydii* requires very sharply drained, poor soil, and tolerates partial shade. In an alpine house, grow in 3 parts grit or sharp sand and 1 part peat or leaf mould. Dislikes hot, dry conditions.

• **PROPAGATION** Sow seed in containers in a cold frame in autumn. Divide *S. subulata* in spring. Root individual rosettes of *S. boydii* as cuttings in early summer.

• **PESTS AND DISEASES** Prone to aphids or red spider mites under glass.

S. boydii ▣ Very slow-growing, dense, cushion-forming perennial producing crowded rosettes of rigid, linear to narrowly wedge-shaped, recurved, glossy, dark green leaves, to 2cm (¾in) long. Bears tiny, solitary, normally petalless, mid-green flowers in summer. Best in an alpine house. ↕2.5cm (1in), ↔ 8cm (3in). Scotland. ❄❄❄

***S. glabra* 'Aurea'** see *S. subulata* 'Aurea'.

***S. subulata* 'Aurea'**, syn. *S. glabra* 'Aurea'. Mat-forming perennial with slender, rooting stems clothed in pointed, linear, yellow-green leaves, to 1cm (½in) long. In summer, bears solitary, 5-petalled white flowers, 4mm (⅛in) across, on stems to 4cm (1½in) long. Effective low ground cover in a rock garden or between paving stones. ↕1cm (½in), ↔ 20cm (8in) or more. W. and C. Europe. ❄❄❄

SAGITTARIA

Arrowhead

ALISMATACEAE

Genus of 20 species of marginal and submerged, herbaceous aquatic perennials and annuals, found mainly on muddy banks or in shallow water in temperate and tropical Europe, Asia, and North, Central, and South America. The often decorative leaves are aerial, floating, or submerged, and linear to elliptic, lance-shaped, ovate, or arrow-shaped. Panicles or racemes of whorled, 3-petalled, saucer-shaped white flowers are borne in summer. Most are excellent for the margins of a wildlife pool, where their tuberous rootstocks may spread; some (including *S. latifolia* and *S. sagittifolia*) produce walnut-sized tubers that attract waterfowl. Grow *S. subulata* in an aquarium for its attractive submerged leaves. In frost-prone areas, grow tender species in a pool in a cool or temperate greenhouse.

• **HARDINESS** Fully hardy to frost tender.

• **CULTIVATION** Outdoors, grow at the margins of a pool, in water no deeper than 22–30cm (9–12in), in full sun. Trim back spreading growth in late summer and remove faded flowers to prevent seeding. In an aquarium, grow in groups of 4 or 5 in a gravelly soil in bright indirect light, with a minimum temperature of 16°C (61°F). Under glass, grow in baskets at the margins of an indoor pool in bright filtered light, with a water temperature of 10°C (50°F). See also pp.52–53.

• **PROPAGATION** Sow seed as soon as ripe in containers standing in trays of shallow water. Remove runners, or collect and plant overwintering tubers, in spring.

• **PESTS AND DISEASES** Leaves may be damaged by water-lily aphid.

S. japonica see *S. sagittifolia* 'Flore Pleno'.

S. lancifolia. Stoloniferous, marginal aquatic perennial producing lance-shaped, leathery, pale green aerial leaves, 15–45cm (6–18in) long. In summer, bears several whorls of white flowers, 3–5cm (1¼–2in) across, on scapes to 2m (6ft) tall. ↕↔ 1.5m (5ft). Tropical and subtropical North, Central, and South America. ❀ (min. 10°C/50°F)

S. latifolia ▣ (Duck potato, Wapato). Marginal aquatic perennial with large tubers and variable, mainly arrow-shaped aerial leaves, 10–30cm (4–12in) long. In summer, racemes of whorled white flowers, 3–4cm (1¼–1½in) across, are produced on the triangular flower stems, to 1.2m (4ft) tall. ↕45–90cm (18–36in), ↔ 90cm (36in). USA. ❄❄❄

S. sagittifolia (Japanese arrowhead). Marginal aquatic perennial bearing arrow-shaped aerial leaves, 25cm (10in) long, with 2 long, acute, basal lobes. In deep water, produces ribbon-like floating leaves, to 80cm (32in) long. In summer, scapes to 1m (3ft) tall bear racemes of white flowers, to 2.5cm (1in) across, with a purple spot at the base of each petal. ↕90cm (36in), ↔ indefinite. Eurasia. ❄❄❄. **'Flore Pleno'**, syn. *S. japonica*, is double-flowered.

S. subulata. Stoloniferous aquatic perennial bearing variable, usually linear, frequently bent or crooked submerged leaves, to 1m (3ft) long (depending on the depth of the water), with long, sharp-pointed or rounded tips. In shallow water, produces elliptic floating leaves, 5cm (2in) long. White flowers, 1.5–2cm (½–¾in) across, are borne in floating whorls of 1–3, in summer. ↕to 60cm (24in), ↔ indefinite. E. USA. ❄

Sagittaria latifolia

▷**Sago, False** see *Cycas circinalis*
▷**Sago fern** see *Cyathea medullaris*
▷**Sago palm** see *Caryota urens, Cycas, C. circinalis*
Japanese see *C. revoluta*
▷**Saguaro cactus** see *Carnegia gigantea*
▷**Sailor caps** see *Dodecatheon hendersonii*
▷**St. Barbara's herb** see *Barbarea*
▷**St. Bernard's lily** see *Anthericum liliago*
▷**St. Bruno's lily** see *Paradisea*
▷**St. Catherine's lace** see *Eriogonum, E. giganteum*
▷**St. Dabeoc's heath** see *Daboecia cantabrica*
▷**St. John's wort** see *Hypericum*
Perforate see *H. perforatum*
▷**St. Joseph's lily** see *Hippeastrum vittatum*
▷**St. Lucie cherry** see *Prunus mahaleb*

SAINTPAULIA

African violet

GESNERIACEAE

Genus of 20 species of low-growing, evergreen perennials found on banks, streamsides, on or among rocks, or as epiphytes on trees in a very small area of tropical E. Africa. Most are virtually stemless or have very short stems, and form rosettes of rounded to elliptic, somewhat succulent, usually hairy leaves. Trailing African violets produce the rosettes on extended stems, with the leaf-stalks usually longer than the leaf-blades. Flowers normally have 2 smaller petals at the top and 3 larger ones below, and are borne singly or in cymes.

There are over 2,000 cultivars, mainly derived from *S. ionantha*, with white, pink, red, blue, violet, bi- or multi-coloured flowers, 1–6cm (½–2½in) across, borne throughout the year. They may be single (5-petalled), semi-double (with small crests or lobes in the middle of the 5 petals), or fully double (with 2 or more layers of petals). The flowers are star-shaped, with all 5 petals of the same shape and size, or bell-shaped. Petal edges may be ruffled, rounded, frilled, or fringed. The leaves are usually mid- or dark green, and may be subtly feathered or flecked, or strongly variegated white, pink, or cream; most are broadly ovate to oval, and 4–20cm (1½–8in) long, including the stalks. Grow African violets as houseplants; most greenhouses or conservatories are too hot in summer and too cold in winter.

African violet cultivars are classified by rosette size into 5 groups (see below). The measurement given is the diameter of the rosette; the spread of each cultivar is the same as this.

MICRO-MINIATURE	less than 8cm (3in)
MINIATURE	8–16cm (3–6in)
SEMI-MINIATURE	16–21cm (6–8in)
STANDARD	21–40cm (8–16in)
LARGE	over 40cm (16in)

• **HARDINESS** Frost tender. Ideal temperature is 18–24°C (64–75°F).

• **CULTIVATION** Under glass, grow in well-drained loamless potting compost in bright filtered light and moderate to

S

Saintpaulia 'Bright Eyes'

Saintpaulia 'Chantabent'

Saintpaulia 'Delft'

Saintpaulia 'Dorothy'

Saintpaulia 'Fancy Pants'

Saintpaulia 'Garden News'

Saintpaulia 'Ice Maiden'

Saintpaulia 'Kristi Marie'

Saintpaulia 'Ms. Pretty'

Saintpaulia 'Rococo Anna'

Saintpaulia 'Starry Trail'

Saintpaulia 'Zoja'

high humidity. At least 12 hours of light per day is needed for long-term flowering. Avoid direct summer sun, but position in the brightest light in winter; artificial light is useful. From early to late summer, water moderately and apply a high potash and phosphate liquid fertilizer every 2 weeks, or add a quarter-strength fertilizer at every watering. Repot at least once a year, keeping to virtually the same container size; do not overpot.

• **PROPAGATION** Sow seed at 19–24°C (66–75°F) as soon as ripe or in early spring. Root leaf cuttings or suckers of cultivars at 24–27°C (75–81°F) in summer. Chimaeras (graft hybrids) will not come true from leaf cuttings.

• **PESTS AND DISEASES** Prone to aphids, mealybugs, thrips, tarsonemid mites, vine weevil larvae, grey mould (*Botrytis*), crown rot, and powdery mildew.

***S.* 'Bright Eyes'** ■ (Standard group) Rosetted perennial with dark green leaves and single, deep blue flowers with prominent yellow pollen sacs. ↕ to 15cm (6in). ❄ (min. 15°C/59°F)

***S.* 'Chantabent'** ■ (Semi-miniature group) Rosetted perennial bearing dark green leaves with deep red undersides. Bears large, single, violet-blue flowers. ↕ 10–15cm (4–6in). ❄ (min. 15°C/59°F)

***S.* 'Chantiana'.** (Miniature group) Rosetted perennial with light green leaves and fully double, light coral-pink flowers. ↕ 8–10cm (3–4in). ❄ (min. 15°C/59°F)

***S.* 'Chantora'.** (Miniature group) Rosetted perennial bearing pointed, dark green leaves with dark red undersides, and single, deep red flowers. ↕ 8–10cm (3–4in). ❄ (min. 15°C/59°F)

***S.* 'Colorado'** ■ syn. *S.* 'Optimara Colorado'. (Standard group) Rosetted perennial with mid-green leaves. The single red flowers have frilled margins and bold yellow pollen sacs. ↕ 15–20cm (6–8in). ❄ (min. 15°C/59°F)

***S.* 'Dancin' Trail'.** (Semi-miniature group) Trailing, rosetted perennial with pointed, shiny, dark green leaves, red beneath, and fully double, magenta-red flowers. ↕ 10–15cm (4–6in). ❄ (min. 15°C/59°F)

***S.* 'Delft'** ■ (Standard group) Strong-growing, rosetted perennial bearing mid-green leaves and large, semi-double, cornflower-blue flowers. ↕ 15cm (6in). ❄ (min. 15°C/59°F)

***S.* 'Dina Mo'.** (Standard group) Rosetted perennial bearing mid-green leaves and fully double, fuchsia-red flowers with narrow white margins. ↕ 15cm (6in). ❄ (min. 15°C/59°F)

***S.* 'Dorothy'** ■ (Standard group) Rosetted perennial bearing long-stalked, light green leaves and large, single, rich pink flowers with frilled white margins. ↕ 15cm (6in). ❄ (min. 15°C/59°F)

***S.* 'Dyn-O-Mite'.** (Standard group) Rosetted perennial producing mid-green leaves with red undersides, and semi-double red flowers. ↕ 15cm (6in). ❄ (min. 15°C/59°F)

***S.* 'Fancy Pants'** ■ (Standard group) Rosetted perennial bearing mid-green leaves and single white flowers with frilled red margins. ↕ 15–20cm (6–8in). ❄ (min. 15°C/59°F)

***S.* 'Fancy Trail'** (Standard group) Compact, rosetted, trailing perennial with shiny, variegated green and white leaves and fully double pink flowers. ↕ 15cm (6in). ❄ (min. 15°C/59°F)

***S.* 'Garden News'** ■ (Standard group) Rosetted perennial bearing light green leaves and producing fully double white flowers, sometimes tinged pale lilac. ↕ 15cm (6in). ❄ (min. 15°C/59°F)

***S.* 'Granger's Wonderland'** see *S.* 'Wonderland'.

S. grotei. Trailing, branching perennial with stems to 40cm (16in) long, rooting at the nodes. Rounded leaves, 8cm (3in) long, have prominent veins and coarsely scalloped margins, and are held on leaf-stalks to 25cm (10in) long. Cymes of 2 or 3 pale mauve flowers, 3cm (1¼in) across, with violet throats, are borne intermittently throughout the year. A parent of the trailing hybrids. ↕ 15–20cm (6–8in), ↔ 30–50cm (12–20in). Tanzania. ❄ (min. 15°C/59°F)

***S.* 'Ice Maiden'** ■ (Standard group) Rosetted perennial bearing mid-green leaves and single white flowers with purple-blue markings. ↕ 15cm (6in). ❄ (min. 15°C/59°F)

S. ionantha. Stemless, rosette-forming perennial producing ovate to oblong-ovate, scalloped, mid-green leaves, to 5cm (2in) long, paler beneath, on leaf-stalks 6cm (2½in) long. Cymes of 8–10 light to dark blue flowers, 2.5cm (1in) across, are produced intermittently throughout the year. ↕ to 10cm (4in), ↔ 15cm (6in). Tanzania. ❄ (min. 15°C/59°F)

***S.* 'King's Treasure'.** (Standard group) Rosetted perennial bearing mid-green leaves and fully double, dark lavender-blue flowers, margined purple, each with a fine white, often green-tinged line at the extreme edges. ↕ 15cm (6in). ❄ (min. 15°C/59°F)

***S.* 'Kiwi Dazzler'.** (Standard group) Rosetted perennial with mid-green leaves. Bears fringed, single, bright red flowers, each with a central white stripe. A chimaera (graft hybrid), so propagate from suckers. ↕ 15cm (6in). ❄ (min. 15°C/59°F)

***S.* 'Kristi Marie'** ■ (Standard group) Rosetted perennial bearing dark green leaves and producing fully double, dusky-red flowers, with white margins. ↕ 15–20cm (6–8in). ❄ (min. 15°C/59°F)

***S.* 'Lila'.** (Standard group) Rosetted perennial producing dark green leaves with red undersides and single, white-

Saintpaulia 'Colorado'

Saintpaulia 'Pip Squeek'

margined, lavender-blue flowers. ↕ 15cm (6in). ❄ (min. 15°C/59°F)
S. 'Maria'. (Standard group) Rosetted perennial bearing dark green leaves and large, single, clear pink flowers with frilled margins. ↕ 15cm (6in). ❄ (min. 15°C/59°F)
S. 'Midget Valentine'. (Miniature group) Rosetted perennial bearing shiny leaves, variegated green and white, and single, fuchsia-red flowers. ↕ 8–10cm (3–4in). ❄ (min. 15°C/59°F)
S. 'Moon Kissed'. (Semi-miniature group) Rosetted perennial bearing dark green leaves and fully double white flowers with fuchsia-pink markings. ↕ 8–13cm (3–5in). ❄ (min. 15°C/59°F)
S. 'Ms. Pretty' ▣ (Standard group) Rosetted perennial bearing dark green leaves and single white flowers with fringed, pink margins. ↕ 15cm (6in). ❄ (min. 15°C/59°F)
S. 'Nortex's Snowkist Haven'. (Standard group) Rosetted perennial with pointed, quilted, mid-green leaves and fringed, single white flowers. ↕ 15cm (6in). ❄ (min. 15°C/59°F)
S. 'Optimara Colorado' see *S.* 'Colorado'.
S. 'Pip Squeek' ▣ (Micro-miniature group) Rosetted, semi-trailing perennial with tiny, pointed, dark green leaves and bearing single, light pink flowers. ↕ 8–10cm (3–4in). ❄ (min. 15°C/59°F)
S. 'Rococo Anna' ▣ syn. *S.* 'Rococo Pink'. (Standard group) Rosetted perennial bearing mid-green leaves with very light green bases and pale undersides, and fully double, deep pink flowers. ↕ 15cm (6in). ❄ (min. 15°C/ 59°F)
S. 'Rococo Pink' see *S.* 'Rococo Anna'.
S. shumensis. Compact, rosette-forming perennial with very short stems. Bears ovate to almost round, toothed leaves, 3.5cm (1½in) long, often with red-tinged veins beneath. Bears cymes of up to 5 pale mauve, almost white flowers, 2.5cm (1in) across, with deep purple eyes, intermittently throughout the year. ↕ 6–8cm (2½–3in), ↔ 8–12cm (3–5in). Tanzania. ❄ (min. 15°C/59°F)
S. 'Snuggles'. (Miniature group) Rosetted perennial with dark green leaves, feathered and margined white, and large, semi-double pink flowers. ↕ 8–10cm (3–4in). ❄ (min. 15°C/59°F)
S. 'Starry Trail' ▣ (Standard group) Rosetted, trailing perennial with dark green leaves. Bears narrow-petalled, semi-double to fully double white flowers, sometimes flushed pale pink. ↕ 15cm (6in). ❄ (min. 15°C/59°F)
S. 'Tomahawk'. (Standard group) Rosetted perennial producing dark green leaves and semi-double to fully double, dark red flowers, with fluted petals. ↕ 15–20cm (6–8in). ❄ (min. 15°C/59°F)
S. 'Wonderland', syn. *S.* 'Granger's Wonderland'. (Large group) Rosetted perennial with wavy-margined, olive-green leaves and ruffled, semi-double, light blue flowers. ↕ 15cm (6in). ❄ (min. 10°C/50°F)
S. 'Zoja' ▣ (Standard group) Rosetted perennial with mid-green leaves and large, single to semi-double, purple-blue flowers with a bold white line at the margin of each petal. ↕ 15cm (6in). ❄ (min. 10°C/50°F)

▷**St. Vincent lilac** see *Solanum seaforthianum*
▷**Salal** see *Gaultheria shallon*

S

SALIX

Willow

SALICACEAE

Genus of approximately 300 species of normally dioecious, deciduous trees and shrubs found in habitats ranging from lowland meadows and riverbanks to sand dunes and mountain screes worldwide, except in Australia. They have simple, entire or toothed, usually alternate leaves, and bear very small flowers in usually erect catkins, before or with the foliage. Of diverse form, willows are cultivated for their habit (particularly the weeping willows), catkins (of which the males are usually the most striking), foliage, and sometimes coloured winter shoots. The largest willows are suitable only for a garden of large proportions; those with a weeping habit are especially effective by water. Grow smaller willows as specimen trees in a small garden, shrubby willows in a shrub border, and dwarf willows in a rock garden or trough.

• **HARDINESS** Fully hardy.

• **CULTIVATION** Grow in any deep, moist but well-drained soil in full sun; willows dislike shallow chalk soil. *S.* 'Erythroflexuosa' needs well-drained soil; the dwarf and alpine species need gritty, sharply drained soil. Pruning group 1 for most; group 7, every 1–3 years, for those grown for coloured winter shoots, and to rejuvenate old plants.

• **PROPAGATION** Root greenwood cuttings in early summer, or hardwood cuttings in winter.

Salix alba var. *vitellina* 'Britzensis'

• **PESTS AND DISEASES** Aphids, caterpillars, leaf beetles, sawflies, willow scale, anthracnose, honey fungus, and rust may be a problem.

S. acutifolia ♀ Spreading tree with slender, arching, deep purple, white-bloomed shoots and narrowly lance-shaped, tapered, dark green leaves, to 10cm (4in) long. Silvery male catkins, 5cm (2in) long, with golden anthers, or pale green female catkins, 2–3cm (¾–1¼) long, are produced in early spring, before the leaves. ↕ 10m (30ft), ↔ 12m (40ft). Russia to E. Asia. ❄❄❄. **'Blue Streak'** is a male clone, and has blue-black shoots with a vivid blue-white bloom.
S. aegyptiaca ♀ syn. *S. medemii* (Musk willow). Strong-growing, bushy shrub or

Salix alba var. *vitellina*

Salix apoda

tree with stout, red-purple shoots and oblong, toothed, dark green leaves, to 15cm (6in) long, with glaucous, hairy undersides. Fragrant grey catkins are produced in early spring, before the leaves: males are up to 4cm (1½in) long, with yellow anthers; females are up to 8cm (3in) long. ↕ 4m (12ft), ↔ 5m (15ft). Turkey, Armenia, Iraq, Iran, Afghanistan. ❄❄❄
S. alba ♀ (White willow). Very fast-growing, spreading tree with grey-pink to brown shoots and lance-shaped, saw-toothed, slender-pointed, dull green leaves, to 10cm (4in) long, silky-hairy when young, blue-green beneath. Yellow male catkins, to 5cm (2in) long, or stalkless, yellow-green female catkins, 3cm (1¼in) long, are produced in spring, with the leaves. ↕ 25m (80ft), ↔ 10m (30ft). Europe, N. Africa, C. Asia. ❄❄❄. **f. *argentea*** see var. *sericea*. **var. *caerulea*** (Cricket-bat willow) has upright branches and blue-green leaves. **var. *sericea***, syn. f. *argentea*, 'Sericea', 'Splendens' (Silver willow) has silvery grey leaves; ↕ 15m (50ft), ↔ 8m (25ft). **'Splendens'** see var. *sericea*. **'Tristis'** ♀ syn. *S. vitellina* 'Pendula', has a more weeping habit, and only produces female catkins. **'Tristis' of gardens** see *S.* x *sepulcralis* 'Chrysocoma'. **var. *vitellina*** ▣ (Golden willow) produces bright yellow to orange winter shoots. **var. *vitellina* 'Britzensis'** ▣ is a male clone, with bright orange-red winter shoots. **var. *vitellina* 'Chermesina'** is a male clone, with carmine-red young winter shoots.
S. apoda ▣ Prostrate shrub with obovate, leathery, dark green leaves, 2–8cm (¾–3in) long, hairy when young. Silky, silvery grey male catkins, 3cm (1¼in) long, which become pink-orange with maturity, are borne in early spring, before the leaves. Female clones are rarely cultivated. Suitable for large rock gardens. ↕ 20cm (8in), ↔ to 60cm (24in). E. Europe, Caucasus. ❄❄❄
S. arenaria see *S. repens* var. *argentea*.
S. babylonica ♀ (Weeping willow). Rounded, weeping tree with slender, pendent, green to brown shoots. Lance-shaped, saw-toothed, tapered, mid-green leaves, to 10cm (4in) long, are grey-green beneath. Slender, silvery green catkins are produced in spring, with the leaves: the males to 5cm (2in) long with yellow anthers, the females to 2.5cm (1in) long. Largely replaced in gardens by *S.* x *sepulcralis* 'Chrysocoma'. ↕↔ 12m (40ft). N. China. ❄❄❄. **'Annularis'** see

Salix babylonica var. *pekinensis* 'Tortuosa'

'Crispa'. **'Crispa'** syn. 'Annularis', is slow-growing and upright, and has curiously twisted leaves. **var. *pekinensis* 'Tortuosa'** ■ syn. *S. matsudana* 'Tortuosa', is fast-growing and upright. It has curiously twisted shoots that are particularly striking in winter, bright green, twisted leaves, and yellow-green catkins; ↕ 15m (50ft), ↔ 8m (25ft).
***S.* 'Blanda'** syn. *S.* x *pendulina* var. *blanda*. Spreading tree with weeping shoots and lance-shaped, tapered, glossy, dark green leaves, to 15cm (6in) long. Slender, silvery green, usually female catkins, to 3cm (1¼in) long, are produced in spring, with the leaves. ↕↔ 12m (40ft). ✲✲✲
S. bockii. Bushy shrub with slender, upright, grey-hairy shoots and oblong, glossy, bright green leaves, to 1.5cm (½in) long, with silky-hairy undersides. Usually female in cultivation; bears green catkins, 4cm (1½in) long, in early and mid-autumn. ↕↔ 2.5m (8ft). W. China. ✲✲✲
***S.* 'Boydii'** see *S.* x *boydii*.
S.* x *boydii ■ (*S. lapponum* x *S. reticulata*) syn. *S.* 'Boydii'. Very slow-growing, upright shrub with gnarled branches bearing almost rounded, rough-textured, prominently veined, grey-green leaves, 1–2cm (½–¾in) long. Occasionally produces insignificant female catkins on bare branches in early spring. Suitable for a rock garden or trough. ↕ 30cm (12in), ↔ 20cm (8in). Scotland (Angus Mountains). ✲✲✲
***S. caprea* 'Kilmarnock'** ■ syn. *S. caprea* 'Pendula' (Kilmarnock willow). Weeping tree with a dense head of stout, yellow-brown shoots and broadly elliptic, toothed leaves, to 10cm (4in) long, dark green above, grey-green beneath. Grey male catkins, 3cm (1¼in) long, studded with yellow anthers, are produced on the bare shoots in mid- and late spring. ↕ 1.5–2m (5–6ft), depending on grafting height, ↔ 2m (6ft). ✲✲✲
***S. caprea* 'Pendula'** see *S. caprea* 'Kilmarnock'.
S.* x *chrysocoma see *S.* x *sepulcralis* 'Chrysocoma'.
S. daphnoides (Violet willow). Initially upright, later spreading tree with purple young shoots, which are white-bloomed in winter, and narrowly oblong, saw-toothed, clearly stalked, dark green leaves, to 12cm (5in) long. Silky grey catkins, to 4cm (1½in) long, are produced in late winter and early spring, before the leaves; male catkins have yellow anthers. ↕ 8m (25ft), ↔ 6m (20ft). Europe to C. Asia. ✲✲✲. **'Aglaia'** ■ has glossy red shoots.
S. elaeagnos, syn. *S. incana* (Hoary willow). Dense, upright shrub with slender, grey-velvety, later red-yellow to almost brown shoots. The linear, entire, dark green leaves, to 20cm (8in) long, are grey when young, white-hairy beneath, and turn yellow in autumn. Produces slender green catkins, 3–6cm (1¼–2½in) long, in spring, as the leaves emerge; male catkins have yellow anthers. ↕ 3m (10ft), ↔ 5m (15ft). C. and S. Europe, S.W. Asia. ✲✲✲
***S.* 'Erythroflexuosa'** syn. *S.* 'Golden Curls', *S. matsudana* 'Tortuosa Aureopendula'. Spreading tree with arching branches and spirally twisted, orange-yellow young shoots. The twisted, lance-shaped, glossy, mid-green leaves, to 8cm (3in) long, are glaucous beneath. Produces slender, pale yellow catkins, 3–4cm (1¼–1½in) long, in spring, with the leaves. ↕↔ 5m (15ft). ✲✲✲
S. exigua ■ (Coyote willow). Upright, thicket-forming, suckering shrub bearing slender shoots. Produces narrowly lance-shaped, tapered, grey-green leaves, to 10cm (4in) long, covered in silky, silvery grey hairs when young. Grey-yellow catkins, the males to 5cm (2in) long, the females to 6cm (2½in) long, are borne in spring, with the leaves. Grows well on sandy soils. ↕ 4m (12ft), ↔ 5m (15ft) or more. W. North America. ✲✲✲
S. fargesii ■ Open, upright, stoutly branched shrub (often confused with *S. moupinensis*) with glossy green young shoots that turn red-brown, and red winter buds. Produces oblong, finely saw-toothed, glossy, dark green leaves, to 18cm (7in) long, silky beneath. Slender green catkins, the males to 12cm (5in) long, the females to 18cm (7in) long, are borne in spring, at the same time as the leaves. ↕↔ 3m (10ft). C. China. ✲✲✲
S. fragilis (Crack willow). Spreading tree with brittle, olive-brown shoots. Bears lance-shaped, finely toothed, glossy, dark green leaves, to 15cm (6in) long, blue-green beneath. Bears slender, pendent green catkins, to 7cm (3in) long, in early spring, as the leaves emerge; male catkins have yellow anthers. ↕↔ 15m (50ft). Europe, N. Turkey, Russia (W. Siberia). ✲✲✲
***S.* 'Golden Curls'** see *S.* 'Erythroflexuosa'.
S. gracilistyla. Spreading, bushy shrub with arching shoots, silky-hairy when young, and oval, entire to finely toothed, silky-hairy, grey-green leaves, to 10cm (4in) long, turning glossy green. Silky grey catkins, to 4cm (1½in) long, are produced in early and mid-spring, before the leaves; male catkins have red anthers that turn bright yellow. ↕ 3m (10ft), ↔ 4m (12ft). E. Asia. ✲✲✲. **'Melanostachys'** ■ syn. var. *melanostachys*, *S. melanostachys*, is an upright male variant that bears black catkins with brick-red anthers.
***S. hastata* 'Wehrhahnii'** ■ Slow-growing, upright shrub with dark purple-brown shoots and oval, entire to finely toothed, bright green leaves, to 6cm (2½in) long. In early spring, bears conspicuous, silvery grey male catkins, to 7cm (3in) long, before the leaves. ↕↔ 1m (3ft). ✲✲✲
S. helvetica ■ (Swiss willow). Upright, many-branched shrub with oblong to ovate-lance-shaped, grey-green leaves, 1–3.5cm (½–1½in) long, smooth above, silver-downy beneath. In early spring, silver-grey catkins, to 5cm (2in) long, open from small golden buds, before the

Salix daphnoides 'Aglaia' (inset: male catkins)

Salix x *boydii*

Salix caprea 'Kilmarnock'

Salix exigua

leaves. ↕ 60cm (24in), ↔ 40cm (16in). Alps. ***
S. hylematica of gardens see *S. lindleyana.*
S. incana see *S. elaeagnos.*
S. irrorata. Upright shrub producing slender purple shoots, which are white-bloomed in winter, and narrowly oblong, entire to sparsely toothed, short-stalked, bright green leaves, to 10cm (4in) long, glaucous beneath. Grey catkins, to 2.5cm (1in) long, are borne in early or mid-spring, before the leaves; male catkins have red anthers that turn yellow. ↕ 3m (10ft), ↔ 5m (15ft). S.W. USA. ***
S. lanata ▣ (Woolly willow). Compact, rounded, bushy shrub bearing stout shoots, white-woolly when young. The leaves are broadly rounded, wavy-margined, dull, dark green, to 6cm (2½in) long, and covered with silvery grey wool. Golden yellow male catkins, to 5cm (2in) long, or grey-yellow female catkins, to 8cm (3in) long, are produced in late spring, with the leaves. ↕ 1m (3ft), ↔ 1.5m (5ft). N. Europe. ***. **'Stuartii'** see *S.* 'Stuartii'.
S. lindleyana, syn. *S. hylematica* of gardens, *S. nepalensis.* Dwarf, procumbent shrub with ovate-spoon-shaped, very glossy, pale green leaves, to 1cm (½in) long, densely set on short branchlets. Bears pinkish brown male catkins, to 1cm (½in) long, or short female catkins, 5mm (¼in) long, in spring, with the leaves. Spreads widely in moist, fertile soils, in partial shade. Much confused with *S. fruticulosa.* ↕ 4cm (1½in), ↔ 60cm (24in) or more. Himalayas. ***
S. magnifica Q Broadly upright shrub or tree bearing stout, red-purple shoots and broadly oval, blue-green leaves, to 20cm (8in) long. Slender green catkins, the males to 18cm (7in) long, the females to 25cm (10in) long, are produced in late spring, after the leaves. ↕ 5m (15ft), ↔ 3m (10ft). W. China. ***
S. 'Mark Postill'. Spreading shrub with stout green shoots, turning brown-purple, and broadly elliptic to rounded, glossy, dark green leaves, to 7cm (3in) long. Stout, initially silvery white, later green female catkins, to 5cm (2in) long, are produced over a long period in spring, before and with the leaves. ↕ 1m (3ft), ↔ 2m (6ft). ***

Salix reticulata

S. matsudana 'Tortuosa' see *S. babylonica* var. *pekinensis* 'Tortuosa'.
S. matsudana 'Tortuosa Aureopendula' see *S.* 'Erythroflexuosa'.
S. medemii see *S. aegyptiaca.*
S. melanostachys see *S. gracilistyla* 'Melanostachys'.
S. nepalensis see *S. lindleyana.*
S. x pendulina var. blanda see *S.* 'Blanda'.
S. pentandra Q (Bay willow). Spreading, bushy-headed tree with brown-green shoots and oval, finely glandular-toothed leaves, to 12cm (5in) long, glossy, dark green above, pale green beneath. Catkins, 5cm (2in) long, are produced in early summer, after the leaves: male catkins are yellow and very showy, with yellow anthers; female catkins are green. ↕↔ 10m (30ft). Eurasia. ***
S. purpurea Q (Purple osier). Spreading shrub to upright tree with arching, frequently red-tinged shoots and often opposite, oblong, almost entire, dark green to blue-green leaves, to 8cm (3in) long. Slender, silvery green catkins, to 3cm (1¼in) long, are produced in early and mid-spring, before the leaves; male catkins have purple anthers that turn yellow. ↕↔ 5m (15ft). Europe, N. Africa, C. Asia. ***. **'Nana'**, syn. 'Gracilis', f. *gracilis*, is compact, bearing slender shoots and small, grey-green leaves, to 3.5cm (1½in) long. Suitable for growing as a low hedge; ↕ 1m (3ft), ↔ 1.5m (5ft).
S. repens ▣ (Creeping willow). Prostrate shrub with slender shoots and

Salix fargesii

Salix gracilistyla 'Melanostachys'

Salix hastata 'Wehrhahnii'

Salix helvetica

Salix lanata

Salix repens

Salix x *sepulcralis* 'Chrysocoma'

oblong to oval, grey-green to bright green leaves, to 3.5cm (1½in) long, silvery beneath. Grey male catkins, to 2cm (¾in) long, with golden yellow anthers, are produced in mid- and late spring, before the leaves. ↕ to 60cm (24in), ↔ 1.5m (5ft) or more. Europe. ***. **var. argentea**, syn. *S. arenaria,* is spreading, with creeping, initially upright, later arching shoots, and obovate, silky grey leaves, to 4cm (1½in) long. Catkins appear in mid-spring; ↕ 1m (3ft), ↔ 2m (6ft); N.W. Europe.
S. reticulata ▣ Dwarf, prostrate shrub with rooting stems bearing rounded-ovate, glossy, dark green leaves, 1–4cm (½–1½in) long, conspicuously veined above, white-hairy beneath. In spring, bears slender yellow catkins, 2.5cm (1in) long, with pink tips. ↕ 8cm (3in), ↔ 30cm (12in). N. Europe, N. Asia, North America. ***
S. retusa. Prostrate, carpeting shrub with rooting stems and ovate-oblong, notched, glossy, mid-green leaves, 1–3cm (½–1¼in) long, mostly clustered towards the twig tips. Bears upright grey catkins, to 2cm (¾in) long, in spring, as the leaves emerge. ↕ 10cm (4in), ↔ to 40cm (16in). Mountains of C. Europe. ***
S. sachalinensis 'Sekka' see *S. udensis* 'Sekka'.
S. x sepulcralis 'Chrysocoma' ▣ Q syn. *S. alba* 'Tristis' of gardens, *S.* x *chrysocoma, S.* x *sepulcralis* var. *chrysocoma* (Golden weeping willow). Fast-growing, wide-spreading tree with slender, golden yellow shoots, pendent to the ground, and narrowly lance-shaped, tapered, bright green leaves, to 12cm (5in) long. Slender catkins, to 5cm (2in) long, both yellow males and green females often present on the same plant, are produced with the leaves, in spring. ↕↔ 15m (50ft). ***
S. x sepulcralis var. chrysocoma see *S.* x *sepulcralis* 'Chrysocoma'.
S. serpyllifolia (Thyme-leaved willow). Prostrate, carpeting shrub with rooting stems and obovate, glossy, mid-green leaves, 1cm (½in) long, that overlap and are pressed closely to the soil. Silvery green catkins, to 5mm (¼in) long, are borne with the leaves, in spring. Very similar to *S. retusa.* ↕ 2.5cm (1in), ↔ 30cm (12in). Alps. ***
S. 'Stuartii', syn. *S. lanata* 'Stuartii'. Dwarf, slow-growing, bushy shrub with yellow-green winter shoots. Bears oblong, dark green leaves, to 5cm (2in) long, woolly when young, densely white-hairy beneath. Yellow-green, initially silky female catkins, to 5cm (2in) long, are borne from orange buds in early and mid-spring. ↕ 1m (3ft), ↔ 2m (6ft). ***
S. udensis 'Sekka', syn. *S. sachalinensis* 'Sekka'. Vigorous, spreading shrub, forming large, dense thickets, with lance-shaped, shallowly scalloped, bright green leaves, to 12cm (5in) long. In early spring, bears showy, silvery grey male catkins, to 4cm (1½in) long, with golden anthers, on often curiously flattened, twisted red shoots. ↕ 5m (15ft), ↔ 10m (30ft). ***
S. viminalis Q (Common osier). Fast-growing, upright shrub or tree with glossy, yellow-green shoots and slender, linear, tapered, dark green leaves, to 15cm (6in) or more long, silver-hairy beneath. Dense, crowded green catkins, to 3.5cm (1½in) long, are produced in late winter and early spring, before the leaves; male catkins have yellow anthers. ↕ 6m (20ft), ↔ 5m (15ft). Eurasia. ***
S. vitellina 'Pendula' see *S. alba* 'Tristis'.

▷ **Sallee, White** see *Eucalyptus pauciflora*

SALPIGLOSSIS

SOLANACEAE

Genus of 2 erect to spreading, bushy, sticky-hairy annuals or short-lived perennials found on disturbed ground, in dry canyons, and on rocky slopes in the southern Andes. They have entire to wavy-margined or lobed, oval to lance-shaped, bright mid-green leaves, and produce funnel-shaped, richly coloured,

Salpiglossis sinuata Casino Series

red, yellow, bronze, violet-blue, or purple flowers from summer to autumn. Suitable for an annual, herbaceous, or mixed border where summers are warm, sunny, and reasonably dry. In cool-temperate regions, they are effective long-flowering container plants in a warm greenhouse or conservatory, and may be bedded out in summer. They provide moderately long-lasting cut flowers.

• **HARDINESS** Half hardy.

• **CULTIVATION** Under glass, grow in loamless or loam-based potting compost (JI No.2) in full light with shade from hot sun. During the growing season, maintain low to moderate humidity, water moderately, and apply a balanced liquid fertilizer every 2 weeks. Keep just moist in winter. Overwinter at 16–18°C (61–64°F). Outdoors, grow in moderately fertile, humus-rich, moist but well-drained soil in full sun; shelter from cold, drying winds. Dead-head to prolong flowering and maintain flower size. Provide brushwood support if grown in a slightly exposed site.

• **PROPAGATION** Sow seed at 18–24°C (64–75°F) in mid-spring, or in autumn or late winter for winter- or early spring-flowering container plants. In very mild areas, sow *in situ* in mid-spring.

• **PESTS AND DISEASES** Aphids, grey mould (*Botrytis*), and foot and root rots may be troublesome.

S. sinuata. Erect annual with slender, branching stems bearing alternate, long-stalked, narrowly to broadly lance-shaped, wavy-margined leaves, to 10cm (4in) long. From summer to autumn, broadly funnel-shaped, 5-lobed flowers, to 5cm (2in) across, in a wide variety of colours, and heavily veined in deeper or contrasting colours, are produced singly in the leaf axils of flowering stems. ↕ to 60cm (24in), ↔ to 30cm (12in). Peru, Argentina. ❄. **Bolero Hybrids** are less floriferous and more straggling than the other cultivars listed, and flower in shades of blue, orange, purple, red, or yellow. Cultivars of **Casino Series** ■ have good weather tolerance, and are compact, branching freely from the bases. Flowers are blue, purple, red, yellow, or orange, often heavily veined. **'Kew Blue'** has clear purple-blue flowers, conspicuously veined.

▷**Salt-and-pepper ivy** see *Hedera helix* 'Minor Marmorata'

▷**Salt tree** see *Halimodendron halodendron*

SALVIA

Sage

LABIATAE/LAMIACEAE

Genus of about 900 species of annuals, biennials, herbaceous and evergreen perennials, and shrubs, some rhizomatous or tuberous. Distributed worldwide in temperate and tropical regions (except in very hot, humid areas), they usually grow in sunny sites, including dry meadows, rocky slopes, scrub, light woodland, and moist grassland. They are frequently aromatic and often hairy; some species are very woolly, and others silver in appearance. The usually square stems bear opposite pairs of simple to pinnate, entire, toothed, notched, or scalloped leaves; basal leaves sometimes differ from stem leaves. Flowers are 2-lipped, the upper lips erect and hooded, the lower ones 2-toothed and more spreading. The calyces are sometimes colourful, and tubular to bell- or funnel-shaped; the often leaf-like, colourful bracts are ovate to diamond-shaped. The flowers are borne in panicles, or in axillary whorls on erect stems, forming more or less interrupted terminal spikes or racemes. Sages are effective in a sunny border, light woodland, or wildflower meadow. Annuals, and perennials grown as annuals, provide brilliant colour for bedding, infilling, or containers; less hardy sages may be grown in a cool or temperate greenhouse, either in a border or in large containers. *S. caespitosa* is suitable for a scree bed or alpine house. Many species attract bees; some have culinary or medicinal uses.

• **HARDINESS** Fully hardy to frost tender.

• **CULTIVATION** Under glass, grow in well-drained, loamless or loam-based potting compost (JI No.2 or 3) in full light with shade from hot sun. While in growth, water freely and apply a balanced liquid fertilizer monthly; water very sparingly in winter, except *S. canariensis*, *S. elegans* and its cultivars, and *S. leucantha*, which should be watered moderately. Maintain low to moderate humidity. Outdoors, grow in light, moderately fertile, humus-rich, moist but well-drained soil in full sun to light dappled shade. Small species with densely hairy or woolly leaves need sharp drainage and full sun. Protect these and frost-hardy species from excessive winter wet, and shelter from cold, drying winds. Pruning group 9, in spring.

Salvia argentea

• **PROPAGATION** Sow seed as follows: annuals at 16–18°C (61–64°F) in mid-spring, biennials in containers in a cold frame in summer, and perennials in containers in a cold frame in spring; annuals and biennials may be sown *in situ* after all danger of frost has passed. Divide perennials in spring. For perennials and subshrubs, root basal or softwood cuttings in spring or early summer, or semi-ripe cuttings in late summer or autumn, with bottom heat.

• **PESTS AND DISEASES** Slugs and snails will attack young growth, as well as the fleshy rhizomes of *S. uliginosa*. Under glass, may be prone to aphids, red spider mites, whiteflies, and foot and root rots.

S. aethiopis. Rosette-forming, monocarpic perennial or biennial with broadly ovate or elliptic to oblong, deeply toothed, white-woolly leaves, to 20cm (8in) long, clasping the erect upper stems. White, sometimes yellow-lipped flowers, 1.5cm (¾in) long, with persistent, broad, spiny bracts, are borne in branching, flat-topped, terminal panicles in mid- and late summer. ↕↔ 60cm (24in). C. and S. Europe to W. Asia. ❄❄❄

S. africana-lutea see *S. aurea*.

S. ambigens see *S. guaranitica* 'Blue Enigma'.

S. angustifolia see *S. azurea*.

S. argentea ■ Rosette-forming biennial or short-lived perennial producing ovate to oblong, toothed, silver-woolly leaves, to 20cm (8in) long. In mid- and late summer, bears many-branched, terminal panicles of white or pinkish-white flowers, to 3cm (1¼in) long, with grey calyces. ↕ 90cm (36in), ↔ 60cm (24in). S. Europe, N. Africa. ❄❄❄

S. aurea, syn. *S. africana-lutea* (Sandsalie). Erect to spreading, rounded, evergreen shrub with sparsely to densely downy stems and rounded to narrowly obovate, densely white-woolly leaves, 1–4cm (½–1½in) long, sometimes minutely scalloped, and dotted with glands. From summer to late autumn, bears dense, terminal racemes of golden brown to red-brown or mauve flowers, 3–5cm (1¼–2in) long, with bell-shaped, purple-tinted calyces. ↕↔ to 1m (3ft). Sandy places in South Africa (Northern Cape, Eastern Cape, Western Cape). ❄

S. azurea, syn. *S. angustifolia*. Erect, woody-based perennial with several to many simple or sparsely branched stems bearing linear, elliptic, or lance-shaped, hairless or softly hairy, sometimes

Salvia cacaliifolia

Salvia coccinea 'Coral Nymph'

toothed, mid- to deep green leaves, 5–10cm (2–4in) long. From late summer to autumn, pure blue or white flowers, 1.5–2cm (½–¾in) long, are produced in dense, terminal racemes. ↕ to 1.5m (5ft), ↔ 60–90cm (24–36in). S.E. USA. ❄❄. **var. *grandiflora***, syn. subsp. *pitcheri*, has very hairy stems; flowers are to 2.5cm (1in) long; S. USA.

***S. bacheriana* of gardens** see *S. buchananii*.

S. blepharophylla. Spreading, sub-shrubby, rhizomatous perennial bearing ovate to triangular, irregularly toothed, finely hairy, dark green leaves, 5cm (2in) long. From early summer to early autumn, branched stems bear loose, terminal racemes of bright scarlet flowers, to 2cm (¾in) long, with large lower lips and maroon calyces. ↕ 40cm (16in), ↔ 45cm (18in). Mexico. ❄

S. buchananii, syn. *S. bacheriana* of gardens. Woody-based perennial, spreading by runners, with erect, branching stems bearing spoon-shaped to ovate-lance-shaped, finely toothed, leathery, dark green leaves, to 7cm (3in) long. Velvet-hairy, magenta-red flowers, to 5cm (2in) long, with dark purplish brown calyces, are borne in loose, terminal racemes from midsummer to mid-autumn. ↕ 60cm (24in), ↔ 30cm (12in). Mexico. ❄

S. bulleyana, syn. *S. flava* var. *megalantha* of gardens. Clump-forming perennial with ovate or triangular-ovate, scalloped, prominently veined, sparsely hairy, wrinkled, mostly basal, mid-green leaves, to 12cm (5in) long. In mid- and late summer, bears terminal racemes of paired yellow flowers, to 3cm (1¼in) long, with purple-brown lower lips and bright green calyces. ↕ 40–90cm (16–36in), ↔ 60cm (24in). W. China. ❄❄❄

S. cacaliifolia ■ Erect, hairy perennial with more or less triangular, entire, mid-green leaves, to 10cm (4in) long. In early summer, branched stems bear terminal panicles of paired, slightly hairy, deep blue flowers, to 2cm (¾in)

Salvia coccinea 'Lady in Red'

long, with much shorter, bell-shaped calyces. ↕ 90cm (36in), ↔ 30cm (12in). Mexico, Guatemala. ❄
S. caerulea of gardens see *S. guaranitica* 'Black and Blue'.
S. caespitosa. Woody-based, mat-forming perennial producing obovate, pinnatisect, silver-hairy leaves, 5cm (2in) long, each with a lance-shaped terminal segment. In summer, bears dense, terminal racemes of wide-tubed, lilac-pink flowers, to 3cm (1¼in) long, with broad lower lips. Resents winter wet. Suitable for an alpine house; can be grown in a scree bed if overhead protection provided in winter. ↕ 15cm (6in), ↔ 30cm (12in). Turkey (Anatolia). ❄❄
S. campanulata. Upright, robust-stemmed perennial with opposite, broadly ovate, mid-green leaves, to 12cm (5in) long, softly hairy on both surfaces and heart-shaped at the bases. In summer, whorls of yellow, rarely blue or purple flowers, 2.5cm (1in) long, each with a bell-shaped calyx, are borne in pairs on spreading panicles. ↕ to 1m (3ft), ↔ to 60cm (24in). Himalayas. ❄❄
S. canariensis. Erect, open, evergreen shrub with sparsely branched, white-downy stems. Lance-shaped to triangular, entire or notched, mid-green leaves, 6–15cm (2½–6in) long, each have 2 spreading lobes at the bases; they are covered with dense white down, at least beneath. From winter to spring, bears small, white to violet or purple flowers, to 2cm (¾in) long, in terminal panicles or racemes. ↕ 1–2m (3–6ft), ↔ 0.6–1.2m (2–4ft). Canary Islands. ❀ (min. 7°C/45°F)
S. cardinalis see *S. fulgens.*
S. chamaedryoides. Low-growing, woody-based perennial with branching stems. Elliptic, finely scalloped, mid- to grey-green leaves, to 2cm (¾in) long, are covered in fine hairs, giving them a sage-green appearance. Deep blue flowers, 2.5cm (1in) long, with widely spreading lips, are borne in terminal racemes in late summer. ↕ 30cm (12in), ↔ 60cm (24in). USA (Texas), Mexico. ❄❄
S. clevelandii (Jim sage). Dwarf, rounded, evergreen shrub, branching mainly from the base, with usually downy stems, and ovate or oblong to elliptic or lance-shaped, wrinkled, toothed, mid-green leaves, to 2.5cm (1in) long. In summer, white, blue, or violet flowers, 1.5cm (½in) long, are borne in terminal whorls or short, simple to branched spikes. ↕ 40–60cm (16–24in), ↔ 30–60cm (12–24in). USA (California). ❄❄
S. coccinea. Erect, bushy annual or perennial with oval to heart-shaped, toothed, hairy, dark green leaves, to 6cm (2½in) long. From summer to autumn, soft cherry-red flowers, to 2cm (¾in) long, are borne in slender, open, terminal spikes. ↕ 60–75cm (24–30in), ↔ to 30cm (12in). Tropical South America. ❄. **'Coral Nymph'** ▣ has coral-pink flowers; ↕ 40cm (16in). **'Lady in Red'** ▣ produces red flowers; ↕ 40cm (16in). **'Snow Nymph'**, syn. 'White Lady', bears white flowers. **'Starry Eyed'** bears white, red, or coral-pink flowers. **'White Lady'** see 'Snow Nymph'.
S. concolor of gardens see *S. guaranitica.*
S. confertiflora ▣ Woody-based perennial with ovate, scalloped, yellow-green leaves, to 20cm (8in) long, that are densely woolly, especially beneath, and unpleasantly scented if crushed. From late summer to mid-autumn, the unbranched stems bear terminal spikes of orange-red flowers, 1cm (½in) long, with hairy, deep red calyces. ↕ to 1.2m (4ft), ↔ 60cm (24in). Brazil. ❄
S. deserta see *S. nemorosa.*
S. discolor ▣ Erect perennial with densely white-woolly, branched stems. Oblong-ovate, entire, mid-green leaves, to 6cm (2½in) long, are densely white-woolly beneath, less hairy above. In late summer and early autumn, bears long, terminal racemes of deep indigo-black flowers, to 2.5cm (1in) long, with finely white-hairy calyces. ↕ 45cm (18in), ↔ 30cm (12in). Peru. ❄
S. elegans. Soft-stemmed herbaceous perennial or subshrub with branching stems and ovate or almost triangular, hairless or softly hairy, toothed, mildly pineapple-scented, mid-green leaves, to 10cm (4in) long. Loose, terminal panicles of bright scarlet flowers, 2.5cm (1in) long, softly hairy inside, are borne from winter to spring. ↕ 2m (6ft), ↔ 1m (3ft). Mexico, Guatemala. ❀ (min. 5°C/41°F). **'Scarlet Pineapple'** ▣ syn. *S. rutilans* (Pineapple sage), has leaves that smell strongly of pineapple when crushed, and more densely hairy stems; it bears larger flowers, to 3.5cm (1½in) long; ↕ 90cm (36in), ↔ 60cm (24in).
S. farinacea (Mealy sage). Erect, bushy perennial, usually grown as an annual, with white-mealy stems bearing pointed, narrowly to broadly lance-shaped, wavy-margined, glossy, mid-green leaves, to 8cm (3in) long, white-hairy beneath. From summer to autumn, produces deep lavender-blue flowers, to 2cm (¾in) long, in tall, slender, dense, purple-stemmed, terminal or axillary spikes. It may be overwintered in moist peat, if kept frost-free. ↕ to 60cm (24in), ↔ to 30cm (12in), as an annual. USA (Texas), Mexico. ❄. **f. *alba*** ▣ bears white flowers. **'Rhea'** is compact and early flowering, with intense dark blue flowers; ↕ to 35cm (14in). **'Strata'** has blue and white flowers. **'Victoria'** ▣ has deep blue flowers and dense basal branching. **'White Porcelain'** has white flowers.

Salvia farinacea f. *alba*

***S. flava* var. *megalantha* of gardens** see *S. bulleyana.*
S. forsskaohlei. Clump-forming perennial producing ovate or deeply lobed, toothed, softly bristly, mostly basal, mid-green leaves, 5–30cm (2–12in) long, with heart-shaped bases. Stems are sometimes branched and, from early summer to early autumn, bear long, terminal or axillary spikes of white-tubed flowers, to 3cm (1¼in) long, with wide-spreading violet lips, the lower lips marked yellowish white. ↕ to 90cm (36in), ↔ 50cm (20in). Bulgaria, Turkey (Black Sea coast). ❄❄❄
S. fruticosa, syn. *S. triloba.* Bushy, evergreen shrub or subshrub with white-hairy, branched stems bearing simple or pinnate, mid-green leaves, to 5cm (2in) long; the pinnate leaves each have 3 or 5 oblong-elliptic leaflets. In summer, produces purple, lilac-pink, or pink, rarely white flowers, to 2.5cm (1in) long, in terminal or axillary racemes.

S

Salvia confertiflora

Salvia discolor

Salvia elegans 'Scarlet Pineapple'

Salvia farinacea 'Victoria'

Salvia fulgens

Salvia involucrata 'Bethellii'

Salvia microphylla

↕ to 1.2m (4ft), ↔ to 80cm (32in). C. and E. Mediterranean. ❄❄

S. fulgens ■ syn. *S. cardinalis.* Woody-based perennial or evergreen subshrub, branching mainly from the base, with ovate to narrowly triangular, toothed or notched leaves, 6–12cm (2½–5in) long, rich green above, densely white-woolly beneath. Terminal or axillary spikes or racemes of red flowers, to 3cm (1¼in) long, with densely downy lower lips, are produced in summer. ↕ 50–100cm (20–39in), ↔ 40–90cm (16–36in). Mexico. ❄

S. gesneriiflora. Subshrubby perennial bearing ovate, scalloped, hairy, mid-green leaves, to 10cm (4in) long, with heart-shaped bases. From early spring to mid-autumn, many-branched stems bear terminal racemes of numerous softly hairy red flowers, 5cm (2in) long, with flattened upper lips. ↕ 60cm (24in), ↔ 20cm (8in). Mexico, Colombia. ❄

S. glutinosa (Jupiter's distaff). Clump-forming, sticky-hairy perennial with branched or unbranched stems and heart-shaped, toothed, mid-green leaves, to 20cm (8in) long. From midsummer to mid-autumn, bears loose, terminal racemes of softly hairy, pale yellow flowers, to 4cm (1½in) long, heavily spotted maroon and with reddish brown markings on the brighter yellow lower lips. ↕↔ 90cm (36in). C. and S. Europe to W. Asia. ❄❄❄

S. grahamii see *S. microphylla.*

S. greggii (Autumn sage). Dwarf, evergreen shrub or sometimes erect, woody-based perennial, branching mainly from the base, with glandular-hairy stems. Ovate or elliptic to oblong or linear, leathery, entire, mid- to deep green leaves, 2–3cm (¾–1¼in) long, are hairless to softly hairy and dotted with glands. Paired, red to purple, pink, yellow, or violet flowers, 2cm (¾in) long, are borne in terminal racemes from late summer to autumn. ↕↔ 30–50cm (12–20in). USA (Texas), Mexico. ❄❄. **'Raspberry Royale'** has bright raspberry-red flowers; ↕ to 60cm (24in), ↔ 30cm (12in).

S. guaranitica, syn. *S. concolor* of gardens. Subshrubby perennial with branched, dark green stems and ovate, pointed, slightly toothed, hairy, wrinkled, mid-green leaves, to 13cm (5in) long. Deep blue flowers, to 5cm (2in) long, with purplish blue calyces, are borne in terminal or axillary spikes from late summer to late autumn. ↕ 1.5m (5ft), ↔ 60cm (24in). Brazil, Uruguay, Argentina. ❄. **'Black and Blue'**, syn. *S. caerulea* of gardens, bears rich blue flowers with very dark purple-blue calyces; ↕ to 2.5m (8ft), ↔ 90cm (36in). **'Blue Enigma'** ■ syn. *S. ambigens*, bears fragrant, deep blue flowers with bright green calyces; ↔ 90cm (36in). **'Purple Splendour'** bears hairless leaves and purple flowers; ↔ 90cm (36in).

S. haematodes see *S. pratensis* Haematodes Group.

S. hians. Erect, sticky-hairy, pleasantly scented, somewhat short-lived perennial with ovate, toothed, prominently veined, wrinkled, dark green leaves, to 15cm (6in) long. Branched stems bear terminal spikes of purplish blue flowers, to 3.5cm (1½in) long, with spreading lips, the lower lips white-marked, from early to late summer. ↕↔ 60cm (24in). Himalayas (mainly Kashmir). ❄❄❄

***S. hispanica* of gardens** see *S. lavandulifolia.*

S. horminum see *S. viridis.*

S. involucrata. Subshrubby perennial with sparsely branched stems and ovate, tapering, entire or notched, softly hairy, rich green leaves, to 12cm (5in) long. From late summer to mid-autumn, bears dense, terminal racemes of purplish red flowers, to 5cm (2in) long, with pink bracts that fall as the flowers open. ↕ 1.5m (5ft), ↔ 1m (3ft). Mexico. ❄❄. **'Bethellii'** ■ has slightly larger, more velvety leaves, and bright purplish crimson flowers. **'Deschampsiana'** has leaves that are narrowly acute at the tips, and more ovoid racemes of rose-pink flowers with bright red bracts and calyces; ↕ 90cm (36in).

S. x jamensis (*S. greggii* x *S. microphylla*). Bushy shrub with opposite, ovate to elliptic, toothed, mid-green leaves, 2–3.5cm (¾–1½in) long. In summer and autumn, red, rose-pink, salmon-pink, orange, or rarely creamy yellow flowers, 1–2.5cm (½–1in) long, are borne in opposite pairs in terminal racemes. ↕ 0.5–1m (20–39in), ↔ 50cm (20in). Mexico. ❄. **'Fuego'** bears bright, flame-red flowers. **'James Compton'** has leaves to 2cm (¾in) long, and bears deep crimson flowers, 2.5cm (1in) long; ↕ to 1m (3ft), ↔ 75cm (30in); ⊛ (min. 5°C/41°F). **'La Luna'** bears creamy yellow flowers, the upper lips covered in buff-coloured hairs. **'Pat Vlasto'** has ovate-elliptic, entire leaves, 2cm (¾in) long, and pink-suffused orange flowers, 2–2.5cm (¾–1in) long; ↕ 1m (3ft), ↔ 75cm (30in); ⊛ (min. 5°C/41°F)

S. jurisicii. Low-growing, hairy perennial with basal rosettes of ovate, scalloped, mid-green leaves, 10cm (4in) long, and many-branched stems bearing pinnate leaves, 10cm (4in) long, each divided into 4–6 pairs of linear leaflets. From early to late summer, produces a profusion of terminal racemes of apparently upside-down, violet-blue flowers, to 1cm (½in) long, the upper lips covered with long, violet-blue hairs. ↕ to 60cm (24in), ↔ 45cm (18in). Yugoslavia (Serbia), Macedonia. ❄❄❄

S. lavandulifolia, syn. *S. hispanica* of gardens. Woody-based perennial with mostly basal, long-stalked, narrowly oblong, entire, grey- to white-woolly leaves, to 2.5cm (1in) long. In midsummer, blue-violet flowers, to 2.5cm (1in) long, are produced in terminal and axillary racemes. ↕ to 50cm (20in), ↔ 60cm (24in). Spain. ❄❄❄ (borderline)

S. lemmonii see *S. microphylla var. wislizenii.*

S. leucantha ■ (Mexican bush). Bushy, evergreen subshrub with white-downy stems when young, and ovate or lance-shaped to oblong or linear, toothed or scalloped, mid-green leaves, to 15cm (6in) long, wrinkled above, white-downy beneath. From winter to spring, produces terminal racemes of white flowers, to 1.5–2cm (½–¾in) long, with bell-shaped, downy, purple to lavender-blue calyces. ↕ 60–100cm (24–39in), ↔ 40–90cm (16–36in). Mexico, tropical Central America. ❄

S. microphylla ■ syn. *S. grahamii.* Moderately bushy, evergreen shrub or shrubby perennial bearing triangular-ovate to elliptic, softly hairy or hairless, mid- to deep green leaves, 1.5–4cm (½–1½in) long, with rounded teeth. From late summer to autumn, paired or whorled, deep crimson or, less commonly, magenta, pink, or purple flowers, 2.5cm (1in) long, are produced in terminal racemes. ↕ 90–120cm (3–4ft), ↔ 60–100cm (24–39in). USA (Arizona, New Mexico), Mexico. ❄❄. **'Newby Hall'**, often grown as var. *neurepia*, has pale green leaves, 3.5–5cm (1¼–2in) long, and produces cherry-red flowers, to 3cm (1¼in) long, mainly in autumn. **'Oxford'** bears deep rose-crimson flowers. **'Ruth Stungo'** has white-splashed leaves. **var. *wislizenii***, syn. *S. lemmonii*, is more compact, with triangular leaves, to 3cm (1¼in) long, and dense spikes of vermilion or magenta flowers; ↕↔ 1m (3ft).

S. nemorosa, syn. *S. deserta.* Erect, many-branched perennial with ovate or lance-shaped to oblong, notched, wrinkled, mid-green leaves, to 10cm (4in) long. From summer to autumn, bears violet to purple, or white to pink flowers, to 1cm (½in) long, with violet to purple bracts, in dense, terminal racemes. ↕ to 1m (3ft), ↔ 60cm (24in). Europe to C. Asia. ❄❄❄. **'East Friesland'** see 'Ostfriesland'. **'Lubecca'**, syn. *S. x superba* 'Lubecca', is dwarf and clump-forming, with greyish green leaves. From midsummer to early autumn, bears violet flowers with reddish purple bracts that persist long after the flowers fall; ↕↔ 45cm (18in). **'Ostfriesland'**, syn. 'East Friesland', produces deep blue-violet flowers; ↕ 45cm (18in).

S

Salvia guaranitica 'Blue Enigma'

Salvia leucantha

Salvia officinalis 'Tricolor'

Salvia patens 'Cambridge Blue'

S. officinalis (Common sage). Subshrubby, erect, hairy, evergreen perennial with oblong-ovate, entire, grey-green-woolly, aromatic leaves, to 8cm (3in) long. Branched stems bear terminal or axillary racemes of lilac-blue flowers, 1.5cm (½in) long, in early and midsummer. A popular culinary herb. ↕ to 80cm (32in), ↔ 1m (3ft). Mediterranean, N. Africa. ❄❄❄. **'Aurea'** has a more compact habit, with oblong yellow leaves, and produces small spikes of purplish blue flowers in early summer; ↕ 30cm (12in), ↔ 45cm (18in). **'Icterina'** has variegated yellow and green leaves. **'Kew Gold'** produces golden yellow leaves, sometimes flecked with green, and bears mauve flowers; ↕ 20–30cm (8–12in), ↔ 30cm (12in). **'Purpurascens'** (Purple sage) has red-purple young leaves. **'Tricolor'** ■ bears grey-green leaves, zoned cream and pink to purple; ❄❄

S. patens. Tuberous perennial with erect, branched stems bearing ovate, broadly ovate to triangular, or pentagonal, toothed, hairy, mid-green leaves, to 20cm (8in) long, with spear-shaped bases. From midsummer to mid-autumn, produces few-flowered, loose, sometimes branched, terminal racemes of paired, deep blue flowers, 5cm (2in) long, with wide open mouths. ↕ 45–60cm (18–24in), ↔ 45cm (18in). Mexico. ❄❄. **'Cambridge Blue'** ■ produces pale blue flowers.

S. pratensis (Meadow clary). Clump-forming, woody-based perennial with ovate, blunt-tipped, toothed, wrinkled, mid-green basal leaves, to 15cm (6in) long, and few smaller stem leaves. In early and midsummer, erect, branched or unbranched, slightly sticky-hairy stems bear terminal spikes of violet, rarely pink or white flowers, 2–3cm (¾–1¼in) long. ↕ to 90cm (36in), ↔ 30cm (12in). Europe, Morocco. ❄❄❄. Cultivars of **Haematodes Group** ■ syn. *S. haematodes*, are short-lived plants with basal rosettes of large, broadly ovate, wavy-margined, dark green leaves, to 20cm (8in) long. Branched, reddish brown stems bear loose, spreading panicles of bluish violet flowers, with hairy upper lips and paler throats; Greece. **'Mittsommer'** produces loose spikes of sky-blue flowers with long, arched upper lips and darker blue calyces and bracts, throughout summer.

S. rutilans see *S. elegans* 'Scarlet Pineapple'.

S. sclarea (Biennial clary). Erect, many-branched, glandular-hairy perennial or biennial with ovate to oblong, notched to irregularly toothed, wrinkled, mid-green leaves, to 23cm (9in) long, with heart-shaped or perfoliate bases. From spring to summer, bears many-flowered, terminal panicles or racemes of cream and lilac to pink or blue flowers, to 3cm (1¼in) long, with prominent lilac bracts. ↕ to 1m (3ft), ↔ 30cm (12in). Europe to C. Asia. ❄❄❄. **var. *turkestanica* of gardens** ■ has pink stems bearing spikes of pink-flecked white flowers.

Salvia sclarea var. *turkestanica* of gardens

Salvia splendens 'Scarlet King'

S. splendens (Scarlet sage). Erect, bushy perennial, usually grown as an annual, with oval, pointed, toothed, slightly hairy, pale to dark green leaves, to 7cm (3in) long. Long-tubed, bright red flowers, 1.5–5cm (½–2in) long, enclosed in red bracts, are borne in dense, terminal spikes from summer to autumn. ↕ to 40cm (16in), ↔ 23–35cm (9–14in). Brazil. ❄. The best of modern seed selections are compact, with very erect flower spikes. Grow red cultivars in full sun; pastel shades need shade from the hottest sun. **'Blaze of Fire'**, syn. 'Fireball', has pale green leaves and red flowers; ↕ 30–40cm (12–16in). Cultivars of **Cleopatra Series** ■ produce flowers in red, salmon-pink, purple, or white; ↕ 30–40cm (12–16in). **'Fireball'** see 'Blaze of Fire'. **Phoenix Series** cultivars produce flowers in dark salmon-pink, pale salmon-pink, purple, white, red, or lilac; ↕ 26–30cm (10–12in). **'Rambo'** is very tall-growing, vigorous, and bushy, with dark green leaves and scarlet flowers; ↕ to 60cm (24in). **'Red Arrow'** has very dark green leaves, and produces scarlet flowers; ↕ to 30cm (12in). **'Red Riches'**, syn. 'Ryco', bears dark green leaves and scarlet flowers; ↕ 30–40cm (12–16in). **'Ryco'** see 'Red Riches'. **'Scarlet King'** ■ is compact and long-flowering, with dark green leaves and scarlet flowers; ↕ to 25cm (10in). **'Scarlet Queen'** bears bright scarlet flowers in early summer; ↕ 25cm (10in). **Sizzler Series** ■ cultivars have flowers in bright shades of cerise-red, lavender-blue, salmon-pink, purple, scarlet, or white. They are early flowering, and available as single colours; ↕ 25–30cm (10–12in).

S. x superba (*S. nemorosa* x *S.* x *sylvestris*). Clump-forming, erect, branched perennial with lance-shaped to oblong, scalloped, mid-green leaves, to 10cm (4in) long, slightly hairy beneath; the basal leaves are stalked, the stem leaves stalkless and sometimes stem-clasping. From midsummer to early autumn, bears slender, terminal racemes of bright violet or purple flowers, to 1.5cm (½in) long. ↕ 60–90m (26–36in), ↔ 45–60cm (18–24in). Garden origin. ❄❄❄. **'Lubecca'** see *S. nemorosa* 'Lubecca'.

S. x sylvestris (*S. nemorosa* x *S. pratensis*). Clump-forming, erect, branched perennial bearing oblong-lance-shaped, scalloped, wrinkled, softly hairy, mid-green leaves, to 7cm (3in) long. Pinkish violet flowers, 1cm (½in) long, are produced in dense, terminal racemes in early and midsummer. ↕ 80cm (32in), ↔ 30cm (12in). Garden origin. ❄❄❄. **'Blauhügel'**, syn. 'Blue Mound', produces pure blue flowers; ↕ 50cm (20in), ↔ 45cm (18in). **'Blaukönigin'**, syn. 'Blue Queen', bears rich blue-violet flowers; ↕ 70cm (28in), ↔ 45cm (18in). **'Blue Mound'** see 'Blauhügel'. **'Blue Queen'** see 'Blaukönigin'. **'Mainacht'** ■ syn. 'May Night', bears large, indigo-blue flowers, 2cm (¾in) long; ↕ 70cm (28in), ↔ 45cm (18in). **'May Night'** see 'Mainacht'.

S

Salvia pratensis Haematodes Group

Salvia splendens Cleopatra Series

Salvia splendens Sizzler Series

Salvia x *sylvestris* 'Mainacht'

'Rose Queen' has rose-pink flowers and grey-tinted leaves; ↕75cm (30in).
S. triloba see *S. fruticosa.*
S. uliginosa ■ (Bog sage). Clump-forming, moisture-loving, rhizomatous perennial with oblong-lance-shaped, deeply toothed, mid-green leaves, to 7cm (3in) long; they are well spaced out and become progressively smaller up the slender, branching stems. From late summer to mid-autumn, bears short, terminal racemes of clear blue flowers, 2cm (¾in) long. Needs moist soil and full sun. ↕ to 2m (6ft), ↔ 90cm (36in). Brazil, Uruguay, Argentina. ❄❄
S. verticillata. Erect herbaceous perennial with opposite, ovate or elliptic to oblong, softly glandular-hairy, mid-green leaves, to 13cm (5in) long, pinnatifid with a larger terminal lobe. In summer, produces branched racemes of violet to lilac-blue, rarely white flowers, 8mm (⅜in) long, in whorls of 20–40 blooms. ↕ to 90cm (36in), ↔ to 45cm (18in). Europe to W. Asia. ❄❄❄
S. viridis, syn. *S. horminum* (Annual clary). Erect, bushy annual with ovate to oblong, notched, hairy, mid-green leaves, 5cm (2in) long. In summer, bears terminal spikes of insignificant, whorled, pink to pale purple flowers, 8–15mm (⅜–½in) long, each whorl enclosed in 2 persistent, violet bracts, to 1cm (½in) long, with darker veins. Grow as a cut flower for the very long-lasting bracts. May also be dried. ↕45–50cm (18–20in), ↔ 23cm (9in). Mediterranean. ❄❄❄. The following cultivars with long-lasting bracts, 2–4cm (¾–1½in) long, are grouped under **var. *comata*. 'Bouquet'**, syn. 'Monarch

Salvia uliginosa

Salvia viridis var. *comata* 'Claryssa'

Bouquet', has blue, rose-pink, white, deep carmine-pink, or purple bracts; also available as single colours.
'Claryssa' ■ is compact and very well-branched, and produces bracts in rose-pink, blue, purple, or white; also available as single colours; ↕ to 40cm (16in). **'Monarch Bouquet'** see 'Bouquet'. **'Oxford Blue'** has violet-blue bracts; ↕30cm (12in). **'Pink Sundae'** has bright carmine-pink bracts. **'White Swan'** produces white bracts with green veins; ↕30cm (12in).

SALVINIA

SALVINIACEAE

Genus of 10 species of aquatic annual ferns found in stagnant or slow-moving water, with a wide tropical and sub-tropical distribution, especially in tropical Africa and Central and South America; they are also naturalized in some warm-temperate areas. Floating, rootless plants, they have very slender, irregularly branched stems, and bear mostly rounded to ovate leaves in pairs, with a third, finely dissected, root-like, submerged leaf. They are useful for an aquarium, where fish fry can hide in the submerged leaves. In tropical areas, grow in an outdoor pool. In frost-prone areas, grow in an outdoor pool during summer, then lift and store in winter.
• **HARDINESS** Frost tender.
• **CULTIVATION** In an aquarium, grow in nutrient-rich water at 18–24°C (64–75°F) in full light. Tilt the aquarium cover to prevent condensation forming on the leaves, as this may cause scorch in artificial light. Very invasive, so thin regularly. Outdoors, float on the surface of a still-water pool in full sun. In frost-prone areas, lift before the first frosts and store in shallow trays of sandy loam covered with 2.5–5cm (1–2in) of water, in a cool or temperate green-house. See also pp.52–53.
• **PROPAGATION** Separate stems in spring or summer.
• **PESTS AND DISEASES** Trouble free.

S. auriculata. Floating aquatic fern with whorls of 3 leaves, each consisting of an opposite pair of oval to ovate floating leaves, 3–4cm (1¼–1½in) long, covered with fine hairs, and one root-like submerged leaf adapted to a root function. ↔ indefinite. Central and South America. ❀ (min. 10°C/50°F)
S. natans ■ Floating aquatic fern bearing paired, elliptic, pale green leaves,

Salvinia natans

to 1.5cm (½in) long, with shiny brown hairs beneath, and a submerged, root-like frond, 2–7cm (¾–3in) long. ↔ indefinite. S. Europe, N. Africa, Asia. ❀ (min. 10°C/50°F)

SAMBUCUS

Elder

CAPRIFOLIACEAE

Genus of about 25 species of herbaceous perennials and deciduous shrubs and trees from woodland and thickets in temperate and subtropical regions of Eurasia, N. and tropical E. Africa, Australia, and North and South America. They are cultivated for their foliage, flowers, and fruits. They bear opposite, pinnate leaves and dense, flat-topped umbels or panicles of small, white to ivory flowers, followed by red, black, or white fruits. Elders are suitable for a mixed or shrub border, or a wild garden. Those with coloured leaves are effective as free-standing specimens. All parts may cause severe discomfort if ingested, although fruits are safe when cooked; contact with the leaves may irritate skin.
• **HARDINESS** Fully hardy.
• **CULTIVATION** Grow in moderately fertile, humus rich, moist but well-drained soil in full sun or partial shade; those with coloured leaves colour well in sun, but retain colour best in dappled shade. Pruning group 7, for those grown for their coloured or cut leaves; group 1 for the rest. Elders tolerate hard pruning as necessary to restrict size.
• **PROPAGATION** Sow seed in containers in an open frame in autumn. Take hardwood cuttings in winter, or green-wood cuttings in early summer.
• **PESTS AND DISEASES** Black fly infest the young shoots and foliage, and *Verticillium* wilt may be a problem.

S. canadensis (American elder). Upright shrub with stout shoots and pinnate leaves, to 30cm (12in) long, each composed of 9 or more elliptic to lance-shaped, toothed, light green leaflets. In midsummer, bears small white flowers in flattened panicles, to 20cm (8in) across, followed by spherical, purple-black fruit, to 5mm (¼in) across. ↕↔ 4m (12ft). North America. ❄❄❄. **'Aurea'** has golden yellow foliage and red fruit.
S. nigra (Black elder, Bourtree, Common elder, Elderberry, European elder). Upright, bushy shrub with stout shoots. Pinnate leaves, to 25cm (10in) long, each have 5 ovate, toothed, mid-green leaflets. Bears musk-scented white flowers in flattened panicles, to 20cm (8in) across, in early summer, followed by spherical, glossy black fruit, to 8mm (⅜in) across. ↕↔ 6m (20ft). Europe, N. Africa, S.W. Asia. ❄❄❄. **'Aurea'** has golden yellow leaves borne on pink-flushed leaf-stalks. **'Aureomarginata'** bears yellow-margined, dark green leaves. **'Guincho Purple'** ■ has dark green leaves, turning blackish purple then red in autumn, and pink-tinged flowers with purple stalks. **f. *laciniata***, syn. 'Laciniata', has irregularly and finely cut leaflets.
S. racemosa (Red-berried elder). Bushy shrub with arching shoots and pinnate

Sambucus nigra 'Guincho Purple'

S

Sambucus racemosa 'Plumosa Aurea'

Sanchezia speciosa

Sanguinaria canadensis

leaves, to 22cm (9in) long, each with usually 5 oval or ovate, toothed, dark green leaflets. In mid-spring, bears small, creamy yellow flowers in conical panicles, 8cm (3in) long, followed in summer by spherical, glossy red fruit, 4mm (⅛in) across. ↕↔ 3m (10ft). Europe, Russia (W. Siberia). ❄❄❄. **'Plumosa'** has purple new growth and finely cut leaflets. **'Plumosa Aurea'** ▣ has finely cut leaflets, bronze when young, turning golden yellow. Foliage may burn in hot sun. **'Sutherland Gold'** is similar to 'Plumosa Aurea', but less susceptible to sun scorch. **'Tenuifolia'** is mound-forming, with leaflets very finely cut into long, slender lobes; ↕ 1m (3ft), ↔ 2m (6ft).

SANCHEZIA

ACANTHACEAE

Genus of about 20 species of soft-stemmed evergreen shrubs and shrubby perennials from tropical rainforest in Central and South America. They have opposite pairs of simple, often entire leaves, and bear terminal or axillary spikes or panicles of tubular, showy, yellow, orange, red, or purple flowers, each with 5 small, rounded lobes, often with coloured bracts. Where temperatures drop below 15°C (59°F), grow in a warm greenhouse or conservatory, or as houseplants. In tropical areas, grow at the base of a warm, sunny wall, or in a shrub border.
• **HARDINESS** Frost tender.
• **CULTIVATION** Under glass, grow in loam-based potting compost (JI No.2) in bright filtered or full light, with shade from hot sun. In growth, water freely and apply a balanced liquid fertilizer every 2 or 3 weeks; water sparingly in winter. Outdoors, grow in moderately fertile, humus rich, moist but well-drained soil, in full sun with some midday shade, or in light dappled shade. Pruning group 8; plants under glass may need restrictive pruning in late winter.
• **PROPAGATION** Root softwood cuttings in spring or semi-ripe cuttings in summer, both with gentle bottom heat.
• **PESTS AND DISEASES** Red spider mites and scale insects may be a problem under glass.

S. glaucophylla see *S. speciosa*.
S. nobilis see *S. speciosa*.
S. speciosa ▣ syn. *S. glaucophylla*, *S. nobilis*, *S. spectabilis*. Moderately bushy shrub with sparsely branched, sturdy, sometimes obscurely angled, smooth, bright green stems and ovate-elliptic to oblong-lance-shaped, glossy, dark green leaves, 15–30cm (6–12in) long, with yellow-, ivory-, or white-banded midribs and main veins. In summer, bears terminal spikes of 6–10 yellow flowers, 4–5cm (1½–2in) long, with red bracts. ↕ 1.2–2.2m (4–7ft), ↔ 90–150cm (3–5ft). Ecuador, Peru. ❀ (min. 13–15°C/55–59°F)
S. spectabilis see *S. speciosa*.

SANDERSONIA

COLCHICACEAE/LILIACEAE

Genus of one species of tuberous, perennial climber from rocky areas and light woodland in South Africa. Related to *Gloriosa* and *Littonia*, it has alternate leaves, often tipped with tendrils, and solitary flowers. In frost-prone areas, grow in a temperate greenhouse or a conservatory. In frost-free areas, grow in a herbaceous border or among low shrubs.
• **HARDINESS** Half hardy.
• **CULTIVATION** Under glass, plant tubers 7–10cm (3–4in) deep in late winter or early spring, in 4 parts loam-based potting compost (JI No.2) and 1 part grit, in full light with some midday shade. In growth, water freely and apply a balanced liquid fertilizer every 4 weeks; dry off as leaves fade and keep dry while dormant. Stems need support. Outdoors, grow in moderately fertile to humus-rich, well-drained soil in full sun. Protect from excessive winter wet. In frost-prone areas, lift tubers in autumn and store in dry, frost-free conditions.
• **PROPAGATION** Sow seed at 18–24°C (64–75°F) as soon as ripe. Divide in autumn or winter.
• **PESTS AND DISEASES** Trouble free.

S. aurantiaca. Perennial climber with slender stems bearing scattered, lance-shaped, mid-green leaves, to 10cm (4in) long, some of which are tipped with tendrils. In summer, pendent, urn-shaped, bright orange flowers, 2.5cm (1in) long, are borne on downcurved stalks, 2–3cm (¾–1¼in) long, from the upper leaf axils. ↕ to 75cm (30in), ↔ 10cm (4in). South Africa. ❄

▷ **Sandsalie** see *Salvia aurea*
▷ **Sandwort** see *Arenaria*
Corsican see *A. balearica*
Pink see *A. purpurascens*

SANGUINARIA

Bloodroot, Red puccoon

PAPAVERACEAE

Genus of one species of rhizomatous perennial occurring in moist woodland in E. North America. It is cultivated for its cup-shaped, white or pink-tinted flowers, which emerge from between the vertically folded leaves as they unfurl, in spring. *S. canadensis* is excellent for growing in a damp, shaded site in a rock garden, wild or woodland garden, or peat bed. The rhizomes exude red sap when cut, giving rise to the common name, bloodroot.
• **HARDINESS** Fully hardy.
• **CULTIVATION** Grow in moderately fertile, humus rich, moist but well-drained soil in deep or partial shade. Thrives in part-day sun where soils remain reliably moist.
• **PROPAGATION** Sow seed in containers in a cold frame in autumn, or divide rhizomes immediately after flowering.
• **PESTS AND DISEASES** Trouble free.

S. canadensis ▣ Rhizomatous perennial producing variably lobed, heart- to kidney-shaped, scalloped, bluish grey-green leaves, 15–30cm (6–12in) across when fully expanded. Solitary, cup-shaped, white, occasionally pink-tinted flowers, to 8cm (3in) across, emerge in spring as the leaves unfold. ↕ 15cm (6in), ↔ 30cm (12in) or more. E. North America. ❄❄❄. **'Plena'** produces many-petalled, double white flowers, which are longer-lasting than those of the species.

SANGUISORBA

Burnet

ROSACEAE

Genus of approximately 18 species of rhizomatous perennials, most occurring in damp meadows, with a few from dry, grassy or rocky sites, in temperate and cooler regions of the N. hemisphere. They produce alternate, pinnate leaves, with mostly oblong to elliptic, toothed, neatly veined leaflets, which in some species are glaucous. The leafy, wiry stems bear dense or loose, bottlebrush-like, terminal spikes of small, fluffy flowers, with red, pink, white, or greenish white sepals and prominent stamens, but no petals. Burnets are suitable for growing in a herbaceous or mixed border, and for naturalizing in a damp meadow garden or by water. Many species provide unusual flowers and foliage for cutting.
• **HARDINESS** Fully hardy.
• **CULTIVATION** Grow in any moderately fertile, moist but well-drained soil that does not dry out, in full sun or partial shade. Taller species usually require support. May become invasive.
• **PROPAGATION** Sow seed in containers in a cold frame in spring or autumn. Divide in spring or autumn.
• **PESTS AND DISEASES** Slugs may damage young leaves.

S. canadensis ▣ (Canadian burnet). Spreading, clump-forming, rhizomatous perennial with upright, simple or branched stems and pinnate, hairy leaves, to 25cm (10in) long, each composed of 7–17 oblong-lance-shaped to ovate leaflets. From midsummer to mid-autumn, long "cones" of green buds open from the bottom up, to form bottlebrush-like spikes, to 20cm (8in) long, of small, fluffy white flowers. ↕ to 2m (6ft), ↔ 1m (3ft). N.E. North America. ❄❄❄
S. obtusa. Rhizomatous perennial with upright stems, branched near the ends, bearing numerous pinnate, greyish green leaves, to 40cm (16in) long, each with 13–17 crowded, oblong-elliptic, almost stalkless leaflets. From mid- or late summer to early autumn, bears small, fluffy, rich pink flowers in short, nodding, bottlebrush-like spikes, 7cm (3in) long. ↕↔ to 60cm (24in). Japan. ❄❄❄
S. officinalis (Greater burnet). Clump-forming, rhizomatous perennial producing pinnate basal leaves, 50cm (20in) long, each with 7–25 oblong-elliptic leaflets; leaves on the erect, branching, often red stems are smaller. The small, red-brown to maroon flowers are borne in erect, very short, dense, ovoid spikes, 1.5–3cm (¾–1¼in) long, from early summer to mid-autumn. ↕ to 1.2m (4ft), ↔ 60cm (24in). Europe, N. and W. Asia, North America. ❄❄❄

Sanguisorba canadensis

S

SANSEVIERIA

Bowstring hemp

AGAVACEAE/DRACAENACEAE

Genus of about 60 species of usually stemless, xerophytic, rhizomatous, evergreen perennials from dry, rocky habitats in tropical and subtropical Africa, Madagascar, India, and Indonesia. They are grown for their stiff, fleshy, linear to broadly ovate, upright or more or less spreading leaves, which may be flat, concave, or cylindrical; these are produced in clumps or squat rosettes from spreading, underground or partially exposed rhizomes. Mature plants infrequently bear low racemes or panicles of fragrant, nectar-rich, tubular, 6-lobed flowers in spring. In frost-prone areas, grow in a warm greenhouse or conservatory, or use as houseplants. In warmer areas, grow in a desert garden, in containers on a patio, or in a small courtyard garden. Tolerant of neglect.

- **HARDINESS** Frost tender.
- **CULTIVATION** Under glass, grow in 2 parts loam-based potting compost (JI No.2) and 1 part coarse grit, in bright filtered light or indirect light. In growth, water moderately and apply a half-strength balanced liquid fertilizer monthly; water sparingly in winter. Pot on only when pot-bound; leaf growth may stop if leaf-tips are damaged. Outdoors, grow in poor to moderately fertile, neutral to slightly alkaline, gritty soil in full sun. Protect from excessive winter wet.
- **PROPAGATION** Remove suckers, or divide, in spring. Root leaf sections with bottom heat from spring to autumn. Offspring from variegated cultivars will lack variegation if raised from leaf cuttings.
- **PESTS AND DISEASES** Vine weevil grubs may be a problem.

S. cylindrica. Very slow-growing, woody, rhizomatous perennial with 2-ranked, erect, cylindrical, fleshy, dark green leaves, to 1m (3ft) or more long, with lighter crossbands. Intermittently bears spike-like racemes, 35–75cm (14–30in) long, of tubular, pink or white flowers, 1.5–2.5cm (½–1in) long, the lobes with margins rolled outwards. ↕ to 1.5m (5ft), ↔ 60cm (24in). Angola. ❄ (min. 13°C/55°F)
S. trifasciata (Mother-in-law's tongue). Erect, rhizomatous perennial with pointed, lance-shaped, fleshy leaves, to

Sansevieria trifasciata 'Laurentii'

1.2m (4ft) or more long, horizontally marbled and banded dark and light green. Racemes, 30–75cm (12–30in) long, of tubular, green or greenish white flowers, 6–10mm (¼–½in) long, are produced intermittently. Dwarf cultivars are suitable for growing in bowls and pans. ↕ 1.2m (4ft), ↔ 50cm (20in). W. tropical Africa. ❄ (min. 13°C/55°F).
'Bantel's Sensation' has variable, slender, slightly spiralled, dark green leaves, to 60cm (24in) long, with intermittent, vertical cream stripes.
'Golden Hahnii' ▣ forms dwarf rosettes of broad leaves, to 20cm (8in) long, with bold, golden yellow, vertical stripes, particularly at the margins; rarely flowers; ↕↔ 12cm (5in). **'Hahnii'** (Bird's nest) is dwarf, with rosettes of broad, mid-green leaves, 25cm (10in) long, crossbanded with darker green; rarely flowers; ↕ to 15cm (6in), ↔ 18cm (7in).
'Laurentii' ▣ has upright leaves, 45cm (18in) long, horizontally marbled mid- and dark green, with broad yellow margins; ↕ 1–1.2m (3–4ft). **'Silver Hahnii'** ▣ is dwarf, with rosettes of broad, dark green leaves, to 25cm (10in) long, banded silver; flowers are rarely borne; ↕↔ 12cm (5in).

Sansevieria trifasciata 'Golden Hahnii'

Sansevieria trifasciata 'Silver Hahnii'

SANTOLINA

ASTERACEAE/COMPOSITAE

Genus of 18 species of evergreen shrubs occurring in dry, rocky habitats in the Mediterranean. They have alternate, entire, pinnatisect, or pinnate, aromatic leaves, and tiny flowers borne in long-stemmed, dense, button-like heads, surrounded by several rows of involucral bracts. Each individual floret is tubular, usually hermaphrodite, and yellow or white; there are no ray-florets. They are grown mainly for their ornamental and aromatic foliage, and are suitable for a mixed or shrub border or a rock garden; they may also be used for ground cover, edging, or as low hedges.

- **HARDINESS** Frost hardy.
- **CULTIVATION** Grow in poor to moderately fertile, well-drained soil in full sun. Pruning group 10, in spring.
- **PROPAGATION** Sow seed in containers in a cold frame in autumn or spring. Root semi-ripe cuttings with bottom heat in late summer.
- **PESTS AND DISEASES** Trouble free.

S. chamaecyparissus, syn. *S. incana* (Cotton lavender). Compact, rounded shrub producing white-woolly young shoots, densely covered with slender, narrowly oblong, toothed to pinnatisect, grey-white leaves, to 4cm (1½in) long, with very fine, toothed divisions. Bright yellow flowerheads, to 1cm (½in) across, are borne on slender stems in mid- and late summer. ↕ 50cm (20in), ↔ 1m (3ft). W. and C. Mediterranean. ✻✻.
'Lambrook Silver' has silver-grey leaves.

Santolina pinnata subsp. *neapolitana* 'Sulphurea'

'Lemon Queen' ▣ is compact, with lemon-yellow flowerheads; ↕↔ 60cm (24in). **'Pretty Carol'** is compact, with soft grey foliage; ↕↔ 40cm (16in).
'Small-Ness' is dwarf; ↕↔ 20cm (8in).
subsp. *tomentosa* see *S. pinnata*.
'Weston' is very dwarf, with very silvery foliage; ↕ 15cm (6in), ↔ 20cm (8in).
S. incana see *S. chamaecyparissus*.
S. neapolitana see *S. pinnata* subsp. *neapolitana*.
S. pinnata, syn. *S. chamaecyparissus* subsp. *tomentosa*. Rounded, bushy shrub with slender, pinnate, hairless, slightly aromatic, mid-green leaves, to 4cm (1½in) long, with many cylindrical leaflets. Creamy white flowerheads, 2cm (¾in) across, are borne in midsummer. ↕ 75cm (30in), ↔ 1m (3ft). Italy. ✻✻.

Santolina chamaecyparissus 'Lemon Queen'

Mainly represented in gardens by the following subspecies and its forms. **subsp. *neapolitana***, syn. *S. neapolitana*, *S. tomentosa*, has aromatic, grey-green foliage and bright yellow flowerheads. **subsp. *neapolitana* 'Edward Bowles'** has grey-green foliage and creamy white flowerheads. **subsp. *neapolitana* 'Sulphurea'** ▣ has grey-green foliage and primrose-yellow flowerheads.
S. rosmarinifolia, syn. *S. virens*, *S. viridis*. Dense, rounded, bushy shrub with slender, finely cut, aromatic, bright green leaves, to 5cm (2in) long. Bright yellow flowerheads, 2cm (¾in) across, are produced at the end of slender shoots in midsummer. ↕ 60cm (24in), ↔ 1m (3ft). S.W. Europe. ❄❄. **'Primrose Gem'** has pale yellow flowerheads.
S. tomentosa see *S. pinnata* subsp. *neapolitana*.
S. virens see *S. rosmarinifolia*.
S. viridis see *S. rosmarinifolia*.

SANVITALIA
Creeping zinnia

ASTERACEAE/COMPOSITAE

Genus of 7 species of creeping and spreading annuals and perennials from rocky slopes and dry river washes in S.W. USA and Mexico. They have opposite, simple, oval leaves, and bear daisy-like, bright yellow, orange, or white flowerheads. Creeping zinnias provide colourful ground cover in an annual or herbaceous border, raised bed, or rock garden, or at the edge of a path. They are also suitable for a trough, or for containers on a patio. Modern cultivars are good for hanging baskets.
• **HARDINESS** Fully hardy.
• **CULTIVATION** Grow in moderately fertile, humus-rich, well-drained soil in full sun.
• **PROPAGATION** Sow seed *in situ* in autumn or spring. Delay thinning autumn-sown seedlings until spring.
• **PESTS AND DISEASES** Trouble free.

S. procumbens ▣ (Creeping zinnia). Prostrate, mat-forming annual with pointed, oval, mid-green leaves, to 6cm (2½in) long. Bears single, black-centred, bright yellow flowerheads, to 2cm (¾in) across, over a long period from early summer to early autumn. ↕ to 20cm (8in), ↔ to 45cm (18in). Mexico. ❄❄❄. **'Gold Braid'** is compact, producing golden yellow flowerheads; ↕ 5–10cm

Sanvitalia procumbens

Sanvitalia procumbens 'Mandarin Orange'

(2–4in), ↔ 35cm (14in). **'Golden Carpet'** is dwarf, producing very dark green leaves and small, lemon-yellow flowerheads; ↕ to 10cm (4in). **'Mandarin Orange'** ▣ is compact, with semi-double orange flowerheads; ↕ to 10cm (4in), ↔ 35cm (14in).

SAPINDUS

SAPINDACEAE

Genus of 13 species of deciduous or evergreen trees, shrubs, and climbers, widely distributed in woodland and on riverbanks in warm-temperate, sub-tropical, and tropical regions. They are cultivated for their alternate, simple or pinnate leaves, axillary or terminal racemes or panicles of small, 4- or 5-petalled flowers, and fleshy, spherical fruits. They grow best in a continental climate, with long, hot summers, where they are effective shade trees. Useful for gardens with poor, dry soil.
• **HARDINESS** Fully hardy to frost tender.
• **CULTIVATION** Grow in poor to moderately fertile, well-drained soil in full sun, sheltered from cold winds. Pruning group 1.
• **PROPAGATION** Sow seed of hardy species in containers in a cold frame in spring, after cold stratification for 8 weeks. Sow seed of tender species at 16–18°C (61–64°F) in spring.
• **PESTS AND DISEASES** Trouble free.

S. drummondii ♀ (Western soapberry). Spreading, deciduous tree producing pinnate leaves, to 40cm (16in) long, with up to 18 lance-shaped, glossy, mid-green leaflets, turning golden yellow in autumn. Small, creamy white flowers are borne in conical, terminal panicles, to 25cm (10in) long, in late spring and early summer; they are followed by spherical, orange-yellow fruit, 1cm (½in) across. ↕ 15m (50ft), ↔ 10m (30ft). S. USA, N. Mexico. ❄❄❄ (borderline)

SAPONARIA
Soapwort

CARYOPHYLLACEAE

Genus of about 20 species of annuals and perennials, some with a woody rootstock, mostly from meadows or rocky areas in the mountains of Europe and S.W. Asia. Closely related to *Lychnis* and *Silene*, they differ in having flowers with 2 styles rather than 3 or 5.

Saponaria caespitosa

They have opposite, entire, variably shaped, narrow leaves and abundant flat, 5-petalled, clawed flowers, usually in shades of pink, borne in loose or dense heads, panicles, or cymes. The genus includes compact plants, suitable for a rock garden, trough, or raised bed, and taller, spreading plants, useful for a herbaceous or mixed border.
• **HARDINESS** Fully hardy.
• **CULTIVATION** Grow border perennials in moderately fertile, well-drained, neutral to slightly alkaline soil in full sun. More compact species, such as *S. caespitosa*, require gritty, sharply drained soil. Cut *S. ocymoides* back hard after flowering, to maintain a compact habit.
• **PROPAGATION** Sow seed in containers in an open frame in autumn or spring. Divide border perennials in autumn or spring. Root softwood cuttings in early summer.
• **PESTS AND DISEASES** May be damaged by slugs and snails.

***S.* 'Bressingham'**, syn. *S.* 'Bressingham Hybrid'. Loose, mat-forming perennial with hairy, narrowly ovate-lance-shaped, mid-green leaves, to 1.5cm (½in) long. Bears many short-stemmed, panicle-like cymes of brilliant deep pink flowers, to 1cm (½in) across, in summer. Ideal for a trough or rock garden. ↕ 8cm (3in), ↔ 30cm (12in). ❄❄❄
***S.* 'Bressingham Hybrid'** see *S.* 'Bressingham'.
S. caespitosa ▣ Compact, densely tufted, mat-forming perennial with a woody rootstock and narrowly lance-shaped, mid-green leaves, 5mm (¼in)

Saponaria ocymoides

long. Few-flowered heads of pink to purple flowers, 1cm (½in) across, are borne just above the leaves in summer. ↕↔ 15cm (6in). Pyrenees. ❄❄❄
S. ocymoides ▣ (Tumbling Ted). Spreading, mat-forming perennial with ovate-lance-shaped, hairy, bright green leaves, to 1cm (½in) long. A profusion of pink flowers, 1cm (½in) across, opens in loose, panicle-like cymes, in summer. May swamp smaller plants. ↕ 8cm (3in), ↔ 45cm (18in) or more. Mountainous areas from Spain to Yugoslavia. ❄❄❄. **'Alba'** is less vigorous, with white flowers. **'Rubra Compacta'** has a neat, dense habit, and dark red flowers.
S. officinalis (Bouncing Bet, Soapwort). Upright perennial, spreading rapidly by rhizomes, with narrowly ovate, rough, prominently veined, mid-green leaves, 4–7cm (1½–3in) long. From summer to autumn, bears panicle-like cymes of pink, red, or white flowers, to 2cm (¾in) across. ↕ 60cm (24in), ↔ 50cm (20in). Europe. ❄❄❄. **'Alba Plena'** produces abundant double white flowers, pink in bud. **'Dazzler'**, syn. 'Taff's Dazzler', 'Variegata', has single pink flowers, and leaves heavily variegated cream. It is less invasive than the species. **'Rubra Plena'** tends to spread, and produces double red flowers that fade to pink. **'Taff's Dazzler'** see 'Dazzler'. **'Variegata'** see 'Dazzler'.
S.* x *olivana ▣ (*S. pumilio* x *S. ocymoides*). Cushion-forming perennial with narrowly lance-shaped, mid-green leaves, 7mm (¼in) long. Produces branching stems around the edges of the cushion, each bearing heads of several pale pink flowers, 1.5cm (½in) across, in summer. ↕ 5cm (2in), ↔ 15cm (6in). Garden origin. ❄❄❄

▷ **Sapphire berry** see *Symplocos paniculata*
▷ **Sapphire flower** see *Browallia speciosa*
▷ **Sarana, Black** see *Fritillaria camschatcensis*

Saponaria x *olivana*

S

SARCOCAPNOS

PAPAVERACEAE

Genus of 3 or 4 species of dwarf, tufted annuals or perennials from cliff crevices in mountains throughout S.W. Europe and N. Africa. They are grown for their fleshy, simple or 2- or 3-ternate, finely divided leaves, to 15cm (6in) long, and for their terminal racemes of spurred flowers, similar to those of *Corydalis*, which are borne in spring and summer. Grow in a scree bed, raised bed, or in tufa; they are also delicate, short-lived plants for an alpine house.

- **HARDINESS** Frost hardy.
- **CULTIVATION** Grow in moderately fertile, sharply drained, alkaline soil, in full sun with some midday shade; protect from excessive winter wet. In an alpine house, grow in a mix of 2 parts grit and 1 part each loam and leaf mould, with additional tufa chippings.
- **PROPAGATION** Sow seed in containers in a cold frame as soon as ripe. Plants grown under glass often self-seed.
- **PESTS AND DISEASES** Aphids and red spider mites may be a problem under glass.

S. enneaphylla. Tuft-forming annual or short-lived perennial with brittle, branching stems bearing fern-like, 2- or 3-ternate, blue-green leaves, to 10cm (4in) long, consisting of ovate to elliptic leaflets with heart-shaped bases. In spring, produces racemes of 5–15 white or pink flowers, to 2cm (¾in) long, with short spurs. ↕↔ 15cm (6in). S. Spain, Morocco. ✻✻

SARCOCAULON

GERANIACEAE

Genus of about 15 species of freely branching, deciduous, succulent perennials and subshrubs from very dry areas of Angola, Namibia, and South Africa. Stem branches are armed with usually small thorns and have hard, resinous bark. The opposite leaves are of 2 types: primary, with long stalks that become spines, and secondary, with shorter stalks that may persist as blunt stumps in the axils of the primary leaves. Solitary, trumpet-shaped flowers are borne mostly from winter to summer. Where temperatures fall below 10°C (50°F), grow in a temperate or warm greenhouse or conservatory; in warmer climates, use in a desert garden.

- **HARDINESS** Frost tender.
- **CULTIVATION** Under glass, grow in standard cactus compost in full light with low humidity. In growth, water moderately, and apply a half-strength balanced liquid fertilizer monthly; water sparingly in winter, but mist lightly on warmer days. Outdoors, grow in poor to moderately fertile, sharply drained soil in full sun. Protect from excessive winter wet. See also pp.48–49.
- **PROPAGATION** Sow seed at 24°C (75°F) as soon as ripe.
- **PESTS AND DISEASES** Susceptible to mealybugs.

S. herrei. Shrubby, succulent perennial with spreading branches marked with leaf scars, and bearing thorns to 2.5cm (1in) long. Triangular to rounded, fleshy, 2- or 3-pinnatisect leaves, 1.5–2cm (½–¾in) long, are yellowish green with silky hairs. White and yellow flowers, 2cm (¾in) across, are borne in winter. ↕↔ to 30cm (12in). South Africa (Western Cape). ❀ (min. 10°C/50°F)

SARCOCOCCA

Christmas box, Sweet box

BUXACEAE

Genus of about 14 species of monoecious, evergreen, sometimes rhizomatous shrubs found in moist, shady places, forest, and thickets from China to the Himalayas and S.E. Asia. They are grown for their foliage, usually fragrant flowers, and berry-like fruits. The leaves are mainly alternate, rarely opposite, entire, and narrowly lance-shaped to broadly ovate or elliptic. Tiny, fragrant, petalless, white or whitish green male and female flowers, 5mm (¼in) long, are borne in small clusters or spikes in the leaf axils. The male flowers have conspicuous anthers; the females are produced below the males in the inflorescence. Grow as ground cover in a woodland garden, or use as a low, informal hedge. Tolerant of atmospheric pollution, dry shade, and neglect.

- **HARDINESS** Fully hardy to frost hardy.
- **CULTIVATION** Grow in moderately fertile, humus-rich, moist but well-drained soil in deep or partial shade. Full sun is tolerated if the soil remains moist. Shelter from cold, drying winds. Pruning group 8.
- **PROPAGATION** Sow seed in containers outdoors in autumn or spring. Take semi-ripe cuttings in late summer. Remove suckers in late winter.
- **PESTS AND DISEASES** Trouble free.

S. confusa ■ Dense, rounded, bushy shrub with elliptic, tapered, glossy, dark green leaves, to 6cm (2½in) long. Clusters of about 5 very fragrant white flowers are borne in winter, followed by spherical, glossy black fruit, 5mm (¼in) across. ↕ 2m (6ft), ↔ 1m (3ft). Probably W. China. ✻✻✻

Sarcococca hookeriana var. *digyna* 'Purple Stem'

Sarcococca humilis

S. hookeriana. Rhizomatous, thicket-forming, suckering, compact shrub with lance-shaped to oblong, mid- to dark green leaves, to 9cm (3½in) long. Clusters of fragrant white flowers are borne in winter, followed by spherical, black or blue-black fruit, 5mm (¼in) across. ↕ 1.5m (5ft), ↔ 2m (6ft). W. China. ✻✻✻. **var. *digyna*** has slender, tapered leaves, and male flowers with cream anthers. **var. *digyna* 'Purple Stem'** ■ has young shoots flushed dark purple-pink, and pink-tinged flowers. **var. *humilis*** see *S. humilis*.

S. humilis ■ syn. *S. hookeriana* var. *humilis*. Dwarf, clump-forming shrub, spreading by suckers, with erect shoots and oblong, glossy, dark green leaves, to 8cm (3in) long. In winter, bears clusters of fragrant, pink-tinged white flowers, the males with pink anthers, followed by spherical, dark blue-black fruit, 5mm (¼in) across. ↕ 60cm (24in), ↔ 1m (3ft). W. China. ✻✻✻

S. ruscifolia. Dense, bushy shrub with arching shoots and ovate, tapered, glossy, dark green leaves, to 6cm (2½in) long. Clusters of fragrant, creamy white flowers are produced in winter, and are followed by spherical, dark red fruit, 5mm (¼in) across. ↕↔ 1m (3ft). W. and C. China. ✻✻. **var. *chinensis*** has narrowly ovate to lance-shaped leaves.

S. saligna. Thicket-forming shrub with erect shoots and narrowly lance-shaped, finely tapered leaves, to 14cm (5½in) long, dark green above, pale green beneath. In winter and early spring, bears spikes, to 1.5cm (½in) long, of unscented, greenish white flowers, followed by ovoid purple fruit, to 1cm (½in) long. ↕ 1m (3ft), ↔ 2m (6ft). Afghanistan to Nepal (Himalayas). ✻✻

Sarcococca confusa

SARITAEA

BIGNONIACEAE

Genus of a single species of woody-stemmed, evergreen tendril climber from woodland in N. South America. It produces opposite pairs of leaves and cyme-like panicles of tubular-bell-shaped flowers, with 5 spreading petal lobes. Where temperatures fall below 10°C (50°F), grow in a temperate or warm greenhouse. In warmer regions, grow over a pergola or arch, or through the branches of a tree.

- **HARDINESS** Frost tender.
- **CULTIVATION** Under glass, grow in loam-based potting compost (JI No.2) in bright filtered light. When in growth, water freely and apply a balanced liquid fertilizer monthly; maintain moderate to high humidity. Water sparingly in winter. Outdoors, grow in moderately fertile, humus-rich, moist but well-drained soil, in full sun with some midday shade, or in partial shade. Pruning group 11, in early spring.
- **PROPAGATION** Sow seed at about 16°C (61°F) in spring. Root semi-ripe cuttings with bottom heat in late summer. Layer in early spring.
- **PESTS AND DISEASES** Red spider mites may be a problem under glass.

S. magnifica, syn. *Arrabidaea magnifica*. Vigorous, erect climber with leaves composed of 2 obovate, rich green leaflets, to 10cm (4in) long, those on the main climbing stems having hook-tipped tendrils. Cyme-like panicles of tubular-bell-shaped, pale purple to rose-pink flowers, 7–9cm (3–3½in) across, with light yellow to white, V-shaped markings inside, are borne in several flushes throughout the year. ↕ to 10m (30ft) or more. Colombia, Ecuador. ❀ (min. 10°C/50°F)

S

SARMIENTA

GESNERIACEAE

Genus of one species of small, shrubby, creeping, evergreen perennial growing epiphytically on trees in cool rainforest in temperate Chile. It has simple leaves in opposite pairs, and 5-lobed, tubular, axillary flowers. Where temperatures fall below 5°C (41°F), grow in a cool or temperate greenhouse, or conservatory. In milder areas, grow over mossy rocks, or epiphytically on a tree.

• **HARDINESS** Frost tender, but may survive short spells down to 0°C (32°F).

• **CULTIVATION** Under glass, grow in 2 parts loamless potting compost and 1 part each fine-grade granulated bark and leaf mould, or grow epiphytically. Provide bright indirect light. In growth, water freely, applying a balanced liquid fertilizer monthly. Mist daily in summer. Water sparingly in winter. Outdoors, grow in fertile, humus-rich soil, ideally mixed with sphagnum moss, in light dappled shade or partial shade.

• **PROPAGATION** Sow seed at 16–21°C (61–70°F) in spring. Root stem-tip cuttings in late summer, with bottom heat. Separate rooted stems in spring.

• **PESTS AND DISEASES** Red spider mites may infest plants grown under glass.

S. repens, syn. *S. scandens.* Creeping or low-climbing perennial with semi-woody, rooting stems and obovate to elliptic, minutely glandular, light to mid-green leaves, to 2.5cm (1in) long, with 3–5 shallow to deep teeth at the tips. In summer, bears solitary, pendent, tubular scarlet flowers, 2–2.5cm (¾–1in) long. ↕ prostrate, ↔ to 30cm (12in) or more. S. Chile. ❀ (min. 5°C/41°F)
S. scandens see *S. repens.*

SARRACENIA

Pitcher plant

SARRACENIACEAE

Genus of 8 species of evergreen or deciduous, carnivorous perennials found in acid and nutrient-deficient bogs from the Canadian Arctic to Florida, USA. Short, stout rhizomes bear sparse, wiry roots and rosettes of phyllodes, some or all of which are modified into nectar-secreting, insect-catching pitchers. The mostly vertical, sometimes horizontal, attractively marked pitchers, 5–90cm (2–36in) long, have lateral wings and hooded lids. Mainly in spring, solitary, nodding or pendent, more or less cup-shaped flowers, with 4 or 5 sepals and 5 petals, are borne above the pitchers. Where temperatures fall below -5°C (23°F), grow in a cold or cool greenhouse or on a sunny window-sill. In warmer areas, grow on a damp, shaded peat terrace.

• **HARDINESS** Fully hardy to frost hardy.

• **CULTIVATION** Under glass, grow in half pots of 3 parts sphagnum moss and 1 part each leaf mould and lime-free coarse sand or grit, in full light with shade from hot sun. In growth, apply a balanced liquid fertilizer monthly. In summer, stand containers in trays of lime-free water. In winter, keep just moist, cool, and well ventilated. Outdoors, grow in humus-rich, moist but sharply drained, acid soil in full sun. Irrigate with lime-free water.

• **PROPAGATION** Sow seed of species at 16–21°C (61–70°F) in spring, after cold stratification for 2 weeks; place the pot in a tray of lime-free water. Prick out seedlings when 3 tiny pitchers appear. Divide in spring.

• **PESTS AND DISEASES** Prone to scale insects, mealybugs, aphids, and tortrix moth caterpillars.

S. drummondii see *S. leucophylla.*
S. flava ■ (Yellow trumpet). Very variable perennial bearing erect, yellow-green pitchers, 30–90cm (12–36in) long, with round mouths and raised lids, often veined red. Phyllodes that do not produce pitchers are linear, and persist throughout the winter. In spring, bears yellow flowers, to 10cm (4in) across. ↕ 50–100cm (20–39in), ↔ to 1m (3ft). USA (Virginia to Alabama, Florida). ✻✻. **'Burgundy'** has pitchers plum-coloured outside. **'Maxima'** has pitchers 90cm (36in) long, with purple-veined lids and stems.
S. leucophylla, syn. *S. drummondii* (White trumpet). Semi-evergreen perennial bearing erect, slender pitchers, 25–100cm (10–39in) long, with narrow wings and erect lids with wavy margins. The lids and tops are typically white, often with light or heavy purple-red netting, gradually merging into green bases. In spring, bears purple flowers, to 7cm (3in) across. ↕ 50–90cm (20–39in), ↔ to 1m (3ft). USA (Missouri to Florida). ✻✻
S. purpurea (Huntsman's cup). Very variable perennial bearing horizontal, purple-veined, purple or green pitchers, 5–50cm (2–20in) long, with upcurved ends, broad wings, and erect, entire, smooth, often glossy, broad lids. Dark purple-red and pink to dark red flowers, occasionally yellow, to 5cm (2in) across, are produced in spring. ↕ 10–15cm (4–6in), ↔ 1m (3ft). Canadian Arctic to USA (New Jersey). ✻✻✻. **subsp. *venosa*** has more inflated, rough, green to purple pitchers, with broader, wavy lids that extend beyond the mouths; flowers are purple or rose-pink; USA (New Jersey to Louisiana), naturalized in Ireland; ✻✻

SASA

GRAMINEAE/POACEAE

Genus of 40–50 species of small to medium-sized bamboos, with running rhizomes, closely related to *Sasaella*, to which several species of *Sasa* have now been transferred. They are found in damp hollows and woodland in Japan, Korea, and China. The ascending canes are smooth and cylindrical, with persistent, bristly sheaths and a white-waxy bloom beneath the nodes. The large, usually broad, thick, toothed, and tessellated leaves often wither at the margins in winter, giving a variegated effect. Use as ground cover under trees, or as a hedge; sasas tolerate deep shade.

• **HARDINESS** Fully hardy.

• **CULTIVATION** Grow in fertile, humus-rich, moist but well-drained soil in full sun to deep shade; tolerant of most soils, but avoid dry soils when planting in full sun. To restrict spread, plant in containers and plunge into the soil.

• **PROPAGATION** Divide or cut sections of the youngest rhizomes in spring.

Sarracenia flava

Sasa veitchii

• **PESTS AND DISEASES** Emergent shoots may be eaten by slugs.

S. albomarginata see *S. veitchii.*
S. humilis see *Pleioblastus humilis.*
***S. masamuneana* 'Albostriata'**, syn. *Sasaella masamuneana* 'Albostriata'. Low-growing, moderately spreading bamboo with very slender, green or brown canes, producing a single branch at each node. The narrowly elliptic, mid-green leaves, 10–19cm (4–7in) long, are conspicuously white-striped when young, becoming yellow as they mature in autumn, and fading in winter. ↕ to 1.5m (5ft), ↔ indefinite. ✻✻✻
***S. palmata* f. *nebulosa*.** Vigorous bamboo with wide-spreading rhizomes and stout, upward-curved, usually purple-streaked canes that produce a single branch at each node. The broadly elliptic, tapered, smooth, glossy, bright green leaves, 35–40cm (14–16in) long, are paler green beneath, and have yellow midribs. The leaves generally wither at the margins and tips in winter. ↕ to 2m (6ft), ↔ indefinite. Japan. ✻✻✻
S. ramosa, syn. *Arundinaria vagans, Sasaella ramosa.* Extremely vigorous, low-growing bamboo with slender, glossy, bright green canes producing a single branch at each node. Elliptic, mid-green leaves, to 20cm (8in) long, have yellow midribs, and wither at the margins and tips in winter. ↕ 0.6–1.5m (2–5ft), ↔ indefinite. Japan. ✻✻✻
S. ruscifolia see *Shibataea kumasasa.*
S. tessellata see *Indocalamus tessellata.*
S. veitchii ■ syn. *S. albomarginata.* Moderately spreading bamboo producing slender, glaucous, usually purple canes, with a single branch at each node. The broadly lance-shaped-ovate, ribbed leaves are glossy, dark green, to 25cm (10in) long, and wither at the margins from late autumn. ↕ to 2m (6ft), usually 1–1.2m (3–4ft), ↔ indefinite. Japan. ✻✻✻

▷ ***Sasaella masamuneana* 'Albostriata'** see *Sasa masamuneana* 'Albostriata'
▷ ***Sasaella ramosa*** see *Sasa ramosa*

Sassafras albidum

SASSAFRAS

LAURACEAE

Genus of 3 species of generally dioecious, deciduous trees from woodland and thickets in China, Taiwan, and North America. They are grown for their stately habit and glossy, aromatic foliage, which colours attractively in autumn. They have deeply fissured bark, and alternate, often 1- to 3-lobed, elliptic, oval, ovate, or obovate leaves. Clustered racemes of small, yellow-green flowers are borne in spring, either before or as the leaves emerge. Where plants of both sexes are grown together, the flowers on female plants are followed by ovoid fruits. Grow as specimen trees in a woodland garden or at woodland margins.
• **HARDINESS** Fully hardy.
• **CULTIVATION** Grow in moist but well-drained, moderately fertile, humus-rich, preferably acid, deep soil in full sun or partial shade. Cut out suckers as they arise. Pruning group 1.
• **PROPAGATION** Sow seed in containers in a cold frame as soon as ripe. Take root cuttings in winter.
• **PESTS AND DISEASES** Trouble free.

S. albidum ▣ ♀ Broadly columnar to upright tree, spreading by suckers. The elliptic to ovate, entire or shallowly to deeply 3-lobed, aromatic, dark green leaves, to 15cm (6in) long, turn yellow to orange or purple in autumn. Racemes to 5cm (2in) across, of tiny yellow flowers open in spring, as the leaves emerge. If pollinated, the flowers on female plants are followed by red-stalked, ovoid, dark blue fruit, 1cm (½in) long. ↕ 25m (80ft), ↔ 15m (50ft). E. North America. ✻✻✻

▷ **Sassafras, Australian** see *Atherosperma moschatum*
▷ ***Sassamorpha tessellata*** see *Indocalamus tessellata*
▷ **Satin flower** see *Clarkia amoena, Lunaria, L. annua*
▷ **Satinwood** see *Phebalium squameum*

SATUREJA

Savory

LABIATAE/LAMIACEAE

Genus of approximately 30 species of annuals, perennials, and subshrubs, widely distributed throughout the N. hemisphere, occurring in dry, sunny sites and often found on cliffs. They are cultivated for their aromatic leaves, which are opposite, linear to lance-shaped, or oblong-obovate to spoon-shaped, and for their cyme-like or spike-like inflorescences; these consist of whorls of stalkless, tubular, 2-lipped flowers, borne in summer, which are attractive to bees and other insects. Suitable for growing in a mixed border or rock garden. *S. hortensis* and *S. montana* are used as culinary herbs.
• **HARDINESS** Fully hardy to frost hardy.
• **CULTIVATION** Grow in moderately fertile, well-drained, neutral to slightly alkaline soil in full sun. Protect from excessive winter wet. Cut back old shoots of subshrubs in early spring.
• **PROPAGATION** Sow seed at 13–16°C (55–61°F) in late winter or early spring; seed of *S. hortensis* may be sown *in situ* in spring or, in mild climates, in autumn. Take greenwood cuttings of subshrubs in summer.
• **PESTS AND DISEASES** Trouble free.

S. hortensis (Summer savory). Bushy, aromatic annual with linear to narrowly lance-shaped, fresh green leaves, to 3cm (1¼in) long. In summer, bears crowded or lax, whorl-like spikes of 2–5 white or pink flowers, to 7mm (¼in) long. ↕ 25cm (10in), ↔ to 30cm (12in). S.E. Europe. ✻✻
S. montana ▣ (Winter savory). Dwarf subshrub producing stalkless, linear to inversely lance-shaped, leathery, smooth or sparsely hairy, dark greyish green leaves, 0.5–3cm (¼–1¼in) long. For long periods throughout summer, bears whorls of up to 14 lavender-pink to purple flowers, to 8mm (⅜in) long, in dense, upright spikes. ↕ 40cm (16in), ↔ 20cm (8in). S. Europe. ✻✻✻.
'Prostrate White' ▣ is more compact, with erect white flower spikes; ↕↔ to 15cm (6in).
S. repanda see *S. spicigera.*
S. reptans see *S. spicigera.*
S. spicigera, syn. *S. repanda, S. reptans.* Creeping, aromatic subshrub with procumbent stems and linear to lance-shaped, mid-green leaves, to 2.5cm (1in) long. In summer, bears lax cymes of white flowers, 1cm (½in) long, in whorls of up to 16. ↕ 15cm (6in), ↔ 30cm (12in). Turkey, Iran, Caucasus. ✻✻✻

Satureja montana 'Prostrate White'

Satureja montana

SAUROMATUM *syn.* TYPHONIUM

ARACEAE

Genus of 2 species of tuberous perennials from woodland and shady cliffs in the Himalayas and E. and W. Africa, grown for their large spathes, borne in spring or early summer, and single, long-stalked leaves. In frost-prone areas, grow in a cool greenhouse, or outside in summer; elsewhere, grow in a woodland garden.
• **HARDINESS** Frost tender.
• **CULTIVATION** Plant tubers 15cm (6in) deep in late winter. Under glass, grow in loam-based potting compost in bright filtered or indirect light. In growth, water moderately; keep completely dry in winter. Tubers will flower on a saucer without soil or water. Outdoors, grow in well-drained, fertile, humus-rich, neutral to slightly acid soil in partial shade.
• **PROPAGATION** Remove offsets when dormant in winter.
• **PESTS AND DISEASES** Trouble free.

Sauromatum venosum

S. guttatum see *S. venosum.*
S. venosum ▣ syn. *S. guttatum* (Monarch of the East, Voodoo lily). Tuberous perennial with an oblong-lance-shaped, yellowish or greenish white spathe, 30–70cm (12–28in) long, heavily spotted purple, with a foul-smelling, greenish purple spadix, to 35cm (14in) long, produced in late spring and early summer. The spathe is followed by a single, rounded leaf, to 35cm (14in) long, with many oblong-lance-shaped segments. ↕ 30–45cm (12–18in), ↔ 15cm (6in). Himalayas. ❀ (min. 5°C/41°F)

▷ **Sausage tree** see *Kigelia*
▷ **Savin** see *Juniperus sabina*
▷ **Savory** see *Satureja*
Summer see *S. hortensis*
Winter see *S. montana*
▷ **Saw palm** see *Acoelorraphe*
Silver see *A. wrightii*

SAXEGOTHAEA

PODOCARPACEAE

Genus of one species of monoecious, evergreen, coniferous tree or shrub from dense forest in Chile and Argentina. It has whorled branches with irregularly set, yew-like foliage, and bears fleshy, spherical green female cones and tiny male cones. Grow in a woodland garden among other conifers, or as a free-standing specimen.
• **HARDINESS** Fully hardy.
• **CULTIVATION** Grow in moderately fertile, well-drained, neutral to slightly acid soil, in full sun with some midday shade, or in partial shade. Shelter from cold, drying winds.
• **PROPAGATION** Take semi-ripe cuttings in late summer or early autumn.
• **PESTS AND DISEASES** Trouble free.

S. conspicua ▣ ◊ (Prince Albert's yew). Slender, conical, coniferous tree or shrub, bushy in cold areas, with smooth, purple-brown bark and whorled branches bearing green shoots. Linear to linear-lance-shaped, dark green leaves, to 3cm (1¼in) long, each have 2 silver crossbands beneath, and persist for 5 or 6 years. Fleshy, spherical, prickly, glaucous-green female cones, 1.5cm (½in) across, contain about 6 seeds, and develop from terminal clusters of scales in autumn. Male cones are cylindrical, dark purple, and borne at the bases of the shoots. ↕ to 20m (70ft), ↔ 5–8m (15–25ft). S. Chile to Argentina. ✻✻✻

Saxegothaea conspicua

SAXIFRAGA

Saxifrage

SAXIFRAGACEAE

Genus of about 440 species of mostly mat- or cushion-forming, evergreen, semi-evergreen, or deciduous perennials, biennials, and a few annuals, mostly from mountains in the N. hemisphere. Those described are evergreen and perennial unless stated. Varying greatly in habit and leaf form, they produce flat, star-shaped, or shallowly cup-shaped flowers, either singly or in cymes, racemes, or panicles. The rosettes of monocarpic saxifrages die after flowering and are replaced by daughter rosettes. Saxifrages are suitable for rock gardens, mixed borders, and woodland gardens.

Saxifrages are classified botanically into sections, subsections, and series. Those of most horticultural value are as follows.

Section Gymnopera (Robertsonia) Saxifrages with evergreen, rosetted leaves, and flowers in panicles on leafless flower stems. Contains London pride (*S.* x *urbium*) and similar shade-lovers.
Section Irregulares (Diptera) Woodland plants with rosettes of basal, usually deciduous leaves (often evergreen under glass); flower panicles, on leafless stems, appear in summer and autumn.
Section Ligulatae (Euaizoonia) The silver or encrusted saxifrages, which have evergreen, monocarpic rosettes with a conspicuous calcareous (lime) encrustation. Cushion- or mat-forming; flower panicles are borne on leafy stems.
Section Porphyrion (Porophyllum) Cushion- or mat-forming, evergreen perennials with rosettes or leafy shoots, usually with lime-encrusted leaves. The section includes the following horticulturally important subsections. ***Engleria*** – saxifrages with rosettes of leaves alternately arranged, the margins translucent. Flower stems are leafy and distinct, with coloured bracts, and flowers have erect sepals largely hiding the pink, purple, white, or yellow petals, which have basal fringes of hairs; they are borne singly or in small cymes or racemes. ***Kabschia*** – saxifrages with leafy shoots, and alternate leaves with translucent margins. The leafy flowering stems are short or distinct (with up to 15 flowers), and bear white, pink, purple, or yellow flowers, singly or in small cymes or racemes. ***Oppositifoliae*** – saxifrages with opposite leaves, usually without translucent margins. Purple, pink, or white flowers are borne in short cymes of up to 3. Flowering stems are short and leafy or absent.
Section Saxifraga (Dactyloides) Perennial, rarely annual or biennial, usually evergreen saxifrages, sometimes summer-dormant; they produce bulbils. Of varied habit, their often leafy shoots form cushions or mats, with soft, lobed or scalloped leaves, lacking chalk glands. Bears cymes of white, rarely red, pink, or yellow flowers on usually leafy stems. Includes the mossy saxifrages.
Section Xanthizoon are mat- or cushion-forming, evergreen perennials with fleshy, narrow, stalkless leaves, with or without functional chalk glands. Yellow or orange flowers are borne in loose cymes on leafy stems.

S

Saxifraga x *apiculata*

• **HARDINESS** Fully hardy; *S. stolonifera* and its cultivars are frost hardy.
• **CULTIVATION** Requirements fall broadly into 4 groups.
1. Grow in moist but well-drained, humus-rich soil in deep or partial shade. Suitable for a border or rock garden.
2. Grow in humus-rich, moist but very sharply drained, neutral to alkaline soil in light shade. Suitable for a rock crevice, scree bed, or alpine house.
3. Grow in moderately fertile, very well-drained, neutral to alkaline soil; keep roots moist. Tolerant of full sun in cool areas, but protect from hot sun in warm areas to prevent leaf scorch. Suitable for a rock garden or trough.
4. Grow in moderately fertile, very sharply drained, alkaline soil or scree in full sun. Suitable for a rock garden, trough, alpine house, or tufa. Some are intolerant of winter wet. In an alpine house, grow in shallow pans in 2 parts loam-based compost (JI No.1) and 1 part limestone chippings.
• **PROPAGATION** Sow seed in autumn in containers in an open frame. Divide herbaceous perennials in spring. Detach individual rosettes and root as cuttings in late spring or early summer.

Saxifraga x *boydii* 'Hindhead Seedling'

• **PESTS AND DISEASES** Aphids, slugs, vine weevil grubs, and red spider mites may be a problem.

S. aizoides (Yellow mountain saxifrage). Mat-forming Xanthizoon saxifrage with branching stems bearing tight rosettes of linear to oblong, fleshy, glossy, mid- to dark green leaves, 0.4–2cm (⅛–¾in) long, with 2 short teeth near the tips, and bristly margins. In summer and early autumn, erect, hairy stems bear star-shaped, red-spotted, deep orange flowers, 8mm (⅜in) across, in few-flowered cymes. Cultivation group 2. ↕15cm (6in), ↔ 20cm (8in). Arctic, alpine areas of Europe, Asia, North America. ❄❄❄
S. aizoon see *S. paniculata*.
S.* x *anglica (*S. aretioides* x *S. lilacina* x *S. media*). Dense, mat- or rosette-forming Kabschia saxifrage with linear-oblong to spoon-shaped, dark green or grey-green to silver, encrusted leaves, 0.3–1.5cm (⅛–½in) long. Cup-shaped, pink to pink-purple flowers, to 2cm (¾in) across, are borne singly or in 2- or 3-flowered cymes in early and mid-spring. Cultivation group 3 or 4. ↕2–6cm (¾–2½in), ↔ 5–30cm (2–12in). Garden origin. ❄❄❄. **'Cranbourne'** has linear, grey-green leaves and, in early summer, bears solitary, almost stemless, deep rose-pink flowers; ↕2.5cm (1in), ↔ 20cm (8in). **'Myra'**, syn. *S.* 'Myra', is very compact and slow-growing, with narrowly lance-shaped leaves, to 1cm (½in) long. Bears deep red-purple flowers, 1cm (½in) across, in early spring; ↕5cm (2in), ↔ 10cm (4in).
S.* x *apiculata ■ (*S. marginata* x *S. sancta*). Cushion-forming Kabschia saxifrage with tight rosettes of linear-lance-shaped, slightly lime-encrusted, deep green leaves, 1cm (½in) long. Produces cymes of 4–12 cup-shaped yellow flowers, 8mm (⅜in) across, in early spring. Cultivation group 3. ↕10cm (4in) ↔ 30cm (12in). Garden origin. ❄❄❄. **'Gregor Mendel'** has glossy, pale green leaves and pale yellow flowers. Good for a rock garden or wall.
S. aretioides. Compact Kabschia saxifrage bearing rosettes of pointed, oblong-lance-shaped, blue-green leaves, 5mm (¼in) long. Produces flat-topped cymes of up to 5 open cup-shaped yellow flowers, 8–10mm (⅜–½in) across, in early spring. Cultivation group 3. ↕8cm (3in), ↔ 15cm (6in). N.W. Spain, Pyrenees. ❄❄❄
***S.* 'Bob Hawkins'.** Mossy, mat-forming Saxifraga saxifrage with large, soft rosettes of deeply divided, linear, white-variegated, mid-green leaves, to 2cm (¾in) long. In summer, bears cymes of 5–12 upturned, cup-shaped, greenish white flowers, to 2cm (¾in) across, on upright stems. Cultivation group 2. ↕15cm (6in), ↔ 30cm (12in). ❄❄❄
S.* x *boydii (*S. aretioides* x *S. burseriana*). Dense, rosette-forming Kabschia saxifrage with linear to lance-shaped, often pointed, grey-green to silver-green leaves, 3–10mm (⅛–½in) long. In spring, cup-shaped yellow flowers, to 1.5cm (½in) across, are borne singly or in 2- or 3-flowered cymes. Cultivation group 3 or 4. ↕3–8cm (1¼–3in), ↔ 15cm (6in). Garden origin. ❄❄❄. **'Faldonside'** is vigorous, with irregular cymes of star-shaped, bright yellow flowers, to 2.5cm (1in) across; ↕5cm (2in). **'Hindhead Seedling'** ■ syn. *S.* 'Hindhead Seedling', has spiny, blue-green leaves, 5–10mm (¼–½in) long, and mostly solitary, yellow-centred, creamy white flowers, to 2.5cm (1in) across; ↕5cm (2in).
S. burseriana ■ Kabschia saxifrage with firm rosettes of pointed, narrowly lance-shaped, lime-encrusted, grey-green leaves, to 1cm (½in) long. Solitary, cup-shaped white flowers, 1cm (½in) across, open on short red stems in early spring. Cultivation group 3 or 4. ↕ to 5cm (2in), ↔ 15cm (6in). E. Alps. ❄❄❄. **'Gloria'** has larger flowers, 3cm (1¼in) across, with yellow centres, on bright red stems.
S. callosa, syn. *S. lingulata*. Rosette-forming Ligulatae saxifrage with linear, lime-encrusted silver leaves, to 8cm (3in) long. In early summer, arching stems bear narrow panicles, 5–20cm (2–8in) long, of 3–7 star-shaped white flowers, 1cm (½in) across. Cultivation group 4. ↕25cm (10in), ↔ 20cm (8in). N.E. Spain, S.W. Alps, Apennines to S. Italy, Sicily, Sardinia. ❄❄❄
S. cochlearis. Dense, cushion-forming Ligulatae saxifrage with compact rosettes of spoon-shaped, mid-green leaves, 4cm

Saxifraga burseriana

Saxifraga cotyledon

(1½in) long, with lime-encrusted margins. In early summer, bears densely hairy panicles, 6–10cm (2½–4in) long, of 15–25 (occasionally up to 60) rounded, sometimes red-spotted white flowers, 1cm (½in) or more across. Cultivation group 3 or 4. ↕ 20cm (8in), ↔ 15cm (6in). France (Maritime Alps). ❄❄❄. **'Minor'** is lower-growing, and has smaller rosettes; ↕ 10cm (4in).
S. cortusifolia. Deciduous or evergreen Irregulares saxifrage with loose rosettes of kidney-shaped to rounded, 5- or 7-lobed, fleshy, glossy, mid-green leaves, 5–8cm (2–3in) long, with scalloped margins. In late summer, produces pyramidal panicles, to 20cm (8in) long, of cup-shaped white flowers, to 3.5cm (1½in) across, spotted yellow or red.

Saxifraga exarata subsp. *moschata* 'Cloth of Gold'

Saxifraga fortunei

Saxifraga federici-augusti subsp. *grisebachii* 'Wisley Variety'

Each flower has 3 or 4 upper petals and 1 or 2 much longer lower petals. Cultivation group 1. ↕ 15cm (6in), ↔ 20cm (8in). Japan. ❄❄❄. **var. *fortunei*** see *S. fortunei.*
S. cotyledon ■ Rosette-forming Ligulatae saxifrage with oblong to inversely lance-shaped, pale green leaves, to 8cm (3in) long, with lime-encrusted teeth. In late spring and early summer, bears loose, pyramidal panicles, to 70cm (28in) long, of cup-shaped white flowers, to 1cm (½in) across, often marked red. Cultivation group 3 or 4. ↕ 30–70cm (12–28in), ↔ 20cm (8in). Iceland, Scandinavia, Alps, Pyrenees. ❄❄❄
S. cuneifolia. Mat-forming Gymnopera saxifrage bearing rosettes of stalked, usually wedge-shaped, occasionally ovate to rounded, leathery, fresh green leaves, to 2.5cm (1in) long, purple beneath. In spring and early summer, produces loose panicles, 5–18cm (2–7in) long, of 3–12 (rarely up to 30) star-shaped white flowers, 7mm (¼in) across, frequently spotted yellow, sometimes red, on red-tinted stems. Cultivation group 1. ↕ 20cm (8in), ↔ 30cm (12in). Europe (Carpathians to Pyrenees). ❄❄❄
S. exarata* subsp. *moschata, syn. *S. moschata*. Mossy, mat- or cushion-forming Saxifraga saxifrage with rosettes of variably shaped, entire or 3-lobed, pale green leaves, 0.4–2cm (⅛–¾in) long. From late spring to early autumn, bears flat-topped cymes of 1–7 star-shaped, cream or yellow, occasionally pink-tinted flowers, to 8mm (⅜in) across. Cultivation group 2. ↕ 10cm (4in), ↔ 30cm (12in). C. and S. Europe. ❄❄❄. **'Cloth of Gold'** ■ has golden foliage; best grown in shade.
S. federici-augusti. Cushion-forming Engleria saxifrage with flat rosettes of obovate to spoon-shaped, grey-green, usually lime-encrusted leaves, 1–3.5cm (½–1½in) long. The red stems, which bear several leaves, and flower-stalks are partially covered in long, bright cherry-red to dark purple, glandular hairs. In late spring, produces slender racemes, 3–10cm (1¼–4in) long, of 15–25 cup-shaped, purplish pink flowers, 6mm (¼in) across. Cultivation group 4. ↕ 7–20cm (3–8in), ↔ to 15cm (6in). Macedonia, Albania, Greece, Bulgaria. ❄❄❄. **subsp. *grisebachii* 'Wisley Variety'** ■ has spoon-shaped, silver-grey leaves, arching stems clothed in green-tipped, red-purple bracts, and red-purple flowers; ↕ 10cm (4in).

S. ferdinandi-coburgi. Dense, irregular cushion-forming Kabschia saxifrage with rosettes of oblong-lance-shaped, chalk-grey, lime-encrusted leaves, to 8mm (⅜in) long, incurved at the tips. In early spring, bears cymes of 7–12 open cup-shaped, yellow flowers, 1cm (½in) across, on red-tinged stems. Cultivation group 3. ↕ 10cm (4in), ↔ 15cm (6in). E. Bulgaria, N. Greece, Macedonia. ❄❄❄
S. fortunei ■ syn. *S. cortusifolia* var. *fortunei*. Deciduous or semi-evergreen, clump-forming Irregulares saxifrage with kidney-shaped to rounded, 7-lobed, mid-green leaves, 6–10cm (2½–4in) across, often red-purple beneath or purple-tinged with age; they have deeply heart-shaped bases and scalloped margins. In late summer or autumn, bears loose, pendent, red-stemmed panicles, to 50cm (20in) long, of white flowers, 1cm (½in) across, with 3 upper petals and 1 or 2 longer lower petals. Cultivation group 1. ↕↔ 30cm (12in). Japan. ❄❄❄. **'Rubrifolia'** is compact, with strongly red-suffused leaves and deep red stems; ↕↔ 20cm (8in).
S. x geum ■ (*S. hirsuta* x *S. umbrosa*). Mat-forming Gymnopera saxifrage with rosettes of long-stalked, sparsely hairy, spoon-shaped, scalloped, mid-green leaves, to 8cm (3in) long. In summer, bears loose panicles, 6–20cm (2½–8in) long, of 2–12 star-shaped white flowers, 7–8mm (¼–⅜in) across, spotted with red. Cultivation group 1. ↕↔ 20cm (8in). Pyrenees. ❄❄❄
S. granulata ■ (Fair maids of France, Meadow saxifrage). Clump-forming, summer-dormant Saxifraga saxifrage with stem and root bulbils, and loose rosettes of kidney-shaped, toothed or scalloped, pale to mid-green leaves, to 3cm (1¼in) long. In late spring, bears panicles, 8–20cm (3–8in) long, of 10–20 rounded white flowers, to 1.5cm (½in) across, on sticky, erect stems. May be naturalized in grass. Cultivation group 2; tolerates full sun in moist soil. ↕ 20–35cm (8–14in), ↔ 30cm (12in). Europe (mostly W.), N. Africa. ❄❄❄. **'Flore Pleno'**, syn. 'Plena', has double flowers. **'Plena'** see 'Flore Pleno'.
***S.* 'Hindhead Seedling'** see *S.* x *boydii* 'Hindhead Seedling'.
***S. x irvingii* 'Jenkinsiae'** ■ syn. *S.* x *jenkinsiae*. Dense, mound-forming, slow-growing Kabschia saxifrage with tight rosettes of wedge-shaped, lime-encrusted, grey-green leaves, 7mm (¼in) long. In early spring, bears abundant solitary, open cup-shaped, dark-centred,

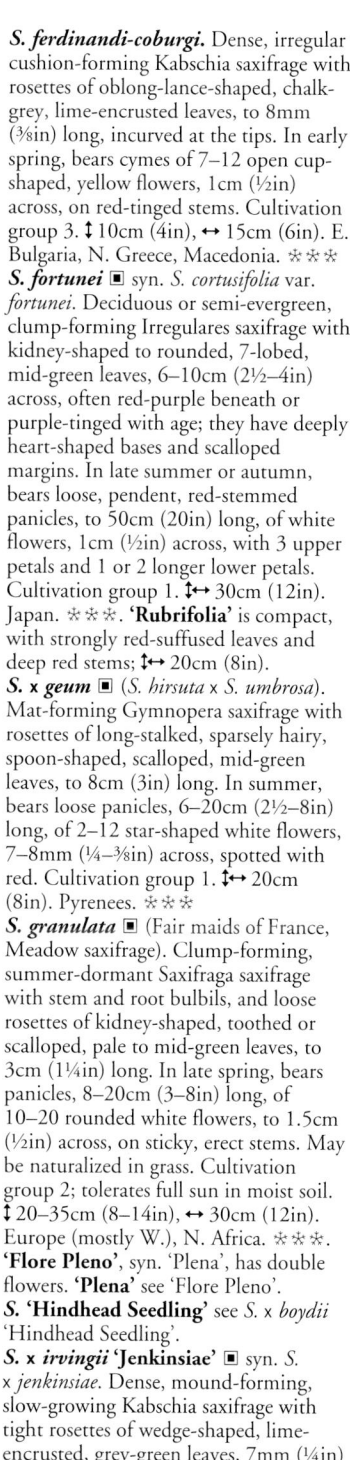

Saxifraga x *geum*

Saxifraga granulata

pale pink flowers, to 2cm (¾in) across, on short red stems. Cultivation group 3. ↕ 5cm (2in), ↔ 20cm (8in). ❄❄❄
S. x jenkinsiae see *S.* x *irvingii* 'Jenkinsiae'.
S. juniperifolia* subsp. *sancta see *S. sancta.*
***S.* 'Kathleen Pinsent'** ■ Rosette-forming Ligulatae saxifrage with narrowly spoon-shaped, silvery leaves, 2–7cm (¾–3in) long, recurved at the tips. In late spring and early summer, bears arching panicles, to 20cm (8in) long, of open cup-shaped, rose-pink flowers, to 2cm (¾in) across. Cultivation group 3 or 4. ↕↔ to 20cm (8in). ❄❄❄
S. lingulata see *S. callosa.*
S. longifolia ■ (Pyrenean saxifrage). Ligulatae saxifrage with a single rosette of linear, lime-encrusted silver leaves, 6–11cm (2½–4½in) long, silver-grey beneath. After 3 or 4 years, produces a huge pyramidal panicle, to 70cm (28in) long, of up to 80 rounded, 5-petalled, open cup-shaped white flowers, 1cm (½in) across, in summer. Cultivation group 4. May only be propagated from seed. ↕ 60cm (24in), ↔ 20cm (8in). Pyrenees. ❄❄❄. **'Tumbling Waters'** see *S.* 'Tumbling Waters'.
S. marginata. Vigorous, cushion- to mat-forming Kabschia saxifrage with rosettes of narrowly elliptic to obovate, lime-encrusted, silver-grey leaves, to 1.5cm (½in) long. Compact panicles, 1–5cm (½–2in) long, of 5–9 open cup-shaped, white, sometimes pink-flushed flowers, to 2cm (¾in) across, are borne in early spring. Cultivation group 3. ↕ 8cm (3in), ↔ 30cm (12in). S. Italy, Balkans, Romania. ❄❄❄

Saxifraga x *irvingii* 'Jenkinsiae'

Saxifraga 'Kathleen Pinsent'

S. moschata see *S. exarata* subsp. *moschata.*
S. 'Myra' see *S.* x *anglica* 'Myra'.
S. oppositifolia ▣ (Purple saxifrage). Flat mat-forming Oppositifoliae saxifrage with rosettes of stiff, oblong or elliptic, dark green leaves, to 5mm (¼in) long, on branching stems. In early summer, bears solitary, almost stemless, cup-shaped, deep red-purple to pale pink or white flowers, to 2cm (¾in) across. Cultivation group 2. ↕ 2.5cm (1in), ↔ 20cm (8in) or more. Arctic, Europe, W. Asia, North America. ❄❄❄. **'Ruth Draper'** has large, bright rose-pink flowers, to 3cm (1¼in) across.
S. paniculata, syn. *S. aizoon.* Variable, mat-forming Ligulatae saxifrage bearing rosettes of incurved, broadly linear or narrowly obovate, grey-green leaves, 0.5–6cm (¼–2½in) long, with lime-encrusted margins. In early summer, numerous cup-shaped flowers open in narrow, flat panicles, 3–20cm (1¼–8in) long. The primary branches each have 1–3, rarely 4, rounded, creamy white, rarely pink flowers, to 1cm (½in) across. Cultivation group 4. ↕ 15cm (6in), ↔ 25cm (10in). Norway, C. and S. Europe, Caucasus, Canada, Greenland,

Saxifraga longifolia

Saxifraga oppositifolia

Iceland. ❄❄❄. **var. *baldensis***, syn. 'Baldensis', 'Minutifolia', produces much smaller rosettes and red-tinged flower stems; ↕ 10cm (4in), ↔ 15cm (6in). **'Baldensis'** see var. *baldensis.* **'Minutifolia'** see var. *baldensis.*
S. porophylla var. thessalica see *S. sempervivum* f. *stenophylla.*
S. 'Primulaize' see *S.* x *primulaize.*
S. x primulaize (*S. aizoides* x *S.* x *urbium* or *S. umbrosa*), syn. *S.* 'Primulaize'. Loose, rosette-forming saxifrage, a hybrid of Section Xanthizoon and Section Gymnopera, resembling a miniature *S.* x *urbium.* Fleshy, narrowly ovate, glossy, mid-green leaves are 2–6cm (¾–2½in) long. In summer, bears loose panicles, 15cm (6in) long, of star-shaped, crimson- or salmon-pink flowers, to 1.5cm (½in) across. Cultivation group 1. ↕ 8cm (3in), ↔ 15cm (6in). Garden origin. ❄❄❄
S. 'Primuloides' see *S. umbrosa* var. *primuloides.*
S. primuloides 'Clarence Elliott' see *S. umbrosa* var. *primuloides* 'Elliott's Variety'.
S. primuloides 'Elliott's Variety' see *S. umbrosa* var. *primuloides* 'Elliott's Variety'.
S. sancta ▣ syn. *S. juniperifolia* subsp. *sancta.* Cushion-forming Kabschia saxifrage with rosettes of narrowly lance-shaped, lime-encrusted, bright green leaves, to 1cm (½in) long. Cymes of 3–7 upward-facing, open cup-shaped, deep yellow flowers, 7–9mm (¼–⅜in) across, with prominent anthers, are borne in spring. Cultivation group 3. ↕ 5cm (2in), ↔ 20cm (8in). N.E. Greece. ❄❄❄
S. sarmentosa 'Tricolor' see *S. stolonifera* 'Tricolor'.

Saxifraga sancta

Saxifraga 'Southside Seedling'

S. scardica. Dense, cushion-forming, slow-growing Kabschia saxifrage with firm rosettes of fleshy, oblong, lime-encrusted, blue-green leaves, to 1.5cm (½in) long. In spring, bears cymes of 4–13 upward-facing, cup-shaped white flowers, to 1.5cm (½in) across, on red-tinted stems. Prefers light dappled shade. Cultivation group 3. ↕ 8cm (3in), ↔ 15cm (6in). Balkans. ❄❄❄
S. sempervivum f. stenophylla, syn. *S. porophylla* var. *thessalica.* Loose, cushion-forming Engleria saxifrage with rosettes of linear, lime-encrusted, silvery green leaves, to 2cm (¾in) long. In spring, crozier-like, silver-hairy stems bear 7–20 pendent, open cup-shaped, deep reddish purple flowers, to 6mm (¼in) across, in racemes, 2–8cm (¾–3in) long. Cultivation group 4. ↕ 10cm (4in), ↔ 20cm (8in). Balkans, N.W. Turkey. ❄❄❄
S. 'Southside Seedling' ▣ Mat-forming Ligulatae saxifrage similar to, and possibly a cultivar of, *S. cotyledon*, with rosettes of oblong to spoon-shaped, pale green leaves, to 12cm (5in) long. Arching panicles, 30cm (12in) long, of open cup-shaped white flowers, 1cm (½in) across, heavily spotted red, are borne in late spring and early summer. Cultivation group 3 or 4. ↕ 30cm (12in), ↔ 20cm (8in). ❄❄❄
S. spruneri. Cushion-forming, slow-growing Kabschia saxifrage. Hairy, oblong or spoon-shaped, lime-encrusted, mid-green leaves, to 7mm (¼in) long, are in small rosettes. In late spring, bears flat-topped cymes of 6–10 star-shaped, yellowish white flowers, to 1cm (½in) across. Cultivation group 3. ↕ 8cm (3in), ↔ 10cm (4in). Balkans. ❄❄❄

Saxifraga stolonifera 'Tricolor'

Saxifraga stribrnyi

Saxifraga 'Tumbling Waters'

S. stolonifera 'Magic Carpet' see *S. stolonifera* 'Tricolor'.
S. stolonifera 'Tricolor' ▣ syn. *S. sarmentosa* 'Tricolor', *S. stolonifera* 'Magic Carpet' (Mother of thousands). Stoloniferous, rosette- or tuft-forming Irregulares saxifrage with kidney-shaped to rounded, deeply cut, mid- to dark green leaves, 4–9cm (1½–3½in) long, strongly patterned in red and white. In summer, bears loose panicles, 20–40cm (8–16in) long, of tiny white flowers, to 8mm (⅜in) across, spotted yellow or red, with 3 or 4 upper petals and 1 or 2 longer lower petals, on slender, upright stems. Cultivation group 1. ↕↔ to 30cm (12in). ❄❄
S. stribrnyi ▣ Mound-forming Engleria saxifrage producing tight rosettes of pointed, inversely lance-shaped to spoon-shaped, lime-encrusted, blue-green leaves, 1–2.5cm (½–1in) long. Branched, arching, crozier-like stems bear racemes, 2–5cm (¾–2in) long, of 10–30 open cup-shaped, deep violet-purple flowers, to 1cm (½in) across, during late spring and early summer. Cultivation group 4. ↕ 10cm (4in), ↔ 20cm (8in). Balkans. ❄❄❄
S. 'Tumbling Waters' ▣ syn. *S. longifolia* 'Tumbling Waters'. Slow-growing Ligulatae perennial producing large, clustered rosettes of narrow, linear, lime-encrusted, silvery green leaves, to 15cm (6in) long. Dense, arching, conical panicles, 30–70cm (12–28in) long, of small, open cup-shaped white flowers, to 1cm (½in) across, are borne in spring, after several years. Cultivation group 4. ↕ 45cm (18in), ↔ 30cm (12in). ❄❄❄

S. umbrosa* var. *primuloides, syn. *S.* 'Primuloides'. Gymnopera saxifrage with neat, compact rosettes of ovate to spoon-shaped, crinkled, regularly scalloped leaves, to 8cm (3in) long, mid-green above, reddish green beneath. Bears loose panicles, to 25cm (10in) long, of star-shaped, red-spotted white flowers, 6–8mm (¼–⅜in) across, in summer. Cultivation group 1. ↕↔ 30cm (12in). Pyrenees. ❄❄❄. **'Clarence Elliott'** see 'Elliott's Variety'. **'Elliott's Variety'**, syn. *S. primuloides* 'Clarence Elliott', *S. primuloides* 'Elliott's Variety', *S. umbrosa* var. *primuloides* 'Clarence Elliott', is more compact, with leaves to 6cm (2½in) long, and red-stemmed, rose-pink flowers, 8–10mm (⅜–½in) across; ↕↔ 15cm (6in).
S.* x *urbium (*S. spathularis* x *S. umbrosa*) (London pride). Vigorous, spreading Gymnopera saxifrage with large rosettes of spoon-shaped, toothed, leathery, mid-green leaves, 2–4cm (¾–1½in) across. Upright, branching stems bear loose panicles, to 30cm (12in) long, of tiny, star-shaped, pink-flushed white flowers, to 8mm (⅜in) across, in summer. Good ground cover, even in poor soil. Cultivation group 1. ↕ 30cm (12in), ↔ indefinite. Garden origin. ❄❄❄

▷**Saxifrage** see *Saxifraga*
Elephant-eared see *Bergenia*
Golden see *Chrysosplenium*
Meadow see *Saxifraga granulata*
Purple see *Saxifraga oppositifolia*
Pyrenean see *Saxifraga longifolia*
Yellow mountain see *Saxifraga aizoides*

SCABIOSA

Pincushion flower, Scabious

DIPSACACEAE

Genus of about 80 species of annuals, biennials, and perennials from sunny sites, dry meadows, and rocky slopes, mostly in the Mediterranean region, but also in the rest of Europe, the Caucasus, Africa, Asia, and Japan. They have mainly basal leaves, which are simple and entire or lobed, pinnatifid, or pinnatisect, and produce compound or solitary, blue, white, yellow, or pink flowerheads with domed, pincushion-like central florets and larger marginal florets. The smaller perennial species are ideal for a rock garden, while the taller ones are suitable for a sunny herbaceous or mixed border, or a wild garden; the annuals are excellent in borders. Long-flowering species and cultivars are ideal for window-boxes or containers on a patio. Many are also good for cutting. All are attractive to bees and butterflies.

- **HARDINESS** Fully hardy to frost hardy.
- **CULTIVATION** Grow in moderately fertile, well-drained, neutral to slightly alkaline soil in full sun. Protect from excessive winter wet. Dead-head to prolong flowering. Divide and replant perennials in fresh or replenished soil every 3 years.
- **PROPAGATION** Sow seed of annuals and biennials at 6–12°C (43–54°F) in early spring, or *in situ* in mid-spring; sow seed of perennials in containers in a cold frame as soon as ripe or in spring. Divide, or take basal cuttings of perennials, in spring.
- **PESTS AND DISEASES** Trouble free.

Scabiosa atropurpurea 'Blue Cockade'

Scabiosa caucasica 'Clive Greaves'

S. alpina see *Cephalaria alpina.*
S. arvensis see *Knautia arvensis.*
S. atropurpurea (Pincushion flower, Sweet scabious). Erect, branching, wiry-stemmed biennial or short-lived perennial with mid-green leaves, 3–12cm (1¼–5in) long: the basal leaves are oblong-spoon-shaped and entire or coarsely toothed; the stem leaves are pinnatifid, composed of entire or toothed segments. Solitary, fragrant, dark purple to lilac flowerheads, to 5cm (2in) across, are borne in summer. ↕ to 90cm (36in), ↔ to 23cm (9in). S. Europe. ❄❄❄. **'Blue Cockade'** ■ has lavender-blue to purple-blue flowerheads, sometimes over 5cm (2in) across. **'Double'** is a mixture with fully double, white, dark purple, blue, or pink flowerheads, which need support. **'Dwarf Double'** is a mixture with fully double flowerheads in white, dark purple, blue, or pink; ↕ to 45cm (18in).
***S.* 'Butterfly Blue'** see *S. columbaria* 'Butterfly Blue'.
***S.* 'Butterfly Pink'** see *S. columbaria* 'Pink Mist'.
S. caucasica. Clump-forming perennial with lance-shaped, entire, grey-green basal leaves, to 15cm (6in) long, with partly winged stalks, and usually unbranched stems bearing pinnatifid leaves. Solitary, pale blue or lavender-blue flowerheads, to 8cm (3in) across, are borne in mid- and late summer. ↕↔ 60cm (24in). Caucasus, N.E. Turkey, N. Iran. ❄❄❄. **'Bressingham White'** has white flowerheads. **'Clive Greaves'** ■ produces lavender-blue flowerheads. **'Floral Queen'** has pale blue flowerheads; ↕ to 75cm (30in). **'Miss Willmott'** ■ has white flowerheads; ↕ to 90cm (36in).
S. columbaria (Small scabious). Branched, hairy perennial with long-stalked, ovate to lance-shaped, simple or pinnatifid basal leaves, 5–15cm (2–6in) long, and pinnatifid, 2-pinnatifid, or pinnatisect stem leaves, the uppermost very finely divided; all are light, mid-, or greyish green. From summer to early autumn, bears solitary, bluish lilac flowerheads, to 4cm (1½in) across. ↕ 50–70cm (20–28in), ↔ to 1m (3ft) or more. Europe, W. Asia. ❄❄❄. The following cultivars are probably hybrids of *S. columbaria.* **'Butterfly Blue'** ■ syn. *S.* 'Butterfly Blue', has grey-green leaves, and produces lavender-blue flowerheads in mid- and late summer; ↕↔ to 40cm (16in). **'Pink Mist'**, syn. *S.* 'Butterfly Pink', *S.* 'Pink Mist', is similar to 'Butterfly Blue', with grey-green leaves and deep pink flowerheads, paler in the centres, borne over long periods in summer; ↕↔ to 40cm (16in).
S. gigantea see *Cephalaria gigantea.*
S. graminifolia. Evergreen, clump-forming perennial with tufts of silver-hairy, entire, linear-lance-shaped, mid-green leaves, to 15cm (6in) long. In summer, solitary, spherical, lilac to violet flowerheads, to 4cm (1½in) across, are borne on stiff, slender stems. ↕ 25cm (10in), ↔ 30cm (12in). S. Europe. ❄❄❄. **'Pinkushion'** is mat-forming, with rose-pink flowerheads.
S. lucida ■ Clump-forming, occasionally branched perennial with tufts of ovate-lance-shaped, toothed basal leaves and pinnatifid stem leaves; both are

Scabiosa columbaria 'Butterfly Blue'

Scabiosa caucasica 'Miss Willmott' (inset: flower detail)

Scabiosa lucida

Scabiosa stellata 'Paper Moon'

S

silvery green and to 12cm (5in) long. In summer, solitary, pale lilac flowerheads, to 4cm (1½in) across, are borne on slender, erect stems. ↕ 20cm (8in), ↔ 30cm (12in). C. Europe. ✻✻✻

***S.* 'Pink Mist'** see *S. columbaria* 'Pink Mist'.

S. rumelica see *Knautia macedonica.*

S. stellata. Erect, branching, wiry-stemmed, hairy annual with lance-shaped to ovate, pinnatifid, mid-green leaves, 18cm (7in) long. Solitary, spherical, pale blue flowerheads, to 3cm (1¼in) across, are borne in summer. They are followed by silvery cream seed heads, to 8cm (3in) across, formed by clustered, cup-shaped, green- or maroon-centred bracts, enlarged after flowering. The seed heads are good for dried flower arrangements. ↕ to 45cm (18in), ↔ 23cm (9in). S. Europe. ✻✻✻. **'Drum Stick'** has light blue flowerheads, turning bronze; ↕ to 30cm (12in). **'Paper Moon'** ■ has pale, watery blue seed heads. **'Ping Pong'** bears small white seed heads.

S. succisa see *Succisa pratensis.*

S. tatarica see *Cephalaria gigantea.*

▷**Scabious** see *Scabiosa*
- **Devil's bit** see *Succisa pratensis*
- **Field** see *Knautia arvensis*
- **Giant** see *Cephalaria gigantea*
- **Sheep's bit** see *Jasione laevis*
- **Shepherd's** see *Jasione laevis*
- **Small** see *Scabiosa columbaria*
- **Sweet** see *Scabiosa atropurpurea*
- **Yellow** see *Cephalaria gigantea*

SCADOXUS

Blood lily

AMARYLLIDACEAE

Genus of 9 species of bulbous and rhizomatous perennials found on rocky cliffs and in woodland in tropical regions of Africa and the Arabian Peninsula. They are closely related to *Haemanthus*, but are distinguished by the spiral arrangement of their leaves, and by their rhizomatous bulbs. They are cultivated for their spectacular, crowded, conical to spherical flowerheads of cylindrical red flowers, with 6 spreading or erect tepals, borne on leafless stems from spring to summer, and followed by spherical, yellow, orange, or red berries. In frost-prone areas, grow blood lilies in a temperate or warm greenhouse or conservatory; elsewhere, use in a border, or at the base of a warm, sunny wall.

S

• **HARDINESS** Frost tender.

Scadoxus multiflorus subsp. *katherinae*

• **CULTIVATION** Plant bulbs in autumn or winter with the necks at soil level. Under glass, grow in loam-based potting compost (JI No.2) in full light with shade from hot sun. Move into partial shade as buds open. When in active growth, water freely and apply a half-strength balanced liquid fertilizer monthly. Dry off as leaves fade. Pot on in spring if necessary. Outdoors, grow in moderately fertile, humus-rich, moist but well-drained soil in full sun or light shade.

• **PROPAGATION** Sow seed at 19–24°C (66–75°F) as soon as ripe. Separate offsets in spring.

• **PESTS AND DISEASES** Trouble free.

S. multiflorus, syn. *Haemanthus multiflorus.* Bulbous perennial with semi-erect, broad, lance-shaped to ovate, basal leaves, to 30cm (12in) long. In summer, produces spherical heads, 10–15cm (4–6in) across, of up to 200 narrow-tepalled red flowers, with conspicuous stamens, followed by small orange berries, 5–10mm (¼–½in) across. ↕ to 60cm (24in), ↔ 15cm (6in). Tropical Africa, South Africa, Yemen. ❁ (min. 10–15°C/50–59°F). **subsp. *katherinae*** ■ syn. *Haemanthus katherinae*, has wavy-margined leaves; ↕ to 1.2m (4ft); E. southern Africa.

S. puniceus, syn. *Haemanthus magnificus, H. natalensis, H. puniceus.* Bulbous perennial with semi-erect, elliptic, wavy-margined, basal leaves, to 30cm (12in) long, that form a "stem", to 50cm (20in) long, of sheathed leaf-stalks. From spring to summer, bears conical heads, 10cm (4in) across, of up to 100 tiny, yellowish green to pink or scarlet flowers, surrounded by conspicuous red bracts; they are followed by yellow berries, 1cm (½in) across. ↕ 50cm (20in), ↔ 15cm (6in). E. and southern Africa. ❁ (min. 10–15°C/50–59°F)

SCAEVOLA

GOODENIACEAE

Genus of about 96 species of mostly short-lived, mainly evergreen perennials, but also scrambling climbers, shrubs and small trees, occurring in habitats ranging from coastal dunes to damp, subalpine regions in Australia and Polynesia. They have alternate, rarely opposite, rounded to linear, entire or toothed leaves, and produce solitary or few-flowered cymes or racemes of distinctive, fan-shaped flowers. In frost-prone areas, grow in a cool greenhouse or conservatory, or grow outdoors in containers or hanging baskets during summer. In warmer climates, grow in a border.

• **HARDINESS** Frost tender, but may tolerate falls in temperature to around -3°C (27°F), or perhaps lower, if soil is very sharply drained.

• **CULTIVATION** Under glass, grow in loam-based potting compost (JI No.2) in bright indirect light. During the growing season, water freely and apply a balanced liquid fertilizer monthly. Keep just moist in winter. Outdoors, grow in moderately fertile, humus-rich, moist but well-drained soil in full sun or light dappled shade.

• **PROPAGATION** Sow seed at 19–24°C (66–75°F) in spring. Root softwood cuttings in late spring or summer, with bottom heat.

• **PESTS AND DISEASES** Trouble free.

Scaevola aemula

S. aemula ■ (Fairy fan-flower). Variable, tufted, evergreen perennial with spoon-shaped, toothed basal leaves, to 9cm (3½in) long, and smaller stem leaves, borne on erect or sometimes procumbent stems, with yellow or brown hairs. Leafy racemes of purple-blue or blue flowers, to 2.5cm (1in) across, are borne during summer. ↕↔ to 50cm (20in). S. and E. Australia. ❁ (min. 5°C/41°F). **'Blue Wonder'**, syn. *S.* 'Blue Wonder', is shrubby, with vigorous, trailing stems and inversely lance-shaped leaves, 1cm (½in) long. Lilac-blue flowers, 1cm (½in) across, are borne almost continuously and in great profusion from spring to autumn; ↕ to 15cm (6in), ↔ to 1.5m (5ft).

***S.* 'Blue Wonder'** see *S. aemula* 'Blue Wonder'.

***S.* 'Mauve Clusters'.** Vigorous, shrubby, evergreen perennial with a trailing habit and inversely lance-shaped leaves, 1cm (½in) long. Leafy racemes of lilac-mauve flowers, 1cm (½in) across, are borne freely for much of the year, but particularly in summer. ↕ 10–15cm (4–6in), ↔ to 1.5m (5ft). Australia. ❁ (min. 5°C/41°F)

▷**Scarlet runner** see *Kennedia prostrata*

SCHEFFLERA *syn.* BRASSAIA

ARALIACEAE

Genus of at least 900 species of mostly evergreen shrubs, trees, and climbers (some epiphytic when juvenile) from warm-temperate and tropical areas of S.E. Asia to the Pacific islands and Central and South America. They are grown mainly for their spiralled, fine, long-stalked, usually rounded, fully divided leaves, each with 3–30 stalked leaflets. In summer, autumn, or winter, mature trees bear compound umbels, panicles, racemes, or spikes of usually tiny flowers with 4 or 5 yellow-green to greenish red petals. The flowers are followed by mostly spherical or ovoid, black or purple fruits. In frost-prone areas, grow in a warm greenhouse or as houseplants. In warmer areas, grow at the back of a shrub border or as an informal hedge or windbreak.

• **HARDINESS** Half hardy to frost tender.

• **CULTIVATION** Under glass, grow in loam-based potting compost (JI No.2) in bright filtered or indirect light. In growth, water moderately and apply a balanced liquid fertilizer monthly; keep just moist in winter. Pot on in spring.

Schefflera actinophylla

Outdoors, grow in fertile, humus-rich, moist but well-drained soil in partial to deep shade. Shelter from cold, drying winds. Pruning group 1; clip hedges in late summer.

• **PROPAGATION** Sow seed at 19–24°C (66–75°F) in spring. Root semi-ripe cuttings with bottom heat in summer. Air layer in spring.

• **PESTS AND DISEASES** Scale insects, thrips, and mealybugs may be a problem under glass.

S. actinophylla ■♀ syn. *Brassaia actinophylla* (Australian ivy palm, Octopus tree, Queensland umbrella tree). Erect, large shrub or small tree with stiff, thick, sparsely branched stems. Large leaves, 10–30cm (4–12in) long, divided into 7–16 ovate-oblong, leathery, glossy, deep bright green leaflets, to 30cm (12in) long, are borne in terminal rosettes on the branches. Leaves of juvenile plants have fewer, smaller leaflets than adult plants. Bears upright, terminal, compound panicles, to 80cm (32in) long, of tiny, brownish pink to red flowers in summer, followed by spherical black fruit. Often grown as juvenile plants. ↕ to 12m (40ft), ↔ to 6m (20ft). N. and N.E. Australia, S. and S.E. New Guinea. ❁ (min. 13°C/55°F)

S. elegantissima ■♀ syn. *Aralia elegantissima, Dizygotheca elegantissima* (False aralia). Erect, sparsely branched, large shrub or small tree with leaves, 8–40cm (3–16in) long, composed of 7–11 linear, deeply toothed leaflets, 15–23cm (6–9in) long; when young, they are glossy, dark green above, dark brown-green beneath, with white

Schefflera elegantissima

midribs; adult plants have broader, stiffer, less glossy leaflets. In autumn and winter, bears yellowish green flowers in terminal umbels, to 30cm (12in) long, followed by spherical black fruit. ↕ 8–15m (25–50ft), ↔ 2–3m (6–10ft). New Caledonia. ❄ (min. 13–15°C/ 55–59°F)

S. heptaphylla ♀ syn. *S. octophylla* (Fukanoki, Ivy tree). Dense, spreading, evergreen or semi-evergreen tree with loose rosettes of leaves, to 13cm (5in) long, each composed of 6–8 elliptic to oblong-elliptic, glossy, deep green leaflets, 10–20cm (4–8in) long, often white beneath. From autumn to early winter, produces yellowish green flowers in terminal panicles, to 30cm (12in) long, followed by spherical, blue-black fruit. ↕ 12–25m (40–80ft), ↔ 5–10m (15–30ft). E. Asia, Philippines. ❄ (min. 13–15°C/55–59°F)

S. octophylla see *S. heptaphylla.*

SCHIMA

THEACEAE

Genus of one very variable species of evergreen tree or shrub extensively distributed in forest from S.W. China and the E. Himalayas to S.E. Asia. It is grown for the attractive spiral arrangement of its simple, glossy leaves, and for its fragrant, camellia-like flowers, usually solitary, sometimes in raceme-like inflorescences. In frost-prone areas, grow in a cool greenhouse; elsewhere, use as a specimen tree in a woodland garden.

- **HARDINESS** Half hardy.
- **CULTIVATION** Under glass, grow in lime-free (ericaceous) potting compost in bright filtered light or indirect light; provide moderate humidity. During the growing season, water freely and apply a balanced liquid fertilizer monthly; keep just moist in winter. Outdoors, grow in humus-rich, leafy, moist but well-drained, neutral to acid soil in full sun with some midday shade, or in partial shade. Shelter from cold, drying winds. Pruning group 1.
- **PROPAGATION** Sow seed at 6–12°C (43–54°F) in autumn. Root semi-ripe cuttings with bottom heat in late summer.
- **PESTS AND DISEASES** Trouble free.

S. argentea see *S. wallichii.*
S. khasiana see *S. wallichii.*
S. wallichii ♤ syn. *S. argentea, S. khasiana.* Broadly conical tree or shrub. The oblong, lance-shaped, ovate, or obovate, tapered leaves are entire, shallowly scalloped, or toothed, 7–24cm (3–10in) long, papery or leathery in texture, and glossy, dark green, with red veins, often reddish beneath. From late summer to autumn, red-tinged buds open to solitary, cup-shaped, fragrant white flowers, to 7cm (3in) across, with 5 or 6 rounded petals. ↕ 10m (30ft), ↔ 6m (20ft). Himalayas to S.E. Asia. ✲

SCHINUS

ANACARDIACEAE

Genus of about 30 species of usually dioecious, evergreen shrubs and trees occurring in woodland from Mexico to Uruguay. They are grown mainly for their alternate leaves, which may be simple or pinnate, entire or toothed. Tiny, 4- or 5-petalled flowers are borne

Schinus molle

in terminal or axillary panicles. When plants of both sexes are grown together, the flowers are followed on female plants by small, red to purple fruits (drupes). In frost-prone areas, grow in a temperate greenhouse or conservatory; elsewhere, use smaller species in a shrub border and larger ones as specimen trees.

- **HARDINESS** Half hardy to frost tender.
- **CULTIVATION** Under glass, grow in loam-based potting compost (JI No.2) in full light with shade from hot sun. When in active growth, water freely and apply a balanced liquid fertilizer monthly; water sparingly in winter. Outdoors, grow in moderately fertile, humus-rich, moist but well-drained soil in full sun, or with some midday shade. Pruning group 1.
- **PROPAGATION** Sow seed at 19–21°C (66–70°F) in spring. Root semi-ripe cuttings with bottom heat during late summer. Air layer in spring.
- **PESTS AND DISEASES** Scale insects and red spider mites may be troublesome under glass.

S. molle ▣ ♀ (Pepper tree, Peruvian mastic tree). Usually broad-headed tree with slender, pendent branches. The arching or semi-pendent, pinnate leaves, 10–30cm (4–12in) long, are composed of 19–41 narrow, lance-shaped, toothed, glossy, mid- to deep green leaflets. Pendent panicles, 8–20cm (3–8in) long, of tiny, whitish yellow flowers are borne from late winter to summer, followed by rose-pink fruit. ↕ 10–25m (30–80ft), ↔ 3–5m (10–15ft). Mexico, Brazil, Bolivia, Chile, N. Argentina, Paraguay, Uruguay. ❄ (min. 10°C/50°F)

S. terebinthifolius ♀ (Brazilian pepper tree, Christmas berry tree). Moderately bushy, large shrub or small tree with erect to spreading stems bearing pinnate leaves, 10–17cm (4–7in) long, with winged midribs and 3–13 (normally 7) oblong, deep green leaflets, which are paler beneath. From summer to autumn, produces panicles, to 15cm (6in) long, of tiny white flowers, followed by red fruit. Contact with the seeds may irritate skin and cause respiratory problems. ↕ 5–7m (15–22ft), ↔ 3–5m (10–15ft). Venezuela to Argentina, S. Brazil. ❄ (min. 7°C/45°F)

SCHISANDRA

SCHISANDRACEAE

Genus of about 25 species of twining, woody, monoecious or dioecious, deciduous or evergreen climbers found in woodland in E. Asia, with one species from S.E. USA. They are grown for their cup-shaped, red, pink, yellow, or white flowers, borne singly or in clusters or short spikes in the leaf axils, and for their spikes of spherical, brightly coloured fruits. Leaves are alternate, entire or toothed, and usually lance-shaped or ovate to elliptic. Both male and female plants of dioecious species must be grown to obtain fruit. Grow in woodland, or train on a wall or pergola.

- **HARDINESS** Fully hardy.
- **CULTIVATION** Grow in fertile, moist but well-drained soil in full sun or partial shade. Tie in shoots of young plants until established. Pruning group 12, in early spring.

Schisandra rubriflora

- **PROPAGATION** Sow seed in containers in a cold frame as soon as ripe. Take greenwood cuttings in early or mid-summer; root semi-ripe cuttings in summer.
- **PESTS AND DISEASES** Trouble free.

S. chinensis. Twining, woody, deciduous climber with red shoots and producing elliptic to obovate, minutely toothed, glossy, dark green leaves, to 14cm (5½in) long. From late spring to summer, bears small clusters of cream to pale pink flowers, to 2cm (¾in) across; these are followed, on female plants, by pendent spikes, to 15cm (6in) long, of fleshy, red or pink fruit. ↕ 10m (30ft). E. Asia. ✲✲✲

S. henryi. Twining, woody, deciduous climber with angled shoots, winged when young, and oval, finely toothed, leathery, glossy, mid-green leaves, to 10cm (4in) long. In spring, bears small clusters of white flowers, 1cm (½in) across; these are followed, on female plants, by pendent spikes, to 7cm (3in) long, of fleshy red fruit. ↕ 3–4m (10–12ft). W. China. ✲✲✲

S. rubriflora ▣ Twining, woody, deciduous climber with slender red shoots and lance-shaped to narrowly elliptic or inversely lance-shaped, slightly toothed to entire, dark green leaves, to 12cm (5in) long, yellow in autumn. Produces solitary, dark crimson flowers, to 2.5cm (1in) across, from late spring to summer, followed, on female plants, by pendent spikes, to 15cm (6in) long, of fleshy red fruit. ↕ 10m (30ft). India, W. China, Burma. ✲✲✲

SCHIZACHYRIUM

GRAMINEAE/POACEAE

Genus of about 100 species of deciduous, perennial grasses native to grasslands worldwide. Closely related to *Andropogon*, they are distinguished by their solitary, terminal, obliquely branched racemes of stalked spikelets. Suitable for a herbaceous or mixed border. The flowerheads may be dried.

- **HARDINESS** Fully hardy.
- **CULTIVATION** Grow in moderately fertile, sharply drained soil in full sun. Cut down old stems in early winter.
- **PROPAGATION** Sow seed at 13–15°C (55–59°F), or divide, in spring.
- **PESTS AND DISEASES** Trouble free.

S. scoparium, syn. *Andropogon scoparius* (Little bluestem). Densely tufted, perennial grass, spreading slowly to form clumps of upright stems with linear, mid-green to grey-green leaves, to 45cm (18in) long, that turn purple to orange-red in autumn. From late summer to mid-autumn, bears narrow racemes, to 15cm (6in) long, of wispy, long-awned spikelets. ↕ to 1m (3ft), ↔ 30cm (12in). North America. ✲✲✲

SCHIZANTHUS

Butterfly flower, Poor man's orchid

SOLANACEAE

Genus of 12–15 erect to spreading, bushy, soft-stemmed, downy annuals, and some biennials, from dry, rocky slopes and canyons in Chile. They have alternate, pinnatisect to 3-pinnatisect or deeply lobed leaves. They are cultivated for their terminal cymes of showy, 2-

Schizanthus pinnatus 'Hit Parade'

lipped, orchid-like flowers of various colours, which are borne from spring to winter. In cool-temperate regions, grow either in a conservatory or cool greenhouse, as half-hardy annuals in a sheltered annual border, or in containers on a patio or in a courtyard garden. In warmer climates, grow in a border. They provide long-lasting cut flowers.

• **Hardiness** Frost tender.
• **Cultivation** Under glass, grow in loam-based potting compost (JI No.2) in full light with shade from hot sun, or in bright filtered light. In growth, water moderately, and apply a high-potash liquid fertilizer every 2 weeks. Support flowering stems. Excessive heat produces elongated plants. Outdoors, grow in fertile, moist but well-drained soil in full sun. Pinch back young growth to promote bushiness.
• **Propagation** Sow seed at 16°C (61°F) in mid-spring for summer- to autumn-flowering plants. Sow in late summer at 16°C (61°F) for winter-flowering container plants.
• **Pests and diseases** Aphids may be a problem under glass.

S. pinnatus (Poor man's orchid). Erect annual with almost fern-like, lance-shaped to inversely lance-shaped, pinnatisect to 3-pinnatisect, light green leaves, to 12cm (5in) long. From spring to autumn, bears terminal, open cymes of tubular, then flared, 2-lipped, white, yellow, pink, purple, or red flowers, to 8cm (3in) across; they often have yellow throats with violet markings, streaked and spotted in contrasting colours. ↕ 20–50cm (8–20in), ↔ 23–30cm (9–12in). Chile. ❀ (min. 5°C/41°F). **'Hit Parade'** ▣ has flowers with clear, contrasting markings; ↕ 23–30cm (9–12in). **'Star Parade'** has a compact, pyramidal habit; ↕ 20–25cm (8–10in).
S. x wisetonensis (*S. grahamii* x *S. pinnatus*). Erect annual with lance-shaped to inversely lance-shaped, pinnatisect to 3-pinnatisect, light green leaves, to 12cm (5in) long. From spring to summer, bears terminal, open cymes of tubular, then flared, 2-lipped, white, pale blue, pink, or red-brown flowers, to 8cm (3in) across, often flushed yellow on the central lobe of the upper lips. ↕ to 45cm (18in), ↔ 23–30cm (9–12in). Garden origin. ❀ (min. 5°C/41°F)

▷ ***Schizocasia portei*** see *Alocasia portei*
▷ ***Schizocodon*** see *Shortia*

Schizopetalon

Brassicaceae/Cruciferae

Genus of about 8 species of erect, slender-stemmed, hairy annuals from rocky slopes and disturbed ground in Chile. They have alternate, wavy-margined, toothed, simple or pinnatifid, linear to ovate leaves. From late spring to early autumn, they bear leafy racemes of star-shaped, white or purple flowers, each with 4 fringed petals. Grow at the edge of a border, in a rock garden or raised bed, or in containers. They are particularly effective grown near a patio or paved area where the evening scent of the blooms may be best appreciated.

• **Hardiness** Frost hardy.
• **Cultivation** Grow in moderately fertile, well-drained soil in full sun.
• **Propagation** Sow seed at 19–21°C (66–70°F) in mid-spring.
• **Pests and diseases** Trouble free.

S. walkeri. Upright, slightly branching annual producing deeply pinnatifid, linear to lance-shaped leaves, to 14cm (5½in) long. Terminal racemes of almond-scented, spreading, deeply cut, star-shaped, pure white flowers, to 4cm (1½in) across, are borne from summer to early autumn. ↕ 15–35cm (6–14in), ↔ 20cm (8in). Chile. ✲✲

Schizophragma

Hydrangeaceae

Genus of 2 species of woody, deciduous root climbers from woodland and cliffs in China, Korea, and Japan. They bear opposite pairs of simple, long-stalked, entire or toothed, ovate, dark green leaves. Schizophragmas are cultivated for their showy flowerheads, similar to those of "lacecap" hydrangeas, but with large, conspicuous, bract-like, sterile, outer flowers. Best grown against a wall, fence, or large tree, to which the plant will attach itself by aerial roots.

• **Hardiness** Fully hardy to frost hardy.
• **Cultivation** Grow in moderately fertile, humus-rich, moist but well-drained soil, in full sun or partial shade. Plant at least 60cm (24in) away from a host plant or support. Tie in to a support and train until established. Pruning group 11, in spring.
• **Propagation** Take greenwood cuttings in early or midsummer; take semi-ripe cuttings in late summer.
• **Pests and diseases** Trouble free.

S. hydrangeoides. Woody root climber with long-stalked, broadly ovate, sharply toothed, dark green leaves, to 15cm (6in) long. In midsummer, small, slightly fragrant, creamy white flowers are borne in broad, flattened, terminal cymes, to 25cm (10in) across, with conspicuous, ovate, creamy, marginal bracts, to 6cm (2½in) long. ↕ 12m (40ft). Korea, Japan. ✲✲✲. **'Roseum'** has pink bracts.

Schizophragma integrifolium

S. integrifolium ▣ Woody root climber with long-stalked, ovate, entire or finely toothed, dark green leaves, to 18cm (7in) long. In midsummer, small, slightly fragrant, creamy white flowers are borne in broad, flattened, terminal cymes, to 30cm (12in) across, with conspicuous, ovate, creamy, marginal bracts, to 9cm (3½in) long. ↕ 12m (40ft). C. and W. China. ✲✲
S. viburnoides see *Pileostegia viburnoides.*

Schizostylis

Kaffir lily

Iridaceae

Genus of a single species of virtually evergreen, rhizomatous perennial from damp water-meadows and streambanks in southern Africa. Kaffir lilies are cultivated for their showy, gladiolus-like spikes of open cup-shaped flowers, which are produced from late summer to early winter. They are suitable for growing at the front of a herbaceous or mixed border, at the base of a warm, sunny wall, or in a small courtyard garden. *S. coccinea* and its cultivars are also effective grown *en masse* in large

Schizostylis coccinea 'Major'

Schizostylis coccinea 'Sunrise'

containers in a cool greenhouse, where they will flower for long periods during the winter months. Excellent for cut flowers.

• **Hardiness** Hardy to -10°C (14°F), although flower spikes will be damaged by frost.
• **Cultivation** Grow in moderately fertile, moist but well-drained soil in full sun. Keep the roots moist. Shelter from cold, drying winds. Provide an organic mulch in winter.
• **Propagation** Sow seed at 13–16°C (55–61°F) in spring. Divide species and cultivars in spring.
• **Pests and diseases** Trouble free.

S. coccinea. Vigorous, clump-forming, rhizomatous perennial with erect, keeled, narrow, sword-shaped leaves, to 40cm (16in) long, with distinct midribs. Spikes of 4–14 open cup-shaped scarlet flowers, 2cm (¾in) across, are produced in autumn. ↕ to 60cm (24in), ↔ 30cm (12in). South Africa, Lesotho, Swaziland. ✲✲. **f. *alba*** bears white flowers. **'Grandiflora'** see 'Major'. **'Jennifer'** is robust, bearing large, mid-pink flowers, 5–6cm (2–2½in) across, in late summer. **'Major'** ▣ syn. 'Grandiflora', is robust, producing large red flowers, 5–6cm (2–2½in) across, on stiff stems in late summer. **'Sunrise'** ▣ syn. 'Sunset', produces large, salmon-pink flowers, 5–6cm (2–2½in) across, in autumn. **'Sunset'** see 'Sunrise'. **'Viscountess Byng'** ▣ produces pale pink flowers, 3cm (1¼in) across, with narrow petals, in late autumn; its flowers are particularly vulnerable to damage by frost.

Schizostylis coccinea 'Viscountess Byng'

S

SCHLUMBERGERA

Christmas cactus

CACTACEAE

Genus of about 6 species of bushy, epiphytic or rock-dwelling, perennial cacti from tropical rainforest in S.E. Brazil, cultivated for their attractive flowers. Erect then pendent, fleshy stems are divided into flattened, oblong or obovate, normally truncate, leaf-like segments, usually with marginal, often prominent notches, almost tooth-like in some species. The areoles often have a few fine bristles; those near the tips of the upper segments bear open trumpet-shaped, narrow-petalled flowers, most in late winter and early spring, others in summer or autumn. Where temperatures fall below 10°C (50°F), grow Christmas cacti as houseplants, or in a temperate or warm greenhouse. In warmer areas, they are suitable for growing in a raised bed in a courtyard garden.

- **HARDINESS** Frost tender.
- **CULTIVATION** Under glass, grow in epiphytic cactus compost in bright indirect light. Water moderately and maintain moderate humidity. Apply a high-potash liquid fertilizer every 4 weeks when in growth; keep just moist after flowering. Repot every 3 or 4 years in spring. Outdoors, grow in humus-rich, acid to neutral, moist but well-drained soil, with added leaf mould and grit, in light dappled to partial shade. Protect from excessive rain; shelter from strong winds. Buds may drop in dry conditions. See also pp.48–49.
- **PROPAGATION** Sow seed at 19–21°C (66–70°F) in spring, or take cuttings of stem sections in spring or early summer.
- **PESTS AND DISEASES** Susceptible to mealybugs.

S. bridgesii see *S.* x *buckleyi.*

***S.* 'Bristol Beauty'.** Epiphytic cactus with oblong, bright green stem segments, 2.5cm (1in) long, with 4–6 marginal notches. In late winter and early spring, produces reddish purple flowers, 7cm (3in) long, with silvery white tubes. ↕ to 35cm (14in), ↔ 30cm (12in). ❀ (min. 10°C/50°F)

S.* x *buckleyi (*S. russelliana* x *S. truncata*) syn. *S. bridgesii* (Christmas cactus). Epiphytic cactus with oblong or obovate, truncate, scalloped, mid-green stem segments, 2–5cm (¾–2in) long. Produces bright red flowers, to 7cm (3in) long, in late winter. ↕ to 35cm (14in), ↔ 1m (3ft). Garden origin. ❀ (min. 10°C/50°F)

Schlumbergera 'Spectabile Coccineum'

***S.* 'Gold Charm'** ■ Epiphytic cactus with oblong, mid-green stem segments, 3–5cm (1¼–2in) long, with 6–8 prominent, tooth-like marginal notches. Flowers, 6cm (2½in) long, are yellow in autumn but may turn pinkish if kept below 14°C (57°F). ↕ to 30cm (12in), ↔ 30cm (12in). ❀ (min. 10°C/50°F)

S. opuntioides, syn. *Epiphyllanthus obovatus.* Epiphytic or rock-dwelling cactus with thick, obovate to oblong, deep green stem segments, 5–7cm (2–3in) long, often tinged red, bearing white areoles, with minute spines, on both surfaces and margins. Deep pink flowers, 6cm (2½in) long, are borne in spring. Allow houseplants a brief, dry period after flowering. ↕ to 40cm (16in), ↔ 22cm (9in). S.E. Brazil. ❀ (min. 10°C/50°F)

S. orssichiana. Epiphytic cactus with oblong, dark green stem segments, to 5cm (2in) long, with 4–6 prominent, tooth-like marginal notches, with areoles set in the angles. White flowers, to 9cm (3½in) long, purplish pink towards the petal tips, are borne from late summer to winter. ↕ to 30cm (12in), ↔ to 35cm (14in). S.E. Brazil. ❀ (min. 10°C/50°F)

***S.* 'Spectabile Coccineum'** ■ Epiphytic cactus with oblong, dark green stem segments, to 2.5cm (1in) long, with 3–5 tooth-like marginal notches. Bears bright red flowers, to 8cm (3in) long, in late winter and early spring. ↕ to 28cm (11in), ↔ 25cm (10in) or more. ❀ (min. 10°C/50°F)

S. truncata ■ syn. *Zygocactus truncatus* (Crab cactus). Epiphytic cactus with oblong, bright green stem segments, 4–6cm (1½–2½in) long, with 4–8 prominent, tooth-like marginal notches. Deep pink, red, orange, or white flowers, to 8cm (3in) long, are borne from late autumn to winter. ↕ to 30cm (12in), ↔ 30cm (12in). S.E. Brazil. ❀ (min. 10°C/50°F)

***S.* 'Wintermärchen'.** Epiphytic cactus bearing oblong, glossy, mid-green stem segments, 4cm (1½in) long, with 4–6 tooth-like marginal notches. Delicate pale pink, almost white flowers, 6–7cm (2½–3in) long, are produced in late autumn, and turn pinkish white in winter. ↕ to 35cm (14in), ↔ 30cm (12in). ❀ (min. 10°C/50°F)

Schlumbergera 'Gold Charm'

Schlumbergera truncata

Schoenoplectus lacustris subsp. *tabernaemontani* 'Zebrinus'

SCHOENOPLECTUS

CYPERACEAE

Genus, formerly included in *Scirpus*, of 80 species of evergreen, rhizomatous, marginal aquatic perennials and annuals usually found on the banks of lakes and slow-running streams, almost worldwide. Leaves are grass-like and are often borne under water. Insignificant flowers are borne in inflorescences on cylindrical or 3-angled stems, in summer. The plant described is grown for its striped stems, and is suitable for cultivation in a bog garden, or as a marginal aquatic plant in still or slow-moving water.

- **HARDINESS** Fully hardy.
- **CULTIVATION** Grow in fertile, wet soil, or in water up to 30cm (12in) deep, in full sun. In small pools, restrict growth by cutting back the rhizomes annually. See also pp.52–53.
- **PROPAGATION** Root sections of rhizome from mid-spring to mid-summer.
- **PESTS AND DISEASES** Trouble free.

***S. lacustris* subsp. *tabernaemontani* 'Zebrinus'** ■ (Club-rush). Rhizomatous perennial with virtually leafless, grey-green stems banded creamy white, arising at intervals along the rhizome. Bears branched clusters, 5–10mm (¼–½in) across, of brown spikelets from early to late summer. Cut reverting stems back to the rhizomes. ↕ 1m (3ft), ↔ 60cm (24in) or more. ❀❀❀

SCHOMBURGKIA

ORCHIDACEAE

Genus, closely related to *Laelia*, of about 12–15 species of large, evergreen, epiphytic or lithophytic orchids from rainforest and moist cliffs or rocks, at low to medium altitudes in the West Indies and tropical America. They have stout, elongated, spindle-shaped to cylindrical, sometimes hollow pseudo-

bulbs, each with 1–3 leathery, semi-rigid, ovate to oblong leaves. Racemes or panicles of showy flowers are produced from the tips of the pseudobulbs, and may be extremely long.
• **HARDINESS** Frost tender.
• **CULTIVATION** Intermediate-growing orchids. Grow in epiphytic orchid compost in containers or slatted baskets. In the growing season, water freely and apply a half-strength balanced liquid fertilizer every 4 weeks; provide high humidity and bright indirect light. Water sparingly and provide full light in winter. See also p.46.
• **PROPAGATION** Divide when the plant "overflows" the sides of the container. Remove backbulbs and pot them up separately.
• **PESTS AND DISEASES** Scale insects, red spider mites, aphids, whiteflies, and mealybugs may be troublesome.

S. tibicinis, syn. *Myrmecophila tibicinis*. Epiphytic orchid with stoutly cylindrical, hollow pseudobulbs and 2 or 3 elliptic to oblong leaves, 45cm (18in) long. Variable, fragrant, brown to rich purple flowers, 6cm (2½in) across, with yellow, white, and purple lips, are produced in extended racemes, 1.5m (5ft) or more long, in summer. ↕↔ 60cm (24in). Mexico to Panama. ❀ (min. 13°C/55°F; max. 30°C/86°F)

SCHOTIA

CAESALPINIACEAE/LEGUMINOSAE

Genus of 4 or 5 species of deciduous or semi-evergreen shrubs and trees from open deciduous woodland, dry woodland, and scrub in southern Africa. They are cultivated for their pinnate leaves, and for their 5-petalled, red or pink flowers, which are borne in summer in axillary or terminal panicles, often on bare stems and sometimes directly from older wood. Where temperatures regularly fall below 0°C (32°F), grow in a cool or temperate greenhouse. In milder climates, use in a shrub border or as specimen plants.
• **HARDINESS** Half hardy to frost tender, but may withstand temperatures down to -5°C (23°F) if the wood has been well ripened in summer.
• **CULTIVATION** Under glass, grow in loam-based potting compost (JI No.2) in full light. During the growing season, water moderately and apply a balanced liquid fertilizer monthly; water sparingly in winter. Outdoors, grow in moderately fertile, well-drained soil in full sun with shelter from cold, drying winds. Pruning group 1.
• **PROPAGATION** Sow seed at 13–16°C (55–61°F) in spring. Root semi-ripe cuttings with bottom heat in summer.
• **PESTS AND DISEASES** Whiteflies and red spider mites may be troublesome under glass.

S. brachypetala ♀ (African walnut, Tree fuchsia, Weeping boerboon). Spreading to arching, semi-evergreen, large shrub or small tree with red-brown bark and grey twigs. The pinnate leaves, to 18cm (7in) long, each have 8–15 oblong or oval leaflets, which emerge rose-red and mature through copper to bright green. From summer to late autumn, bears fragrant flowers in nodding to pendent, usually crowded panicles, to 13cm (5in) across, on leafless or almost leafless twigs; each flower has 5 minute petals and 4 spreading crimson sepals, to 1cm (½in) long. Produces bean-like pods, 5–17cm (2–7in) long, containing large seeds that are edible when roasted. ↕ 10–15m (30–50ft), ↔ 5–10m (15–30ft). Zimbabwe, Mozambique, South Africa (Limpopo, KwaZulu/Natal), Swaziland. ❄ (borderline)

SCHWANTESIA

AIZOACEAE

Genus of 10 species of dwarf, compact, cushion-forming, perennial succulents from hillsides and lowlands of Namibia and S. South Africa. They have unequal pairs of fleshy, keeled, bluish green leaves, and bear daisy-like, bright yellow flowers, which open during the day, in summer. Where temperatures fall below 10°C (50°F), grow in a temperate or warm greenhouse; in warmer climates, schwantesias are suitable for cultivation in a desert garden.
• **HARDINESS** Frost tender.
• **CULTIVATION** Under glass, grow in standard cactus compost in full light with shade from hot sun; provide low humidity. During the growing season, water moderately and apply a balanced liquid fertilizer monthly; keep just moist in winter. Outdoors, grow in poor to moderately fertile, humus-rich, sharply drained soil in full sun. Protect from excessive rain in summer and winter. See also pp.48–49.
• **PROPAGATION** Sow seed at 19–21°C (66–70°F) in spring. Divide offsets from spring to early summer.
• **PESTS AND DISEASES** Prone to aphids while flowering.

S. herrei. Cushion-forming, succulent perennial with 2 or 3 pairs of 3-angled, keeled, fleshy, pale blue-green leaves, 2.5–3.5cm (1–1½in) long, sometimes with a few terminal teeth. Bright yellow flowers, 4cm (1½in) across, are borne in summer. ↕↔ 14cm (5½in). Namibia, South Africa (Northern Cape, Western Cape). ❀ (min. 10°C/50°F)
S. ruedebuschii ▣ Clump-forming, succulent perennial producing slightly angular, very fleshy, white-mottled, greyish green leaves, 3–5cm (1¼–2in) long, the upper surfaces slightly convex, the lower ones more rounded, and the tips widening and bearing 3–7 thick blue teeth, to 4mm (⅛in) long. Bright pale yellow flowers, to 4cm (1½in) across, are borne in summer. ↕ 10cm (4in), ↔ 15cm (6in). Namibia, South Africa (Northern Cape, Western Cape). ❀ (min. 10°C/50°F).

Schwantesia ruedebuschii

SCIADOPITYS

SCIADOPITYACEAE/TAXODIACEAE

Genus of one species of monoecious, evergreen, coniferous tree from forest in Japan. It has peeling, red-brown bark, and the glossy, linear leaves, sometimes in fused pairs, are borne in whorls at the shoot-tips, like the spokes of an umbrella. Use as a specimen tree.
• **HARDINESS** Fully hardy.
• **CULTIVATION** Grow in moderately fertile, moist but well-drained, neutral to slightly acid soil, in full sun with some midday shade, or in partial shade. May need several years training to maintain a central leader.
• **PROPAGATION** Sow seed in containers in a cold frame in spring, or take semi-ripe cuttings in late summer.
• **PESTS AND DISEASES** Trouble free.

S. verticillata ▣ ◊ (Japanese umbrella pine). Conical or columnar-conical tree with red-brown bark, peeling in ribbons, and brown shoots. Linear, grooved, glossy, dark green leaves, 5–12cm (2–5in) long, olive-green beneath, are borne in terminal whorls of 15–25, and persist for 3 or 4 years. Single, ovoid female cones, 5–8cm (2–3in) long, ripen in the second year. Spherical male cones, 3–8mm (⅛–⅜in) across, are borne in clusters. ↕ 10–20m (30–70ft), ↔ to 6–8m (20–25ft). S. Japan. ❄❄❄

Sciadopitys verticillata (inset: female cone detail)

SCILLA

HYACINTHACEAE/LILIACEAE

Genus of about 90 species of bulbous perennials found in a range of habitats including subalpine meadows, rocky slopes, woodland, and sea shores in Europe, southern Africa, and Asia. They are grown for their terminal racemes or corymbs of small, usually blue but also pink, purple, or white, bell-shaped to flat, or star-shaped flowers, borne in spring, summer, and autumn. Most have semi-erect, linear to elliptic, sometimes channelled, basal leaves. Naturalize under trees and shrubs or in grass; small species are suitable for an alpine house.
• **HARDINESS** Fully hardy to half hardy.
• **CULTIVATION** Plant bulbs 8–10cm (3–4in) deep in late summer or early autumn. Under glass, grow in 2 parts loam-based potting compost (JI No.2) and 1 part each leaf mould and grit. Provide full light. When in growth, water freely; keep dry during summer dormancy. Outdoors, grow in moderately fertile, humus-rich, well-drained soil in full sun or partial shade.
• **PROPAGATION** Sow seed in containers in a cold frame as soon as ripe. Divide and pot up offsets when dormant.
• **PESTS AND DISEASES** Prone to viruses.

S. adlamii see *Ledebouria cooperi*.
S. amethystina see *S. litardierei*.
S. amoena. Small, bulbous perennial with 3–5 flaccid, linear, basal leaves, 15–22cm (6–9in) long, emerging before the small, compact racemes of 3–6 star-shaped blue flowers, 1.5–2cm (½–¾in)

S

Scilla bifolia

across, in spring. Good for naturalizing. ↕15–20cm (6–8in), ↔ 5cm (2in). Probably S.E. Europe. ❄❄❄

S. bifolia ■ Small, bulbous perennial with 2 semi-erect, broadly linear, basal leaves, 5–20cm (2–8in) long, borne in early spring, at the same time as slightly one-sided racemes of up to 10 star-shaped, blue to purple-blue flowers, 2.5–4cm (1–1½in) across. Excellent for naturalizing. ↕8–15cm (3–6in), ↔ 5cm (2in). C. and S. Europe, Turkey. ❄❄❄

S. bithynica. Small, bulbous perennial with 3–5 flaccid, linear, basal leaves, to 20cm (8in) long, borne in spring, at the same time as compact, conical racemes of 6–12 star-shaped blue flowers, to 2cm (¾in) across. ↕10–15cm (4–6in), ↔ 8cm (3in). Bulgaria, Turkey. ❄❄❄

S. campanulata see *Hyacinthoides hispanica.*

S. chinensis see *S. scilloides.*

S. cilicica. Bulbous perennial, sometimes confused with *S. hohenackeri*, producing 3 or 4 erect, broadly linear, basal leaves, 15–25cm (6–10in) long, in autumn. In spring, bears loose racemes of 5–15 star-shaped, pale or lavender-blue flowers, 2–3cm (¾–1¼in) across, with reflexed segments. Easily grown in a bulb frame or alpine house. ↕15–35cm (6–14in), ↔ 8cm (3in). Turkey. ❄❄

S. cooperi see *Ledebouria cooperi.*

S. hispanica see *Hyacinthoides hispanica.*

S. hohenackeri. Bulbous perennial, similar to *S. cilicica*, with 3–5 flaccid, linear, basal leaves, 10–25cm (4–10in) long, produced in spring before loose racemes of 4–12 star-shaped, pale blue flowers, 1.5cm (½in) across, with reflexed segments. ↕10–20cm (4–8in), ↔ 5cm (2in). Azerbaijan, Iran. ❄❄❄

S. japonica see *S. scilloides.*

S. liliohyacinthus. Small, clump-forming, bulbous perennial with relatively large, lily-like bulbs, with yellow scales. In late spring, produces a basal cluster of 6–10 erect, inversely lance-shaped, glossy leaves, 15–30cm (6–12in) long, and dense, conical racemes of 5–20 star-shaped, bright lilac-blue to purplish blue, rarely white flowers, 1.5cm (½in) across. Prefers a cool site. ↕15–25cm (6–10in), ↔ 7cm (3in). S.W. France, Spain. ❄❄❄

S. litardierei, syn. *S. amethystina, S. pratensis.* Clump-forming, bulbous perennial with a basal cluster of 3–6 semi-erect, linear leaves, 15–30cm (6–12in) long, borne in early summer, at the same time as dense racemes of 15–35 star-shaped, pale bluish violet flowers, 6mm (¼in) across. ↕10–20cm (4–8in), ↔ 5cm (2in). Coast of former Yugoslavia. ❄❄❄

S. mischtschenkoana, syn. *S. tubergeniana.* Dwarf, bulbous perennial with 3–5 semi-erect, linear to inversely lance-shaped, basal leaves, 4–10cm (1½–4in) long, borne in late winter or early spring. At the same time, racemes of 2–6 star-shaped, silvery blue flowers, 2cm (¾in) across, with darker stripes, open just above the ground. Stems and racemes gradually elongate. ↕10–15cm (4–6in), ↔ 5cm (2in). Georgia, Armenia, Azerbaijan, Iran. ❄❄❄

S. natalensis. Bulbous perennial with 4–8 semi-erect, lance-shaped, basal leaves, to 20cm (8in) long when they emerge at flowering time, later growing to 30–60cm (12–24in). Tall racemes of up to 100 flattish, light violet-blue, pink, or white flowers, 1.5cm (½in) across, are produced in summer. The flowering stems gradually elongate. ↕30–120cm (12–48in), ↔ 8cm (3in). South Africa, Lesotho. ❄

S. non-scripta see *Hyacinthoides non-scripta.*

S. nutans see *Hyacinthoides non-scripta.*

S. peruviana. Virtually evergreen, clump-forming, bulbous perennial with a basal cluster of 5–15 semi-erect, lance-shaped leaves, 40–60cm (16–24in) long, developing in autumn as older leaves fade. In early summer, produces tall, conical racemes of 50–100 star-shaped, deep purplish blue or white flowers, 1.5cm (½in) across. ↕15–30cm (6–12in), ↔ 10cm (4in). Portugal, Spain, Italy, N. Africa. ❄❄. **f. *alba*** ■ has large heads of white flowers.

Scilla peruviana f. *alba*

Scilla siberica 'Spring Beauty'

S. pratensis see *S. litardierei.*

S. scilloides, syn. *S. chinensis, S. japonica.* Slender, bulbous perennial with 2–7 semi-erect, flaccid, linear, basal leaves, 15–25cm (6–10in) long, borne in late summer and early autumn, with slender racemes of 40–80 star-shaped, mauve-pink flowers, 4mm (⅛in) across. Easily grown in full sun or in an alpine house. ↕15–20cm (6–8in), ↔ 5cm (2in). China, Korea, Taiwan, Japan (including Ryukyu Islands). ❄❄❄

S. siberica (Siberian squill). Bulbous perennial with 2–4 semi-erect, broadly linear, basal leaves, 10–15cm (4–6in) long, produced in spring, at the same time as loose racemes of up to 4 or 5 pendent, bowl-shaped, bright blue flowers, 1.5cm (½in) across. Stems gradually elongate. ↕10–20cm (4–8in), ↔ 5cm (2in). Ukraine, Russia, Georgia, Azerbaijan, N. Iran. ❄❄❄. **'Alba'** has white flowers. **'Atrocoerulea'** see 'Spring Beauty'. **'Spring Beauty'** ■ syn. 'Atrocoerulea', has deep blue flowers; ↕to 20cm (8in).

S. socialis see *Ledebouria socialis.*

S. tubergeniana see *S. mischtschenkoana.*

S. violacea see *Ledebouria socialis.*

SCINDAPSUS

ARACEAE

Genus of about 40 species of evergreen climbers, closely related and similar in appearance to *Epipremnum*, occurring in tropical forests in Asia, N. Australia, and the Pacific islands. They are grown for their alternate, entire, dull green to dark green leaves, which are pointed at the tips, and may be lance-shaped, elliptic, ovate to obovate, or sickle-shaped, and range from 10–20cm (4–8in) long. In juvenile plants, the leaf-blades are smaller, sometimes heart-shaped, and overlapping flat against the climbing surface. The solitary inflorescences, which are rarely produced in cultivation except in the tropics, are mostly yellow or white, with canoe-shaped spathes that scarcely open and enclose a cylindrical spadix. The flowers are followed by a dense, ellipsoid cluster of fleshy white, green-yellow, or orange berries, 2–10mm (1/16–½in) in diameter. In frost-prone areas, grow in a temperate or warm greenhouse, or as houseplants. In warmer areas, grow against a wall, over a pergola, or through a tree. All parts may cause severe discomfort if ingested. Contact with sap or plant tissues can cause irritation to skin and mucous membranes.

• **HARDINESS** Frost tender.

• **CULTIVATION** Under glass, grow in loamless potting compost in bright, filtered light. During the growing season, water freely and apply a balanced liquid fertilizer every month; water sparingly in winter. Provide the support of a moss pole. Outdoors, grow in fertile, moist but well-drained soil in shade or partial shade. Pruning group 11, in early spring.

• **PROPAGATION** Root leaf-bud or stem-tip cuttings with bottom heat in summer. Layer in spring or summer.

• **PESTS AND DISEASES** Trouble free.

S. aureus see *Epipremnum aureum.*

S. pictus ■ syn. *Epipremnum pictum* (Satin pothos, Silver vine). Slender climber with dull green, sickle-shaped leaves, to 18cm (7in) long, and white

Scindapsus pictus 'Argyraeus'

spathes, to 7cm (3in) long. It is usually grown in its juvenile form, which is known in cultivation as **'Argyraeus'** ■ syn. var. *argyraeus*, and has satin-textured, heart-shaped, deep green leaves, 7–10cm (3–4in) long, with silver margins and irregular silver blotches on the upper surface. ↕45–90cm (18–36in) if grown in a container; 1–3m (3–10ft) or more if grown in open ground. Borneo, Indonesia. ❀ (min. 15°C/59°F)

SCIRPOIDES

CYPERACEAE

Genus, formerly included in *Scirpus*, of one species of deciduous or semi-evergreen, fleshy-rooted, rhizomatous, perennial sedge found in damp, sandy, coastal areas and damp or wet meadows inland, from Europe to S.W. Asia. *S. holoschoenus* has almost leafless stems, and produces long-stalked, spherical flowerheads from midsummer to early autumn. It is suitable for a wild garden. Grow *S. holoschoenus* 'Variegatus' at the margins of a pool or in a bog garden.

• **HARDINESS** Fully hardy.

• **CULTIVATION** Grow in moderately fertile, constantly moist soil in full sun. Submerge in water to 23cm (9in) deep if grown as a marginal aquatic plant. Cut back stems left for winter effect by early spring. See also pp.52–53.

• **PROPAGATION** Sow seed at 6–12°C (43–54°F) in spring, in permanently moist seed compost. Divide between mid-spring and early summer.

• **PESTS AND DISEASES** Trouble free.

S. holoschoenus, syn. *Scirpus holoschoenus* (Round-headed club-rush). Tufted perennial with upright, smooth, rounded, mid-green stems, to 1m (3ft) long, turning orange-brown in autumn; they occasionally bear linear, round-tipped, rough-margined, mid-green, basal leaves. From midsummer to early autumn, produces lax, terminal umbels of dense, long-stalked, spherical heads, 1cm (½in) long, consisting of ovoid, pale brown spikelets. ↕1m (3ft), ↔ 45cm (18in). Europe, S.W. Asia. ❄❄❄. **'Variegatus'** has leaves and stems ringed yellow.

▷ ***Scirpus cernuus*** see *Isolepis cernua*
▷ ***Scirpus holoschoenus*** see *Scirpoides holoschoenus*
▷ ***Scirpus lacustris* 'Spiralis'** see *Juncus effusus* f. *spiralis*
▷ ***Scirpus setaceus*** see *Isolepis setacea*

S

SCLEROCACTUS

syn. ANCISTROCACTUS

CACTACEAE

Genus, closely allied to and sometimes merged with *Pediocactus*, of 3 or 4 species of depressed-spherical to club-shaped or cylindrical, perennial cacti from relatively arid areas of the USA and Mexico. They have a long, fleshy tap root and deeply notched or warty ribs. The areoles are nectar-secreting and bear prominent spines, the centrals often slightly hooked; flowering areoles extend in a furrow. Diurnal, trumpet-shaped flowers are borne in summer, followed by juicy, ovoid to cylindrical or club- or barrel-shaped, mid-green fruits, scaly on the upper part, smooth below. Where temperatures fall below 7–10°C (45–50°F), grow in a temperate greenhouse; elsewhere, use in a desert garden.

• **HARDINESS** Frost tender.

• **CULTIVATION** Under glass, grow in standard cactus compost in full light with shade from hot sun. When in growth, water moderately and apply a half-strength balanced liquid fertilizer monthly; keep completely dry in winter. Outdoors, grow in poor to moderately fertile, sharply drained, neutral to slightly alkaline soil in full sun with some midday shade. See also pp.48–49.

• **PROPAGATION** Sow seed at 16–21°C (61–70°F) in spring. Graft on to a sturdy rootstock of *Cereus peruvianus* or *Hylocereus undatus* in early summer.

• **PESTS AND DISEASES** Prone to mealybugs.

S. scheeri ■ syn. *Ancistrocactus megarhizus, A. scheeri, Echinocactus scheeri.* Spherical to narrowly club-shaped, dark green, perennial cactus bearing about 13 ribs with warts that have areoles at the tips, and yellow spines (12–20 radials to 1cm (½in) long and 1–4 centrals to 5cm (2in) long, the lowest hooked). Bears greenish yellow flowers, 3cm (1¼in) across, in summer. ↕12cm (5in), ↔ 8cm (3in). USA (Texas), Mexico. ⊛ (min. 7–10°C/45–50°F)

S. uncinatus, syn. *Ancistrocactus uncinatus, Echinocactus uncinatus, Glandulicactus uncinatus, Hamatocactus uncinatus.* Depressed-spherical to short-cylindrical, bluish green, perennial cactus with 13 ribs. Hairy areoles bear prominently hooked, reddish brown spines (7–11 radials to 5cm (2in) long; 1–4 centrals, the upper 3, where present, nearly straight or incurved, and to 2.5cm (1in) long, the lowest one strongly hooked, ascending, and to 9cm (3½in) long). In summer, bears deep pinkish red to brownish red flowers, 2.5cm (1in) across. ↕ 20cm (8in), ↔ 10cm (4in). USA (Texas), N. to C. Mexico. ⊛ (min. 7–10°C/45–50°F). **var. *crassihamatus***, syn. *Ancistrocactus crassihamatus, Ferocactus crassihamatus, Glandulicactus crassihamatus, Hamatocactus crassihamatus*, has large areoles with red spines (7 or 8 radials to 3cm (1¼in) long and 1–4 centrals to 5cm (2in) long, the lowest spine hooked). Flowers, 2cm (¾in) across, have white-margined purple tepals; ↕ to 10cm (4in), ↔ to 15cm (6in); Mexico.

Sclerocactus scheeri

SCOLIOPUS

LILIACEAE/TRILLIACEAE

Genus, allied to *Trillium*, of 2 species of herbaceous perennials found in woodland in the W. USA. Short, underground stems produce usually paired, ovate or oblong to elliptic, boldly veined, basal leaves, sometimes with brown-purple markings. In spring, stalkless umbels of flowers, each with 3 narrow, upright inner tepals and 3 spreading outer tepals, arise directly from buds on the rootstock. Grow for their unusual but malodorous flowers and attractive foliage in a rock garden, peat bed, or alpine house.

• **HARDINESS** Hardy to -10°C (14°F).

• **CULTIVATION** Grow in humus-rich, leafy, moist but well-drained, acid to neutral soil in deep to partial shade. Provide a dry winter mulch. In an alpine house, grow in loamless potting compost with added leaf mould in filtered light.

• **PROPAGATION** Sow seed in containers in a cold frame as soon as ripe.

• **PESTS AND DISEASES** Young foliage may be damaged by slugs and snails.

S. bigelovii see *S. bigelowii.*

S. bigelowii ■ syn. *S. bigelovii* (Footed adder's tongue, Stink pod). Compact herbaceous perennial producing pairs of broadly oblong to elliptic, boldly veined, purple-mottled, dull, dark green leaves, 10–20cm (4–8in) long. In early spring, bears umbels of 3–12 trillium-like flowers, to 5cm (2in) across, with narrow, erect, deep purple inner tepals, and greenish white outer tepals, striped brown-purple. ↕ 10cm (4in), ↔ 15cm (6in). USA (California). ❄❄

▷***Scolopendrium vulgare*** see *Asplenium scolopendrium*

Scoliopus bigelowii

Scopolia carniolica

SCOPOLIA

SOLANACEAE

Genus of 5 species of rhizomatous, creeping perennials from woodland in C. and S. Europe, and Siberia (Russia) to the Himalayas, China, and Japan. Scopolias have alternate, simple, entire, boldly veined leaves. They die back after producing solitary, pendent, bell-shaped flowers in spring. Grow in woodland. All parts are highly toxic if ingested.

• **HARDINESS** Fully hardy.

• **CULTIVATION** Grow in humus-rich, leafy, moist but well-drained, neutral to slightly alkaline soil in partial shade.

• **PROPAGATION** Sow seed in containers in a cold frame in autumn, or *in situ* in autumn or spring. Divide in spring.

• **PESTS AND DISEASES** Trouble free.

S. carniolica ■ Creeping, rhizomatous perennial with ovate or ovate-oblong, pointed, veined, wrinkled leaves, to 20cm (8in) long. Solitary, 5-pointed, bell-shaped, brownish purple to red flowers, 2.5cm (1in) long, yellow-green inside, are borne from the leaf axils in mid- and late spring. ↕↔ to 60cm (24in). C. and S.E. Europe, Caucasus. ❄❄❄. **subsp. *hladnikiana*** has brighter, buff-yellow flowers, greenish yellow inside.

▷**Scorpion orchid** see *Arachnis*
▷**Scorpion senna** see *Coronilla emerus*
▷**Scorpion weed** see *Phacelia*
▷**Scotch laburnum** see *Laburnum alpinum*
▷**Scotch rose** see *Rosa pimpinellifolia*
▷**Scotch thistle** see *Onopordum*
▷**Scots heather** see *Calluna vulgaris*
▷**Scots pine** see *Pinus sylvestris*
▷**Scottish bluebell** see *Campanula rotundifolia*

SCROPHULARIA

Figwort

SCROPHULARIACEAE

Genus of about 200 species of subshrubs and herbaceous perennials, mainly found in marshes, moist meadows, woodland, scrub, and drier wasteland in N. temperate regions, with a few species in tropical North and Central America. Often coarse and unpleasantly scented, they have erect, square stems, opposite, simple, entire or toothed, scalloped or lobed leaves, and small, 2-lipped, foxglove-like, greenish yellow, purple, or red flowers, borne in terminal, panicle-like cymes. Suitable for a wild or woodland garden. *S. auriculata* may also be grown as a marginal aquatic plant.

Scrophularia auriculata 'Variegata'

• **HARDINESS** Fully hardy to half hardy.

• **CULTIVATION** Grow in humus-rich, moist but well-drained soil in dappled to partial shade. If *S. auriculata* and its cultivars are grown as marginal aquatic plants, submerge to about 15cm (6in) deep. See also pp.52–53. To maintain *S. auriculata* 'Variegata' as a foliage plant, remove flowering stems as they form.

• **PROPAGATION** Sow seed of perennials *in situ* in autumn or spring. *S. auriculata* 'Variegata' will not come true from seed. Divide in spring. Root basal cuttings in a cold frame in spring, or root softwood cuttings in summer.

• **PESTS AND DISEASES** Prone to slugs, caterpillars, and figwort weevils.

S. aquatica see *S. auriculata.*

S. auriculata, syn. *S. aquatica* (Water betony, Water figwort). Marginal aquatic perennial, or moisture-loving herbaceous perennial. Erect, square, winged stems produce ovate, wrinkled, toothed, dark green leaves, 5–25cm (2–10in) long. Panicle-like cymes of 2-lipped, yellowish green flowers, to 1cm (½in) long, each with a brown upper lip, are borne above the leaves from early summer to early autumn. ↕↔ 90cm (36in). W. Europe. ❄❄❄. **'Variegata'** ■ has leaves marked cream.

SCUTELLARIA

Helmet flower, Skullcap

LABIATAE/LAMIACEAE

Genus of about 300 species of erect or spreading annuals, rhizomatous and clump-forming herbaceous perennials, and, more rarely, subshrubs, widespread in temperate regions and on mountains in tropical areas. Leaves are opposite and entire, rarely pinnatifid or toothed. The tubular, 2-lipped, blue, violet, yellow, or white flowers, often with coloured bracts, are borne singly or in pairs from the leaf axils, or in terminal spikes or racemes. Grow smaller species in a rock garden or alpine house; use taller species at the front of a herbaceous border.

• **HARDINESS** Fully hardy to frost hardy.

• **CULTIVATION** Grow in moderately fertile, light, gravelly, well-drained, neutral to alkaline soil in full sun or light dappled shade. In very cold areas, apply a deep winter mulch. In an alpine house, grow in equal parts loam, leaf mould, and grit.

S

Scutellaria orientalis

• **PROPAGATION** Sow seed in containers in a cold frame in autumn. Divide in autumn or spring. Take basal and softwood cuttings in late spring or early summer.
• **PESTS AND DISEASES** Prone to aphids and red spider mites under glass.

S. alpina. Spreading, tuft-forming perennial with ovate, toothed, hairy, grey-green leaves, to 2.5cm (1in) long. In summer, bears erect purple flowers, 2.5cm (1in) long, with yellow-white lower lips, in dense, 4-angled racemes. ↕15cm (6in), ↔30cm (12in). S. Europe to Russia (Siberia). ❄❄❄
S. baicalensis. Bushy perennial with angular, decumbent then erect, purple-tinged stems, and short-stalked, lance-shaped, hairy-margined, mid-green leaves, to 4cm (1½in) long. From early summer to early autumn, produces dense, one-sided racemes of hairy flowers, to 2.5cm (1in) long, upper lips dark blue, lower lips paler. ↕↔20–30cm (8–12in). Mongolia, China, Japan. ❄❄❄
S. indica. Slender, upright, rhizomatous perennial with white-hairy, shallowly toothed, broadly ovate to heart-shaped, mid-green leaves, to 2.5cm (1in) long. Bears dense, 4-angled racemes of long-tubed, grey-blue or rarely white flowers, to 2cm (¾in) long, in summer. ↕↔ to 20cm (8in). Mountains of China, Korea, Japan. ❄❄❄. **var. *parvifolia***, syn. var. *japonica*, has lilac-blue flowers; ↕25cm (10in), ↔30cm (12in).
S. orientalis ■ Woody-based, rhizomatous perennial with grey-hairy, rooting stems, and ovate-oblong to broadly ovate, deeply toothed to pinnatisect, dark green leaves, 1.5cm (½in) long, grey-woolly beneath. In summer, bears dense, erect, 4-angled racemes of bright yellow flowers, 1.5–3cm (½–1¼in) long, marked red on the lower lips, and with yellow-green or purple-tinted bracts. ↕25cm (10cm), ↔30cm (12in). S.E. Europe. ❄❄❄

▷**Sea buckthorn** see *Hippophae rhamnoides*
▷***Seaforthia elegans*** see *Ptychosperma elegans*
▷**Sea kale** see *Crambe maritima*
▷**Sea lavender** see *Limonium, L. latifolium*
▷**Sea onion** see *Urginea maritima*
  False see *Ornithogalum longibracteatum*
▷**Sea pink** see *Armeria*
▷**Sedge** see *Carex*
  Bowles' golden see *Carex elata* 'Aurea'
  Drooping see *Carex pendula*
  Hook see *Uncinia*
  Leatherleaf see *Carex buchananii*
  Mace see *Carex grayi*
  Palm branch see *Carex muskingumensis*
  Pendulous see *Carex pendula*
  Variegated russet see *Carex saxatilis* 'Ski Run'
  Weeping see *Carex pendula*
▷**Sedges** see p.54
▷***Sedirea japonica*** see *Aerides japonica*

SEDUM *syn.* HYLOTELEPHIUM

Stonecrop

CRASSULACEAE

Genus of about 400 species of usually succulent annuals and evergreen, semi-evergreen, or deciduous biennials, perennials, subshrubs, and shrubs, a few of which are sometimes included in the genus *Hylotelephium*. They are widely distributed, most found in mountains of the N. hemisphere, but some in arid areas of South America. Stonecrops are very variable, with alternate, opposite, or whorled, fleshy, cylindrical or flattened leaves and usually terminal, often compound, cymes, panicles, or corymbs of generally star-shaped and 5-petalled flowers, borne mostly in summer and autumn. Grow hardy species in a rock garden or at the front of a herbaceous or mixed border. In frost-prone climates, grow tender species as houseplants, or in a temperate greenhouse or conservatory. All parts of the plants may cause mild stomach upset if ingested; contact with the sap may irritate skin.
• **HARDINESS** Fully hardy to frost tender.
• **CULTIVATION** Under glass, grow tender species in a mix of 3 parts loam-based potting compost (JI No.2), 2 parts grit, and 1 part leaf mould, in full light with good ventilation. In growth, water moderately and apply a half-strength balanced liquid fertilizer every month; water sparingly in winter. Outdoors, grow in moderately fertile, well-drained, neutral to slightly alkaline soil in full sun. Vigorous species tolerate light shade. Cut back spreading species after flowering, to maintain shape. Divide larger, herbaceous species every 3 or 4 years to improve flowering.
• **PROPAGATION** Sow seed of hardy species in containers in a cold frame in autumn. Sow seed of annuals and biennials at 13–16°C (55–61°F) in early spring, or *in situ* in mid-spring. Sow tender species at 15–18°C (59–64°F) in early spring. Divide in spring. For perennials, subshrubs, and shrubs, take softwood cuttings of non-flowering shoots in early summer.
• **PESTS AND DISEASES** Outdoors, prone to slugs and snails; may be affected by fungal and bacterial crown and root rots. Under glass, prone to aphids, and may be infested by scale insects, mealybugs, and vine weevil grubs.

S. acre ■ (Biting stonecrop, Common stonecrop, Wallpepper). Mat-forming, evergreen perennial with erect or trailing stems densely clothed in overlapping, triangular, pale green leaves, to 6mm (¼in) long. Flat-topped cymes, 2.5–4cm (1–1½in) across, of star-shaped, yellow-green flowers, 1.5cm (½in) across, are produced in abundance over long periods in summer. ↕5cm (2in), ↔60cm (24in) or more. Europe, Turkey, N. Africa. ❄❄❄. **'Aureum'** ■ bears bright yellow leaves.
S. aizoon, syn. *S. maximowiczii*. Rhizomatous, deciduous perennial with a stout rootstock and upright, unbranched, hairless stems bearing alternate, stalkless, ovate-lance-shaped, coarsely toothed, light green leaves, to 8cm (3in) long. In summer, produces star-shaped yellow flowers, 1.5cm (½in) across, with conspicuous stamens, in terminal, flattened, cyme-like clusters, to 4cm (1½in) across. ↕↔45cm (18in). Russia (Siberia), China, Japan. ❄❄❄. **'Aurantiacum'** ■ has dark red stems, dark green leaves, and red-tinted buds opening to yellow-orange flowers, followed by spherical to ovoid red fruit. **'Euphorbioides'** is more compact, and has deeper yellow flowers; ↕35cm (14in), ↔30cm (12in).
S. alboroseum see *S. erythrostictum*.
***S.* 'Autumn Joy'** see *S.* 'Herbstfreude'.
S. caeruleum. Branching, spreading annual with alternate, spoon-shaped, ovate to oblong-ovate, pale green leaves, 1–2cm (½–¾in) long. In summer, bears star-shaped, 7-petalled, pale blue flowers, 6mm (¼in) across, in cymes to 2.5cm (1in) across. Leaves and stems flush red during flowering. Self-seeds freely. ↕10–15cm (4–6in), ↔ to 15cm (6in). France (Corsica), Italy (Sardinia, Sicily), coastal Tunisia and Algeria. ❄❄❄
S. cauticola. Trailing, stoloniferous, sometimes woody-based, deciduous perennial with purple-tinged stems and opposite, bluntly toothed, rounded to spoon-shaped or obovate, grey-green leaves, to 2.5cm (1in) long. In early autumn, branching stems bear terminal, slightly rounded, panicle-like cymes, to 10cm (4in) across, of star-shaped, pink-purple flowers, to 9mm (⅜in) across, ageing to carmine-red. ↕8cm (3in), ↔30cm (12in). Japan. ❄❄❄
S. crassipes see *Rhodiola wallichiana*.
S. erythrostictum, syn. *Hylotelephium erythrostictum, S. alboroseum*. Clump-forming, deciduous perennial, similar to *S. spectabile*, with unbranched, spreading, woody stems bearing usually opposite, ovate, sometimes toothed, glaucous, grey-green leaves, to 8cm (3in) long. In late summer, bears terminal, corymb-like clusters, to 15cm (6in) across, of star-shaped, greenish white

Sedum acre

Sedum acre 'Aureum'

flowers, 1cm (½in) across, with pink carpels. ↕30cm (12in), ↔60cm (24in). E. Asia. ❄❄❄. **'Mediovariegatum'** bears larger flower clusters, and leaves with central, creamy white splashes, which are especially striking in spring. Grow in partial shade and cut out reverting green shoots; ↔45cm (18in).
S. ewersii. Low-branching, deciduous perennial with opposite, stalkless, rounded to broadly ovate, entire or slightly toothed, grey-blue leaves, to 2cm (¾in) long, heart-shaped at the bases. In summer, produces dense, rounded cymes, to 10cm (4in) across, of star-shaped, pinkish red flowers, to 8mm (⅜in) across. Similar to, but often later flowering than *S. cauticola*. ↕8cm (3in), ↔30cm (12in). C. Asia, Himalayas, Mongolia, China. ❄❄❄
S. frutescens. Shrubby, semi-evergreen perennial bearing woody, branching stems, to 1cm (½in) thick, clothed in papery, peeling bark. Alternate, pointed, linear-elliptic, bright green leaves, 2–6cm (¾–2½in) long, are usually produced in terminal clusters. In summer, star-shaped white flowers, to 1.5cm (½in) across, are produced in few-flowered, terminal cymes. ↕ to 1m (3ft), ↔40cm (16in). Mexico. ❀ (min. 5–7°C/41–45°F)
***S.* 'Herbstfreude'**, syn. *S.* 'Autumn Joy'. Clump-forming, bushy deciduous perennial with unbranched, glaucous, mid-green stems bearing alternate, oblong to obovate, toothed, glaucous, dark green leaves, to 12cm (5in) long. In early autumn, produces flat corymbs, to 20cm (8in) across, of star-shaped flowers, 5mm (¼in) across, deep pink

S

Sedum aizoon 'Aurantiacum'

Sedum humifusum

at first, then turning pinkish bronze to copper-red. ↕↔ to 60cm (24in). ***
S. heterodontum see *Rhodiola heterodonta.*
S. humifusum ■ Mat-forming, evergreen perennial with creeping stems and tight rosettes of overlapping, blunt, obovate, mid-green leaves, 4mm (⅛in) long, ageing to red. Solitary, terminal, bright yellow flowers, 9mm (⅜in) across, are borne in early summer. ↕ 1cm (½in), ↔ 10cm (4in). Mexico. **
S. kamtschaticum. Clump-forming, semi-evergreen perennial with stout rhizomes and alternate, inversely lance-shaped to spoon-shaped, glossy, deep green leaves, to 4cm (1½in) long, coarsely toothed towards the tips. In late summer, bears short-stemmed, flat cymes, to 5cm (2in) across, of star-shaped, golden yellow flowers, 1.5cm (½in) across, opening from pink buds. ↕ 10cm (4in), ↔ 25cm (10in). Russia (Siberia, Kamchatka), N. and C. China, Japan. ***. **'Variegatum'** ■ has pink-tinted, mid-green leaves with cream margins, and yellow flowers, ageing to crimson. Tolerates partial shade.
S. lydium ■ Stem-rooting, mat-forming, evergreen perennial with tight rosettes of cylindrical, red-tipped, bright to mid-green leaves, to 6mm (¼in) long. In summer, bears flat-topped, terminal corymbs, 2.5cm (1in) across, of star-shaped white flowers, 6mm (¼in) across. ↕ 5cm (2in), ↔ 20cm (8in). W. and C. Turkey. ***
S. maximowiczii see *S. aizoon.*
S. morganianum ■ Pendent, evergreen perennial (prostrate in the wild) with fleshy, woody-based stems and alternate, oblong-lance-shaped, fleshy, glaucous, greenish blue leaves, to 2cm (¾in) long. In spring and summer, bears star-shaped, pale pink to scarlet-purple flowers, 1cm (½in) across, in cymes to 2.5cm (1in) across. ↕↔ 30cm (12in). Mexico. ❀ (min. 5–7°C/41–45°F)
S. obtusatum ■ syn. *S. rubroglaucum.* Evergreen perennial with terminal rosettes of spoon-shaped, blunt-tipped, glaucous, mid-green leaves, 0.5–2.5cm (¼–1in) long, flushed crimson in autumn. In summer, bears star-shaped, bright yellow flowers, to 1cm (½in) across, in flat, panicle-like cymes, to 10cm (4in) across. ↕ 5cm (2in), ↔ 20cm (8in). USA (California). ***
S. oxypetalum. Many-branched, semi-evergreen perennial with fleshy, woody stems, clothed in papery, peeling bark. The alternate, inversely lance-shaped to obovate, minutely papillose, greyish green leaves are 5cm (2in) long. Diurnal, star-shaped, fragrant, pink or dull red flowers, to 1.5cm (½in) across, usually with pink-marked petals, open in cymes 4cm (1½in) across, in summer. ↕ 50–90cm (20–36in), ↔ 45cm (18in). Mexico. ❀ (min. 5–7°C/41–45°F)

Sedum morganianum

S. pilosum. Densely grey-hairy, rosette-forming, evergreen biennial. Incurved, oblong to narrowly spoon-shaped, dark green leaves are to 2cm (¾in) long. Bears dense, flat corymbs, 5cm (2in) across, of many short-stemmed, bell-shaped, rose-red flowers, 9mm (⅜in) across, in summer. ↕ 8cm (3in), ↔ 15cm (6in). W. Asia (Turkey to Iran). **
S. populifolium ■ Slowly spreading, deciduous subshrub with slightly decumbent, branched, dark brown stems bearing alternate, ovate, toothed, light green leaves, to 4cm (1½in) long, heart-shaped at the bases. Corymb-like cymes, 5cm (2in) across, of star-shaped, fragrant white flowers, 1cm (½in) across, pink-tinged on the reverse, are borne in late summer and early autumn. ↕ 20–30cm (8–12in), ↔ 45cm (18in). Russia (Siberia). ***
S. reflexum see *S. rupestre.*
S. rhodiola see *Rhodiola rosea.*
S. rosea see *Rhodiola rosea.*
S. rosea* var. *heterodontum see *Rhodiola heterodonta.*
S. rubroglaucum see *S. obtusatum.*
S. rubrotinctum. Evergreen subshrub with numerous arching, rooting, branching stems bearing alternate, blunt, cylindrical, mid-green leaves, 1.5cm (½in) long, often flushed red. Loose, many-flowered cymes, 4cm (1½in) across, of star-shaped, pale yellow flowers, 1cm (½in) across, are borne in winter. ↕ 24cm (10in), ↔ 20cm (8in). Mexico. ** (borderline)

Sedum populifolium

***S.* 'Ruby Glow'** ■ Low-growing deciduous perennial with spreading, unbranched red stems bearing opposite, elliptic, toothed, green-purple leaves, 5cm (2in) long. Many loose cymes, 6cm (2½in) across, of star-shaped, ruby-red flowers, 1cm (½in) across, are produced from midsummer to early autumn. ↕ 25cm (10in), ↔ 45cm (18in). ***
S. rupestre ■ syn. *S. reflexum* (Stone orpine). Vigorous, mat-forming, evergreen perennial with alternate, pointed, cylindrical, grey-green leaves, to 1–2cm (½–¾in) long. Upright, leafy, woody

Sedum 'Ruby Glow'

S

Sedum kamtschaticum 'Variegatum'

Sedum lydium

Sedum obtusatum

Sedum rupestre

Sedum sieboldii 'Mediovariegatum'

stems bear terminal, umbel-like cymes, 6cm (2½in) across, of star-shaped yellow flowers, 1.5cm (½in) across, pendent in bud, but erect as they open in summer. Spreads freely; best in a large rock garden. ↕ 10cm (4in), ↔ 60cm (24in) or more. C. and W. Europe. ❄❄❄
S. sarcocaule see *Crassula sarcocaulis.*
S. sempervivoides. Rosette-forming, evergreen biennial with pointed, ovate to diamond-shaped, hairy, blue-green leaves, to 3cm (1¼in) long, flushed red-purple at the bases. In summer, bears domed, corymb-like panicles, 4–5cm (1½–2in) across, of many star-shaped, carmine-red flowers, 1.5cm (½in) across. Dislikes winter wet; best in an alpine house. ↕ 10cm (4in), ↔ 15cm (6in). Caucasus, Georgia, N. Iran, S.W. Asia. ❄❄

Sedum spathulifolium 'Cape Blanco'

Sedum spathulifolium 'Purpureum'

S. sieboldii. Spreading, tuberous, tufted, deciduous perennial with whorls of 3 rounded, glaucous, blue-green, occasionally purple-tinted leaves, to 2cm (¾in) long, some irregularly toothed and red-margined towards the tips. Star-shaped pink flowers, to 1.5cm (½in) across, are borne in flat-topped cymes, 6cm (2½in) across, in late summer. Use as a houseplant, or in an alpine house. ↕ 10cm (4in), ↔ 20cm (8in). Japan. ❄❄. **'Mediovariegatum'** ▣ syn. 'Foliis Mediovariegatis', 'Foliis Variegatis', 'Variegatum', has glaucous-blue leaves, marbled cream and occasionally with red margins.
S. spathulifolium. Vigorous, mat-forming, evergreen perennial with branching, fleshy stems bearing terminal rosettes of brittle, spoon-shaped, silvery or mid-green leaves, to 2cm (¾in) long, usually tinted bronze-purple. Short-stemmed, star-shaped, bright yellow flowers, 1.5cm (½in) across, are borne in flat cymes, 2.5cm (1in) across, in summer. Tolerates light shade. ↕ 10cm (4in), ↔ 60cm (24in). W. North America. ❄❄❄. **'Cape Blanco'** ▣ syn. 'Cappa Blanca', has the innermost leaves of its rosettes heavily powdered with white bloom. **'Purpureum'** ▣ produces leaves richly suffused reddish purple.
S. spectabile (Ice plant). Clump-forming, deciduous perennial. Upright, unbranched green stems bear opposite or whorled, ovate to elliptic or obovate, slightly scalloped, toothed, grey-green leaves, to 8cm (3in) long. In late summer, star-shaped pink flowers, to 1cm (½in) across, with prominent stamens, are borne in dense, flat cymes, to 15cm (6in) across. Attractive to bees. ↕↔ 45cm (18in). China, Korea. ❄❄❄. **'Brilliant'** ▣ bears flowers with bright pink petals and darker pink carpels and anthers. **'Carmen'** is a slightly darker mauve-pink. **'Iceberg'** has paler green leaves than the species, and pure white flowers; ↕ 30–45cm (12–18in), ↔ 35cm (14in). **'Septemberglut'**, syn. 'September Glow', has glowing, rich pink flowers; ↕ to 50cm (20in).
S. spurium. Vigorous, mat-forming, evergreen perennial with branching red stems bearing opposite, obovate, toothed, mid-green leaves, to 2.5cm (1in) long. Star-shaped, pinkish purple or white flowers, 2cm (¾in) across, are produced in rounded corymbs, 4cm (1½in) across, in late summer. ↕ 10cm (4in), ↔ 60cm (24in) or more. Caucasus, Armenia, N. Iran. ❄❄❄.

Sedum spectabile 'Brilliant'

'Dragon's Blood' see 'Schorbuser Blut'.
'Purple Carpet' see 'Purpurteppich'.
'Purpurteppich', syn. 'Purple Carpet', is compact, with deep plum-purple leaves and dark purplish red flowers.
'Schorbuser Blut' ▣ syn. 'Dragon's Blood', has green leaves, purple-tinted when mature, and deep pink flowers.
S. telephium (Orpine). Clump-forming, rhizomatous, deciduous perennial. Erect, unbranched, pale green stems bear alternate, oblong to oblong-ovate, toothed, glaucous, grey-green leaves, to 8cm (3in) long. Dense, axillary and terminal cymes, to 12cm (5in) across, of star-shaped, purplish pink flowers, to 1cm (½in) across, are borne in late summer and early autumn. ↕ to 60cm (24in), ↔ 30cm (12in). Europe, Russia (Siberia), China, Japan. ❄❄❄. **subsp. *maximum* 'Atropurpureum'** ▣ has glaucous, very dark purple stems and leaves, and smaller cymes of pink flowers with orange-red centres, appearing buff-white; ↕ 45–60cm (18–24in). **'Munstead Dark Red'** has purple-tinted, dark green leaves and dark purplish red flowers, becoming even darker with age; ↕ to 60cm (24in).

Sedum spurium 'Schorbuser Blut'

Sedum telephium subsp. *maximum* 'Atropurpureum'

S. 'Vera Jameson'. Deciduous perennial with spreading purple stems and opposite, ovate, toothed, glaucous, purple-pink leaves, to 10cm (4in) long. In late summer and early autumn, bears rounded cymes, 6cm (2½in) across, of star-shaped, soft rose-pink flowers, 6–10mm (¼–½in) across. ↕ 20–30cm (8–12in), ↔ 45cm (18in). ❄❄❄
S. wallichianum see *Rhodiola wallichiana.*
S. weinbergii see *Graptopetalum paraguayense.*

▷ ***Seemannia gymnostoma*** see *Gloxinia gymnostoma*

SELAGINELLA

SELAGINELLACEAE

Genus of approximately 700 species of evergreen, rhizomatous perennials found in a range of habitats, from semi-desert to rainforest, mostly in tropical regions, with some species in temperate and alpine zones. Grown for their foliage, they vary from small, moss-like tufts to tall, scrambling plants. They have long, creeping, branched stems, often rooting

Selaginella kraussiana

Selaginella lepidophylla

along their length, which are clothed in scale-like leaves, to 3mm (⅛in) long. Spores form in small, leafy, terminal spikes. Use as ground cover or in hanging baskets. In frost-prone areas, grow in a cool, temperate, or warm greenhouse, or as houseplants.
• **HARDINESS** Frost tender.
• **CULTIVATION** Under glass, grow in a mix of 2 parts loam-based potting compost (JI No.2) and 1 part leaf mould, in bright filtered or indirect light; *S. uncinata* and *S. willdenovii* are best in bright filtered light. In growth, water freely and apply a balanced liquid fertilizer monthly. Maintain high humidity. Keep just moist in winter. Outdoors, grow in moderately fertile, humus-rich, moist but well-drained, neutral to slightly acid soil in partial shade. *S. lepidophylla* tolerates drier conditions and prefers alkaline soil. Shelter from cold, drying winds.
• **PROPAGATION** Sow spores at 21°C (70°F) as soon as ripe. Divide rhizomes or rooted stems in spring.
• **PESTS AND DISEASES** Trouble free.

S. emmeliana see *S. pallescens*.
S. kraussiana ▣ (Krauss's spikemoss). Mat-forming perennial producing trailing stems clothed in pinnatisect, bright green foliage. ↕ 2.5cm (1in), ↔ indefinite. Tropical and southern Africa, Azores. ❀ (min. 5–7°C/41–45°F). **'Aurea'** has yellow-green foliage. **'Brownii'** forms small cushions; ↕ 5cm (2in), ↔ 15cm (6in). **'Variegata'** produces cream-splashed foliage.
S. lepidophylla ▣ (Resurrection plant, Rose of Jericho). Small, spreading

Selaginella martensii

Selaginella willdenovii

perennial with dense tufts of dark green leaves. When dry, curls into a ball that opens into a flat rosette when soaked with water. ↕ to 8cm (3in), ↔ 15cm (6in). USA (Arizona, Texas) to Peru. ❀ (min. 5–7°C/41–45°F)
S. martensii ▣ Trailing perennial with many-branched stems bearing frond-like, glossy, bright green foliage. ↕ to 15cm (6in), ↔ 20cm (8in). Central America. ❀ (min. 5–7°C/41–45°F). **'Variegata'** has white-flecked foliage.
S. pallescens, syn. *S. emmeliana*. Perennial with a densely tufted stem, branching from the base, with short, much-divided branches. Leaves are light yellow-green, white beneath. ↕ to 15cm (6in), ↔ 30cm (12in). North America to N. Colombia and Venezuela. ❀ (min. 10–15°C/50–59°F)
S. umbrosa. Perennial with erect, regularly branched, red-tinged stems, and triangular, 3-pinnate branches with light green leaves. ↕ to 40cm (16in), ↔ indefinite. Central and South America. ❀ (min. 10–15°C/50–59°F)
S. uncinata. Perennial with slender, trailing, rooting stems bearing alternate, short, pinnate branches and leaves with a distinct metallic blue sheen. ↕ 2.5–5cm (1–2in), ↔ indefinite. China. ❀ (min. 5–7°C/41–45°F)
S. willdenovii ▣ Perennial climber with a nearly leafless stem bearing densely branched, leafy sideshoots. Leaves are mid-green, ageing to pinkish yellow or plum, with a metallic blue sheen. ↕ 3–6m (10–20ft) or more. Himalayas to S. China and Indonesia. ❀ (min. 10–15°C/50–59°F)

SELAGO

SCROPHULARIACEAE

Genus of about 150 species of evergreen shrubs, subshrubs, and annuals from grassland, rocky places, moist sites, and forest margins in tropical Africa and South Africa. Their simple, often very narrow leaves are usually clustered or solitary, and borne at alternate nodes or occasionally in opposite pairs. Selagos are grown mainly for their heads, spikes, corymbs, or panicles of usually small, tubular flowers, each with 5 spreading petal lobes. In frost-prone climates, grow in a temperate greenhouse. In milder areas, grow at the front of a shrub border, in a raised bed, or at the base of a warm, sunny wall. *S. serrata* is also effective grown in a container in a courtyard garden.
• **HARDINESS** Frost tender, although some may survive temperatures near 0°C (32°F).
• **CULTIVATION** Under glass, grow in loam-based potting compost (JI No.2) in full light with shade from hot sun, or in bright filtered light. In growth, water freely, and apply a balanced liquid fertilizer monthly; maintain low to moderate humidity. Keep just moist in winter. Outdoors, grow in moderately fertile, humus-rich, moist but well-drained soil in full sun. Dead-head regularly. Pruning group 9.
• **PROPAGATION** Sow seed at 13–15°C (55–59°F) in spring. Root softwood cuttings in spring or early summer, with bottom heat. Layer or air layer in spring or early summer.
• **PESTS AND DISEASES** Red spider mites may be a problem under glass.

S. serrata. Initially erect, then becoming spreading to decumbent, evergreen shrub with crowded, stalkless, obovate or oblong, boldly toothed, firm, deep green leaves, to 2.5cm (1in) long. Fragrant purple to pale blue flowers are produced in compact corymbs, to 5cm (2in) across, in summer. ↕↔ 30–90cm (12–36in). South Africa. ❀ (min. 5°C/41°F)

SELENICEREUS

CACTACEAE

Genus of approximately 20 species of mostly scandent or semi-pendent, epiphytic or rock-dwelling, perennial cacti from forest and woody areas of Texas (USA), Mexico, Central America, Colombia, and the West Indies. They produce short-hairy, generally spiny areoles, and most have aerial roots. Stems are slender, ribbed, or, more rarely, angled or flattened. The large, trumpet-shaped, mainly nocturnal flowers are usually borne in summer. In areas where temperatures fall below 15°C (59°F), grow in a warm greenhouse, in hanging baskets or in containers with support for climbing stems. In warmer climates, grow in containers in a courtyard garden, or at the base of a warm, sunny wall.
• **HARDINESS** Frost tender.
• **CULTIVATION** Under glass, grow in epiphytic cactus compost in bright indirect to moderate light. In the growing season, water freely and apply a half-strength balanced liquid fertilizer monthly; keep just moist in winter. Maintain moderate to high humidity. Outdoors, grow in moderately fertile, humus-rich, moist but sharply drained, neutral to slightly alkaline soil, with additional grit and leaf mould, in light dappled to partial shade. See also pp.48–49.
• **PROPAGATION** Sow seed at 16–19°C (61–66°F) as soon as ripe or in spring. Root cuttings of stem segments in a

Selenicereus grandiflorus

closed, slightly shaded propagating case in spring or summer.
• **PESTS AND DISEASES** Scale insects and mealybugs may be a problem.

S. anthonyanus, syn. *Cryptocereus anthonyanus*. Semi-pendent, scandent, epiphytic cactus with flattened, leaf-like, bright green stems, 7–15cm (3–6in) across, with prominent marginal notches, 4.5cm (1¾in) deep, forming lobes. The areoles bear 2–4 short, pale brown spines. In summer, produces nocturnal, fragrant, yellowish or creamy white flowers, 12cm (5in) long, with maroon-red outer segments. ↕ to 75cm (30in), ↔ indefinite. S.E. Mexico. ❀ (min. 15°C/59°F)
S. chrysocardium see *Epiphyllum chrysocardium*.
S. grandiflorus ▣ (Queen of the night). Scandent, epiphytic cactus producing 5- to 8-ribbed, mid-green stems, 1–2.5cm (½–1in) thick, with areoles bearing 6–18 yellow spines that turn grey. The nocturnal, fragrant white flowers, 30cm (12in) long, with spreading, pale yellowish brown outer segments, are borne in summer. ↕ 5m (15ft). Mexico, West Indies. ❀ (min. 15°C/59°F)
S. hamatus. Scandent, epiphytic cactus with 3- or 4-angled, dark green stems, 1.5cm (½in) thick, bearing hooked warts. The areoles have 5–9 white or brown spines. Bears nocturnal, scented white flowers are 20–35cm (8–14in) long, with yellow and red outer segments, in summer. ↕ 4m (12ft). Mexico, West Indies. ❀ (min. 15°C/59°F)
S. innesii. Scandent or trailing, epiphytic cactus with 4- or 5-ribbed, mid-green stems, 1cm (½in) thick, and woolly areoles bearing 1 or 2 thick, pale yellow spines and 3–7 slender ones. In summer, bears diurnal white flowers, 4–5cm (1½–2in) long, with extended petals, to 6cm (2½in) across, the outer petals tinged magenta-pink; some plants have only male flowers, others only female. ↕ to 2m (6ft). West Indies (St. Vincent). ❀ (min. 15°C/59°F)
S. pteranthus. Scandent, epiphytic cactus with 4- to 6-angled, purplish green stems, 2.5–5cm (1–2in) thick, and white-woolly areoles bearing 6–12 thick, yellowish grey spines. Nocturnal, white or pale cream flowers, 30cm (12in) long, with long, slender, recurved, pale purple outer segments, are produced in summer. ↕ 4m (12ft). Mexico. ❀ (min. 15°C/59°F)

S. wercklei. Semi-pendent, freely branching, epiphytic cactus with mid-green stems, 1cm (½in) thick, each with up to 12 shallow ribs. Areoles are mostly spineless, but a few brown spines form on the flower tubes. Nocturnal white flowers, 15cm (6in) long, with red outer segments, are produced in summer. ↕75cm (30in), ↔ indefinite. Costa Rica. ❀ (min. 15°C/59°F)

▷**Self-heal** see *Prunella*
Large see *P. grandiflora*

SELINUM

APIACEAE/UMBELLIFERAE

Genus of 6 species of tap-rooted perennials from rocky slopes, mountain meadows, and scrub in temperate areas of Europe and the Himalayas. The tall stems bear finely cut leaves and large, flattish umbels of small, star-shaped white flowers, rarely purple-tinged. Few *Selinum* species are cultivated, but *S. wallichianum* is suitable for an informal, mixed or shrub border or a woodland garden, and is effective grown as a specimen to display the tiered effect of its floral umbels.

- **HARDINESS** Fully hardy.
- **CULTIVATION** Grow in moderately fertile, moist but well-drained soil in full sun or partial shade. Tolerant of a wide range of conditions.
- **PROPAGATION** Sow seed in containers in a cold frame as soon as ripe; prick out into deep containers as soon as possible to avoid tap-root damage. Divide carefully in early spring; selinums resent disturbance.
- **PESTS AND DISEASES** Overwintering buds are especially prone to slug and snail damage. Powdery mildew may be a problem in dry conditions.

S. tenuifolium see *S. wallichianum.*
S. wallichianum ▣ syn. *S. tenuifolium.* Clump-forming perennial with erect, branched stems, usually shaded or lined reddish purple, as are the leaf-stalks, which are 20–30cm (8–12in) long. Triangular leaf-blades, to 50cm (20in) long, are 2- or 3-pinnate, the final segments elliptic and toothed. Tiny, star-shaped white flowers are borne in terminal umbels, to 20cm (8in) across, from midsummer to early autumn. ↕ to 1.8m (6ft), ↔ 60cm (24in). W. Pakistan, Himalayas, India. ❄❄❄

Selinum wallichianum

SEMELE

Climbing butcher's broom

LILIACEAE/RUSCACEAE

Genus of one species of evergreen, woody climber from laurel forest in S. Spain, S.E. France, Sicily, N. Africa, and the Canary Islands. The true leaves are scale-like, their function taken over by leaf-like stems, on which clusters of tiny, star-shaped, 6-tepalled flowers are borne in late spring and early summer. These are sometimes followed by single-seeded, orange-red berries. In frost-prone areas, grow as a foliage plant in a cool greenhouse. In warmer climates, use to provide handsome foliage cover on a warm, sunny wall.

- **HARDINESS** Half hardy.
- **CULTIVATION** Under glass, grow in loam-based potting compost (JI No.2) in full light with shade from hot sun, or in bright filtered light. In the growing season, water moderately and apply a balanced liquid fertilizer monthly; water sparingly in winter. Maintain low to moderate humidity. Outdoors, grow in moderately fertile, well-drained soil in full sun. Provide the stems with support. Pruning group 11, in late winter or early spring.
- **PROPAGATION** Sow seed at 16–19°C (61–66°F) in spring. Divide in spring.
- **PESTS AND DISEASES** Trouble free.

S. androgyna (Liana). Moderately bushy, twining climber, with the main stems arising at ground level, bearing lance-shaped to ovate, sometimes shallowly lobed, glossy, mid-green, leaf-like stems, to 2.5cm (1in) long. Clusters of 2–6 tiny, star-shaped cream flowers are produced in late spring and early summer; the females are 6mm (¼in) across, the males 9mm (⅜in) across. ↕5–7m (15–22ft). S. Spain, S.E. France (Hyères Isles), Sicily, N. Africa, Canary Islands. ❄

SEMIAQUILEGIA

RANUNCULACEAE

Genus of 7 species of small, sometimes short-lived perennials from mountain habitats in E. Asia. They resemble columbines (*Aquilegia*), but have spurless flowers, swollen or pouched at the bases, borne in corymb-like panicles in spring or summer. Leaves are ternate or 2-ternate, and often further divided. They are most effective when grown in a rock garden.

- **HARDINESS** Fully hardy.
- **CULTIVATION** Grow in moderately fertile, humus-rich, moist but well-drained, neutral to slightly acid soil in full sun with some midday shade, or in partial shade. Provide shelter from cold, drying winds.
- **PROPAGATION** Sow seed in containers in a cold frame as soon as ripe.
- **PESTS AND DISEASES** Susceptible to damage by slugs and snails.

Semiaquilegia ecalcarata

S. ecalcarata ▣ Short-lived, erect perennial with long-stalked, 2-ternate, mid-green leaves, to 8cm (3in) long, the leaflets purple beneath. In early summer, produces loose, corymb-like panicles of pendent, open bell-shaped, dusky pink to deep purple-red flowers, 1.5cm (½in) long. ↕30cm (12in), ↔ 20cm (8in). W. China. ❄❄❄

SEMIARUNDINARIA

GRAMINEAE/POACEAE

Genus of 10–20 species of tall, upright bamboos from deciduous woodland, upland slopes, and ravines in China and Japan. They generally have running rhizomes, but form dense clumps in cool climates. Smooth, cylindrical canes, with short-lived cane-sheaths, some with upper internodes grooved or flattened, produce 3–7 branches at each node, with tessellated, narrowly lance-shaped leaves. Grow in a woodland garden, as a specimen plant, or as an informal hedge.

- **HARDINESS** Fully hardy to frost hardy.
- **CULTIVATION** Grow in moderately fertile, humus-rich, moist but well-drained soil in full sun or light dappled shade.

Semiarundinaria fastuosa

- **PROPAGATION** Divide, or cut up sections of youngest rhizomes, in spring.
- **PESTS AND DISEASES** Young shoots may be damaged by slugs.

S. fastuosa see *Brachystachyum densiflorum*
S. fastuosa ▣ syn. *Arundinaria fastuosa* (Narihira bamboo). Tall, erect, tree-like bamboo, either with spreading rhizomes or forming dense clumps. The shining, mid-green canes are striped purple-brown, markedly so when young; cane-sheaths open to reveal polished, deep red-purple interiors. Bears lance-shaped, glossy, mid-green leaves, 12–15cm (5–6in) long, mainly on the upper part of the plant. ↕ to 7m (22ft), ↔ 2m (6ft) or more. Japan. ❄❄❄
S. tootsik see *Sinobambusa tootsik.*

▷**Seminole bread** see *Zamia pumila*
▷***Sempervivella sedoides*** see *Rosularia sedoides*

SEMPERVIVUM

Houseleek

CRASSULACEAE

Genus of about 40 species of dense, mat-forming, evergreen succulent perennials, mainly from mountains in Europe and Asia. Rosettes of thick, pointed leaves, often with bristle-fringed margins, are sometimes covered with a web of white hairs. Erect stems bear flat, branching, terminal, panicle-like cymes of star-shaped, white, yellow, red, or purple flowers in summer. The rosettes die after flowering, but are replaced by offsets on lateral runners. Numerous cultivars of hybrid origin are available. Grow in a rock garden, scree bed, wall crevice, or trough, or in pots in an alpine house.

- **HARDINESS** Fully hardy.
- **CULTIVATION** Grow in full sun in poor to moderately fertile, sharply drained soil, with added grit. Softly hairy species resent winter wet and are best grown in an alpine house in areas with wet winters. In an alpine house, grow in a mix of equal parts loam-based potting compost (JI No.2) and grit. See also pp.48–49.
- **PROPAGATION** Sow seed in containers in a cold frame in spring. Root offsets in spring or early summer.
- **PESTS AND DISEASES** May be affected by *Endophyllum sempervivi* (rust).

S. arachnoideum ▣ (Cobweb houseleek). Mat-forming, rosetted succulent with fleshy, obovate, mid-green to red

Sempervivum arachnoideum

Sempervivum ciliosum

leaves, to 1cm (½in) long. The rosettes, 1–2.5cm (½–1in) across, are covered in cobwebs of white hairs. In summer, produces flat cymes, to 2.5cm (1in) across, of reddish pink flowers on leafy stems. ↕8cm (3in), ↔ 30cm (12in). Europe (Alps, Apennines, Carpathians). ❄❄❄

S. arboreum see *Aeonium arboreum.*

S. balsamiferum see *Aeonium balsamiferum.*

S. ciliosum ▣ Mat-forming succulent with very hairy rosettes, to 5cm (2in) across, of incurved, inversely lance-shaped, grey-green leaves, 2.5cm (1in) long, convex on both surfaces. Bears flat, compact cymes, 2.5cm (1in) across, of greenish yellow flowers in summer. Best in an alpine house. ↕8cm (3in), ↔ 30cm (12in). Former Yugoslavia, Bulgaria, N.W. Greece. ❄❄❄

***S.* 'Commander Hay'.** Succulent, similar to *S. tectorum*, bearing rosettes, to 10cm (4in) across, of inversely lance-shaped, glossy, deep red-purple leaves, to 4cm (1½in) long, with mid-green tips. In summer, produces cymes, 5–10cm (2–4in) across, of greenish red flowers. ↕10cm (4in), ↔ 30cm (12in). ❄❄❄

S

Sempervivum giuseppii

S. complanatum see *Aeonium tabuliforme.*

S. giuseppii ▣ Vigorous, mat-forming succulent with rosettes, 2.5–3.5cm (1–1½in) across, of ovate, pea-green leaves, 1.5cm (½in) long, hairy when young, and dark-spotted at the tips. Red flowers are produced in cymes, 3.5cm (1½in) across, in summer. ↕8cm (3in), ↔ 30cm (12in). Spain. ❄❄❄

S. grandiflorum. Variable, mat-forming succulent bearing rosettes, 5–10cm (2–4in) across, of sharp-pointed, oblong-triangular, very hairy, dark green leaves, 2.5–5cm (1–2in) long, which are often tipped with brown. In summer, yellow flowers, stained purple at the bases, are produced in cymes 10cm (4in) across. Prefers acid soil. ↕10cm (4in), ↔ 30cm (12in). Europe (W. and C. Alps). ❄❄❄

S. haworthii see *Aeonium haworthii.*

S. helveticum see *S. montanum.*

S. hirtum see *Jovibarba hirta.*

S. masferreri see *Aeonium sedifolium.*

S. montanum ▣ syn. *S. helveticum.* Vigorous, mat-forming succulent with clustered, open rosettes, 2–8cm (¾–3in) across, of sharp-pointed, inversely lance-shaped, finely hairy, fleshy, dull, dark

Sempervivum montanum

Sempervivum tectorum

green leaves, to 1cm (½in) long. Red-purple flowers are borne in loose cymes, to 6cm (2½in) across, in summer. Hybridizes freely. ↕10cm (4in), ↔ 30cm (12in) or more. C. Europe. ❄❄❄

S. nobile see *Aeonium nobile.*

S. patens see *Jovibarba heuffelii.*

S. soboliferum see *Jovibarba sobolifera.*

S. tectorum ▣ (Common houseleek). Mat-forming succulent with open rosettes, to 10cm (4in) across, of thick, obovate to narrowly oblong, bristle-tipped, blue-green leaves, to 4cm (1½in) long, often suffused red-purple. In summer, bears cymes, 5–10cm (2–4in) across, of red-purple flowers on upright, hairy stems. ↕15cm (6in), ↔ 50cm (20in). Mountains of S. Europe. ❄❄❄

▷**Seneca** see *Polygala*

SENECIO

ASTERACEAE/COMPOSITAE

Large genus of more than 1,000 species of annuals, biennials, herbaceous perennials, climbers, shrubs, and small trees, some of them succulent. They are found worldwide in habitats ranging from mountains to sea shores, and in dry to moist soils. Basal leaves are entire or variably lobed, sometimes white or silver; stem leaves, if present, are smaller and alternate. The flowerheads, either solitary or borne in corymbs, are usually terminal and daisy-like (some species lack ray-florets), and yellow, white, red, blue, or purple, sometimes orange; they mainly have yellow, sometimes purple disc-florets. Use annuals for bedding, or in containers; grow small perennials in a scree bed or rock garden, and tall ones in a border or wild garden. In frost-prone areas, grow tender species in a cool or temperate greenhouse. All parts may cause severe discomfort if ingested.

• **HARDINESS** Fully hardy to frost tender.

• **CULTIVATION** For ease of reference, cultivation has been grouped as follows:

1. Grow in poor, gritty, sharply drained soil in full sun.

2. Grow in moderately fertile, well-drained soil in full sun.

3. Grow in moderately fertile, moist to boggy soil (such as in a bog garden) in full sun or partial shade.

4. Under glass, grow in a mix of 2 parts loam-based potting compost (JI No.1) and 1 part each leaf mould and grit in full light with good ventilation. When in growth, water moderately and apply a balanced liquid fertilizer monthly. Maintain moderate humidity. Keep just moist in winter. Outdoors, in frost-free areas, grow as for group 2.

5. Under glass, grow in a mix of 2 parts loam-based potting compost (JI No.1) and 1 part each leaf mould and grit in full light with good ventilation. When in growth, water moderately, maintain low humidity, and apply a half-strength balanced liquid fertilizer monthly. Keep just moist in winter at a minimum of 7–10°C (45–50°F). Outdoors, in frost-free areas, grow as for group 1, in neutral to slightly alkaline soil.

Pruning group 8 or 9 for shrubs; group 11, after flowering, for climbers.

• **PROPAGATION** Sow seed in spring: for cultivation groups 2, 4, and 5 at 19–24°C (66–75°F); for groups 1 and 3 in containers in a cold frame. Divide groups 1 and 3 and *S. doronicum* in spring; take basal cuttings in early spring. Divide groups 4 and 5 as growth begins; take softwood cuttings in early summer or semi-ripe cuttings in mid- or late summer. Take semi-ripe cuttings of silver and white forms of group 2 in mid- or late summer.

• **PESTS AND DISEASES** Prone to rust, particularly *S. cineraria* and its cultivars. Whiteflies, aphids, and red spider mites may be a problem under glass.

S. abrotanifolius. Evergreen subshrub with spreading or erect, hairless or downy stems, and 2- or 3-pinnatisect, glossy, dark green leaves, to 8cm (3in) long, the upper leaves less divided. From midsummer to early autumn, bears yellow to orange-scarlet flowerheads, to 4cm (1½in) across, singly or in few-flowered corymbs. Cultivation group 1. ↕15–45cm (6–18in), ↔ 30cm (12in). Mountains of C. and E. Europe. ❄❄❄

S. articulatus (Candle plant). Erect, perennial succulent with cylindrical, jointed, fleshy, grey-veined, silvery blue stems, each segment to 15cm (6in) long. Bears ovate, 3- to 5-lobed, stalked, blue-green leaves, to 5cm (2in) long. Yellow flowerheads, 1cm (½in) across, are

Senecio articulatus 'Variegatus'

SENECIO

Senecio cineraria 'Cirrus'

Senecio confusus

Senecio grandifolius

Senecio pulcher

borne in small corymbs from spring to autumn. Cultivation group 5. ↕ to 60cm (24in), ↔ indefinite. South Africa. ❀ (min. 7°C/45°F). **'Variegatus'** ■ has bold, pink or cream marks and shading on the leaves and flowerheads.
S. bicolor* subsp. *cineraria see *S. cineraria.*
S. bidwillii see *Brachyglottis bidwillii.*
S. candicans see *S. cineraria.*
S. cineraria, syn. *Cineraria maritima, S. bicolor* subsp. *cineraria, S. candicans, S. maritimus.* Mound-forming, evergreen subshrub or shrub, usually grown as an annual, with ovate to lance-shaped or elliptic, shallowly to deeply pinnatisect or pinnate, felted, silvery grey leaves, to 15cm (6in) long. Loose corymbs of mustard-yellow flowerheads, to 2.5cm (1in) across, are borne in midsummer, in the second year after sowing. Cultivation group 2. Dead-head regularly. ↕↔ to 60cm (24in). W. and C. Mediterranean. ❄❄. Dwarf cultivars, with a range of foliage characteristics, are popular. **'Alice'** has deeply cut, silver-stained white leaves; ↕↔ 30cm (12in). **'Cirrus'** ■ produces elliptic, finely toothed or lobed, silvery green to white leaves; ↕↔ 30cm (12in). **'Silver Dust'** ■ has deeply pinnatisect, lacy, almost white leaves; ↕↔ 30cm (12in). **'White Diamond'** has deeply divided, almost oak-like, grey-white leaves; usually grown as a perennial; ↕ 30–40cm (12–16in), ↔ 30cm (12in).
S. clivorum see *Ligularia dentata.*
S. compactus see *Brachyglottis compacta.*
S. confusus ■ syn. *Pseudogynoxys chenopodioides.* Moderately bushy, evergreen, twining climber with lance-shaped to narrowly ovate, thick, toothed, mid-green leaves, to 8cm (3in) long. Fragrant flowerheads, 5cm (2in) across, are bright orange fading to red, and are profusely borne in small, axillary and terminal corymbs, mainly in summer. Cultivation group 4. ↕ to 6m (20ft) or more. Mexico to Honduras. ❀ (min. 7–10°C/45–50°F)
S. cruentus see *Pericallis* x *hybrida.*
S. doronicum (Leopard's bane ragwort). Clump-forming, deciduous perennial with upright, sometimes branched stems and ovate to lance-shaped or elliptic, toothed, dark green leaves, to 25cm (10in) long, cobweb-hairy beneath. Bright orange-yellow to rich yellow flowerheads, to 6cm (2½in) across, are borne singly or in loose corymbs in early and midsummer. Cultivation group 2. ↕ 15–40cm (6–16in), ↔ 30cm (12in). Mountainous regions of C. and S. Europe. ❄❄❄
***S.* Dunedin Hybrids** see *Brachyglottis* Dunedin Group.
S. elaeagnifolius see *Brachyglottis elaeagnifolia.*
S. elegans. Erect annual with branched stems and oblong-ovate, pinnately lobed or coarsely toothed, deep green leaves, to 8cm (3in) long. In summer, bears corymbs of flowerheads, 2.5cm (1in) across, with yellow disc-florets and purple, reddish purple, or occasionally white ray-florets. Cultivation group 2. ↕ to 60cm (24in), ↔ to 35cm (14in). South Africa. ❄❄
S. grandifolius ■ syn. *Telanthophora grandifolia.* Evergreen shrub, rounded when young, but becoming erect with age, with very thick, sparsely branched, purple-downy stems bearing ovate to elliptic, usually wavy-lobed, sometimes toothed, semi-lustrous, mid- to deep green leaves, 20–45cm (8–18in) long, downy, rust-brown beneath. Small, 5-rayed, bright yellow flowerheads, to 1cm (½in) across, are produced in dense, widely domed corymbs, to 30cm (12in) across, mainly in winter. Cultivation group 4. ↕↔ 2–3m (6–10ft), sometimes more. Mexico. ❀ (min. 7–10°C/45–50°F)
S. greyi see *Brachyglottis greyi.*
***S. greyi* of gardens** see *Brachyglottis* Dunedin Group.
S. hectoris see *Brachyglottis hectoris.*
S. huntii see *Brachyglottis huntii.*
S.* x *hybridus see *Pericallis* x *hybrida.*
S. laxifolius see *Brachyglottis laxifolia.*
***S. laxifolius* of gardens** see *Brachyglottis* Dunedin Group.
S. leucostachys see *S. viravira.*
S. macroglossus (Cape ivy, Natal ivy). Evergreen, twining climber with semi-succulent growth at first, then eventually woody stems, which branch moderately. Triangular to spear-shaped, mid-green leaves, to 8cm (3in) long, have 3–5 pointed lobes. Flowerheads, 5–6cm (2–2½in) across, with white to pale yellow ray-florets, are usually borne singly, sometimes in twos or threes, in summer and winter. Cultivation group 4, with shade from midday sun. ↕ to 3m (10ft), sometimes more. Zimbabwe to Mozambique, E. South Africa. ❀ (min. 5–7°C/41–45°F). **'Variegatus'** ■ has foliage with irregular, cream to light yellow margins.
S. maritimus see *S. cineraria.*
S. mikanioides, syn. *Delairea odorata* (German ivy, Parlour ivy). Evergreen, twining climber with succulent young stems, woody when mature. Fleshy, bright green leaves, 8–10cm (3–4in) across, are triangular to triangular-ovate, with 5–7 broad, pointed lobes. Small, groundsel-like yellow flowerheads, 8mm (⅜in) across, without ray-florets, are

Senecio cineraria 'Silver Dust'

Senecio macroglossus 'Variegatus'

Senecio rowleyanus

S

Senecio smithii

borne in dense, axillary and terminal corymbs, 8cm (3in) across, from autumn to early winter. Cultivation group 4. ↕ to 6m (20ft). South Africa. ❁ (min. 3–5°C/37–41°F)
S. 'Moira Read' see *Brachyglottis* Dunedin Group 'Moira Read'.
S. monroi see *Brachyglottis monroi.*
S. przewalskii see *Ligularia przewalskii.*
S. pulcher ■ Erect, deciduous or semi-evergreen perennial, woolly in early growth, becoming hairless, with leathery, mid-green leaves, to 20cm (8in) long. Basal leaves are elliptic with scalloped margins; stem leaves are lance-shaped with toothed margins. In mid- and late autumn, bears solitary corymbs of carmine-purple flowerheads, 5–8cm (2–3in) across. Cultivation group 4; may survive outdoors in a sheltered, sunny site, in cool, deep, fertile soil; severe weather harms leaves and flowers. ↕ 45–60cm (18–24in), ↔ 50cm (20in). S. Brazil, Uruguay, Argentina. ❄❄
S. radicans. Mat-forming, perennial succulent with prostrate, rooting stems and cylindrical, straight or slightly curved, fleshy, glaucous, mid-green leaves, to 2.5cm (1in) long, each with a darker stripe down the middle. Solitary or paired white flowerheads, 3–5mm (⅛–¼in) across, are borne sporadically during the year. Cultivation group 5. ↕ 8–10cm (3–4in), ↔ 15–30cm (6–12in). South Africa. ❄❄
S. reinholdii see *Brachyglottis rotundifolia.*
S. reniformis see *Cremanthodium reniforme.*
S. rotundifolius see *Brachyglottis rotundifolia.*

Senecio viravira

S. rowleyanus ■ syn. *Kleinia rowleyana* (String of beads). Pendent or creeping, perennial succulent with adventitious roots on the stems and spherical, slightly pointed, mid-green leaves, to 1cm (½in) long. Bears solitary, funnel-shaped, cinnamon-scented white flowerheads, to 1cm (½in) long, with protruding brown stamens, in summer. Cultivation group 5. ↕ 60cm (24in) or more, ↔ indefinite. S.W. Africa. ❁ (min. 7–10°C/45–50°F)
S. scandens. Evergreen, twining climber, woody-based and usually bushy when mature, with ovate or narrowly triangular, almost entire to sharply toothed or lobed, bright green leaves, to 10cm (4in) long. From autumn to winter, bears yellow flowerheads, 1.5cm (½in) across, in panicle-like corymbs, 13cm (5in) across. Cultivation group 4. ↕ 2.5–5m (8–15ft). E. Asia. ❁ (min. 7°C/45°F)
S. serpens, syn. *Kleinia repens.* Shrubby, perennial succulent with semi-erect, fleshy, blue-frosted shoots, 7mm (¼in) thick. Cylindrical, fleshy, waxy, bluish grey leaves, to 3cm (1¼in) long, grooved on the upper surfaces, are crowded at the stem and branch tips. In summer, bears whitish yellow flowerheads, 1cm (½in) long, lacking ray-florets. Cultivation group 5. ↕↔ 30cm (12in). South Africa. ❁ (min. 7°C/45°F)
S. smithii ■ Vigorous, deciduous, clump-forming, woolly perennial with oblong-ovate, toothed, leathery, glossy, dark grey-green basal and stem leaves, to 30cm (12in) long. From early to late summer, stout, upright, unbranched stems bear large corymbs, 10–15cm (4–6in) across, of numerous yellow-centred white flowerheads, to 5cm (2in) across. Cultivation group 3, but best in moist soil. ↕ to 1.2m (4ft), ↔ 60cm (24in). S. Chile, W. Argentina, Falkland Islands. ❄❄❄
S. stapeliiformis see *Kleinia stapeliiformis.*
S. 'Sunshine' see *Brachyglottis* Dunedin Group 'Sunshine'.
S. tanguticus see *Sinacalia tangutica.*
S. viravira ■ syn. *S. leucostachys.* Open, spreading, evergreen subshrub with densely white-hairy shoots and deeply pinnatisect, silvery white leaves, to 8cm (3in) long, with 5–9 linear lobes that are usually further divided. Loose corymbs of small, pale yellow flowerheads, 5mm (¼in) across, without ray-florets, are produced from summer to autumn. Cultivation group 2. ↕ 60cm (24in), ↔ 1m (3ft). Argentina. ❄❄

SENNA

CAESALPINIACEAE/LEGUMINOSAE

Genus, often included in *Cassia*, of about 260 species of evergreen and deciduous trees, shrubs, and perennials from semi-desert, scrub, and savannah in dry, tropical and warm-temperate regions. Leaves are alternate and pinnate, with linear to nearly rounded leaflets. Sennas are cultivated for their yellow or rarely white, pea-like flowers, borne in terminal or axillary racemes, corymbs, or panicles. In frost-prone climates, grow in a temperate or warm greenhouse. In frost-free areas, grow in a shrub border.
• **HARDINESS** Frost tender.
• **CULTIVATION** Under glass, grow in loam-based potting compost (JI No.2) in full light and moderate humidity. In

Senna artemisioides

growth, water moderately and apply a balanced liquid fertilizer monthly; water sparingly in winter. Outdoors, grow in moist but well-drained, moderately fertile soil in full sun. Pruning group 1; may need restrictive pruning under glass.
• **PROPAGATION** Sow seed at 18–24°C (64–75°F) in spring. Divide perennials in spring. Root semi-ripe cuttings with bottom heat in summer.
• **PESTS AND DISEASES** Trouble free.

S. alata ♀ syn. *Cassia alata* (Empress candle plant). Erect to spreading, evergreen shrub or small tree. Broadly oblong to obovate, pinnate leaves, 20–75cm (8–30in) long, produce 14–28 oblong, bright green leaflets. Bears numerous bright yellow flowers, to 2.5cm (1in) across, in tall, erect, axillary racemes, 15–60cm (6–24in) long, predominantly from late summer to autumn; flowers are protected by broad, yellowish green bracts when in bud. ↕ 2–10m (6–30ft), ↔ 2–5m (6–15ft). Africa to S.E. Asia, Pacific islands, tropical America. ❁ (min. 5–7°C/41–45°F)
S. artemisioides ■ syn. *Cassia artemisioides* (Silver cassia). Erect to spreading, evergreen shrub with pinnate leaves, 3–6cm (1¼–2½in) long, composed of 6–8 short, narrowly linear, thickly downy, grey-green leaflets. Stems are covered in ash-white hairs. Produces axillary racemes, to 8cm (3in) long, of 4–12 fragrant, pale to rich yellow flowers, to 1cm (½in) across, intermittently throughout the year. ↕ 1–2m (3–6ft), ↔ 1m (3ft). Australia (Northern Territory, South Australia, New South Wales). ❁ (min. 10–13°C/50–55°F)
S. corymbosa ■ ♀ syn. *Cassia corymbosa.* Erect to spreading, evergreen shrub or small tree producing pinnate, yellowish-green leaves, 40–90cm (16–36in) long, with 6–8 oblong-lance-shaped leaflets. Axillary corymbs, 10cm (4in) across, of up to 20 golden yellow flowers, to 2cm (¾in) across, are borne in late summer. ↕ 2–4m (6–12ft), ↔ 1.5–3m (5–10ft). Argentina, Uruguay. ❁ (min. 5–7°C/41–45°F)
S. didymobotrya ♀ syn. *Cassia didymobotrya.* Erect to spreading, evergreen shrub or small tree with pinnate, mid-green leaves, 10–50cm (4–20in) long, composed of 16–32 elliptic-obovate leaflets. Numerous golden yellow flowers, to 3cm (1¼in) across, with blackish brown bracts covering the buds, are borne in tall, erect, terminal or axillary racemes, 15–60cm (6–24in) long, mainly from late summer to autumn. ↕ 2.5m (8ft), ↔ 1.5–3m (5–10ft). Tropical Africa; naturalized in India, Malaysia. ❁ (min. 13°C/55°F)
S. x floribunda (*S. multiglandulosa* x *S. septentrionalis*) syn. *Cassia corymbosa* var. *plurijuga*, *C.* x *floribunda.* Many-branched, evergreen or deciduous shrub with pinnate, mid-green leaves, 6–8cm (2½–3in) long, comprising 12 oblong-elliptic leaflets. From summer to winter, often-branched, axillary racemes, 10cm (4in) long, produce up to 20 rich yellow flowers, to 2cm (¾in) across. ↕ 1–3m (3–10ft), ↔ 1–2.5m (3–8ft). Garden origin. ❁ (min. 7°C/45°F)

Senna corymbosa

S

S. siamea ♀ syn. *Cassia siamea* (Kassod tree). Fast-growing, evergreen tree with an open habit and hairless young stems. Pinnate, deep yellow-green leaves, 10–35cm (4–14in) long, each have 14–24 narrowly elliptic to oblong leaflets. Dense, erect, terminal, corymb-like panicles, 15–35cm (6–14in) long, each bearing 10–60 yellow flowers, to 2cm (¾in) across, are produced from spring to summer. ↕ 10m (30ft), ↔ 7m (22ft). Indonesia, Malay Peninsula. ❀ (min. 16–18°C/61–64°F)

S. sturtii, syn. *Cassia sturtii*. Spreading or rounded, evergreen shrub. Pinnate, mid-green leaves, 4–5cm (1½–2in) long, have 4–16 linear to elliptic leaflets. In early summer, produces short, axillary racemes, to 10cm (4in) across, each bearing 4 or 5 yellow flowers, 1cm (½in) across. ↕ 1–2m (3–6ft), ↔ 1–1.5m (3–5ft). Australia. ❀ (min. 10°C/50°F)

▷ **Senna,**
Bladder see *Colutea, C. arborescens*
Scorpion see *Coronilla emerus*
▷ **Sensitive plant** see *Mimosa pudica*
▷ **September bells** see *Rothmannia globosa*

SEQUOIA

TAXODIACEAE

Genus of one species of very tall, fast-growing, monoecious, evergreen, coniferous tree from coastal forest in California and Oregon, USA. Sequoia has thick, soft bark, whorled branches when young, and yew-like foliage. It is useful where a tall, evergreen tree is needed quickly. Sequoia thrives in climates with cool, damp summers, and is tolerant of pollution and wind. It is one of the few conifers that will coppice, or make new shoots from the base if cut down. The genus contains the tallest tree and also some of the oldest trees in the world.

- **HARDINESS** Fully hardy.
- **CULTIVATION** Grow in moderately fertile, moist but well-drained soil in full sun to light dappled shade.
- **PROPAGATION** Sow seed in containers in a cold frame in spring. Root softwood cuttings in summer, or semi-ripe cuttings in late summer or autumn.
- **PESTS AND DISEASES** Trouble free.

S. sempervirens ▣ ◊ (Coastal redwood). Columnar-conical tree with horizontal or downcurved branches, thick, fissured, soft, red-brown bark, and mid-green, later red-brown shoots with decurrent leaf bases. The hard, linear, sharp-pointed, deep green leaves, 2cm (¾in) long, silvery white beneath, are 2-ranked. On very strong shoots, the leaves are scale-like. Cones are spherical-cylindrical: the terminal, mid-green female cones, 3cm (1¼in) long, ripen in their first autumn; the tiny, terminal and axillary, brownish green male cones are to 4mm (⅛in) long. ↕ to 112m (365ft), but mainly 20–30m (70–100ft), ↔ 6–9m (20–28ft). USA (coastal California and Oregon). ✻✻✻. **'Adpressa'** has short, broad leaves, to 1cm (½in) long, creamy white when young and lying flat along the shoots; ↕ 6–9m (20–28ft), ↔ 4–6m (12–20ft). **'Pendula'** produces arching branches with pendent branchlets. **'Prostrata'** is a dwarf cultivar, with spreading branches and broader, glaucous, dark green leaves; ↕ to 1.5m (5ft), ↔ 2–3m (6–10ft).

SEQUOIADENDRON

TAXODIACEAE

Genus of one species of monoecious, evergreen, coniferous tree from forest in the mountains of California, USA. It is related to *Sequoia* but has narrowly wedge-shaped leaves and thicker, harder bark, and cones that ripen in the second year rather than the first; it also thrives in a cooler, drier atmosphere than *Sequoia*. An excellent, but very tall specimen tree.

- **HARDINESS** Fully hardy.
- **CULTIVATION** Grow in moderately fertile, well-drained soil in full sun or light dappled shade.
- **PROPAGATION** Sow seed in containers in a cold frame in spring. Root softwood cuttings in summer, or semi-ripe cuttings in late summer.
- **PESTS AND DISEASES** Susceptible to honey fungus.

S. giganteum ▣ ◊ (Big tree, Giant redwood, Sierra redwood, Wellingtonia). Conical tree, becoming columnar, with downcurved branches, very thick, fissured, red-brown bark, and mid-green, later red-brown shoots. Awl-shaped, grey-green leaves, to 7mm (¼in) long, are arranged radially and point forwards on the shoots. Bears ovoid, mid-green female cones, 4.5cm (1¾in) long, ripening brown and persisting for several years. ↕ 25–80m (80–260ft), ↔ 7–10m (22–30ft). USA (Sierra Nevada, California). ✻✻✻. **'Pendulum'** has pendent side branches, giving a curtain-like effect, although the main shoot grows rather erratically.

SERAPIAS

Tongue orchid

ORCHIDACEAE

Genus of 6 species of deciduous, terrestrial orchids found in open, sunny sites, from Ukraine (Crimea) through the Mediterranean to the Azores. The near-spherical tubers produce linear to lance-shaped, channelled, glossy leaves, up to 15cm (6in) long, in late autumn. Between 2 and 10 typically purple-red, occasionally yellow-green, flowers emerge from prominent, upright, purple-flushed bracts in mid-spring. The sepals and petals form a forward-pointing hood, approximately 2.5cm (1in) long, above a pendent, 3-lobed lip, 2–3cm (¾–1¼in) long, with a prominent, pointed, often hairy, apex. In frost-prone, wet climates, grow in an alpine house; in warmer areas, grow in full sun in a rock garden, in a scree or raised bed, or in short grass.

- **HARDINESS** Frost hardy to frost tender.
- **CULTIVATION** Outdoors, grow in a well-drained scree bed, raised bed, or in thin, short turf in full sun or partial shade. Protect from excessive summer rain. In an alpine house, grow in terrestrial orchid compost in full light. Water moderately during the growing season; keep dry and frost-free when dormant. See also p.46.
- **PROPAGATION** Separate tubers in late summer.
- **PESTS AND DISEASES** Susceptible to slugs and snails outdoors and aphids under glass.

S. cordigera ▣ (Heart-lipped tongue orchid). Terrestrial orchid with 2–3 tubers, one stalkless and the others on short runners, each bearing 3–8 lance-

Sequoia sempervirens (inset: leaf and cone detail)

Sequoiadendron giganteum

Serapias cordigera

S

Serapias neglecta

shaped leaves. The leaf bases and stem bracts are typically spotted or veined purple. Spikes, 25–45cm (10–18in) high, bear 4–10 flowers, each with a deep purple to maroon hood and a heart-shaped, dark purple, hairy lip with 2 purple-black ridges at its base. ↕45cm (18in), ↔ 20cm (8in). S. and W. Europe. ✲

S. lingua. Terrestrial orchid, often colony-forming, with 2–5 tubers, one stalkless, the others on short runners, each bearing 3–6 linear to lance-shaped leaves. Spikes, 10–30cm (4–12in) tall, bear 2–8 flowers, each with a green to purple-red hood and an ovate, dark purple (rarely yellow) lip with a solitary, purple-black ridge at its base. ↕30cm (12in), ↔ 15cm (6in). Mediterranean, S.W. Europe. ✲✲

S. neglecta ▣ Terrestrial orchid with 2 stalkless tubers bearing 4–10 lance-shaped leaves. Spikes, 10–30cm (4–12in) tall, produce 2–8 flowers, each with a red-purple, sometimes yellow-green, hood and a heart-shaped, yellow to orange, hairy lip with red or purple side lobes and 2 purple-black ridges at its base. ↕30cm (12in), ↔ 20cm (8in). C. Mediterranean. ✲

S

SERIPHIDIUM

ASTERACEAE/COMPOSITAE

Genus of 60–130 species of annuals, herbaceous or evergreen perennials, and mainly evergreen subshrubs from dry steppes, chaparral, and rocky or stony ground in Europe, N. Africa, temperate Asia, and North America. They are grown for their silver or grey, alternate, simple, pinnatisect, often aromatic leaves. Yellow to purple flowerheads, consisting only of disc-florets, are borne in terminal or axillary spikes, panicles, or racemes in summer or autumn. Grow in a shrub border. Tolerant of neglect.

- **HARDINESS** Fully hardy to half hardy.
- **CULTIVATION** Grow in poor to moderately fertile, dry, sharply drained soil in full sun. Pruning group 9.
- **PROPAGATION** Sow seed in containers in a cold frame in spring. Root semi-ripe cuttings in late summer, with bottom heat.
- **PESTS AND DISEASES** Trouble free.

S. nutans, syn. *Artemisia nutans.* Woody-based, evergreen perennial producing 2- or 3-pinnatisect, aromatic, silvery grey leaves, 5–10cm (2–4in) long, with small, linear lobes. In late summer and early autumn, bears pale yellow flowerheads, 6mm (¼in) across, in dense, leafy, pyramidal panicles, to 12cm (5in) long. ↕ to 1m (3ft), ↔ 60cm (24in). S.E. Russia. ✲✲✲

S. tridentatum ▣ syn. *Artemisia tridentata* (Sagebrush). Woody-based, evergreen perennial or spreading sub-shrub with a short trunk or few stems, white-woolly at first, becoming pale brown as bark forms. Densely clustered, wedge-shaped, aromatic, silvery grey-downy leaves, 1–4cm (½–1½in) long, often have 3-toothed tips. In mid-autumn, bears feathery, greyish white or yellow flowerheads, to 4mm (⅛in) across, in slender panicles, to 45cm (18in) long. ↕↔ to 2.5m (8ft). USA (S. California). ✲✲✲ (borderline)

Seriphidium tridentatum

SERISSA

RUBIACEAE

Genus of one species of small, evergreen shrub from moist, open woodland in S.E. Asia. Its leaves are simple, borne in opposite pairs, and foetid when crushed. Small, funnel-shaped flowers, with tubular calyces and 4–6 spreading petal lobes, are borne singly or in clusters in summer. Where temperatures fall below 7°C (45°F), grow in a temperate greenhouse, mainly as a foliage plant. In warmer areas, grow at the base of a house wall, in a shrub border, or as a low hedge.

- **HARDINESS** Frost tender.
- **CULTIVATION** Under glass, grow in loam-based potting compost (JI No.2) in full light with shade from hot sun. When in growth, water moderately and apply a balanced liquid fertilizer monthly; water sparingly in winter. Outdoors, grow in moderately fertile, moist but well-drained soil in full sun. Shelter from cold, drying winds. Pruning group 9. Trim hedges after flowering or in late winter.
- **PROPAGATION** Root softwood cuttings in spring or early summer, or semi-ripe cuttings in late summer, both with bottom heat. Layer in spring.
- **PESTS AND DISEASES** Scale insects may be a problem under glass.

S. foetida, syn. *S. japonica.* Wiry-stemmed, eventually domed, bushy shrub producing crowded, tiny, ovate, leathery, deep green leaves, to 2cm (¾in) long. In summer, pink buds open to star-shaped white flowers, to 1.5cm (½in) across. ↕30–60cm (12–24in), ↔ 30–75cm (12–30in). S.E. Asia. ❀ (min. 7°C/45°F). **'Flore Pleno'** is smaller, with double flowers; ↕ to 45cm (18in), ↔ 30cm (12in). **'Variegata'** has leaves with cream margins. **'Variegated Pink'** has cream-margined foliage and bears a profusion of pink flowers.

S. japonica see *S. foetida.*

SERRATULA

Saw-wort

ASTERACEAE/COMPOSITAE

Genus of 70 species of perennials growing in dry, grassy places or roadsides from Europe and N. Africa to E. Asia. Generally clump-forming or rhizomatous, they have ovate to elliptic or lance-shaped, simple to deeply pinnatisect, alternate, mid-green to dark green leaves. The flowerheads, borne in panicles in summer and autumn, consist of a bell- or urn-shaped to cylindrical involucre containing a cluster of elongated, tubular, purple or pinkish purple (rarely white to yellow) florets, usually with protruding styles. Grow the smaller species in a rock garden and the taller ones in a border or in grass.

- **HARDINESS** Fully hardy.
- **CULTIVATION** Grow in well-drained soil in full sun or partial shade.
- **PROPAGATION** Sow seed in containers in a cold frame in autumn or spring. Divide in autumn or spring.
- **PESTS AND DISEASES** Powdery mildew may be a problem.

S. coronata. Spreading perennial with creeping, woody rhizomes and erect stems bearing ovate to elliptic, pinnatisect, dark green leaves, 10–40cm (4–16in) long, with 3–8 pairs of oblong, sharply toothed lobes. Purple flowerheads, 3–4cm (1¼–1½in) across, each with a bell-shaped involucre, are borne from late summer to mid-autumn. ↕30–140cm (1–4½ft), ↔ to 1m (3ft) or more. N.E. Asia. ✲✲✲

S. seoanei ▣ syn. *S. shawii* of gardens. Clump-forming perennial with erect stems bearing ovate to lance-shaped, pinnatisect, dark green leaves, to 10cm (4in) long, with 2–7 pairs of lance-shaped, sharply toothed lobes. Pinkish purple flowerheads, 1.5cm (½in) across, each with a cylindrical, purple-flushed involucre, are borne from late summer to late autumn. ↕ to 50cm (20in),

Serratula seoanei

↔ to 20cm (8in). S.W. France, N.W. Spain, N. Portugal. ❄❄❄
***S. shawii* of gardens** see *S. seoanei*.
S. tinctoria. Clump-forming perennial with erect stems bearing ovate to lance-shaped, dark green leaves, 10–25cm (4–10in) long. Leaves are very variable, ranging from toothed to pinnatisect, with up to 7 pairs of oblong to lance-shaped, sharply toothed lobes. From late summer to early autumn, bears purple flowerheads, 1.5–2cm (½–¾in) across, each with a cylindrical, purple-flushed involucre. ↕ to 1m (3ft), ↔ to 40cm (16in). Eurasia, N. Africa. ❄❄❄

SERRURIA

PROTEACEAE

Genus, related to *Protea*, of about 55 species of evergreen shrubs from dry heathland scrub in South Africa. They have alternate, usually finely divided leaves, and bear dense heads of small, 4-petalled flowers from early spring to autumn, surrounded in *S. florida* by showy, petal-like bracts. In frost-prone areas, grow in a temperate greenhouse. In warmer areas, grow in a shrub border or at the base of a warm, sunny wall.
• **HARDINESS** Frost tender, but may survive short spells at about 0°C (32°F).
• **CULTIVATION** Under glass, grow in 1 part loam-based potting compost (JI No.1) and 3 parts 50/50 mix of perlite and peat (or coir) in full light, with good ventilation. During the growing season, water moderately; after the first year, apply a half-strength phosphate-free liquid fertilizer monthly. Water sparingly in winter. Outdoors, grow in poor to moderately fertile, well-drained, neutral to slightly acid soil in full sun. May become chlorotic if deficient in magnesium. Pruning group 1; may need restrictive pruning under glass.
• **PROPAGATION** Sow seed singly in pots at 16–21°C (61–70°F) as soon as ripe or in spring. Root semi-ripe cuttings in late summer, with bottom heat.
• **PESTS AND DISEASES** Trouble free.

S. florida ▣ (Blushing bride). Airy shrub with erect, purple-tinged branches bearing pinnate or 2-pinnate, greyish green leaves, 4–6cm (1½–2½in) long, with almost cylindrical, sharp-pointed leaflets. From spring to autumn, bears salmon-pink flowerheads, 2–2.5cm (¾–1in) across, each with a cup-shaped ring of pink-tinted white bracts. ↕ 1.5–2m (5–6ft), ↔ 1–1.5m (3–5ft). South Africa (Western Cape, Eastern Cape). ❄ (min. 7–10°C/45–50°F)

▷**Serviceberry**
Alder-leaved see *Amelanchier alnifolia*
Allegheny see *Amelanchier laevis*
▷**Service tree** see *Sorbus domestica*
▷**Service tree of Fontainebleau** see *Sorbus latifolia*

SESBANIA syn. DAUBENTONIA

LEGUMINOSAE/PAPILIONACEAE

Genus of about 50 species of short-lived, evergreen perennials, shrubs, and small trees found on streambanks and on moist soils in tropical and subtropical regions worldwide. Sesbanias are cultivated for their showy, pea-like flowers, borne in loose racemes from the leaf axils in summer. The leaves are alternate and pinnate, with many leaflets, each leaf terminating in a short extension of the axis. In frost-prone areas, grow in a cool to warm greenhouse, or in a conservatory. In warmer areas, grow in a shrub border, or at the base of a warm, sunny wall.
• **HARDINESS** Frost tender, but a few species, including *S. punicea*, may survive temperatures around 0°C (32°F), if wood has been well ripened in summer.
• **CULTIVATION** Under glass, grow in loam-based potting compost (JI No.2) in full light. In growth, water freely and apply a balanced liquid fertilizer monthly. Water sparingly in winter. Outdoors, grow in moderately fertile, moist but well-drained soil in full sun. Pruning group 9.
• **PROPAGATION** Sow seed at 15–19°C (59–66°F) in spring. Root semi-ripe cuttings in late summer, with bottom heat.
• **PESTS AND DISEASES** Prone to red spider mites and whiteflies under glass.

S. punicea ♀ syn. *Daubentonia punicea*. Erect to spreading, large shrub or small tree. Pinnate leaves, 20–30cm (8–12in) long, have 6–20 pairs of oblong, mid- to deep green leaflets. In summer, bears pea-like, red-purple flowers, 2cm (¾in) across, in racemes to 10cm (4in) long. ↕ 2–4m (6–12ft), ↔ 1.5–2.5m (5–8ft). S. Brazil, N.E. Argentina, Uruguay. ❄ (min. 5°C/41°F)

SESELI

Moon carrot

APIACEAE/UMBELLIFERAE

Genus of about 100 species of biennials and herbaceous perennials from grasslands and rocky or mountainous areas in Europe and N. Asia, grown mainly for their umbels of white or pink flowers and finely divided foliage. They have solid stems with fibrous remains of old leaf-stalks at their bases. Mid- to dark green leaves are 1- to 4-pinnate or 1- to 3-ternate, with usually linear or thread-like (rarely oblong or ovate) lobes. There may be up to 15 bracts, sometimes none, and 5–12 bracteoles. In summer, bears compound umbels of 5-petalled, occasionally lobed flowers, with broad white petals, often tinged pink; the calyx is absent or reduced to small teeth. The fruit is oblong to ellipsoid or ovoid, slightly compressed, and pale to mid-brown. Grow in a border or rock garden.
• **HARDINESS** Fully hardy.
• **CULTIVATION** Grow in moderately fertile, well-drained soil in full sun. Although tolerant of most soil types, they usually grow best in alkaline soils.
• **PROPAGATION** Sow seed in containers in a cold frame as soon as ripe; prick out into deep pots as soon as possible to avoid damage to the tap root.
• **PESTS AND DISEASES** Prone to slug and snail damage.

S. dichotomum. Upright, downy, herbaceous perennial with 2-pinnate, minutely hairy, mid-green leaves, 3–15cm (1¼–6in) long, with narrowly linear leaflets. 5–7 rayed umbels, to 2cm (¾in) across, bear white flowers, 2–4mm (1/16–⅛in) across, in summer, then ovoid, pale to mid-brown fruit, to 3mm (⅛in) long. ↕ 80–100cm (32–39in), ↔ 30–40cm (12–16in). Ukraine (Crimea), Georgia (Caucasus). ❄❄❄
S. gummiferum ▣ Upright biennial or variable herbaceous perennial with stout stems covered in fine, downy hairs, and 2- or 3-pinnate, ovate-oblong, silvery hairy, glaucous green leaves, to 20cm (8in) long, with linear to linear-oblong lobes that are slightly wedge-shaped at the bases. Hairy-stalked umbels, to 15cm (6in) across, bear white flowers, some-times tinged pink or red, in summer, followed by oblong, pale to mid-brown fruit, 3mm (⅛in) long. ↕ 80–100cm (32–39in), ↔ 30–50cm (12–20in). Ukraine (Crimea), Turkey, Greece (including Crete). ❄❄❄
S. montanum. Upright, hairless herbaceous perennial with 2- or 3-pinnate, glaucous to dark green leaves, 20–40cm (8–16in) long, with linear to obovate lobes. White flowers, often pink in bud, with conspicuous pink stamens, are borne in umbels, 2–4cm (¾–1½in) across, in summer, then oblong-ovoid, pale to mid-brown fruit, to 4mm (⅛in) long. ↕ 40–70cm (16–28in), ↔ 20–70cm (8–28in). S.E. Europe. ❄❄❄

SESLERIA

GRAMINEAE/POACEAE

Genus of 33 species of tufted or clump-forming, evergreen, perennial grasses found mainly in damp or dry grasslands in the hills and mountains of Europe. They bear narrow, usually linear leaves and dense, spherical to cylindrical, spike-like panicles of flowers. Cultivated

Serruria florida

Seseli gummiferum

S

Sesleria nitida

mainly for their colourful foliage, they are suitable for the front of a herbaceous or mixed border, for a rock garden, or for a wildflower meadow.
• **Hardiness** Fully hardy.
• **Cultivation** Grow in moderately fertile, well-drained, neutral to slightly alkaline soil in full sun or dappled shade.
• **Propagation** Sow seed in containers in a cold frame in spring or autumn. Divide in spring.
• **Pests and diseases** Trouble free.

S. albicans, syn. *S. caerulea* subsp. *calcarea* (Blue moor grass). Vigorous, densely tufted, mound-forming, evergreen perennial with round-tipped, flat or channelled, linear, pale blue-grey leaves, to 30cm (12in) long, glossy, dark green beneath. Bears bluish purple, rarely greenish white spikelets, in dense, ovoid panicles, to 1–3cm (½–1¼in) long, just above the foliage from mid-spring to early summer. ↕ to 30cm (12in), ↔ 25cm (10in). Europe. ❄❄❄
S. caerulea* subsp. *calcarea see *S. albicans*.
S. heufleriana (Balkan moor grass). Densely tufted, mound-forming, evergreen perennial with linear, bright green leaves, to 45cm (18in) long, greyish green beneath, and initially glaucous. White spikelets, ageing to deep purple, are borne in panicles 1–3cm (½–1¼in) long, from late spring to late summer. ↕ to 60cm (24in), ↔ 45cm (18in). S.E. Europe. ❄❄❄
S. nitida ■ (Nest moor grass). Densely tufted, mound-forming, evergreen perennial with smooth, linear, sharp-pointed, pale grey-green to grey-blue leaves, to 45cm (18in) long. In late spring and early summer, long stems bear panicles, 2–3cm (¾–1¼in) long, of whitish green spikelets. ↕ to 60cm (24in), ↔ 40cm (16in). C. and S. Italy. ❄❄❄

S

SETARIA
Bristle grass

GRAMINEAE/POACEAE

Genus of about 150 species of annual or perennial grasses that occur in grasslands and woodlands in the tropics, subtropics, and warm-temperate zones. The leaves of different species vary greatly in shape, from linear to lance-shaped, or elliptic-lance-shaped, or occasionally cylindrical. They have long, narrow spikes of green, sometimes purple-flushed flowers, becoming straw-coloured or sometimes yellow with age,

Setaria palmifolia 'Rubra'

usually arching well above the foliage. In frost-prone areas, grow in a temperate greenhouse; in warmer areas, grow in a mixed or herbaceous border. Setarias are also good for dried flower arrangements.
• **Hardiness** Frost hardy to half hardy.
• **Cultivation** Under glass, grow in loam-based potting compost (JI No.3) in full light; when in growth, water freely and apply a balanced liquid fertilizer every 3 weeks. Water sparingly in winter. Outdoors, grow in any well-drained soil in full sun or partial shade.
• **Propagation** For annuals, sow seed *in situ* in spring. Divide perennials in spring. Root stem cuttings with small pieces of shoot attached in spring.
• **Pests and diseases** Red spider mites, caterpillars, and rust may be a problem.

S. palmifolia (Palm grass). Upright to spreading, dense, clump-forming perennial grass with elliptic-lance-shaped, longitudinally pleated leaves, to 45cm (18in) long. Bears arching, narrow stems with bottlebrush-like spikes, 8–13cm (3–5in) long, of green to beige flowers in late summer. ↕ 2–3m (6–10ft), ↔ 1–2m (3–6ft). Tropical Asia, Africa. ❄. **'Rubra'** ■ has purple-red midribs and leaf sheaths.

▷***Setcreasea purpurea*** see *Tradescantia pallida* 'Purpurea'
▷***Setcreasea striata*** see *Callisia elegans*
▷**Sevenbark** see *Hydrangea arborescens*
▷**Seven son flower of Zhejiang** see *Heptacodium, H. miconioides*
▷**Seville orange** see *Citrus aurantium*
▷**Shadbush** see *Amelanchier, A. canadensis*
▷**Shallon** see *Gaultheria shallon*
▷**Shamrock** see *Oxalis, Trifolium repens*
▷**Shamrock pea** see *Parochetus africanus*
▷**Shasta daisy** see *Leucanthemum* x *superbum*
▷**Shaving brush plant** see *Haemanthus albiflos*
▷**Sheepberry** see *Viburnum lentago*
▷**Sheep's bit** see *Jasione*
▷**Shell flower** see *Moluccella laevis, Pistia, P. stratiotes*

SHEPHERDIA

ELAEAGNACEAE

Genus of 3 species of dioecious, evergreen or deciduous shrubs or small trees found in rocky and sandy habitats, and on streambanks, in North America. They have opposite, simple, ovate or oblong leaves and, in spring, before the leaves appear, bear short spikes or racemes of tiny, tubular, petalless flowers, each with a 4-lobed calyx. On female plants, the flowers are followed by spherical or ovoid, red or yellowish red fruits. Valued for their ornamental fruit and foliage, shepherdias are suitable for the back of a mixed or shrub border; they are particularly useful on poor, dry soils, and excellent for sites in exposed coastal regions. Male and female plants must be grown together to obtain fruit.
• **Hardiness** Fully hardy.
• **Cultivation** Grow in moderately fertile, well-drained, neutral to slightly alkaline soil in full sun. Pruning group 1.
• **Propagation** Sow seed in containers in a cold frame in autumn. Root greenwood cuttings in early summer, with gentle bottom heat.
• **Pests and diseases** Trouble free.

S. argentea (Buffalo berry). Upright, bushy, deciduous shrub, often tree-like, with oblong leaves, to 5cm (2in) long, covered in silvery scales. In spring, produces insignificant, yellow-green flowers, followed on female plants by ovoid, sour-tasting, bright red fruit, 5mm (¼in) long. ↕↔ 4m (12ft). North America. ❄❄❄

SHIBATAEA

GRAMINEAE/POACEAE

Genus of about 5 species of low-growing, clump-forming, evergreen bamboos from deciduous woodland and valley slopes in China and Japan. They have slowly spreading rhizomes and slender canes, slightly flattened on one side and slightly bent at the nodes, creating a zigzag effect. Each node bears 2–5 short branches with narrowly ovate to elliptic, tessellated leaves. Grow for their foliage in a mixed border, a gravel planting, or a container on a patio, or, if densely planted, as ground cover.
• **Hardiness** Fully hardy.
• **Cultivation** Grow in moderately fertile, moist but well-drained or damp soil in partial shade, or in full sun where the soil stays damp in spring and summer.
• **Propagation** Divide or transplant sections of young rhizomes in spring.
• **Pests and diseases** Young shoots may be damaged by slugs.

Shibataea kumasasa

S. kumasasa ■ syn. *Sasa ruscifolia*. Evergreen, clump-forming bamboo with short-jointed, greenish brown canes and abundant long-stalked, broadly lance-shaped, taper-pointed, rich dark green leaves, 5–11cm (2–4½in) long. New shoots appear very early in spring. ↕ 0.6–1.5m (2–5ft), ↔ 60cm (24in). Japan. ❄❄❄

▷**Shield, Carolina water** see *Cabomba caroliniana*
▷**Shield fern** see *Polystichum*
  Hard see *P. aculeatum*
  Prickly see *P. aculeatum*
  Soft see *P. setiferum*
▷**Shingle plant** see *Rhaphidophora korthalsii*
▷**Shinleaf** see *Pyrola*
▷**Shoo-fly** see *Nicandra, N. physalodes*
▷**Shooting star** see *Dodecatheon, D. meadia, Thymophylla tenuiloba*

SHORTIA *syn.* SCHIZOCODON

DIAPENSIACEAE

Genus of 6 species of evergreen perennials, spreading by runners, from woodland in E. Asia, with one species from North America. The rounded, heart-shaped, or elliptic, toothed, leathery, glossy, usually dark green leaves often turn red in autumn and winter. Bell-, trumpet-, or funnel-shaped, white or deep pink flowers, with toothed or deeply fringed petals, are borne either singly or in terminal racemes, in spring. These attractive, shade-loving plants are suitable for cultivation in a rock garden, peat bed, open glade in a woodland garden, or an alpine house. They grow best in areas with cool, damp summers.
• **Hardiness** Fully hardy; without snow cover, buds may be damaged by frost.
• **Cultivation** Grow in humus-rich, leafy, moist but well-drained, acid soil in deep to partial shade. Difficult to grow in dry climates, even with frequent watering. Under glass, grow in lime-free (ericaceous) potting compost, and keep cool and well ventilated, with moderate to high humidity.
• **Propagation** Sow seed in containers in a cold frame as soon as ripe; keep

Shortia uniflora 'Grandiflora'

moist at all times. Remove small, rooted runners carefully in spring; shortias dislike root disturbance. Take basal cuttings in early summer.
• **PESTS AND DISEASES** Prone to slugs and snails outdoors; may be infested with aphids under glass.

S. galacifolia (Oconee bells). Clump-forming perennial with rounded, blunt-toothed, glossy, dark green leaves, 2–7cm (¾–3in) long, with wavy margins, turning bronze-red in autumn. In late spring, bears solitary, funnel-shaped white flowers, to 2.5cm (1in) across, often flushed pink, with toothed petals and pink calyces. ↕ 15cm (6in), ↔ 25cm (10in). E. USA. ❄❄❄
S. soldanelloides. Mat-forming perennial producing ovate to rounded, coarsely toothed, glossy, dark green leaves, 5cm (2in) long, rounded or heart-shaped at the bases. In late spring, bears narrowly trumpet-shaped, deep pink flowers, to 2.5cm (1in) across, with deeply fringed petals, usually in one-sided racemes. ↕ 10–30cm (4–12in), ↔ 25cm (10in). Japan. ❄❄❄. **var. *ilicifolia*** has smaller leaves with triangular teeth, and white or rarely pink flowers.
***S. uniflora* 'Grandiflora'** ■ Vigorous, mat-forming perennial with rounded, toothed, glossy, mid-green leaves, 2–7cm (¾–3in) long, heart-shaped at the bases and with wavy margins. In spring, bears a profusion of solitary, widely bell-shaped, shell-pink flowers, 5cm (2in) across, with toothed petals. ↕ 15cm (6in), ↔ 25cm (10in). Japan. ❄❄❄

▷**Shot plant, Indian** see *Canna*
▷**Shower tree, Golden** see *Cassia fistula*
▷**Shrimp bush** see *Justicia brandegeeana*
▷**Shrimp plant** see *Justicia brandegeeana*
▷**Shrubs** see pp.34–35

SIBIRAEA

ROSACEAE

Genus, closely related to *Spiraea*, of one species of deciduous shrub found on cliffs and in rocky places in E. Europe, Russia (Siberia), and China. The leaves are alternate (occasionally appearing whorled on short, lateral shoots), entire, linear-oblong to narrowly obovate, and mid- or blue-green. Racemes of tiny, cup-shaped, white or yellowish green flowers are produced in summer; the flowers are usually either male or female. Grow *S. laevigata* for its foliage and flowers in a mixed or shrub border.
• **HARDINESS** Fully hardy.
• **CULTIVATION** Grow in moderately fertile, well-drained, neutral to slightly alkaline soil in full sun. Pruning group 2 or 4.
• **PROPAGATION** Sow seed in containers in a cold frame in autumn or spring. Root softwood cuttings in spring or summer, with gentle bottom heat.
• **PESTS AND DISEASES** Trouble free.

S. altaiensis see *S. laevigata.*
S. laevigata, syn. *S. altaiensis.* Spreading, sparsely branched shrub with stout, purple-brown shoots and linear-oblong to narrowly obovate, mid- or blue-green leaves, to 10cm (4in) long. Tiny, cup-shaped, white or yellowish green flowers are borne in terminal racemes, to 12cm (5in) long, in early summer. ↕ 1m (3ft), ↔ 1.5m (5ft). Russia (Siberia), Balkans, W. China. ❄❄❄

SIDALCEA

False mallow, Prairie mallow

MALVACEAE

Genus of approximately 20–25 species of annuals and perennials, some rhizomatous, occurring in grassland, woodland glades, and on mountain streamsides in W. and C. North America. They form clumps of rounded to kidney-shaped, palmately lobed or toothed, mid-green basal leaves, from which arise erect, sometimes branched, stiff, flowering stems. These produce palmately lobed, mid-green leaves and long-lasting, hollyhock-like, white, pink, or purple-pink flowers in dense, upright, terminal racemes. Each flower has 5 spreading, sometimes fringed, silky petals and many prominent stamens. Sidalceas are suitable for a mixed or herbaceous border, and provide good cut flowers.
• **HARDINESS** Fully hardy.
• **CULTIVATION** Grow in moderately fertile, humus-rich, moist but well-drained, light, sandy, neutral to slightly acid soil in full sun. Sidalceas will tolerate a wide range of soil conditions, but resent waterlogging. Provide a dry winter mulch of bracken or straw during prolonged frosty periods without protective snow cover. Cut stems back hard after flowering.
• **PROPAGATION** Sow seed in containers in a cold frame in autumn or spring. Divide cultivars in autumn or spring.
• **PESTS AND DISEASES** Prone to slug damage and susceptible to rust.

S. candida. Rhizomatous perennial with rounded, 7-lobed basal leaves, to 20cm (8in) long, and smaller, rounded leaves on the erect, unbranched stems. Dense racemes of open funnel-shaped, white or cream flowers, to 2.5cm (1in) across, are produced in mid- and late summer. ↕ 30–80cm (12–32in), ↔ 45cm (18in). USA (Wyoming, Nevada, Utah, Colorado, New Mexico). ❄❄❄
S. malviflora (Checkerbloom). Erect to slightly decumbent perennial producing rounded to kidney-shaped, shallowly lobed basal leaves, 4–8cm (1½–3in) long, and more deeply lobed stem

Sidalcea malviflora 'William Smith'

Sidalcea malviflora 'Oberon'

leaves. In early and midsummer, bears racemes of funnel-shaped, pink or lilac-pink flowers, 5cm (2in) across. ↕ to 1.2m (4ft), ↔ 45cm (18in). USA (Oregon, California), Mexico (Baja California). ❄❄❄. Most of the cultivars described are hybrids between *S. candida* and *S. malviflora.* **'Croftway Red'** has rich reddish pink flowers; ↕ 90cm (36in). **'Elsie Heugh'** has large, satin-textured, purple-pink flowers, the petals fringed; ↕ 90cm (36in). **'Loveliness'** is compact, with pale pink flowers; ↕ 75cm (30in). **'Oberon'** ■ has clear rose-pink flowers. **'Puck'** is compact and upright, bearing deep pink flowers in midsummer; ↕ to 40cm (16in). **'Reverend Page Roberts'** has silvery, pale rose-pink flowers. **'Sussex Beauty'** has satin-textured, clear pink flowers. **'William Smith'** ■ has deep rose-pink flowers, tinted salmon-pink; ↕ 90cm (36in).

SIDERITIS

LABIATAE/LAMIACEAE

Genus of about 100 species of annuals, perennials, and evergreen shrubs and subshrubs from coastal plains to forest or laurel-covered clifftops in the Mediterranean and Atlantic islands. They are grown mainly for their simple, often softly hairy or white-woolly leaves, arranged in opposite pairs. Tubular to bell-shaped, 2-lipped flowers are borne in whorled spikes in summer. They need long, hot summers to thrive. In warm, dry climates, grow at the front of a mixed or shrub border, in a rock garden, or in a small courtyard garden. Where winters are cold and damp, grow as foliage plants in a cool greenhouse.
• **HARDINESS** Half hardy to frost tender.
• **CULTIVATION** Under glass, grow in loam-based potting compost (JI No.1) in full light. When in growth, water moderately and apply a balanced liquid fertilizer monthly; water sparingly in winter. Outdoors, grow in moderately fertile, sharply drained, neutral to slightly alkaline soil in full sun. Provide a dry winter mulch. Pruning group 9.
• **PROPAGATION** Sow seed of tender species at 13–16°C (55–61°F) in spring; sow seed of hardier species in containers in a cold frame in spring. Divide perennials in early spring. Root softwood cuttings of shrubs in late spring, with bottom heat; take semi-ripe cuttings in late summer.
• **PESTS AND DISEASES** Trouble free.

S. candicans. Erect to spreading, many-branched shrub with ovate to heart-shaped, densely white-woolly, scalloped leaves, 5–10cm (2–4in) long. In summer, bears erect, terminal spikes, 15–28cm (6–11in) long, of 20–30 small, light yellow flowers, 8mm (⅜in) long, tipped orange and red-brown. ↕ 60–90cm (24–36in), ↔ 45–80cm (18–32in). Canary Islands (Tenerife). ❄

▷***Sieversia reptans*** see *Geum reptans*
▷***Sigmatostalix radicans*** see *Ornithophora radicans*

SILENE

Campion, Catchfly

CARYOPHYLLACEAE

Genus of about 500 species of annuals, biennials, and deciduous or evergreen perennials, some subshrubby, widely distributed in habitats ranging from open woodland to meadows and mountain screes in the N. hemisphere; most occur around the Mediterranean, but some are found in the mountains of tropical Africa and in South America. The variable leaves are opposite, linear to ovate or obovate, and entire. The flowers have 5 often notched or split, clawed petals and a tubular, often conspicuously inflated calyx; they are borne singly or in sprays, clusters, broad or narrow panicle-like cymes, or corymb-like panicles. Most silenes are easily grown, and often self-seed freely. Smaller perennials are excellent for a rock garden, and taller ones for the front of a herbaceous border, or for a wild garden. Use annuals as bedding in mixed or annual borders. Some silenes resent winter wet and are best grown in a scree bed or alpine house.
• **HARDINESS** Fully hardy to half hardy.
• **CULTIVATION** Grow in moderately fertile, well-drained, neutral to slightly alkaline soil in full sun or light dappled shade. *S. hookeri* needs acid soil. *S. dioica* 'Rosea Plena' needs moist but well-drained soil in light dappled shade. Grow smaller alpine species in sharply drained, gritty soil in a scree bed, or in a mix of equal parts loam-based potting compost (JI No.2) and sharp grit, in containers in an alpine house.
• **PROPAGATION** Sow seed of perennials in containers in a cold frame in autumn. Sow seed of hardy annuals *in situ* in autumn or spring; sow half-hardy annuals at 16–19°C (61–66°F) in spring and harden off before planting out after last frosts. Divide rooted offshoots of *S. dioica* 'Rosea Plena' from midsummer to autumn. Root basal cuttings of perennials in spring.
• **PESTS AND DISEASES** Outdoors, prone to slug and snail damage; under glass, often infested by aphids, whiteflies, and red spider mites. *S. dioica* 'Rosea Plena' is susceptible to smut fungus and, in dry conditions, to powdery mildew.

S. acaulis (Moss campion). Very dwarf, evergreen perennial forming moss-like cushions of tiny, linear, bright green leaves, 6–10mm (¼–½in) long. In summer, produces solitary, almost stemless, deep pink, sometimes white flowers, to 1cm (½in) across, with entire or notched petals. Suitable for a scree bed, but rarely bears abundant flowers in cultivation. ↕5cm (2in), ↔20cm (8in). Arctic, mountains of Eurasia, North America. ❄❄❄

S. alpestris ▣ syn. *Heliosperma alpestris.* Loosely tufted, branching, evergreen perennial with linear-lance-shaped, mid-green leaves, to 3cm (1¼in) long. In early summer, bears open sprays of rounded, white, sometimes pink-flushed flowers, 1cm (½in) across, with fringed petals. ↕15cm (6in), ↔20cm (8in). Europe (E. Alps). ❄❄❄

S. armeria. Sticky-hairy annual or biennial with upright stems. Produces grey-green leaves, 1–4cm (½–1½in) long, the basal leaves spoon-shaped, the stem leaves lance-shaped. In late summer, bears broad, dense, rounded, corymb-like panicles of deep carmine-pink flowers, to 1.5cm (½in) across, with shallowly notched petals. Treat as an annual. ↕30cm (12in), ↔15cm (6in). C. and S. Europe. ❄❄❄. **'Electra'** ▣ is particularly free-flowering.

S. coeli-rosa ▣ syn. *Agrostemma coeli-rosa, Lychnis coeli-rosa, Viscaria elegans* (Rose of heaven). Erect, slender, hairless annual with oblong to lance-shaped, grey-green leaves, 1–5cm (½–2in) long. In summer, bears loose, long-stalked clusters of spreading, white-centred, rose-pink flowers, to 2.5cm (1in) across, with deeply notched petals and prominently toothed calyces. Good for cut flowers. ↕to 50cm (20in), ↔to 15cm (6in). Mediterranean. ❄❄❄. **Angel Series** cultivars flower in 2 separate, soft, clear colours; ↕25–30cm (10–12in). **'Blue Angel'** has lavender-blue flowers. **'Rose Angel'** ▣ has deep pink-magenta flowers.

Silene armeria 'Electra'

***S. conica* 'Balletje Balletje'.** Erect, slender, sticky-stemmed annual with narrowly lance-shaped, grey-green leaves, 1–4cm (½–1½in) long. In summer, produces cymes of 5–30 rose-pink flowers, to 5mm (¼in) across, but is grown for its oval, sticky-hairy, grey-green calyces, with bright green ribs, which enlarge in fruit and are good for flower arrangements. ↕15–50cm (6–20in), ↔to 15cm (6in). ❄❄❄

***S. dioica* 'Rosea Plena'.** Clump-forming, semi-evergreen perennial with erect, branched flowering stems. Bears dark green leaves, most to 9cm (3½in) long, the basal leaves obovate, the stem leaves oblong-obovate, becoming smaller and almost stalkless towards the stem tips. From late spring to midsummer, bears loosely branched, panicle-like cymes of large, rounded, double flowers, 4cm (1½in) across, with notched, dusky-pink petals, white at the bases. ↕to 80cm (32in), ↔45cm (18in). ❄❄❄

S. elisabethae, syn. *Melandrium elisabethae.* Tufted, semi-evergreen perennial with loose rosettes of lance-shaped, glossy, mid-green leaves, 6cm (2½in) long. In early summer, spreading stems bear usually solitary, large, deep red-purple flowers, 5cm (2in) across, with 2-lobed petals. Resents winter wet. ↕to 25cm (10in), ↔15cm (6in). Limestone screes in the Italian Alps. ❄❄❄

Silene alpestris

Silene coeli-rosa

S. hookeri. Tufted, prostrate, deciduous perennial with lance-shaped, grey-hairy, mid-green leaves, 5–7cm (2–3in) long. In late summer, produces solitary, clear pale pink to salmon-pink flowers, to 6cm (2½in) across, with very deeply lobed white petals. Resents winter wet; needs acid soil. ↕to 5cm (2in), ↔to 15cm (6in). USA (California). ❄❄❄

S. keiskei* var. *minor ▣ Tufted, evergreen perennial, similar to *S. elisabethae*, with hairy, narrowly lance-shaped, dark green leaves, to 3cm (1¼in) long, on slender stems. Bears loosely branching sprays of deep rose-pink flowers, 2–3cm (¾–1¼in) across, with shallowly notched petals, in late summer. ↕10cm (4in), ↔20cm (8in). Japan. ❄❄❄

***S. maritima* 'Flore Pleno'** see *S. uniflora* 'Robin Whitebreast'.

S. pendula (Nodding catchfly). Erect to spreading, glandular-hairy, bushy annual with ovate to lance-shaped, hairy, mid-green leaves, to 6cm (2½in) long. In summer, produces loose clusters of slightly pendent, single or double, pale pink flowers, to 1.5cm (½in) across, with prominently toothed calyces. Suitable for use as an edging plant and also good for hanging baskets. ↕↔15–23cm (6–9in). Mediterranean. ❄❄❄. **'Peach Blossom'** has double flowers, opening deep rose-pink and maturing through pale pink to white, showing a range of colours on a single plant; ↕15cm (6in). **'Snowball'** has double white flowers. **'Triumph'** has double, deep pinkish red flowers.

Silene coeli-rosa 'Rose Angel'

Silene keiskei var. *minor*

Silene schafta

S. schafta ▣ Clump-forming, slender-stemmed, semi-evergreen perennial with lance-shaped, bright green leaves, 1–2cm (½–¾in) long. Profusely bears sprays of long-tubed, deep magenta flowers, 2cm (¾in) across, with notched petals, from late summer to autumn. Suitable for a rock garden. ↕25cm (10in), ↔30cm (12in). W. Asia. ❄❄❄. **'Shell Pink'**, syn. 'Ralph Haywood', has clear pale pink flowers.

***S. uniflora* 'Flore Pleno'** see *S. uniflora* 'Robin Whitebreast'.

***S. uniflora* 'Robin Whitebreast'**, syn. *S. maritima* 'Flore Pleno', *S. uniflora* 'Flore Pleno', *S. vulgaris* subsp. *maritima* 'Flore Pleno' (Double sea campion). Lax, prostrate, deeply rooting, semi-evergreen perennial with fleshy, lance-shaped, grey-green leaves, to 2cm (¾in) long, fringed with fine hairs. In summer, erect, branching stems produce double white flowers, to 2.5cm (1in) across, with deeply cut petals, either singly or in few-flowered clusters. ↕15cm (6in), ↔20cm (8in). ❄❄❄

***S. vulgaris* subsp. *maritima* 'Flore Pleno'** see *S. uniflora* 'Robin Whitebreast'.

▷ **Silk cotton tree** see *Bombax, Ceiba*
  Red see *Bombax ceiba*
  White see *Ceiba pentandra*
▷ **Silk-tassel bush** see *Garrya elliptica*
▷ **Silk tree** see *Albizia julibrissin*
  Floss see *Chorisia speciosa*
▷ **Silk vine** see *Periploca graeca*
▷ **Silkweed** see *Asclepias*

Silphium perfoliatum

SILPHIUM

Prairie dock, Rosinweed

ASTERACEAE/COMPOSITAE

Genus of about 20 species of tall herbaceous perennials from fields, prairies, and open woodland and scrub (some in moister areas) in Canada and C. and E. USA. Their erect, sparsely branched stems exude resinous sap with a strong turpentine-like scent. The opposite or alternate, coarse leaves, sometimes all basal, are lance-shaped to ovate or triangular, some toothed or pinnatifid. Sunflower-like yellow flowerheads are borne in branching corymbs. Excellent for naturalizing in a wild or woodland garden.

- **HARDINESS** Fully hardy.
- **CULTIVATION** Grow in moderately fertile, moist, deep, neutral to slightly alkaline soil in full sun or partial shade; best in heavy soil. *S. perfoliatum* prefers damper soil.
- **PROPAGATION** Sow seed in containers in a cold frame as soon as ripe. Divide in spring.
- **PESTS AND DISEASES** Trouble free.

S. laciniatum (Compass plant, Pilot plant, Polar plant). Upright, clump-forming perennial with stiffly hairy stems bearing alternate, erect, pinnatifid or 2-pinnatifid, fern-like, hairy leaves, to 50cm (20in) long, becoming smaller up the stems; the flat sides face east and west, hence the plant's common names. In late summer and early autumn, bears terminal, narrow, raceme-like corymbs of nodding yellow, eastward-facing flowerheads, to 12cm (5in) across, with darker disc-florets. ↕ to 3m (10ft), ↔ 60cm (24in). E. and C. USA. ❄❄❄

S. perfoliatum ▣ (Cup plant). Erect, hairless or nearly hairless, clump-forming perennial producing opposite, triangular-ovate, coarsely toothed, bristly leaves, to 35cm (14in) long, with winged stalks. The upper leaves are perfoliate. From midsummer to early autumn, bears terminal, open-branched, corymb-like inflorescences of yellow flowerheads, to 8cm (3in) across, with darker disc-florets. ↕ to 2.5m (8ft), ↔ 1m (3ft). North America (Ontario to Oklahoma and Georgia). ❄❄❄

▷ **Silver bell** see *Halesia*
▷ **Silver berry** see *Elaeagnus commutata*
▷ **Silver fir** see *Abies, A. alba*
European see *A. alba*

Silybum marianum

▷ **Silver net leaf** see *Fittonia albivenis* Argyroneura Group
▷ **Silver torch** see *Cleistocactus strausii*
▷ **Silver tree** see *Leucadendron argenteum*
▷ **Silver vine** see *Actinidia polygama, Scindapsus pictus*

SILYBUM

ASTERACEAE/COMPOSITAE

Genus of 2 species of erect, rosette-forming, thistle-like annuals or biennials from mountains of E. Africa and from stony slopes, steppes, and thickets in W. Africa, the Mediterranean, and Europe to C. Asia. They have broad, shallowly to deeply lobed, obovate to inversely lance-shaped, spiny, light to dark green leaves, and spherical, single, purple-pink flowerheads, enclosed in spiny bracts. Grown for their foliage and flowers, they are good for a mixed or herbaceous border or a gravel garden.

- **HARDINESS** Fully hardy.
- **CULTIVATION** Grow in poor to moderately fertile, well-drained, neutral to slightly alkaline soil in full sun. Protect from excessive winter wet. Remove flowering stems as they form, to retain foliage effect.
- **PROPAGATION** Sow seed *in situ* in late spring or early summer and thin seedlings to 60cm (24in) apart. To grow for foliage effect alone, sow in a cold greenhouse in late winter or very early spring; prick out into 9cm (3½in) containers and grow on to plant out in late spring.
- **PESTS AND DISEASES** Prone to slug and snail damage.

S. marianum ▣ (Blessed Mary's thistle). Rosette-forming biennial with a flat, basal rosette of deeply lobed, obovate, spiny, heavily white-veined and marbled, glossy, dark green leaves, to 50cm (20in) long. Two years after sowing, bears thistle-like, slightly scented, purple-pink flowerheads, to 5cm (2in) across, from summer to autumn. ↕ to 1.5m (5ft), ↔ 60–90cm (24–36in). S.W. Europe to Afghanistan, N. Africa. ❄❄❄

SINACALIA

ASTERACEAE/COMPOSITAE

Genus of 4 species of robust, deciduous perennials, with tuberous rhizomes, inhabiting forest margins, grassy slopes, cliffs, and streamsides in China. They have ovate to rounded leaves that are often deeply lobed or pinnatisect and borne in decreasing size alternately up

Sinacalia tangutica

the stem. Erect stems bear terminal panicles or corymbs of few to many flowerheads, consisting of a narrowly cylindrical or bell-shaped involucre with yellow disc florets and 2–8 yellow ray florets. Grow in a woodland garden, or naturalize in areas where a large colony can be appreciated.

- **HARDINESS** Fully hardy.
- **CULTIVATION** Grow in moderately fertile, moist to boggy soil in full sun or partial shade.
- **PROPAGATION** Sow seed in containers outdoors in autumn or spring. Divide in autumn or spring.
- **PESTS AND DISEASES** Young growth is prone to damage from slugs and snails.

S. tangutica ▣ syn. *Ligularia tangutica, Senecio tanguticus* (Chinese groundsel, Chinese ragwort). Vigorous, spreading, rhizomatous, deciduous perennial with erect, unbranched dark stems and ovate, deeply pinnatisect, dark green leaves, to 18cm (7in) long. From late summer to mid-autumn, bears pyramidal panicles of narrow, 2–4 rayed, bright yellow flowerheads, to 3mm (⅛in) across. These are followed by persistent, pale brown, fluffy seedheads. ↕ to 1.5m (5ft), ↔ indefinite. N. and W. China. ❄❄❄

▷ ***Sinarundinaria fangiana*** see *Bashania faberi*
▷ ***Sinarundinaria jaunsarensis*** see *Yushania anceps*
▷ ***Sinarundinaria murieliae*** see *Fargesia murielae*
▷ ***Sinarundinaria nitida*** see *Fargesia nitida*

SINNINGIA

GESNERIACEAE

Genus, including species formerly classified under *Gloxinia* and *Rechsteineria*, of about 40 species of tuberous perennials and deciduous or evergreen, low-growing shrubs from tropical forest in Central and South America. They have usually ovate to elliptic, fleshy leaves, in opposite pairs or in whorls of 6 or more, often crowded at the stem bases. They are grown for their showy, solitary or clustered, tubular, trumpet-shaped, or bell-shaped flowers, generally borne in summer. In frost-prone areas or in areas with high winter rainfall, grow as houseplants or in a warm greenhouse or conservatory. In frost-free areas, they are suitable for a trough, raised bed, peat bed, terrace, or woodland garden.

- **HARDINESS** Frost tender.
- **CULTIVATION** Under glass, grow in loamless potting compost in bright filtered or indirect light. Most are best maintained with high humidity at 18–24°C (64–75°F); grow *S. cardinalis* and *S. pusilla* at 19°C (66°F) or more. In the growing season, water moderately and apply a half-strength high-potash fertilizer every 2 weeks. Dry off tubers in autumn and keep completely dry in winter. Start into growth in early spring in shallow trays of peat; pot up individually into 9–10cm (3½–4in) containers when young shoots are 5–7cm (2–3in) long. Outdoors, grow in moist but well-drained, humus-rich, acid to neutral soil in light dappled or partial shade.
- **PROPAGATION** Surface-sow seed at 15–21°C (59–70°F) in spring. Divide tubers in spring. Take stem-tip cuttings of miniature species and cultivars in late spring or early summer. Root leaf cuttings in spring or summer, with bottom heat.
- **PESTS AND DISEASES** Leafhoppers and western flower thrips may be a problem.

S. canescens, syn. *Rechsteineria leucotricha, S. leucotricha* (Brazilian edelweiss). Upright, densely woolly, tuberous perennial. Whorls of obovate, sage-green leaves, to 15cm (6in) long, are covered with silvery white hairs. In summer, short-lived, nodding, narrowly tubular, pinkish orange-red to rose-pink flowers, 2.5cm (1in) long, are borne in clusters of 3–5. ↕ 30cm (12in), ↔ 35cm (14in). Brazil. ❀ (min. 15°C/59°F)

S. cardinalis ▣ (Cardinal flower, Helmet flower). Tuberous perennial with short white hairs covering both the stems and the pairs of ovate, scalloped, mid-green leaves, 7–15cm (3–6in) long. Clustered, upwardly angled, hooded, tubular, blood-red flowers, 5cm (2in) long, open in succession for up to 3 months from late summer to autumn. ↕↔ to 30cm (12in). Brazil. ❀ (min. 15°C/59°F)

S. leucotricha see *S. canescens*.

***S.* 'Mont Blanc'.** Rosette-forming, tuberous perennial with ovate, velvety, mid-green leaves, 20–24cm (8–10in) long. In summer, bears solitary, erect, trumpet-shaped, pure white flowers, 4cm (1½in) long. ↕ to 30cm (12in), ↔ 45cm (18in). ❀ (min. 15°C/59°F)

S. pusilla. Prostrate, miniature perennial with pea-sized tubers, bearing pairs of ovate, hairy, dark olive-green leaves, to 1cm (½in) long, red-veined beneath. Solitary, nodding, tubular lilac flowers, 2cm (¾in) long, with white throats, are borne on hairy stalks, 1cm (½in) long, in summer. Blooms almost continuously in a terrarium. ↕↔ 2.5–5cm (1–2in). Brazil. ❀ (min. 15°C/59°F). **'White Sprite'** has white flowers.

Sinningia cardinalis

S. regina (Cinderella slippers). Tuberous perennial with pairs of ovate to elliptic, finely scalloped, dark green leaves, 10–20cm (4–8in) long, velvety above and pale green in the vein areas. Clusters of 4–6 nodding, trumpet-shaped, rich purple flowers, 5cm (2in) long, each with a pale yellow band, are produced in summer. ↕ 20cm (8in), ↔ 35cm (14in). Brazil. ❀ (min. 15°C/59°F)
S. speciosa, syn. *Gloxinia speciosa* (Florists' gloxinia). Tuberous perennial with rosettes of ovate to oblong, scalloped, dark green leaves, 20–30cm (8–12in) long, covered with velvety hairs, and red-flushed beneath. Produces solitary or clustered, nodding, tubular-bell-shaped, red, violet-blue, or white flowers, 3.5cm (1½in) long, in summer. ↕↔ 30cm (12in). Brazil. ❀ (min. 15°C/59°F)
***S.* 'Switzerland'** ▣ Tuberous perennial with rosettes of ovate, velvety, mid-green leaves, 20–24cm (8–10in) long. In summer, produces solitary, upright, trumpet-shaped, bright scarlet flowers, 4cm (1½in) long, with wavy white margins. ↕ to 30cm (12in), ↔ 45cm (18in). ❀ (min. 15°C/59°F)

S

 Sinningia 'Switzerland'

***S.* 'Waterloo'.** Rosette-forming, tuberous perennial with ovate, velvety, mid-green leaves, 20–24cm (8–10in) long. In summer, bears solitary, upright, trumpet-shaped, bright scarlet flowers, 4cm (1½in) long. ↕ to 30cm (12in), ↔ 45cm (18in). ❀ (min. 15°C/59°F)

SINOBAMBUSA

GRAMINEAE/POACEAE

Genus of 20 or more species of spreading, deciduous bamboos found in woodland margins in S. China, N. Vietnam, and Taiwan. They are grown for their elegant, upright habit and tall, erect, round, hollow canes, which may be smooth or rough. The canes have distinctive, usually swollen scars at the nodes, from which 1–7 slender branches emerge bearing alternate, ovate to oblong-lance-shaped, mid-green leaves; they have long internodes flattened above the nodes. They are ideal in a woodland garden but may become invasive.
• **HARDINESS** Frost hardy to half hardy.
• **CULTIVATION** Grow in moist but well-drained, humus-rich soil in full sun or partial shade. Shelter from cold, drying winds.
• **PROPAGATION** Divide established clumps, preferably in spring.
• **PESTS AND DISEASES** Trouble free.

S. intermedia. Spreading bamboo with rough, light green canes, to 2.5cm (1in) across, covered with a white powdery coating when young, and with internodes to 60cm (24in) long. Each node produces 3 branches bearing ovate to lance-shaped leaves, to 20cm (8in) long, with deciduous, hairy, mid-green cane sheaths. ↕ to 5m (15ft), ↔ indefinite. S. China. ❄❄
S. orthotropa, syn. *Pseudosasa orthotropa*. Spreading bamboo with smooth, mid-green canes, about 1.5cm (½in) across, sometimes tinged purple, and with internodes about 40cm (16in) long. Each node, occasionally slightly swollen, produces 1–3 branches bearing ovate to lance-shaped, finely toothed leaves, 15–30cm (6–12in) long, and deciduous, finely hairy, mid-green to brown cane sheaths. ↕ 4m (12ft), ↔ indefinite. S. China. ❄❄
S. rubroligula. Spreading bamboo with smooth, grey-green canes, 8mm (⅜in) across, maturing to brownish purple on exposed sides, and with internodes about 25cm (10in) long. Each node produces 3 branches, or 5–7 on upper nodes, bearing lance-shaped to oblong-lance-shaped leaves, to 20cm (8in) long, and deciduous, finely hairy, green to brown cane sheaths. ↕ 2m (6ft), ↔ indefinite. S.E. China. ❄❄
S. tootsik, syn. *Arundinaria tootsik, Semiarundinaria tootsik* (Chinese temple bamboo). Vigorous, spreading bamboo with smooth, dark green canes, 3–4cm (1¼–1½in) across, with internodes 40–60cm (16–24in) long. Each node produces 3 or more branches bearing variable, lance-shaped to narrowly lance-shaped leaves, about 20cm (8in) long, with conspicuous, deciduous, hairy, reddish brown cane sheaths. Avoid dry conditions. ↕ 4–7m (12–21ft), ↔ indefinite. S.E. China. ❄❄.
f. *albovariegata*, syn. 'Albostriata' of gardens, has mid-green leaves with cream stripes and occasionally a few white stripes on the canes.

▷ ***Sinocalamus giganteus*** see *Dendrocalamus giganteus*

SINOCALYCANTHUS

CALYCANTHACEAE

Genus of one species of deciduous shrub, related to *Calycanthus*, occurring in woodland in China. It produces simple, opposite leaves and is grown for its showy, single white flowers, borne in early summer. Use in a shrub border or wild garden.
• **HARDINESS** Fully hardy.
• **CULTIVATION** Grow in moderately fertile, humus-rich, moist but well-drained soil in full sun, or with some midday shade. Shelter from cold, drying winds. Pruning group 1.
• **PROPAGATION** Sow seed in containers in a cold frame in autumn. Root softwood cuttings in late spring or early summer, with bottom heat.
• **PESTS AND DISEASES** Trouble free.

S. chinensis, syn. *Calycanthus chinensis.* Spreading shrub with broadly oval, short-tapered, glossy, mid-green leaves, to 15cm (6in) long. Cup-shaped, slightly pink-flushed white flowers, 7cm (3in) across, marked white and maroon inside, are produced singly, close to the shoot-tips, in early summer. ↕ 3m (10ft), ↔ 4m (12ft). E. China. ❄❄❄

SINOFRANCHETIA

LARDIZABALACEAE

Genus of one species of twining, woody, dioecious, deciduous climber occurring in woodland in China. It has alternate, 3-palmate leaves, and produces pendent racemes of tiny white flowers; on female plants, these are followed by grape-like berries. Cultivated for its attractive foliage and fruit, it may be grown through a tree, over a large shrub, or against a wall. Female plants can bear fruit without a male.
• **HARDINESS** Fully hardy.
• **CULTIVATION** Grow in moderately fertile, humus-rich, moist but well-drained soil in full sun or partial shade. Pruning group 11, in spring.
• **PROPAGATION** Sow seed in containers in a cold frame in autumn. Root softwood cuttings in late spring or early summer.
• **PESTS AND DISEASES** Trouble free.

S. chinensis. Twining, woody climber with glaucous, purple-spotted stems and long-stalked leaves, to 15cm (6in) long, composed of 3 ovate, dark green leaflets, glaucous beneath. In late spring, bears tiny white flowers in pendent racemes, to 10cm (4in) long. In summer, female plants produce spherical, grape-like purple berries, to 2cm (¾in) long. ↕ 12m (40ft). W. and C. China. ❄❄❄

SINOJACKIA

STYRACACEAE

Genus of 2 species of deciduous shrubs or small trees from woodland in China. They are valued for their small racemes of white flowers, which are borne close to the tips of short, leafy shoots in late spring and early summer. The leaves are simple and alternate. Grow sinojackias in a woodland garden.
• **HARDINESS** Fully hardy.
• **CULTIVATION** Grow in moderately fertile, humus-rich, moist but well-drained, acid soil in full sun with some midday shade, or in partial shade. Avoid very exposed sites. Pruning group 1.
• **PROPAGATION** Sow seed in containers in a cold frame in autumn. Root greenwood cuttings in early summer, with bottom heat.
• **PESTS AND DISEASES** Trouble free.

S. rehderiana ▣ ♀ Bushy shrub, or sometimes spreading tree, with elliptic to elliptic-obovate, glossy, dark green leaves, to 9cm (3½in) long. In late spring and early summer, produces pendent, star-shaped white flowers, 2cm (¾in) across, with yellow stamens. ↕↔ to 5m (15ft). E. China. ❄❄❄
S. xylocarpa ♀ Bushy shrub, or sometimes spreading tree, with obovate, glossy, dark green leaves, to 8cm (3in) long, wedge-shaped at the bases and with pointed tips. Star-shaped white flowers, 2.5cm (1in) across, with yellow stamens, are borne in late spring and early summer. ↕↔ to 6m (20ft). E. China. ❄❄❄

Sinojackia rehderiana

SINOWILSONIA

HAMAMELIDACEAE

Genus of one species of monoecious, deciduous shrub or small tree, related to witch hazels (*Hamamelis*), found on streambanks in the mountains of China. It has simple, alternate leaves, and is mainly cultivated for its catkin-like racemes of small flowers, borne in late spring before the leaves. Grow in a shrub border or woodland garden.

- **HARDINESS** Fully hardy.
- **CULTIVATION** Grow in moist but well-drained, moderately fertile, humus-rich, acid soil, in full sun with some midday shade, or in partial shade. Shelter from cold, drying winds. Pruning group 1.
- **PROPAGATION** Sow seed in containers in a cold frame in autumn. Root greenwood cuttings with bottom heat in early summer.
- **PESTS AND DISEASES** Trouble free.

S. henryi Spreading shrub or small tree with broadly oval to elliptic, tapered, bristle-toothed leaves, to 18cm (7in) long. In late spring, bears catkin-like racemes of small green flowers: males are 6cm (2½in) long, females are to 3cm (1¼in) long, and elongate to 15cm (6in) in fruit. The fruit are woody, 2-valved capsules, 2cm (¾in) across. ↕ 8m (25ft), ↔ 5m (15ft). C. and W. China. ❄❄❄

▷ ***Siphonosmanthus delavayi*** see *Osmanthus delavayi*

SISYRINCHIUM

IRIDACEAE

Genus of about 90 species of annuals and rhizomatous perennials, some of which are semi-evergreen. Native to North and South America (although some are widely naturalized elsewhere), they thrive in habitats ranging from mountainous areas to meadows and coastal sands. They produce clumps of linear to sword-shaped, mostly basal leaves, often forming fans. In spring and summer, upright, often winged stems bear star-, cup-, or shallowly trumpet-shaped, blue, yellow, mauve, white, or rarely pink flowers, either singly or in umbel-like clusters of 2–8; each cluster is enclosed in a pair of spathe bracts. Grow smaller species in a rock garden or gravel planting, taller species in a herbaceous border. In frost-prone areas, grow half-hardy plants in a cool green-

Sisyrinchium 'E.K. Balls'

Sisyrinchium graminoides

house or alpine house. Some species self-seed freely. A few species, especially the larger perennials, are shallow rooted, and may die suddenly after several years.

- **HARDINESS** Fully hardy to half hardy.
- **CULTIVATION** Grow in poor to moderately fertile, well-drained, neutral to slightly alkaline soil in full sun. Protect from excessive winter wet.
- **PROPAGATION** Sow seed in containers in a cold frame in autumn or early spring. Divide in spring.
- **PESTS AND DISEASES** May be affected by root rot outdoors, and infested by aphids and red spider mites under glass.

S. angustifolium see *S. graminoides*.
***S.* 'Ball's Mauve'** see *S.* 'E.K. Balls'.
***S. bellum* of gardens** see *S. idahoense*.
S. bermudiana see *S. graminoides*.
***S. birameum* of gardens** see *S. graminoides*.
***S.* 'Biscutella'.** Clump-forming, semi-evergreen perennial with linear leaves, to 18cm (7in) long. In summer, upright stems bear a succession of individually short-lived, shallowly trumpet-shaped, dull yellow flowers, 2cm (¾in) across, heavily veined and suffused brownish purple. ↕ 30cm (12in), ↔ 15cm (6in). ❄❄❄
S. boreale see *S. californicum*.
S. brachypus see *S. californicum*.
S. californicum, syn. *S. boreale*, *S. brachypus*. Short-lived, semi-evergreen perennial with sword-shaped, grey-green leaves, to 15cm (6in) long. In summer, broadly winged stems bear a succession of star-shaped, dark-veined, bright yellow flowers, 1–2cm (½–¾in) across. Self-seeds freely. ↕ 60cm (24in), ↔ to 15cm (6in). W. North America (Vancouver to California). ❄❄
S. douglasii see *Olsynium douglasii*.
***S.* 'E.K. Balls'** ■ syn. *S.* 'Ball's Mauve'. Clump-forming, semi-evergreen perennial with fans of narrow, sword-shaped leaves, to 25cm (10in) long. Erect stems bear individually short-lived, star-shaped mauve flowers, 2cm (¾in) across, in summer. ↕ 25cm (10in), ↔ 15cm (6in). ❄❄❄
S. graminoides ■ syn. *S. angustifolium*, *S. bermudiana*, *S. birameum* of gardens (Blue-eyed grass). Clump-forming, semi-evergreen perennial with linear leaves, to 50cm (20in) long. In summer, erect stems bear a long succession of individually short-lived, iris-like, deep blue, yellow-throated flowers, 2cm (¾in) across. Self-seeds freely. ↕ 50cm (20in), ↔ 15cm (6in). North America. ❄❄❄

Sisyrinchium striatum

S. grandiflorum see *Olsynium douglasii*.
S. idahoense, syn. *S. bellum* of gardens, *S. macounii*. Clump-forming, semi-evergreen perennial with narrowly linear leaves, 7–30cm (3–12in) long. Upright stems bear star-shaped, deep violet-blue flowers, 2.5cm (1in) across, with yellow throats, during summer. Self-seeds freely. ↕ 12cm (5in), ↔ 15cm (6in). USA (Washington and Idaho to California). ❄❄❄. **'Album'**, syn. *S.* 'May Snow', has white flowers with yellow throats.
S. macounii see *S. idahoense*.
***S.* 'May Snow'** see *S. idahoense* 'Album'.
***S.* 'North Star'** see *S.* 'Pole Star'.
S. odoratissimum see *Olsynium biflorum*.
***S.* 'Pole Star'**, syn. *S.* 'North Star'. Clump-forming, semi-evergreen perennial with linear leaves, to 40cm (16in) long. In summer, erect stems bear a succession of star-shaped white flowers, to 3cm (1¼in) across. ↕↔ to 15cm (6in). ❄❄❄
S. striatum ■ syn. *Phaiophleps nigricans*. Clump-forming, evergreen perennial with linear to lance-shaped, iris-like but 2-ranked, stiff, greyish green leaves, to 40cm (16in) long. In early and midsummer, unbranched stems bear stalkless clusters of open cup-shaped, pale yellow flowers, 2.5cm (1in) across, with tepal backs striped purple-brown. ↕ to 90cm (36in), ↔ 25cm (10in). Chile, Argentina. ❄❄❄. **'Aunt May'** ■ syn. 'Variegatum', is less vigorous, with leaves striped creamy yellow; ↕ to 50cm (20in). **'Variegatum'** see 'Aunt May'.

Sisyrinchium striatum 'Aunt May'

▷ **Sitka spruce** see *Picea sitchensis*

SKIMMIA

RUTACEAE

Genus of 4 species of monoecious or dioecious, occasionally hermaphrodite, evergreen shrubs and trees found in woodland from the Himalayas to S.E. Asia, China, and Japan. They are grown for their attractive leaves, flowers, and fruits. Leaves are alternate, simple, aromatic, obovate to inversely lance-shaped or elliptic, and mainly borne in terminal clusters. In spring, they bear terminal panicles of star-shaped flowers, strongly scented in some species, followed, on female and hermaphrodite plants, by fleshy, spherical, red or black fruits. Skimmias are suitable for a shrub border or woodland garden. With dioecious species, both male and female plants are needed to obtain fruit. Skimmias tolerate shade, atmospheric pollution, and neglect. The fruits may cause mild stomach upset if ingested.

- **HARDINESS** Fully hardy.
- **CULTIVATION** Grow in moderately fertile, humus-rich, moist but well-drained soil in light dappled shade to deep shade; *S.* x *confusa* 'Kew Green' tolerates full sun. May become chlorotic

Skimmia x *confusa* 'Kew Green'

Skimmia japonica

S

Skimmia japonica 'Bronze Knight'

on poor, dry soil or if over-exposed to sun. Pruning group 8, if necessary.
• **PROPAGATION** Sow seed in containers in a cold frame in autumn. Root semi-ripe cuttings with bottom heat in late summer.
• **PESTS AND DISEASES** Prone to scale insects.

S. anquetilia. Creeping or erect, dome-shaped shrub producing inversely lance-shaped to oblong-elliptic, leathery, strongly aromatic, dark or yellowish green leaves, to 18cm (7in) long. In mid- and late spring, bears small, yellow-green flowers, 4mm (⅛in) across, in compact, nearly spherical panicles, 5cm (2in) across, followed on female plants by scarlet fruit, 1cm (½in) across. ↕↔ 2m (6ft). W. Himalayas. ❄❄❄
***S. x confusa* 'Kew Green'** ■ Compact, dome-shaped shrub with inversely lance-shaped to elliptic, pointed, aromatic, mid-green leaves, to 11cm (4½in) long. Fragrant, creamy white male flowers, 3–5mm (⅛–¼in) across, open in dense, conical panicles, to 15cm (6in) long, in spring. ↕ 0.5–3m (1½–10ft), ↔ 1.5m (5ft). ❄❄❄
***S.* 'Foremanii' of gardens** see *S. japonica* 'Veitchii'.
S. japonica ■ Dome-shaped to erect or creeping shrub with oval to obovate or inversely lance-shaped, slightly aromatic, dark green leaves, to 10cm (4in) long. Fragrant white flowers, 6mm (¼in) across, sometimes tinged pink or red, often opening from red buds, are borne in dense panicles, to 8cm (3in) long, in mid- and late spring; they are followed on female plants by red fruit, 8mm

S

Skimmia japonica 'Fructu Albo'

Skimmia japonica subsp. *reevesiana*

(⅜in) across. ↕↔ to 6m (20ft). China, Japan, S.E. Asia. ❄❄❄. **'Bowles' Dwarf'** is compact, with leaves to 4cm (1½in) long, and red winter flower buds; both male and female clones are available; ↕ 15cm (6in), ↔ 45cm (18in). **'Bronze Knight'** ■ is a male clone of open habit, with dark red winter buds. **'Cecilia Brown'** has large fruit clusters. **'Foremanii'** see 'Veitchii'. **'Fragrans'**, syn. 'Fragrant Cloud', is an erect, compact, free-flowering male clone, with narrowly oval leaves; ↕↔ 1m (3ft). **'Fragrant Cloud'** see 'Fragrans'. **'Fructu Albo'** ■ has green flower buds and white fruit; ↕ 60cm (24in), ↔ 1m (3ft). **'Nymans'** is a spreading female clone, with inversely lance-shaped leaves; ↕ 1m (3ft), ↔ 2m (6ft). **subsp. *reevesiana*** ■ syn. *S. reevesiana*, is hermaphrodite, with narrowly elliptic, tapered leaves and ovoid fruit; ↕ to 7m (22ft), ↔ 90cm (36in); China, Taiwan. **subsp. *reevesiana* 'Robert Fortune'** is hermaphrodite, with pale green leaves margined dark green. **'Rogersii'** is a dense female clone, with thick, twisted leaves and abundant fruit; ↕↔ 75cm (30in). **'Rubella'** ■ is a compact male clone, with red-margined leaves, and dark red flower buds in autumn and winter. **'Veitchii'**, syn. *S.* 'Foremanii' of gardens, 'Foremanii', is a vigorous, upright female clone. **'Wakehurst White'** has white fruit.
S. reevesiana see *S. japonica* subsp. *reevesiana*.

Skimmia japonica 'Rubella'

▷**Skullcap** see *Scutellaria*
▷**Skunk cabbage** see *Lysichiton*
White see *L. camtschatcensis*
Yellow see *L. americanus*
▷**Sky flower** see *Duranta erecta*
▷**Slime lily** see *Albuca*
▷**Slipper flower** see *Calceolaria*
▷**Slipperwort** see *Calceolaria*
▷**Sloe** see *Prunus spinosa*
▷**Smallweed** see *Calamagrostis*

SMILACINA

False Solomon's seal

CONVALLARIACEAE/LILIACEAE

Genus of 25 species of mainly rhizomatous perennials from woodland in Asia and North and Central America. Similar to Solomon's seal (*Polygonatum*), they have unbranched, often arching stems with alternate, ovate-lance-shaped, stalkless or short-stalked leaves, and bear terminal racemes or panicles of star-shaped, short-stalked, scented, creamy white flowers, followed by green berries, usually ripening to red. Excellent in a woodland garden or shaded border.
• **HARDINESS** Fully hardy.
• **CULTIVATION** Grow in moderately fertile, humus-rich, lime-free, moist but well-drained soil in light dappled shade or deep shade. Shelter from cold winds.
• **PROPAGATION** Sow seed in containers in a cold frame in autumn. Divide rhizomes in spring.
• **PESTS AND DISEASES** Trouble free.

S. racemosa ■ syn. *Maianthemum racemosum* (False spikenard). Clump-forming, rhizomatous perennial with narrowly ovate or elliptic, pointed, prominently veined, mid-green leaves, to 15cm (6in) long, downy beneath and

Smilacina racemosa

yellow in autumn. Terminal panicles of many white to creamy white, sometimes green-tinged flowers, 6mm (¼in) across, are produced in mid- and late spring, occasionally followed by green, later red berries. ↕ to 90cm (36in), ↔ 60cm (24in). North America, Mexico. ❄❄❄

SMILAX

LILIACEAE/SMILACACEAE

Genus of about 200 species of usually dioecious, woody, deciduous or evergreen climbers, and herbaceous perennials, grown for their foliage and fruits. They are widespread in tropical and temperate regions, in woodland and thickets. The alternate, simple, sometimes shallowly lobed leaves are lance-shaped to elliptic, or broadly ovate to rounded, some truncate or heart-shaped at the bases; they have curled tendrils, and are often borne on prickly stems. The small, star-shaped flowers are green, greenish white, yellow, or brown, and are followed by spherical, black or red berries. Train into a tree, on to a pillar, or against a warm, sunny wall. In frost-prone areas, grow tender species in a temperate or warm greenhouse.
• **HARDINESS** Frost hardy to frost tender.
• **CULTIVATION** Grow against a support in moderately fertile, well-drained soil in full sun or partial shade. Pruning group 11, after flowering.
• **PROPAGATION** Sow seed in containers in a cold frame in autumn. Divide in autumn or spring.
• **PESTS AND DISEASES** Trouble free.

S. china. Scrambling, woody, deciduous climber with sparsely prickly shoots and broadly ovate to rounded, tapered, dark green leaves, to 8cm (3in) long. Small umbels of tiny, yellow-green flowers, 2–3mm (1/16–⅛in) across, are borne in spring, followed on female plants by spherical, bright red berries, 8mm (⅜in) across, in autumn. ↕ 5m (15ft). China, Korea, Japan. ❄❄

SMITHIANTHA

Temple bells

GESNERIACEAE

Genus of 4 species of rhizomatous perennials from moist, tropical woodland and rocks in Mexico, grown for their flowers and foliage. They have opposite, heart-shaped, fleshy leaves, with a velvet sheen of fine, red or purple hairs. Terminal racemes of nodding,

Smithiantha 'Orange King'

tubular to tubular-bell-shaped, red, orange, or yellow flowers are borne in summer and autumn. In frost-prone climates, grow in a temperate or warm greenhouse, in a conservatory, or as houseplants. In frost-free areas grow in a border or lightly shaded raised bed; they grow best in areas with dry winters.

• **HARDINESS** Frost tender.

• **CULTIVATION** Under glass, grow in half pots of well-drained, loamless potting compost. Provide high humidity and bright filtered to indirect light. In growth, water moderately and apply a quarter-strength high-potash liquid fertilizer at each watering; maintain at 19°C (66°F). Keep completely dry when dormant in winter. Pot on each spring, and water sparingly until in full growth. Do not overwater. Outdoors, grow in moderately fertile, humus-rich, moist but well-drained, neutral to slightly acid soil, in full sun with some midday shade, or in light dappled shade. Protect from winter wet.

• **PROPAGATION** Sow seed at 15–18°C (59–64°F), or divide rhizomes, in spring.

• **PESTS AND DISEASES** Prone to aphids.

S. cinnabarina, syn. *Naegelia cinnabarina*. Rhizomatous perennial with stem-sheathing, heart-shaped, densely red-hairy, deep green leaves, 15cm (6in) long, marked purple along the veins. From summer to autumn, bears brick-red flowers, 3.5cm (1½in) long, paler or white-spotted in the throats. ↕ to 45cm (18in), ↔ 30cm (12in). Mexico. ❄ (min. 10°C/50°F)

***S.* 'Orange King'** ■ Rhizomatous perennial with heart-shaped, scalloped, densely red-purple-hairy, rich mid-green leaves, 15cm (6in) long, marked dark red along the veins. From summer to autumn, bears orange flowers, 3–4cm (1¼–1½in) long, with red-spotted throats and yellow lips. ↕↔ 60cm (24in). ❄ (min. 10°C/50°F)

S. zebrina, syn. *Gesneria zebrina, Naegelia zebrina*. Rhizomatous perennial producing heart-shaped, deep green leaves, 18cm (7in) long, marked darker green and purple-brown along the veins. Scarlet and yellow flowers, 3.5cm (1½in) long, with red-spotted yellow throats, are borne in summer. ↕ to 75cm (30in), ↔ 35cm (14in). Mexico. ❄ (min. 10°C/50°F)

▷**Smoke bush** see *Cotinus, C. coggygria*
▷**Smoke tree, American** see *Cotinus obovatus*

Smyrnium perfoliatum

SMYRNIUM

APIACEAE/UMBELLIFERAE

Genus of approximately 8 erect, branching biennials or short-lived, monocarpic perennials found in rocky places, scrub, fields, and at woodland margins in Europe, Africa, and W. Asia. They produce broadly oblong, divided basal leaves and rounded, usually entire upper leaves. In late spring and early summer, they bear branched, terminal umbels of numerous tiny, greenish yellow flowers. Ideal for naturalizing in a large border or in a wild or woodland garden. They also provide unusual cut flowers.

• **HARDINESS** Fully hardy.

• **CULTIVATION** Grow in moderately fertile, moist but well-drained soil in full sun to partial shade. Will also naturalize well in grass.

• **PROPAGATION** Sow seed *in situ* in autumn or late spring, or in containers in a cold frame in spring. Germination is often erratic.

• **PESTS AND DISEASES** Trouble free.

S. perfoliatum ■ (Perfoliate Alexanders). Upright biennial with stout, ribbed stems, pinnate or 2-pinnate basal leaves, 5–20cm (2–8in) long, and perfoliate, simple, rounded, bract-like, bright yellow-green upper leaves, 3–10cm (1¼–4in) long, borne on the flowering stems. Many tiny flowers are produced in dome-shaped, 7- to 12-rayed umbels, to 10cm (4in) across, in spring of the second year after germination. ↕ 0.6–1.5m (2–5ft), ↔ 60cm (24in). N. Czech Republic, Slovakia, S. Europe, N. Africa, S.W. Asia. ❄❄❄

▷**Snail bean** see *Vigna caracalla*
▷**Snail flower** see *Vigna caracalla*
▷**Snakeroot** see *Polygala*
White see *Eupatorium rugosum*
▷**Snake root, Black** see *Cimicifuga racemosa*
▷**Snapdragon** see *Antirrhinum*
Dwarf see *Chaenorhinum*
Violet twining see *Maurandella antirrhiniflora*
▷**Sneezeweed** see *Helenium autumnale*
▷**Sneezewort** see *Achillea ptarmica*
▷**Snowball bush** see *Viburnum macrocephalum*
Japanese see *Viburnum plicatum* f. *plicatum*
▷**Snowball tree** see *Viburnum opulus* 'Roseum'
▷**Snowbell** see *Soldanella*
Alpine see *Soldanella alpina*
American see *Styrax americanus*
Fragrant see *Styrax obassia*
Japanese see *Styrax japonicus*
Least see *Soldanella minima*
▷**Snowberry** see *Symphoricarpos, S. albus* var. *laevigatus*
▷**Snow bush** see *Breynia disticha*
▷**Snowdrop** see *Galanthus*
Common see *G. nivalis*
▷**Snowdrop tree** see *Halesia*
▷**Snowflake** see *Leucojum*
Spring see *Leucojum vernum*
Summer see *Leucojum aestivum*
Water see *Nymphoides indica*
▷**Snow in summer** see *Cerastium tomentosum, Ozothamnus thyrsoideus*
▷**Snow in the jungle** see *Porana paniculata*
▷**Snow on the mountain** see *Euphorbia marginata*
▷**Soapberry, Western** see *Sapindus drummondii*
▷**Soapwort** see *Saponaria, S. officinalis*

SOBRALIA

ORCHIDACEAE

Genus of about 50 species of mostly large, evergreen, terrestrial, occasionally epiphytic orchids from Central America and tropical South America, occurring at altitudes of up to 3,400m (11,300ft), sometimes on rocks by streams. They have slender, cane-like stems, with foliage borne along almost all the stem length. The leathery, mid-green leaves are oblong to broadly oval or lance-shaped, and often folded. Short-lived, cattleya-like blooms, with a delicate, papery texture, are borne in succession every 3–4 days, at the stem tips.

• **HARDINESS** Frost tender.

• **CULTIVATION** Cool-growing orchids. Grow in containers of terrestrial orchid compost in bright filtered light, and maintain moderate to high humidity. When in active growth, water freely, mist the foliage daily, and apply a quarter-strength balanced liquid fertilizer monthly. Water sparingly in winter. Pot on when the plant fills the container and "flows" over the sides. See also p.46.

• **PROPAGATION** Divide after flowering. Offshoots may be rooted successfully in spring.

• **PESTS AND DISEASES** Red spider mites, aphids, whiteflies, and mealybugs may be troublesome.

S. macrantha. Terrestrial or epiphytic orchid with lance-shaped leaves, 15–30cm (6–12in) long. Bears papery white to pink-purple flowers, 15–18cm (6–7in) across, with yellow on the lips, from spring to summer. ↕ 2m (6ft), ↔ 1.2m (4ft). Mexico to Costa Rica. ❄ (min. 11–13°C/52–55°F; max. 30°C/86°F)

SOLANDRA

Chalice vine

SOLANACEAE

Genus of 8 species of woody-stemmed, evergreen, scrambling climbers found in tropical forest in Mexico, the West Indies, and South America. They are grown for their large, solitary, funnel- or trumpet-shaped, night-scented flowers, each with 5 reflexed lobes. The lustrous, rich green leaves are alternate, simple, ovate to obovate, and usually leathery. Where temperatures fall below 7–10°C (45–50°F), grow in a temperate greenhouse. In warmer climates, use to clothe a pergola, arch, or wall. All parts are highly toxic if ingested.

• **HARDINESS** Frost tender.

• **CULTIVATION** Under glass, grow in loam-based potting compost (JI No.2) in full light with shade from hot sun. During the growing season, water moderately and apply a balanced liquid fertilizer every 4 weeks. Water more sparingly in winter. Outdoors, grow in moderately fertile, humus-rich, moist but well-drained soil in full sun. Provide support for the climbing stems. Pruning group 11, in late winter or early spring, if necessary to restrict size.

• **PROPAGATION** Sow seed at 16–18°C (61–64°F) in spring. Root semi-ripe cuttings with bottom heat in summer. Air layer in spring.

• **PESTS AND DISEASES** Red spider mites and scale insects may be troublesome under glass.

S. grandiflora. Vigorous, semi-scandent climber with robust, sparsely branched stems clothed in elliptic to obovate leaves, to 13cm (5in) long. In spring, produces funnel-shaped, violet-tinged white flowers, 15–24cm (6–10in) long, which become tawny yellow with age. ↕ to 12m (40ft) or more. Jamaica. ❄ (min. 7–10°C/45–50°F)

S. hartwegii see *S. maxima.*

S. maxima ■ syn. *S. hartwegii, S. nitida* (Cup of gold). Scandent, moderately dense climber producing branching stems clothed in elliptic leaves, to 15cm (6in) long. Trumpet-shaped yellow flowers, 15–20cm (6–8in) long, with purple veins, are produced in summer; the inside of each flower is marked with purple ridges. ↕ to 12m (40ft). Mexico to Colombia and Venezuela. ❄ (min. 7–10°C/45–50°F)

S. nitida see *S. maxima.*

Solandra maxima

SOLANUM

SOLANUM syn. LYCIANTHES

SOLANACEAE

Genus of about 1,400 species of annuals, biennials, herbaceous perennials, and evergreen, semi-evergreen, and deciduous shrubs, trees, and twining climbers from a range of habitats worldwide. The genus includes vegetables, such as potato (*S. tuberosum*) and aubergine (*S. melongena*), and also ornamental plants, described below, grown for their flowers and fruits. The leaves are alternate, and entire, lobed, or pinnate. Small, 5-petalled, bell- or shallowly trumpet-shaped, sometimes star-shaped, yellow-anthered flowers are borne singly or in cymes, cyme-like umbels, corymbs, or panicles, from spring to autumn, and are followed by fruits. Train climbers on a wall. Grow shrubs in a sheltered border. In frost-prone regions, grow tender species in a cool or temperate greenhouse. All parts of most species, especially the fruits of *S. capsicastrum* and *S. pseudocapsicum*, can cause severe discomfort if ingested.

- **HARDINESS** Frost hardy to frost tender.
- **CULTIVATION** Under glass, grow in loam-based potting compost (JI No.2) in full light with shade from hot sun, or in bright indirect light. In growth, water freely, apply a balanced liquid fertilizer monthly, mist daily, and maintain moderate humidity. Apply a high-potash liquid fertilizer every 2 or 3 weeks to *S. capsicastrum* and *S. pseudocapsicum* until fruit ripens. Water sparingly when dormant. Outdoors, grow in moderately fertile, moist but well-drained, neutral to slightly alkaline soil in full sun. Support plants and tie in young shoots regularly. Pruning group 9 for shrubs; group 12 for climbers, after flowering.
- **PROPAGATION** Sow seed at 18–20°C (64–68°F) in spring. Root semi-ripe cuttings of shrubs and climbers with gentle bottom heat from summer to early autumn.
- **PESTS AND DISEASES** Prone to aphids, red spider mites, tomato spotted wilt, and grey mould (*Botrytis*), under glass.

Solanum laxum 'Album'

S. aviculare (Kangaroo apple). Erect to spreading, open, evergreen shrub with narrowly lance-shaped, simple to irregularly pinnatifid, deep green leaves, 12–20cm (5–8in) long. In spring and summer, bears axillary cymes, 5–13cm (2–5in) across, of 3–8 shallowly lobed, blue-purple or white flowers, 3–4cm (1¼–1½in) across, then ovoid, orange-red to scarlet fruit, 1.5cm (½in) long, ripening yellow. ↕ 1.8–3.5m (6–11ft), ↔ 1.5–2.5m (5–8ft). Australia (Queensland to Tasmania), New Zealand. ❄
S. capsicastrum (False Jerusalem cherry, Winter cherry). Erect, bushy, evergreen, downy-stemmed shrub, often grown as a winter-fruiting annual. Oblong to lance-shaped, wavy-margined leaves, 5–7cm (2–3in) long, are downy, dark green. In summer, bears axillary cymes, 5cm (2in) long, of star-shaped white flowers, to 1.5cm (½in) across, followed by oblong-ellipsoid to ovoid, pointed, red or orange-red fruit, 2cm (¾in) or more long. ↕↔ 30–60cm (12–24in), in containers. Brazil. ❀ (min. 5°C/41°F)
S. crispum (Chilean potato tree). Fast-growing, scrambling, evergreen or semi-evergreen climber with ovate, dark green leaves, to 12cm (5in) long. In summer, bears fragrant, lilac- to purple-blue flowers, 2.5cm (1in) across, in terminal corymbs, to 15cm (6in) across; they are followed by yellowish white fruit, 6–9mm (¼–⅜in) across. ↕ 6m (20ft). Peru, Chile. ❄❄. **'Glasnevin'** ■ syn. 'Autumnale', bears deep purple-blue flowers from summer to autumn.
S. jasminoides see *S. laxum*.
S. laciniatum (Kangaroo apple). Vigorous, erect, evergreen shrub with purple-tinged shoots and lance-shaped to deeply pinnatisect, mid-green leaves, to 20cm (8in) long. In summer and autumn, bears dark blue flowers, 5cm (2in) across, in axillary cymes, to 15cm (6in) long. Has ovoid, yellow to brownish yellow fruit, 2cm (¾in) long. ↕ 2m (6ft), ↔ 1.5m (5ft). Australia, New Zealand. ❄
S. laxum, syn. *S. jasminoides* (Potato vine). Scrambling, evergreen or semi-evergreen climber with narrowly ovate to lance-shaped, glossy, dark green leaves, to 5cm (2in) long, sometimes 3- to 5-lobed or with separate ovate leaflets at the bases. In summer and autumn, bears fragrant, blue-white flowers, 2.5cm (1in) across, with yellow anthers, in terminal and axillary clusters, 5–7cm (2–3in) across, followed by ovoid black fruit, 9mm (⅜in) across. ↕ 6m (20ft). Brazil. ❄. **'Album'** ■ has white flowers.
S. pseudocapsicum (Christmas cherry, Jerusalem cherry, Winter cherry). Erect, bushy, evergreen shrub, often grown as a winter-fruiting annual. Wavy-margined, elliptic leaves, to 8cm (3in) long, are glossy, dark green. In summer, bears axillary cymes, 5cm (2in) across, of up

Solanum wendlandii

to 3 star-shaped white flowers, to 1.5cm (½in) across, followed by long-lasting, spherical, red, yellow, or orange-red fruit, 1.5–2cm (½–¾in) across. ↕↔ 30–45cm (12–18in), in containers. E. South America. ❀ (min. 5°C/41°F). **'Cherry Jubilee'** has white, yellow, or orange fruit. **'Fancy'** is compact, with bright scarlet fruit; ↕ to 30cm (12in). **'Joker'** is dwarf, with yellow fruit turning orange and red; ↕↔ 20cm (8in). **'Jubilee'** is dwarf, with pale lime-green fruit, ripening deep orange; ↕↔ 15cm (6in). **'Red Giant'** ■ has large, orange-red fruit, to 2.5cm (1in) across.
S. rantonnei, syn. *Lycianthes rantonnetii*, S. *rantonnetii* (Blue potato bush). Lax, evergreen shrub, usually many-branched when mature, producing ovate to lance-shaped, often wavy-margined, smooth, mid- to deep green leaves, 6–10cm (2½–4in) long. In summer and autumn, bears axillary clusters, to 6cm (2½in) across, of 2–5 shallowly trumpet-shaped, dark blue to violet-blue or pale blue flowers, 1–2.5cm (½–1in) across, with paler blue or yellow-tinged centres, followed by ovoid red fruit, 2.5cm (1in) long. ↕↔ 1–2m (3–6ft). Paraguay, Argentina. ❀ (min. 7°C/45°F). **'Royal Robe'** ■ has fragrant, deep violet-blue flowers with yellow centres.
S. rantonnetii see *S. rantonnei*.
S. seaforthianum (Italian jasmine, St. Vincent lilac). Spreading, evergreen, hairless, scandent climber with broadly elliptic, rich green leaves, 10–20cm (4–8in) long, either entire or pinnatifid with 3–9 lobes. In summer, bears blue, purple, pink, or white flowers, to 2cm (¾in) across, in pendent panicles, to 15cm (6in) across, followed by ovoid red fruit, 6–10mm (¼–½in) across. ↕ to 6m (20ft). Tropical South America. ❀ (min. 7–10°C/45–50°F)
S. wendlandii ■ (Paradise flower, Potato vine). Spreading, evergreen or semi-evergreen, scrambling climber with hooked barbs on the stems and foliage. Bright green leaves, 10–25cm (4–10in) long, are pinnate (with 8–13 leaflets), oblong with heart-shaped bases, or 3-palmate. In summer, bears shallowly trumpet-shaped, lilac-blue flowers, 4–6cm (1½–2½in) across, in terminal, pendent, cyme-like panicles, to 15cm (6in) long, followed by spherical to ovoid orange fruit, 8–10cm (3–4in) across. ↕ 5m (15ft) or more. Costa Rica. ❀ (min. 7–10°C/45–50°F). **'Albescens'** has off-white flowers.

Solanum crispum 'Glasnevin'

Solanum pseudocapsicum 'Red Giant'

Solanum rantonnei 'Royal Robe'

SOLDANELLA
Snowbell
PRIMULACEAE

Genus of about 10 species of small, spring-flowering, evergreen perennials from the mountains of Europe, usually found in alpine turf or among rocks, often flowering through the melting snow. They have basal rosettes of long-stalked, rounded or kidney-shaped, leathery leaves. The nodding to pendent, funnel- or bell-shaped, purple to white flowers have fringed petals and are borne in umbels, rarely singly. Grow in a rock garden, alpine house, or peat bed.
- **HARDINESS** Fully hardy.
- **CULTIVATION** Grow in humus-rich, moist, sharply drained soil in full sun with some midday shade, or in partial shade in warm areas. Top-dress with sharp grit, and protect from excessive winter wet. Under glass, grow in shallow pans of equal parts lime-free (ericaceous) potting compost, leaf mould, and grit.
- **PROPAGATION** Sow seed as soon as ripe in containers in a cold frame. Divide in early spring.
- **PESTS AND DISEASES** Young growth is prone to slug and snail damage.

S. alpina ■ (Alpine snowbell). Clump-forming perennial with thick, rounded to kidney-shaped, dark green leaves, 4cm (1½in) long. In early spring, each erect scape bears 2–5 nodding, funnel-shaped, bluish violet flowers, to 1.5cm (½in) long, with fringed petals cut to half their lengths and marked red inside. ↕↔ 12cm (5in). C. and S. Europe. ✲✲✲
S. carpatica. Clump-forming perennial with rounded, dark green leaves, 5cm (2in) long, violet-purple beneath. In early spring, each scape bears 2–5 funnel-shaped, violet-blue flowers, to 1.5cm (½in) across, resembling those of *S. alpina*, but more freely borne, with fringed petals cut to two-thirds of their lengths. ↕↔ 15cm (6in). E. Europe (W. Carpathians). ✲✲✲

Soldanella alpina

Soldanella villosa

S. minima (Least snowbell). Dwarf, clump-forming perennial with rounded, glossy, mid-green leaves, 1cm (½in) long. In early spring, scapes bear usually solitary, narrowly bell-shaped, white or pale blue flowers, to 1.5cm (½in) long, with darker streaks, the fringed petals cut to a quarter of their lengths. ↕ 10cm (4in), ↔ 20cm (8in). S. central Europe (E. Alps, C. Apennines). ✲✲✲
S. montana. Mound-forming perennial producing shallowly toothed, rounded or kidney-shaped, bright green leaves, 2–7cm (¾–3in) long, violet-tinted beneath. In early spring, each scape bears 3–10 pendent, bell-shaped, lavender-blue flowers, to 2cm (¾in) long, with fringed petals cut to three-quarters of their lengths. ↕ 30cm (12in), ↔ 20cm (8in). S. central Europe (N. Alps, Carpathians, Balkan peninsula). ✲✲✲
S. villosa ■ Vigorous, clump-forming perennial with rounded, hairy-stalked, mid-green leaves, 7cm (3in) long, paler green beneath. In early spring, each scape bears 3 or 4 nodding, bell-shaped violet flowers, 1.5cm (½in) long, with fringed petals cut to three-quarters of their lengths. Relatively easy to grow. ↕ 30cm (12in), ↔ 20cm (8in). S.W. Europe (W. Pyrenees). ✲✲✲

▷**Soldiers and sailors** see *Pulmonaria officinalis*

SOLEIROLIA *syn.* HELXINE
URTICACEAE

Genus of one species of vigorous, dwarf, monoecious, evergreen perennial from moist, shaded sites in W. Mediterranean islands. It is cultivated for its fresh green foliage, and tolerates a wide range of conditions. Where temperatures fall below -5°C (23°F), grow as a houseplant, in a terrarium, or in a cool to warm greenhouse or conservatory. In warmer areas, it provides ground cover in difficult sites outdoors, but is often invasive; it is difficult to eradicate.
- **HARDINESS** Fully hardy (borderline); becomes deciduous below 0°C (32°F).
- **CULTIVATION** Under glass, grow in loam-based potting compost (JI No.1) with added grit, in full light with shade from hot sun, or in partial shade. When in growth, water freely; water sparingly in winter. Outdoors, grow in any soil in sun or shade. May be damaged by frost, but quickly recovers in spring.
- **PROPAGATION** Divide in late spring.
- **PESTS AND DISEASES** Trouble free.

Soleirolia soleirolii

S. soleirolii ■ syn. *Helxine soleirolii* (Baby's tears, Mind your own business, Mother of thousands). Slender, mat-forming perennial with branched, translucent, pale green, sometimes pink-tinted stems and alternate, rounded, minutely hairy, short-stalked leaves, 2–6mm (1/16–¼in) long. Produces tiny, solitary, tubular, 4-lobed, pink-tinged white flowers from the leaf axils in summer. ↕ 5cm (2in), ↔ indefinite. W. Mediterranean islands. ✲✲✲ (borderline). **'Aurea'**, syn. 'Golden Queen', has gold-green leaves. **'Golden Queen'** see 'Aurea'. **'Silver Queen'** see 'Variegata'. **'Variegata'**, syn. 'Silver Queen', has variegated silver leaves.

▷***Solenopsis*** see *Isotoma*
S. axillaris see *I. axillaris*

SOLENOSTEMON
Coleus, Flame nettle, Painted nettle
LABIATAE/LAMIACEAE

Genus of about 60 species of evergreen, bushy, erect to spreading, subshrubby perennials from forest in tropical and subtropical Africa and Asia. They are mainly cultivated for their opposite, coarsely to finely toothed, often hairy, mostly ovate, colourful leaves. The light to dark green leaves can be freckled or banded with pink, red, yellow, purple, and brown, or creamy white. Throughout the year, *Solenostemon* bears raceme-like whorls of tiny, tubular, 2-lipped, blue, white, or purple flowers. In frost-prone climates, grow in a temperate greenhouse or as houseplants, or use outdoors as summer bedding or in containers. In warmer areas, coleus are good bedding plants, particularly for shady positions.
- **HARDINESS** Frost tender.
- **CULTIVATION** Under glass, grow in loam-based potting compost (JI No.3) or loamless potting compost in bright filtered or moderate light. In growth, water freely and apply a high-nitrogen fertilizer every 2 weeks. Keep just moist in winter and give an occasional feed of high potash fertilizer. If required as large specimens, pot on annually in spring and summer. Outdoors, grow in humus-rich, moist but well-drained soil. Provide a sheltered position in full sun or partial shade. Water freely in dry weather. Pinch out young shoots regularly to maintain foliage colour and compact plant shape. It is best to remove emerging flower spikes to maintain shapely plants.
- **PROPAGATION** Surface-sow seed at 16–22°C (61–72°F) in spring and early summer. Root softwood cuttings with bottom heat in spring or summer, or in a warm greenhouse in early autumn. Seed selections tend to produce more free-flowering and smaller plants. Cutting-raised cultivars have been selected to give larger specimens that are more shapely, provided that they are regularly pinched out.
- **PESTS AND DISEASES** Mealybugs, scale insects, and whiteflies may be a problem under glass.

S. scutellarioides, syn. *Coleus blumei*, *C. blumei* var. *verschaffeltii* (Flame nettle, Painted nettle). Finely hairy, evergreen perennial, usually grown as an annual or short-lived perennial for its foliage. Semi-succulent, 4-angled stems bear broadly to narrowly ovate, toothed, sometimes frilly-margined, multi-coloured leaves, to 15cm (6in) long, often heart-shaped at the bases and hairy beneath. Terminal, whorled racemes, 15–23cm (6–9in) long, of tiny, blue, white, or purple flowers, 1.5cm (½in) long, are borne at any time of year. ↕↔ 60–75cm (24–30in), in containers. S.E. Asia (including Malaysia). ⊛ (min. 4°C/39°F). **'Display'**, a cutting-raised cultivar, has hairy, dark orange leaves, to 7cm (3in) long, with black veins and green margins; ↕↔ 60cm (24in). **'Pineapple Beauty'** ■ a cutting-raised cultivar, is very vigorous, with yellow-green leaves, to 8cm (3in) long, that turn gold, and with brown-purple markings at the centres, bases, and on the stems; ideal for large specimens and for training into pyramids or standards; ↕↔ 50–100cm (20–39in). **Rainbow Series** cultivars are vigorous and seed-raised, with strongly coloured leaves, to 5cm (2in) long; good for summer bedding; ↕↔ to 40cm (16in). **'Royal Scot'**, a cutting-raised cultivar, is bushy, with pointed, triangular leaves, to 6cm (2½in) long, orange to red with bright

Solenostemon scutellarioides 'Pineapple Beauty'

Solenostemon scutellarioides Wizard Series

Solenostemon scutellarioides 'Wisley Tapestry'

yellow edges; ↕↔ 60cm (24in). **'Winsome'**, a cutting-raised cultivar, produces a combination of pink, orange, and red leaves, to 6cm (2½in) long, edged greenish yellow; leaves darken with age; ↕↔ 75cm (30in). **'Wisley Tapestry'** ▣ is a prostrate, cutting-raised cultivar, with distinctive, finely cut leaves, to 2cm (¾in) long, in red, green, and yellow; very suitable for bedding and containers; ↕ 23cm (9in), ↔ 45cm (18in). Cultivars of seed-raised **Wizard Series** ▣ are compact and bushy, with small, strongly coloured leaves, to 5cm (2in) long; ↕ to 20cm (8in), ↔ 30cm (12in).

S. thyroideus see *Plectranthus thyroideus*.

SOLIDAGO

Aaron's rod, Golden rod

ASTERACEAE/COMPOSITAE

Genus of about 100 species of woody-based perennials occurring on roadsides, prairies, and riverbanks; most are found in North America, a few in South America and Eurasia. They are valued for their small, elongated flowerheads, borne in racemes, panicles, or corymbs. Stiff, branched stems produce alternate, narrowly elliptic to lance-shaped, entire or toothed, prominently veined, usually mid-green leaves, 10–30cm (4–12in) or more long. Most species are coarse and invasive and are best cultivated in a wild garden, although *S. virgaurea* subsp. *minuta* is suitable for a rock garden. Named hybrids are robust, less invasive, and more colourful, with slightly larger flowerheads. They are ideal for growing in a late-summer border or wild garden, and provide good cut flowers.

- **HARDINESS** Fully hardy.
- **CULTIVATION** Grow in poor to moderately fertile, preferably sandy, well-drained soil in full sun. Remove flowered stems to prevent seeding.

Solidago 'Goldenmosa'

Solidago 'Golden Wings'

- **PROPAGATION** Divide in autumn or spring.
- **PESTS AND DISEASES** Powdery mildew may be a problem.

***S.* 'Crown of Rays'**, syn. *S.* 'Strahlenkrone'. Erect, clump-forming perennial with mid-green leaves. Bears golden yellow flowerheads in flattened, radiating, corymb-like panicles, to 25cm (10in) long, in mid- and late summer. ↕ 60cm (24in), ↔ 45cm (18in). ❄❄❄

***S.* 'Goldenmosa'** ▣ Compact, bushy perennial with wrinkled, mid-green leaves. In late summer and early autumn, bears yellow-stalked, bright yellow flowerheads in conical panicles, to 30cm (12in) long. ↕ to 75cm (30in), ↔ 45cm (18in). ❄❄❄

***S.* 'Golden Wings'** ▣ Erect perennial with mid-green leaves, and spreading, corymb-like panicles, to 25cm (10in) long, of golden yellow flowerheads borne in late summer and early autumn. Thrives in poor soil. ↕ to 1.8m (6ft), ↔ 90cm (36in). ❄❄❄

***S.* 'Lemore'** see x *Solidaster luteus* 'Lemore'.

***S.* 'Loddon Gold'.** Erect perennial with mid-green leaves. In late summer and early autumn, bears deep yellow flowerheads in conical panicles, to 20cm (8in) long. ↕ to 90cm (36in), ↔ 45cm (18in). ❄❄❄

***S.* 'Strahlenkrone'** see *S.* 'Crown of Rays'.

S. virgaurea* subsp. *alpestris see *S. virgaurea* subsp. *minuta*.

S. virgaurea* subsp. *minuta, syn. *S. virgaurea* subsp. *alpestris*. Mound-forming perennial with leathery, lance-shaped, toothed, mid-green leaves, 2–10cm (¾–4in) long. From late summer to autumn, bears compact, erect, spike-like racemes, 3cm (1¼in) long, of deep yellow flowerheads, 6–8mm (¼–⅜in) across. Good for a rock garden, in moist soil. ↕ 5–20cm (2–8in), ↔ 20cm (8in). N., C., and E. Europe. ❄❄❄

x SOLIDASTER

ASTERACEAE/COMPOSITAE

Hybrid genus of one clump-forming perennial, possibly the result of a cross between *Solidago canadensis* and *Aster ptarmicoides*. It is valued for its daisy-like yellow flowerheads, which are profusely borne from midsummer to early autumn. The leaves are alternate, and lance-shaped to linear-elliptic or narrowly inversely lance-shaped. It is suitable for a mixed or herbaceous border, and the flowers are good for cutting.

x *Solidaster luteus*

- **HARDINESS** Fully hardy.
- **CULTIVATION** Grow in moderately fertile, well-drained soil in full sun.
- **PROPAGATION** Divide, or take basal cuttings, in spring.
- **PESTS AND DISEASES** Prone to powdery mildew in dry summers.

x *S. hybridus* see x *S. luteus*.

x *S. luteus* ▣ syn. x *S. hybridus*. Clump-forming perennial with erect, branched stems bearing leaves to 15cm (6in) long, toothed at the tips. From midsummer to early autumn, bears branched, corymb-like panicles of daisy-like flowerheads, to 1cm (½in) across, with pale yellow ray-florets and golden yellow disc-florets. ↕ to 90cm (36in), ↔ 30cm (12in). Garden origin. ❄❄❄. **'Lemore'**, syn. *Solidago* 'Lemore', has pale lemon ray-florets; ↕↔ to 80cm (32in).

SOLLYA

PITTOSPORACEAE

Genus, related to *Billardiera*, of 3 species of evergreen, twining climbers or scandent shrubs or subshrubs found in light woodland in Australia. They are cultivated for their 5-petalled, bell-shaped, usually blue flowers, which are terminally borne, either singly or in pendent cymes, from summer to autumn. Stalkless, narrow, entire or slightly wavy-margined, oblong to ovate or obovate leaves are arranged alternately or in spirals. Where temperatures fall below 5°C (41°F), grow in a cool or temperate greenhouse. In warmer areas, train over an arch, pergola, or shrub.

- **HARDINESS** Frost tender, but may survive temperatures near to 0°C (32°F).
- **CULTIVATION** Under glass, grow in loam-based potting compost (JI No.2) in full light with shade from hot sun, or in bright filtered light. During the growing season, water moderately

S

Sollya heterophylla

and apply a balanced liquid fertilizer monthly; maintain low to moderate humidity. Water sparingly in winter. Outdoors, grow in moderately fertile, humus-rich, moist but well-drained soil in full sun with some midday shade, or in light dappled shade. Apply a dry winter mulch. Support the climbing stems. Pruning group 12, in late winter or early spring.

• **PROPAGATION** Sow seed at 10–16°C (50–61°F) in spring. Root softwood cuttings in late spring or early summer.

• **PESTS AND DISEASES** Red spider mites may be troublesome under glass.

S. fusiformis see *S. heterophylla*.

S. heterophylla ▣ syn. *S. fusiformis* (Bluebell creeper). Weak-stemmed, later bushy, twining climber with ovate to narrowly oblong or obovate, mid- to deep green leaves, 2.5–5cm (1–2in) long, paler beneath. Bell-shaped blue flowers, 1.5cm (½in) across, are borne singly or in cymes of 4–8 or more, from early summer to autumn, followed by edible, cylindrical blue berries, to 2.5cm (1in) long. ↕ 1.5–2m (5–6ft). Australia (Western Australia). ✽ (borderline)

▷ **Solomon's seal** see *Polygonatum*
  Common see *Polygonatum* x *hybridum*
  False see *Smilacina*
  Whorled see *Polygonatum verticillatum*

SONERILA

MELASTOMATACEAE

Genus of about 175 species of evergreen perennials and small shrubs from tropical woodland in Asia, cultivated for their foliage and flowers. The leaves are opposite, whorled, or in basal rosettes, and mainly oval to elliptic, with bold veins. Flowers are star-, saucer-, or cup-shaped, and are borne in curved, spike-like racemes or corymbs. In frost-prone regions, grow in a warm greenhouse or conservatory, as houseplants, or in a terrarium. In warmer climates, use as ground cover among shrubs.

• **HARDINESS** Frost tender.

• **CULTIVATION** Under glass, grow in half pots or shallow pans of loamless potting compost with added fine-grade, granulated bark, in bright filtered light. Maintain steady temperatures and high humidity to prevent leaf drop. When in growth, water moderately and apply a half-strength balanced liquid fertilizer

Sonerila margaritacea 'Hendersonii'

monthly. Keep just moist in winter. Pot on in spring; trim regularly to maintain dense growth. Outdoors, grow in humus-rich, moist but well-drained, acid to neutral soil with added leaf mould and grit, in light dappled to partial shade. Shelter from cold, drying winds.

• **PROPAGATION** Root softwood cuttings with bottom heat in spring or summer.

• **PEST AND DISEASES** Trouble free.

S. margaritacea. Evergreen perennial with weak, 4-angled red stems bearing opposite, ovate to lance-shaped, glossy, dark green leaves, 10cm (4in) long, with numerous oval, pearl-white spots above, purple veins beneath, and purple-red leaf-stalks. Racemes of 8–10 star-shaped, 3-petalled, reddish pink flowers, 1cm (½in) long, are borne from summer to autumn. ↕↔ 25cm (10in). Burma to Indonesia (Java). ❀ (min. 19°C/66°F). **'Argentea'** (Pearly sonerila) has claret-red leaves, densely spotted silver. **'Hendersonii'** ▣ has dark olive-green leaves, covered with white spots above, and purple-red beneath.

▷ **Sonerila, Pearly** see *Sonerila margaritacea* 'Argentea'

SOPHORA

LEGUMINOSAE/PAPILIONACEAE

Genus of about 50 species of herbaceous perennials and deciduous and evergreen trees and shrubs, widely distributed in tropical and temperate regions, found mostly in dry valleys and woodland, and on rocky slopes of hills and mountains. They are cultivated for their elegant,

Sophora davidii

Sophora japonica 'Violacea'

alternate, pinnate leaves and racemes or panicles of pea-like flowers, with upright standards or with all petals forward-pointing. Grow in a shrub border, or as specimen plants. In frost-prone areas, grow tender sophoras at the base of a warm, sunny wall, or in a temperate or warm greenhouse. They need long, hot summers to flower well.

• **HARDINESS** Fully hardy to frost tender.

• **CULTIVATION** Grow in moderately fertile, well-drained soil in full sun. Pruning group 1.

• **PROPAGATION** Sow seed in containers in a cold frame as soon as ripe. Root semi-ripe cuttings of evergreen species with bottom heat in summer or autumn. Graft *S. japonica* cultivars in late winter.

• **PESTS AND DISEASES** Trouble free.

S. davidii ▣ syn. *S. viciifolia*. Bushy or spreading, deciduous shrub with pinnate leaves, to 9cm (3½in) long, each composed of up to 17 oval or obovate, grey-green leaflets. In late spring and early summer, produces terminal racemes, to 15cm (6in) long, of small, pea-like, purple-blue and white flowers, to 2cm (¾in) long. ↕ 2.5m (8ft), ↔ 3m (10ft). China. ✽✽✽

S. japonica ♀ (Japanese pagoda tree). Spreading, deciduous tree with pinnate leaves, to 25cm (10in) long, composed of up to 17 ovate to lance-shaped, glossy, dark green leaflets that turn yellow in autumn. In late summer and early autumn, mature trees bear small, fragrant, pea-like white flowers, 1.5cm (½in) long, in terminal panicles to 30cm (12in) long. ↕ to 30m (100ft), ↔ 20m (70ft). China, Korea. ✽✽✽. **'Pendula'** ♀ has long, pendent branches, and rarely flowers; ↕↔ 3m (10ft). **'Violacea'** ▣ has white flowers tinged lilac-pink.

S. microphylla ♀ syn. *Edwardsia microphylla*. Spreading, evergreen, small tree or shrub producing pinnate leaves, to 15cm (6in) long, each with up to 40 pairs of ovate or elliptic-oblong, dark green leaflets, borne on silky shoots. In spring, bears small, axillary, pendent racemes, to 5cm (2in) long, of pea-like, dark yellow flowers, 5cm (2in) long, with all petals pointing forwards. ↕↔ 8m (25ft). New Zealand, Chile. ✽✽. **'Sun King'** ▣ is bushy, and bears long-lasting flowers in late winter and early spring; ↕↔ 3m (10ft); ✽✽✽

S. tetraptera ♀ (Kowhai). Spreading, evergreen tree or shrub with pinnate leaves, to 17cm (7in) long, each composed of up to 20 pairs of ovate or elliptic-oblong, dark green leaflets. In late spring, produces racemes, to 6cm (2½in) long, of 4–10 golden yellow flowers, to 5cm (2in) long, with all the petals pointing forwards. ↕ 10m (30ft), ↔ 5m (15ft). New Zealand. ✽✽

S. viciifolia see *S. davidii*.

X SOPHROLAELIO-CATTLEYA

ORCHIDACEAE

Trigeneric hybrid genus of evergreen orchids derived from crosses between *Sophronitis*, *Laelia*, and *Cattleya*. They are vegetatively similar to laeliocattleyas and brassolaeliocattleyas, and all are loosely referred to as cattleyas. The spindle-shaped or elongated pseudo-

Sophora microphylla 'Sun King' (inset: flower detail)

S

x *Sophrolaeliocattleya* Hazel Boyd 'Apricot Glow'

x *Sophrolaeliocattleya* Trizac 'Purple Emperor'

bulbs support 1 or 2 semi-rigid, elliptic leaves, to 15cm (6in) long. Flowers 10cm (4in) across, in a range of rich colours from vibrant reds to fiery oranges and yellows, are borne singly or in racemes of up to 6 blooms; they are produced from the bases of the pseudobulbs at any time of year.

- **HARDINESS** Frost tender.
- **CULTIVATION** Intermediate-growing orchids. Grow in containers of terrestrial orchid compost. During the growing season, provide bright indirect light, and water freely; apply a half-strength balanced liquid fertilizer monthly; mist daily and maintain high humidity. In winter, provide full light and water sparingly. See also p.46.
- **PROPAGATION** Divide when the plant "overflows" the container. Remove backbulbs and pot them up separately.
- **PESTS AND DISEASES** Scale insects, red spider mites, aphids, and mealybugs may be troublesome.

S

x *S.* Hazel Boyd 'Apricot Glow' ■ Evergreen orchid with spindle-shaped pseudobulbs and elliptic leaves, 10cm (4in) long. Bears racemes of rich orange-red flowers, marked red on the lips, at any time of year. ↕ 20cm (8in), ↔ 30cm (12in). ❀ (min. 13°C/55°F; max. 30°C/86°F)

x *S.* Jewel Box 'Dark Waters'. Evergreen orchid with spindle-shaped pseudobulbs and elliptic-ovate leaves, 10cm (4in) long. Produces racemes of deep vibrant red flowers at any time of year. ↕↔ 30cm (12in). ❀ (min. 13°C/55°F; max. 30°C/86°F)

x *S.* Trizac 'Purple Emperor' ■ Evergreen orchid with spindle-shaped pseudobulbs and elliptic leaves, 10cm (4in) long. Bears racemes of deep purple flowers at any time of year. ↕↔ 30cm (12in). ❀ (min. 13°C/55°F; max. 30°C/86°F)

SOPHRONITIS

ORCHIDACEAE

Genus of about 8 species of small, evergreen, epiphytic or lithophytic orchids from E. Brazil and Paraguay, found at medium altitudes in humid, shady cloud forest. They have small, elongated to oval, often clustered pseudobulbs, each with a single leathery, ovate to elliptic or oblong, purple-tinted, dark green leaf. Richly coloured flowers are borne singly, or in short-stemmed racemes of up to 5 flowers, at any time of year. The plants resemble miniature cattleyas, and will interbreed with them and other related genera to produce brilliantly coloured hybrids, such as the sophrolaeliocattleyas.

- **HARDINESS** Frost tender.
- **CULTIVATION** Cool-growing orchids. Grow in epiphytic orchid compost in small containers or wooden slatted baskets, or epiphytically on bark. When in growth, provide bright indirect light, water moderately, and maintain high humidity; apply a half-strength balanced liquid fertilizer monthly. In winter, admit full light and water more sparingly. See also p.46.
- **PROPAGATION** Divide when the plant "overflows" the sides of the container.
- **PESTS AND DISEASES** Prone to red spider mites, aphids, and mealybugs.

S. coccinea, syn. *S. grandiflora.* Epiphytic orchid with small, oval or spindle-shaped pseudobulbs and elliptic to ovate, purple-tinted, sometimes glaucous, dark green leaves, 3–6cm (1¼–2½in) long. Bears yellow to red or pinkish red flowers, 6–7cm (2½–3in) across, at any time of year. ↕ 5cm (2in), ↔ 10cm (4in). E. Brazil. ❀ (min. 11–13°C/52–55°F; max. 30°C/86°F)

S. grandiflora see *S. coccinea.*

SORBARIA

ROSACEAE

Genus of 10 species of suckering, deciduous shrubs, often with star-shaped hairs, mainly occurring on riverbanks from the Himalayas to E. Asia. They are cultivated for their elegant foliage and flowers. The leaves are alternate and pinnate; the 5-petalled, star-like white flowers are produced in large, conical, terminal panicles in mid- and late summer. Sorbarias are suitable for a large shrub border, or a wild or woodland garden, where they may form thickets. They are also good for a waterside planting.

- **HARDINESS** Fully hardy.
- **CULTIVATION** Grow in moderately fertile, moist but well-drained, neutral to slightly alkaline soil in full sun to partial shade. Remove excess suckers to restrict spread. Pruning group 2 or 6.
- **PROPAGATION** Sow seed in containers in a cold frame in autumn. Take semi-ripe cuttings in midsummer. Transplant rooted suckers in autumn or winter.
- **PESTS AND DISEASES** Trouble free.

Sorbaria kirilowii

S. aitchisonii see *S. tomentosa* var. *angustifolia.*

S. arborea see *S. kirilowii.*

S. kirilowii ■ syn. *S. arborea, Spiraea arborea.* Vigorous, spreading shrub with arching shoots and pinnate leaves, to 30cm (12in) long, each composed of 13–17 (rarely 9) lance-shaped, tapered, dark green leaflets. In mid- and late summer, bears white flowers, to 6mm (¼in) across, in terminal, arching, conical panicles, to 40cm (16in) long. ↕↔ 1.3–8m (4½–25ft). W. China, S.E. Tibet. ❄❄❄

S. lindleyana see *S. tomentosa.*

S. sorbifolia ■ syn. *Spiraea sorbifolia.* Upright, thicket-forming shrub with erect branches and pinnate leaves, to 25cm (10in) long, each with up to 25 lance-shaped or oblong, tapered, dark green leaflets. In mid- and late summer, produces small white flowers, to 8mm (⅜in) across, in erect, terminal, conical panicles, to 25cm (10in) long. ↕ 2m (6ft), ↔ 3m (10ft). N. Asia, Japan. ❄❄❄

S. tomentosa, syn. *S. lindleyana.* Strong-growing, spreading shrub with pinnate leaves, to 45cm (18in) long, composed of up to 23 lance-shaped, tapered, dark green leaflets. In mid- and late summer, bears small, creamy white flowers, 6mm (¼in) across, in terminal, conical panicles, to 40cm (16in) long. ↕↔ 6m (20ft). Himalayas. ❄❄❄. **var. *angustifolia***, syn *S. aitchisonii, Spiraea aitchisonii*, is shorter, with red shoots and slender leaflets; ↕↔ 3m (10ft); Afghanistan to W. Nepal.

Sorbaria sorbifolia

SORBUS

ROSACEAE

Genus of about 100 species of deciduous trees and shrubs, widely distributed in N. temperate regions, found in woodland, on hills and mountains, and on scree. *Sorbus* species and cultivars are valued for their ornamental leaves, which are alternate, variable, and either simple and toothed to lobed, or pinnate; they often colour well in autumn. They are also grown for their terminal, sometimes panicle-like corymbs of small, white, rarely pink flowers, 0.8–2cm (⅜–¾in) across, borne in spring or early summer, and for their mostly spherical, white, yellow, orange, red, or brown fruit (berries). Tolerant of atmospheric pollution, they are ideal as specimen trees in a small garden, or wild or woodland garden. The raw fruit may cause mild stomach upset if ingested.

- **HARDINESS** Fully hardy to frost hardy.
- **CULTIVATION** Grow in moderately fertile, humus-rich, well-drained soil in full sun or light dappled shade. *Sorbus* species and cultivars with pinnate leaves grow best in moist but well-drained, acid to neutral soil. *S. aria* will thrive on dry, chalky soil as well as on acid soil. Pruning group 1, if necessary.
- **PROPAGATION** Sow seed in containers in a cold frame in autumn. Take greenwood cuttings in early summer; not all will root readily. Bud in summer. Graft in winter.
- **PESTS AND DISEASES** Prone to aphids, blister beetles, red spider mites, scale insects, sawfly larvae, canker, silver leaf, honey fungus, and fireblight.

S. alnifolia ♤ (Korean mountain ash). Broadly conical tree with simple, ovate to lance-shaped, toothed, dark green leaves, to 10cm (4in) long, turning yellow to orange or red in autumn. In mid-spring, bears dense corymbs, 8cm (3in) across, of small white flowers, followed in autumn by spherical, deep pink to red berries, 1cm (½in) across. ↕ 20m (70ft), ↔ 8m (25ft). E. Asia. ❄❄❄

Sorbus americana

Sorbus aria 'Lutescens' (inset: flower detail)

S. americana ■ (American mountain ash). Rounded tree or shrub producing pinnate leaves, to 25cm (10in) long, each with up to 15 oblong to lance-shaped, toothed, light green leaflets, turning yellow or red in autumn. In late spring and early summer, bears dense corymbs, 14cm (5½in) across, of white flowers, followed by spherical, orange-red berries, 8mm (⅜in) across. ↕ 10m (30ft), ↔ 7m (22ft). E. North America. ❄❄❄

S. aria (Whitebeam). Broadly columnar tree producing simple, elliptic to broadly ovate or obovate, toothed, glossy, dark green leaves, to 12cm (5in) long, white-hairy beneath. White flowers are borne in corymbs 8cm (3in) across, in late spring; they are followed by ovoid to spherical, brown-speckled, dark red berries, 1cm (½in) across. ↕ 10–25m (30–80ft), ↔ 10m (30ft). Europe. ❄❄❄. **'Chrysophylla'** has golden yellow juvenile leaves; ↕ 10m (30ft), ↔ 7m (22ft). **'Decaisneana'** see 'Majestica'. **'Lutescens'** ■ is compact in habit, with silvery grey, later grey-green foliage; ↕ 10m (30ft), ↔ 8m (25ft). **'Magnifica'** has large, very glossy leaves, to 12cm (5in) long. **'Majestica'**, syn. 'Decaisneana', has leaves to 15cm (6in) or more long.

S. aucuparia ■ (Mountain ash, Rowan). Broadly conical to rounded tree with mid- to dark green leaves, turning red or yellow in autumn. Leaves are oblong-lance-shaped to elliptic, to 20cm (8in) long, with 1 or 2 pairs of separate leaflets at the bases, or pinnate, with up to 12 oblong-lance-shaped, sharply toothed leaflets. In late spring, bears white flowers in corymbs to 12cm (5in) across, followed by spherical, orange-red berries, 8mm (⅜in) across. ↕ 15m (50ft), ↔ 7m (22ft). Europe, Asia. ❄❄❄. **'Aspleniifolia'** has leaflets pinnately divided at the bases. **'Beissneri'** syn. *S. moravica* 'Laciniata', is upright, with coppery bark, and red shoots and leaf-stalks; yellow-green leaves turn yellow in autumn; ↕ 10m (30ft), ↔ 5m (15ft). **'Cardinal Royal'** is upright and vigorous, and fruits profusely. **'Fastigiata'** syn. *S. decora* var. *nana*, *S. scopulina* of gardens, is dense in habit, with upright branches, conical when mature; it bears dark red berries, 1cm (½in) across; ↕ 8m (25ft), ↔ 5m (15ft). **'Fructu Luteo'** see var. *xanthocarpa*. **var. *pluripinnata*** see *S. scalaris*. **'Sheerwater Seedling'** is narrowly upright; ↕ 10m (30ft), ↔ 5m (15ft). **var. *xanthocarpa*** syn. 'Fructu Luteo', is spreading, with orange-yellow berries; ↕↔ 8m (25ft).

S. cashmiriana ■ Spreading tree or shrub with pinnate leaves, to 20cm (8in) long, composed of 17–21 lance-shaped, dark green leaflets. In late spring, bears pink or white flowers in corymbs 12cm (5in) across, followed by spherical white berries, to 1.5cm (½in) across, pink-tinged at first. ↕ 8m (25ft), ↔ 7m (22ft). W. Himalayas. ❄❄❄

S. 'Chinese Lace' Upright tree with pinnate leaves, to 20cm (8in) long, composed of numerous deeply cut, elliptic to oblong, dark green leaflets. Small white flowers, in corymbs to 15cm (6in) across, are produced in late spring, followed by spherical, orange-red berries, 1cm (½in) across. ↕ 6m (20ft), ↔ 5m (15ft). ❄❄❄

Sorbus aucuparia

S. commixta ■ syn. *S. discolor* of gardens, *S. reflexipetala*. Compact, broadly conical tree or shrub with erect branches and pinnate leaves, to 25cm (10in) long, each with up to 17 elliptic to lance-shaped, tapered, dark green leaflets, turning yellow to red or purple in autumn. In late spring, bears white flowers in corymbs 15cm (6in) across, followed by spherical, orange-red or red berries, 8mm (⅜in) across. ↕ 10m (30ft), ↔ 7m (22ft). Korea, Japan. ❄❄❄. **'Embley'** has bright red leaves in late autumn, and fruits profusely.

S. conradinae see *S. esserteauana*.

S. conradinae of gardens see *S. pohuashanensis*.

S. cuspidata see *S. vestita*.

S. decora ■ Upright tree or shrub with pinnate leaves, to 15cm (6in) long, composed of up to 15 elliptic to oval-lance-shaped, dark blue-green leaflets, turning orange-red in autumn. In late spring, bears white flowers in corymbs to 10cm (4in) across, followed by spherical, bright red berries, 1cm (½in) across. ↕ 8m (25ft), ↔ 5m (15ft). Canada (Newfoundland), Greenland, N.E. USA. ❄❄❄. **var. *nana*** see *S. aucuparia* 'Fastigiata'.

S. discolor of gardens see *S. commixta*.

S. domestica (Service tree). Broadly columnar tree with pinnate leaves, to 20cm (8in) long, composed of up to 21 narrowly oblong, dark green leaflets, turning yellow or red in autumn. In late spring, bears white flowers in conical corymbs, 10cm (4in) across; they are followed by spherical or pear-shaped, yellow-green, red-flushed berries, to 3cm (1¼in) across. ↕ 20m (70ft), ↔ 12m (40ft). C. and S. Europe, N. Africa, Turkey, Caucasus, Ukraine (Crimea), Moldavia. ❄❄❄. **'Maliformis'** see f. *pomifera*. **f. *pomifera***, syn. 'Maliformis', bears spherical berries. **f. *pyriformis*** ■ syn. var. *pyrifera*, var. *pyriformis*, produces pear-shaped berries.

S. esserteauana syn. *S. conradinae*. Spreading tree with large, pinnate leaves, to 25cm (10in) long, composed of up to 15 oblong-lance-shaped, tapered, dark green leaflets, white-felted beneath, turning red in autumn. In late spring, bears white flowers in corymbs 12cm (5in) across, followed by spherical, dark red berries, 8mm (⅜in) across. ↕↔ 10m (30ft). China (W. Sichuan). ❄❄❄. **'Flava'** has orange-yellow berries.

S. folgneri 'Lemon Drop' Arching tree with slightly pendent branches and simple, narrowly ovate, dark green leaves, to 10cm (4in) long, white beneath. In late spring, produces white flowers, in corymbs 10cm (4in) across, followed by ovoid, bright yellow berries, 1cm (½in) across. ↕↔ 8m (25ft). ❄❄❄

S. forrestii Spreading tree with pinnate leaves, to 20cm (8in) long, composed of up to 19 elliptic-oblong, dark blue-green leaflets. In late spring, bears white flowers in corymbs 10cm (4in) across, followed by spherical white berries, 1cm (½in) across, tinged dark pink at the tips. ↕↔ 6m (20ft). China (N.W. Yunnan). ❄❄❄

S. glabrescens see *S. hupehensis*.

S. hupehensis syn. *S. glabrescens* (Hubei rowan). Broadly columnar tree with pinnate leaves, to 15cm (6in) long, each with up to 15 ovate, blue-green leaflets, turning red in autumn. In late spring, bears pyramidal, panicle-like corymbs, to 12cm (5in) long, of white flowers, followed by spherical white berries, 8mm (⅜in) across, slightly flushed pink. ↕↔ to 8m (25ft). China (Hubei). ❄❄❄. **var. *obtusa*** ■ syn. 'Rosea', produces berries that ripen to dark pink.

S

Sorbus cashmiriana

Sorbus commixta

SORBUS

Sorbus decora (inset: fruit detail)

***S.* x *hybrida* of gardens** see *S.* x *thuringiaca.*

S. intermedia ♀ (Swedish whitebeam). Compact, rounded tree with elliptic to oblong-elliptic, toothed, dark green leaves, to 12cm (5in) long, lobed near the bases. In late spring, bears dense corymbs, 12cm (5in) across, of white flowers, followed by ovoid-oblong, bright red berries, 1.5cm (½in) long. ↕↔ 12m (40ft). N.W. Europe. ❄❄❄

***S.* 'Joseph Rock'** ■♀ Broadly upright tree with pinnate leaves, to 15cm (6in) long, composed of up to 21 narrowly oblong, sharply toothed, bright green leaflets, turning orange, red, and purple in autumn. In late spring, bears white flowers, in corymbs 10cm (4in) across, followed by spherical, pale yellow, later orange-yellow berries, 1cm (½in) across. Prone to fireblight. ↕ 10m (30ft), ↔ 7m (22ft). ❄❄❄

S.* x *kewensis ♀ (*S. pohuashanensis* x *S. aucuparia*) syn. *S. pohuashanensis* of gardens. Slow-growing, rounded, shrubby tree with pinnate leaves, to 30cm (12in) long, composed of 4–9 pairs of oblong-elliptic or oblong-lance-shaped, coarsely toothed, mid-green leaflets. In late spring, bears white flowers in corymbs 13cm (5in) across, followed by ovoid, bright red berries, 8mm (⅜in) across. ↕ 2.5m (8ft), ↔ 2m (6ft). Garden origin. ❄❄❄

S. koehneana ♀ Spreading, small tree or shrub with pinnate leaves, to 15cm (6in) long, composed of up to 25 or more oblong to ovate, sharply toothed, dark green leaflets. In late spring, produces small corymbs, 8cm (3in) across, of white flowers, followed by small, spherical, mid-green berries, 6mm (¼in) across, ripening to white, on red stalks. Often confused with *S. fruticosa*, which is very similar but considerably smaller, growing only to 2m (6ft) in height. ↕ 5m (15ft), ↔ 6m (20ft). China. ❄❄❄

***S. lanata* of gardens** see *S. vestita.*

Sorbus domestica f. *pyriformis*

Sorbus hupehensis var. *obtusa*

Sorbus 'Joseph Rock'

S. latifolia ♀ (Service tree of Fontainebleau). Broadly columnar tree with broadly elliptic, sharply toothed, glossy, dark green leaves, to 10cm (4in) long, lobed towards the bases. In late spring, bears white flowers in corymbs 8cm (3in) across, followed by spherical, yellow-brown berries, 1cm (½in) across. ↕ 10–20m (30–70ft), ↔ 5–8m (15–25ft). W. Europe. ❄❄❄

S. megalocarpa ♀ Spreading tree or shrub with arching branches and oval, finely toothed, dark green leaves, to 25cm (10in) long, red when young and in autumn. In early spring, bears pungent, creamy white flowers in dense corymbs, to 15cm (6in) across, before or with the young leaves, followed by ovoid, russet-brown berries, 3cm (1¼in) long. ↕ 8m (25ft), ↔ 10m (30ft). C. to S. China. ❄❄❄

S. microphylla ♀ Elegant, spreading tree or shrub with pinnate leaves, to 17cm (7in) long, each with up to 33 oblong, sharply toothed, dark green leaflets, red in autumn. In late spring, bears small corymbs, to 8cm (3in) across, of pale pink to almost crimson flowers, followed by spherical, white or pink berries, 8mm (⅜in) across. ↕↔ 6m (20ft). W. China, E. Himalayas. ❄❄❄

***S.* 'Mitchellii'** see *S. thibetica* 'John Mitchell'.

***S. moravica* 'Laciniata'** see *S. aucuparia* 'Beissneri'.

S. pohuashanensis ♀ syn. *S. conradinae* of gardens. Spreading tree with pinnate leaves, to 18cm (7in) long, composed of up to 15 elliptic to oblong-lance-shaped, dark green leaflets. In late spring, produces dense corymbs, to 12cm (5in) across, of white flowers, followed by spherical red berries, 8mm (⅜in) across. ↕ to 20m (70ft), ↔ 8m (25ft). Probably N. China. ❄❄❄

Sorbus prattii

Sorbus reducta

***S. pohuashanensis* of gardens** see *S.* x *kewensis.*

S. prattii ■♀ Spreading tree with pinnate leaves, to 15cm (6in) long, composed of up to 31 oblong, sharply toothed, dark green leaflets. In late spring, bears small corymbs, 8cm (3in) across, of white flowers, followed by spherical green berries, 8mm (⅜in) across, ripening to white. ↕↔ 6m (20ft). China (Sichuan). ❄❄❄

S. reducta ■ Thicket-forming, usually suckering shrub with upright shoots. Pinnate leaves, to 10cm (4in) long, composed of up to 15 ovate, glossy, dark green leaflets, turn red and purple in autumn. In late spring, bears white flowers in small, open corymbs, to 8cm (3in) across, followed by spherical, crimson then white berries, 1cm (½in) across. ↕ 1–1.5m (3–5ft), ↔ 2m (6ft) or more. W. China. ❄❄❄

S. reflexipetala see *S. commixta.*

S. sargentiana ■♀ Broadly upright, slow-growing tree with stout shoots and large, sticky red winter buds. Large,

Sorbus sargentiana

S

Sorbus scalaris

pinnate leaves, to 35cm (14in) long, each with up to 13 oblong-lance-shaped, dark green leaflets, turn orange and red in autumn. In early summer, bears white flowers in broad corymbs, 20cm (8in) across, followed by spherical red berries, 8mm (3/8in) across. ↕↔ 10m (30ft). W. China. ❄❄❄
S. scalaris ▣ ♤ syn. *S. aucuparia* var. *pluripinnata*. Spreading tree with pinnate leaves, to 20cm (8in) long, composed of up to 33 narrowly oblong, glossy, dark green leaflets, turning red and purple in late autumn. In late spring and early summer, bears flattened corymbs, 15cm (6in) across, of white flowers, followed by spherical red berries, 6mm (1/4in) across. ↕↔ 10m (30ft). China (W. Sichuan). ❄❄❄
S. scopulina. Erect shrub with pinnate leaves, 3–6cm (1¾–2½in) long, each composed of up to 15 oblong-lance-shaped, dark green leaflets. In late spring and early summer, bears white flowers in corymbs to 10cm (4in) across, followed by spherical, glossy red berries, 1cm (½in) across. ↕ to 2m (6ft), ↔ 1.5m (5ft). North America (British Columbia to New Mexico). ❄❄❄
S. scopulina of gardens see *S. aucuparia* 'Fastigiata'.
S. thibetica ♤ Broadly conical tree with elliptic to rounded, sharply toothed, dark green leaves, to 13cm (5in) long, densely white-hairy when young, and later white-hairy beneath. In late spring and early summer, bears white flowers in corymbs to 6cm (2½in) across, followed by spherical to pear-shaped green berries, 1.5cm (½in) across, ripening orange or yellow. ↕ 20m (70ft), ↔ 15m

Sorbus x *thuringiaca*

Sorbus vilmorinii

(50ft). S.W. China, Himalayas. ❄❄❄. **'John Mitchell'**, syn. *S.* 'Mitchellii', produces broadly rounded leaves.
S. x thuringiaca ▣ ♤ (*S. aria* x *S. aucuparia*) syn. *S.* x *hybrida* of gardens. Compact, broadly conical tree with ovate to elliptic, deeply lobed, glossy, dark green leaves, warm yellow-brown in autumn, to 15cm (6in) long, often with separate leaflets at the bases. In late spring, bears white flowers in corymbs to 12cm (5in) across, followed by spherical to ellipsoid, bright red berries, 1cm (½in) across. ↕ to 15m (50ft), ↔ 8m (25ft). Europe. ❄❄❄. **'Fastigiata'** ♤–♤ is very compact and narrowly upright, becoming broadly conical with age.
S. vestita ♤ syn. *S. cuspidata*, *S. lanata* of gardens. Broadly conical tree with simple, elliptic, sharply toothed, sometimes shallowly lobed leaves, to 20cm (8in) long. Leaves are white-hairy when young; mature leaves are glossy, dark green above, white-hairy beneath. In late spring, bears white-woolly corymbs, to 8cm (3in) across, of white flowers, followed by spherical, brown-speckled, yellow-green berries, 2cm (¾in) across. ↕ to 25m (80ft), ↔ 10m (30ft). Himalayas, N. Burma. ❄❄❄
S. vilmorinii ▣ ♤ Spreading shrub or tree with arching branches and pinnate leaves, to 15cm (6in) long, composed of up to 29 glossy, dark green leaflets. In late spring and early summer, bears white flowers in corymbs 10cm (4in) across, followed by spherical, dark red berries, 1cm (½in) across, ageing pink then white. ↕↔ 5m (15ft). S.W. China. ❄❄❄
S. 'Wilfrid Fox' ♤–♤ Upright tree, broadly conical when mature, with elliptic, glossy, dark green leaves, to 12cm (5in) long, densely white-hairy beneath. White flowers are produced in corymbs 10cm (4in) across, in late spring, followed by spherical, yellow-brown, red-flushed berries, to 1.5cm (½in) across. ↕ 15m (50ft), ↔ 10m (30ft). ❄❄❄

SORGHASTRUM

GRAMINEAE/POACEAE

Genus of about 16 species of clump-forming, annual and perennial grasses from prairies and savannah in Africa and tropical and temperate North, Central, and South America. They are cultivated for their open or narrow, terminal panicles of late-summer flowerheads (which may be dried and dyed), and for their linear, flat or rolled leaves. Suitable for a mixed or herbaceous border.
• **HARDINESS** Fully hardy to frost tender.
• **CULTIVATION** Grow in moderately fertile, well-drained soil in full sun. Protect from excessive winter wet.
• **PROPAGATION** Sow seed in containers in a cold frame in spring. Divide in mid-spring or early summer.
• **PESTS AND DISEASES** Trouble free.

S. avenaceum see *S. nutans*.
S. nutans, syn. *S. avenaceum* (Indian grass, Wood grass). Slowly spreading, perennial grass forming loose clumps of erect stems with arching, broadly linear, bluish green leaves, to 60cm (24in) long. From summer to autumn, produces narrow, terminal panicles, to 35cm (14in) long, of golden brown spikelets. ↕ 1.2m (4ft), ↔ 60cm (24in). E. and C. USA. ❄❄❄. **'Sioux Blue'** is strongly erect, with metallic blue-green leaves, turning purple in autumn, and glossy, red-brown spikelets with yellow anthers.

▷ **Sorrel** see *Oxalis*
▷ **Sorrel tree** see *Oxydendrum arboreum*
▷ **Sourwood** see *Oxydendrum arboreum*
▷ **Southernwood** see *Artemisia abrotanum*
▷ **Sowbread** see *Cyclamen*
▷ **Spanish bayonet** see *Yucca aloifolia*
▷ **Spanish chestnut** see *Castanea sativa*
▷ **Spanish dagger** see *Yucca gloriosa*
▷ **Spanish shawl** see *Heterocentron elegans*

SPARAXIS

Harlequin flower

IRIDACEAE

Genus of 6 species of cormous perennials from moist, rocky sites in South Africa. They are grown for their loose spikes of up to 5 widely funnel-shaped, brightly coloured flowers, borne in spring or summer. The sword-, sickle-, or lance-shaped, ribbed leaves, are often produced in an erect, basal fan. In frost-prone regions, grow in a cool greenhouse or conservatory, or outdoors at the base of a warm, sunny wall in summer. In warmer areas, use in a raised bed or at the front of a border.
• **HARDINESS** Half hardy.
• **CULTIVATION** Plant corms 10cm (4in) deep. Under glass, plant in early to late autumn in loam-based potting compost (JI No.2), with added sand and leaf mould, in full light with shade from hot sun. Water sparingly when in growth, and keep cool; dry off as flowers fade. Keep completely dry when dormant. Outdoors, plant in late autumn in moderately fertile, well-drained soil in full sun. Shelter from cold, drying winds. Provide a dry winter mulch.
• **PROPAGATION** Sow seed in containers in a cold frame as soon as ripe. Remove offsets when corms are dormant.
• **PESTS AND DISEASES** Trouble free.

S. elegans, syn. *Streptanthera cuprea*, *Streptanthera elegans*. Cormous perennial with basal fans of sword-shaped leaves, 8–25cm (3–10in) long. In spring and summer, bears up to 5 stems, each with a spike of up to 5 widely funnel-shaped, orange or red, rarely white flowers, 4cm (1½in) long, fading to pink, and marked with yellow and violet. ↕ 10–30cm (4–12in), ↔ 8cm (3in). South Africa (Western Cape). ❄
S. fragrans. Cormous perennial with basal fans of lance- or sickle-shaped leaves, to 30cm (12in) long. In spring and summer, bears spikes of up to 6 flattish, widely funnel-shaped flowers, 5–6cm (2–2½in) long, with cream, yellow, red-purple, or violet-purple lobes, sometimes with darker markings, and yellow, purple, or black tubes. ↕ 8–45cm (3–18in), ↔ 8cm (3in). South Africa (Western Cape). ❄. **subsp. *grandiflora***, syn. *S. grandiflora*, is less vigorous, bearing reddish purple flowers with yellow tubes.
S. grandiflora see *S. fragrans* subsp. *grandiflora*.
S. pillansii. Cormous perennial with basal fans of 8 or 10 narrowly sword-

Sparaxis tricolor

S

shaped leaves, to 35cm (14in) long. In spring, bears 2–4 stems, each with spikes of 4–9 flattish, widely funnel-shaped flowers, to 6cm (2½in) across, with rose-pink lobes, marked yellow and purple-edged at the bases, and yellow tubes. ↕ to 60cm (24in), ↔ 8cm (3in). South Africa (Western Cape, Northern Cape). ❄

S. tricolor ▣ Cormous perennial with basal fans of erect, lance-shaped leaves, to 30cm (12in) long. From spring to early summer, produces 1–5 stems that bear 2–5 widely funnel-shaped, orange, red, or purple flowers, 5–8cm (2–3in) across, each with a black or dark red central mark. ↕ 10–40cm (4–16in), ↔ 8cm (3in). South Africa (Western Cape). ❄

SPARGANIUM

Burr reed

SPARGANIACEAE/TYPHACEAE

Genus of 21 species of deciduous or semi-evergreen, rhizomatous, marginal aquatic perennials, widely distributed in temperate regions worldwide, where they form vigorous stands of lush growth at the edges of lakes and rivers. Strong rhizomes support erect, linear, deep green, sometimes brown-green leaves, and produce spikes or racemes of inconspicuous, spherical, male and female flowerheads, followed by fleshy, burr-like fruits. Best grown in the shallows of a large wildlife pool.

- **HARDINESS** Fully hardy.
- **CULTIVATION** Grow in large drifts in a shallow pool margin, to 45cm (18in) deep, in full sun or partial shade. In winter, leave the foliage to provide shelter for wildlife. Remove dead foliage in spring. See also pp.52–53.
- **PROPAGATION** Sow seed at 15°C (59°F) as soon as ripe. Divide in spring.
- **PESTS AND DISEASES** Trouble free.

S. emersum. Vigorous, submerged, floating, or erect, semi-evergreen, marginal aquatic perennial with erect, boldly keeled, linear leaves, 20–50cm (8–20in) long, longer and wider on sterile plants. In summer, erect, unbranched flower spikes, 20–80cm (8–32in) long, bear densely packed, spherical, white to yellow-green flowerheads, to 2.5cm (1in) across, followed by ellipsoid, spiky brown fruit, 4–6mm (⅛–¼in) across. ↕ 20–70cm (10–28in), ↔ indefinite. Eurasia, North America. ❄❄❄

S. erectum, syn. *S. ramosum*. Vigorous, erect, rarely floating or submerged, semi-evergreen, marginal aquatic perennial with keeled, linear leaves, 1.5m (5ft) long. In summer, branched flower spikes, 20–100cm (8–39in) long, bear spherical, greenish brown flowerheads, 1–2cm (½–¾in) across, followed by ellipsoid to conical, prickly brown fruit, 6–9mm (¼–⅜in) across. ↕ 1.5m (5ft), ↔ indefinite. Eurasia. ❄❄❄

S. minimum see *S. natans*.

S. natans, syn. *S. minimum*. Slender, floating, deciduous or semi-evergreen, marginal aquatic perennial with thin, flat, translucent, dark green, submerged, sometimes floating leaves, 6–40cm (2½–16in) long. In summer, floating stems, 8–40cm (3–16in) long, bear unbranched spikes, 50–150cm (20–60in) or more long, of spherical, brownish green flowerheads, 1–2cm (½–¾in) across, followed by ovoid, spiky, green or brown fruit, 6–10mm (¼–½in) across. ↔ indefinite. Arctic, Eurasia, North America. ❄❄❄

S. ramosum see *S. erectum*.

▷ ***Sparmannia*** see *Sparrmannia*

SPARRMANNIA

syn. SPARMANNIA

TILIACEAE

Genus of 3–7 species of evergreen shrubs and small trees found in open woodland in tropical Africa, South Africa, and Madagascar. They are grown for their 4-petalled, white or pink to purple flowers, each with a showy boss of stamens, produced in long-stalked umbels from the upper leaf axils. Leaves are alternate, simple or palmately 3- to 7-lobed, toothed, narrow to broadly ovate, and often heart-shaped at the bases. In frost-prone climates, grow in a cool or temperate greenhouse. In warmer areas, grow sparrmannias in a shrub border.

- **HARDINESS** Frost tender.
- **CULTIVATION** Under glass, grow in loam-based potting compost (JI No.3) in full light. When in growth, water freely and apply a balanced liquid fertilizer monthly. Water sparingly in winter. Outdoors, grow in fertile, moist but well-drained soil in full sun. Pruning group 9, in late winter. Needs restrictive pruning under glass.
- **PROPAGATION** Sow seed at 15–18°C (59–64°F) in spring. Root semi-ripe cuttings with bottom heat in summer. Air layer in spring.
- **PESTS AND DISEASES** Whiteflies and red spider mites may be troublesome under glass.

S. africana ▣ ♀ (African hemp). Large shrub or small, upright tree with vigorous, many-branched, hairy stems and long-stalked, ovate to broadly ovate or rounded, shallowly palmately lobed, hairy, light green leaves, to 21cm (8in) long. In late spring and early summer, bears umbels of up to 20 cup-shaped white flowers, 3–4cm (1¼–1½in) across, with long, yellow and red-purple stamens. ↕ 3–6m (10–20ft), ↔ 2–4m (6–12ft). South Africa. ❁ (min. 7°C/45°F). **'Flore Pleno'**, syn. 'Plena', produces double flowers. **'Plena'** see 'Flore Pleno'. **'Variegata'** has leaves marked with white.

Sparrmannia africana

Spartium junceum

SPARTIUM

Broom, Spanish broom

LEGUMINOSAE/PAPILIONACEAE

Genus of a single species of deciduous shrub occurring in dry places, open woodland, and on roadsides mainly in the Mediterranean region, including Portugal. *S. junceum* is cultivated for its terminal racemes of fragrant, pea-like yellow flowers and rich dark green, broom-like stems. The leaves are sparse, alternate, simple, and dark green. It is suitable for a shrub border, or for growing against a warm, sunny wall.

- **HARDINESS** Frost hardy.
- **CULTIVATION** Grow in moderately fertile, well-drained soil in full sun. Thrives in coastal sites and on chalky soils. Pruning group 9. Cut back older specimens to the ground in spring.
- **PROPAGATION** Sow seed in containers in a cold frame in autumn or spring. May self-seed.
- **PESTS AND DISEASES** Young plants may be damaged by rabbits.

S. junceum ▣ Upright shrub with slender, dark green shoots and few linear-oblong to narrowly lance-shaped, dark green leaves, to 3cm (1¼in) long, silky-hairy beneath. A profusion of fragrant, pea-like, golden yellow flowers, 2.5cm (1in) long, is borne in terminal racemes, to 45cm (18in) long, from early summer to early autumn; flowers are followed by flattened, dark brown seed pods, to 8cm (3in) long. ↕↔ 3m (10ft). S. Europe, Ukraine (Crimea), Turkey, Syria, N. Africa. ❄❄

SPATHIPHYLLUM

Peace lily

ARACEAE

Genus of 41 species of erect, sometimes rhizomatous, evergreen perennials from damp tropical forest in Indonesia, the Philippines, and tropical North, Central, and South America. They are cultivated for their stately, long-stemmed, white spathes, set against dark green, elliptic or lance-shaped leaves with prominent midribs. In frost-prone climates, grow in a warm greenhouse or conservatory. In warmer areas, use in a humid, shady border. *Spathiphyllum* hybrids make excellent houseplants. All parts of the plants may cause mild stomach upset if ingested, and contact with the sap may irritate skin.

Spathiphyllum 'Mauna Loa'

- **HARDINESS** Frost tender.
- **CULTIVATION** Under glass, grow in well-drained, loamless compost or loam-based potting compost (JI No.2). Water freely in growth, applying a balanced liquid fertilizer monthly; maintain high humidity. Provide low light throughout the year. Pot on when root growth "overflows" the sides of the container. Outdoors, grow in moist but well-drained, humus-rich soil in shade.
- **PROPAGATION** Sow seed at 23–27°C (73–81°F) as soon as ripe, or in spring on sphagnum moss. Divide in winter or immediately after flowering.
- **PESTS AND DISEASES** Trouble free.

***S.* 'Mauna Loa'** ▣ Vigorous, compact, rhizomatous perennial with lance-shaped, glossy, dark green leaves, to 22cm (9in) long. Bears oval white spathes, 10–15cm (4–6in) long, with ivory spadices, to 8cm (3in) long, in spring and summer. ↕ 60–100cm (2–3ft), ↔ 60cm (24in). ❁ (min. 15°C/59°F)

S. wallisii ▣ (Peace lily). Rhizomatous perennial with lance-shaped-elliptic to oblong-elliptic, dark green leaves, 24–35cm (10–14in) long. Ovate to oblong-elliptic, slightly fragrant white spathes, to 17cm (7in) long, with white, spiky spadices, 3–8cm (1¼–3in) long, are borne above the foliage in spring and summer. ↕ 65cm (26in), ↔ 50cm (20in). Costa Rica, Panama, Colombia, Venezuela. ❁ (min. 10°C/50°F). **'Clevelandii'**, often grown as *S. wallisii*, is free-flowering, with white spathes, to 18cm (7in) long, on long stalks. Leaves are drooping, oblong-lance-shaped, and glossy, 30–45cm (12–18in) long.

Spathiphyllum wallisii

S

SPATHODEA

African tulip tree

BIGNONIACEAE

Genus of one species of usually evergreen tree from forest margins and gorges in tropical Africa. It is grown for its showy, bell-shaped flowers and large, pinnate leaves. Where temperatures fall below 13°C (55°F), grow *S. campanulata* in a warm greenhouse; it seldom blooms in containers. In tropical climates, use as a specimen tree.

• **HARDINESS** Frost tender.

• **CULTIVATION** Under glass, grow in large containers or in a greenhouse border, in loam-based potting compost (JI No.3) in full light. When in growth, water freely and apply a balanced liquid fertilizer monthly; water sparingly in winter. Outdoors, grow in fertile, moist soil in full sun. Pruning group 1; needs restrictive pruning under glass, in late winter or after flowering.

• **PROPAGATION** Sow seed at 18–24°C (64–75°F) in spring. Root semi-ripe cuttings with bottom heat in summer. Air layer in spring.

• **PESTS AND DISEASES** Red spider mites may be troublesome under glass.

S. campanulata ■ ♀ Moderately branched, open, leafy tree with opposite, pinnate leaves, to 45cm (18in) long, each comprising 9–19 oblong to ovate, leathery, deep green leaflets. Terminal racemes or panicles of asymmetrical, bell-shaped, yellow-rimmed, scarlet to blood-red flowers, 5–10cm (2–4in) long, yellowish green inside, are borne mainly in spring and summer; they have a crêpe-like texture, fox-like scent, and abundant nectar. Large, woody, canoe-shaped seed pods release papery-winged seeds. ↕ 18–25m (60–80ft), ↔ 10–18m (30–60ft). Tropical Africa. ❀ (min. 13–15°C/55–59°F)

Spathodea campanulata (inset: flower detail)

▷**Spatterdock** see *Nuphar*
American see *N. advena*
▷**Speargrass** see *Aciphylla, A. colensoi*
▷**Spearmint** see *Mentha spicata*
▷**Spearwort,**
Greater see *Ranunculus lingua*
Lesser see *Ranunculus flammula*
▷***Specularia speculum-veneris*** see *Legousia speculum-veneris*
▷**Speedwell** see *Veronica*
Digger's see *Parahebe perfoliata*
Germander see *Veronica chamaedrys*
Prostrate see *Veronica prostrata*
Rock see *Veronica fruticans*
Silver see *Veronica spicata* subsp. *incana*

SPHAERALCEA

syn. ILIAMNA

False mallow, Globe mallow

MALVACEAE

Genus of about 60 species of downy annuals, perennials, and deciduous or evergreen subshrubs and shrubs found in well-drained sites (many on mountain slopes, in wasteland, or in scrub) in warmer regions of North America, with a few in South America and southern Africa. The upright or decumbent stems bear spirally arranged, linear-lance-shaped to rounded, simple or lobed to palmate, toothed leaves. Saucer- or cup-shaped, mallow-like flowers, the stamens joined into a column around the styles, are borne singly or in racemes or panicles from summer to autumn. Suitable for a gravel garden, raised bed, or stony bank, with protection from excessive winter wet; may also be grown in a cold greenhouse.

Sphaeralcea munroana

• **HARDINESS** Fully hardy to half hardy.

• **CULTIVATION** Outdoors, grow in moderately fertile, sharply drained, gravelly soil in full sun; in colder areas, plant in a warm, dry, sheltered position, and protect from winter wet. Under glass, grow in loam-based potting compost (JI No.2) with added grit, in full light. When in growth, water moderately and apply a balanced liquid fertilizer monthly. Water sparingly in winter. Repot annually in early spring.

• **PROPAGATION** Sow seed at 13°C (55°F) in spring. Divide perennials as growth begins in spring. Root basal or softwood cuttings with bottom heat in spring or early summer.

• **PESTS AND DISEASES** Hollyhock rust may be a problem.

S. coccinea, syn. *Malvastrum coccineum* (Prairie mallow). Spreading, grey- or white-hairy perennial with rounded, deeply 3- to 5-lobed, mid-green leaves, to 4cm (1½in) long, each lobe further divided. Decumbent, branching stems bear short, terminal racemes of cup-shaped, orange to red flowers, to 4cm (1½in) across, throughout summer. ↕ to 60cm (24in), ↔ 35cm (14in). S. Canada, C. and S.W. USA. ❄❄❄

S. fendleri. Hairy, subshrubby perennial with upright, branching stems and ovate to oblong, 3-lobed, toothed leaves, to 6cm (2½in) long, mid-green above, paler and often densely white-hairy beneath. From early summer to mid-autumn, saucer-shaped, reddish orange to pinkish violet flowers, to 2.5cm (1in) across, are borne in tight, axillary panicles, forming long, interrupted spikes. ↕ 1.2m (4ft), ↔ 45cm (18in). S.W. USA. ❄❄

S. munroana ■ Grey-hairy perennial with upright, unbranched stems and ovate to almost diamond-shaped, shallowly 3- to 5-lobed or scalloped, mid-green leaves, to 6cm (2½in) long. From midsummer to early autumn, bears saucer-shaped, reddish orange flowers, 2.5cm (1in) across, in many-flowered, axillary and terminal panicles. ↕ to 80cm (32in), ↔ 45cm (18in). W. North America. ❄❄❄

▷**Spicebush** see *Calycanthus*
▷**Spice bush** see *Lindera benzoin*
▷**Spider flower** see *Cleome*
Brazilian see *Tibouchina urvilleana*
▷**Spider lily** see *Hymenocallis*
Golden see *Lycoris aurea*
Red see *Lycoris radiata*
▷**Spider orchid** see *Brassia lawrenceana*
▷**Spider plant** see *Chlorophytum comosum, Cleome hassleriana*
▷**Spignel** see *Meum athamanticum*
▷**Spikemoss, Krauss's** see *Selaginella kraussiana*
▷**Spikenard, False** see *Smilacina racemosa*
▷***Spiloxene capensis*** see *Hypoxis capensis*
▷**Spinach,**
Chinese see *Amaranthus tricolor*
Lincolnshire see *Chenopodium bonus-henricus*
Red mountain see *Atriplex hortensis*
Tree see *Chenopodium giganteum*
▷**Spindle,**
Japanese see *Euonymus japonicus*
Winged see *Euonymus alatus*
▷**Spindle tree** see *Euonymus*

SPIRAEA

ROSACEAE

Genus of about 80 species of deciduous or semi-evergreen shrubs found in rocky places, thickets, woodland, at woodland margins, and on riverbanks, in N. temperate regions of Europe, Asia, and North America, including Mexico. The alternate leaves are entire, toothed, scalloped, or lobed. Spiraeas are grown mainly for their terminal, umbel-like racemes, panicles, cymes, or corymbs of small, mostly saucer-, cup-, or bowl-shaped, white, yellow, pink, or purple flowers; these are 0.5–1cm (¼–½in) across, sometimes slightly larger, and are profusely borne in spring or summer. Grow in a mixed or shrub border. Compact spiraeas are ideal for a rock garden; use low-growing variants of *S. japonica* as ground cover; use taller spiraeas as informal hedging.

• **HARDINESS** Fully hardy, although new growth on early-flowering species and cultivars may be damaged by late frosts.

• **CULTIVATION** Grow in fertile, moist but well-drained soil in full sun. Pruning group 2 for spiraeas flowering on previous year's wood; group 6 for those flowering on current season's wood (*S. douglasii* and *S. japonica*).

• **PROPAGATION** Take greenwood cuttings in summer. Divide suckering

Spiraea 'Arguta'

S

Spiraea canescens

species, such as *S.* x *billiardii* and *S. douglasii*, in late autumn or early spring.
• **Pests and diseases** Trouble free.

S. aitchisonii see *Sorbaria tomentosa* var. *angustifolia.*
S. albiflora see *S. japonica* var. *albiflora.*
***S. alpina* var. *lobata* of gardens** see *Filipendula multijuga.*
S. arborea see *Sorbaria kirilowii.*
***S.* 'Arguta'** ▣ (Bridal wreath, Foam of May). Dense, rounded, deciduous shrub with slender, arching shoots and lance-shaped to narrowly oblong, toothed, bright green leaves, to 4cm (1½in) long. In spring, produces saucer-shaped white flowers in corymbs, to 6cm (2½in) across, on short, leafy, lateral branches. ↕↔ 2.5m (8ft). ❄❄❄
S. aruncus see *Aruncus dioicus.*
S. betulifolia. Dense, rounded, deciduous shrub with rounded to angled, red-brown shoots and ovate to elliptic or oblong-elliptic leaves, the margins partially or completely, singly or doubly scalloped, dark green above, greyish green beneath, 2–4cm (¾–1½in) long. The small white, sometimes pink, saucer-shaped flowers, with prominent stamens and the sepals reflexed in fruit, are produced in dense corymbs, 2.5–9cm (1–3½in) across, in summer. ↕↔ 0.5–1m (20–39in). N.E. Asia to C. Japan. ❄❄❄
S.* x *billiardii (*S. douglasii* x *S. salicifolia*). Upright, thicket-forming, suckering, deciduous shrub with oval to narrowly oblong, toothed, mid- or dark green leaves, to 10cm (4in) long. Cup-shaped, purple-pink flowers are borne in dense panicles, to 20cm (8in) long, in mid- and late summer. ↕ 1–2m (3–6ft), ↔ to 2m (6ft). Garden origin. ❄❄❄. **'Triumphans'** has dark green leaves, 6cm (2½in) long; ↕↔ 2.5m (8ft).
S.* x *bumalda see *S. japonica* 'Bumalda'.
S. canescens ▣ Upright, deciduous shrub with arching shoots and elliptic to obovate, grey-green leaves, to 2.5cm (1in) long, toothed at the tips. Bowl-shaped, creamy white flowers, in corymbs to 5cm (2in) across, are borne at the tips of short, lateral shoots in mid- and late summer. ↕ 3m (10ft), ↔ 2m (6ft). Himalayas. ❄❄❄
S. cantoniensis ▣ Spreading, deciduous or semi-evergreen shrub with arching shoots and lance-shaped, toothed, blue-green leaves, to 6cm (2½in) long. In early summer, short, lateral shoots bear corymbs, to 5cm (2in) across, of bowl-shaped white flowers. ↕ 2m (6ft), ↔ 3m (10ft). ❄❄❄. **'Flore Pleno'**, syn. 'Lanceata', has double white flowers. **'Lanceata'** see 'Flore Pleno'.
S. crispifolia see *S. japonica* 'Bullata'.
S. digitata see *Filipendula palmata.*
***S. digitata* 'Nana' of gardens** see *Filipendula multijuga.*
S. douglasii. Vigorous, suckering, erect, thicket-forming, deciduous shrub with narrowly oblong, dark green leaves, to 10cm (4in) long, toothed at the tips and densely grey-felted beneath. In early and midsummer, bears bowl-shaped, purple-pink flowers in dense panicles, to 20cm (8in) long. ↕ 2.5m (8ft), ↔ 1.5m (5ft). W. North America. ❄❄❄. **subsp. *menziesii***, syn. *S. menziesii*, produces pink flowers, and leaves without felt beneath.
S. japonica. Clump-forming, deciduous shrub with erect shoots. Ovate to lance-shaped, sharply toothed, dark green leaves, to 12cm (5in) long, are grey-green beneath. In mid- and late summer, bears bowl-shaped, pink or white flowers in corymbs to 20cm (8in) across. ↕ 2m (6ft), ↔ 1.5m (5ft). China, Japan. ❄❄❄. **'Alba'** see var. *albiflora*. **var. *albiflora***, syn. 'Alba', *S. albiflora*, has pale green leaves, and white flowers in corymbs 10cm (4in) across; ↕ 60cm (24in), ↔ 90cm (36in). **'Allgold'** has golden yellow leaves and pink flowers; ↕ 45cm (18in), ↔ 60cm (24in). **'Anthony Waterer'**, has pink flowers, and leaves often margined creamy white, bronze-red when young; ↕ to 1.5m (5ft). **'Bullata'**, syn. *S. crispifolia*, is slow-growing and compact, with small, very dark green leaves, to 2.5cm (1in) long, and pink flowers in corymbs 8cm (3in) across; ↕ to 40cm (16in), ↔ to 50cm (20in). **'Bumalda'**, syn. *S.* x *bumalda*, has bronze young leaves and pink flowers; ↕↔ 1m (3ft). **'Froebelii'** ▣ has bronze-red young leaves and pink flowers. **'Golden Princess'** ▣ has bronze-red, later bright yellow leaves, red in autumn, and bright purplish pink flowers. **'Goldflame'** ▣ has bronze-red young leaves, turning bright yellow then mid-green, and pink flowers; ↕↔ 75cm (30in). **'Little Princess'** ▣ forms a dense mound, with small leaves, 2.5cm (1in) long, and rose-pink flowers in corymbs 4cm (1½in) across; ↕ 50cm (20in), ↔ 1m (3ft). **'Nana'**, syn. 'Nyewoods', forms a dwarf mound, with small leaves, to 1cm (½in) long, and pink flowers in corymbs 2.5cm (1in) across; ↕ 45cm (18in), ↔ 60cm (24in). **'Nyewoods'** see 'Nana'. **'Shiburi'** see 'Shirobana'. **'Shirobana'**, syn. 'Shiburi', has both dark pink and white flowers on the same plant; ↕↔ 60cm (24in).
***S. lobata* 'Nana' of gardens** see *Filipendula multijuga.*
S. menziesii see *S. douglasii* subsp. *menziesii.*
S. nipponica. Upright to spreading, deciduous shrub with arching branches and ovate to rounded, dark green leaves, 1.5–3cm (½–1¼in) long, entire or with a few teeth at the tips, bluish green beneath. In midsummer, bowl-shaped white flowers open in corymbs 2.5–4cm (1–1½in) across. ↕↔ 1.2–2.5m (4–8ft). Japan. ❄❄❄. **'Halward's Silver'** is erect but compact, and flowers freely; ↕↔ 1m (3ft). **'Snowmound'** ▣ syn. var. *tosaensis* of gardens, is fast-growing and spreading. **var. *tosaensis* of gardens** see 'Snowmound'.
S. opulifolius see *Physocarpus opulifolius.*
S. palmata see *Filipendula palmata.*
***S. palmata* 'Purpurea' of gardens** see *Filipendula purpurea* 'Purpurascens'.
S. prunifolia, syn. *S. prunifolia* 'Plena'. Arching, deciduous shrub with ovate, finely toothed leaves, to 4.5cm (1¾in) long, glossy, bright green above, grey-downy beneath, turning bronze-yellow to red in autumn. Double white flowers are produced in stalkless corymbs, to 6cm (2½in) across, on short laterals along the shoots, in mid- and late spring. ↕↔ 2m (6ft). China, Taiwan, Japan. ❄❄❄. **'Plena'** see *S. prunifolia.*
S. salicifolia (Bridewort). Erect, strongly suckering, deciduous shrub with angular, red-brown shoots and elliptic to oblong-lance-shaped, dark green, sharply and often doubly toothed

Spiraea japonica 'Goldflame'

leaves, 4–8cm (1½–3in) long. In summer, bears small white flowers, tinted pink, in dense, pyramidal panicles, to 20cm (8in) long. ↕ 2m (6ft), ↔ 2–3m (6–10ft) or more. C. and S.E. Europe to N.E. Asia (Russia, Mongolia, N. China, Korea, Japan). Naturalized in N. Europe. ❄❄❄
***S.* 'Snow White'**, syn. *S. trichocarpa* 'Snow White'. Bushy, deciduous shrub with arching shoots and ovate, bright mid-green leaves, to 5cm (2in) long, with a few teeth at the tips. Small, cup-shaped white flowers are borne in dense corymbs, to 5cm (2in) across, on short laterals, in late spring and early summer. ↕↔ 2m (6ft). ❄❄❄
S. sorbifolia see *Sorbaria sorbifolia.*
S. thunbergii. Dense, bushy, deciduous or semi-evergreen shrub with arching

Spiraea japonica 'Little Princess'

Spiraea cantoniensis

Spiraea japonica 'Froebelii'

Spiraea japonica 'Golden Princess'

Spiraea nipponica 'Snowmound'

Spiraea x *vanhouttei*

branches and slender, lance-shaped, sparsely toothed, light green leaves, to 4cm (1½in) long. In spring and early summer, bears bowl- or saucer-shaped white flowers in stalkless corymbs, to 5cm (2in) across, on short laterals along the shoots. ↕ 1.5m (5ft), ↔ 2m (6ft). China, Japan. ❄❄❄
S. trichocarpa. Spreading, deciduous shrub with rigid, distinctly angled shoots and inversely lance-shaped to oblong-inversely-lance-shaped, pointed, entire or slightly toothed leaves, bright green above, glaucous beneath, 2.5–6cm (1–2½in) long. In summer, clusters of many, rounded corymbs, 2.5–6cm (1–2½in) across, of saucer-shaped white flowers are borne on short, leafy shoots of the previous year's growth to form arching sprays of bloom. ↕↔ 1–2m (3–6ft). Korea. ❄❄❄. **'Snow White'** see *S.* 'Snow White'.
S. ulmaria see *Filipendula ulmaria.*
S.* x *vanhouttei ▣ (*S. cantoniensis* x *S. trilobata*). Compact, bushy, deciduous shrub with slender, arching shoots. The diamond-shaped to obovate leaves, to 4.5cm (1¾in) long, are scalloped or coarsely toothed, occasionally 3- to 5-lobed at the tips, and dark green above, blue-green beneath. Bowl-shaped white flowers are borne in dense corymbs, to 5cm (2in) across, on short laterals along the shoots, in early summer. ↕ 2m (6ft), ↔ 1.5m (5ft). Garden origin. ❄❄❄. **'Pink Ice'** is slow-growing, with white-flecked leaves.
S. veitchii. Upright, deciduous shrub with long, arching shoots, red when young, and elliptic to oblong, entire, mid-green leaves, to 5cm (2in) long, glaucous beneath. In early and mid-summer, bears bowl-shaped white flowers in dense corymbs, 6cm (2½in) across, on short laterals along the shoots. ↕ 4m (12ft), ↔ 3m (10ft). W. and C. China. ❄❄❄

▷**Spiraea, Rock** see *Petrophytum*

SPIRANTHES

ORCHIDACEAE

Genus of about 50 species of usually small, evergreen or deciduous, terrestrial or rarely epiphytic orchids from grassland or woodland habitats, often close to water, in temperate and tropical regions, mainly in North America, with a few in Europe and Asia. They have tuberous roots and basal rosettes of papery or fleshy, lance-shaped or ovate to almost rounded leaves. Tiny white flowers are produced in spiral racemes along erect stems. May form large colonies outdoors.

- **HARDINESS** Fully hardy to frost tender.
- **CULTIVATION** Cool-growing orchids. Under glass, grow in terrestrial orchid compost in bright filtered light. In the growing season, water freely and apply fertilizer at every third watering. Keep almost dry and frost-free when dormant. Outdoors, plant hardy species, when dormant, in moist but well-drained, fertile, humus-rich, leafy soil in a sheltered site in partial shade. Provide a deep, dry winter mulch in frost-prone areas. See also p.46.
- **PROPAGATION** Divide tubers when dormant.
- **PESTS AND DISEASES** Susceptible to red spider mites and aphids under glass.

S. cernua ▣ (Nodding ladies' tresses). Deciduous, terrestrial orchid producing broadly linear, acute leaves, 5–24cm (2–10in) long. Bears spiral racemes of almost translucent white flowers, 5mm (¼in) long, with yellow centres, in autumn. ↕ 60cm (24in), ↔ 8cm (3in). E. Canada, USA. ❄ (min. 2°C/36°F) in containers.

▷***Spironema fragrans*** see *Callisia fragrans*
▷**Spleenwort** see *Asplenium*
Maidenhair see *A. trichomanes*
Mother see *A. bulbiferum*
Shining see *A. oblongifolium*
▷**Spotted dog** see *Pulmonaria officinalis*
▷**Spotted orchid** see *Dactylorhiza*
Heath see *D. maculata*

Spiranthes cernua

SPREKELIA

AMARYLLIDACEAE

Genus of a single species of bulbous perennial occurring on rocky slopes in Mexico and Guatemala. It has semi-erect, strap-shaped, basal leaves, and is grown for its large, showy, 6-tepalled red flowers, sometimes marked or striped yellow, borne in spring. In frost-prone areas, grow in a temperate greenhouse or conservatory; in warmer areas, grow in a sunny border.

- **HARDINESS** Frost tender.
- **CULTIVATION** Plant in autumn with the neck and shoulders of the bulb above soil level. Under glass, grow in loam-based potting compost (JI No.3) in full light. When in growth, water moderately and apply a half-strength balanced liquid fertilizer every 2 weeks after flowering. Reduce water as foliage fades; keep almost dry when dormant. Repot every 2–3 years. Outdoors, grow in well-drained, moderately fertile soil in full sun. Roots resent disturbance.
- **PROPAGATION** Separate offsets when dormant in early autumn.
- **PESTS AND DISEASES** Trouble free.

S. formosissima ▣ (Aztec lily, Jacobean lily). Bulbous perennial with strap-shaped leaves, to 50cm (20in) long. In spring, produces solitary, bright scarlet to deep crimson flowers, 12cm (5in) across, each with a broad, erect upper tepal, 2 narrower, horizontal tepals, and 3 narrow, pendent tepals. ↕ 15–35cm (6–14in), ↔ 15cm (6in). Mexico, Guatemala. ❄ (min. 7–10°C/45–50°F)

▷**Spring beauty** see *Claytonia*
▷**Spruce** see *Picea*
Black see *P. mariana*
Brewer see *P. breweriana*
Caucasian see *P. orientalis*
Colorado see *P. pungens*
Dragon see *P. asperata*
Engelmann see *P. engelmannii*
Hondo see *P. jezoensis* subsp. *hondoensis*
Lijiang see *P. likiangensis*
Morinda see *P. smithiana*
Norway see *P. abies*
Oriental see *P. orientalis*
Purple-cone see *P. purpurea*
Sargent see *P. brachytyla*
Serbian see *P. omorika*
Sitka see *P. sitchensis*
Taiwan see *P. morrisonicola*
White see *P. glauca*

Sprekelia formosissima

▷**Spurge** see *Euphorbia*
Caper see *E. lathyris*
Cypress see *E. cyparissias*
Hairy see *E. pilosa*
Honey see *E. mellifera*
Portland see *E. portlandica*
Wood see *E. amygdaloides*
▷**Squill,**
Sea see *Urginea maritima*
Siberian see *Scilla siberica*

STACHYS syn. BETONICA

Betony, Hedge nettle, Woundwort

LABIATAE/LAMIACEAE

Genus of about 300 species of annuals, mostly rhizomatous and stoloniferous perennials, and a few evergreen shrubs, widely distributed in a range of habitats, including mountains, dry, rocky hills, scrub, wasteland, meadows, forest clearings, and streamsides, especially in N. temperate regions. The leaves on the square stems are short-stalked or stalkless, opposite, and become progressively smaller up the stems; basal leaves are lance-shaped or elliptic to ovate, entire to scalloped or toothed, wrinkled, prominently veined, hairy, and stalked. Many species are aromatic, occasionally unpleasantly so. The tubular, 2-lipped, often hooded, usually white, yellow, pink, red, or purple flowers are borne in racemes or spikes of axillary whorls. Most are attractive to bees and butterflies. Grow taller perennials in a mixed or herbaceous border. *S. byzantina* is ideal as edging or as ground cover. Low-growing, hairy-leaved species, such as *S. candida*, *S. citrina*, and *S. lavandulifolia*, are suitable for a dry bank, gravel garden, raised bed, or rock garden, but need protection from excessive winter wet; they are best grown in an alpine house. Grow *S. sylvatica* in a wild garden.

- **HARDINESS** Fully hardy to frost hardy.
- **CULTIVATION** Outdoors, grow in well-drained, moderately fertile soil in full sun; *S. macrantha*, *S. officinalis*, and *S. sylvatica* tolerate partial shade. Grow rock-garden species in sharply drained, gritty soil in a sunny site; protect from excessive winter wet. In an alpine house, grow in loam-based potting compost (JI No.2) with added grit, in full light.
- **PROPAGATION** Sow seed in containers in a cold frame in autumn or spring. Divide or remove rooted sections of perennials in spring as growth begins. Take greenwood cuttings of shrubs and subshrubs in early summer.

Stachys byzantina

Stachys byzantina 'Big Ears'

• **PESTS AND DISEASES** Slugs may be a problem. *S. byzantina*, in particular, is susceptible to powdery mildew.

S. betonica see *S. officinalis.*
S. byzantina ■ syn. *S. lanata, S. olympica* (Lambs' ears, Lambs' lugs, Lambs' tails, Lambs' tongues). Mat-forming, densely white-woolly perennial with rosettes of entire, oblong-elliptic to lance-shaped, thick, wrinkled, veined, grey-green leaves, to 10cm (4in) long. Erect stems bear interrupted spikes of woolly, pink-purple flowers, 1.5cm (½in) long, from early summer to early autumn. ↕45cm (18in), ↔60cm (24in). Caucasus to Iran. ✽✽✽. **'Big Ears'** ■ has large, greyish white-felted, mid-green leaves, 25cm (10in) long, and purple flowers. **'Cotton Boll'**, syn. 'Sheila McQueen', has leaves 11cm (4½in) long, and clusters of modified flowers forming cotton-wool-like balls along the stems. **'Primrose Heron'** ■ syn. *S.* 'Primrose Heron', has yellowish grey leaves. **'Sheila McQueen'** see 'Cotton Boll'. **'Silver Carpet'** ■ syn. *S.* 'Silver Carpet', is non-flowering, and produces intensely silvered, greyish white leaves.

Stachys byzantina 'Primrose Heron'

S. candida ■ Spreading subshrub producing rounded, white-felted, grey-green leaves, to 2.5cm (1in) long. In summer, bears leafy spikes of hooded white flowers, 1cm (½in) or more long, streaked and spotted purple. ↕15cm (6in), ↔30cm (12in). S. Greece. ✽✽✽
S. citrina. Spreading, woody-based perennial producing elliptic to ovate-oblong, minutely round-toothed, grey-hairy, soft, lime-green leaves, to 5cm (2in) long. Short, dense, sometimes interrupted spikes of sulphur-yellow flowers, 2–2.5cm (¾–1in) long, are borne in summer. ↕20cm (8in), ↔30cm (12in). Turkey. ✽✽✽
S. coccinea. Spreading, softly hairy perennial with entire, ovate-lance-shaped or oblong-triangular, wrinkled, veined, mid-green leaves, to 7cm (3in) long. Upright stems bear slender spikes of narrow scarlet flowers, to 2cm (¾in) long, from mid-spring to mid-autumn. ↕60cm (24in), ↔45cm (18in). USA (Arizona, Texas) to Mexico. ✽✽
S. discolor see *S. nivea.*
S. grandiflora see *S. macrantha.*
S. lanata see *S. byzantina.*
S. lavandulifolia. Spreading, woody-based perennial with oblong-lance-

Stachys byzantina 'Silver Carpet'

Stachys candida

shaped, toothed, grey-hairy, grey-green leaves, 2–6cm (¾–2½in) long. Upright spikes of purplish pink flowers, to 1.5cm (½in) long, are produced in summer. ↕↔30cm (12in). Turkey, Iraq. ✽✽✽
S. macrantha, syn. *S. grandiflora, S. spicata.* Erect, hairy perennial with rosettes of broadly ovate, scalloped, wrinkled, veined, dark green leaves, to 7cm (3in) long, heart-shaped at the bases. Dense spikes of hooded, pinkish purple flowers, 3cm (1¼in) long, are produced on erect stems from early summer to early autumn. ↕60cm (24in), ↔30cm (12in). Caucasus, N.E. Turkey, N.W. Iran. ✽✽✽. **'Superba'** ■ has slightly deeper pinkish purple flowers.
S. nivea, syn. *Betonica nivea, S. discolor.* Erect, hairy perennial with basal rosettes of oblong-lance-shaped to narrowly lance-shaped, coarsely scalloped, white-downy leaves, 12cm (5in) long, densely covered with simple, bristle-like hairs; the long-stalked stem leaves are similar but shorter. Congested whorls of hooded yellow flowers, to 2.5cm (1in) long, with curved tubes, are borne in spikes in summer. ↕30cm (12in), ↔25cm (10in). Caucasus. ✽✽✽
S. officinalis ■ syn. *Betonica officinalis, S. betonica* (Bishop's wort, Wood betony). Erect, almost hairless to densely hairy perennial with rosettes of ovate-oblong to oblong, scalloped, wrinkled, veined, mid-green leaves, to 12cm (5in) long, heart-shaped at the bases. Upright stems bear dense, oblong spikes of pink, white, or reddish purple flowers, to 1.5cm (½in) long, from early summer to early autumn. ↕60cm (24in), ↔30cm (12in). Europe. ✽✽✽. **'Rosea Superba'** has rose-pink

Stachys macrantha 'Superba'

Stachys officinalis

flowers and slightly paler leaves.
S. olympica see *S. byzantina.*
S. 'Primrose Heron' see *S. byzantina* 'Primrose Heron'.
S. 'Silver Carpet' see *S. byzantina* 'Silver Carpet'.
S. spicata see *S. macrantha.*
S. sylvatica (Hedge woundwort). Strong-smelling, creeping, glandular-hairy perennial with heart- to lance-shaped, toothed, mid-green leaves, 4–14cm (1½–5½in) long. Bears spikes of usually white-marked, dull reddish purple, occasionally pink or white flowers, to 1.5cm (½in) long, from summer to autumn. ↕ to 1m (3ft), ↔40–120cm (16–48in). Europe, W. Asia. ✽✽✽

STACHYURUS

STACHYURACEAE

Genus of about 6 species of deciduous or semi-evergreen shrubs, occasionally small trees, found in woodland and thickets in the Himalayas and E. Asia. They are grown for their pendent racemes of small, 4-petalled flowers, produced from the leaf axils on bare shoots, before the leaves emerge. The alternate, simple, usually lance-shaped-oblong to broadly ovate, toothed leaves are borne on slender, glossy, red-brown shoots. Good for a shrub border, or for growing in a woodland garden or against a wall.

• **HARDINESS** Fully hardy.
• **CULTIVATION** Grow in light, moist but well-drained, humus-rich, fertile, acid soil in full sun or partial shade, with shelter from cold, drying winds. Pruning group 1; cut out flowered shoots to the base on mature plants, after flowering.
• **PROPAGATION** Sow seed in containers in a cold frame in autumn. Take heeled, semi-ripe cuttings in summer.
• **PESTS AND DISEASES** Trouble free.

S. chinensis. Spreading, deciduous shrub with arching shoots and ovate, abruptly pointed, dark green leaves, to 12cm (5in) long. Bell-shaped, pale yellow flowers, 8mm (⅜in) across, are borne in racemes to 13cm (5in) long, in late winter and early spring. ↕2m (6ft), ↔4m (12ft). China. ✽✽✽. **'Magpie'** see *S. praecox* 'Magpie'.
S. praecox. Open, spreading, deciduous shrub with arching, red-purple shoots and ovate, tapered, mid-green leaves, to 18cm (7in) long. Bell-shaped, pale yellow-green flowers, 8mm (⅜in) across, are borne in racemes to 10cm (4in) long, in late winter and early spring.

S

Stachyurus praecox 'Magpie' (inset: flower detail)

↕ 1–4m (3–12ft), ↔ 3m (10ft). Japan. ✲✲✲. **'Magpie'** ■ syn. *S. chinensis* 'Magpie', is less vigorous, with broad, creamy white margins to the leaves; ↕ 1.5m (5ft), ↔ 2m (6ft).

▷ **Staff tree** see *Celastrus scandens*
▷ **Stagger-bush** see *Lyonia mariana*
▷ **Staghorn, South American** see *Platycerium alcicorne*
▷ **Staghorn fern** see *Platycerium*
Common see *P. bifurcatum*

STANGERIA

STANGERIACEAE

Genus of one species of fern-like cycad found in dry, open woodland and scrub in South Africa. It has a swollen, woody, largely underground stem, from the tip of which it produces rosettes of oval to oblong, pinnate leaves, which lack the leathery texture typical of cycads. Separate male and female, cone-like spikes ("cones") of flowers are borne from the centres of the rosettes, usually in summer. In frost-prone regions, grow in a warm greenhouse or as a houseplant. In warmer climates, grow in a border, or as a specimen plant.

Stangeria eriopus

• **HARDINESS** Frost tender.
• **CULTIVATION** Under glass, grow in a mix of equal parts loam, grit, coarse bark, and leaf mould, in bright filtered light with high humidity. In growth, water freely and apply a foliar fertilizer monthly. Water sparingly in winter. Pot on or top-dress in spring. Outdoors, grow in fertile, humus-rich, moist but well-drained soil in dappled shade.
• **PROPAGATION** Surface-sow seed on damp sand at 24–30°C (75–86°F) in spring. Pot up as soon as the tap root begins to form.
• **PESTS AND DISEASES** Susceptible to mealybugs and scale insects under glass.

S. eriopus ■ Fern-like cycad with a cylindrical to turnip-shaped stem or trunk, to 10cm (4in) across, with only the tip above ground. Bears one to several rosettes of long-stalked, pinnate leaves, 0.25–2m (¾–6ft) long, each with 10–40 lance-shaped to oblong, wavy, often papery, olive- to deep green leaflets, with entire or toothed margins. Cylindrical, felted, grey to yellow-brown flowering cones, to 18cm (7in) long, are borne mainly in summer. ↕ to 1m (3ft) or more, ↔ 1–2m (3–6ft). South Africa (Eastern Cape, KwaZulu/Natal). ❄ (min. 15°C/59°F)

STANHOPEA

ORCHIDACEAE

Genus of about 30 species of evergreen, epiphytic orchids from moist forest, 1,000–2,000m (3,250–7,000ft) high, in Mexico and Central and South America. The conical, ribbed pseudobulbs each bear a single, large, semi-rigid, folded, elliptic to oblong-lance-shaped leaf. Pendent racemes of 2–10 very fragrant, short-lived flowers arise from the bases of the pseudobulbs over a long period.
• **HARDINESS** Frost tender.
• **CULTIVATION** Cool- to intermediate-growing orchids. Grow epiphytically on bark, or in epiphytic orchid compost in moss-lined, slatted baskets, to allow the pendent racemes to spread freely downwards. Provide high humidity and bright filtered light in summer, and full light in winter. In full growth, water and mist freely, and apply a half-strength balanced liquid fertilizer monthly. Water sparingly when inactive, which may be in early summer. See also p.46.
• **PROPAGATION** Divide when the plants "overflow" their containers, or remove backbulbs and pot up separately.
• **PESTS AND DISEASES** Susceptible to red spider mites, aphids, and mealybugs.

Stanhopea tigrina

S. oculata. Epiphytic orchid with one broadly elliptic or broadly lance-shaped leaf, 45cm (18in) long. Pendent racemes of waxy, maroon-spotted, light yellow, orange, or white flowers, 12cm (5in) across, are borne in summer or autumn. ↕ 45cm (18in), ↔ 60cm (24in). S. Mexico to Venezuela, N. Peru. ❄ (min. 11–13°C/52–55°F; max. 30°C/86°F)
S. tigrina ■ Epiphytic orchid with one broad, oblong leaf, 40cm (16in) long. Pendent racemes of fleshy yellow flowers, 15cm (6in) across, with dark red markings, are borne from summer to autumn. ↕ 45cm (18in), ↔ 60cm (24in). Mexico. ❄ (min. 11–13°C/52–55°F; max. 30°C/86°F)
S. wardii. Epiphytic orchid with one elliptic leaf, 30–45cm (12–18in) long. Pendent racemes of yellow-orange flowers, 12cm (5in) across, lightly spotted purple, are borne in summer. ↕ 45cm (18in), ↔ 60cm (24in). S. Mexico to Venezuela, N. Peru. ❄ (min. 11–13°C/52–55°F; max. 30°C/86°F)

STAPELIA

Carrion flower

ASCLEPIADACEAE

Genus of about 45 species of perennial succulents from low, hilly, often rocky terrain, mainly in tropical and southern Africa. They have generally erect, angular, coarsely toothed, fleshy stems, which branch from the bases to form large clumps. The rudimentary, fleshy leaves are borne at the tips of the stem teeth. Diurnal, star-shaped, often foul-smelling, solitary or clustered flowers, pollinated by blowflies and bluebottles, are produced in summer, usually from the stem bases. Where temperatures fall below 11°C (52°F), grow in a temperate or warm greenhouse. In warm, dry areas, grow in a raised bed or desert garden. Many species originally included in *Stapelia* are now classified as *Orbea*, *Orbeopsis*, or *Huernia*, as well as various other genera.

Stapelia gigantea

• **HARDINESS** Frost tender.
• **CULTIVATION** Under glass, grow in a mix of equal parts loam-based potting compost (JI No.2) and grit; top-dress with grit. Provide full light with shade from hot sun, and low humidity. When in growth, water moderately and apply a low-nitrogen fertilizer monthly. Water very sparingly at other times. Outdoors, grow in moderately fertile, gritty, sharply drained soil, in full sun with some midday shade. See also pp.48–49.
• **PROPAGATION** Sow seed at 18–21°C (64–70°F) in spring. Separate rooted sections, or take cuttings of stem sections, from spring to summer.
• **PESTS AND DISEASES** Susceptible to mealybugs, root mealybugs, and black root rot.

S. europaea see *Caralluma europaea*.
S. flavirostris see *S. grandiflora*.
S. gigantea ■ syn. *S. nobilis*. Very variable, clump-forming succulent producing erect, 4-angled, velvety, light green stems, 3cm (1¼in) thick, with small teeth. In summer, produces malodorous, pale ochre-yellow and dark red flowers, 25–35cm (10–14in) across, with silky red hairs, numerous minute, transverse red wrinkles, and petals with white-hairy margins. ↕ to 20cm (8in), ↔ indefinite. E. southern Africa. ❄ (min. 11°C/52°F)
S. grandiflora ■ syn. *S. flavirostris*. Clump-forming succulent with erect, toothed, mid-green stems, 2–3cm (¾–1¼in) thick, with slightly winged angles, and covered with minute, velvety

S

Stapelia grandiflora

hairs. In summer, bears dull, purplish red flowers, to 22cm (9in) across, with hairy margins and wrinkled lobes, lined with purple and yellow, becoming rich dull purple at the tips. ↕ to 30cm (12in), ↔ indefinite. South Africa (Western Cape, Eastern Cape), Lesotho. ❄ (min. 11°C/52°F)
S. nobilis see *S. gigantea.*
S. variegata see *Orbea variegata.*

STAPELIANTHUS

ASCLEPIADACEAE

Genus, closely related to *Huernia*, of about 8 species of perennial succulents from hilly lowlands in S. and S.W. Madagascar. They have often prostrate, 4- to 8-angled, fleshy, branching stems, which root down as the plant spreads; the stems sometimes have rudimentary leaves. Diurnal flowers are borne singly or in clusters from leaf axils at the bases of the stems in summer; each flower has a corona forming an erect, 5-lobed head above the staminal column. Where temperatures fall below 10°C (50°F), grow in a temperate or warm greenhouse. In warm, dry areas, use in a desert garden.
• **HARDINESS** Frost tender.
• **CULTIVATION** Under glass, grow in shallow pans in a mix of equal parts loam-based potting compost (JI No.2) and grit; top-dress with grit. Provide bright filtered light and low humidity. In growth, water moderately and apply a low-nitrogen fertilizer monthly. Water sparingly at other times. Outdoors, grow in gritty, sharply drained, moderately fertile soil in full sun with some midday shade. See also pp.48–49.
• **PROPAGATION** Sow seed at 18–21°C (64–70°F) in spring. Take cuttings of stem sections in spring and summer.
• **PESTS AND DISEASES** Trouble free.

S. madagascariensis. Semi-erect or creeping succulent with 6- to 8-angled, red-spotted, grey-green stems, to 8mm (3/8in) thick, with tubercles bearing small, thin, linear, scale-like leaves. In summer, produces bell-shaped, pale yellow, red-marked flowers, to 2cm (3/4in) across; they have triangular, broadly spreading lobes with red papillae on the upper surfaces. ↕ to 5cm (2in), ↔ 12cm (5in). Madagascar. ❄ (min. 10°C/50°F)

STAPELIOPSIS

ASCLEPIADACEAE

Genus of 5 or 6 species of perennial succulents from hilly lowlands of Namibia and South Africa. They have 4-angled, fleshy, minutely hairy, usually toothed, purple-spotted, mid-green stems; in some species these bear tiny leaves. Diurnal, stalked, urn-shaped flowers develop from the bases of new shoots in summer. Where temperatures fall below 10°C (50°F), grow in a temperate or warm greenhouse. In warm, dry areas, use in a desert garden.
• **HARDINESS** Frost tender.
• **CULTIVATION** Under glass, grow in shallow pans in a mix of equal parts loam-based potting compost (JI No.2) and grit; top-dress with grit. Provide bright filtered light and low humidity. In the growing season, water moderately and apply a low-nitrogen fertilizer monthly. Water sparingly at other times. Outdoors, grow in moderately fertile, gritty, sharply drained soil in full sun, with midday shade. See also pp.48–49.
• **PROPAGATION** Sow seed at 18–21°C (64–70°F) in spring. Take cuttings of stem sections in spring and summer.
• **PESTS AND DISEASES** Trouble free.

S. pillansii, syn. *Pectinaria pillansii.* Clustering succulent with usually prostrate, 4-angled, dark green stems, 1cm (1/2in) thick, with prominent brown teeth. Red flowers, 7mm (1/4in) across, pale red inside, with watery papillae, are produced at ground level in summer. ↕ 8cm (3in), ↔ 18cm (7in). South Africa (Eastern Cape). ❄ (min. 10°C/50°F)

STAPHYLEA

Bladdernut

STAPHYLEACEAE

Genus of about 11 species of deciduous shrubs or small trees found in woodland and thickets in N. temperate regions. They are grown for their bell- or cup-shaped, white, cream, or pink flowers, borne in terminal panicles, and for their curious, bladder-like, 2- or 3-lobed fruits. The opposite leaves are pinnate or 3- to 5-palmate. Suitable for a shrub border or woodland garden.
• **HARDINESS** Fully hardy.
• **CULTIVATION** Grow in any moist but well-drained soil in full sun or partial shade. Pruning group 1 or 2.
• **PROPAGATION** Sow seed in containers in a cold frame in autumn. Root greenwood cuttings in early summer, or semi-ripe cuttings in midsummer, both with bottom heat.
• **PESTS AND DISEASES** Trouble free.

S. colchica. Upright shrub with stout shoots and pinnate, glossy, mid-green leaves, each with 3–5 ovate-oblong leaflets, 4–9cm (1½–3½in) long. In late spring, bears bell-shaped, fragrant white flowers, to 2cm (3/4in) long, in panicles to 12cm (5in) long; they are followed by greenish white fruit, to 10cm (4in) long. ↕↔ 3.5m (11ft). Caucasus. ***

Staphylea pinnata

S. holocarpa ♀ Upright shrub or spreading, small tree bearing 3-palmate, blue-green leaves with oblong to lance-shaped leaflets, 3–10cm (1¼–4in) long. Bell-shaped, white to pink flowers, to 1.5cm (½in) long, are produced in nodding panicles, to 10cm (4in) long, in mid- and late spring, before the leaves; they are followed by greenish white fruit, to 5cm (2in) long. ↕ 10m (30ft), ↔ 6m (20ft). China. ***. **'Rosea'** bears bronze young leaves and pink flowers.
S. pinnata ▣ (Bladdernut). Upright shrub with stout shoots and pinnate leaves, each composed of 5–7 ovate-oblong leaflets, 5–10cm (2–4in) long, dark green above, slightly glaucous beneath. In late spring and early summer, bears bell-shaped, fragrant, pink-tinged white flowers, 1cm (½in) long, in pendent panicles, to 10cm (4in) long; they are followed by greenish white fruit, to 4cm (1½in) long. ↕↔ 5m (15ft). Europe, Turkey, Caucasus. ***

▷**Star cluster** see *Pentas lanceolata*
Egyptian see *P. lanceolata*
▷**Starfish plant** see *Cryptanthus*
▷**Starflower** see *Calytrix, Hypoxis, Mentzelia*
▷**Starfruit** see *Damasonium*
▷**Star glory** see *Ipomoea quamoclit*
▷**Star-of-Bethlehem** see *Campanula isophylla, Ornithogalum, O. umbellatum*
▷**Star of the veldt** see *Dimorphotheca sinuata*
▷**Starwort,**
Autumn see *Callitriche hermaphroditica*
Water see *Callitriche*
▷**Statice** see *Limonium, L. sinuatum, Psylliostachys*
Tatarian see *Goniolimon tataricum*
▷***Statice bellidifolia*** see *Limonium bellidifolium*
▷***Statice minuta*** see *Limonium minutum*
▷***Statice spicata*** see *Psylliostachys spicata*
▷***Statice suworowii*** see *Psylliostachys suworowii*

STAUNTONIA

LARDIZABALACEAE

Genus of up to 16 species of twining, woody, mostly dioecious, evergreen climbers occurring in woodland from Burma to Taiwan and Japan. They are cultivated for their handsome, alternate, palmate leaves, for their bell-shaped flowers, borne in few-flowered, axillary racemes, and for their ellipsoid, edible fruits. Grow over a large shrub or through a tree, or train on wires against a wall. In areas of severe frost, grow stauntonias in a cool greenhouse.
• **HARDINESS** Frost hardy to frost tender.
• **CULTIVATION** Under glass, grow in loam-based potting compost (JI No.3) in full light, with shade from hot sun. When in full growth, water freely and apply a balanced liquid fertilizer every 4 weeks. Water sparingly in winter. Outdoors, grow in fertile, well-drained soil, in a warm, sheltered site in full sun or partial shade, with suitable support. Pruning group 11, in early spring.
• **PROPAGATION** Sow seed at 13–16°C (55–61°F) in spring. Take semi-ripe cuttings in summer.
• **PESTS AND DISEASES** Trouble free.

Stauntonia hexaphylla

S. hexaphylla ▣ Fast-growing, dioecious, evergreen climber producing 3- to 7-palmate, mid- to dark green leaves, to 15cm (6in) long, with oval to elliptic, leathery leaflets. Racemes of cup-shaped, fragrant, violet-tinged white flowers, 2cm (3/4in) across, are borne in spring. If pollinated, females produce ellipsoid, edible purple fruit, 5cm (2in) long. ↕ 10m (30ft) or more. S. Korea, Japan. **

▷***Steironema ciliata*** see *Lysimachia ciliata*
▷**Stemless Carline thistle** see *Carlina acaulis*

STEMMACANTHA

ASTERACEAE/COMPOSITAE

Genus of 20 species of perennials, closely related to *Centaurea*, from dry, open grassland and alpine habitats in S. Europe, N. Africa, Asia, and Australia. Erect stems produce ovate to lance-shaped leaves, which are finely to coarsely toothed to very deeply pinnatifid. The foliage is either dark green above and densely felted beneath, or mid-green above and pale green with fine hairs beneath. The flowerheads, which are produced in midsummer on long stems or directly from a basal rosette of leaves in the alpine species, are spherical or hemispherical and consist of tubular white, pink, lilac, or purple florets. Each flowerhead has a conspicuous involucre of overlapping bracts, which are often scaly or papery. Grow stemmacanthas in a sunny border or in a large rock garden or scree bed.
• **HARDINESS** Fully hardy to frost hardy.
• **CULTIVATION** Grow in well-drained, moderately fertile soil in full sun.
• **PROPAGATION** Sow seed *in situ* in spring, or divide in spring.
• **PESTS AND DISEASES** Trouble free.

S. centauroides, syn. *Centaurea centauroides, C.* 'Pulchra Major', *Leuzea centauroides, Rhaponticum centauroides, Serratula cynaroides.* Clump-forming perennial with numerous pinnatifid, narrowly ovate leaves, 15–45cm (6–18in) long, dark green above and grey-green felted beneath. In midsummer, tall stems bear striking buds, with bristly, glossy, silvery green bracts, which open to flowerheads, 8cm (3in) across, with bright purplish red florets. ↕ 1.2m (4ft), ↔ 60cm (24in). S.W. Europe. ***

S

STENANTHIUM

LILIACEAE / MELANTHIACEAE

Genus of about 5 species of bulbous perennials from moist slopes in grassland or open woodland on Sakhalin Island (Russia), and in North America, including Mexico. They have arching, grass-like, mostly basal leaves and erect, slender stems bearing terminal racemes or panicles of small, bell- or star-shaped flowers. Grow in a border, peat bed, or in woodland.

• **HARDINESS** Fully hardy to frost hardy.
• **CULTIVATION** Plant bulbs 10cm (4in) deep in autumn, in moist but well-drained, moderately fertile, humus-rich, neutral to acid soil, in a sheltered site in partial shade. They dislike hot, dry conditions.
• **PROPAGATION** Sow seed in containers in a cold frame as soon as ripe.
• **PESTS AND DISEASES** Trouble free.

S. angustifolium see *S. gramineum*.
S. gramineum, syn. *S. angustifolium*. Bulbous perennial with 4 erect, linear, keeled, channelled, bright green, basal leaves, 30–40cm (12–16in) long. In summer, bears star-shaped, fragrant, white or greenish white to purple flowers, to 2cm (¾in) across, in dense, often arching panicles, to 60cm (24in) long. ↕ 1–2m (3–6ft), ↔ 30cm (12in). S.E. USA. ✻✻. **var. *robustum***, syn. *S. robustum*, has broader leaves and white or green flowers; ↕ to 1.8m (6ft)
S. robustum see *S. gramineum* var. *robustum*.

STENOCACTUS

syn. ECHINOFOSSULOCACTUS

CACTACEAE

Genus of about 10 species of variable, simple, rarely clustering, spherical, perennial cacti from shaded lowlands in Mexico. The stems have numerous, frequently undulating ribs, often with tubercles, and well-spaced areoles bearing variable spines, which are curved or straight, sometimes flat and dagger-like. Bell- or funnel-shaped, sometimes striped flowers develop from the crowns in spring, often in clusters. In frost-prone areas, grow as houseplants or in a temperate greenhouse. In warm, dry climates, use in a desert garden.

• **HARDINESS** Frost tender.
• **CULTIVATION** Under glass, grow in standard cactus compost in full light with low humidity. When in growth, water moderately and apply a low-nitrogen liquid fertilizer at every third or fourth watering. Keep completely dry at other times. Outdoors, grow in poor, humus-rich, gritty, sharply drained soil in full sun, with some midday shade. See also pp.48–49.
• **PROPAGATION** Sow seed at 21°C (70°F) in early spring.
• **PESTS AND DISEASES** Susceptible to aphids while flowering.

Stenocactus coptonogonus

Stenocactus obvallatus

S. coptonogonus ■ syn. *Echinofossulocactus coptonogonus*. Simple cactus producing a depressed-spherical to spherical, grey to blue-green stem with 10–14 deeply scalloped, acute ribs. White areoles bear 3–5 flat, upward-curving, pale brownish red spines, fading to very pale brown, the upper spines to 3cm (1¼in) long, the lower ones to 1.5cm (½in). In spring, bears clusters of funnel-shaped, white to purple flowers, 3cm (1¼in) long, with a pink-purple or violet mid-stripe on each petal. ↕ to 10cm (4in), ↔ 16cm (6in). C. Mexico. ❄ (min. 7°C/45°F)
S. crispatus, syn. *Echinofossulocactus lamellosus*. Simple or clustering cactus with spherical, dark green to blue-green stems, each with 26–60 wavy ribs. White-woolly areoles bear brown-tipped white spines: 6–10 flat, straight radials, to 2.5cm (1in) long; 3 or 4 flattened, slightly curved centrals, 3.5cm (1½in) long. Solitary, funnel-shaped, carmine-red flowers, 4cm (1½in) long, are borne in spring. ↕ 10cm (4in), ↔ 8cm (3in). C. to S. Mexico. ❄ (min. 7°C/45°F)
S. multicostatus, syn. *Echinofossulocactus multicostatus*. Simple or clustering cactus producing flattened-spherical to spherical, pale green stems with 100 or more wavy ribs; each rib bears about 2 white-woolly areoles with 6–18 flat, straight or curved, yellow or grey spines, the upper ones to 8cm (3in) long, the lower to 1.5cm (½in). In spring, bears clusters of funnel-shaped flowers, 2.5cm (1in) long, pinkish purple or white with a purplish violet or faint pink stripe on each petal. ↕↔ 10cm (4in). N.E. Mexico. ❄ (min. 7°C/45°F)
S. obvallatus ■ syn. *Echinofossulocactus pentacanthus*, *E. violaciflorus*. Simple cactus producing a spherical, greyish blue-green stem with 20–50 wavy-margined ribs. White areoles bear 5–12 flat, straight or curved, greyish brown spines, the upper and lateral ones to 5cm (2in) long, the lower to 1cm (½in). In spring, bears solitary, funnel-shaped, pale yellow or pale pink flowers, 2cm (¾in) long, with a purplish red stripe on each petal. ↕↔ 8cm (3in). N. and E. central Mexico. ❄ (min. 7°C/45°F)

STENOCARPUS

PROTEACEAE

Genus of up to 22 species of evergreen shrubs and trees from Malaysia, New Caledonia, and Australia. The trees usually grow in rainforest; the shrubs are found in open scrub, often along watercourses. They have alternate, simple to pinnatifid leaves and, in summer, bear axillary umbels of tubular, cream to red flowers, each with a knob-shaped stigma protruding through a split on the lower side of the tube. In frost-prone areas, use in a temperate greenhouse as foliage plants (flowering is rare in containers). In warmer areas, use as specimen plants.

Stenocarpus sinuatus

• **HARDINESS** Frost tender, but some species may survive brief drops in temperature to around 0°C (32°F).
• **CULTIVATION** Under glass, grow in loam-based potting compost (JI No.3) in full light, shaded from hot sun. When in growth, water moderately and apply a balanced liquid fertilizer every month. Water sparingly in winter. Outdoors, grow in fertile, humus-rich, moist but well drained soil in full sun, with some midday shade; shelter from cold, drying winds. Pruning group 1; may need restrictive pruning under glass.
• **PROPAGATION** Sow seed at 15–20°C (59–68°F) as soon as ripe or in spring (seedlings take about 7 years to flower). Root semi-ripe cuttings with bottom heat in summer.
• **PESTS AND DISEASES** Trouble free.

S. sinuatus ■ ◊ (Firewheel tree). Slow-growing, columnar tree with erect branches and branchlets. The leathery, wavy-margined, glossy, deep green leaves, 60cm (24in) long, are sometimes red beneath, and may be oblong-lance-shaped or deeply lobed, with up to 8 lance-shaped lobes, to 10cm (4in) long. Plants over 3m (10ft) tall bear wheel-like umbels of 12–20 scarlet flowers, to 2.5cm (1in) long, in summer. ↕ 20–30m (70–100ft), ↔ 5–15m (15–50ft). Australia (Queensland, New South Wales). ❄ (min. 7–10°C/45–50°F)

STENOCEREUS

CACTACEAE

Genus of about 25 species of tree-like or shrubby, sometimes clump-forming, perennial cacti found on low hillsides in the USA (Arizona), Mexico, Central America, Colombia, Venezuela, and the West Indies. The prominently ribbed stems are often densely spined. The funnel- or bell-shaped, usually nocturnal flowers, borne in spring or summer, are followed by ovoid, fleshy, spiny fruits. Where temperatures fall below 13°C (55°F), grow in a warm greenhouse. In warmer climates, use in a desert garden.

• **HARDINESS** Frost tender.
• **CULTIVATION** Under glass, grow in a mix of 3 parts standard cactus compost and 1 part leaf mould, in full light with low humidity. From mid-spring to early autumn, water moderately and apply a

Stenocereus eruca

low-nitrogen liquid fertilizer monthly. Keep completely dry at other times. Outdoors, grow in poor to moderately fertile, humus-rich, sharply drained, gritty soil in full sun. See also pp.48–49.
• **PROPAGATION** Sow seed at 21°C (70°F) in spring. Take cuttings of stem sections in summer.
• **PESTS AND DISEASES** Prone to scale insects and aphids while flowering.

S. eruca ▣ syn. *Machaerocereus eruca* (Creeping devil). Bushy, creeping cactus rooting all along its prostrate, 10- to 12-ribbed, mid-green stems, 4–10cm (1½–4in) thick, with only the stem tips erect. Brown areoles bear pale yellow to white spines (about 20 radials, 1 flattened, dagger-like central). In spring, produces nocturnal, funnel-shaped, white or pale yellow, sometimes pink-tinged flowers, 10–14cm (4–5½in) long. ↕ to 30cm (12in), ↔ indefinite. N.W. Mexico. ❀ (min. 13°C/55°F)
S. marginatus, syn. *Marginatocereus marginatus, Pachycereus marginatus.* Tree-like cactus with erect, freely branching, 5- to 7-ribbed, dark greyish green stems, to 30cm (12in) thick. Brown-woolly areoles bear brown spines (7–9 radials, 1 or 2 centrals), which fall as the plant matures. Diurnal, bell-shaped white flowers, red outside, 4–5cm (1½–2in) long, are produced at the stem tips in summer. ↕↔ 6m (20ft). C. and S. Mexico. ❀ (min. 13°C/55°F)

▷ ***Stenolobium stans*** see *Tecoma stans*

STENOMESSON

syn. URCEOLINA

AMARYLLIDACEAE

Genus of about 20 species of bulbous perennials from rocky, upland slopes and meadows in the Andes, South America. They are grown for their umbels of pendent, tubular, brightly coloured flowers, borne on solid, sometimes 4-angled stems mainly from spring to summer. The semi-erect, linear to lance-shaped, occasionally channelled or keeled, basal leaves often elongate after flowering. In frost-prone areas, grow in a temperate greenhouse or conservatory. In warmer areas, grow in a border.
• **HARDINESS** Half hardy to frost tender.
• **CULTIVATION** Plant in autumn with the neck and shoulders of the bulb above soil level. Under glass, grow in loam-based potting compost (JI No.2) in full light, shaded from hot sun. Water

S

Stenomesson miniatum

sparingly until in active growth, then water moderately and apply a balanced liquid fertilizer every 2 weeks. Reduce water as leaves wither, and keep barely moist when dormant. Pot on every 3 years. Outdoors, grow in well-drained, moderately fertile soil in a sheltered site in full sun; protect with a mulch in winter. Roots resent disturbance.
• **PROPAGATION** Sow seed at 16–18°C (61–64°F) in spring. Divide in autumn.
• **PESTS AND DISEASES** Trouble free.

S. incarnatum see *S. variegatum*.
S. miniatum ▣ syn. *Urceolina pendula.* Bulbous perennial bearing umbels of 3–6 pendent, tubular, bright red or orange flowers, 3–3.5cm (1¼–1½in) long, with protruding stamens, from spring to summer. Narrow, strap-shaped leaves, to 40cm (16in) long, develop after the flowers. ↕ 30cm (12in), ↔ 15cm (6in). Peru, Bolivia. ❀ (min. 7–10°C/45–50°F)
S. variegatum, syn. *S. incarnatum.* Bulbous perennial with strap-shaped leaves elongating to 60–75cm (24–30in) long after flowering. In spring, usually 4-angled stems bear umbels of up to 6 pendent, tubular, white, yellow, pink, or scarlet flowers, to 13cm (5in) long, sometimes with bands of another colour, all with a green mark on each tepal. ↕ 40–60cm (16–24in), ↔ 24cm (10in). Ecuador, Peru, Bolivia. ❀ (min. 7–10°C/45–50°F)

STENOTAPHRUM

GRAMINEAE/POACEAE

Genus of about 6 species of annual and perennial grasses, widespread in tropical and subtropical regions worldwide, on seashores or near the coast, occasionally inland. The creeping or ascending stems root at the nodes, and bear linear to lance-shaped, flat or folded, upright leaves, sheathing at the bases. Greenish brown spikelets are borne in axillary and terminal racemes. *S. secundatum* and *S. secundatum* 'Variegatum' are the most commonly grown, and are valued for their foliage. In frost-prone climates, treat perennials as annuals, or grow in a cool greenhouse as ground cover or in hanging baskets. Use as lawn grasses in tropical and subtropical climates; *S. secundatum* 'Variegatum' is also suitable for a border.
• **HARDINESS** Frost tender.
• **CULTIVATION** Under glass, grow in loam-based potting compost (JI No.2) in full light. When in growth, water freely and apply a balanced liquid fertilizer every 2 weeks. Water sparingly in winter. Container-grown plants thrive and continue to look attractive if given a winter minimum temperature of 12°C (54°F). Outdoors, grow in moist but well-drained, fertile soil in full sun. In frost-prone areas, plant out only when danger of frost has passed.
• **PROPAGATION** Divide in spring. Take nodal cuttings in late spring or during summer.
• **PESTS AND DISEASES** Trouble free.

S. secundatum (Buffalo grass, St. Augustine grass). Stoloniferous, prostrate, evergreen, perennial grass. Almost rigid, flattened, branching stems bear linear-oblong, flat to folded, bluish green leaves, to 15cm (6in) long. In late summer and early autumn, produces greenish brown, flattened, spike-like racemes, to 10cm (4in) long. ↕ 15cm (6in), ↔ indefinite. Central America, tropical South America. ❀ (min. 5°C/41°F). **'Variegatum'** has pale green leaves with ivory-white stripes.

STENOTUS

ASTERACEAE/COMPOSITAE

Genus of 18 species of tufted, evergreen subshrubs found in dry, rocky places in W. North America. They produce mainly basal, alternate, leathery, simple, entire leaves and solitary, daisy-like flowerheads. Grow in a rock garden.
• **HARDINESS** Fully hardy to frost hardy.
• **CULTIVATION** Grow in gritty, poor to moderately fertile, sharply drained soil in full sun.
• **PROPAGATION** Sow seed in containers in a cold frame in spring.
• **PESTS AND DISEASES** Trouble free.

S. acaulis, syn. *Haplopappus acaulis.* Mat-forming subshrub producing erect, slender stems and inversely lance-shaped, tapered, dark green leaves, to 6cm (2½in) long. Solitary, daisy-like yellow flowerheads, to 2.5cm (1in) across, are borne in summer. ↕ 15cm (6in), ↔ 45cm (18in). W. USA. ❄❄❄

STEPHANANDRA

ROSACEAE

Genus, related to *Spiraea*, of 4 species of suckering, deciduous shrubs from thickets and woodland margins in E. Asia. They have attractive leaves, which are alternate, narrowly ovate to ovate, lobed, and sharply toothed, with good autumn colour. The tiny, star-shaped, greenish white or yellow-green flowers are borne in terminal, corymb-like panicles during summer. Good for a shrub border.
• **HARDINESS** Fully hardy.
• **CULTIVATION** Grow in moist but well-drained, fertile soil in full sun or partial shade. Pruning group 2.

Stephanandra tanakae

• **PROPAGATION** Separate rooted suckers from autumn to early spring. Take greenwood cuttings in early summer, semi-ripe cuttings in summer, or hardwood cuttings in late autumn.
• **PESTS AND DISEASES** Trouble free.

S. incisa. Thicket-forming shrub producing arching shoots, rich brown in winter, and ovate, sharply lobed, toothed, mid-green leaves, to 8cm (3in) long, turning orange-yellow in autumn. Greenish white flowers are borne in panicles, to 8cm (3in) long, in early summer. ↕ to 2m (6ft), ↔ 3m (10ft). Korea, Japan, Taiwan. ❄❄❄. **'Crispa'** ▣ produces deeply lobed, wavy-margined leaves; ↕ 60cm (24in).

Stephanandra incisa 'Crispa'

S. tanakae ■ Thicket-forming shrub with arching, orange-brown shoots and broadly ovate, 3- to 5-lobed, sharply toothed, mid-green leaves, to 12cm (5in) long, turning orange and yellow in autumn. In early and midsummer, bears yellow-green flowers in panicles to 10cm (4in) long. ↕↔ 3m (10ft). Japan. ❄❄❄

STEPHANOCEREUS

CACTACEAE

Genus of one species of columnar, rarely branching, ribbed, perennial cactus from stony, rocky sites in E. Brazil. The stems, with rings of bristles at the joints, eventually develop woolly cephaliums at the tips; during summer, the tips bear tubular, nocturnal flowers, followed by ovoid, mid-green fruit, 5cm (2in) long, which take many weeks to ripen. Where temperatures fall below 13°C (55°F), grow *S. leucostele* in a warm greenhouse. In warmer areas, use in a desert garden.
• **HARDINESS** Frost tender.
• **CULTIVATION** Under glass, grow in standard cactus compost with added limestone chips, in full light with low humidity. In spring and summer, water moderately and apply a low-nitrogen liquid fertilizer every 4–5 weeks. Water sparingly at other times. Outdoors, grow in sharply drained, gritty, poor, humus-rich, neutral to alkaline soil in full sun. See also pp.48–49.
• **PROPAGATION** Sow seed at 24°C (75°F) in spring.
• **PESTS AND DISEASES** Trouble free.

S. leucostele. Erect, columnar cactus with 12- to 18-ribbed, blue-green stems, to 10cm (4in) thick. Close-set, white-hairy areoles each bear about 22 spines (20 white to yellow radials, 1 or 2 longer yellow centrals). In summer, the densely woolly cephalium produces white flowers, to 7cm (3in) long, with scaly yellow tubes. ↕ to 3m (10ft), ↔ 45cm (18in). E. Brazil. ❀ (min. 13°C/55°F)

STEPHANOTIS

ASCLEPIADACEAE

Genus of 5–15 species of evergreen, woody-stemmed climbers from tropical woodland in Africa, Madagascar, and Asia. They are grown for their strongly perfumed, waxy, tubular, usually white flowers, each with 5 spreading lobes, borne in short-stalked, axillary cymes. Leaves are opposite, ovate to elliptic, and leathery. Where temperatures fall below 15°C (59°F), grow in a warm greenhouse or as houseplants. In warmer areas, train over a pergola or on a wall.
• **HARDINESS** Frost tender.
• **CULTIVATION** Under glass, grow in loamless or loam-based potting compost (JI No.3) in full light, with shade from hot sun. In the growing season, water and mist freely, and apply a balanced liquid fertilizer every 2 or 3 weeks. Water sparingly in winter. Outdoors, grow in moderately fertile, humus-rich, moist but well-drained soil in full sun, with some midday shade. Support climbing stems. Pruning group 11, in late winter or early spring.
• **PROPAGATION** Sow seed at 18–21°C (64–70°F) in spring. Root semi-ripe cuttings with bottom heat in summer.
• **PESTS AND DISEASES** Under glass, may be infested by red spider mites, scale insects, mealybugs, and root mealybugs.

Stephanotis floribunda

S. floribunda ■ syn. *S. jasminoides* (Bridal wreath, Floradora, Madagascar jasmine). Sparsely branched, twining climber with oval to broadly elliptic, thick, glossy, mid- to deep green leaves, to 10cm (4in) or more long. From spring to autumn, bears cymes of 3–6 fragrant, waxy white flowers, 4–6cm (1½–2½in) long. ↕ 3–6m (10–20ft) or more. Madagascar. ❀ (min. 15°C/59°F)
S. jasminoides see *S. floribunda.*

▷ ***Sterculia acerifolia*** see *Brachychiton acerifolius*
▷ ***Sterculia diversifolia*** see *Brachychiton populneus*
▷ ***Sterculia platanifolia*** see *Firmiana simplex*

STERNBERGIA

Autumn daffodil

AMARYLLIDACEAE

Genus of about 8 species of bulbous perennials found on stony hillsides, in fields, and in sparse scrub or pine woodland from S. Europe and Turkey to C. Asia. They are grown for their crocus-like, mainly solitary, funnel- or goblet-shaped, occasionally narrow-tepalled and star-like, usually bright yellow flowers, borne on leafless stems. The erect, basal leaves are linear or strap-shaped to narrowly lance-shaped. Grow in a sunny rock garden. In frost-prone areas, grow all species except *S. lutea* and *S. sicula* in an alpine house or bulb frame; they are intolerant of winter wet.
• **HARDINESS** Frost hardy.
• **CULTIVATION** Plant bulbs 15cm (6in) deep in late summer; plant *S. candida* and *S. fischeriana* 20cm (8in) deep. Under glass, grow in equal parts loam, leaf mould, and sharp sand, in full light. Water sparingly in growth, reduce water as leaves wither, and keep completely dry when dormant. Outdoors, grow in sharply drained, moderately fertile soil in full sun. Allow large clumps to form; divide only if flowering is impaired.
• **PROPAGATION** Sow seed at 13–16°C (55–61°F) as soon as ripe. Separate offsets when dormant.
• **PESTS AND DISEASES** Prone to narcissus viruses. May be infested with large and small narcissus bulb flies and eelworms.

Sternbergia candida

S. candida ■ Bulbous perennial with lance- to strap-shaped, grey-green leaves, 15cm (6in) long, followed in late winter and early spring by cup-, goblet-, or funnel-shaped, fragrant white flowers, 5cm (2in) across. ↕ 10–20cm (4–8in), ↔ 10cm (4in). S.W. Turkey. ❄❄
S. clusiana, syn. *S. macrantha*. Bulbous perennial producing funnel-shaped yellow flowers, 7cm (3in) across, in autumn, before the strap-shaped, grey-green leaves, to 30cm (12in) long, develop. ↕ 10cm (4in), ↔ 8cm (3in). Turkey, Israel, Jordan, Iran. ❄❄
S. fischeriana. Bulbous perennial with goblet-shaped, pale yellow flowers, 3.5cm (1½in) across, borne in winter, after the strap-shaped, glossy, dark grey-green leaves, to 35cm (14in) long. Tends to divide into small, non-flowering bulbs. ↕ 8–15cm (3–6in), ↔ 8cm (3in). Caucasus to India (Kashmir). ❄❄
S. lutea ■ Very free-flowering, bulbous perennial producing goblet-shaped, deep yellow flowers, 4cm (1½in) across, in autumn, at the same time as narrowly lance-shaped, deep green leaves, to 30cm (12in) long. ↕ 15cm (6in), ↔ 8cm (3in). Spain to Afghanistan. ❄❄
S. macrantha see *S. clusiana.*
S. sicula. Variable, bulbous perennial with very narrow, strap-shaped, dark green leaves, 25cm (10in) long, with central grey stripes; these emerge before or with the star-shaped, deep yellow flowers, 1.5–3.5cm (½–1½in) across, with rounded or pointed segments, in autumn. ↕ 7cm (3in), ↔ 5cm (2in). Italy (including Sicily), Greece (including Aegean Islands, Crete), W. Turkey. ❄❄

Sternbergia lutea

STEWARTIA *syn.* STUARTIA

THEACEAE

Genus, related to *Camellia*, of 15–20 species of deciduous or evergreen trees and shrubs from woodland in E. Asia and S.E. USA. They are grown for their often peeling bark, their simple, usually toothed leaves, which colour well in autumn, and their cup-shaped white flowers with bold stamens, borne in the leaf axils. Use as specimens in woodland.
• **HARDINESS** Fully hardy to frost hardy.
• **CULTIVATION** Grow in moist but well-drained, moderately fertile, humus-rich, neutral to acid soil in full sun or dappled shade, with shelter from strong winds. Resent transplanting. Pruning group 1.
• **PROPAGATION** Sow seed in containers in a cold frame in autumn. Take green-wood cuttings in early summer, or semi-ripe cuttings in mid- to late summer. Layer in autumn.
• **PESTS AND DISEASES** Trouble free.

S. koreana see *S. pseudocamellia* Koreana Group.
S. malacodendron ♀ Broadly columnar, deciduous tree or upright, bushy shrub with ovate, finely toothed, dark green leaves, to 10cm (4in) long, downy beneath. Rose-like white flowers, 10cm (4in) across, cup-shaped at first, with purple stamens and often purple streaks on the petals, are borne singly along the shoots in midsummer. ↕ 7m (22ft), ↔ 3m (10ft). S.E. USA. ❄❄
S. monadelpha ■ ♀–♠ Broadly columnar to conical, deciduous tree or shrub with peeling, grey and red-brown bark. Ovate, elliptic, or lance-shaped, toothed, glossy, dark green leaves, to 10cm (4in) long, turn orange and red in autumn. In midsummer, cup-shaped white flowers, 4cm (1½in) across, with creamy filaments and violet anthers, are borne singly or in pairs along the shoots. ↕ to 25m (80ft), ↔ 8m (25ft). Korea, S. Japan. ❄❄❄
S. ovata. Broadly upright, bushy, deciduous shrub bearing ovate to lance-shaped, toothed or entire, dark green leaves, to 15cm (6in) long, red-tinged when young, downy beneath, turning

Stewartia monadelpha

Stewartia pseudocamellia

orange and red in autumn. Rose-like, cup-shaped white flowers, to 10cm (4in) across, with creamy yellow or rose-pink stamens, are produced singly along the shoots in mid- and late summer. ↕6m (20ft), ↔4m (12ft). S.E. USA. ❄❄❄

S. pseudocamellia ▣ ⚲ Broadly columnar, deciduous tree with peeling, pink to red-brown and grey bark. Ovate to elliptic, finely toothed, dark green leaves, to 10cm (4in) long, turn yellow to orange and red in autumn. Rose-like, cup-shaped white flowers, 6cm (2½in) across, with creamy yellow stamens, are borne singly or in pairs along the shoots in midsummer. ↕20m (70ft), ↔8m (25ft). Japan. ❄❄❄. **Koreana Group**, syn. S. *koreana*, *S. pseudocamellia* var. *koreana*, has flowers that open more widely, to 7cm (3in) across; Korea.

S. sinensis ⚲ Broadly conical, deciduous tree with peeling, red-brown bark and ovate or elliptic, toothed, dark green leaves, to 10cm (4in) long, turning bright red in autumn. Rose-like, cup-shaped, fragrant white flowers, 5cm (2in) across, are borne singly along the shoots in midsummer. ↕20m (70ft), ↔7m (22ft). C. and E. China. ❄❄❄

STIGMAPHYLLON

MALPIGHIACEAE

Genus of about 110 species of evergreen, woody-stemmed climbers, shrubs, and perennials from tropical woodland in Central and South America, the Caribbean, and West Africa. They have simple or lobed, sometimes toothed leaves, borne in opposite pairs or nearly alternately. From spring to autumn, wide open, 5-petalled flowers are borne in short, dense, corymb-like racemes. In frost-prone areas, grow in a temperate greenhouse. In warmer climates, grow over a pergola or arch, or through a tree.

- **HARDINESS** Frost tender.
- **CULTIVATION** Under glass, grow in loamless or loam-based potting compost (JI No.3) in full light, shaded from hot sun. In growth, water freely and apply a balanced liquid fertilizer every 4 weeks. Water sparingly in winter. Outdoors, grow in fertile, moist soil in full sun with some shade. Support climbing stems. Pruning group 11, in late winter.
- **PROPAGATION** Root semi-ripe cuttings with bottom heat in summer. Layer in autumn or spring.
- **PESTS AND DISEASES** Trouble free.

Stigmaphyllon ciliatum

S. ciliatum ▣ Twining, evergreen climber with slender, branched stems and broadly ovate, hairy-margined, light green leaves, 4–10cm (1½–4in) long, each with 2 ear-shaped lobes at the bases. Axillary, corymb-like racemes of 3–7 saucer-shaped, rich bright yellow flowers, 3–4cm (1¼–1½in) across, are produced in autumn; each flower has 1 small and 4 large, rounded, clawed, fringed petals. ↕5–8m (15–25ft). Belize to Uruguay. ❀ (min. 7–10°C/45–50°F)

▷**Stinking Benjamin** see *Trillium erectum*
▷**Stinking gladwyn** see *Iris foetidissima*
▷**Stinking madder** see *Putoria calabrica*
▷**Stinking nightshade** see *Hyoscyamus niger*
▷**Stink pod** see *Scoliopus bigelowii*
▷**Stinkwort** see *Helleborus foetidus*

STIPA syn. ACHNATHERUM

Feather grass, Needle grass, Spear grass

GRAMINEAE/POACEAE

Genus of about 300 species of bristly, tufted, evergreen or deciduous, perennial (rarely annual) grasses from open woodland and stony slopes in temperate and warm-temperate areas worldwide. They have linear, pleated, inrolled, sometimes flat leaves, and bear narrow panicles of

Stipa calamagrostis

flat spikelets, often with long, feathery or bristly awns, from early summer to autumn. They are grown for their habit, and also for their inflorescences, which may be dried and dyed for use in flower arrangements. Use in a mixed or shrub border. *S. gigantea* is effective set against a dark backdrop of shrubs or conifers.

- **HARDINESS** Fully hardy to frost hardy; *S. arundinacea* will withstand short periods around -10°C (14°F).
- **CULTIVATION** Grow in moderately fertile, medium to light, well-drained soil in full sun; *S. arundinacea* tolerates heavier soils and partial shade. Cut back deciduous species in early winter; remove dead leaves on evergreens in early spring.
- **PROPAGATION** Sow seed in containers in a cold frame in spring. Divide from mid-spring to early summer.
- **PESTS AND DISEASES** Trouble free.

S. arundinacea ▣ syn. *Anemanthele lessoniana*, *Calamagrostis arundinacea* (Pheasant's tail grass). Loosely tufted, rhizomatous, evergreen perennial with arching, flat or inrolled, leathery, dark green leaves, to 30cm (12in) long, streaked orange-brown in summer, and turning orange-brown all over in winter.

Stipa arundinacea

Stipa gigantea

From midsummer to early autumn, bears pendent panicles, to 75cm (30in) long, of purplish green spikelets. ↕1m (3ft), ↔1.2m (4ft). New Zealand. ❄❄

S. calamagrostis ▣ syn. *S. lasiogrostis.* Densely tufted, deciduous perennial with mounds of arching, linear, inrolled, blue-green leaves, to 30cm (12in) long. In summer, bears silvery, purple-tinted to buff spikelets in nodding, feathery, lax panicles, to 80cm (32in) long. ↕1m (3ft), ↔1.2m (4ft). S. Europe. ❄❄❄

S. gigantea ▣ (Giant feather grass, Golden oats). Densely tufted, evergreen or semi-evergreen perennial forming lax clumps of linear, inrolled, mid-green leaves, to 70cm (28in) long. Bristled, silvery, purplish green spikelets, turning gold when ripe, are borne in long-stemmed, oat-like panicles, to 50cm (20in) long, in summer. ↕to 2.5m (8ft), ↔1.2m (4ft). Spain, Portugal. ❄❄❄

S. lasiogrostis see *S. calamagrostis.*

S. splendens. Densely tufted, deciduous perennial forming large mounds of arching, linear, pleated, dark green leaves, to 50cm (20in) long. Purple-tinted white spikelets, in large, loose panicles, to 50cm (20in) long, are borne above the foliage in early and mid-

Stipa tenuissima

S

summer. ↕ to 2.5m (8ft), ↔ 1.2m (4ft). C. Asia, Russia (Siberia), Chile. ❄❄❄
S. tenuissima ■ Densely tufted, deciduous perennial with erect, narrowly linear to filament-like, tightly inrolled, bright green leaves, 30cm (12in) or more long. In summer, bears many narrow, nodding, softly feathery panicles, to 30cm (12in) long, greenish white at first, becoming buff. ↕ 60cm (24in), ↔ 30cm (12in). USA (Texas, New Mexico), Mexico, Argentina. ❄❄❄

▷**Stock** see *Matthiola, M. incana*
Night-scented see *Matthiola longipetala* subsp. *bicornis*
Virginia see *Malcolmia maritima*

STOKESIA

Stokes' aster

ASTERACEAE/COMPOSITAE

Genus of one species of erect perennial from conifer woods on moist, acid soil in S.E. USA. The evergreen, simple, smooth leaves are entire, sometimes with spines towards the bases, and are borne in basal rosettes. The long-lasting, colourful, terminal, cornflower-like flowerheads are solitary or produced in few- to many-flowered corymbs; they are good for cutting. Grow in a warm position in a herbaceous border.
• **HARDINESS** Fully hardy.
• **CULTIVATION** Grow in light, fertile, moist but well-drained, acid soil in full sun. Liable to rot in damp, heavy soils. Provide twiggy support. Dead-head to prolong flowering. Provide a deep, dry mulch in areas with severe winters.
• **PROPAGATION** Sow seed in containers in a cold frame in autumn. Divide in spring, or take root cuttings in late winter.
• **PESTS AND DISEASES** Trouble free.

S. laevis ■ Rosette-forming, evergreen perennial with elliptic to lance-shaped, mid-green basal leaves, to 20cm (8in) long, slightly spiny near the bases, and with pale greenish white midribs. From midsummer to early autumn, upright stems, with smaller, stalkless leaves, bear solitary, terminal, cornflower-like flowerheads, to 10cm (4in) across; these have spreading, fringed ray-florets in purplish blue, pink, or white, and disc-florets in paler or darker shades of the same colours. ↕ to 60cm (24in), ↔ 45cm (18in). S.E. USA. ❄❄❄. **'Blue Star'** has large, light blue flowerheads with whitish blue disc-florets. **'Silver Moon'** has silvery white flowerheads.

Stokesia laevis

STOMATIUM

AIZOACEAE

Genus of about 40 species of mainly mat-forming, perennial succulents from semi-desert areas of Botswana and South Africa. They have very short stems and unequal pairs of angular or rounded, often keeled, rough, fleshy leaves, sometimes with marginal teeth and white or transparent dots. Solitary, daisy-like, scented flowers are borne in the middle of the stems in summer; they often open in late afternoon and stay open all night. In frost-prone areas, grow in a temperate greenhouse. In warm, dry areas, use in a desert garden or raised bed.
• **HARDINESS** Frost tender.
• **CULTIVATION** Under glass, grow in standard cactus compost in full light. From spring to summer, apply a low-nitrogen fertilizer monthly and water moderately. Water very sparingly at other times. Outdoors, grow in sandy, poor, humus-rich, sharply drained soil in full sun. See also pp.48–49.
• **PROPAGATION** Sow seed at 19–24°C (66–75°F), or take cuttings of stem sections, from spring to summer.
• **PESTS AND DISEASES** Susceptible to aphids while flowering.

S. agninum. Clustering succulent with pairs of 3-angled to semi-cylindrical, oblong, obtuse, very convex and keeled, dull grey-green leaves, 4–5cm (1½–2in) long, roughened by green papillae, and sometimes with 3–5 short, marginal teeth. Pale yellow flowers, 2–2.5cm (¾–1in) across, open in late afternoon or early evening in summer. ↕ 5cm (2in), ↔ 45cm (18in). South Africa (Western Cape). ❁ (min. 7°C/45°F). **var. *integrifolium*** ■ has smooth leaves.
S. patulum. Clustering succulent with crowded pairs of 3-angled to semi-cylindrical, pale greyish green leaves, 2cm (¾in) long, with rough white dots, and with 2–9 pointed tubercles on the upper surfaces. Pale yellow flowers, 2cm (¾in) across, open in the evening in summer. ↕ 3cm (1¼in), ↔ 45cm (18in). South Africa. ❁ (min. 7°C/45°F)

▷**Stone cress** see *Aethionema*
▷**Stonecrop** see *Sedum*
Biting see *S. acre*
Common see *S. acre*
▷**Stone orpine** see *Sedum rupestre*
▷**Stone pine** see *Pinus pinea*
▷**Stone plant** see *Lithops*

Stomatium agninum var. *integrifolium*

▷**Storax** see *Styrax officinalis*
▷**Stork's bill** see *Erodium*
▷***Strangweja spicata*** see *Bellevalia hyacinthoides*
▷***Stranvaesia*** see *Photinia*
S. davidiana see *P. davidiana*
S. nussia see *P. nussia*

STRATIOTES

HYDROCHARITACEAE

Genus of one species of vigorous, dioecious, submerged aquatic perennial found in still and slow-moving water in Eurasia. It has rosettes of narrow, prickly, saw-toothed, submerged leaves, which rise to the surface at flowering time. An attractive foliage plant for a sunny pool, it acts to some extent as a filter and oxygenator, but must be kept in check.
• **HARDINESS** Fully hardy.
• **CULTIVATION** In summer, scatter new plants into a pool of slightly alkaline water over 30cm (12in) deep. Remove runners as necessary to control spread.
• **PROPAGATION** Detach winter buds or young plantlets in spring.
• **PESTS AND DISEASES** Trouble free.

S. aloides (Water soldier). Aquatic perennial with short runners producing stalkless rosettes of linear to lance-shaped, sharp-pointed, toothed, deep olive-green leaves, to 50cm (20in) long. In midsummer, bears cup-shaped, white, sometimes pink-tinged flowers, 3cm (1¼in) across, from 2-leaved bracts: the males in pairs or threes, the females solitary. ↔ indefinite. Eurasia. ❄❄❄

▷**Strawberry** see *Fragaria*
Indian see *Duchesnea indica*
Mock see *Duchesnea indica*
▷**Strawberry bush** see *Calycanthus floridus*
▷**Strawberry tree** see *Arbutus, A. unedo*
Grecian see *A. andrachne*
▷**Strawflower** see *Rhodanthe, Xerochrysum bracteatum*

STRELITZIA

Bird of paradise

STRELITZIACEAE

Genus of about 5 species of clump-forming, evergreen perennials found in habitats ranging from riverbanks to open glades in the bush of South Africa. They have large, long-stalked, mostly oblong to lance-shaped leaves with woody bases forming a "trunk" that may reach 10m (30ft) tall. Their exotic inflorescences, produced intermittently from the leaf axils, consist of usually horizontal, waxy, stiff, boat-shaped spathes, from the top of which crest-like flowers arise sequentially, often in contrasting colours; they are very long-lasting when cut. In frost-prone areas, grow in a warm greenhouse; move outdoors in summer. In warmer areas, grow as specimen plants.
• **HARDINESS** Frost tender.
• **CULTIVATION** Under glass, grow in large containers or in a greenhouse border in loam-based potting compost (JI No.3). Provide full light with shade from hot sun, and ventilate freely when temperatures exceed 20°C (68°F). In the growing season, water freely and apply a balanced liquid fertilizer monthly. Water sparingly in winter. Top-dress annually and repot every second year.

Strelitzia nicolai

Outdoors, grow in fertile, moist but well-drained soil in full sun or partial shade, with shelter from strong winds.
• **PROPAGATION** Sow seed at 18–21°C (64–70°F), or divide rooted suckers, in spring. Seed-raised plants may take 3 or more years to flower.
• **PESTS AND DISEASES** Susceptible to scale insects.

S. alba. Clump-forming perennial with oblong to lance-shaped leaf-blades, 2m (6ft) long, on leaf-stalks 1m (3ft) long. Bears purple-glaucous spathes, 25–30cm (10–12in) long, with white flowers, 20cm (8in) long, usually in spring. ↕ to 10m (30ft), ↔ to 3m (10ft). South Africa (Western Cape, Northern Cape, Eastern Cape). ❁ (min. 10°C/50°F)
S. juncea, syn. *S. reginae* var. *juncea*. Clump-forming perennial with rush-like leaves, 50cm (20in) long, without leaf-blades. From winter to spring, produces green spathes, 12cm (5in) long, and flowers, 3–4cm (1¼–1½in) long, with orange calyces and blue corollas. ↕ to 1.5m (5ft), ↔ 1m (3ft). South Africa (Eastern Cape). ❁ (min. 10°C/50°F)
S. nicolai ■ Clump-forming perennial with oblong leaf-blades, 1.5m (5ft) long,

Strelitzia reginae

S

rounded or heart-shaped at the bases, on leaf-stalks 2m (6ft) long. In spring, bears 3–5 brownish red spathes, 40–45cm (16–18in) long, and white flowers, 20cm (8in) long, with light purplish blue corollas. Needs ample space. ↕ to 10m (30ft), ↔ to 5m (15ft). South Africa (Northern Cape, Eastern Cape, KwaZulu/Natal). ❄ (min. 10°C/50°F)
S. reginae ▣ (Crane flower). Clump-forming perennial with oblong-lance-shaped leaf-blades, to 50cm (20in) long, with round or tapered bases, on stalks to 1m (3ft) long. From winter to spring, bears purple- and orange-flushed green spathes, 12cm (5in) long, and flowers 10cm (4in) long, with orange or yellow calyces and blue corollas. ↕ to 2m (6ft), ↔ to 1m (3ft). South Africa. ❄ (min. 10°C/50°F). **'Humilis'**, syn. 'Pygmaea', is dwarf, forming dense clumps, and has ovate-oblong leaves; it grows well in containers; ↕ 80cm (32in). **'Pygmaea'** see 'Humilis'. **var. *juncea*** see *S. juncea.*

▷ ***Streptanthera cuprea*** see *Sparaxis elegans*
▷ ***Streptanthera elegans*** see *Sparaxis elegans*

STREPTOCARPUS
Cape primrose
GESNERIACEAE

Genus of about 130 species of annuals and perennials, some monocarpic, or rarely subshrubs, often found in rainforest, sometimes as epiphytes, and on damp banks and rocks or in grassland. They occur from tropical to southern Africa, in Madagascar, and in China, with 4 species from S.E. Asia. Linear to rounded, hairy, often mid-green, veined, wrinkled leaves are borne singly or in opposite pairs on erect, fleshy stems, or in stemless rosettes. Cymes of tubular, often 2-lipped flowers, with 5 spreading lobes, are axillary or borne from the leaf rosettes. In frost-prone areas, grow in a temperate or warm greenhouse. Use in a humid, shady border in warmer areas.
• **HARDINESS** Frost tender.
• **CULTIVATION** Under glass, grow in loamless potting compost in bright filtered light, with shade from hot sun. When in growth, water freely, allowing compost to dry out between waterings (overwatering results in basal rot); apply a high-potash fertilizer every 2 weeks. Reduce humidity and keep just moist in winter. Repot annually in spring. Remove faded flowers and stalks to

S

Streptocarpus caulescens

Streptocarpus 'Constant Nymph'

discourage seeding. Outdoors, grow in fertile, leafy, humus-rich, moist but well-drained soil in partial shade.
• **PROPAGATION** Surface-sow seed in late winter or spring, at 18°C (64°F). Divide, or take leaf cuttings, in spring or early summer. Root stem-tip cuttings, 5–8cm (2–3in) long, of bushy and trailing plants in spring, with bottom heat.
• **PESTS AND DISEASES** Leafhoppers, mealybugs, thrips, tarsonemid mites, and vine weevil larvae may be a problem.

***S.* 'Albatross'.** Robust, rhizomatous perennial with rosettes of broad, strap-shaped, finely hairy leaves, 25cm (10in) long. Cymes of up to 5 yellow-throated white flowers, 6cm (2½in) across, open from spring to autumn. ↕ 30cm (12in), ↔ 55cm (22in). ❄ (min. 10°C/ 50°F)
S. caulescens ▣ Erect perennial with fleshy, deep brown stems and opposite, elliptic to ovate, softly hairy leaves, 6cm (2½in) long. Cymes of 6–12 violet or white flowers, 1.5–2cm (½–¾in) across, with purple throats, are borne throughout the year. ↕↔ to 60cm (24in). Kenya, Tanzania. ❄ (min. 10°C/50°F)
***S.* 'Concord Blue'.** Erect, bushy perennial producing fleshy stems and

Streptocarpus 'Lisa'

opposite, rounded, softly hairy leaves, 2.5cm (1in) long. Cymes of many mid-blue flowers, 2cm (¾in) across, open from spring to autumn. ↕ 30cm (12in), ↔ 50cm (20in). ❄ (min. 10°C/50°F)
***S.* 'Constant Nymph'** ▣ Stemless, rhizomatous perennial with rosettes of lance-shaped, finely hairy leaves, to 30cm (12in) long. From spring to autumn, bears cymes of up to 5 blue flowers, 6cm (2½in) across, with pale yellow throats and deep violet veins on the 3 lower lobes. ↕ 30cm (12in), ↔ 60cm (24in). ❄ (min. 10°C/50°F)
***S.* 'Heidi'.** Rhizomatous perennial with rosettes of strap-shaped, finely hairy leaves, to 22cm (9in) long. From spring to autumn, bears cymes of up to 5 clear blue flowers, 6cm (2½in) across, with purple markings on the lower 3 lobes. ↕ 24cm (10in), ↔ 45cm (18in). ❄ (min. 10°C/50°F)
***S.* 'Joanna'.** Vigorous, rhizomatous perennial with rosettes of strap-shaped, finely hairy leaves, 35cm (14in) long. From spring to autumn, bears cymes of up to 5 frilled, deep velvet-red flowers, 8cm (3in) across, with darker markings. ↕ 30cm (12in), ↔ 75cm (30in). ❄ (min. 10°C/50°F)

Streptocarpus 'Kim'

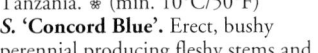

Streptocarpus 'Nicola'

***S.* 'Kim'** ▣ Rhizomatous perennial with rosettes of strap-shaped, finely hairy leaves, 15cm (6in) long. From spring to summer, bears cymes of many dark purple flowers, 3.5cm (1½in) across, with white throats. ↕ 20cm (8in), ↔ 35cm (14in). ❄ (min. 10°C/50°F)
***S.* 'Lisa'** ▣ Rhizomatous perennial with rosettes of strap-shaped, finely hairy leaves, 30cm (12in) long. Many cymes of up to 5 white-throated, shell-pink flowers, 6cm (2½in) across, open from spring to autumn. ↕ 35cm (14in), ↔ 65cm (26in). ❄ (min. 10°C/50°F)
***S.* 'Nicola'** ▣ Rhizomatous perennial with erect rosettes of strap-shaped, finely hairy leaves, 20cm (8in) long. From spring to autumn, bears many cymes of up to 5 semi-double, deep pink flowers, 3cm (1¼in) across. ↕ 35cm (14in), ↔ 45cm (18in). ❄ (min. 10°C/50°F)
S. rexii. Rhizomatous perennial with rosettes of strap-shaped, blunt-tipped, finely hairy leaves, to 30cm (12in) long. Violet-tinged white, or violet flowers, 3.5–4.5cm (1½–1¾in) across, with violet lines on the lower lobes, are borne usually singly or in pairs, or in cymes of up to 6, from spring to autumn. ↕ to 25cm (10in), ↔ to 50cm (20in). South Africa (Western Cape, Eastern Cape, S. KwaZulu/Natal). ❄ (min. 10°C/50°F)
S. saxorum ▣ Prostrate, sparsely branched, woody-based perennial with opposite, elliptic to ovate, finely hairy, thick, grey-green leaves, 2.5cm (1in) long. Axillary, pale lilac, white-throated flowers, 3cm (1¼in) across, are borne singly or in pairs, in spring and early summer. ↕ 15cm (6in), ↔ 60cm (24in). E. Africa. ❄ (min. 10°C/50°F)

Streptocarpus saxorum

STREPTOSOLEN

SOLANACEAE

Genus of one species of evergreen shrub found in open woodland from Colombia to Peru and Ecuador, grown for its clusters of colourful, salverform flowers. It is loosely scrambling, with alternate, simple leaves. Below 7°C (45°F), grow in a cool or temperate greenhouse. In warmer areas, grow against a wall or among other shrubs.

- **HARDINESS** Frost tender; may survive temperatures near to 0°C (32°F).
- **CULTIVATION** Under glass, grow in loam-based potting compost (JI No.3) in full light with shade from hot sun. When in growth, water freely and apply a balanced liquid fertilizer monthly. Water sparingly in winter. Outdoors, grow in fertile, moist but well-drained soil in full sun. Pruning group 8 or 9, in late winter or early spring; group 13 if wall-trained; may need restrictive pruning under glass.
- **PROPAGATION** Root softwood cuttings in early summer, or semi-ripe cuttings in mid- to late summer, both with bottom heat. Layer in late summer.
- **PESTS AND DISEASES** Whiteflies, red spider mites, and aphids may be troublesome under glass.

S. jamesonii ▣ (Marmalade bush). Tall, slender-stemmed shrub, semi-scandent unless annually pruned, with ovate to elliptic, finely wrinkled, mid- to deep green leaves, 2.5–5cm (1–2in) long. From late spring to late summer, produces yellow to orange-yellow flowers, 3–4cm (1¼–1½in) long, with slender, twisted tubes and spreading petal lobes, in large, terminal corymbs, to 15cm (6in) across. ↕ 2–3m (6–10ft), ↔ 1–2.5m (3–8ft). Colombia, Ecuador, Peru. ❀ (min. 7°C/45°F)

Streptosolen jamesonii

▷**String of beads** see *Senecio rowleyanus*

STROBILANTHES

ACANTHACEAE

Genus of 250 species of evergreen or deciduous perennials or soft-stemmed shrubs from woodland margins in Asia and Madagascar. They are grown for their tubular to funnel-shaped, 2-lipped, often hooded, 5-lobed, blue to purple, white, or rarely yellow flowers, borne in terminal or axillary, usually cone-shaped inflorescences, sometimes loose panicles or spikes. The leaves are opposite, ovate to lance-shaped or elliptic, entire or toothed, often in unequal pairs. In frost-prone areas, grow hardy species in a herbaceous border; grow tender species as summer bedding or in a warm greenhouse. In warmer areas, use in a border.

- **HARDINESS** Mostly frost tender; *S. atropurpureus* is fully hardy.
- **CULTIVATION** Under glass, grow in loam-based potting compost (JI No.2) in full light with shade from hot sun. When in growth, water freely; apply a balanced liquid fertilizer monthly. Water moderately in winter. Outdoors, grow in light, fertile, free-draining soil in full sun or partial shade. Pinch out young growth to induce bushiness. In frost-prone climates, protect *S. atropurpureus* with a dry winter mulch. Pruning group 9 for shrubs; they may need restrictive pruning under glass.
- **PROPAGATION** Sow seed at 13–18°C (55–64°F) in spring. Root basal or softwood cuttings in spring or early summer, with bottom heat.
- **PESTS AND DISEASES** Red spider mites may be troublesome.

Strobilanthes atropurpureus

S. anisophyllus. Small subshrub with unequal pairs of lance-shaped, toothed, dark green leaves, 9cm (3½in) long. Tubular, lavender-blue flowers, 2.5cm (1in) long, with curved corolla tubes, are borne in cone-shaped inflorescences in spring and winter. ↕ 1–2m (3–6ft), ↔ 75cm (30in). Himalayas. ❀ (min. 12°C/54°F)

S. atropurpureus ▣ Erect, branching perennial with long-stalked, ovate, toothed, dark green leaves, 10cm (4in) long. Dense spikes of tubular, indigo or purple flowers, 4cm (1½in) long, are produced in summer. ↕ 1.2m (4ft), ↔ 1m (3ft). N. India. ❄❄❄

S. dyerianus (Persian shield). Soft-stemmed shrub with unequal pairs of elliptic, toothed, dark green leaves, to 15cm (6in) long, flushed purple with a silver overlay above, dark purple beneath. Bears short spikes of funnel-shaped, pale blue flowers, 3cm (1¼in) long, in autumn. ↕ 1.2m (4ft), ↔ 1m (3ft). Burma. ❀ (min. 12°C/54°F)

STROMANTHE

MARANTACEAE

Genus of 13 species of evergreen, rhizomatous herbaceous perennials from forest floors and clearings in Central and South America. They are grown for their foliage and showy flower bracts. Obovate, ovate, elliptic, or lance-shaped to linear-lance-shaped leaves are borne basally and on the slender, often many-branched stems. Cup-shaped, yellow, red, or white flowers, with colourful bracts, are borne in racemes or panicles, often several on a stem, in winter, spring, and summer. In frost-prone areas, grow in a warm greenhouse. In warmer areas, use in a damp, humid border.

- **HARDINESS** Frost tender.
- **CULTIVATION** Under glass, grow in a greenhouse border in loamless or loam-based potting compost (JI No.3) in bright filtered light, allowing a free root run. When in growth, water freely, maintain high humidity, and apply a low-nitrogen liquid fertilizer every 2 or 3 weeks. Water moderately in winter. Outdoors, grow in moist, fertile soil in full sun or dappled shade.
- **PROPAGATION** Sow seed at 18°C (64°F) in early spring. Divide when dormant or after flowering, to minimize root damage.
- **PESTS AND DISEASES** Red spider mites may be troublesome in dry conditions.

S. jacquinii, syn. *S. lutea*. Rhizomatous perennial with branching stems and oblong-ovate to elliptic, mid-green leaves, 35cm (14in) long. In winter and spring, bears pale yellow flowers, 9mm (⅜in) long, with bright yellow bracts, in panicles 5–8cm (2–3in) across. ↕ 3m (10ft), ↔ 1m (3ft). Panama, Colombia, Venezuela. ❀ (min. 10°C/50°F)

S. lutea see *S. jacquinii*.

S. sanguinea. Erect, rhizomatous perennial. Branching stems bear lance-shaped to linear-lance-shaped, dark olive-green leaves, 50cm (20in) long, red beneath and 2-ranked at the bases. Bears white-petalled flowers, to 1cm (½in) long, with orange-red sepals, among red bracts, in panicles 5–8cm (2–3in) across, in winter and spring. ↕ to 1.5m (5ft), ↔ 1m (3ft). Brazil. ❀ (min. 10°C/50°F)

STROMBOCACTUS

CACTACEAE

Genus of one species of perennial cactus from rocky fissures in C. Mexico. It has a mainly flattened-spherical stem, with ribs divided into prominent tubercles, spirally arranged; the areoles produce a few bristles, which fall as the plant matures. It produces solitary, funnel-shaped flowers from the crown in summer, followed by thin-walled, dry fruit containing minute seeds. Where temperatures drop below 10°C (50°F), grow in a warm greenhouse; in warmer climates, use in a desert garden.

- **HARDINESS** Frost tender.
- **CULTIVATION** Under glass, grow in standard cactus compost, with added limestone chips, in full light and low humidity. Water moderately in spring and summer, applying a balanced liquid fertilizer every 3 or 4 weeks. Keep completely dry at other times. Outdoors, grow in gritty, sharply drained, poor, humus-rich, preferably neutral to slightly alkaline soil in full sun. See also pp.48–49.
- **PROPAGATION** Sow seed at 21°C (70°F) in spring; seedlings may be difficult to establish.
- **PESTS AND DISEASES** Trouble free.

Strombocactus disciformis

S. disciformis ■ Simple, occasionally offsetting, flattened-spherical, greyish green cactus, bearing a few persistent, off-white, dark-tipped spines at the crown and 12–18 ribs closely set with diamond-shaped tubercles. Each tubercle has a central white areole bearing 1–5 bristly white radial spines (there are no centrals). Produces funnel-shaped, white or yellow flowers, with red throats, 3cm (1¼in) across, by day in summer. ↕↔ to 12cm (5in). C. Mexico. ❀ (min. 10°C/50°F)

STRONGYLODON

LEGUMINOSAE/PAPILIONACEAE

Genus of about 20 species of evergreen shrubs or woody-stemmed, twining climbers from tropical woodland in S.E. Asia and the Pacific islands. Alternate, 3-palmate leaves have lance-shaped to rounded leaflets, the terminal one largest. From winter to summer, they bear pendent racemes of pea-like, red, orange, blue, or bluish green flowers with pointed, upturned keel petals. Below 15°C (59°F), grow in a warm greenhouse or conservatory. In warmer areas, train over an arch or pergola.

Strongylodon macrobotrys

- **HARDINESS** Frost tender.
- **CULTIVATION** Under glass, grow in loam-based potting compost (JI No.3) in full light with shade from hot sun. In growth, water freely; apply a balanced liquid fertilizer every 2 or 3 weeks. Water moderately to sparingly in winter. Outdoors, grow in fertile, humus-rich, neutral to acid soil in full sun or partial shade. Support climbing stems. Pruning group 11; or 12, after flowering.
- **PROPAGATION** Sow seed at 27–30°C (81–86°F) as soon as ripe. Root semi-ripe stem sections in summer, with bottom heat. Air layer in spring.
- **PESTS AND DISEASES** Scale insects may be troublesome under glass.

S. macrobotrys ■ (Emerald creeper, Jade vine). Strong-growing, evergreen, twining climber. Leaves, to 15cm (6in) long, with 3 oblong to elliptic leaflets, are pinkish bronze, turning rich green. From winter to spring, rarely summer, bears pea-like, luminous, blue-green flowers, 8cm (3in) long, in dense racemes, 40–90cm (16–36in) long. ↕ to 20m (70ft). Philippines. ❀ (min. 15°C/59°F)

▷ ***Stuartia*** see *Stewartia*

STYLIDIUM

STYLIDIACEAE

Genus of about 150 species of annuals, herbaceous perennials, and subshrubs from dry scrub in Australia (one species from New Zealand). They are grown for their glossy, grass-like foliage and their flowers. The usually very narrow leaves, to 50cm (20in) long, are alternate or in basal rosettes. Pink, white, yellow, or purple flowers are borne in racemes, panicles, or corymbs in summer. The flowers are asymmetrical: each has 5 petals, one very small, with a central column combining stamens and style. In frost-prone areas, grow in a cool to temperate greenhouse. In warmer areas, use in a sunny border.

- **HARDINESS** Frost tender.
- **CULTIVATION** Under glass, grow in loamless or loam-based potting compost (JI No.2) in full light. When in growth, water sparingly and apply a balanced liquid fertilizer monthly. Keep almost dry in winter. Outdoors, grow in well-drained, fertile soil in full sun.
- **PROPAGATION** Sow seed at 13–18°C (55–64°F), or divide, in spring.
- **PESTS AND DISEASES** Often affected by fungal diseases.

S. graminifolium (Trigger plant). Tufted, short-lived perennial with basal rosettes of stiffly erect to arching, linear leaves, to 24cm (10in) long. Produces tiny, pink to magenta flowers in terminal, erect, narrow racemes, to 30cm (12in) long, in summer. ↕ 30–80cm (12–32in), ↔ 45cm (18in). Australia. ❀ (min. 7°C/45°F)

STYLOPHORUM

PAPAVERACEAE

Genus of 3 species of herbaceous perennials from woodland in E. Asia and E. North America. The pinnatisect leaves have long stalks in the basal rosettes, and are stalkless on the upright, branching, ridged stems. The flowers are saucer-shaped, poppy-like, and yellow or orange, borne in terminal umbels in spring and summer. Stylophorums are attractive plants for a woodland garden, a shady border among shrubs, or a large rock garden. They may self-seed.

Stylophorum diphyllum

- **HARDINESS** Fully hardy.
- **CULTIVATION** Grow in moist, moderately fertile, humus-rich soil in deep or partial shade.
- **PROPAGATION** Sow seed in containers in a cold frame in autumn. Divide in spring; may be slow to re-establish.
- **PESTS AND DISEASES** May be attacked by slugs and snails.

S. diphyllum ■ (Celandine poppy). Downy, rosette-forming perennial with deeply incised, hairy, mid-green leaves, 20–30cm (8–12in) long, each with 5–7 oblong-obovate, irregularly scalloped and toothed lobes. Bright golden yellow flowers, to 2.5cm (1in) across, are borne in summer. ↕↔ to 30cm (12in). E. USA. ❄❄❄

STYPHELIA

EPACRIDACEAE

Genus of 12 species of wiry-stemmed, evergreen shrubs from dry forest and woodland; they occur in Australia, except for one species found in New Guinea. They have small, simple, aromatic, rigidly leathery leaves, arranged alternately or in spirals. Long, slender, tubular flowers, each with 5 reflexed or rolled-back lobes, are borne singly or in small groups from the upper leaf axils in summer. In frost-prone areas, grow in a cool greenhouse. In milder climates, grow in a shrub border.

- **HARDINESS** Half hardy to frost tender.
- **CULTIVATION** Under glass, grow in lime-free (ericaceous) potting compost in full light with good ventilation. In the growing season, water moderately and apply a balanced liquid fertilizer monthly. Water sparingly in winter. Outdoors, grow in fertile, humus-rich, neutral to acid soil in full sun. Pruning group 10, after flowering.
- **PROPAGATION** Sow seed at 6–12°C (43–54°F) as soon as ripe or in spring. Root semi-ripe cuttings in summer, with bottom heat. Layer in spring.
- **PESTS AND DISEASES** Trouble free.

S. colensoi see *Cyathodes colensoi.*
S. triflora (Pink fivecorner). Erect, moderately dense shrub bearing elliptic to oblong-elliptic leaves, 1.5–3cm (½–1¼in) long, with sharp points. In summer, tubular, 5-angled, usually pink to red, occasionally cream or pale yellow-green flowers, 2cm (¾in) long, with strongly rolled-back lobes, are produced singly or in twos or threes. ↕ 0.4–2m (16–72in), ↔ 60–90cm (24–36in). S.W. Australia. ❄

STYRAX

STYRACACEAE

Genus of approximately 100 species of deciduous or evergreen shrubs and small trees found in woodland and thickets in Europe, Asia, and North America, including Mexico. Of graceful habit, they have alternate, short-stalked, variably shaped, entire or toothed leaves. The dainty, nodding, bell-shaped or cup-shaped, fragrant white flowers may be solitary, borne in pendent, terminal or axillary racemes or panicles, or produced in clusters on short branchlets; they appear on the previous year's wood in spring or summer. Grow in a woodland garden.

- **HARDINESS** Fully hardy to frost hardy.
- **CULTIVATION** Grow in moist but well-drained, fertile, humus-rich, neutral to acid soil in full sun or partial shade, with shelter from cold, drying winds. Pruning group 1.
- **PROPAGATION** Sow seed as soon as ripe; keep at 15°C (59°F) for 3 months, then at 0–5°C (32–41°F) for 3 months; keep seedlings frost-free until they are established. Take greenwood cuttings in summer.
- **PESTS AND DISEASES** Trouble free.

S. americanus (American snowbell). Rounded, deciduous shrub with elliptic to oblong, entire or toothed, dark green leaves, to 8cm (3in) long. Nodding, bell-shaped white flowers, 2cm (¾in) long, with narrow, backward-curving petals, are produced singly or in small clusters of up to 4 from the leaf axils, in early and midsummer. ↕ 3m (10ft), ↔ 2.5m (8ft). S.E. USA. ❄❄❄
S. hemsleyanus ♀ Broadly columnar, deciduous tree with oval to obovate, toothed, dark green leaves, to 12cm (5in) long. Bell-shaped white flowers, 1.5cm (½in) long, are borne in terminal racemes or few-branched panicles, to 15cm (6in) long, in early summer. ↕ 8m (25ft), ↔ 5m (15ft). C. China. ❄❄❄
S. japonicus ■♀ (Japanese snowbell). Graceful, spreading, deciduous tree bearing elliptic-oblong, minutely toothed, glossy, mid- to dark green

Styrax japonicus

S

Styrax obassia (inset: flower detail)

leaves, to 10cm (4in) long, turning yellow or red in autumn. Bell-shaped, white, sometimes pink-tinged flowers, 1.5cm (½in) long, are produced singly or in clusters of 3–6 along the undersides of the branches, in early and midsummer. ↕ 10m (30ft), ↔ 8m (25ft). China, Korea, Japan. ❄❄❄. **'Pink Chimes'** bears a profusion of pink flowers.

S. obassia ■ ♀ (Fragrant snowbell). Broadly columnar, deciduous tree bearing elliptic to rounded, dark green leaves, 7–15cm (3–6in) long, distinctly toothed except towards their bases, and blue-grey beneath, turning yellow in autumn. Bell-shaped white flowers, 2.5cm (1in) long, are produced in spreading, terminal racemes, to 20cm (8in) long, in early and midsummer. ↕ 12m (40ft), ↔ 7m (22ft). N. China, Korea, Japan. ❄❄❄

S. officinalis ■ ♀ (Storax). Spreading, deciduous shrub or tree with ovate, entire, dark green leaves, grey-white beneath, to 8cm (3in) long. Bell-shaped white flowers, 2.5cm (1in) long, are produced in pendent clusters of 3–8 near the shoot tips, in early summer. ↕ 6m (20ft), ↔ 5m (15ft). S. Europe, S.W. Asia. ❄❄

S. wilsonii. Rounded, bushy, deciduous shrub with slender shoots and oval to diamond-shaped, dark green leaves, to 2.5cm (1in) long, with a few teeth near the tips. Broadly bell-shaped white flowers, 1.5cm (½in) across, are borne singly or in clusters of up to 4 along the shoots, in early summer. ↕↔ 2.5m (8ft). W. China. ❄❄❄

Styrax officinalis

SUCCISA

DIPSACACEAE

Genus of one species of perennial found in boggy meadows and moorland from Europe to W. Siberia, and in N.W. Africa. Minutely hairy, it bears rosettes of obovate to elliptic basal leaves and erect or decumbent stems with smaller, narrower leaves. Its pincushion-like flowerheads, late- and long-flowering, are similar to those of *Scabiosa*. Grow in a damp wild garden or meadow.

- **HARDINESS** Fully hardy.
- **CULTIVATION** Grow in poor to moderately fertile, peaty soil that is moist at least through the growing season, in full sun or partial shade.
- **PROPAGATION** Sow seed in containers in a cold frame in autumn or spring. Root basal cuttings in spring.
- **PESTS AND DISEASES** Trouble free.

S. pratensis, syn. *Scabiosa succisa* (Blue buttons, Devil's bit scabious). Rosette-forming, rhizomatous perennial with obovate to elliptic, usually entire, mainly basal leaves, to 30cm (12in) long. From midsummer to late autumn, bears solitary, pincushion-like, violet, rarely white or pink flowerheads, to 2.5cm (1in) across. ↕ 15–60cm (6–24in), ↔ to 60cm (24in). Europe, N.W. Africa, Caucasus, Russia (W. Siberia). ❄❄❄

▷ **Succulents** see pp.48–49
▷ **Sugar-almond plant** see *Pachyphytum oviferum*
▷ **Sugarberry** see *Celtis occidentalis, C. reticulata*
▷ **Sugarbush** see *Protea repens*
▷ ***Sulcorebutia*** see *Rebutia*
▷ **Sulphur flower** see *Eriogonum gracilipes, E. umbellatum*
▷ **Sumach** see *Rhus*
Dwarf see *Rhus copallina*
Fragrant see *Rhus aromatica*
Scarlet see *Rhus glabra*
Shining see *Rhus copallina*
Smooth see *Rhus glabra*
Stag's horn see *Rhus typhina*
Velvet see *Rhus typhina*
Venetian see *Cotinus coggygria*
▷ **Summer-sweet** see *Clethra*
▷ **Sundew** see *Drosera*
Cape see *D. capensis*
▷ **Sundrops** see *Oenothera, O. fruticosa, O. perennis*
Ozark see *O. macrocarpa*
▷ **Sunflower** see *Helianthus, H. annuus*
Dark-eye see *Helianthus atrorubens*
Mexican see *Tithonia, T. rotundifolia*
Thin-leaved see *Helianthus decapetalus*
Willow-leaved see *Helianthus salicifolius*
Woolly see *Eriophyllum*
▷ **Sun plant** see *Portulaca grandiflora*
▷ **Supple Jack** see *Berchemia scandens*

SUTERA

SCROPHULARIACEAE

Genus of 49 species of annuals, soft-stemmed evergreen perennials, and small, evergreen shrubs or subshrubs, mostly from woodland margins in South Africa. They have opposite, broadly ovate to broadly elliptic, toothed, lobed, or scalloped, pale to dark green leaves. From summer to autumn, salverform, white, pale mauve, or blue flowers, with tubular corollas and 5 spreading lobes, are borne singly from the leaf axils or in axillary or terminal cymes, racemes, spikes, or panicles. In frost-prone areas, use as summer bedding or in a container or hanging basket, or grow in a temperate greenhouse. In warmer areas, use as edging or in bedding schemes.

- **HARDINESS** Frost tender.
- **CULTIVATION** Under glass, grow in loam-based potting compost (JI No.2) in full light. In the growing season, water freely and apply a balanced liquid fertilizer monthly. Water sparingly in winter. Outdoors, grow in well-drained, fertile soil in full sun.
- **PROPAGATION** Sow seed at 13–18°C (55–64°F), or divide, in spring. Root stem-tip cuttings in spring or summer, with bottom heat.
- **PESTS AND DISEASES** Prone to aphids.

S. cordata, syn. *Bacopa cordata* of gardens. Prostrate to trailing, evergreen perennial with a woody rootstock and loosely branched stems with long white hairs, often rooting at the nodes. Broadly ovate or sometimes broadly elliptic, scalloped or toothed, pale to mid-green leaves, 6–25mm (¼–1in) long, abruptly narrow at their base into short stalks. Solitary, tubular, salverform, yellow-throated white or pale to mid-blue flowers, 8–10mm (¾–½in) long, are borne in the leaf axils in summer. South Africa (Western Cape, Eastern Cape). ↕ to 10cm (4in), ↔ indefinite. ❄

S. grandiflora see *Jamesbrittenia grandiflora.*

S. jurassica see *Jamesbrittenia jurassica.*

S. pristisepala see *Jamesbrittenia pristisepala.*

SUTHERLANDIA

LEGUMINOSAE/PAPILIONACEAE

Genus of 5 species of evergreen shrubs found on dry slopes and grassland in southern Africa. They are grown for their showy, pea-like, red to purple flowers, borne in slender, axillary racemes from late spring to summer, and for their bladder-like fruits. Leaves are alternate and pinnate. In frost-prone climates, grow in a cool greenhouse; in milder areas, plant at the base of a sunny wall.

- **HARDINESS** Frost tender; may survive short periods close to 0°C (32°F).
- **CULTIVATION** Under glass, grow in loam-based potting compost (JI No.2), with added sharp sand, in full light.

Sutherlandia frutescens

S

During growth, water moderately and apply a balanced liquid fertilizer monthly. Water sparingly in winter. Outdoors, grow in well-drained, poor to moderately fertile soil in full sun; tolerates dry soils. Pruning group 8; may need restrictive pruning under glass, in late winter.
• **PROPAGATION** Sow seed at 15°C (59°F) in spring. Root semi-ripe cuttings in summer, with bottom heat.
• **PESTS AND DISEASES** Earwigs and red spider mites may be a problem.

S. frutescens ■ (Balloon pea, Duck plant). Evergreen shrub with slender, erect, twiggy, white-downy stems and pinnate, hairy, grey-green leaves, 6–10cm (2½–4in) long, each with 13–21 small, oblong to linear-elliptic leaflets on densely white-downy midribs. From late spring to summer, bears racemes, to 8cm (3in) long, of pea-like, bright red flowers, 2.5–5cm (1–2in) long, followed by inflated, broadly ellipsoid to almost spherical, greenish yellow, occasionally red-flushed seed pods, to 5cm (2in) long. ↕0.6–2m (2–6ft), ↔ 1–1.5m (3–5ft). Southern Africa. ❄ (min. 5°C/41°F)

SWAINSONA

syn. SWAINSONIA

LEGUMINOSAE/PAPILIONACEAE

Genus of 50 species of perennials, subshrubs, and annuals from stony slopes and grassland and in open woodland, mainly in Australia. They have alternate, pinnate leaves and pea-like, usually purple, sometimes white, pink, yellow, orange, or red flowers, with very broad standard petals, borne in erect, axillary racemes from spring to summer. In frost-prone areas, grow in a cool greenhouse. Elsewhere, use in a border.
• **HARDINESS** Frost tender.
• **CULTIVATION** Under glass, grow in loam-based potting compost (JI No.2), with added sharp sand, in full light. In growth, water moderately and apply a low-phosphate fertilizer monthly. Water sparingly in winter. Outdoors, grow in sharply drained, moderately fertile soil in full sun. Pruning group 10, after flowering (or late winter, if under glass).
• **PROPAGATION** Sow pre-soaked seed at 15°C (59°F) in spring. Root semi-ripe cuttings in summer, with bottom heat.
• **PESTS AND DISEASES** Red spider mites may be a problem under glass.

S. galegifolia ■ Evergreen subshrub with spreading to semi-scandent stems. Pinnate leaves, 5–8cm (2–3in) long, have 11–21 small, oblong, grey- to deep green leaflets. From spring to summer, bears red, pink, purple, or blue flowers, 1.5cm (½in) long. ↕↔1–2m (3–6ft). Australia (Queensland, New South Wales). ❄ (min. 5–7°C/41–45°F). **'Albiflora'** has pure white flowers and pale green leaves. **'Violacea'** bears rose-red to purple flowers.

▷ ***Swainsonia*** see *Swainsona*
▷ **Swallow-wort** see *Asclepias curassavica*
▷ **Swan plant** see *Gomphocarpus physocarpus*
▷ **Sweet basil** see *Ocimum basilicum*
▷ **Sweetbells** see *Leucothoe racemosa*
▷ **Sweet briar** see *Rosa rubiginosa*
▷ **Sweet chestnut** see *Castanea sativa*

Swainsona galegifolia

▷ **Sweet Cicely** see *Myrrhis, M. odorata*
▷ **Sweetcorn** see *Zea mays*
▷ **Sweet gale** see *Myrica gale*
▷ **Sweet gum** see *Liquidambar styraciflua*
Oriental see *L. orientalis*
▷ **Sweetheart plant** see *Philodendron hederaceum*
▷ **Sweetheart vine** see *Ceropegia linearis* subsp. *woodii, Philodendron hederaceum*
▷ **Sweet pea** see *Lathyrus odoratus*
▷ **Sweet pepper bush** see *Clethra, C. alnifolia*
▷ **Sweetshrub, Common** see *Calycanthus floridus*
▷ **Sweetspire** see *Itea virginica*
▷ **Sweet sultan** see *Amberboa, A. moschata*
▷ **Sweet William** see *Dianthus barbatus*
Wild see *Phlox divaricata*
▷ **Sweetwood** see *Glycyrrhiza glabra*
▷ ***Swida alba*** see *Cornus alba*
▷ ***Swida alternifolia*** see *Cornus alternifolia*
▷ ***Swida amomum*** see *Cornus amomum*
▷ ***Swida controversa*** see *Cornus controversa*
▷ **Swiss chard** see *Beta vulgaris* subsp. *cicla*
▷ **Swiss cheese plant** see *Monstera deliciosa*

SYAGRUS syn. ARECASTRUM

ARECACEAE/PALMAE

Genus of 32 species of often low-growing, single- or cluster-stemmed, sometimes stemless palms, from shrubby vegetation to woodland, often on rocky ridges, in South America. Leaves are pinnate, arranged in spiralling, terminal tufts; the ovoid, 3-petalled flowers appear in spikes or panicles between them. In frost-prone climates, grow in a warm or temperate greenhouse, or as houseplants. In warmer areas, use tall species as lawn specimens, and smaller ones in a shrub border.
• **HARDINESS** Frost tender.
• **CULTIVATION** Under glass, grow in loam-based potting compost (JI No.3) in bright filtered light. In growth, water freely; apply a balanced liquid fertilizer monthly. Water sparingly in winter. Pot on or top-dress in spring. Outdoors, grow in fertile, moist but well-drained soil in full sun or partial shade.
• **PROPAGATION** Sow seed at 27°C (81°F) in spring.
• **PESTS AND DISEASES** Red spider mites may be troublesome under glass.

Syagrus flexuosa

S. flexuosa ■ ✲ (Palmito do campo). Small palm with slender, single or clustered stems bearing pinnate leaves, 1–2m (3–6ft) long, composed of many linear, mid- to deep green leaflets each side. Green flowers appear in panicles, to 45cm (18in) or more long, usually in summer. ↕2–5m (6–15ft), ↔ 2–4m (6–12ft). Brazil. ❄ (min. 13°C/55°F)
S. romanzoffiana ✲ syn. *Arecastrum romanzoffianum* (Queen palm). Small to medium-sized palm with a sturdy trunk, sometimes swollen around the middle. Pinnate leaves are 3–5m (10–15ft) long, each with many linear, mid-green leaflets borne singly or in clusters of 2–5. Orange-glanded green flowers are borne in panicles, to 1m (3ft) long, usually in summer. ↕ to 20m (70ft), ↔ 6–10m (20–30ft). Brazil. ❄ (min. 13°C/55°F)
S. weddelliana see *Lytocaryum weddellianum.*

▷ **Sycamore** see *Acer pseudoplatanus*
American see *Platanus occidentalis*
California see *Platanus racemosa*

x SYCOPARROTIA

HAMAMELIDACEAE

Hybrid genus of one species of semi-evergreen shrub with alternate, simple, glossy, dark green leaves and dense clusters of flowers. Grow in a shrub border, as a specimen plant on a lawn, or in light woodland.
• **HARDINESS** Fully hardy.
• **CULTIVATION** Grow in moderately fertile, moist but well-drained, neutral to acid soil in full sun or partial shade. Pruning group 1.
• **PROPAGATION** Take semi-ripe cuttings in summer.
• **PESTS AND DISEASES** Trouble free.

x *S. semidecidua* (*Parrotia persica* x *Sycopsis sinensis*). Spreading shrub with oblong-elliptic, glossy, dark green leaves, to 8cm (3in) long; some turn yellow in autumn. In spring, brown-woolly flower buds reveal dense clusters, 2.5cm (1in) across, of bright red anthers surrounded by small brown bracts. ↕4m (12ft), ↔ 6m (20ft). Garden origin. ✻✻✻

SYCOPSIS

HAMAMELIDACEAE

Genus of 7 species of evergreen shrubs and trees from woodland in China, the Himalayas, and S.E. Asia. They bear alternate, simple, ovate to oblong, entire or finely toothed leaves and, in spring, racemes or heads of small, petalless, male or bisexual flowers. Only *S. sinensis* is

Sycopsis sinensis

generally cultivated, for its flowers; use in a shrub border or woodland garden.
• **HARDINESS** Frost hardy to frost tender.
• **CULTIVATION** Grow in moist but well-drained, moderately fertile, humus-rich, neutral to acid soil in full sun or partial shade, sheltered from strong, and cold, drying winds. Pruning group 1.
• **PROPAGATION** Sow seed as soon as ripe, in lime-free (ericaceous) seed compost in containers in a cold frame. Take semi-ripe cuttings in summer.
• **PESTS AND DISEASES** Trouble free.

S. sinensis ■ Conical shrub with upright branches and oblong, leathery, dark green leaves, to 10cm (4in) long, pale green beneath. In spring, short, dense clusters, 2.5cm (1in) across, of brown-felted buds open to reveal petalless flowers with red anthers and yellow filaments. ↕ 6m (20ft), ↔ 4m (12ft). C. China. ❄❄

SYMPHORICARPOS

Snowberry

CAPRIFOLIACEAE

Genus of about 17 species of deciduous shrubs found in woodland and thickets and on prairies and plains in W. China and North and Central America. They are grown for their spherical or ovoid, fleshy, white to pink, or dark blue or purple fruits, which last well into winter, and their tiny, bell- or funnel-shaped, nectar-rich, white to pink flowers, which attract bees. The flowers are borne singly or in terminal or axillary clusters, spikes, or dense racemes. The leaves are simple

Symphoricarpos albus var. *laevigatus*

Symphoricarpos x *doorenbosii* 'White Hedge'

and opposite. Very hardy, and tolerant of poor soil, pollution, and exposed sites. Good for a shrub border, screen, or informal hedge. Use *S.* x *chenaultii* 'Hancock' as ground cover. Fruits may cause mild stomach upset if ingested; contact with them may irritate skin.
• **HARDINESS** Fully hardy.
• **CULTIVATION** Grow in any fertile, reasonably well-drained soil in full sun or partial shade. Pruning group 1 or 2.
• **PROPAGATION** Divide in autumn if suckering. Take greenwood cuttings in summer, or hardwood cuttings in autumn.
• **PESTS AND DISEASES** Trouble free.

S. albus* var. *laevigatus ■ syn. *S. rivularis* (Snowberry). Thicket-forming shrub with upright, arching shoots and oval to oval-oblong, rarely lobed, dark green leaves, to 5cm (2in) long. Tiny, bell-shaped pink flowers are produced in pairs on spike-like racemes in summer, followed by spherical, pure white fruit, 1cm (½in) across. ↕↔ 2m (6ft). W. North America. ❄❄❄
S.* x *chenaultii (*S. microphyllus* x *S. orbiculatus*). Upright, many-branched shrub with ovate, dark green leaves, to 2.5cm (1in) long, glaucous and densely hairy beneath. In late summer, bears short spikes of small, open bell-shaped, greenish white flowers, followed by spherical, red-stippled white fruit, 6mm (¼in) across. ↕ 2m (6ft), ↔ 1.2m (4ft). Garden origin. ❄❄❄. **'Hancock'** is low and spreading, self-layering to form a broad mound; bears white flowers and sparse, dark pink fruit; ↕↔ 3m (10ft).
S.* x *doorenbosii (*S. albus* var. *laevigatus* x *S.* x *chenaultii*). Thicket-forming shrub with elliptic to broadly ovate, dark green leaves, 2–4cm (¾–1½in) long, lighter beneath. In mid- and late summer, bears short racemes of small, bell-shaped, greenish white flowers, followed by dense clusters of spherical white fruit, to 1.5cm (½in) across, with a pink blush. ↕ 2m (6ft), ↔ indefinite. Garden origin. ❄❄❄. **'Mother of Pearl'** has arching shoots bearing dense crops of fruit. **'White Hedge'** ■ is compact and upright, with white fruit; ↕ 1.5m (5ft).
S. microphyllus. Upright shrub with ovate, blue-green leaves, to 6cm (2½in) long, with pointed tips, softly hairy beneath. In late summer, bears small, cup-shaped white flowers, which are solitary, in axillary pairs, or in short, terminal spikes, followed by spherical,

Symphoricarpos orbiculatus 'Foliis Variegatis'

semi-translucent, pink or white fruit, 8mm (⅜in) across. ↕ 1–2m (3–6ft), ↔ 0.6–1.2m (2–4ft). Mexico. ❄❄❄
S. orbiculatus (Coralberry, Indian currant). Dense, bushy shrub with broadly elliptic to ovate, dark green leaves, to 3cm (1¼in) long. In late summer and early autumn, bears dense clusters of tiny, bell-shaped, white, sometimes pink-tinged flowers, followed by ovoid-spherical, dark purple-red fruit, 6mm (¼in) across. Fruits most freely after a hot summer. ↕↔ 2m (6ft). E. USA, Mexico. ❄❄❄. **'Foliis Variegatis'** ■ syn. 'Variegatus', has irregularly yellow-margined leaves.
S. rivularis see *S. albus* var. *laevigatus.*

SYMPHYANDRA

CAMPANULACEAE

Genus of about 12 species of often monocarpic, sometimes rhizomatous perennials from mountains in the E. Mediterranean and the Caucasus to C. Asia and Korea. They are grown for their tubular-bell-shaped or bell-shaped flowers, borne on branched stems in racemes, corymbs, or panicles over long periods in summer. Leaves are long-stalked, often heart-shaped, toothed, hairy, and mainly basal. Grow in a herbaceous or mixed border, or rock garden. They are very free-flowering, but usually short-lived. May self-seed.
• **HARDINESS** Fully hardy.
• **CULTIVATION** Grow in light, fertile, well-drained soil in full sun or light dappled shade. Often die after flowering; collect seed and propagate regularly.

Symphyandra hofmannii

• **PROPAGATION** Sow seed at 13°C (55°F) in winter or early spring, or in containers in a cold frame when ripe.
• **PESTS AND DISEASES** Susceptible to slugs and snails, especially new growth.

S. armena. Upright or spreading, densely hairy, rhizomatous perennial with long-stalked, pointed, heart-shaped, velvety-hairy, irregularly lobed and toothed leaves, to 25cm (10in) long. During summer, produces pendent, bell-shaped, velvet-textured, white or pale blue flowers, to 2cm (¾in) long, usually in terminal corymbs, sometimes solitary. ↕ to 50cm (20in), ↔ to 30cm (12in). Caucasus, Turkey, Iran. ❄❄❄
S. hofmannii ■ Rosette-forming, usually short-lived, often monocarpic perennial with ovate to lance-shaped, toothed basal leaves, 15cm (6in) long, with winged stalks. Erect stems produce a few alternate, shorter-stalked leaves, and, from early to late summer, they bear terminal racemes of long-lasting, pendent, tubular-bell-shaped, hairy, white to cream flowers, to 3cm (1¼in) long. ↕ 30–60cm (12–24in), ↔ 30cm (12in). Bosnia & Herzegovina. ❄❄❄
S. pendula. Arching, spreading, often woody-based perennial with broadly ovate, hairy, pale green leaves, to 15cm (6in) long, heart-shaped at the bases, and with round-toothed margins. In summer, bears short panicles of bell-shaped, velvet-textured, creamy white flowers, to 5cm (2in) long. ↕ to 50cm (20in), ↔ to 30cm (12in). Caucasus. ❄❄❄
S. wanneri ■ syn. *Campanula wanneri.* Upright, downy, monocarpic perennial with rosettes of lance-shaped, roughly hairy, irregularly toothed leaves, to 10cm (4in) long, stalkless or with winged stalks. Bears pendent, narrowly bell-shaped, deep violet-blue flowers, to 3.5cm (1½in) long, in pyramidal, terminal or axillary panicles, over long periods in summer. ↕↔ to 30cm (12in). Mountains of Romania, Bulgaria, Serbia, Montenegro, Macedonia. ❄❄❄

Symphyandra wanneri

S

SYMPHYTUM

Comfrey

BORAGINACEAE

Genus of 25–35 species of coarse, sometimes invasive, bristly or hairy, rhizomatous perennials from damp, often shady habitats, including woodland, scrub, wasteland, streamsides, and roadsides, in Europe, N. Africa, and W. Asia. Some are used medicinally or for liquid plant food or green manure. They have fleshy roots and long-stalked, oblong- to ovate-lance-shaped or elliptic, wrinkled, prominently veined, mostly basal leaves. Erect, usually branched stems often become decumbent; they bear smaller, more or less stalkless leaves and terminal cymes of pendent, tubular flowers in blue, purple, pink, yellowish white, or white. Excellent ground-cover plants for a shady border or woodland garden, but they can be rampant. Roots and leaves may cause severe discomfort if ingested; contact with foliage may irritate skin.

- **HARDINESS** Fully hardy.
- **CULTIVATION** Grow in moist, moderately fertile soil in full sun or partial shade. Site carefully as all but variegated cultivars may be very invasive; even small pieces of detached root will form new plants. Remove flower stems of variegated cultivars as they form, to keep the foliage attractive. For plant food, grow *S. officinale* and *S.* x *uplandicum* in a permanent, sunny site in a vegetable garden; mulch with well-rotted manure in spring; compost the leaves, or steep in water until decayed, in summer; then use the liquid obtained diluted 1:20.
- **PROPAGATION** Sow seed in containers in a cold frame in autumn or spring. Divide in spring. Take root cuttings in early winter.
- **PESTS AND DISEASES** Trouble free.

S. caucasicum ■ Clump-forming, hairy, rhizomatous perennial with rosettes of oblong-lance-shaped to ovate-lance-shaped, mid-green leaves, to 25cm (10in) long. Bears cymes of bright blue flowers, to 1.5cm (½in) long, on erect then decumbent stems from early to late summer. ↕↔ 60cm (24in), later spreading widely. Caucasus, Iran. ***

***S.* 'Goldsmith'** ■ syn. *S. ibericum* 'Jubilee', *S. ibericum* 'Variegatum', *S.* 'Jubilee'. Spreading, hairy, rhizomatous perennial with ovate-lance-shaped, dark green leaves, to 25cm (10in) long, with gold and cream markings. Bears cymes of pale blue, cream, or pink flowers, to 1.5cm (½in) long, in mid- and late spring. ↕↔ 30cm (12in). ***

Symphytum caucasicum

Symphytum 'Goldsmith'

***S. grandiflorum* of gardens** see *S. ibericum.*

***S.* 'Hidcote Blue'.** Erect then decumbent, hairy, rhizomatous perennial with ovate to elliptic, mid-green leaves, to 25cm (10in) long. In mid- and late spring, cymes of red buds open to pale blue flowers, to 1.5cm (½in) long, fading with age. ↕↔ 45cm (18in). ***

***S.* 'Hidcote Pink'**, syn. *S.* 'Roseum'. Erect then decumbent, hairy, rhizomatous perennial with ovate to elliptic, mid-green leaves, to 25cm (10in) long. Cymes of pale pink and white flowers, to 1.5cm (½in) long, fading with age, are produced in mid- and late spring. ↕↔ 45cm (18in). ***

Symphytum tuberosum

S. ibericum, syn. *S. grandiflorum* of gardens. Erect then decumbent, hairy, rhizomatous perennial. Ovate to elliptic or ovate-lance-shaped, mid-green leaves, are to 25cm (10in) long. In late spring and early summer, cymes of red-tipped buds open to pale yellow flowers, to 1.5cm (½in) long. ↕ 40cm (16in), ↔ 60cm (24in), later more. Turkey (N.E. Anatolia), Georgia. ***. **'Jubilee'** see *S.* 'Goldsmith'. **'Variegatum'** see *S.* 'Goldsmith'.

***S.* 'Jubilee'** see *S.* 'Goldsmith'.

S. officinale (Common comfrey). Vigorous, clump-forming perennial with winged, upright stems and coarse, hairy, ovate to lance-shaped, dark green leaves, 25cm (10in) long, with winged stalks. From late spring to summer, bears forked cymes of purple-violet, pink, or creamy yellow flowers, to 2cm (¾in) long. ↕ to 1.5m (5ft), ↔ to 2m (6ft) or more. Europe, W. Asia. ***. Non-invasive, sterile clones, such as **'Bocking'**, are available.

***S. peregrinum* of gardens** see *S.* x *uplandicum.*

***S.* 'Roseum'** see *S.* 'Hidcote Pink'.

S. tuberosum ■ (Tuberous comfrey). Coarse, creeping perennial producing tuberous rhizomes. Upright, hairy stems bear ovate to lance-shaped, dark green leaves, to 25cm (10in) long, and in early summer produce spiralled cymes of pale yellow flowers, 1.5–2cm (½–¾in) long. ↕ 40–60cm (16–24in), ↔ to 1m (3ft). Europe (Pyrenees to Balkans), N.W. Turkey. ***

S.* x *uplandicum (*S. asperum* x *S. officinale*), syn. *S. peregrinum* of gardens. Erect, bristly perennial bearing oblong to elliptic-lance-shaped, mid-green, basal leaves, to 35cm (14in) long, decurrent at the bases. From late spring to late summer, many-branched stems bear cymes of pinkish blue buds, opening to blue-purple flowers, to 2cm (¾in) long. ↕ 2m (6ft), ↔ 1.2m (4ft) or more. Garden origin (naturalized in N. Europe). ***. **'Variegatum'** ■ has greyish green leaves with broad and irregular cream margins, and pale lilac-pink flowers. Liable to revert, especially if roots are damaged or in poor soil; ↕ 90cm (36in), ↔ 60cm (24in).

Symphytum x *uplandicum* 'Variegatum'

SYMPLOCOS

SYMPLOCACEAE

Genus of about 250 species of evergreen or deciduous trees and shrubs widely distributed, mainly in woodland, from E. Asia to Australasia and in North and South America. Leaves are alternate and simple. Star-shaped, 5-petalled, usually yellow or white flowers are produced singly or in racemes, panicles, or spikes, followed by blue, black, purple, or white ovoid fruits. Only *S. paniculata* is generally cultivated, for its flowers and fruit; grow in a shrub border. It fruits best when several seedlings are planted together, and in hot summers.

- **HARDINESS** Fully hardy to frost tender.
- **CULTIVATION** Grow in fertile, moist but well-drained, neutral to acid soil in full sun, avoiding very exposed positions. Pruning group 1.
- **PROPAGATION** Sow seed in containers in a cold frame in autumn. Take greenwood cuttings in summer.
- **PESTS AND DISEASES** Trouble free.

Symplocos paniculata

S. paniculata ■ ☼ (Sapphire berry). Deciduous, upright, bushy shrub or spreading tree with elliptic to oblong-obovate, finely toothed, sparsely hairy, dark green leaves, to 8cm (3in) long. In late spring and early summer, small, star-shaped, fragrant white flowers, with many prominent stamens, are borne in terminal panicles, to 8cm (3in) long, before ovoid, metallic blue fruit, 8mm (3/8in) across. ↕↔ 5m (15ft), rarely to 12m (40ft). Himalayas, E. Asia. ❄❄❄

SYNADENIUM

EUPHORBIACEAE

Genus of about 20 species of evergreen shrubs and small trees from dry slopes and banks in tropical Africa to the Mascarene Islands. Their smooth, fleshy stems contain a milky sap. Leaves are alternate, simple, obovate or lance-shaped, and fleshy; insignificant, petal-less flowers are borne from the upper leaf axils. *S. compactum* var. *rubrum* is most often grown, for its foliage. Where temperatures fall below 10°C (50°F), grow in a temperate or warm greenhouse, or as a houseplant. In warmer, dry areas, grow in a shrub border. All parts of *Synadenium* species are highly toxic if ingested; sap may irritate skin.

- **HARDINESS** Frost tender.
- **CULTIVATION** Under glass, grow in loam-based potting compost (JI No.2), with added sharp sand, in full light. In growth, water moderately and apply a balanced liquid fertilizer monthly. Water sparingly in winter. Outdoors, grow in moderately fertile, well-drained soil in full sun. Pruning group 9; may need restrictive pruning under glass.
- **PROPAGATION** Sow seed at 15–20°C (59–68°F) in spring. Root semi-ripe cuttings in summer, with bottom heat.
- **PESTS AND DISEASES** Root mealybugs may be a problem under glass.

S. compactum* var. *rubrum, syn. *S grantii* 'Rubrum', *S. grantii* var. *rubrum*. Erect, succulent shrub, eventually moderately bushy, with obovate, finely toothed red leaves, 8–18cm (3–7in) long, red-purple beneath. Throughout the year, bears cup-shaped, yellow-green floral bracts with red glands, in cymes 10–15cm (4–6in) long. ↕ to 3m (10ft), ↔ to 2m (6ft). ❀ (min. 10°C/50°F)

***S. grantii* 'Rubrum'** see *S. compactum* var. *rubrum*.

S. grantii* var. *rubrum see *S. compactum* var. *rubrum*.

SYNGONIUM

Arrowhead vine, Goosefoot plant, Goosefoot vine

ARACEAE

Genus of about 36 species of evergreen root climbers from woodland in tropical Central and South America. The alternate leaves are initially simple and ovate to triangular, becoming larger, long-stalked, arrow-shaped, then 3- to 5-lobed or pedate as the plants mature. Tiny, petalless flowers are borne on spadices surrounded by pale green and cream to purplish green spathes, which often become bright red at fruiting time. Arrowhead vines rarely flower in cultivation, and are grown for foliage. Where temperatures fall below 15°C (59°F), grow in a warm greenhouse or as houseplants. In warmer climates, use as ground cover, or to clothe a wall. All parts may cause mild stomach upset if ingested; contact with the sap may irritate skin and eyes.

- **HARDINESS** Half hardy to frost tender.
- **CULTIVATION** Under glass, grow in loamless potting compost, in bright indirect light for green-leaved plants, or in bright filtered light for variegated ones. Provide moderate humidity. When in growth, water freely and apply a balanced liquid fertilizer every 3 or 4 weeks. Water moderately in winter. Support with a moss pole. Outdoors, grow in fertile, moist soil in light dappled or partial shade. Pruning group 11, in late winter or early spring.
- **PROPAGATION** Root stem-tip cuttings or leaf-bud cuttings in summer, with bottom heat.
- **PESTS AND DISEASES** Mealybugs and red spider mites may be a problem under glass.

S. auritum, syn. *Philodendron auritum* of gardens, *P. trifoliatum* (Five fingers). Sparsely branched trailer or climber. Juvenile leaves are ovate-heart-shaped to triangular, becoming arrow-shaped,

Syngonium podophyllum

Syngonium podophyllum 'Trileaf Wonder'

mid- to deep green, and to 15cm (6in) long; mature leaves are pedate, each with 3–5 elliptic, deep green leaflets, the central one broadly elliptic and 16–40cm (6–16in) long, the others much smaller. In summer, green to yellowish inflorescences, about 11cm (4½in) long, are borne in clusters from the leaf axils. ↕ to 3m (10ft) or more. Cuba, Jamaica, Haiti, Dominican Republic. ❀ (min. 15°C/59°F). **'Fantasy'** has white-mottled leaves.

S. podophyllum ■ syn. *Nephthytis triphylla* of gardens (Arrowhead vine, Goosefoot plant). Sparsely branched climber, compact or trailing when young. Juvenile leaves, 7–14cm (3–5½in) long, are ovate with heart-shaped bases, becoming arrow-shaped. Mature leaves are pedate, each with 5–11 elliptic leaflets, the largest leaflet to about 35cm (14in) long; all are dark green above, sometimes with grey-green markings, and paler beneath. In summer, green to cream inflorescences, about 11cm (4½in) long, are produced in clusters of 4–11 in the leaf axils. ↕ 2m (6ft) or more. Mexico to Brazil. ❀ (min. 15°C/59°F). **Allusion Series** is compact and well branched, with broad, pink-veined leaves. **'Emerald Gem'** produces arrow-shaped, bright green juvenile leaves with pale veins. **'Imperial White'** has arrow-shaped, cream juvenile leaves with green margins. **'Lemon Lime'**, syn. 'Robusta', is compact and non-climbing, with broad leaves, heavily marked white along the veins. **'Maya Red'** has pearly pink leaves. **'Robusta'** see 'Lemon Lime'. **'Trileaf Wonder'** ■ produces leaves with silvery grey veins. **'Variegatum'** bears arrow-shaped leaves splashed creamy white. **'White Butterfly'** has pale green juvenile leaves, heavily marked cream along the veins.

SYNNOTIA

IRIDACEAE

Genus, sometimes included in *Sparaxis*, of 5 species of small, spring-flowering, cormous perennials from low-altitude grassland and scrub in South Africa. They have basal fans of 2-ranked, linear or oblong to lance-shaped leaves. Branched or unbranched stems bear short spikes of funnel-shaped, cream, yellow, lilac, or mauve flowers, hooded like gladioli. In frost-prone areas, grow in a cool greenhouse or bulb frame. In warmer areas, grow in a sunny border.

- **HARDINESS** Half hardy.
- **CULTIVATION** Plant corms in autumn, 10cm (4in) deep. Under glass, grow in loam-based potting compost (JI No.2), with added sand and leaf mould, in full light. Keep cool and only slightly moist until roots are well developed. Water sparingly when in growth, and dry off as the leaves wither; keep dry and frost-free when dormant in summer. Outdoors, grow in a warm, sheltered site in moderately fertile, well-drained soil in full sun. Provide a dry winter mulch, and keep dry in summer.
- **PROPAGATION** Sow seed at 16°C (61°F) as soon as ripe, or in spring. Remove offsets when dormant.
- **PESTS AND DISEASES** Trouble free.

S. variegata. Cormous perennial with a fan of oblong, basal leaves, each to 15cm (6in) long. In spring, an unbranched or 1- to 3-branched stem produces up to 7 hooded flowers, 3cm (1¼in) across, evenly coloured yellow and violet, or lavender-blue to deep purple with yellow stripes on the lower lips and in the throats. ↕ 15–40cm (6–16in), ↔ 8cm (3in). South Africa (Western Cape). ❄. **var. *metelerkampiae*** has a branched stem, each branch producing a sparse spike of violet flowers, marked orange on each of the lower 3 petals.

SYNTHYRIS

SCROPHULARIACEAE

Genus of about 14 species of tufted, low-growing, usually rhizomatous perennials, mainly from woodland in W. and C. North America. They have radical, heart-shaped, kidney-shaped, or pinnatifid leaves. Unbranched, leafy, upright stems produce narrow, upright, spike-like racemes of small, tubular to bell-shaped, violet to blue, or rarely pink or white flowers, mainly in spring. Grow in a woodland or rock garden, or at the front of a shady, herbaceous border. Grow *S. pinnatifida* var. *lanuginosa* in a scree bed or alpine house; it is difficult to cultivate and flower buds often abort.

- **HARDINESS** Fully hardy, but intolerant of winter wet.
- **CULTIVATION** Grow in fertile, moist but well-drained, humus-rich soil in partial or deep shade. Grow *S. pinnatifida* var. *lanuginosa* in a scree bed in gritty, poor to moderately fertile, humus-rich soil in full sun with some

Synthyris missurica

midday shade; in an alpine house, use a mix of equal parts loam, leaf mould, and grit, water moderately when in growth, and keep just moist in winter.

• **PROPAGATION** Sow seed in containers in an open frame in autumn. Divide in early spring as growth begins.

• **PESTS AND DISEASES** Prone to attack by slugs and snails. Aphids and red spider mites may damage *S. pinnatifida* var. *lanuginosa* under glass.

S. missurica ▣ Clump-forming herbaceous perennial with rounded-heart-shaped to kidney-shaped, shallowly lobed, bluntly toothed, leathery, dark green leaves, to 5cm (2in) across. Over long periods in spring, bears tubular-bell-shaped, deep lavender-blue flowers, to 2cm (¾in) long, with prominent styles and anthers, in abundant dense, upright, spike-like racemes, 5–10cm (2–4in) long. ↕ to 25cm (10in), ↔ to 30cm (12in). Arctic Canada to N. and C. USA. ❄❄❄

S. pinnatifida. Clump-forming herbaceous perennial bearing ovate, pinnate, mid-green leaves, to 10cm (4in) long, with linear, toothed segments. In late spring, produces racemes 10–15cm (4–6in) long, of tubular, lavender-blue flowers, to 5cm (2in) long, with silver calyces. ↕↔ to 15cm (6in). USA (Washington). ❄❄❄. **var. *lanuginosa*** forms a low mound, with silvery grey leaves, and bears deep blue flowers, to 2cm (¾in) long, in racemes 3–6cm (1¼–2½in) long; ↕ to 10cm (4in).

S. reniformis. Clump-forming, evergreen perennial with shallowly round-lobed, rounded-heart-shaped, dark green leaves, to 5cm (2in) long, paler beneath. In spring, bears bell-shaped, blue, pink, or white flowers, to 9mm (⅜in) long, in short racemes, to 3cm (1¼in) long. ↕ to 15cm (6in), ↔ to 25cm (10in). USA (Washington, Oregon). ❄❄❄

S. stellata ▣ Clump-forming herbaceous perennial with rounded-heart-shaped, hairy, dark green leaves, to 5cm (2in) across, deeply and doubly toothed. From spring to early summer, bears dense, spike-like racemes, 8–15cm (3–6in) long, of bell-shaped, violet-blue flowers, to 6mm (¼in) long, with conspicuous, sharply toothed bracts. ↕ to 15cm (6in), ↔ to 25cm (10in). USA (Washington, Oregon). ❄❄❄

Synthyris stellata

SYRINGA

Lilac

OLEACEAE

Genus of about 20 species of deciduous shrubs and trees found in woodland and scrub from S.E. Europe to E. Asia. They are grown for their often pyramidal or conical panicles of small, tubular, usually very fragrant flowers, which may be white, pink, almost red to magenta, lilac (light purplish pink), or blue. They have opposite, entire, lance-shaped to rounded, usually ovate, rarely pinnate leaves. Most garden cultivars are grouped under *S. vulgaris*. Grow lilacs in a shrub border or as specimen trees.

• **HARDINESS** Fully hardy, but late frosts may damage new growth.

• **CULTIVATION** Grow in fertile, humus-rich, well-drained, neutral to alkaline soil in full sun. Mulch regularly. Dead-head newly planted lilacs before fruit forms. Pruning group 1 or 2, but prune only lightly; group 1 for *S. reticulata*, *S. vulgaris*, and cultivars; *S. vulgaris* tolerates hard renovation pruning.

• **PROPAGATION** Sow seed in containers in a cold frame as soon as ripe or in spring. Take greenwood cuttings, or layer, in early summer. Graft in winter or bud in midsummer.

• **PESTS AND DISEASES** May be affected by lilac blight, honey fungus, leaf miners, thrips, and willow scale.

***S. afghanica* of gardens** see *S. protolaciniata*.

S. x chinensis (*S.* x *persica* x *S. vulgaris*) (Rouen lilac). Bushy shrub with arching branches and oval leaves, to 8cm (3in) long. In late spring, produces fragrant, lilac-purple flowers in large, nodding panicles, to 15cm (6in) long. ↕↔ 4m (12ft). Garden origin. ❄❄❄. **'Alba'** ▣ bears white flowers. **'Saugeana'** has lilac-red flowers.

S. emodi (Himalayan lilac). Vigorous, upright shrub with stout shoots and elliptic-oblong leaves, to 15cm (6in) long. Unpleasantly scented, pale lilac flowers are produced in large, upright panicles, to 15cm (6in) long, in early summer. ↕ 5m (15ft), ↔ 4m (12ft). Afghanistan, Himalayas. ❄❄❄

***S.* 'Fountain'.** Upright shrub with ovate, tapered leaves, 5–15cm (2–6in) long, mid-green above, blue-green and softly hairy beneath. In early summer, bears single, pale pink flowers in narrow, conical, nodding panicles, to 15cm (6in) long. ↕ 3–4m (10–12ft), ↔ 2–3m (6–10ft). ❄❄❄

S. x hyacinthiflora (*S. oblata* x *S. vulgaris*). Spreading shrub, upright when young, with broadly heart-shaped leaves, bronze when young, often purple in autumn. In mid- and late spring, bears fragrant, single or double, variably coloured flowers, in large panicles, to 12cm (5in) long. ↕↔ 5m (15ft). Garden origin. ❄❄❄. **'Alice Eastwood'** bears double, claret-purple flowers in slender panicles. **'Blue Hyacinth'** ▣ has single, lilac to blue flowers. **'Clarke's Giant'** ▣ has large, single flowers, purple in bud, opening lilac, in panicles to 30cm (12in) long. **'Cora Brandt'** ▣ has double white flowers in large, open panicles, 20–23cm (8–9in) long. **'Esther Staley'** ▣ is vigorous, with profuse single, lilac-pink flowers opening from mauve-red buds.

***S.* 'Isabella'** see *S.* x *prestoniae* 'Isabella'.

S. x josiflexa (*S. josikaea* x *S. komarowii* subsp. *reflexa*). Upright shrub with ovate to oblong-lance-shaped, mid-green leaves, 8–15cm (3–6in) long, white-hairy beneath. In early summer, bears fragrant, lavender-pink flowers in conical to cylindrical panicles, 10–20cm (4–8in) long. ↕ 3m (10ft), ↔ 2m (6ft). Garden origin. ❄❄❄. **'Bellicent'** has tapered, dark green leaves, and bears clear pink flowers in late spring and early summer; ↕ 4m (12ft), ↔ 5m (15ft).

S. komarovii* subsp. *reflexa see *S. reflexa*.

S. x laciniata ▣ (*S. protolaciniata* x *S. vulgaris*). Spreading shrub with lance-shaped to pinnate leaves, to 8cm (3in) long, composed of up to 9 narrowly elliptic, dark green leaflets. Fragrant lilac flowers, in panicles to 10cm (4in) long, are produced in late spring. ↕ 2m (6ft), ↔ 3m (10ft). Garden origin. ❄❄❄

S. meyeri. Compact, rounded shrub with oval leaves, 1–3cm (½–1¼in) long. Bears fragrant, bluish pink or lavender-

Syringa x *chinensis* 'Alba' (inset: flower detail)

Syringa x *hyacinthiflora* 'Blue Hyacinth'

Syringa x *hyacinthiflora* 'Clarke's Giant'

Syringa x *hyacinthiflora* 'Cora Brandt'

Syringa x *hyacinthiflora* 'Esther Staley'

Syringa x *laciniata*

Syringa meyeri 'Palibin'

S

Syringa x *persica*

pink flowers in small panicles, 3–8cm (1¼–3in) long, in late spring and early summer. ↕ 1.5–2m (5–6ft), ↔ 1.2m (4ft). ❄❄❄. **'Palibin'** ■ syn. *S. palibiniana* of gardens, *S. patula* of gardens, *S. velutina* of gardens, is slow-growing, with lavender-pink flowers in dense panicles, to 10cm (4in) long; ↔ 1.5m (5ft).

S. microphylla see *S. pubescens* subsp. *microphylla*.

S. oblata* subsp. *dilatata ♀ Vigorous, upright, later spreading shrub or small tree with broadly heart-shaped, tapered leaves, to 8cm (3in) long, bronze when young, then glossy, mid-green, turning purple in autumn. Fragrant, pale lilac flowers, in broad panicles, to 12cm (5in) long, are produced in mid-spring. ↕↔ 5m (15ft). Korea. ❄❄❄

***S. palibiniana* of gardens** see *S. meyeri* 'Palibin'.

S. patula see *S. pubescens* subsp. *patula*.

***S. patula* of gardens** see *S. meyeri* 'Palibin'.

S. pekinensis see *S. reticulata* subsp. *pekinensis*.

S.* x *persica ■ (*S. afghanica* x *S. laciniata*) (Persian lilac). Compact, bushy shrub with lance-shaped, rarely 3-lobed, dark green leaves, to 6cm (2½in) long. In late spring, profusely bears fragrant purple flowers in small, dense panicles, to 5cm (2in) long. ↕↔ 2m (6ft). Garden origin. ❄❄❄. **'Alba'** has white flowers.

S. pinnatifolia. Open, upright shrub with peeling bark on older branches. Each pinnate leaf, to 6cm (2½in) long, has up to 11 ovate to lance-shaped, dark green leaflets. In late spring, bears fragrant, lilac-flushed white flowers, in panicles to 7cm (3in) long. ↕ to 4m (12ft), ↔ 2.5m (8ft). W. China. ❄❄❄

S.* x *prestoniae ♀ (*S. reflexa* x *S. villosa*). Vigorous, upright shrub or small tree with oval, dark green leaves, to 15cm (6in) long. In early summer, bears fragrant, white, pink, lavender-pink, lavender-blue, violet, magenta, or deep purple flowers in large, erect to nodding panicles, 10–16cm (4–6in) long. ↕↔ 4m (12ft). Garden origin. ❄❄❄. **'Audrey'** has dark pink flowers. **'Coral'** bears pale pink flowers, fading to nearly white. **'Elinor'** bears pale lavender-blue flowers from purple buds. **'Isabella'**, syn. *S.* 'Isabella', has purple-pink flowers.

S. protolaciniata, syn. *S. afghanica* of gardens. Graceful, open, spreading shrub with slender, purplish brown shoots and pinnate leaves, to 7cm (3in) long, each with 3–9 narrowly elliptic to lance-shaped, dark green leaflets. In late spring, bears fragrant lilac flowers, in panicles to 7cm (3in) long. ↕ 3m (10ft), ↔ 1.5m (5ft). W. China. ❄❄❄

S. pubescens. Erect, spreading, often bushy shrub with slender branches, red-green when young, and lance-shaped to ovate or elliptic, glossy, dark green leaves, to 9cm (3½in) long, densely grey-white-hairy beneath. In spring and early summer, bears strongly scented, white-throated, purplish lilac flowers, in panicles to 12cm (5in) long. ↕ to 6m (20ft), ↔ 6m (20ft). N. central China. ❄❄❄. **subsp. *microphylla***, syn. *S. microphylla*, is conical and spreading or upright. Lilac-pink flowers are borne in small panicles, to 7cm (3in) long, in early summer, often again in autumn; W. China. **subsp. *microphylla* 'Superba'** ■ has rose-pink flowers. After initial flowering, it blooms irregularly until autumn. **subsp. *patula***, syn. *S. patula*, has dull green leaves, 5–11cm (2–4½in) long, with purple young shoots. Purplish lilac flowers, in nodding panicles, open from lilac buds; ↕ 4m (12ft), ↔ 2m (6ft); N. China, Korea. **subsp. *patula* 'Miss Kim'** is similar to subsp. *patula*, but has a mound-forming habit; the leaves may turn purple in autumn; ↕ 2m (6ft), ↔ 1.5m (5ft).

Syringa vulgaris 'Monge' (inset: flower detail)

S. reflexa, syn. *S. komarovii* subsp. *reflexa*. Vigorous, upright shrub with stout shoots and oval, dark green leaves, to 15cm (6in) long. Bears rich purple-pink flowers in slender, nodding panicles, to 16cm (6in) long, in late spring and early summer. ↕↔ 4m (12ft). C. China. ❄❄❄

S. reticulata ♀ Upright shrub or broadly conical tree with an oval crown and reddish brown, shining bark when young. Leaves are lance-shaped to ovate, sharp-pointed, and to 15cm (6in) long. Bears fragrant, creamy white flowers, in large, showy panicles, to 20cm (8in) long, in early and midsummer. ↕ 10m (30ft), ↔ 6m (20ft). Japan. ❄❄❄. **'Ivory Silk'** has a compact habit, and flowers profusely, even when young; ↕ 3–4m (10–12ft), ↔ 2m (6ft). **subsp. *pekinensis*** ♀ syn. *S. pekinensis*, is spreading, with arching branches and dark green leaves, to 8cm (3in) long; ↕↔ 5m (15ft); Mongolia, N. China.

S. sweginzowii ■ Upright shrub with red-purple shoots and elliptic-oblong to lance-shaped leaves, to 10cm (4in) long. Fragrant, pale pink to lilac-pink or white flowers, in upright panicles, to 20cm (8in) long, are produced in late spring and early summer. ↕ 4m (12ft), ↔ 2.5m (8ft). S.W. China. ❄❄❄

Syringa pubescens subsp. *microphylla* 'Superba'

Syringa sweginzowii

Syringa vulgaris 'Charles Joly'

Syringa vulgaris 'Charles X'

Syringa vulgaris 'Congo'

Syringa vulgaris 'Decaisne'

Syringa vulgaris 'Jan van Tol'

Syringa vulgaris 'Katherine Havemeyer'

Syringa vulgaris 'Maréchal Foch'

Syringa vulgaris 'Michel Buchner'

Syringa vulgaris 'Mme Antoine Buchner'

Syringa vulgaris 'Mme Florent Stepman'

Syringa vulgaris 'Président Grévy'

***S. velutina* of gardens** see *S. meyeri* 'Palibin'.
S. villosa. Compact, rounded shrub with upright shoots and ovate to oblong leaves, to 20cm (8in) long. Fragrant pink flowers, in large, conical panicles, to 20cm (8in) long, are produced in late spring and early summer. ↕↔ 4m (12ft). N. China. ❄❄❄
S. vulgaris ♀ (Common lilac). Spreading shrub or small tree, upright when young, with heart-shaped to ovate leaves, to 10cm (4in) long. Very fragrant, single or double lilac flowers are produced in dense, conical panicles, to 10–20cm (4–8in) long, in late spring and early summer. ↕↔ 7m (22ft). E. Europe. ❄❄❄. **'Alphonse Lavallée'** bears double, lilac-blue flowers, from purple buds. **'Ami Schott'** bears double, cobalt-blue flowers. **'Andenken an Ludwig Späth'**, syn. 'Souvenir de Louis Spaeth', produces slender panicles, to 30cm (12in) long, of single, dark purple-red flowers. **'Belle de Nancy'** produces large panicles of double, mauve-pink flowers, from purple buds. **'Cavour'** bears upright panicles of single, violet-blue flowers. **'Charles Joly'** ■ bears double, dark purple flowers. **'Charles X'** ■ produces single, purple-red flowers. **'Christophe Colomb'**, syn. 'Christopher Columbus', bears single, deep lilac-pink flowers. **'Congo'** ■ bears large, single, dark lilac-purple flowers, from purple-red buds. **'Decaisne'** ■ is compact, with many single, light purplish blue flowers; ↕ to 2.5m (8ft), ↔ 1.5m (5ft). **'Edith Cavell'** bears panicles, to 30cm (12in) long, of large, double, creamy white flowers. **'Firmament'** produces single, light blue flowers. **'Glory of Horstenstein'** see 'Ruhm von Horstenstein'. **'Jan van Tol'** ■ bears panicles, to 35cm (14in) long, of single, pure white flowers. The vigorous **'Katherine Havemeyer'** ■ bears double, lavender-blue flowers, from purple buds. **'Lucie Baltet'** bears single, pale pink flowers, from purple-pink buds. **'Maréchal Foch'** ■ bears single, carmine-pink flowers. **'Maréchal Lannes'** bears double, pale violet flowers. **'Masséna'** bears loose panicles of large, single, dark purple flowers. **'Maud Notcutt'** produces single, pure white flowers. **'Michel Buchner'** ■ bears large panicles, to 30cm (12in) long, of double, rose-lilac, white-centred flowers. **'Mme Antoine Buchner'** ■ bears slender panicles of double, pale mauve-pink flowers, from dark purple-red buds. **'Mme Florent Stepman'** ■ bears large panicles, to 25cm (10in) long, of single white flowers. **'Mme F. Morel'** ■ produces large panicles of single, dark mauve-pink flowers. **'Mme Lemoine'** ■ bears compact panicles of large, double white flowers, from creamy buds. **'Monge'** ■ bears a profusion of very large, single, dark purple-red flowers. **'Montaigne'** bears double, pale pink flowers, from purple-pink buds. **'Mont Blanc'** produces large panicles, to 35cm (14in) long, of single white flowers. **'Mrs. Edward Harding'** ■ bears large panicles, to 25cm (10in) long, of double, purple-red flowers. **'Night'** bears single, dark purple flowers. **'Olivier de Serres'** bears large panicles, to 35cm (14in) long, of large, double, lavender-blue flowers, from purple-blue buds. **'Paul Hariot'** bears slender panicles of large, double, dark violet-red flowers. **'Paul Thirion'** ■ produces double, lilac-pink flowers, from dark purple-red buds. **'Président Grévy'** ■ bears very large panicles, to 25cm (10in) long, of double, lilac-blue flowers, from red-violet buds. **'Primrose'** ■ bears small panicles of fragrant, single, pale creamy yellow flowers. **'Ruhm von Horstenstein'**, syn. 'Glory of Horstenstein', is vigorous, with compact panicles of single, dark lilac-red flowers. **'Souvenir de Louis Spaeth'** see 'Andenken an Ludwig Späth'. **'Vestale'** produces many single, pure white flowers. **'Victor Lemoine'** bears slender panicles of double, pale lavender-pink to lilac-blue flowers. **'Violetta'** produces long, slim panicles of double, dark violet flowers.
S. yunnanensis ■ Upright shrub with elliptic-oblong leaves, to 10cm (4in) long. Fragrant, pale pink to nearly white flowers, in large, upright or semi-pendent panicles, to 15cm (6in) long, are produced in early summer. ↕ 3m (10ft), ↔ 2.5m (8ft). W. China. ❄❄❄

S

Syringa vulgaris 'Mme F. Morel'

Syringa vulgaris 'Mme Lemoine'

Syringa vulgaris 'Mrs. Edward Harding'

Syringa vulgaris 'Paul Thirion'

Syringa vulgaris 'Primrose'

Syringa yunnanensis

SYZYGIUM

MYRTACEAE

Genus of 400–500 species of aromatic, evergreen shrubs and trees, mostly from woodland and rainforest throughout tropical regions. They have opposite, leathery leaves and terminal or axillary cymes or panicles of saucer-shaped, 4- or 5-petalled flowers, each with a prominent boss of stamens. These are followed by fleshy, spherical to pear-shaped or oblong, red, purple, or white berries. The dried flower buds of *S. aromaticum* are the cloves of commerce. In frost-prone areas, grow in a temperate or warm greenhouse. In warmer climates, grow in a shrub border.
• **HARDINESS** Half hardy to frost tender.
• **CULTIVATION** Under glass, grow in loam-based potting compost (JI No.3) in full or bright indirect light. In spring and summer, water moderately; apply a balanced liquid fertilizer monthly.

Syzygium aromaticum

Water sparingly in winter. Outdoors, grow in deep, fertile, moist, but well-drained soil in full sun or partial shade. Pruning group 1.
• **PROPAGATION** Sow seed at 15–18°C (59–64°F), or 27°C (81°F) for *S. aromaticum*, in spring. Root greenwood cuttings in early summer, or semi-ripe cuttings in mid- to late summer, both with bottom heat. Air layer in spring.
• **PESTS AND DISEASES** Trouble free.

S. aromaticum ■♀ syn. *Eugenia aromatica* (Clove). Small, bushy, roughly conical to columnar tree, with oval-lance-shaped, clove-scented leaves, 8–13cm (3–5in) long, pink-flushed when young, then lustrous, deep green above. In late summer, bears terminal panicles of 3–20 flowers, 1.5–2cm (½–¾in) long, with tiny, pink-tinted petals, which fall on opening, and a small brush of slender yellow stamens; flowers are followed by ellipsoid purple fruit, 8mm (⅜in) long. ↕ to 15m (50ft), ↔ 3–5m (10–15ft). Indonesia (Moluccas). ❀ (min. 22–25°C/72–77°F)
S. paniculatum ■♀ syn. *Eugenia australis* of gardens, *E. paniculata* (Brush cherry). Erect to spreading, bushy, large shrub or small tree with flaky, patterned, cream, pink, and light brown bark. Obovate to elliptic or lance-shaped leaves, 5–9cm (2–3½in) long, reddish bronze when young, become shiny, deep green. In summer, bears a few small white flowers, 1–2.5cm (½–1in) long, with many yellow stamens, in terminal and axillary panicles, followed by ovoid, pink, red, purple, or white fruit, to 2cm (¾in) long. ↕ to 10m (30ft) or more, ↔ 3–10m (10–30ft). Australia (Queensland). ❀ (min. 7°C/45°F)

Syzygium paniculatum

T

TABEBUIA

BIGNONIACEAE

Genus of about 100 species of evergreen or deciduous trees and shrubs found in a variety of habitats, from swamp margins to thickets and rainforest, in Central and South America, and the West Indies. They are grown mainly for their foliage, although flowers may form once plants reach about 3m (10ft) tall. They have mostly opposite, long-stalked, simple or fully divided, 3- to 7-palmate leaves, with the central leaflet longer than the others. The 3- to 5-lobed, tubular to bell-shaped flowers are produced in showy, terminal panicles, usually in spring. Where temperatures fall below 8–15°C (46–59°F), grow in a temperate or warm greenhouse. In warmer areas, grow the larger species as specimens, the shrubby ones in a border.

- **HARDINESS** Frost tender.
- **CULTIVATION** Under glass, grow in loam-based potting compost (JI No.3), in full light with shade from hot sun. In the growing season, water freely and apply a balanced liquid fertilizer monthly; water sparingly in winter. Outdoors, grow in fertile, moist soil in full sun. Pruning group 1; may need restrictive pruning under glass.
- **PROPAGATION** Sow seed at 16°C (61°F) as soon as ripe or in spring. Insert semi-ripe cuttings with bottom heat in summer. Air layer in spring.
- **PESTS AND DISEASES** Red spider mites may be a problem under glass.

T. chrysantha ▣ ♀ Rounded to spreading, deciduous tree bearing 5-palmate leaves, consisting of lance-shaped to obovate, entire or toothed leaflets, the central ones to 18cm (7in) long; the leaflets are mid-green, with a light covering of star-shaped hairs on the upper surfaces, more densely hairy beneath. Trumpet-shaped, sweetly scented, golden yellow flowers, 2.5–8cm

Tabebuia chrysantha

Tabebuia serratifolia

(1–3in) long, are produced in panicles in spring. ↕ 25m (80ft), ↔ 18m (60ft). Mexico to Colombia, Venezuela. ❄ (min. 8°C/46°F)

T. donnell-smithii see *Cybistax donnell-smithii.*

***T. pentaphylla* of gardens** see *T. rosea.*

T. rosea ♀ syn. *T. pentaphylla* of gardens (Pink poui, Pink tecoma, Rosy trumpet tree). Broadly upright, evergreen or deciduous tree with a long, smooth trunk, branching near the top. The 5-palmate leaves have oblong to ovate-elliptic, leathery, scaly, mid- to dark green leaflets, the central ones to 30cm (12in) long. Funnel-shaped, white, pink, or lilac flowers, 5–10cm (2–4in) long, with yellow eyes fading to white, are produced in pairs in dense panicles, in spring. ↕ 20–25m (70–80ft), ↔ 10–15m (30–50ft). Mexico to Colombia, Venezuela. ❄ (min. 10–15°C/50–59°F)

T. serratifolia ▣ ♀ (Guayacan polvillo, Yellow poui). Ascending to spreading, deciduous shrub or medium-sized tree bearing 3- to 5-palmate leaves with oblong-lance-shaped, mid-green leaflets, to 17cm (7in) long, with rounded teeth. From winter to spring, produces dense panicles of funnel-shaped yellow flowers, 5–6cm (2–2½in) long, each with 5 crimped lobes. ↕ to 12m (40ft) (but slow-growing), ↔ to 20m (70ft). Trinidad, Colombia, Venezuela. ❄ (min. 10–15°C/50–59°F)

TABERNAEMONTANA

APOCYNACEAE

Genus of at least 100 species of rounded to upright, evergreen trees and shrubs found in tropical areas worldwide, in a variety of habitats, from rocky coppices to forests. They have opposite, simple, usually oblong to elliptic leaves, and are grown for their salverform flowers, each with 5 wide-spreading lobes, produced in sparsely branched, terminal cymes over a long period in summer. In areas where temperatures fall below 10–13°C (50–55°F), grow in a temperate or warm greenhouse. Elsewhere, grow in a shrub border or small courtyard garden.

- **HARDINESS** Frost tender.
- **CULTIVATION** Under glass, grow in loam-based potting compost (JI No.3) in full light. In the growing season, water moderately and apply a balanced liquid fertilizer monthly; water sparingly in winter. Outdoors, grow in moist, fertile soil in full sun. Pruning group 9, in early spring.
- **PROPAGATION** Sow seed at 16–20°C (61–68°F) in spring. Insert semi-ripe cuttings in summer, with bottom heat in cool areas. Layer or air layer in spring.
- **PESTS AND DISEASES** Scale insects and aphids may be a problem under glass.

T. coronaria see *T. divaricata.*

T. divaricata, syn. *Ervatamia coronaria, T. coronaria* (Crepe jasmine, East Indian rosebay, Paper gardenia). Spreading, bushy, many-branched shrub with elliptic-oblong, wavy-margined, thin, glossy, mid- to dark green leaves, 7–15cm (3–6in) long, paler beneath. In summer, bears cymes of 4–6 salverform, waxy, pure white flowers, 5cm (2in) across, fragrant at dusk and after dark. ↕ 2–3m (6–10ft) or more, ↔ 1.5–2.5m (5–8ft). India to China (Yunnan), Thailand. ❄ (min. 10–13°C/50–55°F). **'Flore Pleno'** has double flowers.

▷ **Tacamahac** see *Populus balsamifera*

TACCA

TACCACEAE

Genus of 10 species of stemless perennials, with solid tubers or upright, scarred rhizomes, from semi-evergreen, monsoon forest in West Africa and S.E. Asia, grown for their handsome foliage and unusual flowers. Lance-shaped to elliptic or obovate, entire or palmately or pinnately lobed leaves, often with purplish green leaf-stalks, are widely spaced or crowded on the rootstock. Nodding, bell-shaped flowers are borne in umbels, each umbel surrounded by 4 leaf-like floral bracts. Each flower also has a distinctive, narrow, thread-like appendage, to 25cm (10in) long. In frost-prone areas, grow in a warm greenhouse; in humid tropical climates, grow in a shady border.

- **HARDINESS** Frost tender.
- **CULTIVATION** Under glass, grow in a mix of equal parts leaf mould and coarse bark, with added slow-release fertilizer, in bright filtered light. Water freely all year; in summer, mist regularly and apply a half-strength foliar fertilizer monthly. Pot on every 2 or 3 years, removing old, decaying rhizomes. Outdoors, grow in fertile, moist but well-drained, leafy, acid soil in partial shade.
- **PROPAGATION** Surface-sow seed at 22–27°C (72–81°F) in spring. Divide, or take transverse sections of rhizomes with at least one bud, in spring. Dust cut surfaces with fungicide.
- **PESTS AND DISEASES** Red spider mites, tarsonemid mites, and grey mould (*Botrytis*) may be a problem.

Tacca chantrierei

T. chantrierei ▣ (Bat flower, Cat's whiskers, Devil flower). Erect, rhizomatous perennial with oblong or lance-shaped leaves, 17–55cm (7–22in) long, dark green above and paler beneath. In summer, umbels of 5-petalled green flowers, each with 2 pairs of green, brown, or black floral bracts and dark green, maroon, or black, thread-like appendages, 25cm (10in) long, are borne on scapes to 65cm (26in) long. ↕↔ 1m (3ft). N.E. India, S.E. Asia. ❄ (min. 13°C/55°F)

T. integrifolia (Bat flower). Erect, rhizomatous perennial with oblong or lance-shaped leaves, 7–65cm (3–26in) long, dark green above and mid-green beneath. In summer, umbels of purple-red or brown flowers, surrounded by 4 green or deep purple floral bracts, are borne on scapes to 1m (3ft) long; the inner 2 flowers are white, green, or purple, with pale green, thread-like appendages, 20cm (8in) long, suffused violet and darkening with age. ↕ to 1.2m (4ft), ↔ 75cm (30in). E. India to S. China, Thailand, Malaysia, Indonesia (Sumatra, Java), Borneo. ❄ (min. 13°C/55°F)

▷ ***Tacitus bellus*** see *Graptopetalum bellum*

▷ ***Tacsonia* x *exoniensis*** see *Passiflora* x *exoniensis*

▷ ***Tacsonia mollissima*** see *Passiflora mollissima*

▷ ***Tacsonia van-volxemii*** see *Passiflora antioquiensis*

TAGETES

ASTERACEAE/COMPOSITAE

Genus of about 50 species of erect, bushy, strongly aromatic annuals and herbaceous perennials. They are found on hot, dry slopes and in valley bottoms from New Mexico, USA, to Argentina; one species occurs in Africa. The many hybrids and cultivars are derived mainly from *T. erecta, T. patula,* and *T. tenuifolia.* The almost fern-like leaves are usually opposite, pinnatifid to pinnate, with conspicuous glands, and mid- to dark green. Daisy-like or double, carnation-like flowerheads are produced singly or in cyme-like clusters from late spring to autumn. Germination from the large, easily handled seeds is rapid, and blooms appear within a few weeks of sowing. The African marigolds are excellent for formal bedding, whereas the French, Afro-French, and Signet marigolds are more suitable for the edge of a mixed border. All are good in containers and provide long-lasting cut flowers. Contact with the foliage may aggravate skin allergies. Four main hybrid groups are in cultivation:

African marigolds (African Group) Compact annuals, derived from *T. erecta*, with angular, hairless stems and pinnate, sparsely glandular leaves, 5–10cm (2–4in) long, each with 11–17 narrowly lance-shaped, pointed, sharply toothed leaflets, to 5cm (2in) long. Large, densely double, pompon-like, terminal flowerheads, usually to 12cm (5in) across, each with 5–8 or more ray-florets and numerous orange to yellow disc-florets, are produced from late spring to autumn. ↔ to 45cm (18in).

French marigolds (French Group) Compact annuals, derived from *T. patula*, with hairless, purple-tinged stems and pinnate leaves, to 10cm (4in) long, with lance-shaped to narrowly lance-shaped, toothed leaflets, to 3cm (1¼in) long. Solitary, usually double flowerheads, typically to 5cm (2in) across, with few to many red-brown, yellow, orange, or parti-coloured ray-florets and usually several disc-florets in a wide range of colours, are borne singly or in cyme-like inflorescences from late spring to autumn. ↔ to 30cm (12in).

Afro-French marigolds (Afro-French Group) Bushy annuals, derived from crosses of *T. erecta* and *T. patula*, with angular to rounded stems, branched and sometimes stained purple, and pinnate leaves, 5–13cm (2–5in) long, with lance-shaped leaflets, to 5cm (2in) long. Numerous small, single or double, yellow or orange flowerheads, usually 2.5–6cm (1–2½in) across, often marked red brown, are borne singly or in cyme-like inflorescences from late spring to autumn. ↔ 30–40cm (12–16in).

Signet marigolds (Signet Group) Upright annuals, derived from *T. tenuifolia*, with cylindrical, simple or many-branched stems and pinnate leaves, 5–13cm (2–5in) long, with narrowly lance-shaped, toothed leaflets, to 2cm (¾in) long. Many single flowerheads, usually to 2.5cm (1in) across, with yellow or orange florets (few ray-florets and several disc-florets), are borne in cyme-like inflorescences from late spring to autumn. ↔ to 40cm (16in).

• **HARDINESS** Half hardy.
• **CULTIVATION** Grow in moderately fertile, well-drained soil in full sun. Dead-head to prolong flowering and water freely during dry seasons. The densely double flowerheads of the African marigolds tend to rot in wet seasons. In containers, use a loam-based potting compost (JI No.2); during the growing season, water freely and apply a balanced liquid fertilizer weekly.
• **PROPAGATION** Sow seed *in situ* in late spring, or at 21°C (70°F) in early spring.
• **PESTS AND DISEASES** Red spider mites, whiteflies, slugs, snails, foot rot, and grey mould (*Botrytis*) may cause problems under glass.

Tagetes Antigua Series 'Antigua Gold'

Tagetes Boy Series

Tagetes Gem Series 'Tangerine Gem'

***T.* Antigua Series.** African marigolds producing orange, lemon-yellow, golden yellow, or primrose-yellow flowerheads, from late spring to early autumn. ↕ to 30cm (12in). ✲. **'Antigua Gold'** ▣ has rich golden yellow flowerheads.

***T.* Aurora Series.** French marigolds bearing densely double, broad-petalled, light to golden yellow, orange, or mahogany-red flowerheads, with some unusual bicolours, from late spring to early autumn. ↕ 20–25cm (8–10in). ✲

***T.* Beaux Series.** Afro-French marigolds bearing double flowerheads in shades of rich golden yellow, orange with a red splash, or copper-red, from late spring to early autumn. ↕ 35cm (14in). ✲

***T.* Bonanza Series.** French marigolds that produce double flowerheads in deep orange-mahogany with gold margins, golden orange-mahogany, or orange-yellow-mahogany, in summer. ↕ 30cm (12in). ✲

***T.* Boy Series** ▣ Compact French marigolds that produce double, crested flowerheads in a range of colours, including shades of golden yellow, yellow, orange, or reddish brown, with deep orange or yellow crests, in late spring and early summer. ↕ to 15cm (6in). ✲. **'Boy O'Boy'** is available as a mixture. **'Golden Boy'** has deep red flowerheads with orange crests. **'Spry Boy'** has deep mahogany flowerheads with bright yellow crests.

***T.* Disco Series.** French marigolds that produce single, weather-resistant flowerheads in a range of colours, including yellow, golden yellow with mahogany markings, golden red, and red-orange, from late spring to early autumn. ↕ 20–25cm (8–10in). ✲

***T.* Excel Series.** African marigolds bearing primrose-yellow, yellow, golden yellow, or orange flowerheads, from late spring to early autumn. ↕ to 30cm (12in). ✲

***T.* Gem Series.** Signet marigolds that bear flowerheads in lemon-yellow, deep orange, or bright orange with darker markings, from late spring to early autumn. ↕ to 23cm (9in). ✲. **'Lemon Gem'** ▣ has lemon-yellow flowerheads. **'Tangerine Gem'** ▣ has deep orange flowerheads.

Tagetes Gem Series 'Lemon Gem'

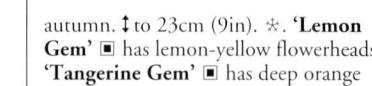

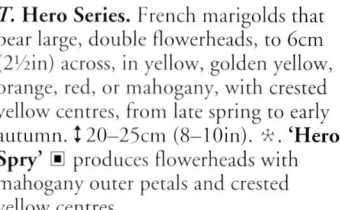

Tagetes Hero Series 'Hero Spry'

***T.* Hero Series.** French marigolds that bear large, double flowerheads, to 6cm (2½in) across, in yellow, golden yellow, orange, red, or mahogany, with crested yellow centres, from late spring to early autumn. ↕ 20–25cm (8–10in). ✲. **'Hero Spry'** ▣ produces flowerheads with mahogany outer petals and crested yellow centres.

***T.* Lady Series.** African marigolds bearing orange, primrose-yellow, yellow, or golden yellow flowerheads, from late spring to early autumn. ↕ 40–45cm (16–18in). ✲

***T.* Marvel Series.** Compact African marigolds bearing densely double flowerheads in gold, orange, yellow, lemon-yellow, or in a formula mixture of colours, from late spring to early autumn. ↕ 45cm (18in). ✲

***T.* Mischief Series.** French marigolds bearing single flowerheads in mahogany-red, yellow, or golden yellow, with some bicolours, from late spring to early autumn. ↕ to 30cm (12in) or more. ✲

***T.* 'Naughty Marietta'** ▣ French marigold producing single, deep yellow flowerheads, with maroon-red markings at the petal centres, from late spring to early autumn. ↕ 30–40cm (12–16in). ✲

***T.* Safari Series.** French marigolds bearing double, broad-petalled flowerheads in a range of colours, including golden yellow with mahogany-red splashes, soft pale yellow, tangerine-orange, and scarlet, from late spring to early autumn. ↕ 20–25cm (8–10in). ✲.

Tagetes 'Naughty Marietta'

Tagetes Safari Series 'Safari Tangerine'

'Safari Tangerine' ■ produces rich tangerine-orange flowerheads.
***T.* Solar Series** ■ Afro-French marigolds bearing large, densely double flowerheads, to 8cm (3in) across, in colours including orange with red flecking, sulphur-yellow, and golden yellow, some with crested centres, from late spring to early autumn. ↕ 35cm (14in). ❄. **'Solar Gold'** has abundant non-crested, golden yellow flowerheads.
***T.* 'Starfire'.** Signet marigold producing flowerheads in a range of colours that includes yellow, golden yellow, and red, with some bicolours, in late spring and early summer. ↕ 15–20cm (6–8in). ❄
***T.* 'Vanilla'** ■ African marigold producing creamy white flowerheads, from late spring to early autumn. ↕ to 35cm (14in). ❄

Tagetes Solar Series

Tagetes 'Vanilla'

***T.* Voyager Series.** Compact African marigolds producing large, yellow or orange flowerheads, to 10cm (4in) across, from late spring to early autumn. ↕ 30–35cm (12–14in). ❄
***T.* Zenith Series.** Afro-French marigolds producing flowerheads in yellow, golden yellow, lemon-yellow, red, or orange, from late spring to early autumn. ↕ 30cm (12in). ❄

▷ **Tail flower** see *Anthurium*
▷ ***Talbotia elegans*** see *Vellozia elegans*

TALINUM

Fameflower

PORTULACACEAE

Genus of 50 species of annuals, biennials, and often succulent and woody-based perennials, found in dry grassland and scrub in tropical and subtropical regions of Africa and North and Central America. The smooth, often succulent, usually deciduous but sometimes semi-evergreen leaves are arranged in attractive rosettes or in opposite pairs on short or elongated stems arising from a tuberous or fleshy rootstock. Showy, cup- to saucer-shaped flowers are borne singly or in cymes or panicles; although short-lived, they may be produced over a long period in summer. Grow in a rock garden. In cool areas, grow tender species in a temperate or warm greenhouse, or on a sunny window-sill.

• **HARDINESS** Fully hardy to frost tender.
• **CULTIVATION** Under glass, grow in standard cactus compost in full light and with good ventilation. In the growing season, water moderately, applying a balanced liquid fertilizer once or twice; keep just moist at other times. Outdoors, grow in well-drained, poor to moderately fertile soil in full sun.
• **PROPAGATION** Sow seed at 15–18°C (59–64°F) in spring or as soon as ripe. Divide mat- or rosette-forming species in spring.
• **PESTS AND DISEASES** Susceptible to greenfly.

T. caffrum. Succulent, deciduous perennial, sometimes biennial, with a thickened, tuberous, caudex-like rootstock, short, erect or prostrate stems, and inversely lance-shaped, linear, or oval, fleshy, mid-green leaves, 2.5–13cm (1–5in) long. Solitary, cup-shaped, pale lemon-yellow flowers, 1–2cm (½–¾in) across, open during daytime in summer. ↕↔ 15cm (6in). Namibia and Angola to Kenya. ❀ (min. 10°C/50°F)
T. okanoganense ■ Prostrate, mat- or cushion-forming, semi-evergreen perennial with succulent stems bearing cylindrical, fleshy, grey-green leaves, to 1cm (½in) long. The basal portions of the leaf midribs are retained as bristles in winter. Solitary, short-stemmed, saucer-shaped white flowers, to 2cm (¾in) across, tinged pink or yellow and with yellow stamens, are borne over several weeks in summer. Grow in an alpine house or trough. ↕ to 5cm (2in), ↔ to 20cm (8in). W. North America. ❄❄❄
T. paniculatum (Jewels of Opar). Tuberous-rooted, deciduous perennial with erect, usually unbranched stems, becoming somewhat woody with age, and elliptic or obovate, mid-green leaves, to 10cm (4in) long. Many-flowered, terminal panicles of bowl-

Talinum okanoganense

shaped, red or yellow flowers, to 2.5cm (1in) across, are produced in summer. ↕ 1m (3ft), ↔ 60cm (24in). S. USA to Central America. ❀ (min. 15°C/59°F)
T. spinescens. Dense, cushion-forming, semi-evergreen perennial with succulent stems, clothed in spines and thickening with age, and cylindrical, fleshy, grey-green leaves, 1–3cm (½–1¼in) long. The basal portions of the leaf midribs are usually retained as bristles in winter. Produces loose, cyme-like panicles of 1–5 short-stemmed, saucer-shaped, dark magenta flowers, to 1.5cm (½in) across, in summer. ↕ to 10cm (4in), ↔ to 15cm (6in). W. North America. ❄❄❄

▷ **Tamarisk** see *Tamarix*

TAMARIX

Tamarisk

TAMARICACEAE

Genus of 54 species of deciduous shrubs and small trees from coastal sites and dry or marshy, often salt-rich areas inland, from W. Europe and the Mediterranean to E. Asia and India. They are grown for their attractive, feathery foliage, consisting of small, scale- or needle-like leaves, and their plume-like, often leafy racemes of small flowers. They are useful for a shrub border in an inland garden, but may also be used as a windbreak or hedge in an exposed coastal area, and for growing on light, sandy soils.

• **HARDINESS** Fully hardy.
• **CULTIVATION** Grow in full sun, in well-drained soil in coastal areas, or in moister soil inland. Shelter from cold, drying winds in inland gardens; in

Tamarix ramosissima

Tamarix ramosissima 'Pink Cascade'

coastal areas, they are resistant to strong winds. Prune regularly, or they may become top-heavy and unstable. Cut back young plants almost to ground level after planting. Pruning group 2 for spring-flowering species; group 6 for those flowering in late summer.
• **PROPAGATION** Sow seed as soon as ripe in containers in a cold frame. Take hardwood cuttings in winter, or semi-ripe cuttings in summer.
• **PESTS AND DISEASES** Trouble free.

T. parviflora. Spreading shrub with arching purple shoots and pointed leaves, 3mm (⅛in) long. In late spring, 4-petalled, pale pink flowers are borne in dense, lateral racemes, to 5cm (2in) long, on the old shoots. ↕ 5m (15ft), ↔ 6m (20ft). S.E. Europe. ❄❄❄
T. pentandra see *T. ramosissima.*
T. ramosissima ■ ♀ syn. *T. pentandra.* Graceful shrub or small tree with arching, red-brown shoots and pointed leaves, to 4mm (⅛in) long. In late summer and early autumn, 5-petalled pink flowers are produced in dense racemes, to 7cm (3in) long, on the new shoots. ↕↔ 5m (15ft). S.E. Europe to Asia. ❄❄❄. **'Pink Cascade'** ■ has rich pink flowers.
T. tetrandra. Shrub or small tree with arching, purple-brown shoots and needle- or scale-like leaves, to 4mm (⅛in) long. Bears 4-petalled, light pink flowers in lateral racemes, to 5cm (2in) long, on the old shoots, in mid- and late spring. ↕↔ 3m (10ft). E. Balkans, W. Asia, S. former USSR. ❄❄❄

▷ **Tampala** see *Amaranthus tricolor*

TANACETUM

syn. BALSAMITA, PYRETHRUM

ASTERACEAE/COMPOSITAE

Genus of about 70 species of annuals and evergreen and herbaceous perennials and subshrubs from mountains, cliffs, meadows, and dry slopes in N. temperate regions. They have simple or pinnate to 3-pinnate, entire, toothed, or scalloped, mostly aromatic, mainly basal leaves that are sparsely to densely hairy and sometimes silver. Stem leaves, where present, are spirally arranged, usually smaller and less divided, and may be stalkless. Terminal, daisy- or button-like flowerheads, borne singly or in corymbs, have yellow disc-florets and sometimes barely discernible, white, red, or yellow ray-florets. This diverse genus includes

TANACETUM

Tanacetum argenteum

Tanacetum coccineum 'Eileen May Robinson'

Tanacetum densum subsp. *amani*

Tanacetum parthenium 'Golden Moss'

species suitable for a rock garden, a herb garden, or border edging. *T. coccineum* and its cultivars are suitable for a border and produce good cut flowers. Some have aromatic foliage, which may be dried for use in pot-pourri; several have medicinal qualities. Contact with the foliage may aggravate skin allergies.

• **HARDINESS** Fully hardy to half hardy.

• **CULTIVATION** Grow in well-drained, preferably sandy soil in full sun, although most will tolerate any soil that is not wet and heavy. *T. balsamita* produces leafier growth in partial shade. Grow mound-forming, dwarf, white- or silver-leaved species in sharply drained, poor to moderately fertile soil. Cut back *T. coccineum* and its cultivars as the flowers fade, in order to encourage a second flowering. *T. parthenium* and its cultivars self-seed prolifically.

• **PROPAGATION** Sow seed at 10–13°C (50–55°F) in late winter or early spring. Divide perennials, or root basal cuttings, in spring. Insert softwood cuttings of *T. parthenium* and *T. ptarmiciflorum* in early summer; in winter, young plants of *T. ptarmiciflorum* are best kept in a cool greenhouse.

• **PESTS AND DISEASES** Aphids, chrysanthemum eelworm, and leaf miners may be a problem.

T. argenteum ■ syn. *Achillea argentea.* Mat-forming, usually evergreen, woody-based perennial with branching, densely white-woolly stems. Ovate, 2-pinnate, bright silvery white leaves, 2–7cm (¾–3in) long, have 5–9 pairs of divided to narrowly lance-shaped leaflets. In summer, daisy-like white flowerheads, 4mm (⅛in) across, are borne singly or in corymbs. Suitable for a rock garden or border edging. ↕ to 20cm (8in), ↔ to 30cm (12in). Mediterranean. ***

T. balsamita, syn. *Balsamita major, Chrysanthemum balsamita* (Alecost, Costmary). Mat-forming, woody-based, rhizomatous perennial with oblong to elliptic, scalloped, softly silver-hairy basal leaves, to 30cm (12in) long, and smaller, stalkless leaves on erect stems. Numerous flowerheads, to 1.5cm (½in) across, with tiny white ray-florets and yellow disc-florets, are borne in corymbs in late summer and early autumn. Grown for its balsam-scented foliage (used in pot-pourri), and suitable for a herb garden. ↕ to 90cm (36in), ↔ 45cm (18in). Europe to C. Asia. ***

T. coccineum, syn. *Chrysanthemum coccineum, Pyrethrum coccineum, P. roseum* (Painted daisy, Pyrethrum). Bushy, hairless, herbaceous perennial with erect stems and elliptic-oblong, pinnatisect or 2-pinnatisect, dark green, mainly basal leaves, to 12cm (5in) long, consisting of 10–14 narrowly lance-shaped, toothed segments. Daisy-like flowerheads to 7cm (3in) across, with white, pink, or red ray-florets and yellow disc-florets are produced in early summer. ↕ 45–75cm (18–30in), ↔ 45cm (18in). Caucasus, S.W. Asia. ***. **'Brenda'** ■ bears deep cerise-pink flowerheads; ↕ 70–80cm (28–32in). **'Eileen May Robinson'** ■ has pale, rich pink flowerheads; ↕ 70–80cm (28–32in). **'James Kelway'** produces brilliant deep crimson-pink flowerheads; ↕ 60cm (24in). **'Snow Cloud'** has white flowerheads; ↕ 60cm (24in).

T. densum* subsp. *amani ■ syn. *Chrysanthemum densum.* Mound-forming, usually evergreen, woody-based perennial with white-downy stems and ovate to broadly elliptic, 2-pinnatisect, downy, grey-white leaves, 2–5cm (¾–2in) long, finely cut into 10–25 inversely lance-shaped segments. In summer, bears flat corymbs of 3–7 daisy-like yellow flowerheads, 5–10mm (¼–½in) across, each with 12–15 yellow ray-florets, to 4mm (⅛in) long. *T. densum* is similar to *T. haradjanii*, but female ray-florets are absent on the latter. Grow in a rock garden. ↕ to 25cm (10in), ↔ to 20cm (8in). Turkey. ***

T. haradjanii, syn. *Chrysanthemum haradjanii.* Mat-forming, woody-based, evergreen perennial with silver-white, downy stems. Oblong-elliptic to ovate, 2- or 3-pinnatisect, silvery grey leaves, to 5cm (2in) long, are composed of 4 or 5 pairs of narrowly lance-shaped, entire or further divided segments. Daisy-like yellow flowerheads, 2–4mm (1/16–⅛in) across, are borne in loose corymbs in late summer. Suitable for a rock garden. ↕ to 15cm (6in), ↔ to 20cm (8in). Syria, Turkey. ***

T. parthenium ■ syn. *Chrysanthemum parthenium, Pyrethrum parthenium* (Feverfew). Short-lived, bushy, aromatic, woody-based perennial with ovate, pinnatisect or 2-pinnatisect, softly hairy basal leaves, to 8cm (3in) long, with 3–5 paired, scalloped or entire segments; smaller, less divided, shorter-stalked leaves are produced on the erect stems. Daisy-like flowerheads, to 2.5cm (1in) across, with yellow disc-florets and white ray-florets, are borne in dense corymbs in summer. Suitable for border edging. ↕ 45–60cm (18–24in), ↔ 30cm (12in). Europe, Caucasus. ***. **'Aureum'** has golden yellow leaves, and produces single, yellow-tinted white flowerheads. **'Ball's Double White'** has double white flowerheads. **'Butterball'** bears double yellow flowerheads. **'Golden Moss'** ■ is dwarf and carpet-forming, with moss-like yellow leaves; ↕ to 10cm (4in). **'Plenum'** ■ has fully double white flowerheads; ↕ 35cm (14in). **'Santana'** is dwarf, producing double flowerheads, and will flower at any time of year when grown in

T

Tanacetum coccineum 'Brenda'

Tanacetum parthenium

Tanacetum parthenium 'Plenum'

Tanacetum parthenium 'Snowball'

Tanacetum ptarmiciflorum

containers; ↕20cm (8in), ↔ 15cm (6in). **'Snowball'** ▣ has pompon-like, fully double, ivory-white flowerheads; ↕30cm (12in), ↔ 15cm (6in).
T. ptarmiciflorum ▣ syn. *Pyrethrum ptarmiciflorum.* Woody-based perennial, often grown as an annual, with erect stems. Elliptic to oblong-ovate, 2- or 3-pinnatisect, silver-hairy basal and stem leaves, to 10cm (4in) long, have 8–22 linear-elliptic, scalloped segments. Daisy-like white flowerheads, to 2.5cm (1in) across, with yellow disc-florets, are borne in dense corymbs in late summer. Suitable for border edging. ↕60cm (24in), ↔ 40cm (16in). Canary Islands (Gran Canaria). ✻
T. vulgare, syn. *Chrysanthemum vulgare* (Common tansy). Vigorous, erect, deciduous perennial with alternate, oblong, pinnate leaves, to 10cm (4in) long, comprising up to 12 oblong or lance-shaped, pinnately lobed or toothed leaflets. Bears button-shaped, bright yellow flowerheads, to 1cm (½in) across, in flat-topped corymbs, 14cm (5½in) across, in summer. Suitable for a herb garden. ↕60–90cm (24–36in), ↔ 45cm (18in). Europe. ✻✻✻

TANAKAEA syn. TANAKEA

Japanese foam flower

SAXIFRAGACEAE

Genus of one species of dioecious, rhizomatous, evergreen perennial that occurs in wet, rocky, shaded sites in Japan. *T. radicans* is an attractive creeping plant, producing basal leaf rosettes and upright, leafless stems bearing dense panicles of minute white flowers in late spring and early summer. Grow in a moist, shaded site in a woodland or rock garden.

- **HARDINESS** Fully hardy.
- **CULTIVATION** Grow in moist, humus-rich, peaty soil in full or partial shade.
- **PROPAGATION** Separate rooted portions of rhizome in spring.
- **PESTS AND DISEASES** Trouble free.

T. radicans. Dense, spreading perennial with basal rosettes of ovate to broadly lance-shaped or oblong, leathery leaves, 2–8cm (¾–3in) long, rounded or heart-shaped at the bases, dark green above, paler beneath. In late spring and early summer, mainly unisexual, star-shaped white flowers, to 3mm (⅛in) across, with prominent anthers, are borne in dense panicles, 5–15cm (2–6in) long. ↕ to 10cm (4in), ↔ to 30cm (12in). Japan (Shikoku, Kyushu). ✻✻✻

▷**Tanakea** see *Tanakaea*
▷**Tanekaha** see *Phyllocladus trichomanoides*
▷**Tangerine** see *Citrus reticulata*
▷**Tanguru** see *Olearia albida*
▷**Tannia** see *Xanthosoma, X. sagittifolium*
Blue see *X. nigrum*
▷**Tansy, Common** see *Tanacetum vulgare*

TAPEINOCHILUS

COSTACEAE/ZINGIBERACEAE

Genus of about 15 species of evergreen, rhizomatous perennials from tropical forest in Malaysia, Indonesia, New Guinea, and N.E. Australia. They are cultivated mainly for their spectacular inflorescences of red bracts. The obovate leaves, to 15cm (6in) long, are spirally arranged on bamboo-like stems. In frost-prone areas, grow in a warm greenhouse; in humid tropical climates, grow in a shady border.

- **HARDINESS** Frost tender.
- **CULTIVATION** Under glass, grow in loam-based potting compost (JI No.3), with added leaf mould, in bright indirect light or deep shade, with high humidity. In spring and summer, water freely and apply a balanced liquid fertilizer monthly; water moderately in winter. Outdoors, grow in fertile, leafy, humus-rich soil in deep shade.
- **PROPAGATION** Sow seed at 20°C (68°F) in early spring. Divide in spring.
- **PESTS AND DISEASES** Trouble free.

T. ananassae. Clump-forming perennial producing long, narrowly obovate, sharply pointed leaves, 15cm (6in) long. In summer, leafless stems, 45–120cm (18–48in) long, bear cone-like inflorescences of numerous recurved, overlapping, vivid red bracts, 10cm (4in) across, resembling red pineapples; they often cover the small yellow flowers. ↕ to 2m (6ft), ↔ 1m (3ft). Indonesia (Moluccas). ❀ (min. 20°C/68°F)

▷**Tarata** see *Pittosporum eugenioides*
▷**Taro** see *Colocasia, C. esculenta*
Blue see *Xanthosoma nigrum*
Giant see *Alocasia macrorrhiza*
Imperial see *Colocasia esculenta* 'Illustris'
▷**Tarragon** see *Artemisia dracunculus*
▷**Tarweed** see *Grindelia*
▷***Tasmannia*** see *Drimys*
T. aromatica see *D. lanceolata*
▷**Tassel flower** see *Amaranthus caudatus, Emilia*
▷**Tassel-white** see *Itea virginica*

TAXODIUM

Swamp cypress

TAXODIACEAE

Genus of 2 species of upright, conical, monoecious, deciduous or semi-evergreen, coniferous trees found in swampy forest or by river margins from S.E. USA to Guatemala. The shoots are of 2 types: deciduous (without buds), which fall in autumn, and persistent (with buds), from which only the leaves fall. The narrowly lance-shaped or linear leaves are arranged alternately, radially, or in 2 ranks. Male cones occur in groups; female cones are scattered. They are late to come into leaf and to assume their spectacular autumn colours. Grow as specimen trees; they are especially suited to very wet sites, where they grow aerial roots (known as pneumatophores or "knees") at water level.

- **HARDINESS** Fully hardy.
- **CULTIVATION** Grow in any moist or wet, preferably acid soil in full or partial shade.
- **PROPAGATION** Sow seed in containers in a cold frame in spring. Graft cultivars in late winter.
- **PESTS AND DISEASES** Trouble free.

T. ascendens see *T. distichum* var. *imbricarium.*
T. distichum ▣◊ (Swamp cypress). Conical tree, becoming columnar and often ragged with age, due to its brittle branches and pale brown, shallowly fissured bark. The alternate (almost opposite), narrowly lance-shaped, pale green leaves, 2cm (¾in) long, turning rust-brown in autumn, are 2-ranked on deciduous shoots. On persistent shoots, leaves are small and scale-like. Spherical green female cones, 3cm (1¼in) across, ripen to brown in autumn; pendent red

Taxodium distichum

Taxodium distichum var. *imbricarium* 'Nutans'

male cones expand in winter. ↕20–40m (70–130ft), ↔ 6–9m (20–28ft). S.E. USA. ✻✻✻. **var. *imbricarium***, syn. *T. ascendens, T. distichum* var. *imbricatum* (Pond cypress) is narrowly conical, with dull brown bark and radial leaves, 5–10mm (¼–½in) long, lying flat on erect shoots; ↕10–20m (30–70ft), ↔ to 6m (20ft). **var. *imbricarium* 'Nutans'** ▣ produces erect foliage shoots, becoming pendent when mature. **var. *imbricatum*** see var. *imbricarium.*

TAXUS

Yew

TAXACEAE

Genus of 5–10 species of broadly rounded to upright, dioecious, evergreen, coniferous, large shrubs or small trees found in forest extending from N. temperate areas to the Philippines and Central America. Yews are grown for their reddish-brown, frequently peeling bark, and their linear, dark green leaves, often paler beneath; these are spirally arranged but often appear 2-ranked. On the female plants, single-seeded, oblong-ovoid fruits are produced in open, fleshy arils. Grow as specimen plants or use for hedging and topiary; the prostrate forms make good ground cover, even in dense, dry shade. Most tolerate exposure, dry soils, and urban pollution. All parts (but not the arils) are highly toxic if ingested.

- **HARDINESS** Fully hardy.
- **CULTIVATION** Grow in any well-drained, fertile soil, including chalky or acid soils, in sun or deep shade. Trim hedging in summer and early autumn. Can withstand renovation pruning.
- **PROPAGATION** Sow seed as soon as ripe in containers in a cold frame, or in a seedbed; seed may take 2 or more years to germinate. Insert semi-ripe cuttings in late summer or early autumn; take cuttings from strongly upright shoots (except for prostrate cultivars), otherwise they may not form a strong leading shoot. Graft cultivars in early autumn.

Taxus baccata 'Adpressa'

• **Pests and diseases** Resistant to most diseases, except *Phytophthora* root rot. May be damaged by tortrix moth caterpillars, vine weevil, and yew scale.

T. baccata ♢ (Yew). Broadly conical tree with spreading, horizontal branches, scaly, purple-brown bark, and shoots that remain green for several years. Linear, glossy or matt, dark green leaves, 2–3cm (¾–1¼in) long, paler beneath, are 2-ranked and parted either side of the shoots. Yellow male cones are borne in spring. Fruit consist of single green seeds with juicy, sweet, usually red arils, 1cm (½in) across. ↕ 10–20m (30–70ft), ↔ 8–10m (25–30ft). Europe, N. Africa to Iran. ✲✲✲. **'Adpressa'** ▣♢ is a dense, spreading, female shrub, with short, wide, abruptly pointed leaves, to 1.5cm (½in) long; ↕ 6m (20ft), ↔ 4m (12ft). **'Dovastonii Aurea'** ▣♢ is a small, female tree, with spreading branches, pendent branchlets, and yellow-margined leaves borne on golden yellow shoots; ↕ 3–5m (10–15ft), ↔ 2m (6ft). **'Fastigiata'** ▣♢ (Florence Court yew, Irish yew) is columnar and female, with radially set leaves; ↕ to 10m (30ft), ↔ 6m (20ft). **'Fastigiata Aurea'** ♢ is female, similar to 'Fastigiata', but has variegated leaves with gold patches; ↕ 6m (20ft), ↔ 3m (10ft). **'Fastigiata Aureomarginata'** ♢ is female, similar to 'Fastigiata', but with leaves margined bright yellow; ↕ 3–5m (10–15ft), ↔ 1–2.5m (3–8ft). **'Repandens'** is a female shrub, and does not form leaders but spreads over the ground, forming a mound; ↕ to 60cm (24in), ↔ 5m (15ft). **'Repens Aurea'** is a female shrub that is

Taxus baccata 'Fastigiata'

similar to, and may even be the same as 'Dovastonii Aurea', but is propagated from sideshoots and thus forms only spreading ground cover; ↕↔ 1–1.5m (3–5ft). **'Standishii'** ♢ is narrow and columnar, a miniature female selection of 'Fastigiata', and has golden yellow leaves; ↕ 1.5m (5ft), ↔ 60cm (24in).
T. cuspidata ▣♢ (Japanese yew). Broadly columnar shrub or small tree with linear, spiny-tipped, dark green leaves, 1.5–2.5cm (½–1in) long, tawny or yellow-green beneath, turning red-green over winter, and narrowly parted either side of the shoots. Scarlet arils are 0.5–1cm (¼–½in) across. Much hardier in cold areas than *T. baccata.* ↕ 10–15m (30–50ft), ↔ 6–8m (20–25ft). N.E. China, Japan. ✲✲✲. **var. *nana*** is a spreading shrub, with erect shoots and radial leaves, and is mainly male in cultivation; ↕ 2–4m (6–12ft); Japan (Honshu). **var. *nana* 'Densa'** is a low-growing, broad, flattened, female shrub; ↕ 1.2m (4ft), ↔ to 6m (20ft).
T.* x *media ♢–♢ (*T. baccata* x *T. cuspidata*). Rounded to upright tree with the vigour of *T. baccata* and the hardiness of *T. cuspidata.* Distinctly 2-ranked, oblong to needle-like, pointed, flat, olive- to dark green leaves, 1.5–3cm (½–1¼in) long, have prominent white midribs and are slightly red-flushed in winter. Scarlet arils are 5–10mm (¼–½in) across. ↕↔ to 6–8m (20–25ft). Garden origin. ✲✲✲. **'Brownii'** ♢ is female, dense and spherical, with short, parted, widely spaced, dark green leaves, 1.5–2cm (½–¾in) long; ↕ to 2.5m (8ft), ↔ to 3.5m (11ft). **'Hicksii'** ♢ is probably male, and columnar in habit, similar to *T. baccata* 'Fastigiata' but more open, with more radially set, dark green leaves; ↕ 6–8m (20–25ft), ↔ 2–3m (6–10ft), later to 6m (20ft).

▷**Tea,**
Labrador see *Ledum groenlandicum*
Oswego see *Monarda didyma*
Sweet see *Osmanthus fragrans*
▷**Teasel** see *Dipsacus*
▷**Tea tree** see *Leptospermum*
Duke of Argyll's see *Lycium barbarum*
New Zealand see *Leptospermum scoparium*
Woolly see *Leptospermum lanigerum*

Tecoma syn. Tecomaria

Bignoniaceae

Genus of about 12 species of evergreen climbers, scrambling shrubs, and upright trees, found on rocky slopes and in valleys in southern Africa and from S. USA to Argentina. The opposite leaves are pinnate or sometimes 3-pinnate, with ovate-oblong to rounded leaflets. Narrowly bell- to funnel-shaped, 5-lobed, yellow, orange, or red flowers are produced in dense, terminal racemes or panicles between winter and summer. In frost-prone areas, grow in a cool or temperate greenhouse or conservatory. In warmer climates, grow as specimen plants; the scrambling species may be trained over an arch.
• **Hardiness** Frost tender; *T. capensis* may survive brief spells near 0°C (32°F).
• **Cultivation** Under glass, plant directly into a border, or grow in large tubs of loam-based potting compost (JI No.3), in full light. During the growing season, water freely and apply a half-strength balanced liquid fertilizer monthly; water sparingly in winter. Outdoors, grow in moist but well-drained, fertile soil in full sun. Pruning group 8 for early-flowering species; group 9 for late-flowering species, in early spring. Under glass, prune plants to restrict growth; thin overcrowded stems.

Tecoma stans

• **Propagation** Sow seed at 18–21°C (64–70°F) in spring. Insert semi-ripe cuttings with bottom heat in summer. Layer *T. capensis* in spring or autumn.
• **Pests and diseases** Red spider mites and whiteflies may be troublesome under glass.

T. australis see *Pandorea pandorana.*
T. capensis, syn. *Bignonia capensis, Tecomaria capensis, T. petersii* (Cape honeysuckle). Erect, scrambling, evergreen shrub with slender stems and pinnate, lustrous, mid- to dark green leaves, to 15cm (6in) long, each with 5–7 elliptic-ovate to roughly diamond-shaped, toothed leaflets. Racemes, to 15cm (6in) long, of slender, tubular, orange to scarlet flowers, 6–7cm (2½–3in) long, are produced mainly in summer. ↕ 2–7m (6–22ft), ↔ 1–3m (3–10ft). Southern Africa. ❀ (min. 5°C/41°F). **'Apricot'** is compact, with vivid apricot-orange flowers; ↕ to 1.5m (5ft), ↔ 1m (3ft). **'Aurea'** ▣ bears yellow flowers, to 5cm (2in) long; ↕ 4m (12ft), ↔ 2m (6ft). **'Lutea'** is slow-growing, with dark yellow flowers; ↕ 2m (6ft), ↔ 1m (3ft).
T. grandiflora see *Campsis grandiflora.*
T. radicans see *Campsis radicans.*
T. ricasoliana see *Podranea ricasoliana.*
T. stans ▣♢ syn. *Bignonia stans, Stenolobium stans* (Trumpet bush, Yellow bells, Yellow elder). Open, ascending, large shrub or small tree, often with several slim trunks if grown as a tree. Pinnate leaves, to 35cm (14in) long, each have 5–13 oblong-ovate to lance-shaped, toothed, bright green leaflets. Funnel-shaped, bright yellow flowers, 5cm (2in) long, are produced in terminal racemes or panicles, to 15cm (6in) long, from late winter to summer. ↕ 5–9m (15–28ft), ↔ 3–5m (10–15ft). S. USA to Guatemala, Argentina. ❀ (min. 7–10°C/45–50°F)

▷**Tecoma, Pink** see *Tabebuia rosea*

Tecomanthe

Bignoniaceae

Genus of 5 species of woody-stemmed, evergreen, twining climbers from tropical woodland in Indonesia, New Guinea, the Solomon Islands, and Australasia. They bear funnel-shaped, 5-lobed flowers, in pendent racemes from the bare branches, below the leafy stems. The opposite leaves are pinnate or sometimes 3-palmate. Where

Taxus baccata 'Dovastonii Aurea'

Taxus cuspidata

Tecoma capensis 'Aurea'

T

temperatures fall below 15°C (59°F), grow in a warm greenhouse. In tropical areas, train over an arch or pergola, or grow against a warm wall.
• **HARDINESS** Frost tender.
• **CULTIVATION** Under glass, grow in loam-based potting compost (JI No.3) in full light with shade from hot sun. Provide strong support. In the growing season, water freely, applying a balanced liquid fertilizer monthly; water sparingly in winter. Outdoors, grow in fertile, moist but well-drained soil, in full sun with some midday shade. Pruning group 11, in spring.
• **PROPAGATION** Sow seed at 18–21°C (64–70°F) in spring. Insert semi-ripe cuttings with bottom heat in summer. Layer in spring.
• **PESTS AND DISEASES** Red spider mites and mealybugs may be troublesome under glass.

T. dendrophila. Evergreen, twining climber with sparsely branched stems, particularly when young, and pinnate leaves, 7cm (3in) long, each consisting of 3–5 ovate or oblong-lance-shaped, rich green leaflets. In summer, produces racemes of 1–12 flowers, 7–11cm (3–4½in) long, with deep pink to rose-purple tubes, becoming yellow at the top, and yellow lobes, suffused and veined pink or purple. ↕ to 15m (50ft) or more. Indonesia (Moluccas), New Guinea, Solomon Islands. ❀ (min. 13–15°C/55–59°F)
T. speciosa. Evergreen, twining climber with sparsely branched stems when young, and pinnate leaves, to 6cm (2½in) long, each with 5 broadly obovate, thick, lustrous, deep green leaflets. In autumn, bears light, almost luminous, yellow-green flowers, 6–8cm (2½–3in) long, with downy lobes, in dense racemes of 1–10. ↕ 10m (30ft) or more. New Zealand (Three Kings Islands). ❀ (min. 13–15°C/55–59°F)

▷ ***Tecomaria*** see *Tecoma*
T. capensis see *T. capensis*
T. petersii see *T. capensis*

TECOPHILAEA

LILIACEAE/TECOPHILAEACEAE

Genus of 2 species of cormous perennials, originally from subalpine grassland in South America but probably now extinct in the wild. They have narrowly lance-shaped, basal leaves, and bear crocus-like, brilliantly coloured flowers on leafless stems in spring. They are suitable for a rock garden or raised bed, but, in all except completely frost-free areas, should be grown in a bulb frame, cold greenhouse, or alpine house to protect the early growth from frost.
• **HARDINESS** Frost hardy, but early leaves are liable to frost damage.
• **CULTIVATION** Under glass, plant 5cm (2in) deep, in a mix of equal parts loam-based potting compost (JI No.2) and sharp sand in full light. In the growing season, water moderately; reduce water gradually as the leaves die down to keep corms warm and dry during summer dormancy. Outdoors, grow in well-drained, sandy soil in full sun.
• **PROPAGATION** Sow seed in pots in a frost-free frame, in autumn or as soon as ripe. Remove offsets in late summer.
• **PESTS AND DISEASES** Trouble free.

Tecophilaea cyanocrocus

T. cyanocrocus ▣ (Chilean blue crocus). Small, cormous perennial with semi-erect, narrowly lance-shaped, basal leaves, to 13cm (5in) long. In spring, bears 1 or 2 open funnel-shaped, intense gentian-blue flowers, 4–5cm (1½–2in) long, with white throats and faint white veins. ↕ 8–10cm (3–4in), ↔ 5cm (2in). Chile. ❄❄. **var. *leichtlinii*** has pale blue flowers with large white centres. **var. *violacea*** has deep violet flowers.

▷ **Teddy bear plant** see *Cyanotis kewensis*
▷ ***Telanthophora grandifolia*** see *Senecio grandifolius*

TELEKIA

ASTERACEAE/COMPOSITAE

Genus of 2 species of imposing, erect, herbaceous perennials found in moist woodland and beside streams in scrub, from C. and S. Europe to the Caucasus, Turkey, Ukraine, Belorussia, and Russia. The basal leaves are long-stalked, ovate and coarsely toothed; the alternate stem leaves have shorter stalks. Solitary flowerheads, with long, narrow yellow ray-florets, tubular yellow disc-florets, ageing to brown, and 3 or 4 rows of overlapping involucral bracts, are produced in branching sprays from early summer to early autumn. *Telekia* species make effective specimen plants for a damp woodland and wild garden, or beside water.
• **HARDINESS** Fully hardy.
• **CULTIVATION** Grow in moist, not too fertile soil, in partial shade with shelter from strong winds. They may self-seed.
• **PROPAGATION** Sow seed in containers as soon as ripe. Divide in spring.
• **PESTS AND DISEASES** Young leaves may be damaged by slugs.

T. speciosa, syn. *Buphthalmum speciosum.* Spreading, rhizomatous perennial with ovate, coarsely scalloped to toothed, aromatic, somewhat limp leaves, 30cm (12in) or more long, heart-shaped at the bases, on stalks to 20cm (8in) long. The coarse, upright stems have smaller, almost clasping leaves. In late summer and early autumn, loose, branching sprays of solitary, daisy-like yellow flowerheads, 6–9cm (2½–3½in) across, are produced on long peduncles. ↕ to 2m (6ft), ↔ 1m (3ft). S.E. Europe, Caucasus, Ukraine, Belorussia, Russia. ❄❄❄

▷ ***Telesonix jamesii*** see *Boykinia jamesii*

TELLIMA

Fringe cups

SAXIFRAGACEAE

Genus of one species of rosette-forming, hairy herbaceous perennial from cool, moist woodland in W. North America. The mainly basal leaves are heart-shaped or triangular to kidney-shaped, scalloped or toothed, and 5- to 7-lobed. Small, bell-shaped flowers, with 5 tiny petals, fringed into linear segments, relatively large calyces, and 10 stamens, are borne in terminal racemes in late spring and midsummer. Fringe cups are drought-tolerant and suitable for ground cover in a shrub border or woodland garden.
• **HARDINESS** Fully hardy.

Tellima grandiflora

• **CULTIVATION** Grow in moist, humus-rich soil in partial shade, although will tolerate dry soil and full sun. Self-seeds freely.
• **PROPAGATION** Sow seed in containers in a cold frame as soon as ripe or in spring. Divide in spring.
• **PESTS AND DISEASES** Leaves may be attacked by slugs.

T. grandiflora ▣ Rosette-forming perennial with hairy, heart-shaped or triangular to kidney-shaped, 5- to 7-lobed, scalloped leaves, 5–10cm (2–4in) long. From late spring to midsummer, erect, hairy stems bear terminal racemes, to 30cm (12in) long, of 15–30 white to greenish white flowers, to 8mm (⅜in) long, with greenish white calyces. ↕ to 80cm (32in), ↔ 30cm (12in). North America (Alaska to California). ❄❄❄. **'Perky'** has smaller leaves, and bears red flowers; ↕ to 40cm (16in), ↔ 25cm (10in). **'Purpurteppich'** has leaves tinged purplish red in summer, dark purple leaf-stalks, and pink-fringed green flowers; ↕ to 60cm (24in).

TELOPEA

Waratah

PROTEACEAE

Genus of 4 species of evergreen shrubs or small trees occurring in drought-prone woodland in Australia. The alternate leaves are simple, leathery, and sometimes toothed or lobed. *Telopea* species are cultivated mainly for their paired, tubular flowers, 2–2.5cm (¾–1in) long, which are split on the lower sides. Each flower has 4 short lobes, with the margins rolled under, and a prominent stigma. The flowers are surrounded by overlapping, coloured bracts and are produced in dense, terminal, umbel-like heads in spring or summer; they are followed by boat-shaped, woody seed pods. In frost-prone climates, grow in a cool greenhouse. In warmer areas, they are suitable for a shrub border.
• **HARDINESS** Half hardy to frost tender.
• **CULTIVATION** Under glass, grow in loam-based potting compost (JI No.2), with additional sharp sand, in full light or bright filtered light. During the growing season, water freely and apply a low-nitrate, low-phosphate fertilizer monthly; water sparingly in winter. Outdoors, grow in moist but well-drained, sandy, slightly acid soil in full sun or partial shade. Pruning group 8.

• **PROPAGATION** Sow seed in containers in a cold frame as soon as ripe. Insert semi-ripe or leaf-bud cuttings with bottom heat in summer.
• **PESTS AND DISEASES** Trouble free.

T. mongaensis ■ (Braidwood waratah, Monga waratah). Erect, bushy shrub producing inversely lance-shaped, round-tipped, matt, dark green leaves, 10–15cm (4–6in) long. From late spring to summer, produces flowerheads 8–10cm (3–4in) across, each consisting of a ring of pale green to pale pink bracts and abundant tubular red flowers. ↕ 2–3m (6–10ft) or more, ↔ 1.5–2.5m (5–8ft). Australia (New South Wales). ✻
T. oreades ■ ♀ (Gippsland waratah, Victorian waratah). Large, moderately bushy shrub or sometimes small, broadly upright tree with inversely lance-shaped to obovate, matt, dark green leaves, 15–20cm (6–8in) long, with pointed tips. In late spring and summer, bears flowerheads 9cm (3½in) across, each consisting of a ring of light green or pink bracts and tubular red flowers. ↕ to 3m (10ft) as a shrub, to 10m (30ft) as a tree, ↔ 1.5–3m (5–10ft) or more. Australia (Victoria). ✻
T. speciosissima (Common waratah, Sydney waratah). Large shrub, bushy when young, often becoming untidy with age, with narrowly obovate, round-tipped, mid-green leaves, to 25cm (10in) long, usually toothed above the middle. Flowerheads, 10–15cm (4–6in) across, each consisting of a ring of red bracts and many tubular red flowers, the outer flowers maturing first, are borne in spring. ↕ 3m (10ft), ↔ 1.5–2m (5–6ft). Australia (New South Wales). ✻
T. truncata ♀ (Tasmanian waratah). Many-branched shrub or, rarely, small tree with lance-shaped to obovate, usually entire leaves with recurved margins, to 10cm (4in) long, dull green and hairless above, silver-hairy beneath. In early summer, produces flowerheads 5–8cm (2–3in) across, each consisting of

Telopea oreades

a ring of inconspicuous, hairy, rust-red bracts and 10–20 tubular red, rarely yellow flowers, all maturing at the same time. ↕ to 8m (25ft), ↔ 1.5–3m (5–10ft). Australia (Tasmania). ✻

▷**Temple bells** see *Smithiantha*

TEMPLETONIA

LEGUMINOSAE/PAPILIONACEAE

Genus of 11 species of upright to rounded, evergreen shrubs and sub-shrubs found in dry, open scrub and drought-prone woodland in Australia. Angular or grooved, sometimes spiny branches bear alternate, simple, obovate to oblong leaves. They are grown for their pea-like flowers, borne singly or in clusters from the leaf axils, between autumn and spring. Where temperatures fall below 5–7°C (41–45°F), grow in a cool or temperate greenhouse. Elsewhere, grow in a shrub border.
• **HARDINESS** Frost tender.
• **CULTIVATION** Under glass, grow in loam-based potting compost (JI No.2) in full light. In the growing season, water freely, applying a balanced liquid fertilizer monthly; water sparingly in

Telopea mongaensis (inset: flowerhead detail)

Templetonia retusa

winter. Outdoors, grow in moist but well-drained, fertile soil in full sun. Pruning group 8; plants under glass may need restrictive pruning.
• **PROPAGATION** Sow pre-soaked seed at 16°C (61°F) in spring. Insert semi-ripe cuttings with bottom heat in summer. Layer in spring.
• **PESTS AND DISEASES** Red spider mites may be troublesome under glass.

T. retusa ■ (Cockies' tongues, Coral bush, Flame bush). Evergreen shrub, bushy when young, with alternate, obovate to oblong, leathery, glaucous, deep green leaves, 1.5–4cm (½–1½in) long. Crimson, sometimes pink or yellow-white flowers, 3–5cm (1¼–2in) long, are borne singly from the leaf axils from winter to spring. ↕ 1–3m (3–10ft), ↔ 1–2m (3–6ft). S. and W. Australia. ❀ (min. 5–7°C/41–45°F)

▷**Terebinth** see *Pistacia terebinthus*

TERMINALIA

COMBRETACEAE

Genus of 200 species of deciduous and evergreen trees, frequently buttressed, found in tropical woodland worldwide. The attractive, simple, entire, broadly obovate to oblong or elliptic leaves are either transparent or minutely pitted with transparent spots, and arranged alternately, in spirals, or in nearly opposite pairs. Insignificant, petalless, tubular flowers are borne in axillary or terminal spikes or panicles, followed by one-seeded fruits. Where temperatures fall below 13°C (55°F), grow in a temperate or warm greenhouse. In tropical climates, grow as specimen or shade trees, hedges, or windbreaks.
• **HARDINESS** Frost tender.
• **CULTIVATION** Under glass, grow in loam-based potting compost (JI No.2), with additional sharp sand, in full light. During the growing season, water moderately and apply a balanced liquid fertilizer monthly; water sparingly in winter. Outdoors, grow in moderately fertile, sandy soil in full sun. Pruning group 1; plants grown under glass need restrictive pruning.
• **PROPAGATION** Sow seed at 18–24°C (64–75°F) in spring. Layer in spring.
• **PESTS AND DISEASES** Trouble free.

T. catappa ♀ (Indian almond). Dense, spreading, deciduous tree, the branches of young specimens forming horizontal whorls. Broadly obovate to obovate, lustrous, dark green leaves, to 25cm (10in) long, borne in rosette-like clusters at the branch tips, turn red before falling. Petalless flowers have white calyces, with tubes to 1cm (½in) long, and are borne in axillary spikes, to 16cm (6in) long, in summer; they are followed by narrowly winged, ellipsoid, red, yellow, or green fruit, 5–7cm (2–3in) long, with edible seeds. ↕ 20–35m (70–120ft), ↔ 15–20m (50–70ft). Tropical Asia, Malaysia, N. Australia, Polynesia. ❀ (min. 13–15°C/55–59°F)

TERNSTROEMIA

THEACEAE

Genus of 85 species of evergreen trees and shrubs occurring in woodland in mainly tropical regions of Asia, Africa, and North and South America. They are cultivated for their handsome, usually entire, leathery leaves, their many-stamened flowers, produced singly or sometimes in small clusters, and their usually pendent, spherical, fleshy, greenish yellow then bright red fruit. *T. gymnanthera* is the most commonly cultivated species. Grow as a specimen plant, in a shrub border, or against a shady wall, or use for hedging. In frost-prone climates, grow tender species in a conservatory or cool greenhouse.
• **HARDINESS** Frost hardy to frost tender.
• **CULTIVATION** Under glass, grow in lime-free (ericaceous) compost in bright filtered light. In the growing season, water freely, applying a balanced liquid fertilizer monthly; water sparingly in winter. Outdoors, grow in moist but well-drained, humus-rich, acid soil in partial shade. Pruning group 8; plants grown under glass may need restrictive pruning. Trim hedges after flowering.
• **PROPAGATION** Sow seed as soon as ripe in containers in a cold frame. Insert semi-ripe cuttings with bottom heat in late summer.
• **PESTS AND DISEASES** Trouble free.

T. gymnanthera, syn. *T. japonica.* Rounded, evergreen shrub. Elliptic to inversely lance-shaped, leathery, glossy, very dark green leaves, to 10cm (4in) long, turning bronze in cold weather, are usually clustered at the shoot tips. White flowers, 1cm (½in) across, are produced singly or in small clusters from the leaf axils, in late spring and early summer; they are followed by spherical, greenish yellow berries, 2.5cm (1in) long, ripening to red. ↕↔ 3m (10ft). China, Taiwan, Japan. ✻✻ (borderline).
'Variegata' has leaves margined with creamy white, and tinged pink in winter; ✻
T. japonica see *T. gymnanthera.*

▷***Testudinaria elephantipes*** see *Dioscorea elephantipes*

TETRACENTRON

TETRACENTRACEAE

Genus of one species of deciduous tree found in mountain woodland in S.W. and C. China, the Himalayas, and N. Burma, cultivated for its attractive foliage and flower spikes. The alternate, simple leaves have stipule-like flanges on the stalks. Small, petalless, bisexual yellow flowers are produced in pendent

spikes in summer. *T. sinense* is suitable for a woodland garden.
- **HARDINESS** Fully hardy, but young growth may be damaged by late frosts.
- **CULTIVATION** Grow in well-drained soil in sun or partial shade. Shelter from cold, drying winds. Pruning group 1.
- **PROPAGATION** Sow seed in a seedbed in autumn. Insert semi-ripe cuttings with bottom heat in summer.
- **PESTS AND DISEASES** Trouble free.

T. sinense ♀ Graceful, spreading, deciduous tree with ovate or heart-shaped, tapered, scalloped, dark green leaves, to 12cm (5in) long, turning red in autumn. Tiny yellow flowers are borne in slender, pendent spikes, to 15cm (6in) long, from the shoot tips in summer. ↕ 17–30m (56–100ft), ↔ 10m (30ft). Himalayas, S.W. and C. China, N. Burma. ❄❄❄

TETRADIUM *syn.* EUODIA, EVODIA

RUTACEAE

Genus of 9 species of upright to rounded, deciduous or evergreen trees and shrubs found in woodland from the Himalayas to E. and S.E. Asia, and cultivated for their attractive foliage, flowers, and dense clusters of fruit. They have opposite, usually pinnate leaves. Cup-shaped flowers, each with 4 or 5 usually hooded petals, are borne in terminal or axillary corymbs or panicles. Oval to pear-shaped or spherical green fruits, with 1–5 follicles, each 1- or 2-seeded, are produced in late summer or autumn. Tetradiums make handsome specimen trees for a lawn or woodland garden. In frost-prone areas, grow tender species in a cool or temperate greenhouse.
- **HARDINESS** Fully hardy to frost tender.
- **CULTIVATION** Grow in well-drained soil in full sun or partial shade. Pruning group 1.
- **PROPAGATION** Sow seed in a seedbed in autumn. Insert root cuttings in midwinter.
- **PESTS AND DISEASES** Trouble free.

T. daniellii ▣ ♀ syn. *Euodia daniellii, E. hupehensis.* Spreading, deciduous tree bearing pinnate leaves, to 40cm (16in) or more long, each with up to 11 elliptic, ovate, or lance-shaped, glossy, dark green leaflets, turning yellow in autumn. Small, aromatic white flowers, with yellow anthers, are produced in domed, terminal corymbs, to 15cm (6in) across, in late summer and early autumn; they are followed by dense clusters of spherical, red-brown to black fruit, 8mm (3/8in) across. ↕↔ 15m (50ft). S.W. China, Korea. ❄❄❄

Tetradium daniellii

TETRANEMA

SCROPHULARIACEAE

Genus of 2 species of shrubby, evergreen perennials from moist, shady situations at altitudes up to 1,200m (4,000ft) in Mexico and Guatemala. They are cultivated for their decorative flowers, produced over a long period in summer. The many flower stems bear terminal clusters of trumpet-shaped, 2-lipped, violet, lilac, or mauve flowers, the upper lips 2-lobed, the lower ones 3-lobed; the stems arise from neat rosettes of obovate or oblong, scalloped, leathery leaves. In frost-prone areas, grow in a warm greenhouse or as houseplants. In warmer areas, grow in a shady border.
- **HARDINESS** Frost tender.
- **CULTIVATION** Under glass, grow in loam-based potting compost (JI No.2) in bright filtered light with moderate to high humidity. In summer, water freely and apply a balanced liquid fertilizer monthly; water moderately at other times. Pot on in spring. Outdoors, grow in well-drained soil in partial shade.
- **PROPAGATION** Sow seed at 18–21°C (64–70°F) as soon as ripe or in spring. Divide established clumps in spring.
- **PESTS AND DISEASES** Aphids may be a problem.

T. mexicanum see *T. roseum.*
T. roseum ▣ syn. *T. mexicanum* (Mexican foxglove, Mexican violet). Evergreen perennial with obovate, dark green leaves, to 12cm (5in) long. In summer, trumpet-shaped, 2-lipped, lilac or mauve flowers, 1.5cm (1/2in) across, with darker markings, are produced on stems to 20cm (8in) long. ↕ 20cm (8in), ↔ 15cm (6in). Mexico. ❀ (min. 13°C/55°F)

Tetranema roseum

TETRANEURIS

ASTERACEAE/COMPOSITAE

Genus of about 35 species of aromatic annuals and short-lived herbaceous perennials from plains, prairies, and mountain screes in W. and C. USA. They are grown for their aromatic foliage and flowers. Alternate, narrowly linear to lance-shaped or inversely lance-shaped, occasionally lobed, very hairy leaves are usually arranged in basal rosettes, but are occasionally distributed along the stems. The mostly solitary, daisy-like yellow flowerheads are borne in early summer. Grow in a sunny scree bed or alpine house.
- **HARDINESS** Fully hardy.
- **CULTIVATION** Outdoors, grow in sharply drained, gritty soil in full sun, protected from excessive winter wet. In an alpine house, use a mix of 2 parts grit and 1 part each loam and leaf mould. Water moderately when in growth, avoiding the foliage, and sparingly in winter.
- **PROPAGATION** Sow seed as soon as ripe in an open frame.
- **PESTS AND DISEASES** Aphids and red spider mites may prove troublesome under glass.

T. acaulis, syn. *Hymenoxys acaulis.* Tap-rooted perennial with crowded, basal rosettes of narrowly inversely lance-shaped, very hairy, grey-green leaves, 2–8cm (1/4–3in) long. Usually solitary yellow flowerheads, to 5cm (2in) across, are borne on upright, hairy stems in early summer. ↕↔ to 15cm (6in). USA (Idaho to N. Dakota, Texas, and New Mexico). ❄❄❄

TETRAPANAX

ARALIACEAE

Genus of one species of suckering, evergreen shrub or small tree occurring in woodland in S. China and Taiwan. It is grown for its large, alternate, palmately lobed leaves, its umbels of flowers, borne in panicle-like, woolly inflorescences with conspicuous bracts, and its clusters of black fruit. In frost-prone areas, grow against a warm wall, in a container moved under cover in winter, or in a cool greenhouse. In warmer climates, grow in a sheltered border. The flowers are particularly attractive to bees.
- **HARDINESS** Frost hardy (borderline).
- **CULTIVATION** Under glass, grow in loam-based potting compost (JI No.2), in full light with shade from hot sun. During the growing season, water freely and apply a balanced liquid fertilizer monthly; water sparingly in winter. Outdoors, grow in any well-drained soil in full sun, sheltered from strong winds. In order to restrict the spread of established clumps, remove suckers at the extremities. Where top-growth is killed by frost, *T. papyrifer* may be almost herbaceous, growing again from below ground. Pruning group 1 or 7.
- **PROPAGATION** Sow seed in containers in a cold frame in autumn. Remove suckers in spring or summer.
- **PESTS AND DISEASES** Trouble free.

T. papyrifer ♀ syn. *Aralia papyrifer, Fatsia papyrifera, T. papyriferus* (Rice-paper plant). Thicket-forming, sparsely branched, evergreen shrub or small tree with stout shoots. The 5- to 11-lobed leaves, to 50cm (20in) or more across, scaly, mid-green above and felted pale green beneath, are clustered at the shoot tips. In autumn, produces umbels, 1cm (1/2in) across, of white flowers in panicle-like inflorescences, to 50cm (20in) long, followed by spherical fruit, to 3mm (1/8in) across. ↕↔ 5m (15ft) or more. S. China, Taiwan. ❄❄ (borderline)
T. papyriferus see *T. papyrifer.*

TETRASTIGMA

VITACEAE

Genus of about 90 species of evergreen and deciduous tendril climbers found in tropical woodland from Indonesia and Malaysia to N. Australia. They are grown mainly for their alternate, mostly fully divided, sometimes lobed, palmate to pedate leaves. Tiny, 4-petalled flowers are borne in cyme-like, axillary umbels or clusters in summer, followed by grape-like black berries. In areas where temperatures fall below 15°C (59°F), grow in a warm greenhouse or as houseplants. In tropical climates, train over a wall or a tree stump.
- **HARDINESS** Frost tender.
- **CULTIVATION** Under glass, grow in loam-based potting compost (JI No.3), with additional leaf mould, in bright filtered or bright indirect light, with moderate to high humidity. In the growing season, water freely, applying a balanced liquid fertilizer monthly; water moderately in winter. The climbing stems need support. Outdoors, grow in moist, fertile soil in partial or dappled shade. Pruning group 11, in spring.
- **PROPAGATION** Insert semi-ripe cuttings with bottom heat in summer. Layer in spring.
- **PESTS AND DISEASES** Red spider mites may be a problem under glass.

T. voinierianum ▣ syn. *Cissus voinieriana, Vitis voinieriana* (Chestnut vine, Lizard plant). Strong-growing,

Tetrastigma voinierianum

T

evergreen climber with sturdy, hairy, densely red-brown stems. Leaves are 3- to 5-palmate, 15–40cm (6–16in) long, with broadly diamond-shaped to obovate, coarsely toothed leaflets, to 25cm (10in) long, lustrous, dark green above and brownish yellow-hairy beneath. Yellowish green flowers are borne in dense, axillary umbels or clusters, 5cm (2in) across, on mature plants in summer; they are followed by small, acidic berries. ↕ to 15m (50ft) or more. Laos. ❀ (min. 15°C/59°F)

TETRATHECA

TREMANDRACEAE

Genus of at least 20 species of small, evergreen shrubs from heathland and drought-prone forest in Australia, grown for their flowers and attractive, heather-like habit. The tiny, linear to rounded leaves are arranged alternately, in whorls, or in opposite pairs. Solitary, nodding, cross-, star-, or cup-shaped, 4- or 5-petalled flowers are borne from the upper leaf axils in spring and summer. In frost-prone regions, grow in a cool greenhouse. In milder areas, grow in a shrub border.

• **HARDINESS** Half hardy; *T. ciliare* may survive brief spells at a few degrees below 0°C (32°F).

• **CULTIVATION** Under glass, grow in lime-free (ericaceous) potting compost in full light, with shade from hot sun, and with good ventilation. In growth, water freely and apply a half-strength balanced liquid fertilizer monthly; water sparingly in winter. Outdoors, grow in humus-rich, neutral to acid soil in full sun with some midday shade. Pruning group 10, after flowering.

• **PROPAGATION** Surface-sow seed at 13–16°C (55–61°F) in spring. Insert semi-ripe cuttings with bottom heat in summer. Air layer in spring.

• **PESTS AND DISEASES** Trouble free.

T. ciliata. Twiggy, tufted shrub with wiry, densely hairy stems and whorls of 3 broadly ovate, mid- to dark green leaves, 5mm (¼in) long, fringed with hairs. From spring to summer, cup-shaped, rose-pink flowers, 1–2cm (½–¾in) across, each with 4 oblong petals, are produced from the upper leaf axils. ↕↔ 40–50cm (16–20in). S. Australia. ❄

TEUCRIUM

LABIATAE/LAMIACEAE

Genus of approximately 300 species of herbaceous perennials and evergreen and deciduous shrubs and subshrubs, found mainly in thickets, woodland, dry, rocky places, and mountainous areas worldwide, especially in the Mediterranean region. Teucriums are grown for their attractive habit, aromatic foliage, and whorled clusters or racemes of 2–6 tubular to bell-shaped, sometimes 2-lipped flowers. The leaves, arranged in opposite pairs, are simple or lobed, and entire or toothed. Teucriums have a variety of garden uses: the small species, to 30cm (12in) tall, are suitable for a rock garden, raised bed, or trough; grow the shrubs, such as *T. fruticans*, in a sheltered border or against a warm, sunny wall, or use for hedging in mild climates.

Teucrium fruticans

• **HARDINESS** Fully hardy to frost hardy.

• **CULTIVATION** Grow in well-drained, preferably neutral to alkaline soil in full sun; the smallest species retain their compact habit better on poor, gritty soil. Pruning group 7 for *T. fruticans.*

• **PROPAGATION** Sow seed in containers in a cold frame as soon as ripe. Insert softwood cuttings in early summer, or semi-ripe cuttings in midsummer, both with bottom heat. Overwinter young plants of frost-hardy species in a cool greenhouse.

• **PESTS AND DISEASES** Trouble free.

T. aroanium, syn. *T. aroanum.* Low-growing, evergreen subshrub producing branching, stoloniferous, densely hairy stems and ovate or elliptic to oblong, aromatic, silver-hairy leaves, to 2cm (¾in) long. In summer, 2-lipped purple flowers, to 2cm (¾in) long, are borne in short-stemmed, axillary clusters. ↕ to 8cm (3in), ↔ to 20cm (8in). S. Greece. ❄❄❄

T. aroanum see *T. aroanium.*

T. fruticans ▣ (Shrubby germander, Tree germander). Bushy, evergreen shrub with arching, white-woolly shoots and aromatic, ovate to lance-shaped, grey-green leaves, to 2cm (¾in) long, white-woolly beneath. In summer, whorls of pale blue flowers, 2.5cm (1in) long, with prominent stamens, are borne in terminal racemes, to 10cm (4in) long. ↕ 60–100cm (24–39in), ↔ 4m (12ft). W. Mediterranean. ❄❄. **'Azureum'** has dark blue flowers.

Teucrium polium

T. polium ▣ Mound-forming, deciduous subshrub with decumbent to erect, white- to tawny-woolly stems. Bears stemless, linear or oblong to lance-shaped, wrinkled, white-woolly, grey-green leaves, to 3.5cm (1½in) long. In summer, 2-lipped, purple or yellow flowers, to 1cm (½in) long, are borne in abundant dense, flat-topped, terminal clusters. ↕↔ 30cm (12in). Mediterranean to W. Asia. ❄❄❄

T. subspinosum. Shrubby perennial with ascending, twisted, branching, white-woolly stems; there are short spines on the branchlets. The diamond-shaped to lance-shaped or linear, grey-green leaves, to 7mm (¼in) long, are often densely white-woolly beneath. In summer, 2-lipped pink flowers, to 8mm (⅜in) long, are produced in loose, terminal racemes, to 5cm (2in) long. ↕↔ 20cm (8in). Balearic Islands (Majorca). ❄❄❄

THALIA

MARANTACEAE

Genus of 12 species of evergreen or herbaceous, marginal aquatic perennials found at the swampy margins of lakes and ponds from S.E. USA to Argentina, including the West Indies, with one species in tropical Africa. They have handsome, long-stalked, ovate-lance-shaped leaves, and bear unusual violet flowers, with enlarged staminodes, in 2 ranks in long-stalked, branched panicles. In frost-prone areas, grow in a pool in a cool greenhouse. In warmer areas, grow as specimen plants in and around a tropical pool or bog garden.

• **HARDINESS** Half hardy to frost tender; if well below water level, *T. dealbata*

Thalia dealbata

survives occasional temperatures to -5°C (23°F) but then becomes deciduous.

• **CULTIVATION** Grow in a large aquatic planting basket of fertile, loamy soil, or in deep, humus-rich mud in water up to 15cm (6in) deep, at the edge of a sunny pool. In summer, apply a proprietary aquatic plant fertilizer monthly. Remove old leaves and flowers regularly. Under glass, grow in baskets of loam-based potting compost (JI No.3) in full light, with a minimum temperature of 10°C (50°F). See also pp.52–53.

• **PROPAGATION** Sow seed at 16–21°C (61–70°F) in moist propagating compost, as soon as ripe or in spring. Divide in spring.

• **PESTS AND DISEASES** Trouble free.

T. dealbata ▣ Evergreen, marginal aquatic perennial with ovate to lance-shaped, white-floury, grey-green leaves, 50cm (20in) long, on leaf-stalks 30–60cm (12–24in) long. In summer, produces violet flowers, 1.5–2cm (½–¾in) across. They are borne in slender panicles, to 20cm (8in) long. ↕ 2–3m (6–10ft), ↔ 2m (6ft). S. USA, Mexico. ❄ (borderline)

T. geniculata. Evergreen, marginal aquatic perennial bearing ovate to lance-shaped, grey-green leaves, to 60cm (24in) long, on leaf-stalks to 1.8m (6ft) long. In summer, bears violet flowers, 1.5–2cm (½–¾in) across, in lax, pendent panicles, to 20cm (8in) long. ↕↔ 2m (6ft). Tropical Africa, USA (Florida) to Argentina, West Indies. ❄ (borderline)

THALICTRUM

Meadow rue

RANUNCULACEAE

Genus of about 130 species of rhizomatous or tuberous perennials found by streams, in meadows, and in moist, shady, often mountainous areas worldwide (except Australasia), mainly in N. temperate regions. The usually erect stems bear alternate, ternate to 4-ternate or 2- to 4-pinnate, sometimes glaucous leaves with lobed or toothed leaflets, the end leaflet longer than the others. The many tiny, petalless flowers are borne in axillary or terminal corymbs, racemes, or panicles; they have petal-like sepals and often numerous showy stamens and pistils in white, yellow, pink, lilac-pink, or violet, giving a fluffy effect. Grown for their attractive foliage and flowers, the taller species are

T

excellent background plants for a border, or a wild or woodland garden; the smaller species are suitable for a shady rock garden, peat bed, or alpine house. Except for *T. aquilegiifolium* and *T. flavum*, most grow best in areas with cool, damp summers. In frost-prone climates, grow tender species in a cool greenhouse.

- **HARDINESS** Fully hardy to frost tender.
- **CULTIVATION** Grow in moist, humus-rich soil in partial shade; *T. flavum* subsp. *glaucum* tolerates drier soil and more sun. Grow smaller, alpine species in moist, humus-rich, acid soil in cool partial shade. Tall species and cultivars need staking. Divide and replant *T. delavayi* 'Hewitt's Double' every 2 or 3 years to maintain vigour. All start into growth in mid- or late spring, so take care to avoid damage to dormant plants when cultivating earlier in the year.
- **PROPAGATION** Sow seed in containers in a cold frame as soon as ripe or in early spring. Divide as new growth begins in spring; divisions may be slow to re-establish. *T. delavayi* 'Hewitt's Double' is sterile, and may be increased only by division.
- **PESTS AND DISEASES** Susceptible to powdery mildew in dry conditions. Slugs may be a problem.

T. aquilegiifolium ■ Erect, clump-forming, rhizomatous perennial with 2- or 3-pinnate, hairless leaves, to 30cm (12in) long, composed of obovate, wavy-margined leaflets. Clustered, fluffy flowers, 8–10mm (3/8–1/2in) long, with greenish white sepals, falling to reveal numerous bright purple-pink or white stamens, are produced in spreading, flat-topped, terminal panicles on glaucous stems in early summer. ↕ to 1m (3ft), ↔ 45cm (18in). Europe to temperate Asia. ✻✻✻. **'Purple Cloud'** see 'Thundercloud'. **'Thundercloud'**, syn. 'Purple Cloud', has dark purple stamens. **'White Cloud'** has yellow-tipped white stamens.

T. chelidonii. Erect, clump-forming, rhizomatous perennial bearing 2- or 3-pinnate or ternate, hairless leaves, to 45cm (18in) long, with ovate to almost rounded, many-toothed leaflets. During late summer and early autumn, fluffy flowers, to 2.5cm (1in) across, with conspicuous mauve sepals and shorter, pendent yellow stamens, are produced in terminal and axillary panicles. ↕ 0.3–2.5m (1–8ft), ↔ 60cm (24in). C. and E. Himalayas. ✻✻✻

Thalictrum aquilegiifolium

Thalictrum delavayi 'Album'

T. delavayi, syn. *T. dipterocarpum* of gardens. Erect, hairless, clump-forming, rhizomatous perennial with slender stems, shaded dark purple, and usually 2- or 3-pinnate or ternate leaves, to 35cm (14in) long, with entire or 3-lobed leaflets. From midsummer to early autumn, numerous long-stalked, fluffy flowers, to 2.5cm (1in) across, with large, lilac to white sepals, 1.5cm (1/2in) long, and clusters of yellowish white stamens, are borne in widely branching, pyramidal, terminal and axillary panicles. ↕ 1.2m (4ft) or more, ↔ 60cm (24in). E. Tibet to W. China. ✻✻✻. **'Album'** ■ has flowers with white sepals. **'Hewitt's Double'** ■ lacks stamens but has more numerous rich mauve sepals, forming long-lasting, rounded, pompon-like flowers.

T. diffusiflorum. Erect, clump-forming, rhizomatous perennial, similar to *T. chelidonii*, bearing 2- or 3-pinnate or ternate, greyish green leaves, to 20cm (8in) long, with rounded, almost circular, slightly toothed, finely hairy leaflets. In summer, bears fluffy flowers, 2.5cm (1¼in) across, with light pinkish mauve sepals and much shorter, pendent yellow stamens, in loose, few- to many-

Thalictrum delavayi 'Hewitt's Double'

Thalictrum flavum subsp. *glaucum*

flowered, axillary and terminal panicles. ↕ 90cm (36in) or more, ↔ 30cm (12in). S.E. Tibet. ✻✻✻

***T. dipterocarpum* of gardens** see *T. delavayi.*

T. flavum (Yellow meadow rue). Clump-forming, rhizomatous perennial producing 2- or 3-pinnate, hairless leaves, to 40cm (16in) long, composed of obovate, 3- or 4-lobed leaflets. In summer, numerous fragrant flowers, 5mm (1/4in) long, with small yellow sepals and longer, erect, bright yellow stamens, are produced in erect, compact, narrowly ovoid, axillary and terminal panicles on stout, furrowed stems. ↕ to 1m (3ft), ↔ 45cm (18in). Europe to Caucasus, Russia (Siberia). ✻✻✻. **subsp. *glaucum*** ■ syn. *T. speciosissimum*, has glaucous stems and foliage, the leaflets with prominent veins beneath, and larger panicles of paler, sulphur-yellow flowers; ↔ 60cm (24in); Portugal, Spain, N.W. Africa. **'Illuminator'** has bright green leaves, emerging yellow-green, and lemon-yellow flowers; ↕ 1.2m (4ft).

T. kiusianum ■ Mat-forming perennial with short rhizomes and fern-like, ternate or 2-ternate, dark blue-green leaves, to 12cm (5in) long, with ovate, 3- to 5-lobed leaflets. Pale pinkish mauve flowers, 1cm (1/2in) across, with conspicuous stamens, are borne in few-flowered, short-stemmed corymbs in early summer. Grow in a damp, shady peat bed, trough, rock garden, or alpine house. Prefers peaty soil. ↕ to 10cm (4in), ↔ to 30cm (12in). Japan. ✻✻✻

T. orientale. Slow-growing, clump-forming, rhizomatous perennial with

Thalictrum kiusianum

Thalictrum rochebruneanum

fern-like, 2-ternate, blue-green leaves, to 12cm (5in) long, with rounded, 3-lobed leaflets. Deep pinkish blue flowers, 1.5cm (1/2in) long, are produced in few-flowered, wiry-stemmed corymbs in late spring and early summer. Difficult to propagate. ↕↔ to 30cm (12in). Greece to Caucasus. ✻✻✻

T. rochebruneanum ■ Upright, hairless, clump-forming, rhizomatous perennial with 3- or 4-ternate leaves, to 45cm (18in) long, composed of obovate to elliptic, entire or lobed leaflets. White or lavender-pink flowers, 1.5cm (1/2in) long, with pendent stamens, are produced in loose panicles in summer. ↕ 90cm (36in), ↔ 30cm (12in). Japan. ✻✻✻

T. speciosissimum see *T. flavum* subsp. *glaucum.*

THAMNOCALAMUS

GRAMINEAE/POACEAE

Genus of about 4 species of vigorous, clump-forming, evergreen bamboos occurring in damp mountain woodland, mainly in the Himalayas and China, with one in South Africa. They are deep-rooted plants with round, many-branched, thick, hollow canes, often covered with a waxy blue or glaucous white bloom. The alternate, linear or lance-shaped, mid- to greyish green leaves are small, generally 12–20cm (5–8in) long, thin-textured, tessellated, and sometimes glaucous. With their graceful, erect to arching habit, they are valuable as large specimen plants or for screening.

- **HARDINESS** Fully hardy to frost hardy.
- **CULTIVATION** Tolerant of most soils in full sun or partial shade but avoid waterlogged conditions. Thin clumps by removing older canes in spring as young canes emerge.
- **PROPAGATION** Divide established clumps, preferably in spring.
- **PESTS AND DISEASES** Mostly trouble free.

T. aristatus, syn. *Arundinaria aristata*. Erect to arching bamboo with yellow-green canes, 2cm (3/4in) across, later speckled brown. Each swollen node produces up to 5 branches, bearing linear to lance-shaped, mid-green leaves, to about 12cm (5in) long. Deciduous, hairy cane sheaths are papery, cream to pale green. ↕ 3–6m (10–20ft), ↔ 3m (10ft) or more. N.E. Himalayas to China. ✻✻

Thamnocalamus spathiflorus

***T. aristatus* of gardens** see *T. spathiflorus*.
T. crassinodus see *T. spathiflorus* f. *crassinodus*.
T. falconeri see *Himalayacalamus falconeri*.
***T. spathaceus* of gardens** see *Fargesia murielae*.
T. spathiflorus ■ syn. *Arundinaria spathiflora*, *T. aristatus* of gardens. Erect to arching bamboo, sometimes confused with *Fargesia murieliae*, with flexible grey canes, 2cm (¾in) across, glaucous at first, later flushed pink in bright light. Each swollen node produces 2–5 branches bearing lance-shaped, soft greyish green leaves, 12cm (5in) long, with deciduous, almost hairless, cream to pale green cane sheaths. ↕ to 6m (20ft), ↔ 3m (10ft) or more. N.W. Himalayas. ✲✲. **f. *crassinodus*** ■ syn. *T. crassinodus*, has an arching habit, olive-green canes, 1–2cm (½–¾in) across, glaucous when young, with more swollen nodes and smaller leaves, 6cm (2½in) long; ↕ 3–4m (10–12ft).
f. *crassinodus* 'Kew Beauty' produces erect, blue-grey young canes, which age to brownish red then deep red, and very small leaves, 5cm (2in) long.
f. *crassinodus* 'Merlyn' has green canes and branches turning to yellow-green.
T. tessellatus, syn. *Arundinaria tessellata*. Erect bamboo with yellowish green canes, 1.5–3cm (½–1¼in) across, turning purple, especially in bright light. Each swollen node produces 5–8 branches bearing finely tapered, linear to lance-shaped, glaucous, mid-green leaves, 10–20cm (4–8in) long, and conspicuous, persistent, papery, pale cream to white cane sheaths. Leaves are not produced on first year canes, but eventually the canes become densely leafy. ↕ 4m (12ft) or more, ↔ 2m (6ft) or more. South Africa (Eastern Cape, Western Cape, Northern Cape, KwaZulu/Natal), Lesotho. ✲✲

Thamnocalamus spathiflorus f. *crassinodus*

THAMNOCHORTUS

RESTIONACEAE

Genus of 34 species of rhizomatous or tufted, evergreen perennials, growing in stony or sandy soils in S.W. and South Africa, and cultivated for their elegant graceful culms and delicate, grassy flowerheads. In some species, short, thread-like, feathery sterile branchlets are clustered around the culm nodes. The brown spikelets are borne in summer, the males and females on separate plants. The leaves are reduced to sheath-like structures that are split to the base, and the unbranched culms are covered in the lower part by persistent sheaths. The sheaths are membranous above and often become frayed with age. In frost-prone climates, grow as specimen plants in containers; in

Thamnochortus lucens

warmer climates, grow as specimen plants or in borders.
• **HARDINESS** Frost hardy to half hardy.
• **CULTIVATION** Grow in moderately fertile, well-drained, acid soil in full sun. *T. insignis* tolerates alkaline soil.
• **PROPAGATION** Sow seed at 16–18°C (61–64°F) in spring, after soaking for 24 hours in warm water. Divide rhizomes in early spring.
• **PESTS AND DISEASES** Red spider mites and whiteflies may cause problems under glass.

T. insignis (Roof reed). Tufted perennial with sterile, unbranched, smooth, dark green culms arising from vigorous rhizomes. Erect, mid-brown female spikelets and pendent, mid-brown male spikelets are borne in tight clusters in summer. Each floret is at least as wide as long, 2–3mm (1⁄16–⅛in). Tolerates sand- and salt-laden winds. ↕ 1.5–2m (5–6ft), ↔ 2.5–3m (8–10ft). South Africa (Western Cape). ✲✲
T. lucens ■ Tufted perennial arising from a short rhizome, often with tangled clusters of sterile, short, unbranched, smooth, mid-green branchlets at the base and at the nodes in the year after flowering. Erect, purplish brown female spikelets and pendent, chestnut-brown male spikelets are borne in almost horizontal clusters in summer. Each floret is at least as wide as long, 4–5mm (⅛–¼in). ↕ 70–90cm (28–36in), ↔ 40–60cm (16–24in). South Africa (Western Cape). ✲

▷**Thatch,**
Brittle see *Thrinax morrisii*
Buffalo see *Thrinax morrisii*
Silver see *Coccothrinax fragrans*
▷**Thatch palm** see *Coccothrinax, Thrinax, T. parviflora*

THELOCACTUS

CACTACEAE

Genus of about 11 species of spherical to short-cylindrical, ribbed or warty, perennial cacti occurring in arid regions of S.W. USA and C., E., and N. Mexico. In summer, large, funnel- to bell-shaped, diurnal flowers are borne on or near the slightly depressed crowns. In areas where temperatures fall below 7°C (45°F), grow *Thelocactus* species as houseplants, or in a cool or temperate greenhouse. In warm, dry climates, they are suitable for a border with other cacti, or for a desert garden.

• **HARDINESS** Frost tender.
• **CULTIVATION** Under glass, grow in standard cactus compost in full light, with low humidity. From mid-spring to early autumn, water moderately, applying fertilizer 2 or 3 times; keep completely dry at other times of year. Outdoors, grow in poor to moderately fertile, gritty, sharply drained soil in full sun. See also pp.48–49.
• **PROPAGATION** Sow seed at 21°C (70°F) in spring. Detach offsets in spring or early summer.
• **PESTS AND DISEASES** Mealybugs may be a problem.

T. bicolor ■ syn. *Ferocactus bicolor*. Simple, rarely clustering cactus bearing spherical, often slightly elongated, bluish green stems. Each rib has 8–13 straight or spirally arranged, warty ribs. Areoles, which have nectar-secreting glands, produce red, yellow, or white spines (8–18 radials and 4 slightly longer centrals, the uppermost of which is flat). Funnel-shaped, red-throated, dark purple-pink flowers, 4–8cm (1½–3in) across, are produced in summer. ↕ 15–20cm (6–8in), ↔ 10cm (4in). USA (Texas), N. and E. Mexico. ❀ (min. 7°C/45°F)
T. leucacanthus. Frequently offsetting cactus producing spherical to cylindrical, pale green stems, each bearing 7–14 straight or slightly spiralling, conical, warty ribs. The areoles, which have nectar-secreting glands, produce yellow, red, grey, or black spines (6–20 yellow, sometimes red-tinged radials and 1–3 yellow, red, or black centrals). The short-tubed and

Thelocactus bicolor

T

funnel-shaped flowers, 4–5cm (1½–2in) across and varying from pale to deep yellow or magenta, are produced in summer. ↕ to 15cm (6in), ↔ to 20cm (8in). C. Mexico. ❀ (min. 7°C/45°F)
T. macdowellii, syn. *Echinocactus macdowellii.* Sometimes clustering cactus producing spherical to club-shaped, pale green stems, each bearing 20–25 conical, warty ribs. The white-felted areoles are densely arranged, and produce glassy, transparent, white or pale yellow spines (15–20 radials and 3 or 4 yellowish white centrals, the centrals longer than the radials). Funnel-shaped magenta flowers, 5cm (2in) or more across, are produced in summer. ↕ to 15cm (6in), ↔ 10cm (4in). N.E. Mexico. ❀ (min. 7°C/45°F)
T. setispinus, syn. *Ferocactus setispinus, Hamatocactus setispinus.* Solitary cactus, later offsetting, producing spherical to short-cylindrical, dark green stems. Each stem has 12–15 notched, often wavy ribs. Rounded to elliptic, straw-coloured areoles produce white or brown spines (9–17 white or red-tinged radials and 1 pale yellow, sometimes red-tinged, hooked central). Funnel-shaped, red-throated yellow flowers, to 5cm (2in) across, are produced from summer to autumn. ↕ 20cm (8in), ↔ 12cm (5in). USA (Texas), N.E. Mexico. ❀ (min. 7°C/45°F)

▷ ***Thelycrania*** see *Cornus*
T. alba see *C. alba*

THELYPTERIS

THELYPTERIDACEAE

Genus of 2 species of deciduous, terrestrial ferns found in swamps and bogs in temperate regions throughout the world. The lance-shaped, pinnate fronds, comprising deeply lobed pinnae, arise from creeping rhizomes. Sori, which have no protective indusia, form on the undersides of the fronds. Grow in a moist border, or plant at the edge of a pond; *T. palustris* may be invasive.
• **HARDINESS** Fully hardy.
• **CULTIVATION** Grow in any moist, moderately fertile soil in full sun or partial shade.
• **PROPAGATION** Sow spores at 15°C (59°F) as soon as ripe. Divide in spring or summer. See also p.51.
• **PESTS AND DISEASES** Trouble free.

T. hexagonoptera see *Phegopteris hexagonoptera.*

Thelypteris palustris

T. palustris ▣ (Marsh fern). Deciduous fern producing long, creeping rhizomes and long-stalked, erect, lance-shaped, pinnate, pale green sterile fronds, to 40cm (16in) long, each consisting of up to 25 pairs of narrowly lance-shaped, deeply lobed pinnae. Fertile fronds, 90cm (36in) long, which are produced only in good light, have pinnae with narrower lobes. The abundant sori may produce a brown haze over the colony in late summer. ↕ 60cm (24in), ↔ to 1m (3ft). Europe, Asia. ❄❄❄
T. phegopteris see *Phegopteris connectilis.*

THERMOPSIS

LEGUMINOSAE/PAPILIONACEAE

Genus of approximately 20 species of rhizomatous perennials that grow on grassy mountainsides, in light woodland, and at streamsides in Siberia (Russia), N. India, E. Asia, and North America. They are cultivated for their attractive foliage and racemes of lupin-like flowers. Erect stems bear alternate, stalked, 3-palmate leaves, sometimes silver-hairy, with persistent, leafy stipules; the similar basal leaves are produced in smaller numbers. The pea-like, yellow or purple flowers, with rounded standard petals and roughly equal-sized keel and wing petals, are borne in terminal or axillary racemes. Suitable for growing in a mixed or herbaceous border, or a wildflower garden; *T. rhombifolia* is invasive and best in a wild garden. The flowers are attractive to bees.
• **HARDINESS** Fully hardy.
• **CULTIVATION** Grow in light, well-drained, fertile, loamy soil in full sun or partial shade, although they will tolerate a range of conditions. Usually long-lived, they have tough roots that resent disturbance.
• **PROPAGATION** Sow seed at 10–13°C (50–55°F) in spring, transplanting seedlings to their final growing position as soon as they are large enough to be

Thermopsis villosa

handled. Division is difficult, and divisions are very slow to re-establish.
• **PESTS AND DISEASES** Slugs and aphids may be a problem.

T. caroliniana see *T. villosa.*
T. montana see *T. rhombifolia.*
T. rhombifolia ▣ syn. *T. montana.* Rhizomatous perennial producing unbranched stems and 3-palmate leaves, to 11cm (4½in) long, with broadly ovate leaflets. The stems and lower leaf surfaces are softly silver-hairy. In early summer, yellow flowers, 2.5cm (1in) long, are produced in erect, terminal racemes. ↕ 90cm (36in), ↔ 60cm (24in). USA (Rocky Mountains to New Mexico). ❄❄❄
T. villosa ▣ syn. *T. caroliniana* (Carolina lupin). Rhizomatous perennial with stout, few-branched or branchless, hairless stems. The 3-palmate leaves, to 10cm (4in) long, have elliptic, obovate, or lance-shaped leaflets, hairless above, glaucous and silky-hairy beneath. In late spring and early summer, downy yellow flowers, to 2cm (¾in) long, are borne in erect, compact, terminal racemes. ↕ 1–1.5m (3–5ft), ↔ 60cm (24in). USA (North Carolina to Georgia). ❄❄❄

Thermopsis rhombifolia

THESPESIA

MALVACEAE

Genus of 17 species of mainly evergreen shrubs and trees, closely allied to *Hibiscus*, occurring throughout the world in a wide range of habitats, often in coastal areas of tropical regions. They are grown for their cup-shaped flowers, each with 5 spreading petals, produced singly or in clusters from the leaf axils. The leaves are alternate, simple, mainly lance-shaped to broadly ovate, or palmately 5- to 9-lobed. In areas where temperatures fall below 13–15°C (55–59°F), grow in a warm greenhouse. In tropical climates, grow as specimen plants, screens, or windbreaks, especially in coastal areas.
• **HARDINESS** Frost tender.
• **CULTIVATION** Under glass, grow in loam-based potting compost (JI No.3) in full light. In growth, water freely, applying a balanced liquid fertilizer monthly; water sparingly in winter. Outdoors, grow in moist but well-drained, fertile soil in full sun. Pruning group 1; plants under glass may need restrictive pruning.
• **PROPAGATION** Sow seed at 16°C (61°F) in spring. Insert semi-ripe cuttings with bottom heat in summer. Air layer in spring or summer.
• **PESTS AND DISEASES** Susceptible to red spider mites and whiteflies under glass.

T. populnea ♀ (Portia tree). Erect to spreading, bushy, evergreen tree bearing long-stalked, heart-shaped to ovate, light to mid-green leaves, 6–12cm (2½–5in) long, with nectar-bearing zones at the bases of the midribs. Solitary yellow flowers, 5–8cm (2–3in) across, with maroon-marked centres, open in sequence throughout the year in warm areas; they fade to dull purple. ↕ 10–15m (30–50ft), ↔ 5–8m (15–25ft). Coastal tropics. ❀ (min. 13–15°C/55–59°F)

THEVETIA

APOCYNACEAE

Genus of 8 species of evergreen shrubs and small trees from woodland, often near coastal areas, in tropical North and South America and the West Indies. They are cultivated for their showy, funnel-shaped flowers, with 5 overlapping petals, produced singly or in cymes from spring to autumn. They have alternate, simple, mostly linear to ovate leaves. Where temperatures fall below 13–15°C (55–59°F), grow in a temperate or warm greenhouse. In warmer climates, grow in a shrub border. The seeds are highly toxic if ingested.
• **HARDINESS** Frost tender.
• **CULTIVATION** Under glass, grow in loam-based potting compost (JI No.2) in full light and with good ventilation. During the growing season, water freely and apply a balanced liquid fertilizer monthly; water sparingly in winter. Outdoors, grow in moist but well-drained, fertile soil in full sun. Pruning group 1; plants under glass need restrictive pruning.
• **PROPAGATION** Sow seed at 18–21°C (64–70°F) in spring. Insert semi-ripe cuttings with bottom heat in summer.
• **PESTS AND DISEASES** Trouble free.

Thevetia peruviana

T. neriifolia see *T. peruviana.*
T. peruviana ▣ ◊ syn. *T. neriifolia.* Erect, open shrub or small tree with narrowly lance-shaped, lustrous, mid- to dark green leaves, 8–15cm (3–6in) long. Bears fragrant, apricot-yellow flowers, to 7cm (3in) long, in few-flowered cymes near the shoot-tips from spring to autumn, followed by triangular-ovoid, semi-fleshy, red, later black seed pods, each containing 1 or 2 nut-like seeds. ↕ 2–8m (6–25ft), ↔ 1–3m (3–10ft). Tropical America. ❀ (min. 13–15°C/ 55–59°F). **'Alba'** has white flowers.

▷**Thistle,**
Blessed Mary's see *Silybum marianum*
Carline see *Carlina*
Cotton see *Onopordum*
Globe see *Echinops*
Mountain see *Acanthus montanus*
Mountain sow see *Cicerbita alpina*
Scotch see *Onopordum*
Stemless Carline see *Carlina acaulis*

THLADIANTHA

CUCURBITACEAE

Genus of 23 species of annual climbers and herbaceous, dioecious, tuberous climbing perennials, found in forest margins and scrub from E. Asia to Malaysia. The fast-growing, annual, hairy stems bear tendrils and alternate leaves that are usually heart-shaped and toothed. They are grown for their showy racemes of bell-shaped, yellow male flowers, borne in the axils in early and midsummer, and are ideal for clothing a wall or fence with foliage. The female flowers are also yellow, but are solitary or occasionally borne in small clusters, and may be followed by oblong-ovoid to globose fruit, 3–5cm (1¼–2in) long.
• **HARDINESS** Fully hardy to frost hardy.
• **CULTIVATION** Grow in fertile, well-drained soil in a sheltered site in full sun or partial shade. Provide support and protect young shoots of small tubers.
• **PROPAGATION** Sow seed at 13–18°C (55–64°F) in late winter or early spring. Take basal cuttings or divide tubers in spring.
• **PESTS AND DISEASES** Trouble free.

T. dubia. Tuberous, climbing perennial with unbranched tendrils and shortly pointed, heart-shaped to ovate, toothed leaves, 5–10cm (2–4in) long. Bears racemes of reflexed, bell-shaped, yellow male flowers, to 2.5cm (1in) long. Female flowers are similar but borne singly on short stalks in the leaf axils. ↕ 3m (10ft). Korea, N.E. China. ❄❄❄
T. oliveri. Tuberous, climbing perennial bearing branched tendrils and rounded, heart-shaped, toothed leaves, 10–25cm (4–10in) long. Bears bell-shaped, yellow male flowers, to 2.5cm (1in) long, with reflexed petals, in many-flowered axillary racemes; female flowers are solitary. ↕ 4m (12ft). China. ❄❄

THLASPI

BRASSICACEAE/CRUCIFERAE

Genus of about 60 species of annuals, biennials, and short-lived perennials found in alpine pasture, in mountain woodland, or among rocks and screes in N. temperate regions. They produce oblong or spoon-shaped to broadly ovate or rounded, entire or toothed leaves, usually in rosettes, and are grown for their racemes of 4-petalled, cross-shaped flowers, borne from spring to early summer. Suitable for a sunny rock garden, scree bed, or alpine house.
• **HARDINESS** Fully hardy.
• **CULTIVATION** Grow in gritty, humus-rich, sharply drained soil in full sun with some midday shade. In an alpine house, use a mix of equal parts loam, leaf mould, and sharp grit.
• **PROPAGATION** Sow seed as soon as ripe in pots in an open frame. May self-seed.
• **PESTS AND DISEASES** Slugs and snails may be a problem.

T. bulbosum. Tufted, tuberous-rooted perennial with rosettes of ovate to ovate-oblong or rounded, entire or toothed, glaucous, dark green leaves, to 2.5cm (1in) long. Deep purple-violet flowers, 6–8mm (¼–⅜in) across, with spoon-shaped petals, are produced in loose, spike-like racemes in spring. ↕ to 10cm (4in), ↔ to 20cm (8in). C. Greece, Aegean Islands. ❄❄❄
***T. cepaeifolium* subsp. *rotundifolium*.** Short-lived, tufted perennial bearing broadly ovate to almost rounded, deep green leaves, to 1.5cm (½in) long. From spring to early summer, fragrant, deep violet-blue flowers, 1cm (½in) long, are produced in short-stemmed, congested, head-like racemes. ↕↔ to 10cm (4in). Europe (Alps, Apennines). ❄❄❄
T. macrophyllum see *Pachyphragma macrophyllum.*

▷**Thorn,**
Chinese box see *Lycium barbarum*
Christ's see *Euphorbia milii* var. *splendens, Paliurus spina-christi*
Cockspur see *Crataegus crus-galli*
Glastonbury see *Crataegus monogyna* 'Biflora'
Goat's see *Astragalus*
Jerusalem see *Paliurus spina-christi, Parkinsonia aculeata*
Kangaroo see *Acacia paradoxa*
Tansy-leaved see *Crataegus tanacetifolia*
Washington see *Crataegus phaenopyrum*
▷**Thorns, Crown of** see *Euphorbia milii*
▷**Thorow-wax** see *Bupleurum*
▷**Thousand mothers** see *Tolmiea menziesii*
▷**Three-men-in-a-boat** see *Tradescantia spathacea*
▷**Thrift** see *Armeria*
Sea see *A. maritima*

THRINAX

Thatch palm

ARECACEAE/PALMAE

Genus of 7 species of single-stemmed palms, found in forested areas on well-drained, often limestone soils, from sea-level to 1,200m (4,000ft), in the USA (Florida), Mexico, Belize, and the Caribbean islands. Long-stalked, fan-shaped, palmately lobed leaves are borne in a terminal, almost spherical head. Produces small, cup-shaped flowers, composed of a fused, 3-lobed calyx and a 3-lobed corolla, in panicles between the leaves. In frost-prone areas, grow in a warm greenhouse or as houseplants. In tropical regions, grow in a shrub border or as specimen plants on a lawn.
• **HARDINESS** Frost tender.
• **CULTIVATION** Under glass, grow in loam-based potting compost (JI No.3) in full light or bright filtered light. During growth, water freely and apply a balanced liquid fertilizer monthly; water sparingly in winter. Pot on or top-dress in spring. Outdoors, grow in moist but well-drained, fertile soil in full sun.
• **PROPAGATION** Sow seed at 27°C (81°F) in spring.
• **PESTS AND DISEASES** Red spider mites may be a problem under glass.

T. bahamensis see *T. morrisii.*
T. microcarpa see *T. morrisii.*
T. morrisii ▣ ✝ syn. *T. bahamensis, T. microcarpa, T. ponceana* (Brittle thatch, Buffalo thatch, Key palm). Small palm with a slim, erect stem. Leaves, 75cm (30in) long, are divided to halfway into 33–58 narrow lobes, densely white- to tan-scaly beneath when young, then glabrous blue-green above; they have fibrous-based leaf-stalks, to 80cm (32in) long. White to yellow or orange flowers are borne in loose, arching panicles, to 1.5m (5ft) long, usually in summer. ↕ 5–10m (15–30ft), ↔ 2–3.5m (6–11ft). USA (Florida), Cuba, West Indies. ❀ (min. 16°C/61°F)

Thrinax morrisii

T. parviflora ✝ (Broom palm, Thatch palm). Small to medium-sized palm with a slim stem. Leaves, to 1m (3ft) long, are divided to halfway into 35–60 narrow lobes, sparsely scaly beneath, rich green above; they have leaf-stalks 40–130cm (16–54in) long. Fragrant, cream to yellow flowers are produced in panicles, 0.5–1.7m (20–66in) long, usually in summer. ↕ 6–13m (20–43ft), ↔ 1.5–3.5m (5–11ft). Jamaica. ❀ (min. 16°C/61°F)
T. ponceana see *T. morrisii.*

▷**Throatwort** see *Campanula trachelium*
Blue see *Trachelium caeruleum*

THRYPTOMENE

Heath myrtle

MYRTACEAE

Genus of 25 species of upright to spreading, evergreen shrubs, found on rocky slopes and heathland in Australia, and grown for their flowers and foliage. The wiry stems bear small, simple, oblong or obovate to inversely lance-shaped leaves in opposite pairs, and produce an abundance of saucer-shaped flowers, each with 5 petals and 5 tepals, from winter to summer. In frost-prone areas, grow in a cool greenhouse. In milder climates, grow heath myrtles in a shrub border.
• **HARDINESS** Frost tender.
• **CULTIVATION** Under glass, grow in lime-free (ericaceous) potting compost in full light with good ventilation. During the growing season, water moderately and apply a half-strength, balanced liquid fertilizer monthly; water sparingly in winter. Outdoors, grow in light, well-drained, moderately fertile, neutral to acid soil in full sun. Pruning group 10, after flowering.
• **PROPAGATION** Surface-sow seed at 13°C (55°F) in spring. Insert semi-ripe cuttings with bottom heat in summer.
• **PESTS AND DISEASES** Trouble free.

T. calycina. Spreading, bushy shrub with crowded, tiny, oblong to inversely lance-shaped, aromatic, dark green leaves, 0.8–1.5cm (⅜–½in) long. From winter to spring, axillary, white, pink, or pink and white flowers, 6mm (¼in) across, with yellow centres that age to red, are borne singly or in clusters of 2 or 3. ↕↔ 1.5–2.5m (5–8ft). Australia (Victoria). ❀ (min. 4–5°C/39–41°F)

THUJA

Arborvitae

CUPRESSACEAE

Genus of 5 species of narrowly to broadly conical, sometimes columnar, monoecious, evergreen, coniferous trees found in forests in E. Asia and North America. Scale-like, narrowly wedge- to diamond-shaped leaves, borne in 2 ranks of opposite pairs, are usually aromatic when bruised. The small, erect, variably shaped female cones, which lack spines, have scales that hinge from the base; male cones are small and ovoid. Grow as specimen trees; most are suitable for hedging. The dwarf cultivars may be grown in a rock garden. Contact with the foliage may aggravate skin allergies.
• **HARDINESS** Fully hardy.
• **CULTIVATION** Grow in deep, moist but well-drained soil in full sun. Shelter

Thuja koraiensis

from cold, drying winds, especially when young. Trim hedging in spring and late summer.

• **PROPAGATION** Sow seed in late winter in containers in a cold frame. Insert semi-ripe cuttings in late summer.

• **PESTS AND DISEASES** Prone to scale insects, aphids, and *Coryneum* canker. Leaves are susceptible to *Keithia* disease, which may be fatal in young seedlings.

T. koraiensis ■ ◊–△ Small, conical tree with often trailing branchlets and flattened shoots. Scale-like leaves are triangular on the main shoots and diamond-shaped on the young shoots. They are bright mid-green above and vivid silver beneath. Ellipsoid brown female cones, 0.8–1.5cm (⅜–½in) long, each have 4 pairs of scales. ↕ to 10m

Thuja occidentalis 'Hetz Midget' (inset: leaf detail)

(30ft), ↔ to 5m (15ft). N.E. China, Korea. ❄❄❄

T. occidentalis ◊ (White cedar). Small, rounded, conical tree with billowing branches and shredding, orange-brown bark. Scale-like, ovate, yellowish green leaves, pale or greyish green beneath, each with a prominent, raised dorsal gland, are apple-scented. Ovoid female cones, 1cm (½in) long, each have 8–10 pairs of smooth scales. ↕ 10–20m (30–70ft), ↔ 3–5m (10–15ft). E. North America. ❄❄❄. **'Caespitosa'** ■ is a very slow-growing, cushion- or bun-shaped shrub; ↕ to 30cm (12in), ↔ to 40cm (16in). **'Filiformis'** is mound-forming, with pendent, whip-like shoots; ↕ to 8m (25ft). **'Golden Globe'** is a dwarf, spherical shrub, with bright golden yellow leaves; ↕↔ 1m (3ft). **'Hetz Midget'** ■ is a slow-growing, spherical, dwarf bush; ↕↔ 80cm (32in). **'Holmstrup'** is a dense, conical bush, with vertical sprays of mid-green leaves; ↕ to 4m (12ft). **'Little Champion'** is a spherical shrub, with bright green leaves; ↕↔ 1m (3ft). **'Rheingold'** ■ is a conical bush, with golden yellow leaves, pink-tinted when young; ↕ 1–2m (3–6ft). **'Smaragd'** is a dwarf, conical, compact shrub, with bright green leaves; ↕ 1m (3ft), ↔ 80cm (32in). **'Wansdyke Silver'** is dwarf and conical, with variegated, silver-white leaves; ↕ 1.5m (5ft), ↔ 60cm (24in).

T. orientalis see *Platycladus orientalis*.

T. plicata ■ ◊–◊ (Western red cedar). Tall, columnar-conical tree, developing billowing lower branches with fissured, red-brown bark and flat, horizontal or hanging sprays of foliage. Scale-like, ovate, mid- to dark green leaves, whitish green beneath, have small dorsal glands. Oblong-ellipsoid female cones, to 1.5cm (½in) long, have 4 or 5 pairs of scales, with a small, terminal hook on each scale. ↕ 20–35m (70–120ft), ↔ 6–9m (20–30ft). W. North America. ❄❄❄. All of the following, except 'Zebrina',

Thuja plicata 'Stoneham Gold'

are shrubs. **'Atrovirens'** is good for hedging, and has very dark green leaves. **'Aurea'** has golden yellow leaves. **'Hillieri'** is dwarf, with blue-green leaves; ↕↔ 2–3m (6–10ft). **'Stoneham Gold'** ■ is conical, with bright gold new leaves, ageing to dark green; ↕↔ to 2m (6ft). **'Zebrina'** △ is a broadly conical tree, with yellow-striped leaves; ↕ 12–15m (40–50ft), ↔ 4m (12ft).

THUJOPSIS

CUPRESSACEAE

Genus of one species of monoecious, slow-growing, evergreen, coniferous tree, related to *Thuja*, found in forest in Japan. *T. dolabrata* has shredding bark, 4-ranked, scale-like leaves, and a large, prominent, central prickle on each cone scale. A fine specimen tree in woodland.

• **HARDINESS** Fully hardy.

• **CULTIVATION** Grow in moist but well-drained, fertile, humus-rich soil in full sun with shelter from cold, dry winds.

• **PROPAGATION** Sow seed in containers in a cold frame in late winter or early spring. Insert semi-ripe cuttings in late summer.

• **PESTS AND DISEASES** Trouble free.

T. dolabrata ◊–◊ (Hiba). Conical to cylindrical tree with brown bark, shredding in grey strips, and 4-ranked, thick, scale-like, shiny-margined, glossy, dark green leaves, silvery white beneath; spreading side leaves are hatchet- or boat-shaped. Spherical, blue-grey female cones, 1cm (½in) across, with leathery scales, ripen to brown; cylindrical male cones are dark violet. ↕ to 20m (70ft),

Thuja occidentalis 'Caespitosa'

Thuja occidentalis 'Rheingold'

Thuja plicata

Thujopsis dolabrata 'Variegata'

↔ 6–9m (20–30ft). Japan. ✲✲✲. **'Nana'** is dwarf, with lighter leaves; ↕ 1m (3ft), ↔ 80cm (32in). **'Variegata'** ▣ has mid-green foliage with white patches; ↕ 10m (30ft), ↔ 4m (12ft).

THUNBERGIA

ACANTHACEAE

Genus of about 100 species of annuals, evergreen perennials, including many twining climbers, and some shrubs, from tropical and southern Africa, Madagascar, and warm to tropical Asia. They occur on forest floors or in rocky areas, or climb trees or shrubs. The salverform to trumpet-shaped flowers are blue, yellow, orange, red, or white, each with 5 usually spreading lobes. They are borne singly from the leaf axils or in terminal racemes, mainly in summer. Opposite, elliptic or ovate to almost rounded leaves may be lobed or toothed. In frost-prone areas, grow in a temperate or warm greenhouse; *T. alata*, *T. gregorii*, and their cultivars may be grown outdoors as annuals in a sheltered site. In warmer areas, grow shrubs and perennials in a border; the climbers are suitable for an arch, pergola, or tree.

• **HARDINESS** Half hardy to frost tender.
• **CULTIVATION** Under glass, grow in loam-based potting compost (JI No.3) in full light with shade from hot sun. Support the climbing stems. In growth, water freely, applying a balanced liquid fertilizer monthly; water sparingly in winter. Outdoors, grow in moist but well-drained, fertile soil in full sun. Tropical climbers require partial shade. Pruning group 11 for climbers, in early spring; group 9 for shrubs. All may need restrictive pruning under glass.
• **PROPAGATION** Sow seed at 16–18°C (61–64°F) in spring. Insert greenwood cuttings in early summer, or semi-ripe cuttings in mid- or late summer, both with bottom heat. Layer in spring.
• **PESTS AND DISEASES** Red spider mites, whiteflies, and scale insects may be a problem under glass.

T. alata ▣ (Black-eyed Susan). Evergreen, perennial, twining climber, often grown as an annual, with ovate-triangular, toothed, mid-green leaves, to 8cm (3in) long, usually with angular basal lobes and narrowly winged stalks. Produces numerous axillary, solitary, salverform flowers, 3–4cm (1¼–1½in) across, usually bright orange or yellow, sometimes creamy white, either with or

Thunbergia grandiflora

without chocolate-purple centres, from summer to autumn. ↕ to 2.5m (8ft) as a perennial, 1.5–2m (5–8ft) as an annual. Tropical Africa. ❀ (min. 7–10°C/ 45–50°F). **Suzie Hybrids** have dark-centred, orange-yellow or white flowers.

T. coccinea. Moderately to sparsely branched, evergreen, perennial, twining climber with narrowly elliptic-ovate, toothed, dark green leaves, to 20cm (8in) long. Tubular, orange-red flowers, 2.5cm (1in) long, with reflexed lobes, are produced in loose, pendent racemes, 15–45cm (6–18in) long, from winter to spring. ↕ 3–8m (10–25ft). India, Burma. ❀ (min. 10–13°C/50–55°F)

T. erecta (Bush clock vine, King's mantle). Often creeping or mat-forming, evergreen perennial or bushy, spreading shrub, with ovate to oblong, semi-lustrous, dark green leaves, 3–8cm (1¼–3in) long, sometimes with a few broad teeth. Solitary, trumpet-shaped, creamy yellow flowers, to 7cm (3in) long, with deep blue-purple lobes, are produced from the leaf axils in summer. ↕↔ to 2m (6ft). Tropical W. Africa to South Africa. ❀ (min. 7°C/45°F)

T. gibsonii see *T. gregorii.*

T. grandiflora ▣ (Bengal clock vine, Blue trumpet vine). Vigorous, woody-stemmed, evergreen, perennial, twining climber. Ovate-elliptic to heart-shaped, toothed or lobed, dark green leaves, 10–20cm (4–8in) long, are softly hairy. Bears trumpet-shaped, lavender-blue to violet-blue, rarely white flowers, 8cm (3in) long, with yellow throats, singly or in pendent racemes, to 10cm (4in) long, in summer. ↕ 5–10m (15–30ft). N. India. ❀ (min. 10–13°C/ 50–55°F)

Thunbergia mysorensis

T. gregorii ▣ syn. *T. gibsonii.* Woody-based, evergreen, perennial, twining climber, often grown as an annual, with slender, bristly-hairy stems and ovate-triangular, softly hairy, mid-green leaves, to 8cm (3in) long. In summer, bears solitary, salverform, clear orange flowers, 4.5cm (1¾in) across. ↕ to 4m (12ft) or more as a perennial, to 2.2m (7ft) as an annual. Tropical Africa. ❀ (min. 10–13°C/50–55°F)

T. mysorensis ▣ Vigorous, woody-stemmed, evergreen, perennial, twining climber with slender, sparsely branched shoots, at least when young. Narrowly elliptic, slender-pointed, toothed, dark green leaves, 10–15cm (4–6in) long, are prominently veined. In spring, hooded, 2-lipped yellow flowers, 5cm (2in) long, with brownish red to purple tubes, and almost erect, arching, tongue-like upper lips, are produced in pendent racemes, to 18cm (7in) long. ↕ to 6m (20ft) or more. India (Nilgiri Hills). ❀ (min. 13–15°C/55–59°F)

▷ **Thyme** see *Thymus*
Basil see *Acinos arvensis*
Caraway see *Thymus herba-barona*
Curly water see *Lagarosiphon*
Garden see *Thymus vulgaris*
Lemon-scented see *Thymus* x *citriodorus*
Mother of see *Acinos arvensis*

THYMOPHYLLA

ASTERACEAE/COMPOSITAE

Genus of 10–12 species of erect to spreading, bushy, strongly aromatic annuals, biennials, perennials, and sub-shrubs from dry slopes and prairies in the USA, Mexico, and Central America. Alternate or opposite leaves are entire to pinnatisect. The abundant small, daisy-like, bright yellow or orange flowerheads are borne from spring to summer. Use *T. tenuiloba* for summer bedding, or grow in a container or hanging basket.

• **HARDINESS** Frost hardy.
• **CULTIVATION** Grow in well-drained, moderately fertile soil in full sun.
• **PROPAGATION** Sow seed at 10–13°C (50–55°F) in mid-spring, and plant out after last frosts. Alternatively, sow seed *in situ* in mid- to late spring.
• **PESTS AND DISEASES** Trouble free.

T. tenuiloba ▣ (Dahlberg daisy, Golden fleece, Shooting star). Branching annual, rarely a short-lived perennial, with almost fern-like, pinnatisect,

Thymophylla tenuiloba

pungent leaves, 0.8–2.5cm (⅜–1in) long, with 7–15 long, linear lobes. From spring to summer, produces upturned, star-shaped, bright yellow flowerheads, to 1.5cm (½in) across. ↕↔ to 30cm (12in). USA (Texas), Mexico. ✲✲

THYMUS

Thyme

LABIATAE/LAMIACEAE

Genus of approximately 350 species of woody-based, aromatic, evergreen perennials, shrubs, and subshrubs, found mainly on calcareous soils and in dry grassland throughout Eurasia. They have small, opposite, oval to linear leaves. In summer, they produce usually terminal, whorled racemes, heads, or clusters of tubular, 2-lipped, usually pink, purple, or white flowers, mostly 4–8mm (⅛–⅜in) long, often with conspicuous bracts. Some thymes, such as *T.* x *citriodorus*, *T. herba-barona*, and *T. vulgaris*, have culinary uses. Most are ideal low shrubs or mat-forming plants for a sunny border or rock garden. The prostrate species, such as *T. polytrichus* or *T. serpyllum*, are suitable for planting in paving crevices. Some, such as *T. cilicicus*, need protection from winter wet and are best grown in an alpine house. All are attractive to bees. Many cultivars described here under *T. serpyllum* are probably of hybrid origin, and their status is botanically uncertain.

• **HARDINESS** Fully hardy to frost hardy.
• **CULTIVATION** Grow in well-drained, neutral to alkaline soil in full sun. After flowering, cut vigorous thymes back hard to retain compactness. In an alpine house, use a mix of equal parts loam, leaf mould, and grit. Pruning group 10, in spring, for upright, shrubby species.
• **PROPAGATION** Sow seed in containers in a cold frame in spring. Divide in spring. Insert semi-ripe cuttings in mid- or late summer, or softwood cuttings in early summer. Separate rooted stem sections in spring or summer, and pot on until re-established.
• **PESTS AND DISEASES** Trouble free.

T. azoricus see *T. caespititius.*

T. caespititius, syn. *T. azoricus*, *T. micans.* Dense, mat- or mound-forming subshrub with branching, woody stems and hairy, narrowly spoon-shaped, dark green leaves, to 1cm (½in) long. In late spring and early summer, bears whorled heads of pale rose-pink, lilac, or white flowers, pressed against the foliage.

T

Thunbergia alata

Thunbergia gregorii

↕ to 5cm (2in), ↔ to 30cm (12in). Spain, Portugal. ❄❄❄
T. cilicicus ■ Compact, cushion- to tussock-forming subshrub with upright, minutely hairy shoots bearing stalkless, linear, prominently veined, dark green leaves, to 1cm (½in) long, finely hairy beneath and at the margins. In early summer, bears lilac or mauve flowers in dense, hemispherical heads. ↕ to 15cm (6in), ↔ to 20cm (8in). Turkey. ❄❄
T. x citriodorus (*T. pulegioides* x *T. vulgaris*) (Lemon-scented thyme). Bushy, rounded shrub with branching stems and narrow, oval-diamond-shaped to lance-shaped, more or less hairless, mid-green leaves, to 1cm (½in) long. In summer, pale lavender-pink flowers, with leaf-like bracts, are borne in irregular, oblong heads. ↕ to 30cm (12in), ↔ to 25cm (10in). Garden origin. ❄❄❄. **'Anderson's Gold'** see 'Bertram Anderson'. **'Archer's Gold'** has mid-green leaves with narrow, golden yellow margins. **'Aureus'** ■ has gold-dappled leaves. **'Bertram Anderson'** ■ syn. 'Anderson's Gold', has grey-green leaves, strongly suffused yellow. **'Golden King'** is upright, with gold-margined leaves; ↕ 25cm (10in), ↔ to 45cm (18in). **'Silver Posie'** see *T. vulgaris* 'Silver Posie'. **'Silver Queen'** has cream-variegated leaves.
T. doerfleri. Compact, spreading subshrub with prostrate, hairy stems and linear, fragrant, mid- to dark green, hairy leaves, 0.8–1.5cm (⅜–½in) long. Purplish pink flowers are produced in whorled racemes in summer. ↕ 15cm (6in), ↔ 45cm (18in). Albania. ❄❄❄. **'Bressingham'** ■ is prostrate and mat-forming, with grey-green leaves and clear pink flowers; ↕ 10cm (4in), ↔ 35cm (14in).
T. 'Doone Valley' ■ Mat-forming subshrub with lance-shaped, dark olive-green leaves, to 1cm (½in) long, with yellow spots. Lavender-pink flowers, opening from crimson-red buds, are borne in rounded heads in summer. ↕ 12cm (5in), ↔ 35cm (14in). ❄❄❄
T. herba-barona (Caraway thyme). Dwarf, loosely mat-forming, wiry-branched subshrub bearing ovate to lance-shaped, caraway-scented, dark green leaves, to 7mm (¼in) long. Pale pink flowers are produced in loose, irregular, oblong to hemispherical heads

Thymus pulegioides

in midsummer. ↕ to 10cm (4in), ↔ to 20cm (8in). Corsica, Sardinia. ❄❄❄
T. leucotrichus ■ Dwarf, creeping subshrub with narrowly lance-shaped, hairy, grey-green leaves, 4–9mm (⅛–⅜in) long. Whorled clusters of pale purplish pink flowers are produced in late spring. ↕ to 15cm (6in), ↔ to 20cm (8in). Greece, Turkey. ❄❄❄
T. longiflorus ■ Densely branched subshrub with ascending, hairy shoots bearing hairy, narrowly elliptic to linear, greyish green leaves, to 1cm (½in) long, with the margins rolled under. Pink flowers with ovate, leathery, greenish purple bracts are borne in spike-like whorls in summer. ↕ to 30cm (12in), ↔ to 25cm (10in). S. Spain. ❄❄
T. mastichina. Vigorous, erect subshrub with upright, hairy shoots and ovate to elliptic-lance-shaped, often shallowly scalloped, mid-green leaves, 1.5cm (½in) long. In summer, bears spherical heads of abundant white flowers. ↕ to 30cm (12in), ↔ to 40cm (16in). Spain, Portugal. ❄❄❄

T. membranaceus. Spreading, rounded shrub with ascending shoots and linear, grey-green leaves, to 1.5cm (½in) long. In summer, bears ovoid heads of long-tubed white flowers, to 1cm (½in) long, with conspicuous, greenish white bracts. Grow in an alpine house or a warm garden. ↕↔ to 20cm (8in). S. Spain. ❄❄
T. micans see *T. caespititius.*
T. polytrichus. Creeping, mat-forming subshrub with woody, prostrate, branching stems and narrowly obovate, dark green leaves, 8mm (⅜in) long, fringed with minute hairs. Pale to deep purple, occasionally off-white flowers are borne in terminal heads in summer. ↕ to 5cm (2in), ↔ to 60cm (24in) or more. S. Europe. ❄❄❄. **subsp. *britannicus* var. *albus***, syn. *T. praecox* subsp. *arcticus* var. *albus*, has softly hairy stems, obovate leaves, and white flowers.
T. praecox* subsp. *arcticus* var. *albus see *T. polytrichus* subsp. *britannicus* var. *albus.*
***T. praecox* 'Coccineus'** see *T. serpyllum* var. *coccineus.*

T. pulegioides ■ Spreading subshrub with semi-erect, 4-angled stems and oblong-lance-shaped, very aromatic, mid-green leaves, 0.6–2cm (¼–¾in) long. In late spring and early summer, bears short, irregular, whorled racemes of pink to purple flowers. ↕ 5–25cm (2–10in), ↔ 30cm (12in). Europe. ❄❄❄. **'Goldentime'**, syn. *T. vulgaris* 'Aureus' of gardens, has leaves suffused yellow.
T. richardii. Spreading to loosely mat-forming subshrub with ovate, aromatic, mid-green leaves, 0.9–1.5cm (⅜–½in) long. Whorled racemes of purple flowers are produced in late spring. ↕ 12cm (5in), ↔ 30cm (12in). Spain (Balearic Islands), Italy (Sicily), Croatia. ❄❄❄. **subsp. *nitidus*** has narrowly ovate leaves, to 1cm (½in) long; Italy (Sicily). **subsp. *nitidus* 'Peter Davis'** ■ is bushy, with grey-green leaves, to 8mm (⅜in) long, and numerous pink flowers; ↕ 15cm (6in), ↔ 5cm (2in).
T. serpyllum. Mat-forming subshrub with finely hairy, trailing stems and linear to elliptic or elliptic-ovate, mid-green leaves, 4–8mm (⅛–⅜in) long. In summer, has congested whorls of purple flowers. ↕ 25cm (10in), ↔ 45cm (18in). Europe. ❄❄❄. **'Annie Hall'** ■ has pale purple-pink flowers. **var. *coccineus*** ■ syn. *T. praecox* 'Coccineus', produces crimson-pink flowers. **'Elfin'** ■ forms dense leafy mounds, and seldom flowers freely; ↕ to 8cm (3in), ↔ to 10cm (4in). **'Minimus'** is compact, with lance-shaped leaves, to 4mm (⅛in) long, and pink flowers; ↕ 5cm (2in), ↔ 10cm (4in). **'Minus'** is compact, with lance-shaped leaves, to 5mm (¼in) long, and pink flowers; ↕ 12cm (5in). **'Pink Chintz'** has grey-green leaves and flesh-pink flowers. **'Snowdrift'** bears clear white flowers.
T. 'Silver Posie' see *T. vulgaris* 'Silver Posie'.
T. vulgaris (Garden thyme). Bushy, cushion-forming, spreading subshrub with linear to elliptic, finely hairy, aromatic, grey-green leaves, 0.6–1.5cm (¼–½in) long. In late spring and early summer, bright purple to white flowers are produced in whorled racemes. ↕ 15–30cm (6–12in), ↔ 40cm (16in). W. Mediterranean to S. Italy. ❄❄❄. **'Aureus' of gardens** see *T. pulegioides* 'Goldentime'. **'Silver Posie'** ■ syn. *T. x citriodorus* 'Silver Posie', *T.* 'Silver Posie', has white-margined leaves.

Thymus cilicicus

Thymus x *citriodorus* 'Aureus'

Thymus x *citriodorus* 'Bertram Anderson'

Thymus doerfleri 'Bressingham'

Thymus 'Doone Valley'

Thymus leucotrichus

Thymus longiflorus

Thymus richardii subsp. *nitidus* 'Peter Davis'

Thymus serpyllum 'Annie Hall'

Thymus serpyllum var. *coccineus*

Thymus serpyllum 'Elfin'

Thymus vulgaris 'Silver Posie'

T

TIARELLA

Foam flower

SAXIFRAGACEAE

Genus of about 7 species of rhizomatous herbaceous perennials from woodland and streambanks in E. Asia and North America. The mainly basal, ovate to heart-shaped or rounded, toothed, sometimes long-stalked leaves are simple or palmately 3- to 5-lobed, occasionally 7-lobed, or 3-palmate; they are pale to mid-green, often turning shades of reddish copper in autumn and winter, and have conspicuous veins and sparse, bristly hairs. The tiny, star-shaped, fluffy, white or pinkish white flowers, 5–10mm (¼–½in) across, are borne in terminal panicles or racemes over a long period from spring to summer. Grow as ground cover in a woodland garden or shady border; *T. cordifolia* spreads freely.

• **HARDINESS** Fully hardy.

• **CULTIVATION** Grow ideally in cool, moist, humus-rich soil, although they tolerate a wide range of soil conditions. Provide deep or partial shade. Protect from excessive winter wet.

• **PROPAGATION** Sow seed in containers in a cold frame in spring or as soon as ripe. Divide in spring.

• **PESTS AND DISEASES** Leaves may be damaged by slugs.

T. cordifolia ■ (Foam flower). Vigorous, rhizomatous perennial, spreading by stolons, with hairy, 3- to 5-lobed, ovate, pale green leaves, to 10cm (4in) long, heart-shaped at the bases, tinted bronze-red in autumn. Creamy white flowers are borne in a profusion of upright, spike-like racemes, 10–30cm (4–12in) long, in summer. ↕ 10–30cm (4–12in), ↔ to 30cm (12in) or more. North America. ❄❄❄. **var. *collina*** see *T. wherryi*.

***T.* 'Maple Leaf'.** Clump-forming, herbaceous or semi-evergreen perennial, without stolons, producing rosettes of broadly ovate, 5-lobed, mid-green, red-flushed leaves, 5–12cm (2–5in) long. From late spring to midsummer, bears white, pink-flushed flowers in racemes, 15–30cm (6–12in) long. ↕↔ to 30cm (12in). ❄❄❄

T. trifoliata ■ Clump-forming, rhizomatous perennial, without stolons, producing 3-palmate basal leaves, to 8cm (3in) long, with 3-lobed, hairy, mid-green leaflets, veined dark green; the 2 or 3 stem leaves have short stalks.

T

Tiarella cordifolia

Tiarella trifoliata

Pendent white flowers are produced in loose panicles, 15–50cm (6–20in) long, opening from pinkish white buds from late spring to midsummer. ↕ to 50cm (20in), ↔ 30cm (12in). North America (Alaska to Oregon). ❄❄❄

T. wherryi, syn. *T. cordifolia* var. *collina*. Compact, slow-growing, clump-forming perennial, without stolons, producing hairy, ovate, sharply 3-lobed, maroon-tinted, pale green leaves, to 14cm (5½in) long, heart-shaped at the bases. White, sometimes pink-tinged flowers are borne in brown-stemmed, slender, spike-like racemes, 15–35cm (6–14in) long, in late spring and early summer. Prefers moist shade. ↕ to 20cm (8in), ↔ to 15cm (6in). USA (Appalachians). ❄❄❄. **'Bronze Beauty'** has dark red-bronze foliage and light pinkish white flowers.

TIBOUCHINA

MELASTOMATACEAE

Genus of about 350 species of evergreen shrubs and subshrubs or herbaceous perennials, some of them climbing, found in rainforest in Mexico, the West Indies, and from tropical South America to N. Argentina (mainly Brazil). Large, elliptic, ovate, or lance-shaped, leathery leaves, usually with 1–3 pairs of prominent, primary veins, are borne in opposite pairs. Saucer- to cup-shaped, mostly 5-petalled flowers are produced singly, in threes, or in long panicles. Where temperatures fall below 7°C (45°F), grow in a cool or temperate greenhouse. In warmer areas, grow in a shrub border.

• **HARDINESS** Frost tender.

• **CULTIVATION** Under glass, grow in loam-based potting compost (JI No.3) in full light with shade from hot sun. During growth, water freely and apply a balanced liquid fertilizer monthly; water sparingly in winter. Outdoors, grow in moist, fertile soil in full sun. Pruning group 9; plants grown under glass need restrictive pruning in late winter.

Tibouchina urvilleana

• **PROPAGATION** Sow seed at 16°C (61°F) in spring. Root softwood cuttings in late spring or semi-ripe cuttings in summer, both with bottom heat.

• **PESTS AND DISEASES** Prone to oedema, red spider mites, and aphids under glass.

T. organensis, syn. *T. semidecandra* subsp. *floribunda* (Glory bush). Open, erect shrub with 4-angled, hairy stems and ovate-oblong, velvety-hairy, greyish green leaves, to 15cm (6in) long, sometimes maturing to bright scarlet. From summer to autumn, produces open, leafy panicles of satin-textured, saucer-shaped, bluish purple flowers, 10cm (4in) or more across. ↕ 3–6m (10–20ft), ↔ 2–3m (6–10ft). S.E. Brazil. ❁ (min. 5–7°C/41–45°F)

***T. semidecandra* of gardens** see *T. urvilleana*.

T. semidecandra* subsp. *floribunda see *T. organensis*.

T. urvilleana ■ syn. *Pleroma macrantha*, *T. semidecandra* of gardens (Brazilian spider flower, Glory bush). Erect to spreading shrub with 4-angled, red-hairy stems and oblong-ovate to ovate or elliptic, velvety-hairy, mid- to dark green leaves, 5–7cm (2–3in) long. From summer to autumn, bears leafy panicles of satin-textured, saucer-shaped, reddish purple flowers, 7–10cm (3–4in) across, with dark, hooked stamens. ↕ 3–6m (10–20ft), ↔ 2–3m (6–10ft). Brazil. ❁ (min. 3–5°C/39–41°F)

▷ **Tickseed** see *Coreopsis*
▷ **Tidy tips** see *Layia platyglossa*
▷ **Tiger flower** see *Tigridia*, *T. pavonia*
▷ **Tiger jaws** see *Faucaria*

TIGRIDIA

Peacock flower, Tiger flower

IRIDACEAE

Genus of 23 species of bulbous perennials from seasonally dry sands and grassland, occasionally among rocks, in Mexico and Guatemala. They have mostly basal, narrowly lance-shaped to sword-shaped leaves. The attractive, short-lived, brightly coloured summer flowers, either upright and iris-like or pendent and bell-shaped, have 3 large, spreading outer segments and 3 shorter inner ones. In frost-free climates, grow in a border; in frost-prone areas, grow outdoors and lift in autumn, or grow permanently as container plants in a cool greenhouse or conservatory.

• **HARDINESS** Frost tender.

Tigridia pavonia

• **CULTIVATION** Plant 10cm (4in) deep. Outdoors, grow in well-drained, preferably sandy, fertile soil in full sun. In cold areas, lift bulbs after flowering and overwinter in dry sand at about 10°C (50°F). Under glass, grow in loam-based potting compost (JI No.2), with added sharp sand. Water freely when in growth and keep dry when dormant; repot annually in spring.

• **PROPAGATION** Sow seed at 13–18°C (55–64°F) in spring. Separate offsets when dormant (taking care to avoid plants affected by viruses).

• **PESTS AND DISEASES** Prone to viruses.

T. meleagris. Bulbous perennial with branched stems bearing 1 or 2 lance-shaped leaves, 20–30cm (8–12in) long; basal leaves are only rarely produced. In summer, bears 2–6 pendent, widely bell-shaped, pale pink to maroon flowers, 3cm (1¼in) across, with darker spots. ↕ 25–60cm (10–24in), ↔ 10cm (4in). Mexico. ❁ (min. 8–12°C/46–54°F)

T. pavonia ■ (Peacock flower, Tiger flower). Bulbous perennial with lance-shaped leaves, 20–50cm (8–20in) long, borne in a basal fan. In summer, bears occasionally branched stems, each with 1–3 stem leaves and a succession of iris-like, orange to pink, red, yellow, or white flowers, 10–15cm (4–6in) across, mostly with contrasting central marks. ↕ 1.5m (5ft), ↔ 10cm (4in). Mexico. ❁ (min. 8–12°C/46–54°F)

TILIA

Lime, Linden

TILIACEAE

Genus of 20–45 species of deciduous trees occurring in woodland in Europe, Asia, and North America. They are cultivated for their stately habit, their foliage and flowers, and, in some cases, for their colourful winter shoots. The ovate to rounded leaves, arranged alternately on slender stalks, are toothed or lobed, with tapered to pointed tips and heart-shaped bases. On old trees, the smooth, silver-grey bark becomes fissured. Small, cup-shaped, fragrant, creamy white to yellow flowers are borne in slender, axillary cymes with long stalks; the stalks are fused with the upper surfaces of large, narrowly elliptic or inversely lance-shaped, membranous bracts, usually pale yellow or green, to 15cm (6in) long. The flowers are followed by dry, nut-like fruits. Grow as free-standing specimens or avenue trees.

Tilia cordata 'Rancho'

The flowers attract bees, although the nectar of *T. tomentosa* and *T.* 'Petiolaris' may be toxic, especially to bumblebees.

• **HARDINESS** Fully hardy.

• **CULTIVATION** Grow in moist but well-drained soil in full sun or partial shade. Avoid very dry conditions and exposure to strong winds. Limes prefer alkaline or neutral soil, but they tolerate acid soil. *T.* x *europaea* often produces dense thickets of shoots from the base and from burrs on the trunk; remove these every few years by cutting back to the trunk in early spring. Pruning group 1.

• **PROPAGATION** Stratify seed for 3–5 months and sow in containers in a cold frame in spring, or sow as soon as ripe in a seed bed in autumn; garden-collected seed may yield hybrids of variable quality. Bud in late summer on to seedling understock of *T. platyphyllos* or *T. tomentosa.* Remove suckers in winter.

• **PESTS AND DISEASES** Susceptible to honey fungus, *Phytophthora* root rot, gall mites on the leaves, scale insects on the bark, and aphids that produce sticky honeydew.

T. americana (American lime, Basswood). Broadly columnar tree with broadly ovate to rounded, dark green leaves, matt above, glossy beneath, to 20cm (8in) long. Pendent cymes of 10–15 yellow flowers, 1.5cm (½in) across, are produced in midsummer. ↕25m (80ft), ↔15m (50ft). C. and E. North America. ❄❄❄. **'Fastigiata'** is conical, with upright branches; ↔8m (25ft). **'Redmond'** syn. *T.* x *euchlora* 'Redmond', is dense and broadly conical; ↕14m (46ft), ↔7m (22ft).

Tilia henryana

T. caroliniana (Carolina basswood). Dense, rounded tree with ovate, dark green leaves, to 9cm (3½in) long, paler and hairy beneath. In early summer, bears pale yellow flowers, 1.5cm (½in) across, in pendent cymes of 10–15. ↕10–12m (30–40ft), ↔8m (25ft). S.E. USA. ❄❄❄

T. cordata (Small-leaved lime). Broadly columnar tree with rounded, dark green leaves, to 8cm (3in) long, blue-green and smooth beneath except for tufts of brown hairs in the leaf axils; leaves turn yellow in autumn. Produces cymes of up to 10 pale yellow flowers, 2cm (¾in) across, in midsummer. ↕25m (90ft), ↔15m (50ft). Europe, Caucasus. ❄❄❄. **'Greenspire'** is vigorous and conical; ↕15m (50ft), ↔7m (22ft). **'Rancho'** ▣ is open in habit when young, becoming narrowly conical, with glossy leaves; ↕15m (50ft), ↔8m (25ft).

***T. dasystyla* of gardens** see *T.* x *euchlora.*

T.* x *euchlora syn. *T. dasystyla* of gardens. Rounded tree with branches that become slightly pendent with age. The rounded to broadly ovate, toothed leaves, 5–10cm (2–4in) long, are heart-shaped at the bases, glossy, dark green above and pale green with tufts of hairs in the axils of the veins beneath. Cymes of 3–7 yellowish white flowers, 1.5cm (½in) across, are borne in midsummer. Remains free of aphids, and therefore also of sticky honeydew. ↕20m (70ft), ↔15m (50ft). Garden origin. ❄❄❄. **'Redmond'** see *T. americana* 'Redmond'.

T.* x *europaea (*T. cordata* x *T. platyphyllos*) syn. *T. intermedia*, *T.* x *vulgaris* (Common lime). Broadly columnar tree with broadly ovate to rounded, dark green leaves, to 10cm (4in) long, paler beneath. Cymes of up to 10 pale yellow flowers, 2cm (¾in) across, are borne in midsummer. ↕35m (120ft), ↔15m (50ft). Europe. ❄❄❄. **'Wratislaviensis'** has bright yellow young leaves, turning yellowish green; ↕20m (70ft), ↔12m (40ft).

Tilia 'Petiolaris'

T. henryana ▣ Spreading tree with broadly ovate, glossy, bright green leaves, to 12cm (5in) long, brown-hairy and paler beneath, red-tinged when young, and with long, bristle-like teeth. In late summer and early autumn, bears cymes of up to 25 small, creamy white flowers, 1.5cm (½in) across. ↕↔ to 25m (80ft). C. China. ❄❄❄

T. intermedia see *T.* x *europaea.*

T. japonica (Japanese lime). Broadly columnar tree with rounded, dark green leaves, to 8cm (3in) long, blue-green beneath. Pendent cymes of 4–10 pale yellow flowers, 1.5cm (½in) across, are produced in midsummer. ↕20m (70ft), ↔6m (20ft). E. China, Japan. ❄❄❄

T. mongolica (Mongolian lime). Rounded tree or shrub with glossy, dark green leaves, to 4cm (1½in) long, blue-green beneath, and red when young; they are rounded to triangular, and deeply cut into 3 sharply toothed lobes, often with 2 lateral lobes. Pale yellow flowers, 2cm (¾in) across, are produced in pendent cymes of up to 30 in early summer. ↕18m (60ft), ↔12m (40ft). Mongolia, N. China. ❄❄❄

Tilia oliveri (inset: leaf and fruit detail)

Tilia platyphyllos

T. oliveri ▣ Spreading tree with broadly ovate, dark green leaves, to 12cm (5in) long, tapering to sharp points at the tips, densely white-hairy beneath. Pendent cymes of 6–10 pale yellow flowers, 1cm (½in) across, are produced in midsummer. ↕15m (50ft), ↔10m (30ft). C. China. ❄❄❄

T. petiolaris see *T.* 'Petiolaris'.

***T.* 'Petiolaris'** ▣ syn. *T. petiolaris*, *T. tomentosa* 'Petiolaris' (Pendulous silver lime). Broadly columnar tree with weeping branches, pendent shoots, and long-stalked, rounded, dark green leaves, to 8cm (3in) long, densely white-hairy beneath. Produces pendent cymes of up to 10 fragrant, pale yellow flowers, to 1.5cm (½in) across, in late summer. ↕30m (100ft), ↔20m (70ft). ❄❄❄

T. platyphyllos ▣ (Large-leaved lime). Broadly columnar tree with rounded to broadly ovate, dark green leaves, 8–15cm (3–6in) long, paler and usually densely hairy beneath, turning yellow in autumn. Produces pendent cymes of 3–5 pale yellow flowers, 2cm (¾in) across, in midsummer. ↕30m (100ft), ↔20m (70ft). Europe. ❄❄❄. **'Princes Street'** is upright, with bright red winter shoots. **'Rubra'** (Red-twigged lime) has red winter shoots.

T. tomentosa (European white lime, Silver lime). Broadly columnar tree with rounded to broadly ovate, sometimes lobed, dark green leaves, to 10cm (4in) long, densely white-hairy beneath. In summer, bears cymes of up to 10 very fragrant white flowers, to 1.5cm (½in) across. ↕30m (100ft), ↔20m (70ft). S.E. Europe, S.W. Asia. ❄❄❄. **'Petiolaris'** see *T.* 'Petiolaris'.

T.* x *vulgaris see *T.* x *europaea.*

T

TILLANDSIA

Air plant

BROMELIACEAE

Genus of over 400 species of epiphytic, terrestrial, or rock-dwelling, evergreen perennials (bromeliads) from scrub and woodland in S. USA, the West Indies, and Central and South America. The entire, often scaly leaves are strap-shaped to narrowly triangular to linear, sometimes tapering to fine threads; they are mainly borne in rosettes, with a few along the slender stems, and sometimes have prominent sheaths. Most species have tubular to funnel-shaped flowers, each with 3 sepals and 3 petals, often with spreading terminal lobes; they are borne among usually colourful floral bracts, generally opening in daytime in spring or autumn. The flowers may be solitary but are usually in 2 or more opposite rows, forming small, dense racemes or spikes, which are sometimes grouped into compound inflorescences; the flowers are borne mainly at the ends of scapes that have sometimes dense or colourful bracts. Where temperatures fall below 7°C (45°F), grow in a temperate greenhouse or conservatory, or as houseplants. In warmer areas, grow the epiphytic species on a tree; the rock-dwelling and terrestrial species may also be grown in a rock garden, on bark or tree branches placed on the ground, or beneath trees or shrubs.

• **HARDINESS** Frost tender.

• **CULTIVATION** Under glass, grow epiphytically in bright indirect light, with moderate to high humidity; rock-dwelling species prefer full light with shade from hot sun, and will tolerate low humidity. From late spring to mid-autumn, mist daily with rainwater and apply a quarter-strength low-nitrogen liquid fertilizer monthly. In winter, mist once or twice a week. Grow terrestrial species, and *T. cyanea* and *T. lindenii*, in containers of terrestrial bromeliad compost, with the bases of the leaves at or just above the surface, in bright filtered light. In growth, water freely and apply a half-strength, low-nitrogen fertilizer monthly; keep just moist in winter. Outdoors, grow epiphytic species in a tree in moist, partial shade. Grow terrestrial and rock-dwelling species in coarse, open, leafy soil in partial or dappled shade. See also p.47.

• **PROPAGATION** Sow seed at 27°C (81°F) in spring, on to bundles of

T

Tillandsia argentea

Tillandsia brachycaulos

conifer twigs and sphagnum moss; mist daily. Detach offsets in spring.

• **PESTS AND DISEASES** Vulnerable to aphids while flowering.

T. aeranthos, syn. *T. dianthoidea.* Epiphytic, cushion-forming perennial with fine-scaly stems bearing narrowly lance-shaped, often keeled, rigid, densely grey-scaly, mid-green leaves, 10cm (4in) or more long. In spring, bears cylindrical spikes of 5–20 slender, funnel-shaped, dark blue flowers, 2.5cm (1in) long, with bright rose-pink floral bracts. ↕↔ to 30cm (12in). S. Brazil, N.E. Argentina, Paraguay, Uruguay. ❀ (min. 7°C/45°F)

T. argentea ▣ Epiphytic perennial with a rhizomatous, curved, short, branched stem bearing dense rosettes of narrowly linear, silvery white-scaly, pale green leaves, 6–9cm (2½–3½in) long. Bears simple spikes of 6–8 tubular, bright red or blue flowers, 3cm (1¼in) long, with salmon-pink floral bracts, in spring. ↕↔ to 25cm (10in). Mexico, Guatemala, Cuba, Jamaica. ❀ (min. 7°C/45°F)

T. bergeri. Rock-dwelling perennial with rosettes of narrowly triangular, grey-scaly, mid-green leaves, 10cm (4in) long. In spring, produces simple spikes of 7–12 funnel-shaped, blue and white flowers, 3cm (1¼in) long, fading to rose-pink, with grey-green floral bracts. ↕ to 18cm (7in), ↔ 15cm (6in). Argentina. ❀ (min. 7°C/45°F)

T. brachycaulos ▣ Stemless, epiphytic perennial with rosettes of slender, linear to lance-shaped, arching, densely green-scaly or silver-grey-scaly, dark green leaves, 12–26cm (5–10in) long, with thread-like tips and prominent sheaths, turning bright red when in flower. In spring, bears short spikes of 1 or 2 erect, tubular violet flowers, to 7cm (3in) long, with red floral bracts, clustered into a head. ↕↔ 25cm (10in). S. Mexico, Central America. ❀ (min. 7°C/45°F)

T. caput-medusae ▣ Stemless, epiphytic perennial with rosettes of narrowly awl-shaped, tapered, recurved, pale green leaves, 15cm (6in) or more long; the leaf-blades are covered with spreading, coarse, silver-grey hairs, and have ovate sheaths inflated to form hollow pseudobulbs. Suberect or curved spikes of 6–12 slender, tubular blue flowers, 3–4cm (1¼–1½in) long, with red floral bracts, are produced in late spring. ↕ 15–40cm (6–16in), ↔ to 24cm (10in). Mexico, Central America. ❀ (min. 7°C/45°F)

Tillandsia caput-medusae

T. crocata. Short-stemmed, untidy, sometimes branched, epiphytic or rock-dwelling perennial with 2 rows of linear, coarse, grey-hairy, mid-green leaves, 10–15cm (4–6in) long. In spring or autumn, produces simple spikes of 3 or 4 funnel-shaped, bright canary-yellow flowers, 2cm (¾in) long, with green, heavily grey-scaled floral bracts. ↕ to 20cm (8in), ↔ to 15cm (6in). Brazil, Argentina. ❀ (min. 7°C/45°F)

T. cyanea ▣ Epiphytic perennial with stemless rosettes of linear-triangular, semi-erect then recurved, dark green leaves, to 35cm (14in) long, red-striped near the bases. Flattened, paddle-shaped, almost stalkless spikes of 20 funnel-shaped, rich violet flowers, to 3cm (1¼in) long, with spreading petals and rose-pink floral bracts, are produced in late spring or autumn. ↕ to 30cm (12in), ↔ to 40cm (16in). Ecuador. ❀ (min. 7°C/45°F)

T. dianthoidea see *T. aeranthos.*

T. fasciculata ▣ Epiphytic perennial with stemless rosettes of narrowly triangular, spreading, sparsely hairy or silver-grey-hairy, brittle, pale grey-green leaves, to 30cm (12in) long, with brown sheaths. In late spring, spikes of red to yellow floral bracts and erect, tubular, white and purple flowers, to 6cm (2½in) long, usually 3 or 4 at a time, are borne in compound inflorescences. ↕↔ 30cm (12in) or more. S. USA, West Indies, Mexico to Colombia and Peru. ❀ (min. 7°C/45°F)

T. gardneri. Epiphytic or rock-dwelling perennial bearing dense rosettes of narrowly triangular, densely scaly, silver-

Tillandsia cyanea

Tillandsia fasciculata

Tillandsia lindenii

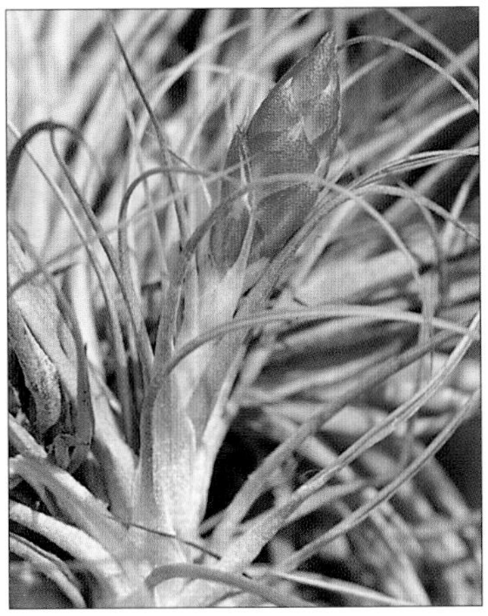

Tillandsia stricta

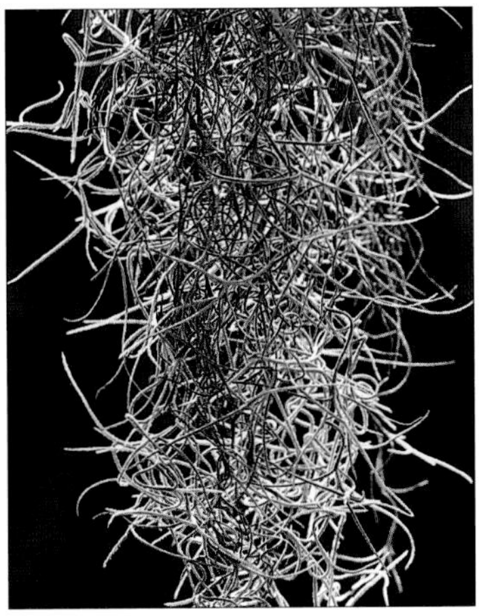

Tillandsia usneoides

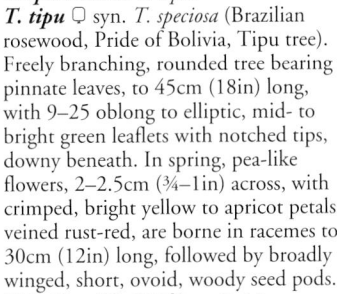

grey leaves, 10–27cm (4–11in) long, the lower ones recurved. Compound inflorescences, each consisting of 4–12 spikes of 3–12 slender, funnel-shaped, rose-pink to pale lavender-pink flowers, to 2cm (¾in) long, with green to pink floral bracts, are produced in late spring. ↕↔ 25cm (10in). Colombia to E. Brazil, Trinidad. ❄ (min. 7°C/45°F)

T. imperialis. Stemless, epiphytic or rock-dwelling perennial producing dense rosettes of slender, lance-shaped, sparsely scaly, mid-green or slightly purple leaves, to 40cm (16in) long. In autumn, spikes of 3 or 4 erect, tubular violet flowers, to 6cm (2½in) long, with brilliant red floral bracts, are borne in compound, cone-shaped inflorescences. ↕↔ 50cm (20in). C. and S. Mexico. ❄ (min. 7°C/45°F)

T. ionantha. Freely clustering, epiphytic or terrestrial perennial with dense rosettes of linear, incurved or recurved, coarsely scaly, greyish green leaves, to 4cm (1½in) long, turning red in late spring. Solitary, tubular, violet-blue and white flowers, to 4.5cm (1¾in) long, with white floral bracts, are borne in simple spikes in spring. ↕ 12cm (5in), ↔ 10cm (4in) or more. Mexico, Central America. ❄ (min. 7°C/45°F)

T. leiboldiana. Stemless, epiphytic perennial with funnel-shaped rosettes of slender, lance-shaped, mid-green leaves, to 15cm (6in) long, with flat, brown-scaly sheaths. Branched spikes of 3–8 tubular violet flowers, 3cm (1¼in) long, with red or purple floral bracts, are produced in late spring. ↕↔ 30–60cm (12–24in). Mexico, Central America. ❄ (min. 7°C/45°F)

T. lindenii ▣ (Blue-flowered torch). Epiphytic perennial with funnel-shaped rosettes of linear-triangular, arching, dark green leaves, 40cm (16in) long, striped reddish purple. In late spring or autumn, green to purple-pink floral bracts and funnel-shaped, white-eyed, deep purple-blue flowers, 7cm (3in) long, with spreading petals, are borne in lance-shaped spikes, each with 2 ranks of up to 20 flowers. ↕ 40cm (16in), ↔ 60cm (24in). N.W. Peru. ❄ (min. 7°C/45°F)

T. multicaulis ▣ Epiphytic perennial with dense, funnel-shaped rosettes of linear, pale brown-scaly, mid-green leaves, 30–40cm (12–16in) long. In late spring, simple, sword-shaped spikes of 9–12 tubular blue flowers, 7cm (3in) long, with greenish white sepals and red floral bracts, are produced from the leaf axils on scapes with green bracts. ↕↔ 40cm (16in). Mexico, Central America. ❄ (min. 7°C/45°F)

T. punctulata. Stemless, epiphytic perennial forming symmetrical rosettes of linear, bright green and purplish green leaves, to 45cm (18in) long, with almost black sheaths. In late spring, bears erect spikes of 4–6 tubular, white-tipped violet flowers, 3–5cm (1¼–2in) long, with green floral bracts, sometimes grouped into compound inflorescences; scapes have red bracts. ↕↔ 45cm (18in). Mexico to Panama. ❄ (min. 7°C/45°F)

T. recurvata. Epiphytic or terrestrial perennial with simple or branched stems bearing linear, recurved, grey-scaly, mid-green leaves, 3–17cm (1¼–7in) long, in 2 rows. In autumn, produces simple spikes of 1–5 slender, funnel-shaped, erect, pale violet or white flowers, to 1.5cm (½in) long, with green sepals and green or silver, grey-scaly floral bracts. ↕↔ 10–20cm (4–8in). S. USA, Central and South America. ❄ (min. 7°C/45°F)

T. stricta ▣ Clump-forming, short-stemmed, epiphytic perennial with dense rosettes of narrowly triangular, grey-scaly, pale green leaves, 6–18cm (2½–7in) long. In spring, bears slender, pendent, cone-shaped spikes of 40 or more slender, funnel-shaped, blue or purple flowers, 2cm (¾in) or more long, with yellowish white to rose-pink floral bracts. ↕↔ 10–20cm (4–8in). Venezuela and Trinidad to N. Argentina. ❄ (min. 7°C/45°F)

T. usneoides ▣ (Spanish moss). Pendent, epiphytic perennial with branching, rootless, wiry stems, to 3mm (⅛in) thick, bearing cylindrical, densely grey-scaly, grey-green leaves, 2.5–5cm (1–2in) long. Solitary, tubular, fragrant, greenish yellow or pale blue flowers, to 1cm (½in) long, with green or silver, grey-scaly floral bracts, are produced in late spring or autumn. ↕ 8m (25ft), ↔ indefinite. S. USA, Central and South America, West Indies. ❄ (min. 7°C/45°F)

Tillandsia multicaulis

TIPUANA

Tipu tree

LEGUMINOSAE/PAPILIONACEAE

Genus of one species of semi-evergreen tree found in tropical forest in South America, and cultivated for its attractive habit and flowers. *T. tipu* has mainly alternate, pinnate leaves and arching to pendent, terminal or axillary racemes or panicles of pea-like flowers. Where temperatures fall below 10°C (50°F), grow in a cool or temperate greenhouse; flowers are seldom produced when grown in a container. In warmer areas, grow as a shade or avenue tree.

- **HARDINESS** Frost tender.
- **CULTIVATION** Under glass, grow in loam-based potting compost (JI No.2) in full light. From late spring to early autumn, water freely and apply a balanced liquid fertilizer monthly; water sparingly in winter. Outdoors, grow in moist but well-drained, fertile soil in full sun. Pruning group 1; plants grown under glass need restrictive pruning after flowering.
- **PROPAGATION** Sow seed at 15°C (59°F) in spring.
- **PESTS AND DISEASES** Red spider mites may be troublesome under glass.

T. speciosa see *T. tipu.*

T. tipu ♀ syn. *T. speciosa* (Brazilian rosewood, Pride of Bolivia, Tipu tree). Freely branching, rounded tree bearing pinnate leaves, to 45cm (18in) long, with 9–25 oblong to elliptic, mid- to bright green leaflets with notched tips, downy beneath. In spring, pea-like flowers, 2–2.5cm (¾–1in) across, with crimped, bright yellow to apricot petals, veined rust-red, are borne in racemes to 30cm (12in) long, followed by broadly winged, short, ovoid, woody seed pods. ↕ 10–30m (30–100ft), ↔ 8–15m (25–50ft). Bolivia, Brazil, Argentina. ❄ (min. 7–10°C/45–50°F)

▷**Tipu tree** see *Tipuana, T. tipu*

TITANOPSIS

AIZOACEAE

Genus of 5 or 6 species of short-stemmed, fleshy-rooted, succulent herbaceous perennials, readily forming dense mats or clumps, found in semi-desert areas of Namibia and South Africa. The erect, spoon-shaped to 3-angled, fleshy leaves, thickly crowded with tubercles at the tips, are arranged in attractive basal rosettes. Solitary, daisy-like, yellow or orange flowers are borne during daytime from late summer to early spring. In areas where temperatures fall below 10°C (50°F), grow in a bowl garden indoors or in a warm greenhouse. In warmer climates, grow in a desert garden.

- **HARDINESS** Frost tender.
- **CULTIVATION** Under glass, grow in deep containers in a mix of 3 parts standard cactus compost and 1 part limestone chippings; provide full light and low humidity. From spring to late summer, water moderately, applying a balanced liquid fertilizer 3 or 4 times; keep dry at other times. Outdoors, grow in sharply drained, gritty, alkaline soil in full sun. See also pp.48–49.
- **PROPAGATION** Sow seed at 21°C (70°F) in spring or early summer.
- **PESTS AND DISEASES** Vulnerable to greenfly while flowering.

T. calcarea ▣ Clump-forming succulent with crowded, basal rosettes of spoon-shaped, bluish green, sometimes white-tinged leaves, 6–8cm (2½–3in) long, with reddish or greyish white tubercles. Bears bright golden yellow to orange flowers, 2cm (¾in) across, from late summer to autumn. ↕ 3cm (1¼in),

Titanopsis calcarea

↔ 10cm (4in). South Africa (Western Cape). ❀ (min. 10°C/50°F)

T. schwantesii. Clump-forming succulent with basal rosettes of spoon-shaped, light grey-blue, sometimes red-tinged leaves, 3cm (1¼in) long, with rounded bases, 3-angled tips, and yellowish brown tubercles. Pale yellow flowers, to 2cm (¾in) across, are borne from autumn to early winter. ↕ 3cm (1¼in), ↔ 10cm (4in). Namibia. ❀ (min. 10°C/50°F)

TITHONIA

Mexican sunflower

ASTERACEAE/COMPOSITAE

Genus of 10 erect, bushy, stout-stemmed, sometimes woody-based, frequently hairy annuals, perennials, and shrubs, found in thickets and scrub in Mexico and Central America. Alternate, occasionally opposite, entire or lobed leaves each have 3 prominent veins. Large, long-stemmed, mostly solitary flowerheads are borne from late summer to autumn. *T. rotundifolia*, the most commonly grown species, lends height to a mixed or annual border, and provides long-lasting cut flowers.

- **HARDINESS** Half hardy.
- **CULTIVATION** Grow in well-drained, moderately fertile soil in full sun, with shelter from strong winds. Support tall cultivars, water in dry weather, and dead-head to prolong flowering. They grow poorly in cool, overcast weather.
- **PROPAGATION** Sow seed at 13–18°C (55–64°F) in mid- to late spring. Plant out when all danger of frost has passed. Alternatively, sow seed *in situ* in late spring. If seedlings are subjected to cold, leaves turn yellow.
- **PESTS AND DISEASES** Young foliage may be attacked by slugs and snails.

T. rotundifolia, syn. *T. speciosa* (Mexican sunflower). Robust, branching annual with long, triangular-ovate, entire or occasionally 3-lobed, toothed leaves, 8–30cm (3–12in) long, hairy beneath. Bright orange or orange-red flowerheads, to 8cm (3in) across, similar to those of single-flowered dahlias, are borne from late summer to autumn. ↕ to 2m (6ft), ↔ 30cm (12in). Mexico to Central America. ✲. **'Goldfinger'** is compact, with vivid, rich orange flowerheads; ↕ to 75cm (30in). **'Sundance'** has bright orange flowerheads. **'Torch'** ▣ has vivid red or orange-red flowerheads.

T. speciosa see *T. rotundifolia*.

T

Tithonia rotundifolia 'Torch'

▷**Ti tree** see *Cordyline fruticosa*
▷**Toadflax** see *Linaria, L. vulgaris*
Alpine see *Linaria alpina*
Ivy-leaved see *Cymbalaria muralis*
Purple-net see *Linaria reticulata*
▷**Toad-shade** see *Trillium sessile*
▷**Tobacco plant** see *Nicotiana*

TODEA

OSMUNDACEAE

Genus of 2 species of large, terrestrial, evergreen ferns found in open places in tropical and warm-temperate rainforest in South Africa, Australia, New Guinea, and New Zealand. Massive, erect, hairy rhizomes bear crowns of upright 2-pinnate, leathery fronds, with spores along the veins. In frost-prone climates, grow *T. barbara* in a temperate or warm greenhouse. In warmer areas, grow as a specimen plant or in light woodland.

- **HARDINESS** Frost tender.
- **CULTIVATION** Under glass, grow in 1 part each of loam, medium-grade bark, and charcoal, 2 parts sharp sand, and 3 parts leaf mould, in bright filtered light, with moderate humidity. In growth, water freely and apply a balanced liquid fertilizer monthly; water moderately to sparingly in winter. Outdoors, grow in moist, fertile soil in partial shade.
- **PROPAGATION** Sow spores at 21°C (70°F) as soon as ripe. Divide in early summer, but only after several trunks have developed. See also p.51.
- **PESTS AND DISEASES** Susceptible to mealybugs under glass.

T. barbara ♈ Tree-like fern with stout black rhizomes and short, thick trunks, to 80cm (32in) tall. Glossy, bright green fronds, to 2m (6ft) long, have lance-shaped, pinnatifid pinnae. ↕ to 2m (6ft), ↔ to 1.5m (5ft). South Africa, Australia, New Zealand. ❀ (min. 5°C/41°F)

▷**Toe toe** see *Cortaderia richardii*

TOLMIEA

Pick-a-back plant, Youth-on-age

SAXIFRAGACEAE

Genus of one species of fast-spreading herbaceous perennial from coniferous woodland in W. North America. It is unusual in that young plants grow on its leaves, where leaf-stalk and blade meet. Leafy stems bear erect racemes of small, cup-shaped flowers with 3 stamens. Grow as ground cover in a woodland garden or as a foliage houseplant.

- **HARDINESS** Fully hardy.
- **CULTIVATION** Grow in cool, moist, humus-rich soil in partial or deep shade. Sun will scorch the leaves. Under glass, grow in fertile, loam-based potting compost (JI No.2) in bright filtered or indirect light. In growth, water freely and apply a balanced liquid fertilizer monthly; water sparingly in winter.
- **PROPAGATION** Sow seed in containers in a cold frame in autumn. Divide in spring. Remove and pot up plantlets from the leaves in mid- to late summer, or peg leaves into potting compost and remove plantlets when rooted.
- **PESTS AND DISEASES** Trouble free.

T. menziesii (Thousand mothers). Clump-forming, hairy perennial with creeping rhizomes and mainly basal,

Tolmiea menziesii 'Taff's Gold'

long-stalked, kidney-shaped, shallowly lobed, toothed, conspicuously veined, pale to lime-green leaves, to 12cm (5in) long. In late spring and early summer, produces one-sided racemes of 20–50 slightly scented flowers, to 1cm (½in) long, with orange anthers; the sepals are pale green, heavily shaded and lined purple-brown, with thread-like, purple-brown petals recurved between them. ↕ 30–60cm (12–24in), ↔ 1–2m (3–6ft). W. North America. ✲✲✲. **'Goldsplash'** see 'Taff's Gold'. **'Maculata'** see 'Taff's Gold'. **'Taff's Gold'** ▣ syn. 'Goldsplash', 'Maculata', has paler green leaves, spotted and mottled cream and pale yellow.

TOLPIS

ASTERACEAE/COMPOSITAE

Genus of 20 frequently mat-forming annuals and perennials from dry, sandy areas in the Azores and the Canary Islands, the Mediterranean region, N.E. Africa, and Ethiopia. The mainly ovate to lance-shaped, toothed or lobed, bright green basal leaves are usually arranged in rosettes, while the branching stems support pinnate or lobed leaves. Leaves and stems contain a milky latex. Daisy-like, bright yellow flowerheads emerge over a long period from spring to summer. Suitable for the front of a mixed or annual border.

- **HARDINESS** Fully hardy.
- **CULTIVATION** Grow in well-drained, light, moderately fertile soil in full sun. Dead-head to prolong flowering.
- **PROPAGATION** Sow seed *in situ* in mid-spring.
- **PESTS AND DISEASES** Trouble free.

Tolpis barbata

T. barbata ▣ Annual with mostly basal, lance-shaped to oblong, toothed, hairy, bright green leaves, 2–10cm (¾–4in) long. From spring to summer, solitary or clustered, bright yellow flowerheads, 1–3cm (½–1¼in) across, with fringed margins and dark maroon centres, are borne singly or in clusters, on sparsely leaved, branching stems. ↕ to 60cm (24in), usually less, ↔ 30cm (12in). Mediterranean. ✲✲✲

▷**Tongue orchid** see *Serapias*
Heart-lipped see *S. cordigera*

TOONA

MELIACEAE

Genus of about 6 species of deciduous or semi-evergreen trees found in woodland from E. Asia to Australasia. They have alternate, pinnate leaves and large, terminal or axillary panicles of small, cup-shaped, fragrant, greenish white or white flowers. *T. sinensis* is an effective specimen tree. Best where summers are hot, it is a useful shade or street tree.

- **HARDINESS** Fully hardy.
- **CULTIVATION** Grow in fertile, well-drained soil in full sun. Pruning group 1.
- **PROPAGATION** Sow seed in containers in a cold frame in autumn. Insert root cuttings in late winter.
- **PESTS AND DISEASES** Trouble free.

T. sinensis ▣♀ syn. *Cedrela sinensis*. Broadly columnar, deciduous tree with peeling brown bark. Aromatic leaves, to 60cm (24in) long, have up to 26 ovate-lance-shaped to oblong, papery leaflets, bronze-red to pink when young, turning yellow in autumn. In midsummer, bears small, fragrant, white or greenish white flowers in pendent, terminal panicles, to 30cm (12in) long. ↕ 15m (50ft), ↔ 10m (30ft). China. ✲✲✲. **'Flamingo'** has vivid pink young leaves, turning creamy yellow then bright green.

▷**Toothwort, Purple** see *Lathraea clandestina*

Toona sinensis

Torenia fournieri

TORENIA

Wishbone flower

SCROPHULARIACEAE

Genus of 40–50 erect to spreading, bushy, sometimes softly hairy annuals and perennials found in woodland, at altitudes up to 3,000m (10,000ft), in tropical Africa and Asia. They are grown for their short, showy, terminal or axillary racemes of tubular then flaring, 2-lipped flowers, the upper lips slightly 2-lobed, the lower ones markedly 3-lobed, produced in summer. The opposite leaves are mostly broadly to narrowly ovate or lance-shaped, and may be entire or toothed. *T. fournieri* is the most commonly cultivated species: use for summer bedding, or grow at the front of an annual or mixed border; it is also grown as a summer-flowering houseplant or cool-greenhouse plant.

• **HARDINESS** Frost tender.

• **CULTIVATION** Under glass, grow in loam-based potting compost (JI No.2) in bright filtered light, providing good ventilation. In the growing season, water freely and apply a high-potash liquid fertilizer every 2 or 3 weeks. Pinch out stem tips to promote bushiness. Outdoors, grow in fertile, moist but well-drained soil in partial shade.

• **PROPAGATION** Sow seed at 18°C (64°F) in mid-spring; harden off and plant out when all danger of frost has passed.

• **PESTS AND DISEASES** Trouble free.

T. fournieri ▣ (Wishbone flower). Erect, smooth annual with long-stalked, pointed, ovate to narrowly ovate, toothed, pale green leaves, 4–5cm (1½–2in) long. In summer, produces abundant lilac-blue flowers, to 3.5cm (1½in) long, the lower lips deep purple and the throats marked yellow. ↕ 30cm (12in), ↔ 15–23cm (6–9in). Tropical Asia. ❀ (min. 5°C/41°F). Cultivars of **Clown Series** ▣ are compact, and produce white, pink, deep purple, or lavender-blue flowers; ↕ 20–25cm (8–10in). **Panda Series** cultivars are more compact, producing white, pink, purple, or lavender-blue flowers; ↕ 10–20cm (4–8in).

▷ **Tormentil** see *Potentilla erecta*

TORREYA

Nutmeg yew

TAXACEAE

Genus of 7 species of dioecious, evergreen, coniferous shrubs or trees found in woodland in Asia and North America. The flattened, lance-shaped, 2-ranked leaves are yew-like, but hard and spine-tipped. The common name refers to the single-seeded, ovoid or ovoid-ellipsoid female, cone-like structures ("cones"); they may take 2 years to ripen, maturing to olive- or plum-like fruits. The male "cones" are white and spherical. Nutmeg yews are vigorous, small to medium-sized specimen trees. *T. californica* thrives in areas with cool, damp summers, whereas other species grow best in areas with summers that are warm and humid.

• **HARDINESS** Fully hardy.

Torenia fournieri Clown Series

Torreya californica

• **CULTIVATION** Grow in fertile, moist but well-drained soil in full sun or light dappled shade. Provide shelter from cold, drying winds.

• **PROPAGATION** Sow seed in pots in a cold frame or seed bed, as soon as ripe; the seed may take 2 or more years to germinate. Insert semi-ripe cuttings in late summer; use cuttings from strongly upright growth to form leading shoots.

• **PESTS AND DISEASES** Trouble free.

T. californica ▣ ♢ (California nutmeg tree). Broadly conical tree with whorled branches, red-brown or brown bark, becoming scaly, and green shoots with pointed buds. Produces spreading, 2-ranked, narrowly lance-shaped, tapered, yellowish green leaves, 3–5cm (1¼–2in) long, and ellipsoid or obovoid, purplish green female "cones", to 4cm (1½in) long. ↕ to 25m (80ft), ↔ to 8m (25ft). USA (C. California). ✻✻✻

T. nucifera ♢–♢ Upright to broadly conical tree with opposite branchlets and producing linear, glossy, dark green leaves, 2–3cm (¾–1¼in) long, in 2 opposite ranks, separated by a broad, V-shaped channel. The ellipsoid female "cones" are olive-green, 2.5cm (1in) long. ↕ to 15m (50ft), ↔ 8m (25ft). S. Japan. ✻✻✻

▷ **Totara, Alpine** see *Podocarpus nivalis*
▷ ***Tovara*** see *Persicaria*
T. virginiana see *P. virginiana*

TOWNSENDIA

ASTERACEAE/COMPOSITAE

Genus of about 20 species of compact, occasionally stemless annuals and evergreen, often monocarpic perennials found in open, freely draining habitats in mountainous areas of W. North America. The alternate leaves are linear to spoon-shaped, entire, and smooth to densely hairy. Solitary, short-stemmed, aster-like flowerheads are produced in summer. Suitable for a rock garden, trough, or alpine house.

• **HARDINESS** Fully hardy.

• **CULTIVATION** Grow in gritty, sharply drained soil in full sun. Protect from excessive winter wet. In an alpine house, grow in a mix of equal parts loam, leaf mould, and sharp sand.

• **PROPAGATION** Sow seed as soon as ripe in containers in a cold frame. Propagate regularly as plants are often short-lived.

• **PESTS AND DISEASES** Susceptible to aphids and red spider mites under glass.

Townsendia formosa

T. formosa ▣ Upright, clump-forming, rhizomatous perennial with spoon-shaped to inversely lance-shaped leaves, to 8cm (3in) long, with finely hairy midribs and margins. In summer, one to several solitary flowerheads, 3cm (1¼in) across, with pale violet ray-florets, mauve beneath, and yellow disc-florets, are produced on upright stems, 10cm (4in) long. ↕ to 60cm (24in), ↔ to 15cm (6in). S.W. USA. ✻✻✻

T. parryi. Clump-forming, short-lived perennial with spoon-shaped, slightly fleshy leaves, to 10cm (4in) long, smooth above and bristly-hairy beneath. One to several solitary flowerheads, to 3cm (1¼in) across, with violet-blue or lavender-blue ray-florets and yellow disc-florets, are borne on upright stems, 5–15cm (2–6in) long, in early summer. ↕ to 15cm (6in), ↔ to 10cm (4in). N.W. North America. ✻✻✻

▷ ***Toxicodendron*** see *Rhus*
T. succedaneum see *R. succedanea*
T. vernicifluum see *R. verniciflua*
▷ **Toyon** see *Heteromeles salicifolia*

TRACHELIUM

syn. DIOSPHAERA

CAMPANULACEAE

Genus of about 7 species of small, sometimes cushion-forming, often woody-based perennials, usually found in calcareous soils in the Mediterranean region. The tiny, narrowly lance-shaped to oblong or almost rounded leaves are alternate and simple. Tubular flowers, each with 5 spreading petal lobes, are solitary or, more usually, produced in corymbs. Grow *T. caeruleum* and other tall species and cultivars in an annual, mixed, or herbaceous border; their flowers are excellent for cutting. Dwarf tracheliums, such as *T. asperuloides*, are suitable for a rock garden, scree bed, trough, or alpine house.

• **HARDINESS** Fully hardy to half hardy.

• **CULTIVATION** Grow in well-drained soil in full sun with some midday shade. *T. asperuloides* prefers sharply drained, alkaline soil, and needs protection from excessive winter wet. In an alpine house, grow in deep containers in equal parts loam, leaf mould, and sharp sand.

• **PROPAGATION** Sow seed of half-hardy species at 13–16°C (55–61°F) in early spring, or *in situ* in late spring. Sow seed of fully hardy species as soon as ripe in containers in a cold frame. Insert softwood cuttings in early summer.

Trachelium asperuloides

• **PESTS AND DISEASES** Aphids and red spider mites may prove troublesome under glass.

T. asperuloides ■ syn. *Diosphaera asperuloides*. Dense, cushion-forming perennial with thread-like stems bearing minute, overlapping, ovate-rounded, glossy, mid-green leaves, 6mm (¼in) long. In late summer, bears abundant, tubular, lavender-blue or white flowers, 6mm (¼in) across, singly or in corymbs of up to 5, on very short flower-stalks in the upper leaf axils. ↕ to 5cm (2in), ↔ to 15cm (6in). S. Greece. ✻✻✻

T. caeruleum (Blue throatwort). Erect perennial, grown as an annual in frost-prone climates, with pointed, oval to lance-shaped, toothed, mid-green leaves, 8cm (3in) long. In summer, bears lightly scented, deep violet-blue or white flowers, to 7mm (¼in) across, in dense, dome-shaped, terminal corymbs on long, branching, red-flushed stalks. ↕ 1–1.2m (3–4ft), ↔ 30cm (12in). W. and C. Mediterranean. ✻. **'Purple Umbrella'** has deep purple flowers. **'White Veil'** has white flowers.

TRACHELOSPERMUM

APOCYNACEAE

Genus of about 20 species of woody, evergreen, twining climbers found in woodland from India to Japan. They are grown for their attractive foliage and fragrant flowers. Opposite, lance-shaped to broadly ovate leaves are borne on stems that contain a milky latex. Small, salverform flowers, with cylindrical tubes and 5 spreading, slightly twisted lobes, are produced in terminal or axillary cymes, followed by pendent, pod-like fruits (seldom borne in areas with cool summers). Grow against a warm, sunny wall; in areas prone to severe frosts, grow in a cool greenhouse.

• **HARDINESS** Frost hardy.

• **CULTIVATION** Outdoors, grow in fertile, well-drained soil in full sun or partial shade; provide shelter from cold, drying winds. Under glass, grow in loam-based potting compost (JI No.3) in full light with shade from hot sun. During the growing season, water freely and apply a balanced liquid fertilizer monthly. Water sparingly in winter. Pruning group 11, in early spring.

• **PROPAGATION** Insert semi-ripe cuttings with bottom heat in summer. Layer in autumn.

• **PESTS AND DISEASES** Trouble free.

Trachelospermum jasminoides

T. asiaticum. Woody, evergreen, twining climber bearing oval, glossy, dark green leaves, to 5cm (2in) long. Fragrant, creamy white flowers, 2cm (¾in) across, which age to yellow, are produced in terminal cymes in mid- and late summer. ↕ 6m (20ft). Korea, Japan. ✻✻

T. jasminoides ■ (Confederate jasmine, Star jasmine). Woody, evergreen, twining climber with oval, glossy, dark green leaves, to 10cm (4in) long, turning bronze-red in winter. In mid- and late summer, pure white flowers, 2.5cm (1in) across, are produced in terminal and axillary cymes. ↕ 9m (28ft). China, Korea, Japan. ✻✻

TRACHYCARPUS

ARECACEAE/PALMAE

Genus of 6 species of usually single-stemmed, sometimes clustering, dioecious, evergreen palms occurring in temperate and mountain forest in sub-tropical Asia. They are cultivated for their attractive habit, their terminal, fan-shaped leaves, palmately lobed to half their length or more, and their cup-shaped flowers, surrounded by bowl-shaped, white or brown bracts. The flowers are followed by spherical or kidney-shaped fruits. Fan palms are small enough to be grown in a restricted area, such as a courtyard; they are also effective specimen trees.

• **HARDINESS** Frost hardy.

• **CULTIVATION** Grow in well-drained, fertile soil in full sun or light dappled shade, sheltered from strong or cold, drying winds.

Trachycarpus fortunei

• **PROPAGATION** Sow seed in spring or autumn at 24°C (75°F).

• **PESTS AND DISEASES** Trouble free.

T. fortunei ■ 🌴 (Chusan palm). Unbranched, single-stemmed, evergreen palm with a head of fan-shaped, dark green leaves, 45–75cm (18–30in) long, with numerous pointed segments variously lobed to half their length or more. Small yellow flowers are borne in large, pendent panicles, 60cm (24in) or more long; they emerge from close to the leaf bases in early summer. Female plants bear spherical, blue-black fruit, 1cm (½in) across. ↕ to 20m (70ft), ↔ 2.5m (8ft). C. China. ✻✻. **'Nanus'** has a short or almost non-existent trunk and stiffer leaf-blades, to 30cm (12in) long.

TRACHYMENE

syn. DIDISCUS

APIACEAE/UMBELLIFERAE

Genus of 12 or more species of erect, branching annuals, biennials, and perennials from moist woodland and swamps to dry sandhills and subalpine areas in Australia and the W. Pacific. The lacy leaves are ternate or 2-ternate, usually with linear leaflets, or rarely with 2 leaflets or palmately divided. Dainty, terminal umbels of tiny, star-shaped, white, pink, or blue flowers are borne in summer. Grow *T. coerulea*, the species most commonly cultivated, at the front of an annual or mixed border, or in a cool greenhouse. It provides long-lasting cut flowers.

• **HARDINESS** Half hardy.

• **CULTIVATION** Under glass, grow in loam-based potting compost (JI No.2) in full light with shade from hot sun. In summer, water moderately and apply a high-potash liquid fertilizer every 2 or 3 weeks. Outdoors, grow in light, well-drained, moderately fertile soil in a sheltered site in full sun. Provide twiggy support.

• **PROPAGATION** Sow seed at 15°C (59°F) in mid-spring, or sow *in situ* in late spring. Germination is slow.

• **PESTS AND DISEASES** Trouble free.

T. coerulea, syn. *Didiscus coeruleus* (Blue lace flower). Stiff-stemmed annual or biennial with pale green leaves, to 10cm (4in) long, divided into 2 or 3 narrow, 3-lobed leaflets. Lightly scented, lavender-blue flowers are produced in long-stemmed, rounded umbels, to 5cm (2in) across, in summer. ↕ to 60cm (24in), ↔ 23cm (9in). W. Australia. ✻

TRADESCANTIA

COMMELINACEAE

Genus of about 65 species of creeping, trailing, or tuft-forming, fibrous- or tuberous-rooted, evergreen perennials from woodland, scrub, or disturbed ground in North, Central, and South America. The leaves are alternate, usually fleshy, lance-shaped to ovate, often purple-flushed or variegated, and hairy or hairless. Short-lived, spreading, usually saucer-shaped flowers, each with 3 petals and 3 sepals, are produced in terminal or axillary cymes, which are fused in pairs, with paired, boat-shaped bracts. Hardy tradescantias are suitable for a mixed or herbaceous border. In

Tradescantia Andersoniana Group 'J.C. Weguelin'

warm regions, grow the tender species beneath shrubs or for ground cover; in frost-prone areas, grow in a temperate or cool greenhouse, as houseplants, or in a conservatory; they are especially effective in hanging baskets. Contact with the foliage may irritate skin.

• **HARDINESS** Fully hardy to frost tender.

• **CULTIVATION** Under glass, grow in loamless or loam-based potting compost (JI No.2) in bright filtered light. When in active growth, water moderately and apply a balanced liquid fertilizer every 4 weeks; water sparingly in winter. Pinch growing tips to encourage bushiness, and remove plain green foliage from variegated cultivars. Pot on each spring. Outdoors, grow in moist, fertile soil in full sun or partial shade. After flowering, cut back flowered stems to prevent seeding and to encourage further flowers.

• **PROPAGATION** Insert stem-tip cuttings, 5–8cm (2–3in) long, of the tender tradescantias at any time; root in cutting compost or water, then pot up into soil-based compost (JI No.1). Divide hardy species and cultivars in autumn or spring.

• **PESTS AND DISEASES** Susceptible to aphids, grubs, and vine weevil.

T. albiflora **'Albovittata'** see *T. fluminensis* 'Albovittata'.

T. albiflora **'Variegata'** see *T. fluminensis* 'Variegata'.

T. x andersoniana see *T.* Andersoniana Group.

T. **Andersoniana Group**, syn. *T. x andersoniana*. Tufted, clump-forming perennials with erect, branching stems and arching, narrowly lance-shaped, pointed, hairless, slightly fleshy, mid-green, often purple-tinted leaves, to 35cm (14in) long. Blue, purple, rose-pink to rose-red, or white flowers, 2.5–4cm (1–1½in) across, each have 3 wide-open, triangular petals and fluffy-hairy stamen filaments; they are borne in succession in paired, terminal cymes from early summer to early autumn. ↕ 40–60cm (16–24in), ↔ 45–60cm (18–24in). ✻✻✻. **'Carmine Glow'** see 'Karminglut'. **'Iris Prichard'** has white flowers, shaded pale blue. **'Isis'** produces large, dark blue flowers. **'J.C. Weguelin'** ■ has large, pale blue flowers. **'Karminglut'**, syn. 'Carmine Glow', has carmine-red flowers. **'Osprey'** ■ has large white flowers with blue stamen filaments. **'Purewell Giant'** ■ produces

T

Tradescantia Andersoniana Group 'Osprey'

Tradescantia Andersoniana Group 'Purple Dome'

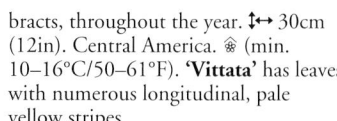

Tradescantia fluminensis 'Albovittata'

Tradescantia pallida 'Purpurea'

large, purple to rose-red flowers; ↕↔ 45cm (18in). **'Purple Dome'** ■ produces large, rich purple flowers. **'Red Cloud'** has cerise-red flowers; ↕↔ 45cm (18in). **'Zwanenburg Blue'** has large, dark blue flowers.
T. blossfeldiana see *T. cerinthoides.*
T. cerinthoides, syn. *T. blossfeldiana.* Vigorous, creeping or ascending perennial with stout, branching stems and elliptic-oblong to narrowly ovate, very fleshy, deep green leaves, 15cm (6in) long, hairless above, and deep purple and densely hairy beneath. Paired, terminal or axillary cymes of pink and white flowers are produced intermittently throughout the year. ↕ 90cm (36in), ↔ 45cm (18in). Brazil. ❀ (min. 10–16°C/50–61°F).
'Variegata' has leaves with bold buff stripes, light pink above.
T. fluminensis (Wandering Jew). Trailing perennial with thin, pointed, ovate to ovate-oblong, usually hairless, light green leaves, 2–10cm (¾–4in) long, often stained purple beneath. White flowers are produced in paired, terminal or axillary cymes intermittently throughout the year. ↕ 15cm (6in), ↔ 20cm (8in). Brazil to N. Argentina. ❀ (min. 10–16°C/50–61°F).
'Albovittata' ■ syn. *T. albiflora* 'Albovittata', has light green leaves with white longitudinal stripes, and purple undersides that partially show through the almost transparent upper surfaces.
'Aurea' has yellow-striped leaves.
'Variegata' ■ syn. *T. albiflora* 'Variegata', has leaves variably striped green, white, purple, or cream.
T. navicularis see *Callisia navicularis.*
***T. pallida* 'Purple Heart'** see *T. pallida* 'Purpurea'.
***T. pallida* 'Purpurea'** ■ syn. *Setcreasea purpurea, T. pallida* 'Purple Heart'. Trailing perennial producing ascending purple stems. Large, pointed, narrowly oblong leaves, 8–15cm (3–6in) long, are V-shaped in section, and fleshy, hairless, rich violet-purple. In summer, bears bright pink flowers in paired, terminal cymes. Leaves colour best in bright sunlight and when the root zone is slightly dry and cramped. ↕ 20cm (8in), ↔ to 40cm (16in). E. Mexico. ❀ (min. 10–16°C/50–61°F)
T. pexata see *T. sillamontana.*
T. purpusii see *T. zebrina* 'Purpusii'.
T. sillamontana ■ syn. *T. pexata, T. velutina* (White velvet). Trailing perennial producing upright, later spreading, silky-hairy stems and ovate, fleshy, silky-hairy, grey-green leaves, 4–6cm (1½–2½in) long. Magenta-pink flowers are borne in paired, terminal cymes in summer. ↕ 30cm (12in), ↔ to 45cm (18in). N. Mexico. ❀ (min. 10–16°C/50–61°F)
T. spathacea ■ syn. *Rhoeo discolor, R. spathacea* (Moses-in-the-cradle, Three-men-in-a-boat). Clump-forming perennial with rosettes of semi-erect, linear-lance-shaped, fleshy, hairless leaves, 20–35cm (8–14in) long, dark green above and deep purple beneath. White flowers are produced in paired, axillary cymes, which are surrounded by prominent, long-lasting purple bracts, throughout the year. ↕↔ 30cm (12in). Central America. ❀ (min. 10–16°C/50–61°F). **'Vittata'** has leaves with numerous longitudinal, pale yellow stripes.
T. velutina see *T. sillamontana.*
T. zanonia, syn. *Campelia zanonia.* Clump-forming perennial with erect or decumbent stems and broadly elliptic to inversely lance-shaped, hairless, membranous, dark green leaves, 24cm (10in) long. White flowers are borne in paired, axillary cymes, surrounded by 2 leafy bracts, from summer to winter. ↕ 2.2m (7ft), ↔ 1m (3ft). Mexico to Brazil, West Indies. ❀ (min. 10–16°C/50–61°F). **'Mexican Flag'** has leaves with longitudinal white stripes and red margins, sometimes silvery beneath.

Tradescantia Andersoniana Group 'Purewell Giant'

Tradescantia sillamontana

T

Tradescantia fluminensis 'Variegata'

Tradescantia spathacea

Tradescantia zebrina

Tradescantia zebrina 'Purpusii'

T. zebrina ■ syn. *Zebrina pendula* (Wandering Jew). Trailing perennial with ovate-oblong to broadly ovate, fleshy, hairless, bluish green leaves, to 10cm (4in) long; 2 longitudinal stripes, silver-green above and rich purple beneath, mark each leaf. Purple-pink to purple-blue flowers are produced in paired, terminal cymes intermittently throughout the year. ↕15cm (6in), ↔ 20cm (8in). S. Mexico. ❀ (min. 10–16°C/50–61°F). **'Purpusii'** ■ syn. *T. purpusii*, *Zebrina purpusii*, has rich bronze-purple leaves and pink flowers. **'Quadricolor'** has leaves striped green, cream, pink, and silver.

TRAPA

Water chestnut

TRAPACEAE

Genus of about 30 species of submerged aquatic annuals from still or slow-moving water in C. Europe, E. Asia, and Africa. The creeping, floating stems bear linear submerged leaves and rosettes of ovate or almost triangular to diamond-shaped, toothed, mottled floating leaves, hairy beneath, with spongy, swollen leaf-stalks. Small, solitary, tubular, white or lilac flowers are followed by inflated, spiny fruits. In frost-prone areas, grow in baskets in a cold-greenhouse pool, or float rosettes on the surface of an outdoor pool after last frosts. In warmer climates, grow in an outdoor pool.
• **HARDINESS** Half hardy to frost tender.
• **CULTIVATION** Plant in baskets of loam-based potting compost (JI No.3) in full light, at no less than 10°C (50°F); or, in frost-prone areas, float rosettes on

Trapa natans

still, shallow, nutrient-rich, acid water in full sun. See also pp.52–53.
• **PROPAGATION** Collect seed in autumn. Store frost-free in water or wet moss over winter; sow in spring, at 13–18°C (55–64°F), in wet compost.
• **PESTS AND DISEASES** Trouble free.

T. natans ■ (Jesuit's nut, Water caltrops, Water chestnut). Clump-forming, aquatic annual. Roughly diamond-shaped, floating leaves, 2.5cm (1in) across, have red-tinged leaf-stalks, 5–8cm (2–3in) long. White flowers are borne from the leaf axils in summer, followed by 4-angled, spiny, hard black fruit, to 5cm (2in) across. ↔ indefinite. Eurasia, Africa. ❄ (borderline)

▷ **Traveller's joy** see *Clematis*
▷ **Traveller's tree** see *Ravenala*
▷ **Tree fern** see *Cyathea*
  Black see *Cyathea medullaris*
  Hawaiian see *Cibotium glaucum*
  Soft see *Dicksonia antarctica*
  Woolly see *Dicksonia antarctica*
▷ **Tree heath** see *Erica arborea*
▷ **Tree-ivy** see x *Fatshedera lizei*
▷ **Tree of heaven** see *Ailanthus altissima*
▷ **Trees** see pp.32–33
▷ **Tree spinach** see *Chenopodium giganteum*
▷ **Tree tomato** see *Cyphomandra*
▷ **Trefoil,**
  Double bird's foot see *Lotus corniculatus* 'Plenus'
  Moon see *Medicago arborea*
▷ ***Trichinium manglesii*** see *Ptilotus manglesii*
▷ ***Trichocereus bridgesii*** see *Echinopsis lageniformis*
▷ ***Trichocereus candicans*** see *Echinopsis candicans*
▷ ***Trichocereus grandiflorus*** see *Echinopsis huascha*
▷ ***Trichocereus huascha*** see *Echinopsis huascha*
▷ ***Trichocereus shaferi*** see *Echinopsis schickendantzii*
▷ ***Trichocereus spachianus*** see *Echinopsis spachiana*

TRICHODIADEMA

AIZOACEAE

Genus of about 30 species of mainly small, tuberous, fibrous, or woody-based, shrubby, succulent perennials found in dry, hilly areas in Namibia, South Africa, and Ethiopia. The long-lasting, solitary, short-stalked, daisy-like, terminal flowers are borne on long or

Trichodiadema mirabile

short stems in daytime, from spring to autumn. Semi-cylindrical to cylindrical leaves are sparsely covered with minute papillae, creating a glistening effect; the leaf tips bear clusters of stiff, spreading or erect, shiny bristles. Below 7°C (45°F), grow in a temperate greenhouse. In warm, dry areas, grow in a border.
• **HARDINESS** Frost tender.
• **CULTIVATION** Under glass, grow in standard cactus compost in full light, with low humidity. In growth, water moderately and apply a low-nitrogen fertilizer every 3 or 4 weeks; keep dry at other times. Outdoors, grow in gritty, sharply drained, poor to moderately fertile soil in full sun. See also pp.48–49.
• **PROPAGATION** Sow seed at 19–24°C (66–75°F), or insert cuttings of stem sections, in spring or summer.
• **PESTS AND DISEASES** Susceptible to mealybugs early in the season.

T. bulbosum. Semi-erect, short- to long-stemmed succulent with an almost caudex-like, tuberous rootstock and semi-cylindrical, grey-papillose leaves, to 8mm (3/8in) long, with white bristles. Deep red flowers, 2cm (3/4in) across, are borne from spring to autumn. ↕20cm (8in), ↔ 30cm (12in). South Africa (Eastern Cape). ❀ (min. 7°C/45°F)
T. mirabile ■ Short-stemmed, often prostrate succulent with a fibrous rootstock, and stems covered with bristly white hairs. Semi-cylindrical, finger-like leaves, to 2.5cm (1in) long, are flat above, and have blunt tips with stiff, dark brown bristles. White flowers, 4cm (1½in) across, are produced in summer. ↕10cm (4in), ↔ 12cm (5in) or more. South Africa (Eastern Cape, Karoo). ❀ (min. 7°C/45°F)

TRICHOSANTHES

CUCURBITACEAE

Genus of 15 species of monoecious or dioecious, annual and perennial tendril climbers found in woodland and scrub from Indonesia and Malaysia to the Pacific islands. Colourful, ornamental, mostly ovoid or spherical gourd fruits are edible when young. The alternate leaves are ovate to rounded, and simple or palmately 3- to 9-lobed. Parasol-like, fringed, 5-lobed flowers are produced from the upper leaf axils in summer, the females singly, the males in racemes or, rarely, singly. In frost-prone areas, grow in a warm greenhouse; elsewhere, train over a pergola, arch, or tree stump.
• **HARDINESS** Frost tender.
• **CULTIVATION** Under glass, grow in loam-based potting compost (JI No.3) in full light with shade from hot sun, with high humidity. During growth, water freely and apply a balanced liquid fertilizer every 2 weeks. Water sparingly in winter. For good fruit production, pollinate by hand. Outdoors, grow in moist but well-drained, fertile soil in full sun. Provide support for climbing stems.
• **PROPAGATION** Sow seed at 20°C (68°F) in spring. Insert softwood cuttings with bottom heat in summer.
• **PESTS AND DISEASES** Susceptible to red spider mites and whiteflies under glass.

T. anguina see *T. cucumerina* var. *anguina*.
T. cucumerina. Dioecious, annual climber with slender, 5-angled stems and rounded-kidney-shaped to broadly ovate, 5- to 7-lobed, toothed, rich green leaves, 6–13cm (2½–5in) long. Bears pure white flowers, 5cm (2in) across, in summer. Ovoid to conical fruit, 6cm (2½in) long, are yellowish green with red seeds. ↕3–5m (10–15ft) or more. India to Malaysia and N. Australia. ❀ (min. 15°C/59°F). **var. *anguina***, syn. *T. anguina* (Serpent cucumber, Snake gourd), has shallowly to deeply 3- to 7-lobed leaves, to 15cm (6in) long, and slender, twisted, pointed fruit, 0.3–2m (1–6ft) long, white-striped when young, orange when ripe; Pakistan to India.

▷ ***Trichosma suavis*** see *Eria coronaria*
▷ ***Tricuspidaria lanceolata*** see *Crinodendron hookerianum*

TRICYRTIS

Toad lily

CONVALLARIACEAE/LILIACEAE

Genus of about 16 species of rhizomatous or stoloniferous herbaceous perennials occurring in moist woodland and on mountains and cliffs from the E. Himalayas to the Philippines. Erect or arching, usually hairy stems bear alternate, sometimes 2-ranked, oblong to lance-shaped, pointed, pale to dark green, usually stem-clasping leaves; they are often glossy, sometimes spotted darker green, and have prominent veins. The flowers are star-shaped, open bell-shaped, or funnel-shaped with the tips opened out. They each have 6 tepals, the outer 3 with basal bulges, and are borne singly or in clusters from the leaf axils, or in terminal or axillary cymes. Toad

Tricyrtis formosana

Tricyrtis hirta var. *alba*

lilies are suitable for a woodland garden, a shady border, or a peat bank.
• **HARDINESS** Fully hardy.
• **CULTIVATION** Grow in moist but well-drained, humus-rich soil in deep or partial shade. *T. latifolia* tolerates drier conditions and may spread widely. *T. macrantha* and *T. macrantha* subsp. *macranthopsis* prefer deep shade and very moist soil. In colder areas, grow the late-blooming species in a sheltered, warm but not sunny position to encourage flowering before frosts. Provide a deep winter mulch in areas where prolonged cold is not accompanied by snow cover.
• **PROPAGATION** Sow seed as soon as ripe in containers in a cold frame; where frost is severe, overwinter young plants in a cold greenhouse for the first winter. Divide in early spring, when dormant.
• **PESTS AND DISEASES** Slugs and snails may attack young spring growth.

T. bakeri see *T. latifolia.*
T. flava. Clump-forming perennial with short rhizomes, erect, softly hairy stems, and broadly ovate, veined, mid-green leaves, to 14cm (5½in) long, often with dark purplish green spots. In early autumn, upward-facing, star-shaped yellow flowers, to 2.5cm (1in) across, spotted brownish-purple, are borne singly or in clusters from the upper leaf axils. ↕ 30–50cm (12–20in), ↔ 30cm (12in). Japan. ❄❄❄. **subsp. *ohsumiensis*** see *T. ohsumiensis.*
T. formosana ■ syn. *T. stolonifera.* Rhizomatous perennial, spreading by stolons, with erect, somewhat zig-zagging, softly hairy stems, and inversely lance-shaped to ovate, veined, glossy, dark green leaves, to 12cm (5in) long, spotted darker purplish green. In early autumn, produces branched, terminal cymes of upward-facing, star-shaped, white to pinkish white or pinkish purple flowers, 2.5–3cm (1–1¼in) across; they are spotted reddish purple inside, with yellow tepal bases and heavily red-spotted white stigmas. ↕ to 80cm (32in), ↔ 45cm (18in). Taiwan. ❄❄❄
T. hirta, syn. *T. japonica.* Clump-forming, rhizomatous perennial with densely hairy stems and lance-shaped, veined, hairy, pale green leaves, to 15cm (6in) long, heart-shaped at the bases. From late summer to mid-autumn, erect, funnel-shaped, purple-spotted white flowers, to 3cm (1¼in) long, with purple stigmas and spreading then recurved tepals, are produced singly or in clusters from the leaf axils, or in

Tricyrtis macrantha subsp. *macranthopsis*

terminal or axillary cymes. ↕ to 80cm (32in), ↔ 60cm (24in). Japan. ❄❄❄. **var. *alba*** ■ has green-flushed white flowers with pink-tinged anthers. **'Miyazaki'** bears white flowers, spotted lilac-purple, in the leaf axils all along the stems; ↕ to 90cm (36in), ↔ 45cm (18in). **'White Towers'** has erect stems, and bears upward-facing white flowers, with pink-tinged stamens, in most of the leaf axils; ↕ to 60cm (24in), ↔ 30cm (12in).
T. japonica see *T. hirta.*
T. latifolia, syn. *T. bakeri.* Spreading, clump-forming perennial with short rhizomes, erect to arching, hairy stems, and broadly ovate-oblong, veined, glossy, mid-green leaves, to 15cm (6in) long, with heart-shaped bases, spotted darker green when young. In early and midsummer, produces upward-facing, trumpet- then star-shaped flowers, to 2.5cm (1in) across, with spreading, brown-spotted tepals, yellow inside and greenish yellow outside, in branched, terminal cymes. ↕ to 80cm (32in), ↔ 90cm (36in). China, Japan. ❄❄❄
T. macrantha. Tufted perennial with short rhizomes, arching or decumbent, brown-hairy stems, and ovate to lance-shaped, veined, glossy, dark green leaves, 10–15cm (4–6in) long, heart-shaped at the bases. In early and mid-autumn, bears pendent, bell-shaped, deep yellow flowers, 3–4cm (1¼–1½in) long, with thick, fleshy tepals, spotted red-brown inside, in few-flowered cymes from the upper leaf axils. ↕ 40–80cm (16–32in), ↔ 30cm (12in). Japan. ❄❄❄. **subsp. *macranthopsis*** ■ syn. *T. macranthopsis*, has hairless stems, with leaves to 17cm (7in) long, and bears axillary or terminal cymes in mid- and late autumn.
T. macranthopsis see *T. macrantha* subsp. *macranthopsis.*
T. ohsumiensis ■ syn. *T. flava* subsp. *ohsumiensis.* Clump-forming perennial with short rhizomes, erect to arching, hairy stems, and oblong-lance-shaped, veined, pale green leaves, 5–20cm (2–8in) long, marked darker green, the lower ones larger and elliptic-oblong. In early autumn, upward-facing, broadly bell-shaped yellow flowers, 2.5–3cm (1–1¼in) long, faintly brown-spotted inside, especially the stigmas, are borne singly or in axillary clusters. ↕ to 50cm (20in), ↔ 23cm (9in). Japan. ❄❄❄
T. perfoliata. Spreading, rhizomatous perennial with almost decumbent, zig-zagging, hairless stems. Perfoliate, broadly lance-shaped, veined, leathery, glossy, mid-green leaves, 7–18cm (3–7in) long, have long, tapered tips. Upward-facing, funnel-shaped yellow flowers, to 3cm (1¼in) long, sparsely spotted brownish red, are borne singly from the upper leaf axils in late spring. ↕ to 70cm (28in), ↔ 25cm (10in). Japan. ❄❄❄
T. stolonifera see *T. formosana.*

TRIFOLIUM

Clover

LEGUMINOSAE/PAPILIONACEAE

Genus of about 240 species of erect or creeping annuals, biennials, and herbaceous perennials, usually found on scree or in grassy meadows or scrub worldwide, except in Australasia, and mainly in the N. hemisphere. The 3-

Tricyrtis ohsumiensis

Trifolium repens 'Purpurascens Quadrifolium'

palmate leaves, rarely up to 7-palmate, have entire or toothed leaflets, usually with stipules. Small, pea-like flowers are produced in heads or in short, terminal or axillary spike-like racemes (or, rarely, singly), in spring or summer, and are attractive to bees. Many clovers are invasive weeds. The others are suitable for a border or a wildflower garden.
• **HARDINESS** Fully hardy.
• **CULTIVATION** Grow in moist but well-drained, neutral soil in full sun.
• **PROPAGATION** Sow seed in containers in a cold frame in spring. Divide, or detach and replant rooted stems, in spring.
• **PESTS AND DISEASES** Trouble free.

T. incarnatum (Crimson clover, Italian clover). Erect, bushy, downy-stemmed annual with 3-palmate leaves, to 3cm (1¼in) long, with obovate-wedge-shaped leaflets, finely toothed towards the tips. In spring and summer, bears oblong, spike-like racemes, to 1.5cm (½in) across, of 5–8 deep red to creamy yellow flowers. ↕↔ 20–50cm (8–20in). S. and W. Europe. ❄❄❄
***T. pratense* 'Dolly North'** see *T. pratense* 'Susan Smith'.
***T. pratense* 'Goldnet'** see *T. pratense* 'Susan Smith'.
***T. pratense* 'Susan Smith'**, syn. *T. pratense* 'Dolly North', *T. pratense* 'Goldnet'. Mat-forming perennial with 3-palmate leaves, to 3.5cm (1½in) long, with obovate to broadly elliptic, entire leaflets, usually notched at the tips, with vein-like gold markings, hairy beneath. In early and midsummer, bears dense, spherical to ovoid, axillary, spike-like racemes, to 2cm (¾in) across, of 5–9 pink flowers. ↕ 15cm (6in), ↔ 45cm (18in). ❄❄❄
T. repens (Dutch clover, Shamrock, White clover). The species is very invasive, and a weed of lawns. **'Purpurascens Quadrifolium'** ■ is a vigorous, rhizomatous, stem-rooting perennial with 4-palmate leaves, 2–3cm (¾–1¼in) long, divided into inversely heart-shaped leaflets with deep purple-maroon centres and narrow, mid-green margins. Small, pea-like white flowers are produced in dense, umbel-like racemes, 1.5–2cm (½–¾in) across, in summer. ↕ to 10cm (4in), ↔ indefinite. Europe. ❄❄❄.

▷**Trigger plant** see *Stylidium graminifolium*

TRILLIUM

Trinity flower, Wake robin, Wood lily

LILIACEAE/TRILLIACEAE

Genus of about 30 species of rhizomatous, deciduous perennials occurring mainly in woodland and scrub in North America, with a few species in the W. Himalayas and N.E. Asia. Erect, rarely procumbent, short stems each bear an apical whorl of 3 lance-shaped or elliptic to ovate or diamond-shaped, net-veined, often silver- or purple-marbled leaves. Upright or nodding, terminal, solitary, funnel- or cup-shaped flowers, with whorls of 3 leaf-like, often reflexed outer sepals, and 3 inner petals, are either stalkless supported by the leaves, or stalked and borne above or below the leaves. Suitable for a moist, shady border or woodland garden. Grow the smallest species, *T. nivale* and *T. rivale*, on a peat bank, where they will not be overwhelmed by other plants.

- **HARDINESS** Fully hardy.
- **CULTIVATION** Grow in moist but well-drained, deep, humus-rich, preferably acid to neutral soil, although some will grow in moderately alkaline soils, in deep or partial shade. Mulch annually in autumn with leaf mould.
- **PROPAGATION** Sow seed as soon as ripe in containers in a shaded cold frame; leaves will not usually appear until the second spring, and plants take 5–7 years to reach flowering size. Divide rhizomes after flowering, ensuring that each section has at least one growing point; divisions may be slow to re-establish. Alternatively, cut out the growing point from the rhizome after flowering, which stimulates formation of offsets.
- **PESTS AND DISEASES** Young leaves may be damaged by slugs and snails.

T. catesbaei see *T. catesbyi.*
T. catesbyi, syn. *T. catesbaei*, *T. nervosum*, *T. stylosum.* Slender, clump-forming perennial with red-pink-tinted stems and almost stalkless, elliptic to

Trillium cernuum

Trillium chloropetalum

ovate, deeply veined leaves, to 7cm (3in) long. Stalked, nodding, pale to deep pink flowers, with ovate to heart-shaped petals, to 5cm (2in) long, reflexed, mid-green sepals, and pale green ovaries, are borne beneath or among the leaves in spring and summer. ↕ to 50cm (20in), ↔ to 15cm (6in). S.E. USA. ✻✻✻
T. cernuum ▣ Clump-forming perennial with short-stalked, broadly diamond-shaped, abruptly pointed, mid-green leaves, 5–15cm (2–6in) long, with moderately conspicuous veining. Pale pink, sometimes reddish brown, occasionally white flowers, with recurved, wavy petals, to 2cm (¾in) long, prominent purple stamens, and dark red ovaries, are borne on reflexed, pendent stalks, beneath or among the leaves, in spring. ↕ to 60cm (24in), ↔ to 25cm (10in). E. North America. ✻✻✻. **f. *album*** has white flowers.
T. chloropetalum ▣ Robust, clump-forming perennial with thick, hairless, red-green stems. Stalkless, broadly ovate to diamond-shaped, dark green leaves, 10–20cm (4–8in) long, are variably marbled greyish cream or maroon. Upright, stalkless, fragrant flowers, with obovate, greenish white, yellow, or brownish purple petals, 5–10cm (2–4in) long, and spreading, lance-shaped sepals, are borne above or among the leaves, in spring. ↕ to 40cm (16in), ↔ to 20cm (8in). USA (California). ✻✻✻
T. cuneatum, syn. *T. sessile* of gardens. Robust, upright, clump-forming perennial with stalkless, broadly ovate-rounded, often pointed, mid-green leaves, to 20cm (8in) long, marked pale or silver-green. In spring, upright, stalkless, musk-scented, dark maroon flowers, with wedge-shaped petals, 5cm (2in) or more long, and purple-tipped, olive-green sepals, are borne above the leaves. Similar to *T. sessile*; often sold under that name. ↕ 30–60cm (12–24in), ↔ to 30cm (12in). S.E. USA. ✻✻✻
T. erectum ▣ (Birth root, Stinking Benjamin). Vigorous, upright perennial with stalkless, broadly ovate, mid-green leaves, to 20cm (8in) long. In spring, stalked, upright or outward-facing flowers, with pointed, elliptic, spreading or incurved petals, to 8cm (3in) long, are borne above the leaves; flowers are deep red-purple, occasionally white or yellow, with purple-tinted green sepals and purple ovaries. ↕ to 50cm (20in), ↔ to 30cm (12in). E. North America. ✻✻✻. **f. *albiflorum*** has white or pale pink petals with dark purple ovaries.

Trillium erectum

T. grandiflorum ▣ (Wake robin). Vigorous, clump-forming perennial with almost stalkless, ovate to rounded, dark green leaves, to 30cm (12in) long. In spring and summer, pure white flowers, often fading to pink, with green sepals, are produced above the leaves; they are stalked, erect or outward-facing, cupped at first, then opening widely, with broadly ovate, slightly wavy petals, to 8cm (3in) long, reflexing near the tips. ↕ to 40cm (16in), ↔ 30cm (12in) or more. E. North America. ✻✻✻. **'Flore Pleno'** is slower-growing, with very attractive, formal double flowers. Several variants with slightly differing double flowers are grown under this name.
T. kamtschaticum. Upright perennial with stalkless, ovate to diamond-shaped, abruptly pointed, dark green leaves, to

Trillium luteum

15cm (6in) long. Stalked, upright flowers, with ovate white petals, to 4.5cm (1¾in) long, sometimes purple-flushed with age, and dark green sepals, are produced above the leaves in late spring and early summer. ↕ to 25cm (10in), ↔ to 20cm (8in). E. Asia. ✻✻✻
T. luteum ▣ Upright, clump-forming perennial with stalkless, elliptic to broadly ovate, abruptly pointed, mid-green leaves, to 15cm (6in) long, heavily marked paler green. Stalkless, upright, sweet-scented, golden- or bronze-green flowers, with inversely lance-shaped to obovate or narrowly elliptic petals, to 9cm (3½in) long, and lance-shaped, mid-green sepals, are produced above the leaves in spring. ↕ to 40cm (16in), ↔ to 30cm (12in). S.E. USA. ✻✻✻
T. nervosum see *T. catesbyi.*

Trillium grandiflorum

Trillium ovatum

T. nivale (Dwarf white wood lily, Snow trillium). Compact, clump-forming perennial with stalked, ovate, dark bluish green leaves, to 3.5cm (1½in) long. Bears short-stalked, upright, pure white flowers, with oblong petals, to 4cm (1½in) long, and green sepals and ovaries, above the leaves in early spring. Not easy to grow. ↕ to 12cm (5in), ↔ to 10cm (4in). S.E. USA. ❄❄❄
T. ovatum ▣ Clump-forming perennial with red-green stems and stalkless, diamond-shaped, pointed, dark green leaves, to 15cm (6in) long, each with 5 conspicuous sunken veins. In spring, stalked, upright, musk-scented, pure white flowers, fading to pink or red, with spreading, ovate petals, 2.5–7cm (1–3in) long, and green sepals, are borne above the leaves. ↕ to 50cm (20in), ↔ to 20cm (8in). W. North America. ❄❄❄
T. recurvatum. Upright, clump-forming perennial with lance-shaped to elliptic, mottled, mid-green leaves, to 8cm (3in) long, tapering to short stalks. In spring, upright, stalkless, deep maroon, occasionally white or yellow flowers are produced above the leaves; they have lance-shaped to ovate petals, to 5cm (2in) long, clawed at the bases, and strongly recurving green sepals. ↕ to 40cm (16in), ↔ to 30cm (12in). E. USA. ❄❄❄
T. rivale ▣ Dwarf, upright perennial with stalked, ovate, pointed, mid-green leaves, to 3cm (1¼in) long. In spring, stalked, upright, white or pale pink flowers, spotted purple at the bases, with diamond-shaped to ovate petals, to 2.5cm (1in) long, and green sepals, are produced above the leaves. Similar to

Trillium rivale

Trillium sessile

T. nivale, but easier to grow. ↕ to 12cm (5in), ↔ to 15cm (6in). W. USA. ❄❄❄
T. sessile ▣ (Toad-shade, Wake robin). Upright, clump-forming perennial with stalkless, broadly elliptic to rounded, deep green leaves, to 12cm (5in) long, marbled pale green, grey-white, and bronze-maroon. Stalkless, upright, red-maroon, rarely greenish yellow flowers, with lance-shaped petals, to 4.5cm (1¾in) long, and spreading, maroon-flushed green sepals, are borne above the leaves in late spring. ↕ to 30cm (12in), ↔ to 20cm (8in). N.E. USA. ❄❄❄
T. sessile of gardens see *T. cuneatum.*
T. stylosum see *T. catesbyi.*
T. undulatum (Painted trillium, Painted wood lily). Graceful, clump-forming perennial with erect, pale green stems, flushed pink at the bases, and stalked, narrowly ovate, tapered, dark blue-green leaves, to 15cm (6in) long. In late spring, stalked, upright, white or very pale pink flowers, with wavy petals, to 3cm (1¼in) long, with dark red, V-shaped marks at the bases and maroon-margined, dark green sepals, are borne above the leaves. Not easy to grow; needs moist, acid soil. ↕ to 30cm (12in), ↔ to 15cm (6in). E. USA. ❄❄❄
T. viride. Upright perennial with sometimes downy stems, and stalkless, lance-shaped to elliptic, mid-green leaves, 8–15cm (3–6in) long, spotted white above. Stalkless, upright, malodorous, yellow-green flowers, sometimes maroon at the bases, occasionally completely maroon, with narrowly lance-shaped petals, to 7cm (3in) long, and green sepals, are borne above the leaves in spring. ↕ to 40cm (16in), ↔ to 20cm (8in). USA (Illinois, Missouri). ❄❄❄

▷ **Trillium,**
Painted see *Trillium undulatum*
Snow see *Trillium nivale*
▷ **Trinity flower** see *Trillium*

TRIPETALEIA

syn. ELLIOTTIA

ERICACEAE

Genus of 2 species of deciduous shrubs found in mountain woodland in Japan. They are cultivated for their terminal panicles of attractive, 3-petalled, sometimes 4- or 5-petalled flowers. Grow in a peat, rock, or woodland garden.
• **HARDINESS** Fully hardy.
• **CULTIVATION** Grow in moist but well-drained, humus-rich, acid soil in partial shade. Pruning group 1.
• **PROPAGATION** Sow seed in containers in a cold frame in autumn. Insert softwood cuttings in summer.
• **PESTS AND DISEASES** Trouble free.

T. paniculata, syn. *Elliottia paniculata.* Upright, deciduous shrub with alternate, obovate to narrowly ovate-elliptic, dark green leaves, to 6cm (2½in) long. From midsummer to early autumn, pink-tinged white flowers, 2cm (¾in) across, with 3 or 5 narrow, twisted petals, are borne in upright, terminal panicles, to 15cm (6in) long. ↕↔ 1.5m (5ft). Japan. ❄❄❄

TRIPTERYGIUM

CELASTRACEAE

Genus of 2 or 3 species of deciduous, scrambling to twining climbers from deciduous woodland in E. Asia. They have large, alternate, ovate or broadly ovate to elliptic leaves. Abundant tiny, 5-petalled, saucer-shaped flowers are borne in terminal panicles, followed by prominently winged fruits. *T. regelii*, the most commonly cultivated species, is suitable for training on a house wall or over a pergola, tree, or tall tree stump. In frost-prone areas, grow half-hardy species in a cool greenhouse.
• **HARDINESS** Frost hardy to half hardy.
• **CULTIVATION** Grow in moist but well-drained, fertile soil in full sun. Pruning group 11, in spring.
• **PROPAGATION** Sow seed in containers in a cold frame as soon as ripe. Root semi-ripe cuttings in summer with bottom heat. Layer in early spring.
• **PESTS AND DISEASES** Trouble free.

T. regelii. Bushy, twining climber, often loosely shrubby when young, producing slightly angled, warty stems and long-stalked, ovate or broadly ovate to elliptic, slender-pointed, toothed, bright green leaves, 8–13cm (3–5in) long. In summer, small, saucer-shaped, green-tinted white flowers are borne in leafy panicles, to 25cm (10in) long, followed by 3-winged, pale green to light brown fruit, 1.5–2cm (½–¾in) long. ↕ to 10m (30ft). China, Korea, Japan. ❄❄

▷ **Tristagma 'Rolf Fiedler'** see *Ipheion* 'Rolf Fiedler'
▷ **Tristagma uniflorum** see *Ipheion uniflorum*
▷ **Tristania conferta** see *Lophostemon confertus*

TRITELEIA

ALLIACEAE/LILIACEAE

Genus of about 15 species of cormous perennials, closely related to *Brodiaea*, mainly found in grassland, chaparral, and pine woodland in W. USA. They are cultivated for their umbels of funnel-shaped flowers, borne on leafless stems. The semi-erect, narrowly linear, basal leaves usually die away by flowering time. Suitable for a warm, sunny, mixed or herbaceous border. In areas prone to severe frosts, grow in a cold greenhouse or alpine house.
• **HARDINESS** Frost hardy.
• **CULTIVATION** Plant corms 8cm (3in) deep in autumn. Outdoors, grow in light, sandy, fertile soil in full sun. Under glass, grow in loam-based potting compost (JI No.2), with added sharp

Triteleia hyacinthina

sand, in full light. After planting, water sparingly until leaves appear. In growth, water freely and apply a half-strength balanced liquid fertilizer monthly. Reduce water gradually after flowering; keep warm and dry when dormant.
• **PROPAGATION** Sow seed at 13–16°C (55–61°F) as soon as ripe or in early spring; seed-grown plants take 3–5 years to reach maturity. Separate corms when dormant.
• **PESTS AND DISEASES** Trouble free.

T. hyacinthina ▣ syn. *Brodiaea hyacinthina, B. lactea.* Cormous perennial with linear, basal leaves, 10–40cm (4–16in) long. Flat umbels, 10cm (4in) across, of up to 20 or more white or pale blue flowers, 1.5cm (½in) long, are produced in late spring and early summer. ↕ to 70cm (28in), ↔ 5cm (2in). W. USA. ❄❄
T. ixioides, syn. *Brodiaea ixioides, B. lutea.* Cormous perennial with linear, basal leaves, 10–40cm (4–16in) long. Open umbels, 12cm (5in) across, of up to 25 yellow flowers, 1–2.5cm (½–1in) long, with purple midribs, are produced in early summer. ↕ to 60cm (24in), ↔ 8cm (3in). W. USA. ❄❄
T. laxa ▣ syn. *Brodiaea laxa.* Showy, cormous perennial with linear, basal leaves, 20–40cm (8–16in) long. In early summer, produces loose umbels, 16cm (6in) across, of up to 25 pale to deep purple-blue flowers, 2–5cm (¾–2in) long, rarely white or shading to white at the bases. ↕ to 70cm (28in), ↔ 5cm (2in). W. USA. ❄❄. **'Koningin Fabiola'**, syn. 'Queen Fabiola', has purple-blue flowers, 5cm (2in) long.

Triteleia laxa

T. peduncularis, syn. *Brodiaea peduncularis.* Cormous perennial with linear, basal leaves, 20–40cm (8–16in) long. In summer, produces lax umbels, 35cm (14in) across, of up to 20 white or pale blue flowers, 3cm (1¼in) long. ↕ to 40cm (16in), ↔ 8cm (3in). USA (California). ❄❄

TRITONIA

IRIDACEAE

Genus of 28 species of cormous perennials, closely related to *Crocosmia*, found mainly on grassy or stony hillsides in South Africa and Swaziland. They are grown for their slender spikes of funnel- or cup-shaped, colourful flowers. The 2-ranked leaves are usually linear to lance-shaped. Grow in a warm, sunny, mixed or herbaceous border. In frost-prone areas, grow half-hardy species in a cool greenhouse or conservatory.

- **HARDINESS** Frost hardy to half hardy.
- **CULTIVATION** Plant 10cm (4in) deep. Under glass, grow in loam-based potting compost (JI No.2), with added sharp sand, in full light. After flowering, water sparingly, until leaves appear; in full growth, water freely. As leaves wither after flowering, reduce water gradually to ensure a warm, dry dormancy. Repot annually. Outdoors, grow in light, well-drained, preferably sandy soil, in a sheltered site in full sun. Provide a deep, dry winter mulch. Avoid excessive moisture, especially when dormant.
- **PROPAGATION** Sow seed at 13–16°C (55–61°F) as soon as ripe. Remove offsets when dormant
- **PESTS AND DISEASES** Trouble free.

T. crocata, syn. *T. fenestrata, T. hyalina.* Cormous perennial with erect, lance-shaped, basal leaves, 5–30cm (2–12in) long. Spikes of up to 10 cup-shaped, orange to pinkish red flowers, 1.5cm (½in) long, are produced on arching, wiry stems in spring. ↕ 20–50cm (8–20in), ↔ 8cm (3in). South Africa (Western Cape, Eastern Cape). ❄. **'Princess Beatrix'** ■ bears brilliant orange-red flowers. **'White Glory'** has amber-tinged white flowers.
T. disticha, syn. *Crocosmia rosea.* Cormous perennial with erect, linear or lance- or sword-shaped, basal leaves, 25–70cm (10–28in) long. In mid- and late summer, irregular, funnel-shaped, orange-red, red, or pink flowers, 2cm (¾in) long, are borne in many-flowered spikes, on arching, branched stems.

T

Tritonia crocata 'Princess Beatrix'

Tritonia disticha subsp. *rubrolucens*

↕ 50–100cm (20–39in), ↔ 5cm (2in). South Africa (Western Cape, Eastern Cape, Kwazulu/Natal). ❄❄. **subsp. *rubrolucens*** ■ syn. *T. rosea, T. rubrolucens*, bears a succession of open funnel-shaped pink flowers, 2.5–3.5cm (1–1½in) across, in one-sided spikes on wiry stems; South Africa (Eastern Cape, Free State, Kwazulu/Natal, Mpumalanga), Swaziland.
T. fenestrata see *T. crocata.*
T. hyalina see *T. crocata.*
T. longiflora see *Ixia paniculata.*
T. rosea see *T. disticha* subsp. *rubrolucens.*
T. rubrolucens see *T. disticha* subsp. *rubrolucens.*

TROCHODENDRON

TROCHODENDRACEAE

Genus of one species of evergreen tree or large shrub from forest in Japan, Korea, and Taiwan. *T. aralioides* is grown for its handsome, spirally arranged leaves and its racemes of unusual, vivid green flowers. Grow in a woodland garden among other trees and shrubs.

- **HARDINESS** Frost hardy.
- **CULTIVATION** Grow in moist but well-drained, neutral to slightly acid soil in full sun or dappled shade. Shelter from cold, drying winds. Pruning group 1.
- **PROPAGATION** Sow seed in containers in a cold frame in autumn. Insert semi-ripe cuttings in summer.
- **PESTS AND DISEASES** Trouble free.

T. aralioides ■ Q Broadly columnar tree or large, rounded shrub with broadly ovate to elliptic, tapered, glossy, dark green leaves, to 12cm (5in) long. Racemes, to 12cm (5in) long, of 10–20 or more flowers are borne at the shoot-tips in late spring and early summer; the petalless, bright green flowers, 2cm (¾in) across, each consist of numerous stamens radiating from a central green disc. ↕ 10m (30ft), ↔ 8m (25ft). Japan (including Ryukyu Islands), Korea, Taiwan. ❄❄

Trochodendron aralioides

TROLLIUS

Globeflower

RANUNCULACEAE

Genus of about 24 species of buttercup-like, hairless, clump-forming herbaceous perennials from moist or wet meadows in cool-temperate areas of Europe, Asia, and North America. They produce numerous fibrous roots, and basal rosettes of stalked, palmately lobed leaves, the lobes further divided or toothed. Erect stems usually bear a few, mainly stalkless leaves. Both the basal and stem leaves are usually mid-green, sometimes glossy. Terminal, solitary, spherical to bowl-shaped flowers, with reduced or linear, petal-like sepals, nectary-bearing petals, and numerous stamens, are borne in spring or summer. Grow in a moist border or bog garden, or beside a pond or stream, or naturalize in a damp meadow garden.

- **HARDINESS** Fully hardy.
- **CULTIVATION** Grow in moist, deep, fertile, preferably heavy soil, which does not dry out, in full sun or partial shade. Cut stems back hard after first flush of flowers; apply a balanced liquid fertilizer to encourage further blooming. Earlier-flowering species and cultivars may be forced gently in a temperate greenhouse, to produce early flowers for cutting.
- **PROPAGATION** Sow seed in containers in a cold frame as soon as ripe or in spring; seed may take 2 years to germinate. Divide as new growth begins or immediately after flowering.
- **PESTS AND DISEASES** Powdery mildew may be a problem.

Trollius chinensis

Trollius x *cultorum* 'Alabaster'

T. chinensis ■ syn. *T. ledebourii* of gardens. Clump-forming perennial bearing 5-lobed basal leaves, to 12cm (5in) long, with broadly lance-shaped lobes divided into sharply toothed segments; the stem leaves are smaller. In midsummer, shallowly bowl-shaped, light orange-yellow flowers, 5cm (2in) across, with long petals, are produced on stout, furrowed stems. ↕ to 90cm (36in), ↔ 45cm (18in). N.E. China. ❄❄❄
***T. x cultorum* cultivars.** Clump-forming perennials bearing 5-lobed, toothed, glossy basal leaves, 18cm (7in) long, with lance-shaped lobes divided into toothed segments; stem leaves are smaller and more finely divided. Bowl-shaped flowers, 2.5–6cm (1–2½in) across, are borne from mid-spring to midsummer. ↕ to 90cm (36in), ↔ 45cm (18in). ❄❄❄. **'Alabaster'** ■ is less vigorous than most cultivars, and bears pale primrose-yellow flowers in mid- and late spring; ↕ to 60cm (24in), ↔ to 40cm (16in). **'Earliest of All'** ■ bears clear yellow flowers, 7cm (3in) across, in mid-spring; ↕ 50cm (20in), ↔ 40cm (16in). **'Feuertroll'**, syn. 'Fireglobe', produces rich orange-yellow flowers, with deeper orange stamens, in late

Trollius x *cultorum* 'Earliest of All'

Trollius x *cultorum* 'Orange Princess'

spring; ↕ to 65cm (26in), ↔ 40cm (16in). **'Fireglobe'** see 'Feuertroll'. **'Gold Fountain'** see 'Goldquelle'. **'Goldquelle'**, syn. 'Gold Fountain', bears yellow flowers, 7cm (3in) across, in early and midsummer; ↕ to 70cm (28in). **'Lemon Queen'** bears pale yellow flowers, 7cm (3in) across, in late spring and early summer; ↕ 60cm (24in). **'Orange Princess'** ▣ bears orange-gold flowers in late spring and early summer.
T. europaeus (Common European globeflower). Clump-forming, very variable perennial bearing 5-lobed basal leaves, to 12cm (5in) long, with wedge-shaped, deeply divided and toothed lobes. Erect, rarely branched stems produce smaller leaves and spherical, lemon-yellow flowers, 5cm (2in) across, in early and midsummer. ↕ 80cm (32in), ↔ 45cm (18in). Europe, Caucasus, North America. ✲✲✲. **'Canary Bird'** bears pale lemon-yellow flowers over a long period.
***T. ledebourii* of gardens** see *T. chinensis*.
T. pumilus ▣ Clump-forming, tufted perennial bearing 5-lobed, glossy basal leaves, 2–7cm (¾–3in) long, with oblong to lance-shaped, toothed lobes. In late spring and early summer, produces cup-shaped, deep golden yellow flowers, 2–3.5cm (¾–1½in) across, often red or purple-crimson on the outside. ↕ to 30cm (12in), ↔ to 20cm (8in). Himalayas, E. Tibet, China. ✲✲✲
T. yunnanensis. Clump-forming, tufted perennial bearing 3- to 5-lobed, glossy basal leaves, 5–12cm (2–5in) long, with ovate, toothed lobes; the stem leaves are similar but smaller. In late spring and early summer, produces cup-shaped, golden yellow flowers, 2–6cm (¾–2½in) across. ↕ to 70cm (28in), ↔ to 30cm (12in). S.W. China. ✲✲✲

Trollius pumilus

▷ **Trompetilla, Scarlet** see *Bouvardia ternifolia*

TROPAEOLUM

TROPAEOLACEAE

Genus of 80–90 species of hairless, climbing, trailing, or bushy annuals and herbaceous perennials, many with tuberous roots, found mainly in cool, mountainous areas in Central and South America. The alternate, rounded, peltate leaves are entire or palmately lobed to palmate with 5–7 lobes or leaflets; they have long leaf-stalks, which are used as the method of attachment in climbing species. Roughly funnel-shaped flowers, with 5 showy, clawed petals, often with prominent spurs, and 5 inconspicuous, pointed sepals, are borne singly from the leaf axils. Grow climbing tropaeolums over a fence, trellis, pergola, or non-flowering shrub, or allow to trail on a bank or dry wall. *T. polyphyllum* is suitable for a raised or scree bed, or a large rock garden. The dwarf, bushy *T. majus* hybrids and cultivars are effective in an annual bed or border; the trailing or semi-trailing variants are excellent for hanging baskets or other containers. In frost-prone areas, grow tender perennials in a cool greenhouse or conservatory. The leaves and flowers of annual tropaeolums are edible, and the young fruits of *T. majus* can be pickled.

• **HARDINESS** Frost hardy to frost tender.

• **CULTIVATION** Grow in moist but well-drained, moderately fertile soil in full sun. *T. majus* and its hybrids and cultivars flower best in poorer soils; *T. speciosum* prefers moist, humus-rich, neutral to acid soil in full sun or partial shade, but with roots and lower stems in cool shade. Support the climbing stems. In frost-prone areas, lift the tubers of *T. tuberosum* and store in a frost-free place until the following spring. Under glass, grow in loam-based potting compost (JI No.2), with added fine grit, in full light with shade from hot sun. Plant those with running rootstocks directly into a border; tuberous tropaeolums need deep containers. During growth, water freely and apply a balanced liquid fertilizer monthly; reduce water as leaves wither and keep barely moist when dormant. *T. azureum* and *T. tricolorum* are both dormant in summer; start into growth in early autumn, and water sparingly in autumn and winter.

• **PROPAGATION** Sow seed of annuals at 13–16°C (55–61°F) in early spring, or *in situ* in mid-spring. Sow seed of perennials in containers in a cold frame as soon as ripe; germination is often erratic. Separate tubers in autumn, when dormant. Divide *T. speciosum* carefully in early spring. Insert stem-tip cuttings in late summer with bottom heat. Root basal or stem-tip cuttings of selected cultivars, such as *T. majus* 'Hermine Grasshoff', in spring or early summer.

• **PESTS AND DISEASES** Caterpillars of cabbage white butterflies, flea beetles, black fly, and slugs may be troublesome. *T. majus* and its hybrids and cultivars are susceptible to whiteflies and viruses.

Tropaeolum Alaska Series

T. aduncum see *T. peregrinum*.
***T.* Alaska Series** ▣ Dwarf, bushy annuals, derived from *T. majus*, with light green leaves, speckled and marked creamy white. Single flowers, in shades of yellow, orange, mahogany, or cream, are borne from summer to autumn. ↕ to 30cm (12in), ↔ to 45cm (18in). ✲
T. azureum. Perennial climber with an ovoid tuber and 5- to 9-palmate or palmately lobed, pale or mid-green leaves, 2cm (¾in) across, with lance-shaped leaflets or lobes. Short-spurred, sky-blue flowers, 1.5–2cm (½–¾in) across, with whitish cream or yellow centres, are borne in late spring. ↕ 60–100cm (24–39in). Chile. ✲
T. canariense see *T. peregrinum*.
***T.* 'Empress of India'.** Dwarf, bushy annual, derived from *T. majus*, with purple-green leaves. From summer to autumn, produces semi-double, velvety, rich scarlet flowers. ↕ to 30cm (12in), ↔ to 45cm (18in). ✲
***T.* Gleam Series.** Vigorous, semi-trailing annuals, derived from *T. majus*, bearing semi-double flowers in scarlet, orange, yellow, or pastel shades from summer to autumn. ↕ to 40cm (16in), ↔ to 60cm (24in). ✲
***T.* Jewel Series** ▣ Dwarf, bushy annuals, derived from *T. majus*, bearing semi-double and double, yellow, pink-orange, scarlet, or crimson flowers from early summer to autumn; flowers are sometimes covered by the foliage. ↕ to 30cm (12in), ↔ to 45cm (18in). ✲
T. majus (Indian cress, Nasturtium). Strong-growing, annual climber, sometimes scrambling, with rounded to kidney-shaped, wavy-margined, light green leaves, 2.5–6cm (1–2½in) long. From summer to autumn, bears long-spurred, red, orange, or yellow flowers, 5–6cm (2–2½in) across. Many cultivars often attributed to *T. majus*, and with similar characteristics to the species, are of hybrid origin, and are described here under their cultivar names. ↕ 1–3m (3–10ft), ↔ 1.5–5m (5–15ft). Bolivia to Colombia. ❀ (min. 3°C/37°F). **'Hermine Grashoff'** has double, bright red flowers, and may only be propagated by stem-tip cuttings.
***T.* 'Peach Melba'** ▣ Dwarf, bushy annual, derived from *T. majus*, bearing semi-double, creamy yellow flowers with orange-red centres, from summer to autumn. Best in a container. ↕ 23–30cm (9–12in), ↔ to 45cm (18in). ✲

Tropaeolum Jewel Series

Tropaeolum 'Peach Melba'

Tropaeolum peregrinum (inset: flower detail)

T. peregrinum ■ syn. *T. aduncum, T. canariense* (Canary creeper). Strong-growing, annual climber with 5-lobed, light to greyish green leaves, 2.5–5cm (1–2in) long. From summer to autumn, produces hook-spurred, bright yellow flowers, 2.5cm (1in) across; they have 3 tiny lower petals and 2 large, erect upper ones, which are toothed and fringed like tiny birds' wings. ↕2.5–4m (8–12ft). Ecuador, Peru. ⌂ (min. 3°C/37°F)

T. polyphyllum ■ Trailing herbaceous perennial with an elongated, rhizome-like tuber and deeply 5- to 9-lobed, glaucous, blue-green leaves, to 8cm (3in) long. Long-spurred, rich yellow to orange flowers, 4cm (1½in) across, are produced among long, trailing masses of foliage over a long period in summer. ↕5–8cm (2–3in), ↔ to 1m (3ft). Chile, Argentina. ❄❄

T. speciosum ■ (Flame creeper, Flame nasturtium). Slender, perennial climber with deep-rooting, long, thin, fleshy white rhizomes. The 5- to 7-palmate, mid- to dark green leaves, 4cm (1½in) long, are composed of obovate to wedge-shaped leaflets. From summer to autumn, bears long-spurred, bright vermilion flowers, 2cm (¾in) across, with long-clawed petals, the lower 3 of which are larger than the others; flowers are followed by spherical blue fruit with persistent red calyces. ↕ to 3m (10ft) or more. Chile. ❄❄

***T.* Tom Thumb Series.** Dwarf, bushy annuals, derived from *T. majus*, bearing single, yellow, orange, red, salmon-pink, or rose-pink flowers from summer to autumn; flowers are sometimes covered by the foliage. ↕ to 24cm (10in), ↔ to 35cm (14in). ❄

T. tricolor see *T. tricolorum.*

T. tricolorum, syn. *T. tricolor.* Tuberous-rooted, perennial climber with ovoid, often irregular tubers. Very slender stems bear rounded, 5- to 7-palmate, light green leaves, to 4cm (1½in) long, with narrowly elliptic to narrowly obovate, 5- to 7-lobed leaflets. From winter to early summer, bears flowers, 3cm (1¼in) long, with lantern-shaped, maroon-tipped, orange-scarlet calyces, short, orange to yellow petals, and long, upturned, red to yellow or purple spurs. ↕1–2m (3–6ft). Chile. ❄

T. tuberosum. Perennial climber with large, purple-marbled yellow tubers and 3- to 6-lobed, greyish green leaves, 5cm (2in) long. Long-spurred, cup-shaped

Tropaeolum polyphyllum

Tropaeolum speciosum

Tropaeolum tuberosum var. *lineamaculatum* 'Ken Aslet'

flowers, 3–4cm (1¼–1½in) long, with orange-red sepals and deep yellow to orange-yellow petals, with brown veins inside, are produced from midsummer to autumn. ↕2–4m (6–12ft). Colombia, Ecuador, Peru, Bolivia. ❄. **var. *lineamaculatum* 'Ken Aslet'** ■ is the most common cultivar, and has orange flowers. **var. *piliferum* 'Sidney'** has more slender, rhizome-like tubers and orange flowers, 2–3cm (¾–1¼in) long.

***T.* Whirlybird Series.** Dwarf, bushy annuals, derived from *T. majus*. Non-spurred, single to semi-double flowers, in colours including reds, pinks, yellows, and oranges, are produced well above the foliage, from summer to autumn. ↕ to 24cm (10in), ↔ to 35cm (14in). ❄. **'Whirlybird Cream'** has creamy yellow flowers; ⌂ (min. 3–5°C/37–41°F)

▷**Trumpet,**
Evening see *Gelsemium sempervirens*
Golden see *Allamanda cathartica*
Herald's see *Beaumontia grandiflora*
Water see *Cryptocoryne*
White see *Sarracenia leucophylla*
Yellow see *Sarracenia flava*
▷**Trumpet bush** see *Tecoma stans*
▷**Trumpet creeper** see *Campsis*
Chinese see *C. grandiflora*
Common see *C. radicans*
▷**Trumpet tree, Rosy** see *Tabebuia rosea*
▷**Trumpet vine** see *Campsis*
Blue see *Thunbergia grandiflora*
Chinese see *Campsis grandiflora*
Pink see *Podranea ricasoliana*

TSUGA

Hemlock

PINACEAE

Genus of 10 or 11 species of evergreen, monoecious, coniferous trees found in forest from the Himalayas to N. Burma, W. Vietnam, China, Taiwan, and Japan, and in North America. Flattened, usually linear leaves, with silvery white bands beneath, are radially arranged or 2-ranked, and vary in length along the shoots. The small, ovoid-oblong to almost spherical, terminal, pale to mid-brown female cones become pendent, similar to those of *Picea*, but with few scales; male cones are almost spherical, 3–5mm (⅛–¼in) across, and borne at the tips of lateral shoots. The leading shoot is pendent. Tsugas are excellent specimen trees and very shade-tolerant, especially when young. *T. heterophylla* is suitable for hedging. The dwarf cultivars are all suitable for bonsai work.

• **HARDINESS** Fully hardy.

• **CULTIVATION** Grow in humus-rich, moist but well-drained, acid to slightly alkaline soil in full sun or partial shade, providing shelter from cold, drying winds. Trim hedges from early to late summer.

• **PROPAGATION** Sow seed in containers in a cold frame in spring. Root semi-ripe cuttings in late summer or early autumn.

• **PESTS AND DISEASES** Susceptible to butt rot fungus.

T. canadensis ■ △ (Eastern hemlock). Broadly conical tree, often having several stems, with deeply furrowed, purplish grey bark and small-budded, slender, grey-hairy shoots. Linear, finely toothed, mid-green leaves, to 2cm (¾in) long, taper from the bases and are 2-ranked with a wide parting below; a few very short leaves lie flat along the shoots with their silver undersides uppermost. Oblong-conical female cones are 2cm (¾in) long. ↕ to 25m (80ft), ↔ to 10m (30ft). E. North America. ❄❄❄. **'Aurea'** is compact and slow-growing, with golden yellow young foliage, turning greener with age; ↕8m (25ft), ↔ 4m (12ft). **'Bennett'** is dwarf and vase-shaped, forming a central "nest", with short, light green leaves; ↕1.5m (5ft), ↔ 2m (6ft). **'Cole's Prostrate'**, syn. 'Coles', is low-growing and suitable for ground cover; ↕30cm (12in), ↔ 1m (3ft). **'Gracilis'** is a slow-growing, dwarf shrub with pendent branch tips; ↕↔ 1m (3ft). **'Jeddeloh'** ■ is hemispherical, and similar to 'Bennett', with bright green leaves; ↕1.5m (5ft), ↔ 2m (6ft). **'Pendula'**, syn. f. *pendula*, is a slow-growing, spreading, mound-forming shrub, with pendent branches, and is very effective hanging over a bank or wall; ↕ to 4m (12ft), ↔ to 8m (25ft).

T. caroliniana △ (Carolina hemlock). Conical or ovoid, twiggy tree with shallowly fissured, red-brown bark and shiny, red-brown shoots with short hairs in the grooves. Round-tipped, entire, dark green leaves, 1–2cm (½–¾in) long, are 2-ranked, widely parted above, and somewhat irregular and sparse. Ovoid to ellipsoid female cones are 2.5–3.5cm (1–1½in) long. ↕15–20m (50–70ft), ↔ to 8m (25ft). USA (Appalachians from Virginia to Georgia). ❄❄❄

T. diversifolia △ (Northern Japanese hemlock). Broadly conical, later domed tree, usually having several stems, with

Tsuga canadensis

Tsuga canadensis 'Jeddeloh'

orange-brown bark and orange shoots with short, fine hairs. Linear leaves are very glossy, dark green, 0.5–1.5cm (¼–½in) long, and 2-ranked with a wide parting above, broader and more densely packed towards the rounded, notched shoot-tips. Ovoid female cones are up to 2cm (¾in) long. ↕ to 15m (50ft), ↔ to 8m (25ft). N. Japan. ❄❄❄

T. heterophylla ◊ (Western hemlock). Narrowly conical tree with cracked, purple-brown bark, horizontal branches with pendent tips, and brownish grey shoots with long brown hairs. Blunt, round-tipped, narrowly elliptic-oblong, finely toothed, very glossy, dark green leaves, 0.5–2cm (¼–¾in) long, are 2-ranked with a wide parting beneath. Ovoid female cones are 2cm (¾in) long. Very shade-tolerant but requires shelter from wind. ↕ 20–40m (70–130ft), ↔ 6–10m (20–30ft). W. North America (Alaska to California). ❄❄❄

T. mertensiana ◊ (Mountain hemlock). Columnar-conical tree with scaly, purple to red-brown bark and hairy, red-brown shoots. Thick, blunt-tipped, linear, entire, glaucous blue or grey-green leaves, 1.5–2.5cm (½–1in) long, are convex on both sides, and radially arranged. Female cones are oblong-cylindrical, 4–8cm (1½–3in) long, and have reflexed scales when fully open. ↕ 15m (50ft), ↔ 6m (20ft). W. North America (Alaska to California). ❄❄❄. **'Glauca'** ▣ ◊–⌂ is slow-growing and dwarf, with glaucous, silver-grey foliage; ↕ 3m (10ft), ↔ 2m (6ft).

T. sieboldii ⌂ (Southern Japanese hemlock). Broadly conical tree having several stems with smooth, dark grey bark, later cracked, and stiff, shiny, buff shoots. Linear, entire leaves, 0.7–2cm (¼–¾in) long, with notched tips, glossy, dark green above and pale green or dull white beneath, are variable in length and arrangement. Ovoid female cones are 2.5cm (1in) long. ↕ 15m (50ft), ↔ to 8m (25ft). S. Japan. ❄❄❄

TSUSIOPHYLLUM

ERICACEAE

Genus of one species of dwarf, semi-evergreen shrub found in woodland in Japan. It is cultivated for its umbel-like clusters of small, tubular-bell-shaped white flowers, borne in early summer, and is an attractive addition to a peat bed or woodland garden.

- **HARDINESS** Frost hardy.
- **CULTIVATION** Grow in moist, humus-rich, acid soil in partial shade. Provide shelter from cold, drying winds. Pruning group 8.
- **PROPAGATION** Sow seed as soon as ripe in containers in a cold frame. Insert semi-ripe cuttings in summer.
- **PESTS AND DISEASES** Trouble free.

T. tanakae. Prostrate, spreading shrub with short, hairy branches and alternate, ovate to lance-shaped or inversely lance-shaped, very hairy, dark green leaves, 1–3cm (½–1¼in) or more long. Dense clusters of 2–6 silky-hairy white flowers, 7–10mm (¼–½in) long, each with 4 or 5 spreading petal lobes, are produced at the shoot-tips in early summer. ↕ to 50cm (20in), ↔ to 20cm (8in). Japan (Honshu). ❄❄

Tsuga mertensiana 'Glauca'

TUBERARIA

CISTACEAE

Genus of about 12 species of annuals and perennials from scrub, heath, and woodland in C. and S. Europe. The simple, lance-shaped to almost rounded leaves are borne in basal rosettes, and occasionally on the upright flowering stems. Terminal cymes of shallowly cup-shaped yellow flowers, sometimes with purple or red spots, are borne in late spring and summer. Grow annuals in a mixed or annual border, and perennials in a sunny border or warm rock garden.

- **HARDINESS** Fully hardy to frost hardy.
- **CULTIVATION** Grow in any well-drained soil in full sun.
- **PROPAGATION** Sow seed at 13–16°C (55–61°F) in early spring. Seed of annuals may also be sown *in situ* in mid- to late spring. Separate rooted rosettes, or take rosettes as cuttings, in spring.
- **PESTS AND DISEASES** Leaves may be damaged by slugs and snails.

T. guttata, syn. *Helianthemum guttatum.* Erect, rosette-forming, hairy annual with wavy-margined, mid-green, prominently 3-veined leaves, 2.5–8cm (1–3in) long; the basal leaves are elliptic or obovate, the stem leaves linear-oblong or linear-lance-shaped. In summer, bears terminal cymes of short-lived, long-stalked, cup-shaped yellow flowers, to 3cm (1¼in) across, each petal spotted maroon-red at the base. ↕↔ to 30cm (12in). C. and S. Europe. ❄❄❄

T. lignosa, syn. *Helianthemum tuberaria.* Spreading, rosette-forming, woody-based perennial with hairy, obovate to lance-shaped or elliptic, dark green leaves, to 6cm (2½in) long. Loose, terminal cymes of bright yellow flowers, 2.5–3cm (1–1¼in) across, without spots, are produced from early to late summer. ↕ to 40cm (16in), ↔ 40cm (16in). W. Mediterranean. ❄❄

▷**Tuberose** see *Polianthes tuberosa*

TULBAGHIA

ALLIACEAE/LILIACEAE

Genus of about 24 species of clump-forming, mainly deciduous, sometimes semi-evergreen, rhizomatous or bulbous perennials found in various habitats, some mountainous, in tropical and temperate southern Africa. Basal, strap-shaped to linear, hairless, occasionally grey-green leaves have a smell like that of onions or garlic. Umbels of dainty, usually purple or white flowers, some fragrant, especially at night, are borne over a long period from late spring to autumn. The flowers are tubular, each with 6 spreading tepals and a small, trumpet-like corona. In frost-prone areas, grow in a cool green-house, particularly *T. alliacea*, which has overwintering leaves. Elsewhere, grow in a sunny border or rock garden.

- **HARDINESS** Frost hardy to frost tender; most frost-hardy species tolerate short periods at temperatures to -10°C (14°F).
- **CULTIVATION** Under glass, grow in well-drained, loam-based potting compost (JI No.2) in full light. Water freely when in growth; reduce water when in flower, and again as the leaves wither; keep almost dry when dormant. Outdoors, grow in well-drained, moderately fertile, humus-rich, loamy soil in full sun. In frost-prone areas, provide a dry winter mulch.
- **PROPAGATION** Sow seed in containers in a cold frame as soon as ripe, or in spring. Seed germinates easily, and the seedlings quickly reach flowering size. Divide most species in spring; divide *T. alliacea* in late summer.
- **PESTS AND DISEASES** Susceptible to aphids and whiteflies under glass.

Tulbaghia simmleri

T. alliacea. Semi-evergreen, rhizomatous perennial bearing clusters of narrowly linear leaves, to 20cm (8in) long. In late spring and early summer, bears terminal umbels of fragrant, purple-tinged, greenish white flowers, 1cm (½in) long; the flowers have brownish red coronas. ↕ to 45cm (18in), ↔ 20cm (8in). Zimbabwe, South Africa (Northern Cape, Eastern Cape, Western Cape). ❄❄

T. capensis. Rhizomatous perennial with clusters of narrowly linear leaves, to 30cm (12in) long. Terminal umbels of greenish purple flowers, to 1.5cm (½in) long, with purplish brown coronas, are produced in early and midsummer. ↕ to 60cm (24in), ↔ 25cm (10in). South Africa (Namaqualand to Western Cape). ❄❄

T. fragrans see *T. simmleri.*

T. pulchella see *T. simmleri.*

T. simmleri ▣ syn. *T. fragrans*, *T. pulchella.* Bulbous perennial with clusters of linear leaves, 30–60cm (12–24in) long (wider than in most species). Large, terminal umbels of fragrant, light to deep purple flowers, to 2cm (¾in) long, are produced in early and midsummer. ↕ to 60cm (24in), ↔ 25cm (10in). South Africa (Mpumalanga). ❄❄

T. violacea. Vigorous, clump-forming perennial with corm-like rhizomes and narrowly linear, greyish green leaves, to 30cm (12in) long. Large, terminal umbels of fragrant lilac flowers, 2cm (¾in) long, are produced from mid-summer to early autumn. ↕ 45–60cm (18–24in), ↔ 25cm (10in). South Africa (Eastern Cape, KwaZulu/Natal, Mpumalanga). ❄❄. **'Silver Lace'**, syn. 'Variegata', has cream-striped leaves and larger flowers, 2–4cm (¾–1½in) long.

▷**Tulip** see *Tulipa*
Cape see *Haemanthus coccineus*
Lady see *Tulipa clusiana*
Mariposa see *Calochortus*
Water-lily see *Tulipa kaufmanniana*
▷**Tulip tree** see *Liriodendron, L. tulipifera*
Chinese see *L. chinense*

TULIPA *syn.* AMANA

Tulip

LILIACEAE

Genus of about 100 species of bulbous perennials found in usually hot, dry habitats, from sea level and steppes to alpine areas, in temperate Europe, Asia and the Middle East; they are at their most diverse in C. Asia. Tulips have linear to broadly ovate, either hairy or hairless, sometimes channelled or wavy-margined, mostly mid- or grey-green leaves; they are generally borne at the base, although in some species and cultivars they are arranged alternately on the usually hairless, sometimes hairy or downy flower stems, and decrease in size up the stem. The upright, terminal flowers, each with 6 tepals (often referred to as petals), are borne singly or in clusters of up to 12. Tulip cultivars have single or double flowers, mainly ovoid or goblet- to bowl-shaped or lily-like, sometimes fringed (see panel below), and are available in a wide range of single, mixed, or variegated colours. Variegation (i.e. breaks in colour) may be caused by a virus, although healthy tulips may also be variegated.

Tulips are valued in beds and borders for their brilliant colours. Some smaller species, such as *T. kaufmanniana* and *T. tarda*, are suitable for a rock garden. If ingested, all parts may cause mild stomach upset, and contact with any part may aggravate skin allergies.

For horticultural purposes, tulips are divided into the following groups, which are chiefly defined by their flower characteristics. This replaces the older divisions (given in brackets below).

Single Early Group (Division 1)
Cup-shaped flowers, to 7cm (3in) across, are white to dark purple, often margined, "flamed", or flecked with a contrasting colour. Early and mid-spring-flowering. Leaves are 10–35cm (4–14in) long. Suitable for bedding or a mixed border; use low-growing cultivars in containers. ↕15–45cm (6–18in).

Double Early Group (Division 2)
Fully double, bowl-shaped flowers, to 8cm (3in) across, are dark red to yellow or white, often margined or flecked with another colour. Mid-spring-flowering. Leaves are 10–35cm (4–14in) long. Suitable for bedding and containers. ↕30–40cm (12–16in).

Triumph Group (Division 3)
Single, cup-shaped flowers, to 6cm (2½in) across, are produced in a wide range of colours, including dark purple to red, pink, yellow, or white, often margined or flecked with a contrasting colour. Mid- or late spring-flowering. Leaves are 10–35cm (4–14in) long. Suitable for bedding, and good for cut flowers. ↕35–60cm (14–24in).

Darwin Hybrid Group (Division 4)
Single, ovoid flowers, to 7cm (3in) across, are often very brightly coloured in shades of yellow, pink, orange, or red, usually flushed, "flamed", or margined with a different colour, and often with contrasting bases. Mid- or late spring-flowering. Leaves are upright, 10–35cm (4–14in) long. Not to be confused with the old Darwin tulips (see Single Late Group). Suitable for bedding, and good for cut flowers. ↕50–70cm (20–28in).

Single Late Group (Division 5)
Cup- or goblet-shaped flowers, to 7cm (3in) across, sometimes several to a stem, are white to yellow, pink, red, or almost black, often with contrasting margins. Late spring-flowering. Leaves are 10–35cm (4–14in) long. Includes the old Darwin and cottage tulips. Suitable for bedding, and good for cut flowers. ↕45–75cm (18–30in).

Lily-flowered Group (Division 6)
Elegant, single, goblet-shaped flowers, to 8cm (3in) across, with reflexed, pointed tips to the tepals, are white to yellow, or pink to shades of red and magenta, sometimes margined, "flamed", or flushed with a contrasting colour. Late spring-flowering. Leaves are 10–40cm (4–16in) long. Excellent for formal bedding. ↕45–65cm (18–26in).

Fringed Group (Division 7)
Single, cup-shaped flowers, to 8cm (3in) across, are white, yellow, pink, red, or violet, with fringed margins, usually in a different colour. Late spring-flowering. Leaves are 10–40cm (4–16in) long. Suitable for a border, and good for cut flowers. ↕35–65cm (14–26in).

Viridiflora Group (Division 8)
Single, cup- or almost closed bowl-shaped flowers, to 8cm (3in) across, are sometimes entirely green, margined with another colour, or white to yellow, red, or purple, "flamed" or striped green, with contrasting centres. Late spring-flowering. Leaves are 10–40cm (4–16in) long. Ideal for a mixed border, and good for cut flowers. ↕40–55cm (16–22in).

Rembrandt Group (Division 9)
Single, cup-shaped flowers, to 8cm (3in) across, are white, yellow, or red, with black, brown, bronze, purple, red, or pink stripes or "feathers", caused by a virus. Often termed "broken" tulips. Late spring-flowering. Leaves are 10–35cm (4–14in) long. Suitable for a mixed border, and good for cut flowers. ↕45–65cm (18–26in).

Parrot Group (Division 10)
Single, cup-shaped flowers, to 10cm (4in) across, are white to pink or violet-blue, often unevenly striped with different colours, including green. The tepals are finely and irregularly cut. Late spring-flowering. Leaves are 10–35cm (4–14in) long. Ideal for a border; good for cut flowers. ↕35–65cm (14–26in).

Double Late Group (peony-flowered) (Division 11)
Fully double, bowl-shaped flowers, to 12cm (5in) across, are white to purple, sometimes margined or "flamed" in a different colour. Late spring-flowering. Leaves are 10–40cm (4–16in) long. Suitable for bedding or a border. ↕35–60cm (14–24in).

Kaufmanniana Group (Division 12)
T. kaufmanniana and hybrids mainly derived from it. Single, bowl-shaped flowers, 8–10cm (3–4in) across, are frequently multicoloured, usually with distinctively coloured bases. Early or mid-spring-flowering. Leaves, 8–25cm (3–10in) long, are sometimes marked bronze, red, or purple. Ideal for a rock garden or border. ↕15–30cm (6–12in).

Fosteriana Group (Division 13)
T. fosteriana and hybrids mainly derived from it. Single, bowl-shaped flowers, to 12cm (5in) across, are white to yellow or dark red, sometimes margined or "flamed" in another colour, and with contrasting bases. Mid-spring-flowering.

Tulipa 'Abba'

Tulipa acuminata

Tulipa 'African Queen'

Tulipa 'Ancilla'

Tulipa 'Angélique'

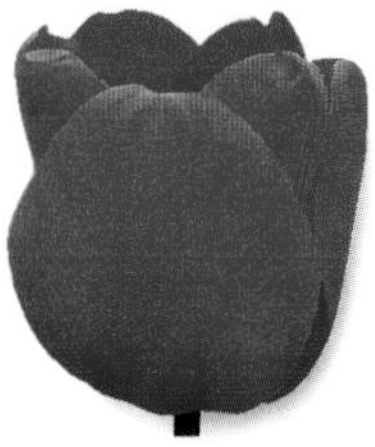
Tulipa 'Apeldoorn'

Leaves, 5–30cm (2–12in) long, are usually light bright green to dark green, sometimes marked red-purple. Suitable for a border. ↕20–65cm (8–26in).

Greigii Group (Division 14)
T. greigii and hybrids mainly derived from it. Single, bowl-shaped flowers, to 10cm (4in) across, are yellow to red, sometimes "flamed" or margined in a different colour, and with contrasting bases. Usually early or mid-spring-flowering. Broad, spreading, usually wavy-margined, blue-grey leaves, 5–18cm (2–7in) long, have dark bluish maroon markings. Grow in a rock garden or border. ↕15–30cm (6–12in).

Miscellaneous Group (Division 15)
All species and hybrids not included in other divisions. There are two informal sections: low-growing, 10–20cm (4–8in) tall, with star-shaped flowers, 5–8cm (2–3in) across, with pointed tepals; and taller-growing, 20–35cm (8–14in) or more tall, with mainly bowl-shaped flowers, 6–15cm (2½–6in) across, mostly with rounded bases and tepals. Late winter- to late spring-flowering. Grow in a rock garden. Keep dry in summer. The smallest ones may also be grown in a bulb frame or alpine house. *T. sprengeri* and *T. sylvestris* are suitable for naturalizing in fine grass.

• **HARDINESS** Fully hardy.
• **CULTIVATION** Grow in fertile, well-drained soil in full sun, sheltered from strong winds: *T. sprengeri* and *T. tarda* prefer humus-rich, peaty soil; rock garden species and cultivars prefer more sharply drained soil. All dislike excessive wet. Plant at a depth of 10–15cm (4–6in) in late summer or autumn; allow for a spread of 8–13cm (3–5in) for most tulips, and 13–15cm (5–6in) for Greigii and Kaufmanniana Group tulips, which have spreading leaves. Dead-head and remove any fallen tepals after flowering. The species, and many Greigii and Kaufmanniana Group tulips, may be left in the ground for several years. For those belonging to other groups, lift bulbs annually, once the leaves have died down, and ripen in a cold greenhouse. Replant the largest bulbs, and grow on smaller ones in a nursery bed for a year. Smaller tulips may be grown in containers in a bulb frame or alpine house, in a mix of equal parts loam, leaf mould, and sharp sand. In growth, water moderately, applying a balanced liquid fertilizer weekly for 3 or 4 weeks after flowering; keep dry in summer, and repot annually. Early-flowering and Triumph Group tulips are sometimes prepared for forcing, in a

TULIP FLOWERS

Tulips are valued for their brightly coloured, upright flowers, mainly produced in spring. The flowers may be single or double, and vary in shape from simple cups, bowls, and goblets to more complex forms produced by twisted or rounded tepals.

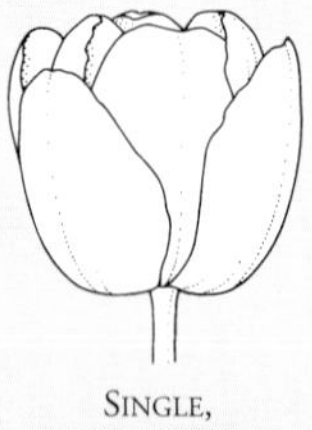
SINGLE, CUP-SHAPED

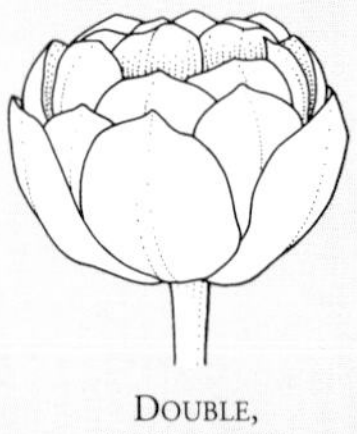
DOUBLE, BOWL-SHAPED

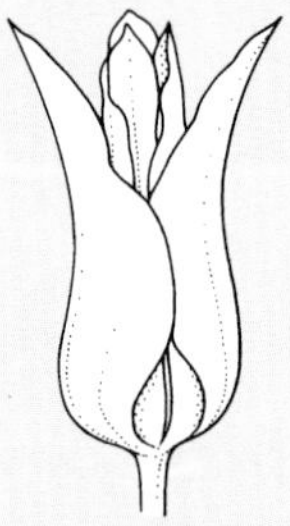
GOBLET-SHAPED

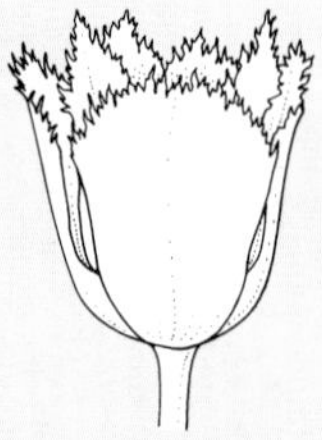
FRINGED

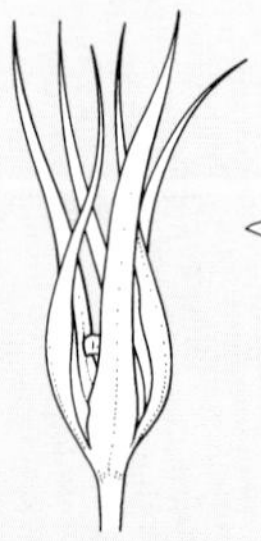
LONG, SLENDER-TEPALLED

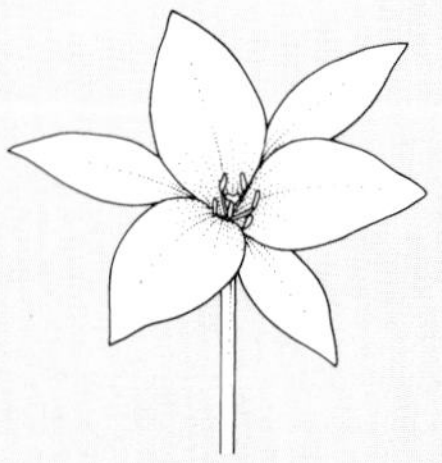
STAR-SHAPED

TULIPA

Tulipa 'Apricot Beauty'

Tulipa 'Arabian Mystery'

Tulipa 'Attila'

Tulipa 'Balalaika'

Tulipa 'Ballade'

Tulipa batalinii

Tulipa biflora

Tulipa 'Bing Crosby'

Tulipa 'Bird of Paradise'

Tulipa 'Blue Heron'

Tulipa 'Blue Parrot'

Tulipa 'Burns'

similar manner to hyacinths (see *Hyacinthus*), except that tulip bulbs should be kept in a cool, dark place until leaf tips show, then brought indoors or into a greenhouse at 10°C (50°F). Raise the temperature gradually to no more than 18°C (64°F) when leaves reach 10cm (4in) long.

• **PROPAGATION** Sow seed of species in containers in a cold greenhouse or frame in autumn; it may take 4–7 years for flowers to be produced. Separate offsets of species and cultivars after lifting in summer, replant, and grow on.

• **PESTS AND DISEASES** Bulb rots may affect tulips in poorly drained soil. Aphids spread tulip-breaking virus from Rembrandt Group tulips to other tulips. Also prone to tulip fire, slugs, and stem and bulb eelworms.

***T.* 'Abba'** ▣ Double Early Group tulip producing glowing tomato-red flowers, flushed dull cardinal-red and sometimes irregularly feathered yellow. Mid-spring-flowering. ↕30cm (12in). ✻✻✻

***T.* 'Abra'.** Triumph Group tulip bearing yellow-margined, reddish brown flowers in mid-spring. ↕40cm (16in). ✻✻✻

T. acuminata ▣ Miscellaneous Group tulip with 2–7 linear to lance-shaped, sometimes wavy-margined, hairless, glaucous, grey-green leaves, to 30cm (12in) long. Solitary flowers, 10cm (4in) long, with long, pointed tepals and rounded bases, are produced on hairless or finely downy stems in early and mid-spring. Flowers are pale red or yellow, usually tinged red or green. Stamens have reddish brown anthers and yellow or white filaments. ↕50cm (20in). Garden origin. ✻✻✻

***T.* 'African Queen'** ▣ Triumph Group tulip bearing dark purplish red flowers, fading at the margins, with purple-margined, primrose-yellow basal marks. Insides are dark ruby-red with yellowish white or white margins and purple anthers. Mid-spring-flowering. ↕40cm (16in). ✻✻✻

T. aitchisonii see *T. clusiana.*

***T.* 'Aladdin'.** Lily-flowered Group tulip bearing yellow-margined scarlet flowers in late spring. ↕45cm (18in). ✻✻✻

***T.* 'Ancilla'** ▣ Kaufmanniana Group tulip producing soft pink flowers, flushed rose-red, with red inner and outer basal rings. Mid-spring-flowering. ↕15cm (6in). ✻✻✻

***T.* 'Angélique'** ▣ Double Late Group tulip with pale pink flowers, flushed with paler and darker shades of pink, with lighter margins and, occasionally, green or yellow bases. Mid-spring-flowering. ↕30cm (12in). ✻✻✻

***T.* 'Apeldoorn'** ▣ Darwin Hybrid Group tulip bearing cherry-red flowers with signal-red margins. Insides are signal-red with yellow-bordered black marks and black anthers. Mid-spring-flowering. ↕60cm (24in). ✻✻✻

***T.* 'Apeldoorn's Elite'.** Darwin Hybrid Group tulip with red-feathered, buttercup-yellow flowers, flushed yellowish green at the bases outside, with black anthers and black basal marks inside. Mid-spring-flowering. ↕60cm (24in). ✻✻✻

***T.* 'Apricot Beauty'** ▣ Single Early Group tulip producing soft salmon-pink flowers, later with orange margins, in mid-spring. Good for forcing. ↕35cm (14in). ✻✻✻

***T.* 'Apricot Jewel'.** Miscellaneous Group tulip bearing apricot flowers, flushed orange at the bases, in early and mid-spring. ↕35cm (14in). ✻✻✻

***T.* 'Arabian Mystery'** ▣ Triumph Group tulip bearing dark purple flowers, with white margins, in mid-spring. ↕45cm (18in). ✻✻✻

***T.* 'Aristocrat'.** Single Late Group tulip producing white-margined, soft purplish violet flowers in late spring. ↕60cm (24in). ✻✻✻

***T.* 'Artist'** ▣ Viridiflora Group tulip bearing purple and salmon-pink flowers, green-flushed salmon-pink inside, in late spring. ↕45cm (18in). ✻✻✻

Tulipa 'Artist'

***T.* 'Attila'** ▣ Triumph Group tulip bearing light purplish violet flowers in mid-spring. Good for forcing. ↕40cm (16in). ✻✻✻

T. aucheriana. Miscellaneous Group tulip with 2–5 linear, channelled, hairless, glaucous, mid-green leaves, to 15cm (6in) long. In mid-spring, bears star-shaped pink flowers, to 7cm (3in) across, with yellow centres and stamens, singly or, occasionally, in twos or threes. ↕10–25cm (4–10in). Iran. ✻✻✻

T. australis see *T. sylvestris.*

***T.* 'Avignon'.** Single Late Group tulip producing red flowers, shading fire-red towards the margins and flushed yellowish white at the bases. Insides are tomato-red with yellow basal marks, greenish red at the margins, and with yellow anthers. Late spring-flowering. ↕50cm (20in). ✻✻✻

***T.* 'Balalaika'** ▣ Single Late Group tulip bearing glowing bright red flowers with yellow basal marks inside and black anthers. Late spring-flowering. ↕55cm (22in). ✻✻✻

***T.* 'Ballade'** ▣ Lily-flowered Group tulip bearing white-margined, reddish magenta flowers with white-margined yellow basal marks inside. Late spring-flowering. ↕50cm (20in). ✻✻✻

***T.* 'Ballerina'.** Lily-flowered Group tulip producing lemon-yellow flowers with blood-red flames, orange-yellow veins at the margins, and star-shaped yellow bases. Insides are capsicum-red, feathered marigold-orange, with pale golden yellow anthers. Late spring-flowering. ↕60cm (24in). ✻✻✻

***T.* 'Baronesse'.** Single Late Group tulip producing rose-red flowers with broad white margins and bluish white bases. Insides are white with red feathers, pale blue and yellow basal marks, and dark brown anthers. Late spring-flowering. ↕45cm (18in). ✻✻✻

T. batalinii ▣ Miscellaneous Group tulip with 3–9 linear, sickle-shaped, hairless, grey-green leaves, to 15cm (6in) long, with wavy red margins. In early and mid-spring, produces solitary, bowl-shaped, pale yellow flowers, to 8cm (3in) across, with rounded bases and dark yellow or bronze marks inside. Stamens have yellow anthers and black or yellow filaments. ↕35cm (14in). Uzbekistan. ✻✻✻

***T.* 'Bellona'.** Triumph Group tulip bearing scented, golden yellow flowers in mid-spring. ↕40cm (16in). ✻✻✻

***T.* 'Bestseller'.** Single Early Group tulip producing bright copper-orange flowers in mid-spring. ↕35cm (14in). ✻✻✻

***T.* 'Bienvenue'.** Darwin Hybrid Group tulip bearing canary-yellow flowers with dark yellowish pink flames and yellow-green bases. Insides are bright golden yellow, flamed capsicum-red, with black basal marks. Mid-spring-flowering. ↕60cm (24in). ✻✻✻

T. biflora ▣ syn. *T. polychroma.* Miscellaneous Group tulip with 1 or 2 linear, hairless, grey-green leaves, to 18cm (7in) long. Star-shaped, fragrant, red-margined white flowers, to 4cm (1½in) across, have yellow bases, and are flushed greenish grey or greenish pink outside. Stamens have yellow anthers, often tipped dark purple or black, and yellow filaments. Flowers are borne singly or in twos or threes, on upright stems from late winter to spring. ↕10cm (4in). Kazakhstan, E. Turkey, Iran, Afghanistan, Tajikistan. ✻✻✻

***T.* 'Bing Crosby'** ▣ Triumph Group tulip producing glowing scarlet flowers in mid-spring. ↕40cm (16in). ✻✻✻

***T.* 'Bird of Paradise'** ▣ Parrot Group tulip with orange-margined, cardinal-red flowers. Insides are scarlet, feathered dark red, with bright yellow bases and purple anthers. Late spring-flowering. ↕55cm (22in). ✻✻✻

***T.* 'Blue Heron'** ▣ Fringed Group tulip producing purple-fringed, violet-purple flowers. Insides are cobalt-violet with white stripes and bases, and black anthers. Late spring-flowering. ↕60cm (24in). ✻✻✻

***T.* 'Blue Parrot'** ▣ Parrot Group tulip with bright violet-blue flowers, bronze-purple inside. Late spring-flowering. ↕60cm (24in). ✻✻✻

***T.* 'Bright Gem'.** Miscellaneous Group tulip bearing orange-flushed, sulphur-yellow flowers with bronze-orange basal marks. Early and mid-spring-flowering. ↕35cm (14in). ✻✻✻

***T.* 'Brilliant Star'.** Single Early Group tulip bearing bright vermilion flowers in mid-spring. ↕20cm (8in). ✻✻✻

***T.* 'Burgundy Lace'.** Fringed Group tulip bearing fringed, wine-red flowers in late spring. ↕60cm (24in). ✻✻✻

***T.* 'Burns'** ▣ Fringed Group tulip bearing bright light pink flowers, with

Tulipa 'Candela'

Tulipa 'Cape Cod'

Tulipa 'Carnaval de Nice'

Tulipa 'China Pink'

Tulipa 'Clara Butt'

Tulipa clusiana

Tulipa clusiana var. *chrysantha*

Tulipa 'Don Quichotte'

Tulipa 'Dreamboat'

Tulipa 'Dreaming Maid'

Tulipa 'Estella Rijnveld'

Tulipa 'Flaming Parrot'

greyish white bases outside, in late spring. Insides are pinkish red with ivory-white bases, violet margins, and yellow anthers. ↕50cm (20in). ✱✱✱
T. 'Buttercup'. Greigii Group tulip bearing yellow-margined, carmine-red flowers, dark golden yellow inside, with red-marked yellow bases. Mid-spring-flowering. Leaves are marked dark bluish maroon. ↕25cm (10in). ✱✱✱
T. 'Candela' ■ Fosteriana Group tulip producing large, pure yellow flowers, with black anthers, in mid-spring. ↕35cm (14in). ✱✱✱
T. 'Cape Cod' ■ Greigii Group tulip bearing apricot-yellow flowers, with red central stripes on the tepals, in mid-spring. Leaves are marked dark bluish maroon. ↕20cm (8in). ✱✱✱
T. 'Carnaval de Nice' ■ Double Late Group tulip bearing white flowers, with dark red feathers and markings, in late spring. ↕40cm (16in). ✱✱✱
T. 'China Pink' ■ Lily-flowered Group tulip bearing pink flowers, with white bases inside, in late spring. ↕50cm (20in). ✱✱✱
T. chrysantha see *T. clusiana* var. *chrysantha.*
T. 'Clara Butt' ■ Single Late Group tulip bearing deep salmon-pink flowers in late spring. ↕60cm (24in). ✱✱✱

Tulipa 'Dreamland'

T. clusiana ■ syn. *T. aitchisonii* (Lady tulip). Miscellaneous Group tulip with 2–5 linear, hairless, glaucous, grey-green leaves, to 15cm (6in) long, sometimes wavy-margined. Bowl-shaped, later star-shaped flowers, to 10cm (4in) across, with rounded bases, are produced singly or in pairs in early and mid-spring. Flowers are white, striped dark pink outside, with purple or crimson basal marks and purple stamens. ↕30cm (12in). Iran to Himalayas. ✱✱✱. **var. *chrysantha*** ■ syn. *T. chrysantha*, *T. stellata* var. *chrysantha*, has up to 3 yellow flowers, tinged red or brownish purple outside, with yellow anthers. **var. *stellata***, syn. *T. stellata*, has star-shaped flowers with yellow basal marks.
T. 'Cordell Hull'. Single Late Group tulip bearing white-flamed red flowers in late spring. ↕60cm (24in). ✱✱✱
T. 'Corona'. Kaufmanniana Group tulip bearing red flowers, pale yellow inside, in mid-spring. Leaves are marked purple. ↕25cm (10in). ✱✱✱
T. 'Corsage'. Greigii Group tulip bearing rose-pink flowers, with yellow margins and bronze bases, in mid-spring. Insides are rose-red with golden yellow feathers. Leaves are marked dark bluish maroon. ↕25cm (10in). ✱✱✱
T. 'Couleur Cardinal'. Triumph Group tulip producing plum-purple flowers, dark crimson-scarlet inside, in mid-spring. ↕35cm (14in). ✱✱✱
***T. dasystemon* of gardens** see *T. tarda.*
T. 'Dawnglow'. Darwin Hybrid Group tulip bearing pale apricot flowers, flushed carmine-pink, with greenish yellow bases. Insides are yellow-orange with purple anthers. Mid-spring-flowering. ↕60cm (24in). ✱✱✱
T. 'Destiny'. Parrot Group tulip producing carmine-pink flowers, with creamy white bases and bronze anthers, in late spring. ↕45cm (18in). ✱✱✱
T. 'Diana'. Single Early Group tulip producing white flowers in mid-spring. ↕35cm (14in). ✱✱✱
T. 'Don Quichotte' ■ Triumph Group tulip producing cherry-pink flowers in late spring. ↕40cm (16in). ✱✱✱
T. 'Dreamboat' ■ Greigii Group tulip producing red-tinged, amber-yellow flowers with red-marked, green-bronze bases. Mid-spring-flowering. Leaves are marked dark bluish maroon. ↕20cm (8in). ✱✱✱
T. 'Dreaming Maid' ■ Triumph Group tulip producing white-margined violet flowers in mid-spring. ↕50cm (20in). ✱✱✱
T. 'Dreamland' ■ Single Late Group tulip producing cream-flamed red flowers. Insides are pinkish red with white bases and yellow anthers. Late spring-flowering. ↕60cm (24in). ✱✱✱
T. 'Early Harvest'. Kaufmanniana Group tulip bearing dark pinkish red flowers with yellow margins and bases, and bronze-green basal marks. Insides are yellow with vivid, reddish orange markings and pale yellow anthers. Mid-spring-flowering. Leaves are marked purple. ↕25cm (10in). ✱✱✱
T. edulis, syn. *Amana edulis.* Miscellaneous Group tulip with 6 linear, hairless, mid-green leaves, 15–25cm (6–10in) long. In late winter and early spring, star-shaped white flowers, 6cm (2½in) across, veined reddish brown or purple outside, with yellow-margined, dark purple basal marks and yellow anthers, are borne singly or in pairs. The 2 or 3 linear bracts below each flower distinguish it from other species. ↕20cm (8in). N.E. China, Korea, Japan. ✱✱✱
T. 'Elizabeth Arden'. Darwin Hybrid Group tulip producing violet-flushed, dark salmon-pink flowers with yellow and white bases. Mid-spring-flowering. ↕55cm (22in). ✱✱✱
T. 'Engadin'. Greigii Group tulip bearing yellow-margined, blood-red flowers, dark golden yellow with blood-red stripes inside. Mid-spring-flowering. Leaves are marked dark bluish maroon. ↕20cm (8in). ✱✱✱
T. 'Esperanto'. Viridiflora Group tulip bearing pinkish red flowers with green-flamed midveins, which fade to reddish brown, greenish brown bases, and greenish yellow anthers. Late spring-flowering. Leaves are margined white. ↕50cm (20in). ✱✱✱
T. 'Estella Rijnveld' ■ syn. *T.* 'Gay Presto'. Parrot Group tulip producing fringed, white-flamed red flowers in late spring. ↕55cm (22in). ✱✱✱
T. 'Fancy Frills'. Fringed Group tulip producing deep rose-red flowers with whitish pink fringes, ivory-white bases, and pale yellow anthers. Late spring-flowering. ↕45cm (18in). ✱✱✱
T. 'Flaming Parrot' ■ Parrot Group tulip with deep yellow flowers, flamed

Tulipa 'Fringed Beauty'

Tulipa 'Fringed Elegance'

Tulipa 'Generaal de Wet'

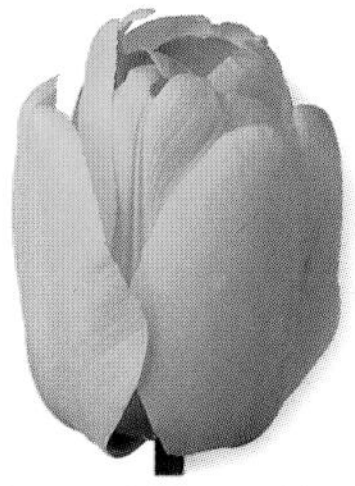
Tulipa 'Golden Apeldoorn'

Tulipa 'Golden Artist'

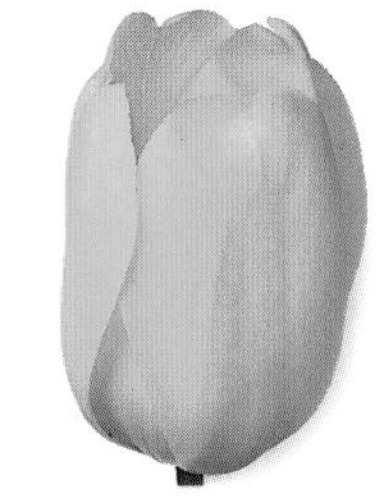
Tulipa 'Golden Oxford'

Tulipa 'Gordon Cooper'

Tulipa 'Groenland'

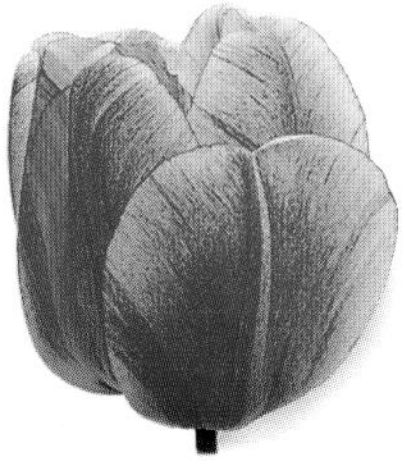
Tulipa 'Gudoshnik'

Tulipa hageri 'Splendens'

Tulipa 'Hamilton'

Tulipa humilis

dark red, and with primrose-yellow bases. Insides are primrose-yellow with glowing blood-red flames, and purple-black anthers. Late spring-flowering. ↕55cm (22in). ❄❄❄

T. fosteriana. Fosteriana Group tulip with 3–6 oblong to broadly ovate, light grey-green leaves, to 30cm (12in) long, downy above. Bowl-shaped, slightly fragrant flowers, to 20cm (8in) across, with rounded bases, are borne singly on slightly downy stems in early and mid-spring. Flowers are bright red with yellow-margined, purplish black basal marks. Stamens have purplish black anthers and black or yellow filaments. ↕45cm (18in). Kazakhstan, Uzbekistan, Tajikistan. ❄❄❄. **'Princeps'** has orange-scarlet flowers, scarlet inside, with greenish bronze basal marks.

***T.* 'Fringed Beauty'** ■ Fringed Group tulip producing vermilion flowers, with golden yellow fringes, in late spring. ↕35cm (14in). ❄❄❄

***T.* 'Fringed Elegance'** ■ Fringed Group tulip bearing primrose-yellow flowers, with paler fringes, and sometimes with pink markings, in late spring. Insides are brilliant greenish yellow with bronze-green basal marks and purple anthers. ↕35cm (14in). ❄❄❄

***T.* 'Garden Party'.** Triumph Group tulip bearing white flowers, carmine-red at the margins. Insides are feathered carmine-red with white bases. Mid-spring-flowering. ↕45cm (18in). ❄❄❄

***T.* 'Gay Presto'** see *T.* 'Estella Rijnveld'.

***T.* 'Generaal de Wet'** ■ syn. *T.* 'General de Wet'. Single Early Group tulip bearing fragrant, golden orange flowers, with dark orange shading, in mid-spring. ↕40cm (16in). ❄❄❄

***T.* 'General de Wet'** see *T.* 'Generaal de Wet'.

***T.* 'Georgette'.** Single Late Group tulip producing red-margined yellow flowers, several per stem, in late spring. ↕45cm (18in). ❄❄❄

***T.* 'Gerbrand Kieft'.** Double Late Group tulip bearing glowing purple-red flowers, with pure white margins, in late spring. ↕45cm (18in). ❄❄❄

T. gesneriana. Miscellaneous Group tulip with 2–7 lance-shaped to ovate-lance-shaped, hairless or finely downy, mid-green leaves, to 30cm (12in) long. Solitary flowers, to 12cm (5in) across, cup-shaped at first, opening to star-shaped, with rounded bases, are borne on hairless or finely downy stems in early to late spring. Flowers are red, orange, yellow, or purplish red, sometimes marked yellow or black at the bases, with purple or yellow stamens. The original parent of many garden cultivars. ↕45cm (18in). Probably garden origin; naturalized in parts of the Mediterranean. ❄❄❄

***T.* 'Giuseppe Verdi'** ■ Kaufmanniana Group tulip bearing yellow-margined, carmine-red flowers, golden yellow with small red marks inside, in mid-spring. Leaves are marked purple. ↕20cm (8in). ❄❄❄

***T.* 'Golden Apeldoorn'** ■ Darwin Hybrid Group tulip producing golden yellow flowers, with black anthers, in mid-spring. Inside, star-shaped black bases have bronze-green borders. ↕60cm (24in). ❄❄❄

***T.* 'Golden Artist'** ■ Viridiflora Group tulip producing golden orange flowers, with green stripes on the tepals, in late spring. ↕45cm (18in). ❄❄❄

Tulipa 'Giuseppe Verdi'

***T.* 'Golden Mirjoran'.** Triumph Group tulip producing dark rose-red flowers, with light yellow margins, in mid-spring. Insides are sulphur-yellow with broad, cherry-red margins and purple-brown anthers. ↕45cm (18in). ❄❄❄

***T.* 'Golden Oxford'** ■ syn. *T.* 'Topic'. Darwin Hybrid Group tulip producing pure yellow flowers, sometimes narrowly margined red, with black anthers, in mid-spring. ↕60cm (24in). ❄❄❄

***T.* 'Gordon Cooper'** ■ Darwin Hybrid Group tulip with red flowers, maturing to pink, with signal-red margins and bluish black and yellow basal marks. Insides are glowing signal-red with black anthers. Mid-spring-flowering. ↕60cm (24in). ❄❄❄

***T.* 'Grand Duc'** see *T.* 'Keizerskroon'.

***T.* 'Greenland'** see *T.* 'Groenland'.

T. greigii. Greigii Group tulip with 2–7 oblong-lance-shaped to lance-shaped, sometimes wavy-margined, glaucous, grey-green leaves, to 25cm (10in) long, streaked or marked reddish or dark purple, and often downy above. In early spring, densely downy, pink- or brown-tinged stems bear solitary, bowl-shaped, red or yellow flowers, to 14cm (5½in) across; they are often orange-stained outside, with yellow-rimmed, blackish purple basal marks and black stamens. ↕50cm (20in). Tajikistan. ❄❄❄

***T.* 'Greuze'.** Single Late Group tulip producing violet-purple flowers in late spring. ↕55cm (22in). ❄❄❄

***T.* 'Groenland'** ■ syn. *T.* 'Greenland'. Viridiflora Group tulip producing green flowers, with rose-pink margins, in late spring. ↕45cm (18in). ❄❄❄

***T.* 'Gudoshnik'** ■ Darwin Hybrid Group tulip bearing yellow flowers with red spots, rose-pink flames, bluish black basal marks, and black anthers. Mid-spring-flowering. ↕60cm (24in). ❄❄❄

T. hageri. Miscellaneous Group tulip with 2–7 lance-shaped, hairless, light green leaves, to 20cm (8in) long, often margined reddish purple. In early and mid-spring, bears star-shaped flowers, 6–9cm (2½–3½in) across, singly or in clusters of up to 4, on hairless stems. The buff flowers are mostly green-tinged outside. Inside, they are dull red with black, sometimes yellow-margined basal marks, dark green or brown anthers, and green filaments, sometimes tinged purple. ↕35cm (14in). Bulgaria, Greece, W. Turkey. ❄❄❄. **var. *nitens*** has orange-scarlet flowers and glaucous leaves. **'Splendens'** ■ has crimson-scarlet flowers, brownish red inside.

***T.* 'Hamilton'** ■ Fringed Group tulip producing buttercup-yellow flowers, with darker yellow fringes and anthers, in late spring. ↕50cm (20in). ❄❄❄

***T.* 'Hans Mayer'.** Darwin Hybrid Group tulip bearing buttercup-yellow flowers, flamed translucent vermilion, with light green bases. Insides are golden yellow with vermilion flames and dark brown bases. Brown anthers have a violet glow. Mid-spring-flowering. ↕60cm (24in). ❄❄❄

***T.* 'Heart's Delight'.** Kaufmanniana Group tulip. Flowers dark rose-red with pale rose-pink margins and red-marked, golden yellow bases. Insides are ivory-white. Early spring-flowering. Leaves are marked purple. ↕20cm (8in). ❄❄❄

***T.* 'Hollywood'.** Viridiflora Group tulip producing green-tinged red flowers, with yellow basal marks, in late spring. ↕50cm (20in). ❄❄❄

T. humilis ■ Miscellaneous Group tulip with 2–5 linear, channelled, hairless, glaucous, grey-green leaves, to 15cm (6in) long. In early and mid-spring, star-shaped flowers, to 7cm (3in) across, are borne singly, or sometimes in twos or threes. Flowers are pale pink to purplish pink or magenta, often tinged greyish green outside, with yellow, olive-green, or blue-black basal marks, and frequently margined yellow or white. Stamens have yellow, brown, purple, or black anthers and yellow filaments. ↕to 25cm (10in). S. and E. Turkey, N. Iraq, N. and W. Iran, Azerbaijan. ❄❄❄. **var. *pulchella*** see *T. pulchella*. **var. *violacea*** see *T. violacea*.

***T.* 'Ile de France'.** Triumph Group tulip producing cardinal-red flowers with dark bronze-green basal marks and narrow, yellowish brown margins. Insides are blood-red. Mid- and late spring-flowering. ↕60cm (24in). ❄❄❄

***T.* 'Inzell'.** Triumph Group tulip producing ivory-white flowers, with yellow anthers, in mid-spring. ↕45cm (18in). ❄❄❄

***T.* 'Jewel of Spring'.** Darwin Hybrid Group tulip producing red-margined, sulphur-yellow flowers, with greenish black bases and black anthers, in mid-spring. ↕60cm (24in). ❄❄❄

Tulipa 'Juan'

Tulipa linifolia

Tulipa 'Lustige Witwe'

Tulipa 'Margot Fonteyn'

Tulipa 'Mariette'

Tulipa marjolletii

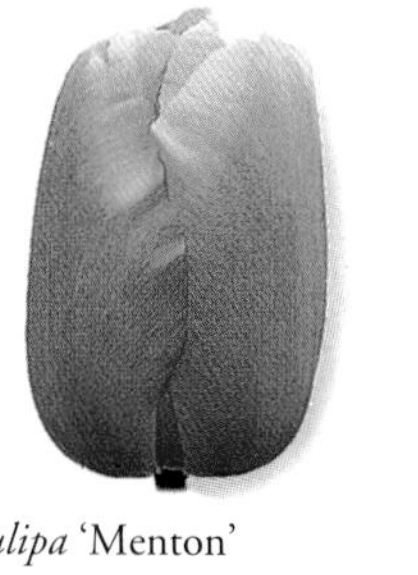

Tulipa 'Menton'

Tulipa 'Mme. Lefeber'

Tulipa 'Orange Monarch'

Tulipa 'Oriental Splendour'

Tulipa orphanidea

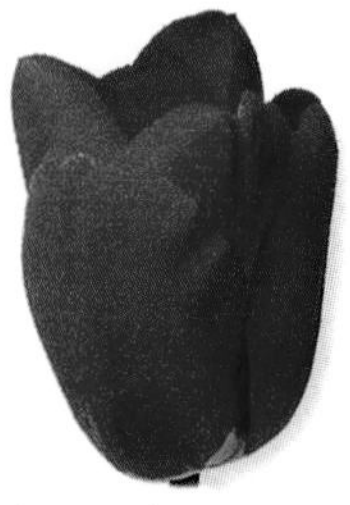

Tulipa 'Oxford'

***T.* 'Joffre'.** Single Early Group tulip producing yellow flowers, with subtle, light to dark red shades, in early spring. ↕30cm (12in). ❄❄❄

***T.* 'Johann Strauss'.** Kaufmanniana Group tulip bearing currant-red flowers, margined sulphur-yellow, with golden yellow bases. Insides are ivory-white. Early spring-flowering. Leaves are marked purple. ↕20cm (8in). ❄❄❄

***T.* 'Juan'** ■ Fosteriana Group tulip producing pink-tinged, dark orange flowers, with yellow bases and anthers, in mid-spring. Leaves are marked reddish brown. ↕25cm (10in). ❄❄❄

T. kaufmanniana (Water-lily tulip). Kaufmanniana Group tulip with 3–5 lance-shaped to inversely lance-shaped, slightly wavy-margined, hairless, grey-green leaves, to 25cm (10in) long. Bowl-shaped flowers, 3–12cm (1¼–5in) across, are borne singly or in clusters of up to 5, on slightly downy, often red-tinged stems in early and mid-spring. Flowers are cream or yellow, flushed pink or greyish green outside, or pink, orange, or red, often with contrasting basal marks. Stamens are yellow with twisted anthers. ↕to 25cm (10in). Kazakhstan, Uzbekistan, Tajikistan, Kyrgyzstan. ❄❄❄

***T.* 'Kees Nelis'.** Triumph Group tulip bearing blood-red flowers, with orange-yellow margins, in mid-spring. ↕40cm (16in). ❄❄❄

***T.* 'Keizerskroon'** ■ syn. *T.* 'Grand Duc'. Single Early Group tulip bearing broadly yellow-margined scarlet flowers in mid-spring. ↕30cm (12in). ❄❄❄

***T.* 'Kingsblood'.** Single Late Group tulip bearing cherry-red flowers, with scarlet margins, in late spring. ↕60cm (24in). ❄❄❄

T. kolpakowskiana. Miscellaneous Group tulip with 2–4 erect, linear, deeply channelled, hairless, wavy-margined, grey-green leaves, to 20cm (8in) long. In early and mid-spring, bowl-shaped yellow flowers, 3.5–7cm (1½–3in) across, marked crimson, orange, or olive-green outside, with yellow stamens, are produced singly or in clusters of up to 4. ↕20cm (8in). Uzbekistan, Afghanistan. ❄❄❄

T. linifolia ■ Miscellaneous Group tulip with 3–9 linear-sickle-shaped, hairless, grey-green leaves, to 8cm (3in) long, with wavy red margins. Bowl-shaped red flowers, to 8cm (3in) across, are produced in early and mid-spring. The rounded flower bases have blackish purple, often yellow-margined marks; stamens have dark purple or yellow anthers and black or yellow filaments. ↕20cm (8in). Uzbekistan, N. Iran, Afghanistan. ❄❄❄

***T.* 'Longfellow'.** Greigii Group tulip bearing black-based vermilion flowers, striped lighter red, and signal-red inside, in mid-spring. Leaves are marked dark bluish purple. ↕30cm (12in). ❄❄❄

***T.* 'Lustige Witwe'** ■ syn. *T.* 'Merry Widow'. Triumph Group tulip bearing glowing dark red flowers, margined pure white, in mid-spring. ↕40cm (16in). ❄❄❄

***T.* 'Magician'** see *T.* 'Magier'.

***T.* 'Magier'**, syn. *T.* 'Magician'. Single Late Group tulip bearing white flowers, with violet-blue margins, in late spring. ↕55cm (22in). ❄❄❄

***T.* 'Maja'.** Fringed Group tulip bearing fringed, pale mimosa-yellow flowers, brilliant greenish yellow inside, with bronze-yellow bases and yellow anthers, in late spring. ↕50cm (20in). ❄❄❄

Tulipa 'Keizerskroon'

***T.* 'Margot Fonteyn'** ■ Triumph Group tulip bearing yellow-margined, cardinal-red flowers with yellow bases. Insides are bright red with lighter margins and black anthers. Mid-spring-flowering. ↕40cm (16in). ❄❄❄

***T.* 'Mariette'** ■ Lily-flowered Group tulip bearing satin-textured, dark rose-pink flowers, with white bases inside, in late spring. ↕50cm (20in). ❄❄❄

T. marjolettii see *T. marjolletii.*

T. marjolletii ■ syn. *T. marjolettii.* Miscellaneous Group tulip with 2–7 lance-shaped to ovate-lance-shaped, hairless, grey-green leaves, to 30cm (12in) long. In early and mid-spring, hairless stems bear solitary, bowl-shaped, creamy white flowers, to 12cm (5in) across, with rounded bases, margined dark pink and flushed purple on the outside. Stamens have yellow anthers and blue-black filaments. ↕45cm (18in). Probably garden origin; naturalized in S.W. Europe. ❄❄❄

***T.* 'Martine Bijl'.** Triumph Group tulip bearing glowing blood-red flowers, with yellow bases and bluish black anthers, in mid-spring. ↕45cm (18in). ❄❄❄

***T.* 'Maytime'.** Lily-flowered Group tulip bearing reddish violet flowers, with narrowly white-margined yellow bases, in late spring. ↕50cm (20in). ❄❄❄

***T.* 'Maywonder'.** Double Late Group tulip bearing rose-pink flowers in late spring. ↕45cm (18in). ❄❄❄

***T.* 'Menton'** ■ Single Late Group tulip bearing pinkish red flowers with pale orange stripes at the margins, and green-marked, yellow and white bases. Insides are poppy-red with white veins and yellow anthers. Late spring-flowering. ↕60cm (24in). ❄❄❄

***T.* 'Merry Widow'** see *T.* 'Lustige Witwe'.

***T.* 'Miss Holland'.** Triumph Group tulip bearing blood-red flowers with signal-red flames and buttercup-yellow bases with greenish yellow margins. Insides are signal-red with dark brown anthers. Mid-spring-flowering. ↕45cm (18in). ❄❄❄

***T.* 'Mme Lefeber'** ■ syn. *T.* 'Red Emperor'. Fosteriana Group tulip bearing fire-red flowers in early spring. ↕35cm (14in). ❄❄❄

***T.* 'Monsella'.** Double Early Group tulip bearing canary-yellow flowers with blood-red flames, sulphur-yellow inside, in mid-spring. ↕30cm (12in). ❄❄❄

T. montana, syn. *T. wilsoniana.* Miscellaneous Group tulip with 3–6 narrowly lance-shaped, wavy-margined, channelled, hairless, grey-green leaves, to 15cm (6in) long. In early and mid-spring, produces solitary, bowl-shaped red flowers, to 8cm (3in) across, with rounded bases, sometimes with a small, dark green central mark on each flower. Stamens have yellow anthers and red filaments. ↕25cm (10in). Turkmenistan, N. Iran. ❄❄❄

***T.* 'Monte Carlo'.** Double Early Group tulip producing sulphur-yellow flowers, with small red feathers, in mid-spring. ↕30cm (12in). ❄❄❄

***T.* 'Mount Tacoma'.** Double Late Group tulip producing pure white flowers in late spring. ↕40cm (16in). ❄❄❄

***T.* 'New Design'.** Triumph Group tulip bearing light yellow flowers, the outsides fading to pinkish white and having pale fuchsia-red margins. Insides have apricot flames, buttercup-yellow bases, and dark brown anthers. Mid-spring-flowering. Leaves have pinkish white margins. ↕45cm (18in). ❄❄❄

***T.* 'Noranda'.** Fringed Group tulip bearing dark blood-red flowers with fringed, orange-tinted margins, green-yellow bases, and black anthers. Late spring-flowering. ↕50cm (20in). ❄❄❄

***T.* 'Orange Favourite'.** Parrot Group tulip producing fragrant, green-marked orange flowers, with yellow bases, in late spring. ↕55cm (22in). ❄❄❄

***T.* 'Orange Monarch'** ■ Triumph Group tulip bearing orange flowers, tinged red-pink, with orange-yellow bases. Insides are apricot-orange with purple anthers. Mid-spring-flowering. ↕40cm (16in). ❄❄❄

***T.* 'Oranje Nassau'.** Double Early Group tulip bearing blood-red flowers, flushed fire-red, in mid-spring. ↕30cm (12in). ❄❄❄

***T.* 'Oratorio'.** Greigii Group tulip bearing rose-pink flowers, with black bases, in early spring. Insides are apricot-pink. Leaves are marked dark bluish purple. ↕20cm (8in). ❄❄❄

***T.* 'Oriental Splendour'** ■ Greigii Group tulip with carmine-red flowers, lemon-yellow at the margins and inside, and with green and red basal markings. Early spring-flowering. Leaves are marked dark bluish purple. ↕30cm (12in). ❄❄❄

Tulipa 'Page Polka'

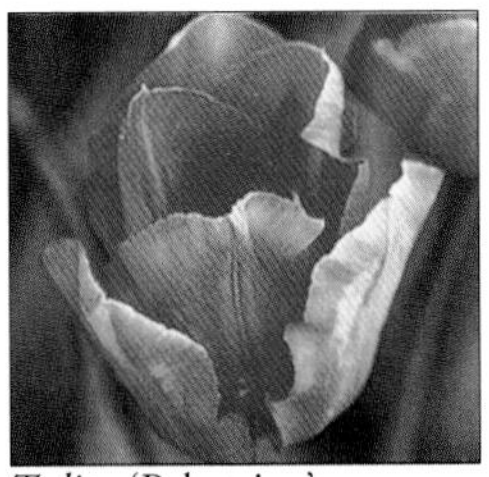

Tulipa 'Palestrina'

Tulipa 'Peach Blossom'

Tulipa 'Pink Diamond'

Tulipa 'Plaisir'

Tulipa praestans 'Van Tubergen's Variety'

Tulipa 'Prinses Irene'

Tulipa 'Queen of Night'

Tulipa 'Queen of Sheba'

Tulipa 'Red Riding Hood'

Tulipa saxatilis

Tulipa 'Schoonoord'

T. orphanidea ■ Miscellaneous Group tulip with 2–7 lance-shaped, hairless, mid-green leaves, to 20cm (8in) long, often margined reddish purple. Star-shaped flowers, 3–6cm (1¼–2½in) across, are borne singly or in twos or threes, on hairless or downy stems in mid- and late spring. Flowers are buff, usually green-tinged outside; insides are pale to bright orange or brownish red, flushed red or rarely yellow, with black or dark green basal markings. Stamens have dark green or brown anthers and green, sometimes purple-tinged filaments. ↕35cm (14in). Bulgaria, Greece, W. Turkey. ❄❄❄

***T.* 'Oxford'** ■ Darwin Hybrid Group tulip producing scarlet flowers, flushed purple-red, with sulphur-yellow bases. Insides are capsicum-red. Mid-spring-flowering. ↕60cm (24in). ❄❄❄

***T.* 'Page Polka'** ■ Triumph Group tulip producing dark red flowers, striped white outside, with white basal marks and yellow anthers. Mid-spring-flowering. ↕40cm (16in). ❄❄❄

***T.* 'Palestrina'** ■ Triumph Group tulip bearing salmon-pink flowers, green-tinged outside, in late spring. ↕50cm (20in). ❄❄❄

***T.* 'Passionale'.** Triumph Group tulip producing lilac-purple flowers, with dark purplish red flames, in mid-spring. Insides are beetroot-purple with purple-margined, tawny-yellow bases and light yellow anthers. ↕45cm (18in). ❄❄❄

***T.* 'Peach Blossom'** ■ Double Early Group tulip producing dark rose-pink flowers in mid-spring. Young flowers often have greenish white bases. ↕30cm (12in). ❄❄❄

Tulipa praestans 'Unicum'

***T.* 'Peer Gynt'.** Triumph Group tulip bearing purple-margined, bright rose-pink flowers with yellow-spotted white bases. Insides are pink with purple-grey anthers. Mid-spring-flowering. ↕45cm (18in). ❄❄❄

***T.* 'Pink Diamond'** ■ Single Late Group tulip producing pink-purple flowers with paler margins. Insides are bright mid-pink with grey-yellow bases and yellow-green anthers. Late spring-flowering. ↕60cm (24in). ❄❄❄

***T.* 'Plaisir'** ■ Greigii Group tulip bearing carmine-red flowers with sulphur-yellow margins and black and yellow bases. Insides are vermilion with sulphur-yellow margins. Early spring-flowering. Leaves are marked dark bluish maroon. ↕15cm (6in). ❄❄❄

T. polychroma see *T. biflora.*

T. praestans. Miscellaneous Group tulip with 3–6 erect, oblong or lance-shaped, keeled, downy, grey-green leaves, to 20cm (8in) long. In early and mid-spring, bowl-shaped, scarlet-orange flowers, 10–12cm (4–5in) across, are produced singly or in clusters of up to 5 on each of the minutely downy stems; stamens have yellow or purplish red anthers, and red filaments shading to yellow at the bases. Easily grown. ↕30cm (12in). Kazakhstan (Pamir Altai), Tajikistan. ❄❄❄. **'Fusilier'** produces several very bright red flowers. **'Unicum'** ■ has variegated leaves with creamy white margins, and bears up to 5 capsicum-red flowers with small, light yellow bases and blue-black anthers. **'Van Tubergen's Variety'** ■ has up to 3 larger, bright orange-scarlet flowers, flushed yellow at the bases, with reddish brown anthers. ↕50cm (20in).

***T.* 'Prinses Irene'** ■ Triumph Group tulip bearing unusual, orange and purple flowers in mid-spring. ↕35cm (14in). ❄❄❄

T. pulchella, syn. *T. humilis* var. *pulchella.* Miscellaneous Group tulip with 2–5 linear, hairless, glaucous, grey-green leaves, to 15cm (6in) long. In early and mid-spring, produces star-shaped, light crimson or purple flowers, to 7cm (3in) across, with blue-black basal marks. They are borne singly or sometimes in twos or threes. The stamens have purple anthers and blue filaments. ↕35cm (14in). Turkey, N. Iran, Turkmenistan, Uzbekistan, Afghanistan. ❄❄❄. **'Odalisque'** bears pale purple flowers with yellow basal marks. **'Persian Pearl'** produces rose-red flowers with yellow basal marks.

***T.* 'Purissima'** ■ syn. *T.* 'White Emperor'. Fosteriana Group tulip that produces pure white flowers in mid-spring. ↕35cm (14in). ❄❄❄

***T.* 'Queen of Night'** ■ Single Late Group tulip producing velvety, dark maroon flowers in late spring. ↕60cm (24in). ❄❄❄

***T.* 'Queen of Sheba'** ■ Lily-flowered Group tulip that produces glowing brownish red flowers, with orange margins, in late spring. ↕60cm (24in). ❄❄❄

***T.* 'Red Emperor'** see *T.* 'Mme Lefeber'.

***T.* 'Red Parrot'.** Parrot Group tulip producing raspberry-red flowers in late spring. ↕55cm (22in). ❄❄❄

***T.* 'Red Riding Hood'** ■ Greigii Group tulip producing carmine-red flowers, scarlet inside, with black bases, in early spring. Leaves are marked dark bluish maroon. ↕20cm (8in). ❄❄❄

Tulipa 'Purissima'

***T.* 'Reginald Dixon'.** Fosteriana Group tulip with yellow-margined scarlet flowers. Insides are lemon-yellow with red-marked black bases. Mid-spring-flowering. ↕30cm (12in). ❄❄❄

***T.* 'Renown'.** Single Late Group tulip producing light carmine-red flowers with paler margins and blue-margined yellow bases. Late spring-flowering. ↕50cm (20in). ❄❄❄

***T.* 'Rococo'.** Parrot Group tulip bearing carmine-red flowers, margined fire-red, in late spring. ↕35cm (14in). ❄❄❄

***T.* 'Rondo'.** Fosteriana Group tulip producing yellow-margined vermilion flowers, golden yellow inside, with red-marked yellow bases. Mid-spring-flowering. ↕30cm (12in). ❄❄❄

***T.* 'Rosario'.** Triumph Group tulip producing dark pink flowers with large white bases. Insides are rose-pink with smaller, ivory-white bases. Mid-spring-flowering. ↕45cm (18in). ❄❄❄

T. saxatilis ■ Miscellaneous Group tulip, spreading by runners, producing 2–4 linear, hairless, shiny, mid-green leaves, to 30cm (12in) long. In mid- and late spring, star-shaped, fragrant flowers, 6–8cm (2½–3in) across, are borne singly or in clusters of up to 4. The flowers are pink to lilac-purple with white-margined yellow marks and the stamens have yellow, purple, or brown anthers and yellow filaments. ↕35cm (14in). Crete, W. Turkey. ❄❄❄

***T.* 'Schoonoord'** ■ Double Early Group tulip bearing pure white flowers in mid-spring. ↕30cm (12in). ❄❄❄

***T.* 'Shakespeare'.** Kaufmanniana Group tulip bearing carmine-red flowers, with salmon-pink margins and golden yellow bases, in mid-spring. Insides are scarlet-flushed salmon-pink. ↕25cm (10in). ❄❄❄

***T.* 'Shirley'.** Triumph Group tulip bearing ivory-white flowers, with narrow purple margins, white bases spotted pale purple, and brownish violet anthers, in late spring. ↕60cm (24in). ❄❄❄

***T.* 'Solva'.** Fosteriana Group tulip bearing pale vermilion flowers, yellow at the bases, in mid-spring. ↕35cm (14in). ❄❄❄

***T.* 'Sorbet'.** Single Late Group tulip bearing pinkish white flowers, creamy white at the bases, in late spring. Insides

Tulipa sprengeri

Tulipa 'Spring Green'

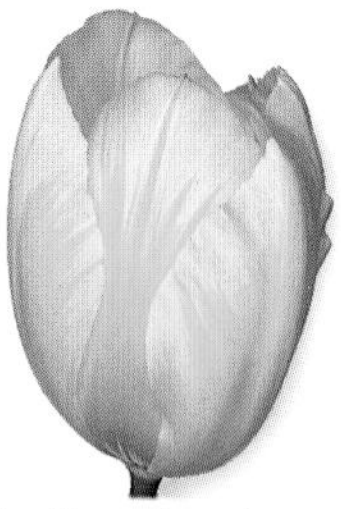
Tulipa 'Sweetheart'

Tulipa sylvestris

Tulipa tarda

Tulipa turkestanica

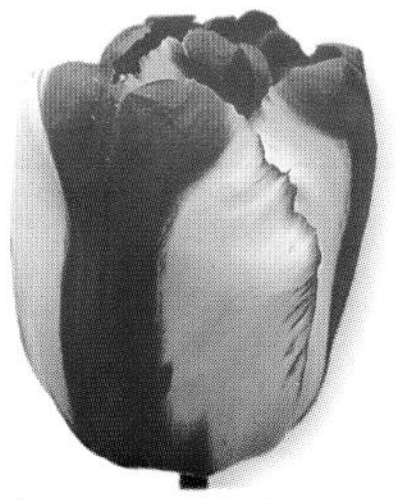
Tulipa 'Union Jack'

Tulipa violacea

Tulipa 'West Point'

Tulipa 'White Parrot'

Tulipa whittallii

Tulipa 'Yokohama'

are white with carmine-red flames and yellow anthers. ↕60cm (24in). ❄❄❄
T. sprengeri ■ Miscellaneous Group tulip with 5 or 6 linear, hairless, shiny, erect, mid-green leaves, to 25cm (10in) long. In early summer, solitary, goblet-shaped, red to orange-red flowers, 4.5–6cm (1¾–2½in) long, with yellow-buff bases, yellow anthers, and red filaments, are borne on smooth stems. One of the latest tulips to flower. Will self-seed and naturalize in sun or light woodland. ↕50cm (20in). Turkey (but no longer known in the wild). ❄❄❄
***T.* 'Spring Green'** ■ Viridiflora Group tulip bearing green-feathered, ivory-white flowers, with light green anthers, in late spring. ↕40cm (16in). ❄❄❄
T. stellata see *T. clusiana* var. *stellata.*
T. stellata* var. *chrysantha see *T. clusiana* var. *chrysantha.*
***T.* 'Sweetheart'** ■ Fosteriana Group tulip bearing ivory-white flowers with lemon-yellow flames, broad, ivory-white margins, and yellow bases. Insides are deep yellow with ivory-white margins and yellow anthers. Mid-spring-flowering. ↕30cm (12in). ❄❄❄
***T.* 'Sweet Lady'.** Greigii Group tulip with leaves marked dark bluish maroon. In mid-spring, bears peach-pink flowers with yellow-tinged, bronze-green bases and yellow anthers. ↕20cm (8in). ❄❄❄
T. sylvestris ■ syn. *T. australis.* Miscellaneous Group tulip with 2–4 linear, channelled, glaucous, light green leaves, to 20cm (8in) long. In mid- and late spring, star-shaped, fragrant flowers, 6–8cm (2½–3in) across, pendent in bud then erect, are borne singly or in pairs. Flowers are yellow, occasionally cream, with green-flushed bases outside and yellow anthers. Easily grown. ↕45cm (18in). Origin unknown; naturalized in Europe and from N. Africa to the Middle East and Russia (Siberia). ❄❄❄
T. tarda ■ syn. *T. dasystemon* of gardens. Miscellaneous Group tulip with 3–7 lance-shaped, recurved, often finely fringed, shiny, bright green leaves, to 12cm (5in) long. Produces 4–6 star-shaped flowers, to 6cm (2½in) across, in early and mid-spring. Flowers are white with a green tinge, sometimes red-tinged outside and yellow on the lower half inside. Stamens are yellow. ↕15cm (6in). C. Asia (Tien Shan). ❄❄❄
***T.* 'Texas Gold'.** Parrot Group tulip producing red-margined, bright golden yellow flowers. Late spring-flowering. ↕55cm (22in). ❄❄❄
***T.* 'Topic'** see *T.* 'Golden Oxford'.
***T.* 'Toronto'.** Greigii Group tulip bearing vermilion-tinged, pinkish red flowers, several to a stem, in mid-spring; insides are tangerine-red with buttercup-yellow bases, tinged bronze-green, and bronze anthers. Leaves are marked dark bluish maroon. ↕20cm (8in). ❄❄❄
T. turkestanica ■ Miscellaneous Group tulip with 2–4 linear, grey-green leaves, to 15cm (6in) long. In early and mid-spring, up to 12 star-shaped, malodorous white flowers, 3–5cm (1¼–2in) across, flushed greenish grey or greenish pink outside, yellow or orange at the centres, are borne on hairy stems. Stamens have purple, brown, or purple-tipped yellow anthers, and yellow filaments. ↕30cm (12in). Kazakhstan, Tajikistan, N.W. China. ❄❄❄
***T.* 'Union Jack'** ■ Single Late Group tulip bearing ivory-white flowers, with raspberry-red flames and blue-margined white bases, in late spring. ↕60cm (24in). ❄❄❄
T. urumiensis. Miscellaneous Group tulip with 2–4 linear, sometimes slightly glaucous, mid-green leaves, to 12cm (5in) long. Star-shaped yellow flowers, 5–7cm (2–3in) across, flushed lilac or reddish brown outside, with yellow stamens, are produced singly or in pairs in early spring. ↕15cm (6in). N.W. Iran. ❄❄❄
***T.* 'Viking'.** Double Early Group tulip bearing scarlet-flamed, greenish red flowers. Insides are signal-red with slight yellow feathering, canary-yellow bases, and purple anthers. Mid-spring-flowering. ↕30cm (12in). ❄❄❄
T. violacea ■ syn. *T. humilis* var. *violacea.* Miscellaneous Group tulip with 2–5 linear, channelled, hairless, glaucous, grey-green leaves, to 15cm (6in) long. Produces star-shaped violet-purple flowers, 7cm (3in) across, with yellow or blue-black basal marks and purple stamens, singly or sometimes in clusters of 3, in early and mid-spring. ↕25cm (10in). S. and E. Turkey, N. Iraq, N. and W. Iran, Azerbaijan. ❄❄❄
T. vvedenskyi. Miscellaneous Group tulip with 4 or 5 lance-shaped, reflexed, often very finely downy, glaucous, grey-green, crimped leaves, to 30cm (12in) long. Solitary, bowl-shaped flowers, to 20cm (8in) across, with rounded bases, are borne on bristly, sometimes purple-tinged stems in early and mid-spring. Flowers are red with black or yellow basal marks, violet or yellow anthers, and brown or yellow filaments. ↕50cm (20in). Kazakhstan, C. Asia (Tien Shan). ❄❄❄. **'Tangerine Beauty'** has bright red flowers, orange inside, with pale yellow basal marks; stamens have purple anthers and yellow filaments.
***T.* 'West Point'** ■ Lily-flowered Group tulip producing primrose-yellow flowers in late spring. ↕50cm (20in). ❄❄❄
***T.* 'White Emperor'** see *T.* 'Purissima'.
***T.* 'White Parrot'** ■ Parrot Group tulip producing pure white flowers in late spring. ↕55cm (22in). ❄❄❄
T. whittallii ■ Miscellaneous Group tulip with 2–7 lance-shaped, hairless, mid-green leaves, to 20cm (8in) long, often with reddish purple margins. In early and mid-spring, bears star-shaped flowers, 3–6cm (1¼–2½in) across, singly or in clusters of up to 4 on hairless stems. Flowers are bright bronze-orange, usually green-tinged outside, with black, sometimes yellow-margined basal marks inside. Stamens have dark green or brown anthers, and purple or green filaments. ↕35cm (14in). Bulgaria, Greece, W. Turkey. ❄❄❄
***T.* 'Willemsoord'.** Double Early Group tulip bearing carmine-red and white flowers in mid-spring. ↕30cm (12in). ❄❄❄
T. wilsoniana see *T. montana.*
***T.* 'Wirosa'.** Double Late Group tulip with cream-margined, wine-red flowers in late spring. ↕40cm (16in). ❄❄❄
***T.* 'Yellow Purissima'.** Fosteriana Group tulip with canary-yellow flowers, broadly flamed deep yellow. Insides are bright golden yellow with greenish yellow anthers. Mid-spring-flowering. ↕35cm (14in). ❄❄❄
***T.* 'Yokohama'** ■ Single Early Group tulip producing tapered yellow flowers, with yellow anthers, in mid-spring. ↕30cm (12in). ❄❄❄
***T.* 'Zampa'.** Greigii Group tulip producing primrose-yellow flowers, with bronze and green bases, in mid-spring. Leaves are marked dark bluish maroon. ↕25cm (10in). ❄❄❄

▷**Tulip tree** see *Liriodendron, L. tulipifera*
African see *Spathodea*
Chinese see *Liriodendron chinense*
▷**Tumbling Ted** see *Saponaria ocymoides*
▷***Tunica saxifraga*** see *Petrorhagia saxifraga*
▷**Tunic flower** see *Petrorhagia saxifraga*
▷**Tupelo** see *Nyssa, N. sylvatica*
Chinese see *N. sinensis*
▷***Turbinicarpus schmiedickeanus*** see *Neolloydia schmiedickeana*
▷**Turkscap lily,**
American see *Lilium superbum*
Common see *Lilium martagon*
Scarlet see *Lilium chalcedonicum*
▷**Turpentine tree** see *Pistacia terebinthus*
▷**Turtlehead** see *Chelone, C. glabra*
▷**Tussock grass** see *Cortaderia, Deschampsia cespitosa*
Plumed see *Chionochloa conspicua*
▷**Tutsan** see *Hypericum androsaemum*

TWEEDIA *syn.* OXYPETALUM

ASCLEPIADACEAE

Genus of one species of evergreen, twining, scrambling subshrub from scrub and rocky areas in S. Brazil and Uruguay. It has simple, opposite leaves and stalked, axillary and terminal cymes of short, tubular, 5-petalled, salverform flowers. In frost-prone areas, grow as an annual or in a cool greenhouse. In warmer climates, grow in a border or among other small shrubs.
• **HARDINESS** Frost tender.
• **CULTIVATION** Under glass, grow in loam-based potting compost (JI No.2) in full light. In the growing season,

Tweedia caerulea

T

water freely and apply a balanced liquid fertilizer monthly; water sparingly in winter. Outdoors, grow in moist but well-drained, fertile soil in full sun. Support the climbing stems. Pruning group 13, in early spring.
• **PROPAGATION** Sow seed at 15°C (59°F) in spring. Insert softwood cuttings with bottom heat in summer.
• **PESTS AND DISEASES** Trouble free.

T. caerulea ■ syn. *Amblyopetalum caeruleum, Oxypetalum caeruleum.* Erect, evergreen subshrub with twining, white-hairy stems and oblong-lance-shaped, downy, light green leaves, 5–10cm (2–4in) long, usually heart-shaped at the bases. From summer to early autumn, oblong-petalled, sky-blue flowers, 2–2.5cm (¾–1in) across, pink-flushed in bud and ageing to purple, are borne in small, 3- or 4-flowered cymes. ↕ 60–100cm (24–39in). S. Brazil to Uruguay. ❀ (min. 3–5°C/39–41°F)

▷**Twinberry** see *Lonicera involucrata*
▷**Twin-flower** see *Linnaea*
▷**Twin leaf** see *Jeffersonia*

TYLECODON

CRASSULACEAE

Genus of 20–30 species of bushy, succulent, deciduous shrubs, similar to *Cotyledon* and at one time included in that genus. They occur in deserts and partially shaded areas of Namibia and South Africa. Linear to ovate, spoon-shaped, or almost cylindrical leaves are alternate or in crowded spirals. Mainly bell-shaped, upright to pendent flowers have calyces with club-shaped hairs, in complex, many-branched, panicle-like cymes. In warm, dry, winter-rainfall areas, they are summer-dormant and suitable for a succulent border. In areas where temperatures fall below 7°C (45°F), grow in a temperate greenhouse. The leaves of *T. papillaris* subsp. *wallichii* are highly toxic if ingested.
• **HARDINESS** Frost tender.
• **CULTIVATION** Under glass, grow in standard cactus compost in full light, with low humidity. In growth, water moderately and apply a half-strength, low-nitrogen liquid fertilizer every 4–6 weeks; keep dry when leafless, and water moderately as growth resumes. Pot on as or just before new growth begins. Outdoors, grow in sharply drained, humus-rich, sandy or gritty soil in full sun. Pruning group 1. See also pp.48–49.

Tylecodon reticulatus

• **PROPAGATION** Sow seed at 19–24°C (66–75°F), or insert cuttings of stem sections, in late spring or summer.
• **PESTS AND DISEASES** Prey to mealybugs.

T. paniculatus, syn. *Cotyledon paniculata* (Butter tree). Succulent shrub producing soft, swollen, fleshy stems and short, thick, fleshy, warty branches, all covered with papery yellow bark. Obovate-spoon-shaped, fleshy, bright green leaves, to 11cm (4½in) long, are initially hairy with smooth margins, becoming completely hairless before falling. In spring, nodding, yellow-striped, dark reddish brown flowers, 1.5cm (½in) long, are borne in panicle-like cymes, 60cm (24in) long. ↕ to 2m (6ft), ↔ 1m (3ft). Namibia, South Africa (Northern Cape, Western Cape, Eastern Cape). ❀ (min. 7°C/45°F)
T. papillaris* subsp. *wallichii, syn. *Cotyledon wallichii, T. wallichii.* Succulent shrub with fleshy stems and branches, covered with prominent, persistent leaf bases. Short-lived, linear-cylindrical, grey-green leaves, 5–12cm (2–5in) long, grooved above, die back from the branch tips. Pendent, tubular, pale greenish yellow flowers, 2cm (¾in) long, are borne in panicle-like cymes, to 70cm (28in) long, in autumn and winter. ↕↔ 30cm (12in). South Africa (Western Cape, Karoo). ❀ (min. 7°C/45°F)
T. reticulatus ■ syn. *Cotyledon reticulata* (Barbed-wire plant). Stumpy, succulent shrub with short, thick, fleshy stems, covered with peeling grey-brown bark, and soft, spongy branches covered in leaf scars. Linear to almost cylindrical, downy, soft, brown-tipped, yellowish green leaves, 1.5–5cm (½–2in) long, are compressed or grooved above. In winter, bears erect, yellowish green flowers, 1cm (½in) long, in panicle-like cymes, to 30cm (12in) long. Dead inflorescences persist, forming a tangle of weak, silvery thorns that envelops the plant. ↕↔ 30cm (12in). Namibia, South Africa (Western Cape, Karoo). ❀ (min. 7°C/45°F)
T. wallichii see *T. papillaris* subsp. *wallichii*

TYPHA

Bulrush, Cat's tail, Reedmace

TYPHACEAE

Genus of 10–15 species of monoecious, marginal aquatic herbaceous perennials from temperate and tropical regions worldwide. They form dense, robust stands of vegetation around lakes and large ponds. Thick rhizomes spread in shallow water, producing long, linear, mostly basal leaves and poker-like brown flower spikes, borne among the foliage but overtopped by the leaf tips. Clusters of male and female flowers are produced on the same spike. Grow only around a large wildlife pool, where deep water prevents their spread; *T. minima* is the only species suitable for a small pool or tub. The flower spikes are used in dried flower arrangements.
• **HARDINESS** Fully hardy.
• **CULTIVATION** Grow in water to 30–40cm (12–16in) deep, with ample space and depth of mud for the root system. Flexible liners may be punctured by the rhizome tips of the larger species. Pick flowerheads for drying early in the season, and seal them with lacquer.

Typha latifolia

• **PROPAGATION** Divide rootstock in spring.
• **PESTS AND DISEASES** Trouble free.

T. angustifolia (Lesser bulrush, Narrow-leaved reedmace, Soft flag). Aquatic perennial with linear leaves, to 1.5m (5ft) long, sheathed at the bases. Brown flower spikes, 8–20cm (3–8in) long, are borne in midsummer; male and female flowers are 3–8cm (1¼–3in) apart, the females with dark reddish brown scales. ↕ 1.5m (5ft), ↔ indefinite. Europe, N. and C. Asia, N. Africa, North to South America. ❄❄❄
T. latifolia ■ (Bulrush, Cat's tail). Aquatic perennial with strap-shaped leaves, to 2m (6ft) or more long, with open-sheathed bases. Dark brown flower spikes, 15–22cm (6–9in) long, are borne in summer; male and female flowers are close together, no more than 2.5cm (1in) apart, the females becoming white-mottled with age. ↕ 2m (6ft) or more, ↔ indefinite. Europe, Asia, N. Africa, North America. ❄❄❄. **'Variegata'** ■ is much less vigorous, and has leaves with longitudinal cream stripes; ↕ 0.9–1.2m (3–4ft).
T. minima ■ Slender, aquatic perennial with narrowly linear leaves, 20–75cm (8–30in) long. Dark brown flowers are produced in cylindrical spikes, 1.5–5cm (½–2in) long, the female flowers borne immediately above the males, in mid- and late summer. ↕ to 75cm (30in), ↔ 30–45cm (12–18in). Eurasia. ❄❄❄

▷ ***Typhonium*** see *Sauromatum*

Typha latifolia 'Variegata'

Typha minima

T

U

UEBELMANNIA

CACTACEAE

Genus of 3–5 species of simple, perennial cacti found in humid, moist areas in the mountains of E. Brazil. The mostly spherical to cylindrical stems have smooth or finely warty, sometimes scaly ribs, and spiny areoles. Diurnal, solitary, funnel-shaped yellow flowers are produced near the crown in summer. In areas where temperatures drop below 15°C (59°F), grow in a warm greenhouse; in warmer climates, they are useful in a border.

- **HARDINESS** Frost tender.
- **CULTIVATION** Under glass, grow in acid standard cactus compost in full light. From mid-spring to early autumn, water moderately and apply a low-nitrogen liquid fertilizer every 6–8 weeks. Mist daily in summer. In winter, keep completely dry, but mist frequently on warm days. Outdoors, grow in gritty, moderately fertile, sharply drained, acid soil in full sun. See also pp.48–49.
- **PROPAGATION** Sow seed at 24°C (75°F) in spring. Often difficult to grow unless grafted.
- **PESTS AND DISEASES** Trouble free.

U. buiningii. Cactus with spherical, sometimes slightly elongated, greenish red-brown to deep chocolate stems, each with about 18 ribs, totally covered with minute, waxy scales. Close-set areoles each bear 6–8 semi-erect (some slightly curved), black-tipped, yellow-brown spines. Funnel-shaped, bright yellow flowers, 2cm (¾in) across, are borne in summer. ↕ 10–12cm (4–5in), ↔ 8cm (3in). E. Brazil. ❀ (min. 15°C/59°F)
U. pectinifera ▣ Cactus with spherical to cylindrical, reddish green to reddish brown stems, later elongating, each with 15–20 prominently margined, smooth ribs and minute, off-white scales (sometimes absent in cultivation). Close-set areoles each bear 3–6 comb-like, light grey to nearly black spines. Funnel-shaped yellow flowers, to 1cm (½in) across, are borne in summer. ↕ 50–80cm (20–32in), ↔ 15cm (6in). E. Brazil. ❀ (min. 15°C/59°F)

Uebelmannia pectinifera

UGNI

MYRTACEAE

Genus of 5–15 species of densely leafy, evergreen shrubs or trees found in forest and scrub in South America. They have opposite, small, elliptic to ovate, simple, leathery leaves, and produce solitary, cup- or bowl-shaped flowers from the leaf axils of young shoots, followed by edible, spherical berries. *U. molinae*, the only species usually cultivated, is valued for its foliage, flowers, and fruit. Grow in a sheltered border or use as hedging. In frost-prone areas, grow tender species in a cool greenhouse.

- **HARDINESS** Frost hardy to frost tender.
- **CULTIVATION** Grow in any moist but well-drained soil in full sun or partial shade. In frost-prone climates, shelter from cold, dry winds. Pruning group 1.
- **PROPAGATION** Root semi-ripe cuttings in late summer, with bottom heat.
- **PESTS AND DISEASES** Trouble free.

U. molinae ♀ syn. *Eugenia ugni*, *Myrtus ugni* (Chilean guava). Upright shrub or tree with elliptic to ovate, glossy, dark green leaves, to 3.5cm (1½in) long. Nodding, bowl-shaped, fragrant, pink-tinged white flowers, 1cm (½in) across, are produced singly from the leaf axils in late spring, followed by spherical, aromatic, dark red berries, 1cm (½in) across, in autumn. ↕ 1.5m (5ft), ↔ 1m (3ft). Chile, W. Argentina. ✲✲

ULEX

Furze, Gorse

LEGUMINOSAE/PAPILIONACEAE

Genus of about 20 species of spiny, evergreen shrubs from heaths and hill-sides, woodland margins, and rocky sites in W. and C. Europe and N. Africa. As young seedlings, they have alternate leaves, which are quickly replaced by long-lasting green spines. They are grown for their axillary, pea-like yellow flowers, borne singly, in clusters, or in racemes, virtually all year round in mild climates. Suitable for a shrub border and as a low hedge. The seeds may cause mild stomach upset if ingested.

- **HARDINESS** Fully hardy.
- **CULTIVATION** Grow in poor, sandy, acid to neutral, well-drained soil in full sun. May become very leggy on rich soil. Pruning group 10, after flowering, every 2 or 3 years.
- **PROPAGATION** Sow seed in containers in a cold frame in autumn or spring. Take semi-ripe cuttings in summer.
- **PESTS AND DISEASES** Trouble free.

U. europaeus ▣ (Furze, Gorse, Whin). Upright to rounded, densely bushy shrub with spine-tipped green shoots and rigid leaves reduced to deeply grooved spines, to 2.5cm (1in) long. Solitary, axillary, pea-like, coconut-scented, bright yellow flowers, 2cm (¾in) long, are produced intermittently throughout the year but mainly over a long period in spring. Dark brown seed pods, to 2cm (¾in) long, are borne in summer. ↕ to 2.5m (8ft), ↔ 2m (6ft).

Ulex europaeus

W. and C. Europe. ✲✲✲. **'Flore Pleno'** has double flowers and no fruit. **'Strictus'** (Irish gorse) is less spiny, with upright shoots.
U. gallii (Dwarf gorse). Spreading shrub with spine-tipped green shoots and rigid leaves reduced to slightly grooved spines, to 2.5cm (1in) long. From late summer to autumn, bears solitary, axillary, pea-like, bright yellow flowers, 1.5cm (½in) long; dark brown seed pods, to 1.5cm (½in) long, are produced in spring. ↕ 1.5–2m (5–6ft), ↔ 1.5m (5ft). W. Europe. ✲✲✲

▷**Ulmo** see *Eucryphia cordifolia*

ULMUS

Elm

ULMACEAE

Genus of about 45 species of deciduous, rarely semi-evergreen trees and, very rarely, shrubs, occurring in woodland, thickets, and hedgerows in N. temperate regions. They have alternate, ovate to elliptic, obovate, or rounded, toothed leaves, usually with very unequally sized bases, and often attractively coloured in autumn. Clusters of tiny, bell-shaped flowers, each with 4–9 segments joined at the bases, are usually produced from axillary buds in spring, but sometimes from leafy buds in autumn; the flowers are very quickly followed by fruits, each consisting of a seed surrounded by a green to brown, rounded to elliptic, membranous wing. Cultivated for their habit and foliage, elms are mainly grown as specimen trees. *U.* x *hollandica* 'Jacqueline Hillier' is suitable for a shrub border and for hedging.

- **HARDINESS** Fully hardy.
- **CULTIVATION** Grow in any well-drained soil in full sun or partial shade. Pruning group 1.
- **PROPAGATION** Sow seed in containers outdoors in autumn or spring. Take greenwood cuttings in summer, or remove rooted suckers in autumn. Bud weeping trees in summer, or graft in winter.
- **PESTS AND DISEASES** Dutch elm disease is usually fatal; *U.* x *hollandica* 'Jacqueline Hillier', *U. parvifolia* and its cultivars, *U. pumila*, and *U.* 'Sapporo Autumn Gold' are partially resistant. A number of Asiatic species are, at present, the most disease-resistant. Elms may also be affected by honey fungus. Aphids, leafhoppers, and gall mites may be a problem.

U. americana ♀ (American white elm). Graceful, rounded, deciduous tree with pendent branch tips and ovate to elliptic, toothed, dark green leaves, to 15cm (6in) long, turning bright yellow in autumn. Tiny red flowers are produced in early spring, followed in mid- and late spring by winged green fruit, 1cm (½in) across. ↕↔ 30m (100ft). E. North America (E. of the Rocky Mountains). ✲✲✲
U. angustifolia see *U. minor* subsp. *angustifolia*.
U. angustifolia* var. *cornubiensis see *U. minor* 'Cornubiensis'.
***U.* 'Camperdownii'** see *U. glabra* 'Camperdownii'.
U. carpinifolia see *U. minor*.

Ulmus glabra 'Exoniensis' (inset: leaf detail)

U

Ulmus x *hollandica* 'Jacqueline Hillier'

U. carpinifolia* var. *cornubiensis see *U. minor* 'Cornubiensis'.
U. carpinifolia* var. *sarniensis see *U. minor* subsp. *sarniensis*.
***U.* 'Commelin'** see *U.* x *hollandica* 'Commelin'.
***U.* 'Dicksonii'** see *U. minor* 'Dicksonii'.
***U.* x *elegantissima* 'Jacqueline Hillier'** see *U.* x *hollandica* 'Jacqueline Hillier'.
U. glabra ○ (Wych elm). Rounded, deciduous tree with broadly obovate, double-toothed, dark green leaves, to 15cm (6in) long, lobed at the tips, and rough above, downy beneath, turning yellow in autumn. Tiny red flowers are produced in early spring, followed by clustered, winged green fruit, 2.5cm (1in) across, in late spring. ↕35–40m (120–130ft), ↔25m (80ft). Europe, S.W. Asia. ❄❄❄. **'Camperdownii'** ○ syn. *U.* 'Camperdownii' (Camperdown elm) is weeping, with twisted branches and toothed to double-toothed, dark matt green leaves, to 20cm (8in) long; ↕↔8m (25ft). **'Exoniensis'** ■◊–○ (Exeter elm) is narrowly columnar when young, broadening with age, and has upright branches bearing clustered, twisted, and folded leaves; ↕15m (50ft), ↔8m (25ft).
U.* x *hollandica ◊ (probably *U. glabra* x *U. minor*) (Dutch elm). Broadly columnar, deciduous tree with a short trunk and wide-spreading to often arching or pendent branches. Broadly elliptic, pointed, double-toothed, dark green leaves, 7–12cm (3–5in) long, initially rough above, becoming glossy, turn yellow in autumn. Tiny red flowers are produced in early spring, followed by winged green fruit, 2cm (¾in) across, in late spring. ↕35m (120ft), ↔25m (80ft). Europe. ❄❄❄. **'Commelin'** △ syn. *U.* 'Commelin', is narrower in habit, with more upright branches and oval, toothed, bright green leaves, to 10cm (4in) long, smooth above, downy beneath, turning yellow in autumn. Flowers are produced in late spring, followed by fruit 1cm (½in) across, in late summer. ↕25m (80ft), ↔15m (50ft). **'Jacqueline Hillier'** ■ syn. *U.* x *elegantissima* 'Jacqueline Hillier', is a slow-growing, rounded, bushy shrub with elliptic-lance-shaped, double-toothed leaves, to 3.5cm (1½in) long, rough above, densely arranged in 2 rows along the shoots, and lasting until early winter; flowers are not usually produced. ↕↔2.5m (8ft). **'Vegeta'** ◊ syn. *U. vegeta* (Huntingdon elm) is fast-growing and broadly upright, with erect branches, pendent outer shoots, and broadly elliptic, ovate, or obovate, toothed, slightly rough leaves that turn yellow in autumn.
U. minor ◊ syn. *U. carpinifolia* (European field elm, Smooth-leaved elm). Broadly columnar, deciduous tree with arching branches and pendent shoots. Bears ovate, glossy, mid-green leaves, to 10cm (4in) long, smooth above, downy along the veins beneath and in the vein axils, and with double-toothed margins; they turn yellow in autumn. Very small red flowers are produced in early and mid-spring, followed by winged green fruit, 1cm (½in) across, in late spring. ↕30m (100ft), ↔20m (70ft). Europe, N. Africa, S.W. Asia. ❄❄❄. **subsp. *angustifolia*** ○ syn. *U. angustifolia* (Goodyer's elm) has a rounded canopy and elliptic or obovate to inversely lance-shaped, double-toothed, glossy, mid- to deep green leaves, 5–13cm (2–5in) long, paler beneath. Flowers are produced in early spring, followed by fruit to 1.5cm (½in) across, in summer. S. Europe, N. Africa, S.W. Asia. **'Cornubiensis'** ◊–◊ syn. *U. angustifolia* var. *cornubiensis*, *U. carpinifolia* var. *cornubiensis* (Cornish elm), sometimes considered a synonym of subsp. *angustifolia*, is conical when young, becoming columnar and round-topped when mature, with upright branches. S.W. England. ↔15m (50ft). **'Dicksonii'** ■△ syn. *U.* 'Dicksonii', *U. sarniensis* 'Aurea', *U.* 'Wheatleyi Aurea' (Cornish golden elm, Dickson's golden elm) is slow-growing, compact, and broadly conical, with broadly oval, toothed, glossy, bright golden yellow leaves, to 6cm (2½in) long; flowers are produced in spring, but only rarely. ↕10m (30ft), ↔6m (20ft). **subsp. *sarniensis*** ◊ syn. *U. carpinifolia* var. *sarniensis* (Jersey elm, Wheatley elm) is compact and conical, with upright branches and broadly elliptic to obovate, toothed, smooth, glossy, mid-green leaves, to 7cm (3in) long; flowers are produced in early spring. ↔10m (30ft).
U. parvifolia ■○ (Chinese elm). Spreading, deciduous or semi-evergreen tree with pendent shoots and flaking bark marked orange and brown. Elliptic, toothed, leathery, glossy, dark green leaves, to 6cm (2½in) long, with bases of almost equal size with matted hair beneath, may turn yellow or red in late autumn or early winter. Tiny red flowers are produced from late summer to autumn; they are followed by winged green fruit, 8mm (⅜in) across, in late autumn. ↕18m (60ft), ↔8–12m (25–40ft). China, Korea, Japan. ❄❄❄. **'Frosty'** is slow-growing and shrubby, with small, white-margined leaves, less than 2.5cm (1in) long; ↕↔2.5m (8ft). **'Hokkaido'**, syn. 'Pygmaea', is slow-growing, with small leaves, to 4cm (1½in) long, and corky bark; ↕↔2.5m (8ft). **'Pygmaea'** see 'Hokkaido'.
U. procera ◊ (English elm). Broadly upright, deciduous tree with a dense crown, broadest at the top. Broadly ovate to obovate, dark green leaves, to 10cm (4in) long, are rough above, paler and thinly hairy beneath, with coarsely double-toothed margins; they turn yellow in late autumn. Tiny red flowers are produced in early spring, followed by winged green fruit, to 1.5cm (½in) across, in late spring. ↕40m (130ft), ↔15m (50ft). UK. ❄❄❄
U. pumila ◊ (Siberian elm). Broadly upright, deciduous tree with narrowly elliptic to lance-shaped or ovate, tapered, toothed, dark green leaves, 3–10cm (1¼–4in) long, smooth above, hairy beneath, especially when young. Bears tiny red flowers in early spring, followed by winged green fruit, 1cm (½in) across, in late spring. ↕20–30m (70–100ft), ↔12m (40ft). Russia (E. Siberia), S. Kazakhstan, N. China. ❄❄❄
***U.* 'Sapporo Autumn Gold'** △ Fast-growing, broadly conical, deciduous tree with upright branches. Oval, toothed, smooth, glossy, dark green leaves, to 8cm (3in) long, red-tinged when young, turn yellow-green in autumn. Flowers are not usually produced. ↕18m (60ft), ↔12m (40ft). ❄❄❄
***U. sarniensis* 'Aurea'** see *U. minor* 'Dicksonii'.
U. vegeta see *U.* x *hollandica* 'Vegeta'.
***U.* 'Wheatleyi Aurea'** see *U. minor* 'Dicksonii'.

Ulmus minor 'Dicksonii'

Ulmus parvifolia

UMBELLULARIA

LAURACEAE

Genus of one species of evergreen tree, with alternate, entire leaves, from coniferous forest in W. USA. It is grown for its aromatic foliage, although the scent of the crushed leaves may induce headaches and nausea in some people. Grow as a specimen tree in a woodland garden or other sheltered site.

- **HARDINESS** Frost hardy.
- **CULTIVATION** Grow in any well-drained soil in full sun. In frost-prone climates, shelter from cold, drying winds. Pruning group 1.
- **PROPAGATION** Sow seed in containers in a cold frame in autumn. Insert semi-ripe cuttings in summer.
- **PESTS AND DISEASES** Trouble free.

Umbellularia californica

U. californica ■○ (California laurel, Headache tree). Rounded, evergreen tree with elliptic to oblong, leathery, very aromatic, bright green leaves, to 10cm (4in) long. Bears umbels of up to 10 small, salverform, yellow-green flowers, 1cm (½in) across, from the leaf axils in late winter and spring, then ovoid purple berries, 2.5cm (1in) long. ↕18m (60ft), ↔12m (40ft). USA (S. Oregon, N. California). ❄❄❄ (borderline)

▷**Umbrella leaf** see *Diphylleia cymosa*
▷**Umbrella pine** see *Pinus pinea*
Japanese see *Sciadopitys verticillata*
▷**Umbrella plant** see *Cyperus alternifolius*
▷**Umbrella tree** see *Magnolia macrophylla, M. tripetala*
Queensland see *Schefflera actinophylla*

UNCINIA

Hook sedge

CYPERACEAE

Genus of about 35–45 species of tufted, evergreen, monoecious perennials, some rhizomatous, found in damp, tussocky grassland, moist woodland, or swamps throughout S. temperate zones, except southern Africa. They have smooth, 3-angled to cylindrical stems and flat or shallowly channelled, grass-like leaves. The flowering stems bear spikes, with the male flowers at the top of the spike and the females beneath. The female flowers give rise to hooked, nut-like fruits. Several species are grown for their colourful leaves; they are suitable for the front of a border, or gravel plantings. In frost-prone climates, grow frost-tender species in a cool greenhouse.

- **HARDINESS** Frost hardy to frost tender; those described here will tolerate temperatures to about -10°C (14°F) for short periods.
- **CULTIVATION** Grow in moderately fertile, humus-rich, moist but well-drained soil in full sun or light dappled shade.
- **PROPAGATION** Sow seed at 13°C (55°F) in spring. Divide between late spring and midsummer.
- **PESTS AND DISEASES** Trouble free.

Uncinia rubra

U. rubra ■ Evergreen perennial, loosely tufted or with short rhizomes. Rigid, upright, 3-angled stems bear flat or inrolled, abruptly pointed, shiny leaves, to 35cm (14in) long; both stems and leaves are greenish red to rich reddish brown. Dark brown to black flowers are produced in narrow spikes, to 6cm (2½in) long, in mid- and late summer. ↕ 30cm (12in), ↔ 35cm (14in). New Zealand. ❄❄
U. uncinata. Densely tufted, evergreen perennial, similar to *U. rubra* but smaller, with rigid, upright stems and flat, rough-margined, pale brown to red-brown leaves, 5–10cm (2–4in) long. Bears dark brown flowers in narrow spikes, 15cm (6in) long, in mid- and late summer. ↕ 25cm (10in), ↔ 30cm (12in). New Zealand. ❄❄

▷ **Unicorn plant** see *Proboscidea*
Common see *P. louisianica*
▷ ***Uniola latifolia*** see *Chasmanthium latifolium*
▷ ***Urceolina*** see *Stenomesson*
U. pendula see *S. miniatum*

URGINEA

HYACINTHACEAE/LILIACEAE

Genus of about 100 species of bulbous perennials found on dry, rocky hillsides, on sandy soils near coasts, or on plains or savannah, mostly in tropical Africa, with a few in the Mediterranean. They have narrowly linear, basal leaves, and are grown for their star- or saucer-shaped flowers, produced in long, erect, dense racemes on leafless stems in summer and autumn. Grow in a sunny border. In frost-prone areas, grow half-hardy and frost-tender species in a cool greenhouse.

- **HARDINESS** Frost hardy to frost tender.
- **CULTIVATION** Under glass, grow in loam-based potting compost (JI No.2), with added sharp sand, in full light. Water freely when in growth. Keep just moist when dormant. Outdoors, grow in sandy or stony, poor to moderately fertile, sharply drained soil in full sun. Protect from winter wet.
- **PROPAGATION** Sow seed at 13–18°C (55–64°F) when ripe. Remove offsets in summer.
- **PESTS AND DISEASES** Trouble free.

U. maritima (Sea onion, Sea squill). Bulbous perennial producing dense racemes, 30cm (12in) or more long, of many tiny, star-shaped white flowers, 6mm (¼in) across, with green or purple midveins, in late summer and early autumn. Erect, narrow, basal leaves, 30–100cm (12–39in) long, appear in autumn, after the flowers. ↕ 1.5m (5ft), ↔ 30cm (12in). Mediterranean. ❄

URSINIA

ASTERACEAE/COMPOSITAE

Genus of about 40 species of annuals and evergreen perennials and subshrubs from dry savannah in South Africa, Namibia, Botswana, and Ethiopia. They are cultivated mainly for their flowers; a few species are grown for their foliage. The alternate leaves may occasionally be simple, but are usually pinnatifid, pinnatisect, or pinnate, often hairy or downy, and frequently aromatic. Daisy-like, yellow, orange, or red flowerheads, usually solitary, sometimes in corymbs, are borne on long stalks well above the foliage. Grow annual species at the front of a border or at the base of a house wall. Where winter temperatures fall below 0°C (32°F), grow perennials and subshrubs in a cool greenhouse or treat as annuals. Alternatively, lift before the first frosts and overwinter in frost-free conditions. In milder areas, grow in a border or small courtyard garden.

- **HARDINESS** Half hardy to frost tender.
- **CULTIVATION** Under glass, grow in loam-based potting compost (JI No.1) in full light. In growth, water freely and apply a balanced liquid fertilizer every 4 weeks. Water sparingly in winter. Outdoors, grow in sandy, fertile, well-drained soil in full sun.
- **PROPAGATION** Sow seed at 13–18°C (55–64°F) in spring. Take softwood cuttings in summer.
- **PESTS AND DISEASES** Trouble free.

U. anethoides. Bushy, evergreen perennial, usually grown as an annual, with crowded, pinnatisect, thinly hairy or hairless leaves, 2.5–4cm (1–1½in) long, with linear, almost cylindrical lobes. In summer, bears solitary, golden yellow flowerheads, 2.5cm (1in) across, with purple disc-florets. ↕ 45cm (18in), ↔ 35cm (14in). South Africa. ❄
U. anthemoides ■ Erect, bushy annual with pinnatisect, slightly hairy, scented, light green leaves, 2–6cm (¾–1½in) long, with slender, flat or thread-like lobes. In summer, produces solitary, purple-centred, yellow-orange flowerheads, to 6cm (2½in) across, each ray-floret zoned in maroon-red or copper-purple on the underside. ↕ to 40cm (16in), ↔ to 30cm (12in). South Africa (Northern Cape, Western Cape, Eastern Cape). ❄

Ursinia anthemoides

U. chrysanthemoides. Erect, spreading, woody-based, evergreen, short-lived perennial, sometimes grown as an annual, with rooting stems. Bears softly hairy or hairless, scented, silvery grey-green leaves, 5cm (2in) long, which may be pinnate, 2-pinnate, or occasionally entire, all on the same plant. Produces solitary flowerheads, 3–6cm (1¼–2½in) across, with yellow or occasionally red or white ray-florets, sometimes copper-tinted beneath, mainly in summer. ↕ 30–45cm (12–18in), ↔ 60–75cm (24–30in). South Africa (Northern Cape, Western Cape, Eastern Cape). ❁ (min. 5–7°C/41–45°F). **var. *geyeri***, syn. 'Geyeri', *U. geyeri*, has dull green leaves, very white-woolly at first. Rich crimson-red flowerheads, 2.5–6cm (1–2½in) across, with red-black disc-florets, are produced in summer. ↕ to 90cm (36in), ↔ to 30cm (12in)
U. geyeri see *U. chrysanthemoides* var. *geyeri.*
U. sericea. Bushy, evergreen subshrub with pinnate or pinnatisect, silver-silky-hairy leaves, to 8cm (3in) long. In summer, produces solitary yellow flowerheads, to 3cm (1¼in) across, on very long stalks. ↕↔ to 70cm (30in). South Africa (Northern Cape, Western Cape, Eastern Cape). ❁ (min. 5–7°C/41–45°F)

UTRICULARIA

Bladderwort

LENTIBULARIACEAE

Genus of approximately 180 species of terrestrial, epiphytic, or free-floating aquatic annuals and perennials found worldwide in stagnant, shallow water, or growing on rainforest trees. They are insectivorous, and thrive in water that attracts mosquito larvae. Generally rootless, they have mainly submerged stems, either loosely anchored or free-floating, and thread-like or linear to rounded leaves with traps (bladders) adapted to catch and absorb insects. The flowers, solitary or in racemes, are usually borne on leafless stems above the water, and are supported by a whorl of spongy, floating leaves. Grow in an outdoor pool. In frost-prone areas, grow tender species in a warm aquarium. The hardy species may also be grown in a cold-water aquarium.

- **HARDINESS** Fully hardy to frost tender.
- **CULTIVATION** Outdoors, grow in acid water that warms up quickly in spring, in full sun. In an aquarium, grow in full light in soft, algae-free water; frost-tender species need a water temperature of 19°C (66°F), hardy species 12–15°C (54–59°F). See also pp.52–53.
- **PROPAGATION** Collect buds that sink to the bottom of the pool or aquarium after flowering and replant. Divide mats of floating foliage in summer.
- **PESTS AND DISEASES** Trouble free.

U. exoleta see *U. gibba.*
U. gibba, syn. *U. exoleta.* Floating aquatic annual or perennial with mat-forming stolons. Slender stems produce feathery, bladder-bearing leaves, to 8cm (3in) long. In midsummer, pouched, red-veined yellow flowers, to 6mm (¼in) long, are borne above the water, either singly or in a 2- to 5-flowered raceme, 20cm (8in) long. ↔ 20cm (8in). Spain, Portugal, Israel, southern Africa, China, Japan, Australia, New Zealand, North America, Argentina. ❁ (min. 7°C/45°F)

UVULARIA

Merrybells

CONVALLARIACEAE/LILIACEAE

Genus of 5 species of rhizomatous perennials from woodland in E. North America. They have erect, simple or branched stems, the upper parts bearing alternate, stalkless or perfoliate, ovate to lance-shaped, hairless or downy leaves. Pendent, tubular-bell-shaped, 6-tepalled yellow flowers are produced on long, slender stalks, and are usually solitary (occasionally in pairs) and terminal. Excellent for a peat bed, shady border, or woodland garden.

- **HARDINESS** Fully hardy.
- **CULTIVATION** Grow in fertile, humus-rich, moist but well-drained soil in deep or partial shade.
- **PROPAGATION** Sow seed in containers in a cold frame as soon as ripe. Divide in early spring.
- **PESTS AND DISEASES** Very susceptible to slugs and snails, especially in spring.

U. grandiflora ■ (Large merrybells). Slowly spreading, rhizomatous perennial with sometimes 2-branched stems bearing ovate-lance-shaped, downward-pointing, perfoliate, mid-green leaves, to 13cm (5in) long, softly hairy beneath. Solitary or paired, pendent, tubular-bell-shaped, sometimes green-tinted, yellow flowers, 5cm (2in) long, with free, slightly twisted tepals, and stamens longer than styles, are borne in mid- and late spring. ↕ to 75cm (30in), ↔ 30cm (12in). E. North America. ❄❄❄. **var. *pallida*** has paler yellow flowers.
U. perfoliata. Slowly spreading, creeping, rhizomatous perennial with sometimes 2-branched stems bearing downward-pointing, ovate-lance-shaped, perfoliate, mid-green, hairless leaves, to 10cm (4in) long. A few solitary or paired, pendent, tubular-bell-shaped, pale yellow flowers, to 3.5cm (1½in) long, with free, slightly twisted tepals, the tips spreading, and stamens shorter than styles, are borne in late spring and early summer. ↕ to 60cm (24in), ↔ 30cm (12in). E. North America. ❄❄❄

Uvularia grandiflora

U

VACCINIUM

V

VACCINIUM

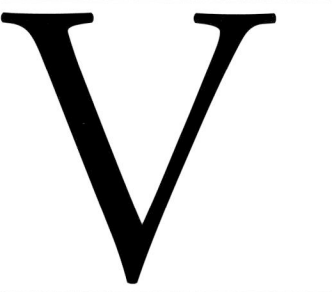

Bilberry, Blueberry, Cranberry, Whortleberry

ERICACEAE

Genus of about 450 species of evergreen, semi-evergreen, or deciduous shrubs and trees, widely distributed throughout arctic and tropical regions, occurring in a variety of habitats from heath and moorland to bogs and woodland. They are valued for their ornamental foliage, flowers, and berries. The leathery leaves are alternate, and may be lance-shaped to elliptic, ovate, or rounded, with entire or toothed margins; in some of the deciduous species, the leaves provide brilliant autumn colour. The small, urn- or bell-shaped to cylindrical flowers are white, green, pink, or red, and are produced either singly in the leaf axils or in terminal or axillary racemes in spring and summer. The flowers are followed by edible, usually spherical berries; some species, including *V. angustifolium* var. *laevifolium*, *V. corymbosum*, and *V. macrocarpon*, are grown primarily for their fruits (blueberries and cranberries). Vacciniums are best suited to a woodland garden.

• **HARDINESS** Fully hardy to frost hardy.

• **CULTIVATION** Grow in acid, peaty or sandy, moist but well-drained soil in full sun or partial shade. Pruning group 1 for deciduous species; group 8 for evergreens.

• **PROPAGATION** Sow seed in containers in a cold frame in autumn. Take greenwood cuttings of deciduous species in early summer, and semi-ripe cuttings of evergreens in mid- to late summer. Layer in late summer.

• **PESTS AND DISEASES** May be affected by *Phytophthora* crown and root rot.

V. angustifolium* var. *laevifolium ▣ (Lowbush blueberry). Spreading, densely branched, deciduous shrub with lance-shaped, minutely toothed, glossy,

Vaccinium angustifolium var. *laevifolium*

Vaccinium arctostaphylos

dark green leaves, to 4cm (1½in) long, turning red in autumn. Bell-shaped, white, sometimes pink-tinged flowers, 1cm (½in) long, are borne in pendent, axillary and terminal racemes, to 5cm (2in) long, in mid- and late spring; they are followed by edible, sweet, spherical, blue-black berries, to 1.5cm (½in) across. ↕↔ 10–60cm (4–24in). E. North America. ❄❄❄

V. arctostaphylos ▣ (Caucasian whortleberry). Erect, densely branched, deciduous shrub with red-brown young shoots and elliptic, entire, dark green leaves, to 10cm (4in) long, coloured red and purple in autumn. Bell-shaped, pink-tinged white flowers, 8mm (⅜in) long, are produced in pendent, axillary racemes, to 5cm (2in) long, in early summer; they are followed by edible, spherical, purple-black berries, 8mm (⅜in) across. ↕ 3m (10ft), ↔ 2m (6ft). Bulgaria, Turkey, Caucasus. ❄❄❄

V. caespitosum (Dwarf bilberry). Low-growing, rapidly spreading, densely branched, deciduous shrub with elliptic to obovate, entire or toothed, dark green leaves, 1.5–3.5cm (½–1½in) long. In late spring and early summer, produces pendent, urn-shaped, white to pink flowers, 5mm (¼in) long, singly from the leaf axils; flowers are followed by edible, spherical, blue-black fruit, 6mm (¼in) across. ↕ to 15cm (6in), ↔ 60cm (24in), or more. N. and W. North America. ❄❄❄

V. corymbosum ▣ (Highbush blueberry, Swamp blueberry). Upright, dense, many-branched, deciduous shrub with arching shoots and lance-shaped to elliptic, entire or toothed, mid-green

Vaccinium corymbosum

Vaccinium glaucoalbum

leaves, to 9cm (3½in) long, turning yellow or red in autumn. In late spring and early summer, produces pendent, terminal racemes, to 5cm (2in) long, of cylindrical, white, sometimes pink-tinged flowers, 1cm (½in) long; they are followed by edible, sweet, spherical, blue-black berries, to 1cm (½in) across. ↕↔ 1.5m (5ft). E. North America. ❄❄❄

V. crassifolium (Creeping blueberry). Vigorous, procumbent, mat-forming, evergreen shrub with oval-elliptic to rounded, finely toothed, thick, leathery, dark green leaves, 0.8–1.5cm (⅜–½in) long, paler beneath. In late spring and early summer, bears pendent, urn-shaped, white to pink or rose-red flowers, 4mm (⅛in) long, in loose, terminal and axillary racemes, to 5cm (2in) long; they are followed by edible, spherical, purple-black fruit, to 1cm (½in) across. ↕ to 45cm (18in), ↔ 1m (3ft). S.E. USA. ❄❄❄ (borderline). **'Well's Delight'** has a looser, broader habit, and prefers partial shade; ↕ to 20cm (8in), ↔ 60cm (24in) or more.

V. cylindraceum. Upright, semi-evergreen shrub with lance-shaped, finely toothed, glossy, dark green leaves, to 6cm (2½in) long, retained until shortly before new growth begins in spring. In late summer and early autumn, bears cylindrical, red-tinged green flowers, 9–15mm (⅜–½in) long, in pendent, dense, axillary racemes, 5cm (2in) long; they are followed by edible, spherical, blue-black berries, 1cm (½in) long. ↕ 2.5m (8ft), ↔ 2m (6ft). Azores. ❄❄

V. delavayi. Compact, spreading, evergreen shrub with densely arranged, obovate to elliptic, entire, leathery, dark green leaves, to 1.5cm (½in) long, red-tinged when young. Tiny, pendent, urn-shaped, pink-flushed, creamy white flowers, 6mm (¼in) long, are produced singly or in clusters of 2–4 from the leaf axils in early summer; they are followed by edible, spherical, deep red berries, 5mm (¼in) across. ↕ 60cm (24in), ↔ 90cm (36in). S.W. China. ❄❄

V. floribundum, syn. *V. mortinia* (Mortiña). Spreading, evergreen shrub bearing arching shoots densely covered with ovate, glandular-toothed, dark green leaves, to 1cm (½in) long, red when young. In early summer, produces dense, pendent, axillary racemes, to 5cm (2in) long, of cylindrical pink flowers, 6mm (¼in) long; they are followed by edible, spherical red berries, 5mm (¼in) across. ↕ 1m (3ft), ↔ 2m (6ft). Ecuador, Peru. ❄❄

V. glaucoalbum ▣ Spreading, mound-forming, dense, evergreen shrub producing elliptic, dark green leaves, to 6cm (2½in) long, bright bluish white beneath, either entire or with bristle-like teeth. Cylindrical, pink-tinged white flowers, 6mm (¼in) long, are borne in pendent, axillary racemes, to 7cm (3in) long, in late spring and early summer; they are followed by edible, spherical, white-bloomed, blue-black berries, 8mm (⅜in) across. ↕ 50–120cm (20–48in), ↔ 1m (3ft). E. Himalayas to China, Tibet, N. Burma. ❄❄

V. macrocarpon (Cranberry). Prostrate, mat-forming, evergreen shrub with slender shoots and elliptic-oblong, entire, dark green leaves, to 2cm (¾in) long, bronze in winter. In summer, pendent, slender-stalked, bell-shaped pink flowers, 1cm (½in) across, with 4 slender, reflexed lobes, are produced singly from the leaf axils or in clusters of 2–10; they are followed by edible, spherical red berries, to 2cm (¾in) across. Best in cool, moist soil in sun. ↕ 15cm (6in), ↔ indefinite. E. North America. ❄❄❄

V. mortinia see *V. floribundum*.

V. moupinense. Compact, rounded, evergreen shrub with densely arranged, elliptic-oblong to obovate, entire, leathery, glossy, dark green leaves, to 1cm (½in) long. Tiny, urn-shaped, dark red-brown flowers, 5mm (¼in) long, are produced in pendent, axillary racemes, to 2.5cm (1in) long, in late spring and early summer; they are followed by edible, spherical, purple-black berries,

Vaccinium myrtillus

Vaccinium vitis-idaea subsp. *minus*

6mm (¼in) across. ↕ 60cm (24in), ↔ 90cm (36in). W. China. ✼✼✼
V. myrtillus ■ (Bilberry, Whinberry, Whortleberry). Vigorous, creeping, deciduous shrub with dense, upright stems and oval-elliptic, finely toothed, glossy, bright green leaves, 1–3cm (½–1¼in) long, often colouring red in autumn. In late spring and early summer, pendent, axillary, rounded, urn-shaped pink flowers, 6mm (¼in) long, are produced singly or in pairs. Flowers are followed by edible, spherical, blue-black berries, 6–10mm (¼–½in) across. May be invasive in fertile soils. ↕ to 30cm (12in), ↔ indefinite. Europe to N. Asia. ✼✼✼
V. nummularia. Spreading, low-growing, evergreen shrub with arching, brown-bristly stems. Rounded to elliptic, finely toothed, leathery, wrinkled, glossy, bright green leaves, 1–2.5cm (½–1in) long, are margined with red-brown bristles. In late spring, urn-shaped, red-tipped, pale pink flowers, 5mm (¼in) long, are produced in pendent racemes, to 5cm (2in) long, from leaf axils near the shoot tips; they are followed by edible, broadly ovoid black berries, 6mm (¼in) across. ↕ to 30cm (12in), ↔ to 60cm (24in). Himalayas (Sikkim, Bhutan). ✼✼✼ (borderline)
V. ovatum (Box blueberry). Upright, bushy, evergreen shrub with arching shoots and densely arranged, ovate, finely toothed, leathery, glossy, dark green leaves, to 3cm (1¼in) long, bronze when young. In late spring and early summer, produces cylindrical or urn-shaped, pink-flushed white flowers, 6mm (¼in) long, in dense, nodding, axillary racemes, 2.5cm (1in) long; flowers are followed by edible, spherical, glossy black berries, 6mm (¼in) across. ↕ 4m (12ft), ↔ 3m (10ft). W. North America (British Columbia to California). ✼✼
V. parvifolium (Red whortleberry). Upright, deciduous shrub with oblong, entire, blue-green leaves, to 3cm (1¼in) long, turning brilliant red in autumn. Small, rounded, urn-shaped, white, sometimes pink-tinged flowers, 4–6mm (⅛–¼in) long, are produced singly or in pairs from the leaf axils in late spring and early summer. Flowers are followed by edible, spherical, coral-red berries, 1cm (½in) across. ↕ 3m (10ft), ↔ 2m (6ft). W. North America (Alaska to California). ✼✼✼

Vaccinium vitis-idaea 'Koralle' (inset: fruit detail)

V. praestans. Dwarf, deciduous shrub with sparse, creeping and ascending shoots. Broadly elliptic to obovate, indistinctly toothed, pale green leaves, 2.5–5cm (1–2in) long, are blunt or sharp-pointed at the tips and tapering at the bases, turning red in autumn. In early summer, produces bell-shaped, pink-flushed white flowers, 6mm (¼in) long, either singly or in few-flowered, pendent, axillary racemes, to 5cm (2in) long; they are followed by edible, spherical, bright red berries, 1cm (½in) across. ↕ to 10cm (4in), ↔ to 30cm (12in). N.E. Asia. ✼✼✼
V. vitis-idaea (Cowberry). Creeping, evergreen shrub, spreading by means of underground rhizomes, and bearing obovate, glossy, dark green leaves, to 2.5cm (1in) long, often shallowly notched at the tips. In late spring and early summer, produces bell-shaped, white to deep pink flowers, 6mm (¼in) long, in dense, nodding, terminal racemes, to 2.5cm (1in) long; they are followed by edible but acidic, spherical, bright red berries, 6mm (¼in) across. ↕ 25cm (10in), ↔ indefinite. Arctic and alpine regions of N. Eurasia, Japan, North America. ✼✼✼. **'Koralle'** ■ produces abundant fruit, to 9mm (⅜in) across. **subsp. *minus*** ■ is shorter, with smaller leaves, to 1.5cm (½in) long, and deep pink flowers; ↕ 20cm (8in); Arctic and alpine North America.

▷**Valerian** see *Centranthus, Valeriana*
Common see *Valeriana officinalis*
Greek see *Polemonium caeruleum*
Red see *Centranthus ruber*

VALERIANA

Valerian

VALERIANACEAE

Genus of 200 or more species of annuals, often rhizomatous or tap-rooted herbaceous perennials, semi-evergreen subshrubs, and usually evergreen shrubs. They are found throughout the world, except in Australasia, and occur in moist woodland, meadows, or at streamsides, often in mountainous regions; the alpine species grow in scree or rock crevices. The opposite leaves are often aromatic, but not always pleasantly so; they are generally simple, although the non-shrubby species often produce pinnate or pinnatifid stem leaves as well as basal rosettes of simple leaves. The small, unisexual or bisexual, salverform flowers are pink to lavender-pink, white, or yellow, and are borne in terminal, panicle- or corymb-like cymes in summer. The few species in cultivation are herbaceous perennials, grown for their attractive flowers. Valerians are suitable for growing in an informal, cottage-style garden, herbaceous border, or herb garden, or for naturalizing in a wild garden.

- **HARDINESS** Fully hardy.
- **CULTIVATION** Grow in any, preferably moist soil in full sun or dappled shade. Tall-stemmed species and cultivars may require support.
- **PROPAGATION** Sow seed in containers outdoors, or take basal cuttings, in spring. Divide in spring or autumn.
- **PESTS AND DISEASES** Trouble free.

Valeriana phu 'Aurea'

V. officinalis (All heal, Common valerian). Upright, clump-forming perennial with short rhizomes producing fleshy, branching stems. The aromatic, bright green, basal and stem leaves are pinnate, to 20cm (8in) long, each with 7–10 pairs of lance-shaped, toothed leaflets. Branched, rounded, corymb-like cymes of salverform, bisexual, pink or white flowers, to 5mm (¼in) long, are borne throughout summer. ↕ 1.2–2m (4–6ft), ↔ 40–80cm (16–32in). W. Europe. ✼✼✼
***V. phu* 'Aurea'** ■ Clump-forming, rhizomatous perennial with simple or pinnatifid, elliptic to inversely lance-shaped, aromatic basal leaves, to 20cm (8in) long, and pinnatifid, pinnatisect, or pinnate stem leaves; pinnate leaves have 3 or 4 pairs of elliptic leaflets. All leaves are soft yellow in spring, turning lime- to mid-green by summer. In early summer, branching stems bear panicle-like corymbs of small, salverform, bisexual white flowers, 4mm (⅛in) long. ↕ to 1.5m (5ft), ↔ 60cm (24in). ✼✼✼

VALLEA

ELAEOCARPACEAE

Genus of one species of evergreen shrub or tree found in scrub in the Andes from Colombia to Bolivia. It has spirally arranged, simple or occasionally lobed leaves, and produces cup-shaped flowers, each with 5 sepals and 5 petals, in small, axillary and terminal cymes. Where temperatures fall below 0°C (32°F), grow in a cool greenhouse. In warmer areas, use in a courtyard garden or border, or plant against a warm, sunny wall.

- **HARDINESS** Frost hardy (borderline).
- **CULTIVATION** Under glass, grow in lime-free (ericaceous) potting compost in full or bright filtered light. When in growth, water moderately and apply a balanced liquid fertilizer monthly. Water sparingly in winter. Outdoors, grow in moderately fertile, neutral to acid, moist but well-drained soil in full sun or partial shade. Pruning group 9; may require restrictive pruning under glass.
- **PROPAGATION** Sow seed at 6–12°C (43–54°F), ideally as soon as ripe. Root semi-ripe cuttings with bottom heat in mid- or late summer.
- **PESTS AND DISEASES** Red spider mites may be a problem under glass.

V. stipularis ♀ Erect to spreading shrub or tree, freely branching, at least when mature. Almost fleshy, leathery, deep green leaves, 3–12cm (1¼–5in) long, are lance-shaped to broadly ovate,

V

rounded to heart-shaped at the bases, and sometimes lobed. Cymes of cup-shaped, crimson to dark rose-red flowers, 2–2.5cm (¾–1in) across, with darker veins, are produced from spring to summer. ↕3–5m (10–15ft), ↔ 2–4m (6–12ft). N. South America (Colombia to Bolivia). ❄❄ (borderline)

▷ ***Vallota speciosa*** see *Cyrtanthus elatus*

VANCOUVERIA

BERBERIDACEAE

Genus, closely allied to *Epimedium*, of about 3 species of creeping, rhizomatous perennials, some of them evergreen, from rocky hillside scrub or coniferous woodland in W. USA. They are grown for their ternate or 2-ternate, thick, sometimes leathery, basal leaves, and for their loose panicles of nodding flowers, each with 6 reflexed petals and 12 sepals, borne on wiry stems in late spring and summer. Suitable for ground cover in a large rock garden or woodland garden.

- **HARDINESS** Fully hardy to frost hardy.
- **CULTIVATION** Grow in moderately fertile, humus-rich, leafy, moist but well-drained soil in partial shade. Shelter from cold, drying winds.
- **PROPAGATION** Sow seed in containers in a cold frame as soon as ripe. Divide in spring.
- **PESTS AND DISEASES** Vine weevil may be a problem.

V. chrysantha. Creeping, evergreen, rhizomatous perennial with ternate or 2-ternate, thick, leathery, glossy, dark green, basal leaves, to 45cm (18in) long, glaucous and paler beneath, composed of usually 9, rarely 3 or 5, rounded, diamond-shaped leaflets, 4cm (1½in) long, with thickened, wavy margins. From late spring to summer, leafless stems bear loose panicles of 4–15 yellow flowers, to 1cm (½in) long. ↕to 30cm (12in), ↔ to 60cm (24in) or more. USA (S.W. Oregon, N. California). ❄❄❄
V. hexandra ▣ Creeping, deciduous, rhizomatous perennial with 2-ternate, normally basal leaves, to 45cm (18in) long, each composed of 9 or more variable, ovate, smooth-textured, bright green leaflets, 7cm (3in) long, white-hairy when young. In late spring and early summer, leafless stems bear loose panicles of 6–45 white flowers, to 1.5cm (½in) long. Seldom spreads as widely as *V. chrysantha*. ↕↔ to 40cm (16in). USA (Washington to California). ❄❄❄

Vancouveria hexandra

VANDA

ORCHIDACEAE

Genus of 30–40 species of evergreen, epiphytic, monopodial orchids found in exposed sites in scrub forest at altitudes of 1,500m (5,000ft) from India to S.E. Asia and the Philippines, and south to Australia. Their stout, simple stems have aerial roots on the lower parts; the tips bear 2-ranked, strap-shaped to linear, leathery, semi-rigid, mid-green leaves, often lobed or toothed at the tips. The flowers, borne in axillary, occasionally terminal racemes, are often large, showy, and intricately coloured on their sepals, with small lips. A range of richly coloured hybrids is available.

- **HARDINESS** Frost tender.
- **CULTIVATION** Intermediate-growing orchids. Grow in epiphytic orchid compost in slatted baskets in full light with shade from hot sun. In summer, water freely, apply fertilizer at every third watering, and mist plants twice daily. Water moderately in winter. See also p.46.
- **PROPAGATION** Remove offsets that arise at the base of the plants, or root cuttings of stem sections, in spring.
- **PESTS AND DISEASES** Susceptible to red spider mites, aphids, and mealybugs.

V. caerulea. Unbranched, epiphytic orchid with curved, linear leaves, to 25cm (10in) long. In autumn and winter, bears long, pendent racemes of clear blue flowers, 5–10cm (2–4in) across, often chequered darker blue; lips are dark violet-blue with whitish blue lateral lobes. ↕60cm (24in), ↔ 30cm (12in). India, Burma, Thailand. ❀ (min. 13–16°C/55–61°F; max. 30°C/86°F)
***V.* Kasem's Delight** (*V.* Sun Tan x *V.* Thospol). Unbranched, epiphytic orchid with linear leaves, 15cm (6in) long. Flowers, 10cm (4in) across, in a combination of deep mauve and indigo, are borne in long, pendent racemes intermittently throughout the year. ↕60cm (24in), ↔ 30cm (12in). ❀ (min. 13–16°C/55–61°F; max. 30°C/86°F)
***V.* Rothschildiana** ▣ (*Euanthe sanderiana* x *V. caerulea*). Unbranched, epiphytic orchid with curved, linear leaves, 15cm (6in) long. Dark-veined, violet-blue flowers, 10cm (4in) across, are borne in long, pendent racemes intermittently throughout the year. ↕60cm (24in), ↔ 30cm (12in). ❀ (min. 13–16°C/55–61°F; max. 30°C/86°F)

Vanda Rothschildiana

V. sanderiana see *Euanthe sanderiana*.
V. tessellata. Unbranched, epiphytic orchid with curved, linear leaves, to 45cm (18in) long. In autumn, produces long, pendent racemes of variable flowers, 5cm (2in) across, yellow-green or very pale blue, chequered brown, with white-margined, violet to blue lips. ↕60cm (24in), ↔ 30cm (12in). India, Sri Lanka, Burma, Malaysia. ❀ (min. 13–16°C/55–61°F; max. 30°C/86°F)
V. tricolor. Unbranched, epiphytic orchid with curved, linear leaves, 45cm (18in) long. Fragrant flowers, 5–7cm (2–3in) across, are usually pale yellow, heavily patterned red-brown, with purple-striped, violet-red lips; they are borne in long, erect to spreading racemes in winter. ↕1m (3ft), ↔ 30cm (12in). Laos, Indonesia (Java). ❀ (min. 13–16°C/55–61°F; max. 30°C/86°F)

▷**Vaquero blanco** see *Cydista aequinoctialis*
▷**Varnish tree** see *Rhus verniciflua*
▷**Vase plant** see *Aechmea fasciata*
▷**Vegetable sheep** see *Haastia*, *H. pulvinaris*, *Raoulia eximia*

VEITCHIA

ARECACEAE/PALMAE

Genus of 18 species of single-stemmed palms found in tropical rainforest, from sea level to 650m (2,100ft), from the Philippines and New Caledonia to Fiji and the New Hebrides. Oblong, pinnate leaves are produced in terminal tufts above a distinctive crownshaft; bowl-shaped, 3-petalled flowers are borne in panicles just beneath the foliage, and are followed by showy, red to orange fruits. In frost-prone climates, grow in a warm greenhouse or as houseplants. In warmer areas, use small species in a courtyard or border, and grow tall species on a lawn.

- **HARDINESS** Frost tender.
- **CULTIVATION** Under glass, grow in loam-based potting compost (JI No.3) with added peat and sharp sand, in full light. Pot on or top-dress in spring. When in growth, water freely and apply a balanced liquid fertilizer monthly. Water sparingly in winter. Outdoors, grow in fertile, moist but well-drained soil in full sun.
- **PROPAGATION** Sow seed at 24°C (75°F) in spring.
- **PESTS AND DISEASES** Red spider mites may be troublesome under glass.

V. joannis 🌴 syn. *Kentia joannis*. Tall palm with a slender, columnar trunk, to 28cm (11in) across. Erect to arching, mid- to deep green leaves, to 3m (10ft) or more long, each have 70–80 narrowly linear, arching leaflets. Greenish yellow flowers, 1cm (½in) across, are produced in panicles to 1m (3ft) long, usually in summer; they are followed by ovoid, orange-red fruit, 5–6cm (2–2½in) long. ↕to 30m (100ft), ↔ to 6m (20ft). Fiji. ❀ (min. 15°C/59°F)
V. merrillii ▣🌴 syn. *Adonidia merrillii* (Christmas palm, Manila palm). Small palm with a slender trunk, to 26cm (10in) across, which tapers towards the crownshaft. Strongly arching, matt, mid- to deep green leaves, 1–2m (3–6ft) long, each have 40–60 strap-shaped leaflets, pale green and scaly beneath. Green to yellow-green flowers, 2cm (¾in) across, are borne in panicles to 1m (3ft) long,

Veitchia merrillii

usually in summer; they are followed by ovoid crimson fruit, to 3cm (1¼in) long, which are at their most colourful during winter. ↕to 5–6m (15–20ft), ↔ 2–3.5m (6–11ft). Philippines (Palawan Islands). ❀ (min. 15°C/59°F)

VELLOZIA

VELLOZIACEAE

Genus of 124 species of xerophytic, sometimes tree-like, evergreen perennials occurring on rocky, windswept cliffs or outcrops in scrub or woodland in tropical Africa, Madagascar, and tropical N., C., and S. America. They are grown for their fragrant, white, yellow, blue, purple, or violet flowers, which are bell-, funnel-, or star-shaped, and borne singly on long stalks. The narrowly elliptic to lance-shaped, toothed, rigid, often sharp-edged leaves are produced in tufts at the tops of woody stems, which can reach 4m (12ft) high. In frost-prone regions, grow in a warm greenhouse in containers or in hanging baskets. In dry, tropical areas, grow in a rock garden or desert garden. Vellozias often appear dead in drought conditions but quickly bear new leaves after watering or rainfall.

- **HARDINESS** Frost tender.
- **CULTIVATION** Under glass, grow in loam-based potting compost (JI No.2) with added peat and sharp sand, in full light. Water sparingly during the growing season; keep almost dry in winter. Outdoors, grow in moderately fertile, sharply drained soil in full sun.
- **PROPAGATION** Sow seed at 19–24°C (66–75°F), or divide, in spring.
- **PESTS AND DISEASES** Trouble free.

V. elegans, syn. *Barbacenia elegans, Talbotia elegans.* Evergreen perennial with firm, arching stems and narrow, lance-shaped, mid-green leaves, to 21cm (8in) long, with slender points. Pale lilac buds open to solitary, star-shaped, pure white flowers, 3cm (1¼in) across, in spring. ↕ 15–20cm (6–8in), ↔ 20cm (8in). South Africa (KwaZulu/Natal). ❀ (min. 16°C/61°F)

▷**Velour philodendron** see *Philodendron melanochrysum*

VELTHEIMIA

HYACINTHACEAE/LILIACEAE

Genus of 2 species of bulbous perennials from grassy and rocky hillsides in South Africa. They are grown for their rosettes of thick, wavy leaves, and for their terminal racemes of pendent, spring flowers, similar in form to those of red hot pokers (*Kniphofia*). In frost-prone areas, grow in a temperate greenhouse or as houseplants. In warmer areas, grow in a warm, sunny border.

- **HARDINESS** Frost tender.
- **CULTIVATION** Plant in autumn with the neck of each bulb just above the soil surface. Under glass, grow in loam-based potting compost (JI No.2) with added sharp sand, in full sun. In growth, water moderately and apply a low-nitrogen liquid fertilizer every 2 weeks. Reduce watering as the leaves fade, and keep just moist when dormant. Repot only when congested, to avoid root disturbance. Outdoors, grow in moderately fertile, well-drained soil in full sun.
- **PROPAGATION** Sow seed at 19–24°C (66–75°F) in autumn. Remove offsets in late summer.
- **PESTS AND DISEASES** Trouble free.

V. bracteata ▣ syn. *V. capensis* of gardens, *V. undulata, V. viridifolia.* Robust, bulbous perennial with basal rosettes of broad, strap-shaped, thick, spreading, wavy, glossy, dark green leaves, to 35cm (14in) long and 10cm (4in) across. In spring, bears dense, terminal racemes of up to 60 pendent, tubular, yellow-spotted, pinkish purple flowers, 4cm (1½in) long, on stout, erect, yellow-spotted purple stems. ↕ 45cm (18in), ↔ 30cm (12in). South Africa. ❀ (min. 5–7°C/41–45°F). **'Rosalba'** has red-tinted yellow flowers.
V. capensis, syn. *V. glauca, V. roodeae, V. viridifolia* of gardens. Bulbous perennial with basal rosettes of erect, narrowly lance-shaped, wavy-margined, thick, glaucous, bluish green leaves, to 30cm (12in) long and 4cm (1½in) across. In spring, stout green stems, flecked purple, bear terminal racemes of pendent, tubular flowers, 2–3cm (¾–1¼in) long, varying from white with red spots to pink with green or red markings. Similar to *V. bracteata*, but more delicate and less easy to grow. ↕ 45cm (18in), ↔ 30cm (12in). South Africa (Western Cape). ❀ (min. 5–7°C/ 41–45°F)
***V. capensis* of gardens** see *V. bracteata.*
V. glauca see *V. capensis.*
V. roodeae see *V. capensis.*
V. undulata see *V. bracteata.*
V. viridifolia see *V. bracteata.*
***V. viridifolia* of gardens** see *V. capensis.*

Veltheimia bracteata

▷**Velvet, White** see *Tradescantia sillamontana*
▷**Velvet bent** see *Agrostis canina*
▷**Velvet plant** see *Gynura aurantiaca*
Purple see *Gynura aurantiaca*
Royal see *Gynura aurantiaca*
Trailing see *Ruellia makoyana*
▷**Venetian sumach** see *Cotinus coggyria*
▷ **x *Venidioarctotis*** see *Arctotis, A.* Harlequin Hybrids
▷***Venidium*** see *Arctotis*
V. fastuosum see *A. fastuosa*
▷**Venus fly trap** see *Dionaea, D. muscipula*
▷**Venus's looking glass** see *Legousia speculum-veneris*

VERATRUM

LILIACEAE/MELANTHIACEAE

Genus of about 45 species of imposing, vigorous perennials, with poisonous black rhizomes, from damp meadows and open woodland throughout the N. hemisphere. The alternate, pleated, prominently veined, mid- to dark green leaves are broadly elliptic to ovate at the bases of the stout, erect stems, usually becoming smaller and more lance-shaped further up the stems. Numerous small, star-shaped, white, green, reddish brown, or almost black flowers are borne in summer, followed by spherical seed heads. The flowers are borne in large, terminal panicles, with unisexual (male) and bisexual flowers in the same inflorescence. Grow in a moist, shady site in a mixed or herbaceous border, a peat bed, or in a woodland or wild garden. All parts are highly toxic if ingested. Contact with the foliage may irritate the skin.

- **HARDINESS** Fully hardy.

Veratrum album

Veratrum nigrum

- **CULTIVATION** Grow in deep, fertile, moist but well-drained soil, with added well-rotted organic matter, in a site in partial shade, or in full sun where the soil does not dry out; *V. viride* tolerates wet soil. Provide shelter from cold, drying winds.
- **PROPAGATION** Sow seed in containers in a cold frame as soon as ripe. Divide in autumn or early spring.
- **PESTS AND DISEASES** Susceptible to slug and snail damage.

V. album ▣ (False hellebore, White hellebore). Rhizomatous perennial with ovate to broadly elliptic, pleated basal leaves, to 30cm (12in) long, and a few stem leaves. All leaves are hairless above, hairy-veined beneath. In early and mid-summer, bears numerous star-shaped, greenish white to white flowers, 1.5–2cm (½–¾in) across, in erect, terminal, freely branched panicles, to 60cm (24in) long. ↕ to 2m (6ft), ↔ 60cm (24in). Europe, N. Africa, N. Asia. ✱✱✱
V. nigrum ▣ Rhizomatous perennial producing broadly elliptic, pleated basal leaves, to 35cm (14in) long, and a few stem leaves. All foliage is hairless. In mid- and late summer, numerous star-shaped, unpleasantly scented, reddish brown to almost black flowers, 1.5cm (½in) across, with green-striped backs, are borne in terminal panicles, 45cm (18in) long; the lower branches are often horizontal or slightly pendent. ↕ 60–120cm (24–48in), ↔ 60cm (24in). Europe to Russia (Siberia), China, Korea. ✱✱✱
V. viride (Indian poke). Rhizomatous perennial with ovate to broadly elliptic, pleated basal leaves, to 30cm (12in) long, and a few stem leaves. All leaves are hairless above and hairy beneath. In early and midsummer, numerous star-shaped, green to yellowish green flowers, to 2cm (¾in) across, are produced in terminal panicles, to 60cm (24in) long, with slightly pendent lower branches. ↕ to 2m (6ft), ↔ 60cm (24in). E. North America. ✱✱✱

VERBASCUM *syn.* CELSIA

Mullein

SCROPHULARIACEAE

Genus of 360 species, most of which are biennials, with a few annuals, perennials, and subshrubs, some semi-evergreen or evergreen. They are found mainly on dry, stony hillsides, wasteland, and in open woodland in Europe, N. Africa, and W. and C. Asia. Usually hairy, sometimes woolly plants, they have large, alternate, simple, entire, scalloped, lobed, or toothed, soft-textured basal leaves, which often form large rosettes, and smaller, often stalkless stem leaves. Most produce one or a few tall, erect stems bearing flowers in dense spikes or racemes, but some may have flowers clustered within the rosette centres. The generally short-stemmed or stemless, outward-facing, saucer-shaped flowers are usually yellow, occasionally purple, red, brownish red, or white; each has a short tube with 5 wide-spreading lobes, and sometimes coloured filament hairs. Individual flowers are short-lived, but they are very numerous and flowering takes place over a long period. Semi-evergreen species are grown as much for their overwintering rosettes of white-woolly leaves, built up during the first year, as for their flowers.

Most cultivated mulleins are hybrids. Rosette-forming and short-lived, they have ovate to oblong, mid- to greyish green leaves, and generally bear large, showy, saucer-shaped flowers, to 4cm (1½in) across, in more or less branched racemes, 30–100cm (12–39in) long.

Hybrids and larger species are good for growing in a large, mixed or herbaceous border or gravel bed, or for naturalizing in a wild or woodland garden. Smaller species, including *V. dumulosum, V. pestalozzae*, and *V. spinosum*, are suitable for a rock garden or alpine house.

- **HARDINESS** Fully hardy to frost hardy.
- **CULTIVATION** Grow in alkaline, poor, well-drained soil in full sun. In fertile soil, they grow larger and need support. Protect alpines from winter wet. In an alpine house, use a mix of equal parts loam-based potting compost (JI No.2) and grit.
- **PROPAGATION** Sow seed of biennials and perennials in containers in a cold frame in late spring or early summer; biennials sown at 13–18°C (55–64°F) in early spring may flower and die in their first year. Divide perennials in spring, or take root cuttings in winter. Take semi-ripe cuttings of shrubby species in late summer.
- **PESTS AND DISEASES** Powdery mildew, some moth caterpillars, and figwort weevil may be a problem.

V. acaule, syn. *Celsia acaulis.* Rosette-forming, evergreen perennial producing ovate, rough, grey-green, basal leaves, to 5cm (2in) long, with coarsely toothed margins. In midsummer, bears saucer-shaped yellow flowers, 2cm (¾in) across, either singly or in clusters, from the centres of the rosettes. Best in a dry wall or alpine house. ↕ to 5cm (2in), ↔ to 15cm (6in). Mediterranean. ✱✱✱
V. arcturus, syn. *Celsia arcturus.* Rosette-forming, evergreen subshrub or semi-evergreen, woody-based perennial, usually grown as an annual or biennial.

Verbascum chaixii f. *album*

Oblong to lance-shaped, pinnatifid, softly downy, grey-green, basal leaves, to 15cm (6in) long, each have a large terminal lobe, and lateral lobes that are progressively smaller towards the base. In summer of the second year, bears saucer-shaped yellow flowers, to 2.5cm (1in) across, in erect, loose racemes, to 20cm (8in) long. Protect against frost in winter. ↕ 30–60cm (12–24in), ↔ 30cm (12in). Greece (Crete). ✲✲

V. bombyciferum, syn. *V. broussa*. Rosette-forming biennial or short-lived, evergreen perennial covered with silky silver hairs. It has ovate-oblong, densely white-woolly, basal leaves, to 35cm (14in) long. Saucer-shaped, sulphur-yellow flowers, to 4cm (1½in) across, are borne in erect, dense, sparsely branched spikes, 60–120cm (24–48in) long, in summer. ↕ to 1.8m (8ft), ↔ to 60cm (24in). Turkey. ✲✲✲. **'Silver Lining'**, often cultivated as an annual, has silvery white, very silky-hairy foliage.

V. broussa see *V. bombyciferum*.

V. chaixii (Nettle-leaved mullein). Rosette-forming, semi-evergreen perennial producing long-stalked, ovate-oblong, grey-hairy, mid-green basal leaves, 5–25cm (2–10in) long, with scalloped margins, and sometimes lobed towards the bases. Densely white-woolly stems bear short-stalked leaves on the middle section of the stem, and more rounded, stalkless upper leaves. Saucer-shaped, pale yellow flowers, to 2.5cm (1in) across, with purple filament hairs, are borne in slender panicles, to 40cm (16in) long, from mid- to late summer. ↕ to 90cm (36in), ↔ 45cm (18in). C., E., and S. Europe. ✲✲✲. **f. *album*** ▣ produces white flowers with mauve centres.

***V.* 'C.L. Adams'.** Erect, semi-evergreen perennial with ovate to lance-shaped, wrinkled, mid-green leaves, to 20cm (8in) long. Saucer-shaped, deep yellow flowers, 3cm (1¼in) across, with reddish purple filament hairs, are borne in erect, branched spikes, 30–60cm (12–24in) long, from early to late summer. ↕ to 2m (6ft), ↔ 30cm (12in). ✲✲✲

***V.* 'Cotswold Queen'** ▣ Erect, semi-evergreen perennial with ovate to lance-shaped, wrinkled, grey-green leaves, to 20cm (8in) long. From early to late summer, bears erect, unbranched spikes, 30–60cm (12–24in) long, of saucer-shaped yellow flowers, to 4cm (1½in) across, with purple filament hairs. ↕ 1.2m (4ft), ↔ 30cm (12in). ✲✲✲

Verbascum 'Cotswold Queen'

Verbascum dumulosum

V. densiflorum, syn. *V. thapsiforme*. Rosette-forming biennial or short-lived, semi-evergreen perennial with a dense covering of grey-yellow hairs and oblong to elliptic, wavy-margined, mid- to dark green, basal leaves, to 45cm (18in) long. In summer, produces erect, branching spikes, 60–90cm (24–36in) long, of closely set clusters of saucer-shaped, bright yellow, sometimes white flowers, to 5cm (2in) across. ↕ 1.2–1.5m (4–5ft), ↔ to 60cm (24in). Europe, Russia (Siberia). ✲✲✲

V. dumulosum ▣ Spreading, evergreen subshrub with white-downy stems and elliptic, entire to scalloped, felted-hairy, grey or grey-green leaves, 1.5–5cm (½–2in) long. In late spring and early summer, produces a succession of short racemes, to 15cm (6in) long, of saucer-shaped yellow flowers, to 1.5cm (½in) across, with small, red-purple eyes. Grow on its side in a wall crevice, or in a gravel or scree bed. ↕ to 25cm (10in), ↔ to 40cm (16in). S.W. Turkey. ✲✲✲

***V.* 'Gainsborough'** ▣ Rosette-forming, semi-evergreen perennial with ovate to elliptic, wrinkled, grey-green leaves, 25cm (10in) long. From early to late summer, bears pyramidal panicles, to 75cm (30in) long, of saucer-shaped, soft yellow flowers, 2.5cm (1in) across. ↕ to 1.2m (4ft), ↔ 30cm (12in). ✲✲✲

***V.* 'Helen Johnson'.** Rosette-forming, evergreen perennial producing ovate to lance-shaped, wrinkled, finely downy, grey-green leaves, 20cm (8in) long. From early to late summer, bears saucer-shaped, light pinkish brown flowers, 3cm (1¼in) across, with purple filament hairs, in erect, branched spikes to 45cm (18in) long. ↕ 90cm (36in), ↔ 30cm (12in) or more. ✲✲✲

Verbascum 'Gainsborough'

Verbascum 'Letitia'

***V.* 'Letitia'** ▣ Dense, rounded, evergreen subshrub with stiff, branching stems bearing oblong-lance-shaped, irregularly toothed or lobed, grey-green leaves, 3cm (1¼in) long. Produces an abundance of almost flat, clear yellow flowers, 1.5cm (½in) across, with reddish purple centres, in short racemes, 10cm (4in) long, over long periods in summer. Suitable for a raised bed, rock garden, or alpine house. Needs sharply drained soil. ↕ to 25cm (10in), ↔ to 30cm (12in). ✲✲✲

V. longifolium* var. *pannosum see *V. olympicum.*

***V.* 'Mont Blanc'.** Rosette-forming, semi-evergreen perennial producing ovate to lance-shaped, wrinkled, finely white-downy, pale grey-green, basal leaves, to 30cm (12in) long. Upright, unbranched, slender racemes, to 50cm (20in) long, of saucer-shaped, pure white flowers, to 3cm (1¼in) across, are borne from early to late summer. ↕ 90cm (36in), ↔ 30cm (12in). ✲✲✲

V. nigrum ▣ (Dark mullein). Rosette-forming, deciduous or semi-evergreen perennial with ovate-oblong, scalloped,

Verbascum nigrum

long-stalked, mid- to dark green basal leaves, 15–40cm (6–16in) long; the leaves become progressively shorter-stalked up the stems, then stalkless and more rounded; all leaves are heart-shaped at the bases, hairless above, and slightly grey-woolly beneath. From midsummer to early autumn, usually unbranched, ridged stems, with long hairs, bear slender racemes, 50cm (20in) long, of clustered, saucer-shaped, dark yellow flowers, to 2.5cm (1in) across, with violet filament hairs. ↕ 90cm (36in), ↔ 60cm (24in). Europe to Russia (Siberia). ❄❄❄

V. olympicum ■ syn. *V. longifolium* var. *pannosum.* Rosette-forming, densely grey-white-woolly, often monocarpic perennial with broadly lance-shaped, entire, short-stalked, mid-green, mainly basal leaves, usually 15cm (6in) long, sometimes to 60cm (24in). Branching stems, which form a candelabra shape, bear stalkless leaves; from early to late summer of the second or third year, they bear panicles, to 75cm (30in) or more long, of clustered, saucer-shaped, golden yellow flowers, 3cm (1¼in) across, with yellowish white filament hairs. Often dies after flowering. ↕ to 2m (6ft), ↔ 60cm (24in). Greece. ❄❄❄

V. pestallozae. Dwarf, many-branched, evergreen subshrub with stems and mid-green leaves clothed in densely felted, white, yellow, or tawny-brown hairs. In summer, bears elliptic to lance-shaped, entire, basal leaves, 2.5–4cm (1–1½in) long, and short racemes, to 15cm (6in) long, of saucer-shaped yellow flowers, 2cm (¾in) across. ↕ to 25cm (10in), ↔ to 40cm (16in). Turkey. ❄❄❄

V. phoeniceum (Purple mullein). Rosette-forming biennial or short-lived, evergreen perennial with short-stalked, ovate, slightly scalloped, wrinkled, conspicuously veined, dark green basal leaves, to 15cm (6in) long, sparsely softly hairy or hairless, and a few stalkless stem leaves. In late spring and early summer, bears slender racemes, 75cm (30in) long, of saucer-shaped, white, pink, or violet to dark purple flowers, to 3cm (1¼in) across, with violet filament hairs. ↕ to 1.2m (4ft), ↔ 45cm (18in). S. Europe, N. Africa to C. Asia (Altai Mountains). ❄❄❄

Verbascum olympicum

***V.* 'Pink Domino'.** Rosette-forming, semi-evergreen perennial with ovate to lance-shaped, wrinkled, dark purplish green leaves, 20cm (8in) long. From early to late summer, produces saucer-shaped, deep rose-pink flowers, 3cm (1¼in) long, with darker purple filament hairs, in erect, unbranched spikes, 70cm (28in) long. ↕ 1.2m (4ft), ↔ 30cm (12in). ❄❄❄

V. spinosum. Slow-growing, hummock-forming, intricately branched, semi-evergreen subshrub with woody grey shoots terminating in sharp spines. The oblong-lance-shaped, woolly, grey-white leaves, 1.5–5cm (½–2in) long, are irregularly toothed or lobed. In summer, bears twiggy panicles, to 5cm (2in) long, of saucer-shaped yellow flowers, to 2cm (¾in) across, with short lilac filament hairs. ↕ to 25cm (10in), ↔ to 40cm (16in) or more. Greece (Crete). ❄❄❄

V. thapsiforme see *V. densiflorum.*

V. thapsus (Aaron's rod, Great mullein). Robust, grey- or white-woolly, rosette-forming biennial with elliptic to oblong, entire or finely scalloped, mid-green, basal leaves, to 50cm (20in) long. In the summer of the second year, produces a stout, erect, usually unbranched, densely woolly stem, terminating in a spike-like raceme, to 75cm (30in) long, of saucer-shaped yellow flowers, to 3cm (1¼in) across. Suitable for a wildflower border. ↕ 1.2–2m (4–6ft), ↔ to 45cm (18in). Eurasia. ❄❄❄

VERBENA *syn.* GLANDULARIA

VERBENACEAE

Genus of about 250 species of annuals, perennials, and subshrubs, some of them tuberous or rhizomatous, occurring in usually open and sunny habitats, such as prairies, wasteland, and roadsides, and in open woodland (some species prefer dry sites, others moist). Almost all are from tropical and temperate regions of North, Central, and South America; a few are from S. Europe. The erect or procumbent, square stems have usually opposite, toothed, sometimes lobed to pinnatifid leaves, and bear small flowers in dense, terminal spikes, panicles, cymes, or corymbs, occasionally singly. The flowers, often brightly coloured, are salverform, each with a tubular corolla spreading at the mouth, and slightly 2-lipped, with 2 upper petals and 3 lower ones. Verbenas are long-flowering, but only a few species are fully hardy. There are numerous hybrids, which are ideal for an annual border, for edging, or for growing in containers, including hanging baskets; a few are suitable for a herbaceous border.

• **HARDINESS** Fully hardy to frost tender. Frost-hardy species often survive falls in temperature to -10°C (14°F).

• **CULTIVATION** In containers, grow in loam-based potting compost (JI No.2) with added sharp sand, in full sun. Water freely in growth, and apply a balanced liquid fertilizer monthly. Water more sparingly in winter. Outdoors, grow in moist but well-drained, moderately fertile soil in full sun. In frost-prone areas, protect with a dry winter mulch.

Verbena bonariensis

• **PROPAGATION** Sow seed at 18–21°C (64–70°F) in autumn or early spring. Divide perennials in spring. Take stem-tip cuttings in late summer.

• **PESTS AND DISEASES** Aphids, thrips, and leafhoppers may be a problem, especially in dry conditions. Vulnerable to slug damage. Most verbenas are very susceptible to powdery mildew.

***V. alpina* of gardens** see *V.* x *maonettii.*

V. bonariensis ■ syn. *V. patagonica.* Stiff, upright, open clump-forming perennial with rough, branching stems bearing a few oblong-lance-shaped, wrinkled, clasping leaves, to 13cm (5in) long, with toothed margins and hairy beneath. Salverform, lilac-purple flowers, 6mm (¼in) across, are borne in panicle-like cymes, to 5cm (2in) across, from midsummer to early autumn. ↕ to 2m (6ft), ↔ 45cm (18in). South America (Brazil to Argentina). ❄❄

V. chamaedrifolia see *V. peruviana.*

V. chamaedrioides see *V. peruviana.*

V. corymbosa ■ Spreading, rhizomatous perennial with erect, branched stems and stalkless, oblong or ovate, toothed, rough leaves, 2.5–6cm (1–2½in) long, often lobed at the bases. From early to late summer, bears salverform, red-purple flowers, 1cm (½in) across, in dense, corymb-like panicles, 5–8cm (2–3in) across. ↕ 1–2m (3–6ft), ↔ 60cm (24in). South America (S. Chile, Argentina). ❄❄

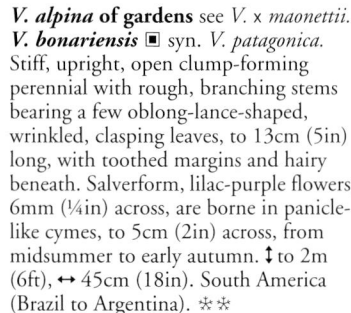

Verbena corymbosa

Verbena x *hybrida* 'Imagination'

V. hastata. Upright, clump-forming perennial with stems sometimes branched near the top. Bears stalked, mainly lance-shaped, pointed, toothed leaves, to 15cm (6in) long, the lowest ones spear-shaped. From early summer to early autumn, produces stiff panicles, 5–10cm (2–4in) across, of numerous salverform, violet-blue to pinkish purple, occasionally white flowers, 5mm (¼in) across. ↕ to 1.5m (5ft), ↔ 60cm (24in). E. North America. ❄❄❄

V.* x *hortensis see *V.* x *hybrida* cultivars.

***V.* x *hybrida* cultivars**, syn. *V.* x *hortensis.* Erect and bushy, or spreading and mat-forming, hairy perennials, usually grown as annuals, with ovate to oblong, toothed, rough, mid- to dark green leaves, 5–10cm (2–4in) long, either stalkless or with short stalks. In summer and autumn, they bear tight, corymb-like panicles, to 8cm (3in) or more across, of tiny, salverform, sometimes scented, white, pink, red, yellow,

Verbena x *hybrida* Novalis Series 'White'

Verbena x *hybrida* 'Peaches and Cream'

or purple-blue flowers, 1–2.5cm (½–1in) across, each usually with a white eye. ↕ to 45cm (18in), ↔ 30–50cm (12–20in). ❄. Cultivars of **Derby Series** are erect and bushy, producing flowers in a full range of colours, biased slightly towards pink and red shades; ↕ to 25cm (10in). **'Imagination'** ■ is spreading and mound-forming, with pinnatifid leaves and deep violet-blue flowers; good for hanging baskets. It is sometimes listed under *V. speciosa*. Cultivars of **Novalis Series** are erect and bushy, with almost spherical corymbs, 5–8cm (2–3in) across, of white-eyed flowers in rose-pink, deep blue, pinkish red, and scarlet, as well as single-colours in bright scarlet, white, or rose-pink; ↕ to 25cm (10in). **Novalis Series 'White'** ■ has pure white flowers. **'Peaches and Cream'** ■ is spreading and branching, with pastel orange-pink flowers, ageing to apricot-yellow, then creamy yellow. **Romance Series** ■ cultivars are erect and bushy, producing white-eyed flowers in deep wine red, intense scarlet, carmine-rose-red, and blue-purple, as well as single colours of white, bright scarlet, dark rose, or lavender-pink; ↕ to 25cm (10in). **Sandy Series** ■ cultivars are compact and erect, with flowers in rose-pink, rose-pink with white eyes, magenta, scarlet, or white; colour mixtures are available. **'Showtime'** is bushy and fairly slow-growing, bearing flowers in a wide range of colours.
***V.* 'Lawrence Johnston'.** Spreading perennial with ovate to oblong, toothed leaves, to 10cm (4in) long. Salverform, cardinal-red flowers, 1cm (½in) across, are borne in large corymbs, 5cm (2in)

Verbena x *hybrida* Sandy Series

across, in summer and early autumn. ↕ 45cm (18in), ↔ 60cm (24in). ❄❄
***V.* 'Mahonettii'** see *V.* x *maonettii.*
***V.* x *maonettii*,** syn. *V. alpina* of gardens, *V.* 'Mahonetti' (Italian verbena). Spreading, prostrate perennial with finely cut, pinnatifid leaves, to 2.5cm (1in) long. Produces short spikes of red-violet flowers, to 1cm (½in) across, with white-margined lobes, in summer. ↕ to 5cm (2in), ↔ to 30cm (12in). ❄❄
V. patagonica see *V. bonariensis.*
***V. peruviana*,** syn. *V. chamaedrifolia, V. chamaedrioides.* Fast-growing, mat-forming, semi-evergreen perennial with slender, ascending stems clothed in closely set, oblong-lance-shaped, toothed leaves, 5cm (2in) long, with short stalks. From summer to autumn, bears salver-form, rich scarlet flowers, 1cm (½in) across, in flat-topped, corymb-like spikes, 5cm (2in) across. ↕ to 7cm (3in), ↔ 1m (3ft). South America (S. Brazil to Argentina). ❄❄. **'Alba'** ■ produces white flowers.
***V. rigida*,** syn. *V. venosa.* Erect to spreading, hairy, tuberous perennial, grown as an annual, with stalkless, oblong, toothed, rough leaves, to 8cm (3in) long. In summer, bears salverform, fragrant, bright purple or magenta flowers, 5mm (¼in) across, in lax corymbs, to 5cm (2in) across, gradually lengthening and becoming spike-like with age. ↕ 45–60cm (18–24in), ↔ to 40cm (16in). South America (S. Brazil, Argentina). ❄❄. **'Lilacina'** has violet-blue flowers. **'Polaris'** forms dense clumps, and has rigid leaves to 7cm (3in) long; from early summer to early autumn, bears silver-blue flowers, 8mm (⅜in) across, in corymbs 5cm (2in) across; ↕ to 60cm (24in), ↔ 30cm (12in).
***V.* 'Saint Paul'** see *V.* 'Sissinghurst'.
***V.* 'Silver Anne'.** Upright, spreading perennial with ovate-oblong, shallowly cut, rough, stalked leaves, 10cm (4in) long. Corymbs, 4cm (1½in) across, of salverform, sweetly scented flowers, 1cm (½in) across, bright pink at first and fading to silver-white with age, open in succession in summer and autumn, giving a multi-toned effect. ↕ to 30cm (12in), ↔ 60cm (24in). ❄❄
***V.* 'Sissinghurst'** ■ syn. *V.* 'Saint Paul'. Mat-forming perennial with ovate, pinnatifid, dark green leaves, to 3cm (1¼in) long. Salverform, magenta-pink flowers, 1cm (½in) across, are borne in corymbs, 2.5cm (1in) across, from late spring to autumn, but most prolifically in summer. ↕ to 20cm (8in), ↔ to 1m (3ft). ❄❄
V. tenuisecta. (Moss verbena). Usually prostrate to decumbent, sometimes erect, aromatic annual or perennial with 3-lobed leaves, to 3.5cm (1½in) long, the lobes pinnatifid, with linear, entire or toothed segments. Salverform, lilac, mauve, purple, white, or blue flowers are borne in corymb-like spikes, to 5cm (2in) across, from summer to autumn. ↕ to 50cm (20in), ↔ to 23cm (9in). S. South America. ❄❄❄
V. venosa see *V. rigida.*

▷**Verbena,**
Italian see *Verbena* x *maonettii*
Lemon see *Aloysia triphylla*
Moss see *Verbena tenuisecta*

VERNONIA
Ironweed

ASTERACEAE/COMPOSITAE

Genus of about 1,000 species of annuals, perennials, climbers, subshrubs, shrubs, and trees from mainly tropical and subtropical habitats, ranging from moist meadows to dry woodland. Most occur in South America, some in Africa, Asia, Australasia, and North America. Species from more northerly habitats are usually annuals or herbaceous perennials; those from the tropics are mainly woody. Only the perennials are cultivated. They have upright stems bearing alternate, simple, entire or toothed, stalkless leaves, and flat, corymb-like cymes of tubular, purple or reddish pink, rarely white flowerheads, becoming rust-coloured with age. Grow in a wild garden or mixed border.

- **HARDINESS** Fully hardy to frost tender.
- **CULTIVATION** Grow in any light, moderately fertile, moist soil in full sun or partial shade. Dead-head regularly.
- **PROPAGATION** Sow seed in containers in a cold frame in spring. Divide in spring or autumn.
- **PESTS AND DISEASES** Slugs may be a problem.

V. noveboracensis. Upright herbaceous perennial with branching stems bearing lance-shaped, entire to toothed leaves, to 20cm (8in) long. From late summer to mid-autumn, bears loose, flat, corymb-like cymes of tubular, red-purple or white florets, in fluffy heads, 1cm (½in) across. ↕ to 2m (6ft), ↔ 60cm (24in). USA (Massachusetts to Mississippi and Georgia). ❄❄❄

Verbena x *hybrida* Romance Series

Verbena peruviana 'Alba'

Verbena 'Sissinghurst'

VERONICA

Speedwell

SCROPHULARIACEAE

Genus of about 250 species of annuals, perennials (including some marginal aquatics), and mostly deciduous subshrubs, some of them rhizomatous. They occur in swamps and moist meadows and grassland, or in open woodland to dry, sunny meadows, rocky hills, and scree, mainly in Europe. The linear to broadly lance-shaped, or oblong to rounded, entire or toothed, stalkless or short-stalked leaves are usually produced in opposite pairs, although those on the flowering stems can be alternate or whorled. Small, outward-facing flowers, 5–15mm (¼–½in) across, in purple, blue, pink, or white, are borne in long, axillary or terminal racemes or spikes, or singly from the leaf axils, from spring to autumn. The petals form a short tube, with 4 or 5 spreading, often unequally sized lobes; each flower has only 2 functional stamens. Good for a mixed or herbaceous border. Use cushion- or mat-forming veronicas in a rock garden; grow less vigorous species and cultivars in a trough or in an alpine house.

• **HARDINESS** Fully hardy to frost hardy.

• **CULTIVATION** Outdoors, grow alpines and rock garden veronicas in poor to moderately fertile, well-drained soil in full sun. Protect species with felted leaves from winter wet. In an alpine house, grow in a mix of equal parts loam, leaf mould, and grit. Grow border veronicas in loamy, moderately fertile, moist but well-drained soil in full sun or partial shade. Grow *V. beccabunga* in wet soil, or in water to 12cm (5in) deep, in full sun; see also pp.52–53.

• **PROPAGATION** Sow seed in containers in a cold frame in autumn. Divide perennials in autumn or spring; for *V. beccabunga*, divide, or take stem-tip cuttings, in summer. Take softwood cuttings of subshrubs in spring.

• **PESTS AND DISEASES** May suffer from downy mildew, powdery mildew, and leaf spot.

Veronica gentianoides

Veronica peduncularis

Veronica prostrata 'Trehane'

Veronica austriaca subsp. *teucrium* 'Kapitän'

V. austriaca* subsp. *teucrium, syn. *V. teucrium.* Mat-forming perennial with ovate to oblong, scalloped or deeply toothed, hairy, greyish green leaves, to 7cm (3in) long. Upright stems bear abundant erect, terminal, spike-like racemes, 10–15cm (4–6in) long, of saucer-shaped, deep bright blue flowers over a long period in summer. ↕ to 90cm (36in), ↔ to 60cm (24in). N. temperate Europe. ❄❄❄. **'Kapitän'** ■ has gentian-blue flowers; ↕ to 30cm (12in), ↔ to 40cm (16in). **'Shirley Blue'** bears erect racemes, 6–10cm (2½–4in) long, of vivid blue flowers from late spring to midsummer; ↕ to 25cm (10in), ↔ 30cm (12in).

V. beccabunga ■ (Brooklime). Usually evergreen, marginal aquatic perennial with creeping, branching, hollow, fleshy stems, rooting at the nodes, and ovate to rounded, entire or toothed, fleshy mid-green leaves, 1–4cm (½–1½in) long. Saucer-shaped, white-centred blue flowers are borne in loose, erect, axillary racemes, to 12cm (5in) long, from late spring to late summer. ↕ 10cm (4in), ↔ indefinite. Eurasia. ❄❄❄

V. chamaedrys (Germander speedwell). Spreading, slender-stemmed, branching, rhizomatous perennial with stalkless, ovate to lance-shaped, toothed, bright green leaves, to 4cm (1½in) long. From summer to autumn, bears saucer-shaped, white-eyed, bright blue flowers in erect, slender, paired, axillary racemes, 8–15cm (3–6in) long. ↕ 30–50cm (12–20in), ↔ 50–80cm (20–32in). Europe, Caucasus, Russia (Siberia). ❄❄❄

V. cinerea. Woody-based, white-felted, subshrubby, evergreen perennial with prostrate, branching stems and linear, entire, mid-green, densely silvery white-woolly leaves, to 1.5cm (½in) long. In early summer, bears abundant terminal racemes, 2–3cm (¾–1¼in) long, of saucer-shaped, deep blue or blue-purple flowers. ↕ to15cm (6in), ↔ to 30cm (12in). E. Mediterranean, Turkey. ❄❄❄

V. fruticans, syn. *V. saxatilis* (Rock speedwell). Mat-forming, woody-based, branching perennial or subshrub with obovate to narrowly oblong, entire or slightly scalloped, mid-green leaves, to 2cm (¾in) long. In summer, bears erect, terminal racemes, to 5cm (2in) long, of saucer-shaped, deep blue flowers with dark red eyes. ↕ to 8cm (3in), ↔ to 20cm (8in). N.W. Europe, mountains of Spain to C. Europe, Balkans. ❄❄❄

V. gentianoides ■ Mat-forming perennial with basal rosettes of broadly lance-shaped, entire or slightly scalloped, thick, dark green leaves, to 8cm (3in) long. In early summer, bears shallowly cup-shaped, pale blue, rarely darker blue or white flowers in erect, terminal racemes, 8–25cm (3–10in) long. ↕↔ 45cm (18in). Ukraine (Crimea), N. and C. Turkey, Caucasus. ❄❄❄. **'Variegata'** has white-variegated leaves and blue flowers.

V. incana see *V. spicata* subsp. *incana*.

***V. incana* 'Saraband'** see *V. spicata* subsp. *incana* 'Saraband'.

***V. incana* 'Wendy'** see *V. spicata* subsp. *incana* 'Wendy'.

V. kellereri see *V. spicata.*

V. longifolia ■ Variable, upright perennial with lance-shaped to linear, pointed, toothed, mid-green leaves, to 12cm (5in) long, either opposite or in whorls of 3, usually on unbranched stems. In late summer and early autumn, bears tubular, 5-lobed, lilac-blue flowers in dense, erect, terminal racemes, to 25cm (10in) long. ↕ to 1.2m (4ft), ↔ 30cm (12in). N. and C. Europe to Russia (Siberia), E. Asia. ❄❄❄. **'Blauriesin'**, syn. 'Foerster's Blue', is bushy, with bright, deep blue flowers; ↕ to 75cm (30in).

V. pectinata. Dense, mat-forming, evergreen, subshrubby perennial with elliptic to oblong, deeply toothed, grey leaves, to 2.5cm (1in) long. Saucer-shaped, white-eyed, deep blue flowers are borne in short, erect, axillary racemes, 6–25cm (2½–10in) long, in summer. ↕ to 8cm (3in), ↔ to 20cm (8in). E. Balkans, Turkey. ❄❄❄. **'Rosea'** has pink flowers.

V. peduncularis ■ Mat-forming perennial with branching rhizomes and prostrate to ascending, freely branched stems bearing ovate to lance-shaped, toothed, glossy, purple-tinged, mid-green leaves, 0.5–2.5cm (¼–1in) long. Produces abundant erect, axillary racemes, 4–8cm (1½–3in) long, of saucer-shaped, deep blue flowers, with

V

Veronica beccabunga

Veronica longifolia

Veronica prostrata

Veronica spicata subsp. *incana*

Veronica spicata 'Rotfuchs'

small white eyes, over a long period from early spring to summer. ↕ to 10cm (4in), ↔ 60cm (24in) or more. Turkey, Caucasus, Ukraine. ✻✻✻. **'Georgia Blue'**, syn. 'Oxford Blue', is vigorous, very free-flowering, and easily grown.
V. perfoliata see *Parahebe perfoliata*.
V. prostrata ▣ syn. *V. rupestris* (Prostrate speedwell). Mat-forming perennial with short, branched, decumbent stems bearing linear-oblong to ovate, toothed, bright to mid-green leaves, 0.8–2.5cm (⅜–1in) long. In early summer, produces erect, terminal, spike-like racemes, 2–4cm (¾–1½in) long, of saucer-shaped, pale to deep blue flowers. ↕ to 15cm (6in), ↔ to 40cm (16in). Europe. ✻✻✻. **'Loddon Blue'** bears bright blue flowers; ↕ to 20cm (8in). **'Mrs. Holt'** produces pale pink flowers. **'Trehane'** ▣ has yellow-green or golden leaves and deep blue flowers.
V. rupestris see *V. prostrata*.
V. saxatilis see *V. fruticans*.
V. spicata, syn. *V. kellereri*. Mat-forming perennial with decumbent, simple, rooting stems, and ascending to erect, flowering stems bearing oblong-lance-shaped to linear, toothed, hairy leaves, to 8cm (3in) long. Star-shaped, bright blue flowers, with long purple stamens, open in erect, dense, pyramidal, terminal racemes, to 30cm (12in) long, from early to late summer. ↕ 30–60cm (12–24in), ↔ 45cm (18in). Europe to Turkey, C. and E. Asia. ✻✻✻. **'Barcarolle'** freely bears pink flowers; ↕ 30cm (12in). **'Heidekind'** has silver-grey leaves and short spikes of raspberry-pink flowers; ↕ 30cm (12in). **'Icicle'**, syn. 'White Icicle', has white flowers; ↕ 60cm (24in). **subsp. *incana*** ▣ syn. *V. incana* (Silver speedwell), is entirely silver-hairy, and has purple-blue flowers; ↕↔ 30cm (12in); Russia. **subsp. *incana* 'Saraband'**, syn. *V. incana* 'Saraband', has violet-blue flowers above densely hairy, silver-grey foliage. **subsp. *incana* 'Wendy'**, syn. *V. incana* 'Wendy', has a looser habit, with grey leaves and bright blue flowers; ↕ 45cm (18in). **'Red Fox'** see 'Rotfuchs'. **'Romiley Purple'** is bushy, with lateral racemes of dark violet flowers; ↕ 45cm (18in). **'Rotfuchs'** ▣ syn. 'Red Fox', has very deep pink flowers; ↕↔ 30cm (12in). **'White Icicle'** see 'Icicle'.
V. teucrium see *V. austriaca* subsp. *teucrium*.
V. virginica see *Veronicastrum virginicum*.

VERONICASTRUM

SCROPHULARIACEAE

Genus of 2 species of erect perennials, one from Siberia, one from North America, occurring in open woodland, scrub, prairies, meadows, and grassy mountain sites. Imposing in stature, they have whorls of 3–7 more or less horizontal, simple, toothed leaves. They bear veronica-like racemes of salverform, white to pale pink or bluish purple flowers, terminally and from the upper leaf axils; each flower has a long, slender tube and 4 or 5 short lobes. Use to add height to a mixed summer border.
• **HARDINESS** Fully hardy.
• **CULTIVATION** Grow in moderately fertile, humus-rich, moist soil in full sun or partial shade.

Veronicastrum virginicum f. *album*

• **PROPAGATION** Sow seed in pots in a cold frame in autumn. Divide in spring.
• **PESTS AND DISEASES** Prone to downy mildew, powdery mildew, and leaf spot.

V. virginicum, syn. *Veronica virginica* (Culver's root). Erect, usually hairless perennial with unbranched stems bearing lance-shaped to inversely lance-shaped, pointed, toothed, dark green leaves, to 15cm (6in) long, in whorls of 3–7. From midsummer to early autumn, bears tubular, white to pink or bluish purple flowers, 7mm (¼in) long, with protruding stamens, in slender, dense, terminal and axillary racemes. ↕ to 2m (6ft), ↔ 45cm (18in). North America (Ontario to Texas). ✻✻✻. **f. *album*** ▣ has white flowers.

VERTICORDIA

MYRTACEAE

Genus of about 50 species of heath-like, evergreen shrubs from usually sandy or gravel heathland in Australia. They are grown for their leafy racemes or corymbs of showy flowers, produced terminally or from the upper leaf axils; each flower has 5 feathery, often coloured sepals and 5 entire or toothed petals. The leathery leaves are small, simple, and usually borne in opposite pairs. Where winter temperatures fall below 7°C (45°F), grow in a temperate greenhouse. In warmer, dry climates, use in a border.
• **HARDINESS** Frost tender.
• **CULTIVATION** Under glass, grow in lime-free (ericaceous) potting compost with added sharp sand, in full light. In growth, water moderately and apply a low-phosphate, low-nitrogen fertilizer monthly. Water sparingly in winter. Outdoors, grow in moderately fertile, neutral to acid, sharply drained soil in full sun. Pruning group 8 or 9; may need restrictive pruning under glass.
• **PROPAGATION** Sow seed at 13–18°C (55–64°F) in spring. Take semi-ripe cuttings in summer.
• **PESTS AND DISEASES** Red spider mites may be a problem under glass.

V. grandis (Scarlet featherflower). Usually erect, sparsely branched, open shrub with crowded, rounded, semi-glossy, greyish to deep green leaves, 0.8–1.5cm (⅜–½in) long. From spring to summer, bears deep bright scarlet to pink flowers, 2–2.5cm (¾–1in) across, in dense corymbs, to 12cm (5in) across, either terminally or from the upper leaf axils. ↕↔ 1–2m (3–6ft). W. Australia. ❁ (min. 7°C/45°F)
V. plumosa ▣ (Featherflower). Erect, bushy shrub with crowded, linear, cylindrical, grey-green leaves, 1cm (½in) long. Terminal corymbs, 3cm (1¼in) across, of many pink or white flowers, to 9mm (⅜in) wide, are borne from spring to autumn. ↕↔ to 90cm (36in). Granite outcrops in S.W. Australia. ❁ (min. 7°C/45°F)

Verticordia plumosa

VESTIA

SOLANACEAE

Genus of one species of evergreen shrub found in woodland in Chile, cultivated for its attractive but malodorous foliage and flowers. The leaves are alternate, obovate to elliptic, and glossy, dark green. The pendent, pale yellow flowers are borne singly or in clusters. Best grown in a sheltered border or against a sunny wall in frost-prone areas. Where temperatures fall much below -5°C (23°F), grow in a cool greenhouse.
• **HARDINESS** Frost hardy.
• **CULTIVATION** Under glass, grow in loam-based potting compost (JI No.2) in full light, shaded from hot sun. In growth, water moderately and apply a balanced liquid fertilizer monthly. Water sparingly in winter. Outdoors, grow in any well-drained soil in full sun. In frost-prone areas, shelter from cold, drying winds in winter. Pruning group 8.
• **PROPAGATION** Sow seed in containers in a cold frame in autumn, or take semi-ripe cuttings in summer.
• **PESTS AND DISEASES** Trouble free.

V. foetida ▣ syn. *V. lycioides*. Erect, evergreen shrub with glossy, dark green leaves, to 5cm (2in) long, unpleasantly scented when crushed. Pendent, tubular, pale yellow flowers, to 3cm (1¼in) long, with protruding stamens, are produced singly or in clusters from the leaf axils from mid-spring to midsummer. ↕ 2m (6ft), ↔ 1.5m (5ft). Chile. ✻✻
V. lycioides see *V. foetida*.

▷**Vetch** see *Hippocrepis*
Bitter see *Lathyrus linifolius* var. *montanus*
Horseshoe see *Hippocrepis*
Kidney see *Anthyllis vulneraria*
Milk see *Astragalus*
▷**Vetchling,**
Common see *Lathyrus pratensis*
Meadow see *Lathyrus pratensis*
Spring see *Lathyrus vernus*

Vestia foetida

VIBURNUM

CAPRIFOLIACEAE

Genus of 150 or more species of evergreen, semi-evergreen, and deciduous shrubs, sometimes trees, from thickets and woodland, mainly in N. temperate regions, but extending to S.E. Asia and South America. They are cultivated for their foliage, flowers, and fruits. The mostly lance-shaped to rounded, entire or toothed, sometimes lobed leaves are arranged in opposite pairs, occasionally in whorls of 3; they are often rough and prominently veined, and, in most deciduous species, colour attractively in autumn. The sometimes fragrant, white or cream, pink-flushed, or wholly pink flowers are salverform to tubular, or tubular-trumpet-shaped, each with 5 usually spreading lobes. They are borne in terminal or axillary panicles, clusters, corymbs, or cymes, which are often spherical or domed. Some species have flowers in flattened heads, similar to those of "lacecap" hydrangeas, in which the small, fertile central flowers are surrounded by larger, flat or saucer-shaped, sterile ray-florets. The ornamental fruits are usually spherical or ovoid, and may be red, blue, or black.

Viburnums are suitable for a shrub border or woodland garden. Grow *V. macrocephalum* against a wall. Many show self-incompatibility; fruiting is often best if several seedlings of the same species are planted together so that cross-pollination can occur. The fruits of viburnums may cause mild stomach upset if ingested.

- **HARDINESS** Fully hardy to frost hardy.
- **CULTIVATION** Grow in any moderately fertile, moist but well-drained soil in full sun or partial shade. *V. lantanoides* needs lime-free soil. In frost-prone regions, shelter evergreen viburnums from cold, drying winds. Pruning group 1 for evergreens; group 8 for deciduous viburnums. *V. tinus* and most deciduous viburnums tolerate hard pruning.
- **PROPAGATION** Sow seed in containers in a cold frame, or in a seed bed, in autumn. Take greenwood cuttings of deciduous viburnums, and semi-ripe cuttings of evergreens, in summer.
- **PESTS AND DISEASES** Aphids and viburnum beetles may be a problem, particularly on *V. lantana*, *V. opulus*, and *V. tinus*. *V. tinus* is susceptible to whiteflies. All are prone to honey fungus and leaf spot.

V. acerifolium ■ (Dockmackie, Possum-haw). Upright, deciduous shrub with maple-like, 3-lobed, dark green leaves, to 12cm (5in) long, turning orange, red, and purple in autumn. In early summer, bears small, tubular white flowers, 5mm (¼in) across, in long-stalked cymes, 8cm (3in) across, at the shoot-tips. Ovoid red fruit, 8mm (⅜in) long, ripen to purple-black. ↕ 1–2m (3–6ft), ↔ 1.2m (4ft). E. North America. ✻✻✻

V

V. alnifolium see *V. lantanoides.*

V. betulifolium. Upright, deciduous shrub with arching branches and ovate, tapered, toothed, glossy, dark green leaves, to 10cm (4in) long. In early summer, bears small, salverform white flowers, 5mm (¼in) across, in domed terminal corymbs, to 10cm (4in) across; they are followed by pendent clusters of spherical, bright red fruit, 6mm (¼in) across. ↕↔ 3m (10ft). W. and C. China. ✻✻✻

V. x bodnantense (*V. farreri* x *V. grandiflorum*). Upright, deciduous shrub with ovate to oblong, toothed, dark green leaves, to 10cm (4in) long, bronze when young. Heavily scented, tubular, rich rose-red to white-pink flowers, to 1cm (½in) across, are borne in dense, terminal and axillary clusters, to 7cm (3in) across, on bare wood, over a long period from late autumn to spring. Virtually sterile, producing a few small, spherical, blue-black or purple fruit, 3–6mm (⅛–¼in) across. ↕ 3m (10ft), ↔ 2m (6ft). Garden origin. ✻✻✻. Mainly grown as the following cultivars. **'Charles Lamont'** bears bright pink flowers. **'Dawn'** ■ has dark pink flowers, ageing to white, strongly flushed pink. **'Deben'** bears white flowers, faintly pink-flushed in winter.

V. x burkwoodii (*V. carlesii* x *V. utile*). Open, rounded, bushy, evergreen shrub producing ovate, sparsely toothed, glossy, dark green leaves, to 10cm (4in) long. Tubular, fragrant white flowers, 1cm (½in) across, in domed, terminal corymbs, to 9cm (3½in) across, open from pink buds in mid- and late spring; the flattened, ellipsoid red fruit, 1cm (½in) long, ripen to black in autumn. ↕↔ 2.5m (8ft). Garden origin. ✻✻✻. **'Anne Russell'** ■ is compact and deciduous, with fragrant flowers; ↕ 2m (6ft), ↔ 1.5m (5ft). **'Chenaultii'** is compact, with pale pink flowers and leaves that turn bronze in autumn; ↕↔ 1.5m (5ft). **'Fulbrook'**, syn. *V.* 'Fulbrook', has very fragrant white flowers. **'Park Farm Hybrid'** has dark pink flowers, fading to white, in broad corymbs, to 12cm (5in) across; some leaves turn orange and red in autumn.

V. x carlcephalum ■ (*V. carlesii* x *V. macrocephalum*). Rounded, bushy, deciduous shrub with broadly heart-shaped, irregularly toothed, dark green leaves, 12cm (5in) long, turning red in autumn. Tubular-trumpet-shaped, fragrant white flowers, 1.5cm (½in) across, in domed, terminal corymbs, 15cm (6in) across, open from pink buds in late spring. ↕↔ 3m (10ft). Garden origin. ✻✻✻

V. carlesii ■ Dense, bushy, deciduous shrub with ovate, irregularly toothed, dark green leaves, to 10cm (4in) long, often turning red in autumn. In mid- and late spring, pink buds open to

Viburnum acerifolium

Viburnum x *bodnantense* 'Dawn'

tubular, very fragrant, white or pink-flushed white flowers, 1cm (½in) across, produced in domed, terminal corymbs, to 8cm (3in) across; they are followed by ellipsoid red fruit, 6mm (¼in) long, ripening to black. ↕↔ 2m (6ft). Korea, Japan (Tsushima Island). ✻✻✻. **'Aurora'** has red buds, opening to pink flowers. **'Diana'** has bronze young leaves, and red buds opening to purple-pink flowers that fade to white.

***V.* 'Chesapeake'** ■ Compact, dense mound-forming, semi-evergreen shrub with ovate, slightly wavy-margined, leathery, glossy, dark green leaves, to 10cm (4in) long. Pink buds open to salverform, fragrant white flowers, 1cm (½in) across, borne in domed, terminal corymbs, 9cm (3½in) across, in mid- and late spring. It is virtually sterile, bearing no fruit. ↕ 2m (6ft), ↔ 3m (10ft). ✻✻✻

V. cinnamomifolium ☉ Rounded, open, evergreen shrub, sometimes a small tree, with elliptic, tapered, sparsely toothed, conspicuously 3-veined, dark green leaves, dark green above, paler beneath, to 15cm (6in) long. In early summer, produces tiny, tubular white flowers, 4mm (⅛in) across, in loose, terminal cymes, 12–17cm (5–7in) across. Flowers are followed by ovoid, glossy, blue-black fruit, 4mm (⅛in) long. ↕↔ 5m (15ft), to 6m (20ft) high as a tree. W. China. ✻✻

V. davidii ■ Dome-shaped, compact, evergreen shrub with oval, indistinctly toothed, 3-veined, dark green leaves, to 15cm (6in) long. Tiny, tubular white flowers, 4mm (⅛in) across, are borne in flattened, terminal cymes, 7cm (3in)

Viburnum x *burkwoodii* 'Anne Russell'

Viburnum x *carlcephalum*

across, in late spring; they are followed by ovoid, metallic-blue fruit, 6mm (¼in) long. Both male and female plants are needed to produce fruit. ↕↔ 1–1.5m (3–5ft). W. China. ✻✻✻

V. dentatum ■ (Southern arrow-wood). Upright, deciduous shrub with arching branches and ovate to rounded, coarsely toothed, dark green leaves, to 11cm (4½in) long, turning yellow or red in autumn. Tiny, tubular white flowers, 4mm (⅛in) across, are borne in flattened, terminal corymbs, 10cm (4in) across, in late spring and early summer; they are followed by ovoid, blue-black fruit, 8mm (⅜in) long. ↕↔ 3m (10ft). E. North America. ✻✻✻

V. dilatatum. Upright, deciduous shrub producing broadly ovate to rounded or obovate, coarsely toothed, dark green leaves, to 12cm (5in) long, turning bronze to red in autumn. Small, salverform white flowers, 5mm (¼in) across, are borne in domed, terminal corymbs, to 12cm (5in) across, in late spring and early summer. The flowers are followed by ovoid, bright red fruit, 8mm (⅜in) long. ↕ 3m (10ft), ↔ 2m (6ft). China, Japan. ✻✻✻. **'Catskill'** ■ is compact, with leaves turning yellow, orange, and red in autumn, and bears dark red fruit; ↕ 1.5m (5ft), ↔ 2.5m (8ft). **'Erie'** is mound-forming, bearing large cymes, to 15cm (6in) across, and a profusion of fruit, turning pink in winter; ↕ 2m (6ft), ↔ 3m (10ft). **f. *xanthocarpum*** bears yellow fruit.

***V.* 'Eskimo'.** Mound-forming, compact, semi-evergreen shrub producing ovate, leathery, glossy, dark green leaves, to 10cm (4in) long. In mid- and late

Viburnum carlesii

Viburnum 'Chesapeake'

Viburnum dentatum

Viburnum farreri

Viburnum x *juddii*

spring, pink-tinged cream buds open to tubular, pure white flowers, 1cm (½in) across, borne in dense, terminal, almost spherical corymbs, 10cm (4in) across. ↕↔ 1.5m (5ft). ❄❄❄
V. farreri ▣ syn. *V. fragrans*. Erect, deciduous shrub with oval, toothed, dark green leaves, to 10cm (4in) long, bronze when young, turning red-purple in autumn. Tubular, fragrant, white or pink-tinged white flowers, 1cm (½in) long, are borne in dense, terminal and lateral clusters, to 5cm (2in) across, in late autumn and, in mild weather, in winter and early spring on bare stems; they are followed by spherical, bright red fruit, 5mm (¼in) long. ↕ 3m (10ft), ↔ 2.5m (8ft). N. China. ❄❄❄.
'Album' see 'Candidissimum'.
'Candidissimum', syn. 'Album', has leaves that are pale green when young, and bears white flowers followed by pale yellow fruit. **'Nanum'** forms a dense mound, but is not free-flowering; ↕ 75cm (30in), ↔ 1m (3ft).
V. foetens, syn. *V. grandiflorum* f. *foetens*. Upright, deciduous shrub with oblong, dark green leaves, to 10cm (4in) long. From late autumn to early spring, produces tubular, fragrant, white or pink-tinged white flowers, 5cm (2in) long, in flattened, terminal clusters, to 5cm (2in) across, on bare stems; they are followed by ovoid red fruit, to 1cm (½in) long, ripening to black. ↕↔ 2m (6ft). Himalayas. ❄❄❄
V. fragrans see *V. farreri*.
***V.* 'Fulbrook'** see *V.* x *burkwoodii* 'Fulbrook'.
***V.* x *globosum* 'Jermyns Globe'** ▣ Dense, rounded, evergreen shrub with narrowly elliptic, tapered, dark green leaves, to 9cm (4½in) long, 3-veined at the bases. Masses of small, tubular white flowers, to 12mm (½in) across, are borne in flattened, terminal corymbs, 6cm (2½in) across, in late spring; they are followed by ovoid, metallic-blue fruit, 6mm (¼in) long. ↕ 2.5m (8ft), ↔ 3m (10ft). ❄❄❄
V. grandiflorum. Open, upright, deciduous shrub with stout shoots and elliptic, finely and irregularly toothed, dark green leaves, to 10cm (4in) long, turning dark purple in autumn. From winter to early spring, tubular, fragrant, pink-flushed white flowers, to 2cm (¾in) across, are borne on bare stems in flattened, terminal clusters, to 8cm (3in) across, followed by ovoid, black-purple fruit, to 2cm (¾in) long. ↕↔ 2m (6ft). Himalayas, W. China. ❄❄❄. **f. *foetens*** see *V. foetens*. **'Snow White'** has white flowers, flushed pink on the backs of the lobes, opening from dark pink buds.
V. harryanum. Upright, bushy, evergreen shrub with rounded, dark green leaves, to 2.5cm (1in) long, often in whorls of 3. Bears tiny, tubular white flowers, 3mm (⅛in) across, in flattened, terminal, umbel-like cymes, 4cm (1½in) across, in late spring, then ovoid, glossy black fruit, 4mm (⅛in) long. ↕ 3m (10ft), ↔ 2.5m (8ft). W. China. ❄❄❄
V. japonicum. Rounded, evergreen shrub with stout shoots and ovate to rounded, leathery, sparsely toothed, glossy, dark green leaves, to 15cm (6in) long. Small, tubular, fragrant white flowers, 1cm (½in) across, in spherical cymes, to 10cm (4in) across, are borne in early summer, followed by ovoid, bright red fruit, 8mm (⅜in) long, which last into winter. ↕ 2m (6ft), ↔ 2.5m (8ft). Japan. ❄❄❄
V.* x *juddii ▣ (*V. bitchiuense* x *V. carlesii*). Rounded, bushy, deciduous shrub with oval, dark green leaves, to 6cm (2½in) long, sometimes turning red in autumn. Small, salverform, fragrant, pink-tinged white flowers, 6mm (¼in) across, in almost spherical corymbs, to 9cm (3½in) across, open from pink buds in mid- and late spring. ↕ 1.2m (4ft), ↔ 1.5m (5ft). Garden origin. ❄❄❄
V. lantana (Wayfaring tree). Vigorous, upright, deciduous shrub with broadly ovate, finely toothed, grey-green leaves, to 12cm (5in) long, often turning red in autumn. Small, tubular white flowers, 6mm (¼in) across, in loosely domed cymes, to 10cm (4in) across, are borne in late spring and early summer; they are followed by ovoid-oblong red fruit, 8mm (⅜in) long, ripening to black. ↕ 5m (15ft), ↔ 4m (12ft). Europe, N. Africa, S.W. Asia. ❄❄❄. **'Mohican'** is compact, with dark green foliage and orange-red fruit; ↕↔ 2.5m (8ft)
V. lantanoides, syn. *V. alnifolium* (Hobble bush). Spreading, deciduous shrub, the outer branches prostrate and rooting in the soil. Broadly ovate to rounded, irregularly toothed, dark green leaves, to 20cm (8in) long, turn yellow to red or purple in autumn. In late spring and early summer, bears lacecap-like, terminal cymes, to 12cm (5in) wide, of tubular, white, fertile central flowers, 3–4mm (⅛in) across, surrounded by saucer-shaped, white, sterile ray-florets,

Viburnum davidii

Viburnum dilatatum 'Catskill'

Viburnum x *globosum* 'Jermyns Globe' (inset: flower detail)

V

Viburnum macrocephalum

Viburnum opulus 'Compactum'

Viburnum plicatum f. *tomentosum* 'Mariesii'

Viburnum rhytidophyllum

to 2.5cm (1in) across; they are followed by ovoid red fruit, 8mm (⅜in) long, ripening to black-purple. Prefers partial shade. ↕ 2.5m (8ft), ↔ 4m (12ft). E. North America. ✻✻✻

V. lentago ◇ (Sheepberry). Vigorous, upright, deciduous shrub or small tree, producing oval, finely toothed, glossy, dark green leaves, to 10cm (4in) long, turning red and purple in autumn. Small, tubular, fragrant, creamy white flowers, to 5mm (¼in) across, are borne in flattened, terminal cymes, to 11cm (4½in) across, in late spring and early summer, followed by ovoid, blue-black fruit, 1cm (½in) long. ↕ 4m (12ft), ↔ 3m (10ft). E. North America. ✻✻✻

V. macrocephalum ■ (Snowball bush). Rounded shrub, sometimes tree-like, semi-evergreen or evergreen in mild climates, deciduous where winters are severe, with ovate to elliptic, toothed, dark green leaves, to 10cm (4in) long. In late spring, salverform, sterile white flowers, 3cm (1¼in) across, are borne in dense, terminal cymes, to 15cm (6in) across. Does not bear fruit. ↕↔ 5m (15ft). Garden origin. ✻✻

V. mariesii see *V. plicatum* f. *tomentosum* 'Mariesii'.

V. odoratissimum. Vigorous, bushy, evergreen shrub with oval, glossy, dark green leaves, to 20cm (8in) long. Small, tubular, fragrant white flowers, 6mm (¼in) across, are produced in broadly conical panicles, 8–10cm (3–4in) long, in late spring, followed by ovoid red fruit, 1cm (½in) long, ripening to black. ↕↔ 5m (15ft). India, China, Burma, Philippines, Japan. ✻✻

V. opulus (Guelder rose). Vigorous, bushy, deciduous shrub with maple-like, usually 3-lobed, dark green leaves, to 10cm (4in) long, turning red in autumn. In late spring and early summer, bears flat, lacecap-like, terminal cymes, to 8cm (3in) across, composed of tubular, white, fertile central flowers, 2cm (¾in) across, surrounded by showy, flat, white, sterile ray-florets, to 2cm (¾in) across; they are followed by spherical, fleshy, bright red fruit, 8mm (⅜in) across. ↕ 5m (15ft), ↔ 4m (12ft). Europe, N. Africa, C. Asia. ✻✻✻. **var. *americanum*** see *V. trilobum*. **'Compactum'** ■ is slow-growing and very dense; ↕↔ 1.5m (5ft). **'Roseum'**, syn. 'Sterile' (Snowball tree), has a rounded habit, with leaves that become purple-tinted in autumn; it bears large, white or green-tinted white, sterile flowers, 1cm (½in) long, sometimes turning pink, in spherical cymes, 5–6cm (2–2½in) across; ↕↔ to 4m (12ft). **'Sterile'** see 'Roseum'. **'Xanthocarpum'** ■ produces bright yellow fruit.

V. plicatum* f. *plicatum (Japanese snowball bush). Spreading, bushy, deciduous shrub with heart-shaped, tapered, toothed, deeply veined, dark green leaves, to 10cm (4in) long, turning red-purple in autumn. In late spring, bears saucer-shaped, sterile white flowers, to 3cm (1¼in) across, in dense, spherical, terminal cymes, 8cm (3in) across. Does not produce fruit. ↕ 3m (10ft), ↔ 4m (12ft). Garden origin. ✻✻✻. **'Nanum'** see f. *tomentosum* 'Nanum Semperflorens'. **f. *plicatum* 'Grandiflorum'** has larger double flowerheads, to 10cm (4in) across. **f. *tomentosum***, syn. *V. tomentosum*, has flattened, lacecap-like cymes, to 10cm (4in) across, with tiny, fertile central flowers and larger, sterile outer florets, to 3cm (1¼in) across. Ovoid red fruit, 8mm (⅜in) long, ripen to black; China, Japan. The following cultivars have fertile central flowers and sterile outer florets; they are grouped under f. *tomentosum*. **f. *tomentosum* 'Lanarth'** has large, sterile florets, to 5cm (2in) or more across, and bears few fruit. **f. *tomentosum* 'Mariesii'** ■ syn. *V. mariesii*, has distinctly layered, tiered branches, and produces few fruit. **f. *tomentosum* 'Nanum Semperflorens'**, syn. 'Nanum', 'Watanabe', *V. semperflorens, V. watanabei*, is low-growing and compact, blooming over a long period from late spring to autumn; ↕ 2m (6ft), ↔ 1.5m (5ft). **f. *tomentosum* 'Pink Beauty'** ■ has white sterile florets, maturing to pink, and fruits freely. **f. *tomentosum* 'Rowallane'** is compact, with leaves turning dark red-purple in autumn, and bears abundant red fruit; ↕↔ 2m (6ft). **f. *tomentosum* 'Watanabe'** see f. *tomentosum* 'Nanum Semperflorens'.

V. x pragense see *V.* 'Pragense'.

***V.* 'Pragense'** ■ syn. *V.* x *pragense*. Rounded, bushy, evergreen shrub with elliptic, deeply veined, wrinkled, wavy-margined, glossy, dark green leaves, to 10cm (4in) long. Tubular white flowers, 5–8mm (¼–⅜in) across, opening from pink buds, are produced in domed, terminal, umbel-like cymes, to 10cm (4in) across, in late spring. ↕↔ 3m (10ft). ✻✻✻

Viburnum opulus 'Xanthocarpum'

Viburnum plicatum f. *tomentosum* 'Pink Beauty'

Viburnum 'Pragense'

Viburnum sieboldii

Viburnum tinus

V. propinquum. Compact, bushy, evergreen shrub with ovate-lance-shaped to elliptic, sparsely toothed, 3-veined, glossy, dark green leaves, to 9cm (3½in) long. Tiny, tubular, greenish white flowers, 4mm (⅛in) across, in flattened, terminal cymes, to 8cm (3in) across, are borne in late spring, sometimes followed by ovoid, blue-black fruit, 5mm (¼in) long. ↕3m (10ft), ↔2m (6ft). C. and W. China, Taiwan, Philippines. ✻✻
V. x rhytidophylloides (*V. lantana* x *V. rhytidophyllum*). Spreading, semi-evergreen shrub with arching shoots clothed in oblong, wavy-margined, dark green leaves, to 20cm (8in) long. In late spring, small, tubular, creamy white flowers, 5mm (¼in) across, are borne in flattened, terminal, umbel-like cymes, to 10cm (4in) across; they are followed by ovoid red fruit, 8mm (⅜in) long, which ripen to black. ↕3m (10ft), ↔4m (12ft). Garden origin. ✻✻✻. **'Willowwood'** has deeply veined, glossy leaves.
V. rhytidophyllum ▣ Vigorous, erect, evergreen shrub with oblong to lance-shaped, wavy-margined, very deeply veined, glossy, dark green leaves, 20cm (8in) or more long. In late spring, bears tubular, creamy white flowers, 5mm (¼in) across, in dense, domed, terminal, umbel-like cymes, to 20cm (8in) across. Ovoid red fruit, 8mm (⅜in) long, ripens to glossy black. ↕5m (15ft), ↔4m (12ft). C. and W. China. ✻✻✻
V. sargentii. Bushy, deciduous shrub with maple-like, 3-lobed, toothed leaves, to 12cm (5in) long, bronze when young, often turning yellow or red in autumn. Flat, lacecap-like cymes, to 10cm (4in) across, with a central mass of tiny, tubular, white, fertile flowers surrounded by saucer-shaped, white, sterile ray-florets, 2cm (¾in) across, are borne in late spring. The flowers are followed by spherical, bright red fruit, 1cm (½in) across. ↕↔3m (10ft). N.E. Asia. ✻✻✻. **f. *flavum*** produces yellow fruit. **'Onondaga'** has an upright habit, and bears dark bronze-purple foliage ageing to dark green, then red-purple. Fertile flowers are dark red in bud, opening pink-flushed white; ↔2m (6ft)
V. semperflorens see *V. plicatum* f. *tomentosum* 'Nanum Semperflorens'.
V. sieboldii ▣ Compact, spreading, large, deciduous shrub with arching shoots and elliptic to obovate, coarsely toothed, glossy, dark green leaves, to 12cm (5in) long. Bears small, tubular white flowers, 6mm (¼in) across, in flattened, terminal cymes, to 10cm (4in) across, in late spring, and followed by ovoid pink fruit, 1cm (½in) long, which ripen to black. ↕4m (12ft), ↔6m (20ft). Japan. ✻✻✻
V. tinus ▣ (Laurustinus). Compact, bushy, evergreen shrub with narrowly ovate to oblong, dark green leaves, to 10cm (4in) long. Bears small, salverform white flowers, 6mm (¼in) across, in flattened, terminal cymes, to 10cm (4in) across, over a long period in late winter and spring; they are followed by ovoid, dark blue-black fruit, 6mm (¼in) long. ↕↔3m (10ft). Mediterranean. ✻✻✻. **'Eve Price'** ▣ is dense, with leaves to 8cm (3in) long, and pink flower buds. **'Gwenllian'** bears a profusion of pink-flushed white flowers opening from dark pink buds, and fruits freely. **'Lucidum'** is vigorous, with glossy leaves; each flower is 1cm (½in) across. **'Pink Prelude'** has white flowers opening from pink buds and ageing to pink. **'Purpureum'** has young foliage tinged dark bronze-purple. **'Variegatum'** ▣ has leaves broadly margined with creamy yellow; needs more shelter than green-leaved forms.
V. tomentosum see *V. plicatum* f. *tomentosum*.
V. trilobum, syn. *V. opulus* var. *americanum*. Dense, rounded, deciduous shrub producing maple-like, 3-lobed, dark green leaves, to 12cm (5in) long, bronze when young, turning yellow to red in autumn. In late spring, bears flattened, lacecap-like, terminal cymes, to 10cm (4in) across, of tiny, tubular, white, fertile central flowers, 2cm (¾in) across, surrounded by showy, flat, white, sterile florets, to 2cm (¾in) across. The flowers are followed by edible, spherical red fruit, 8mm (⅜in) across. ↕5m (15ft), ↔4m (12ft). North America. ✻✻✻
V. watanabei see *V. plicatum* f. *tomentosum* 'Nanum Semperflorens'.

Viburnum tinus 'Variegatum'

Viburnum tinus 'Eve Price'

VICTORIA

Giant water lily

NYMPHAEACEAE

Genus of 2 species of rhizomatous, submerged, deep-water aquatic annuals or perennials occurring in tropical South America, in the slow-moving backwaters of the Amazon. Their stout rhizomes support enormous, rounded, floating leaves, and bear night-blooming, water-lily-like flowers. In tropical gardens, grow in a large pool; elsewhere, grow as annuals in a heated pool in a warm greenhouse.

• **HARDINESS** Frost tender.
• **CULTIVATION** Outdoors, grow in a pool at least 1m (3ft) deep in full sun; grow in baskets, 1m (3ft) across and 60cm (24in) deep, of rich, loamy soil, with added well-rotted organic matter. Under glass, grow in baskets of loamy soil in a water temperature of 21–24°C (70–75°F) in summer; provide full light. During the growing season, add pellets of slow-release fertilizer to the soil every 6 weeks. See also pp.52–53.
• **PROPAGATION** Collect the seeds when ripe and overwinter in distilled water. In early spring, sow at 29–32°C (84–90°F), covering the seeds with 5–8cm (2–3in) of water.
• **PESTS AND DISEASES** Trouble free.

V. amazonica ▣ (Amazon water lily, Royal water lily). Submerged, deep-water aquatic annual or perennial with stout rhizomes supporting rounded, mid-green, floating leaves, to 2m (6ft) long, reddish purple beneath; they have large prickles and vertical rims, to 10cm (4in), or occasionally 15cm (6in) high. In summer, bears many-petalled, water-lily-like white flowers, to 30cm (12in) across, ageing pink, with prickly sepals. ↔6m (20ft). South America (Amazon). ❀ (min. 25°C/77°F to remain perennial)
V. cruziana, syn. *V. trickeri* (Santa Cruz water lily). Submerged, deep-water aquatic annual or perennial with stout rhizomes supporting rounded, floating leaves, to 1.4m (4½ft) long, with vertical rims, to 20cm (8in) high. Leaves are mid-green above, densely softly hairy and reddish purple beneath, but the undersides are less highly coloured than those of *V. amazonica*. In summer, bears many-petalled, water-lily-like white flowers, to 10cm (4in) across, the sepals with basal prickles only. ↔6m (20ft). South America (Bolivia, Brazil, N. Argentina, Paraguay). ❀ (min. 22–25°C/72–77°F to remain perennial)
***V.* 'Longwood Hybrid'** (*V. amazonica* x *V. cruziana*). Submerged, deep-water aquatic annual or perennial with a stout rhizome supporting rounded, mid-green, floating leaves, to 2.5m (8ft) long, with reddish purple outer margins on the upturned rims. In summer, produces many-petalled, water-lily-like white flowers, to 30cm (12in) across, the sepals with basal prickles only. More free-flowering and hardier than its parents. ↔7m (22ft). Garden origin. ❀ (min. 22°C/72°F to remain perennial)
V. trickeri see *V. cruziana*.

Victoria amazonica

VIGNA

LEGUMINOSAE / PAPILIONACEAE

Genus of about 150 species of erect and climbing or trailing annuals and evergreen perennials from woodland, scrub, and rocky areas in tropical regions of Africa, Asia, S. USA, and Central and South America. Most are cultivated as agricultural crops, for their edible pods and seeds (beans); the climbers are also grown as ornamentals, for their flowers, foliage, and seed pods. The alternate leaves are palmately lobed or 3-palmate with entire leaflets. Pea-like flowers with distinctive, coiled keel petals are borne in axillary clusters or racemes, often in alternate pairs, followed by linear, straight or curved pods. Where summer temperatures average less than 16°C (61°F), grow as annuals in a warm greenhouse. Elsewhere, grow over a pergola, arch, or tall tree stump.

- **HARDINESS** Frost tender.
- **CULTIVATION** Under glass, grow in loam-based potting compost (JI No.2) in full light. In the growing season, water freely and apply a balanced liquid fertilizer monthly; water sparingly in winter. Outdoors, grow in fertile, moist but well-drained soil in full sun. Support climbing stems. Pruning group 11, in early spring.
- **PROPAGATION** Sow seed at 13–18°C (55–64°F) in autumn or spring.
- **PESTS AND DISEASES** Susceptible to red spider mites and whiteflies under glass.

V. caracalla, syn. *Phaseolus caracalla* (Corkscrew flower, Snail bean, Snail flower). Fast-growing, evergreen, twining, perennial climber with sparsely branched stems and 3-palmate leaves, 15cm (6in) long, with ovate, downy, light to mid-green leaflets, 7–13cm (3–5in) long. From summer to autumn, and into winter if warm enough, bears erect, axillary racemes, to 30cm (12in) long, of pink, white, or yellow flowers 3–5cm (1¼–2in) across, with elongated and coiled keel and standard petals, the keels coiled like a snail's shell; flowers are followed by nearly cylindrical, green then brown fruit, 15–18cm (6–7in) long. ↕ 6–8m (20–25ft). Tropical South America. ❀ (min. 10–15°C/50–59°F)

▷ ***Villarsia nymphoides*** see *Nymphoides peltata*

VINCA

Periwinkle

APOCYNACEAE

Genus of 7 species of slender-stemmed, evergreen subshrubs and herbaceous perennials from woodland in Europe, N. Africa, and C. Asia. They are grown for their opposite, simple, lance-shaped to elliptic or ovate, often variegated leaves, and for their showy, long-stalked, star-like or salverform flowers, each with 5 petal lobes, borne singly in the leaf axils. Useful ground cover for a woodland garden, shrub border, or shady bank, but may be invasive. All parts may cause mild stomach upset if ingested.

- **HARDINESS** Fully hardy to frost hardy.
- **CULTIVATION** Grow in any but very dry soil, in full sun (for best flowering) or partial shade. To restrict growth, cut back hard in early spring.

Vinca difformis

- **PROPAGATION** Divide from autumn to spring. Take semi-ripe cuttings in summer.
- **PESTS AND DISEASES** Prone to rust.

V. difformis ■ Prostrate, evergreen subshrub with usually narrowly lance-shaped, glossy, dark green leaves, to 7cm (3in) long. In late winter and early spring, upright shoots produce pale blue to nearly white flowers, to 4cm (1½in) across. ↕ 30cm (12in), ↔ indefinite. S.W. Europe, N. Africa. ❄❄
***V. herbacea* 'Hidcote Purple'** see *V. major* var. *oxyloba.*
***V. hirsuta* of gardens** see *V. major* var. *oxyloba.*
V. major (Greater periwinkle). Prostrate, evergreen shrub with arching shoots and ovate to lance-shaped, dark green leaves, to 9cm (3½in) long. Blue-violet or dark violet flowers, to 5cm (2in) across, are produced over a long period from mid-spring to autumn. ↕ 45cm (18in), ↔ indefinite. W. Mediterranean. ❄❄❄. **'Dartington Star'** see var. *oxyloba*. **'Elegantissima'** see 'Variegata'. **subsp. *hirsuta***, syn. var. *pubescens*, produces lance-shaped, distinctly hairy leaves; Georgia, Turkey. **'Maculata'** has leaves with yellow-green centres. **var. *oxyloba***, syn. 'Dartington Star', *V. herbacea* 'Hidcote Purple', *V. hirsuta* of gardens, produces dark violet-blue flowers with narrow, pointed lobes. **var. *pubescens*** see subsp. *hirsuta.* **'Reticulata'** has leaves conspicuously veined with yellow or cream when young, later dark green. **'Variegata'** ■ syn. 'Elegantissima' has leaves margined creamy white.

Vinca major 'Variegata'

Vinca minor

V. minor ■ (Lesser periwinkle). Prostrate, mat-forming, evergreen shrub with long, trailing shoots and elliptic or lance-shaped, sometimes ovate, dark green leaves, to 5cm (2in) long. Over a long period from mid-spring to autumn, bears usually blue-violet, sometimes pale blue, reddish purple, or white flowers, 2.5–3cm (1–1¼in) across. ↕ 10–20cm (4–8in), ↔ indefinite. Europe, S. Russia, N. Caucasus. ❄❄❄. **f. *alba*** has white flowers. **'Alba Aureavariegata'** see 'Alba Variegata'. **'Alba Variegata'**, syn. 'Alba Aureavariegata', has leaves with pale yellow margins, and bears white flowers. **'Argenteovariegata'**, syn. 'Variegata', has leaves with creamy white margins, and produces light violet-blue flowers. **'Atropurpurea'**, syn. 'Purpurea', 'Rubra', has dark plum-purple flowers. **'Azurea Flore Pleno'**, syn. 'Caerulea Plena', has double, sky-blue flowers. **'Bowles' Blue'** see 'La Grave'. **'Bowles' Variety'** see 'La Grave'. **'Bowles' White'** bears white flowers, opening from pinkish white buds. **'Caerulea Plena'** see 'Azurea Flore Pleno'. **'Double Burgundy'** see 'Multiplex'. **'Gertrude Jekyll'** is very compact, and profusely bears white flowers. **'La Grave'**, syn. 'Bowles' Blue', 'Bowles' Variety', bears lavender-blue flowers, 3cm (1¼in) across. **'Multiplex'**, syn. 'Double Burgundy', has double, plum-purple flowers. **'Purpurea'** see 'Atropurpurea'. **'Rubra'** see 'Atropurpurea'. **'Variegata'** see 'Argenteovariegata'.
V. rosea see *Catharanthus roseus.*

▷ **Vine** see *Vitis*
Allegheny see *Adlumia fungosa*
Arrowhead see *Syngonium, S. podophyllum*
Balloon see *Cardiospermum halicacabum*
Bengal clock see *Thunbergia grandiflora*
Blue trumpet see *Thunbergia grandiflora*
Bush clock see *Thunbergia erecta*
Cat's claw see *Macfadyena*
Chalice see *Solandra*
Chestnut see *Tetrastigma voinierianum*
Chinese trumpet see *Campsis grandiflora*
Chocolate see *Akebia*
Common cat's claw see *Macfadyena unguis-cati*
Common coral see *Kennedia coccinea*
Confederate see *Antigonon leptopus*
Coral see *Antigonon*

▷ **Vine cont.**
Cross see *Bignonia*
Firecracker see *Manettia cordifolia*
Goosefoot see *Syngonium*
Grape see *Vitis*
Hemp see *Mikania scandens*
Jade see *Strongylodon macrobotrys*
Kangaroo see *Cissus antarctica*
Kudzu see *Pueraria lobata*
Lipstick see *Aeschynanthus radicans* var. *lobbianus*
Macquarie see *Muehlenbeckia adpressa*
Madeira see *Anredera cordifolia*
Mignonette see *Anredera cordifolia*
Pink trumpet see *Podranea ricasoliana*
Potato see *Solanum laxum, S. wendlandii*
Rattan see *Berchemia scandens*
Rosary see *Ceropegia linearis* subsp. *woodii*
Russian see *Fallopia baldschuanica*
Silk see *Periploca graeca*
Silver see *Actinidia polygama, Scindapsus pictus*
Staff see *Celastrus, C. orbiculatus, C. scandens*
Sweetheart see *Ceropegia linearis* subsp. *woodii, Philodendron hederaceum*
Tara see *Actinidia arguta*
Trumpet see *Campsis*
Water see *Cissus hypoglauca*
Wonga wonga see *Pandorea pandorana*

VIOLA *syn.* ERPETION

Pansy, Violet

VIOLACEAE

Genus of about 500 species of annuals, biennials, evergreen, semi-evergreen, and deciduous perennials (some tufted or rhizomatous), and a few deciduous subshrubs, found in varied habitats in temperate regions worldwide. They have variable, entire to finely pinnatisect, mostly mid-green leaves with stipules. Some South American species are rosette-forming, and are very similar to sempervivums. The mostly unscented flowers, borne in the leaf axils, are usually solitary, rarely paired. Each has 5 petals: a spurred lower petal, 2 lateral petals, and 2 upward-facing upper petals. Most flower profusely over long periods in summer, and may self-seed freely.

Many cultivars within the genus are informally referred to as garden pansies, violas, or violettas; all are derived from the complex hybridization of *V. tricolor, V. lutea, V. cornuta*, and other species. Garden pansies (*V.* x *wittrockiana* cultivars) are biennials or very short-lived perennials, with faintly scented or unscented, more or less rounded flowers with patterned "faces", and a single-stemmed root system. Violas, often called "tufted pansies", are compact, tufted perennials with usually scented, more or less rounded, often patterned flowers with rays (lines in a deeper or contrasting colour), and a multi-stemmed root system. Violettas are more compact than violas, with small, sweetly fragrant, oval flowers, each with a central yellow mark and no rays.

The perennials and subshrubs are suitable for a rock garden, a scree bed, or the front of a border; a few are best in an alpine house. Treat garden pansies as annuals, biennials, or short-lived

V

Viola

Viola biflora

perennials: they are good for containers; some are suitable for summer bedding; plant winter- or spring-flowering types with spring-flowering bulbs.

• **Hardiness** Fully hardy to half hardy.

• **Cultivation** Grow in fertile, humus-rich, moist but well-drained soil in full sun or partial shade. In a rock garden, grow in poor to moderately fertile, gritty, sharply drained soil in full sun or partial shade; protect from winter wet. In an alpine house, use a mix of equal parts loam, leaf mould, and grit or tufa chips. Dead-head to prolong flowering. After flowering, cut back vigorous plants, especially *V. cornuta*, to keep compact.

• **Propagation** Sow seed in containers in a cold frame as soon as ripe or in spring; for garden pansies sow seed in late winter for early spring and summer flowering, or in summer for winter flowering. Divide *V. biflora*, *V. cornuta*, *V. elatior*, *V. glabella*, *V. hederacea*, *V. obliqua*, and *V. odorata* in spring or autumn. Take stem-tip cuttings of perennials and subshrubs in spring or late summer. Many viola species are short-lived, so propagate them regularly.

• **Pests and diseases** May be damaged by slugs, snails, aphids, red spider mites, and violet leaf midges. Susceptible to leaf spot; may also be affected by mosaic viruses, rust, and powdery mildew.

V. adunca (Hooked-spur violet, Western dog violet). Compact, tuft-forming, semi-evergreen perennial with procumbent stems bearing ovate to broadly ovate, finely toothed, smooth to slightly hairy leaves, to 4cm (1½in) long. In spring, bears scented, violet to lavender-blue flowers, 2cm (¾in) across, with white spurs, to 2cm (¾in) long, and white eyes. Suitable for a rock garden; self-seeds freely. ↕↔ to 8cm (3in). N. USA. ❄❄❄. **var. *minor*** see *V. labradorica*.

V. aetolica. Neat, clump-forming, short-lived, evergreen perennial with short, spreading stems and ovate to lance-shaped, scalloped leaves, to 2cm (¾in) long. In late spring and early summer, produces yellow flowers, to 2cm (¾in) across; the slightly darker lower petals have spurs to 6mm (¼in) long. ↕ to 8cm (3in), ↔ to 15cm (6in). E. Europe. ❄❄❄

V. beckwithii (Great Basin violet). Small, tufted, evergreen perennial with spreading stems and palmately 3-lobed, hairy, conspicuously veined leaves, 3cm (1¼in) long, each lobe pinnatifid with linear segments. In spring, bears solitary, slightly scented flowers, 2cm (¾in) across, with spurs to 2mm (1/16in) long; the 2 upper petals are deep reddish violet, the 3 lower ones pale lavender-blue with purple-veined yellow bases. Best in an alpine house; difficult to grow. ↕ 5–13cm (2–5in), ↔ to 10cm (4in). North America (Great Basin area). ❄❄❄

V. biflora ▣ (Twin-flowered violet). Dwarf, creeping herbaceous perennial with slender rhizomes and thin stems bearing kidney- to heart-shaped, toothed, pale green leaves, 3–4cm (1¼–1½in) long, with scalloped margins. In late spring and summer, bears solitary or paired, deep lemon

Viola canina

flowers, 1.5cm (½in) across, veined dark purple-brown on the lower petals and with spurs to 3mm (⅛in) long. Prefers moist soil in partial shade. ↕ to 8cm (3in), ↔ to 20cm (8in). Europe to N. Asia, North America (Alaska, Rocky Mountains). ❄❄❄

V. canina ▣ (Dog violet, Heath violet). Rhizomatous, semi-evergreen perennial with decumbent to erect stems and ovate to ovate-lance-shaped, entire leaves, 1–2cm (½–¾in) long, shallowly heart-shaped at the bases. In spring and early summer, bears solitary, bright blue or violet flowers, to 2.5cm (1in) across, each with a straight, pale yellowish green or white spur, 1cm (½in) long. ↕↔ 15–30cm (6–12in). Temperate Europe and W. Asia. ❄❄❄

V. cazorlensis ▣ Dwarf, woody-based, evergreen perennial with crowded, upright stems bearing very narrow, linear to inversely lance-shaped, entire leaves, to 1.5cm (½in) long. In late spring and early summer, produces narrow-petalled, pinkish purple flowers, 2cm (¾in) across, with notched lower petals, and slender spurs, to 3cm (1¼in) long. Difficult to grow; best in tufa or in an alpine house. ↕ to 8cm (3in), ↔ to 10cm (4in). S.E. Spain. ❄❄❄

V. cornuta ▣ (Horned violet, Viola). Spreading, rhizomatous, evergreen perennial with ascending stems and ovate, toothed leaves, 2–5cm (¾–2in) long, truncate at the bases. From spring to summer, produces abundant slightly scented flowers, to 3.5cm (1½in) across; they have widely separated, usually violet to lilac-blue petals, the lower ones with white markings, and slender spurs, to 1.5cm (½in) long. ↕ to 15cm (6in), ↔ to 40cm (16in) or more. Spain (Pyrenees). ❄❄❄. **var. *minor*** is smaller in all its parts, and has lavender-blue or white flowers, 1.5–2cm (½–¾in) across; ↕ to 7cm (3in), ↔ to 20cm (8in).

V. cucullata see *V. obliqua*.

V. elatior, syn. *V. erecta*. Upright, sparsely branched, subshrubby perennial with deciduous, lance-shaped, toothed leaves, to 9cm (3½in) long, slightly heart-shaped at the bases. Bears scented, pale lavender-blue flowers, 2.5cm (1in) across, with spurs 2–4mm (1/16–⅛in) long, over long periods in late spring and early summer. Easily grown in moist soil. ↕ to 30cm (12in), ↔ to 15cm (6in). C., S., and E. Europe to W. Asia. ❄❄❄

V. erecta see *V. elatior*.

V. glabella (Stream violet). Vigorous, spreading, rhizomatous, deciduous or

Viola cazorlensis

Viola cornuta

semi-evergreen perennial with upright or spreading stems and long-stalked, ovate or rounded, toothed, bright green leaves, 3–9cm (1¼–3½in) long, with heart-shaped bases. In late spring, bears deep yellow flowers, 2.5cm (1in) across, veined purple on the lower petals, and with short spurs, 2mm (1/16in) long. Prefers partial shade. ↕ to 20cm (8in), ↔ to 30cm (12in) or more. N.E. Asia, N.W. USA. ❄❄❄

V. gracilis, syn. *V. velutina*. Mat-forming, evergreen perennial with erect or ascending stems and oblong to broadly ovate, variably toothed leaves, 2–3cm (¾–1¼in) long, with finely divided stipules. In summer, bears yellow-eyed, deep violet, occasionally yellow flowers, to 3cm (1¼in) across, with slender spurs, to 7mm (¼in) long. Needs full sun. ↕ to 10cm (4in), ↔ to 20cm (8in). Balkan Peninsula, Greece, Turkey. ❄❄❄

***V.* 'Haslemere'** see *V.* 'Nellie Britton'.

V. hederacea, syn. *Erpetion hederaceum*, *E. reniforme*, *V. reniforme* (Australian violet, Ivy-leaved violet, Trailing violet). Mat-forming, evergreen perennial with slender stolons and short, erect, tufted stems bearing broadly ovate to kidney-shaped, entire or coarsely toothed, dark green leaves, to 3.5cm (1½in) long, with scalloped margins. In late summer, bears sometimes slightly scented flowers, to 2.5cm (1in) across, either spurless or with inconspicuous spurs, and with a rather flattened appearance; they may be white, cream, pale to dark violet, or sometimes white with violet patches. Best in an alpine house; prefers partial shade. Very vigorous; good ground

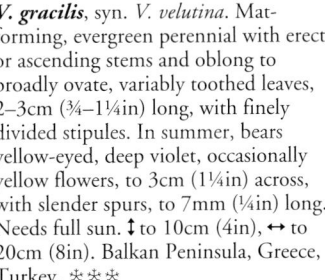

Viola 'Huntercombe Purple'

Viola 'Jackanapes'

cover in warm climates. ↕ to 10cm (4in), ↔ 20–30cm (8–12in). Australia. ✻✻

***V.* 'Huntercombe Purple'** ■ Spreading, clump-forming, evergreen perennial with upright stems and ovate, toothed leaves, to 2.5cm (1in) long. In spring and late summer, produces abundant deep violet-purple flowers, to 2.5cm (1in) across, with spurs 4–6mm (⅛–¼in) long. ↕ to 15cm (6in), ↔ to 30cm (12in). ✻✻✻

***V.* 'Irish Molly'.** Evergreen, usually short-lived perennial with spreading stems and broadly ovate, deeply cut leaves, to 3cm (1¼in) long. In summer, produces a long succession of dark gold flowers, to 3cm (1¼in) across, with brown centres, and spurs 4–6mm (⅛–¼in) long. Propagate regularly. ↕ to 15cm (6in), ↔ to 20cm (8in). ✻✻✻

***V.* 'Jackanapes'** ■ Robust, clump-forming, evergreen perennial with spreading stems and ovate, toothed, bright green leaves, to 2.5cm (1in) long. In late spring and summer, produces flowers to 2cm (¾in) across, the upper petals deep violet-purple to almost brown, the lower ones golden yellow, streaked purple at the centres, and with spurs 1.5cm (½in) long. Propagate regularly. ↕ to 12cm (5in), ↔ to 30cm (12in). ✻✻✻

V. labradorica, syn. *V. adunca* var. *minor* (Labrador violet). Spreading, clump-forming, semi-evergreen perennial with prostrate stems and heart- to kidney-shaped, finely toothed, dark green leaves, 2cm (¾in) long, flushed bronze-purple when young. Solitary, pale purple flowers, 1.5cm (½in) across, with short spurs, 6mm (¼in) long, are borne in spring and summer. ↕ to 8cm (3in), ↔ indefinite. Canada, N. USA, Greenland. ✻✻✻. **var. *purpurea* of gardens** see *V. riviniana* 'Purpurea'.

V. lutea, syn. *V. lutea* subsp. *elegans* (Mountain pansy). Slender, creeping, rhizomatous, evergreen perennial bearing ovate lower stem leaves and ovate to lance-shaped, shallowly scalloped or almost entire upper leaves, to 2cm (¾in) long. In late spring and early summer, bears flowers to 3cm (1¼in) across, in bright yellow, blue-violet, or red-violet, or all three colours combined, and with short spurs, 3–6mm (⅛–¼in) long. ↕↔ 7–15cm (3–6in). W. and C. Europe. ✻✻✻. **subsp. *elegans*** see *V. lutea.*

***V.* 'Nellie Britton'** ■ syn. *V.* 'Haslemere'. Clump-forming, evergreen perennial with spreading stems bearing ovate to lance-shaped, toothed, glossy leaves, 3cm (1¼in) long. Pinkish mauve flowers, to 2.5cm (1in) across, with spurs 1cm (½in) long, are profusely borne over long periods in summer. ↕ to 15cm (6in), ↔ to 30cm (12in). ✻✻✻

V. obliqua, syn. *V. cucullata* (Marsh blue violet). Spreading, stemless, rhizomatous, deciduous perennial with heart-shaped, toothed leaves, to 9cm (3½in) long. In late spring, solitary, blue-violet flowers, to 2cm (¾in) across, with short spurs to 2mm (1/16in) long, are borne above the leaves. Occasionally produces white flowers with blue eyes and blue veins. ↕ to 8cm (3in), ↔ to 25cm (10in). North America. ✻✻✻

V. odorata (English violet, Garden violet, Sweet violet). Rhizomatous, semi-evergreen perennial with slender stolons and short, erect stems that bear tufts of heart-shaped to rounded, toothed, bright green leaves, to 6cm (2½in) long. In late winter and early spring, produces sweetly scented, blue or white flowers, 2cm (¾in) or more across, with spurs to 5mm (¼in) long. Self-seeds freely. ↕ to 20cm (8in), ↔ 30cm (12in) or more. Probably W. and S. Europe; very widely naturalized elsewhere. ✻✻✻

V. papilionacea see *V. sororia.*

V. pedata ■ (Bird's-foot violet, Crow-foot violet). Stemless, clump-forming, semi-evergreen perennial with short, stout rhizomes and 3-lobed leaves, to 3cm (1¼in) long, the 2 lateral lobes themselves divided into 3–5 linear or spoon-shaped lobes. In late spring and early summer, bears yellow-centred, pale violet flowers, 3cm (1¼in) across, with widely spaced petals and short spurs, to 2mm (1/16in) long. Flowers are sometimes white or bicoloured, with deep purple upper petals and pale lavender-blue or white lower ones. Best in an alpine house. Needs well-drained, peaty, sandy soil. ↕ to 5cm (2in), ↔ to 10cm (4in). E. North America. ✻✻✻

V. pedatifida (Larkspur violet, Purple prairie violet). Small, clump-forming, semi-evergreen to deciduous perennial with 5- to 11-palmate leaves, to 3cm (1¼in) long, with very narrow leaflets. In spring and summer, bears deep violet-blue flowers, to 2cm (¾in) across, with bearded lower petals and short spurs, 4mm (⅛in) long. Self-seeds freely. ↕ to 12cm (5in), ↔ to 15cm (6in). C. North America. ✻✻✻

Viola sororia 'Freckles'

V. reniforme see *V. hederacea.*

V. riviniana (Common dog violet, Wood violet). Tufted, semi-evergreen perennial with basal tufts of ovate-rounded, toothed leaves, to 4cm (1½in) long, deeply heart-shaped at the bases. In late spring and early summer, bears pale violet-blue flowers, 1.5–2.5cm (½–1in) across, with notched, white or pale purple spurs, to 5mm (¼in) long. Suitable for a wild garden, in deep or partial shade. ↕ 10–20cm (4–8in), ↔ 20–40cm (8–16in). Europe, N. Africa. ✻✻✻. **'Purpurea'** ■ syn. *V. labradorica* var. *purpurea* of gardens, has dark purplish green leaves. Invasive, but excellent in a wild or woodland garden.

V. sororia, syn. *V. papilionacea* (Sister violet, Woolly blue violet). Stemless, rhizomatous herbaceous perennial with ovate to rounded, sharp-pointed, scalloped leaves, to 10cm (4in) long, densely hairy beneath. In spring and summer, bears flowers to 2cm (¾in) across, with short spurs, to 3mm (⅛in) long. The flowers are sometimes deep violet-blue, but usually white, heavily speckled and streaked violet-blue around the centres. Self-seeds freely. ↕ to 10cm (4in), ↔ to 20cm (8in). E. North America. ✻✻✻. **'Freckles'** ■ bears white flowers, speckled violet-purple.

V. tricolor ■ (Heartsease, Love-in-idleness, Wild pansy). Tufted annual, biennial, or short-lived, evergreen perennial, sometimes rhizomatous, with spreading stems and ovate to heart-shaped, toothed leaves, to 3cm (1¼in) long. From spring to autumn, bears flowers, 2.5cm (1in) or more across, in shades of purple, lavender-blue, white,

Viola 'Nellie Britton'

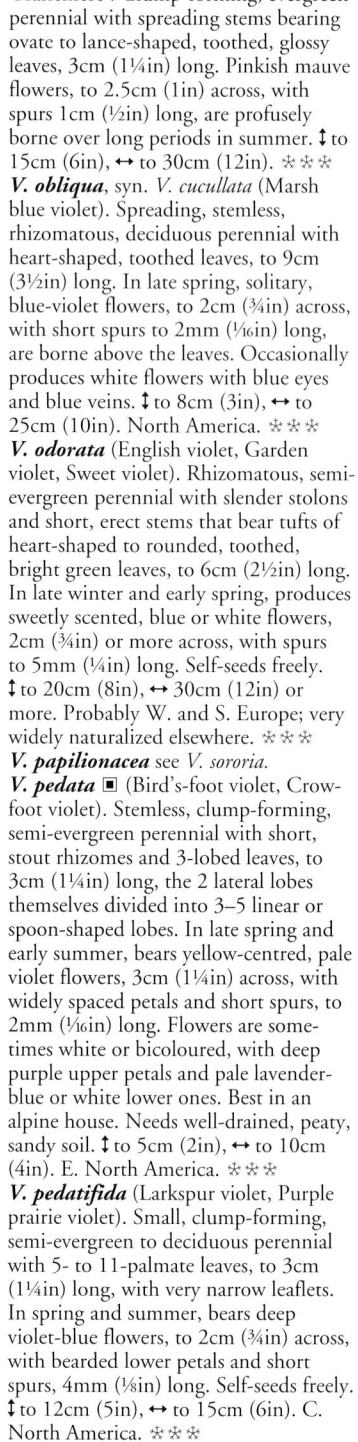

Viola pedata

Viola riviniana 'Purpurea'

Viola tricolor

Viola tricolor 'Bowles' Black'

or yellow, with usually dark purple upper petals, lower petals often streaked dark purple, and spurs to 7mm (¼in) long. Very short-lived, but self-seeds prolifically. ↕ to 8–12cm (3–5in), ↔ to 10–15cm (4–6in). Europe, Asia. ❄❄❄. **'Bowles' Black'** ■ has velvety, almost black flowers with small, golden yellow eyes. Seeds freely and comes almost true from seed; ↕ to 10cm (4in), ↔ to 20cm (8in). **'Prince Henry'** bears small, very dark purple flowers, 1.5–2cm (½–¾in) across, from spring to summer. **'Prince John'** bears small, bright yellow flowers, 1.5–2cm (½–¾in) across, from spring to summer.

V. velutina see *V. gracilis*.

***V. x wittrockiana* cultivars** (Pansy). Erect, bushy evergreen perennials, grown as annuals or biennials, derived from cross-breeding *V. altaica*, *V. cornuta*, *V. lutea*, and *V. tricolor*; they are usually larger and more robust than their parents. They have spreading stems and ovate to almost heart-shaped, shallowly lobed, shiny, mid- to deep green leaves, to 3.5cm (1½in) or more long. Flowers are 6–10cm (2½–4in) across, with the lateral petals overlapping the lower and upper petals, and with very short spurs. They may be either self-coloured, usually in blue, white, yellow, orange, pink, red, or purple; bicoloured; or the more traditional pansy type, bicoloured with central, face-like markings. Flowers are borne mainly from early spring to summer, some from autumn to winter. Other, usually smaller-flowered cultivars have been bred for winter and early spring flowering, and are excellent bedding

Viola x *wittrockiana* Fama Series

Viola x *wittrockiana* Forerunner Series

plants. ↕ 16–23cm (6–9in), ↔ 23–30cm (9–12in). ❄❄❄. **Allegro Series** cultivars bear large flowers in a broad colour range, with or without markings, in winter and spring. **'Baby Lucia'** produces small, yellow-eyed, clear blue flowers in spring and summer. **'Bambini'** has small flowers, borne in spring and summer, in a wide colour range, most with contrasting white or yellow faces and "whiskered" central markings. **Bingo Series** cultivars flower in winter and spring, producing large blooms in a broad colour range, some with darker markings. **Clear Crystal Series** cultivars bear medium-sized flowers in summer, in a wide range of clear, single colours, without central markings. **'Cornetto'** produces small, very long-spurred, clear white flowers in spring and summer. **Crown Series** cultivars produce large flowers in a broad range of clear colours, in early spring and summer. **Crystal Bowl Series** cultivars are compact, and bear medium-sized, unmarked flowers in a wide range of clear colours, including white, in summer; ↕ 23cm (9in), ↔ 30cm (12in). **'Cuty'** bears small, yellow-eyed white flowers, with deep violet-purple upper petals, from spring to summer. **Delta Series** cultivars are compact and robust, bearing large flowers in a wide range of colours, some with darker markings, in early spring. **Fama Series** ■ cultivars produce large flowers in winter and spring, in a wide range of single colours and in mixed colours. **Fanfare Series** cultivars are compact, producing medium-sized flowers in winter and spring, available in

Viola x *wittrockiana*
Joker Series 'Jolly Joker'

Viola x *wittrockiana* Princess Series

a range of single colours and bicolours; excellent for hanging baskets. Cultivars of **Forerunner Series** ■ bloom in winter and spring, bearing medium-sized flowers in a range of bright single colours and bicolours. Cultivars of **Imperial Series** produce large flowers in a broad colour range, almost all with a deeper central mark, in winter and early spring; **'Imperial Frosty Rose'** is an unusual rose-pink with a deeper central mark; **'Imperial Gold Princess'** is bicoloured yellow and red. **Jewel Series** cultivars are compact and free-flowering, bearing small blooms in winter and spring, in yellow, blue, purple with pansy faces, and white with pansy faces. Cultivars of **Joker Series** produce medium-sized, bicoloured flowers in light blue, mahogany-gold, violet-gold, and mixed colours, with very strongly marked pansy faces, in summer; **'Jolly Joker'** ■ blooms in spring and summer, and has medium-sized orange flowers, with deep purple upper petals and purple-margined lower petals. **'Pretty'** bears small yellow flowers, with rich mahogany-red upper petals, in spring and summer. **Princess Series** ■ cultivars are neat in habit, and produce small flowers in blue, cream, dark purple, bicoloured purple and white, or yellow, in spring and summer. **Rally Series** cultivars are free-flowering, producing medium-sized blooms in a broad range of colours, in winter and spring. Cultivars of **Regal Series** are compact, producing medium-sized flowers in a wide range of separate colours and a mixture of colours, all with darker markings, in winter and

Viola x *wittrockiana* Universal Series

spring. **Super Chalon Giants** bears medium-sized to large, bicoloured flowers, with wavy, ruffled margins, in summer. **Ultima Series** cultivars, blooming in winter and spring, have medium-sized flowers in a very broad range of colours, including bicolours. **Universal Series** ■ cultivars bear medium-sized flowers in winter and spring, in a broad range of colours, including bicolours, and sometimes with patterned faces. Cultivars of **Velours Series** have a neat habit, and bear small flowers in violet-blue, pale blue with deep blue markings, purple, and yellow, in spring and summer.

▷**Viola** see *Viola cornuta*
▷**Violet** see *Viola*
African see *Saintpaulia*
Amethyst see *Browallia*
Australian see *Viola hederacea*
Bird's-foot see *Viola pedata*
Bush see *Browallia*
Common dog see *Viola riviniana*
Crow-foot see *Viola pedata*
Dame's see *Hesperis matronalis*
Dog see *Viola canina*
Dog's-tooth see *Erythronium*
English see *Viola odorata*
European dog's-tooth see *Erythronium dens-canis*
Flame see *Episcia*
Garden see *Viola odorata*
Great Basin see *Viola beckwithii*
Heath see *Viola canina*
Hooked-spur see *Viola adunca*
Horned see *Viola cornuta*
Ivy-leaved see *Viola hederacea*
Labrador see *Viola labradorica*
Larkspur see *Viola pedatifida*
Marsh blue see *Viola obliqua*
Mexican see *Tetranema roseum*
Persian see *Exacum affine*
Philippine see *Barleria cristata*
Purple prairie see *Viola pedatifida*
Sister see *Viola sororia*
Stream see *Viola glabella*
Sweet see *Viola odorata*
Trailing see *Viola hederacea*
Twin-flowered see *Viola biflora*
Water see *Hottonia palustris*
Western dog see *Viola adunca*
Wood see *Viola riviniana*
Woolly blue see *Viola sororia*
▷**Viper's bugloss** see *Echium vulgare*

VIRGILIA

LEGUMINOSAE/PAPILIONACEAE

Genus of 2 species of small, evergreen trees from forest edges and river valleys in coastal areas of South Africa. They have alternate, pinnate leaves, and are grown for their abundant pea-like flowers, borne in axillary or terminal racemes, occasionally in panicles. Where winter temperatures fall below 5–7°C (41–45°F), grow in a cool greenhouse. In milder areas, use as specimen trees.

• **HARDINESS** Frost tender, but may survive to 0°C (32°F) provided the wood has been well ripened in summer.

• **CULTIVATION** Under glass, grow in ericaceous potting compost with added sharp sand, in full light. In growth, water moderately and apply a balanced liquid fertilizer every month; water sparingly in winter. Outdoors, grow in neutral to acid, poor to moderately fertile, moist but well-drained soil in full sun. Pruning group 1; may need restrictive pruning under glass.

Virgilia oroboides

• **PROPAGATION** Sow seed at about 15°C (59°F) in spring, after soaking in hot water or after scarification.
• **PESTS AND DISEASES** Trouble free.

V. capensis see *V. oroboides.*
V. oroboides ■ ◊–◊ syn. *V. capensis.* Fast-growing shrub or small, rounded to broadly columnar tree, usually with several main stems, and with red-downy young growth. Pinnate leaves, 10–20cm (4–8in) long, each have 13–21 narrowly oblong, leathery, mid- to deep green leaflets, pale and densely woolly beneath, with thorn-like points. From spring to summer, bears racemes of up to 12 pea-like, fragrant, white, pink, purple, or crimson flowers, to 2cm (¾in) across. ↕5–9m (15–28ft), ↔ 3–5m (10–15ft). South Africa (Western Cape, Eastern Cape). ❄ (borderline)

▷**Virginia creeper** see *Parthenocissus, P. quinquefolia*
Chinese see *P. henryana*
▷**Virgin's bower** see *Clematis*
▷***Viscaria*** see *Lychnis*
V. elegans see *Silene coeli-rosa*
V. vulgaris see *Lychnis viscaria*

VITALIANA syn. DOUGLASIA

PRIMULACEAE

Genus of one species of tufted, mat- or cushion-forming, evergreen perennial, occurring in alpine and subalpine screes, rocks, and meadows in the mountains of C. and S. Europe. It has rosettes of small leaves, and is cultivated for its solitary flowers, produced in spring. Grow in a rock garden, scree bed, or alpine house.

Vitaliana primuliflora

• **HARDINESS** Fully hardy, but dislikes excessive winter wet.
• **CULTIVATION** Grow in leafy, moderately fertile, gritty, moist but sharply drained soil in full sun. Protect from winter wet. In an alpine house, grow in a mix of 1 part each loam and leaf mould, and 3 parts grit.
• **PROPAGATION** Sow seed in containers in an open frame as soon as ripe. Detach and root offsets in spring and early summer.
• **PESTS AND DISEASES** Susceptible to aphids and red spider mites under glass.

V. primuliflora ■ syn. *Androsace vitaliana, Douglasia vitaliana.* Tufted, mat- or cushion-forming, evergreen perennial with creeping stems and tight rosettes of linear to oblong-lance-shaped, pointed, usually hairy, pale green leaves, to 1cm (½in) long, with silver margins. In spring, bears solitary, almost stemless, tubular yellow flowers, to 2cm (¾in) across, with 5 spreading lobes. ↕ to 2.5cm (1in), ↔ to 25cm (10in). Mountains of S.W. and C. Europe, to S.E. Alps, and C. Apennines. ❄❄❄

VITEX

VERBENACEAE

Widespread genus of 250 species of deciduous or evergreen trees and shrubs, occurring mainly in tropical regions, often in woodland or dried-up river beds. They have opposite, fully divided, 3- to 7-palmate leaves, and produce terminal panicles, racemes, or cymes of tubular, 2-lipped flowers. *V. agnus-castus* and *V. negundo* are cultivated for their elegant foliage and late flowers, and may be grown in a shrub border or against a wall. In frost-prone areas, cultivate tender species in a warm greenhouse.
• **HARDINESS** Frost hardy to frost tender.
• **CULTIVATION** Grow in any well-drained soil in full sun. In frost-prone areas, shelter frost-hardy species from cold, drying winds. Pruning group 6.
• **PROPAGATION** Sow seed at 6–12°C (43–54°F) in autumn or spring. Take semi-ripe cuttings in summer.
• **PESTS AND DISEASES** Trouble free.

V. agnus-castus (Chaste tree). Open, spreading, deciduous shrub with 5- or 7-palmate leaves composed of slender, narrowly elliptic, pointed, entire or slightly toothed, aromatic, dark green

Vitex agnus-castus var. *latifolia*

leaflets, to 10cm (4in) or more long. Small, tubular, fragrant, lilac- to dark blue, sometimes white flowers are borne in slender upright, terminal panicles, to 13–18cm (5–7in) long, in early and mid-autumn. ↕↔ 2–8m (6–25ft). Mediterranean to C. Asia. ❄❄. **var. *latifolia*** ■ is more vigorous, with broader leaflets.
V. negundo. Bushy, deciduous shrub with 3- to 5-palmate, dark green leaves composed of lance-shaped, pointed, sharply toothed or entire leaflets, to 10cm (4in) long. In late summer and early autumn, bears small, tubular, pale violet-blue flowers in terminal panicles, to 22cm (9in) long. ↕↔ 3m (10ft). E. Africa, E. Asia. ❄❄

VITIS

Grape vine, Vine

VITACEAE

Genus of about 65 species of woody, deciduous tendril climbers, occasionally shrubs, found in woodland, woodland margins, and thickets in N. temperate regions. They have flaking bark and alternate, simple to lobed, sometimes toothed leaves. Tiny green flowers are produced in panicles from the leaf axils in summer, and are followed by fruits (grapes), which in some species are edible or are used to make wine. The ornamental vines are cultivated for their foliage and fruits; grow over a trellis, pergola, or fence, or through a large shrub or tree, or train against a wall.
• **HARDINESS** Fully hardy.
• **CULTIVATION** Grow in well-drained, preferably neutral to alkaline, humus-rich soil in full sun or partial shade. Pruning group 11, in midwinter, and again in midsummer if necessary, to restrict growth; pruning group 12, if more formal training required.
• **PROPAGATION** Sow seed in containers in a cold frame in autumn or spring. Take hardwood cuttings in late winter, or root "vine eye" cuttings (with a single bud) in early spring. Layer in autumn.
• **PESTS AND DISEASES** May be affected by powdery mildew and honey fungus. Scale insects and mealybugs may be troublesome under glass.

V. aconitifolia see *Ampelopsis aconitifolia.*
V. amurensis (Amur grape). Vigorous, woody, deciduous climber, sometimes a shrub, with red-tinged young shoots and broadly ovate, often shallowly 3-lobed, sharply toothed, dark green leaves, to 30cm (12in) long, heart-shaped at the bases, and turning red and purple in autumn. Produces small and unpalatable, ovoid, white-bloomed black grapes, 1.5cm (½in) across, in late summer. ↕15m (50ft). China, Korea, Japan. ❄❄❄
V. 'Brant'. Vigorous, woody, deciduous climber with rounded, palmately 3- to 5-lobed, toothed, bright green leaves, to 22cm (9in) long, which turn bronze-red with green veins in autumn. In autumn, produces large bunches of edible, spherical, blue-black grapes, 1.5cm (½in) across. ↕7m (22ft) or more. ❄❄❄
V. capensis see *Rhoicissus capensis.*
V. coignetiae ■ Vigorous, woody, deciduous climber with large, heart-shaped, shallowly 3- to 5-lobed,

Vitis coignetiae

shallowly to coarsely toothed, dark green leaves, to 30cm (12in) long, with deeply impressed veins above and thickly brown-felted beneath; they turn bright red in autumn. Small, unpalatable, spherical, blue-black grapes, 1cm (½in) across, are produced in autumn. ↕15m (50ft). Korea, Japan. ❄❄❄
V. davidii. Woody, deciduous climber producing young shoots densely covered with short, rigid spines. Heart-shaped, shallowly lobed, toothed, glossy, dark green leaves, to 25cm (10in) long, blue-green or blue-grey beneath, turn scarlet in autumn. Produces edible, spherical black grapes, 1.5cm (½in) across, in autumn. ↕8m (25ft) or more. China. ❄❄❄
V. henryana see *Parthenocissus henryana.*
V. heterophylla see *Ampelopsis brevipedunculata* var. *maximowiczii.*
V. quinquefolia see *Parthenocissus quinquefolia.*
V. striata see *Cissus striata.*
V. thomsonii see *Parthenocissus thomsonii.*
***V. vinifera* 'Purpurea'** ■ Woody, deciduous climber with rounded, 3- to 5-lobed, toothed leaves, to 15cm (6in)

Vitis vinifera 'Purpurea'

V

long, grey-hairy at first, turning plum-purple, then dark purple in autumn. In autumn, produces small, unpalatable, spherical purple grapes, to 2cm (¾in) across. ↕ 7m (22ft). ❄❄❄
V. voinieriana see *Tetrastigma voinierianum.*

VRIESEA

BROMELIACEAE

Genus of about 250 species of rosette-forming, evergreen, mostly epiphytic perennials (bromeliads), closely related to *Tillandsia*. They occur in forested and rocky areas, to 2,500m (8,000ft) high, in Mexico, Central America, the West Indies, and South America. The mostly lance-shaped or linear leaves have smooth margins, are often finely scaly, and frequently have coloured cross-bands and other markings. Bract-like sheaths, sometimes colourful, are present at the leaf bases. The short-stalked flowers are variously shaped, with petals free or fused into a tube, often shorter than the sepals, each petal with 2 scales at the base on the inner surface; the flowers are usually borne in flattened, 2-ranked, spike-like racemes or panicles, with prominent floral bracts, produced on more or less erect scapes from the rosette centres, in summer or autumn. Where temperatures drop below 15°C (59°F), grow in a warm greenhouse or as houseplants. In tropical gardens, grow epiphytically in trees, or on mossy rocks.

- **HARDINESS** Frost tender.
- **CULTIVATION** Under glass, grow attached to pieces of bark or tree branches, or in containers of standard epiphytic bromeliad compost, in moderate light. During the growing season, keep the rosette centres filled with water, mist daily, and apply quarter-strength foliar fertilizer every 4–5 weeks. Keep just moist in winter. Outdoors, grow epiphytically in partial shade. See also p.47.
- **PROPAGATION** Sow seed at 19–24°C (66–75°F) when ripe. Remove offsets in spring.
- **PESTS AND DISEASES** Susceptible to scale insects.

V. carinata ▣ (Lobster claw, Painted feather). Epiphytic bromeliad with funnel-shaped rosettes of arching, lance-shaped, pale green leaves, to 20cm (8in) long, broadly acute or rounded at the tips, and with broadly elliptic, red-tinged sheaths, 5–6cm (2–2½in) long.

Vriesea carinata

Vriesea hieroglyphica

In summer or autumn, scapes with green, purple, or red bracts bear spike-like racemes, 4–5cm (1½–2in) long, of tubular flowers, to 5cm (2in) long; the flowers have green-tipped yellow petals, keeled sepals, and red-based, yellow-green floral bracts. ↕ to 30cm (12in), ↔ 15–20cm (6–8in). Brazil. ❀ (min. 15°C/59°F)
V. fenestralis. Rock-dwelling or epiphytic bromeliad with funnel-shaped rosettes of recurved or arching, broadly linear, pale green leaves, to 40cm (16in) long, with rounded tips, each with a recurved thorn; the leaf-blades have dark green lines and purple circles beneath, and the broadly oval, yellowish green sheaths, 9–10cm (3½–4in) long, are spotted reddish brown. In summer, bears loose, spike-like racemes, to 30cm (12in) long, of green floral bracts and spreading, yellowish green or greenish white flowers, 6–7cm (2½–3in) long. ↕ to 1m (3ft), ↔ 35–50cm (14–20in). Brazil. ❀ (min. 15°C/59°F)
V. fosteriana. Epiphytic, probably also terrestrial bromeliad with stiff, dense, funnel-shaped rosettes of arching, broadly tongue-shaped, yellowish to deep green leaves, to 70cm (28in) long;

Vriesea platynema

they are cross-banded with purple or maroon, especially beneath, and have broadly oval, dark brown sheaths, 10–15cm (4–6in) long. In summer, bears loose, spike-like racemes, 40cm (16in) or more long, of yellow floral bracts and tubular flowers, 4.5cm (1¾in) long, with yellow petals and green sepals, all with reddish brown tips. ↕ to 1.5m (5ft), ↔ 1m (3ft). Brazil. ❀ (min. 15°C/59°F)
V. hieroglyphica ▣ (King of bromeliads). Epiphytic bromeliad with dense, funnel-shaped rosettes of arching, strap-shaped, minutely scaly, yellowish green leaves, 50–80cm (20–32in) long, marked dark green above, purplish brown beneath; dark brown sheaths are 8–10cm (3–4in) long. In summer, produces branching, spike-like racemes or panicles, to 80cm (32in) long, of greenish yellow floral bracts and tubular-trumpet-shaped, sulphur-yellow flowers, to 6cm (2½in) long. ↕ to 1m (3ft), ↔ 80–100cm (32–39in). E. Brazil. ❀ (min. 15°C/59°F)
V. imperialis (Giant vriesea). Rock-dwelling bromeliad with funnel-shaped rosettes of flat or arching, lance-shaped, leathery, pale reddish green leaves, 1.5m (5ft) long, with broadly oval, green sheaths, to 20cm (8in) long. In summer, erect scapes bear glossy, maroon-red bracts and branching, pyramidal, spike-like racemes or panicles, 2m (6ft) or more long, with red floral bracts and tubular, yellow or white flowers, 10cm (4in) or more long. ↕ 3–5m (10–15ft), ↔ 1.5m (5ft) or more. E. Brazil. ❀ (min. 15°C/59°F)
V. platynema ▣ Variable, epiphytic bromeliad with very dense, funnel-shaped rosettes of flaccid, strap-shaped, violet-tipped, dull green, often violet-striped leaves, 60cm (24in) long, often margined purple, and with broadly oval, dark brown sheaths, to 12cm (5in) long. In summer, bears loose, spike-like racemes, to 40cm (16in) long, of red or yellow floral bracts and tubular green flowers, to 4.5cm (1¾in) long, with yellow sepals. ↕ to 1m (3ft), ↔ 60cm (24in). West Indies, E. South America. ❀ (min. 15°C/59°F). **'Variegata'** has mid-green leaves, pale reddish purple beneath, with pale lines near the tips; E. Brazil.
V. psittacina. Variable, epiphytic bromeliad with broadly funnel-shaped rosettes of arching, strap-shaped, pale green leaves, 50cm (20in) long; the leaves have elliptic, green or pale brown sheaths, 7–9cm (3–3½in) long. In summer, produces slender, erect, spike-like racemes, to 30cm (12in) long, with yellow-tipped red, or entirely red or green, floral bracts, and spreading, sometimes green-tipped yellow flowers, 6cm (2½in) long. ↕ to 60cm (24in), ↔ 40–60cm (16–24in). Brazil, Paraguay. ❀ (min. 15°C/59°F)
V. saundersii. Rock-dwelling bromeliad with dense rosettes of arching, linear, thorn-tipped, grey-scaly, grey-green leaves, 30cm (12in) long; they have fine maroon spots beneath, and oval, yellowish brown sheaths, to 15cm (6in) long, with reddish brown spots. In summer, bears dense, spike-like racemes or panicles, 14cm (5½in) long, of pale or yellowish green floral bracts and tubular yellow flowers, 3.5cm (1½in) long, with pale or yellowish green sepals. ↕ 60–70cm (24–28in), ↔ 40cm (16in). E. Brazil. ❀ (min. 15°C/59°F)
V. splendens ▣ (Flaming sword). Variable, terrestrial or epiphytic bromeliad producing dense, funnel-shaped rosettes of arching, linear, bluish green leaves, to 80cm (32in) long, with broad, dark green, purple, or reddish brown cross-banding, and with indistinct sheaths. In summer, bears lance-shaped, spike-like racemes, to 55cm (22in) long, of thin, bright red floral bracts and tubular yellow flowers, 8cm (3in) long, with often red-tipped yellow sepals. ↕ to 1m (3ft), ↔ 30cm (12in). E. Venezuela to French Guiana. ❀ (min. 15°C/59°F)

▷**Vriesea, Giant** see *Vriesea imperialis*

Vriesea splendens

W

WACHENDORFIA

HAEMODORACEAE

Genus of about 25 species of tuberous, evergreen perennials found on grassy slopes in South Africa. They have bright red tubers and large, broadly linear, pleated, parallel-veined, erect, basal leaves, sheathing one another at their bases and arranged in 2 opposite rows. They are grown for their large, terminal panicles of irregular, flat, star-shaped yellow flowers, with 6 tepals, borne on leafless stems. In frost-prone areas, grow in a cool greenhouse; for optimum flowering, plant directly into a greenhouse border. In frost-free areas, grow in a sheltered border.

• **HARDINESS** Half hardy.

• **CULTIVATION** Under glass, grow in loam-based potting compost (JI No.2), with additional sharp sand and peat or leaf mould, in full light. During the growing season, water freely and apply a balanced liquid fertilizer every month. Keep just moist when dormant. Outdoors, grow in fertile, reliably moist soil in full sun.

• **PROPAGATION** Sow seed at 13–18°C (55–64°F) in autumn or spring. Separate tubers in spring.

• **PESTS AND DISEASES** Susceptible to slug and snail damage.

W. thyrsiflora ■ Clump-forming, tuberous perennial with furry red roots and tubers. Arching, broadly linear, pleated, parallel-veined, basal leaves, to 1m (3ft) long, are hairless and fairly brittle. In early summer, produces dense panicles of star-shaped yellow flowers, to 3cm (1¼in) across. ↕ 1.5–2m (5–6ft), ↔ 45cm (18in). South Africa (Northern Cape, Western Cape, Eastern Cape). ❄

Wachendorfia thyrsiflora

▷**Waffle plant, Purple** see *Hemigraphis* 'Exotica'

WAHLENBERGIA

CAMPANULACEAE

Genus of about 150 species of mat-forming to upright annuals and perennials from mountains in Europe, South Africa, and Australasia. They have variable, usually alternate leaves, and are grown for their conspicuous, funnel-, bell-, saucer-, or star-shaped, usually violet, blue, or white flowers, borne singly or in cymes, in summer. Grow in a rock garden, peat bed, or alpine house.

• **HARDINESS** Fully hardy (borderline) to frost hardy.

• **CULTIVATION** Grow in well-drained, sandy, humus-rich soil in a sheltered site in partial shade. In an alpine house, grow in a mix of equal parts loam, leaf mould, and sharp sand.

• **PROPAGATION** Sow seed at 13–15°C (55–59°F) in early spring. Divide in spring. Propagate regularly.

• **PESTS AND DISEASES** May be damaged by slugs and snails.

W. albomarginata (New Zealand bluebell). Tufted, spreading, short-lived, rhizomatous perennial producing basal rosettes of elliptic to lance-shaped or ovate-spoon-shaped, hairy, leathery, mid-green leaves, to 2cm (¾in) long, with reddish brown margins, often purplish green beneath. Solitary, slender-stemmed, upward-facing, bell-shaped, blue, sometimes white flowers, 2.5cm (1in) across, usually with green veins, are produced in summer. ↕ 5–20cm (2–8in), ↔ to 20cm (8in). New Zealand. ❄❄❄ (borderline)

W. gloriosa ■ Tufted, rhizomatous perennial bearing lance-shaped, thick, dark green leaves, 2–3cm (¾–1¼in) long, with wavy, toothed margins. Solitary, upward-facing, widely bell-shaped, deep violet-blue flowers, 2cm (¾in) across, with darker veins, are produced in summer. ↕ to 5cm (2in), ↔ to 15cm (6in). Australia. ❄❄

W. pumilio see *Edraianthus pumilio.*

W. serpyllifolia see *Edraianthus serpyllifolius.*

Wahlenbergia gloriosa

▷**Wake robin** see *Trillium, T. grandiflorum, T. sessile*

WALDSTEINIA

ROSACEAE

Genus of about 6 species of tufted, rhizomatous, herbaceous perennials found in woodland throughout N. temperate regions. They are grown mainly for their alternate, 3-palmate or palmately 3- to 7-lobed leaves, and for their saucer-shaped yellow flowers, borne singly or in cymes in late spring and early summer. They provide good ground cover in a woodland garden, on dry, shady banks, or at the front of a herbaceous border, but may be invasive.

• **HARDINESS** Fully hardy.

• **CULTIVATION** Grow in any moderately fertile soil in full or partial shade.

• **PROPAGATION** Sow seed in containers in a cold frame in autumn or spring. Divide in early spring.

• **PESTS AND DISEASES** Trouble free.

W. ternata ■ syn. *W. trifolia.* Vigorous, semi-evergreen perennial, spreading by rhizomes and stolons, with 3-palmate, shallowly lobed and toothed leaves, to 6cm (2½in) long, each composed of 2 almost diamond-shaped lateral leaflets and a rounded terminal leaflet. In late spring and early summer, bears loose cymes of 3–7 saucer-shaped, bright yellow flowers, 1.5cm (½in) across. ↕ to 10cm (4in), ↔ 60cm (24in) or more. C., E., and S. Europe, Russia (E. Siberia), China, Japan. ❄❄❄

W. trifolia see *W. ternata.*

Waldsteinia ternata

▷**Wallflower** see *Erysimum, E. cheiri*
Siberian see *E.* x *allionii*
Western see *E. asperum*

▷**Wallpepper** see *Sedum acre*

▷**Walnut** see *Juglans*
African see *Schotia brachypetala*
Black see *Juglans nigra*
Californian see *Juglans californica*
Common see *Juglans regia*
Japanese see *Juglans ailantifolia*
Manchurian see *Juglans mandshurica*
Texan see *Juglans microcarpa*

▷**Wandering Jew** see *Tradescantia fluminensis, T. zebrina*

▷**Wandflower** see *Dierama, Galax*

▷**Wapato** see *Sagittaria latifolia*

▷**Waratah** see *Telopea*
Braidwood see *T. mongaensis*
Common see *T. speciosissima*
Gippsland see *T. oreades*
Monga see *T. mongaensis*
Sydney see *T. speciosissima*
Tasmanian see *T. truncata*
Victorian see *T. oreades*

WASHINGTONIA

ARECACEAE/PALMAE

Genus of 2 species of single-stemmed palms from rocky, arid areas in S.W. USA and N. Mexico. Deeply lobed, fan-shaped leaves are borne in terminal heads that form a dense, shaggy thatch on the trunk as they die back. Because of fire risk, this dead material is often removed in cultivation. Tubular, creamy white or creamy pink flowers, each with 3 petal lobes, are borne in slender, arching panicles between the leaves. In frost-prone climates, grow young plants as houseplants or in a temperate or warm greenhouse. In warmer areas, use as lawn specimens or as avenue trees.

• **HARDINESS** Frost tender.

• **CULTIVATION** Under glass, grow in loam-based potting compost (JI No.3), with added leaf mould and sharp sand, in full light. When in growth, water moderately and apply a balanced liquid fertilizer monthly; keep almost dry in winter. Outdoors, grow in fertile, well-drained soil in full sun.

• **PROPAGATION** Sow seed at 24°C (75°F) in spring.

• **PESTS AND DISEASES** Red spider mites and scale insects may be troublesome under glass.

W. filamentosa see *W. filifera.*

W. filifera 🌴 syn. *W. filamentosa* (Desert fan palm, Northern washingtonia). Medium-sized to large palm with a robust, columnar trunk. Leaf-stalks are sharply toothed at the bases, and the fan-shaped, grey-green blades, 1.5–3m (5–10ft) long, are erect at first, then spreading and arching, with filaments hanging from the slender lobes. Dead foliage forms an even skirt that clothes the trunk from top to bottom. Bears tubular, creamy white flowers in panicles to 5m (15ft) long, usually in summer. ↕ 15–20m (50–70ft), ↔ 3–6m (10–20ft). USA (S. California, S. Arizona). ❁ (min. 8–10°C/46–50°F)

W. robusta ■ 🌴 (Thread palm). Tall, fast-growing palm with a slender trunk that gradually tapers from ground level to the crown. Leaf-stalks are sharply toothed throughout their length, and the fan-shaped, bright green blades, to

Washingtonia robusta

1m (3ft) long, have arching lobe tips, with inconspicuous or no filaments. Dead foliage forms a shaggy skirt that clothes the trunk. Tubular, creamy pink flowers are borne in panicles to 3m (10ft) long, usually in summer. Suitable for coastal gardens. ↕ to 25m (80ft), ↔ 2.5–5m (8–15ft). N. Mexico. ❀ (min. 8–10°C/46–50°F)

▷ **Washingtonia, Northern** see *Washingtonia filifera*
▷ **Water fringe** see *Nymphoides peltata*
▷ **Water hyssop** see *Bacopa*
▷ **Water lily** see *Nymphaea*
Amazon see *Victoria amazonica*
Australian see *Nymphaea gigantea*
Cape blue see *Nymphaea capensis*
Egyptian see *Nymphaea lotus*
Giant see *Victoria*
Royal see *Victoria amazonica*
Santa Cruz see *Victoria cruziana*
White see *Nymphaea alba*
Yellow see *Nymphaea mexicana*
▷ **Watermint** see *Mentha aquatica*
▷ **Water shield, Carolina** see *Cabomba caroliniana*
▷ **Water soldier** see *Stratiotes aloides*

WATSONIA

IRIDACEAE

Genus of approximately 60 species of cormous perennials, usually found on rocky or grassy slopes and plateaux in South Africa and Madagascar. They have erect, usually sword-shaped, basal leaves, and are cultivated for their showy spikes of horizontal, tubular, red, orange, pink, or white flowers, with curved tubes and 6 tepal lobes; the flowers are borne on erect stems at various times of the year. They are only suitable for outdoor cultivation in areas where there is little or no frost. In frost-prone areas, grow in a cool greenhouse or conservatory; spring- and summer-growing species may be grown in a border outdoors, and lifted in autumn for storage in a dry, frost-free place.

• **HARDINESS** Half hardy.
• **CULTIVATION** Under glass, grow in loam-based potting compost (JI No.2), with added sharp sand and leaf mould, in full sun. In growth, water freely and apply a balanced liquid fertilizer every month. Keep just moist when dormant. Outdoors, grow in light, well-drained soil that does not dry out in summer. Where frost is likely, protect with a dry winter mulch.

Watsonia pillansii

Watsonia 'Stanford Scarlet'

• **PROPAGATION** Sow seed at 13–18°C (55–64°F) in autumn. Divide in spring.
• **PESTS AND DISEASES** Trouble free.

W. aletroides. Clump-forming, cormous perennial with sword-shaped, glossy leaves, 20–40cm (8–16in) long, overtopped from late winter to spring by unbranched spikes of up to 12 tubular, orange-red flowers, 5cm (2in) long, the tepal lobes not spreading. ↕ 60cm (24in), ↔ 10cm (4in). South Africa (Western Cape). ✲
W. ardernei see *W. borbonica* subsp. *ardernei.*
W. beatricis see *W. pillansii.*
W. borbonica, syn. *W. pyramidata.* Clump-forming, cormous perennial with narrowly sword-shaped leaves, to 75cm (30in) long. In summer, bears branched spikes of up to 20 slightly irregular, bright pink flowers, 3cm (1¼in) long, with spreading tepal lobes and white lines at the base of each tepal. ↕ 1–1.5m (3–5ft), ↔ 10cm (4in). South Africa (Western Cape). ✲. **subsp. *ardernei***, syn. *W. ardernei*, has usually white, rarely pink flowers.
W. bulbillifera see *W. meriania* var. *bulbillifera.*
W. fourcadei. Robust, clump-forming, cormous perennial with sword-shaped leaves, 30–60cm (12–24in) long. Dense, branched spikes of 20–40 tubular, pink, orange, or red flowers, 6cm (2½in) long, are produced in spring and summer. ↕ 1.5m (5ft), ↔ 10cm (4in). South Africa (Western Cape). ✲
W. humilis. Slender, clump-forming, cormous perennial with lance-shaped leaves, to 30cm (12in) long. In spring or early summer, produces unbranched spikes of up to 12 tubular flowers, 3–4.5cm (1¼–1¾in) long, either white with pink outside, or pink with darker pink outside. ↕ 30cm (12in), ↔ 8cm (3in). South Africa (Western Cape). ✲
W. marginata. Clump-forming, cormous perennial with sword-shaped leaves, 75cm (30in) long. From spring to early summer, bears dense, branched spikes of few to many tubular, mauve-pink flowers, 2cm (¾in) long, with spreading tepal lobes and white and purple markings. ↕ to 2m (6ft), ↔ 15cm (6in). South Africa (Western Cape). ✲
W. meriania. Clump-forming, cormous perennial with sword-shaped leaves, 30–60cm (12–24in) long. In summer, produces branched spikes of up to 25 tubular flowers, 2–2.5cm (¾–1in) long, with spreading tepal lobes, in bright rose-red, rarely scarlet or white. ↕ 0.5–2m (1¾–6ft), ↔ 15cm (6in). South Africa. (Eastern Cape, Western Cape, KwaZulu/Natal). ✲. **var. *bulbillifera***, syn. *W. bulbillifera*, has flowers 3cm (1¼in) long, and bears bulbils among the flower spikes.
W. pillansii ■ syn. *W. beatricis.* Slender, clump-forming, cormous perennial producing sword-shaped leaves, 25–60cm (10–24in) long. From summer to autumn, bears branched spikes of 20–25 tubular, bright orange to orange-red flowers, to 5cm (2in) long, with spreading tepal lobes. ↕ 50–120cm (20–48in), ↔ 10cm (4in). South Africa (Western Cape, Eastern Cape, KwaZulu/Natal, Mpumalanga). ✲
W. pyramidata see *W. borbonica.*
***W.* 'Stanford Scarlet'** ■ Slender, clump-forming, cormous perennial with sword-shaped leaves, 40–100cm (16–39in) long. Bears unbranched spikes of 10–12 tubular, orange-scarlet flowers, 3cm (1¼in) long, with spreading tepal lobes, in late spring or summer. ↕ 0.8–1.4m (32–54in), ↔ 15cm (6in). ✲

▷ ***Wattakaka*** see *Dregea*
W. sinensis see *D. sinensis*
▷ **Wattle** see *Acacia*
Black see *Acacia mearnsii*
Cape see *Paraserianthes lophantha*
Cootamundra see *Acacia baileyana*
Drummond's see *Acacia drummondii*
Early black see *Acacia decurrens*
Green see *Acacia decurrens*
Hedge see *Acacia paradoxa*
Knife-leaf see *Acacia cultriformis*
Ovens see *Acacia pravissima*
Queensland silver see *Acacia podalyriifolia*
Silver see *Acacia dealbata, A. retinodes*
Swamp see *Acacia retinodes, Paraserianthes lophantha*
White sallow see *Acacia floribunda*
▷ **Wax flower** see *Eriostemon, Hoya, Jamesia americana*
Long-leaf see *Eriostemon myoporoides*
Philippine see *Etlingera elatior*
▷ **Wax, Geraldton** see *Chamelaucium uncinatum*
▷ **Wax plant** see *Hoya carnosa*
▷ **Wax tree** see *Rhus succedanea*
▷ **Wayfaring tree** see *Viburnum lantana*
▷ **Weather prophet** see *Dimorphotheca pluvialis*

WEBEROCEREUS

CACTACEAE

Genus of about 5 species of climbing or pendent, epiphytic or rock-dwelling, perennial cacti from mostly rainforest habitats in Mexico, Guatemala, Nicaragua, Costa Rica, and Panama. They have aerial roots and spiny, fleshy stems that may be 3- or 4-angled, slender and cylindrical, or flat and leaf-like with scalloped margins. Nocturnal, cup- or funnel-shaped, pink or greenish or yellowish white flowers are produced in midsummer, followed by spherical to oblong, warty fruits with short, spiny or hairy areoles. Where temperatures drop below 15°C (59°F), grow in a warm greenhouse; in warmer climates, use outdoors in a courtyard garden or against a wall.

• **HARDINESS** Frost tender.

Weberocereus biolleyi

• **CULTIVATION** Under glass, grow in epiphytic cactus compost, with added leaf mould, in bright filtered light and high humidity. From spring to early autumn, water freely, apply a half-strength, balanced liquid fertilizer every 4 or 5 weeks, and mist daily with tepid water. Keep just moist at other times. Outdoors, grow in gritty, moderately fertile, sharply drained soil in partial shade. See also pp.48–49.
• **PROPAGATION** Sow seed at 19–24°C (66–75°F), or take cuttings of stem sections, both in spring or summer.
• **PESTS AND DISEASES** Scale insects may attack plants if left dry.

W. biolleyi ▣ Mainly pendent cactus with cylindrical or irregularly 4-angled stems, 5mm (¼in) thick, sometimes branching. Small, white-woolly areoles occasionally bear 1–3 very short, fine yellow spines. Funnel-shaped, whitish pink flowers, 3–5cm (1¼–2in) long, with dark pink outer petals, are borne in midsummer. ↕ 80cm (32in), ↔ 30cm (12in). Costa Rica. ❄ (min. 15°C/59°F)
W. bradei, syn. *Eccremocactus bradei*. Pendent cactus with flat, leaf-like, wavy-margined, jointed branches, to 10cm (4in) across; these produce small, pale brown-woolly areoles, each with one dark brown spine. Funnel-shaped white flowers, 6–7cm (2½–3in) long, with slightly expanding, fleshy petals, pale pink outside, are borne from the upper areoles from spring to autumn. ↕↔ 60cm (24in). Costa Rica. ❄ (min. 15°C/59°F)
W. glaber, syn. *Werckleocereus glaber*. Climbing cactus with 3-angled, toothed, pale green stems, 2.5–4.5cm (1–1¾in) thick. Small, brown-woolly areoles bear 2–4 yellow or brown spines. Cup-shaped white flowers, 10–12cm (4–5in) long, with pale greenish brown outer petals, are borne in midsummer. ↕ 3m (10ft), ↔ 60cm (24in). Mexico, Guatemala, Costa Rica. ❄ (min. 15°C/59°F)

WEDELIA

ASTERACEAE/COMPOSITAE

Genus of about 70 species of erect, prostrate, or climbing, hairy annuals, evergreen perennials and soft-stemmed or woody shrubs, found near coasts in tropical and subtropical regions. They have opposite, usually oblong to elliptic or obovate, toothed or lobed leaves, and are grown for their daisy-like yellow flowerheads, borne either singly or in few-headed clusters in summer. In frost-

Wedelia trilobata

prone areas, grow as houseplants, or in a warm greenhouse, or use outdoors in summer in containers. In warmer areas, *W. trilobata* is a rampant ground-cover plant, and is also useful for growing in dry shade under trees.
• **HARDINESS** Frost tender.
• **CULTIVATION** Grow in any well-drained soil or potting compost.
• **PROPAGATION** Sow seed at 18°C (64°F), divide, or root stem-tip cuttings, at any time.
• **PESTS AND DISEASES** Trouble free.

W. trilobata ▣ Creeping, evergreen perennial, rooting at the leaf nodes and spreading widely. The elliptic or obovate, mid- to dark green leaves, 12cm (5in) long, are usually 3-lobed, sometimes entire or barely lobed. Solitary, daisy-like yellow flowerheads, 2cm (¾in) across, are borne from late spring to autumn. ↕ 15–20cm (6–8in), ↔ 2m (6ft) or more. USA (Florida), West Indies, Central America, tropical South America. ❄ (min. 13°C/55°F)

▷ **Weeping willow** see *Salix babylonica*
Golden see *Salix* x *sepulcralis* 'Chrysocoma'

WEIGELA

CAPRIFOLIACEAE

Genus of 12 species of mostly spreading to upright, deciduous shrubs found in scrub and woodland margins in E. Asia. They have opposite, oblong to ovate or elliptic, toothed leaves, usually up to 10cm (4in) long. Weigelas are cultivated for their showy, bell- to funnel-shaped, pink to red, sometimes white or yellow flowers; these are usually 4cm (1½in) long, and are borne singly or in corymbs or cymes of 3 or 4, usually on short lateral twigs on the previous year's branches. Suitable for a mixed or shrub border, or for open woodland.
• **HARDINESS** Fully hardy.
• **CULTIVATION** Grow in any fertile, well-drained soil in full sun or partial shade. Pruning group 2.
• **PROPAGATION** Sow seed in containers in a cold frame in autumn; weigelas hybridize readily, so seed may not come true. Root greenwood cuttings in early summer; semi-ripe cuttings with bottom heat in midsummer; hardwood cuttings from autumn to winter.
• **PESTS AND DISEASES** Leaves may be attacked by leaf and bud eelworm, and honey fungus.

Weigela 'Eva Rathke' (inset: flower detail)

***W.* 'Abel Carrière'.** Spreading shrub with oval, dark green leaves. Bell-shaped, dark pinkish red flowers, with yellow-spotted throats, open from purple-red buds in late spring and early summer. ↕↔ 2m (6ft). ❄❄❄
***W.* 'Briant Rubidor'**, syn. *W.* 'Olympiade'. Spreading shrub with oval, leaves, to 8cm (3in) long, yellow-green at first, turning bright yellow or sometimes becoming margined with yellow. In late spring and early summer, bears bell-shaped, dark ruby-red flowers, 3cm (1¼in) long. Best in partial shade. ↕↔ 2m (6ft). ❄❄❄
***W.* 'Bristol Ruby'.** Vigorous, upright shrub with oval, dark green leaves and usually bell-shaped, dark red flowers, opening from very dark red buds, in late spring and early summer. ↕ 2.5m (8ft), ↔ 2m (6ft). ❄❄❄
***W.* 'Bristol Snowflake'** see *W.* 'Snowflake'.
***W.* 'Candida'.** Spreading, bushy shrub with oval, bright green leaves and bell-shaped, pure white flowers, borne in late spring and early summer. ↕↔ 2.5m (8ft). ❄❄❄
***W.* 'Carnaval'.** Vigorous, upright shrub with oval, dark green leaves, to 10cm

Weigela florida 'Foliis Purpureis'

(4in) or more long. Bell-shaped flowers, to 5cm (2in) long, in a combination of pale pink, white, and dark pink, are borne in late spring and early summer. ↕ 2.5m (8ft), ↔ 2m (6ft). ❄❄❄
***W.* 'Eva Rathke'** ▣ Compact, upright shrub with oval, dark green leaves and broadly funnel-shaped, dark crimson flowers, opening from dark red buds in late spring and early summer. ↕↔ 1.5m (5ft). ❄❄❄
***W. florida*.** Spreading shrub with arching shoots and oval, tapered, dark green leaves. Produces corymbs of funnel-shaped, dark pink flowers, 3cm (1¼in) long, pale pink to nearly white inside, in late spring and early summer. ↕↔ 2.5m (8ft). N. China, Korea. ❄❄❄. **'Foliis Purpureis'** ▣ has bronze-green

Weigela florida 'Variegata'

Weigela 'Looymansii Aurea'

foliage; ↕1m (3ft), ↔1.5m (5ft).
'Variegata' ■ is compact, with white-margined, grey-green leaves; ↕↔ 2–2.5m (6–9ft).
***W.* 'Looymansii Aurea'** ■ Slow-growing, spreading shrub with arching shoots and oval, golden yellow leaves, 8cm (3in) long, narrowly margined with red. Bears bell-shaped, pale pink flowers in late spring and early summer. Best in partial shade. ↕↔ 1.5m (5ft). ❄❄❄
W. middendorffiana. Upright shrub with oval, bright green leaves, to 8cm (3in) long. Bell-shaped, pale yellow flowers, often with conspicuous, orange or red throat markings, are borne in terminal cymes from mid-spring to midsummer. ↕↔ 1.5m (5ft). N.E. Russia, N. China, Korea, Japan. ❄❄❄
***W.* 'Minuet'.** Compact, spreading shrub with oval, bronze-green leaves, to 8cm (3in) long. Bears bell-shaped, slightly fragrant, dark pink flowers, with yellow throats, in late spring and early summer. ↕75cm (30in), ↔1.2m (4ft). ❄❄❄
***W.* 'Olympiade'** see *W.* 'Briant Rubidor'.
W. praecox. Upright shrub with oval, dark green leaves, hairy beneath. In late spring and early summer, bears corymbs of funnel-shaped, fragrant pink flowers with yellow throats. ↕2.5m (8ft), ↔2m (6ft). N.E. Russia, Korea, Japan. ❄❄❄.
'Variegata' has leaves with creamy yellow margins that turn white with age.
***W.* 'Snowflake'**, syn. *W.* 'Bristol Snowflake'. Spreading shrub with ovate, dark green leaves and bell-shaped, pure white flowers, borne profusely in late spring and early summer. ↕1.2m (4ft), ↔1.5m (5ft). ❄❄❄

▷ ***Weingartia*** see *Rebutia*
W. neocumingii see *R. neocumingii*

WELDENIA

COMMELINACEAE

Genus of one species of tuberous perennial occurring in the mountains of Mexico and Guatemala. *W. candida* is grown for its rosettes of large, simple leaves and its stalkless cymes of cup-shaped white flowers. Grow in a raised bed; in regions with cool, damp winters, it is best grown in an alpine house.

- **HARDINESS** Frost hardy.
- **CULTIVATION** Grow in gritty, moderately fertile, sharply drained soil in full sun. Protect from winter wet. In an alpine house, grow in deep containers in a mix of equal parts loam, leaf mould,

Weldenia candida

and grit. Water freely in growth; reduce water as leaves wither, and keep barely moist when dormant in winter. Repot annually in autumn.

- **PROPAGATION** Sow seed as soon as ripe in containers in a cold frame. Divide in spring. Take root cuttings in winter.
- **PESTS AND DISEASES** Aphids and whiteflies may be a problem under glass.

W. candida ■ Tuberous perennial with rosettes of lance-shaped, pointed, wavy-margined, slightly leathery leaves, 5–20cm (2–8in) long. In late spring and early summer, bears a long succession of upright, cup-shaped, pure white flowers, to 3cm (1¼in) across. ↕↔ to 15cm (6in). Mexico, Guatemala. ❄❄

▷ **Wellingtonia** see *Sequoiadendron giganteum*

WELWITSCHIA

WELWITSCHIACEAE

Genus of one species of prostrate, dioecious, evergreen perennial from deserts, mainly coastal, in Angola and Namibia. It has a large but relatively shallow tap root with many lateral roots just below ground level. The fleshy, leathery, mid- or grey-green leaves are strap-shaped, and the inflorescences are cone-like. In their natural habitat, male plants produce masses of pollen, which is carried on the wind to female plants. In summer, females can produce up to 100 conical to spherical floral cones, but there is no record of welwitschias blooming in cultivation, except in botanic gardens. Where temperatures

Welwitschia mirabilis

drop below 19°C (66°F), grow in a warm greenhouse; in warmer climates, use in a desert garden. Its adaptation to the extreme conditions of its natural habitat means it is difficult to cultivate.

- **HARDINESS** Frost tender.
- **CULTIVATION** Under glass, grow in a mixture of 2 parts sharp, granitic sand and 1 part each loam-based potting compost (JI No.2), peat, and leaf mould. Provide full light and low humidity. Grow in deep containers, or in a clay drainpipe, and top-dress with crushed limestone. From spring to autumn, water moderately and apply a balanced liquid fertilizer every 6–8 weeks. Keep completely dry in winter. Outdoors, grow in gritty, poor, sharply drained soil, with added leaf mould, in full sun. See also pp.48–49.
- **PROPAGATION** Sow seed at 19–24°C (66–75°F) as soon as ripe; sow in tall, narrow containers that allow for the growth of the tap root.
- **PESTS AND DISEASES** Trouble free.

W. bainesii see *W. mirabilis.*
W. mirabilis ■ syn. *W. bainesii.* Prostrate, dioecious, evergreen perennial with a short, conical caudex becoming swollen with age, often 1m (3ft) across in very old plants, and divided in half by a groove. The 2 strap-shaped, often curling, leathery, fleshy, mid- or grey-green leaves, 2m (6ft) or more long, grow from marginal grooves on the crown. Cones are produced in axillary cymes from the top of the caudex in summer: female cones, 5cm (2in) long, are brownish green; male cones, 3cm (1¼in) long, are reddish brown. ↕45cm (18in) or more, ↔4m (12ft). Angola, Namibia. ❀ (min. 19°C/66°F)

▷ ***Werckleocereus glaber*** see *Weberocereus glaber*

WESTRINGIA

LABIATAE/LAMIACEAE

Genus of about 25 species of rounded to erect, evergreen shrubs from dry coastal heathland, scrub, sands, and dry forest in Australia. They are cultivated for their flowers and foliage. The crowded, narrowly linear to ovate, rosemary-like leaves are produced in whorls of 3–5. The tubular, white to pale blue or mauve flowers are 2-lipped, the upper lip longer, erect and 2-lobed, the lower lip divided into 3 spreading lobes; the flowers are borne singly in the uppermost leaf axils or in terminal clusters. In frost-prone areas, grow in a cool greenhouse. In milder regions, use in a border, or as a hedge or screen.

- **HARDINESS** Frost tender; some species (including *W. fruticosa*) may survive short spells just below 0°C (32°F).
- **CULTIVATION** Under glass, grow in loam-based potting compost (JI No.2), with added leaf mould and sharp sand, in full light. When in growth, water moderately and apply a balanced liquid fertilizer monthly. Water sparingly in winter. Outdoors, grow in moderately fertile, moist but well-drained soil in full sun. Pruning group 9; trim hedges in late spring and late summer. May need restrictive pruning under glass.
- **PROPAGATION** Sow seed at 13–18°C (55–64°F) in spring. Root greenwood cuttings in early summer, or semi-ripe

Westringia fruticosa

cuttings with some bottom heat in midsummer.

- **PESTS AND DISEASES** Trouble free.

W. fruticosa ■ syn. *W. rosmariniformis* (Australian rosemary). Erect, bushy, rounded shrub, becoming more open as it matures, with linear to narrowly lance-shaped leaves, 1.5–2.5cm (½–1in) long, mid- to deep green above, white-felted beneath. Solitary, tubular, white to very pale blue flowers, 1.5cm (½in) across, with darker freckling in the throats, are borne in axillary cymes from late spring to early autumn. ↕↔ 1–1.5m (3–5ft). Australia (coastal New South Wales). ❀ (min. 5°C/41°F)
W. rosmariniformis see *W. fruticosa.*

▷ **Whauwhaupaku** see *Pseudopanax arboreus*
▷ **Wheat, Puffed** see *Briza maxima*
▷ **Wheatgrass, Intermediate** see *Elymus hispidus*
▷ **Whin** see *Ulex europaeus*
▷ **Whinberry** see *Vaccinium myrtillus*
▷ **Whitebeam** see *Sorbus aria*
Swedish see *S. intermedia*
▷ **White cup** see *Nierembergia repens*
▷ **White paint brush** see *Haemanthus albiflos*
▷ **White pine,**
Eastern see *Pinus strobus*
Japanese see *Pinus parviflora*
Mexican see *Pinus ayacahuite*
Western see *Pinus monticola*
▷ **White rose of York** see *Rosa* 'Alba Maxima'
▷ **Whitethorn, Coast** see *Ceanothus incanus*
▷ **White trumpet** see *Sarracenia leucophylla*
▷ **Whitey wood** see *Acradenia frankliniae*
▷ **Whitlow-wort** see *Paronychia*
▷ **Whorlflower** see *Morina longifolia*
▷ **Whortleberry** see *Vaccinium, V. myrtillus*
Caucasian see *V. arctostaphylos*
Red see *V. parvifolium*
▷ **Widow's tears** see *Commelina*

WIGANDIA

HYDROPHYLLACEAE

Genus of 5 species of evergreen, upright to spreading perennials, subshrubs, shrubs, and small trees occurring in woodland and roadsides in tropical USA, Central America, and South America. They are cultivated for their flowers and foliage. The large, alternate,

Wigandia caracasana

simple, oblong to broadly ovate, toothed leaves are covered in stinging hairs. Tubular-based, bell-shaped, usually lilac to violet flowers, with 5 broad, wide-spreading lobes, are borne in terminal panicles. Where temperatures fall below 5–7°C (41–45°F) in winter, grow in a cool or temperate greenhouse or use as annuals for summer bedding. In milder areas, grow as specimen plants. Contact with foliage may aggravate skin allergies.
• **HARDINESS** Frost tender.
• **CULTIVATION** Under glass, grow in loam-based potting compost (JI No.2) in full light. During the growing season, water moderately and apply a balanced liquid fertilizer monthly. Water sparingly in winter. Outdoors, grow in fertile, moist but well-drained soil in full sun. Pruning group 1; may need restrictive pruning under glass.
• **PROPAGATION** Sow seed at 13–18°C (55–64°F) in spring. Take greenwood cuttings in early summer.
• **PESTS AND DISEASES** Red spider mites may be troublesome under glass.

W. caracasana ▣ syn. *W. macrophylla*. Open, soft-stemmed, evergreen sub-shrub with robust, sparsely branched, yellow- to white-woolly stems. Long-stalked, ovate, coarsely toothed leaves, 30–60cm (12–24in) long, heart-shaped at the bases, are mid- to deep green above, hoary beneath. Bears bell-shaped, white-tubed, light violet flowers, 2cm (¾in) across, in large, terminal panicles, to 30cm (12in) or more long, mainly in summer. ↕ 3–4m (10–12ft), ↔ 2–3.5m (6–11ft). Mexico to Colombia. ❀ (min. 7°C/45°F)
W. macrophylla see *W. caracasana*.

▷ ***Wigginsia*** see *Parodia*
W. erinacea see *P. erinacea*
W. vorwerkiana see *P. erinacea*

WIKSTROEMIA

THYMELAEACEAE

Genus of approximately 70 species of deciduous or evergreen, spreading to upright shrubs and trees, closely related to *Daphne*. They are usually found in habitats ranging from dry slopes to wet woodland in mountainous areas from the Himalayas to E. Asia, Sri Lanka, Australia, and the Pacific islands. The alternate or opposite leaves are oblong-lance-shaped to broadly ovate. Tubular or salverform, usually yellow flowers are produced in terminal spikes, racemes, cymes, or, occasionally, panicles. *W. canescens*, valued for its flowers, will grow in a sheltered position in a woodland garden. In frost-prone areas, grow the tender species in a cool or temperate greenhouse.
• **HARDINESS** Fully hardy to frost tender.
• **CULTIVATION** Grow in any well-drained soil in full sun to partial shade. In frost-prone areas, shelter from cold, drying winds. Pruning group 1.
• **PROPAGATION** Sow seed in containers in a cold frame in autumn.
• **PESTS AND DISEASES** Trouble free.

W. canescens. Upright, deciduous shrub with slender, arching shoots. Alternate to nearly opposite, elliptic leaves are up to 8cm (3in) long. In late summer and early autumn, purple flower buds open to tubular, yellow to greenish yellow flowers, 1.5cm (½in) long, each with a slender, slightly curved tube and 4 short lobes, in terminal cymes. ↕ 1.8m (6ft), ↔ 1.5m (5ft). Sri Lanka, Himalayas, China. ❄❄

▷ ***Wilcoxia albiflora*** see *Echinocereus leucanthus*
▷ ***Wilcoxia schmollii*** see *Echinocereus schmollii*
▷ **Wild flowers** see p.43
▷ **Wild Irishman** see *Discaria toumatou*
▷ **Wild liquorice** see *Astragalus glycyphyllos*
▷ **Wild Spaniard** see *Aciphylla colensoi*
▷ **Willow** see *Salix*
Bay see *Salix pentandra*
Coyote see *Salix exigua*
Crack see *Salix fragilis*
Creeping see *Salix repens*
Cricket-bat see *Salix alba* var. *caerulea*
Desert see *Pittosporum phillyreoides*
Golden see *Salix alba* var. *vitellina*
Golden weeping see *Salix* x *sepulcralis* 'Chrysocoma'
Hoary see *Salix elaeagnos*
Kilmarnock see *Salix caprea* 'Kilmarnock'
Musk see *Salix aegyptiaca*
Silver see *Salix alba* var. *sericea*
Swiss see *Salix helvetica*
Thyme-leaved see *Salix serpyllifolia*
Violet see *Salix daphnoides*
Weeping see *Salix babylonica*
White see *Salix alba*
Woolly see *Salix lanata*
▷ **Willow-bell** see *Campanula persicifolia* var. *planiflora*
▷ **Willow herb** see *Epilobium*

x WILSONARA

ORCHIDACEAE

Hybrid genus of evergreen orchids, derived from crosses between *Cochlioda*, *Odontoglossum*, and *Oncidium*. Conical, flattened pseudobulbs grow from a rhizome, each pseudobulb producing 1 or 2 soft, linear to lance-shaped leaves at its apex. The inflorescences, either tall panicles with 100 or more flowers, or shorter panicles of larger flowers, are produced from the bases of the pseudobulbs. The rounded, sometimes star-shaped flowers are very variably coloured, often having conspicuous markings.
• **HARDINESS** Frost tender.
• **CULTIVATION** Cool-growing orchids. Grow in epiphytic orchid compost in

x *Wilsonara* Hambühren Stern 'Cheam'

containers that restrict the roots. In summer, provide bright filtered light and high humidity, water freely, applying a fertilizer at every third watering, and mist twice daily. In winter, admit full light, water sparingly, provide moderate humidity, and mist daily. See also p.46.
• **PROPAGATION** Divide when plants fill their containers and "flow" over the sides.
• **PESTS AND DISEASES** Aphids, red spider mites, and mealybugs may be a problem.

x *W.* Hambühren Stern 'Cheam' ▣ (*Oncidium tigrinum* x x *Odontioda* Lippestern). Evergreen orchid with 1 or 2 linear leaves, 23cm (9in) long. Almost circular flowers, 6cm (2½in) across, are rich brown and yellow, and are borne in long panicles at any time of year. ↕ 60cm (24in), ↔ 30cm (12in). ❀ (min. 10°C/50°F; max. 30°C/86°F)

▷ **Windflower** see *Anemone*, *A. nemorosa*, *Zephyranthes*
▷ **Winecups** see *Geissorhiza radians*
▷ **Wing nut** see *Pterocarya*
Caucasian see *P. fraxinifolia*
Chinese see *P. stenoptera*
Japanese see *P. rhoifolia*
▷ ***Wintera aromatica*** see *Drimys winteri*
▷ **Winter aconite** see *Eranthis*, *E. hyemalis*
▷ **Winterberry** see *Ilex verticillata*
Japanese see *Ilex serrata*
▷ **Wintergreen** see *Gaultheria procumbens*, *Pyrola*
Round-leaved see *Pyrola rotundifolia*
▷ **Winter heath** see *Erica carnea*
▷ **Winter's bark** see *Drimys winteri*
▷ **Wintersweet** see *Acokanthera oblongifolia*, *Chimonanthus*, *C. praecox*
▷ **Wire-netting bush** see *Corokia cotoneaster*
▷ **Wishbone flower** see *Torenia*, *T. fournieri*
▷ **Wistaria** see *Wisteria*

WISTERIA

Wistaria

LEGUMINOSAE/PAPILIONACEAE

Genus of about 10 species of twining, woody, deciduous climbers found in moist woodland and on streambanks in China, Korea, Japan, and C. and S. USA. They have alternate, pinnate, dark green leaves, to 35cm (14in) or more long, with ovate to lance-shaped or elliptic leaflets. They are cultivated for their showy, pea-like, fragrant flowers, borne in usually pendent racemes in spring or summer, followed by pendent, bean-like green seed pods. Train a wistaria against a wall, into a tree, over an arch or pergola, or as a free-standing half-standard. The stems twine anticlockwise around the support. All parts may cause severe discomfort if ingested.
• **HARDINESS** Fully hardy, but flower buds may be damaged by late frosts.
• **CULTIVATION** Grow in fertile, moist but well-drained soil in full sun or partial shade. Wisterias growing into trees need no training. To train formally, after planting, prune back the leading shoot to 75–90cm (30–36in) above ground level. During the first growing season, tie in lateral shoots to the framework and cut back sublaterals to 2 or 3 buds. In the first winter, cut back laterals by one-third of their length, and sublaterals to 2 or 3 buds; cut back the leading shoot again, to 75–90cm (30–36in) above the point from which the topmost laterals branch. In subsequent years, repeat the pruning of the leader and selection of lateral shoots until the framework has been completed. Once the plant is established, in late summer cut back all shoots not needed to extend the framework, to within 15cm (6in) of the main branches; leave 4–6 leaves on each shoot. In midwinter, reduce these spurs further to 8–10cm (3–4in), leaving only 2 or 3 buds.
• **PROPAGATION** Take basal cuttings from sideshoots in early to midsummer and root with bottom heat. Layer in autumn, or graft in winter.
• **PESTS AND DISEASES** May be attacked by leaf spot, aphids, honey fungus, and brown scale.

W. brachybotrys (Silky wisteria). Twining climber with pinnate, softly hairy leaves, to 35cm (14in) long, each

Wisteria brachybotrys 'Shiro-kapitan'

W

Wisteria floribunda 'Alba'

composed of 9–13 ovate to lance-shaped leaflets. Pea-like, fragrant, yellow-marked, violet to white flowers are produced in racemes, to 15cm (6in) long, in early summer; they are followed by bean-like, velvety green seed pods, to 20cm (8in) long. ↕9m (28ft) or more. Garden origin. ❄❄❄. **'Alba'** see 'Shiro-kapitan'. **f. *alba*** see 'Shiro-kapitan'. **'Alba Plena'** see 'Shiro-kapitan'. **'Murasaki-kapitan'**, syn. *W. venusta* 'Violacea', *W. venusta* f. *violacea*, has deep blue-violet flowers with prominent white, slightly yellow-tinged markings on the standards. **f. *plena*** see 'Shiro-kapitan'. **'Shiro-kapitan'** ■ syn. 'Alba', f. *alba*, 'Alba Plena', f. *plena*, *W. venusta*, *W. venusta* 'Alba', *W. venusta* f. *alba*, *W. venusta* 'Alba Plena', produces white flowers with a yellow stain at the base of each standard. Double flowers are occasionally produced.

W. chinensis see *W. sinensis*.

W. floribunda (Japanese wisteria). Vigorous, twining climber with pinnate leaves, each composed of 11–19 ovate to lance-shaped leaflets. In early summer, pea-like, fragrant, blue to violet, pink, or white flowers, the standards marked with white and yellow, are produced in pendent racemes, to 30cm (12in) or more long, the flowers opening gradually from the bases to the tips; they are often followed by bean-like, velvety green seed pods, to 15cm (6in) long. ↕9m (28ft) or more. Japan. ❄❄❄. **'Alba'** ■ syn. 'Shiro-noda', bears white flowers in racemes to 60cm (24in) long. **'Black Dragon'** see *W.* x *formosa* 'Yae-kokuryu'. **'Double Black Dragon'** see 'Violacea Plena'. **'Hon-beni'** see 'Rosea'. **'Honko'** see 'Rosea'. **'Kyushaku'** see 'Multijuga'. **'Multijuga'** ■ syn. 'Kyushaku', 'Macrobotrys', has lilac-blue flowers in racemes 0.9–1.2m (3–4ft) long. **'Macrobotrys'** see 'Multijuga'. **f. *rosea*** see 'Rosea'. **'Rosea'**, syn. 'Hon-beni', 'Honko', f. *rosea*, has pink flowers in racemes to 45cm (18in) long. **'Shiro-noda'** see 'Alba'. **'Violacea Plena'**, syn. 'Double Black Dragon', has double, violet-blue flowers.

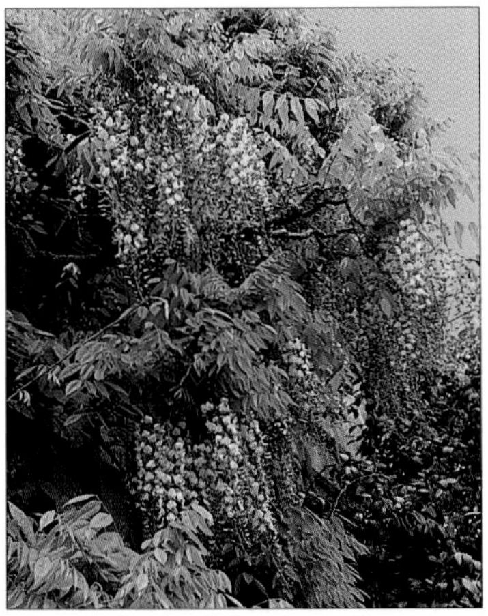

Wisteria floribunda 'Multijuga'

Wisteria x *formosa*

Wisteria sinensis 'Alba'

W.* x *formosa ■ (*W. floribunda* x *W. sinensis*). Vigorous, twining climber with pinnate leaves, each composed of 9–15, broadly ovate to elliptic leaflets. Pea-like, fragrant, violet-blue flowers, with white and yellow markings, are borne in pendent racemes, to 25cm (10in) long, in late spring and early summer, often followed by bean-like, velvety green seed pods, to 15cm (6in) long. ↕9m (28ft) or more. Garden origin. ❄❄❄. **'Yae-kokuryu'**, syn. *W. floribunda* 'Black Dragon', has racemes, 30–50cm (12–20in) long, with purple-violet flowers.

W. sinensis, syn. *W. chinensis* (Chinese wisteria). Vigorous, twining climber with pinnate leaves, each composed of 7–13 elliptic or ovate leaflets. Pea-like, fragrant, lilac-blue to white flowers, in dense, pendent racemes to 30cm (12in) long, are borne in late spring and early summer; they are often followed by bean-like, velvety green seed pods, to 15cm (6in) long. ↕9m (28ft) or more. China. ❄❄❄. **'Alba'** ■ has white flowers. **'Prolific'** bears many lilac-blue to pale violet-blue flowers. **'Sierra Madre'** produces very fragrant, lavender-violet flowers with white-flushed standards.

W. venusta see *W. brachybotrys* 'Shiro-kapitan'.

***W. venusta* 'Alba'** see *W. brachybotrys* 'Shiro-kapitan'.

W. venusta* f. *alba see *W. brachybotrys* 'Shiro-kapitan'.

***W. venusta* 'Alba Plena'** see *W. brachybotrys* 'Shiro-kapitan'.

***W. venusta* 'Violacea'** see *W. brachybotrys* 'Murasaki-kapitan'.

W. venusta* f. *violacea see *W. brachybotrys* 'Murasaki-kapitan'.

▷**Wisteria,**
Chinese see *Wisteria sinensis*
Japanese see *Wisteria floribunda*
Silky see *Wisteria brachybotrys*
South African see *Bolusanthus*
Water see *Hygrophila difformis*

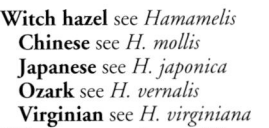

▷**Witch hazel** see *Hamamelis*
Chinese see *H. mollis*
Japanese see *H. japonica*
Ozark see *H. vernalis*
Virginian see *H. virginiana*

▷***Wittia amazonica*** see *Disocactus amazonicus*

▷***Wittiocactus amazonicus*** see *Disocactus amazonicus*

WITTROCKIA

BROMELIACEAE

Genus, closely related to *Nidularium*, of 7 species of rosetted, stemless, evergreen, terrestrial, epiphytic, or rock-dwelling perennials (bromeliads) from mountain areas, to 900m (3,000ft) high, in Brazil. The linear, spiny-margined, scaly leaves, smooth near the tips, are often wide and colourful. In summer, spikes of tubular, usually blue flowers, with 3 separate sepals and 3 petals joined only at their tips, are produced among clusters of leaf-like bracts within the leaf rosettes. In areas where temperatures drop below 18°C (64°F), grow as houseplants or in a warm greenhouse; in warmer climates, use in a humid, moist border.

- **HARDINESS** Frost tender.
- **CULTIVATION** Under glass, grow in standard epiphytic or terrestrial bromeliad compost in bright filtered light. From late spring to early autumn, mist daily with tepid water to maintain moderate humidity, and apply a low-nitrogen liquid fertilizer every 3 or 4 weeks. Outdoors, grow in peaty, leafy, moderately fertile, moist but well-drained soil in a site in partial shade. See also p.47.
- **PROPAGATION** Sow seed at 19–24°C (66–75°F) in spring. Detach offsets in spring or summer.
- **PESTS AND DISEASES** Susceptible to mealybugs.

W. superba ■ Terrestrial, epiphytic, or rock-dwelling, evergreen bromeliad producing linear, pointed, mid-green leaves, to 1m (3ft) long, narrower at the bases, and with brown scales, red tips, and spiny, red or green teeth. Compact, sunken inflorescences, 12cm (5in) wide, consisting of cone-shaped spikes of tubular blue flowers with pointed petals, surrounded by red bracts, are produced on very short scapes in summer. ↕↔1m (3ft) or more. E. Brazil. ❀ (min. 18°C/64°F)

▷**Wood** see *Isatis tinctoria*

Wittrockia superba

W

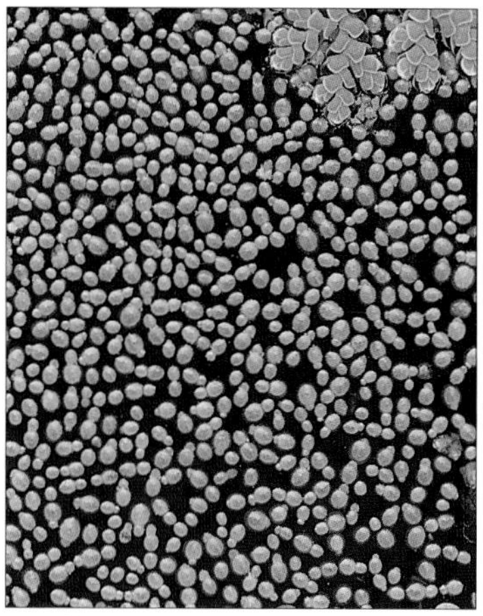

Wolffia arrhiza

Woodsia polystichoides

Woodwardia radicans

WOLFFIA

ARACEAE

Genus of 8 species of semi-evergreen, floating aquatic perennials, similar to duckweeds (*Lemna*) but much smaller and lacking a root, with a wide distribution in Europe, Africa, W. Asia, India, Australia, North America, and E. Brazil. They are the smallest known flowering plants, grown mainly for their curiosity value. In frost-prone areas, grow in an aquarium. In warmer climates, grow in an outdoor pool.

- **HARDINESS** Half hardy to frost tender.
- **CULTIVATION** In an outdoor pool, grow in full sun. In an aquarium, grow at 15–28°C (59–82°F) in full light. See also pp.52–53.
- **PROPAGATION** Detach plantlets as they form.
- **PESTS AND DISEASES** Trouble free.

W. arrhiza ■ Semi-evergreen, floating aquatic perennial with rootless, rounded, bright green fronds, 1mm (1/16in) across. Insignificant, green-tinged white flowers are produced in summer. ↔ indefinite. Europe, Africa, W. Asia, Australia. ✲

▷**Wolf's bane** see *Aconitum lycoctonum*
▷**Wombat berry** see *Eustrephus*
▷**Wonga wonga vine** see *Pandorea pandorana*
▷**Wood anemone** see *Anemone nemorosa*
▷**Woodbine** see *Lonicera periclymenum*
▷**Wood fern, Wallich's** see *Dryopteris wallichiana*
▷**Woodland star** see *Lithophragma*
▷**Wood lily** see *Trillium*
Dwarf white see *T. nivale*
Painted see *T. undulatum*
▷**Wood rose** see *Merremia tuberosa*
▷**Woodruff** see *Asperula*
Sweet see *Galium odoratum*
▷**Woodrush** see *Luzula*
Greater see *L. sylvatica*
Snowy see *L. nivea*

W

WOODSIA

DRYOPTERIDACEAE

Genus of approximately 25 species of small, tufted, deciduous, terrestrial or rock-dwelling ferns occurring in upland and mountainous regions, mainly in the N. hemisphere. They have erect, short rhizomes, and pinnate to 2-pinnate fronds with the pinnae sometimes pinnatifid. Sporangia are in cup-shaped indusia, which have often deeply cut fringes. Suitable for a rock garden.

- **HARDINESS** Fully hardy to frost hardy.
- **CULTIVATION** Grow in sharply drained but moist, fertile soil in partial shade. Position crowns above soil level and surround with small stones. *W. ilvensis* prefers acid soil.
- **PROPAGATION** Sow spores at 15–16°C (59–61°F) as soon as ripe. Divide when dormant. See also p.51.
- **PESTS AND DISEASES** Trouble free.

W. ilvensis (Rusty woodsia). Dwarf, tufted, terrestrial or rock-dwelling fern. In early spring, produces lance-shaped to oblong, pinnate, dull green fronds, to 15cm (6in) long, each composed of 7–25 pairs of ovate to lance-shaped, lobed pinnae, clothed with reddish brown hairs and scales. ↕15cm (6in), ↔ 10cm (4in). Arctic, Europe, North America. ✲✲✲

W. polystichoides ■ (Holly-fern woodsia). Tufted, terrestrial or rock-dwelling fern. In early spring, produces lance-shaped, pinnate, pale green fronds, to 35cm (14in) long, softly hairy on both surfaces and scaly beneath; each is composed of 15–30 pairs of narrowly sickle-shaped or oblong pinnae, with slightly toothed margins. May be damaged by late frosts. ↕10–30cm (4–12in), ↔ 20–40cm (8–16in). E. Asia. ✲✲✲

▷**Woodsia,**
Holly-fern see *Woodsia polystichoides*
Rusty see *Woodsia ilvensis*

WOODWARDIA

Chain fern

BLECHNACEAE

Genus of approximately 10 species of evergreen or deciduous, terrestrial ferns found in damp, sheltered places in warm-temperate regions of Eurasia and North America. Some are creeping plants, found in acid bogs. Most are large, often with spreading and arching, usually pinnate fronds with pinnatifid pinnae, unfurling in spring; bulbils may be produced towards the tips of the fronds or on their upper surfaces. The chain-like arrangement of the sori on the undersides of the pinnae gives rise to the common name. Use to clothe a moist, shady bank, ideally near water.

- **HARDINESS** Fully hardy to frost hardy.
- **CULTIVATION** Grow in neutral, moderately fertile, damp soil in partial shade. In frost-prone climates, shelter from cold, drying winds and protect in winter with a dry mulch.
- **PROPAGATION** Sow spores at 16°C (61°F) in late summer or early autumn. Remove bulbils in autumn. Divide in spring. See also p.51.
- **PESTS AND DISEASES** Trouble free.

W. radicans ■ (European chain fern). Evergreen fern with arching, broadly lance-shaped, pinnate, dark green fronds, to 2m (6ft) tall, producing bulbils near the tips; the pinnatifid pinnae, to 30cm (12in) long, are ovate-lance-shaped, with curved, lance-shaped, finely toothed segments. ↕1.8m (6ft), ↔ 3m (10ft). Atlantic islands, S.W. Europe. ✲✲

W. unigemmata (Asian chain fern). Evergreen fern very similar to *W. radicans*. New foliage emerges brilliant red and fades to brown then green. ↕1m (3ft), ↔ 3m (10ft). Himalayas, E. Asia. ✲✲✲ (borderline)

▷**Wormwood** see *Artemisia, A. absinthium*

WORSLEYA

Blue amaryllis

AMARYLLIDACEAE

Genus of one species of bulbous, evergreen perennial from moist mountain forests in Brazil. It has strap-shaped leaves, and is grown for its large umbels of funnel-shaped flowers, borne on leafless stems in winter. In frost-prone climates, it is suitable for a warm greenhouse or conservatory, although it does not easily flower. In warmer climates, grow in a warm, sunny border.

- **HARDINESS** Frost tender.
- **CULTIVATION** Plant bulbs with the necks just above soil level. Under glass, grow in loam-based potting compost (JI No.2), with added leaf mould and bark chips or sharp sand, in full light. In growth, water freely and apply a balanced liquid fertilizer monthly. Keep barely moist in winter, but do not allow the compost to dry out. Outdoors, grow in fertile, reliably moist but sharply drained soil in full sun.
- **PROPAGATION** Sow seed at 19–24°C (66–75°F) in spring.
- **PESTS AND DISEASES** Trouble free.

W. procera see *W. rayneri*.
W. rayneri, syn. *Hippeastrum procerum, W. procera*. Robust, bulbous, evergreen perennial with arching, strap-shaped leaves, to 1m (3ft) long. In winter, bears umbels of up to 14 funnel-shaped flowers, lilac-blue to white at the bases, 4cm (1½in) across, speckled mauve within; the tubes are 2cm (¾in) long, the curving lobes to 15cm (6in) long. ↕1–1.2m (3–4ft), ↔ 30cm (12in). Brazil. ❀ (min. 15°C/59°F)

▷**Woundwort** see *Stachys*
Hedge see *S. sylvatica*
▷**Wreath,**
Bridal see *Francoa, Spiraea* 'Arguta', *Stephanotis floribunda*
Purple see *Petrea volubilis*
Queen's see *Antigonon, Petrea volubilis*

WULFENIA

SCROPHULARIACEAE

Genus of about 6 species of rosette-forming, evergreen perennials from alpine meadows in C. and S.E. Europe, W. Asia, and the Himalayas. They are grown mainly for their spike-like racemes of tubular, 2-lipped, blue to pinkish purple or occasionally white flowers borne in summer. Leaves are inversely lance-shaped to broadly ovate or oblong. Suitable for a rock garden or wall crevice.

- **HARDINESS** Fully hardy.
- **CULTIVATION** Grow in gritty, humus-rich, moist but well-drained soil in full sun. Protect from winter wet.
- **PROPAGATION** Sow seed in containers in a cold frame in spring or autumn. Divide in spring.
- **PESTS AND DISEASES** Trouble free.

W. amherstiana ■ Evergreen perennial with rosettes of obovate-oblong, coarsely scalloped, conspicuously veined, dark green leaves, 5–15cm (2–6in) long, sparsely hairy beneath. In summer, produces erect stems bearing lax, one-sided racemes, 4–20cm (1½–8in) long, of many small, narrowly tubular, pinkish purple flowers. ↕↔ to 20cm (8in). Afghanistan, W. Himalayas. ✲✲✲

W. carinthiaca. Evergreen perennial with rosettes of scalloped, inversely lance-shaped to obovate, shiny, dark green leaves, to 20cm (8in) long. In summer, bears dense, one-sided racemes, 6–10cm (2½–4in) long, of small, narrowly tubular, deep violet-blue flowers on erect stems. ↕↔ 25cm (10in) or more. S.E. Alps, Albania. ✲✲✲

Wulfenia amherstiana

X

XANTHOCERAS

SAPINDACEAE

Genus of one species of erect, deciduous shrub found in scrub and at woodland margins in N. China. An unusual plant and rare in gardens, *X. sorbifolium* is cultivated for its alternate, pinnate leaves and attractive star-shaped, 5-petalled white flowers, borne in late spring. Suitable for a shrub border, for training against a wall, or for a sunny position in a woodland garden.

- **HARDINESS** Fully hardy.
- **CULTIVATION** Grow in fertile, well-drained soil in full sun; grows best in areas with very hot summers. In frost-prone climates, provide shelter from cold, drying winds in winter. Pruning group 1.
- **PROPAGATION** Sow seed in containers outdoors in autumn. Take root cuttings, or remove rooted suckers, in winter.
- **PESTS AND DISEASES** May be affected by coral spot.

X. sorbifolium ■ Upright, deciduous shrub with stout shoots and pinnate leaves, to 30cm (12in) long, composed of up to 17 narrowly elliptic to lance-shaped, toothed, glossy, dark green leaflets. As the young leaves emerge in late spring, star-shaped white flowers, 3cm (1¼in) across, are terminally borne in upright panicles, 15–20cm (6–8in) long; yellow-green marks at the petal bases mature to brown. ↕ 4m (12ft), ↔ 3m (10ft). N. China. ❄❄❄

Xanthoceras sorbifolium

Xanthophthalmum segetum

XANTHOPHTHALMUM

ASTERACEAE/COMPOSITAE

Genus of 2 species of vigorous, bushy, erect annuals, widespread in dry fields and wasteland in Europe. The alternate, oblong to obovate, light or grey-green leaves are mainly pinnatisect, although towards the stem tips they may be entire. Solitary, daisy-like flowerheads, to 5cm (2in) across, with usually yellow ray-florets and yellow disc-florets, are borne at the ends of the branched shoots in spring and summer. Suitable for an annual border, or for infilling in a herbaceous border. *X. segetum* is also suitable for a wildflower garden.

- **HARDINESS** Fully hardy.
- **CULTIVATION** Grow in well-drained, moderately fertile soil, ideally in full sun.
- **PROPAGATION** Sow seed under glass in spring or *in situ* from spring to early summer.
- **PESTS AND DISEASES** Trouble free.

X. coronarium, syn. *Chrysanthemum coronarium.* Many-branched annual chrysanthemum with pinnatisect, fern-like, light green leaves, 5–7cm (2–3in) long. From late spring to summer, bears daisy-like yellow flowerheads, to 5cm (2in) across. ↕ to 80cm (32in), ↔ to 40cm (16in). Mediterranean. ❄❄❄. **'Primrose Gem'** has primrose-yellow, golden-eyed flowerheads; ↕ to 30–45cm (12–18in).

X. segetum ■ syn. *Chrysanthemum segetum* (Corn marigold). Fleshy annual chrysanthemum, sometimes single-stemmed, with grey-green leaves, 3–5cm (1¼–2in) long, entire towards the stem tips, pinnatisect lower down the stems. Daisy-like yellow flowerheads, to 5cm (2in) across, are produced in summer. Often included in wildflower seed mixtures. ↕ to 80cm (32in), ↔ 30cm (12in). Mediterranean. ❄❄❄. **'Prado'** produces large, golden yellow flowerheads, to 8cm (3in) across, with dark brown central discs.

Xanthorhiza simplicissima

XANTHORHIZA

RANUNCULACEAE

Genus of one species of suckering, deciduous shrub found in moist woodland and on streambanks in E. USA. It is cultivated for its alternate, pinnate leaves, clustered at the shoot tips. Tiny, 5-petalled, star-shaped, brown-purple flowers are produced in pendent clusters of racemes or panicles in spring. *X. simplicissima* provides excellent ground cover in a shady position.

- **HARDINESS** Fully hardy.
- **CULTIVATION** Grow in moist but not waterlogged soil in full or partial shade. Pruning group 1 or 3.
- **PROPAGATION** Sow seed in containers outdoors in autumn. Divide in spring or autumn.
- **PESTS AND DISEASES** Trouble free.

X. apiifolia see *X. simplicissima.*

X. simplicissima ■ syn. *X. apiifolia* (Yellowroot). Thicket-forming shrub with erect shoots and bright green leaves to 30cm (12in) long, bronze at first, often red-purple in autumn, each with 3–5 ovate, deeply lobed, irregularly toothed leaflets. In early to mid-spring, as the leaves emerge, produces brown-purple flowers in pendent racemes or panicles, to 10cm (4in) long. ↕ 60cm (24in), ↔ 1.5m (5ft) or more. E. USA (Pennsylvania to Florida). ❄❄❄

XANTHOSOMA

Malanga, Tannia, Yautia

ARACEAE

Genus of about 60 species of tuberous or clump-forming, small to very large perennials with often very thick stems, from forests and wet places in tropical and subtropical North, Central, and South America and the West Indies. They are cultivated for their handsome, fleshy, long-stalked leaves, which may be arrow- to spear-shaped or pedately divided into 3–18 segments. Their cylindrical or spherical tubers, which are white, orange, pink, or purple inside, are sometimes edible if cooked, as are the stems and leaves of some species. Inflorescences consist of a spadix within a taller spathe, and are borne intermittently throughout the year. In frost-prone areas, grow in a warm greenhouse or conservatory. In warmer areas, grow in a shady border. All parts are toxic if ingested raw; contact with the sap may irritate skin and eyes.

- **HARDINESS** Frost tender.
- **CULTIVATION** Under glass, grow in containers that allow a free root run, in loam-based potting compost (JI No.2), with added well-rotted manure and leaf mould, in moderate light. In growth, water freely and apply a balanced liquid fertilizer every 2–3 weeks. Water moderately in winter. Outdoors, grow in slightly acid, leafy, humus-rich, fertile, well-drained soil in partial shade. Avoid waterlogging.
- **PROPAGATION** Separate tubers at any time of year. Take sections of stems as cuttings in non-tuberous species from spring to autumn.
- **PESTS AND DISEASES** Trouble free.

Xanthosoma 'Hilo Beauty'

Xanthosoma nigrum

***X.* 'Hilo Beauty'** ■ syn. *Alocasia* 'Hilo Beauty'. Robust tuberous perennial with thin-textured, bluntly arrow-shaped leaves, to 40cm (16in) long, mid-green irregularly marked chartreuse-green, and glaucous, blue-black leaf-stalks. Inflorescences not known. Grown particularly for the very attractive foliage. ↕90cm (36in), ↔ 60cm (24in). Garden origin. ❀ (min. 13°C/55°F)

X. nigrum ■ syn. *X. violaceum* (Blue tannia, Blue taro). Robust tuberous perennial with arrow-shaped leaves, 70cm (28in) long, glaucous and purple-flushed, with purple veins and margins and dark purple leaf-stalks, to 2m (6ft) long. Inflorescences, which appear intermittently, have yellow-white spathes and violet to burgundy or white spadices. Purple-grey tubers are edible. ↕2–2.5m (6–8ft), ↔ 2m (6ft). Tropical USA, Central America, South America, West Indies. ❀ (min. 13°C/55°F)

X. sagittifolium (Coco-yam, Malanga blanca, Tannia). Thick-stemmed, tuberous perennial with arrow-shaped, often white-spotted leaves, to 1m (3ft) long, with broad basal lobes, and leaf-stalks 1m (3ft) long. Greenish white spathes, 25cm (10in) long, surrounding white spadices, are borne intermittently. Stems and tubers are edible. ↕↔ 2m (6ft). Tropical USA, Central America, South America, West Indies. ❀ (min. 13°C/55°F)

X. violaceum see *X. nigrum.*

XERANTHEMUM

ASTERACEAE/COMPOSITAE

Genus of 6 species of erect, white-woolly, branching annuals from steppes and stony banks in the Mediterranean to S.W. Asia. They have alternate, linear to linear-elliptic, entire leaves, and are cultivated for their daisy-like, crimson-red, pink, white, lilac-blue, or mauve-blue flowerheads, which are enclosed within papery bracts and are produced in summer and autumn. Xeranthemums are suitable for an annual border, and are useful in providing attractive, long-lasting cut flowers for both fresh and dried arrangements.

- **HARDINESS** Half hardy.
- **CULTIVATION** Grow in moderately fertile, well-drained soil in full sun. Provide support in exposed sites. Cut flowers for drying before they have fully opened and hang them upside down in a cool, dark, well-ventilated area.

Xeranthemum annuum

- **PROPAGATION** Sow seed at 16°C (61°F) in spring.
- **PESTS AND DISEASES** Trouble free.

X. annuum ■ Slender, upright annual, branched at the bases of the wiry stems, bearing linear-elliptic, entire, woolly, silver-green leaves, 2–6cm (¾–2½in) long. Branched heads of delicate, daisy-like, single to double, white, bright pink, crimson-red, or deep purple flowerheads, to 5cm (2in) across, are produced from summer to autumn. ↕25–75cm (10–30in), ↔ 45cm (18in). S.E. Europe to Caucasus, Iran. ✻. **'Snow Lady'** produces single white flowerheads.

XEROCHRYSUM

syn. BRACTEANTHA

ASTERACEAE/COMPOSITAE

Genus of 6 or 7 species of herbaceous perennials and annuals occurring in open grassland and scrub in Australia. The stalkless, ovate to broadly lance-shaped, glandular-hairy leaves, 5–15cm (2–6in) long, are borne on erect, branching stems. Daisy-like flower-heads have papery, white, yellow, or pink involucral bracts and central yellow disc-florets. They are suitable for growing in an annual border, or may be used to fill gaps in a mixed or herbaceous border. Low-growing cultivars may also be used for edging, or in a window-box. *X. bracteatum* is often grown for cutting and drying.

- **HARDINESS** Frost hardy to half hardy.

Xerochrysum bracteatum Bright Bikinis Series

Xerochrysum bracteatum 'Dargan Hill Monarch'

- **CULTIVATION** Grow in moderately fertile, moist but well-drained soil in full sun. Cultivars 90cm (36in) or more tall require staking.
- **PROPAGATION** Sow seed at 18°C (64°F) in spring.
- **PESTS AND DISEASES** Susceptible to downy mildew.

X. bracteatum, syn. *Bracteantha bracteata, Helichrysum bracteatum* (Golden everlasting, Strawflower). Erect annual or short-lived perennial with broadly lance-shaped, grey-green leaves, to 12cm (5in) long. From late spring to autumn, produces terminal, solitary, papery, bright white, yellow, pink, or red flowerheads, 1.5–5cm (½–2in) across. ↕10–100cm (4–39in), ↔ 30cm (12in). Australia. ✻. Cultivars of **Bright Bikinis Series** ■ have double, red, pink, orange, yellow, or white flowerheads, to 8cm (3in) across; ↕ to 30cm (12in). **'Dargan Hill Monarch'** ■ has golden yellow flowerheads, 5–7cm (2–3in) across; ✻✻. **'Frosted Sulphur'** has double, silvery, pale sulphur-yellow flowerheads; ↕ to 1m (3ft). **King Size Series** cultivars have fully double flowerheads, to 10cm (4in) across, in yellow, orange, red, pink, or silvery white (available in single colours or a mix); ↕ 1m (3ft). **Monstrosum Series** ■ cultivars have fully double flowerheads, to 8cm (3in) across, in pink, red, orange, yellow, or white; ↕ to 90cm (36in). **'Silvery Rose'** ■ has double, silvery rose-pink flowerheads; ↕ to 75cm (30in). **'Skynet'**

Xerochrysum bracteatum Monstrosum Series

Xerochrysum bracteatum 'Silvery Rose'

has pink-flushed, creamy white flowerheads, to 8cm (3in) across. **Tetraploid Double Series** cultivars are extremely vigorous, with pink, crimson-red, yellow, orange, or white flowerheads, to 8cm (3in) across.

XEROPHYLLUM

LILIACEAE/MELANTHIACEAE

Genus of 2 or 3 species of upright, rhizomatous, clump-forming perennials from dry slopes and open woodland in hilly and mountainous areas of North America. They are cultivated for their attractive flowers and bold, architectural foliage. Woody, stem-like rhizomes produce numerous densely tufted, linear, finely tapered leaves, mid-green above and glaucous, blue-green beneath, with hard, rough or finely toothed margins. The leaves become progressively smaller towards the tips of the unbranched stems, each of which bears a dense, terminal raceme of small, funnel-shaped, white or yellowish white flowers in summer. They are suitable for growing in a sunny herbaceous border or in a Mediterranean garden.

- **HARDINESS** Fully hardy.
- **CULTIVATION** Grow in moderately fertile, moist but well-drained soil in full sun. In frost-prone areas, protect crowns with a dry winter mulch.
- **PROPAGATION** Sow seed in containers in a cold frame in autumn or spring. Divide crowns just before growth commences in spring.
- **PESTS AND DISEASES** Trouble free.

X. asphodeloides. Upright perennial with linear leaves, to 45cm (18in) long, mid-green above, glaucous, blue-green beneath, with rough margins. During summer, produces funnel-shaped, fragrant, yellow-white flowers, 1cm (½in) across, in dense, broad, rounded racemes, to 30cm (12in) long. ↕ to 1.5m (5ft), ↔ to 60cm (24in). E. Canada to USA (New Jersey to Tennessee, Georgia). ✻✻✻

X. tenax. Upright perennial with tufted, linear, stiff leaves, to 90cm (36in) long, mid-green above, glaucous, blue-green beneath, with rough margins. Produces funnel-shaped, white to cream flowers, 5mm (¼in) across, in dense racemes, to 60cm (24in) long, in summer. ↕↔ 75cm (30in). W. North America. ✻✻✻

Y

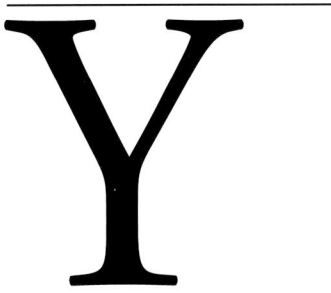

▷**Yam, Ornamental** see *Dioscorea discolor*
▷**Yanquapin** see *Nelumbo lutea*
▷**Yarrow** see *Achillea*
  Golden see *Eriophyllum*
▷**Yautia** see *Xanthosoma*
▷**Yellow archangel** see *Lamium galeobdolon*
▷**Yellow bells** see *Tecoma stans*
▷**Yellowroot** see *Xanthorhiza simplicissima*
▷**Yellow trumpet** see *Sarracenia flava*
▷**Yellow wood** see *Cladrastis kentukea*
▷**Yesterday, today, and tomorrow** see *Brunfelsia pauciflora*
▷**Yew** see *Taxus, T. baccata*
  Florence Court see *Taxus baccata* 'Fastigiata'
  Fortune plum see *Cephalotaxus fortunei*
  Irish see *Taxus baccata* 'Fastigiata'
  Japanese see *Taxus cuspidata*
  Nutmeg see *Torreya*
  Plum see *Cephalotaxus, C. harringtonii*
  Prince Albert's see *Saxegothaea conspicua*
▷**Ylang-ylang** see *Cananga odorata*
▷**Youth-on-age** see *Tolmiea*

YUCCA syn. HESPEROYUCCA

AGAVACEAE

Genus of about 40 species of rosette-forming or woody-based perennials (some species monocarpic), evergreen shrubs, and erect, eventually spreading, evergreen trees from hot, dry places, such as deserts, sand dunes, and plains, in North and Central America and the West Indies. They are cultivated for their bold, linear to lance-shaped or inversely lance-shaped, neatly or loosely rosetted leaves, and for their erect or rarely pendent panicles of bell-shaped to hemispherical, usually white flowers. Use as architectural specimens in a border or courtyard. In frost-prone areas, grow tender yuccas in a cool or temperate greenhouse, or a conservatory.

• **HARDINESS** Fully hardy to frost tender.

• **CULTIVATION** Under glass, grow in loam-based potting compost (JI No.2) in full light. When in growth, water moderately and apply a balanced liquid fertilizer monthly. Water sparingly in winter. Outdoors, grow in any well-drained soil in full sun. Flowers may require hand-pollination to set seed. Remove spent flowering stems.

• **PROPAGATION** Sow seed in spring, at 13–18°C (55–64°F) for hardy yuccas, or at 19–24°C (66–75°F) for tender ones. Remove rooted suckers in spring. Take root cuttings in winter.

• **PESTS AND DISEASES** Susceptible to leaf spot; aphids may infest flowers.

Yucca aloifolia

Y. aloifolia ▣ ♀ (Spanish bayonet). Slow-growing, rounded shrub or small tree with a simple or branched stem and densely arranged, linear to narrowly lance-shaped, toothed, dark green leaves, to 50cm (20in) long, each ending in a sharp, stiff point. From summer to autumn, bears stout, erect panicles, to 45cm (18in) long, of pendent, bell-shaped, white, sometimes purple-tinged flowers, 3cm (1¼in) long, held above the foliage. ↕ 8m (25ft), ↔ 4–5m (12–15ft). S.E. USA, Mexico, West Indies. ❀ (min. 7°C/45°F)

Y. elephantipes ♀ syn. *Y. guatemalensis* (Giant yucca, Spineless yucca). Large, upright shrub or usually small tree with several to many sparsely branched trunks arising near ground level. Narrowly lance-shaped, light to mid-green leaves, 60–100cm (24–39in) long, are stiffly leathery, with toothed margins. On mature plants, pendent, hemispherical, white to cream flowers, 3–4cm (1¼–1½in) long, are borne in dense, erect panicles, to 1m (3ft) long, from summer to autumn. ↕ to 10m (30ft), ↔ 5–8m (15–25ft). Mexico. ❀ (min. 10°C/50°F). **'Variegata'** ▣ has leaves with creamy white margins.

Yucca filamentosa 'Bright Edge'

Y. filamentosa (Adam's needle). Clump-forming shrub, stemless or almost so, with basal rosettes of inversely lance-shaped, rigid, dark green leaves, to 75cm (30in) long, margined with curly white threads. Nodding, bell-shaped white flowers, 5cm (2in) long, tinged green or cream, are borne in upright panicles, to 2m (6ft) or more long, in mid- and late summer. ↕ 75cm (30in), ↔ 1.5m (5ft). USA (New Jersey to Florida). ❄❄❄. **'Bright Edge'** ▣ has leaves with broad yellow margins. **'Variegata'** has white-margined, blue-green leaves, tinged pink in winter.

Yucca elephantipes 'Variegata'

Y. flaccida. Clump-forming, almost stemless shrub bearing basal rosettes of lance-shaped, dark blue-green leaves, to 55cm (22in) long, fringed with curly or straight threads. Bears nodding, bell-shaped white flowers, 5cm (2in) long, in upright panicles, to 1.5m (5ft) or more long, in mid- and late summer. ↕ 55cm (22in), ↔ 1.5m (5ft). USA (N. Carolina to Alabama). ❄❄❄. **'Golden Sword'** has yellow-margined leaves. **'Ivory'** bears a profusion of spreading, green-tinged, creamy white flowers.

Y. gloriosa ▣ (Spanish dagger). Erect shrub with a stout stem, simple at first, later sparsely branched, bearing terminal tufts of narrowly lance-shaped, stiffly pointed, arching, leaves, to 60cm (24in) long, blue-green maturing to dark green, with entire to few-toothed margins. From late summer to autumn, produces pendent, bell-shaped, sometimes purple-tinged, white flowers, 5cm (2in) long, in upright panicles, to 2.5m (8ft) long. ↕↔ 2m (6ft). USA (N. Carolina to Florida). ❄❄. **'Nobilis'** has flowers with red petal backs, and blue-green leaves, the outer ones arched. **'Variegata'** has yellow-margined leaves.

Y. guatemalensis see *Y. elephantipes.*

Y. longifolia see *Beaucarnia longifolia.*

Y. parviflora see *Hesperaloe parviflora.*

Y. recurvifolia. Robust, tree-like shrub, sometimes with several trunk-like stems, sparsely branched with age. Bears lance-shaped, arching to strongly recurved, stiffly leathery, mid- to deep green

Yucca gloriosa

Yucca whipplei

leaves, to 90cm (36in) long, blue-green when young, with entire to slightly toothed margins. Pendent, bell-shaped cream flowers, 6–8cm (2½–3in) long, open in upright panicles, to 2m (6ft) long, from late summer to autumn. ↕1.5–2.5m (5–8ft), ↔ 1.2–2m (4–6ft). USA (Georgia to Missouri). ❄❄❄

Y. whipplei ▣ (Our Lord's candle). Clump-forming, stemless, monocarpic shrub with dense tufts of slender, linear, finely toothed, rigid, grey-green leaves, to 90cm (36in) long. Pendent, bell-shaped or hemispherical, fragrant, creamy white, sometimes purple-tinged flowers, 3.5cm (1½in) long, are borne in summer in upright panicles, to 2m (6ft) or more long. Propagate by seed; it may take many years to flower. ↕1m (3ft), ↔ 1.2m (4ft). USA (S. California, Arizona), N.W. Mexico. ❄❄

▷**Yucca,**
Giant see *Yucca elephantipes*
Spineless see *Yucca elephantipes*
▷**Yulan** see *Magnolia denudata*

YUSHANIA

Anceps bamboo

GRAMINEAE/POACEAE

Genus of 2 species of tall, evergreen, clump-forming bamboos found at high altitudes in the N.W. and C. Himalayas, Taiwan, and the Philippines. Cultivated for their lance-shaped to linear leaves, yushanias are suitable for use as hedging or screening, or as specimen plants, but they can be invasive.

• **HARDINESS** Fully hardy, although foliage may be damaged in extreme cold.

• **CULTIVATION** Grow in fertile, humus-rich, moist but well-drained soil in full sun or partial shade. In frost-prone areas, shelter from cold winds. Plant in large tubs plunged into soil to restrict spread.

• **PROPAGATION** Divide in spring.

• **PESTS AND DISEASES** Young shoots may be damaged by slugs.

Y. anceps, syn. *Arundinaria anceps, Arundinaria jaunsarensis, Sinarundinaria jaunsarensis* (Anceps bamboo). Tall, evergreen, rhizomatous bamboo forming dense, scattered clumps of shiny, dark green canes, straight and erect at first, arching with age. Pendent branchlets bear narrowly lance-shaped, mid-green leaves, 6–14cm (2½–5½in) long, rounded at the bases, with purple-tinted stalks. ↕4m (12ft) or more, ↔ indefinite. N.W. and C. Himalayas. ❄❄❄

Z

ZALUZIANSKYA

SCROPHULARIACEAE

Genus of about 35 species of sticky, low-growing annuals and evergreen perennials or subshrubs from grassland and rocky slopes in South Africa. They are grown for their terminal spikes of tubular, salverform, heavily scented flowers, with 5 spreading petal lobes; the flowers are usually deep red in bud, opening to white with red petal backs. The variably shaped leaves are entire or toothed, the lower ones opposite, the upper ones alternate. Suitable for a sunny rock garden or alpine house.

• **HARDINESS** Frost hardy.

• **CULTIVATION** Grow in moist but sharply drained, humus-rich soil in full sun. Cut back hard after flowering. In an alpine house, grow in a mix of equal parts loam, leaf mould, and grit. Water freely when in growth. Keep barely moist in winter.

• **PROPAGATION** Propagate regularly as plants are short-lived. Take stem-tip cuttings in summer, overwinter in frost-free conditions, and plant out in spring. Seed is not regularly produced in gardens; if available, sow at 10–13°C (50–55°F) as soon as ripe or in spring.

• **PESTS AND DISEASES** Aphids and red spider mites may be troublesome under glass.

Z. ovata ▣ Clump-forming, evergreen perennial with branching, brittle stems bearing ovate, toothed, sticky, grey-green leaves, 4cm (1½in) long. Produces terminal spikes of salverform, crimson-backed white flowers, 2–2.5cm (¾–1in) across, each with 5 petal lobes, cleft into 2 further lobes; they open in sunshine, and are produced over a long period in summer. ↕ to 25cm (10in), ↔ to 60cm (24in). South Africa (Western Cape, Northern Cape, Eastern Cape, KwaZulu/Natal, Free State), Lesotho. ❄❄

Zaluzianskya ovata

ZAMIA

ZAMIACEAE

Genus of about 30 species of mainly small, dioecious cycads found in scrub and pine woodland and on dry slopes from North to South America. Most have short, swollen stems, some similar to palms; others, with tuberous, underground stems, resemble ferns. Zamias are grown for their habit and pinnate leaves, borne in terminal whorls or rosettes and often composed of many narrow, oblong or linear to ovate leaflets. They produce usually felted, single-sexed, cone-like flower spikes ("cones"), with male and female flowers borne on separate plants; the insignificant male cones are cylindrical, the females ovoid. In frost-prone areas, grow in a warm greenhouse or as houseplants. In tropical areas, site large species on a lawn and small ones in a shrub border.

• **HARDINESS** Frost tender.

• **CULTIVATION** Under glass, grow in loam-based potting compost (JI No.3), with added leaf mould and sharp sand, in full light with shade from hot sun. During the growing season, water freely and apply a balanced liquid fertilizer monthly. Water sparingly in winter. Outdoors, grow in fertile, moist but well-drained soil in full sun with some midday shade, or in partial shade.

• **PROPAGATION** Sow seed at 24°C (75°F) in spring.

• **PESTS AND DISEASES** Susceptible to scale insects and mealybugs under glass.

Z. floridana see *Z. pumila.*

Z. furfuracea (Cardboard palm). Small cycad with a partly underground, simple or rarely branched, cylindrical trunk. Bears terminal whorls of semi-erect to spreading, pinnate leaves, to 1m (3ft) long, each with up to 24 oblong or inversely lance-shaped to obovate, stiff, pale green leaflets, later olive-green, with red-brown hairs. Produces felted, red-brown female flower cones, 10–13cm (4–5in) long, usually in summer. ↕ to 1m (3ft), ↔ to 2m (6ft). Coast of E. Mexico. ❀ (min. 15°C/59°F)

Z. integrifolia see *Z. pumila.*

Z. loddigesii. Small cycad with a largely underground, sometimes branching trunk. Bears terminal whorls of semi-erect to spreading, pinnate leaves, to 1m (3ft) long, each with up to 54 narrowly lance-shaped, lustrous, bright green leaflets, toothed on their upper halves. Brownish green female flower cones, 5cm (2in) or more long, are generally produced in summer. ↕1.5m (5ft), ↔ to 1.7m (5½ft). Mexico, Guatemala. ❀ (min. 15°C/59°F). **var. *latifolia*** has lance-shaped to obovate leaflets.

Z. pumila ▣ syn. *Z. floridana, Z. integrifolia* (Florida arrowroot, Guayiga, Seminole bread). Small cycad with a mainly underground, unbranched or branched trunk. Bears terminal rosettes of ascending to spreading, pinnate leaves, 60–120cm (24–48in) long, each with up to 60 linear to inversely lance-shaped, leathery, deep green leaflets, frequently toothed on their upper halves. Large, russet-green female flower cones, to 15cm (6in) long, are usually produced in summer. ↕ to 1.2m (4ft), ↔ 1.2–2m (4–6ft). USA (Florida), Cuba, West Indies. ❀ (min. 15°C/59°F)

Zamia pumila

ZAMIOCULCAS

ARACEAE

Genus of one species of evergreen or partially deciduous perennial, found in forests or savannah, often on stony ground, in tropical E. and subtropical S.E. Africa. It has a short, thick rhizome and succulent, persistent leaf-stalks that bear alternate to almost opposite leaflets. During prolonged drought, leaflets are shed. Detached leaflets can develop roots at the base and form new plants. Valued for its stiffly erect, succulent, glossy foliage, it is best grown as a houseplant in frost-prone climates. In warm areas, grow as a drought-resistant perennial in a shady border.

• **HARDINESS** Frost tender.

• **CULTIVATION** Under glass, grow in well-drained, loam-based potting compost (JI No.3), with added grit, in moderate light. When in growth, water moderately and apply a balanced liquid fertilizer every 2–3 weeks; maintain moderate humidity. Water sparingly in winter. Avoid waterlogging, since susceptible to rot. Outdoors, grow in well-drained, even stony, soil in partial shade.

• **PROPAGATION** Divide in spring as new growth begins. Root detached leaflets with bottom heat at any time.

• **PESTS AND DISEASES** Trouble free.

Z. zamiifolia ▣ (Z-Z plant). Clump-forming, succulent evergreen or seasonally dormant perennial with pinnate, glossy, dark emerald-green to dark green leaves, 30cm (12in) long,

Zamioculcas zamiifolia

Z

composed of stout leaf-stalks, thickened at the base, and glossy, leathery, alternate to almost opposite, oblong-elliptic to ovate-elliptic leaflets, to 15cm (6in) long. Green spathes, to 7cm (3in) long, are borne at ground level on short stalks, to 4cm (1½in) long; the spadix is white and shorter than the spathe. ↕90cm (36in), ↔45cm (18in). E. and S.E. Africa. ❀ (min. 13°C/55°F)

ZANTEDESCHIA

Arum lily

ARACEAE

Genus of 8 species of tuberous or rhizomatous perennials, found in moist soils and swamps or at lake margins in southern and E. Africa. They are grown for their unusual, white or brightly coloured spathes, borne in spring and summer. Most bear lance-shaped or narrowly to broadly arrow- or heart-shaped leaves. A number of hybrids has been developed. **Elliottiana hybrids** have usually broadly heart-shaped, usually mid- to dark green leaves, most covered with translucent white dots, and usually yellow spathes, 15cm (6in) long, surrounding golden yellow spadices. **Rehmannii hybrids** have lance-shaped, rarely spotted, mid- to dark green leaves, and white to pink or dark purple spathes, 12cm (5in) long, surrounding yellow spadices.

Z. aethiopica may be cultivated as a marginal aquatic. Where temperatures fall below 10°C (50°F), grow less hardy arum lilies in a warm greenhouse or as houseplants, or plant out in a sunny site in summer. All parts may cause mild stomach upset if ingested, and contact with the sap may irritate the skin.

Zantedeschia albomaculata

Zantedeschia elliottiana

Zantedeschia aethiopica 'Crowborough'

Zantedeschia aethiopica 'Green Goddess'

• **HARDINESS** Fully hardy to frost tender.
• **CULTIVATION** Under glass, grow in loam-based potting compost (JI No.2) in full light. When in growth, water freely and apply a balanced liquid fertilizer every 2 weeks until the flowers have faded. Keep just moist in winter. Outdoors, grow in humus-rich, moist soil in full sun. In frost-prone areas, protect *Z. aethiopica* with a deep winter mulch. As a marginal aquatic, grow *Z. aethiopica* in a planting basket 25–30cm (10–12in) across, filled with heavy loam, in water up to 30cm (12in) deep; see also pp.52–53.
• **PROPAGATION** Sow seed at 21–27°C (70–81°F) when ripe. Divide in spring.
• **PESTS AND DISEASES** Prone to aphids and thrips. Susceptible to various fungal and bacterial rots, and viruses.

Z. aethiopica (Arum lily). Clump-forming, rhizomatous perennial, evergreen in mild areas, with semi-erect, arrow-shaped, glossy, bright green leaves, to 45cm (18in) long. From late spring to midsummer, bears a succession of large, pure white spathes, to 25cm (10in) long, with creamy yellow spadices. ↕↔ 90cm (36in). South Africa, Lesotho. ✻✻. **'Apple Court Babe'** is small-growing; ↕60cm (24in). **'Crowborough'** ■ has spathes 10–15cm (4–6in) long; ✻✻✻ (borderline). **'Green Goddess'** ■ has dull green leaves and white-centred, dull green spathes, 15–20cm (6–8in) long. **'Little Gem'** is dwarf and floriferous; ↕45cm (18in). **'Marshmallow Pink'** has pale pink spathes, 10–15cm (4–6in) long. **'Pink Mist'** has pale pink spathes, 10–15cm (4–6in) long; ↕↔ 60cm (24in); ✻✻✻. **'White Sail'** has open white spathes, 10cm (4in) long.

Z. albomaculata ■ syn. *Z. melanoleuca*. Rhizomatous perennial with semi-erect, arrow-shaped, mid-green, basal leaves, to 45cm (18in) long, with translucent white spots. In summer, bears white to cream, pale yellow, or pale pink spathes, to 12cm (5in) long, each with a purple mark inside at the base, surrounding yellow spadices. ↕↔ 30–40cm (12–16in). Tropical E. Africa, southern Africa. ❀ (min. 10°C/50°F)

Z. angustiloba see *Z. pentlandii.*

***Z.* 'Anneke'**, syn. 'Silver Lining'. Elliottiana hybrid with heavily white-spotted leaves. Bears deep purplish mauve spathes with a silvery white rim in summer. ↕60–75cm (24–30in), ↔20cm (8in). ❀ (min. 10°C/50°F)

***Z.* 'Aztec Gold'.** Elliottiana hybrid with unspotted leaves. Golden yellow spathes are borne in summer, maturing to burnt orange. ↕55cm (22in), ↔20cm (8in). ❀ (min. 10°C/50°F)

***Z.* 'Black Eyed Beauty'.** Elliottiana hybrid with heavily white-spotted leaves. In summer, produces cream spathes, each with a black central mark in the throat. ↕30–40cm (12–16in), ↔15cm (6in). ❀ (min. 10°C/50°F)

***Z.* 'Black Magic'.** Elliottiana hybrid with heavily white-mottled leaves. Bears yellow spathes, with black throats, in summer. ↕75cm (30in), ↔20cm (8in). ❀ (min. 10°C/50°F)

Zantedeschia 'Crystal Blush'

***Z.* 'Cameo'.** Elliottiana hybrid with white-spotted leaves and straw-yellow to salmon-orange spathes produced in summer. ↕60cm (24in), ↔20cm (8in). ❀ (min. 10°C/50°F)

***Z.* 'Captain Rodin'.** Elliottiana hybrid with white-mottled leaves. Bears creamy white spathes with a pink flush in summer. ↕40–60cm (16–24in), ↔25cm (10in). ❀ (min. 10°C/50°F)

***Z.* 'Celeste'.** Elliottiana hybrid with white-mottled leaves and dark pink spathes in summer. ↕to 60cm (24in), ↔25cm (10in). ❀ (min. 10°C/50°F)

***Z.* 'Crystal Blush'** ■ Elliottiana hybrid with unspotted leaves and creamy white spathes, delicately flushed pink, in summer. ↕55cm (22in), ↔20cm (8in). ❀ (min. 10°C/50°F)

Z. elliottiana ■ (Golden arum). Rhizomatous perennial with erect, heart-shaped, dark green, basal leaves, to 28cm (11in) long, covered with translucent white spots. In summer, produces yellow spathes, 15cm (6in) long, with yellow spadices. ↕60–90cm (24–36in), ↔30cm (12in). Origin unknown. ❀ (min. 10°C/50°F)

***Z.* 'Flame'** ■ Elliottiana hybrid with white-spotted leaves and red-orange to

Zantedeschia 'Flame'

Z

Zantedeschia 'Garnet Glow'

yellow spathes produced in late summer. ↕↔ 30–40cm (12–16in). ❀ (min. 10°C/50°F)
Z. 'Florex Gold'. Elliottiana hybrid with white-mottled leaves. Deep golden yellow spathes are produced in summer. ↕ 40–60cm (16–24in), ↔ 25cm (10in). ❀ (min. 10°C/50°F)
Z. 'Galaxy'. Elliottiana hybrid with arrow-shaped, heavily white-mottled leaves. Dark red spathes with buff-yellow spadices are produced in summer. ↕ 30–40cm (12–16in), ↔ 20cm (8in). ❀ (min. 10°C/50°F)
Z. 'Garnet Glow' ■ Elliottiana hybrid with white-spotted leaves and light red spathes produced in summer. ↕ 60cm (24in), ↔ 20cm (8in). ❀ (min. 10°C/50°F)
Z. 'Little Suzie'. Compact Rehmannii hybrid with unspotted leaves and numerous small pink spathes, to 5cm (2in) long, borne in summer. ↕ 30–45cm (12–18in), ↔ 30cm (12in). ❀ (min. 10°C/50°F)
Z. 'Majestic Red'. Elliottiana hybrid with white-spotted leaves and pointed, purple-red spathes, borne in summer. ↕ 65cm (26in), ↔ 20cm (8in). ❀ (min. 10°C/50°F)
Z. 'Mango' ■ Elliottiana hybrid with white-spotted leaves and deep orange spathes, tinged red, borne in summer. ↕ 65cm (26in), ↔ 20cm (8in). ❀ (min. 10°C/50°F)
Z. melanoleuca see *Z. albomaculata.*
Z. pentlandii, syn. *Z. angustiloba.* Upright, rhizomatous perennial with erect, oblong-elliptic to oblong-lance-shaped, mid- to dark green, rarely spotted leaves, to 30cm (12in) long,

Zantedeschia 'Zwartzwalder'

arrow- or heart-shaped at the bases. In summer, produces golden to yellow spathes, to 12cm (5in) long, each marked dark purple inside at the base, and golden yellow spadices. ↕ 60–90cm (24–36in), ↔ 20cm (8in). South Africa (Mpumalanga, Northern Cape). ✲✲✲
Z. 'Pink Persuasion'. Elliottiana hybrid with white-spotted leaves and rich pink spathes produced in summer. ↕ 65cm (26in), ↔ 20cm (8in). ❀ (min. 10°C/50°F)
Z. rehmannii (Pink arum). Rhizomatous perennial with semi-erect, lance-shaped, dark green, basal leaves. In summer, produces slender, white to pink or dark purple spathes, 12cm (5in) long, with yellow spadices. ↕ 40cm (16in), ↔ 28cm (11in). South Africa (Mpumalanga, Northern Cape), Swaziland. ❀ (min. 10°C/50°F)
Z. 'Silver Lining' see *Z.* 'Anneke'.
Z. 'Zwartzwalder' ■ Elliottiana hybrid with heavily white-spotted leaves and blackish maroon purple spathes produced in summer. ↕ 60cm (24in), ↔ 20cm (8in). ❀ (min. 10°C/50°F)

Zantedeschia 'Mango'

Zanthoxylum piperitum

ZANTHOXYLUM

RUTACEAE

Genus of about 250 species of broadly rounded to upright, spiny, deciduous or evergreen trees and shrubs, mainly from forest in Asia, Australia, North to South America, and Africa. They have aromatic bark, and alternate, usually pinnate leaves, dotted with tiny glands. Their fruits split to reveal seeds attached by short threads. They bear cymes or panicles of small, cup-shaped, green or yellowish green flowers from spring to summer; plants may be dioecious, or bear both unisexual and bisexual flowers. Good for a shrub border or as specimen trees. In frost-prone areas, grow tender species in a cool greenhouse.

- **HARDINESS** Fully hardy to frost tender.
- **CULTIVATION** Grow in fertile, well-drained soil in full sun or light dappled shade. Pruning group 1.
- **PROPAGATION** Sow seed in containers in a cold frame in autumn. Root semi-ripe cuttings in midsummer, with bottom heat. Take root cuttings in late winter.
- **PESTS AND DISEASES** Trouble free.

Zanthoxylum simulans

Z. piperitum ■ (Japan pepper). Bushy, spiny, deciduous shrub with pinnate, aromatic, glossy, dark green leaves, to 15cm (6in) long, each with 11–23 ovate, toothed leaflets, turning yellow in autumn. In early summer, bears panicles, 5cm (2in) long, of small, cup-shaped, yellow-green flowers from the leaf axils; they are followed by tiny, spherical, berry-like red fruit, which split to reveal black seeds. ↕↔ 2.5m (8ft). China, Korea, Japan, Taiwan. ✲✲✲
Z. simulans ■ ♀ Spreading, deciduous shrub or small tree with broad spines, sometimes with pendent shoots. Pinnate leaves, to 20cm (8in) long, each with up to 11 ovate-oblong, saw-toothed, glossy, dark green leaflets, become yellow to reddish yellow in autumn. In early summer, bears tiny, cup-shaped green flowers in cymes 5cm (2in) across, followed by spherical, warty red fruit, 5mm (¼in) across, which split to reveal glossy black seeds. ↕ 6m (20ft), ↔ 5m (15ft). China, Japan, Taiwan. ✲✲✲

ZAUSCHNERIA

Californian fuchsia

ONAGRACEAE

Genus of 4 species of subshrubby, evergreen or deciduous perennials, sometimes included in *Epilobium*, from dry slopes and chaparral or coastal sage brush in W. North America. The small, opposite or alternate, linear-lance-shaped to broadly ovate leaves are stalkless or virtually so. Californian fuchsias are grown for their profusion of tubular to funnel-shaped, usually scarlet flowers, borne in terminal racemes in late summer and autumn. They are suitable for a rock garden, dry-stone wall, or a mixed or herbaceous border.

- **HARDINESS** Fully hardy to frost hardy.
- **CULTIVATION** Grow in moderately fertile, well-drained soil in full sun, with shelter from cold, dry winds.
- **PROPAGATION** Sow seed in containers in a cold frame in spring. Root basal cuttings in spring, with bottom heat.
- **PESTS AND DISEASES** Young growth may be damaged by slugs.

Z. californica, syn. *Epilobium californicum.* Clump-forming, woody-based, evergreen or semi-evergreen, rhizomatous perennial producing lance-shaped to linear-lance-shaped, hairy, grey-green leaves, 1–4cm (½–1½in) long. Bears terminal racemes of tubular, brilliant scarlet flowers, 2.5–4cm (1–1½in) long, over long periods in late summer and early autumn. ↕ to 30cm (12in), ↔ to 50cm (20in). USA (California). ✲✲✲ (borderline). **subsp. *angustifolia*** has linear, densely woolly leaves, and slightly shorter flowers; ↕ to 50cm (20in). **subsp. *cana***, syn. *Epilobium canum, Z. cana*, is deciduous, with linear to oblong, grey-woolly to white silky-hairy leaves and funnel-shaped, vermilion to scarlet flowers; ↕ to 60cm (24in), ↔ 45cm (18in). **'Dublin'** ■ is deciduous, with bright red flowers; ↕ to 25cm (10in), ↔ to 30cm (12in). **subsp. *latifolia*** is spreading, with a non-woody base, and has ovate to lance-shaped-ovate, finely hairy, mid-green to greyish green leaves. **'Solidarity Pink'** is less vigorous, and has pale pink flowers; ↔ to 30cm (12in).
Z. cana see *Z. californica* subsp. *cana.*

Zauschneria californica 'Dublin'

Z. septentrionalis, syn. *Epilobium septentrionale*. Mat-forming, non-woody, deciduous perennial with oval or lance-shaped to ovate, hairy, grey to grey-green leaves, 1–2.5cm (½–1in) long. Racemes of short-stalked, tubular scarlet flowers, to 3cm (1¼in) long, are borne in profusion in late summer. ↕ 10–20cm (4–8in), ↔ to 20cm (8in). ❄❄❄

ZEA

GRAMINEAE/POACEAE

Genus of 4 species of annual, rarely perennial grasses from field margins and disturbed ground in Central America. Sturdy stems bear lance-shaped leaves in 2 ranks and terminal, spike-like male panicles, each with a solitary, stemless spikelet or "ear" on the inter-nodes; axillary female inflorescences consist of numerous spikelets in longitudinal rows on a thickened axis. The female flowers, each with a long, silky style, are enclosed within a spathe bract or "husk", and are followed by a "cob" of fleshy kernels. *Z. mays* (maize) is an important cereal crop in tropical and temperate regions. The ornamental cultivars are valued for their variegated leaves and multi-coloured cobs. Grow in a sheltered border or as dot plants in summer bedding schemes.

- **HARDINESS** Half hardy.
- **CULTIVATION** Grow in a warm, sheltered site in fertile, moist but well-drained soil in full sun.
- **PROPAGATION** Sow seed at 18°C (64°F) in late winter or early spring, or *in situ* in late spring.
- **PESTS AND DISEASES** Occasionally attacked by aphids and sweetcorn smut.

Zea mays 'Strawberry Corn'

Z. mays (Maize, Sweetcorn). Robust, erect, annual grass with pointed, lance-shaped, arching, wavy leaves, to 90cm (36in) long. In midsummer, produces a terminal panicle of spike-like male racemes, to 20cm (8in) long, and female inflorescences, also to 20cm (8in) long, enclosed within spathe bracts. The female flowers are followed in late summer and early autumn by cobs with flattened, usually yellow, sweet-tasting, edible grains, to 1cm (½in) long. ↕ to 4m (12ft), ↔ 60cm (24in) or more. Mexico. ❄. **'Harlequin'** has foliage striped green, red, and white, and cobs with deep red grains; ↕ 1.2m (4ft). **'Strawberry Corn'** ▣ produces cobs with small, yellow to burgundy-red grains enclosed within yellow-green spathe bracts; ↕ 1.2m (4ft). **'Variegata'** has leaves boldly striped with creamy white; ↕ 90cm (36in).

▷ **Zebra plant** see *Aphelandra squarrosa, Calathea zebrina, Cryptanthus zonatus*

▷ ***Zebrina pendula*** see *Tradescantia zebrina*

▷ ***Zebrina purpusii*** see *Tradescantia zebrina* 'Purpusii'

ZELKOVA

ULMACEAE

Genus of about 6 species of deciduous, monoecious or hermaphrodite trees, occasionally shrubby, occurring in scrub and woodland in Sicily (Italy), Crete (Greece), N.E. Turkey, the Caucasus, N. Iran, and E. Asia. They are grown for their attractive habit and alternate, oval-

Zelkova serrata

oblong to ovate or elliptic, toothed, dark green leaves, which change colour to yellow, then orange-brown or red, in autumn. *Zelkova* species are closely related to, and often confused with elms (*Ulmus*), differing in their unwinged fruits and in their leaves, which are not oblique at the bases. The very small, inconspicuous, male or hermaphrodite green flowers are borne singly or in small clusters in spring, the males from the lower axils of the shoots, the hermaphrodites higher up; the flowers are followed by small, spherical green fruits. *Zelkova* species and cultivars are imposing specimen and avenue trees, most of them suitable for open parkland and larger gardens; *Z. abelicea* and dwarf cultivars of *Z. serrata* are better suited for use in smaller gardens.

Zelkova carpinifolia (inset: leaf detail)

- **HARDINESS** Fully hardy.
- **CULTIVATION** Grow in deep, fertile, moist but well-drained soil in sun or partial shade. In frost-prone areas, protect from cold, drying winds. Pruning group 1.
- **PROPAGATION** Sow seed in containers outdoors in autumn. Take greenwood cuttings in summer (preferably from young plants). Graft in winter. Remove rooted suckers in winter.
- **PESTS AND DISEASES** Prone to bacterial canker, Dutch elm disease, and horse-chestnut scale.

Z. abelicea 🌳 syn. *Z. cretica*. Spreading, bushy-headed tree with white-hairy young shoots and ovate, thick-textured, glossy, dark green leaves, to 2.5cm (1in) long, each with up to 6 or 7 teeth on either side. ↕ 5m (15ft), ↔ 7m (22ft). Greece (Crete). ❄❄❄

Z. carpinifolia ▣🌳 (Caucasian elm). Broadly upright tree, normally with a short, stout trunk from which arise many erect branches. Ovate, dark green leaves, slightly rough above, to 10cm (4in) long, each with about 10 broad teeth on either side, are orange-brown in autumn. ↕ 30m (100ft), ↔ 25m (80ft). Caucasus, N.E. Turkey, N. Iran. ❄❄❄

Z. cretica see *Z. abelicea*.

Z. keaki see *Z. serrata*.

Z. serrata ▣🌳 syn. *Z. keaki* (Japanese zelkova). Spreading tree with smooth grey bark, peeling to reveal orange patches. Thin, narrowly ovate, tapered leaves, to 12cm (5in) long, each with up to 16 teeth on either side, are dark green, becoming yellow, orange, or red in autumn. ↕ to 30m (100ft), ↔ 18m (60ft). S. Korea, Japan, Taiwan. ❄❄❄. **'Goblin'** is dwarf and slow-growing, forming a dense, bushy shrub; ↕↔ 1m (3ft). **'Green Vase'** is vase-shaped, fast-growing, and graceful, with upright, arching branches, and leaves that turn orange-brown to bronze-red in autumn. **'Village Green'** is fast-growing, with red autumn coloration; it is resistant to Dutch elm disease.

Z. sinica 🌳 Broadly upright tree with a short trunk, numerous ascending branches, and peeling bark marked grey, orange, and brown. Ovate, thin, dark green leaves, to 9cm (4½in) long, each with up to 10 teeth on either side and entire at the tapered base, turn yellow or orange in autumn. ↕ 18m (60ft), ↔ 15m (50ft). C. and E. China. ❄❄❄

▷ **Zelkova, Japanese** see *Zelkova serrata*.

Zenobia pulverulenta

ZENOBIA

ERICACEAE

Genus of one species of spreading, deciduous or semi-evergreen shrub occurring in moist, sandy places and bogs in S.E. USA. It has oblong-ovate, toothed leaves, and is grown for its bell-shaped, fragrant white flowers. Suitable for a woodland garden.

• **HARDINESS** Fully hardy.
• **CULTIVATION** Grow in a sheltered site, in acid, humus-rich, moist soil in sun or partial shade. Plant in shade in areas where the soil dries out in summer. Pruning group 2 or 5, in midsummer.
• **PROPAGATION** Sow seed in containers outdoors in late winter. Take semi-ripe cuttings in summer.
• **PESTS AND DISEASES** Trouble free.

Z. pulverulenta ▣ Spreading shrub with slender, arching shoots producing alternate, oblong-ovate, glaucous, blue-green to glossy, dark green leaves, to 8cm (3in) long, with toothed margins. Pendent, bell-shaped, scented white flowers, 1.2cm (½in) long, are borne in erect racemes, to 20cm (8in) long, in early and midsummer. ↕ 2m (6ft), ↔ 1.5m (5ft). USA (Virginia to South Carolina). ✻✻✻

ZEPHYRANTHES

syn. COOPERIA

Rain flower, Windflower

AMARYLLIDACEAE

Genus of about 71 species of bulbous perennials, some evergreen, found in grassland from North to South America. Closely related to *Habranthus*, they are grown for their erect, funnel-shaped to tubular, often crocus-like, white, yellow, pink, or red flowers, borne from spring to autumn, usually when the linear leaves emerge. In frost-prone areas, grow in an alpine house or cool greenhouse; *Z. candida* will thrive outside in a rock garden. Elsewhere, use in a rock garden or at the front of a sunny border.

• **HARDINESS** Frost hardy to frost tender.
• **CULTIVATION** Under glass, grow 10cm (4in) deep in loam-based potting compost (JI No.2), with added sharp sand, in full light. When in growth, water freely and apply a balanced liquid fertilizer every 4 weeks. Keep just moist in winter. Outdoors, grow in moist but well-drained soil in full sun. Protect from winter wet.

Zephyranthes grandiflora

• **PROPAGATION** Sow seed at 13–18°C (55–64°F) as soon as ripe. Separate offsets in spring.
• **PESTS AND DISEASES** Trouble free.

Z. andersonii see *Habranthus tubispathus*.
Z. atamasca (Atamasco lily). Deciduous, bulbous perennial with semi-erect, strap-shaped, basal leaves, to 40cm (16in) long. In spring or summer, bears funnel-shaped white flowers, 7cm (3in) long, the petals sometimes flushed with purple. ↕ 20–30cm (8–12in), ↔ 5cm (2in). S.E. USA. ✻
Z. candida. Deciduous, bulbous perennial with upright, narrowly linear, basal leaves, to 40cm (16in) long. Bears a succession of crocus-like, pure white flowers, 3cm (1¼in) long, occasionally tinted with red on the petal backs, from summer to early autumn. ↕ 10–20cm (4–8in), ↔ 8cm (3in). Argentina, Uruguay. ✻✻
Z. carinata see *Z. grandiflora*.
Z. citrina. Deciduous, bulbous perennial producing crocus-like, bright yellow flowers, 5cm (2in) long, above the erect, rush-like, basal leaves, to 30cm (12in) long, in autumn. ↕ 10–15cm (4–6in), ↔ 5cm (2in). Tropical South America. ✻
Z. grandiflora ▣ syn. *Z. carinata, Z. rosea* of gardens. Deciduous, bulbous perennial with semi-erect, slender, linear, glossy, basal leaves, to 30cm (12in) long. In late summer and early autumn, bears funnel-shaped, bright pink flowers, 7cm (3in) long. An attractive greenhouse container plant. ↕ 20–30cm (8–12in), ↔ 5cm (2in). Central America. ✻
Z. robusta see *Habranthus robustus*.
Z. rosea. Deciduous, bulbous perennial with semi-erect, narrowly linear, basal leaves, to 20cm (8in) long. Short-tubed, funnel-shaped pink flowers, to 3cm (1¼in) long, are borne in autumn. ↕ 15–20cm (6–8in), ↔ 8–10cm (3–4in). Cuba, West Indies, Guatemala. ✻
***Z. rosea* of gardens** see *Z. grandiflora*.

ZIGADENUS

LILIACEAE/MELANTHIACEAE

Genus of 18 species of bulbous or rhizomatous, deciduous perennials from grassland and open woodland in North America, Mexico, and N.E. Asia. They are cultivated for their upright, terminal racemes or panicles of small, star-shaped, 6-tepalled, greenish white or yellowish

Zigadenus fremontii

white flowers, produced in summer. The leaves are mainly basal and linear, and often folded or keeled. Good for a shady border or woodland garden; grow *Z. fremontii* in a bulb frame. All parts are highly toxic if ingested.

• **HARDINESS** Frost hardy.
• **CULTIVATION** Grow in deep, fertile, moist but well-drained soil in full sun or partial shade; *Z. fremontii* prefers full sun. In a bulb frame, grow 15–20cm (6–8in) deep in equal parts loam-based potting compost (JI No.2) and grit.
• **PROPAGATION** Sow seed at 13–18°C (55–64°F) when ripe or in spring. Divide in spring or autumn.
• **PESTS AND DISEASES** Trouble free.

Z. elegans. Bulbous perennial with semi-erect, narrowly linear, grey-green, basal leaves, to 30cm (12in) long. Bears spikes of many star-shaped, greenish white flowers, 8mm (⅜in) across, with prominent, yellowish green nectaries, in mid- and late summer. ↕ 70cm (28in), ↔ 8cm (3in). North America (Alaska, Minnesota to Arizona). ✻✻
Z. fremontii ▣ Robust, bulbous perennial with semi-erect, narrowly linear, greyish green, basal leaves, to 60cm (24in) long. Racemes or panicles of many star-shaped, creamy white flowers, 1.5cm (½in) across, are borne in early summer. Requires dry summer dormancy; best in a bulb frame. ↕ 70cm (28in), ↔ 8cm (3in). USA (S. Oregon) to Mexico (N. Baja California). ✻✻
Z. glaucus. Bulbous perennial with semi-erect, narrowly linear, greyish green, basal leaves, to 30cm (12in) long. In summer, bears racemes or panicles of many star-shaped, creamy white flowers, to 1cm (½in) across, suffused brown or purple. ↕ to 60cm (24in), ↔ to 8cm (3in). E. Canada, N.E. USA. ✻✻
Z. nuttallii. Slender, bulbous perennial with semi-erect, narrowly linear, mid- to dark green, basal leaves, to 45cm (18in) long. In summer, bears dense racemes of numerous tiny, star-shaped, creamy yellow flowers, 6–8mm (¼–⅜in) across. ↕ 30–60cm (12–24in), ↔ 8cm (3in). W. North America. ✻✻
Z. venenosus (Death camas). Bulbous perennial with semi-erect, narrowly linear, mid- to dark green, basal leaves, to 30cm (12in) long. In summer, produces slender racemes of numerous small, star-shaped, off-white flowers, 3–6mm (⅛–¼in) across. ↕ 70cm (28in), ↔ 8cm (3in). North America (W. Canada to Utah, New Mexico). ✻✻

ZINNIA

ASTERACEAE/COMPOSITAE

Genus of 20 species of spreading to erect annuals, perennials, and subshrubs from scrub and desert grassland, mainly in Mexico, but also in S.W. USA, and Central and South America. They have branching, angled or rounded stems and opposite, stalkless or almost stalkless, linear to ovate or elliptic, pale to mid-green leaves. Zinnias are cultivated for their solitary, long-stemmed, daisy-like, terminal flowerheads in a wide range of colours, including white, yellow, orange, red, purple, and lilac, some with white eyes. Use in an annual or mixed border, and for cutting. Smaller cultivars are suitable for edging, and for window-boxes or other containers.

• **HARDINESS** Frost tender.
• **CULTIVATION** Grow in fertile, humus-rich, well-drained soil in full sun. Dead-head to prolong flowering.
• **PROPAGATION** Sow seed at 13–18°C (55–64°F) in early spring, or *in situ* in late spring. Sow in succession for a longer flowering display.
• **PESTS AND DISEASES** Trouble free if grown in an open position to minimize attack by mildew.

***Z. angustifolia* of gardens** see *Z. haageana*.
***Z. angustifolia* 'Orange Star'** see *Z. haageana* 'Orange Star'.
***Z. angustifolia* 'Persian Carpet'** see *Z. haageana* 'Persian Carpet'.
Z. elegans. Upright, bushy annual bearing lightly hairy, ovate to lance-

Zinnia elegans Dreamland Series 'Dreamland Scarlet'

Zinnia elegans 'Envy'

Z

Zinnia elegans
Peter Pan Series 'Peter Pan Gold'

Zinnia haageana 'Orange Star'

shaped leaves, to 8cm (3in) long. Daisy-like, broad-petalled purple flowerheads, to 4.5cm (1¾in) across, are produced in summer. ↕ 60–75cm (24–30in), ↔ 30cm (12in). Mexico. ❀ (min. 10°C/50°F). **'Belvedere'** is dwarf, with double, weather-resistant flowerheads in a broad colour range; ↕ to 30cm (12in). **Cactus-flowered Group** cultivars are tall-growing, with large, semi-double flowerheads, to 12cm (5in) across, like those of cactus dahlias, with long, narrow, quilled petals in a broad colour range; ↕ 60–90cm (24–36in). **Dreamland Series 'Dreamland Scarlet'** ▣ is dwarf and compact, produces scarlet-orange blooms, and is ideal for containers or bedding; ↕ 20–25cm (8–10in). **'Envy'** ▣ has semi-double, chartreuse-green flowerheads, and tolerates shade; ↕ to 75cm (30in). **Hobgoblin Series** cultivars are dwarf, sturdy, and bushy, with small, single, weather-resistant flowerheads in a broad colour range; good for bedding; ↕ to 45cm (18in). **Peter Pan Series** cultivars are extremely dwarf and compact; early-flowering with large flowers, to 10cm (4in) across; use in containers or as bedding plants; **'Peter Pan Gold'** ▣ has golden yellow flowers. **'Ruffles'** has ruffled, fully double flowerheads, like those of pompon dahlias, in a wide colour range; good for cut flowers; ↕ to 60cm (24in). **Short Stuff Series** cultivars are dwarf and compact, with double flowerheads, to 6cm (2½in) across, in a broad colour range; ↕ to 25cm (10in). **Small World Series** cultivars are dwarf, with double flowerheads in a wide colour range, including pale pink; ↕ to 45cm (18in). **'State Fair'** is tall-growing and very vigorous, with large, double, lavender, rose-pink, orange, purple, or scarlet flowerheads, to 8cm (3in) across; ↕ to 75cm (30in). **Thumbelina Series** ▣ cultivars are very dwarf and spreading, with single or semi-double, weather-resistant, yellow, red, magenta, or pale pink flowerheads; ↕ to 15cm (6in).

Z. haageana, syn. *Z. angustifolia* of gardens, *Z. mexicana* (Mexican zinnia). Erect, bushy annual with oblong to linear or linear-lance-shaped leaves, to 7cm (3in) long, lightly covered in bristly hairs. Daisy-like, broad-petalled, bright orange flowerheads, to 3.5cm (1½in) across, are produced in summer. ↕ to 60cm (24in), ↔ to 30cm (12in). S.E. USA, Mexico. ✲. **'Classic'** see 'Orange Star'. **'Orange Star'** ▣ syn. 'Classic', *Z. angustifolia* 'Orange Star', is dwarf and bushy in habit, and produces orange flowerheads; mildew-resistant and good for ground cover; ↕ to 25cm (10in). **'Persian Carpet'** ▣ syn. *Z. angustifolia* 'Persian Carpet', is dwarf, compact, and spreading; produces small, semi-double and double, weather-resistant flowerheads, to 4cm (1½in) across, in a range of bicolours and tricolours; excellent for summer bedding; ↕ to 40cm (16in). **'Star White'** has white flowerheads with golden yellow centres.

Z. mexicana see *Z. haageana*.

▷**Zinnia,**
Creeping see *Sanvitalia, S. procumbens*
Mexican see *Zinnia haageana*

ZIZANIA

Water oats, Wild rice

GRAMINEAE/POACEAE

Genus of 3 species of annual or perennial, marginal aquatic grasses from marshland and lake margins in E. Asia and North America. They are cultivated for their flat, linear leaves, produced on tall, reedy stems. Conical or pyramidal, feathery panicles of spikelets are borne from summer to autumn, followed by edible, rice-like seeds. Suitable for a large pond or wildlife pool. In frost-prone areas, grow tender species in a warm greenhouse.

- **HARDINESS** Fully hardy to frost tender.
- **CULTIVATION** Outdoors, grow at the edges of a large pool in full sun, in water to 23cm (9in) deep. See also pp.52–53.
- **PROPAGATION** Overwinter seed in trays of damp loam, and sow at 18°C (64°F) in early spring. As the seedlings emerge, cover with 5cm (2in) of water and maintain at the same temperature.
- **PESTS AND DISEASES** Trouble free.

Z. aquatica (Annual wild rice, Canadian wild rice, Water rice). Marginal aquatic annual with grass-like, linear, deep green leaves, to 1.2m (4ft) long. Pale green flowers are borne in pyramidal panicles, to 75cm (30in) long, in summer, followed by edible, rice-like seeds. ↕ 3m (10ft), ↔ 45cm (18in). North America. ✲✲✲

▷***Zygocactus truncatus*** see *Schlumbergera truncata*

ZYGOPETALUM

ORCHIDACEAE

Genus of about 20 species of evergreen, epiphytic or terrestrial orchids native to South America, occurring in warm, moist rainforest, sometimes on rocky outcrops or in leaf litter. They have conical to ovoid pseudobulbs, from the tops of which are produced 2 or more narrowly elongated, lance-shaped, leathery or fleshy leaves. Racemes of delicate, highly fragrant flowers, most of which are richly coloured with an attractive combination of green-brown and indigo-blue, arise from the bases of the pseudobulbs from autumn to spring.

- **HARDINESS** Frost tender.
- **CULTIVATION** Cool- to intermediate-growing orchids. Grow in standard epiphytic orchid compost in containers that will easily accommodate the root system, or in slatted baskets. During the growing season, provide high humidity and bright filtered light; water freely, and apply a quarter- to half-strength balanced liquid fertilizer at every third watering. In winter, admit full light and water sparingly. See also p.46.
- **PROPAGATION** Divide when the roots of the plant fill the container and "flow" over the sides. Alternatively, remove backbulbs and pot them up separately.
- **PESTS AND DISEASES** Susceptible to red spider mites, aphids, and mealybugs.

Z. mackaii ▣ syn. *Z. mackayi.* Epiphytic orchid with fleshy, ovoid pseudobulbs and 2 or 3 pendent, lance-shaped, leathery, apical leaves, 30–50cm (12–20in) long. Upright racemes of 5–7 green flowers, to 8cm (3in) across, each one strongly barred in brown and with a heavily veined indigo-blue lip, are borne from autumn to winter. ↕ 30cm (12in), ↔ 45cm (18in). Brazil. ❀ (min. 11–13°C/52–55°F; max. 30°C/86°F)

Z. mackayi see *Z. mackaii.*

***Z.* Perrenoudii** (*Z. intermedium* x *Z. maxillare*). Epiphytic orchid with fleshy, ovoid pseudobulbs and 2 pendent, lance-shaped, leathery, apical leaves, 30cm (12in) long. Upright racemes of 5–12 green flowers, 5–7cm (2–3in) across, each one lightly barred in brown and with a heavily veined indigo lip, are produced from autumn to spring. ↕↔ 30cm (12in). ❀ (min. 11–13°C/ 52–55°F; max. 30°C/86°F)

▷**Z-Z plant** see *Zamioculcas zamiifolia*

Zinnia elegans Thumbelina Series

Zinnia haageana 'Persian Carpet'

Zygopetalum mackaii

Z

COMMON NAMES INDEX

A

B

Banyan see *Ficus benghalensis*
Baobab tree see *Adansonia digitata*
Barbados cherry see *Malpighia glabra*
Barbados gooseberry see *Pereskia aculeata*
Barbados maidenhair fern see *Adiantum tenerum* 'Farleyense'
Barbados pride see *Caesalpinia pulcherrima*
Barbed-wire plant see *Tylecodon reticulatus*
Barbel palm see *Acanthophoenix*
Barberry see *Berberis*
Barberton daisy see *Gerbera jamesonii*
Barley see *Hordeum*
Barrenwort see *Epimedium*
Basil see *Ocimum basilicum*
Basil thyme see *Acinos arvensis*
Basswood see *Tilia americana*
Bastard balm see *Melittis*
Bastard indigo see *Amorpha fruticosa*
Bat flower see *Tacca chantrierei, T. integrifolia*
Bats-in-the-belfry see *Campanula trachelium*
Bath asparagus see *Ornithogalum pyrenaicum*
Bay laurel see *Laurus nobilis*
Bayonet plant see *Aciphylla*
Bay willow see *Salix pentandra*
Beach aster see *Erigeron glaucus*
Beach pine see *Pinus contorta*
Bead plant see *Nertera granadensis*
Bead-tree see *Melia azedarach*
Bearberry see *Arctostaphylos*
Bearded bellflower see *Campanula barbata*
Beardlip penstemon see *Penstemon barbatus*
Bear's breeches see *Acanthus*
Bear's foot see *Helleborus foetidus*
Bear's paw fern see *Aglaomorpha meyeniana*
Beautiful fir see *Abies amabilis*
Beauty berry see *Callicarpa*
Beauty bush see *Kolkwitzia*
Bedstraw see *Galium*
Bee balm see *Melissa officinalis, Monarda didyma*
Beech see *Fagus*
Beech fern see *Phegopteris, P. connectilis*
Beefsteak begonia see *Begonia* 'Erythrophylla'
Beefsteak plant see *Iresine herbstii*
Bee orchid see *Ophrys apifera*
Beet see *Beta*
Bejuco Colorado see *Cydista aequinoctialis*
Belladonna lily see *Amaryllis belladonna*
Belle de nuit see *Ipomoea alba*
Bellflower see *Campanula*
Bell-flowered cherry see *Prunus campanulata*
Bell heather see *Erica cinerea*
Bell pepper see *Capsicum annuum* Grossum Group
Bells of Ireland see *Moluccella laevis*
Bengal clock vine see *Thunbergia grandiflora*
Bentham's cornel see *Cornus capitata*
Bergamot see *Monarda, M. didyma*
Berlin poplar see *Populus* x *berolinensis*
Bermuda grass see *Cynodon dactylon*
Besom heath see *Erica scoparia*
Betel nut palm see *Areca catechu*
Betony see *Stachys*
Bhutan pine see *Pinus wallichiana*
Bidi-bidi see *Acaena*
Biennial clary see *Salvia sclarea*
Bigberry manzanita see *Arctostaphylos glauca*
Big bluestem see *Andropogon gerardii*
Big-cone pine see *Pinus coulteri*
Big-leaf maple see *Acer macrophyllum*
Bigtooth aspen see *Populus grandidentata*
Big tree see *Sequoiadendron giganteum*
Bilberry see *Vaccinium, V. myrtillus*
Billy buttons see *Craspedia, Pycnosorus*
Bindweed see *Convolvulus*
Birch see *Betula*
Bird catcher tree see *Pisonia umbellifera*
Bird cherry see *Prunus padus*
Bird of paradise see *Strelitzia*
Bird of paradise shrub see *Caesalpinia gilliesii*
Bird's eye see *Gilia tricolor*
Bird's eye bush see *Ochna*
Bird's foot ivy see *Hedera helix* 'Pedata'
Bird's-foot violet see *Viola pedata*
Bird's nest see *Sansevieria trifasciata* 'Hahnii'
Bird's-nest bromeliad see *Nidularium*
Bird's-nest fern see *Asplenium australasicum, A. nidus*
Birth root see *Trillium erectum*
Birthwort see *Aristolochia clematitis*
Bishop pine see *Pinus muricata*
Bishop's cap see *Astrophytum myriostigma, Mitella*
Bishop's mitre see *Epimedium*
Bishop's wort see *Stachys officinalis*
Bistort see *Persicaria amplexicaulis, P. bistorta*
Biting stonecrop see *Sedum acre*
Bittercress see *Cardamine*
Bitternut see *Carya cordiformis*
Bitternut hickory see *Carya cordiformis*
Bitterroot see *Lewisia rediviva*
Bittersweet see *Celastrus*
Bitter vetch see *Lathyrus linifolius* var. *montanus*
Bitterwort see *Gentiana lutea*
Black alder see *Ilex verticillata*
Black bamboo see *Phyllostachys nigra*
Black bean tree see *Castanospermum australe*
Black beech see *Nothofagus solanderi*
Blackberry lily see *Belamcanda chinensis*
Black birch see *Betula nigra*
Black cherry see *Prunus serotina*
Black chokeberry see *Aronia melanocarpa*
Black cohosh see *Cimicifuga racemosa*
Black coral pea see *Kennedia nigricans*
Black cottonwood see *Populus trichocarpa*
Black elder see *Sambucus nigra*
Black-eyed Susan see *Rudbeckia fulgida, R. hirta, Thunbergia alata*
Black fritillary see *Fritillaria biflora*
Black gold philodendron see *Philodendron melanochrysum*
Black gum see *Nyssa sylvatica*
Black henbane see *Hyoscyamus niger*
Black huckleberry see *Gaylussacia baccata*
Black Jack oak see *Quercus marilandica*
Black kangaroo paw see *Macropidia fuliginosa*
Black locust see *Robinia pseudoacacia*
Black mulberry see *Morus nigra*
Black oak see *Quercus velutina*
Black pepper see *Piper nigrum*
Black poplar see *Populus nigra*
Black sarana see *Fritillaria camschatcensis*
Black snake root see *Cimicifuga racemosa*
Black spruce see *Picea mariana*
Blackthorn see *Prunus spinosa*
Black tree fern see *Cyathea medullaris*
Black walnut see *Juglans nigra*
Black wattle see *Acacia mearnsii*
Blackwood see *Acacia melanoxylon*
Bladder fern see *Cystopteris*
Bladdernut see *Staphylea, S. pinnata*
Bladderpod see *Physaria*
Bladder senna see *Colutea, C. arborescens*
Bladderwort see *Utricularia*
Blanket flower see *Gaillardia, G. pulchella*
Blazing star see *Chamaelirion luteum, Liatris, Mentzelia lindleyi*
Bleeding heart see *Dicentra spectabilis*
Blessed Mary's thistle see *Silybum marianum*
Blood flower see *Asclepias curassavica*
Blood leaf see *Iresine lindenii*
Blood lily see *Haemanthus, Scadoxus*
Blood-red heath see *Erica cruenta*
Bloodroot see *Sanguinaria*
Bloody cranesbill see *Geranium sanguineum*
Bloody dock see *Rumex sanguineus*
Blue amaryllis see *Worsleya*
Blue Atlas cedar see *Cedrus atlantica* f. *glauca*
Bluebell see *Hyacinthoides*
Bluebell creeper see *Sollya heterophylla*
Blue bells see *Mertensia virginica*
Blueberry see *Vaccinium*
Blueblossom see *Ceanothus thyrsiflorus*
Blue-bottle see *Centaurea cyanus*
Blue bugle see *Ajuga genevensis*
Blue buttons see *Succisa pratensis*
Blue cardinal flower see *Lobelia siphilitica*
Blue cohosh see *Caulophyllum thalictroides*
Blue cowslip see *Pulmonaria angustifolia*
Blue cupidone see *Catananche*
Blue daisy see *Felicia, F. amelloides*
Blue dawn flower see *Ipomoea indica*
Blue Douglas fir see *Pseudotsuga menziesii* var. *glauca*
Blue-eyed African daisy see *Arctotis venusta*
Blue-eyed grass see *Sisyrinchium graminoides*
Blue-eyed Mary see *Omphalodes verna*
Blue fan palm see *Brahea armata*
Blue fern see *Phlebodium aureum* 'Mandaianum'
Blue fescue see *Festuca glauca*
Blue flag see *Iris versicolor*
Blue-flowered torch see *Tillandsia lindenii*
Blue glory bower see *Clerodendrum ugandense*
Blue grama see *Bouteloua gracilis*
Blue gum see *Eucalyptus leucoxylon*
Blue hesper palm see *Brahea armata*
Blue holly see *Ilex* x *meserveae*
Blue lace flower see *Trachymene coerulea*
Blue lotus see *Nymphaea caerulea*
Blue moor grass see *Sesleria albicans*
Blue oat grass see *Helictotrichon sempervirens*
Blue palmetto see *Rhapidophyllum hystrix*
Blue passion flower see *Passiflora caerulea*
Blue pea see *Clitoria ternatea*
Blue phlox see *Phlox divaricata*
Blue pimpernel see *Anagallis monellii*
Blue pine see *Pinus wallichiana*
Blue potato bush see *Solanum rantonnei*
Blue sage see *Eranthemum pulchellum*
Blue tannia see *Xanthosoma nigrum*
Blue taro see *Xanthosoma nigrum, X. violaceum*
Blue throatwort see *Trachelium caeruleum*
Blue trumpet vine see *Thunbergia grandiflora*
Bluets see *Hedyotis*
Blushing bride see *Serruria florida*
Blushing bromeliad see *Neoregelia carolinae, Nidularium fulgens*
Blushing philodendron see *Philodendron erubescens*
Bobie-bobie see *Phebalium squameum*
Bog arum see *Calla palustris*
Bogbean see *Menyanthes trifoliata*
Bog myrtle see *Myrica gale*
Bog rosemary see *Andromeda*
Bog sage see *Salvia uliginosa*
Bog star see *Parnassia*
Bonin Island juniper see *Juniperus procumbens*
Boojum tree see *Fouquieria columnaris*
Borage see *Borago officinalis*
Bosnian pine see *Pinus heldreichii*
Boston fern see *Nephrolepis exaltata* 'Bostoniensis'
Boston ivy see *Parthenocissus tricuspidata*
Bo tree see *Ficus religiosa*
Bottlebrush see *Callistemon*
Bottlebrush buckeye see *Aesculus parviflora*
Bottle gentian see *Gentiana andrewsii*
Bottle palm see *Beaucarnea recurvata, Hyophorbe, H. lagenicaulis*
Bottletree see *Brachychiton*
Bouncing Bet see *Saponaria officinalis*
Bourtree see *Sambucus nigra*
Bower plant see *Pandorea jasminoides*
Bowles' golden grass see *Milium effusum* 'Aureum'
Bowles' golden sedge see *Carex elata* 'Aurea'
Bowles' mint see *Mentha* x *villosa* var. *alopecuroides*
Bowman's root see *Gillenia trifoliata*
Bowstring hemp see *Sansevieria*
Box see *Buxus*
Box blueberry see *Vaccinium ovatum*
Box elder see *Acer negundo*
Box-leaved holly see *Ilex crenata*
Boxwood see *Buxus*
Braidwood waratah see *Telopea mongaensis*
Brake see *Pteris*
Brass buttons see *Cotula coronopifolia*
Brazilian edelweiss see *Sinningia canescens*
Brazilian firecracker see *Manettia luteorubra*
Brazilian pepper tree see *Schinus terebinthifolius*
Brazilian plume see *Justicia carnea*
Brazilian red cloak see *Megaskepasma erythrochlamys*
Brazilian rosewood see *Tipuana tipu*
Brazilian spider flower see *Tibouchina urvilleana*
Brewer spruce see *Picea breweriana*
Bridal bouquet see *Porana paniculata*
Bridal wreath see *Francoa, Spiraea* 'Arguta', *Stephanotis floribunda*
Bride's bonnet see *Clintonia uniflora*
Bridewort see *Spiraea salicifolia*
Bristle club-rush see *Isolepis setacea*
Bristlecone fir see *Abies bracteata*
Bristle cone pine see *Pinus aristata*
Bristle grass see *Setaria*
Bristly locust see *Robinia hispida*
Brittle bladder fern see *Cystopteris fragilis*
Brittle gum see *Eucalyptus mannifera* subsp. *maculosa*
Brittle maidenhair fern see *Adiantum tenerum*
Brittle thatch see *Thrinax morrisii*

Broad beech fern see *Phegopteris hexagonoptera*
Broad buckler fern see *Dryopteris dilatata*
Broadleaf see *Griselinia littoralis*
Broad-leaf drumsticks see *Isopogon anemonifolius*
Broad-leaved cotton grass see *Eriophorum latifolium*
Broad-leaved kindling bark see *Eucalyptus dalrympleana*
Brooklime see *Veronica beccabunga*
Broom see *Cytisus, Genista, Ruscus, Spartium*
Broom palm see *Thrinax parviflora*
Brown boronia see *Boronia megastigma*
Brush box see *Lophostemon confertus*
Brush cherry see *Syzygium paniculatum*
Buckeye see *Aesculus*
Buckler fern see *Dryopteris*
Buddha's belly bamboo see *Bambusa ventricosa*
Buffalo berry see *Shepherdia argentea*
Buffalo currant see *Ribes odoratum*
Buffalo grass see *Stenotaphrum secundatum*
Buffalo thatch see *Thrinax morrisii*
Buffalo-wood see *Burchellia*
Bugbane see *Cimicifuga*
Bugle see *Ajuga*
Bulbous buttercup see *Ranunculus bulbosus*
Bulbous oat grass see *Arrhenatherum elatius* subsp. *bulbosum* 'Variegatum'
Bull bay see *Magnolia grandiflora*
Bullock's heart ivy see *Hedera colchica*
Bulrush see *Typha, T. latifolia*
Bunchgrass see *Beaucarnea texana*
Bunny ears see *Opuntia microdasys* var. *pallida*
Bunya-bunya see *Araucaria bidwillii*
Burmese fish-tail palm see *Caryota mitis*
Burnet see *Sanguisorba*
Burnet rose see *Rosa pimpinellifolia*
Burning bush see *Bassia scoparia* f. *trichophylla, Dictamnus albus*
Burrawong see *Macrozamia communis*
Burr reed see *Sparganium*
Burr rose see *Rosa roxburghii*
Bush clock vine see *Thunbergia erecta*
Bush clover see *Lespedeza*
Bush groundsel see *Baccharis halimifolia*
Bush honeysuckle see *Diervilla*
Bush pea see *Pultenaea procumbens*
Bush violet see *Browallia*
Busy Lizzie see *Impatiens, I. walleriana*
Butcher's broom see *Ruscus aculeatus*
Butterbur see *Petasites*
Buttercup see *Ranunculus*
Butterfly bush see *Buddleja davidii*
Butterfly flower see *Schizanthus*
Butterfly orchid see *Orchis papilionacea*
Butterfly palm see *Chrysalidocarpus lutescens*
Butterfly weed see *Asclepias tuberosa*
Butternut see *Juglans cinerea*
Butter tree see *Tylecodon paniculatus*
Butterwort see *Pinguicula*
Buttonbush see *Cephalanthus occidentalis*
Button fern see *Pellaea rotundifolia*
Button-willow see *Cephalanthus occidentalis*
Buttonwood see *Platanus occidentalis*
Byfield fern see *Bowenia spectabilis*

C

Cabbage gum see *Eucalyptus pauciflora*
Cabbage palm see *Cordyline, Livistona australis*
Cabbage palmetto see *Sabal palmetto*
Cabbage tree see *Cordyline*
Calamint see *Acinos, Calamintha*
Calamondin see x *Citrofortunella microcarpa*
Calico bush see *Kalmia latifolia*
Calico flower see *Aristolochia littoralis*
Calico plant see *Alternanthera bettzichiana*
California buckeye see *Aesculus californica*
California laurel see *Umbellularia californica*
California lilac see *Ceanothus*
Californian allspice see *Calycanthus occidentalis*
Californian black oak see *Quercus kelloggii*
Californian bluebell see *Phacelia campanularia*
Californian firecracker see *Dichelostemma ida-maia*
Californian fuchsia see *Zauschneria*
Californian live oak see *Quercus agrifolia*
Californian poppy see *Platystemon, P. californicus*
California nutmeg tree see *Torreya californica*
Californian walnut see *Juglans californica*
California poppy see *Eschscholzia, E. californica*
California redbud see *Cercis occidentalis*
California red fir see *Abies magnifica*
California sycamore see *Platanus racemosa*
Camellia rose see *Rosa laevigata*
Camperdown elm see *Ulmus glabra* 'Camperdownii'
Campernelle jonquil see *Narcissus* x *odorus*
Camphor tree see *Cinnamomum camphora*
Campion see *Lychnis, Silene*
Canadian burnet see *Sanguisorba canadensis*
Canadian moonseed see *Menispermum canadense*
Canadian pondweed see *Elodea canadensis*
Canadian poplar see *Populus* x *canadensis*
Canadian wild rice see *Zizania aquatica*
Canadian wild rye see *Elymus canadensis*
Canary bellflower see *Canarina canariensis*
Canary bird bush see *Crotalaria agatiflora*
Canary creeper see *Tropaeolum peregrinum*
Canary Island date palm see *Phoenix canariensis*
Canary Island ivy see *Hedera canariensis*
Canary Islands pine see *Pinus canariensis*
Candle plant see *Plectranthus oertendahlii, Senecio articulatus*
Candlewood see *Rothmannia capensis*
Candy carrot see *Athamanta cretensis*
Candytuft see *Iberis*
Canebrake see *Arundinaria gigantea*
Canoe birch see *Betula papyrifera*
Cantabrian heath see *Daboecia cantabrica*
Canterbury bells see *Campanula medium, C. medium* 'Calycanthema'
Canyon maple see *Acer saccharum* subsp. *grandidentatum*
Canyon oak see *Quercus chrysolepis*
Cape blue water lily see *Nymphaea capensis*
Cape cowslip see *Lachenalia*
Cape figwort see *Phygelius capensis*
Cape grape see *Rhoicissus capensis*
Cape honeysuckle see *Tecoma capensis*
Cape ivy see *Senecio macroglossus*
Cape jasmine see *Gardenia augusta*
Cape kaffirboom see *Erythrina caffra*
Cape leadwort see *Plumbago auriculata*
Cape myrtle see *Myrsine africana, Phylica*
Cape pondweed see *Aponogeton distachyos*
Cape primrose see *Streptocarpus*
Caper spurge see *Euphorbia lathyris*
Cape sundew see *Drosera capensis*
Cape tulip see *Haemanthus coccineus*
Cape wattle see *Paraserianthes lophantha*
Cappadocian maple see *Acer cappadocicum*
Caraway see *Carum, C. carvi*
Caraway thyme see *Thymus herba-barona*
Cardamom see *Elettaria cardamomum*
Cardboard palm see *Zamia furfuracea*
Cardinal climber see *Ipomoea* x *multifida*
Cardinal flower see *Lobelia cardinalis, Sinningia cardinalis*
Cardinal's guard see *Pachystachys coccinea*
Cardoon see *Cynara cardunculus*
Caricature plant see *Graptophyllum pictum*
Carline thistle see *Carlina*
Carmel ceanothus see *Ceanothus griseus*
Carnation see *Dianthus*
Carolina allspice see *Calycanthus floridus*
Carolina basswood see *Tilia caroliniana*
Carolina hemlock see *Tsuga caroliniana*
Carolina jasmine see *Gelsemium sempervirens*
Carolina lupin see *Thermopsis villosa*
Carolina water shield see *Cabomba caroliniana*
Carpet plant see *Episcia*
Carrion flower see *Stapelia*
Carthusian pink see *Dianthus carthusianorum*
Cascade penstemon see *Penstemon serrulatus*
Caspian locust see *Gleditsia caspica*
Cast-iron plant see *Aspidistra elatior*
Castor oil plant see *Ricinus communis*
Catalina ironwood see *Lyonothamnus floribundus*
Catchfly see *Lychnis, Silene*
Cathedral bell see *Cobaea scandens*
Cathedral windows see *Calathea makoyana*
Catherine's pincushion see *Leucospermum catherinae*
Catmint see *Nepeta*
Cat's claw vine see *Macfadyena*
Cat's ears see *Antennaria, Calochortus*
Cat's paw see *Anigozanthos*
Cat's tail see *Typha, T. latifolia*
Cat's whiskers see *Tacca chantrierei*
Caucasian elm see *Zelkova carpinifolia*
Caucasian fir see *Abies nordmanniana*
Caucasian maple see *Acer cappadocicum*
Caucasian peony see *Paeonia mlokosewitschii*
Caucasian spruce see *Picea orientalis*
Caucasian whortleberry see *Vaccinium arctostaphylos*
Caucasian wing nut see *Pterocarya fraxinifolia*
Cayenne pepper see *Capsicum annuum* Longum Group
Cedar see *Cedrus*
Cedar of Goa see *Cupressus lusitanica*
Cedar of Lebanon see *Cedrus libani*
Celandine crocus see *Crocus korolkowii*
Celandine poppy see *Stylophorum diphyllum*
Celery pine see *Phyllocladus*
Centaury see *Centaurium*
Ceriman see *Monstera deliciosa*
Chain fern see *Woodwardia*
Chain plant see *Callisia fragrans, C. navicularis*
Chalice vine see *Solandra*
Chalk false brome see *Brachypodium pinnatum*
Chamomile see *Chamaemelum*
Channelled heath see *Erica canaliculata*
Chaste tree see *Vitex agnus-castus*
Chatham Island forget-me-not see *Myosotidium hortensia*
Checkerberry see *Gaultheria procumbens*
Checkerbloom see *Sidalcea malviflora*
Cheddar pink see *Dianthus gratianopolitanus*
Cheesewood see *Pittosporum undulatum*
Cherokee rose see *Rosa laevigata*
Cherry birch see *Betula lenta*
Cherry laurel see *Prunus laurocerasus*
Cherry pepper see *Capsicum annuum* Cerasiforme Group
Cherry pie see *Heliotropium arborescens*
Cherry plum see *Prunus cerasifera*
Chestnut see *Castanea*
Chestnut-leaved oak see *Quercus castaneifolia*
Chestnut rose see *Rosa roxburghii*
Chestnut vine see *Tetrastigma voinierianum*
Chickasaw rose see *Rosa bracteata*
Chickling pea see *Lathyrus sativus*
Chicory see *Cichorium, C. intybus*
Chilean bellflower see *Lapageria rosea*
Chilean blue crocus see *Tecophilaea cyanocrocus*
Chilean fire bush see *Embothrium, E. coccineum*
Chilean glory flower see *Eccremocarpus, E. scaber*
Chilean guava see *Ugni molinae*
Chilean hazel see *Gevuina avellana*
Chilean incense cedar see *Austrocedrus chilensis*
Chilean jasmine see *Mandevilla laxa*
Chilean pine see *Araucaria araucana*
Chilean potato tree see *Solanum crispum*
Chilean wine palm see *Jubaea*
Chile nut see *Gevuina avellana*
Chilli pepper see *Capsicum, C. annuum, C. annuum* Longum Group
Chimney bellflower see *Campanula pyramidalis*
China aster see *Callistephus*
China fir see *Cunninghamia, C. lanceolata*
Chincherinchee see *Ornithogalum thyrsoides*
Chinese anise see *Illicium anisatum, I. verum*
Chinese box see *Murraya paniculata*

Coriander see *Coriandrum*
Corkbark fir see *Abies lasiocarpa* var. *arizonica*
Cork oak see *Quercus suber*
Corkscrew flower see *Vigna caracalla*
Corkscrew hazel see *Corylus avellana* 'Contorta'
Corkscrew rush see *Juncus effusus* f. *spiralis*
Corn cockle see *Agrostemma*
Cornel see *Cornus*
Cornelian cherry see *Cornus mas*
Cornflower see *Centaurea cyanus*
Cornish elm see *Ulmus minor* 'Cornubiensis'
Cornish golden elm see *Ulmus minor* 'Dicksonii'
Cornish heath see *Erica vagans*
Corn lily see *Clintonia borealis, Ixia*
Corn marigold see *Xanthophthalmum segetum*
Corn poppy see *Papaver rhoeas*
Corsican heath see *Erica terminalis*
Corsican hellebore see *Helleborus argutifolius*
Corsican mint see *Mentha requienii*
Corsican pine see *Pinus nigra* subsp. *laricio*
Corsican sandwort see *Arenaria balearica*
Costmary see *Tanacetum balsamita*
Cotton grass see *Eriophorum*
Cotton lavender see *Santolina chamaecyparissus*
Cotton-pole cactus see *Opuntia vestita*
Cotton rose see *Hibiscus mutabilis*
Cotton thistle see *Onopordum*
Cottonwood see *Populus*
Coulter pine see *Pinus coulteri*
Cowberry see *Vaccinium vitis-idaea*
Cow itch tree see *Lagunaria patersonii*
Cow parsley see *Anthriscus sylvestris*
Cowslip see *Primula veris*
Cowtail pine see *Cephalotaxus harringtonii*
Coyote willow see *Salix exigua*
Crab apple see *Malus*
Crab cactus see *Schlumbergera truncata*
Crab grass see *Panicum*
Crack willow see *Salix fragilis*
Cradle orchid see *Anguloa*
Cranberry see *Vaccinium, V. macrocarpon*
Crane flower see *Strelitzia reginae*
Cranesbill see *Geranium*
Crazy-leaf begonia see *Begonia* 'Phyllomanica'
Creamcups see *Platystemon, P. californicus*
Creeping blueberry see *Vaccinium crassifolium*
Creeping blueblossom see *Ceanothus thyrsiflorus* var. *repens*
Creeping bluets see *Hedyotis michauxii*
Creeping box see *Mitchella repens*
Creeping buttons see *Peperomia rotundifolia*
Creeping Charlie see *Pilea nummulariifolia*
Creeping devil see *Stenocereus eruca*
Creeping dogwood see *Cornus canadensis*
Creeping fig see *Ficus pumila*
Creeping forget-me-not see *Omphalodes verna*
Creeping gloxinia see *Lophospermum erubescens*
Creeping juniper see *Juniperus horizontalis*
Creeping phlox see *Phlox stolonifera*
Creeping willow see *Salix repens*
Creeping zinnia see *Sanvitalia, S. procumbens*
Crepe flower see *Lagerstroemia indica*
Crepe ginger see *Costus speciosus*
Crepe jasmine see *Tabernaemontana divaricata*
Crepe myrtle see *Lagerstroemia indica*
Crested moss rose see *Rosa* x *centifolia* 'Cristata'
Cretan dittany see *Origanum dictamnus*
Cricket-bat willow see *Salix alba* var. *caerulea*
Crimson bottlebrush see *Callistemon citrinus*
Crimson clover see *Trifolium incarnatum*
Crimson damask rose see *Rosa gallica* var. *officinalis*
Cross-leaved heath see *Erica tetralix*
Cross vine see *Bignonia*
Croton see *Codiaeum*
Crowfoot see *Ranunculus*
Crow-foot violet see *Viola pedata*
Crown fern see *Blechnum discolor*
Crown imperial see *Fritillaria imperialis*
Crown of thorns see *Euphorbia milii*
Cruel plant see *Araujia sericifera*
Cuckoo flower see *Cardamine pratensis*
Cucumber tree see *Magnolia acuminata*
Culver's root see *Veronicastrum virginicum*
Cumin see *Cuminum, C. cyminum*
Cup and saucer see *Campanula medium* 'Calycanthema'
Cup and saucer plant see *Cobaea scandens*
Cup flower see *Nierembergia*
Cupid's bower see *Achimenes*
Cupid's dart see *Catananche*
Cup of gold see *Solandra maxima*
Cup plant see *Silphium perfoliatum*
Curled pondweed see *Potamogeton crispus*
Curly water thyme see *Lagarosiphon*
Curry plant see *Helichrysum italicum* subsp. *serotinum*
Curtain fig see *Ficus microcarpa*
Cushion bush see *Leucophyta*
Cypress see *Chamaecyparis, Cupressus*
Cypress pine see *Callitris*
Cypress spurge see *Euphorbia cyparissias*
Cyprus cedar see *Cedrus brevifolia*

D

Daffodil see *Narcissus*
Dahlberg daisy see *Thymophylla tenuiloba*
Daily dew see *Drosera*
Daimio oak see *Quercus dentata*
Daisy see *Bellis*
Daisy bush see *Olearia*
Dalmatian bellflower see *Campanula portenschlagiana*
Dalmatian laburnum see *Petteria ramentacea*
Damask rose see *Rosa* x *damascena*
Dame's violet see *Hesperis matronalis*
Dancing doll orchid see *Oncidium flexuosum*
Dark-eye sunflower see *Helianthus atrorubens*
Dark mullein see *Verbascum nigrum*
Darley Dale heath see *Erica* x *darleyensis*
Dasheen see *Colocasia esculenta*
Date palm see *Phoenix dactylifera*
Date plum see *Diospyros lotus*
Dawn redwood see *Metasequoia glyptostroboides*
Day flower see *Commelina*
Daylily see *Hemerocallis*
Dead nettle see *Lamium*
Death camas see *Zigadenus venenosus*
Delta maidenhair fern see *Adiantum raddianum*
Deodar cedar see *Cedrus deodara*
Deptford pink see *Dianthus armeria*
Desert candle see *Eremurus*
Desert evening primrose see *Oenothera deltoides*
Desert fan palm see *Washingtonia filifera*
Desert lily see *Hesperocallis undulata*
Desert rose see *Adenium*
Desert willow see *Pittosporum phillyreoides*
Devil flower see *Tacca chantrierei*
Devil-in-a-bush see *Nigella, N. damascena*
Devil's apples see *Mandragora officinarum*
Devil's bit see *Chamaelirion*
Devil's bit scabious see *Succisa pratensis*
Devil's fig see *Argemone mexicana*
Devil's ivy see *Epipremnum aureum*
Devil's tongue see *Amorphophallus, A. konjac*
Devil's walking stick see *Aralia spinosa*
Dhak see *Butea monosperma*
Diamond-leaved laurel see *Pittosporum rhombifolium*
Diamond maidenhair fern see *Adiantum trapeziforme*
Diamond milfoil see *Myriophyllum aquaticum*
Dickie's fern see *Cystopteris dickieana*
Dickson's golden elm see *Ulmus minor* 'Dicksonii'
Digger pine see *Pinus sabineana*
Digger's speedwell see *Parahebe perfoliata*
Dill see *Anethum, A. graveolens*
Diss grass see *Ampelodesmos mauritanica*
Dittany see *Dictamnus albus*
Dock see *Rumex*
Dockmackie see *Viburnum acerifolium*
Dog's-tooth violet see *Erythronium*
Dog violet see *Viola canina*
Dogwood see *Cornus*
Doll's eyes see *Actaea pachypoda* f. *pachypoda*
Dorset heath see *Erica ciliaris*
Double bird's foot trefoil see *Lotus corniculatus* 'Plenus'
Double coconut see *Lodoicea*
Double creeping buttercup see *Ranunculus repens* var. *pleniflorus*
Double sea campion see *Silene uniflora* 'Robin Whitebreast'
Double velvet rose see *Rosa* 'Tuscany Superb'
Double white banksian rose see *Rosa banksiae*
Douglas fir see *Pseudotsuga menziesii*
Doum palm see *Hyphaene, H. coriacea*
Dove tree see *Davidia*
Downy birch see *Betula pubescens*
Dragon arum see *Dracunculus vulgaris*
Dragon's head see *Dracocephalum*
Dragon's mouth see *Horminum pyrenaicum*
Dragon spruce see *Picea asperata*
Dragon tree see *Dracaena draco*
Drooping coneflower see *Ratibida pinnata*
Drooping sedge see *Carex pendula*
Dropwort see *Filipendula vulgaris*
Drummond's wattle see *Acacia drummondii*
Drumstick primula see *Primula denticulata*
Drumsticks see *Isopogon, Pycnosorus, P. globosus*
Drunkard's dream see *Hatiora salicornioides*
Duck plant see *Sutherlandia frutescens*
Duck potato see *Sagittaria latifolia*
Duke of Argyll's tea tree see *Lycium barbarum*
Dumb cane see *Dieffenbachia*
Dumpling cactus see *Lophophora williamsii*
Dune manzanita see *Arctostaphylos pumila*
Dungwort see *Helleborus foetidus*
Dunkeld larch see *Larix* x *marschlinsii*
Dusky coral pea see *Kennedia rubicunda*
Dusky cranesbill see *Geranium phaeum*
Dusty miller see *Lychnis coronaria*
Dutch clover see *Trifolium repens*
Dutch crocus see *Crocus vernus*
Dutch elm see *Ulmus* x *hollandica*
Dutchman's breeches see *Dicentra cucullaria, D. spectabilis*
Dutchman's pipe see *Aristolochia, A. macrophylla*
Dwarf apple see *Angophora hispida*
Dwarf azalea see *Rhododendron atlanticum*
Dwarf bearded iris see *Iris pumila*
Dwarf bilberry see *Vaccinium caespitosum*
Dwarf birch see *Betula nana*
Dwarf cornel see *Cornus canadensis*
Dwarf fan palm see *Chamaerops*
Dwarf ginger lily see *Kaempferia roscoeana*
Dwarf gorse see *Ulex gallii*
Dwarf Japanese rush see *Acorus gramineus* var. *pusillus*
Dwarf maidenhair fern see *Adiantum aleuticum* var. *subpumilum*
Dwarf mountain pine see *Pinus mugo*
Dwarf palmetto see *Sabal minor*
Dwarf Russian almond see *Prunus tenella*
Dwarf Siberian pine see *Pinus pumila*
Dwarf snapdragon see *Chaenorhinum*
Dwarf Spanish heath see *Erica umbellata*
Dwarf sumach see *Rhus copallina*
Dwarf white wood lily see *Trillium nivale*
Dyer's greenweed see *Genista tinctoria*

E

Eagle's claw maple see *Acer platanoides* 'Laciniatum'
Early black wattle see *Acacia decurrens*
Early Dutch honeysuckle see *Lonicera periclymenum* 'Belgica'
Early purple orchid see *Orchis mascula*
Early spider orchid see *Ophrys sphegodes*
Earth star see *Cryptanthus*
East African laburnum see *Calpurnia aurea*
Easter cactus see *Hatiora rosea*
Easter lily see *Lilium longiflorum*
Eastern bog laurel see *Kalmia polifolia*
Eastern cottonwood see *Populus deltoides*
Eastern hemlock see *Tsuga canadensis*

F

Fuchsia-flowered currant see *Ribes speciosum*
Fuji cherry see *Prunus incisa*
Fukanoki see *Schefflera heptaphylla*
Full-moon maple see *Acer japonicum*
Fumewort see *Corydalis solida*
Furze see *Ulex, U. europaeus*

G

Galingale see *Cyperus longus*
Gallberry see *Ilex glabra*
Gardeners' garters see *Phalaris arundinacea* var. *picta*
Garden myrrh see *Myrrhis odorata*
Garden thyme see *Thymus vulgaris*
Garden violet see *Viola odorata*
Garland flower see *Daphne cneorum, Hedychium coronarium*
Garland lily see *Hedychium*
Garlic see *Allium sativum*
Gayfeather see *Liatris, L. spicata*
Gean see *Prunus avium*
Gentian see *Gentiana*
Geraldton wax see *Chamelaucium uncinatum*
Geranium aralia see *Polyscias guilfoylei*
German catchfly see *Lychnis viscaria*
Germander speedwell see *Veronica chamaedrys*
German ivy see *Senecio mikanioides*
Ghost tree see *Davidia*
Ghost weed see *Euphorbia marginata*
Giant bellflower see *Ostrowskia*
Giant Burmese honeysuckle see *Lonicera hildebrandiana*
Giant buttercup see *Ranunculus lyallii*
Giant cowslip see *Primula florindae*
Giant crepe myrtle see *Lagerstroemia speciosa*
Giant feather grass see *Stipa gigantea*
Giant fennel see *Ferula*
Giant fir see *Abies grandis*
Giant granadilla see *Passiflora quadrangularis*
Giant helleborine see *Epipactis gigantea*
Giant hogweed see *Heracleum mantegazzianum*
Giant lily see *Cardiocrinum*
Giant maidenhair fern see *Adiantum formosum, A. trapeziforme*
Giant marsh marigold see *Caltha palustris* var. *palustris*
Giant pineapple flower see *Eucomis pallidiflora*
Giant redwood see *Sequoiadendron giganteum*
Giant reed see *Arundo donax*
Giant scabious see *Cephalaria gigantea*
Giant Spaniard see *Aciphylla scott-thomsonii*
Giant taro see *Alocasia macrorrhiza*
Giant timber bamboo see *Phyllostachys bambusoides*
Giant vriesea see *Vriesea imperialis*
Giant water lily see *Victoria*
Giant yucca see *Yucca elephantipes*
Gillyflower see *Matthiola, M. incana*
Gingerbread palm see *Hyphaene thebaica*
Ginger lily see *Alpinia, Hedychium*
Ginger mint see *Mentha* x *gracilis* 'Variegata'
Gippsland waratah see *Telopea oreades*
Glastonbury thorn see *Crataegus monogyna* 'Biflora'
Glaucous hair grass see *Koeleria glauca*
Globe amaranth see *Gomphrena globosa*
Globe artichoke see *Cynara scolymus*
Globe daisy see *Globularia*
Globeflower see *Trollius*
Globe mallow see *Sphaeralcea*
Globe thistle see *Echinops*
Glory bower see *Clerodendrum chinense* var. *chinense, C. speciosissimum, C. thomsoniae*
Glory bush see *Tibouchina organensis, T. urvilleana*
Glory fern see *Adiantum tenerum* 'Farleyense'
Glory flower see *Clerodendrum bungei*
Glory lily see *Gloriosa*
Glory of the snow see *Chionodoxa*
Glory of the sun see *Leucocoryne ixioides*
Glory pea see *Clianthus formosus, C. puniceus*
Goatsbeard see *Aruncus dioicus*
Goat's horn cactus see *Astrophytum capricorne*
Goat's rue see *Galega*
Goat's thorn see *Astragalus*
Goldback fern see *Pityrogramma triangularis*
Gold dust see *Aurinia saxatilis*
Golden arum see *Zantedeschia elliottiana*
Golden bamboo see *Phyllostachys aurea*
Golden barrel cactus see *Echinocactus grusonii*
Golden bell see *Forsythia suspensa*
Golden chain orchid see *Dendrochilum*
Golden chervil see *Chaerophyllum aureum*
Golden chinkapin see *Chrysolepis chrysophylla*
Golden club see *Orontium*
Golden creeping Jenny see *Lysimachia nummularia* 'Aurea'
Golden dewdrop see *Duranta erecta*
Golden eardrops see *Dicentra chrysantha*
Golden everlasting see *Xerochrysum bracteatum*
Golden feather palm see *Chrysalidocarpus lutescens*
Golden flax see *Linum flavum*
Golden fleece see *Thymophylla tenuiloba*
Golden garlic see *Allium moly*
Golden groundsel see *Ligularia dentata*
Golden heather see *Cassinia leptophylla* subsp. *fulvida*
Golden larch see *Pseudolarix amabilis*
Golden male fern see *Dryopteris affinis*
Golden marguerite see *Anthemis tinctoria*
Golden oats see *Stipa gigantea*
Golden polypody see *Phlebodium aureum*
Golden pothos see *Epipremnum aureum*
Golden privet see *Ligustrum ovalifolium* 'Aureum'
Golden rain see *Laburnum*
Golden-rain tree see *Koelreuteria paniculata*
Golden-rayed lily see *Lilium auratum*
Golden rod see *Solidago*
Golden rose of China see *Rosa xanthina* f. *hugonis*
Golden saxifrage see *Chrysosplenium*
Golden shower see *Pyrostegia venusta*
Golden shower tree see *Cassia fistula*
Golden spider lily see *Lycoris aurea*
Golden top see *Lamarckia aurea*
Golden trumpet see *Allamanda cathartica*
Golden weeping willow see *Salix* x *sepulcralis* 'Chrysocoma'
Golden wild marjoram see *Origanum vulgare* 'Aureum'
Golden willow see *Salix alba* var. *vitellina*
Golden wood millet see *Milium effusum* 'Aureum'
Golden yarrow see *Eriophyllum*
Goldie's fern see *Dryopteris goldieana*
Goldilocks see *Aster linosyris*
Gold lace cactus see *Mammillaria elongata*
Gold lobelia see *Monopsis lutea*
Gold thread see *Coptis*
Good King Henry see *Chenopodium bonus-henricus*
Good luck plant see *Oxalis tetraphylla*
Good luck tree see *Cordyline fruticosa*
Goodyer's elm see *Ulmus minor* subsp. *angustifolia*
Goosefoot see *Chenopodium*
Goosefoot plant see *Syngonium, S. podophyllum*
Goosefoot vine see *Syngonium*
Gorgon plant see *Euryale*
Gorse see *Ulex, U. europaeus*
Granadilla see *Passiflora*
Grand fir see *Abies grandis*
Granite bottlebrush see *Melaleuca elliptica*
Granny's bonnet see *Aquilegia vulgaris*
Grape hyacinth see *Muscari*
Grape ivy see *Cissus rhombifolia*
Grape vine see *Vitis*
Grass of Parnassus see *Parnassia, P. palustris*
Grass widow see *Olsynium douglasii*
Grassy bells see *Edraianthus*
Great Basin violet see *Viola beckwithii*
Greater burnet see *Sanguisorba officinalis*
Greater celandine see *Chelidonium majus*
Greater knapweed see *Centaurea scabiosa*
Greater periwinkle see *Vinca major*
Greater quaking grass see *Briza maxima*
Greater spearwort see *Ranunculus lingua*
Greater woodrush see *Luzula sylvatica*
Great-leaved magnolia see *Magnolia macrophylla*
Great mullein see *Verbascum thapsus*
Great white cherry see *Prunus* 'Taihaku'
Great white rose see *Rosa* 'Alba Maxima'
Grecian strawberry tree see *Arbutus andrachne*
Greek bush basil see *Ocimum basilicum* var. *minimum*
Greek fir see *Abies cephalonica*
Greek maple see *Acer heldreichii* subsp. *trautvetteri*
Greek valerian see *Polemonium caeruleum*
Green alder see *Alnus viridis*
Green alkanet see *Pentaglottis, P. sempervirens*
Green arrow arum see *Peltandra virginica*
Green ash see *Fraxinus pennsylvanica*
Green bottlebrush see *Callistemon viridiflorus*
Green earth star see *Cryptanthus acaulis*
Green hellebore see *Helleborus viridis*
Green kangaroo paw see *Anigozanthos viridis*
Greenleaf manzanita see *Arctostaphylos patula*
Green osier see *Cornus alternifolia*
Green rose see *Rosa* x *odorata* 'Viridiflora'
Green-veined orchid see *Orchis morio*
Green wattle see *Acacia decurrens*
Grey alder see *Alnus incana*
Grey birch see *Betula populifolia*
Grey fescue see *Festuca glauca*
Grey goddess palm see *Brahea armata*
Grey-head coneflower see *Ratibida pinnata*
Grey poplar see *Populus* x *canescens*
Grizzly bear cactus see *Opuntia erinacea* var. *ursina*
Ground cherry see *Physalis*
Ground elder see *Aegopodium*
Ground ivy see *Glechoma*
Ground pink see *Linanthus dianthiflorus*
Guadalupe cypress see *Cupressus guadalupensis*
Guayacan polvillo see *Tabebuia serratifolia*
Guayiga see *Zamia pumila*
Guelder rose see *Viburnum opulus*
Guernsey lily see *Nerine sarniensis*
Guinea-wing begonia see *Begonia albopicta*
Gum see *Eucalyptus*
Gum plant see *Grindelia*
Gutta-percha tree see *Eucommia ulmoides*

H

Hackberry see *Celtis, C. occidentalis*
Hairawn muhly see *Muhlenbergia capillaris*
Hair grass see *Aira, A. elegantissima, Deschampsia*
Hairy canary clover see *Lotus hirsutus*
Hairy couch see *Elymus hispidus*
Hairy golden aster see *Heterotheca villosa*
Hairy lip fern see *Cheilanthes tomentosa*
Hairy spurge see *Euphorbia pilosa*
Hamburg parsley see *Petroselinum crispum* var. *tuberosum*
Handkerchief tree see *Davidia*
Hard fern see *Blechnum, B. spicant*
Hardheads see *Centaurea*
Hard shield fern see *Polystichum aculeatum*
Harebell see *Campanula rotundifolia*
Harebell poppy see *Meconopsis quintuplinervia*
Hare's foot fern see *Davallia canariensis, Phlebodium aureum*
Hare's tail see *Lagurus, L. ovatus*
Harlequin flower see *Sparaxis*
Harry Lauder's walking stick see *Corylus avellana* 'Contorta'
Hart's tongue fern see *Asplenium scolopendrium*
Hattie's pincushion see *Astrantia*
Hawaiian hibiscus see *Hibiscus rosa-sinensis*
Hawaiian tree fern see *Cibotium glaucum*
Hawk's beard see *Crepis*
Hawkweed see *Hieracium*
Hawthorn see *Crataegus*
Hawthorn maple see *Acer crataegifolium*
Hazel see *Corylus*
Headache tree see *Umbellularia californica*
Heart leaf see *Philodendron hederaceum*
Heart-leaved flame pea see *Chorizema cordatum*

Heart-lipped tongue orchid see *Serapias cordigera*
Heart of flame see *Bromelia balansae*
Heart of Jesus see *Caladium bicolor*
Heart pea see *Cardiospermum halicacabum*
Heartsease see *Viola tricolor*
Heart seed see *Cardiospermum*
Hearts on a string see *Ceropegia linearis* subsp. *woodii*
Heath see *Erica*
Heath banksia see *Banksia ericifolia*
Heather see *Calluna*
Heath myrtle see *Thryptomene*
Heath spotted orchid see *Dactylorhiza maculata*
Heath violet see *Viola canina*
Heavenly bamboo see *Nandina domestica*
Hedge bamboo see *Bambusa multiplex*
Hedgehog broom see *Erinacea anthyllis*
Hedgehog fir see *Abies pinsapo*
Hedgehog holly see *Ilex aquifolium* 'Ferox'
Hedgehog rose see *Rosa rugosa*
Hedge nettle see *Stachys*
Hedge wattle see *Acacia paradoxa*
Hedge woundwort see *Stachys sylvatica*
Helen's flower see *Helenium*
Heliotrope see *Heliotropium*, *H. arborescens*
Hellebore see *Helleborus*
Helleborine see *Epipactis*
Helmet flower see *Scutellaria*, *Sinningia cardinalis*
Hemlock see *Tsuga*
Hemp agrimony see *Eupatorium*, *E. cannabinum*
Hemp vine see *Mikania scandens*
Hen-and-chicken fern see *Asplenium bulbiferum*
Hen and chickens houseleek see *Jovibarba sobolifera*
Henbane see *Hyoscyamus*, *H. niger*
Henna tree see *Lawsonia*
Herald's trumpet see *Beaumontia grandiflora*
Herb Christopher see *Actaea spicata* var. *spicata*
Herb Robert see *Geranium robertianum*
Hercules' club see *Aralia spinosa*
Heron's bill see *Erodium*
Herringbone plant see *Maranta leuconeura* 'Erythroneura'
Hesper palm see *Brahea*
Hiba see *Thujopsis dolabrata*
Hickory see *Carya*
Higan cherry see *Prunus* x *subhirtella*
Highbush blueberry see *Vaccinium corymbosum*
Hill cherry see *Prunus jamasakura*
Himalayan birch see *Betula utilis*
Himalayan blue poppy see *Meconopsis betonicifolia*, *M. grandis*
Himalayan box see *Buxus wallichiana*
Himalayan cinquefoil see *Potentilla atrosanguinea*
Himalayan cowslip see *Primula sikkimensis*
Himalayan holly see *Ilex dipyrena*
Himalayan honeysuckle see *Leycesteria formosa*
Himalayan lilac see *Syringa emodi*
Himalayan maidenhair fern see *Adiantum venustum*
Himalayan peony see *Paeonia emodi*
Himalayan weeping juniper see *Juniperus recurva*
Hinoki cypress see *Chamaecyparis obtusa*
Hoary willow see *Salix elaeagnos*
Hobble bush see *Viburnum lantanoides*
Hognut see *Carya glabra*
Holford pine see *Pinus* x *holdfordiana*
Holly see *Ilex*
Holly fern see *Polystichum*
Holly-fern woodsia see *Woodsia polystichoides*
Holly flame pea see *Chorizema ilicifolium*
Hollyhock see *Alcea*, *A. rosea*
Hollyhock begonia see *Begonia gracilis* var. *martiana*
Hollyhock mallow see *Malva alcea*
Hollyleaf ceanothus see *Ceanothus purpureus*
Holly-leaved cherry see *Prunus ilicifolia*
Holly-leaved hovea see *Hovea chorizemifolia*
Holm oak see *Quercus ilex*
Hondo spruce see *Picea jezoensis* subsp. *hondoensis*
Honesty see *Lunaria*, *L. annua*
Honey-balls see *Cephalanthus occidentalis*
Honey bush see *Melianthus major*
Honey locust see *Gleditsia triacanthos*
Honey palm see *Jubaea chilensis*
Honey spurge see *Euphorbia mellifera*
Honeysuckle see *Lonicera*
Honeywort see *Cerinthe*
Hooked-spur violet see *Viola adunca*
Hook sedge see *Uncinia*
Hoop-petticoat daffodil see *Narcissus bulbocodium*
Hoop pine see *Araucaria cunninghamii*
Hop see *Humulus*, *H. lupulus*
Hop bush see *Dodonaea viscosa*
Hop-headed barleria see *Barleria lupulina*
Hop hornbeam see *Ostrya carpinifolia*
Hop marjoram see *Origanum dictamnus*
Hop tree see *Ptelea trifoliata*
Horehound see *Marrubium*
Hornbeam see *Carpinus*
Hornbeam maple see *Acer carpinifolium*
Horned holly see *Ilex cornuta*
Horned poppy see *Glaucium*
Horned rampion see *Phyteuma*
Horned violet see *Viola cornuta*
Hornwort see *Ceratophyllum*, *C. demersum*
Horse chestnut see *Aesculus*, *A. hippocastanum*
Horsemint see *Mentha longifolia*
Horseradish see *Armoracia rusticana*
Horseshoe vetch see *Hippocrepis*
Horsetail tree see *Casuarina equisetifolia*
Hottentot fig see *Carpobrotus edulis*
Hot water plant see *Achimenes*
Hound's tongue see *Cynoglossum*, *C. nervosum*, *C. officinale*
Houpara see *Pseudopanax lessonii*
Houseleek see *Sempervivum*
Hubei rowan see *Sorbus hupehensis*
Huckleberry see *Gaylussacia*
Humble plant see *Mimosa pudica*
Hungarian oak see *Quercus frainetto*
Huntingdon elm see *Ulmus* x *hollandica* 'Vegeta'
Huntsman's cup see *Sarracenia purpurea*
Hyacinth see *Hyacinthus*
Hybrid larch see *Larix* x *marschlinsii*
Hyssop see *Hyssopus*, *H. officinalis*

I

Ice fescue see *Festuca glacialis*
Icelandic poppy see *Papaver croceum*
Ice plant see *Dorotheanthus*, *Sedum spectabile*
Ilang-ilang see *Cananga odorata*
Illawarra palm see *Archontophoenix cunninghamiana*
Impala lily see *Adenium*
Imperial taro see *Colocasia esculenta* 'Illustris'
Incense cedar see *Calocedrus*, *C. decurrens*
Incense plant see *Calomeria*, *C. amaranthoides*, *Olearia moschata*
Incense rose see *Rosa primula*
Indian almond see *Terminalia catappa*
Indian bean see *Lablab purpureus*
Indian bean tree see *Catalpa bignonioides*
Indian blanket see *Gaillardia pulchella*
Indian cress see *Tropaeolum majus*
Indian currant see *Symphoricarpos orbiculatus*
Indian fig see *Ficus benghalensis*, *Opuntia ficus-indica*
Indian ginger see *Alpinia calcarata*
Indian grass see *Sorghastrum nutans*
Indian hawthorn see *Rhaphiolepis indica*
Indian hemp see *Hibiscus cannabinus*
Indian horse chestnut see *Aesculus indica*
Indian laburnum see *Cassia fistula*
Indian laurel see *Ficus microcarpa*
Indian mallow see *Abutilon*
Indian physic see *Gillenia trifoliata*
Indian pink see *Dianthus chinensis*
Indian plum see *Oemleria cerasiformis*
Indian poke see *Veratrum viride*
Indian rhododendron see *Melastoma malabathricum*
Indian root see *Asclepias curassavica*
Indian shot plant see *Canna*
Indian strawberry see *Duchesnea indica*
India rubber fig see *Ficus elastica*
India rubber tree see *Ficus elastica*
Inkberry see *Ilex glabra*
Intermediate wheatgrass see *Elymus hispidus*
Interrupted fern see *Osmunda claytoniana*
Irish gorse see *Ulex europaeus* 'Strictus'
Irish heath see *Erica erigena*
Irish ivy see *Hedera hibernica*
Irish yew see *Taxus baccata* 'Fastigiata'
Ironbark see *Eucalyptus*
Iron-cross begonia see *Begonia masoniana*
Ironweed see *Vernonia*
Ironwood see *Ostrya virginiana*
Italian alder see *Alnus cordata*
Italian bellflower see *Campanula isophylla*
Italian buckthorn see *Rhamnus alaternus*
Italian clover see *Trifolium incarnatum*
Italian cypress see *Cupressus sempervirens*
Italian honeysuckle see *Lonicera caprifolium*
Italian ivy see *Hedera helix* f. *poetarum*
Italian jasmine see *Solanum seaforthianum*
Italian maple see *Acer opalus*
Italian parsley see *Petroselinum crispum* var. *neapolitanum*
Italian verbena see *Verbena* x *maonettii*
Ivory bells see *Campanula alliariifolia*
Ivy see *Hedera*
Ivy-leaf peperomia see *Peperomia griseoargentea*
Ivy-leaved toadflax see *Cymbalaria muralis*
Ivy-leaved violet see *Viola hederacea*
Ivy of Uruguay see *Cissus striata*
Ivy tree see *Schefflera heptaphylla*

J

Jaburan lily see *Ophiopogon jaburan*
Jack-in-the-pulpit see *Arisaema triphyllum*
Jack pine see *Pinus banksiana*
Jacobean lily see *Sprekelia formosissima*
Jacobite rose see *Rosa* 'Alba Maxima'
Jacob's ladder see *Polemonium*, *P. caeruleum*
Jacob's rod see *Asphodeline*
Jade plant see *Crassula ovata*
Jade tree see *Crassula ovata*
Jade vine see *Strongylodon macrobotrys*
Jaggery palm see *Caryota urens*
Japanese alder see *Alnus japonica*
Japanese anemone see *Anemone hupehensis* var. *japonica*, *A.* x *hybrida*
Japanese angelica tree see *Aralia elata*
Japanese apricot see *Prunus mume*
Japanese aralia see *Fatsia japonica*
Japanese arrowhead see *Sagittaria sagittifolia*
Japanese arrowroot see *Pueraria lobata*
Japanese banana see *Musa basjoo*
Japanese beech see *Fagus crenata*
Japanese big-leaf magnolia see *Magnolia obovata*
Japanese bitter orange see *Poncirus trifoliata*
Japanese black pine see *Pinus thunbergii*
Japanese cedar see *Cryptomeria*, *C. japonica*
Japanese cherry birch see *Betula grossa*
Japanese climbing fern see *Lygodium japonicum*
Japanese crab apple see *Malus floribunda*
Japanese fatsia see *Fatsia japonica*
Japanese felt fern see *Pyrrosia lingua*
Japanese foam flower see *Tanakaea*
Japanese holly see *Ilex crenata*
Japanese holly fern see *Cyrtomium falcatum*
Japanese honeysuckle see *Lonicera japonica*
Japanese horse chestnut see *Aesculus turbinata*
Japanese ivy see *Hedera rhombea*
Japanese lantern see *Hibiscus schizopetalus*, *Physalis alkekengi*
Japanese larch see *Larix kaempferi*
Japanese lime see *Tilia japonica*
Japanese maple see *Acer japonicum*, *A. palmatum*
Japanese mock orange see *Pittosporum tobira*
Japanese muhly see *Muhlenbergia japonica*
Japanese pagoda tree see *Sophora japonica*
Japanese painted fern see *Athyrium niponicum*
Japanese persimmon see *Diospyros kaki*
Japanese pond lily see *Nuphar japonica*

Japanese primrose see *Primula japonica*
Japanese privet see *Ligustrum japonicum*
Japanese quince see *Chaenomeles, C. japonica*
Japanese red pine see *Pinus densiflora*
Japanese rose see *Rosa rugosa*
Japanese rush see *Acorus gramineus*
Japanese sago palm see *Cycas revoluta*
Japanese snowball bush see *Viburnum plicatum* f. *plicatum*
Japanese snowbell see *Styrax japonicus*
Japanese spindle see *Euonymus japonicus*
Japanese tassel fern see *Polystichum polyblepharum*
Japanese umbrella pine see *Sciadopitys verticillata*
Japanese walnut see *Juglans ailantifolia*
Japanese white pine see *Pinus parviflora*
Japanese wing nut see *Pterocarya rhoifolia*
Japanese winterberry see *Ilex serrata*
Japanese wisteria see *Wisteria floribunda*
Japanese witch hazel see *Hamamelis japonica*
Japanese yew see *Taxus cuspidata*
Japanese zelkova see *Zelkova serrata*
Japonica see *Chaenomeles, C. japonica*
Japan pepper see *Zanthoxylum piperitum*
Jasmine see *Jasminum*
Java glorybean see *Clerodendrum speciosissimum*
Jeffrey pine see *Pinus jeffreyi*
Jelly palm see *Butia capitata*
Jersey elm see *Ulmus minor* subsp. *sarniensis*
Jerusalem cherry see *Solanum pseudocapsicum*
Jerusalem cowslip see *Pulmonaria officinalis*
Jerusalem cross see *Lychnis chalcedonica*
Jerusalem sage see *Phlomis fruticosa, Pulmonaria saccharata*
Jerusalem thorn see *Paliurus spina-christi, Parkinsonia aculeata*
Jessamine see *Jasminum*
Jesuit's nut see *Trapa natans*
Jewel orchid see *Goodyera*
Jewels of Opar see *Talinum paniculatum*
Jew's mantle see *Kerria*
Jim sage see *Salvia clevelandii*
Job's tears see *Coix lacryma-jobi*
Joe Pye weed see *Eupatorium purpureum*
Jointed rush see *Juncus articulatus*
Judas tree see *Cercis siliquastrum*
Juneberry see *Amelanchier*
Jungle brake see *Pteris umbrosa*
Jungle flame see *Ixora coccinea*
Jungle geranium see *Ixora coccinea*
Juniper see *Juniperus*
Jupiter's distaff see *Salvia glutinosa*

K

Kaffir bread see *Encephalartos caffer*
Kaffir fig see *Carpobrotus edulis*
Kaffir lily see *Schizostylis*
Kahili ginger see *Hedychium gardnerianum*
Kaki see *Diospyros kaki*
Kangaroo apple see *Solanum aviculare, S. laciniatum*
Kangaroo paw see *Anigozanthos*
Kangaroo thorn see *Acacia paradoxa*
Kangaroo vine see *Cissus antarctica*
Kansas feather see *Liatris pycnostachya*
Kapok see *Ceiba pentandra*
Kapokkie heath see *Erica peziza*
Karaka see *Corynocarpus laevigatus*
Karo see *Pittosporum crassifolium*
Karum oil tree see *Pongamia pinnata*
Kashmir cypress see *Cupressus torulosa* 'Cashmeriana'
Kassod tree see *Senna siamea*
Katsura tree see *Cercidiphyllum japonicum*
Kauri pine see *Agathis, A. australis*
Kawaka see *Libocedrus plumosa*
Kawa kawa see *Macropiper excelsum*
Kenaf see *Hibiscus cannabinus*
Kentia palm see *Howea forsteriana*
Kentucky coffee tree see *Gymnocladus dioica*
Kermes oak see *Quercus coccifera*
Kerosene bush see *Ozothamnus ledifolius*
Key palm see *Thrinax morrisii*
Kidney vetch see *Anthyllis vulneraria*
Kilmarnock willow see *Salix caprea* 'Kilmarnock'
King anthurium see *Anthurium warocqueanum*
King begonia see *Begonia rex*
Kingcup see *Caltha, C. palustris*
Kingfisher daisy see *Felicia bergeriana*
King of bromeliads see *Vriesea hieroglyphica*
King palm see *Archontophoenix*
King protea see *Protea cynaroides*
King's crown see *Justicia carnea*
King's mantle see *Thunbergia erecta*
King's spear see *Asphodeline lutea*
King William pine see *Athrotaxis selaginoides*
Kinnikinnick see *Arctostaphylos uva-ursi*
Kiss-me-over-the-garden-gate see *Persicaria orientale*
Kiwi fruit see *Actinidia deliciosa*
Klapperbos see *Nymania capensis*
Knapweed see *Centaurea*
Knife-leaf wattle see *Acacia cultriformis*
Knobcone pine see *Pinus attenuata*
Kohuhu see *Pittosporum tenuifolium*
Korean fir see *Abies koreana*
Korean forsythia see *Forsythia ovata*
Korean maple see *Acer pseudosieboldianum*
Korean mountain ash see *Sorbus alnifolia*
Korean pine see *Pinus koraiensis*
Korean rock fern see *Polystichum tsussimense*
Korokio see *Corokia buddlejoides*
Kowhai see *Sophora tetraptera*
Krauss's spikemoss see *Selaginella kraussiana*
Kris plant see *Alocasia sanderiana*
Kudzu vine see *Pueraria lobata*
Kumquat see *Fortunella*
Kurrajong see *Brachychiton, B. discolor, B. populneus*
Kusamaki see *Podocarpus macrophyllus*
Kybean gum see *Eucalyptus parvifolia*
Kyo-Chiku see *Dendrocalamus giganteus*

L

Labrador tea see *Ledum groenlandicum*
Labrador violet see *Viola labradorica*
Lace aralia see *Polyscias guilfoylei* 'Victoriae'
Lace-bark see *Hoheria populnea*
Lacebark pine see *Pinus bungeana*
Lace plant see *Aponogeton madagascariensis*
Lad's love see *Artemisia abrotanum*
Lady fern see *Athyrium, A. filix-femina*
Lady of the night see *Brunfelsia americana*
Lady palm see *Rhapis*
Lady's mantle see *Alchemilla*
Lady's slipper orchid see *Cypripedium, C. calceolus*
Lady's smock see *Cardamine pratensis*
Lady tulip see *Tulipa clusiana*
Lambs' ears see *Stachys byzantina*
Lambs' lugs see *Stachys byzantina*
Lambs' tails see *Stachys byzantina*
Lambs' tongues see *Stachys byzantina*
Lancewood see *Pseudopanax crassifolius*
Lantern tree see *Crinodendron hookerianum*
Larch see *Larix*
Large blue fescue see *Festuca amethystina*
Large-leaved holly fern see *Cyrtomium macrophyllum*
Large-leaved lime see *Tilia platyphyllos*
Large merrybells see *Uvularia grandiflora*
Large self-heal see *Prunella grandiflora*
Larkspur see *Consolida, C. ajacis*
Larkspur violet see *Viola pedatifida*
Latan palm see *Latania*
Late Dutch honeysuckle see *Lonicera periclymenum* 'Serotina'
Late spider orchid see *Ophrys holoserica*
Lattice leaf plant see *Aponogeton madagascariensis*
Laudanum see *Cistus ladanifer*
Laurel see *Prunus laurocerasus, P. lusitanica*
Laurustinus see *Viburnum tinus*
Lavandin see *Lavandula* x *intermedia*
Lavender see *Lavandula, L. angustifolia*
Lawn chamomile see *Chamaemelum nobile*
Lawson cypress see *Chamaecyparis lawsoniana*
Lead plant see *Amorpha canescens*
Leadwort see *Plumbago*
Leafy hawkweed see *Hieracium umbellatum*
Least snowbell see *Soldanella minima*
Leather fern see *Rumohra adiantiformis*
Leatherleaf see *Chamaedaphne calyculata*
Leatherleaf sedge see *Carex buchananii*
Leatherwood see *Cyrilla racemiflora, Dirca palustris*
Leathery polypody see *Polypodium scouleri*
Lebanon oak see *Quercus libani*
Lebombo cycad see *Encephalartos lebomboensis*
Lemon see *Citrus limon*
Lemon balm see *Melissa officinalis*
Lemon bottlebrush see *Callistemon pallidus*
Lemon grass see *Cymbopogon citratus*
Lemon ironwood see *Backhousia citriodora*
Lemon mint see *Mentha* x *piperita* f. *citrata*
Lemon-scented myrtle see *Backhousia citriodora, Darwinia citriodora*
Lemon-scented thyme see *Thymus* x *citriodorus*
Lemon verbena see *Aloysia triphylla*
Lemonwood see *Pittosporum eugenioides*
Lenten rose see *Helleborus orientalis*
Lentisc see *Pistacia lentiscus*
Lent lily see *Narcissus pseudonarcissus*
Leopard begonia see *Begonia manicata*
Leopard lily see *Belamcanda chinensis, Lilium pardalinum*
Leopard's bane see *Doronicum*
Leopard's bane ragwort see *Senecio doronicum*
Lesser bulrush see *Typha angustifolia*
Lesser calamint see *Calamintha nepeta*
Lesser celandine see *Ranunculus ficaria*
Lesser periwinkle see *Vinca minor*
Lesser quaking grass see *Briza minor*
Lesser spearwort see *Ranunculus flammula*
Lettuce leaf begonia see *Begonia* 'Crestabruchii'
Leyland cypress see x *Cupressocyparis leylandii*
Liana see *Semele androgyna*
Licorice fern see *Polypodium glycyrrhiza*
Lijiang spruce see *Picea likiangensis*
Lilac see *Syringa*
Lilac fuchsia see *Fuchsia arborescens*
Lillypilly see *Acmena smithii*
Lily see *Lilium*
Lily-of-the-valley see *Convallaria*
Lily-of-the-valley tree see *Clethra arborea*
Lily tree see *Magnolia denudata*
Lilyturf see *Liriope, Ophiopogon*
Limber pine see *Pinus flexilis*
Lime see *Tilia*
Limestone polypody see *Gymnocarpium robertianum*
Lincolnshire spinach see *Chenopodium bonus-henricus*
Linden see *Tilia*
Ling see *Calluna, C. vulgaris*
Lion's ear see *Leonotis leonurus*
Lip fern see *Cheilanthes*
Lipstick palm see *Cyrtostachys lakka*
Lipstick plant see *Aeschynanthus pulcher*
Lipstick tree see *Bixa orellana*
Lipstick vine see *Aeschynanthus radicans* var. *lobbianus*
Liquorice see *Glycyrrhiza glabra*
Little bluestem see *Schizachyrium scoparium*
Little kangaroo paw see *Anigozanthos bicolor*
Little pickles see *Othonna capensis*
Living baseball see *Euphorbia obesa*
Living granite see *Pleiospilos*
Living rock see *Ariocarpus fissuratus*
Livingstone daisy see *Dorotheanthus, D. bellidiformis*
Living stones see *Lithops*
Lizard plant see *Tetrastigma voinierianum*
Lizard tail see *Crassula muscosa*
Lobel's maple see *Acer cappadocicum* subsp. *lobelii*
Loblolly bay see *Gordonia lasianthus*
Lobster claw see *Clianthus puniceus, Vriesea carinata*
Locust see *Robinia pseudoacacia*
Lodgepole pine see *Pinus contorta, P. contorta* var. *latifolia*
Lollipop plant see *Pachystachys lutea*
Lombardy poplar see *Populus nigra* var. *italica*
London plane see *Platanus* x *hispanica*
London pride see *Saxifraga* x *urbium*
Long-headed poppy see *Papaver dubium*

Long-leaf wax flower see *Eriostemon myoporoides*
Looking glass plant see *Coprosma repens*
Loosestrife see *Lysimachia, Lythrum*
Loquat see *Eriobotrya japonica*
Lord Anson's blue pea see *Lathyrus nervosus*
Lords and ladies see *Arum*
Lotus see *Nelumbo*
Lovage see *Levisticum*
Love apple see *Mandragora officinarum*
Love grass see *Eragrostis*
Love-in-a-mist see *Nigella, N. damascena*
Love-in-a-puff see *Cardiospermum halicacabum*
Love-in-idleness see *Viola tricolor*
Love-lies-bleeding see *Amaranthus caudatus*
Lovely penstemon see *Penstemon venustus*
Lowbush blueberry see *Vaccinium angustifolium* var. *laevifolium*
Lucerne see *Medicago sativa*
Lucky bean tree see *Erythrina caffra, E. lysistemon*
Lucky clover see *Oxalis tetraphylla*
Lucombe oak see *Quercus* x *hispanica* 'Lucombeana'
Lungwort see *Pulmonaria*
Lupin see *Lupinus*
Lyre flower see *Dicentra spectabilis*

M

Macartney rose see *Rosa bracteata*
Macassar oil tree see *Cananga odorata*
Macaw fat palm see *Elaeis guineensis*
Macedonian pine see *Pinus peuce*
Mace sedge see *Carex grayi*
Mackay's heath see *Erica mackaiana*
Macquarie vine see *Muehlenbeckia adpressa*
Macqui see *Aristotelia chilensis*
Madagascar jasmine see *Stephanotis floribunda*
Madagascar periwinkle see *Catharanthus, C. roseus*
Madeira vine see *Anredera cordifolia*
Madonna lily see *Lilium candidum*
Madroño see *Arbutus menziesii*
Maiden grass see *Miscanthus sinensis* 'Gracillimus'
Maidenhair fern see *Adiantum*
Maidenhair spleenwort see *Asplenium trichomanes*
Maidenhair tree see *Ginkgo, G. biloba*
Maiden pink see *Dianthus deltoides*
Maiten see *Maytenus boaria*
Maize see *Zea mays*
Majorcan peony see *Paeonia cambessedesii*
Malanga see *Xanthosoma*
Malanga blanca see *Xanthosoma sagittifolium*
Malay banyan see *Ficus microcarpa*
Male fern see *Dryopteris filix-mas*
Mallow see *Lavatera, Malva*
Maltese cross see *Lychnis chalcedonica*
Manchurian cherry see *Prunus maackii*
Manchurian crab apple see *Malus baccata* var. *mandshurica*
Manchurian walnut see *Juglans mandshurica*
Mandarin see *Citrus reticulata*
Mandrake see *Mandragora*
Man fern see *Dicksonia antarctica*
Mangles' kangaroo paw see *Anigozanthos manglesii*
Manila palm see *Veitchia merrillii*
Manna ash see *Fraxinus ornus*
Manna gum see *Eucalyptus viminalis*
Manuka see *Leptospermum scoparium*
Manzanita see *Arbutus, Arctostaphylos, A. manzanita*
Maple see *Acer*
Maple-leaf begonia see *Begonia dregei, B.* 'Weltoniensis'
Maracuja de refresco see *Passiflora alata*
Marbled rainbow plant see *Billbergia* Fantasia Group
Marguerite see *Leucanthemum vulgare*
Marigold see *Calendula*
Mariposa tulip see *Calochortus*
Maritime pine see *Pinus pinaster*
Marjoram see *Origanum*
Marlberry see *Ardisia japonica*
Marlborough rock daisy see *Pachystegia insignis*
Marmalade bush see *Streptosolen jamesonii*
Marsh andromeda see *Andromeda polifolia*
Marsh blue violet see *Viola obliqua*
Marsh cinquefoil see *Potentilla palustris*
Marsh fern see *Thelypteris palustris*
Marsh hypericum see *Hypericum elodes*
Marsh ledum see *Ledum palustre*
Marsh mallow see *Althaea officinalis*
Marsh marigold see *Caltha, C. palustris*
Marsh orchid see *Dactylorhiza*
Marvel of Peru see *Mirabilis jalapa*
Mask flower see *Alonsoa*
Masterwort see *Astrantia*
Mastic tree see *Pistacia lentiscus*
Matilija poppy see *Romneya*
Mat rush see *Lomandra*
Maule's quince see *Chaenomeles japonica*
Mauritania vine reed see *Ampelodesmos mauritanica*
May see *Crataegus laevigata, C. monogyna*
May apple see *Podophyllum peltatum*
Mayflower see *Epigaea repens*
May lily see *Maianthemum*
Maypops see *Passiflora incarnata*
Meadow beauty see *Rhexia, R. virginica*
Meadow buttercup see *Ranunculus acris*
Meadow clary see *Salvia pratensis*
Meadow cranesbill see *Geranium pratense*
Meadow grass see *Poa*
Meadow lily see *Lilium canadense*
Meadow phlox see *Phlox maculata*
Meadow rue see *Thalictrum*
Meadow saffron see *Colchicum autumnale*
Meadow saxifrage see *Saxifraga granulata*
Meadowsweet see *Filipendula ulmaria*
Meadow vetchling see *Lathyrus pratensis*
Mealie heath see *Erica patersonia*
Mealy sage see *Salvia farinacea*
Medick see *Medicago*
Mediterranean cypress see *Cupressus sempervirens*
Mediterranean heath see *Erica erigena*
Medlar see *Mespilus germanica*
Medusa's head see *Euphorbia caput-medusae*
Melick see *Melica*
Memorial rose see *Rosa wichurana*
Menzies' banksia see *Banksia menziesii*
Merrybells see *Uvularia*
Metallic-leaf begonia see *Begonia metallica*
Mexican breadfruit see *Monstera deliciosa*
Mexican bush see *Salvia leucantha*
Mexican creeper see *Antigonon leptopus*
Mexican cypress see *Cupressus lusitanica*
Mexican fern palm see *Dioon edule*
Mexican firecracker see *Echeveria setosa*
Mexican flame bush see *Calliandra tweedii*
Mexican flame leaf see *Euphorbia pulcherrima*
Mexican foxglove see *Tetranema roseum*
Mexican grass plant see *Dasylirion longissimum*
Mexican hat see *Ratibida*
Mexican hat plant see *Kalanchoe daigremontiana*
Mexican horncone see *Ceratozamia mexicana*
Mexican lily see *Hippeastrum reginae*
Mexican muhly see *Muhlenbergia mexicana*
Mexican orange blossom see *Choisya, C. ternata*
Mexican piñon see *Pinus cembroides*
Mexican sunflower see *Tithonia, T. rotundifolia*
Mexican tulip poppy see *Hunnemannia fumariifolia*
Mexican violet see *Tetranema roseum*
Mexican weeping pine see *Pinus patula*
Mexican white pine see *Pinus ayacahuite*
Mexican zinnia see *Zinnia haageana*
Meyer's lemon see *Citrus limon* 'Meyer'
Mezereon see *Daphne mezereum*
Michaelmas daisy see *Aster novi-belgii*
Mickey Mouse plant see *Ochna serrulata*
Midland hawthorn see *Crataegus laevigata*
Mignonette see *Reseda*
Mignonette tree see *Lawsonia*
Mignonette vine see *Anredera cordifolia*
Mile-a-minute plant see *Fallopia aubertii, F. baldschuanica*
Milfoil see *Myriophyllum*
Milk bush see *Gomphocarpus fruticosus*
Milkmaids see *Burchardia*
Milk vetch see *Astragalus*
Milkweed see *Asclepias, Euphorbia*
Milkwort see *Polygala, P. calcarea*
Milky bellflower see *Campanula lactiflora*
Millet see *Panicum miliaceum*
Mimosa see *Acacia dealbata*
Mind your own business see *Soleirolia soleirolii*
Miniature date palm see *Phoenix roebelenii*
Miniature fan palm see *Rhapis excelsa*
Miniature fish-tail palm see *Chamaedorea metallica*
Miniature holly see *Malpighia coccigera*
Mint see *Mentha*
Mint bush see *Prostanthera*
Mintleaf see *Plectranthus madagascariensis*
Mirbeck's oak see *Quercus canariensis*
Mirror orchid see *Ophrys vernixia*
Mission bells see *Fritillaria biflora*
Mississippi hackberry see *Celtis laevigata*
Miss Willmott's ghost see *Eryngium giganteum*
Mistletoe cactus see *Rhipsalis baccifera*
Mistletoe fig see *Ficus deltoidea*
Mitrewort see *Mitella*
Mock orange see *Philadelphus, P. coronarius*
Mock strawberry see *Duchesnea indica*
Modjadji cycad see *Encephalartos transvenosus*
Mole plant see *Euphorbia lathyris*
Monarch birch see *Betula maximowicziana*
Monarch of the East see *Sauromatum venosum*
Monarch of the veldt see *Arctotis fastuosa*
Monga waratah see *Telopea mongaensis*
Mongolian lime see *Tilia mongolica*
Monkey cup see *Nepenthes*
Monkey flower see *Mimulus*
Monkey musk see *Mimulus luteus*
Monkey plant see *Ruellia makoyana*
Monkey puzzle see *Araucaria araucana*
Monkshood see *Aconitum, A. napellus*
Montbretia see *Crocosmia, C.* x *crocosmiiflora*
Monterey ceanothus see *Ceanothus rigidus*
Monterey cypress see *Cupressus macrocarpa*
Monterey pine see *Pinus radiata*
Montezuma pine see *Pinus montezumae*
Montpellier maple see *Acer monspessulanum*
Montpellier rock rose see *Cistus monspeliensis*
Moon carrot see *Seseli*
Moonflower see *Ipomoea alba*
Moonlight holly see *Ilex aquifolium* 'Flavescens'
Moonseed see *Menispermum*
Moon trefoil see *Medicago arborea*
Moosewood see *Acer pensylvanicum*
Mop-head acacia see *Robinia pseudoacacia* 'Umbraculifera'
Moreton Bay chestnut see *Castanospermum australe*
Moreton Bay fig see *Ficus macrophylla*
Moreton Bay pine see *Araucaria cunninghamii*
Morinda spruce see *Picea smithiana*
Morning glory see *Ipomoea, I. tricolor*
Morning star lily see *Lilium concolor*
Mortiña see *Vaccinium floribundum*
Moses-in-the-cradle see *Tradescantia spathacea*
Mosquito bills see *Dodecatheon hendersonii*
Mosquito grass see *Bouteloua gracilis*
Mosquito plant see *Azolla filiculoides*
Moss campion see *Silene acaulis*
Moss phlox see *Phlox subulata*
Moss verbena see *Verbena tenuisecta*
Mother-in-law's cushion see *Echinocactus grusonii*
Mother-in-law's tongue see *Dieffenbachia, Sansevieria trifasciata*
Mother of pearl plant see *Graptopetalum paraguayense*
Mother of thousands see *Saxifraga stolonifera* 'Tricolor', *Soleirolia soleirolii*
Mother of thyme see *Acinos arvensis*
Mother spleenwort see *Asplenium bulbiferum*
Moth orchid see *Phalaenopsis*
Mottlecah see *Eucalyptus macrocarpa*
Mountain alder see *Alnus tenuifolia*
Mountain ash see *Sorbus aucuparia*
Mountain avens see *Dryas, D. octopetala*
Mountain beech see *Nothofagus solanderi* var. *cliffortioides*
Mountain devil see *Lambertia formosa*
Mountain ebony see *Bauhinia variegata*
Mountain flax see *Phormium cookianum*
Mountain fringe see *Adlumia fungosa*

Mountain gum see *Eucalyptus dalrympleana*
Mountain hakea see *Hakea lissosperma*
Mountain hemlock see *Tsuga mertensiana*
Mountain holly see *Olearia ilicifolia*
Mountain laurel see *Kalmia latifolia*
Mountain maple see *Acer spicatum*
Mountain melick see *Melica nutans*
Mountain pansy see *Viola lutea*
Mountain pepper see *Drimys lanceolata*
Mountain phlox see *Linanthus grandiflorus*
Mountain pine see *Pinus uncinata*
Mountain sow thistle see *Cicerbita alpina*
Mountain thistle see *Acanthus montanus*
Mount Cook lily see *Ranunculus lyallii*
Mount Etna broom see *Genista aetnensis*
Mount Wellington peppermint see *Eucalyptus coccifera*
Mourning iris see *Iris susiana*
Mourning widow see *Geranium phaeum*
Mouse plant see *Arisarum proboscideum*
Moutan see *Paeonia suffruticosa*
Mrs. Frizell's lady fern see *Athyrium filix-femina* 'Frizelliae'
Mrs. Robb's bonnet see *Euphorbia amygdaloides* var. *robbiae*
Mugga see *Eucalyptus sideroxylon*
Mugwort see *Artemisia*
Muhly see *Muhlenbergia*
Mulberry see *Morus*
Mullein see *Verbascum*
Musk see *Mimulus*
Musk mallow see *Abelmoschus moschatus, Malva moschata*
Musk rose see *Rosa moschata*
Musk willow see *Salix aegyptiaca*
Myriad leaf see *Myriophyllum verticillatum*
Myrobalan see *Prunus cerasifera*
Myrrh-scented rose see *Rosa* 'Splendens'
Myrtle see *Myrtus*
Myrtle beech see *Nothofagus cunninghamii*

N

Naked ladies see *Colchicum*
Nankeen lily see *Lilium* x *testaceum*
Narihira bamboo see *Semiarundinaria fastuosa*
Narrow buckler fern see *Dryopteris carthusiana*
Narrow-leaved ash see *Fraxinus angustifolia*
Narrow-leaved black peppermint see *Eucalyptus nicholii*
Narrow-leaved bottlebrush see *Callistemon linearis*
Narrow-leaved reedmace see *Typha angustifolia*
Nasturtium see *Tropaeolum majus*
Natal bottlebrush see *Greyia sutherlandii*
Natal cycad see *Encephalartos atalensis*
Natal grass see *Melinis repens*
Natal ivy see *Senecio macroglossus*
Natal laburnum see *Calpurnia aurea*
Natal plum see *Carissa macrocarpa*
Navelwort see *Omphalodes*
Necklace poplar see *Populus deltoides*
Needle grass see *Stipa*
Needle palm see *Rhapidophyllum*
Nepal ivy see *Hedera nepalensis*
Nerve plant see *Fittonia*
Nest moor grass see *Sesleria nitida*
Net bush see *Calothamnus*
Nettle-leaved bellflower see *Campanula trachelium*
Nettle-leaved mullein see *Verbascum chaixii*
Nettle tree see *Celtis*
Never-never plant see *Ctenanthe oppenheimiana* 'Tricolor'
New Caledonian pine see *Araucaria columnaris*
New England aster see *Aster novae-angliae*
New Guinea creeper see *Mucuna bennettii*
New Mexico locust see *Robinia neomexicana*
New South Wales Christmas tree see *Ceratopetalum gummiferum*
New York aster see *Aster novi-belgii*
New Zealand bluebell see *Wahlenbergia albomarginata*
New Zealand burr see *Acaena*
New Zealand cabbage palm see *Cordyline australis*
New Zealand daisy see *Celmisia*
New Zealand edelweiss see *Leucogenes*
New Zealand flax see *Phormium tenax*
New Zealand honeysuckle see *Knightia excelsa*
New Zealand tea tree see *Leptospermum scoparium*
Ngaio see *Myoporum laetum*
Night-scented stock see *Matthiola longipetala* subsp. *bicornis*
Nikau palm see *Rhopalostylis sapida*
Nikko fir see *Abies homolepis*
Nikko maple see *Acer maximowiczianum*
Ninebark see *Physocarpus opulifolius*
Nirre see *Nothofagus antarctica*
Noble bamboo see *Himalayacalamus falconeri*
Noble fir see *Abies procera*
Nodding catchfly see *Silene pendula*
Nodding ladies' tresses see *Spiranthes cernua*
Nodding lily see *Lilium cernuum*
Nodding onion see *Allium cernuum*
Nootka cypress see *Chamaecyparis nootkatensis*
Nootka rose see *Rosa nutkana*
Nordmann fir see *Abies nordmanniana*
Norfolk Island hibiscus see *Lagunaria*
Norfolk Island pine see *Araucaria heterophylla*
Norfolk reed see *Phragmites australis*
Norse fire plant see *Columnea* 'Stavanger'
North African ivy see *Hedera canariensis*
North American hay-scented fern see *Dennstaedtia punctiloba*
Northern bangalow palm see *Archontophoenix alexandrae*
Northern catalpa see *Catalpa speciosa*
Northern Japanese hemlock see *Tsuga diversifolia*
Northern maidenhair fern see *Adiantum aleuticum*
Northern pin oak see *Quercus ellipsoidalis*
Northern rata see *Metrosideros robustus*
Northern washingtonia see *Washingtonia filifera*
Norway maple see *Acer platanoides*
Norway spruce see *Picea abies*
Nutmeg yew see *Torreya*

O

Oak see *Quercus*
Oak fern see *Gymnocarpium dryopteris*
Oak-leaved hydrangea see *Hydrangea quercifolia*
Oat grass see *Arrhenatherum*
Obedient plant see *Physostegia, P. virginiana*
Ocean spray see *Holodiscus discolor*
Oconee bells see *Shortia galacifolia*
Ocotillo see *Fouquieria splendens*
Octopus tree see *Schefflera actinophylla*
Ohio buckeye see *Aesculus glabra*
Oil palm see *Elaeis*
Old black rose see *Rosa* 'Nuits de Young'
Old blush China rose see *Rosa* x *odorata* 'Pallida'
Old glory rose see *Rosa* 'Gloire de Dijon'
Old lady cactus see *Mammillaria hahniana*
Old maid see *Catharanthus roseus*
Old man see *Artemisia abrotanum*
Old man cactus see *Cephalocereus senilis*
Old-man-live-forever see *Pelargonium cotyledonis*
Old man's beard see *Clematis*
Old pheasant's eye see *Narcissus poeticus* var. *recurvus*
Oleander see *Nerium*
Oleaster see *Elaeagnus angustifolia*
Olive see *Olea, O. europaea*
One-leaved ash see *Fraxinus excelsior* f. *diversifolia*
Onion see *Allium*
Onion couch see *Arrhenatherum elatius* subsp. *bulbosum* 'Variegatum'
Opium poppy see *Papaver somniferum*
Orange ball tree see *Buddleja globosa*
Orange hawkweed see *Pilosella aurantiaca*
Orange jasmine see *Murraya paniculata*
Orange lily see *Lilium bulbiferum*
Orchid cactus see *Epiphyllum*
Orchid tree see *Amherstia nobilis, Bauhinia variegata*
Oregano see *Origanum, O. vulgare*
Oregon alder see *Alnus rubra*
Oregon ash see *Fraxinus latifolia*
Oregon grape see *Mahonia aquifolium*
Oregon maple see *Acer macrophyllum*
Oregon oak see *Quercus garryana*
Oregon plum see *Oemleria cerasiformis*
Oriental beech see *Fagus orientalis*
Oriental bittersweet see *Celastrus orbiculatus*
Oriental plane see *Platanus orientalis*
Oriental poppy see *Papaver orientale*
Oriental spruce see *Picea orientalis*
Oriental sweet gum see *Liquidambar orientalis*
Oriental thuja see *Platycladus*
Ornamental cabbage see *Brassica oleracea* cultivars
Ornamental cherry see *Prunus*
Ornamental yam see *Dioscorea discolor*
Orpine see *Sedum telephium*
Orris root see *Iris germanica* 'Florentina'
Osage orange see *Maclura pomifera*
Oso berry see *Oemleria cerasiformis*
Ostrich fern see *Matteuccia struthiopteris*
Oswego tea see *Monarda didyma*
Our Lord's candle see *Yucca whipplei*
Oval-leaved mint bush see *Prostanthera ovalifolia*
Ovens wattle see *Acacia pravissima*
Owl's eyes see *Huernia zebrina*
Ox eye see *Heliopsis*
Ox-eye chamomile see *Anthemis tinctoria*
Ox-eye daisy see *Leucanthemum vulgare*
Oxlip see *Primula elatior*
Oyster Bay cypress pine see *Callitris rhomboidea*
Oyster plant see *Mertensia maritima*
Ozark sundrops see *Oenothera macrocarpa*
Ozark witch hazel see *Hamamelis vernalis*

P

Pacific dogwood see *Cornus nuttallii*
Pacific fir see *Abies amabilis*
Pacific grindelia see *Grindelia stricta*
Pagoda dogwood see *Cornus alternifolia*
Pagoda flower see *Clerodendrum paniculatum*
Pagoda tree see *Plumeria*
Painted brake see *Pteris tricolor*
Painted daisy see *Chrysanthemum carinatum, Tanacetum coccineum*
Painted damask rose see *Rosa* 'Leda'
Painted drop-tongue see *Aglaonema crispum*
Painted feather see *Vriesea carinata*
Painted leaf see *Euphorbia cyathophora*
Painted-leaf begonia see *Begonia rex*
Painted net leaf see *Fittonia*
Painted nettle see *Solenostemon, S. scutellarioides*
Painted trillium see *Trillium undulatum*
Painted wood lily see *Trillium undulatum*
Palas see *Butea monosperma*
Pale mat rush see *Lomandra glauca*
Palm branch sedge see *Carex muskingumensis*
Palmetto see *Sabal*
Palm grass see *Setaria palmifolia*
Palmito do campo see *Syagrus flexuosa*
Palm-leaf begonia see *Begonia luxurians*
Palm Springs daisy see *Cladanthus*
Palmyra palm see *Borassus flabellifer*
Pampas grass see *Cortaderia, C. selloana*
Panama hat palm see *Carludovica palmata*
Panama orange see x *Citrofortunella microcarpa*
Panamiga see *Pilea involucrata*
Panda plant see *Philodendron bipennifolium*
Pansy see *Viola, V.* x *wittrockiana*
Pansy orchid see *Miltoniopsis*
Panther lily see *Lilium pardalinum*
Paperbark see *Melaleuca*
Paper-bark maple see *Acer griseum*
Paper birch see *Betula papyrifera*
Paper bush see *Edgeworthia*
Paper gardenia see *Tabernaemontana divaricata*
Paper mulberry see *Broussonetia papyrifera*
Paper-white narcissus see *Narcissus papyraceus*
Paprika see *Capsicum annuum*
Papyrus see *Cyperus papyrus*
Parachute plant see *Ceropegia sandersonii*
Paradise flower see *Solanum wendlandii*

Paradise lily see *Paradisea*
Parapara see *Pisonia umbellifera*
Parlour ivy see *Senecio mikanioides*
Parlour maple see *Abutilon*
Parlour palm see *Chamaedorea elegans*
Parrot feather see *Myriophyllum aquaticum*
Parrot leaf see *Alternanthera ficoidea*
Parrot's beak see *Lotus berthelotii*
Parrot's bill see *Clianthus puniceus*
Parrot's flower see *Heliconia psittacorum*
Parrot's plantain see *Heliconia psittacorum*
Parry manzanita see *Arctostaphylos manzanita*
Parsley see *Petroselinum, P. crispum*
Parsons' pink China rose see *Rosa* x *odorata* 'Pallida'
Partridge berry see *Mitchella, M. repens*
Partridge-breasted aloe see *Aloe variegata*
Pasque flower see *Pulsatilla vulgaris*
Passion flower see *Passiflora*
Passion fruit see *Passiflora edulis*
Pawpaw see *Asimina triloba*
Peace lily see *Spathiphyllum, S. wallisii*
Peach see *Prunus persica*
Peach-leaved bellflower see *Campanula persicifolia*
Peach palm see *Bactris gasipaes*
Peacock flower see *Tigridia, T. pavonia*
Peacock lily see *Kaempferia roscoeana*
Peacock plant see *Calathea makoyana*
Peanut cactus see *Echinopsis chamaecereus*
Pear see *Pyrus*
Pearl berry see *Margyricarpus pinnatus*
Pearl bush see *Exochorda*
Pearl everlasting see *Anaphalis*
Pearl plant see *Haworthia pumila*
Pearlwort see *Sagina*
Pearly sonerila see *Sonerila margaritacea* 'Argentea'
Pea tree see *Caragana arborescens*
Pecan see *Carya illinoinensis*
Pedunculate oak see *Quercus robur*
Peepul see *Ficus religiosa*
Pelican's beak see *Lotus berthelotii*
Pencil cedar see *Juniperus virginiana*
Pendulous sedge see *Carex pendula*
Pendulous silver lime see *Tilia* 'Petiolaris'
Pennyroyal see *Mentha pulegium*
Pennywort see *Hydrocotyle*
Peony see *Paeonia*
Pepper see *Capsicum, Piper*
Pepper face see *Peperomia obtusifolia*
Peppermint-scented geranium see *Pelargonium tomentosum*
Pepper tree see *Macropiper excelsum, Schinus molle*
Pepperwort see *Marsilea*
Père David's maple see *Acer davidii*
Perennial centaury see *Centaurium scilloides*
Perennial flax see *Linum perenne*
Perennial honesty see *Lunaria rediviva*
Perennial pea see *Lathyrus latifolius, L. sylvestris*
Perennial phlox see *Phlox paniculata*
Perfoliate Alexanders see *Smyrnium perfoliatum*
Perforate St. John's wort see *Hypericum perforatum*
Periwinkle see *Vinca*
Persian buttercup see *Ranunculus asiaticus*
Persian everlasting pea see *Lathyrus rotundifolius*
Persian ironwood see *Parrotia persica*
Persian ivy see *Hedera colchica*
Persian lilac see *Melia azedarach, Syringa* x *persica*
Persian shield see *Strobilanthes dyerianus*
Persian violet see *Exacum affine*
Persian yellow rose see *Rosa foetida* 'Persiana'
Peruvian daffodil see *Hymenocallis narcissiflora*
Peruvian lily see *Alstroemeria*
Peruvian mastic tree see *Schinus molle*
Petticoat palm see *Copernicia macroglossa*
Phanera see *Bauhinia corymbosa*
Pheasant's eye see *Adonis annua*
Pheasant's tail grass see *Stipa arundinacea*
Philippine violet see *Barleria cristata*
Philippine wax flower see *Etlingera elatior*
Piccabeen palm see *Archontophoenix cunninghamiana*
Pick-a-back plant see *Tolmiea*
Pickerel weed see *Pontederia, P. cordata*
Pigeon berry see *Duranta erecta*
Pigmy date palm see *Phoenix roebelenii*
Pignut see *Carya glabra*
Pignut hickory see *Carya glabra*
Pikake see *Jasminum sambac*
Pilewort see *Ranunculus ficaria*
Pilot plant see *Silphium laciniatum*
Pimpernel see *Anagallis*
Pinang see *Areca catechu*
Pin cherry see *Prunus pensylvanica*
Pincushion see *Leucospermum*
Pincushion flower see *Isopogon dubius, Scabiosa, S. atropurpurea*
Pine see *Pinus*
Pineapple see *Ananas*
Pineapple broom see *Cytisus battandieri*
Pineapple flower see *Eucomis*
Pineapple guava see *Acca sellowiana*
Pineapple lily see *Eucomis*
Pineapple mint see *Mentha suaveolens* 'Variegata'
Pineapple sage see *Salvia elegans* 'Scarlet Pineapple'
Pine bottlebrush see *Callistemon pinifolius*
Pine-mat manzanita see *Arctostaphylos nevadensis*
Pink see *Dianthus*
Pink arum see *Zantedeschia rehmannii*
Pink broom see *Notospartium carmichaeliae*
Pink dandelion see *Crepis incana*
Pink fivecorner see *Styphelia triflora*
Pink muhly see *Muhlenbergia capillaris*
Pink mulla mulla see *Ptilotus exaltatus*
Pink porcelain lily see *Alpinia zerumbet*
Pink poui see *Tabebuia rosea*
Pink sandwort see *Arenaria purpurascens*
Pink shower see *Cassia javanica*
Pink tecoma see *Tabebuia rosea*
Pink trumpet vine see *Podranea ricasoliana*
Pin oak see *Quercus palustris*
Pistachio see *Pistacia*
Pitcher plant see *Sarracenia*
Pitch pine see *Pinus rigida*
Plane see *Platanus*
Plantain see *Musa, Plantago*
Plantain lily see *Hosta*
Plumed tussock grass see *Chionochloa conspicua*
Plume grass see *Saccharum*
Plume plant see *Calomeria amaranthoides*
Plume poppy see *Macleaya, M. cordata*
Plum yew see *Cephalotaxus, C. harringtonii, Prumnopitys andina*
Plush plant see *Echeveria pulvinata*
Poached egg plant see *Limnanthes, L. douglasii*
Poet's ivy see *Hedera helix* f. *poetarum*
Poet's narcissus see *Narcissus poeticus*
Pohutakawa see *Metrosideros*
Poinsettia see *Euphorbia pulcherrima*
Poison arrow plant see *Acokanthera oblongifolia*
Poison bulb see *Crinum asiaticum*
Pokeweed see *Phytolacca, P. americana*
Polar plant see *Silphium laciniatum*
Policeman's helmet see *Impatiens glandulifera*
Polka dot plant see *Hypoestes, H. phyllostachya*
Polyanthus see *Primula* Polyanthus Group
Pomegranate see *Punica, P. granatum*
Pompon rose see *Rosa* 'De Meaux'
Pond cypress see *Taxodium distichum* var. *imbricarium*
Ponderosa pine see *Pinus ponderosa*
Pondweed see *Elodea*
Ponytail see *Beaucarnea recurvata*
Poona oil tree see *Pongamia pinnata*
Poor man's orchid see *Schizanthus, S. pinnatus*
Poplar see *Populus*
Poppy see *Papaver*
Poppy mallow see *Callirhoe*
Porcupine palm see *Rhapidophyllum hystrix*
Portia tree see *Thespesia populnea*
Port Jackson fig see *Ficus rubiginosa*
Portland rose see *Rosa* 'Portlandica'
Portland spurge see *Euphorbia portlandica*
Portugal laurel see *Prunus lusitanica*
Portuguese broom see *Cytisus multiflorus*
Portuguese heath see *Erica lusitanica*
Possum haw see *Ilex decidua, Viburnum acerifolium*
Potato vine see *Solanum laxum, S. wendlandii*
Pot marigold see *Calendula*
Pot marjoram see *Origanum onites*
Pouch flower see *Calceolaria*
Powdered gum see *Eucalyptus pulverulenta*
Powder-puff tree see *Calliandra*
Prairie coneflower see *Ratibida*
Prairie dock see *Silphium*
Prairie mallow see *Sidalcea, Sphaeralcea coccinea*
Prairie poppy mallow see *Callirhoe involucrata*
Prairie star see *Lithophragma parviflorum*
Prayer peperomia see *Peperomia dolabriformis*
Prayer plant see *Maranta leuconeura*
Prickle ear see *Acanthostachys*
Prickly cycad see *Encephalartos altensteinii*
Prickly Moses see *Acacia verticillata*
Prickly pear see *Opuntia ficus-indica*
Prickly poppy see *Argemone, A. mexicana*
Prickly shield fern see *Polystichum aculeatum*
Pride of Bolivia see *Tipuana tipu*
Pride of Burma see *Amherstia nobilis*
Pride of India see *Koelreuteria paniculata, Lagerstroemia speciosa, Melia azedarach*
Pride of Madeira see *Echium candicans*
Primavera see *Cybistax donnell-smithii*
Primrose see *Primula, P. vulgaris*
Primrose jasmine see *Jasminum mesnyi*
Prince Albert's yew see *Saxegothaea conspicua*
Prince of Wales heath see *Erica perspicua*
Prince's feather see *Amaranthus cruentus, Persicaria orientale*
Prince's pine see *Chimaphila*
Princess feather see *Persicaria orientale*
Princess palm see *Dictyosperma*
Princess tree see *Paulownia tomentosa*
Privet see *Ligustrum*
Proboscis flower see *Proboscidea*
Propeller plant see *Crassula perfoliata* var. *minor*
Prophet flower see *Arnebia pulchra*
Prostrate speedwell see *Veronica prostrata*
Provins rose see *Rosa gallica* var. *officinalis*
Pudding pipe-tree see *Cassia fistula*
Puffed wheat see *Briza maxima*
Purging cassia see *Cassia fistula*
Purple amaranth see *Amaranthus cruentus*
Purple anise see *Illicium floridanum*
Purple apple berry see *Billardiera longiflora*
Purple broom see *Chamaecytisus purpureus*
Purple chokeberry see *Aronia* x *prunifolia*
Purple-cone spruce see *Picea purpurea*
Purple coral pea see *Hardenbergia violacea*
Purple glory plant see *Jamesbrittenia grandiflora*
Purple granadilla see *Passiflora edulis*
Purple-leaved ivy see *Hedera helix* 'Atropurpurea'
Purple loosestrife see *Lythrum salicaria*
Purple moor grass see *Molinia caerulea*
Purple mullein see *Verbascum phoeniceum*
Purple-net toadflax see *Linaria reticulata*
Purple osier see *Salix purpurea*
Purple prairie violet see *Viola pedatifida*
Purple sage see *Salvia officinalis* 'Purpurascens'
Purple saxifrage see *Saxifraga oppositifolia*
Purple toothwort see *Lathraea clandestina*
Purple velvet plant see *Gynura aurantiaca*
Purple waffle plant see *Hemigraphis* 'Exotica'
Purple wreath see *Petrea volubilis*
Purslane see *Claytonia, Portulaca*
Pussy ears see *Cyanotis somaliensis*
Pussy-toes see *Antennaria*
Pygmy bamboo see *Pleioblastus pygmaeus*
Pygmy date palm see *Phoenix roebelenii*
Pyjama lily see *Crinum macowanii*
Pyramidal bugle see *Ajuga pyramidalis*
Pyrenean dead nettle see *Horminum pyrenaicum*
Pyrenean saxifrage see *Saxifraga longifolia*
Pyrethrum see *Tanacetum coccineum*

Q

Quaking aspen see *Populus tremuloides*
Quaking grass see *Briza*
Quamash see *Camassia, C. quamash*
Quassia see *Picrasma quassioides*
Queen Anne's double daffodil see *Narcissus* 'Eystettensis'
Queen Anne's lace see *Anthriscus sylvestris*
Queen Anne's thimbles see *Gilia capitata*
Queen anthurium see *Anthurium veitchii*
Queencup see *Clintonia uniflora*
Queen lily see *Curcuma petiolata, Phaedranassa*
Queen of the meadows see *Filipendula ulmaria*
Queen of the night see *Selenicereus grandiflorus*
Queen of the prairies see *Filipendula rubra*
Queen palm see *Syagrus romanzoffiana*
Queen's crepe myrtle see *Lagerstroemia speciosa*
Queensland lacebark see *Brachychiton discolor*
Queensland pyramid tree see *Lagunaria patersonia*
Queensland silver wattle see *Acacia podalyriifolia*
Queensland umbrella tree see *Schefflera actinophylla*
Queen's tears see *Billbergia nutans*
Queen's wreath see *Antigonon, Petrea volubilis*
Queen Victoria's lady fern see *Athyrium filix-femina* Cruciatum Group 'Victoriae'
Quick see *Crataegus monogyna*
Quickthorn see *Crataegus monogyna*
Quince see *Cydonia*

R

Rabbit's foot see *Maranta leuconeura* 'Kerchoveana'
Rabbit's foot fern see *Davallia fejeensis, Phlebodium aureum*
Rabbit's tracks see *Maranta leuconeura* 'Kerchoveana'
Radiata pine see *Pinus radiata*
Radiator plant see *Peperomia maculosa*
Raffia see *Raphia*
Ragged robin see *Lychnis flos-cuculi*
Rainbow star see *Cryptanthus bromelioides*
Rain daisy see *Dimorphotheca pluvialis*
Rain flower see *Zephyranthes*
Raisin-tree see *Hovenia dulcis*
Ramanas rose see *Rosa rugosa*
Ram's horn see *Proboscidea louisianica*
Rangoon creeper see *Quisqualis indica*
Rata see *Metrosideros, M. robustus*
Rat's tail cactus see *Aporocactus*
Rattan cane see *Calamus rotang*
Rattan vine see *Berchemia scandens*
Rattlebox see *Crotalaria*
Rattlesnake plant see *Calathea lancifolia*
Rattlesnake root see *Chamaelirion luteum*
Rauli see *Nothofagus procera*
Red alder see *Alnus rubra*
Red amaranth see *Amaranthus cruentus*
Red angels' trumpets see *Brugmansia sanguinea*
Red ash see *Fraxinus pennsylvanica*
Red banana passion flower see *Passiflora antioquiensis*
Red baneberry see *Actaea rubra*
Red-barked dogwood see *Cornus alba*
Red-berried elder see *Sambucus racemosa*
Red box see *Eucalyptus polyanthemos*
Red buckeye see *Aesculus pavia*
Red bud maple see *Acer heldreichii* subsp. *trautvetteri*
Red chokeberry see *Aronia arbutifolia*
Red cole see *Armoracia rusticana*
Red cone pepper see *Capsicum annuum* Fasciculatum Group
Red fan palm see *Livistona mariae*
Red flame ivy see *Hemigraphis alternata*
Red-flowering gum see *Eucalyptus ficifolia*
Red ginger see *Alpinia purpurata*
Red ginger lily see *Hedychium coccineum*
Red granadilla see *Passiflora coccinea*
Red horned poppy see *Glaucium corniculatum*
Red horse chestnut see *Aesculus* x *carnea*
Red-hot cat's tail see *Acalypha hispida*
Red hot poker see *Kniphofia*
Red ink plant see *Phytolacca americana*
Red ironbark see *Eucalyptus sideroxylon*
Red justicia see *Megaskepasma erythrochlamys*
Red-leaf philodendron see *Philodendron erubescens*
Red maple see *Acer rubrum*
Red mint see *Mentha* x *gracilis* 'Variegata'
Red morning glory see *Ipomoea coccinea*
Red moss rose see *Rosa* 'Henri Martin'
Red mountain spinach see *Atriplex hortensis*
Red mulberry see *Morus rubra*
Red oak see *Quercus rubra*
Red orache see *Atriplex hortensis*
Red osier dogwood see *Cornus stolonifera*
Red passion flower see *Passiflora racemosa*
Red pepper see *Capsicum annuum* Conioides Group
Red pine see *Pinus resinosa*
Red pineapple see *Ananas bracteatus*
Red puccoon see *Sanguinaria*
Red raripila see *Mentha* x *smithiana*
Red river gum see *Eucalyptus camaldulensis*
Red rose of Lancaster see *Rosa gallica* var. *officinalis*
Red silk cotton tree see *Bombax ceiba*
Red spider lily see *Lycoris radiata*
Red tree see *Peperomia metallica*
Red-twigged lime see *Tilia platyphyllos* 'Rubra'
Red valerian see *Centranthus ruber*
Red-veined dock see *Rumex sanguineus*
Red whortleberry see *Vaccinium parvifolium*
Reed see *Phragmites*
Reed canary grass see *Phalaris arundinacea*
Reed grass see *Calamagrostis*
Reedmace see *Typha*
Reed palm see *Chamaedorea seifrizii*
Regal lily see *Lilium regale*
Restharrow see *Ononis*
Resurrection fern see *Polypodium polypodioides*
Resurrection lily see *Kaempferia rotunda, Lycoris squamigera*
Resurrection plant see *Selaginella lepidophylla*
Rewarewa see *Knightia excelsa*
Rheumatism root see *Jeffersonia diphylla*
Rhubarb see *Rheum*
Ribbon bush see *Homalocladium, Hypoestes aristata*
Ribbon grass see *Phalaris arundinacea*
Ribbon gum see *Eucalyptus viminalis*
Ribbon plant see *Chlorophytum comosum, Dracaena sanderiana*
Ribbonwood see *Hoheria sexstylosa*
Rice see *Oryza*
Rice-grain fritillary see *Fritillaria affinis*
Rice-paper plant see *Tetrapanax papyrifer*
Rimu see *Dacrydium cupressinum*
River birch see *Betula nigra*
Roblé see *Nothofagus obliqua*
Robust marsh orchid see *Dactylorhiza elata*
Rockcap fern see *Polypodium virginianum*
Rock cress see *Arabis*
Rock daisy see *Brachyscome multifida*
Rock jasmine see *Androsace*
Rock maple see *Acer saccharum*
Rock penstemon see *Penstemon rupicola*
Rock purslane see *Calandrinia umbellata*
Rock rose see *Cistus, Helianthemum*
Rock speedwell see *Veronica fruticans*
Rock spiraea see *Petrophytum*
Rocky Mountain columbine see *Aquilegia saximontana*
Rocky Mountain juniper see *Juniperus scopulorum*
Rocky Mountain piñon see *Pinus edulis*
Roman chamomile see *Chamaemelum nobile*
Roof iris see *Iris tectorum*
Roof reed see *Chondropetalum tectorum, Thamnochortus insignis*
Rooistompie see *Mimetes cucullatus*
Rope grass see *Ampelodesmos mauritanica*
Rosa mundi rose see *Rosa gallica* var. *officinalis* 'Versicolor'
Rosary vine see *Ceropegia linearis* subsp. *woodii*
Rose see *Rosa*
Rose acacia see *Robinia hispida*
Rose bay see *Nerium oleander*
Rosebud cherry see *Prunus* x *subhirtella*
Rose campion see *Lychnis coronaria*
Rose coneflower see *Isopogon dubius*
Rose geranium see *Pelargonium* 'Graveolens' of gardens
Rosemary see *Rosmarinus, R. officinalis*
Rose moss see *Portulaca, P. grandiflora*
Rose of Castille see *Rosa* x *damascena* var. *semperflorens*
Rose of China see *Hibiscus rosa-sinensis*
Rose of heaven see *Silene coeli-rosa*
Rose of Jericho see *Selaginella lepidophylla*
Rose of Sharon see *Hypericum calycinum*
Roseroot see *Rhodiola rosea*
Rosinweed see *Grindelia, Silphium*
Rosy garlic see *Allium roseum*
Rosy trumpet tree see *Tabebuia rosea*
Rouen lilac see *Syringa* x *chinensis*
Round-headed club-rush see *Scirpoides holoschoenus*
Roundheaded leek see *Allium sphaerocephalon*
Round kumquat see *Fortunella japonica*
Round-leaved mint bush see *Prostanthera rotundifolia*
Round-leaved snow gum see *Eucalyptus perriniana*
Round-leaved wintergreen see *Pyrola rotundifolia*
Rowan see *Sorbus aucuparia*
Royal fern see *Osmunda regalis*
Royal palm see *Roystonea*
Royal velvet plant see *Gynura aurantiaca*
Royal water lily see *Victoria amazonica*
Rubber plant see *Ficus elastica*
Rue see *Ruta*
Rue anemone see *Anemonella thalictroides*
Ruffle palm see *Aiphanes*
Running postman see *Kennedia prostrata*
Rush see *Juncus*
Rush-leaved jonquil see *Narcissus assoanus*
Russian pea shrub see *Caragana frutex*
Russian vine see *Fallopia baldschuanica*
Rusty-back fern see *Asplenium ceterach*
Rusty foxglove see *Digitalis ferruginea*
Rusty leaf see *Menziesia ferruginea*
Rusty lyonia see *Lyonia ferruginea*
Rusty woodsia see *Woodsia ilvensis*

S

Sacramento rose see *Rosa stellata* var. *mirifica*
Sacred fig see *Ficus religiosa*
Sacred flower of the Incas see *Cantua buxifolia*
Sacred lotus see *Nelumbo nucifera*
Safflower see *Carthamus, C. tinctorius*
Saffron buckwheat see *Eriogonum crocatum*
Saffron crocus see *Crocus sativus*
Saffron-spike see *Aphelandra squarrosa*
Sage see *Salvia*
Sagebrush see *Artemisia, Seriphidium tridentatum*
Sago fern see *Cyathea medullaris*
Sago palm see *Caryota urens, Cycas, C. circinalis*
Saguaro cactus see *Carnegiea gigantea*
Sailor caps see *Dodecatheon hendersonii*
St. Augustine grass see *Stenotaphrum secundatum*
St. Barbara's herb see *Barbarea*
St. Bernard's lily see *Anthericum liliago*
St. Bruno's lily see *Paradisea*
St. Catherine's lace see *Eriogonum, E. giganteum*
St. Dabeoc's heath see *Daboecia cantabrica*
St. John's wort see *Hypericum*
St. Joseph's lily see *Hippeastrum vittatum*
St. Lucie cherry see *Prunus mahaleb*
St. Vincent lilac see *Solanum seaforthianum*
Salal see *Gaultheria shallon*
Salt-and-pepper ivy see *Hedera helix* 'Minor Marmorata'
Salt tree see *Halimodendron halodendron*
Sand dollar cactus see *Astrophytum asterias*
Sand myrtle see *Leiophyllum buxifolium*

South American staghorn see *Platycerium alcicorne*
Southern arrow-wood see *Viburnum dentatum*
Southern beech see *Nothofagus*
Southern blue flag see *Iris virginica*
Southern catalpa see *Catalpa bignonioides*
Southern Japanese hemlock see *Tsuga sieboldii*
Southern nettle tree see *Celtis australis*
Southern polypody see *Polypodium cambricum*
Southernwood see *Artemisia abrotanum*
Spangle grass see *Chasmanthium latifolium*
Spanish bayonet see *Yucca aloifolia*
Spanish bluebell see *Hyacinthoides hispanica*
Spanish broom see *Spartium*
Spanish chestnut see *Castanea sativa*
Spanish dagger see *Yucca gloriosa*
Spanish fir see *Abies pinsapo*
Spanish flag see *Ipomoea lobata*
Spanish gorse see *Genista hispanica*
Spanish heath see *Erica australis*
Spanish iris see *Iris xiphium*
Spanish morning glory see *Merremia tuberosa*
Spanish moss see *Tillandsia usneoides*
Spanish shawl see *Heterocentron elegans*
Spatterdock see *Nuphar*
Spear grass see *Poa, Stipa*
Speargrass see *Aciphylla, A. colensoi*
Spear lily see *Doryanthes*
Spearmint see *Mentha spicata*
Speedwell see *Veronica*
Spicebush see *Calycanthus*
Spice bush see *Lindera benzoin*
Spider brake see *Pteris multifida*
Spider flower see *Cleome*
Spider lily see *Hymenocallis*
Spider orchid see *Brassia lawrenceana*
Spider plant see *Chlorophytum comosum, Cleome hassleriana*
Spignel see *Meum athamanticum*
Spike heath see *Erica spiculifolia*
Spike lavender see *Lavandula latifolia*
Spindle tree see *Euonymus*
Spine aster see *Machaeranthera*
Spineless yucca see *Yucca elephantipes*
Spine palm see *Aiphanes caryotifolia*
Spinning gum see *Eucalyptus perriniana*
Spiny club palm see *Bactris*
Spiny-headed mat rush see *Lomandra longifolia*
Spiral ginger see *Costus malortieanus*
Spleenwort see *Asplenium*
Spotted dog see *Pulmonaria officinalis*
Spotted emu bush see *Eremophila maculata*
Spotted gentian see *Gentiana punctata*
Spotted laurel see *Aucuba japonica*
Spotted orchid see *Dactylorhiza*
Spring beauty see *Claytonia*
Spring gentian see *Gentiana verna*
Spring snowflake see *Leucojum vernum*
Spring vetchling see *Lathyrus vernus*
Spruce see *Picea*
Spurge see *Euphorbia*
Spurge laurel see *Daphne laureola*
Square-stemmed bamboo see *Chimonobambusa quadrangularis*
Squirrel's foot fern see *Davallia mariesii*
Squirrel tail grass see *Hordeum jubatum*
Squirting cucumber see *Ecballium*
Staff tree see *Celastrus scandens*
Staff vine see *Celastrus, C. orbiculatus, C. scandens*
Stagger-bush see *Lyonia mariana*
Staghorn fern see *Platycerium*
Stag's horn sumach see *Rhus typhina*
Stanford manzanita see *Arctostaphylos stanfordiana*
Star anise see *Illicium verum*
Star cluster see *Pentas lanceolata*
Star daisy see *Lindheimera, L. texana*
Starfish cactus see *Orbea variegata*
Starfish plant see *Cryptanthus*
Starflower see *Calytrix, Hypoxis, Mentzelia*
Starfruit see *Damasonium*
Star gentian see *Gentiana verna*
Star glory see *Ipomoea quamoclit*
Star grass see *Cynodon aethiopicus*
Star jasmine see *Trachelospermum jasminoides*
Star magnolia see *Magnolia stellata*
Star morning glory see *Ipomoea coccinea*
Star-of-Bethlehem see *Campanula isophylla, Ornithogalum, O. umbellatum*
Star of the veldt see *Dimorphotheca sinuata*
Statice see *Limonium, L. sinuatum, Psylliostachys*
Stemless Carline thistle see *Carlina acaulis*
Stiff bottlebrush see *Callistemon rigidus*
Stinking Benjamin see *Trillium erectum*
Stinking gladwyn see *Iris foetidissima*
Stinking hellebore see *Helleborus foetidus*
Stinking iris see *Iris foetidissima*
Stinking madder see *Putoria calabrica*
Stinking nightshade see *Hyoscyamus niger*
Stink pod see *Scoliopus bigelowii*
Stinkwort see *Helleborus foetidus*
Stitched-leaf begonia see *Begonia mazae* f. *viridis*
Stock see *Matthiola, M. incana*
Stokes' aster see *Stokesia*
Stone cress see *Aethionema*
Stonecrop see *Sedum*
Stone orpine see *Sedum rupestre*
Stone pine see *Pinus pinea*
Stone plant see *Lithops*
Storax see *Styrax officinalis*
Stork's bill see *Erodium*
Strawberry see *Fragaria*
Strawberry bush see *Calycanthus floridus*
Strawberry tree see *Arbutus, A. unedo*
Strawflower see *Rhodanthe, Xerochrysum bracteatum*
Stream violet see *Viola glabella*
String of beads see *Senecio rowleyanus*
Striped inch plant see *Callisia elegans*
Striped Japanese muhly see *Muhlenbergia japonica* 'Cream Delight'
Striped maple see *Acer pensylvanicum*
Sturt's desert pea see *Clianthus formosus*
Sugar-almond plant see *Pachyphytum oviferum*
Sugarberry see *Celtis occidentalis, C. reticulata*
Sugarbush see *Protea repens*
Sugar hackberry see *Celtis laevigata*
Sugar maple see *Acer saccharum*
Sugar palm see *Arenga pinnata*
Sulphur flower see *Eriogonum gracilipes, E. umbellatum*
Sumach see *Rhus*
Summer cypress see *Bassia scoparia* f. *trichophylla*
Summer damask rose see *Rosa* x *damascena*
Summer holly see *Arctostaphylos diversifolia*
Summer savory see *Satureja hortensis*
Summer snowflake see *Leucojum aestivum*
Summer-sweet see *Clethra*
Sundew see *Drosera*
Sundrops see *Oenothera, O. fruticosa, O. perennis*
Sunflower see *Helianthus, H. annuus*
Sun plant see *Portulaca grandiflora*
Sunrise horse chestnut see *Aesculus* x *neglecta* 'Erythroblastos'
Sun rose see *Cistus, Helianthemum*
Supple Jack see *Berchemia scandens*
Suurberg cycad see *Encephalartos longifolius*
Swallow-wort see *Asclepias curassavica*
Swamp blueberry see *Vaccinium corymbosum*
Swamp bottlebrush see *Beaufortia sparsa*
Swamp cypress see *Taxodium, T. distichum*
Swamp hickory see *Carya cordiformis*
Swamp lobelia see *Lobelia paludosa*
Swamp maple see *Acer rubrum*
Swamp milkweed see *Asclepias incarnata*
Swamp pink see *Helonias bullata*
Swamp rose mallow see *Hibiscus moscheutos*
Swamp wattle see *Acacia retinodes, Paraserianthes lophantha*
Swamp white oak see *Quercus bicolor*
Swan orchid see *Cycnoches*
Swan plant see *Gomphocarpus physocarpus*
Swan river daisy see *Brachyscome, B. iberidifolia*
Swan river pea see *Brachysema celsianum*
Swedish ivy see *Plectranthus oertendahlii, P. verticillatus*
Swedish whitebeam see *Sorbus intermedia*
Sweet Alison see *Lobularia*
Sweet alyssum see *Lobularia*
Sweet azalea see *Rhododendron arborescens*
Sweet basil see *Ocimum basilicum*
Sweet bay see *Laurus nobilis, Magnolia virginiana*
Sweetbells see *Leucothoe racemosa*
Sweet birch see *Betula lenta*
Sweet box see *Sarcococca*
Sweet briar see *Rosa rubiginosa*
Sweet chestnut see *Castanea, C. sativa*
Sweet Cicely see *Myrrhis, M. odorata*
Sweet coltsfoot see *Petasites*
Sweetcorn see *Zea mays*
Sweet gale see *Myrica gale*
Sweet gum see *Liquidambar styraciflua*
Sweetheart ivy see *Hedera hibernica* 'Deltoidea'
Sweetheart peperomia see *Peperomia marmorata*
Sweetheart plant see *Philodendron hederaceum*
Sweetheart vine see *Ceropegia linearis* subsp. *woodii, Philodendron hederaceum*
Sweet marjoram see *Origanum majorana*
Sweet orange see *Citrus sinensis* 'Washington'
Sweet pea see *Lathyrus odoratus*
Sweet pepper bush see *Clethra, C. alnifolia*
Sweet rocket see *Hesperis matronalis*
Sweet scabious see *Scabiosa atropurpurea*
Sweet-scented geranium see *Pelargonium* 'Graveolens' of gardens
Sweetspire see *Itea virginica*
Sweet sultan see *Amberboa, A. moschata*
Sweet tea see *Osmanthus fragrans*
Sweet violet see *Viola odorata*
Sweet William see *Dianthus barbatus*
Sweetwood see *Glycyrrhiza glabra*
Sweet woodruff see *Galium odoratum*
Swiss chard see *Beta vulgaris* subsp. *cicla*
Swiss cheese plant see *Monstera deliciosa*
Swiss stone pine see *Pinus cembra*
Swiss willow see *Salix helvetica*
Switch grass see *Panicum virgatum*
Switch ivy see *Leucothoe fontanesiana*
Sword brake see *Pteris ensiformis*
Sword fern see *Nephrolepis, Polystichum munitum*
Sycamore see *Acer pseudoplatanus*
Sydney peppermint see *Eucalyptus piperita*
Sydney rock rose see *Boronia serrulata*
Sydney waratah see *Telopea speciosissima*
Syrian juniper see *Juniperus drupacea*
Szechuan birch see *Betula szechuanica*

T

Tacamahac see *Populus balsamifera*
Tail flower see *Anthurium*
Taiwan cherry see *Prunus campanulata*
Taiwan spruce see *Picea morrisonicola*
Talipot palm see *Corypha umbraculifera*
Tamarisk see *Tamarix*
Tampala see *Amaranthus tricolor*
Tanakea see *Tanakaea*
Tanbark oak see *Lithocarpus densiflorus*
Tanekaha see *Phyllocladus trichomanoides*
Tangerine see *Citrus reticulata*
Tanguru see *Olearia albida*
Tannia see *Xanthosoma, X. sagittifolium*
Tansy-leaved thorn see *Crataegus tanacetifolia*
Tarata see *Pittosporum eugenioides*
Tara vine see *Actinidia arguta*
Tarentum myrtle see *Myrtus communis* subsp. *tarentina*
Taro see *Colocasia, C. esculenta*
Tarragon see *Artemisia dracunculus*
Tarweed see *Grindelia*
Tasmanian blue gum see *Eucalyptus globulus*
Tasmanian cedar see *Athrotaxis, A.* x *laxifolia*
Tasmanian Christmas bells see *Blandfordia punicea*
Tasmanian cypress pine see *Callitris oblonga*
Tasmanian laurel see *Anopterus glandulosus*
Tasmanian podocarp see *Podocarpus lawrencii*
Tasmanian snow gum see *Eucalyptus coccifera*
Tasmanian waratah see *Telopea truncata*
Tasmanian yellow gum see *Eucalyptus johnstonii*
Tassel flower see *Amaranthus caudatus, Emilia*
Tassel grape hyacinth see *Muscari comosum*
Tassel maidenhair fern see *Adiantum raddianum* 'Grandiceps'
Tassel-white see *Itea virginica*
Tatarian maple see *Acer tataricum*

Tatarian statice see *Goniolimon tataricum*
Tatting fern see *Athyrium filix-femina* 'Frizelliae'
Teasel see *Dipsacus*
Tea tree see *Leptospermum*
Teddy bear plant see *Cyanotis kewensis*
Temple bells see *Smithiantha*
Temple juniper see *Juniperus rigida*
Tenby daffodil see *Narcissus obvallaris*
Tender brake see *Pteris tremula*
Terebinth see *Pistacia terebinthus*
Texan bluebell see *Eustoma grandiflorum*
Texan walnut see *Juglans microcarpa*
Texas bluebonnet see *Lupinus texensis*
Texas palmetto see *Sabal mexicana*
Thatch leaf palm see *Howea forsteriana*
Thatch palm see *Coccothrinax, Thrinax, T. parviflora*
Thick-leaf phlox see *Phlox carolina*
Thinleaf alder see *Alnus tenuifolia*
Thin-leaved sunflower see *Helianthus decapetalus*
Thornless rose see *Rosa* 'Zéphirine Drouhin'
Thorow-wax see *Bupleurum*
Thousand mothers see *Tolmiea menziesii*
Thread palm see *Washingtonia robusta*
Three-men-in-a-boat see *Tradescantia spathacea*
Three-toothed maple see *Acer buergerianum*
Thrift see *Armeria*
Throatwort see *Campanula trachelium*
Thyme see *Thymus*
Thyme-leaved willow see *Salix serpyllifolia*
Tibetan blue poppy see *Meconopsis betonicifolia*
Tickseed see *Coreopsis*
Tidy tips see *Layia platyglossa*
Tiger flower see *Tigridia, T. pavonia*
Tiger jaws see *Faucaria*
Tiger lily see *Lilium lancifolium*
Tiger orchid see *Rossioglossum grande*
Tingiringi gum see *Eucalyptus glaucescens*
Tipu tree see *Tipuana, T. tipu*
Ti tree see *Cordyline fruticosa*
Titan arum see *Amorphophallus titanum*
Toad cactus see *Orbea variegata*
Toadflax see *Linaria, L. vulgaris*
Toad lily see *Tricyrtis*
Toad-shade see *Trillium sessile*
Tobacco plant see *Nicotiana*
Toddy palm see *Borassus flabellifer, Caryota urens*
Toe toe see *Cortaderia richardii*
Tonghi bottlebrush see *Callistemon subulatus*
Tongue fern see *Pyrrosia lingua*
Tongue orchid see *Serapias*
Toothbrush grass see *Lamarckia aurea*
Toothed lancewood see *Pseudopanax ferox*
Topel holly see *Ilex* x *attenuata*
Torch ginger see *Etlingera elatior*
Torch lily see *Kniphofia*
Tor grass see *Brachypodium pinnatum*
Tormentil see *Potentilla erecta*
Toyon see *Heteromeles salicifolia*
Trailing abutilon see *Abutilon megapotamicum*
Trailing arbutus see *Epigaea repens*
Trailing azalea see *Loiseleuria*
Trailing fuchsia see *Fuchsia procumbens*
Trailing maidenhair fern see *Adiantum caudatum*
Trailing phlox see *Phlox nivalis*
Trailing velvet plant see *Ruellia makoyana*
Trailing violet see *Viola hederacea*
Transcaucasian birch see *Betula medwedewii*
Transvaal daisy see *Gerbera jamesonii*
Transvaal kaffirboom see *Erythrina lysistemon*
Traveller's joy see *Clematis*
Traveller's tree see *Ravenala*
Tree fern see *Cyathea*
Tree fuchsia see *Schotia brachypetala*
Tree germander see *Teucrium fruticans*
Tree heath see *Erica arborea*
Tree-ivy see x *Fatshedera lizei*
Tree lavatera see *Lavatera thuringiaca*
Tree lupin see *Lupinus arboreus*
Tree mallow see *Lavatera arborea*
Tree of heaven see *Ailanthus altissima*
Tree philodendron see *Philodendron bipinnatifidum*
Tree poppy see *Dendromecon, Romneya*
Tree purslane see *Atriplex halimus*
Tree spinach see *Chenopodium giganteum*
Tree tomato see *Cyphomandra*
Trembling grass see *Briza media*
Trident maple see *Acer buergerianum*
Trifoliate bittercress see *Cardamine trifolia*
Trigger plant see *Stylidium graminifolium*
Trinity flower see *Trillium*
Tropical pitcher plant see *Nepenthes*
Trout-leaved begonia see *Begonia* x *argenteoguttata*
Trout lily see *Erythronium*
True maidenhair fern see *Adiantum capillus-veneris*
Trumpet bush see *Tecoma stans*
Trumpet creeper see *Campsis*
Trumpet gentian see *Gentiana acaulis, G. clusii*
Trumpet honeysuckle see *Lonicera sempervirens*
Trumpet vine see *Campsis*
Tuberose see *Polianthes tuberosa*
Tuberous comfrey see *Symphytum tuberosum*
Tufted fescue see *Festuca amethystina*
Tufted hair grass see *Deschampsia cespitosa*
Tulip see *Tulipa*
Tulip orchid see *Anguloa*
Tulip tree see *Liriodendron, L. tulipifera*
Tumbling Ted see *Saponaria ocymoides*
Tunic flower see *Petrorhagia saxifraga*
Tupelo see *Nyssa, N. sylvatica*
Turkey oak see *Quercus cerris*
Turkish hazel see *Corylus colurna*
Turk's cap cactus see *Melocactus*
Turpentine tree see *Pistacia terebinthus*
Turtlehead see *Chelone, C. glabra*
Tussock grass see *Cortaderia, Deschampsia cespitosa*
Tutsan see *Hypericum androsaemum*
Twiggy baeckea see *Baeckea virgata*
Twinberry see *Lonicera involucrata*
Twin-flower see *Linnaea*
Twin-flowered violet see *Viola biflora*
Twining brodiaea see *Dichelostemma volubile*
Twin leaf see *Jeffersonia*
Twinspur see *Diascia barberae*

U

Ulmo see *Eucryphia cordifolia*
Umbrella arum see *Amorphophallus konjac*
Umbrella bamboo see *Fargesia murielae*
Umbrella grass see *Cyperus involucratus*
Umbrella leaf see *Diphylleia cymosa*
Umbrella palm see *Hedyscepe*
Umbrella pine see *Pinus pinea*
Umbrella plant see *Cyperus alternifolius*
Umbrella tree see *Magnolia macrophylla, M. tripetala*
Unicorn plant see *Proboscidea*
Upright bugle see *Ajuga genevensis*
Urn-fruited gum see *Eucalyptus urnigera*
Urn gum see *Eucalyptus urnigera*

V

Valerian see *Centranthus, Valeriana*
Vaquero blanco see *Cydista aequinoctialis*
Variegated ginger see *Alpinia vittata*
Variegated goutweed see *Aegopodium podagraria* 'Variegatum'
Variegated ground elder see *Aegopodium podagraria* 'Variegatum'
Variegated ground ivy see *Glechoma hederacea* 'Variegata'
Variegated Japanese rush see *Acorus gramineus* 'Variegatus'
Variegated lemon-scented pelargonium see *Pelargonium crispum* 'Variegatum'
Variegated russet sedge see *Carex saxatilis* 'Ski Run'
Varnish tree see *Rhus verniciflua*
Vase plant see *Aechmea fasciata*
Vegetable sheep see *Haastia, H. pulvinaris, Raoulia eximia*
Veitch fir see *Abies veitchii*
Veitch's heath see *Erica* x *veitchii*
Vejar fir see *Abies vejarii*
Velour philodendron see *Philodendron melanochrysum*
Velvet ash see *Fraxinus velutina*
Velvet bent see *Agrostis canina*
Velvet plant see *Gynura aurantiaca*
Velvet sumach see *Rhus typhina*
Venetian sumach see *Cotinus coggygria*
Venus fly trap see *Dionaea, D. muscipula*
Venus's looking glass see *Legousia speculum-veneris*
Venus's navelwort see *Omphalodes linifolia*
Vetch see *Hippocrepis*
Victorian waratah see *Telopea oreades*
Vine see *Vitis*
Vine maple see *Acer circinatum*
Viola see *Viola cornuta*
Violet see *Viola*
Violet cabbage see *Moricandia moricandioides*
Violet twining snapdragon see *Maurandella antirrhiniflora*
Violet willow see *Salix daphnoides*
Viper's bugloss see *Echium vulgare*
Virginia cowslip see *Mertensia virginica*
Virginia creeper see *Parthenocissus, P. quinquefolia*
Virginian bird cherry see *Prunus virginiana*
Virginian polypody see *Polypodium virginianum*
Virginian witch hazel see *Hamamelis virginiana*
Virginia stock see *Malcolmia maritima*
Virgin's bower see *Clematis*
Voodoo lily see *Sauromatum venosum*

W

Wake robin see *Trillium, T. grandiflorum, T. sessile*
Walking fern see *Asplenium rhizophyllum*
Walking maidenhair fern see *Adiantum caudatum*
Walking stick palm see *Linospadix monostachya*
Wallflower see *Erysimum, E. cheiri*
Wallich's wood fern see *Dryopteris wallichiana*
Wallpepper see *Sedum acre*
Walnut see *Juglans*
Wandering heath see *Erica vagans*
Wandering Jew see *Tradescantia fluminensis, T. zebrina*
Wandflower see *Dierama, Galax*
Wapato see *Sagittaria latifolia*
Waratah see *Telopea*
Warminster broom see *Cytisus* x *praecox* 'Warminster'
Washington thorn see *Crataegus phaenopyrum*
Water betony see *Scrophularia auriculata*
Water caltrops see *Trapa natans*
Water chestnut see *Trapa, T. natans*
Water chinquapin see *Nelumbo lutea*
Water clover see *Marsilea, M. quadrifolia*
Water crowfoot see *Ranunculus aquatilis*
Water figwort see *Scrophularia auriculata*
Water forget-me-not see *Myosotis scorpioides*
Water fringe see *Nymphoides peltata*
Water gladiolus see *Butomus*
Water hawthorn see *Aponogeton distachyos*
Water heath see *Erica curviflora*
Water hyacinth see *Eichhornia, E. crassipes*
Water hyssop see *Bacopa*
Water lettuce see *Pistia, P. stratiotes*
Water lily see *Nymphaea*
Water-lily tulip see *Tulipa kaufmanniana*
Water lobelia see *Lobelia dortmanna*
Watermelon peperomia see *Peperomia argyreia*
Watermint see *Mentha aquatica*
Water oak see *Quercus nigra*
Water oats see *Zizania*
Water plantain see *Alisma*
Water poppy see *Hydrocleys nymphoides*
Water purslane see *Ludwigia palustris*
Water rice see *Zizania aquatica*
Water snowflake see *Nymphoides indica*
Water soldier see *Stratiotes aloides*
Water sprite see *Ceratopteris thalictroides*
Water starwort see *Callitriche*

Water trumpet see *Cryptocoryne*
Water vine see *Cissus hypoglauca*
Water violet see *Hottonia palustris*
Water wisteria see *Hygrophila difformis*
Watson's heath see *Erica* x *watsonii*
Wattle see *Acacia*
Wavy hair grass see *Deschampsia flexuosa*
Wax flower see *Eriostemon*, *Hoya*, *Jamesia americana*
Wax mallow see *Malvaviscus arboreus*
Wax myrtle see *Myrica cerifera*
Wax palm see *Copernicia*
Wax plant see *Hoya carnosa*
Wax privet peperomia see *Peperomia glabella*
Wax tree see *Rhus succedanea*
Wayfaring tree see *Viburnum lantana*
Weather prophet see *Dimorphotheca pluvialis*
Weddell palm see *Lytocaryum weddellianum*
Weeping ash see *Fraxinus excelsior* 'Pendula'
Weeping aspen see *Populus tremula* 'Pendula'
Weeping beech see *Fagus sylvatica* f. *pendula*
Weeping boerboon see *Schotia brachypetala*
Weeping bottlebrush see *Callistemon viminalis*
Weeping broom see *Chordospartium stevensonii*
Weeping fig see *Ficus benjamina*
Weeping gum see *Eucalyptus pauciflora*
Weeping myall see *Acacia pendula*
Weeping pittosporum see *Pittosporum phillyreoides*
Weeping sedge see *Carex pendula*
Weeping willow see *Salix babylonica*
Wellingtonia see *Sequoiadendron giganteum*
Welsh poppy see *Meconopsis cambrica*
Western balsam poplar see *Populus trichocarpa*
Western catalpa see *Catalpa speciosa*
Western dog violet see *Viola adunca*
Western hackberry see *Celtis reticulata*
Western hemlock see *Tsuga heterophylla*
Western larch see *Larix occidentalis*
Western laurel see *Kalmia microphylla*
Western milfoil see *Myriophyllum hippuroides*
Western mugwort see *Artemisia ludoviciana*
Western prickly Moses see *Acacia pulchella*
Western redbud see *Cercis occidentalis*
Western red cedar see *Thuja plicata*
Western soapberry see *Sapindus drummondii*
Western tea myrtle see *Melaleuca nesophila*
Western wallflower see *Erysimum asperum*
Western white pine see *Pinus monticola*
Western yellow pine see *Pinus ponderosa*
West Indian holly see *Leea coccinea*
West Indian jasmine see *Plumeria*, *P. alba*
Weymouth pine see *Pinus strobus*
Whauwhaupaku see *Pseudopanax arboreus*
Wheatley elm see *Ulmus minor* subsp. *sarniensis*
Whin see *Ulex europaeus*
Whinberry see *Vaccinium myrtillus*
White alder see *Alnus rhombifolia*, *Clethra*
White arrow arum see *Peltandra sagittifolia*
White ash see *Fraxinus americana*
White bachelor's buttons see *Ranunculus aconitifolius* 'Flore Pleno'
White baneberry see *Actaea pachypoda* f. *pachypoda*
Whitebark pine see *Pinus albicaulis*
Whitebeam see *Sorbus aria*
White bottlebrush see *Callistemon salignus*
White cedar see *Thuja occidentalis*
White clover see *Trifolium repens*
White corallita see *Porana paniculata*
White cup see *Nierembergia repens*
White cypress see *Chamaecyparis thyoides*
White fir see *Abies concolor*
White forsythia see *Abeliophyllum*
White gardenia see *Gardenia thunbergia*
White ginger lily see *Hedychium coronarium*
White gum see *Eucalyptus viminalis*
White hellebore see *Veratrum album*
White hoop-petticoat daffodil see *Narcissus cantabricus*
White ironbark see *Eucalyptus leucoxylon*
White lilyturf see *Ophiopogon jaburan*
White mugwort see *Artemisia lactiflora*
White mulberry see *Morus alba*
White paint brush see *Haemanthus albiflos*
White pepper see *Piper nigrum*
White poplar see *Populus alba*
White rose of York see *Rosa* 'Alba Maxima'
White sallee see *Eucalyptus pauciflora*
White sallow wattle see *Acacia floribunda*
White silk cotton tree see *Ceiba pentandra*
White skunk cabbage see *Lysichiton camtschatcensis*
White snakeroot see *Eupatorium rugosum*
White Spanish broom see *Cytisus multiflorus*
White spruce see *Picea glauca*
White trumpet see *Sarracenia leucophylla*
White velvet see *Tradescantia sillamontana*
White water lily see *Nymphaea alba*
White willow see *Salix alba*
Whitey wood see *Acradenia frankliniae*
Whitlow grass see *Draba*
Whitlow-wort see *Paronychia*
Whorled heath see *Erica manipuliflora*
Whorled Solomon's seal see *Polygonatum verticillatum*
Whorlflower see *Morina longifolia*
Whortleberry see *Vaccinium*, *V. myrtillus*
Widow iris see *Hermodactylus tuberosus*
Widow's tears see *Commelina*
Wild angelica see *Angelica sylvestris*
Wild bergamot see *Monarda fistulosa*
Wild bleeding heart see *Dicentra formosa*
Wild buckwheat see *Eriogonum*
Wild carnation see *Dianthus caryophyllus*
Wild cherry see *Prunus avium*
Wild cotton see *Cochlospermum vitifolium*
Wild crab apple see *Malus sylvestris*
Wild daffodil see *Narcissus pseudonarcissus*
Wild ginger see *Asarum*
Wild hyacinth see *Camassia scilloides*
Wild indigo see *Baptisia*
Wild Irishman see *Discaria toumatou*
Wild jonquil see *Narcissus jonquilla*
Wild lily-of-the-valley see *Pyrola rotundifolia*
Wild liquorice see *Astragalus glycyphyllos*
Wild marjoram see *Origanum vulgare*
Wild onion see *Allium cernuum*
Wild pansy see *Viola tricolor*
Wild pineapple see *Ananas bracteatus*
Wild pomegranate see *Burchellia bubalina*
Wild rice see *Zizania*
Wild rosemary see *Dampiera rosmarinifolia*
Wild rum cherry see *Prunus serotina*
Wild rye see *Elymus*
Wild Spaniard see *Aciphylla colensoi*
Wild sweet crab apple see *Malus coronaria*
Wild sweet William see *Phlox divaricata*
Williams' heath see *Erica* x *williamsii*
Willow see *Salix*
Willow-bell see *Campanula persicifolia* var. *planiflora*
Willow bottlebrush see *Callistemon salignus*
Willow gentian see *Gentiana asclepiadea*
Willow herb see *Epilobium*
Willowleaf podocarp see *Podocarpus salignus*
Willow-leaved hakea see *Hakea salicifolia*
Willow-leaved jessamine see *Cestrum parqui*
Willow-leaved magnolia see *Magnolia salicifolia*
Willow-leaved sunflower see *Helianthus salicifolius*
Willow oak see *Quercus phellos*
Windflower see *Anemone*, *A. nemorosa*, *Zephyranthes*
Window palm see *Reinhardtia*, *R. gracilis*
Winecups see *Geissorhiza radians*
Wine palm see *Borassus flabellifer*, *Caryota urens*
Winged everlasting see *Ammobium*, *A. alatum*
Winged spindle see *Euonymus alatus*
Winged-stem passion flower see *Passiflora alata*
Winged thorn rose see *Rosa sericea* subsp. *omeiensis* f. *pteracantha*
Wing nut see *Pterocarya*
Winter aconite see *Eranthis*, *E. hyemalis*
Winterberry see *Ilex verticillata*
Winter cherry see *Cardiospermum halicacabum*, *Solanum capsicastrum*, *S. pseudocapsicum*
Wintergreen see *Gaultheria procumbens*, *Pyrola*
Winter heath see *Erica carnea*
Winter heliotrope see *Petasites fragrans*
Winter jasmine see *Jasminum nudiflorum*
Winter savory see *Satureja montana*
Winter's bark see *Drimys winteri*
Wintersweet see *Acokanthera oblongifolia*, *Chimonanthus*, *C. praecox*
Wire-netting bush see *Corokia cotoneaster*
Wirestem muhly see *Muhlenbergia mexicana*
Wishbone flower see *Torenia*, *T. fournieri*
Wistaria see *Wisteria*
Witch alder see *Fothergilla gardenii*
Witch grass see *Panicum capillare*
Witch hazel see *Hamamelis*
Woad see *Isatis tinctoria*
Wolf's bane see *Aconitum lycoctonum*
Wolgan snow gum see *Eucalyptus gregsoniana*
Wombat berry see *Eustrephus*
Wonga wonga vine see *Pandorea pandorana*
Wood anemone see *Anemone nemorosa*
Wood betony see *Stachys officinalis*
Woodbine see *Lonicera periclymenum*
Wood cranesbill see *Geranium sylvaticum*
Wood false brome see *Brachypodium sylvaticum*
Wood grass see *Sorghastrum nutans*
Woodland star see *Lithophragma*
Wood lily see *Trillium*
Wood melick see *Melica nutans*
Wood rose see *Merremia tuberosa*
Woodruff see *Asperula*
Woodrush see *Luzula*
Wood spurge see *Euphorbia amygdaloides*
Wood violet see *Viola riviniana*
Woolly-bearded protea see *Protea magnifica*
Woolly blue violet see *Viola sororia*
Woolly foxtail grass see *Alopecurus lanatus*
Woolly morning glory see *Argyreia nervosa*
Woolly sunflower see *Eriophyllum*
Woolly tea tree see *Leptospermum lanigerum*
Woolly tree fern see *Dicksonia antarctica*
Woolly willow see *Salix lanata*
Wormwood see *Artemisia*, *A. absinthium*
Woundwort see *Stachys*
Wych elm see *Ulmus glabra*

Y

Yanquapin see *Nelumbo lutea*
Yarrow see *Achillea*
Yautia see *Xanthosoma*
Yellow adder's tongue see *Erythronium americanum*
Yellow archangel see *Lamium galeobdolon*
Yellow asphodel see *Asphodeline lutea*
Yellow banksian rose see *Rosa banksiae* 'Lutea'
Yellow bells see *Tecoma stans*
Yellow birch see *Betula alleghaniensis*
Yellow buckeye see *Aesculus flava*
Yellow elder see *Tecoma stans*
Yellow flag see *Iris pseudacorus*
Yellow flamboyant tree see *Peltophorum pterocarpum*
Yellow flax see *Linum flavum*, *Reinwardtia indica*
Yellow floating heart see *Nymphoides peltata*
Yellow foxglove see *Digitalis grandiflora*
Yellow fritillary see *Fritillaria pudica*
Yellow gentian see *Gentiana lutea*
Yellow-groove bamboo see *Phyllostachys aureosulcata*
Yellow gum see *Eucalyptus leucoxylon*
Yellow haw see *Crataegus flava*
Yellow horned poppy see *Glaucium flavum*
Yellow jasmine see *Jasminum humile*

Z

GLOSSARY OF TERMS

This glossary provides concise definitions of terms used throughout the encyclopedia, as well as a number of others commonly found in horticulture. For the sake of clarity, many of the terms are narrowly defined here, but may be interpreted differently in non-horticultural contexts. For an illustrated account of plant botany, cultivation, and ornamental plant groups, see the introductory pages (pp.10–54); an index for these appears on p.1128. Pests and diseases are defined on pp.30–31.

A

Accent plant Plant used in a formal bed or border to emphasize contrasts of height, colour, and/or texture.
Acicular *see* Needle-shaped.
Acid With a pH value below 7.
Acuminate With a long, tapering point.
Acute Ending in a short, sharp point.
Adpressed Pressed flat to the axis to which it is attached.
Adventitious Refers to a plant organ that occurs in an unusual location.
Aeration Loosening of the soil structure to allow free circulation of air.
Aerial root Root that emerges from the stem above ground level.
Air-layering Method of propagation whereby a cut in an aerial stem is covered with moist sphagnum moss and sealed in a plastic sleeve in order to induce rooting. *See also p.28.*
Alkaline With a pH value above 7.
Alpine 1. High-altitude plant from above the tree-line and usually snow-covered in winter. 2. Loosely, any plant suitable for a rock garden. *See also pp.40–41.*
Alpine house Unheated, well-ventilated greenhouse used to grow alpines and other perennial plants.
Alternate Used to describe organs, usually leaves, borne singly at each node, in 2 vertical rows, on either side of an axis.
Androdioecious Having male and hermaphrodite flowers on separate plants of the same species. *See also* Dioecious, Gynodioecious, Monoecious.
Angiosperm Flowering plant that bears ovules, later seeds, enclosed in ovaries (as opposed to a gymnosperm, which bears naked ovules, then seeds, in cones). *See also p.10.*
Annual Plant that completes its life-cycle in one growing season. *See also pp.42–43.*
Annulus 1. Corona or rim of the corolla in the plants of the Asclepiadaceae family. 2. In ferns, the part of the sporangium involved in spore dispersal.
Anther Part of the stamen that releases pollen; usually borne on a filament.
Apex (*pl.* apexes; *adj.* apical) Tip or growing point of an organ.
Apomixis (*adj.* apomictic) Asexual production of ripe seed. Offspring are clones – that is, genetically identical to the parent.
Aquatic plant Plant that lives in water; free-floating, submerged, or rooted on the bottom with the leaves and flowers above water. *See also pp.52–53.*
Arching Curving gently downwards, but less markedly so than when described as pendent. *See also* Pendent.
Areole 1. Depressed or raised area bearing spines, branches, or flowers in cacti. 2. Small space outlined on a surface, such as an area of leaf between veins.
Aril Coat covering some seeds, often fleshy and brightly coloured.
Aroid Member of the Araceae family, characterized by an inflorescence composed of a spadix and spathe.
Arrow-shaped (sagittate) With a narrow, blunt or pointed tip, and widening at the base into 2 acute, downward-pointing lobes.
Asexual reproduction Process of producing new individuals by apomixis or vegetative propagation. *See also* Reproduction.
Auricle (*adj.* auricular) Ear-like lobe, often in pairs at the base of an organ.
Awn Stiff, bristle-like projection often found on grass seeds and spikelets.
Axil Upper angle between a part of a plant and the stem that bears it.
Axillary Borne in an axil. *See also* Terminal.
Axis (*pl.* axes) Rachis, stalk, or stem on which organs such as flowers, leaves, or leaflets are arranged.

B

Backbulb Dormant pseudobulb unique to orchids.
Bamboo Woody-caned plant belonging to the Gramineae family. *See also p.54.*
Bark Outermost layers of a woody stem, including all the living and non-living tissues outside the cambium.
Basal At the base of an organ or structure.
Basal leaf Leaf that grows from the lowest part of the stem.
Basal stem cutting Cutting taken from the base of a plant, usually herbaceous, in spring.
Beard 1. Awn. 2. Tuft or zone of hair.
Bed Area of ground, often set into a lawn, in which plants are grown.
Bedding plant Annual, biennial, or perennial planted to provide a temporary display of foliage and/or flowers.
Bell-shaped (campanulate) Used to describe a flower with a broad tube terminating in flared lobes.
Berry Fruit with soft flesh surrounding one or more seeds.
Bicoloured With 2 distinct colours.
Biennial Plant that completes its life-cycle in 2 years, growing in the first year, and flowering and fruiting in the second. *See also pp.10, 42–43.*
Bigeneric hybrid Offspring derived from crossing 2 different genera.
Binomial Two-part name derived from Latin or Greek, consisting of a genus name and a species, cultivar, group, series, or hybrid epithet, denoting an individual within a genus. *See also p.11.*
Bipinnate (2-pinnate) *see* Pinnate.
Bisexual (hermaphrodite) Refers to a flower that bears both male and female reproductive organs.
Biternate (2-ternate) *see* Ternate.
Bleed To weep sap.
Blind 1. Refers to a plant in which the growing point has been damaged. 2. Refers to plants, particularly bulbs, that do not flower.
Bloom 1. Flower or blossom. 2. Fine, waxy, whitish or bluish white coating. *See also* Glaucous, White-frosted.
Bog garden Waterlogged area used to grow plants found in bogs, marshes, wet pasture, and at water margins.
Bolt To produce flowers and seed prematurely.
Bonsai Production of dwarf trees or shrubs by pruning and root restriction.
Bottom heat Warmth radiated from below, usually via electrical cables, used in propagating cases to assist the rooting of cuttings and the germination of seed.
Bowl-shaped Used to describe a flower that is hemispherical with the sides straight or very slightly spreading at the tips.
Bract Modified leaf at the base of a flower or flowerhead. May be small and scale-like, or large, brightly coloured, and petal-like, or resemble normal foliage.
Bracteole Secondary bract sheathing a flower in an inflorescence, itself enclosed within a primary bract.
Branch Division of a stem, a trunk, or the axis of an inflorescence.
Branched-head standard Standard tree with a clear stem of 1.8m (6ft); the leader is cut back to develop an open crown. *See also p.33,* Central-leader standard.
Break To produce new growth as a result of pinching out.
Broad-leaved Used to describe trees and shrubs that have broad, flat, usually deciduous leaves – in contrast to the narrow, linear, usually evergreen needles of conifers.
Broken Type of marking in which the ground colour is striped with one or more contrasting colours, usually caused by viral infection; particularly applied to tulips.
Bromeliad Member of the Bromeliaceae family, characterized by showy inflorescences, frequently with brightly coloured bracts, and rosettes of often colourful leaves. *See also p.47.*
Bud Immature organ or shoot enclosing an embryonic branch, leaf, inflorescence, or flower.
Budding Method of propagation in which a vegetative bud of one plant is grafted on to another plant.
Bulb Modified, subterranean bud, with a short, thick stem and fleshy, scale leaves or leaf bases.
Bulb frame Glass or plastic frame used to provide a dry environment for bulbs during dormancy.
Bulbiferous Bearing bulbs or bulbils.
Bulbil Small, bulb-like organ borne in the axil of a leaf, bract, or occasionally flowerhead.
Bulbiliferous Bearing bulbils.
Bulblet Small bulb produced at the base of a parent bulb, often inside the tunic.
Bulbous 1. Used to describe a stem that is swollen at the base, usually underground. 2. Describes a plant with bulbs. 3. Loosely, refers to a plant with an underground storage organ such as a bulb, corm, tuber, or rhizome. *See also pp.44–45.*
Burr 1. Prickly, spiny, or hooked fruit, seed head, or flowerhead. 2. Woody outgrowth on the trunk of some trees.
Buttress root Fluted or swollen tree trunk that aids stability in shallow rooting conditions. *See also* Stilt root.

C

Cactus (*pl.* cacti) Stem succulent, member of the Cactaceae family. *See also pp.48–49.*
Calcareous Refers to soil with a high content of calcium carbonate (chalk) or magnesium carbonate. *See also* Lime.
Calcicole A lime-loving plant that lives on and favours calcareous soils.
Calcifuge A lime-hating plant that is harmed by calcareous soils.
Callus Thickened tissue that is formed by the cambium layer to aid healing around a wound.
Calyx (*pl.* calyces) Collective name for sepals, joined or separate, which form the outer whorl of the perianth.
Cambium Growth tissue directly below the bark of woody plants; its increase adds to the girth of roots and stems.
Campanulate *see* Bell-shaped.
Cane Hollow, slender, jointed stem, particularly characteristic of bamboos.
Cane sheath The basal section of a leaf that surrounds a bamboo cane as a tube, or a tube-like sheath with overlapping margins that is distinct from the leaf-blade.
Capitulum *see* Flowerhead.
Capsule Dry fruit that splits open to disperse ripe seed.
Carnivorous (insectivorous) Applied to a plant that obtains nutrients by trapping and ingesting insects or other small creatures.
Carpel Female part of a flower consisting of a style, a stigma, and an ovary. *See also* Pistil.
Catkin Form of inflorescence, often pendent, consisting of scale-like bracts and tiny, unisexual, usually petalless flowers arranged in a spike.
Caudex (*pl.* caudices) Swollen stem base of a woody-based plant such as a palm, a cycad, or some succulents.
Caudiciform Resembling or possessing a caudex.
Cauliflory (*adj.* cauliflorous) The production of flowers directly from a branch or stem, as in *Cercis* (Judas tree).
Central Spine of a cactus, growing from the centre of an areole.
Central-leader standard Standard tree with a clear stem of 1.8m (6ft) or more,

and lateral branches that taper from an erect central leader. *See also p.33*, Branched-head standard.
Central vein *see* Midrib.
Cephalium Woody, flower-bearing, densely spined area at the stem apex of some cacti. *See also* Pseudocephalium.
Chalky *see* Calcareous.
Channelled Lined with one or more longitudinal grooves.
Chimaera Plant composed of 2 or more genetically different tissues; the result of a mutation or of a graft hybrid.
Chipping *see* Scarify.
Chlorophyll Green pigment that absorbs energy from sunlight. *See also* Photosynthesis.
Chlorosis (adj. chlorotic) Loss of chlorophyll, and consequently the loss of green leaf coloration, caused by mineral deficiency, poor light levels, or disease.
Ciliate Bearing a marginal fringe of fine hairs.
Cladode *see* Phylloclade.
Cladophyll *see* Phylloclade.
Clay Very fertile, heavy, moisture-retentive soil, prone to compaction and surface capping.
Clay granules Moisture-retentive pellets of expanded clay. In hot, dry weather, the evaporation of water poured on to these granules increases humidity around houseplants.
Cleft Divided almost halfway to the centre. *See also* Sinus.
Climber Plant that climbs or clings by means of modified stems, roots, leaves, or leaf-stalks, using other plants or objects as support. *See also pp.36–37*, Scandent, Tendril.
Cloche Structure of glass or plastic panes or plastic sheeting, mainly used for cold-weather protection or for forcing early crops in open ground.
Clone A genetically identical group of plants derived from one individual by vegetative propagation or apomixis.
Cluster (fascicle) Arrangement of several inflorescences, leaves, stems, roots, or flowers that arise from a single point, or appear to do so.
Cold frame Unheated frame used for growing on fully hardy, frost-hardy, and half-hardy plants, usually situated outdoors.
Cold greenhouse Unheated but frost-free greenhouse. *See also p.24.*
Column Flower organ, mainly found in orchids, consisting of fused male and female reproductive parts.
Compaction Compression of soil and deterioration of its structure, particularly saturated clay and silt soils, resulting in poor aeration and drainage; usually a result of treading or excessive cultivation, especially on wet soils of heavy texture. *See also* Surface-capping.
Compost *see* Cutting compost, Garden compost, JI No.1/2/3, Loam, Peat, Potting compost, Seed compost.
Compound Consisting of several parts, but still identifiable as single unit, for example a compound leaf is one divided into 2 or more leaflets.
Cone Woody, seed-bearing structure in gymnosperms, generally composed of an axis with many lateral scales.
Conic, conical Refers to a solid form; cone-shaped, tapering evenly base to tip.
Conifer (*adj.* coniferous) Mostly evergreen trees or shrubs, usually with needle-like, linear leaves, and seeds borne naked on the scales of cones. Often from cool-temperate zones.
Conservatory Glazed, heated or unheated structure attached to a house; often has poorer ventilation than a greenhouse. *See also p.24.*
Conspicuous Seen easily with the naked eye; frequently used to mean showy or enlarged. *See also* Prominent.
Continental climate Weather conditions in the centre of a landmass, distant from coastal areas; the seasons are well defined, with hot summers and cold winters. *See also pp.18–19.*
Contractile Used to describe a root that is able to draw a bulb, corm, rhizome, or seedling deeper into the soil or closer to the surface.
Cool greenhouse Greenhouse with a minimum temperature of 2°C (35°F). *See also p.24.*
Cool-temperate Refers to a temperate climate with cold winters and warm summers.
Coppice (stool) To prune trees or shrubs close to ground level annually to promote strong growth.
Cordate *see* Heart-shaped.
Cordon Trained plant (usually a fruit tree) generally restricted to one main stem, occasionally 2–4 stems, by a careful system of training and pruning.
Corm (*adj.* cormous) Subterranean storage organ consisting of a solid stem or stem base, often enclosed in a tunic. Corms are replaced annually.
Cormel, cormlet Small corm that arises at or near the base of a mature one.
Corolla 1. Collective name for petals. 2. Inner whorl of perianth segments in some monocotyledons.
Corona A crown- or cup-like growth on a flower, between the corolla and the stamens, formed either by fused stamen filaments or by the perianth segments.
Corymb Broad, flat-topped or domed inflorescence of stalked flowers or flower-heads arising at different levels on alternate sides of an axis.
Cotyledon *see* Seed-leaf.
Creeper, creeping Used to describe a plant that spreads over the soil surface, usually rooting as it grows.
Crenate *see* Scalloped.
Crest 1. Tuft of hairs or soft bristles. 2. Raised ridge on a surface. *See also* Beard.
Cristate 1. Crested, or with a terminal tuft of hairs or other tissue. 2. Describes ferns with ruffled, usually forked fronds.
Crocks Broken pieces of clay pot, used to cover drainage holes in containers in order to provide free drainage and improve air circulation to the roots.
Cross To interbreed. *See also* Hybrid.
Cross-pollination When the stigma of a flower on one plant is dusted with the pollen from a different plant.
Cross-shaped (cruciform) Used to describe a flower with 4 petals, usually set at right-angles to each other in the form of a cross when viewed from above.
Crown 1. Growing point of a plant from which new shoots arise, at or just below the soil surface, at the junction with the roots. 2. Uppermost part of a tree or shrub. 3. Corona of a flower.
Crown bud Central flower bud growing at the tip of a shoot among other, usually smaller buds.
Crownshaft Upper section of a palm or cycad trunk, bearing leaves and inflorescences.
Crozier Coiled juvenile frond of a fern, similar in form to a bishop's crozier.
Cruciform *see* Cross-shaped.
Culm Jointed flowering stem of a grass.
Cultigen Plant known only in cultivation.
Cultivar (*abbrev.* cv., contraction of "cultivated variety") Plant raised or selected in cultivation that retains distinct, uniform characteristics when propagated by appropriate means. *See also pp.11, 42.*
Cuneate *see* Wedge-shaped.
Cup Corona of *Narcissus*, but only when shorter than the surrounding tepals.
Cup-shaped Used to describe a flower that is hemispherical with the sides straight or very slightly spreading at the tips; slightly narrower than bowl-shaped.
Cupule Cup-shaped whorl of hard, fused bracts surrounding the base of a fruit, as in beech nuts (*Fagus*).
Cutting Section of leaf, stem, or root separated from a plant and used for propagation. *See also p.29*, Basal stem cutting, Greenwood cutting, Hardwood cutting, Heel cutting, Leaf-bud cutting, Leaf cutting, Root cutting, Semi-ripe cutting, Softwood cutting, Stem-tip cutting.
Cutting compost Free-draining, low-nutrient compost that is used to root cuttings; usually based on fine-grade granulated bark, soil, peat (or peat substitute), perlite, or sand.
Cyathium (*pl.* cyathia) Inflorescence of *Euphorbia*, in which a cup-like involucre surrounds a single pistil and several male flowers, each with a single stamen; flowers are sometimes bisexual.
Cycad Member of the Cycadaceae family, mainly with stiff, palm-like leaves borne terminally from a short, stout trunk. *See also p.50.*
Cyme Flat or round-topped, branched inflorescence with each axis ending in a flower, the oldest at the centre, and the youngest arising in succession from the axils of bracteoles.

D

Damp down To wet the floor and staging in a greenhouse in order to raise humidity and lower the temperature. *See also* Mist.
Damping off Collapse of seedlings and young plants caused by soil- or water-borne fungi, which rot the bases of stems and roots.
Dead-head To remove spent flowerheads in order to prolong flowering and prevent self-seeding.
Deciduous 1. Shedding leaves annually at the end of the growing season. 2. Falling away when no longer functional, as with the petals of many flowers.
Decumbent Growing close to the ground but usually with upward-growing tips.
Decurrent Extending downwards from the point of attachment; often used to describe the attachment of a leaf to a stem.
Decurved Curved downwards.
Decussate *see* Rank.
Deep-water aquatic Plant that roots in water 30–90cm (12–36in) deep, and produces foliage and flowers at or above surface level.
Deltoid *see* Triangular.
Demersed Rising up out of the water (of parts of an aquatic plant). *See also* Emersed.
Dentate *see* Toothed.
Depressed Used to describe a flattened, solid form.
Diamond-shaped (rhomboidal) Roughly oval but with acute angles at the base and tip, and obtuse angles midway down both sides.
Dicotyledon Angiosperm with 2 seed-leaves, net-veined leaves, a cambium layer (in many species), and floral parts usually in fours or fives. *See also* Monocotyledon.
Die-back Death of a shoot, beginning at the tip, due to damage or disease.
Digitate *see* Palmate.
Dioecious Bearing male and female flowers on separate plants, so that both male and female plants must be grown if fruit is required. *See also* Androdioecious, Gynodioecious, Monoecious.
Disbud To remove surplus buds so that better quality flowers or fruit are borne.
Disc-floret Tiny, usually tubular flower, one of many that normally comprise the centre of a (composite) flowerhead.
Dissected *see* Divided.
Distichous *see* Rank.
Diurnal With activity taking place only in daylight, e.g. a flower that opens only during the day. *See also* Nocturnal.
Divide To propagate a plant by splitting it into 2 or more parts, each with its own section of root system and one or more shoots or dormant buds.
Divided (dissected) Deeply cut into segments or lobes.
Dormancy (*adj.* dormant) Suspension of active growth in unfavourable conditions.
Dot plant Usually tall-growing plant, used singly in the design of a formal bed or border to accentuate contrasts of height, colour, and/or texture.
Double Used to describe a flower with more petals than in the normal wild state, and with few, if any, stamens.
Drainage 1. Movement of excess water through the soil or compost. 2. System designed to remove excess water rapidly from the soil.
Drill Narrow, straight furrow in the soil, in which seeds are sown.
Drupe Fruit consisting of one or several hard seeds (stones) surrounded by a fleshy outer covering.
Dwarf Small or slow-growing variant of a species resulting from hybridization, mutation, or specific cultivation methods. *See also* Bonsai.

E

Earth up To draw soil up around a plant to exclude light, promote the formation of roots from the stem, or provide winter protection.
Ellipsoid Used to describe a solid form, broadest at the centre, tapering towards each end; length is 2 times the width. It is wider than a spindle-shaped form, with the sides more curved.
Elliptic Used to describe a flat structure, broadest at the centre, tapering towards each end; length is 2 times the width.

Embryo Part of a seed from which a new plant develops.
Emersed Permanently submersed in water (of parts of an aquatic plant). *See also* Demersed.
Ensiform *see* Strap-shaped.
Entire Used to describe a continuous, untoothed, and unlobed margin, usually of a leaf.
Ephemeral 1. Lasting for one day only, as with some flowers. 2. Short-lived, as with plants that live only for a few weeks, but which may produce several generations in a single growing season.
Epicalyx (*pl.* epicalyces) 1. Whorl of bracts surrounding the calyx. 2. False calyx.
Epicormic Refers to strong shoots that develop from latent or adventitious buds under the bark of a tree or shrub, usually close to pruning cuts or wounds.
Epigeal *See* Germination.
Epiphyte (*adj.* epiphytic) Plant that grows on another plant without obtaining food from it.
Erect Upright; perpendicular to the ground or to the point of attachment.
Ericaceous 1. Belonging to the Ericaceae family. 2. Heath-like or allied to the genus *Erica*. 3. Used to describe lime-free potting compost with a pH of 6.5 or less, suitable for growing acid-loving, lime-hating plants. *See also* Calcifuge.
Espalier Fruit tree with pairs of branches trained horizontally from the central stem, in a single plane.
Etiolated Used to describe a plant that has abnormally elongated, often bleached shoots as a result of poor light levels.
Evergreen 1. Retaining leaves for more than one growing season. 2. Plant with the above characteristic.
Everlasting (immortelle) Plant with often papery bracts, flowers, or flowerheads that retain their form and/or colour on drying.
Exfoliating Peeling off in thin flakes, shreds, plates, or layers; usually refers to bark.
Exserted Extending beyond or projecting from a surrounding organ or parts, as when stamens protrude beyond a corolla.
Eye 1. Centre of a flower, usually contrasting with the ground colour. 2. A latent bud, especially on tuberous plants, such as dahlias and potatoes.

F

F1 hybrid Vigorous and uniform, first-generation offspring, derived from crossing 2 distinct, pure-bred lines. F2 hybrids result from self-pollination within a population of F1 hybrids; they do not come true.
Falcate *see* Sickle-shaped.
Fall Semi-pendent or spreading tepal of *Iris* flower.
Family Primary category in plant classification, between order and genus, encompassing genera that have natural characteristics that allow them to be grouped together. *See also p.11.*
Fancy Used to describe a flower that is flaked, flecked, or striped in contrast to the ground colour.
Fan palm Palm with fan-like, palmate rather than pinnate leaves.
Fan-shaped (flabellate) Wedge-shaped or semi-circular, with a pleated or boldly veined surface.
Farina (*adj.* farinaceous, farinose) *see* White-mealy.
Fascicle *see* Cluster.
Fastigiate Used to describe the habit of a tree or shrub with a strongly upright, narrow crown of more or less erect branches, growing almost parallel with the main stem or trunk.
Feathered 1. Used to describe a standard tree with a stem or trunk that is branched to the base with lateral "feathers". *See also p.33*, Central-leader standard. 2. Used to describe a flower with feather-like markings contrasting with the ground colour, particularly of some tulips.
Fern Non-flowering, vascular plant, often with feather-like fronds. *See also p.51.*
Fertile 1. Refers to organs that produce functional pollen, spores, or viable seed. 2. Used to describe soil with a high content of nutrients essential to plant growth.
Fertilization Sexual fusion of male and female elements, initiating seed development. *See also* Reproduction.
Fertilizer Nutrients added to soil or potting compost to promote the vigour of a plant. Nitrogen (N), phosphorus (P), and potassium (K) are the chief elements used in inorganic fertilizers. Organic fertilizers are based on decomposed plant or animal matter.
Filament 1. Stalk of the stamen attached to the anther. 2. Thread-like extension or hair.
Filiform *see* Thread-like.
Fimbriate Fringed at the margin, for example, of a leaf or petal, where the fringe is formed by very slender extensions of the tissue rather than attached as hairs. *See also* Ciliate.
Flabellate *see* Fan-shaped.
Flaked Used to describe a flower in which another colour overlies the ground colour in large splashes; particularly applied to some carnations (*Dianthus*) and tulips.
Flamed Used to describe a flower in which another colour overlies the ground colour in a combination of fine feathering with a solid band of colour at the centre of the petal; particularly applied to tulips.
Floret Tiny, individual flower within a dense inflorescence, such as a grass flower in a spikelet, or a disc- or ray-floret in a (composite) flowerhead.
Florist flower Highly bred flower usually grown for exhibition, as with auriculas (primulas) and chrysanthemums.
Flower Reproductive structure of angiosperms, usually consisting of an ovary or stamens, or both, most frequently encircled by a perianth of differentiated petals and sepals or undifferentiated tepals, and usually borne on a flower-stalk. *See also pp.16–17.*
Flowerhead (capitulum) Inflorescence consisting of a central group of tiny disc-florets, usually ringed by ray-florets, borne on a compressed axis or stem. Also referred to as a composite flowerhead.
Flowering plant *see* Angiosperm.
Flower-stalk (pedicel) Stalk supporting an individual flower or fruit singly or in an inflorescence.
Fluted With long, rounded, vertical grooves.
Foliage plant Used to describe a plant grown primarily for the colour, pattern, or texture of its leaves rather than its flowers.
Foliar feed Dilute solution of fertilizer applied to leaves.
Follicle Dry fruit, formed from a single carpel, that splits along one side to release one or more seeds.
Force To induce unseasonal growth, flowering, or fruiting of a plant, usually under glass; achieved by manipulating the plant's environment.
Forma (*abbrev.* f.) Variant of a species, ranked below *varietas* (var.) in the nomenclatural hierarchy, distinguished by minor characteristics such as habit or the colour of the leaves, flowers, or fruits. *See also p.11.*
Formative pruning Training of young trees or shrubs to produce a framework of strong, evenly spaced stems or branches. *See also p.25.*
Frame Structure with a glass or plastic cover used for forcing, hardening off, propagation, or winter protection. *See also* Bulb frame, Cold frame, Propagating frame.
Free-tipped Refers to a conifer needle that is pressed flat to an axis with the tip extending beyond it.
Frond 1. Leaf of a fern. 2. Loosely, a large, compound leaf, such as a palm leaf.
Frost hardy Able to withstand temperatures down to -5°C (23°F).
Frost tender May be damaged by temperatures below 5°C (41°F).
Fruit Ripened ovary and any attached structures that ripen with it.
Fully hardy Able to withstand temperatures down to -15°C (5°F).
Fungus (*pl.* fungi; *adj.* fungal) Non-vascular, non-photosynthetic organism, such as a mould or mushroom, that obtains nutrients by absorbing organic compounds from its surroundings.
Funnel-shaped Used to describe a flower in which the perianth widens gradually from the base into a spreading, often lobed mouth, like a funnel.
Fusiform *see* Spindle-shaped.

G

Garden compost Humus-rich material formed by the decay of organic matter. Used as a mulch or to improve soil structure and nutrition.
Garden origin Applied to a plant that has been artificially bred or selected, rather than occurring in the wild.
Garigue Exposed Mediterranean habitat covered with scrub vegetation.
Genus (*pl.* genera; *adj.* generic) Primary category in plant classification, ranked between family and species. Encompasses species that share a wide range of characteristics. *See also p.11*, Binomial.
Germination Physical and biochemical changes that occur as a seed begins to generate into a young plant, resulting in the development of a radicle (rudimentary root) and plumule (rudimentary shoot). When the seed-leaf or seed-leaves remain within the seedcoat below ground during germination, as with broad bean (*Vicia faba*), it is known as hypogeal germination. When the seed-leaves emerge above ground and turn green during germination, as with sycamore (*Acer pseudoplatanus*), it is known as epigeal germination.
Gesneriad Member of the Gesneriaceae family, including perennials, climbers, subshrubs, and small trees, many of which are epiphytic. *See also p.40.*
Glabrous Smooth and hairless.
Gland Cell, organ, or pore that secretes oils or other substances.
Glandular-hairy With gland-tipped hairs.
Glaucous With a blue-green, blue-grey, grey, or white bloom; usually refers to stems and leaves.
Globose *see* Spherical.
Globular *see* Spherical.
Glochid Small, barbed bristle or hair borne on the areole of a cactus.
Glume Thin, dry, membrane-like bract in the inflorescence of a grass or sedge, usually arranged in 2 ranks; may be a perianth segment, or support a spikelet or flower, depending on the species.
Graft hybrid Plant resulting from the combination of tissues from both scion and rootstock after grafting. *See also* Chimaera.
Grafting Method of propagation in which the scion of one plant and the rootstock of another, closely related plant are artificially united so that they eventually function as one plant.
Granulated bark Bark ground to fine, medium, or coarse grade, often used in potting compost.
Grass Member of the Gramineae family, with round, hollow, or solid stems that have usually regularly spaced, solid nodes. The basic inflorescence is a spikelet, grouped into a panicle, raceme, or spike. *See also p.54.*
Greenhouse (glasshouse) Structure glazed with glass or plastic, providing a controlled environment for the cultivation of plants. *See also p.24*, Cold greenhouse, Cool greenhouse, Temperate greenhouse, Warm greenhouse.
Green manure Practice of sowing quick-growing crops, e.g. clover (*Trifolium*), and digging them into the soil to decompose and improve the humus content.
Greenwood cutting Cutting taken from the shoot-tip of a plant once the initial flush of spring growth has slowed; stems are slightly harder than those used for softwood cuttings.
Grex A collective term applied to all the progeny of an artificial cross from known parents of different taxa. Mainly applied to orchids. *See also p.11.*
Ground cover Applied to (usually) low-growing plants that quickly spread over the soil surface, helping to suppress weeds.
Ground frost Climatic effect when the temperature at or just beneath the surface of the soil falls to 0°C (32°F) or below.
Group Category of cultivated plants that denotes a collection of similar, named cultivars. *See also p.11*, Series.
Growing point (shoot-tip) Tip of a shoot from which new extension growth develops.
Growing season Part of the year when a plant is in active growth.
Grow on To grow young plants to a stage where they are ready to plant out or flower.
Growth habit *see* Habit.
Gymnosperm Tree or shrub, generally evergreen, that bears naked

seeds in cones rather than enclosed in ovaries, e.g. conifers, cycads. *See also p.10.*
Gynodioecious Bearing hermaphrodite and female flowers on separate plants of the same species. *See also* Androdioecious, Dioecious, Monoecious.

H

Habit Characteristic form, appearance, or mode of growth of a mature plant.
Habitat Natural environment in which a plant occurs in the wild.
Haft Narrow or constricted base of an organ, particularly the fall and standard petals of *Iris* flowers.
Half hardy Able to withstand temperatures down to 0°C (32°F).
Half-pot Container that is half the depth of a standard plant pot.
Half-standard Standard tree or shrub with a clear stem of 1–1.5m (3–5ft) from ground level to the lowest lateral branches.
Harden off To acclimatize young plants reared in a protective environment to cooler conditions outdoors by gradually introducing them to a cooler environment.
Hardiness Capacity of a cultivated plant to withstand adverse conditions; in general usage, its tolerance of low temperatures. *See pp.18–19.*
Hardwood Mature wood used for cuttings.
Hardwood cutting Cutting taken from mature wood from early autumn (after leaf fall) to early winter.
Hastate *see* Spear-shaped.
Heart-shaped (cordate) 1. Roughly ovate, pointed at the tip, and with a deep cleft at the centre of a rounded base. 2. Used to describe a base that is rounded with a deep cleft at the centre, which in leaves is where the leaf-stalk attaches.
Heel cutting Cutting consisting of a vigorous sideshoot from a stem of the current season's growth, with a small piece of bark or older wood at the base.
Herb 1. Plant with practical properties, such as for culinary or medicinal use. 2. Botanically, any herbaceous plant.
Herbaceous border Area of land set aside for the cultivation of herbaceous plants.
Herbaceous plant Non-woody plant that dies back (loses top-growth and becomes dormant) at the end of the growing season, usually in autumn, overwintering by means of underground rootstocks. Some may develop a woody base. Growth resumes in spring.
Herbicide Chemical treatment used to control or eradicate weeds.
Hermaphrodite *see* Bisexual.
Hip Fleshy fruit of a rose.
Hose-in-hose Used to describe a double flower in which the corolla or calyx is duplicated, with one inserted in the throat of the other.
Houseplant Any plant grown for long periods indoors, often frost-tender species that would not survive outside in cold climates.
Humidity Measure of the air's moisture content as a percentage of saturated air (relative humidity/RH). In this encyclopedia, low humidity is below 50% RH; moderate humidity is 51–60% RH; high humidity is 61% RH and above. *See also p.24.*
Humus Slowly decomposed organic material found in soil; may also refer to rotted garden compost or leaf mould. Where lacking or deficient, it may be dug into soil to increase bacterial activity and improve structure. Humus increases a soil's ability to retain nutrients and moisture, and acts as a reserve of slowly released plant nutrients, including nitrogen and phosphorus.
Hybrid (cross) Naturally or artificially produced offspring of genetically distinct parents of different taxa. Hybrids show new characteristics and are often vigorous in growth. *See also* F1 hybrid, Graft hybrid, Intergeneric hybrid, Interspecific hybrid, Multigeneric hybrid, Trigeneric hybrid.
Hypogeal *See* Germination.

I

Immortelle *see* Everlasting.
Incised Deeply, irregularly, and sharply toothed or lobed.
Incurved Bending inwards.
Indumentum Covering of hair or, more rarely, scales.
Indusium (*pl.* indusia) Tissue covering a sorus on a fern frond.
Infertile 1. Refers to a soil that is very low in nutrients. 2. More loosely, applied to plants that do not flower or fruit for various reasons, but may do so if the conditions are right. *See also* Sterile.
Inflorescence Arrangement of flowers on a single axis. *See also* Catkin, Cluster, Corymb, Cyme, Flowerhead, Panicle, Raceme, Spadix, Spike, Umbel.
Insecticide Chemical treatment used to control or eradicate insect pests.
Insectivorous *see* Carnivorous.
Insert To place cuttings in a growing medium.
Intergeneric hybrid Result of crossing plants of 2 distinct, usually closely related genera.
Internode Section of stem between 2 nodes.
Interrupted Refers to a structure, usually an inflorescence, that is not continuous, such as the inflorescences of *Salvia* species.
Interspecific hybrid Result of crossing 2 species within the same genus.
Invasive Used to describe a vigorous plant that rapidly overwhelms more delicate neighbours, unless restricted in spread.
Inversely heart-shaped (obcordate) Inversely ovate, with a deep cleft at the centre of a rounded tip, and pointed at the base.
Inversely lance-shaped (oblanceolate) Broadest above the centre, tapering to a narrow basal point; length is 3–6 times the width.
Involucre (*adj.* involucral) Ring of crowded bracts (sometimes only one), sometimes conspicuous and often overlapping, around the base of a flowerhead or umbel.

JK

JI No.1/2/3 (John Innes composts) Series of standardized potting composts containing 7 parts sterilized loam, 3 parts peat (or substitute), and 2 parts sand, to which are added varying amounts of ground limestone, hoof and horn, superphosphate, and potassium sulphate. JI Nos.1, 2, and 3 contain increasing amounts of fertilizer to suit plants of varying vigour and seasonal changes in growth rate. *See also p.24.*
Juvenile The early phase of a plant's life before adulthood, characterized by sexual immaturity, and/or a different growth habit or foliage form, as in most *Eucalyptus* and *Juniperus*.
Keel 1. Prominent longitudinal ridge, usually on the underside of an organ such as a leaf, similar to the keel of a boat. 2. Two lower, fused petals of a pea-like flower.
Kidney-shaped (reniform) Roughly quarter-moon-shaped with blunt ends (on a leaf, the stalk is attached at the notched centre of the concave margin).

L

Labellum Lip, particularly applied to prominent third petal of *Iris* or orchid flowers. *See also* Lip.
Laced Used to describe a flower in which the colour of the petal margins and centre contrast with the ground colour.
Laciniate Used to describe a margin that is finely and irregularly cut.
Lamina *see* Leaf-blade.
Lanceolate *see* Lance-shaped.
Lance-shaped (lanceolate) Broadest below the centre, tapering to a narrow tip; length is 3–6 times the width.
Latent bud Used to describe a bud that remains inactive or dormant until stimulated into growth.
Lateral 1. Located on or to the side of an axis or organ, such as lateral veins that arise from the midrib on a leaf surface. 2. Sideshoot from the stem of a plant.
Latex Milky-white sap or fluid that bleeds from some plants when the stem is cut or damaged; may be irritant.
Lath house Structure composed of light planks (laths) or trellis work used to protect plants from sun, wind, and rain and to acclimatize young, usually woody, plants before planting out in the garden.
Lax Loose, not compact.
Layering Method of propagation whereby a stem is pegged to the soil while still attached to the parent plant, to induce rooting. *See also* Air-layering, Mound-layering.
Leaching Removal of soluble nutrients from soil by the passage of water.
Leader 1. Main, usually central stem of a plant. *See also* Central-leader standard. 2. Terminal shoot of a main branch.
Leaf Plant organ, usually flattened and green, borne on a stem or branch, that fulfils the functions of photosynthesis, respiration, and transpiration. *See also pp.14–15.*
Leaf axil Angle formed between a leaf or leaf-stalk and the stem of a plant.
Leaf-blade (lamina) Thin, usually flat part of a leaf, excluding the leaf-stalk.
Leaf-bud cutting Cutting taken from a stem section, including a leaf-bud and leaf-stalk.
Leaf cutting Cutting taken from a leaf or section of a leaf.
Leaflet Single division of a compound leaf. Botanically, a pinna.
Leaf mould Fibrous, flaky, organic material composed of decayed leaves. Found naturally in woodland, and made from stacked leaves in gardens for use as a peat substitute. *See also* Humus, Leaf-rich.
Leaf node Point at which a leaf arises from a stem.
Leaf-rich Used to describe soil that has a high proportion of humus or leaf mould.
Leaf scar Raised area on a tree trunk, branch, or twig, where a leaf once grew.
Leaf-stalk (petiole) Part of a leaf, attached to the base or centre of the leaf-blade, that connects it to a stem or branch.
Legume *see* Pod.
Lenticel Raised pore on the surface of bark or some fruits, which provides access for air to the inner tissues.
Liana, liane Woody-stemmed, climbing plant.
Ligulate *see* Strap-shaped.
Limb 1. Broadened, flattened, and expanded part of a plant organ, usually a leaf or flower, extending from a narrower base. 2. Larger branch of a tree.
Lime Loosely, refers to compounds of calcium. Calcium content is used to measure soil pH. *See also* Calcareous.
Lime-free Refers to acidic soil. *See also* Peat.
Lime-tolerant Capable of growing in calcareous soil. *See also* Calcicole.
Linear Long and narrow, with parallel margins, or almost so; length is 12 or more times the width.
Lingulate Shaped like a tongue.
Lip Prominent lower lobe on a flower, formed by one or more fused petals or sepals. *See also* Labellum.
Liquid feed Water-diluted solution of fertilizers, often used for houseplants.
Lithophytic (saxicolous) Growing on or among rocks or stones.
Loam Highly fertile, well-drained but moisture-retentive soil, usually fibre- and humus-rich, and containing more or less equal parts of clay, sand, and silt.
Lobe Usually rounded segment, separated from adjacent segments by clefts extending halfway or less to the centre of an organ, such as a leaf. *See also* Palmately lobed.
Lorate *see* Strap-shaped.

M

Maquis Habitat consisting of dense shrub thickets, particular to Corsican and other Mediterranean coastlines.
Marginal aquatic Plant that requires permanently moist conditions, from pure mud to water 30–45cm (12–18in) deep.
Maritime climate Weather conditions experienced in coastal areas. Proximity to the sea or ocean brings exposure to strong winds, but usually moderates seasonal temperatures; rainfall occurs regularly throughout the year. *See also pp.18–19.*
Meristem Tip of a shoot or root in which cell division takes place. Undifferentiated cells are formed or differentiated into tissues that eventually become leaves, flowers, stems, or even whole plants.
Microclimate Local environmental conditions in a specific and limited area, which may differ markedly from the general conditions that pertain in the locality, for example, by virtue of greater shelter from or exposure to the elements.
Midrib (midvein) Primary, usually central vein running from the stalk to the tip of a leaf or leaflet.

Midvein *see* Midrib.
Mist To increase humidity under glass in summer by spraying very fine droplets of water into the air. *See also* Damp down.
Mixed border Area of ground in which herbaceous plants, annuals, bulbs, and shrubs are grown.
Monocarpic Refers to plants that flower and fruit once and then die. Monocarpic perennials may grow for several or many years before flowering.
Monocotyledon Angiosperm with a single seed-leaf, parallel-veined leaves, no cambium layer, and floral parts usually in threes. *See also* Dicotyledon.
Monoecious With separate male and female flowers borne on the same plant. *See also* Androdioecious, Dioecious, Gynodioecious.
Monopodial Refers to a stem or rhizome growing indefinitely from an apical or terminal bud, not usually producing secondary branches.
Monotypic Having only one component, e.g. a genus containing a single species.
Mound-layering Method of propagation whereby the basal section of a stem is earthed-up to induce rooting.
Mulch Layer of material spread on the top of the soil around plants. Loose mulches, such as leaf mould and garden compost, retain moisture, insulate roots, and can improve soil structure and add nutrients. Sheet mulches, such as black polythene, suppress weeds and also conserve moisture. *See also p.21.*
Multigeneric hybrid Result of crossing 3 or more genera, often over more than one generation.
Mutation *see* Sport.
Mycorrhizal Refers to a mutually beneficial association between a fungus and the roots of a plant.

N

Native Species that naturally grows wild in a particular area.
Naturalized Used to describe a species that apparently grows wild in a particular area, but is introduced and not native.
Neck **1.** The upper part of a bulb from where the leaves and flowering stem emerge. **2.** The junction between top growth and root growth of a plant, usually at soil level.
Nectar Sugary, liquid secretion that attracts some pollinators.
Nectary Gland, often a modified sepal, petal, or stamen, that secretes nectar.
Needle Stiff, linear leaf of a conifer.
Needle-shaped (acicular) Long, narrow, and rounded rather than flat in cross-section; narrower than linear.
Neutral With pH7, neither acid nor alkaline.
Nocturnal With activity taking place at night, e.g. a flower that opens only at night. *See also* Diurnal.
Node Point on a stem, sometimes swollen, at which leaves, leaf buds, and shoots arise.
Nodule Small, rounded swelling on the roots or other plant part, frequently associated with nitrogen-fixing bacteria. May also be a symptom of eelworm (nematode) infestation.
Nomenclature Standard system of naming plants and providing for the formation and use of the names. Cultivated plants are named in accordance with the International Code of Nomenclature for Cultivated Plants and the International Code for Botanical Nomenclature. *See also p.11.*
Non-vascular Used to describe plants that lack conductive tissue for the circulation of water and nutrients, for example fungi and mosses. *See also p.10.*
Non-woody *see* Soft-stemmed.
Nut Dry, non-splitting fruit with a hard or leathery shell surrounding a single seed (kernel).
Nutrients Minerals necessary for healthy metabolism and growth.

O

Obcordate *see* Inversely heart-shaped.
Oblanceolate *see* Inversely lance-shaped.
Oblong With 2 parallel sides of roughly equal length; length is 2–4 times the width.
Oblong-ovate Roughly oblong, rounded at both ends, and broader at one end than the other.
Obovate Refers to a flat form, egg-shaped in outline and broadest above the middle; length is 1½–2 times the width.
Obovoid Refers to a solid form, egg-shaped and broadest above the middle; length is 1½ times the width.
Offset Small plant that arises naturally by vegetative increase, as with many bulbous plants and succulents.
Of gardens Term used after the Latin name of a plant to denote that the name is commonly but incorrectly used.
Open pollination Natural pollination without the intervention of the gardener or plant breeder.
Opposite Used to describe organs, usually leaves, borne in pairs at each node, in the same plane but on opposite sides of an axis.
Orbicular *see* Rounded.
Orchid Member of the Orchidaceae family, which contains 835 genera of perennials, more than half epiphytic, the rest terrestrial; they are characterized by their unique flower structure. *See also p.46.*
Organic **1.** Carbon-based matter of plant or animal origin. **2.** Gardening practices using only natural materials.
Osmunda fibre Chopped, dried roots of the fern genus *Osmunda*, used in orchid cultivation.
Oval Broadly elliptic, rounded at both ends, with slightly parallel sides in the middle; length is 1½–2 times the width.
Ovary Female organ of a flower, containing ovules.
Ovate Refers to a flat form, egg-shaped in outline and broadest below the middle; length is 1½ times the width.
Overpotting When a plant is potted in too large a pot. If the volume of soil in the pot is too large for the existing rootball to exploit within a growing season, the unused potting mixture may become waterlogged and sour, leading eventually to root death and failure to thrive. *See also* Pot-bound.
Overwintering **1.** Refers to annuals and biennials sown late in one season, which then survive over winter as young plants and go on to flower early in the next season. **2.** The survival over winter of any plant in a state that differs from the normal growth mode, as with herbaceous perennials.
Ovoid Refers to a solid form, egg-shaped, and broadest below the middle.
Ovule Part of the ovary from which seed develops after fertilization.
Oxygenator Fully submerged aquatic plant that releases oxygen into the water.

PQ

Palm Member of the Palmae or Arecaceae family. Usually solitary, sometimes multi-stemmed trees or shrubs with characteristic terminal rosettes of palmate or pinnate leaves. *See also p.50,* Fan palm.
Palmate Used to describe a compound leaf that is fully divided into leaflets arising from a single basal point; it is often also used loosely to mean lobed in a hand-like form. 3-palmate leaves are divided into 3 leaflets, and are often also referred to as trifoliolate, ternate, or, incorrectly, trifoliate. 5-palmate leaves are divided into 5 leaflets, and may also be described as digitate. *See also* Trifoliate.
Palmately lobed Used to describe a leaf that is deeply divided into 3–7, sometimes more, lobes. It is distinct from a palmate leaf in that the divisions do not extend to the basal point, so remain lobes rather than leaflets.
Pan Shallow dish used for growing alpine plants and sowing seed; often set into a raised bed.
Panicle Branched raceme. Loosely applied to freely branched, corymb-like or cyme-like inflorescences.
Papilla (*pl.* papillae, *adj.* papillose) Small, soft, wart-like projection.
Pappus A tuft or whorl of scales or delicate bristles, often found in place of the calyx in the flowers of some members of the family Compositae.
Parasite Organism that derives nutrients directly from a host species, often to the detriment of the latter.
Pea-like Used to describe a flower structure found in many genera of the Leguminosae and Papilionaceae family, with an erect standard petal, 2 large, usually lateral wing petals, and 2 lower, keeled petals that may be fused at the base or on the lower side, enclosing the stamens and pistil.
Peat Moisture-retentive, humus-rich, acid, partially decayed organic matter, with a pH up to 6.5. Used mainly for potting compost. Derived from sedges (sedge peat) or sphagnum moss (sphagnum peat) and occurring in boggy, waterlogged conditions. Increasingly, due to environmental concerns regarding the diminishing number of peat bogs, peat substitutes are used for preference where appropriate; they include animal wastes, coconut fibre (coir), garden compost, mushroom compost, worm-worked compost, granulated bark, and leaf mould.
Peat bed Area edged with peat blocks and filled with moist, peaty soil, for growing acid-loving plants.
Pectinate Arrangement of plant organs, usually leaves, in regular, comb-like rows, either in a single row or 2-ranked.
Pedate Used to describe a palmate or palmately divided leaf in which the basal lobes or leaflets are themselves lobed.
Pedicel *see* Flower-stalk.
Peduncle Stalk of an inflorescence.
Peltate Attached to the stalk at the centre or other point on the underside of a structure, such as a leaf, rather than at the margin.
Pendent Hanging downwards. Used synonymously with pendulous.
Perennial Plant that lives for more than 2 growing seasons; in horticulture, usually only applied to non-woody plants. *See also pp.10, 38–39.*
Perfoliate Used to describe stalkless leaves, arranged singly or in opposite pairs, with the bases united around the stem.
Perianth Collective term for the corolla and calyx, whether these are distinct from each other or undifferentiated.
Perianth segment Undifferentiated petal or sepal.
Perlite Light granules of volcanic minerals added to soil or to potting and seed compost to improve aeration.
Permeability Ease with which water passes through soil.
Perpetual-flowering Used to describe a plant that bears flowers more or less continuously throughout the year. *See also* Remontant.
Persistent Remaining attached to the plant.
Pesticide Chemical treatment used to control or eradicate pests, diseases, or weeds.
Pests Loosely, vermin that feed on plants, and often transmit disease. *See also pp.30–31.*
Petal Modified leaf that makes up the corolla of a flower; generally brightly coloured. *See also* Perianth segment, Tepal.
Petaloid Similar to a petal in colour, shape, and texture; most often used of flower parts modified into the form of petals, as in petaloid stamen.
Petiole *see* Leaf-stalk.
pH Measure of acidity or alkalinity. Many garden plants prefer neutral to slightly acid soil with pH5.5–7.5. *See also* Acid, Alkaline, Neutral.
Photosynthesis Complex series of chemical reactions in green plants and some bacteria, in which energy from sunlight is absorbed by chlorophyll, and carbon dioxide and water are converted into sugars and oxygen.
Phylloclade (cladode, cladophyll) Stem that looks like and takes on the functions of a leaf.
Phyllode Expanded leaf-stalk that takes on the functions of a leaf.
Picotee Used to describe a flower with narrow petal margins contrasting with the ground colour.
Pinch out (stop) To remove soft growing points to encourage the bushy growth of sideshoots.
Pinna (*pl.* pinnae) Leaflet of a pinnate leaf or of a fern frond. *See also* Pinnate.
Pinnate Used to describe a compound leaf with leaflets (pinnae) arranged alternately or in opposite pairs on a central axis, with or without a terminal leaflet. 2-pinnate (bipinnate) leaves have pinnately divided leaflets. 3-pinnate (tripinnate) leaves have pinnately divided leaflets that are themselves pinnately divided.
Pinnatifid Used to describe a simple leaf with usually opposite pairs of lobes cut no deeper than halfway to the midrib.
Pinnatisect Used to describe a simple leaf

with usually opposite pairs of deep lobes cut almost to the midrib.
Pinnule *see* Segment.
Pistil Female reproductive organ of a flower, composed of one or several fused or separate carpels.
Plant Breeder's Rights (*abbr.* PBR) Patented legal protection afforded to the breeder of a new plant cultivar, which allows the breeder to obtain royalties and which prohibits unauthorized propagation of the new plant. *See also* Cultivar, Trade designation, and p.11.
Plantlet 1. Older seedling. 2. Young, small plant that develops on a mature plant. *See also* Offset, Plug, Viviparous.
Pleach To intertwine the branches of a tree or shrub and clip them to form a hedge or screen.
Plug A seedling or young plant raised in a modular tray in order that it can be planted out or potted on with minimal root disturbance.
Plumose 1. Feather-like, with long, fine, often branched hairs. 2. Applied to plume-like, finely branched inflorescences.
Plumule The rudimentary stem or shoot of a germinating seed.
Plunge To sink a container to its rim in ashes, peat, sand, or soil to insulate the roots and prevent the plant drying out.
Pod (legume) 1. One-celled fruit of the Leguminosae family that splits along 2 sides to disperse ripe seed. 2. Loosely, any dry fruit that splits to disperse seed.
Pollard To cut branches back hard to the main trunk of a tree in order to restrict growth.
Pollen Grains released from anthers containing the male element necessary for fertilization.
Pollination Transfer of pollen from the anthers to the stigma of the same or a different flower. Can be performed by animals, insects, wind, or water, and, in the garden, by hand. *See also* Open pollination, Wind pollination.
Pompon Used to describe a roughly spherical flower with tightly packed florets that are often curved inwards.
Pot-bound Used to describe a plant with roots that have totally filled and are now constricted by its container. *See also* Overpotting, Pot on.
Pot on To remove a plant (usually a cutting or seedling) from an outgrown container, and place it with fresh compost in a larger container, with room for further growth. *See also* Overpotting.
Potting compost Well-drained but moisture-retentive growing medium used mainly for container-grown plants. Loam-based potting compost is based on loam mixed with peat (or substitute), and perlite, vermiculite, or sharp sand. Loamless potting composts are based on peat (or substitute), mixed with sphagnum moss and perlite or vermiculite. *See also p.24*, Ericaceous, JI No.1/2/3.
Pot up To insert a seedling or rooted cutting in potting compost in a container. *See also* Overpotting.
Pre-chill *see* Stratify.
Prepared Usually used to describe bulbs that have been treated to induce them into growth and flower before their normal season, as with *Freesia* and *Hyacinthus orientalis* cultivars. *See also* Vernalization.
Pre-soak To soak seed in recently boiled water for between 10 minutes and 72 hours, depending on the species, to soften the seedcoat prior to sowing, thus hastening germination.
Prick out To transfer seedlings or small cuttings from where they have been propagated into appropriate containers and compost, where they have room to grow.
Procumbent *see* Prostrate.
Proliferation 1. Development of an abnormal number of organs in a flower, or an abnormal number of flowerheads. 2. The viviparous habit of vegetative reproduction, whereby plant species characteristically produce plantlets or offsets. *See also* Viviparous.
Prominent Clearly visible, standing out from a surface; usually used to describe veins or other surface features. *See also* Conspicuous.
Propagate To increase plants by seed or by vegetative means. *See also pp.28–29*, Vegetative propagation.
Propagating case (propagator) Small, closed case with a transparent lid, used to provide a humid atmosphere indoors, usually with bottom heat, for rooting cuttings, germinating seed, or raising other plants.
Propagating frame Large, usually glazed or partially glazed case, normally unheated, used outdoors to root cuttings, germinate seed, or raise other plants.
Propagator *see* Propagating case.
Prostrate (procumbent) Used to describe a plant with spreading or trailing stems lying flat on the ground.
Pruinose *see* White-frosted.
Prune To remove twigs or branches from woody plants in order to maintain health, control size, train to a desired shape, or stimulate growth or the production of flowers or fruit. *See also pp.25–27*, Formative pruning, Renovation pruning, Restrictive pruning.
Pseudobulb Swollen, bulb-like stem, sometimes jointed, that acts as a storage organ for some sympodial orchids. *See also* Backbulb.
Pseudocephalium Woody, flower-bearing, densely spined area near the apex of some cacti. *See also* Cephalium.
Pteridophyte Ferns and their primitive allies, such as club mosses and horsetails; non-flowering, vascular plants increasing sexually by means of spores.
Quilled Used to describe a flowerhead consisting of narrow, tubular ray-florets.

R

Raceme Inflorescence of stalked flowers radiating from a single, unbranched axis, the youngest flowers near the tip.
Rachis Main axis of a compound leaf or inflorescence.
Radial Spine at the perimeter of an areole on a cactus.
Radical Refers to basal leaves that grow from or near ground level. *See also* Rosette.
Radicle The rudimentary root of a germinating seed.
Rank Refers to a linear arrangement of leaves. 2-ranked (distichous) leaves are arranged in opposite pairs along a stem. 4-ranked (decussate) leaves are arranged in opposite pairs, each pair at right angles to the pair next to it.
Ray-floret Tiny, usually strap-shaped, tubular-based, outer flower of a (composite) flowerhead.
Receptacle Enlarged or elongated tip of the stem from which all parts of a simple flower arise.
Recurved Arched backwards.
Reflexed Arched or bent sharply back upon itself.
Remontant Refers to a plant that flowers more than once within a growing season, at distinct times.
Renewal pruning *see* Renovation pruning.
Reniform *see* Kidney-shaped.
Renovation pruning (renewal pruning) Hard pruning to rejuvenate an old or overgrown shrub. *See also p.25.*
Repeat-flowering *See* Remontant.
Repot To remove a plant (usually mature) from an outgrown container, and re-establish it in a larger container.
Reproduction Process of producing new individuals by either sexual or asexual (vegetative) methods.
Respiration Absorption of oxygen and breakdown of carbohydrates within cells, releasing carbon dioxide and water and providing energy for metabolism.
Resting period *see* Dormancy.
Restrictive pruning Annual pruning to limit growth. *See also p.25.*
Reversion Genetic change within a sport or chimaera in which a plant or part of a plant reverts to its original character.
Rhizome (*adj.* rhizomatous) Horizontal, usually branching and fleshy stem, growing underground or, less often, at ground level.
Rhomboidal *see* Diamond-shaped.
Rib 1. Ridge, normally vertical, formed on the stem of a cactus. 2. Refers to the primary vein on a leaf.
Ripening 1. Maturing of fruit. 2. Maturing of young shoots (wood) on trees and shrubs, or of bulbs.
Ripewood cutting Cutting of a mature shoot taken from an evergreen plant, from late summer to early winter.
Rock-dwelling *see* Lithophytic.
Rock garden Area for growing alpines and rock plants among rocks, ideally set out naturally as rock outcrops.
Rock plant Any small plant grown in association with alpines, and with similar cultivation requirements. *See also pp.40–41.*
Root 1. Part of a plant, usually underground, that anchors it and absorbs water and nutrients from the soil. 2. To insert cuttings in a compost where they will produce roots. *See also pp.12–13*, Aerial root, Buttress root, Stilt root, Tap root.
Root ball Mass of roots and soil or compost attached to them, formed by a plant in a container or in the ground.
Root cutting Cutting taken from vigorous, young roots during winter.
Rootstock 1. Underground part of a plant. 2. Loosely, the crown and root system of any herbaceous perennial, from which new plants arise. 3. Plant upon which a scion is grafted.
Rosette 1. Dense whorl of leaves arising from the central point or crown of a plant, usually at or near ground level. 2. Whorled arrangement of petals or tepals.
Rosulate Used to describe leaves arranged in a basal rosette or rosettes.
Rotate *see* Wheel-shaped.
Rounded (orbicular) Roughly or fully circular in outline.
Runner 1. Trailing stem, growing above ground and rooting at the nodes, where plantlets are produced. 2. Underground, spreading shoot producing upright shoots that form new plants at intervals. *See also* Stolon.

S

Sac Space or chamber inside an ovary, anther, or fruit.
Sagittate *see* Arrow-shaped.
Salverform Used to describe a flower with a long, slim, tubular corolla that spreads out into more or less horizontal, flat lobes.
Sandy Used to describe dry, light, free-draining soil, low in nutrients, derived from quartz or sandstone.
Sap Juice that flows through conductive tissue of vascular plants.
Sapling Young tree.
Saprophyte (*adj.* saprophytic) Plant, usually lacking in chlorophyll, that absorbs nutrients from dead or decaying organic matter.
Saucer-shaped Used to describe a flat flower with the corolla lobes slightly upturned at the tips.
Savannah Flat, dry grassland habitat covered with low shrubs and dotted with small trees.
Saxicolous *see* Lithophytic.
Scale 1. Flat, membranous structure. 2. Dry leaf or bract, usually pressed flat to the axis to which it is attached.
Scale leaves Specialized leaves resembling scales, such as those that cover buds or form bulbs.
Scalloped (crenate) Refers to a margin, generally of a leaf, with shallow, rounded teeth.
Scandent Used to describe a plant that climbs by means of flexible stems that grow over or through supports, attaching themselves loosely, if at all. *See also pp.36–37*, Climber.
Scape Leafless stem of a solitary flower or inflorescence.
Scarify 1. To treate chemically or abrade the hard outer casing of a seed before sowing, to increase rate of water uptake and thus rate of germination. 2. To remove moss and old grass from a lawn by raking. *See also p.28.*
Scion Shoot or part of a shoot that is bonded to the rootstock of a second plant by grafting.
Scree 1. Slope of unstable, rocky fragments, with excellent drainage, but often with freshwater springs running beneath, found on mountainsides and at the bottom of mountain cliffs and escarpments. 2. In gardens, a deep layer of stone chippings with a small proportion of loam, providing very sharp drainage for alpines and rock plants.
Scrub Habitat with poor or dry soil, covered with bushes and small trees.
Seed Ripened, fertilized ovule containing a dormant embryo capable of developing into an adult plant.
Seedbed Area of ground that has been dug over, raked, and firmed in preparation for sowing seed.
Seedcoat Outer casing of seed. *See also* Aril.

Seed compost Fine-textured, low-nutrient, moisture-retentive compost, formulated for the healthy germination and development of seeds and seedlings; also used for rooting cuttings.
Seed head Loosely refers to dry fruits. *See also* Capsule.
Seed-leaf (cotyledon) First leaf, pair of leaves, or occasionally group of leaves produced by a germinating seed. The seed-leaf (or seed-leaves) may remain within the seedcoat, or emerge and turn green during germination. *See also* Germination.
Seedling Young plant raised from seed.
Segment 1. Subdivision of pinna on a pinnate leaf or frond; botanically known as a pinnule. 2. Any division of an organ, such as the lobe of a leaf or flower.
Selection A distinct form of a plant that is selected for its ornamental qualities, for which it is propagated and given a cultivar name and/or a trade designation. *See also* Cultivar, Trade designation.
Self *see* Self-coloured.
Self-clinging Used to describe a climber that can climb without the support of other plants, clinging to a surface by means of aerial roots or adhesive pads.
Self-coloured (self) Used to describe a flower with a uniform colour.
Self-fertile (self-setting) Used to describe a plant that does not need pollen from a second individual in order to fertilize and set fruit. *See also* Self-pollinate.
Self-pollinate Process whereby pollen from the anthers of one flower reaches the stigma of a second flower on the same plant. *See also* Self-fertile.
Self-seed To regenerate from seed that is dispersed in the garden without human intervention.
Self-setting *see* Self-fertile.
Self-sterile Used to describe a plant that requires pollen from a second individual of the species, but not the same clone, to fertilize its flowers.
Semi-deciduous *see* Semi-evergreen.
Semi-double Used to describe a flower with 2 or 3 times the number of petals of a single flower, usually arranged in 2 or 3 rows.
Semi-evergreen Used to describe a plant that retains most or some of its foliage throughout the year.
Semi-ripe cutting Cutting taken from semi-mature wood in mid- or late summer, occasionally in early autumn.
Semi-ripe wood Refers to stems or shoots that have slowed down in growth and become semi-woody.
Senescent Refers to the physiological processes following maturity that lead eventually to the natural death of a plant.
Sepal One part of the calyx, when it is composed of separate parts. Usually green and smaller than petals, but sometimes colourful and petal-like.
Series Name applied to a group of cultivars of annuals that share most of the same characteristics but differ from one another by one character (rarely more), usually colour. *See also pp.11, 42.*
Serrate Used to describe a finely toothed margin, usually of a leaf, with the teeth slightly curved as in a saw blade.
Sessile Refers to a stalkless or almost stalkless plant organ.
Set Refers to fertilized flowers that have developed fruit.
Sharp drainage Very free movement of excess water through the soil.
Sheath Tubular structure around a part of a plant, such as a leaf base around a stem.
Shoot 1. First, erect growth of a seedling, before it becomes a stem. 2. Loosely applied to side-growths, twigs, or branches. *See also* Branch, Sideshoot, Stem.
Shoot-tip *see* Growing point.
Shrub Deciduous or evergreen perennial with multiple woody stems or branches, generally bearing branches from or near its base. *See also pp.34–35.*
Shrub border Area of ground set aside for the cultivation of shrubs.
Shrublet *see* Subshrub.
Shy-flowering 1. Reluctant to come into flower. 2. Bearing few blooms.
Sickle-shaped (falcate) Curving sideways in the manner of a scythe or sickle.
Sideshoot Lateral shoot that develops from the side of a main shoot.
Silt Moderately fertile, moisture-retentive soil, prone to compaction and surface-capping. Has finer soil particles than clay.
Simple Not divided into secondary units; for example, a leaf with a continuous surface, not cut into leaflets.
Single Used to describe a flower with the normal number of petals or tepals for the species, arranged in a single whorl. Also applied to (composite) flowerheads that have a single row of outer ray-florets with the centre filled with disc-florets.
Sinus Deep cleft between 2 lobes.
Slipper-shaped Used to describe a flower in which the corolla has a pouch-like form.
Soft-stemmed With a non-woody stem.
Soft-tip cutting *see* Stem-tip cutting.
Softwood Young, soft, unripened shoots of woody plants.
Softwood cutting Cutting taken from young, non-woody growth, from spring to early summer.
Soilless medium Growing medium based on substances other than soil. *See also* Clay granules, Perlite, Vermiculite.
Solitary Flower borne singly rather than in an inflorescence.
Sorus (*pl.* sori) Cluster of sporangia usually on the underside of a fern frond, almost always surrounded or covered by an indusium.
Spadix (*pl.* spadices) Fleshy axis of a spike or spike-like inflorescence, embedded with tiny sessile flowers, usually borne within a spathe.
Spathe Often prominent, fleshy, hood-like bract, surrounding a spadix.
Spathulate *see* Spoon-shaped.
Spear-shaped (hastate) Triangular, with 2 equal, roughly triangular, outward-pointing, basal lobes.
Species Basic category in plant classification, ranked below genus and consisting of similar individual plants that breed true in the wild. Characterized by a binomial. *See also p.11.*
Specimen plant Ornamental plant, normally a tree or shrub, grown usually in a prominent position, where it may be viewed from different angles.
Speculum Glossy raised area, varying from square- to diamond- or horseshoe-shaped, on the lip of some orchid flowers.
Sphagnum Genus of mosses which, when decomposed in bog conditions, is called sphagnum (or moss) peat. In fresh form, it is used to line hanging baskets, or is finely chopped and added to orchid compost.
Spherical (globose, globular) Applied to a round or almost round solid form.
Spike Inflorescence in which stalkless flowers are arranged on an unbranched axis.
Spikelet Small spike forming part of a compound inflorescence, particularly in grasses and bromeliads.
Spindle-shaped (fusiform) Applied to a solid form, broadest at the centre, tapering towards each end (narrower and with straighter sides than ellipsoid forms).
Spine Stiff, sharp-tipped, modified leaf or stem.
Spinose, Spiny Bearing stiff, sharp-tipped spines.
Spoon-shaped (spathulate) Narrow at the base, gradually broadening into a blunt, rounded tip.
Sporangium (*pl.* sporangia) Spore-producing organ on the underside of the fronds of all ferns (and other members of the order Pteridophyta). *See also p.51.*
Spore Basic unit of reproduction in many non-flowering plants, such as ferns, fungi, and mosses. *See also p.51.*
Sporeling Young plant raised from a spore.
Sporophyll A leaf, modified leaf, or leaf-like structure that bears spores.
Sport (mutation) Natural or induced genetic change, often exhibited as a variegated shoot or flower from the parent plant. Sports may be vegetatively propagated to give rise to new cultivars. *See also p.11.*
Spray Cluster of flowers or flowerheads arranged on a single, branched stem.
Spread Measure of an individual plant's horizontal growth. Spreads given in this encyclopedia correspond to the diameter of a mature plant (in perennials, after 3 years' growth) in an appropriate garden site.
Spur 1. Modified petal with a hollow, basal projection, often containing nectar. 2. Short branches or branchlets along the main branches, on which flowers and fruit are produced.
Stalk Stem-like organ joining a leaf, flower, flowerhead, or inflorescence to the stem of a plant. *See also* Flower-stalk, Leaf-stalk, Peduncle, Sessile.
Stamen Male part of a flower, composed of an anther, normally borne on a filament.
Staminode Sterile, modified stamen, either inconspicuous or resembling a narrow petal.
Standard 1. Tree or shrub trained to form a rounded head of branches at the top of a clear stem. *See also* Branched-head standard, Central-leader standard, Half-standard. 2. Uppermost petal of a pea-like flower, often large and brightly coloured. 3. Erect inner tepal of an *Iris* flower.
Star-shaped (stellate) Refers to a flower with widely spaced, narrow petals or tepals that radiate from a common central point.
Stellate *see* Star-shaped.
Stem Main axis of a plant, usually above ground, that supports structures such as branches, leaves, flowers, and fruit.
Stem-tip cutting (soft-tip cutting) Cutting taken from the soft tip of a non-flowering stem, usually from spring to autumn.
Sterile 1. Refers to any flower that is incapable of producing seeds. 2. Applied to trees in which the flowers may be self-sterile. 3. Refers to soils that have been deliberately treated with a chemical to kill weed seeds, pests, and diseases.
Stigma Tip of the pistil, which receives pollen to fertilize the ovules.
Stilt root Stabilizing, obliquely angled, adventitious root produced from the trunks of trees adapted to shallow or waterlogged soil. *See also* Buttress root.
Stipule Leaf-like or bract-like structure borne, usually in pairs, at the point where a leaf-stalk arises from a stem.
Stolon (*adj.* stoloniferous) Arching, horizontal or trailing stem producing roots and new shoot at its tips.
Stoloniform Resembling a stolon.
Stomata Microscopic pores in the surface of the aerial parts of plants, allowing gaseous exchange. *See also* Transpiration.
Stool *see* Coppice.
Stop *see* Pinch out.
Strap-shaped (ensiform, ligulate, lorate) Narrow, with straight or curving sides; length is 6 (or more) times the width.
Stratify (pre-chill) To expose seed to cold in order to break dormancy, either by refrigeration before sowing, or by sowing outdoors in autumn or winter.
Strobilus (*pl.* strobili) Reproductive organ of a conifer. Male strobili resemble catkins; female ones resemble mature cones in miniature.
Style Part of the carpel or pistil connecting the ovary and the stigma.
Subalpine Applied to mountain areas between the foothills and the alpine slopes.
Submerged aquatic Plant that remains totally submerged below water.
Subshrub (shrublet) 1. Woody-based plant with soft-wooded stems. 2. Low-growing, woody-stemmed plant.
Subsoil Layer of soil below the topsoil, usually less fertile and of poor structure.
Subspecies (*abbrev.* subsp.) Category of plant classification, below species but higher in rank than *varietas* or *forma*. *See also p.11.*
Subtropical Refers to the high-temperature zone located between tropical and temperate regions. Rainfall occurs mainly as heavy downpours during the monsoon season.
Succulent Plant with fleshy leaves, roots, or stems (not bulbs, corms, rhizomes, or tubers) that are adapted for water storage; often native to arid areas. *See also pp.48–49.*
Sucker 1. Adventitious shoot arising below soil level, usually from the roots rather than from the stem or crown of the plant. 2. Shoot that arises from the stock of a grafted or budded plant.
Surface-capping When the soil surface bakes dry in summer, especially on clay and silt soils, resulting in poor aeration. *See also* Compaction.
Swamp Spongy, waterlogged habitat.
Sympodial Form of growth in which the terminal bud dies or ends in an inflorescence, and growth continues from lateral buds.
Synonym Name or epithet that is not the accepted one for the plant. *See also p.11.*

T

Tap root 1. Primary, sometimes swollen, downward-growing root of a plant from which the root system extends. 2. Where a plant is described as tap-rooted, the strongly downward-growing root penetrates the soil deeply and remains unbranched or scarcely branched.
Taxon (*pl.* taxa) Named group of organisms that is defined by a set of shared characters. Taxonomy is the science of classification, nomenclature, and identification of organisms. *See also p.10–11.*
Temperate Refers to zones located between the subtropics and the polar circles, which experience distinct seasons, without temperature extremes. Rainfall occurs throughout the year. *See also* Cool-temperate, Warm-temperate.
Temperate greenhouse Greenhouse with a minimum temperature of 7°C (45°F). *See also p.24.*
Tender Applied to plants that may be damaged by temperatures below 5°C (41°F). *See also* Frost tender.
Tendril Coiling, thread-like, modified leaf, leaflet, inflorescence, or shoot used by a climbing plant to attach itself to an adjacent support.
Tepal Petal or sepal of a flower, where the calyx and corolla are not clearly distinguished. *See also* Perianth segment, Petaloid.
Terminal Located at the end of a stem, shoot, or other organ. *See also* Axillary.
Ternate Arranged in groups of 3 around a common axis. In a 2-ternate (biternate) leaf, these divisions are themselves divided into 3; in a 3-ternate (triternate) leaf, these parts are further divided into 3. *See also* Palmate.
Terrarium An enclosed, glass or plastic container in which plants are grown.
Terrestrial Used to describe a land plant that grows in soil, rather than epiphytically, as a parasite, or in water.
Tessellated With a bold, chequered pattern that contrasts with the ground colour; usually describes markings on a corolla.
Thin To remove a number of buds, flowers, seedlings, or shoots to improve the growth and quality of remaining ones.
Thread-like (filiform) Long, very slender like a filament, and rounded rather than flat in cross section; narrower than linear.
Throat Opening of the tubular part of a flower, from where the petals or tepals spread.
Tilth The crumbly structure of well-cultivated soil; usually used to describe a surface prepared for seed sowing.
Tissue culture The growth of plant cells in an artificial growing medium under sterile laboratory conditions.
Toothed (dentate) Used to describe a margin, usually of a leaf, with tooth-like, triangular indentations. Double-toothed margins have alternate large and small teeth.
Top-dress 1. To apply fertilizers or mulches to the soil surface around plants. 2. To apply organic and inorganic dressing to lawns to feed and improve the texture of the grass. 3. To apply material such as stone or grit, usually decorative, to the surface of the soil or potting compost around a plant, in order to improve drainage and reduce moisture loss. 4. To renew the upper layers of potting compost in a container instead of potting on the plant.
Topiary Clipping and training of shrubs or trees into free, geometric, or representational forms.
Topsoil Uppermost layer of the soil, usually the most fertile.
Trace elements Chemical elements essential for healthy plant growth, but only in minute quantities.
Trade designation Name used in addition to the registered name of a plant awarded Plant Breeder's Rights protection. It is common practice that the approved name registered for such a plant is a code or "nonsense" name; this is the true cultivar name. An additional selling name, the trade designation, which is chosen to be more attractive at the point of sale, is also given. It is distinguished from a true cultivar name in that it is not enclosed in single quotation marks and, in this encyclopedia, it is printed in a contrasting typeface. For example, *Choisya* SUNDANCE ('Lich'); the former is a trade designation, the latter (in brackets) the cultivar name. *See also* Plant Breeder's Rights.
Trailing Used to describe stems that are prostrate but not rooting.
Train To prune and shape the growth of any plant.
Transpiration Evaporation of water from the leaves and stems of plants (mostly through stomata).
Tree Woody perennial with a crown of branches developing from the top of a usually single stem or trunk. *See also pp.32–33.*
Tree fern Large fern that develops a tree-like trunk in maturity. *See also p.51.*
Triangular (deltoid) With 3 sides of equal length. A triangular leaf is attached to the stem at a point midway along one side.
Trifoliate Arrangement of leaves that arise in groups of 3 from a single point.
Trifoliolate *see* Palmate.
Trigeneric hybrid Offspring of 3 genera, crossed over 2 generations.
Tripartite Divided almost to the base into 3 lobes or segments.
Tripinnate (3-pinnate) *see* Pinnate.
Triternate (3-ternate) *see* Ternate.
Tropical Refers to the zone between the Tropics of Cancer and Capricorn, with a hot, steamy climate that encourages lush plant growth. Rainfall may occur throughout the year or mainly during a monsoon season. *See also* Subtropical.
True (true-breeding) Term applied to plants that, when raised from seed, virtually reproduce the characteristics of the parents.
Trumpet-shaped Refers to a flower with a long, narrow tube, flaring at the throat into corolla lobes, which are usually arched backwards.
Truncate Ending abruptly as though cut off at a right-angle.
Trunk Rigid, woody, bark-covered stem of a tree.
Truss Compact cluster of flowers or fruit, particularly of rhododendrons.
Tuber (*adj.* tuberous) Swollen root or underground stem with storage tissue.
Tubercle (*adj.* tuberculate) Small, wart-like projection.
Tuberiferous, tuberous Bearing tubers.
Tubular Refers to a plant organ, usually a flower, with perianth segments fully or partially fused to form a hollow tube.
Tufa Porous, moisture-retentive limestone rock, used for the cultivation of alkaline-loving, rock-dwelling alpines.
Tunic Membrane covering bulbs and corms, often papery but sometimes thick and leathery.
Turion Detached, often fleshy bud of an aquatic plant that overwinters at the bottom of a pond, regenerating in spring.
Turkscap Refers to a flower resembling a traditional Turkish cap with petals strongly reflexed.
Twiner Climbing plant that twines around its host or support.

UV

Umbel Flat- or round-topped inflorescence in which numerous stalked flowers are terminally borne from a single point.
Unarmed Devoid of spines.
Undulate Used to describe the wavy surface or margin of a leaf or flower.
Unisexual Applied to a flower that is either male or female only, requiring pollination from a flower of the other sex.
Upright *see* Erect.
Urceolate *see* Urn-shaped.
Urn-shaped (urceolate) Used to describe a spherical to cylindrical or tubular flower contracted at or just below the mouth.
Variant Plant form that varies to some degree from the norm. Often loosely applied to any naturally occurring or artificially selected form of species.
Variegation Irregular arrangement of pigments, usually as result of mutation or sometimes disease.
Varietas (variety; *abbrev.* var.) Naturally occurring variant of a species, ranked taxonomically between subspecies and *forma*. *See also p.11.*
Variety *see* Varietas.
Vascular Containing conductive tissue, enabling sap to circulate through the plant. *See also p.10,* Non-vascular.
Vegetative propagation Asexual techniques for increasing plants, by cuttings, division, grafting, or layering.
Vein Fibrous strand of vascular tissue that conducts sap through the plant.
Venation Pattern of leaf veins.
Ventilation Control of air movement under glass to avoid atmospheric stagnation and regulate temperature.
Vermiculite Light, mica-like mineral added to potting compost to improve aeration and moisture retention.
Vernal Appearing in spring.
Vernalization The treatment of bulbs, seeds, or plants to break dormancy and initiate growth or flowering, usually by means of exposure to low temperatures or plant hormones. *See also* Stratify.
Verrucose *see* Warty.
Viable Applied to seed capable of germination.
Viviparous Used to describe a plant that forms plantlets on leaves, inflorescences, or stems. Also applied loosely to plants that produce bulbils or bulblets on these organs.

WX

Warm greenhouse Greenhouse with a minimum temperature of 13°C (55°F). *See also p.24.*
Warm-temperate Refers to a temperate climate with mild winters and hot summers.
Warty (verrucose) Used to describe wart-like projections from a surface, such as that of a leaf.
Wasteland Weed-infested, desolate habitat.
Waterlogged Refers to soil that is saturated as a result of excessive rainfall, overwatering, or proximity to a water source, and which often drains very slowly.
Water plant *see* Aquatic plant.
Wedge-shaped (cuneate) Inversely triangular, or with straight sides tapering to the base.
Weed 1. Vigorous, invasive, or self-seeding plant competing with desired garden plants for moisture and nutrients. 2. Any plant growing where it is not wanted.
Weeping Used to describe a tree or shrub that is pendent in habit.
Wheel-shaped (rotate) Used to describe a flower with a short tube and segments or petal limbs spreading evenly in a circle.
White-frosted (pruinose) With a whitish bloom. *See also* Glaucous.
White-mealy (farinaceous, farinose) With a white or yellow, floury or starchy texture.
Whorl Circular arrangement of 3 or more flowers, parts of a flower, leaves, or shoots, arising from a single point.
Wildflower garden Informal garden used to grow mainly indigenous plants.
Wild garden Informal area intended to resemble a natural habitat, such as a woodland or alpine meadow. *See also* Woodland garden.
Wind pollination Transfer of pollen by wind; wind-pollinated flowers are often pendulous, with reduced perianth segments, and frequently emerge before the leaves, as in the catkins of *Alnus, Betula,* and *Corylus*. *See also* Open pollination, Pollination.
Wing 1. Thin, flat or membranous extension of an organ. 2. Lateral petal in many orchids and members of the Leguminosae family. *See also* Pea-like.
Witches' broom Abnormal, very congested growth in trees and shrubs, often densely twiggy and resembling a bird's nest in deciduous trees, which results from infection by various mites or fungi, or low-temperature injury.
Woodland garden Woodland in which non-indigenous trees and shrubs are grown with underplantings of shade-loving herbaceous plants and bulbs, and often with artificially created open glades.
Woody Used to describe the fibrous stems of certain perennials, such as trees and shrubs, that persist above ground throughout the year.
Woody-based perennial Perennial with a woody base but herbaceous stems.
Xerophytic Used to describe a plant adapted to survive in arid conditions, by the reduction of stems and leaves to minimize water loss, or by having water-storage tissue, as in succulents.

ACKNOWLEDGEMENTS

Dorling Kindersley would like to thank the following:

Jane Aspden, for her initial planning and management of the project.

Additional editorial assistance
Louise Abbott, Cathy Buchanan, Rebecca Davies, Claire Folkard, Robert Graham, Lindsay Harber, Lesley Malkin, Carla Masson, Andrew Mikolajski, Gillian Emerson Roberts, Ray Rogers, Lyn Saville, Sue Spielberg.

Additional design assistance
Stephen Josland, Geoff Manders, Alistair Wardle.

Additional administrative assistance
Esther Beaton, David Bruce, Caroline Fanshawe, Melissa Gould, Angela-Marie Graham, Ros Searle, Meryl Silbert, Roma Sinclair.

Additional consultants
John Amand, Darrell Apps, Nicola Brown, Tony Clements, Philip Eden, Martin F. Gardner, Mark Griffiths, Andrew Halstead, A.P. Hamilton, Barbara Haynes, Ronald Hedge, P. Francis Hunt, Frances Hutchison, Sally Kington, Alan Leslie, Suzanne Maxwell, Susanne Mitchell, Diana Percy, Chris Prior, James E. Richardson, Dr Johan van Scheepen, Nicola J. Sinclair, Philip Thomas, Peter Valder.

Additional photographers
Peter Anderson, Bill Balham, Paul Barker, Peter Chadwick, Roger Foley, Paul Goff, Steve Gorton, David Harding, Dr Alan Hemsley, Julian Holland, Neil Holmes, David Karonides, Jonathan Metcalf, Les Saucier, Roger Scruton, Steven Still, Darryl Sweetland, Alex Watson.

Colour correction
Pelican Graphics, London EC2.

Dorling Kindersley would also like to thank the private individuals and staff at the locations and organizations listed below for their help with the photography for this encyclopedia. Unless otherwise stated, all are located in the UK.

Ingrid Adler, Canberra, A.C.T., Australia; African Violet Centre, Terrington St. Clement, Norfolk; Albert's Garden, Pialligo, A.C.T., Australia; I. Allen, Wraxall, Bristol, Avon; The Alpine Garden Society Centre, Pershore, Hereford & Worcs; Jacques Amand Ltd., Stanmore, Middx; Anglo Aquarium Plants, Enfield, Middx; Apple Court, Lymington, Hants; Arcadia Lily Ponds, Arcadia, N.S.W., Australia; Architectural Plants, Horsham, W. Sussex; David Austin Roses Ltd., Wolverhampton, W. Midlands; Australian National Botanic Gardens, Canberra, A.C.T., Australia; Aylett Nurseries Ltd., St. Albans, Herts; Steven Bailey Ltd., Lymington, Hants; Bill Baker, Tidmarsh, Reading, Berks; Bankstown Native Gardens, Picnic Point, N.S.W., Australia; Batsford Arboretum, Moreton-in-Marsh, Glos; Les & Nancy Beard, Warriewood, N.S.W., Australia; Bedgebury Pinetum, Bedgebury, Kent; Birch Farm Nursery, Gravetye, W. Sussex; Birmingham Botanic Gardens, Birmingham, W. Midlands; Joy Bishop, Lightwater, Surrey; Blackthorn Nurseries, (Sue & Robin White), Alresford, Hants; Bloomsbury Nursery and Garden, (Susan & Michael Oakley), Padworth Common, Reading, Berks; Bourne Brook Nurseries, (B. & H.M. Baker), Halstead, Essex; Rupert Bowlby, Reigate, Surrey; Bressingham Gardens, Diss, Norfolk; Bridgemere Nurseries, Nantwich, Cheshire; Brighton Town Council, Brighton, E. Sussex; British Gladiolus Society; British Orchid Growers' Association; Broadleigh Gardens, Taunton, Somerset; Brockings Exotics, North Petherwin, Cornwall; Bromeliad Society of N.S.W., (Bob Christoffel, Alice Williams), Australia; Brooklyn Botanic Garden, New York, USA; Mrs. Ruth Buckley, Clunton, Shropshire; Burncoose Nursery, Gwennap, Cornwall; Burnham Nurseries, Newton Abbott, Devon; Bushyfield Nursery, Herne, Kent; Buskers End, Bowral, N.S.W., Australia; Calwell Garden Connection, Calwell, A.C.T., Australia; Cambridge Alpines, Cottenham, Cambs; Cambridge Bulbs, Newton, Cambs; Cambridge Garden Plants, Horningsea, Cambs; Carnon Downs Garden Centre, Truro, Cornwall; Coby Causer, Sydney, N.S.W., Australia; Colin Chapman, Wyverstone, Suffolk; Beth Chatto Gardens, Elmstead Market, Colchester, Essex; Claylane Nursery, South Nutfield, Redhill, Surrey; Cloudhill Nursery, Olinda, VIC, Australia; Colegrave Seeds, Hallam, VIC, Australia; Colegraves Seeds Ltd., Banbury, Oxon; Colonial Cottage Nursery, Dural, N.S.W., Australia; Conifer Gardens Nursery, Ferny Creek, VIC, Australia; Coolwyn Conifers, Monbulk, VIC, Australia; Cottage Garden Roses, (John Scarman), Stretton, Staffs; Dr & Mrs. A.J. Cox, Marcliff, Warks; C.S.I.R.O. Forestry, (Nathan Caesar, David Spencer), Yarralumla, A.C.T., Australia; Derby City Council Leisure Services, Derby; Dibley's Nurseries, Llanelidan, Ruthin, Clwyd; Diggers Seeds, Dromana, VIC, Australia; Dingle Plants & Gardens, Pilsgate, Stamford, Lincs; Drummond Castle, Crieff, Perthshire; Drysdale Nursery, Fordingbridge, Hants; Drywood Nursery, (Ian Kirby), Holton, Northants; Duchy College, Camborne, Cornwall; Mr. & Mrs. E.W. Dyer, Welford-on-Avon, Warks; Eastgrove Cottage Garden Nursery, (Carol & Malcolm Skinner), Sankyns Green, Hereford & Worcs; E.C.C. International, St. Austell, Cornwall; Alan Edwards, Dorking, Surrey; Mrs. Sally Edwards, Horningsea, Cambs; Exbury Gardens, (Nicholas de Rothschild), Exbury, Hants; Fairchild Tropical Garden, (Mary E. Collins), Miami, Florida, USA; A.T. Farmer, Hanslope, Bucks; Fibrex Nurseries, Pebworth, Stratford-on-Avon, Warks; Field House Nurseries, Gotham, Nottingham; Floranova Ltd., Foxley, Dereham, Norfolk; Fortescue Garden Trust, Buckland, Monachorum, Devon; Four Seasons, Forncett St. Mary, Norwich, Norfolk; Derek Fox, Hockley, Essex; Jeremy Francis, Olinda, VIC, Australia; Fulbrooke Nursery, Westley Waterless, Newmarket, Suffolk; The Garden, Mawson, A.C.T., Australia; *Gardening Which?*, Capel Manor, Enfield, Middx; Garden of St. Erth, Blackwood, VIC, Australia; Garden World, Keysborough, VIC, Australia; Douglas Gardiner, Wimbledon, London; Glasgow Botanic Garden, Glasgow; Glebe Cottage Nursery, (Carol Klein), Warleigh, Devon; David Glen, Ascot, VIC, Australia; Glenedd Violets, Sutton Bridge, Lincs; Goldbrook Plants, Hoxne, Suffolk; Goscote Nurseries, Cossington, Leics; Pam Gossage, Oakenlea, Yeoville, Somerset; Hadspen Gardens, (Norrie & Sandra Pope), Castle Cary, Somerset; Hall Farm Nursery, Kinnerley, Shropshire; Johan Harder, Arcadia, N.S.W., Australia; Hardy Exotics Nursery, Whitecross, Cornwall; Hardy's Cottage Garden Plants, Whitchurch, Hants; Harvey & Son, Little Shelford, Cambs; Martin Harwood, Chobham, Surrey; Hayward's Carnations, Waterlooville, Hants; The Hon. Mrs. Peter Healing, Kemerton, Hereford & Worcs; Hibiscus Park Nursery, Warriewood, N.S.W., Australia; Sir Harold Hillier Gardens & Arboretum, Ampfield, Romsey, Hants; Malcolm Hillier, London; Hilltop Cottage, Guildford, VIC, Australia; Hinton Nurseries, Christchurch, Dorset; Judith Hitchings, Swalcliffe, Oxon; Mr. & Mrs. D. Hodges, Alkerton, Oxon; Holkam Gardens, Holkam, Norfolk; Holly Gate Nurseries, Ashington, W. Sussex; Honeysome Aquatic Nursery, Sutton, Cambs; Hopleys Plants Ltd., Much Hadham, Herts; The Hon. & Mrs. Simon Howard, Castle Howard, N. Yorks; Howard & Kooij's Nurseries, Wortham, Diss, Norfolk; J. Huish, Wraxall, Bristol; V.H. Humphrey, (Pauline Brown), Dorking, Surrey; Annie Huntington, Sudborough, Northants; Huntington Botanical Gardens, San Marino, CA., USA; Essie Huxley, Longley, TAS, Australia; Ian Huxley, Guildford, VIC, Australia; Brenda Hyatt, Chatham, Kent; Idon Croft Herbs, Staplehurst, Kent; W.E.Th. Ingwersen Ltd., East Grinstead, W. Sussex; Susan Irvine, Gisborne, VIC, Australia; Russell & Sue Jenner, Gould Farm Nurseries, Cranbrook, Kent; Barbara Jennings, Sandy Bay, TAS, Australia; Sally Johannsohn, Neika, TAS, Australia; Mr. & Mrs. Roy Joseph, Welshpool, Powys; Karoo Botanic Gardens, Cape Town, South Africa; Mr. S. Keeble, Wickhambrook, Suffolk; Kelways Nurseries, Langport, Somerset; Lisse Keukenhof, Holland; Kiftsgate Court Gardens, (Mr. & Mrs. J. Chambers), Chipping Campden, Glos; Kirstenboch Gardens, Worcester, South Africa; Lakeland Horticultural Society, Windermere, Cumbria; Lambley Nursery, Ascot, VIC, Australia; Langthorns Plantery, Little Canfield, Dunmow, Essex; Wendy Lauderdale, Kilmington, Wiltshire; Ledora Water Gardens, (Mr. Kuring-Gai), N.S.W., Australia; Leonardslee Gardens, Lower Beeding, W. Sussex; Pam & Peter Lewis, Buckland Newton, Dorset; Littlebrook Fuschias, (Carol Gubler), Aldershot, Hants; Little Treasures Nursery, Horsedowns, Cornwall; London Aquatic Company, Enfield, Middx; Longacres Nursery & Florist, Bagshot, Surrey; Lower Kennegy Nursery, Germoe Crossroads, Cornwall; Rob Magnus, Woodbridge, TAS, Australia; Mansell & Hatcher Ltd., Rawdon, Leeds; Marwood Hill Gardens, Marwood, Devon; Colin Mason, Kenilworth, Warks; Mattocks Roses, Courtney, Oxford; Dr Ronald McKenzie, Shilton, Burford, Oxon; Moidart Wholesale Nursery, Burradoo, N.S.W., Australia; Moles Seeds, Colchester, Essex; Monksilver Nursery, Cottenham, Cambs; National Chrysanthemum Society, Tamworth, Staffs; National Herb Garden, (Janet Walker), Washington, D.C., USA; The National Trust, Powis Castle, Welshpool, Powys; The National Trust, Tintinhull House, Yeovil, Somerset; Ness Gardens, Neston, South Wirral, Cheshire; The New York Botanical Garden (Gregory Piotrowski, Michael Ruggiero, Mobee Weinstein), New York, USA; Nielsen Plants, Hellingly, E. Sussex; Norgate's Plant Farm, (Dennis Norgate), Trentham, VIC, Australia; Northern Horticultural Society, Harrogate, N. Yorks; The Nurseries, (Ian Roger), Pickering, N. Yorks; Odiham Waterlily Collection, Basingstoke, Hants; Margaret Farquhar Ogilvie, The House of Pitmuies, by Forfar, Tayside; Old Court Nurseries, (Mr. & Mrs. P. Picton), Colwall, Malvern, Hereford & Worcs; Mr. M. Oviatt-Ham, Willingham, Cambs; Mr. & Mrs. R. Paice, Bourton-on-the-Hill, Glos; Pan-American Seeds, Abington, Cambs; Paradise Centre, Lamarsh, Bures, Suffolk; Paradise Park, Hayle, Cornwall; Park Green Nurseries, (Richard Ford), Stowmarket, Suffolk; *Passiflora* National Collection, Clevedon, Avon; Wendy & Michael Perry, Truro, Cornwall; Perryhill Nurseries, (Peter Chapman), Hartfield, E. Sussex; Pine Lodge Gardens, Cuddra, Cornwall; Pirianda Garden, Olinda, VIC, Australia; Michael Pitkin, Arcadia, N.S.W., Australia; Roger Platts, Mavesfield, E. Sussex; Potash Nursery, (R.J. Blythe), Stowmarket, Suffolk; Suz Price, Daylesford, VIC, Australia; Probus Gardens, Probus, Cornwall; Mr. & Mrs. T. Ratcliff, Little Thakeham, Storrington, W. Sussex; Reads Nursery, Loddon, Norfolk; Rhodes & Rockliffe Nursery, Nazeing, Essex; Mr. & Mrs. E.J. Rice, Saxlingham, Norfolk; Rickards Hardy Ferns, Tenbury Wells, Hereford & Worcs; Noel Riley, Arcadia, N.S.W., Australia; Dr M. Rogers, Ramsden, Oxon; Romantic Cottage Garden, Dromana, VIC, Australia; Royal Botanic Garden, Edinburgh; Royal Botanic Gardens, (Sue Wells), Hobart, TAS, Australia; Royal Botanic Gardens, (Jenny Evans), Kew, Surrey; Royal Botanic Gardens, Melbourne, VIC, Australia; Royal Botanic Gardens, Peradeniya, Sri Lanka; Royal Botanic Gardens, Sydney, N.S.W., Australia; Royal Canberra Golf Club, Yarralumla, A.C.T., Australia; Royal Horticultural Society, Vincent Square, London; Royal Horticultural Society, Hyde Hall Garden, Chelmsford, Essex; Royal Horticultural Society, Rosemoor Garden, Great Torrington, Devon; Royal Horticultural Society's Gardens, Wisley, Surrey; Royal National Rose Society, St. Albans, Herts; The Savill Garden & Valley Gardens, (John Bond), Windsor Great Park, Berks; Lord Saye & Sele, Broughton Castle, Banbury, Oxon; R.A. Scamp, Falmouth, Cornwall; Scarletts Nursery, West Bergholt, Suffolk; Scotts Nurseries Ltd., Merriott, Somerset; Rob & Dawn Senior, Marazion, Cornwall; Peter Simmons, North Chailey, E. Sussex; Singapore Botanic Gardens, Singapore; Springfield Gardens, (Andrew Boynton), Spalding, Lincs; Ashley Stephenson, Sydney, N.S.W., Australia; Stonecrop Gardens, (Caroline Burgess), Cold Spring, New York, USA; Stonehurst Nursery, Ardingly, W. Sussex; Stony Range Flora Reserve, Dee Why, N.S.W., Australia; Strybing Arboretum & Botanical Gardens, San Francisco, CA., USA; Sudeley Castle Gardens, (Lady Ashcombe), Winchcombe, Glos; Suttons Seeds Ltd., Torquay, Devon; Mr. & Mrs. R.J. Taylor, Dolton, Devon; Sue Templeton, Albury, N.S.W., Australia; Andrew Thompson, Cheltenham, VIC, Australia; David Trehane, Probus, Truro, Cornwall; Trehane Camellia Nursery, Wimborne, Dorset; Trewhella House, Daylesford, VIC, Australia; Trinidad Botanic Gardens, Trinidad; Tropical Botanic Gardens & Research Institute, Palode, Kerala, India; University Botanic Garden, Cambridge; University Botanic Gardens, Oxford; University of California Arboretum, Santa Cruz, CA., USA; University Parks, Oxford; University of Reading Botanic Garden, Reading, Berks; Unlimited Perennials, Albury, N.S.W., Australia; Unwins Seeds Ltd., Histon, Cambs; Rosemary Verey, Barnsley, Glos; Viburnum Gardens, Arcadia, N.S.W., Australia; Wakehurst Place, (Royal Botanic Gardens, Kew), Ardingly, W. Sussex; Walnut Tree Gardens, (Mrs. M. Oldaker), Little Chart, Kent; Graham Warwick, Burradoo, N.S.W., Australia; Peter Waster, Invergowrie, Perthshire; Waterperry Gardens, Wheatley, Oxon; Theresa Watts, Canberra, A.C.T., Australia; Mr. A. West, Hailey, Oxon; Westonbirt Arboretum (Hugh Angus), Westonbirt, Glos; Whitehouse Ivies, Fardham, Colchester, Essex; Garry Wood, Baxter, VIC, Australia; Ray Wood, Castle Howard, N. Yorks; Woodbank Nursery, (Ken & Lesley Gillanders), Longley, TAS, Australia; Wylde Court Rainforest, Newbury, Berks; Arthur Yates & Co., Milperra, N.S.W., Australia.

PHOTOGRAPHY CREDITS

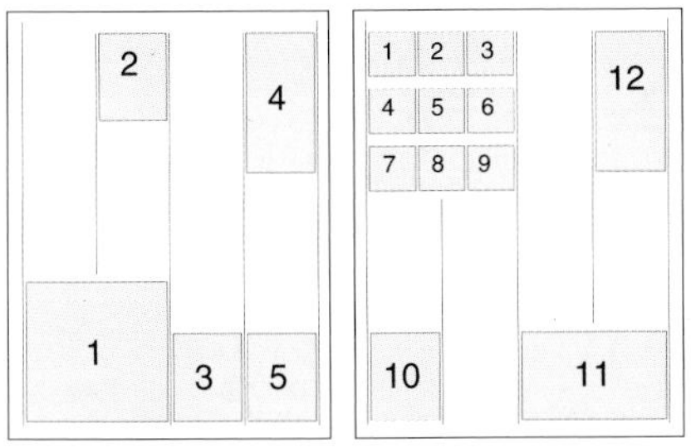

With the exception of those listed below, all photographs in the encyclopedia were taken by the photographers listed on p.6. Dorling Kindersley is grateful to the following agencies and photographers for their kind permission to reproduce images in the encyclopedia. To locate the photographs credited below, use the reference numbers given. The first in each pair of numbers is the page number on which the photograph appears; the second is its position number, determined by the order of photographs on each page (see left).

How to use the photography grid (above)

Photographs are numbered from top to bottom within each column of text, then left to right across the page. In the feature panels, photographs are numbered from left to right across each row, working from the top row to the bottom row (see panel on right-hand page above).

Abraxas Gardens
523/5 • 523/9 • 524/14 • 525/5 • 525/8 • 527/5

The Alpine Garden Society
546/10 • 585/1 • 740/1

John Amand
1095/5 • 1096/1 • 1096/3

Roger Aylett Nurseries
348/5 • 348/17 • 349/5 • 349/6 • 349/11 • 350/7 • 351/1 • 351/5 • 351/9 • 352/11

A-Z Botanical Collection
710/8 • 711/8 • 780/12 • 782/2 • Dr Bob Gibbons 337/2 • Bruno Petriglia 337/4 • Dan Sams 252/2
Moira C. Smith 661/2 • Adrian Thomas 709/10

George Bartlett
462/8

Gillian Beckett
104/6 • 260/3 • 358/3 • 391/1 • 409/1 • 500/1 • 529/2 • 557/3 • 993/2

Biofotos
10/5 • 18/1 • 40/3 • 56/1 • 61/1 • 73/5 • 109/3 • 304/2 • 549/4 • 705/3 • 942/1

John Bowers Daylilies
522/4 • 523/7 • 525/7 • 526/7 • 526/8

Deni Bown
1091/4

Christopher Brickell
87/2 • 177/6 • 178/3 • 223/4 • 264/1 • 307/1 • 365/1 • 372/3 • 394/1 • 954/3 • 995/4

Pat Brindley
369/4 • 446/4 • 635/1

Eric Catterall
171/7

Leigh Clapp
333/3

Bruce Coleman Limited
18/2

Eric Crichton Photos
171/2 • 261/3 • 337/3 • 779/4 • 883/1 • 979/4

Brian Duncan
710/3 • 711/3 • 711/6 • 711/12 • 713/3 • 715/6

Jack Elliott
143/1 • 286/5 • 425/4 • 471/6 • 575/10 • 690/1 • 754/2 • 1079/3

Nigel Farr
273/7

John Fielding
103/4 • 158/7 • 362/7

Fleurmerc B.V.
83/3 • 304/1 • 561/1 • 603/3 • 664/9 • 694/4

John Galbally
369/8 • 369/9 • 370/1 • 370/14 • 371/5

Garden Matters
575/6

Garden Picture Library
35/2 • 40/2 • 42/2 • 43/1 • 46/2 • 48/2 • 51/3 • 52/2 • 92/1 • 139/2 • 199/3 • 223/6 • 301/4 • 352/1
443/2 • 475/1 • 634/2 • 681/3 • 696/3 • 729/3 • 786/5 • 850/9 • 929/14 • 997/4 • 1003/4 • 1006/1
Mark Bolton 1032/2 • Philippe Bonduel 925/7 • Chris Burrows 166/1 • 633/11 • Densey Clyne 573/10
Christopher Fairweather 532/6 • John Glover 665/1
Neil Holmes 903/1• J. S. Sira-G.P.L. 783/7 • 903/3

Garden and Wildlife Matters
461/12 • 546/10 • 585/1 • 740/1• 780/3• 781/5•
783/10 • 783/12 • John Feltwell 462/1, 531/2, 782/3
Martin P. Land 633/6

Garden World Images
109/1 • 154/4 • 154/5 • 155/7 • 156/1 • 167/2 • 253/2
253/3 • 260/4 • 263/5 • 264/3 • 283/11 • 460/8 • 463/1
463/2 • 463/8 • 523/4 • 523/8 • 526/5 • 527/7 • 531/3
543/8 • 546/10 • 570/6 • 574/1 • 575/1 • 585/1
662/3 • 702/2 • 702/3 • 702/4 • 710/9 • 711/4 • 711/9
713/1 • 713/3 • 713/5 • 740/1 • 778/5 • 779/1 • 779/9 • 780/8 • 780/9 • 781/2 • 781/3 • 783/1
783/4 • 783/9 • 831/1 • 831/4 • 883/2 • 905/2 • 918/1 • 921/9 • 924/3 • 927/12 • 928/7 • 929/7
930/3 • 931/3 • 931/10 • 933/3 • 933/7 • 933/12 • 934/5 • 935/10 • 936/2 • 1032/3

John Glover
44/2 • 128/1 • 315/2 • 330/2 • 570/3 • 782/7 • 918/13, 922/1 • 992/2 • 1095/6

Derek Gould
175/3 • 321/2 • 381/2 • 386/1 • 388/1 • 518/2 • 570/4 • 583/1 • 585/2 • 587/4 • 600/7 • 681/2
947/3 • 1024/7 • 1091/2

Peter Harkness
912/1 • 912/5 • 912/13 • 914/10 • 918/3 • 922/6 • 924/6 • 925/4 • 925/5 • 925/6 • 927/8 • 930/11
932/1 • 933/13 • 935/1

Jerry Harpur
36/2 • 38/1 (designer: Beth Chatto) • 43/2 • 54/6

Derek Hewlett
348/7 • 348/12 • 351/2 • 351/10 • 352/3

Neil Holmes
666/5

Clive Innes
58/6 • 191/3 • 191/4 • 280/4 • 393/2 • 397/1 • 401/1 • 437/2 • 438/1 • 496/3 • 503/2 • 540/2 • 550/2
550/3 • 550/4 • 608/3 • 727/5 • 733/1 • 733/2 • 771/1 • 870/2 • 1005/4 • 1041/2

International Flower Bulb Centre
482/9 • 483/4 • 484/4

Andrew Lawson
44/3 • 125/1 • 129/4 • 195/3 • 227/1 • 246/5 • 259/2 • 261/4 • 280/1 • 281/1 • 283/12 • 283/14 • 285/7
396/1 • 423/2 • 427/2 • 463/6 • 463/7 • 522/7 • 528/4 • 533/2 • 631/15 • 633/10 • 638/2 • 709/4
711/10 • 763/3 • 764/1 • 778/4 • 885/2 • 904/4 • 927/7 • 933/5 • 934/2 • 981/2 • 991/4 • 1094/4
1095/2 • 1095/4

Brian Mathew
122/2

Peter Maynard
574/2 • 577/4 • 577/8 • 579/7 • 580/2

Clive Nichols
34/2 • 53/1 (designer: Roger Platts) • 54/7 • 227/3 • 359/2 • 711/1 • 713/8

Oxford Scientific Films
546/10 • 585/1 • 740/1 • Dr Raymond Parks 830/4

Vincent Page
918/8 • 926/12 • 929/2

Jerry Pavia Photography Inc.
525/3 • 546/10 • 585/1 • 740/1

Photos Horticultural
75/3 • 76/3 • 78/1 • 83/1 • 86/3 • 106/2 • 107/3 • 110/1 • 140/4 • 141/1 • 142/7 • 154/3 • 167/1
168/13 • 168/19 • 170/4 • 170/14 • 170/19 • 196/2 • 208/1 • 216/2 • 233/3 • 266/1 • 266/2 • 279/2
286/2 • 287/1 • 287/2 • 296/2 • 300/5 • 301/2 • 305/2 • 340/2 • 345/1 • 371/10 • 378/3 • 385/1
394/2 • 396/2 • 400/1 • 408/1 • 421/1 • 430/2 • 442/2 • 446/2 • 448/2 • 450/2 • 459/1 • 460/9
462/2 • 462/4 • 506/6 • 507/3 • 527/8 • 532/3 • 537/1 • 540/1 • 549/1 • 549/3 • 565/2 • 566/3
567/4 • 569/3 • 578/9 • 579/6 • 590/1 • 595/1 • 595/2 • 596/1 • 596/4 • 597/3 • 622/2 • 663/6
679/2 • 682/1 • 688/3 • 699/1 • 700/2 • 702/1 • 709/8 • 710/2 • 710/11 • 705/1 • 779/2 • 779/3
780/1 • 780/7 • 780/14 • 782/5 • 782/8 • 791/3 • 828/3 • 828/4 • 876/4 • 892/6 • 903/2 • 915/5
917/2 • 918/2 • 919/12 • 924/1 • 924/2 • 925/8 • 925/13 • 929/10 • 930/9 • 934/4 • 934/7 • 935/1
935/13 • 936/3 • 948/1 • 953/3 • 959/2 • 962/2 • 980/1 • 980/3 • 985/3 • 1025/1 • 1028/4 • 1029/1
1030/1 • 1032/1 • 1037/3 • 1037/12 • 1043/4 • 1053/2 • 1088/1 • 1095/3 • 1096/2 • MJK 533/4

Planet Earth Pictures
47/2 • 50/2

Plant Portraits Worldwide
61/5 • 73/1 • 74/3 • 77/2 • 91/2 • 102/2 • 109/1 • 114/4 • 119/1 • 122/1 • 139/1 • 139/3 • 139/4 • 159/3
160/2 • 163/3 • 179/1 • 193/1 • 196/1 • 209/3 • 225/3 • 264/4 • 275/3 • 280/2 • 296/3 • 319/2 • 327/2
333/1 • 358/1 • 360/1 • 360/2 • 378/4 • 386/2 • 387/1 • 389/3 • 392/2 • 430/7 • 472/1 • 474/10 • 485/4
506/4 • 524/3 • 541/2 • 542/2 • 626/1 • 656/2 • 667/3 • 704/4 • 716/2 • 723/6 • 750/2 • 766/2 • 769/1
770/1 • 810/2 • 824/3 • 835/3 • 1080/5

Martin Rickard
837/4

Sakata Seeds
442/1

Mike Shadrack
542/4 • 542/6 • 542/7 • 542/11 • 543/7 • 544/1 • 544/9 • 545/2 • 546/10 • 585/1 • 740/1

Christine Skelmersdale
325/12 • 909/3 • 1007/2

Harry Smith Collection
63/1 • 72/6 • 73/2 • 77/4 • 123/3 • 125/4 • 126/4 • 129/2 • 135/4 • 138/2 • 163/1 • 181/4 • 186/2 • 190/3
194/3 • 206/4 • 207/4 • 230/4 • 246/1 • 291/2 • 296/1 • 353/10 • 376/6 • 381/4 • 383/1 • 385/2 • 418/9
423/3 • 446/3 • 474/11 • 475/2 • 479/5 • 485/11 • 518/4 • 534/4 • 576/8 • 589/3 • 615/1 • 633/5 • 633/19
644/4 • 681/4 • 720/2 • 761/14 • 761/17 • 787/2 • 797/1 • 915/3 • 952/4 • 959/3 • 981/1 • 986/2 • 990/3
999/3 • 1057/12 1081/6 • 1099/2

Van Staaveren Aalsmeer B.V.
456/1 • 456/2

W.B. Wade
268/2 • 268/4 • 268/6 • 268/8 • 269/2 • 269/5 • 269/11 • 269/13 • 270/1 • 270/2 • 270/3 • 270/8
270/9 • 270/11 • 271/10 • 272/2 • 272/5 • 272/11 • 273/6 • 546/10 • 585/1 • 740/1

GENERAL INDEX

This index provides quick access to the general horticultural topics featured in the main introduction to the encyclopedia (pp.10–54). Plant names are not listed here, as these are presented in alphabetical sequence throughout the plant directory, together with cross-references to all synonyms and common names.

Visual glossary: Pruning groups

Group 1

Action In late winter or early spring, when dormant, remove misplaced or crossing shoots to maintain permanent, healthy framework.

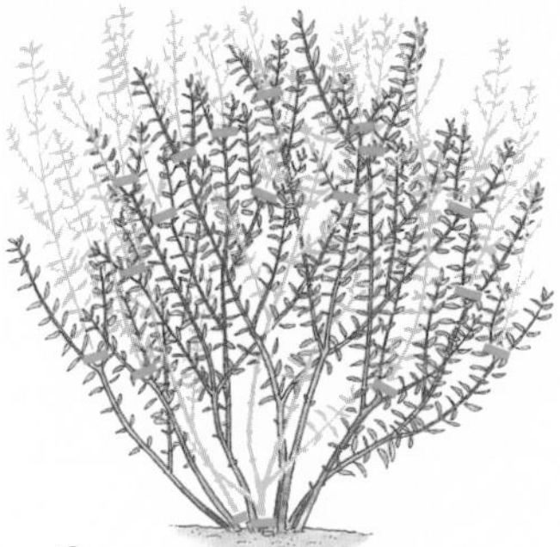

Group 2

Action After flowering, cut back flowered shoots to strong buds or young lower growth; on mature plants, also cut back a quarter to a fifth of old shoots to base.

Group 3

Action After flowering, cut back flowered shoots to young sideshoots or to strong buds low down on branch framework.

Group 4

Action Cut back to first bud or pair of buds below each flowerhead. Once established, cut back a third to a quarter of old shoots to base in early or mid-spring.

Group 5

Action After flowering, cut back all stems to strong buds, or to developing shoots close to base.

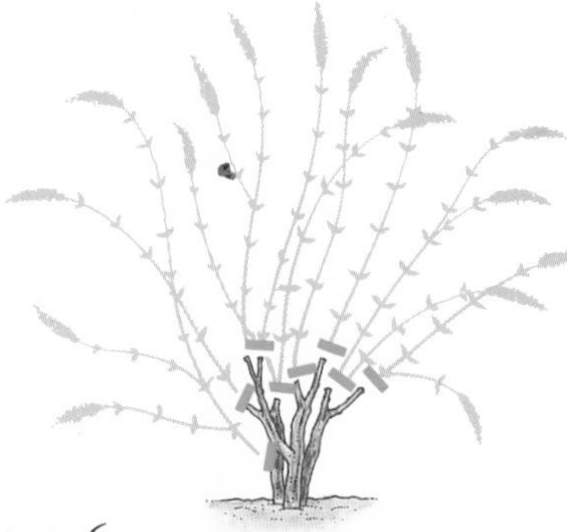

Group 6

Action In early spring, cut back to permanent framework or, for subshrubs and for drastic renovation, cut back flowered stems close to base.

Group 7

Action In early spring, cut back stems to within 2 or 3 buds of base (suckering species close to base), or to permanent framework.

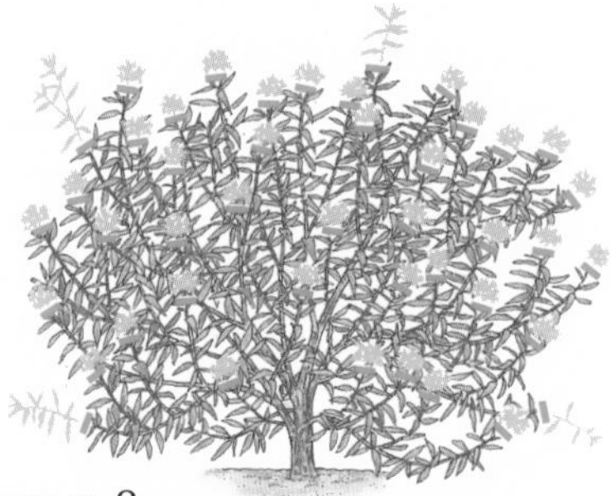

Group 8

Action After flowering, lightly trim or prune back shoots that spoil symmetry. Dead-head regularly if practical (unless fruit required).

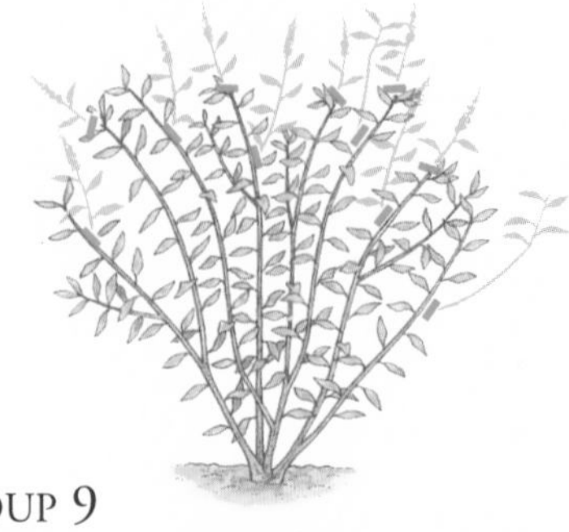

Group 9

Action In mid- or late spring, lightly trim or prune back shoots that spoil symmetry. Dead-head regularly if practical (unless fruit required).

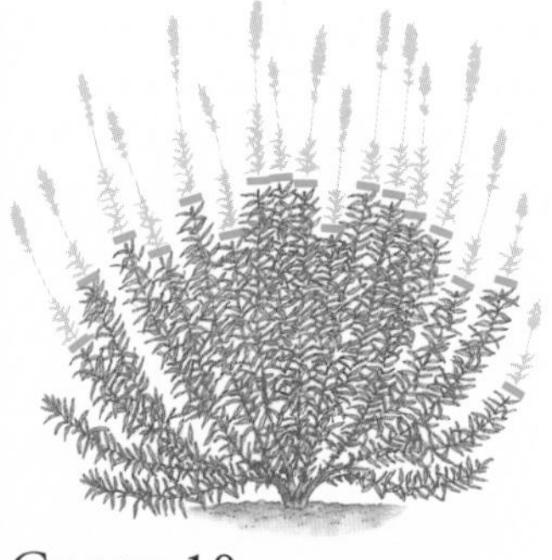

Group 10

Action After flowering, or in early or mid-spring, cut back flowered shoots to within 2.5cm (1in) of old growth.

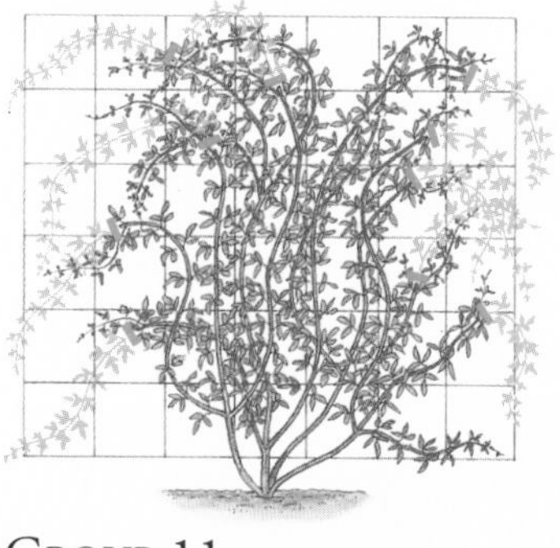

Group 11

Action After flowering, or in late winter or early spring, trim to fit available space; carry out renovation pruning as needed.

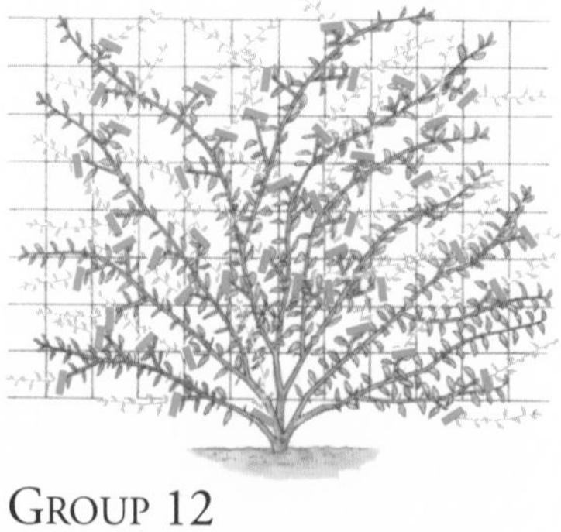

Group 12

Action After flowering, or in late winter or early spring, "spur prune" sideshoots to within 3 or 4 buds of permanent framework.

Group 13

Action After flowering, or in late winter or early spring, cut back flowered shoots to within 2–4 buds of permanent framework.

Visual glossary: Leaves

Structure of a leaf

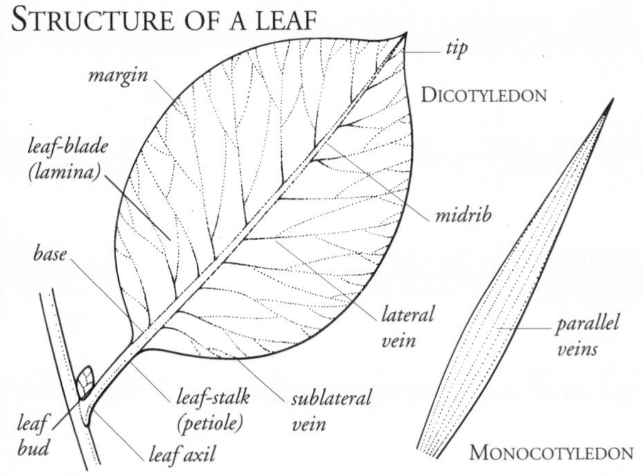

Arrangements

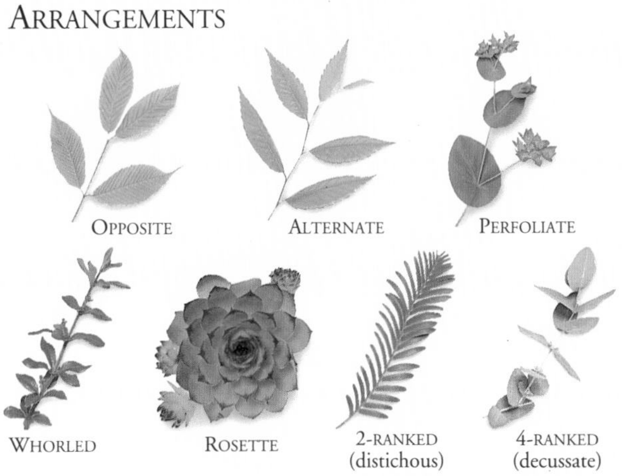

Coniferous leaves

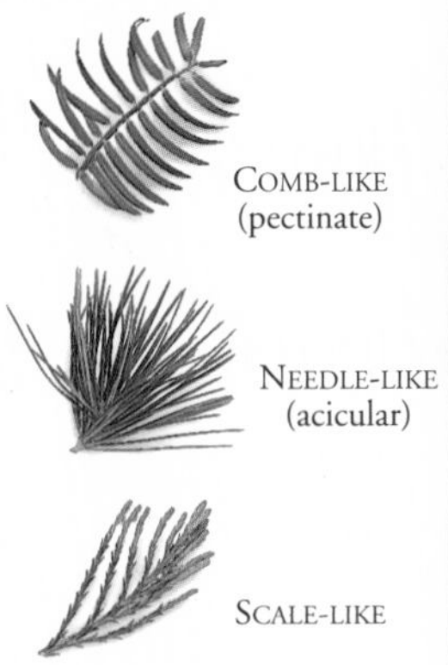

Lobing and division

Shapes

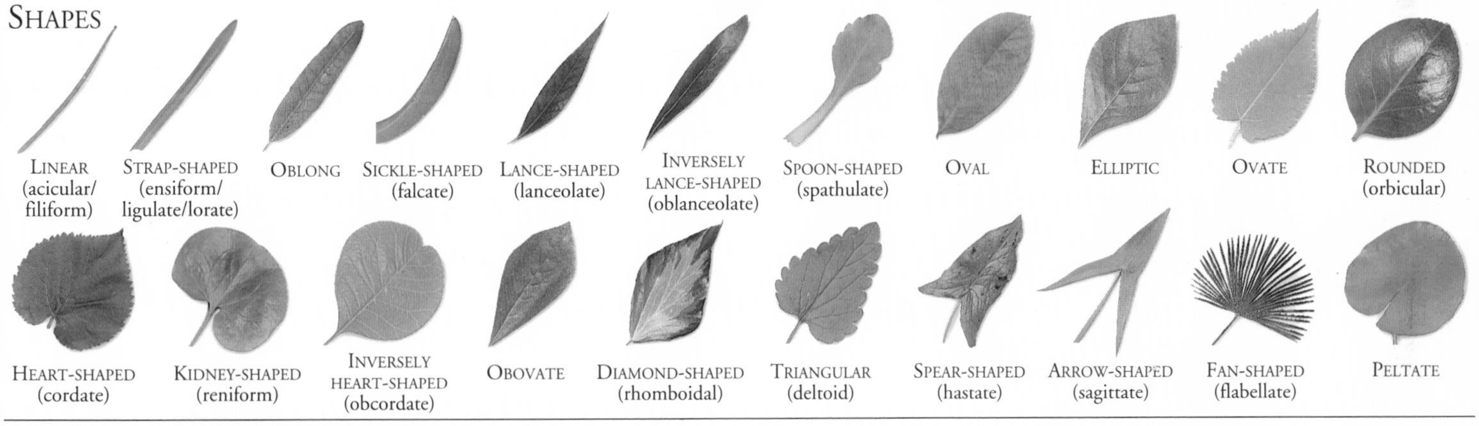

Margins

Tips

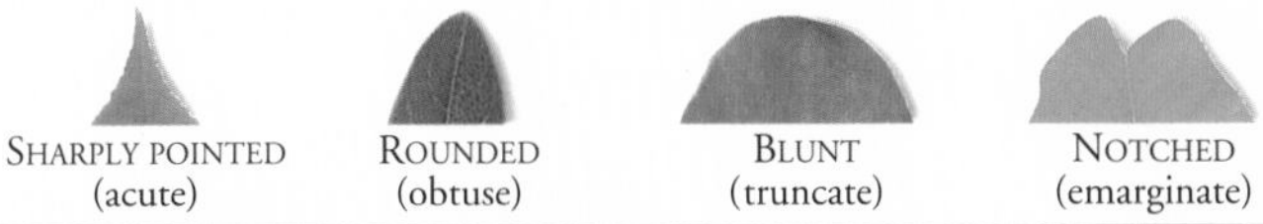

Bases

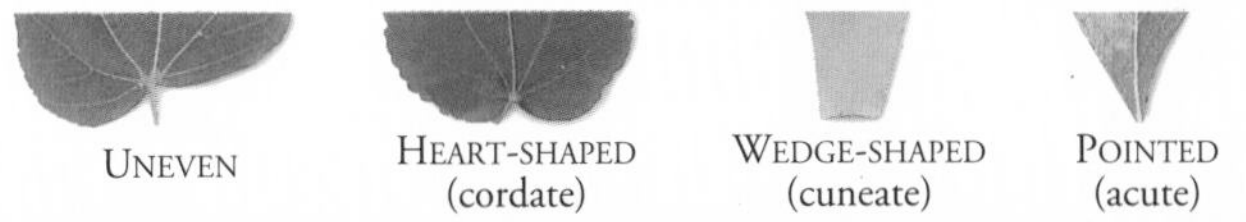

Key to symbols

Miscellaneous	Plant dimensions
Cross-reference	Typical height
Plant is pictured (on same page as entry or adjacent ones)	Typical spread
	Typical height and spread (if the same)

Tree shapes		
Rounded to broadly spreading	Broadly conical	Small weeping
Rounded to broadly columnar	Narrowly conical	Single-stemmed palm, cycad, or similar tree
Broadly columnar	Narrowly conical (flame-shaped)	Multi-stemmed palm, cycad, or similar tree
Narrowly columnar	Large weeping	

Hardiness ratings

Frost tender: plant may be damaged by temperatures below 5°C (41°F)	Half hardy: plant can withstand temperatures down to 0°C (32°F)	Frost hardy: plant can withstand temperatures down to -5°C (23°F)	Fully hardy: plant can withstand temperatures down to -15°C (5°F)